Fodor's 2000

Europe

The complete guide, thoroughly up-to-date

Packed with details that will make your trip

What to see, what to skip

City strolls, countryside adventures

Smart lodging and dining options

Transportation tips, distances and directions

Key contacts, savvy travel tips

When to go, what to pack

Clear, accurate, easy-to-use maps

Fodor's Travel Publications, Inc. • New York, Toronto, London, Sydney, Auckland
www.fodors.com

Fodor's EUROPE

EDITOR: Nancy van Itallie

Editorial Contributors: Robert Andrews, Catherine Belonogoff, John Bigley, Toula Bogdanos, Jacqueline Brown, Jules Brown, Jeffrey Carson, Daniel Cash, Christine Cipriani, Peter Collis, Nancy Coons, Roderick Craig, Fionn Davenport, Martha de la Cal, Bonnie Dodson, Jon Eldan, Robert Fisher, Jane Foster, Brent Gregston, Katrin Gygax, Lucy Hawking, Simon Hewitt, Rebecca Hirschfield, Rhoda Holmes, Alannah Hopkin, Anto Howard, Beth Ingpen, Tania Inowlocki, Vincent Jamison, Gareth Jenkins, Nicola Keegan, Suzanne Rowan Kelleher, Michael Kissane, Christina Knight, Martha Lagace, Natasha Lesser, Carla Lionello, Mark Little, Alexander Lobrano, Joan Lofgren, Gerry Madigan, Andrew May, Jennifer McDermott, Christopher Mooney, Lauren Myers, Jennifer Paull, Paris Permenter, Ian Phillips, Ian Plenderleith, Karina Porcelli, Tatiana Repkova, Kristin Rimington, Caragh Rockwood, Patricia Rucidlo, Eva Marquez Salmerón, Jürgen Scheunemann, Helayne Schiff, George Semler, Ted Shoemaker, Dawn Smith, Gilbert Summers, Robert Tilley, Julie Tomasz, Goril Trondsen, Susan Tuttle-Laube, Annie Ward, Devin Wilson, Stephen Wolf

Editorial Production: Tom Holton
Maps: David Lindroth, *cartographer*; Robert Blake, *map editor*
Design: Fabrizio La Rocca, *creative director*; Guido Caroti, *art director*; Jolie Novak, *photo editor*
Cover Design: Pentagram
Production/Manufacturing: Robert B. Shields
Cover Photograph: BKA Network/Aspen

Copyright

ISBN 0–679–00328–2

ISSN 0362–0204

Special Sales

Fodor's Travel Publications are available at special discounts for bulk purchases for sales promotions or premiums. Special editions, including personalized covers, excerpts of existing guides, and corporate imprints, can be created in large quantities for special needs. For more information, contact your local bookseller or write to Special Markets, Fodor's Travel Publications, 201 East 50th Street, New York, NY 10022. Inquiries from Canada should be directed to your local Canadian bookseller or sent to Random House of Canada, Ltd., Marketing Department, 2775 Matheson Boulevard East, Mississauga, Ontario L4W 4P7. Inquiries from the United Kingdom should be sent to Fodor's Travel Publications, 20 Vauxhall Bridge Road, London SW1V 2SA, England.

PRINTED IN THE UNITED STATES OF AMERICA

10 9 8 7 6 5 4 3 2 1

CONTENTS

⊕ *Italic entries are maps.*

ON THE ROAD WITH FODOR'S

EVERY Y2K TRIP IS A SIGNIFICANT trip. So if there was ever a time you needed excellent travel information, it's now. Acutely aware of that fact, we've pulled out all stops in preparing *Fodor's Europe*. To guide you in putting together your European experience, we've chosen the best of both city and countryside. And to direct you to the places that are truly worth your time and money in this important year, we've rallied the team of endearingly picky know-it-alls we're pleased to call our writers. Having seen all corners of Europe, they're real experts. If you knew them, you'd poll them for tips yourself.

How to Use This Book

The section following this one, **New and Noteworthy,** cues you in on trends and happenings. Following that is Chapter 1, **Smart Travel Tips,** arranged alphabetically by topic. Under each listing you'll find tips and information that will help you accomplish what you need to in Europe. You'll also find addresses and telephone numbers of organizations and companies that offer destination-related services and detailed information and publications.

Chapters in *Europe 2000* are in alphabetical order by country. Each covers the country's essential information A to Z, exploring, dining lodging, nightlife and the arts, shopping, and side trips in cities and regions. Sites in major cities accompanied by maps are arranged alphabetically, but they are num-

bered on the maps according to the suggested sequence of a walk or tour. Within regional sections, all restaurants and lodgings are grouped with the town. The A to Z list that ends all city or regional sections covers getting there and getting around. It also provides helpful contacts and resources.

Important Tip

Although all prices, opening times, and other details in this book are based on information supplied to us at press time, changes occur all the time in the travel world, and Fodor's cannot accept responsibility for facts that become outdated or for inadvertent errors or omissions. So **always confirm information when it matters,** especially if you're making a detour to visit a specific place.

Don't Forget to Write

Keeping a travel guide fresh and up-to-date is a big job. So we love your feedback—positive and negative—and follow up on all suggestions. Contact the Europe editor at editors@fodors.com or c/o Fodor's, 201 East 50th Street, New York, New York 10022. And have a wonderful trip!

Karen Cure

Karen Cure
Editorial Director

NEW AND NOTEWORTHY

A NEW UNIT OF CURRENCY MADE its debut on January 1, 1999, when the conversion to the **euro** (€) began for 11 of the 15 members of the European Union (EU). Some payment systems (mainly in trade) began using the euro immediately. The rates of conversion between the euro and local currencies are irrevocably fixed, eliminating commission charges in currency exchange. Consumers continue to use their own national currency because euro banknotes and coins are not yet available, but the gradual introduction of dual pricing of goods and services is enabling people to get used to the new money. Eventually, the euro will become a currency in its own right and participating national currencies will no longer be listed on foreign exchange markets. By January 1, 2002, new euro banknotes and coins will be put into circulation and the old national currencies will be withdrawn.

From July 1, 1999, purchases aboard planes or boats between countries of the EU were **no longer duty-free,** as the EU continues to move toward a border-free status.

In honor of the millennium, Europe in 2000 will have **nine cultural capitals** instead of the usual one. The cities are Avignon, France; Bergen, Norway; Bologna, Italy; Brussels, Belgium; Helsinki, Finland; Krakow, Poland; Prague, Czech Republic; Reykjavík, Iceland; and Santiago de Compostela, Spain. The nine are collaborating to establish improved public access to each of their museum and exhibition collections, using technology to help create a "virtual cultural infrastructure" linking their resources electronically.

Andorra

The new **telecabina** (cable car) from Encamp up to the Grau Roig ski resort has been named Funicamp. A new telecabina network is being installed to connect hotels in the valley with the upper slopes and ski runs, alleviating the wicked winter traffic jams for which Andorra has become notorious.

Montserrat Caballe now gives a mid-June voice master class that includes concerts, competitions, and performances. The classical music festival—Narciso Yepes en Ordino—takes place during the last week of September and first week of October.

Austria

Top musical events in 2000 include a **Joseph Haydn** festival and a special **Vienna Philharmonic** *Oster Klang* (Sound of Easter) series of concerts under the direction of Nikolaus Harnoncourt. Getting tickets to the glamorous **Opernball** in Vienna depends on luck, speed, and lots of spare cash. Earmark March 2, 2000, to take part in this quintessentially Viennese occasion.

The new year also marks the 500th birthday of **Kaiser Karl V,** Holy Roman Emperor and King of Spain (as Charles I) during the first half of the 16th century. Madrid, Bonn and Ghent will be hosting concurrent exhibits on different aspects of the ruler's life, with Vienna concentrating on his artistic and cultural contributions. Other important upcoming events in the **Vienna art world** include exhibits featuring artists **Cezanne** and **El Greco** and the Italian architect **Francesco Borromini.**The founder of psychoanalysis, **Sigmund Freud,** will be the focus of a joint venture by the Vienna National Library and the Freud Museum in early 2000. The London Freud Museum is lending Freud's original couch, which he took with him into exile (the Vienna Freud Museum possesses a copy).

Baltic States

Estonia, Latvia and Lithuania are attractive vacation spots for travel because they are relatively inexpensive, undiscovered, and provide the quality found in most Western European tourist destinations. The states are spending more and more on infrastructure improvements and Old Town maintenance. Estonia plows steadily forward in European Union talks—the only Baltic state chosen to begin negotiations. Riga, although struggling with its sometimes politically unpleasant neighbor Russia, is the most cosmopolitan of the three capitals, with new Armenian, French, and Italian restaurants as well as many luxurious hotels. In 1998 Vilnius completely renovated its Baroque historic district, one of the largest in Europe.

Belgium

As one of the nine **Cultural Capitals of Europe** designated for 2000, Brussels is hosting a series of cultural events and entertainments throughout the year, as well as undertaking myriad civic regeneration projects designed to make the city a brighter place for the new millennium. For visitors, a highlight should be the massive Zinneke Parade in mid-June. While Brussels looks to the future, Ghent is celebrating the 500th birthday of its most famous son, **Emperor Charles V**—although many Ghent residents believe the Habsburg monarch did them more harm than good. For sports fans, the year's highlight is the **Euro 2000** soccer championships in June, co-hosted with the Netherlands and featuring the cream of European footballing talent.

Bulgaria

In Bulgaria the currency is undergoing some huge changes. In spring 1999 the lev "lost its zeros," making conversion calculations much easier. As the economy improves, new businesses, restaurants, hotels, and shops are opening up, and towns and landscapes alike are getting a face-lift.

Cyprus

The attempt to **reunite** Cyprus with the Turkish-controlled northern sector continues but so far has not been successful. Construction projects are underway on the island, including a major **highway** that extends the route between Nicosia and Limassol on to Paphos. The Cyprus Tourism Organization is supporting revitalization of popular destinations with changes such as **pedestrian areas** in the major cities. Recently the organization instituted a new **agritourism** project to encourage the renovation of traditional homes in villages as guest accommodations. The island is increasingly becoming a magnet for sports tourism, particularly **birding** tours.

Czech Republic

The Czech Republic, pursuing economic and cultural revitalization, aims for eventual membership in the EU and in NATO. Prague's Ruzyně airport has a spacious and spiffy **new terminal.** The arrival of visitors and long-term residents from all over the world has brought forth **new restaurants** offering Cajun, Indian, vegetarian, and other exotic fare alongside the traditional ones serving pork and dumplings. At the end of 1998, Prague added another glorious site to its must-see list: the gorgeously renovated **Spanish Synagogue** in Old Town, originally built in 1868 on the site of the ancient Old Synagogue (which had been destroyed by anti-Jewish riots in 1389). The restored Spanish Synagogue is an excellent example of Moorish architecture and decoration.

The annual mid-May–early June **Prague Spring Music Festival** is attracting record numbers of music lovers. The less-hyped **Prague Autumn festival** has begun to bring in equally strong performers and orchestras, and the State Opera's annual **Verdi Festival** in August is gaining popularity. The country and Prague in particular also highlight the newest in films from Eastern Europe and the world through regular film festivals. (There are at least six annually.)

Denmark

Copenhagen's massive infrastructure projects will be close to completion in mid-2000, making intercontinental–Scandinavian travel much simpler. The first of these colossal projects, the Storebæltsbro (the Great Belt Bridge) rail and automobile link between Fyn and Sjælland has reduced crossing times by at least an hour and eliminated, for better or worse, many of the enormous ferries that used to ply the Danish waters. By June 2000, the construction of the Øresunds bridge between Copenhagen and Malmö, Sweden, will be completed, linking the two countries and creating what many hope will be a new binational metropolis. Plans to celebrate this union include the Cultural Bridge, a 3½-month celebration that kicks off September 15 on both sides of the Sound, with a flurry of activities, including concerts, theater, and expositions, in the Lund-Malmö-Copenhagen-Skagen region.

Streamlined travel between Copenhagen Airport and the city center should serve as a primer for urban planners everywhere: If there are no traffic delays, cars can zip from city center to the airport on the new highway in 10 minutes; the newest subway of the city train system can get you between the airport and the city's main train station in about 12 minutes.

As transportation becomes easier, hotel capacity is increasing: In the center of town, just next door to Tivoli, a four-star First Hotel was opened in May 1999 with 403 rooms. Among the biggest new projects underway, a new four-star Hilton hotel will be completed in 2000 next door to the Copenhagen Airport's Air Rail Terminal. The hotel will cover 25,000 square meters and will include 375 rooms and suites. Finally, Marriott is also building its first Scandinavian hotel in Copenhagen. The five-star, 395-room harbor-front hotel, to open in the summer of 2001, is expected to include extensive conference facilities.

Finland

The year 2000 marks Helsinki's 450th anniversary, which the city is celebrating as a **European City of Culture,** or "cultural capital." Key exhibits include the Kide (Crystal) sound-and-light sculpture installation, divided among the nine cultural capitals in 1999 and connected by a live link-up. At the turn of the millennium the crystal will be rejoined in Helsinki to form a tunnel of light 3 m (10 ft) high and 18 m (59 ft) long at Senate Square. FIND is an extensive exhibition of Finish design and applied arts set to open in all cultural capitals in February. Finland's Science Center, Heureka, presents a high-tech interactive exhibition on communication with counterparts in the other capitals.

The **history of St. Petersburg,** Finland's neighboring Russian metropolis, is highlighted through music, literature, films, science, and research in April–May. Helsinki also "calls the stars home" in 2000, bringing internationally acclaimed conductors and musicians home for special **performances.** A parade and a variety of concerts and performances throughout the city mark **Helsinki's 450th anniversary** on June 12, 2000. The Cutty Sark **Tall Ships Race** set for July attracts some 120 sailing ships to the city.

On the Esplanade, the luxurious, turn-of-the-century landmark **Kämp Hotel** reopened in spring 1999 after extensive renovations, again one of the finest hotels in the Nordic countries.

Festivals throughout Finland continue to attract elite performers in opera, jazz, dance, folk music, and theater, yet ticket prices remain affordable.

France

France is approaching celebrations for the Year 2000 with typical last-minute panache—plans for events for **Paris,** for instance, include decorating the **Champs-Élysées** with a series of giant archways on New Year's Eve, to symbolize the gateway to the new millennium. Perhaps the capital's most durable legacy will be an uninterrupted **walkway along the Seine** from the Parc André-Citroën, near the Eiffel Tower, to the new National Library at Tolbiac.

The **Pompidou Center** heads an impressive list of Paris museums set to reopen in 2000 after extensive renovation. Others include the National Technical Museum, or **Conservatoire National des Techniques,** also in the Marais; the **Musée Guimet,** with one of the world's most lavish collections of Oriental art; the **Musée des Monuments Français** at Trocadéro; the **Musée de la Poste**; and the **Musée des Arts Décoratifs** in one wing of the Louvre, whose ongoing renovation should be finally over by 2000. New museums in the capital include the **Musée de l'Art et de l'Histoire du Judaïsme,** in the Marais, and the **Musée de l'Erotisme** in Montmartre. It's now possible to take a backstage visit to the city's largest and most famous cinema, the Art Deco **Rex.**

Paris continues to spruce itself up for the new millennium. The top of the Concorde **obelisk** (which is to be converted into a giant sundial in summer 2000) has been gilded; the ornate facade of the **Opéra Garnier** is being cleaned; the adjacent triumphal arches at the **Porte St-Denis** and **Porte St-Martin** have been cleaned also.

Ongoing redevelopment at **Bercy** in east Paris has seen a streetful of former wine warehouses transformed into trendy boutiques and restaurants, with Frank Gehry's quirky American Center, closed in 1994, set to reopen as a Maison du Cinéma (movie center) sometime during 2000 if all goes well. A **footbridge** will soon link the Parc de Bercy to the grand new Bibliothèque François-Mitterrand (National Library) across the Seine. Bercy and the Library are now linked to central Paris by a new, fully automated, state-of-the-art Métro line, **No. 14,** complete with several impressive new stations. Just as grand is the new RER Line E, also known as **Eole,** with two new stations, Haussmann St-Lazare and Magenta, linking Gare St-Lazare with Gare du Nord/Gare de l'Est—a boon for many travelers changing stations in Paris.

Restoration of the gardens at **Versailles** continues, with replanting schemes continuing through at least 2000 to bring some of Louis XIV's original groves back to their original glory. Extra palace rooms, celebrating French history, were opened to the public in 1999.

Double-decker TGV trains have been widely introduced and help you combine high-speed travel with far-reaching views. The **A16** expressway north of Paris now goes all the way to **Boulogne-sur-Mer,** whose Nausicaä aquarium (the north of France's top tourist attraction) was expanded to twice its original size in 1998. The giant art museum in nearby **Lille** has reopened after six years of painstaking renovation, and the city's main church, Notre-Dame de la Treille, finally got itself a facade nearly 150 years after its foundation stone was laid. A new modern art museum has opened in **Strasbourg** and the arts museum in **Nancy** has been granted a spectacular extension.

Germany

Berlin is again the capital of Germany and you can watch parliament members debating the country's future under the restored **Reichstag**'s glass dome. Internationally renowned architects continue to fill in the scar left by the disappeared Wall; the jagged building creating the most buzz is that of the **Jewish Museum,** by Daniel Libeskind. Hannover has spruced itself up to host the international **Expo 2000** between May and October. Countries from all continents will showcase their cultures, ecologies, and technological achievements. Germany celebrates **Bach** in the year 2000 with concerts country-wide, with particularly special events in Leipzig, where Bach was once choirmaster. Munich plans to open its new museum, **Pinakothek der Moderne,** which will house the city's most prestigious collections of 20th-century art. The Olympic Park outside Munich added an **Olympic Spirit** theme park in 1999, which offers an adrenaline-pumping array of virtual-reality experiences for the would-be athlete. If you don't get tickets this

year, you'll have to wait until 2010 to see the alpine town of Oberammergau's **Passion Play.** In thanks for escaping the Black Death, the town residents perform the religious pageant every ten years.

Great Britain

From the vantage point of 1999—a.k.a. the precursor to the big 2000—Great Britain is poised to embrace the turning of the century. The question is: Is everything in London ready? Due to open on December 31, 1999, is the **Millennium Dome** at Greenwich, set on the eastern outskirts of London. Whether this multimillion-pound 320-meter structure designed by architect-provocateur Richard Rogers is a must-see or an expensive mistake is not possible to say at press time, but it is certainly the most costly monument to the advent of the new millennium. Almost 1,200 ft in diameter and more than 150 ft high, it is also very large indeed. With 14 themed zones inside leading into the world of the 21st century, this extravaganza could prove to be peerless in its foresight. Other major building projects in London include the new **Tate Gallery of Modern Art** being installed in the former Bankside Power Station. Opening in May 2000, the new Tate will house the huge numbers of works of art that were formerly hidden from public view due to lack of space in the old Millbank Gallery. Also going up on the south side of the Thames is the **British Airways London Eye**—the world's tallest ferris wheel.

Among London's other attractions, check out the new **British Library** and its public-friendly offerings: the Italianate piazza-style entrance, the touchscreen access to important manuscripts from the Magna Carta to the Beatles' sheet music, and the glass edifice that houses King George's library. The staid bastion of the **British Museum** is putting a bold new face on its ownership of the Elgin Marbles. These controversial treasures are now shown in a grand, modern setting and their history brought up-to-date with a tactile, interactive display in the Parthenon Galleries. The **Natural History Museum** is perfecting its biggest project since it opened in 1881, the Earth Galleries, which examine earthly phenomena—volcanoes, tornadoes, deserts—and then take you out into space and onto other planets.

At **Westminster Abbey,** the earth is positively moving, as a recent visitor discovered when the floor gave way beneath him and brought him too close to the corpses of ancient history for comfort. Too many old bones crumbling beneath, and the weight of too many tourists have weakened the floor in areas; if remedial work is carried out, disruption will be minimal. Last but far from least, in July 1999, Queen Elizabeth II presided over the opening ceremonies in Edinburgh of **Scotland**'s first Parliament in 300 years, revived by the current Labour government.

Greece

Dubbed the "airport for the new millennium," **Eleftherios Venizelos airport outside Athens** at Sparta is on schedule for a spring 2001 opening. Athens's much-needed beautification continues in preparation for the 2004 Olympics: the city plans to remodel **Omonia Square** in time for the opening of the new **Metro** line in 2000. The square will be covered over with a translucent dome, illuminating train platforms below with natural light, and sightseers will be able to view the Acropolis from specially positioned stands on the square.

In **Thessaloniki** the landmark White Tower will house a new **City Museum** in 2000, with exhibits mapping out the city's history from its founding in the 4th century BC to the 1922 Asia Minor disaster. One section will trace Thessaloniki's history through its monuments, another will highlight its commercial activities, demography, and native customs, and a third will focus on inhabitants' daily life. Built in the 15th century as part of the city fortifications, the White Tower became known as the Tower of Blood in the 19th century when it served as a prison. In the mid-1990s, the Byzantine works it housed were relocated to the nearby new Museum of Byzantine Civilization.

Archaeologists will replace the 2,600-year-old **marble lions of Delos** to prevent further damage from the Aegean sun and wind. Uninhabited Delos was one of ancient Greece's most sacred sites and the center of the Delian Confederacy. Still guarding the Sacred Lake are five of the original lions; after their removal they will be placed on display in the island's museum.

Hungary

With a new NATO membership and an invitation into the European Union on the more distant, but likely, horizon, Hungary stands at the center of Europe more and more prominently. The year 2000 marks the **Magyar Millennium,** the 1,000th anniversary of Hungary's founding as a state. In celebration, the government has allotted significant funds for improvements and restoration work on important sites throughout the country. Highlights include renovations for Budapest's National Museum, Museum of Fine Arts, and Museum of Applied Arts, as well as on 49 historic castles nationally.

Grand old **Budapest** is seeing more and more improvements and development, from private restoration of crumbling, once-elegant buildings to more pedestrian-only zones, as well as new restaurants and shops sprouting around the city.

Hungary continues to improve its **infrastructure.** In Budapest a fourth metro line through southern Buda was on hold at press time but still in the city's plans. Budapest's Ferihegy Airport has undergone a major expansion; its brand-new Terminal 2b opened in late 1998. Major highways continue to be upgraded and extended, and the antiquated telephone system is being overhauled.

Hungary's annual inflation rate has decreased dramatically from more than 25% to 10%, and with continued significant devaluation of the forint, exchange rates keep improving for visitors. Yet, while Hungary remains a bargain compared to Western Europe, strictly rock-bottom **prices** are a thing of the past as restaurant and hotel rates creep upward to compensate for the nation's shrinking currency.

Iceland

This year marks the **1000th anniversary of Icelander Leifur Eiríksson's discovery of North America.** To commemorate the event, Iceland is reawakening Viking culture in a big way, cooperating with, among others, the United States and Norway in **festivities celebrating Viking discoveries.** Eiríksson's birthplace farm, Eiríkstöð, near the village of Dalvík, has been the focus of intensive anthropological research, and it promises to be a major attraction this year. An **International Viking Festival 2000** includes saga tours that visit historic sites mentioned in Iceland's great sagas. And hoteliers and **Icelandic Farm Holidays** are busy adding new and better accommodations to welcome the travelers of the new millennium.

Nature advocates recently discovered that tiny Iceland has Europe's largest surviving block of intact wilderness, and for the adventuresome, highland and glacier safaris are spectacular and memorable experiences.

Another spectacle is **Keiko,** the Orca whale star of the film *Free Willy,* now in a wide-water pen off the Westman Island of Heimaey. He appears well on his way toward full rehabilitation for complete freedom. His celebrity status has brought attention to, and fostered other **whale-watching** ventures, notably in Húsavík on the north coast and Hafnarfjörður and Keflavík in the southwest.

Reykjavík is spruced up as one of the European Cultural Cities for the Year 2000 with a special version of the **Reykjavík Arts Festival** as a highlight. Kópavogi, the capital's immediate neighbor to the south, now boasts Iceland's first purpose-built concert hall. Much farther north, as if to more than match the capital's new covered ice-skating rink, **Akureyri** plans to meet the millennium with a new winter sports center.

Ireland

Ireland's **economy** continues to **boom** and the extraordinary expansion of Dublin progresses without any sign of abating. With standards of living soaring and unemployment at an all time low of around 6%, Ireland, and especially Dublin, is for the first time experiencing a net inflow of immigration over emigration. For the visitor this means a much more cosmopolitan city, where your waitress is as likely to be from Budapest as Blarney. New construction continues throughout the city, with the luxury Morrison Hotel yet another addition to the high-end lodging sector.

A major upgrading of Ireland's national routes is drawing near completion, yet as the **infrastructure** improves, traffic conditions seem to worsen. Cork, Galway, and Limerick are all seeing major increases in the number of cars but it is in Dublin that congestion has begun to approach the level of that in other major European cities.

Millennium celebrations in Ireland center on the country's biggest-ever fireworks display along the banks of the Liffey on New Year's Eve. The Millennium Needle, the tallest man-made structure in the country, is a giant monument that replaces the old Nelson's Pillar on O'Connell Street.

In **Northern Ireland** the all-party cease-fire has held for two years and the 1998 Good Friday agreement is close to being implemented. Assembly elections offered the historic outcome of a government containing both Unionists and Republican ministers. But last-minute disagreements about the issue of disarmament are threatening to topple the whole process. If implemented in full, the agreement will result in devolved government in the form of an assembly for Northern Ireland, an end to the South's constitutional claim to the North, a North-South Council to oversee cooperation on matters of mutual interest, and adherence to the principle that Northern Ireland will not leave the U.K. without the consent of a majority of the people of the province.

Italy

Rome marks the beginning of the third millennium after the birth of Christ with **Jubilee 2000** (Giubileo 2000), which is projected to bring 30 million tourists and religious pilgrims to the Eternal City. During 1999, Rome sprinted to the finish with large-scale public works and infrastructure projects, including the cleaning of the facade of St. Peter's Basilica itself. Rome will issue 12 million high-tech "Pilgrim ID" cards with special microchips to facilitate access to public transportation and religious sites and events. A multilingual Web site has been set up at www.Jubil2000.org. The **Shroud of Turin** (Sacra Sindone), arguably Italy's most famous holy relic, will be on display from August 26 to October 22, 2000.

Milan's new **Malpensa 2000** airport (MXP), now Italy's biggest aerial gateway to the rest of the world, finally opened amid much hoopla in late 1998. Malpensa 2000 was almost immediately plagued by problems ranging from sticky runway tar to lost luggage, topped off by reliably long delays that continued into 1999.

Bologna will serve as one of Europe's nine official Cultural Capitals for the year 2000, benefiting from improvements in infrastructure in anticipation of the festivities.

The **telephone number system** in Italy has changed: It is now always necessary to dial the 3-digit regional code, even when dialing locally, and you no longer drop the "0" in the regional code. For instance, to call Florence from within Florence, you dial "055" plus the local number.

Luxembourg

In Luxembourg City, from fall 1999 through March 2000, 19 **sculptures by Henry Moore** will be on display, 12 in the streets and parks of the city and seven in the Bank de Luxembourg headquarters on the Kirchberg. The new **sports center** under construction next to the Olympic swimming pool on the Kirchberg should open in 2000. The opening of the I. M. Pei–designed Grand Duke Jean Modern Art Museum has been postponed to 2001 or even 2002. From 3rd to 12th August 2000, Luxembourg hosts the European Hot Air Ballooning Championships near Larochette.

Malta

Diving schools are poppping up on Malta's quieter sister island, **Gozo,** where construction goes on apace, making it ever more visitor-friendly.

Netherlands

The Netherlands continues to be one of the most economically and socially stable countries in Europe. The Dutch feel comfortable with the move to the euro, though the logistics of the transition are daunting. Despite environmental issues, a serious consideration in a country that is so densely populated, **Schiphol Airport** is set to expand. In Amsterdam, the construction of the **Noord-Zuidlijn** (the North–South metro line) is about to start, using innovative boring techniques to prevent damage to historic buildings along the route.

The transformation of Amsterdam's central **Museumplein** was completed in mid-1999, creating a landscaped recreation area with stunning modernistic waterscapes as a backdrop for the newly completed extension to the Van Gogh Museum and the ongoing development of the Stedelijk Museum of Modern Art. **Exhibitions** to watch for in 2000 include 17th- and 18th-century still lifes from June to September at the Rijksmuseum in Amsterdam.

SAIL 2000 will bring a spectacular flotilla of three-masted ships up the North-Sea Canal to the Dutch capital at the conclusion of the World Tall Ships' Race. The Parade of Sail will take place on August 24—accompanied by a stunning fireworks display and other street events.

Among the year's other important cultural events are the annual, multidisciplinary **Holland Festival** throughout June, during which the **Netherlands Opera** will present its first-ever complete cycle of Wagner's four-part Ring music-drama. The three-day, star-studded **North Sea Jazz Festival** is held in The Hague on the second weekend in July, while the world-famous **Holland Festival of Early Music,** for lovers of music of the Renaissance and Baroque eras, is held in Utrecht during the last week of August.

Norway

A coalition of three centrist parties (Christian Democrat, Center, and Liberal) elected to power in 1997 still governs the country, although the opposition Labour party maintains its majority in Parliament. Norway has experienced more economic uncertainty than is usual over the last few years, especially when oil prices weakened during 1998. The country remains stable, however, and is for the time being committed to staying outside the European Union. The next general election takes place in 2001.

Although Oslo's new international **airport** at Gardermoen is among Europe's most modern, it still suffers from a score of teething problems. Delays are common, especially at busy periods in winter, when aircraft must wait in line for de-icing. The new high-speed airport express train operates from the heart of the airport complex direct to Oslo Central Station, with a journey time of around half an hour.

As one of nine European Cities of Culture in 2000, **Bergen** is hosting three season-based programs of art and folk events: Bergen will be celebrated in spring and autumn, while Norway's western fjord region is the focus of the summer festivities. Particular **annual events** that are worth attending are the National Day held every May 17, with celebrations in every village, town, and city throughout the country. In Oslo there is a three-hour long and very festive Children's Parade. Most adults wear national costume and a sense of restrained national pride abounds. Other events include the Ski-jumping World Cup held at the awe-inspiring and recently renovated Hol-menkollen International Ski Jump in March. Meanwhile, the Oslo Horse Show is held in October and the Oslo Marathon in September.

Poland

A tourism law, enacted in July 1998, is expected to improve facilities and service throughout the country. Existing hotels have two years to comply with the new system, which enforces standards for each star rating. Nevertheless, top hotels are still dodging the five-star rating, which carries 22% value-added tax, instead of 7% for lower ratings. **An increasing number of business travelers** continue to visit Poland, demanding more luxurious accommodations with high-tech facilities. Holiday Inn opened a hotel in Gdańsk across from the main train station in spring 1999. Meanwhile, a Hyatt International hotel is planned for construction in the attractive ulica Belwederska area of Warsaw.

The government has also rejuvenated the five-year-old **Polish Tourism Development Agency,** to promote construction of mid-range hotels for tourists. The action is part of an overall movement to improve Poland's infrastructure, from roads to highways to telecommunications. Further privatization of the Orbis chain, which owns more than 10,000 hotels nationwide, should bring improvements to them.

The big picture finds Poland approaching a number of European structures: It joined NATO in early 1999, while EU accession is projected for 2002 or 2003. Further down the line, EMU membership is planned for 2006.

Portugal

Portugal's program to digitalize its **phone network** continues. Not all recordings stating the new number are in English, so you may need the assistance of an international operator.

Many new stations on Lisbon's expanded **metro** (subway) system are operational and additional stations will continue to open through the year 2000. The opening of two ring road systems, completion of a north–south cross-city highway linking the Ponte 25 de Abril with the toll high-way to the north, the opening of a second bridge, the **Ponte Vasco de Gama,** and the start-up of a light suburban rail using the Ponte 25 de Abril crossing have all contributed to easing traffic congestion in and around the capital.

Development in Lisbon's **Chiado shopping district** continues, as the historic facades—destroyed in a 1988 fire—are slowly restored. The left-in-place nucleus of Lisbon's World Exposition, EXPO'98, has become the leisure hub of an ambitious riverfront development site. Baptized **Parque das Nações,** the area has waterfront restaurants and Europe's biggest oceanarium among its attractions. Vasco da Gama Shopping, a huge shopping center with a multiscreen cinema, opened there in April 1999. In addition, the Feira Internacional de Lisboa (FIL), or trade fair center, moved there from Alcantara in 1999. **New hotels** are springing up throughout Lisbon. In addition to the Meliá Confort Oriente at Parque das Naçóes, and the new hotels in the Chiado, the Dom Pedro Lisboa, near Amoreiras, is also set for completion by 2000. In the Parque Eduardo VII, a **public swimming pool** is planned alongside the new tennis courts. Lisbon's camping site in the Monsanto woods has reopened as a deluxe spot with vastly improved facilities.

Out along the **Estoril coast,** renovations and landscaping to the seawall and promenade came to fruition during 1999. In a joint program with the EU, the **Algarve** region is currently replacing its many (and often confusing) road signs with clear, color-coded, easy-to-read markers.

Romania

The strict guidelines for its coveted admission to NATO and the EU have helped Romania to look realistically at what is necessary to rebuild the nation following its years under a dictatorship. The number of private establishments is increasing steadily. The government has agreed to discourage the country's long-standing policy of charging foreigners higher rates than Romanians. An increase in competition among travel agencies has helped to strengthen efforts to attract visitors.

Slovakia

A new pro-democratic government that resulted from parliamentary elections in fall 1998 is firmly leading the country toward **European Union membership.** Since its 1993 separation from the Czechs, Slovakia has seen a fast **privatization** process followed by **renovations** of buildings of any historical value throughout the country. Groups of opera fans from Vienna often come to see performances at the Slovak National Theater in Bratislava. Musicians and music lovers from around the world come to the annual **Classical Music Festival of Bratislava** in the fall.

Bratislava has a **new railway terminal** that will soon be served by a new, faster railway track to Vienna. Since 1997 the country's 6% to 7% inflation rate has been the lowest among the post-communist countries of Central and Eastern Europe.

Slovenia

In the nine years since gaining independence, Slovenia has done all it could to shrug off the Yugoslav image. Now at the top of the list among countries queuing up for NATO and EU membership, this tiny nation identifies more closely with Austria than with its Slav neighbors.

Spain

Barcelona's opera house, the **Gran Teatre del Liceu,** is one of the most beautiful in Europe. First built in 1847, it was gutted in early 1994 by a fire of still-uncertain origins but has finally reopened after a spectacular restoration. Even if you don't see an opera, inquire about tours of the building; some of the Liceu's oldest and most spectacular halls and rooms were unharmed by the fire.

The gleaming **Guggenheim Museum Bilbao,** designed by American architect Frank Gehry, has transformed Bilbao, capital of the Basque country, from an industrial blot to a Place to Be. This titanium landmark houses cubist, expressionist, surrealist, and geometrical and abstract expressionist works. In Catalonia, the Spanish Ministry of Tourism is now operating a **Dalí triangle,** which includes not only the Museu Dalí, in Figueres, but the artist's fishing shack

in Port Lligat, near Cadaqués, and his castle in Pubol. Starting from Barcelona, the triangular tour of Dalí's personal world covers roughly 140 miles and crosses some of the most beautiful countryside in Catalonia.

Sweden

A much-anticipated **airport high-speed express train** started operation between Stockholm's Central Station and Arlanda Airport in August 1999. Traveling at speeds of 160–200 kph (100–125 mph), the train makes the trip in only 20 minutes and runs four times an hour. A one-way ticket costs SKr120. Spending the night out in the **Stockholm archipelago** is easier and cheaper than ever as hotels and youth hostels are spreading throughout the islands. More information and guided English-language tours are available through the Stockholm Information Service.

Switzerland

Recent dips in the the Swiss franc's clout have eased the pain for American visitors. Skiers who annually converge on Graubünden resorts will have their path considerably smoothed; the **Vereina Tunnel,** stretching from Klosters to Susch/Lavin, is slated for completion in late fall 1999. The railway will load cars and whisk away twice an hour from each terminal—an especially big blessing when the Flüela Pass is closed by snow.

Luzern's **Kultur- und Kongresszentrum,** the new home of the prestigious International Music Festival, plans to open a museum in its stunning complex by summer 2000.

Little visible damage remains from the series of severe avalanches in winter 1998–99, even though in some resorts and villages such as Wengen, buildings were demolished by snow slides.

Turkey

In early 1999 there appeared little prospect of an end to the **political instability** that has dogged Turkey throughout the 1990s. Turks went to the polls in April 1999 to elect their eighth government in less than four years. The election produced neither a stable government nor an end to the deepening social polarization between Turkey's grassroots nationalist/Islamist movement and its secular establishment, headed by the country's powerful military.

Europe

Political instability and the repercussions of the Asian financial crisis produced a sharp economic slowdown in late 1998 and early 1999. But the downturn in economic activity helped curb country's long-term **chronic inflation.** By early 1999 annual consumer inflation rate had fallen to under 70% for the first time in five years. But in dollar terms Turkey nevertheless remained one of the least expensive countries in Europe.

At press time it was still too early to assess the full impact of the earthquake that shook northwestern Turkey in mid-August 1999. All of the tourist sites and major hotels in central Istanbul and Bursa escaped virtually unscathed, but there was considerable damage to the infrastructure, particularly land and sea communications east of Istanbul, linking the city with Ankara, Yalova, and Bursa. However, there was no damage to Istanbul airport and flights continued to operate normally. Nor was there any damage in the Aegean, Mediterranean, Eastern Black Sea, Central, or Eastern Anatolian regions. Travelers planning to visit, or pass through, the area east of the Sea of Marmara should check carefully with the Turkish embassy, consulate, or tourist office before embarking.

FINLAND

Gulf of Bothnia

Oslo SWEDEN

Helsinki *Gulf of Finland* **St. Petersburg**

Tallinn ESTONIA

Stockholm

rrak *Kattegat* **Göteborg**

Riga LATVIA

Moscow

Copenhagen LITHUANIA

Baltic Sea **Kaunas** RUSSIA

Vilnius

Kaliningrad **Minsk**

Berlin POLAND BELARUS

MANY **Warsaw**

Kraków

Prague UKRAINE **Kiev**

CZECH REPUBLIC

SLOVAKIA

ich **Vienna** **Bratislava**

Salzburg **Budapest** MOLDOVA

AUSTRIA HUNGARY **Chişinău**

EIN SLOVENIA

Ljubljana **Zagreb** ROMANIA

nice CROATIA **Novi Sad**

BOSNIA AND **Bucharest**

HERZEGOVINA **Belgrade** *Black Sea*

Adriatic Sea **Sarajevo** SERBIA

YUGOSLAVIA BULGARIA

Rome MONTENEGRO KOSOVO

Podgorica **Priština** **Sofia**

ITALY **Skopje** **Istanbul**

Tiranë MACEDONIA

Naples ALBANIA **Ankara**

TURKEY

ian Sea GREECE

Aegean Sea

Ionian Sea

Sicily **Athens**

MALTA *Crete* CYPRUS

Mediterranean Sea

World Time Zones

Numbers below vertical bands relate each zone to Greenwich Mean Time (0 hrs.).
Local times frequently differ from these general indications,
as indicated by light-face numbers on map.

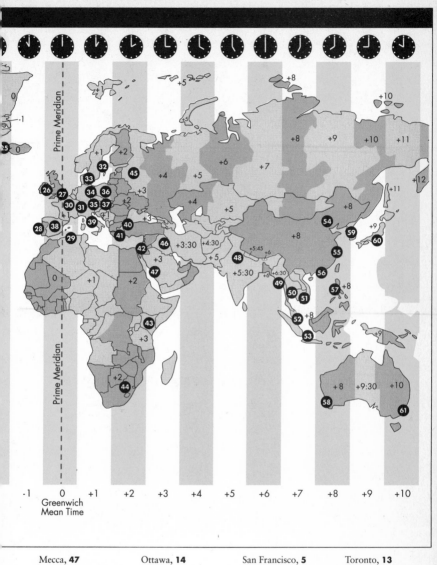

1 SMART TRAVEL TIPS A TO Z

SMART TRAVEL TIPS

Before booking, **compare different modes of transportation.** Many city pairs are so close together that flying hardly makes sense. For instance, it may take just half an hour to fly between London and Paris, but you must factor in time spent getting to and from the airports, plus check-in time. A 3-hour train ride from city center to city center seems a better alternative. It makes sense to **save air travel for longer distances**—say, between London and Rome, Paris and Vienna, Brussels and Stockholm—and do your local traveling from these hubs.

If you're flying so-called **national carriers,** full-fare tickets often remain the only kind available for one-way trips and restriction-free round-trips, and they are prohibitively expensive for most leisure travelers. On most European flights, your choice is between Business Class (which is what you get when paying full fare) and Economy (coach). Some flights are all Economy. First Class has ceased to exist in Europe. The most reasonable fares have long been non-refundable and non-transferable round trips (APEX fares), which require a Saturday night at the destination. But the near-monopoly that used to be enjoyed by these airlines is crumbling, and they have had to start offering less restrictive fares. Check before you fly.

Some national carriers reward transatlantic passengers with fixed-price flight coupons (priced at $100–$120) to destinations from their respective hubs and/or domestic or area air passes. These must be bought before leaving home. If you're young, **ask about youth stand-by fares,** which are available on a number of domestic and some international services.

Over the last few years, a substantial number of local airlines have been created to provide feeder services to major hubs and services between secondary city pairs. Do not, however, expect rock-bottom prices. **Seek advice from local branches of interna-tional travel agencies** like American Express or Carlson/Wagonlit.

Low-cost no-frills airlines base their fares on one-way travel, and a return ticket is simply twice the price. Advertised fares are always preceded by the word "from." To get the lowest fare, book two weeks ahead of time; it also helps to be flexible about your date of travel. In general, you have to book directly by calling the airline, credit card in hand. Some also accept reservations by fax. Reservation via Internet is available with companies such as SABRE (http://www.easysabre .com). You can make secure payments via the net and hunt the cheapest flight deals, as well as reserve hotels. You get a reservation number and pick up your boarding pass at the airport. Note that some flights use relatively distant secondary airports.

ARRIVALS

Passport control has become a perfunctory affair within most of the European Union (EU). The nine signatories to the Schengen Agreement (Austria, Belgium, France, Germany, Italy, Luxembourg, The Netherlands, Portugal and Spain) have abolished passport controls for travelers between countries in that area, but individual countries can temporarily suspend it.

The most notable exception is Great Britain; when a number of flights from the U.S. arrive at Heathrow or Gatwick close together in the morning, **be prepared for a longish wait** (though rarely as long as Europeans have to wait at JFK in New York).

The Green Channel/Red Channel customs system in operation at most Western European airports and other borders is basically an honor system. If you have nothing to declare, walk through the Green Channel, where there are only spot luggage checks; if in doubt, go through the Red Channel. If you fly between two EU-member countries, go through the new **Blue Channel,** where there are no customs officers except the one who glances at baggage labels to make sure only people off EU flights get through. On average, you need to **count on at least half an hour from deplaning to getting out of the airport.**

BOOKING YOUR FLIGHT

When you book **look for nonstop flights** and **remember that "direct" flights stop at least once.** Try to avoid connecting flights, which require a change of plane.

CARRIERS

When flying internationally, you must usually choose between a domestic carrier, the national flag carrier of the country you are visiting, and a foreign carrier from a third country. National flag carriers have the greatest number of nonstops. Domestic carriers may have better connections to your home town and serve a greater number of gateway cities. Third-party carriers may have a price advantage.

➤ U.S. AIRLINES: **American** (☎ 800/ 433–7300). **Continental** (☎ 800/525– 0280). **Delta** (☎ 800/221–1212). **Northwest** (☎ 800/225–2525). **TWA** (☎ 800/221–2000). **United** (☎ 800/ 241–6522). **US Airways** (☎ 800/428– 4322).

➤ EUROPEAN AIRLINES: Austria: **Austrian Airlines** (☎ 800/843–0002). Belgium: **Sabena Belgian World Airlines** (☎ 800/955–2000). The Czech Republic and Slovakia: **Czech Airlines** (CSA, ☎ 212/765–6022). Denmark: **Scandinavian Airlines** (SAS, ☎ 800/221–2350). Finland: **Finnair** (☎ 800/950–5000). France: **Air France** (☎ 800/237–2747). Germany: **Lufthansa** (☎ 800/645– 3880). Great Britain: **British Airways** (☎ 800/247–9297). **Virgin Atlantic** (☎ 800/862–8621). Greece: **Olympic Airways** (☎ 212/838–3600 or 800/ 223–1226). Hungary: **Malév Hungarian Airlines** (☎ 212/757–6446, 800/ 223–6884 outside NY only). Iceland: **Icelandair** (☎ 800/223–5500). Ireland: **Aer Lingus** (☎ 888/474–7424 or 800/223–6537). Italy: **Alitalia** (☎ 800/223–5730). Netherlands: **KLM Royal Dutch Airlines** (☎ 800/ 447–4747). Norway: **SAS** (☎ 800/ 221–2350). Poland: **LOT Polish Airlines** (☎ 212/869–1074). Portugal: **TAP Air Portugal** (☎ 800/221–7370).

Romania: **Tarom Romanian Air Transport** (☎ 212/687–6013). Spain: **Iberia Airlines** (☎ 800/772–4642). Sweden: **SAS** (☎ 800/221–2350). Switzerland: **Swissair** (☎ 800/221– 4750). Turkey: **THY Turkish Airlines** (☎ 212/339–9650).

➤ FROM CANADA: **Air Canada** (☎ 800/776–3000). **Air Transat** (☎ 877/ 872–6728).

➤ FROM THE U.K.: **British Airways** (✉ 156 Regent St., London W1R 5TA, ☎ 0345/222–111). **British Midland** (☎ 0345/554–554). **Debonair** (☎ 0541/500–300. **EasyJet** (☎ 0990/29–29–29 or 01582/44–55– 55). **KLMuk** (☎ 0990/750–900). **Ryanair** (☎ 0541/569–569). **Virgin Express** (☎ 0800/89–11–99).

➤ FROM AUSTRALIA: **Qantas Airways** (☎ within Sydney 2/957–0111; from outside Sydney 008/112121).

➤ FROM IRELAND: **Aer Lingus** (☎ 01/ 705–3333).

➤ FROM NEW ZEALAND: **Air New Zealand** (☎ 0800–737–000).

➤ NO-FRILLS CARRIER RESERVATIONS WITHIN EUROPE: Belgium: **Virgin Express** (☎ 32/2/752–0505) from Brussels to Milan, Rome, Nice, Madrid, Barcelona, Copenhagen, and London; from Rome to Barcelona and Madrid; and all **Sabena** flights to London, Barcelona, and Rome. Ireland: **Ryanair** (☎ 01/844–4400 in Ireland; 0541/569–569, FAX 0541/ 580–588 in the U.K.) from Dublin to 12 U.K. destinations, to Paris (Beauvais) and Brussels (Charleroi); from London (Stansted, Luton, and Gatwick) to Dublin; from London (Stansted) to Stockholm (Skavsta) and Oslo (Torp). United Kingdom: **Debonair** (☎ 0541/500–300) from London (Luton) to Düsseldorf (Mönchengladbach), Barcelona, Copenhagen, Madrid, Munich, Nice, Milan (Bergamo), and Rome (Ciampino); from Munich to Copenhagen, Düsseldorf, Nice, Madrid, and Rome; from Barcelona to Madrid and Rome; and from northern Italian cities to Calabria. **EasyJet** (☎ 01582/ 700–059) from London (Luton) to Amsterdam, Athens, Barcelona, Nice,

Palma de Mallorca and four Scottish destinations; from Liverpool to Amsterdam and Nice. **Go** (☎ 08456/054–321) from London (Stansted) to Edinburgh, Lisbon, Munich, Copenhagen, and four Italian destinations.

CHECK-IN & BOARDING

Assuming that not everyone with a ticket will show up, airlines routinely overbook planes. When that happens, airlines ask for volunteers to give up their seats. In return these volunteers usually get a certificate for a free flight and are rebooked on the next flight out. If there are not enough volunteers, the airline must choose who will be denied boarding. The first to get bumped are passengers who checked in late and those flying on discounted tickets, so **get to the gate and check in as early as possible,** especially during peak periods.

Always **bring a government-issued photo ID to the airport.** You may be asked to show it before you are allowed to check in.

Also, **be sure baggage is ticketed properly** and that the correct ticket/stub/coupon is taken for the current leg of your trip.

CUTTING COSTS

The least-expensive airfares to Europe must usually be purchased in advance and are non-refundable. It's smart to **call a number of airlines, and when you are quoted a good price, book it on the spot**—the same fare may not be available the next day. Always **check different routings** and look into using different airports. Travel agents, especially low-fare specialists (☞ Discounts & Deals, *below*), are helpful.

Consolidators are another good source. They buy tickets for scheduled international flights at reduced rates from the airlines, then sell them at prices that beat the best fare available directly from the airlines, usually without restrictions. Sometimes you can even get your money back if you need to return the ticket. Carefully read the fine print detailing penalties for changes and cancellations, and **confirm your consolidator reservation with the airline.**

When you **fly as a courier** you trade your checked-luggage space for a ticket deeply subsidized by a courier service. There are restrictions on when you can book and how long you can stay.

Ask your airline about purchasing discount passes for intra-European flights before you leave the United States to save significantly on travel between European cities.

➤ CONSOLIDATORS: **Cheap Tickets** (☎ 800/377–1000). **Up & Away Travel** (☎ 212/889–2345). **Discount Airline Ticket Service** (☎ 800/576–1600). **Unitravel** (☎ 800/325–2222). **World Travel Network** (☎ 800/409–6753).

➤ COURIERS: **Air Courier Association** (✉ 15000 W. 6th Ave., Suite 203, Golden, CO 80401, ☎ 800/282–1202, www.aircourier.org).

International Association of Air Travel Couriers (✉ 220 South Dixie Highway #3, P.O. Box 1349, Lake Worth, FL, 33460, ☎ 561/582–8320, FAX 561/582–1581, www.courier.org).

Now Voyager Travel (✉ 74 Varick St., Suite 307, New York, NY 10013, ☎ 212/431–1616, FAX 212/219–1753 or 212/334–5243, www.nowvoyager-travel.com).

➤ DISCOUNT PASSES: **British Airways** (☎ 800/247–9297). **KLM Royal Dutch Airlines** (☎ 800/447–4747). **Sabena Belgian World Airlines** (☎ 800/955–2000). **Swissair** (☎ 800/221–4750).

ENJOYING THE FLIGHT

For more legroom **request an emergency-aisle seat.** Don't sit in the row in front of the emergency aisle or in front of a bulkhead, where seats may not recline. If you have dietary concerns, **ask for special meals when booking.** These can be vegetarian, low-cholesterol, or kosher, for example. On long flights, try to maintain a normal routine, to help fight jet lag. At night **get some sleep.** By day **eat lightly, drink water** (not alcohol), and **move around the cabin** to stretch your legs.

Choose a flight that leaves the east coast of the United States in the evening and start the day in Europe with more time in your destination and reduced sleep disruption.

FLYING TIMES

Flights from New York to London take about 6½ hours, to Paris 7½ hours, to Frankfurt 7½ hours, and to Rome 8½ hours. From Sydney to London, flights take about 23 hours via Bangkok, to Paris 22¾ hours via Singapore, to Frankfurt 22 hours via Singapore, and to Rome 25 hours via Bangkok. Flights from Auckland to London take about 24 hours and to Frankfurt 23 hours.

HOW TO COMPLAIN

If your baggage goes astray or your flight goes awry, complain right away. Most carriers require that you **file a claim immediately.**

➤ AIRLINE COMPLAINTS: U.S. Department of Transportation **Aviation Consumer Protection Division** (✉ C-75, Room 4107, Washington, DC 20590, ☎ 202/366–2220). **Federal Aviation Administration Consumer Hotline** (☎ 800/322–7873).

RECONFIRMING

Depending on the airline or on whether your ticket was bought through a consolidator, you may have to reconfirm your flights a specified number of hours before departure. **Check with your travel agent or airline** when you buy your ticket.

AIRPORTS

☞ Essentials *in* city sections of country chapters.

DUTY-FREE SHOPPING

Duty-free shopping was eliminated in EU countries as of July 1, 1999. In non-EU countries, if you're looking for good deals associated with duty-free airport shopping, **check out liquor and beauty products,** although prices vary considerably. The amount of liquor you may buy is restricted, generally to two bottles.

Some airport concourses, notably in Amsterdam, Copenhagen, and Shannon, have practically been transformed into shopping malls, selling everything from electronics and chocolates to fashion and furs. These are tax-free rather than duty-free shops; if this is your last stop before leaving the EU there's no VAT and you can **avoid the tax-refund rigmarole.**

BIKE TRAVEL

Some ferry lines transport bicycles free, but others charge a nominal fee, so **shop around.** You can also transport your bicycle by air as checked baggage (☞ Bikes in Flight, *below*). Most European rail lines will transport bicycles free of charge or for a nominal fee, but **book ahead** with the main booking office.

Local and regional tourist information offices will have information about renting bicycles, camping sites, cycling tracks, and local bike tours. (For bike tours of Europe, ☞ Tours & Packages, *below*.)

BIKES IN FLIGHT

Most airlines accommodate bikes as luggage, provided they are dismantled and boxed. For bike boxes, often free at bike shops, you'll pay about $5 (at least $100 for bike bags) from airlines. International travelers can sometimes substitute a bike for a piece of checked luggage at no charge; otherwise, the cost is about $100. Domestic and Canadian airlines charge $25–$50.

BOAT & FERRY TRAVEL

Ferry routes for passengers and vehicles link the countries surrounding the North Sea, the Irish Sea, and the Baltic Sea; Italy with Greece; and Spain, France, Italy, and Greece with their respective islands in the Mediterranean. Longer ferry routes—between, for instance, Britain and Spain or Scandinavia—can help you **reduce the amount of driving and often save time.** A number of modern ships offer improved comfort and entertainment ranging from one-armed bandits to gourmet dining and from swimming pools to magicians to keep the kids happy.

FARES & SCHEDULES

☞ Individual country chapters, or contact operators for specific information on fares and schedules.

➤ BOAT & FERRY INFORMATION: Ferry operators between the British Isles and the Continent include: **Brittany**

Ferries (✉ Millbay Docks, Plymouth PL1 3EW, ☎ 0990/360–360) from Plymouth to Roscoff (Brittany) and Santander (Spain), from Poole to Cherbourg, and from Portsmouth to Caen and St. Malo; **Fjord Line** (✉ International Ferry Terminal, Royal Quays, North Shields NE29 6EE, ☎ 0191/296–1313), from Newcastle to Bergen/Stavanger/Haugesund (Norway); **Hoverspeed** (✉ International Hoverport, Marine Parade, Dover, Kent CT17 9TG, ☎ 0990/240–241), Dover–Calais, Dover–Oostend, Folkestone–Boulogne, Newhaven–Dieppe, Stranraer–Belfast, and Liverpool–Dublin; **Irish Ferries** (✉ Reliance House, Water St., Liverpool L2 8TP, ☎ 0990/171–717), Holyhead–Dublin and Pembroke–Rosslare; also Rosslare (Ireland; reservations 01/638–3333) to Cherbourg, and Roscoff; **P&O Stena Line** (✉ Channel House, Channel View Rd., Dover, Kent CT17 9TJ, ☎ 0870/600–0600), Dover–Calais; **P&O European Ferries** (☎ 0870/242–4999 sails Portsmouth to Le Havre and Bilbao (Spain), and Cairnyarn (Scotland)–Larne (Belfast); **P&O North Sea Ferries** (✉ King George Dock, Hedon Rd., Hull HU9 5QA, ☎ 01482/377–177), from Hull to Rotterdam; **Scandinavian Seaways** (✉ Scandinavia House, Parkeston Quay, Harwich, Essex CO12 4QG, ☎ 01255/240–240), from Harwich to Esbjerg (Denmark), Hamburg, and Gothenburg and from Newcastle-upon-Tyne to IJmuiden, 20 miles west of Amsterdam and (summer season) Gothenburg and Hamburg; **SeaFrance** (✉ Eastern Docks, Dover, Kent CT16 1JA, ☎ 01304/212–696), Dover–Calais; **Stena Line** (✉ Charter House, Park St., Ashford, Kent TN24 8EX, ☎ 0990/707–070), Harwich–Hook of Holland, Holyhead–Dun Laoghaire (Dublin), Fishguard–Rosslare, and Stranraer (Scotland)–Belfast; and **Swansea Cork Ferries** (✉ Harbour Office, Kings Dock, Swansea SA1 1SF, ☎ 01792/456–116), Swansea–Cork (March–Jan.).

BUS TRAVEL

International bus travel is rapidly expanding in Europe, thanks to changing EU rules and the Channel Tunnel, but it still has some way to go before it achieves the status of a natural choice, except in Britain and Sweden. In other northern European countries, bus services exist mostly to supplement railroads. Some bus routes between northern Europe and the Mediterranean area cater mostly to low-income immigrants visiting their home countries.

Within several southern European countries—including Portugal, Greece, parts of Spain, and Turkey—the bus has supplanted the train as the main means of public transportation, and is often quicker and more comfortable, with more frequent service, than the antiquated national rolling stock. Be prepared to discover that the bus is more expensive. Competition among lines is keen, so **ask about air-conditioning and reclining seats before you book.**

Eurolines comprises 30 motor-coach operators of international scheduled services. They also transport passengers within each country. The 30-nation network serves 1500 cities with services ranging from twice weekly to five times daily. Eurolines has its own coach stations in Paris (✉ 28 av. du Général de Gaulle at Bagnelot; Métro: Gallieni), Brussels (80 rue du Progrès, next to the Gare du Nord), and Amsterdam (adjacent to the Amstel Railway Station). In other cities, coaches depart from railway stations or municipal bus terminals.

From the U.K., Eurolines links London with 400 destinations on the European Continent and Ireland, from Stockholm to Rome, from Dublin to Bucharest. All are via Calais, using either ferry services or Le Shuttle/Eurotunnel under the English Channel. Buses leave from Victoria Coach Station (adjoining the railway station). Services link up with the National Express network covering the U.K.

Busabout service has passes that are not time limited and can be used throughout the April-to-October season. Starting from Paris, Zone 1 takes in Copenhagen and central Europe, Zone 2 extends south to Italy and Zone 3 to Spain. There are also links to London and Athens.

The same company offers **Bedabout,** providing accommodation in tent cities in 10 key locations at peak season when other low-budget accommodations tend to be fully booked; 10 nights cost $125.

National or regional tourist offices have information about bus services. For reservations on major lines before you go, **contact your travel agent at home.**

CUTTING COSTS

The **Eurolines Pass** allows unlimited travel between 40 European cities on scheduled bus services. A 30-day summer pass costs $379 ($329 for those under 26 or over 60); a 60-day pass costs $449 ($409). Passes can be bought from Eurolines offices and travel agents in Europe and from the companies listed below.

➤ DISCOUNT PASSES: In the U.S.: Eurolines Passes can be purchased from **DER Travel Services** (✉ 9501 W. Devon Ave., Rosemont, IL 60018, ☎ 800/782–2424, 847/692–6300 in Illinois), and from most Hostelling International and all STA offices (☞ Students in Europe, *below*).

FARES & SCHEDULES

For specific fares and schedules, ☞ individual country chapters, or contact bus operators.

➤ BUS INFORMATION: **Busabout (UK) Ltd.** (✉ 258 Vauxhall Bridge Rd., London, SW1V 1BF, ☎ 020/7950–1661, ℻ 020/7950–1661). **Eurolines** (✉ 52 Grosvenor Gardens, London SW1 WOAU, ☎ 0990/143–219 or 020/7730–8235). **Eurolines (UK)** (✉ 4 Cardiff Rd., Luton LU1 1HX, ☎ 01582/404–511, ℻ 01582/400–694). For brochures and timetables, contact the **Eurolines Pass Organization** (✉ Keizersgracht 317, 1016 EE Amsterdam, Netherlands, ☎ 020/625–3010, ℻ 020/420–6904).

CAMERAS & PHOTOGRAPHY

➤ PHOTO HELP: **Kodak Information Center** (☎ 800/242–2424). *Kodak Guide to Shooting Great Travel Pictures,* available in bookstores or from Fodor's Travel Publications (☎ 800/533–6478; $16.50 plus $4 shipping).

EQUIPMENT PRECAUTIONS

Always **keep your film and tape out of the sun.** Carry an extra supply of batteries, and **be prepared to turn on your camera or camcorder** to prove to security personnel that the device is real. Always **ask for hand inspection of film,** which becomes clouded after successive exposures to airport X-ray machines, and **keep videotapes away from metal detectors.**

CAR RENTAL

The great attraction of renting is obviously that you become independent of public transport. Cost-wise, you should **consider renting a car only if you are with at least one other person;** single travelers pay a tremendous premium. Car rental costs vary from country to country; rates in Scandinavia and Eastern Europe are particularly high. If you're visiting a number of countries with varying rates, it makes sense to **rent a vehicle in the cheapest country.** For instance, if you plan to visit Normandy, the same company that rents you a car for a weekly rate of $246 in Paris will rent you one for $159 in Brussels, adding a few hours to your trip but at a 35% savings.

Picking up a car at an airport is convenient but often costs extra (up to 10%) as rental companies pass along the fees charged to them by airports.

Rates in London begin at $39 a day and $136 a week for an economy car with air conditioning, a manual transmission, and unlimited mileage. Rates in Paris begin at $60 a day and $196 a week. Rates in Madrid begin at $37 a day and $132 a week. Rates in Rome begin at $49 a day and $167 a week. Rates in Frankfurt begin at $18 a day and $91 a week. These figures do not include tax on car rentals, which ranges from 15% to 21%.

➤ MAJOR AGENCIES: **Alamo** (☎ 800/522–9696; 020/8759–6200 in the U.K.). **Avis** (☎ 800/331–1084; 800/879–2847 in Canada; 02/9353–9000 in Australia; 09/525–1982 in New Zealand). **Budget** (☎ 800/527–0700; 0144/227–6266 in the U.K.). **Dollar** (☎ 800/800–6000; 020/8897–0811 in the U.K., where it is known as

SMART TRAVEL TIPS

Eurodollar, 02/9223–1444 in Australia). **Hertz** (☎ 800/654–3001; 800/263–0600 in Canada; 020/8897–2072 in the U.K.; 02/9669–2444 in Australia; 03/358–6777 in New Zealand). **National InterRent** (☎ 800/227–3876; 0345/222525 in the U.K., where it is known as Europcar InterRent).

CUTTING COSTS

If you think you'll need a car in Europe but are unsure about when or where, ask your travel agent to check out Kemwel's CarPass. This gives the benefit of pre-paid vouchers with the flexibility of last-minute bookings in Europe. Unused vouchers are refunded. To get the best deal **book through a travel agent who will shop around.**

Do **look into wholesalers,** companies that do not own fleets but rent in bulk from those that do and often offer better rates than traditional car-rental operations. Payment must be made before you leave home. Short-term leasing can save money if you need a rental for more than 17 days. Kemwel and Europe by Car are among the wholesalers offering such deals.

➤ WHOLESALERS: **Auto Europe** (☎ 207/842–2000 or 800/223–5555, FAX 800/235–6321). **Europe by Car** (☎ 212/581–3040 or 800/223–1516, FAX 212/246–1458). **DER Travel Services** (✉ 9501 W. Devon Ave., Rosemont, IL 60018, ☎ 800/782–2424, FAX 800/282–7474 for information; 800/860–9944 for brochures). **Kemwel Holiday Autos** (☎ 914/835–3000 or 800/678–0678, FAX 914/835–5126).

INSURANCE

When driving a rented car you are generally responsible for any damage to or loss of the vehicle. Before you rent see what coverage your personal auto-insurance policy and credit cards already provide.

Collision policies that car-rental companies sell for European rentals usually do not include stolen-vehicle coverage. Before you buy it, check your existing policies—you may already be covered. Note that in Italy, all car-rental companies make you buy theft-protection policies.

REQUIREMENTS & RESTRICTIONS

Your own driver's license is acceptable virtually everywhere. An International Driver's Permit is a good idea, especially if your travel is likely to include Eastern Europe; it's available from the American or Canadian automobile association, and, in the United Kingdom, from the Automobile Association or Royal Automobile Club. These international permits are universally recognized, and having one in your wallet may save you a problem with the local authorities.

SURCHARGES

Before you pick up a car in one city and leave it in another **ask about drop-off charges or one-way service fees,** which can be substantial. Note, too, that some rental agencies charge extra if you return the car before the time specified in your contract. To avoid a hefty refueling fee **fill the tank just before you turn in the car,** but be aware that gas stations near the rental outlet may overcharge.

CAR TRAVEL

Unless you're in a rush to get from A to B, you will find it rewarding to **avoid the freeways and use the alternative and toll-free main routes.** Wherever you're driving, **be sure to carry a good road map.** You can purchase maps in bookshops and many newsstands at home and throughout Europe. City maps of major cities are generally available at service stations close to the destination.

Motorway tolls can easily add $25 a day to your costs in driving through France, and there are toll roads throughout southern Europe, as well as charges for many tunnels. When crossing borders into Switzerland, you're charged 40 Swiss francs (about $30) for a *vignette* that entitles you to use Swiss freeways for a year. To get a handle on costs, **ask the national tourist office or car rental firm about tolls before you travel.**

If you are driving a rented car, **be sure to carry the necessary papers provided by the rental company.** For U.K. citizens, if the vehicle is your own, you will need proof of ownership, a certificate of roadworthiness (known as a Ministry of Transport, or MOT, road vehicle certificate), up-to-date vehicle registration or tax certificate, and a Green Card proof of insurance, available from your insurance company (fees vary depending on destination and length of stay).

Border controls have been abolished within the EU (except in the U.K., Ireland, Scandinavia, and Greece). The border posts are still standing, but drivers whiz through them without slowing down. Truck traffic is generally routed to separate checkpoints.

Drivers traveling between Great Britain and the Continent can now **consider using the Eurotunnel,** the train carrying cars, buses, motorbikes and trucks, plus their passengers, through the Channel Tunnel between Folkestone and Calais in 35 minutes. The loading areas have an almost space-age feel, as you drive your car into the silver sheet-metal wagons. The shuttle trains operate continuously—three to four trains per hour—and reservations are not needed, but to avoid queueing, tickets can be bought in advance from travel agents or by credit card from **Eurotunnel** (☎ 321006400 in France, 0990/353–535 in the U.K.). Prices vary according to length of stay on the continent, as well as the time of travel. Prices given are for return fares throughout most of the year, but do not account for the summer peak fares during July and August. Depending on travel dates, a short break (less than 5 days) costs Euro 165–265, and a standard return costs Euro 259–425. Club Class gives you the right to priority queueing and entry to the Club Class lounge for a premium of about 35%. To calculate single fares simply divide by two. Note that you must make advance reservations to benefit from promotional fares and special offers. *See* The Channel Tunnel, *below,* and Ferries, *above.*

AUTO CLUBS

➤ In Australia: **Australian Automobile Association** (☎ 02/6247–7311).

➤ In Canada: **Canadian Automobile Association** (CAA, ☎ 613/247–0117).

➤ In New Zealand: **New Zealand Automobile Association** (☎ 09/377–4660).

➤ In the U.K.: **Automobile Association** (AA, ☎ 0990/500–600). **Royal Automobile Club** (RAC, ☎ 0990/722–722 for membership; 0345/121–345 for insurance).

➤ In the U.S.: **American Automobile Association** (☎ 800/564–6222).

EMERGENCIES

You must carry a reflecting red triangle (to be placed well behind your car in case of breakdown). A first-aid kit and fire extinguisher are strongly recommended.

GASOLINE

Be prepared: Gasoline costs three to four times more than in the United States, due to heavy taxes. The better fuel economy of European cars offsets the higher price to some extent.

ROAD CONDITIONS

During peak vacation periods, main routes can be jammed with holiday traffic. In the United Kingdom, **try to avoid driving during any of the long bank-holiday (public holiday) weekends,** when motorways are invariably clogged. The tunnels carrying traffic between Italy and the countries to the north are often overburdened with truck traffic; cross the Alps on a weekend, if you can. In France, Greece, Spain, and Italy, huge numbers of people still take a fixed one-month vacation in August, so **avoid driving during** le départ, the first weekend in August, when vast numbers of drivers head south; or le retour, when they head back.

RULES OF THE ROAD

Establishing a speed limit for German motorways has proved a tougher nut than any successive government could crack. On the rest of the Continent, the limit is generally 130 kph (80 mph), but the cruising speed is mostly about 140 kph (about 87 mph). In the United Kingdom, the speed limit is 70 mph (112 kph), but there, too, passing at considerably higher speed is not uncommon. For safe driving, **stay in the slower lane unless you want to pass, and make way for faster cars wanting to pass you.** Much of the time traffic is heavier than is common on U.S. freeways outside major city rush hours.

In the United Kingdom, the Republic of Ireland, Malta, Cyprus, and Gibraltar, cars drive on the left. In other European countries, traffic is on the right. If you're coming off the Eurotunnel shuttle, or ferries from Britain or Ireland to the Continent (or vice versa), beware the transition. Green signs indicate access to freeways everywhere except in France, where they are blue.

THE CHANNEL TUNNEL

Short of flying, the "Chunnel" is the fastest way to cross the English Channel: 35 minutes from Folkestone to Calais, 60 minutes from motorway to motorway, or 3 hours from London's Waterloo Station to Paris's Gare du Nord.

➤ CAR TRANSPORT: **Eurotunnel** (☎ 0990/353–535 in the U.K.).

➤ PASSENGER SERVICE: In the U.K.: **Eurostar** (☎ 0990/186–186), **InterCity Europe** (✉ Victoria Station, London, ☎ 0990/848–848 for creditcard bookings). In the U.S.: **BritRail Travel** (☎ 800/677–8585), **Rail Europe** (☎ 800/942–4866).

CHILDREN IN EUROPE

Be sure to plan ahead and **involve your youngsters** as you outline your trip. When packing, include things to keep them busy en route. On sightseeing days try to schedule activities of special interest to your children. If you are renting a car don't forget to **arrange for a car seat** when you reserve.

FLYING

If your children are two or older **ask about children's airfares.** As a general rule, infants under two not occupying a seat fly at greatly reduced fares or even for free. When booking **confirm carry-on allowances** if you're traveling with infants. In general, for babies charged 10% of the adult fare, you are allowed one carry-on bag and a collapsible stroller; if the flight is full

the stroller may have to be checked or you may be limited to less.

Experts agree that it's a good idea to use safety seats aloft for children weighing less than 40 pounds. Airlines set their own policies: U.S. carriers usually require that the child be ticketed, even if he or she is young enough to ride free, since the seats must be strapped into regular seats. Do **check your airline's policy about using safety seats during takeoff and landing.** And since safety seats are not allowed just everywhere in the plane, get your seat assignments early.

When reserving, **request children's meals or a freestanding bassinet** if you need them. But note that bulkhead seats, where you must sit to use the bassinet may lack an overhead bin or storage space on the floor.

LODGING

Most hotels in Europe allow children under a certain age to stay in their parents' room at no extra charge, but others charge for them as extra adults; be sure to **find out the cutoff age for children's discounts.**

Club Med has "Baby Clubs" (from age four months), "Mini Clubs" (for ages four to six or eight, depending on the resort), and "Kids Clubs" (for ages eight and up during school holidays) at many of its resort villages in France, Italy, Switzerland, and Spain.

SIGHTS & ATTRACTIONS

Places that are especially good for children are indicated by a rubber duckie icon in the margin.

CONSUMER PROTECTION

Whenever shopping or buying travel services in Europe, **pay with a major credit card** so you can cancel payment or get reimbursed if there's a problem. If you're doing business with a particular company for the first time, **contact your local Better Business Bureau and the attorney general's offices** in your state and the company's home state, as well. Have any complaints been filed? Finally, if you're buying a package or tour, always **consider travel insurance that** includes default coverage (☞ Insurance, *below*).

➤ LOCAL BBBs: **Council of Better Business Bureaus** (⊠ 4200 Wilson Blvd., Suite 800, Arlington, VA 22203, ☎ 703/276–0100, FAX 703/525–8277).

Europe is a major cruise center, with six seas (Aegean, Baltic, Black, Mediterranean, North, and Tyrrhenian) and the Atlantic Ocean. From the majesty of Norway's fjords to the ruins of ancient Greece, the region has more than one could possibly hope to see on one cruise vacation. **Select your ship as carefully as you choose your itinerary.** Cruises sail in Europe from April to November.

➤ CRUISE LINES: **Abercrombie & Kent** (⊠ 1520 Kensington Rd., Oak Brook, IL 60521, ☎ 630/954–2944 or 800/323–7308); **Celebrity Cruises** (⊠ 1050 Caribbean Way, Miami, FL 33132, ☎ 800/437–3111); **Clipper Cruise Line** (⊠ 7711 Bonhomme Ave., St. Louis, MO 63105, ☎ 800/325–0010); **Crystal Cruises** (⊠ 2049 Century Park E, Suite 1400, Los Angeles, CA 90067, ☎ 800/446–6620); **Cunard Line Limited** (6100 Blue Lagoon Dr., Suite 400, Miami, FL 33126, ☎ 800/929–9595); **Holland America Line** (⊠ 300 Elliott Ave. W, Seattle, WA 98119, ☎ 800/426–0327); **Orient Lines** (⊠ 1510 S.E. 17th St., Fort Lauderdale, FL 33316, ☎ 954/527–6660 or 800/333–7300); **Princess Cruises** (⊠ 10100 Santa Monica Blvd., Los Angeles, CA 90067, ☎ 310/553–1770 or 800/774–6237 for brochures); **Radisson Seven Seas Cruises** (⊠ 600 Corporate Dr., Suite 410, Fort Lauderdale, FL 33334, ☎ 800/333–3333); **Royal Caribbean International** (⊠ 1050 Caribbean Way, Miami, FL 33132, ☎ 305/539–6000 or 800/255–4373 for brochures); **Royal Olympic Cruises** (⊠ 805 Third Ave., 18th Floor, New York, NY 10022, ☎ 212/397–6400 or 800/872–6400; 800/368–3888 in Canada); **Silversea Cruises** (⊠ 110 E. Broward Blvd., Fort Lauderdale, FL 33301, ☎ 954/522–4477 or 800/722–9955); **Special Expeditions** (⊠ 720 5th Ave., New York, NY 10019, ☎ 212/765–7740 or 800/762–0003); **Windstar Cruises** (⊠ 300 Elliott Ave. W, Seattle, WA 98119, ☎ 800/258–7245).

When shopping, **keep receipts** for all purchases. Upon reentering the country, **be ready to show customs officials what you've bought.** If you feel a duty is incorrect or object to the way your clearance was handled, note the inspector's badge number and ask to see a supervisor. If the problem isn't resolved, write to the appropriate authorities, beginning with the port director at your point of entry.

IN EUROPE

Since the EU's 1992 agreement on a unified European market, the same customs regulations apply to all 15 member states (Austria, Belgium, Denmark, Finland, France, Germany, Great Britain, Greece, Ireland, Italy, Luxembourg, the Netherlands, Portugal, Spain, and Sweden). If you arrive from another EU country, you do not have to pass through customs.

Duty-free allowances for visitors from outside the EU are the same whatever your nationality (but you have to be over 17): 200 cigarettes or 50 cigars or 100 cigarillos or 250 grams of pipe tobacco; 1 liter of spirits or 2 liters of fortified or sparkling wine or liqueurs; 2 liters of still table wine; 60 milliliters of perfume; 250 milliliters of toilet water (note: 1 U.S. quart equals 0.946 liters); plus $200 worth of other goods, including gifts and souvenirs. Unless otherwise noted in individual country chapters, there are no restrictions on the import or export of currency. These limits remained in force after June 30, 1999, when duty-free shopping for travel within the EU was abolished.

See individual country chapters on non-EU countries for information on their import limits.

SMART TRAVEL TIPS

IN AUSTRALIA

Australia residents who are 18 or older may bring home A$400 worth of souvenirs and gifts (including jewelry), 250 cigarettes or 250 grams of tobacco, and 1,125 ml of alcohol (including wine, beer, and spirits). Residents under 18 may bring back A$200 worth of goods. Prohibited items include meat products. Seeds, plants, and fruits need to be declared upon arrival.

➤ INFORMATION: **Australian Customs Service** (Regional Director, ⊠ Box 8, Sydney, NSW 2001, ☎ 02/9213–2000, FAX 02/9213–4000).

IN CANADA

Canadian residents who have been out of Canada for at least 7 days may bring home C$500 worth of goods duty-free. If you've been away less than 7 days but more than 48 hours, the duty-free allowance drops to C$200; if your trip lasts 24–48 hours, the allowance is C$50. You may not pool allowances with family members. Goods claimed under the C$500 exemption may follow you by mail; those claimed under the lesser exemptions must accompany you. Alcohol and tobacco products may be included in the 7-day and 48-hour exemptions but not in the 24-hour exemption. If you meet the age requirements of the province or territory through which you reenter Canada, you may bring in, duty-free, 1.14 liters (40 imperial ounces) of wine or liquor *or* 24 12-ounce cans or bottles of beer or ale. If you are 16 or older you may bring in, duty-free, 200 cigarettes and 50 cigars. Check ahead of time with Revenue Canada or the Department of Agriculture for policies regarding meat products, seeds, plants, and fruits.

You may send an unlimited number of gifts worth up to C$60 each duty-free to Canada. Label the package UNSOLICITED GIFT—VALUE UNDER $60. Alcohol and tobacco are excluded.

➤ INFORMATION: **Revenue Canada** (⊠ 2265 St. Laurent Blvd. S, Ottawa, Ontario K1G 4K3, ☎ 613/993–0534; 800/461–9999 in Canada).

IN NEW ZEALAND

Homeward-bound residents 17 or older may bring back $700 worth of souvenirs and gifts. Your duty-free allowance also includes 4.5 liters of wine or beer; one 1,125-ml bottle of spirits; and either 200 cigarettes, 250 grams of tobacco, 50 cigars, or a combination of the three up to 250 grams. Prohibited items include meat products, seeds, plants, and fruits.

➤ INFORMATION: **New Zealand Customs** (Custom House, ⊠ 50 Anzac Ave., Box 29, Auckland, New Zealand, ☎ 09/359–6655, FAX 09/359–6732).

IN THE U.K.

If you are a U.K. resident and your journey was wholly within the European Union (EU), you won't have to pass through customs when you return to the United Kingdom. If you plan to bring back large quantities of alcohol or tobacco, check EU limits beforehand. From countries outside the EU, you may bring home, duty-free, 200 cigarettes or 50 cigars; 1 liter of spirits or 2 liters of fortified or sparkling wine or liqueurs; 2 liters of still table wine; 60 milliliters of perfume; 250 milliliters of toilet water; plus £136 worth of other goods, including gifts and souvenirs. If you're returning from outside the EU, prohibited items include meat products, seeds, plants, and fruits.

➤ INFORMATION: **HM Customs and Excise** (⊠ Dorset House, Stamford St., Bromley Kent BR1 1XX, ☎ 020/7202–4227).

IN THE U.S.

U.S. residents who have been out of the country for at least 48 hours (and who have not used the $400 allowance or any part of it in the past 30 days) may bring home $400 worth of foreign goods duty-free. U.S. residents 21 and older may bring back 1 liter of alcohol duty-free. In addition, regardless of your age, you are allowed 200 cigarettes and 100 non-Cuban cigars. Antiques, which the U.S. Customs Service define as objects more than 100 years old, enter duty-free, as do original works of art done entirely by hand, including paintings, drawings, and sculptures.

You may also send packages home duty-free: up to $200 worth of goods for personal use, with a limit of one parcel per addressee per day (and no alcohol or tobacco products or perfume worth more than $5); label the package PERSONAL USE and attach a list of its contents and their retail value. Do not label the package UNSOLICITED GIFT or your duty-free exemption will drop to $100. Mailed items do not affect your duty-free allowance on your return.

➤ INFORMATION: **U.S. Customs Service** (inquiries, ✉ 1300 Pennsylvania Ave. NW, Washington, DC 20229, ☎ 202/927–6724; complaints, ✉ Office of Regulations and Rulings, 1300 Pennsylvania Ave. NW, Washington, DC 20229; registration of equipment, ✉ Resource Management, 1300 Pennsylvania Ave. NW, Washington, DC 20229, ☎ 202/927–0540).

DINING

See discussions of dining in individual country chapters. The restaurants we list are the cream of the crop in each price category.

RESERVATIONS & DRESS

Reservations are always a good idea: we mention them only when they're essential or are not accepted. Book as far ahead as you can, and reconfirm as soon as you arrive. We mention dress only when men are required to wear a jacket or a jacket and tie.

DISABILITIES & ACCESSIBILITY

Getting around in many European cities and towns can be difficult if you're using a wheelchair, as cobblestone-paved streets and sidewalks are common in older, historic districts. Some that have been renovated have a flagstone track along with the cobblestones. Generally, newer facilities (including museums, transportation, hotels) provide easier access for people with disabilities.

LODGING

When discussing accessibility with an operator or reservations agent **ask hard questions.** Are there any stairs, inside *or* out? Are there grab bars next to the toilet *and* in the shower/tub? How wide is the doorway to the room? To the bathroom? For the most extensive facilities meeting the latest legal specifications **opt for newer accommodations.**

➤ COMPLAINTS: **Disability Rights Section** (✉ U.S. Department of Justice, Civil Rights Division, Box 66738, Washington, DC 20035-6738, ☎ 202/514–0301; 800/514–0301; 202/514–0301 TTY; 800/514–0301 TTY, FAX 202/307–1198) for general complaints. **Aviation Consumer Protection Division** (☞ Air Travel, *above*) for airline-related problems.

TRAVEL AGENCIES

In the United States, although the Americans with Disabilities Act requires that travel firms serve the needs of all travelers, some agencies specialize in working with people with disabilities.

➤ TRAVELERS WITH MOBILITY PROBLEMS: **Access Adventures** (✉ 206 Chestnut Ridge Rd., Rochester, NY 14624, ☎ 716/889–9096), run by a former physical-rehabilitation counselor. **Accessible Vans of the Rockies, Activity and Travel Agency** (✉ 2040 W. Hamilton Pl., Sheridan, CO 80110, ☎ 303/806–5047 or 888/837–0065, FAX 303/781–2329). **CareVacations** (✉ 5-5110 50th Ave., Leduc, Alberta T9E 6V4, ☎ 780/986–6404 or 780/986–8332) has group tours and is especially helpful with cruise vacations. **Flying Wheels Travel** (✉ 143 W. Bridge St., Box 382, Owatonna, MN 55060, ☎ 507/451–5005 or 800/535–6790, FAX 507/451–1685). **Hinsdale Travel Service** (✉ 201 E. Ogden Ave., Suite 100, Hinsdale, IL 60521, ☎ 630/325–1335).

➤ TRAVELERS WITH DEVELOPMENTAL DISABILITIES: **Sprout** (✉ 893 Amsterdam Ave., New York, NY 10025, ☎ 212/222–9575 or 888/222–9575, FAX 212/222–9768).

DISCOUNTS & DEALS

Be a smart shopper and **compare all your options** before making decisions. A plane ticket bought with a promotional coupon from travel clubs, coupon books, and direct-mail offers may not be cheaper than the least expensive fare from a discount ticket agency. And always keep in mind that what you get is just as important as what you save.

DISCOUNT RESERVATIONS

To save money **look into discount-reservations services** with toll-free numbers, which use their buying power to get a better price on hotels, airline tickets, even car rentals. When booking a room, always **call the hotel's local toll-free number** (if one is available) rather than the central reservations number—you'll often get a better price. Always ask about special packages or corporate rates.

When shopping for the best deal on hotels and car rentals **look for guaranteed exchange rates,** which protect you against a falling dollar. With your rate locked in, you won't pay more, even if the price goes up in the local currency.

➤ AIRLINE TICKETS: **Fly 4 Less** (☎ 800/359–4537). **Fly ASAP** (☎ 800/359–2727).

➤ HOTEL ROOMS: **Hotel Reservations Network** (☎ 800/964–6835). **International Marketing & Travel Concepts** (☎ 800/790–4682). **Steigenberger Reservation Service** (☎ 800/223–5652). **Travel Interlink** (☎ 800/888–5898).

PACKAGE DEALS

Don't confuse packages and guided tours. When you buy a package, you travel on your own, just as though you had planned the trip yourself. Fly/drive packages, which combine airfare and car rental, are often a good deal. If you **buy a rail/drive pass** you may save on train tickets and car rentals. All Eurail- and Europass holders get a discount on Eurostar fares through the Channel Tunnel. A German Rail Pass is also good for travel aboard some KD River Steamers and some Deutsche Touring/Europabus routes. Greek Flexipass options may include sightseeing, hotels, and plane tickets.

ELECTRICITY

To use your U.S.-purchased electric-powered equipment **bring a converter and adapter.** The electrical current in Europe is 220 volts, 50 cycles alternating current (AC); wall outlets in most of Europe take plugs with two round prongs; Great Britain (and also Malta) uses plugs with three oblong prongs.

If your appliances are dual-voltage you'll need only an adapter. Don't use 110-volt outlets, marked FOR SHAVERS ONLY, for high-wattage appliances such as blow-dryers. Most laptops operate equally well on 110 and 220 volts and so require only an adapter.

GAY & LESBIAN TRAVEL

Although big cities like Amsterdam and Paris have a visible and happening gay scene, most of Europe has a view of homosexuality similar to that found away from big cities in the U.S.

➤ GAY- AND LESBIAN-FRIENDLY TRAVEL AGENCIES: **Different Roads Travel** (✉ 8383 Wilshire Blvd., Suite 902, Beverly Hills, CA 90211, ☎ 323/651–5557 or 800/429–8747, FAX 323/651–3678). **Kennedy Travel** (✉ 314 Jericho Turnpike, Floral Park, NY 11001, ☎ 516/352–4888 or 800/237–7433, FAX 516/354–8849). **Now Voyager** (✉ 4406 18th St., San Francisco, CA 94114, ☎ 415/626–1169 or 800/255–6951, FAX 415/626–8626). **Yellowbrick Road** (✉ 1500 W. Balmoral Ave., Chicago, IL 60640, ☎ 773/561–1800 or 800/642–2488, FAX 773/561–4497). **Skylink Travel and Tour** (✉ 1006 Mendocino Ave., Santa Rosa, CA 95401, ☎ 707/546–9888 or 800/225–5759, FAX 707/546–9891), serving lesbian travelers.

INSURANCE

The most useful travel insurance plan is a comprehensive policy that includes coverage for trip cancellation and interruption, default, trip delay, and medical expenses (with a waiver for preexisting conditions).

Without insurance you will lose all or most of your money if you cancel your trip, regardless of the reason. Default insurance covers you if your tour operator, airline, or cruise line goes out of business. Trip-delay covers expenses that arise because of bad weather or mechanical delays. Study the fine print when comparing policies.

If you're traveling internationally, a key component of travel insurance is coverage for medical bills incurred if you get sick on the road. Such expenses are not generally covered by Medicare and by some private policies. U.K. residents can buy a travel-insurance policy valid for most vacations taken during the year in which it's purchased (but check preexisting-condition coverage). British and Australian citizens need extra medical coverage when traveling overseas.

Always **buy travel policies directly from the insurance company**; if you buy a policy from a cruise line, airline, or tour operator that goes out of business you probably will not be covered for the agency or operator's default, a major risk. Before you make any purchase **review your existing health and home-owner's policies** to find what they cover away from home.

➤ TRAVEL INSURERS: In the U.S. Access **America** (✉ 6600 W. Broad St., Richmond, VA 23230, ☎ 804/285–3300 or 800/284–8300), **Travel Guard International** (✉ 1145 Clark St., Stevens Point, WI 54481, ☎ 715/345–0505 or 800/826–1300). In Canada **Voyager Insurance** (✉ 44 Peel Center Dr., Brampton, Ontario L6T 4M8, ☎ 905/791–8700; 800/668–4342 in Canada).

➤ INSURANCE INFORMATION: In the U.K. the **Association of British Insurers** (✉ 51–55 Gresham St., London EC2V 7HQ, ☎ 020/7600–3333, FAX 020/7696–8999). In Australia the **Insurance Council of Australia** (☎ 03/9614–1077, FAX 03/9614–7924).

LANGUAGE

LANGUAGES FOR TRAVELERS

A phrase book and language-tape set can help get you started.

➤ PHRASE BOOKS & LANGUAGE-TAPE SETS: *Fodor's French for Travelers, Fodor's German for Travelers, Fodor's Italian for Travelers, Fodor's Spanish for Travelers* (☎ 800/733–3000 in the U.S.; 800/668–4247 in Canada; $7 for phrasebook, $16.95 for audio set).

LODGING

For discussions of accommodations in Europe, ☞ Lodging sections in individual country chapters. The lodgings we list are the cream of the crop in each price category. When pricing accommodations, always ask what facilities are included and what costs extra.

Assume that hotels operate on the European Plan (EP, with no meals) unless we specify that they use the Continental Plan (CP, with a Continental breakfast daily), Modified American Plan (MAP, with breakfast and dinner daily), or the Full American Plan (FAP, with all meals).

APARTMENT & VILLA RENTALS

If you want a home base that's roomy enough for a family and comes with cooking facilities **consider a furnished rental.** These can save you money, especially if you're traveling with a group. Home-exchange directories sometimes list rentals as well as exchanges. Some services search for a house or apartment for you (even a castle if that's your fancy) and handle the paperwork. Some send an illustrated catalog; others send photographs only of specific properties, sometimes at a charge. Up-front registration fees may apply.

➤ INTERNATIONAL AGENTS: **At Home Abroad** (✉ 405 E. 56th St., Suite 6H, New York, NY 10022, ☎ 212/421–9165, FAX 212/752–1591). **Drawbridge to Europe** (✉ 5456 Adams Rd., Talent, OR 97540, ☎ 541/512–8927 or 888/268–1148, FAX 541/512–0978). **Europa-Let/Tropical Inn-Let** (✉ 92 N. Main St., Ashland, OR 97520, ☎ 541/482–5806 or 800/462–4486, FAX 541/482–0660). **Hometours International** (✉ Box 11503, Knoxville, TN 37939, ☎ 423/690–8484 or 800/367–4668). **Interhome** (✉ 1990 N.E. 163rd St., Suite 110, Miami Beach, FL 33162, ☎ 305/940–2299 or 800/882–6864, FAX 305/940–2911). **Rental Directories International** (✉ 2044 Rittenhouse Sq., Philadelphia, PA 19103, ☎ 215/985–4001, FAX 215/985–0323). **Rent-a-Home International** (✉ 7200 34th Ave. NW, Seattle, WA 98117, ☎ 206/789–9377, FAX 206/789–9379). **Vacation Home Rentals Worldwide** (✉ 235 Kensington Ave., Norwood, NJ 07648, ☎ 201/767–9393 or 800/633–3284, FAX 201/767–5510). **Villas and Apartments Abroad** (✉ 420 Madison Ave., Suite 1003, New York, NY 10017, ☎ 212/759–1025 or 800/

433–3020, FAX 212/755–8316). **Villas International** (✉ 950 Northgate Dr., Suite 206, San Rafael, CA 94903, ☎ 415/499–9490 or 800/221–2260, FAX 415/499–9491). **Hideaways International** (✉ 767 Islington St., Portsmouth, NH 03801, ☎ 603/430–4433 or 800/843–4433, FAX 603/430–4444; membership $99).

HOME EXCHANGES

If you would like to exchange your home for someone else's **join a home-exchange organization,** which will send you its updated listings of available exchanges for a year and will include your own listing in at least one of them. It's up to you to make specific arrangements.

➤ EXCHANGE CLUBS: **HomeLink International** (✉ Box 650, Key West, FL 33041, ☎ 305/294–7766 or 800/638–3841, FAX 305/294–1448; $88 per year). **Intervac U.S.** (✉ Box 590504, San Francisco, CA 94159, ☎ 800/756–4663, FAX 415/435–7440; $83 per year).

HOSTELS

No matter what your age you can **save on lodging costs by staying at hostels.** In some 5,000 locations in more than 70 countries around the world, Hostelling International (HI), the umbrella group for a number of national youth-hostel associations, offers single-sex, dorm-style beds and, at many hostels, couples rooms and family accommodations. Membership in any HI national hostel association, open to travelers of all ages, allows you to stay in HI-affiliated hostels at member rates (one-year membership is about $25 for adults; hostels run about $10–$25 per night). Members also have priority if the hostel is full; they're eligible for discounts around the world, even on rail and bus travel in some countries.

➤ ORGANIZATIONS: **Hostelling International—American Youth Hostels** (✉ 733 15th St. NW, Suite 840, Washington, DC 20005, ☎ 202/783–6161, FAX 202/783–6171). **Hostelling International—Canada** (✉ 400–205 Catherine St., Ottawa, Ontario K2P 1C3, ☎ 613/237–7884, FAX 613/237–7868). **Youth Hostel Association of England and Wales** (✉ Trevelyan

House, 8 St. Stephen's Hill, St. Albans, Hertfordshire AL1 2DY, ☎ 01727/855215 or 01727/845047, FAX 01727/844126). **Australian Youth Hostel Association** (✉ 10 Mallett St., Camperdown, NSW 2050, ☎ 02/9565–1699, FAX 02/9565–1325). **Youth Hostels Association of New Zealand** (✉ Box 436, Christchurch, New Zealand, ☎ 03/379–9970, FAX 03/365–4476). Membership in the U.S. $25, in Canada C$26.75, in the U.K. £9.30, in Australia $44, in New Zealand $24.

HOTELS

All hotels listed have private bath unless otherwise noted.

Admission prices throughout this guide are for attractions that charge more than $10 or the equivalent. Admission and transportation prices are given for adults. Substantially reduced fees are almost always available for children, students, and senior citizens. For information on taxes, *see* Taxes, *below.*

ATMS

ATMs are ubiquitous throughout Europe; you can even draw local currency from an ATM in most airports just about as soon as you deplane.

➤ ATM LOCATIONS:

Cirrus (☎ 800/424–7787).

CREDIT CARDS

Should you use a credit card or a debit card when traveling? Both have benefits. A credit card allows you to delay payment and gives you certain rights as a consumer (☞ Consumer Protection, *above*). A debit card, also known as a check card, deducts funds directly from your checking account and helps you stay within your budget. When you want to rent a car, you may still need an old-fashioned credit card. You can always *pay* for your car with a debit card, but some agencies will not allow you to *reserve* a car with a debit card.

Otherwise, the two types of plastic are virtually the same. Both will get you cash advances at ATMs worldwide if your card is properly programmed with your personal identification number (PIN). Both offer excellent, wholesale exchange rates. And both protect you against unauthorized use if the card is lost or stolen. Your liability is limited to $50, as long as you report the card missing.

Throughout this guide, the following abbreviations are used: **AE**, American Express; **DC**, Diner's Club; **MC**, Master Card; and **V**, Visa.

CURRENCY

The euro, or single European currency, was launched on January 1, 1999. The rates of conversion between the euro (which uses the symbol €) and local currencies were irrevocably fixed at that time. Eleven EU nations have joined the system in the first wave—all but the U.K., Sweden, Denmark, and Greece, which aims to join in 2001. At the moment the euro is mainly used for trade transactions. Bank notes and coins won't disappear until 2002, but in the meantime, dual pricing of goods and services will enable people to become accustomed to the new currency before its eventual introduction as a physical entity. From January 1, 2002, new euro banknotes and coins will be put into circulation and the old national currencies will be withdrawn. In some countries this will be a gradual process over a period of three months, while in others it will be a swifter transition, after which euro banknotes and coins alone will have legal tender status.

CURRENCY EXCHANGE

Conversions between non-euro currencies and currencies in the euro zone are now calculated via the euro rate vis à vis the third currency rather than directly between the third currency and the euro-zone currency. Once the euro has been introduced as a currency, visitors to Europe will incur no currency exchange charges within the participating countries. For the most favorable rates, **change money through banks.** Although ATM transaction fees may be higher abroad than at home, ATM rates are excellent because they are based on wholesale rates offered only by major banks. You won't do as well at exchange booths in airports or rail and bus stations, in hotels, in restaurants, or in stores. To avoid lines at airport exchange booths in countries whose currency is traded internationally, **get a bit of local currency before you leave home.**

➤ EXCHANGE SERVICES: **International Currency Express** (☎ 888/842–0880 on East Coast; 888/278–6628 on West Coast). **Thomas Cook Currency Services** (☎ 800/287–7362 for telephone orders and retail locations).

TRAVELER'S CHECKS

Do you need traveler's checks? It depends on where you're headed. If you're going to rural areas and small towns, go with cash; traveler's checks are best used in cities. Lost or stolen checks can usually be replaced within 24 hours. To ensure a speedy refund, buy your own traveler's checks— don't let someone else pay for them: irregularities like this can cause delays. The person who bought the checks should make the call to request a refund.

PACKING

You should **pack more for the season than for any particular dress code.** In general, northern and central Europe have cold, snowy winters, and the Mediterranean countries have mild winters, though parts of southern Europe can be bitterly cold, too. In the Mediterranean resorts **bring a warm jacket for mornings and evenings,** even in summer. The mountains usually are warm on summer days, but the weather is unpredictable, and the nights are generally cool.

For European cities, **pack as you would for an American city:** formal outfits for first-class restaurants and nightclubs, casual clothes elsewhere. Jeans are perfectly acceptable for sightseeing and informal dining. Sturdy walking shoes are appropriate for the cobblestone streets and gravel paths that fill many of the parks and surround some of the historic buildings. For visits to churches, cathedrals, and mosques, **avoid shorts and revealing outfits.** In Italy, women cover their shoulders and arms (a shawl will do). Women, however, no longer need to cover their heads in Roman Catholic churches. In Greece

SMART TRAVEL TIPS

many monasteries bar women wearing pants; long skirts are often provided at the entrance as a cover-up for both women wearing pants and men dressed in shorts. In Turkey, though, women must have a head covering; a long-sleeved shirt and a long skirt or slacks are required.

To discourage purse snatchers and pickpockets, **take a handbag with long straps** that you can sling across your body, bandolier-style, and with a zippered compartment for money.

If you stay in budget hotels, **take your own soap.**

In your carry-on luggage **bring an extra pair of eyeglasses or contact lenses** and **enough of any medication you take** to last the entire trip. You may also want your doctor to write a spare prescription using the drug's generic name, since brand names may vary from country to country. In luggage to be checked, **never pack prescription drugs or valuables.** To avoid customs delays, carry medications in their original packaging. And don't forget to copy down and carry addresses of offices that handle refunds of lost traveler's checks.

CHECKING LUGGAGE

How many carry-on bags you can bring with you is up to the airline. Most allow two, but not always, so make sure that everything you carry aboard will fit under your seat, and get to the gate early. Note that if you have a seat at the back of the plane, you'll probably board first, while the overhead bins are still empty.

If you are flying internationally, note that baggage allowances may be determined not by piece but by weight—generally 88 pounds (40 kilograms) in first class, 66 pounds (30 kilograms) in business class, and 44 pounds (20 kilograms) in economy.

Airline liability for baggage is limited to $1,250 per person on flights within the United States. On international flights it amounts to $9.07 per pound or $20 per kilogram for checked baggage (roughly $640 per 70-pound bag) and $400 per passenger for unchecked baggage. You can buy additional coverage at check-in for about $10 per $1,000 of coverage, but it excludes a rather extensive list of items, shown on your airline ticket.

Before departure **itemize your bags' contents** and their worth, and label the bags with your name, address, and phone number. (If you use your home address, cover it so that potential thieves can't see it readily.) Inside each bag **pack a copy of your itinerary.** At check-in **make sure that each bag is correctly tagged** with the destination airport's three-letter code. If your bags arrive damaged or fail to arrive at all, file a written report with the airline before leaving the airport.

PASSPORTS & VISAS

When traveling internationally **carry a passport even if you don't need one** (it's always the best form of I.D.), and **make two photocopies of the data page** (one for someone at home and another for you, carried separately from your passport). If you lose your passport promptly call the nearest embassy or consulate and the local police.

ENTERING EUROPE

Citizens of the U.S., Canada, U.K., Ireland, Australia, and New Zealand need passports for travel in Europe. Visas may also be required for visits to or through Turkey, Poland, Estonia, Latvia, Romania, Hungary, and the Czech and Slovak Republics even for short stays or train trips, and in some cases must be obtained before you'll be allowed to enter. Check with the nearest consulate of the country you'll be visiting for visa requirements. Austria and Italy require that you register with the local police shortly after arriving.

PASSPORT OFFICES

The best time to apply for a passport or to renew is during the fall and winter. Before any trip, check your passport's expiration date, and, if necessary, renew it as soon as possible.

➤ AUSTRALIAN CITIZENS: **Australian Passport Office** (☎ 131–232).

➤ CANADIAN CITIZENS: **Passport Office** (☎ 819/994–3500 or 800/567–6868).

➤ New Zealand Citizens: **New Zealand Passport Office** (☎ 04/494–0700 for information on how to apply; 04/474–8000 or 0800/225–050 in New Zealand for information on applications already submitted).

➤ U.K. Citizens: **London Passport Office** (☎ 0990/210–410) for fees and documentation requirements and to request an emergency passport.

➤ U.S. Citizens: **National Passport Information Center** (☎ 900/225–5674; calls are 35¢ per minute for automated service, $1.05 per minute for operator service).

SENIOR-CITIZEN TRAVEL

Radisson SAS Hotels in Europe offer discounts of 25% or more to senior citizens, subject to availability. You need a confirmed reservation.

To qualify for age-related discounts **mention your senior-citizen status up front** when booking hotel reservations (not when checking out) and before you're seated in restaurants (not when paying the bill). When renting a car ask about promotional car-rental discounts, which can be cheaper than senior-citizen rates.

➤ Educational Programs: **Elderhostel** (✉ 75 Federal St., 3rd fl., Boston, MA 02110, ☎ 877/426–8056, ℻ 877/426–2166). **Interhostel** (✉ University of New Hampshire, 6 Garrison Ave., Durham, NH 03824, ☎ 603/862–1147 or 800/733–9753, ℻ 603/862–1113). **Folkways Institute** (✉ 14600 Southeast Aldridge Rd., Portland, OR 97236-6518, ☎ 503/658–6600 or 800/225–4666, ℻ 503/658–8672).

STUDENTS IN EUROPE

Students in Europe are entitled to a wide range of discounts on admission and transportation. **An International Student Identity Card** (☞ CIEE *in* Student I.D.s &Services, *below*) helps.

Many U.S. colleges and universities have study-abroad programs or can link you up with one, and numerous institutions of higher learning in Europe accept foreign students for a semester or year's study. Check with your college administration or contact the CIEE (☞ Student I.D.s & Services *below*) for contacts and brochures.

If you're between 18 and 26, the Ibis hotel chain will let you have a room for $50 or less, provided you show up after 9 PM and they have a room free. You'll be asked for your student ID. Your chances are best on weekends. There are more than 400 Ibis hotels in Europe, most of them in France.

➤ Student I.D.s & Services: **Council on International Educational Exchange** (CIEE, ✉ 205 E. 42nd St., 14th fl., New York, NY 10017, ☎ 212/822–2600 or 888/268–6245, ℻ 212/822–2699) for mail orders only, in the U.S. **Hostelling International–New York** (891 Amsterdam Ave., New York, NY 10025, ☎ 212/932–2300). **STA Travel** (U.S., ☎ 800/781–4040; London, ☎ 020/7361–6262; Frankfurt, ☎ 69/979–07460; Auckland, ☎ 0800/100–677; Melbourne, ☎ 3/9349–4344; Johannesburg, ☎ 11/447–5414). **Travel Cuts** (✉ 187 College St., Toronto, Ontario M5T 1P7, ☎ 416/979–2406 or 800/667–2887) in Canada.

TAXES

VALUE-ADDED TAX (V.A.T.)

Global Refund arranges V.A.T. refunds for more than 130,000 shops world-wide. In participating stores, **ask for a Global Refund Cheque when making a purchase**—this Cheque will clearly state the amount of your refund in local currency, with the service charge already incorporated (the service charge equals approximately 3%–4% of the purchase price of the item). When you leave the European Union, get your Global Refund Cheque and any customs forms stamped by the customs official. You can take them to the refund office at the airport, where your money will be refunded in cash, by check, or to your credit card. Alternatively, you can mail your validated Cheque to Global Refund, and your credit card account will automatically be credited within three billing cycles. Global Refund has a fax-back service further clarifying the process.

➤ VAT Refunds: **Global Refund** (✉ 707 Summer St., Stamford, CT 06901, ☎ 800/566–9828, www.globalrefund.com).

TELEPHONES

Telephone systems in Europe are in flux; expect new area codes and extra digits in numbers. Keep in mind that some countries now rely on phone cards; it's a good idea to buy one so you don't have to hunt for a phone that takes coins. Country codes appear in the A to Z listings at the beginning of each country chapter.

INTERNATIONAL CALLS

Consult individual country chapters for information on dialing international calls.

AT&T, MCI, and Sprint international access codes make calling the United States relatively convenient, but you may find the local access number blocked in many hotel rooms. First ask the hotel operator to connect you. If the hotel operator balks, ask for an international operator, or dial the international operator yourself. One way to improve your odds of being connected to your long-distance carrier is to travel with more than one company's calling card (a hotel may block Sprint, for example, but not MCI). If all else fails, call from a pay phone in the hotel lobby. Check individual country chapters for local access numbers or call your carrier for the number before you go.

➤ ACCESS CODES: **AT&T Direct** (☎ 800/435–0812). **MCI WorldPhone** (☎ 800/444–4141). **Sprint International Access** (☎ 913/624–5336).

TOURS & PACKAGES

On a prepackaged tour or independent vacation everything is prearranged so you'll spend less time planning—and often get it all at a good price.

BOOKING WITH AN AGENT

Travel agents are excellent resources. But it's a good idea to collect brochures from several agencies because some agents' suggestions may be influenced by relationships with tour and package firms that reward them for volume sales. If you have a special interest **find an agent with expertise in that area**; ASTA (☞ Travel Agencies, *below*) has a database of specialists worldwide.

Make sure your travel agent knows the accommodations and other services of the place they're recommending. Ask about the hotel's location, room size, beds, and whether it has a pool, room service, or programs for children, if you care about these. Has your agent been there in person or sent others whom you can contact?

Do some homework on your own, too: Local tourism boards can provide information about lesser-known and small-niche operators, some of which may sell only direct.

BUYER BEWARE

Each year consumers are stranded or lose their money when tour operators—even large ones with excellent reputations—go out of business. So **check out the operator.** Ask several travel agents about its reputation, and try to **book with a company that has a consumer-protection program.** (Look for information in the company's brochure). In the United States, members of the National Tour Association and United States Tour Operators Association are required to set aside funds to cover your payments and travel arrangements in case the company defaults. It's also a good idea to choose a company that participates in the American Society of Travel Agent's Tour Operator Program (TOP); ASTA will act as mediator in any disputes between you and your tour operator.

Remember that the more your package or tour includes the better you can predict the ultimate cost of your vacation. Make sure you know exactly what is covered, and **beware of hidden costs.** Are taxes, tips, and transfers included? Entertainment and excursions? These can add up.

➤ TOUR-OPERATOR RECOMMENDATIONS: **American Society of Travel Agents** (☞ Travel Agencies, *below*). **National Tour Association** (NTA, ✉ 546 E. Main St., Lexington, KY 40508, ☎ 606/226–4444 or 800/682–8886). **United States Tour Operators Association** (USTOA, ✉ 342 Madison Ave., Suite 1522, New York, NY 10173, ☎ 212/599–6599 or 800/468–7862, FAX 212/599–6744).

TRAIN TRAVEL

Some national high-speed train systems have begun to link up to form the nucleus of a pan-European system. On a long journey, you still have to change trains a couple of times, for the national railways are jealously guarding their prerogatives. Deregulation, so far achieved only in Britain, is vigorously pushed by the European Commission. Even so, French TGV (Trains à Grande Vitesse), which serve most major cities in France, have been extended to Geneva, Lausanne, Bern, Zurich, Turin, and Milan. They link up with the latest generation of Italy's tilting Pendolino trains, also called Eurostar Italia. They extend beyond the country's borders with a service from Turin to Lyon and, in a joint venture with the Swiss Railways, from Milan to Geneva and Zurich. The TGV–like Thalys trains operate from Brussels to Paris on high-speed tracks and from Brussels to Amsterdam and Cologne on conventional track. Germany's equally fast ICE trains connect Hamburg and points in between with Basel, and Mannheim with Munich.

High-speed trains cover the distance from Paris to Marseille in just over 4 hours, Hamburg to Munich in less than 6, traveling at speeds of up to 190 mph on dedicated track and over 150 mph on old track. They have made both expensive sleeper compartments and budget *couchettes* (seats that convert into bunks) all but obsolete. Their other attraction is the comfort of a super-smooth ride. The flip side is the reservations requirement; rather than just hopping on the next train, you need to **reserve in advance or allow enough time to make a reservation at the station.**

The **Orient Express,** a glamorous recreation of a sumptuous past, takes two days to cover the distance from London to Venice, and if you want to know the price you can't afford it. The Swiss Railways operate special services that allow you to enjoy superb scenery and railway buffs to admire the equally superb railroad technology. The **Panoramic Express** takes 3 hours to travel from Montreux via Gstaad to Interlaken; the **Glacier Express** (7½ hours) runs from Zermatt to St. Moritz and also offers en-route gourmet dining as befits these famous resorts; and the **Bernina Express,** the most spectacular, runs from Chur over the 7,400-ft Bernina Pass (where you can turn around;

each leg takes 2½ hours), or you can continue to Tirano in Italy (4 hours, with connections to Lugano and Milan). Holders of a Swisspass can travel on all three, but reservations are needed. For additional information on rail services and special fares, contact the national tourist office of the country (☞ Visitor Information, *below*).

CLASSES

Virtually all European systems, including the high-speed ones, operate a two-tier class system. First class costs substantially more and is usually a luxury rather than a necessity. Some of the poorer European countries retain a third class, but avoid it unless you're an adventure-minded budget traveler.

CUTTING COSTS

To save money **look into rail passes.** But be aware that if you don't plan to cover many miles, you may come out ahead by buying individual tickets.

Before you invest in a discount pass, ask for a comparison of the cost against the point-to-point fares on your actual itinerary. (Rates given in this section are for 1999, the latest available at press time.) EurailPasses provide unlimited first-class rail travel for the duration of the pass in 17 European countries: Austria, Belgium, Denmark, Finland, France, Germany, Greece, Hungary, the Irish Republic, Italy, Luxembourg, the Netherlands, Norway, Portugal, Spain, Sweden, and Switzerland (but not the United Kingdom). If you plan to rack up the miles, get a standard pass. These are available for 15 days ($554, £390), 21 days ($718, £506), one month ($890, £627), two months ($1,260, £887), and three months ($1,558, £1,097). Note that you will have to pay a supplement for certain high-speed trains—half the fare on Eurostar.

In addition to standard EurailPasses, check out special rail-pass plans. Among these are the Eurail Youthpass (in second class for those under-26, from $388/£273 to $1,089/£767), the Eurail Saverpass (which gives a discount for 2 to 5 people traveling together; a minimum of two persons

SMART TRAVEL TIPS

Oct. through March, three April through Sept.; from $470/£332 to $1,324/£932 per person), and the Eurail Flexipass (which allows 10 or 15 travel days within a two-month period, $654/£461 and $862/£607 respectively). If you're going to travel in just one part of Europe, look into a regional pass, such as the East Europe Pass.

If your plans call for only limited train travel, consider Europass, which costs less money than a EurailPass and is available in first class only for adults and second class only for travelers under 26. It has a number of conditions. It is valid only in France, Germany, Italy, Spain, and Switzerland, but "associated countries" can be added at an extra charge. These are Austria/Hungary, the Benelux area, Greece and Portugal, to a maximum of 2 extensions. You also get from 5 to 15 travel days during a two-month time period. The other side of the coin is that a Europass costs a couple of hundred dollars less than the least expensive EurailPass. A Europass Adult ranges in price from $348 to $728 (£254 to £603), a Europass Youth from $233 to $513 (£170 to £431).

It used to be the rule that you had to **purchase your pass before you leave** for Europe. This remains the recommended option, but in case of need you can now buy a pass in person within six months of your arrival in Europe from Rail Europe (✉ 179 Piccadilly, London). Also remember that you need to **book seats ahead even if you are using a rail pass**; seat reservations are required on European high-speed trains, and are a good idea on other trains that may be crowded—particularly around Easter and at the beginning and end of European vacation periods. You will also need to purchase sleeper or couchette (sleeping berth) reservations separately.

European nationals and others who have resided in Europe for at least six months qualify for the **InterRail Pass.** It used to be exclusively for young people but can now also be purchased, at a premium, by older travelers. This entitles you to unlimited second-class travel within up to eight zones you

have preselected. One zone for 22 days, for instance, costs UK£159 for -26's (£229 for 26+); all zones for one month, £259 (£349). InterRail Passes can be bought only in Europe at main railway stations or in the U.K. from Rail Europe in London (☞ Train Information, *below*).

FROM THE U.K.

Sleek, high-speed Eurostar trains use the Channel Tunnel to link London (Waterloo) with Paris (Gare du Nord) in 3 hours and with Brussels (Gare du Midi) in 2 hours, 40 minutes. When the British build their high-speed rail link to London (St. Pancras), probably in 2003, another half-hour will be shaved off travel time. There are a minimum of 14 daily services to Paris and 10 to Brussels.

Many of the trains stop at Ashford (Kent), and all at the Lille-Europe station in northern France, where you can change to French TGV trains to Brittany, southwest France, Lyon, the Alps, and the Riviera, eliminating the need to transit between stations in Paris.

Passengers headed for Germany and the Netherlands can buy through tickets via Brussels to Cologne (5½ hours) and Amsterdam (5 hours, 45 minutes).Eurostar does not accept EurailPasses but allows discounts of 40%–50% to passholders. Check for special prices and deals before you book. Or, if money is no object, you can choose the Premium First Class (to Paris only), complete with limo delivery and pick-up at the stations, improved catering, and greater comfort.

Conventional boat trains from London are timed to dovetail with ferry departures at Channel ports. The ferries connect with onward trains at the main French, Belgian, Dutch and Irish ports. Be sure to ask when making your reservation which London railway station to use.

INDIVIDUAL COUNTRY PASSES

Single-country passes are issued by most national railways, and the majority are sold by Rail Europe (☞ EurailPasses, *above*, and individual country chapters).

➤ TRAIN INFORMATION: **CIT Tours Corp.** (✉ 15 West 44th St., 10th Floor, New York, NY 10036, ☎ 800/248–7245 for rail or 800/248–8687 for tours and hotels), **DER Travel Services** (☞ Discount Passes, Eurolines, *in* Bus Travel, *above*), **Eurostar** (☎ 800/942–4866 or 805/482–8210 in U.S.; 0990/186–186 in the U.K.; 01233/617–575 from other countries), **Rail Europe** (✉ 226–230 Westchester Ave., White Plains, NY 10604, ☎ 800/438–7245, FAX 800/432–1329 in U.S.; ✉ 2087 Dundas E., Suite 105, Mississauga, Ontario L4X 1M2, ☎ 905/602–4195 in Canada; ✉ 179 Piccadilly and Victoria Station, London W1V 8BA, ☎ 0990/848–848 or 020/7647–4900 in U.K.).

Venice Simplon-Orient Express (✉ Sea Containers House, 20 Upper Ground, London SE1 9PF, ☎ 020/7805–5100 reservations; 0123/3211–772 brochures; 800/524–2420 reservations in U.S.).

FARES & SCHEDULES

A good rail timetable is indispensable if you're doing extensive rail traveling. The Thomas Cook Timetables are updated monthly. There's also an annual summer edition (limited to Britain, France, and the Benelux).

TRAVEL AGENCIES

A good travel agent puts your needs first. Look for an agency that has been in business at least five years, emphasizes customer service, and has someone on staff who specializes in your destination. In addition **make sure the agency belongs to a professional trade organization.** The American Society of Travel Agents (ASTA), with 27,000 agents in some 170 countries, is the largest and most influential in the field. Operating under the motto "Integrity in Travel," it maintains and enforces a strict code of ethics and will step in to help mediate any agent-client disputes if necessary. ASTA also maintains a website that includes a directory of agents. (Note that if a travel agency is also acting as your tour operator *see* Buyer Beware *in* Tours & Packages, *above*.)

➤ LOCAL AGENT REFERRALS: **American Society of Travel Agents** (ASTA,

☎ 800/965–2782 24-hr hot line, FAX 703/684–8319). **Association of Canadian Travel Agents** (✉ 1729 Bank St., Suite 201, Ottawa, Ontario K1V 7Z5, ☎ 613/521–0474, FAX 613/521–0805). **Association of British Travel Agents** (✉ 55–57 Newman St., London W1P 4AH, ☎ 020/7637–2444, FAX 020/7637–0713). **Australian Federation of Travel Agents** (✉ Level 3, 309 Pitt St., Sydney 2000, ☎ 02/9264–3299, FAX 02/9264–1085). **Travel Agents' Association of New Zealand** (✉ Box 1888, Wellington 10033, ☎ 04/499–0104, FAX 04/499–0786).

VISITOR INFORMATION

For general information before you go, contact the national tourism offices.

➤ AUSTRIAN NATIONAL TOURIST OFFICE: **U.S.** (✉ Box 1142, Times Square Station, New York, NY 10108-1142, ☎ 212/944–6880, FAX 212/730–4568). **Canada** (✉ 2 Bloor St. E, Suite 3330, Toronto, Ontario M4W 1A8, ☎ 416/967–3381, FAX 416/967–4101; ✉ 1010 Ouest Rue, Sherbrooke, Ste. 1410, Montréal, Québec, H3A 2R7, ☎ 514/849–3709, FAX 514/849–9577; ✉ Granville Sq., 200 Granville St., Ste. 1380, Vancouver, British Columbia, V6C 1S4, ☎ 604/683–5808, FAX 604/662–8528). **U.K.** (14 Cork St., London, W1X 1PF, ☎ 020/7629–0461, FAX 020/7499–6038, oewlon@easynet.co.uk). **Australia and New Zealand** (✉ 36 Carrington St., 1st floor, Sydney, NSW 2000, ☎ 02/9299–3621, FAX 02/9299–3808, oewsyd@world.net). **Ireland** (✉ Merrion Hall, Strand Rd., Sandymount, P.O. Box 2506, Dublin 4, ☎ 01/283–0488, FAX 01/283–0531).

➤ BELGIAN NATIONAL TOURIST OFFICE: **U.S.** (✉ 780 3rd Ave., New York, NY 10017, ☎ 212/758–8130, FAX 212/355–7675, info@visitbelgium.com). **Canada** (✉ Box 760 NDG, Montréal, Québec H4A 3S2, ☎ 514/484–3594, FAX 514/489–8965). **U.K.** (✉ 31 Pepper St., London E14 9RW, ☎ 0891/887–799, FAX 020/7458–2999, info@belgiumtourism.org). Calls cost 50p per minute.

SMART TRAVEL TIPS

➤ British Tourist Authority: **U.S.:** Nationwide (✉ 551 5th Ave., 7th floor, New York, NY 10176, ☎ 212/986–2200 or 800/462–2748, FAX 212/986–1188); 24-hour fax information line (FAX 818/441–8265); (✉ 625 N. Michigan Ave., Suite 1510, Chicago, 60611; walk-in service only). **Canada** (✉ 111 Avenue Rd., Suite 450, Toronto, Ontario M5R 3J8, ☎ 416/925–6326 or 888/847–4885, FAX 416/961–2175). **Britain Visitors Centre** (✉ 1 Lower Regent St., London SW1Y 4PQ, ☎ 0800/192–192 or ✉ Thames Tower, Black's Rd., London W6 9EL[no information by phone]). **Australia** (✉ Level 16, Gateway, 1 Macquarie Place, Sydney, NSW 2000, ☎ 02/9377–4400, FAX 02/9377–4499). **New Zealand** (✉ Dilworth Bldg., Suite 305, 3rd floor, Corner of Queen & Customs Streets, Auckland 1, ☎ 09/303–1446, FAX 09/377–6965). **Ireland** (✉ 18-19 College Green, Dublin 2, ☎ 01/670–8000, FAX 01/670–8244).

➤ Bulgaria: **U.S. and Canada** (Balkan Tourist USA, authorized agent, ✉ 20 E. 46th St., Suite 1003, New York, NY 10017, ☎ 212/338–6838, 800/822–1106, FAX 212/822–5910). **U.K.** (Balkan Tourist UK ✉ 111 Bartholomew Rd., London NW2 BJ, ☎ 020/7485–4584; Balkan Holidays, ✉ 19 Conduit St., London W1R 9TD, ☎ 020/7491–4499, FAX 020/7543–5577).

➤ Cyprus Tourist Office: **U.S. and Canada** (✉ 13 E. 40th St., New York, NY 10016, ☎ 212/683–5280, FAX 212/683–5282). **U.K.** (✉ 213 Regent St., London W1R 8DA, ☎ 020/7734–9822, FAX 020/7287-6534; 821 UN Plaza, 6th fl., New York NY 10017, ☎ 212/687–2350). North Cyprus Tourist Office (✉ 28 Cockspur St., London SW1Y 5BN, ☎ 020/7930–5069).

➤ Czech Center: **U.S. and Canada** (✉ 1109 Madison Ave., New York, NY 10028, ☎ 212/288–0830). **U.K.** (✉ 95 Great Portland St., London W1N 5RA, ☎ 020/7291–9920, FAX 020/7436–1300).

➤ Danish Tourist Board: **U.S. and Canada** (✉ Box 4649, Grand Central Station, New York, NY 10163-4649, ☎ 212/885–9700, FAX 212/885–9710).

U.K. (✉ 55 Sloane St., London SW1X 9SY, ☎ 020/7259–5959 or 0891/600–109 for 24-hour brochure line, costs 50p per minute peak rate or 45p per minute cheap rate, FAX 020/7259–5955, dtb.london@dt.dk).

➤ Estonian Tourist Office: **U.S.** (Consulate, ✉ 630 Fifth Ave., Suite 2415, New York, NY 10011, ☎ 212/247–7634, FAX 212/262–0893). **Canada** (Consulate, ✉ 958 Broadview Ave., Suite 202, Toronto, ON M4K 2R6, ☎ 416/461–0764, FAX 416/461–0353, estconsu@inforamp.net). **U.K.** (Embassy, ✉ 16 Hyde Park Gate, London, SW7 5DG, ☎ 020/7589–3428, FAX 020/7589–3430, loa@estonia.gov.uk). **Australia** (Consulate, ✉ 86 Louisa Rd., Birchgrove, NSW 2041, ☎ 02/9810–7468, FAX 02/9818–1779, eestikon@ozemail.com.au).

➤ Finnish Tourist Board: **U.S. and Canada** (✉ Box 4649, Grand Central Station, New York, NY 10163-4649, ☎ 212/885–9700, FAX 212/885–9710). **U.K.** (✉ 30–35 Pall Mall, London SW1Y 5LP, ☎ 020/7930–5871, FAX 020/73210696).

➤ French Government Tourist Office: **U.S.** Nationwide (☎ 900/990–0040; costs 50¢ per minute); New York City (✉ 444 Madison Ave., 10022, ☎ 212/838–7800); Chicago (✉ 676 N. Michigan Ave., 60611, ☎ 312/751–7800); Beverly Hills (✉ 9454 Wilshire Blvd., 90212, ☎ 310/271–6665, FAX 310/276–2835). **Canada** (✉ 1981 Ave., McGill College, Suite 490, Montréal, Québec H3A 2W9, ☎ 514/288–4264, FAX 514/845–4868; ✉ 30 St. Patrick St., Suite 700, Toronto, Ontario M5T 3A3, ☎ 416/491–7622, FAX 416/979–7587). **U.K.** (✉ 178 Piccadilly, London W1V OAL, ☎ 0891/244–123, FAX 020/7493–6594). Calls cost 50p per minute. **Australia** (✉ 25 Bligh St., Sydney, NSW 2000, ☎ 02/9231–5244, FAX 02/9221–8682, frencht@ozemail.com.au. **Ireland** (✉ 35 Lower Abbey St., Dublin 1, ☎ 01/703–4046, FAX 01/874–7324.

➤ German National Tourist Office: **U.S.** Nationwide (✉ 122 E. 42nd St., New York, NY 10168, ☎ 212/661–7200, FAX 212/661–7174, gntony@aol.com). **Canada** (✉ 175 Bloor St. E, Suite 604, Toronto,

Ontario M4W 3R8, ☎ 416/968–1570, ℻ 416/968–1986, germanto@idirect.com). **U.K.** (✉ 18 Conduit St., London W1R 0DT, ☎ 020/7495–0081 or 0891/600–100 for brochures, costs 50p per minute peak rate or 45p per minute cheap rate, ℻ 020/7495–6129, 106167.3216@compuserve.com). **Australia** (✉ P.O. Box A980, Sydney, NSW 1235, ☎ 02/9267–8148, ℻ 02/9267–9035).

➤ GIBRALTAR INFORMATION BUREAU: **U.S. and Canada** (✉ 1156 15th St. NW, Suite 1100, Washington, DC 20005, ☎ 202/452–1108, ℻ 202/452–1109). **U.K.** (Gibraltar Tourist Board, ✉ Arundel Great Court, 179 The Strand, London WC2R 1EH, ☎ 020/7836–0777, ℻ 020/7240–6612, giblondon@aol.com).

➤ GREEK NATIONAL TOURIST ORGANIZATION: **U.S.:** Nationwide (✉ 645 5th Ave., New York, NY 10022, ☎ 212/421–5777, ℻ 212/826–6940); Los Angeles (✉ 611 W. 6th St., Suite 2198, 92668, ☎ 213/626–6696, ℻ 213/489–9744); Chicago (✉ 168 N. Michigan Ave., Suite 600, 60601, ☎ 312/782–1084, ℻ 312/782–1091). **Canada** (✉ 1233 Rue de la Montagne, Suite 101, Montréal, Québec H3G 1Z2, ☎ 514/871–1535, ℻ 514/871–1498; ✉ 1300 Bay St., Toronto, Ontario M5R 3K8, ☎ 416/968–2220, ℻ 416/968–6533). **U.K.** (✉ 4 Conduit St., London W1R 0DJ, ☎ 020/7734–5997, ℻ 020/7287–1369). **Australia** (✉ 51-57 Pitt St., Sydney, NSW 2000, ☎ 9241–1663, ℻ 9235–2174.

➤ HUNGARIAN NATIONAL TOURIST OFFICE: **U.S. and Canada** (✉ 150 E. 58th St., 33rd Floor, New York, NY 10155, ☎ 212/355–0240, ℻ 212/207–4103, htnewyork@hungary-tourism.hu). **U.K.** (✉ Embassy of the Republic of Hungary, Commercial Section, 46 Eaton Pl., London SW1X 8AL, ☎ 020/7823–1032, ℻ 020/7823–1459, htlondon@hungary-tourism.hu).

➤ ICELAND TOURIST BOARD: **U.S. and Canada** Scandinavia Tourism Inc. (✉ Box 4649, Grand Central Station, New York, NY 10163–4649, ☎ 212/885–9700, ℻ 212/885–9710). **U.K.** (✉ 172 Tottenham Court Rd., 3rd floor, London W1P 9LG, ☎ 020/

7388–7550 for brochures, or contact IcelandAir at 020/7388–5599).

➤ IRISH TOURIST BOARD: **U.S.** (✉ 345 Park Ave., New York, NY 10154, ☎ 212/418–0800 or 800/223–6470, ℻ 212/371–9052). **Canada** (✉ 160 Bloor St. E, Suite 1150, Toronto, Ontario M4W 1B9, ☎ 416/487–3335, ℻ 416/929–6783). **U.K.** (✉ Ireland House, 150 New Bond St., London W1Y 0AQ, ☎ 020/7493–3201 or, ℻ 020/7493–9065). **Australia** (✉ 5th floor, 36 Carrington St., Sydney, NSW 2000, ☎ 02/9299–6177, ℻ 02/9299–6323).**Ireland** (✉ Baggot Street Bridge, Dublin 2, ☎ 01/602–4000, 850/230–330 or, ℻ 01/602–4000).

➤ ITALIAN GOVERNMENT TRAVEL OFFICE (ENIT): **U.S.** Nationwide (✉ 630 5th Ave., Suite 1565, New York, NY 10111, ☎ 212/245–4822, ℻ 212/586–9249, enitny@bway.net); Chicago (✉ 500 N. Michigan Ave., Suite 2240, 60611, ☎ 312/644–0996, ℻ 312/644–3019); Los Angeles (✉ 12400 Wilshire Blvd., Suite 550, 90025, ☎ 310/820–1898, ℻ 310/820–6357). **Canada** (✉ 1 Pl. Ville Marie, Suite 1914, Montréal, Québec H3B 3M9, ☎ 514/866–7667, ℻ 514/392–1429, 739145@icam.net). **U.K.** (Italian State Tourist Board, ✉ 1 Princes St., London W1R 9AY, ☎ 020/7408–1254, ℻ 020/7493–6695, enitlond@globalnet.co.uk).

➤ LITHUANIAN TOURIST BOARD: **U.S.** (Embassy, ✉ 2622 Sixteenth St., NW, Washington, DC 20009–4202, ☎ 202/234–5860, ℻ 202/328–0466). **U.K.** (Consulate, ✉ 84 Gloucester Pl., London WIH 3HN, ☎ 020/7486–6401, ℻ 020/7468–6403).

➤ LUXEMBOURG NATIONAL TOURIST OFFICE: **U.S. and Canada** (✉ 17 Beekman Pl., New York, NY 10022, ☎ 212/935–8888, ℻ 212/935–5896, luxnto@aol.com or tourism@ont.smtp.etat.lu). **U.K.** (✉ 122 Regent St., London W1R 5FE, ☎ 020/7434–2800, ℻ 020/7734–1205, tourism@luxembourg.co.uk).

➤ MALTA NATIONAL TOURIST OFFICE: **U.S. and Canada** (✉ 350 5th Ave., Suite 4412, New York, NY 10118, ☎ 212/695–9520, ℻ 212/695–8229, office.us@tourism.org.mt). **U.K. and Ireland** (✉ 36–38 Piccadilly, London W1V 0PP, ☎ 020/7292–4900, FAX 020/7734–1880, office.uk@tourism.org.mt). **Australia** (✉ 403 George St., Sydney, NSW 2000, ☎ 020/7292–4900, FAX 02/9290–3641, office.au@tourism.org.mt, **Ireland** (14 Leeson Park, Dublin 6, ☎ 0353/496–0244, FAX 0353/497–5183).

➤ MONACO GOVERNMENT TOURIST OFFICE AND CONVENTION BUREAU: **U.S. and Canada** (✉ 565 5th Ave., New York, NY 10017, ☎ 212/286–3330, FAX 212/286–9890). **U.K.** (✉ The Chambers, Chelsea Harbour, London SW10 0XF, ☎ 020/7352–9962, FAX 020/7352–2103).

➤ NETHERLANDS BOARD OF TOURISM: **U.S.** (✉ 225 N. Michigan Ave., Suite 1854, Chicago, IL 60601, ☎ 888/464–6552 or 312/819–1500, FAX 312/819–1740). **Canada** (✉ Box 1078, Toronto, Ontario M5C 2K5, ☎ 888/464–6552 in English, or 888/729–7227 in French, FAX 416/363–1470). **U.K.** (✉ 18 Buckingham Gate, London SW1E 6LD, ☎ 0891/717–777, cost 50p per minute, FAX 020/7828–7941).

➤ NORWEGIAN TOURIST BOARD: **U.S. and Canada** (✉ Box 4649, Grand Central Station, New York, NY 10163–4649, ☎ 212/885–9700, FAX 212/885–9710, usa@nortra.no). **U.K.** (✉ Charles House, 5 Regent St., London SW1Y 4LR, ☎ 020/7839–2650, FAX 020/7839–6014, greatbritain@nortra.no).

➤ POLISH NATIONAL TOURIST OFFICE: **U.S. and Canada** (✉ 275 Madison Ave., Suite 1711, New York, NY 10016, ☎ 212/338–9412, FAX 212/338–9283). **U.K.** (✉ 310–312 Regent St., Remo House, 1st floor, London W1R 5AJ, ☎ 020/7580–8811, FAX 020/7580–8866).

➤ PORTUGUESE NATIONAL TOURIST OFFICE: **U.S.** (✉ 590 5th Ave., 4th floor, New York, NY 10036, ☎ 212/354–4403, FAX 212/764–6137). **Canada** (✉ 60 Bloor St. W, Suite 1005, Toronto, Ontario M4W 3B8, ☎ 416/921–7376, FAX 416/921–1353, iceptor@idirect.com). **U.K.** (✉ 2nd floor, 22–25A Sackville St., London

W1X 2LY, ☎ 020/7494–1441 or 0891/600–370 [24-hour brochure line, costs 50p per minute peak rate or 45p per minute cheap rate], FAX 020/7494–1868, iceplond@dircon.co.uk). **Ireland** (✉ 54 Dawson St., Dublin 2, ☎ 01/670–9133, FAX 01/670–9141, info@icep.ie).

➤ ROMANIAN NATIONAL TOURIST OFFICE: **U.S. and Canada** (✉ 342 Madison Ave., Suite 210, New York, NY 10173, ☎ 212/545–8484). **U.K.** (✉ 83A Marylebone High St., London W1M 3DE, ☎ 020/7935–6435, FAX 020/7224–3692).

➤ SLOVAK TOURIST OFFICE: **U.S. and Canada:** (Embassy, ✉ 2201 Wisconsin Ave., NW, Suite 250, Washington, DC 20007, ☎ 202/965–5160, FAX 202/965–5166); **U.K.:** (Embassy, Information Dept., ✉ 25 Kensington Palace Gardens, London W8 4QY, ☎ 020/7243–0803, FAX 020/7727–5824). Czech and Slovak Tourist Centre (✉ 16 Frognal Parade, Finchley Rd., London NW3 5HG, ☎ 020/7794–3263, FAX 020/7794–3265).

➤ TOURIST OFFICE OF SPAIN: **U.S.:** Nationwide (✉ 666 5th Ave., 35th floor, New York, NY 10103, ☎ 212/265–8822, FAX 212/265–8864); Chicago (✉ 845 N. Michigan Ave., Suite 915 E, 60611, ☎ 312/642–1992, FAX 312/642–9817); Los Angeles (✉ 8383 Wilshire Blvd., Suite 960, 90211, ☎ 213/658–7188, FAX 213/658–1061); Miami (✉ 1221 Brickell Ave., Suite 1850, 33131, ☎ 305/358–1992, FAX 305/358–8223). **Canada** (✉ 2 Bloor St. W, 34th floor, Toronto, Ontario M4W 3E2, ☎ 416/961–3131, FAX 416/961–1992). **U.K.** (✉ 22–23 Manchester Sq., London W1M 5AP, ☎ 020/7486–8077 or 0891/669–920 [24-hour brochure line], FAX 020/7486–8034); calls to the brochure line cost 50p per minute.

➤ SWEDISH TRAVEL AND TOURISM COUNCIL: **U.S. and Canada:** (✉ Box 4649, Grand Central Station, New York, NY 10163–4649, ☎ 212/885–9700, FAX 212/885–9764, info@gosweden.org). **U.K.** (✉ 11 Montagu Pl., London W1H 2AL, ☎ 020/7870–5600, FAX 020/7724–5872, info@swetourism.org.uk).

➤ SWITZERLAND TOURISM: **U.S.:** New York (✉ 608 5th Ave., 10020, ☎ 212/757–5944, FAX 212/262–6116; El Segundo, CA (✉ 222 N. Sepulveda Blvd., Suite 1570, 90245, ☎ 310/335–5980, FAX 310/335–5982); Chicago (✉ 150 N. Michigan Ave., Suite 2930, 60601, ☎ 312/630–5840, FAX 312/630–5848). **Canada** (✉ 926 The East Mall, Etobicoke, Ontario M9B 6KI, ☎ 416/695–2090, FAX 416/695–2774). **U.K.** (✉ Swiss Centre, 1 New Coventry St., London W1V 8EE, ☎ 020/7734–1921, FAX 020/7437–4577, london@switzerlandvacation.ch).

➤ TURKISH TOURIST OFFICE: **U.S.:** Nationwide (✉ 821 UN Plaza, New York, NY 10017, ☎ 212/687–2194, FAX 212/599–7568); Washington DC (✉ 1717 Massachusetts Ave. NW, Suite 306, 20036, ☎ 202/429–9844, FAX 202/429–5649). **Canada** (✉ 360 Albert St., Suite 801, Ottawa, Ontario K1R 7X7, ☎ 613/230–8654, FAX 613/230–3683). **U.K.** (✉ 1st floor, Egyptian House, 170–173 Piccadilly, London W1V 9DD, ☎ 020/7629–7771, FAX 020/7491–0773).

➤ U.S. GOVERNMENT ADVISORIES: **U.S. Department of State** (✉ Overseas Citizens Services Office, Room 4811 N.S., 2201 C St. NW, Washington, DC 20520; ☎ 202/647–5225 for interactive hot line; 301/946–4400 for computer bulletin board; FAX 202/647–3000 for interactive hot line); enclose a self-addressed, stamped, business-size envelope.

WHEN TO GO

For information about travel seasons and for the average daily maximum and minimum temperatures of the major European cities, *see* the A to Z section *in* each country chapter.

➤ FORECASTS: **Weather Channel Connection** (☎ 900/932–8437), 95¢ per minute from a Touch-Tone phone.

ANDORRA

ANDORRA LA VELLA AND BEYOND

The co-principality of Andorra has carved itself a niche in the world's imagination as a trout-fishing, through-the-looking-glass Pyrenean paradise. Though this perception may cause some disappointment when you find yourself in a 20-mile traffic jam of bargain hunters on the one road through the country, don't give up: Andorra's upper reaches are still pristine.

In 1993, this 495-sq-km (191-sq-mi) tax haven, commercial oasis, winter sport station, and mountain hideaway drafted a constitution and held elections, converting one of Europe's last pockets of feudalism into a modern democratic state and member of the United Nations. The bishop of Urgell and the president of France assumed even more symbolic roles as the co-princes of this unique Pyrenean country. The area originally fell through the cracks between France and Spain when Charlemagne founded Andorra as an independent entity during his 8th-century battles with the Moors. In the 9th century, his heir, Charles the Bald, made the bishop of Urgell overlord of Andorra, a role contested by the French counts of Foix until a treaty providing for joint suzerainty was agreed upon in 1278. During the 16th century the French monarchy inherited these rights and eventually passed them on to the presidents of France.

This dual protection long allowed Andorra to thrive as a low-tax, duty-free haven. Europe's new semi-borderless unity, however, has changed this special status, and Andorra is now in the process of developing an improved tourist industry and a more conventional economy.

Winter sports, mountain climbing and hiking, and the architectural and cultural heritage represented by its many Romanesque chapels, bridges, and medieval farm and town houses are Andorra's once and future stock in trade, although numbered bank accounts will surely not be disappearing anytime soon.

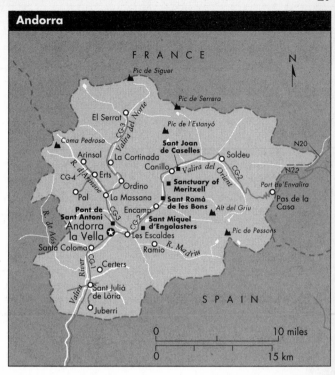

Andorra

ANDORRA A TO Z

Customs

Non-Europeans need a passport to cross the border; Europeans enter with only an identity card. Crossing out of Andorra, however, can be a problem. The French customs officers between Pas de la Casa and the Puymorens Tunnel sporadically stage mammoth roadblocks and may search anything. Spanish customs between Andorra la Vella and Seu d'Urgell can also be tricky. The established limits for all varieties of goods are specified in "Franquicias dels Viatgers," a leaflet in French, Catalan, Spanish, and English that is distributed by the Andorra National Tourist Office in Barcelona or Andorra la Vella (☞ Visitor Information, *in* Andorra Essentials, *below*). No one seems to mind how often you pass customs on a given day, however. So one way to score significant savings is to stay in a hotel on the Spanish side and make a half dozen trips through.

Dining

Andorra is developing a growing reputation for fine dining. There are good restaurants serving French, Spanish, or Catalan cuisine and plenty of spots where you can eat hearty Pyrenean fare at no great cost. Local dishes worth trying include *trinchat,* a typical mountain specialty of potatoes and cabbage with bacon; *estofat d'isard* (stewed mountain goat); *truite de carreroles* (omelet with wild mushrooms); local cheeses, such as *formatge de tupí;* and *rostes amb mel* (ham baked with honey). Most restaurants offer prix-fixe menus, but some more expensive establishments are only à la carte.

MEALTIMES

Andorrans eat late: Dinners don't usually get under way until 8 or 9, and lunch is a substantial meal served between 1:30 and 4.

RATINGS
The following price ratings are for a three-course meal for one person, not including wine.

CATEGORY	COST
$$$$	over 5,000 ptas.
$$$	3,500 ptas.–5,000 ptas.
$$	1,500 ptas.–3,500 ptas.
$	under 1,500 ptas.

WHAT TO WEAR

Casual dress is acceptable in all restaurants in Andorra, regardless of price category.

Language

Although more than three-quarters of the country's population of about 65,000 are not native speakers of Catalan, it is the co-principality's official language. Spanish, French, and English are also commonly spoken by merchants and service personnel.

Lodging

The number of Andorran hotels continues to increase, and standards are rising. The decor is usually functional, but service is friendly and the facilities are excellent. Most hotels are open year-round. Reservations are necessary during July and August. Hotel rates often include at least two meals.

RATINGS

The following price ratings apply for two people in a double room.

CATEGORY	COST
$$$$	over 10,000 ptas.
$$$	7,500 ptas.–10,000 ptas.
$$	4,500 ptas.–7,500 ptas.
$	3,500 ptas.–4,500 ptas.

Mail

You can buy Andorran stamps with French francs or Spanish pesetas, though the postal service within the country is free. The Spanish post office in Andorra la Vella is at Carrer Joan Maragall 10; the French post office is at 1 rue Père d'Urg. There are no postal codes in Andorra, but be sure to write "Principat d'Andorra" to distinguish the country from the Spanish town of the same name. The abbreviation "s/n" in an address means that the building has no number.

Money Matters

CURRENCY

The Spanish peseta (pta.) is the major Andorran currency, but French francs are equally acceptable, and all prices are quoted in both currencies. For exchange rates and coinage information, ☞ Currency *in* Chapters 11 *and* 28.

SAMPLE PRICES

Soft drink, 175 ptas.; cup of coffee, 125 ptas.; 1½-km (1-mi) taxi ride, 350 ptas.; ham sandwich, 500 ptas.

TIPPING

Restaurant and café prices always include a 10%–15% service charge; it's customary to leave a similar amount in addition to the charge, but this is completely optional.

WHAT IT WILL COST

Prices in Andorra are similar to those in neighboring France and Spain. The best bargains still available are products subject to state tax, such as tobacco, alcohol, perfume, and gasoline. Such staples as butter, cheese, and milk sold as surplus by member countries of the European Union (EU) are also cheaper in Andorra.

National Holidays

January 1; March 14 (Constitution Day); April 23 (St. George's Day); April 24 (Easter Monday); May 1 (Labor Day); June 12 (Pentecost Monday); June 24 (St. John); September 8 (La Verge de Meritxell); November 1 (All Saints' Day); December 8 (Immaculate Conception); December 25; December 26 (St. Stephen's Feast).

Opening and Closing Times

Banks are open weekdays 9–1 and 3–5, and Saturday 9–noon. They are closed Sunday. Andorra is predominantly Catholic; most chapels and **churches** are kept locked around the clock, the key being left at the closest house. Check with the local tourist office. **Shops** are open daily 9–8, though many are closed between 1 and 4.

Telephoning

COUNTRY CODE

The country code for Andorra is 376.

INTERNATIONAL CALLS

For assistance, call the local operator at 111. To call Andorra from Spain, dial 00–376 and the six-digit local number; from France, dial 00–376.

LOCAL CALLS

For local directory assistance, dial 111. Andorra has no regional area codes. Most pay phones take phone cards issued by the telephone company, which may be purchased at *tabacs* (stores that sell tobacco and stamps).

Transportation

BY BUS

A bus service runs twice daily from Barcelona (✉ Ronda Universidad 4). In summer direct buses run from Perpignan and Toulouse to Andorra. The ride from Barcelona, Perpignan, or Toulouse to Andorra la Vella takes about three hours.

Minibuses connect the towns and villages, and fares are low; 150 ptas. will take you 5 km (3 mi). Details on fares and services are available at hotels and from tourist offices.

BY CAR

Road maintenance varies. The one main artery from France into Spain via Andorra la Vella is curvy but good and handles the heaviest traffic. The spur north toward the ski resorts at La Massana and Ordino is also excellent. Once you leave the valley floor, the roads are narrow, winding, and best suited to four-wheel-drive vehicles, especially in snow. In winter, snow tires or chains are essential. Although the Puymorens Tunnel does not surface in Andorra, it does eliminate the switchbacks of the Puymorens mountain pass going through toward Spain from the northern entrance at L'Hospitalet, France. This pass is either dangerous or closed in bad weather and adds an extra 30 minutes to the Barcelona–Pas de la Casa trip. In good weather, the drive is spectacularly scenic.

The fastest, most direct route from Barcelona to Andorra la Vella— with the fewest curves and the most tolls (about 4,500 ptas. in all)— runs through the Tunel del Cadí and the Cerdanya Valley via Bellver and La Seu d'Urgell. Slightly longer but cheaper, more beautiful, and often free of holdups is the western approach to La Seu d'Urgell via N-II to Igualada, then through Cervera, Pons, and Oliana on C-1311.

The back way through Puigcerdà to Pas de la Casa is often a good way to avoid traffic. Andorra is 620 km (385 mi) from Madrid via Zaragoza, Lleida, and the C-1311, a six- to seven-hour drive.

BY PLANE

The nearest international airports are at Barcelona (200 km/125 mi) and, in France, at Perpignan (136 km/85 mi) and Toulouse-Blagnac (180 km/112 mi).

BY TRAIN

From Barcelona, take the train to Puigcerdà, then the bus to La Seu d'Urgell and Andorra la Vella; from Madrid, take the train to Lleida and then a bus to La Seu d'Urgell and Andorra la Vella. From Toulouse, take the train to Ax-les-Thermes and L'Hospitalet, where the bus to Pas de la Casa and Andorra la Vella meets the morning train. Alternatively, go on to Latour-de-Carol and take the bus from Puigcerdà to La Seu d'Urgell and Andorra la Vella.

ON FOOT

Mountainous Andorra is a playground for hikers and backpackers. The mountains are high and the terrain is wild, so a degree of care and experience is advisable. There are three long-distance trails: the GR7, which runs from the French border near Pas de la Casa to Les Escaldes on the road from Andorra la Vella to Spain; the GR11, also called the Ordino Route, a high-mountain trail that stretches across the central range; and the GR P1, a perimeter route running the crests around the Andorran border. There are 26 mountain refuges distributed throughout Andorra so you can plan day treks and travel light. Get details on treks and walks from tourist offices.

Weather

With a reliable snowfall from December to early April, Andorra has excellent ski resorts at Soldeu, Arinsal, Pal, Pas de la Casa–Grau Roig, and Ordino–Arcalis and a cross-country center at La Rabassa. Winter brings a huge influx of skiing buffs, but consumers are eager to take advantage of Andorra's tax- and duty-free shopping all year long. Holidays and weekends can make getting into, out of, or through Andorra a nightmare any time of year. In early April, the bird migrations from Africa begin, and the first flush of spring flowers livens the slopes and valleys. Be warned that even in summer the nighttime temperatures can drop to freezing.

CLIMATE

The following are the average daily maximum and minimum temperatures for Andorra.

Jan.	43F	6C	**May**	62F	17C	**Sept.**	71F	22C
	30	1		43	6		49	10
Feb.	45F	7C	**June**	73F	23C	**Oct.**	60F	16C
	30	1		39	4		42	6
Mar.	54F	12C	**July**	79F	26C	**Nov.**	51F	10C
	35	2		54	12		35	2
Apr.	58F	14C	**Aug.**	76F	24C	**Dec.**	42F	6C
	39	4		53	12		31	1

EXPLORING ANDORRA

Exploring Andorra takes time. The roads are narrow and steep, the views compel frequent stops, and every village is worth examining. If possible, do as much sightseeing on foot as time permits.

Andorra la Vella

The capital's pivotal attraction, outside of its shops and restaurants, is the **Casa de la Vall** (House of the Valley) overlooking the town's main square. Constructed in 1580, this massive and medieval bulk of stone is the seat of the Andorran government. Charmingly rustic, the Casa de la Vall contains many notable religious frescoes, some of which were carefully moved here from village churches high in the Pyrenees. The kitchen is particularly interesting, with its splendid array of ancient copper pots and other culinary implements. ⊠ *Carrer de la Vall s/n.* ☉ *Tours weekdays 9–1 and 3–7. Closed weekends.*

$$$ ✕ **Moli dels Fanals.** This quiet restaurant occupies an antique *borda*
★ (a typical stone Andorran mountain refuge) with a fireplace and wooden paneling. The Catalan cuisine here uses consistently high-quality ingredients. Try the *magret de canard* (breast of duck) with grapes and port. ⊠ *Carrer Dr. Vilanova 9 (Borda Casadet),* ☎ *821381. AE, DC, MC, V. Closed Mon. and last 2 wks in Aug. No dinner Sun.*

$$–$$$ ✕ **Borda Estevet.** A borda with a very Pyrenean feel, this simple spot offers a selection of Spanish and Andorran dishes, beef cooked and served *a la llosa* (on hot slabs of slate), and three private dining rooms in addition to the main dining room. ⊠ *Ctra. Comella 2,* ☎ *864026. AE, DC, MC, V. Closed Sun. in Aug.*

$$–$$$ ✕ **Versailles.** A tiny and authentic French bistro with only 10 tables,
★ the Versailles is nearly always packed. The cuisine is primarily French with occasional Andorran specialties—such as *escudella barrejada,* a thick vegetable and meat soup, or *civet de jabali,* stewed wild boar. ⊠ *Cap del Carrer 1,* ☎ *821331. AE, DC, MC, V.*

$$ ✕🏨 **Celler d'En Toni.** This small, rustic hotel and restaurant in the cen-
★ ter of Andorra la Vella offers good value on rooms and serves some of the best food in the co-principality, a blend of Mediterranean and Pyrenean cuisines. The rooms, while not luxurious, are adequate and the quality of the restaurant more than compensates. ⊠ *Verge del Pilar 4,* ☎ *821252,* 📠 *821872. 17 rooms. Restaurant. AE, DC, MC, V.*

$$$$ 🏨 **Andorra Park.** The Park is a grand building away from the city's congestion of traffic and pedestrians. The hotel bar is a popular watering hole for local society. There's a pretty garden, a pitching and putting green, and an ample terrace. The deluxe guest rooms have private balconies. ⊠ *Carrer Les Canals 24,* ☎ *820979,* 📠 *820983. 40 rooms. Restaurant, pool. AE, DC, MC, V.*

$$$$ 🏨 **Hotel Eden Roc.** Besides having all the amenities of larger hotels, the smaller Eden Roc offers an exceptional dining room, a terrace, and attentive personal service. ⊠ *Av. Dr. Mitjavila 1,* ☎ *821000,* 📠 *860319. 56 rooms. Restaurant. AE, V.*

$$$$ 🏨 **Hotel Mercure.** The large, modern Mercure is widely considered one
★ of the capital's best hotels. The rooms are spacious and the furnishings smartly contemporary. The outdoor terrace is a pleasant spot to relax and watch the bustle below. ⊠ *Carrer de la Roda,* ☎ *820773,* 📠 *828195. 150 rooms. Restaurant, bar, cafeteria, pool, fitness room, parking. AE, DC, MC, V.*

$$$ 🏨 **Hotel Ibis.** This hotel is part of the new Accor chain that includes the neighboring Novotel and the Mercure. The hotel restaurant, the Brasserie, is a bright and friendly spot with quick and convenient service and fare. The rooms, sleek and modern, are impeccable but characterless. ⊠ *Av. Meritxell 58,* ☎ *820777,* 📠 *828245. 63 rooms. Restaurant, bar, cafeteria, parking. AE, DC, MC, V.*

Les Escaldes

The spa town, now virtually one with Andorra la Vella, is a 15-minute
★ walk from the Casa de la Vall. The Romanesque church of **Sant Miquel d'Engolasters** stands on a ridge northeast of the capital and can be

reached on foot—allow half a day for the round-trip—or by automobile up a mountain road. The views are well worth the climb.

★ **Caldea** is an elaborate thermal spa complex barely 1 km (½ mi) from the center of Andorra la Vella, complete with steam rooms, Turkish baths, and snow patios. There are three restaurants, boutiques, an art gallery, and a cocktail bar open until 2 AM. Charges for the treatments vary; a five-day Andorra ski ticket will get you in for free. ⊠ *Parc de la Mola 10, Les Escaldes*, ☎ 865777, ℻ 865656.

$$$$ ✕▥ **Roc Blanc.** Sleek, modern, and luxurious, with a wealth of facilities
★ to pamper the body, from mud baths to acupuncture—that's what the Roc Blanc is all about. The rooms are large, there's a terrace, and the hotel's restaurants, La Brasserie, L'Entrecôte, and El Pi, serve Andorran and international specialties. ⊠ *Plaça dels Co-Prínceps 5*, ☎ 871400, ℻ *860244. 250 rooms. 3 restaurants, 2 pools. AE, DC, MC, V.*

Encamp

Just beyond the town, which is 6 km (4 mi) northeast of Andorra la
★ Vella, is the 12th-century church of **Sant Romà de les Bons,** in a particularly picturesque setting combining medieval buildings and mountain scenery. The new Funitel, a 20-passenger combination funicular car and *telecabine* or gondola, connects Encamp with the ski slopes of Grau Roig and Pas de la Casa. ⊠ *Old part of town.*

$$ ▥ **Hotel La Mola.** This friendly spot, midway between the ski slopes and the bright lights of Andorra la Vella, is a comfortable choice that has all the basic facilities at half the price of some of the better-known Andorran hotels. ⊠ *Av. Co-Princep Episcopal 62*, ☎ 831181, ℻ *833046. 48 rooms. Restaurant, pool. AE, DC, MC, V.*

Canillo

The **Santuari de Meritxell** is the focal point of Andorran religious life. The Blessed Virgin of Meritxell is the principality's patron saint, yet, oddly enough for such a religious country, her patronage wasn't declared until the late 19th century. The original sanctuary was destroyed by fire in 1972; the new gray-stone building that replaced it looks remarkably like a factory, but the mountain setting is superb. ⊠ *CG-2, between Encamp and Canillo.* ▨ *Free.* ☽ *Wed.–Mon. 9–1 and 3–7.*

Just outside Canillo stands a **seven-armed Gothic cross** of stone (in fact, it has only six arms; one has been broken off). The Romanesque church of **Sant Joan de Caselles,** 2 km (1½ mi) east of Canillo, is one of Andorra's treasures, with its ancient walls of stone that has turned a lovely dappled gingerbread color over the centuries. The bell tower is stunning: three stories of weathered stone punctuated by rows of round-arch windows. Inside, a fine reredos (a wall or screen behind an altar), dating from 1525, depicts the life of St. John the Evangelist.

La Massana

★ **Pont de Sant Antoni** (St. Anthony Bridge), a Romanesque stone bridge spanning a narrow river, is just 3 km (2 mi) north of Andorra la Vella on the CG-3 road toward La Massana. The rustic streets of the picturesque mountain town are good for strolling.

$$$$ ✕ **El Rusc.** A smallish flower-covered chalet 1 km (½ mi) from La Massana, El Rusc may be Andorra's top restaurant in both cost and quality. Chef Antoni Garrallá serves Basque cuisine and French and international specialties. Try the foie gras with onions or *besugo* (baked sea bream), a standard treat from the Basque country. ⊠ *Ctra. de Arinsal, La Massana*, ☎ 838200, ℻ *835180. Reservations essential. AE, DC, MC, V. Closed Mon. No dinner Sun.*

$$ ✕ **La Borda de l'Avi.** This popular place specializes in lamb, goat,
★ beef, quail, partridge, and trout cooked over coals. The three dining
rooms can hold some 200 diners and, during the high season, often
do. ✉ *Ctra. de Arinsal, La Massana,* ☎ *835154. AE, DC, MC, V.*

Ordino

The tiny village 5 km (3 mi) northeast of La Massana is known for its
medieval church, **Sant Martíde la Cortinada.** Romanesque with Baroque
altarpieces, the church also has 12th-century frescoes and unusual
wooden furnishings. To see it properly, go at night between 7 and 8,
when Mass is celebrated.

$$ 🏨 **Hotel Coma.** Surrounded by woods and meadows, this Swiss chalet-
style hideaway just outside the village offers scenery, silence, and sim-
ple Andorran fare at affordable prices. ✉ *Ctra. General,* ☎ *835116,*
FAX *837909. 48 rooms. Restaurant, pool. AE, DC, MC, V.*

La Cortinada

In this village is **Can Pal,** a fine example of medieval Andorran architecture. It is a privately owned manor house (strictly no admittance)
with a dovecote attached. Note the turret perched high on the far side.

Santa Coloma

★ Santa Coloma's pre-Romanesque **Santa Coloma de les Bons** hermitage,
the only Andorran church with a round tower, is the main attraction
in this village 4 km (2½ mi) south of Andorra la Vella on CG-1. Parts
of the church date from the 9th and 10th centuries. Twelfth-century
Romanesque frescoes fill the interior walls, while an 18th-century
Baroque altarpiece presides.

$$ ✕ **El Bon Racó.** Exactly what the name says it is—a good corner, nook,
or retreat—it is a traditional borda in design. The place turns out fine
Pyrenean *cuina cassolana* (home cooking) at encouraging prices. Try
to arrive early; it fills quickly, especially on weekends. ✉ *Av. Salou 86,*
☎ *822085. AE, DC, MC, V. Closed Sept. 8 and Dec. 25.*

Pas de la Casa

This conglomeration of high-rises and supermarkets is a sort of An-
dorran Smuggler's Notch, traditionally a place for French and Span-
ish shoppers to effect a quick sting while the kids are skiing and then
retreat back to their respective countries. Known to be colder and snowier
than any other point around, Pas de la Casa is a favorite ski resort, es-
pecially for visitors from the Cerdanya valley in Spain.

$$–$$$ 🏨 **Esqui d'Or.** At the very foot of the lift of what may be the snowiest
ski resort in the Pyrenees (certainly in Andorra), this modern hotel is
a handy resource if you can get a reservation for rooms overlooking
the slopes. The restaurant evolves from buffet breakfast and lunch to
serious cuisine at dinner. ✉ *Catalunya 9,* ☎ *855127,* **FAX** *855178. 62
rooms. Restaurant, cafeteria. AE, DC, MC, V.*

Sant Julià de Lòria

Sant Julià de Lòria is the first parish you encounter coming into An-
dorra from Spain. It is the site of Andorra's only Nordic skiing facil-
ity. Around and above it are a number of unspoiled small villages.

$$$ 🏨 **Pol.** Gracefully modern surroundings and a friendly staff help make
★ this hotel popular. A garden and terrace are part of the Pol's appeal,
and its dance club is a busy nightspot. ✉ *Av. Verge de Canólich 52,*
☎ *841122,* **FAX** *841852. 80 rooms. Restaurant. AE, MC, V.*

Shopping

Shopping has traditionally been one of Andorra's main attractions, but be careful: Not all the goods displayed are at bargain prices. Good buys are such consumables as gasoline, perfume, butter, cheese, cigarettes, wine, whiskey, and gin. For cameras, tape recorders, and other imported items, compare prices and models carefully. Ask for the *precio último* (final price) and insist politely on *el descuento,* the 10% discount to which you are entitled as a visitor to Andorra.

The main shopping area is **Andorra la Vella.** There are also stores in all the new developments and in the towns close to the frontiers, namely Pas de la Casa and Sant Julià de Lòria. The **Punt de Trobada** center (⊠ Ctra. d'Espanya, ☎ 843433), 2 km (1¼ mi) from the Spanish border, is bright, modern, and immense. **La Casa del Formatge** (⊠ Av. Carlemany s/n, ☎ 821689) in Les Escaldes has more than 500 different kinds of cheeses from all over the world.

Andorra Essentials

Consulates

U.S. (⊠ Pg. Reina Elisenda 23, Barcelona, Spain, ☎ 93/2802227). **Canadian** (⊠ Nuñez de Balboa 35, Madrid, Spain, ☎ 91/2259119). **U.K.** (⊠ Apartado de Correos 12111, Barcelona, Spain, ☎ 93/3222151).

Emergencies

Police (☎ 110). **Mountain rescue** (☎ 112). **Ambulance** (☎ 118). **Doctor** (☎ 868000). **Dentist** (☎ 868000). **Pharmacy** (☎ 868000).

Guided Tours

Tours of Andorra la Vella and the surrounding countryside are offered by several firms; check with the tourist office for details or call **Excursion Nadal** (☎ 821138) or **Sol i Neu Excursion** (☎ 823653).

Travel Agency

Relax Travel Agency/American Express (⊠ Mossen Tremosa 12, Andorra la Vella, ☎ 822044, FAX 827055).

Visitor Information

Andorra La Vella (Sindicat d'Iniciativa/National Tourist Office; ⊠ Carrer Dr. Vilanova, ☎ 820214, FAX 825823; Barcelona office, ⊠ Carrer Marià Cubí 159 08021, ☎ 93/200–0655 or 93/200–0787; city tourist office, ⊠ Plaça de la Rotonda, ☎ 827117). **Canillo** (Unió Pro-Turisme, ⊠ Caseta Pro-Turisme, ☎ FAX 851002). **Encamp** (Unió Pro-Foment i Turisme, ⊠ Plaça Consell General, ☎ 831405, FAX 831878). **Escaldes-Engordany** (Unió Pro-Turisme, ⊠ Plaça dels Co-Príncceps, ☎ 820963). **La Massana** (Unió Pro-Turisme, ⊠ Plaça del Quart, ☎ 835693). **Ordino** (Oficina de Turisme, ⊠ Cruïlla d'Ordino, ☎ 836963). **Pas de la Casa** (Unió Pro-Turisme, ⊠ C. Bernat III, ☎ 855292). **Sant Julià de Lòria** (Unió Pro-Turisme, ⊠ Plaça de la Germandat, ☎ 841352).

3 AUSTRIA

VIENNA, DANUBE VALLEY, SALZBURG, INNSBRUCK

An oft-told story concerns an airline pilot whose prelanding announcement advised, "Ladies and gentlemen, we are on the final approach to Vienna Airport. Please make sure your seat belts are fastened, please refrain from smoking until you are inside the terminal, and please set your watches back 100 years."

Apocryphal or not, the pilot's observation suggests the allure of a country where visitors can sense something of what Europe was like before the pulse of the 20th century quickened to a beat that would have dizzied our great-grandparents. Today, the occasional gentleman will kiss a lady's hand just as in the days of the Habsburgs, and Lipizzaner stallions still dance to Mozart minuets—in other words, Austria is a country that has not forgotten the elegance of its past.

Look beyond the postcard clichés of dancing white horses, the zither strains, and the singing of the Vienna Boys Choir, however, and you'll find a conservative-mannered yet modern country, one of Europe's richest, in which the juxtaposition of old and new often creates excitement—even controversy. Vienna has its sumptuous palaces, but it is also home to an assemblage of U.N. organizations housed in a wholly modern complex. Tucked away between storybook villages are giant industrial plants, one of which turns out millions of compact discs for Sony. The world's largest penicillin producer is hidden away in a Tirolean valley. And those countless glittering crystal objects you see in jewelry and gift stores around the world originate in a small village outside Innsbruck. By no means is the country frozen in a time warp: Rather, it is the contrast between the old and the new—experiencing an Andrew Lloyd Webber musical in the theater where Mozart's *Magic Flute* premiered—that makes Austria such a fascinating place to visit.

So, too, does the fact that, poised as it is between East and West, Austria shares a culture with Europe but has deep roots as well in the lands that lie beyond to the east. It was Metternich who declared that "Asia begins at the Landstrasse," referring to Vienna's crucial role as the meeting place of East and West for 2,000 years. Today, Vienna's spectacular historical and artistic heritage—exemplified by the legacies of

Austria (Österreich)

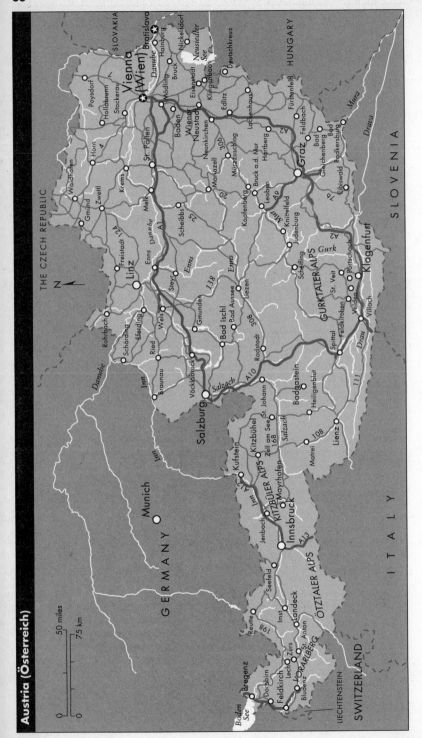

Beethoven, Freud, Klimt, and Mahler—lures travelers to this grande dame of a city. Between the Apfelstrudel and psychoanalysis, Schubert and sausages, lies a definite old-world charm that natives would be the last to underplay.

But as with most countries, the capital is only a small part of what Austria has to offer. A grand tour of the country reveals considerably more Austrias than the nine provinces would suggest: Salzburg—home every summer to one of the world's ritziest music festivals—is a departure point for the Salzkammergut lake country and the mountains of Land Salzburg; as the hub of the Alps, Innsbruck beckons skiers to explore the resorts of Lech, St. Anton, and Kitzbühel; finally, there's the scenic Wachau stretch of the Danube Valley.

In the end, the way to get the most out of Austria is to come armed with a taste for history, an appreciation for the quirks in human nature, and a thirst for art and wonderful music. A taste for good wine comes in handy, too—as you'll discover when you're sitting in a wine garden in the heart of a lush vineyard, enjoying a mug of Grüner Veltliner to the gentle background music of a Schrammel quartet.

AUSTRIA A TO Z

Customs
Austria's duty-free allowances are as follows: 200 cigarettes or 50 cigars or 250 grams of tobacco; 2 liters of wine and 1 liter of spirits; 1 bottle of toilet water (about 250-milliliter size); and 50 milliliters of perfume for those age 17 and over arriving from non–European Union countries. Tourists also do not have to pay duty on personal articles brought into Austria temporarily for their own use.

Dining
Take your choice among sidewalk *Wurstl* (frankfurter) stands, *Imbissstuben* (quick-lunch stops), cafés, *Heuriger* (wine taverns), self-service restaurants, modest *Gasthäuser* (neighborhood establishments featuring local specialties), and full-fledged restaurants in every price category. Most places post their menus outside. Shops (such as Eduscho) that sell coffee beans also offer coffee by the cup at prices considerably lower than those in cafés. Many Anker bakery shops also offer tasty *Schmankerl* (snacks) and coffee, and some offer a full breakfast. *Würstelstands* offer a tempting array of grilled sausages, including *Käsekrainer* (beef and melted cheese), served with a roll and mustard. A growing number of shops and snack bars offer pizza by the slice.

MEALTIMES
A typical Austrian breakfast consists of rolls, cold cuts, cheese, and coffee. Lunch is usually the big meal of the day for Austrians unless they're dining out in the evening. *Jause* (coffee with cake) is taken in the late afternoon, and a light supper ends the day.

RATINGS
Prices are per person and include appetizer and a main course, usually with salad, and a small beer or glass of wine. Meals in the top price categories will include a dessert or cheese with coffee. Prices include taxes and service (but adding another 3%–5% to the bill as a tip is customary).

CATEGORY	MAJOR CITY	OTHER AREAS
$$$$	over AS750	over AS500
$$$	AS350–AS750	AS300–AS500
$$	AS200–AS350	AS170–AS300
$	under AS200	under AS170

WHAT TO WEAR

A jacket and tie are generally advised for restaurants in the top two price categories. Otherwise casual dress is acceptable. When in doubt, it's best to dress up.

Language

German is the official national language. In larger cities and most resort areas you will have no problem finding English speakers; hotel and restaurant employees, in particular, speak English reasonably well. Most younger Austrians speak at least passable English.

Lodging

CAMPING

Most campsites are well equipped, with water and toilet facilities. Some have hookups for RVs. Few campsites are open year-round. Summer or winter, make reservations well in advance to be sure of a site. In addition to campsites, mountain cabins are available on an overnight basis to Alpine hikers. For information, contact **Österreichischer Alpenverein** (⌧ Wilhelm-Greil-Str. 15, A-6020 Innsbruck, ☎ 0512/5954734, FAX 0512/575528). Information on camping is available from the National Tourist Office (☞ Visitor Information, *below*).

HOTELS

Austrian hotels and pensions are officially classified using from one to five stars. These grades broadly coincide with our own four-point rating system. No matter what the category, standards for service and cleanliness are high. All hotels in the upper three categories have either a bath or shower in the room; even the most inexpensive accommodations provide hot and cold water. Accommodations include castles and palaces, conventional hotels, *Gasthöfe* (country inns), and the more modest pensions. In summer, student dormitories offer a reasonably priced option to guests of all ages.

RATINGS

All prices quoted here are for two people in a double room and include taxes. Although exact rates vary, a single room generally costs more than half the price of a comparable double. Breakfast at the roll-and-coffee level is often included in the room rate; full and sumptuous breakfast buffets, however, can involve a supplementary charge. Keep in mind that hotels outside Vienna may offer comprehensive rates that include breakfast *and* dinner; these are often excellent deals.

CATEGORY	MAJOR CITY	OTHER AREAS
$$$$	over AS2,700	over AS2,000
$$$	AS1,700–AS2,700	AS1,500–AS2,000
$$	AS1,000–AS1,700	AS900–AS1,500
$	under AS1,000	under AS900

YOUTH HOSTELS

Hosteling is well developed, although most locations are outside city centers. For information, contact **Österreichischer Jugendherbergsverband** (Austrian Hostel Association; ⌧ Schottenring 28, A-1010 Vienna, ☎ 01/533–5353, FAX 01/535–0861).

Mail

POSTAL RATES

Airmail letters and postcards to the United States and Canada cost AS13 minimum. Airmail letters and postcards to the United Kingdom cost AS7, and an aerogram costs AS13.

RECEIVING MAIL

American Express offices in Vienna (⌧ Kärntner Strasse 21-23, ☎ 01/515–40–0), Linz (⌧ Bürgerstrasse 14, ☎ 0732/669013), Salzburg (⌧

Mozartplatz 5-7, ☎ 0662/8080), and Innsbruck (⊠ Brixnerstrasse 3, ☎ 0512/582491) will hold mail at no charge for those carrying an American Express credit card or American Express traveler's checks.

Money Matters

COSTS

Austria has become expensive, but as inflation is relatively low, the currency has remained fairly stable. Vienna and Salzburg are the most expensive cities, along with fashionable resorts at Kitzbühel, Seefeld, Badgastein, Velden, Zell am See, Pörtschach, St. Anton, Zürs, and Lech. Many smaller towns near these resorts offer virtually identical facilities at half the price. Drinks in bars and clubs cost considerably more than in cafés or restaurants. Austrian prices include service and tax.

CREDIT CARDS

Credit cards are not as widely used in Austria as they are in other European countries, and not all establishments that accept plastic take all cards. Some may require a minimum purchase if payment is to be made by card. Many restaurants take cash only. **American Express** has money machines in Vienna at its main office (⊠ Kärntnerstr. 21–23) and at the airport. Many of the **Bankomat** money dispensers will also accept Visa cards if you have an encoded international PIN.

CURRENCY

The unit of currency is the Austrian schilling (AS), divided into 100 groschen. There are AS20, 50, 100, 500, 1,000, and 5,000 bills; AS1, 5, 10, and 20 coins; and 1-, 2-, 5-, 10-, and 50-groschen coins. The 1-, 2-, and 5-groschen coins are rare, and the AS20 coins are unpopular, though useful for some cigarette machines. The 500- and 100-schilling notes look similar; confusing the two can be an expensive mistake. At press time (summer 1999), the exchange rate was AS13.27 to the dollar, AS9.03 to the Canadian dollar, and AS20.99 to the pound sterling. You may bring in any amount of either foreign currency or schillings and take out any amount with you.

Exchange traveler's checks at a bank, a post office, or the American Express office to get the best rate. All charge a small commission; some smaller banks or "change" offices may give a poorer rate *and* charge a higher fee. All change offices at airports and at main train stations in major cities cash traveler's checks. In Vienna, bank-operated change offices with extended hours are found on Stephansplatz and at the main rail stations. Bank Austria machines on Stephansplatz, at Kärntnerstrasse 51 (to the right of the Opera), and at the Raiffeisenbank on Kohlmarkt (at Michaelerplatz) change bills from other currencies into schillings, but rates are poor and the commission hefty.

SAMPLE PRICES

Cup of coffee in a café or restaurant, AS35–AS45; ½ liter of draft beer, AS28–AS48; small glass of wine, AS35; Coca-Cola, AS28; open sandwich, AS25; theater ticket, AS200–AS300; concert ticket, AS250–AS500; opera ticket, AS600 and up; 2-km (1-mi) taxi ride, AS60.

TIPPING

In restaurants, 10% service is included. Add anything from AS5 to AS50, depending on the restaurant and the size of the bill, or about 3–5%. Leave the actual tip by telling the waiter the total amount you wish to pay—that is, the bill plus the tip—then remit the tip with the payment to the waiter (do not leave it on the table). Railroad porters and hotel porters or bellhops get AS10 per bag. Doormen get AS20 for hailing a cab and assisting. Room service gets AS20 for snacks and AS20–AS40 for full meals; in more expensive establishments, expect to tip on the higher side. Maids get no tip unless you stay a week or more, or unless special service is rendered.

National Holidays

January 1; January 6 (Epiphany); April 24 (Easter Monday); May 1 (May Day); June 1 (Ascension); June 11, 12 (Pentecost); June 22 (Corpus Christi); August 15 (Assumption); October 26 (National Day); November 1 (All Saints' Day); December 8 (Immaculate Conception); December 25–26. On the December 8 holiday, banks and offices are closed but most shops are open.

Opening and Closing Times

Banks are open weekdays 8–noon or 12:30, and 1:30–3; until 5 on Thursday; closed Saturday. Hours vary from one city to another. Principal offices in cities stay open during lunch. **Museum** opening days and times vary considerably from one city to another and depend on the season and other factors. Monday is often a closing day. Your hotel or the local tourist office will have current details. **Shops** are open weekdays from 8 or 9 until 6, in shopping centers to 7:30, and Saturday until 5, although some may still close at noon or 1. Many smaller shops close for one or two hours at midday. Larger food markets are open weekdays from 7:30 to 7:30, Saturday to 5.

Shopping

SALES TAX REFUNDS

A value-added tax (VAT) of 20% is charged on all sales and is automatically included in prices. If you purchase goods worth AS1,000 or more and are not a citizen of an EU country, you can claim a refund of the tax either as you leave or after you've returned home. Ask the store clerk to fill out the necessary papers. Get them stamped at the airport or border crossing by customs officials (who may ask to see the goods). You can get an immediate refund of the VAT, less a service charge, at international airports or at main border crossings, or you can return the papers by mail to the shop(s). The VAT refund can be credited to your credit card account or remitted by check.

Telephoning

COUNTRY CODE

The country code for Austria is 43. When dialing an Austrian number from abroad, drop the initial 0 from the local area code.

INTERNATIONAL CALLS

It costs considerably more to telephone *from* Austria than it does *to* Austria. Calls from post offices are least expensive. To avoid hotel charges, call overseas and ask to be called back; use an international credit card, available from AT&T, MCI, and others; or use access codes to reach operators for **AT&T** (☎ 022/903–011), **MCI World Phone** (☎ 022/903–012), or **Canada Direct** (☎ 022/903–013). To make a collect call—you can't do this from pay phones—dial the operator and ask for an *R*-Gespräch (pronounced air-ga-*shprayk*). For international information dial 11812 for numbers in Germany, 11813 for numbers in other European countries, and 11814 for overseas numbers. Most operators speak English; if yours doesn't, you'll be passed along to one who does.

LOCAL CALLS

Pay telephones take AS1, 5, 10, and 20 coins. Emergency calls are free. Instructions are in English in most booths. The initial connection for a local call costs AS2. Insert AS1 or more to continue the connection when you hear the tone warning that your time is up. Phone cards. available at post offices, work in all phones marked *Wertkartentele-*

fon. The cost of the call will be deducted from the card automatically. Cards cost AS190 for AS200 worth of calls, AS95 for AS100 worth, and AS48 for calls totaling AS50. Phone numbers throughout Austria are currently being changed. A sharp tone indicates either no connection or that the number has been changed. Dial 11811 for numbers in Austria.

Transportation

BY BUS

Austria has an extensive national bus network run by the post office and railroads. Where trains don't go, buses do, and you'll find them (bright yellow for easy recognition) in the remotest regions. You can buy tickets on board and in the off season there is no problem getting a seat, but on routes to favored ski areas during holiday periods reservations are essential. Bookings can be handled at the ticket office (there's one in most towns with bus service) or by travel agents. In most communities, bus routes begin and end at or near the railroad station, making transfers easy. Increasingly, coordination of bus service with railroads means that many of the discounts and special tickets available for trains apply to buses as well.

BY CAR

Gasoline. Gas prices are the most expensive in Europe, though eventually they will have to be lowered to conform with other EU countries. Currently it costs roughly AS11 a liter for unleaded gasoline and AS8.50 a liter for diesel, and at nearly four liters to the gallon, the final tally can be quite hefty.

Parking. Traffic congestion in major cities means that driving generally takes longer than public transportation. City planners' solutions have been to make driving as difficult as possible, with one-way streets and other tricks, and a car in town is far more of a burden than a pleasure. Daytime parking is very difficult. A Parkschein (available at most tobacconists and magazine stands) allows you to park for 90 minutes. Display the paper on your dashboard. Parking in smaller towns and villages is much easier and not as restricted.

Road Conditions. The Austrian highway network is excellent and roads are well-maintained and well-marked. Secondary roads may be narrow and winding and very picturesque. The main routes (Autobahns), especially the A10 down to Carinthia and Italy, are packed during both Austrian and German school holidays.

Rules of the Road. Drive on the right. Seat belts are compulsory in front. Children under 12 must sit in the back, and smaller children must have a restraining seat. Speed limits are as posted; otherwise, 130 kph (80 mph) on expressways, 100 kph (62 mph) on other main roads, 50 kph (31 mph) in built-up areas. Some city areas have speed limits of 30 kph (19 mph). Be aware that speed is checked by radar, even in small towns, and fines are heavy. The right-of-way is for those coming from the right (especially in traffic circles) unless otherwise marked. All vehicles using the autobahn (divided, mostly limited-access main highways, including the main highway from Vienna airport to the city) must display an Autobahn-Vignette toll sticker on the inside of the windshield. If you're renting a car in Austria it's already included, but if you're coming from another country you need to buy a one-week sticker for AS70. Two-month stickers cost AS150. If you're caught without a sticker, the fine is AS1,100. To apply, contact the **ÖAMTC/Österreichischer Automobile-, Motorrad- und Touringclub** (✉ Schubertring 3, A-1010, Vienna, ☎ 01/711997).

Travel by air within Austria is expensive. Austria's national airline, **Austrian Airlines** (☎ 01/1789; main office, ✉ Kärtner Ring 18, 1010 Vienna), and its subsidiary, Tyrolean Airlines, offer service from Vienna to Graz, Linz, Innsbruck, Salzburg and points outside Austria. **Rheintalflug** (☎ 01/ 7007-36911) has service between Vienna and Altenrhein (Switzerland, near Bregenz) with bus connections to points in Voralberg.

Austrian train service is excellent and efficient. The IC (InterCity) or EC (EuroCity) trains are the fastest, with a supplement of AS50 included in the price of the ticket. If you are traveling outside the country, be sure to check at the station if an additional supplement is required. Some trains require it and it costs more to buy it on-board. It's also a good idea to pay the extra AS30 per ticket for a seat reservation, especially at peak holiday times, and year-round for travel to major destinations. If you're planning on doing a lot of traveling within Austria, a Bundesnetzkarte (full-network pass) grants you unlimited travel for a month and is also good for discounts on boat excursions on the Wolfgansee and Bodensee, and on all funiculars and cog railways.

Visitor Information
Central Tourist Office (national tourist office; ✉ Margaretenstr. 1, A-1040 Vienna, ☎ 01/211140, FAX 01/216–8492) for phone inquiries and hotel assistance. **City Tourist Office** (✉ Kärnterstr. 38, A-1010 Vienna).

Weather
Austria has two tourist seasons. The summer season technically starts around Easter, reaches its peak in July, and winds down in September. In summer, Vienna literally moves outdoors. May, June, September, and October are the most temperate months, and the most affordable. The winter cultural season starts in October and runs into June; winter sports get under way in December and last until the end of April, although you can ski in certain areas well into June and on some of the highest glaciers year-round. Some events—the Salzburg Festival is a prime example—occasion a substantial increase in hotel and other prices.

Summer can be warm; winter, bitterly cold. The southern region is usually several degrees warmer in summer, several degrees colder in winter. Winters north of the Alps can be overcast and dreary, whereas the south basks in winter sunshine. The following are the average daily maximum and minimum temperatures for Vienna.

Jan.	34F	1C	May	67F	19C	Sept.	68F	20C
	25	– 4		50	10		53	11
Feb.	38F	3C	June	73F	23C	Oct.	56F	14C
	28	– 3		56	14		44	7
Mar.	47F	8C	July	76F	25C	Nov.	45F	7C
	30	– 1		60	15		37	3
Apr.	58F	15C	Aug.	75F	24C	Dec.	37F	3C
	43	6		59	15		30	– 1

VIENNA

Vienna has been characterized as an "old dowager of a town"—an Austro-Hungarian empress widowed in 1918 by the Great War. It's not just the aristocratic and courtly atmosphere, with monumental doorways and facades of former palaces at every turn. Nor is it just that Vienna (Wien in German) has a higher proportion of middle-aged and older citizens than any other city in Europe, with a concomitant air of stability, quiet, and respectability. Rather, it's this factor—combined with a love of music; a discreet weakness for rich food (especially cakes); an adherence to old-fashioned and formal forms of address; a high regard for the arts; and a gentle mourning for lost glories—that preserves the stiff elegance of old-world dignity.

Exploring Vienna

Numbers in the margin correspond to points of interest on the Vienna map.

Most main sights are in the inner zone, the oldest part of the city, encircled by the Ring, once the course of the city walls and today a broad tree-lined boulevard. Carry a ready supply of AS10 coins; many places of interest have coin-operated tape-recording machines that provide English commentaries. As you wander around, train yourself to look upward; some of the most memorable architectural delights are found on upper stories and along roof lines. Note that addresses throughout the chapter ending with "-strasse" or "-gasse" (both meaning "street") are abbreviated "str." or "g." respectively (Augustinerstrasse will be "Augustinerstr."; Dorotheergasse will be "Dorotheerg.").

The Heart of Vienna

❶ Albertina. Some of the greatest old master drawings—including Dürer's *Praying Hands*—are housed in this unassuming building, home to the world's largest collection of drawings, sketches, engravings, and etchings. Other highlights include works by Rembrandt, Michelangelo, and Correggio. The building is undergoing restoration and at press time (spring 1999) the collection was being housed in the Akademiehof (✉ Makartpl. 3, opposite Secession; Karlspl. U-bahn stop), possibly until 2001. ✉ *Augustinerstr. 1,* ☎ *01/581–3060–21.* ☉ *Tues.–Fri. 10–6, weekends 10–4.*

❸ Augustinerkirche (St. Augustine's Church). The interior of this 14th-century church has undergone restoration; while much of the earlier Baroque ornamentation was removed in the 1780s, the gilt organ decoration and main altar remain as visual sensations. This was the court church; the Habsburg rulers' hearts are preserved in a chamber here. On Sunday, the 11 AM mass here is sung in Latin. ✉ *Josefspl.*

⓲ Donner Brunnen (Donner Fountain). Marking the center of Neuer Markt square since 1739, this fountain is a Baroque showpiece adorned with florid sculpted figures. The characters represent the main rivers that flow into the Danube. Empress Maria Theresa thought the figures were scandalously underclad and wanted them removed. ✉ *Neuer Markt.*

㉕ Freud Museum. The original famous couch is gone (there's a replica), but the apartment in which Sigmund Freud developed modern psychiatry and treated his first patients is otherwise generally intact. Other rooms include a reference library. ✉ *Bergg. 19,* ☎ *01/319–1596.* ☉ *July–Sept., daily 9–6; Oct.–June, daily 9–4.*

㉜ Heeresgeschichtliches Museum (Museum of Military History). Designed by Theophil Hansen, this impressive neo-Gothic building houses war artifacts ranging from armor and Turkish tents confiscated from the Turks during the 16th-century siege of Vienna to fighter planes and tanks. Also on display is the bullet-riddled car that Archduke Franz Ferdinand and his wife were riding in when they were assassinated in Sarajevo in 1914. ✉ *Arsenal 3, Bldg. 18,* ☎ *01/795–610.* ☉ *Sat.–Thurs., 10–4. Tram 18/Ghegastr., near the Belvedere.*

46

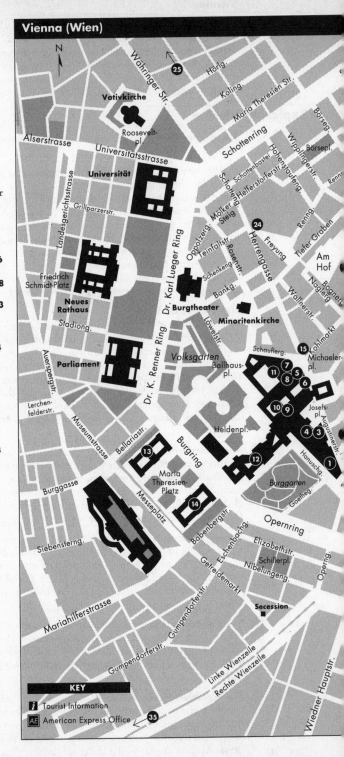

Vienna (Wien)

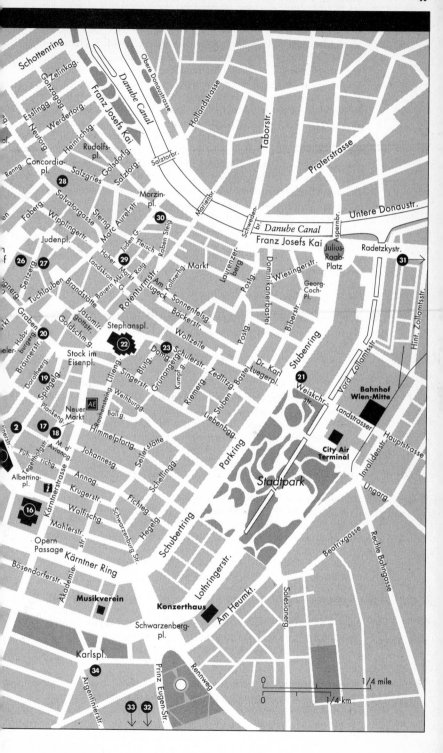

★ **⑦ Hofburg** (Imperial Palace). This centerpiece of Imperial Vienna is actually a vast complex comprising numerous buildings, courtyards, and must-sees. Start with the magnificent domed entry—**Michaelertor** (St. Michael's Gate), the principal gateway to the Hofburg—and go through the courtyards to the vast grassy plaza, Heldenplatz (Hero's Square), on the front. The palace complex, with sections dating from the 13th through 18th centuries, includes the ☞ **Augustinerkirche**, the ☞ **Nationalbibliothek**—its central room is one of the most spectacular Baroque showpieces anywhere—and the ☞ **Hofburgkapelle**, home to the Vienna Boys Choir. Here, too, are the famous ☞ **Spanische Reitschule**—where the Lipizzaners go through their paces—and three fascinating museums: ☞ **Hofsilber-und Tafelkammer Museum**, the ☞ **Schauräume in der Hofburg**, and the ☞ **Schatzkammer**, as well as the **Schmetterlinghaus** (Butterfly House), alive with unusual butterflies. The complex also houses the office of the federal presidency, a glittering chandelier-lit convention center, an elegant multipurpose hall (Redoutensaal), and private apartments as well as lesser government offices. The complex of the Hofburg is centered around the ☞ **Neue Burg** palace. ⊠ *Hofburg: main streets circling complex—Opernring, Augustinerstr., Schauflerg., and Dr. Karl Renner-Ring Str. Schmetterlinghaus: entrance in Burggarten,* ☎ *01/533–8570.* ⊙ *Apr.–Oct., daily 10–5; Nov.–Mar., daily 10–4.*

⑩ Hofburgkapelle (Court Chapel). Home to the renowned Vienna Boys Choir, this Gothic chapel dates from 1449. You'll need tickets to hear the angelic boys sing mass (only 10 side balcony seats afford views) at 9:15 AM on Sunday, mid-September through June; tickets are available from travel agencies at a substantial markup, at the chapel itself (open daily 11:30–1 and 3–5), or by writing two months in advance to the Hofmusikkapelle (Hofburg, Schweizerhof, A-1010 Vienna). General seating costs AS60, prime seats in the front of the church AS340. The City Tourist Office (☞ Visitor Information *in* Vienna Essentials, *below*) can sometimes help with ticket applications. Limited standing room is available for free; get to the chapel by at least 8:30 AM on Sunday for a shot at a spot. ⊠ *Hofburg, Schweizer Hof,* ☎ *01/533–9927–71,* FAX *01/533–9927–75.*

★ **⑪ Hofsilber-und Tafelkammer Museum** (Court Silver and Tableware Museum). See how royalty dined in this brilliant showcase of imperial table settings. Little wonder Marie Antoinette—who, as a child of Maria Theresa, grew up in Schloss Schönbrunn (☞ *below*)—had a taste for extreme luxury. You can buy a combined ticket, which includes the imperial apartments around the corner. ⊠ *Burghof inner court, Michaelertrakt,* ☎ *01/533–7570.* ⊙ *Daily 9–4:30.*

⑲ Jüdisches Museum der Stadt Wien (Jewish Museum). Housed in the former Eskeles town palace, the city's Jewish Museum offers permanent and changing exhibits that portray the richness of the Jewish culture and heritage that contributed so much to Vienna and Austria. On the top floor is a staggering collection of Judaica. ⊠ *Dorotheerg. 11,* ☎ *01/535–0431.* ⊙ *Sun.–Wed. and Fri. 10–6, Thurs. 10–9.*

⑰ Kapuzinerkirche (Capuchin Church). The ground-level church is nothing unusual, but the basement crypt holds the imperial vault, the **Kaisergruft**, the final resting place of many sarcophagi of long-dead Habsburgs. The oldest tomb is that of Ferdinand II; it dates from 1633. The most recent one is that of Empress Zita, widow of the last of the kaisers, who died in 1989. ⊠ *Neuer Markt 1,* ☎ *01/512–6853–12.* ⊙ *Daily 9:30–4.*

★ **㉞ Karlskirche** (St. Charles's Church). The classical Baroque facade and dome flanked by vast twin columns instantly identify the Karlskirche, one of the city's best-known landmarks. The church was built around 1715 by Fischer von Erlach. In the surprisingly small oval interior, the ceiling has airy frescoes, while the Baroque altar is adorned with a magnificent sunburstlike array of gilded shafts. ⊠ *Karlspl.*

★ ⑭ **Kunsthistorisches Museum** (Art History Museum). One of the finest art collections in the world, housed in palatial splendor, this is the jewel of Vienna's museums. Its glories are the Italian and Flemish collections, assembled by the Habsburgs over many centuries. The group of paintings by Pieter Bruegel the Elder is the largest in existence. The large-scale works concentrated in the main galleries shouldn't distract you from the masterworks in the more intimate side wings. One level down is the remarkable *Kunstkammer,* displaying priceless objects created for the Habsburg emperors. These include curiosities made of gold, silver, and crystal (including Cellini's salt cellar). ⊠ *Maria-Theresien-Pl.,* ☎ *01/525–240.* ☉ *Tues.–Sun. 10–6, Thurs. 10–9.*

Ⓒ ⑥ **Lipizzaner Museum.** To learn more about the extraordinary Lipizzan horses of the Spanish Riding School, visit this museum in what used to be the old imperial pharmacy. Exhibits document the history of the Lipizzaners through paintings, photographs, and videos giving an overview from the 16th century to the present. A visit to the stables allows you to see the horses up close through a window. ⊠ *Reitschulg. 2,* ☎ *01/526–4184–30,* ﬀ︎ *01/526–4186.* ✉ *AS50; combined ticket with morning training session AS130.* ☉ *Daily 9–6.*

⑮ **Looshaus** (Loos Building). This monument of 20th-century architecture, designed by Adolf Loos and built in 1911, is tellingly located opposite the Baroque-era Michaelertor (☞ Hofburg, *above*). Step inside—it's now a bank—to see the remarkable restoration of the foyer. Outside, it's no more than a simple stucco-and-glass structure, but architectural historians point to it as one of the earliest "modern" buildings—with style determined by function—in Europe. ⊠ *Michaelerpl. 3.*

㉓ **Mozart Errinerungsräume** (Mozart Memorial Rooms). A commemorative museum occupies the small apartment in the house on a narrow street just east of St. Stephen's cathedral where Mozart lived from 1784 to 1787. It was here that the composer wrote *The Marriage of Figaro* (hence the nickname Figaro House), and, some claim, spent the happiest years of his life. Fascinating Mozart memorabilia are on view, unfortunately displayed in an inappropriately modern fashion. ⊠ *Domg. 5,* ☎ *01/513–6294.* ☉ *Tues.–Sun. 9–12:15 and 1–4:30.*

㉑ **Museum für angewandte Kunst (MAK)** (Museum of Applied Arts). This fascinating museum contains a large collection of Austrian furniture, porcelain, art objects, and priceless Oriental carpets; the Jugendstil display devoted to Josef Hoffman and his followers at the Wiener Werkstätte is particularly fine. The museum puts on changing exhibitions of contemporary art, with artists ranging from Chris Burden to Nam June Paik. The museum also houses the popular MAK Cafe (☞ Dining and Lodging, *below*). ⊠ *Stubenring 5,* ☎ *01/711–36–0.* ☉ *Tues.– Wed. and Fri.–Sun. 10–6, Thurs. 10–9. U-bahn: U3 Stubentor.*

★ ④ **Nationalbibliothek** (National Library). The focus here is on the stunning Baroque central hall—one of Europe's most magnificently decorated spaces. Don't overlook the fascinating collection of globes on the third floor. ⊠ *Josefspl. 1. Library:* ☎ *01/534–100.* ☉ *Hrs vary: generally mid-May–Oct., Mon.–Sat. 10–4; Nov.–mid-May, Mon.–Sat. 10–2; Sun. and holidays 10–1. Globe museum:* ☎ *01/534–10–297.* ☉ *Mon.– Wed. and Fri. 11–noon, Thurs. 2–3.*

⑬ Naturhistorisches Museum (Natural History Museum). The twin buildings opposite the art-filled Kunsthistorisches Museum (☞ *above*) house ranks of assorted showcases filled with stuffed animals, but such special collections as butterflies are better presented. There are dinosaur skeletons, of course. Here also is the Venus of Willendorf, a 25,000-year-old statuette discovered in Lower Austria. ⊠ *Maria-Theresien-Pl.,* ☏ *01/521-77-0.* ☉ *Wed.–Mon. 9–6.*

⑫ Neue Burg (New Wing of the Imperial Palace). This ponderous 19th-century edifice—Hitler announced the annexation of Austria from its balcony in 1938—now houses a series of museums, ranging from musical instruments (Beethoven's piano) to weapons (tons of armor) to the collections of the **Völkerkunde** (Ethnological; Montezuma's headdress) and **Ephesus** (classical antiquity) museums. ⊠ *Heldenpl. 1,* ☏ *01/525-240.* ☉ *Wed.–Mon. 10–6. Ethnological and Ephesus museums: Jan.–Mar., Wed.–Mon. 10–6; Apr.–Dec., Wed.–Mon. 10–4.*

⑳ Pestsäule (Plague Column). Shooting up from the middle of the broad Graben square like a geyser of whipped cream touched with gold, this heavily ornate Baroque-era column commemorates the Black Death of the plague epidemic of 1697. ⊠ *Graben.*

★ **⑨ Schatzkammer** (Imperial Treasury). An almost overpowering display includes the magnificent crown jewels, the imperial crowns, the treasure of the Order of the Golden Fleece, regal robes, and other secular and ecclesiastical treasures. The imperial crown of the Holy Roman Empire is over 1,000 years old. ⊠ *Hofburg, Schweizer Hof,* ☏ *01/533-7931.* ☉ *Wed.–Mon. 10–6.*

⑧ Schauräume in der Hofburg (Imperial Apartments). The long, repetitive suite of conventionally luxurious rooms has a poignant feel. The decoration (19th-century imitation of 18th-century rococo) tries to look regal, but ends up looking merely official. Among the few signs of genuine life are Emperor Franz Josef's spartan, iron field bed, and Empress Elizabeth's wooden gymnastics equipment. Obsessed with her looks, she suffered from anorexia and was fanatically devoted to exercise. ⊠ *Michaelerpl. 1; entrance under Michaelertor dome* (☞ *Hofburg, above*), ☏ *01/533-7570.* ☉ *Daily 9–4:30.*

★ **⑤ Spanische Reitschule** (Spanish Riding School). Probably the most famous interior in Vienna, the riding arena of the Spanish Riding School—wedding-cake white and crystal-chandeliered—is where the beloved white Lipizzaner horses train and perform dressage when they are not stabled in stalls across the Reitschulgasse to the east side of the school. Due to renovations, the school entrance has been temporarily moved from Josefsplatz to the main courtyard next to the Swiss Gate, beyond the Michaelertor rotunda dome; when renovations are done, the main entrance will be moved back, so double-check. For performance schedules and tickets, write to the Spanische Reitschule (⊠ Hofburg, A-1010 Vienna) *at least* three months in advance. The AmEx office sometimes has a few last-minute tickets, but expect a 22% service charge. You can watch the 10 AM–noon training sessions Tuesday–Saturday during much of the performance season (tickets only at the door). ⊠ *Michaelerpl. 1, Hofburg,* ☏ *01/533-9031-0,* ☏ *01/535-0186.* ☜ *AS250–AS900, standing room AS200, morning training sessions AS100; Sat.-morning training sessions with music, AS250, available only through travel agencies.* ☉ *Mar.–June and Sept.–mid-Dec; closed tour wks.*

⑯ Staatsoper (State Opera House). Considered one of the best opera houses in the world, the Staatsoper is a focus of Viennese social life as well. Almost totally destroyed in the last days of World War II (only the walls and front foyers were saved), it was rebuilt in its present simpler elegance and reopened in 1955. Tickets for seats can be expensive and scarce, but among the very best bargains in Vienna are the Staatsoper standing-room tickets, available for each performance at delightfully affordable prices— as low as AS50 ($4.50)! Backstage tours also are available. The repertory schedule is one of the most ambitious in Europe; as many as four different operas are performed in a single week during the September– June season. ⊠ *Opernring 2,* ☎ *01/514–4426–13.*

★ ㉒ **Stephansdom** (St. Stephen's Cathedral). The towering Gothic spires and gaudy 19th-century tile roof of the city's central landmark still dominate the skyline. The oldest parts of the structure are the 13th-century entrance, the soaring **Riesentor** (Great Entry), and the **Heidentürme** (Heathens' Towers). Inside, the church is mysteriously shadowy, filled with an array of monuments, tombs, sculptures, paintings, and pulpits. Despite numerous Baroque additions—and extensive wartime damage—the atmosphere seems authentically medieval. Climb the 343 steps of the south tower—Alte Steffl (Old Stephen) as the Viennese call it—for a stupendous view over the city. An elevator goes up the north tower to the Pummerin, a 22-ton bell cast in part from cannons captured from the Turks in 1683. If you take a 30-minute tour of the crypt, you can see the copper jars in which the entrails of the Habsburgs are carefully preserved. ⊠ *Stephanspl.,* ☎ *01/515–52–3526.* ☉ *Catacombs (guided tour only): Mon.–Sat. 10, 11, 11:30, 2, 2:30, 3:30, 4, 4:30; Sun. and holidays 2, 2:30, 3:30, 4, 4:30. North tower: Apr.–Sept., daily 9–6; Oct.–Mar., daily 8–5. South tower: daily 9–5:30.*

☾ ❷ **Theater Museum.** Housed in the noted 18th-century Palais Lobkowitz— Beethoven was a regular visitor here—this museum covers the history of theater in Vienna and the rest of Austria. A children's museum in the basement—alas, open only by appointment—is reached by a slide! ⊠ *Lobkowitzpl. 2,* ☎ *01/512–8800–0.* ☉ *Tues.–Sun. 10–5.*

Other Corners of Vienna

㉖ **Am Hof.** The name of this remarkable square translates simply as "at court." On the east side of Am Hof, most of the Baroque overlay both inside and out on the massive **Kirche am Hof** (Church of the Nine Choirs of Angels) dates from the 1600s. The somewhat dreary interior is curiously reminiscent of those of many Dutch churches. In the northeast corner of the square check out what is possibly the most ornate fire station in the world. You'll find an open-air antiques market in the square on Thursday and Friday in summer and frequent seasonal markets at other times. ⊠ *Bounded by Tiefer Graben on west, Naglerg. on south, and Seitzerg. on east.*

㉙ **Hoher Markt.** This ancient cobblestone square with its imposing central monument celebrating the betrothal of Mary and Joseph sits atop **Roman ruins** (⊠ Hoher Markt 3, ☎ 01/535–5606), remains of the 2nd-century Roman legion encampment. On the north side of Hoher Markt is the amusing **Anker-Uhr,** a clock that marks the hour with a parade of moving figures. The figures are identified on a plaque at the lower left of the clock. ⊠ *Judeng. and Fisch-hof Str.*

㉛ **Hundertwasserhaus** (Hundertwasser House). This structure is an eccentric modern masterpiece envisioned by artist Friedenreich Hundertwasser (b. 1928)—an astonishing apartment complex marked by turrets, towers, unusual windows, and uneven floors. The nearby **Kunst-Haus Wien** (Vienna House of Art; ⊠ KunstHaus Wien, Untere Weissgerberstr. 13, ☎ 01/712–0491) is an art museum designed by the artist; it offers a floor of Hundertwasser plus changing exhibits of other modern works. ⊠ *Kegelg. and Köweng.* ☉ *Daily 10–7.*

㉘ Maria am Gestade (St. Mary's on the Bank). When built around 1400, this was a church for fishermen from the nearby canal, hence the name. Note the arched stone doorway and the ornate carved stone latticework "folded hands" spire. ⊠ *Salvatorg./Passauer Pl.*

㉚ Ruprechtskirche (St. Rupert's Church). Vienna's oldest church, dating from the 11th century, is usually closed, but sometimes opens for local art shows and summer evening classical concerts. ⊠ *Ruprechtspl.*

★ **㉝ Schloss Belvedere** (Belvedere Palace). On a rise overlooking the city, this Baroque-era palace is one of the showpieces of Vienna. It was commissioned by Prince Eugene of Savoy and built by Johann Lukas von Hildebrandt in 1721–22. The palace consists of two separate buildings, one at the foot of the hill and the other at the top. The Upper Belvedere houses a gallery of 19th- and 20th-century Viennese art, featuring works by Klimt (including his world-famous painting *The Kiss*), Kokoschka, Schiele, Waldmüller, and Makart; the Lower Belvedere has a Baroque museum together with exhibits of Austrian art of the Middle Ages. Take Streetcar D toward the Südbahnhof to reach the Belvedere. ⊠ *Prinz-Eugen-Str. 27,* ☎ *01/795–570.* ⊙ *Tues.–Sun. 10–5.*

★ **㉟ Schloss Schönbrunn** (Schönbrunn Palace). The Versailles of Vienna, this magnificent Baroque residence with grandly formal gardens was built for the Habsburgs between 1696 and 1713. The complex has been a summer residence for such personages as Maria Theresa and Napoléon. Kaiser Franz Josef I was born and died here. His "office" (kept as he left it in 1916) is a touching reminder of his Spartan life. In contrast, other rooms are filled with truly spectacular imperial elegance. Six-year-old Mozart played here in the Hall of Mirrors for Maria Theresa and the court. The ornate reception areas are still used for state occasions. A guided tour leading through more than 40 of the palace's 1,441 rooms is the best way to see inside the palace (the most dazzling salons start at No. 21). Ask to see the **Berglzimmer,** ornately decorated ground-floor rooms generally not included in tours. To get to the palace, take the U4 subway line from the city center, five stops from Karlsplatz. ⊠ *Schönbrunner Schlosstr.,* ☎ *01/81113.* ⊟ *AS140 with guided tour; AS110 without tour (40 rooms).* ⊙ *Nov.–Mar., daily 8:30–4:30; Apr.–Oct., daily 8:30–5.*

☾ On the grounds of the Schönbrunn Palace is the **Tiergarten** (zoo), Europe's oldest menagerie, established in 1752 to amuse and educate the court. It houses an extensive assortment of animals; the original Baroque enclosures now serve as viewing pavilions, with the animals housed in effective, modern settings. ☎ *01/877–9294–0.* ⊙ *Nov.–Jan., daily 9–4:30; Feb. and Oct., daily 9–5; Mar., daily 9–5:30; Apr., daily 9–6; May–Sept., daily 9–6:30.*

Pathways lead up through the formal gardens to the **Gloriette,** an 18th-century Baroque folly on the rise behind Schloss Schönbrunn built to afford superb views of the city. A café is inside. ⊙ *Daily 9–5.*

☾ The **Wagenburg** (Imperial Coach Collection), near the entrance to the palace grounds, displays splendid examples of bygone conveyances, from ornate children's sleighs to the grand carriages built to carry the coffins of deceased emperors in state funerals. ☎ *01/877–3244.* ⊙ *Apr.–Oct., daily 9–6; Nov.–Mar., Tues.–Sun. 10–4.*

Wander the grounds to discover the **Schöner Brunnen** (Beautiful Fountain) for which the Schönbrunn Palace is named; the re-created but convincing massive **Römische Ruinen** (Roman Ruins); and the great glass **Palmenhaus** (Palmery), with its orchids and exotic plants. *Palm House:*

✉ *Nearest entrance Hietzing,* ☎ *01/877–5087–406.* ⊙ *May–Sept., daily 9:30–5:30; Oct.–Apr., daily 9:30–4:30.*

㉔ Schottenkirche, Museum im Schottenstift (Scottish Church and Museum). Despite its name, the monks who founded this church around 1177 were actually Irish, not Scots. The present imposing building dates from the mid-1600s. In contrast to the plain exterior, the interior bubbles with cherubs and angels. The Benedictines have set up a small but worthwhile museum of mainly religious art, including a late-Gothic winged altarpiece removed from the church when the interior was given a Baroque overlay. The museum entrance is in the courtyard. ✉ *Freyung 6,* ☎ *01/534–98–600.* ⊙ *Thurs.–Sat. 10–5, Sun. noon–5.*

㉗ Uhrenmuseum (Clock Museum). Tucked away on several floors of a lovely Renaissance structure is an amazing collection of clocks and watches. Try to be here when the hundreds of clocks strike the noon hour. ✉ *Schulhof 2,* ☎ *01/533–2265.* ⊙ *Tues.–Sun. 9–4:30.*

Vienna Environs

Wienerwald (Vienna Woods). You can reach a small corner of the historic Vienna Woods by streetcar and bus: Take a streetcar or the U-2 subway line to Schottentor/University and, from there, Streetcar 38 (Grinzing) to the end of the line. To get into the woods, change in Grinzing to Bus 38A. This will take you to the Kahlenberg, which provides a superb view out over the Danube and the city. You can take the bus or hike to the Leopoldsberg, the promontory over the Danube from which Turkish invading forces were repulsed during the 16th and 17th centuries. Grinzing itself is a village out of a picture book. Unfortunately, much of the wine offered in its wine taverns, or Heuriger, is less than enchanting. For better wine and ambience, try the area around Pfarrplatz and Probusgasse in Hohe Warte (Streetcar 37, Bus 39A) or the suburb of Nussdorf (Streetcar D).

Dining and Lodging

In the mid-1990s Vienna, once a culinary backwater, produced a new generation of chefs willing to slaughter sacred cows and create a *Neue Küche,* a new Vienna cuisine. The movement relies on lighter versions of the old standbys and clever combinations of such traditional ingredients as liver pâtés and sour cream.

In a first-class restaurant you will pay as much as in most other Western European capitals. But you can still find good food at refreshingly low prices in the simpler restaurants, particularly at neighborhood Gasthäuser (rustic inns) in the suburbs. Remember if you eat your main meal at noon (as the Viennese do), you can take advantage of the luncheon specials available at most restaurants and in cafés. For details and price-category definitions, *see* Dining *in* Austria A to Z, *above.*

As for hotels, Vienna's first district (A-1010) is the best base for visitors because it's so close to most of the major sights, restaurants, and shops. This accessibility translates, of course, into higher prices. Try bargaining for discounts at the larger international chain hotels during the off-season. For details and price-category definitions, *see* Lodging *in* Austria A to Z, *above.*

$$$$ ✕ **Steirereck.** Generally conceded to be the most famous restaurant in
★ Austria, it consistently ranks high on critics' lists. The setting is elegant, and extra touches include a bread trolley overflowing with freshly baked loaves and, at the end of the meal, an outstanding selection of cheeses from Steirereck's own cheese cellar. Fish choices are plentiful and may include delicate smoked catfish or turbot in an avocado crust.

Also good is the lamb with crepes and spinach cooked simply with garlic and olive oil. ⊠ *Rasumofskyg. 2,* ☎ *01/713–3168. Reservations essential. Jacket and tie. AE, DC, MC, V. Closed weekends.*

$$$ ✕ **Do & Co.** The spectacular setting at the top of the modern Haas-Haus building smack in the middle of Stephansplatz would make this worthwhile for the view alone, but the food is also excellent and varied, with a nouvelle-Oriental slant that produces fragrant, tangy wok creations. Among the numerous meat choices, the combination king crab and Uruguayan steak is the most popular. In the evenings, book a table by the window so you can see the sunset over the spires of St. Stephen's, and in warm weather, ask for a table outside on the balcony. ⊠ *In Haas-Haus, Stephanspl. 12,* ☎ *01/535–3969. Reservations essential. Jacket and tie. V.*

$$$ ✕ **Fadinger.** Near the *Börse* (the Vienna Stock Exchange), this unpretentious restaurant serves some of the best nouvelle Austrian cuisine in the city. The widely varied menu includes light-as-a-feather fish dishes, such as salmon in a crisp potato crust, as well as hearty, but never heavy, meat courses. The *Zwiebelrostbraten,* skirt steak topped with crisp fried onions, is outstanding. ⊠ *Wipplingerstr. 29,* ☎ *01/533–4341. Reservations essential. No credit cards. Closed weekends.*

$$$ ✕ **Zu ebener Erde und erster Stock.** This gem of a historic house near the Volkstheater was named for a play by Nestroy (the title translates as "the ground level and first floor"). Upstairs is the cozy Biedermeier room with crocheted pillows and old family photos on the walls, and downstairs is an informal room where the focus is on light, pretheater meals. *Kürbis* (pumpkin) figures prominently on the seasonal menu, and selections include pumpkin cream soup and pumpkin risotto paired with branzino (sea bass) in rosemary broth. The beef roulade stuffed with mozzarella and eggplant is also wonderful. ⊠ *Burgg. 13,* ☎ *01/523–6254. Reservations essential. AE, V. Closed Mon. and late July–late Aug. No lunch Sat.*

$$ ✕ **Artner.** This modern, nicely lit restaurant has one of the most in-
★ novative menus in the city; in addition, it is unique in showcasing fantastic wines and goat cheese from its own 350-year-old winery in the Carnuntum region east of Vienna. Start with a salad of field greens and grilled goat cheese, then go on to mahimahi wrapped in a palm leaf and served with red rice in a mango-coconut sauce, or sesame-crusted pike perch with Oriental noodles and cilantro pesto. Lamb and veal dishes are also temptingly offered. ⊠ *Florag. 6 (entrance on Neumanng.),* ☎ *01/503–5033,* 𝖥𝖠𝖷 *01/503–5034. AE, DC, MC, V. No lunch weekends. U-bahn: U1/Taubstummeng.*

$$ ✕ **Figlmüller.** Known for its gargantuan schnitzel, which is so large it overflows the plate, Figlmüller is always packed with diners sharing benches and long tables. Food choices are limited, and everything is à la carte. The small enclosed "greenhouse" in the passageway entry is more popular than the inside rooms. ⊠ *Wollzeile 5 (passageway from Stephansdom),* ☎ *01/512–6177. No credit cards. Closed Aug.*

$$ ✕ **Hansen.** Housed downstairs in the Börse (Vienna Stock Exchange)
★ and named for the building's 19th-century architect, Theophil Hansen, this unique restaurant is also an exotic, upscale flower market. Guests dine on Mediterranan-inspired dishes such as scampi risotto or spaghettini with oven-dried tomatoes in a black olive cream sauce. Lunch is the main event here, though you can also come for breakfast or a pretheater dinner. ⊠ *Wipplingerstr. 34,* ☎ *01/532–0542. Reservations essential. AE, DC, MC, V. Closed Sun. and after 8 PM.*

$$ ✕ **Lebenbauer.** Vienna's premier vegetarian restaurant even has a no-smoking room, rare in this part of Europe. Specialties include *Hirseg-röstl* (millet hash with pumpkin seeds in an oyster mushroom sauce) and gluten-free pasta with smoked salmon and shrimp in a dill cream sauce. ⊠ *Teinfaltstr. 3, near Freyung,* ☎ *01/533–5556–0. AE, DC, MC, V. Closed 3–5 weekdays, Sat. eve., Sun., and first 2 wks Aug.*

$$ ✕ **Leopold.** This modern, convivial restaurant takes its name from the
★ church of St. Leopold next door. Walls are a deep ochre and decorated with local artists' paintings. The eclectic menu offers several vegetarian choices and updated variations of Austrian cuisine, such as beef with hash browns and creamed green beans. The warm hazelnut cake doused with caramel chocolate sauce is sublime. ⊠ *Grosse Pfarrg. 11,* ☎ *01/214–2170. Reservations essential. AE, DC, MC, V. No lunch. No breakfast Sun. mid-June–mid-Sept. U-bahn: U1, U4/Schwedenpl., Tram N/Obere Augarten.*

$$ ✕ **Livingstone.** If you're homesick for a hamburger and fries, this is the place to go. Buns are homemade and the Austrian beef is of the finest quality. But if the tropical-colonial setting straight out of a 1940s Bogart movie makes you want to try something more adventurous—such as pasta with smoked tofu, tiger shrimp, and squash—you won't be disappointed. ⊠ *Zelinkag. 4, near the Börse,* ☎ *01/533–3393. AE, DC, MC, V. No lunch.*

$$ ✕ **MAK Cafe.** In the Museum of Applied Arts (☞ Exploring Vienna, *above*), also known as MAK, this is one of the "scene" places in Vienna. The menu changes frequently and includes lots of vegetarian items. One staple is the delicious pierogi stuffed with either potatoes or minced beef. In summer sit outside in the shaded inner courtyard. ⊠ *Stubenring 3–5,* ☎ *01/714–0121. No credit cards. Closed Mon.*

$$ ✕ **Neu Wien.** As the name says, this is a taste of the new Vienna. The
★ vaulted interior is enlivened by cheeky modern art. The eclectic menu changes frequently, but look for the herbed goat cheese salad with basil oil dressing or veal with tagliatelle in a truffle sauce. ⊠ *Bäckerstr. 5, near St. Stephen's,* ☎ *01/512–0999. Reservations essential. MC, V. Closed weekends in summer. No lunch.*

$ ✕ **Brezl Gwölb.** Housed in a medieval pretzel factory between Am Hof and Judenplatz, this snug restaurant fills up fast at night. Try the scrumptious *Tyroler G'röstl,* a kind of hash with ham served in a blackened skillet. Try to get a table downstairs in the genuine medieval cellar, which looks like a set from *Phantom of the Opera.* ⊠ *Ledererhof 9,* ☎ *01/533–8811. AE, DC, MC, V.*

$ ✕ **Spatzennest.** This is simple, hearty Viennese cooking at its best, served in a restaurant on a quaint, cobblestone, pedestrian street in Old Vienna. Tasty dishes include schnitzel and roast chicken with spaetzle and slivers of ham and melted cheese. It's delightful in summer, when tables are set outside. It can be smoky indoors. ⊠ *Ulrichspl. 1, near the Volkstheater,* ☎ *01/520–1659. No credit cards. Closed Fri.–Sat.*

$$$$ ⊞ **Bristol.** Opposite the Staatsoper (State Opera House), the Bristol has one of the finest locations in the city. The accent here is on tradition, from the brocaded walls to the Biedermeier period furnishings in the public rooms and some of the bedrooms. The building dates from 1892, and during the 1945–55 occupation it was the U.S. military headquarters. ⊠ *Kärntner Ring 1, A-1010,* ☎ *01/515–16–0,* 🅵🅰🆇 *01/515–16–550. 141 rooms. 2 restaurants, café, health club. AE, DC, MC, V.*

$$$$ ⊞ **Das Triest.** This is a little off the beaten track but still within easy walking distance of the city center. Totally redone by Sir Terence Conran, it evokes the feeling of being aboard an ultrasleek new ocean liner, which is surprising, considering it was once the stable of the old Vienna-Trieste posthouse. Little extras in the rooms are plentiful; even the doorknobs feel nice to the touch. Breakfast is included in the room rate. ⊠ *Wiedner Hauptstr. 12, A-1010,* ☎ *01/589–180,* 🅵🅰🆇 *01/589–1818. 73 rooms. Restaurant, bar, health club. AE, DC, MC, V.*

$$$$ 🏨 **Imperial.** The hotel is as much a palace today as when it was formally opened in 1873 by Emperor Franz Josef. The emphasis is on Old Vienna elegance and privacy, which accounts for the heads of state and celebrities staying here. The beautiful rooms are furnished in antique style, though only the first three floors are part of the original house and have high ceilings; subsequent floors were added in the late 1930s. ✉ *Kärntner Ring 16, A–1010,* ☎ *01/501–10–0,* FAX *01/501–10–410. 128 rooms. Restaurant, café, piano bar, no-smoking rooms. AE, DC, MC, V.*

$$$$ 🏨 **Palais Schwarzenberg.** Set against a vast formal park, the palace,
★ built in the early 1700s, seems like a country estate. Each room is individual and luxuriously appointed, with the family's original artwork adorning the walls. A renovated wing has ultramodern suites by Italian designer Paolo Piva. You don't have to be a guest here to come for a drink, coffee, or light lunch, served outside on the terrace in summer or beside a roaring fireplace in the main sitting room in winter. ✉ *Schwarzenbergpl. 9, A–1030,* ☎ *01/798–4515–0,* FAX *01/798–4714. 44 rooms. Restaurant, bar, pool. AE, DC, MC, V.*

$$$$ 🏨 **Sacher.** The grand old Sacher dates from 1876, and it has retained
★ its sense of history over the years while providing luxurious, modern-day comfort. The corridors are a veritable art gallery, and the exquisitely furnished bedrooms also contain original artwork. The location directly behind the Opera House could hardly be more central. The ratio of staff to guests is more than two to one, and among the traditional luxury hotels, the Sacher probably offers the best value. Meals in the Red Room or Anna Sacher Room are first-rate; the Café Sacher, of course, is legendary. ✉ *Philharmonikerstr. 4, A-1010,* ☎ *01/514–56–0,* FAX *01/ 514–57–810. 108 rooms. Restaurant, bar. AE, DC, MC, V.*

$$$ 🏨 **Altstadt.** A real gem, this small hotel was once a patrician home.
★ Rooms are large, with all the modern comforts, though they retain an antique feel. The English-style lounge has a fireplace and plump floral sofas. The breakfast room is bright. You're one streetcar stop or a pleasant walk from the main museums. ✉ *Kircheng. 41, A-1070,* ☎ *01/526–3399–0,* FAX *01/523–4901. 25 rooms. AE, DC, MC, V.*

$$$ 🏨 **König von Ungarn.** This utterly charming hotel is tucked away in the shadow of the cathedral. Rooms are furnished with country antiques (some have Styrian wood-paneled walls) and come with walk-in closets and double sinks in the sparkling bathrooms. The two suites are two-storied. ✉ *Schulerstr. 10, A-1010,* ☎ *01/515–84–0,* FAX *01/515– 848. 33 rooms. Restaurant. DC, MC, V.*

$$–$$$ 🏨 **Altwienerhof.** Don't be put off by this small hotel's rather unappealing neighborhood, just one subway stop away from the Westbahnhof. The spacious, comfortable rooms, most with modern, ultraluxurious bathrooms and some with a view over the lovely inner courtyard, more than make up for it. A rich buffet breakfast is included in the room price. ✉ *Herklotzg. 6, A–1150,* ☎ *01/892–6000,* FAX *01/892– 6000–8. 23 rooms. AE, DC, MC, V.*

$$–$$$ 🏨 **Regina.** This dignified old hotel sits regally on the edge of the Alt-
★ stadt, commanding a view of Sigmund Freud Park. The high-ceilinged rooms are quiet, spacious and attractively decorated, and most have charming sitting areas. Freud, who lived nearby, used to eat breakfast in the hotel's café every morning. Buffet breakfast is included. ✉ *Rooseveltpl. 15, A-1090,* ☎ *01/404–460,* FAX *01/408–8392. 125 rooms. Restaurant. AE, DC, MC, V.*

$$ 🏨 **Austria.** Tucked away on a tiny cul-de-sac, this older house offers
★ the ultimate in quiet only five minutes' walk from the heart of the city. The high-ceilinged rooms are pleasing in their combination of dark wood and lighter walls; the decor is mixed, with Oriental carpets on many floors. The nice courtyard terrace is a perfect place to sip coffee. ✉

Wolfeng. 3/Fleischmarkt 20, A-1010, ☎ 01/515–23–0, FAX 01/515–23–506. 46 rooms, 42 with bath or shower. AE, DC, MC, V.

$$ 🏨 **Kärntnerhof.** Behind the "Schönbrunn yellow" facade of this elegant 100-year-old house on a quiet cul-de-sac lies one of the friendliest small hotels in the center of the city. The dated lobby is cheered by a gorgeously restored Biedermeier elevator. The rooms are functionally decorated but clean and serviceable. Pets are welcome here. ⊠ *Grashofg. 4, A-1010, ☎ 01/512–1923–0, FAX 01/513–2228–33. 43 rooms, 41 with bath or shower. AE, DC, MC, V.*

$$ 🏨 **Zur Wiener Staatsoper.** A great deal of loving care has gone into this family-owned hotel near the State Opera, reputed to be one of the Viennese settings in John Irving's *The Hotel New Hampshire*. Rooms are small but have high ceilings and are charmingly decorated with pretty fabrics. ⊠ *Krugerstr. 11, A-1010, ☎ 01/513–1274, FAX 01/513–1274–15. 22 rooms with shower. AE, MC, V.*

$ 🏨 **Pension Riedl.** On the upper floors of a lovely 19th-century building designed by Otto Wagner, this small establishment offers comfortable rooms with shower and TV. As an added touch, breakfast is delivered ★ en suite. Friendly owner Maria Felser is happy to arrange concert tickets and tours. ⊠ *Georg–Coch–Pl. 3/4/10 (near Julius–Raab Pl.), A-1010, ☎ 01/512–7919, FAX 01/512–7919–8. 7 rooms with bath, 1 with shower. DC, MC, V. Closed last wk Jan. and first 2 wks Feb.*

$ 🏨 **Reimer.** The cheery, comfortable Reimer is in a prime location just off the Mariahilferstrasse. Rooms have high ceilings and large windows. Breakfast is included. ⊠ *Kircheng. 18, A-1070, ☎ 01/523–6162, FAX 01/524–3782. 14 rooms with bath or shower. MC, V.*

Nightlife and the Arts

The Arts

MUSIC

Most classical concerts are held in the **Konzerthaus** (⊠ Lothringerstr. 20, ☎ 01/712–1211) or the **Musikverein** (⊠ Bösendorferstr. 12, ☎ 01/505–8190). Tickets can be bought at their box offices or ordered by phone. Pop concerts are scheduled from time to time at the **Austria Center** (⊠ Am Hubertusdamm 6, U-1 subway to Vienna International Center stop, ☎ 01/236–9150). Tickets to various musical events are sold through **Vienna Ticket Service** (☎ 01/534–1775, FAX 01/534–1726) and the Salettl gazebo ticket office (⊠ Kärntnerstrasse, next to Staatsoper, ☎ 01/588–85), which is open daily 10–7. At the same office, same-day half-price tickets to many musical events—*but not the Staatsoper, Volksoper, or symphony concerts*—go on sale at 2 PM.

THEATER AND OPERA

Check the monthly program published by the city; posters also show opera and theater schedules. The **Staatsoper,** one of world's great opera houses, presents major stars in its almost-nightly original-language performances. The **Volksoper** offers lighter operas, operettas, and musicals, all in German. Performances at the **Akadamietheater** and **Burgtheater** are also in German. Tickets for the Staatsoper, the Volksoper, and the Burg and Akademie theaters are available at the central ticket office (⊠ Bundestheaterkassen, Hanuschg. 3, ☎ 01/514–44–2959 or 01/514–44–2969), open weekdays 8–6, weekends and holidays 9–noon, to the left rear of the Staatsoper. Tickets go on sale a month before performances. Unsold tickets can be obtained at the evening box office. Tickets can be ordered three weeks or more in advance in writing (or by fax) or a month in advance by phone (☎ 01/513–1513). Standing room tickets for the Staatsoper are a great bargain.

Theater is offered in English at **Vienna's English Theater** (⊠ Josefsg. 12, ☎ 01/402–1260) and the **International Theater** (⊠ Porzellang. 8, ☎ 01/319–6272).

Nightlife

The central district for nightlife in Vienna is nicknamed the **Bermuda-Dreieck** (Bermuda Triangle). Centered around Judengasse/Seitenstettengasse, next to St. Ruprecht's, a small Romanesque church, the area is jammed with everything from good bistros to jazz clubs.

CABARETS

Most cabarets are expensive and unmemorable. One leading option is **Casanova** (⊠ Dorotheerg. 6, ☎ 01/512–9845), which emphasizes striptease. A popular cabaret/nightclub is **Moulin Rouge** (⊠ Walfischg. 11, ☎ 01/512–2130), where there are floor shows and some striptease.

CAFÉS

A quintessential Viennese institution, the coffeehouse, or café, is club, pub, and bistro all rolled into one. To savor the atmosphere of the coffeehouses you must take your time: Set aside an afternoon, a morning, or at least a couple of hours, and settle down in one of your choice. There is no need to worry about overstaying your welcome, even over a single small cup of Mokka—although in some of the more opulent coffeehouses, this cup of coffee can cost as much as a meal.

Alte Backstube (⊠ Langeg. 34, ☎ 01/406–1101), in a gorgeous Baroque house—with a café in front and restaurant in back—was once a bakery and is now a museum as well. **Café Central** (⊠ Herreng. 14, ☎ 01/535–4176–0) is where Trotsky played chess; in the Palais Ferstel, it's one of Vienna's most beautiful cafés. **Cafe Landtmann** (⊠ Dr. Karl Leuger Str. 4, ☎ 01/532–0621), next to the dignified Burgtheater, with front-row views of the Ringstrasse, was reputedly Freud's favorite café. A 200-year-old institution, **Demel** (⊠ Kohlmarkt 14, ☎ 01/535–1717–0) is the *grande dame* of Viennese cafés. Order their famous coffee, brought with hot milk in a dainty creamer, to go along with their Senegal torte, a scrumptious hazelnut cake. The elegant front rooms have more atmosphere than the airy modern atrium, and the first room is reserved for nonsmokers. **Gerstner** (⊠ Kärtnerstr. 15, ☎ 01/496377) is in the heart of the bustling Kärntnerstrasse, and one of the more modern Viennese cafés. Popular here is the Bruegel torte, a marzipan pastry. **Museum** (⊠ Friedrichstr. 6, ☎ 01/586–5202), with its original interior by the architect Adolf Loos, draws a mixed crowd and has an ample supply of newspapers. **The Sacher** (⊠ Philharmonikerstr. 4, ☎ 01/514–56–0) is hardly a typical Vienna café; more a shrine to plush gilt and marzipan, it's both a must-see and a must-eat, despite the crowds of tourists here to order the world's ultimate chocolate cake.

DISCOS

Atrium (⊠ Schwarzenbergpl. 10, ☎ 01/505–3594) is open Thursday through Sunday and draws a lively young crowd. Live bands, dancing, and snacks are offered at **Chattanooga** (⊠ Graben 29A, ☎ 01/533–5000). **First Floor** (⊠ Corner of Seitenstetteng./Rabensteig., ☎ 01/533–7866) is actually one floor up from ground level and garners the attractive thirtysomething crowd. **P 1** (⊠ Rotg. 9, ☎ 01/535–9995) is a spot for the MTV crowd. The **U-4** (⊠ Schönbrunnerstr. 222, ☎ 01/815–8307) ranks high among the young set.

NIGHTCLUBS

A casual '50s atmosphere pervades the popular **Café Volksgarten** (⊠ Burgring 1, ☎ 01/532–0907), in the city park of the same name; tables are set outdoors in summer. The more formal **Eden Bar** (⊠ Lilieng.

2, ☎ 01/512–7450) is among Vienna's classier nightspots; don't expect to be let in unless you're dressed to kill.

WINE TAVERNS

Some of the city's atmospheric Heuriger, or wine taverns, date from as far back as the 12th century. Open at lunchtime as well as evenings, the **Augustinerkeller** (⊠ Augustinerstr. 1, ☎ 01/533–1026), in the Albertina building, is a cheery wine tavern with live, schmaltzy music after 6 PM. The **Esterházykeller** (⊠ Haarhof 1, ☎ 01/533–3482), in a particularly mazelike network of rooms, has good wines. The **Zwölf Apostelkeller** (⊠ Sonnenfelsg. 3, ☎ 01/512–6777), near St. Stephen's, has rooms that are down, down, down underground.

Shopping

Boutiques

Famous names line the **Kohlmarkt** and **Graben** and their respective side streets, as well as the side streets off **Kärntnerstrasse.**

Folk Costumes

The main resource for exquisite Austrian *Trachten* (native dress) is **Loden-Plankl** (⊠ Michaelerpl. 6, ☎ 01/533–8032).

Food and Flea Markets

The **Naschmarkt** (foodstuffs market; ⊠ between Rechte and Linke Wienzeile) is a sensational open-air market offering specialties from around the world. The fascinating **Flohmarkt** (flea market; subway U-4 to Kettenbrückeng.; ☉ Sat. 8–4) operates year-round beyond the Naschmarkt. An **Arts and Antiques Market** (⊠ beside Danube Canal near Salztorbrücke; open May–Sept., Sat. 2–6, Sun. 10–6) has a mixed selection, including some high-quality offerings. Check Am Hof square for antiques and collectibles (late spring–early fall, Thurs. and Fri.). Also look for the seasonal markets in Freyung Square.

Shopping Districts

Kärntnerstrasse is lined with luxury boutiques and large emporiums. The Viennese do much of their in-town shopping in the many department and specialty stores of **Mariahilferstrasse.**

Vienna Essentials

Arriving and Departing

BY CAR

The main access routes are the expressways to the west and south (Westautobahn A1, Südautobahn A2). Routes leading to the downtown area are marked ZENTRUM.

BY PLANE

All flights use **Schwechat Airport** (☎ 01/7007–0), about 16 km (10 mi) southwest of Vienna.

Between the Airport and Downtown. Buses leave the airport for the city air terminal, Wien-Mitte Landstrasse Hauptstrasse (⊠ Am Stadtpark, ☎ 01/5800–33369), by the Hilton, on every half hour from 5 to 6:30 AM and every 20 minutes from 6:50 AM to 11:30 PM; after that, buses depart every hour until 5 AM. Buses also run every hour (Apr.–Sept., weekends and hols, every ½ hr) from the airport to the Westbahnhof (West Train Station) and the Südbahnhof (South Train Station). The one-way fare for all buses is AS70. The S7 **train** (called the *Schnellbahn*) shuttles every half hour between the airport and the Landstrasse/Wien-Mitte (city center) and Wien-Nord (north Vienna) stations; the fare is AS34 and it takes about 35 minutes. Follow the signs picturing a train to the basement of the airport. A **taxi** from the airport to downtown Vienna costs about AS350–AS450; agree on a price in advance. Cabs (legally) do not meter this drive, as airport fares are more or less fixed (legally again) at about double the meter fare. The cheapest cab service is C+K Airport Service (☎ 01/1731, 01/689–6969), charging a set price of AS270. C+K will also meet your plane at no extra charge if you let them know in advance.

BY TRAIN

Vienna has four train stations. The Westbahnhof is for trains to and from Linz, Salzburg, and Innsbruck, and to and from Germany, France, and Switzerland. The Südbahnhof is for trains to and from Graz, Klagenfurt, Villach, and Italy. The Franz-Josefs-Bahnhof, or Nordbahnhof, is for trains to and from Prague, Berlin, and Warsaw. Go to the Wien-Mitte/Landstrasse Hauptstrasse station for local trains to and from the north of the city. Budapest trains use both the Westbahnhof and Südbahnhof, and Bratislava trains both Wien-Mitte and the Südbahnhof, so check.

Getting Around

Vienna addresses include a roman numeral that designates in which of the city's 23 districts the address is located. The first district (I; the inner city) is bounded by the Ringstrasse and the Danube Canal. The 2nd through 9th (II through IX) districts surround the inner city, starting with the 2nd district across the Danube Canal and running clockwise; the 10th through the 23rd districts form a second concentric ring of suburbs.

Vienna is fairly easy to explore on foot; much of the heart of the city—the area within the Ringstrasse—is a pedestrian zone. Public transportation is comfortable, convenient, and frequent, though not cheap. **Tickets for buses, subways, and streetcars** are available in subway stations and from dispensers on buses and streetcars. Tickets in multiples of five are sold at cigarette shops—look for the sign TABAK-TRAFIK—or at the window marked VORVERKAUF at such central stations as Karlsplatz or Stephansplatz. A block of five tickets costs AS95, a single ticket AS19, a 24-hour ticket AS60, a three-day tourist ticket AS150, and an eight-day ticket AS300. Tariffs may be slightly higher in 2000. Maps and information in English are available at the Stephansplatz, Karlsplatz, and Praterstern U-bahn stations.

The Vienna Card, available for AS210 at tourist and transportation information offices and most hotels, will give you unlimited travel for 72 hours on city buses, streetcars, and the subway, reductions on selected museum entry fees, plus tips and discounts on various attractions and selected shopping throughout the city.

BY BICYCLE

Vienna has hundreds of kilometers of marked cycle routes, including reserved routes through the center of the city. Paved cycling routes parallel the Danube. For details, get the city brochure on cycling. Bicycles can be rented at a number of locations and can be taken on the Vienna subway (with the exception of the U-6 line) year-round all day Sunday and holidays, from 9 to 3, and after 6:30 on weekdays, and, from May through September, after 9 AM Saturday. You'll need a half-fare ticket for the bike (☞ By Subway, *below*).

BY BUS OR STREETCAR

Inner-city buses are numbered 1A through 3A and operate weekdays until about 7:40 PM, Saturday until 7 PM. Reduced fares are available for these routes (buy a **Kurzstreckenkarte;** it allows you four trips for AS34) as well as designated shorter stretches (roughly two to four stops) on all other bus and streetcar lines. Streetcars and buses are numbered or lettered according to route, and they run until about midnight. Night buses marked *N* follow 22 special routes every half hour between 12:30 AM and 4:30 AM. Get a route plan from any of the public transport or VORVERKAUF offices. The fare is AS25, payable on the bus unless you have a 24-hour, three-day, or eight-day ticket; then you need only pay an AS10 supplement. The central terminus is Schwedenplatz. Streetcars 1 and 2 run the circular route around the Ring clockwise and counterclockwise, respectively.

BY CAR

Unless you know your way around the city, a car is more of a nuisance than a help. The center of the city is a pedestrian zone, and city on-street parking is a problem. Observe signs; tow-away is expensive. In winter, overnight parking is forbidden on city streets with streetcar lines. Overnight street parking in districts I, VI, VII, VIII, and IX is restricted to residents with stickers; check before you leave a car on the street, even for a brief period.

BY SUBWAY

Subway (U-bahn) lines—stations are marked with a huge blue U—are designated U-1, U-2, U-3, U-4, and U-6, and are clearly marked and color-coded. Trains run daily until about 12:30 AM. Additional services are provided by fast suburban trains, the S-bahn, indicated by a stylized blue *S* symbol. Both are tied into the general city fare system.

BY TAXI

Cabs can be flagged on the street if the FREI (free) sign is lit. You can also dial ☎ 60160, 31300, or 40100 to request one. All rides around town are metered. The initial fare is AS35, but expect to pay AS80–AS100 for an average city ride. There are additional charges for luggage, and a surcharge of AS16 is added at night, on Sunday, and for telephone orders. Tip the driver AS5–AS8 by rounding up the fare.

Contacts and Resources

EMBASSIES AND CONSULATES

U.S. (✉ Boltzmanng. 16, ☎ 01/313–39); **consulate** (✉ Gartenbaupromenade, Parkring 12A, in Marriott building, ☎ 01/313–39). **Canadian** (✉ Laurenzerberg 2, 3rd floor of Hauptpost building complex, ☎ 01/531–38–3000). **U.K. embassy and consulate** (✉ Jauresg. 10, near Schloss Belvedere, ☎ 01/71613–5151, embassy and consulate).

EMERGENCIES

Police (☎ 133). **Ambulance** (☎ 144). **Doctor:** ask your hotel, or in an emergency, phone your embassy or consulate (☞ *above*). **Pharmacies:** In each neighborhood, one pharmacy (Apotheke) in rotation is open all night and weekends; the address is posted on each area pharmacy.

ENGLISH-LANGUAGE BOOKSTORES

Big Ben Bookshop (✉ Serviteng. 4a, ☎ 01/319–6412). **British Bookshop** (✉ Weihburgg. 24–26, ☎ 01/512–1945–0). **Shakespeare & Co.** (✉ Sterng. 2, ☎ 01/535–5053).

GUIDED TOURS

Guided walking tours in English are available almost daily and include such topics as "Jewish Vienna." Tours will take you to cultural events and nightclubs, and there are daytime bus trips to the Danube Valley, Salzburg, and Budapest, among other spots. Check with the City Tourist Office (☞ Visitor Information, *below*) or your hotel.

The following are city orientation tours. Prices are similar, but find out whether you will visit or just drive past Schönbrunn and Belvedere palaces and whether admission fees are included. **Cityrama** (☎ 01/534–1332) provides city tours with hotel pickup. **CityTouring Vienna** (☎ 01/894–

1417–0), with hotel pickup, starts from the city air terminal behind the Hilton Hotel (✉ Am Stadtpark). **Vienna Sightseeing Tours** (☎ 01/712–4683–0) offers a short highlights tour or a lengthier one to the Vienna Woods, Mayerling, and other sights near Vienna. Tours start in front of or beside the Staatsoper on the Operngasse.

TRAVEL AGENCIES
American Express (✉ Kärntnerstr. 21–23, ☎ 01/515–40–0). **Ökista** (✉ Reichsratsstr. 3, ☎ 01/402–1561). **Österreichisches Verkehrsbüro** (Austrian Travel Agency; ✉ Taborstr. 13, A-1020, ☎ 01/588–000, FAX 01/586–8533).

VISITOR INFORMATION
City Tourist Office (✉ Kärntnerstr. 38, behind Staatsoper).

THE DANUBE VALLEY

Austria contains some of the most beautiful stretches of the Danube (Donau), extending about 88 km (55 mi) west of Vienna. The river rolls through the celebrated Wachau—a gloriously scenic valley that offers magnificent countryside, some of Austria's best food and wine, and comfortable—in some cases elegant—accommodations. Above the river are the ruins of ancient castles. The abbeys at Melk and Göttweig, with their magnificent libraries, dominate their settings. Vineyards sweep down to the river, which is lined with fruit trees that burst into blossom every spring. People here live close to the land, and at certain times of year vintners open their homes to sell their own wines and produce. Roadside stands offer flowers, fruits, vegetables, and wines. This is also a region of legend: The Danube shares with the Rhine the story of the mythical Nibelungen, defenders of Siegfried, hero of German myth.

The most delightful way to approach the Wachau is by boat, but car and train routes are also scenically splendid (☞ Getting Around *in* The Danube Valley Essentials, *below*). From Vienna you can follow the southern Danube bank, crossing at Melk and returning along the north bank. Vienna to Melk is about 112 km (70 mi), the return along the north bank about 109 km (68 mi).

Klosterneuburg

The massive **Stift Klosterneuburg** (abbey) dominating this market town was established in 1114; treasures in its museum include an enameled altar dating from 1181. The abbey is a major agricultural landowner in the region, and its extensive vineyards produce excellent wines. ✉ *Stiftspl. 1,* ☎ *02243/411–212.* ☉ *Daily guided tours every hr 9–12 and 1:30–4:30; in winter 10–12 and 1:30–4:30.*

Göttweig

You will see **Stift Göttweig** high above the Danube Valley opposite Krems long before you reach it. This impressive 11th-century Benedictine abbey affords sensational panoramas of the Danube Valley; you can stroll the grounds and visit the chapel. ✉ *Rte. 303, on south bank of Danube, opposite Krems, Furth bei Göttweig,* ☎ *02732/85581–231.*

$$$$ ✕ **Landhaus Bacher.** This is one of Austria's best restaurants, elegant
★   but entirely lacking in pretension. The menu is seasonal and innovative, but lamb and fish dishes are always present. Dining in the garden during summer adds to the experience. It's on the riverbank opposite Krems. ✉ *Südtirolerpl. 208, Mautern,* ☎ *02732/82937–0. Reservations essential. DC, V. Closed Mon.–Tues. and mid-Jan.–mid-Feb.*

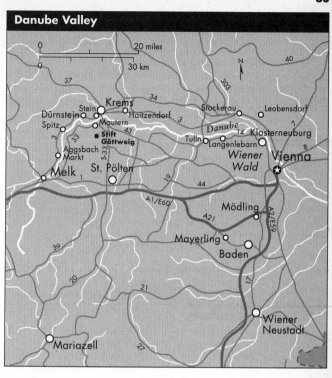

Danube Valley

0 20 miles
0 30 km

N

37
40
303
Krems
34
Stein
Dürnstein
Haitzendorf
Stockerau
Leobensdorf
Spitz
Mautern
3
Danube
14
Klosterneuburg
43
Stift
Tulln
Langenlebarn
8
Göttweig
Aggsbach
Markt
Wiener
Vienna
St. Pölten
Wald
Melk
1
9
44
A1/E60
Mödling
A21
A2/E59
Mayerling
39
Baden
20
17
21
Wiener
Neustadt
Mariazell
23

\$–\$\$ ✕ **Stiftskeller.** Have lunch at the abbey's restaurant. If the weather is clear, sit on the open terrace and enjoy magnificent views of the Danube in the distance. The local wines are excellent. ⊠ *Stift Göttweig,* ☎ *02732/ 84663. AE, DC, MC, V. Closed Nov.–Mar.*

Melk

The **Benediktinerstift Melk** (Benedictine abbey of Melk) is one of the most impressive in Europe, commandingly perched above the Danube. This is one of Austria's monumental, major sights, with its library rich in art as well as books; the ceiling frescoes are particularly memorable. ⊠ *Abt Berthold Dietmayr-Str. 1,* ☎ *02752/52312–255,* FAX *02752/ 52312–226.* ☉ *May–Sept., daily 9–6; Oct.–Apr., daily 9–5.*

Dürnstein

Across the river from Melk, the romantic road hugs the Danube, heading north toward Dürnstein and Krems. The beautiful medieval town of Dürnstein is associated with Richard the Lionhearted, who was imprisoned in its now-ruined castle for 13 months in 1192–93. The town is also known for its fine hotels, restaurants, and wines, and for its gloriously Baroque Stiftskirche church.

\$\$\$\$ 🏨 **Richard Löwenherz.** This former cloister, justifiably a Romantik hotel
★ member, sits above the Danube. Room furnishings include antiques and every comfort. The restaurant is excellent, as are the house wines. ⊠ *Dürnstein 8, A-3061,* ☎ *02711/222,* FAX *02711/222–18. 40 rooms. Restaurant, bar, pool. AE, DC, MC, V. Closed Nov.–Mar.*

Krems/Stein an der Donau

Remnants of the ancient city wall are prominent in this town over 1,000 years old, with its Renaissance, Gothic, and Baroque monuments. Krems and Stein sit at the center of Austria's foremost wine-growing region. You can explore the town center, the churches, and the **Weinkolleg**

Kloster Und, a wine museum in a beautifully restored cloister in Und, tucked between Krems and Stein. ⊠ *Undstr. 6,* ☎ *02732/73073–0.* ⌨ *AS130, including tasting.* ⊙ *Wed.–Sun. 1–7. Closed Dec. 23–Mar.*

Stein, with its 16th-century houses, is virtually part of adjacent Krems. Look for the former **Imperial Toll House** and the 14th-century **Minoritenkirche,** a church that now serves as an exhibition showcase, just off the main street.

$$ ⛫ **Alte Post.** A 16th-century house with an arcade courtyard, the inn is conveniently positioned right in the center of Krems. In good weather the courtyard is used for dining. ⊠ *Obere Landstr. 32, A–3500, Krems,* ☎ *02732/82276–0,* ⁀⁀ *02732/84396. 26 rooms, 1 with bath. Restaurant (closed Wed.). No credit cards. Closed Jan.–mid-Mar.*

Haitzendorf

A worthwhile detour from Route 3 at Grafenwörth leads to the moated, turreted **Schloss Grafenegg.** The original 1533 castle was rebuilt in the 1800s with wonderful Disneyesque English Gothic Revival overtones, gargoyles and all. ☎ *02735/2205–13.*

$$ ✕ **Schlosstaverne Mörwald.** Here you'll find excellent food either in the Biedermeier-style dining rooms or on the garden terrace. ⊠ *Schloss Grafenegg,* ☎ *02735/2616–0. No credit cards. Closed Mon., Jan.–Feb.*

Korneuburg

Here an imposing neo-Gothic city hall towers over the town square. About 3 km (2 mi) north of Korneuburg off Route 3 sits **Burg Kreuzenstein,** perched prominently upon a hilltop. The 19th-century castle includes a small museum of armor. ⊠ *Leobendorf bei Korneuburg,* ☎ *02262/66102.* ⊙ *Mid-Mar.–mid-Nov. Tours daily 9–4.*

The Danube Valley Essentials

Getting Around

BY BOAT

Travel upstream, with stops at Krems, Dürnstein, Melk, and points between. Return to Vienna by boat or by train from Melk (combination tickets available). Check in Vienna with DDSG Blue Danube Schiffahrt (⊠ Friedrichstr. 7, ☎ 01/588–800) for ferry schedules.

BY CAR

If you're pressed for time, take the autobahn to St. Pölten, turn north onto Route S-33, and follow the signs to Melk. For a more scenic route, follow the south shore of the Danube via Klosterneuburg and Greifenstein, taking Routes 14, 19, 43, and 33. Cross the Danube at Melk, then return to Vienna along the north bank of the river (Rte 3).

BY TRAIN

Depart from the Westbahnhof for Melk, then take the bus along the north bank of the Danube to Dürnstein and Krems. Side bus trips can be made from Krems to Göttweig.

Contacts and Resources

GUIDED TOURS

Vienna travel agencies (☞ Vienna Essentials, *above*) offer tours of the Wachau ranging from one-day outings to longer excursions.

VISITOR INFORMATION

Lower Austria Tourist Office (⊠ Walfischg. 6, Vienna, ☎ 01/513–8022–0, ⁀⁀ 01/513–8022–30). **Dürnstein** (⊠ Parkpl. Ost, ☎ 02711/219). **Klosterneuburg** (⊠ Niedermarkt 4, Postfach 6, ☎ 02243/4440). **Krems/Stein an der Donau** (⊠ Undstr. 6, ☎ 02732/85620). **Melk** (⊠ Babenbergerstr. 1, ☎ 02752/52307–32).

SALZBURG

Salzburg, best known as the birthplace of Wolfgang Amadeus Mozart, receives its greatest number of visitors every summer during its music festival, the world-famous Salzburger Festspiele. Dominated by a fortress on one side and the Kapuzinerberg, a small mountain, on the other, this Baroque city is best explored on foot, for many of its most interesting areas are pedestrian precincts. Besides the festival, the city has innumerable other attractions. Thanks to the powerful prince-arch-bishops of the Habsburg era, few other places offer an equivalent abundance of Baroque splendor. Many sites are identifiable from the film that made Salzburg a household name in the United States, *The Sound of Music*. No matter what season you visit, bring an umbrella: Salzburg is noted for sudden, brief downpours.

Exploring Salzburg

Numbers in the margin correspond to points of interest on the Salzburg map.

The Salzach River separates Salzburg's old and "new" towns; for the best perspective on the old, climb the Kapuzinerberg (follow pathways from Linzergasse or Steingasse). For another postcard view, look toward the fortress through the Mirabell gardens, behind Mirabell palace. The sweeping panorama from the fortress itself offers the reverse of both perspectives. Wander along Getreidegasse, with its quaint wrought-iron shop signs and the Mönchsberg standing sentinel at the far end. Don't neglect the warren of interconnecting side alleys: These shelter a number of fine shops and often open onto impressive inner court-yards that are guaranteed to be overflowing with flowers in summer.

⑭ Alter Markt (Old Market Square). In the heart of the Altstadt (Old City) is the Alter Markt, the old marketplace and center of secular life in past centuries. Salzburg's narrowest house is squeezed into the north side of the picturesque 17th-century square, filled in summer with flower stalls. Look into the former court pharmacy (Hof-apotheke) for a touch of centuries past. ⊠ *Judeng., Getreideg., Goldg.*

⑥ Carolino Augusteum Museum (Historical Museum). The city museum is devoted to art, archaeology, and fascinating musical instruments. ⊠ *Museumspl. 1,* ☎ *0662/841134–0.* ⏲ *Tues. 9–8, Wed.–Sun. 9–5.*

★ ⑩ Dom (Cathedral). The cathedral square setting is close to perfection, while the sheer mass of the cathedral itself gives a suggestion of the one-time power of the prince-archbishops who ruled the region. You enter through great bronze doors. A small museum shows off centuries of church treasures. ⊠ *Dompl. 1,* ☎ *0662/844189.* ⏲ *May 2–end Oct., Mon.–Sat. 10–5, Sun. and holidays 1–6.*

★ ⓒ ⑪ Festung Hohensalzburg (Fortress Salzburg). To reach the 12th-century fortress that dominates the city, walk up the narrow Festungsgasse at the back end of Kapitalplatz. From here, you can either follow the foot-path up the hill or take a five-minute ride on the funicular, or Fes-tungsbahn. On a sunny day, you can hike up Festungsgasse, turning frequently to enjoy the changing panorama of the city below. The ter-race restaurant overlooks a *stunning* panorama. A main attraction is **St. George's Chapel**, built in 1501. A year later, in 1502, the chapel acquired the 200-pipe barrel organ, which is played daily in summer at 7 AM, 11 AM, and 6 PM. ⊠ *Mönchsberg 34,* ☎ *0662/842430.* ⏲ *Nov.–Mar., daily 9–5; Apr.–June and Oct., daily 9–6; July–Sept., daily 8–7.*

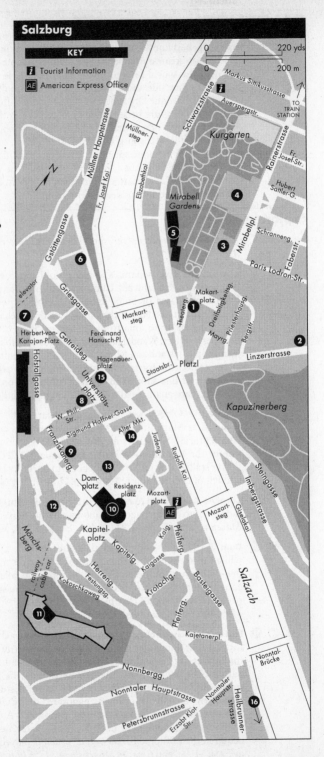

Salzburg

KEY

ℹ️ Tourist Information

AE American Express Office

❾ Franziskanerkloster (St. Francis Monastery). A tall, graceful spire marks this 13th-century church, a mix of architectural styles with Romanesque and Gothic accents. The Baroque altar is by Fisher von Erlach. Check for mass—frequently one of Mozart's—on Sunday at 9. ⊠ *Franziskanerg. 5,* ☎ *0662/843629–0.* ☺ *Daily 6:30 AM–7:30 PM.*

❷ Friedhof St. Sebastian (Cemetery of St. Sebastian). This secluded spot is where the scene near the end of *The Sound of Music* when the von Trapps are nearly captured takes place. The cemetery was commissioned in the late 16th century by Prince-Archbishop Wolf Dietrich and built in the arcaded style of an Italian *campo santo.* Wolf Dietrich's brightly tiled mausoleum is unusual for Austria. Also buried here are Mozart's widow, Constanze, and his father, Leopold (by the central path leading to the mausoleum). ⊠ *Linzerg. 41.* ☺ *Daily 7–7.*

★ **❽ Kollegienkirche** or Universitätskirche (Collegiate/University Church). The work of Fischer von Erlach in 1707, this is one of the best examples of Baroque architecture anywhere. ⊠ *Universitätspl.,* ☎ *0662/841–327.* ☺ *Oct.–Mar., Mon.–Fri. 8–4, Sat.–Sun. 10–4; Apr.–Sept., daily 8 AM–7 PM.*

☚ **❶ Mozart-Wohnhaus** (Mozart Residence). The house where the Mozart family lived for some years includes a small recital hall and the Mozart Audio and Film Museum. Combination tickets with Mozarts Geburtshaus (☞ *below*) are cheaper than buying tickets at each place individually. ⊠ *Makartpl. 8,* ☎ *0662/883454–0.* ☺ *Daily 10–6.*

❺ Mozarteum und Marionettentheater (Mozart Center and Marionette Theater). This is the main research facility devoted to the work of Salzburg's most famous native son, Wolfgang Amadeus Mozart. Inside the complex are the University Mozarteum (☎ 0662/88908–0); the International Mozarteum Foundation (⊠ Schwarzstr. 26, ☎ 0662/88940), whose courtyard contains the summerhouse (accessible only by special appointment) in which Mozart wrote *The Magic Flute*; and the **Marionettentheater,** home to the extraordinary Salzburg Marionette Theater. The south end of the Mozarteum complex on Makartplatz includes the **Landestheater** (Provincal Theater; ☞ Opera, Music, and Art *in* The Arts, *below*) where operas, operetta, ballet, and dramas are staged during winter months when the winter festival buildings are closed. ⊠ *Marionettentheater, Schwarzstr. 24,* ☎ *0662/872406–0,* FAX *0662/882141.* ☎ *AS250–480.* ☺ *Box office, Mon.–Sat. 9–1 and 2 hrs before marionette performance; Salzburg season May–Sept., Dec. 25, Mozart Week (Jan.), Easter.*

★ ☚ **⓯ Mozarts Geburtshaus** (Mozart's Birthplace). The house at the head of the tiny Hagenauerplatz in which the famed composer was born is now a museum, packed with Mozart memorabilia. Combination tickets with the Mozart-Wohnhaus (☞ *above*) are cheaper than buying tickets at each place individually. ⊠ *Getreideg. 9,* ☎ *0662/844313.* ☺ *Daily 9–6.*

⓭ Residenz (Residence). The palatial complex on Residenzplatz includes the prince-archbishops' historic and sumptuous living quarters and ceremonial reception rooms. The **Residenzgalerie** has an outstanding collection of 16th- through 19th-century European art. Combination tickets can provide entry to both sites. ⊠ *Residenzpl. 1,* ☎ *0662/8042–2690; 0662/840451 art collection.* ☺ *Residence: Tours Sept.–June, daily 10, 11, noon, 2, and 3; July–Aug., daily 10–4:30, every 30 mins. Art Collection: Apr.–Sept., daily 10–5; Oct.–Mar., Thurs.–Tues. 10–5.*

❸ Salzburger Barockmuseum (Salzburg Baroque Museum). A focal point of the celebrated Mirabell Gardens, the museum stands between Mirabellplatz and the Orangerie. The museum displays 17th- and

18th-century paintings and sketches, including works by the Neopolitan painter Luca Giordano and the Austrian Baroque painter Johann Michael Rottmayr, as well as a Bernini sculpture. You can wander through the Baroque gardens behind the city's main theater complex and discover a dramatic view of the Old City with the fortress in the background. ⊠ *Orangeriegarten,* ☎ *0662/877432.* ⊙ *Tues.–Sat. 9–noon and 2–5, Sun. and holidays 9–noon.*

16 Schloss Hellbrunn (Hellbrunn Castle). Take Bus 55 from the city center about 5 km (3 mi) to Hellbrunn, 6 km (4 mi) south of Salzburg, to reach this popular attraction. The castle was built during the 17th century, and its rooms have some fine trompe l'oeil decorations. To entertain Salzburg's great prince-archbishops, its gardens contain an ingenious system of **Wasserspiele**—hidden jets of water conceived by someone with an impish sense of humor: Expect to get sprinkled by surprise. ⊠ *Fürstenweg, 37, Hellweg,* ☎ *0662/820372.* ⊙ *Tours daily 9–5. Call for information on evening tours in July–Aug.*

In the Hellbrunn park complex is the **Tiergarten** (zoo), outstanding for the way in which the animals are housed in natural surroundings. The **Monatsschlössl,** the historic hunting lodge, houses a small folklore museum. ⊠ *Zoo:* ☎ *0662/820176.* ⊙ *Oct.–Mar., daily 8:30–4; Apr. and Sept., daily 8:30–5:30; May–Aug., daily 8:30–7.*

4 Schloss Mirabell (Mirabell Palace and Gardens). Built by Prince-Archbishop Wolf Dietrich for his mistress, the elegant complex now houses public offices, including that of the city's registrar; many couples come here to be married. The foyer and staircase, decorated with cherubs, are splendid examples of Baroque excess. The gardens are where the von Trapp children "Do-re-mi-ed" in *The Sound of Music.* ⊠ *Mirabellpl., off Makartpl.,* ☎ *no phone.* ⊙ *Mon.–Thurs. 8–4, Fri. 8–1.*

7 Spielzeugmuseum (Toy Museum). Once a hospital, the Bürgerspital now houses a toy and musical instruments museum within its Renaissance arcades. There's a combined ticket with the Carolino Augusteum Museum (☞ *above*), cathedral excavations, and the Folklore Museum at Schloss Hellbrunn (☞ *above*). Nearby on Herbert-von-Karajan-Platz is the 15th-century royal **Pferdeschwemme** (Horse Drinking Trough). ⊠ *Bürgerspitalg. 2,* ☎ *0662/847560.* ⊙ *Tues.–Sun. 9–5.*

12 Stift St. Peter (St. Peter's Abbey). Late-Baroque style marks this sumptuous edifice tucked beneath the mountain. The cemetery lends an added air of mystery to the monks' caves cut into the cliff. The catacombs attached to the church can be visited by guided tour. ⊠ *St. Peter Bezirk, just off Kapitalpl.,* ☎ *0662/844578–0.* ⊙ *Tours daily 10:30, 11:30, 1:30, 2:30, and 3:30.*

The Arts

Festivals

Information and tickets for the main **Salzburger Festspiele** (Salzburg Festival), held in late July and August, as well as the Easter Festival (early April) and the Pentecost Concerts (late May), can be obtained from Salzburger Festspiele (⊠ Postfach 140, A-5010 Salzburg, FAX 0662/8045–760). Write or fax ahead, as it is difficult (but not impossible) to obtain tickets for festival performances once you are in Salzburg.

Opera, Music, and Art

Theater and opera are presented in the three auditoriums of the **Festspielhaus** (⊠ Hofstallg. 1, ☎ 0662/8045–579, ticket office). Opera, operettas, ballet, and drama are offered at the **Landestheater** (⊠

Schwarzstr. 22, ☎ 0662/871–5120). Concerts are the specialty at the **Mozarteum** (⊠ Schwarzstr. 26, ☎ 0662/873154). Chamber music has a grand venue at the **Schloss Mirabell** (⊠ Mirabellpl., off Makartpl., ☎ 0662/848586 for tickets). Special art exhibitions are often held in the **Rupertinum** (⊠ Wiener-Philharmoniker-Gasse 9). Another outstanding venue is the **Galerie Welz** (⊠ Sigmund-Haffner-G. 16).

Dining and Lodging

This is a tourist town, and popular restaurants are always crowded, so make reservations well ahead, particularly during festival times. Most restaurants are open daily during festival season. For details and price-category definitions, *see* Dining *in* Austria A to Z, *above.*

As for hotels, reservations are always advisable and are imperative at festival times (both Easter and summer). Be aware that many hotels charge higher prices during festival times. For details and price-category definitions, *see* Lodging *in* Austria A to Z, *above.*

$$$$ ✕ **Bei Bruno.** A short walk from Schloss Mirabell, this intimate restaurant in the Bristol Hotel is a perfect choice for after-concert dining. The food is nouvelle Austrian, specializing in fresh fish, lightly prepared, and the menu changes frequently to showcase what's in season, such as the delicious *Steinpilze* (porcini mushrooms) and potato casserole. ⊠ *Makartpl. 4,* ☎ *0662/878417. AE, DC, MC, V, Closed Sun.*

$$$ ✕ **K+K am Waagplatz.** This upstairs restaurant has white linen tablecloths, candles, flowers, and windows opening onto the street. The fare includes locally caught fish, chicken breast medallions in a cheese crust with pasta and basil-tomato sauce, and lentil salad with strips of goose breast, as well as traditional Austrian dishes and game in season. ⊠ *Waagpl. 2,* ☎ *0662/842156. AE, DC, MC, V.*

$$$ ✕ **Zum Eulenspiegel.** Delicious food matches the unique setting in this
★ house, which is hundreds of years old. Tables are set with white linen in wonderful nooks and crannies reached by odd staircases. Try the potato goulash with chunks of sausage and beef in a creamy paprika sauce or fish stew Provençale. These are served at lunch, or all day in the bar downstairs. ⊠ *Hagenauerpl. 2,* ☎ *0662/843180. Reservations essential. AE, MC, V. Closed Sun., Feb.–mid-Mar.*

$$ ✕ **Salome Alt.** This all-organic restaurant named for the comely woman who bore Prince-Archbishop Wolf Dietrich 15 children, offers a tempting array of dishes such as *Kürbiscremesuppe* (pumpkin cream soup), *Welsfilet* (catfish) in paprika sauce, or lamb in an herb crust with rosemary ravioli. ⊠ *In Wolf Dietrich Hotel, Wolf Dietrich-Str. 7,* ☎ *0662/ 871275. AE, DC, MC, V. Closed Sun. No lunch.*

$$ ✕ **St. Peter Stiftskeller.** This is one of oldest restaurants in Europe. The courtyard, with its gray stone archways and vine-trellised walls, couldn't be more dramatic. The food, however, tends to be on the heavy side with an emphasis on pork, sauerkraut, and dumplings. Still, it's worth the experience. ⊠ *St. Peter District I/4,* ☎ *0662/848481. Reservations essential. MC, V.*

$ ✕ **Bistro Bio Terra.** Inside the Rupertinum Galerie, this vegetarian restaurant serves imaginative dishes entirely free of animal products or preservatives. The chef takes Italian recipes and creates his own vegetarian versions. The blackboard menu changes daily, but look for bruschetta with a variety of toppings or red beet risotto. ⊠ *Philharmonikerg. 9,* ☎ *06222/849414. No credit cards. Closed Mon.*

$ ✕ **Zum Fidelen Affen** The name means "At the Faithful Ape," which
★ explains the ape motifs in this *Gasthaus,* dominated by a large circular bar and stone pillars under a vaulted ceiling. Besides the microbrewed beer on tap, the kitchen offers tasty, filling dishes, such as *Gemuse gröstl*

(home-fried potatoes with vegetables and polenta) and the outstanding garlic cream soup with black-bread croutons. ✉ *Priesterhausg. 8,* ☎ *0662/877361. No credit cards. Closed Sun. No lunch.*

$$$$ 🏨 **Bristol.** No two rooms are alike in this luxurious turn-of the-century hotel, which has superb views of the river and fortress. Guest rooms are furnished in sumptuous style, right down to the marble bathrooms, which have all the little extras. It is close to both the Old City and Schloss Mirabell. ✉ *Makartpl. 4, A-5020,* ☎ *0662/873557,* ℻ *0662/873–5576. 63 rooms. Restaurant. AE, DC, MC, V.*

$$$$ 🏨 **Goldener Hirsch.** The "Golden Stag" has the best location of all Salzburg's luxury hotels, right down the street from Mozart's Birthplace. Rooms in this nearly 600-year-old town house have a simple, rustic charm with bright rag rugs; the stag motif is everywhere, including the lamp shades, which were hand-painted by an Austrian countess. ✉ *Getreideg. 37, A-5020,* ☎ *0662/8084–0,* ℻ *0662/843–349. 70 rooms. Restaurant. AE, DC, MC, V.*

$$$$ 🏨 **Österreichischer Hof.** Clientele at this beautiful hotel on the banks
★ of the Salzach River have ranged from the Beatles and the Rolling Stones to, more recently, Hillary and Chelsea Clinton. It's owned by the Gürtler family, who also own the Hotel Sacher in Vienna. Each room is different, but all are exquisitely decorated, with care and attention given to every possible whim or need, and the staff is warm and friendly. Room prices include a delicious buffet breakfast, complete with Sekt (Austrian sparkling wine). ✉ *Schwarzstr. 5–7, A-5020,* ☎ *0662/88977–0,* ℻ *0662/88977–551. 120 rooms. 4 restaurants. AE, DC, MC, V.*

$$$$ 🏨 **Schloss Fuschl.** Just 16 km (10 mi) from Salzburg, this 15th-century castle was built as a hunting lodge for the bishop-princes of the city; it was owned by Baron von Ribbentrop, Hitler's foreign minister, before it became a hotel in the 1950s. Ringed by mountains and on three sides by the pristine Fuschlsee, it has one of the most magical settings in Austria. Suites and superior rooms are regally splendid, and though the standard rooms are more modern, most have spectacular views of the lake. ✉ *Hof bei Salzburg A-5322,* ☎ *06229/2253–0,* ℻ *06229/2253–531. 62 rooms, 22 apartments. Restaurant, pool. AE, DC, MC, V.*

$$–$$$ 🏨 **Wolf Dietrich.** Rooms in this small hotel are charmingly decorated,
★ some with Laura Ashley fabrics, and have extra amenities, such as VCRs and sitting areas. Rooms in the back look out over the looming Gaisberg and the cemetery of St. Sebastian (☞ Exploring Salzburg, *above*). ✉ *Wolf Dietrich-Str. 7, A-5020,* ☎ *0662/871275,* ℻ *0662/882320. 30 rooms. Restaurant, pool. AE, DC, MC, V.*

$$ 🏨 **Blaue Gans.** This longtime favorite was renovated in 1998, but the prices haven't gone up. The newly whitewashed rooms are appealing in their rustic simplicity; some have skylights. Its location right on Getreidegasse makes this 500-year-old hotel a top choice, so reserve early. ✉ *Getreideg. 43, A–5020,* ☎ *0662/841317,* ℻ *0662/841317–9. 88 rooms. Restaurant. AE, DC, MC, V.*

$ 🏨 **Haus Kernstock.** This alpine chalet near the airport offers peace and quiet in a pretty setting. Rooms have a cheerful, homespun touch. Frau Kernstock has two bikes that she lends for exploring the countryside, and she'll also meet you at the bus stop if you let her know in advance. ✉ *Karolingerstr. 29, A-5020,* ☎ *0662/827469,* ℻ *0662/827469. 5 rooms with bath. MC, V. From city, Bus 27/Kugelhof stop; from train station, Bus 77/Karolingerstr. stop.*

Shopping

Shopping centers around Griesgasse, Getreidegasse, and Alter Markt in the Old City, and Platzl and Linzer Strasse on the other side of the river. Look for quality handicrafts at **Salzburger Heimatwerk** (⊠ Residenzpl. 9, ☎ 0662/844119).

Salzburg Essentials

Arriving and Departing

BY BUS

The central bus terminal (⊠ Südtirolerplatz, ☎ 0662/167 for postal bus information; ☎ 0662/872150 for railway bus information) is in front of the train station, the Salzburg Hauptbahnhof.

BY CAR

Salzburg has several autobahn exits; study the map. Parking is available in the cavernous garages under the Mönchsberg, near the city center, and in other garages around the city; look for the large blue P signs.

BY PLANE

All flights go via Salzburg Airport (☎ 0662/8580–0), 4 km (2½ mi) west of the city.

Between the Airport and Downtown. Buses leave for the Salzburg train station at Südtirolerplatz every 15 minutes during the day, every half hour at night to 10 PM. Journey time is about 20 minutes. Taxi fare runs about AS150–AS170.

BY TRAIN

Salzburg's main train station is at Südtirolerplatz. For train information, call ☎ 0662/1717; for telephone ticket orders and seat reservations, call ☎ 0662/1700.

Getting Around

Salzburg is compact and most distances are short. This is a city to explore on foot, but take an umbrella, as surprise showers are legendary. Consider purchasing the Salzburg Card. **SalzburgKarten** are good for 24, 48, or 72 hours at AS200, AS290, and AS380, respectively, and allow no-charge entry to most museums and sights, use of public transport, and special discount offers.

BY BICYCLE

A bicycle is useful only if you want to tackle some of the outlying areas. Marked bicycle paths show the way.

BY BUS AND TROLLEYBUS

Service is frequent and reliable; route maps are available from the tourist office or your hotel. Save money by buying an **Umweltkarte,** a 24-hour ticket that is good on all trolley and bus lines. For local transportation information, call ☎ 0662/620551–552.

BY CAR

Don't even think of it! The old part of the city is a pedestrian zone. Many other parts of the city have restricted parking (indicated by a blue pavement stripe), reserved either for residents with permits or for a restricted period. Get parking tickets from coin-operated dispensers on street corners; instructions are also in English.

BY FIAKER

*Fiaker*s (horse-drawn cabs) on the Residenzplatz cost AS380 (up to four people) for 20–25 minutes, AS740 for 50 minutes.

BY TAXI

At festival time, taxis are too scarce to hail on the street, so order through your hotel porter or call ☎ 0662/8111 or ☎ 0662/1716.

Contacts and Resources

CONSULATES

U.S. (⊠ Alter Markt 1/3, ☎ 0662/848776, ℻ 0662/849777). **U.K.** (⊠ Alter Markt 4, ☎ 0662/848133).

EMERGENCIES

Police (☎ 133). **Ambulance** (☎ 144). **Pharmacies** (Apotheken) stay open nights and weekends on rotation; a sign is posted outside each pharmacy listing which are open.

ENGLISH-LANGUAGE BOOKSTORES

American Discount (⊠ Alter Markt 1, ☎ 0662/845640) concentrates on popular paperbacks and magazines. Most good bookstores have some books in English.

GUIDED TOURS

Orientation. Guided bus tours of the city and its environs are given by: **Bob's Special Tours** (⊠ Kaig. 19, ☎ 0662/849511–0, ℻ 0662/849512); **Panorama Tours** (⊠ Schranneng. 2/2, ☎ 0662/883211–0); and **Salzburg Sightseeing Tours** (⊠ Mirabellpl. 2, ☎ 0662/881616). Note that buses cannot enter much of the Altstadt (Old City).

Special-Interest. Many tour operators offer *Sound of Music* excursions through the city; those given by Bob's Special Tours (☞ *above*) are among the friendliest. All tour operators can organize chauffeur-driven tours for up to eight people. Your hotel will have details.

Walking. The city tourist office's folder "Salzburg—The Art of Taking It All In at a Glance" describes a one-day self-guided walking tour.

TRAVEL AGENCIES

American Express (⊠ Mozartpl. 5–7, ☎ 0662/8080, ℻ 0662/8080–148). **Wagon-Lits Travel** (⊠ Münzg. 1, ☎ 0662/842755, ℻ 0662/842755–5).

VISITOR INFORMATION

City Tourist Offices (Stadtverkehrsbüro; ⊠ Mozartpl. 5, walk-ins only; Hauptbahnhof/main train station, ⊠ Bahnsteig 2A, inside station, ☎ 0662/88987; Central Office, ☎ 0662/88987–0, ℻ 0662/88987–32, phone/fax inquiries only).

INNSBRUCK

Squeezed by mountains and sharing the valley with the Inn River, Innsbruck is compact and very easy to explore on foot. The medieval city—it received its municipal charter in 1239—owes much of its fame and charm to its unique location. To the north, the steep, sheer sides of the Alps rise like a shimmering blue-and-white wall from the edge of the city, an awe-inspiring backdrop for the mellow green domes and red roofs of the picturesque Baroque town.

Exploring Innsbruck

Numbers in the margin correspond to points of interest on the Innsbruck map.

Modern-day Innsbruck retains close associations with three historic figures: Emperor Maximilian I and Empress Maria Theresa (both responsible for much of the city's architecture), and Andreas Hofer, a Tyrolean patriot. You will find repeated references to these names as you tour the city and its historic core—the Altstadt.

OFF THE
BEATEN PATH

Alpenzoo. This is a unique opportunity to see 150 species of Alpine animals in their natural habitat, some of which are extinct in the wild. To get there without a car, take Tram 1, Hungerburgbahn or Bus O, N, D, or E, or the shuttle from Maria-Theresien Strasse in front of the Alter Landhaus and Hofburg. ⊠ *Weiherburgg. 37,* ☎ *0512/292323.* ⊙ *Daily 9–6, in winter 9–5.*

❽ Annasäule (St. Anna's Column). This memorial commemorates the withdrawal of Bavarian forces in the war of the Spanish Succession in 1703 on St. Anna's Day. From here you'll have a classic view of Innsbruck and the glorious mountains. ⊠ *Maria-Theresien-Str.*

❸ Domkirche (Cathedral). Built in 1722 and dedicated to St. James, the church has an interior with dramatic painted ceilings and a high-altar portrait of the Madonna by Lucas Cranach the Elder dating from about 1520. ⊠ *Dompl. 6.* ⊙ *Sat.–Thurs. 6–noon, Fri. 2–5.*

❻ Ferdinandeum (Tyrolean Provincal Museum). Austria's largest collection of Gothic art is here as well as paintings from the 19th and 20th centuries. ⊠ *Museumstr. 15,* ☎ *0512/59489.* ⊙ *May–Sept., daily 10–5 and Thurs. 7 PM–9 PM; Oct.–Apr., Tues.–Sat. 10–noon and 2–5, Sun. and holidays 10–1.*

★ **❶ Goldenes Dachl** (The Golden Roof). The ancient mansion with its gold-roof (copper tiles gilded with 31 pounds of gold) balcony is the city's foremost landmark. The balcony was a reviewing stand. The building now houses a **Museum Maximilianeum** (Maximilian Museum), which focuses on the life and works of the Habsburg ruler between 1490 and 1519. A combined ticket also gives you entry to the Ferdinandeum (☞ *above*) and the Stadtturm, the 15th-century city tower, across the street. ⊠ *Herzog Friedrich-Str. 21,* ☎ *0512/581111.* ⊙ *Daily 10–6.*

❾ Helblinghaus (Helbling House). Dating from 1560, this Gothic town house in a 1730 makeover received a facade of ornate blue-and-white rococo decoration that remains one of Innsbruck's most beautiful sights. ⊠ *Herzog Friedrich-Str.*

★ **❷ Hofburg** (Imperial Palace). Dating from 1460, the rococo palace has an ornate reception hall decorated with portraits of Maria Theresa's ancestors. ⊠ *Rennweg 1,* ☎ *0512/587186.* ⊙ *Daily 9–5.*

★ **❹ Hofkirche** (Court Church). Maximilian's mausoleum is surrounded by 24 marble reliefs portraying his accomplishments, as well as 28 oversize bronze statues of his ancestors. Andreas Hofer is also buried here. Don't miss the heavily decorated altar of the 16th-century **Silberne Kapelle** (Silver Chapel). ⊠ *Universitätsstr. 2,* ☎ *0512/584302.* ⊙ *Sept.–June, daily 9–5; July–Aug., daily 9–5:30.*

OFF THE
BEATEN PATH

Schloss Ambras. When Archduke Ferdinand II fell in love with a commoner, Philippine Welser, the court allowed them to marry, but they were forced to live outside the city limits. Ferdinand revamped a 10th-century castle, completing it in 1556 for his bride. In acres of gardens and woodland, it is a curiously inviting castle, with cheery red and white shutters on its many windows. The upper castle now houses rooms lined with noble portraits and the lower section has a collection of weaponry and armor. Be sure to inspect Philippine's sunken bath, a luxury for its time. The Schloss is 3 km (2 mi) southeast of the city. Take Tram 3 to Ambras or the shuttle (AS30 round-trip, leaves on the hour) from Maria-Theresien-Str. 45. ⊠ *Schloßstr. 20,* ☎ *0512/348446.* ⊙ *Apr.–Oct., Wed.–Mon. 10–5. Check with tourist office for winter hrs.*

Innsbruck

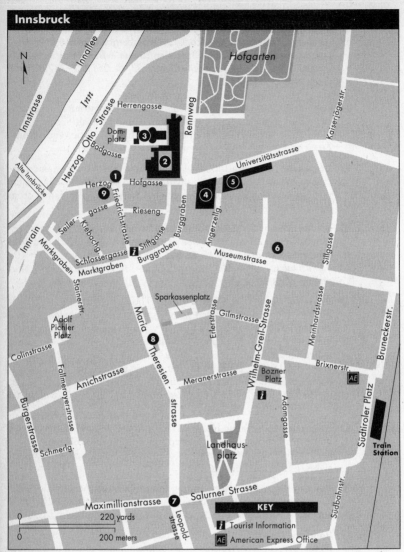

Annasäule, **8**
Domkirche, **3**
Ferdinandeum, **6**
Goldenes Dachl, **1**
Helblinghaus, **9**
Hofburg, **2**

Hofkirche, **4**
Tiroler Volkskunst-
museum, **5**
Triumphpforte, **7**

❺ **Tiroler Volkskunstmuseum** (Tyrolean Folk Art Museum). In the Hofkirche complex (☞ *above*), this fascinating museum exhibits costumes and farmhouse rooms decorated in styles ranging from Gothic to rococo. There's a combined ticket with the Hofburg. ⊠ *Universitätsstr. 2,* ☎ *0512/584302.* ☉ *Sept.–June, Mon.–Sat. 9–5, Sun. and holidays 9–noon; July–Aug., Mon.–Sat. 9–5:30, Sun. and holidays 9–noon.*

❼ **Triumphpforte** (Triumphal Arch). In honor of the marriage of Leopold (son of Maria Theresa and Francis I, brother of Marie Antoinette, and later Kaiser Leopold II) to Maria Ludovica of Tuscany, the arch was built in 1765. It expresses the joy of the marriage on one side and the sadness of the death Francis I, who died suddenly during the wedding celebrations, on the other. ⊠ *Maria-Theresien-Str.*

The Arts

Most hotels have a monthly calendar of events (in English). The City Tourist Office (☞ Visitor Information *in* Innsbruck Essentials, *below*) sells tickets to most events. The leading venue for operas, musicals, and concerts is the **Tiroler Landestheater** (⊠ Rennweg 2, ☎ 0512/520744). Other major performances are held at the **Kongresshaus** (⊠ Rennweg 3, ☎ 0512/5936–0).

Dining and Lodging

Innsbruck gives you a chance to sample hearty Tyrolean cooking, such as *Tyroler G'röstl,* a tasty potato hash with onion and bacon, and *Schlutzkrapferln,* a local version of ravioli. Don't forget to check out some of the city's delightful coffeehouses. For details and price-category definitions, *see* Dining *in* Austria A to Z, *above.*

Many travelers use Innsbruck hotels as home bases for excursions into the surrounding countryside—book far in advance for accommodations. Most hotels offer or can arrange transport to ski areas. For details and price-category definitions, *see* Lodging *in* Austria A to Z, *above.*

\$\$\$\$ ✕ **Schwarzer Adler.** The lead-paned windows and rustic Tirolean
★ decor of this intimate, romantic restaurant in the Schwarzer Adler Hotel provide the perfect backdrop for a memorable meal. Specialties include lobster ragout with tagliatelle in a red wine sauce and grilled freshwater trout. ⊠ *Kaiserjägerstr. 2,* ☎ *0512/587109. Reservations essential. Jacket and tie. AE, DC, MC, V. Closed Sun. and mid-Jan.*

\$\$\$ ✕ **Sweet Basil.** Passersby often pause to look through the big window of this new, always-crowded restaurant. Cozily arranged tables are topped with squat golden candles, made more dramatic because they're the only lighting used. Every month a different style of cuisine is featured, from Tex-Mex to Chinese to Italian, but traditional Austrian dishes are offered as well. ⊠ *Herzog-Friedrich-Str. 31,* ☎ *0512/584996. AE, DC, MC, V.*

\$\$\$ ✕ **Tiroler Stuben.** This restaurant has a broad seasonal menu, includ-
★ ing lots of vegetarian choices. Try the *Schlutzkrapferln* (Tyrolean ravioli) or a simple, succulent roast chicken with potato salad. ⊠ *Alpotel Tirol, Innrain 13 (Ursulinenhof),* ☎ *0512/577931. AE, MC, V.*

\$\$ ✕ **Ottoburg.** You can sit in a bay window in one of the upstairs rooms overlooking the Altstadt in this medieval gray stone town house with charming red and white shutters. The lunch menu changes daily, but look for *Tyroler G'röstl* (potato hash with chunks of pork and slivered onion). ⊠ *Herzog Friedrich-Str. 1A,* ☎ *0512/574652. Reservations essential. AE, DC, MC, V.*

\$\$ ✕ **Philippine.** The food here is exclusively vegetarian, with so many tempting items to choose from it's hard to make a decision. You might start with polenta topped with Gorgonzola and ruby red tomatoes and then go on to cannelloni stuffed with potatoes and smoked tofu, or pumpkin risotto with pumpkin seeds, ginger, and Parmesan. The restaurant has a light, cheerful ambience, and tables are candlelit at night. ⊠ *Müllerstr. and Templestr.,* ☎ *0512/589157. MC, V.*

$ ✕ **Theresien Bräu.** This multilevel brewhouse in the center of town is decorated to give the appearance of the inside of a ship. An assortment of seafaring gear is scattered throughout, such as fishnets, steamer trunks, and even rowboats. But the focus here is on beer, brewed right on the premises. Meals and snacks include zucchini ragout with polenta gratiné, or *Tafelspitz,* a boiled beef dish. People of any age can be found here, but be prepared for loud music. ⊠ *Maria-Theresien-Str. 51–53,* ☎ *0512/587580,* 𝐅𝐀𝐗 *0512/587580–5. AE, DC, MC, V.*

$$$$ ▥ **Goldener Adler.** Mozart, Goethe, and more recently John Glenn and the king and queen of Norway have stayed here. This traditional hotel, a 600-year-old house with stone walls, winding staircases, and a variety of nooks and crannies, has mostly spacious rooms, though a few readers have complained about closetlike rooms on the upper floors. The location is ideal, in the heart of the Old City. ⊠ *Herzog Friedrich-Str. 6, A-6020,* ☎ *0512/586334,* 𝐅𝐀𝐗 *0512/584409. 40 rooms. 2 restaurants. AE, DC, MC, V.*

$$$ ▥ **Alpotel Tirol.** Abundant space, comfort, and modern style are the keys in this hotel on the edge of the Altstadt. The staff is particularly helpful. Many rooms have balconies overlooking the quiet garden and mountains. The Tiroler Stuben restaurant is unusually good (☞ *above*). ⊠ *Innrain 13 (Ursulinenpassage), A-6020,* ☎ *0512/577931,* 𝐅𝐀𝐗 *0512/577931–15. 75 rooms. Restaurant. AE, DC, MC, V.*

$$$ ▥ **Hotel Central.** Halfway between the train station and the Altstadt (about a 10-minute walk from each), the hotel has rooms that are modern and spare, though spacious. The hotel's elegant café carries a tempting choice of pastries and offers a selection of international newspapers. ⊠ *Gilmstr. 5, A-6020,* ☎ *0512/5920,* 𝐅𝐀𝐗 *0512/580310. 87 rooms. Restaurant. AE, DC, MC, V.*

$$$ ▥ **Hotel Maria Theresia.** Ideally situated in the center of the shopping district, this Best Western hotel with a 1920s facade is yet just a five-minute walk from the Altstadt. The rooms, which are decorated with Baroque-style or modern furniture, are comfortable and spacious. ⊠ *Maria-Theresien-Str. 31, A-6020,* ☎ *0512/5933,* 𝐅𝐀𝐗 *0512/575619. 105 rooms. Restaurant, bar. AE, DC, MC, V.*

$$ ▥ **Weisses Kreuz.** Occupying an honored position in the Altstadt, the
★   White Cross is a lovely inn that dates from 1465. Mozart stayed here. ⊠ *Herzog Friedrich-Str. 31, A-6020,* ☎ *0512/59479,* 𝐅𝐀𝐗 *0512/59479–90. 39 rooms, 28 with bath or shower. Restaurant. AE, V.*

$ ▥ **Tautermann.** You're within walking distance of the center in this spacious house above the city (take Bus A from the main station to Höttinger Kirchenplatz). The rooms are in natural woods and white. ⊠ *Stamser Feld/Höttingerg., A-6020,* ☎ *0512/281572,* 𝐅𝐀𝐗 *0512/281572–10. 28 rooms with bath or shower. AE, DC, MC, V.*

Shopping

The main central shopping district is concentrated around the Old City, along Maria-Theresien-Strasse, Maximilianstrasse, Anichstrasse, Burggraben, Museumstrasse, and Wilhelm-Greil-Strasse and their side streets. For local handicrafts, try **Tiroler Heimatwerk** (⊠ Meraner Str. 2–4, ☎ 0512/582320).

Innsbruck Essentials

Arriving and Departing

BY BUS

The terminal (⊠ Südtiroler-Pl., ☎ 0512/585155) is to the right of the main train station. Routes extend from here throughout the Tirol.

BY CAR

Exit from the east–west autobahn or from the Brenner autobahn running south to Italy.

BY PLANE

The airport is 4 km (2½ mi) to the west of the city. For flight information, phone ☎ 0512/22525–304.

Between the Airport and Downtown. Buses (Line F) to the city center (⊠ Maria-Theresien-Str.) run every 20 minutes and take about 20 minutes. Get your ticket from the bus driver; it costs AS21. Taxis should take no more than 10–15 minutes into town, and the fare is between AS120 and AS150.

BY TRAIN

The city's main station is at Südtiroler-Platz. For train information, call ☎ 0512/1717; for ticket reservations, call ☎ 0512/1700.

Getting Around

BY BUS AND STREETCAR

Service is frequent and efficient. Most bus and streetcar routes begin or end at Südtiroler-Platz, in front of the main train station. Bus is the most convenient way to reach the six major ski areas outside the city. From the Old City, the buses leave from in front of the Tiroler Landestheater (☞ The Arts, *above*).

BY CAR

A car is a burden except for getting out of town. Much of the downtown area is a pedestrian zone or paid-parking only; get parking vouchers at tobacco shops, coin-operated dispensers, or the City Tourist Office (☞ Visitor Information, *below*).

BY TAXI

Taxis are not much faster than walking, particularly along the one-way streets and in the Altstadt. To order a radio cab, phone ☎ 0512/1718, 0512/5311, or 0512/45500.

Contacts and Resources

EMERGENCIES

Police (☎ 133). **Ambulance** (☎ 144). **Pharmacies** (Apotheken) stay open nights and weekends on a rotation system. Signs outside each pharmacy list which ones will be open.

GUIDED TOURS

Orientation. Two-hour bus tours covering the city's highlights leave from the hotel information office at the railroad station (⊠ Südtiroler-Pl.) daily at noon. In summer, additional buses are scheduled at 10 and 2, and there are shorter tours Monday through Saturday at 10:15, noon, 2, and 3:15. Contact your hotel or the tourist office.

TRAVEL AGENCIES

American Express (⊠ Brixnerstr. 3, ☎ 0512/582491, FAX 0512/573385). **Wagons-Lits Travel** (⊠ Brixnerstr. 2, ☎ 0512/520790, FAX 0512/520–7985).

Visitor Information

City Tourist Office (⊠ Burggraben 3, ☎ 0512/5356–0, FAX 0512/535643). **Österreichischer Alpenverein** (⊠ Wilhelm-Greil-Str. 15, ☎ 0512/

59547–34, FAX 0512/575528) has information on Alpine huts and mountaineering. Pick up a free *Club Innsbruck* card at your hotel for free use of ski buses and discount ski-lift passes. The *Innsbruck Card* (good for 24, 48, and 72 hours at AS230, AS300, and AS370, respectively) gives you free admission to all the museums, mountain cable cars, the Alpenzoo, and Schloss Ambras, plus free bus and tram transportation.

4 BALTIC STATES

ESTONIA, LATVIA, LITHUANIA

Estonia, Latvia, Lithuania: These three small countries in northeastern Europe have weathered centuries of domination by Germans, Swedes, Russians, and Poles; fought countless battles to preserve at least their dignity; and won their independence twice in the 20th century. The three countries share terrain and history. Nevertheless, since breaking free of the Soviet Union in 1990 and 1991, the Baltics have been quietly reconstructing their individual national identities, societies, and economies, and each is quite resolute about its distinctness from the others.

While building sustainable democracies out of the rubble of post-Soviet republics, Estonia, Latvia, and Lithuania have pursued very different alliances. Estonia, with linguistic and geographic affinities to Helsinki, looks every bit as Scandinavian and Western as its neighbor across the Gulf of Finland. Latvia, with a huge Russian population, still retains some of the chaos of its eastern former nemesis but has emerged as the most cosmopolitan country of the three. Lithuania was slower in embracing the West but since 1996 has made great strides, renewing contacts and relations with Poland in an effort to hitch itself to the EU and NATO's rising star.

Although there aren't many world-famous attractions in the Baltics, the region's obscurity may actually be the best thing about it. Another plus for the English-speaker is that it is becoming increasingly easy to roam the three Baltic capitals of Tallinn, Rīga (Riga), and Vilnius without encountering language barriers. The landscape itself is also free of barriers; everywhere in the Baltics you'll find unspoiled forests and beaches, as well as people whose initial aloofness toward strangers often gives way to genuine friendliness.

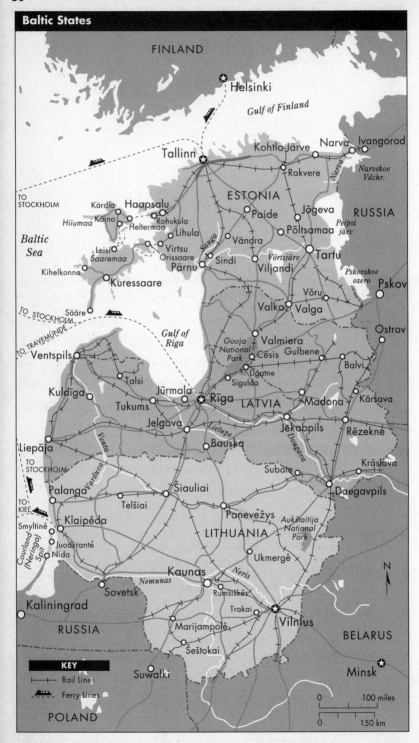

Baltic States

FINLAND

Helsinki

Gulf of Finland

TO STOCKHOLM

Tallinn

Kohtla-Järve

Narva

Ivangorod

Rakvere

Narvskoe Vdchr.

RUSSIA

ESTONIA

Kärdla

Haapsalu

Paide

Jõgeva

Hiiumaa

Käina

Rohukula

Heltermaa

Lihula

Põltsamaa

Peipsi järv

Baltic Sea

Leisi

Saaremaa

Virtsu

Orissaare

Vändra

Tartu

Kihelkonna

Pärnu

Sindi

Viljandi

Võrtsjärv

Pskovskoe ozero

Kuressaare

Sääre

Võru

Pskov

TO STOCKHOLM

Gulf of Riga

Valka

Valga

Ostrov

TO TRAVEMÜNDE

Gauja National Park

Valmiera

Gulbene

Ventspils

Cēsis

Balvi

Talsi

Līgatne

Sigulda

Kuldīga

Jūrmala

Rīga

LATVIA

Madona

Kārsava

Tukums

Jelgava

Jēkabpils

Rēzekne

Bauska

Lielupe

Daugava

Liepāja

Venta

Subate

Krāslava

TO STOCKHOLM

Vārduva

Palanga

Šiauliai

Daugavpils

TO KIEL

Telšiai

Panevėžys

Aukštaitija National Park

Smyltinė

Klaipėda

LITHUANIA

Juodkrantė

Nida

Ukmergė

Courland (Neringa) Spit

Kaunas

Neris

N

Nemunas

Rumšiškės

Kaliningrad

Sovetsk

Trakai

Vilnius

RUSSIA

Marijampolė

BELARUS

Šeštokai

KEY

Minsk

Rail Lines

Ferry Lines

Suwałki

0   100 miles

0   150 km

POLAND

Baltic States A to Z

For country-specific details (money, phones, and so on), *see* the appropriate sections *below*; the following is general information on all three Baltic states.

Customs

Duty-free allowances are: 250 grams of tobacco, 1 liter of spirits, 1 liter of wine, and 10 liters of beer (3 liters of wine and 5 liters of beer in Lithuania).

The export of antiques and historic artifacts is strictly controlled. Contact the **Division of Export of Culture Objects** (☎ 2/448–501) in Estonia, the **Ministry of Culture** (☎ 721–4100) in Latvia, or the **Committee of Cultural Heritage** (☎ 2/724–005) in Lithuania. Generally a 10%–20% duty is charged on goods more than 50 years old and native to the country; up to 100% duty is charged on goods more than 100 years old made in a foreign country but bought in the Baltics.

Dining

Native dishes predominate: usually meat, potatoes, and root-vegetable salad. Nevertheless, the dining scene in the capitals has much improved in recent years. All three cities—Tallinn, Riga, and Vilnius—offer an astonishing array of authentic international cuisine. Riga has the most upscale restaurants while Vilnius has the best array of international cuisine. In Tallinn a group of new restaurants concentrate on national cuisine served in medieval stone cellars.

RATINGS

Prices are for a three-course meal for one person, not including drinks or tip.

CATEGORY	COST
$$$	over $20
$$	$10–$20
$	under $10

WHAT TO WEAR

Casual dress is acceptable in all restaurants in the Baltics. However, jeans, sweat suits, and tennis shoes are generally not appropriate for high-priced establishments.

Embassies

ESTONIA

U.S. (✉ Kentmanni 20, Tallinn, ☎ 631–2021, FAX 631–2025). **Canadian** (✉ Toom-kooli 13, Tallinn, ☎ 631–7978, FAX 631–3573). **U.K.** (✉ Kentmanni 20, Tallinn, ☎ 631–3461, FAX 631–3354).

LATVIA

U.S. (✉ Raiņa 7, Riga, ☎ 722–0005, FAX 722–6530). **Canadian** (✉ Doma laukums 4, Riga, ☎ 783–0141 or 722–6315, FAX 783–0140). **U.K.** (✉ Alunāna 5, Riga, ☎ 733–8126, FAX 733–8132). **Australian** (✉ Raiņa 3, Riga, ☎ 722–2383, FAX 722–5228).

LITHUANIA

U.S. (✉ Akmenų 6, Vilnius, ☎ 2/222–737, FAX 2/312–819). **Canadian** (✉ Gedimino 64, Vilnius, ☎ 2/220–853, FAX 2/220–884). **U.K.** (✉ Antakalnio 2, Vilnius, ☎ 2/222–070, FAX 2/727–579). **Australian** (✉ Karmelitu 4/12, Vilnius, ☎ 2/223–369, FAX 2/223–369).

Lodging

Rooms in all hotels listed have private bath or shower unless otherwise noted. Most have air-conditioning, but verify this in summer.

RATINGS

Prices are for two people sharing a double room and include breakfast.

CATEGORY	COST
$$$$	over $120
$$$	$80–$120
$$	$40–$80
$	under $40

Opening and Closing Times

Banks are open weekdays 9–4, but some open as early as 8 and close as late as 7 in Latvia and Estonia. In Lithuania banks are open weekdays 8–4:30, though some close at 3 on Fridays. Most are closed on Saturday, but some stay open 9–3. **Museums** are generally open 11–5 and are closed on Monday and Tuesday. Some stay open until 6. **Shops** open between 10 and 11 and close between 5 and 7, with shorter hours on Saturday. Most shops are closed on Sunday.

Visas

American, Australian, British, Irish, and New Zealand citizens can stay in Estonia visa-free for up to 90 days. Canadian citizens now need a visa to enter Estonia. Australians, Canadians, and New Zealanders need visas for Latvia; a 90-day visa can be purchased from consulates outside Latvia, and 10-day visas can be purchased for 12Ls at the Riga airport. Citizens of New Zealand and Ireland need visas to enter Lithuania. A 10-day visa can be issued at the Vilnius airport for 160Lt if your country of citizenship does not have a Lithuanian embassy or consulate or you are a citizen of an EU country.

Visitor Information

Estonia: **Tallinn** (⊠ Raekoja plats 10, ☎ 631–3940, ℻ 631–3941). Latvia: **Riga** (⊠ Skārņu 22, ☎ 955–8438, ℻ 722–7680). Lithuania: **Vilnius** (⊠ Pilies 42, ☎ ℻ 2/620–762; ⊠ Airport arrivals hall, Rodūnės kelias 2, ☎ 99/99721).

Weather

Mid-summer in the capital cities sees an influx of tourists and an exodus by locals. For local color and temperate weather, visit in late spring or early autumn. Always be prepared for cold weather and rain.

CLIMATE

The Baltic states' climate is temperate, but tends to be cool and damp. Coastal regions tend to be colder by a few degrees in winter and warmer by a few in summer. The rainy season is in early summer. The snowy, cold winter season lasts from November through March. Summers, though warm, are generally wet and humid. August tends to see the smallest amount of rain in all three Baltic States. The average daily temperatures for Estonia, Latvia, and Lithuania, in that order, are:

Jan.	30.9F	-0.6C	**May**	46.6F	8.1C	**Sept.**	52.5F	11.4C
	31.6	-0.2		52.3F	11.3C		52.2F	11.2C
	30.7	-0.7		55.4F	13C		53.4F	11.9C
Feb.	27.1F	-2.7C	**June**	59.5F	15.3C	**Oct.**	39.7F	4.3C
	31.2F	-0.4C		62.4F	16.9C		40.1F	4.5C
	32.3F	0.2C		55.4F	13C		41.2F	5.1C
Mar.	31.6F	-0.2C	**July**	64.4F	18C	**Nov.**	33.6F	0.9C
	26.8F	-2.9C		62F	16.7C		34.5F	1.4C
	30.9F	-0.6C		61.3F	16.3C		35F	1.7C
Apr.	36.3F	2.4C	**Aug.**	65.8F	18.8C	**Dec.**	26.4F	-3.1C
	43.3F	6.3C		59F	15C		23.9F	-4.5C
	46.8F	8.2C		58.1F	14.5C		24.3F	-4.3C

ESTONIA

The country's history is sprinkled liberally with long stretches of foreign domination, beginning in 1219 with the Danes, followed without interruption by the Germans, Swedes, and Russians. Only after World War I, with Russia in revolutionary wreckage, was Estonia able to declare its independence. But shortly before the Second World War, in 1940, that independence was usurped by the Soviets, who—save for a brief three-year occupation by Hitler's Nazis—proceeded to suppress all forms of national Estonian pride for the next 50 years. Estonia finally regained independence in 1991. In the early 1990s Estonia's own Riigikogu (Parliament), not some other nation's puppet ruler, handed down from the Upper City reforms that—though occasionally unpleasant—forced Estonia to blaze its post-Soviet trail to the European Union. In 1997 the country got the nod from Brussels to join the EU, an endorsement of Estonia's progress toward a sustainable market economy.

Estonia A to Z

Emergencies

Police (☎ 002). **Ambulance** (☎ 003). **Doctor: Tallinn Central Hospital** (☎ 620–7010); **ESMED Medical Center** (☎ 657–9118); **Medica Arstikeskus** (☎ 26/444–4231). **Dentist: Baltic Medical Partners** (☎ 631–1222); **Kentmanni hambaravi** (☎ 26/455–785). **Pharmacy: Koduapteek** (☎ 26/430–220); **Tallinna Linna Apteek** (☎ 644–2262).

Guided Tours

CDS Tours (✉ Raekoja plats 17, ☎ 627–6797, ℻ 631–3666). **Estonian Holidays** (✉ Pärnu maantee 12, ☎ 631–4106, ℻ 631–4109). **Reisiekspert** (✉ Roosikrantsi 17, ☎ 610–8600).

Language

Estonian, which belongs to the Finno-Ugric family, is the official language. However, many people in cities speak English perfectly. Most Estonians will ignore attempts to communicate in Russian, though the 30% of the population that is ethnically Russian is happy to speak it.

Mail

A 20-gram letter to the United States costs 7EEK, a postcard 6.70EEK. To Europe a 20-gram letter costs 5.50EEK, a postcard 5.20EEK. The **main post office** (✉ Narva 1, Tallinn, ☎ 625–7300) is open weekdays 8–7, Saturday 9–5. Stamps are sold at post offices only.

Money Matters

COSTS

A cup of coffee or tea costs 10EEK; a glass of beer 20EEK–25EEK; a main dish at a local, medium-priced restaurant 50EEK–60EEK. Admission to museums and galleries costs 10EEK or 20EEK. If you're staying in Tallinn from one to three days, the best deal is the Tallinn Card, which can be purchased at Visitor Information, all points of entry, and some hotels. It allows visitors free access to public transportation, free admission to museums, a free bus and walking tour, and discounts at shops and restaurants in Tallinn.

CURRENCY

The monetary unit in Estonia is the kroon, which is divided into 100 senti. There are notes of 1, 2, 5, 10, 25, 50, 100, and 500EEK and coins of 5, 10, 20, and 50 senti and 1EEK. At press time (summer 1999) the rate of exchange was 14.98EEK to the U.S. dollar, 10.20EEK to the Canadian dollar, 23.71EEK to the pound sterling, 8EEK to the Australian dollar, and 8EEK to the New Zealand dollar. The Estonian kroon is pegged 8EEK to the German mark. National banks, with branches in all major and most minor cities, change cash and traveler's checks at fair commissions; most also give advances on a Visa or MasterCard. Credit cards are widely accepted in Estonia.

TIPPING

At restaurants a 10% service charge is sometimes added and an 18% VAT is included in the price of dishes on the menu but may be listed separately on your bill. Tipping is not obligatory; for excellent service, add 10%.

National Holidays

January 1; February 24 (Independence Day); April 21 (Good Friday); April 23 (Easter); May 1 (May Day); May 31 (Whitsuntide); June 23 (Victory Day); June 24 (St. John's Day/Midsummer); December 25, 26.

Telephoning

COUNTRY CODE

The country code for Estonia is ☎ 372. For seven-digit phone numbers in Tallinn, there is no city code. For six-digit numbers dialed from abroad or outside the city, you must add an additional "2" for Tallinn.

INTERNATIONAL CALLS

To reach an **AT&T** long-distance operator, dial 8–008001001.

LOCAL CALLS

Pay phones take phone cards worth 30, 50, or 100 EEK. Buy cards at any kiosk. **Telephone information** (☎ 626–1111 or ☎ 8–1182).

Transportation

BY BOAT

Passenger ships—including frequent ferries and hydrofoils to nearby Helsinki—connect Tallinn with various Scandinavian cities.

BY BUS

Public transport costs 5–9 EEK. Buy tickets from nearly any kiosk or from the driver. A single type of ticket is valid on buses, trolleys, and streetcars. Express buses and tickets purchased from the driver rather than at a kiosk cost more. Punch your ticket upon boarding or be fined 360EEK. Public transport operates 6 AM to midnight. Domestic bus trips cost 40EEK–90EEK. For bus schedules call **Express Hotline** (☎ 631–3222).

BY CAR

An international or national driver's license bearing a photo is acceptable in Estonia. Drive on the right. Most roads are not up to Western standards, but major thoroughfares tend to be in better condition than secondary roads, where potholes and unpaved ways are common. Gas costs 7EEK per liter. Cars may be rented from 700EEK a day.

BY PLANE

There are no direct flights between Estonia and the United States. Estonian Air operates from Amsterdam, Copenhagen, Hamburg, Helsinki, London, Stockholm, and Vilnius. American carriers partnered with Finnair, Lufthansa, SAS, and LOT have good connections.

BY PRIVATE TAXI

Taxis operate 24 hours throughout the city. Taxis are expensive around hotels and ferry, bus, and train stations, cheaper within the city center; it's best to telephone for one. Taxi fares generally start at 6EEK or 8EEK and increase by 4EEK or 6EEK per km (½ mi) in the daytime, more at night or in bad weather. Drivers are bound by law to display an operating license and a meter. In-town journeys cost up to 50EEK. **Esra** (☎ 642–5425) and **Tulika** (☎ 612–0000) are by and large trustworthy taxi companies.

Exploring Estonia

Tallinn

Tallinn's tiny Old Town, the most stunning and impressive in the region, has romantic towers, ankle-wrenching cobblestone streets, cozy nooks, city-wall cafés, and a dozen other attractions—all within 1 square kilometer. In the 1990s, Vanalinn (the lower Old Town)—historically the domain of traders, artisans, and ordinary citizens—has sprouted glitzy neon signs in otherwise charming alleys and sights. The stately, sedate Toompea (Upper Town), a hillock that was the site of the original Estonian settlement, is on the burial mound of Kalev, the epic hero of Estonia. Toompea Castle, crowning the hill, is now the seat of the country's parliament and is not open to visitors.

The 19th-century Russian Orthodox **Aleksandr Nevski Khram** (Alexander Nevsky Cathedral), which houses the country's largest bell, is symbol of the centuries of Russification this country has endured. ⊠ *Lossi pl. 10, Toompea,* ☎ *2/443–484.* ☉ *Daily 8–7:30.*

In an 18th-century noble's house, the **Eesti Kunstimuuseum** (Estonian National Art Museum) contains an impressive array of Estonian art from the last 200 years. ⊠ *Kiriku pl. 1, Toompea,* ☎ *644–1478.* ☉ *Wed.–Sun. 11–6.*

The Lutheran **Toomkirik,** the oldest church in the country, was founded by the occupying Danes in the 13th century and rebuilt in 1686. ⊠ *Toom-kooli 6, Toompea,* ☎ *2/444–140.* ☉ *Daily 9–4:30.*

★ At the southern end of the Old Town looms the magnificent, six-story tower **Kiek-in-de-Kök** (Low German for "peep in the kitchen"), so called because during the 15th century one could peer into the kitchens of lower-town houses from here. The tower houses a museum of contemporary art and ancient maps and weapons. ⊠ *Komandandi 1, Vanalinn,* ☎ *2/446–686.* ☉ *Tues.–Fri. 10:30–5:30, weekends 11–4:30.*

The 15th-century **Niguliste kirik** (Church of St. Nicholas) is famed for its fragment of a treasured frieze, Bernt Notke's (1440–1509) *Danse Macabre,* a haunting depiction of death. ⊠ *Niguliste 13, Vanalinn,* ☎ *2/449–911.* ☉ *Thurs.–Sun. 11:30–6, Tues. 5–8, Wed. 2–6.*

The stocky guardian of the northernmost point of the Old City, **Paks Margareeta** (Fat Margaret) is a 16th-century fortification named for a particularly hefty cannon it housed. Now it contains a **Maritime Museum.** ⊠ *Pikk 70, Vanalinn,* ☎ *641–1413.* ☉ *Wed.–Sun. 10–6.*

★ For a completely raw and untranslated look at the country's musical past, peek into the **Teatri ja Muusikamuuseum** (Theater and Music Museum), where displays span the folksy and the freaky. ⊠ *Müürivahe 12,* ☎ *2/446–407.* ☉ *Wed.–Sun. 10–6.*

★ **Raekoja plats** (Town Hall Square) has a long, illustrious history of intrigue, executions, and salt (Tallinn's main export in the Middle Ages). Take a guided tour of the only surviving original Gothic **town hall** in Northern Europe. Old Thomas, its weather vane, has been atop the town hall since 1530. Across the square stands the town **apothecary** (⊠ Raekoja plats 11), which dates from 1422. Near the center of the square, an L-shape stone marks the site of a 17th-century execution, where a priest was beheaded for killing a waitress who had offered him a rock-hard omelet. ⊠ *Vanalinn,* ☎ *2/440–819.* ☉ *Weekdays 10–4.*

DINING AND LODGING

$$$ ✕ **Gloria.** The premier dining establishment in Tallinn has hosted many a distinguished guest, including the pope. As one would expect, the food—sole meunière, three tenors salad (tomato, mozzarella, and olives)—rarely fails to please. ⊠ *Müürivahe 2,* ☎ *644–6950. Reservations essential. Jacket and tie. MC, V.*

$$$ ✕ **Tanduur.** One of the fanciest restaurants in the capital serves astoundingly good Indian food. The tangerine-color walls and the strings of white lights covering the ceiling create a warm atmosphere in this cellar restaurant. ⊠ *Vene 7,* ☎ *631–3084. MC, V.*

$$ ✕ **Möökkala.** A superior seafood restaurant tucked away in an Old Town cellar, it has everything from crab salad to caviar to perch. The decor is an odd mix of ancient stone walls and passé pastel furnishings. ⊠ *Rüütli 16/18,* ☎ *631–3583. MC, V.*

$$ ✕ **Olde Hansa.** In a 15th-century building in the Old Town, this medieval-style restaurant creates an authentic ancient atmosphere with waiters in period costume, candlelit tables, and historic recipes for such dishes as nobleman's smoked filet mignon in mushroom sauce and wild boar with game sauce and forest berries. The honey beer is out of this world and the food always fresh and tasty. ⊠ *Vanaturg 1,* ☎ *26/445–438. No credit cards.*

$$ ✕ **Toomkooli.** Enjoy such local dishes as reindeer with apple-cranberry jam in this snug hilltop dining room on Toompea. ⊠ *Toom-kooli 13,* ☎ *644–6613. AE, MC, V.*

$ ✕ **Creperie Chez Grigou.** A bit of Paris in Tallinn: The black-clad waitresses are friendly and the crepes, though diminutive, are enticing with ham, cheese, mushrooms, zucchini, or even banana fillings. Candlelight and soft jazz music greet a hip, laid-back clientele. ⊠ *Müürivahe 23,* ☎ *631–4337. No credit cards.*

$$$$ 🏨 **Olümpia.** This high-rise offers a variety of rooms. Amenities include a conference hall, a top-floor sauna overlooking the city, and a splendid breakfast buffet. Request a room with a view of the Old Town. ⊠ *Liivalaia 33, EE0001,* ☎ *631–5315 or 631–5333,* 𝔉𝔄𝔛 *631–5675. 405 rooms. 2 restaurants, pool, sauna, exercise room. AE, DC, MC, V.*

$$$$ 🏨 **Park Consul Schlösse.** In three medieval warehouses in the Old Town, Tallinn's most luxurious hotel has unparalleled charm. The rooms are furnished with quaint English furniture. ⊠ *Pühavaimu 13–15, EE10123,* ☎ *699–7700,* 𝔉𝔄𝔛 *699–7777. 23 rooms. Restaurant, sauna. DC, MC, V.*

$$ 🏨 **Hotel Central.** Winning service, a breakfast buffet, and special rooms for allergy sufferers are attractions here. The luxury rooms are a better value than the economy rooms. ⊠ *Narva 7c, EE0001,* ☎ *633–9800,* 𝔉𝔄𝔛 *633–9900. 124 rooms. 2 restaurants. AE, DC, MC, V.*

$$ 🏨 **St. Barbara.** On the edge of Old Town, the St. Barbara occupies an unassuming building and offers standard hotel rooms. Its location makes it a good value. ⊠ *Roosikrantsi 2a, EE0001,* ☎ *631–3991,* 𝔉𝔄𝔛 *631–3992. 53 rooms. Restaurant. AE, DC, MC, V.*

$ 🏨 **Eeslitall.** Right in the middle of Old Town, this budget hotel has sparely furnished rooms with common showers and toilets. Double rooms have a choice of one double bed or two singles. ⊠ *Dunkri 4/6, EE0001,* ☎ *631–3755,* 𝔉𝔄𝔛 *631–3210. 9 rooms. Restaurant. No credit cards.*

The Islands

Some 1,500 time machines float off the western coast of Estonia, embodying what the country was all about before World War II. Because the Soviets feared a mass exodus to the West, these islands have largely been off-limits for the past 50 years. Only two islands, Saaremaa and Hiiumaa, are easily accessible, through port towns about 100 km (62 mi) south of Tallinn. **Kruessaare**, the capital of **Saaremaa**, is a town of only 16,000, but proudly lays claim to an almost wholly intact **Gothic castle**, complete with turrets and moat. Some modest cliffs and beaches round out a trip to the island. **Hiiumaa**, and its center of **Kärdla**, is quieter still, with nothing more audacious than some windmills and a few birds to disturb this perfect retreat.

LATVIA

Latvia, and particularly Riga, is fiercely distinct from the other two Baltic states in a number of ways. German influence was stronger here than elsewhere, as the 14th-century Knights of the Sword used this as their base. When the Soviets forcibly incorporated Latvia into the Soviet Union, in 1944, the effects of Russification—coupled with the White Russians who had been arriving since 1710, when Russia first invaded Latvia—were more devastating. Today 45% of Latvia is Russian-speaking; in Riga, Russians, Ukrainians, and Belorussians are the majority. This has created a palpable tension: Latvians are angered because their culture has been suppressed for 50 years and Russian continues to be used on the street; Russians are peeved that most of them have yet to be given citizenship here.

Latvia A to Z

Emergencies
Police (☎ 02). **Ambulance** (☎ 03). **Doctor: Ars** (☎ 720–1001 or 720–1007). **Dentist: A + S Health Center** (☎ 728–9516). **Pharmacy: Kamēlijas aptieka** (☎ 2/293–514).

Guided Tours
Latvia Tours (☎ 708–5001).

Language
Latvian belongs to the Baltic branch of the Indo-European family of languages. The country's official language is Latvian; the unofficial language is Russian. Most Latvians will answer you if addressed in Russian, but more and more speak perfect English.

Mail
A 20-gram letter to the United States costs 30s, a postcard 25s. To Europe a 20-gram letter costs 20s, a postcard 16s. The **main post office** (✉ Brīvības 19, Riga, ☎ 701–8738) is open 24 hours.

Money Matters
COSTS
A cup of coffee or tea costs 40s; a glass of local beer 1Ls; a medium-priced local dish will cost 2Ls to 4Ls. Admission to museums and galleries costs around 50s.

CURRENCY
The monetary unit in Latvia is the lat (Ls), which is divided into 100 santīmi(s). There are notes of 5, 10, 20, 50, 100, and 500 lat, coins of 1 and 2 lat and 1, 2, 5, 10, 20, and 50 santīmi. At press time (summer 1999) the rate of exchange was 60s to the U.S. dollar, 41s to the Canadian dollar, 94s to the pound sterling, 37s to the Australian dollar, and 32s to the New Zealand dollar. Banks, with branches in all major and most minor cities, change cash and traveler's checks at fair commissions; most also give advances on a Visa or MasterCard. Credit cards are widely accepted.

TIPPING
At restaurants a service charge of 10% is sometimes added and an 18% VAT is automatically included. Tipping is not obligatory, but for excellent service, add 10%.

National Holidays
January 1; April 21 (Good Friday); April 23 (Easter); May 1 (Labor Day); June 23, 24 (St. John's Day/Midsummer); November 18 (Independence Day, 1918); December 25, 26 (Christmas); December 31.

Telephoning

COUNTRY CODE

The country code for Latvia is 371.

INTERNATIONAL CALLS

To reach an **AT&T** long-distance operator, dial 700–7007.

LOCAL CALLS

Pay phones take phone cards worth 2, 5, or 10 Ls. Buy cards at any kiosk. **Telephone information** (☎ 900–0000 or 777–0777).

Transportation

BY BOAT

Passenger ships connect Riga with various Scandinavian ports.

BY BUS

Public transport costs 18s. Buy bus tickets from the conductor on the bus. Tram and trolleybus tickets are sold at kiosks. Public transport runs from 5:30 AM to 12:30 AM. Some routes have 24-hour service. Domestic bus trips cost less than 5Ls. For bus schedules call the 24-hour **Ekspress Hotline** (☎ 777–0777).

BY CAR

An international or national driver's license bearing a photo is acceptable in Latvia. Drive on the right. Roads are not up to Western standards. Gas costs 30s per liter. Cars may be rented from 40Ls a day; lower rates are available for longer rental terms.

BY PLANE

Air Baltic operates from Copenhagen, Frankfurt, Geneva, Hamburg, Helsinki, Munich, Stockholm, Tallinn, Vilnius, and Warsaw. Finnair, LOT, and British Airways connect from the United States.

BY PRIVATE TAXI

Taxis operate 24 hours throughout Riga. They are expensive around hotels and ferry, bus, and train stations, cheaper within the city center; for best results, telephone for one. The official rate is 25s per km (½ mi) in the daytime and 35s at night or in bad weather. Drivers must display an operating license and a meter. Stick to the state cabs with orange and black markings. Insist that the meter be turned on; if there is no meter, choose another taxi or decide on a price beforehand. **Riga Taxi** (☎ 739–1881) and **State Taxis** (☎ 707–7077 or 733–4041) are by and large trustworthy taxi companies.

BY SERVICE TAXI

Shared taxis accommodate up to 10 people and are cheap and comfortable. They operate on virtually every bus and trolleybus line. Tariffs are 15s and 25s. Passengers may embark at any regular bus stop and disembark anywhere along the route.

BY TRAIN

Electric trains are by far the preferable mode of transport for getting around Latvia. Tickets cost less than 5Ls. For train schedule information call the 24-hour **Ekspress Hotline** (☎ 777–0777).

Exploring Latvia

Riga

Riga has an upscale, big-city feel unmatched in the region. The capital is almost as large as Tallinn and Vilnius combined and is the business center of the area. Original, high-quality restaurants and hotels have given Riga something to brag about.

Although Riga's Old Town is its calling card, it is also the city of Art Nouveau. Long avenues of complex and sometimes whimsical interwar Jugendstil facades hint at Riga's grand past. Many were designed by Mikhail Eisenstein, the father of Soviet director Sergei. This style dominates the city center; you can see the finest examples at Alberta 2, 2a, 4, 6, 8, and 13 and Strēlnieku 4a.

Currently ensconced in scaffolding, the fiercely Gothic **Melngavlvju Nams** (Blackheads House) was built in 1344 as a hotel for wayfaring merchants (who wore black hats). Partially destroyed during World War II and leveled by the Soviets in 1948, it is being reconstructed for Riga's 800th anniversary in 2001. ✉ *Strēlnieku laukums.*

The **Brīvdabas muzejs** (Open-air Ethnographic Museum) is well worth the 9-km (5-mi) trek from downtown. At this countryside living museum farmsteads and villages have been crafted to look like those in 18th- and 19th-century Latvia; folk-costumed workers engage in traditional activities (beekeeping, smithery, and so on). ✉ *Brīvības 440,* ☎ *799–4510.* ⊘ *Daily 11–5.*

★ The central **Brīvības piemineklis** (Freedom Monument), a 1935 statue whose upheld stars represent Latvia's united peoples (the Kurzeme, Vidzeme, and Latgale), was the rallying point for many nationalist protests during the late 1980s and early 1990s. ✉ *Brīvības and Raiņa.*

In **Doma laukums** (Dom Square), the nerve center of the Old Town, the stately 1210 **Doma Baznīca** (Dome Cathedral) dominates. Reconstructed over the years with bits of Romanesque, Gothic, and Baroque, this place of worship is astounding for its architecture as much as for its size. The massive 6,768-pipe organ is among the largest in Europe. ✉ *Doma laukums,* ☎ *721–3213.* ⊘ *Tues.–Fri. 1–5, Sat. 10–2.*

★ The **Okupācijas Muzejs** (Latvian Occupation Museum) details the devastation of Latvia at the hands of the Nazis and Soviets during World War II as well as the Latvians' struggle for independence in September 1991. In front of the museum is a monument to the Latvian sharpshooters who protected Lenin during the 1917 revolution. ✉ *Strēlnieku laukums 1,* ☎ *721–2715.* ▣ *Free.* ⊘ *Tues.–Sun. 11–5.*

★ At **Rīgas Motormuzejs** (Motor Museum) the Western cars on display can impress, but the Soviet models—including Stalin's iron-plated limo and a Rolls Royce totaled by Brezhnev himself—are the most fun. ✉ *Eizenšteina 6,* ☎ *709–7170.* ⊘ *Tues.–Sun. 10–6.*

Latvia's restored 18th-century **Nacionālā Opera Doms** (Opera House), where Richard Wagner once conducted, is just off Freedom Square. ✉ *Box office, Teatra 10/12,* ☎ *722–5747 or 722–5803.*

Towering **Pētera baznīca** (St. Peter's Church), originally built in 1209, had a long history of annihilation and conflagration before being destroyed most recently in 1941. Rebuilt by the Soviets, it lacks authenticity but has a good observation deck on the 200-ft spire. ✉ *Skārņu 19.* ⊘ *Tues.–Sun. 10–7.*

The **Trīs Brāļi** (Three Brothers)—a trio of houses on Mazā Pils—show what the city looked like before the 20th century. The three oldest stone houses in the capital (No. 17 is the oldest, dating from the 15th century) span several styles, from the medieval to the Baroque. The middle house is the city's **architecture museum.** ✉ *Mazā Pils 17, 19, 21,* ☎ *7/220–779.* ⊘ *Mon.–Fri. 9–5, Sat. noon–4.*

The **Valsts mākslas muzejs** (National Art Museum) has a gorgeous interior equipped with imposing marble staircases linking several large halls of 19th- and 20th-century Latvian art. ⊠ *Kr. Valdemara 10a,* ☎ *732–5021.* ⊙ *Wed.–Mon. 11–5.*

DINING AND LODGING

$$$ ✕ **Reformātu Klubs.** The international menu is tasty, but it's the nightly live jazz music after 10 that draws the crowds. Candlelight glows in the sepia-tone dining room—the converted basement of a church hall. ⊠ *Mārstaļu 10,* ☎ *721–0027. AE, DC, MC, V.*

$$$ ✕ **Symposium.** One of Riga's premiere dining establishments, Symposium serves outstanding Continental cuisine, with an emphasis on seafood dishes, in a softly lit dining room to the strains of classical music. ⊠ *Dzirnavu 84/1,* ☎ *724–2545. MC, V.*

$$$ ✕ **Vincents.** Named for the Dutch Impressionist, this restaurant has fed the likes of Prince Charles, B. B. King, and Mstislav Rostropovich. The menu is a sensational collection of international delicacies, such as ostrich fillet or smoked salmon, all with a French flair. ⊠ *Elizabetes 19,* ☎ *733–2634. MC, V.*

$$ ✕ **Osiris.** Next to the Aperto Libro English-language bookstore, this is a favorite meeting spot of diplomats and ex-pats. It's famed for its weekend brunches, but any meal is super here, from sesame and spinach omelets to Greek salads. ⊠ *Kr. Barona 31,* ☎ *724–3002. MC, V.*

$$ ✕ **Staburags.** In an Art Nouveau building in downtown Riga, Staburags may be the capital's best place to sample Latvian national cuisine, with such dishes as roast leg of pork, sauerkraut, all manner of potato dishes, and smoked chicken. The ceramic tableware is authentic and the food more than satisfying. ⊠ *Čaka 55,* ☎ *299–787. No credit cards.*

$ ✕ **Rāma.** The resident Hare Krishna community offers out-of-this-world vegetarian Indian fare in a preach-free environment. ⊠ *Kr. Barona 56,* ☎ *2/274–120. No credit cards.*

$$$$ 🏬 **Hotel De Rome.** With warm and classy service, it is elegant and worth the cost. Some rooms are decorated with turn-of-the-century antiques. Amenities include conference facilities, an outstanding breakfast, and a roomy sauna. ⊠ *Kaļķu 28, LV1050,* ☎ *708–7600,* FAX *708–7606. 90 rooms. 2 restaurants, sauna. AE, DC, MC, V.*

$$$$ 🏬 **Radisson SAS Daugava.** In this hotel across the river from Old Town, the simple, modern rooms have spectacular views. The staff is probably the most gracious in town and the quality is all that you would expect from an international chain. ⊠ *Kugu 24, LV1050,* ☎ *706–1111,* FAX *706–1100. 361 rooms. Restaurant, pool, sauna. AE, DC, MC, V.*

$$$ 🏬 **Konventa Sēta.** In a charming complex of buildings dating from the Middle Ages, this hotel has rooms with a clean, white, Scandinavian aesthetic and medieval details. ⊠ *Kalēju 9/11, LV1050,* ☎ *708–7501,* FAX *708–7506. 140 rooms. Restaurant. AE, DC, MC, V.*

$$$ 🏬 **Latvija.** At this efficient, sleek, modern hotel the VIP floors offer spectacular views and luxurious rooms. Standard rooms are well appointed. Amenities include a business center and a Turkish sauna. ⊠ *Elizabetes 55, LV1050,* ☎ *722–9020,* FAX *782–0240. 354 rooms. 3 restaurants. AE, DC, MC, V.*

$$ 🏬 **Raudi un Draugi.** Run by British-Latvians, this small hotel affords a great location for a low price; it's clean, efficiently run, and simple. Large rooms for families are available. ⊠ *Mārstaļu 1/3, LV1050,* ☎ *722–0372,* FAX *724–2239. 47 rooms. MC, V.*

$ 🏬 **Saulīte.** Don't expect much, but the location (between the train station and Old Town) and low cost make it an option. Renovated rooms are a tad overpriced but more comfortable. ⊠ *Merķeļa 12, LV1050,* ☎ *722–4546,* FAX *722–3629. 38 rooms.*

Jūrmala

The Latvian name of this string of four small towns means "seaside" in English, and for a 20-km (12-mi) stretch that is exactly what you get. Mostly Latvians and local Russians enjoy the chilly Baltic sea here. Recent efforts by the Swedes helped clean up the beaches. Frequent electric trains (crowded in summer) make the 40-minute trip.

Gauja nacionälais parks

Only about one hour east of the capital, Gauja National Park, populated by friendly people and a helpful forestry staff, feels light-years away. Latvia's deepest river valley, at 280 ft, is little more than a dip, but the gently flowing Gauja and the 13th-century ruins of **Turaidas Pils** (Turaida Castle), built by the Knights of the Sword, near Sigulda provide amusement, a few local legends, ancient graffiti, a bobsled track, and bungee-jumping tourists. ⊠ *53 km (33 mi) east of Riga; Sigulda visitor center: Raiņa 15,* ☎ *2/971–345.*

LITHUANIA

Lithuania was historically the invader, not the invaded. In 1386, the country formed a union with Poland, and over the following 400 years the joint kingdom stretched from the Baltic to the Black Sea. Though Poland took the leading role until the late 18th century, Lithuanians still remember their time as a European superpower. Russification ensued, followed by a short period of independence (during which Kaunas was the capital, as Vilnius was occupied by Poland). Although hundreds of thousands of Lithuanians were deported by the Soviets in the 1940s and 1950s, today 80% of the population is Lithuanian, with only 10% Russian-speaking. However, the Jewish population—which had thrived here since the 1400s—was almost entirely decimated during the Nazi occupation of World War II.

Lithuania A to Z

Emergencies

Police (☎ 02). **Ambulance** (☎ 03). **Doctor: Baltic-American Clinic** (☎ 2/342–020). **Dentist: Dentamed** (☎ 2/227–582). **Pharmacy: Gedimino Vaistinė** (☎ 2/624–930).

Guided Tours

Astrida (☎ 2/614–459) and **Piligrimas ir Kompanija** (☎ 8/611–800) run two-hour walking tours in Vilnius.

Language

Lithuanian is the official language; however, English, Russian, and to a certain degree Polish are spoken in Vilnius.

Mail

A 20-gram letter to the United States or Europe costs 1.35Lt, a postcard 1Lt. The **main post office** (⊠ Gedimino 7, ☎ 2/616–759) is open weekdays 7–7, Saturday 9–4.

Money Matters

COSTS

A cup of coffee or tea costs 3Lt to 5Lt; a glass of local beer 8Lt; a medium-priced dish at a local restaurant 12Lt to 15Lt. Admission to museums and galleries costs about 4Lt.

CURRENCY

The monetary unit in Lithuania is the litas, which is divided into 100 centas. There are notes of 1, 2, 5, 10, 20, 50, 100, and 200 litas and coins of 1, 2, and 5 litas and 1, 2, 5, 10, 20, and 50 centas. At press time (summer 1999) the rate of exchange was 3.98Lt to the U.S. dollar, 2.71Lt to the Canadian dollar, 6.29Lt to the pound sterling, 2.62Lt to the Australian dollar, 2.12Lt to the New Zealand dollar, and 5.24Lt to the Irish punt. National banks, with branches in all major and most minor cities, change cash and traveler's checks at fair commissions; most also give advances on a Visa card. Credit cards are widely accepted.

TIPPING

At restaurants a service of charge of 7% is sometimes added and an 18% VAT is included in the price of dishes on the menu but may be listed separately on your bill. Tipping is not obligatory; if you've received excellent service, round up or add 10%.

National Holidays

January 1; February 16 (Independence Day); March 11 (Restoration of Lithuania's Independence); April 23 (Easter); May 1 (Labor Day); July 6 (Day of Statehood); November 1 (All Saints' Day); December 25, 26 (Christmas).

Telephoning

COUNTRY CODE

The country code for Lithuania is 370.

INTERNATIONAL CALLS

To reach an **AT&T** long-distance operator dial 8–196.

LOCAL CALLS

Rectangular pay phones accept magnetic strip cards worth 3.54Lt, 7.08Lt, 14.16Lt, or 28.32Lt. Square pay phones accept chip cards worth 7.08Lt. The phone cards are not interchangeable; pictures displaying the proper combination are on most phones. Buy either kind of phone card from any post office or Lietuvos Spauda kiosk. **Telephone information** (☎ 2/704–000 or 2/757–009).

Transportation

BY BUS

Public transport costs 60c at kiosks and 75c from the driver. Buy tickets separately for buses and trolleybuses. Punch your ticket upon boarding or be fined 20Lt. Most public transport operates 5:30 AM to midnight. Domestic bus trips cost between 8Lt and 40Lt. For bus schedules try **Infolinija** (☎ 2/704–000) or the bus station (☎ 2/262–482).

BY CAR

An international or national driver's license bearing a photo is acceptable in Lithuania. Drive on the right. Main roads tend to be in good condition, better than those in Latvia or Estonia; however, secondary roads are commonly unpaved and have potholes. Gas costs 2Lt per liter. Cars may be rented from 250Lt a day; lower rates are available for longer rental terms.

BY PLANE

No direct flights link Lithuania and the United States. Lithuanian Airlines operates from Amsterdam, Berlin, Copenhagen, Frankfurt, Helsinki, London, Paris, Stockholm, and Warsaw.

BY PRIVATE TAXI

Taxis operate 24 hours throughout the city. Taxis can be expensive around hotels and the bus and train stations. It's best to telephone for one. Taxi fares generally start at 1.30Lt and increase by 1Lt to 1.30Lt per km (0.6 mi) in the daytime, more at night or in bad weather. Drivers must display an operating license and a meter. In-town journeys cost up to 10Lt. **Express Taxi** (☎ 2/631–111 or 2/250–000) and **Vilniaus Taxi** (☎ 2/228–888 or 2/229–403) are by and large trustworthy.

BY SERVICE TAXI
Shared taxis accommodate up to 10 people and are cheap and comfortable. They operate on virtually every bus and trolleybus line. Tariffs are 1Lt to 2Lt. Passengers may embark at any regular bus stop and disembark anywhere along the route.

BY TRAIN
Domestic train trips cost between 8Lt and 40Lt. For schedules call the **train station** (☎ 2/630–086). Beware that certain trains running from Vilnius to Poland cross Belarus. Avoid these trains, as you need a Belarusian transit visa to cross a mere 48 km (30 mi) of Belarus along the way. Trains are slower and less comfortable than buses.

Exploring Lithuania

Vilnius

What Vilnius has is *soul*. Good jazz and friendly faces are a way of life here. A few relaxed eateries make their customers regulars. Though the Old Town is somewhat shabby around the edges—it is, after all, the biggest in Central and Eastern Europe—those structures that have been renovated shine, and some that haven't been renovated possess a living pulse as homes for the city's artsy squatters.

Founded by Lithuanian Grand Duke Gediminas in the 14th century, Vilnius was an important center of Lithuanian, Polish, and Jewish culture until World War II. Now this former "Jerusalem of the East" is Lithuania's bustling capital—a national symbol to extradited Poles, a ghost town to the 150,000 Jews who once lived here, and home to 100,000 displaced Russians. It has museums, lush parks, a wealth of Baroque churches, and myriad courtyards, many with cafés.

★ Vilnius's main cathedral, **Arkikatedra Bazilika,** has been a major national symbol for centuries; inside is the dazzling 17th-century Chapel of St. Kazimieras. Originally a temple to Perkūnas, one of Lithuania's many pagan gods, the building became a church during the 13th century, when Lithuania converted from paganism to Christianity; it was the last European country to do so. The cathedral was used for other purposes under Communism; the church reclaimed the cathedral in the 1980s. ✉ *Katedros 1,* ☎ 2/611–127. ☉ *Daily 2–6.*

★ The **Aušros Vartai** (Gates of Dawn) is the only one remaining of Vilnius's nine 16th-century gates. Beyond it to the right, a door leads to the **Chapel of Our Lady of Vilnius** (☉ daily 9–6), a room whose walls are covered with small metal and silver hearts and which contains an icon of the Virgin Mary renowned for its healing powers. Many of the devout climb on their knees up the steps to this holy place, converted into a chapel in 1671 and remade in neoclassical style in 1829. ✉ *Aušros Vartų.*

Wind past the good-natured, beer-drinking youth of Kalnų Parkas and mount Castle Hill, topped by the 13th-century **Gedimino bokštas** (Gedimino Tower), once part of the city's fortifications. Inside the tower is the **Vilniaus pilies muziejus** (Vilnius Castle Museum; ✉ Arsenalo 5, ☎ 2/617–453; ☉ daily 11–6), which has outstanding city views. To the east you can see the **Trijų Kryžių Kalnas** (Hill of Three Crosses), which are said to commemorate seven Franciscan monks killed on the hill by pagans; four of them were thrown into the river below (hence only three crosses).

During the early 1900s Vilnius was Europe's major center of Yiddish education and literature. By the end of World War II, all but 600 of Vilnius's 100,000 Jews had been killed. Today the **Jewish quarter** contains almost no trace of the once-thriving culture. The single remaining **synagogue** (✉ Pylimo 39) survived only because the Nazis used it as a medical-supply warehouse. To learn about Vilnius's Jewish heritage, visit the **Valstybinis ǎydų muziejus** (State Jewish Museum). ✉ *Pylimo 4,* ☎ *2/617–917.* ۞ *Mon.–Thurs. 9–5, Fri. 9–4.*

★ In the New Town, at the **Genocido Aukų Muziejus** (KGB Museum), plaques take you through a litany of horrors in the basement of the former KGB prison. Hundreds of Lithuanians were killed here, with hundreds of thousands deported to Siberia by the Soviet regime during the 1940s and '50s. ✉ *Aukų 4,* ☎ *2/622–449.* ۞ *Tues.–Sun. 10–4.*

The amazing Gothic facade of the 16th-century **Šv Onos Bažnyčia** (St. Anne's Church) was created using 33 different types of brick. It's said that when Napoléon passed through town, he wanted to take the church back to Paris "in the palm of his hand." ✉ *Maironio 8,* ☎ *2/ 611–236.* ۞ *Mon.–Fri. 6:30 PM–8:30 PM, weekends 9–7:30.*

The Baroque 17th-century **Šv Kazimiero bažnyčia** (St. Casimir's Church) is named for the city's patron saint, Prince Casimir Jagiellon. During Russia's reign a cupola replaced the familiar crown. Today it's a popular spot for Sunday-afternoon organ recitals. ✉ *Didžioji 34,* ☎ *2/ 221–715.* ۞ *Mon.–Sat. 4–5:30, Sun. 9–2.*

The **Šv Petro ir Povilo** (Church of Saints Peter and Paul) has an astounding Baroque interior, with nearly 2,000 ornate, white-stucco figures and an extraordinary boat-shape glass chandelier. ✉ *Antakalnio 1,* ☎ *2/ 340–229.* ۞ *Mon.–Sat. 7 PM–8 PM, Sun. 10–8.*

The best collection of Lithuanian fine art is at the **Vilniaus Paveikslų Galerija** (Vilnius Picture Gallery), which displays 16th- to 19th-century paintings, as well as a number of sculptures and some early pottery and folk art. The interior, which was a palace from the 17th through the 19th centuries, has been handsomely restored. ✉ *Didžioji 4,* ☎ *2/224–258.* ۞ *Tues.–Sun. noon–6.*

Vilniaus Universiteto (Vilnius University), founded by the Jesuits in 1570, is a fascinating complex of 12 courtyards. Highlights include the **observatory**, with its 18th-century zodiac engravings, and the Gothic **Sts. Johns' Church** (☎ 2/611–795), begun in 1387. ✉ *Šv Jono 12.*

DINING AND LODGING

$$$ ✕ **Freskos.** The pleasant dining room is filled with antiques and props from the opera and theater. The menu offers such delights as pepper steak or grilled chicken breast salad. There's also a salad bar, a dessert cart, and local beer. ✉ *Didžioji 31,* ☎ *2/618–133. MC, V.*

$$ ✕ **Da Antonio.** This welcome addition to the dining scene is upscale but relaxed. The fare is Italian: great pies, pastas, and meat dishes, and the city's top cappuccino. ✉ *Vilniaus 23,* ☎ *2/620–109. MC, V.*

$$ ✕ **Ritos Sleptuvė.** Lithuanian-American Rita Dapkus, who gave up political life to start cooking, serves authentic Chicago-style pizza, great steaks, the best Tex-Mex in Lithuania, and Vilnius's best breakfast. ✉ *Goštauto 8,* ☎ *2/626–117. AE, MC, V.*

$$ ✕ **Stikliai Aludė Stikliai Taverna.** The dining room here is in a medieval cellar full of museum-quality antiques and has live folk music nightly. The menu offers Lithuanian potato and meat dishes such as *cepeliniai* (potatoes stuffed with meat) and local wines and beers. ✉ *Gaono 7,* ☎ *2/624–501. AE, MC, V.*

$ ✕ **Amatininkų Užeiga.** This cozy restaurant's forte is authentic Lithuanian food, from stews to roasted meats, not found on most Vilnius menus. The decor oozes fin-de-siècle charm, with wicker baskets, wooden furniture, and wrought-iron everything. ⊠ *Didžioji 19/2*, ☎ *2/617–968. MC, V.*

$$$$ 🛏 **Radisson SAS Astorija Hotel Vilnius.** Radisson-quality rooms in this turn-of-the-century building have a touch of the antique thrown in. As the only international chain property in town, this hotel sets the standard for service in Vilnius. ⊠ *Didžioji 35/2, 2001*, ☎ *2/220–110*, 📠 *2/221–762. 61 rooms. Restaurant. AE, DC, MC, V.*

$$$$ 🛏 **Stikliai.** Rooms at this inn dating from the 17th century are lavish and elegant, with a hint of British colonial meets Martha Stewart: comfortable, with lots of flower prints, antique baskets, and knickknacks. Service is impeccable and amenities include a sauna. ⊠ *Gaono 7, 2001*, ☎ *2/627–971*, 📠 *2/223–870. 29 rooms. 2 restaurants. AE, MC, V.*

$$$ 🛏 **Narutis.** On the pedestrian street, this Old Town hotel has spacious, well-appointed rooms. The restored building dates from the 16th century. ⊠ *Pilies 24, 2001*, ☎ *2/222–894*, 📠 *2/622–882. 30 rooms. 2 restaurants, sauna, exercise room. AE, MC, V.*

$$$ 🛏 **Villon.** A free shuttle connects this deluxe hotel/spa/convention center with town, 20 minutes away. The spacious rooms range from wood-paneled with a cozy country feel to pristine-white and warm-gold elegance. Amenities include a satisfying breakfast buffet and Turkish and Finnish saunas. ⊠ *Box 2590, 2015, 19 km (12 mi) north of Vilnius on Riga-Vilnius hwy*, ☎ *2/739–600*, 📠 *2/651–385. 65 rooms. 2 restaurants, pool. AE, DC, MC, V.*

$$ 🛏 **AAA Mano Liza Guest House.** The charming guest house has a Victorian aura and delightfully accommodating service. Rooms provide all the perks of a more upscale hotel, including cable television and high-quality beds. The café below serves refreshingly light Continental fare. ⊠ *Ligonines 5, 2001*, ☎ *2/222–225 or 2/222–545*, 📠 *2/222–608. 8 rooms. Restaurant. AE, DC, MC, V.*

$ 🛏 **JNN Hostel.** This completely renovated hostel across the river from the Old Town has a youthful ambience. The rooms are impeccably clean and each has its own shower and toilet. ⊠ *Ukmergės 25, 2600*, ☎ *2/722–270*, 📠 *2/725–651. 10 rooms. Restaurant, pool. MC, V.*

Neringa

Also known as the Courland Spit, this tiny 100-km- (60-mi-) long fingernail of land 315 km (195 mi) west of Vilnius via ferry from Klaipeda ranks among Europe's most fascinating natural features. Although only half of the spit is Lithuanian—the other half belongs to the Russian exclave of Kaliningrad—there's plenty of space for playing on the beach. Of the two tiny villages, **Nida,** about 50 km (31 mi) down the two-lane road, is the more developed, with bigger dunes and a more popular beach. The sleepy town of **Juodkrante,** 25 km (15 mi) out on the spit, feels less like a resort.

5 BELGIUM

BRUSSELS, ANTWERP, GHENT, BRUGGE

Belgium is a connoisseur's delight. The land of Bruegel and Van Eyck, Rubens and Van Dyck, and Ensor and Magritte is where their best work can still be seen. Belgian culture was and remains that of a bourgeois, mercantile society. Feudal lords may have built Belgium's many castles, and prelates its splendid churches, but merchants and craftsmen are responsible for the guild houses and sculpture-adorned town halls of Brussels, Antwerp, Ghent, and Brugge.

This small country offers surprising variety, from the beaches and dunes of the North Sea coast and the tree-lined canals and big sky of the "platte (flat) land" to the rolling Bruegel country around Brussels and the sheer cliffs and dense woods of the Ardennes. The state of Belgium is one of Europe's youngest, but its territory has been fought over for centuries by invaders from all sides. Julius Caesar called the Belgae the bravest of the tribes that defied the Roman legions. His conquerors were followed by Huns and Vikings, the Spanish, and the French. The Battle of the Golden Spurs, in 1302, when mounted French knights were defeated by Flemish foot soldiers, is still commemorated in Flanders as the date when Flemish identity came into its own. The greatest battleground, though, was Waterloo, just south of Brussels, where Napoléon was defeated by the British and Prussians in 1815.

With independence in 1830, Belgium began forging a national identity. The Belgians are inveterate individualists—witness the endless variations of Art Nouveau in the Belle Epoque town houses that line many a prosperous street. The art of living well has been cultivated since the days of the great Burgundian wedding feasts, when members of the ruling dynasty were joined with other royal houses. The country continues to claim an amazing number of eating places dedicated to haute cuisine. Whole families often celebrate a first communion, an engagement, or a birthday in an expensive restaurant. That generosity of spirit is also manifested in the comfortable proportions of private homes and in the spacious public squares and avenues.

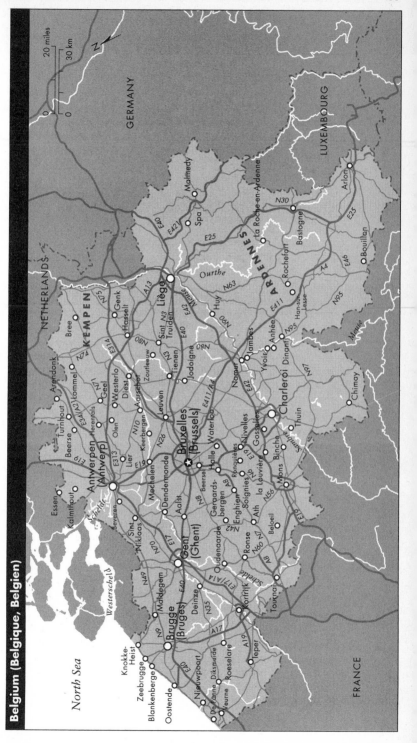

Belgium packs just over 5 million Dutch-speaking Flemings and almost as many French-speaking Walloons into a country the size of Vermont or Wales. The presence of two language cultures enriches its intellectual life but also creates constant political tension. The creation in the '90s of three largely self-governing regions—Flanders, Wallonia, and the City of Brussels, which is bilingual and multicultural—has only emphasized the divisions between the cultures.

Belgium's neutrality was violated during both world wars, when much of its architectural heritage was destroyed and great suffering was inflicted by the occupying forces. This may be why Belgium staunchly supports the European Union (EU), which has guaranteed peace in Western Europe for the past 50 years. As the home of most of the EU institutions, Brussels has to some become a synonym for a faceless bureaucracy, but this is unfair to both the city and the so-called Eurocrats. For the Belgian government, maintaining the trust of the people without pandering to extremist linguistic/political divisions looks to be a tall order.

BELGIUM A TO Z

Customs
For details on imports and duty-free limits for visitors from outside the EU, *see* Customs & Duties *in* Chapter 1.

Dining
Most Belgians take eating seriously and are discerning about fresh produce and innovative recipes. At the top end of the scale, *menus de dégustation* (tasting menus) offer a chance to sample a large selection of the chef's finest dishes. Many brasseries and neighborhood restaurants have risen to the challenge of making eating out affordable, and animated ambience amply compensates for a more limited cuisine.

Belgian specialties include *lapin à la bière* (rabbit in beer), *faisan à la brabançonne* (pheasant with braised endives), *waterzooi* (a rich fish or chicken hotpot), and *moules marinières* with *frites* (marinated mussels, served with french fries). Other local specialties are endives; marvelous asparagus from Mechelen, at its best in May; and tiny, sweet shrimp fresh from the North Sea. For lunch, cold cuts, a *croque-monsieur* (toasted ham-and-cheese sandwich), and *jambon d'Ardennes* (Ardennes ham) are popular, as is creamy *fromage blanc* (similar to cottage cheese) with radishes and spring onions on rye.

Fixed-price menus are widely available and often represent considerable savings. Menus and prices should always be posted outside a restaurant, although it's a good idea to check availability before you sit down in restaurants in tourist areas.

MEALTIMES
Most hotels serve breakfast until 10 AM. Belgians usually eat lunch between 1 and 3 PM. The main meal of the day is dinner, which most Belgians eat between 7 and 10 PM; peak dining time used to be about 8 but is now creeping closer to 9:30. Dining well after 11 PM is something of a challenge.

RATINGS
Prices are per person, à la carte, and include a first course, main course, dessert, 16% service, and a whopping 21% value-added tax, but no wine. Look for fixed-price menus; if you sacrifice choice, you can eat well for less than BF700 in many good restaurants. Restaurant prices are roughly the same in Brussels and other cities.

CATEGORY	COST
$$$$	over BF3,500
$$$	BF2,500–BF3,500
$$	BF1,500–BF2,500
$	under BF1,500

WHAT TO WEAR

Jacket and tie are required only in the most expensive establishments. Younger Belgians favor casual dress in most restaurants.

Language

Language is a sensitive subject and is beginning to exert an unhealthy influence on politics at the national and regional level. There are three national languages in Belgium: French, spoken primarily in the south of the country (Wallonia); Dutch, spoken in the north (Flanders); and German, spoken in a small area in the east. Brussels is bilingual, with both French and Dutch officially recognized, though the majority of residents are francophones. Many people speak English in Brussels and in Flanders; in Wallonia, English-speakers tend to be thin on the ground. Belgian French and Dutch both contain slight local differences in vocabulary and pronunciation from the corresponding languages spoken in the neighboring countries to the south and north.

Lodging

As the capital of Europe, Brussels attracts high-powered visitors, and many luxury hotels have been built to accommodate them. Over weekends and during July and August, business travelers are few and far between, so prices come down to BF5,000 or less. New hotels catering to cost-conscious travelers have also been built, where doubles cost less than BF3,000.

BED-AND-BREAKFAST

This has recently become an attractive option, thanks to self-regulation and higher standards. Contact local tourist offices (☞ Visitor Information *in* Contacts and Resources *in each region, below*).

CAMPING

Belgium is well supplied with camping and caravan (trailer) sites. For details contact the **Royal Camping and Caravaning Club of Belgium** (✉ Av. Villa 5, 1060 Brussels, ☎ 02/537–3681).

HOTELS

You can trust Belgian hotels, almost without exception, to be clean and of a high standard. The more ritzy hotels in city centers tend to be like luxury hotels around the globe. Smaller, family-owned hotels are much more personal. Brugge is especially well endowed with romantic hideaways. **BTR** (Belgian Tourist Reservations; ✉ Bd. Anspach 111, 1000 Brussels, ☎ 02/513–7484, FAX 02/513–9277) handles reservations free.

RATINGS

Hotel prices, including a 16% service charge and 6% sales tax, are usually posted in each room. All prices are for two people in a standard double room, excluding service charges and 14.9% room tax. The tax is slightly lower at suburban hotels.

CATEGORY	BRUSSELS	OTHER CITIES
$$$$	Over BF9,000	Over BF7,500
$$$	BF6,500–BF9,000	BF5,500–BF7,500
$$	BF3,500–BF6,500	BF2,500–BF5,500
$	under BF3,500	under BF2,500

For information about youth hostels in Brussels and Wallonia, contact **Les Auberges de la Jeunesse** (✉ Rue de la Sablonnière 28, 1000 Brussels, ☎ 02/219–5676). For Flanders, contact **Vlaamse Jeugdherbergcentrale** (✉ Van Stralenstraat 40, 2060 Antwerp, ☎ 03/232–7218). The youth organization **Acotra World** (✉ Rue de la Madeleine 51, ☎ 02/512–8607) makes travel arrangements for young people.

Mail

POSTAL RATES

First-class (airmail) letters and postcards to the United States cost BF34, second-class (surface) BF20. Airmail letters and postcards to the United Kingdom cost BF17. All international first-class mail must be marked with a blue A-PRIOR sticker (available in post offices).

Money Matters

COSTS

Costs in Brussels are on a par with those in London and New York. All taxes and service charges are included in hotel and restaurant bills. Restaurant prices are inflated by value-added tax. Gasoline prices are high, but the highways are toll-free.

CURRENCY

The unit of currency in Belgium is the franc (BF). There are bills of 100, 200, 500, 1,000, 2,000, and 10,000 francs, and coins of 1, 5, 20, and 50 francs. At press time (summer 1999), the exchange rate was BF38.90 to the U.S. dollar, BF26.48 to the Canadian dollar, BF61.55 to the pound sterling, BF25.59 to the Australian dollar, BF20.73 to the New Zealand dollar, and BF40.3399 to the euro.

SAMPLE PRICES

A cup of coffee in a café will cost BF50–BF70; a glass of draft beer, BF50–BF85; and a glass of wine, about BF80–BF120. A single bus/metro/tram ride costs BF50, and theater tickets cost about BF500.

National Holidays

January 1; April 24 (Easter Monday); May 1 (May Day); June 1 (Ascension); June 12 (Pentecost Monday); July 21 (National Day); August 15 (Assumption); November 1 (All Saints' Day); November 11 (Armistice Day); December 25.

Opening and Closing Times

Banks are usually open weekdays 9–4; some close for an hour at lunch. Exchange facilities (Bureaux de Change) are usually open on weekends, but you'll get a better rate in banks during the week. **Museums** are generally open 10–5 Tuesday through Sunday. **Shops** are open weekdays and Saturday 10–6 and generally stay open later on Friday. Bakeries are open Sunday and closed Monday.

Shopping

VALUE-ADDED TAX REFUNDS

See Taxes *in* Chapter 1, *above*; there are variations simpler than that described in Chapter 1, but they require trust. One often suggested by diamond jewelers in Antwerp is that you pay the full amount by credit card. After you have had the invoice stamped by customs at your last port of call in the EU, you mail it back to the store before boarding your plane, and the VAT amount will be credited to your card account.

Telephoning

COUNTRY CODE

The country code for Belgium is 32. When dialing Belgium from outside the country, drop the first zero in the regional telephone code.

INTERNATIONAL CALLS

Buy a high-denomination telecard (☞ Local Calls, *below*) and make a direct call from a phone booth. For credit card and collect calls, dial **AT&T** (☎ 0800–10010), **MCI Worldphone** (☎ 0800–10012), or **Sprint** (☎ 0800–10014).

LOCAL CALLS

Pay phones work mostly with telecards, available at post offices and at many newsstands. An average local call costs BF20. Coin-operated phones (on the platforms of metro stations) take 5- and 20-franc coins.

Tipping

A service charge is always included in restaurant and hotel bills. The tip is also included in taxi fares. Railway porters expect a minimum of BF60 per suitcase. For bellhops and doormen, BF100 is adequate. Give movie ushers BF10, whether or not they show you to your seat. Tip washroom attendants in public places BF10. And tip doormen at bars, nightclubs, or discos around BF40 if you're planning to go back.

Transportation

BY BICYCLE

You can rent a bicycle from Belgian Railways at 48 stations throughout the country; train travelers get reduced rates. These bikes are serviceable, but not the state-of-the-art mountain bikes you can rent in specialized outlets. Bicycling is especially easy in the flat northern and coastal areas; in the hilly south and east it's much more strenuous. There are bicycle lanes in many Flemish cities, where car use is being discouraged, but cycling in Brussels takes a lot of guts.

BY BUS

Intercity bus services are rudimentary; bus routes often operate as an adjunct to the train. Getting between Flanders and Wallonia by bus is nigh-on impossible. Check at the tourist office or train station.

BY CAR

Parking. On-street parking often requires you to display a ticket dispensed from not-always-obvious machines generally located in the middle of the block. Old-fashioned meters taking 5- or 20-franc coins still line some streets. Parking garages provide an expensive option. On no account park in front of a garage or a building bearing a towing sign: Being towed is expensive and time-consuming.

Road Conditions. Belgium has an excellent system of toll-free expressways, most of them illuminated at night, and the main roads are generally very good. Road numbers for main roads have the prefix *N*; expressways, the prefix *A* or *E*. Watch for potholes in city streets.

Road Signs. Road signs are written in the language of the region, so you need to know that Antwerp is Antwerpen in Dutch and Anvers in French; likewise, Brugge is Bruges in French and Brussels is Bruxelles in French and Brussel in Dutch; Ghent is Gent (Flemish) and Gand (French). Even more confusing, Liège and Luik are the same place, as are Louvain and Leuven, and Namur and Namen. Yet more difficult is Mons (French) and Bergen (Dutch), or Tournai (French) and Doornik (Dutch). On the Brussels-Liège/Luik motorway, signs change language with alarming frequency as you crisscross the Wallonia-Flanders border. Finally, Uitrit is Dutch for exit.

Rules of the Road. Drive on the right and pass on the left; passing on the right is forbidden. Seat belts are compulsory in both front and rear seats. Every car must have a triangle-shaped warning sign to be used in the event of a breakdown or accident. At intersections, traffic on the right has right-of-way. Adhere strictly to this rule, as there are few stop or yield signs. Never, ever assume that someone with priority will stop if you don't. Pedestrians have priority on marked crossings, and vehicles in traffic circles have priority over those entering them—even if they're coming from the right. Buses have priority over cars, and trams have abslolute priority; they will ring bells or sound horns if you're obstructing them, and they will hit you if they can't stop. Maximum speed limits are 120 kph (75 mph) on highways, 90 kph (55 mph) on major roads, and 50 kph (30 mph) in cities.

BY PLANE
There are no domestic air services.

BY TRAIN
Fast and frequent trains connect all main towns and cities. A **Benelux Tourrail Ticket** allows unlimited travel throughout Belgium, Luxembourg, and the Netherlands for any five days during a one-month period. The **Belgian Tourrail Ticket** allows unlimited travel for five days in a one-month period. People from 12 to 26 can purchase a **Go Pass,** valid for 10 one-way trips in a six-month period. Special weekend round-trip tickets are valid from Friday morning to Monday night: A 40% reduction is available on the first traveler's ticket and a 60% reduction on companions' tickets. Sample full-price round-trip fares (second class) from Brussels are: to Antwerp, BF380; to Brugge, BF740; and to Ghent, BF470.

Visitor Information

Each region has its own tourist office. The **national Flemish office** (☎ 02/504–0355) and the **national French-speaking office** (☎ 02/504–0205) are at the same address in Brussels and share a ground-floor **Tourist Information Office** (✉ Rue Marché-aux-Herbes 63, ☎ 02/504–0390).

Weather

The tourist season runs from early May to late September and peaks in July and August, when the weather is warmest. May and September offer the advantage of generally clear skies and smaller crowds.

CLIMATE
Temperatures range from around 65°F in May to an average of 73°F in July and August. In winter they drop to an average of about 40°F to 45°F. Snow is unusual except in the mountains of the Ardennes, where cross-country and alpine skiing are popular. On the coast and in the Ardennes, frozen fogs can reduce visibility to 5 yards and render road surfaces glassy.

The following are the average daily maximum and minimum temperatures for Brussels.

Jan.	40F	4C	May	65F	18C	Sept.	69F	21C
	30	– 1		46	8		51	11
Feb.	44F	7C	June	72F	22C	Oct.	60F	15C
	32	0		52	11		45	7
Mar.	51F	11C	July	73F	23C	Nov.	48F	9C
	36	25		4	12		38	3
Apr.	58F	14C	Aug.	72F	22C	Dec.	42F	6C
	41	5		54	12		32	0

BRUSSELS

Brussels is rising to its status as a focal point of national tensions and international politics. Known as the capital of Europe, Brussels has become synonymous with the European Union and the project to unite the continent, but while diplomats, politicians, lobbyists, businesses, and journalists have flocked to the city, it's far from becoming gray, faceless, or functional. Brussels's strength is its diversity; a bilingual city where French- and Dutch-speaking cultures are too often divided, it's home to all the cultures of Europe, east and west, as well as Americans, Congolese, Rwandans, Vietnamese, Turks, and Moroccans. In the new millennium, Brussels is preparing to embrace its eclecticism and recapture the cosmopolitan charm it had at the turn of the 20th century. In Brussels, Art Nouveau flourished as nowhere else, and its spirit lives on in gloriously individualistic town houses. Away from the winding alleys of the city center, parks and squares are plentiful, and the wooded Bois de la Cambre, at the end of Avenue Louise, leads straight into a forest as large as the city itself.

Exploring Brussels

You need to give yourself at least two days to explore the many riches of Brussels, devoting one day to the Old Town (whose cobblestones call for comfortable walking shoes), and the other to the great museums and uptown shopping streets.

Around the Grand'Place

Numbers in the margin correspond to points of interest on the Brussels map.

⑨ Cathédrale St-Michel et Ste-Gudule. The names of the archangel and an obscure 7th-century local saint have been joined for the cathedral of Brussels. Begun in 1226, it combines architectural styles from the Romanesque to full-blown Gothic. The chief treasures are the stained-glass windows designed by Bernard van Orley, an early 16th-century court painter. The ornately carved pulpit (1699) depicts Adam and Eve being expelled from the Garden of Eden. In the crypt are remnants of the original 11th-century Romanesque church. The interior restoration of the nave is complete, and the choir is due to be renovated by summer 2000. ⊠ *Parvis Ste-Gudule,* ☎ *02/217–8345.* ⊙ *Nov.–Mar., daily 7–6; Apr.–Oct., Mon.–Sat. 7–7, Sun. 2–7.*

★ ⑦ Centre Belge de la Bande Dessinée (Belgian Comic Strip Center). This unique museum celebrates the comic strip, focusing on such famous Belgian graphic artists as Hergé, Tintin's creator; Morris, the progenitor of Lucky Luke; and many others. There's a lending library, a bookshop, and a splendidly airy brasserie. The display is housed in an imposing Art Nouveau department store from 1903, designed down to the smallest detail by that movement's leading figure, Victor Horta (1861–1947). ⊠ *Rue des Sables 20,* ☎ *02/219–1980.* ⊙ *Tues.–Sun. 10–6.*

⑤ Galeries St-Hubert. The oldest covered shopping arcade in western Europe—and still one of its most elegant—was constructed in 1847 and is filled with shops, restaurants, and theaters. Diffused daylight penetrates the gallery from the glassed arches high above, flags of many nations billow ever so slightly, and neoclassical gods and heroes look down on the crowded scene from their sculpted niches. Midway through, the gallery is traversed by **Rue des Bouchers,** which forms the main restaurant area in the tourist maelstrom. Caveat: The more lavish the display of food outside, the poorer the cuisine inside. ⊠ *Between Rue du Marché-aux-Herbes and Rue d'Arenberg.*

★ ① Grand'Place. The ornate Baroque guild houses here, with their burnished facades, were completed in 1695, just three years after a French bombardment destroyed everything but the Town Hall. The houses are topped by gilded statues of saints and heroes, so vividly rendered that they seem to call out to each other. Thus the end result of Louis XIV's folly is Europe's most sumptuous market square. There is a daily

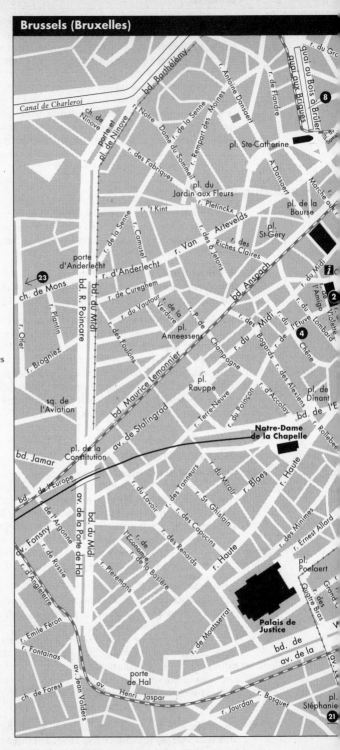

Brussels (Bruxelles)

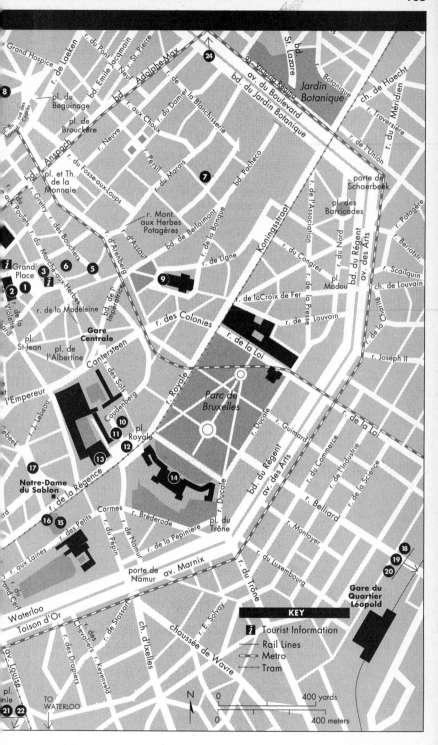

r. de Laeken
Grand Hospice
r. du Pont Neuf
r. St-Pierre
bd. Emile Jacqmain
Adolphe-Max
r. de la Blanchisserie
r. du Damier
av. Victoria Regina
av. du Boulevard
bd. du Jardin Botanique
bd. St-Lazare
Botanique
Jardin Botanique
ch. de Haecht
r. Traversière
r. du Méridien

pl. du Béguinage
bd.
Anspach
r. aux Choux
r. Neuve
r. du Fosse-aux-Loups
r. Persil
r. du Marais
bd. Pacheco
r. de l'Union
porte de Schaerbeek
r. de l'Association
pl. des Barricades
r. Potagère
r. Berlotstr.

pl. de Brouckère
pl. et Th. de la Monnaie
r. Grétry
r. des Bouchers
r. Mont. aux Herbes Potagères
r. d'Arenberg
r. d'Assaut
bd. de Berlaimont
r. de la Banque
r. de Ligne
Koningsstraat
r. du Congres
r. de la Presse
r. du Nord
bd. du Régent
av. des Arts
r. Scailquin
ch. de Louvain

Grand' Place
r. du Marché-aux-Herbes
r. de la Madeleine
bd. de l'Impératrice
r. des Colonies
de la Croix de Fer
r. de Louvain
r. de la Charité
pl. Madou

Gare Centrale
Cantersteen
r. des Sols
Coudenberg
r. Royale
Parc de Bruxelles
r. de la Loi
r. Ducale
r. Guimard
r. Joseph II

pl. St-Jean
pl. de l'Albertine
l'Empereur
r. Lebeau
pl. Royale
r. de la Régence
bd. du Régent
av. des Arts
r. du Commerce
r. de l'Industrie
r. de la Science
r. Belliard

Notre-Dame du Sablon
Carmes
r. Bréderode
pl. du Trône
r. Montoyer

r. des Petits
r. du Pépin
r. de Namur
r. de la Pepinière
Gare du Quartier Léopold

r. aux Laines
porte de Namur
av. Marnix
r. du Trône
r. du Luxembourg

Waterloo
Toison d'Or
r. de Stassart
r. des Chevaliers
r. Keyenveld
ch. d'Ixelles
chaussée de Wavre
r. E. Solvay

TO WATERLOO
av. Louise
pl. nie

KEY
i Tourist Information
— Rail Lines
═ Metro
━ Tram

N
0   400 yards
0   400 meters

flower market from spring to fall. On summer nights, music and colored light flood the entire square. Shops, restaurants, and taverns occupy most ground floors. The Maison des Brasseurs houses the **Brewery Museum** (⊠ Grand'Place 10, ☎ 02/511–4987). The Grand'Place comes enchantingly alive during local festivals like the *Ommegang,* a magnificent historical pageant re-creating Emperor Charles V's reception in the city (first Tues. and Thurs. in July), and the European Christmas Market, with stalls representing many different nations and a life-size crèche with real animals. ⊠ *Rue au Beurre, Rue du Chair et du Pain, Rue des Harengs, Rue de la Colline, Rue de l'Etuve, Rue de la Tête d'Or.*

② **Hôtel de Ville** (Town Hall). Dominating the Grand'Place, the Town Hall is around 300 years older than the guild houses that line the square. Over the gateway are statues of the prophets and effigies of long-gone dukes and duchesses. The slender central tower, combining boldness and light, is topped by a statue of St. Michael crushing a figure of the devil under his feet. The halls are embellished with some of the finest examples of Brussels and Mechelen tapestries. ⊠ *Grand'Place,* ☎ 02/279–4365. ⊙ *English-speaking tours Tues. 11:30 and 3:15, Wed. 3:15, Sun. 12:15. No individual visits.*

③ **Maison du Roi** (King's House). Despite the name, no king ever lived in this 16th-century palace facing the Town Hall. It contains the **Musée de la Ville de Bruxelles** (City Museum), whose collections include Gothic sculptures, porcelain, silverware, and paintings such as Bruegel's *Marriage Procession.* On the top floor is an extravagant wardrobe of costumes for Manneken Pis (☞ *below*), starting with one donated by the self-same Louis XIV who destroyed the original Grand'Place. ⊠ *Grand'Place,* ☎ 02/279–4355. ⊙ *Mon.–Thurs. 10–12:30 and 1:30– 5 (Oct.–Mar. until 4), weekends 10–1.*

④ **Manneken Pis.** Originally, this was one of many public fountains. The first mention of him dates from 1377, but the present version, a small bronze statue of a chubby little boy peeing, was made by Jerome Duquesnoy in 1619. The statue is in fact a copy; the original was kidnapped by 18th-century French soldiers. ⊠ *Corner Rue de l'Etuve and Rue du Chêne, 3 blocks southwest of Grand'Place.*

Rue Antoine Dansaert. This is the flagship street of Brussels's fashionable quarter, which extends south to the Place Saint-Géry. Boutiques sell Belgian-designed men's and women's fashions along with other high-fashion names. Inexpensive restaurants, trendy bars, and cozy cafés rub shoulders with avant-garde galleries and stylish furniture shops. ⊠ *Between Rue Van Artevelde at Grand'Place and Porte de Flandre.*

☝ ⑥ **Théâtre de Marionettes Toone** (Toone Marionette Theater). Brussels folklore lives on in this tiny, family-run puppet theater, with a cozy adjoining pub and a small museum. The puppeteers irreverently tackle anything from *Hamlet* to the *Three Musketeers* in the broadest of Brussels dialect. There are occasional performances in French, Dutch, and even English. ⊠ *Impasse Schuddeveld off Petite Rue des Bouchers,* ☎ 02/ 511–7137 or 02/513–7486. ☜ *performances, BF400; museum free with ticket for show.* ⊙ *Daily; performances, 8:30 PM.*

⑧ **Vismet** (Fish Market). The canals around which this lively quay district sprang up have been filled in, but the many seafood restaurants remain, making it a pleasantly animated area, highly popular with the *Bruxellois* (residents of Brussels) despite the often unjustified high prices. When the weather is good, the restaurants all set up tables and chairs on the wide promenade, where cargoes of fish were once unloaded. ⊠ *Quai au Bois-à-Brûler and Quai aux Briques.*

Around the Place Royale

★ **⑰** **Grand Sablon.** A well-to-do, sophisticated square, it's alive with cafés, restaurants, art galleries, and antiques shops. At the upper end of the square stands the church of **Notre Dame du Sablon,** built in flamboyant Gothic style in 1304 by the crossbowmen who used to train here. The stained-glass windows are illuminated from within at night, creating an extraordinary effect of kindly warmth. Weekend mornings, a lively antiques market takes place below the church. Downhill from the Grand Sablon stands the 12th-century **Eglise Notre-Dame de la Chapelle** (⊠ Pl. de la Chapelle). Its Gothic exterior and surprising Baroque belfry have been splendidly restored. This was the parish church of Pieter Bruegel the Elder (1520–69), and he is buried here in an imposing marble tomb amid much statuary. ⊠ *Jct. Rue des Minimes, Rue des Pigeons, Rue Stevens, Rue de Rollebeek, Rue Libeau, Rue de la Paille, Rue Sainte-Anne, Rue Rodenbroek, Rue des Sablons.*

⑬ **Musée d'Art Ancien** (Fine Arts Museum). The collection of old masters focuses on Flemish and Dutch paintings from the 15th to the 19th centuries. In the Bruegel Room is one of the world's finest collections of his works, including the *Fall of Icarus*; the Rubens Room holds paintings by that master. The museum displays works by Hieronymus Bosch, Memling, Rubens, Van Dyck, and many others. An underground passage links it with the adjacent Museum of Modern Art. ⊠ *Rue de la Régence 3,* ☎ *02/508–3211.* ☉ *Tues.–Sun. 10–5.*

★ **⑪** **Musée d'Art Moderne** (Modern Art Museum). Housed in an exciting feat of modern architecture, it descends eight floors into the ground around a central light well. The museum's strength lies in the quality of Belgian modern art: not only Magritte's luminous fantasies, Delvaux's nudes in surrealist settings, and James Ensor's hallucinatory carnival scenes, but also the works of artists such as Léon Spilliaert, Constant Permeke, Leo Brusselmans, and Rik Wouters from the first half of the century; the post-war COBRA group, including Pierre Alechinsky and Henri Michaux; and on to contemporary works. ⊠ *Pl. Royale 1,* ☎ *02/508–3211.* ☉ *Tues.–Sun. 10–1 and 2–5.*

⑯ **Musée Instrumental** (Musical Instruments Museum). Six thousand instruments, from the Bronze Age to today, make up this extraordinary collection. The saxophone family is well represented, as befits the country of its inventor, Adolphe Sax (1814–94). The museum is scheduled to move by spring 2000 to the Art Nouveau ☞ Old England building, a few blocks away. ⊠ *Pl. du Petit Sablon 17,* ☎ *02/511–3595.* 🎟 *Free.* ☉ *Tues., Thurs., Sat. 2:30–4:30, Wed. 4–6, Sun 10:30–12:30.*

★ **⑩** **Old England.** This glass-and-steel Art Nouveau masterpiece, designed by Paul Saintenoy (1862–1952) for the British-owned department store Old England in 1899, has a fanciful corner turret. ⊠ *Rue Montagne-de-la-Cour 94.*

⑭ **Palais Royal** (Royal Palace). The palace facing the Royal Park was rebuilt in 1904 to suit the expansive tastes of Leopold II (1835–1909). The king's architect, Alphonse Balat, achieved his masterpiece with the monumental stairway and the Throne Hall. The Belgian Royal Family uses this address only on state occasions. ⊠ *Pl. des Palais,* ☎ *02/ 551–2020.* 🎟 *Free.* ☉ *July 22–early Sept., Tues.–Sun. 10–4.*

⑮ **Petit Sablon.** Statues of the counts Egmont and Hoorn, who were executed by the Spanish in 1568, hold pride of place here. The square is surrounded by a magnificent wrought-iron fence, topped by 48 small statues representing Brussels's medieval guilds. Each craftsman carries an object that reveals his trade: The furniture-maker holds a chair; the wine merchant, a goblet. ⊠ *Rue de la Régence.*

⑫ **Place Royale.** This white, symmetrical square is neoclassical Vienna transposed to Brussels. From here you have a superb view over the lower town. The Coudenberg Palace once stood here. Underneath the square, excavations have revealed the *Aula Magna* (Great Hall), where the Flanders-born King of Spain and Holy Roman Emperor Charles V (1500–58) was crowned and where he also announced his abdication two years before his death. The name of the palace lives on in the 18th-century church, St-Jacques-sur-Coudenberg. In the center of the square stands the equestrian statue of Godefroy de Bouillon (1060–1100), leader of the First Crusade and ruler of Jerusalem. ⊠ *Jct. Rue de la Régence, Rue Royale, Rue de Namur, and Rue Mont de la Cour.*

Elsewhere in Brussels

⑱ **Autoworld.** This mecca for vintage car aficionados comprises a collection of more than 450 vehicles. The surprise star of the show is the Belgian-made Minerva, a luxury car from the early '30s. ⊠ *Parc du Cinquantenaire 11,* ☎ *02/736–4165.* ⊙ *Daily 10–6.*

⑲ **European Union Institutions.** The various offices of the European Commission are centered on Rond Point Schuman (Metro: Schuman). The rounded glass summit of the **European Parliament** building (⊠ Rue Wiertz 43) looms behind the Gare de Luxembourg. ⊠ *Rond Point Schuman, Rue de la Loi, RueArchimède, Bd. Charlemagne, Rue Wiertz.*

㉑ **Hôtel Hannon** (Hannon Mansion). The flowering of Art Nouveau produced this handsome, original town house by Jules Brunfaut (1903), now a gallery devoted to contemporary photography. In the interior note the staircase with its romantic fresco, as well as the stained glass. ⊠ *Av. de la Jonction 1,* ☎ *02/538–4220.* ⊙ *Tues.–Sun. 1–6. Closed July 15–Aug. 15. Near Musée Horta; trams 91 and 92 from Place Louise.*

★ ㉓ **Maison d'Erasme** (Erasmus House). In the middle of a nondescript neighborhood, this remarkable redbrick 15th-century house was home to the great humanist Erasmus in 1521. Every detail is authentic, with period furniture, paintings by Holbein and Hieronymus Bosch, prints by Albrecht Dürer, and first editions of Erasmus's works, including *In Praise of Folly.* ⊠ *Rue du Chapître 31,* ☎ *02/521–1383.* ⊙ *Wed.–Thurs. and Sat.–Mon., 10–noon and 2–5. Metro: St-Guidon.*

㉔ **Mini-Europe.** This popular attraction in a 5-acre park is a collection of 300 models (on a 1:25 scale) of buildings from the 15 European Union countries. ⊠ *Bd. du Centenaire 20,* ☎ *02/478–0550.* ▦ *BF395.* ⊙ *Sept.–June, daily 9:30–5; July–Aug., daily 9:30–8. Metro: Heysel.*

Musée des Enfants (Children's Museum). Few kids don't fall in love with this educational center for 2- to 12-year-olds. They get to plunge their arms into sticky goo, dress up in eccentric costumes, walk through a hall of mirrors, crawl through tunnels, and take photographs with an oversize camera. ⊠ *Rue du Bourgmestre 15,* ☎ *02/640–0107.* ⊙ *Sept.–July, Wed. and weekends 2:30–5. Trams 93 and 94.*

★ ㉒ **Musée Horta** (Horta Museum). Victor Horta, the Belgian master of Art Nouveau, designed this building for himself and lived and worked here until 1919. From cellar to attic—the staircase is a great work of art—every detail of the house displays the exuberant curves of the Art Nouveau style. Horta's aim was to put nature and light back into daily life, and here his floral motifs give a sense of opulence and spaciousness where in fact space is very limited. ⊠ *Rue Américaine 25,* ☎ *02/537–1692.* ⊙ *Tues.–Sat. 2–5:30. Tram 91 or 92 from Pl. Louise.*

⑳ **Musée Royal de l'Afrique Centrale** (Africa Museum). King Leopold II (1835–1909) didn't do things by halves. He was sole owner of the Congo, later Zaire, and now the Republic of Congo—a colonial adventure that brought great wealth to the exploiters and untold misery to the exploited. He built a museum outside Brussels to house some 250,000 objects emanating from his domain. The museum has since become a leading research center for African studies, with 13 specialized libraries. ⊠ *Leuvensesteenweg 13, Tervuren,* ☏ *02/769–5401.* ⊙ *Mid-Mar.–mid-Oct., Tues.–Sun. 9–5:30; mid-Oct.–mid-Mar., Tues.–Sun. 10–4:30. Tram 44 from Square Montgomery.*

Dining and Lodging

You can eat as well in Brussels as anywhere else in the world. Brussels's 3,000-odd restaurants are supplemented by a multitude of fast-food establishments and snack bars, and most cafés also offer *petite restauration* (light meals)—omelets, pastas, and the like. Check out fixed-price menus, especially in top-dollar restaurants. They sometimes cost only half of what you would pay dining à la carte, and the quality of your meal is likely to be just as good. There's much less smoking than in the past, but dedicated no-smoking areas are rare. For price categories, *see* Dining *in* Belgium A to Z, *above.*

The main hotel districts are around the Grand'Place and in the Avenue Louise shopping area. If you have a problem finding accommodations, go to the TIB tourist office in the Hôtel de Ville at the Grand'-Place. Weekend and summer discounts, often of 50% or more, are available in almost all hotels; be sure to check when you book. Most new hotels have set aside rooms or floors for nonsmokers and offer a limited number of rooms equipped for people with disabilities. For price categories, *see* Lodging *in* Belgium A to Z, *above.*

$$$$ ★ ✕ **Comme Chez Soi.** Pierre Wynants runs Brussels's most celebrated restaurant, where the kitchen is larger than the Art Nouveau dining room. One all-time favorite, fillet of sole with a white wine mousseline and shrimp, is always on the menu, but the chef likes to chop and change, constantly creating new culinary masterpieces. Go in a party of four; tables for two are too close for comfort, and the intimate surrounds can be tough if you can't stand smoke. Reserve well ahead; you may have to wait six weeks for a table. ⊠ *Pl. Rouppe 23,* ☏ *02/512–2921. Reservations essential. Jacket and tie. AE, DC, MC, V. Closed Sun., Mon., July, Dec. 25–Jan. 1.*

$$$$ ★ ✕ **La Truffe Noire.** Luigi Ciciriello's "Black Truffle" is a spacious eatery with a cuisine that draws on classic Italian and modern French cooking. Carpaccio, prepared at the table, comes with long strips of truffle and Parmesan, while entrées include Vendé pigeon with truffles and steamed John Dory with truffles and leeks. ⊠ *Bd. de la Cambre 12,* ☏ *02/640–4422. Reservations essential. Jacket and tie. AE, DC, MC, V. Closed Sun., Easter wk, 2nd ½ of Aug., Christmas wk. No lunch Sat.*

$$$$ ★ ✕ **Sea Grill.** Gigantic etched-glass murals convey the cool of the Arctic fjords that provide inspiration and ingredients for Belgium's best seafood restaurant. Chef Yves Mattagne's gift for applying meat preparations to fish is showcased in dishes like noisettes of tuna Rossini, while house classics include whole sea bass baked in salt and Brittany lobster pressed at your table. ⊠ *Radisson SAS Hotel, Rue du Fossé-aux-Loups 47,* ☏ *02/227–3120. Jacket and tie. AE, DC, MC, V. Closed Sun., 1st wk of April, and 4 wks in July/Aug. No lunch Sat.*

$$$ ★ ✕ **Ogenblik.** With green-shade lamps over marble-top tables, sawdust on the floor, ample servings, and a great ambience, Ogenblik is a true bistro. The long and imaginative menu changes frequently but generally includes such specialties as millefeuille with lobster and salmon and saddle of lamb with fresh, young vegetables. ⊠ *Galerie des Princes 1,* ☏ *02/511–6151. AE, DC, MC, V. Closed Sun.*

$$ ✕ **Au Stekerlapatte.** In the shadow of the monstrous Palais de Justice, this bustling Marolles bistro is packed nightly with diners craving liberal portions of Belgian specialties. Try black pudding with caramelized apples, sauerkraut, beef fried with shallots, grilled pig's trotters, or spareribs. ⊠ *Rue des Prêtres 4,* ☎ *02/512–8681. MC, V. Closed Sun. No lunch.*

$$ ✕ **Au Vieux St-Martin.** Belgian specialties dominate the menu here, and portions are generous. The restaurant claims to have invented the now ubiquitous *filet américain,* the well-seasoned Belgian version of steak tartare. The walls are hung with bright contemporary paintings, and picture windows face the pleasant square. ⊠ *Pl. du Grand Sablon 38,* ☎ *02/512–6476. Reservations not accepted. MC, V.*

$$ ✕ **Aux Armes de Bruxelles.** One of the few restaurants to escape the "tourist trap" label in this hectic street, it has three rooms with a lively atmosphere: The most popular section overlooks the street theater outside, but locals prefer the cozy rotunda. It offers the classics of Belgian cooking—tomatoes stuffed with freshly peeled shrimp, waterzooi (creamy rich fish stew), and mussels in white wine. ⊠ *Rue des Bouchers 13,* ☎ *02/511–5550. AE, DC, MC, V. Closed Mon.*

$ ✕ **Chez Jean.** This old-timer next to the Grand'Place has been dishing up good, honest Belgian food for nearly 70 years, in an unpretentious, old-fashioned setting with waitresses in black and white and the daily specials chalked up on the mirrors. Expect large, tasty portions of shrimp croquettes, salmon and endives cooked with beer, and chicken with *kriek* (cherry beer) and cherries. ⊠ *Rue des Chapeliers 6,* ☎ *02/511–9815. AE, DC, MC, V. Closed Sun. and June.*

$ ✕ **El Yasmine.** One of the best of the capital's many North African restaurants offers delicate Moroccan-Tunisian dishes in a setting where the billowy sky-blue sheets and glittery cushions recall a Berber tent. Couscous and *tajines* (Moroccan casseroles with fish or meat, usually involving fruit and spices) are the order of the day. ⊠ *Ch. d'Ixelles 234,* ☎ *02/647–5181. No credit cards. Closed Sun.*

$ ✕ **Falstaff.** This huge tavern with an Art Nouveau interior fills up for
★   lunch and keeps going until 5 AM. The ever-changing crowd, from students to pensioners, consumes onion soup, filet mignon, salads, and other brasserie fare. On the outside terrace, a favorite meeting point for groups, the surliness of the waiters is a local legend. ⊠ *Rue Henri Maus 19,* ☎ *02/511–8789. AE, DC, MC, V.*

$ ✕ **Léon de Bruxelles.** Critics deride it as McMoules-frites, but this century-old eatery is popular, with franchises across Belgium and even in Paris. The secret is vast plates of mussels and specialties such as eels in green sauce served from noon to midnight, a free children's menu, and great french fries. ⊠ *Rue des Bouchers 18,* ☎ *02/511–1415. Reservations not accepted. AE, DC, MC, V.*

$ ✕ **Le Pain Quotidien.** These bakeries-cum-snack bars have spread like wildfire all over Brussels (and even to New York and Boston in the U.S.) with the same formula: copious salads and delicious open sandwiches on farm-style bread, served at a communal table from 7 AM to 7 PM. Service at peak hours tends to be slow or nonexistent. ⊠ *Rue des Sablons 11,* ☎ *02/513–5154;* ⊠ *Rue Antoine Dansaert 16,* ☎ *02/502–2361; and other locations. Reservations not accepted. No credit cards.*

$ ✕ **Les Salons de Wittamer.** The elegant upstairs rooms at Brussels's best-
★   known patisserie house a stylish breakfast and lunch restaurant, where meals are topped off with the establishment's celebrated pastry or ice-cream concoctions. ⊠ *Pl. du Grand Sablon 12,* ☎ *02/512–3742. AE, DC, MC, V. Closed Mon.*

$$$$ ▣ **Brussels Hilton.** The 27-story Hilton was one of the capital's first high-rises in the '60s and remains a distinctive landmark with great views of the inner town. Corner rooms are the most desirable; there are four floors of executive rooms and superb business facilities. The second-floor Maison du Boeuf restaurant is much appreciated by Brussels gourmets. The hotel is in the luxury shopping area, overlooking the Parc d'Egmont. ⊠ *Bd. de Waterloo 38, 1000,* ☎ *02/504–1111,* ℻ *02/504–2111. 390 rooms, 39 suites. 2 restaurants. AE, DC, MC, V.*

$$$$ ⛨ **Conrad.** Opened by the Hilton group in 1993, the Conrad, seeking to combine the European grand hotel tradition with American tastes and amenities, has quickly become *the* place to stay for visiting dignitaries. Rooms are spacious, with three telephones, bathrobes, and in-room checkout. The Maison de Maître restaurant maintains the same high standard, and the large bar is pleasantly clublike. ⊠ *Av. Louise 71, 1050,* ☎ *02/542–4242,* ℻ *02/542–4200. 244 rooms, 15 suites. 2 restaurants. AE, DC, MC, V.*

$$$$ ⛨ **Le Méridien.** Opened in 1995, Le Méridien is Brussels's newest lux-★ ury hotel, in a drab but convenient area opposite Gare Centrale. The marble and gilt-edged lobby recalls palatial Parisian hotels, and the restaurant sets out brightly colored Limoges china. Rooms, in dark blue or green, come with three telephones, large desks, and data ports. ⊠ *Carrefour de l'Europe 3, 1000,* ☎ *02/548–4211,* ℻ *02/548–4080. 212 rooms, 12 suites. Restaurant. AE, DC, MC, V.*

$$$$ ⛨ **Radisson SAS.** This excellent 1990 hotel has guest rooms decorated with great panache in four different styles: Scandinavian, Asian, Italian, and Art Deco. A portion of the city wall from 1134 forms part of the atrium. Children under 15 stay free; check weekend rates. ⊠ *Rue du Fossé-aux-Loups 47, 1000,* ☎ *02/219–2828,* ℻ *02/219–6262. 263 rooms, 18 suites. 3 restaurants. AE, DC, MC, V.*

$$$ ⛨ **Amigo.** Although it was built in the 1950s, this family-owned hotel ★ off the Grand'Place has the charm of an earlier age. It's a favorite among the titled and famed who relish privacy. Each room is individually decorated, often in silk, velvet, and brocades, and most have marble bathrooms. Some 60 rooms, omitted from the most recent refurbishment, are more modestly priced. ⊠ *Rue d'Amigo 1–3, 1000,* ☎ *02/547–4747,* ℻ *02/513–5277. 178 rooms, 7 suites. Restaurant. AE, DC, MC, V.*

$$$ ⛨ **Metropole.** Built in 1895, this restored Belle Epoque masterpiece is the last trace of elegance in what was once one of Brussels's most charming squares. The lobby sets the tone, with its high coffered ceiling, chandeliers, and Oriental rugs, while the staircase and original lift are as stunning as they were when Sarah Bernhardt stayed here. The theme extends seamlessly to the restaurant and to the café, which opens onto a heated terrace. Most guest rooms are in discreet pastel shades and Art Deco style, but the very high ceilings take getting used to. ⊠ *Pl. de Brouckère 31, 1000,* ☎ *02/217–2300,* ℻ *02/218–0220. 404 rooms, 6 suites. 2 restaurants. AE, DC, MC, V.*

$$ ⛨ **Le Dixseptième.** In this stylish, 17th-century hotel, originally the residence of the Spanish ambassador, each room is named for a Belgian artist. Suites are up a splendid Louis XV staircase, and the standard rooms surround an interior courtyard. Whitewashed walls, bare floors, exposed beams, and colorful textiles are the style here. Some rooms have kitchenettes; suites have working fireplaces and fax machines. ⊠ *Rue de la Madeleine 25, 1000,* ☎ *02/502–5744,* ℻ *02/502–6424. 12 rooms, 12 suites. AE, DC, MC, V.*

$$ **Manos Stéphanie.** This former town house, opened as a hotel in 1992, has a marble lobby, Louis XV furniture, and elegant rooms full of character. Service is friendly, breakfast is included, and children under 12 stay free. ⊠ *Chaussée de Charleroi 28,* ☎ *02/539–0250,* ℻ *02/537–5729. 48 rooms, 7 suites. Restaurant, bar. AE, DC, MC, V.*

$ ⛨ **Bed & Brussels.** This upscale B&B accommodations service arranges stays with 100 host families, most of them with room to spare after children have flown the coop. Many rooms come with private bath, and breakfast with the hosts is included. ⊠ *Rue Gustave Biot 2, 1050,* ☎ *02/646–0737,* ℻ *02/644–0114. MC, V.*

$ 🏨 **Matignon.** Only the Belle Epoque facade of this family-run hotel opposite the Bourse was preserved when it was converted into a hotel in 1993. The lobby is tiny to make room for the bustling café-brasserie. Rooms are small but have large beds (and large TVs), and the duplex suites are good value for families. It's noisy but very central. ⊠ *Rue de la Bourse 10, 1000,* ☎ *02/511–0888,* ℻ *02/513–6927. 37 rooms, 8 suites. Restaurant. AE, DC, MC, V.*

$ 🏨 **Orion.** This residential apartment hotel accepts overnight guests and is a good choice for families. The exterior is plain, but the location on the Vismet is plum. Rooms have pull-out twin beds; junior suites sleep four. All have kitchenettes. ⊠ *Quai au Bois-à-Brûler 51, 1000,* ☎ *02/221–1411,* ℻ *02/221–1599. 169 rooms. Breakfast room. AE, DC, MC, V.*

$ 🏨 **Welcome Hotel/Truite d'Argent.** Among the charms of Brussels's small-
★ est hotel are owners Michel and Sophie Smeesters. The six rooms, with king- or queen-size beds, would be a credit to far more expensive establishments; it's essential to book well ahead. There's a charming breakfast room, and Michel doubles as chef of the excellent seafood restaurant La Truite d'Argent, where hotel guests get a discount. ⊠ *Rue du Peuplier 5, 1000,* ☎ *02/219–9546,* ℻ *02/217–1887. 6 rooms. Restaurant. AE, DC, MC, V.*

Nightlife and the Arts

The Arts

The best way to find out what's going on in Brussels—and throughout the country—is to buy a copy of the English-language weekly magazine *The Bulletin.* It's published every Thursday.

FILM

Movies are mainly shown in their original language. Complete listings appear in *The Bulletin.* First-run movies are shown at the multiscreen **Kinepolis** (⊠ Av. du Centenaire 1) and the **UGC Acropole** (⊠ Galeries de la Toison d'Or, ⊠ Pl. de Brouckère). For unusual movies or screen classics, visit the **Musée du Cinéma** (Cinema Museum; ⊠ Rue Baron Horta 9, ☎ 02/507–8370), where three movies with sound and two silents are shown daily.

MUSIC

Major symphony concerts and recitals are held at the **Palais des Beaux-Arts** (⊠ Rue Ravenstein 23, ☎ 02/507–8200). Chamber music is best enjoyed at the intimate **Conservatoire Royal de Musique** (⊠ Rue de la Régence 30, ☎ 02/507–8200). Free Sunday morning and lunchtime concerts take place at various churches, including the Cathédrale St-Michel et Ste-Gudule (☞ Exploring Brussels, *above*) and the Eglise des Minimes (⊠ Rue des Minimes 62). **Ancienne Belgique** (⊠ Bd. Anspach 110, ☎ 02/548–2424) hosts rock and pop concerts.

OPERA AND DANCE

The national opera company, based at the handsome **Théâtre Royal de la Monnaie** (⊠ Pl. de la Monnaie, ☎ 02/219–1211), stages productions of international quality. Touring dance and opera companies often perform at **Cirque Royal** (⊠ Rue de l'Enseignement 81, ☎ 02/218–2015).

THEATER

The **Théâtre Royal du Parc** (⊠ Rue de la Loi 3, ☎ 02/512–2339) stages productions of Molière and other French classics. Avant-garde theater is performed at: **Théâtre Varia** (⊠ Rue du Sceptre 78, ☎ 02/

640–8258) and at **Théâtre de Poche** (⊠ 1 Chemin du Gymnase, in Bois de la Cambre, ☎ 02/649–1727).

Nightlife

BARS

There's a café on virtually every corner in Brussels, and all of them serve beer from morning to late at night. If you crave a young crowd, try the sidewalk spillout of **Au Soleil** (⊠ Rue Marché au Charbon 86, ☎ 02/513–3430). The Flemish venue **Beurs Café** (⊠ Rue Auguste Orts 20–26, ☎ 02/513–8290) attracts the earnestly trendy young. **Cirio** (⊠ Rue de la Bourse 18, ☎ 02/512–1395) is a pleasant old Art Nouveau bar. On the Grand'Place, **Le Cerf** (⊠ Grand'Place 20, ☎ 02/511–4791) is particularly pleasant. **La Fleur en Papier Doré** (⊠ Rue des Aléxiens 53, ☎ 02/511–1659) is a quiet bar with surrealist decor that attracts an artsy crowd. **Rick's Café Américain** (⊠ Av. Louise 344, ☎ 02/648–1451) is a favorite with the American and British expat community. Like most western European cities, Brussels has a sizable number of "Irish" bars. **James Joyce** (⊠ Rue Archimède 34, ☎ 02/230–9894) was the first in Brussels and is the most genuinely Gaelic. **Kitty O'Shea's** (⊠ Bd. de Charlemagne 42, ☎ 02/230–7875) is a favorite with Eurocrats and young Commission trainees (*stagiaires*).

DANCE CLUBS

In all the clubs the action starts after midnight. Electronica fans prefer **Fuse** (⊠ 208 Rue Blaes, ☎ 02/511–9789), a bunker-style techno haven with regular gay and lesbian nights. **Griffin's** (⊠ Rue Duquesnoy 5, ☎ 02/505–5555), at the Royal Windsor Hotel, appeals to young adults and business travelers. **Mirano Continental** (⊠ Chaussée de Louvain 38, ☎ 02/227–3970) remains the glitzy hangout of choice for the self-styled beautiful people. **Who's Who's Land** (⊠ Rue du Poincon 17, ☎ 02/512–6343) has made big waves among good-time house fans.

JAZZ

Most of Brussels's dozen or so jazz haunts present live music only on certain nights; check before you go. **New York Café Jazz Club** (⊠ Chaussée de Charleroi 5, ☎ 02/534–8509) is an American restaurant by day and a modern jazz hangout by night. **Sounds** (⊠ Rue de la Tulipe 28, ☎ 02/512–9250), a big café, emphasizes jazz-rock, blues, and other modern trends. **Travers** (⊠ Rue Traversière 11, ☎ 02/218–4086), a café-cum-jazz club, is a cramped but outstanding showcase for the country's leading players.

Shopping

Gift Ideas

For beer, **400 bières artisanales** (⊠ Chaussé de Wavre 175, ☎ 02/511–3742) offers a well-judged, continually surprising selection of Belgium's 400 beers.

Belgium is where the *praline*—rich chocolate filled with flavored creams, liqueur, or nuts—was invented. Try Godiva, Neuhaus, or the lower-priced Leonidas, available at shops throughout the city. **Le St. Aulaye** (⊠ Rue Jean Chapelie 4, ☎ 02/345–7785) is an excellent patisserie with a sideline in superb chocolates. **Pierre Marcolini** (⊠ Pl. du Grand Sablon 39, ☎ 02/511–3321) is the boy wonder of the chocolate world. Exclusive handmade pralines can be bought at **Wittamer** (⊠ Pl. du Grand Sablon 12, ☎ 02/512–3742).

Only the Val-St-Lambert mark guarantees handblown, hand-carved crystal tableware. Many stores sell crystal, including **Art and Selection** (⊠ Rue Marché-aux-Herbes 83, ☎ 02/511–8448) near the Grand'Place.

In shopping for lace, ask whether it is handmade Belgian or made in East Asia. **Maison F. Rubbrecht** (⊠ Grand'Place 23, ☎ 02/512–0218) sells authentic Belgian lace. For a choice of old and modern lace, try **Manufacture Belge de Dentelle** (⊠ Galerie de la Reine 6–8, ☎ 02/511–4477).

Markets

On Saturday (9–6) and Sunday (9–2), the upper end of the Grand Sablon square becomes an **antiques and book market** with more than 100 stalls. The **Vieux Marché** (⊠ Pl. du Jeu de Balle), open daily 7–2, is a flea market worth visiting for the authentic atmosphere of the working-class Marolles district. If you hope to make real finds, get here early.

Shopping Districts

The shops in the **Galeries St-Hubert** sell mostly luxury goods or gift items. The **Rue Neuve** and the **City 2** mall are good for less expensive boutiques and department stores. Avant-garde clothes by the Antwerp Six and their successors are sold in boutiques in the **Rue Antoine Dansaert.**

Uptown, **Avenue Louise,** with the arcades Galerie Louise and Espace Louise, counts a large number of boutiques selling expensive men's and women's wear, accessories, leather goods, and jewelry. The **Boulevard de Waterloo** is home to the same fashion names as Bond Street and Rodeo Drive. The **Grand Sablon** has more charm; this is the center for antiques, oriental carpets, and art galleries.

Side Trip

Waterloo, where Napoléon was finally defeated by the British and German armies on June 18, 1815, lies 19 km (12 mi) to the south of the city; take a bus from Place Rouppe or a train from Gare Centrale to Waterloo station. The **Waterloo Tourist Office** (⊠ Chaussée de Bruxelles 149, ☎ 02/354–9910) is in the center of town.

The **Wellington Museum,** in the building where the general established his headquarters, displays maps and models of the battle and military memorabilia. ⊠ Ch. de Bruxelles 147, ☎ 02/354–7806. ☉ Apr.–mid-Nov., daily 9:30–6:30; mid-Nov.–Mar., daily 10:30–5.

Just south of town is the battlefield. The **Visitors' Center** has an audiovisual presentation showing scenes of the battle. You can also book guides to take you around the battlefield. ⊠ Rte. du Lion 252–254, Braine–l'Alleud, ☎ 02/385–1912. ☉ Apr.–Oct., daily 9:30–5:30; Nov.–Feb., daily 10:30–4; Mar., daily 10–5. Guides 1815: ⊠ Rte. du Lion 250, ☎ 02/385–0625. ⊞ BF1,400, 1 hr; BF2,200, 3 hrs.

Overlooking the battlefield is the **Butte de Lion,** a 28-ton pyramid-shape monument erected by the Dutch. After climbing 226 steps, you will be rewarded with a great view of the site, especially the quadrangular fortified farms where British troops broke the French assault.

Brussels Essentials

Arriving and Departing

BY BUS

Eurolines (⊠ Place de Brouckère 50, ☎ 02/217–0025) operates up to three daily express services from and to Amsterdam, Berlin, Frankfurt, Paris, and London. The Eurolines Coach Station (⊠ Rue du Progrès 80, ☎ 02/203–0707) in Brussels adjoins the Gare du Nord.

BY CAR

If you use Le Shuttle under the English Channel or a ferry to Calais, note that the E40 (via Oostende and Brugge) connects with the French highway, cutting driving time from Calais to Brussels to under two hours.

BY FERRY

Hoverspeed (☎ 01304/240241 in the U.K.; 059/559911 in Belgium) operates Seacat catamaran services between Dover and Oostende, carrying cars and foot passengers. Travel time is less than two hours. Trains at either end connect with London and Brussels. **P&O Stena** (☎ 0990/ 980980 in the U.K.; 050/542222 in Europe) operates an overnight ferry service between Hull and Zeebrugge.

BY PLANE

All international flights arrive at Brussels National Airport at Zaventem (sometimes called simply Zaventem), northeast of the city center. For flight information, call ☎ 0900–00747.

Between the Airport and Downtown. Trains run between Brussels Airport and all three main railway stations in Brussels: South, Central, and North. The Airport City Express runs four times per hour, from about 6 AM to about midnight. The journey takes just over 15 minutes. A one-way ticket costs BF140 (1st class) or BF90 (2nd class). A taxi to the city center takes about a half hour and costs about BF1,000.

BY TRAIN

Ten **Eurostar** (☎ 02/555–2525 for information; 0900/10–177 for telephone sales) passenger trains a day link Brussels's Gare du Midi with London's Waterloo station via the Channel Tunnel in two hours, 40 minutes. A one-way trip costs BF8,700 in business class and from BF3,490 in economy; rail pass holders qualify for 50% discounts.

All rail services between Brussels and Paris are on **Thalys** (☎ 0800/95– 777 for information; 0900/10–177 for reservations) high-speed trains (1 hr, 25 min). A one-way trip costs BF3,200 ("Confort 1"), BF2,070 ("Confort 2"). Reservations are required.

Getting Around

BY METRO, TRAM, AND BUS

The metro (subway), trams (streetcars), and buses run as parts of the same system. All are clean and efficient, and a single ticket costs BF50. The best buy is a 10-trip ticket for BF330 or a one-day card costing BF130. Tickets are sold in any metro station or at newsstands. Single tickets can be purchased on the bus or tram.

BY TAXI

To call a cab, phone **Taxis Verts** (☎ 02/349–4949) or catch one at a cab stand. It's not always possible to hail cruising taxis. Typical downtown rides cost BF250–BF500.

Contacts and Resources

EMBASSIES

U.S. (✉ Bd. du Régent 27, 1000 Brussels, ☎ 02/508–2111). **Canadian** (✉ Av. de Tervuren 2, 1040 Brussels, ☎ 02/741–0611). **U.K.** (✉ Rue d'Arlon 85, 1040 Brussels, ☎ 02/287–6211). **Australian** (✉ Rue Guimard 6–8, 1040 Brussels, ☎ 02/286–0500). **New Zealand** (✉ Bd. du Régent 47, 1000 Brussels, ☎ 02/512–1040).

EMERGENCIES

Police (☎ 101). **Ambulance and Fire Brigade** (☎ 100). **Doctor** (☎ 02/ 479–1818). **Dentist** (☎ 02/426–1026). **Pharmacy:** For information about all-night and weekend services, call ☎ 02/479–1818.

ENGLISH-LANGUAGE BOOKSTORES

Librairie de Rome (✉ Av. Louise 50b, ☎ 02/511–7937). **Sterling Books** (✉ Rue du Fossé-aux-Loups 38, ☎ 02/223–6223). **Waterstones** (✉ Bd. Adolphe Max 71–75, ☎ 02/219–2708).

Orientation. Chatterbus (⊠ Rue des Thuyas 12, ☎ 02/673–1835 for reservations) tours (early June–Sept.) include visits on foot or by minibus to the main sights (BF600) and a walking tour with a visit to a bistro (BF250). **De Boeck Sightseeing Tours** (⊠ Rue de la Colline 8, Grand'Place, ☎ 02/513–7744) operates city tours (BF790) with multilingual cassette commentary. **Walking Tours** organized by the tourist office (BF350) depart from the Tourist Information Brussels (TIB) office in the Town Hall, May–September, Monday–Saturday at 10.

Qualified guides are available for individual tours from the TIB (☎ 02/513–8940). Three hours costs BF3,000 for up to 20 people.

Side Trips. De Boeck Sightseeing Tours (☞ *above*) visits Antwerp, the Ardennes, Brugge, Ghent, Ieper, and Waterloo.

Special-Interest Bus Tours. Expertly guided half-day English-language coach tours are organized by **ARAU** (⊠ Bd. Adolphe Max 55, ☎ 02/219–3345 information and reservations), from March through November, including "Brussels 1900: Art Nouveau" (every Sat.) and "Brussels 1930: Art Deco" (every 3rd Sat.). Admission is BF600. Tours begin in front of Hotel Métropole on Place Brouckère.

American Express (⊠ Houtweg 24, 1170 Brussels, ☎ 02/245–2250). **Carlson Wagonlit Travel** (⊠ Bd. Clovis 53, 1040 Brussels, ☎ 02/287–8811).

Tourist Information Brussels (TIB; ⊠ Hôtel de Ville, Grand'Place, ☎ 02/513–8940); here you can buy a **Tourist Passport** (BF300)—a one-day transport card and BF1,000 worth of museum admissions.

ANTWERP

Antwerp's Dutch name is Antwerpen, close enough to be confused with *handwerpen*, and thereby hangs a tale. The Roman soldier Silvius Brabo is said to have cut off and flung into the water the hand of the giant who exacted a toll from boatmen on the river. *Hand* is hand, and *werpen* means throwing. The tale explains the presence of severed hands on the city's coat of arms.

Great prosperity came to Antwerp in the 16th century, during the reign of Charles V. A hundred years later, Rubens and his contemporaries made the city an equally important center of the arts. Craftsmen began practicing diamond-cutting at about this time, and the city is still the world leader in the diamond trade, with an annual turnover of more than $20 billion. In spite of being 88 km (55 mi) up the River Scheldt, it is Europe's second-largest port after Rotterdam. Antwerp is the principal city of Flanders, and the Antwerpers, convinced they are a cut above most others, don't mind at all their Spanish-derived nickname: *Sinjoren* (señores).

Exploring Antwerp

Numbers in the margin correspond to points of interest on the Antwerp map.

The Old City—a short subway ride from the Central Station—is the heart of Antwerp and best explored on foot. Rubens and his contemporaries seem to be everywhere, in churches, art museums, and splendid Renaissance mansions. Antwerp is also known as the City of Madonnas. You'll see a statuette of Our Lady on many a street corner.

⑧ **Bourlaschouwburg** (Bourla Theater). Dating from the 1830s, this handsome neoclassical theater was allowed to fall into neglect before being restored to gold-and-velvet glory in 1995. Sunday brunch in the supremely opulent café is booked up weeks in advance. ⊠ *Komedieplaats 18,* ☎ *03/231–0750.*

⑫ **Centraal Station** (Central Station). This railway station is special. Leopold II (1835–1909), a monarch not given to understatement, had it built in 1905 as a neo-Baroque cathedral to the railway age, with splendid staircases and a magnificently vaulted ticket-office hall. ⊠ *Koningin Astridplein,* ☎ *03/233–3915.*

☺ ⑪ **Dierentuin** (Antwerp Zoo). The residents are housed in style in this huge, well-designed complex: giraffes and ostriches in an Egyptian temple, rhinoceroses in a Moorish villa, okapis around an Indian temple. There's also a winter garden, a planetarium, an aquarium, a dolphin pool, and a good restaurant. ⊠ *Koningin Astridplein 26,* ☎ *03/202– 4540.* ▭ *BF450.* ☉ *Dec.–Jan., daily 9–4:30; Feb. and mid-Oct.–Nov., daily 9–4:45; 1st ½ Mar. and 1st ½ Oct., daily 9–5:15; mid-Mar.–June and Sept., daily 9–5:45; July and Aug., daily 9–6:15.*

❶ **Grote Markt.** The heart of the Old City, a three-sided square, is dominated by a huge fountain topped by a statue of Silvius Brabo, the giant-killer. The Renaissance **Stadhuis** (City Hall) flanks one side of the square, and guild houses the other two. ⊠ *Jct. Suikerrui, Oude Koornmarkt, Handschoenmarkt, Kaasrui, Hofstraat, and Nosestraat.*

❻ **Koninklijk Museum voor Schone Kunsten** (Royal Museum of Fine Arts). This huge museum south of the Old City contains more than 1,500 paintings by old masters, including magnificent works by Van Eyck, Memling, Rubens, Van Dyck, Jordaens, Hals, and Bruegel. The second floor houses an outstanding collection of Flemish paintings from the 15th and 16th centuries; the first floor has more modern paintings, including works by Emile Claus, Rik Wouters, Constant Permeke, Magritte, Delvaux, and James Ensor. ⊠ *Leopold de Waelplaats 2,* ☎ *03/238–7809.* ☉ *Tues.–Sun. 10–5, Wed. to 9.*

★ ❼ **Museum Mayer van den Bergh.** A passionate 19th-century collector, Mayer van den Bergh amassed almost 4,000 works of art, the best of which are displayed in the small museum that bears his name. The masterpiece is Bruegel's great *Dulle Griet (Mad Meg)*, an antiwar allegory. In 1894 Mayer van den Bergh bought the painting for a mere BF488. ⊠ *Lange Gasthuisstraat 19,* ☎ *03/232–4237.* ☉ *Tues.–Sun. 10–5.*

★ ❺ **Museum Plantin-Moretus.** Religious dissident, humanist, and printer extraordinaire, Christophe Plantin (1514–89) founded a printing house that flourished for three centuries. Two typefaces designed here, Plantin and Garamond, are still in use. The presses continue to work. Among the treasures are portraits by Rubens as well as many first editions, engravings, and a copy of the Gutenberg Bible. The luxurious private apartments and editorial offices can also be visited. ⊠ *Vrijdagmarkt 22,* ☎ *03/233–0294.* ☉ *Tues.–Sun. 10–5.*

★ ❸ **Onze-Lieve-Vrouwekathedraal** (Cathedral of Our Lady). You'll see the white, 404-ft spire of Antwerp's Gothic masterpiece from far away. Starting in 1352, a succession of architects worked on it for more than 200 years, but the ensemble is completely coherent. The paintings and statuary it contained have repeatedly been plundered, most recently by the army of the French Revolution. The cathedral's many treasures still include four Rubens altarpieces. His *Descent from the Cross* is flanked by panels showing Mary's visit to Elizabeth and the presentation of Jesus in the Temple; these are among the tenderest and most

Antwerp (Antwerpen)

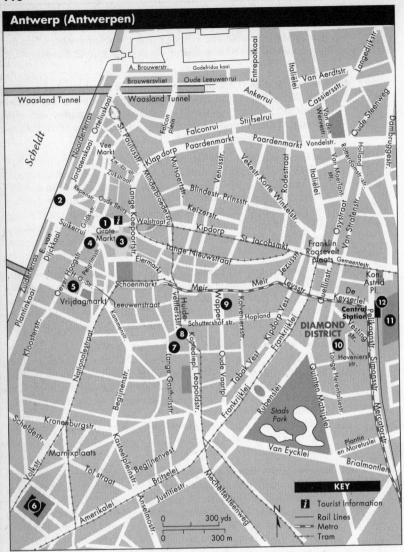

Bourlaschouwburg, **8**
Centraal Station, **12**
Dierentuin, **11**
Grote Market, **1**
Koninklijk Museum
voor Schone
Kunsten, **6**
Museum Mayer
van den Bergh, **7**

Museum Plantin-
Moretus, **5**
Onze-Lieve-
Vrouwekathedraal, **3**
Provinciaal
Diamantmuseum, **10**
Rubenshuis, **9**
Steen, **2**
Vlaeykensgang, **4**

delicate Biblical scenes ever painted. ⊠ *Handschoenmarkt,* ☎ *03/231–3033.* ☉ *Weekdays 10–5, Sat. 10–3, Sun. 1–4.*

⑩ Provinciaal Diamantmuseum (Provincial Diamond Museum). This remarkable museum traces the long and often bloody history of the search for mankind's most precious stones. You are guided through the entire diamond production process, from extraction to the sparkling gem. There's also a 19th-century diamond workshop and a treasure room of outstanding jewelry. The museum is around the corner from the **diamond district** (⊠ Hoveniersstraat), thronged with diamond dealers of every extraction—Orthodox Jews, Russians, Armenians, Indians, Africans, Lebanese—for here is where Antwerp's four diamond *bourses* and most of the diamond firms and polishing and cutting workshops are located. ⊠ *Lange Herentalsestraat 31–33,* ☎ *03/202–4890.* ☉ *Daily 10–5; cutting demonstrations Sat. afternoon.*

⑨ Rubenshuis (Rubens House). Rubens lived here from 1610 until his death in 1640. The mansion, a reconstruction based on his original designs, gives a vivid impression of the artist's life as wealthy court painter and diplomat. The mezzanine overlooks the studio where Rubens and his pupils worked. His widow promptly sold 300 paintings when he died, but a few Rubens originals do hang in the house. ⊠ *Wapper 9,* ☎ *03/232–4747.* ☉ *Tues.–Sun. 10–5.*

② Steen. This 9th-century fortress is the oldest building in Antwerp. It was used as a prison for centuries, and the crucifix where condemned men said their final prayers is still in place. The Steen now houses the **National Scheepvaartmuseum** (National Maritime Museum). ⊠ *Steenplein,* ☎ *03/232–0850.* ☉ *Tues.–Sun. 10–4:45.*

④ Vlaeykensgang. Time has stood still in this cobblestone alley in the center of town, which captures the mood and style of the 16th century. There's no better place to linger on a Monday night, when the carillon concert rings out from the Cathedral.

Dining and Lodging

Dining in Antwerp's many fine restaurants has a distinctly French flavor, making full use of the excellent ingredients from the surrounding farmland. Naturally, seafood has pride of place on the dinner tables of this port city. For details and price-category definitions, *see* Dining *in* Belgium A to Z, *above.*

The Antwerp City Tourist Office(☞ Visitor Information *in* Antwerp Essentials, *below*) keeps track of the best hotel prices and can make reservations for you up to a week in advance. Write or fax for a reservation form. It also maintains a list of some 25 recommended bed-and-breakfast accommodations from BF1,200 to BF2,000. For details and price-category definitions, *see* Lodging *in* Belgium A to Z, *above.*

$$$$ ✕ **'t Fornuis.** In the heart of Old Antwerp, this old and cozy restaurant, decorated in traditional Flemish style, serves some of the best food in the city. The menu changes frequently, but truffled sweetbreads with wild truffle sauce are a house classic. ⊠ *Reyndersstraat 24,* ☎ *03/233–6270. Reservations essential. Jacket and tie. AE, DC, MC, V. Closed weekends and 3 wks in Aug.*

$$$ ✕ **De Matelote.** The gifted chef at this tiny restaurant in a narrow, Old
★ City street concocts such inventive dishes as grilled asparagus with fresh morels and a poached egg, or langoustines in a light curry sauce. The chef knows how to ennoble fish like brill or skate, making this the best fish restaurant in town. ⊠ *Haarstraat 9,* ☎ *03/231–3207. Reservations essential. AE, DC, MC, V. Closed Sun., July.*

$$$ ✕ **Neuze Neuze.** Five tiny houses cobbled together form a handsome,
★ split-level restaurant with whitewashed walls, dark-brown beams, and
a blazing fireplace. The inventive dishes include sautéed goose liver with
caramelized pineapple, or scallops with rhubarb preserve. ⊠ *Wijn-
gaardstraat 19,* ☎ *03/232–5783. AE, DC, MC, V. Closed Sun. 2 wks
in July and 2 wks in Jan. No lunch Sat.*

$$ ✕ **Hungry Henrietta.** Father and son run this stylish Antwerp institution, next to the church where Rubens is buried. You can dine in the
garden when the weather's good. Fillet of salmon with endives, quail
salad, and leg of lamb are on the menu. ⊠ *Sint-Jacobsstraat 17,* ☎
03/232–2928. AE, DC, MC, V. Closed weekends and Aug.

$$ ✕ **Sir Anthony Van Dijck.** On Antwerp's most famous and romantic
★ alley is a classy brasserie, with an interior courtyard and tables grouped
around stone pillars under high, massive beams. The menu changes
monthly, but expect such items as salad liègeoise with smoked salmon
and caramelized onions, duck à l'orange, and tuna steak. There are two
seatings a night. ⊠ *Vlaeykensgang, Oude Koornmarkt 16,* ☎ *03/
231–6170. Reservations essential. AE, DC, MC, V. Closed Sun., Aug.*

$ ✕ **Cirque Belge.** A replica of the Atomium, a facsimile of the Manneken
Pis, portraits of famous Belgians, and paintings of national products
from beer to Rizla papers: Here's Belgium's answer to Belgian-bash-
ers, a knowingly kitsch extravaganza with well-executed, locally in-
spired cuisine and a huge range of beers. Try fish soup, rabbit in beer,
or fried beef in shallots. ⊠ *Ernest Van Dijckkaai 13-14,* ☎ *03/232–
9439. No credit cards.*

$ ✕ **Kiekekot.** Antwerp students satisfy their craving for spit-roasted
chicken and french fries at this no-frills "chicken coop," which offers
a juicy half chicken for about BF250 nearly all night. ⊠ *Grote Markt
35,* ☎ *03/232–1502. MC, V. Closed Tues.*

$ ✕ **'t Hofke.** This restaurant is worth visiting for its location alone—
it's in the Vlaeykensgang alley, where time seems to have stood still.
The cozy dining room has the look and feel of a private home, and the
menu includes a large selection of salads and omelets, as well as scampi
in cream with cognac and calf liver with Roquefort. ⊠ *Oude Koorn-
markt 16,* ☎ *03/233–8606. AE, MC, V. Closed Mon.*

$ ✕ **Zuiderterras.** A stark glass-and-black-metal construction, this river-
side café and restaurant was designed by avant-garde architect bOb
(his spelling) Van Reeth in 1993. You can have a light meal for about
$15 and enjoy seeing the river traffic on one side and, on the other, a
view of the cathedral and the Old Town. ⊠ *Ernest Van Dijckkaai 37,*
☎ *03/234–1275. Reservations not accepted. AE, MC, V.*

$$$$ 🛏 **Antwerp Hilton.** Incorporating the turn-of-the-century Grand Bazaar
building, the five stories of the Hilton (from 1993) are architecturally
compatible with the much older buildings on Groenplaats. Rooms are
equipped with three telephones, safes, and desks. Afternoon tea is
served in the marble-floored lobby. The restaurant, Het Vyfde Seizoen,
will satisfy gourmets. ⊠ *Groenplaats, 2000,* ☎ *03/204–1212,* FAX *03/
204–1213. 183 rooms, 18 suites. 2 restaurants. AE, DC, MC, V.*

$$$$ 🛏 **De Witte Lelie.** Three step-gabled 16th-century houses have been com-
★ bined to make the White Lily Antwerp's most exclusive hotel (opened
in 1993). Personal service is the watchword in the 10-room hotel, dec-
orated mostly in white, with colorful carpets and modern art on the
walls. Sumptuous breakfasts are served on a loggia opening up on the
inner courtyard. ⊠ *Keizerstraat 16-18, 2000,* ☎ *03/226–1966,* FAX *03/
234–0019. 4 rooms, 6 suites. Breakfast room. AE, DC, MC, V.*

$$$ 🛏 **Classic Hotel Villa Mozart.** This small, modern hotel in an old build-
ing in a pedestrian area could not be more central: next door to the
cathedral. The rooms, equipped with business-class features, air-conditioning, and electronic safes, are slightly cramped, but many over-

look the cathedral. ⊠ *Handschoenmarkt 3, 2000,* ☎ *03/231–3031,* FAX *03/231–5685. 25 rooms. Restaurant. AE, DC, MC, V.*

$$
★ **Firean.** An Art Deco gem built in 1929, Firean is family operated. Rooms are decorated in pastels, offset by rich fabrics. There's a tiny bar-cum–breakfast room, where eggs are served in floral-print cozies. The location is not central, but a tram to the Old Town runs outside the door. ⊠ *Karel Oomsstraat 6, 2018,* ☎ *03/237–0260,* FAX *03/238– 1168. 9 rooms, 6 in annex next door. AE, DC, MC, V.*

$$ **Hyllit.** The Hyllit (1995) stands on the corner of De Keyserlaan, Antwerp's prestige shopping street, with its entrance on Appelmansstraat, the gateway to the diamond district (reception on second floor). Rooms are decorated in muted colors and equipped with office-type desks; suites have a fax as well. There's a roof-top buffet breakfast room and full room service. ⊠ *De Keyserlei 28–30, 2018,* ☎ *03/202–6800,* FAX *03/ 202–6890. 24 rooms, 56 suites. Breakfast room. AE, DC, MC, V.*

$ **Pension Cammerpoorte.** The rooms (some with a view of the cathedral) are decorated in bright pastels and sad-clown art, and many can comfortably house a family of four. A buffet breakfast, included in the price, is served in the tidy brick-and-lace café. There's no elevator for the four floors. ⊠ *Steenhouwersvest 55, 2000,* ☎ *03/231–2836,* FAX *03/226–2843. 16 rooms with shower. AE, DC, MC, V.*

Shopping

In fashion, Antwerp has become a center second only to Milan, thanks to a group of designers who burst on the scene as the Antwerp Six. Inspired by their success, other young designers of fashion items have achieved prominence; check out the boutiques in the De Wilde Zee district and along Huidevetterstraat and Schuttershofstraat. Ready-to-wear by Raf Simons and Martin Margiela can be found at **Louis** (⊠ Lombardenstraat 2, ☎ 03/232–9872). **Dries Van Noten** (⊠ Nationalestraat 16, ☎ 03/233–9437) has a beautiful boutique, Modepaleis, that's not to be confused with the drab Van Noten shop opposite.

If you plan to invest in diamonds, it makes sense to do so in the world's leading diamond center. If you're not an expert, your best bet is **Diamondland** (⊠ Appelmansstraat 33a, ☎ 03/234–3612), in whose spectacular showrooms you can see both loose and mounted diamonds.

Antwerp Essentials

Arriving and Departing

BY CAR

Expressways from Amsterdam, Eindhoven, Aachen, Liège, Brussels, and Ghent converge on Antwerp's inner-city ring expressway. It's a 10-lane racetrack, so be sure you're in the correct lane well before you exit.

BY PLANE

Antwerp International Airport (☎ 03/218–1211 for flight information) is 5½ km (3 mi) southeast of the city. There are several flights a day to and from London City Airport. Most passengers arrive via Brussels National Airport (Zaventem), which is linked with Antwerp by hourly bus service (50 minutes one-way).

Between Antwerp Airport and Downtown. Buses to Antwerp's Centraal Station leave every 20 minutes; travel time is about 15 minutes.

BY TRAIN

Frequent fast trains run between Antwerp (Centraal Station, ☎ 03/204– 2040) and Brussels; the trip takes 35 minutes.

Getting Around

In the downtown area, the tram is the most convenient means of transportation. Some lines have gone underground (look for signs marked M); the most useful line runs between Centraal Station (Metro: Diamant) and the Groenplaats (for the old city). A single ride costs BF40, a 10-ride ticket BF290, and a day pass BF110. For detailed transportation maps, stop at the tourist office.

Contacts and Resources

GUIDED TOURS

Orientation. Touristram (Groenplaats, ☎ 03/480–9388) operates 50-minute tram tours with cassette commentary in the Old City and old harbor area. Tickets (BF125) are sold on the tram. Qualified **personal guides** can be engaged through the City Tourist Office (below), which requires a couple of days' notice. The price for two hours is BF1,500.

Special Interest. Flandria (☎ 03/231–3100) operates 90-minute boat trips on the River Scheldt, departing from the Steenplein pontoon (next to the Steen) from Easter through September (BF250), as well as boat tours of the enormous port (2½ hours), which leave from Quay 13 near Londonstraat, May–October (BF400).

VISITOR INFORMATION

Toerisme Stad Antwerpen (Antwerp City Tourist Office; ✉ Grote Markt 15, ☎ 03/232–0103, FAX 03/231–1937).

GHENT

Ghent—spelled Gent in Dutch and known to French-speakers as Gand—is the home of one of the world's greatest works of art, Van Eyck's *Adoration of the Mystic Lamb*. The city center may come straight out of the Middle Ages, but this is a dynamic, modern town with a long-established rebellious streak. It was weavers from Ghent, joined by others from Brugge, who took up arms to defeat the French cavalry in 1302. Charles V (1500–58) was born here, but that did not prevent an uprising against Spanish rule from being cruelly crushed. Centuries later, a weaver saved Ghent from decline by stealing a new-fangled spinning mule from England and starting Ghent's industrial revolution. Later, socialists battled here for workers' rights, and Ghent became the site of Belgium's first Flemish-speaking university. The militant tradition continues to this day: While the city celebrates Charles's 500th birthday in 2000, many academics and locals vehemently oppose the festivities.

Exploring Ghent

The best spot to start a walk around the center is Sint-Michielsbrug (St. Michael's Bridge), with its view of Ghent's three glorious medieval steeples. The closest is the severe early Gothic Sint-Niklaaskerk (St. Nicholas's Church); behind it is the Belfort (Belfry) from 1314. In the background rises the honey-color tower of Sint-Baafskathedraal (St. Bavo's Cathedral) in Brabant Gothic. The classic walk around the Old City takes you up to the Gravensteen (Castle of the Counts), and then, on the opposite shore of the River Leie, to the Stadhuis (Town Hall) and the Cathedral. Many historic buildings are lit up every night from May through October (and Friday and Saturday nights the rest of the year), making an evening walk a memorable experience.

Belfort (The Belfry). Three hundred feet high, it symbolizes the power of the guilds during the 14th century. The spire was added for the World's Fair of 1913, based on the original plans. A 52-bell carillon hangs on the fifth floor, but can only be visited with a guide. ⊠ *Sint-Baafsplein,* ☎ *09/233–3954.* ⊙ *Mid-Apr.–mid-Nov., daily 10–12:30 and 2–5:30; guided visits at 10 min past hr, weekends afternoons only.*

★ **Graslei.** This quay along the Leie River, between St. Michael's Bridge and Gras Bridge, is best seen from the Korenlei across the river. Once the center of Ghent's trade, it is lined with a row of Baroque guild houses and other buildings, among them the 12th-century **Koornstapelhuis** (Granary), used for 600 years.

Gravensteen. The ancient Castle of the Counts of Flanders hulks up like an enormous battleship near the confluence of the Leie with the Lieve Canal, the 700-year-old waterway that links the city with Brugge, and offers splendid views from its battlements. First erected in 1180, the castle has been rebuilt a number of times, most recently in the 19th century. A gruesome display of torture instruments indicates how feudal power was maintained. The spinning mules that made Ghent a textile center were first installed here. ⊠ *Sint-Veerleplein,* ☎ *09/225–9306.* ⊙ *Apr.–Sept., daily 9–6; Oct.–Mar., daily 9–5.*

Museum voor Schone Kunsten (Fine Arts Museum). Paintings and sculptures from the Middle Ages to the early 20th century are displayed here. The collection includes two outstanding paintings by Hieronymus Bosch, *St. Jerome* and *The Bearing of the Cross,* and a fine selection of Belgian art from the turn of the century. ⊠ *Nicolaas de Liemaeckereplein 3,* ☎ *09/222–1703.* ⊙ *Tues.–Sun. 9:30–5.*

★ **Sint-Baafskathedraal** (St. Bavo's Cathedral). In the De Villa Chapel is the stupendous 24-panel *Adoration of the Mystic Lamb,* completed on May 6, 1432, by Jan Van Eyck (1389–1441), who is said to have invented the technique of painting with oil. The painting's central panel is based on Revelation 14:1: "And I looked, and, lo, a Lamb stood on Mt. Sion, and with him a hundred forty and four thousand." To the medieval viewer, the painting was a theological summation of all things revealed about the relationship between God and the world. Over the centuries, the painting has been stolen and recovered a number of times. The cathedral has several other treasures, notably a Rubens masterpiece, *The Vocation of St. Bavo,* in which the artist painted himself as a convert in a red cloak. ⊠ *Sint-Baafsplein,* ☎ *09/225–4985.* ⊙ *Cathedral: daily 8:30–6. Chapel: Apr.–Oct., Mon.–Sat. 9:30–noon and 2–6, Sun. 1–6; Nov.–Mar., Mon.–Sat., 10:30–noon and 2:30–4, Sun. 2–5. No visits to cathedral or chapel during services.*

Stadhuis (Town Hall). You notice immediately that this 16th-century building reflects two distinct architectural styles, the result of crippling tax rises imposed by Charles V that forced a halt in construction. The older Gothic section, with its lacelike tracery, was begun early in the 16th century. The structure was finished at the end of the same century in a more sober Renaissance style. ⊠ *Botermarkt,* ☎ *09/233–0772.* ⊙ *Guided visits only, May–Oct., Mon.–Thurs. at 3.*

Dining and Lodging

Ghent's contribution to Belgian gastronomy is a creamy fish and vegetable stew called waterzooi, which most menus offer. For details and price-category definitions, *see* Dining *in* Belgium A to Z, *above.*

A number of Ghent hotels catering to exhibition and trade-fair visitors stand near the Expo Center. There are not so many in the Old Town, but they do include the oldest hotel in Europe. For details and price-category definitions, *see* Lodging *in* Belgium A to Z, *above.*

$$$ ✕ **Waterzooi.** This tiny restaurant stands on a square distinguished by
★   16th- and 17th-century buildings. It serves such specialties as turbot
      with pepper sauce or lobster-filled ravioli with tarragon. ⊠ *Sint-Veer-*
      leplein 2, ☎ *09/225–0563. Reservations essential. Jacket and tie. AE,*
      DC, MC, V. Closed Wed., Sun., and 3 wks in Aug.

$$ ✕ **'t Buikske Vol.** Patershol, formerly a district where textile workers
★   lived, has become a charming residential area. Probably the best among
      nouveau-chic Patershol's trendy eateries, the Buikske Vol presents such
      well-prepared dishes as grilled turbot, fillet of beef with onion confit,
      or sweetbreads with rabbit. ⊠ *Kraanlei 17*, ☎ *09/225–1880. AE,*
      MC, V. Closed Sun., Wed., Easter wk, and 1st ½ Aug. No lunch Sat.

$$ ✕ **Het Cooremetershuis.** One flight up in an ancient guild house on the
★   Graslei is this small, adventurous restaurant. It's noted for well-exe-
      cuted contemporary dishes, including fillet of lamb with lentils, sole
      in Riesling wine, and John Dory with a parsley coulis. ⊠ *Graslei 12*,
      ☎ *09/223–4971. Reservations essential. AE, DC, MC, V. Closed Wed.,*
      Sun., and July 15–Aug. 15.

$–$$ ✕ **Pakhuis.** An old warehouse has been skillfully converted into an enor-
      mously popular brasserie, with marble-top tables, parquet flooring,
      dozens of overhead fans, and a huge oak bar as the centerpiece. There's
      an oyster-and-shellfish bar to supplement such basic brasserie fare as
      knuckle of ham with mustard and steak tartare. ⊠ *Schuurkenstraat*
      4, ☎ *09/223–5555. AE, DC, MC, V. Closed Sun.*

$ ✕ **Taverne Keizershof.** Touristy taverns are much the same all over Bel-
      gium, but this one is popular with locals—always a good sign. The daily
      plates are large portions of good, solid foods, and all-day snacks in-
      clude toasted sandwiches and spaghetti. ⊠ *Vrijdagmarkt 47*, ☎ *09/*
      223–4446. MC, V. Closed Sun.

$$$ ▦ **Sofitel.** The Ghent outpost of this classy and comfortable French
      hotel chain is a converted Art Nouveau building, decorated in warm
      brown and beige and excellently situated in the heart of the Old City.
      The bathrooms are palatial. ⊠ *Hoogpoort 63, 9000*, ☎ *09/233–3331*,
      FAX *09/233–1102. 124 rooms, 3 suites. Restaurant. AE, DC, MC, V.*

$$ ▦ **Gravensteen.** This handsome, 19th-century mansion, restored to its
      original Second Empire style, has a superb canal-front location, a few
      steps from the Castle of the Counts. Some of the rooms are small but
      indivdual, while 10 more luxurious rooms overlook the canal. ⊠ *Jan*
      Breydelstraat 35, 9000, ☎ *09/225–1150*, FAX *09/225–1850. 42 rooms,*
      3 suites. AE, DC, MC, V.

$$ ▦ **Sint-Jorishof.** Napoléon stayed here, and so, before him, did Mary
      of Burgundy and Emperor Charles V, for this hotel has been operat-
      ing since 1228, making it the oldest in Europe. Much of its Gothic spirit
      has been preserved, especially in the reception area and the restaurant,
      which serves classic French fare. There are only four rooms in the main
      building; the rest are in two converted 18th-century houses across the
      street. ⊠ *Botermarkt 2, 9000*, ☎ *09/224–2424*, FAX *09/224–2640. 4*
      rooms in main building, 24 in annex. Restaurant. AE, DC, MC, V.

$ ▦ **Erasmus.** From the flagstone and wood-beam library-lounge to the
★   stone mantels in the bedrooms, every inch of this noble 16th-century
      house has been scrubbed, polished, and bedecked with period orna-
      ments. Even the tiny garden has been carefully manicured. ⊠ *Poel 25*,
      9000, ☎ *09/224–2195*, FAX *09/233–4241. 11 rooms. AE, DC, MC, V.*

Ghent Essentials

Arriving and Departing

BY CAR

Ghent is just off the six-lane E40 from Brussels, which continues to
Brugge and the coast. Traffic can be bumper-to-bumper on summer

weekends. It is generally lighter on the E17 from Antwerp, which continues to Lille and Paris. Finding your way in and out of the city center can be extremely tricky; advance preparation is a good idea.

BY TRAIN

Nonstop trains depart for Gent-Sint-Pieters on the hour and 27 minutes past the hour from Gare du Midi in Brussels (☎ 02/203–3640 or 09/221–4444). Travel time to Ghent is 28 minutes.

Getting Around

Most of the sights are within a radius of 1 km (½ mi) from the Town Hall, and by far the best way to see them is on foot. You can rent bikes at the train station, and parts of the city center are closed to cars.

Contacts and Resources

GUIDED TOURS

Sightseeing boats, operating Easter–October, depart from landing stages at Graslei (☎ 09/282–9248) and Korenlei (☎ 09/223–8853) for 35-minute trips. Admission is BF150. Your Ghent experience can be much enhanced by a personal guide; call **Gidsenbond van Gent** (Association of Ghent Guides; ☎ 09/233–0772, FAX 09/233–0865). The charge is BF1,500 for the first two hours; BF750 per additional hour.

VISITOR INFORMATION

Dienst voor Toerisme (Tourist Office; ✉ Belfort, Botermarkt 17a, ☎ 09/266–5232).

BRUGGE

Brugge (or Bruges, as it is known to French- and most English-speakers) represents the flowering of commerce and culture in the Middle Ages. The city had the good fortune to be linked with the North Sea by a navigable waterway and became a leading member of the Hanseatic League during the 13th century. Splendid marriage feasts were celebrated here; that of Charles the Bold, Duke of Burgundy (1433–77), to Margaret of York in 1468 is commemorated in the annual Holy Blood Procession. Disaster struck when the link with the sea silted up during the 15th century, but this past misfortune is responsible for Brugge's present glory. Little has changed in this city of interlaced canals overhung with humpback bridges.

Exploring Brugge

Numbers in the margin correspond to points of interest on the Brugge (Bruges) map.

The center of Brugge is virtually reserved for pedestrians; you need to remember that cobbled streets call for good walking shoes. Brugge draws visitors in droves, but there's always a quiet corner away from the madding crowd. Try to do your exploring in the early evening when the day trippers have left and the city is at its most magical.

★ **❾ Begijnhof** (Beguinage). The Begijnhof has been an oasis of peace for 750 years. The first Beguines were widows of fallen crusaders. They were not nuns but lived a devout life while serving the community. Although the last Beguines left the close of small, whitewashed houses in 1930, a Benedictine community has replaced them, and you may join them, discreetly, for vespers in their small church. ✉ *Off Wijngaardstraat,* ☎ *050/330011.* ☉ *Apr.–Sept., daily 10–noon and 1:45–5:30; Oct.–Nov. and Mar., daily 10:30–noon and 1:45–5; Dec.–Feb., Wed.–Thurs. and weekends 2:45–4:45, Fri. 1:45–6.*

Brugge (Bruges)

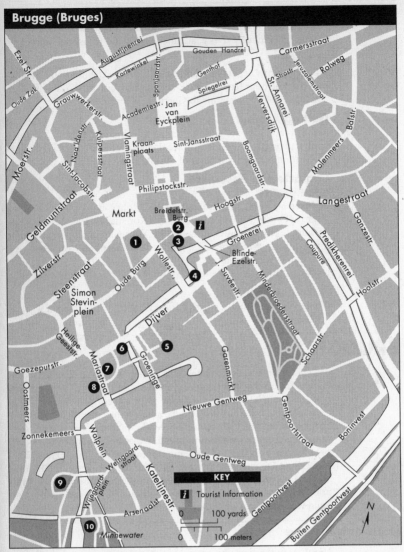

Begijnhof, **9**

Belfort, **1**

Brangwyn Museum, **6**

Burg, **2**

Groeninge
Museum, **5**

Heilig-Bloed
Basiliek, **3**

Memling
Museum, **8**

Minnewater, **10**

Onze-Lieve
Vrouwekerk, **7**

Reien, **4**

❶ Belfort (The Belfry). There's a panoramic view of the town from the top of the 270-ft-high (366 steps!) Belfort, which dominates the Markt, the city's ancient market square. The Belfort has a carillon notable even in Belgium, where they are a matter of civic pride. ⊠ *Markt 7.* ☉ *Apr.–Sept., daily 9:30–5; Oct.–Mar., daily 9:30–12:30 and 1:30–5. Carillon concerts: Oct.–mid-June, Wed. and weekends 2:15–3; mid-June–Sept., Mon., Wed., and Sat. 9 PM–10 PM, Sun. 2:15–3.*

❻ Brangwyn Museum. The Brugge-born English artist Frank Brangwyn (1867–1956) was one of several British Romantics who lived in the city and influenced the reconstruction of many buildings in a pseudo-Gothic style. Many of his brooding paintings of Brugge are on view here. On the ground floor is the **Kantmuseum** (Lace Museum), containing outstanding examples of a craft long and lovingly practiced in Brugge. ⊠ *Dijver 16,* ☎ *050/448711.* ☉ *Apr.–Sept., daily 9:30–5; Oct.–Dec. and Feb.–Mar., Wed.–Mon. 9:30–12:30 and 2–5.*

★ **❷ Burg.** This magic, medieval square is the focal point of ancient Brugge. The **Stadhuis** (Town Hall), a jewel of Gothic architecture in white sandstone from the 14th century and the model for town halls across Belgium, has an ornate facade adorned with a multitude of statues. It is linked with the graceful, Renaissance **Oude Griffie** (Old Recorder's House) by a bridge arching over the narrow Blinde Ezelstraat, which leads down to the canal. ⊠ *Stadhuis: Burg 12.* ☉ *Apr.–Sept., daily 9:30–5; Oct.–Mar., daily 9:30–12:30 and 2–5.*

★ **❺ Groeninge Museum.** This small museum enjoys a worldwide reputation for its superb and wide-ranging collection of Flemish Primitives, including Van Eyck's realistic *Virgin and Canon Van der Paele*; Memling's *Moreel Triptych*, arguably his most intensely spiritual work; Hieronymus Bosch's surrealistic *Last Judgment*; and Pieter Bruegel's *Preaching of John the Baptist*. ⊠ *Dijver 12,* ☎ *050/448711.* ☉ *Apr.–Sept., daily 9:30–5; Oct.–Mar., Wed.–Mon. 9:30–12:30 and 2–5.*

❸ Heilig-Bloed Basiliek (Basilica of the Holy Blood). The Basilica stands on a corner of the Burg, next to the Town Hall. The Lower Chapel has kept its pure, austere 12th-century Romanesque character. The upper chapel, however, was rebuilt during the 15th century and again, with an ultraflamboyant Gothic stairway, in the 19th century. The vial thought to contain a few drops of the blood of Christ is exposed here every Friday. The **Heilig-Bloed Museum** (Museum of the Holy Blood) has a reliquary and paintings. The **Procession of the Holy Blood** on Ascension Day (May 14 in 2000) combines religious and historical pageantry. ⊠ *Burg.* ☉ *Museum: Apr.–Sept., daily 9:30–11:50 and 2–5:50; Oct.–Mar., daily 10–noon and 2–4. Closed Wed. afternoon.*

★ **❽ Memling Museum.** The museum is dedicated to the work of the Brugge painter Hans Memling (c. 1430–94), perhaps the greatest and certainly the most spiritual of all early Flemish painters. The six masterpieces in the museum include the altarpiece *St. John the Baptist and St. John the Evangelist* and the miniatures adorning the St. Ursula shrine. The museum is housed in the former **Sint-Janshospitaal,** where the sick were nursed for 700 years. The 17th-century pharmacy can be visited. ⊠ *Mariastraat 38,* ☎ *050/448711.* ☉ *Apr.–Sept., daily 9:30–5; Oct.–Mar., Thurs.–Tues. 9:30–12:30 and 2–5.*

❿ Minnewater. The enchanting body of water, created in the 13th century, was once the city harbor and more recently has been known as the "Lake of Love." The adjoining 16th-century lockkeeper's house is usually surrounded by white swans, the symbol of the city. ⊠ *Off Wijngaardplein, next to Begijnhof.*

❼ Onze-Lieve-Vrouwekerk (Church of Our Lady). At 381 ft, the severe spire is the tallest brick construction in the world. Inside the church, you'll find a notable collection of paintings and carvings—including Michelangelo's small *Madonna and Child*—and splendid tombs with the effigies of Duke Charles the Bold of Burgundy, who died on the battlefield in 1477 and his daughter, Mary, who married into the Habsburg family and died in a horseback-riding accident at the age of 25. ⊠ *Gruuthusestraat.* ⊙ *Apr.–Sept., weekdays 10–11:30 and 2:30–5, Sat. 10–11:30 and 2:30–4, Sun. 2:30–5; Oct.–Mar., weekdays 10–11:30 and 2:30–5, Sat. 10–11:30 and 2:30–4:30, Sun. 2:30–4:30.*

★ **❹ Reien** (Canals). The canals of Brugge with their old, arching stone bridges can be explored both by boat and on foot along the quays. They give the city its special character. From **Steenhouwersdijk** you see the brick rear gables, which are all that remains of the old county hall. Next to the little **Huidenvettersplein**, with its 17th-century guild houses, is **Rozenhoedkaai**; from here the view of the heart of Brugge includes the pinnacles of the Town Hall, the Basilica, and the Belfry.

Dining and Lodging

Along Brugge's quiet streets stand some of Belgium's finest restaurants. The Markt, however, is ringed with unremarkable restaurants catering to the tourist trade. For details and price-category definitions, *see* Dining *in* Belgium A to Z, *above.*

In proportion to its size, Brugge has a large number of hotels, many of them romantic, canal-side residences, for this is a town where people like to come for a second honeymoon. Prices are relatively high, but so are standards. Many hotels offer package deals. For details and price-category definitions, *see* Lodging *in* Belgium A to Z, *above.*

$$$$ ✕ **De Karmeliet.** Owner-chef Geert Van Hecke, one of Belgium's best, ★ works in this lovely 18th-century house. His inventive, elaborate kitchen serves a festival of flavors: goose liver with truffled potatoes, roast langoustines with endives in an apple-and-curry juice, cod carpaccio with asparagus. ⊠ *Langestraat 19,* ☎ *050/338259. Reservations essential. Jacket and tie. AE, DC, MC, V. Closed Mon. No dinner Sun.*

$$ ✕ **Breydel–De Coninck.** Famed for fresh mussels and other seafood, this no-frills, untouristy restaurant stands between the Markt and the Burg. While there are token offerings of eel and steak, the focus is on the basics—a huge crock heaped high with shiny, blue-black shells. ⊠ *Breidelstraat 24,* ☎ *050/339746. AE, MC, V. Closed Wed. and June.*

$ ✕ **Straffe Hendrik.** This daytime pub is attached to the brewery, dating from 1546, that produces the potent, crystal-clear, natural beer of the same name. It also serves quite acceptable pub grub, and you can tour the facilities. The square is among Brugge's most charming. ⊠ *Walplein 26,* ☎ *050/332697. No credit cards.*

$ ✕ **Taverne Oud Handbogenhof.** Here's an authentic Flemish inn, with a big courtyard shaded by linden trees. It's much favored by locals, always a good sign. Specialties are spareribs with garlic sauce and salmon with scallops and shrimp in white sauce. ⊠ *Baliestraat 6,* ☎ *050/331945. MC, V. Closed Mon., 1st wk July, Jan. No lunch Tues.*

$$$ ✕▥ **'t Bourgoensche Cruyce.** In a romantic canal-side setting, this restaurant has salmon-and-copper decor that is reflected in the water. The cuisine is equally romantic: panfried langoustines with wild mushrooms, tournedos of salmon with bacon, turbot medallions with coriander and caramelized leeks (reservations essential; closed Tues., Wed., and 1st wk in July). The establishment has eight cozy guest rooms furnished in traditional Flemish style; four face the canal. ⊠ *Wollestraat 41*, ☎ *050/337926*, ℻ *050/341968. 8 rooms. Restaurant. AE, DC, MC, V. Closed mid-Nov.–mid-Dec.*

$$$ ✕🏠 **Die Swaene.** This hotel has "romantic" written all over it: canal-side location, oxblood wallpaper, four-poster beds, candles, and marble nymphs in every nook and cranny: honeymoon heaven. The restaurant ($$$$; closed Wed., 3 wks in July, 3 wks in Jan.; no lunch Thurs.) is a serious contender as one of the best in this gourmet city: goose liver, sweetbreads, and grilled turbot are among its treats. ⊠ *Steenhouwersdijk 1, 8000,* ☎ *050/342798,* ℻ *050/336674. 22 rooms, 2 suites. Restaurant, pool. AE, DC, MC, V.*

$$ ✕🏠 **De Castillion.** This restaurant and hotel was the residence of 18th-century bishop Jean-Baptiste de Castillion. Predinner drinks and postprandial coffee are served in a handsome Art Deco salon. Fillet of venison in a Pomerol stock and turbot and scampi on a bed of tagliatelle with a curry sauce are among the offerings (reservations essential; jacket and tie required; no dinner Sun., no lunch Mon. and Tues.). The rooms in the hotel side vary considerably in size and price. Their decor ranges from rustic to modern. ⊠ *Heilige Geeststraat 1,* ☎ *050/343001,* ℻ *050/339475. 18 rooms, 2 suites. Restaurant. AE, DC, MC, V.*

$$$ 🏠 **De Tuileriëen.** A 15th-century mansion with Venetian glass windows
★ has been converted into a patrician hotel and decorated with discreet antique reproductions. The breakfast room has a coffered ceiling. Canal-side rooms have great views; courtyard rooms are quieter. ⊠ *Dijver 7, 8000,* ☎ *050/343691,* ℻ *050/340400. 20 rooms, 6 suites. Pool. AE, DC, MC, V.*

$$$ 🏠 **Walburg.** One of Brugge's grandest 19th-century town houses, a few blocks from the Burg, was converted into a hotel in 1996. The rooms, decorated in different color schemes, with period Marie Antoinette furniture and marble bathrooms, are a generous 750 square ft—and the suite twice as large. ⊠ *Boomgaardstraat 13, 8000,* ☎ *050/349414,* ℻ *050/336884. 12 rooms, 1 suite. Restaurant, bar. AE, DC, MC, V.*

$$ 🏠 **Egmond.** Every room in this manorlike inn on Minnewater has gar-
★ den views, as well as parquet floors and the odd fireplace or dormer ceiling. The hotel is a pleasant retreat from the bustle of the center, 10 minutes away. The bathrooms are tiny. ⊠ *Minnewater 15, 8000,* ☎ *050/341445,* ℻ *050/342940. 9 rooms. No credit cards.*

$ 🏠 **De Pauw.** At this family-run hotel, the warmly furnished rooms have
★ names rather than numbers, and breakfast comes with six kinds of bread, cold cuts, and cheese. The two rooms that share a shower down the hall are a super value. ⊠ *Sint-Gilliskerkhof 8, 8000,* ☎ *050/337118,* ℻ *050/345140. 8 rooms, 6 with bath. AE, DC, MC, V.*

Brugge Essentials

Arriving and Departing

BY CAR

Brugge is about an hour's drive from Brussels on the E40 motorway to the coast. Holiday weekend traffic is often heavy. Unless you are driving to a hotel, leave your car at one of the parking lots or garages at the entrance to the Old City.

BY TRAIN

Trains run hourly at 28 and 59 minutes past the hour from Brussels (Gare du Midi) to Brugge. The station is south of the canal that circles the downtown area; for train information, call ☎ *050/382382.* Travel time from Brussels is 53 minutes.

Getting Around

The center of Brugge is best explored on foot, as car and bus access is severely restricted. This makes for bicycle heaven; ask the tourist office (☞ *below*) for information on where to rent one.

Contacts and Resources

GUIDED TOURS

Boat trips along the city canals are run by several companies and depart from five separate landings. Boats ply the waters March–November, daily 10–6. They leave every 10–15 minutes, and a 30-minute trip costs BF175. The **horse-drawn carriages** that congregate in the Markt are an expensive way of seeing the sights. They are available March–November, daily 10–6; a 35-minute trip will cost BF900. The carriages take up to five people. Fifty-minute **minibus tours** of the city center leave every hour on the hour from the Markt in front of the post office.

VISITOR INFORMATION

Toerism Brugge (Brugge Tourist Office; ✉ Burg 11, ☏ 050/448686, FAX 050/448600). Contact them well in advance for tickets to the Holy Blood Procession (☞ Heilig-Bloed Basiliek *in* Exploring Brugge, *above*).

6 BULGARIA

SOFIA, THE BLACK SEA COAST, INLAND BULGARIA

Bulgaria, with mountains and seasides, modern cities and medieval villages, is an enigmatic land where rustic beauty coexists with decaying remnants of a Communist past. Lying in the eastern half of the Balkan Peninsula, Bulgaria was the closest ally of the former Soviet Union until the 1989 overthrow of Communist party head Todor Zhivkov. Since then, Bulgaria, which is striving to become a member of the European Union, has struggled toward democracy and a free-market economy.

Corruption, massive unemployment, and skyrocketing inflation resulting in a decreasing standard of living severely tested the patience of Bulgarians after 1989. The national desire for change was reflected in the victory of opposition candidate Peter Stoyanov in the presidential elections of late 1996. In January of 1997, as the lev plunged, the people of Bulgaria took to the streets. Protests and strikes immobilized the country and forced the Socialist party government to hold early elections (although it still officially had two years to go in power). April 1997 elections gave the opposition coalition (UDF; Union of Democratic Forces) a plurality. Though it is still doubtful that the fledgling government can pull Bulgaria out of the economic crisis that's made it one of the poorest countries in Europe, the lev is finally somewhat stable, and the country and people are enjoying the most optimistic atmosphere in years. Foods and goods are plentiful and, for those living on a Western salary, very inexpensive.

Endowed with long Black Sea beaches, the rugged interior Balkan Range, and fertile Danube plains, Bulgaria has much to offer year-round. The Black Sea coast, the country's eastern border, is particularly alluring, with secluded coves and fishing villages built amid Byzantine and Roman ruins, and wide, shallow beaches that have been developed into resorts. The terrain of the beautiful interior is ideal for hiking and skiing. In the more remote areas hides a tranquil world of forested ridges,

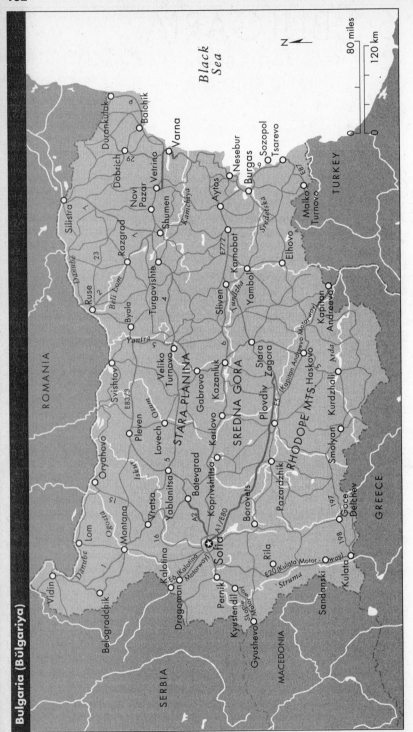

Bulgaria (Bŭlgariya)

spectacular valleys, and small villages where donkey-drawn carts are still the primary transport.

Founded in AD 681 by the Bulgars, a Turkic tribe from Central Asia, Bulgaria was already a crossroads. Archaeological finds in Varna, on the Black Sea coast, give proof of civilization from as early as 4600 BC. Part of the Byzantine Empire from 1018 to 1185, Bulgaria was occupied by the Turks from 1396 until 1878. Today, Bulgaria has Eastern-influenced architecture, Turkish fast-food aromas, Greek ruins, Soviet monuments, and European outdoor cafés. Five hundred years of Muslim occupation and nearly half a century of Communist rule did not wipe out Christianity. The country's 120 monasteries, with their icons and numerous frescoes, chronicle the development of Bulgarian cultural and national identity.

The capital, Sofia, sits picturesquely in a valley near Mt. Vitosha. Rich with history and culture, the city also has good hotels, a variety of restaurants, and a vibrant Mediterranean-style nightlife. Veliko Turnovo, just north of the Balkan Range in the center of the country and the capital from the 12th through the 14th centuries during the Second Bulgarian Empire, still has medieval ramparts and vernacular architecture. Plovdiv, a university town southeast of Sofia, has a particularly picturesque Old Quarter as well as one of the world's best-preserved Roman amphitheaters. Varna, the site of one of Europe's first cultural settlements, is a summer beach playground and among the most important ports on the Black Sea.

BULGARIA A TO Z

Customs
You may import duty-free into Bulgaria 250 grams of tobacco products, plus 1 liter of hard liquor and 2 liters of wine. Declare items of greater value—computers, camcorders, and the like—so there will be no problems with Bulgarian customs officials on departure. Failure to declare items of value can result in a fine or even police detainment when you attempt to leave.

Dining
In Bulgaria you have a choice between predictable hotel dining, which often includes international cuisines, and more adventurous outings to private restaurants or cafés where the menu may be in Cyrillic. The best bets are the small folk-style restaurants called *mehanas* that serve regional specialties often at shared tables.

Bulgarian national dishes are closely related to their Greek and Slav counterparts: basic Balkan cooking includes lamb and potatoes, pork sausages called *kebapche,* and a popular salad called *shopska salata* made with feta-style sheep cheese, tomatoes, cucumbers, peppers, and onions. Bulgaria produces sumptuous fruits and vegetables. Try the rich, amber-color *bolgar* grapes and orange-red apricots. Bulgaria invented *kiselo mlyako* (yogurt), and there is excellent *tarator* (cold yogurt soup with sliced cucumber and garlic) in summer. *Banitsa* (butter, cheese, and phyllo dough pastry) is often eaten for breakfast. Syrupy baklava and chocolate or *palachinki* (nut- and honey-stuffed crepes) are favorite desserts.

Bulgarian wines are good, usually full-bodied, dry, and inexpensive. The national drink is *rakia*—either *slivova* (plum) or *grozdova* (grape) brandy—but other hard alcohol and beer are popular, too. Coffee is strong and is often drunk along with a cold beverage, such as cola or a lemon drink. Tea is taken with lemon rather than milk.

Prices are per person and include a first course, main course, dessert, and tip, but no alcohol.

CATEGORY	COST
$$$$	over 20,000 leva
$$$	12,000 leva–20,000 leva
$$	7,000 leva–12,000 leva
$	under 7,000 leva

WHAT TO WEAR

In Sofia, formal dress (jacket and tie) is customary at $$$$ restaurants. Casual dress is appropriate elsewhere.

Language

The official language, Bulgarian, is written in Cyrillic and is close to Old Church Slavonic, the root of all Slavic languages. English, though becoming popular with the young, is rarely understood outside major hotels and restaurants. It is essential to remember that in Bulgaria a nod of the head means "no" and a shake of the head means "yes."

Lodging

There is a wide choice of accommodations, ranging from the old, state-run hotels—most of them dating from the '60s and '70s—to new, private hotels, apartment rentals, rooms in private homes, and campsites. Although hotels are improving, the older ones still tend to suffer from temperamental wiring and erratic plumbing; pack a universal drain plug, as plugs are often missing in bathrooms.

HOTELS

At press time most of the formerly government-owned or operated hotels had been privatized or were in the process. During the conversion, hotels may be closed for renovation. Private hotels are opening as well. Outside Sofia call ahead to hotels to get the latest information. Most hotels have restaurants and bars; the large, modern ones have swimming pools, shops, and other facilities.

PRIVATE ACCOMMODATIONS

Staying in private homes, with arrangements made by private-room agencies, is becoming a popular alternative to hotels; it not only cuts costs but also means increased contact with Bulgarians. Booking offices are located in most main tourist areas. In Sofia contact **Balkantour Ltd.** (✉ 27 bul. Stamboliiski, ☎ 02/988–5543 or 02/987–7233). **Balkan Tourist** (✉ 1 bul. Vitosha, ☎ 02/87–51–92) can help with Sofia lodgings. Bring your own towels, soap, and other necessities.

RENTED ACCOMMODATIONS

Rented accommodations are a growth industry, with planned modern complexes as well as picturesque cottages. Cooking facilities tend to be meager, and meal vouchers are included in the deal. An English-speaking manager is generally on hand. Such accommodations usually aren't offered in Sofia but can often be found on the Black Sea coast and in Plovdiv and Veliko Turnovo. Check with the agencies listed under Visitor Information (☞ *below*).

RATINGS

Prices are for two people in a double room with half board (breakfast and a main meal). At the leading hotels you can pay in either U.S. dollars or leva; the less expensive hotels accept only leva. Foreign currency can be exchanged for leva at the reception desk in most hotels. The price categories below are listed in U.S. dollars, as that is how hotel prices are usually quoted.

CATEGORY	SOFIA	OTHER AREAS
$$$$	over $200	over $100
$$$	$130–$200	$70–$100
$$	$70–$130	$40–$70
$	under $70	under $40

Mail

Letters up to 10 grams to North America cost 900 leva; to the United Kingdom, 760 leva. Rates change constantly with inflation, so ask for the current price at the post office.

Money Matters

COSTS

The favorable exchange rate makes prices seem extremely low by international standards. The greatest expense is lodging, but it is possible to cut costs by choosing the more moderate hotels or staying in a private room in a Bulgarian house or apartment. Taxi and public transport fares, museum and theater admissions, and meal prices in most restaurants are quite low.

CREDIT CARDS

The major international credit cards are accepted in a few larger stores and in the most expensive hotels and restaurants, but before you place an order, check to see whether or not you can use your card. Outside of Sofia, and at any small restaurant or hotel, credit cards are almost always worthless. Bring cash.

CURRENCY

The unit of currency in Bulgaria is the lev (plural leva). There are bills of 100, 200, 500, 1,000, 2,000, 5,000, 10,000, 20,000, and 50,000 leva. Although prices are sometimes quoted in dollars, all goods and services (except the most expensive hotels and international airline tickets) must be paid for in leva. You may import any amount of foreign currency, including traveler's checks, and exchange foreign currency at banks, hotels, airports, border posts, and the plentiful private exchange offices (which offer the best rates and take no commission). Bring new, clean U.S. bills, as counterfeiting is a recent phenomenon, and torn or marked currency will be turned away. Though it is possible to change traveler's checks at a few select locations, such as the airport and some major hotels, commissions are exorbitant. In small towns traveler's checks are worthless. ATMs are found only in Sofia. The value of the lev continues to fluctuate, though a currency board has pegged it at 1000 leva to 1 DM, and the exchange rate and price information quoted here may be outdated very quickly. At press time (summer 1999) the rate quoted by the Bulgarian State Bank was 1,875 leva to the U.S. dollar, 1,276 leva to the Canadian dollar, 2,971 leva to the pound sterling, 1,234 leva to the Australian dollar, and 1,001 leva to the New Zealand dollar. Monetary reform is on the horizon, and by the year 2000, Bulgarian bills will "lose their zeros" and 1 lev will equal 1 DM.

SAMPLE PRICES

Because of fluctuating exchange rates, the following price list can be used only as a rough guide. A trip on a tram, trolley, or bus, 250 leva; theater ticket, 2,000–7,500 leva; coffee in a moderate restaurant, 300 leva; bottle of wine in a moderate restaurant, 4,000–9,000 leva; museum admission, 500–2,000 leva.

TIPPING

Tips of 10% of the bill are appropriate for waiters and taxi drivers; hotel employees also receive tips ($1 or the equivalent for bellhops and 10%–20% at expensive hotels; 10% in leva at smaller hotels).

National Holidays

January 1; March 3 (Liberation Day); April 22, 23 (Orthodox Easter); May 1 (Labor Day); May 24 (Saints Cyril and Methodius—creators of the Cyrillic alphabet—Commemoration Day); December 24–26.

Opening and Closing Times

Banks are open weekdays 9–5. **Museums** are usually open 9–5 but are often closed on Monday or Tuesday. **Shops** are open Monday through Saturday 9–7; some are open on Sunday. A few *denonoshni magazini* (day and night minimarkets) in the city center are open 24 hours.

Passports and Visas

All visitors need a valid passport. Americans do not need visas when traveling as tourists for 30 days or less. Other tourists, traveling independently, should inquire about visa requirements at a Bulgarian embassy or consulate before entering the country. Many package tours are exempt from the visa requirement.

Telephoning

Local calls cost 2 leva and can be made from your hotel, from pay phones, or from the two types of card phones, *Betkom* and *Bulfon,* both of which can also be used for long-distance calls throughout Bulgaria and Europe. Phone cards can be purchased at post offices, hotels, and numerous street kiosks. Calls to the United States can be made from Bulfon or Betkom phones by using a local calling card to reach the international operator and then a long-distance calling card to reach the States. They can also be made from your hotel, for a surcharge, or placed from a post office. In Sofia direct-dial calls to the United States can also be made from the international phone office (½ block west of the main post office). To place a call using an **AT&T USA Direct** international operator, dial 00–800–0010.

COUNTRY CODE

For international calls to Bulgaria, the country code is 359. The access code for Sofia is 2 from outside Bulgaria and 02 from within.

Transportation

Bulgaria uses the following abbreviations in addresses: *ul.* (*ulitsa*) is street; *bul.* (*bulevard*) is boulevard; *pl.* (*ploshtad*) is square.

BY BOAT

Modern luxury vessels cruise the Danube from Passau in Austria to Ruse. Hydrofoils link main communities along the Bulgarian stretches of the Danube and the Black Sea, and there are coastal excursions from some Black Sea resorts. A ferry from Vidin to Calafat links Bulgaria with Romania. Contact a travel agent for reservations.

BY BUS

An increasing number of private bus firms link all the major towns. Buses tend to be luxurious, air-conditioned, and faster than trains. Bus stations are generally close to the train station. Buy tickets a day or two in advance (but no more than a week). Within the cities a regular system of trams and trolley buses operates for a single fare of 200 leva. In Sofia booths at bus stops sell tickets; outside the city you can pay the driver. **Group Travel** (✉ Novotel Europa Sofia, 131 bul. Maria Luisa, 11202 Sofia, ☎ 02/83–29–10) is the chief bus service in the country.

BY CAR

For motorist information contact the **Bulgarian Automobile Touring Association** (SBA; ✉ 3 ul. Pozitano Sofia, ☎ 02/980–33–08).

Breakdowns. In case of breakdown call ☎ 146. The **SBA** trucks carry essential spares. Fiat, Ford, Volkswagen, Peugeot, and Mercedes-Benz all have car-service operations in Bulgaria. Other important numbers for drivers are ☎ 165 for road police and ☎ 150 for ambulance.

Car Rental. Three international car-rental firms have offices in Sofia and other major towns: **Avis** (Sheraton Sofia Hotel, ⊠ 5 pl. St. Nedelya, ☎ 02/988–81–67; Sofia airport, ☎ 02/73–80–23). **Eurodollar** (Hotel Kempinski Zografski, ⊠ 100 bul. James Bourchier, ☎ 02/87–57–79). **Hertz** (☎ 02/980–04–61 reservations, ☎ 02/79–14–77 airport). Two agencies rent cars with drivers: **Balkantour** (⊠ 27 bul. Stamboliiski, ☎ 02/988–55–43), **Balkantourist** (⊠ 1 bul. Vitosha, ☎ 02/87–51–92).

Gasoline. Stations are regularly spaced on main roads but may be few and far between. All are marked on Balkantourist's motoring map and sell unlimited quantities of fuel. A listing of 24-hour petrol stations in Sofia can be found in the **Sofia City Guide,** an English-language brochure for sale at news kiosks and free at major hotels.

Parking. Bulgaria's parking laws are liberal, and if there's not a place on the street, you can often park on the sidewalk. Just be sure you're not blocking a driveway or another car, and never park where there's a NO PARKING sign (a red circle with a line through it). If you are in doubt, check with the hotel, restaurant, or sight you are visiting.

Road Conditions. Main roads are generally well engineered, although some routes are poor and narrow for the volume of traffic they have to carry. A large-scale expressway construction program has begun to link the main towns. Completed stretches run from Kalotina—on the Serbian border—to Sofia, and from Sofia to Plovdiv.

Rules of the Road. Drive on the right. The speed limit is 50 or 60 kph (31 or 36 mph) in built-up areas, and 80 kph (50 mph) elsewhere, except on highways, where it is 120 kph (70 mph). Balkantourist recommends that you take out collision, or Casco, insurance. You are required to carry a first-aid kit, fire extinguisher, and triangle-shaped breakdown sign in the vehicle. Front seat belts must be worn. The drunk-driving laws are strict—you are expected not to drive after you have had more than one drink. If you're pulled over, be prepared to pay on the spot a fine determined by the officer.

BY PLANE

Balkan Airlines (⊠ 12 pl. Narodno Subranie Sofia, ☎ 02/880–663) has regular services to Varna and Burgas, the biggest ports on the Black Sea. Group-travel and air-taxi services are available through **Hemus Air** (⊠ Sofia International Airport, ☎ 02/72–07–54), which also arranges business flights to other destinations in the country.

BY TRAIN

In Sofia buy tickets in advance at the ticket office (in the underpass below the National Palace of Culture) to avoid long lines at the station. In other cities get your tickets at the station. It's best to take an *ekspresni* (express) or *burzi* (fast) train, as they are the fastest and most comfortable. *Putnicheski* (slow) trains are very old and painfully slow. Trains tend to be crowded; seat reservations are obligatory on expresses. *Purva clasa* (first class) is not much more expensive than second class and is worth it. From Sofia there are six main routes—to Varna or Burgas on the Black Sea coast, to Plovdiv and beyond to the Turkish border, to Dragoman and the Serbian border, to Kulata and the Greek border, and to Ruse on the Romanian border.

Visitor Information

Balkan Tour Sofia (⊠ 27 bul. Stamboliiski, ☎ 02/988–55–43). **Balkan Tourist** (⊠ 1 bul. Vitosha, ☎ 02/87–51–92).

Weather

The ski season lasts from mid-December through March; the Black Sea coast season runs from May through October, reaching its peak in July and August. Fruit trees blossom in April and May; in May and early June the blossoms are gathered in the Valley of Roses; in October the fall colors are at their best.

CLIMATE

Summers are warm; winters are crisp and cold. The coastal areas enjoy considerable sunshine. March and April are the wettest months inland. Even when the temperature climbs, the Black Sea breezes and the cooler mountain air prevent the heat from being overwhelming.

The following are the average daily maximum and minimum temperatures for Sofia.

Jan.	35F	2C	May	69F	21C	Sept.	70F	22C
	25	− 4		50	10		52	11
Feb.	39F	4C	June	76F	24C	Oct.	63F	17C
	27	− 3		56	14		46	8
Mar.	50F	10C	July	81F	27C	Nov.	48F	9C
	33	1		60	16		37	3
Apr.	60F	16C	Aug.	79F	26C	Dec.	38F	4C
	42	5		59	15		28	− 2

SOFIA

Bulgaria's bustling capital stands on the high Sofia Plain, ringed by mountain ranges: the Balkan Range to the north; the Lyulin Mountains to the west; part of the Sredna Gora Mountains to the southeast; and, to the southwest, Mt. Vitosha—the city's playground—which rises to more than 7,600 ft. The area has been inhabited for about 7,000 years, but your first impression may be of a city besieged by urban development dominated by an expanse of nightmarish Socialist-era block housing. This soon gives way to spacious parks, open-air cafés, and broad streets filled with an incongruous mix of Western sports cars and old-fashioned farmer's wagons laden with firewood. In 1998, for the first time in eight years, Sofia was able to afford to pump water to its many neglected city fountains, if only for a few hours a day. Ploshtad Slaveikov, one of the most heavily traveled squares in the city center, has just received a face-lift from the European Union and is repainted in bright colors, with a brand new marble fountain. In the 1870s Sofia was still part of the Ottoman Empire, and one mosque still remains. Most of the city was planned after 1880, and following the destruction of World War II, many of the main buildings were rebuilt in the Socialist style.

Exploring Sofia

Numbers in the margin correspond to points of interest on the Sofia map.

There are enough intriguing museums and musical performances to merit a lengthy stay, but, you can see the main city sights in two days and enjoy the serenity of Mt. Vitosha on a third day.

❻ **Banya Bashi Dzhamiya** (Banya Bashi Mosque). This distinctive building, consisting of a large dome and a lone minaret, a legacy from the centuries of Turkish rule, was built during the 16th century and closed between the mid-1980s and 1993. Now that it is open for worship, loudspeakers on the minaret call the city's Muslim minority to prayer. ✉ *bul. Maria Luiza at ul. Triyaditsa.*

Sofia

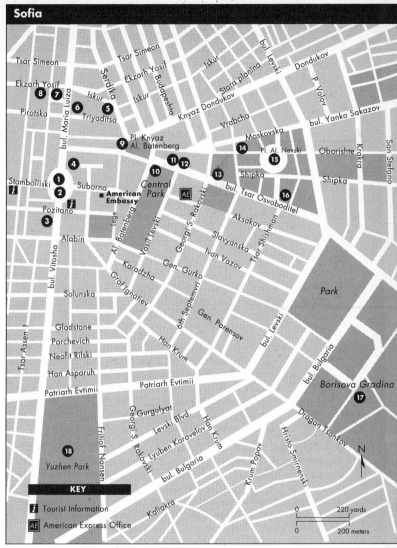

KEY

ℹ️ Tourist Information

A/E American Express Office

Banya Bashi
Dzhamiya, **6**

Borisova Gradina, **17**

Hram-pametnik
Alexander Nevski, **15**

Mavsolei Georgi
Dimitrov, **10**

Narodno
Subranie, **16**

Natsionalen Dvorets
na Kulturata, **18**

Natsionalen
Etnografski
Muzei, **12**

Natsionalen
Istoricheski Muzei, **3**

Natsionalna
Hudozhestvena
Galeria, **11**

Partiyniyat Dom, **9**

Ploshtad Sveta
Nedelya, **1**

Rotonda Sveti
Georgi, **4**

Tsentralna
Sinagoga, **8**

Tsentralnata
Banya, **5**

Tsentralni Hali, **7**

Tsurkva Sveta
Nedelya, **2**

Tsurkva Sveta
Sofia, **14**

Tsurkva Sveti
Nikolai, **13**

🐾 ⑰ **Borisova Gradina** (Boris's Garden). Dilapidated benches, stray dogs, overflowing garbage dumpsters, an empty lake, a dry fountain, and neglected statues of Communist leaders mar this former haven. Nevertheless, it is huge, central, and important to the city's inhabitants. The wild woods surrounding it are good for a stroll. In summer, ice-cream vendors, children in rented battery-operated minicars, a first-class outdoor disco, and a surprisingly pristine public pool with water slides for children bring life to the park. ⌧ *bul. Bulgaria between bul. Tsar Osvoboditel and bul. Dragan Tsankov.*

★ ⑮ **Hram-pametnik Alexander Nevski** (Alexander Nevski Memorial Church). The neo-Byzantine structure with glittering onion domes dominates the city. It was built by the Bulgarian people at the beginning of the 20th century as a mark of gratitude to their Russian liberators. Inside are decorations in alabaster, onyx, and Italian marble; Venetian mosaics; magnificent frescoes; and space for a congregation of 5,000. Attend a service to hear the superb choir, and, above all, don't miss the fine collection of icons in the **Crypt Museum.** ⌧ *pl. Alexander Nevski,* ☎ *02/981–57–75.* ⊙ *Wed.–Mon. 10–5.*

⑩ **Mavsolei Georgi Dimitrov** (Georgi Dimitrov Mausoleum). In 1990 the remains of the first general secretary of the Bulgarian Communist party, who died in Moscow in 1949, were moved to the Central Cemetery. As of now, the mausoleum serves as the site of Sofia's annual summer outdoor opera performance. ⌧ *South side of pl. Alexander Batenberg.*

⑯ **Narodno Subranie** (National Assembly). Topped by the Bulgarian national flag, this squat building is adorned with an inscription reading "Unity makes strength," referring to the unification of the country in 1885, a few years after the defeat of the Turks. In front of the building is a monument to the Russians, who helped in the battle against the Turks, surmounted by an equestrian statue of Russian Tsar Alexander II. ⌧ *bul. Tsar Osvoboditel at pl. Narodno Subranie.*

🐾 ⑱ **Natsionalen Dvorets na Kulturata** (National Palace of Culture). The large modern building houses halls for conventions and cultural events. Its multilevel underpass is equipped with a train-ticket office, shops, restaurants, discos, and a bowling alley. The park to the north draws crowds of roller-blading, skateboarding, and bike-riding teenagers. Younger children skitter around in rented battery-operated minicars. ⌧ *Yuzhen Park, 1 pl. Bulgaria,* ☎ *02/5159–2841.*

⑫ **Natsionalen Etnografski Muzei** (National Ethnographic Museum). The former palace of the Bulgarian tsar currently houses displays of costumes, crafts, and tools illustrating the life of the country's rural areas as late as the 19th century. ⌧ *1 pl. Alexander Batenberg,* ☎ *02/87–41–91.* ⊙ *Wed.–Sun. 10:30–noon and 1:30–5:30.*

★ ③ **Natsionalen Istoricheski Muzei** (National History Museum). The museum has vast collections vividly illustrating the art history of Bulgaria, including priceless Thracian treasures, Roman mosaics, enameled jewelry from the First Bulgarian Kingdom (AD 600–AD 1018), and glowing religious art that survived the years of Ottoman oppression. ⌧ *2 bul. Vitosha,* ☎ *02/980–3889.* ⊙ *Weekdays 9:30–6:30.*

⑪ **Natsionalna Hudozhestvena Galeria** (National Art Gallery). In the west wing of the former tsar's palace is a collection of outstanding Bulgarian works, as well as a section devoted to foreign art. ⌧ *1 pl. Alexander Batenberg,* ☎ *02/89–28–41.* ⊙ *Tues.–Sun. 10:30–6.*

⑨ **Partiyniyat Dom** (The Party House). The former headquarters of the Bulgarian Communist party is prominent on a vast square. The imposing Stalinist-style building now houses the administrative offices of the parliament. The pole on top of the building looks bare without the gigantic red star it once supported. ⊠ *pl. Alexander Batenberg.*

① **Ploshtad Sveta Nedelya** (St. Nedelya Square). From this large, bustling, and open square in center of town, the shopping street Bulevardi Vitosha stretches south and Bulevardi Maria Luisa north. Vendors sell flowers, nuts, and toys, fortune-tellers use hamsters to predict your future, and Gypsies congregate to perform. The square is a good starting point for an exploration of the main sights. ⊠ *Bordered by bul. Vitosha, bul. Maria Luiza, and bul. Stamboliiski.*

④ **Rotonda Sveti Georgi** (Rotunda of St. George). On the northeast side of St. Nedelya Square, in the courtyard of the Sheraton Sofia Balkan Hotel, stands this unusual artifact. Built during the 4th century as a Roman temple, it has served as both a mosque and a church, and recent restoration has revealed medieval frescoes. ⊠ *2 pl. St. Nedelya.*

⑧ **Tsentralna Sinagoga** (Central Synagogue). This spectacular structure topped with an enormous dome is surrounded by five smaller domes and six towers. Constructed in 1909, it has recently been renovated after decades of disuse. ⊠ *ul. Ekzarh Yosif.* ⊙ *Daily 11–2, 4–6.*

⑤ **Tsentralnata Banya** (The Central Baths). For years this former Ottoman mineral bathhouse was in ruins. Renovations, begun in 1997, have restored the outside of the splendid building, and the domes gleam once again. The amazing interior is still closed, but repairs are under way and by the summer of '99, it should open again as a public bathhouse. At the spring in the adjacent park, Sofians line up to fill plastic bottles with hot mineral water, thought to cure respiratory diseases and ensure longevity. ⊠ *bul. Maria Luiza at ul. Triyaditsa.*

⑦ **Tsentralni Hali** (Central Market Hall). Once one of the most beautiful buildings in Sofia, the hall served as the central market during Communist times. Allowed to fall into ruin, is currently closed for renovations. ⊠ *bul. Maria Luiza at ul. Ekzarh Yosif.*

② **Tsurkva Sveta Nedelya** (St. Nedelya Church). This 19th-century church, with its huge dome ringed by small windows, dominates the south side of St. Nedelya Square. It is the latest in a series of churches that have occupied the site since the Middle Ages. Behind it is bulevard Vitosha, a lively pedestrian street with stores and cafés. ⊠ *pl. St. Nedelya.*

⑭ **Tsurkva Sveta Sofia** (Church of St. Sofia). This simple brick edifice dating from the 6th century became in the mid-14th century the namesake for the city of Sofia. ⊠ *North side of pl. Alexander Nevski.*

⑬ **Tsurkva Sveti Nikolai** (Church of St. Nicholas). This ornate Russian structure was erected between 1912 and 1914. ⊠ *bul. Tsar Osvoboditel at ul. Rakovski.*

Dining and Lodging

Suddenly Sofia is teeming with new restaurants and cafés, offering high-quality but inexpensive international cuisines. Still, if you can tolerate cigarette smoke and crowded seating, the most authentic eating experience is in a mehana, or tavern, where the music is loud and diners relax for hours over rakia and salads. For details and price-category definitions, *see* Dining *in* Bulgaria A to Z, *above.*

The hotels below are comfortable, with a high standard of cleanliness, and are open year-round. You shouldn't have trouble finding a room, even if you arrive in town without a reservation. If you want help, **Balkantourist** (⊠ 1 bul. Vitosha, ☎ 02/87–51–92) will book you in a state-owned hotel. For details and price-category definitions, *see* Lodging *in* Bulgaria A to Z, *above.*

$$$$ ✕ **Nad Aleyata, Zad Shkafut** (Beyond the Alley, Behind the Cupboard). In a beautiful old house this small, casually elegant restaurant serves such Bulgarian and European dishes as chicken Kiev, Russian salad, veal medallions, beef with béchamel sauce, and grilled pork stuffed with mushrooms and cheese. The staff speaks English, there are menus in English, and it is one of the few places that provide the kind of Western service that foreigners tend to expect—such as taking back a cold or undercooked dish. ✉ *31 ul. Budapeshta,* ☎ *02/83–55–81. Reservations essential. No credit cards.*

$$$$ ✕ **Rotiserie Nationale.** Brand new as of 1998, the Rotiserie eclipses all
★ other Sofia restaurants for high-caliber atmosphere and first-class cuisine. Expect to be greeted with a free cocktail, and to be escorted into a cellar outfitted for medieval dining decadence. You can feast on duck in orange sauce, succulent roast lamb, paté de foie gras, Caesar salads, and pears flambé as musicians stroll between the long banquet tables adorned with golden candelabras. Nowhere in the west can you experience such luxury, complete with carafes of excellent homemade wine, at the Rotiserie's price of less than $20 per person. You won't get past the host without reservations, a jacket, and dress shoes. ✉ *ul. Hristo Belchev at ul. Neofit Rilski,* ☎ *02/980–1717. Reservations essential. V.*

$$$$ ✕ **33 Stoli** (33 Chairs). Classy and intimate, this candlelit cellar has a changing menu specializing in such fine European cuisine as frogs' legs and Swiss fondue, as well as a wide range of appetizers and salads. The desserts are irresistible: Try *shokolade palachinka sus presni plodove* (chocolate crepe with fresh fruit). ✉ *14 ul. Assen Zlatarov,* ☎ *02/44–29–81. Reservations essential. No credit cards.*

$$$ ✕ **Bai Gencho.** A favorite with Sofians, this traditional Bulgarian mehana is a classic tavern with the added elegance of candles, fresh flowers on each table, and a basement fireplace. The *etspetsialitet na gotvachka za dvama* (mixed grill of sausages, steaks, and shish kebabs) is a carnivore's dream. ✉ *15 ul. Kniaz Alexander Dondukov,* ☎ *02/81–74–54. Reservations essential. No credit cards.*

$$$ ✕ **Mexicano (Casa del Arquitecto).** Pseudo-Mexican food and Cuban musicians make this quirky place popular. It also serves traditional Bulgarian dishes, including a spicy moussaka. In summer the outdoor candlelit patio, with its canopy of leafy trees, draws crowds who put up with the inflated prices and snobby service. ✉ *11 ul. Krakra,* ☎ *02/44–65–98 or 02/44–17–24. No credit cards.*

$$$ ✕ **Planet.** Launched with much fanfare in 1998, this Planet Hollywood rip-off is a brilliant, if amusing, Eastern European approximation of the real thing. It is one of the first places in Sofia to provide excellent food, top-notch live music, and a vibrant ambience. A favorite with local celebrities as well as visiting filmmakers (who appreciate the Hollywood film decor and location next door to the art cinema), the restaurant features a rolling appetizer cart heaped with caviar, smoked salmon, Bulgarian salads, and miniquiches as well as a menu that mixes Bulgarian specialties with Pan-European and American dishes. ✉ *ul. Ekzarh Josif 37,* ☎ *02/981–1713. V.*

$$ ✕ **Art Club Lucky.** A trendy café and renowned Mafia hangout, Art Club Lucky serves excellent pizzas, quiches, salads, and sandwiches. Bright windows facing lively ulitsa Tsar Shishman make it an ideal spot for a daytime cappuccino and delicious dessert while you people-watch. ✉ *38 ul. Gurko,* ☎ *02/980–77–12. No credit cards.*

$ ✕ **Baalbeck.** Local businesspeople like this Middle Eastern restaurant just off central Slaveikov Square. Though it's seedy in appearance, it prepares fast lunches of delicious falafel, hummus, and tabouli. Sit downstairs for a quick bite wrapped in pita bread to go, or dine upstairs if you want your *doner kebap* (a lamb, beef, or chicken skewer) on a plate. ✉ *6 ul. Vasil Levski. No credit cards.*

$$$$ 🏨 **Castle Hotel Hrankov.** This new hotel at the foot of Mt. Vitosha is a cross between a beige-and-white mountain chalet and a castle (with turrets and oversize doorways). It has windows facing the mountain, plush carpets, chandeliers, and a clean bright ambience as well as the best fitness center in the city, with squash courts, an Olympic-size swimming pool, tennis courts, and ski facilities. ✉ *53 ul. Krusheva Gradina, Dragalevtsi 1415,* ☎ *02/91–909,* 𝖥𝖠𝖷 *02/67–29–85. 360 rooms. 4 restaurants, pool. AE, DC, MC, V.*

$$$$ 🏨 **Hotel Kempinski Zografski–Sofia.** The towering, luxurious hotel is
★ designed in Japanese minimalist style. Guest rooms are rather basic: big beds, televisions, large bathrooms with bathtubs, mini-refrigerators, and desks. The hotel also has a shopping arcade and the most expensive restaurant in the entire country, Sakura, Bulgaria's one and only spot for sushi. ✉ *100 bul. James Bourchier, 1407,* ☎ *02/62–518,* 𝖥𝖠𝖷 *02/68–12–25. 454 rooms. 5 restaurants, pool. AE, DC, MC, V.*

$$$$ 🏨 **Hotel Maria Luiza.** The closest thing Sofia has to a modern yet cozy bed-and-breakfast, this upscale private hotel has comfortable, cheery rooms, and a friendly staff. The hotel is a narrow six stories, in a renovated stretch of turn-of-the-century buildings. Fruit baskets and chocolates greet guests in the rooms, windows face out toward the Banya Bashi Mosque, and the bathrooms have big, glass, Western-style showers. ✉ *29 bul. Maria Luiza, 1000,* ☎ *02/9–10–44,* 𝖥𝖠𝖷 *02/980–33–55. 21 rooms with bath or shower. Restaurant. AE, DC, MC, V.*

$$$$ 🏨 **Sheraton Sofia Hotel Balkan.** This first-class hotel has a central lo-
★ cation that is hard to match. Rooms are basic and businesslike with dark decor. Suites are more lavish, with brighter decor, bigger bathtubs, and views of the Plaza Sveta Nedelya. The excellent Viennese café has outdoor seating in summer. ✉ *5 pl. St. Nedelya, 1000,* ☎ *02/981–65–41,* 𝖥𝖠𝖷 *02/980–64–64. 187 rooms. 3 restaurants. AE, DC, MC, V.*

$$$ 🏨 **Bulgaria.** Despite its central location, this small hotel is quiet and old-fashioned. Dark and decorated with antiques, it is private, somber, and serious. Guests are more likely to be Eastern European business travelers than Westerners or tourists on holiday. ✉ *4 bul. Tsar Osvoboditel, 1000,* ☎ *02/87–19–77 or 02/87–01–91,* 𝖥𝖠𝖷 *02/88–41–77. 85 rooms with bath or shower. Restaurant. No credit cards.*

$$$ 🏨 **Gloria Palace.** Just south of the Plaza Sveta Nedelya stands the brightly painted purple Gloria Palace. With marble floors, rich purple curtains, and gold accents, the lobby reflects the decor of the ornate guest rooms. Large beds, fluffy towels, two stellar suite apartments, and room service presented with flair show that this new palace is striving to be fit for a king. ✉ *20 bul. Maria Luiza, 1000,* ☎ *02/980–7895,* 𝖥𝖠𝖷 *02/980–7894. 28 rooms. 2 restaurants. AE, DC, MC, V.*

$$ 🏨 **Grand Hotel Sofia.** This central, five-story Interhotel is comfortable, pleasant, and intimate. The decor is austere, and the amenities are basic: TV, phone, bath, and shower. Suites are better; some have office and kitchen areas. The Panorama Restaurant affords a fine view of Sofia but provides mechanical, unfriendly service. Still popular with former Communist leaders, the stately hotel transports you back to Bulgaria before MTV. ✉ *4 pl. Narodno Subranie, 1000,* ☎ *02/987–0602,* 𝖥𝖠𝖷 *02/988–13–08. 106 rooms. 2 restaurants. AE, DC, MC, V.*

$$ 🏨 **Rila.** A rather unattractive, squat structure in the center of the city, the Rila has basic rooms (bed, bath, TV, phone, desk, and shower) decorated in drab brown and orange. The hotel and its Bulgarian tavern, bingo parlor, and cafeteria are frequented mostly by other Eastern Europeans. ✉ *6 ul. Kaloyan, 1000,* ☎ *02/980–88–65,* 𝖥𝖠𝖷 *02/981–33–86. 138 rooms with bath or shower. Restaurant. AE, DC, MC, V.*

$$ 🖫 **Sun Hotel.** Cozy and comparatively inexpensive, this private hotel offers small but comfortable rooms and a business center in a beautiful old building with lots of character. It is directly across from the Lion's Bridge, Sofia's most notorious red-light district and hunting ground for pickpockets. ⊠ *89 bul. Maria Luiza, 1000,* ☎ *02/83–36–70,* FAX *02/83–53–89. 16 rooms with bath or shower. No credit cards.*

Nightlife and the Arts

The Arts

The standard of music in Bulgaria is high, whether it's performed in opera houses, or symphony halls, or at concerts of folk music, with its close harmonies and colorful stage displays. For a list of cultural events in Sofia, pick up a copy of *Sofia City Info Guide* at the American Express office (☞ Contacts and Resources *in* Sofia Essentials, *below*) or at hotels. Newsstands in Sofia now carry two helpful English-language newspapers: the *Sofia Independent* and the *Sofia Echo,* which publish current news and entertainment listings. For ballet and opera tickets, go to the **Sofia National Opera House** (⊠ 1 ul. Vrabcha at 58 bul. Dondukov, ☎ 02/987–7011). Buy concert and symphony tickets at the **Bulgarian Concert Hall** (⊠ 1 ul. Aksokov, ☎ 02/987–7656), where the Sofia Philharmonic Orchestra performs every Thursday night at 7:30.

There are a number of good art galleries: The **City Art Gallery** (⊠ 1 ul. Gen. Gurko, ☎ 02/87–21–81) has permanent exhibits of both 19th-century and modern Bulgarian paintings as well as changing exhibits showcasing contemporary artists. The art gallery of the **Sts. Cyril and Methodius International Foundation** (⊠ pl. Alexander Nevski, ☎ 02/80–44–37) has a collection of Indian, African, Japanese, and Western European paintings and sculptures. The art gallery of the **Union of Bulgarian Artists** (⊠ 6 ul. Shipka, ☎ 02/43–351) has exhibitions of contemporary Bulgarian art.

Most movie theaters show recent foreign films in their original languages with Bulgarian subtitles: **Dom na Kinoto** (House of Cinema; ⊠ 37 ul. Ekzarh Yosif, ☎ 02/88–06–76). **Serdika** (⊠ pl. Pametnik V. Levski, ☎ 02/43–17–97). **Vitosha** (⊠ 62 bul. Vitosha, ☎ 02/988–58–78).

Nightlife

BARS AND NIGHTCLUBS

The **Blaze Club** (⊠ 36 ul. Slavianska, ☎ 02/988-1423) is where the young and hip go for dance music after the bars on ulitsa Shishman shut their doors. **La Strada Jazz Club** (⊠ 4 ul. 6 Septemvri, ☎ no phone) draws a sophisticated, international crowd. The **703 Club** (⊠ 38 ul. Gurko, at ul. Tsar Shishman, ☎ 02/981–97–75) is a contemporary, mellow, evening bar for trendy twentysomethings. For live music, check out the lineup at **Swingin' Hall** (⊠ 8 bul. Dragan Tsankov, ☎ 02/66–63–23).

CASINOS

You can try your luck at the **International Casino Club Sheraton** (⊠ 5 pl. St. Nedelya, ☎ 02/981–5747). **Las Vegas** (Novotel Europa, ⊠ 131 bul. Maria Luiza, ☎ 02/931–00–72) also offers gambling.

DISCOS

Aliby (⊠ Borisova Gradina, ☎ no phone) is Sofia's hippest summertime club, where a college crowd gathers to dance to electronic music in a carnival atmosphere. For year-round all-night dancing action, try **Chervilo** (Lipsticks; ⊠ 48 bul. Tsar Osvoboditel, ☎ no phone) for beautiful people, salsa lessons, and sangria at the Wednesdays Latino party. **Neron** (⊠ 1 pl. Bulgaria, ☎ 02/80–34–38), in the National Palace of

Culture, is a huge, flashy underground disco popular with the local Mafia; metal detectors screen for guns as you enter, and you must check your mobile phone with your coat. **Spartacus** (✉ bul. Vasil Levski and bul. Tsar Osvoboditel, in underpass in front of Sofia University) is Sofia's first gay club, attracting the city's avant garde, both gay and straight.

Shopping

Department Stores

Bonjour (✉ 2 pl. Slaveikov; 93 ul. Alabin; 97 bul. Levski) stocks everything from food and wine to sporting goods, gifts, and cosmetics. The drab Tsentralen Universalen Magazin—**TSUM** (Central Department Store; ✉ 2 bul. Maria Luiza) is Sofia's biggest department store.

Gifts and Souvenirs

The **Bulgarian Folk Art Shop** (✉ 14 bul. Vitosha) carries an excellent assortment of national arts. **Prizma Magazin** (✉ 1 ul. Vasil Levski) offers many souvenirs. There is a good selection of arts and crafts at the shop of the **Union of Bulgarian Artists** (✉ 6 ul. Shipka). The outdoor **arts and crafts market** around Alexander Nevski Cathedral specializes in lace and linen at reasonable prices. For a large variety of **crafts and souvenirs,** visit the underpass between St. Nedelya Church and the Central Department Store.

For furs or leather, try the shops along bulevard Vitosha, such as the **Agressia Boutique** (✉ 59 bul. Vitosha), as well as those on bulevard Levski and bulevard Tsar Osvoboditel. Specialized Western boutiques are popping up: **Bally** (✉ 11 ul. Graf Ignatiev) has a new boutique. **Benetton** (12 pl. Slaveikov, ☎ 02/980–8709) is now a big presence on ploshtad Slaveikov. For men, **Hugo Boss** (✉ 1 ul. Legue) is a pricey alternative to Bulgarian designs.

For recordings of Bulgarian music, go to the underpass below the National Palace of Culture (☞ Exploring Sofia, *above*), where there are stalls selling music.

There are still some rare antiques deals in Sofia; ulitsa Rakovski is particularly full of antiques dealers. **Letostrui** (✉ 157 ul. Rakovski) is a reputable (if expensive) place to start your search. For excellent regional wines and tobacco, **Bai Gencho** (✉ 24, bul. Yanko Sakazov) has one of the best selections.

Shopping Districts

Bulevard Vitosha is a lively street with many upscale shops. Moderately priced and stylish boutiques are on **ulitsa Graf Ignatiev.** The quintessential shopping excursion is to the outdoor **Zhenski Pazaar** (✉ ul. Stefan Stambolov, bet ul. Tsar Simeon and bul. Slivnitsa), the women's market, so-called for the endless stalls worked by women from neighboring villages who hawk everything from homemade brooms and lace to produce and used electronic equipment.

Side Trips

Both Boyana (8 km/5 mi southwest of Sofia) and Dragalevtsi (9 km/5½ mi south of Sofia) are pleasant day trips to the Mt. Vitosha vicinity and can be reached by Bus 64 from Sofia.

Boyana

The little medieval **Boyana Church** is well worth a visit, as is the small, elegant restaurant of the same name, next door. The church is closed for restoration, but a replica, complete with copies of the exquisite 13th-century frescoes, is open to visitors. ✉ *ul. Belite Brezi.* ☉ *Daily approx. noon–4.*

$ ✕ Chepishev. At the foot of Mt. Vitosha, this eatery offers Bulgarian specialties and live folk music in the evenings. ⊠ *Boyana district, 25 ul. Kumata,* ☎ *02/56–50–35. No credit cards.*

Dragalevtsi

The **Dragalevtsi Monastery** stands in beech woods above the village. The complex is still used as a convent, but you can visit the 14th-century church with its outdoor frescoes. ⊠ *3 km (2 mi) past Vodenicharski Mehani Restaurant, Dragalevtsi.*

You can take chairlifts (beside Vodenicharski Mehani Restaurant) from Dragalevtsi to the delightful resort complex of **Aleko.** From Aleko you can continue on foot for about an hour to the top of **Rezen Maluk,** the nearest peak. There are well-marked walking and ski trails.

$$ ✕ Vodenicharski Mehani (Miller's Tavern). Made up of three old mills linked together, it stands at the foot of Mt. Vitosha. A folklore show and a menu of Bulgarian specialties provide an authentic atmosphere. Try the *gyuvech* (potatoes, tomatoes, peas, and onions baked in an earthenware dish). ⊠ *Dragalevtsi district (Bus 64), at southern end of town next to chairlift,* ☎ *02/67–10–21 or 02/67–10–01. No credit cards.*

Sofia Essentials

Arriving and Departing

BY CAR

From Greece, take E-20, passing through the checkpoint at Kulata; from Turkey, take E-5, passing through the checkpoint Kapitan-Andreevo. Border crossings to Romania are at Vidin on E-79 and at Ruse on E-97 and E-85.

BY PLANE

All international flights arrive at Sofia airport. For information on international flights, call ☎ 02/79–80–35 or ☎ 02/72–06–72; for domestic flights, ☎ 02/72–24–14.

Between the Airport and Downtown. Bus 84 from Sofia University serves the airport. At the airport taxi stand fares to the center are fixed at $20. If you speak some Bulgarian and know where you're going, private taxis outside the terminal will get you there for less than half the official price. Agree on the fare before starting. The **Tourist Service Travel Agency** (⊠ 127 ul. Rakovski, ☎ 02/988–8108) operates a $5 (or 9,000-leva) airport shuttle, with service *to* the airport *from* the city center only.

BY TRAIN

Tsentralna Gara (Central Station; ⊠ northern edge of city, ☎ 02/3–11–11 or 02/843–33–33). Ticket offices (⊠ in underpass below National Palace of Culture, ☎ 02/59-01-36; ⊠ 1 pl. Bulgaria, ☎ 02/59-01–36; Rila International Travel Agency, ⊠ 5 ul. Gurko, ☎ 02/87–07–77).

Getting Around

The main sights are concentrated in the center, so the best way to see the city is on foot.

BY BUS

Buses, trolleys, and trams run fairly often. Buy a ticket from the ticket stand near the streetcar stop and punch it into the machine on board. (Watch how other people do it.) For information (in Bulgarian), call ☎ 02/312–42–63 or 02/88–13–53.

BY RENTAL CAR

You can hire a car with a driver through Balkantourist, Balkantour Ltd., or your hotel (☞ Transportation *in* Bulgaria A to Z, *above*); you can also rent a car at the airport or from one of the city's car-rental agencies.

BY TAXI
Hail cabs in the street or at a stand—or ask the hotel to call one (☎ 2121, 1280, or 1282). Always take a taxi with a phone number written on the side. The rate should be 300 leva–400 leva per kilometer during the day, and 400 leva–500 leva at night. There is a 10-leva surcharge for taxis ordered by phone in Sofia (☎ 2121, 1280, or 1282). To tip, round out the fare by 5%–10%.

Contacts and Resources

EMBASSIES
U.S. (✉ 1 ul. Suborna, ☎ 02/980–52–41). **U.K.** (✉ 38 bul. Levski, ☎ 02/980–1220).

EMERGENCIES
Police (☎ 166). **Fire** (☎ 160). **Ambulance** (☎ 150). **Doctor: Pirogov Emergency Hospital** (☎ 02/5–15–31). **Pharmacy: Apteka** (✉ 5 pl. St. Nedelya, ☎ 02/87–59–89) is open daily 24 hours.

GUIDED TOURS
Orientation. Guided tours of Sofia and environs are arranged by Balkantourist or Balkantour Ltd. (☞ Visitor Information, *below*) or by major hotels. Among the possibilities are three- to four-hour tours of the principal city sights by car or minibus or a longer four- to five-hour tour that goes as far as Mt. Vitosha.

Side Trips. Balkantourist and Balkantour Ltd. (☞ Visitor Information, *below*) offer special-interest tours to monasteries, to museum towns, to sports areas and spas, and more.

TRAVEL AGENCIES
American Express (✉ 1 ul. Vasil Levski, ☎ 02/981–42–01). **Carlson Wagonlit Travel** (✉ 10 ul. Lege, ☎ 02/980–81–26). **Shipka Travel Agency** (✉ 6 ul. Sveta Sofia, ☎ 02/884–293).

VISITOR INFORMATION
Balkantourist (✉ 1 bul. Vitosha, ☎ 02/87–51–92). **Balkantour Ltd.** (✉ 27 bul. Stamboliiski, ☎ 02/988–55–43 or 02/987–72–33).

THE BLACK SEA COAST

Bulgaria's most popular resort area attracts visitors from all over Europe. Its sunny, sandy beaches are backed by the easternmost slopes of the Balkan Range and, to the south, by the Strandzha Mountains. Although the tourist centers tend to be huge, state-built complexes with a somewhat lean feel, they have modern amenities. Slunchev Bryag (Sunny Beach), the largest of the resorts, with more than 100 hotels, has plenty of children's amusements and play areas but is closed from November through April.

The historic port of Varna is a good center for exploration. A focal point of land and sea transportation for the region, it has museums, a variety of restaurants, and a lively nightlife in summer. The nearby fishing villages of Nesebâr and Sozopol to the south are more attractive and tranquil. Hotels tend to be scarce in these villages, but private lodgings are easily arranged through local accommodation agencies. Besides water sports, tennis and horseback riding are available.

Varna

Bulgaria's third-largest city is easily reached by rail (about 7½ hours by express) or road from Sofia. If you plan to drive, allow time to see

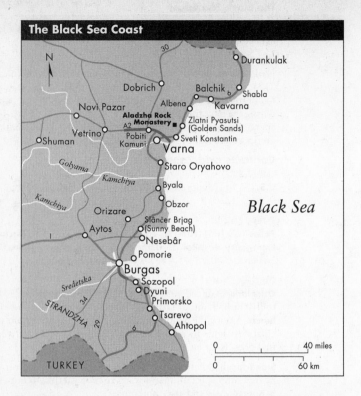

The Black Sea Coast

Durankulak

Dobrich · Balchik · Shabla

Albena · Kavarna

Novi Pazar

Aladzha Rock Monastery · Zlatni Pyasutsi (Golden Sands)

Vetrino · Pobiti Kamuni · Sveti Konstantin

Shuman

Varna

Golyama

Kamchiya · Staro Oryahovo

Kamchiya · Byala

Orizare · Obzor

Aytos · Slâncer Brjag (Sunny Beach)

Nesebâr

Pomorie

Burgas

Sredetska · Sozopol

Dyuni

STRANDZHA · Primorsko

Tsarevo

Ahtopol

TURKEY

Black Sea

0   40 miles

0   60 km

the **Pobiti Kamuni** (Stone Forest), monumental petrified tree trunks just off the Sofia–Varna road between Devnya and Varna. The ancient city of Varna, named Odyssos by the Greeks, became a major Roman trading center and is now an important shipbuilding and industrial city. With its beaches and tourism, Varna has become cosmopolitan; it even holds an international Film Festival each August.

The **Archeologicheski Muzei** (Archaeological Museum) is one of the great—if lesser known—museums of Europe. The splendid collection includes the world's oldest gold treasures from the Varna necropolis of the 4th millennium BC, as well as Thracian, Greek, and Roman artifacts and richly painted icons. ☒ *41 bul. Maria Luiza, in park,* ☎ *052/23–70–57 or 052/212–41.* ◷ *Tues.–Sat. 10–5.*

The pedestrian-only **ploshtad Nezavisimost** marks the center of town. To the east, **ulitsa Knyaz Boris I** is lined with shops, cafés, and restaurants. Take a look at the lavish murals in the monumental **Tsurkva Yspenie Bogorodichno** (Cathedral of the Assumption), built between 1880 and 1886. ☒ *pl. Mitropolit Simeon.* ◷ *May–Sept., daily 10–6; Oct.–Apr., daily 10–1 and 4–5:30.*

In the extensive and luxuriant **Primorski Park** (Seaside Park) are restaurants, an open-air theater, and the fascinating **Copernicus Astronomy Complex** (☎ 052/22–28–90), open weekdays 8–noon and 2–5, near the main entrance. ☒ *Southern end of bul. Primorski.*

Wander through the remains of the **Rimski Termi** (Roman Baths), dating from the 2nd through the 3rd centuries. Signs in English detail the various steps of the bath ritual. ☒ *ul. Han Krum just south of Tsurkva Sveta Bogoroditsa.*

The 1602 **Tsurkva Sveta Bogoroditsa** (Church of the Holy Virgin) is worth a look for its beautifully carved iconostasis. ⊠ *ul. Han Krum at ul. Knyaz Alexander Batenberg.*

Running north from the cathedral is **ulitsa Vladislav Varnenchik,** with shops, movie theaters, and eateries. In the city gardens stands the **starata chasovnikuh kula** (Old Clock Tower; ⊠ pl. Nezavisimost), built in 1880 by the Varna Guild Association. The magnificent Baroque **Stoyan Buchvarov Dramatichen Teatur** (Stoyan Bucharov Drama Theater; ⊠ pl. Nezavisimost) presents local and national theater productions, as well as opera and symphonic concerts.

The restored **ulitsa Stari Druzhi** is comfortingly lined with restaurants, taverns, and coffeehouses. The **Morski Muzei** (Marine Museum) has displays on the early days of navigation on the Black Sea and the Danube. ⊠ *2 bul. Primorski,* ☎ *052/22–26–55.* ☉ *Weekdays 8–4.*

$$ ✕ **Horizont.** This restaurant in the north end of Primorski Park has a wide selection of seafood as well as a view of the Black Sea from its outside tables. It's not too busy during the day, but at night the live Greek music draws a crowd. ⊠ *ul. Morska Gradina, just inside the front entrance to the park,* ☎ *052/88–45–30. No credit cards.*

$$ ✕ **Paraklisa.** Antiquated and charming, this unique garden dining spot has a friendly mehana atmosphere. The menu offers classic Bulgarian cuisine and a wide variety of rakias and wines. The *pulneni chushki* (peppers stuffed with cardamom-spiced pork and rice) are especially good, though the restaurant is best known for its delicious vegetarian dishes such as *tarator* (cold yogurt and cucumber soup) and *tikvichki sus kiselo mlyako* (panfried zucchini in buttery yogurt sauce). ⊠ *bul. Primorski s/n opposite Marine Museum,* ☎ *052/223–495. No credit cards.*

$$ ▥ **Cherno More.** The dark, four-story structure with a 22-story tower
★ stands on a bright, tree-lined street packed with cafés, bars, and shops. Although its decor is a bit dated, this is still one of the more modern hotels in Varna. Rooms are spartan: low beds, fading carpet, inexpensive wooden furniture, and small bathrooms. You can expect panoramic vistas from the top floors of the tower. ⊠ *33 bul. Slivnitsa, 9000,* ☎ *052/23–21–19,* 𝕱𝕬𝕏 *052/236–311. 230 rooms with bath or shower. 3 restaurants. AE, DC, MC, V.*

Albena

The newest and most modern Black Sea resort has a long, wide beach and clean sea. Some of its 35 hotels have extensive hydrotherapy facilities. The contemporary conveniences of this present-day tourist village come with a smaller dose of local charm, inflated prices, and menus and street signs in German and Russian. This is a resort for people seeking amenities but not necessarily the true Bulgaria.

$$ ✕ **Bambuka.** This open-air restaurant serves mainly grilled, picnic-style Bulgarian seafood and salads, but the dinner menu includes earthenware pots of *kavarma* (meat and vegetable stew) and *gyuvech* (stewed chunks of vegetables and lamb). ⊠ *bul. Bryag, off E-87, Albena exit,* ☎ *05722/24–04. No credit cards.*

$$$ ▥ **Albena Resort Dobrudzha.** The mineral-water health spa is the main attraction at this big, comfortable hotel. ⊠ *bul. Bryag, off E-87, Albena exit, 9620,* ☎ *05722/20–20,* 𝕱𝕬𝕏 *05722/22–16. 275 rooms. 3 restaurants, 2 pools. AE, DC, MC, V.*

Slunchev Bryag

This enormous popular resort, known as **Sunny Beach** in English, offers safe beaches, gentle tides, and facilities for children. It has a variety of beachside restaurants, kiosks, and playgrounds. Rapid Socialist construction left behind huge, ugly hotels that line a gorgeous crescent-shape beach.

$$ ✕ **Hanska Shatra** (Tent Inn). In the coastal hills above the sea, this combination restaurant and nightclub has been built to resemble the tents of the *Hans* (Bulgarian rulers) of old. It has entertainment well into the night. Take a taxi or have someone from your hotel draw a map. Like many Bulgarian beach resort restaurants, it is in the woods off poorly marked, unlit roads. ✉ *Off E-87, 4¼ km (3 mi) west of Slunchev Bryag,* ☎ *0554/28–11. No credit cards.*

$$ ✕ **Ribarska Hizha** (Fisherman's Hut). The lively beachside restaurant specializes in fried fish and has music until 1 AM. ✉ *Northern end of Slunchev Bryag,* ☎ *0554/21–86. No credit cards.*

$$ ☷ **Chaika.** Among the bargain hotels (though rates double June–September), the Chaika is cozy, with a sea-facing location, just off the cleanest and prettiest stretch of beach. It is close to the best restaurants and cafés, on the way out of town toward the quaint neighboring village of Nesebur. ✉ *Slunchev Bryag 8240,* ☎ *0554/23–08. 36 rooms with bath or shower. No credit cards.*

$$ ☷ **Globus.** Popular with tour groups and usually full, with a lively, hol-
★ iday atmosphere, the hotel is among the best in the resort. The rooms are brighter, cleaner, and more modern (with bigger, better-equipped bathroom facilities, such as enclosed showers) than those in many other hotels. ✉ *Slunchev Bryag 8240,* ☎ *0554/22–45. 100 rooms with bath or shower. Restaurant, pool. AE, DC, MC, V.*

★ Nesebâr

Just 10 minutes by bus or car south of Sunny Beach is a painter's and poet's retreat. It would be hard to find a town that exudes a greater sense of age than this ancient settlement, founded by the Greeks 25 centuries ago on a rocky peninsula reached by a narrow causeway. Among its vine-covered houses are richly decorated medieval churches. Don't miss the frescoes and the dozens of small, private, cozy pubs.

$$ ✕ **Kapitanska Sreshta.** The ancient charm of this old fisherman's restaurant makes it one of the most photographed buildings in Nesebur. Its authentic interior and top-quality seafood draw Bulgarian tourists, and the waiters in naval costumes provide friendly service to boisterous holiday crowds. ✉ *ul. Chaika,* ☎ *0554/34–29. No credit cards.*

Burgas

Bulgaria's second main port on the Black Sea, Burgas was until 1998 known chiefly as a chaotic, industrial, and polluted port town. Following massive local renovations starting in 1997, the city's two main streets, ulitsa Aleksandrovska and bulevard Bogoridi, intersect to form a quaint town center teeming with freshly painted outdoor cafés, bars, shops, and excellent seafood restaurants. Burgas is now famed for spectacular windsurfing as well as for the summer '98 Eastern European electronic music festival, "Metropolis," which drew tens of thousands of young people. An especially pleasant walk is through the **Primorska Gradina** (Seaside Park), with its expansive beach and pedestrian alleyways winding through the adjacent gardens. There still seems little reason to subject yourself to this summer seaside city during off-season when the streets are empty and cafés closed.

$$ ✕ **Cheren Peter.** This elegant and inexpensive hideaway is on the more sedate side of town. The cuisine is Bulgarian—everything from a big *ovcharska salata* (shepherd salad: tomatoes, cucumbers, mushrooms, peppers, feta cheese, and boiled eggs) to moussaka, grilled meats, and dessert crepes. ✉ *26 ul. Gurko,* ☎ *no phone. No credit cards.*

$$ ⊞ **Bulgaria.** Rooms at this high-rise Interhotel in the center of town are modern but basic, with televisions, showers, and desks. Popular with tour groups and business travelers, it has its own nightclub and a restaurant set in a mock winter garden. ⊠ *21 ul. Aleksandrovska, 8000,* ☎ *056/4–28–20,* ℻ *056/4–72–91. 200 rooms with bath or shower. Restaurant. DC, MC, V.*

★ **Sozopol**

Nestled in Byzantine ruins, the fishing port of Sozopol, with narrow, cobbled streets leading down to the harbor, was Apollonia, the oldest of the Greek colonies in Bulgaria. It is now a popular haunt for Bulgarian and, increasingly, foreign writers and artists, who find private accommodations (through Lotos, ⊠ ul. Ropotamo, ☎ 05514/429) in the rustic Black Sea–style houses, so picturesque with their rough stone foundations and unpainted wood slats on the upper stories. It also hosts the **Apollonia Arts Festival** each September, which draws musicians, playwrights, painters, dancers, and actors from all of Europe.

Black Sea Coast Essentials

Getting Around

Buses make frequent runs up and down the coast. **Cars** and **bicycles** can be rented. A regular **boat** service travels the Varna–Sveti Konstantin (St. Konstantin)–Zlatni Pyasutsi (Golden Sands)–Albena–Balchik route.

Guided Tours

Excursions can be arranged from all resorts. There are bus excursions to Sofia from Albena and Slânčer Brjag; a one-day bus and boat trip along the Danube from neighboring resorts Zlatni Pyasutsi and Sveti Konstantin, as well as Albena; and a multiday bus tour of Bulgaria, including the Valley of Roses, departing from Zlatni Pyasutsi, Sveti Konstantin, and Albena. All tours are run by local tourist agencies (☞ Visitor Information, *below,* or check with your hotel information desk). In Varna, the recently launched **Adonis 45 Travel Agency** (⊠ 51 ul. Slivnitsa, ☎ 052/603–051, ℻ 052/658–215) arranges individual tours.

Visitor Information

Albena (☎ 05722/27–21). **Burgas** (Hotel Primorets, ⊠ 1, ul. Knyaz Batenberg, ☎ 056/4–54–96). **Nesebâr** (⊠ 8 ul. Chaika, ☎ 0554/58–30). **Slunchev Bryag** (☎ 0554/23–25). **Varna** (Varnenski Brjag, ⊠ 3 ul. Moussala, ☎ 052/22–55–24 or 052/22–22–72).

INLAND BULGARIA

Inland Bulgaria, despite limited hotel facilities and sometimes complicated public transportation, has its own distinctive flavor. Wooded and mountainous, the interior is dotted with attractive museum villages (entire settlements listed for preservation because of their historic cultural value) and ancient towns. The foothills of the Balkan Range, Stara Planina (old mountains), lie parallel to the lower Sredna Gora Mountains, with the verdant Rozova Dolina (Valley of Roses) between them. In the Balkan Range is the ancient capital of Veliko Turnovo; south of the Sredna Gora stretches the fertile Thracian plain, home to Bulgaria's second-largest city, Plovdiv. Between Sofia and Plovdiv lies the enchanting old town of Koprivshtitsa. To the south, in the Rila Mountains, is Borovets, the first of the mountain resorts.

★ **Koprivshtitsa**

One of Bulgaria's showpiece villages, Koprivshtitsa is set in mountain pastures and pine forests, about 3,050 ft up in the Sredna Gora range. It is 105 km (65 mi) from Sofia, reached by a minor road south from

Inland Bulgaria

the Sofia–Kazanluk expressway. Koprivshtitsa became a prosperous trading center with close ties to Istanbul during the 19th century. The architecture of this period, called the National Revival or Bulgarian Renaissance style, is marked by carved woodwork on broad verandas and overhanging eaves, brilliant colors, and courtyards with studded wooden gates. For centuries artists, poets, and wealthy merchants have made their homes here, and many of the historic houses are now open as museums.

$ ✕ **Byaloto Kouche.** Uphill from the town square, this intimate, family-owned restaurant is decorated in the National Revival style and offers traditional Bulgarian dishes. ✉ *ul. Generilo 2,* ☎ *07184/22–50. No credit cards.*

$ 🏠 **Hotel Byaloto Kouche.** This charming inn offers rustic rooms furnished in the traditional National Revival style, with woven rugs and low beds. One room has a fireplace, but none have adjoining baths. ✉ *ul. Generilo 2, 2090,* ☎ *07184/22–50. 6 rooms without bath. Restaurant. No credit cards.*

$ 🏠 **Koprivshtitsa.** This good-value hotel, popular with vacationing Bulgarians, is just across the river from the center of town. ✉ *12 ul. G. Benkovski, 2090,* ☎ *07184/21–82. 30 rooms with bath or shower. No credit cards.*

Troyan

Troyan is a tiny, sleepy, old town. A few kilometers from town stands the **Troyanski Monastir** (Troyan Monastery), built during the 1600s in the heart of the mountains. Its church was painstakingly remodeled during the 19th century, and its icons, wood carvings, and frescoes are classic examples of National Revival art. Here at the monastery, monks still brew the nation's most famous brand of rakia, *Troyankso Slivova*. ✉ *5 km (3 mi) east of Troyan.* ☉ *Daily 8–6.*

Veliko Turnovo

This town of panoramic vistas, about 200 km (124 mi) northeast of Sofia, rises up against steep mountain slopes through which the Yantra River runs its jagged course. From the 12th through the 14th centuries, Veliko Turnovo was the capital of the Second Bulgarian Kingdom. Damaged by repeated Ottoman attacks, and again by an earthquake in 1913, it has been reconstructed and is now a museum city of marvelous relics. Ideally, you should begin at a vantage point above the town in order to get an overview of its design and character.

In a large, National Revival–style house, the **Muzei Vuzrazhdanei Uchereditelno Subranie** (Museum of the National Revival and Constitutional Assembly) has three floors of exhibits. The first floor holds a collection of medieval icons and local craftwork; the second has photos and documents detailing the national liberation movement; the third houses the hall where the first Bulgarian parliament drafted the country's first constitution. ⊠ *2 ul. Nicola Picolo,* ☏ *062/2–98–21.* ⊙ *Wed.–Sun. 8–noon and 1–5.*

☺ **Tsarevets,** a hill on the east end of town, almost encircled by the Yantra River, is where the palace and patriarchate of the Second Bulgarian Kingdom stood. The area is under restoration, and steep paths and stairways provide opportunities to view the extensive ruins of the royal palace. Thursday through Saturday in the summer, the hill is illuminated at 10 PM with a spectacular laser light show. Every day during the summer on the bridge leading to the castle ruins, surreal, life-size puppets enact scenes relating to the castle and Bulgarian history. The prominent feature on the south side of Tsarevets is **Balduinova Kula** (Baldwin's Tower), the 13th-century prison of Baldwin of Flanders, onetime Latin emperor of Constantinople. On the west side of the hill stands the 13th-century **Tsurkva na Chetirideset Muchenitsi** (Church of the Forty Martyrs), with its Turnovo-school frescoes and two inscribed columns, one dating from the 9th century. On the north side of Tsarevets, the **Tsurkva na Sveti Petur i Pavel** (Church of Sts. Peter and Paul) has vigorous murals both inside and out. Across the river to the west, reached by a bridge near the Forty Martyrs, the restored **Tsurkva na Sveti Dimitur** (Church of St. Dimitrius) was built on the spot where the Second Bulgarian Kingdom was proclaimed in 1185.

Near the center of town is **ulitsa Samovodene,** lined with restored crafts workshops—a fascinating place to linger and a good place to find souvenirs, Turkish candy, or a charming café.

$ ✕ **Bolyarska Izba** (Bolyar's Hut). In the center of the busy district just north of the river, this unpretentious eatery is a favorite with locals, many of whom order the house *sarmi* (vine leaves stuffed with pork). ⊠ *ul. St. Stambolov,* ☏ *no phone. No credit cards.*

$$$$ ⛨ **Veliko Turnovo.** Right in the middle of the most historic part of the town, this modern Interhotel offers some of the best facilities in its class. Rooms, though not bright, are big and airy with all the amenities, such as televisions, phones, desks, and modern bathrooms. ⊠ *2 ul. Al. Penchev, 5000,* ☏ *062/3–05–71. 195 rooms with bath or shower. 2 restaurants, pool. AE, DC, MC, V.*

$$ ⛨ **Etur.** Despite its dark and state-owned atmosphere, this moderate-size hotel is still a good value and the best base for sightseeing within the city. ⊠ *1 ul. Ivailo, 5000,* ☏ *062/268–51. 80 rooms with shower. Restaurant. AE, DC, MC, V.*

$$ ⛨ **Yantra.** The Yantra has some of the best views in town, looking across the river to Tsarevets. It also has a decent restaurant with a balcony that provides the best vantage point on the great vista. ⊠ *1 pl. Vel-*

chova Zavera, 5000, ☎ *062/2–03–91,* FAX *062/218–07. 60 rooms, most with shower. Restaurant. AE, DC, MC, V.*

Etur

This museum village sits on the banks of the Sivek, a small branch of the Yantra River, 9 km (6 mi) south of Gabrovo. The mill here is still powered by a stream, and local craftspeople continue to be trained in traditional skills. ⊠ *ul. Aprilov.*

Shipka Pass

This 49-km (30-mi) stretch of highway through treacherous and majestic mountain terrain between Kazanluk and Gabrovo is 225 km (140 mi) east of Sofia at the eastern edge of the Sredna Gora mountains. A mighty monument on the peak honors the thousands of Russian soldiers and Bulgarian volunteers who died here in 1877, during the Russian-Turkish Wars.

Kazanluk

In this town at the eastern end of the Valley of Roses, you can trace the history of rose cultivation, Bulgaria's oldest industry. Each June the town hosts the Festival of Roses, which features folk dancing, art exhibits, and rose-picking demonstrations.

★ Plovdiv

Bustling with college students and new businesses, Bulgaria's second-largest city, Plovdiv, is one of the oldest settlements in Europe and now a major industrial, cultural, and intellectual center. Closed to cars to preserve the original cobble work, the breathtaking, lantern-lit **starata grad** (old town) lies on the hillier southern side of the Maritsa River.

Below the medieval gateway of Hisar Kapiya, the **Georgiadieva Kushta** (Georgiadi House) is a grandiose example of National Revival–style architecture; it also contains a small museum dedicated to the April 1876 uprising against the Turks. ⊠ *1 ul. Starinna.* ☉ *Wed.–Sun. 9:30–12:30 and 2–5.*

The old **Kapana District** (⊠ northwest of pl. Stamboliiski) has narrow, winding streets lined with restored shops and cafés. The exquisite hilltop **Rimski amfiteatur** (Roman amphitheater), only discovered and excavated in 1981, has been sensitively renovated. In summer the theater is used for dramatic and musical performances. ⊠ *ul. Tsar Ivailo.*

The **Natsionalen Archeologicheski Muzei** (National Archaeological Museum) holds a replica of the 4th-century BC Panajuriste Gold Treasure and a wealth of ancient Thracian artifacts from Plovdiv and the surrounding region. ⊠ *1 pl. Suedinenie,* ☎ *032/55-82-98.* ☉ *Tues.–Sun. 9–12:30 and 2–5:30.*

The **Natsionalen Etnografski Muzei** (National Ethnographic Museum) in the former home of a Greek merchant, Arghir Kuyumdzhioglu, is an elegant example of the National Revival style, which made its first impact in Plovdiv. The museum is filled with artifacts from that fertile period. ⊠ *2 ul. Chomakov,* ☎ *032/22–56–56.* ☉ *Tues.–Sun. 9–noon and 2–5.*

The steep, narrow **ulitsa Strumna** is lined with workshops and boutiques, some reached through little courtyards. Beyond the railings and past the jewelry and leather vendors in the center of Stamboliiski Square stand the remains of a 2nd-century **Rimski stadion** (Roman stadium). ⊠ *ul. Saborna and ul. Knyaz Alexander I.*

$$$ ✕ **Puldin.** On a hill in the center of old town, this folk restaurant has a romantic subterranean dining room complete with a waterfall and live piano music. Order the excellent *pulneni chushki* (peppers stuffed with meat, spices, and rice) served with yogurt for a taste of Bulgarian home cooking. ⊠ *3 ul. Knyaz Tseretelev,* ☎ *032/23–17–20. AE, DC, MC, V.*

$$ ✕ **Alafrangite.** This charming mehana is in a restored 19th-century house with carved wood ceilings and a vine-covered courtyard in the old part of town. One of the specialties is *kuopoolu* (vegetable puree of baked eggplant, peppers, and tomatoes). ⊠ *17 ul. Nektariev,* ☎ *032/22–98–09 or 032/26–95–95. No credit cards.*

$$ ✕ **Restaurant Starata Kushta.** In a renovated Renaissance house in the old quarter, this restaurant presents such traditional fare as *cirene po shopski* (hot feta cheese with herbs, tomatoes, and peppers in an earthenware pot). ⊠ *19 ul. Nektariev,* ☎ *032/26–68–42. No credit cards.*

$$$ ▦ **Trimontsium.** This central Interhotel built during the 1950s is comfortable and ideal as a base for exploring the old town. ⊠ *2 ul. Kapitan Raicho, 4000,* ☎ *032/2–34–91. 163 rooms with bath or shower. Restaurant. AE, DC, MC, V.*

$$ ▦ **Hotel S and M.** This brand-new family-run bed-and-breakfast (opened in 1997) just outside the old town has bright, airy rooms with bay windows and private baths. ⊠ *28 Hristo Duckmedjiev, 4000,* ☎ *032/26–01–35. 4 rooms. Café. AE, MC, V.*

$$ ▦ **Novotel Plovdiv.** The large, modern, and well-equipped Novotel lies across the river from the main town, near the fairgrounds. ⊠ *2 ul. Zlatyu Boyadzhiev, 4000,* ☎ *032/558–92,* ℻ *032/551–979. 322 rooms. Restaurant, pool. AE, DC, MC, V.*

Borovets

Slightly more than 4,300 ft up the northern slopes of the Rila Mountains, this is an excellent walking center and winter-sports resort. It is well equipped with hotels, folk-style taverns, and ski schools. The winding mountain road leads back to Sofia, 70 km (43 mi) from here, past **Iskur Reservoir,** the largest lake in the country.

Rila

★ **Rilski Monastir** (Rila Monastery), founded by Ivan of Rila in the 10th century, lies in a steep, forested valley past the village of Rila. The monastery has suffered so frequently from fire that most of it is now a grand National Revival reconstruction, although a rugged 14th-century tower has survived. The striking mountain retreat is home to flocks of storks. Part of the complex has been turned into a museum, and some of the monks' cells are now guest rooms. You can see 14 small chapels with frescoes from the 15th and 17th centuries, a lavishly carved altarpiece in the new Church of the Assumption, the sarcophagus of Ivan of Rila, icons, and ancient manuscripts.

Inland Bulgaria Essentials

Getting Around

Rail and bus services cover all parts of inland Bulgaria, but the best bet is to rent a car. To hire a driver, check with Balkantourist or Balkantour Ltd. (☞ Visitor Information *in* Sofia Essentials, *above*).

Guided Tours

Organized tours set out from Sofia, each covering different points of interest. Check with your hotel information desk or with Balkantourist or Balkantour Ltd. (☞ Visitor Information *in* Sofia Essentials, *above*).

Visitor Information

Plovdiv (Puldin Tours, ⊠ 106 bul. Bulgaria, ☎ 032/55–38–48). **Veliko Turnovo** (E.A.D. Yantra, ⊠ 2 ul. Al. Penchev, ☎ 062/3–05–71).

7 CYPRUS

THE REPUBLIC OF CYPRUS, NORTHERN CYPRUS

The Mediterranean island of Cyprus was once a center for the cult of the Greek goddess Aphrodite. Wooded and mountainous, with a 751-km-long (466-mi-long) coastline, Cyprus lies just off the southern coast of Turkey. Fruits and fish are plentiful. The summers are hot and dry, the springs gentle. Winter snow in the Troodos Mountains permits skiing in the morning and sunbathing on a beach in the afternoon.

Cyprus's strategic position in the eastern Mediterranean has made it subject to regular invasions by powerful empires. Greeks, Phoenicians, Assyrians, Egyptians, Persians, Romans, and Byzantines—all have ruled here. In the Middle Ages King Richard I of England took Cyprus from the Byzantine Empire by force and gave it to Guy of Lusignan. Guy's descendants ruled the island until the late 15th century, when it was annexed by the Venetians. From the 16th century through the 19th century it was ruled by the Turks. It became a British colony in 1914.

Vestiges of the diverse cultures that have ruled here dot the island. Many fortifications built by the Crusaders and the Venetians still stand. The tomb of the prophet Muhammad's aunt (Hala Sultan Tekke), on the shore of the great salt lake, is one of Islam's most important shrines. A piece of the true cross is said to be kept in the monastery of Stavrovouni, and Paphos has the remains of a pillar to which St. Paul was allegedly tied when he was beaten for preaching Christianity.

The upheavals are not over. Following independence in 1960, the island became the focus of contention between Greeks and Turks. Currently some 80% of the population is Greek and 12.3% Turkish. Since 1974 Cyprus has been divided by a thin buffer zone—occupied by United Nations (UN) forces—between the Turkish Cypriot north and the Greek Cypriot south. The zone cuts right through the capital city of Nicosia. Talks aimed at uniting the communities into one bizonal federal state have been going on for years. Both communities have comfortable tourist facilities, but entry through the northern part, which is recognized only by Turkey, makes access to the south impossible.

Cyprus (Kypros, Kibrís)

THE REPUBLIC OF CYPRUS

The Republic of Cyprus A to Z

Customs

Duty-free allowances are: 250 grams of tobacco, 1 liter of spirits or 2 liters of wine, 0.6 liters of perfume, and up to C£100 in other goods.

The export of antiques and historic artifacts is strictly forbidden unless a license is obtained from the Department of Antiquities in Nicosia.

Dining

The top hotels offer a good variety of both local and international food at competitive prices; large buffets are especially popular. Meals in local restaurants or tavernas usually start with a variety of *mezes* (appetizers), followed by kebabs, dolmas, stews, fresh fish, and various lamb dishes. Meals end with fruit or honey pastries and Greek coffee. By law, all establishments must display a menu with government-approved prices, which include the 10% service charge and 8% value-added tax. Food is relatively cheap and the quality is good.

RATINGS

Prices are for a three-course meal for one person, not including drinks or tip.

CATEGORY	COST
$$$	over C£12
$$	C£6–C£12
$	under C£6

Casual dress is acceptable in most restaurants in Cyprus, regardless of price category, although those in major hotels may require more formal clothing.

Embassies or High Commissions

U.S. (⊠ Gonia Metochiou and Ploutarchou, Egkomi, 2406 Lefkosia, Nicosia, ☎ 02/476100, 𝖥𝖠𝖷 02/465944). **Consulate of Canada** (⊠ 4 Annis Komninis, Nicosia, ☎ 02/766699, 𝖥𝖠𝖷 02/459096). **U.K. British High Commission** (⊠ Alexandrou Palli, Box 1978, Nicosia, ☎ 02/473131–7, 𝖥𝖠𝖷 02/367198).

Emergencies

Police, Ambulance, and **Fire Brigade** (☎ 199). **Doctor:** Nicosia General Hospital (☎ 02/451111); Limassol Hospital (☎ 05/330333); Paphos Hospital (☎ 06/240111). **Pharmacies** (for information in English about those open late and on holidays, ☎ 1412 in Nicosia, 1415 in Limassol, 1414 in Larnaca, or 1416 in Paphos).

Guided Tours

Licensed guides can be hired for half-day (starting at about C£29) and full-day (starting at C£46) tours; a list of licensed guides is available from the Cyprus Tourism Orgnization. Try **National Sightseeing Tours** (⊠ c/o Louis Tourist Agency, 54–58 Evagoras Ave., Nicosia, ☎ 02/442114) for half-day and full-day trips—expect to pay C£7–C£19. Night tours typically include dinner at a local taverna, folk dancing, and bouzouki music. In seaside resorts hotels or travel agencies can arrange coastal cruises.

Language

Greek is the main language, but English is widely spoken in hotels, tavernas, and other tourist haunts. Off the beaten path, sign language may have to do.

The Republic of Cyprus government has carried out a controversial exercise to spell all place names as they are pronounced in Greek. Hence Nicosia becomes Lefkosia, Larnaca is Larnaka, Limassol is Lemesos, and Paphos is Pafos. Internationally, the original names remain, and in Cyprus both spellings are currently in use. To avoid confusion we have retained the original spellings.

Lodging

All hotels listed have private bath or shower, but check when making reservations. Most have at least partial air-conditioning. In resort areas many hotel/apartments have kitchens.

Prices are for two people sharing a double room and include breakfast.

CATEGORY	COST
$$$$	over C£80
$$$	C£60–C£80
$$	C£40–C£60
$	under C£40

Mail

A 20-gram letter to the United States costs 36¢, a postcard, 31¢. To Europe a 20-gram letter costs 31¢, and a postcard 26¢. Post offices are open weekdays 7:30–1:30 and 3–5 (except Wednesday), and Saturday 9–11. Stamps are also sold at hotels, newsstands, and kiosks. Every item of mail must carry a separate 1¢ refugee stamp, which is included in the above costs.

Money Matters

COSTS

A cup of coffee or tea costs Cyprus 60¢–C£1; a glass of beer 75¢–C£1; a kebab around C£1.25–C£1.75; a bottle of local wine C£1.75–C£4.50. Admission to museums and galleries costs 50¢–C£1.

CURRENCY

The monetary unit in the Republic of Cyprus is the Cyprus pound (C£), which is divided into 100 cents. There are notes of C£20, C£10, C£5, and C£1 and coins of 50, 20, 10, 5, 2, and 1 Cyprus cents. At press time (summer 1999) the rate of exchange was C£0.55 to the U.S. dollar, C£0.38 to the Canadian dollar, C£0.87 to the pound sterling, C£0.36 to the Australian dollar, C£0.29 to the New Zealand dollar, and C£0.73 to the Irish punt.

TIPPING

A service charge of 10% and an 8% VAT are automatically included in all bills. If service has been especially good, add 5%.

National Holidays

January 1; January 6 (Epiphany); March 13 (Green Monday); March 25 (Greek National Day); April 1 (Greek Cypriot National Day); April 28–May 1 (Greek Orthodox Easter); May 1 (Labor Day); June 19 (Pentecost Monday); August 15 (Assumption); October 1 (Cyprus Independence Day); October 28 (Greek National Day); December 24, 25, 26.

Opening and Closing Times

Banks are open September–June, weekdays 8:30–12:30 and Monday afternoons 3:15–4:45; July and August, weekdays 8:15–12:30. Some have special afternoon tourist services and will cash traveler's checks weekdays 3–6 in winter, 4–7 in summer, and Saturday 8:30–noon year-round. **Museum** hours vary; it pays to check ahead. Generally, museums are closed for lunch and on Sunday. Most ancient monuments are open from dawn to dusk. **Shops** open between 8 and 9 and close at 6 PM November–March, 7 PM April–May and mid-September–October, 7:30 PM June–mid-September. Between June and mid-September, they close for the afternoon summer break 1–4, and throughout the year at 2 on Wednesday and Saturday, and all day Sunday. In tourist areas shops may stay open late and on Sunday in summer.

Telephoning

COUNTRY CODE

The country code for Cyprus is 357.

INTERNATIONAL CALLS

To reach an **AT&T** long-distance operator, dial 080–90010; for **MCI,** 080–90000; for **Sprint,** 080–90001. Public phones may require the deposit of a coin or use of a phone card when you call these services.

LOCAL CALLS

Pay phones take 2¢, 5¢, 10¢, and 20¢ coins, but most popular these days are those taking Telecards. These have values of C£3, C£5, or C£10 and can be purchased at post offices, banks, souvenir shops, and kiosks. Cheaper rates apply from 10 PM to 8 AM and all day Sunday. For telephone information dial 192 in all towns.

Transportation

BY BOAT

Passenger ships connect Cyprus (Limassol and Larnaca) with various Greek, Italian, Egyptian, and Middle Eastern ports.

This is the cheapest form of transportation in urban areas; the fare is 40¢. Buses operate every half hour and cover an extensive network. In Nicosia, buses run until 7:30 PM (6:30 PM in winter). In tourist areas during the summer services are extended until midnight. Intercity bus fares range between C£2 and C£3. For information on the Nicosia–Limassol–Paphos route, call 02/463989; for the Limassol–Larnaca–Ayia Napa route, dial 04/654890.

BY CAR

An international or national license is acceptable in Cyprus. Drive on the left. Main roads between large towns are good. Minor roads can be unsurfaced, narrow, and winding. Gas costs about 38¢ per liter. Cars may be rented from C£17 per day, less off season.

BY PLANE

There are no direct flights between Cyprus and the United States. Cyprus Airways and British Airways fly direct from London to Larnaca and Paphos. Cyprus Airways also operates from Manchester and many Continental and Mediterranean cities.

BY PRIVATE TAXI

Private taxis operate 24 hours throughout the island. They are generally very cheap within towns but far more expensive than service taxis between towns. Telephone from your hotel or hail one in the street. Urban taxis have an initial charge of 65¢ and charge 22¢ per km (½ mi) in the daytime, more at night. Drivers are bound by law to display and run a meter. In-town journeys range from C£1.50 to about C£3.

BY SERVICE TAXI

Shared taxis accommodate four to seven passengers and are a cheap, fast, and comfortable way to travel between the main towns: Nicosia, Limassol, Larnaca, and Paphos. Tariffs are from C£1.65 to C£4.25. Seats must be booked by phone, and passengers may embark/disembark anywhere within the town. The taxis run every half hour (Monday–Saturday 5:45 AM–6:30 PM). Sunday service is less frequent and must be booked one day ahead. Contact **Karydas** (☎ 02/463126), **Kypros Taxi Office** (☎ 02/464811), or **Kyriakos** (☎ 02/444141).

Visas

No visas are necessary for holders of valid passports from the United States, Canada, the United Kingdom, or mainland European countries.

VISITOR INFORMATION

Nicosia (national office, ✉ 19 Limassol Ave., ☎ 02/337715, FAX 02/331644; local, ✉ Laiki Yitonia, ☎ 02/444264). **Larnaka** (✉ Democratias Sq., ☎ 04/654322). **Limassol** (✉ Spyros Araouzos St., ☎ 05/362756). **Paphos** (✉ Gladstone St., ☎ 06/232841).

Weather

The tourist season runs throughout the year, though prices tend to be lower from November through March. Spring and fall are best, usually warm enough for swimming but not uncomfortably hot.

CLIMATE

The rainy season is in January and February, and it often snows in the highest parts of the Troodos Mountains from January through March. January and February can be cold and wet; July and August are always very hot and dry. The following are the average daily maximum and minimum temperatures for Nicosia.

Jan.	59F	15C	May	85F	29C	Sept.	92F	33C
	42	5		58	14		65	18
Feb.	61F	16C	June	92F	33C	Oct.	83F	28C
	42	5		65	18		58	14
Mar.	66F	19C	July	98F	37C	Nov.	72F	22C
	44	7		70	21		51	10
Apr.	75F	24C	Aug.	98F	37C	Dec.	63F	17C
	50	10		69	21		45	7

Exploring the Republic of Cyprus

Nicosia

The capital is twice divided. Its picturesque Old City is contained within 16th-century Venetian fortifications that separate it from the wide, tree-lined streets, large hotels, and high-rises of the modern section. The second division is political and more noticeable. The so-called Green Line (set up by the UN) divides the island between the Republic of Cyprus and Turkish-occupied Northern Cyprus. It is possible, at press time (spring 1999), to arrange a day trip from the Greek to the Turkish sector through the official checkpoint in Nicosia (Ledra Palace), though it is essential to return by 5 PM. There is no official representation from countries other than Turkey in the northern sector so contact your consulate before crossing the line to confirm safety.

★ In the Greek sector **Laiki Yitonia,** at the southern edge of the Old City, is an area of winding alleys and traditional architecture that is being completely renovated. Among its important sites is the **Archbishopric,** which houses several museums. Tavernas, cafés, and crafts workshops line the shaded, cobbled streets. Just to the west lies Ledra Street, where modern shops alternate with yet more crafts shops. Head north to visit the tiny Greek Orthodox **Tripiotis** church (⊠ Solonos 47–49), with its ornately carved golden iconostasis and silver-covered icons, which dates from 1690.

The **Leventis Municipal Museum of Nicosia** traces the city's history from 3000 BC to the present, with exhibits on crafts and daily life. ⊠ *17 Ippocratous St.,* ☎ *02/451475.* ☒ *Free.* ☉ *Tues.–Sun. 10–4:30.*

Housed in a wing of the archiepiscopal palace built in 1960 in neo-Byzantine style, the **Archbishop Makarios III Cultural Foundation** consists of the **Byzantine Art Museum,** with fine displays of icons spanning 1,000 years, and the **Greek War of Independence Gallery,** with a collection of maps, paintings, and mementos of 1821. ⊠ *Archbishop Kyprianou Sq.,* ☎ *02/430008.* ☉ *Weekdays 9–4:30, Sat. 8–12.*

The **Museum of the National Struggle** has dramatic displays of the Cypriot campaigns against the British from 1955 to 1959. ⊠ *Archbishop Kinyras 7,* ☎ *02/304550.* ☉ *Weekdays 8–2:30 and 3–6.*

★ The **Cyprus Folk Art Museum,** housed in the 14th-century part of the archiepiscopal palace, has demonstrations of ancient weaving techniques and displays of ceramics and olive and wine presses. ⊠ *Archbishop Kyprianou Sq.,* ☎ *02/432578.* ☉ *Weekdays 8–2:30 and 3–5.*

Don't miss **Ayios Ioannis** (St. John's) Cathedral, built in 1662 within the courtyard of the archiepiscopal palace. Look for the 18th-century wall paintings illustrating important moments in Cypriot religious history and including a depiction of the tomb of St. Barnabas. ⊠ *Archbishop Kyprianou Sq.* ☉ *Weekdays 8–12 and 2–6, Sat. 8–12.*

The **Famagusta Gate,** now a cultural center, houses exhibitions, a lecture hall, and a theater. ⊠ *Athina St.,* ☎ *02/430877.* ⊘ *Weekdays 8–12 and 2–4, Sat. 8–12.*

★ Outside the city walls near the western Paphos Gate stands the **Cyprus Museum.** It has archaeological displays ranging from Neolithic to Roman times. This stop is essential to an understanding of the island's ancient sites. ⊠ *Museum St.,* ☎ *02/305320.* ⊘ *Mon.–Sat. 9–5, Sun. 10–1.*

The neoclassical **Municipal Theater** (⊠ Museum St.) seats 1,200 people and stages events throughout the year, including Greek-language dramas and concerts. The lush **Municipal Gardens** (⊠ opposite Cyprus Museum) are a well-maintained oasis of greenery in the city.

$$$ ✕ **Plaka Tavern.** One of the oldest eating establishments in the city, in the heart of Engomi, offers up to 30 different meze dishes, including some unusual items, such as snails and okra with tomatoes. ⊠ *8 Stylianou Lena,* ☎ *02/352898. AE, DC, MC, V.*

$$$ ✕ **Trattoria Romantica.** The fare, like the owner, is Italian, and the atmosphere is distinctly friendly, with no shortage of advice available on any topic relating to Cyprus. There's a roaring fire in winter and service in the courtyard outside in summer. ⊠ *13 Evagora Pallikaridi,* ☎ *02/376161. AE, DC, MC, V. Closed Sun.*

$$$$ 🏨 **Cyprus Hilton.** The Hilton is among the island's best hotels, with extensive sports facilities, a skylit indoor pool, and dancing. An executive wing with 84 rooms offers separate check-in, a business center, a club room, and exercise rooms. ⊠ *Archbishop Makarios Ave., Box 2023, 1516,* ☎ *02/377777,* 𝔽𝔸𝕏 *02/377788. 281 rooms, 17 suites. 2 restaurants, 2 pools. AE, DC, MC, V.*

$$$ 🏨 **Holiday Inn.** In the Old City, near commercial and historic districts, this member of the chain opened in 1995. Its amenities include Japanese, international, and health-food restaurants and a rooftop pool with a garden. ⊠ *70 Regina St., Box 1212, 1507,* ☎ *02/475131,* 𝔽𝔸𝕏 *02/473337. 140 rooms. 4 restaurants, 2 pools. AE, DC, MC, V.*

$$ 🏨 **Cleopatra Hotel.** This hostelry offers a convenient location, cordial service, and well-prepared food served poolside. ⊠ *8 Florina St., Box 1397, 1507,* ☎ *02/445254,* 𝔽𝔸𝕏 *02/452618. 90 rooms. Restaurant, pool. AE, DC, MC, V.*

Ayia Napa

Once a small fishing village, 30 km (19 mi) east of Larnaca, it is anchored by a 16th-century monastery and renowned for its white, sandy beaches and views of the brilliant sea. Today its many restaurants and hotels reflect the town's transformation into Cyprus's premier vacationland. Ayia Napa maintains the flavor of its historic past, however, and beneath the monastery's 14th-century sycamore tree, you can still enjoy the panoramic view of the Mediterranean.

$$$ 🏨 **Nissi Beach.** This modern, air-conditioned hotel is set in magnificent gardens overlooking a sandy beach 3 km (2 mi) outside town. Some accommodations are in bungalows, which do not have kitchens. Amenities include a dive shop, an indoor heated pool, a health club, and more. ⊠ *Nissi Ave., Box 10, 5340,* ☎ *03/721021,* 𝔽𝔸𝕏 *03/721623. 270 rooms, 166 bungalows. Restaurant, pool. AE, DC, MC, V.*

$$ 🏨 **Pernera Beach Sun Hotel.** This budget hotel has a view of the beach. All rooms are air-conditioned. ⊠ *Pernera Beach, Box 38, 5340,* ☎ *03/831011,* 𝔽𝔸𝕏 *03/831020. 156 rooms. AE, DC, MC, V.*

Larnaca

The seaside resort with its own airport, 51 km (32 mi) southeast of Nicosia, has a flamboyant Whitsuntide celebration, Cataklysmos, as well as fine beaches, palm trees, and a modern harbor. In the marina district the **Larnaca Museum** displays treasures, including outstanding sculptures and Bronze Age seals. ⊠ *Kimon and Kilkis Sts.,* ☎ *04/630169.* ⊙ *Weekdays 7:30–2:30.*

Kition, the old Larnaca of biblical times, was one of the most important ancient city-kingdoms. Architectural remains of temples date from the 13th century BC. ⊠ *Kyman St., north of Larnaca Museum.* ⊙ *Sept.–June, weekdays 7:30–2:30 (until 6 on Thurs.); July–Aug., 7:30–noon.*

The **Pierides Collection** is a private assemblage of more than 3,000 pieces distinguished by its Bronze Age terra-cotta figures. ⊠ *Paul Zenon Kitieos St. 4, near Lord Byron St.,* ☎ *04/651345.* ⊙ *Mid-June–Sept., Mon.–Sat. 9–1 and 4–7; Oct.–mid-June, weekdays 9–1 and 3–5, Sat. 9–1.*

The 17th-century **Turkish fort** contains finds from Hala Sultan Tekke (☞ *below*) and Kition (☞ *above*). ⊠ *Within sight of marina on seafront.* ⊙ *June–Sept., daily 7:30–7; Oct.–May, weekdays 7:30–5, Thurs. 7:30–6.*

In the town center stands one of the island's more important churches, **Ayios Lazarus,** resplendent with icons. It has a fascinating crypt containing Lazarus's sarcophagus. ⊠ *Plateia Agiou Lazarou.* ⊙ *Oct.–May, daily 8–12:30 and 2:30–5; June–Sept., daily 8–12:30 and 3:30–6:30.*

South of Larnaca on the airport road is the 2½-sq-mi **Salt Lake.** In winter it's a refuge for migrating birds. On the lake's edge a mosque stands ★ in an oasis of palm trees guarding the **Hala Sultan Tekke**—burial place of the prophet Muhammad's aunt, Umm Haram, and an important Muslim shrine. ⊠ *Salt Lake.* ☜ *Free.* ⊙ *June–Sept., daily 7:30–7:30; Oct.–May, daily 7:30–5.*

The 11th-century **Panayia Angeloktistos** church, 11 km (7 mi) south of Larnaca, has extraordinary Byzantine wall mosaics that date from the 6th and 7th centuries. ⊠ *Rte. B4, Kiti.* ⊙ *Daily 9–5.*

On a mountain 40 km (25 mi) west of Larnaca stands the **Stavrovouni** (Mountain of the Cross) monastery. It was founded by St. Helena in AD 326; the present buildings date from the 19th century. The views from here are splendid. Ideally, the monastery should be visited in a spirit of pilgrimage rather than sightseeing, out of respect for the monks. Male visitors are allowed inside the monastery daily from sunrise to sunset, except between noon and 3 (noon and 1, Oct.–May).

$$ ✕ **Monte Carlo.** The outdoor seating at this spot along the road to the airport is on a balcony extending over the sea. Service is efficient, and the dining area is clean. Try the fish and meat mezes and casseroles. ⊠ *28 Pigiale Pasa Ave.,* ☎ *04/653815. AE, DC, MC, V.*

$ ✕ **Omiros.** This family-owned restaurant is best known for its fish meze, a true feast of 24 dishes fresh from the sea. Menu items also include red mullet, calamari, octopus, lamb chops, pork kebabs, and more. ⊠ *Pigiale Pasa Ave., Stadem Court 3,* ☎ *04/653521. AE, DC, MC, V.*

$$$$ 🏨 **Golden Bay.** Comfort is paramount at this beach hotel east of the town center. All rooms have balconies and views of the sea. The extensive sports facilities make it an ideal spot for summer or winter vacations. ⊠ *Larnaca-Dhekelia Rd., Box 741, 6306,* ☎ *04/645444,* FAX *04/645451. 194 rooms. 2 restaurants, 2 pools. AE, DC, MC, V.*

$$$ 🏨 **Sandy Beach Hotel.** Between Larnaca and Dhekelia, this beach hotel has a large pool area as well as a health club and tennis court. All rooms have twin beds and a partial sea view. ⊠ *Larnaca–Dekeleia Rd., 8 km/5 mi from Larnaca, Box 857, 6307,* ☎ *04/646333,* FAX *04/646900. 195 rooms, 5 suites. 3 restaurants, 2 pools. AE, DC, MC, V.*

$$ 🏨 **Pasithea.** This apartment/hotel near Salt Lake is a short stroll from the sandy beach. The management is friendly, and the one-bedroom

apartments are spacious. ⊠ *4 Michael Angelou, Box 309, 6028,* ☎ *04/658264,* F̅A̅X̅ *04/625848. 14 apartments. AE, DC, MC, V.*

$ ⌶ **Cactus Hotel.** The Cactus, near the airport, has a restaurant and bar. It's 20 minutes from the seafront and Larnaca's tavernas. ⊠ *6–8 Shakespeare St., Box 188, 6027,* ☎ *046/27400,* F̅A̅X̅ *046/26966. 58 rooms. Restaurant, pool. AE, MC, V.*

Phikardou

In this museum village south of Nicosia, many of the rural houses, outstanding examples of folk architecture, have remarkable woodwork; they also contain the household furnishings used a century ago. Official tour guides are available in the village. ⊠ *Machairas Alicosia Rd. via Klirou; 1½ km (1 mi) east of Gourri,* ☎ *02/337715 in Nicosia.* ⊙ *Hrs vary.*

Limassol

A commercial port and wine-making center on the south coast, Limassol, 75 km (47 mi) from Nicosia, is a bustling, cosmopolitan town. Luxury hotels, apartments, and guest houses stretch along 12 km (7 mi) of seafront. The town's nightlife is the liveliest on the island. In the center, the elegant, modern shops of Makarios Avenue contrast with those of the old part of town, where local handicrafts prevail.

★ The 14th-century **Limassol Fort,** was built on the site of a Byzantine fortification. Richard the Lion-Hearted and Berengaria of Navarre are said to have married here in 1191. The **Cyprus Medieval Museum** in the castle displays medieval armor and relics. ⊠ *Near old port,* ☎ *05/330132.* ⊙ *Weekdays 7:30–5, Sat. 9–5, Sun. 10–1.*

For a glimpse of Cypriot folklore, visit the **Folk Art Museum.** The collection includes national costumes and fine examples of weaving and other crafts. ⊠ *Agiou Andreou 253,* ☎ *05/362303.* ⊙ *Oct.–May, Mon.–Wed., Fri. 8:30–1:30 and 3:30–5:30, Thurs. 8:30–1:30; June–Sept., Mon.–Wed., Fri. 8:30–1:30 and 4–6:30, Thurs. 8:30–1:30.*

At the annual **Limassol Wine Festival** in September, local wineries offer free samples and demonstrate traditional grape-pressing methods. There are open-air music and dance performances. The **KEO Winery,** just west of the town, welcomes visitors. ⊠ *Roosevelt Ave., toward the new port,* ☎ *05/362053.* ▧ *Free.* ⊙ *Tours weekdays, 10.*

★ **Kolossi Castle,** a Crusader fortress of the Knights of St. John, was constructed during the 13th century and rebuilt during the 15th. ⊠ *Road to Paphos.* ⊙ *June–Sept., daily 7:30–7:30; Oct.–May, daily 7:30–5.*

Kourion (Curium), west of Limassol, has Greek and Roman ruins. In the amphitheater, classical and Shakespearean plays are sometimes staged. Next to the theater is the **Villa of Eustolios,** a summerhouse built by a wealthy Christian. A nearby **Roman stadium** has been partially rebuilt. The **Apollo Hylates** (Sanctuary of Apollo of the Woodlands), an impressive archaeological site, stands 3 km (2 mi) farther on. ⊠ *Main Paphos Rd.* ⊙ *June–Sept., daily 7:30–7:30; Oct.–May, daily 8–4:45.*

$$$ ✕ **Scottis Steak House.** Just off the city's main thoroughfare, Makarios Avenue, this restaurant's plain-looking exterior hides some of the best steaks available in Cyprus, all served with tasty fresh vegetables. ⊠ *38 Souli St.,* ☎ *05/335173. AE, DC, MC, V.*

$$ ✕ **Porta.** A varied menu of international and Cypriot dishes, such as *foukoudha* barbecue (grilled strips of steak) and trout baked in prawn and mushroom sauce, is served in this restored warehouse. On many nights you'll be entertained by soft, live music. ⊠ *17 Yenethliou Mitella, Old Castle,* ☎ *05/360339. MC, V.*

$$$$ 🏨 **Four Seasons Hotel.** One of the premier hotels in Cyprus, this property is not part of the international chain but offers comparable elegance. The spacious rooms have marble baths; many also have balconies with sea views. Guest services include a spa, a dive shop, a children's club, tennis and squash courts, and a gym. ✉ *Old Limassol–Nicosia Rd., Box 7222, 3313,* ☎ *05/310222,* 🖷 *05/310887. 190 rooms, 18 suites. 3 restaurants, 3 pools. AE, DC, MC, V.*

$$$$ 🏨 **Le Meridien.** The striking lobby of this large, luxurious hotel is pink marble and glass. The amenities are first-class, and the hotel has Larnaca's largest swimming pool. Guest options include scuba diving, a kids' center, a health club, and a heated indoor pool. ✉ *Old Limassol–Nicosia Rd., Box 6560, 3308,* ☎ *05/634000,* 🖷 *05/634222. 232 rooms, 69 suites. 3 restaurants, 2 pools. AE, DC, MC, V.*

$$ 🏨 **Azur Beach.** This fine apartment/hotel has a good sandy beach and helpful management. ✉ *Potamios Yermasoyias, Box 1318, 3504,* ☎ *05/322667,* 🖷 *05/321897. 24 1-bedroom apartments, 12 studios, 60 rooms. 2 restaurants. DC, MC, V.*

$ 🏨 **Continental.** A great sea view adds to the appeal of this family hotel close to the castle. ✉ *137 Spyros Araouzos Ave., Box 398, 3604,* ☎ *05/362530,* 🖷 *05/373030. 30 rooms. AE, V.*

Troodos Mountains

North of Limassol, these mountains, which rise to 1,950 m (6,500 ft), have shady cedar and pine forests and cool springs. Small, painted churches in the Troodos and Pitsilia Foothills are rich examples of a rare indigenous art form. **Asinou Church,** near the village of Nikitari, and **Agios Nikolaos tis Stegis** (St. Nicholas of the Roof), south of Kakopetria, are especially noteworthy. Nearby is the **Tall Trees Trout Farm,** an oasis serving delicious meals of fresh fish. In winter, skiers take over; **Platres,** in the foothills of Mt. Olympus, is the principal resort. At the **Kykkos** monastery, founded in 1100, the prized icon of the Virgin is reputed to have been painted by St. Luke.

Petra tou Romiou

The legendary **birthplace of Aphrodite**—Greek goddess of love and beauty—is just off the main road between Limassol and Petra. Signs in Greek and English identify it.

Paphos

In the west of the island 142 km (88 mi) southwest of Nicosia, the town combines superb sea swimming with archaeological sites and a rich history. The center is modern.

The **Paphos District Archaeological Museum** displays pottery, jewelry, and statuettes from Cyprus's Roman villas. ✉ *43 Grivas Dighenis Ave., Ktima,* ☎ *06/240215.* ☉ *Weekdays 7:30–5 (until 6 on Thurs.), weekends 10–1.*

★ There are notable icons in the **Byzantine Museum** in the archiepiscopal palace. ✉ *7 Andreas Ioannou St.,* ☎ *06/232092.* ☉ *Oct.–May, weekdays 9–5, Sat. 9–2; June–Sept., weekdays 9–7, Sat. 9–2.*

The charming **Ethnographical Museum** provides a fascinating review of history with various rooms of typical old houses re-created in their original state, including furnishings, fabrics, and kitchen and agricultural utensils. ✉ *1 Exo Vrysi,* ☎ *06/232010.* ☉ *June–Sept., Mon—Sat. 9–1 and 2–7; Oct.–May, Mon–Sat. 9–1 and 2–5, Sun. 10–1.*

Don't miss the elaborate **Roman mosaics** in the **Roman Villa of Theseus,** the **House of Dionysos,** and the **House of Aion.** The town bus stops nearby. ✉ *Kato Paphos (New Paphos), near harbor.* ☉ *June–Sept., daily 7:30–7:30; Oct.–May, daily 7:30–5.*

★ The **Tombs of the Kings,** an early necropolis, date from 300 BC. Though the coffin niches are empty, a powerful sense of mystery remains. ⊠ *Kato Paphos (New Paphos).* ☉ *June–Sept., daily 7:30–7:30; Oct.–May, daily 7:30–5.*

$$ ✕ **Chez Alex Fish Tavern.** The well-established tavern serves only fresh fish (the catch of the day) and fish mezes. ⊠ *7 Constantia St., Kato Paphos,* ☎ *06/234767. AE, DC, MC, V.*

$$$ ⛱ **Azia Beach Hotel.** Ninety percent of the rooms at this expansive hotel perched up on rugged cliffs have a sea view. Along with a large, lagoon-shape pool, the resort offers tennis, squash, and a health center. ⊠ *Akamas Ave., Box 2108, 8061,* ☎ *06/247800,* ℻ *06/246883. 179 rooms, 4 suites. 3 restaurants, 2 pools. AE, DC, MC, V.*

$$$ ⛱ **Coral Beach Hotel and Resort.** Just 10 minutes from the town of Paphos, this luxurious seaside hotel has rooms decorated with the colors of the Mediterranean. Guest facilities include a complete spa with an indoor heated pool, scuba diving, and an arts and crafts workshop. ⊠ *Coral Bay, Box 2422, 8099,* ☎ *06/621711,* ℻ *06/621742. 420 rooms. 5 restaurants, 2 pools. AE, DC, MC, V.*

$$$ ⛱ **Paphos Beach.** Surrounded by gardens, this hotel has a wealth of facilities. Water sports are a major draw here. Accommodations are either in the main hotel or in roomy bungalows on the grounds. ⊠ *Posidonos St., Box 136, 8125,* ☎ *06/233091,* ℻ *06/242818. 224 rooms, 20 bungalows. 3 restaurants, pool. AE, DC, MC, V.*

$$ ⛱ **Amalthea Beach Hotel.** This hotel on the beach amid banana groves has a friendly, personal atmosphere fostered by the resident owner-managers. The impressive, open lobby, furnished with gray leather couches and large plants, overlooks the water, and the rooms have balconies with sea views. ⊠ *8574 Kissonerga Rd., Box 323, 8102,* ☎ *06/245709,* ℻ *06/245963. 168 rooms. Restaurant, 2 pools. AE, DC, MC, V.*

$$ ⛱ **Hilltop Gardens Hotel Apartments.** All apartments have a view of the sea, just 500 yards away. The decor is a pleasant mixture of traditional Cypriot village style, including wooden furniture, and modern touches. ⊠ *Off Tombs of the Kings Rd., Box 185, 8046,* ☎ *06/243111,* ℻ *06/248229. 48 apartments. Pool. AE, DC, MC, V.*

Polis

Just past the town's fishing harbor of Latchi, and 48 km (30 mi) north of Paphos, are the **Baths of Aphrodite,** where the goddess is said to have seduced her swains. The wild, undeveloped Akamas Peninsula is perfect for a hike.

NORTHERN CYPRUS

There are two important things to bear in mind in Northern Cyprus. One is to obey the "no photographs" signs wherever they appear. The other is to note that as Turkish is the language used here, Turkish names designate the cities and towns: Nicosia is known as Lefkoşa, Kyrenia as Girne, and Famagusta as Gazimagusa. A useful map showing these and other Turkish names is available free from tourist offices.

Northern Cyprus A to Z

Money Matters

COSTS

Prices for food and accommodations tend to be lower than those in the Republic of Cyprus. However, with the exception of Turkish wines and spirits, most foreign drinks will be slightly more expensive as they will have been imported via Turkey.

CURRENCY
The monetary unit in Northern Cyprus is the Turkish lira (TL; ☞ Chapter 31, Turkey). There are bills for 5,000,000; 1,000,000; 500,000; 250,000; 100,000; and 50,000 and coins for 50,000; 25,000; 10,000; and 5,000 TL. The Turkish lira is subject to considerable inflation, so most of the prices in this section are quoted in U.S. dollars.

SAMPLE PRICES
A cup of coffee costs around $1, a glass of beer about $1.50. Wine is around $3 per glass. An 80-km (50-mi) taxi ride costs about $30. Admission to museums costs about $1.

Opening and Closing Times
In the hot summer months (May–September), weekday museum hours are usually 8–1:30 and 4–6, but check before you visit.

Transportation
BY BUS AND DOLMUŞ
Buses and the shared dolmuş (taxis) are the cheapest forms of transportation. Service is frequent on main routes. A bus from Nicosia to Kyrenia costs about 90¢, and to Famagusta about $1.50. A seat in a dolmuş for the same trips would cost about $1.50 and $3, respectively.

BY CAR
☞ By Car *in* The Republic of Cyprus A to Z, *above*.

BY PLANE
Cyprus Turkish Airlines, Istanbul Airlines, and Turkish Airlines run all flights via mainland Turkey, usually with a change of plane at Istanbul. There are also nonstop flights from Adana, Ankara, Antalya, and İzmir to Ercan Airport near Nicosia. Ferries run from Mersin and Tasucu in Turkey to Famagusta and Kyrenia, respectively. It is not possible to enter Cyprus from Northern Cyprus unless you are returning from a day trip from Nicosia.

Visitor Information
Department of Tourism Marketing (⊠ Selçuklu Caddesi, Lefkoşa/Nicosia; postal address, Selçuklu Cad., Lefkoşa-KKTC, Mersin 10, Turkey, ☎ 90/392/228–1057, FAX 90/392/228–5625). Regional tourism offices: Famagusta (☎ 90/392/366–2864), Kyrenia (☎ 90/392/815–2145), and Nicosia (☎ 90/392/228 1057).

Weather
☞ Weather *in* The Republic of Cyprus A to Z, *above*.

Exploring Northern Cyprus

Lefkoşa (Nicosia)
The Turkish half of the city is the capital of Northern Cyprus. A walk around the Old City, within the encircling walls, is rich with glimpses from the Byzantine, Lusignan, and Venetian past. In addition to Venetian fortifications (☞ Exploring the Republic of Cyprus, *above*), it contains the **Selimiye Mosque** (⊠ Selimiye St.), originally the 13th-century Cathedral of St. Sophia and a fine example of Gothic architecture to which a pair of minarets has been added. Near the Girne Gate is the **Mevlevi Tekke ve Etnografi Müzesi** (Mevlevi Shrine and Ethnographic Museum), the former home of the Mevlevi Dervishes, a Sufi order. The building now houses a museum of Turkish history and culture. ⊠ *Girne St.* ☉ *Weekdays 8–1 and 2–5, Sat. 8–1, Sun. 10–1.*

Girne (Kyrenia)
Of the coastal resorts, Girne, with its yacht-filled harbor, is the most appealing. There are excellent beaches to the east and west of the

town. **Girne Castle,** overlooking the harbor, is Venetian. It now houses the **Batık Gemi Müzesi** (Shipwreck Museum), whose prize possession is the remains of a ship that sank around 300 BC. ⊙ *Weekdays 8–1 and 2–5, Sat. 8–1, Sun. 10–1.*

The fantastic ruins of the **Castle of St. Hilarion** stand on a hilltop 11 km (7 mi) southwest of Girne. It's a strenuous walk, so take a taxi; the views are breathtaking. The romantic ruins of the former **Abbey of Bellapais,** built during the 12th century by the Lusignans, are just as impressive. They lie on a mountainside 6 km (4 mi) southeast of Girne, overlooking the coastal plain.

$$$ ✕ **Jashan.** An idyllic mountain village with starlit views across the coastal
★   plain to the Mediterranean may seem an incongruous location for an Indian restaurant, but the food and service, both provided by native Indians, are superb and the setting exquisite. ⊠ *Karaman, 6 km (4 mi) west of Girne,* ☎ *90/392/822–2514. MC, V. Closed Mon.*

$ ✕ **Harbour Club.** On the waterfront at Girne's picturesque harbor, this two-story restaurant offers French cuisine upstairs and local food on the open ground-floor terrace. Try the *şeftali kebab* (specially prepared meatballs), a Turkish Cypriot speciality. ⊠ *Girne Harbor,* ☎ *90/392/ 815–5320. No credit cards.*

$$$$ 🏨 **Jasmine Court.** Next to its own beach in Girne, the luxurious hotel is a resort in its own right, with air-conditioned rooms, palm-tree–shaded poolside terraces, sports facilities, a casino, and a disco. ⊠ *Temmuz Cad. 20, Girne, Mersin 10, Turkey,* ☎ *90/392/815–1450,* 🆋 *90/392/ 815–1488. 143 rooms. Restaurant, pool. MC, V.*

$$ 🏨 **Dome Hotel.** Despite the renovation of the lobby and restaurant, this doyen of Girne's hotels still has a nostalgic air of faded 1960s grandeur. Rooms on the seaside may have a slightly battered decor but are superbly located almost literally over the water. ⊠ *Kordonboyu Caddesi, Girne, Mersin 10, Turkey,* ☎ *90/392/815–2453,* 🆋 *90/392/815–2772. 170 rooms. Restaurant, pool. MC, V.*

Gazimagusa (Famagusta)

The chief port of Northern Cyprus, Gazimagusa, has massive and well-preserved Venetian walls and the late-13th-century Gothic Cathedral of St. Nicholas, now Lala Mustafa Pasha Mosque. The Old Town, within the walls, is the most intriguing district to explore.

Salamis, on the seashore north of Gazimagusa, is an ancient ruined city and perhaps the most dramatic archaeological site on the island. St. Barnabas and St. Paul arrived in Salamis and established a church near here. Most of the ruins date from the Roman Empire, including a well-preserved theater, an amphitheater, villas, colonnades, and superb mosaic floors. After surviving earthquakes and pirate raids, the city was abandoned in the 7th century AD when the population moved to what is now Famagusta. Much of ancient city is overgrown with a tangle of bushes and stiff dune grass, which serve only to enhance the site's serene, poignant beauty.

CZECH REPUBLIC

PRAGUE, SIDE TRIPS: BOHEMIA AND MORAVIA

For all its history, the Czech Republic is a very young nation. After a peaceful revolution overthrew a Communist regime that had been in power for 40 years, Czechoslovakia split in 1993 as its two constituent republics, Czech and Slovak, formed independent countries.

Formed from the ruins of the Austro-Hungarian empire at the end of World War I, Czechoslovakia appeared to withstand the threat of divisive nationalism and brought stability to the potentially volatile region. During the difficult 1930s, the Czechoslovak republic stood as the model democracy in central Europe. In the 1960s a courageous Slovak, Alexander Dubček, led the 1968 Prague Spring, an intense period of national renewal. Students and opponents of the Communist regime in both Prague and Bratislava toppled the ruling party in 1989.

Czechoslovakia proved to be an artificial creation that masked important and long-standing cultural differences between two outwardly similar peoples. The old Czech lands of Bohemia and Moravia, whose territory makes up most of the Czech Republic, can look to a rich cultural history that goes back a millennium, and they played pivotal roles in the great religious and social conflicts of European history. Slovakia, by contrast, languished for centuries as an agrarian outpost of the Hungarian empire. Given the state of the Slovaks' national ego, independence was probably inevitable.

Since the 1989 revolution, Prague, the Czech capital, has become one of Europe's top destinations. Forget old impressions of neglect and melancholy; Prague exudes an atmosphere of enthusiasm and provides such conveniences as English-language newspapers, attentive service, loads of upscale shopping choices, and restaurateurs who will try to find you a seat even if you don't have a reservation. Musicians and writers find new inspiration in the city that once harbored Mozart and Kafka. Spectacular Gothic, Baroque, and Art Nouveau treasures stand in glorious counterpoint to drab remnants of socialist architecture.

Outside the capital you can discover everything from imperial spas to modern industrial cities. Don't pass up the lovely towns and castles of

Czech Republic (Česká Republika)

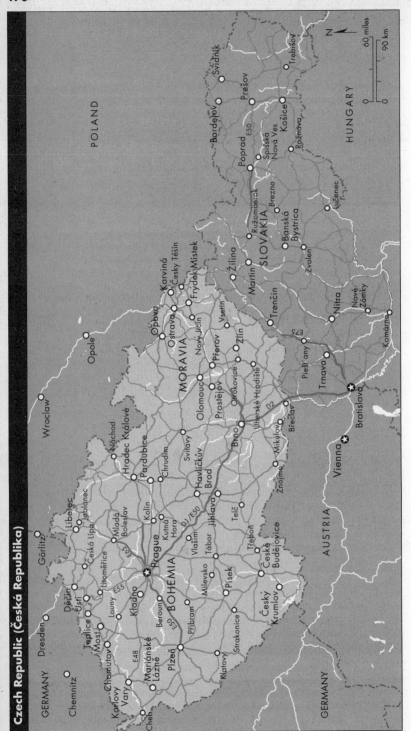

southern Bohemia: the Renaissance river town of Český Krumlov
ranks among Central Europe's grandest sights.

CZECH REPUBLIC A TO Z

Customs

You may import duty-free 200 cigarettes, 50 cigars, 1 liter of spirits,
2 liters of wine, and gifts with a total value of 1,000 Kč. Goods worth
up to 3,000 Kč (aprox. 90 USD) are not liable for duty upon arrival.
Declare items of greater value (jewelry, computers, and so on) on arrival to avoid problems with customs officials on departure. You may
only export antiques that are certified as not of historical value. Reputable dealers will advise. Play safe, and also save your receipts.

Dining

Dining options include restaurants; the *vinárna* (wine cellar), which
covers anything from inexpensive wine bars to swank restaurants; the
more down-to-earth *pivnice* or *hospody* (beer taverns); cafeterias; and
coffee shops and snack bars. Make reservations at all but the humblest
places during high season. Privatization has brought more culinary variety, especially in Prague. Be wary of food bought from street vendors,
as sanitary conditions may not be ideal.

Prague ham makes a favorite first course. The most typical main dish
is roast pork (or duck or goose) with sauerkraut. Also try the outstanding
trout, carp, and other freshwater fish. Crepes, here called *palačinky,*
are ubiquitous and may come with savory or sweet fillings. Dumplings
in various forms, generally with a rich gravy, accompany many dishes.
A typical Czech breakfast is cold cuts and spreadable cheese or jam
with rolls, washed down with coffee.

MEALTIMES

Lunch is usually from 11:30 to 2 or 3; dinner from 6 to 9:30 or 10.
At places open all day, it's easier to get a table during off-hours.

RATINGS

Prices are reasonable, even in some of the more expensive restaurants.
The following prices apply for a first course, main course, and dessert
(prices are per person, excluding wine and tip).

CATEGORY	PRAGUE	OTHER AREAS
$$$$	over 1,440 Kč	over 1,260 Kč
$$$	900 Kč–1,440 Kč	720 Kč–1,260 Kč
$$	540 Kč–900 Kč	360 Kč–720 Kč
$	under 540 Kč	under 360 Kč

WHAT TO WEAR

A jacket and tie are recommended for $$$$ and $$$ restaurants. In-
formal dress is appropriate elsewhere.

Language

Czech, which belongs to the Slavic family of languages along with Rus-
sian, Polish, and Slovak, uses the Latin alphabet like English but adds
special diacritical marks to make certain sounds: č is written for the
"ch" sound, for instance. Unlike words in many other languages,
Czech words are spelled phonetically, and the emphasis is almost al-
ways on the first syllable. You'll find a growing number of English-
speakers, especially among young people and in the tourist industry.
German is generally understood throughout the country.

Lodging

Accommodations in the Czech Republic range from hotels, motels, pri-
vate lodgings, and hostels to campsites. Renovated older properties have

great character and style. There is a shortage of reasonably affordable hotel rooms during the peak season, so make reservations well in advance. Private room agencies offer a variety of lodgings. The standards of facilities and services in the less expensive categories hardly match those in the West, so don't be surprised by faulty plumbing or indifferent reception clerks. Unless otherwise noted, rooms include bath.

CAMPING

Maps showing the locations of the many campgrounds around the country are available at bookstores and tourist offices. Several campgrounds in Prague operate year-round; the Prague Information Service (PIS) (☞ Visitor Information *in* Prague Essentials, *below*) has a list.

HOTELS

These are officially graded with from one to five stars, using the international classification system. Outside Prague and the spa resorts, few hotels carry more than three stars.

Bills can be paid in koruny (check to see if your hotel insists on hard currency; some hotels refuse to accept credit cards). Breakfast is often included in the room price.

PRIVATE LODGINGS

Many travel agencies in Prague offer accommodation in private homes. Such rooms are invariably cheaper and often more comfortable than hotel rooms, though you may have to sacrifice some privacy. The largest room-finding service is probably **AVE** (☎ 02/2422–3226) in the main and Holešovice train stations and at the airport (all branches are open daily). Insist on a room in the city center, however, or you may find yourself in a dreary, far-off suburb. Another helpful agency is **City of Prague Accommodation Service** (⊠ Haštalská 7, ☎ 02/231–6663). Elsewhere, look along main roads for signs that read ROOM FREE (i.e., room available), or in German, ZIMMER FREI or PRIVATZIMMER. Offices of the travel bureau Čedok and the Prague Information Service (PIS) (☞ Visitor Information *in* Prague Essentials, *below*) can also help you find private accommodations.

RATINGS

Prices are for double rooms, generally including breakfast. Prices at the lower end of the scale apply to low season. Expect a 15%–25% rate increase at certain periods, such as Christmas, New Year's, Easter, or during festivals.

CATEGORY	PRAGUE	OTHER AREAS
$$$$	over 5,200 Kč	over 2,600 Kč
$$$	2,600 Kč–5,200 Kč	1,300 Kč–2,600 Kč
$$	1,300 Kč–2,600 Kč	650 Kč–1,300 Kč
$	under 1,300 Kč	under 650 Kč

YOUTH HOSTELS

IYH members can book reservations at any of 25-odd hostels across the country, including three in Prague (350 Kč and up, including breakfast), at **KMC** (⊠ Karoliny Světlé 30, 160 00 Prague 6, ☎ 02/9000–1458). IYH cards are also sold here (250 Kč) and at **CKM Youth Travel Service** (⊠ Jindřišská 28, Prague 1, ☎ 02/268623).

In Prague most hostels are open to everyone and generally operate year-round. One of these is **Hostel Estec** (⊠ Vaníčkova 5, 160 00 Prague 6, ☎ 02/5721–0410 or 02/527344, FAX 02/5721–5263). Ask at accommodation agencies about hostels outside Prague. Rates start at 300 Kč per person at hostels not affiliated with IYH.

Mail

POSTAL RATES

First-class (airmail) letters to the United States and Canada cost 11 Kč up to 20 grams, postcards 7 Kč. First-class (airmail) letters to the United Kingdom cost 8 Kč up to 20 grams, postcards 5 Kč.

RECEIVING MAIL

Mail can be labeled "poste restante" and sent to the main post office in Prague (⊠ Jindřišská 14, Prague) or to any other main post office. There's no charge. The American Express office (⊠ Václavské nám. 56/Wenceslas Sq. 56, Prague, ☎ 02/2280–0251) will hold letters to card-holders or holders of American Express traveler's checks.

Money Matters

COSTS

Costs are highest in Prague and only slightly lower in the main Bohemian resorts and spas, though even in these places you can now find inexpensive accommodations in private homes. The least expensive area is southern Moravia. Note that many public venues in Prague and the Czech Republic continue the odious practice of adhering to a separate pricing system for Czechs and for foreigners. (Foreigners may be charged double or more on museum admission, for example.)

CURRENCY

The unit of currency in the Czech Republic is the crown, or *koruna* (plural *koruny*), written as Kč, and divided into 100 *haléřů* (hellers). There are bills of 20, 50, 100, 200, 500, 1,000, and 5,000 koruny and coins of 10, 20, and 50 hellers and 1, 2, 5, 10, 20, and 50 koruny. At press time (summer 1999), the rate of exchange was 35.30 Kč to the U.S. dollar, 24.03 Kč to the Canadian dollar, 55.92 Kč to the pound sterling, 23.23 Kč to the Australian dollar, and 18.85 Kč to the New Zealand dollar. Banks and ATMs give the best rates. Banks and private exchange outlets, which litter Prague's tourist routes, charge either a set fee or a percentage of the transaction or both, and for small transactions (US$100 or less) the charge at a bank may be more than you would pay for the same transaction at a private exchange outlet. It's wise to compare. The koruna is fully convertible and can be purchased outside the country and changed into other currencies, but you should keep your receipts and convert your koruny before you leave the country just to be sure.

SAMPLE PRICES

Cup of coffee, 30 Kč; beer (½ liter), 10 Kč–25 Kč; Coca-Cola, 20 Kč; ham sandwich, 30 Kč; 1½-km (1-mi) taxi ride, 50 Kč–100 Kč; museum and castle admission, 20 Kč–300 Kč.

TIPPING

A service charge is rarely added to restaurant bills. Give a tip for good service directly to the waiter when you pay your bill. As a rule of thumb, round up to the next multiple of 10 (i.e., if the bill comes to 83 Kč, give the waiter 90 Kč). Give 10% on big or group tabs. For taxis, consider 10% a reasonable tip. In the better hotels doormen should get 20 Kč for each bag they carry to the check-in desk; bellhops get up to 40 Kč each for taking them up to your rooms. In $$ or $ hotels plan to lug your own baggage.

National Holidays

January 1; April 23 and 24 (Easter Sunday and Monday); May 1 (Labor Day); May 8 (Liberation Day); July 5 (Sts. Cyril and Methodius); July 6 (Jan Hus); October 28 (Czech National Day); December 24–26.

Opening and Closing Times

Banks are open weekdays 8–5. **Museums** are usually open Tuesday–Sunday 10–5. **Shops** are generally open weekdays 9–6; some close for lunch between noon and 2. Many are also open Saturday mornings.

Passports and Visas

United States, Canadian, and British citizens need only a valid passport to visit the Czech Republic as tourists. United States citizens may stay for 30 days without a visa; British and Canadian citizens, six months. Australians need tourist visas to enter the Czech Republic; the visa is free if obtained at a Czech embassy or consulate outside the Czech Republic; at the Czech Republic border, it costs 1,600 Kc.

Telephoning

To use a public phone buy a phone card at a newsstand or tobacconist. Cards cost 100 Kč for 50 units or 190 Kč for 100 units. CzechMate cards worth 750 Kč of telephoning—ideal for long-distance calls—are also sold at post offices. To place a call, lift the receiver, insert the card, and dial.

COUNTRY CODE

The Czech Republic's country code is 420.

INTERNATIONAL CALLS

Some special international pay phone booths in central Prague will take 5-Kč coins or accept phone cards that allow automatic dialing. You will also find coin and card booths at the main post office (⌧ Jindřišská 14), near Václavské náměstí (Wenceslas Square); the entrance for telephone service is in this building but around the corner on Politických vězňů Street. The international dialing code is 00. Dial 0132 for international inquiries to the United States, Canada, or the United Kingdom. To place a call via an **AT&T USA Direct** international operator, dial 0042–000101; for **MCI,** dial 0042–000112; for **Sprint,** dial 0042–087187. International rates vary according to destination.

LOCAL CALLS

Local calls cost one unit.

Transportation

Traveling in the Czech Republic is relatively simple once you know the basic street sign words: *ulice* (street), abbreviated to *ul.* (note that common usage often drops ulice in a printed address), *náměstí* (square), abbreviated to *nám.,* and *třída* (avenue). In most cases blue signs on buildings mark the street address.

BY BUS

An excellent bus network provides quicker service than trains at somewhat higher prices (low by Western standards). Buses are always full. Reserve your seat in advance, especially on long-distance routes.

BY CAR

Breakdowns. The Yellow Angels (☎ 123 or 124) operate a patrol service on main highways. The emergency number for motorists is 1054.

Gasoline. At about 93 Kč ($2.60) a gallon, gasoline is expensive. Look for service stations along main roads on the outskirts of towns and cities.

Road Conditions. Main roads are usually good, if sometimes narrow. An expressway links Plzeň, Prague, Brno, and Bratislava. If you plan to do much exploring, pick up an *Auto Atlas,* available in bookstores and souvenir shops.

Rules of the Road. Drive on the right. Speed limits are 60 kph (37 mph) in urban areas, 90 kph (55 mph) on open roads, and 110 kph (68 mph) on expressways. Seat belts are compulsory outside urban areas; drinking and driving is strictly prohibited. A permit is required to drive on expressways and other four-lane highways. It costs 800 Kč and is sold at border crossings, post offices, and some service stations.

BY PLANE

Good air service links Prague with several other towns, including Ostrava in Moravia and Bratislava and Poprad (for the High Tatras) in Slovakia. Prices are reasonable. Make reservations at Čedok offices or directly at **ČSA**, Czech Airlines (☎ 02/2010–4310).

BY TRAIN

The country has an extensive rail network. Fares are relatively low and trains are crowded. You have to pay a small supplement on EuroCity (EC) and·InterCity (IC) trains. Most long-distance trains have dining cars; overnight trains between main centers have sleeping cars.

Visitor Information

Many towns have an information office ("Infocentrum") or private tourist bureau, often in the main square. The ubiquitous Čedok (main office, ⊠ Na Příkopě 18, 111 35 Prague 1, ☎ 02/2419–7643 or 02/2419–7111), now a private travel agency, has offices in all larger towns.

Weather

Organized sightseeing tours run from April or May through October (year-round in Prague). Some monuments, especially castles, either close entirely or curtail their hours in winter. Hotel rates may decrease in the off-season except during festivals. May, the month of fruit blossoms, is the time of the Prague Spring International Music Festival. Huge crowds clog Prague sites in spring, summer, and early fall.

CLIMATE

The following are the average daily maximum and minimum temperatures for Prague.

Jan.	36F	2C	**May**	66F	19C	**Sept.**	68F	20C
	25	– 4		46	8		50	10
Feb.	37F	3C	**June**	72F	22C	**Oct.**	55F	13C
	27	– 3		52	11		41	5
Mar.	46F	8C	**July**	75F	24C	**Nov.**	46F	8C
	32	0		55	13		36	2
Apr.	58F	14C	**Aug.**	73F	23C	**Dec.**	37F	3C
	39	4		55	13		28	– 2

PRAGUE

Poets, philosophers, and the Czech-in-the-street have long sung the praises of Praha (Prague), also referred to as the "Golden City of a Hundred Spires." Like Rome, Prague is built on seven hills, which slope gently or tilt precipitously down to the Vltava (Moldau) River. The riverside location, enhanced by a series of graceful bridges, makes a great setting for two of the city's most notable features: its extravagant, fairy-tale architecture and its memorable music. Mozart claimed that no one understood him better than the citizens of Prague, and he was only one of several great masters who lived or lingered here.

It was under Karel IV (Charles IV), during the 14th century, that Prague first became the seat of the Holy Roman Empire—virtually the capital of Western Europe—and acquired its distinctive Gothic imprint. The medieval inheritance is still here under the overlays of graceful Renaissance and exuberant Baroque. Prague escaped serious wartime damage, but it didn't escape neglect. During the 1990s, however, artisans and their workers have restored dozens of the city's historic buildings with care and sensitivity.

Exploring Prague

Shades of the five medieval towns that combined to form Prague linger in the divisions of its historic districts. On the flat eastern shore of the Vltava River are three areas arranged like nesting boxes: **Josefov** (the old Jewish Quarter) within **Staré Město** (Old Town) within **Nové Město** (New Town). **Malá Strana** (the Lesser Quarter) and **Hradčany** (Castle District) perch along the river's hillier west bank. Spanning the Vltava is **Karlův most** (the Charles Bridge), which links the Old Town to the Lesser Quarter; everything within the historic center can be reached on foot in a half hour or less from here.

Nové Město and Staré Město (New Town and Old Town)

Numbers in the margin correspond to points of interest on the Prague map.

⑪ **Betlémská kaple** (Bethlehem Chapel). The martyr and national hero Jan Hus thundered his reform teachings from the chapel pulpit during the early 15th century. The structure was rebuilt in the 1950s, but the little door through which Hus came to the pulpit is original, as are some of the inscriptions on the wall. ⊠ *Betlémské nám.* ☉ *Apr.–Sept. daily 9–6; Oct.–Mar. daily 9–5.*

❸ **Celetná ulice.** Medieval kings took this street on their way to their coronation at Prague Castle. The **Royal Route** continues past the Gothic spires of the Týn Church in Old Town Square; it then crosses Charles Bridge and goes up to the castle. Along the route stands every variety of Romanesque, Gothic, Renaissance, and Baroque architecture.

⑩ **Clam-Gallas palác** (Clam-Gallas Palace). Squatting on a constricted site in the heart of the Old Town, this pompous Baroque palace was designed by the great Viennese architect J. B. Fischer von Erlach. All the sculptures, including the Titans that struggle to support the two doorways, are the work of one of the great Bohemian Baroque artists, Matthias Braun. Peek inside at the superb staircase or attend an evening concert. ⊠ *Husova 20.*

❹ **Dům U černé Matky Boží** (House of the Black Madonna). This Cubist building adds a decided jolt to the architectural styles along Celetná ulice. In the second decade of the 20th century, several leading Czech architects boldly applied Cubism's radical reworking of visual space to structures. The Black Madonna, designed by Josef Gočár, is unflinchingly modern yet topped with an almost Baroque tile roof. ⊠ *Celetná ul. (at Ovocnýtrh),* ☎ *2421–1732.* ☉ *Tues.–Sun. 10–6.*

❻ **Expozice Franze Kafky** (Franz Kafka's birthplace). Since the 1989 revolution, Kafka's popularity has soared, and the works of this German Jewish writer are now widely available in Czech. A museum in the house displays photos, editions of Kafka's books, and other memorabilia. (Kafka's grave lies in the overgrown New Jewish Cemetery at the Želivského Metro stop.) ⊠ *U radnice 5.* ☉ *Tues.–Fri. 10–6, Sat. 10–5.*

❷ **Na Příkopě.** Once part of the moat surrounding the Old Town, this street is now an elegant (in places) pedestrian mall. It leads from the bottom of Wenceslas Square to the **Obecní dům** (Municipal House), Prague's most lavish Art Nouveau building, which reopened in 1997 after a controversial, two-year refurbishment. A bridge links it to the

Prašná brána (Powder Tower), a 19th-century neo-Gothic restoration of the medieval original. ⊠ *Nám. Republiky.*

★ ⑤ **Staroměstské náměstí** (Old Town Square). The old commercial center of the Old Town is now a remarkably harmonious hub—architecturally beautiful and relatively car-free and quiet. Looming over the center, the twin towers of **Kostel Panny Marie před Týnem** (the Church of the Virgin Mary before Týn) look forbidding despite Disneyesque lighting. The large Secession-style **sculptural group** in the square's center commemorates the martyr Jan Hus, whose followers completed the Týn Church during the 15th century. The white Baroque **Kostel svatého Mikuláše** (Church of St. Nicholas) is tucked into the square's northwest angle. It was built by Kilian Ignatz Dientzenhofer, co-architect also of the Lesser Quarter's church of the same name. Every hour, mobs converge on the Clock Tower of the **Staroměstská radnice** (Old Town Hall) as the clock's 15th-century mechanism activates a procession that includes the 12 Apostles. A skeleton figure of Death tolls the bell. ⊠ *Pařížská, Dlouhá, Celetná, Železná, Melantrichova, and Kaprova.*

⑧ **Staronová synagóga** (Old-New Synagogue). A small congregation still attends the little Gothic Old-New Synagogue, one of Europe's oldest surviving houses of Jewish prayer. Men are required to cover their heads upon entering; skull caps are sold for a small fee at the door. ⊠ *Červená 3 at Pařížská.* ☉ *Sun.–Thurs. 9–5, Fri. 9–2.*

★ ⑨ **Starý židovský hřbitov** (Old Jewish Cemetery). The crowded cemetery is part of **Josefov**, the former Jewish quarter, and is one of Europe's most unforgettable sights. Here, ancient tombstones lean into one another; below them, piled layer upon layer, are thousands of graves. Many gravestones—they date from the mid-14th to the late 18th centuries—are carved with symbols indicating the name, profession, and attributes of the deceased. If you visit the tomb of the 16th-century scholar Rabbi Löw, you may see scraps of paper covered with prayers or requests stuffed into the cracks. In legend the rabbi protected Prague's Jews with the help of a *golem*, or artificial man; today he still receives appeals for assistance. ⊠ *Entrance at Pinkas Synagogue, Široká 3.*

❶ **Václavské náměstí** (Wenceslas Square). In the Times Square of Prague hundreds of thousands voiced their disgust for the Communist regime in November 1989 at the outset of the "Velvet Revolution." The "square" is actually a broad boulevard that slopes down from the **Národní muzeum** (National Museum) and the equestrian **statue of St. Václav** (Wenceslas). ⊠ *Between Wilsonova and jct. Na příkopě and 26 Října.*

❼ **Židovské muzeum** (Jewish Museum). The rich exhibits in Josefov's Pinkas Synagogue, Maisel Synagogue, Klaus Synagogue, Ceremonial Hall, and newly renovated Spanish Synagogue, along with the Old Jewish Cemetery, make up the museum. Jews, forced to fulfill Adolf Hitler's plan to document the lives of the people he was trying to exterminate, gathered the collections. They include ceremonial objects, textiles, and displays covering the history of Bohemia's and Moravia's Jews. The interior of the Pinkas Synagogue is especially poignant, as it is painted with the names of 77,297 Jewish Czechs killed during World War II. Pinkas Synagogue also contains a permanent exhibition of drawings by children who were interned at the Terezín (Theresienstadt) concentration camp from 1942 to 1944. *Museum ticket offices:* ⊠ *U starého hřbitova 3a and Široká 3.* ☉ *Sun.–Fri. 9–6 (9–4 in winter; last tour of cemetery at 3 in winter). Closed Sat. and religious holidays.*

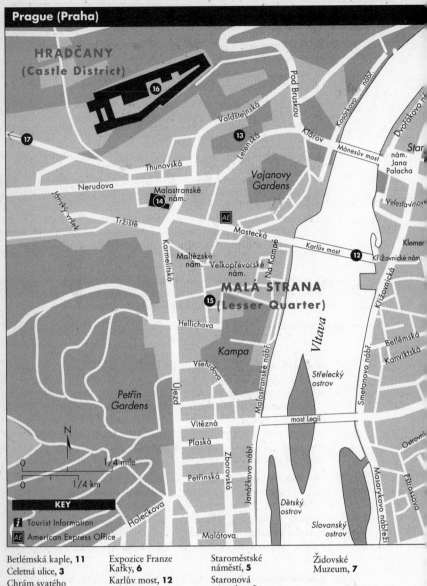

Prague (Praha)

HRADČANY
(Castle District)

16

17

Valdštejnská

Pod Bruskou

Klárov

Košárkovo nábř.

Dvořákovo ná

13

Letenská

Mánesův most

Star
nám.
Jana
Palacha

Thunovská

Vojanovy
Gardens

Nerudova

Malostranské
nám.

14

AE

Mostecká

Veleslavínov

Karlův most

12

Klemer

Jánský vršek

Tržiště

Karmelitská

Na Kampě

Křižovnické nám

Maltézské
nám. Velkopřevorské
nám.

MALÁ STRANA

Křižovnická

15

(Lesser Quarter)

Hellichova

Vltava

Betlémská

Kampa

Všehrdova

Malostranské nábř.

Střelecký
ostrov

Konvíktská

Petřín
Gardens

Újezd

Smetanovo nábř.

N

Vítězná

most Legií

Ostrovní

Plaská

1/4 mile

Zborovská

Petřínská

Janáčkovo nábř.

Dětský
ostrov

Masarykovo nábřeží

Příčrossova

0   1/4 km

Slovanský
ostrov

KEY

ℹ️ Tourist Information

Holečkova

AE American Express Office

Malátova

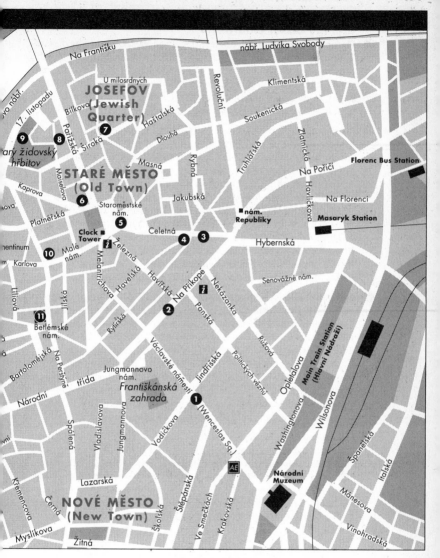

Na Františku

nábř. Ludvíka Svobody

U milosrdných

JOSEFOV
(Jewish
Quarter)

17. listopadu

Bílkova

Klimentská

Haštalská

Dlouhá

Soukenická

Revoluční

Pařížská

Široká

ová nábř.

9

8

ary židovský
hřbitov

Maiselova

Masná

Rybná

Truhlářská

Zlatnická

Na Poříčí

Havlíčkova

Florenc Bus Station

STARÉ MĚSTO
(Old Town)

Kaprova

Platnéřská

6

Jakubská

Na Florenci

Masaryk Station

ová.

Staroměstské
nám.

5

Celetná

■ **nám.**
Republiky

Clock
Tower ■

i

Železná

4

3

Hybernská

nentinum

Karlova

10

Malé
nám.

Melantrichova

Havelská

Havířská

Na Příkopě

Nekázanka

Senovážné nám.

Liliová

Jilská

Rytířská

2

i

Panská

Růžová

11

Betlémské
nám.

Bartolomějská

Na Perštýně

Jungmannovo
nám.

Františkánská
zahrada

Václavské náměstí

Jindřišská

Politických vězňů

Opletalova

Main Train Station
(Hlavní Nádraží)

Wilsonova

Národní

třída

1

[Wenceslas Sq.]

Spálená

Vladislavova

Jungmannova

Vodičkova

Washingtonova

Křemencová

Černá

NOVÉ MĚSTO
(New Town)

Lazarská

Štěpánská

Školská

AE

Ve Smečkách

Kralovská

Národní
Muzeum

Španělská

Italská

Mánesova

Myslíkova

Žitná

Vinohradská

Karlův most and Malá Strana (Charles Bridge and the Lesser Quarter)

⑭ Chrám svatého Mikuláše (Church of St. Nicholas). Designed by the late-17th-century Dietzenhofer architects, father and son, this is among the most beautiful examples of the Bohemian Baroque, an architectural style that flowered in Prague after the Counter-Reformation. On clear days you can enjoy great views from the tower. ⊠ *Malostranské nám.* ⏱ *Sept.–May, daily 9–4; June–Aug., daily 9–6.*

★ **⑫ Karlův most** (Charles Bridge). As you stand on this statue-lined stone bridge, unsurpassed in grace and setting, you see views of Prague that would be familiar to its 14th-century builder Peter Parler and to the artists who started adding the 30 sculptures during the 17th century. Today, nearly all the sculptures on the bridge are skillful copies of the originals, which have been taken indoors to be protected from the polluted air. The 12th on the left (starting from the Old Town side of the bridge) depicts St. Luitgarde (Matthias Braun sculpted the original, circa 1710). In the 14th on the left, a Turk guards suffering saints (F. M. Brokoff sculpted the original, circa 1714). The bridge itself is a gift to Prague from the Holy Roman Emperor Charles IV. ⊠ *Between Mostecká ul. on Malá Strana side and Karlova ul. on Old Town side.*

⑮ Malá Strana (Lesser Quarter). One of Prague's most intriguing neighborhoods, the "Little Town" lolls indolently below Prague Castle. Two events, above all, made possible the quarter's aristocratic architectural visage: the fire of 1541 and the expulsions of Czech nobles and townspeople defeated in the Protestant rebellion against the Catholic Habsburgs in 1620. Each of these catastrophes cleared the way for extensive rebuilding and new construction of palaces and gardens. On Malostranské náměstí (Lesser Quarter Square), you'll find the **Church of St. Nicholas** (☞ Chrám svatého Mikuláše, *above*). ⊠ *Bordered by Pražský hrad, Petřín Hill, Vítězná ul.*

⑬ Valdštejnská zahrada (Wallenstein Gardens). This is one of the most elegant of the many sumptuous Lesser Quarter gardens. During the 1620s the Habsburgs' victorious commander, Czech nobleman Albrecht of Wallenstein, demolished a wide swath of existing structures in order to build his oversize palace with its charming walled garden. A covered outdoor stage of late-Renaissance style dominates the western end. ⊠ *Entrance, Letenská 10.* ⊡ *Free.* ⏱ *May–Sept., daily 9–7.*

OFF THE BEATEN PATH
Villa Bertramka. While in Prague Mozart liked to stay at the secluded estate of his friends the Dušeks. The house is now a small museum packed with Mozart memorabilia. From Karmelitská ulice in Malá Strana, take Tram 12 south to the Anděl Metro station; walk down Plzeňská ulice a few hundred yards, and take a left at Mozartova ulice. ⊠ *Mozartova ul. 169, Smíchov,* ☎ *02/543893.* ⏱ *Daily 9:30–6.*

Pražský hrad and Hradčany (Prague Castle and the Castle District)

⑰ Loreta. This Baroque church and shrine are named for the Italian town to which angels supposedly transported the Virgin Mary's house from Nazareth to save it from the infidel. The glory of its fabulous treasury is the monstrance, the *Sun of Prague*, with its 6,222 diamonds. Arrive on the hour to hear the 27-bell carillon. ⊠ *Loretánské nám. 7.* ⏱ *Tues.–Sun. 9–noon and 1–4:30.*

★ **⑯ Pražský hrad** (Prague Castle). From its narrow hilltop, the monumental castle complex has witnessed the changing fortunes of the city for more than 1,000 years. The castle's physical and spiritual core, **Chrám** svatého Víta (St. Vitus Cathedral), took from 1344 to 1929 to build, so you can trace in its lines architectural styles from high Gothic to Art Nouveau. The eastern end, mostly the work of Peter Parler, builder of the Charles Bridge, is a triumph of Bohemian Gothic. "Good King" Wenceslas (in reality a mere prince, later canonized) has his own chapel in the south transept, dimly lit and decorated with fine medieval wall paintings. Note the fine 17th-century carved wooden panels on either side of the chancel. The left-hand panel shows a view of the castle and town in November 1620 as the defeated Czech Protestants flee into exile. The three easternmost chapels house tombs of Czech princes and kings of the 11th to the 13th centuries, while Charles IV and Rudolf II lie in the crypt, the former in a bizarre modern sarcophagus.

Behind St. Vitus's, don't miss the miniature houses of **Zlatá ulička** (Golden Lane). Its name, and the apocryphal tale of how Holy Roman Emperor Rudolf II used to lock up alchemists here until they transmuted lead into gold, may come from the gold-beaters who once lived here. Knightly tournaments often accompanied coronation ceremonies in the **Královský palác** (Royal Palace), next to the cathedral, hence the broad Riders' Staircase leading up to the grandiose **Vladislavský sál** (Vladislav Hall), with its splendid late-Gothic vaulting and Renaissance windows. Oldest of all the castle's buildings, though much restored, is the complex of **Bazilika svatého Jiří** (St. George's Basilica and Convent). The basilica's cool Romanesque lines hide behind a glowing salmon-color Baroque facade. The ex-convent houses a superb collection of Bohemian art from medieval religious sculptures to Baroque paintings. The castle **ramparts** afford glorious vistas of Prague's fabled hundred spires rising above the rooftops. ⊠ *Approach via Nerudova, Staré zámecké schody, or Keplerova. Main castle ticket office in Second Courtyard.* ▦ *100 Kč; tickets valid 3 days; admits visitors to cathedral, Royal Palace, and St. George's Basilica (but not convent gallery), and Powder Tower.* ⊙ *Oct.–Mar., daily 9–4; Apr.–Sept., daily 9–5. Castle gardens, Apr.–Oct., daily 9–5.*

Dining and Lodging

Eating out is important to Prague residents; make reservations whenever possible. For details and price-category definitions, *see* Dining *in* Czech Republic A to Z, *above.*

Many of Prague's older hotels have been renovated, and new establishments in old buildings ornament the Old Town and Lesser Quarter. Very few hotel rooms in the more desirable districts go for less than $100 per double room in high season; most less-expensive hotels are far from the center of Prague. Private rooms and pensions remain the best budget deal. For details and price-category definitions, *see* Lodging *in* Czech Republic A to Z, *above.*

$$$$ ✕ **Circle Line Brasserie.** Elegant yet decidedly un-stuffy, this dining spot tucked into a restored Baroque palace in Malá Strana offers delicious nouvelle cuisine specialties. Appetizers and main courses may include hare terrine with sun-dried plums and apricots; roasted lamb sweetbreads with truffle sauce; and grilled veal ribs with mustard seed sauce. A pianist plays unintrusively each evening; service is gracious and discreet. ⊠ *Malostranské nám. 12, Malá Strana,* ☎ *02/530308. Reservations essential. AE, DC, MC, V.*

$$$$ ✕ **U Zlaté Hrušky.** Careful restoration has returned this restaurant to its original 18th-century style. It specializes in Moravian wines, which are well matched with fillet steaks and goose liver. ⊠ *Nový Svět 3, Hradčany,* ☎ *02/2051–5356. Reservations essential. AE, V.*

$$$$ ✕ **Vinárna V Zátiši.** Impeccably gracious service and serene sur-
★ roundings make an evening at the Still Life one of Prague's most memorable dining experiences. Continental cuisine is exquisitely prepared
and presented—fish and game specialities are outstanding. The wine
list is extensive, with special emphasis on French vintages. ⊠ *Liliová
1, Staré Město,* ☎ *02/2422–8977. Reservations essential. AE, MC, V.*

$$$ ✕ **U Mecenáše.** This wine restaurant manages to be both medieval and
elegant despite the presence of an ancient gallows. Try to get a table
in the back room. The chef specializes in thick, juicy steaks, served with
a variety of sauces. ⊠ *Malostranské nám. 10, Malá Strana,* ☎ *02/
533881. Reservations essential. AE, MC, V. No lunch.*

$$$ ✕ **U Modré Kachničky.** The exuberant, eclectic decor is as attractive
★ as the Czech and international dishes, which include steaks, duck, and
game in autumn, and Bohemian trout and carp. ⊠ *Nebovidská 6, Malá
Strana,* ☎ *02/5732–0308. Dinner reservations essential. AE, V.*

$$$ ✕ **Zlatý kohout.** One of the city's best-kept secrets, the Golden Rooster,
★ in the shadow of Prague's gorgeous Baroque New Town Hall, offers
delectable Continental dishes in unpretentious yet elegant surround-
ings. Especially good is the creamy carrot-orange soup. Zlatý kohout
is the restaurant of choice for habitués and employees of the nearby
French and Belgian cultural institutes. ⊠ *Karlovo nám. 24, Nové
Město,* ☎ *02/2223–2382. Reservations essential. AE, MC, V.*

$$ ✕ **Amadé.** In this cellar restaurant near Old Town's St. Agnes Cloister, Czech cooking meets Swiss and Austrian cuisines, with marvelous
results. The wine list offers Czech wines plus a carefully selected range
from Chile, Bulgaria, Spain, and France. Recommended dishes: Zurich
Geschnetzeltes (slivers of veal in a white wine sauce with hints of
tangy mustard) and dessert pancakes filled with bitter chocolate. ⊠ *U
Milosrdných 10, Staré Město,* ☎ *02/2318867. No credit cards.*

$$ ✕ **Chez Marcel.** This authentic French bistro on a quiet, picturesque
street offers a little taste of Paris in the center of Prague's Old Town.
French owned and operated, Chez Marcel has an extensive menu suit-
able for lingering over a three-course meal (French cheeses, salads, patés,
rabbit, and some of the best steaks in Prague) or just a quick espresso.
⊠ *Haštalská 12, Staré Město,* ☎ *02/231–5676. No credit cards.*

$$ ✕ **Dynamo.** With a consistent clientele of beautiful people, this little
green diner is one of the trendiest spots on what is fast becoming a ver-
itable restaurant row. Dynamo's quirky menu offers tasty variations
on Continental themes, such as liver and apples on toast, and succulent eggplant filled with grilled vegetables. ⊠ *Pštrossova 221/29, Nové
Město,* ☎ *02/294224. AE, MC, V.*

$$ ✕ **Palffy palác.** The faded charm of an old-world palace makes this a
★ lovely, romantic spot for a meal. Very good Continental cuisine is
served with elegance that befits the surroundings. Try the potatoes au
gratin or chicken stuffed with goat cheese. Surprisingly, brunches here
are not worth the price. Dining is also possible on the terrace in sum-
mer. ⊠ *Valdštejnská 14, Malá Strana,* ☎ *02/5732–0570. AE, MC, V.*

$$ ✕ **Pezinok.** You'll get good, filling Slovak fare at this relaxed, no-frills
restaurant behind Národní třída in the New Town. The homemade
sausage, accompanied by hearty wine, is excellent. ⊠ *Purkyňova 4,
Nové Město,* ☎ *02/2494–6537. AE, MC, V.*

$–$$ ✕ **Novoměstský pivovar.** Always packed with out-of-towners and lo-
cals alike, this microbrewery-restaurant is a maze of rooms, some
painted in mock-medieval style, others decorated with murals of Prague
street scenes. Pork knuckle *(vepřové koleno)* is a favorite dish. The beer
is the cloudy, fruity, fermented style exclusive to this venue. ⊠ *Vodičkova
20, Prague 1,* ☎ *02/2423–3533. AE, MC, V.*

$ ✕ **Bohemia Bagel.** The casual, American-owned and child-friendly
Bohemia Bagel serves a good assortment of fresh bagels from raisin-

walnut to "supreme" with all kinds of spreads and toppings. The thick soups are among the best in Prague for the price, and the bottomless cups of coffee (from gourmet blends) are a further draw. ⊠ *Újezd 16, Malá Strána,* ☏ *02/531002. No credit cards.*

$ ✕ **Česká hospoda v Krakovské.** Right off Wenceslas Square, this clean pub noted for its excellent traditional fare is the place to try Bohemian duck. Pair it with cold Krušovice beer. ⊠ *Krakovská 20, Nové Město,* ☏ *02/2221–0204. No credit cards.*

$ ✕ **Country Life.** A godsend for Praguers and travelers, this health-food cafeteria offers a bounteous (and fresh!) salad bar and daily rotating meat-free specials. The dining area has that rare Prague luxury for a low-end eating establishment: no blaring techno music. There's table service evenings after 6:30. It's off the courtyard connecting Melantrichova and Michalská streets. ⊠ *Melantrichova 15, Staré Město,* ☏ *02/ 2421–3366. No credit cards. Closed Sat.*

$ ✕ **Kavárna Slavia.** This legendary hangout for the best and brightest of
★ the Czech arts world—from composer Bedřich Smetana and poet Jaroslav Seifert to then-dissident Václav Havel—is back in business after real-estate wrangles held it hostage for most of the '90s. Its Art Deco decor is a perfect backdrop for people-watching, and the vistas (the river and Prague Castle or the National Theater) are a compelling reason to linger over an espresso. You can also order a light meal here. ⊠ *Smetanovo nábřeží 1012/2, Nové Město,* ☏ *02/2422–0957. No credit cards.*

$ ✕ **U Zlatého Tygra.** This crowded hangout is the last of a breed of authentic Czech pivnice. The smoke and stares preclude a long stay, but it's worth a visit for such pub staples as ham and cheese plates or roast pork. The service is surly, but the beer is good. ⊠ *Husova 17, Staré Město,* ☏ *02/2422–9020. Reservations not accepted. No credit cards.*

$$$$ 🛏 **Diplomat.** Completed in 1990, the Diplomat fuses style with Western efficiency. A 10-minute taxi or subway ride from the Old Town, it's convenient to the airport. The hotel is modern and tasteful, with a huge, sunny lobby and comfortable rooms. ⊠ *Evropská 15, 160 00 Prague 6,* ☏ *02/2439–4111,* ℻ *02/2439–4215. 369 rooms, 13 suites. 2 restaurants. AE, DC, MC, V.*

$$$$ 🛏 **Dům U Červeného Lva.** In Malá Strana, a five-minute walk from
★ Prague Castle's front gates, the Baroque House at the Red Lion is an intimate, immaculately kept hotel. The spare but comfortable guest rooms have parquet floors, 17th-century painted-beam ceilings, superb antiques, and all-white bathrooms with brass fixtures. The two top-floor rooms can double as a suite. There is no elevator, and stairs are steep. ⊠ *Nerudova 41, 118 00 Prague 1,* ☏ *02/537–239 or 02/538–192,* ℻ *02/538–193. 11 rooms. 2 restaurants. AE, MC, V.*

$$$$ 🛏 **Hoffmeister.** On a picturesque (if a bit busy) corner near the Mal-
★ ostranská Metro station, this is one of the most stylish small hotels in the city. Rooms, done in a soothing palette of blues, grays, and purples, have finely crafted wood built-ins and luxuriously appointed bathrooms. Museum-quality prints by the proprietor's father hang throughout the hotel. ⊠ *Pod Bruskou 7, 118 00 Prague 1,* ☏ *02/5731–0942,* ℻ *02/ 530959 or 02/5732–0906. 42 rooms. Restaurant. AE, DC, MC, V.*

$$$$ 🛏 **Palace Praha.** The Art Nouveau–style Palace is Prague's most ele-
★ gant and luxurious hotel, though it now faces tougher competition from other luxury hotels. Rooms have high ceilings, marble baths with phones, and minibars with complimentary snacks and beverages. Its central location just off Wenceslas Square offers more convenience than local character. ⊠ *Panská 12, 110 00 Prague 1,* ☏ *02/2409–3111,* ℻ *02/2422–1240. 125 rooms. Restaurant. AE, DC, MC, V.*

$$$ 🛏 **Hotel U staré paní.** "The Old Lady" is a delightfully cozy hotel only five minutes by foot from Old Town Square, in a renovated building on one of Prague's most atmospheric Old Town lanes. Comfortable rooms are decorated in soft tones with simple Scandinavian-style furnishings. One of Prague's best jazz clubs has concerts nightly here in the basement. (Yes, it is soundproofed.) ✉ *Michalská 9, 110 00 Prague 1,* ☎ *02/267267, 02/264920, or 02/261655,* FAX *02/267–9841, 02/267267, or 02/264920. 18 rooms. Restaurant, jazz club. AE, MC, V.*

$$$ 🏨 **Kampa.** An early Baroque armory-turned-hotel, the Kampa is tucked away in a residential corner of the Lesser Quarter. The rooms are clean, if spare, but the bucolic setting one block from the river as well as a lovely park compensate for its relative remoteness. ✉ *Všehrdova 16, 118 00 Prague 1,* ☎ *02/5732–0508 or 02/732–0404,* FAX *02/5732–0262. 85 rooms. Restaurant. AE, DC, MC, V.*

$$$ 🏨 **Opera.** Once the lodging of choice for divas performing at the nearby State Theater, the Opera greatly declined under the Communists. The mid-'90s saw the grand fin de siècle facade rejuvenated with a perky pink-and-white paint job and the installation of bathrooms and TVs in all rooms. Comfy wing chairs add to the rooms, which are decorated in tan and white. ✉ *Těšnov 13, 110 00 Prague 1,* ☎ *02/231–5609,* FAX *02/231–1477. 64 rooms. Restaurant, bar. AE, DC, MC, V.*

$$ 🏨 **Central.** Quite conveniently, this hotel lives up to its name, with a site near Celetná ulice and Náměstí Republiky. Rooms are sparely furnished, but all have baths. The Baroque glories of the Old Town are steps away. ✉ *Rybná 8, 110 00 Prague 1,* ☎ *02/2481–2041,* FAX *02/232–8404. 62 rooms, 4 suites. Restaurant, bar. AE, DC, MC, V.*

$ 🏨 **Balkan.** The hotel is a spiffy yellow building on an otherwise drab street not far from the Lesser Quarter. Rooms are small, simple, clean: white speads and walls, tan paneling, lacy curtains. Request a room at the back, as the hotel is on a major street, one block from the tram stop. ✉ *Svornosti 28, 150 00 Prague 5,* ☎ FAX *02/540777. 24 rooms. Breakfast not included. Restaurant. AE.*

$ 🏨 **Pension Unitas.** Operated by the Christian charity Unitas in an Old Town convent, this well-run establishment has sparely furnished rooms, all of which are nonsmoking. Note that an adjacent 3-star hotel, Cloister Inn, shares the same address and phone number. ✉ *Bartolomějská 9, 110 00 Prague 1,* ☎ *02/2327700,* FAX *02/2327709. 34 rooms without bath. Reserve well in advance, even for off-season. Restaurant. AE, MC, V.*

$ 🏨 **Penzion Sprint.** Basic, clean, no-frills rooms, most of which have their own bathrooms (however tiny), make the Sprint a fine budget choice. The rustic-looking pension is on a quiet residential street in the outskirts of Prague about 20 minutes from the airport; tram 18 rumbles directly to Old Town. ✉ *Cukrovárnická 64, 160 00 Prague 6,* ☎ *02/312–3338,* FAX *02/312–4871. 12 rooms, 8 with bath. AE, MC, V.*

Nightlife and the Arts

The Arts

Prague's cultural life is one of its top attractions—and its citizens like to dress up and participate; performances can be booked far ahead. Monthly programs of events are available at the PIS (☞ Visitor Information *in* Prague Essentials, *below*), Čedok (☞ Visitor Information *in* Prague Essentials, *below*), or hotels. The English-language newspaper *The Prague Post* carries detailed entertainment listings. The main ticket agencies are **Bohemia Ticket International** (✉ Na Příkopě 16, ☎ 02/2421–5031) and **Ticketpro** (✉ Salvátorská 10, ☎ 02/2481–4020, FAX 02/2481–4021). For major concerts, opera, and theater, it's much cheaper to buy tickets at the box office.

CONCERTS

Performances are held in many palaces and churches. Too often, programs lack originality (how many different ensembles can play the *Four*

Seasons at once?), but the settings are lovely and the acoustics can be superb. Concerts at the **churches of St. Nicholas** in both the Old Town Square and the Lesser Quarter are especially enjoyable. At **St. James's Church** on Malá Stupartská (Old Town) cantatas are performed amid a flourish of Baroque statuary. At the Prague Castle's **Garden on the Ramparts,** music in summer comes with a view.

The excellent Czech Philharmonic plays in the intimate, lavish Dvořák Hall in the **Rudolfinum** (✉ Nám. Jana Palacha, ☎ 02/2489–3352). The lush home of the Prague Symphony, **Smetana Hall,** reopened in 1997 along with the rest of the Obecní dům building (✉ Nám. Republiky 5, ☎ 02/2200–2100 or 02/2200–2101).

OPERA AND BALLET
Opera is of an especially high standard in the Czech Republic. One of the main venues in the grand style of the 19th century is the beautifully restored **National Theater** (✉ Národní třída 2, ☎ 02/2421–5001). The **State Opera of Prague** (✉ Wilsonova 4, ☎ 02/265353), formerly the Smetana Theater, is another historic site for opera lovers. The **Theater of the Estates** (✉ Ovocný trh 1, ☎ 02/2421–5001) hosts opera, ballet, and theater performances by the National Theater ensembles. Mozart conducted the premiere of *Don Giovanni* here.

PUPPET SHOWS
This traditional form of Czech entertainment, generally adaptations of operas performed to recorded music, has been given new life at the **National Marionette Theater** (✉ Žatecká 1, ☎ 02/2324565).

THEATER
A dozen or so professional companies play in Prague to packed houses. Nonverbal theater abounds as well, notably "black theater," a melding of live acting, mime, video, and stage trickery that, despite signs of fatigue, continues to draw crowds. The popular **Archa Theater** (✉ Na Poříčí 26, ☎ 02/232–8800) offers avant-garde and experimental theater, music, and dance and hosts world-class visiting ensembles, including the Royal Shakespeare Company. **Laterna Magika** (Magic Lantern; ✉ Národní třída 4, ☎ 02/2491–4129) is one of the more established producers of black theater extravaganzas.

Nightlife

DISCOS AND CABARET
Discos catering to a young crowd blast sound onto lower Wenceslas Square. **Corona Club and Latin Café** (✉ Novotného lávká, ☎ 02/2108–2357) has Latin, Gypsy, and other dance-friendly music. A classier act, where the newest dance music plays, is the ever-popular **Radost FX** (✉ Bělehradská 120, Prague 2, ☎ 02/251210).

JAZZ AND ROCK CLUBS
Jazz clubs are a Prague institution, although foreign customers keep them in business. Excellent Czech groups play the tiny **AghaRTA** (✉ Krakovská 5, ☎ 02/2221–1275); arrive well before the 9 PM show time to get a seat with a sight line. Top jazz groups (and the odd world-music touring ensemble) play **Jazz Club U staré paní** (✉ Michalská 9, ☎ 02/264920) in Old Town. **Malostranská Beseda** (✉ Malostranské nám. 21, ☎ 02/539024) is a funky hall for rock, jazz, and folk. At the alt **Palác Akropolis** (✉ Kubelíkova 27, ☎ 02/9000–2310) you can hear folk, rock, and jazz. **Reduta** (✉ Národní třída 20, ☎ 02/2491–2246), the city's best-known jazz club for three decades, stars mostly local talent. Hip locals congregate at **Roxy** (✉ Dlouhá 33, ☎ 02/2481–0951) for everything from punk to funk to New Age tunes.

Shopping

Many of the main shops are in and around Old Town Square and Na Příkopě, as well as along Celetná ulice and Pařížská. On the Lesser Quarter side, Nerudova has the densest concentration of shops.

Department Stores

The biggest department store is **Kotva** (⊠ Nám. Republiky 8), which grows flashier and more expensive every year. **Bílá Labuť'** (⊠ Na Poříčí 23) is a good-value option. The basement supermarket at **Tesco** (⊠ Národní třída 26) is the best and biggest in the city.

Specialty Shops

Shops specializing in Bohemian crystal, porcelain, ceramics, and antiques abound in Old Town and Malá Strana, and on Golden Lane at Prague Castle. Look for the name **Dílo** (⊠ Staroměstské nám. 15, Old Town; U Lužického semináře 14, Malá Strana) for glass and ceramic sculptures, prints, and paintings by local artists. **Lidová Řemesla** (folk art; ⊠ Jilská 22, Old Town; Mostecká 17, Malá Strana) shops stock wooden toys, elegant blue-and-white textiles, and charming Christmas ornaments made from straw or pastry. **Moser** (⊠ Na Příkopě 12, ☎ 02/2421–1293) is the source for glass and porcelain.

Side Trips

The castle and spa region of Bohemia or the history-drenched villages of Moravia make excellent (and convenient) excursions from Prague. Buses or trains link the capital with every corner of the Bohemian region; transportation to towns in Moravia takes longer (three hours or more from the capital) but is also dependable.

Bohemia's Spas and Castles

The Bohemian countryside is a restful world of gentle hills and thick woods. It is especially beautiful during fall foliage season or in May, when the fruit trees that line the roads are in blossom. Two of the most famous of the Czech Republic's scores of spas lie in such settings: Karlovy Vary (Karlsbad) and Mariánské Lázně (Marienbad). During the 19th and early 20th centuries, European royalty and aristocrats came to ease their overindulged bodies (or indulge them even more) at these spas.

South Bohemia, a country of lonely castles, green hills, and quiet fish ponds, is sprinkled with exquisite medieval towns, many of them undergoing much-needed rehabilitation. In such towns as Tábor, the Hussite reformist movement was born during the early 15th century, sparking a series of religious conflicts that engulfed all of Europe. Countering the Hussites from Český Krumlov was the powerful Rožmberk family, who scattered castles over the countryside and created lake-size "ponds" in which to breed highly prized carp, still the focus of a Czech Christmas dinner.

Praguers love to spend weekends in the **Berounka Valley,** where two magnificent castles rise up over the river.

Karlštejn, less than an hour from Prague off Route E50 (direction Beroun), is an admirable restoration of the 14th-century castle built by Charles IV. It protects the crown jewels of the Holy Roman Empire, housed in the castle's stunning **Kaple svatého kříže** (Chapel of the Holy Rood), which is filled with 128 Gothic paintings and 2,000 dazzling gems. ⊠ *Karlštejn,* ☎ *0311/684617 or 0311/681617.* ⊙ *Nov.–Mar., Tues.–Sun. 9–3; Apr. and Oct., Tues.–Sun. 9–4; May, June, and Sept., Tues.–Sun. 9–5; July and Aug., Tues.–Sun. 9–6.*

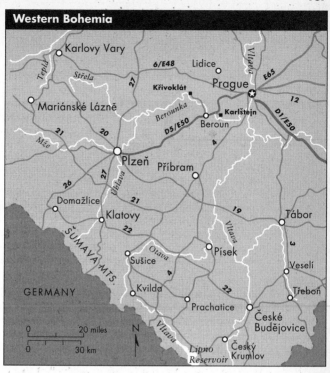

Western Bohemia

Karlovy Vary · Střela · 6/E48 · Lidice · Vltava · Prague · E65 · Mariánské Lázně · Křivoklát · Berounka · Karlštejn · 12 · D1/E50 · Beroun · D5/E50 · Tepla · 27 · 21 · 20 · Mže · Plzeň · Příbram · 26 · 27 · Vltava · 21 · Domažlice · 22 · 19 · Tábor · Klatovy · Otava · Písek · 3 · ŠUMAVA MTS. · Sušice · Veselí · GERMANY · Kvilda · 22 · Třeboň · Prachatice · České Budějovice · 20 miles · 30 km · N · Vltava · Lipno Reservoir · Český Krumlov

The main attractions of **Křivoklát** are its glorious woodlands, a favorite royal hunting ground in times past. The castle is about an hour from Prague. ⊠ *Křivoklát,* ☎ *0313/558440.* ⊘ *Apr.–May and Sept.–Dec., Tues.–Sun. 9–4; June–Aug., Tues.–Sun. 9–6.*

★ About two hours from Prague by car on route E48, **Karlovy Vary,** or Karlsbad, was named for the Holy Roman Emperor Charles IV. While he was in pursuit of a deer during a hunt, the animal supposedly led him to the main spring of Vřídlo. Over the years the spa attracted not only many of the crowned heads and much of the blue blood of Europe, but also leading musicians and writers. Its confident bourgeois architecture nestles in a deep, forested valley; the meandering Tepla River divides the town down the middle. The elegant, old spa part of town is lined with fanciful turn-of-the-century buildings in soft colors. Four colonnades (free-standing covered pedestrian walkways), one of wrought iron, one of carved wood, one of stone, and one of steel and glass, allow leisurely strolling and sipping of mineral waters. The waters from the spa's 12 springs are uniformly foul-tasting: Sip them while nibbling rich Karlovy Vary *oplatky* (wafers), then resort to the "13th spring," Karlovy Vary's tangy herbal liqueur known as Becherovka.

$$$$ 🏨 **Dvořák.** Opened in 1991, this Austrian-built hotel in the center of town has imaginative decor, with whimsical white furniture, pale peach walls, and lacy curtains. The view from the front rooms looks out onto the Tepla River and rose gardens in season. The lobby is bright, and the staff is cheerful and utterly professional. ⊠ *Nova louka 11, 360 21,* ☎ *017/322–4145,* 𝖥𝖠𝖷 *017/322–2814. 76 rooms, 3 suites. Restaurant. AE, DC, MC, V.*

$$$–$$$$ 🏨 **Grandhotel Pupp.** Founded in 1701, the Pupp still has a fine 18th-
★ century hall, the Slavností sál. It's one of the oldest surviving hotels in Europe, with glittering names—past and present—in its guest register.

For more elegance, request a room furnished in 19th-century period style; other rooms were redecorated in a functional way under Communism. ⊠ *Mírové nám. 2, 360 91,* ☎ *017/310–9111,* 𝔽𝔸𝕏 *017/322–4032. 214 rooms, 10 suites. 2 restaurants. AE, DC, MC, V.*

$$–$$$ 🏨 **Thermal.** An unappealing gray high-rise, the hotel, built during the 1970s, is solidly anchored at one end of Karlovy Vary's colonnade. Its rooms are not special—narrow and simply furnished with basic white furniture and lots of mirrors—but the balconies of all front-facing rooms afford a magical view over the entire colonnade and the rolling hills of the town. The Thermal's heated outdoor pool, built into a hillside and open year-round, allows similar gorgeous vistas. ⊠ *I. P. Pavlova 11, 360 00 Karlovy Vary,* ☎ *017/321–1111,* 𝔽𝔸𝕏 *017/322–6992. 145 rooms. 2 restaurants, pool. AE, DC, MC, V.*

The sanatoriums and colonnades of **Mariánské Lázně** (Marienbad) are impressively arrayed around an oblong park; it's not hard to conjure up visions of Chopin or Goethe retreating here from the comparatively noisy Karlovy Vary. Nowadays, the town has one of the Czech Republic's best golf courses and hosts a PGA European Tour event. The resort is about three hours from Prague, on Route 21 off Route E50.

$$$–$$$$ 🏨 **Palace.** Built during the spa's heyday in 1875, this elegant five-story building is in the resort center. Turrets sprout at the top of the bright white-and-canary-yellow hotel, and the myriad balconies have swirling metal railings. Chandeliers and gold-color plating glisten in the public rooms. The comfortable guest rooms are less ostentatious, decorated in peach tones, with simple light fixtures and fluted white furniture. No-smoking rooms are available, as are complete spa services on-site. ⊠ *Hlavní třída 67, 353 01,* ☎ *0165/622222,* 𝔽𝔸𝕏 *0165/624262. 40 rooms, 5 suites. Restaurant, spa. AE, DC, MC, V.*

$$$ 🏨 **Bohemia.** At this lemon-yellow spa resort beautiful crystal chandeliers in the main hall set the stage for a comfortable and elegant stay. The rooms are well appointed in soothing pale tones. To be really decadent request one of the enormous suites overlooking the park. The staff can arrange spa treatments and horseback riding. Rates are significantly lower in fall and winter. ⊠ *Hlavní třída 100, 353 01,* ☎ *0165/623251,* 𝔽𝔸𝕏 *0165/622943. 73 rooms, 4 suites. Restaurant. AE, DC, MC, V.*

★   Once the main seat of the Rožmberks, Bohemia's noblest family, **Český Krumlov,** about four hours south of Prague (on Route 55 to České Budějovice and then on Route 159), is an enchanting town with its imposing Renaissance **Hrad** (castle; ☎ 0337/711465; ⊙ Apr., Oct, Tues.–Sun. 9–4; May–Aug., Tues.–Sun. 8–5; Sept., Tues.–Sun. 9–5), complete with romantic elevated walkways, a round, pastel-hue tower, and an 18th-century theater that still hosts performances. The Vltava River snakes through the town, which has steeply stacked steps on either bank linking various levels and twisting narrow lanes that converge on **Náměstí Svornosti,** the Old Town's main square. A number of notable Renaissance houses add an air of formality to this exquisite place. The **Mezinárodní kulturní centrum Egona Schieleho** (Egon Schiele Center) exhibits the work of the painter, a frequent visitor to the town, and other 20th-century artists. ⊠ *Široká 70–72,* ☎ *0337/711224.* ⊙ *Daily 10–6 (11–5 in low season).*

$$$ ✕🏨 **Na louži.** Homey wooden shutters on street level set the old-but-
★   cared-for atmosphere of this friendly pub-restaurant and the five immaculate small rooms upstairs, which are furnished with cozy country-style beds and wardrobes. ⊠ *Kájovská 66, 381 01,* ☎ 𝔽𝔸𝕏 *0337/711280. 5 rooms. Restaurant. No credit cards.*

$$$ 🏨 **Růže.** The stone exterior clearly shows its Renaissance monastery past, but the lobby is modern. Most of the (smallish) rooms were modernized in the '70s with violet as the color of choice; they have tiny Gothic windows. ⊠ *Horní ul. 153, 381 01,* ☎ *0337/711141,* ℻ *0337/711128. 50 rooms, 38 with bath. Restaurant. AE, DC, MC, V.*

After Jan Hus's death at the stake in 1415, his proto-Protestant followers established an egalitarian commune on a fortified bluff above the Lužnice river. The zealots of **Tábor** (1½ hr from Prague on Route E55) were shaped into Europe's most-feared army. The town itself became a weapon of defense: Its twisting streets were designed to confuse the enemy. A labyrinth of tunnels and cellars below the town served as both living quarters and link with the outer defenses. The story is told in the **Husitské muzeum** (Hussite Museum) just off Žižkovo náměstí. ⊠ *Křivkova 31.* ⊙ *Apr.–Nov. 8:30–4 (in winter on request).*

Moravian Towns

Moravia, with its peaceful villages and small towns three to four hours southeast of Prague, is the easternmost of the historic Czech Lands, sharing a lightly populated border with Bohemia.

A former center of Jewish life and learning in the Habsburg empire, **Mikulov** (about 4 hrs southeast of Prague on Route 620 off E55) now bears few traces of its scholarly past. Today, the town is known for its wine making. During the grape harvest in October, head for the limestone hills surrounding the town—tradition dictates that a knock on the door of a private *sklípek* (wine cellar) will lead to a tasting session. The town's Baroque-and-Gothic **Zámek Mikulov** (château) contains a wine-making museum where you can see a 22,000-gallon wine cask from 1643. ⊠ ☎ *0625/2255.* ⊙ *Apr.–Oct., Tues.–Sun. 9–4.*

$–$$$ ╳⛩ **Rohatý Krokodýl.** This classic hotel (the Horned Crocodile) is perfectly in keeping with the town's look in that it is a long, low white building on a street that dates back to the Renaissance. Furnishings are simple, modern, and immaculately clean. The restaurant—with terrace dining in summer and hearty Czech specialties—is outstanding. ⊠ *Husova 8, 692 01,* ☎ *0625/2692,* ℻ *0625/3695. 10 rooms, 3 suites. Restaurant. AE, MC, V.*

Amid the farmlands and industrial centers of middle Moravia, **Olomouc,** three hours from Prague on Route 462 off E50, comes as an unexpected joy. The city retains its rambling Old Town, partially circled by high brick fortifications. The Renaissance town hall and the tall, impossibly ornate Trinity column compete for attention on **Horní náměstí,** the main square. At the eastern end of the Old Town are the neo-Gothic **Dóm svatého Václava** (Cathedral of St. Wenceslas; ⊠ Václavské nám.), one of the glories of Moravia, and a ruined 12th-century **palace** (⊠ Dómská ul.) with an exquisite row of Romanesque stone windows.

$$$ ⛩ **Hotel U Dómu.** This cozy, well-cared-for establishment run by the Jiříček family is steps from the cathedral. Spacious rooms (all including kitchenettes and large bathrooms) are furnished with simple, Scandinavian-style furniture, pastel carpeting, and white walls; tasteful, original watercolors decorating the rooms are by local artists. Service is friendly and obliging. ⊠ *Dómská 4, 772 00,* ☎ *068/522–0502,* ℻ *068/522–0501. 6 rooms. Café-bar. MC, V.*

It is a surprise to come upon trim little **Telč,** with its neat, formal architecture, nestled in such bucolic countryside on Route 406 (E50 and 19). Only the Renaissance facades, each fronted by arcades and topped with rich gables, are visible, and although these are colorful, cute, and well maintained, often the buildings behind them are falling apart. The Renaissance theme carries over to the **Zámek Telč** (château), whose architecture and

decoration form a rare pre-Baroque example of stylistic unity. ☎ 066/
962821. ⊙ Apr.–Oct., Tues.–Sun. 9–4.

Prague Essentials

Arriving and Departing

BY BUS

The Czech bus network (**ČSAD**) operates from a station (⊠ Křižíkova
4, ☎ 02/1034) near Prague's main train station. Take Metro B or C
to the Florenc stop.

BY PLANE

All international flights arrive at Prague's Ruzyně Airport, about 20
km (12 mi) from downtown. For arrival and departure times, call ☎
02/367760 or 02/2011–3314.

Between the Airport and Downtown. The private Cedaz **minibus shuttle** links the airport and Náměstí Republiky. Shuttles run every 30 to
60 minutes between 5:30 AM and 9 PM daily. The trip costs 90 Kč one-
way and takes about 30 minutes. On regular **Bus** 119 the cost is 12
Kč, but you'll need to change to the subway at the Dejvická station to
reach the center. By **taxi,** expect to pay 600 Kč to the center. Only one
city-authorized firm, FIX (unmetered: the fee is up to the drivers; negotiate before stepping into the car), is permitted to pick up customers
at the airport. (You may take any taxi *to* the airport, however.)

BY TRAIN

The main station is Hlavní Nádraží (⊠ Wilsonova ul.), not far from
Wenceslas Square. Some international trains use Nádraží Holešovice
(⊠ Vrbenského ul.), on the same Metro line (C) as the main station.
Call ☎ 02/2422–4200, 02/2461–4030, or 02/2461–4031 for domes-
tic and international schedules for both stations.

Getting Around

BY CAR

In the center of the city meters with green stripes let you park up to
six hours; an orange stripe indicates a two-hour limit. Blue-marked spaces
are reserved for local residents. (Parking boots may be attached to of-
fending vehicles.) There is an underground lot (⊠ Alšovo nábřeží) near
Old Town Square.

BY PUBLIC TRANSPORT

Public transportation is a bargain. *Jízdenky* (tickets) can be bought at
hotels, newsstands, and dispensing machines in Metro stations. Transport passes for unlimited use of the system for one day (70 Kč) up to
15 days (280 Kč) are sold at some newsstands and at the windows
marked DP or *Jízdenky* in the main Metro stations. Be sure to validate
your pass by signing it where indicated. A basic 12-Kč ticket allows
one hour's travel, with unlimited transfers (90 minutes on weekends
and between 8 PM and 5 AM weekdays) on the Metro, tram, and bus
network within the city limits. Cheaper 8-Kč tickets are good for a tram
or bus ride up to 15 minutes without transferring, or 30 minutes on
the Metro including transfers between lines; on the Metro, though, you
cannot travel more than four stops from your starting point. For the
Metro punch the ticket in the station before getting onto the escala-
tors; for buses and trams punch the ticket inside the vehicle (enter the
tram or bus through any door and stick the tickets horizontally—and
gently—into the little yellow machines, which should "stamp" them
with the date and time; it's an acquired trick of hand-eye coordination; ask for help from another passenger if your machine is not cooperating, which is often the case). If you fail to validate your ticket
you may be fined 200 Kč by a ticket inspector.

Note: Prague has quite a pickpocketing racket, to which the police apparently turn a blind eye. Be very wary of raucous groups of people making a commotion as they get on and off trams and metros; generally they are working the passengers. Keep close watch on your belongings and purses on crowded streets and in crowded sites.

Subway. Prague's three modern Metro lines are easy to use and relatively safe. They provide the simplest and fastest means of transportation, and most new maps of Prague mark the routes. The Metro runs from 5 AM to midnight, seven days a week.

Tram and Bus. Trams are often more convenient than the Metro for short hops. Most bus lines connect outlying suburbs with the nearest Metro station. Trams 50–59 and buses numbered 500 and above run all night—at, however, intervals of up to an hour—after the Metro stops.

BY TAXI
Each of Prague's countless taxi operators is allowed to set its own fares; the rates should be posted on the cab doors. The average basic charge is 20–30 Kč and per-kilometer rates range from 15 Kč to 30 Kč. Order them in advance by telephone. Try **AAA** (☎ 02/1080) or **Profitaxi** (☎ 02/1035). Some larger hotels have their own fleets, which are a little more expensive.

Note: Do not pick up cabs on the street, especially in the tourist areas: taxi drivers in Prague are notorious for doctoring their meters and for being in with the mafia, and many drivers will not hesitate to rip you off, threaten you if you balk at paying their exorbitant prices, or worse.

Contacts and Resources

EMBASSIES AND CONSULATE
U.S. (⊠ Tržiště 15, Malá Strana, ☎ 02/5732–0663). **Canadian** (⊠ Mickiewiczova 6, Hradčany, ☎ 02/2431–1108). **U.K.** (⊠ Thunovská 14, Malá Strana, ☎ 02/5732–0355). **Australian** (The Honorary Consulate and Trade Commission of Australia, ⊠ Na Ořechovce 38, ☎ 02/2431–0071 or 02/2431–0743).

EMERGENCIES
Police (☎ 158). **Ambulance** (☎ 155). **Foreigners' Department of Na Homolce Hospital** (weekdays ☎ 02/5292–2146, evenings and weekends ☎ 02/5221–1111 or 02/5292–2403). **First Medical Clinic of Prague** (☎ 02/292286 or 02/2421–6200; 24-hr emergency ☎ 02/0601–225050, mobile phone). **American Medical Center** (☎ 02/807756, 02/807757, 02/807758 weekdays). Be prepared to pay in cash for medical treatment, whether you are insured or not. **24-Hour Pharmacies** (⊠ Lékárna U Anděla, Štefánikova 6, Prague 5, ☎ 02/537039; ⊠ Lékárna Palackého, Palackého 5, Prague 1, ☎ 02/2494–6982).

ENGLISH-LANGUAGE BOOKSTORES
Anagram Bookshop (⊠ Týn 4, Prague 1). **Big Ben Bookshop** (⊠ Malá Štupartská 5, Prague 1). **Globe Bookstore and Coffeehouse** (⊠ Janovského 14, Prague 7). **Knihkupectví U černé Matky Boží** (⊠ Celetná ul. 34 at Ovocnýtrh Prague; good for hiking maps and atlases; go downstairs). **U Knihomola** (⊠ Mánesova 79, Prague 2).

GUIDED TOURS
Excursions. Čedok's (☞ Visitor Information, *below*) one-day tours out of Prague include excursions to the lovely medieval town of Kutná Hora, the unusual sandstone formations of the "Bohemian Paradise" region, famous spa towns and castles, wineries, and the Terezín ghetto.

Orientation. Čedok offers a daily three-hour tour of the city, starting at 10 AM from two (⊠ Na Příkopě 18 and Pařížská 6, ☎ 02/2419–

7111 and 02/2419–7643) offices. **Martin-Tour** (☎ 02/2421–2473) offers a tour departing from Náměstí Republiky and three other Old Town
points four times daily. **PIS** (☎ 02/2448–2569) arranges guided tours
at its Na Příkopě and Old Town Square locations.

Personal Guides. Contact Čedok (☞ Visitor Information, *below*) or
PIS (☞ Visitor Information, *below*) to arrange a personal walking tour
of the city. Prices start at around 400 Kč per hour.

Special-Interest. For cultural tours call **Čedok** (☞ Visitor Information,
below). These include visits to the Jewish quarter, performances of folk
troupes, Laterna Magika (☞ Nightlife and the Arts, *above*), opera, and
concerts. **Shalom** (☎ 02/2423–0126) specializes in tours of the Jewish quarter.

TRAVEL AGENCIES
American Express (✉ Václavské nám. 56, ☎ 02/2280–0223, FAX 02/
2221–1131; lost or stolen credit cards, ☎ 02/2280–0222). **Thomas Cook**
(✉ Národní třída 28, ☎ 02/2110–5371).

VISITOR INFORMATION
Čedok (✉ main office, Na Příkopě 18, near Wenceslas Sq., ☎ 02/2419–
7111; other branches, ✉ Rytířská 16 and ✉ Pařížská 6). **Prague Information Service** (PIS; ✉ Na Příkopě 20 and Staroměstské nám. 22,
☎ 02/2448–2569).

The English-language weekly *The Prague Post* lists current events and
entertainment programs.

Tourist bureaus outside Prague are found in: **Český Krumlov** (✉ In-
focentrum, Nám. Svornosti 1, ☎ 0337/711183). **Karlovy Vary** (✉ Ul.
Dr. Bechera 21–23, ☎ 017/22281). **Mariánské Lázně** (✉ Infocentrum,
Hlavní 47, ☎ 0165/622474 or 0165/5892). **Mikulov** (✉ Regional
Tourist Center, Nám. 32, ☎ FAX 0625/2855). **Olomouc** (✉ Horní nám.,
☎ 068/551–3385). **Tábor** (✉ Žižkovo nám., ☎ 0361/252385). **Telč**
(✉ Town hall, Nám. Zachariáše z Hradce 10, ☎ 066/962233).

9 DENMARK

COPENHAGEN, FYN AND THE CENTRAL ISLANDS, JYLLAND AND THE LAKES

Ebullience and a sense of humor have always been Danish trademarks. Though one might expect a country comprising more than 400 islands to develop an island mentality, the Danes are famous for their friendliness. They even have a word—*hyggelig*—for the feeling of well-being that comes from their own brand of cozy hospitality.

The stereotype of melancholic Scandinavia simply doesn't hold here: neither in the café-studded streets of the larger cities, where musicians and fruit vendors hawk their wares to passersby, nor in the tiny coastal towns, where the fishing boats are as brightly painted as fire trucks. Even the country's indoor/outdoor museums, where history is brought to life in clusters of reconstructed buildings out in the open, indicate that Danes don't choose to keep experience behind glass.

This is a land of well-groomed agriculture, where every available acre is planted in orchards, forests, or crops. Nowhere are you far from water as you drive on and off the ferries and bridges linking the three regions of Jylland (Jutland), Fyn (Funen), and Sjælland (Zealand).

The surrounding sea has shaped Denmark's history. The Vikings, unparalleled seafarers, had seen much of the world by the 8th century. Today the Danes remain expert navigators, using their 4,480 km (2,800 mi) of coastline both for sport—there are regattas around Sjælland and Fyn—and for fishing and trading. Copenhagen is also proving itself as one of the most popular cruise ports in northern Europe.

Long one of the world's most liberal countries, Denmark has a highly developed social welfare system. Hefty taxes are the subject of grumbling and jokes, but Danes remain proud of their state-funded medical and educational systems.

The country that gave the world Isak Dinesen, Hans Christian Andersen, and Søren Kierkegaard has a long-standing commitment to culture and the arts. In what other nation does the royal couple translate the writings of Simone de Beauvoir or the queen design costumes for the bal-

Denmark (Danmark)

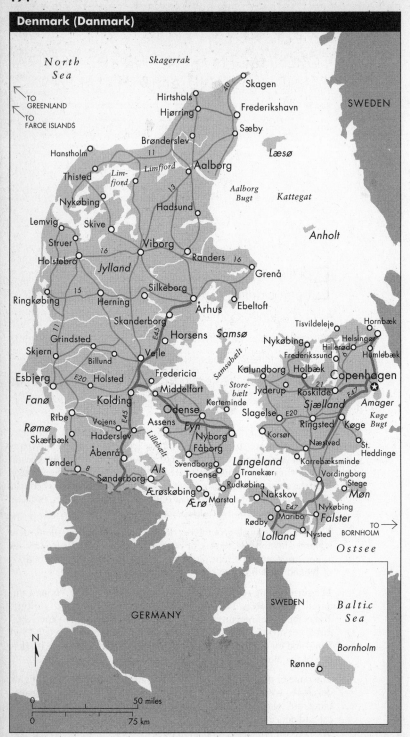

North
Sea

Skagerrak

Skagen

TO
GREENLAND

TO
FAROE ISLANDS

Hirtshals
Hjørring
Frederikshavn
Sæby

SWEDEN

Brønderslev
Hanstholm
11
Aalborg
Læsø

Thisted
Lim-
fjord
Limfjord
Aalborg
Bugt
Kattegat

Nykøbing
13
Hadsund

Lemvig
Skive
Anholt

Struer
Viborg
16
Randers
16

Holstebro
Jylland
Grenå

Ringkøbing
15
Herning
Silkeborg
Århus
Ebeltoft

Skanderborg
Horsens
Samsø
Tisvildeleje
Hornbæk

Grindsted
Vejle
Helsingør
Nykøbing
Hillerød
Humlebæk

Skjern
Billund
Frederikssund

Esbjerg
E20
Holsted
Fredericia
Kalundborg
Holbæk
Copenhagen

Fanø
Middelfart
Store-
bælt
Jyderup
Roskilde
Amager

Ribe
Kolding
Odense
Kerteminde
Sjælland
Køge
Bugt

Rømø
Vojens
Assens
Fyn
Slagelse
E20
Ringsted
Køge

Skærbæk
Haderslev
Nyborg
Korsør
Næsved
St.
Heddinge

Åbenrå
Fåborg
Langeland
Karrebæksminde

Tønder
8
Svendborg
Tranekær
Vordingborg
Stege

Sønderborg
Als
Troense
Rudkøbing
Møn

Ærøskøbing
Marstal
Nakskov
Nykøbing
Falster

Ærø
Rødby
Maribo
TO
BORNHOLM

Lolland
Nysted
Ostsee

GERMANY

N

SWEDEN
Baltic
Sea

Bornholm

Rønne

0   50 miles
0   75 km

let? The Royal Danish Ballet is world renowned, and even in the provinces there are numerous theater groups and opera houses.

Perhaps Denmark's greatest charm is its manageable size—about half that of Maine or 4½ times the size of Wales (53,485 sq km/33,215 sq mi). The combined ferry and train ride from Esbjerg, on the western coast of Jylland, to Copenhagen, on the eastern coast of Sjælland, takes just over three hours. From the capital you can make comfortable, unhurried expeditions by boat, car, bus, or train to explore one of the world's most civilized countries.

DENMARK A TO Z

Customs

For details on imports and duty-free limits, *see* Customs & Duties *in* Chapter 1.

Dining

Danes take their eating seriously, and traditional Danish food, however simple, is excellent, with an emphasis on fresh ingredients, few spices, and careful presentation. Fish and meat are both of top quality in this fishing and farming country, and both are staple ingredients of the famous *smørrebrød* (open-faced sandwiches). Some smørrebrød are huge meals in themselves: You may be faced with a dauntingly large (but nonetheless delicious) mound of fish or meat, slathered with condiments, all atop either *rugbrød* (rye bread) or *franskbrød* (French bread). Another specialty is *wienerbrød,* a confection far superior to anything billed as "Danish pastry" elsewhere.

All Scandinavian countries have versions of the cold table, but Danes claim that theirs, *det store kolde bord,* is the original and the best. It's a celebration meal; the setting of the long table is a work of art—often with lighted candles and silver platters—and the food itself is a minor miracle of design and decoration.

In hotels and restaurants the cold table is served at lunch only, though you will find a more limited version at hotel breakfasts—a good bet for budget travelers, since you can eat as much as you like.

Denmark boasts more than 50 varieties of beer, made by as many breweries; the best-known suds are Carlsberg and Tuborg, both made by the same company. If you like harder stuff, try *snaps,* the aquavit traditionally drunk with cold food, especially herring. A note about smoking: Danes, like many Europeans, regard smoking as an inalienable right. Militant insistence that they abstain will be regarded as either hysteria or comedy. A polite tone requesting they blow their smoke away from you may prove more effective.

MEALTIMES

The Danes start work early, which means they generally eat lunch at noon. Evening meals are also eaten early, so make sure you have dinner reservations for 9 at the latest. Bars and cafés stay open later, and most offer at least light fare.

RATINGS

Meal prices vary little between town and country. While approximate price ranges are given below, remember that careful ordering, especially when it comes to beer, wine, and liquor, can get you a moderate ($$) meal at a very expensive ($$$$) restaurant. Prices are per person and include a first course, main course, and dessert, plus taxes and tip, but not wine.

CATEGORY	COPENHAGEN	OTHER AREAS
$$$$	over DKr400	over DKr350
$$$	DKr200–DKr400	DKr200–DKr350
$$	DKr120–DKr200	DKr100–DKr200
$	under DKr120	under DKr100

WHAT TO WEAR

The Danes are fairly casual, and few restaurants require a jacket and tie. Even in the most chic establishments, the tone is elegantly casual.

Language

Danish is a difficult tongue for foreigners—except those from Norway and Sweden—to understand, let alone speak. Danes are good linguists, however, and almost everyone, except perhaps elderly people in rural areas, speaks English well in addition to a third language, usually French or German.

Lodging

Accommodations in Denmark range from the spare and comfortable to the resplendent. Even inexpensive hotels have invested in good materials and good, firm beds in simple designs. However, when you make reservations, pin down details so that you get what you want. Many hotels are in century-old buildings; room sizes, even in top hotels, can vary enormously; the smallest have sloping ceilings and cubbyhole-size doubles. Also ask about noise caused by traffic or adjacent rooms. If you have preferences, ask for them specifically and get a confirmation in writing. The staff at the hotels will almost always try to accommodate you. Also, many Danes prefer a shower to a bath, so if you particularly want a tub, ask for it, but be prepared to pay more. Except in the case of rentals, breakfast and taxes are usually included in prices, though this seems to be changing. Check when making a reservation.

CAMPING

Denmark has more than 500 approved campsites, with a rating system of one, two, or three stars. To camp you need an International Camping Carnet or Danish Camping Pass (available at any campsite and valid for one year). For more details on camping and discounts for groups and families, contact **Campingrådet** (⊠ Hesseløg. 16, DK 2100 Copenhagen Ø, ☎ 39/27–88–44).

FARM VACATIONS

This is perhaps the best way to see how the Danes live and work. You stay on a farm and share meals with the family; you can even help with the chores. The minimum stay is three nights; bed-and-breakfast is about DKr150, and half board (an overnight with breakfast and one hot meal) runs DKr245. (Full board, an overnight with three meals, can be arranged.) There is a 50% discount for children under 11. Contact **Ferie på Landet** (Holiday in the Country; ⊠ Søndergade 26, DK 8700 Horsens, ☎ 70/10–41–90, FAX 75/60–21–90) for details.

HOTELS

Luxury hotels in the city or countryside offer rooms of a high standard; in a manor-house hotel you may find yourself sleeping in a four-poster bed. Less expensive accommodations, however, are uniformly clean and comfortable.

INNS

A cheaper and charming alternative to hotels are the old stagecoach *kroer*—inns scattered throughout Denmark. You can save money by contacting **Kro Ferie** (Inn Holiday, ⊠ Vejlevej 16, DK 8700 Horsens, Jylland, ☎ 75/64–87–00) to invest in a book of Inn Checks, valid at 84 inns. Each check costs about DKr640 per couple and includes one overnight stay in a double room, breakfast included. Family checks, for three (DKr720) and four (DKr800), are also available. Order a free catalog from Kro Ferie and choose carefully; the organization includes some chain hotels bereft of even a smidgen of inn-related charm. Some also tack a DKr150 surcharge on the price of a double.

RATINGS

Prices are for two people in a double room and include service and taxes and usually breakfast.

CATEGORY	COPENHAGEN	OTHER AREAS
$$$$	over DKr1,300	over DKr950
$$$	DKr800–DKr1,300	DKr700–DKr950
$$	DKr670–DKr800	DKr450–DKr700
$	under DKr670	under DKr450

All prices are for a standard double room, excluding service charges and 14.9% room tax. The tax is slightly lower at suburban hotels.

RENTALS

Many Danes rent out their summer homes—an ideal option if you want to see the countryside in a more relaxed way. A simple house with room for four costs from DKr1,000 per week to twice that much during the summer high season. Contact the Danish Tourist Board (☞ Visitor Information, *below*) for details.

YOUTH HOSTELS

The 101 youth hostels in Denmark are open to everyone regardless of age. If you have an International Youth Hostels Association card (obtainable before you leave home), the rate is roughly DKr90 for a single bed, DKr150–DKr300 for a private double room. Without the card, there's a surcharge of about DKr25 per person. For more information contact **Danhostel Danmarks Vandrehjem** (✉ Vesterbrog. 39, DK 1620 Copenhagen V, ☎ 31/31–36–12, FAX 31/31–36–26) or American Youth Hostels (☞ Students *in* Chapter 1).

Mail

POSTAL RATES

Surface and airmail letters, aerograms, and postcards to the United States and Canada cost DKr5.50 for 20 grams. Letters and postcards to the United Kingdom and other EU countries cost DKr4.50. Stamps are sold at post offices and some shops.

RECEIVING MAIL

If you do not know where you will be staying, your mail can be addressed to "poste restante" and sent to any post office. If no post office is specified, letters will be sent to the main post office in Copenhagen (✉ Tietgensg. 37, DK 1704).

Money Matters

COSTS

Denmark's economy is stable, and inflation remains reasonably low, without wild fluctuations in exchange rates. The standard and the cost of living is high, especially for such luxuries as hard alcohol and cigarettes. Prices are highest in Copenhagen; the least expensive areas are Fyn and Jylland.

CURRENCY

The monetary unit in Denmark is the krone (kr., DKr, or DKK), which is divided into 100 øre. At press time (summer 1999), the krone stood at DKr7.17 to the U.S. dollar, DKr4.88 to the Canadian dollar, DKr11.35 to the pound sterling, DKr4.72 to the Australian dollar, and DKr3.83 to the New Zealand dollar. Most well-known credit cards are accepted in Denmark, though the American Express card is accepted less frequently than others. Traveler's checks can be cashed in banks and in many hotels, restaurants, and shops.

SAMPLE PRICES

Cup of coffee, DKr14–DKr25; bottle of beer, DKr15–DKr30; soda, DKr10–DKr15; ham sandwich, DKr22–DKr40; 1½-km (1-mi) taxi ride, DKr30.

TIPPING

The egalitarian Danes do not expect to be tipped. The exceptions are hotel porters, who get around DKr5 per bag; you should also leave DKr1 or DKr2 for the use of a public toilet if there is an attendant.

National Holidays

January 1; April 23–24 (Easter); May 19 (Common Prayer); June 1 (Ascension); June 5 (Constitution Day; shops close at noon); June 11 (Pentecost), and December 24–26.

Opening and Closing Times

Banks in Copenhagen are open weekdays 9:30–4 and Thursday until 6. Several *bureaux de change,* including those at Copenhagen's central station and airport, stay open until 10 PM. Outside Copenhagen, banking hours vary. **Museums** are generally open 10–3 or 11–4 and closed Monday. In winter opening hours are shorter, and some museums close for the season. Check the local papers or ask at tourist offices. **Small shops** and boutiques are open weekdays 10–5:30; most stay open Thursday and Friday until 7 or 8 and close on Saturday at 1 or 2. On the first and last Saturday of every month, most shops stay open until 4 or 5. Call to double-check weekend opening hours for specific stores to avoid disappointment.

Shopping

SALES-TAX REFUNDS

Visitors from a non-EU country can save about 18% on purchases over DKr300 by obtaining a refund of the value-added tax (VAT) at the more than 1,500 shops displaying TAX FREE signs. If the shop sends your purchase directly to your home address, you pay only the sales price, exclusive of VAT. If you want to take the goods home yourself, pay the full price in the shop and get a VAT refund at the Danish duty-free shopping center at the Copenhagen airport. Get a copy of the *Tax-Free Shopping Guide* from the Danish Tourist Board (☞ Visitor Information, *below*).

Telephoning

COUNTRY CODE

The country code for Denmark is 45.

INTERNATIONAL CALLS

Dial 00, then the country code, area code, and the desired number. To reach an **AT&T** long-distance operator, dial ☎ 800/10010; for **MCI WorldCom,** dial ☎ 800/10022; and for **Sprint,** ☎ 800/10877.

LOCAL CALLS

Pay phones take 1-, 2-, 5-, and 10-DKr coins. You must use area codes even when dialing a local number. Calling cards, which are sold at Danish State Railways stations, post offices, and some kiosks, cost DKr25, DKr50, or DKr100, and are increasingly necessary as pay phones become a thing of the past.

OPERATORS AND INFORMATION

To ask an operator, most of whom speak English, for local assistance, dial 118; for an international operator, dial 113.

Transportation

BY BICYCLE

Some say the Danes have the greatest number of bikes per capita in the world. Indeed, with its flat landscape and uncrowded roads, Denmark is a cyclist's paradise. You can rent bikes at some train stations and many tourist offices, as well as from private firms. Contact the **Danish Cyclists' Association** (Dansk Cyklist Forbund; ✉ Rømersg. 7, DK 1362 Copenhagen, ☎ 33/32–31–21) for additional information. The Danish Tourist Board (☞ Visitor Information, *below*) publishes the pamphlet "Cycling Holiday in Denmark." In the warmer months, you'll also see Bycykler (City Bikes) parked at special bike stands around town; the one at the top of Nyhavn usually has a couple available. Deposit DKr20 and pedal away. Though the bikes are often dented, they do function. You'll get your deposit back when you return the bike.

BY BOAT

There is frequent service to Germany, Poland, Sweden, Norway, and the Faroe Islands (in the Atlantic Ocean, north of Scotland), as well as to Britain. Domestic ferries provide service between Jylland, Fyn, and Sjælland and to the smaller islands, 100 of which are inhabited. Danish State Railways and several private shipping companies publish timetables in English; you should reserve on both domestic and overseas routes. Ask about off-season discounts.

BY CAR

Roads here are good and largely traffic-free (except around Copenhagen); you can reach many islands by toll-free bridges.

Breakdowns. Members of organizations affiliated with Alliance International de Tourisme (AIT), including American AAA and British AA, can get technical and legal assistance from the **Danish Motoring Organization** (FDM, ✉ Firskovvej 32, DK 2800 Lyngby, ☎ 45/27–07–07). All highways have emergency phones, and you can also phone your car-rental company for help. If you cannot drive your car to a garage for repairs, the rescue corps, **Falck** (☎ 44/92–22–22), can help anywhere, night or day.

Gasoline. Gas costs about DKr6 a liter. Reality check: That's US$4 a gallon.

Parking. In areas with signs reading PARKERING/STANDSNING FORBUDT (no parking and no stopping) you are allowed a three-minute grace period to load and unload. In towns automatic parking-permit machines are used. Drop in coins, push the silver button, and a ticket marked with the expiration time will drop down. Display the ticket clearly on the dashboard. Parking for an hour costs DKr6–Dkr15 in Copenhagen, DKr7 elsewhere. In some areas signs post parking regulations. All cars have a plastic dial on the inside of their windshields. Set the dial to the time you leave your car.

Rules of the Road. To drive you will need a valid license, and if you're using your own car it must have a certificate of registration and national plates. A triangular hazard-warning sign is compulsory in every car and is provided with rentals. The driver and all passengers must wear seat belts. Headlights must always be on—even in the daytime. Motorcyclists must always wear helmets and use headlights. All drivers must pay attention to cyclists, who use the outer right lane and have the right-of-way.

Drive on the right and give way to traffic from the left. A red-and-white triangular yield sign, or a line of white triangles across the road, means you must yield to traffic on the road you are entering. Do not turn right on a red light. Speed limits are 50 kph (30 mph) in built-up areas; 100

kph (60 mph) on highways; and 80 kph (50 mph) on other roads. If you are towing a trailer, you must not exceed 70 kph (40 mph). Speeding, and drinking and driving, especially, are punished severely.

BY TRAIN AND BUS

Traveling by train or bus is easy, as **Danish State Railways** (DSB, ☎ 70/13–14–15 for information) and a few private companies cover the country with a dense network of train services, supplemented in remote areas by buses. Hourly intercity trains connect the main towns in Jylland and Fyn with Copenhagen and Sjælland, using high-speed diesels, called IC-3s, on the most important stretches. All these trains make the seven-minute tunnel crossing of the Store Bælt (Great Belt), the waterway separating Fyn and Sjælland. Seat reservations on intercity trains and IC-3s are optional, but you must have a reservation if you plan to cross the Great Belt. Buy tickets at stations for trains, buses, and connecting ferry crossings (buses allow you to buy tickets on board). For most cross-country trips, children between 4 and 11 accompanied by an adult travel free, though they must have a seat reservation (DKr15). Ask about discounts for senior citizens and groups.

Fares. The **ScanRail** pass affords unlimited train travel throughout Denmark, Finland, Norway, and Sweden, as well as restricted ferry passage in and beyond Scandinavia. It is available for five days of travel within 15 days, 10 days within a month, or 21 days. In the United States call RailEurope (☎ 800/438–7245), or DER (☎ 800/782–2424). Buy your tickets in the United States: Though they are available in Denmark, they are more expensive. Various discounts are offered to holders of the pass by hotel chains and other organizations; ask DER, RailEurope, or your travel agent for details.

Visitor Information

The main tourist information office is the **Danish Tourist Board** (✉ Danmarks Turistråd, Bernstoffsg. 1, DK 1577 Copenhagen V, ☎ 33/11–13–25; ✉ Tivoli grounds, plus Helsingør, Hillerød, Køge, Roskilde, Gilleleje, Hundersted, and Tisvildeleje). Youth information is available in Copenhagen at **Ungdoms Information** (✉ Rådhusstraede 13, ☎ 33/73–06–50).

Weather

Most travelers visit Denmark during the warmest months, July and August, but there are advantages to going in May, June, or September, when sights are less crowded and many establishments offer off-season discounts. However, few places in Denmark are ever unpleasantly crowded, and when the Danes make their annual exodus to the beaches, the cities have even more breathing space. In the winter months days are short and dark, and important attractions, including Copenhagen's Tivoli Gardens, are closed for most of the season. It's worth noting, however, that winter holidays are beautiful and especially cozy—even Tivoli reopens with its special Christmas market.

CLIMATE

The following are the average daily maximum and minimum temperatures for Copenhagen.

Jan.	36F	2C	May	61F	16C	Sept.	64F	18C
	28	– 2		46	8		51	11
Feb.	36F	2C	June	67F	19C	Oct.	54F	12C
	28	– 2		52	11		44	7
Mar.	41F	5C	July	71F	22C	Nov.	45F	7C
	31	– 1		57	14		38	3
Apr.	51F	11C	Aug.	70F	21C	Dec.	40F	4C
	38	3		56	14		34	1

COPENHAGEN

If you arrive in Copenhagen Airport on the isle of Amager, as you taxi into the city you are met with no startling skyline, no seething metropolis. Instead, elegant spires and central cobbled streets characterize Scandinavia's most populous capital and one of its oldest towns. It is not divided like most other cities into single-purpose districts; instead it is a rich, multilayered capital where people work, play, shop, and live throughout its central core. Surrounded by water, be it sea or canal, and connected by bridges and drawbridges, it has a maritime atmosphere that is indelible.

Exploring Copenhagen

Numbers in the margin correspond to points of interest on the Copenhagen map.

When Denmark ruled Norway and Sweden during the 15th century, Copenhagen was the capital of all three countries. Today it is still a lively northern capital, with about 1 million inhabitants. It's a city meant for walking, the first in Europe to recognize the value of pedestrian streets in fostering community spirit. As you stroll through the cobbled streets and squares, you'll find that Copenhagen combines the excitement and variety of big-city life with a small-town atmosphere. If there's such a thing as a cozy metropolis, this is it.

In Copenhagen you're never far from water, whether sea or canal. The city itself is built upon two main islands, Slotsholmen and Christianshavn, connected by drawbridges. The ancient heart of the city is intersected by two heavily peopled walking streets—part of the five such streets known collectively as Strøget—and around them curls a maze of cobbled streets packed with tiny boutiques, cafés, and restaurants—all best explored on foot. In summer, when Copenhagen moves outside, the most engaging views of city life are from sidewalk cafés in the sunny squares. Walk down Nyhavn Canal, once the haunt of a salty crew of sailors, now gentrified and filled with chic restaurants.

⑯ Amalienborg (Amalia's Castle). During the fall and winter, when the royal family has returned to its principal residence since 1784, the Royal Guard and band march through the city at noon to change the palace guard. Amelienborg's other main attraction is the second division of the Royal Collection (the first is at Rosenborg), housed inside the **Amalienborg Museum.** Among the collection's offerings are the study of King Christian IX (1818–1906) and the drawing room of his wife, Queen Louise. Also included are a set of rococo banquet silver, highlighted by a bombastic Viking ship centerpiece, and a small costume exhibit. Afterward, you can view visiting yachts along the castle's harbor, as well as the modern sculptures and manicured flower beds of **Amalienhaven** (Amalia's Gardens). ⌧ *Amalienborg Pl.,* ☏ *33/12–21–86.* ☉ *May–late Oct., daily 11–4; late Oct.–Apr., Tues.–Sun. 11–4.*

⑩ Børsen (the Stock Exchange). This edifice is believed to be the oldest such structure still in use, though it functions only on special occasions. It was built by the 16th-century monarch King Christian IV, a scholar and warrior, and the architect of much of the city. The king is said to have had a hand in twisting the tails of the four dragons that form the structure's distinctive green copper spire. With its steep roofs, tiny windows, and gables, the building is one of Copenhagen's treasures. ⌧ *Christiansborg Slotspl. Not open to public.*

㉕ Botanisk Have (Botanical Garden). Copenhagen's 25-acre botanical gardens, with a rather spectacular Palm House containing tropical and subtropical plants, upstages the palatial gardens of **Rosenborg Slot** (Rosenborg Castle; ☞ *below*). Also on the grounds are an observatory and a geological museum. ⊠ *Gothersg. 128,* ☎ *33/32–22–40.* ☒ *Free.* ☽ *Grounds: May–Aug., daily 8:30–6; Sept.–Apr., daily 8:30–4. Palm House: daily 10–3.*

㉜ Carlsberg Bryggeri (Carlsberg Brewery). Four giant Bornholm granite elephants guard the entrance to this world-famous brewery; a tour of the draft-horse stalls and **Carlsberg Museum** begins at the front gate. ⊠ *Ny Carlsbergvej 140,* ☎ *33/27–13–14.* ☽ *Tours: weekdays at 11 and 2 or by arrangement for groups.*

★ ❺ Christiansborg Slot (Christiansborg Castle). This massive gray complex contains the Folketinget (Parliament House) and the Royal Reception Chambers. It is on the site of the city's first fortress, built by Bishop Absalon in 1167. While the castle was being built at the beginning of the 20th century, the National Museum excavated the ruins beneath the site. ⊠ *Christiansborg. Christiansborg ruins:* ☎ *33/92–64–92;* ☽ *May–Sept., daily 9:30–3:30; Oct.–Apr., Tues., Thurs., Fri., Sun. 9:30–3:30. Folketinget:* ☎ *33/37–55–00;* ☒ *free;* ☽ *tour times vary; call ahead. Reception chambers:* ☎ *33/92–64–92;* ☽ *hrs and tour times vary; call.*

❷⓿ Den Lille Havfrue (The Little Mermaid). In 1913 this statue was erected to commemorate Hans Christian Andersen's lovelorn creation. It's now the subject of hundreds of travel posters. On Sunday **Langelinie**, the lick of land you follow to reach the famed nymph, is thronged with promenading Danes and tourists—the pack of whom are often much more absorbing to watch than the somewhat overrated sculpture. She has been mysteriously decapitated a couple of times since she was set on her perch; the most recent incident took place in early 1998, and though her head was returned within a week, she gained much more publicity without it. ⊠ *Langelinie promenade.*

⓲ Frihedsmuseet (Liberty Museum). Evocative displays commemorate the heroic World War II Danish resistance movement, which saved 7,000 Jews from the Nazis by hiding and then smuggling them across to Sweden. ⊠ *Churchillparken,* ☎ *33/13–77–14.* ☒ *Free.* ☽ *Sept. 16–Apr., Tues.–Sat. 11–3, Sun. 11–4; May–Sept. 15, Tues.–Sat. 10–4, Sun. 10–5.*

㉛ Heligånds Kirken (Church of the Holy Ghost). This church on Strøget contains a marble font by the sculptor Bertel Thovaldsen (1770–1844) in its 18th-century choir. ⊠ *Niels Hemmingsensg. 5, Amagertorv section,* ☎ *33/12–95–55.* ☒ *Free.* ☽ *Weekdays 9–1, Sat. 10–noon.*

㉗ Hirschsprungske Samling (Hirschsprung Collection). This cozy museum displays works from Denmark's Golden Age of Painting, the mid-19th-century school of Naturalism pioneered by C.W. Eckersberg, whose pictures contain a remarkable wealth of detail and technical skill combined with limpid, cool, luminescent color. Other prominent painters of the trend include Christian Kobke and Julius Exner. The Hirschsprungske also has a collection of paintings by the late-19th-century artists of the Danish Skagen school, as well as interiors with furnishings from the artists' homes. ⊠ *Stockholmsg. 20,* ☎ *31/42–03–36.* ☽ *Thurs.–Mon. 11–4, Wed. 11–9.*

⓳ Kastellet (The Citadel). Once surrounded by two rings of moats, this building was the city's main fortress during the 18th century, but, in a grim reversal during World War II, the Germans used it as their headquarters during their occupation of Denmark. The lovely green area around it, **Churchillparken,** cut throughout with walking paths, is a favorite among the Danes, who flock here on weekends. If you have time, walk past the spired **St. Alban's,** an English church that stands at the park's entrance. ✉ *Churchillparken. Grounds:* ⊙ *Daily 6* AM–*sunset.*

㉒ **Københavns Synagoge** (Copenhagen Synagogue). This synagogue was designed by the contemporary architect Gustav Friedrich Hetsch, who borrowed from the Doric and Egyptian styles in creating the arklike structure. ✉ *Krystalg. 12.* ⊙ *Daily services 4:15.*

⑬ **Kongelig Teater** (Royal Theater). The home of Danish opera and ballet as well as theater occupies the southeast side of Kongens Nytorv. The Danish Royal Ballet remains one of the world's great companies, with a repertory ranging from classical to modern. On the western side of the square you'll see the stately facade of the **D'Angleterre,** the grandest of Copenhagen's hotels. ✉ *Tordenskjoldsg. 3,* ☎ *33/69–69–69. Not open for tours.*

❼ **Kongelige Bibliotek** (Royal Library). This library houses the country's largest collection of books, newspapers, and manuscripts. Look for early records of the Viking journeys to America and Greenland and the statue of the philosopher Søren Kierkegaard in the garden. A dark marble annex next door, also known as the Black Diamond, opens in the fall of 1999. It has special reading rooms, a ground-floor performance space, and a bookstore. ✉ *Slotsholmen,* ☎ *33/93–01–11.* ▦ *Free.* ⊙ *June–Aug., weekdays 9–7, Sat. 10–7; Sept.–May, Mon. 9–7, Tues.–Thurs. 9–9, Fri. 9–7, Sat. 10–7.*

⑰ **Kunstindustrimuseet** (Museum of Decorative Art). The highlights of this museum's collection are a large assortment of European and Asian handicrafts, as well as ceramics, silver, and tapestries. The quiet library full of design tomes and magazines doubles as a primer for Danish functionalism with its Le Klint paper lamp shades and wooden desks. ✉ *Bredg. 68,* ☎ *33/14–94–52.* ⊙ *Permanent exhibition, Tues.–Sun. 1–4; special exhibitions, Tues.–Sat. 10–4, Sun. 1–4.*

❷ **Lurblæserne** (Lur Blower Column). Topped by two Vikings blowing an ancient trumpet called a *lur,* this column erected in 1914 displays a good deal of artistic license—the lur dates from the Bronze Age, 1500 BC, whereas the Vikings lived a mere 1,000 years ago. The monument is a starting point for sightseeing tours of the city. ✉ *East side of Rådhus Pl.*

⑮ **Marmorkirken** (The Marble Church). The ponderous Frederikskirke, commonly called the Marmorkirken, is a Baroque church begun in 1749 in high-priced Norwegian marble that stood unfinished (because of budget constraints) from 1770 to 1874. It was finally completed and consecrated in 1894. Perched around the exterior are 16 statues of various religious leaders from Moses to Luther, and below them stand sculptures of outstanding Danish ministers and bishops. ✉ *Frederiksgade 4,* ☎ *33/15–01–44.* ▦ *Free Wed.* ⊙ *Mon.–Tues. and Thurs.–Fri. 11–2, Wed. 11–6, Sat. 11–4, Sun. noon –4, with service at 10:30.*

☙ ❹ **Nationalmuseet** (National Museum). This museum has extensive collections chronicling Danish cultural history to modern times and displays of Egyptian, Greek, and Roman antiquities. You can see Viking Runic stones in the Danish cultural history section. The children's museum is an excellent place to ease kids into joys of history; though the original relics are secured behind glass, there is plenty of stuff, including clothing and a school, to play in and with. ✉ *Ny Vesterg. 10,* ☎ *33/13–44–11.* ⊙ *Tues.–Sun. 10–5.*

⑫ **Nikolaj Kirken** (St. Nicholas Church). In Østergade, the easternmost of the streets that make up Strøget, you cannot miss the green spire of St. Nicholas Church. The present structure was built in the 20th century; the previous one, dating from the 13th century, was destroyed

204

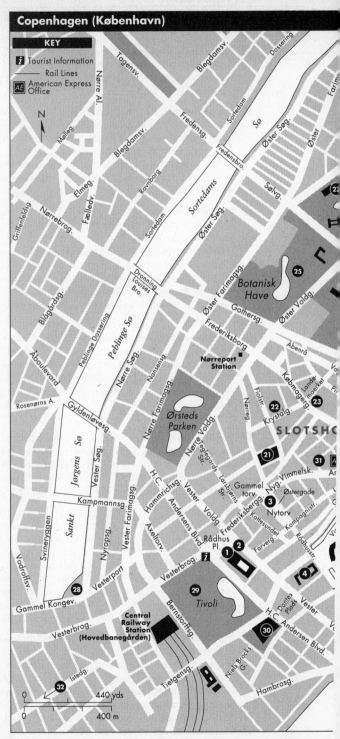

Copenhagen (København)

Farimagsg.
Dag Hammarskjölds Al.
Kristianiag.
Langelliniebrd.
Østbaneg.
Stockholmsg.
Østerport Station
Oslo Plads
Folke Bernadottes Al.
Langelinie
Forbindelsev.
Yderhavn
27
26
Øster Anlæg
Grønningen
St. Kongensg.
Churchill-parken
19
20
Sølvg.
Rigensg.
Fredericiag.
Bredg.
Esplanaden
18
Amalieg.
17
24
Kongens Have
Kronprinsesseg.
Store Kongensg.
Bredg.
15
Toldbodg.
Dronningens Tværg.
16
Adelg.
Borgerg.
Amalieg.
Sankt Annæ Plads
Vognmagerg.
Gammelmønt
Ny Østerg.
Gothersg.
Pilestræde
Kongens Nytorv
14
Nyhavn
HOLMEN
Østerg.
Kr. Bernikg.
Bremerholm
Nyhavn
Canal
AF
Amagertorv
12
Hojbro
13
Heibergsg.
Holmenskanal
Inderhavn
Læderstr.
Gammel Strand
Holbergsg.
Vindelbrog.
Holmenskanal
Havnegade
6
Christiansborg Slotsplads
5
10
Chr. IV's Bro
Børsg.
8
Tøjhusgade
7
Knippelsbro
CHRISTIANSHAVN
9
Frederiksholms Kanal
Christians Brygge
Sankt Annæg.
11
Voldg.
Torveg.
Dronningensg.
Princessg.
Christianshavns Voldg.
Langerbro.
Langebro
Langerbrog.
Christianshavns
Amagerbrog.
Voldg.
Amager Blvd.
Stadsgraven
Vermlandsg.

by fire in 1728. Today the building is no longer a church but an art gallery and exhibition center. ⊠ *Nikolaipl.*, ☎ *33/93–16–26.* ▦ *Changing admission for special exhibitions.* ⊙ *Daily noon–5.*

★ ㉚ **Ny Carlsberg Glyptotek** (New Carlsberg Sculpture Museum). This elaborate neoclassical building houses one of Europe's greatest collections of Greek and Roman antiquities and sculpture. In 1996 a new modern wing, envisioned as a three-story treasure chest and designed by the acclaimed Danish architect Henning Larsen, was completed. It houses an impressive pre-Impressionist collection including works from the Barbizon school; Impressionist paintings, including works by Monet, Sisley, and Pissarro; and a post-Impressionist section, with 50 Gauguin paintings plus 12 of his very rare sculpures. ⊠ *Dantes Pl. 7,* ☎ *33/41–81–41.* ▦ *Free Wed. and Sun.* ⊙ *Tues.–Sun. 10–4.*

★ ⑭ **Nyhavn** (New Harbor). You can relax with a beer in one of the most gentrified parts of the city, a longtime haunt of sailors. Now restaurants and cafés outnumber tattoo shops. The name refers to both the street and the canal leading southeast out of Kongens Nytorv—but to Danes, it could as well mean the general feeling of tipsy euphoria that erupts here every warm, sunny day. Long into the hot summer nights, the area still gets rowdy, with Scandinavians reveling against the backdrop of a fleet of old-time sailing ships and well-preserved 18th-century buildings. Hans Christian Andersen lived at numbers 18 and 20. Nearer to the harbor are old shipping warehouses, including two—Nyhavn 71 and the Admiral—that have been converted into comfortable hotels. ⊠ *East of Kongens Nytorv.*

★ ❶ **Rådhus Pladsen** (City Hall Square). This hub of Copenhagen's commercial district is the best place to start a stroll. The Renaissance-style building dominating it is the **Rådhus** (City Hall), completed in 1905. A statue of Copenhagen's 12th-century founder, Bishop Absalon, sits atop the main entrance. Inside, you can see the first World Clock, an astrological timepiece invented and built by Jens Olsen and set in motion in 1955. You can take a guided tour partway up the 350-ft **tower** for a panoramic view. ⊠ *Square in Strøget at eastern end of Vesterbrog. and western end of Frederiksbergg.,* ☎ *33/66–25–82.* ⊙ *Rådhus: Mon.–Wed., Fri. 9:30–3, Thurs. 9:30–4, Sat. 9:30–1. Tours in English, weekdays at 3, Sat. at 10. Tower tours: Oct.–May, Mon.–Sat. at noon; June–Sept. at 10, noon, and 2. Call to confirm hrs.*

★ ㉔ **Rosenborg Slot** (Rosenborg Castle). This Renaissance palace—built by jack of all trades Christian IV—houses the Crown Jewels, as well as a collection of costumes and royal memorabilia. Don't miss Christian IV's pearl-studded saddle. ⊠ *Øster Voldg. 4A,* ☎ *33/15–32–86.* ⊙ *Castle, late Oct.–Apr., Tues., Fri., and Sun. 11–2; treasury, Tues.–Sun. 11–3; both, May, Sept.–late Oct., daily 11–3; June–Aug., daily 10–4.*

㉓ **Rundetårn** (Round Tower). It is said that Peter the Great of Russia drove a horse and carriage up the 600 ft of the inner staircase of this round tower, built as an observatory in 1642 by Christian IV. It's a formidable walk, but the view is worth it. At the base of the tower is the university church, Trinitas; halfway up the tower you can take a break at the tower's art gallery. ⊠ *Købmagerg. 52A,* ☎ *33/93–66–60.* ⊙ *Tower, Sept.–May, Mon.–Sat. 10–5, Sun. noon–4; June–Aug., Mon.–Sat. 10–8, Sun. noon–8. Observatory and telescope, with astronomer to answer questions, mid-Oct.–mid-Mar., Tues.–Wed. 7 PM–10 PM.*

↻ ㉖ **Statens Museum for Kunst** (National Art Gallery). This museum reopens in the fall of 1999 with a complete refurbishment of the original 100-year-old building and a new, modern building that doubles the exhibition space. Though the collection remains the same—including works of Danish art from the Golden Age (early 19th century) to the present, as well as paintings by Rubens, Dürer, the Impressionists, and other European masters—the space also includes a children's museum, an amphitheater, a documentation center and study room, a bookstore, and a restaurant. ☒ *Sølvg. 48–50,* ☎ *33/74–84–94.* ☉ *Tues.–Sun. 10–5, Wed. until 9.*

❸ Strøget. Frederiksberggade is the first of the five pedestrian streets that make up Strøget, Copenhagen's shopping district and promenade area. Walk past the cafés and trendy boutiques to the double square of **Gammeltorv** and **Nytorv,** where, farther along, the street is paved with mosaic tiles. Outside the posh displays of the fur and porcelain shops the sidewalks have the festive aura of a street fair. **Kongens Nytorv** (King's New Market) is the square marking the end of Strøget.

❽ Teatermuseum (Theater Museum). Built in 1767 in the Royal Court, this museum is devoted to exhibits on theater and ballet history. You can wander around the boxes, stage, and dressing rooms to see where it all happened. ☒ *Christiansborg Ridebane 18,* ☎ *33/11–51–76.* ☉ *Wed. 2–4, weekends noon–4.*

★ **❻ Thorvaldsen Museum.** The Danish 19th-century sculptor Bertel Thorvaldsen, whose tomb stands in the center of the museum, was greatly influenced by the statues and reliefs of classical antiquity. In addition to his own works, the collection includes drawings and paintings by others that illustrate the influence of Italy on the artists of Denmark's Golden Age. ☒ *Porthusg. 2,* ☎ *33/32–15–32.* ☒ *Free Wed.* ☉ *Tues.–Sun. 10–5.*

★ ☺ **㉙ Tivoli.** In the 1840s the Danish architect Georg Carstensen persuaded King Christian VIII that an amusement park would be the perfect opiate for the masses, arguing that "when people amuse themselves, they forget politics." In the season from May through September, about 4 million people come through the gates. Tivoli is more sophisticated than a mere funfair: It offers a pantomime theater and an open-air stage, elegant restaurants, and frequent classical, jazz, and rock concerts in addition to a museum chronicling its own history. On weekends there are elaborate fireworks displays. Try to see Tivoli at least once by night, when the trees are illuminated along with the Chinese Pagoda and the main fountain. In recent years Tivoli has also been opened a month before Christmas with a gift and decorations market and children's rides. Do take the little ones, even in the winter; the luminescence of this place is magical. Most of the restaurants are also open, but there are plenty of less expensive food stalls serving everything from Oriental specialties to mulled wine. ☒ *Vesterbrog. 3,* ☎ *33/15–10–01.* ☉ *May–mid-Sept., daily 11 AM–midnight.*

❾ Tøjhusmuseet (Royal Armory). The Renaissance structure was built by King Christian IV, a scholar and a warrior as well as the architect of much of the city. It houses impressive displays of uniforms, weapons, and armor in an arched hall 200 yards long. ☒ *Tøjhusg. 3,* ☎ *33/11–60–37.* ☒ *Free Wed.* ☉ *Tues.–Sun. 12–4.*

㉘ Tycho Brahe Planetarium. This modern, cylindrical building is filled with astronomy exhibits and an Omnimax theater that takes visitors on a simulated journey up into space and down into the depths of the seas; reservations are advised for the theater. Because these films can be disorienting, planetarium officials do not recommend them for children under seven. ☒ *Gammel Kongevej 10,* ☎ *33/12–12–24.* ☒ *Exhibition and theater Dkr70.* ☉ *Daily 10:30–9.*

⓫ **Vor Frelsers Kirken** (Our Savior's Church). Local legend has it the stair-case encircling the fantastic green-and-gold spire of this 1696 Gothic structure was built curling the wrong way around and that when its architect reached the top and saw what he had done, he jumped. ⊠ *Skt. Annæg. 9,* ☎ *31/57–63–25.* ⬚ *Free.* ☽ *Weekdays 9–1. Closed during services and special functions; call ahead.*

㉑ **Vor Frue Kirken** (Church of Our Lady). Though this has been Copen-hagen's cathedral since 1924, the site itself has been a place of wor-ship since the 13th century, when Bishop Absalon built a chapel here. The spare, neoclassical facade is a 19th-century innovation repairing damage suffered during Nelson's bombing of the city in 1801. If the church is open, you can see Thorvaldsen's marble sculptures of Christ and the Apostles. Afterwards, if you're on your way to the Nørreport train station, you'll pass the stoic, columned **Kobenhavns Universitet** (Copenhagen University; ⊠ Norregade 10). It was built during the 19th century on the site of the medieval bishops' palace. ⊠ *Pilestræde 67,* ☎ *33/14–41–28.* ☽ *Irregular hrs; call ahead.*

Dining and Lodging

Food remains one of the great pleasures in Copenhagen, a city with more than 2,000 restaurants. Traditional Danish fare spans all the price categories: You can order a light lunch of smørrebrød, snack from a store kolde bord, or dine out on lobster and Limfjord oysters. You can also enjoy fast food Danish style, in the form of *pølser* (hot dogs) sold from trailers on the street. Team any of this with some pastry from a bakery (the shops displaying an upside-down gold pretzel), and you've got yourself a meal on the go. Many restaurants close for Christmas, roughly from December 24 through December 31. For details and price-category information, *see* Dining *in* Denmark A to Z, *above.*

Copenhagen is well served by a wide range of hotels, which are almost always clean, comfortable, and well run. Most but not all Danish ho-tels include a substantial breakfast in the room rate. Summertime reservations are a good idea, but if you should arrive without one, try the hotel booking service at the Danish Tourist Board (☞ Visitor In-formation *in* Copenhagen Essentials, *below*). They can also give you a "same-day, last-minute price," which is about DKr320 to DKr400 for a double hotel room. This service will also locate rooms in private homes, with rates starting at about DKr260 for a double. Try the **Ung-doms Information** lodging service (⊠ Rådhusstr. 13, ☎ 33/73–06–50) for budget accommodations. For details and price-category defini-tions, *see* Lodging *in* Denmark A to Z, *above.*

$$$$ ✕ **Kong Hans Kaelder.** Five centuries ago this was a Nordic vineyard, ★ but now it's one of Scandinavia's finest restaurants. Continuing in the footsteps of legendary (in Denmark) chef Daniel Letz, chef Thomas Rode Andersen continues to serve superb French-inspired dishes. The set-ting is subterranean and mysterious, with whitewashed, arching ceil-ings, candles, and wood carvings. ⊠ *Vingårdstr. 6,* ☎ *33/11–68–68. AE, DC, MC, V. Closed Sun. and Mon. June–mid-July and Aug.; mid-end July; and Easter wk. No lunch.*

$$$$ ✕ **Krogs.** This elegant canal-front restaurant commands a loyal clien-tele, both foreign and local. It's decorated with pale green walls and paintings of old Copenhagen. The menu (printed in five languages) lists such specialties as a rich, dark bouillabaisse and a generous cold plat-ter heaped with sea scallops, lobster, and local fish. ⊠ *Gammel Strand 38,* ☎ *33/15–89–15. Reservations essential. AE, DC, MC, V.*

$$$$ ✕ **Sct. Gertruds Kloster.** The history of this monastery goes back 700 ★ years. The dining room, bedecked with hundreds of icons, is illumi-

nated by 2,000 candles. The extensive French menu lists such specials as fillet of halibut with lobster glacé and duck breast in tarragon sauce. ⊠ *Hauser Pl. 32,* ☎ *33/14–66–30. Reservations essential. AE, DC, MC, V. No lunch.*

$$$ ✕ **Els.** When it opened in 1853, the intimate Els was the place to be
★ seen before the theater, and the painted Muses on the walls still watch diners rush to make an 8 o'clock curtain. Antique wooden columns and Royal Copenhagen tile tables complement a nouvelle Danish and French menu that changes daily, offering game, fish, and market-fresh produce. ⊠ *Store Strandstr. 3,* ☎ *33/14–13–41. Reservations essential. AE, DC, MC, V.*

$$$ ✕ **L'Alsace.** In the cobbled courtyard of Pistolstraede and hung with paintings by Danish surrealist Wilhelm Freddie, this restaurant is peaceful and quiet, attracting such diverse diners as Queen Margrethe and Pope Paul II. The hand-drawn menu includes a hearty *choucroute* (sauerkraut) with sausage and pork, plus fruit tarts and cakes for dessert. ⊠ *Ny Østerg. 9,* ☎ *33/14–57–43. AE, DC, MC, V. Closed Sun.*

$$$ ✕ **Pakhuskælderen.** Surrounded by thick white walls and raw timbers, the Nyhavn 71 hotel's (☞ *below*) intimate restaurant attracts a mix of business and holiday guests. It is known for its fresh, classically prepared range of Danish-French specialties. ⊠ *Nyhavn 71,* ☎ *33/11–85–85. Reservations essential. AE, DC, MC, V. Closed Sun. No lunch.*

$$ ✕ **Copenhagen Corner.** Diners here are treated to a superb view of the Rådhus Pladsen, as well as to a terrific store kolde bord, both of which compensate for the often harried staff. Specialties include fried veal with bouillon gravy and fried potatoes; entrecôte in garlic and bordelaise sauce, served with creamed potatoes; and a herring plate with three types of spiced and marinated herring and boiled potatoes. ⊠ *Rådhus Pl.,* ☎ *33/91–45–45. AE, DC, MC, V.*

$$ ✕ **El Meson.** Ceiling-hung pottery, knowledgeable waiters, and a top-notch menu make this Copenhagen's best Spanish restaurant. Choose carefully for a moderately priced meal, which might include beef spiced with spearmint, lamb with honey sauce, or paella for two. ⊠ *Hauser Pl. 12,* ☎ *33/11–91–31. AE, DC, MC, V. Closed Sun. No lunch.*

$$ ✕ **Havfruen.** A life-size wooden mermaid swings decorously from the ceiling in this small, rustic fish restaurant in Nyhavn. Natives love the maritime-bistro ambience and the daily evolving French and Danish menu. ⊠ *Nyhavn 39,* ☎ *33/11–11–38. DC, MC, V. Closed Sun.*

$$ ✕ **Ida Davidsen.** Five generations old (counting Ida's children Oscar
★ and Ida Maria), this world-renowned lunch spot has become synonymous with smørrebrød. Choose from these creative open-face sandwiches, piled high with such ingredients as pâté, bacon, and steak tartare, or even kangaroo, or opt for smoked duck served with a beet salad and potatoes. ⊠ *St. Kongensg. 70,* ☎ *33/91–36–55. Reservations essential. AE, DC, MC, V. Closed weekends and July. No dinner.*

$$ ✕ **Peder Oxe.** This countrified, lively bistro welcomes you with rustic antiques, 15th-century Portuguese tiles, and damask-covered tables set with heavy cutlery. Grilled steaks and fish—and some of the best burgers in town—come with an excellent salad bar. ⊠ *Gråbrødretorv 11,* ☎ *33/11–00–77. DC, MC, V.*

$$ ✕ **Victor.** This French-style corner café has great people-watching and bistro fare. It's best during weekend lunches, when Danes gather for such specialties as rib roast, homemade pâté, smoked salmon, and cheese platters. Careful ordering here can get you an inexpensive meal. Unfortunately, the waiters can be obnoxious. ⊠ *Ny Østerg. 8,* ☎ *33/13–36–13. AE, DC, MC, V.*

$ ✕ **Flyvefisken.** Silvery stenciled fish swim along blue-and-yellow stenciled walls in this funky Thai eatery. Among the city's more experimental (and spicy) restaurants, it offers chicken with cashews, spicy shrimp soup with lemongrass, and herring shark in basil sauce. A less-expensive health-food café is in the basement. ☒ *Larsbjørnsstr. 18,* ☎ *33/14–95–15. AE, DC, MC, V. Closed Sun.*

$ ✗ **Quattro Fontane.** On a corner west of the lakes, one of Copenhagen's busiest Italian restaurants is a noisy, two-story affair, packed tight with marble-top tables and a steady flow of young Danes. Chatty Italian waiters serve cheese or beef ravioli, cannelloni, linguine with clam sauce, and thick pizzas. ☒ *Guldbersg. 3,* ☎ *31/39–39–31. Reservations essential weekends. No credit cards.*

$ ✗ **Riz Raz.** On a corner off Strøget, this Middle Eastern restaurant packs
★ in young and old, families, and singles every night and on weekends. The very inexpensive all-you-can-eat buffet is heaped with healthy dishes, including lentils, falafel, bean salads, and occasionally pizza. ☒ *Kompagnistr. 20,* ☎ *33/15–05–75. Reservations essential weekends. DC, MC, V.*

$$$$ ▥ **D'Angleterre.** The grande dame of Copenhagen hotels has under-
★ gone major changes this century, but the hotel still retains its old-world, old-money aura. The rooms are done in pinks and blues, with over-stuffed chairs and antique escritoires and armoires. Bathrooms sparkle with brass, mahogany, and marble. If you are a light sleeper, choose a back room; some guests complain of noise from the nearby bars, as well as early morning deliveries. ☒ *Kongens Nytorv 34, DK 1051 KBH K,* ☎ *33/12–00–95,* ℻ *33/12–11–18. 110 rooms, 20 suites. 2 restaurants, pool. AE, DC, MC, V.*

$$$$ ▥ **Nyhavn 71.** In a 200-year-old warehouse overlooking the old ships of Nyhavn, this quiet hotel is a good choice for privacy-seekers. In 1998, the hotel underwent a renovation, but wisely, the management maintained the charm of the place. The maritime interiors have been preserved with their original plaster walls and exposed brick. Rooms are tiny but cozy, with warm woolen spreads, dark woods, soft leather furniture, and crisscrossing timbers. ☒ *Nyhavn 71, DK 1051 KBH K,* ☎ *33/11–85–85,* ℻ *33/93–15–85. 84 rooms. Restaurant. AE, DC, MC, V.*

$$$$ ▥ **SAS Scandinavia.** Near the airport, this is one of northern Europe's largest hotels and Copenhagen's token skyscraper. An immense lobby, with cool, recessed lighting and streamlined furniture, gives access to the city's first (and only) casino. Guest rooms are large and somewhat institutional but offer every modern convenience. Breakfast is not included in the rates. ☒ *Amager Blvd. 70, DK 2300 KBH S,* ☎ *33/11–24–23,* ℻ *31/57–01–93. 542 rooms, 52 suites. 4 restaurants, pool. AE, DC, MC, V.*

$$$ ▥ **Kong Frederik.** West of Rådhus Pladsen, near Strøget, this intimate hotel is a cozy version of its big sister, D'Angleterre (☞ *above*). The sunny Queen's Garden restaurant serves a breakfast buffet (not included in the rate); rooms are elegant with Oriental vases, mauve carpets, and all modern amenities. ☒ *Vester Voldg. 25, DK 1552 KBH K,* ☎ *33/12–59–02,* ℻ *33/93–59–01. 110 rooms, 17 suites. Restaurant. AE, DC, MC, V.*

$$$ ▥ **Neptun.** The centrally sited Neptun has been in business for nearly 150 years and shows no signs of flagging. Guest rooms decorated with blond wood are favored by Americans. Though charming, this Best Western Hotel can become very busy with tour groups. Moreover, because it is housed in a old building, room sizes vary greatly, and so does the noise from the street. Ask for details when booking a room. ☒ *Skt. Annæ Pl. 18, DK 1250 KBH K,* ☎ *33/13–89–00,* ℻ *33/14–12–50. 123 rooms, 14 suites. Restaurant. AE, DC, MC, V.*

$$$ ▥ **The Phoenix.** This luxury hotel welcomes guests with automatic glass doors, crystal chandeliers, and gilt touches everywhere. The staff switches languages as they register business and cruise guests. Suites and executive-class rooms have Biedermeier-style furniture and 18-karat-gold-plated bathroom fixtures, but the standard rooms are very small,

at barely 9 ft × 15 ft. If you're a light sleeper, ask for a room above the second floor to avoid street noise. ⊠ *Bredg. 37, DK 1260 KBH K,* ☎ *33/95–95–00,* FAX *33/33–98–33. 208 rooms, 7 suites. Restaurant. AE, DC, MC, V.*

$$ 🏨 **Ascot.** A charming old building downtown, this family-owned hotel has a classically columned entrance and an excellent breakfast buffet. Rooms have colorful geometric-pattern bedspreads and cozy bathrooms. A few have kitchenettes. Repeat guests often ask for their regular rooms. Be warned: In recent years, a nearby late-night disco has disturbed some guests. Be sure to ask for a room as far away from it as possible. ⊠ *Studiestr. 61, DK 1554 KBH K,* ☎ *33/12–60–00,* FAX *33/14–60–40. 113 rooms, 30 apartments. Restaurant (breakfast only). AE, DC, MC, V.*

$$ 🏨 **Copenhagen Admiral.** Overlooking old Copenhagen and Amalienborg, the monolithic Admiral, once a grain warehouse, now affords historic but airy accommodations. With massive stone walls broken by rows of tiny windows, it's one of the less expensive top hotels, though in recent years it's been upping both frills and prices. Guest rooms are spare, with jutting beams and modern prints. ⊠ *Toldbodg. 24–28, DK 1253 KBH K,* ☎ *33/11–82–82,* FAX *33/32–55–42. 365 rooms. Restaurant. AE, DC, MC, V.*

$$ 🏨 **Triton.** Despite seedy surroundings, this streamlined hotel attracts a cosmopolitan clientele thanks to a central location in Vesterbro. The large rooms, in blond wood and warm tones, have new bathrooms and state-of-the-art fixtures. The buffet breakfast included in the price is exceptionally generous, the staff friendly. There are also family rooms, each with a separate bedroom and fold-out couch. ⊠ *Helgolandsg. 7–11, DK 1653 KBH K,* ☎ *31/31–32–66,* FAX *31/31–69–70. 123 rooms. Restaurant (breakfast only). AE, DC, MC, V.*

$ 🏨 **Cab-Inn Scandinavia.** Winter business travelers and kroner-pinching summer backpackers and families alike flock to Copenhagen's answer to Japanese-style hotel minirooms. More cozy than futuristic, shiplike "berths" are brightly decorated, all with standard furnishings, including a small wall-hung desk with chair. Around the corner, at Danasvej 32, is a sister hotel, the Cab-Inn Copenhagen, with 86 rooms. ⊠ *Vodroffsvej 55, DK 1900 FR C,* ☎ *35/36–11–11,* FAX *35/36–11–14. 201 rooms with shower. AE, DC, MC, V.*

$ 🏨 **Missionhotellet Nebo.** This budget hotel is between the main train station and Istedgade's seediest porn shops. Nonetheless, it's a prim hotel, comfortable and well maintained by a friendly staff. The dormlike guest rooms are furnished with industrial carpeting, polished pine furniture, and soft duvet covers. Baths, showers, and toilets are clustered at the center of each hallway, and the breakfast restaurant downstairs has a tiny courtyard. ⊠ *Istedg. 6, DK 1650 KBH V,* ☎ *31/21–12–17,* FAX *31/23–47–74. 96 rooms, 40 with bath. AE, DC, MC, V.*

Nightlife and the Arts

Copenhagen This Week has good information on musical and theatrical happenings, as well as on special events and exhibitions. Concert and festival information is available from the **Dansk Musik Information Center** (DMIC; ⊠ Gråbrødretorv 16, ☎ 33/11–20–66). Copenhagen's main theater and concert season runs from September through May, and tickets can be obtained either directly from theaters and concert halls or from ticket agencies; ask your hotel concierge for advice. **Billetnet** (⊠ Main post office: Tietgensg. 37, ☎ 38/88–70–22), a box-office service available at all large post offices, has tickets for most major events. Keep in mind that same-day purchases at the box office at **Tivoli** (⊠ Vesterbrogade 3, ☎ 33/15–10–12) are half price if you pick them up after noon.

The Arts

FILM AND TELEVISION

Copenhagen natives are avid **movie** buffs, and as the Danes rarely dub films or television imports, you can often see original American and British movies and TV shows with Danish subtitles.

MUSIC

Tivoli Concert Hall (⊠ Tietensg. 20, ☎ 33/15–10–12) offers more than 150 concerts each summer, presenting a host of Danish and foreign soloists, conductors, and orchestras.

THEATER

The **Royal Theater** (⊠ Kongens Nytorv, ☎ 33/14–10–02) regularly holds theater, ballet, and opera performances. For English-language theater, try to catch a performance of the professional **London Toast Theatre** (☎ 33/22–86–86).

Nightlife

Many of the city's restaurants, cafés, bars, and clubs stay open after midnight, some as late as 5 AM. Copenhagen is famous for jazz, but you'll find nightspots catering to musical tastes ranging from bop to ballroom music. In the inner city most discos open at 11 PM, have a cover charge (about DKr40), and pile on steep drink prices. A few streets behind the railway station is Copenhagen's red-light district, where sex shops share space with grocers. Although the area is fairly well lighted and lively, women may feel uncomfortable here alone at night.

JAZZ

Many of Copenhagen's sophisticated jazz clubs have closed in the past couple of years. The upscale **Copenhagen Jazz House** (⊠ Niels Hemmingsensg. 10, ☎ 33/15–26–00) attracts European and some international talent to its chic, modern barlike ambience. **La Fontaine** (⊠ Kompagnistr. 11, ☎ 33/11–60–98) is Copenhagen's quintessential jazz dive, with sagging curtains, impenetrable smoke, crusty lounge lizards, and the random barmaid nymph; for jazz lovers the bordello mood and Scandinavian jazz talent make this a must. **Tivoli Jazzhouse Mantra** (⊠ Vesterbrog. 3, ☎ 33/11–11–13), Tivoli's jazz club, lures some of the biggest names in the world.

NIGHTCLUBS AND DANCING

The young set gets down on the disco floor in the fashionable **Park Café** (⊠ Østerbrog. 79, ☎ 35/26–63–42). The mellower folks come for brunch when the place transforms back to its old-world roots, or to check out the movie theater next door. **Rosie McGees** (⊠ Vesterbrog. 2A, ☎ 33/32–19–23) is a very popular English-style pub with Mexican food and dancing. **Sabor Latino** (⊠ Vester Voldg. 85, ☎ 33/11–97–66) is the UN of discos, with an international crowd dancing to salsa and other Latin beats. Among the most enduring clubs is **Woodstock** (⊠ Vesterg. 12, ☎ 33/11–20–71), where a mixed audience grooves to '60s classics.

Shopping

Strøget's pedestrian streets are synonymous with shopping.

Specialty Shops

Just off Østergade is **Pistolstræde,** a typical old courtyard filled with intriguing boutiques. Farther down the street toward the town hall square is a compound that includes several important stores: **Georg Jensen** (⊠ Amagertorv 4, ☎ 33/11–40–80), one of the world's finest silversmiths, gleams with a wide array of silver patterns and jewelry. Don't miss the **Georg Jensen Museum** (⊠ Amagertorv 6, ☎ 33/14–02–29), which showcases glass and silver creations ranging from tiny, twisted-glass shot glasses to an $85,000 silver fish dish. **Royal Copenhagen Porcelain** (⊠ Amagertorv 6, ☎ 33/13–71–81) carries both old and new china, plus porcelain patterns and figurines.

A. C. Bang (⊠ Østerg. 27, ☎ 33/15–17–26) upholds its old-world, old-money aura with impeccable quality; midsummer and after-Christmas fur sales offer real savings. **Bang & Olufsen** (⊠ Østerg. 3–5, ☎ 33/15–04–22) offers reasonable prices for radios, TVs, and stereo equipment in its own upscale shop. Along Strøget, at furrier **Birger Christensen** (⊠ Østerg. 38, ☎ 33/11–55–55), you can peruse designer clothes and chic furs. **FONA** (⊠ Østerg. 47, ☎ 33/15–90–55) carries stereo equipment, including the superior design and sound of Bang & Olufsen. **Illum** (⊠ Østerg. 52, ☎ 33/14–40–02) is a department store that has a fine basement grocery and eating arcade. Don't confuse Illum with **Illums Bolighus** (⊠ Amagertorv 10, ☎ 33/14–19–41), where designer furnishings, porcelain, quality clothing, and gifts are displayed in near-gallery surroundings. **Magasin** (⊠ Kongens Nytorv 13, ☎ 33/11–44–33), one of the largest department stores in Scandinavia, offers all kinds of clothing and gifts, as well as an excellent grocery department.

Side Trips

Heslingør

Shakespeare immortalized both the town and the castle when he chose Helsingør's **Kronborg Slot** (Kronborg Castle) as the setting for *Hamlet*. Completed in 1585, the present gabled and turreted structure is about 600 years younger than the fortress we imagine as the setting of Shakespeare's tragedy. Inside are a 200-ft-long dining hall, the luxurious chapel and the royal chambers. The ramparts and 12-ft-thick walls are a reminder of the castle's role as a coastal bulwark—Sweden is only a few kilometers away. Helsingør town—about 47 km (29 mi) north of Copenhagen—possesses a number of picturesque streets with 16th-century houses. Frequent trains stop at Helsingør station, and then it's a 20-minute walk around the harbor to the castle. ⊠ *Kronborg Slot,* ☎ *49/21–30–78.* ⊙ *Easter and May–Sept., daily 10:30–5; Oct. and Apr., Tues.–Sun. 11–4; Nov.–Mar., Tues.–Sun. 11–3.*

Humlebæk

The town, 35 km (22 mi) and a half-hour train ride from Copenhagen, is part of the "Danish Riviera" on the North Sjælland coast. Its chief
★ ℭ landmark is **Louisiana,** a world-class modern art collection housed in a spectacular building. Even if you can't tell a Rauschenberg from a Rembrandt, you should make the trip to see the setting: It's an elegant, rambling structure in a large park with views of the sound and, on a clear day, Sweden. The children's wing houses pyramid-shape chalkboards, kid-proof computers, and weekend activities under the guidance of an artist or museum coordinator. A combined train fare (from Copenhagen) and admission (DKr94) is available from DSB (☞ Arriving and Departing by Train *in* Copenhagen Essentials, *below*). A 10-minute walk from the station, the museum is also accessible by the E4 highway and the more scenic Strandvejen, or coastal road. ⊠ *Gammel Strandvej 13,* ☎ *49/19–07–19.* ⊙ *Daily 10–5, Wed. 10–10.*

Roskilde

For a look into the past, head 30 km (19 mi) west of Copenhagen to the bustling market town of Roskilde. A key administrative center during Viking times, it remained one of the largest towns in northern Europe through the Middle Ages. Today the legacy of its 1,000-year history lives on in its spectacular cathedral. Built on the site of one of Denmark's first churches, the **Domkirke** (cathedral) has been the burial place of Danish royalty since the 15th century. The combined effect of their tombs is striking—from the magnificent shrine of Christian IV to the simple brick chapel of Frederik IX. ✉ *Domkirkepl.,* ☎ *46/35–27–00.* ☉ *Subject to change; call ahead.*

★ A 10-minute walk south and through the park takes you to the water and the **Vikingeskibshallen** (Viking Ship Museum). Inside are five exquisitely reconstructed Viking ships, discovered at the bottom of Roskilde Fjord in 1962. Detailed placards in English chronicle Viking history. There are also English-language films on the excavation and reconstruction. ✉ *Strandengen,* ☎ *46/35–65–55.* ☉ *Apr.–Oct., daily 9–5; Nov.–Mar., daily 10–4.*

Copenhagen Essentials

Arriving and Departing

BY PLANE

The main airport for both international and domestic flights is Copenhagen Airport, 10 km (6 mi) southeast of town.

Between the Airport and Downtown. Trains from the airport's sleek new subterranean train station take less than 10 minutes to zip into Copenhagen's main station. Buy a ticket upstairs in the airport train station (Dk16.50); three trains an hour go into Copenhagen, while a fourth travels farther to Roskilde. Bus service to the city is frequent. The airport bus to the central station leaves every 15 minutes: The trip takes about 25 minutes; the fare is about DKr40 (pay on the bus). Public buses cost about DKr18 and run as often but take longer. Bus 250S takes you to Rådhus Pladsen, the city hall square. A taxi ride takes 15 minutes and costs about DKr150.

BY TRAIN

Copenhagen's clean and convenient central station, **Hovedbanegården** (✉ Just south of Vesterbrog., ☎ 33/14–88–00) is the hub of the country's train network. Intercity express trains leave hourly, on the hour, from 6 AM to 10 PM for principal towns in Fyn and Jylland. Find out more from DSB Information (☎ 70/13–14–15) at the central station. You can make reservations at the central station as well as most other stations, and through travel agents. Public shower facilities at the central station are open 4:30 AM–2 AM and cost DKr15.

Getting Around

BY BICYCLE

More than half the 5 million Danes are said to ride bikes, which visitors use as well. Bike rental costs DKr25 to DKr60 a day, with a deposit of DKr100 to DKr200. Contact **Københavns Cykler** (✉ Central Station, ☎ 33/33–86–13) or **Østerport Cykler** (✉ Oslo Plads, ☎ 33/33–85–13).

BY BUS AND SUBURBAN TRAIN

The best bet for visitors is the **Copenhagen Card,** affording unlimited travel on buses and suburban trains (S-trains), admission to some 60 museums and sights around metropolitan Copenhagen, and a reduction on the ferry crossing to Sweden. Buy the card, which costs about DKr155 (24 hours), Dkr255 (48 hours), or DKr320 (72 hours)—half price for children ages 5 to 11—at tourist offices or hotels or from travel agents.

Buses and suburban trains operate on the same ticket system and divide Copenhagen and environs into three zones. Tickets are validated on the time system: On the basic ticket, which costs DKr11 for an hour, you can travel anywhere in the zone in which you started. You can buy a discount *klip cort* (clip card), equivalent to 10 basic tickets, for DKr75. Call the 24-hour information service for zone information (☏ 36/45–45–45 for buses, ☏ 70/13–14–15 for S-trains; wait for the Danish message to end and a live operator will answer). Buses and S-trains run from 5 AM (6 AM on Sunday) to 12:30 AM. A reduced network of buses drives through the night.

BY CAR

Copenhagen is a city for walkers, not drivers. The charm of its pedestrian streets is paid for by a complicated one-way road system and difficult parking. Leave your car in the garage: Attractions are relatively close together, and public transportation is excellent.

BY TAXI

The computer-metered Mercedeses and Volvos are not cheap. The base charge is DKr15, plus DKr8–DKr10 (DKr11 at night) per km (½ mi). A cab is available when it displays the sign FRI (free); you can either hail a cab (though this can be difficult outside the center), pick one up at a taxi stand, or call (☏ 35/35–35–35); there's a surcharge of DKr20.

Contacts and Resources

EMBASSIES

U.S. (✉ Dag Hammarskjöldsallé 24, ☏ 35/55–31–44). **Canadian** (✉ Kristen Benikowsg. 1, ☏ 33/12–22–99). **U.K.** (✉ Kastelsvej 40, ☏ 35/44–52–00). **Australian** (Kristianiagade 21, 2100 KBH O, ☏ 35/26–22–44. **Irish** (Ostbanegade 21, 2100 KBH, O, ☏ 31/42–32–33).

EMERGENCIES

Police, fire, ambulance (☏ 112). **Auto Rescue/Falck** (☏ 31/14–22–22). **Doctor** (☏ 33/93–63–00 weekdays 8–4; 38/84–00–41 daily after 4 PM); fees payable in cash only, night fees around DKr120–DKr350. **Dentist:** Dental Emergency Service (✉ Tandlægevagten 14, Oslo Pl., near Østerport station, ☏ no phone); emergencies only, cash only. **Pharmacies** open 24 hours: **Steno Apotek** (✉ Vesterbrog. 6C, ☏ 33/14–82–66); **Sønderbro Apotek** (✉ Amagerbrog. 158, Amager area, ☏ 32/58–01–40).

ENGLISH-LANGUAGE BOOKSTORES

Arnold Busck (✉ Købmagerg. 49, ☏ 33/73–35–00). **Boghallen** (✉ Rådhus Pl. 37, ☏ 33/47–25–60).

GUIDED TOURS

Orientation. The "Harbor and Canal Tour" by boat leaves from Gammel Strand and the east side of Kongens Nytorv; it runs from May through mid-September, daily every half hour from 10 to 5. Several bus tours, conducted by **Copenhagen Excursions** (☏ 32/54–06–06), leave from the Lur Blowers' Column in Rådhus Pladsen.

Personal Guides. The Danish Tourist Board (☞ Visitor Information, *below*) can recommend multilingual guides for individual needs; travel agents have details on hiring a limousine and guide.

Regional. The Danish Tourist Board (☞ Visitor Information, *below*) has full details relating to excursions outside the city, including visits to castles (such as Hamlet's castle), the Viking Ship Museum, and Sweden.

Special-Interest. The "Royal Copenhagen Porcelain" tour (✉ Smalleg. 45, ☏ 31/86–48–59) is given on weekdays at 9, 10, 11, 1, and 2. If you're a beer aficionado, try the "Carlsberg Brewery Tour" (☞ Exploring Copenhagen, *above*).

Walking. The Danish Tourist Board (☞ Visitor Information, *below*) supplies maps and brochures and can recommend a walking tour.

Carlson Wagonlit Travel (⊠ Ved Vesterport 6, ☎ 33/63–78–78). **DSB Rejsebureau Terminus** (⊠ Central Station, ☎ 33/14–11–26). **Spies** (⊠ Nyropsg. 41, ☎ 33/32–15–00).

Danish Tourist Board (Danmarks Turistråd; ⊠ Bernstoffsg. 1, Tivoli Grounds, DK 1577 KBH V, ☎ 33/11–13–25).

FYN AND THE CENTRAL ISLANDS

It was Hans Christian Andersen, the region's most famous native, who dubbed Fyn (Funen) the "Garden of Denmark." Part orchard, part farmland, Fyn is sandwiched between Sjælland and Jylland. With its tidy, rolling landscape, seaside towns, manor houses, and castles, it is one of Denmark's loveliest islands. Its capital—1,000-year-old Odense, in the north—is the birthplace of Hans Christian Andersen; his life and works are immortalized here in two museums. Fyn is also the site of two of Denmark's best-preserved castles: 12th-century Nyborg Slot, in the east, and 16th-century Egeskov Slot, near Svendborg, in the south. From Svendborg it's easy to hop on a ferry and visit some of the smaller islands, such as Tåsinge, Langeland, and Ærø, whose main town, Ærøskøbing, with its twisting streets and half-timber houses, seems caught in a time warp.

Fyn has a wide range of hotels and inns, many of which offer off-season (October through May) rates, as well as special weekend deals. The islands also have numerous campsites and youth hostels, all clean and attractively located. Some, like Odense's youth hostel, are set in old manor houses. Contact local tourist offices for information (☞ Visitor Information *in* Fyn and the Central Islands Essentials, *below*).

Nyborg

This 13th-century town was Denmark's capital during the Middle Ages, as well as an important stop on a major trading route between Sjælland and Jylland. From 1200 to 1413, Nyborg housed the Danehof, the early Danish parliament. Nyborg's major landmark is its 12th-century **Nyborg Slot** (Nyborg Castle). It was here that Erik Glipping granted the first Danish constitution, the Great Charter, in 1282. ⊠ *Slotspl.*, ☎ *65/31–02–07.* ☉ *Mar.–May, Tues.–Sun. 10–3; June–Aug., daily 10–5; Sept.–Oct., Tues.–Sun. 10–3.*

$$$ 🏨 **Hesselet.** This modern hotel tucked into the Fyn landscape affords views of the Store Belt bridge and paths down to the sea. Inside it's a refined English-cum-Asian sanctuary with impeccable service. The guest rooms are furnished with cushy, modern furniture, and most have splendid views. ⊠ *Christianslundsvej 119, DK 5800,* ☎ *65/31–30–29,* ℻ *65/31–29–58. 43 rooms, 3 suites. Restaurant, indoor pool. AE, DC, MC, V.*

Kerteminde

Coastal Kerteminde is Fyn's most important fishing village and a picturesque summer resort. Stroll down Langegade to see its half-timber houses.

$$$ ✕ **Rudolf Mathis.** You can enjoy delectable fish and seafood specialties and a splendid view of Kerteminde Harbor at this traditional Danish restaurant. ⊠ *Dosseringen 13, 13 km (8 mi) northeast of Odense on Rte. 165,* ☎ *65/32–32–33. AE, DC, MC, V. Closed Mon. Jan.–Mar., and Sun. Oct. and Dec.*

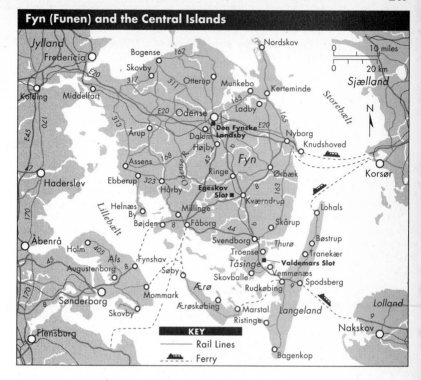

Fyn (Funen) and the Central Islands

Ladby

If you're a Viking enthusiast, stop in the village of Ladby to see the **Ladbyskibet** (Ladby ship), the 1,100-year-old underground remains of a Viking chieftain's burial, complete with his 72-ft-long ship. The warrior was equipped for his trip to Valhalla (the afterlife) with his weapons, four hunting dogs, and 11 horses. ⊠ *Vikingevej 123,* ☎ *65/ 32–16–67.* ☉ *Mar.–May and Sept.–Oct., Tues.–Sun 10–4; June–Aug., daily 10–5; Nov.–Feb., Wed.–Sun. 11–3.*

Odense

Plan to spend at least one night in Denmark's third-largest city. In addition to its museums and pleasant pedestrian streets, Odense is an especially charming provincial capital. If you can't take quaintness, don't go to the **H. C. Andersens Hus** (Hans Christian Andersen Museum). The surrounding district has been carefully preserved, with cobbled pedestrian streets and low houses with lace curtains. Inside, exhibits use photos, diaries, drawings, and letters to convey a sense of the man and the time in which he lived. Attached to the museum is an extensive library with Andersen's works in more than 127 languages (he was in fact one of the most widely published authors in the history of literature), where you can listen to fairy tales on tape. The museum includes child-friendly exhibits. ⊠ *Hans Jensenstr. 37–45,* ☎ *66/13–13–72, ext. 4611.* ☉ *Mid-June–Aug., daily 9–7; Sept.–mid-June, Tues.–Sun. 10–4.*

The **Børnekulturehuset Fyretøjet** (The Children's Culture House, The Tinderbox) museum includes walk-through fairy-tale exhibits as well as studios where children can draw and write their own tales and plays and then dress up and perform them. ⊠ *Hans Jensenstr. 21,* ☎ *66/14–44–11.* ☉ *Feb.–Dec., Tues.–Sun., 10–4.*

The modern **Carl Nielsen Museum** has multimedia exhibits of Denmark's most famous composer (1865–1931) and his wife, the sculptor Anne

Marie Carl Nielsen (1863–1945). ✉ *Claus Bergsg. 11,* ☎ *66/13–13–72, ext. 4671.* ☉ *Apr.–May and Sept.–Oct., Thurs.–Sun. noon–4; June–Aug., Tues.–Sun. noon–4; Nov.–Mar., Thurs.–Fri 4–8, weekends noon–4.*

Odense's **Møntergården** (Museum of Cultural and Urban History) fills four houses representing Danish architectural styles from the Renaissance to the 18th century, all grouped around a shady, cobbled courtyard. Inside are dioramas, an extensive coin collection, clothed dummies, toys, and tableaux. ✉ *Overg. 48–50,* ☎ *66/13–13–72, ext. 4611.* ☉ *Tues.–Sun. 10–4.*

Brandts Passage, off Vestergade, is a heavily boutiqued walking street. At the end of the Passage, in what was once a textile factory, is a four-★ story art gallery, the **Brandts Klædefabrik,** incorporating the **Museet for Foto Kunst** (Museum for Photographic Art), **Danmarks Grafiske Museum** (the Danish Graphics Museum), and **Kunst Hallen** (Art Hall), with temporary exhibits for video art. It's well worth the short walk to see Fyn's rendition of a New York SoHo loft. ✉ *37–43 Brandts Passage,* ☎ *66/13–78–97.* ☉ *Sept.–June, Tues.–Sun. 10–5; July–Aug., daily 10–5.*

Ⓒ Don't neglect **Den Fynske Landsby** (Fyn Village); an enjoyable way to get here is to travel down the Odense River by boat. The open-air museum village is made up of 20 farm buildings, including workshops, a vicarage, a water mill, and a windmill. There's a theater, too, with summertime adaptations of Andersen's tales. ✉ *Sejerskovvej 20,* ☎ *66/13–13–72, ext. 4642.* ☉ *Apr.–mid-June and mid-Aug.–Oct., Tues.–Sun. 10–5; mid-June–mid-Aug., daily 9:30–7; Nov.–Mar., Sun. and holidays 11–3.*

$$ ✕ **Le Provence.** A few minutes from the pedestrian street, this restaurant, with its cozy orange-and-yellow–clad dining room, puts a Danish twist on Provençal cuisine, with such specialties as venison in blackberry sauce and duck breast cooked in sherry. ✉ *Pogstr. 31,* ☎ *66/12–12–96. DC, MC, V.*

$ ✕ **Målet.** A lively crowd calls this sports club its neighborhood bar. Next to steaming plates of schnitzel served in a dozen ways, soccer is the delight of the house. ✉ *Jernbaneg. 17,* ☎ *66/17–82–41. Reservations not accepted. No credit cards.*

$$$$ 🏨 **Grand Hotel.** They don't make spacious, gracious places like this anymore. Dating from 1897, the Grand offers spruced-up fin de siècle elegance. The lobby decor is cool and green, with a sweeping staircase and a spectacular Pompeian-red dining room. Guest rooms are ample and comfortable. ✉ *Jernbaneg. 18, DK 5000,* ☎ *66/11–71–71,* FAX *66/14–11–71. 137 rooms. Restaurant. AE, DC, MC, V.*

$$ 🏨 **Hotel Ansgar.** Though completely renovated in 1995, this hotel still maintains a cozy, modest, English-style ambience. The rooms—done in rather dark colors—have a mix of old and new furniture. ✉ *Østre Stationsvej 32, DK 5000,* ☎ *66/11–96–93,* FAX *66/11–96–75. 44 rooms. Restaurant. AE, MC, V.*

$ 🏨 **Hotel Ydes.** If you're a student or budget-conscious and tired of barracks-type accommodations, this bright, colorful hotel is a good bet. The plain, white, hospital-style rooms are clean and comfortable. ✉ *Hans Tausensg. 11, DK 5000,* ☎ *66/12–11–31. 30 rooms, 24 with shower. Restaurant. AE, DC, MC, V.*

Fåborg

Four times a day, the lovely little 12th-century town of Fåborg echoes with the dulcet chiming of the Klokketårnet (Bell Tower)'s carillon, the largest in Fyn. Dating from 1725, the **Gamla Gård** (Old Merchant's

House) presents the cultural history of Fyn. ⊠ *Holkeg. 1,* ☎ *62/61–33–38.* ⊙ *Mid-May–Sept., daily 10:30–4:30.*

The **Fåborg Museum for Fynsk Malerkunst** (Fyn Painting Museum) displays the compositions—dating mainly from 1880 to 1920—of Fyn painters, filled with the dusky light that so often illuminates Scandinavian painting. ⊠ *Grønneg. 75,* ☎ *62/61–06–45.* ⊙ *Apr.–May and Sept.–Oct., daily 10–4; June–Aug., daily 10–5; Nov.–Mar., daily 11–3.*

$$$$ 🏨 **Falsled Kro.** Once a smuggler's hideaway, this 500-year-old institution is one of Denmark's most elegant inns. A favorite among well-heeled Europeans, it has sumptuously appointed cottages with European antiques and stone fireplaces. The restaurant combines French and Danish cuisines, employing ingredients from its own garden and markets in faraway Lyon. ⊠ *Assensvej 513, DK 5642 Millinge, 13 km (8 mi) northwest of Fåborg on Millinge-Assens Hwy.,* ☎ *62/68–11–11,* FAX *62/68–11–62. 14 rooms, 3 apartments. Restaurant. AE, DC, MC. Closed Jan.–Feb.*

$$$ 🏨 **Steensgård Herregårdspension.** A long avenue of beeches leads to this 700-year-old moated manor house 7 km (4½ mi) northwest of Fåborg. Rooms are elegant, with antiques, four-poster beds, and yards of silk damask. The fine restaurant serves wild game from the manor's own preserve. ⊠ *Steensgård 4, DK 5642 Millinge,* ☎ *62/61–94–90,* FAX *62/61–78–61. 15 rooms, 13 with bath. Restaurant. AE, DC, MC, V. Closed Jan.*

Ærø

Take the car ferry to **Søby** at the northern tip of Ærø island, the "Jewel of the Archipelago," where roads wend thier way through fertile fields and past thatched farmhouses. South from Søby is the charming town of **Ærøskøbing,** on the island's north coast. Once you've spent an hour walking through its cobbled 17th- and 18th-century streets, you'll understand its great appeal.

$$ 🏨 **Ærøhus.** The half-timber building with a steep red roof looks like a rustic cottage on the outside and a great aunt's house on the inside. Hanging pots and slanted walls highlight the public areas; pine furniture and cheerful curtains and duvets keep the guest rooms simple and bright. Apartments, all with kitchenettes, occupy an annex. The garden's eight cottages have small terraces. ⊠ *Vesterg. 38, DK 5970 Ærøskøbing,* ☎ *62/52–10–03,* FAX *62/52–21–23. 30 rooms, 18 with bath; 8 cottages; 37 apartments. Restaurant. AE, V. Closed Dec. 24 and Jan.*

Svendborg

The southernmost town in Fyn is the gateway to the country's south-
★ ern islands. Just north of Svendborg is **Egeskov Slot** (Egeskov Castle), one of the best-preserved island castles in Europe. Egeskov means "oak forest," and an entire one was felled around 1540 to form the piles on which the rose-stone structure was erected. The park contains noteworthy Renaissance, Baroque, English, and peasant gardens and an antique-car museum. Though this is still a private home, a few rooms, including the trophy-filled hunting room, are open to the public. ⊠ *Egeskovg. 18, Kværndrup, 15 km/9 mi north of Svendborg,* ☎ *62/27–10–16.* 🎫 *Castle and museum, DKr100.* ⊙ *Castle: May–June, Aug.–Sept., daily 10–5; July, daily 10–7. Museum: May and Sept., daily 10–5; June and Aug., daily 9–6; July, daily 9–8.*

$ ✕ **Ærø.** A dim hodgepodge of ship parts and maritime doodads, this harborside restaurant is peopled by brusque waitresses and serious local trenchermen. The menu remains staunchly old-fashioned, focusing on *frikadeller* (fried meatballs), fried *rødspætte* (plaice) with hollandaise sauce, and dozens of smørrebrød options. ✉ *Brøg. 1 ved Ærøfærgen,* ☎ *62/21–07–60. DC, MC, V. Closed Sun.*

Troense

On the island of Tåsinge, pretty Troense is one of Denmark's best-preserved villages. Once the home port for countless sailing ships, both Viking and, later, commercial, today the harbor is stuffed with pleasure yachts. Dating from around 1640, **Valdemars Slot** (Valdemars Castle), now a sumptuously furnished home, is one of Denmark's oldest privately owned castles. Upstairs rooms are appointed to the smallest detail. Downstairs is the castle church, illuminated only by candlelight. There's a restaurant (☞ *below*) beneath the church. The sister café overlooks Lunkebugten, a bay with one of south Fyn's best stretches of beach. ✉ *Slotsalleen 100, Troense,* ☎ *62/22–61–06.* ☉ *May and Sept.–Oct., daily 10–5; June–Aug. daily 10–6. Call first to confirm opening hrs.*

$$$ ✕ **Restaurant Valdemars Slot.** Beneath the castle, this domed restaurant is all romance and prettiness, with pink carpet and candlelight. Fresh ingredients from France and Germany and wild game from the castle's preserve are the essentials for an ever-changing menu, which includes such specialties as wild venison with cream sauce and duck breast à l'orange. The less expensive café, Den Grå Dame, serves traditional Danish food. ✉ *Slotsalleen 100, Troense,* ☎ *62/22–59–00. AE, MC, V. Closed Nov.–Mar. except to groups of 4 or more with several days' notice.*

Langeland

Tåsinge is connected with the island of Langeland by a causeway bridge. The largest island in the southern archipelago, Langeland is rich in relics of the past, and the beaches are worth scouting out.

Fyn and the Central Islands Essentials

Getting Around

The best starting point is Nyborg, on Fyn's east coast, just across the Great Belt from Korsør, on Sjælland. "The other Chunnel"—this one connecting Sjælland to Fyn—opened for rail traffic in 1997 and for cars in 1998. From Nyborg the easiest way to travel is by car, though public transportation is good. Distances on Fyn and its islands are short, but there is much to see and you can easily spend two or three days here, circling the islands from Nyborg or using Odense or Svendborg as a base from which to make excursions.

Guided Tours

At the tourist board (☞ Visitor Information, *below*), pick up a copy of the free booklet "In the Footsteps of Hans Christian Andersen"; it describes a very enjoyable walking tour that you take at your own pace. "From Medieval Odense to the Odense of Today," offered July–August, Tuesday–Thursday at 11, also organized by the tourist board (☞ Visitor Information, *below*), takes you on a tour of the town through the ages.

A day trip to Odense leaves from Copenhagen's city hall square at 9 AM every Sunday from mid-May to mid-September. Lasting about 11 hours, the trip includes stops at several picturesque villages and a lightning-speed visit to Egeskov Castle.

Visitor Information

South Fyn Tourist Board (✉ Centrumpl., Svendborg, ☎ 62/21–09–80). **Nyborg** (✉ Torvet 9, ☎ 65/31–02–80). **Odense** (✉ Rådhuset, ☎ 66/12–75–20).

JYLLAND AND THE LAKES

A region of carefully groomed pastures punctuated by stretches of rugged beauty, the peninsula of Jylland (Jutland) is the only part of Denmark that is naturally attached to the mainland of Europe; its southern boundary forms the frontier with Germany. Moors and sand dunes cover a tenth of the peninsula—the windswept landscapes of Isak Dinesen's short stories can be seen in the northwest—and the remaining land is devoted to agriculture and forestry. On the east side of the peninsula, facing Fyn, well-wooded fjords run inland for kilometers. Beyond rustic towns and stark countryside, Jylland possesses gracious castles, parklands, and the famed Legoland. Ribe, Denmark's oldest town, lies to the south; to the east is Århus, Denmark's second-largest city, with superb museums and a new concert hall. If you are in this region directly after touring Fyn, head northwest from Odense through Middlefart and then on to Vejle. By train, either from Odense or Copenhagen, the starting point is Kolding, to the south of Vejle.

Kolding

Don't miss the well-preserved 13th-century **Koldinghus** castle, a royal residence during the Middle Ages. Rebuilt in the 15th century, it was destroyed by fire in the early 1800s. Modern restoration took nearly 20 years, ending in 1993. Perched at the edge of the Kolding Fjord is a massive redbrick quadrangle centered on a courtyard. The castle floors are made of raw oak, and its walls are alternately spare and white or lined with iron plates. The construction reveals how Danish design bridges the old and the new: The building was awarded the European Nostra Prize in 1993 for restoration. ⊠ *Markdanerg.,* ☎ *75/50–15–00.* ☉ *Daily 10–5.*

The **Geografiske Have** (Geographical Garden) has a rose garden with more than 120 varieties, as well as some 2,000 other plants from all parts of the world, arranged geographically. ⊠ *Christian den IV Vej,* ☎ *75/50–38–80.* ☉ *May–Sept., daily 10–6; Oct.–Apr., Mon.–Fri., 8–2:30, weekends 9–5.*

Vejle

Beautifully positioned on the fjord amid forest-clad hills, Vejle looks toward the Kattegat, the strait that divides Jylland and Fyn. You can hear an old Dominican monastery clock chiming the hours; the clock survives, but the monastery itself was long ago torn down to make room for the town's imposing 19th-century city hall.

$$$$ 🏨 **Munkebjerg.** Seven kilometers (4½ miles) southeast of town, surrounded by a thick beech forest and majestic views of the Vejle Fjord, this elegant hotel provides privacy. Overlooking the forest, rooms are furnished in blond pine and soft green; the lobby is rustic. Of the two top-notch restaurants, one specializes in French cuisine, the other in very Danish fare. Amenities include a heliport. ⊠ *Munkebjergvej 125, DK 7100,* ☎ *76/42–85–00,* FAX *75/72–08–86. 148 rooms. 2 restaurants, pool. AE, DC, MC, V.*

Jelling

Here lie two 10th-century burial mounds, all that remains from the court of King Gorm the Old and his wife, Thyra. Between the mounds are the Jelling **Runestener** (runic stones), one of which, "Denmark's Certificate of Baptism," is decorated with the oldest known figure of Christ in Scandinavia. The stone was erected by Gorm's son, King Harald Bluetooth, who brought Christianity to the Danes in AD 960.

Jutland (Jylland)

0 ——————— 40 miles

0 ——————— 60 km

N

KEY

🚢 Ferry

Skagerrak

Skagen

TO SWEDEN

Hirtshals

Tuen

55 · E39 · 40 · 35

Hjørring

Frederikshavn

55 · 13

Sæby

Brønderslev

E39 · E45 · 541

Nørresundby

Limfjord

Aalborg

Kattegat

Hanstholm

29

11

Thisted

26

181 · 11

Mors

Lim-fjord

Løgstør

Nibe

26

Nykøbing Mors

29

13

E45

Hadsund

507 · 541

Hobro

Lemvig

Venø Bugt

Skive

Mariager

28

Struer

Råsted

Holstebro

16

Viborg

16

Randers

Nissum Fjord

Hald Sø

13

Auning

Grenå

Ribe

Gudenå

Storå

18

26

E45

15

Ringkøbing

15

15

Århus

Ebeltoft

Herning

Silkeborg

Ringkøbing Fjord

Skjern

18

Brande

13

Skanderborg

E45

Skjernå

11

Grindsted

Givskud

Horsens

Samsø

Varde

Jelling

TO KALUNDBORG

Varde Å

Billund

Vejle

30

Vejle Fjord

Esbjerg

E20

Holsted

Fredericia

Fyn

Storebælt

E133

Fanø

Sønderho

Kongeå

Kolding

Middelfart

311

Odense

TO HARWICH, NEWCASTLE

Ribe

Christiansfeld

E45

Rømø

Ribe Å

Vojens

168

E20

Skærbæk

Haderslev

Nyborg

11

Åbenrå

Fåborg

6

8

Svendborg

Silkeborg

The region between Silkeborg, on the banks of the Gudenå in Jylland's lake district, and Skanderborg to the east reveals some of Denmark's loveliest scenery. The best way to explore the area is by water; the Gudenå winds its way some 160 km (100 mi) through lakes and wooded hillsides down to the sea. You can take an excursion boat or, better still, a rare old coal-fired paddle steamer, the **Hjejlen,** which runs in summer and is based at Silkeborg. Ever since 1861 it has been paddling its way through narrow stretches of fjord where the treetops meet overhead to the foot of Denmark's highest hill, the Himmelbjerget, which rises all of 438 ft at Lake Julso. You can clamber up the narrow paths through the heather and trees to the top of the hill, where there is an 80-ft tower erected in 1875 in memory of King Frederik VII. ⊠ *Havnen, Silkeborg,* ☎ *86/82–07–66 (reservations).* 🎟 *Round-trip DKr39– DKr76.* ⊙ *Departs Silkeborg Harbor 10 and 1:45 Sun. in June, daily mid-June–July.*

One of Silkeborg's chief attractions can be seen in the **Kulturhistoriske Museum** (Museum of Cultural History)—the 2,200-year-old Tollund Man, whose corpse was preserved by the natural chemicals in a nearby bog. ⊠ *Hovedgaardsvej 7,* ☎ *86/82–14–99.* ⊙ *Mid-Apr.–late Oct., daily 10–5; late Oct.–mid-Apr., Wed. and weekends noon–4.*

Århus

Denmark's second-largest city is at its liveliest during the 10-day **Århus Festival** in late August, which brings together everything from classical concerts to jazz and folk music, clowning, theater, exhibitions, beer tents, and sports. The town's cathedral, the 15th-century **Domkirke,** is Denmark's longest church; it contains a beautifully executed three-panel altarpiece. Whimsical sketches enliven the ceiling. ⊠ *Bispetorv,* ☎ *86/ 12–38–45.* ⊙ *Jan.–Apr., Mon.–Sat. 10–3; May–Sept., Mon.–Sat. 9:30– 4; Oct.– Dec., Mon.–Sat. 10–3. Closed Sun. and holidays for services.*

Århus's 13th-century **Vor Frue Kirken** (Church of Our Lady), formerly attached to a Dominican abbey, has an eerie but interesting crypt church rediscovered in 1955 and dating from 1060, one of the oldest preserved stone churches in Scandinavia. The vaulted space contains a replica of an old Roman crucifix. ⊠ *Frue Kirkepl.,* ☎ *86/12–12–43.* ⊙ *Sept.–Apr., weekdays 10–2, Sat. 10–noon; May–Aug., weekdays 10– 4, Sat. 10–2. Closed Sun. and holidays for services.*

The town's open-air museum, the **Gamle By** (Old Town), is composed of 65 half-timber houses, a mill, and a millstream. The meticulously recreated period interiors range from the 15th to the early 20th centuries. ⊠ *Viborgvej,* ☎ *86/12–31–88.* ⊙ *Jan.–Mar., daily 11–3; Apr., May, Sept., Oct., daily 10–5; June–Aug., daily 9–6; Nov.–Dec., daily 10–4.*

★ In a 250-acre forest just south of Århus, the indoor-outdoor **Moesgård Forhistorisk Museum** (Prehistoric Museum) displays ethnography and archaeology, including the Grauballe Man, a well-preserved corpse from 2,000 years ago. Take the Prehistoric Trail through the forest, which leads past Stone and Bronze Age displays to some reconstructed houses from Viking times. ⊠ *Ny Moesgård Allé 20, Højbjerg,* ☎ *89/42–11– 00.* ⊙ *Jan.–mid-Mar. and Oct.–Dec., Tues.–Sun. 10–4; mid-Mar.– Sept., daily 10–5.*

$ ✗ **Rio Grande.** Full of the standard-issue blankets, straw hats, and bright colors ubiquitous in Mexican restaurants all over the world, Rio Grande is a favorite with youngsters, families, and even businesspeople. Heaping plates of tacos, enchiladas, and chili are a good value— and tasty, too. ⊠ *Vesterg. 39,* ☎ *86/19–06–96. AE, MC, V.*

$$$$ 🏨 **Royal Hotel.** Open since 1838, Århus's grand hotel has hosted such greats as Arthur Rubinstein and Marian Andersen. Guests are welcomed into a stately lobby appointed with Chesterfield sofas, modern paintings, and a winding staircase leading to the accommodations above. The plush rooms vary in style and decor, but all have rich drapery, velour- and brocade-covered furniture, and marble bathrooms. ⊠ *Store Torv 4, DK 8100,* ☎ *86/12–00–11,* ꜰᴀx *86/76–04–04. 98 rooms, 7 suites. Restaurant. AE, DC, MC, V.*

$ 🏨 **Youth Hostel Pavilionen.** As in all Danish youth and family hostels, rooms here are clean, bright, and functional, and the secluded, wooded setting near the fjord is downright beautiful. Keep in mind that it does get noisy, with carousing business parties mixed in with budget-conscious backpackers. There's a kitchen for guests' use. The cafeteria serves breakfast only. ⊠ *Marienlundsvej 10, DK 8240,* ☎ *86/16–72–98,* ꜰᴀx *86/10–55–60. 30 rooms, 11 with shower; 4 communal showers and toilets. AE, MC, V. Closed mid-Dec.–mid-Jan.*

Aalborg

This city guards the narrowest point of the Limfjord, the great waterway of northern Jylland and the gateway between north and south. Here you'll find charming combinations of new and old; twisting lanes filled with medieval houses and, nearby, broad modern boulevards. Jomfru Ane Gade, a tiny cobbled street in the center of Aalborg, is lined with restaurants, inns, and sidewalk cafés. The magnificent five-story **Jens Bangs Stenhus** (Jens Bang's Stone House; ⊠ Østerågade 9, ☎ 98/12–50–56), dating from 1624, has an atmospheric restaurant and an excellent wine cellar. The Baroque cathedral, **Budolfi Kirken** (⊠ Gammel Torv), is consecrated to the English St. Butolph. The 15th-century **Helligaandsklosteret** (Monastery of the Holy Ghost; ⊠ C. W. Obelspl., next to Budolfi Kirken), one of Denmark's best preserved, is now a home for the elderly.

$$ ✗ **Duus Vinkælder.** This amazing cellar is part alchemist's den, part
★ neighborhood bar. Though most people come for a drink before or after dinner, you can also get a light bite. In summer the menu is chiefly smørrebrød, but during the winter you can order such specialties as pølser, frikadeller, *biksemad* (cubed potato, meat, and onion hash), and the restaurant's specialty, pâté. ⊠ *Østerå 9,* ☎ *98/12–50–56. Reservations essential. No credit cards. Closed Sun.*

$$ ✗ **Spisehuset Kniv og Gaffel.** In a 400-year-old building parallel to Jomfru Ane Gade, the busy Knife and Fork is crammed with oak tables balancing on crazy slanting floors and lit by candles. Its year-round courtyard is a veritable greenhouse. Young waitresses negotiate the mayhem to deliver inch-thick steaks, the house specialty. ⊠ *Maren Turisg. 10,* ☎ *98/16–69–72. DC, MC, V. Closed Sun.*

$$$$ 🏨 **Helnan Phønix.** In a sumptuous old mansion, this hotel is popular with international and business guests. Rooms are luxuriously furnished with plump chairs and polished dark-wood furniture; in some the original raw beams are still intact. The Brigarden restaurant serves excellent Danish cuisine. ⊠ *Vesterbro 77, DK 9000,* ☎ *98/12–00–11,* ꜰᴀx *98/16–31–66. 208 rooms, 2 suites. Restaurant. AE, DC, MC, V.*

Skagen

The picturesque streets and luminous light of the town have inspired both painters and writers. Here the Danish artist Holger Drachmann (1846–1908) and his friends founded what has become known as the Skagen school of painting; you can see their work in the **Skagens Museum.** ⊠ *Brøndumsvej 4,* ☎ *98/44–64–44.* ☉ *Apr. and Oct., Tues.– Sun. 11–4; May and Sept., daily 10–5; June–Aug., daily 10–6; Nov.– Mar., Wed.–Fri. 1–4, Sat. 11–4, Sun. 11–3.*

$$$ ⚏ **Brøndums Hotel.** A few minutes from the beach, this 150-year-old gabled inn is furnished with antiques and Skagen-school paintings. The 21 guest rooms in the main building, without TVs or phones, are old-fashioned, with wicker chairs, Oriental rugs, and pine and four-poster beds. Some are beginning to show their age, but 25 annex rooms are more modern. The hotel has a fine Danish-French restaurant with a lavish cold table. ⊠ *Anchersvej 3, DK 9990,* ☎ *98/44–15–55,* FAX *98/45–15–20. 46 rooms, 12 with bath. Restaurant. AE, DC, MC, V.*

Viborg

Dating from the 8th century, the town started out as a trading post and a place of pagan sacrifice. Later it became a center of Christianity, with monasteries and its own bishop. The 1,000-year-old **Haervejen,** the old military road that starts near here, was once Denmark's most important connection with the outside world. Legend has it that during the 11th century, King Canute set out from Viborg to conquer England, which he subsequently ruled from 1016 to 1035. Built in 1130, Viborg's **Domkirke** (cathedral; ⊠ Mogensg., ☎ 86/62–10–60) was once the largest granite church in the world. The crypt, restored and reopened in 1876, is all that remains of the original building. Its 20th-century biblical frescoes were painted by Danish artist Joakim Skovgaard.

Hald Sø

There's terrific walking country beside Hald Sø (Hald Lake) and on the nearby heather-clad **Dollerup Bakker** (Dollerup Hills). At a small kiosk near the lake that sells snacks and sweets you can pick up a map.

Herning

In this old moorland town, you'll find a remarkable circular building with an exterior frieze by Carl-Henning Pedersen (born 1913); it houses the **Carl–Henning Pedersen and Else Afelt Museum.** Just next door is the **Herning Art Museum.** The concave outer wall of the collar-shape building, a shirt factory until 1977, is lined with another enormous frieze 722 ft long. The two museums are set within a sculpture park. ⊠ *Birk Centerpark 1–3,* ☎ *97/12–10–33.* ⊘ *Nov.–Apr., Tues.–Sun. noon–5; May–June, Sept.–Oct., Tues.–Sun. 10–5; July, daily 10–5.*

Ribe

The medieval center in Denmark's oldest town is preserved by the Danish National Trust. From May to mid-September, a night watchman walks around the town telling of its ancient history and singing traditional songs. Visitors can join him in the main square each night at 10.

$$$ ⚏ **Hotel Dagmar.** In the middle of Ribe's quaint center, this cozy, half-timber hotel encapsulates the charm of the 16th century, with stained-glass windows, frescoes, sloping floors, and carved chairs. The lavish rooms are all appointed with antique canopy beds, fat armchairs, and chaise longues. The fine French restaurant serves such specialties as fillet of salmon in sorrel cream sauce and marinated *foie gras de canard* (duck liver). ⊠ *Torvet 1, DK 6760,* ☎ *75/42–00–33,* FAX *75/42–36–52. 50 rooms. Restaurant. AE, DC, MC, V.*

Billund

★ ☺ **Legoland** is a park filled with scaled-down versions of cities, towns, and villages, working harbors and airports, a Statue of Liberty, a statue of Sitting Bull, a Mt. Rushmore, a safari park, even a Pirate Land—all constructed of millions of Lego bricks. There are also exhibits of toys from pre-Lego days, including Legoland's showpiece, Titania's Palace, a sumptuous dollhouse built in 1907 by Sir Neville Wilkinson for his daughter. The park also has a massive theme-building-ride-restaurant extravaganza: It all takes place within the double-football-field-size Castleland, where guests arrive through a serpentine dragon ride.

Everything inside is made of 45 million Lego bricks, including the wizards and warlocks, dragons and knights that inhabit it. That is until you get to the theme restaurant, the Knight's Barbeque, where waiters in Middle Ages garb hustle skewered haunches of beef, "loooong sausages," and typical fare of the period. ⊠ *Legoland,* ☎ *75/33–13–33.* 💷 *DKr120–DKr130.* ☾ *Mid-Apr.–Oct., daily 10–8.*

Jylland and the Lakes Essentials

Getting Around

Although there is good train and bus service between all the main cities, this region is best visited by car. The delightful offshore islands are suitable only if you have ample time, as many involve an overnight stay.

Guided Tours

Guided tours are scarce in these parts; stop by any tourist office for maps and suggestions for a walking tour. Århus also offers a "Round and About the City" tour, which leaves from the tourist board (☞ Visitor Information, *below*) daily at 10 AM from mid-June to mid-August.

Visitor Information

Aalborg (⊠ Østerå 8, ☎ 98/12–60–22). **Århus** (⊠ Rådhuset, ☎ 89/40–67–00). **Billund** (⊠ c/o Legoland A/S, ☎ 75/33–19–26). **Herning** (⊠ Bredg. 2, ☎ 97/12–44–22). **Kolding** (⊠ Axeltorv 8, ☎ 76/33–21–00). **Randers** (⊠ Erhvervens Hus, Tørvebryggen 12, ☎ 86/42–44–77). **Ribe** (⊠ Torvet 3–5, ☎ 75/42–15–00). **Silkeborg** (⊠ Åhavevej Haven, Godthåbsvej 4, ☎ 86/82–19–11). **Vejle** (⊠ Banegaardspl. 6, ☎ 75/82–19–55). **Viborg** (⊠ Nytorv 9, ☎ 86/61–16–66).

If you like majestic open spaces, fine architecture, and the Nordic quality of life, Finland is for you. It is a land of lakes—187,888 at the last count—and forests, whose people prize their natural surroundings while expanding the frontiers of modern design and high technology.

The music of Sibelius echoes the mood of this Nordic landscape. Both can swing from the somber nocturne of midwinter darkness to the tremolos of sunlight slanting through pine and bone-white birch, ending with the diminuendo of a sunset as it fades into the next day's dawn. Similarly, the Finnish people reflect the changing moods of their land and climate. Their affinity with nature has produced some of the world's greatest designers and architects. Many American cities have buildings designed by Alvar Aalto and the Saarinens, Eliel and his son Eero. Today Finland is also increasingly known for its high-tech achievements, especially by the mobile phone giant, Nokia.

While Internet and e-mail connections in Finland are more numerous per capita than anywhere else, the country's 5.1 million inhabitants continue to treasure their vast silent spaces. They won't always appreciate back-slapping familiarity—least of all in the sauna, widely regarded in the land that gave the traditional bath its name as a spiritual, as well as a cleansing, experience. Nevertheless, Finns are not unlikely to strike up impromptu conversations in pubs or provide generous help for a lost tourist.

Until 1917 Finland (in Finnish, *Suomi*) was under the domination of Sweden and Russia. After more than 600 years under the Swedish crown and 100 under the tsars, the country bears marks of the two cultures, such as a small but influential Swedish-speaking minority and a scattering of onion-dome Orthodox churches. The Finns themselves, neither Scandinavian nor Slavic, are descendants of the wandering Finno-Ugric peoples, who settled on the swampy shores of the Gulf of Finland before the Christian era. Finnish is one of the Finno-Ugric languages; it is related to Estonian and, distantly, to Hungarian.

There is a tough, resilient quality to the Finns. No other people fought the Soviets to a standstill as the Finns did in the Winter War of 1939–40. This resilience stems partly from the turbulence of the country's past, but it also comes from the people's strength and determination to work the land and survive the long, dark winters. They are stubborn, self-sufficient, and patriotic, yet not aggressively nationalistic. Having over-come a severe recession and a daunting rate of unemployment during the early 1990s, Finland became assertive in international markets, proud of its technology leaders as well as such sports figures as Formula One champ Mika Häkkinen, and increasingly aware of what it has to offer the rest of Europe. In 1995 Finland joined the European Union, aiming for greater economic and political security and strength-ening its profile by promoting the Union's "northern dimension."

Finland's extensive public transport system offers an efficient and af-fordable way to cover beautiful expanses of lakeland and forest. The atmosphere in the capital, Helsinki, with its outdoor summer bars and cafés and multilingual population, is far more cosmopolitan than was the case a decade ago. A conspicuous influx of Russians and Estoni-ans is also evidence of Finland's new, more open relationship with its eastern neighbors.

"The strength of a small nation lies in its culture," noted Finland's lead-ing 19th-century statesman and philosopher, Johan Vilhelm Snellman. As though inspired by this thought, Finns—who are among the world's top readers—continue to nurture a rich cultural climate, as is illustrated by 900 museums and a slew of summer festivals. In 2000 Helsinki cel-ebrates its 450th anniversary while in the limelight as a European Cul-tural Capital, prompting an array of special art, design, and technology exhibits.

FINLAND A TO Z

Customs
For details on imports and duty-free limits, *see* Customs & Duties *in* Chapter 1.

Dining
As in other parts of Scandinavia, the *seisovapöytä* (buffet table) is often a work of art as well as a feast. Some special Finnish dishes are *poronkäristys* (reindeer casserole); salmon, herring, and various fresh-water fish; and *lihapullat* (meatballs with a creamy sauce). Crayfish parties are popular between the end of July and early September. In the autumn local mushrooms such as the *suppelovahvero* (funnel-shape chanterelle) are a nice complement to meat and game. For a de-licious dessert, try *lakka* (cloudberries), which grow in the midnight sun above the Arctic Circle and are frequently used in sauces for ice cream. Most restaurants close for major holidays. Inexpensive lunches are served in *kahvila* (coffee shops) and *baari* (usually cafés, not bars).

MEALTIMES
The Finns eat early; lunch runs from 11 or noon to 1 or 2, dinner from 4 to 7, but restaurants also serve meals after 7.

RATINGS
Prices are per person and include first course, main course, dessert, and *palvelupalkkio* (service charge), which is included on the check. If you want to leave an additional tip—though it really isn't necessary—round the figure off to the nearest FIM 5 or FIM 10.

Finland (Suomi)

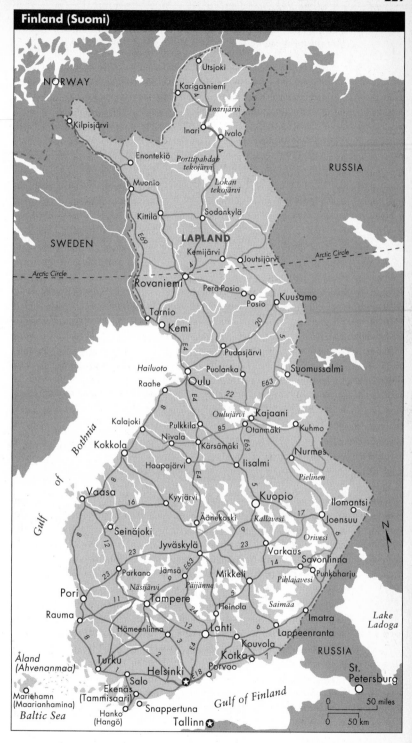

NORWAY

Utsjoki

Karigasniemi

Inarijärvi

Kilpisjärvi

Inari

Ivalo

Enontekiö

Porttipahdan tekojärvi

RUSSIA

Muonio

Lokan tekojärvi

Kittilä

Sodankylä

SWEDEN

E69

LAPLAND

Kemijärvi

Arctic Circle

Joutsijärvi

Arctic Circle

Rovaniemi

Perä-Posio

Posio

Kuusamo

Tornio

20

Kemi

E4

Pudasjärvi

Suomussalmi

Hailuoto

Puolanka

Raahe

Oulu

E63

E4

22

8

Oulujärvi

Kajaani

Kalajoki

Pulkkila

85

Otanmäki

Kuhmo

Nivala

Kärsämäki

E63

Nurmes

Kokkola

Haapajärvi

E4

Iisalmi

Pielinen

Vaasa

Kyyjärvi

5

Kuopio

Ilomantsi

16

Äänekoski

Kallavesi

17

Joensuu

8

Seinäjoki

9

Orivesi

6

12

Jyväskylä

23

Varkaus

23

Parkano

Jämsä

E63

14

Savonlinna

Näsijärvi

9

Päijänne

Mikkeli

Punkaharju

Pori

11

Tampere

5

Pihlajavesi

Rauma

Heinola

Saimaa

8

Hämeenlinna

24

Lahti

6

Imatra

Lake Ladoga

12

Lappeenranta

3

Kouvola

RUSSIA

Turku

2

E4

Kotka

1

St. Petersburg

Åland (Ahvenanmaa)

Salo

Helsinki

Porvoo

E18

Mariehamn (Maarianhamina)

Ekenäs (Tammisaari)

Snappertuna

N

Baltic Sea

Hanko (Hangö)

Gulf of Finland

Tallinn

Gulf of Bothnia

0   50 miles

0   50 km

If you select the prix-fixe menu, which usually covers two courses and coffee and is served at certain hours in many establishments, the cost of the meal can be as little as half the prices shown below.

CATEGORY	HELSINKI	OTHER AREAS
$$$$	over FIM 200	over FIM 170
$$$	FIM 150–FIM 200	FIM 140–FIM 170
$$	FIM 80–FIM 150	FIM 80–FIM 140
$	under FIM 80	under FIM 80

WHAT TO WEAR

Except for the most elegant establishments, where a jacket and tie are preferred, casual attire is acceptable for restaurants in all price categories; jeans are not allowed in some more expensive dining rooms.

Language

The official languages of Finland are Finnish and Swedish. A little more than 6% of the total population speak Swedish, but in some areas, such as the west coast and in pockets close to Helsinki, Swedish speakers form a local majority. English is widely spoken in Helsinki and by young Finns around the country. In Finnish Lapland the native Sámi (pronounced Sah-me) population speaks three different dialects of a language distantly related to Finnish. Note that the Finnish letters ä and ö and the Swedish å come at the end of the alphabet.

Lodging

Finland offers a full range of accommodations: hotels, motels, boardinghouses, bed-and-breakfasts, rental chalets and cottages, farmhouses, youth hostels, and campsites. There is no official rating system, but standards are generally high. If you haven't reserved a room before arriving in Helsinki, you can make reservations through a travel agency or at the **Hotel Booking Centre** (✉ Rautatieasema , ☎ 09/171–133, 🖷 09/175–524, hotel@helsinkiexpert.fi); the booking service is free by phone, fax, or e-mail; if booked in person, the charge is FIM 30 per room or FIM 15 per hostel bed in Helsinki, FIM 40 for all other reservations outside Helsinki.

BOARDINGHOUSES AND RENTALS

Found mainly outside Helsinki, these provide the least expensive accommodations; local tourist offices have lists. The selection is huge; chalets and cottages are nearly always in delightful lakeside or seashore settings. Comfortable (not luxurious) accommodations cost FIM 1,200–FIM 4,000 per week for a four-person rental. A central reservations agency is **Lomarengas** (✉ Hämeentie 105D, 00550 Helsinki, ☎ 09/5766–3300; or ✉ Eteläesplanadi 4, 00130 Helsinki, ☎ 09/170–611 May–Sept. only).

CAMPING

Finland has about 350 campsites. All offer showers and cooking facilities, and many include cottages for rent. Lists, with sites graded according to a three-grade system, are available from the Finnish Youth Hostel Association and the Finnish Tourist Board.

FARMHOUSES

Farmhouses are in attractive settings, usually near water. A central reservations agency is **Suomen 4H-liitto** (✉ Abrahaminkatu 7, 00180 Helsinki, ☎ 09/642–233, 🖷 09/642–274).

HOTELS

Most hotels in Finland are modern or recently renovated; a few occupy fine old manor houses. Rooms usually have a bath or shower, and virtually all hotels have saunas. Prices generally include breakfast and often a morning sauna and swim. The **Finncheque** voucher system (mid-May through September) offers good discounts. Only the first night can be reserved from outside Finland, but subsequent reservations can be made free from any Finncheque hotel. For additional information inquire at Suomen Hotellivaraukset Oy (HVO; ⊠ Dagmarinkatu 4, 00100 Helsinki, ☎ 09/499–155 or toll-free in Finland 9800/55155, FAX 09/440–383, suomen.hotellivaraukset@co.inet.fi).

RATINGS

Prices are for two people in a double room on a weekday and include breakfast and service charges. Weekend and summer rates tend to be significantly lower.

CATEGORY	HELSINKI	OTHER AREAS
$$$$	over FIM 900	over FIM 700
$$$	FIM 600–FIM 900	FIM 550–FIM 700
$$	FIM 400–FIM 600	FIM 400–FIM 550
$	under FIM 400	under FIM 400

SUMMER HOTELS

Some university student housing is turned into "summer hotels" from June through August; they offer modern facilities at slightly lower-than-average prices. The Finnish Youth Hostel Association publishes "Hostel-lit," which lists summer hotels as well as youth hostels. Free copies are available at the Finnish Tourist Board (☞ Visitor Information, *below*) and the Finnish Youth Hostel Association (☞ *below*).

YOUTH HOSTELS

Hostels range from empty schools to small manor houses. The Finnish Tourist Board (☞ Visitor Information, *below*) and the Finnish **Youth Hostel Association** (YHA; ⊠ Yrjönkatu 38B, 00100 Helsinki, ☎ 09/694–0377, FAX 09/693–1349) can provide a list of hostels. There are no age restrictions, and prices range from FIM 60 to FIM 250 per bed, with a discount of FIM 15 for YHA members. Single and double rooms are also available in some locations.

Mail

POSTAL RATES

Airmail rates to North America are FIM 3.40 for postcards or letters weighing up to 20 grams. Letters to the United Kingdom and the rest of the European Union cost FIM 3.20.

RECEIVING MAIL

If you're uncertain about where you'll be staying, have mail sent to you marked "poste restante" and addressed to the post office in the appropriate town (Helsinki's main post office: ⊠ Mannerheimintie 11, 00100). American Express offers free mail service to cardholders (⊠ Clients' Mail, American Express, Mikonkatu 2D, 00100 Helsinki).

Money Matters

COSTS

Prices are highest in Helsinki. Taxes are already included in hotel and restaurant charges. The prices of many goods include an 18% sales tax; the tax on food is less (☞ Shopping, *below*).

CURRENCY

The unit of currency in Finland is the Finnish mark, divided into 100 penniä. There are bills of FIM 20, 50, 100, 500, and 1,000. Coins are 10 and 50 penniä, and FIM 1, FIM 5, and FIM 10. At press time (summer 1999), the exchange rate was about FIM 5.73 to the U.S. dollar, FIM 3.90 to the Canadian dollar, FIM 9.08 to the pound sterling, FIM 3.77 to the Australian dollar, and FIM 3.06 to the New Zealand dollar. Finland is one of the "first wave" countries in the European Monetary Union project, so expect to see parallel pricing in marks and euros; actual exchange rates listed here are based on the euro. Credit cards are widely accepted, even in many taxicabs. Traveler's checks can be cashed only in banks.

Finland is making advances in the use of a "smart" prepaid electronic cash card, called the Avant card, that processes even the smallest of anonymous cash transactions; at press time such transactions could be made at designated public pay phones, vending machines, and McDonald's, of all places. Disposable prepaid cards can be purchased at kiosks. Reloadable purse cards will eventually be integrated with existing ATM and debit cards.

SAMPLE PRICES
Cup of coffee, FIM 8; glass of beer, FIM 15–FIM 25; soft drink, FIM 10; ham sandwich, FIM 15–FIM 20; 2-km (1-mi) taxi ride, FIM 30.

TIPPING
You can give taxi drivers small coins. Train and airport porters have a fixed charge. It's not necessary to tip hotel doormen for carrying bags to the check-in counter, but give bellhops FIM 5–FIM 10 for carrying bags to your room. The coat-check room fee of FIM 5 is usually clearly posted; if not, give FIM 10, depending on the number in your party. FIM 5 is a standard tip for minor services.

National Holidays
January 1; January 6 (Epiphany); April 21, 23–24 (Good Friday, Easter, and Easter Monday); May 1 (May Day); June 1 (Ascension); June 11(Pentecost/Whit Sunday); June 23–24 (Midsummer's Eve and Day); October 31–November 1 (All Saints' Day); December 6 (Independence Day); December 25–26 (Christmas and Boxing Day).

Opening and Closing Times
Banks are open weekdays 9:15–4:15; exchange offices are open longer. Opening hours for **museums** vary considerably, so check individual listings. Many museums in the countryside are open only in summer. **Shops** are generally open weekdays 9–6, Saturday 9–2. Department stores and supermarkets stay open until 8 or 9 on weekdays and 5 or 6 on Saturdays. Shops may also open on Sunday during June, July, and August and on four other Sundays in the year—usually in December for Christmas shopping. Shops in the tunnel complex beneath Helsinki's main railway station are open daily, including holidays, until 10 PM.

Shopping
Non-EU residents who purchase goods worth more than FIM 250 in any shop marked "tax free for tourists" can get a 12%–16% refund (10% on food). Show your passport and the store will give you a check for the appropriate amount, which you can cash at your final point of departure from the EU.

Telephoning
COUNTRY CODE
The country code for Finland is 358.

INTERNATIONAL CALLS
You can dial Britain and North America directly from anywhere in Finland. Calls to other countries can be made from telegraph offices, which are marked TELE or LENNÄTIN and are usually next to a post office. An operator will assign you a private booth and collect payment at the end of the call. To dial numbers from outside Finland, omit the zero at the beginning of the city code. To make a direct international phone call from Finland, dial 00, or 999, or 990, then the appropri-

ate country code and phone number. You can reach long-distance operators by dialing the following numbers: **AT&T** (☎ 9800–10010), **MCI** (☎ 9800–10280), and **Sprint** (☎ 9800–10284). For **directory assistance** abroad, dial 020–208.

LOCAL CALLS

To avoid exorbitant hotel surcharges on calls, use public pay phones, and have some FIM 1 and FIM 5 coins ready. Many pay phones only accept a phone card; the *Sonera Kortti, HPY Kortti,* and other cards are available at post offices, R-kiosks (small convenience stores), and some grocery stores. They come in increments of FIM 30, FIM 50, FIM 100, and FIM 150. Be aware that several local phone companies also offer cards and that some pay phones only accept certain cards. For information about telephone service, call HPY/HTF at 6061 or Sonera at 02–0401. For **directory assistance** dial 118 or 10013 (English-speaking operator).

Transportation

BY BICYCLE

Well-marked cycle paths run into the heart of Helsinki and other towns and cities, making cycling safe and fast. Bikes can be rented at some youth hostels. The **Finnish Youth Hostel Association** (⊠ Yrjönkatu 38B, 00100 Helsinki, ☎ 09/694–0377) offers round-trip packages from Helsinki, including bike rental and hostel accommodation, for FIM 1,280 (seven days) or FIM 2,200 (14 days).

BY BOAT

Helsinki and Turku have regular sea links with the Finnish Åland Islands in the Baltic Sea. Ferry and hydrofoil traffic between Helsinki and Tallinn is also convenient for one–two-day side trips. From mid-June to mid-August you can cruise the lakes of the Finnish interior. Complete timetables are available from the Finnish Tourist Board (☞ Visitor Information, *below*).

BY BUS

Finland's bus system can take you virtually anywhere. A Coach Holiday Ticket, available from bus stations and travel agencies, entitles you to 1,000 km (625 mi) of bus travel within two weeks for FIM 390.

BY CAR

Breakdowns and Accidents. The Automobile and Touring Club of Finland (Autoliitto; ⊠ Hämeentie 105 A, 00550 Helsinki, ☎ 09/774–761) operates a 24-hour information service (☎ 09/7747–6400; 9700–8080 on weekends) for club members and members of foreign auto clubs. If an accident requires an ambulance or fire squad, call the national emergency number, 112. Report accidents without delay to the insurance company listed on rental-car documents or to the Finnish Motor Insurers' Centre (Liikennevakuutuskeskus; ⊠ Bulevardi 28, 00120 Helsinki, ☎ 09/680–401) as well as to the police (☎ 10022).

Gasoline. Gasoline costs about FM 5.54 per liter.

Parking. Finding parking is difficult only in some city centers. Major cities offer multistory garages; most towns have on-street meters. In Helsinki there is no free on-street parking. In areas with no meters drivers must display a *pysäköintilippu* (parking voucher), for sale at R-kiosks and gas stations, on their dashboard. Illegally parked cars may be towed.

Road Conditions. Finland has an expanding network of efficient major roads, some of which are multi-lane. In the north, you can expect long stretches of dirt road, which become difficult to negotiate during the spring thaw. Away from the larger towns, traffic is light, but take elk and reindeer warning signs seriously.

Rules of the Road. Drive on the right. At intersections cars coming from the right have the right-of-way. Speed limits (usually marked) are 50 kph (30 mph) in built-up areas and 80–100 kph (50–62 mph) in the country and on main roads, 120 kph (74 mph) in summer on some highways. Low-beam headlights must be used at all times outside city areas, seat belts are compulsory (for all seats), and you must carry a warning triangle in case of a breakdown.

BY PLANE

Finnair (☎ 09/818–800 or 9800/3466) operates an elaborate network of flights linking 25 towns in Finland. Finnair grants visitors under age 25 a youth discount on flights booked ahead, with reductions as much as 50% or more. These tickets are available in most countries and in Finland at major travel agencies.

BY TRAIN

Finland's comfortable and clean rail system extends to all main centers of the country. A special **Finnrail Pass** entitles you to unlimited travel for 3, 5, or 10 days within a four-week period. In Finland the Finnrail Pass is available from VR Finnish Railways (☎ 09/707–5700, FAX 09/707–3700, www.vr.fi). In the United States and Canada it can be purchased from Rail Europe (☎ 800/438–7245), and in the United Kingdom, from Norvista (☎ 0171/409–7334). The **ScanRail** and **ScanRail Flexi** passes allow unlimited train travel throughout Denmark, Finland, Norway, and Sweden, as well as restricted ferry passage in and beyond Scandinavia. The ScanRail pass is available for 21 days, the ScanRail Flexipass for 5 out of 15 days. Certain hotel chains and organizations offer discounts to pass holders. In the United States call Rail Europe (☞ *above*), or DER (☎ 800/782–2424), which also offers a 21-day pass.

Visitor Information

Finnish Tourist Board **Tourist Information Office** (✉ Eteläesplanadi 4, 00100 Helsinki, ☎ 09/4176–9300, FAX 09/4176–9301, www.mek.fi).

Weather

The summer season from mid-June to mid-August is marked by long hours of sunlight and cool nights. Though many establishments and sights close or drastically reduce hours off-season, the advantages to off-season travel are many: avoiding the mosquitoes, especially fearsome in the north; spectacular fall foliage; and cross-country skiing.

CLIMATE

You can expect warm days in Helsinki from mid-May, and in Lapland from mid-June. Hot weather, with temperatures well into the 80s, is not uncommon in July and August. The midnight sun can be seen from May through July, depending on the region. For a period in midwinter, the northern lights in Lapland almost make up for the fact that the sun does not rise at all. Even in Helsinki, summer nights are brief and never really dark; in midwinter daylight lasts only a few hours.

The following are average daily maximum and minimum temperatures for Helsinki.

Jan.	30F	– 1C	**May**	64F	18C	**Sept.**	53F	11C
	26	– 3		48	9		39	4
Feb.	34F	1C	**June**	60F	16C	**Oct.**	46F	8C
	24	– 4		48	9		36	2
Mar.	36F	2C	**July**	68F	20C	**Nov.**	32F	0C
	26	– 3		55	13		26	– 3
Apr.	46F	8C	**Aug.**	64F	18C	**Dec.**	32F	0C
	32	0		53	12		24	– 4

HELSINKI

Built on the peninsulas and islands of the Baltic shoreline, Helsinki is a city of the sea. Streets curve around bays, bridges arch between islands, and ferries carry traffic to islands farther offshore. The smell of the sea hovers over the city, and there is a constant bustle in the city's harbors as the huge ships that ply the Baltic drop and lift anchor.

Helsinki has grown dramatically since World War II; it now has a population of well over 500,000, accounting for more than 1/10th of Finland's population. The city covers a total of 1,140 square km (433 square mi), including some 315 islands, with at least 30% of the metropolitan area reserved for parks and other open spaces. Most of Helsinki's sights, hotels, and restaurants, however, are crowded onto a single peninsula.

During the 16th century the Swedish king Gustav Vasa, at that time ruler of Finland as well, was determined to woo trade away from the Estonian city of Tallinn and the Hanseatic League. Helsinki was founded next to the rapids of the Vantaa River on June 12, 1550, by a group of Finns who had settled here upon the king's orders.

Over the next three centuries, Turku, on Finland's west coast, was the country's political and intellectual capital. Helsinki took center stage only when Sweden ceded Finland to Russia in 1809. Tsar Alexander I turned Finland into an autonomous grand duchy, proclaiming Helsinki its capital in 1812. Around the same time, much of Turku burned to the ground, and its university was forced to move to Helsinki. From then on Helsinki's position as Finland's first city was assured.

Just before the tsar's proclamation, a fire destroyed many of Helsinki's traditional wooden buildings, making it necessary to build a new city center. The German-born architect Carl Ludvig Engel was entrusted with the project, and thanks to him Helsinki has some of the purest neoclassical architecture in the world. Add to this foundation the stunning outlines of the Jugendstil (Art Nouveau) period of the early 20th century and more modern buildings designed by native Finnish architects, and you have a capital city as architecturally eye-catching as it is unlike those of the rest of Europe.

Exploring Helsinki

Numbers in the margin correspond to points of interest on the Helsinki map.

⑰ Eduskuntatalo (Parliament House). This imposing, colonnaded, red-granite structure was built between 1927 and 1931. The legislature has one of the world's highest ratios of women to men. ⊠ *Mannerheimintie 30,* ☎ *09/432–2027.*

⑲ Finlandiatalo (Finlandia Hall). The lake Töölönlahti forms the backdrop of this important cultural venue, which has hosted hundreds of concerts, meetings, and congresses per year since its completion in 1971. Architect Alvar Aalto designed this creative, marble and black-granite building to be functional: The tower and inclined roof enhance acoustics in the concert hall. ⊠ *Mannerheimintie 13,* ☎ *09/402–4246.* ☺ *Concerts usually Wed. and Thurs. nights.*

Kaivopuisto (Well Park). This elegant district was favored by Russian high society during the 19th century. Now it is a residential area for diplomats and a popular strolling ground. ⊠ *Close to ferry terminals.*

Katajanokka. Nineteenth-century brick warehouses in this district have been converted into boutiques, galleries, crafts studios, and restaurants. ⊠ *Harbor district east of Kanavaranta and the Greek Orthodox cathedral.*

❸ Katumuseo/Helsingin Kaupunginmuseo (Street Museum/Helsinki City Museum). Walk down this block of Sofiakatu from the esplanade to Senate Square and step through various periods of Helsinki's history. The Helsinki City Museum is on the same street. ⊠ *Sofiankatu 4,* ☎ *09/169–3933.* ⊙ *City Museum: weekdays 9–5, weekends 11–5.*

★ **❶ Kauppatori** (Market Square). The colorful, bustling market beside the South Harbor attracts customers for freshly cut flowers, fruit, and vegetables trucked in from the hinterland, as well as handicrafts from small country villages—all sold by vendors in bright orange tents. Closer to the dock are fresh fish from the waters of the Baltic. You can't miss the curvaceous *Havis Amanda* statue watching over the busy square. ⊠ *Eteläranta and Pohjoisesplanadi.* ⊙ *Market: year-round, Mon.–Fri. 6:30–2, Sat. 6:30–3; June–Aug., also open Mon.–Fri. 3:30–8 and Sun. 9–4 (except on Midsummer).*

❷ Kaupungintalo (City Hall). This light-blue building on Pohjoisesplanadi (North Esplanade), the political center of Finland, is the home of city government offices. ⊠ *Pohjoisesplanadi 1,* ☎ *09/1691.*

⊙ ㉔ Korkeasaari Eläintarha (Helsinki Zoo). Here snow leopards and reindeer thrive in the cold Finnish climate and children can climb on outdoor play equipment. The ferry departs from the Market Square approximately every 30 minutes from May through September. Alternatively, you can catch the bus at Erottaja or Herttoniemi (weekends), or take the metro to the Kulosaari stop, cross under the tracks, and then follow the signs 20 minutes to the zoo. ⊠ *Korkeasaari Island,* ☎ *09/169–5969.* ⊙ *Jan.–Feb., daily 10–4; Mar.–Apr., daily 10–6; May–Sept., daily 10–8; Oct.–Dec., daily 10–4.*

⓯ Mannerheimin patsas (statue of Marshal Mannerheim). In front of the main post office, the bronze equestrian gazes down Mannerheimintie, named in his honor. No man in Finnish history is as revered as Baron Carl Gustaf Mannerheim, the military and political leader who guided Finland through the first half of the 20th century. ⊠ *Mannerheimintie.*

⓰ Nykytaiteenmuseo (Kiasma) (Museum of Contemporary Art). Praised for the boldness of its curved steel shell, but also condemned for its encroachment on the territory of the Mannerheim statue, this striking museum opened in 1998 and displays a wealth of Finnish and foreign art from the 1960s to the present. Look for the "butterfly" windows and don't miss the view of Töölönlahti from the café. ⊠ *Mannerheiminaukio 2.* ☎ *09/1733–6501.* ⊙ *Year-round Tues. 9–5, Wed.–Sun. 10–10.*

❻ Presidentinlinna (President's Palace). Built as a private home in 1818, the palace was converted for use by tsars in 1843. It served as the official residence of Finnish presidents from 1919 to 1993; now its rooms are used as offices and reception halls. ⊠ *Pohjoisesplanadi 1,* ☎ *09/ 601–966.* ⊙ *Tours by appointment, Wed., Sat. 11–4.*

⓭ Rautatieasema (train station). The station and the adjoining square are the city's bustling commuter hub. The solid building was designed by Eliel Saarinen, one of the founders of the early 20th-century National Romantic style. ⊠ *Kaivokatu,* ☎ *09/7071 or 09/707–5700 for reservations.*

★ **❹ Senaatintori** (Senate Square). The heart of neoclassical Helsinki, the square designed by Carl Ludvig Engel is a harmonious blend of Europe's ancient architectural styles. In addition to **Tuomiokirkko** (☞ *below*), the main building of Helsinki University and the State Council Building flank the square. **Kiseleff Bazaar Hall,** with cafés and gift and crafts shops, is on the south side of the square. ⊠ *Bordered by Aleksanterinkatu to south and Hallituskatu to north.*

⓫ **Stockmann's.** This huge department store, which fills an entire block, was a target for Russian consumers in Soviet times. ⊠ *Aleksanterinkatu 52,* ☏ *09/1211.* ⊙ *Mon.–Fri. 9–9, Sat. 9–6.*

★ ⓲ **Suomen Kansallismuseo** (National Museum). Eliel Saarinen and his partners blend allusions to Finnish medieval churches and castles with elements of Art Nouveau in this vintage example of the National Romantic style. The museum is closed for renovations until spring 2000, when it will reopen its archaeological, cultural, and ethnological collection to the public. ⊠ *Mannerheimintie 34,* ☏ *09/405–0470.*

⓴ **Suomen Kansallisooppera** (Finnish National Opera). The splendid state-of-the-art opera house opened in 1993 in a park overlooking Töölönlahti. The striking white exterior has clean modern lines. ⊠ *Helsinginkatu 58,* ☏ *09/4030–2210.*

⓮ **Suomen Kansallisteatteri** (National Theater). Productions in the three theaters inside are in Finnish. The elegant granite facade overlooking the railway station square is decorated with quirky relief typical of the Finnish National Romantic style. In front is a statue of writer Aleksis Kivi. ⊠ *North side of Rautatientori,* ☏ *09/1733–1331.*

★ ❾ **Suomenlinna** (Finland's Castle). Frequent ferries link Kauppatori (☞ *above*) with this island fortress, which was begun in 1748 by Finnish units of the Swedish army. Its six islands were Sweden's shield against Russia until a Swedish commander surrendered to Russia during the War of Finland (1808–19). A heavy British naval attack in 1855, during the Crimean War, damaged the fortress. Today Suomenlinna, a UNESCO World Heritage site, continues as a military garrison but has museums and parks as well. In early summer it is awash with purple lilacs. ⊠ *Island southeast of harbor,* ☏ *09/668–880 (castle and tour information).* ⊙ *Tours: June–Aug. 12:30 and 2:30.*

⓾ **Svenska Teatern** (Swedish Theater). All performances at this circular theater are in Swedish; many are musicals. ⊠ *Pohjoisesplanadi 2,* ☏ *09/6162–1411.* ⊙ *Box office: daily noon–performance time.*

★ ㉑ **Temppeliaukion Kirkko** (Temple Square Church). In a labyrinth of streets west of the Opera, this strikingly modern church is carved out of rock and topped with a copper dome. ⊠ *Lutherininkatu 3,* ☏ *09/ 494–698.* ⊙ *Weekdays 10–8, Sat. 10–6, Sun. 12–1:45 and 3:15–5:45. Closed Tues. 12:45–2 and during weddings, concerts, and services.*

❺ **Tuomiokirkko** (Lutheran Cathedral). Completed in 1852, the domed cathedral dominates the Senaatintori and serves as a symbol of Helsinki. ⊠ *Yliopistonkatu 7,* ☏ *09/6220–8610.* ⊙ *June–Aug., weekdays 9–5, Sat. 9–7, Sun. 9–8; Sept.–May, weekdays 10–4, Sat. 10–7, Sun. 10–4.*

★ ❼ **Uspenskin Katedraali** (Uspenski Cathedral). The redbrick Orthodox cathedral looms over the east side of Kauppatori. ⊠ *Kanavakatu 1,* ☏ *09/634–267.* ⊙ *May–Sept., Mon. and Wed.–Fri. 9:30–4, Tues. 9:30–6, Sat. 10–4, Sun. noon–3; Oct.–Apr., Tues. and Thurs. 9–2, Wed. noon–6, Fri. noon–4, Sun. noon–3.*

⓬ **Valtion Taidemuseo** (Finnish National Gallery). The best traditional Finnish art is housed in this complex, which includes the **Ateneum,** with Finnish art from the 18th century to the 1960s, as well as changing shows, an excellent bookshop, and a café. ⊠ *Kaivokatu 2–4,* ☏ *09/ 173–361.* ⊙ *Tues. and Fri. 9–6, Wed. and Thurs. 9–8, weekends 11–5.*

238

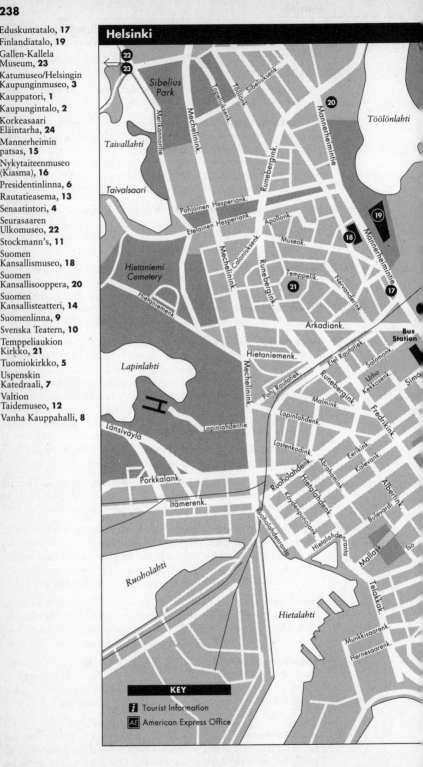

Helsinki

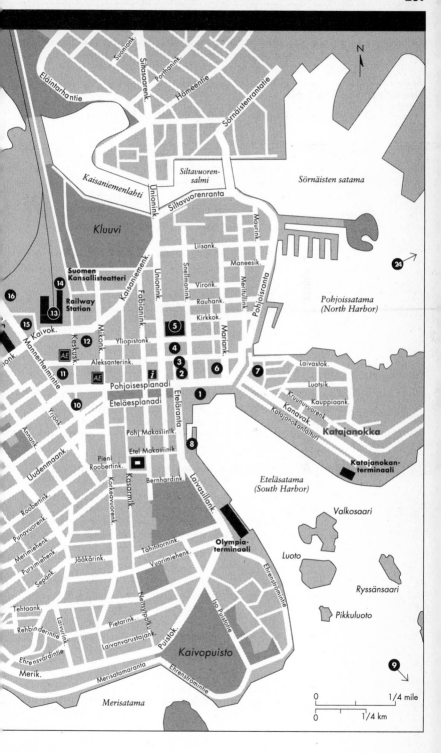

N

Eläintarhantie

Suoniank.
Sillasaarenk.
Porthanink.
Hämeentie
Sörnäistenrantatie

Kaisaniemenlahti
Unionk.

Siltavuoren-
salmi

Siltavuorenranta

Sörnäisten satama

Kluuvi

Maurink.

Liisank.

Maneesik.

**Suomen
Kansallisteatteri**

Kaisaniemenk.

Unionk.

Fabianink.

Snellmanink.

Virronk.

Meritullink.

Rauhank.

Kirkkok.

Pohjoisranta

Pohjoissatama
(North Harbor)

14

**Railway
Station**

16

13

Yliopistonk.

5

Mariank.

15

Kaivok.

Keskusk.

Miikonk.

12

4

3
2

6

Laivastok.

7

Luotsik.

Mannerheimintie

AE

Aleksanterink.

AE

i

Pohjoisesplanadi

Eteläesplanadi

Eteläranta

1

Kauppaank.

Kruununvuorenk.

Kanavak.

Katajanokanlaituri

Katajanokka

11

10

Vironk.

Pohj Makasiink.

Etel Makasiink.

8

Annank.

Pieni
Roobertink.

Bernhardink.

**Katajanokan-
terminaali**

Kasarmk.

Eteläsatama
(South Harbor)

Uudenmaank.

Korkeavuorenk.

Laivasillank.

Valkosaari

Roobertink.

Punavuorenk.

Tähtitornink.

Merimiehenk.

Pursimiehenk.

Jääkärink.

Vuorimiehenk.

Luoto

Neitsytpolku

**Olympia-
terminaali**

Ryssänsaari

Sepänk.

Tehtaank.

Laivurink.

Pietarink.

Iso Puistotie

Ehrenströmintie

Pikkuluoto

Rehbinderintie

Laivanvarustajank.

Puistok.

Ehrensvärdintie

Kaivopuisto

Merik.

Merisatamaranta

Ehrenströmintie

9

Merisatama

0   1/4 mile

0   1/4 km

⑧ Vanha Kauppahalli (Old Market Hall). On the western shore of the South Harbor, near the huge ferry dock for boats from Sweden, Poland, and Estonia, the brick market hall is worth a visit for its amazing spreads of meat, fish, and other delights. ⊠ *Eteläranta, along the South Harbor.* ⊘ *Weekdays 8–8, Sat. 8–3.*

Elsewhere in Helsinki

㉓ Gallen-Kallela Museum. Akseli Gallen-Kallela (1865–1931), one of Finland's greatest artists, lived in this studio-home. To get to the estate, take Tram 4 in front of the City Sokos department store on Mannerheimintie. From the Munkkiniemi stop transfer to Bus 33, or walk the 2 km (1 mi) through the woods. ⊠ *Gallen-Kallelantie 27, Tarvaspää Espoo,* ☎ *09/513–388.* ⊘ *Mid-May–Aug., Mon.–Thurs. 10–8, Fri.–Sun. 10–5; Sept.–mid-May, Tues.–Sat. 10–4, Sun. 10–5.*

㉒ Seurasaaren Ulkomuseo (Seurasaari Open-Air Museum). Evoking the Finnish countryside within the city, this museum showcases traditional rural architecture and lifestyles on a wooded island. A highlight is the ornate **Karunan kirkko** (Karuna Church) from 1686. Seurasaari also has a restaurant and several beaches, including a secluded clothing-optional strand. A long, picturesque bridge connects the island to the city mainland. ⊠ *Seurasaari, island 5 km/3 mi west of city center; Bus 24 from Swedish Theater,* ☎ *09/484–712.* ⊘ *Island: accessible anytime; museum: June–Aug., Mon., Tues., Wed. 11–7, Thurs.–Sun. 11–5; May 15–30 and Sept. 1–15, weekdays 9–3, weekends 11–5. Museum closed in winter.*

Dining and Lodging

Although Russian restaurants are among the star attractions here, do seek out Finnish specialties—pheasant, reindeer, hare, and grouse—accompanied by wildberries and exotic mushrooms. Many expensive establishments close on weekends. For details and price-category information, *see* Dining *in* Finland A to Z, *above.*

Helsinki's hotels have a reputation for being extremely expensive, but this is true only of the very top stratum. Special summer and weekend offers are common. Generous breakfast buffets are nearly always included in the room price. The standards of cleanliness are high, and the level of service usually corresponds to the price. Most hotels cater to business travelers, but standard rooms tend to be small, even at more expensive hotels. For details and price-category information, *see* Lodging *in* Finland A to Z, *above.*

\$\$\$\$ ✕ **Alexander Nevski.** In a city famed for fine Russian cuisine, Alexan-
★   der Nevski has the best. Echoing the Russian-French style of 19th-century St. Petersburg, the decor is dominated by palm trees and shades of green. Sample the game specialties—often baked in clay pots—and blinis. ⊠ *Pohjoisesplanadi 17,* ☎ *09/639–610. AE, DC, MC, V.*

\$\$\$\$ ✕ **Amadeus.** Near the South Harbor, in an old town house with an intimate 19th-century interior, Amadeus specializes in such game dishes as snow grouse, wild duck, and reindeer fillets. ⊠ *Sofiankatu 4,* ☎ *09/626–676. AE, DC, MC, V. Closed Sun.*

\$\$\$\$ ✕ **Havis Amanda.** Across the street from the *Havis Amanda* statue, this neat and gracious restaurant, with its sophisticated turn-of-the-century interior, is a seafood institution. Don't pass up the flamed cloudberry crepes served with ice cream for dessert. ⊠ *Unioninkatu 23,* ☎ *09/666–882. AE, DC, MC, V. Closed Sun., except in summer.*

\$\$\$\$ ✕ **Töölönranta.** Right behind the National Opera House, the new upmarket Töölönranta draws plenty of operagoers. The innovative water-cooled wok is the source of stir-fried specials and, like the rest of the kitchen area, is open to view from the restaurant. The patio catches the evening sun. ⊠ *Helsinginkatu 56,* ☎ *09/454–2100. AE, DC, MC, V. Closed Sun. mid-Sept.–Apr.*

$$$$ ✗ **Troikka.** The Troikka takes you back to tsarist times in decor, paintings, and music. Try the *pelmeny* (small meat pastries). ⊠ *Caloniuksenkatu 3,* ☎ *09/445–229. AE, DC, MC, V. Closed Sun., weekends in July.*

$$$ ✗ **Bellevue.** Established in 1917, Bellevue is one of Helsinki's oldest
★ Russian restaurants, in both decor and cuisine. The fillet à la Novgorod (a traditional ox fillet prepared with carrots, barley, and sauerkraut) and chicken Kiev are the authentic articles here. ⊠ *Rahapajankatu 3,* ☎ *09/179–560. AE, DC, MC, V. No lunch weekends.*

$$$ ✗ **Sipuli.** In a brick warehouse dating from the late 19th century, Sipuli takes its name from the golden onion-shape cupolas that adorn the Orthodox Uspenski Cathedral nearby. The food is French in style with a Finnish flair. ⊠ *Kanavaranta 3,* ☎ *09/179–900. AE, DC, MC, V. Closed weekends except for groups. No lunch weekends.*

$$ ✗ **Kuu.** For the true character of Helsinki, try simple, friendly, and atmospheric Kuu (moon), which has retained its local character and clientele. The menu combines Finnish specialties with creative international fare. ⊠ *Töölönkatu 27,* ☎ *09/2709–0973. AE, DC, MC, V.*

$$ ✗ **Kynsilaukka.** Most imaginative and dominated by garlic—there's
★ even garlic beer—this restaurant appeals to the senses with fresh, beautifully prepared food. Stellar dishes include cold marinated reindeer and pancakes with cloudberry sauce and ice cream. ⊠ *Fredrikinkatu 22,* ☎ *09/651–939. AE, DC, MC, V.*

$$ ✗ **Maxill.** This café-bar hybrid earned its reputation by serving absolutely the best omelets in town. The atmosphere is young and trendy, in keeping with the other shops and restaurants in this colorful, lively street. ⊠ *Korkeavuorenkatu 4,* ☎ *09/638–873. AE, DC, MC, V.*

$$ ✗ **Wellamo.** Unbeatable for cheerful intimacy and local character, the restaurant holds spontaneous piano recitals and often displays art on its walls. Fried Baltic herrings and fried Camembert head the simple but hearty menu. ⊠ *Vyökatu 9,* ☎ *09/663–139. AE, DC, MC, V. Closed Mon.*

$$ ✗ **Zucchini.** For a vegetarian lunch or just coffee and dessert, Zucchini is a cozy hideaway with quiet music, magazines, and a few sidewalk tables. Pizzas, soups, and salads are all tasty here. ⊠ *Fabianinkatu 4,* ☎ *09/622–2907. DC, MC, V. No dinner.*

$ ✗ **Ravintola Perho.** This restaurant is associated with Helsinki's catering school and emphasizes Finnish food; try the fish dishes. ⊠ *Mechelininkatu 7,* ☎ *09/5807–8600. AE, DC, MC, V.*

$$$$ ▥ **Hotel Kämp.** Opposite the Esplanade Park stands this splendid turn-
★ of-the-century cultural landmark, restored in 1999. Expect the ultimate in luxury, service, and decor. ⊠ *Pohjoisesplanadi 29, 00100,* ☎ *09/ 576–1111,* ℻ *09/576–1122. 298 rooms, 59 suites. 2 restaurants. AE, DC, MC, V.*

$$$$ ▥ **Inter-Continental Helsinki.** The host of a Clinton-Yeltsin summit and
★ various diplomatic guests, this hotel offers a host of amenities (faxes, printers) in newly renovated rooms. It's close to Finlandia Hall and the Finnish National Opera; the new restaurant, Olivo, serves Mediterranean dishes and has a separate wine bar. ⊠ *Mannerheimintie 46, 00260,* ☎ *09/40551,* ℻ *09/405–5255. 552 rooms. 2 restaurants, pool. AE, DC, MC, V.*

$$$$ ▥ **Kalastajatorppa.** In the posh western Munkkiniemi neighborhood, this hotel catered to U.S. presidents Ronald Reagan and George Bush. The best rooms are in the seaside annex, and all are large and airy. Rooms in the main building may be equipped with bath and terrace or with showers only; prices vary accordingly. ⊠ *Kalastajatorpantie 1, 00330,*

☎ 09/45811, FAX 09/458–1668. *235 rooms, 8 suites. 2 restaurants, 2 indoor pools. AE, DC, MC, V.*

$$$$ ☷ **Radisson SAS Hesperia Hotel Helsinki.** Built in 1972, the updated hotel remains Finnish with a modern flair. It's just a short stroll from the center of the city. ⊠ *Mannerheimintie 50, 00260,* ☎ 09/43101, FAX 09/431–0995. *383 rooms. Restaurant, pool. AE, DC, MC, V.*

$$$$ ☷ **Scandic Hotel Marski.** Opposite Stockmann's department store, the Marski has suites that are the last word in modern luxury, and all rooms are soundproof, shutting out traffic noise. ⊠ *Mannerheimintie 10, 00100,* ☎ 09/68061, FAX 09/642–377. *236 rooms, 6 suites. Restaurant. AE, DC, MC, V.*

$$$$ ☷ **Strand Inter-Continental.** This waterfront hotel has granite and mar-
★   ble in the lobby and modern designer bedrooms. There is a choice of cuisines—Pamir's elegant offerings of seafood, steak, and game, or the Atrium Plaza's buffet for light meals. ⊠ *John Stenberginranta 4, 00530,* ☎ 09/39351, FAX 09/393–5255. *200 rooms. 2 restaurants, pool. AE, DC, MC, V.*

$$$ ☷ **Cumulus Rantasipi Airport Hotel.** Proximity to the airport and a shuttle for the 3¼ km (2 mi) to town are the keys to this hotel. Rooms are rather small. ⊠ *Robert Huberintie 4, 01510 Vantaa,* ☎ 09/4157–7100, FAX 09/4157–7333. *276 rooms. Restaurant, pool. AE, DC, MC, V.*

$$$ ☷ **Cumulus Seurahuone.** Built in 1914 and renovated in 1992, this tra-
★   ditional hotel has rooms that range from sleek modern to formal classic with crystal chandeliers and brass bedsteads. The street-side rooms are not always quiet. ⊠ *Kaivokatu 12, 00100,* ☎ 09/69141, FAX 09/691–4010. *118 rooms. Restaurant. AE, DC, MC, V.*

$$$ ☷ **Grand Marina.** This renovated early 19th-century customs warehouse sits in the posh Katajanokka Island neighborhood. Friendly service and ample modern facilities have made the hotel a success. ⊠ *Katajanokanlaituri 7, 00160,* ☎ 09/16661, FAX 09/664–764. *462 rooms. 2 restaurants. AE, DC, MC, V.*

$$$ ☷ **Rivoli Jardin.** The newly renovated high-class town house is tucked into the heart of Helsinki's shopping and business center. All rooms face the inner courtyard, free of traffic noise. ⊠ *Kasarmikatu 40, 00130,* ☎ 09/177–880, FAX 09/656–988. *55 rooms. Bar, sauna. AE, DC, MC, V.*

$$$ ☷ **Sokos Hotel Torni.** Be sure to take in the striking views of Helsinki from the the Atelier Bar and from the higher floors of the original part of this hotel, built in 1903. Some old-section rooms on the courtyard have high ceilings with original carved-wood details and wooden writing desks. ⊠ *Yrjönkatu 26, 00100,* ☎ 09/131–131, FAX 09/131–1361. *154 rooms with bath or shower, 9 suites. 2 restaurants. AE, DC, MC, V. Closed Dec. 25.*

$$ ☷ **Arthur.** A property of the Helsinki YMCA, on a quiet, central street, Arthur is unpretentious and comfortable. ⊠ *Vuorikatu 19, 00100,* ☎ 09/173–441, FAX 09/626–880. *144 rooms. Restaurant. AE, DC, MC, V.*

$$ ☷ **Aurora.** About 2 km (1 mi) from the city center, just opposite the Linnanmäki amusement park, the hotel has reasonable prices, cozy rooms, and good facilities. ⊠ *Helsinginkatu 50, 00530,* ☎ 09/770–100, FAX 09/7701–0200. *70 rooms. Restaurant. AE, DC, MC, V.*

$$ ☷ **Cumulus Merihotelli.** Standing right on the seafront, the Merihotelli is a 10-minute walk from the center of town. Rooms are modern but smallish; those with a sea view get some traffic noise. ⊠ *John Stenberginranta 6, 00530,* ☎ 09/69121, FAX 09/691–2214. *87 rooms. 2 restaurants. AE, DC, MC, V.*

$$ ☷ **Marttahotelli.** Run by a century-old women's association, the hotel has small but pleasantly decorated rooms. It is only a 10-minute walk from the railway station. ⊠ *Uudenmaankatu 24, 00120,* ☎ 09/618–7400, FAX 09/618–7401. *44 rooms, 1 suite. AE, DC, MC, V.*

$ **Academica.** This summer hotel is a standard student dormitory during the school year. Its simple rooms and the impressive array of exercise facilities make this an excellent value. ⊠ *Hietaniemenkatu 14, 00100,* ☎ *09/1311–4334,* FAX *09/441–201. 115 rooms. Pool. AE, DC, MC, V. Closed Sept.–May 2.*

Nightlife and the Arts

The Arts

For a list of events pick up *Helsinki This Week,* available in hotels and tourist offices. In summer the guide lists a telephone number for recorded program information in English. Published every two months, *Helsinki Happens* also lists events and provides more detailed cultural background. Tickets are available from **Lippupalvelu** (⊠ Pohjoisesplanadi 19, ☎ 0600–10020, charge FIM 20/call + local call charge; or 0600–10495, charge FIM 4.95/min. + local call charge; 358 9/6138–6246 from abroad). Call **Tiketti** (⊠ Yrjönkatu 29C, ☎ 9700–21204) for small concerts at clubs and restaurants.

CONCERTS

Finlandiatalo (Finlandia Hall; ⊠ Karamzininkatu 4, ☎ 09/40241) is the home of the Helsinki Philharmonic. **Savoy Theater** (⊠ Kasarminkatu 46–48, ☎ 09/169–3703) presents ballet and world music. The **Sibelius Academy** (⊠ Pohjois Rautatiekatu 9, ☎ 09/405–4662) hosts frequent performances, usually by students. **Temppeliaukio Kirkko** (Temppeli-aukion Church; ⊠ Lutherinkatu 3, ☎ 09/494–698) is a favorite venue for choral and chamber music.

FESTIVALS

Many festivals are scheduled throughout the country, especially in summer. For information contact **Finland Festivals** (⊠ Uudenmaankatu 36D, 00120 Helsinki, ☎ 09/612–6760 or 09/6126–7611, FAX 09/6126–7610, www.festivals.fi). The **Helsinki Festival** (⊠ Lasipalatsi, Man-nerheimintie 22-24, 00100 Helsinki, ☎ 09/6126–5100, FAX 09/6126–5161, www.helsinkifestival.fi), one of the largest in the Nordic region, presents scores of music, dance, and poetry performances and art ex-hibits during two weeks in August and September.

THEATER

Summertime productions (in Finnish or Swedish) in such bucolic set-tings as Suomenlinna Island, Keskuspuisto Park, Mustikkamaa Island, and the Rowing Stadium (operettas) make enjoyable entertainment. Check *Helsinki This Week* for listings. Also try the splendid **Suomen Kansallisooppera** (Finnish National Opera; ⊠ Helsinginkatu 58, ☎ 09/4030–2211; ☞ Exploring Helsinki, *above*).

Nightlife

BARS AND LOUNGES

Helsinki This Week (☞ The Arts, *above*) lists all the pubs and clubs. **Cantina West** (⊠ Kasarmikatu 23, ☎ 09/622–0900) is a Tex-Mex bar and restaurant with live music Thursday–Saturday. One of Helsinki's most popular nightspots is **Happy Days** (⊠ Pohjoisesplanadi 2, ☎ 09/657–700), known for its burgers and outdoor summer terrace. **Kaarle XII** (⊠ Kasarmikatu 40, ☎ 09/171–312) is in one of Helsinki's strik-ing Jugendstil buildings: The young and beautiful are drawn here for crowded socializing and dancing on weekends. Founded in 1867, **Kap-peli** (⊠ Eteläesplanadi 1, ☎ 09/179–242) brews its own beer. At **Sto-ryville** (⊠ Museokatu 8, ☎ 09/408–007), Finnish and foreign jazz musicians complement New Orleans–style cuisine.

Popular Irish pubs include **Molly Malone's** (⊠ Kaisaniemenkatu 1C, ☎ 09/171-272), **O'Malley's** (⊠ Yrjökatu 28, ☎ 09/131–131), and

Richard O'Donoghue's (✉ Rikhardinkatu 4, ☎ 09/622–5992).
Angleterre (✉ Fredrikinkatu 47, ☎ 09/647–371) is a cozy English ale
house run by an award-winning cellar master and frequented by the
Helsinki professional crowd. The **William K** (✉ Annankatu 3, ☎ 09/
680–2562; ✉ Mannerheimintie 72, ☎ 09/409–484; ✉ Fleminginkatu
6, ☎ 09/821–816; ✉ Fredrikinkatu 65, ☎ 09/693–1427) bars also offer
an excellent selection of European ales.

NIGHTCLUBS
Fennia (✉ Mikonkatu 17, ☎ 09/621–7170) has dancing on weekends.
Helsinki's largest and most famous club is the **Hesperia Nightclub** (✉
Radisson SAS Hotel Hesperia, Kivelänkatu 2, ☎ 09/43101). **Kaivo-
huone** (✉ Kaivopuisto/Well Park, ☎ 09/177–881) is a summertime favorite in an attractive park setting. The line outside the street-level
entrance to **Tenth Floor** (✉ Asema-aukio, ☎ 09/1311–8232) testifies
to its popularity with the trendy dance-and-party crowd.

Shopping

Department Stores
Stockmann's (☞ Exploring Helsinki, *above*).

Markets
In good weather you'll find a variety of goods at the **Hietalahti Flea
Market** (✉ Hietalahti at west end of Bulevardi). **Kauppatori** (Market
Sq.; ☞ Exploring Helsinki, *above*) next to the South Harbor is an ab-
solute must year-round.

Shopping Districts
Helsinki's prime shopping districts run along **Pohjoisesplanadi** (North
Esplanade) and **Aleksanterinkatu** in the city center. Along **Pohjoisesplanadi** and **Eteläesplanadi** (✉ bordering the gardens), you'll find Finland's design houses. Look for antiques shops in the **Kruununhaka** (✉
behind Senate Sq.) neighborhood.

Specialty Shops
Forum (✉ Mannerheimintie 20, ☎ 09/694–1498) is a modern, multistory shopping mall carrying clothing, gifts, books, and toys. The **Kiseleff Bazaar Hall** (✉ Aleksanterinkatu 22–28) has shops specializing in
handicrafts, toys, knitwear, and children's items. You can shop until
10 PM in stores along the **Tunneli** (✉ underneath the train station).

Aarikka (✉ Pohjoisesplanadi 27, ☎ 09/652–277; ✉ Eteläesplanadi 8,
☎ 09/175–462) offers wooden jewelry, toys, and gifts. **Artek** (✉ Eteläesplanadi 18, ☎ 09/613–250) is known for its Alvar Aalto–designed furniture and ceramics. **Hackman Shop Arabia** (✉ Pohjoisesplanadi 25,
☎ 0204/393–501) sells Finland's Arabia china and Iittala glass. **Kale-
vala Koru** (✉ Unioninkatu 25, ☎ 09/171–520) specializes in jewelry
based on ancient Finnish designs; most jewelers also sell a selection of
the designs. **Marimekko** (✉ Pohjoisesplanadi 31, ☎ 09/177–944; ✉
Eteläesplanadi 14, ☎ 170–704) sells women's clothing, household
items, and gifts made from its textiles. **Pentik** (✉ Pohjoisesplanadi 27,
☎ 09/625–558) has tasteful pottery and household goods.

Side Trip from Helsinki
Hvitträsk, a dramatic and romantic villa designed by Eliel Saarinen and
his partners Herman Gesellius and Armas Lindgren, was their shared
home and studio from the turn of the century and is now a museum.
This forested estate 30 km (19 mi) west of Helsinki has exhibits, a restaurant, a café, a shop, and a lakeside sauna with swimming. Bus 166 will
take you from Helsinki's main bus station, or take the train to Luoma
and follow the signs, about 2 km (1 mi), or to Masala and take a taxi.

✉ *Luoma, Kirkkonummi,* ☎ *09/221–9230.* ⊙ *June–Aug., weekdays 10–7, weekends 10–6; Sept.–May, Tues.–Fri. 11–6, weekends 11–5.*

Helsinki Essentials

Arriving and Departing

BY BOAT

The **Finnjet-Silja and Viking Line** (✉ Mannerheimintie 12, ☎ 09/123–577) terminal for ships arriving from Travemünde, Germany, and Stockholm is at Katajanokanlaituri (✉ east side of South Harbor). **Silja Line** (✉ Mannerheimintie 2, ☎ 09/18–041) ships from Stockholm, Sweden, arrive at Olympialaituri (✉ west side of South Harbor).

BY BUS

The main long-distance bus station is **Linja-autoasema** (✉ off Mannerheimintie, between Salomonkatu and Simonkatu). Many local buses arrive and depart from **Rautatientori** (Railway Station Square). For information on long-distance transport, call ☎ 9600–4000.

BY PLANE

All international flights arrive at **Helsinki–Vantaa Airport** (✉ 20 km/12 mi north of Helsinki, ☎ 9600–8100 information).

Between the Airport and Downtown. Finnair buses make the trip between Helsinki–Vantaa Airport and the city center two–three times an hour, stopping behind the Inter-Continental Helsinki and at the Finnair Terminal next to the train station. The ride takes about 35 minutes and costs FIM 25. A local bus service (Bus 615) will also take you to the train station and costs FIM 15 for the 40-minute ride. Expect to pay between FIM 100 and FIM 140 for a taxi into the city center. The Airport Taxi minivan service drops you at your destination for FIM 60 per person, FIM 80 for two persons. If you are driving, follow the well-placed signs to Highway 137 (Tuusulantie) and KESKUSTA (downtown Helsinki).

BY TRAIN

Helsinki's main rail gateway is the **Rautatieasema** (train station; ✉ city center, off Kaivokatu, ☎ 09/707–5700 information).

Getting Around

The center of Helsinki is compact and best explored on foot. If you want to use public transportation, your best buy is the **Helsinki Kortti** (Helsinki Card), which offers unlimited travel on city public transportation, free entry to many museums, a free sightseeing tour, and a variety of other discounts. It's available for one, two, or three days. You can buy it at some hotels and travel agencies, Stockmann's department store, the Hotel Booking Centre (*see* Lodging *in* Finland A to Z), some R-kiosks in the city center, and the Helsinki City Tourist Office (☞ Visitor Information, *below*. The **Helsinki City Transport tourist ticket** entitles you to unlimited travel on all buses, trams, subways, and local trains in Helsinki. It is valid for one, three, or five days and costs FIM 25, FIM 50, or FIM 75. For timetable and ticket information related to Helsinki's comprehensive, punctual, and generally efficient public transport system, call the 24-hour line (in Finland), ☎ 0100–111.

BY BOAT

In summer regular boat service links the South Harbor Kauppatori (Market Square) with the Suomenlinna and Korkeasaari, site of Helsinki Zoo. Schedules and prices are listed on signboards at the harbor.

BY BUS, STREETCAR, LOCAL TRAIN, OR SUBWAY

Tickets may be purchased at subway stations, R-kiosks, and shops displaying the Helsinki city transport logo (two curving black arrows on a yellow background). Standard single tickets valid on all transport, and permitting transfers within the whole network for within an hour of the time stamped on the ticket, cost FIM 10, and can be bought on trams and buses. Single tickets bought beforehand, at the City Transport office in the railway station tunnel or at one of the many R-kiosk shops, for example, cost FIM 8. A 10-trip ticket sold at R-kiosks costs FIM 75. Most of Helsinki's major points of interest, from Kauppatori to the Opera House, are along the 3T tram line; the Helsinki City Tourist Office (☞ Visitor Information, *below*) distributes a free pamphlet called "Helsinki Sightseeing: 3T."

Helsinki's subway (Metro) line runs from Ruoholahti, just west of the city center, to Mellunmäki, in the eastern suburbs. It operates Monday through Saturday from 5:25 AM, and Sunday from 6:30 AM to 11:20 PM.

BY TAXI

Taxis are all marked TAKSI. Meters start at FIM 30, the fare rising on a kilometer basis. A listing of all taxi companies appears in the white pages; they charge from the point of dispatch. The main phone number for taxi service is ☎ 700–700. Be sure to request a cab that accepts credit cards when ordering a taxi by phone. Car services have a minimum charge and should be ordered well in advance.

Contacts and Resources

EMBASSIES

Australian Consulate (✉ Museokatu 25B, ☎ 09/447-223). **Canadian** (✉ Pohjoisesplanadi 25B, ☎ 09/171–141). **Ireland** (✉ Erottajankatu 7A, ☎ 09/646–006). **U.K.** (✉ Itäinen Puistotie 17, ☎ 09/228–65100). **U.S.** (✉ Itäinen Puistotie 14, ☎ 09/171–931).

EMERGENCIES

Police (☎ 112 or 10022). **Ambulance** (☎ 112). **Doctor** (☎ 10023). **Dentist** (☎ 09/736–166). **General** (☎ 112). **24-hour Pharmacy** (Yliopiston Apteekki; ✉ Mannerheimintie 96, ☎ 09/4178–0300).

ENGLISH-LANGUAGE BOOKSTORES

Akateeminen Kirjakauppa (Academic Bookstore; ✉ Pohjoisesplanadi 39, ☎ 09/12141). **Suomalainen Kirjakauppa** (Finnish Bookstore; ✉ Aleksanterinkatu 23, ☎ 09/651–855).

GUIDED TOURS

Boat. J. L. Runeberg (✉ departs from Kauppatori, ☎ 019/524–3331) has all-day boat tours to the charming old wooden town of Porvoo, with departures at 10 AM six days a week May 31–September 13.

Orientation. Suomen Turistiauto (✉ Kaupintie 8, ☎ 09/588–5116; ✉ Silja Line, South Harbor). **Ageba Travel Agency** (✉ Pohjoisranta 4, 00170 Helsinki, ☎ 09/615–0155).

TRAVEL AGENCIES

American Express (✉ Area Travel Agency, Mikonkatu 2D, 00100 Helsinki, ☎ 09/628–788). **Finland Travel Bureau** (Suomen Matkatoimisto; ✉ Kaivokatu 10A, PL 319, 00100 Helsinki, ☎ 09/18261). **Finnway Inc.** (✉ 228 E. 45th St., 14th floor, New York, NY 10017, ☎ 212/818–1198). **Norvista** (✉ 227 Regent St., London W1R 8PD, ☎ 0171/409–7334).

VISITOR INFORMATION

Helsinki City Tourist Office (✉ Pohjoisesplanadi 19, ☎ 09/169–3757, FAX 09/169–3839). The Finnish Tourist Board **Tourist Information Office** (✉ Eteläesplanadi 4, ☎ 09/4176–9300).

SOUTH COAST

A magical world of 30,000 islands stretches along Finland's coastline, forming a magnificent archipelago in the Gulf of Finland and the Baltic. On the coast, Turku, the former Finnish capital, was the main gateway through which cultural influences reached Finland over the centuries. Westward from Turku lies the rugged and fascinating Åland Islands group, an autonomous province of its own. Many of Finland's oldest towns, chartered by Swedish kings, lie in the southwest—hence the predominance of the Swedish language here. It is a region of flat, often mist-soaked rural farmlands and villages of picturesque, traditional wooden houses.

Snappertuna

Snappertuna, 70 km (43 mi) west of Helsinki, is a farming town with a proud hilltop church, a charming homestead museum, and a castle set in a small dale. The handsome, restored ruin of **Raaseporin Linna** (Raseborg Castle) is believed to date from the 12th century. In summer concerts, dramas, and old-time market fairs are staged here. Guided tours are arranged by the local tourist office (☎ 019/278–6540). ✉ *Keskuskatu 90,* ☎ *019/234–015.* ☉ *May–Aug., daily 10–8.*

Ekenäs (Tammisaari)

Tammisaari, more commonly known by its Swedish name, Ekenäs, has a colorful Old Quarter, 18th- and 19th-century buildings, and a lively marina. In summer the sun glints off the water and marine traffic is at its peak. The **Tammisaaren Museo** (Tammisaari Museum) is the provincial museum of western Uusimaa and provides a taste of the region's culture and history. ✉ *Kustaa Vaasan katu 11,* ☎ *019/263–3161.* ☉ *May 20–July, Tues.–Sun. 11–4; Aug.–May 19, Tues.–Thurs. 6 PM–8 PM.*

$$ ✕🏨 **Ekenäs Stadshotell and Restaurant.** This modern, airy hotel is set amid fine lawns and gardens right in the heart of Tammisaari. Some of the rooms have private balconies, all have wide windows and comfortable modern furnishings. The restaurant offers Continental food and Swedish-Finnish seafood specialties; dine to live music on weekends. ✉ *Pohjoinen Rantakatu 1, 10600 Tammisaari,* ☎ *019/241–3131,* 🄵🄰🄺 *019/246–1550. 16 rooms, 2 suites. Restaurant, indoor pool. AE, DC, MC, V.*

Hanko

In the coastal town of Hanko (Hangö), you'll find long stretches of beach— about 30 km (19 mi) in total—and some of the most fanciful private homes in Finland, their porches edged with gingerbread iron- and woodwork, and whimsical towers sprouting from their roofs. Hanko is also a popular sailing center, with Finland's largest guest harbor.

Fortified in the 18th century, Hanko lost its defenses to the Russians in 1854, during the Crimean War. Later Hanko became a popular spa town for Russians, then the port from which more than 300,000 Finns emigrated to North America between 1880 and 1930.

Turku

Founded at the beginning of the 13th century, Turku is the nation's oldest city and was the original capital of Finland. The city has a long history as a commercial and intellectual center; the site of the first Finnish university, it now has two major universities, the Finnish University of Turku and the Swedish-speaking Åbo Akademi. With a population of more than 170,000, Turku is the fifth-largest city in Finland; its significant commercial harbor is active year-round and is a departure point for daily ferries to Stockholm and the beautiful Åland archipelago.

Known jointly as **Aboa Vetus/Ars Nova,** the Museum of Archeaology and History and the Museum of Contemporary Art exhibit excavated medieval archaeological remains along with the modern art collection of the former Villa von Rettig museum. Look for Picasso's *Swordsman* as well as works by Auguste Herbin (1882–1960) and Max Ernst (1891–1976). ⊠ *Itäinen Rantakatu 4-6,* ☎ *02/250–0552.* ⊙ *May– Sept., daily 11–7; Oct.–Apr., Tues.–Sun. 11–7.*

The **Luostarinmäen Kasityöläismuseo** (Luostarinmäki Handicrafts Museum) is an authentic collection of wooden houses and buildings containing shops and workshops where traditional crafts are demonstrated and sold. ⊠ *Vartiovuorenkatu 4,* ☎ *02/262–0350.* ⊙ *Mid-Apr.–mid-Sept., daily 10–6; mid-Sept.–mid-Apr., Tues.–Sun. 10–3.*

Where the Aura flows into the sea stands **Turun Linna** (Turku Castle), one of the city's most important historical monuments. The oldest part of the fortress was built at the end of the 13th century, and the newer part dates from the 16th century. The vaulted chambers evoke a sense of the domestic lives of the Swedish royals. A good gift shop and a pleasant café are on the castle grounds. ⊠ *Linnankatu 80,* ☎ *02/262–0300.* ⊙ *Mid-Apr.–mid-Sept., daily 10–6; mid-Sept.–mid-Apr., Mon. 2–7, Tues.–Sun. 10–3.*

The **Turun Taidemuseo** (Turku Art Museum) holds some of Finland's most famous paintings, including works by Akseli Gallen-Kallela, and a broad selection of turn-of-the-century Finnish art and contemporary works. Due to renovation, exhibits are temporarily being held on the Vartiovuorenmäki hill, in the Old Observatory (Vartiovuorenmäen Tähtitorni) designed by Carl Ludvig Engel. ⊠ *Aurakatu 26, Puolanpuisto,* ☎ *02/274–7570.* ⊙ *Old Observatory: Apr.–Sept., Tues., Fri., Sat. 10–4, Wed., Thurs. 10–7, Sun. 11–6; Oct.–Mar., Tues., Wed., Fri., Sat. 10–4, Thurs. 10–7, Sun. 11–6.*

The 700-year-old **Turun Tuomiokirkko** (Turku Cathedral) remains the seat of the archbishop of Finland. Although it was partially gutted by fire in 1827, the cathedral has been completely restored and celebrates its 700th anniversary in 2000. The cathedral museum includes a collection of medieval church vestments, silver chalices, and wooden sculptures. ⊠ *Turun Tuomiokirkko,* ☎ *02/251–0651.* ▨ *Free.* ⊙ *Mid-Apr.–mid-Sept., daily 9–8; mid-Sept.–mid-Apr., daily 9–7.*

$$$ ✕ **Calamare.** At this hotel restaurant, try the Delicacy Plate, with Baltic herring, roe in mustard sauce, shrimp, fillet of beef, egg, and marinated mushrooms. Calamare has impressive views of the Auajoki River and a Mediterranean atmosphere with Roman-style statues and palm trees. ⊠ *Linnankatu 32,* ☎ *02/336–2126. AE, DC, MC, V.*

$$ ✕ **Suomalainen Pohja.** Next to the Turku Art Museum, this restaurant has a splendid view of an adjacent park. Seafood, poultry, and game dishes are good here; try the fillet of reindeer with sautéed potatoes or the cold smoked rainbow trout with asparagus. ⊠ *Aurakatu 24,* ☎ *02/251–2000. AE, DC, MC, V. Closed weekends.*

$$ 🏨 **Park Hotel.** The castlelike Park Hotel in the heart of Turku is one of Finland's most unusual lodgings. Rooms have high ceilings and antique furniture. ⊠ *Rauhankatu 1, 20100 Turku,* ☎ *02/273–2555,* ⨍ₐₓ *02/251–9696. 21 rooms. Restaurant. AE, DC, MC, V.*

South Coast Essentials

Getting Around

Turku offers a special 24-hour Tourist Ticket (FIM 20) for unlimited public transport access; it can be purchased on buses.

Regular daily bus services operate between Helsinki and Turku. The trip takes about 2½ hours.

Passenger/car ferries depart daily from Turku's harbor for Stockholm and Åland. Contact **Silja Line** (☏ 09/18–041, ℻ 09/180–4276) or **Viking Line** (☏ 09/12351, ℻ 09/647–075) for details and timetables.

The main route between Helsinki and Turku is fast and normally traffic-free. A parallel, more picturesque route to the south takes you at a leisurely pace through the smaller towns closer to the coast.

Turku Airport is about 7 km (4½ mi) from the city center. Finnair flies to Helsinki, Mariehamn, and Stockholm.

Turku is served by fast train services to Helsinki and Tampere several times a day. The Pendolino high-speed train also operates between Helsinki and Turku, cutting travel time to under two hours.

Guided Tours
Turku TouRing/City Tourist Information Office (✉ Aurakatu 4, 20100 Turku, ☏ 02/262–7444, ℻ 02/233–6488). **Finland Travel Bureau** (☞ Travel Agencies *in* Contacts and Resources *in* Helsinki Essentials, *above*).

Visitor Information
Hanko (✉ Tourist Information Office, Box 14, 5 Raatihuoneentori, 10901, ☏ 019/220–3411, ℻ 019/220–3261). **Turku** (✉ Turku TouRing/City Tourist Information Office, Aurakatu 4, 20100 Turku, ☏ 02/262–7444, ℻ 02/233–6488).

THE LAKELANDS

In southeastern and central Finland, the light has a softness that seems to brush the forests, lakes, and islands, changing the landscape throughout the day. For centuries this beautiful region was a much-contested buffer between the warring empires of Sweden and Russia. The Finns of the Lakelands prevailed by sheer *sisu* (guts), and now their descendants thrive amid the rough beauty of the terrain.

Savonlinna
The center of Savonlinna is a series of islands linked by bridges. An open-air market flourishes alongside the main passenger quay. Savonlinna was once the hub of the passenger fleet serving Saimaa, the largest lake system in Europe. Now cruise boats dominate lake traffic.

★ First built in 1475 to protect Finland's eastern border, the castle **Olavin-linna** rises majestically out of the lake, retaining its medieval character. It is one of Scandinavia's best-preserved historic monuments and houses two museums. The **Savonlinna Opera Festival** is held in the courtyard each July. Make reservations well in advance for both the opera and hotel rooms; contact the Savonlinna Tourist Service (☏ 015/517–510, ℻ 015/517–5123). ✉ *10-min walk southeast from quay,* ☏ *015/531–164.* ▣ *Castle admission includes guided tours in English on the hr.* ☉ *June–mid-Aug., daily 10–5; mid-Aug.–May, daily 10–3.*

Near Olavinlinna is the **Savonlinnan maakunta museo** (Savonlinna Provincial Museum), to which belong the 19th-century steam schooners the SS *Salama,* the SS *Mikko,* and the SS *Savonlinna.* ✉ *Near Olavin-*

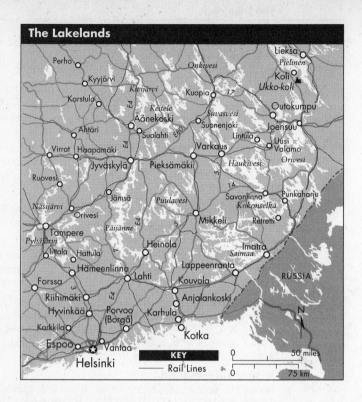

The Lakelands

KEY

—— Rail Lines

0   50 miles

0   75 km

linna. ⊙ *Sept.–June, Tues.–Sun. 11–5; July, daily 11–6; Aug., daily 11–5.*

$$$ ✕ **Rauhalinna.** This romantic turn-of-the-century timber villa was built by a general in the Imperial Russian Army. From town it's 16 km (10 mi) by road, 40 minutes by boat. Both food and atmosphere are Old Russian, touched by Finnish accents. ⊠ *Lehtiniemi,* ☎ *015/523–119. Reservations essential. AE, DC, MC, V. Closed Aug. 7–July 3.*

$$ ✕ **Majakka.** Centrally located, Majakka goes in for home cooking and a family atmosphere. ⊠ *Satamakatu 11,* ☎ *015/531–456. Festival-season reservations essential. AE, DC, MC, V.*

$ ✕ **Paviljonki.** An affiliate of the Savonlinna restaurant school, this convenient spot just 1 km (½ mi) west of the city serves classic Finnish dishes. ⊠ *Rajalahdenkatu 4,* ☎ *015/574–9303. DC, MC, V.*

$$$–$$$$ 🏠 **Seurahuone.** In this hotel near the market and passenger harbor, rooms are small but modern. The open-air summer restaurant has views of the harbor and the market. ⊠ *Kauppatori 4–6, 57130,* ☎ *015/5731,* FAX *015/273–918. 84 rooms. 6 restaurants. AE, DC, MC, V.*

$$$ 🏠 **Casino Spa.** The Casino Spa has a bucolic lakeside setting on an island linked by a pedestrian bridge to the center of town. Rooms are basic with brown cork floors, white walls, and simple furnishings. ⊠ *Kylpylaitoksentie, Kasinosaari, 57130,* ☎ *015/57500,* FAX *015/73–950. 80 rooms. Restaurant, pool. AE, DC, MC, V.*

Punkaharju

This breathtaking ridge of pine-covered rocks predates the Ice Age. Sometimes narrowing to only 25 ft, it rises out of the water to separate the lakes on either side.

Take an excursion (by boat or bus) to **Taidekeskus Retretti** (Retretti Art Centre), the largest privately owned art center in Scandinavia; come to see changing exhibits, multimedia programs, and children's events. ✉ *Just south of Punkaharju,* ☎ *015/644–253,* ℻ *015/644–314.* 🎫 *FIM 65.* ◷ *June and Aug., daily 10–5; July daily 10–6.*

The nearby **Lusto–Suomen Metsämuseo ja Metsätietokeskus** (Lusto Finnish Forest Museum) has displays on every aspect of forestry, from the industrial to the artistic, and all sides of Finland's close relationship with its most abundant natural resource, including demonstrations and theme days. Make an appointment for a guided tour. ✉ *Lustontie 1, 58450, Punkaharju,* ☎ *015/345–100.* ◷ *May–Sept., daily 10–6; Oct.–Apr., Tues.–Sun. 10–5.*

$$$ 🏨 **Punkaharju National Hotel.** Near the Retretti Art Centre, this building was constructed as a gamekeeper's lodge for Tsar Nicholas I in 1845 but has since been enlarged and restored. Now it's a restful spot for a meal or an overnight visit. ✉ *Punkaharju 2, 58450,* ☎ *015/739–611,* ℻ *015/441–784. 24 rooms. Restaurant. AE, DC, MC, V.*

Kuopio

The 11½-hour boat trip from Savonlinna to Kuopio may be the best opportunity you'll get to appreciate the soul of the Finnish Lakelands. Meals are available on board. The boat arrives at Kuopio's passenger harbor, where you'll find a small evening market daily from 3 to 10.

★ Kuopio's tourist office is close to the **Tori** (marketplace), one of the most colorful outdoor markets in Finland. ✉ *City center.* ◷ *May–Sept., weekdays 7–5, Sat. 7–3; Oct.–Apr., weekdays 7–3, Sat. 7–2.*

The **Ortodoksinen Kirkkomuseo** (Orthodox Church Museum) has an unusual collection of religious art from the monasteries of Karelia (the eastern province of Finland, part of which is now in Russia). ✉ *Karjalankatu 1,* ☎ *017/287–2244.* ◷ *May, June, Aug., Tues.–Sun. 10–4; July, Tues.–Fri. 10–5; Sept.–Apr., weekdays noon–3, weekends noon–5.*

Puijo Näkötorni (Puijo Tower) is best visited at sunset, when the lakes shimmer with reflected light. It has two observation decks and a revolving restaurant on top from which you can enjoy the marvelous views. ✉ *3 km (2 mi) northwest of Kuopio,* ☎ *017/209–103.* 🎫 *Free Sept.–Apr.* ◷ *May–Aug., daily 11–11; Sept.–Apr., daily 11–9.*

Valamon Luostari (Valamo Monastery) is a center for Russian Orthodox religious and cultural life in Finland. Precious 18th-century icons and other sacred objects are housed in the main church and in the icon conservation center. On the grounds are a café-restaurant, hotel, and hostel accommodations. ✉ *Uusi Valamo,* ☎ *017/570–111.* 🎫 *Free.* ◷ *Oct.–Feb., daily 8 AM–9 PM; Mar.–Sept., daily 7 AM–9 PM.*

$$$ ✕ **Musta Lammas.** Finnish dishes are served in this former beer cellar. The specialty is the smoked *muikku*—a kind of whitefish—with sour cream and mashed potatoes. ✉ *Satamakatu 4,* ☎ *017/262–3494. AE, DC, MC, V. Closed Sun.*

$$ ✕ **Sampo.** The specialty here is whitefish. The atmosphere is unpretentious and lively, and the location in the town center is convenient. ✉ *Kauppakatu 13,* ☎ *017/261–4677. AE, DC, MC, V.*

$$$ 🏨 **Scandic Hotel Kuopio.** The best equipped of local hotels, the Scandic has all the advantages of a lakefront location while being close to the center of town. Rooms are spacious by European standards, with large beds and generous towels. ✉ *Satamakatu 1, 70100,* ☎ *017/195–111,* ℻ *017/195–170. 134 rooms. Pool. AE, DC, MC, V.*

$$ 🏨 **Hotel-Spa Rauhalahti.** Sports-oriented travelers and families flock to this high-energy setting. Close to the lakeshore and 5 km (3 mi) from the town center, Rauhalahti offers lively activities and conveniences for all ages and interests. ✉ *Katiskaniementie 8, 70700,* ☎ *017/473–111,*

☎ *017/473–470. 106 rooms, 20 apartments, 26 hostel rooms. 3 restaurants. AE, DC, MC, V.*

Tampere

While cotton and textile manufacturers put Tampere on the map as a traditional center of industry, the city is now known for its high-tech companies and large universities. Nevertheless, Tampere's mere 200,000 inhabitants also nurture an unusually sophisticated cultural environment.

From about the year 1000, this part of Finland was a base from which traders and hunters set out on their expeditions to the north. It was not until 1779 that a Swedish king, Gustav III, founded Tampere. A Scotsman by the name of James Finlayson came to the city in 1882 and established a factory for spinning cotton. The firm of Finlayson is still one of the country's large industrial enterprises.

An isthmus, little more than 1 km (½ mi) wide at its narrowest point, separates the lakes Näsijärvi and Pyhäjärvi, and at one spot the waters of one rush through to the other down the Tammerkoski Rapids. Their natural beauty has been preserved despite the factories on either bank, and the distinctive public buildings of the city grouped around them add to the overall effect.

The **Amurin Työläismuseokortteli** (Amuri Museum of Workers' Housing) consists of more than 30 apartments in a collection of wooden houses, plus a sauna, a bakery, a haberdashery, and more from the 1880s to the 1970s. Its cozy café has garden seating in summer. ⊠ *Makasiininkatu 12,* ☎ *03/314–6690.* ⊘ *Mid-May–mid-Sept., Tues.–Sun. 10–6.*

The **Lenin Museo** (Lenin Museum) occupies the hall where Lenin and Stalin first met; photos, memorabilia, and temporary exhibits document the life of Lenin and the Russian Revolution. ⊠ *Hämeenpuisto 28, 3rd fl.,* ☎ *03/276–8100.* ⊘ *Weekdays 9–6, weekends 11–4.*

On the east side of town the modern **Kalevan Kirkko** (Kaleva Church) is a soaring monument to light and space designed by Reima (1923–1993) and Reili (b. 1926) Pietilä, the famous architect couple who also designed the Tampere city library, "Metso." ⊠ *Liisanpuisto 1.* ⊘ *May–Aug., daily 9–6; Sept.–Apr., daily 11–3.*

The **Museokeskus Vapriikki** (Museum Centre Vapriikki) consolidates the collections of five separate museums (700,000 pieces) to illustrate the city's role in Finnish industrial history. Housed in a former textile and turbine factory complex that dates from the 1880s, the permanent exhibit focuses on local history, while other displays cover archaeological finds and modern art. ⊠ *Veturiaukio 4,* ☎ *03/3146–6966.* ⊘ *Tues.–Sun., 10–6.*

Among Reima Pietilä's many unusual structures in Tampere is the **Tampere pääkirjasto** (Tampere Central Library), nicknamed "metso" (wood grouse) for its unusual shape; it houses an exhibit celebrating the Moomintroll books of Finnish author Tove Jansson. ⊠ *Pirkankatu 2,* ☎ *03/314–614.* ⊘ *Sept.–May, Mon.–Fri. 9:30–8, Sat. 9:30–3; June–Aug., Mon.–Fri. 9:30–7, Sat. 9:30–3.*

The **Tuomiokirkko** (cathedral), built in 1907, displays some of the best-known masterpieces of Finnish mural art. ⊠ *Tuomiokirkonkatu 3.* ⊘ *May–Aug., daily 9–6; Sept.–Apr., daily 11–3.*

☙ The **Särkänniemi peninsula** holds many attractions. **Särkänniemen Huvikeskus** (Särkäniemi Amusement Center) is a major recreation complex made up of an amusement park, a children's zoo, a planetarium, and a well-planned aquarium with a separate "dolphinarium." Within

Särkäniemi, the **Sara Hildénin Taidemuseo** (Sara Hildén Art Museum) is a striking example of Finnish architecture, displaying works by such modern artists as Chagall, Klee, Miró, and Picasso. ⊠ *Särkänniemi. Hildén Museum:* ☎ *03/214–3134; 03/248–8111 or 9800–4242 (main complex information).* 🎫 *Joint admission: FIM 130.* ⊙ *Daily 11–6.*

Särkänniemi's 550-ft **Näsinneula Observation Tower,** the tallest in Finland, dominates the Tampere skyline. At the top are an observatory and a revolving restaurant. The contrast between the industrial maze of Tampere at your feet and the serenity of the lakes stretching out to meet the horizon is unforgettable. ⊠ *Särkänniemi.* ☎ *03/248–8111 (main complex information).* ⊙ *Observation tower: June–Aug., daily 10–10; Sept.–May, daily 10–4.*

On the **"Poet's Way"** boat tour along Lake Näsijärvi, the boat passes through the agricultural parish of Ruovesi, where J. L. Runeberg, Finland's national poet, once lived. Many artists and writers spend their summers by the straits of Visuvesi. ⊠ *Finnish Silverline and "Poet's Way," Tampere Tourist Information Centre, Verkatehtaankatu 2,* ☎ *03/3141–3500.* 🎫 *Round-trip fare: FIM 310.*

\$\$\$ ✕ **Tiiliholvi.** A romantic cellar set in an Art Nouveau building with a colorful past, Tiiliholvi offers Finnish haute cuisine and the best wine selection in town. Try the chanterelle soup and the grilled reindeer with cranberry and bread cheese sauce, then indulge in cloudberry crème brûlée. ⊠ *Kauppakatu 10,* ☎ *03/272–0231. AE, DC, MC, V. Closed Sun.*

\$\$ ✕ **Laterna.** Located in a tsarist-era hotel and once the haunt of artists and writers, Laterna offers Russian fare with a Finnish twist in charming surroundings. Head to the downstairs café for live jazz, art exhibits, and poetry evenings. ⊠ *Puutarhakatu 11,* ☎ *03/272–0241. AE, DC, MC, V.*

\$\$ ✕ **Silakka.** In a casual atmosphere, Silakka (which means Baltic herring) serves excellent Finnish fish specialties. ⊠ *Koskikeskus, Hatan-* ★ *pään valtatie 1,* ☎ *03/214–9740. DC, MC, V.*

\$\$\$–\$\$\$\$ 🏨 **Sokos Hotel Ilves.** Soaring above newly gentrified old warehouses near the city center, the hotel has rooms above the sixth floor with spectacular views of the city and Pyhäjärvi and Näsijärvi lakes.⊠ *Hatanpään valtatie 1, 33100,* ☎ *03/262–6262,* ℻ *03/262–6263. 336 rooms. 4 restaurants, pool. AE, DC, MC, V.*

\$\$–\$\$\$ 🏨 **Cumulus Koskikatu.** Overlooking the tame rapids of Tammerkoski, Cumulus Koskikatu is central and modern. ⊠ *Koskikatu 5, 33100,* ☎ *03/242–4111,* ℻ *03/242–4399. 230 rooms. Restaurant, pool. AE, DC, MC, V.*

\$ 🏨 **Iltatähti Apartment Hotel.** In the center of town, this hotel offers pleasant and unpretentious accommodation at budget rates. ⊠ *Tuomiokirkonkatu 19, 33100,* ☎ *03/315–161,* ℻ *03/3151–6262. 40 rooms. No credit cards.*

Iittala

The **Iittala Lasikeskus** (Iittala Glass Center) offers museum tours and has a shop. Top designers produce the magnificent glass; the seconds are bargains you won't find elsewhere. ⊠ *14500 Iittala,* ☎ *0204/396–230.* ⊙ *Museum: May–Aug., daily 10–6; Sept.–Apr., daily 10–5; shop: May–Aug., daily 9–8; Sept.–Apr., daily 10–6.*

Hämeenlinna

Hämeenlinna's secondary school has educated many famous Finns, among them composer Jean Sibelius (1865–1957). The only surviving timber house in the town center is **Sibeliuksen syntymäkoti** (Sibelius's birthplace), a modest dwelling built in 1834. One of the rooms houses the harmonium Sibelius played as a child. ✉ *Hallituskatu 11,* ☎ *03/621–2755.* ☉ *May–Aug., daily 10–4; Sept.–Apr., daily noon–4.*

Hämeen Linna (Häme Castle) is Finland's oldest castle: Swedish crusaders began building it during the 13th century. At times a granary and a prison, the lakeshore castle is now restored and open to the public for tours and exhibitions; it sits 1 km (½ mi) north of Hämeenlinna's town center. ✉ *Kustaa III:n katu 6,* ☎ *03/675–6820.* ☉ *May–Aug. 14, daily 10–6; Aug. 15–Apr., daily 10–4. Closed on major holidays.*

The **Hämeenlinnan Taidemuseo** (Hämeenlinna Art Museum), housed partly in a 19th-century granary designed by Carl Ludvig Engel, exhibits Finnish art from the 19th and 20th centuries and foreign art from the 17th century; works evacuated from Vyborg in 1939 form the core of the collection. ✉ *Viipurintie 2,* ☎ *03/621–2669.* ☉ *Tues., Wed., Fri.–Sun., 12–6; Thurs. 12–8.*

Hattula

The interior of medieval **Hattulan Kirkko** (Hattula Church), 8 km (5 mi) north of Hämeenlinna in Hattula, has frescoes of biblical scenes in which the vicious little devils and soulful saints are still as vivid as when they were first painted around 1510. ✉ *Hattula,* ☎ *03/672–3383 during opening hrs, 03/637–2477 at other times.* ☉ *May 15–Aug. 15, daily 11–5; other times by appointment.*

Riihimäki

The **Suomen Lasimuseo** (Finnish Glass Museum) in Riihimäki, 35 km (22 mi) south of Hämeenlinna, has an outstanding display of the history of glass from early Egyptian times to the present, artfully arranged in an old glass factory. ✉ *Tehtaankatu 23, Riihimäki,* ☎ *019/741–7494.* ☉ *May–Aug., daily 10–6; Sept.–Apr., Tues.–Sun. 10–6.*

$$ ✕ **Lehmushovi.** In a manor house in a park near the Glass Museum, Lehmushovi offers Finnish and international cuisine. ✉ *Lehmustie 5,* ☎ *019/738–113. DC, MC, V.*

$$$ 🏨 **Rantasipi Aulanko.** One of Finland's top hotels, Rantasipi Aulanko
★ sits on the lakeshore in a beautifully landscaped park 6½ km (4 mi) from town. All rooms have wall-to-wall carpeting and overlook the golf course, the park, or the lake. ✉ *Aulanko Puisto (Aulanko Park), 13210,* ☎ *03/658–801,* 🖷 *03/682–1922. 245 rooms. Pool. AE, DC, MC, V.*

The Lakelands Essentials

Getting Around

In Tampere you can buy a 24-hour **Tourist Ticket** from the city tourist office (☞ Visitor Information, *below*) that allows unlimited travel on city transportation.

BY BUS

Buses are the best form of public transport into the region, with frequent connections to lake destinations from most major towns. The ride from Helsinki to Savonlinna takes six hours.

BY CAR

The region is vast, so the route you choose will depend on your destination. Consult the Finnish Automobile Association or tourist boards for route advice.

BY PLANE

Airports in the Lakelands are at Tampere, Mikkeli, Jyväskylä, Varkaus, Lappeenranta, Savonlinna, Kuopio, and Joensuu.

BY TRAIN
Trains run from Helsinki to Lahti, Mikkeli, Imatra, Lappeenranta, Joensuu, and Jyväskylä.

Guided Tours

Friendly Finland Tours (Finland Travel Bureau, ☞ Travel Agencies *in*
Contacts and Resources *in* Helsinki Essentials, *above*).

Visitor Information

Hämeenlinna (✉ Sibeliuksenkatu 5A, 13100, ☎ 03/621–2388). **Kuopio** (✉ Haapaniemenkatu 17, 70110, ☎ 017/182–584). **Savonlinna**
(✉ Puistokatu 1, 57100, ☎ 015/273–492). **Tampere** (✉ Verkatehtaankatu 2, 33211, ☎ 03/212–6652).

FINNISH LAPLAND

Lapland is a region of great silences with endless forests and fells. Settlers in Finnish Lapland have walked gently and left the landscape almost unspoiled. The oldest traces of human habitation in Finland have
been found in Lapland, where hoards of Danish, English, and even Ara-
bian coins indicate active trading many centuries ago. Until the 1930s,
Lapland was still largely unexploited, and any trip to the region was
an expedition. Its isolation ended when the Arctic Highway was completed, connecting Rovaniemi with the Arctic Sea.

Only about 4,000 native Sámi still live in Lapland; the remainder of
the province's population of 203,000 is Finnish. Recent grassroots efforts to preserve Sámi language and traditions have been largely successful. Sámi craftspeople create beautiful objects and clothing out of
the materials readily at hand: wood, bone, and reindeer pelts.

While winter in Lapland brings with it the fascinating northern lights
and reindeer roundups, beautiful weather often complements summer's
nightless days. In early fall nature's colors are spectacular.

Exploring Lapland

Rovaniemi

Rovaniemi is the Lapland administrative and communications hub.
Nearly razed by the retreating German army in 1944, Rovaniemi is
today a modern university town and business center strongly influenced
by Alvar Aalto's architecture. One notable structure is the **Lappia-Talo**
(Lappia House; ✉ Hallituskatu 11, ☎ 016/322–2944), an Aalto-de-
signed concert and congress center with the world's northernmost
professional theater.

★ You can get a good instant introduction to the region and its natural
history at the **Arktikum** (Arctic Research Center), 1 km (½ mi) north
of Lappia-Talo. The Arktikum houses the Lapland Provincial Museum, with exhibits on Sámi culture. ✉ *Pohjoisranta 4,* ☎ *016/317–
840.* ☉ *May and June, daily 10–6; July and Aug., daily 10–8; Sept.–
Apr., Tues.–Sun. 10–6.*

$$ ✕ **Fransmanni.** In the Vaakuna Hotel in downtown Rovaniemi, this
restaurant specializes in international, Finnish, and Sámi dishes. ✉
Koskikatu 4, ☎ *016/332–211. AE, DC, MC, V.*

$$ ✕ **Ounasvaaran Pirtit.** This town favorite, a small restaurant decorated
in traditional Lapp wooden style and focused on a welcoming open
fireplace, serves traditional Finnish and Sámi fare. ✉ *Antinmukka 4,*
☎ *016/369–056. Reservations essential. MC, V.*

$$$ 🏨 **Sky Hotel Rovaniemi.** The views of the town and the surrounding
★ area are fantastic from this tranquil, full-service hotel perched on

Finnish Lapland

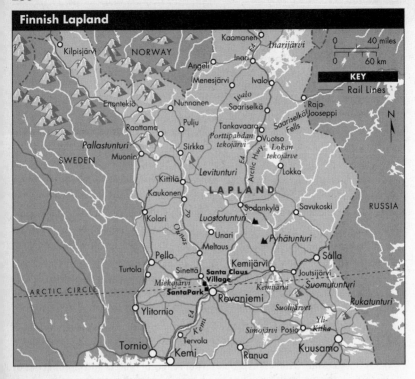

Ounasvaara Mountain, 3 km (2 mi) from town. Most rooms have saunas. ⊠ 96400, ☎ 016/335–3311, 🖷 016/318–789. 69 rooms. Restaurant. AE, DC, MC, V.

$$$ 🏨 **Sokos Hotel Vaakuna.** Opened in 1992, the Vaakuna has small rooms painted in pastel shades. The club here is a center of Rovaniemi nightlife. ⊠ Koskikatu 4, 96200, ☎ 016/332–211, 🖷 016/332–2199. 157 rooms, 2 suites. 2 restaurants. AE, DC, MC, V.

$$ 🏨 **Rantasipi Hotel Pohjanhovi.** With its pleasant location overlooking the Kemi River, this hotel is an old favorite with travelers to the north. It has been expanded and modernized over the years. ⊠ Pohjanpuistikko 2, 96200, ☎ 016/33711, 🖷 016/313–997. 212 rooms, 4 suites. 2 restaurants, pool. AE, DC, MC, V.

$$ 🏨 **Rudolf.** This small, comfortable hotel is close to the center of town and has a traditional restaurant. ⊠ Koskikatu 41, 96100, ☎ 016/342–3222, 🖷 016/342–3226. 41 rooms. Restaurant, pool. AE, DC, MC, V.

$ 🏨 **Oppipoika.** Top-notch service at this branch of the Hotel School of Rovaniemi complements highly memorable food, including a variety of Lapland specialties. Rooms are spacious and comfortable. ⊠ Korkalonkatu 33, 96200, ☎ 016/338–8111, 🖷 016/346–969. 40 rooms. 2 restaurants, pool. AE, DC, MC, V.

Arctic Circle

🕐 **SantaPark,** a Christmas theme park deep inside a rocky cavern, offers a Magic Sleigh Ride, a Puppet Circus, and a Christmas Carrousel, among other attractions. Take the Santa Train from the Park to **Santa Claus Village,** where you can shop for gifts and have your purchases shipped with a special Santa Claus Land stamp; stop along the way at the Reindeer Park to see Santa's sleigh team. ⊠ Artic Circle, 96930, Park: ☎ 016/333–0000 Park; 016/356–2157 Village, 🖷 016/333–0020 Park; 016/348–1418 Village. 🎫 Park: FIM 95, family ticket FIM 90; Vil-

lage: Free. ☉ *Park: Mid-Jan.–mid-Feb. and mid-Mar.–mid-May, week-ends; mid-Feb.–mid-Mar., mid-May–Aug., and Dec.–mid-Jan., daily; closed Sept.–Nov.; call for hrs. Village: June–Aug., daily 8–8; Sept.–May, daily 10–5.*

Tankavaara

Tankavaara is the most accessible and best developed of several gold-panning areas. The **Kultamuseo** (Gold Museum) tells the centuries-old story of Lapland's hardy fortune seekers. In the summer months authentic prospectors will show you how to wash gold dust and tiny nuggets from the dirt of an ice-cold stream. ⊠ *Arctic Hwy. 4, Kultakylä,* ☎ *016/626–158.* ☉ *June–Aug. 15, daily 9–6; Aug. 16–Sept., daily 9–5; Oct.–May, daily 10–4.*

$$ ✗ **Wanha Waskoolimies.** Sámi specialties predominate at this attractive café/restaurant at the Gold Museum; try the gold prospector's reindeer beefsteak. ⊠ *Tankavaaran kultakylä,* ☎ *016/626–158. DC, V.*

Saariselkä

From here you can set off into the true wilderness; during the snowy months, it has some of the finest cross-country and downhill skiing in Finland. More than 2,500 square km (965 square mi) of this magnificent area have been set aside as **Urho Kekkosen kansallispuisto** (Urho Kekkonen National Park; ⊠ Northern Lapland Tourism, Honkapolku 3, 99830 Saariselkä, ☎ 016/668–400, 𝔽𝔸𝕏 016/668–405).

$$$ 🏨 **Riekonlinna.** This is the most recent and best-equipped addition to the developing tourist complex on the fringes of the wilderness fells. Catering to sports enthusiasts, it offers a wide range of facilities, including a children's play room, ski maintenance, and storage room. ⊠ *99830,* ☎ *016/679–4455,* 𝔽𝔸𝕏 *016/679–4456. 124 rooms. Bar, casino. AE, DC, MC, V.*

Ivalo

Just south of here, the highway passes the **Ivalojoki** (Ivalo River). Join a canoe trip down its swift waters to Lake Inari. The modern community of Ivalo is the main center for northern Lapland.

$$ 🏨 **Ivalo.** Modern and fully equipped, the Hotel Ivalo is right on the river about 1 km (½ mi) from the village center. One of its two restaurants serves Lapland specialties, including *poronkäristys,* a reindeer casserole. ⊠ *Ivalontie 34, 99800,* ☎ *016/688–111,* 𝔽𝔸𝕏 *016/661–905. 94 rooms. Restaurant, pool. AE, DC, MC, V.*

$ 🏨 **Kultahippu.** Here, next to the Ivalo River, you can patronize the "northernmost nightclub in Finland." The hotel has cozy rooms. ⊠ *Petsamontie 1, 99800,* ☎ *016/661–825,* 𝔽𝔸𝕏 *016/662–510. 30 rooms. Restaurant. AE, DC, MC, V.*

Inari

The huge island-studded expanses of Inarijärvi (Lake Inari), north of Ivalo, offer endless possibilities for wilderness exploration. Lakeside Inari, home of the Sámi Parliament, is a good base for summer boat excursions. Set in the oldest inhabited region of northern Lapland and named after the Lapp word for village or living space, the new **SIIDA Centre** hosts a variety of exhibits on the Sámi people and the northern seasons. The center houses the **Saamelaismuseo** (Sámi Museum) and the **Ylä-Lapin luontokeskus** (Northern Lapland Nature Centre). The Nature Centre includes the **Metsähallitus** (Forest and Park Service; ☎ 0205/647–740, 𝔽𝔸𝕏 0205/647–750), which can provide camping and fishing permits along with advice on exploring the wilderness. A 17-acre open-air museum complements the indoor exhibits during the summer. ⊠ *Highway 4 by Lake*

Inari, 99870 Inari, ☎ 016/665–212, ℻ 016/665–156. ⊙ Saamelaismuseo: June–Sept., daily 9–8; Oct.–May, Tues.–Sun. 10–5.

$$ 🏠 **Inarin Kultahovi.** This renovated old inn stands on the wooded bank of a swiftly flowing river. ✉ 99870, ☎ 016/671–221, ℻ 016/671–250. *29 rooms. Restaurant. DC, MC, V.*

Lapland Essentials

Getting Around

All but the most remote towns are accessible by bus, train, or plane.

BY BUS

Buses leave five times daily from Rovaniemi to Inari (five hours) and Ivalo (four hours). Taxi stands are at most bus stations.

BY CAR

The Arctic Highway will take you north from Rovaniemi at the Arctic Circle to Inari, just below the 69th parallel.

BY PLANE

Finnair domestic flights link Oulu and Rovaniemi with Ivalo, Enontekiö, Kemi, and Sodankylä. Finnair also has daily flights directly from Helsinki to Kuusamo. The SAS-owned **Air Botnia** (☎ 09/6151–2900) also serves Lapland's airports.

Guided Tours

Friendly Finland Tours (Finland Travel Bureau, ☞ Travel Agencies *in* Contacts and Resources *in* Helsinki Essentials, *above*).

Visitor Information

Inari (✉ Northern Lapland Tourism, Honkapolku 3, 99800 Saariselkä, ☎ 016/668–402, ℻ 016/668–403). **Rovaniemi** (✉ Koskikatu 1, 96200, ☎ 016/346–270 or 016/322–2279, ℻ 016/342–4650). **Saariselkä** (✉ Saariselkätie, PL 22, 99831, ☎ 016/668–122). **Sodankylä** (✉ Jäämerentie 3, 99600, ☎ 016/618–168, ℻ 016/613–478).

11 FRANCE

PARIS, THE ILE-DE-FRANCE, THE LOIRE VALLEY, NORMANDY, BURGUNDY AND LYON, PROVENCE, THE CÔTE D'AZUR

Like the high-speed trains speeding toward the Channel Tunnel, France has been on the move. This is particularly evident in Paris: In the last two decades no other European capital has seen as much building at such a pharaonic pace. I. M. Pei's glass pyramid at the Louvre and the postmodern Grande Arche de la Défense are just two examples of the architecturally dramatic monuments that have shocked purists and set the city abuzz.

But France's attachment to its heritage also persists, as major restorations of the Champs-Élysées and the Tuileries Gardens in Paris have proved. The world's most magnificent châteaux—Versailles and Fontainebleau in the Ile-de-France, Chenonceau and Chambord in the Loire Valley—have remained testaments to France's illustrious nobility. The spires of Chartres and Claude Monet's gardens in Giverny have continued to demonstrate France's glorious artistic and architectural legacy.

The Loire Valley and the Ile-de-France are easily accessible from Paris. But to really experience France, you must travel farther afield. Go west to Normandy, home of Camembert, Calvados (apple brandy), the D-Day landings, and dramatic Mont-St-Michel overlooking the English Channel (*La Manche* to the French). Head southeast to Burgundy, famed for its wine, and explore the hills of Beaujolais, en route to Lyon, a city that competes with Paris—and Dijon—for the title of France's gastronomic capital. Then wend your way south along the towering Rhône Valley to Provence, for the warm colors and the sweet smell of lavender. And continue on to the Côte d'Azur, for the stars, the sun, and the beaches along the bright blue waters of the Mediterranean.

The best way to get by in France is to try out a little French—a simple *"bonjour"* (good day) or a *"Parlez-vous anglais?"* (Do you speak English?) will go a long away. Do as the French do: You'll be surprised, for instance, at how quickly a surly waiter will melt if you fight a smirk with a smirk. Take time out from your busy sightseeing schedule to

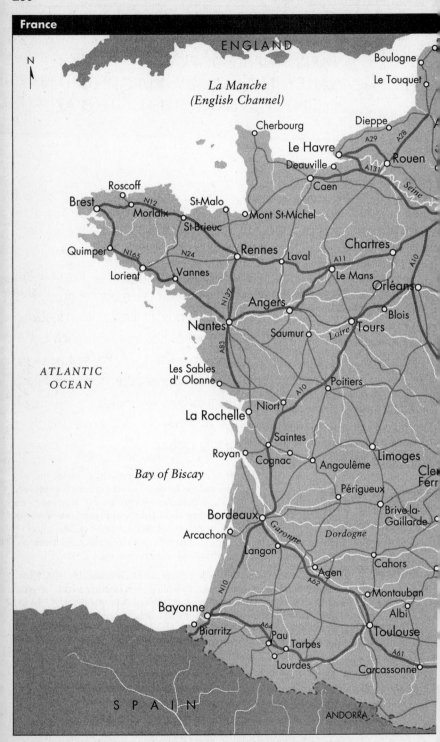

ENGLAND

La Manche
(English Channel)

N

Boulogne

Le Touquet

Dieppe

Cherbourg

Le Havre

Deauville

Rouen

Seine

Roscoff

Brest

Morlaix

St-Malo

Mont St-Michel

Caen

N12

St-Brieuc

Chartres

Quimper

N165

N24

Rennes

Laval

A11

Le Mans

A10

Orléans

Lorient

Vannes

Angers

Blois

Nantes

Saumur

Tours

Loire

N137

A83

Les Sables
d' Olonne

*ATLANTIC
OCEAN*

Poitiers

A10

Niort

La Rochelle

Saintes

Limoges

Royan

Cognac

Angoulême

Cler
Férr

Bay of Biscay

Périgueux

Brive-la-
Gaillarde

Bordeaux

Garonne

Dordogne

Arcachon

Langon

Cahors

Agen

A62

Montauban

N10

Albi

Bayonne

Toulouse

Biarritz

A64

Pau

Tarbes

A61

Lourdes

Carcassonne

SPAIN

ANDORRA

Calais

BELGIUM

A26
Lille

Arras
Amiens
Cambrai
St. Quentin

LUXEMBOURG

A16

Beauvais
Laon

A1

Reims

Paris
Metz

A5
Châlons-en-
Champagne
Nancy

Fontainebleau
Troyes
Strasbourg

A26
Colmar

Sens
A31

Auxerre
Mulhouse

A6
Belfort

Bourges
Dijon
Besançon

A36

Nevers
Beaune

A71
Autun

Saône

Montluçon
Mâcon
Bourg-en-
Bresse

Clermont-
errand
Lyon
Rhône

A72

Aurillac
Le Puy
A43
Chambéry

A49
Grenoble

A75
Rhône

Rodez
Montélimar

Millau
Gap
Sisteron

Nîmes
Avignon
A57

Montpellier
Aix-en-Provence
Monte Carlo
Nice

A9
A8
Cannes

Narbonne
Marseille

A19
Toulon

Perpignan

Mediterranean Sea
Corsica

0   50 mi
0   75 km

GERMANY

SWITZERLAND

ITALY

Corsica
Calvi
Bastia

Corte

Ajaccio
N198

Bonifacio

match that French passion for the daily rituals. Linger over a coffee in the afternoon or a bottle of wine at dinner and your own experience will be all the more authentic and satisfying.

FRANCE A TO Z

Customs
For details on imports and duty-free limits, *see* Customs & Duties *in* Chapter 1.

Dining
Eating in France is serious business, at least for two of the three meals each day. For a light meal try an informal café or brasserie (steak and french fries remain the classic) or a picnic (a baguette with ham, cheese, or pâté is a perfect combination). Reservations are advised at most restaurants, particularly in summer. French breakfasts are relatively modest—strong coffee, fruit juice if you insist, and croissants.

MEALTIMES
Dinner is the main meal and usually begins at 8. Lunch begins at noon in the countryside, and 12:30 or 1 (seldom later) in towns.

PRECAUTIONS
Tap water is perfectly safe, though not always very palatable (least of all in Paris). Mineral water is a good alternative; there's a vast choice of *eau plate* (still) and *eau gazeuse* (fizzy).

RATINGS
Prices are per person and include a first course, main course, and dessert plus tax (20.6%) and service (which are always included in displayed prices), but not wine.

CATEGORY	MAJOR CITY	OTHER AREAS
$$$$	over 600 frs	over 500 frs
$$$	300 frs–600 frs	250 frs–500 frs
$$	175 frs–300 frs	125 frs–250 frs
$	under 175 frs	under 125 frs

WHAT TO WEAR
Jacket and tie are recommended for $$$$ and $$$ restaurants, and at some of the more stylish $$ restaurants as well. When in doubt, it's best to dress up. Otherwise casual dress is appropriate (though be aware that casual in Paris means stylish and no shorts or sneakers).

Language
The French study English for a minimum of four years at school and, although few are fluent, their English is probably better than the French of most Americans. English is widely understood in major tourist areas, and in most hotels there is likely to be at least one person who can converse with you. Even if your own French is rusty, try to master a few words: People will greatly appreciate your efforts.

Lodging
France has a wide range of accommodations, from rambling old village inns to stylishly converted châteaux to modern hotels. Prices must, by law, be posted in the hotel room and include taxes and service. Prices are usually listed by room, not per person, and don't usually include breakfast. In smaller rural hotels, you may be expected to have your evening meal at the hotel, too.

The quality of accommodations, particularly in older properties, can vary greatly from room to room; if you don't like the room you're given, ask to see another. When making reservations, state your preference for twin or double beds and for *douche* (shower) or *baignoire* (tub)—the latter always costs more.

It's always a good idea to make hotel reservations in Paris and other major tourist destinations as far in advance as possible, especially in late spring, summer, or fall. If you arrive without a reservation, tourist offices in major train stations and most towns may be able to find a hotel for you.

BED-AND-BREAKFASTS

Known as *chambres d'hôte,* B&Bs are becoming increasingly popular in rural areas and can be a great bargain. Check local tourist offices for details, or contact the **Maison des Gîtes de France** (✉ 59 rue St-Lazare, 75439 Cedex Paris, ☎ 01–49–70–75–75), a national organization listing B&Bs all over France.

CAMPING

French campsites have a good reputation for organization and amenities but are crowded in July and August. Many campsites welcome reservations, and in summer, it makes sense to book in advance. A guide to France's campsites is published by the **Fédération Française de Camping et de Caravaning** (✉ 78 rue de Rivoli, 75004 Paris, ☎ 01–42–72–84–08).

HOSTELS

Some of the hostels in France are quite nice and even have double rooms; age restrictions may apply. Contact the **Fédération Unie des Auberges de Jeunesse** (✉ 27 rue Pajol, 75018 Paris, ☎ 01–44–89–87–27, FAX 01–44–89–87–10) for information.

HOTELS

First-time travelers to France (or anywhere else in Europe, for that matter), take note: Not only are hotel rooms here small by American standards, they are also rarely as well appointed. Unless you have booked into a top-tier address, do not expect to find a spacious room with all the latest conveniences. The hotels we have chosen can be relied upon to offer clean linens, conscientious service, and considerable charm. Rest assured that the bathrooms, though sometimes small, will be clean and comfortable, but don't be surprised to find the bed a bit saggy, or the carpet in the hall a little threadbare.

RATINGS

Prices are for standard double rooms and include tax (20.6%) and service charges.

CATEGORY	MAJOR CITY	OTHER AREAS
$$$$	over 1,200 frs	over 800 frs
$$$	750 frs–1,200 frs	500 frs–800 frs
$$	450 frs–750 frs	250 frs–500 frs
$	under 450 frs	under 250 frs

VACATION RENTALS

Renting an apartment or a *gîte* (a furnished house) for a week or month can be more convenient and save you money if you're traveling with a group or family. The **French Government Tourist Offices** in New York and London (☞ Visitor Information, *below*) are good sources for information about rentals. **Gîtes de France** (✉ 59 rue St-Lazare, 75009 Paris, ☎ 01–49–70–75–75, FAX 01–42–81–28–53) has a list of gîtes for rent: Indicate the region that interests you or order the annual nationwide guide (140 frs).

The following agencies list houses and apartments for rent: **At Home Abroad** (✉ 405 E. 56th St., Suite 6H, New York, NY 10022, ☎ 212/

421–9165, ⊞ 212/752–1591). **At Home in France** (✉ P.O. Box 643, Ashland, OR 97520, ☎ 541/488–9467, ⊞ 541/488–9468). **Orion** (✉ 30 Pl. d'Italie, 75013, ☎ 01–40–78–54–54; 800/546–4777, 212/688–9538 in the U.S., ⊞ 01–40–78–54–55; 212/688–9467 in the U.S.). **Paris Appartements Services** (✉ 69 rue d'Argout, 75002, ☎ 01–40–28–01–28, ⊞ 01–40–28–92–01). **Ville et Village** (✉ 2124 Kittredge St., Suite 200 Berkeley, CA, ☎ 510/559–8080; ⊞ 510/559–8217).

Mail

POSTAL RATES

Letters and postcards to the United States and Canada cost 4.40 francs for 20 grams. Letters to the United Kingdom cost 3 francs for up to 20 grams, as do letters within France. Postcards cost 2.70 francs within France and to EU countries. Stamps can be bought in post offices (La Poste) and cafés sporting a red TABAC sign outside.

RECEIVING MAIL

If you're uncertain where you'll be staying, have mail sent to American Express (if you're a card member) or Thomas Cook; mail labeled "poste restante" is also accepted at most French post offices.

Money Matters

COSTS

There's no way around it: France is expensive. But many travel basics—hotels, restaurants, plane, and train tickets—can be made more affordable by planning ahead, taking advantage of prix-fixe menus, and staying in smaller, family-run places. Prices are highest in Paris and on the Côte d'Azur, though even in these areas you can find reasonable accommodations and food.

All taxes must be included in posted prices in France. The initials TTC (*toutes taxes comprises,* which means taxes included) are sometimes included on price lists, but they are superfluous. Restaurant and hotel prices must *by law* include taxes and service charges: If they are tacked onto your bill as additional items, you should complain.

CURRENCY

The unit of French currency is the franc, subdivided into 100 centimes. Bills are issued in denominations of 50, 100, 200, and 500 francs (frs); coins are 5, 10, 20, and 50 centimes and 1, 2, 5, 10, and 20 francs. The small, copper-color 5-, 10-, and 20-centime coins have considerable nuisance value, but they can be used for tips in bars and cafés. International credit cards and traveler's checks are widely accepted throughout France, except in rural areas. At press time (summer 1999), the U.S. dollar bought 6.32 francs, the Canadian dollar 4.31 francs, the pound sterling 10.02 francs, the Australian dollar 4.16 francs, the New Zealand dollar 3.38 francs, and the euro 6.55957 francs.

SAMPLE PRICES

Prices vary greatly depending on the region, proximity to tourist sights, and—believe it or not—whether you're sitting down (and where—inside or on the terrace) or standing up in a café! Here are a few samples: cup of coffee, 6–12 francs; glass of beer, 10–25 francs; soft drink, 10–20 francs; ham sandwich, 15–25 francs; 1½-km (1-mi) taxi ride, 35 francs.

TIPPING

The bill in a bar or restaurant includes service, but it's customary to leave some small change unless you're dissatisfied. The amount varies, from 30 centimes for a beer to 10–30 francs after a meal. Tip taxi drivers and hairdressers about 10%. Give ushers in theaters 1–2 francs. Cloakroom attendants will expect nothing if there is a sign saying POUR-

BOIRE INTERDIT (tipping forbidden); otherwise give them 5 francs. Washroom attendants usually get 2 francs—a sum that is often posted. Bellhops should get 10 francs per item. If you stay in a moderately priced hotel for more than two or three days, it is customary to leave something for the chambermaid—perhaps 10 francs per day. Expect to tip 10 francs for room service—but nothing is expected if breakfast is routinely served in your room. Service station attendants get nothing for giving you gas or oil, and 5 or 10 francs for checking tires. Train and airport porters get a fixed sum (6–10 frs) per bag. Museum guides should get 5–10 francs after a guided tour. Tip tour guides (and bus drivers) 10 francs or more after an excursion.

National Holidays

January 1; April 24 (Easter Monday); May 1 (Labor Day); May 8 (VE Day); June 1 (Ascension); June 12 (Pentecost Monday); July 14 (Bastille Day); August 15 (Assumption); November 1 (All Saints' Day); November 11 (Armistice); December 25.

Opening and Closing Times

Banks are open weekdays 9:30–5, with variations; most close for at least an hour at lunch. **Museums** are closed one day a week (often Monday or Tuesday) and on national holidays. Usual hours are from 9:30 to 5 or 6. Many museums close for lunch (noon–2); on Sunday many are open afternoons only. **Shops** in big towns are open from 9 or 9:30 to 7 or 8 without a lunch break; though still rare, an increasing number are now open on Sunday. Smaller shops often open earlier and close later, but take a lengthy lunch break (12:30–4). This siesta-type schedule is more typical in the south of France. Corner grocery stores frequently stay open until around 10 PM.

Precautions

Beware of thieves and pickpockets! Though no one likes to talk about it, burglaries, once confined to major cities, have spread into the countryside. Keep photocopies of your passport and credit cards, just in case.

Shopping

BARGAINING

People don't usually bargain in shops where prices are clearly marked, but they do at outdoor markets and flea markets.

SALES-TAX REFUNDS

A value-added tax of 20.6%, known in France as the TVA, is imposed on most consumer goods. Non–European Union residents aged 15 and over can reclaim part of this tax. To qualify, your purchases in a single shop must total at least 2,000 francs. The amount of the refund varies from shop to shop, but usually hovers between 13% and 16%. The major department stores have simplified the refund process with special desks where the *bordereaux* (export sales invoices) are prepared.

Telephoning

French phone numbers have 10 digits. All phone numbers have a two-digit prefix determined by zone: Paris and the Ile-de-France, 01; the northwest, 02; the northeast, 03; the southeast, 04; and the southwest, 05.

COUNTRY CODE

The country code for France is 33 and for Monaco 337. To call France from the United States, dial 011 (for all international calls), then dial 33 (the country code), and the number in France, minus any initial 0. To dial France from the United Kingdom, dial 00–33, then dial the number in France, minus any initial 0.

INTERNATIONAL CALLS

To call a foreign country from France, dial 00 and wait for the tone, then dial the country code, area code, and number. You can also contact your long distance carrier directly and charge your call to your calling card or make a collect call: **AT&T** (☎ 08–00–99–00–11), **MCI** (☎ 08–00–99–00–19), **Sprint** (☎ 08–00–99–00–87).

LOCAL AND REGIONAL CALLS

To make calls within a region or to another region in France, simply dial the full, 10-digit number. A local call in France costs 74 centimes per three minutes; half-price rates apply between 7 PM and 8 AM and between noon Saturday and 8 AM Monday. Dial 12 for local operators.

Telephone booths can almost always be found at post offices, cafés, and métro stations. Some French pay phones take 1-, 2-, and 5-franc coins (1-franc minimum), but most phones are now operated by *télécartes* (phone cards), sold in post offices, métro stations, and cafés with red TABAC signs by unit (cost: 49 frs for 50 units; 97.50 frs for 120 units).

Transportation

BY BICYCLE

The French are great bicycling enthusiasts—witness the Tour de France—and there are many good bicycling routes in France. For 44 francs a day (55 frs for a 10-gear touring bike) you can rent a bike from one of 240 train stations; you need to show your passport and leave a deposit of 1,000 francs or a Visa or MasterCard. Bikes may be taken as accompanied luggage from any station in France; some trains in rural areas don't even charge for this. Tourist offices supply details on the more than 200 local shops that rent bikes, as well as mountain bikes (known as VTT or *Vélos Touts Terrains*), or you can get the SNCF brochure "Guide du Train et du Vélo" from any station.

BY BOAT

Canal and river vacations are popular: You can either take an organized cruise or rent a boat and plan your own leisurely route. Contact a travel agent for details or ask for a "Tourisme Fluvial" brochure in any French tourist office.

BY BUS

Because of the excellent train service, long-distance buses are rare; they're found mainly where train service is scarce. Bus tours are organized by **SNCF** (☞ By Train, *below*). Long-distance routes to many European cities are covered by **Eurolines** (✉ 28 av. Général-de-Gaulle, 93170 Bagnolet, ☎ 01–49–72–51–51, métro Galliéni).

BY CAR

Breakdowns. If your car breaks down on a highway, go to a roadside emergency telephone and call the breakdown service. If you have a breakdown anywhere else, find the nearest garage or contact the police (dial 17).

Gasoline. Gas is expensive, especially on expressways and in rural areas. Don't let your tank get too low—you can go for many mi in the country without passing a gas station—and keep an eye on pump prices as you go. These vary enormously; from 6.10 to 7 francs per liter. The cheapest gas can be found at *hypermarchés* (super stores).

Parking. Parking is a nightmare in Paris and often difficult in other large towns. Meters and ticket machines (pay and display) are common: Make sure you have a supply of 1-, 2-, 5-, and 10-franc coins. Parking is free during August in most of Paris, but be sure to check the signs. In smaller towns parking may be permitted on one side of the street only—alternating every two weeks—so pay attention to signs.

Road Conditions. France's roads are classified into five types, numbered and prefixed *A, N, D, C,* or *V*. Roads marked *A* (Autoroutes) are expressways. There are excellent links between Paris and most French cities, but poor ones between the provinces (the principal exceptions being A26 from Calais to Reims, A62 between Bordeaux and Toulouse, and A9/A8 the length of the Mediterranean coast). It's often difficult to avoid Paris when crossing France—just try to steer clear of the rush hours (7–9:30 AM and 4:30–7:30 PM). A *péage* (toll) must be paid on most expressways: The rate varies but can be steep. The *N* (Route Nationale) roads—which are sometimes divided highways—and *D* (Route Départementale) roads are usually wide and fast, and driving along them can be a real pleasure. Don't be daunted by smaller (*C* and *V*) roads, either. The yellow regional Michelin maps—on sale throughout France—are invaluable.

Rules of the Road. You may use your own driver's license in France, but you must be able to prove you have third-party insurance. Drive on the right and yield to drivers coming from the right if there is no solid white line. Seat belts are obligatory for all passengers, and children under 12 may not travel in the front seat. Speed limits are 130 kph (80 mph) on expressways, 110 kph (70 mph) on divided highways, 90 kph (55 mph) on other roads, 50 kph (30 mph) in towns. French drivers break these limits and police dish out hefty on-the-spot fines with equal abandon.

BY PLANE

The major gateways to France are the airports outside Paris: **Orly** (☎ 01–49–75–15–15) and **Charles de Gaulle** (☎ 01–48–62–22–80), more commonly known as Roissy. Flying time is 7½ hours from New York, 9 hours from Chicago, and 11 hours from Los Angeles. Many major airlines also have (less frequent) flights to Lyon, Nice, Marseille, Bordeaux, and Toulouse.

Domestic air travel in France is less expensive than it used to be, and there are more flights all over the country. (Train service, however, may be faster when you consider time spent getting to and from the airport.) Most domestic flights from Paris leave from Orly on **Air France** (☎ 800/237–2747 in the U.S., 08–02–80–28–02 in France); it flies all over the country. **Air Liberté** (☎ 08–03–80–58–05) flies from Paris to the Côte d'Azur and the southwest region of France.

BY TRAIN

SNCF (✉ 88 rue St-Lazare, 75009 Paris, ☎ 08–36–35–35–35), the French national railroad, is fast, punctual, comfortable, and comprehensive. The TGV (*Trains à Grande Vitesse*), with a top speed of 300 kph (190 mph), are the best domestic trains, heading southeast from Paris to Lyon, the Côte d'Azur, and Switzerland; west to Nantes; southwest to Bordeaux; and north to Lille and Brussels. TGVs require a seat reservation (easily obtained at the ticket window or from an automatic machine). Prices vary depending on the time of travel. For instance, the cost of a second-class ticket for the Paris–Lyon route usually costs 304 francs but climbs to 384 francs during the morning and evening rush hours. Seat reservations are reassuring but seldom necessary on other French trains, except at holiday times.

You must punch your train ticket in one of the orange machines (*composteurs*) you'll encounter alongside platforms. Slide your ticket in face up and wait for a "clunk" sound. (The small yellow tickets and automatic ticket barriers used for most suburban Paris trains are similar to those in the métro/RER.) The ticket collectors will present you with an on-the-spot fine of 100 francs if your ticket hasn't been validated before boarding.

On overnight trains you choose between *wagons-lits* (private sleeping cars), which are expensive, and *couchettes* (bunks), which sleep six to a compartment in second class and four to a compartment in first class (sheet and pillow provided) and are cheaper (90 frs). Ordinary compartment seats do not pull together to enable you to lie down. In summer special night trains from Paris to Spain and the Côte d'Azur are geared for a younger market, with discos and bars.

Fares. If France is your only destination in Europe, consider purchasing a **France Rail Pass,** which allows three days of unlimited train travel in a one-month period. Prices range from $120 to $198 for one or two adults in first or second class. Additional days may be added for $30 a day in either class. Other options include the France Rail 'n Drive Pass (combining rail and rental car), France Rail 'n Fly Pass (rail travel and one air journey within France), and the France Fly Rail 'n Drive Pass (a rail, air, and rental-car program all in one).

France is one of 17 countries in which you can use **Eurailpasses,** which provide unlimited first-class rail travel, in all of the participating countries, for the duration of the pass. If your plans call for only limited train travel, look into a **Europass,** which costs less money than a Eurailpass.

Various reduced-fare passes are available from major train stations in France and from SNCF travel agents. If you are planning to do a lot of traveling by train in France, consider buying a special **France Vacances** card (1,018 frs for four days, 1,622 frs for nine days). When traveling together, two people (who don't have to be a couple) can save money with the **Découverte à Deux.** Just say you're traveling together when you make a reservation or buy the tickets, and you will get a 25% discount during "périodes bleues" (blue periods; weekdays and not on or near any holidays—calendars are available at stations). Senior citizens (over 60) qualify for the **Carte Senior** (285 frs for four trips), and young people (under 26) qualify for the **Carte 12/25** (270 frs). You can get 50% discounts in blue periods. The **Carte Enfant** (350 frs) enables children and up to four accompanying adults to travel at half- or quarter-price, depending on the travel period. Other discounts are available if you book 30 or 8 days before traveling (**Découverte J30** or **Découverte J8**). If you don't benefit from any of these reductions and plan on traveling at least 1,000 km (620 mi) round-trip (including several stops), look into purchasing a **Billet Séjour.** This ticket gives you a 25% reduction if you stay over a Sunday and travel only during blue periods.

Visas
A valid passport is required for citizens of the United States, Canada, New Zealand, and Australia, but no visa for visits to France of less than three months. A valid passport is all that is required for British nationals.

Visitor Information
France On-Call (☎ 410/286–8310 Mon.–Fri. 9–7, www.france-tourism.com). **Chicago** (676 N. Michigan Ave., Chicago, IL 60611, fgto@mcs.net). **London** 178 Piccadilly, London W1V OAL U.K., ☎ 171/6399–3500, FAX 171/6493–6594. **Los Angeles** (9454 Wilshire Blvd., Suite 715, Beverly Hills, CA 90212, fgto@gte.net). **Montréal** (1981 Ave. McGill College, Suite 490, Montréal, Québec H3A 2W9 Canada). **New York City** (444 Madison Ave., 16th floor, New York, NY 10022, info@francetourism.com).

Weather

June and September, free of midsummer crowds, are the best months to be in France. June has the advantage of long daylight hours; slightly cheaper prices and many warm days (often lasting well into October) make September attractive. The second half of July and all of August are spoiled by inflated prices and huge crowds on the beaches, and the heat can be stifling in southern France. Paris, though pleasantly deserted, can be stuffy in August, too. Anytime between March and November offers a good chance to soak up some sun on the Côte d'Azur. The weather in Paris and the Loire is unappealing before Easter (lots of rain and chilly temperatures). If you're dreaming of Paris in the springtime, May (not April) is your best bet.

CLIMATE

North of the Loire (including Paris), France has a northern European climate—coldish winters, pleasant if unpredictable summers, and frequent rain. Southern France has a Mediterranean climate: mild winters, long, hot summers, and sunshine much of the year. The more Continental climate of eastern and central France is a mixture of these two extremes: Winters can be very cold and summers mighty hot. France's Atlantic coast has a temperate climate even south of the Loire, with the exception of the much warmer Biarritz.

The following are the average daily maximum and minimum temperatures for Paris and Marseille.

PARIS

Jan.	43F	6C	May	68F	20C	Sept.	70F	21C
	34	1		49	10		53	12
Feb.	45F	7C	June	73F	23C	Oct.	60F	16C
	34	1		55	13		46	8
Mar.	54F	12C	July	76F	25C	Nov.	50F	10C
	39	4		58	15		40	5
Apr.	60F	16C	Aug.	75F	24C	Dec.	44F	7C
	43	6		58	15		36	2

MARSEILLE

Jan.	50F	10C	May	71F	22C	Sept.	77F	25C
	35	2		52	11		58	15
Feb.	53F	12C	June	79F	26C	Oct.	68F	20C
	36	2		58	14		51	10
Mar.	59F	15C	July	84F	29C	Nov.	58F	14C
	41	5		63	17		41	5
Apr.	64F	18C	Aug.	83F	28C	Dec.	52F	11C
	46	8		63	17		37	3

PARIS

A city of vast, noble perspectives and winding, hidden streets, Paris remains a combination of the pompous and the intimate. If there's a problem with a trip to Paris, it's the embarrassment of riches that faces you. Whether you've come looking for sheer physical beauty, cultural and artistic diversions, world-famous dining and shopping, history, or simply local color, you will find it here in abundance.

Exploring Paris

Numbers in the margin correspond to points of interest on the Paris map.

Paris is a compact city. With the exceptions of the Bois de Boulogne and Montmartre, you can easily walk from one sight to the next. The city is divided in two by the River Seine, with two islands (Ile de la Cité and Ile St-Louis) in the middle. The south—or Left—Bank has a more intimate, bohemian flavor than the haughtier Right Bank. The east–west axis from Châtelet to the Arc de Triomphe, via the rue de Rivoli and the Champs-Élysées, is the principal thoroughfare for sightseeing and shopping on the Right Bank.

The **Carte Musées–Monuments** pass, which allows you access to most Paris museums and monuments, can be obtained from museums or major métro stations (one-day pass, 80 frs; three days, 160 frs; five days, 240 frs). Note, however, that this pass may only be useful to you if you plan to see *a lot* of museums in the allotted days.

If time is a problem, try to get in several "musts": Explore Notre-Dame and the Latin Quarter; head to Place de la Concorde and enjoy the vista from the Champs-Élysées to the Louvre; then take a boat along the Seine for a waterside rendezvous with the Eiffel Tower. You could finish off with dinner in Montmartre and consider it a day well spent.

From the Eiffel Tower to Pont de l'Alma

The Eiffel Tower lords it over this southwest area of Paris. Across the way, in the Palais de Chaillot on Place du Trocadéro, are a number of museums. In this area, too, is where you get the Bateaux Mouches, the boats that ply the Seine on their tours of Paris by water.

❹ Bateaux Mouches. These popular motorboats set off on their hour-long tours of Paris waters regularly (every half hour in summer). ✉ *Pl. de l'Alma,* ☎ *01–40–76–99–99. Métro: Alma-Marceau.*

❶ Eiffel Tower (Tour Eiffel). What is now the worldwide symbol of Paris nearly became 7,000 tons of scrap-iron when its concession expired in 1909. Only its potential use as a radio antenna saved the day. Architect Gustave Eiffel, whose skill as an engineer earned him renown as a builder of iron bridges, created his Tower for the World Exhibition of 1889. Restoration in the 1980s didn't make the elevators any faster—long lines are inevitable unless you come in the evening (when every girder is lit in glorious detail)—but decent shops and two good restaurants were added. The view from 1,000 ft up will enable you to appreciate the city's layout and proportions. ✉ *quai Branly,* ☎ *01–44–11–23–23.* ۞ *July– Aug., daily 9 AM–midnight; Sept.–June, Sun.–Thurs. 9 AM–11 PM, Fri.– Sat. 9 AM–midnight. Métro: Bir-Hakeim; RER: Champ-de-Mars.*

❸ Musée d'Art Moderne de la Ville de Paris (City of Paris Museum of Modern Art). Both temporary exhibits and a permanent collection of top-quality 20th-century art can be found at this modern art museum. It takes over, chronologically speaking, where the Musée d'Orsay leaves off. ✉ *11 av. du Président-Wilson,* ☎ *01–53–67–40–00.* ۞ *Tues.– Sun. 10–5:30, Wed. 10–8:30. Métro: Iéna.*

❷ Palais de Chaillot (Chaillot Palace). This honey-color, Art Deco culture center facing the Seine, perched atop tumbling gardens with sculpture and fountains, was built in the 1930s. It houses three museums: the **Musée des Monuments Français** (French Monuments Museum), whose painstaking replicas of statues and archways form an excellent introduction to French medieval architecture; the **Musée de la Marine** (Maritime Museum), with a salty collection of seafaring paraphernalia; and the **Musée de l'Homme** (Museum of Mankind), an anthropology museum with an array of prehistoric artifacts. ⊠ *Pl. du Trocadéro.* ☉ *Wed.–Mon. 10–5. Métro: Trocadéro.*

From the Arc de Triomphe to the Louvre

The Arc de Triomphe stands foursquare at the top of the city's most famous avenue, the Champs-Élysées, which slopes gracefully down to Place de la Concorde. Beyond lies the Tuileries Garden and the gleaming glass pyramid of the world's largest museum, the Louvre.

❺ **Arc de Triomphe** (Triumphal Arch). This 164-ft arch was planned by Napoléon to celebrate his military successes. Yet when Empress Marie-Louise entered Paris in 1810, it was barely off the ground. Napoléon had been dead for 15 years when the Arc de Triomphe was finished in 1836. The arch looms over Place Charles-de-Gaulle, referred to by Parisians as **L'Étoile** (The Star), one of Europe's most chaotic traffic circles. Short of a death-defying dash, your only way to get over to the Arc de Triomphe is to take the pedestrian underpass. France's Unknown Soldier is buried beneath the archway; the flame is rekindled every evening at 6:30. Halfway up the arch is a small museum devoted to its history. ⊠ *Pl. Charles-de-Gaulle,* ☎ *01–43–80–31–31.* ☉ *Easter–Oct., daily 9:30 AM–11 PM; Oct.–Easter, daily 10 AM–10:30 PM. Métro, RER: Charles-de-Gaulle–Étoile.*

❻ **Champs-Élysées.** The cosmopolitan pulse of Paris beats strongest along this gracefully sloping, 2-km (1-mi) avenue, originally laid out in the 1660s by André Le Nôtre as a garden sweeping away from the Tuileries. There isn't much sign of that pastoral past these days, as you stroll by the cafés, restaurants, airline offices, car showrooms, movie theaters, and chic arcades that occupy its upper half. *Métro: George-V, Franklin-D.-Roosevelt, Champs-Élysées–Clemenceau.*

❼ **Grand Palais** (Grand Palace). This so-called palace was built for the World Exhibition of 1900 and now houses temporary exhibitions. Unfortunately the main hall, with its Art Nouveau iron banisters and striking glass roof, is closed for renovation and is unlikely to reopen before 2002; but you can still visit the **Palais de la Découverte** (Palace of Discovery), with scientific and mechanical exhibits and a **planetarium.** ⊠ *av. Winston-Churchill,* ☎ *01–42–65–12–73.* ☉ *Palais de la Découverte: Tues.–Sat. 9:30–6, Sun. 10–7. Métro: Franklin-D.-Roosevelt.*

❽ **Jardin des Tuileries** (Tuileries Garden). These enormous formal gardens are lined with trees, ponds, and statues. At the far end of the Tuileries, leading toward the Louvre, is the **Arc du Carrousel,** a dainty triumphal arch erected more quickly (1806–08) than its big brother at the far end of the Champs-Élysées. *Métro: Concorde.*

★ ⑫ **Louvre.** Once a royal palace, now the world's largest and most famous museum, the Louvre has been given fresh purpose by a decade of expansion, renovation, and reorganization, symbolized by I. M. Pei's daring glass pyramid that now serves as the entrance to both the museum and an underground shopping arcade, the **Carrousel du Louvre.**

The Louvre was begun as a fortress around 1200, but the earliest parts still in use date from the 1540s. Building was a regular process until the reign of Napoléon III in the 1860s. Then, the Louvre was even larger; a wing facing the Tuileries Gardens was razed by rampaging revolutionaries during the bloody Paris Commune of 1871.

Pei's new Louvre has emerged less cramped and more rationally organized. Yet its sheer variety can intimidate. The main attraction is Leonardo da Vinci's *Mona Lisa* (known in French as *La Joconde*), painted in 1503. It's smaller than you might have imagined, kept behind glass, and invariably encircled by a mob of tourists. Turn your attention instead to some less-crowded rooms and galleries nearby, where Leonardo's fellow Italians are strongly represented: Fra Angelico, Giotto, Mantegna, Raphael, Titian, and Veronese. El Greco, Murillo, and Velázquez lead the Spanish; Van Eyck, Rembrandt, Frans Hals, Bruegel, Holbein, and Rubens underline the achievements of northern European art. English paintings are highlighted by works of Lawrence, Reynolds, Gainsborough, and Turner. Highlights of French painting include works by Poussin, Fragonard, Chardin, Boucher, and Watteau— together with David's *Oath of the Horatii,* Géricault's *Raft of the Medusa,* and Delacroix's *Liberty Guiding the People.*

Famous statues include the soaring *Victory of Samothrace,* the celebrated *Venus de Milo,* and the realistic Egyptian *Seated Scribe.* New rooms for ancient Persian, Arab, and Greek art were opened in 1997. Also be sure to inspect the Gobelin tapestries, the Crown Jewels (including the 186-carat Regent diamond), and the 9th-century bronze statuette of Emperor Charlemagne. ⊠ *Palais du Louvre (it's faster to enter through the Carrousel du Louvre mall on rue de Rivoli than through the pyramid),* ☎ *01–40–20–51–51 for information.* ☉ *Mon. and Wed. 9 AM–9:45 PM, Thurs.–Sun. 9–6. Métro: Palais-Royal.*

⑪ **Musée du Jeu de Paume.** Renovations transformed this museum, at the entrance to the Tuileries Garden, into an ultramodern, white-walled showcase for excellent temporary exhibits of bold contemporary art. The building was once the spot of *jeu de paume* games (literally, palm game—a forerunner of tennis). ⊠ *Pl. de la Concorde,* ☎ *01–42–60–69–69.* ☉ *Tues. noon–9:30, Wed.–Fri. noon–7, weekends 10–7. Métro: Concorde.*

⑩ **Musée de l'Orangerie** (Orangery Museum). This museum bordering the Tuileries Garden contains fine early 20th-century French works by Monet (including some of his *Water Lilies*), Renoir, Marie Laurencin, and others. ⊠ *Pl. de la Concorde,* ☎ *01–42–97–48–16.* ☉ *Wed.–Mon. 9:45–5:15. Métro: Concorde.*

Petit Palais (Little Palace). Directly opposite the main entrance to the Grand Palais, and built at the same time (1900), this building is home to an attractively presented collection of French paintings and furniture from the 18th and 19th centuries. ⊠ *av. Winston-Churchill,* ☎ *01–42–65–12–73.* ☉ *Tues.–Sun. 10–5:40, Métro: Champs-Élysées–Clemenceau.*

⑨ **Place de la Concorde.** Flanked by elegant neoclassical buildings, this huge square is often choked with traffic and perhaps at its most scenic come nightfall. Over 1,000 people, including Louis XVI and Marie-Antoinette, were guillotined here in the early 1790s. The obelisk, a gift from the viceroy of Egypt, originally stood at Luxor and was erected here in 1833; the top was gilded in 1998. *Métro: Concorde.*

The Faubourg St-Honoré

The Faubourg St-Honoré, north of the Champs-Élysées and the Tuileries, is synonymous with style—as you will see as you progress from the President's Palace to the monumental Madeleine church and on to stately Place Vendôme. Leading names in modern fashion are found farther east on Place des Victoires, close to what was once the city's main market, Les Halles (pronounced *layal*). Now in its place is a modern shopping mall, the Forum des Halles. In contrast, nearby, is the august church of St-Eustache. Similarly, the incongruous black-and-white columns in the classical courtyard of neighboring Palais-Royal present a further case of daring modernity—or architectural vandalism, depending on your point of view.

⑭ Église de la Madeleine. With its uncompromising array of columns, this church, known as La Madeleine, looks more like a Greek temple. Inside, the walls are richly decorated, with plenty of gold glinting through the murk. The church was designed in 1814 but not consecrated until 1842, after futile efforts to turn the site into a train station. ⊠ *Pl. de la Madeleine.* ⊙ *Mon.–Sat. 7:30–7, Sun. 8–7. Métro: Madeleine.*

⑱ Forum des Halles. Since the city's much-lamented central glass-and-iron market halls were torn down during the late '60s, the area has been transformed into a trendy—albeit slightly seedy—shopping complex, the Forum des Halles. A topiary garden basks in the shadow of the nearby **Bourse du Commerce** (Commercial Exchange) and bulky church of **St-Eustache** (☞ *below*). *Métro: Les Halles; RER: Châtelet–Les Halles.*

⑬ Palais de l'Élysée (Élysée Palace). This "palace," known to the French simply as L'Élysée, where the French president lives, works, and receives official visitors, was originally constructed as a private mansion in 1718 and has housed presidents only since 1873. ⊠ *55 rue du Faubourg St-Honoré. Not open to the public. Métro: Miromesnil.*

⑯ Palais-Royal. This erstwhile Royal Palace, built in the 1630s and now occupied by the Ministry of Culture, has a garden bordered by arcades and boutiques, and an adjacent courtyard with modern, candy-stripe columns by Daniel Buren. ⊠ *Pl. André-Malraux. Métro: Palais-Royal.*

⑮ Place Vendôme. This rhythmically proportioned example of 17th-century urban architecture is one of the world's most opulent squares. Top jewelers compete for attention with the limousines that draw up outside the Ritz Hotel. The square's central pillar was made from the melted bronze of 1,200 cannons captured by Napoléon at the Battle of Austerlitz in 1805. That's Napoléon at the top, disguised as a Roman emperor. *Métro: Tuileries.*

⑰ Place des Victoires. This circular square, home to many of the city's top fashion boutiques, was laid out in 1685 by Jules-Hardouin Mansart in honor of the military victories (*victoires*) of Louis XIV. The Sun King gallops along on a bronze horse in the middle. *Métro: Sentier.*

⑲ St-Eustache. This colossal church, also known as the Cathedral of Les Halles, was erected between 1532 and 1637, and testifies to the stylistic transition between Gothic and Classical architecture. ⊠ *2 rue du Jour. Métro: Les Halles; RER: Châtelet–Les Halles.*

The Grand Boulevards

The focal point of this walk is the uninterrupted avenue that runs in almost a straight line from St-Augustin, the city's grandest Second Empire church, to Place de la République, whose very name symbolizes the ultimate downfall of the imperial regime. The avenue's name changes six times along the way, which is why Parisians refer to it as the *Grands Boulevards* (plural).

㉒ Grands Magasins (Department Stores). Paris's most venerable department stores can be found behind the Opéra: **Galeries Lafayette** has an elegant turn-of-the-century glass dome; **Au Printemps** an excellent view from its rooftop cafeteria. ⊠ *bd. Haussmann. Métro: Havre-Caumartin.*

㉑ Opéra Garnier. The original Paris opera house was the flagship building of the Second Empire (1851–70). Architect Charles Garnier fused elements of neoclassical architecture—like the bas-reliefs on the newly cleaned facade—in an exaggerated combination imbued with as much subtlety as a Wagnerian cymbal crash. You can visit the lavishly upholstered auditorium, with its ceiling painted by Marc Chagall in

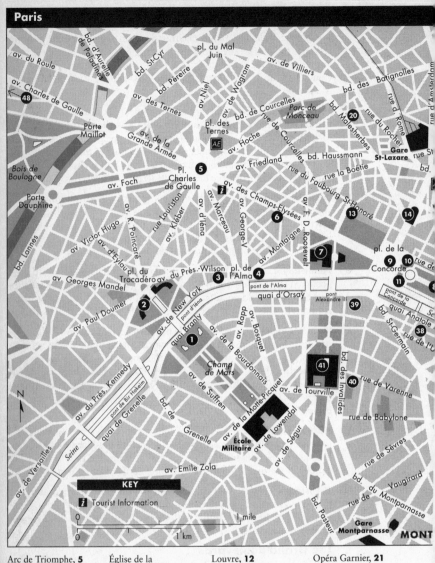

KEY

i Tourist Information

0 ————————— 1 mile

0 ————————— 1 km

Arc de Triomphe, **5**
Arènes de Lutèce, **33**
Bateaux Mouches, **4**
Bercy, **45**
Bibliothèque François-Mitterrand, **46**
Centre Pompidou, **23**
Champs-Elysées, **6**
Cimetière du Père-Lachaise, **47**
Conciergerie, **28**
La Défense, **48**

Église de la Madeleine, **14**
Eiffel Tower, **1**
Forum des Halles, **18**
Grand Palais, **7**
Grands Magasins, **22**
Hôtel des Invalides, **41**
Hôtel de Ville, **24**
Jardin du Luxembourg, **35**
Jardin des Plantes, **34**
Jardin des Tuileries, **8**

Louvre, **12**
Musée d'Art Moderne de la Ville de Paris, **3**
Musée du Jeu de Paume, **11**
Musée de Montmartre, **44**
Musée de l'Orangerie, **10**
Musée d'Orsay, **38**
Musée Picasso, **25**
Musée Rodin, **40**
Notre-Dame, **30**

Opéra Garnier, **21**
Palais Bourbon, **39**
Palais de Chaillot, **2**
Palais de l'Elysée, **13**
Palais-Royal, **16**
Panthéon, **32**
Place des Abbesses, **43**
Place de la Bastille, **27**
Place de la Concorde, **9**

1964. ⊠ *Pl. de l'Opéra,* ☎ *01–40–01–22–63.* ⊙ *Daily 10–5:30. Métro: Opéra.*

⓴ St-Augustin. This domed church was dexterously constructed in the 1860s within the confines of an awkward, V-shape site. It represented a breakthrough in ecclesiastical engineering, insofar as the use of metal pillars and girders obviated the need for exterior buttressing. ⊠ *Pl. St-Augustin. Métro: St-Augustin.*

The Marais and the Bastille

The Marais is one of the city's most historic and sought-after residential districts. The gracious architecture of the 17th and early 18th centuries sets the tone (the buildings here were spared the attentions of Haussmann, the city planner who rebuilt so much of Paris in the mid-19th century). In contrast is the architecturally whimsical Pompidou Center, on the western edge of the Marais. On the eastern side of the neighborhood is Place de la Bastille, site of the infamous prison stormed on July 14, 1789, an event that came to symbolize the beginning of the French Revolution. The surrounding Bastille quarter is filled with galleries, shops, theaters, cafés, restaurants, and bars.

㉓ Centre Pompidou (Pompidou Center). The futuristic, funnel-top Pompidou Center was built in the mid-1970s and named in honor of former French president Georges Pompidou (1911–74). The Center soon attracted over 8 million visitors a year—five times more than intended—and was closed from 1996 to January 2000 for top-to-bottom renovation. The center is most famous for its **Musée National d'Art Moderne** (Modern Art Museum), where the emphasis is largely on French works, from Fauvism and Cubism to postwar abstract art. On the square in front is the **Atelier Brancusi** (Brancusi's Studio), four reconstituted glass-fronted rooms of Romanian-born sculptor Constantin Brancusi. ⊠ *Pl. Georges-Pompidou,* ☎ *01–44–78–12–33.* ⊙ *Wed.–Mon. noon– 10. Métro: Rambuteau, Châtelet–Les Halles, Hôtel de Ville.*

㉔ Hôtel de Ville (City Hall). Overlooking the Seine, the Hôtel de Ville has only been the office of the mayor since 1977—when the seat was first created in Paris. During the Commune of 1871, the building was burned to the ground. Today's structure, based closely on the 16th-century Renaissance original, went up between 1874 and 1884. ⊠ *Pl. de l'Hôtel de Ville.* ⊙ *Open for special exhibitions only. Métro: Hôtel de Ville.*

㉕ Musée Picasso (Picasso Museum). The Hôtel Salé, an elegant mansion, is home to an extensive collection of little-known paintings, drawings, and engravings donated to the state by Picasso's heirs in lieu of death duties. ⊠ *5 rue de Thorigny,* ☎ *01–42–71–25–21.* ⊙ *Wed.–Mon. 9:30–5:30. Métro: St-Sébastien.*

㉗ Place de la Bastille. Nothing remains of the fortress stormed at the outbreak of the French Revolution; the soaring gilt-edge column, topped by the figure of Liberty, commemorates Parisians killed in the long-forgotten uprising of 1830. Also on the square is the modern, glass-fronted **Opéra de la Bastille** (Bastille Opera), opened in 1989 in commemoration of the Revolution's bicentennial. Rather more appealing is the **Viaduc des Arts** (Arts Viaduct) that leads off down avenue Daumesnil: a disused railway viaduct converted into boutiques below and a walkway on top. *Métro: Bastille.*

★ ㉖ Place des Vosges. Built in 1605, this is the oldest square in Paris. Its harmonious proportions, soft pink brick, and cloisterlike arcades give it an aura of calm. In the far corner is the **Maison de Victor Hugo** (Victor Hugo Museum), containing souvenirs of the great poet's life and many of his surprisingly able paintings and ink drawings. ⊠ *Maison de Victor Hugo: 6 Pl. des Vosges.* ⊙ *Tues.–Sun. 10–5:45. Métro: St-Paul.*

The Islands and the Latin Quarter

Of the two islands in the Seine, the Ile St-Louis is today largely residential, whereas the Ile de la Cité remains deeply historic (it was here that the earliest inhabitants of Paris, the Gaulish tribe of the Parisii, settled in about 250 BC). Here you'll find the great, brooding cathedral of Notre-Dame, jewel-like Ste-Chapelle, and the Conciergerie, the former city prison. South of Ile de la Cité on the Left Bank of the Seine is the bohemian Quartier Latin, with its warren of steep sloping streets, populated largely by Sorbonne students and academics.

㉝ Arènes de Lutèce (Lutèce Arena). This Gallo-Roman arena was rediscovered only in 1869; it has since been landscaped and excavated to reveal parts of the original amphitheater. ⊠ *Enter on rue Monge or rue de Navarre.* ⊙ *Daylight hrs. Métro: Monge.*

㉘ Conciergerie. This former prison has a superb vaulted 14th-century hall, the **Salles des Gens d'Armes** (Hall of the Men-at-Arms), that often hosts temporary exhibitions. The **Tour de l'Horloge** (Clock Tower) near the entrance on quai de l'Horloge has a clock that has been ticking off time since 1370. ⊠ *1 quai de l'Horloge,* ☎ *01–53–73–78–50.* ⊙ *Apr.–Sept., daily 9:30–6:30; Oct.–Mar., daily 10–5. Métro: Cité.*

㉞ Jardin des Plantes (Botanical Garden). Established here since the 17th century, Paris's Botanical Garden has a zoo, an aquarium, a maze, an alpine garden, hothouses, and several natural history museums: the **Musée Entomologique** (insects); the **Musée Paléontologique** (fossils and prehistoric animals); and the **Musée Minéralogique** (minerals). Don't miss the **Grande Galerie de l'Évolution** (Great Hall of Evolution) for its mind-blowing collection of stuffed and mounted animals (some now extinct). ⊠ *36 rue Geoffroy-St-Hilaire.* ⊙ *Museums: Wed.–Mon. 10–5 (Musée Entomologique, 1–5). Grande Galerie de l'Évolution: Wed.–Mon. 10–6, Thurs. 10–10. Métro: Monge.*

㉚ Notre-Dame. Notre-Dame Cathedral, Paris's historic and geographic heart, has been a place of worship for more than 2,000 years; the present building is the fourth on this site. It was begun in 1163, making it one of the earliest Gothic cathedrals, but wasn't finished until 1345. The interior is at its lightest and least crowded in the early morning. Window space is limited and filled with shimmering stained glass; the circular rose windows in the transept are particularly delicate. The 387-step climb up the towers is worth the effort for a perfect view of the gargoyles and Paris. ⊠ *Pl. du Parvis.* ⊙ *Cathedral: daily 8–7; treasury (religious and vestmental relics): Mon.–Fri. 9:30–6:30. Métro: Cité.*

㉜ Panthéon. This Temple to the Famous started life as a church (1758–89). Since the Revolution, the crypt has contained the remains of such national heroes as Voltaire, Rousseau, and Zola. The austere interior is ringed with Puvis de Chavannes's late-19th-century frescoes, relating the life of Geneviève, patron saint of Paris, and contains a swinging model of the giant pendulum used here by Léon Foucault in 1851 to prove the earth's rotation. ⊠ *Pl. du Panthéon,* ☎ *01–44–32–18–00.* ⊙ *Daily 10–6:15. Métro: Cardinal-Lemoine.*

㉙ Ste-Chapelle (Holy Chapel). This chapel in the Palais de Justice was built by St-Louis (Louis IX) in the 1240s to house the Crown of Thorns he had just bought from Emperor Baldwin of Constantinople. The somewhat garish lower chapel is less impressive than the upper one, whose walls consist of little else but dazzling 13th-century stained glass. ⊠

4 bd. du Palais. ⓧ *Apr.–Sept., daily 9:30–6:30; Oct.–Mar., daily 10–
5. Métro: Cité.*

㉛ Sorbonne. Students at Paris's ancient university—one of the oldest in
Europe—used to listen to lectures in Latin, which explains why the surrounding area is known as the Latin Quarter. You can visit the main
courtyard and peek into the lecture halls if they're not in use. The Baroque
chapel is only open during exhibitions. ⊠ *rue de la Sorbonne. Métro:
Cluny–La Sorbonne.*

From St-Germain to Les Invalides

This area of the Left Bank extends from the lively St-Germain neighborhood
(named for the oldest church in Paris) to the stately quarter around the
Musée d'Orsay and Les Invalides. Other highlights are the city's most
colorful park, the Jardin du Luxembourg; the Palais Bourbon, home to
the National Assembly; and the Musée Rodin. South of St-Germain is
Montparnasse, which had its cultural heyday in the first part of the 20th
century, when it was *the* place for painters and poets to live.

㊶ Hôtel des Invalides. Soaring above expansive if hardly manicured
lawns, Les Invalides was founded by Louis XIV in 1674 to house
wounded (*invalid*) war veterans. Although only a few old soldiers live
here today, the military link remains in the form of the **Musée de l'Ar-
mée**—a vast, though musty military museum with a collection of arms,
armor, and uniforms. The **Musée des Plans-Reliefs** contains a fascinating
collection of scale models of French towns, dating from the days of
military architect Vauban in the 17th century. The Invalides itself is an
outstanding Baroque ensemble, designed by Bruand and Hardouin-
Mansart. Its second church, the **Église du Dôme**, possesses the city's
most elegant dome and is home to Napoléon's tomb. ⊠ *Pl. des Invalides,*
☎ *01–44–42–37–67.* ⓧ *Apr.–Sept., daily 10–5:45; Oct.–Mar., daily
10–4:45. Métro: La Tour–Maubourg.*

㉟ Jardin du Luxembourg (Luxembourg Garden). Paris's most famous Left
Bank park has tennis courts, flower beds, tree-lined alleys, and a large
pond (with toy boats for rent alongside). The **Palais du Luxembourg**
(Luxembourg Palace), built by Queen Maria de' Medici at the beginning of the 17th century in answer to Florence's Pitti Palace, houses
the French Senate and is not open to the public. *Métro: Odéon; RER:
Luxembourg.*

★ **㊳ Musée d'Orsay** (Orsay Museum). This museum, in a renovated former train station, is one of Paris's star attractions, thanks to its imaginatively housed collections of the arts (mainly French) spanning the
period 1848–1914. The chief artistic attraction is its Impressionist
collection. Other highlights include Art Nouveau furniture, a faithfully
restored Belle Epoque restaurant, and a model of the Opéra quarter
beneath a glass floor. ⊠ *1 rue Bellechasse,* ☎ *01–40–49–48–14.* ⓧ *Tues.–
Sat. 10–6, Thurs. 10–9:45, Sun. 9–6. Métro: Solférino; RER: Musée
d'Orsay.*

㊵ Musée Rodin (Rodin Museum). The splendid, 18th-century Hôtel Biron
makes a gracious setting for the sculpture of Auguste Rodin (1840–
1917). In back is a pretty garden with Rodin sculptures and hundreds
of rosebushes. ⊠ *77 rue de Varenne,* ☎ *01–44–18–61–10.* ⓧ *Tues.–
Sun. 10–5. Métro: Varenne.*

㊴ Palais Bourbon. The 18th-century home of the **Assemblée Nationale**
(French National Legislature) is only open during temporary exhibitions, but its colonnaded facade, commissioned by Napoléon, is a
handsome sight. ⊠ *Pl. du Palais-Bourbon. Métro: Assemblée Nationale.*

㉚ St-Germain-des-Prés. The oldest church in Paris was first built to shelter a relic of the true cross, brought back from Spain in AD 542. The chancel was enlarged and the church consecrated by Pope Alexander III in 1163 (the church tower dates from this period). ⊠ *Pl. St-Germain-des-Prés.* ⊘ *Weekdays 8–7:30, weekends 8 AM–9 PM. Métro: St-Germain-des-Prés.*

㉟ St-Sulpice. Stand back and admire the impressive 18th-century facade of this enormous 17th-century church. The unequal, unfinished towers strike a quirky, fallible note at odds with the chillingly impersonal interior, embellished only by the masterly wall paintings by Delacroix— notably *Jacob and the Angel*—in the first chapel on the right. ⊠ *Pl. St-Sulpice. Métro: St-Sulpice.*

Montmartre

On a dramatic rise above the city is Montmartre, site of the Sacré-Coeur Basilica and home to a once-thriving artistic community. Visiting Montmartre means negotiating a lot of steep streets and flights of steps.

㊹ Musée de Montmartre (Montmartre Museum). In its turn-of-the-century heyday, Montmartre's historical museum was home to an illustrious group of painters, writers, and assorted cabaret artists. ⊠ *12 rue Cortot,* ☎ *01–46–06–61–11.* ⊘ *Tues.–Sun. 11–6. Métro: Lamarck-Caulaincourt.*

㊸ Place des Abbesses. This triangular square is typical of the picturesque, slightly countrified style that has made Montmartre famous. The entrance to the Abbesses métro station, a curving, sensuous mass of delicate iron, is one of Guimard's two original Art Nouveau entrance canopies left in Paris. *Métro: Abbesses.*

㊷ Sacré-Coeur. If you start at the Anvers métro station and head up rue de Steinkerque (full of budget clothing shops), you'll be greeted by the most familiar and spectacular view of the Sacré-Coeur, perched proudly atop the Butte Montmartre. The basilica was built in a bizarre, mock-Byzantine style between 1876 and 1910; although no favorite with aesthetes, it has become a major Paris landmark. It was constructed as an act of national penitence after the disastrous Franco-Prussian War of 1870—a Catholic show of strength at a time of bitter church-state conflict. ⊠ *Pl. du Parvis-du-Sacré-Coeur. Métro: Anvers.*

Off the Beaten Path

㊺ Bercy. This colorful district, tucked away on the Right Bank of the Seine, south of the Gare de Lyon in the 12ᵉ arrondissement and opposite the new national library, was for centuries filled with warehouses storing wine from the provinces. Some of the old warehouses have been renovated, but most have been replaced by the **Parc de Bercy**, a witty, state-of-the art garden. The mighty glass wall of the **Ministère des Finances** (Finance Ministry) looms up at one end, beyond the sloping, grass-walled **Palais Omnisports** indoor stadium. Nearby, Frank Gehry's quirky, cubistic former **American Center** was set to open as a movie theater complex by 2000. ⊠ *rue de Bercy. Métro: Bercy, Cour St-Emilion.*

㊻ Bibliothèque François-Mitterrand (National Library). The last of late president Mitterrand's grand building projects opened in early 1997. Architect Dominique Perault's controversial design features four soaring 24-story L-shape towers (meant to resemble open books) around a stunning interior courtyard of tall evergreens—sunk beneath ground level. ⊠ *11 quai François-Mauriac,* ☎ *01–53–79–59–59.* ⊘ *Tues.–Sat. 10–7, Sun. noon–6. Métro: Bibliothèque.*

㊼ Cimetière du Père-Lachaise (Father Lachaise Cemetery). This cemetery forms a veritable necropolis with cobbled avenues and tombs competing in pomposity and originality. Leading incumbents include Frédéric

Chopin, Marcel Proust, Jim Morrison, Edith Piaf, and Gertrude Stein. Get a map at the entrance and track them down. ⊠ *Entrances on rue des Rondeaux, bd. de Ménilmontant, and rue de la Réunion.* ☉ *Apr.– Sept., daily 8–6; Oct.–Mar., daily 8–5. Métro: Père-Lachaise, Gambetta, Philippe-Auguste.*

㊽ **La Défense.** If you're interested in modern architecture, you'll be stimulated by the variety of skyscrapers clustered around the sculpture-littered plaza in this contemporary suburb, just west of Paris. The most famous building is the **Grande Arche,** a huge hollow cube crowning the majestic vista that extends from the Louvre via the Arc de Triomphe. Tubular glass elevators whisk you to the top. ☉ *Grande Arche: daily 10–7. Métro: Grande Arche de La Défense.*

Dining

Left Bank

$$$ ✕ **Le Violon d'Ingres.** Christian Constant, former head chef of the Hôtel
★ Crillon, has created a hit with his own well-heeled bistro. The regularly revised menu may include such dishes as cream of pumpkin soup with sheep's cheese, and guinea hen on a bed of diced turnips. ⊠ *135 rue St-Dominique,* ☎ *01–45–44–15–05. Reservations essential. AE, DC, MC, V. Closed Sun., Mon. Métro: École-Militaire.*

$$ ✕ **Alcazar.** Englishman Sir Terence Conran's stunning, large new brasserie is one of the chicest spots in town. Young French chef Guillaume Lutard has created a regularly changing, appealingly classic menu. Note that there's a separate and less expensive bar menu—a good option for a quick, casual bite. ⊠ *62 rue Mazarine,* ☎ *01–53–10–19–99. Reservations essential. AE, DC, MC, V. Métro: Odéon.*

$$ ✕ **Campagne et Provence.** On the quai across from Notre-Dame, this pleasant little restaurant serves Provençal cuisine including grilled John Dory with preserved fennel, and peppers stuffed with cod and eggplant. ⊠ *25 quai de la Tournelle, 5ᵉ,* ☎ *01–43–54–05–17. MC, V. Closed Sun. No lunch Sat., Mon. Métro: Maubert-Mutualité.*

$$ ✕ **Philippe Detourbe.** Sample Detourbe's spectacular food at remark-
★ ably good prices amid black lacquer, mirrors, and Burgundy velvet upholstery. The menu of contemporary French cooking changes with every meal. ⊠ *8 rue Nicolas Charlet, 15ᵉ,* ☎ *01–42–19–08–59. Reservations essential. MC, V. Closed Sun. No lunch Sat. Métro: Pasteur.*

$–$$ ✕ **Au Bon Accueil.** Book a table at this popular bistro as soon as you get to town. The excellent *cuisine du marché* (menu based on what's in the markets that day) has made it a hit, as have the delicious, homemade desserts. ⊠ *14 rue de Montessuy, 7ᵉ,* ☎ *01–47–05–46–11. Reservations essential. MC, V. Closed Sun. Métro, RER: Pont l'Alma.*

$ ✕ **Le Bouillon Racine.** Originally a *bouillon,* a Parisian soup restaurant popular at the turn of the century, this two-story place is now a delightfully renovated Belle Epoque oasis with a good Franco-Belgian menu. ⊠ *3 rue Racine, 6ᵉ,* ☎ *01–44–32–15–60. Reservations essential. AE, MC, V. Closed Sun. Métro: Odéon.*

$ ✕ **Le Terroir.** A jolly crowd of regulars makes this little bistro festive. The solidly classical menu includes an assortment of salads, and calves' liver, or monkfish with saffron. ⊠ *11 bd. Arago, 13ᵉ,* ☎ *01–47–07–36–99. AE, MC, V. Closed Sun. No lunch Sat. Métro: Les Gobelins.*

Right Bank

$$$$ ✕ **Le Grand Véfour.** Luminaries from Napoléon to Colette to Jean Cocteau frequented this intimate and sumptuous address under the arcades of the Palais-Royal. Chef Guy Martin impresses with his unique blend of such sophisticated yet rustic dishes as roast lamb in a juice of herbs. ⊠ *17 rue Beaujolais, 1ᵉʳ,* ☎ *01–42–96–56–27. Reservations es-*

sential 1 wk in advance. Jacket and tie. AE, DC, MC, V. Closed weekends and Aug. Métro: Palais-Royal.

$$$$ ✕ **Guy Savoy.** Top chef Guy Savoy's other five bistros have not distracted him too much from his handsome luxury restaurant near the Arc de Triomphe. The oysters in aspic, and grilled pigeon reveal the magnitude of his talent. ✉ 18 rue Troyon, 17e, ☎ 01–43–80–40–61. AE, MC, V. Closed Sun. No lunch Sat. Métro: Charles-de-Gaulle–Étoile.

$$$$ ✕ **Pierre Gagnaire.** Legendary chef Pierre Gagnaire's cooking is at once ★ intellectual and poetic—unexpected tastes and textures are brought together in a sensational experience. The only drawback is the amateurish service and the puzzlingly brief wine list. ✉ 6 rue de Balzac, 8e, ☎ 01–44–35–18–25. Reservations essential. AE, DC, MC, V. Closed Sun. Métro: Charles-de-Gaulle–Étoile.

$$ ✕ **Chardenoux.** A bit off the beaten path but well worth the effort, this cozy neighborhood bistro with etched-glass windows, dark bentwood furniture, and a long zinc bar attracts a cross section of savvy Parisians. The traditional cooking is first rate, from the delicious foie gras salad to the veal chop with morels. ✉ 1 rue Jules-Valles, 11e, ☎ 01–43–71–49–52. AE, V. Closed weekends and Aug. Métro: Charonne.

$$ ✕ **Chez Georges.** The traditional bistro cooking is good—herring, sole, kidneys, steak, and frîtes (fries)—but the atmosphere is better. A wood-paneled entry leads you to an elegant and unpretentious dining room where one long, white-clothed stretch of table lines the mirrored walls. ✉ 1 rue du Mail, 2e, ☎ 01–42–60–07–11. AE, DC, MC, V. Closed Sun. and Aug. Métro: Sentier.

$$ ✕ **Le Repaire de Cartouche.** Near the Cirque d'Hiver in the Bastille, this split-level, '50s-style bistro with dark-wood decor is the latest good-value sensation in Paris. Young chef Rodolphe Paquin is a creative and impeccably trained cook who does a stylish take on earthy French regional dishes. ✉ 99 rue Amelot, 11e, ☎ 01–47–00–25–86. Reservations essential. AE, MC, V. Closed Sun. No dinner Mon. Métro: Filles du Calvaire.

$$ ✕ **Sébillon.** The original Sébillon has nurtured residents of the fashionable suburb of Neuilly for generations; this elegant, polished branch off the Champs-Élysées continues the tradition. The menu includes lobster salad, lots of shellfish, and—the specialty—roast leg of lamb sliced table-side. ✉ 66 rue Pierre Charron, ☎ 01–43–59–28–15. AE, DC, MC, V. Métro: Franklin-D.-Roosevelt.

$–$$ ✕ **Bofinger.** Settle in to one of the tables dressed in crisp white linens, under the gorgeous Art Nouveau glass cupola, and enjoy fine classic brasserie fare, such as oysters, grilled sole, or fillet of lamb. Note that the no-smoking section here is not only enforced, but is also in the prettiest part of the restaurant. ✉ 5–7 rue de la Bastille, ☎ 01–42–72–87–82. AE, DC, MC, V. Métro: Bastille.

$–$$ ✕ **Chez Michel.** If you're willing to go out of your way for excellent food at fair prices, even if the decor and the neighborhood are drab, then this place is for you. Chef Thierry Breton pulls a stylish crowd with his wonderful cuisine du marché and dishes from his native Brittany, including lasagna stuffed with chèvre cheese. ✉ 10 rue Belzunce, 10e, ☎ 01–44–53–06–20. Reservations essential. MC, V. Closed Sun., Mon. No lunch Sat. Métro: Gare du Nord.

Lodging

Left Bank

$$$$ ⊡ **Montalembert.** Whether appointed with traditional or contemporary furnishings, rooms at the Montalembert are all about simple lines and chic luxury. Ask about special packages if you're staying for more than three nights. ✉ 3 rue de Montalembert, 75007, ☎ 01–45–49–

68–68, 800/628–8929 *in the U.S.,* FAX *01–45–49–69–49. 50 rooms, 6 suites. Restaurant, bar. AE, DC, MC, V. Métro: Rue du Bac.*

$$$$ ⊞ **Relais St-Germain.** The interior-designer owners of this hotel have
★ exquisite taste and a superb respect for tradition and detail. Moreover, rooms are at least twice the size of those at other area hotels. Much of the furniture was selected with a knowledgeable eye from the city's *brocantes* (secondhand dealers). Breakfast is included. ⊠ *9 carrefour de l'Odéon, 75006,* ☎ *01–43–29–12–05,* FAX *01–46–33–45–30. 21 rooms, 1 suite. AE, DC, MC, V. Métro: Odéon.*

$$$ ⊞ **Jardin du Luxembourg.** Blessed with a charming staff and a stylish look, this hotel is one of the most sought-after in the Latin Quarter. Rooms are a bit small (common for this neighborhood) but intelligently furnished to save space, and warmly decorated *à la provençale*. Ask for one with a balcony overlooking the street. ⊠ *5 impasse Royer-Collard, 75005,* ☎ *01–40–46–08–88,* FAX *01–40–46–02–28. 27 rooms. AE, DC, MC, V. Métro: Luxembourg.*

$$–$$$ ⊞ **Le Tourville.** Here is a rare find: an intimate, upscale hotel at affordable
★ prices. Each room has crisp, virgin-white damask upholstery set against pastel or ocher walls, a smattering of antiques, original artwork, and fabulous old mirrors. ⊠ *16 av. de Tourville, 75007,* ☎ *01–47–05–62–62, 800/528–3549 in the U.S.,* FAX *01–47–05–43–90. 27 rooms, 3 junior suites. Bar. AE, DC, MC, V. Métro: École Militaire.*

$$ ⊞ **Atelier Montparnasse.** This Art Deco–inspired gem was designed with style and comfort in mind. Rooms are tastefully decorated and spacious; one sleeps three. The hotel is within walking distance of the Luxembourg Gardens and St-Germain-des-Prés. ⊠ *49 rue Vavin, 75006,* ☎ *01–46–33–60–00,* FAX *01–40–51–04–21. 17 rooms. AE, DC, MC, V. Métro: Vavin.*

$$ ⊞ **Latour Maubourg.** In the residential heart of the 7ᵉ arrondissement, a stone's throw from Les Invalides, this hotel is homey and unpretentious. With just 10 rooms, the accent is on intimacy and personalized service. ⊠ *150 rue de Grenelle, 75007,* ☎ *01–47–05–16–16,* FAX *01–47–05–16–14. 9 rooms, 1 suite. MC, V. Métro: La Tour–Maubourg.*

$ ⊞ **Familia.** The hospitable Gaucheron family bends over backwards for you. About half the rooms feature romantic sepia frescoes of celebrated Paris scenes; others have exquisite Louis XV–style furnishings, or nice mahogany pieces. Book a month ahead for one with a walk-out balcony on the second or fifth floor. ⊠ *11 rue des Écoles, 75005,* ☎ *01–43–54–55–27,* FAX *01–43–29–61–77. 30 rooms, 16 with shower. AE, MC, V. Métro: Cardinal Lemoine.*

Right Bank

$$$$ ⊞ **Costes.** Jean-Louis and Gilbert Costes's sumptuous hotel is the darling of the fashion and media set. Conjuring up the palaces of Napoléon III, rooms are swathed in rich garnet and bronze tones and luxurious fabrics. ⊠ *239 rue St-Honoré, 75001,* ☎ *01–42–44–50–50,* FAX *01–42–44–50–01. 85 rooms. Restaurant, bar. AE, DC, MC, V. Métro: Tuileries.*

$$$$ ⊞ **Lancaster.** The Lancaster—one of Paris's most venerable institutions—
★ has been transformed into one of the city's most modish luxury hotels. A seamless blend of the traditional and the contemporary, it has the overall feel of timeless elegance. ⊠ *7 rue de Berri, 75008,* ☎ *01–40–76–40–76, 800/63–SAVOY in the U.S.,* FAX *01–40–76–40–00. 50 rooms, 10 suites. Restaurant, bar. AE, DC, MC, V. Métro: George-V.*

$$$$ ⊞ **Pavillon de la Reine.** This magnificent hotel, filled with Louis XIII–style fireplaces and antiques, is in a mansion reconstructed from original plans. Ask for a duplex with French windows overlooking the first of two flower-filled courtyards behind the historic Queen's Pavilion. ⊠ *28 Pl. des Vosges, 75003,* ☎ *01–40–29–19–19, 800/447–7462 in*

the U.S., FAX *01–40–29–19–20. 30 rooms, 25 suites. Bar, breakfast room, free parking. AE, DC, MC, V. Métro: Bastille, St-Paul.*

$–$$$ 🏨 **Louvre Forum.** This friendly hotel is a find: Smack in the center of town, it has clean, comfortable, well-equipped rooms (with satellite TV) at extremely reasonable prices. ✉ *25 rue du Bouloi, 75001,* ☎ *01–42–36–54–19,* FAX *01–42–33–66–31. 27 rooms, 16 with shower. AE, DC, MC, V. Métro: Louvre.*

$$ 🏨 **Bretonnerie.** This small hotel is in a 17th-century *hôtel particulier* (town house) on a tiny street in the Marais. Rooms are Louis XIII style, complete with upholstered walls, but vary considerably in size from spacious to cramped. ✉ *22 rue Ste-Croix-de-la-Bretonnerie, 75004,* ☎ *01–48–87–77–63,* FAX *01–42–77–26–78. 27 rooms, 3 suites. MC, V. Métro: Hôtel de Ville.*

$$ 🏨 **Caron de Beaumarchais.** The theme of this intimate jewel is the work
★ of Caron de Beaumarchais, who wrote the *Marriage of Figaro* in 1778. Rooms are faithfully decorated to reflect the taste of 18th-century French nobility. The second- and fifth-floor rooms with balconies are the largest; those on the sixth floor have views across Right Bank rooftops. ✉ *12 rue Vieille-du-Temple, 75004,* ☎ *01–42–72–34–12,* FAX *01–42–72–34–63. 19 rooms, 2 with shower. AE, DC, MC, V. Métro: Hôtel de Ville.*

$ 🏨 **Castex.** In a Revolution-era building in the Marais, this hotel is a bargain hunter's dream. Rooms are low on frills but squeaky clean, the owners are friendly, and the prices are rock-bottom, which ensures that the hotel is often booked months ahead by a largely young, American clientele. There's no elevator, and the only TV is on the ground floor. ✉ *5 rue Castex, 75004,* ☎ *01–42–72–31–52,* FAX *01–42–72–57–91. 27 rooms, 23 with shower. MC, V. Métro: Bastille.*

Nightlife and the Arts

For detailed entertainment listings, look for the weekly magazines *Pariscope, L'Officiel des Spectacles,* and *Figaroscope.* The Paris Tourist Office's 24-hour English-language hot line (☎ 08–36–68–31–12) and Web site (www.paris-touristoffice.com) are also good sources of information about weekly events.

Tickets can be purchased at the place of performance (beware of scalpers: counterfeit tickets have been sold); otherwise, try your hotel or a travel agency such as **Paris-Vision** (✉ 1 rue Auber, 9ᵉ, ☎ 01–40–06–01–00, métro Opéra). For most concerts, tickets can be bought at the music stores **FNAC** (✉ 1–5 rue Pierre Lescot, Forum des Halles, 1ᵉʳ, ☎ 01–49–87–50–50, métro Châtelet–Les Halles) or **Virgin Megastore** (✉ 52 av. des Champs-Élysées, 8ᵉ, ☎ 08–03–02–30–24, métro Franklin-D.-Roosevelt). Half-price tickets for same-day theater performances are available at the **Kiosques Théâtre** (✉ across from 15 Pl. de la Madeleine, métro Madeleine), and in front of the Gare Montparnasse (✉ at Pl. Raoul Dautry, 14ᵉ, métro Montparnasse-Bienvenüe). Both are open Tuesday–Saturday 12:30–8, and Sunday 12:30–4. Expect to pay a 16-franc commission per ticket and to wait in line.

The Arts

CLASSICAL MUSIC AND OPERA

Inexpensive organ or chamber music concerts take place in many churches throughout the city. Following are other venues for orchestral concerts and recitals. **Cité de la Musique** (✉ in the Parc de La Villette, 221 av. Jean-Jaurès, 19ᵉ, ☎ 01–44–84–44–84, métro Porte de Pantin). **Opéra de la Bastille** (✉ Pl. de la Bastille, 12ᵉ, ☎ 08–36–69–78–68, métro Bastille). **Salle Pleyel** (✉ 252 rue du Faubourg-St-Honoré, 8ᵉ, ☎ 01–45–61–53–00, métro Ternes). **Théâtre des Champs-**

Élysées (⊠ 15 av. Montaigne, 8ᵉ, ☎ 01–49–52–50–50, métro Alma-Marceau).

Opéra Garnier (⊠ Pl. de l'Opéra, 9ᵉ, ☎ 08–36–69–78–68, métro Opéra), the "old Opéra," now concentrates on dance: In addition to being the home of the well-reputed Paris Ballet, it also bills a number of major foreign troupes. The **Théâtre de la Ville** (⊠ 2 Pl. du Châtelet, 4ᵉ, métro Châtelet, and ⊠ 31 rue des Abbesses, 18ᵉ, métro Abbesses, ☎ 01–42–74–22–77 for both) is the place for contemporary dance.

Paris has hundreds of cinemas. Admission is generally 40–50 francs, with reduced rates at some theaters on Monday. In principal tourist areas such as the Champs-Élysées and Les Halles, and on the boulevard des Italiens near the Opéra, theaters show English films marked *version originale* (v.o., i.e., not dubbed). Classics and independent films often play in Latin Quarter theaters. **Cinémathèque Française** (⊠ 42 bd. de Bonne-Nouvelle, 10ᵉ, ☎ 01–47–04–24–24, métro Bonne-Nouvelle, and ⊠ Palais de Chaillot, 7 av. Albert de Mun, ☎ 01–55–73–16–80, métro Trocadéro) shows classic French and international films Wednesday–Sunday.

There is no Parisian equivalent to Broadway or the West End, although a number of theaters line the grand boulevards between the Opéra and République. Shows are mostly in French. The **Comédie Française** (⊠ Pl. André-Malraux, 1ᵉʳ, ☎ 01–44–58–15–15, métro Palais-Royal) performs distinguished classical drama by the likes of Racine, Molière, and Corneille. The **Théâtre de la Huchette** (⊠ 23 rue de la Huchette, 5ᵉ, ☎ 01–43–26–38–99, métro St-Michel) is a tiny venue where Ionesco's short plays make a deliberately ridiculous mess of the French language. The **Théâtre de l'Odéon** (⊠ Pl. de l'Odéon, 6ᵉ, ☎ 01–44–41–36–36, métro Odéon) has made pan-European theater its primary focus.

Nightlife

The hottest area at the moment is around Ménilmontant and Parmentier, and the nightlife is still hopping in and around the Bastille. The Left Bank tends to be more subdued. The Champs-Élysées is making a strong comeback, though the crowd remains predominantly foreign. Gay and lesbian bars are mostly concentrated in the Marais (especially around rue Ste-Croix-de-la-Bretonnerie) and include some of the most happening addresses in the city.

If you want to dance the night away, some of the best clubs are the following: **Les Bains** (⊠ 7 rue du Bourg-l'Abbé, 3ᵉ, ☎ 01–48–87–01–80, métro Etienne-Marcel). **Le Cabaret** (⊠ 68 rue Pierre-Charron, 8ᵉ, ☎ 01–42–89–44–14, métro Franklin-D.-Roosevelt). **Queen** (⊠ 102 av. des Champs-Élysées, 8ᵉ, ☎ 01–53–89–08–90, métro George-V).

Paris has many bars; following is a sampling: **Amnésia Café** (⊠ 42 rue Vieille-du-Temple, 4ᵉ, ☎ 01–42–72–16–94, métro St-Paul), which attracts a young, professional gay and lesbian crowd. **Café Charbon** (⊠ 109 rue Oberkampf, 11ᵉ, ☎ 01–43–57–55–13, métro St-Maur/Parmentier), in a beautifully restored 19th-century café. **Le Fumoir** (⊠ 6 rue Amiral de Coligny, 1ᵉʳ, ☎ 01–42–92–00–24, métro Louvre), a fashionable spot for cocktails, with comfy leather sofas and a library. **Man Ray** (⊠ 34 rue Marbeuf, 8ᵉ, ☎ 01–56–88–36–36, métro Franklin-D.-Roosevelt), owned by Sean Penn, Johnny Depp, and Mick Hucknall, has a mezzanine bar overlooking the Asian–Art Deco dining room. **Le What's Up** (⊠ 15 rue Daval, 11ᵉ, ☎ 01–48–05–88–33, métro Bastille) is a trendy bar with modern decor and DJs who mix house and garage music from 10:30 PM on.

CABARETS

Paris's cabarets are household names, shunned by Parisians and beloved of foreign tourists, who flock to the shows. Prices range from 200 francs (simple admission plus one drink) to more than 800 francs (dinner plus show). **Crazy Horse** (⊠ 12 av. George V, 8ᵉ, ☎ 01–47–23–32–32, métro Alma-Marceau). **Lido** (⊠ 116 bis av. des Champs-Élysées, 8ᵉ, ☎ 01–40–76–56–10, métro George-V). **Moulin Rouge** (⊠ Pl. Blanche, 18ᵉ, ☎ 01–53–09–82–82, métro Blanche).

JAZZ CLUBS

Paris is one of the great jazz cities of the world. For nightly schedules consult the magazines *Jazz Hot* or *Jazz Magazine*. Nothing gets going till 10 or 11 PM, and entry prices vary widely from about 40 francs to over 100 francs. **New Morning** (⊠ 7 rue des Petites-Ecuries, 10ᵉ, ☎ 01–45–23–51–41, métro Château-d'Eau) is a premier spot for serious fans of avant-garde jazz, folk, and world music. The greatest names in French and international jazz play at **Le Petit Journal** (⊠ 71 bd. St-Michel, 5ᵉ, ☎ 01–43–26–28–59, RER Luxembourg); it's closed Sunday. **Le Petit Opportun** (⊠ 15 rue des Lavandières-Ste-Opportune, 1ᵉʳ, ☎ 01–42–36–01–36, métro Châtelet), in a converted bistro, often has top-flight American soloists with French backup.

ROCK CLUBS

Lists of upcoming concerts are posted on boards in the FNAC stores. Following are the best places to catch big French and international stars: **L'Olympia** (⊠ 28 bd. des Capucines, 9ᵉ, ☎ 01–47–42–25–49, métro Opéra) and **Zenith** (⊠ Parc de La Villette, 19ᵉ, ☎ 01–42–08–60–00, métro Porte-de-Pantin). For emerging talent and lesser known groups, try **Bataclan** (⊠ 50 bd. Voltaire, 11ᵉ, ☎ 01–48–06–28–12, métro Oberkampf) and **L'Élysée Montmartre** (⊠ 72 bd. Rochechouart, 18ᵉ, ☎ 01–44–92–45–45, métro Anvers).

Shopping

Boutiques

Only Milan can compete with Paris for the title of Capital of European Chic. The top designer shops are found on **avenue Montaigne, rue du Faubourg-St-Honoré,** and **Place des Victoires.** The area around **St-Germain-des-Prés** on the Left Bank is a mecca for small specialty shops and boutiques, and has recently seen an influx of the elite names in haute couture. The top names in jewelry are grouped around the **Place Vendôme** and scores of trendy boutiques can be found around **Les Halles.** Between the pre-Revolution mansions and tiny kosher food stores that characterize the **Marais** are numerous gift shops and clothing stores. Search for bargains on the streets around the foot of Montmartre, or in the designer discount shops (Cacharel, Rykiel, Chevignon) along **rue d'Alésia** in Montparnasse.

Department Stores

Au Bon Marché (⊠ 22 rue de Sèvres, 7ᵉ, métro Sèvres-Babylone). **Au Printemps** (⊠ 64 bd. Haussmann, 9ᵉ, métro Havre-Caumartin). **Galeries Lafayette** (⊠ 40 bd. Haussmann, 9ᵉ, métro Chaussée-d'Antin). **La Samaritaine** (⊠ 19 rue de la Monnaie, 1ᵉʳ, métro Pont-Neuf). **Marks & Spencer** (⊠ 35 bd. Haussmann, 9ᵉ, ☎ 01–47–42–42–91, métro Havre-Caumartin, Auber, or Opéra).

Food and Flea Markets

Every *quartier* (neighborhood) has at least one open-air food market. Some of the best are on rue de Buci, rue Mouffetard, rue Montorgueil, rue Mouffetard, and rue Lepic. Sunday morning till 1 PM is usually a good time to go; they are likely to be closed Monday.

The **Marché aux Puces de St-Ouen** (métro Porte de Clignancourt), just north of Paris, is one of Europe's largest flea markets; it's open Saturday–Monday. Best bargains are to be had early in the morning. Smaller flea markets also take place at **Porte de Vanves** and **Porte de Montreuil** (weekends only).

Gifts

Old prints are sold by **bouquinistes** (secondhand booksellers) in stalls along the banks of the Seine. **Le Cave Augé** (✉ 116 bd. Haussmann, 8e, métro St-Augustin) is one of the best wine shops in Paris. **Fauchon** (✉ 30 Pl. de la Madeleine, 8e, métro Madeleine) and **Hédiard** (✉ 21 Pl. de la Madeleine, 8e, métro Madeleine) are two gourmet food shops. **Guerlain** (✉ 47 rue Bonaparte, 6e, métro Mabillon) carries legendary French perfumes. The **Maison du Chocolat** (✉ 56 rue Pierre-Charron, 8e, ☎ 01–47–23–38–25, métro Franklin-D.-Roosevelt; ✉ 8 bd. de la Madeleine, 9e, ☎ 01–47–42–86–52, métro Madeleine; ✉ 225 rue du Faubourg St-Honoré, 8e, ☎ 01–42–27–39–44, métro Ternes) is the place for chocolate. The **Musée des Arts Décoratifs** (✉ 107 rue de Rivoli, 1er, métro Palais-Royal) has state-of-the-art home decorations.

Paris Essentials

Arriving and Departing

BY BUS

See By Bus *in* Transportation *in* France A to Z, *above.*

BY CAR

Expressways converge on the capital from every direction: A1 from the north (225 km/140 mi to Lille); A13 from Normandy (225 km/140 mi to Caen); A4 from the east (500 km/310 mi to Strasbourg); A10 from the southwest (580 km/360 mi to Bordeaux); and A7 from the Alps and Côte d'Azur (466 km/290 mi to Lyon). Each connects with the *périphérique,* the beltway, around Paris. Exits are named by *porte* (gateway), not numbered. The "Périphe" can be fast—but gets very busy; try to avoid it between 7:30 and 10 AM and between 4:30 and 7:30 PM.

BY PLANE

International flights arrive at either **Charles de Gaulle Airport** (known as Roissy to the French), 24 km (15 mi) northeast of Paris, or at **Orly Airport,** 16 km (10 mi) south of the city. Both airports have two terminals.

Between the Airport and Downtown. Both airports have train stations from which you can take the **RER,** the local commuter train, to Paris. The advantages of this are speed, price (48 frs to Paris from Roissy, 57 frs from Orly via the shuttle-train Orlyval with a change to the RER at Antony), and the RER's direct link with the métro system. The disadvantage is having to lug your bags around. **Taxi** fares between the airports and Paris are about 160 francs (Orly) and 230 francs (Roissy), with a 6-franc surcharge per bag. The **Paris Airports Service** (☎ 01–49–62–78–78, FAX 01–49–62–78–79) takes you by eight-passenger van to your destination in Paris from Roissy: 140 francs (one person) or 170 francs (two); Orly: 110 francs (one), 130 francs (two), less for groups. You need to book at least two days in advance (there are English-speaking clerks).

From Roissy **Air France Buses** (open to all) leave every 15 minutes from 5:40 AM to 11 PM. The fare is 60 francs and the trip takes from 40 minutes to 1½ hours during rush hour. You arrive at the Arc de Triomphe or Porte Maillot, on the Right Bank by the Hôtel Concorde-Lafayette.

From Orly, buses operated by Air France leave every 12 minutes from 6 AM to 11 PM and arrive at the Air France terminal near Les Invalides on the Left Bank. The fare is 45 francs, and the trip takes between 30 and 60 minutes, depending on traffic. Alternatively, the **Roissybus,** operated by Paris Transport Authority (RATP), runs directly to and from rue Scribe, by the Opéra, every 15 minutes and costs 45 francs. RATP also runs the **Orlybus** to and from Denfert-Rochereau and Orly every 15 minutes for 35 francs; the trip takes around 35 minutes.

BY TRAIN

Paris has five international stations: **Gare du Nord** (for northern France, northern Europe, and England via Calais or the Channel Tunnel); **Gare de l'Est** (for Strasbourg, Luxembourg, Basel, and central Europe); **Gare de Lyon** (for Lyon, Marseille, the Côte d'Azur, Geneva, and Italy); **Gare d'Austerlitz** (for the Loire Valley, southwest France, and Spain); and **Gare St-Lazare** (for Normandy and England via Dieppe). The **Gare Montparnasse** serves western France (mainly Nantes and Brittany) and is the terminal for the TGV Atlantic service from Paris to Bordeaux. Call **SNCF** (☎ 08–36–35–35–35) for information. You can reserve tickets at any Paris station regardless of the destination. Go to the Grandes Lignes counter for travel within France or to the Billets Internationaux desk if you're heading out of France.

Getting Around

Paris is relatively small as capital cities go, and most of its prize monuments and museums are within walking distance of one another. A river cruise is a pleasant way to get an overview. The most convenient form of public transportation is the métro; buses are a slower alternative, though they do allow you to see more of the city. Taxis are not that expensive, but are not always so easy to find. Car travel within Paris is best avoided because finding parking is difficult and there is often a lot of traffic.

BY BUS

Most buses run from around 6 AM to 8:30 PM; some continue until midnight. Routes are posted on the sides of buses. *Noctambus* (night buses) operate from 1 AM to 6 AM between Châtelet and nearby suburbs. They can be stopped by hailing them at any point on their route. You can use your métro tickets on the buses, or you can buy a one-ride ticket on board. You need to show weekly/monthly/special tickets to the driver; if you have individual tickets, state your destination and be prepared to punch one or more tickets in the red and gray machines on board the bus.

BY MÉTRO

Thirteen métro lines crisscross Paris and the nearby suburbs, and you are seldom more than a five-minute walk from the nearest station. It's essential to know the name of the last station on the line you take, since this name appears on all signs within the system. A connection (you can make as many as you please on one ticket) is called a *correspondânce.* At junction stations illuminated orange signs bearing the names of each line terminus appear over the corridors that lead to the various correspondances.

The métro connects at several points in Paris with RER trains that race across Paris from suburb to suburb: RER trains are a sort of supersonic métro and can be great time-savers. All métro tickets and passes are valid for RER and bus travel within Paris.

The métro runs from 5:30 AM to 1:15 AM. Some lines and stations in the seedier parts of Paris are a bit risky at night—in particular, Line 2 (Porte-Dauphine–Nation) and the northern section of Line 13 from St-

Paris Métro

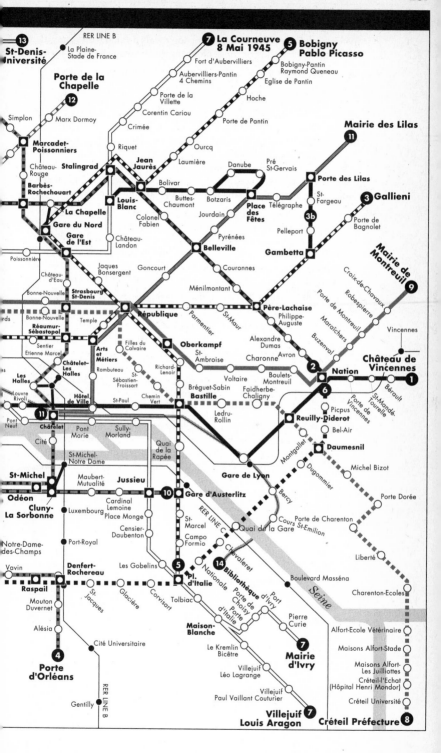

Lazare to St-Denis/Asnières. The long, bleak corridors at Jaurès and Stalingrad are a haven for pickpockets and purse snatchers. But the Paris métro is relatively safe, as long as you don't walk around with your wallet in your back pocket or travel alone (especially women) late at night.

Métro tickets cost 8 francs each, though a *carnet* (10 tickets for 52 frs) is a far better value. If you're staying for a week or more, the best deal is the *coupon jaune* (weekly) or *carte orange* (monthly) ticket, sold according to zone. Zones 1 and 2 cover the entire métro network (80 frs per week or 271 frs per month). If you plan to take a suburban train to visit monuments in the Ile-de-France, you should consider a four-zone ticket (Versailles, St-Germain-en-Laye; 134 frs per week) or a six-zone ticket (Rambouillet, Fontainebleau; 184 frs per week). For these weekly or monthly tickets, you need a pass (available from train and major métro stations), and you must provide a passport-size photograph.

Alternatively there are one-day (*Mobilis*) and two-, three-, and five-day (*Paris Visite*) unlimited travel tickets for the métro, bus, and RER. Unlike the coupon jaune, which is good from Monday morning to Sunday evening, the latter are valid starting any day of the week and give you admission discounts to a limited number of museums and tourist attractions. Prices are 30, 90, 120, and 175 francs for Paris only; 100, 175, 245, and 300 francs for the suburbs, including Versailles, St-Germain-en-Laye, and Disneyland Paris.

Access to métro and RER platforms is through an automatic ticket barrier. Slide your ticket in flat and pick it up as it pops up farther along. Keep your ticket; you'll need it again to leave the RER system. Sometimes green-clad métro authorities will ask to see it when you enter or leave the station: Be prepared—they aren't very friendly, and they will impose a large fine if you can't produce your ticket.

BY TAXI

Taxis in Paris aren't a standard vehicle type or color. Daytime rates (7 to 7) within Paris are about 2.80 francs per km (½ mi), and nighttime rates are around 4.50 francs, plus a basic charge of 13 francs. Rates outside the city limits are about 40% higher. Ask your hotel or restaurant to call for a taxi, since cruising cabs can be hard to find. There are numerous taxi stands, but you have to know where to look. Taxis seldom take more than three people at a time.

Contacts and Resources

EMBASSIES

Australia (4 rue Jean-Rey, 15ᵉ, ☎ 01–40–59–33–00, métro Bir Hakeim). **Canada** (✉ 35 av. Montaigne, 8ᵉ, ☎ 01–44–43–29–00, métro Franklin-D.-Roosevelt). **United Kingdom** (✉ 35 rue du Faubourg–St-Honoré, 8ᵉ, ☎ 01–44–51–31–00, métro Concorde). **United States** (✉ 2 av. Gabriel, 8ᵉ, ☎ 01–43–12–22–22, métro Concorde). **New Zealand** (7 ter rue Léonardo da Vinci, 16ᵉ, ☎ 01–45–00–24–11, métro Victor Hugo).

EMERGENCIES

Police (☎ 17). Automatic phone booths can be found at various main crossroads for use in police emergencies (Police-Secours) or for medical help (Services Médicaux). **Ambulance** (☎ 15 for emergencies, or 01–45–67–50–50). **Dentist** (☎ 01–43–37–51–00), open 24 hrs. **Doctor** (☎ 01–47–37–77–77).

Hospitals: American Hospital (✉ 63 bd. Victor-Hugo, Neuilly, ☎ 01–47–45–71–00); **British Hospital** (✉ 3 rue Barbès, Levallois-Perret, ☎ 01–47–58–13–12).

Pharmacies: Les Champs (⊠ 84 av. des Champs-Élysées, ☎ 01–45–62–02–41), open 24 hrs; **Pharmacie des Arts** (⊠ 106 bd. Montparnasse, 6ᵉ, ☎ 01–43–35–44–88), open until midnight.

ENGLISH-LANGUAGE BOOKSTORES

Most newsstands in central Paris sell *Time, Newsweek,* and the *International Herald Tribune,* as well as the English dailies. Some English-language bookstores include: **Brentano's** (⊠ 37 av. de l'Opéra); **Shakespeare & Co.** (⊠ 37 rue de la Bûcherie); and **W. H. Smith** (⊠ 248 rue de Rivoli).

GUIDED TOURS

Bicycle Tours: Paris à Vélo (⊠ 37 bd Bourdon, 4ᵉ, ☎ 01–48–87–60–01) organizes three-hour cycling tours around Paris and rents bikes for 80 francs a day.

Boat Tours: Boat rides along the Seine are a must if it's your first time in Paris. The price for a 60-minute trip is 40–50 francs. Boats depart in season every half hour from 10:30 to 5 (less frequently in winter). The **Bateaux Mouches** leave from the Pont de l'Alma, at the bottom of avenue George-V. The **Bateaux Parisiens** leave from the Pont d'Iéna, by the Eiffel Tower. The **Vedettes du Pont-Neuf** set off from beneath square du Vert-Galant on the western edge of the Ile de la Cité.

Bus Tours: Bus tours of Paris provide a good introduction to the city. Tours usually start from the tour company's office and are generally given in double-decker buses with either a live guide or tape-recorded commentary. They last two to three hours and cost about 150 francs. Tour operators also have a variety of theme tours (historic Paris, modern Paris, Paris by night) that last from 2½ hours to all day and cost up to 390 francs, as well as half- and full-day excursions to Chartres, Versailles, Fontainebleau, the Loire Valley, and Mont-St-Michel (for a cost of 195–970 francs). **Cityrama** (⊠ 4 Pl. des Pyramides, 1ᵉʳ, ☎ 01–44–55–61–00) is one of the largest bus operators in Paris; it also runs minibus excursions that pick you up and drop you off at your hotel. **Paris Vision** (⊠ 214 rue de Rivoli, 1ᵉʳ, ☎ 01–42–60–31–25) is another large bus tour operator.

Personal Guides: Tours of Paris or the surrounding areas by limousine or minibus for up to seven passengers for a minimum of three hours can be organized. The cost starts at about 250 francs per hour. Contact: **International Limousines** (⊠ 182 bd. Pereire, 17ᵉ, ☎ 01–53–81–14–14); **Paris Bus** (⊠ 22 rue de la Prévoyance, Vincennes, ☎ 01–43–65–55–55); and **Touringscope** (⊠ 11 bis bd. Haussmann, 9ᵉ, ☎ 01–53–34–11–91).

Walking Tours: Numerous special-interest tours concentrate on historical or architectural topics. Most are in French and cost between 40 and 60 francs. Details are published in the weekly magazines *Pariscope* and *L'Officiel des Spectacles* under the heading "Conférences."

TRAVEL AGENCIES

American Express (⊠ 11 rue Scribe, 9ᵉ, ☎ 01–47–77–77–07). **Wagons-Lits** (⊠ 32 rue du Quatre-Septembre, 2ᵉ, ☎ 01–42–66–15–80).

VISITOR INFORMATION

The **Paris Tourist Office** (⊠ 127 av. des Champs-Élysées, ☎ 01–49–52–53–54; 01–49–52–53–56 for recorded information in English) is open daily 9–8. It has branches at all mainline train stations except Gare St-Lazare.

ILE-DE-FRANCE

The region surrounding Paris is called Ile-de-France, although it isn't actually an *île* (island). But the area is figuratively isolated from the rest of France by three rivers—the Seine, the Oise, and the Marne—that weave meandering circles around its periphery. If you are visiting Paris—and France—for the first time, this is an excellent place to get a taste of French provincial life, with its palpably slower pace.

Parts of the area are fighting a losing battle against the encroaching capital, but you can still see the countryside that was the inspiration for the Impressionists and other 19th-century painters, as well as the wealth of architecture dating from the Middle Ages and Renaissance. The most famous sights are Chartres—one of the most beautiful French cathedrals—and Versailles, the monumental château of Louis XIV, the Sun King. Before the completion of Versailles, king and court resided in the delightful château of St-Germain-en-Laye, west of Paris—an easy day trip from the capital, as are the châteaux of Vaux-le-Vicomte, Rambouillet, and Fontainebleau, and Disneyland Paris.

The region can be covered in a series of loops: Travel west from Paris to see Versailles, Rambouillet, and Chartres; east to Disneyland; and southeast to Fontainebleau, Barbizon, and Vaux-le-Vicomte. Most of these sights are under 80 km (50 mi) away from Paris, including Disneyland, which is just 32 km (20 mi) east of the city via A4 (or take the RER-A train, stopping at Marne-la-Vallée-Chessy). Chartres and Giverny are a little farther away, but they're still easily manageable—and particularly enjoyable—side trips from the capital.

Versailles

Versailles is the location of one of the world's grandest palaces—and in fact, a grand town, since the château's opulence had to have a setting to match. Wide, tree-lined avenues, broader than the Champs-Élysées and bordered by massive 17th-century mansions, lead directly to the palace. From the imposing Place d'Armes, you enter the Cour d'Honneur, a sprawling cobbled forecourt. Right in the middle, the statue of Louis XIV, the Sun King, stands triumphant, surveying the town built to house those of the 20,000 noblemen, servants, and hangers-on who weren't quick enough to grab one of the 3,000 beds in the château.

★ The **Château de Versailles** took 50 years to complete. Hills were flattened, marshes drained, forests transplanted, and water from the Seine river was channeled from several mi away to supply the magnificent fountains. Visit the **Grands Appartements** (State Rooms), rooms that made up the royal quarters, and the famous **Galerie des Glaces** (Hall of Mirrors), where the controversial Treaty of Versailles, asserting Germany's responsibility for World War I, was signed in 1919. Both can be visited without a guide, but you can get an audio tour in English. There are also guided tours of the **Petits Appartements** (Private Apartments), where the royal family and friends lived in relative intimacy, and the magnificent opera house—one of the first oval rooms in France, built in the north wing for Louis XV in 1770.

The château's vast **park** is a masterpiece of formal landscaping. At one end of the Petit Canal, which crosses the Grand Canal at right angles, is the **Grand Trianon,** a scaled-down pleasure palace built in the 1680s. The **Petit Trianon,** nearby, is a sumptuously furnished 18th-century mansion, commissioned by Louis XV; Marie-Antoinette would flee here to avoid the stuffy atmosphere of the court. Nearby, she built a model village, complete with dairy and water mill, where she and her companions led a make-believe bucolic life. ☎ *01–30–84–76–18.* ☺

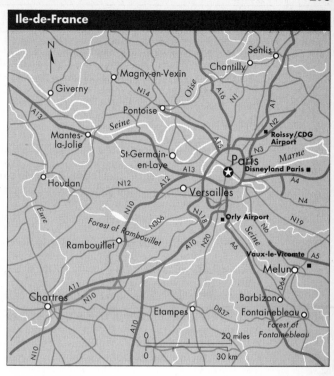

Ile-de-France

*Château: Apr.–Sept., Tues.–Sun. 9–6:30; Oct.–Mar., Tues.–Sun. 9–
5:30. Galerie des Glaces:* ☉ *9:45–5. Opéra:* ☉ *9:45–3:30. Tours of
Petits Appartements and opera house every 15 mins. Park:* ☉ *7–dusk.
Grand Trianon and Petit Trianon:* ☉ *Tues.–Fri. 10–12:30 and 2–5:30,
weekends 10–5:30.*

$$$$ ✕ **Trois Marches.** Don't miss Gerard Vié's nouvelle cuisine at the best
restaurant in town. The view of the château park and the setting—in
the sumptuous Trianon Palace Hotel—add to the experience. ✉ *1 bd.
de la Reine,* ☎ *01–39–50–13–21. Reservations essential. Jacket and
tie. AE, DC, MC, V. Closed Sun., Mon., and Aug.*

$$ ✕ **Quai No. 1.** Barometers, sails, and model boats fill this small, charm-
ing seafood restaurant. In summer you can enjoy your meal on the ter-
race. Home-smoked salmon and sauerkraut with fish are specialties;
any dish on the two prix-fixe menus is a good value. ✉ *1 av. de St-
Cloud,* ☎ *01–39–50–42–26. MC, V. Closed Mon. No dinner Sun.*

Rambouillet

The small town of Rambouillet is home to a château, a park, and 34,000
acres of forest. Since 1897 the **Château de Rambouillet** has been a sum-
mer residence of the French president; today it is also used as a site for
international summits. You can't visit the château if the president is in
residence—fortunately, that's not often. French kings have lived in the
château since it was built in 1375. Highlights include the wood-paneled
apartments, especially the **Boudoir de la Comtesse** (Countess's Dressing
Room); the marble-walled **Salle de Marbre** (Marble Room), dating from
the Renaissance; and the **Salle de Bains de Napoléon** (Napoléon's Bath-
room), adorned with Pompeii-style frescoes. The **park** stretches way be-
hind the château, and includes the Jardin d'Eau (Water Garden), an
English-style garden, and the **Laiterie de la Reine** (Queen's Dairy), named
for Marie-Antoinette: another of her attempts to "get back to nature."

☎ *01–34–94–28–00.* ☉ *Daily 10–11:30 and 2–5:30; park: sunrise–sunset; laiterie: Wed.–Mon. 10–11:30 and 2–4:30 (until 4, Oct.–Mar.).*

$ ✕ **La Poste.** You can bank on traditional, unpretentious cooking at this former coaching inn. The restaurant's two dining rooms are often packed with a lively crowd. Game is a specialty in season. ✉ *101 rue du Général-de-Gaulle,* ☎ *01–34–83–03–01. AE, MC, V. Closed Mon. No dinner Sun.*

Chartres

Long before you reach Chartres, you'll see its famous cathedral towering over the plain. The attractive old town, steeped in religious history and dating from before the Roman conquest, is still laced with

★ winding medieval streets. The Gothic **Cathédral Notre-Dame** is the sixth Christian church on the site; despite a series of fires, it has remained basically the same since the 12th and 13th centuries. The **Portail Royal** (Royal Portal) on the main facade, presenting the life and triumph of the Savior, is one of the country's finest examples of Romanesque sculpture. Inside, the 12th- and 13th-century windows, many of which have been restored over the past decade, come alive even in dull weather, thanks to the deep Chartres blue of the stained glass: Its formula remains a mystery to this day. ✉ *18 rue du Cloître-Notre-Dame.* ☉ *Tours in English daily noon and 2:45; ask at the Maison des Clercs.*

$$$ ✕ **La Vieille Maison.** In a refitted 14th-century building a stone's throw from the cathedral, the Vieille Maison serves both excellent nouvelle cuisine and traditional dishes. Try the regional Menu Beauceron, for the homemade foie gras and duck dishes. ✉ *5 rue au Lait,* ☎ *02–37–34–10–67. AE, MC, V. Closed Mon. No dinner Sun.*

$$ ✕ **Buisson Ardent.** This attractive restaurant, in an old, oak-beamed building opposite the Vieille Maison, serves such dishes as chicken ravioli with leeks or rolled beef with spinach. ✉ *10 rue au Lait,* ☎ *02–37–34–04–66. AE, DC, MC, V. No dinner Sun.*

$$$ 🏨 **Grand Monarque.** The most popular rooms in this 18th-century coaching inn are in a separate turn-of-the-century building overlooking a garden. The hotel also has an excellent restaurant with a good choice of prix-fixe menus for 158, 225, and 280 francs. ✉ *22 Pl. des Épars, 28000,* ☎ *02–37–21–00–72,* 🗛 *02–37–36–34–18. 54 rooms. Restaurant. AE, DC, MC, V.*

Giverny

This small village is a place of pilgrimage for art lovers enticed by the

★ **Maison et Jardin Claude Monet** (Claude Monet's House and Garden). The house where Monet worked and lived for over 40 years has been faithfully restored; the kitchen with its cool blue tiles and the buttercup-yellow dining room are particularly striking. However, the real pull is the colorful garden and especially the famous lily pond with its Japanese bridge, which was one of Monet's favorite subjects. ✉ *84 rue Claude-Monet,* ☎ *02–32–51–94–65.* ☉ *Apr.–Oct., Tues.–Sun. 10–noon and 2–6.*

Fontainebleau

During the early 16th century the flamboyant François I transformed the medieval hunting lodge of Fontainebleau into a magnificent Re-

★ naissance palace, the **Château de Fontainebleau.** His successor, Henri II, covered the palace with his initials, woven into the *D* for his mistress, Diane de Poitiers. When he died, his queen, Catherine de' Medici, carried out further alterations, later continued under Louis XIV. However, it was Napoléon who made a Versailles, as it were, out of the château by spending lavishly to restore the neglected property to its former glory. Before he was exiled to Elba, he bade farewell to his Old Guard in the courtyard now known as the **Cour des Adieux** (Court of Farewell), with its elegant horseshoe staircase. Ask the curator to let you see the **Cour Ovale** (Oval Court), the oldest and perhaps most interesting courtyard. It stands on the site of the original 12th-century fortified building, of which only the keep remains.

The **Grands Appartements** (State Rooms) are the main attractions of any visit to the château; these include the **Galerie François Ier** (Francis I Gallery) and a covered bridge (built 1528–30) looking out over the Cour de la Fontaine. The magnificent **Salle de Bal** (Ballroom) is nearly 100 ft long, with wood paneling, 16th-century frescoes and gilding, and, reputedly, the first coffered ceiling in France, its intricate pattern echoed by the splendid 19th-century parquet floor. If you're here on a weekday, you may also be able to join a guided tour (in French) of the **Petits Appartements** (Private Apartments), used by Napoléon and Joséphine, and the **Musée Napoléon** (Napoleonic Museum), which has some mementos, including the leader's imperial uniform. ⊠ *Pl. du Général-de-Gaulle,* ☎ *01–60–71–50–70.* ☉ *Wed.–Mon. 9:30–5. Call ahead for tour schedule.*

$$$$ ✕⌂ **Aigle-Noir.** This may be Fontainebleau's costliest hotel, but you
★ can't go wrong if you request one of the rooms overlooking either the garden or the château. Late-18th- or early 19th-century reproduction furniture evokes a Napoleonic mood. The restaurant, Le Beauharnais, serves subtle, imaginative cuisine; reservations are essential and jacket and tie are recommended. ⊠ *27 Pl. Napoléon-Bonaparte, 77300,* ☎ *01–64–22–32–65,* ☒ *01–64–22–17–33. 56 rooms. Restaurant, pool. AE, DC, MC, V.*

$$ ⌂ **Londres.** The balconies of this tranquil hotel overlook the palace and the Cour des Adieux; the 1830 facade is preserved by government order. Inside, the decor is dominated by Louis XV furniture. ⊠ *1 Pl. du Général-de-Gaulle, 77300,* ☎ *01–64–22–20–21,* ☒ *01–60–72–39–16. 22 rooms. Restaurant, bar. AE, DC, MC, V. Closed mid-Dec.–early Jan.*

Barbizon

This delightful village is scarcely more than a main street lined with restaurants and boutiques, but a group of landscape painters, including Camille Corot, Jean-François Millet, and Théodore Rousseau, put it on the map in the mid-19th century. Two artists' studios are open to the public—the **Atelier Millet** (⊠ 27 Grand-Rue) and the **Atelier Rousseau** (⊠ 55 Grand-Rue).

Corot and company would often repair to the Auberge du Père Ganne after painting; the inn still stands, and is now the **Musée de l'École de Barbizon** (Barbizon School Museum). The museum contains documents of the village as it was during the 19th century and a few original works by the landscapists—including some paintings done on the inn's walls and furniture. ⊠ *92 Grande-Rue,* ☎ *01–60–66–22–27.* ☉ *Wed.–Mon. 10–12:30 and 2–5.*

$–$$ ✕ **Le Relais.** Enjoy the large portions of delicious specialties—particularly the beef and the game (in season). In summer you can eat in the shade of lime and chestnut trees on the large if noisy terrace. ⊠ *2 av. du Général-de-Gaulle,* ☎ *01–60–66–40–28. Weekend reservations essential June–Sept. MC, V. Closed Wed. No dinner Tues.*

$$ ⌂ **Auberge des Alouettes.** Two acres of grounds stretch around this
★ delightful 19th-century inn. The interior is '30s style, but many rooms still have original oak beams. The restaurant, on a large open terrace, features nouvelle cuisine in sizable portions. Weekend dinner reservations are essential. ⊠ *4 rue Antoine-Barye, 77630,* ☎ *01–60–66–41–98,* ☒ *01–60–66–20–69. 22 rooms. Restaurant. AE, DC, MC, V.*

Vaux-le-Vicomte

★ The **Château de Vaux-le-Vicomte** is one of the greatest monuments of 17th-century France. Too grand for some: When owner Nicolas Fouquet, the royal finance minister, threw a housewarming party in 1661, Sun King Louis XIV threw a fit of jealousy, hurled Fouquet in the slammer on trumped-up fraud charges, and promptly began building Versailles to prove just who was boss—after signing up Fouquet's architectural supergroup (Louis Le Vau for design, André Le Nôtre in the gardens, and Charles Le Brun on all lead murals). From your point of view, though, Fouquet's *folie de grandeur* will probably be a treat. ☎ *01–64–14–41–90.* ▣ *Château and ground: 59 fr; candlelight visits: 80 frs.* ☉ *Mid-Mar.–mid-Nov., daily 10–6. Candlelight visits May–Oct., Sat. 8:30 PM–11 PM.*

Disneyland Paris

Get a dose of American pop culture in between visits to the Louvre and the Left Bank. Disneyland Paris is east of the capital, in Marne-la-Vallée, and easily accessible by RER from the city.

The theme park, less than 1½ km (½ mi) across, is ringed by a railroad with whistling steam engines. In the middle of the park is the soaring Sleeping Beauty Castle, surrounded by a plaza from which you can enter each of the "lands": **Frontierland, Adventureland, Fantasyland,** and **Discoveryland.** In addition **Main Street U.S.A.** connects the castle to the entrance. Also included in the complex is **Disney Village,** an entertainment center with restaurants, a theater, dance clubs, shops, a post office, and a tourist office. ☎ *01–60–30–60–30.* ▣ *Apr.–Sept. and Christmas period: 210 frs (405 frs for 2-day Passport, 570 frs for 3-day Passport); Oct.–Mar., except Christmas period: 160 frs (310 frs for 2-day Passport, 435 frs for 3-day Passport); includes admission to all individual attractions within the park but not meals. AE, DC, MC, V.* ☉ *Mid-June–mid-Sept., daily 9 AM–10 PM; mid-Sept.–mid-June, daily 10–6; Christmas period and spring school holidays, daily 9–8.*

$–$$ ✕ **Disneyland Restaurants.** The park is peppered with places to eat, ranging from snack bars and fast-food joints to full-service restaurants—all with a distinguishing theme. Eateries serve nonstop as long as the park is open. ☎ *01–60–45–65–40. Sit-down restaurants: AE, DC, MC, V; no credit cards at counter-service restaurants.*

$$–$$$$ ▥ **Disneyland Hotels.** The resort has 5,000 rooms in six hotels, all a short distance from the park, ranging from the luxurious Disneyland Hotel to the not-so-rustic Camp Davy Crockett. Free transportation to the park is available at every hotel. To book a room contact the Central Reservations Office. ✉ *Central Reservations Office, Box 100, 77777 Marne-la-Vallée cedex 4,* ☎ *01–60–30–60–30, 407/934–7639 in the U.S.,* ⛶ *01–49–30–71–00. All hotels have at least 1 restaurant and indoor swimming pool. AE, DC, MC, V.*

Ile-de-France Essentials

Getting Around

The region is reached easily from Paris by car and by regular RER train service. But you might find it convenient to group some sights together: Versailles, Rambouillet, and Chartres are all on the Paris–Chartres train line; Fontainebleau, Barbizon, and Vaux-le-Vicomte are all within a few mi of each other.

BY CAR

A13 links Paris (from Porte d'Auteuil) to Versailles. You can get to Chartres on A10 from Paris (Porte d'Orléans). For Fontainebleau take A6 from Paris (Porte d'Orléans) or, for a more attractive route through the Forest of Sénart and the northern part of the Forest of Fontainebleau, take N6 from Porte de Charenton via Melun. Vaux-le-Vicomte is 6 km (4 mi) northeast of Melun via N36 and D215. The 32-km (20-mi) drive along A4 from Paris to Disneyland Paris takes about 30 minutes, longer in heavy traffic. Disneyland is 4 km (2½ mi) off A4; follow the signs for the park.

BY TRAIN

Three lines connect Paris with Versailles; the trip takes about 30 minutes. RER-C5 to Versailles Rive Gauche station takes you closest to the château; trains from Paris (Gare Montparnasse) stop at Versailles Chantiers and continue to Rambouillet and Chartres. Trains from Gare St-Lazare stop at La Défense en route to Versailles Rive Droite. Fontainebleau is served by 20 trains a day from Gare de Lyon; buses for Barbizon leave from the main post office in Fontainebleau. The RER-A4 line goes to Disneyland Paris. Vaux-le-Vicomte is a 7-km (4-mi) taxi ride from the nearest station at Melun, served by regular trains from Paris and Fontainebleau. The taxi ride costs about 80–100 francs.

Guided Tours

Following are two private companies that organize regular half-day and full-day tours from Paris to Chartres, Fontainebleau, Barbizon, and Versailles with English-speaking guides. Tours are subject to cancellation, and reservations are suggested. **Cityrama** (⊠ 4 Pl. des Pyramides, Paris, 1ᵉʳ, ☎ 01–44–55–61–00). **Paris Vision** (⊠ 214 rue de Rivoli, Paris, 1ᵉʳ, ☎ 01–42–60–31–25).

Visitor Information

Barbizon (⊠ 55 Grande-Rue, ☎ 01–60–66–41–87). **Chartres** (⊠ Pl. de la Cathédrale, ☎ 02–37–21–50–00). **Disneyland Paris** (⊠ B.P. 100, 77777 Marne-la-Vallée cedex, ☎ 01–60–30–60–30). **Fontainebleau** (⊠ 4 rue Royale, ☎ 01–60–74–99–99). **Rambouillet** (⊠ 1 Pl. de la Libération, ☎ 01–34–83–21–21). **Versailles** (⊠ 7 rue des Réservoirs, ☎ 01–39–50–36–22).

THE LOIRE VALLEY

The Loire is the longest river in France, rising near Le Puy in the east of the Massif Central and pursuing a broad northwest curve on its 1,000-km (620-mi) course to the Atlantic near Nantes. The meandering Loire has two distinct faces: fast-flowing and spectacular in spring, sluggish and sandy in summer. Château country encompasses the 225-km (140-mi) stretch between Orléans, 113 km (70 mi) south of Paris, and Angers, 96 km (60 mi) from the Atlantic coast. Thanks to its mild climate and lush meadowland, this area is known as the Garden of France.

To the north lies the vast grain plain of the Beauce; to the southeast the marshy, forest-covered Sologne, renowned for mushrooms, asparagus, and game. The star attractions along the rocky banks of the Loire and its tributaries—the Rivers Cher, Indre, Vienne, and Loir (with no *e*)—are the famous châteaux: stately houses, castles, and fairy-tale palaces, where Renaissance elegance is often combined with fortresslike medieval mass. The Loire Valley was fought over by France and England during the Middle Ages until, inspired by Joan of Arc, the "Maid of Orléans" (scene of her most rousing military success), France finally managed to expel the English.

The Loire Valley's golden age came under François I (1515–47), France's flamboyant contemporary of England's Henry VIII. He hired Renaissance craftsmen from Italy and hobnobbed with the aging

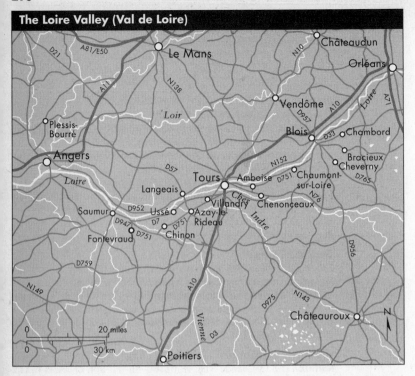

The Loire Valley (Val de Loire)

Leonardo da Vinci, his guest at Amboise. You can see his salamander emblem in many châteaux.

Most of the sights covered here are close to the Loire River along the 170-km (105-mi) stretch between Blois and Angers. If you're coming from Paris, Châteaudun and Vendôme make good stops en route to Blois. Tours, 58 km (36 mi) west of Blois, is the region's major city. Saumur, Chinon, and Amboise are the other main historic towns.

Châteaudun

The **Château de Châteaudun** is a colossal castle, resplendent and impregnable on a steep promontory 200 ft above the Loir. The round, 12th-century **Grosse Tour** (Big Tower) is one of France's beefiest keeps, with walls over 12 ft thick. In the chapel alongside are 15 lifelike statues, mainly of saints, sculpted locally during the late 15th century. ☎ 02–37–94–02–90. ⊙ *Mid-Mar.–Sept., daily 9–12:30 and 2–6; Oct.– mid-Mar., daily 10–12:30 and 2–5.*

Vendôme

At Vendôme the Loir River (not to be confused with the larger and more famous Loire to the south) splits into many arms, giving the town a canal-like charm that harmonizes with its old streets and bridges.

The large main church, the **Église de la Trinité,** is an encyclopedia of different styles, with brilliantly carved choir stalls and an exuberant west front. It is the work of Jean de Beauce, best known for his spire at Chartres Cathedral. Vendôme also has a ruined castle with ramparts and pleasant, uncrowded gardens, open from 9 to dusk.

Blois

With its forest of towers and tumbling alleyways, Blois is the most attractive of the major Loire towns. It is best known for its massive **Château de Blois,** a mixture of four different styles: Feudal (13th century),

Gothic-Renaissance Transition (circa 1500), Renaissance (circa 1520), and Classical (circa 1635). ☎ 02–54–74–16–06. ☉ *Apr.–Aug., daily 9–6; Sept.–Mar., daily 9–12:30 and 2–5:30.*

$$ ✗ **Rendezvous des Pêcheurs.** This restaurant near the Loire, below the château, serves chef Eric Reithler's inventive fish-based specialties. ✉ *27 rue du Foix,* ☎ *02–54–74–67–48. MC, V. Closed Sun. No dinner Mon.*

$$ ✗🏨 **Médicis.** Your best bet in Blois, this smart, friendly hotel 1 km (½ mi) from the château has comfortable rooms. Each is furnished differently, but all share the same joyous color scheme. Chef-owner Christian Garanger's cooking is innovative classical—*coquilles St-Jacques* (scallops) with a pear fondue, for instance. ✉ *2 allée François-I, 41000,* ☎ *02–54–43–94–04,* 🆂 *02–54–42–04–05. 11 rooms, 1 suite. Restaurant. AE, DC, MC, V. Closed Jan.*

Chambord

★ The largest of the Loire châteaux, the palatial **Château de Chambord** (begun in 1519) is in the heart of a vast forest. Another forest is on the roof: 365 chimneys and turrets, representing architectural self-indulgence at its least squeamish. Grandeur or a mere 440-room folly? Judge for yourself, but don't miss the superb spiral staircase or the chance to saunter over the rooftop terrace. ☎ *02–54–50–40–28.* ☉ *Apr.–Aug., daily 9:30–6:30; Sept.–Mar., daily 9:30–5:15.*

$$ 🏨 **Grand St-Michel.** Considering its location across from the château,
★ the St-Michel is reasonably priced. The best rooms are those with a splendid view of the château and the forest backdrop. ✉ *103 Pl. St-Michel, 41250,* ☎ *02–54–20–31–31,* 🆂 *02–54–20–36–40. 39 rooms, 31 with bath or shower. Restaurant. MC, V. Closed mid-Nov.–late Dec.*

Chaumont-sur-Loire

Chaumont is best known for its sturdy castle with famous stables and magnificent panorama of the Loire. The riverside **Château de Chaumont** was built between 1465 and 1510—well before Benjamin Franklin became a regular visitor. The stables, where purebreds dined like royalty, show the importance attached to fine horses, for hunting or just prestige. ☎ *02–54–51–26–26.* ☉ *Apr.–Sept., daily 9:30–6:30; Oct.–Mar., daily 10–5.*

Amboise

This bustling town has two star attractions. The **Château d'Amboise,** dating from 1500, has splendid grounds, a rich interior, and fine views of the river from the battlements. But it wasn't always so peaceful: In 1560, more than 1,000 Protestant "conspirators" were hanged from these battlements during the Wars of Religion. ☎ *02–47–57–00–98.* ☉ *July–Aug., daily 9–6:30; Sept.–June, daily 9–noon and 2–5:30.*

The **Clos-Lucé,** a 15th-century brick manor house, was the last home of Leonardo da Vinci, who was invited to stay by François I and died here in 1519. His engineering genius is illustrated by models based on his plans and sketches. ✉ *2 rue du Clos-Lucé,* ☎ *02–47–57–62–88.* ☉ *Sept.–June, daily 9–6; July–Aug., daily 9–7.*

$–$$ ✗🏨 **Le Blason.** This delightful, small hotel is behind the château; Rooms 109 and 229 are especially nice. The pretty little restaurant has a seasonal menu that begins at 95 francs and might include roast lamb with garlic or medallions of pork. ✉ *11 Pl. Richelieu, 37400,* ☎ *02–47–23–22–41,* 🆂 *02–47–57–56–18. 29 rooms. Restaurant. AE, DC, MC, V.*

Chenonceaux

The small village of Chenonceaux, on the Cher River, is best known as the site of the "most romantic" of all the Loire châteaux. The early
★ 16th-century **Château de Chenonceau** (without the *x*) straddles the

tranquil Cher like a bridge. It's surrounded by elegant gardens and plane trees. Inside are fine paintings, colossal fireplaces, and richly worked ceilings. A museum with wax figures depicting scenes from the château's history is in an outbuilding. ☎ 02–47–23–90–07. ☉ *Feb.–May and Oct.–mid-Nov., daily 9–5; June and Sept., daily 9–6; July–Aug., daily 9–7.*

$$ ✕⊞ **Bon Laboureur & Château.** Since 1882, four generations of the Jeudi family has run this elegant inn. Rooms in the old house are comfortably traditional; those in the former stables are larger and more modern; the biggest are in the converted manor house across the street. Dine on such excellent dishes as *poêlée de St-Jacques* (sautéed scallops) with fresh wild mushrooms. ⊠ *6 rue du Dr-Bretonneau, 37150,* ☎ *02–47–23–90–02,* 🖷 *02–47–23–82–01. 36 rooms. Restaurant, pool. AE, DC, MC, V. Closed mid-Nov.–mid-Dec.*

Tours

The largest city along the Loire, with 250,000 inhabitants, Tours was extensively damaged in World War II. But the timber-framed houses in the medieval center of Tours, the attractive old quarter around Place Plumereau, were tastefully restored.

★ The **Cathédrale St-Gatien** (1239–1484) numbers among France's most impressive churches. The influence of local Renaissance sculptors and craftsmen is evident on the ornate facade. The stained glass in the choir is particularly delicate; some of it dates from 1320. ⊠ *rue Lavoisier.*

$$$ ✕⊞ **Domaine de la Tortinière.** This turreted, mid-19th century man-
★ sion stands on a hill amid vast fields and woodland, 12 km (7 mi) south of Tours on N10 near Montbazon. Rooms vary in styles, ranging from conventionally old-fashioned to brashly modern. The spacious restaurant looks out over the gardens; salmon, pigeon, and rabbit with truffles are menu highlights. ⊠ *10 rte. de Ballan, 37250 Veigné,* ☎ *02–47–34–35–00,* 🖷 *02–47–65–95–70. 14 rooms. Restaurant. AE, MC, V. Closed mid-Dec.–Feb.*

$$$ ⊞ **Univers.** Rooms in this old hotel are all slightly different and all cleverly designed; wood paneling and soft colors give them warmth; most look onto the garden. The lobby has murals depicting some famous guests, among them Winston Churchill and Maurice Chevalier. ⊠ *5 bd. Heurteloup, 37000,* ☎ *02–47–05–37–12,* 🖷 *02–47–61–51–80. 80 rooms, 8 suites. Restaurant. AE, DC, MC, V.*

Villandry

The **Château de Villandry,** near the Cher River, is known for its pains-
★ takingly relaid 16th-century **gardens,** with long avenues of 1,500 manicured lime trees. The château interior was restored in the mid-19th century. Note the painted and gilded ceiling from Toledo and the collection of Spanish pictures. ☎ 02–47–50–02–09. ☉ *June–Sept., château daily 9–6, gardens daily 9–8; Oct.–May, château daily 9:30–12:30 and 2–5:30, gardens daily 9–dusk.*

Langeais

Across the Loire from Villandry is the small, old village of Langeais, which seems to be crushed underfoot by its massive castle. The **Château de Langeais,** built during the 1460s and never altered, is one of the Loire's most uncompromising castles. Its apartments contain a superb collection of tapestries, chests, and beds. ☎ 02–47–96–72–60. ☉ *Easter–Oct., daily 9–6:30; Nov.–Easter, Tues.–Sun. 9–noon and 2–5.*

Azay-le-Rideau

One of the region's prettiest châteaux is the early 16th-century **Château d'Azay-le-Rideau.** Its high roof and cheerful corner turrets are reflected in the Indre River, which surrounds the château like a lake. This graceful ensemble compensates for the château's spartan interior, as does the charm of the surrounding village. ☎ 02–47–45–42–04. ⊙ Apr.–Sept., daily 9:30–6; Oct.–Mar., daily 9:30–noon and 2–5.

Ussé

The **Château d'Ussé**—actually in the village of Rigny-Ussé—claims to be the setting of the French fairy tale *Sleeping Beauty*. Its bristling turrets, terraces, and forest backcloth are undeniably romantic. Be sure to visit the dainty Renaissance chapel in the park. ☎ 02–47–95–54–05. ⊙ Mid-Feb.–mid-Nov., daily 9–noon and 2–6.

Chinon

Chinon is an ancient town nestled by the Vienne River, with a rock-of-ages castle patrolling the horizon. The 12th-century **Château de Chinon,** with walls 400 yards long, is mainly in ruins, though there's a small museum in the **Logis Royal** (Royal Chambers). The **Tour de l'Horloge** (Clock Tower), whose bell has sounded the hours since 1399, contains the **Musée Jeanne d'Arc** (Joan of Arc Museum). ☎ 02–47–93–13–45. ⊙ Nov.–mid-Mar., daily 9–noon and 2–5; mid-Mar.–June and Sept., daily 9–6; July–Aug., daily 9–7; Oct., daily 9–5.

$$$ ✕▦ **Château de Marçay.** In this 15th-century château, 6 km (4 mi) south of Chinon via D49 and D116, Pascal Bodin prepares excellent cuisine—carpaccio of duck, and tournedos of salmon in a Chinon wine sauce. Rooms are furnished with antiques; beams and gables add warmth. Those on the ground floor in the west wing have private patios; the ones in the pavilion near the château, though pleasantly furnished, have less charm. ✉ 37500 Marçay, ☎ 02–47–93–03–47, ℻ 02–47–93–45–33. 35 rooms (27 in château). Restaurant, pool, tennis court. AE, DC, MC, V. Closed Feb.–mid-Mar.

Fontevraud

This quiet village is dominated by its medieval **Abbaye,** where English kings Henry II and Richard the Lionhearted are buried. The church, cloisters, Renaissance chapter house, long-vaulted refectory, and octagonal kitchen are still standing. Guided tours are in French, but you can get a brochure in English. ☎ 02–41–51–71–41. ⊙ May–mid-Sept., daily 9–noon and 2–6:30; mid-Sept.–Apr., daily 9:30–noon and 2–5.

Saumur

The prosperous town of Saumur is famous for its riding school, wines, and castle. The **Château de Saumur**—a white 14th-century castle—towers above the river. It is home to two outstanding museums: the **Musée des Arts Décoratifs** (Decorative Arts Museum), featuring porcelain and enamels; and the **Musée du Cheval** (Horse Museum), with saddles, stirrups, skeletons, and Stubbs engravings. ☎ 02–41–40–24–40. ⊙ July–Sept., daily 9–6:30; Oct. and Apr.–June, daily 9–11:30 and 2–6; Nov.–Mar., Wed.–Mon. 9:30–noon and 2–5:30.

$$ ✕▦ **Anne d'Anjou.** Close to the center of town, this hotel facing the river has a view of the château (floodlit at night) perched above. Inside the 18th-century building, the simple rooms are filled with both old furniture and contemporary decor; Room 102 has wood-panel paintings and Empire furnishings. The outstanding restaurant, Les Ménestrels, serves imaginative regional cuisine. ✉ 32 quai Mayaud, 49400, ☎ 02–41–67–30–30, ℻ 02–41–67–51–00. 50 rooms. Restaurant. AE, DC, MC, V.

Angers

★ This historic city on the Maine River, just north of the Loire, is dominated by its castle. The feudal **Château d'Angers,** built by St-Louis (1228–38), has a dry moat, drawbridge, and 17 round towers along its 1-km-long (½-mi-long) walls. A gallery houses an exquisite tapestry collection, notable for the blockbuster **Apocalypse Tapestry,** gorily evoking scenes from the Book of Revelation. It was woven in Paris around 1380 and restored to almost pristine glory in 1996. ☎ 02–41–87–43–47. ☉ *July–Aug., daily 10–7; Sept.–June, daily 10–5.*

$ ✗ **La Treille.** For traditional, simple fare, try this small, two-story mom-and-pop restaurant just off Place Ste-Croix (next to the cathedral). The prix-fixe menu may start with a *salade au chèvre chaud* (warm goat cheese salad), followed by confit of duck, and an apple tart. The upstairs dining room has a party atmosphere; downstairs is quieter. ⊠ *12 rue Montault,* ☎ *02–41–88–45–51. MC, V. Closed Sun.*

$$$ ✗⌂ **Pavillon Paul Le Quéré.** Paul Le Quéré's luxurious hotel complements his fine restaurant in a mansion off the main avenue. Rooms are in classical, modern style. Le Quéré is an accomplished chef who creates subtle, imaginative dishes like pigeon with licorice. ⊠ *3 bd. du Maréchal-Foch, 49100,* ☎ *02–41–20–00–20,* FAX *02–41–20–06–20. 6 rooms, 4 suites. Restaurant. AE, DC, MC, V.*

The Loire Valley Essentials

Getting Around

The easiest way to visit the Loire châteaux is by car; N152 hugs the riverbank and offers excellent sightseeing possibilities. Trains run along the Loire Valley every two hours, supplemented by local bus services. A peaceful way to explore the region is to rent a bicycle at one of the SNCF train stations.

Guided Tours

Bus tours of the main châteaux leave daily in summer from Tours, Blois, Angers, Orléans, and Saumur: Ask at the relevant tourist offices (☞ *below*) for latest times and prices. Most châteaux insist that you follow one of their tours; try to get a booklet in English before joining the tour, as most are in French.

Visitor Information

Angers (⊠ Pl. du Président-Kennedy, ☎ 02–41–23–51–11). **Blois** (⊠ 3 av. du Dr-Jean-Laigret, ☎ 02–54–90–41–41). **Orléans** (⊠ Pl. Albert-Ier, ☎ 02–38–24–05–05). **Tours** (⊠ 78 rue Bernard-Palissy, ☎ 02–47–70–37–37).

NORMANDY

Jutting out into the Channel, Normandy has had more connections with the English-speaking world, from William the Conqueror to D-Day, than any other part of France. Come here not only to see historic monuments but to explore the countryside, rich with apple orchards, lush meadows, and sandy beaches.

The historic cities of Rouen and Caen, capitals of Upper and Lower Normandy, respectively, are full of churches, well-preserved buildings, and museums. The Seine Valley is lined with abbeys and castles from all periods; along the coast are remnants of the D-Day landings. Normandy also has one of France's most enduring tourist attractions: Mont-St-Michel, a remarkable Gothic abbey perched on a rocky mount off the Cotentin peninsula.

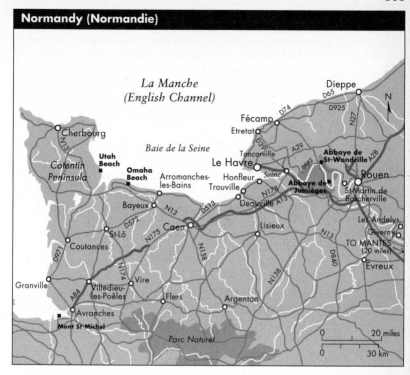

Étretat and Fécamp on the Alabaster Coast and Deauville, Trouville, and Honfleur on the Côte Fleurie (Flower Coast) are among Normandy's many seaside resorts. Normandy is also recognized as one of France's finest gastronomic regions for its excellent cheeses, cider, calvados, and wide range of seafood dishes.

A13 and N13, linking Rouen to Caen, Bayeux, and Cherbourg, are the backbones of Normandy. The expressway goes as far as Caen; it's fast highway thereafter.

Les Andelys

In one of the most picturesque loops of the Seine, the small town of Les Andelys is set against magnificent chalky cliffs. Dominating the town are the imposing ruins of the **Château Gaillard,** a castle built in 1196 by Richard the Lionhearted, king of England and duke of Normandy. It overlooks Les Andelys from the top of the river's chalky cliffs, with spectacular views in both directions. ⊠ *rue Richard-Coeur-de-Lion,* ☎ *02–32–54–41–93.* ⊘ *Mid-Mar.–mid-Nov., Thurs.–Mon. 10–12:30 and 2–5, Wed. 2–5.*

Rouen

Numbers in the margin correspond to points of interest on the Rouen map.

Although blitzed during World War II, Rouen retains much medieval charm. The square where Joan of Arc was burned at the stake in 1431 has been transformed beyond recognition, but the adjacent rue du Gros-Horloge, with its giant Renaissance clock built in 1527, fires the imagination.

❶ You may be familiar with the facade of Rouen's **Cathédrale Notre-Dame** from Claude Monet's famous series of paintings. The facade has suffered badly from war since Monet's days, but its two towers—the older,

12th-century Tour St-Romain and the more intricate Tour de Beurre—retain lofty appeal. The huge metal spire over the crossing is a 19th-century appendage of dubious distinction. Inside, note the 160-ft tower above the crossing on its four massive pillars, and the richly carved staircase in the north transept. ⊠ *Pl. de la Cathédrale.* ☉ *Mon.–Sat. 8–7, Sun. 8–6.*

② The name of the pedestrian rue du Gros-Horloge, Rouen's most popular street, comes from the **Gros-Horloge** itself, a giant Renaissance clock; in 1527 the Rouennais had a splendid arch built especially for it. A 15th-century belfry gives you the chance to study the iron mechanism. ⊠ *rue du Gros-Horloge.* ☉ *Wed.–Mon. 10–1 and 2–6.*

③ The Renaissance **Palais de Justice** (Law Courts), the most impressive civic building in Rouen, dates from the early 16th century. The facade bristles with a forest of turrets, pinnacles, gables, and buttresses. ⊠ *34–36 rue des Juifs,* ☎ *02–35–52–88–70.*

④ The modern, fish-shape **Église Jeanne d'Arc** (Joan of Arc Church), built in the old market square on the site of Joan of Arc's execution, showcases some pleasantly incongruous 16th-century stained glass, rescued from a church bombed in 1944. ⊠ *Pl. du Vieux-Marché.* ☉ *Daily 10–12:15 and 2–6, except Fri. and Sun. mornings.*

⑤ **Abbaye St-Ouen,** an airy, beautifully proportioned 14th-century abbey-church, has splendid medieval stained glass and one of France's most sonorous 19th-century organs. ⊠ *Pl. du Général-de-Gaulle.* ☉ *Mid-Mar.–Oct., Wed.–Mon. 8–noon and 2–6; Nov.–mid-Dec. and mid-Jan.–mid-Mar., Wed., Sat., and Sun. 10–12:30 and 2–6.*

⑥ The **Musée des Beaux-Arts** (Fine Arts Museum) specializes in 17th- and 19th-century French painting, with an emphasis on works by local artists and a collection of macabre paintings by Rouen-born painter Théodore Géricault. ⊠ *26 bis rue Jean-Lecanuet,* ☎ *02–35–71–28–40.* ☉ *Wed.–Mon. 10–6.*

⑦ At the **Musée de la Céramique** (Ceramics Museum), you can see examples of local earthenware; Rouen used to be a renowned faience-making center, reaching its heyday in the early 18th century. ⊠ *rue Faucon,* ☎ *02–35–07–31–74.* ☉ *Wed.–Mon. 10–1 and 2–6.*

$$$ ✕ **La Couronne.** Built in 1345, La Couronne is supposedly the oldest inn in France. Amid the oak beams, leather upholstery, and woodwork is a sculpture collection. The traditional cuisine features homemade foie gras and turbot in flaky pastry; keep to the "menu Normand" or expect a hefty bill. ⊠ *31 Pl. du Vieux-Marché,* ☎ *02–35–71–66–66. Reservations essential. AE, DC, MC, V.*

$$–$$$ 🏨 **Mercure Rouen-Centre.** In the jumble of narrow streets near the cathedral (a challenge if you arrive by car), this modern hotel has small, comfortable rooms in breezy pastels. It's not particularly charming, but it's central and has a bar for an evening aperitif. ⊠ *7 rue de la Croix-de-Fer, 76000,* ☎ *02–35–52–69–52,* FAX *02–35–89–41–46. 125 rooms. Bar. AE, DC, MC, V.*

$–$$ 🏨 **Cathédrale.** This appealing hotel is in a medieval building on a narrow pedestrian street behind the cathedral (you can sleep soundly: The cathedral bells don't boom out the hour at night). Rooms are petite, but neat and comfortable. ⊠ *12 rue St-Romain, 76000,* ☎ *02–35–71–57–95,* FAX *02–35–70–15–54. 24 rooms. MC, V.*

Abbaye de Jumièges

The **Abbaye de Jumièges,** once a powerful Benedictine center, was founded in the 7th century but dismantled during the Revolution. The ruins are substantial and spectacular, and you can also visit the remains

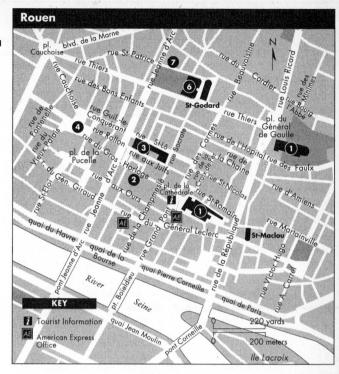

of the chapter house and several chapels. ✉ *24 rue Guillaume-le-Con-*
quérant, ☎ *02–35–37–24–02.* ☉ *Apr.–Sept., daily 9–7; Oct.–Mar., daily*
9:30–1 and 2:30–5:30.

Abbaye de St-Wandrille

The **Abbaye de St-Wandrille** was founded in 649 and still has a Benedictine community. Arrive early in the morning to hear the Gregorian
chants at Mass. ☎ *02–35–96–23–11.* ☉ *Guided tour at 3 and 4 week-*
days, 11:30 Sun.

Fécamp

Fécamp, at the foot of the highest cliffs in Normandy, was the region's
first place of pilgrimage. Legend has it that in the first century, an abandoned boat washed ashore here with a bottle containing Christ's blood.
The 11th-century **Église de la Trinité** was built for all the pilgrims. ✉
rue Leroux. ☉ *Guided tours May–Oct., Sun. at 11, 3, and 5.*

Bénédictine liqueur comes from Fécamp, and the **Palais de la Béné-**
dictine, rebuilt in 1892 after a fire, remains one of the fanciest-look-
ing distilleries in the world. A free sample is thrown in with the tour.
✉ *110 rue Alexandre-le-Grand,* ☎ *02–35–10–26–10.* ☉ *Daily 10–11:15*
and 2–5.

\$\$ ✕⌂ **Auberge de la Rouge.** This quaint inn is in a little hamlet just south
of Fécamp. In the restaurant, classic and modern dishes such as coquilles St-Jacques (scallops in the shell in a sherry cream sauce) and
pressed duck are served; it's closed Sunday dinner and Monday. ✉ *St-*
Léonard, 76400, ☎ *02–35–28–07–59,* 🖷 *02–35–28–70–55. 8 rooms.*
Restaurant. AE, DC, MC, V.

Étretat

Claude Monet painted in Étretat as well as in Rouen and Giverny, im-
mortalizing the site's rough cliff formations long before the advent of

postcards. The white **Falaises d'Étretat** (Étretat Cliffs) are just as famous in France as Dover's are in England. Two immense archways—walls of stone hollowed out by the sea—lead to neighboring beaches at low tide. For a view over the bay and the **Aiguille** (Needle), which is an enormous rock towering in the middle, take the little path up the **Falaise d'Aval** (Aval Cliff).

$$ ✕ **Roches Blanches.** Just off the beach, this family-owned restaurant is a concrete, post–World War II eyesore. But the views and the superbly fresh seafood are another story. ⊠ *rue de l'Abbé-Cochet,* ☎ *02–35–27–07–34. Reservations essential. MC, V. Closed Tues.–Thurs. (Wed. only July–early Sept.), Jan., and Oct.*

$$ 🏨 **Donjon.** This charming little château, in a park overlooking the town, has lovely views of the bay. Rooms are individually furnished, spacious, comfortable, and quiet. Reliable French cuisine is served with flair in the cozy, romantic restaurant. ⊠ *chemin de St-Clair, 76790,* ☎ *02–35–27–08–23,* 🄵🄰🄸 *02–35–29–92–24. 10 rooms, 7 with bath. Restaurant, pool. AE, DC, MC, V.*

Honfleur

Toward the end of the last century, pretty Honfleur, once an important port for maritime expeditions, became a favorite spot for vacationers and painters, including the Impressionists. In summer or on weekends, be prepared for lines at restaurants and cafés. Its lively cobbled streets, harbors full of colorful yachts, and the **Église Ste-Catherine**—a 15th-century wooden church—make it the most picturesque town on the Normandy coast.

$$$ ✕ **Absinthe.** A magnificent 16th-century dining room is the setting for nouvelle and traditional cuisine, with an accent on seafood. In warm weather dine on the quayside terrace. There's also a pub, the Ivanhoe. ⊠ *10 quai de la Quarantaine,* ☎ *02–31–89–39–00. AE, DC, MC, V. Closed mid-Nov.–mid.-Dec.*

$$–$$$ ✕ **L'Assiette Gourmande.** When chef Gérard Bonnefoy comes into the dining room at Honfleur's unsung top restaurant, he decides what you would enjoy after a few minutes of conversation. Maybe you'll be lucky enough to have the superb coquilles St-Jacques grilled with sautéed asparagus in a raspberry vinaigrette and orange sauce. ⊠ *2 quai des Passagers,* ☎ *02–31–89–24–88. AE, DC, MC, V.*

$$ 🏨 **Cheval Blanc.** Friendly owners Alain Petit and his wife run this inn in a renovated 15th-century building on the harbor front. Rooms have fine views of the harbor; No. 34 (slightly more expensive than the others) has gabled ceilings, a small sitting area, and a whirlpool bath. ⊠ *2 quai des Passagers, 14600,* ☎ *02–31–81–65–00,* 🄵🄰🄸 *02–31–89–52–80. 33 rooms, 14 with bath. MC, V. Closed Jan.*

Trouville–Deauville

Although separated only by the little Touques River, the popular resort towns of Trouville and Deauville are vastly different in mood. Deauville is the fancier of the two, with its palaces, casino, horse racing, and film festival. Some would say all the style is artificial: The town was built from scratch in the 1860s, and is invaded each weekend by wealthy Parisians. Neighboring Trouville retains an active fishing fleet and working population, and is less damaging to the wallet. Its beach is arguably larger and more scenic, tucked in beneath a corniche.

$$$$ ✕🏨 **Normandy.** The fashionable and monied from Paris have been attracted to this hotel, with its traditional Norman facade and underground passage to the casino, since it opened in 1912. Request a room with a sea view. The gourmet restaurant, La Potinière, and the large dining room both serve mouthwatering variations of Norman cuisine.

⌧ *38 rue Jean-Mermoz, 14800 Deauville,* ☎ *02–31–98–66–22, 800/
223–5652 for U.S. reservations,* ⬛ *02–31–98–66–23. 271 rooms. 2
restaurants, indoor pool, sauna. AE, DC, MC, V.*

$–$$ ▯ **Carmen.** This straightforward, unpretentious little hotel is around
the corner from the casino and a block from the sea. Rooms range from
plain and inexpensive to comfortable and moderate. The owners, the
Bude family, are on hand to give advice. ⌧ *24 rue Carnot, 14360 Trouville,* ☎ *02–31–88–35–43,* ⬛ *02–31–88–08–03. 18 rooms. Restaurant. AE, DC, MC, V. Closed Jan.–mid-Feb., and 10 days in Oct.*

Caen

Caen, a few mi inland, is the capital of Lower Normandy and one of the
region's few cities. It was badly bombed in 1944 but has been rebuilt
with care. William the Conqueror was responsible for Caen's large
Château, an impregnable-looking fortress glowering down from a hill
above the city center. Its ramparts now encircle a public garden containing
two museums, the **Musée des Beaux-Arts,** a Fine Arts Museum with a
choice collection of old masters, and the **Musée de Normandie,** devoted
to regional history. ⌧ *Museum entrance by castle gateway,* ☎ *Beaux-
Arts: 02–31–86–06–24; Normandie: 02–31–85–28–63.* ☉ *Beaux-Arts:
Wed.–Mon. 9:30–12:30 and 2–6; Normandie: Wed.–Mon. 9:30–6.*

William and his queen, Mathilda, also built Caen's "his and hers" abbeys.
The **Abbaye aux Dames** (Women's Abbey) now houses government
offices; however, its elegant arcaded courtyard and ground-floor reception rooms can be admired during a (free) guided tour, as can its
church. ⌧ *Pl. de la Reine-Mathilde,* ☎ *02–31–06–98–98.* ▱ *Free.* ☉
Guided tours daily at 2:30 and 4.

The **Abbaye aux Hommes** (Men's Abbey), begun in Romanesque style
in 1066 and added to in the 18th century, has a cathedral-size church.
⌧ *Pl. Louis-Guillouard,* ☎ *02–31–30–41–00.* ☉ *Tours daily at 9:30,
11, 2:30, and 4.*

An imaginative introduction to the Normandy landings of June 1944
is to be found at the **Mémorial,** a striking modern museum on the north
side of the city. ⌧ *Esplanade Dwight-D.-Eisenhower,* ☎ *02–31–06–
06–44.* ▱ *72 frs.* ☉ *Nov.–Jan., daily 9–6; Feb.–Oct., daily 9–7.*

$$$ ✕ **Bourride.** Michel Bruneau, chef and owner of this restaurant on one
of the town's oldest streets, bases his inventive recipes almost exclu-
sively on local and regional produce. Specialties include skate caramelized
in honey and cider, and meat pastry cooked in cider vinegar. ⌧ *15 rue
du Vaugueux,* ☎ *02–31–93–50–76. AE, DC, MC, V. Closed Sun., Mon.,
most of Jan., and mid- to late Aug.*

$$ ✕▯ **Dauphin.** Rooms in this old priory are small but clean; many overlook a quiet courtyard. The restaurant serves excellent Norman dishes,
emphasizing seafood with unusually light sauces. ⌧ *29 rue Gémare,
14000,* ☎ *02–31–86–22–26,* ⬛ *02–31–86–35–14. 21 rooms. Restaurant. AE, DC, MC, V.*

Bayeux

Bayeux, a few mi inland from the D-Day beaches, was the first French
town freed by the Allies in June 1944. It's known primarily as the home
★ of **Bayeux Tapestry** (La Tapisserie de la Reine Mathilde, or Queen
Mathilda's Tapestry), which tells the epic story of William's conquest
of England in 1066. You can rent headphones in English (5 frs) with
scene-by-scene commentary. ⌧ *13 bis rue de Nesmond,* ☎ *02–31–51–
25–50.* ☉ *May–mid-Sept., daily 9–6:30; mid-Sept.–Apr., daily 9:30–
12:30 and 2–6.*

The **Musée Baron-Gérard** (Baron Gerard Museum) has a fine collection of Bayeux porcelain and lace, ceramics from Rouen, apothecary jars from the 17th and 18th centuries, and furniture and paintings from the 16th to 19th centuries. ✉ *1 rue de la Chaine*, ☎ *02–31–92–14–21.* ⏰ *June–mid-Sept., daily 9–7; mid-Sept.–May, daily 10–12:30 and 2–6. Closed 2 wks in Jan.*

Dominating the heart of Bayeux is the **Cathédrale Notre-Dame** (✉ rue de Bienvenu), a harmonious mixture of Norman (Romanesque) and Gothic architecture. Note the portal on the south side of the transept, depicting the assassination of English Archbishop Thomas à Becket in Canterbury Cathedral in 1170.

The **Musée de la Bataille de Normandie** (Battle of Normandy Museum), overlooking the British Military Cemetery, traces the Allied advance against the Nazis in June and July of 1944. ✉ *bd. Général-Fabian-Ware*, ☎ *02–31–92–93–41.* ⏰ *May–mid-Sept., daily 9–6:30; mid-Sept.–Apr., daily 10–noon and 2–6.*

$$ ✕ **Les Quatre Saisons.** This restaurant, in the Grand Hôtel du Luxembourg, is one of the best in town. The classical repertoire of Normandy dishes ranges from chicken roasted with cider to veal in a sauce scented with calvados. ✉ *25 rue des Bouchers*, ☎ *02–31–92–00–04. AE, DC, MC, V.*

$ ✕ **Amaryllis.** This small, simple restaurant with fewer than 15 tables serves good, reasonably priced Norman fare. For 110 francs you can get a three-course dinner that might include a half dozen oysters, sole with a cider-based sauce, and dessert. ✉ *32 rue St-Patrice*, ☎ *02–31–22–47–94. AE, DC, MC, V. Closed Mon. and mid-Dec.–mid-Jan.*

$$$ ✕▦ **Chenevière.** In a late-19th-century grand manor in parkland between Bayeux and the coast, this elegant hotel has rooms with modern furnishings, floor-to-ceiling windows, and flowered bedspreads that add a splash of color. The restaurant serves classic Norman cuisine. ✉ *Les Escures, 14520 Commes (9 km/5½ mi north of Bayeux via D6)*, ☎ *02–31–51–25–25*, ⎌ *02–31–51–25–20. 19 rooms. Restaurant. AE, MC, V.*

$$ ▦ **Churchill.** This friendly, family-run inn in an old town house is within walking distance of Bayeux's major attractions. Rooms vary in shape and size; furnishings are modest and functional. ✉ *14 rue St-Jean, 14400*, ☎ *02–31–21–31–80*, ⎌ *02–31–21–41–66. 31 rooms. AE, DC, MC, V. Closed mid-Nov.–mid-Mar.*

Arromanches-les-Bains

Not much remains to mark the furious fighting waged hereabouts. In the bay off Arromanches, however, some elements of the floating harbor are still visible. A few hundred yards out to sea you can see the concrete vestiges of **Mulberry B**, an artificial harbor built for the landings. (American troops landed farther up the coast on Omaha Beach, where Mulberry A was destroyed by a storm soon after.)

The **Musée du Débarquement** (Normandy Landings Museum) on the seafront shows the D-Day landing plan and a film (in English) about the operation. ✉ *Pl. du 6-Juin*, ☎ *02–31–22–34–31.* ⏰ *May–Sept., daily 9–7; Oct.–Dec. and Feb.–Apr., daily 9:30–12:30 and 1:30–5.*

★ Mont-St-Michel

Fabled Mont-St-Michel, an offshore rock crowned by the spire of a medieval abbey, is perhaps the most spectacular site in France—and certainly the most visited outside Paris. The best views can be had on the road from Avranches, to the east. The mount's fame comes not just from its location—until the causeway (soon to be replaced by a bridge to allow the tide to circulate) was built, it was cut off from the mainland at high tide—but also from the dramatic nature of its construction during the 8th century, when tons of granite were brought from the nearby Chausey Islands and hauled up the 265-ft peak. It has been a pilgrimage site ever since.

For most of the year Mont-St-Michel—officially a small village with a permanent population of less than 100—is surrounded by sandy beach. The best time to see it is during the high tides of spring and fall, when the sea comes pounding in—dangerously fast—and encircles the mount. **La Merveille** (The Wonder) is the name given to the collection of Gothic buildings on top. What looks like a fortress is in fact a series of architectural layers that trace the evolution of French architecture from Romanesque to late Gothic. You can join a guided tour (in English). ☎ 02–33–60–14–14. ☉ May–Sept., daily 9:30–11:30 and 1:30–6; Oct.–Apr., Wed.–Mon. 9:30–4:30.

$$$ ✕⊞ **Terrasses Poulard.** In this overpriced collection of town houses, each room is named after a famous Norman personality and styled accordingly. Several have breathtaking views of the bay; others look out onto a little garden. The restaurant is crowded with tourists and lined with posters and photographs recalling illustrious past visitors. ⊠ Grande Rue, 50116, ☎ 02–33–60–14–09, FAX 02–33–60–37–31. 29 rooms. Restaurant. AE, DC, MC, V.

$$ ⊞ **Le Manoir de la Roche Torin.** This small ivy-clad manor house, 9 km (6 mi) east of Mont-St-Michel, is an appealing alternative to the high-priced hotels on the mount. Rooms are pleasantly old-fashioned. ⊠ 34 rte. de la Roche-Torin, 50220 Courtils, ☎ 02–33–70–96–55, FAX 02–33–48–35–20. 11 rooms, 1 suite. Restaurant. MC, V. Closed mid-Nov.–mid-Mar.

Normandy Essentials

Getting Around
Normandy is best visited by car. Though trains leave regularly from Paris to Rouen, Caen, and Bayeux, limited connections make cross-country traveling difficult and time consuming. Visiting many of the historic monuments and towns—such as Honfleur and Mont-St-Michel, which has no train station—means using buses, which run infrequently.

Guided Tours
One-day excursions (970 frs) to Mont-St-Michel from Paris are organized by the following: **Cityrama** (⊠ 4 Pl. des Pyramides, 75001 Paris, ☎ 01–44–55–61–00) and **Paris Vision** (⊠ 214 rue de Rivoli, 75001 Paris, ☎ 01–42–60–31–25).

Visitor Information
Les Andelys (⊠ rue Philippe-Auguste, ☎ 02–32–54–41–93). **Bayeux** (⊠ 3 rue St-Jean, ☎ 02–31–51–28–28). **Caen** (⊠ 12 Pl. St-Pierre, ☎ 02–31–27–14–14). **Deauville** (⊠ rue Victor-Hugo, ☎ 02–31–14–40–00). **Étretat** (⊠ Pl. Maurice-Guillard, ☎ 02–35–27–05–21). **Fécamp** (⊠ 113 rue Alexandre-le-Grand, ☎ 02–35–28–51–01). **Honfleur** (⊠ 9 rue de la Ville, ☎ 02–31–89–23–30). **Mont-St-Michel** (⊠ Corps de Garde des Bourgeois, ☎ 02–33–60–14–30). **Rouen** (⊠ 25 Pl. de la Cathédrale, ☎ 02–32–08–32–40).

BURGUNDY AND LYON

For a region whose powerful, late medieval dukes held sway over the largest tract of Western Europe and whose current image is closely allied to its expensive wine, Burgundy is a place of surprisingly rustic, quiet charm. Its leading religious monument is the Romanesque basilica in Vézelay, once an important pilgrimage center, and today a tiny village hidden in rolling hills. The heart of Burgundy is the dark, brooding Morvan Forest. Dijon, the region's only city, retains something of its medieval opulence, but its present reputation is essentially gastronomic. Top restaurants abound. The vineyards leading down toward Beaune are among the world's most distinguished and picturesque. The vines continue to flourish as you head south along the Saône Valley, through the Mâconnais and Beaujolais, toward Lyon, one of France's most appealing cities.

Burgundy is best visited by car. Its meandering country roads invite leisurely exploration. There are few big towns, and traveling around by train is unrewarding, especially as the infrequent cross-country trains steam along at the speed of a legendary Burgundy snail. However, the TGV (high speed trains) zip out of Paris to Dijon (75 minutes), Mâcon (100 minutes), and Lyon (2 hours). It makes sense for Sens to be your first stop on the way down to Burgundy, as it is just 120 km (75 mi) southeast of Paris on N6—a fast, pretty road that hugs the Yonne Valley south of Fontainebleau. Take A6, if you are in a hurry. Zigzag across N6 and A6, taking the smaller roads that lead off them. A6, which turns into A7, is the highway to the Mediterranean and will take you close to Auxerre, Dijon, Beaune, Mâcon, and Lyon, then down the Rhône valley to Provence.

Sens

Sens is home to France's senior archbishop and is dominated by the 12th-century **Cathédrale St-Étienne.** This is one of the oldest cathedrals in France and has a foursquare facade topped by towers and an incongruous little Renaissance campanile. The vast, harmonious interior contains outstanding stained glass of various periods.

The roof of the 13th-century **Palais Synodal** (Synodal Palace), alongside Sens's cathedral, is notable for its diamond tile motif—misleadingly (and incongruously) added in the mid-19th century by medieval monument restorer Viollet-le-Duc. Annexed to the Palais Synodal is an ensemble of Renaissance buildings. Inside is a museum with archaeological finds from the Gallo-Roman period. The cathedral treasury, on the museum's second floor, is one of the richest in France. ☎ 03–86–64–46–27. ☉ June–Sept., daily 10–noon and 2–6; Oct.–May, Wed. and weekends 10–noon and 2–6, Mon. and Thurs.–Fri. 2–6.

$$ ✕🏨 **Hôtel de Paris et de la Poste.** Owned for the last several decades
★ by the Godard family, the modernized Paris & Poste, which began life as a post house in the 1700s, is a convenient and pleasant stopping point. Rooms are clean and well equipped. But it is the traditional restaurant, padded green leather armchairs in the lounge, and little curved wooden bar that give this place its comfy charm. ✉ 97 rue de la République, 89100, ☎ 03–86–65–17–43, FAX 03–86–64–48–45. 25 rooms. Restaurant. AE, DC, MC, V.

Auxerre

Auxerre is the jewel of Burgundy's Yonne region—a beautifully laid-out town with three imposing and elegant churches climbing the large hill that is its perch over the Yonne River. Its steep, undulating streets are full of half-timbered houses in every imaginable style and shape.

Its main feature is the muscular **Cathédrale St-Étienne,** rising majestically from the squat houses around it. It was built between the 13th and 16th centuries and has a powerful north tower similar to that at Clamecy. ✉ Pl. St-Étienne, ☎ 03–86–52–31–68. ☉ Easter–Nov., Mon.–Sat. 9–noon and 2–6, Sun. 2–6.

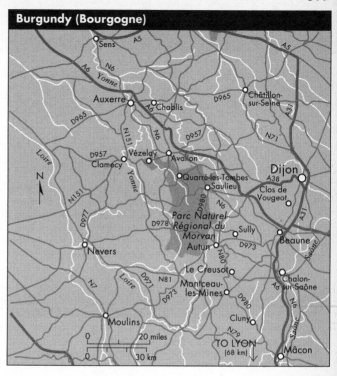

Burgundy (Bourgogne)

The earliest above-ground section of the former **Abbaye de St-Germain** is the 12th-century Romanesque bell tower. But the extensive underground crypt was inaugurated by Charles the Bald in 859, and contains its original Carolingian frescoes and Ionic capitals. ⊠ *Pl. St-Germain,* ☎ *03–86–51–09–74.* ⊙ *Guided tours of the crypt, Oct.–Apr., daily at 10, 11, and 2–5; May–Sept., daily every half hr between 10 and 5:30.*

\$\$ ✕ **Jardin Gourmand.** As its name implies, this restaurant has a pretty garden where you can eat in summer. The interior of this former manor house is equally congenial. Terrine of pheasant breast is a specialty: Hope that the starter of snails with barley and chanterelles and the *gêlée de raisin de chablis* (chablis grape gelatin) dessert are available. ⊠ *56 bd. Vauban,* ☎ *03–86–51–53–52. AE, MC, V. Closed Mon.*

\$\$\$ ⌂ **Château de Ribourdin.** Retired farmer Claude Brodard began building ★ his *chambres d'hôtes* (B&B) in an old stable five years ago, and the result is cozy, comfortable, and reasonably priced. Château de la Borde, named for a small manor nearby, is the smallest, sunniest and most intimate room. ⊠ *89240 Chevannes (8 km/5 mi southwest of Auxerre on D1),* ☎ *03–86–41–23–16,* FAX *03–86–41–23–16. 5 rooms. No credit cards.*

Chablis

Famous for its dry white wine, Chablis makes an attractive excursion 16 km (10 mi) to the east of Auxerre, along D965. Beware of village tourist shops selling local wines at unpalatable prices. The surrounding vineyards are dramatic: Their steeply banked hills stand in contrast to the region's characteristic gentle slopes.

\$\$–\$\$\$ ✕⌂ **Hostellerie des Clos.** The moderately priced, simple yet comfort- ★ able rooms at this inn have floral curtains and wicker tables with chairs. Most of all, come here for chef Michel Vignaud's fine cooking;

it's the best in the region. (The restaurant is closed Wednesday.) ✉ *18 rue Jules-Rathier, 89800,* ☎ *03–86–42–10–63,* 𝔽𝔸𝕏 *03–86–42–17–11. 26 rooms. Restaurant. AE, MC, V. Closed late Dec.–mid-Jan.*

Clamecy

Slow-moving Clamecy's tumbling alleyways and untouched, ancient houses epitomize *"la France profonde"* (the heart of France). The multishape roofs, dominated by the majestic square tower of the church of **St-Martin,** are best viewed from the banks of the Yonne River.

The river played a crucial role in Clamecy's development; trees from the nearby Morvan Forest were chopped down and floated to Paris in huge convoys. The history of this form of transport (*flottage*), which lasted until 1923, is detailed in the Musée Municipal (Town Museum), also known as the **Musée d'Art et d'Histoire Romain Rolland** (Romain Rolland Museum of Art and History). Native son Rolland, Nobel laureate for literature in 1915, spent his final years in nearby Vézelay. Faience and paintings from the 17th–19th centuries are also on display. ✉ *av. de la République,* ☎ *03–86–27–17–99.* ⊙ *Nov.–Easter, Mon. and Wed.– Sat. 10–noon and 3–6; Easter–Oct., Wed.–Mon. 10–noon and 2–6.*

Vézelay

Burgundy's leading religious monument is the Romanesque basilica in Vézelay, once an important pilgrimage center, and today a tiny village hidden in rolling hills. The **Basilique Ste-Madeleine** is perched on a rocky crag, with commanding views of the surrounding countryside. It rose to fame during the 11th century as the resting place of the relics of St. Mary Magdalene and became a departure point for the great pilgrimages to Santiago de Compostela in northwest Spain. The church was rescued from decay by the 19th-century Gothic Revival architect Viollet-le-Duc and counts as one of the foremost Romanesque buildings in existence. ✉ *Pl. de la Basilique,* ☎ *03–86–33–39–50.* ⊙ *Daily 8–8, except during offices Mon.–Sat. 12:30–1:15 and 6–7, Sun. 11–12:15.*

$$$$ ✕🏨 **L'Espérance.** In St-Père-sous-Vézelay, a neighboring village, enjoy chef Marc Meneau's subtle and original cuisine at one of France's premier restaurants (closed Tuesday, Wednesday lunch, and February; reservations and jacket and tie are required). A second restaurant, Le Pré des Marguerites, serves simpler, more traditional, less expensive fare. Rooms in the main house are pretty, but rather small; the others, in nearby buildings, are slightly larger. ✉ *89450 St-Père-sous-Vézelay,* ☎ *03–86–33–39–10,* 𝔽𝔸𝕏 *03–86–33–26–15. 44 rooms. Restaurant. AE, DC, MC, V. Closed Feb.*

Avallon

Avallon's location, on a promontory, is spectacular, and its old streets and ramparts are great places to stroll. At the venerable church of **St-Lazarus,** you can see how the imagination of Romanesque stone carvers ran riot with the portals.

$–$$ ✕🏨 **Les Capucins.** This intimate hotel has rooms in a range of prices. In the lovely restaurant, four prix-fixe menus are dominated by regional fare. ✉ *6 av. Paul-Doumer (also known as av. de la Gare), 89200,* ☎ *03–86–34–06–52,* 𝔽𝔸𝕏 *03–86–34–58–47. 8 rooms, 7 with bath. Restaurant. AE, MC, V. Closed Dec.–Jan.*

Parc Naturel Régional du Morvan

If you're in no rush to get to Dijon, take time to explore the northern part of the huge Morvan Regional Park; roads and trails in the park twist and turn past lovely lakes, hills, and forests. This is where Parisians come to hike the well-marked trails and spend nights in small gîtes (rustic bed-and-breakfasts and refuges). Horseback riding is also popular, and some gîtes have stables.

Saulieu

Saulieu's reputation belies its size (just 3,000 inhabitants). It's renowned for good food (Rabelais, that 16th-century authority, extolled its hospitality) and Christmas trees (a million are harvested each year). The abbey church of **St-Andoche** is almost as old as Vézelay's, though less imposing and more restored. The town museum, the **Musée François Pompon,** contains a room devoted to Pompon, the Art Deco sculptor of animals; another dedicated to local gastronomic lore; and a collection of Gallo-Roman funeral stones and sacred art. ⊠ *rue Sallier,* ☎ *03–80–64–19–51.* ☉ *Apr.–Sept., Wed.–Mon. 10–12:30 and 2–6 (until 5:30 Oct.–Mar.).*

Dijon

Dijon is both the capital of Burgundy and of gastronomy. Testimony to Dijon's bygone splendor is the **Palais des Ducs** (Ducal Palace), now one of France's leading art museums. The tombs of Philip the Bold and John the Fearless head a rich collection of medieval objects and Renaissance furniture. ⊠ *cour de Bar du Palais des Etats,* ☎ *03–80–74–52–70.* ☉ *Wed.–Mon. 10–6.*

With its spindlelike towers, delicate arches gracing its facade, and 13th-century stained glass, **Notre-Dame** (⊠ rue de la Préfecture) church is one of the city's highlights. Among the city's oldest churches, the **Cathédral St-Bénigne** (⊠ Pl. St-Bénigne) is comparatively austere; its chief glory is the 11th-century crypt—a forest of pillars surmounted by a rotunda. The relatively new church of **St-Michel** (⊠ Pl. St-Michel) is notable for its chunky Renaissance facade. Don't miss the exuberant 15th-century gateway at the **Chartreuse de Champmol** (⊠ just off av. Albert 1er beyond the train station)—all that remains of a former charterhouse. Next to the Chartreuse de Champmol is the **Puits de Moïse,** the so-called Well of Moses, with six large, realistic medieval statues. It was designed by Flemish master Claus Sluter, who also created the tombs of the Dukes of Burgundy.

A leisurely trip south of Dijon in the direction of Beaune takes you through some of the world's most famous **vineyards.** Route D122 wends its way past such properties as Gevrey-Chambertin and Chambolle-Musigny, then joins N74 at Chambolle-Musigny.

$ ✗ **Bistrot des Halles.** Of the many restaurants in the area, this one is the best value. Well-prepared dishes range from escargots to beef bourguignon with braised endives. Dine either at the sidewalk tables or inside, where mirrors and polished wood dominate. ⊠ *8 rue Bannelier,* ☎ *03–80–49–94–15. MC, V. No dinner Sun.*

$$–$$$ ✗🏨 **Chapeau Rouge.** A player piano in the bar and elegant staircase give this hotel a charm that the rooms, though clean and well-appointed, lack. The restaurant is renowned as a haven of classic regional cuisine. ⊠ *5 rue Michelet, 21000,* ☎ *03–80–30–28–10,* FAX *03–80–30–33–89. 30 rooms. Restaurant, bar. AE, DC, MC, V.*

$$$–$$$$ 🏨 **Hôtel Sofitel Dijon–La Cloche.** The best hotel in Dijon, in use since the 19th century, La Cloche is a successful cross between luxury chain and grand hotel. Try to get a room overlooking the tranquil back garden, also the backdrop for the greenhoused restaurant, La Rotonde. ⊠ *14 Pl. Darcy, 21000,* ☎ *03–80–30–12–32,* FAX *03–80–30–04–15. 53 rooms, 15 suites. 2 restaurants, bar, exercise room. AE, DC, MC, V.*

Clos de Vougeot

Visit Clos de Vougeot to see its *grange viticole* (wine-making barn), surrounded by its famous vineyard. Constructed by Cistercian monks during the 12th century and completed during the Renaissance, the **Château du Clos de Vougeot** is famous as the seat of Burgundy's elite company of wine lovers, the Confrérie des Chevaliers du Tastevin. They gather here in November at the start of an annual three-day festival, Les Trois Glorieuses. ☏ *03–80–62–86–09*. ⊙ *Apr.–Sept., daily 9–6:30; Oct.–Mar., weekdays and Sun. 9–11:30 and 2–5:30, Sat. 9–5.*

Beaune

★ Despite the hordes of tourists, Beaune remains one of the most attractive French provincial towns. The **Hospices de Beaune** (or Hôtel Dieu), founded in 1443 as a hospital, owns some of the region's finest vineyards. Its history is retraced in a museum that also has Rogier van der Weyden's Flemish masterpiece *The Last Judgment*. ⊠ *Hospices de Beaune,* ☏ *03–80–24–45–00.* ⊙ *Apr.–mid-Nov., daily 9–6:30; mid-Nov.–Mar., daily 9–11:30 and 2–5:30.*

Tapestries, relating the life of the Virgin, hang in Beaune's 12th-century main church, the **Collégiale Notre-Dame** (⊠ off av. de la République). In the candlelit cellars of the **Marché aux Vins** (Wine Market) you can, for the price of admission, taste as many of the regional wines as you wish. ⊠ *rue Nicolas Rolin,* ☏ *03–80–25–08–20.* ⌷ *Entry and tasting 50 frs.* ⊙ *Daily 9:30–12 and 2–6.*

$$ ✕ **L'Écusson.** Don't be put off by its unprepossessing exterior. This is a comfortable, friendly, thick-carpeted restaurant with good value, prix-fixe menus. Showcased is chef Jean-Pierre Senelet's surefooted culinary mastery in dishes like boar terrine with dried apricot and juniper berries. ⊠ *Pl. Malmédy,* ☏ *03–80–24–03–82. Reservations essential. AE, DC, MC, V. Closed Feb., early July, and Sun. No dinner Wed.*

$–$$ ✕ **Le Gourmandin.** Chef Alain Billard and host Isabelle Crotet serve
★ regional fare at their intimate bistro—pork shank and shoulder stewed with beans and cabbage, called *potée Bourguignonne*, is a delicious staple—and a good range of wines from small vineyards. ⊠ *8 Pl. Carnot,* ☏ *03–80–24–07–88. MC, V. Nov.–Feb., closed Tue., no lunch Wed.; Mar.–Oct., closed Tues., no dinner Mon.; Jan.–Feb. (variable).*

$$$ 🛏 **Le Cep.** This top hotel in two old town houses (the oldest is circa 1547) is only five minutes from the main square. The spacious rooms have antiques; those facing the courtyard are quieter. Service can become a little harried when tour groups, albeit of fairly small size, check in and out. ⊠ *27 rue Maufoux, 21200,* ☏ *03–80–22–35–48,* FAX *03–80–22–76–80. 53 rooms. Restaurant. AE, DC, MC, V.*

$$ 🛏 **Hôtel de la Cloche.** In the heart of town, this welcoming hotel in a 15th-century residence has neat rooms decorated with care. The best have full baths; the smaller, delightful attic rooms have shower only. ⊠ *40–42 rue Faubourg-Madeleine, 21200,* ☏ *03–80–24–66–33,* FAX *03–80–24–04–24. 22 rooms. Restaurant. AE, MC, V. Closed late Dec.–mid-Jan.*

Sully

The turreted Renaissance **Château de Sully** stands in a stately park, surrounded by a moat. A monumental staircase leads to the north front and a broad terrace. Marshal MacMahon, president of France from 1873 to 1879, was born here in 1808. ☏ *03–85–82–10–27.* ⊙ *Château: 45-min guided tours June–Sept. (call for times); grounds: daily 10–noon and 2–6.*

Autun

An underrated mecca for lovers of both Gallo-Roman and Romanesque art, Autun has been an important town since Roman times. You'll find the well-preserved archways, Porte St-André and Porte d'Arroux, and the Théâtre Romain, once the largest arena in Gaul.

★ The town's principal monument is the **Cathédrale St-Lazarus** (✉ Pl. St-Louis), a curious Gothic cathedral redone in the Classical style by 18th-century clerics trying to follow fashion. Note the lacy Flamboyant Gothic organ tribune and some of the best Romanesque stonework, including the inspired nave capitals and Gislebertus's tympanum above the main door. The **Salle Capitulaire** houses sculptor Gislebertus's original, 12th-century capitals, distinguished by their relief carving.

The star of the **Musée Rolin** is a Gislebertus masterpiece, the *Temptation of Eve*, which originally topped one of the side doors of the cathedral. Try to imagine the missing elements of the scene: Adam on the left and the Devil on the right. ✉ *3 rue des Bancs,* ☎ *03–85–52–09–76.* ☉ *Oct.–Mar., Wed.–Sat. 10–12 and 2–4, Sun. 10–2 and 2:30–5; Apr.–Sept., Wed.–Mon. 9:30–12 and 1:30–6.*

$$ ✗☷ **St-Louis.** This comfortable hotel on a quiet street dates from the 17th century, but the well-designed wrought-iron furnishings are imported from Mexico and the manager hails from North America. The pleasant patio-garden is a delight and La Rotonde is one of Autun's top restaurants. ✉ *6 rue de l'Arbalète, 71400,* ☎ *03–85–52–01–01,* FAX *03–85–86–32–54. 39 rooms. Restaurant. AE, DC, MC, V.*

Cluny

Famous for its medieval abbey, which was once the center of a vast Christian empire, Cluny is now a tourist mecca. Founded in the 10th century, the **Ancienne Abbaye** was the biggest church in Europe until the 16th century, when St. Peter's was built in Rome. The ruins give an idea of its original grandeur. The **Clocher de l'Eau-Bénite**, a majestic bell tower, crowns the only remaining part of the abbey church, the south transept. The 13th-century **farinier** (flour mill) has a fine oak and chestnut roof and a collection of Romanesque capitals from the disappeared choir. The **Musée Ochier**, in the abbatial palace, contains Europe's foremost Romanesque lapidary museum. Vestiges of both the abbey and the village constructed around it are conserved here, as well as part of the *bibliothèque des moines* (monks' library). ☎ *03–85–59–12–79.* ☉ *Abbey and museum: Nov.–mid-Feb., daily 10–12 and 2–4; mid-Feb.–Mar., daily 10–12 and 2–5; Apr.–June, daily 9:30–noon and 2–6; July–Aug., daily 9–7; Sept., daily 9–6; Oct., daily 9:30–noon and 2–5.*

$$$ ✗☷ **Bourgogne.** The old-fashioned hotel building, dating from 1817, stands where other parts of the abbey used to be. It has a small garden and an atmospheric restaurant serving comfort cuisine, such as *volaille de Bresse au Noilly et morilles* (Bresse chicken with Noilly Prat and morilles). (Lunch is not served on Tuesday and Wednesday.) ✉ *Pl. de l'Abbaye, 71250,* ☎ *03–85–59–00–58,* FAX *03–85–59–03–73. 15 rooms. Restaurant. AE, DC, MC, V. Closed mid-Nov.–early Mar.*

$ ✗☷ **Hôtel de l'Abbaye.** This modest hotel is just five minutes from Cluny's center. Request one of the three rooms to the right of the dining room. The restaurant serves reasonably priced local cuisine, and is closed Sunday night and Monday. ✉ *av. Charles-de-Gaulle, 71250,* ☎ *03–85–59–11–14,* FAX *03–85–59–09–76. 14 rooms, 9 with bath. Restaurant. AE, MC, V. Closed mid-Jan.–mid-Feb.*

Lyon

Numbers in the margin correspond to points of interest on the Lyon map.

Lyon, one of France's "second" cities, is easily accessible by car or train. Much of the city has an enchanting air of untroubled prosperity, and the dining choices are plentiful. It's easy to walk its pedestrian streets and explore its sights. If you have a few days, you can visit Vieux Lyon (Old Lyon) on the western bank of the Saône River; the old Roman

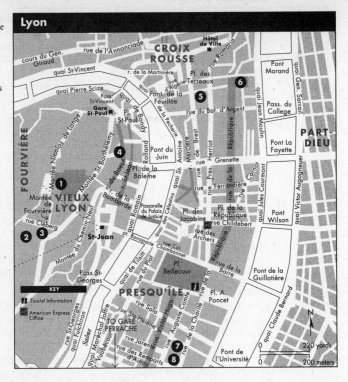

district of Fourvière above it; and La Presqu'île between the Saône and the Rhône, which is the main downtown area, with shops, restaurants, bars, and theaters. For 90 francs, you can purchase a three-day museum pass, the "Clés de Lyon."

It's easy to get around the city on the subway. A single ticket costs 8 francs, a 10-ticket book 68 francs. A day pass for bus and métro is 24 francs (available from bus drivers and machines in the métro).

❶ The cliff-top silhouette of the **Basilique de Notre-Dame-de-Fourvière** is the city's most striking symbol: The 19th-century basilica is a mishmash of styles with an interior that's pure overkill. Climb the observatory heights for the view, instead, and then go to the nearby Roman remains. ✉ *Pl. de Fourvière.* ☽ *Basilica: daily 8–noon and 2–6. Observatory: Easter–Oct., daily 10–noon and 2–6; Nov.–Easter, weekends 2–6.*

❷ Two ruined, semicircular **Théâtres Romains** (Roman Theaters) are tucked into the hillside, just down from the summit of Fourvière. The **Grand Théâtre**, the oldest Roman theater in France, was built in 15 BC. The smaller **Odéon** was designed for music and poetry performances. ✉ *Colline Fourfière.* ☽ *Daily 9–dusk.*

❸ At the **Musée de la Civilisation Gallo-Romaine** (Gallo-Roman Civilization Museum), statues, mosaics, vases, coins, and tombstones from Lyon's Roman precursors are on display. ✉ *17 rue Clébert,* ☎ *04–72–38–81–90.* ☽ *Wed.–Sun. 9:30–noon and 2–6.*

❹ Housed in the city's largest ensemble of Renaissance buildings, the **Musée Historique de Lyon** (Lyon Historical Museum) has a collection of medieval sculpture, furniture, pottery, paintings, and engravings. ✉ *1 Pl. du Petit-Collège* ☎ *04–78–42–03–61.* ☽ *Wed.–Mon. 10:45–6.*

⑤ The best museum in Lyon is the **Musée des Beaux-Arts** (Fine Arts Museum). It houses sculpture, classical relics, and an extensive collection of old masters and Impressionists. ⊠ *20 Pl. des Terreaux,* ☎ *04–72–10–17–40.* ☉ *Wed.–Sun. 10:30–6.*

⑥ The barrel-vaulted **Opéra de Lyon,** a reincarnation of a moribund 1831 building, was built in the early '90s. It incorporates a columned exterior, soaring glass vaulting, neoclassical public spaces, and the latest backstage magic. ⊠ *Pl. de la Comédie,* ☎ *04–72–00–45–00; 04–72–00–45–45 (tickets).*

★ **⑦** In an 18th-century mansion, the **Musée des Arts Décoratifs** (Decorative Arts Museum) has fine collections of silverware, furniture, objets d'art, porcelain, and tapestries. ⊠ *34 rue de la Charité,* ☎ *04–78–38–42–00.* ☉ *Tues.–Sun. 10–5:30.*

⑧ On display at the **Musée Historique des Tissus** (Textile History Museum) is a fascinating exhibit of intricate carpets, tapestries, and silks (silk- and clothmaking made Lyon famous). ⊠ *34 rue de la Charité,* ☎ *04–78–38–42–00.* ☉ *Tues.–Sun. 10–5:30.*

$$$$ ✕ **Léon de Lyon.** Chef Jean-Paul Lacombe's innovative uses of the re-
★ gion's butter, cream, and foie gras put this restaurant, in an old house, at the forefront of the city's gastronomic scene. ⊠ *1 rue Pléney,* ☎ *04–72–10–11–12. Reservations essential. Jacket required. AE, MC, V. Closed Sun., Mon., early–late Aug.*

$$ ✕ **Les Muses.** High up under the glass vault of the Opéra de Lyon is
★ this small restaurant run by Philippe Chavent. The nouvelle cuisine is excellent, especially the salmon in butter sauce with watercress mousse. The best value at dinner is the 159-franc menu. ⊠ *Opéra de Lyon,* ☎ *04–72–00–45–58. Reservations essential. AE, MC, V.*

$ ✕ **Brunet.** Tables are crammed together in this tiny *bouchon* (tavern) with past menus inscribed on mirrors and a few photographs. The food is good, traditional Lyonnais fare. ⊠ *23 rue Claudia,* ☎ *04–78–37–44–31. MC, V. Closed Sun.–Mon. and Aug.*

$$$$ ⌂ **La Cour des Loges.** Young Lyonnais architects teamed with Italian
★ designers to transform four Renaissance mansions into one of Lyon's most stylish hotels. Rooms range from fairly small to comfortably large and are either classic or contemporary in design. ⊠ *6 rue du Boeuf, 69005,* ☎ *04–72–77–44–44,* Ⅸ *04–72–40–93–61. 63 rooms. Restaurant, bar. AE, DC, MC, V.*

$$–$$$ ⌂ **Grand Hôtel des Beaux-Arts.** Half of the rooms at this hotel are "inspired worlds" where an artist has developed a theme through his paintings. Some rooms are traditionally furnished. ⊠ *rue du Président Édouard-Herriot, Pl. des Jacobins, 69002,* ☎ *04–78–38–09–50,* Ⅸ *04–78–42–19–19. 75 rooms. AE, DC, MC, V.*

$ ⌂ **Bed et Breakfast à Lyon.** This nonprofit agency can house you for one night or several: Singles are 120–290 francs; doubles are 170–390 francs. The agency is open weekdays 9:30 AM–8 PM. ⊠ *3 bis rue de la Garenne, 69005,* ☎ *04–72–16–95–01,* Ⅸ *04–78–59–58–62. No credit cards.*

Burgundy and Lyon Essentials

Getting Around

Larger towns can be reached by train, but to see smaller towns you need a car. A6 is the main route through the region (Lyon is 463 km/287 mi south of Paris). N6 is a slower, prettier option.

The TGV to Lyon leaves from Paris (Gare de Lyon) hourly and arrives in just two hours. Six TGVs also go daily between Charles de Gaulle airport and Lyon. From Lyon there is frequent train service to other points. In addition, buses leave Lyon for smaller towns in the region. Dijon has two local train routes: one linking Sens, Joigny, Montbard, Dijon, Beaune, Chalon, Tournus, and Mâcon; and the other connecting Auxerre, Avallon, Clamecy, Autun, and Nevers.

The international airport for the region is in **Satolas** (☎ 04–72–22–72–21 for flight information), 26 km (16 mi) east of Lyon. Air France and other major airlines have connecting services from Paris.

Guided Tours

Write to the **Comité Régional de Tourisme** (✉ B.P. 1602, 21035 Dijon) for information on regional tours using Dijon as a base, including wine tastings and visits to the famous religious sites. Contact the **Comité Régional du Tourisme Rhône-Alpes** (✉ 78 rte. de Paris, 69260 Charbonnières-les-Bains, ☎ 04–72–59–21–59) for information on Lyon (and the Alps).

Visitor Information

Auxerre (✉ 1 quai de la République, ☎ 03–86–52–06–19). **Beaune** (✉ rue de l'Hôtel-Dieu, ☎ 03–80–26–21–30). **Dijon** (✉ 29 Pl. Darcy, 03–80–44–11–44). **Lyon** (✉ Pl. Bellecour, ☎ 04–72–77–69–69; ✉ av. Adolphe Max, near cathedral, ☎ 04–72–77–69–69; ✉ Perrache train station). **Sens** (✉ Pl. Jean-Jaurès, ☎ 03–86–65–19–49).

PROVENCE

As you approach Provence there is a magical moment when the north is finally left behind: Cypresses and red-tile roofs appear; you hear the screech of cicadas and catch the scent of wild thyme and lavender—and all of this is against a backdrop of harsh, brightly lit landscapes that inspired the paintings of Paul Cézanne and Vincent van Gogh. Roman remains litter the ground in well-preserved profusion. The theater and triumphal arch in Orange, the amphitheaters in Nîmes and Arles (both are still used for spectacles that include bullfighting), the aqueduct at Pont du Gard, and the mausoleum in St-Rémy-de-Provence are considered the best of their kind in existence.

A number of towns have grown up along the Rhône Valley owing to its historical importance as a communications artery. The biggest is bustling Marseille; Orange, Avignon, Tarascon, and Arles have more picturesque charm. The Camargue, on the other hand, is the marshy realm of birds and beasts, though its coast attracts flocks of vacationers. North of Marseille lies Aix-en-Provence, with an old-time elegance that reflects its former role as regional capital. Extending the traditional boundaries of Provence westward, historic Nîmes has been included. The Côte d'Azur is also part of this region but has an identity of its own (☞ The Côte d'Azur, *below*).

Orange

Orange is a small, pleasant town that sinks into total siesta somnolence during hot afternoons, but at other times buzzes with visitors keen on admiring its Roman remains.

★ The magnificent, semicircular **Théâtre Antique** (Ancient Theater), in the center of town, is the best-preserved remains of a theater from the ancient world. It was built in the time of Caesar Augustus and still accommodates 7,000 spectators for open-air concerts and operatic performances. ✉ *Pl. des Frères-Mounet*, ☎ *04–90–34–70–88.* ☉ *Apr.–Oct., daily 9–6:30; Nov.–Mar., daily 9–noon and 1:30–5.*

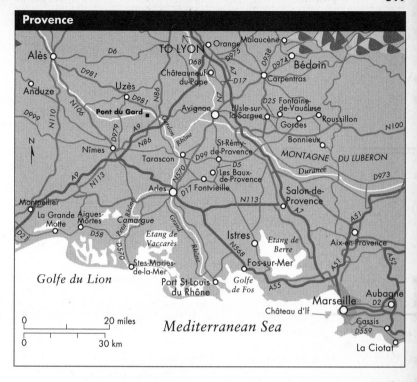

The 70-ft **Arc de Triomphe** (Triumphal Arch) was probably built around AD 25 in honor of the Gallic Wars; it's the third-highest Roman arch still standing.

$ ✕ **La Yaka.** At this intimate, unpretentious bistro, you are greeted by the beaming owner/host/waiter, then pampered with a plethora of menu choices. Specialties are emphatically traditional home cooking and include rabbit stew and *caillette* (pork-liver meat loaf). ✉ *24 Pl. Sylvain,* ☎ *04–90–34–70–03. MC, V. Closed Wed. and Nov. No dinner Tues.*

$$ 🏨 **Arène.** On a quiet square in the old-town center, this comfortable old hotel has attentive owners and a labyrinth of rooms in rich colors and heavy fabrics. The nicest ones look out over the square. There's no elevator. ✉ *Pl. de Langues, 84100,* ☎ *04–90–11–40–40,* 🖷 *04–90–11–40–45. 30 rooms. AE, DC, MC, V.*

Avignon

A warren of medieval alleys nestling behind a protective ring of stocky towers, Avignon is where seven exiled popes camped between 1309 and 1377 after fleeing from the corruption of Rome. The most dominant building within the town walls is the colossal **Palais des Papes** (Papal Palace). It's really two buildings: the severe **Palais Vieux** (Old Palace), built between 1334 and 1342 by Pope Benedict XII, a member of the Cistercian order, which frowned on frivolity; and the more decorative **Palais Nouveau** (New Palace), built in the following decade by the arty, lavish Pope Clement VI. Magnificent frescoes relieve the austere stone, stripped during the Revolution. ✉ *Pl. du Palais-des-Papes,* ☎ *04–90–27–50–00.* ☉ *Apr.–Oct., daily 9–7 (to 8 in Aug.–Sept.); Nov.–Mar., daily 9:30–5:45.*

The 12th-century **Cathédral** near the Palais des Papes contains the Gothic tomb of Pope John XII. Beyond the cathedral is the **Rocher des Doms**

(Bluff of the Doms), a large park from which there are fine views of the town and the river.

The medieval **Petit Palais** (Small Palace) was once home to cardinals and archbishops. Nowadays it contains an outstanding collection of old masters. ☒ *21 Pl. du Palais,* ☎ *04–90–86–44–58.* ☉ *Sept.–June, Wed.–Mon. 9:30–noon and 2–6; July–Aug., Wed.–Mon. 10:30–6.*

The 12th-century **Pont St-Bénezet** (St-Bénezet Bridge) is an easy walk from the Petit Palais if you want a demi-inspection of the bridge—only half of it now remains.

Scattered insouciantly through a crumbling Jesuit church, the **Musée Lapidaire** displays a variety of archaeological finds. ☒ *27 rue de la République,* ☎ *04–90–85–75–38.* ☉ *Wed.–Mon. 10–noon and 2–6.*

The **Musée Calvet,** an 18th-century Palladian-style manor, contains an extensive collection of mainly French paintings from the 16th century on. Greek, Roman, and Etruscan statuettes are also displayed. ☒ *65 rue Joseph-Vernet,* ☎ *04–90–86–33–84.* ☉ *Wed.–Mon. 10–noon and 2–6.*

$$$ ✕ **Hiély-Lucullus.** Among the top 50 restaurants in France, this dignified spot has hyper-traditional delicacies, impeccably presented. The fixed-price menus are a remarkable value. ☒ *5 rue de la République,* ☎ *04–90–86–17–07. Reservations essential. AE, V. Closed most of Jan., last 2 wks in June, and Mon. No lunch Tues.*

$$ ✕ **La Cuisine de Reine.** Glassed into a white-stone cloister, this chic bistro
★ sports a theater dell'arte decor and a young, laid-back waitstaff. The blackboard lists eclectic dishes: duck in rosemary honey, and rosy herbed lamb chops. On Saturday, join the cashmere-and-loafer set for the 120-franc brunch buffet. ☒ *83 rue Joseph-Vernet,* ☎ *04–90–85–99–04. AE, DC, MC, V. Closed Sun. No dinner Mon.*

$$$$ ✕▥ **Hôtel de la Mirande.** Rich with exquisite reproduction fabrics and
★ beeswaxed antiques, this designer's dream of a hotel is just below the Papal Palace. Its enclosed garden is a breakfast and dinner oasis and its central lounge is a skylit and jazz-warmed haven. Rooms are both gorgeous and comfy. ☒ *Pl. de la Mirande, 84000,* ☎ *04–90–85–93–93,* ℻ *04–90–86–26–85. 19 rooms, 1 suite. Restaurant, bar. AE, DC, MC, V.*

$$ ▥ **Hôtel du Blauvac.** Just off rue de la République and Place de l'Horloge, this 17th-century nobleman's home has been divided into guest rooms. Many have exposed stonework, aged-oak detailing, and tall windows that look, alas, onto backstreet walls. Pretty fabrics and a warm, familial welcome more than compensate, however. ☒ *11 rue de la Bancasse, 84000,* ☎ *04–90–86–34–11,* ℻ *04–90–86–27–41. 16 rooms. Bar. AE, DC, MC, V.*

Pont du Gard

Twenty minutes west of Avignon looms the well-preserved Pont du Gard, a huge, three-tier aqueduct, erected 2,000 years ago as part of a 48-km (30-mi) canal supplying water to Roman Nîmes. Its setting, spanning a rocky gorge 150 ft above the Gardon River, is nothing less than spectacular.

Nîmes

Though it's a feisty rat-race of a town today, few cities have preserved such visible links with their Roman past as Nîmes, which is 20 km (12½ mi) southwest of the Pont du Gard (via N86). A three-day, 60-franc "passport," available from the tourist office, admits you to the town's museums and monuments.

★ The flawlessly preserved Roman **Arènes** (Arena) has a seating capacity of 21,000. An inflatable roof covers it in winter for concerts and exhibitions; bullfights and tennis tournaments are held in it in summer. ⊠ *bd. Victor-Hugo,* ☎ *04–66–67–29–11.* ⊙ *May–Mar., daily 9–noon and 2–6; Apr. guided visits only.*

At the **Musée des Beaux-Arts** (Fine Arts Museum), you can admire a vast Roman mosaic and works by Poussin, Bruegel, Rubens, and Rodin. ⊠ *rue de la Cité-Foulc,* ☎ *04–66–67–38–21.* ⊙ *Tues.–Sun. 11–6.*

The **Musée Archéologique et d'Histoire Naturelle** (Museum of Archaeology and Natural History) is rich in local archaeological finds. ⊠ *bd. de l'Amiral-Courbet,* ☎ *04–66–67–25–57.* ⊙ *Tues.–Sun. 11–6.*

The **Musée du Vieux Nîmes** (Museum of Old Nîmes), in a 17th-century bishop's palace, has a vibrant display of textiles, including samples of early denim, which came from Nîmes ("de Nîmes"). ⊠ *Pl. aux Herbes,* ☎ *04–66–36–00–64.* ⊙ *Tues.–Sun. 11–6.*

The **Maison Carrée** (Square House), a superb Roman temple dating from the 1st century AD, is now a gallery for tiny exhibitions. So classically delightful are the lines of this temple that Thomas Jefferson had it copied for Virginia's state capitol. ⊠ *bd. Victor-Hugo.* ⊙ *May–Oct., daily 9–7; Nov.–Apr., daily 9–6.*

$ ✕ **Chez Jacotte.** Duck into an old-town back alley and into this cross-
★ vaulted grotto that embodies Nîmes's Spanish-bohemian flair. Watch for blackboard specials such as scrambled eggs with truffles and asparagus. ⊠ *15 rue Fresque (Impasse),* ☎ *04–66–21–64–59. MC, V. Closed Sun.–Mon. No lunch Sat.*

$$ ⌂ **La Baume.** In the heart of scruffy old Nîmes, this noble 17th-century *hôtel particulier* (mansion) has been reincarnated as a stylish hotel. The stenciled beam ceilings, cross vaults, and archways counterbalance hot ocher tones, swagged raw cotton, leather, and halogen lights. ⊠ *21 rue Nationale, 30000,* ☎ *04–66–76–28–42,* FAX *04–66–76–28–45. 33 rooms. AE, DC, MC, V.*

The Camargue

The Camargue is a haunting, desolate marshy wilderness of endless horizons, vast pools, low flat plains, and innumerable species of migrating birds. **Stes-Maries-de-la-Mer** is the Camargue's main town and now a resort with good, sandy beaches. The town is home to a tiny, dark fortress-church that guards caskets containing relics of the "Holy Maries" for whom the town was named. **Aigues-Mortes,** another Camargue town, was once a coastal fortress, from where Louis IX launched crusades to Jerusalem. Now its shores have silted into plains, but its extraordinary castellated city walls remain, containing a sleepily charming Provencal village.

Arles

Arles was once considered the "Rome of the North" and it was home to both Gauguin and van Gogh. For 55 francs you can purchase a joint ticket to all the monuments and museums.

The town's most notable sight is the 26,000-capacity **Arènes** (Arena), built in the 1st century AD for circuses and gladiator combats. ⊠ *Rond-Point des Arènes,* ☎ *04–90–49–36–74.* ⊙ *Dec.–Jan., daily 10–noon and 2–4:30; Feb., daily 10–noon and 2–5:30; Mar., daily 9–12:30 and 2–5:30; Apr.–mid-June, daily 9–12:30 and 2–7; mid-June–mid-Sept., daily 9–7; late Sept., daily 9–12:30 and 2–7; Oct., daily 10–12:30 and 2–5:30; Nov., daily 10–12:30 and 2–5.*

Close by are the scanty remains of Arles's **Théâtre Antique** (Roman Theater); the bits of marble column scattered around the grassy enclosure hint poignantly at the theater's onetime grandeur. ⊠ *rue du Cloître,* ☎ *04–90–49–36–74.* ⊙ *Dec.–Jan., daily 10–noon and 2–4:30; Feb.,* *daily 10–noon and 2–5:30; Mar., daily 9–12:30 and 2–5:30; Apr.–mid-June, daily 9–12:30 and 2–7; mid-June–mid-Sept., daily 9–7; late Sept., daily 9–12:30 and 2–7; Oct., daily 10–12:30 and 2–5:30; Nov., daily 10–12:30 and 2–5.*

The **Museon Arlaten,** housed in a 16th-century mansion, displays costumes and headdresses, puppets, and waxworks. They were all lovingly assembled by the great 19th-century Provençal poet, Frédéric Mistral. ⊠ *29 rue de la République,* ☎ *04–90–93–58–11.* ☉ *Apr.–May, Tues.–Sun. 9–noon and 2–6; June, Tues.–Sun. 9–noon and 2–6:30; July–Aug., daily 9–noon and 2–7; Sept., daily 9–noon and 2–6; Oct., Tues.–Sun. 9–noon and 2–5:30; Nov.–Mar., Tues.–Sun. 9–noon and 2–5.*

★ Classed as a world treasure by UNESCO, the extraordinary Romanesque **Église St-Trophime** (⊠ Pl. de la République) dates from the 11th century.

★ Tucked discreetly behind St-Trophime is a peaceful haven, the **Cloître St-Trophime** (St-Trophime Cloister). A Romanesque treasure worthy of the church, it is one of the loveliest cloisters in Provence. ☎ *04–90–49–36–74.* ☉ *Dec.–Jan., daily 10–noon and 2–4:30; Feb., daily 10–noon and 2–5:30; Mar., daily 9–12:30 and 2–5:30; Apr.–mid-June, daily 9–12:30 and 2–7; mid-June–mid-Sept., daily 9–7; late Sept., daily 9–12:30 and 2–7; Oct., daily 10–12:30 and 2–5:30; Nov., daily 10–12:30 and 2–5.*

The fountains of the **Jardin d'Hiver** (Winter Garden) figure in several of van Gogh's paintings. Firebrand Dutchman Vincent van Gogh produced much of his best work—and chopped off his ear—in Arles during a frenzied 15-month spell (1888–90) just before his suicide at 37. Markers throughout Arles note settings he painted. ⊠ *East end of bd. des Luces.*

Alongside the Rhône and a little to the west of downtown is the modern **Musée de l'Arles Antique** (Museum of Arles Antiquities), displaying historical artifacts excavated in the region of Arles. ⊠ *Presque'île du Cirque Romain, south side of town (across N113), by the Rhône,* ☎ *04–90–19–88–88.* ☉ *Apr.–mid-Sept., daily 9–7; mid-Sept.–Mar., daily 9:30–noon and 2–5:45.*

$ ✕ **L'Affenage.** A smorgasbord of Provençal hors d'oeuvres draws loyal locals to this former fire-horse shed. They come here for heaping plates of fried eggplant, tapenade, chickpeas in cumin, and lamb chops grilled in the great stone fireplace. ⊠ *4 rue Molière,* ☎ *04–90–96–07–67. AE, MC, V. Closed Sun. and 3 wks in Aug. No dinner Wed.*

$$$$ 🏨 **Nord-Pinus.** J. Peterman would feel right at home in this quintessen-
★ tially Mediterranean hotel on Place du Forum; Hemingway did. Travel relics, kilims, oil jars, wrought iron, and colorful ceramics create a richly atmospheric stage set. ⊠ *Pl. du Forum, 13200,* ☎ *04–90–47–17–16,* FAX *04–90–93–34–00. 26 rooms. Brasserie, bar. AE, DC, MC, V.*

$$$ 🏨 **Arlatan.** Once home to the counts of Arlatan, this 15th-century stone house stands on the site of a 4th-century basilica, and a glass floor reveals the excavated vestiges under the lobby. Rows of rooms—each decorated with a chic, light hand—horseshoe around a lovely fountain courtyard. ⊠ *26 rue du Sauvage, 13200,* ☎ *04–90–93–56–66,* FAX *04–90–49–68–45. 33 rooms, 7 suites. AE, DC, MC, V.*

$ 🏨 **Muette.** With 12th-century exposed stone walls, a 15th-century spi-
★ ral stair, weathered wood, and an old-town setting, a hotelier wouldn't have to try very hard to please. But the couple who own this place do: Hand-stripped doors, antiques, fresh white-and-blue-tile baths, Provençal prints, and fresh sunflowers in every room show they care.

✉ *15 rue des Suisses, 13200,* ☎ *04–90–96–15–39,* 𝖥𝖠𝖷 *04–90–49–73–16. 18 rooms, 17 with bath. AE, MC, V.*

Tarascon

The mythical Tarasque, a monster that would emerge from the Rhône to gobble up children and cattle, came from Tarascon, north of Arles. St. Martha slew it, but no one has slain the paper mill whose fumes wreak havoc on the town. Worth seeing, however, is the town's formidable 12th-century **Château,** with its massive stone walls towering 150 ft above the Rhône, among the most daunting in France. ☎ *04–90–91–01–93.* ☉ *Apr.–Sept., daily 9–7; Oct.–Mar., Wed.–Mon. 9–noon and 2–5.*

St-Rémy-de-Provence

Something felicitous has happened in this market town—a steady infusion of style, of art, of imagination—all brought by people with a respect for local traditions and a love of Provençal ways. Here more than anywhere you can meditate quietly on antiquity, browse redolent markets with basket in hand, peer down the very row of plane trees you remember from a van Gogh, and also enjoy urbane galleries, cosmopolitan shops, and specialty food boutiques.

Founded during the 6th century BC, St-Rémy de Provence was known as Glanum to the Greeks and Romans. Its Roman **Mausolée** (Mausoleum) was erected around AD 100 to the memory of Caius and Lucius Caesar, grandsons of the emperor Augustus. The **Arc Triomphal** (Triumphal Arch) is a few decades older and has suffered more heavily than the mausoleum. All who crossed the Alps entered Roman Glanum through this gate, decorated with reliefs of battle scenes depicting Caesar's defeat and the capture of the Gauls. Excavations of **Glanum** began in 1921, and a tenth of the original Roman town has now been unearthed. The remains are less spectacular than the arch and mausoleum but are still fascinating. ✉ *Off D5, direction Les Baux,* ☎ *04–90–92–64–04.* ☉ *Apr.–Sept., daily 9–7; Oct.–Mar., daily 9–noon and 2–5.*

You can examine many of the finds from Glanum—statues, pottery, and jewelry—at the **Musée Archéologique** (Archaeology Museum) in the center of St-Rémy. ✉ *Hôtel de Sade, rue Parage,* ☎ *04–90–92–64–04.* ☉ *Feb.–Mar. and Oct., Tues.–Sun. 10–noon and 2–5; Apr.–Sept., Tues.–Sun. 10–noon and 2–6; Nov.–Dec., Wed., Sat., and Sun. 10–noon and 2–5.*

$–$$ ✕ **L'Assiette de Marie.** In a bower of attic treasures, choose from the
★ day's specials, all made with Marie Ricco's Corsican-Italian touch—marinated vegetables with tapenade, a cast-iron casserole of superb pasta, and satiny *panetone* (flan). ✉ *1 rue Jaume Roux,* ☎ *04–90–92–32–14. Reservations essential in high season. MC, V. Closed Tues. Nov.–Easter. No lunch Mon., Tues.*

$$$$ ✕🏠 **Domaine de Valmouraine.** In this genteel inn on a broad park, over-
★ stuffed English-country decor mixes cozily with cool Provençal stone and timber. The restaurant features fresh game, seafood, local oils, and truffles. English owner Judith McHugo makes clients feel like weekend guests in a manor house. ✉ *Petite rte. des Baux (D27), 13210,* ☎ *04–90–92–44–62,* 𝖥𝖠𝖷 *04–90–92–37–32. 14 rooms. Restaurant, pool. AE, DC, MC, V.*

Les Baux-de-Provence

Hilly D5 leads south from St-Rémy-de-Provence to the striking medieval village of Les Baux-de-Provence, perched high above the surrounding countryside of vines, olive trees, and bauxite quarries. Half of Les Baux is composed of tiny climbing streets and ancient stone houses inhabited, for the most part, by local craftsmen. The other half, within the hillcrest ramparts of the Château des Baux, is a mass of medieval ruins.

L'Isle-sur-la-Sorgue

Crisscrossed with canals and alive with moss-covered waterwheels that once drove its silk, wool, and paper mills, this charming valley town retains its gentle appeal. Except on Sunday: Then this easygoing old town transforms itself into a Marrakech of marketeers, its streets crammed with antiques and brocantes, its cafés swelling with crowds of bargain browsers. The token sight to see is L'Isle's 17th-century church, the **Collégiale Notre-Dame-des-Anges,** extravagantly decorated with gilt, faux marbre, and sentimental frescoes.

Gordes

Gordes was once an unspoiled hilltop village; it has now become a famous, unspoiled hilltop village surrounded by luxury vacation homes, modern hotels, restaurants, and B&Bs. No matter: The ancient stone village still rises above the valley in painterly hues of honey gold. The only way to see the interior of the **Château** is to view its collection of photo paintings by pop artist Pol Mara, who lived in Gordes. ☎ 04–90–72–02–75. ⊙ Wed.–Mon. 10–noon and 2–6.

$$$ ✕ **Comptoir du Victuailler.** This tiny but deluxe bistro features a smorgasbord of fresh cod and vegetables crowned with pestled garlic mayonnaise, served on the terrace at the foot of Gorde's chateau. ⊠ Pl. du Château, ☎ 04–90–72–01–31. Reservations essential. MC, V. Closed mid-Nov.–mid-Dec., mid-Jan.–mid-Mar., and Wed. Sept.–May. No dinner Tues.

$$$ 🏨 **Domaine de l'Enclos.** A thorough face-lift has left this cluster of stone cottages looking lovelier than ever, with newly laid antique tiles and fresh faux-patinas to keep it looking fashionably old. The atmosphere is surprisingly warm and familial for an inn of this sophistication. ⊠ rte. de Sénanque, 84220, ☎ 04–90–72–71–00, FAX 04–90–72–03–03. 7 rooms, 6 apartments. Restaurant, pool. AE, MC, V.

Bonnieux

Bonnieux rises out of the arid hills in a jumble of honey-color cubes that change color subtly as the day progresses. Most of its sharply raked streets take in wide-angle valley views.

$$–$$$ ✕ **Le Fournil.** In a natural grotto deep in stone, lighted by candles and arty torchères, this restaurant would be memorable even without trendy decor and stylishly presented Provençal cuisine. ⊠ 5 Pl. Carnot, ☎ 04–90–75–83–62. MC, V. Closed mid-Nov.–mid-Dec., mid-Jan.–mid-Feb., and Mon. No lunch Sat. July–Aug.

$$ 🏨 **Hostellerie du Prieuré.** In a former 17th-century priory, this hotel is filled with a mix of antiques and collectibles. A few rooms, such as No. 9, have a private balcony; others have a view of the garden. ⊠ In center of village, 84480, ☎ 04–90–75–80–78, FAX 04–90–75–96–00. 10 rooms. Restaurant. MC, V.

★ Aix-en-Provence

Few towns are as well preserved as the traditional capital of Provence: elegant Aix-en-Provence, birthplace of the Impressionist Paul Cézanne (1839–1906) and the novelist Émile Zola (1840–1902). The celebrated, graceful, lively avenue **cours Mirabeau** is the town's nerve center. It divides Old Aix in half, with narrow medieval streets to the north and 18th-century mansions to the south (particularly along rue Espariat).

The sumptuous Hôtel Boyer d'Éguilles, erected in 1675, is worth a visit for its fine woodwork and murals, but is best known as the **Muséum d'Histoire Naturelle** (Natural History Museum). The highlight is the rare collection of dinosaur eggs. ✉ *6 rue Espariat,* ☎ *04–42–26–23–67.* ☉ *Mon.–Sat. 10–noon and 2–6, Sun. 2–6.*

The **Cathédrale St-Sauveur** (✉ rue Gaston-de-Saporta) houses the re-markable 15th-century *Tryptique du Buisson Ardent* (Burning Bush Triptych) by Nicolas Froment.

The Archbishop's Palace, next to the cathedral, is now home to the **Musée des Tapisseries** (Tapestry Museum). Its highlight is a magnifi-cent series of 17 tapestries made in Beauvais that date, like the palace itself, from the 17th and 18th centuries. ✉ *28 Pl. des Martyrs de la Résistance,* ☎ *04–42–23–09–91.* ☉ *Wed.–Mon. 10–noon and 2–5:45.*

In the **Musée du Vieil Aix** (Museum of Old Aix), in a 17th-century man-sion, is an eclectic assortment of local treasures, from faience to *san-tons* (terra-cotta figurines). ✉ *17 rue Gaston-de-Saporta,* ☎ *04–42–21–43–55.* ☉ *Apr.–Oct., Tues.–Sun. 10–noon and 2–6:30; Nov.–Mar., Tues.–Sun. 10–noon and 2–5.*

At the **Musée-Atelier de Paul Cézanne** (Cézanne's Studio) no major pic-tures are on display, but his studio remains as he left it at the time of his death in 1906. ✉ *9 av. Paul-Cézanne,* ☎ *04–42–21–06–53.* ☉ *Daily 10–noon and 2–6.*

Several of Cézanne's oils and watercolors can be found at the **Musée Granet.** ✉ *13 rue Cardinale,* ☎ *04–42–38–14–70.* ☉ *Wed.–Mon. 10–noon and 2–6.*

$$$ ✕ **Le Clos de la Violette.** Aix's best restaurant is in a residential dis-
★ trict north of the old town. Chef Jean-Marc Banzo uses only fresh, local ingredients in his nouvelle and traditional recipes. The weekday lunch menu is more moderately priced. ✉ *10 av. de la Violette,* ☎ *04–42–23–30–71. AE, MC, V. Closed Sun. No lunch Mon.*

$$ ✕ **Brasserie Les Deux Garcons.** It's standard brasserie fare—stick to the shellfish or the smoked-duck salad—but eating isn't what you come here for. It's the linen-decked sidewalk tables facing onto the cours Mirabeau, and the white-swathed waiters snaking between the chairs. ✉ *53 cours Mirabeau,* ☎ *04–42–26–00–51. MC, V.*

$$–$$$ ☷ **Nègre-Coste.** This elegant 18th-century town house has luxurious old-world decor downstairs, but rooms need updating. Still, where else can you lean over the cours Mirabeau with your morning coffee in hand? ✉ *33 cours Mirabeau, 13100,* ☎ *04–42–27–74–22,* ⊞ *04–42–26–80–93. 37 rooms. AE, DC, MC, V.*

$–$$ ☷ **Quatre Dauphins.** In a noble hôtel particulier in the quiet Mazarin
★ quarter, this modest but impeccable lodging has pretty, comfortable lit-tle rooms spruced up with Provençal decor. ✉ *55 rue Roux Alphéran, 13100,* ☎ *04–42–38–16–39,* ⊞ *04–42–38–60–19. 12 rooms. MC, V.*

Marseille

Much maligned, Marseille is often given wide berth by travelers. What a waste: Its Cubist jumbles of blinding-white stone rise up over a pic-ture-book seaport crowned by larger-than-life neo-Byzantine churches. Its labyrinthine old town paints in broad strokes of saffron and robin's-egg blue. Feisty and fond of broad gestures, Marseille is a dynamic city, as cosmopolitan now as when the Phocaeans first founded it, and with all the exoticism of the international shipping port it has been for 2,600 years.

The picturesque **Vieux Port** (Old Harbor) is the heart of Marseille; av-enue Canebière leads to the water's edge. A short way down the quay on the right (as you look out to sea) is the elegant 17th-century **Hôtel de Ville** (Town Hall). The Maison Diamantée, behind the Town Hall, is a 16th-century mansion housing the **Musée du Vieux Marseille** (Old

Marseille Museum), displaying local costumes, pictures, and figurines. ⊠ *2 rue de la Prison,* ☎ *04–91–13–89–00.* ☉ *Call for hrs.*

Against the backdrop of industrial docks, the various domes of Marseille's pompous, striped neo-Byzantine **Cathédral de la Major** (⊠ Esplanade de la Tourette) look utterly incongruous.

The grid of narrow, tumbledown streets leading off rue du Panier is called simply *Le Panier* (The Basket). Apart from the ambience, Le Panier is worth visiting for the elegantly restored 17th-century hospice now known as the **Centre de la Vieille Charité** (Center of the Old Charity). It now houses a top-drawer archaeology museum and a collection of African, Oceanic, and Native American art. ⊠ *2 rue de la Charité,* ☎ *04–91–14–58–80.* ⌨ *12 frs per museum.* ☉ *May–Sept., Tues.–Sun. 11–6; Oct.–Apr., Tues.–Sun. 10–5.*

The church of **Notre-Dame de la Garde,** with its great gilded statue of the Virgin, stands sentinel over the old port below. Hike to the top or take Bus 60 from cours Jean-Ballard. ⊠ *Pl. du Colonel-Edon,* ☎ *04–91–13–40–80.* ☉ *May–Sept., daily 7 AM–8 PM; Oct.–Apr., daily 7–7.*

Take time to drive the scenic 5-km (3-mi) coast road (corniche du Président-J.-F.-Kennedy) and stop at the magical **Vallon des Auffes,** a tiny castaway fishing port typical of greater Marseille. From the corniche du Président-J.-F.-Kennedy there are breathtaking views across the sea toward the rocky **Îles de Frioul,** which can be visited by ferries that leave from Vieux Port frequently throughout the day.

$ ✕ **Etienne.** This tiny Le Panier hole-in-the-wall has more than just a good fresh-anchovy pizza from the wood-burning oven. There are also a slab of rare-grilled beef and the quintessential *pieds et paquets,* Marseille's earthy classic of pigs' feet and stuffed tripe. ⊠ *43 rue de la Lorette,* ☎ *no phone. No credit cards.*

$$$ ▣ **Mercure Beauvau Vieux Port.** Real antiques, burnished wood, a touch
★   of brass, and deep carpet underfoot give this intimate urban hotel genuine old-world charm. ⊠ *4 rue Beauvau, 13001,* ☎ *04–91–54–91–00, 1–800–MERCURE for U.S. reservations,* FAX *04–91–54–15–76. 71 rooms. Bar. AE, DC, MC, V.*

Provence Essentials

Getting Around

Provence's key attractions are not far apart. Traveling by car is the most rewarding way to get around, especially if you want to go to the smaller villages and explore the landscape. Speedy highways descend from Lyon and split at Orange to go to Nîmes and Montpellier or Aix-en-Provence and Marseille en route to the Côte d'Azur. If you're limited to public transportation, Avignon makes the best base for both train and bus connections. Avignon is where the TGV from Paris and Lyon splits for either the run down to Marseille or Montpellier. From Marseille trains run along the coast to Nice and Monaco.

Guided Tours

The tourist offices (☞ Visitor Information, *below*) in many towns, including Nîmes, Avignon, Aix-en-Provence, and Marseille, give walking tours.

Visitor Information

Aix-en-Provence (⊠ 2 Pl. du Général-de-Gaulle, ☎ 04–42–16–11–61). **Arles** (⊠ esplanade Charles-de-Gaulle, ☎ 04–90–18–41–21). **Avignon** (⊠ 41 cours Jean-Jaurès, ☎ 04–90–82–65–11). **Marseille** (⊠ 4 La Canebière, ☎ 04–91–13–89–00). **Nîmes** (⊠ 6 rue Auguste, ☎ 04–66–67–29–11).

THE CÔTE D'AZUR

Few places in the world have the same pull on the imagination as France's fabled Côte d'Azur, the Mediterranean coastline stretching from St-Tropez in the west to Menton on the Italian border. Cooled by the Mediterranean in the summer and warmed by it in winter, the climate is almost always pleasant. Avoid the area in July and August, however, unless you love crowds.

The Côte d'Azur's coastal resorts may live exclusively for the tourist trade and have often been ruined by high-rises, but the hinterlands remain relatively untarnished. The little villages perched high on the hills behind medieval ramparts seem to belong to another century. One of them, St-Paul-de-Vence, is the home of the Maeght Foundation, one of the world's leading museums of modern art. Artists have played a considerable role in popular conceptions of the Côte d'Azur, and their presence is reflected in the number of art museums: the Musée Picasso in Antibes, the Musée Renoir and the Musée d'Art Moderne Méditerranée in Cagnes-sur-Mer, and the Musée Jean Cocteau in Menton.

Although the tiny principality of Monaco, which lies between Nice and Menton, is a sovereign state, with its own army and police force, its language, food, and way of life are French.

The distance between St-Tropez and the border with Italy is only 120 km (75 mi), so most places are, in fact, within a day's journey. For the drama of mountains and sea, take one of the famous Corniche roads, which traverse the coastline at various heights over the Mediterranean and are especially spectacular from Nice to the Italian frontier (☞ Getting Around *in* The Côte d'Azur Essentials, *below*).

St-Tropez

St-Tropez was just another pretty fishing village until it was "discovered" in the 1950s by the "beautiful people," a fast set of film stars, starlets, and others who scorned bourgeois values while enjoying bourgeois bank balances. Today, its summer population swells from 6,000 to 60,000, and the top hotels and nightclubs are jammed. In winter it's hard to find a restaurant open. The best times to visit, therefore, are early summer or fall. May and June are perhaps the best months, when the town lets its hair down during two local festivals.

The **Vieux Port** (Old Harbor) is the liveliest part of town with plenty of outdoor cafés for good people watching. Between the old and new harbors, in a cleverly converted chapel, is the **Musée de l'Annonciade** (Annunciation Museum), housing paintings by artists drawn to St-Tropez between 1890 and 1940, including Signac, Matisse, Derain, and Van Dongen. ⊠ *quai de l'Épi,* ☏ *04–94–97–04–01.* ☉ *June–Sept., Wed.–Mon. 10–noon and 3–7; Oct.–May, Wed.–Mon. 10–noon and 2–6.*

★ Across Place de l'Hôtel de Ville is the **Vieille Ville** (Old Town), where twisting streets, designed to break the impact of the terrible mistral (the cold, dry, northerly wind common to this region), open onto tiny squares and fountains. The long climb up to the **Citadelle** rewards you with a splendid view across the gulf to Ste-Maxime, a quieter if heavily built-up and less posh family resort with a decent beach and reasonably priced hotels.

Easily visited from St-Tropez is the old Provençal town of **Ramatuelle** on a rocky spur 440 ft above the sea. Six km (4 mi) north of Ramatuelle is the hilltop village of **Gassin,** a lovely place to escape the heat of the shoreline.

The Côte d'Azur

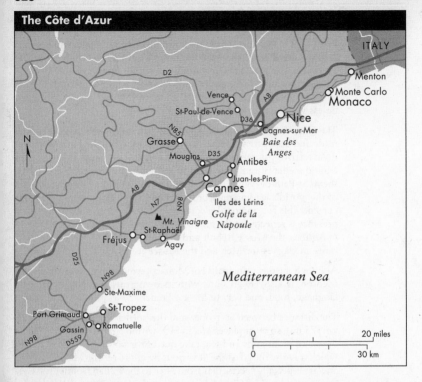

ITALY

Menton
Monte Carlo
Monaco

Vence
St-Paul-de-Vence
Nice
Cagnes-sur-Mer
Baie des Anges
Grasse
Mougins
Antibes
Juan-les-Pins
Cannes
Iles des Lérins
Golfe de la Napoule
Mt. Vinaigre
St-Raphaël
Fréjus
Agay

Mediterranean Sea

Ste-Maxime
St-Tropez
Port Grimaud
Gassin
Ramatuelle

0   20 miles
0   30 km

$$–$$$ ✕🏨 **La Résidence de la Pinède.** This balustraded white villa and its broad annex sprawl elegantly along a private waterfront (pay extra for a seaside room). The fair-sized rooms and the sunny colors add to the charms of this resort. The restaurant features the skills of chef Herve Quesnel: truffle ravioli, sautéed prawns on basil-perfumed scrambled eggs, and fresh fig tarts. ⊠ *Plage de la Bouillabaisse, 83991,* ☎ *04–94–55–91–00,* 🆐 *04–94–97–73–64. 39 rooms, 4 suites. Restaurant, pool. AE, DC, MC, V. Closed mid-Oct.–Mar.*

Fréjus

Fréjus was founded by Julius Caesar as Forum Julii in 49 BC. The Roman remains are modest but impressive, and consist of part of the theater, an arena, a long series of chunks of aqueduct, and city walls. In the heart of the atmospheric hilltop old town, the **Groupe Episcopal** includes an austere early Gothic cathedral, a cloister mixing Gothic and Romanesque styles, and a baptistery dating from the 5th century. ⊠ *Pl. Formigé.* ⊙ *Oct.–Mar., Tues.–Sun. 9–noon and 2–5; Apr.–Sept., daily 9–noon and 2–5.*

Cannes

In 1834 a chance event was to change the town of Cannes forever. Lord Brougham, Britain's lord chancellor, was en route to Nice when an outbreak of cholera forced the authorities to freeze all travel. Trapped in Cannes, he fell in love with the place and built himself a house to use as an annual refuge from the British winter. The English aristocracy, czars, kings, and princes soon caught on, and Cannes became a community for the international elite. Grand palace hotels were built to cater to them, and Cannes came to symbolize dignified luxury. Today, Cannes is also synonymous with the International Film Festival.

Stroll along seafront **La Croisette,** an elegant promenade. Along the promenade are cafés, boutiques, and luxury hotels. Almost all beaches are private, but that doesn't mean you can't use them, only that you must pay for the privilege. Behind the promenade is the town, and beyond, the hills with the villas of the very rich. Only a few steps inland is the ★ old town, known as **Le Suquet,** with its steep, cobbled streets and its 12th-century watchtower.

$$ ✕ **Chez Astoux.** For seafood, this stands out among the other restaurants on the block. The ambience is simple but elegant, both on the terrace and inside. Locals carry home shellfish platters from its portfresh supplies. ⊠ *43 rue Félix-Faure,* ☎ *04–93–39–06–22. AE, DC, MC, V.*

$ ✕ **Bouchon d'Objectif.** Popular and unpretentious, this tiny bistro
★ serves inexpensive Provençal fare prepared with a sophisticated twist. An ever-changing display of photography adds a hip touch to the simple ocher-and-aqua setting. ⊠ *10 rue Constantine,* ☎ *04–93–99–21–76. AE, MC, V. Closed Mon.*

$ ✕ **Montagard.** This extraordinary spot serves elegant, imaginative
★ vegetarian cuisine—nearly nonexistent in France—in a chic, low-key setting. ⊠ *6 rue Maréchal Joffre,* ☎ *04–93–39–98–38. MC, V. Closed Sun. No lunch Mon.*

$$$ ▥ **Majestic.** Of the luxury hotels lining La Croisette, this one has an air of aristocratic discretion (though prices are mega-deluxe). Rooms are spacious and traditional, though refreshingly pastel. ⊠ *14 La Croisette, 06400,* ☎ *04–92–98–77–00,* ℻ *04–93–38–97–90. 298 rooms. Restaurant, pool. AE, DC, MC, V. Closed mid-Nov.–Dec.*

$$ ▥ **Molière.** Plush, intimate and low-keyed, this low-priced hotel has small
★ rooms in cool shades of peach and indigo. Nearly all overlook a vast enclosed front garden. ⊠ *5 rue Molière, 06400,* ☎ *04–93–68–16–16,* ℻ *04–93–68–29–57. 42 rooms. AE, MC, V. Closed mid-Nov.–late Dec.*

$ ▥ **Albert Ier.** In a quiet residential area above the Forville market, this neo–Art Deco mansion is in an enclosed garden. It's a 10-minute walk downhill to La Croisette and the beach. ⊠ *68 av. de Grasse, 06400,* ☎ *04–93–39–24–04,* ℻ *04–93–38–83–75. 11 rooms. MC, V.*

Grasse

Grasse is perched in the hills behind Cannes. Take N85 or just follow your nose to the town that claims to be the perfume capital of the world. A good portion of its 40,000 inhabitants work at distilling and extracting scent from the tons of roses, lavender, and jasmine produced here every year. The various perfumers are only too happy to guide you around their fragrant establishments. **Fragonard** (⊠ 20 bd. Fragonard, ☎ 04–93–77–94–30) is the best known. The old town is attractive, with its narrow alleys and massive, somber **Cathédrale.** Three of the paintings inside the cathedral are by Rubens and one is by Fragonard, who lived here for many years.

Mougins

Quaint, fortified, hilltop Mougins is made up of a cluster of ancient houses dating from the 15th century. Unfortunately, its popularity means that you have to park at the bottom of the hill and hike into the old village, which is a little hard to find behind the new houses and shopping centers that form Cannes's suburban sprawl. Don't be misled by signs for Mougins-le-Haut, a huge real-estate development. Be sure to stop in at the **Notre-Dame-de-Vie** hermitage, one of the village's most interesting sights; Picasso choose to live here until his death.

$$$$ ✕▥ **Moulin de Mougins.** Roger Vergé's fine hotel and restaurant (reservations essential; closed Monday, no lunch Thursday) is in a converted mill a short distance west of Mougins on D3. The cuisine, now created with chef Serge Chollet, ranges from seemingly simple salads to rich sauces for lobster, salmon, and turbot. The atmosphere is surprisingly informal. There are five elegantly rustic guest rooms. ✉ *Quartier Notre-Dame-de-Vie, 424 chemin du Moulin, 06250,* ☎ *04–93–75–78–24,* FAX *04–93–90–18–55. 3 rooms, 2 apartments. Restaurant. AE, DC, MC, V. Closed Feb.–Mar.*

Antibes

On the east side of Cannes and Napoule Bay are Antibes and Juan-les-Pins, two villages that flow into one another with no perceptible boundary on either side of the peninsula, the Cap d'Antibes. Antibes, an older village, dates from the 4th century BC, when it was a Greek trading port. Every morning except Monday, the market on the Cours Masséna comes alive with the colors of roses, carnations, anemones, and tulips.

The Grimaldis, the family that rules Monaco, built the **Château Grimaldi** during the 12th century on the remains of a Roman camp. Today, the château's main attraction is the **Musée Picasso** (Picasso Museum), a bounty of paintings, ceramics, and lithographs inspired by the sea and Greek mythology. ✉ *Pl. du Château,* ☎ *04–93–90–54–20.* ☉ *June–Sept., Tues.–Sun. 10–6; Oct.–May, Tues.–Sun. 10–noon and 2–6.*

$$ ✗ **Le Brûlot.** This busy bistro is one street back from the market. Chef
★ Christian Blancheri hoists anything from suckling pigs to apple pies in and out of his roaring wood oven. ✉ *3 rue Frédéric Isnard,* ☎ *04–93–34–17–76. MC, V. Closed Sun., last 2 wks of Aug., last wk Dec.–1st wk Jan. No lunch Mon.*

$$$$ ✗🏨 **Juana.** At this luxuriously renovated '30s hotel run by the second generation of the Barrache family, service is attentive and rooms are large and individually decorated. Chef Christian Morisset wins praise for his fine seafood and lamb at La Terrasse, one of the best restaurants on the coast. ✉ *av. Georges-Gallice, 06160 Juan-les-Pins,* ☎ *04–93–61–08–70,* FAX *04–93–61–76–60. 45 rooms. Restaurant, pool. AE, MC, V. Closed late Oct.–mid-Apr.*

$$ ✗🏨 **Auberge Provençale.** Rooms in this onetime abbey, complete with
★ beams and canopied beds, are charming. The dining room (closed Monday, no lunch Tuesday) and the garden are decorated with the same impeccable taste. Cuisine includes fine bouillabaisse, fresh seafood, and grilled lamb and duck. ✉ *61 Pl. Nationale, 06600,* ☎ *04–93–34–13–24,* FAX *04–93–34–89–88. 6 rooms. Restaurant. AE, DC, MC, V.*

Nice

Numbers in the margin correspond to points of interest on the Nice map.

With a population of 350,000 and its own university, Nice is the undisputed capital of the Côte d'Azur. Founded by the Greeks as Nikaia, it has lived through several civilizations and was attached to France only in 1860. It consequently has a profusion of Greek, Italian, British, and French styles, and a raffish, seductive charm. It also has a labyrinthine old town, an opera house, museums, and flourishing markets—all strung along an open stretch of pebble beach. During the pre-Lent Carnival, the town is especially lively.

① **Place Masséna** is a fine square built in 1815 to celebrate a local hero: one of Napoléon's most successful generals. Stroll through the Jardin
② Albert to get to the **Promenade des Anglais** (English Promenade), built by the English community here in 1824. The promenade is very busy, but it's a pleasant strand between town and sea with fine views of the Baie des Anges (Bay of Angels).

③ In the **Palais Masséna** (Masséna Palace) is a museum of city history with eclectic treasures ranging from Garibaldi's death sheet to Empress

Josephine's tiara. ✉ *65 rue de France*, ☎ *04–93–88–11–34*. ☉ *Wed.– Mon. 10–noon and 2–6.*

❹ The **Musée des Beaux-Arts Jules-Chéret** (Jules Chéret Fine Arts Museum) was built in 1878 as a palatial mansion for a Russian princess. The rich collection has paintings by Sisley, Bonnard, and Vuillard; sculptures by Rodin; and ceramics by Picasso. ✉ *33 av. des Baumettes*, ☎ *04–92–15–28–28.* ☉ *May–Sept., Tues.–Sun. 10–noon and 2–6; Oct.– Apr., Tues.–Sun. 10–noon and 2–5.*

The Cours Saleya flower market and the narrow streets in Vieux Nice (Old Nice) are the prettiest parts of town: While you're market-brows-
★ ❺ ing, stop in to see the 18th-century **Chapelle de la Miséricorde,** renowned for its ornate Baroque interior and sculpted decoration. At the north-
❻ ern end of the old town is the vast Italian-style **Place Garibaldi**—all
❼ yellow-ocher buildings and formal fountains. The **Musée d'Art Modern** (Modern Art Museum), off Place Garibaldi, has an outstanding collection of French and international abstract and figurative art from the late 1950s onward. ✉ *Promenade des Arts*, ☎ *04–93–62–61–62.* ☉ *Wed.–Mon. 11–6, Fri. 11–10.*

❽ The **Musée National Message Biblique Chagall** (Marc Chagall Museum of Biblical Themes) has a superb, life-affirming collection of Chagall's (1887–1985) late works, including the 17 huge canvases of *The Message of the Bible,* which took 13 years to complete. ✉ *av. du Dr-Mé-nard*, ☎ *04–93–53–87–20.* ☉ *July–Sept., Wed.–Mon. 10–6; Oct.– June, Wed.–Mon. 10–5.*

❾ A 17th-century Italian villa amid Roman remains contains the **Musée Matisse** (Matisse Museum) with paintings and bronzes by Henri Matisse (1869–1954), who lived nearly 40 years in Nice. ✉ *164 av. des Arènes-de-Cimiez.* ☎ *04–93–81–08–08.* ☉ *Apr.–Oct., Wed.–Mon. 10–6; Nov.–Mar. 10–5.*

❿ Next door to the Matisse museum, the **Musée Archéologique** displays findings from the Roman city that once flourished here. ☎ *04–93–81–59–57.* ☉ *Apr.–Sept., Tues.–Sun. 10–noon and 2–6; Oct.–Mar., 10–1 and 2–5.*

$$ ✗ **La Mérenda.** The back-to-bistro boom climaxed here when super-
★ star chef Dominique Le Stanc took over this tiny, unpretentious landmark of Provençal cuisine. Now he and his wife work in the miniature open kitchen creating the ultimate versions of stuffed sardines, pistou, and slow-simmered *daubes* (beef stews). Stop by in person to reserve entry to the inner sanctum. ✉ *4 rue de la Terrasse*, ☎ *no phone. No credit cards. Closed weekends, last wk in July, 1st 2 wks in Aug., and school holidays.*

$–$$ ✗ **Lou Pistou.** This mom-and-pop shoebox of a restaurant serves real, authentically prepared Niçoise home cooking. ✉ *4 rue de la Terrasse (just off Espace Masséna)*, ☎ *04–93–62–21–82. MC, V. Closed weekends.*

$$$$ ✗🏨 **Château des Ollières.** The genteel owner of this fantastical neo-Moroccan palace, once the dream house of Prince Lobnov-Rostowsky, has financed its restoration by conceding to modern commerce. Its eight rooms are furnished with period details—herringbone parquet, crown moldings, and chandeliers. Deluxe rooms have vast marble baths and fine old furniture; standard rooms are filled with toile de Jouy. The candlelit restaurant functions as a table d'hôte—one prix-fixe menu each day. ✉ *39 av. des Baumettes, 06000*, ☎ *04–92–15–77–99*, FAX *04–93–88–35–68. 8 rooms. Restaurant. AE, MC, V.*

$$ 🏨 **Windsor.** This is a memorably eccentric hotel with a vision: Most
★ of its white-on-white rooms either have frescoes of mythic themes or

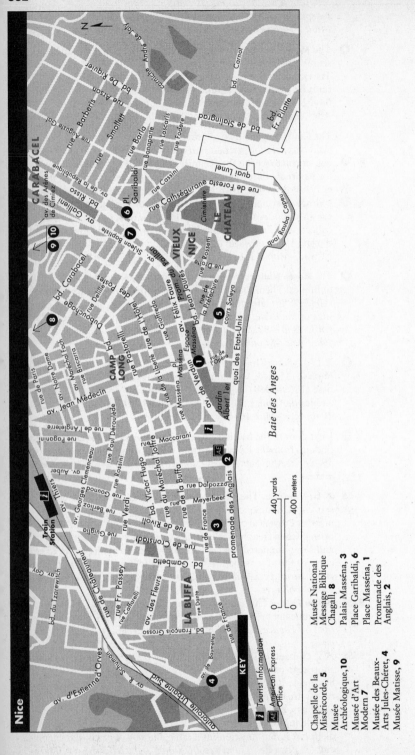

are works of artists' whimsy. But the real draw of this otherworldly place is its astonishing city-center garden. ⊠ *11 rue Dalpozzo, 06000,* ☎ *04–93–88–59–35,* FAX *04–93–88–94–57. 57 rooms. Restaurant, bar, pool. AE, DC, MC, V.*

Monaco

Sixteen km (10 mi) along the coast east of Nice lies tiny Monaco. Though there is no frontier, it is a different country; when dialing numbers from outside Monaco, including France, you must prefix the call with "377."

For more than a century Monaco's livelihood was centered beneath the copper roof of its splendid **casino.** The oldest section dates from 1878 and was conceived by Charles Garnier, architect of the Paris opera house. ⊠ *Pl. du Casino,* ☎ *92–16–21–21. Persons under 21 not admitted.* ☑ *European rooms, 50 frs; English Club and Monte-Carlo Sporting Club rooms, 100 frs; access to slot machines, free.* ⊙ *Daily noon–4* AM. *Closed May 1.*

Monaco Town, the principality's old quarter, has many vaulted passageways and exudes an almost tangible medieval feel. The magnificent **Palais du Prince** (Prince's Palace), a grandiose Italianate structure with a Moorish tower, was largely rebuilt in the last century. Here, since 1297, the Grimaldi dynasty has lived and ruled. The spectacle of the **Changing of the Guard** occurs each morning at 11:55; inside, guided tours take you through the state apartments and a wing containing the **Palace Archives** and **Musée Napoléon** (Napoleonic Museum), which remains open throughout the year. ⊠ *Pl. du Palais,* ☎ *93–25–18–31.* ⊙ *June–Oct., daily 9:30–6:30; Musée Napoléon and Palace Archives: Tues.–Sun. 9:30–6:30.*

Monaco's **Cathédrale** (⊠ 4 rue Colonel Bellando de Castro) is a late-19th-century neo-Romanesque confection in which Philadelphia-born Princess Grace lies entombed in splendor along with past members of the Grimaldi dynasty.

At the **Musée Océanographique** (Oceanography Museum and Aquarium), also an internationally renowned research institute founded by Prince Albert and run for years by underwater explorer Jacques Cousteau (1910–97), the aquarium is the undisputed highlight. ⊠ *av. St-Martin,* ☎ *93–15–36–00.* ⊙ *July–Aug., daily 9–8; Sept. and Apr.–June, daily 9–7; Oct.–Mar., daily 9:30–7; Nov.–Feb., daily 10–6.*

The Moneghetti area is the setting for the **Jardin Exotique** (Exotic Plants Garden), where 600 varieties of cacti and succulents cling to the rock face. Your ticket to the Jardin Exotique also allows you to explore the caves next door, and to visit the adjacent **Musée d'Anthropologie Préhistorique** (Museum of Prehistoric Anthropology). ⊠ *bd. du Jardin Exotique,* ☎ *93–15–80–06.* ⊙ *Mid-May–mid-Sept., daily 9–7; mid-Sept.–mid-May, daily 9–6.*

$$$$ ✕ **Louis XV.** The opulent decor never manages to upstage chef Alain
★ Ducasse's beautifully conceived "country cooking," where ravioli with foie gras and truffles slum happily alongside salt cod and tripe. ⊠ *Hôtel de Paris, Pl. du Casino,* ☎ *92–16–30–01. Reservations essential. AE, DC, MC, V. Closed Tues. and Wed. (except dinner July–Aug.), mid-Feb.–early Mar., and late Nov.–late Dec.*

$$–$$$ ✕ **Castelroc.** With its pine-shaded terrace across from the entrance to the Prince's Palace, this is one of the more popular lunch spots in town. The cuisine is a mix of classic and regional flavors, from *anchoïade* (anchovy paste) to tender grilled scampi. ⊠ *Pl. du Palais,* ☎ *93–30–36–68. MC, V. Closed Sat. and end Nov.–Dec.*

$$$$ ⊞ **Hôtel de Paris.** At this famed establishment, elegance, expense, luxury, dignity, and old-world charm are the watchwords. Built in 1864, it still exudes the gold-plated splendor of an era when kings and grand dukes were pampered here. You, on the other hand, may be ignored. ⊠ *Pl. du Casino, 98000,* ☎ *92–16–30–00,* FAX *92–16–38–50. 245 rooms. 4 restaurants, 2 pools. AE, DC, MC, V.*

$$ ⊞ **Alexandra.** The friendly proprietress, Madame Larouquie, makes you feel right at home in this central, comfortable spot. Who cares if the color schemes clash and decor is spare, when the baths are big and newly redone? ⊠ *35 bd. Princesse-Charlotte, 98000,* ☎ *93–50–63–13,* FAX *92–16–06–48. 55 rooms. AE, DC, MC, V.*

Menton

Menton also once belonged to the Grimaldis and, like Nice, became part of France only in 1860. Because of its popularity among British visitors, the western side of the town was developed at the turn of the century to cater to the influx of the rich and famous, with spacious avenues, first-class hotels, and the inevitable casino. The eastern side of town long remained the domain of the local fishermen but has also been developed. A large marina was built and the Sablettes, once a tiny beach, has been artificially extended.

Down by the harbor is a small 17th-century fort, where Jean Cocteau, the artist, writer, and filmmaker, once worked. It now houses the **Musée Jean Cocteau,** with a collection of his work. ⊠ *111 quai Napoléon,* ☎ *04–93–57–72–30.* ☉ *Wed.–Sun. 10–noon and 2–6.*

$$–$$$ ✕⊞ **Aiglon.** Sweep down the curving stone stair to the terrazzo mosaic lobby of this lovely 1880 garden-villa; or settle onto your little balcony overlooking the grounds and a tiny wedge of sea. There's a room for every whim, all soft-edged, comfortable, and romantic. The poolside restaurant, Le Riaumont, serves up classic seafood and candlelight. ⊠ *7 av. de la Madone, 06502,* ☎ *04–93–57–55–55,* FAX *04–93–35–92–39. 28 rooms, 2 apartments. Restaurant, bar, pool. AE, MC, V.*

The Côte d'Azur Essentials

Getting Around

A8 is the only way to get around the Côte d'Azur quickly (keep lots of change handy for tolls). A car is best for exploring the hill towns perched behind the Côte d'Azur, but a train line follows the coast from Marseille to the Italian border, providing excellent access to the seaside resort towns. Taking local buses (marked GARE ROUTIÈRE) or a guided tour (☞ *below*) is necessary to visit Grasse, Vence, and other inland areas if you're traveling by public transportation.

Guided Tours

SNCF runs many organized tours (contact the Nice Tourist Office, ☞ *below*) to areas otherwise hard to reach. Boats operate from Nice to Marseille; from St-Tropez to the charming Hyères Islands; and from Antibes, Cannes, and Juan-les-Pins to the Lérins Islands.

Visitor Information

Antibes (⊠ 11 Pl. Général-de-Gaulle, ☎ 04–92–90–53–00). **Cannes** (⊠ Palais des Festivals La Croisette, ☎ 04–93–39–01–01). **Fréjus** (⊠ 325 rue Jean-Jaurès, ☎ 04–93–39–24–53). **Grasse** (⊠ 22 cours Honoré-Cresp, ☎ 04–93–36–03–56). **Juan-les-Pins** (⊠ 51 bd. Charles-Guillaumont, ☎ 04–92–90–53–05). **Menton** (⊠ Palais de l'Europe, av. Boyer, 04–92–41–76–76). **Monaco** (⊠ 2a bd. des Moulins, ☎ 377/92–16–61–16). **Nice** (⊠ av. Thiers, ☎ 04–92–14–48–00; ⊠ 5 av. Gustave-V, ☎ 04–93–87–60–60). **St-Tropez** (⊠ quai Jean-Jaurès, ☎ 04–94–97–45–21).

12 GERMANY

MUNICH, THE BLACK FOREST, FRANKFURT, THE RHINE, HAMBURG, BERLIN, SAXONY AND THURINGIA

October 3, 2000, marks the 10th anniversary of Germany's unification. Forty years of division wrought many differences between the eastern and western states, but the country is well past getting to know itself and is moving on to defining its future, led by a new government in the restored capital of Berlin.

Unification has been easier politically than economically, yet unemployment in the eastern states is what contributed greatly to 16-year incumbent chancellor Helmut Kohl's downfall and the election of Gerhard Schröder, a Social Democrat, to replace him. The new left-of-center government is expected to re-engerize the country, much as Americans hoped Clinton would theirs in 1992. The new chancellor's government and the Bundestag (lower house of parliament) returned to Berlin in April 1999. Although some federal ministries will remain on the Rhine, the move ends Bonn's 50-year reign as capital of West Germany.

One of the touchiest domestic issues remains unemployment, which has hovered at the record level of 4 million nationwide and has been twice as bad in the five states of the east as in the west (18.3% versus 9.5% in November 1998, for example). Most eastern Germans earn less than their counterparts to the west, but many of their basic living costs are lower. Overall, eastern shops may be less stylish, but they are filled with the sorts of material goods that were unobtainable under the Communist regime.

Eastern Germany's emergence from Communism has not so much inspired a new sense of nationhood as it has revived regional traditions and identities. The villages south of Leipzig and Dresden have more in common with their neighbors in northern Bavaria, from whom they were cut off for four decades, than with Berlin bureaucrats.

Germans are industrious. But while they may hammer away at a building site by 7 AM or seat themselves at a desk by 8 AM, they take their leisure time just as seriously. Annual vacations of up to six weeks are the norm, and secular and religious festivals occupy at least another

12 days. Every town and village, and many a city neighborhood, manages at least one "Fest" a year, when the beer barrels are rolled out and sausages are thrown on the grill. The seasons have their own festivities: Fasching (carnival) heralds the end of winter, beer gardens open up with the first warm rays of sunshine; fall is celebrated with the Munich Oktoberfest; and Advent brings Christkindlmärkte, colorful pre-Christmas markets held in town and city squares.

The great outdoors has always been an important escape for Germans. A Bavarian mountain inn, on a gentle slope rising to the Alps, is only a short drive from boisterous Munich. The busy industrial city of Stuttgart lies at the gateway to the *Schwarzwald* (Black Forest), a region of spas, hiking trails, and cuckoo clocks. Sprawling Berlin is filled with its own lakes and green parklands. The German trains that link these various regions are fast, clean, and punctual, and a drive on a speed limit–free autobahn will give you an idea of just how fast those BMWs and Mercedeses are built to go.

GERMANY A TO Z

Customs
For details on imports and duty-free limits, *see* Customs & Duties *in* Chapter 1.

Dining
The range of dining experiences in Germany is vast: everything from high-priced nouvelle cuisine to varieties of sausages. Countrywide, seek out *Gaststätten, Gasthäuser,* or *Gasthöfe*—local inns—for atmosphere and regional specialties. Beer gardens in Bavaria, *Apfelwein* (alcoholic apple cider) taverns in Frankfurt, and *Kneipen*—the pubs–cum–local cafés on the corner—in Berlin nearly always offer the best value and local atmosphere. Just about every town will have a *Ratskeller,* a cellar restaurant in the town hall, where exposed beams, huge fireplaces, sturdy tables, and immense portions are the rule.

The natural accompaniment to German food is either beer or wine. Munich is the beer capital of Germany, though there's no part of the country where you won't find a local brew. Say *"Helles"* or *"Export"* if you want light beer; *"Dunkles"* if you want dark beer. In Bavaria try the sour but refreshing beer brewed from wheat, called *Weissbier.*

Germany is also a major producer of wine (mostly white), and much of it is of superlative quality. All wines are graded in one of three basic categories: *Tafelwein* (table wine); *Qualitätswein* (fine wine); and *Qualitätswein mit Prädikat* (top-quality wine).

MEALTIMES
Breakfast, served from 6:30 to 10 (in some cafés and Kneipen, until as late as 2 or 4 PM), is often a substantial meal, with cold meats, cheeses, rolls, and fruit. Many city hotels offer Sunday brunch, and the trend is rapidly catching on. Lunch is served from around 11:30 (especially in rural areas) to around 2; dinner is generally from 6 until 9:30, or earlier in some quiet country areas. Big-city hotels and popular restaurants serve later. Lunch tends to be the main meal. Try something from the lunchtime *Tageskarte,* or suggested menu, for maximum nourishment at minimum outlay.

RATINGS
The following chart gives price ranges for restaurants in the western part of Germany. Food prices in the former East Germany are slightly lower and still somewhat unstable, although many city restaurants match

rates in western Germany. Prices are per person and include a first course, main course, dessert, and tip and 10% tax.

CATEGORY	MAJOR CITIES AND RESORTS	OTHER AREAS
$$$$	over DM 100	over DM 90
$$$	DM 75–DM 100	DM 55–DM 90
$$	DM 50–DM 75	DM 35–DM 55
$	under DM 50	under DM 35

WHAT TO WEAR

Jacket and tie are advised for restaurants in the $$$ and $$$$ categories. Casual dress is appropriate elsewhere.

Language

English has long been taught in high schools in the western part of Germany. Consequently, many people under age 40 speak some English. Older people in rural areas are less familiar with English, although some may remember the language from contacts with American and British forces who occupied portions of the country after World War II.

Among Germany's many dialects, probably the most difficult to comprehend is Bavaria's. Except for older people in remote, rural districts, virtually everyone can also speak *Hochdeutsch,* the German equivalent of Oxford English. Hochdeutsch is always used on TV and radio.

Lodging

The standard of German hotels, from top-notch luxury spots (of which the country has more than its fair share) to the humblest pension, is excellent. You can expect courteous service; clean and comfortable rooms; and, in rural areas especially, considerable old-German atmosphere.

The country has numerous *Gasthöfe* or *Gasthäuser* (country inns); pensions or *Fremdenheime* (guest houses); and, at the lowest end of the scale, *Zimmer,* meaning rooms, normally in private houses. Look for the sign ZIMMER FREI (rooms free) or ZU VERMIETEN (for rent). A red sign reading BESETZT means there are no vacancies.

Lists of hotels are available from the **Deutsche Hotel- und Gaststättenverband** (✉ Kronprinzenstr. 46, D-53173 Bonn, ☎ 0228/82008–0, FAX 0228/82008–46) and from all regional and local tourist offices. Tourist offices will also make reservations for you—they usually charge a nominal fee—but may have difficulty doing so after 4 PM in peak season and on weekends. There is also an excellent, nationwide reservations service, **Turistische Informations-und Buchungssystem** (TIBS, ✉ Yorckstr. 32, Freiburg im Breisgau, ☎ 0761/885810, FAX 0761/8858129), which is open weekdays 9–6, and Saturday 9–1.

Most hotels have restaurants, but those describing themselves as *Garni* will provide breakfast only. Many larger hotels offer no-smoking rooms, and some even have no-smoking floors, so ask. We classify an apartment here as having two separate rooms and cooking facilities; otherwise a larger-than-standard unit with a sitting room is considered a suite.

Accommodations in eastern Germany are blossoming under private enterprise, though top-level hotels remain fairly scarce. If you want to stay in a good hotel, book well in advance. Hotel rooms in the cities are in demand year-round because of the high volume of business travel.

CAMPING

There are some 5,000 campsites in Germany, about 2,700 of which are listed by the **German Camping Club** (DCC, ✉ Mandlstr. 28, D-80802

Germany (Deutschland)

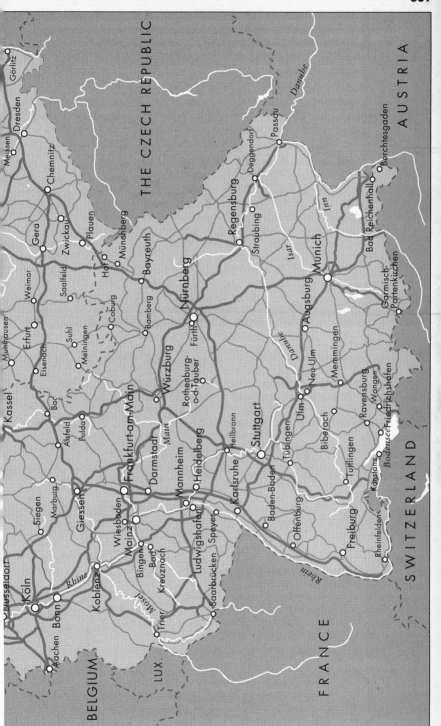

Munich, ☎ 089/380–1420, ℻ 089/334737). Most are open from May through October, with about 400 staying open year-round. They tend to be crowded in summer, so make reservations a day or two ahead. Prices at ordinary campsites range from DM 20 to DM 50 per night for two adults, a car, and a tent or trailer. There are also some higher-priced facilities, replete with pool, sports facilities, and entertainment programs.

CASTLE HOTELS

Germany's *Schloss,* or castle, hotels are privately owned and run, and prices are mostly moderate; some of the simpler establishments, however, may lack a little in the way of comfort, and furnishings can be basic. On the whole they're delightful, with antiques, imposing interiors, and out-of-the-way locations. For a brochure listing castle hotels, contact **European Castle Hotels** (✉ Postfach 1111, D-67142 Deidesheim an der Weinstrasse, ☎ 06326/70000, ℻ 06326/700022).

FARM VACATIONS

Taking an *Urlaub auf dem Bauernhof* (farm vacation) has increased dramatically in popularity over the past decade. Almost every regional tourist office has listings of farms, by area, offering bed-and-breakfast, apartments, or whole farmhouses to rent. The **German Agricultural Association** (DLG; ✉ Eschborner Landstr. 122, D-60489 Frankfurt/Main, ☎ 069/247–880, ℻ 069/247–88–110) produces an annual catalog of more than 1,500 farms, all of them inspected and graded, that offer lodging. The brochure costs DM 14.50 in bookstores, and DM 20 postpaid.

HOTEL GROUPS

Ringhotels (✉ Belfortstr. 6–8, D-81667 Munich, ☎ 089/458–70354, ℻ 089/45870331) groups 154 individually owned and managed hotels in the medium price range. Many are in the countryside or in pretty villages. Package deals of two to three days are available.

Among the most delightful places to stay and eat in Germany are the aptly named **Romantik Hotels and Restaurants.** All are in historic buildings—this is a precondition of membership—and are personally run by the owners. The emphasis generally is on solid comfort, good food, and style. A listing of all Romantik Hotels is available outside Germany from German National Tourist Offices (☞ Visitor Information *in* Chapter 1).

RATINGS

Breakfast is usually, but not always, included in the room rate, so check before you book. Major hotels in cities often have lower rates on weekends or when business is quiet. If you're lucky, you can find reductions of up to 60%. Likewise, rooms reserved after 10 PM will often carry a discount.

The following chart is for hotels throughout Germany. In Berlin and Hamburg, price categories are about DM 50 higher than those for major cities, indicated below. Prices are for standard double rooms and include tax.

CATEGORY	MAJOR CITIES AND RESORTS	OTHER AREAS
$$$$	over DM 300	over DM 200
$$$	DM 200–DM 300	DM 160–DM 200
$$	DM 140–DM 200	DM 100–DM 160
$	under DM 140	under DM 100

RENTALS

Apartments and houses, most accommodating from two to eight guests, can be rented throughout Germany. Rates are reasonable, with reductions for longer stays. Rates for short- or medium-term stays usually include charges for gas and electricity. Local and regional tourist offices have lists of apartments in their areas; otherwise contact the Deutsche Hotel- und Gaststättenverband (DEHOGA) (☞ *above*).

YOUTH HOSTELS

Germany's more than 600 *Jugendherberge* (youth hostels) are among the most efficient and up-to-date in Europe. Many are in castles. There's an age limit of 27 in Bavaria; elsewhere, there are no restrictions, though those under 20 take preference if space is limited. You must be a member of a national hosteling association or Hostelling International (HI) in order to stay at a hostel. Rates range from $10 to $25 per night. The **JH Service GmbH** (✉ Postfach 1462, D-32704 Detmold, ☎ 05231/74010, ℻ 05231/7401–49) provides a complete list of German hostels for DM 16 and has information on regional offices around the country. Hostels must be reserved well in advance for midsummer, especially in eastern Germany. Bookings for hostels can be made only by calling hostels directly.

Mail

POSTAL RATES

Airmail letters to the United States and Canada cost DM 3; postcards cost DM 2. Airmail letters to the United Kingdom cost DM 1.10; postcards cost DM 1.

RECEIVING MAIL

You can arrange to have mail sent to you in care of any German post office; have the envelope marked "Postlagernd." This service is free. Alternatively, if you have an American Express card or have booked a vacation with American Express you can have mail sent to any American Express office in Germany; there's no charge.

Money Matters

COSTS

Inflation crept up in the 1990s (although at press time the annual rate of inflation was being held below 1%). The most expensive areas to visit are the major cities, notably Berlin, Frankfurt, Hamburg, and Munich. Costs are somewhat lower in eastern Germany, but businesses that cater specifically to visitors are increasingly charging western German rates.

CURRENCY

Although the new European monetary unit, the euro, officially made its appearance in 1999, it won't replace the Deutschmark as a currency until the year 2002. Deutschmark banknotes and coins are still the means of exchange. However, stores, restaurants, and other businesses increasingly show their prices in both the D-mark and the euro. Read all prices carefully and be sure that bills, credit card charges, and so on, indicate whether the price is in the euro (EUR) or the mark (DM). There are roughly two marks in a euro. The Deutschmark, generally referred to as the mark, is divided into 100 pfennige. There are bills of 5 (rare), 10, 20, 50, 100, 200, 500, and 1,000 marks and coins of 1, 2, 5, 10, and 50 pfennige and 1, 2, and 5 marks. At press time (spring 1999), the mark stood at DM 1.91 to the U.S. dollar, DM 1.30 to the Canadian dollar, and DM 2.99 to the pound sterling.

SAMPLE PRICES

Cup of coffee in a café, DM 3.50, in a stand-up snack bar DM 1.80; mug of beer in a beer hall, DM 4.50, bottle of beer from a supermarket, DM 1.50; soft drink, DM 2; ham sandwich, DM 4; 3-km (2-mi) taxi ride, DM 13.

TIPPING

Overtipping is as frowned upon as not tipping at all. In restaurants service is included (under the heading *Bedienung*, at the bottom of the check), and it is customary to round out the check to the next mark or two, a practice also commonplace in cafés, beer halls, and bars. For taxi drivers, also round out to the next mark or two: for DM 11.20, make it DM 12; for DM 11.80, make it DM 13. Railway and airport porters (if you can find any) have their own scale of charges, but round out the requested amount to the next mark. Hotel porters get DM 1 per bag. Doormen are tipped the same amount for small services, such as calling a cab. Room service should be rewarded with at least DM 2 every time you use it. Maids should get about DM 2 per day. Double all these figures at luxury hotels. Service-station attendants get 50 pf or DM 1 for checking oil and tires or cleaning windshields.

National Holidays

January 1; January 6 (Epiphany—Bavaria, Baden-Württemberg, and Sachsen-Anhalt only); April 21 (Good Friday); April 24 (Easter Monday); May 1 (Worker's Day); June 1 (Ascension); June 12 (Pentecost Monday); June 22 (Corpus Christi—south Germany only); August 15 (Assumption Day—Bavaria and Saarland only); October 3 (German Unity Day); November 1 (All Saints' Day); December 24–26.

Opening and Closing Times

Banks. Times vary from state to state and city to city, but banks are usually open weekdays from 8:30 or 9 to 2 or 3 (5 or 6 on Thursday). Some banks close from 12:30 to 1:30. Branches at airports and main train stations open as early as 6:30 AM and close as late as 10:30 PM. **Museums** are generally open from Tuesday through Sunday 10–5. Some close for an hour or more at lunch, and some are open on Monday. Many stay open until 8 or 9 on Wednesday and/or Thursday. Larger **shops** and department stores open weekdays 9:30–8, and Saturday 9:30–4. Many smaller shops, however, close around 6:30 PM.

Shopping

SALES TAX

German goods carry a 16% value-added tax (VAT). You can claim the tax back either as you leave the country or once you've returned home. When you make a purchase, ask the shopkeeper for a form known as an *Ausfuhr-Abnehmerbescheinigung*; he or she will help you fill it out. As you leave the country present the form, plus the goods and receipts, to German customs, which will give you an official export certificate or stamp and point you in the direction of a refund point where you can recover the tax in cash. Alternatively, send the form back to the shop, and it will send the refund.

Telephoning

COUNTRY CODE

Germany's country code is 49. When dialing a number in Germany from outside the country, drop the initial 0 in the regional code.

INTERNATIONAL CALLS

A four-minute call to the United States costs DM 3.40 between 2 PM and 3 AM and DM 2.92 the rest of the day. Calls can be made from just about any telephone booth, most of which are card operated. If you expect to do a lot of calling, international or local, purchase a telephone card (☞ Local Calls, *below*). You can also make international calls from post offices, even those in small country towns. Pay the clerk at the end of your call, adding a DM 2 service fee. To reach an **AT&T** long-distance operator, dial 0130–0010; for **MCI WorldCom,** dial 0130–0012; for **Sprint,** 0130–0013. Dial 0010 for a local operator who handles international calls.

LOCAL CALLS

Card phones have almost entirely replaced coin-operated phones: Cards cost DM 12 or DM 50 (the latter good for DM 60 worth of calls) and are sold at all post offices and many exchange places. The rare coin-operated phone takes 10 pf, DM 1, and DM 5 pieces. If you need an operator, dial 010. You'll get six minutes for a 30pf local call.

Transportation

BY BICYCLE

Bicycles can be rented at more than 160 train stations throughout Germany from April through October. The cost is DM 6 to DM 25 per day. You may have to leave cash or your passport or other identification as a deposit, depending on the arrangement with the private contractors who now handle the service. You can pick up a bike at one station and return it to another, provided both stations rent bikes. Mountain bikes can be rented for DM 20 to DM 40 a day at the Alpine stations of Garmisch-Partenkirchen, Immenstadt, Oberstdorf, and Sonthofen. You can usually take a bike on local or regional transportation systems at no extra charge. Buses and rail cars almost always have a "cargo space" that can be used. You will need to buy a *Fahrradkarte,* or bicycle ticket (DM 6 for journeys up to 50 km/32 mi; DM 12 for longer trips), to take your bike on the railway; InterCity Express trains do not carry bikes. Most cities also have companies that rent bikes for about DM 15 per day or DM 80 to DM 90 a week. The nationwide bicycle hotline is ☎ 0180/319-4194.

BY BOAT

You can cruise rivers and lakes throughout Germany. The biggest fleet belongs to the Köln-based **Köln-Düsseldorfer Rheinschiffahrt** (KD Rhine Line; ⊠ Frankenwerft 15, D-50667 Köln, ☎ 0221/208-8288), which operates on the Rhine, Mosel, Saar, Neckar, Danube, Elbe, and Main rivers. Its U.S. representative is **JFO CruiseShip Corp.** (⊠ 2500 Westchester Ave., Purchase, NY 10577, ☎ 914/696-3600 or 800/346-6525; ⊠ 323 Geary St., Suite 603, San Francisco, CA 94102, ☎ 415/392-8817 or 800/858-8587).

Services on the 160-km (100-mi) stretch of the Danube (Donau) between the spectacular Kelheim Gorge and Passau on the Austrian border are operated by **Donauschiffahrt Wurm & Köck** (⊠ Höllgasse 26, D-94032 Passau, ☎ 0851/929-292, ﬀ 0851/33518). The Bodensee (Lake Constance), the largest lake in Germany, has up to 40 ships crisscrossing it in summer. **Bodensee-Schiffsbetriebe** (⊠ Hafenstr. 6, D-78462 Konstanz, ☎ 07531/281389, ﬀ 07531/281373) also has information on cruises. For details on regular summer cruises on Bavaria's five largest lakes—Ammersee, Chiemsee, Königsee, Tegernsee, and Starnbergersee—contact local tourist offices.

BY BUS

Long-distance bus services in Germany are part of the Europe-wide Europabus network. Services are neither as frequent nor as comprehensive as those on the rail system, so make reservations. All Europabus services have a bilingual attendant and offer small luxuries that you won't find on the more basic, though still comfortable, regular services. For details and reservations contact **Deutsche Touring** (DTG, ⊠ Am Römerhof 17, D-60486 Frankfurt/Main, ☎ 069/7903261, ﬀ 069/706079). Travel agents and Deutsche Touring offices in Köln, Hannover, Hamburg, Munich, Nürnberg, and Wuppertal can also take reservations. Rural bus services are operated by local municipalities and some private firms.

BY CAR

Breakdowns. The **ADAC** (⊠ Am Westpark 8, D-81373 Munich, ☎ 089/76760, ﬀ 089/76762500), the major German automobile organization, gives free help and advice to tourists, though you have to pay for any spare parts you need, plus labor and mileage if a tow truck has to be called. All autobahns have regularly spaced telephones at which you can call for help, and if you have a mobile phone, you can get help by calling ☎ 222–222.

Gasoline. Unleaded gas and diesel are generally available all over Germany, and leaded fuel is being phased out. The price of a liter of gas may range from DM 1.20 to DM 1.70, depending on the grade.

Parking. Daytime parking in cities is very difficult. If you can find a parking garage or lot, use it or you'll risk having your car towed. Parking restrictions are not always clearly marked and can be hard to understand when they are. Parking-meter spaces are free at night.

Road Conditions. The autobahn system in Germany is of the highest standard. These roads are marked either A (on blue signs), meaning intra-German highways, or E (on green signs), meaning they form part of the Europe-wide *Europastrasse* network. All autobahns are toll free. Local roads are called *Bundesstrassen* and are marked by their number on a yellow sign. Most local roads are single lane and slower than autobahns.

Rules of the Road. Officially, there's no speed limit on autobahns, although you'll find signs recommending that motorists stay below 130 kph (80 mph). Blue signs on autobahns recommend the minimum speed on that stretch. Germans are fast drivers, and autobahn speeds of more than 160 kph (100 mph) are common. Unless you're driving at that speed, stay in the right-hand lane on autobahns, and use the left-hand lanes only for passing. There are speed limits on other roads—100 kph (60 mph) on Bundesstrassen, 80 kph (50 mph) on country roads, between 30 kph (18 mph) and 60 kph (36 mph) in built-up urban areas. Fines for exceeding the speed limit can be heavy. Penalties for driving under the influence of alcohol are even more severe, so make sure to keep within the legal limit—equivalent to the consumption of two small beers or a glass of wine.

BY PLANE

Germany's national airline, **Lufthansa** (☎ 800/645–3880 in the U.S., 0171/495–2044 in Great Britain, 0180/380–3803 in Germany), serves all major cities. **LTU International Airways** (☎ 800/546–7334 in the U.S., 0211/941–8888 in Germany) has connections between Düsseldorf and Munich and between Frankfurt and Munich. Regular fares are high, but you can save up to 40% with *Flieg und Spar* (fly-and-save) specials; several restrictions apply, such as a DM 100 penalty for changing flights. A British Airways subsidiary, **Deutsche BA** (based at Munich's Franz Josef Strauss Airport, ☎ 089/9759–320), competes with Lufthansa on many domestic routes, including those between Berlin and Munich, Munich and Hamburg, and Köln/Bonn and Düsseldorf. Deutsche BA fares are often substantially lower than Lufthansa's.

BY TRAIN

The German railway system is being privatized, so routes and timetables may change in some areas. The two separate rail networks of the former East and West Germany merged in 1994 into one entity known as **Deutsche Bahn** (DB) (German Rail, ☎ 01805/996-633), bringing Berlin and the cities of the old DDR much closer to the main railheads of the west.

Train journeys between the centers of many cities—Munich–Frankfurt, for example—can be completed faster by rail than by plane. InterCity Night trains are true "rolling hotels" with dining cars and shower and lavatory in each sleeping compartment, and overnight D-class trains also have sleepers. All InterCity trains have restaurant cars, and InterCity and EuroCity trains have either restaurant cars or trolley service. Seat reservations (highly advisable on InterCity, EuroCity, and InterCity Express trains) cost DM 3. Bikes cannot be transported on InterCity Express services, but InterCity, EuroCity, and most D-class trains have onboard storage, and InterRegio trains even have compartments where cyclists can travel next to their bikes.

Fares. The **German Rail Pass,** not available to Germans, allows travel over the entire German rail network for 4 to 10 days within a single month. It can be purchased for first- or second-class travel. A **Twin Pass** discounts these rates for two people traveling together. A **Youth Pass,** sold to those age 12–25, is for second-class travel. These passes are also good for a 75% discount on tour routes, such as the ones along the Romantic and Castle roads served by **Deutsche Touring** (☞ By Bus, *above*) and Rhine, Main, and Mosel river cruises operated by the **Köln-Düsseldorfer Rheinschiffahrt** (☞ By Boat, *above*). Passes are sold by travel agents and **DER Tours** (✉ Box 1606, Des Plaines, IL 60017, ☎ 800/782–2424) in the United States and by Deutsche Bahn in Germany.

The popular **Inter Rail** ticket can be complicated, but there are big savings for travelers touring just one area of Europe. Young travelers (26 years old or younger) touring only Germany can get an even better deal with a **Euro Domino** ticket, but must purchase the ticket outside Germany. No age limit is linked to the Inter Rail and other special deals, such as the Sparpreis and ICE-Super Sparpreis, which offer big savings on return journeys made on off-peak days.

If you intend to stay in one region of Germany, you can save on fares by buying a *FerienTicket* (Holiday Ticket), valid for unlimited train travel in any one region for one, two, or three weeks. The ticket costs DM 40 for one week, DM 60 for two weeks, and DM 80 for three weeks.

Weather

The main tourist season in Germany runs from May to late October, when the weather is best. Hundreds of folk festivals take place during this period. Winter-sports season in the Bavarian Alps runs from Christmas to mid-March. Prices are generally higher in summer. Most resorts have *Zwischensaison* (between season) and *Nebensaison* (edge-of-season) rates, and tourist offices can provide lists of hotels offering *Pauschalangebote* (special low-price inclusive weekly packages). Similarly, many winter resorts lower their rates for the periods immediately before and after the Christmas and New Year's high season (*weisse Wochen,* or "white weeks"). In the colder months, weather can be gloomy, and, except at ski resorts and in the larger cities, many attractions are closed.

CLIMATE

Germany's climate is generally temperate. Winters vary from mild and damp to very cold and bright. Summers are usually sunny and warm, though be prepared for overcast and wet days too. In Alpine regions spring often comes late, with snow flurries well into April. Only in southern Bavaria (Bayern) will you find strikingly variable weather, which is caused by the *Föhn,* a warm Alpine wind that brings sudden barometric changes and gives rise to clear but oppressive conditions in summer and causes snow to disappear overnight in winter.

The following are the average daily maximum and minimum temperatures for Munich.

Jan.	35F	1C	May	64F	18C	Sept.	67F	20C
	23	– 5		45	7		48	9
Feb.	38F	3C	June	70F	21C	Oct.	56F	13C
	23	– 5		51	11		40	4
Mar.	48F	9C	July	74F	23C	Nov.	44F	7C
	30	– 1		55	13		33	0
Apr.	56F	14C	Aug.	73F	23C	Dec.	36F	2C
	38	3		54	12		26	– 3

MUNICH

Munich (München in German) is sometimes referred to as the nation's "secret capital." Flamboyant and easygoing, the city of beer and Baroque is starkly different from the sometimes stiffly Prussian-influenced Berlin; the gritty and industrial Hamburg; or the hardheaded, commercially driven Frankfurt. Munich is known for its good-natured and relaxed charm—Gemütlichkeit, they call it. The Bavarian city is a crazy mix of high culture (visit its world-class opera house and art galleries) and wild abandon (witness the vulgar frivolity of Oktoberfest). The 19th-century King Ludwig I of Bavaria brought much international prestige to his home city after declaring: "I want to make Munich a town that does such credit to Germany that nobody knows Germany unless he has seen Munich." He kept his promise with an architectural and artistic renaissance—before abdicating in the wake of a wild romance with an Irish-born courtesan, Lola Montez.

Exploring Munich

Numbers in the margin correspond to points of interest on the Munich map.

Munich is unique among German cities because it has no identifiable, homogeneous Old Town center. Clusters of centuries-old buildings that belong to Munich's origins are often separated by postwar developments, of sometimes singular ugliness.

★ ⑳ **Alte Pinakothek** (Old Picture Gallery). This major art gallery contains some of the world's most celebrated old master paintings, including works by Dürer, Rembrandt, Rubens, and Murillo. Built by Leo von Klenze at the beginning of the 19th century to house King Ludwig I's collections, the towering brick edifice is also an architectural treasure in its own right. After extensive renovations, the museum reopened in late 1997 and now displays its treasures in the high style they deserve. ⊠ *Barestr. 27,* ☎ *089/238–05216.* ☉ *Tues., Wed., Fri., weekends 9– 5; Thurs. 9–8.*

⚅ ⑧ **Altes Rathaus** (Old Town Hall). The 1474 medieval building has a fine assembly room used for official functions, although it is rarely open to the general public. Its tower provides a satisfyingly atmospheric setting for a little toy museum. ⊠ *Marienpl.,* ☎ *089/233–22347.* ☉ *Daily 10–5:30.*

★ ⑨ **Asamkirche** (Asam Church). Some consider the Asamkirche a preposterously overdecorated jewel box; others find it one of Europe's finest late-Baroque churches. It was built around 1730 by the Asam brothers—Cosmas Damian and Egid Quirin—next door to their home, the Asamhaus. They dedicated it to St. John Nepomuk, a 14th-century monk. Inside, there is a riot of decoration: gilding, frescoes, statuary, rich rosy marble, and billowing stucco clouds. ⊠ *Sendlingerstr.* ☉ *Daily 9– 5:30.*

❸ Bürgersaal. Behind the modest facade of this unassuming church is an unusual split-level interior. The main Oberkirche (upper level) consists of a richly decorated Baroque oratory. The Unterkirche (lower level) is a cryptlike chapel containing the tomb of the courageous Jesuit priest Rupert Mayer, an outspoken opponent of the Nazis. ⊠ *Neuhauserstr. 14,* ☎ *089/223–884.* ☉ *Oberkirche: Mon.–Sat. 11–1, Sun. 9–12:30; Unterkirche: Mon.–Sat. 6:30 AM–7 PM, Sun. 7–7.*

☾ ⑰ Englischer Garten (English Garden). Count Rumford, a refugee from the American War of Independence, designed this seemingly endless park (5 km/3 mi long and more than ½ km/¼ mi wide) in the open and informal style favored by 18th-century English aristocrats. You can rent boats here, relax in beer gardens (the most famous is at the foot of a Chinese Pagoda), ride your bike (or ski in winter), or simply stroll. Ludwig II loved to wander incognito along the English Garden's serpentine paths. A large section of the park right behind the **Haus der Kunst** (☞ *below*) has been designated a nudist area. ⊠ *Bordering eastern side of Schwabing.*

⑮ Feldherrnhalle (Hall of Generals). This local open-air hall of fame was modeled on the 14th-century Loggia dei Lanzi in Florence. During the '30s and '40s it was a key Nazi shrine, marking the site of Hitler's abortive rising, or putsch, which took place in 1923. All who passed it had to give the Nazi salute. ⊠ *South end of Odeonspl.*

★ ❺ Frauenkirche (Church of Our Lady). This soaring Gothic redbrick masterpiece has two incongruous towers topped by onion-shape domes, symbols of the city (perhaps because they resemble brimming beer mugs, cynics claim). The church was built between 1474 and 1494; the towers were added in 1524–25. The cathedral's interior is stark. The crypt houses the tombs of numerous Wittelsbachs, the family that ruled Bavaria for seven centuries until forced to abdicate in 1918. ⊠ *Frauenpl.,* ☎ *089/290–0820.*

❶ Hauptbahnhof (Main Train Station). The city tourist office is here, with maps and helpful information on events around town. ⊠ *Bahnhofpl.,* ☎ *089/2333–0258.*

⑱ Haus der Kunst (House of Art). The grandiose portico of this vast art gallery identifies the building as one of Munich's few remaining Nazi-era monuments, opened officially in 1938 by Hitler himself. It now stages regular exhibitions of art and sculpture, combining them frequently with theatrical and musical "happenings." ⊠ *Prinzregentenstr. 1,* ☎ *089/2112–7137.* ☉ *Tues., Wed., Fri., weekends 10–5, Thurs. 10–8.*

⑬ Hofgarten (Royal Garden). The formal garden was once part of the royal palace grounds. It is bordered on two sides by arcades designed in the 19th century by the royal architect Leo von Klenze. ⊠ *Hofgartenstr., north of Residenz.*

❷ Karlsplatz (Charles Square). Known locally as Stachus, this busy intersection has one of Munich's most popular fountains, a circle of water jets that cool city shoppers and office workers on hot summer days. Backing the fountain, a semicircle of yellow-front buildings with high windows and delicate cast-iron balconies gives the area a southern, almost Mediterranean, air. ⊠ *Junction Sonnenstr., Bayerstr., Schützenstr., Luisenstr., Prielmayerstr., and Neuhauserstr.*

★ ❻ Marienplatz (Square of Our Lady). Surrounded by shops, restaurants, and cafés, this square is named for the 1638 gilt statue of the Virgin Mary that has been watching over it for nearly four centuries. ⊠ *Bordered by Kaufingerstr., Rosenstr., Weinstr., and Dienerstr.*

Alte Pinakothek, **20**
Altes Rathaus, **8**
Asamkirche, **9**
Bürgersaal, **3**
Englischer Garten, **17**
Feldherrnhalle, **15**
Frauenkirche, **5**
Hauptbahnhof, **1**
Haus der Kunst, **18**
Hofgarten, **13**
Karlsplatz, **2**
Marienplatz, **6**
Michaelskirche, **4**
Nationaltheater, **12**
Neue Pinakothek, **21**
Neues Rathaus, **7**
Pinakothek der
Moderne, **19**
Residenz, **11**
Siegestor, **16**
Theatinerkirche, **14**
Viktualienmarkt, **10**

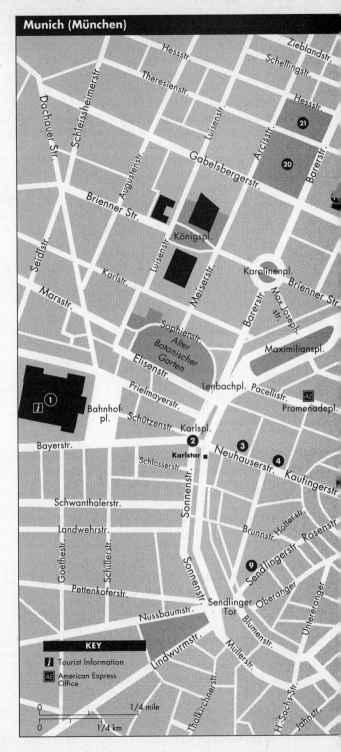

Munich (München)

KEY

ℹ️ Tourist Information

AE American Express Office

0 ___ 1/4 mile

0 ___ 1/4 km

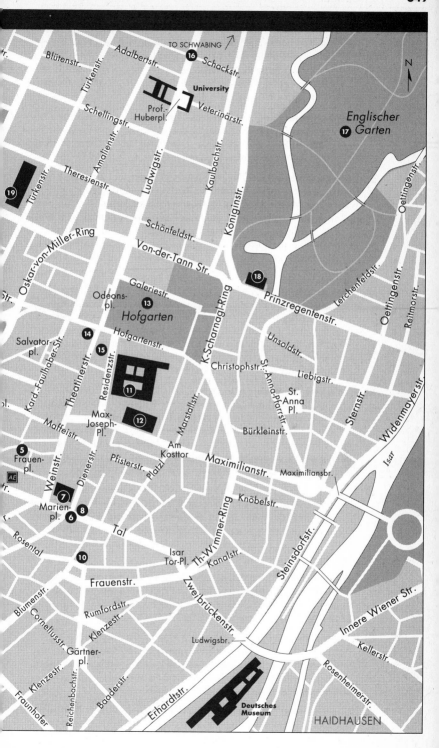

TO SCHWABING

16 Schackstr.

Blütenstr.

Adalbertstr.

Turkenstr.

N

University

Prof.-Huberpl.

Veterinärstr.

Schellingstr.

Amalienstr.

Englischer

17 *Garten*

Theresienstr.

Turkenstr.

Ludwigstr.

Kaulbachstr.

Königinstr.

Oettingenstr.

19

Oskar-von-Miller-Ring

Schönfeldstr.

Von-der-Tann Str.

Lerchenfeldstr.

Oettingenstr.

Reitmorstr.

Galeriestr.

Odeons-pl.

18

Prinzregentenstr.

13

Hofgarten

K-Scharnagl-Ring

Unsoldstr.

14

Hofgartenstr.

Salvator-pl.

Christophstr.

St.-Anna-Pl.str.

Liebigstr.

Kard-Faulhaber-Str.

Theatinerstr.

Residenzstr.

15

Marstallstr.

St. Anna Pl.

Sternstr.

11

Max-Joseph-Pl.

12

Bürkleinstr.

Maffeistr.

Dienerstr.

Pfisterstr.

Platzl

Am Kosttor

Maximilianstr.

Maximiliansbr.

5

Frauen-pl.

AF

7

Weinstr.

Knöbelstr.

Th-Wimmer-Ring

Isar

Marien-pl.

8

6

Tal

Rosental

10

Isar Tor-Pl.

Kanalstr.

Steinsdorfstr.

Widenmayerstr.

Frauenstr.

Zweibrückenstr.

Blumenstr.

Rumfordstr.

Corneliusstr.

Klenzestr.

Innere Wiener Str.

Klenzestr.

Gärtner-pl.

Ludwigsbr.

Kellerstr.

Reichenbachstr.

Baaderstr.

Erhardtstr.

Deutsches Museum

Rosenheimerstr.

Fraunhofer

HAIDHAUSEN

❹ **Michaelskirche** (St. Michael's Church). One of the most magnificent Renaissance churches in Germany, this spacious and handsome structure is decorated throughout in plain white stucco. It was built during the late 16th century for the Jesuits and was closely modeled on Il Gesù, the Jesuit church in Rome. ✉ *Neuhauserstr. 6,* ☎ *089/551–99257.* ☼ *Mon.–Wed., Fri., Sat. 8:30–7; Thurs. 8:30–9; Sun. 6 AM–10 PM. Guided tours Wed. at 2.*

⓬ **Nationaltheater** (National Theater). Constructed at the beginning of the 19th century and twice destroyed, this neoclassical opera house with state-of-the-art facilities is the home of the world-famous Bavarian State Opera and Ballet companies. ✉ *Maximilianstr. 1,* ☎ *089/218–51920.*

㉑ **Neue Pinakothek** (New Picture Gallery). The original art gallery that Ludwig I built to house his "modern" collections (19th-century works) was destroyed during World War II and replaced by a new exhibition hall in 1981. The low, brick structure—some have compared it to a Florentine palazzo—is a superb, skylit setting for one of the finest collections of European 19th-century paintings and sculpture in the world. ✉ *Barerstr. 29, near Königspl.,* ☎ *089/238–05195.* ☼ *Wed., Thurs., Fri., weekends 10–5; Tues. 10–8.*

❼ **Neues Rathaus** (New City Hall). Munich's present city hall was built between 1867 and 1908 in the fussy, turreted, neo-Gothic style so beloved by King Ludwig II. At 11 AM and noon daily (also May–October at 5 PM and 9 PM), the central tower's *Glockenspiel,* or chiming clock, swings into action with two tiers of dancing and jousting figures. An elevator serves an observation point near the top of one of the towers. ✉ *Marienpl.,* ☎ *089/2331.* ☼ *Tower Mon.–Thurs. 9–4, Fri. 9–1.*

⓳ **Pinakothek der Moderne** (Modern Art Gallery). A year-2000 addition to Munich's art gallery and museum scene is an impressive glass-and-concrete ensemble bringing together outstanding collections: modern and graphic art, industrial design and *objets d'art,* the Bavarian State collection of graphic art, and the Technical University museum of architecture. ✉ *Corner of Gabelsberger-Türkenstr.,* ☎ *089/2380–5118.* ☼ *Hours unavailable at press time.*

⓫ **Residenz** (Royal Palace). This mighty yet somber palace dating from the 14th century was the home of the Wittelsbach dukes for more than three centuries. Its main attractions are the glittering Schatzkammer, or treasury, and the glorious rococo theater. ✉ *Max-Joseph-Pl. 3,* ☎ *089/290–671.* ☼ *Schatzkammer: Tues.–Sun. 10–4:30; Cuvilliés Theater: Mon.–Sat. 2–5, Sun. 10–5.*

⓰ **Siegestor** (Victory Arch). The monument has Italian origins—it was modeled on the Arch of Constantine in Rome—and was built to honor the achievements of the Bavarian army during the Wars of Liberation (1813–15) against Napoleon. ✉ *Start of Leopoldstr.*

⓮ **Theatinerkirche** (Theatine Church). This handsome, yellow-stucco church was built for the Theatine monks in the mid-17th century, though its striking facade, with twin eye-catching domes, was added only in the following century. The interior is austerely white. ✉ *Theatinerstr. 22,* ☎ *089/221–650.* ☼ *Daily 7–7.*

★ ⓾ **Viktualienmarkt** (Food Market). The city's open-air market (*Viktualien* is an old German word for vittles, or food) has a wide range of produce—German and international goods, Bavarian beer, and French wines—and is a feast for the eyes as well as the stomach. ✉ *Southeast of Marienpl. via Tal or Rindermarkt.* ☼ *Mon.–Sat. 7–6:30.*

Munich Environs

KZ–Gedenkstätte Dachau (Dachau Concentration Camp Memorial Site). Although the 1,200-year-old town of Dachau attracted hordes of painters and artists from the mid-19th century until World War I, it is now best known as the site of Germany's first concentration camp. From its opening in 1933 until its capture by American soldiers in 1945, the camp held more than 206,000 political dissidents, Jews, homosexuals, clergy, and other "enemies" of the Nazis; more than 32,000 prisoners died here. Photographs, contemporary documents, the few remaining cell blocks, and the grim crematorium create a somber and moving picture of the vicious living and working conditions at the camp. The town of Dachau is a 20-minute ride from Marienplatz on the S-2 suburban railway line. To get to the concentration camp site take Bus 724 or 726 from the train station or town center. Both stop near the entrance to the camp site. ⊠ *Alte Römerstr. 75, Dachau,* ☎ *08121/1741.* ☒ *Free.* ☉ *Tues.–Sun. 9–5; documentary (in English) shown at 11:30 and 3:30.*

☺ **Olympiapark.** The undulating circus-tent-like roofs that cover the stadiums built for the 1972 Olympic Games are part of the Olympic Park on the northern edge of Schwabing. The roofs are made of translucent tiles that glisten in the midday sun and act as amplifiers for visiting rock bands. Train tours of the park run throughout the day from March through November. Take the elevator up the 960-ft **Olympia Tower** for a view of the city and the Alps; there's also a revolving restaurant near the top. The former Olympic cycling stadium was converted in 1999 to an **"Olympic Spirit"** exhibition and "fun-park" where you can participate in virtual-reality Olympic sports. ⊠ *U-bahn 3 to northern edge of Schwabing,* ☎ *089/306–72414.* ☉ *Main stadium: daily 9–4:30; Tower: daily 9* AM*–midnight; "Olympic Spirit": daily 10–6.*

☺ **Schloss Nymphenburg** (Nymphenburg Palace). The summer palace of the Wittelsbachs stands magnificently in its own park in the western suburb of Nymphenburg. The oldest parts date from 1664, but construction continued for more than 100 years, the bulk of the work undertaken during the reign of Max Emmanuel between 1680 and 1730. The interiors are exceptional, especially the **Festsaal** (Banqueting Hall), a rococo masterpiece in green and gold. The **Schönheits Galerie** (Gallery of Beauties) contains more than 100 portraits of women who had caught the eye of Ludwig I. The rococo **Amalienburg** (Hunting Lodge) on the grounds was built by François Cuvilliés, architect of the theater in Munich's **Residenz** (☞ *above*). The palace also contains the **Marstallmuseum** (Museum of Royal Carriages), a sleigh that belonged to Ludwig II is included among the opulently decorated vehicles, and, on the floor above, the **Nymphenburger Porzellan** (Nymphenburg Porcelain Gallery) exhibits porcelain produced here between 1747 and the 1920s. The **Museum Mensch und Natur** (Museum of Man and Nature) in the north wing concentrates on the history of humans, the variety of life on Earth, and our place in the environment. ⊠ *U-bahn 1 from Hauptbahnhof to Rotkreuzpl., then Tram 12, toward Amalienburg,* ☎ *089/179–080.* ☉ *Apr.–Sept., Tues.–Sun. 9–12:30 and 1:30–5; Oct.–Mar., Tues.–Sun. 10–12:30 and 1:30–4; gardens, daily 9–dusk.*

Dining and Lodging

Munich claims some of Europe's best chefs in some of the most noted—and pricey—restaurants in Germany. For local cuisine, Munich's wood-paneled, flagstone beer restaurants and halls serve food sturdy enough to match the large measures of beer served. Münchners love to eat just as much as they love to drink, and the range of food is as varied and rich as the local breweries' output.

Though Munich has a vast number of hotels in all price ranges, many are full year-round. If you plan to visit during the "fashion weeks" (Mode Wochen) in March and September or during Oktoberfest at the end of September, make reservations at least several months in advance. Munich's tourist offices will handle only written or personal requests for reservations assistance. Write or fax the **Fremdenverkehrsamt** (✉ Sendlingerstr. 1, D-80313 Munich, 𝔽𝔸𝕏 089/239–1313). Your best bet for finding a room if you haven't reserved one is the tourist offices at the Hauptbahnhof, on Bahnhofplatz, or at the Rathaus (City Hall) on Marienplatz. There is a small fee.

Rates are often, but not always, lower in suburban hotels—and taking the 15-minute U-bahn or S-bahn ride into town is easy enough. The city tourist office's "Key to Munich" packages include reduced-rate hotel reservations, sightseeing tours, theater admissions, and low-cost travel on the U- and S-bahn. For details and price-category definitions for dining and lodging, *see* Dining *and* Lodging *in* Germany A to Z, *above.*

$$$$ ✕ **Königshof.** On the second floor of the postwar Königshof Hotel, the
★   restaurant is without doubt Munich's most opulent. The neo-Baroque style includes ceiling frescoes, subdued chandelier lighting, and heavy drapery. Nouvelle cuisine is served—breast of goose with truffles, for example, or veal in basil cream and mushroom sauce. ✉ *Karlspl. 25,* ☎ *089/551–36142. AE, DC, MC, V.*

$$$ ✕ **Lenbach.** Michael Käfer's spectacular restaurant is not for the shy: Guests enter the vast dining area along a floor-lit catwalk. Britain's top restaurant designer, Sir Terence Conran, was given a 100-year-old city palace to work on and clearly had a ball. The high, vaulted ceilings, marble pillars, art nouveau wrought-iron, and rich stucco were blended with Conran's typical minimalist decoration, all under the theme of the "Seven Deadly Sins." Outstanding seafood is a feature of a daily buffet in the chandelier-hung main lobby. The bar is Munich's longest. ✉ *Ottostr. 6,* ☎ *089/549–1300. Jacket and tie. AE, MC, V.*

$$$ ✕ **Preysing Keller.** The food here is light and sophisticated but with
★   recognizably Teutonic touches. The over-restored restaurant is in a 16th-century cellar. It's the food, the extensive wine list, and the perfect service that make this place special. ✉ *Innere-Wiener-Str. 6,* ☎ *089/458–45260. Reservations essential. No credit cards. Closed Sun.*

$$–$$$ ✕ **Dukatz.** Join the Munich literati and glitterati in the severely intellectual surroundings of the *Literaturhaus* (House of Literature). The restaurant hums with talk of publishing contracts and literary gossip. Its excellent cuisine combines traditional German with a light Gallic touch: lamb's tripe melting in a rich champagne sauce, for instance, or stuffed pig's trotters with truffles. The light and airy café-bar has a stack of American and British daily papers. ✉ *Salvatorpl. 1,* ☎ *089/291–9600. Reservations essential. No credit cards. No dinner Sun.*

$$ ✕ **Weinhaus Neuner.** Originally a seminary, this early 18th-century building houses Munich's oldest surviving wine hostelry, in the Neuner family since 1852. The high-ceiling dining rooms are lined with dark oak paneling. Look for the herb-filled pork fillets with noodles, and veal with Morchela mushroom sauce. ✉ *Herzogspitalstr. 8,* ☎ *089/260–3954. Reservations essential. AE, DC, MC. Closed Sun. and holidays.*

$–$$ ✕ **Augustiner Keller.** This 19th-century establishment is the flagship beer restaurant of one of Munich's oldest breweries, Augustiner. The decor of the two baronial hall–like rooms emphasizes wood—from the refurbished parquet floors to the wooden barrels from which the beer is drawn. Bavarian specialties such as *Tellerfleisch*—cold roast beef with lashings of horseradish, served on a big wooden board—fill the daily menu. ✉ *Arnulfstr. 52,* ☎ *089/594–393. AE, DC, MC, V.*

$-$$ ✗ **Bamberger Haus.** This historic villa on the edge of Schwabing's Luitpold Park has a rambling, vaulted beer-cellar and a slightly faded upstairs dining room. You dine beneath crystal chandeliers and under the gaze of Baroque statuary. Some of the vegetarian dishes on the imaginative menu, such as the vegetables au gratin, are incredibly cheap and filling. ⊠ *Brunnerstr. 2,* ☎ *089/308–8966. AE, MC, V.*

$-$$ ✗ **Dürnbräu.** A fountain plays outside this picturesque old Bavarian inn. Inside, it's crowded and noisy. Expect to share a table; your fellow diners will range from business sorts to students. The food is resolutely traditional. Try the cream of spinach soup and the boiled beef. ⊠ *Dürnbräug. 2,* ☎ *089/222–195. AE, DC, MC, V.*

$-$$ ✗ **Grüne Gans.** This small, chummy restaurant near the Viktualienmarkt is popular with local entertainers, whose photographs clutter the walls. International fare with regional German influences dominates the menu. Try the chervil cream soup, followed by calves' kidneys in tarragon sauce. ⊠ *Am Einlass 5,* ☎ *089/266–228. Reservations essential. No credit cards. Closed Sun. No lunch.*

$ ✗ **Altes Hackerhaus.** This upscale beer restaurant on one of Munich's
★ ritziest shopping streets is full of bric-a-brac and mementos that hark back to its origins as a medieval brewery. Since 1570, beer has been brewed or served here at the birthplace of one of the city's largest breweries—Hacker-Pschorr. Duck into one of the cozy little rooms and choose from the selection of hearty soups, then try a plate of *Käsespätzle* (egg noodles with melted cheese). ⊠ *Sendlingerstr. 14,* ☎ *089/260–5026. AE, DC, MC, V.*

$ ✗ **Brauhaus zur Brez'n.** This hostelry bedecked in the blue and white of the Bavarian flag spreads over three floors. Everyone from local business lunchers to hungry night owls chooses from a big all-day menu of traditional roasts, to be washed down with a choice of three draft beers. ⊠ *Leopoldstr. 72,* ☎ *089/390–092. AE, DC, MC, V.*

$ ✗ **Franziskaner.** Vaulted archways, cavernous rooms interspersed with intimate dining areas, bold blue frescoes on the walls, and long wooden tables create a spic-and-span medieval atmosphere. Besides the late-morning *Weisswurst* (a delicate white sausage), look for *Ochsenfleisch* (boiled ox meat) and dumplings. ⊠ *Perusastr. 5,* ☎ *089/231–8120. Reservations not accepted. AE, DC, MC, V.*

$ ✗ **Hofbräuhaus.** The cavernous, smoky, stone vaults of the Hofbräuhaus contain crowds of singing, shouting, swaying beer drinkers. If you're not here solely to drink, try the Bavarian food in the more subdued upstairs restaurant, where the service is not so brusque. It's between Marienplatz and Maximilianstrasse. ⊠ *Platzl 9,* ☎ *089/221–676. Reservations not accepted. MC, V.*

$ ✗ **Hundskugel.** History practically oozes from the crooked walls at this tavern, Munich's oldest, which dates from 1440. Order *Spanferkel*—roast suckling pig—if it's on the menu; this is simple Bavarian fare at its best. ⊠ *Hotterstr. 18,* ☎ *089/264–272. No credit cards. Closed Sun.*

$ ✗ **Pfälzer Weinprobierstube.** A warren of stone-vault rooms of vari-
★ ous sizes, wooden tables, glittering candles, dirndl-clad waitresses, and a vast range of wines provide a backdrop for food that's reliable rather than spectacular. Local specialties predominate. ⊠ *Residenzstr. 1,* ☎ *089/225–628. Reservations not accepted. No credit cards.*

$$$$ ▥ **Bayerischer Hof.** This is one of Munich's most traditional luxury hotels. Public rooms are decorated with antiques, paintings, marble, and painted wood. Old-fashioned comfort and class abound in the older rooms; some of the newer rooms are less ornate but functional. ⊠ *Promenadepl. 2–6, D-80333,* ☎ *089/21200,* FAX *089/212–0906. 383 rooms, 45 apartments. 3 restaurants, pool. AE, DC, MC, V.*

$$$$ ▥ **Kempinski Hotel Vier Jahreszeiten.** Close to the heart of the city,
★ the Vier Jahreszeiten—Four Seasons—has been playing host to the

world's wealthy and titled for more than a century. Elegance and luxury set the tone; many rooms have handsome antique pieces. ⊠ *Maximilianstr. 17, D-80539,* ☎ *089/21250, 516/794–2670 reservations in U.S.,* FAX *089/2125–2000. 268 rooms, 30 suites, 1 presidential suite, 17 apartments. 2 restaurants, pool. AE, DC, MC, V.*

$$$$ ⊡ **Rafael.** A character-laden lodging in the heart of the Old Town (close
★ to the Hofbräuhaus), the Rafael, which opened in 1989, retains many of the architectural features of its building's late-19th-century origins, including a sweeping staircase and stucco ceilings. In 1995, Britain's Prince Charles stayed here. Rooms are individually furnished and extravagantly decorated. The hotel restaurant, Mark's, has made a name for itself with its new German cuisine. ⊠ *Neuturmstr. 1, D-80331,* ☎ *089/290–980,* FAX *089/222–539. 54 rooms, 19 suites. Restaurant, pool. AE, DC, MC, V.*

$$$–$$$$ ⊡ **Eden Hotel Wolff.** Chandeliers and dark-wood paneling in the public rooms underline the old-fashioned elegance of this downtown favorite (it's across from the train station and the airport bus terminal). The rooms are comfortable, and most are spacious. Dine on excellent Bavarian specialties in the intimate Zirbelstube restaurant. ⊠ *Arnulfstr. 4, D-80335,* ☎ *089/551–150,* FAX *089/5511–5555. 209 rooms, 2 suites. Restaurant. AE, DC, MC, V.*

$$$–$$$$ ⊡ **Torbräu.** In the shadow of one of Munich's ancient city gates, this snug hotel offers comfortable rooms decorated in plush and ornate Italian style. ⊠ *Tal 41, D-80331,* ☎ *089/225–016,* FAX *089/225–019. 83 rooms, 3 suites. Restaurant, indoor pool. AE, MC, V.*

$$$ ⊡ **Adria.** This modern, comfortable hotel is in the middle of Munich's museum quarter. Rooms are large and tastefully decorated, with old prints on the pale pink walls, Oriental rugs on the floors, and flowers beside the large double beds. A spectacular breakfast buffet (including a glass of sparkling wine) is included in the rate. ⊠ *Liebigstr. 8a, D-80538,* ☎ *089/293–081,* FAX *089/227–015. 46 rooms. AE, MC, V.*

$$$ ⊡ **Admiral.** In the heart of the city, this stylish, small hotel is a haven of peace, with a courtyard garden for breakfast and for evening cocktails (also served at an elegant indoor bar). Most rooms have balconies overlooking the rooftops of the city center. Room rates include a breakfast buffet with homemade jams and in-season strawberries. ⊠ *Kohlstr. 9, D-80469,* ☎ *089/226–641,* FAX *089/216–350. 33 rooms. Bar. AE, DC, MC, V.*

$$ ⊡ **Hotel Europa.** Mention Fodor's at this large but friendly hotel near the main railroad station, and you may be able to get a slight discount. The hotel is on a busy shopping street so try for a room overlooking the small back garden and terrace, where you can also take breakfast in good weather. All rooms are furnished in modern, brightly colored fabrics and light woods and veneers. ⊠ *Dachauerstr. 115, D-80335,* ☎ *089/542–420,* FAX *089/542–42500. 180 rooms. Restaurant. AE, MC, V.*

$ ⊡ **Hotel-Pension am Siegestor.** An ancient, wood-paneled elevator carries you in style to the fourth-floor reception area of this charming little hotel between Schwabing's main boulevard and the university quarter. Rooms on the fifth floor, tucked up under the eaves, are particularly cozy. None has a private bath, but each floor has its own bathroom. ⊠ *Akademiestr. 5, D-80799,* ☎ *089/399–550 or 089/399–551,* FAX *089/ 343–050. 20 rooms with shared bath. No credit cards.*

$ ⊡ **Hotel-Pension Beck.** American and British guests receive a particularly warm welcome from the Anglophile owner of the rambling, friendly Beck. Rooms are furnished in pinewood. The pension is near museums and the Englischer Garten. ⊠ *Thierschstr. 36, D-80538,* ☎ *089/220–708 or 089/225–768,* FAX *089/220–925. 44 rooms, 7 with shower. No credit cards.*

Nightlife and the Arts

The Arts

Details of concerts and theater performances are available from the "Vorschau" or "Monatsprogramm" booklets obtainable at most hotel reception desks. Some hotels will make ticket reservations; otherwise book tickets at the two kiosks on the concourse below Marienplatz, or use one of the ticket agencies in the city center: **Max Hieber Konzertkasse** (⊠ Liebfrauenstr. 1, ☎ 089/290–08014) or the **Residenz Bücherstube** (⊠ Residenzstr. 1, ☎ 089/220–868 concert tickets only).

CONCERTS

Munich's Philharmonic Orchestra performs in one of Germany's finest concert halls, the Philharmonie at the **Gasteig** (⊠ Rosenheimerstr. 5, ☎ 089/5481–8181). Tickets are sold at the box office. The Bavarian Radio Orchestra also performs Sunday concerts here. In summer, concerts are held at Schloss Nymphenburg and in the open-air interior courtyard of the Residenz (☞ Exploring Munich, *above*).

DANCE

The ballet company of the Bavarian State Opera performs at the **Nationaltheater** (⊠ Maximilianstr. 11, ☎ 089/2185–1920). Ballet productions are also staged at the attractive late-19th-century **Staatstheater am Gärtnerplatz** (⊠ Gärtnerpl. 3, ☎ 089/201–6767).

OPERA

Munich's Bavarian State Opera company is world famous, and tickets for major productions in its permanent home, the **Nationaltheater** (⊠ Maximilianstr. 11, ☎ 089/2185–1920), are often difficult to come by. Try at the evening box office, which opens on the south side of the theater one hour before performances. Book far in advance through the tourist office (☞ Visitor Information, *below*) for the annual opera festival held in July and August.

THEATER

The Bavarian state-supported **Residenz Theater** (Royal Theater) concentrates on the classics. More than 20 other theater companies perform throughout the city (some of them in basements). Regular English-language productions of the American Drama Group Europe are staged in the auditorium of **America House** (Amerikahaus; ⊠ Karolinenpl. 3, ☎ 089/343–803). English-language productions also appear from time to time at the **Theater im Karlshof** (⊠ Karlstr. 43, ☎ 089/596–611).

Nightlife

BARS, CABARET, NIGHTCLUBS

Munich's media types have turned the **Alter Simpl** (⊠ Turkenstr. 57, ☎ 089/272–3083) into an unofficial press club. The **Havana** (⊠ Herrnstr. 3, ☎ 089/291–884) does its best to look like a run-down Cuban dive, drawing a chic clientele. **Käfers am Odeonsplatz** (⊠ Odeonspl. 3, ☎ 089/290–7530) attracts a similarly smart and contact-happy crowd. **O'Reilly's Irish Cellar Pub** (⊠ Maximilianstr. 29, ☎ 089/293–311) pours genuine Irish Guinness. Great Caribbean cocktails and a powerful Irish-German Black and Tan (Guinness and strong German beer) are served at the English, nautical-style **Pusser's** bar (⊠ Falkenturmstr. 9, ☎ 089/220–500). The bar **Schumann's** (⊠ Maximilianstr. 36, ☎ 089/229–060) has a shabby New York look, but the clientele is Munich chic.

DANCE CLUBS

Clubs abound in the side streets off **Freilitzschstrasse,** surrounding Münchener Freiheit in Schwabing. Munich's spectacular dance club center, the **Kunstpark Ost** (⊠ Grafingerstr. 6, ☎ 089/490–72113), is in a former pasta factory with 13 "entertainment areas," including several clubs and music bars. At **Maximilian's** (⊠ Maximilianspl. 16, ☎ 089/223–252), the chic crowd packs a throbbing cellar into the early hours. The **Nachtcafe** (⊠ Maximilianspl. 5, ☎ 089/595–900) is open all night on weekends. **P1** (⊠ Haus der Kunst, Prinzregentenstr. 1, ☎ 089/294–252) is the queen of them all, a place to see and be seen, with a series of tiny dance floors and a great sound system. Tops of the lot (quite literally) is the **Skyline** (⊠ Münchner Freiheit, ☎ 089/333–131), at the top of the Hertie department store building, Münchner Freiheit.

JAZZ CLUBS
Munich's longest-established jazz haunt, the **Schwabinger Podium** (⊠ Wagnerstr. 1, ☎ 089/399–482), has taken to offering rock music as well as traditional jazz; it's packed nightly. The **Unterfahrt** (⊠ Kirchenstr. 96, ☎ 089/448–2794), in Munich's latest "quartier Latin," Haidhausen, has traditional and mainstream jazz.

Shopping

Antiques
Blumenstrasse, Türkenstrasse, and Westenriederstrasse have antiques shops of every description, while those that line Prannerstrasse, behind the classy Bayerischer Hof Hotel, concentrate on treasures that usually end up in museums. The open-air Auer Dult fairs sell antiques; they're held on Mariahilfplatz at the end of April, July, and October.

Department Stores
Most of the major department stores are along Maffeistrasse, Kaufingerstrasse, and Neuhauserstrasse. **Hertie** (⊠ Bahnhofpl. 7, ☎ 089/55120) is the largest and, some claim, the best department store in the city; it has a stylish delicatessen, a champagne bar, and a bistro. **Kaufhof** has two central Munich stores (⊠ Karlspl. 2, opposite Hertie, ☎ 089/51250; ⊠ corner Marienpl., ☎ 089/231–851); both offer a wide range of goods in the middle price range. **Karstadt** (⊠ Neuhauserstr. 18, ☎ 089/290–230) is a high-class department store, with an abundance of Bavarian arts and crafts.

Gift Ideas
Munich is a city of beer, and beer mugs and coasters make good gifts to take home. Many shops specialize in beer-related souvenirs, but **Ludwig Mory** (⊠ Marienpl. 8, ☎ 089/224–542) is about the best. Munich is also the home of the famous **Porzellan Manufaktur Nymphenburg** (Nymphenburg Porcelain Factory; ⊠ junction Odeonspl. and Briennerstr., ☎ 089/282–428; ⊠ Nördliche Schlossrondell 8, in front of Schloss Nymphenburg, ☎ 089/1791–9710).

Shopping Districts
Munich has an immense **central shopping area,** 2 km (1 mi) of pedestrian streets stretching from the train station to Marienplatz and north to Odeonsplatz. The two main streets here are Neuhauserstrasse and Kaufingerstrasse. For **upscale shopping** Maximilianstrasse, Residenzstrasse, and Theatinerstrasse are unbeatable and contain a fine array of classy and tempting stores. **Schwabing,** north of the university, has several of the city's most intriguing and offbeat shopping streets—Schellingstrasse and Hohenzollernstrasse are two to try.

Munich Essentials

Arriving and Departing

BY BUS

Munich has no central bus station. Long-distance buses arrive at and depart from the north side of the train station on Arnulfstrasse.

BY CAR

From the north (Nürnberg, Frankfurt), leave the autobahn at the Schwabing exit and follow the STADTMITTE signs. The autobahn from Stuttgart and the west ends at Obermenzing; again, follow the STADT-MITTE signs. The autobahns from Salzburg and the east, from Garmisch and the south, and from Lindau and the southwest all join up with the city beltway, the Mittlerer Ring. The city center is well posted.

BY PLANE

Munich's **Franz Josef Strauss (FJS) Airport,** named for a former state premier, is 28 km (17 mi) northeast of the city center.

Between the Airport and Downtown. The S-8 and S-1 **S-bahn** (suburban train lines) link FJS Airport with the city's main train station (Hauptbahnhof). Trains depart in both directions every 10 minutes from 3:55 AM to 12:55 AM daily. Intermediate stops are made at the Ostbahnhof (good for hotels located east of the River Isar) and city-center stations such as Marienplatz. The 38-minute trip costs DM 11.20 if you purchase a multi-use strip ticket (☞ Getting Around, *below*) and use eight strips; otherwise an ordinary one-way ticket is DM 14 per person. A tip for families: Up to five people (maximum of two adults) can travel to or from the airport for only DM 25 after 9 AM by buying a Tageskarte (☞ Getting Around, *below*).

Bus service is slower and more expensive (DM 15) than the S-bahn; only use it if you're carrying a great deal of luggage. A **taxi** will cost between DM 80 and DM 100. If you are **driving** from the airport into the city, follow the MÜNCHEN autobahn signs to A92 and A9. Once on the A92, watch carefully for the signs to Munich; many motorists miss the sign and end up headed toward Stuttgart.

BY TRAIN

All long-distance services arrive at and depart from the main train station, the Hauptbahnhof. Trains to and from destinations in the Bavarian Alps usually use the adjoining Starnbergerbahnhof. For information on train times call 089/19419. For tickets and information go to the station or to the ABR travel agency on Bahnhofplatz.

Getting Around

BY PUBLIC TRANSPORTATION

Downtown Munich is only about 1.6 km (1 mi) square, so it can easily be explored on foot. Other areas—Schwabing, Nymphenburg, the Olympiapark—are best reached on the efficient and comprehensive public transportation network, which incorporates buses, streetcars, U-bahn (subways), and S-bahn (suburban trains). Tickets are good for the entire network, and you can break your trip as many times as you like using just one ticket, provided you travel in one direction within a given period of time. If you plan to make only a few trips, buy *Streifenkarten* (strip tickets)—blue for adults, red for children. At press time, a 10-strip ticket cost DM 14. All tickets must be validated by time, punching them in the automatic machines at station entrances and on all buses and streetcars.

The best buy is the *Tageskarte* (all-day ticket): Up to two adults and three children can use this ticket for unlimited journeys between 9 AM and the end of the day's service (about 2 AM). It costs DM 12.50 for the inner zone, which covers central Munich. A Tageskarte for the entire system, extending to the Starnbergersee and Ammersee, costs DM 25. Holders of a Eurail Pass, a Youth Pass, an InterRail Card, or a DB Tourist Card travel free on all S-bahn trains.

BY TAXI

Munich's cream-color taxis are numerous. Hail them in the street or call 089/21610 or 089/19410. Rates start at DM 5 and rise by DM 2.20 per km (about DM 4 per 2 km/1 mi). There are additional charges of DM 2 if a taxi is ordered by telephone and DM 1 per piece of luggage. Plan to pay about DM 13 for a short trip within the city.

Contacts and Resources

CONSULATES

U.S. (⊠ Königinstr. 5, ☎ 089/28880). **Canada** (⊠ Tal 29, ☎ 089/219–9570). **U.K.** (⊠ Bürkleinstr. 10, ☎ 089/211–090). **Ireland** (⊠ Mauerkircherstr. 1a, ☎ 089/985–723).

EMERGENCIES

Police (☎ 110). **Ambulance and emergency medical attention** (☎ 089/19222). **Fire Department and Paramedical Aid** (☎ 112). **Dentist** (☎ 089/723–3093). **Pharmacies: Europa-Apotheke** (⊠ Schützenstr. 12, near Hauptbahnhof, ☎ 089/595–423); **Internationale Ludwigs-Apotheke** (⊠ Neuhauserstr. 11, ☎ 089/260–3021).

ENGLISH-LANGUAGE BOOKSTORES

Anglia English Bookshop (⊠ Schellingstr. 3, ☎ 089/283–642). **Hugen-dubel** (⊠ Marienpl. 22, ☎ 089/22890; ⊠ Karlspl. 3, ☎ 089/552–2530).

GUIDED TOURS

Orientation. City bus tours are operated by **Panorama Tours** (⊠ Arnulfstr. 8, ☎ 089/591–504). Tours run daily and take in the city center, the Olympiapark, and Schloss Nymphenburg. Departures are at 10 AM and 2:30 PM (and 11:30 AM in midsummer) from outside the Hertie department store across from the Hauptbahnhof, the main train station. The cost ranges from DM 15 to DM 27 per person.

Walking and Cycling. Walking tours of the old city center set out from Marienplatz every Friday and Saturday at 10:30 and 1. They cost DM 16. **City Hopper Touren** (☎ 089/272–1131) tours of the city, including bike rentals, cost between DM 22 and DM 34 per person depending on the size of the group. **Mike's Bike Tours** (☎ 089/651–4275) organizes tours of the city led by English-speaking guides March through November, daily, starting from the Altes Rathaus at 11:30 and 4. The DM 28 cost includes bike rental and, in fine weather, a beer-garden stop.

Radius Touristik (⊠ Arnulfstr. 3, opposite platforms 30–36 in Hauptbahnhof main concourse, ☎ 089/596–113) has bicycle tours from May through the beginning of October at 10:15 and 2; the cost, including bike rental, is DM 15.

Excursions. Panorama Tours (⊠ Arnulfstr. 8, ☎ 089/591–504) organizes bus trips to most tourist attractions outside the city, including the "Royal Castles Tour" (Schlösserfahrt) of "Mad" King Ludwig's dream palaces; the cost is DM 78.

TRAVEL AGENCIES

ABR (☎ 089/5450–6415), the official Bavarian travel agency, has outlets all over Munich. **American Express** (⊠ Promenadepl. 6, ☎ 089/290–900).

VISITOR INFORMATION

Hauptbahnhof (Main Train Station; ⊠ Bahnhofpl. 2, next to ABR travel agency, ☎ 089/233–30256). **Franz Josef Strauss Airport** (☎ 089/9759–2815). **Rathaus** (⊠ City Hall on Marienpl., ☎ 089/233–30273).

THE BLACK FOREST

Only a century ago the Black Forest (Schwarzwald) was one of the wildest stretches of countryside in Europe. But then the deep hot springs first enjoyed by the Romans were rediscovered, and small, forgotten villages became wealthy spas. The friendly and hospitable region is still extensively forested but with large, open valleys and stretches of verdant farmland. The Black Forest is the southernmost German wine region and the custodian of some of the country's best traditional foods. Black Forest smoked ham and Black Forest cake are its famous exports. The region retains its vibrant clock-making tradition, and wood-carving is still a viable occupation here.

You can tour the region by all means of transportation, taking in parts of the Black Forest High Road, Low Road, Spa Road, Wine Road, and Clock Road. Crossing all the regions of the Black Forest, these roads start in the north in Pforzheim and go as far south as Staufen (approximately 200 km/125 mi) before descending into the Rhine Valley and returning north along the Rhine River to Baden-Baden (approximately 90 km/56 mi).

Pforzheim

The ancient Roman city, almost completely destroyed by wartime bombing, is an example of careful reconstruction. The **Schmuckmuseum** (Jewelry Museum) in the Reuchlinhaus has a magnificent collection of jewelry. ⊠ *Jahnstr. 42,* ☎ *07231/392–126.* ☉ *Tues.–Sun. 10–5.*

$$ ✕ **Silberburg.** This rustic restaurant offers classic and regional cooking. Ask to see the *Tagesempfehlungen*—the chef's daily recommendations. ⊠ *Dietlingerstr. 27,* ☎ *07231/41159. Reservations essential. AE, DC, MC, V. Closed Mon. and 3 wks in Aug. No lunch Tues.*

Bad Liebenzell

The first stop on B463 is one of the Black Forest's oldest spas, with the remains of 15th-century installations. You can take the waters at the **Paracelsusbad lido complex** (Paracelsus Swimming Pool Center) on the Nagold riverbank. ☎ *07052/408–250.* ☉ *Apr.–Oct., Tues., Wed., Fri.–Sun. 7:30 AM–9 PM; Mon., Thurs. 7:30–5; Nov.–Mar., Tues., Wed., Fri.–Sun. 8:30–8; Mon., Thurs. 8:30–5.*

$$$ ✕▥ **Kronen Hotel.** A large modern wing updates this comfortable hotel. The kitchen, which provides the food for the hotel's three different restaurants, prides itself on serving healthful cuisine with lots of fresh vegetables and herbs, whole-grain products, and fruit. ⊠ *Badweg 7, D-75378,* ☎ *07052/4090,* 𝐅𝐀𝐗 *07052/409–420. 43 rooms. 3 restaurants. AE, DC, V.*

Calw

Lovely Calw (pronounced "calve") lies south of Bad Liebenzell. Its famous native son, the novelist and poet Hermann Hesse (1877–1962), called it the "most beautiful [town] of all I know."

The **Neubulach silver mine** was once the most productive in the Black Forest; it closed in 1924 and is now a museum. ⊠ *Talmühle turnoff south of Calw,* ☎ *07053/969510.* ☉ *Apr.–Oct., daily 10–4:15.*

$$$ ✕▥ **Hotel Kloster Hirsau.** This country-house hotel on the wooded out-
★   skirts of Calw stands on the site of a 900-year-old monastery, whose Gothic cloisters are still largely intact. In the restaurant, owner-chef Joachim Ulrich's menu changes daily. The emphasis is on regional dishes enhanced with a French touch such as Swabian farmhouse noodles with truffle vinaigrette. ⊠ *Wildbaderstr. 2, D-75365,* ☎ *07051/5621,* 𝐅𝐀𝐗 *07051/51795. 43 rooms. Restaurant, pool. DC, MC, V.*

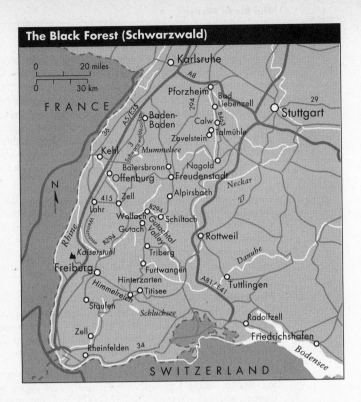

The Black Forest (Schwarzwald)

$$ ✕🏠 **Ratsstube.** Most of the original features, including 16th-century beams and brickwork, are preserved at this historic house in the center of Calw. Rooms aren't spacious but they are brightly decorated with pastel colors and floral patterns. The restaurant offers sturdy, traditional German fare, such as marinated beef and noodles, thick soups, and Black Forest sausage. ⌧ *Marktpl. 12, D-75365,* ☎ 07051/92050, FAX 07051/70826. *13 rooms. Restaurant. AE, D, V.*

Nagold

The town of Nagold lies at the confluence of two gently flowing Black Forest streams, the Nagold and the Waldach. The elliptical street plan harks back to the town's founding 750 years ago; half-timbered buildings, the Romanesque Remigius church, and the modest, hilltop remains of a medieval castle are other reminders of its long history.

$$–$$$ ✕🏠 **Adler.** This 17th-century half-timbered inn has the kind of ambience lesser establishments can't build in with false beams. The menu emphasizes traditional Swabian dishes. Veal in mushroom sauce and venison (in season) are reliable favorites. ⌧ *Badstr. 1 D-72202,* ☎ 07452/67534, FAX 07452/67080. *22 rooms. AE, MC. Restaurant closed Mon.*

Freudenstadt

This small town lies south of Nagold in the middle of lush farmland. Flattened in the war, it was painstakingly restored. The main square, one of Germany's largest, is surrounded by arcaded houses. The imposing **Protestant parish church**'s L-shape ground plan was a daring innovation in the early 17th century.

$$ ✕ **Ratskeller.** If it's cold outside, ask for a place near the Ratskeller's *Kachelofen,* a large, traditional, tile stove. Swabian dishes and venison are prominent on the menu, but if the homemade trout roulade with crab sauce is available, go for it. ⊠ *Marktpl. 8,* ☎ *07441/2693. MC, V. Closed Mon.*

$$ ✕ **Warteck.** Unless you arrive in the dead of winter, you'll find flowers everywhere here, even in the nooks and crannies between the leaded windows. Try the succulent lamb in meadow herbs, venison with Swabian noodles, or veal in mushroom sauce. In season the *Spargel* (asparagus) is dressed in an aromatic hazelnut vinaigrette. ⊠ *Stuttgarter Str. 14, D-72250,* ☎ *07441/7418. DC, V. Closed Tues.*

$$$ ✕🖭 **Schwarzwaldhotel Birkenhof.** Old-fashioned comfort and a woodland setting complement a wide range of sports facilities at this superbly
★ equipped hotel. The two restaurants offer a choice between classic French cuisine and sturdy Black Forest fare. ⊠ *Wildbaderstr. 95, D-72250,* ☎ *07441/8920,* ℻ *07441/4763. 57 rooms. 2 restaurants, indoor pool. AE, DC, MC, V.*

$$-$$$ ✕🖭 **Bären.** Owned by the same family since 1878, the sturdy old Gasthof strives to maintain tradition and service with a personal touch. Rooms are modern but homey with farmhouse-style bedsteads and cupboards. The beam-ceiling restaurant is a favorite with the locals; its menu combines heavy German dishes (roasts and hearty sauces) and lighter international fare. ⊠ *Langestr. 33, D-72250,* ☎ *07441/2779,* ℻ *07441/2887. 33 rooms. Restaurant. No credit cards.*

Baiersbronn

This mountain resort (7 km/4 mi northwest of Freudenstadt), in the midst of the northern Black Forest, is blessed with two of Germany's leading hotel-restaurants—both for hospitality and cuisine. Skiing, golf, and horseback riding are among the area's activities.

$$$$ ✕🖭 **Bareiss.** The luxury hotel has dark-wood furniture, and tapestry-
★ papered walls are warmly lit by candles and traditional lamps. Restaurant Bareiss (closed Monday and Tuesday) serves light, classic cuisine and carefully selected wines (30 brands of champagne alone). The hotel is among the best equipped in the Black Forest. Suites have their own sauna, solarium, and whirlpool baths. ⊠ *Gärtenbühlweg 14, D-07442 Mitteltal/Baiersbronn,* ☎ *07442/470,* ℻ *07442/47320. 53 rooms, 42 apartments, 7 suites. 2 restaurants, 3 pools. AE, DC, MC, V.*

$$$$ ✕🖭 **Traube Tonbach.** The award-winning mountain hotel has three out-
★ standing restaurants—the Schwarzwaldstube (closed Monday and Tuesday), the Köhlerstube, and the Bauernstube. The latter two have beamed ceilings. The hotel is a harmonious blend of old and new, each room enjoying sweeping views of the forest. Guests are nearly outnumbered by a small army of extremely helpful and friendly staff. ⊠ *Tonbachstr. 237, D-72270,* ☎ *07442/4920,* ℻ *07442/492–692. 134 rooms, 58 apartments, 8 suites. 3 restaurants, 3 pools. AE, DC, MC, V.*

$$ ✕🖭 **Hotel Lamm.** The half-timber exterior of this 200-year-old building presents a clear picture of the traditional Black Forest hotel within. Rooms are furnished with heavy oak fittings and some fine antiques. In its beamed restaurant you can order fish taken from the hotel's trout pools. ⊠ *Ellbacherstr. 4, D-072270 Mitteltal/Baiersbronn,* ☎ *07442/ 4980,* ℻ *07442/49878. 48 rooms. Restaurant, pool. AE, DC, MC, V.*

★ Wolfach

South of Freudenstadt on B294, Wolfach has a glass factory, the **Dorotheen-Glashütte,** that is one of the last of its kind—glass is blown by centuries-old techniques once common throughout the region. ⊠ *Glashüttenweg 4,* ☎ *07834/751.* ☉ *Weekdays 9–4:30, Sat. 9–2.*

Gutach

Gutach is best known for the **Vogtsbauernhof,** an outdoor museum consisting of old Black Forest buildings. The town lies in Gutachtal, south of Wolfach, a valley famous for its traditional costumes, and if you're here at the right time (holidays and some Sundays), you'll see the married women sporting black pom-poms on their hats to denote their matronly status (red pom-poms are for the unmarried).

$$–$$$ ✕🏨 **Romantik Hotel Stollen.** The flower-bedecked balconies and low
★   roofs of this hotel disguise a distinctive and luxurious interior, where understated comfort—some rooms have four-poster beds—is combined with attentive service. The restaurant, complete with a roaring log fire, serves regional food with nouvelle touches. ✉ *Elzacherstr. 2, D-79261 Gutach-Bleibach, 21 km (15 mi) northeast of Freiburg,* ☎ *07685/207,* 📠 *07685/1550. 11 rooms, 1 suite. Restaurant. AE, MC, V.*

Triberg

★   This town is the site of Germany's highest **waterfalls,** plunging nearly 509 ft. The area around the falls is also renowned for pom-pom hats, straw-covered farmhouses, cuckoo clocks, and mountain railways. The ride on the **Schwarzwaldbahn** (Black Forest Railway) Offenburg–Villingen line, which passes through Triberg, is one of Germany's most scenic.

The **Schwarzwaldmuseum** (Black Forest Museum) has exhibits related to Black Forest culture. The oldest clock dates from 1640; its simple wooden mechanism is said to have been carved with a bread knife. ✉ *Wallfahrtstr. 4,* ☎ *077722/4434.* ⊙ *May–Oct., daily 9–6; Nov. 1–15 and mid-Dec.–Apr., daily 10–5; mid-Nov.–mid-Dec., weekends 10–5.*

$$–$$$ ✕🏨 **Romantik Parkhotel Wehrle.** The Wehrle family has owned this
★   enchanting building in the center of town since 1707; its vine-covered facade dominates the marketplace. The comfortable rooms are individually furnished, the service is impeccable, and the restaurant's trout is outstanding. ✉ *Gartenstr. 24, D-78098,* ☎ *07722/86020,* 📠 *07722/860–290. 53 rooms, 6 apartments, 1 suite. 2 restaurants, 1 indoor and 1 outdoor pool. AE, DC, MC, V.*

Furtwangen

Clock enthusiasts visit Furtwangen for its **Uhren Museum** (Clock Museum), the largest of its kind in Germany. It charts the development of Black Forest clocks, especially the cuckoo clock. The collection includes an astronomical timepiece weighing more than a ton. ✉ *Gerwigstr. 11,* ☎ *07723/920–117.* ⊙ *Apr.–Oct., daily 9–5; Nov.–Mar., daily 10–5.*

Titisee

The 2½-km-long (1½-mi-long) lake, set in a mighty forest, is the star attraction of the Black Forest's lakeland region. It becomes invariably crowded in summer with boats and windsurfers. Boats and boards can be rented at several points along the shore.

$$ ✕🏨 **Romantik Hotel Adler Post.** In the Neustadt district of Titisee, about 5 km (3 mi) from the lake, the solid, old building has been in the possession of the Ketterer family for more than 140 years. The guest rooms are comfortably and traditionally furnished. The hotel's restaurant is noted for its regional cuisine. ✉ *Hauptstr. 16, D-79822 Titisee–Neustadt,* ☎ *07651/5066,* 📠 *07651/3729. 24 rooms, 4 apartments. Restaurant, pool. AE, DC, MC, V. Closed mid-Mar.–early Apr.*

Hinterzarten

This lovely 800-year-old town is the most popular resort for cross-country skiing and hiking in the southern Black Forest. Some buildings date from the 12th century, among them **St. Oswald's church,** built in 1146. Hinterzarten's oldest inn, **Weisses Rossle,** has been in business since 1347.

$$$ ✗⊞ **Park Hotel Adler.** The hotel, established in 1446, has been managed by the same family for 14 generations. It stands on nearly 2 acres of grounds that are ringed by the Black Forest. Marie Antoinette once ate here, and the highest standards are maintained in the French restaurant and a paneled 17th-century dining room. All rooms are sumptuously appointed. ✉ *Adlerpl. 3, D-79856,* ☎ *07652/1270,* F̄A̱X̱ *07652/ 127–717. 46 rooms, 32 suites. 2 restaurants, pool. AE, DC, MC, V.*

Schluchsee

The largest of the Black Forest lakes, mountain-enclosed Schluchsee is a diverse resort, attracting swimmers, windsurfers, fishers, and, in winter, skiers.

Freiburg

Perched on the western slopes of the Black Forest, this is now one of the region's largest and loveliest cities; it was founded as a free market town during the 12th century. Towering over Freiburg's rebuilt medieval streets is its most famous landmark, the **Münster** (Cathedral). This church, which took three centuries to build, has one of the finest spires in the world. ✉ *Münsterpl.,* ☎ *0761/31099.* ☉ *Münster tours Mon. and Fri. 2:30; Wed., Thurs., weekends 10:30.*

★

On weekdays the square in front of the cathedral, **Münsterplatz,** becomes a mass of color and movement; it's the town market, where you can buy everything from herbs to hot sausage. The Kaufhaus, a 16th-century market house, overlooks it.

$$–$$$ ✗ **Oberkirchs Weinstuben.** Next to the Renaissance Kaufhaus, this wine cellar is a bastion of tradition and local Gemütlichkeit. Approximately 20 Baden wines are served by the glass, from white Gutedel to red Spätburgunder. The proprietor personally bags some of the game that ends up in the kitchen. Fresh trout is another specialty. ✉ *Münsterpl. 22,* ☎ *0761/31011. V. Closed Sun., holidays, and Jan. 10–Feb. 2.*

$$ ✗ **Kleiner Meyerhof.** This has a Weinstube atmosphere, but with more places to sit. It's a good spot to try regional specialties at comfortable prices. In fall and winter come for goose and wild game. ✉ *Rathausg. 27,* ☎ *0761/26941. MC. Closed Sun. June–Aug.*

$$ ✗ **Kühler Krug.** Venison dominates the menu at this restaurant, which has even given its name to a distinctive saddle-of-venison dish. There's also a range of freshwater fish available. ✉ *Torpl. 1,* ☎ *0761/29103. MC. Closed Mon. and 3 wks in June. No lunch Tues.*

$ ✗ **Freiburger Salatstuben.** Healthy vegetarian food is prepared in creative ways—try the homemade whole-wheat noodles with cauliflower in a pepper cream sauce—and served cafeteria style. It gets crowded with university students at peak hours. ✉ *Am Martinstor-Löwenstr. 1,* ☎ *0761/35155. No credit cards. Closed Sun., holidays. No dinner Sat.*

$$$–$$$$ ✗⊞ **Colombi.** Freiburg's most luxurious hotel also has the city's finest and most original restaurant (closed Sunday). In the rustic section you can order hearty local dishes, such as lentil soup and venison, while the more elegant section's menu combines traditional meat and fish dishes with innovative sauces. The two reconstructed 18th-century farmhouse guest cottages are stunningly furnished and decorated with antiques. ✉ *Am Colombi Park/Rotteckring 16, D-79098,* ☎ *0761/21060,* F̄A̱X̱ *0761/ 31410. 80 rooms, 12 suites. Restaurant. AE, DC, MC, V.*

★

$$$ ✗⊞ **Zum Roten Bären.** Now a showpiece of the Ring group, this inn, which dates from 1311, has very comfortable lodging and excellent dining in a cozy warren of four restaurants and taverns. You can tour the two basement floors of cellars, which date from the 12th century and are well stocked with fine wines. ✉ *Oberlinden 12, D-79098,* ☎ *0761/36913,* F̄A̱X̱ *0761/36916. 19 rooms, 3 apartments. 4 restaurants. AE, DC, MC, V.*

★

$$ X🏠 **Markgräfler Hof.** Even the French make the pilgrimage to dine in Hans Leo Kempchen's restaurant, in this old hotel within Freiburg's quaint pedestrian zone. Kempchen rewards travelers with special menus, dishes like bouillabaisse of freshwater fish, and unbeatable two-day deals that include accommodations, a wine tasting, and a guided tour of the city. Reserve rooms well in advance. ⊠ *Gerberau 22, D-79098,* ☎ *0761/32540,* 🅵🅰🆇 *0761/37947. 18 rooms. Restaurant. AE, DC, MC, V.*

$$ 🏠 **Rappen Hotel.** The Rappen is in the center of the traffic-free Old Town overlooking the marketplace and the cathedral (and overhearing the bustle of the former and the bells of the latter). A farmhouse theme prevails, with rustic furnishings in every room. The comfortable restaurant offers more than 200 regional wines. ⊠ *Am Münsterpl. 13, D-79098,* ☎ *0761/31353,* 🅵🅰🆇 *0751/382–252. 25 rooms, 13 with bath. Restaurant. AE, DC, MC, V.*

Staufen

This small town, some 19 km (12 mi) south of Freiburg, claims the inquisitive Dr. Faustus as one of its early burghers. Faustus, who reputedly made a pact with the Devil, was the subject of Goethe's 1808 drama, *Faust.* Faustus lived and died in the inn **Gasthaus zum Löwen** (⊠ Hauptstr. 47).

The Weinstrasse

From Staufen turn northward toward Baden-Baden along the Weinstrasse (Wine Road) skirting the French border to your left, through vineyards that produce the prized Baden wine. All the vineyards offer tastings, so don't hesitate to drop in and try one or two.

The Schwarzwaldhochstrasse

Leave the Wine Road at the town of Lahr and head inland, on B415, through the narrow Schuttertal valley to Zell, and from there to the Schwarzwaldhochstrasse (Black Forest High Road). This is the land of fable and superstition, and if you're here during the misty days of autumn, stop off at the mystery-shrouded lake called the **Mummelsee.**

★ Baden-Baden

The fashionable Baden-Baden, idyllically set in a wooded valley of the northern Black Forest, sits atop the extensive underground hot springs that gave the city its name (*Baden* means baths). The Romans first exploited the springs, which were then rediscovered by wealthy travelers a couple of centuries ago. By the end of the 19th century, there was scarcely a crowned head of Europe who had not dipped into the healing waters.

One of the grand buildings of Baden-Baden's Belle Epoque is the pillared **Kurhaus** (Spa), home of Germany's first casino, which opened its doors in 1853. Visitors are required to sign a declaration that they enter with sufficient funds to settle subsequent debts! Passports are necessary as proof of identity and jacket and tie are required. ⊠ *Werderstr.,* ☎ *07221/21060.*

At Baden-Baden's famous Roman baths, the **Friedrichsbad,** you take the waters just as the Romans did nearly 2,000 years ago—nude. The remains of the Roman baths that lie beneath the Friedrichsbad can be visited from April through October. ⊠ *Römerpl. 1,* ☎ *07221/275–920.* 🖭 *3 hrs, DM 28 (DM 48 with massage).* ☉ *Mon.–Sat. 9 AM–10 PM, Sun. 2–10. Children under 18 not admitted.*

The **Caracalla-Therme** (Caracalla Baths) are a huge, modern complex with five indoor pools, two outdoor pools, numerous whirlpools, a solarium, and a "sauna landscape"—you look out through windows at

the countryside while you bake. ⊠ *Römerpl. 11,* ☎ *07221/275–940.*
⧠ *2 hrs, DM 18; 3 hrs, DM 24.* ⊙ *Daily 8 AM–10 PM.*

$$$ ✕ **Stahlbad.** The Gallo-Germanic menu here is echoed by the restaurant's furnishings—19th-century French oils adorn the walls, and French and German china are reflected in the mahogany gleam of antique tables and sideboards. An abundance of green velvet catches the tone of the parklike grounds of the stately house that accommodates this elegant restaurant. ⊠ *Augustapl. 2,* ☎ *07221/24569. AE, DC, MC, V. Closed Mon.*

$$$ ✕⊞ **Der Kleine Prinz.** Each room of this beautifully modernized 19th-
★ century mansion is decorated in a different style, from romantic Art Nouveau to Manhattan modern. Chef Berthold Krieger combines nouvelle cuisine flair with unmistakable German thoroughness, elevating the restaurant (closed first two weeks of January) to a leading position in demanding Baden-Baden. ⊠ *Lichtentalerstr. 36, D-76530,* ☎ *07221/3464,* ⅎⅩ *07221/38264. 25 rooms, 13 suites. Restaurant. AE, DC, MC, V.*

$$ ✕⊞ **Gasthaus zur Traube.** Regional specialties, such as smoked bacon and homemade noodles, head the menu in this cozy inn, south of the city center in the Neuweier district. You can also spend the night in one of the neat and moderately priced rooms. The restaurant is closed Wednesday. ⊠ *Mauerbergstr. 107, D-76534,* ☎ *07223/96820,* ⅎⅩ *07223/6764. 15 rooms, 1 suite. Restaurant. V.*

$$$$ ⊞ **Brenner's Park Hotel.** This exceptional, stately mansion is set in spacious, private grounds. All rooms are luxuriously furnished and appointed. ⊠ *Schillerstr. 6, D-76530,* ☎ *07221/9000,* ⅎⅩ *07221/38772. 68 rooms, 32 suites. 2 restaurants, pool. AE, DC, MC.*

$ ⊞ **Hotel am Markt.** The Bogner family has run the place for more than three decades—a relatively short amount of time for this 250-plus-year-old building. It's friendly, popular, and right in the center of town. ⊠ *Marktpl. 17–18, D-76530,* ☎ *07221/22747,* ⅎⅩ *07221/391–887. 28 rooms, 14 with bath. Restaurant. AE, DC, MC, V.*

The Black Forest Essentials

Getting Around

The **Rhine Valley autobahn,** the A5, runs the entire length of the Black Forest and connects at Karlsruhe with the rest of the German expressway network. Well-paved, single-lane highways traverse the region. The nearest **airports** are in Stuttgart; Strasbourg, in the neighboring French Alsace; and the Swiss border city of Basel, just 64 km (40 mi) from Freiburg. A main **north–south train line** follows the Rhine Valley, carrying EuroCity and InterCity trains that call at hourly intervals at Freiburg and Baden-Baden, connecting them directly with Frankfurt and many other German cities. Local lines connect most Black Forest towns, and two local east–west services, the Black Forest Railway and the Höllental Railway, are spectacular scenic runs.

Guided Tours

Guided bus tours of the Black Forest begin in Freiburg; contact the visitor information office (☞ *below*). A choice of 25 one-day tours includes the French Alsace region, the Swiss Alps, and various attractions in the Black Forest itself. Prices start at DM 32 and include English-speaking guides.

Visitor Information

The **Fremdenverkehrsverband** (regional tourist authority; ⊠ Bertold-str. 45, D-79098 Freiburg, ☎ 0761/31317) offers a series of scenic routes covering every important attraction.

Baden-Baden (✉ Augustapl. 8, D-76530, ☎ 07221/275–200). **Freiburg** (✉ Rotteckring 14, D-79098, ☎ 0761/388-1880). **Freudenstadt** (✉ Promenadenpl. 1, D-72250, ☎ 07741/8640). **Pforzheim** (✉ Marktpl. 1, D-75175, ☎ 07231/39900). **Schluchsee** (✉ Kurverwaltung, Fischbacherstr. 7, D-79859, ☎ 07656/7732).

FRANKFURT

Virtually flattened by bombs during World War II, Frankfurt-am-Main now bristles with skyscrapers, the visible signs of the city's role as Germany's financial capital. Originally a Roman settlement, Frankfurt later served as one of Charlemagne's two capitals (the other being Aachen). Still later, the electors of the Holy Roman Empire met here to choose and crown the emperor. It is also the birthplace of the poet and dramatist Johann Wolfgang von Goethe (1749–1832).

Exploring Frankfurt

Numbers in the margin correspond to points of interest on the Frankfurt map.

The neighborhood around the Hauptbahnhof (main train station), site of many major hotels, is mostly devoted to business and banking, but do be careful of the seedy red-light district nearby. If you want a sense of the past, or to let the good times roll, head to the Old Town with its restored medieval quarter and to Sachsenhausen across the river, where the pubs and museums greatly outnumber the banks.

🔞 **Alte Oper** (Old Opera House). Built between 1873 and 1880 and destroyed during World War II, Frankfurt's Old Opera House has been beautifully reconstructed in the style of the original. ✉ *Opernpl.,* ☎ *069/134–0400.*

🔞 **Börse** (Stock Exchange). The Börse was founded by Frankfurt merchants in 1558 to establish some order in their often chaotic dealings, but the present building dates from the 1870s. This center for Germany's stock and money market also has a visitors gallery. ✉ *Börsepl.,* ☎ *069/ 21010.* 🎟 *Free.* ⏱ *Weekdays 10:30–1:30.*

🔞 **Fressgasse** (Pig-Out Alley). The proper name of one of the city's liveliest thoroughfares is Grosse Bockenheimer Strasse, but Frankfurters have given it this sobriquet because of the amazing choice of delicatessens, wine merchants, cafés, and restaurants. ✉ *East of Opernpl.*

★ 🔞 **Goethehaus und Goethemuseum** (Goethe's House and Museum). The birthplace of Germany's most famous poet is furnished with many original pieces that belonged to his family. Although the original house was destroyed by Allied bombing, it has been carefully rebuilt and restored in every detail. The adjoining museum contains works of art that inspired Goethe (he was an amateur painter) and works associated with his literary contemporaries. ✉ *Grosser Hirschgraben 23–25,* ☎ *069/ 138–800.* ⏱ *Mon.–Sat. 9–6, Sun. 10–1.*

🔞 **Hauptwache.** This square serves as the hub of the city's transportation network. The attractive Baroque building with a steeply sloping roof is the actual Hauptwache (main guard), a municipal guardhouse built in 1729. Today it houses a café and a tourist information office. ✉ *Junction Zeil and Grosse Eschenheimer Str.*

🔞 **Jüdisches Museum** (Jewish Museum). In the former Rothschild Palace, this museum tells the story of Frankfurt's Jewish quarter. Prior to the Holocaust it was the second largest Jewish community in Germany. ✉ *Untermainkai 14–15,* ☎ *069/2123–4856.* ⏱ *Tues.–Sun. 10–5, Wed. 10–8.*

⑩ Karmeliterkloster (Carmelite Church and Monastery). Secularized in 1803, the church and buildings were renovated in the 1980s and now contain the **Museum für Vor- und Frügeschichte** (Museum of Prehistory and Early History). The main cloister has a **gallery** that houses rotating modern art exhibitions and the largest religious fresco north of the Alps, a 16th-century representation of Christ's birth and death. *Museum: ⊠ Karmeliterg. 1, ☎ 069/2123–5896. ☉ Tues. and Thurs.–Sun. 10–5, Wed. 10–8. Gallery: ⊠ Münzg. 9, ☎ 069/2123–8425. ☉ Daily 11–6.*

❸ Katharinenkirche (St. Catherine's Church). Originally built between 1678 and 1681, it was the first independent Protestant church in the Gothic style. The first Protestant sermon in Frankfurt was given here. *⊠ Junction An der Hauptwache and Katherinenpfad. ☉ Daily 10–5.*

⑯ Kuhhirtenturm (Shepherd's Tower). Built during the 15th century, this is the last of nine towers that formed part of the fortifications for **Sachsenhausen** (☞ *below*). The composer Paul Hindemith lived in the tower from 1923 to 1927 while working at the Frankfurt Opera. *⊠ Grosse Ritter G. at Sachsenhaüser Ufer.*

❾ Leonhardskirche (St. Leonard's Church). This beautifully preserved 13th-century building with five naves has some fine old stained glass. The hanging, ornately carved piece of the ceiling vault was already a major Frankfurt tourist attraction during the 17th century. *⊠ Junction Leonhardstr. and Untermainkai. ☉ Wed., Fri., Sat. 10–noon and 3–6; Tues., Thurs. 10–noon and 3–6:30; Sun. 9–1 and 3–6.*

⑮ Museum für Moderne Kunst (Museum of Modern Art). In a distinctive triangular building designed by Austrian architect Hans Hollein, the collection has American Pop art and works by such German artists as Gerhard Richter and Joseph Beuys. *⊠ Domstr. 10, ☎ 069/2123–0447. ☉ Tues., Thurs.–Sun. 10–5, Wed. 10–8.*

❽ Nikolaikirche (St. Nicholas's Church). This small red sandstone church dates from the late 13th century. The wonderful chimes of the glockenspiel carillon ring out three times a day. *⊠ South side of Römerberg. ☉ Mon.–Sat. 10–5. Carillon chimes daily at 9, noon, and 5.*

❹ Paulskirche (St. Paul's Church). The first all-German parliament meeting, in 1848, took place at this church. The parliament lasted a year, having done little more than offer the Prussian king the crown of Germany. Today the church is used mainly for formal ceremonial events. *⊠ Paulspl. ☉ Daily 11–3.*

❻ Römer (City Hall). Its gabled Gothic facade with an ornate balcony is widely known as the city's official emblem. The mercantile-minded Frankfurt burghers used the complex of three patrician buildings not only for political and ceremonial purposes but also for trade fairs and other commercial ventures. Banquets to celebrate the coronations of the Holy Roman emperors were mounted starting in 1562 in the **Kaisersaal** (Imperial Hall). Impressive, full-length, 19th-century portraits of the 52 emperors of the Holy Roman Empire line the walls of the reconstructed banquet hall. *⊠ West side of Römerberg, ☎ 069/2123–4814. ☉ Daily 10–1 and 2–5. Closed during official functions.*

❺ Römerberg. This square north of the Main River, lovingly restored after wartime bomb damage, is the historical focal point of the city. The **Römer** (☞ *above*) and the **Nikolaikirche** (☞ *above*) are found here. The fine 16th-century **Fountain of Justitia** (Justice) stands in the center of the square. At the coronation of Emperor Matthias in 1612, wine instead of water flowed from the fountain. This practice has recently been revived by the city fathers for special festive occasions. *⊠ Bordered by Domstr., Neue Krämerstr., and Saalg.*

Frankfurt

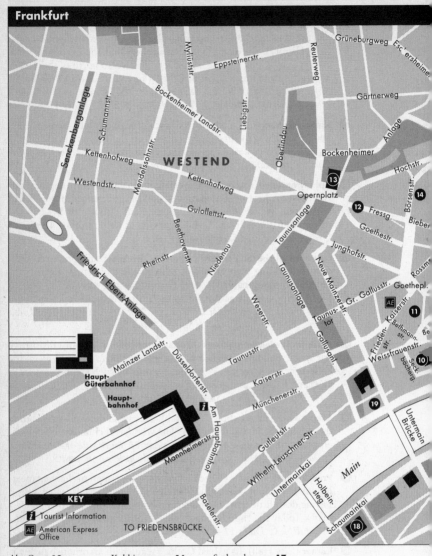

Alte Oper, **13**
Börse, **14**
Fressgasse, **12**
Goethehaus und
Goethemuseum, **11**
Hauptwache, **1**
Jüdisches
Museum, **19**
Karmeliterkloster, **10**
Katharinenkirche, **3**

Kuhhirtenturm, **16**
Leonhardskirche, **9**
Museum für Moderne
Kunst, **15**
Nikolaikirche, **8**
Paulskirche, **4**
Römer, **6**
Römerberg Square, **5**

Sachsenhausen, **17**
St. Bartholomäus, **7**
Städelsches Kunstin-
stitut und Städtische
Galerie, **18**
Zeil, **2**

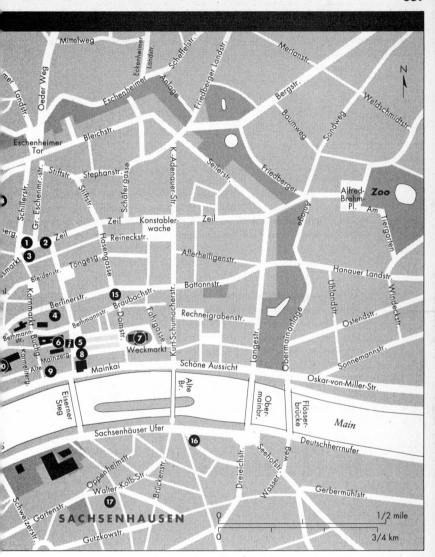

Mittelweg

Oeder Weg

Mer Landstr.

Eschenheimer Landstr.

Eckenheimer Landstr.

Scheffelstr.

Anlage

Friedberger Landstr.

Merianstr.

Bergstr.

Baumweg

Sandweg

Weidschmidtstr.

N

Eschenheimer Tor

Bleichstr.

Stiftstr.

Stephanstr.

Schäfergasse

K.-Adenauer-Str.

Seilerstr.

Friedberger

Anlage

Alfred-Brehm-Pl.

Zoo

Am Tiergarten

Schillerstr.

Gr. Eschenhr.-str.

Stiftstr.

Zeil

Konstablerwache

Zeil

berg.

Zeil

Reineckstr.

Hasengasse

Allerheiligenstr.

Hanauer Landstr.

Uhlandstr.

Ostendstr.

Windeckstr.

Bleidenstr.

Töngesg.

Braubachstr.

Battonnstr.

Obermainanlage

ol.

Berlinerstr.

Bethmannstr.

Damstr.

Kurt-Schumacherstr.

Rechneigrabenstr.

Langestr.

Sonnemannstr.

Kornmarkt

Buchg.

Fahrgasse

Weckmarkt

Schöne Aussicht

Oskar-von-Miller-Str.

Bethmann-str.

Karmeliterg.

Alte Mainzerg.

Mainkai

Alte Br.

Ober-mainbr.

Flösser-brücke

Main

Eiserner Steg

Sachsenhäuser Ufer

Deutschherrnufer

Oppenheimstr.

Walter-Kolb-Str.

Brückenstr.

Dreieichstr.

Seehofstr.

Wasserweg

Gerbermühlstr.

Gartenstr.

SACHSENHAUSEN

Schweizerstr.

Gutzkowstr.

0 1/2 mile

0 3/4 km

★ ⑰ **Sachsenhausen.** The old quarter of Sachsenhausen, on the south bank of the Main River, has been sensitively preserved and continues to be very popular with residents and visitors alike. Charlemagne is said to have established a settlement here during the 8th century with a group of Saxon families. The neighborhood is the home of the famous *Ebbel-woi* (apple wine or cider) taverns. A green pine wreath above the entrance tells passersby that freshly pressed—and alcoholic—apple cider is on tap. You can eat well in these small inns, too, though the menu might seem odd. For example, *Handkas mit Musik* does not promise music at your table. The Musik means that the cheese, or *Kas* (from Käse), will be served with raw onions, oil, vinegar, and bread and butter.

⓻ **St. Bartholomäus** (Church of St. Bartholomew). Also known as the Kaiser-dom (Imperial Cathedral), this impressive structure isn't really a cathedral. It was built largely between the 13th and 15th centuries and survived the bombs of World War II with most of its original treasures intact. The tall, red sandstone tower (almost 300 ft high) was added between 1415 and 1514. Excavations in front of the main entrance in 1953 revealed the remains of a Roman settlement and the foundations of a Carolingian imperial palace. ⊠ *Domstr.* ☉ *Apr.–Oct., Mon. 9–12:30 and 3–6, Tues.–Sun. 8–6; Nov.–Feb., daily 9–noon and 3–5.*

★ ⑱ **Städelsches Kunstinstitut und Städtische Galerie** (Städel Art Institute and Municipal Gallery). One of Germany's important art collections has paintings by Dürer, Vermeer, Rembrandt, Rubens, Monet, Renoir, and other great masters. The section on German Expressionism is particularly strong, with works by Frankfurt artist Max Beckmann. ⊠ *Schaumainkai 63,* ☎ *069/605–0980.* ▨ *Free on Wed.* ☉ *Tues. and Thurs.–Sun. 10–5, Wed. 10–8.*

⓶ **Zeil.** The heart of Frankfurt's shopping district is this ritzy pedestrian thoroughfare, which is Germany's busiest shopping street. ⊠ *East of Hauptwache.*

Dining and Lodging

Businesspeople descend on Frankfurt year-round, so most hotels in the city are expensive (many offer significant reductions on weekends) and frequently book up well in advance. The majority of the larger hotels are around the main train station, a 15- to 20-minute walk from the Old Town. For any of the fancier restaurants in Frankfurt, make reservations in advance. Many serve bargain lunch menus. For example, **Erno's Bistro, Gargantua,** and **Humperdinck** have midday menus for DM 49. Laughter is the only response you'll get if you try to reserve a table at the apple-wine taverns—you're expected to just show up and find space at one of the long tables. For details and price-category definitions on dining and lodging, *see* Dining *and* Lodging *in* Germany A to Z, *above.*

$$$$ ✕ **Humperdinck.** Chef Alfred Friedrich regales the lucky diners at his
★   15 tables with some of the most creative cooking in Frankfurt; rabbit salad with marinated mushrooms, and sea bass with fennel are typical entrées, followed by wild strawberries in cream. ⊠ *Grüneburgweg 95 at Liebigstr.,* ☎ *069/9720–3154. Jacket and tie. AE, MC, V.*

$$$ ✕ **Erno's Bistro.** Small, chic, and popular with visiting power brokers, Erno's has become something of a Frankfurt institution. The menu has classy nouvelle specialties, with fish—flown in daily, often from France—predominating. The waiters speak English. ⊠ *Liebigstr. 15,* ☎ *069/721–997. Reservations essential. AE, DC, MC, V. Closed weekends and July–early Aug.*

$$ ✕ **Altes Zollhaus.** Very good versions of traditional German special-ties are served in this beautiful, 200-year-old half-timber house. Try a game dish. In summer you can eat in the beautiful garden. ⊠ *Fried-berger Landstr. 531,* ☎ *069/472–707. AE, DC, MC, V. Closed Mon. No lunch.*

$$ ✕ **Charlot.** The French cuisine of this very popular restaurant acquired an Italian touch with the arrival of chef Mario. The Alte Oper is just across the street, so after the curtain falls you'll be fighting music buffs for a place in the French bistro–style dining rooms. ⊠ *Opernpl. 10,* ☎ *069/287–007. AE, DC, MC, V. No lunch Sun.*

$$ ✕ **Jaspers.** This is technically a French restaurant, but the many Al-satian specialties give it a German flair. Some better dishes include fish soup with croutons, and snails in Calvados sauce over spinach. The high level of service and cooking puts many better known and more expensive restaurants to shame. ⊠ *Schifferstr. 8 (just off Affentorpl.), Sachsenhausen,* ☎ *069/614–117. AE, DC, V. Closed Sun.*

$$ ✕ **Oscar's.** Although it looks like cross between a Paris bistro and a
★ New York diner, Oscar's actually belongs to a grand hotel, the Frank-furter Hof. It's something of a crossroads where a business lunch rubs shoulders with a romantic rendezvous. The chef will deftly put the world on your plate—nachos, shellfish, Argentine steaks, California cuisine, or something closer to home like grilled blood sausage or stewed beef with Frankfurter sauce. ⊠ *Am Kaiserplatz,* ☎ *069/215150. Reserva-tions essential. AE, DC, MC, V.*

$ ✕ **Café GegenwART.** "Gegenwart" means "the present," and the em-phasis on ART means there are always works of local artists exhib-ited in this friendly, bustling café. The cuisine is also artfully presented. Try the freshly caught angler fish or the tomato fondue when avail-able. ⊠ *Bergerstr. 6,* ☎ *069/497–0544. No credit cards.*

$ ✕ **Germania.** This noisy, smoky apple-wine tavern, one of Sachsen-hausen's most authentic, is filled with long wooden tables at which lo-cals rub—and bend—elbows. Good traditional grub and great cider, but absolutely no beer! ⊠ *16 Textorstr., Sachsenhausen,* ☎ *069/613–336. No credit cards. Closed Mon.*

$ ✕ **Wagner.** The kitchen produces the same hearty German dishes as
★ other apple-wine taverns, only better. Try the *Tafelspitz mit Frankfurter Grüner Sosse* (stewed beef with a sauce of green herbs) or come on Friday for fresh fish. Beer and wine are served as well as cider. This Sachsenhausen classic succeeds in being trendy, touristy, and traditional all at once. ⊠ *Schweizer Str. 71, Sachsenhausen,* ☎ *069/612–565. Reser-vations not accepted. No credit cards.*

$$$$ ⊞ **Gravenbruch Kempinski.** The atmosphere of the 16th-century manor
★ house around which the elegant, sophisticated hotel was built still re-mains at this parkland site in leafy Neu Isenburg (a 15-minute drive south of Frankfurt). Some of the luxuriously appointed rooms and suites are arranged as duplex penthouse apartments. Ask for a room over-looking the lake. ⊠ *An der Bundestr. 459, D-63243 Neu-Isenburg,* ☎ *06102/5050,* ℻ *06102/505–900. 287 rooms. 2 restaurants, 1 indoor and 1 outdoor pool. AE, DC, MC, V.*

$$$$ ⊞ **Hessischer Hof.** In this former palace, still owned by a prince of Hesse, antiques are deftly positioned in many guest rooms. One of the two bars, Jimmy's, numbers among Frankfurt's best, and the hotel restau-rant, Sevres, is prized for its haute cuisine and refined ambience. ⊠ *Friedrich-Ebert-Anlage 40, D-60235,* ☎ *069/7540–2924,* ℻ *069/ 754–0924. 117 rooms. Restaurant. AE, DC, MC, V.*

$$$$ ⊞ **Steigenberger Hotel Frankfurter Hof.** The Victorian Frankfurter
★ Hof is one of the city's oldest hotels. The atmosphere throughout is one of old-fashioned, formal elegance, with burnished woods, fresh flow-ers, and thick-carpeted hush. Kaiser Wilhelm once slept here. ⊠ *Am*

Kaiserpl., D-60311, ☎ 069/21502, ⟨FAX⟩ 069/215–900. 332 rooms, 10 suites. 4 restaurants. AE, DC, MC, V.

$$$ 🖭 **Hotel Robert Mayer.** In a turn-of-the-century villa, each room has ★ been decorated by a different Frankfurt artist, with furniture designs by the likes of Rietveld and Frank Lloyd Wright. The room designed by Therese Traube contrasts abstract newspaper collage with a replica Louis XIV armchair. Breakfast is included in the price of the room. ⊠ *Robert-Mayer-Str. 44, D-60486, ☎ 069/970910. 11 rooms, 1 suite. AE, DC, MC, V.*

$$ 🖭 **Maingau.** You'll find this pleasant hotel-restaurant in the middle of ★ the lively Sachsenhausen quarter. Rooms are modest but spotless, comfortable, and equipped with TVs; the room rate includes a substantial breakfast buffet. Chef Stephan Döpfner has made the restaurant, Maingau-Stuben, one of Frankfurt's best. ⊠ *Schifferstr. 38–40, D-60594, ☎ 069/617–001, ⟨FAX⟩ 069/620–790. 100 rooms. Restaurant. AE, MC.*

$$ 🖭 **Westend.** French antiques are at every turn in this small, elegant, family-run establishment. It's very popular with media types. ⊠ *Westendstr. 15, D-60325, ☎ 069/ 746–702, ⟨FAX⟩ 069/745–396. 15 rooms. AE, MC, V.*

$ 🖭 **Hotel-Schiff** *Peter Schlott.* The hotel ship is moored on the Main River in the suburb of Höchst, a 15-minute train or tram ride from the city center. Guest cabins are on the small side, but the river views more than compensate. ⊠ *Mainberg, D-65929, ☎ 069/315–480, ⟨FAX⟩ 069/307–671. 19 rooms, 10 with shower. Restaurant. AE, MC.*

$ 🖭 **Waldhotel Hensels Felsenkeller.** Helmut Braun's hotel backs onto the woods that ring Frankfurt, and the city center is just a 15-minute train ride away (the nearest stop is a three-minute walk). Rooms are basic; the less expensive ones have shared showers. ⊠ *Buchrainstr. 95, D-60599, ☎ 069/652–086, ⟨FAX⟩ 069/658–379. 15 rooms, 7 with bath. Restaurant. No credit cards.*

Frankfurt Essentials

Arriving and Departing

BY BUS

Long-distance buses connect Frankfurt with more than 200 other European cities. Buses leave from the south side of the Hauptbahnhof. Tickets and information are available from **Deutsche Touring** (⊠ Am Römerhof 17, ☎ 069/79030).

BY CAR

Frankfurt is the junction of many major **autobahns.** The most important are the A-3, running south from Köln and then on to Würzburg, Nürnberg, and Munich; and the A-5, running south from Giessen and then on to Mannheim, Heidelberg, Karlsruhe, and the Swiss-German border at Basel. A complex series of beltways surrounds the city. If you're driving to Frankfurt on the A-5 from either north or south, exit at Nordwestkreuz and follow A-66 to the Nordend district, just north of downtown. Driving south on A-3, exit onto A-66 and follow the signs to Frankfurt-Höchst and then the Nordend district. Driving north on A-3, exit at Offenbach onto A-661 and follow the signs for FRANK-FURT-STADTMITTE (City Center).

BY PLANE

Frankfurt Airport, the busiest and biggest airport in mainland Europe, is about 10 km (6 mi) southwest of the city. A new airport railway station for high-speed InterCity Express (ICE) trains was inaugurated in spring 1999.

Between the Airport and Downtown. Getting into Frankfurt from the airport is easy. The S-8 (S-bahn) runs from the airport to downtown, stopping at the Hauptbahnhof (main train station) and then at the central Hauptwache square. Trains run every 15 minutes and the ride takes about as long; the one-way fare is DM 5.90. InterCity and InterCity Express (ICE) trains to and from most major western German cities also stop at the airport. Taxis from the airport downtown take about 20 minutes (double that in rush hour); the fare averages DM 40. If you're driving, take the B43 main road, following signs for STADTMITTE.

BY TRAIN

EuroCity and InterCity trains connect Frankfurt with all other German cities and many major European ones. The InterCity Express (ICE) line links Frankfurt with Hamburg, Munich, and several other major German cities. All long-distance trains arrive at and depart from the Hauptbahnhof. For information call **Deutsche Bahn** (German Railways; ☎ 069/19419) or ask at the information office in the station.

Getting Around

BY PUBLIC TRANSPORTATION

Frankfurt's efficient, well-integrated public transportation system consists of the U-bahn (subway), S-bahn (suburban railway), and Strassenbahn (streetcars). During rush hours the subway is sometimes the fastest way to get around. Fares for the entire system are uniform but based on a complicated zone system. Tickets may be purchased from automatic vending machines accepting coins and notes at all stations and at most street newsstands; on buses and streetcars, they can also be purchased from the driver. For further information or assistance call 069/269–462. The Frankfurt tourist office sells a Frankfurt Card (DM 12 for one day, DM 19 for two days) entitling you to unlimited inner-zone travel, a trip to the airport, and half-price admission to 15 museums.

BY TAXI

Cabs are not always easy to hail from the sidewalk; some stop, others will pick up only from the city's numerous taxi stands or outside hotels or the train station. Fares start at DM 3.50 and increase by DM 2.15–DM 2.55 per km (½ mi), depending on the time of day. You can call 069/250–001 or 069/230–033 for a taxi to come get you.

Contacts and Resources

CONSULATES

U.S. (⊠ Siesmayerstr. 21, ☎ 069/75350). **U.K.** (⊠ Bockenheimer Landstr. 42, ☎ 069/170–0020). **Australia** (⊠ Gutleustr. 85/IV, ☎ 069/273–9090).

EMERGENCIES

Police (☎ 110). **Fire** (☎ 112). **Medical Emergencies** (☎ 069/7950–2200 or 069/19292). **Dental Emergencies** (☎ 069/660–7271). **Pharmacies** (☎ 069/11500).

ENGLISH-LANGUAGE BOOKSTORES

American Book Center (⊠ Jahnstr. 36, ☎ 069/552–816). **British Bookshop** (⊠ Börsenstr. 17, ☎ 069/280–492).

GUIDED TOURS

Orientation. Two-and-a-half-hour bus tours that take in all the main sights with English-speaking guides, as well as special tours by prior arrangement, are offered by the **main tourist office** (⊠ Römerberg 27, ☎ 069/2123–8953). **Gray Line** (☎ 069/230–492) also offers two-hour city tours. The **city transit authority** (☎ 069/2132–2425) runs a brightly painted old-time streetcar—the *Ebbelwoi Express* (Cider Express)—on weekend and holiday afternoons. Departures are from the Bornheim-Mitte U- and S-bahn station and the fare is DM 4.

Excursions. The **Deutsche Bahn,** German Railways, organizes a number of trips, described in a brochure, "Der Schöne Tag," available at the main train station and the DER tourist office (☞ Visitor Information, *below*). **Deutsche Touring** (✉ Am Römerhof 17, ☎ 069/790–3261) offers excursions outside Frankfurt. Pleasure boats of the Primus Line cruise the Main and Rhine rivers from Frankfurt, sailing as far as the Lorelei and back in a day; for schedules and reservations contact **Frankfurter Personenschiffahrt** (✉ Mainkai 36, ☎ 069/281–884).

MAIL

Note that the official address for Frankfurt includes "Main" after the city name in any variety of ways—Frankfurt/Main, Frankfurt am Main, Frankfurt/M, to cite a few.

TRAVEL AGENCIES

American Express (✉ Kaiserstr. 8, ☎ 069/210–5111).

VISITOR INFORMATION

Main tourist office (✉ Römerberg 27, ☎ 069/2123–8800; mailing address, ✉ Verkehrsamt Frankfurt/Main, Kaiserstr. 52, D-60329, ☎ 069/2123–8800). **Frankfurt Airport** (FAG Flughafen-Information, first floor of Arrivals Hall B; DER Deutsches Reisebüro, Arrivals Hall B-6). **Hauptbahnhof** (Main Train Station; ✉ Am Hauptbahnhof, opposite Track 23, ☎ 069/2123–8849).

THE RHINE

For the Romans, who established forts and colonies along its western bank, the Rhine was the frontier between civilization and the barbaric German tribes. Roman artifacts are exhibited in museums throughout the region. In the Middle Ages the river's importance as a trade artery made it the focus of conflict between princes, nobles, and archbishops. Many of the picturesque castles that crown its banks were the homes of robber barons who held up or exacted tolls on passing ships.

For poets and composers the Rhine—or *Vater Rhein* (Father Rhine), as the Germans call it—has been an endless source of inspiration. As legend has it, the Lorelei, a treacherous, craggy rock, was home to a beautiful and bewitching maiden who lured sailors to a watery grave. The Rhine does not belong to Germany alone, but the German span of it has the most spectacular scenery—especially the 190-km (120-mi) stretch between Mainz and Köln (Cologne) known as the Middle Rhine. This is a land of steep and thickly wooded hills, vineyards, tiny villages hugging the banks, and a succession of brooding castles.

Köln

The largest German city on the Rhine is Köln (Cologne), first settled by the Romans in 38 BC. The Franks and Merovingians followed the Romans before Charlemagne restored the city's fortunes during the 9th century, appointing its first archbishop and ensuring its ecclesiastical prominence for centuries.

By the Middle Ages Köln was the largest city north of the Alps, and, as a member of the powerful Hanseatic League, it was more important commercially than either London or Paris. Ninety percent of the city was destroyed in World War II, and the rush to rebuild it shows in some of the blocky, uninspired architecture. Still, attempts were made to restore many of its old buildings. Whatever the city's aesthetic drawbacks, the Altstadt (Old Town), within the line of the medieval city walls, has great charm, and at night it throbs with life.

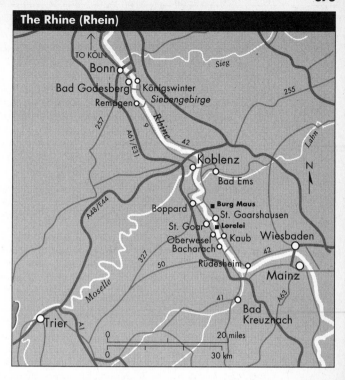

The Rhine (Rhein)

TO KÖLN

Bonn

Sieg

Bad Godesberg · Königswinter
Remagen · *Siebengebirge*

255

257 · 9 · *Rhine* · 42

Lahn

Koblenz

N

Bad Ems

Boppard · ■ Burg Maus
St. Goarshausen
St. Goar · ■ Lorelei
Oberwesel · Kaub
Bacharach · Wiesbaden

A48/E44 · 327 · 50

Rüdesheim

42

Mainz

Moselle

41

463

Trier · A1

Bad Kreuznach

0 _____ 20 miles
0 _____ 30 km

★ Towering over the Old Town is the **Kölner Dom** (Cologne Cathedral), an extraordinary Gothic edifice, dedicated to St. Peter and the Virgin. At 515 ft high, the two western towers of the cathedral were by far the tallest structures in the world when they were finished. The length of the building is 469 ft; the width of the nave is 148 ft; and the highest part of the interior is 139 ft. The cathedral was built to house what were believed to be the relics of the Magi, the three kings or wise men who paid homage to the infant Jesus. Today the relics are kept just behind the altar, in the same enormous gold-and-silver reliquary in which they were originally displayed. The Gero Cross, a monumental oak crucifix, dates from 971. Impressive for its simple grace, it's in the last chapel on the left as you face the high altar. The *Adoration of the Kings* (1440), a triptych by Stephan Lochner, Köln's most famous medieval painter, is to the right. More treasures can be seen in the **Schatzkammer** (Cathedral Treasury), including the silver shrine of Archbishop Engelbert, who was stabbed to death in 1225. ⊠ *Dompl.,* ☎ *0221/135–130.* ⊙ *Mon.–Sat. 9–5, Sun. 1–5.*

★ The ultramodern **Wallraf-Richartz-Museum/Museum Ludwig** complex across the square from the Dom forms the largest art collection in the Rhineland. The Wallraf-Richartz-Museum's pictures span the years 1300–1900, with Dutch and Flemish schools particularly well represented (Rubens, who spent his youth in Köln, has a place of honor). The Museum Ludwig is devoted exclusively to 20th-century art. ⊠ *Bischofsgartenstr. 1,* ☎ *0221/221–22379.* 🎟 *Both museums: DM 10.* ⊙ *Tues. 10–8, Wed.–Fri. 10–6, weekends 11–6.*

★ Opposite the Dom is the **Römisch-Germanisches Museum** (Roman-German Museum), built from 1970 to 1974 around the Dionysus mosaic that was uncovered during the construction of an air-raid shelter in 1941. The huge mosaic, more than 300 ft square, once covered the dining-room floor of a wealthy Roman trader's villa. ⊠ *Roncallipl. 4,* ☎ *0221/ 221–24438.* ☉ *Tues.–Sun. 10–5.*

The **Altes Rathaus** (Old Town Hall) stands in the **Alter Markt** (Old Market Square) south of the Dom. This is the oldest town hall in Germany; there was a seat of local government here in Roman times, and directly below the current Rathaus are the remains of the Roman city governor's headquarters, the Praetorium. Go inside to see the 14th-century **Hansa Saal,** a meeting hall whose tall Gothic windows and barrel-vaulted wooden ceiling are potent expressions of medieval civic pride. The figures of the prophets, standing on pedestals at one end, are all from the early 15th century. ⊠ *Alter Markt,* ☎ *0221/221–23345 for tour information.*

Gross St. Martin (Great St. Martin), the most outstanding of Köln's 12 Romanesque churches, has a massive 13th-century tower, distinctive turrets, and an imposing central spire. ⊠ *Lintg.* ☉ *Daily 9–5.*

Gross St. Martin is the parish church of Köln's colorful old section near the river, the **Martinsviertel** (St. Martin's Quarter), an attractive combination of reconstructed, high-gabled medieval buildings, winding alleys, and tastefully designed modern apartments and business quarters. Head here at night—the place comes alive at sunset. ⊠ *Btw. Lintg. and Gürzenichstr.*

The 12th-century **Cäcilienkirche** (St. Cecilia Church) lies at the edge of the Martinsviertel. Its cool, well-lighted interior now houses one of the world's finest museums of medieval Christian art, the **Schnütgen Museum.** Although the main emphasis of the museum falls on early and medieval sacred art, the collection also covers the Renaissance and Baroque periods. ⊠ *Cäcilienstr. 29,* ☎ *0221/221–22310.* ☉ *Tues.–Fri. 10–5, Wed. 10–8, weekends 11–5. Guided tours (in German) Sun. 11.*

St. Gereon's is one of the most noteworthy early medieval structures still in existence. This exquisite Romanesque church stands on the site of an old Roman burial ground six blocks west of the train station. An enormous dome rests on walls that were once clad in gold mosaics. Roman masonry still forms part of the structure, which is believed to have been built over the grave of its namesake, the 4th-century martyr and patron saint of Köln. ⊠ *Gereonshof 4,* ☎ *0221/579–0950.* ☉ *Daily 10–noon and 3–6.*

$$$ ✕ **Bizim.** The extraordinary chef, Enis Akisik, has made his Bizim a candidate for best Turkish restaurant in Germany. Forget shish kebab and prepare yourself for a leisurely experience that might include scampi with tarragon sauce, quail grilled on a rosemary spit and served in its own juices, or veal with wild mushrooms. The four-course lunch menu (DM 55) is highly recommended. ⊠ *Weidengasse 47–49,* ☎ *0221– 131581. Reservations essential. AE, D. Closed Sat.–Mon.*

$$$ ✕ **Le Moissonnier.** Part of the charm of this restaurant—among the best
★ in the city—is its lack of pretension. In contrast to the gray neighborhood, the turn-of-the-century bistro decor radiates warmth from its mirrors, Tiffany-style lamps, and painted flowers. Chef Eric Menchon serves such dishes as crayfish sautéed in vanilla oil, a gourmet version of stuffed cabbage with veal and squid, and ginger parfait with walnuts and fried bananas. ⊠ *Krefelder Str. 25,* ☎ *0221/729479,* 𝔽𝔸𝕏 *0221/ 7325461. Reservations essential. No credit cards. Closed Sun.–Mon.*

$$ ✕ **Früh am Dom.** For real down-home German food, few places compare with this former brewery. Bold frescoes on the vaulted ceilings establish the mood, and such dishes as *Hämmchen* (pork shank) provide an authentically Teutonic experience. ⊠ *Am Hof 12–14,* ☎ *0221/258– 0389. No credit cards.*

$$$$ ✕⌨ **Dom-Hotel.** The Dom is in a class of its own. Old-fashioned, formal, and gracious, with a stunning location right by the cathedral, it offers elegance and discreet, efficient service. The antiques-filled bedrooms, generally in Louis XV or Louis XVI style, are subdued in color, high-ceilinged, and spacious. Each room is individually furnished. In the glassed-in Atelier am Dom you can enjoy views of the cathedral while dining on anything from wild boar served with chanterelle ragout to tofu piccata with ratatouille and curried rice. ✉ *Domkloster 2A, D-50667,* ☎ *0221/20240,* FAX *0221/202–4444. 112 rooms. 2 restaurants. AE, DC, MC, V.*

$$$$ ✕⌨ **Excelsior Hotel Ernst.** The Empire-style lobby in sumptuous royal
★ blue, bright yellow, and gold is striking, and a similar, boldly conceived grandeur extends to all the public rooms in this 1863 hotel. Old master paintings (including a Van Dyck) are everywhere; you'll be served breakfast in a room hung with Gobelin tapestries. Guest rooms are intimate in scale, with spectacular marble bathrooms and ultramodern fixtures. The lacquered-wood-paneled restaurant serves classic French cuisine imaginatively prepared. ✉ *Trankg. 1–5, D-50667,* ☎ *0221/ 2701,* FAX *0221/135–150. 160 rooms. Restaurant. AE, DC, MC, V.*

$$$$ ⌨ **Hotel im Wasserturm.** What used to be Europe's tallest water tower
★ is now an 11-story luxury hotel-in-the-round. The neoclassic look of the brick exterior was retained by order of Cologne conservationists. The ultramodern interior was the work of the French designer Andrée Putman. The 11th-floor restaurant has a view of the city. ✉ *Kayg. 2, D-50676,* ☎ *0221/20080,* FAX *0221/200–8888. 48 rooms, 40 suites and maisonettes. Restaurant. AE, DC, MC, V.*

$$ ⌨ **Chelsea.** This hotel has a strong following among artists and art dealers, and decor that is a cross between Rietveld, Philippe Starck, and a half dozen others. The bathrooms and bathtubs are luxuriously roomy and there is no end of mirrors. Breakfast is served until noon. It's just 20 minutes away from the city center by foot, 10 by subway or tram. ✉ *Jülicherstr. 1, D-50674,* ☎ *0221/234755,* FAX *0221/239137. 22 rooms. Restaurant. AE, DC, MC, V.*

$$ ⌨ **Das Kleine Stapelhäuschen.** One of the few houses along the riverbank to have survived World War II bombings, this is among the very oldest buildings in Köln. You can't beat the location, overlooking the river and right by Gross St. Martin; rooms make up in quaintness for what they lack in luxury. ✉ *Fischmarkt 1–3, D-50667,* ☎ *0221/257–7862,* FAX *0221/257–4232. 31 rooms. MC, V.*

Bonn

Not far south of Köln is the staid city of Bonn, the former capital of West Germany, which has now handed over most of its legislative and administrative functions to Berlin. The city has a late-Romanesque, 900-year-old **Münster** (Cathedral) with a massive octagonal main tower, a soaring spire, and an ornate rococo pulpit. ✉ *Münsterpl.,* ☎ *0228/ 633–344.* ☉ *Daily 7–7.*

★ The **Beethovenhaus** (Beethoven Museum) displays scores, a grand piano, and ear trumpets in the house where the composer was born. ✉ *Bonng. 20,* ☎ *0228/981–7525.* ☉ *Apr.–Sept., Mon.–Sat. 10–5, Sun. 11–4; Oct.–Mar., Mon.–Sat. 10–4, Sun. 11–4.*

The **Kunst- und Austellungshalle der Bundesrepublik Deutschland** (Art and Exhibition Hall of the German Federal Republic) hosts major traveling exhibitions. ✉ *Friedrich-Ebert-Allee 2,* ☎ *0228/9171200.* ✉ *Free.* ☉ *Tues.–Sun. 10–7.*

The town of Königswinter (12 km/7 mi northeast of Bonn) has one of the most-visited castle sites on the Rhine, **Drachenfels.** Its ruins crown the highest hill in the Siebengebirge (Seven Hills), commanding a spectacular view of the river. The castle was built during the 12th century by the archbishop of Köln.

$$ ✕ **Gasthaus Sutorius.** Just across from the church of St. Margaretha in Königswinter, this wine tavern serves refined variations on traditional German dishes, along with an intelligent selection of local wines. In summer, food is served outdoors beneath the linden trees. ✉ *Oelinghovener Str. 7, Königswinter,* ☎ *02244/4749. AE, D. Closed Mon. No lunch Tues.–Sat.*

$$ ✕ **Haus Daufenbach.** Behind the stark white exterior, the mood is rustic, with simple wooden furniture and antlers on the walls. Specialties include *Spanferkel* (suckling pig) and a range of imaginative salads. Wines come from the restaurant's own vineyards. ✉ *Brüderg. 6,* ☎ *0228/ 637–944. No credit cards. Closed Mon. No dinner Sun. in summer.*

$ ✕ **Em Höttche.** Travelers have been dining at this rustic tavern since the late 14th century; today it offers one of the best-value lunches in town. The food is hearty, and the portions are large. ✉ *Markt 4,* ☎ *0228/690–009. Reservations not accepted. No credit cards.*

$$$$ ▣ **Domicil.** A group of buildings around a courtyard has been stylishly converted into a hotel of great charm and comfort. The rooms are decorated in styles from fin-de-siècle romantic to Italian modern. ✉ *Thomas-Mann-Str. 24–26, D-53115,* ☎ *0228/729–090,* FAX *0228/691– 207. 42 rooms. Restaurant. AE, DC, MC, V. Closed Dec. 25–Jan. 1.*

$$ ▣ **Rheinland.** This modest lodging is a short walk from the center of the Old Town. Rooms are comfortable, and a good buffet breakfast greets the day. ✉ *Berliner Freiheit 11, D-53111,* ☎ *0228/658–096,* FAX *0228/472–844. 31 rooms. AE, MC.*

$$ ▣ **Sternhotel.** For good value, solid comfort, and a central location in the Old Town, the family-run "Star" is tops. Rooms are small, but all are pleasantly furnished. Snacks are available at the bar. ✉ *Markt 8, D-53111,* ☎ *0228/72670,* FAX *0228/726–7125. 81 rooms. Bar. AE, DC, MC, V.*

Koblenz

This ancient city began as a Roman camp more than 2,000 years ago. The sharp peninsula, **Deutsches Eck** (Corner of Germany), is where the Mosel and Lahn rivers flow into the Rhine. On summer evenings concerts are held in the nearby Blumenhof Garden. Most of the city's historic churches are also within walking distance of the Deutsches Eck. The **Liebfrauenkirche** (Church of Our Lady), completed in the 13th century but later much modified, incorporates Romanesque, late-Gothic, and Baroque elements. ✉ *An der Liebfrauenkirche.* ◷ *Daily 7–6.*

The city's most important church, **St. Kastor Kirche** combines Romanesque and Gothic elements and contains some unusual altar tombs and rare Gothic wall paintings. ✉ *Kastorhof.* ◷ *Daily 7–6.*

St. Florin Kirche, a Romanesque church built around 1100, was remodeled in the Gothic style during the 14th century. Gothic windows and a vaulted ceiling were added during the 17th century. The vaults beneath St. Florin's contain an interesting assortment of Roman remains. ✉ *St. Florins Markt at Auf der Danne Str.*

Much of the **Altstadt** (Old Town) of Koblenz is now an attractive pedestrian district. Many of the ancient cellars beneath the houses serve as wine bars and jazz clubs.

The **Museum Ludwig** presents rotating exhibitions of contemporary art, much of it from the enormous collection of Koblenz-born tycoon Peter Ludwig. ✉ *Danziger Freiheit 1,* ☎ *0261/304–040.* ◷ *Tues., Wed., Fri., and Sat. 11–5; Thurs. 11–8; Sun. 11–6.*

The **Mittelrhein Museum** (Middle Rhine Museum) displays Rhenish art and artifacts from the Middle Ages to the present day. ⊠ *15 Florinsmarkt,* ☎ *0261/129–2502.* ⊙ *Tues. and Thurs.–Sat. 11–5, Wed. 11–8, Sun. 11–6.*

Across the river from Koblenz, on the Rhine's east bank, towers the city's most spectacular castle, **Festung Ehrenbreitstein.** The fortifications of this vast structure date from the 1100s, although the bulk of it was built much later, during the 16th and 17th centuries. To reach the fortress take the *Sesselbahn* (cable car) or try walking up. ☎ *0261/97030.* ⊠ *Castle: Free.* ⊙ *Daily 9–12:30 and 1–5. Cable car:* ⊙ *June–Aug., daily 9–6; Sept., daily 10–6; Easter–May, daily 10–5.*

$$ ✕ **Wacht am Rhein.** The name of this attractive riverside restaurant, Watch on the Rhine, sums it up. In summer take a table on the terrace and watch the river traffic pass by; in winter choose a window table and dine with the Rhine outside and the atmospheric warmth of the fin de siècle fittings and furnishings inside. Fish is the basis of the extensive menu. ⊠ *Adenauer-Ufer 6,* ☎ *0261/15313. AE.*

$$$ ✕⊞ **Kurfürstliches Amtshaus.** The yellow walls of the former castle rise
★   above the town of Daun in the picturesque Eifel, a region of volcanic lakes just outside Koblenz. Inside are comforts both baronial and modern. Most bedrooms have views of the surrounding hills and woods. The heated swimming pool uses water from the local springs. The restaurant, "Graf Leopold," has a noted German chef who excels at both traditional and creative Asian-accented dishes. ⊠ *Auf dem Burgberg, D-54550 Daun,* ☎ *06592/9250,* FAX *06592/925255. 35 rooms, 1 suite. Restaurant, pool. AE, DC, V.*

$$–$$$ ⊞ **Kleiner Reisen.** This well-run, straightforward hotel gives value for your money. Another plus is the quiet riverside location that's still within walking distance of the train station and Old Town. ⊠ *Kaiserin-Augusta-Anlagen 18, D-56068,* ☎ *0261/32077,* FAX *0261/160–725. 27 rooms. AE, DC, MC, V.*

Rhine Gorge

Between Koblenz and Mainz, the Rhine flows through the 64-km (40-mi) Rhine Gorge. It is here that the Rhine lives up to its legends and lore, and where in places the river narrows to a mere 200 yards. Vineyards occupy every inch of available soil on the steep, terraced slopes. High above, ancient castles crown the rocky shelves.

South of Koblenz, at a wide, western bend in the river, lies the quiet old town of **Boppard**, once a bustling city of the Holy Roman Empire. Now the remains of its Roman fort and castle are used to house a museum of Roman artifacts and geological specimens. There are also several notable churches, including the **Karmeliterkirche** (Carmelite Church), with its fine Baroque altar, and the Romanesque church of **St. Severus.** From Boppard there is a wonderful view across the Rhine to the ruined castles of **Liebenstein** and **Sterrenberg.**

★   **Marksburg** castle is on the east bank of the river, 500 ft above the town of Braubach. Built during the 12th century to protect silver and lead mines in the area, it is the only castle in the entire Middle Rhine Valley to have survived the centuries without ever being destroyed. Within its massive walls are a collection of weapons and manuscripts, a medieval botanical garden, and a restaurant. ☎ *02627/206.* ⊙ *Easter–Oct., daily 10–5; Nov.–day before Easter, daily 11–4.*

$$$ ⊞ **Bellevue Rheinhotel.** This is one of the Rhineland's most majestic hotels, an imposing turn-of-the-century building whose elegant white-and-yellow facade, under steep slate eaves, faces directly onto the river.

✉ *Rheinallee 41–42, D-56154,* ☎ *06742/1020,* FAX *06742/102–602. 94 rooms. Restaurant, pool. AE, DC, MC, V.*

St. Goar

South of Boppard, this little town is crowded against the steep gorge cliff and shadowed by the imposing ruin of **Burg Rheinfels** (Rhine Cliff Castle), built during the mid-13th century. The ruins are now being restored, and a luxury hotel has been built on the site. ☎ *06741/8020.* ☉ *Apr.–Oct., daily 9–6; Nov.–Mar., daily 10–4.*

Just across from the town of St. Goar, on the east bank of the Rhine, lies its sister village, **St. Goarshausen** (an hourly ferry service links the city to St. Goar). **Burg Katz** (Cat Castle), a massive 13th-century fortress, towers over St. Goarshausen. The top of the cliff offers a great view of the famous Lorelei rock.

The **Lorelei rock** is only a few kilometers from St. Goarshausen; follow the road marked with LORELEI-FELSEN signs. Here the Rhine takes a sharp turn around a rocky, shrub-covered headland. This is the narrowest and shallowest part of the Middle Rhine, full of treacherous currents. According to legend the beautiful maiden, Lore, sat on the rock here, combing her golden hair and singing a song so irresistible that passing sailors forgot the navigational hazards and were swept to their deaths.

$$ ✕ **Roter Kopf.** This is a historic wine restaurant brimming with rustic Rhineland atmosphere. ✉ *Burgstr. 5, St. Goarshausen,* ☎ *06771/ 2698. No credit cards.*

$$$ ✕🏨 **Auf Schönburg.** Above the Rhine and the town of Oberwesel
★ stands this castle-turned-hotel. The modernized rooms are decorated with antiques. The wooden-beamed restaurant serves such satisfying dishes as lentil soup with mushroom ravioli or rack of lamb in an herb crust. ✉ *Burg Schönburg, D-55430 Oberwesel,* ☎ *06744/93930,* FAX *06744/1613. 20 rooms. Restaurant. AE, DC, MC, V. Closed Jan.–Mar.*

$$$ 🏨 **Schlosshotel and Villa Rheinfels.** High above St. Goar, on a hill com-
★ manding spectacular river views, the hotel rises from the ruins of the ad-jacent castle (☞ *above*). ✉ *Schlossberg 47, D-56329 St. Goar,* ☎ *06741/ 8020,* FAX *06741/802802. 58 rooms. Restaurant, pool. AE, DC, MC, V.*

$ 🏨 **Hermannsmühle.** This warm, rustic, chalet-style hotel just outside St. Goarshausen has heavy furniture painted with floral patterns. ✉ *Forstbachstr. 46, D-56346 St. Goarshausen,* ☎ *06771/7317. 10 rooms. Restaurant. MC, V. Closed mid-Nov.–Feb.*

Kaub

This medieval village, south of the Lorelei on the east side of the river, is one of the most-photographed sites of the Middle Rhine region because of its unusual castles. Like a small sailing ship bristling with sharp-pointed towers, the **Pfalzgrafenstein** castle sits on a tiny island in the middle of the Rhine. During the 14th century the resident Pfalzgraf, or Count Palatine, was said to have strung chains across the Rhine to stop riverboats and collect his tolls. A boat takes visitors from Kaub to the island. ☉ *Trips every ½ hr 9–1 and 2–5 (in season).*

The small **Burg Gutenfels** (Good Cliff Castle) perches on a hillside above Kaub. Built during the 13th century, Gutenfels was completely reno-vated at the end of the 18th century and is now a hotel (☞ *below*).

$$$ 🏨 **Burg Gutenfels.** The terrace of this luxurious castle hotel has one of the finest views in the Rhine Valley. Wines come from the hotel's own vineyard. Be sure to reserve well in advance. ✉ *D-56349 Kaub am Rhein,* ☎ *06774/220,* FAX *06774/1760. 10 rooms. Restaurant. AE, DC, MC, V.*

Bacharach

This picturesque village, encircled by 15th-century walls, is the best-preserved town of the Middle Rhine. Bacharach is an important trading center for the region's vintages.

$$ ✕🏨 **Altkölnischer Hof.** This small but cozy half-timber hotel was built at the turn of the century. Its rustic restaurant serves typical local dishes and some excellent wines. ✉ *Blücherstr. 2, D-55422,* ☎ *06743/ 1339,* ℻ *06743/2793. 18 rooms. Restaurant. AE, V. Closed Nov.–Mar.*

Rüdesheim

According to legend, the first vines in this famous wine town were planted by Charlemagne. More recent vintages can be tested in the many taverns lining **Drosselgasse,** a narrow, colorful street in the heart of town. Rüdesheim is in the center of the Rhine Gorge region and the most popular destination on the Rhine—be sure secure lodging well in advance.

$$–$$$ ✕ **Krone.** The restaurant of the 450-year-old Krone hotel is outstand-
★ ing. Chef Herbert Pucher's terrines and pâtés draw regular customers from Frankfurt. His fish dishes are supreme, and the Rhine wines are the best. ✉ *Rheinuferstr. 10, Assmannshausen,* ☎ *06722/4030,* ℻ *06722/3049. AE, DC, MC, V.*

$$ ✕🏨 **Rüdesheimer Schloss.** Modern comforts border on the luxurious
★ in this historic wine tavern that goes back 265 years. Most of the rooms have a view of the hillside vineyards. The three suites have avant-garde decor. Room 20 is popular for its large terrace. ✉ *Steingasse 10, D-65385,* ☎ *06722/90500,* ℻ *06722/47960. 18 rooms, 3 suites. Restaurant. AE, DC, MC, V.*

$$$–$$$$ 🏨 **Hotel Jagdschloss Niederwald.** This is not so much a place to overnight as it is a luxury resort. It's in the hills 5 km (3 mi) outside Rüdesheim, with views over the Rhine and the Rhine Gorge. The former hunting lodge of the dukes of Hesse, it has a lavish, baronial atmosphere. ✉ *Auf dem Niederwald 1, D-65383,* ☎ *06722/1004,* ℻ *06722/47970. 52 rooms. Restaurant, pool. AE, DC, MC, V. Closed Jan.–mid-Mar.*

Mainz

This bustling modern city of nearly 200,000 lies on the west bank of the Rhine, at the mouth of the Main River. Once the seat of powerful
★ archbishops, the city still has as its focal point the **Dom,** one of the finest Romanesque cathedrals in Germany, dating mostly from the late 11th century through the 13th century, with an imposing Baroque spire added in the 18th century. ✉ *Domstr. 3,* ☎ *06131/253–344.* ⊘ *Mon.–Wed. and Fri. 10–4, Thurs. 10–5, Sat. 10–2.*

★ The **Gutenberg Museum** honors the printing pioneer Johannes Gutenberg, who first experimented with movable type around 1450 in Mainz. The museum houses his press and one of the Bibles he printed. ✉ *Liebfrauenpl. 5,* ☎ *06131/122–644.* ⊘ *Tues.–Sat. 10–6, Sun. and holidays 10–1. Closed Jan.*

The **Römisch-Germanisches Museum** (Roman-German Museum) in the Kurfürstliches Schloss (Elector's Palace) contains a notable collection of archaeological finds from a Roman settlement and two ancient Roman ships unearthed in 1981. ✉ *Rheinstr.,* ☎ *06131/91240.* ⊡ *Free.* ⊘ *Tues.–Sun. 10–5.*

★ The **Mittelrheinische Landesmuseum** (Middle Rhine Provincial Museum) covers the culture of the Middle Rhine region from the Stone Age to the present. Its remarkable collection of Roman altars and tombstones includes the Jupitersäule (Jupiter's Pillar), a beautifully preserved column dedicated to the Roman god. The museum is three blocks off the riverfront. ⊠ *Grosse Bleiche 49–51,* ☎ *06131/28570.* ⊙ *Tues. 10–8, Wed.–Sun. 10–5.*

The Gothic church of **St. Stephan** stands on a hilltop to the south; in its choir are six stained-glass windows by painter Marc Chagall (1887–1985). ⊠ *Kleine Weissg. 12,* ☎ *06131/231–640.* ⊙ *Feb.–Nov., weekdays 10–noon and 2–5; Dec.–Jan., weekdays 10–noon and 2–4:30.*

$$ ✕ **Rats und Zunftstuben Heilig Geist.** This popular restaurant incorporates some Roman remains into its decor and offers a traditional atmosphere. The cuisine is hearty German fare. ⊠ *Renteng. 2,* ☎ *06131/225–757. Reservations essential. AE, DC, MC, V. Closed Sun.*

$$$ ✕▥ **Hilton International.** A terrific location by the Rhine and high stan-
★ dards of service and comfort make the Hilton the best choice in Mainz. The buffets in the Römische Weinstube are excellent. The hotel also has a casino. ⊠ *Rheinstr. 68, D-55116,* ☎ *06131/2450,* ℻ *06131/245–589. 433 rooms. 2 restaurants, casino. AE, DC, MC, V.*

$ ▥ **Hotel Stadt Coblenz.** In the heart of the town this attractive hotel offers budget rooms (bath in the hall)—ask for a room facing the back. The rustic restaurant serves local and German specialties. ⊠ *Rheinstr. 49, D-55116,* ☎ *06131/227–602. 17 rooms. Restaurant. No credit cards.*

The Rhine Essentials

Getting Around

BY BICYCLE

Tourist offices in all the larger towns will provide information and route maps. **Deutsche Bahn** (☎ 069/19419) rents bikes at numerous stations. Ask for the *"Fahrrad am Bahnhof"* ("Bikes for Rent") brochure at any station.

BY BOAT

Köln-Düsseldorfer Rheinschiffahrt (KD Rhine Line, ☞ By Boat *in* Germany A to Z, *above*) has daily cruises between Köln and Frankfurt from Easter to late October. From March through November the **Hebel-Line** (☎ 06742/2420) in Boppard cruises the Lorelei Valley; night cruises have music and dancing. For information about Neckar River excursions contact **Neckar Personen Schiffahrt** (☎ 0711/541–073 or 0711/541–074).

BY CAR

For information about Rhineland's comprehensive highway network contact the **Automobilclub von Deutschland** (German Automobile Club; ⊠ Lyonerstr. 16, D-60528 Frankfurt-am-Main, ☎ 069/66060).

BY TRAIN

One of the best ways to visit the Rhineland in very limited time is to take the scenic, two-hour train journey from Mainz north to Köln along the western bank of the river. Contact **Deutsche Bahn** (German Railways; ⊠ Friedrich-Ebert-Anlage 43, Frankfurt, ☎ 069/19419), or get details at any central train station travel office.

Guided Tours

In addition to a number of special-interest cruises, **Köln-Düsseldorfer Rheinschiffahrt** (☞ By Boat *in* Germany A to Z, *above*) operates a series of excursions covering the towns along its routes. The local shipping company, **Personenschiffahrt Merkelbach** (⊠ Emserstr. 87, D-56076 Koblenz-Pfaffendorf, ☎ 0261/76810), has river tours. **Rhein und Moselschiffahrt Gerhard Colée-Hölzenbein** (⊠ Rheinzollstr. 4, D-56068 Koblenz, ☎ 0261/37744) organizes tours of the Mosel and Rhine rivers. The **tourist offices** in Mainz, Köln, and Koblenz (☞ Visitor Information, *below*) offer English-language tours of their respective cities.

Visitor Information

For general information on the region contact the **Fremdenverkehrs-verband Rheinland-Pfalz** (Rhineland Tourist Board, ⊠ Löhrstr. 103, Postfach 1420, D-56014 Koblenz, ☎ 0261/915–200).

Bacharach (Fremdenverkehrsamt, ⊠ Oberstr. 1, D-55422, ☎ 06743/2968). **Boppard** (Verkehrsamt, ⊠ Karmeliterstr. 2, D-54154, ☎ 06742/10325). **Koblenz** (Fremdenverkehrsamt Pavillon am Hauptbahnhof, ⊠ Postfach 2080, D-56020, ☎ 0261/31304). **Köln** (Verkehrsamt, ⊠ Unter Fettenhennen 19, D-50667, ☎ 0221/221–23345). **Mainz** (⊠ Tourist-Zentrale Mainz, Im Brückenturm am Rathaus, D-55116, ☎ 06131/286–210). **Rüdesheim** (Verkehrsamt, ⊠ Rheinstr. 16, D-65385, ☎ 06722/19433). **St. Goarshausen** (Verkehrsamt, ⊠ Bahnhofstr. 8, D-56346, ☎ 06771/9100).

HAMBURG

Water—in the form of the Alster Lakes and the Elbe River—is Hamburg's defining feature. The city-state's official title, the Free and Hanseatic City of Hamburg, reflects its kingpin status in the medieval Hanseatic League, a union that dominated trade on the North and the Baltic seas. The city is still a major port, with 33 individual docks and 500 berths for oceangoing vessels. The seafaring life has created the city's most distinct attractions, from the fish market to the Reeperbahn (the red-light district).

Exploring Hamburg

Numbers in the margin correspond to points of interest on the Hamburg map.

Within the remaining traces of its old city walls, downtown Hamburg combines the seamiest, steamiest streets of dockland Europe with sleek avenues. The city is easy to explore on foot.

★ ❷ **Alter Botanischer Garten** (Old Botanical Gardens). This green and open park in Wallringpark specializes in rare and exotic plants. Tropical and subtropical species grow under glass in hothouses, and specialty gardens—including herbal and medicinal—cluster around an old moat. ⊠ *Stephanspl.,* ☎ *040/232–327.* 🎫 *Free.* ☉ *Daily 8–6.*

❾ **Bismarck-Denkmal** (Bismarck Memorial). The colossal 111-ft granite monument, erected between 1903 and 1906, is a mounted statue of Chancellor Bismarck, the Prussian "Iron Chancellor," who was the force behind the unification of Germany in the 19th century. ⊠ *Helgoländer Allee.*

❽ **Blankenese.** This city suburb on the Elbe is more like a quaint, terraced fishing village. Besides some shops, the town has a small food market on Tuesday, Friday, and Saturday. It's a beautiful, long walk (13 km/8 mi) from the St. Pauli Landungsbrücken to Blankenese, but a ferry and S-bahn also link Blankenese and the St. Pauli district.

★ ❼ **Erotic Art Museum.** Sexually provocative art from 1520 to the present, 500 original works in all, is showcased here with great taste and decorum. Special exhibits of modern erotic photography or comic art are staged in a building on Bernhard-Nocht-Strasse. ⊠ *Nobistor 10a at Reeperbahn and Bernhard-Nocht-Str. 69,* ☎ *040/3174–757. Minimum age 18.* 🎫 *DM 15, combined ticket for both exhibitions DM 20.* ☉ *Tues.–Sun. 10 AM–midnight. U-bahn: St. Pauli.*

★ ❺ **Fischmarkt** (Fish Market). Freshly caught fish are only part of a compendium of wares on sale at the popular Fischmarkt in Altona. In fact

Hamburg

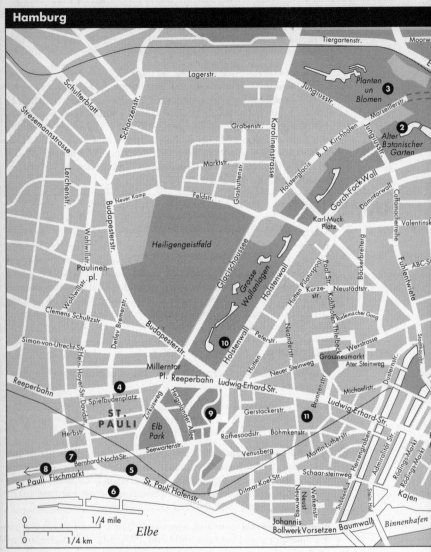

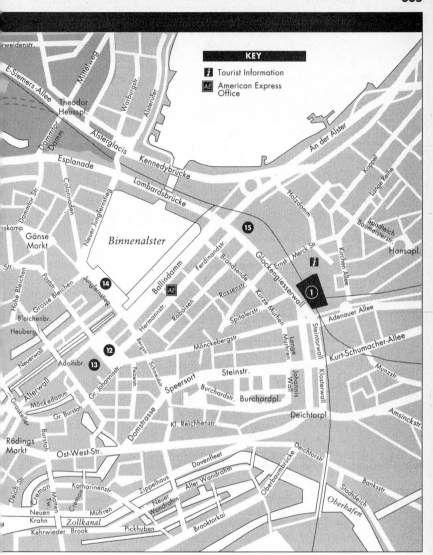

you can find almost anything—from live parrots and palm trees to armloads of flowers and bananas, or valuable antiques to fourth-hand junk. ⊠ *Between Grosse Elbestr. and St. Pauli Landungsbrücken.* ☉ *Apr.–Sept., Sun. 5 AM–10 AM; Oct.–Mar., Sun. 7 AM–10 AM.*

❶ Hauptbahnhof. This train station's impressive architecture of steel and glass is a breathtaking example of imperial German pride. It was opened in 1906 and completely renovated in 1991. The enormous 394-ft-long cast-iron-and-glass building is accentuated by a 460-ft-wide glazed roof that is supported only by pillars at each end. The largest structure of its kind in Europe, it is remarkably spacious and light inside. ⊠ *Steintorpl.*

⓮ Jungfernstieg. This wide promenade looking out over the Alster lakes is the city's premier shopping boulevard, bordering Hamburg's smaller artificial lake, the Binnenalster. It's lined with classy jewelers and chic clothing boutiques. Prices are high, but the quality is first-rate.

★ ⓯ Kunsthalle (Art Gallery). This prestigious exhibition hall's paintings include works by practically all the great northern European masters from the 14th through the 20th centuries. The 1996 postmodern cube, designed by Berlin star architect O. M. Ungers, contains an international modern art collection, with works by Andy Warhol, Joseph Beuys, Georg Baselitz, and David Hockney. ⊠ *Glockengiesserwall,* ☎ *040/2486–2612.* ☉ *Tues.–Wed. and Fri.–Sun. 10–6, Thurs. 10–9.*

❻ Landungsbrücken (Landing Bridges). These main harbor terminals are the start of the many boat trips around the seaport area (☞ Guided Tours *in* Contacts and Resources, *below*). ⊠ *Near St. Pauli and Hafenstr.*

★ ⓫ Michaliskirche (St. Michael's Church). The finest Baroque church in northern Germany serves as Hamburg's principal Protestant house of worship. St. Michael's has a distinctive 433-ft brick-and-iron tower bearing the largest tower clock in Germany, 26 ft in diameter. Just above the clock is the viewing platform, which affords a magnificent panorama of the city, the Elbe River, and the Alster Lakes. ⊠ *Krayenkamp 10,* ☎ *040/3767–8100.* ☉ *Apr.–Sept., Mon.–Sat. 9–6, Sun. 11:30–5:30; Oct.–Mar., Mon.–Sat. 10–4:30, Sun. 11:30–4:30.*

❿ Museum für Hamburgische Geschichte (Museum of Hamburg History). The museum's vast collection of artifacts charts the history of Hamburg from its origins in the 9th century to the present. ⊠ *Holstenwall 24,* ☎ *040/3504–2360.* ☉ *Tues.–Sun. 10–6.*

❸ Planten un Blomen (Plants and Flowers). Opened in 1935, this restful park has beautifully groomed plant, flower, and water gardens. The Japanese Garden is Europe's largest. ⊠ *Stephanspl.* ☎ *Free.* ☉ *Mar.–Oct., daily 9–4:45; Nov.–Feb., daily 9–3:45.*

★ ⓭ Rathaus (Town Hall). To most Hamburgers this pompous neo-Gothic building is the symbolic heart of the city. It has 647 rooms, six more than Buckingham Palace. Only the state rooms are open to visitors. ⊠ *Rathausmarkt,* ☎ *040/3681–2470.* ☉ *English-language tours: Mon.–Thurs. hourly 10:15–3:15, Fri.–Sun. hourly 10:15–1:15.*

⓬ Rathausmarkt (Town Hall Square). The large square, with its surrounding arcades, was laid out after Hamburg's Great Fire of 1842. The architects set out to create an Italian-style piazza, drawing on St. Mark's in Venice for inspiration. The rounded glass arcade bordered by trees was added in 1982. ⊠ *Bordered by Johannesstr., Alter Wall, Adolphsbrücke, and Adolphspl.*

❹ Reeperbahn. The red-light Reeperbahn is the major thoroughfare of the St. Pauli district. It offers a broad menu of entertainment besides striptease and sex shows. Beyond this strip, St. Pauli is dominated by its riverfront, which gives it a maritime, though run-down, appeal.

Dining and Lodging

A flotilla of boats brings a wide variety of fish to Hamburg's harbor. Harborside taverns and sophisticated restaurants serve fresh seafood, cooked in the traditional northern German way. One of the most celebrated of the robust local specialties is *Aalsuppe* (eel soup), a tangy concoction resembling bouillabaisse. *Räucheraal* (smoked eel) is also worth sampling. Another popular dish is the sailors' favorite *Labskaus,* a stew made from pickled meat, potatoes, and sometimes herring; it is usually garnished with a fried egg, sour pickles, and plenty of beets.

The city's hotels range from luxury properties to simple pensions. The nearly year-round conference and convention business keeps most rooms booked, and rates are high, although special weekend reductions are common. The tourist office can help you with reservations; try the HAM-Hotline (☎ 040/3005–1300) to secure a room. A fee of DM 5 is charged when you make your reservation; this is then deducted from your hotel bill. For details and price-category definitions for dining and lodging, *see* Dining *and* Lodging *in* Germany A to Z, *above.*

$$$$ ✕ **Landhaus Dill.** A fin de siècle building with views of the Elbe houses this stylish restaurant, with crisp linen on the tables, glistening tile floors, and exquisite entrées. The lobster salad is prepared at your table, and the rack of lamb comes hot from the kitchen with an aromatic thyme sauce. ⊠ *Elbchaussee 94,* ☎ *040/390–5077. Jacket and tie. AE, DC, MC, V. Closed Mon.*

$$$ ✕ **Landhaus Scherrer.** A popular, country house–style restaurant in the
★ Altona district, Scherrer fuses sophisticated nouvelle specialties with more down-to-earth local dishes. ⊠ *Elbchaussee 130,* ☎ *040/880–1325. Jacket and tie. AE, DC, MC. Closed Sun. and holidays.*

$$$ ✕ **Nil.** Media types, plus the intellectual and cultural elite of Hamburg,
★ inhabit this hip place. Nestled in an old '50s-style shoe shop, it spans three floors. The kitchen turns out high-powered seafood and modern German fare such as *Rinderfilet mit Walnuß-Rosmarinkruste, Schwarzwurzeln und Madeirasauce* (filleted beef in a walnut-rosemary crust, with Madeira sauce) or *Zander in Nussbutter mit Weinkraut und glasierten Trauben* (pike perch in nut butter with wine cabbage and glacéed grapes). ⊠ *Neuer Pferdemarkt 5,* ☎ *040/4397–823. Reservations essential for dinner. AE, DC, MC, V.*

$$$ ✕ **Peter Lembcke.** There's no better place to eat eel soup or the tradi-
★ tional Hamburg Labskaus than this small, traditional restaurant just north of the train station. ⊠ *Holzdamm 49,* ☎ *040/243–290. AE, DC, MC, V. Closed Sun. and holidays. No lunch Sat.*

$$$ ✕ **Rive.** Fresh seafood, including oysters and clams, are served right
★ at the harbor, in a building representing a ship, where mostly media people hang out enjoying spectacular views. ⊠ *Van der Smissen Str. 1, Kreuzfahrt-Center,* ☎ *040/3805–919. Reservations essential. AE.*

$$ ✕ **Ahrberg.** Next to the river in Blankenese, the Ahrberg has a cozy, wood-paneled dining room and a terrace for summer dining. The menu offers traditional German dishes and seafood specialties—often served together. Try the shrimp and potato soup and the fresh carp in season. ⊠ *Strandweg 33, Blankenese,* ☎ *040/860–438. AE, MC. Closed Sun.*

$$ ✕ **Eisenstein.** A sure bet are the daily Italian-Mediterranean dishes, in-
★ cluding pasta and pizzas, but there's also duck, pheasant, and an amazing assortment of fine wines. The crowd is joyful and mostly stylish, and the setting, a 19th-century industrial complex with high ceilings

and dark red brick walls, is very rustic. ⊠ *Friedensallee 9,* ☎ *040/3904–606. Reservations essential for dinner. No credit cards.*

$$ ✕ **Fischerhaus.** Hamburg's fish market is right outside the door of this traditional old restaurant, which accounts for the variety and quality of seafood dishes on its menu. Meat-eaters are also catered to, and the soups (especially fish soup) are legendary. It's always busy, so be sure to reserve a table and arrive on time. ⊠ *St. Pauli Fischmarkt 14,* ☎ *040/314–053. AE, DC, MC, V.*

$$$$ 🏨 **Kempinski Hotel Atlantic Hamburg.** The sumptuous Atlantic has been
★ a focal point of Hamburg's social scene since it opened in 1909. Rooms, whether traditionally furnished or more modern, exude an understated luxury, and suites are just short of palatial; the service is swift and hushed. ⊠ *An der Alster 72–79, D-20099,* ☎ *040/28880,* 🅵🅰🆇 *040/24729. 254 rooms, 13 suites. 2 restaurants. AE, DC, MC, V.*

$$$$ 🏨 **Park Hyatt Hamburg.** This ultramodern hotel is hidden behind the
★ historic walls of the Levanethaus, an old warehouse, located close to the downtown area. Guest rooms have bright and stylish furnishings; the pool and fitness area is breathtaking. If you are bored with the old-world atmosphere of other first-class hotels, this is the place to stay. ⊠ *Bugenhagenstr. 8–10, D-20095,* ☎ *040/3332–1234,* 🅵🅰🆇 *040/3332–1235. 220 rooms, 31 suites. 2 restaurants, pool. AE, DC, MC, V.*

$$$$ 🏨 **Vier Jahreszeiten.** This handsome 19th-century town house hotel
★ has scenic views of the Binnenalster and is rated among the world's best for its old-style rooms, impeccable service, and excellent food. ⊠ *Neuer Jungfernstieg 9–14, D-20354,* ☎ *040/34940,* 🅵🅰🆇 *040/349–4602. 158 rooms, 23 suites. 3 restaurants. AE, DC, MC, V.*

$$$ 🏨 **Aussen Alster.** Crisp and contemporary in design, this boutique hotel gives personal attention to its guests. Rooms are compact; most have a full bathroom, but a few have a shower only. The cool, modern decor is warmed by a fireplace and a friendly bar. ⊠ *Schmilinskystr. 11, D-20099,* ☎ *040/241–557,* 🅵🅰🆇 *040/280–3231. 27 rooms. Restaurant. AE, DC, MC, V.*

$$$ 🏨 **Hotel Prem.** Most guests here are regulars who have their favorite
★ rooms; no two rooms are the same. The Adenauer Suite (named for the chancellor who stayed here), for example, is traditionally furnished, including an antique chaise longue and a period writing desk in a small alcove with a lake view. ⊠ *An der Alster 9, D-20099,* ☎ *040/2417–2628,* 🅵🅰🆇 *040/2803–851. 44 rooms, 11 suites. Restaurant. AE, DC, MC, V.*

$$ 🏨 **Kronprinz.** For its down-market location (on a busy street opposite the railway station) and its moderate price, the Kronprinz is a surprisingly attractive hotel. Rooms are individually styled, modern but homey; ask for Number 45, with its mahogany and red-plush decor. ⊠ *Kirchenallee 46, D-20099,* ☎ *040/243–258,* 🅵🅰🆇 *040/280–1097. 69 rooms. Restaurant. AE, DC, MC, V.*

$$ 🏨 **Wedina.** Rooms at this small hotel are neat, compact, and completely
★ renovated. When making a reservation, ask for a room in the stylish 100-year-old-plus "Yellow House," which is rustic Italian in style and has an elegant parquet floor. ⊠ *Gurlittstr. 23, D-20099,* ☎ *040/243–011,* 🅵🅰🆇 *040/280–3894. 27 rooms. Pool. AE, DC, MC, V.*

Nightlife and the Arts

From about 10 PM on, the Reeperbahn springs to life, and *everything* is for sale. Among the Reeperbahn's even rougher side streets, the most notorious is the Grosse Freiheit, which means "Great Freedom." The area is not just a red-light district, however. Side streets have a mixture of yuppie bars, restaurants, and theaters that are somewhat more refined than the seamen's bars and sex shops. Hans-Albers-Platz is a center of this revival. The **Hans-Albers-Ecke** (⊠ Hans-Albers-Pl., ☎ 040/317–5960) is an old sailors' hangout. The bar **La Paloma** (⊠ Gerhardstr. 2, ☎ 040/314–512) is stylish. The **Theater Schmidt** (⊠ Spielbudenpl. 27–28, ☎ 040/3177–8899) presents variety shows most evenings to a packed house.

Hamburg Essentials

Arriving and Departing

BY BUS

Hamburg's bus station, the **Zentral-Omnibus-Bahnhof** (ZOB; ☎ 040/247–575), is right behind the Hauptbahnhof (☞ By Train, *below*). For more information contact the **Deutsche Touring** (⊠ Am Römerhof 17, D-60486 Frankfurt/Main, ☎ 069/79030).

BY CAR

Hamburg is easier to handle by car than are many other German cities and is relatively uncongested with traffic. Incoming autobahns connect with Hamburg's three beltways, which then take you easily to the downtown area. Follow the signs for STADTZENTRUM (downtown).

BY PLANE

Fuhlsbüttel, Hamburg's international airport, is 11 km (7 mi) northwest of the city.

Between the Airport and Downtown. An Airport-City-Bus runs nonstop between the airport and Hamburg's Hauptbahnhof at 20-minute intervals between 5:40 AM and 10:30 PM. Tickets are DM 8 per person. The Airport-Express (Bus 110) runs every 10 minutes between the airport and the Ohlsdorf U- and S-bahn stations, a 17-minute ride from the main train station. The fare is DM 10. If you're driving from the airport, follow the signs to STADTZENTRUM (downtown).

BY TRAIN

Hamburg is a terminus for main-line service to northern Germany. There are two principal stations: the Hauptbahnhof (main train station; ⊠ Adenauerallee 78, ☎ 040/19419), and Hamburg-Altona.

Getting Around

BY PUBLIC TRANSPORTATION

The comprehensive city and suburban transportation system includes the U-bahn (subway) network, which connects efficiently with the S-bahn (suburban train lines), and an exemplary bus service. Tickets cover travel by all three, as well as by harbor ferry. The one- and three-day Hamburg CARD allows free travel on all public transportation within the city, free admission to state museums, and discounts of approximately 30% on most bus, train, and boat tours. For information about this card inquire at tourist offices (☞ Visitor Information, *below*). Information on the public-transportation system can be obtained directly from the **Hamburg Passenger Transport Board** (HVV; ⊠ Steinstr. 1, ☎ 040/19449).

BY TAXI

Taxi meters start at DM 3.60, and the fare is DM 2.20 per km (½ mi), plus 50 pfennigs for each piece of luggage. To order a taxi call ☎ 040/441–011, ☎ 040/686–868, or ☎ 040/611–061.

Contacts and Resources

CONSULATES

U.S. (⊠ Alsterufer 28, ☎ 040/411–710). **U.K.** (⊠ Harvestehuder Weg 8a, ☎ 040/448–0320). **Ireland** (⊠ Feldbrunnenstr. 43, ☎ 040/4418–6213). **New Zealand** (⊠ Heimhuder Str. 56, ☎ 040/442–5550).

EMERGENCIES

Police (☎ 110). **Ambulance and Fire Department** (☎ 112). **Medical Emergencies** (☎ 040/228–022). **Dentist** (☎ 040/11500).

ENGLISH-LANGUAGE BOOKSTORE
Frensche International (⊠ Spitalerstr. 26c, ☎ 040/327–585).

GUIDED TOURS
Orientation. Bus tours of the city, with a guide who rapidly describes sights in both German and English, leave from Kirchenallee (in front of the Hauptbahnhof) at regular intervals. The 1¾-hour tour costs DM 26. For an additional DM 11, tours can be combined with a one-hour boat trip around Hamburg harbor. For more information contact a city tourist office (☞ Visitor Information, *below*).

Boat. Tours of the harbor leave every half hour in summer, less frequently during the winter, from *Landungsbrücken* (Piers) 1, 2, 3, and 7. The one-hour tour costs DM 15. A special harbor tour with an English-speaking guide leaves Pier 1 at 11:15 daily from March through November (same price). The Störtebeker line (☎ 040/2274–2375) has a special party boat on which you can wine, dine, and dance. For additional information on harbor tours call ☎ 040/311–7070, 040/313–130, 040/313–959, or 040/314–611. Fifty-minute cruises of the Binnenalster and Aussenalster leave from the Jungfernstieg.

TRAVEL AGENCIES
American Express (⊠ Ballindamm 39, ☎ 040/309–080), and at the Airport Fuhlsbüttel (⊠ terminal 4, level 2, ☎ 040/5005–980). **Hapag-Lloyd** (⊠ Verkehrspavillon Jungfernstieg, ☎ 040/3258–5640).

VISITOR INFORMATION
Hauptbahnhof (Central Train Station, ⊠ Steintorpl., at Kirchenallee main exit, ☎ 040/3005–1200). **St. Pauli Landungsbrücken** (Boat Landings; ⊠ between Piers 4 and 5; ☎ 040/300–51200).

BERLIN

In the year 2000 Berlin's role as the renewed German capital is finally secured. A royal residence during the 15th century, Berlin came into its own under the rule of King Friedrich II (1712–86)—Frederick the Great—whose liberal reforms and artistic patronage led the city's development into a major cultural capital. The 20th century should have crushed the city's spirit. Hitler and his supporters destroyed its reputation for tolerance and plunged Berlin headlong into the war that led to its wholesale destruction. After World War II, Berlin was still to face the bitter division of the city and the construction of the infamous Wall in 1961. Today, as ever, life here is on the cutting edge.

Exploring Berlin

With the Berlin Wall relegated to the junk pile of history, you can focus on navigating Berlin's eclectic museums, sprawling parklands, and racy atmosphere. Most of the really stunning parts of the prewar capital are in the historic eastern part of town, which has grand avenues and monumental buildings. The western downtown districts are best known for their shopping boulevards. Berlin is laid out on an epic scale—western Berlin alone is four times the size of Paris—so allow plenty of time to get around.

Berliners come off as brash, witty, no-nonsense types, who speak German with their own piquant dialect and are considered by their fellow countrymen a most rude species. It's attributable to the fact that many residents have faced adversity all their lives, managing by resorting to a mordant wit and cynical acceptance of circumstances.

Downtown Berlin

Numbers in the margin correspond to points of interest on the Downtown Berlin map.

★ **⑬ Ägyptisches Museum** (Egyptian Museum). This small but outstanding museum is home to the portrait bust of Nefertiti known around the world. The 3,300-year-old queen is the centerpiece of a fascinating collection of Egyptian antiquities that includes some of the finest preserved mummies outside Cairo. ✉ *Schlosstr. 70,* ☎ *030/320–911.* ◷ *Mon.–Thurs. 9–6, weekends 11–6.*

⑯ Bildungs- und Gedenkstätte Haus der Wannsee-Konferenz (Educational and Memorial Site House of the Wannsee Conference). This elegant Berlin villa hosted the fateful *Wannsee-Konferenz* held on January 20, 1942, when Nazi leaders planned the systematic deportation and genocide of Europe's Jewish population. This conference and its results are illustrated in an exhibition. From the U-Bahn Wannsee station take bus 114. ✉ *Am Grossen Wannsee 56–58,* ☎ *030/805–0010.* ▦ *Free.* ◷ *Mon.–Fri., 10–6, weekends, 2–6.*

★ **⑥ Brandenburger Tor** (Brandenburg Gate). Berlin's premier historic landmark was built in 1788 to celebrate the triumphant Prussian armies. The monumental gate was cut off from West Berlin by the Wall, and it became a focal point of celebrations marking the reunification of Berlin and of all Germany. The square behind the gate, **Pariser Platz,** has regained its prewar design. Among the new buildings erected here between 1996 and 1999 is the American Embassy. You'll reach the gate by walking along Strasse des 17. Juni (June 17th Street). ✉ *Under den Linden at Pariser Pl.*

⑰ Dahlemer Museen. This unique complex of six museums includes the **Museum für Völkerkunde** (Ethnographic Museum), internationally famous for its arts and artifacts from Africa, Asia, the South Seas, and the Americas. In the year 2000, only this museum is open. ✉ *Lansstr. 8, subway line U-2 to Dahlem-Dorf station,* ☎ *030/83011.* ◷ *Tues.–Fri. 9–6, weekends 11–6.*

⑮ Grunewald (Green Forest). Together with its Wannsee lakes, this splendid forest is the most popular retreat for Berliners, who come out in force, swimming, sailing their boats, tramping through the woods, and riding horseback. In winter a downhill ski run and even a ski jump operate on the modest slopes of Teufelsberg hill. Excursion steamers ply the Wannsee, the Havel River, and the Müggelsee (☞ Guided Tours *in* Berlin Essentials, *below*). ✉ *Southwest of downtown western Berlin.*

★ **⑩ Haus am Checkpoint Charlie** (House at Checkpoint Charlie–The Wall Museum). The museum reviews events leading up to the Wall's construction and displays actual tools and equipment, records, and photographs documenting methods used by East Germans to cross over to the West. The Wall is long gone, but the museum is on the site of the famous Cold War border crossing. ✉ *Friedrichstr. 43–44,* ☎ *030/ 253–7250.* ◷ *Daily 9 AM–10 PM.*

⑪ Jüdisches Museum (Jewish Museum). Berlin's latest addition to the museum scene is its most controversial ever. It will showcase the history and culture of Berlin's Jewish community, though the museum still had no collection at press time. You can take a tour of the impressive building. Its jagged, elongated structure was designed by American architect Daniel Libeskind. ✉ *Lindenstr. 9–14,* ☎ *030/259–933.*

Downtown Berlin

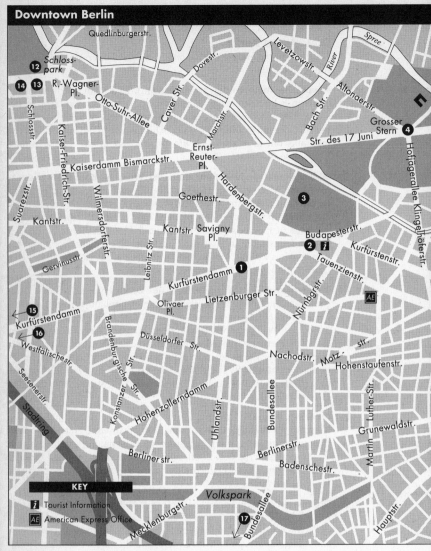

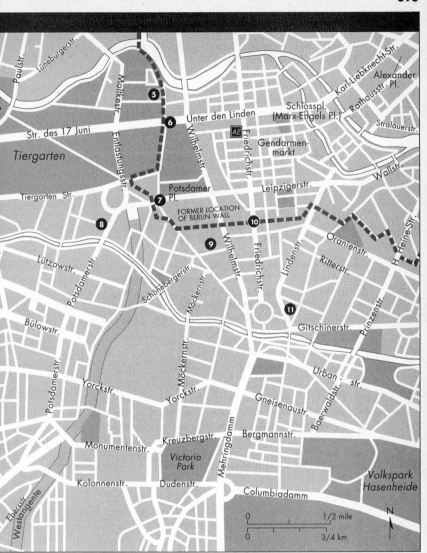

★ ❷ **Kaiser-Wilhelm-Gedächtniskirche** (Kaiser Wilhelm Memorial Church). This landmark, which once symbolized West Berlin, is a dramatic reminder of the futile destructiveness of war. The shell of the tower is all that remains of the 19th-century church dedicated to Kaiser Wilhelm I. Adjoining the tower are a new church and bell tower. ⊠ *Breitscheidpl.,* ☏ *030/218–5023.* ▣ *Free.* ☉ *Old Tower: Mon.–Sat. 10–4; Memorial Church: daily 9–7. Closed holidays.*

★ ❽ **Kulturforum** (Cultural Forum). With its unique ensemble of museums, galleries, and libraries, the complex is a cultural jewel. It includes the **Philharmonie** (Philharmonic Hall), home of the Berlin Philharmonic orchestra. ⊠ *Matthäikirchstr. 1,* ☏ *030/2548–8132.* ☉ *Box office weekdays 3:30–6, weekends 11–2.*

The **Kunstgewerbemuseum** (Museum of Decorative Arts) displays arts and crafts of Europe from the Middle Ages to the present. ⊠ *Matthäikirchpl. 10,* ☏ *030/266–2902.* ☉ *Tues.–Sun. 9–6.*

The **Gemäldegalerie** (painting gallery) reunites formerly separated collections from eastern and western Berlin. One of Europe's finest art galleries, it has an extensive selection of European paintings from the 13th through the 18th centuries, among them works by Dürer, Cranach the Elder, and Holbein, as well as of the Italian masters—Botticelli, Titian, Giotto, Lippi, and Raphael. ⊠ *Matthäikirchpl. 8,* ☏ *030/2660 or 030/2090–555 (for all state museums in Berlin).* ☉ *Tues.–Sun. 10–6.*

The **Neue Nationalgalerie** (New National Gallery), a mid-1960s, glass-and-steel construction designed by Mies van der Rohe, exhibits paintings, sculptures, and drawings from the 19th and 20th centuries. ⊠ *Potsdamer Str. 50,* ☏ *030/266–2662.* ☉ *Tues.–Fri. 9–6, weekends 10–6.*

★ ❶ **Kurfürstendamm.** Ku'damm, as Berliners call it, is one of Europe's busiest thoroughfares, throbbing with activity day and night. The boulevard is being transformed as some of the 1950s buildings are replaced with skyscrapers. The **Europa Center,** a shopping center dating from the early '60s, and the square in front of it is a buzzing, central meeting point.

★ ❼ **Potsdamer Platz.** This huge, entirely reconstructed square was Europe's busiest plaza before World War II. Today Sony, Mercedes Benz, Asea Brown Boveri, and others have built their new company headquarters here. The **Potsdamer Platz Arkaden,** a shopping and entertainment mecca covering 40,000 square yards, houses 140 upscale shops, a musical theater, a variety stage, cafés, a movie complex, a 3D-IMAX cinema, and even a casino. ⊠ *IMAX, Marlene-Dietrich-Pl. 4,* ☏ *030/4431–6131.* ☉ *Daily 10–12 AM.*

The light glass- and steel construction of the neighboring **Sony Center** is an architectural marvel designed by German-American architect Helmut Jahn. The Sony European headquarters are here, as well as the **Marlene Dietrich collection,** a small museum presenting the movie star's personal belongings such as dresses, movie memorabilia, letters, and more. Also in the center is the *Kaisersaal* ("Emperor's Hall"), a café from the prewar Grand Hotel Esplanade that was located on this spot.

The best overview of the ongoing constructions can be found in and on top of the bright-red **Information Center,** at the square's eastern end. Architectural plans and models are exhibited; an English-language tour is available by appointment. The center will close by the end of 2000. ⊠ *Infobox, Leipziger Pl. 21,* ☏ *030/2266–2424.* ☉ *Mon.–Wed. and Fri. 9–7, Thurs. 9–9, weekends 9–7.*

⑨ Prinz-Albrecht-Gelände (Prince Albrecht Grounds). The buildings that once stood here housed the headquarters of the Gestapo, the secret security police, and other Nazi security organizations from 1933 until 1945. After the war, they were leveled; in 1987 what was left of the buildings was excavated and an exhibit documenting their history and Nazi atrocities opened—"Topography of Terrors." ⊠ *Stresemannstr. 110,* ☎ *030/2545–090.* ☜ *Free.* ⊙ *Daily 10–6.*

⑤ Reichstag (German Parliament). The monumental and rather grim-looking building served as Germany's seat of parliament from its completion in 1894 until 1933, when it was gutted by fire under suspicious circumstances. After being remodeled under the direction of British architect Sir Norman Foster, the Reichstag is once again hosting the Deutscher Bundestag, Germany's federal parliament. The restaurant under the cupola is open to the public. ⊠ *Pl. der Republik.*

★ **⑭ Sammlung Berggruen** (Berggruen Collection). This small museum focuses on the history of modern art, with representative work from such artists as Van Gogh, Cézanne, Picasso, Giacometti, Klee, and more contemporary artists. Heinz Berggruen, a businessman who emigrated to the United States in the 1930s, collected the excellent paintings. ⊠ *Schlosstr. 1,* ☎ *030/3269–580.* ⊙ *Tues.–Fri. 9–6, weekends 11–6.*

★ **⑫ Schloss Charlottenburg.** Built at the end of the 17th century by King Frederick I for his wife, Queen Sophie Charlotte, this grand palace and its magnificent gardens were progressively enlarged for later royal residents and now include museums. ⊠ *Luisenpl., U-7 subway line to Richard-Wagner-Pl. station; from station walk east along Otto-Suhr-Allee;* ☎ *030/320–911.* ⊙ *Tues.–Fri. 9–6, weekends 11–6.*

④ Siegessäule (Victory Column). The memorial, erected in 1873, commemorates four Prussian military campaigns. It stands at the center of the 630-acre **Tiergarten** (Animal Park), the former hunting grounds of the Great Elector. After climbing 285 steps to its 213-ft summit, you'll be rewarded with a fine view of Berlin. ⊠ *Am Grossen Stern,* ☎ *030/ 391–2961.* ⊙ *Mon. 1–6; Tues.–Sun., holidays 9–6.*

★ **③ Zoologischer Garten** (Zoological Gardens). Berlin's enchanting zoo has the world's largest variety of individual types of fauna, along with a fascinating aquarium. ⊠ *Hardenbergpl. 8 and Budapester Str. 34,* ☎ *030/254–010.* ☜ *Combined zoo and aquarium ticket, DM 19.* ⊙ *Zoo: Jan.– Feb., daily 9–5; Mar., daily 9–5:30; late Mar.–late Sept., daily 9–6:30; Oct., daily 9–6; Nov. and Dec., daily, 9–5. Aquarium: daily 9–6.*

Historic Berlin

Numbers in the margin correspond to points of interest on the Historic Berlin map.

㉓ Berliner Dom. The impressive 19th-century cathedral with its enormous green copper dome is one of the great ecclesiastical buildings in Germany. Its main nave was reopened in June 1993 after a 20-year renovation. More than 80 sarcophagi of Prussian royals are on display in the cathedral's catacombs. ⊠ *Am Lustgarten,* ☎ *030/202–69111.* ☜ *Museum free.* ⊙ *Church: Mon.–Sat. 9–6:30, Sun. 11:30–6:30; balcony: Mon.–Sat. 10–6, Sun. 11:30–6; museum: Wed.–Sun. 10–6.*

㉖ Berliner Rathaus (Berlin City Hall). After the city's reunification this redbrick symbol of Berlin's 19th-century urban pride again became the seat of the city government. ⊠ *Jüdenstr. at Rathausstr.,* ☎ *030/24010.* ☜ *Free.* ⊙ *Weekdays 9–6.*

㉑ Deutsches Historisches Museum (German Historical Museum). The onetime Prussian Zeughaus (arsenal), a magnificent Baroque building constructed in 1695–1730, houses Germany's National History Museum, a compendium of German history from the Middle Ages to the present. It is currently closed and some of its exhibits are presented at the ☞ **Kronprinzenpalais** across the street. ⊠ *Unter den Linden 2.*

㉕ Fernsehturm. At 1,198 ft high, eastern Berlin's TV tower is 710 ft *taller* than western Berlin's. Its observation deck affords the best view of Berlin; the city's highest café, which revolves, is also up here. ⊠ *Alexanderpl.,* ☎ *030/242–3333.* ⊙ *Daily 9 AM–midnight.*

★ **⑱ Friedrichstrasse** (Frederick Street). Head south on historic Friedrichstrasse from Unter den Linden for chic new shops, including the **Friedrichstadtpassagen,** a gigantic shopping and business complex. At the corner of Französische Strasse is the French department store **Galeries Lafayette** (⊠ Französische Str. 23, ☎ 030/209–480).

★ **㉚ Gedenkstätte Berliner Mauer** (Memorial Site Berlin Wall). This is the only nearly original piece of the Berlin Wall left in the city. The open-air museum shows a 230-ft-long piece of the whole Wall system, which consisted of two walls and a control path used by border guards with their German shepherds or army jeeps.⊠ *Junction Bergstr. and Invalidenstr..*

⑲ Gendarmenmarkt (Gendarme Market). This historic square has the beautifully reconstructed **Schauspielhaus** (Theatre)—built in 1818, and now one of the city's main concert halls—and twin **Deutscher** (German) and **Französischer** (French) cathedrals. The French cathedral houses a museum displaying the history of Huguenot immigrants in Berlin; the German cathedral presents an official exhibit on German history. *Deutscher Dom:* ⊠ *Gendarmenmarkt 1,* ☎ *030/2273–2141.* 🎫 *Free.* ⊙ *Tues.–Sun. 10–5. Französischer Dom:* ⊠ *Gendarmenmarkt,* ☎ *030/229–1760.* ⊙ *Tues.–Sat. noon–5, Sun. 11–5.*

★ **㉘ Hackesche Höfe** (Hackesche Warehouses). Built in 1905–07, the completely restored Hackesche Höfe are the finest example of Art Deco industrial architecture in Berlin. Today it's the center of the bustling nightlife of the Mitte district, with several bars and theaters. ⊠ *Rosenthaler Str. 40–41.*

★ **㉛ Hamburger Bahnhof** (Hamburg Train Station). Berlin's newest museum for contemporary art is housed in an early 19th-century structure, once a major train station. Remodeled and given a huge and spectacular new wing—a stunning interplay of glass, steel, color, and sunlight—it displays an outstanding private collection of works by German artists Joseph Beuys and Anselm Kiefer as well as paintings by Andy Warhol, Cy Twombly, Robert Rauschenberg, and Robert Morris. ⊠ *Invalidenstr. 50–51,* ☎ *030/3978–340.* ⊙ *Tues.–Fri. 10–6, weekends 11–6.*

Kronprinzenpalais (Prince's Palace). Now used as a temporary exhibition hall for the ☞ **Deutsches Historisches Museum,** this magnificent baroque-style building was constructed in 1732 for Crown Prince Friedrich (who later became Frederick the Great). ⊠ *Unter den Linden 3,* ☎ *030/203–040.* 🎫 *Free, English-speaking guide DM 60.* ⊙ *Thurs.–Tues. 10–6.*

★ **㉒ Museumsinsel** (Museum Island). This unique complex contains four world-class museums. The **Nationalgalerie** (National Gallery; ⊠ Bodest.) has 19th- and 20th-century paintings and sculptures, which are temporarily on display at the **Altes Museum** (Old Museum; entrance on ⊠ Lustgarten). The collections here include postwar art from some of Germany's most prominent artists and numerous works by the old masters. The **Pergamonmuseum** (⊠ Am Kupfergraben), one of Europe's

Historic Berlin

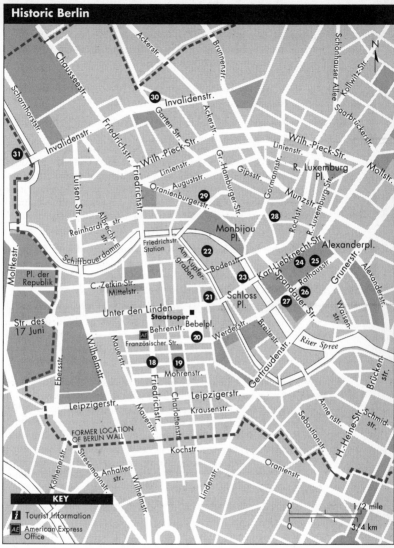

KEY

- **i** Tourist Information
- **AE** American Express Office

0 ___ 1/2 mile
0 ___ 3/4 km

Berliner Dom, **23**

Berliner Rathaus, **26**

Deutsches Historisches Museum, **21**

Fernsehturm, **25**

Friedrichstrasse, **18**

Gedenkstätte Berliner Mauer, **30**

Gendarmenmarkt, **19**

Hackesche Höfe, **28**

Hamburger Bahnhof, **31**

Museumsinsel, **22**

Neue Synagoge, **29**

Nikolaiviertel, **27**

St. Hedwigs-kathedrale, **20**

St. Marienkirche, **24**

greatest museums, takes its name from its principal exhibit, the Pergamon Altar, a monumental Greek sculpture dating from 180 BC that occupies an entire city block. The **Bodemuseum** (✉ Am Kupfergraben; entrance on Monbijoubrücke) has an outstanding collection of early Christian, Byzantine, and Egyptian art, but is currently closed. ✉ *Museumsinsel; right from Unter den Linden along Spree Canal via Am Zeughaus and Am Kupfergraben;* ☎ *030/209–050 for all museums.* 🎟 *Free 1st Sun. of month.* ⊙ *Tues.–Sun. 10–6.*

㉙ Neue Synagoge. Completed in 1866, in Middle Eastern style, this was one of Germany's most beautiful synagogues until it was seriously damaged on *Kristallnacht,* November 9, 1938, when synagogues and Jewish stores across Germany were vandalized, looted, and burned. Today the outside is perfectly restored, and the interior is connected to the **Centrum Judaicum** (Jewish Center)—an institution of Jewish culture and learning that frequently stages exhibitions and other cultural events. ✉ *Oranienburger Str. 28/30,* ☎ *030/2840–1316.* ⊙ *Sun.–Thurs. 10–5:30, Fri. 10–1:30.*

㉗ Nikolaiviertel. Berlin's oldest historic quarter is filled with delightful shops, cafés, and restaurants. Nikolaikirchplatz has Berlin's oldest building, the **Nikolaikirche** (St. Nicholas Church), dating from 1230. ✉ *Nikolaikirchpl.,* ☎ *030/240–020.* ⊙ *Tues.–Sun. 10–6.*

㉔ St. Hedwigskathedrale (St. Hedwig's Cathedral). When Berlin's premier Catholic church was erected in 1747, it was the first built in resolutely Protestant Berlin since the Reformation. ✉ *Hinter der Katholischen Kirche 3,* ☎ *030/203–4810.* ⊙ *Weekdays 10–5, Sun. 1–5.*

㉔ St. Marienkirche (Church of St. Mary). This medieval church, one of the finest in Berlin, is worth a visit for its late-Gothic fresco *Der Totentanz* (*Dance of Death*). Obscured for many years, it was restored in 1950, revealing the original in all its macabre allure. The cross on top of the church tower was an everlasting annoyance to communist rulers, as its golden metal was always mirrored in the windows of the Fernsehturm TV tower, the pride of socialist construction genius. ✉ *Karl-Liebknecht-Str. 8,* ☎ *030/242–4467.* ⊙ *Mon.–Thurs. 10–noon and 1–5, Sat. noon–4:30, Sun. noon–5. Free tours Mon.–Thurs. at 1, Sun. at 11:45.*

Dining and Lodging

Typical Berliner meals include *Eisbein mit Sauerkraut* (knuckle of pork with sauerkraut), *Spanferkel* (suckling pig), *Berliner Schüsselsülze* (potted meat in aspic), *Schlachterplatte* (mixed grill), and *Currywurst* (chubby and very spicy frankfurters sold at wurst stands). For details and price-category definitions, *see* Dining *in* Germany A to Z, *above.*

Year-round business conventions and the influx of summer tourists mean you should make reservations for hotels well in advance. For lodging in Berlin add DM 50 to the price chart categories given in Lodging *in* Germany A to Z, *above.*

$$$$ ✕ **Bamberger Reiter.** At one of the city's best restaurants, Tyrolean chef
  ★   Franz Raneburger relies heavily on fresh market produce for his *Neue Deutsche Küche* (new German cuisine), so the menu changes from day to day. ✉ *Regensburger Str. 7,* ☎ *030/218–4282. Reservations essential. AE, DC, V. Closed Sun., Mon., Jan. 1–15.*

$$$ ✕ **Borchardt.** At this fashionable meeting place, columns, red plush
  ★   benches, and an Art Nouveau mosaic create the impression of a 1920s salon. Entrées are prepared with a French accent. ✉ *Französische Str. 47,* ☎ *030/203–971–17. Reservations essential. AE, V.*

$$$ ✕ **Paris Bar.** This Charlottenburg restaurant attracts a polyglot clientele of film stars, artists, entrepreneurs, and executives. The cuisine is high-powered, but medium-quality French. ✉ *Kantstr. 152,* ☎ *030/313–8052. AE.*

$$$ ✕ **Rockendorf's.** The city's premier restaurant has only fixed-price ★ menus, some with up to nine courses. Exquisitely presented, the mainly nouvelle specialties are sometimes fused with classic German cuisine. The wine list—with 800 choices—has the appropriate accompaniment to any menu. ✉ *Düsterhauptstr. 1,* ☎ *030/402–3099. Reservations essential. AE, DC, MC, V. Closed Sun., Mon., 3–4 wks in summer, and Dec. 25–Jan. 6.*

$$$ ✕ **VAU.** Still a newcomer to Berlin's hip restaurant scene, VAU serves ★ excellent German fish and game dishes prepared by chef Kolja Kleeberg. Among his creations is *Steinbutt mit Kalbbries auf Rotweinschalotten* (turbot with veal sweetbread on shallots in red wine). The VAU's cool interior is all style and modern art. ✉ *Jägerstr. 54/55,* ☎ *030/2029–730. Reservations essential. AE, DC, MC, V. Closed Sun.*

$$ ✕ **Florian.** One of the most popular restaurants in town, the Florian ★ serves a high-gear combination of Swabian cuisine with a slight French accent in a relaxed atmosphere. Writers, artists, and film people flock here. ✉ *Grolmanstr. 52,* ☎ *030/3139–184. Reservations essential. No credit cards.*

$$ ✕ **Hackescher Hof.** The restaurant is without question one of the most ★ *in* places in town and a great place to experience the upswing in the old East firsthand. The food is a mixture of international nouvelle cuisine and beefy German cooking—there is also a special dinner menu with more refined dishes. ✉ *Rosenthaler Str. 40/41,* ☎ *030/2835–293. Reservations essential. AE, MC, V.*

$$ ✕ **Reinhard's.** Berliners of all stripes meet here in the Nikolai Quar- ★ ter to enjoy the carefully prepared entrées and to sample spirits from the amply stocked bar. *Adlon* (honey-glazed breast of duck) is one of the house specialties. Reinhard's has a second restaurant on the Ku'-damm; it's much smaller, but more elegant and one of the trendiest spots in town. ✉ *Poststr. 28,* ☎ *030/242–5295;* ✉ *Kurfürstendamm 190,* ☎ *030/881–1621. Reservations essential on weekends. AE, DC, MC, V. Closed Dec. 24.*

$ ✕ **Alt-Cöllner Schankstuben.** A tiny restaurant and a pub inhabit this charming, historic Berlin house. The menu is relatively limited, but the quality, like the service, is good. ✉ *Friedrichsgracht 50,* ☎ *030/2011–299. AE, DC, MC, V.*

$ ✕ **Blockhaus Nikolskoe.** Prussian King Frederick Wilhelm III built this Russian-style wooden lodge for his daughter Charlotte, wife of Russia's Tsar Nicholas I. It's on the eastern edge of Glienicke Park, with an open terrace (in summer) overlooking the Havel River. Game dishes are the focus. ✉ *Nikolskoer Weg 15,* ☎ *030/805–2914. DC, MC, V. Closed Thurs.*

$ ✕ **Café Oren.** This popular vegetarian eatery is next to the Neue Syn- ★ agoge. The restaurant buzzes with loud chatter all evening, and the atmosphere and service are friendly. The extensive menu offers mostly Israeli and Middle Eastern fare and *Gefillte fish,* a tasty (and very salty) German-Jewish dish. ✉ *Oranienburger Str. 28,* ☎ *030/282–8228. AE, MC, V.*

$ ✕ **Grossbeerenkeller.** The cellar restaurant, with its massive, dark-oak ★ furniture and decorative antlers, is one of the most original dining spots in town. Owner and bartender Ingeborg Zinn-Baier presents such dishes as *Sülze vom Schweinekopf mit Bratkartoffeln und Remoulade* (diced pork with home fries and herb sauce) and *Kasseler Nacken mit Grünkohl* (boiled salt pork meat with green cabbage). ✉ *Grossbeerenstr. 90,* ☎ *030/2513–064. No credit cards. Closed Sun. and holidays.*

$ ✕ **Zur Letzten Instanz.** Established in 1621, Berlin's oldest restaurant combines the charming atmosphere of old-world Berlin with a limited (but tasty) choice of dishes. The emphasis here is on beer, both in the recipes and in the mug. Service can be erratic, though engagingly friendly. ⊠ *Waisenstr. 14–16,* ☎ *030/242–5528. AE, DC, MC, V.*

$$$$ 🏨 **Bristol Hotel Kempinski.** This grand hotel in the heart of the city has the best of Berlin's shopping on its doorstep. All the rooms and suites are luxuriously decorated and equipped, with marble bathrooms, air-conditioning, cable TV, and English-style furnishings. Children under 12 stay for free if they share their parents' room. ⊠ *Kurfürstendamm 27, D-10719,* ☎ *030/884–340,* 🗚 *030/883–6075. 301 rooms, 52 suites. 2 restaurants, pool. AE, DC, MC, V.*

$$$$ 🏨 **Four Seasons Hotel Berlin.** Smooth and up-to-date services such as
★ portable phones and fax machines complement turn-of-the-century luxury here. Thick red carpets, heavy crystal chandeliers, and a romantic restaurant, including an open fireplace, make for a sophisticated and serene atmosphere. ⊠ *Charlottenstr. 49, D-10117,* ☎ *030/20338,* 🗚 *030/2033–6166. 162 rooms, 42 suites. Restaurant. AE, DC, MC, V.*

$$$$ 🏨 **Grand Hotel Esplanade.** The Grand Hotel Esplanade exudes luxury. Uncompromisingly modern architecture, chic rooms, and works of art by some of Berlin's most acclaimed artists are among its delights. ⊠ *Lützowufer 15, D-10785,* ☎ *030/254–780,* 🗚 *030/265–1171. 369 rooms, 33 suites. 3 restaurants, pool. AE, DC, MC, V.*

$$$$ 🏨 **Grand Hyatt Berlin.** Europe's first Grand Hyatt is in the new heart of Berlin, offering large guest rooms with dark cherry-wood furniture, marble bathrooms (accessible through Asian-style sliding doors), and Bauhaus artist photographs. A special attraction of the first-class hotel is the top-floor gym and swimming pool, which have a great view of Berlin's skyline. ⊠ *Marlene-Dietrich-Pl. 2, D-10785,* ☎ *030/2553–1234,* 🗚 *030/ 2553–1235. 340 rooms, 15 suites. Restaurant, pool. AE, DC, MC, V.*

$$$$ 🏨 **Hotel Adlon Berlin.** This elegant hotel on Pariser Platz has to live
★ up to its almost mythical predecessor, the old Hotel Adlon, which, until its destruction during World War II, was considered Europe's premier resort. The new Adlon has impeccable service and an international guest list. Guest rooms are furnished in '20s style with dark-wood trimmings and bathrooms in black granite and bright marble. ⊠ *Unter den Linden 77, D-10117,* ☎ *030/22610,* 🗚 *030/2261–2222. 337 rooms, 51 suites. 2 restaurants, pool. AE, DC, MC, V.*

$$$$ 🏨 **Inter-Continental Berlin.** Rooms and suites are all of the highest standard and their decor shows exquisite taste. The west wing offers the best rooms and overlooks the greenery of the vast Tiergarten area. The west wing rooms have views of the vast Tiergarten park. Rooms in east wing are more recently renovated. ⊠ *Budapester Str. 2, D-10787,* ☎ *030/26020,* 🗚 *030/2602–1182. 510 rooms, 67 suites. 3 restaurants, pool. AE, DC, MC, V.*

$$$$ 🏨 **Steigenberger Berlin.** The Steigenberger group's exemplary Berlin hotel is steps from the Ku'damm but still remarkably quiet. All rooms have elegant maple-wood furniture. Luxury rooms of the executive club provide late check-in, complimentary ironing and shoe-shine service, a special lounge, and a small breakfast. ⊠ *Los-Angeles-Pl. 1, D-10789,* ☎ *030/21270,* 🗚 *030/212–7799. 397 rooms, 11 suites. 2 restaurants, pool. AE, DC, MC, V.*

$$$$ 🏨 **Westin Grand Hotel.** The Westin Hotel Group put this former top East Berlin hotel through a major modernization. Its neoclassical pink-marble lobby, with a soaring six-story atrium, has polished brass accents, stucco work, and rich wall coverings. Standard rooms are done in muted tones; bathrooms have large tubs. ⊠ *Friedrichstr. 158–164, D-10117,* ☎ *030/20270,* 🗚 *030/2027–3413. 323 rooms, 31 suites. 6 restaurants, pool. AE, DC, MC, V.*

$$$ 🏨 **Estrel Residence Congress Hotel.** Europe's largest hotel may seem
★ huge and anonymous, but it's the only place to get upscale rooms and
service for less money. The modern hotel offers countless amenities with
quiet efficiency and comfort. Rooms are decorated with Russian art.
The lobby is a breathtakingly bright atrium with a greenhouse atmo-
sphere. The hotel is in the unappealing working-class district of
Neukölln, some 20 minutes from downtown. ⊠ *Sonnenallee 225, D-
12057,* ☎ *030/68310,* ℻ *030/6831–2346. 1,045 rooms, 80 suites. 9
restaurants, pool. AE, DC, MC, V.*

$$ 🏨 **Hotel Astoria.** This is one of the most traditional privately owned
and run hotels in Berlin and it shows: Rooms, service and the hotel's
restaurant all have a personal touch. Rooms are spacious, though the
1980s furniture may seem outdated. The location is good for exploring Kurfürstendamm and the western downtown area, yet it's a quiet
side street. ⊠ *Fasanenstr. 2, D-10623,* ☎ *030/3124–067,* ℻ *030/
3125–027. 31 rooms, 1 suite. AE, DC, MC, V.*

$$ 🏨 **Hotel-Pension Dittberner.** The Dittberner, close to Olivaer Platz and
★ Kurfürstendamm, is a typical, family-run small hotel in a turn-of-the-
century house. Some of the furniture in the (now mostly renovated)
rooms are a little worn, but the warm atmosphere and the breakfast
buffet more than make up for it. ⊠ *Wielandstr. 26, D-10707,* ☎ *030/
8846–950,* ℻ *030/8854–046. 22 rooms. No credit cards.*

$$ 🏨 **Riehmers Hofgarten.** Surrounded by the bars and restaurants of the
★ colorful Kreuzberg district, this hotel has fast connections to the center
of town. The 19th-century building's high-ceiling rooms are stylishly furnished and completely renovated. ⊠ *Yorckstr. 83, D-10965,* ☎ *030/7809–
8800,* ℻ *030/7809–8808. 21 rooms. Restaurant. AE, DC, MC, V.*

$$ 🏨 **Charlottenburger Hof.** A creative flair, a convenient location across
★ from the Charlottenburg S-bahn station, and low rates make this low-
key hotel an incredible value for no-fuss travelers. The variety of rooms
can suit friends, couples, or families. Kurfürstendamm is a 10-minute
walk, taxis are easy to catch at the S-bahn station, and the bus to and
from Tegel airport stops a block away. ⊠ *Stuttgarter Pl. 14, D-10627,*
☎ *030/32–90–70,* ℻ *030/323–3723. 46 rooms with bath or shower.
AE, MC, V.*

Nightlife and the Arts

The Arts

The quality of opera and classical concerts in Berlin is high. Tickets are
available at the theaters' own box offices, either in advance or an hour
before the performance; at many hotels; and at numerous ticket agen-
cies: **Hekticket office** (⊠ Rathausstr. 1 and Zoo-Palast movie theater at
Alexanderpl., ☎ 030/2431–2431); **Showtime Konzert- und Theaterkassen**
(⊠ Tauentzienstr. 21 at KaDeWe, ☎ 030/217–7754); **Theaterkonz-
ertkasse City Center** (⊠ Kurfürstendamm 16, ☎ 030/882–6563); and
Wertheim (⊠ Kurfürstendamm 181, ☎ 030/8822500). Detailed in-
formation about what's going on in Berlin can be found in *Berlin–the
magazine,* an English-language monthly cultural magazine published by
Berlin's Tourism Board; *Berlin Programm,* a monthly tourist guide to
Berlin arts, museums, and theaters; and the magazines *prinz, tip,* and
zitty, which appear every two weeks and provide full arts listings.

CONCERTS

The Berlin Philharmonic, one of the world's leading orchestras, per-
forms in the **Philharmonie** (⊠ Matthäikirchstr. 1, ☎ 030/254–880 or
030/2548–8132). A more historic venue is the **Konzerthaus Berlin** (⊠
Gendarmenmarkt, ☎ 030/2030–92101).

MUSICALS

For musicals check out: **Estrel Festival Center** (✉ Sonnenallee 225/ Ziegrastr. 21–29, ☎ 030/6831–6831); **Schiller-Theater** (✉ Bismarckstr. 110, ☎ 030/3111–3111); and **Theater des Westens** (✉ Kantstr. 12, ☎ 030/882–2888).

OPERA AND BALLET

The **Deutsche Oper** (German Opera House; ✉ Bismarckstr. 35, ☎ 030/ 343–8401), by the U-bahn stop of the same name, is home to both opera and ballet. The grand **Staatsoper Unter den Linden** (German State Opera; ✉ Unter den Linden 7, ☎ 030/2035–4555) is Berlin's main opera house. The box office is open weekdays 10–6, weekends 2–6; you can reserve by phone weekdays 10–8, weekends 2–8. **Komische Oper** (Comic Opera House; ✉ Behrenstr. 55–57, ☎ 030/4702–1000) schedules opera and dance performances.

VARIETY SHOWS

Variety shows are particularly thriving in Berlin. Intimate and intellectually entertaining is the **Bar jeder Vernuft** (✉ Schaperstr. 24, ☎ 030/ 8831–582). Hilarious shows that even non-German speakers can appreciate are at the **Chamäleon Varieté** (✉ Rosenthaler Str. 40/41, ☎ 030/2827–118). The world's largest circus is at the **Friedrichstadtpalast** (✉ Friedrichstr. 107, ☎ 030/2326–2326). The small but classy **Wintergarten** (✉ Potsdamer Str. 96, ☎ 030/2308–8230 or 030/2500– 8863) pays romantic homage to the '20s.

Nightlife

With more than 6,000 Kneipen (pubs), bars, and clubs, nightlife in Berlin is no halfhearted affair. Almost 50 Kneipen have live music of one kind or another, and there are numerous small cabaret clubs and discos. The centers of this nocturnal scene are around Savignyplatz in Charlottenburg; Nollendorfplatz and its side streets in Schöneberg; Oranienstrasse and Wienerstrasse in Kreuzberg; Kollwitzplatz in the Prenzlauer Berg district; and Oranienburger Strasse, Rosenthaler Platz, and Hackesche Höfe in Mitte.

Berlin is a major center for jazz in Europe. Call the tourist office (☞ Visitor Information *in* Berlin Essentials, *below*) for details on the annual fall international Jazz Fest. Jazz groups appear throughout the year at the **A-Trane** (✉ Pestalozzistr. 105, ☎ 030/3132–550), **Eierschale** (✉ Podbielskiallee 50, ☎ 030/832–7097), and **Quasimodo** (✉ Kantstr. 12a, ☎ 030/312–8086).

Shopping

Antiques

On weekends from 10 to 5, the colorful and lively antiques and handicrafts fair on **Strasse des 17. Juni** swings into action. Not far from **Wittenbergplatz,** several streets are strong on antiques, including Eisenacher Strasse, Fuggerstrasse, Keithstrasse, Kalckreuthstrasse, Motzstrasse, and Nollendorfstrasse.

Department Stores

Galeries Lafayette (✉ Französische Str. 23, ☎ 030/209–480) carries almost exclusively French products, including designer clothes, perfume, and French produce. One of Berlin's classiest department stores is the **Kaufhaus des Westens** (KaDeWe; ✉ Tauentzienstr. 21, ☎ 030/21210); check out the food department, which occupies the whole sixth floor. The main department store in eastern Berlin is **Kaufhof** (✉ North end of Alexanderpl., ☎ 030/247–430). Downtown Berlin's **Wertheim** (✉ Kurfürstendamm 181, ☎ 030/8800–3206) is neither as big nor as attractive as KaDeWe, but it has a large selection of fine wares.

Gift Ideas

Fine porcelain is still produced at the former Royal Prussian Porcelain Factory, now called **Staatliche Porzellan Manufaktur** (State Porcelain Factory) or KPM. This delicate, handmade, hand-painted china is sold at KPM's store (⊠ Kurfürstendamm 26A, ☎ 030/8867–210), and the factory salesroom (⊠ Wegelystr. 1, ☎ 030/390–090), where seconds are sold at reduced prices. The **Gipsformerei der Staatlichen Museen Preussicher Kulturbesitz** (Plaster Sculpture of the Prussian Cultural Foundation State Museums; ⊠ Sophie-Charlotte-Str. 17, ☎ 030/321–7011) sells plaster casts of the Egyptian queen Nefertiti and other museum treasures.

Shopping Districts

The liveliest and most famous shopping area in west Berlin is the **Kurfürstendamm** and its side streets, especially between Breitscheidplatz and Olivaer Platz. The **Europa Center** at Breitscheidplatz encompasses more than 100 stores, cafés, and restaurants—but is not a place to bargain hunt. Running east from Breitscheidplatz is **Tauentzienstrasse.** The **Potsdamer Platz Arkaden** is the city's newest shopping mall on Potsdamer Platz. Eastern Berlin's best shops are along **Friedrichstrasse** and in the area around **Alexanderplatz.**

Berlin Essentials

Arriving and Departing

BY BUS

Berlin is linked by bus to 170 European cities. You can reserve at the central bus terminal (⊠ junction Masurenallee 4–6 and Messedamm, ☎ 030/301–8028) or through DER (state agency) or commercial travel agencies.

BY CAR

The eight roads linking the western part of Germany with Berlin have been incorporated into the country-wide autobahn network, but be prepared for large traffic jams, particularly on weekends.

BY PLANE

Tegel (☎ 01805–000186) airport is only 7 km (4 mi) from downtown. The former military airfield at **Tempelhof** (☎ 030/6951–2288), even closer to downtown, is used for commuter plane traffic. **Schönefeld** (☎ 030/6091–5112) airport is about 24 km (15 mi) outside the downtown area; it is used primarily for charter flights to Asia and southern and eastern Europe.

Between the Airports and Downtown. Buses 109 and X09 run every 10 minutes between **Tegel** airport and downtown. The journey takes 30 minutes; the fare is DM 3.90 and covers all public transportation throughout Berlin. A taxi costs about DM 25. If you're driving from the airport, follow signs for the STADTAUTOBAHN (City Freeway). **Tempelhof** is right on the U-6 subway line, in the center of the city. A shuttle bus leaves **Schönefeld** airport every 10–15 minutes for the nearby S-bahn station. S-bahn trains leave every 20 minutes for the Friedrichstrasse and Zoologischer Garten stations. The trip takes about 30 minutes; the fare is DM 3.60. Taxi fare to your hotel is about DM 40–DM 55, and the trip takes about 40 minutes. By car follow the signs for BERLIN–ZENTRUM (Downtown Berlin).

BY TRAIN

There are major rail routes to Berlin from Hamburg, Hannover, Köln, Frankfurt, Munich, and Nürnberg, and the network has expanded considerably, making the rest of eastern Germany more accessible. For information call **Deutsche Bahn** (☎ 030/19419) or inquire at the local main train station.

Getting Around
The city has an excellent public transportation system: a combination of U-bahn and S-bahn lines, buses, and streetcars (in eastern Berlin only). For DM 3.90, you can buy a ticket that covers travel on the entire downtown system (fare zones A and B) for two hours. Buy a **Kurzstreckentarif** for a short trip; it allows you to ride six bus stops or three U-bahn or S-bahn stops for DM 2.50. The **Day Card,** for DM 7.80, is valid for 24 hours after validation. The **Group Day Card,** for DM 22.50, offers the same benefits for two adults and up to three children.

The **Tourist Pass,** valid for a week and costing DM 40, is the best bargain. The **BerlinWelcomeCard,** at DM 16 for a day (DM 29 for two days), entitles one adult and up to three children to unlimited travel as well as free or reduced sightseeing trips and admission to museums, theaters, and other events and attractions. If you're caught without a validated ticket, the fine is DM 60. Tickets are available from vending machines at U-bahn and S-bahn stations or from bus drivers. For information call the **Berliner Verkehrsbetriebe** (BVG; Berlin Public Transportation; ☎ 030/19449 or 030/7527–020) or go to the information office on Hardenbergplatz, directly in front of the Bahnhof Zoo train station.

Please note: Ticket regulations will probably change in 2000.

The base rate is DM 4, after which prices vary according to a complex tariff system. If your ride will be short, ask in advance for the special Kurzstreckentarif, which is DM 5 for rides of less than 2 km (1 mi) or five minutes. Figure on paying around DM 15 for a ride the length of the Kurfurstendamm. Hail cabs in the street or at taxi stands, or order one by calling ☎ 030/9644, 030/210–202, 030/691–001, or 030/261–026. U-bahn employees will call a taxi for passengers after 8 PM.

Contacts and Resources
U.S. (✉ Neustädtische Kirchstr. 4–5, ☎ 030/2385–174). **Canada** (✉ International Trade Center, Friedrichstr. 95, ☎ 030/261–1161). **U.K.** (✉ Unter den Linden 32–34, ☎ 030/201–840). **Australia** (✉ Uhlandstr. 181–183, ☎ 030/880–0880). **Ireland** (✉ Ernst-Reuter-Pl. 10, ☎ 030/3480–0822).

Please note: The consulates listed above are branch offices of the embassies' head offices in Bonn. By the year 2000, the United States and a number of nations will have moved their main offices to new facilities in Berlin. Phone numbers and addresses shown above are likely to change.

Police (☎ 030/110). **Ambulance** (☎ 030/112). **Dentist emergency assistance** (☎ 030/8900–4333). **Emergency pharmaceutical assistance** (☎ 030/01189).

Buchhandlung Kiepert (✉ Hardenbergstr. 4–5, ☎ 030/311–0090). **Dussmann Kulturkaufhaus** (✉ Friedrichstr. 90, ☎ 030/20250). **Hugendubel** (✉ Tauentzienstr. 13, ☎ 030/214060). **Marga Schoeller** (✉ Knesebeckstr. 33, ☎ 030/881–1112).

Orientation. Berliner Bären Stadtrundfahrt (BBS, ✉ Seeburgerstr. 19b, ☎ 030/3519–5270); **Berolina Stadtrundfahrten** (✉ Kurfürstendamm

22, corner Meinekestr., ☎ 030/8856–8030); **Bus Verkehr Berlin** (BVB, ✉ Kurfürstendamm 225, ☎ 030/885–9880); and **Severin & Kühn** (✉ Kurfürstendamm 216, ☎ 030/8804–190) offer more or less identical tours in English, covering Berlin's major sights, as well as day trips to Potsdam and Dresden. The Berlin tour costs DM 25 to DM 45; Potsdam and Sanssouci Palace, the favorite residence of Frederick the Great, costs DM 54.

Boat. Berlin is a city of waterways, and boats traverse the Spree River, the canals that connect the network of big lakes, and the lakes themselves. For details contact the main city tourist office (☞ Visitor Information, *below*).

TRAVEL AGENCIES
American Express Reisebüro (✉ at Wittenbergpl., Bayreuther Str. 37, ☎ 030/2149–8363; ✉ Uhlandstr. 173, ☎ 030/882–7575; ✉ Friedrichstr. 172, ☎ 030/238–4102). **American Lloyd** (✉ Kurfürstendamm 209, ☎ 030/20740).

VISITOR INFORMATION
The **Berlin Tourismus Marketing GmbH** (main tourist office; Europa Center; Brandenburger Tor; Tegel Airport; by mail, Berlin Tourismus Marketing, ✉ Am Karlsbad 11, D-10785 Berlin). **Berlin-Hotline** (☎ 030/ 250–025, ℻ 030/2500–2424).

SAXONY AND THURINGIA

Saxony and Thuringia—the states' names alone conjure up images of kingdoms and forest legends, of cultural riches and booming industrial enterprises. Since German reunification, the world's admiration has returned to Saxony's museum-rich capital, Dresden, porcelain works in Meissen, and musical and literary traditions in Leipzig.

Largely rural Thuringia has ample tourist accommodations, as it was a popular East German holiday destination. During the 14th century, traders from the dark forested depths of the Thüringer Wald (forest) used the 168-km (104-mi) Rennsteig ("fast trail") to travel along the region's pristine peaks. The German Enlightenment movement was spearheaded in Weimar, as was the short-lived German democracy, the Weimar Republic, in the 1920s.

Dresden
Saxony's capital city sits majestically on the banks of the Elbe River. Although it suffered appalling damage during World War II, it has been lovingly rebuilt. Italianate influences abound, most pronounced in the glorious rococo and Baroque buildings in pastel shades of yellow and green.

The magnificent **Semperoper** (Semper Opera House) was built in 1838–41 by architect Gottfried Semper. The sumptuous reconstructed interior is covered in velvet and brocade in shades of crimson, white, and gold. Wagner's *The Flying Dutchman* and *Tannhäuser* (conducted by the composer) and nine operas by Richard Strauss premiered here. Tickets to performances here are often hard to get; try booking through your travel agent before you go or ask at your hotel. As a last resort, line up at the evening box office, the Abendkasse, left of the main entrance, about ½ hour before the performance. ✉ Theaterpl., ☎ 0351/ 491–1496, 0351/49110, 0351/491–11730 (tickets). ☉ Tour hrs vary but run daily 10–3.

★ The largely 18th-century **Zwinger** palace complex is among the greatest examples of Baroque architecture in Europe. Completely enclosing a central courtyard of lawns and pools, six linked pavilions are

Saxony and Thuringia (Sachsen und Thüringen)

adorned with a riot of sandstone garlands, nymphs, and other Baroque ornamentation and sculpture, created under the direction of Matthäus Daniel Pöppelmann. The complex is home to the world-renowned **Sempergalerie** (Semper Gallery), whose Gemäldegalerie Alte Meister (Gallery of Old Masters) contains works by Dürer, Holbein the Younger, Rembrandt, Vermeer, Raphael, Correggio, and Canaletto. The **Porzellansammlung** (Porcelain Museum) is famous for its Meissen pieces. ⊠ *Theaterpl., follow Sophienstrasse,* ☎ *0351/491–4619.* ☉ *Sempergalerie: Tues.–Sun. 10–6; Porzellansammlung: Fri.–Wed. 10–6.*

Despite its name, the **Neumarkt** (New Market) serves as the historic heart of old Dresden. The mighty Baroque **Frauenkirche** (Church of Our Lady), once Germany's greatest Protestant church but until recently in ruins, is being slowly reconstructed on the square. ⊠ *Bordered by Schlosstr., Landhausstr., Tzschirnerpl., and Brühlsche G.*

Dresden's leading art museum, the **Albertinum,** is housed in a massive, imperial-style building. The **Gemäldegalerie Neue Meister** (New Masters Gallery) displays outstanding 19th- and 20th-century European works. The **Grünes Gewölbe** (Green Vault; entered from Georg-Treu-Platz), named after the collection's original home in the palace of August the Strong, showcases unique objets d'art fashioned from gold, silver, ivory, amber, and other precious and semiprecious materials. Next door, the **Skulpturensammlung** (Sculpture Collection) includes ancient Egyptian and classical objects and Italian Mannerist works. ⊠ *Am Neumarkt at Brühlsche Terrasse,* ☎ *0351/4914–619.* ☉ *Fri.–Wed. 10–6.*

The **Verkehrsmuseum** (Transport Museum), a collection of historic vehicles, including vintage automobiles and engines, occupies the 16th-century Johanneum, once the royal stables. On its outside wall is a prime example of Meissen porcelain art: a 335-ft-long mural of a royal procession. ⊠ *Am Neumarkt,* ☎ *0351/86440.* ☉ *Tues.–Sun. 10–5.*

The **Katholische Hofkirche** (Catholic Court Church), also known as the Cathedral of St. Trinitas, is Saxony's largest church, consecrated in 1754. In the crypt are the tombs of 49 Saxon rulers and a precious vessel containing the heart of August the Strong. ⊠ *Schlosspl.,* ☎ *0351/495–1233.* 🎫 *Free.* ⊙ *Weekdays 9–5, Sat. 10–5, Sun. noon–5.*

The **Sächsische Porzellanmanufaktur Dresden,** 9 km (5.6 mi) southwest of Dresden in Freital, is where Dresden's renowned porcelain is made. Exquisite examples of the porcelain are sold in all Dresden department stores, and the Freital showroom sells items as well. ⊠ *Bachstr. 16, Freital,* ☎ *0351/647–1310.* ⊙ *Mon.–Sat. 8–5.*

$$ ✕ **Ristorante Bellotto im Italienischen Dörfchen.** This Baroque structure on the Elbe was built to house Italian craftsmen working on the nearby Hofkirche. It has been cleverly and tastefully converted into a restaurant and café, with a shady beer garden and fine river views. The Italian influence is still in evidence—in the decor and on the menu, where pasta dishes are heavily favored. ⊠ *Theaterpl. 3,* ☎ *0351/498–1681. AE, DC, MC, V.*

$–$$ ✕ **Sophienkeller.** One of the jolliest and most original restaurants in
★ eastern Germany, the Sophienkeller offers truly Saxon dishes and strong beer. It's tucked in the basement of the Taschenbergpalais. ⊠ *Taschenberg 3,* ☎ *0351/0351/497–260. AE, MC, V.*

$$$$ 🏨 **Kempinski Hotel Taschenbergpalais Dresden.** The rebuilt historic
★ Taschenberg Palace—the work of architect Matthäus Daniel Pöppelmann—reopened as a hotel in early 1995. It provides expensive pampering in the romantic heart of old Dresden. ⊠ *Am Taschenberg 3, D-01067,* ☎ *0351/49120,* 🕾 *0351/491–2812. 188 rooms, 25 suites. 2 restaurants, pool. AE, DC, MC, V.*

$$$$ 🏨 **Westin Bellevue Dresden.** Across the river from the Zwinger palace, the opera, and the main museums, this modern hotel cleverly incorporates an old restored mansion. Most of the recently modernized rooms are more functional than luxurious, but the service is outstanding. ⊠ *Grosse-Meissner-Str. 15, D-01097,* ☎ *0351/8050,* 🕾 *0351/8051–699. 323 rooms, 16 suites. 3 restaurants, pool. AE, DC, MC, V.*

$$$ 🏨 **artotel Dresden.** Inside the artotel are more than 600 works by Dresden-born painter and sculptor A. R. Penck, as well as designs by Italian interior architect Denis Santachiara. The hotel's heavily styled rooms and service have genuine first-class appeal at considerably lower prices. ⊠ *Astra-Allee 33, D-01067,* ☎ *0351/49220,* 🕾 *0351/492–2777. 158 rooms, 16 suites. 3 restaurants, pool. AE, DC, MC, V.*

$$$ 🏨 **Hotel am Terrassenufer.** Dresden's court painter Canaletto Belotto (1720–80) painted the very vistas you can see from this 12-story hotel on the Elbe River terrace. Rooms have bright, cherry-wood veneer furniture and fresh pastel color schemes; all have panoramic views of the river and the Old Town, and on clear days even to the hills of the Sächsische Schweiz, a mountain region south of Dresden. ⊠ *Am Terrassenufer 12, D-01067,* ☎ *0351/440–9500,* 🕾 *0351/440–9600. 190 rooms, 6 suites. Restaurant. AE, DC, MC, V.*

$$ ✕🏨 **Hotelschiff *Florentina*.** From your cabin window in this cleverly converted "hotel ship" you have a better view of the Elbe and Dresden than you would from many of the luxury hotels along the banks. Space is understandably a bit cramped, although all the cabins have satellite TV and bathrooms with showers. The restaurant has the best view in town. ⊠ *Terrassenufer, D-01069,* ☎ *0351/459–0169,* 🕾 *0351/459–5036. 64 cabins. Restaurant. AE, DC, MC, V.*

Meissen

This romantic city on the Elbe River, 25 km (16 mi) northwest of Dresden, is known the world over for its porcelain, bearing the crossed blue swords trademark. The first European porcelain was made in this area, and in 1710 the royal porcelain workshop was established here, close to the local raw materials.

The **Staatliche Porzellan–Manufaktur Meissen** (Meissen's porcelain works) outgrew its castle workshop during the mid-19th century and is now on the outskirts of town. In one of the works' buildings are a **Schauwerkstatt** (production demonstration workshop) and a **Schauhalle** (museum) whose Meissen collection rivals that of the Porcelain Museum in Dresden (☞ Zwinger *in* Dresden, *above*). ✉ *Talstr. 9,* ☎ *03521/ 468–700.* ⊘ *Daily 9–5.*

Leipzig

With a population of about 560,000, Leipzig is the second-largest city (after Berlin) in eastern Germany. Since the Middle Ages, it has been an important market town and a center for printing, book publishing, and the fur business. Its year-round industrial fairs maintain Leipzig's position as a commercial center. Yet it is music and literature that most people associate with Leipzig; Johann Sebastian Bach (1685–1750) was the organist and choir director at St. Thomas's church, and the composer Richard Wagner was born in Leipzig in 1813. One of the greatest battles of the Napoleonic Wars, and one that led to the ultimate defeat of the French general—the Battle of the Nations—was fought here in 1813.

The unique **Hauptbahnhof,** with its 26 platforms, majestic staircase, great arched ceiling, and more than 150 upscale shops, is Europe's largest railway station. ✉ *Willy-Brandt-Pl.,* ☎ *0341/19419.*

Leipzig's showpiece is its **Markt,** an old market square only slightly smaller than St. Mark's Square in Venice. Small streets leading off from the Markt attest to Leipzig's rich trading past. Tucked in among them are glass-roofed arcades of surprising beauty and elegance. One side of the Markt is occupied completely by the recently restored Renaissance **Altes Rathaus** (Old City Hall), which now houses the **Stadtgeschichtliches Museum** (City History Museum), where Leipzig's past is well documented. ✉ *Markt 1,* ☎ *0341/965–130.* ⊘ *Tues. 2–8, Wed.–Sun. 10–6.*

Mädlerpassage (Mädler Mall) is Leipzig's finest shopping arcade, where references to Goethe's *Faust* lurk in every marble corner. Goethe set a scene in the Auerbachs Keller restaurant (☞ *below*) here. ✉ *Grimmaischestr.*

★ Johann Sebastian Bach worked for 27 years at **Thomaskirche** (St. Thomas's Church), composing most of his cantatas for the church's boys' choir. The city celebrates Bach in 2000 with special concerts and events. ✉ *Thomaskirchhof (just off Grimmaischestr.),* ☎ *0341/9602–855.* ▣ *Free.* ⊘ *Apr.–Oct., daily 8–6; Nov.–Mar., daily 9–5.*

★ **Nikolaikirche** (St. Nicholas's Church) is more impressive inside than out; it has an ornate 16th-century pulpit and an unusual diamond-pattern ceiling supported by classical pillars crowned with palm-tree-like flourishes. Demonstrations at the church in 1989 are credited with helping to bring down the Communist regime. ✉ *Nikolaikirchhof,* ☎ *0341/960–5270.* ▣ *Free.* ⊘ *Daily 10–6.*

The **Grassimuseum,** a fine example of German Art Deco, was built between 1925 and 1929 to house three important museums: the **Museum für Kunsthandwerk** (Museum of Arts and Crafts), open Tuesday, Thursday–Sunday 10–6, Wednesday noon–8; the **Museum für Völkerkunde zu Leipzig** (Ethnological Museum), open Tuesday–Friday 10–5:30, weekends 10–4; and the **Musikinstrumenten-Museum** (Musical

Instruments Museum; ⊠ enter from Täubchenweg 2.), open Tuesday–Friday 10–5, Saturday 10–5, Sunday 10–1. *Grassimuseum:* ⊠ *Johannespl. 5–11,* ☎ *0341/21420.*

★ The city's most outstanding museum, the **Museum der Bildenden Künste** (Museum of Fine Arts), is an art gallery of international stature, especially strong in German and Dutch painting. ⊠ *Grimmaischestr. 1–7,* ☎ *0341/216–9914.* ۞ *Tues., Thurs.–Sun. 10–6, Wed. 1–9:30.*

The modernistic **Opernhaus** (Opera House; ⊠ Augustuspl. 12, ☎ 0341/126–1261) is a center of the city's music life. The **Neues Gewandhaus** (⊠ Augustuspl. 8, ☎ 0341/127–0280) is home to a first-class orchestra.

$$ ✕ **Auerbachs Keller.** Established in 1530, this restaurant was made fa-
★ mous by Goethe's *Faust* and became an indispensable part of Leipzig life. Saxon dishes, often with Faustian names, head the menu. ⊠ *Mädlerpassage, Grimmaischestr. 2–4,* ☎ *0341/216–100. Reservations essential. Jacket and tie. AE, MC, V.*

$$ ✕ **Barthels Hof.** The beamed and paneled *Gasthaus* restaurant is a local
★ favorite and serves hearty Saxon food with an international touch. The breakfast buffet is impressive, too. ⊠ *Hainstr. 1,* ☎ *0341/141–310. AE, DC, MC, V.*

$$ ✕ **Paulaner Restaurant.** Munich's Paulaner brewery has transformed a historic corner of Leipzig into a vast complex combining a restaurant, banquet hall, café, and beer garden. There's something for everybody here, from intimate dining to noisy, Bavarian-style tavern-table conviviality. ⊠ *Klosterg. 3–5,* ☎ *0341/211–3115. AE, MC, V.*

$$ ✕ **Zill's Tunnel.** In the barrel-vaulted ground-floor restaurant, friendly
★ staff serve foaming glasses of excellent local beer. The menu carries Old Saxon descriptions of traditional dishes. ⊠ *Barfussgässchen 9,* ☎ *0341/960–2078. AE, MC, V.*

$$$$ ⊞ **Hotel Inter-Continental Leipzig.** The imposing high-rise "Interconti" offers outstanding service, but the place lacks atmosphere, despite a Japanese restaurant and garden. Rooms have every extravagance, including bathrooms with marble floors and walls. ⊠ *Gerberstr. 15, D-04105,* ☎ *0341/9880,* ℻ *0341/988–1229. 447 rooms, 26 suites. 3 restaurants, pool. AE, DC, MC, V.*

$$$$ ⊞ **Kempinski Hotel Fürstenhof Leipzig.** One of the country's most lux-
★ urious hotels is in the *Löhr-Haus,* a revered old mansion. The 19th-century-style banquet section is stunning with red wallpaper and dark mahogany wood. The spacious rooms are decorated with cherry-wood designer furniture. The fitness and swimming pool facilities are among the best in eastern Germany. ⊠ *Tröndlinring 8, D-04105,* ☎ *0341/ 1400,* ℻ *0341/1403–700. 84 rooms, 8 suites. Restaurant, pool. AE, DC, MC, V.*

$$$ ⊞ **Renaissance Leipzig Hotel.** In a city of trade fairs, this large hotel in the heart of old Leipzig attracts business travelers for its hushed atmosphere and its large, elegant rooms. If you reserve a room on the CLUB floor, for about DM 40 a day you get a free continental breakfast and access to the CLUB-Lounge. The hotel's restaurant, Four Seasons, serves light Asian cuisine. ⊠ *Querstr. 12, D-04103,* ☎ *0341/12920,* ℻ *0341/ 1292–800. 295 rooms, 61 suites. Restaurant, pool. AE, DC, MC, V.*

Weimar

Sitting prettily on the Ilm River between the Ettersberg and Vogtland hills, Weimar has a place in German political and cultural history all out of proportion to its size (population 63,000). It is here that Goethe and the poet and dramatist Friedrich von Schiller were neighbors, Carl Maria von Weber (1786–1826) wrote some of his best music, and Liszt presented the first performance of Wagner's *Lohengrin.* Walter Gropius founded his Bauhaus design school in Weimar in 1919, and here in 1919–20 the German National Assembly drew up the constitution of the Weimar Republic.

Theaterplatz, in front of the National Theater, has a statue that shows Goethe placing a patronizing hand on the shoulder of the younger Schiller. ⊠ *Bordered by Dingelstedstr., Gropiusstr., Heinrich-Heine-Str., Schiller-str., and Schützeng.*

★ The **Goethehaus** was Goethe's home for 47 of his 57 years in Weimar. The museum is testimony not only to the great man's literary might but also to his interest in the sciences, particularly medicine, and his administrative skills (and frustrations) as Weimar's exchequer. ⊠ *Frauenplan 1, 2 blocks south of Theaterpl.,* ☎ *03643/545–320.* ☉ *Mar.–Oct., Tues.–Sun. 9–6; Nov.–Feb., Tues.–Sun. 10–4.*

On a tree-shaded square around the corner from Goethe's house is the green-shuttered **Schillerhaus,** in which Friedrich Schiller and his family spent an all-too-brief but happy three years (the poet died here in 1805). His study, dominated by the desk at which he probably completed *Wilhelm Tell,* is tucked up underneath the mansard roof. ⊠ *Schillerstr. 17,* ☎ *03643/545–350.* ☉ *Mar.–Oct., Mon. and Wed.–Sun. 9–6; Nov.–Feb., Mon. and Wed.–Sun. 9–4.*

Weimar's 16th-century castle, the **Stadtschloss** (City Palace), has a restored classical staircase, festival hall, and falcon gallery. The castle's impressive art collection includes paintings by Cranach the Elder and early 20th-century works by such artists as Böcklin, Liebermann, and Beckmann. ⊠ *Burgpl. 4, around corner from market square,* ☎ *03643/5460.* ☉ *Sept.–Mar., Tues. 10–4:30; Apr.–Aug., Tues.–Sun. 10–6.*

Goethe and Schiller are buried in the leafy **Historischer Friedhof** (Historic Cemetery), where virtually every gravestone commemorates a famous citizen. The writers' tombs are in the vault of the chapel. ⊠ *Berkaer Str. and Am Poseckschen Garten; south past Goethe Haus and Wieland Pl.,* ☉ *Mar.–Oct., Wed.–Mon. 9–1 and 2–5; Nov.–Feb., Wed.–Mon. 9–1.*

Goethe's beloved **Gartenhaus,** a country cottage where he spent many happy hours, is set amid parkland on the banks of the river Ilm. He wrote much poetry and began his masterpiece, *Iphigenie,* here. You can soak up the rural atmosphere along the river footpaths. ⊠ *Goethep-ark,* ☎ *03642/545–375.* ☉ *Mar.–Oct., Mon. and Wed.–Sun. 9–6; Nov.–Feb., Mon. and Wed.–Sun. 9–4.*

North of Weimar, in the Ettersberg Hills, is a blighted patch of land that contrasts cruelly with the verdant countryside that so inspired
★ Goethe: **Buchenwald,** where between 1937 and 1945, some 65,000 men, women, and children from 35 countries died from disease, starvation, or gruesome medical experiments. There are three small exhibition areas. ⊠ *Buchenwald Str.; take public Bus No. 6 from Goethepl.;* ☎ *03643/4300.* ▧ *Free.* ☉ *May–Sept., Tues.–Sun. 9:45–5:15; Oct.–Apr., Tues.–Sun. 8:45–4:15.*

$$ ✕ **Hotel Thüringen.** The plush elegance of the hotel's restaurant, complete with velvet drapes and chandeliers, makes it seem expensive, but the menu of international and regional dishes, such as Thüringer roast beef, is remarkably moderately priced. ⊠ *Brennerstr. 42,* ☎ *03643/903–675. AE, DC, MC, V.*

$ ✕ **Scharfe Ecke.** Thuringia's traditional *Knödeln* (dumplings) are best here. But be patient; they're made to order and take at least 20 minutes to prepare. The Knödeln come with just about every dish, from roast pork to venison stew. The ideal accompaniment is the locally brewed beer. ⊠ *Eisfeld 2,* ☎ *03643/202–430. No credit cards. Closed Mon.*

$$$$ ☷ **Hilton Weimar.** Weimar's most modern hotel combines lavishness and smooth-running service. The riverside Belvedere Park that Goethe helped plan is just across the road. Weimar's center is a hike in the other direction, but buses are frequent. ⊠ *Belvederer Allee 25, D-99425,* ☎ *03643/7220,* ℻ *03643/722–741. 294 rooms, 6 suites. 2 restaurants, pool. AE, DC, MC, V.*

$$$$ ☷ **Kempinski Hotel Elephant.** The historic Elephant, dating from 1696,
★ is famous for its charm—even through the Communist years. Goethe,
. Schiller, and Liszt are some of the illustrious names in the hotel register. Book well in advance. ⊠ *Markt 19, D-99423,* ☎ *03643/8020,* ℻ *03643/802–610. 97 rooms, 5 suites. 2 restaurants. AE, DC, MC, V.*

$$ ☷ **Amalienhof VCH Hotel.** Book far ahead to secure a room here. The officially protected building began life in 1826 as a church hostel, but subsequent remodeling turned it into a comfortable, cozy, and friendly little hotel, central to Weimar's attractions. Double rooms have first-rate antique reproductions; public rooms have the real thing. ⊠ *Amalienstr. 2, D-99423,* ☎ *03643/5490,* ℻ *03643/549–110. 22 rooms, 9 apartments. AE, MC, V.*

Saxony and Thuringia Essentials

Getting Around

BY BOAT

The **Weisse Flotte** (White Fleet) of inland boats, including paddle side-wheelers, ply the River Elbe, starting in Dresden or at the beautiful forested border town of Bad Schandau and proceeding on into the Czech Republic. For details contact the tour operator (⊠ Sächsische Dampfschiffahrt, Hertha-Lindner-Str. 10, D-01067 Dresden, ☎ 0351/866–090). **Köln-Düsseldorfer Rheinschiffahrt** (☞ By Boat *in* Germany A to Z, *above*) operates luxury cruises in both directions on the Elbe from May through October.

BY BUS AND STREETCAR

Within Saxony and Thuringia, most areas are accessible by bus, but service is infrequent and connects chiefly with rail lines. In Dresden, Meissen, Leipzig, and Weimar, public buses and streetcars are cheap and efficient.

BY CAR

Some 1,600 km (1,000 mi) of autobahn and 11,300 km (7,000 mi) of secondary roads crisscross the five new federal states in the east. Resurfacing of some of the Communist-built highways has resulted in the lifting of the previous strictly enforced 100-kph (62-mph) speed limits on autobahns. Gas stations can be scarce on back roads.

BY TAXI

Taxis in Dresden are inexpensive. Leipzig has more cabs than any other eastern German city because of the trade fairs. Weimar's chief attractions are close to one another, but you may want to take a taxi from the main train station, which is somewhat removed from the city center.

BY TRAIN

InterCity, EuroCity, and InterCity Express trains connect Dresden, Meissen, Leipzig, and Weimar with Berlin and other major German cities, with InterRegio services completing the express network; older and slower D- and E-class trains connect smaller towns.

Leipzig has an **S-bahn** system. Tickets must be obtained in advance, at various prices according to the number of rides in a block. Get S-bahn tickets at the main railway station.

Guided Tours

In **Dresden** there are 10 daily guided tours by bus, tram, or open carriage, at least two steamer trips on the Elbe, and four walking tours. Consult the tourist office (☞ Visitor Information, *below*) before setting off. The office also sells a one-day Dresden Card (DM 11, or DM 20 for 48 hours) covering various museum admissions and transportation.

The visitor information office in **Leipzig** (☞ Visitor Information, *below*) leads regularly scheduled bus and tram tours of the city; reservations are advised (☎ 0341/79590). Walking tours start from the main tourist office (☞ Visitor Information, *below*) at 4 PM.

Walking tours of **Weimar** start from the main tourist office, daily at 11 and 4. Individual tours can also be arranged. In smaller cities like **Meissen,** tours can be arranged by the tourist offices (☞ Visitor Information, *below*).

Visitor Information

Dresden (✉ Tourist-Information, Prager Str. 10, D-01069, ☎ 0351/491–920). **Leipzig** (✉ Leipzig Tourist Service e.V., Sachsenpl. 1, D-06108, ☎ 0341/7401–260/265). **Meissen** (✉ An der Frauenkirche 3, D-01662, ☎ 03521/454–470). **Weimar** (✉ Tourist-Information, Markt 10, D-99421, ☎ 03643/24000).

13 GREAT BRITAIN

LONDON, WINDSOR TO BATH, CAMBRIDGE, YORK, THE LAKE DISTRICT, EDINBURGH

When you visit London, chances are you'll glimpse St. Paul's Cathedral riding high and white over the rooftops of the city skyline, just as it does in Canaletto's 18th-century views of the Thames. The great cathedral, cleaned, glows honey-gold, breathtakingly floodlit by night, making architect Christopher Wren's detail and proportion evident once again. Then, on second glance, you'll note that St. Paul's is being nudged by modern, glittering skyscrapers, with glass and steel tower blocks marching two abreast the length of London Wall. The juxtaposition should give you pause: Clearly, when you come to see the sights of Britain, you ought not to miss the greatest sight of all, which is the unconquered, nearly 2,000-year-long continuity of English society.

From Baroque-era cathedrals to the latest Postmodern structures, from prehistoric Stonehenge to Regency Bath, from one-pub Cotswold villages to London's Mod Brit restaurants, Great Britain is a spectacular tribute to the strength—and flexibility—of tradition. Here, in this "green and pleasant land," you'll find soaring medieval cathedrals, evidence of the faith of the churchmen and masons who built them; grand country mansions of the aristocracy filled with treasures—paintings, furniture, tapestries—and set in elegantly landscaped grounds; and grim fortified castles, whose gray-stone walls held fast against all challengers. But there is more to Britain than a historical theme park aspect: Many of the pleasures of exploration derive from the ever-changing variety of its countryside. A day's drive from York, for example, will take you through stretches of wild, heather-covered moorland, ablaze with color in the fall; or past the steep, sheep-dotted mountainsides of the Dales, in which isolated hamlets are scattered.

Wandering off the beaten track will also allow you to discover Britain's many distinctive rural towns and villages, which move at a notably slower pace than do the metropolitan centers. A medieval parish church, a high street of 18th-century buildings accented by occasional survivors from earlier centuries, and perhaps a grandiose Victorian town hall, all still in use today, help to convey a sense of a living past. This direct continuity of past into present can be generously experienced in such a celebrated place as Stratford-upon-Avon. It's even more evident in such communities as the little town of Chipping Campden, set in the rolling Cotswold Hills, or Bury St. Edmunds, in the gentle Suffolk countryside east of Cambridge. In such places the visitor's understanding is often aided by small museums devoted to local history, full of intriguing artifacts and information on trade, traditions, and social life. These towns are likely places to look for specialty goods, including knitwear, pottery, and glass, the result of a 1990s renaissance in craftsmanship.

In contrast is the dazzling—at times hectic—pace of life in London. Today, Britain's swinging-again capital is much in the news and the city's sizzling art, dining, style, and fashion scenes have done much to transform London's stodgy and traditional image. Thanks to such figures as artist Damien Hirst, designer-provocateur Alexander McQueen, and, of course, Tony Blair, the new young(ish) Prime Minister, the New London continues to make headlines around the world. On the cusp of the new century, London has become Europe's most future-active capital and, fittingly, will be welcoming the new centuries with a slew of millennium goodies, including the gigantic Millennium Dome and the new Tate Gallery of Modern Art; even age-old landmarks like St. Paul's and the British Museum are getting impressive face-lifts.

Finally, it is important to remember that Great Britain consists of three nations—England, Scotland, and Wales—and that 648 km (400 mi) north of London lies the capital city of Edinburgh, whose streets and monuments bear witness to the often turbulent and momentous history of the Scottish people.

GREAT BRITAIN A TO Z

Customs

For details on imports and duty-free limits, *see* Customs & Duties *in* Chapter 1.

Dining

British food used to be put down for its lack of imagination and its mediocrity. Today, numerous chefs have taken such giant steps that London is now one of the world's greatest cities for dining out. Across Britain, the problem may be not so much bad food as expensive food—you might want to check prices on the menu, which, by law, must be displayed outside the restaurant, before stepping inside. The best of traditional British cooking, deeper into the country, uses top-quality, fresh, local ingredients: wild salmon; spring lamb; distinctive handmade cheeses; myriad, almost forgotten, fruit varieties; and countless types of seasonal vegetables. Nearly all restaurant menus include vegetarian dishes, and interesting ethnic cuisines, especially Asian, can be found in the main street of even the smaller towns and villages.

MEALTIMES

These vary somewhat, depending on the region of the country you are visiting. But in general breakfast is served between 7:30 and 9 and lunch between noon and 2 (in the North the latter meal is called dinner). Tea—a famous British tradition and often a meal in itself—is generally served between 4 and 5:30. Dinner or supper is served between 7:30 and 9:30, sometimes earlier, but rarely later outside the metropolitan areas. High tea, at about 6, replaces dinner in some areas—especially in Scotland—and in large cities, pre- and after-theater suppers are often available. Note that many upscale restaurants close for 10 days during Easter and/or Christmas and for several weeks in July, August, or September. Call ahead.

RATINGS

Prices quoted here are per person and include a first course, a main course, and dessert, but not wine or service.

CATEGORY	LONDON AND SOUTHERN ENGLAND	OTHER AREAS
$$$$	over £50	over £40
$$$	£35–£50	£25–£40
$$	£25–£35	£15–£25
$	under £25	under £15

WHAT TO WEAR

Jacket and tie are suggested for the more formal restaurants in the top price categories, but, in general, casual chic or informal dress is acceptable in most establishments.

Lodging

Britain offers a wide variety of accommodations, ranging from enormous, top-quality, top-price hotels to simple, intimate farmhouses and guest houses. Note that many smaller establishments close for 10 days during Christmas and sometimes for several weeks in July or August. Call ahead.

BED-AND-BREAKFASTS

In Britain these are small, simple establishments, not the upscale option Americans know by this name. They offer modest, inexpensive accommodations, usually in a family home. Few rooms have private bathrooms, and most B&Bs offer no meals other than breakfast. Guest houses are a slightly larger, somewhat more luxurious, version. Both provide the visitor with an excellent glimpse of everyday British life.

CAMPING

Britain offers an abundance of campsites. Some are large and well equipped; others are merely small farmers' fields, offering primitive facilities. For information contact the British Tourist Authority in the United States (☞ Visitor Information *in* Chapter 1) or the **Camping and Caravanning Club** (✉ Greenfields House, Westwood Way, Coventry CV4 8JH, ☎ 01203/694995).

FARMHOUSES

Farmhouses rarely offer professional hotel standards, but they have a special appeal: the rustic, rural experience. Prices are generally very reasonable. A car is vital for a successful farmhouse stay. The **Farm Holiday Bureau** (✉ National Agricultural Centre, Stoneleigh Park, Kenilworth, Warwickshire CV8 2LZ, ☎ 01203/696909), a network of farming and country people who offer B&B accommodation, is a good source for regional tourist board inspected and approved properties. These properties are listed in the "Stay on a Farm" guide, produced by the Bureau.

HISTORIC BUILDINGS

To spend your vacation in a Gothic temple, an old lighthouse on an isolated island, or maybe in an apartment at Hampton Court Palace, contact one of the half dozen organizations in Great Britain that have specially adapted, modernized historic buildings to rent. A leading char-

Great Britain

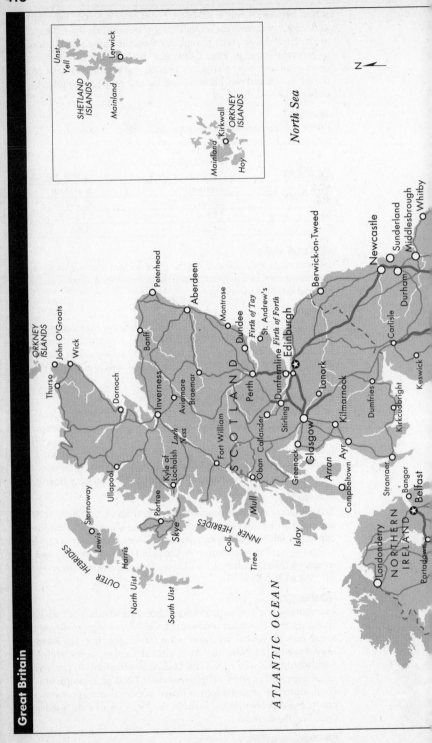

ORKNEY
ISLANDS

SHETLAND
ISLANDS

Unst
Yell
Lerwick
Mainland

Mainland
Kirkwall
ORKNEY
ISLANDS
Hoy

North Sea

N

Peterhead
Aberdeen
Montrose
Banff
Dundee
Firth of Tay
St. Andrew's
Firth of Forth
Inverness
Aviemore
Braemar
Perth
Dunfermline
Edinburgh
Berwick-on-Tweed
Newcastle
Sunderland
Middlesbrough
Whitby
Durham
Carlisle
Keswick

John O'Groats
Wick
ORKNEY
ISLANDS
Thurso
Dornoch
Loch
Ness
Fort William
SCOTLAND
Stirling
Glasgow
Lanark
Kilmarnock
Dumfries
Kirkcudbright

Kyle of
Lochalsh
Oban
Callander
Greenock
Ayr
Arran
Campbeltown
Stranraer
Bangor
Belfast

Portree
Skye
INNER HEBRIDES
Mull
Coll
Islay
NORTHERN
IRELAND
Portadown

Stornoway
Lewis
Harris
OUTER HEBRIDES
Ullapool
Tiree
Londonderry

North Uist
South Uist

ATLANTIC OCEAN

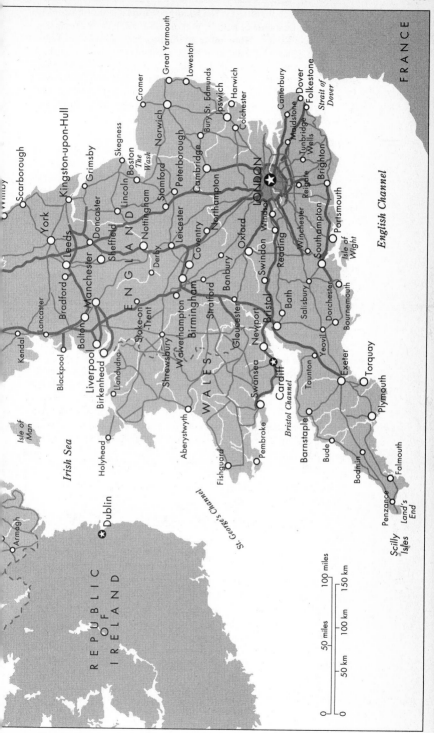

ity that rents such buildings is **The Landmark Trust** (⊠ Shottesbrooke, Maidenhead, Berkshire SL6 3SW, ☎ 01628/825925); these properties do not have TVs. The **National Trust** (⊠ Box 536, Melksham, Wiltshire SN12 8SX, ☎ 01225/705676) is another heritage charity that rents historic buildings. A noted source of such rentals is **Portmeirion Cottages** (⊠ Hotel Portmeirion, Gwynedd, Wales LL48 6ET, ☎ 01766/770228). The rather upscale **Rural Retreats** (⊠ Retreat House, Station Rd., Blockley, Moreton-in-Marsh, Gloucestershire GL56 9DZ, ☎ 01386/701177) has a number of these properties.

HOLIDAY COTTAGES

Furnished apartments, houses, cottages, and trailers are available for weekly rental in all areas of the country. These vary from quaint, cleverly converted farmhouses to brand-new buildings set in scenic surroundings. The British Tourist Authority booklet, "Self Catering Holiday Homes," is available from the BTA office in New York. Lists of rental properties are available free of charge from local Tourist Information Centres in Britain. Discounts of up to 50% apply during the off-season (October through March).

HOTELS

British hotels vary greatly, and there is no reliable official system of classification. Most have rooms with private bathrooms, although there are still many—usually older hotels—that offer some rooms with only washbasins; in this case, showers and bathtubs (and toilets) are usually just down the hall. Many also have "good" and "bad" wings. Be sure to check the room before you take it. Generally, British hotel prices include breakfast, but beware: Many offer only a Continental breakfast—often little more than tea and toast. A hotel that includes a traditional British breakfast in its rates is usually a good bet. Hotel prices in London can be significantly higher than in the rest of the country, and sometimes the quality does not reflect the extra cost. Tourist information centers all over the country will reserve rooms for you, usually for a small fee. A great many hotels offer special weekend and off-season bargain packages.

RATINGS

Prices are for two people in a double room and include all taxes.

CATEGORY	LONDON AND SOUTHERN ENGLAND	OTHER AREAS
$$$$	over £180	over £110
$$$	£120–£180	£60–£110
$$	£70–£120	£50–£60
$	under £70	under £50

UNIVERSITY HOUSING

In larger cities and in some towns, certain universities offer their residence halls to paying vacationers. The facilities available are usually compact sleeping units, and they can be rented on a nightly basis. For information contact the **British Universities Accommodation Consortium** (⊠ Box 1498, University Park, Nottingham NG7 2RD, ☎ 01159/504571).

YOUTH HOSTELS

The more than 350 youth hostels throughout England, Wales, and Scotland range from very basic to very good. Many are in remote and beautiful areas; others are on the outskirts of large cities. Despite the name, there is no age restriction. The accommodations are inexpensive and generally reliable and usually include cooking facilities. For additional information contact the **YHA Headquarters** (⊠ Trevelyan House, 8 St. Stephen's Hill, St. Albans, Hertfordshire AL1 2DY, ☎ 01727/845047).

Mail

POSTAL RATES

Airmail letters to the United States and Canada cost 43p for 10 grams; postcards, 37p; aerograms, 36p. Letters and postcards to Europe weighing up to 20 grams cost 30p. Letters within the United Kingdom: first-class, 26p; second-class and postcards, 20p. These rates are current at press time.

RECEIVING MAIL

If you're uncertain where you'll be staying, you can arrange to have your mail sent to American Express (⊠ 6 Haymarket, London SW1Y 4BS). The service is free to cardholders and AmEx travelers' check holders; all others pay a small fee. You can also collect letters at London's Main Post Office. Ask to have them addressed as the recipient's name appears on their passport, to "Poste Restante" or "To Be Called For" and mailed to the Main Post Office, Trafalgar Square, 24–28 William IV Street, London WC2N 4DL. For collection, hours are Monday–Friday 8 AM–9 PM, Saturday 9 AM–8 PM. You'll need your passport or other official form of identification. This service can be arranged at post offices throughout Britain.

Money Matters

COSTS

In general, transportation in Britain is expensive in comparison to other countries. You would be well advised to take advantage of the many reductions and special fares available on trains, buses, and subways. Always ask about these when buying your ticket.

London now ranks with Tokyo as one of the world's most expensive hotel capitals. Finding budget accommodations—especially during July and August—can be difficult; you should try to book well ahead if you are visiting during these months. Many London hotels offer special off-season (October–March) rates, however. Dining out at top-of-the-line restaurants can be prohibitively expensive, but there are new chains of French-Italian–style café-brasseries, along with a large number of pubs and ethnic restaurants that offer excellent food at reasonable prices. Fast-food facilities of every nationality are widespread.

Remember that the gulf between prices in the capital and outside is wide. Be prepared to pay a value-added tax (VAT) of 17½% on almost everything you buy; in nearly all cases it is included in the advertised price.

CURRENCY

The British unit of currency is the pound sterling, divided into 100 pence (p). Bills are issued in denominations of 5, 10, 20, and 50 pounds (£). Coins are £2, £1, 50p, 20p, 10p, 5p, 2p, and 1p; the 10p and 5p are the size of a quarter and a dime, respectively. Scottish banks issue Scottish currency, of which all coins and notes—with the exception of the £1 notes—are accepted in England. At press time (summer 1999) the pound stood at approximately £.64 to the U.S dollar, £.43 to the Canadian dollar, £.42 to the Australian dollar, and £.34 to the New Zealand dollar.

Traveler's checks are widely accepted in Britain, and many banks, hotels, and shops offer currency-exchange facilities. You will have to pay a £2 commission fee wherever you change them; banks offer the best rates, yet even these fees vary. If you are changing currency, you will have to pay (on top of commission) based on the amount you are changing. In London and other big cities, *bureaux de change* abound, but it definitely pays to shop around: They charge a flat fee and it's often a great deal more than that at other establishments, such as banks.

American Express foreign exchange desks do not charge a commission fee on AmEx traveler's checks. Credit cards are universally accepted, too. The most commonly used are MasterCard and Visa.

SAMPLE PRICES
For London: cup of coffee, £1–£2; pint of beer, £1.80–£2.20; glass of wine, £2–£4; soda, 80p–£1.50; 2-km (1-mi) taxi ride, £3; ham sandwich, £1.75–£3.50.

TIPPING
Some restaurants and most hotels add a service charge of 10%–15% to the bill. If this has been done, you're under no obligation to tip further. If no service charge is indicated, add 10%–15% to your total bill, unless you are totally unhappy with the service given. Taxi drivers should also get 10%–15%, although it's not obligatory. You are not expected to tip theater or cinema ushers, elevator operators, or bartenders in pubs. Hairdressers and barbers should receive 10%–15%.

National Holidays

Parliament isn't the only institution to decide which days are national holidays: Some holidays are actually subject to royal proclamation. England and Wales: New Year's Day (January 3, in lieu of Saturday—there may also be an additional day for millennium celebrations); April 21 and 24 (Good Friday and Easter Monday); May 1 and 29 (May Day—first Monday in May; Spring Holiday—last Monday in May); August 28 (Summer Holiday, last Monday in August); December 25–26 (Christmas Day and Boxing Day).

Opening and Closing Times

Banks. Most banks are open weekdays 9:30–4:30. Some have extended hours on Thursday evening, and a few are open on Saturday morning. **Museums.** Museum hours vary considerably from one part of the country to another. In large cities most are open Tuesday–Saturday 10–5; many are also open on Sunday afternoon. The majority close one day a week. Be sure to double-check the opening times of historic houses, especially if the visit involves a special trip; most stately houses in the countryside are closed November–March. **Shops.** Usual business hours are Monday–Saturday 9–5:30, but many shops are open Sunday. Outside the main centers most shops close at 1 PM once a week, often Wednesday or Thursday. In small villages many also close for lunch. In large cities—especially London—department stores stay open for late-night shopping (usually until 7:30 or 8) one day midweek.

Shopping

SALES-TAX REFUNDS
Foreign visitors from outside Europe can avoid Britain's 17½% value-added tax (VAT) by taking advantage of the following two methods. By the Direct Export method, the shopkeeper arranges the export of the goods and does not charge VAT at the point of sale. This means that the purchases are sent on to your home separately. If you prefer to take your purchase with you, try the Retail Export scheme, run by most large stores: The special Form 407 (provided only by the retailer) is attached to your invoice. You must present the goods, form, and invoice to the customs officer at the last port of departure from the EU. Allow plenty of time to do this at the airport as there are often long lines. The form is then returned to the store and the refund forwarded to you, minus a small service charge. For inquiries call the local Customs & Excise office listed in the telephone directory.

Telephoning

COUNTRY CODE

When you're dialing overseas, the United Kingdom's country code is 44. When dialing a number in Britain from abroad, drop the initial 0 from the local area code.

INTERNATIONAL CALLS

The cheapest way to make an overseas call is to dial it yourself. But be sure to have plenty of coins or phone cards close at hand (newsagents sell budget-rate international phone cards, such as First National and America First, which can be used from any phone by dialing an access number, then pin number). After you have inserted the coins or card, dial 00 (the international code), then the country code—for the United States, it is 1—followed by the area code and local number. To reach an **AT&T** long-distance operator, dial 0500/890011; for **MCI,** dial 0800/890222; and for **Sprint,** dial 0800/890877 (from a British Telecom phone) or 0500/890877 (from a Cable&Wireless phone). To make a collect or other operator-assisted call, dial 155.

LOCAL CALLS

Public telephones are plentiful in British cities, especially London. Other than on the street, the best place to find a bank of pay phones is in a hotel or large post office; pubs and stations usually have a pay phone, too. British Telecom is gradually replacing the distinctive red phone booths with generic glass and steel cubicles, but the traditional boxes still remain in the countryside where the modern versions do not suit the surroundings. The workings of coin-operated telephones vary, but there are usually instructions in each unit. Most take 10p, 20p, 50p, and £1 coins. A phone card is also available; it comes in denominations of 10, 20, 50, and 100 units and can be bought in a number of retail outlets. Card phones, which are clearly marked with a special green insignia, will not accept coins. You can often use your credit card, although this is a more expensive option.

A local call before 6 PM costs 15p for three minutes; this doubles to 30p for the same from a pay phone. A daytime call to the United States will cost 24p a minute on a regular phone (weekends are cheaper); 80p on a pay phone. Each large city or region in Britain has its own numerical prefix, which is used only when you are dialing from outside the city. In provincial areas the dialing codes for nearby towns are often posted in the booth.

NEW LONDON AREA CODES

In order to facilitate expanded telephone access, British Telecom and other British telephone services are in the process of instituting new area codes for all London telephone numbers. The former London area codes of 0171 and 0181 are changing to 0207 and 0208, a procedure beginning June 1999 until the official changeover of April 22, 2000. Until that date London numbers can be accessed with parallel systems using both forms of area codes. Note that the new area codes will impact London's actual telephone numbers—for example, 0171/222–3333 will now become 020/7222-3333. 0800 numbers and national information numbers of 0345 will not change. Portsmouth, Cardiff, and Southampton have also undergone area code changes recently.

OPERATORS AND INFORMATION

For information anywhere in Britain, dial 192. For the operator, dial 100. For assistance with international calls, dial 155.

Transportation

BY BICYCLE

Most towns—including London—offer bike-rental facilities. Any bike shop or tourist information center should be able to direct you to the nearest rental firm. Rental fees can be as little as £5 per day, plus a fairly large deposit, though this can often be put on your credit card. If you're planning a tour and would like information on rental shops and special holidays for cyclists, contact a British Tourist Authority office in the United States before you leave home. In Britain contact the **Cyclists' Touring Club** (⊠ Cotterell House, 69 Meadrow, Godalming, Surrey GU7 3HS, ☎ 01483/417217).

BY BOAT

Britain offers more than 2,430 km (1,500 mi) of navigable inland waterways—rivers, lakes, canals, locks, and loughs—for leisure travel. Particular regions, such as the Norfolk Broads in East Anglia, the Severn Valley in the West Country, and the lochs and canals of Scotland are especially inviting. Although there are no regularly scheduled waterborne services, hundreds of yachts, canal boats, and motor cruises are available throughout the year. The **British Tourist Authority's** free booklet "Inland Waterway Holidays" is a good source of information (available only from offices outside the United Kingdom). The **Inland Waterways Association** (⊠ Box 114, Rickmansworth, Hertfordshire WD3 1ZY, ☎ 01923/711114) is a popular source for maps and guide books. **British Waterways** (⊠ Willow Grange, Church Rd., Watford WD1 3QA, ☎ 01923/226422) can assist with information. For boat-rental operators along Britain's several hundred kilometers of historic canals and waterways, contact the **Association of Pleasure Craft Operators** (⊠ 35A High St., Newport, Shropshire TF10 7AT, ☎ 01952/813572).

BY BUS

Bus prices are invariably half those of train tickets, and the network is just as extensive. There is one important semantic difference to keep in mind when discussing bus travel in Britain. **Buses** (either double- or single-decker) are generally part of the local transportation system in towns and cities and make frequent stops. **Coaches,** on the other hand, are comparable to American Greyhound buses and are used only for long-distance travel.

National Express offers the largest number of routes of any coach operator in Britain. It also offers a variety of discount tickets, including the **Discount Coachcard** and the **Tourist Trail Pass** for overseas visitors. The Discount Coachcard (£8) provides a 20%–30% reduction on journeys made within a year and is only available to students and those under 25 years or over 50. The Tourist Trail Pass offers discounted rates for several ranges of days' travel. Passes can be bought from travel agents in the United States through British Travel International (⊠ Box 299, Elkton, Virginia 22827, ☎ 540/298–2332); in London, at the Victoria Coach Station (⊠ Buckingham Palace Rd., SW1 9TP); or at any of 1,200 National Express agents nationwide. Information about all services can be obtained from the National Express Information Office at Victoria Coach Station (☎ 0990/808080) and in Scotland, from **Scottish Citylink** (⊠ St. Andrew Sq., ☎ 0990/505050) in Edinburgh.

BY CAR

Breakdowns. The Automobile Association (AA; ☎ 0800/887766) runs a 24-hour breakdown service, as does the Royal Automobile Club (☎ 0800/828282). Most motorways have emergency phones along the route that connect the caller to the nearest police station. If you are driving extensively through Britain, membership in the AA (☎

0990/500600) can be useful for many reasons; you can also sign up through car-rental agents.

Gasoline. In Britain gas (called petrol) pumps now measure in liters. Petrol is rarely sold here in gallons; if you do come across gallons, remember that there are 5 American gallons—to 4 British gallons—for that amount, you will get about 20 liters. At press time the price of gasoline was about £2.80 per U.S. gallon, and £2.50 for lead-free. The price generally rises in spring and autumn with government tax rises, and you'll find the cheapest prices at the supermarket pumps. Although you can still buy leaded gas at most stations, the trend is for greener, cleaner lead-free, which is slightly cheaper.

Parking. Parking in London and in other large cities can be a nightmare. On-street meters are hard to find and can be very expensive. Cheaper pay-and-display lots (the driver inserts money into a machine to receive a sticker for the car with the amount of time allowed for parking) are common in smaller towns and suburban areas. But wherever you are, in town or city, beware of yellow or red lines. A single yellow line denotes no parking during the daytime. Double yellow lines or red lines indicate a more extensive prohibition on stopping. The exact times can always be ascertained from nearby signs, usually attached to lampposts. Illegal parking can result in having your vehicle removed or its wheel clamped, which can lead to a great deal of inconvenience as well as a hefty fine. Be sure to check street signs carefully before parking. In central London, where there is a good bus and underground service and taxis are plentiful, the use of a car is not recommended. If you must drive, an indispensable insider's reference book is the *London Parking Guide* (£4.99, Two Heads Publishing), available at good bookstores.

Road Conditions. Britain has superhighways (called motorways) running almost the length of the country, with links connecting them in the South, West, Midlands, and North. Motorways, given the prefix *M* on maps and road signs and shown in blue, have two or three lanes in each direction and are designed for high-speed rather than scenic travel. The main north–south road between London and the north is the M1. Other principal routes are the M3, from southwest London to the south coast and channel port ferries; M4 covers the route from London to Wales via Bristol and is heavily congested by weekenders escaping from the city; M5, running from the Midlands to the deep southwest peninsula; M6, from the Midlands north to Scotland; M11 serves eastward to Cambridge; M20 for southeast to Folkestone ferries and the Eurotunnel; M40 for northwest to Oxford, Stratford, and the Midlands. Encircling London is the M25, which provides access to many of the aforementioned motorways and links into the capital and is, therefore, heavily traveled during work rush hours, with a lull during the day. Be ready for lengthy rush-hour jams and heavy traffic during holiday weekends.

The other primary roads are A roads. Shown on maps as red and green lines, they connect town to town. Some bypass town centers and have fast stretches of divided (two-lane dual carriageway) highway. These are shown as thicker, black-edged lines on maps. Most other routes, yellow B roads, are the early roads once designed for horses and carriages. Although they—and the even narrower, winding white unclassified village roads—will allow you to see much more of the real Britain, your journey could end up taking twice the time. In remote country areas, road travel can be slow, especially in an icy winter. Good planning maps are available from the **AA** (Automobile Association) and the **RAC** (Royal Automobile Club); for in-depth exploring try the Ordnance Survey 1:50,000-series maps. These show every road, track, and footpath in the country. You might also consult the very useful Ordnance Survey *Motoring Atlas,* available at many bookstores.

Rules of the Road. You can use either your driver's license or an International Driving Permit in Britain. Drive on the left-hand side of the road and pay close attention to the varying—and abruptly changing—speed limits. Seat belts are obligatory for front-seat passengers (and back-seat ones when the cars are fitted with them). In general, speed limits are 30 mph in the center of cities and built-up areas, 40 mph in suburban areas, 70 mph on motorways, divided highways, and dual carriageways, and 60 mph on all other roads.

BY PLANE

Britain offers an extensive network of internal air routes, run by about six different airlines. Hourly shuttle services operate every day between London and Glasgow, Edinburgh, Belfast, and Manchester. Seats are available on a no-reservations basis, and you can generally check in about half an hour before flight departure time. Keep in mind, however, that with fast trains and relatively short distances, it is often much cheaper—and not much more time-consuming—to travel by train.

BY TRAIN

Britain's rail system is somewhat overpriced, but it is one of the fastest, safest, and most comfortable rail services in the world. The beloved—and loathed—**British Rail (BR)** has now been broken up into individual private operators. For better or worse, only time will tell. If you need answers on train travel questions before you arrive in Great Britain, the overseas number to dial is ☎ 0161/236–3522. In Great Britain, the number for National Rail Enquiries is ☎ 0345/484950.

The country's principal—and most efficient—service is National Railways (using the old BR InterCity network of tracks and rolling stock), linking London with every major city in the country. The most modern high-speed trains travel up to 140 mph and offer comfortable, fully air-conditioned cars, both first and second class, with restaurant or buffet facilities. Local train services are not quite as reliable, particularly around such congested city centers as London. In general, seat reservations are not necessary except during peak vacation periods and on popular medium- and long-distance routes. Charges for reserving a standard-class seat start from £1, although reservations may be free over some routes.

Fares. Rail fares are high when compared with those in other countries. However, the network does offer a wide, and often bewildering, range of ticket reductions, and these can make a tremendous difference. The information office in each station can help you make the right choice. Information and tickets can also be obtained from Rail Travel Centres within the larger train stations and from selected travel agents displaying the double-arrow old British Rail logo.

One of the best bargains available to overseas visitors is the **BritRail Pass** or the **BritRail Flexi Pass,** the U.K. equivalent of the Eurail ticket. It provides unlimited standard and first-class travel over the entire rail network for periods of 8, 15, or 22 days, or for one month. These passes can be purchased only outside Britain, either in the United States, before you leave, or in one of 46 other countries. British Rail still has an information office in New York City (✉ BritRail Travel International, 1500 Broadway, New York, NY 10036, ☎ 212/575–2542).

If you are planning to travel only short distances, be sure to buy inexpensive **same-day return tickets** ("cheap day returns"). These cost only slightly more than ordinary one-way ("single"), standard-class tickets but can be used *only* after 9:30 AM and on weekends. Other special offers are regional **Rover** tickets, giving unlimited travel within local areas, and **Saver** returns, allowing greatly reduced round-trip travel during off-peak periods. Inquire at main rail stations for details about reduced-price tickets to specific destinations.

Visitor Information

For National Tourist Board addresses and phone numbers, *see* Visitor Information *in* Chapter 1. For regional and city tourist boards, *see* Visitor Information *in* the Essentials directory for the relevant geographic region, *below*.

Weather

CLIMATE

On the whole, Britain's winters are rarely bitter, except in the north and Scotland. Recent summers have been scorchers all over the country. Wherever you are, and whatever the season, be prepared for sudden changes. What begins as a brilliant, sunny day often turns into a damp and dismal one by lunchtime. Take an umbrella and raincoat wherever you go, particularly in Scotland, where the temperatures can be somewhat cooler.

The following are the average daily maximum and minimum temperatures for London.

Jan.	43F	6C	May	62F	17C	Sept.	65F	19C
	36	2		47	8		52	11
Feb.	44F	7C	June	69F	20C	Oct.	58F	14C
	36	2		53	12		46	8
Mar.	50F	10C	July	71F	22C	Nov.	50F	10C
	38	3		56	13		42	6
Apr.	56F	13C	Aug.	71F	22C	Dec.	45F	7C
	42	6		56	13		38	3

LONDON

If London contained only its famous landmarks—Buckingham Palace, Big Ben, Parliament, the Tower of London—it would still rank as one of the world's great destinations. It is a vast city of living history, whose story is still emerging in big events, like the death of Princess Diana in 1997, and small, like the opening of what seems like the millionth new restaurant. A city that loves to be explored, London beckons with great museums, royal pageantry, and history-steeped houses. Marvel at the Duke of Wellington's house, track Jack the Ripper's shadow in Whitechapel, then get Beatle-ized at Abbey Road. East End, West End, you'll find London is a dickens of a place.

Exploring London

Traditionally London has been divided between the City, to the east, where its banking and commercial interests lie, and Westminster, to the west, the seat of the royal court and of government. It is in these two areas that you will find most of the grand buildings that have played a central role in British history: the Tower of London and St. Paul's Cathedral, Westminster Abbey and the Houses of Parliament, Buckingham Palace, and the older royal palace of St. James's.

Visitors who restrict their sightseeing to the well-known tourist areas miss much of the best the city has to offer. Within a few minutes' walk of Buckingham Palace, for instance, lie St. James's and Mayfair, two neighboring quarters of elegant town houses built for the nobility during the 17th and early 18th centuries and now notable for the shopping opportunities they house. The same lesson applies to the City, where, tucked away in quiet corners, stand many of the churches Christopher Wren built to replace those destroyed during the Great Fire of 1666.

Other parts of London worth exploring include Covent Garden, a former fruit and flower market converted into a lively shopping and entertainment center where you can wander for hours enjoying the friendly bustle of the streets. Hyde Park and Kensington Gardens, by contrast, offer a great swath of green parkland across the city center, preserved by past kings and queens for their own hunting and relaxation. A walk across Hyde Park will bring you to the museum district of South Kensington, with three major national collections: the Natural History Museum, the Science Museum, and the Victoria & Albert Museum, which specializes in the fine and applied arts.

The south side of the River Thames has its treats as well. A short stroll across Waterloo Bridge brings you to the South Bank Arts Complex, which includes the National Theatre, the Royal Festival Hall, the Hayward Gallery (with changing exhibitions of international art), the National Film Theatre, and the Museum of the Moving Image (MOMI)—a must for movie buffs. Here also are the exciting reconstruction of Shakespeare's Globe theater and its sister museum; and the future home, at Bankside Power Station, of the Tate Gallery of Modern Art—due for completion for the millennium. The views from the South Bank are stunning—to the west are the Houses of Parliament and Big Ben; to the east the dome of St. Paul's is just visible on London's changing skyline. London, although not simple of layout, is a rewarding walking city, and this remains the best way to get to know its nooks and crannies. The infamous weather may not be on your side, but there's plenty of indoor entertainment to keep you amused if you forget the umbrella!

Westminster

Numbers in the margin correspond to points of interest on the London map.

Westminster is the royal backyard—the traditional center of the royal court and of government. Here, within 1 km (½ mi) or so of one another, are nearly all of London's most celebrated buildings, and there is a strong feeling of history all around you. Generations of kings and queens have lived here since the end of the 11th century—including the current monarch. The Queen resides at Buckingham Palace through most of the year; during summer periods when she visits her country estates, the palace is partially open to visitors.

❼ Banqueting House. On the right side of the grand processional avenue known as Whitehall—site of many important government offices—stands this famous monument of the English Renaissance period. Designed by Inigo Jones in 1625 for court entertainments, it is the only part of Whitehall Palace, the monarch's principal residence during the 16th and 17th centuries, that was not burned down in 1698. It has a magnificent ceiling by Rubens, and outside is an inscription that marks the window through which King Charles I stepped to his execution. ⊠ *Whitehall,* ☎ *020/7930–4179.* ⊘ *Tues.–Sat. 10–5, Sun. 2–5.*

❽ Buckingham Palace. Supreme among the symbols of London, indeed of Britain generally, and of the royal family, Buckingham Palace tops many must-see lists—although the building itself is no masterpiece and has housed the monarch only since Victoria moved here from Kensington Palace at her accession in 1837. Located at the end of the Mall, the palace is the London home of the Queen and the administrative hub of the entire royal family. When the Queen is in residence (normally on weekdays except in January, August, September, and part of June), the royal standard flies over the east front. Inside are dozens of ornate 19th-century-style state rooms used on formal occasions. The private apartments of Queen Elizabeth and Prince Philip are in the north wing. Parts of Buckingham Palace are now open to the public during August and September; during the entire year, the former chapel, bombed during World War II, rebuilt in 1961, is the site of the **Queen's Gallery** (☞ *below*), which shows treasures from the vast royal art collections. The ceremony of the **Changing of the Guard** takes place in front of the palace at 11:30 daily, April through July, and on alternate days during the rest of the year. It's advisable to arrive early, as people are invariably stacked several deep along the railings, whatever the weather. ⊠ *Buckingham Palace Rd.,* ☎ *020/7839–1377; 020/7321–2233 credit-card pre-booking reservations line (AE, MC, V).* ✉ *£9.* ☉ *Early Aug.–early Oct. (confirm specific dates, which are subject to the Queen's mandate), 9:30–4:15.*

⑫ Cabinet War Rooms. It was from this small maze of 17 bomb-proof underground rooms—located in back of the hulking Foreign Office—that Britain's World War II fortunes were directed. During air raids the Cabinet met here—the Cabinet Room is still arranged as if a meeting were about to convene. Among the rooms are the Prime Minister's Room, from which Winston Churchill made many of his inspiring wartime broadcasts, and the Transatlantic Telephone Room, from which he spoke directly to President Roosevelt in the White House. ⊠ *Clive Steps, King Charles St.,* ☎ *020/7930–6961.* ☉ *Daily 10–5:15.*

❻ Carlton House Terrace. This architectural showpiece of the Mall (☞ *below*) is a Regency-era masterpiece, built in 1827–32 by John Nash in imposing white stucco and with massive Corinthian columns. It is home to the Institute of Contemporary Arts.

⑱ Horse Guards Parade. The former tiltyard of Whitehall Palace is the site of the annual ceremony of Trooping the Colour, when the Queen takes the salute in the great military parade that marks her official birthday on the second Saturday in June (her real one is on April 21). Demand for tickets is great, but happily there are Queenless rehearsals on the previous two Saturdays, the later one presided over by Prince Charles; for information, call 020/7414–2497. There is also a daily guard-changing ceremony outside the guard house, on Whitehall, at 11 AM (10 on Sunday)—one of London's best photo-ops. ⊠ *Whitehall, opposite Downing St.*

⑮ Houses of Parliament. The Houses of Parliament are among the city's most famous and photogenic sights. The Clock Tower keeps watch on Parliament Square, in which stand statues of everyone from Richard the Lionhearted to Abraham Lincoln, and, across the way, Westminster Abbey. Also known as the **Palace of Westminster,** this was the site of the monarch's main residence from the 11th century until 1512; the court then moved to the newly built Whitehall Palace. The only parts of the original building to have survived are the Jewel Tower and **Westminster Hall,** which has a fine hammer-beam roof. The rest of the structure was destroyed in a disastrous fire in 1834 and was rebuilt in the newly popular mock-medieval Gothic style to the delight of millions. The architect, Augustus Pugin, designed the entire place, right down to the Gothic umbrella stands. This newer part of the palace con-

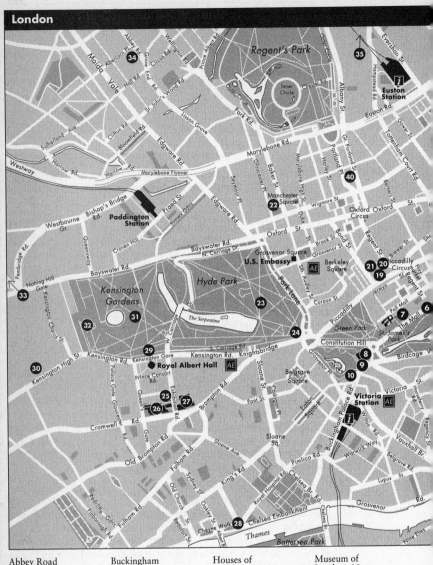

Abbey Road Studios, **34**	Buckingham Palace, **8**	Houses of Parliament, **15**	Museum of London, **44**
Albert Memorial, **29**	Burlington Arcade, **20**	Hyde Park, **23**	Museum of Mankind, **21**
Apsley House, **24**	Cabinet War Rooms, **12**	Kensington Gardens, **31**	National Gallery, **2**
Banqueting House, **17**	Carlton House Terrace, **6**	Kensington Palace, **32**	National Portrait Gallery, **3**
Barbican Centre, **45**	Cheyne Walk, **28**	Kenwood House, **35**	Natural History Museum, **26**
BBC Experience, **40**	Covent Garden, **36**	Linley Sambourne House, **30**	Parliament Square, **14**
British Museum, **41**	Horse Guards Parade, **18**	The Mall, **5**	Portobello Road, **33**
			Queen's Gallery, **9**

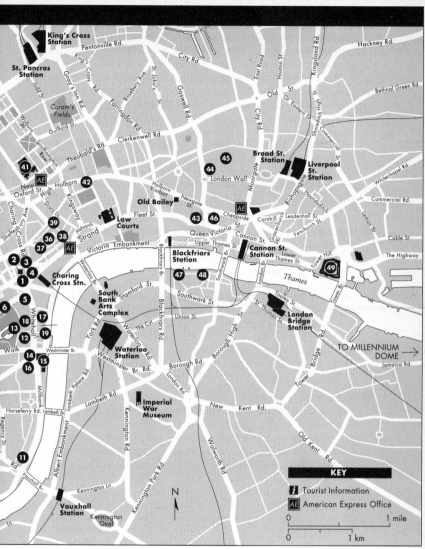

tains the debating chambers and committee rooms of the two Houses of Parliament—the Commons (whose members are elected) and the Lords (whose members are appointed or inherit their seats). There are no tours of the palace, but the public is admitted to the Public Gallery of each House; expect to wait in line for several hours (the line for the Lords is generally much shorter than that for the Commons). The most famous features of the palace are its towers. At the south end is the 336-ft **Victoria Tower.** At the other end is **St. Stephen's Tower,** or the Clock Tower, better known, but inaccurately so, as **Big Ben;** that name properly belongs to the 13-ton bell in the tower on which the hours are struck. Big Ben himself was probably Sir Benjamin Hall, commissioner of works when the bell was installed in the 1850s. A light shines from the top of the tower during a night sitting of Parliament. Come early, as lines are long. ⊠ *St. Stephen's Entrance, St. Margaret St., SW1,* ☎ *020/7219–3000.* ☑ *Free.* ☉ *Commons: Mon.–Thurs. 2:30–10, Fri. 9:30–3; Lords: Mon.–Thurs. 2:30–10. Closed Dec. 22–Jan 20.*

❺ **The Mall.** The splendid and imperial **Admiralty Arch** guards the entrance to The Mall, the noted ceremonial way that leads alongside **St. James's Park** to Buckingham Palace. The Mall takes its name from a game called *palle maille,* a version of croquet that James I imported from France, and Charles II popularized during the late 1600s. The park was developed by successive monarchs, most recently by George IV in the 1820s, having originally been used for hunting by Henry VIII. Join office workers relaxing with a lunchtime sandwich, or stroll here on a summer's evening when the illuminated fountains play and Westminster Abbey and the Houses of Parliament are floodlit. Toward Buckingham Palace, along The Mall, you'll pass the foot of the imposing **Carlton House Terrace** (☞ *above*).

★ ❷ **National Gallery.** Generally ranked right after the Louvre, the National Gallery is one of the world's greatest museums. Occupying the long neoclassical building on the north side of Trafalgar Square (☞ *below*), it contains works by virtually every famous artist and school from the 14th to the 19th centuries. Its galleries overflow with masterpieces, including Jan van Eyck's *Arnolfini Marriage,* Leonardo da Vinci's *Burlington Virgin and Child,* Velásquez's *The Toilet of Venus* (known as "The Rokeby Venus"), and Constable's *Hay Wain.* The gallery is especially strong on Flemish and Dutch masters, Rubens and Rembrandt among them, and on Italian Renaissance works. The museum's Brasserie is an excellent spot for lunch. ⊠ *Trafalgar Sq.,* ☎ *020/7747–2885.* ☑ *Free; admission charge for special exhibitions.* ☉ *Mon.–Sat. 10–6, Sun. 2–6; June–Aug., also Wed. until 9.*

❸ **National Portrait Gallery.** This fascinating collection contains portraits of well-known (and not-so-well-known) Britons, including monarchs, statesmen, and writers. ⊠ *2 St. Martin's Pl., at foot of Charing Cross Rd.,* ☎ *020/7306–0055.* ☑ *Free.* ☉ *Weekdays 10–5, Sat. 10–6, Sun. 2–6.*

❾ **Queen's Gallery.** This is the former chapel at the south side of Buckingham Palace (☞ *above*). On display here are smaller shows drawn from the royal collections, such as Michelangelo drawings; call for information on current exhibits. After October 10, 1999, the gallery is closing for renovation and will not reopen until 2002. ⊠ *Buckingham Palace Rd.,* ☎ *020/7799–2331.* ☑ *Combined ticket for Queen's Gallery and Royal Mews £6.70.* ☉ *Tues.–Sat. 10–5, Sun. 2–5.*

❿ **Royal Mews.** Unmissable children's entertainment, this museum is the home of Her Majesty's Coronation Coach. Here, some of the queen's horses are stabled and the elaborately gilded state coaches are on view.

⌂ *Buckingham Palace Rd.,* ☎ *020/7799–2331.* ▭ *Combined ticket with Queen's Gallery £6.70.* ☉ *Aug. 2–Sept. 30, Mon.–Thurs. 10:30–4:30; Oct. 1–Aug. 1 Mon.–Thurs. 12–4.*

❹ St. Martin-in-the-Fields. Soaring above Trafalgar Square, this landmark church may seem familiar to many Americans because James Gibbs's classical-temple-with-spire design became a pattern for churches in early Colonial America. Built in about 1730, the distinctive neoclassical church is the site for regular lunchtime music recitals. ⌂ *Trafalgar Sq.,* ☎ *020/7930–0089; 020/7839–8362 credit-card bookings for evening concerts.* ☉ *Church: daily 8–8; crypt: Mon.–Sat. 10–8, Sun. noon–6.*

⓫ Tate Gallery. By the river to the north of Chelsea, on traffic-laden Millbank, the Tate Gallery of Modern British Art is the greatest museum devoted to British painting and sculpture. "Modern" is slightly misleading, as one of the three collections here consists of British art from 1545 to the present, including works by William Hogarth, Thomas Gainsborough, Sir Joshua Reynolds, and George Stubbs from the 18th century; and by John Constable, William Blake, and the Pre-Raphaelite painters from the 19th century (don't miss Sir John Everett Millais's unforgettable *Ophelia*). Also from the 19th century is the second of the Tate's collections, the incredible Turner Bequest, consisting of the personal collection of England's greatest romantic painter, J. M. W. Turner. About a 20-minute walk south of the Houses of Parliament, the main Tate is also accessible if you tube it to the Pimlico stop, then take a five-minute walk through Chelsea to the museum. Also see the new Tate Gallery of Modern Art, Bankside, *in* The City and South Bank, *below.*⌂ *Millbank, SW1,* ☎ *020/7821–1313 or 020/7821–7128.* ▭ *Free; special exhibitions £3–£7.* ☉ *Daily 10–5:50. Tube: Pimlico.*

⓭ Ten Downing Street. As you walk along Whitehall, past government offices, you'll note, on the north side of the street, the entrance to Downing Street, a row of unassuming 18th-century houses. The official prime minister's office is at No. 10, with a private apartment on the top floor (although Tony Blair and his family don't use this as their main address). The chancellor of the exchequer, the finance minister, occupies No. 11. The street is now gated off from the main thoroughfare. Not far away in the middle of Whitehall is the **Cenotaph,** a stone national memorial to the dead of both world wars. At 11 AM on the Sunday closest to the 11th day of the 11th month, the Queen and other dignitaries lay flowers in tribute here.

❶ Trafalgar Square. This is the center of London, by dint of a plaque on the corner of the Strand and Charing Cross Road from which distances on U.K. signposts are measured. It is the home of the **National Gallery** (☞ *above*) and of one of London's most distinctive landmarks, **Nelson's Column,** a tribute to one of England's favorite heroes, Admiral Lord Horatio Nelson, who routed the French at the Battle of Trafalgar in 1805. Permanently alive with Londoners and tourists alike, roaring traffic, and pigeons, it remains London's "living room"— great events, such as New Year's, royal weddings, elections, and sporting triumphs will always see the crowds gathering in the city's most famous square.

★ **⓰ Westminster Abbey.** This is the most ancient of London's great churches and the most important, for it is here that Britain's monarchs are crowned. Most of the abbey dates largely from the 13th and 14th centuries. The main nave is packed with atmosphere and memories, as it has witnessed many splendid coronation ceremonies, royal weddings, and more recently, the funeral of Diana, Princess of Wales. It is also packed with crowds—so many, in fact, that the Abbey has now started to charge admission to the main nave (always free, of course, for participants in religious services). **Henry VII's Chapel,** an exquisite example of the heavily decorated late-Gothic style, was not built until the early 1600s, and the twin towers over the west entrance are an 18th-century addition. There is much to see inside, including the tomb of the Unknown Warrior, a nameless World War I soldier buried, in memory of the war's victims, in earth brought with his corpse from France; and the famous Poets' Corner, where England's great writers—Milton, Chaucer, Shakespeare, et al.—are memorialized, and some are actually buried. Behind the high altar are the royal tombs, including those of Queen Elizabeth I; Mary, Queen of Scots; and Henry V. In the Chapel of Edward the Confessor stands the Coronation Chair. Among the royal weddings that have taken place here are those of the present queen and most recently, in 1986, the (ill-starred) duke and duchess of York. It is all too easy to forget, swamped by the crowds trying to see the abbey's sights, that this is a place of worship. Early morning is a good moment to catch something of the building's atmosphere. Better still, take time to attend a service. Note that photography is not permitted except Wednesday 6 PM–8 PM. ⊠ *Broad Sanctuary,* ☎ *020/ 7222–5152.* ⊙ *Mon.—Sat. 9–3:45 (last admission Sat. 1:45). Undercroft, Pyx Chamber, Chapter House, and Treasury: Apr.–Oct., daily 10:30–5:30; Nov.–Mar., daily 10:30–3:45. Closed Sun. except for religious services; Henry VII Chapel closed Sun.*

St. James's and Mayfair

These are two of London's most exclusive neighborhoods, where the homes are fashionable and the shopping is world class. You can start by walking west from Piccadilly Circus along Piccadilly, a busy street lined with some very English shops (including Hatchards, the booksellers; Swaine, Adeney Brigg, the equestrian outfitters; and Fortnum & Mason, the department store that supplies the Queen's groceries).

㉔ Apsley House. Once known, quite simply, as No. 1, London, this was long celebrated as the best address in town. Built by Robert Adam in the 1770s, this was where the Duke of Wellington lived from the 1820s until his death in 1852. It has been kept as the Iron Duke liked it, his uniforms and weapons, his porcelain and plate, and his extensive art collection displayed heroically in opulent 19th-century rooms. Unmissable, in every sense, is the gigantic Canova statue of a nude (but fig-leafed) Napoléon Bonaparte, Wellington's archenemy. ⊠ *149 Piccadilly,* ☎ *020/7499–5676.* ⊙ *Tues.–Sun. 11–5.*

㊵ BBC Experience. To celebrate its 75th anniversary, the BBC has just opened the doors of its own in-house museum. There's an audiovisual show, an interactive section—want to try making your own director's cut of a segment of *EastEnders?*—and, of course, a massive gift shop. Conveniently, admission is on a prebooked and timed system. ⊠ *Broadcasting House, Portland Pl., W1,* ☎ *0870/603–0304, 01222/55771 outside U.K.* ▨ *Free.* ⊙ *Daily 9:30–5:30. Tube: Oxford Circus.*

⑳ Burlington Arcade. This perfectly picturesque covered walkway dates from 1819. Here, shops sell cashmere sweaters, silk scarves, handmade chocolates, and leather-bound books. If not the choice shopping spot it once was, it still makes a great photo-op, particularly if you can snap the uniformed beadle (he ensures that no one runs, whistles, or sings here) on duty. ⊠ *Off Piccadilly.*

㉑ Museum of Mankind. Behind the Royal Academy, this magnificently florid Victorian edifice contains the British Museum's ethnographic collection (though this will soon be transferred to the British Museum when the British Library moves to its new premises in St. Pancras). There are displays on the South Seas, the Arctic, and other regions of the world. ⊠ *6 Burlington Gardens,* ☎ *020/7323–8043.* ⊟ *Free.* ☉ *Mon.–Sat. 10–5, Sun. 2:30–6.*

⑲ Royal Academy of Arts. On the north side of Piccadilly, the grand marble pile of **Burlington House** contains the offices of many learned societies and the headquarters of the Royal Academy. The RA, as it is generally known, stages major visiting art exhibitions. Once most famous for its Summer Exhibition (May–August)—a chaotic hodgepodge of works by living and mostly conservative British artists—the RA has now adopted an impressive schedule of temporary art exhibitions that ranks among the most prestigious and cutting-edge in the country; inquire about current calendar of events. ⊠ *Burlington House,* ☎ *020/ 7439–7438; 020/7439–4996 recorded information.* ⊟ *Admission varies according to exhibition.* ☉ *Sat.–Thurs. 10–6, Fri. 10–8:30.*

❼ St. James's Palace. This historic abode has for centuries been a useful royal address and, today, it still is, as it is the current residence of the future King Charles III (if the current Prince of Wales makes it to Westminster Abbey). Although the earliest parts of the lovely brick building date from the 1530s, it had a relatively short career as the center of royal affairs—from the destruction of Whitehall Palace in 1698 until 1837, when Victoria became queen and moved the royal household down the road to Buckingham Palace. Today, the Palace is closed to the public, but your viewfinder will love the picturesque exterior and regimental guard on duty. ⊠ *Friary Court, Pall Mall.*

㉒ Wallace Collection. A palatial town-house museum, the Wallace is important, exciting, undervisited—and free. As at the Frick Collection in New York, the setting here, Hertford House, is part of the show—built for the Duke of Manchester, and now stuffed with armor, exquisite furniture, and great paintings, including Bouchers, Watteaus, and Fragonard's *The Swing.* Don't forget to smile back at Frans Hals's *Laughing Cavalier* in the Big Gallery. ⊠ *Hertford House, Manchester Sq.,* ☎ *020/ 7935–0687.* ⊟ *Free.* ☉ *Mon.–Sat. 10–5, Sun. 2–5.*

Hyde Park, Kensington, and Beyond

When in need of elbow room, Londoners head for their green "lungs"— Hyde Park and Kensington Gardens. Viewed by natives as their own private backyards, they form an open swath across central London. In and around them are some of London's most noted museums and monuments.

㉙ Albert Memorial. Magnificently restored in 1998 to its original gilded glory, this florid monument of the 19th century commemorates Queen Victoria's much-loved husband, Prince Albert, who died in 1861 at the age of 42. The monument, itself the epitome of high Victorian taste, commemorates the many socially uplifting projects of the prince, among them the Great Exhibition of 1851, whose catalog he is holding. The memorial is directly opposite the Royal Albert Hall. ⊠ *Kensington Gore.*

㉘ Cheyne Walk. The most beautiful spot in Chelsea—one of London's most arty (and expensive) residential districts—this Thamesside street is adorned with Queen Anne houses and legendary addresses. Author George Eliot died at No. 4 in 1880; Pre-Raphaelite artist Dante Gabriel Rossetti lived at No. 16. Two other resident artists were James McNeill Whistler and J. M. W. Turner.

㉓ Hyde Park. Along with the smaller St. James's and Green Parks to the east, Hyde Park started as Henry VIII's hunting grounds. Nowadays, it remains a tranquil oasis from urban London—-tranquil, that is, except for Sunday morning, when the soapbox orators take over **Speakers' Corner,** near the northeast corner of the park. Not far away, along the south side of the park, is **Rotten Row.** It was Henry VIII's royal path to the hunt—hence the name, a corruption of *route du roi.* It's still used by the Household Cavalry, the queen's guard. You can see them leave, in full regalia, plumed helmets and all, at around 10:30, or await the return of the exhausted ex-guard about noon. ⊠ *Bounded by the Ring, Bayswater Rd., Park La., and Knightsbridge.*

③① Kensington Gardens. More formal than neighboring Hyde Park, Kensington Gardens was first laid out as palace grounds and adjoins Kensington Palace (☞ *below*). George Frampton's 1912 **Peter Pan,** a bronze of the boy who lived on an island in the Serpentine and never grew up, overlooks the Long Water. His creator, J. M. Barrie, lived at 100 Bayswater Road, not 500 yards from here. At the **Round Pond,** you can feed the swans. Nearby is boating and swimming in the **Serpentine,** an S-shape lake. Refreshments can be had at the lakeside tearooms. The **Serpentine Gallery** (☎ 020/7402–6075) holds noteworthy exhibitions of modern art. ⊠ *Bounded by The Broad Walk, Bayswater Rd., the Ring, and Kensington Rd.*

③② Kensington Palace. This has been a royal home since the late 17th century. From the outside it looks less like a palace than a country house, which it was until William III bought it in 1689. Queen Victoria spent a less-than-happy childhood at Kensington Palace, Princess Diana a less-than-happy marriage. Called the "royal ghetto," the palace is home to many Windsors (they live in a distant section cordoned off to the public). Kensington Palace's state apartments have been restored to how they were in Princess Victoria's day. Drop in on the Orangery here for a very elegant cup of tea. ⊠ *Kensington Gardens,* ☎ *020/7937–9561.* ⊙ *May–Dec., daily 10–3:30.*

③⓪ Linley Sambourne House. Stuffed with Victorian and Edwardian antiques, fabrics, and paintings, this is one of the most charming 19th-century London houses extant—little wonder it was filmed for Merchant/Ivory's *A Room with A View.* During the 1870s this was home to the political cartoonist Edward Linley Sambourne. ⊠ *18 Stafford Terr.,* ☎ *020/8994–1019.* ⊙ *Mar.–Oct., Wed. 10–4, Sun. 2–5.*

②⑥ Natural History Museum. Housed in an ornate late-Victorian building with striking modern additions, this museum features displays on such topics as human biology and evolution, designed to challenge visitors to think for themselves. ⊠ *Cromwell Rd.,* ☎ *020/7938–9123; 0142/692–7654 recorded information.* ▣ *Free weekdays 4:30–5:50 and weekends 5–5:50.* ⊙ *Mon.–Sat. 10–6, Sun. 2:30–6.*

③③ Portobello Road. North of Kensington Gardens is the lively **Notting Hill** district, full of restaurants and cafés where some of London's most stylish, trend-setting people gather. The best-known attraction in this area is Portobello Road, where the lively antiques and bric-a-brac market is held each Saturday (arrive at 6 AM for the best finds); the southern end is focused on antiques, the northern end on food, flowers, and secondhand clothes. The street is also full of regular antiques shops that are open most weekdays. ⊠ *Pembridge Rd., Notting Hill Gate.* ⊙ *Antiques market Sat. 6–4.*

②⑤ Science Museum. The leading national collection of science and technology, this museum has extensive hands-on exhibits on outer space, astronomy, and hundreds of other subjects. ⊠ *Exhibition Rd.,* ☎ *020/7938–8000.* ⊙ *Mon.–Sat. 10–6, Sun. 11–6.*

★ ㉗ **Victoria & Albert Museum.** The V&A, as it is commonly known, originated during the 19th century as a museum of the decorative arts and has extensive collections of costumes, paintings, jewelry, and crafts from every part of the globe. Don't miss the sculpture court, the vintage couture collections, and the great Raphael Room. ⊠ *Cromwell Rd.,* ☎ *020/7938–8500.* 🖭 *Free after 4:30, except Wed.* ☉ *Mon. noon–5:50, Tues.–Sun. 10–5:50; Wed. Late View 4:30–9:30.*

Covent Garden

The Covent Garden district—which lies just to the east of Soho—has gone from a down-at-heels area to one of the busiest, most raffishly enjoyable parts of the city. Continental-style open-air cafés create a very un-English atmosphere, with vintage fashion boutiques, art galleries, and street buskers attracting crowds.

㊱ **Covent Garden.** You could easily spend several hours exploring the block of streets north of the Strand known as Covent Garden. The heart of the area is a former wholesale fruit and vegetable market—made famous as one of Eliza Doolittle's haunts in *My Fair Lady*—established in 1656. **The Piazza,** the Victorian Market Building, is now a vibrant shopping center, with numerous boutiques, crafts shops, and cafés. On the south side of the market building is the **Jubilee market,** with crafts and clothing stalls. The section is anchored by **St. Paul's Church** (☞ *below*) and the **Royal Opera House** (now undergoing extensive renovations; ☞ *below*). For interesting specialty shops, head north of the Market Building. Shops on **Long Acre** sell maps, art books and materials, and clothing; shops on **Neal Street** sell clothes, pottery, jewelry, tea, housewares, and goods from East Asia. ⊠ *Bounded by the Strand, Charing Cross Rd., Long Acre, and Drury La.*

㊴ **Royal Opera House.** After years of mammoth renovations, this historic theater is set to reopen in December 1999. Until then, the legendary resident troupes of the Royal Ballet and the Royal Opera Company will be performing elsewhere (☞ Nightlife and the Arts, *below*). ⊠ *Bow St.*

㊲ **St. Paul's Church.** A landmark of the Covent Garden market area, this 1633 church, designed by Inigo Jones, is known as the Actors' Church. Inside are numerous memorials to theater people. Look for the open-air entertainers performing under the church's portico. ⊠ *Bedford St.*

㊳ **Theatre Museum.** A comprehensive collection of material on the history of the English theater, this museum traces the history not merely of the classic drama but also of opera, music hall, pantomime, and musical comedy. A highlight is the re-creation of a dressing room filled with memorabilia of former stars. ⊠ *Russell St.,* ☎ *020/7836–7891.* ☉ *Tues.–Sun. 11–7.*

Bloomsbury

Bloomsbury is a semiresidential district to the north of Covent Garden that contains some spacious and elegant 17th- and 18th-century squares. It could be called the intellectual center of London, as both the British Museum and the University of London are here. The area also gave its name to the Bloomsbury Group, a clique of writers and painters who thrived here during the early 20th century.

★ ㊶ **British Museum.** Known as "Mankind's attic," this fabled museum houses a vast and priceless collection of treasures, including Egyptian, Greek, and Roman antiquities; Renaissance jewelry; pottery; coins; glass; and drawings from virtually every European school since the 15th century. It's best to pick out one section that particularly interests you—to try to see everything would be an overwhelming and exhausting task.

Some of the highlights are the **Elgin Marbles,** sculptures that formerly decorated the Parthenon in Athens; the **Rosetta Stone,** which helped archaeologists to interpret Egyptian hieroglyphs; a copy of the **Magna Carta,** the charter signed by King John in 1215 to which is ascribed the origins of English liberty; and the recently restored Reading Room. Changing the face of the museum just in time for the millennium, a vast, modern Great Court entrance, with new galleries and interactive attractions, is scheduled to open in Autumn 2000. ☒ *Great Russell St.,* ☎ *020/7636–1555; 020/7580–1788 recorded information.* ☒ *Free (donation suggested).* ☉ *Mon.–Sat. 10–5, Sun. 2:30–6.*

★ ❷ **Sir John Soane's Museum.** On the border of London's legal district, this museum, stuffed with antique busts and myriad decorative delights, is an eccentric, smile-inducing 19th-century collection of art and artifacts in the former home of the architect of the Bank of England. ☒ *13 Lincoln's Inn Fields,* ☎ *020/7405–2107.* ☒ *Free.* ☉ *Tues.–Sat. 10–5; until 9 on the first Tues. of month.*

The City and South Bank

The City, the commercial center of London, was actually once the site of the great Roman city of Londinium. Since those days, the City has been rebuilt innumerable times and, today, ancient and modern jostle each other elbow to elbow. Several of London's most famous attractions are here, along with the adjacent area across the Thames commonly called the South Bank. Here, Shakespeare's Globe Theatre, the new Tate Museum of Modern Art, and the astonishing British Airways London Eye—the world's largest Ferris wheel—are drawing both natives and visitors in droves. That old London dig about needing a passport to cross the river is no longer heard.

❹ **Barbican Centre.** A vast arts center built by the City of London, the Barbican takes its name from the watchtower that stood here during the Middle Ages. The arts center contains a concert hall, where the London Symphony Orchestra is based, two theaters, an art gallery, a cinema, and several restaurants. The theaters are the London home of the **Royal Shakespeare Company.** ☒ *Silk St.,* ☎ *020/7638–8891; 020/7628–3351 RSC backstage tour.* ☒ *Barbican Centre free.* ☉ *Barbican Centre: Mon.–Sat. 9 AM–11 PM, Sun. noon–11; gallery: Mon.–Sat. 10–7:30, Sun. noon–7:30; conservatory: weekends noon–5:30.*

❹ **Museum of London.** At **London Wall,** so called because it follows the line of the wall that surrounded the Roman settlement, the Museum of London enables you to get the history of London sorted out—although there's a great deal to sort out: Oliver Cromwell's death mask, Queen Victoria's crinolined gowns, Selfridge's Art Deco elevators, and the Lord Mayor's Coach are just some of the goodies here. ☒ *London Wall, EC2,* ☎ *020/7600–0807.* ☒ *Free 4:30–5:50.* ☉ *Mon.–Sat. 10–5:50, Sun. noon–5:50.*

❹ **St. Mary-le-Bow.** This church was rebuilt by Christopher Wren after the Great Fire; it was built again after being bombed during World War II. It is said that to be a true Cockney, you must be born within the sound of Bow bells. The church is a landmark of the **Cheapside** district. This was the marketplace of medieval London (the word *ceap* is Old English for "to barter"), as the street names hereabouts indicate: Milk Street, Ironmonger Lane, and so on. Despite rebuilding, many of the streets still run on the medieval pattern. ☒ *Cheapside.*

★ ❸ **St. Paul's Cathedral.** London's symbolic heart, St. Paul's is Sir Christopher Wren's masterpiece. Its dome—the world's third largest—can be seen from many an angle in other parts of the city. The cathedral was completed in 1710 following the Great Fire. Wren was the architect who was also responsible for designing 50 City parish churches to replace those lost in that disaster. Fittingly, he is buried in the crypt under a simple Latin epitaph, composed by his son, which translates as: "Reader, if you seek his monument, look around you." The cathedral has been the site of many famous state occasions, including the funeral of Winston Churchill in 1965 and the ill-fated marriage of the prince and princess of Wales in 1981. In the ambulatory (the area behind the high altar) is the American Chapel, a memorial to the 28,000 U.S. servicemen and women stationed in Britain during World War II who lost their lives while on active service. The greatest architectural glory of the cathedral is the dome. This consists of three distinct elements: an outer, timber-frame dome covered with lead; an interior dome built of brick and decorated with frescoes of the life of St. Paul by the 18th-century artist Sir James Thornhill; and, in between, a brick cone that supports and strengthens both. There is a good view of the church from the **Whispering Gallery,** high up in the inner dome. The gallery is so called because of its remarkable acoustics, whereby words spoken on one side can be clearly heard on the other, 107 ft away. Above this gallery are two others, both external, from which there are fine views over the City and beyond. ✉ *St. Paul's Churchyard, Paternoster Sq.,* ☎ *020/ 7236–4128.* 🎫 *Combined ticket £7.50.* ◷ *Cathedral: Mon.–Sat. 8:30– 4; ambulatory, crypt, and galleries: Mon.–Sat. 9:30–4:15.*

★ ❹❼ **Shakespeare's Globe Theatre.** This spectacular theater is a replica of Shakespeare's open-roof Globe Playhouse (built in 1599; incinerated in 1613), where most of the playwright's great plays premiered. It stands 200 yards from the original, overlooking the Thames. It has been built with the use of authentic Elizabethan materials, down to the first thatch roof in London since the Great Fire. Plays are presented in natural light (and sometimes rain), to 1,000 people on wooden benches in the "bays," plus 500 "groundlings," standing on a carpet of filbert shells and clinker, just as they did nearly four centuries ago. The main theater season is only from June through September, but throughout the year, you can tour the Globe through admission to the **New Shakespeare's Globe Exhibition,** which opened in September 1999 and is the largest ever to focus on the Bard. In addition, productions are now scheduled throughout the year in a second, indoor theater, built to a design of the 17th-century architect Inigo Jones. ✉ *New Globe Walk, Bankside (South Bank),* ☎ *020/7902–1500.* ◷ *Daily 10–5.* ◷ *Call for performance schedule.*

❹❽ **Tate Gallery of Modern Art, Bankside.** Opposite St. Paul's Cathedral along the banks of the Thames in South Bank, this is the new branch of the Tate Gallery of Modern British Art (☞ *Westminster, above*). The £100-million state-of-the-art transformation of the former Bankside Power Station by Swiss architects Herzog and de Meuron is set for completion in May 2000, and will firmly place this gallery as one of the great world-class modern art museums, continuing the picture—where the National Gallery finishes—from the 19th century on. ✉ *25 Summer St., SE1 9JT,* ☎ *020/7887–8000.* 🎫 *Free.* ◷ *Hours not determined at press time.*

★ ❺⓪ **Tower of London.** A guaranteed spine-chiller, this is one of London's most famous sights and one of its most crowded, too. Come as early in the day as possible and head for the Crown Jewels so you can see them before the crowds arrive. The tower served the monarchs of medieval England as both fortress and palace. Every British sovereign from William the Conqueror in the 11th century to Henry VIII in the 16th lived here, and it remains a royal palace, in name at least. The White Tower is the oldest and also the most conspicuous building in the entire complex. Inside, the Chapel of St. John is one of the few unaltered parts. The Royal Armories, England's national collection of arms and armor, occupies the rest of the White Tower.

The **History Gallery,** south of the White Tower, is a walk-through display designed to answer questions about the inhabitants of the tower and its evolution over the centuries. Among other buildings worth seeing is the **Bloody Tower.** The little princes in the tower—the uncrowned boy-king Edward V and his brother Richard, duke of York, supposedly murdered on the orders of the duke of Gloucester, later crowned Richard III—certainly lived in the Bloody Tower, and may well have died here, too. In the **Wakefield Tower,** Henry VI is alleged to have been murdered in 1471 during England's medieval civil war, the Wars of the Roses. It was a rare honor to be beheaded in private inside the tower; most people were executed outside, on **Tower Hill,** where the rabble could get a much better view.

The **Crown Jewels** are a breathtakingly splendid collection of regalia, precious stones, gold, and silver. The Royal Scepter contains the largest cut diamond in the world. The Imperial State Crown, made for the 1838 coronation of Queen Victoria, contains some 3,000 precious stones, largely diamonds and pearls. The Jewels are housed in the Martin Tower. Look for the ravens—Hardey, George, Hugine, Mumin, Cedric, Odin, Thor and Gwylem (who talks)—whose presence at the tower is traditional. It is said that if they leave, the tower will fall and England will lose her greatness. ⊠ *Tower Hill,* ☎ *020/7709–0765.* ⊠ *£10.50.* ☉ *Mar.–Oct., Mon.–Sat. 9–5, Sun. 10–5; Nov.–Feb., Tues.–Sat. 9–4, Sun.–Mon. 10–4 (the Tower closes 1 hr after last admission time and all internal buildings close 30 mins after last admission). Yeoman Warder guides conduct tours daily from Middle Tower; no charge, but a tip is always appreciated. Subject to weather and availability of guides, tours are conducted about every 30 mins until 3:30 in summer, 2:30 in winter.*

Hampstead

Hampstead is a village within the city, where many famous poets and writers have lived. Today it is a fashionable residential area, with a main shopping street and some rows of elegant 18th-century houses. The heath is one of London's largest and most attractive open spaces.

㉞ Abbey Road Studios. Here, outside the legendary Abbey Road Studios (the facility is closed to the public), is the most famous zebra crossing in the world. Immortalized on the cover of the Beatles' *Abbey Road* album of 1969, this pedestrian crosswalk is a spot beloved to countless Beatlemaniacs and baby boomers, many of whom venture here to leave their signature on the white stucco fence that fronts the adjacent studio facility. Abbey Road is not in Hampstead but in adjacent St. John's Wood, an elegant residential suburb a 10-minute ride on the tube from central London. ⊠ *3 Abbey Rd.*

㉟ Kenwood House. Standing alone in its own landscaped grounds on the north side of the heath is Kenwood House, built during the 17th century and remodeled by Robert Adam at the end of the 18th century. The house contains a collection of superb paintings by such masters as Rembrandt, Turner, Reynolds, Van Dyck, and Gainsborough—and *The Guitar Player,* probably the most beautiful Vermeer in England. Unfortunately, only one grand Adam interior remains. The lovely landscaped grounds provide the setting for symphony concerts in summer. ⊠ *Hampstead La.,* ☎ *020/8348–1286.* ⊠ *Free.* ☉ *Easter–Sept., daily 10–6; Oct.–Easter, daily 10–4.*

Greenwich

Home to the Millennium Dome and a number of historical and maritime attractions, Greenwich—set on the Thames some 8 km (5 mi) east of central London—is an ideal destination for a day out. New transport links to the Millennium borough should make trips there both easy and cheap (provided they are all finished on time, that is). Greenwich is set to join the sprawling Underground network, connecting to central London via the Jubilee line with a new station at North Greenwich, on the Greenwich peninsula. The Docklands train is being extended with a tunnel under the river, coming up to a station at Cutty Sark Gardens and one at Greenwich Railway station. Most people will journey to the Dome via the Millennium Transit Link, a shuttle service that leaves Charlton railway station. Note that the Millennium site itself is car free. You can also get to Greenwich by riverboat from Westminster and Tower Bridge piers and by ThamesLine's high-speed river buses.

Cutty Sark. Now in dry dock is the glorious 19th-century clipper ship *Cutty Sark.* ⊠ *King William Walk,* ☎ *020/8858–3445.* ⊙ *Daily 10–5.*

Millennium Dome. Located on the Prime Meridian, or Longitude Zero, in Greenwich, the Millennium Dome is probably the biggest monument to the advent of the new century. Looking like a futuristic sports arena, this colossus is more than 4 km (2½ mi) in circumference, with a roof 2 km (1 mi) high and strong enough to support a jumbo jet. Inside is a 21st-century version of Prince Albert's famous 1851 Great Exhibition. This ultimate look at what awaits mankind in the next 100 years is organized by themed Disneyesque zones, such as Learning, Work, and Play. Of all the exhibitions, the Body Zone is the most talked about, thanks to its larger-than-the-Statue-of-Liberty representation of the human body, which will allow visitors to journey through myriad passageways to see how bodies function. In the performance area of the Dome, a cast of 200 performers will put on a show with acrobatics, music, and visual effects, up to six times a day. During most of the year, tickets will be for a one-day-long session; during the peak summer season and holidays, days will be split into two sessions. Note that you are not able to buy tickets for admission on site—only at newsagents, lottery ticket agents, stores throughout London, and the hotline telephone service. From center Greenwich and the famous Royal Naval College and Cutty Sark complex, head northeast by the Thames along the new Riverside Walk to walk to the Dome. ⊠ *Millennium Dome, Drawdock St., Greenwich Peninsula,* ☎ *0870/603–2000 public information hotline.* ☞ *£20.* ⊙ *Daily 10–6:30, peak summer months and holidays 9:30–11.*

National Maritime Museum. A treasure house of paintings, maps, models, and, best of all, ships from all ages, this is a fascinating museum. Don't miss the ornate royal barges. ⊠ *Romney Rd.,* ☎ *020/8858–4422.* ⊙ *Mon.–Sat. 10–6, Sun. noon–6.*

Old Royal Observatory. Stand astride both hemispheres in the courtyard of the Old Royal Observatory, where the prime meridian—zero degrees longitude—is set. The Observatory is at the top of the hill, behind the National Maritime Museum and Royal Naval College, in **Greenwich Park**, originally a royal hunting ground and today an attractive open space. The Observatory, founded in 1675, has original telescopes and other astronomical instruments on display. ⊠ *Greenwich Park,* ☎ *020/8858–4422.* ⊙ *Mon.–Sat. 10–6, Sun. noon–6.*

Greenwich

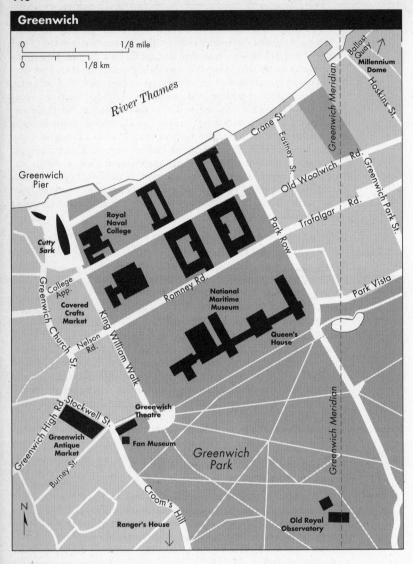

0   1/8 mile

0   1/8 km

River Thames

Greenwich Pier

Crane St.

Easney St.

Old Woolwich Rd.

Greenwich Meridian

Ballast Quay

Millennium Dome

Hoskins St.

Cutty Sark

Royal Naval College

Greenwich Park St.

Trafalgar Rd.

Park Row

College App.

Greenwich Church St.

Covered Crafts Market

Romney Rd.

National Maritime Museum

Park Vista

King William Walk

Nelson Rd.

Queen's House

Greenwich High Rd.

Stockwell St.

Greenwich Theatre

Fan Museum

Greenwich Antique Market

Burney St.

Greenwich Park

Croom's Hill

Greenwich Meridian

Ranger's House

Old Royal Observatory

N

Dining

For details and price-category definitions, *see* Dining *in* Great Britain A to Z, *above.*

Bloomsbury

$$ ✕ **Chez Gérard.** This purveyor of steak-*frîtes* (with french fries) and similarly simple Gallic offerings is reliable, relaxed, and usefully located near Oxford Street. ⊠ *8 Charlotte St.,* ☎ *020/7636–4975. AE, DC, MC, V. Tube: Goodge St.*

$$ ✕ **Museum Street Café.** A convenient spot to the British Museum and worth a special trip in the evening, the Mediterranean-tinged home cooking (spinach-and-olive tart; char-grilled leg of lamb; Valrhona chocolate cake) and minimalist white-wall decor in this little place are satisfying. They now offer a breakfast and wholesome tea on Saturdays. ⊠ *47 Museum St.,* ☎ *020/7405–3211. Reservations essential. AE, V. Closed Sun. Tube: Tottenham Court Rd.*

Chelsea

$$$–$$$$ ✕ **Gordon Ramsay.** A table at Ramsay's restaurant has been London's
★ toughest reservation to score for almost as long as it's been open, because the soccer star–turned–chef has every table gasping in awe at his famous cappuccino of white beans with sautéed girolles and truffles, followed by—well, anything at all. Reserve months ahead; go for lunch (£24) if money is an object. ⊠ *68–69 Royal Hospital Rd.,* ☎ *020/7352–4441 or 020/7352–3334. Reservations essential. AE, DC, MC, V. Closed Sat.–Sun. Tube: Sloane Sq.*

$$$ ✕ **Chutney Mary.** London's only Anglo-Indian restaurant provides a fantasy version of the British Raj, with colonial cocktails and authentic re-creations of comforting, rich dishes, such as Country Captain (chicken with almonds, raisins, chilies, and spices). ⊠ *535 King's Rd.,* ☎ *020/7351–3113. AE, DC, MC, V. Tube: Fulham Broadway.*

$$ ✕ **Bluebird.** Here's Terence Conran's latest "gastrodome"—supermarket, brasserie, fruit stand, butcher shop, boutique, and café-restaurant, all housed in a snappy King's Road former garage. The menu has more than a nod in the Asia-Pacific direction. Go for the synergy and visual excitement—Conran's chefs share a tendency to promise more than they deliver. ⊠ *350 King's Rd.,* ☎ *020/7559–1000. Reservations essential. AE, DC, MC, V. Tube: Sloane Sq.*

$$ ✕ **Cactus Blue.** Southwestern food from America is a hot thing on the London dining scene and this place is one of a flush of new Tex-Mex spots with attitude. You can find the buzz on split levels of ocher hues which offset dramatic cacti. On offer are tequilas, beers, and baja wines, which help slide down the crab stacks and quesadillas. ⊠ *86 Fulham Rd.,* ☎ *020/7283–7858. AE, MC, V. Tube: South Kensington.*

The City

$$$ ✕ **St. John.** Resembling a stark monks' refectory crossed with an art gallery, this modern British innovator has equally uncompromising menus. Some loathe bone marrow and parsley salad, huge servings of braised pheasant with "black cabbage," or deviled crab, or organ meats any which way, with English puddings and Malmsey wine to follow, but newspaper journalists and swank architects love it. ⊠ *26 St John St.,* ☎ *020/7251–0848. Reservations essential. AE, DC, MC, V. No dinner Sun. Tube: Farringdon.*

Covent Garden

$$$ ✕ **The Ivy.** The epitome of style without pretentiousness, this restau-
★ rant beguiles everybody, including media, literary, and theatrical movers and shakers. The menu's got it all—fish-and-chips, sausage-and-mash,

squid-ink risotto, sticky toffee pudding—and all are good. ⊠ *1 West St.,* ☎ *020/7836–4751. Reservations essential. AE, DC, MC, V. Tube: Covent Garden.*

$$$ ✕ **Rules.** This is probably the city's most beautiful restaurant—daffodil-
★ yellow 19th-century walls, Victorian oil paintings, and hundreds of framed engravings make up the history-rich setting—and certainly one of the oldest (it has been here since 1798). Rules is traditional from soup to nuts, or rather, from venison and Dover sole to trifle and Stilton. There's the odd nod to newer cuisines, but the clientele of expense accounters and tourists who want to feast where Dickens and Lillie Langtry once did remains. Note there are three floors to this establishment, with the most opulent salons on the first floor. ⊠ *35 Maiden La.,* ☎ *020/7836–5314. AE, DC, MC, V. Tube: Covent Garden.*

$–$$ ✕ **Joe Allen.** Long hours (thespians flock here after the curtains fall in
★ Theatreland) and a welcoming, if loud, brick-walled interior mean New York Joe's London branch is still swinging after more than two decades. The fun, Cal-Ital menu helps, with barbecued ribs with black-eyed peas, London's only available corn muffins, and roast monkfish with sun-dried-tomato salsa usually on tap. ⊠ *13 Exeter St.,* ☎ *020/7836–0651. Reservations essential. AE, DC, MC, V. Tube: Covent Garden.*

$ ✕ **Food for Thought.** This is a simple downstairs vegetarian restaurant, with seats for only 50. The menu—stir-fries, casseroles, salads, and dessert—changes daily, and each dish is freshly made. No alcohol is served. ⊠ *31 Neal St.,* ☎ *020/7836–0239. Reservations not accepted. No credit cards. Closed 2 wks at Christmas. Tube: Covent Garden.*

Kensington

$$$$ ✕ **Bibendum.** Upstairs in the renovated 1911 Michelin building, this
★ Art Deco dining extravaganza continues to entice with a menu as Gallic and gorgeous as ever. From the scallops in citrus sauce to the passion-fruit *bavarois* (Bavarian cream), all the dishes are unpretentious but admirably done. The separate Oyster Bar, downstairs, is another way to go. ⊠ *81 Fulham Rd.,* ☎ *020/7581–5817. Reservations essential. AE, DC, MC, V. Tube: South Kensington.*

$$ ✕ **Pasha.** Not quite a taste of old Tangiers, Pasha delivers modern Morocco and due east in a very à la mode manner. Waiters in traditional dress drift between piles of silken cushions and flickering candlelight to bring delicacies such as *pastilla* (pie) of pigeon and stylish cross-cuisine desserts (brûlé with exotic North African fruits). ⊠ *1 Gloucester Rd.,* ☎ *020/7589–7969. Reservations essential. AE, MC, V. Tube: Gloucester Rd.*

Knightsbridge

$$$$ ✕ **La Tante Claire.** One of London's best restaurants has upped its pots
★ and pans from Chelsea and moved to the Berkeley Hotel. Chef Pierre Koffmann still holds the reins over the kitchen, so you can expect his haute cuisine fireworks, such as his signature dish of pigs' feet stuffed with mousse of white meat with sweetbreads and wild mushrooms. The set lunch menu is a genuine bargain. Lunch reservations must be made two or three days in advance, dinner reservations three to four in advance. ⊠ *Berkeley Hotel, Wilton Pl.,* ☎ *020/7823–2003. Reservations essential. Jacket and tie. AE, DC, MC, V. Closed weekends. Tube: Knightsbridge.*

$$$ ✕ **Zafferano.** Princess Margaret, Eric Clapton, Joan Collins (she asked
★ that the lights be turned down), and any number of stylish folk have flocked to this Belgravia place, London's best exponent of *cucina nuova.* The fireworks are in the kitchen, not in the brick-wall-and-saffron-hue decor, but *what* fireworks: pumpkin ravioli with a splash of Amaretto, *mondeghini ai crostini di risotto* (minced pork wrapped in Savoy cabbage leaves), and monkfish with walnuts. Be sure to book

early: Even Al Pacino was turned away one night. ⊠ *15 Lowndes St.,* ☎ *020/7235–5800. Reservations essential. AE, MC, V. Tube: Knightsbridge.*

\$–\$\$ ✕ **The Enterprise.** One of the new luxury breed of gastro-pubs, this is perhaps the chicest of the lot—near Harrods and Brompton Cross, it's filled with decorative types. The menu isn't overly pretty—char-grilled squid stuffed with almonds, entrecôte steak, salmon with artichoke hearts—but the ambience certainly is. ⊠ *35 Walton St.,* ☎ *020/7584–3148. AE, MC, V. Tube: South Kensington.*

\$ ✕ **Stockpot.** Speedy service is the mark of this large, jolly restaurant full of students and shoppers. The food is sometimes unstartling, but filling and wholesome: Try the Lancashire hot pot, for example, and the apple crumble. Breakfast is also served Monday–Saturday. ⊠ *6 Basil St.,* ☎ *020/7589–8627. No credit cards. Tube: Knightsbridge.*

Mayfair

\$\$\$\$ ✕ **Oak Room.** Bad boy Marco Pierre White enjoys Jagger-like fame from
★ his TV appearances and gossip column reports of his complicated love life and random eruptions of fury. He should stick to his pans, say superchef critics, meaning it literally in some cases. But, hype aside, Marco may be London's greatest chef and now gets to show off in his most spectacular setting yet—all Belle Epoque soaring ceilings and gilded bits, and palms and paintings. ⊠ *Le Meridien, 21 Piccadilly,* ☎ *020/7437–0202. Reservations essential. Jacket and tie. AE, DC, MC, V. Tube: Piccadilly Circus.*

\$\$\$ ✕ **Criterion.** A spectacular neo-Byzantine palace of gold mosaic, Christo-size turquoise drapes, and white tablecloths, the Criterion is under the aegis of Marco Pierre White, the bigmouthed, bigheaded wunderchef now at the helm of several of London's best restaurants, and features his style of haute-bistro French food: a rich, black squid-ink risotto; intricate assemblies of fish; and delicate salads. ⊠ *Piccadilly Circus,* ☎ *020/7930–0488. AE, DC, MC, V. Tube: Piccadilly Circus.*

\$\$–\$\$\$ ✕ **L'Odéon.** This contribution to London's mania for giant restaurants overlooks Regent Street in a former airline office. Food is elevated French-bistro-style with usual modish Italian additions—grilled fish and meats with imaginative vegetable combinations, such as wild mushrooms on brioche toast. Tables by the huge arched windows are fun for people-watching. ⊠ *65 Regent St.,* ☎ *020/7287–1400. AE, DC, MC, V. Tube: Piccadilly Circus.*

Notting Hill

\$\$\$ ✕ **Kensington Place.** Trendy and loud, this ever-popular place features enormous plate-glass windows through which to be seen, and plenty of fashionable food—grilled foie gras with sweet-corn pancake and baked tamarillo with vanilla ice are perennials—but it's the fun buzz that draws the crowds. ⊠ *201 Kensington Church St.,* ☎ *020/7727–3184. DC, MC, V. Tube: Notting Hill Gate.*

\$\$ ✕ **The Cow.** Slightly tucked away in the backwaters of trendy Portobello-land, this is the nicest of a trio of foodie pubs that feed the neighborhood arty hipsters and media stars. The Cow is the child of Tom Conran, son of Sir Terence (who owns half of London's restaurants). It pretends to be a pub in County Derry, serving oysters, crab salad, and other seafood with the beer, and heartier food in the cozy restaurant upstairs. ⊠ *89 Westbourne Park Rd.,* ☎ *020/7221–5400. Reservations essential. MC, V. No dinner Sun. Tube: Westbourne Park.*

\$\$ ✕ **Pharmacy.** One of London's most photographed scene-arenas, the Pharmacy looks just like its namesake, with waitstaff garbed like hospital orderlies. Even its menu looks fab, but then Damien Hirst, artist extraordinaire, is a co-owner. The menu highlights "comfort food" and ranges from fisherman's pie to spit-roast Landes duck, sauce aigre-doux.

Don't you dare leave the bar without ordering a "Cough Syrup." ⊠ *150 Notting Hill Gate,* ☎ *020/7221–2442. Reservations essential. AE, MC, V. Tube: Notting Hill Gate.*

$ ✕ **Tootsies.** A useful burger joint characterized by loudish rock and vintage advertisements on the walls, Tootsies serves some of London's better burgers, as well as chili, chicken, BLTs, taco salad, apple pie, fudge cake, and ice cream. There are five other branches. ⊠ *120 Holland Park Ave.,* ☎ *020/7229–8567. Reservations not accepted. MC, V. Tube: Holland Park.*

St. James's

$$$ ✕ **Le Caprice.** Fabulously dark and glamorous, with its black walls and
★   stark white tablecloths, Caprice is a perennial that does nothing wrong, from its kind, efficient, nonpartisan (famous folk eat here often) service to its pan-European menu (salmon fish cake with sorrel sauce; confit of goose with prunes). ⊠ *Arlington House, Arlington St.,* ☎ *020/ 7629–2239. Reservations essential. AE, DC, MC, V. No dinner Sun. Tube: Green Park.*

Soho

$$–$$$ ✕ **Titanic.** London's splashiest new restaurant is now riding high on the crest of a media wave, yet Marco Pierre White, the noted chef who opened this—the latest and greatest in the tide of trend-driven dining spots—claims it was not inspired by the blockbuster film. But like the movie, this place has pulled in the crowds, plus a clientele of the young, loud, and fashionable. Decor is Art Deco ocean liner, dinner is fun and casual, ranging from fish-and-chips to squid-ink risotto to sticky toffee, and prices are lower than you'd expect for this corner of town. ⊠ *81 Brewer St.,* ☎ *020/7437–1912. Reservations essential. AE, MC, V. Tube: Piccadilly Circus.*

$–$$$ ✕ **Mezzo.** Sir Terence Conran's 700-seater Mezzo isn't only London's biggest, it's the most gigantic restaurant in all of Europe—you could decant most of Soho inside its three levels. Downstairs is Mezzo, where the soaring, glass-walled kitchen abuts a bustling ocean liner of a dining room; here, the food is French-ish, with the usual Conran seafood platters, and there's a nifty jazz trio and dance floor. Upstairs, the "Mezzonine" and bar are informal, and less expensive. Finally, a separate café stays open till the wee hours. Much maligned and beloved by turns, Mezzo continues to draw the young office and evening crowds. ⊠ *100 Wardour St.,* ☎ *020/7314–4000. AE, DC, MC, V. Tube: Leicester Sq.*

$–$$ ✕ **Villandry.** Heaven for foodies, Villandry recently moved and expanded into a food hall that is nearly larger than the one at Harrods. Lined with handsome dark-wood shelves, this mammoth cave of wonders positively heaves with goodies—French pâtés, Continental cheeses, fruit tarts, biscuits, and breads galore are just some of the tempting offerings. If you must indulge but can't wait to take a bite, there's a tearoom café and dining room in which to enjoy breakfast, lunch, and dinner daily. ⊠ *170 Great Portland St.,* ☎ *020/7631–3131. AE, MC, V. Tube: Great Portland St.*

South Bank

$$–$$$ ✕ **OXO Tower Brasserie and Restaurant.** London finally has a room
★   with a view, and *such* a view. On the eighth floor of the beautifully revived OXO Tower Wharf building, near the South Bank Centre, this elegant space has Euro food with this year's trendy ingredients (acorn-fed black pig charcuterie with tomato and pear chutney is one example). The ceiling slats turn and change from white to midnight blue, but who notices, with St. Paul's dazzling you across the water? ⊠ *Bankside,* ☎ *020/7803–3888. AE, MC, V. Tube: Waterloo.*

Lodging

For details and price-category definitions, *see* Lodging *in* Great Britain A to Z, *above*. Note that although British hotels traditionally included breakfast in their nightly tariff, these days many of London's most expensive establishments charge extra for breakfast.

Bayswater

$$ ★ **Commodore.** This peaceful hotel of three converted Victorians has some amazing (especially for the price) rooms—as superior to the regular ones (which usually go to package tour groups) as Harrods is to KMart. Twenty are miniduplexes, with sleeping gallery. One (Number 11) is a real duplex, entered through a secret mirrored door, with a thick-carpeted, *very* quiet bedroom upstairs and its toilet below. ⊠ *50 Lancaster Gate, W2 3NA,* ☎ *020/7402–5291,* ℻ *020/7262–1088. 90 rooms. Bar. AE, MC, V. Tube: Lancaster Gate.*

$$ **London Elizabeth.** Steps from Hyde Park and the Lancaster Gate tube, this family-owned gem has one of the prettiest hotel facades in London. The charm continues inside—foyer and lounge are crammed with coffee tables and chintz drapery, lace antimacassars, and little chandeliers. There is an exceptionally charming Anglo-Irish staff. ⊠ *Lancaster Terr., W2 3PF,* ☎ *020/7402–6641,* ℻ *020/7224–8900. 55 rooms. Restaurant. AE, DC, MC, V. Tube: Lancaster Gate.*

$ **Columbia.** The public rooms in these five joined Victorians are as big as museum halls, painted in icy hues of powder blue and buttermilk, or paneled in dark wood. At one end of the day they contain the hippest band du jour drinking pints; at the other, there are sightseers sipping coffee. Rooms are clean, high-ceilinged, and sometimes very large—it's just a shame that teak veneer and avocado bathroom suites haven't made it back into the style bible yet. ⊠ *95–99 Lancaster Gate, W2 3NS,* ☎ *020/7402–0021,* ℻ *020/7706–4691. 103 rooms. Restaurant, bar. AE, MC, V. Tube: Lancaster Gate.*

Bloomsbury

$ **Morgan.** This charming family-run hotel in an 18th-century terrace house has rooms that are small and comfortably furnished, but friendly and cheerful. The tiny paneled breakfast room is straight out of a doll's house. The back rooms overlook the British Museum. ⊠ *24 Bloomsbury St., WC1B 3QJ,* ☎ *020/7636–3735. 15 rooms with bath or shower. MC, V. Tube: Russell Sq.*

$ **Ridgemount.** The kindly owners, Mr. and Mrs. Rees, make you feel at home in this tiny hotel by the British Museum. There's a homey, cluttered feel in the public areas and some bedrooms overlook a leafy garden. ⊠ *65 Gower St., WC1E 6HJ,* ☎ *020/7636–1141. 34 rooms, 8 with bath. No credit cards. Tube: Russell Sq.*

Chelsea, Kensington, and Holland Park

$$$$ ★ **Blakes.** Patronized by musicians and film stars, this hotel is one of the most exotic in town. Its Victorian exterior contrasts with the rather 1980s ultrachic interior, an arty mix of Biedermeier and bamboo, four-poster beds, and chinoiserie, all lit as dramatically as film noir. The bedrooms have individual designs ranging from swaths of black moiré silk to an entirely pink suite. ⊠ *33 Roland Gardens, SW7 3PF,* ☎ *020/7370–6701. 52 rooms. Restaurant. AE, DC, MC, V. Tube: Gloucester Rd.*

$$$$ ★ **Halcyon.** Discretion, decadent decor, and disco divas make this expensive, enormous, wedding-cake Edwardian desperately desirable. The Blue Room has moons and stars, the Egyptian Suite is canopied like a bedouin tent, on and on. All guest rooms are different but large, with the high ceilings and big windows of the Holland Park vernacular. ⊠ *81 Holland Park, W11 3RZ,* ☎ *020/7727–7288,* ℻ *020/7229–8516. 42 rooms. Restaurant. AE, DC, MC, V. Tube: Holland Park.*

$$$ **The Gore.** Every wall of every room in this friendly and quiet hotel
★   near the Albert Hall is smothered in prints and etchings, and antiques
pepper the rooms. Some of these are spectacular follies—such as Tudor-
style Room 101, with its minstrel gallery and four-poster. The crowd
here is elegant and arty. ⊠ *189 Queens Gate, SW7 5EX,* ☎ *020/7584–
6601,* FAX *020/7589–8127. 54 rooms. Restaurant. AE, DC, MC, V. Tube:
Gloucester Rd.*

$$–$$$ **Portobello.** A faithful and chic core of visitors returns again and again
to this eccentric hotel in a Victorian terrace near the Portobello Road
antiques market. Some rooms are tiny, but the ambience of '60s swing-
ing London, the ecclesiastical antiques, and the peaceful vista of the
gardens in back make up for it. ⊠ *22 Stanley Gardens, W11 2NG,* ☎
020/7727–2777, FAX *020/7792–9641. 22 rooms with bath or shower.
Restaurant. AE, DC, MC, V. Tube: Ladbroke Grove.*

$ **Abbey House.** Standards are high (some rooms even feature or-
thopedic beds) and the rooms unusually spacious in this hotel in a fine
residential block near Kensington Palace and Gardens. ⊠ *11 Vicarage
Gate, W8 4AG,* ☎ *020/7727–2594. 16 rooms with shared bath. No
credit cards. Tube: Kensington High St.*

$ **The Vicarage.** This has long been a favorite for the budget-minded—
family-owned, set on a leaf-shaded street just off Kensington Church
Street, the Vicarage is set in a large white Victorian house. Bedrooms
are traditional and comfortable, with solid English furniture. Definitely
a charmer—but it is beginning to fray around the edges. ⊠ *10 Vicarage
Gate, W8 4AG,* ☎ *020/7229–4030. 19 rooms without bath. No credit
cards. Tube: Kensington High St.*

Knightsbridge, Belgravia, and Victoria

$$$$ **The Lanesborough.** Brocades and Regency stripes, moiré silks and
fleurs-de-lis, antiques, oils, and reproductions in gilded splendor—
everything undulates with richness in this upscale conversion of the old
St. George's Hospital at Hyde Park Corner. To register you just sign
the book, then retire to your room to find a personal butler, business
cards with your in-room fax and phone numbers, VCR and CD player,
umbrella, robe, huge flacons of unguents for bath time, and a drinks
tray. ⊠ *1 Lanesborough Pl., SW1X 7TA,* ☎ *020/7259–5599,* FAX *020/
7259–5606. 95 rooms. 2 restaurants. AE, DC, MC, V. Tube: Hyde Park
Corner.*

$$$ **Basil Street.** Family run for some 80 years, this is a gracious Ed-
wardian hotel on a quiet street. The rooms are filled with antiques, as
are the various lounges, hushed like libraries with polished wooden floors
and Oriental rugs. It sounds swanky, but Basil Street is more like
home. ⊠ *Basil St., SW3 1AH,* ☎ *020/7581–3311,* FAX *020/7581–
3693. 92 rooms, 72 with bath. 2 restaurants. AE, DC, MC, V. Tube:
Knightsbridge.*

$$$ **The Pelham.** Magnificent 18th-century pine paneling in the draw-
★   ing room, glazed chintz and antique lace, four-posters in some rooms,
fireplaces in others—this hotel run by Tim and Kit Kemp feels more
like an elegant home. It's near the big museums, and 24-hour room
service and business services are available. ⊠ *15 Cromwell Pl., SW7
2LA,* ☎ *020/7589–8288,* FAX *020/7584–8444. 37 rooms. Restaurant.
AE, MC, V. Tube: South Kensington.*

$$$ **The Rubens.** The boast of this hotel is that they treat you like roy-
alty—after all, you're only a stone's throw from the real thing, with Buck-
ingham Palace just across the road. And if this is how Her Majesty lives,
then we've all got reason to be jealous. This elegant hotel, looking out
over the Royal Mews, provides the sort of deep comfort needed to soothe
away a hard's day sightseeing. With well-appointed rooms and a location that could not be more truly central, this hotel is a sightseers' dream.

✉ *39 Buckingham Palace Rd., SW1W OPS,* ☎ *020/7834–6600,* FAX *020/7828–5401. 180 rooms. Restaurant, bar. AE, DC, MC, V.*

$ 🏨 **London County Hall Travel Inn Capital.** Don't get too excited—this neighbor of the luxurious new Marriott in the County Hall complex lacks the fabled river view (it's at the back of the grand former seat of local government, on the south side of the Thames). Still, you get an incredible value, with the standard facilities of the cookie-cutter rooms of this chain, viz: TV, tea/coffeemaker, en suite bath/shower and—wow!—foldout beds that let you accommodate two children at no extra charge. You're looking at £50/night for a family of four, in the shadow of Big Ben. *That's* a bargain. ✉ *Belvedere Rd., SE1 7PB,* ☎ *020/7902–1600,* FAX *020/7902–1619. 312 rooms. Restaurant. AE, MC, V. Tube: Westminster.*

West End

$$$$ 🏨 **Brown's.** Close to Bond Street, Brown's is like a country house in the middle of town, with wood paneling, grandfather clocks, and large fireplaces. Founded in 1837 by Lord Byron's "gentleman's gentleman," James Brown, it has attracted Anglophilic Americans ever since. Both Roosevelts used to stay here. ✉ *34 Albemarle St., W1A 4SW,* ☎ *020/7493–6020,* FAX *020/7493–9381. 132 rooms. Restaurant. AE, DC, MC, V. Tube: Green Park.*

$$$$ 🏨 **Claridge's.** This hotel has one of the world's classiest guest lists. The
★ liveried staff is friendly, not at all condescending, and the rooms are luxurious. The hotel was founded in 1812, but the present decor is either 1930s Art Deco or country-house style. Have a drink or afternoon tea in the Foyer and hear the Hungarian mini-orchestra. The rooms are spacious, the sweeping staircase grand. A £40-million renovation completed in 1998 has given a dazzling face lift to this legendary grande dame. ✉ *Brook St., W1A 2JQ,* ☎ *020/7629–8860,* FAX *020/7499–2210. 200 rooms. Restaurant, bar. AE, DC, MC, V. Tube: Bond St.*

$$$$ 🏨 **Covent Garden Hotel.** Clearly London's most relentlessly chic, extra-
★ stylish hotel, this former 1880s-vintage hospital is located in the midst of the artsy Covent Garden district, and is now the London home-away-from-home for a melange of off-duty celebrities, actors, and style mavens. Theatrically baronial, the public rooms will keep even the most picky atmosphere-hunter happy. Isn't that Helena Bonham Carter having tea in the drawing room? ✉ *10 Monmouth St., WC2H 9HB,* ☎ *020/7806–1000,* FAX *020/7806–1100. 46 rooms, 4 suites. Restaurant, minibars, room service, exercise room, laundry service. AE, MC, V. Tube: Covent Garden.*

$$$$ 🏨 **Dukes.** The refurbishment of this small Edwardian hotel in a cul-de-sac in St. James's has raised its popularity rating several notches. Top-floor suites are among the finds of London for peace, views, antiques, and homeyness. ✉ *35 St. James's Pl., SW1A 1NY,* ☎ *020/7491–4840,* FAX *020/7493–1264. 62 rooms. Restaurant. AE, DC, MC, V. Tube: Green Park.*

$$$$ 🏨 **Savoy.** This grand, historic, late-Victorian hotel has been the by-
★ word for luxury for just over a century. Hemingway loved its American Bar and Elizabeth Taylor spent her first honeymoon here. Spacious bedrooms have antiques and cream plasterwork, and the best ones overlook the Thames. More than a hint of dazzling 1920s style remains. ✉ *Strand, WC2R 0EU,* ☎ *020/7836–4343,* FAX *020/7240–6040. 202 rooms. 3 restaurants. AE, DC, MC, V. Tube: Aldwych.*

$$$ 🏨 **Hazlitt's.** Still Soho's sole hotel, this, the last home of William Hazlitt, the essayist (1778–1830), is crammed with prints on every wall, Victorian claw-foot baths, assorted antiques, plants, and bits of art. There's no elevator, the sitting room is minuscule, floors can be creaky and bedrooms tiny, but Hazlitt's legion of devotees don't mind. And who needs room service when you live on Restaurant Row? ⊠ *6 Frith St., W1V 5TZ,* ☎ *020/7434–1771,* FAX *020/7439–1524. 23 rooms. AE, DC, MC, V. Tube: Piccadilly Circus.*

$$ 🖾 **Bryanston Court.** Three 18th-century houses have been converted into a traditional English family-run hotel with open fires and comfortable armchairs; the bedrooms are more contemporary. ⊠ *56–60 Great Cumberland Pl., W1H 7FD,* ☎ *020/7262–3141,* FAX *020/7262–7248. 56 rooms with bath or shower. Breakfast room, bar. AE, DC, MC, V. Tube: Marble Arch.*

$$ 🖾 **The Fielding.** Tucked away in a quiet alley, steps from the Royal Opera House, this cozy place is so adored by its regulars that you'd better book ahead. It's shabby-homey in decor and attitude—there's no elevator, only one room has a bathtub (most have showers), and there's no room service or restaurant, but it's cute and handy for the theater. ⊠ *4 Broad Ct., Bow St., WC2B 5OZ,* ☎ *020/7836–8305,* FAX *020/7497–0064. 26 rooms, 1 with bath, 23 with showers. AE, DC, MC, V. Tube: Covent Garden.*

Nightlife and the Arts

The Arts

For a list of events in the London arts scene, visit a newsstand or bookstore to pick up the weekly magazine *Time Out.* The city's evening paper, the *Evening Standard,* carries listings, as do the major Sunday papers; the daily *Independent* and *Guardian;* and, on Friday, *The Times.* The London Tourist Board's *Visitor Call* service (calls cost 49p/min.; ☎ 0891/505440 for what's on this week) also offers listings for theater and other arts events.

BALLET

The Royal Opera House has been the traditional home of the world-famous **Royal Ballet,** but the beloved opera house is now closed for a renovation until December 1999. During construction, the Royal Ballet will be performing at Sadler's Wells Theater (☎ 020/7863–8000) and at the Royal Festival Hall in the South Bank Arts Complex (☎ 020/7928–8800); check with the box office of the Royal Opera House (☎ 020/7304–4000) for complete information. The prices are slightly more reasonable than for the opera, but be sure to book well ahead. The **English National Ballet** and visiting companies perform at the Coliseum (☎ 020/7632–8300) but that theater, too, is scheduled for a renovation program lasting several seasons, and resident troupes will be performing elsewhere (call the Coliseum Box Office for further information). **Sadler's Wells Theatre** (☎ 020/7713–6000) hosts regional ballet and international modern dance troupes. Prices here are reasonable.

CONCERTS

Ticket prices for symphony orchestra concerts are still relatively moderate—between £5 and £35, although you can expect to pay more to hear big-name artists on tour. If you can't book in advance, arrive half an hour before the performance for a chance at returns.

The London Symphony Orchestra is in residence at the **Barbican Arts Centre** (☎ 020/7638–8891), although other top symphony and chamber orchestras also perform here. The **South Bank arts complex** (☎ 020/7960–4233), which includes the **Royal Festival Hall** and the **Queen Elizabeth Hall,** is another major venue for choral, symphonic, and chamber concerts. For less expensive concert going, try the **Royal Albert Hall** (☎ 020/7589–8212) during the summer Promenade season; special tickets for standing room are available at the hall on the night of performance. Note, too, that the concerts have begun to be jumbo-screen broadcast in Hyde Park, but even here a seat on the grass requires a paid ticket. Call 020/7589–82122 for further information. **The Wigmore Hall** (☎ 020/7935–2141) is a small auditorium, ideal for recitals. Inexpensive lunchtime concerts take place all over the city in smaller halls and churches, often featuring string quartets, vocalists, jazz ensembles, and gospel choirs. **St. John's, Smith Square** (☎ 020/7222–1061), a converted Queen Anne church, is one of the more popular venues. It has a handy crypt cafeteria.

FILM

Most West End cinemas are in the area around Leicester Square and Piccadilly Circus. Tickets average £7.50. Matinees and Monday evenings are cheaper. Cinema clubs screen a wide range of films: classics, Continental, underground, rare, or underestimated masterpieces. A temporary membership fee is usually about £1. One of the best cinema clubs is the **National Film Theatre** (☎ 020/7928–3232), part of the South Bank arts complex.

OPERA

The **Royal Opera House** (☎ 020/7304–4000) ranks alongside the New York Met. It's one of the grandest sights in London, but the theater is in the final stages of a massive renovation, due to be completed December 1999. The resident opera company will be performing at other venues during this period, in particular the newly refurbished Sadler's Wells Theatre (☎ 020/7713–6000). For ongoing information check with the box office. The **Coliseum** (☎ 020/7632–8300) is the home of the English National Opera Company; productions are staged in English and are often innovative and exciting. The ticket price range is about £8 to £45. Call the box office for the latest information, as the Coliseum is also scheduled for a major renovation.

THEATER

London's theater life can more or less be divided into three categories: the government-subsidized national companies; the commercial, or "West End," theaters; and the fringe. The **Royal National Theatre Company** (NT) shares the laurels as the top national repertory troupe with the Royal Shakespeare Company. In similar fashion to the latter troupe, the NT presents a variety of plays by writers of all nationalities, ranging from the classics of Shakespeare and his contemporaries to specially commissioned modern works. The NT is based at the South Bank arts complex (box office: ☎ 020/7452–3000). The **Royal Shakespeare Company** (RSC) is based at the Barbican Centre (box office: ☎ 020/7638–8891). At press time, the RSC announced it had terminated its summer season in London. That's a pity for summer visitors, but they can always book tickets at the spectacular new reconstruction of the famed Elizabethan-era **Shakespeare's Globe Theatre** (box office: ☎ 020/7401–9919) on the South Bank, which only offers open-air, late-afternoon performances from June through September.

The **West End theaters** largely stage musicals, comedies, whodunits, and revivals of lighter plays of the 19th and 20th centuries, often starring television celebrities. Occasionally there are more serious productions, including successful productions transferred from the subsidized theaters, such as RSC's *Les Liaisons Dangereuses* and *Les Misérables*. The two dozen or so established **fringe theaters**, scattered around central London and the immediate outskirts, frequently present some of London's most intriguing productions, if you're prepared to overlook occasional rough staging and uncomfortable seating.

Most theaters have an evening performance at 7:30 or 8 daily, except Sunday, and a matinee twice a week (Wednesday or Thursday, and Saturday). Expect to pay from £10 for a seat in the upper balcony and at least £25 for a good seat in the stalls (orchestra) or dress circle (mezzanine)—more for musicals. Tickets may be booked in person at the theater box office; over the phone by credit card; or through ticket agents, such as **First Call** (☎ 420–0000) or **Ticketmaster** (☎ 020/7344–0055 or 800/775–2525 from the United States). In addition the **SOLT Kiosk** in Leicester Square sells half-price tickets on the day of performance for about 25 theaters; there is a small service charge. It's open Monday–Saturday 2–6:30, Sunday 12–3. Beware of scalpers!

Nightlife

London's nightspots are legion; here are some of the best known. For up-to-the-minute listings, buy *Time Out* magazine.

CABARET

The best comedy in town can be found in the big, bright, new-look **Comedy Store** (✉ Haymarket House, Oxendon St., near Piccadilly Circus, ☎ 01426/914433). **Madame Jo Jo's** (✉ 8 Brewer St., ☎ 020/7287–1414) is possibly the most fun of any London cabaret, with its outrageous, glittering drag shows. The place is luxurious and civilized.

JAZZ CLUBS

Blue Note (✉ 1 Hoxton Sq., ☎ 020/7729–8440), in an out-of-the-way warehouse on the northern edge of the City (the nearest tube is Old Street), is a cool jazz and world-beat club/restaurant that attracts a young crowd. **Ronnie Scott's** (✉ 47 Frith St., ☎ 020/7439–0747) is the legendary Soho jazz club where international performers regularly take the stage.

NIGHTCLUBS

Café de Paris (✉ 3–4 Coventry St. W1V 7FL, ☎ 020/7734–7700) has been open since 1914 and is one of London's most glamour-puss settings, once the haunt of royals and stars such as Noel Coward, Marlene Dietrich, Fred Astaire, and Frank Sinatra. **Hanover Grand** (✉ 6 Hanover Sq., ☎ 020/7499–7977) is a swank and opulent big West End club, which attracts TV stars and footballers whose exploits here you can later read about in the tabloids. The "Haute Couture" one-nighter takes over on Friday, while Saturday's glam disco "Malibu Stacey" pulls in all those who want to be seen. The lines outside get long, so dress up to impress the bouncers. **Ministry of Sound** (✉ 103 Gaunt St., ☎ 020/7378–6528) is more of an industry than a club, with its own record label, line of apparel, and, of course, DJs. Inside, there are chill-out rooms, dance floors, promotional Sony Playstations, Absolut shot bars—all the club kid's favorite things. If you are one, and you only have time for one night out, make it here. Glitzy **Stringfellows** (✉ 16–19 Upper St. Martin's La., ☎ 020/7240–5534) has an Art Deco upstairs restaurant, mirrored walls, and a dazzling light show in the downstairs dance floor.

ROCK

The Forum (✉ 9–17 Highgate Rd., Kentish Town, ☎ 020/7284–2200), a little out of the way, is a premier venue for medium-to-big acts. **100 Club** (✉ 100 Oxford St., W1, ☎ 020/7636–0933) is a basement dive that's always been there for R&B, rock, jazz, and beer. **The Shepherds Bush Empire** (✉ Shepherds Bush Green, W12, ☎ 020/8740–7474) is a major venue for largish acts in West London.

Shopping

Shopping is one of London's great pleasures. Different areas retain their traditional specialties, but there are also numerous pockets of local shops to explore, and it's fun to seek out the small crafts, antiques, and gift stores, designer-clothing resale outlets, and national department-store chains.

Shopping Districts

Chelsea. Centering on the King's Road, Chelsea was once synonymous with ultrafashion; it still harbors some designer boutiques, plus antiques and home furnishings stores. **Covent Garden.** A something-for-everyone neighborhood, Covent Garden has numerous clothing chain stores, stalls selling crafts, and shops selling gifts of every type—bikes, kites, herbs, beads, hats, you name it. **Kensington.** This area's main drag, Kensington High Street, is a smaller, classier version of Oxford Street (☞ *below*), with Barkers department store, and a branch of Marks & Spencer at the eastern end. Try Kensington Church Street for expensive antiques, plus a little fashion. Venture out to the W11 and W2 neighborhoods around the Holland Park/Westbourne Grove/Notting Hill end, and you'll find specialty shops with must-have status, plus lots of fashionable bistros for sustenance. **Knightsbridge.** Kensington's neighbor, Knightsbridge has Harrods, of course, but also Harvey Nichols, the chicest clothes shop in London, and many expensive designers' boutiques along Sloane Street, Walton Street, and Beauchamp Place. Adjacent Belgravia is also a burgeoning area for posh designer stores.

Mayfair. Bond Street, Old and New, is the elegant lure here, with the hautest of haute couture and jewelry outposts, plus fine art. South Molton Street offers high-price, high-style fashion—especially at Browns—and the tailors of Savile Row are of worldwide repute. **Oxford Street.** Crowded and a bit past its prime, Oxford Street is lined with tawdry discount shops. However, Selfridges, John Lewis, and Marks & Spencer are wonderful department stores, and there are interesting boutiques secreted off Oxford Street, just north of the Bond Street tube stop, in little St. Christopher's Place and Gees Court. Check out the cobbled streets in West Soho, behind Liberty in Regent St., for handcrafted jewelry, designer gear, and stylish cafés. **Regent Street.** Perpendicular to Oxford Street lies this noted shopping avenue—famous for its curving path—with possibly London's most pleasant department store, Liberty's, as well as Hamley's, the capital's toy mecca. Shops around once-famous **Carnaby Street** stock designer youth paraphernalia and at least 57 varieties of T-shirts. **St. James's.** The fabled English gentleman buys much of his gear at stores in this area: handmade hats, shirts, and shoes, silver shaving kits, and hip flasks. Here is also the world's best cheese shop, Paxton & Whitfield. Don't expect any bargains in this neighborhood.

Street Markets

Street markets are one aspect of London life not to be missed. Here are some of the more interesting markets:

Bermondsey. Arrive as early as possible for the best treasure—that's what the dealers do. ⊠ *Tower Bridge Rd., SE1.* ☉ *Fri. 4 AM–1 PM. Tube to London Bridge or Bus 15 or 25 to Aldgate and then Bus 42 over Tower Bridge to Bermondsey Sq.*

Camden Lock. The youth center of the world, apparently, it's good for cheap clothes and boots. The canalside antiques, crafts, and junk markets are also picturesque and very crowded. ⊠ *Chalk Farm Rd., NW1.* ☉ *Shops: Tues.–Sun. 9:30–5:30; stalls: weekends 8–6. Tube or Bus 24 or 29 to Camden Town.*

Camden Passage. The rows of little antiques stalls are a good hunting ground for silverware and jewelry. Stalls open Wednesday and Saturday, but there is also a books and prints market on Thursday. Surrounding shops are open the rest of the week. ⊠ *Islington, N1.* ☉ *Wed., Sat. 8:30–3. Tube or Bus 19 or 38 to Angel.*

Petticoat Lane. Look for budget-priced leather goods, gaudy knitwear, and fashions, plus cameras, videos, stereos, antiques, books, and bric-a-brac. ✉ *Middlesex St., E1.* ☉ *Sun. 9–2. Tube to Liverpool St., Aldgate, or Aldgate East.*

Portobello Market. Saturday is the best day for antiques, though this neighborhood is London's melting pot, becoming more vibrant every year. Find fabulous small shops, the city's trendiest restaurants, and a Friday and Saturday flea market at the far end at Ladbroke Grove. ✉ *Portobello Rd., W11.* ☉ *Fri. 5 AM–3 PM, Sat. 6 AM–5 PM. Tube or Bus 52 to Notting Hill Gate or Ladbroke Grove, or Bus 15 to Kensington Park Rd.*

London Essentials

Arriving and Departing

BY BUS

The **National Express** (✉ Victoria Coach Station, Buckingham Palace Rd., ☎ 0990/808080) coach service has routes to more than 1,200 major towns and cities in the United Kingdom. It's considerably cheaper than the train, although the trips usually take longer. National Express offers two types of service: Ordinary service makes frequent stops for refreshment breaks (although all coaches have toilet and washroom facilities and reclining seats); Rapide and Flightlink service has stewardess and refreshment facilities on board. Day returns are available on both, but booking is advised on the Rapide service.

BY PLANE

International flights to London arrive at either Heathrow Airport, 24 km (15 mi) west of London, or at Gatwick Airport, 43 km (27 mi) south of the capital. Most flights from the United States go to Heathrow. Gatwick is London's second gateway. It has grown from a European airport into an airport that serves 21 scheduled U.S. destinations. A third, new, state-of-the-art airport, Stansted, is to the east of the city. It handles mainly European and domestic traffic, although there is a scheduled service from New York.

Carriers serving Great Britain include **American Airlines** (☎ 800/433–7300; 020/8572–5555 in London) to Heathrow, Gatwick; **British Airways** (☎ 800/247–9297; 0345/222111 in London) to Heathrow, Gatwick; **Continental** (☎ 800/231–0856; 0800/776464 in London) to Gatwick; **Delta** (☎ 800/241–4141; 0800/414767 in London) to Heathrow, Gatwick; **Northwest Airlines** (☎ 800/447–4747; 0990/561000 in London) to Gatwick; **TWA** (☎ 800/892–4141; 020/8814–0707 or 01293/535535 in London) to Gatwick; **United** (☎ 800/241–6522; 0845/8444777 in London) to Heathrow; and **Virgin Atlantic** (☎ 800/862–8621; 01293/747747 in London) to Heathrow, Gatwick.

Between the Airport and Downtown. The Piccadilly Line serves Heathrow (all terminals) with a direct Underground (subway) link. Two special buses also serve Heathrow: Airbus A1 leaves every 30 minutes for west and central London and Victoria Station; Airbus A2 goes to west and north London to Euston and King's Cross Station every 30 minutes. The new Heathrow Express train links the airport with Paddington Station in only 15 minutes.

From Gatwick the quickest way to London is the nonstop rail Gatwick Express, costing (at press time) £9.50 one-way and taking 30 minutes to reach Victoria Station. Trains run every 15 minutes from 5:20 AM to 12:50 AM, then hourly 1:35 AM–4:35 AM. Hourly bus service (6:30 AM to 10 PM) is provided by Flightline 777 to Victoria Coach Station. This takes about 90 minutes and costs £7.50 one-way.

Cars and taxis drive into London from Heathrow on M4; the trip can take more than an hour, depending on traffic. The taxi fare is about £40, plus tip. From Gatwick the taxi fare is at least £60, plus tip; traffic can be very heavy.

BY TRAIN

London is served by no fewer than 15 main-line train stations, so be absolutely certain of the station for your departure or arrival. All have Underground stops either in the train station or within a few minutes' walk from it, and most are served by several bus routes. The principal routes that connect London to other major towns and cities are on an InterCity network. Seats can be reserved by phone only with a credit card. You can, of course, apply in person to any British Rail Travel Centre or directly to the station from which you depart.

Fares. The fare structures are slowly changing as the formerly nationalized British Rail is sold off to various independent operators. Generally speaking, it is less expensive to buy a return (round-trip) ticket, especially for day trips not far from London, and you should always inquire at the information office to find out what discount fares are available for your route. You can hear a recorded summary of timetable and fare information to many destinations by calling the appropriate "dial and listen" numbers listed under British Rail in the telephone book. For travel inquiries call 0345/484950.

Below is a list of the major London rail stations and the areas they serve. One central telephone line gets you through to any of the stations: ☎ 0345/484950.

Charing Cross serves southeast England, including Canterbury, Margate, Dover/Folkestone, and ferry ports. **Euston/St. Pancras** serves East Anglia, Essex, the Northeast, the Northwest, and North Wales, including Coventry, Stratford-upon-Avon, Birmingham, Manchester, Liverpool, Windermere, Glasgow, and Inverness, northwest Scotland. **King's Cross** serves the east Midlands; the Northeast, including York, Leeds, and Newcastle; and north and east Scotland, including Edinburgh and Aberdeen. **Liverpool Street** serves Essex and East Anglia. **Paddington** serves the south Midlands, west and south Wales, and the west country, including Oxford. **Victoria** serves southern England, including Gatwick Airport, Brighton, Dover/Folkestone and ferry ports, and the south coast. **Waterloo** serves the southwestern United Kingdom, including Salisbury, Portsmouth, Southampton, and Isle of Wight. **Waterloo International** is for the Eurostar to Europe. **Via the Channel Tunnel.** If you're combining a trip to Great Britain with stops on the Continent, you can either drive your car onto a Le Shuttle train through the Channel Tunnel (35 minutes from Folkestone to Calais), or book a seat on the Eurostar high-speed train service that zips through the tunnel (three hours from London's Waterloo International Station to Paris, 3¼ hours from London to Brussels). For details, *see* the Channel Tunnel *in* Chapter 1.

Getting Around

BY BUS

London's bus system consists of bright red double- and single-deckers, plus other buses of various colors. Destinations are displayed on the front and back, with the bus number on the front, back, and side. Not all buses run the full length of their route at all times. Some buses are still operated with a conductor whom you pay after finding a seat, but these days you will more often find one-person buses, in which you pay the driver upon boarding.

Buses stop only at clearly indicated stops. Main stops—at which the bus should stop automatically—have a plain white background with a red LT symbol on it. There are also request stops with red signs, a white symbol, and the word REQUEST added; at these you must hail the bus to make it stop. Smoking is not allowed on any bus. Although you can see much of the town from a bus, *don't* take one if you want to get anywhere in a hurry; traffic often slows travel to a crawl, and during peak times you may find yourself waiting at least 20 minutes for a bus and not being able to get on it once it arrives. If you intend to go by bus, ask at a Travel Information Centre for a free bus map.

Fares. Single fares start at 70p for short hops (£1 in the central zone). Travelcards (☞ By Underground, *below*) are good for tube, bus, and British Rail trains in the Greater London Zones. There are also a number of bus passes available for daily, weekly, and monthly use, and prices vary according to zones. A photograph is required for weekly or monthly bus passes.

BY CAR

The best advice is to avoid driving in London because of the ancient street patterns and the chronic parking restrictions. One-way streets also add to the confusion.

BY TAXI

London's black taxis are famous for their comfort and for the ability of their drivers to remember the mazelike pattern of the capital's streets. Hotels and main tourist areas have ranks (stands) where you wait your turn to take one of the taxis that drive up. You can also hail a taxi if the flag is up or the yellow FOR HIRE sign is lighted. Fares start at £1.40 and increase by units of 20p per 281 yards or 55.5 seconds until the fare exceeds £8.60. After that, it's 20p for each 188 yards or 37 seconds. Surcharges are a tricky extra, which range from 40p for additional passengers or bulky luggage to 60p for evenings 8 PM until midnight, and until 6 AM on weekends and public holidays—at Christmas it zooms to £2 and there's 40p extra for each additional passenger. Note that fares are occasionally raised from year to year. As for tipping, taxi drivers should get 10%–15% of the tab.

BY UNDERGROUND

Known as "the tube," London's extensive Underground system is by far the most widely used form of city transportation. Trains run both beneath and above ground out into the suburbs, and all stations are clearly marked with the London Underground circular symbol. (A SUBWAY sign refers to an under-the-street crossing.) Trains are all one class; smoking is *not* allowed on board or in the stations.

There are 10 basic lines—all named. The Central, District, Northern, Metropolitan, and Piccadilly lines all have branches, usually taking you to the outlying sections of the city, so be sure to note which branch is needed for your particular destination. Electronic platform signs tell you the final stop and route of the next train, and some signs conveniently indicate how many minutes you'll have to wait for the train to arrive. Begun in the Victorian era, the Underground is still being expanded and improved. The East London line, which runs from Shoreditch and Whitechapel south to New Cross, reopened in 1998. Autumn 1999 is the latest date for the opening of the Jubilee line extension: This state-of-the-art subway will sweep from Green Park to London Bridge and Southwark, with connections to Canary Wharf and the Docklands and the much-hyped Millennium Dome, and on to the east at Stratford.

From Monday through Saturday, trains begin running just after 5 AM; the last services leave central London between midnight and 12:30 AM. On Sunday trains start two hours later and finish about an hour earlier. The frequency of trains depends on the route and the time of day, but normally you should not have to wait more than 10 minutes. A pocket map of the entire tube network is available free from most Underground ticket counters. There should also be a large map on the wall of each platform, and the new computerized database, "Routes," is available at 14 London Transport (LT) Travel Information Centres (☞ *below*).

Fares. For both buses and tube fares, London is divided into six concentric zones; the fare goes up the farther afield you travel. Ask at Underground ticket counters for the LT booklet "Fares and Tickets," which gives all details; after some experimenting you'll soon know which ticket best serves your particular needs. You must buy a ticket before you travel; many types of travel cards can be bought from Pass Agents that display the sign: tobacconists, confectioners, newsagents, and National Railway stations.

Here is a summary of the major ticket categories, but note that these prices are subject to increases.

Carnet. A convenient book of 10 single tickets to use in central zone 1 only; £10.

Singles and Returns. For one trip between any two stations, you can buy an ordinary single (one-way ticket) for travel anytime on the day of issue; if you're coming back on the same route the same day, then an ordinary return (round-trip ticket) costs twice the single fare. Singles vary in price from 90p for short hops (£1.40 in the central zone) to £3.40 for a six-zone journey—not a good option for the sightseer who wants to make several journeys.

Travelcards. These allow unrestricted travel on the tube, most buses, and British Rail trains in the Greater London zones and are valid weekdays after 9:30 AM, weekends, and all public holidays. They cannot be used on airbuses, night buses, or for certain special services. There are different options available: a **One Day Travelcard** costs £3.80–£4.50; **Weekend Travelcards,** for the two days of the weekend and on any two consecutive days during public holidays, £5.70–£6.70. **Family Travelcards:** one-day ticket for one or two adults with one to four children costs £3–£3.60 with one child; extra children cost 60p each—adults do not have to be related to the children or even to each other.

Visitor's Travelcard. These are the best bet for visitors, but they must be bought before leaving home (they're available in both the United States and Canada). They are valid for periods of three, four, or seven days ($25, $32, $49 respectively) and can be used on the tube and virtually all buses and British Rail services in London. All these cards also include a set of money-saving discounts to many of London's top attractions. Apply to travel agents or to **BritRail Travel International** (✉ 1500 Broadway, New York, NY 10036, ☎ 212/382–3737).

For more information there are **LT Travel Information Centres** at the following tube stations: Euston, Hammersmith, King's Cross, Liverpool St., Oxford Circus, Piccadilly Circus, St. James's Park, Victoria, and Heathrow (in Terminals 1, 2, and 4); open 7:15 AM–10 PM, with Terminal 4's TIC closing at 3 PM. For information on all London tube and bus times, fares, and so on, dial 020/7222–1234 (24 hours). For travelers with disabilities call for the free leaflet, "Access to the Underground" (☎ 020/7918–3312).

Contacts and Resources

U.S. (✉ 24 Grosvenor Sq., W1A 1AE, ☎ 020/7499–9000).

Canadian High Commission (✉ McDonald House, 1 Grosvenor Sq., W1X 0AB, ☎ 020/7258–6600).

Police, fire brigade, or ambulance: ☎ 999. **Late-night pharmacies: Bliss Chemist** (✉ 5 Marble Arch, W1, ☎ 020/7723–6116) and **Boots** (✉ 44 Piccadilly Circus, W1, ☎ 020/7734–6126; ✉ 151 Oxford St., W1, ☎ 020/7409–2857).

By Bus. The **Original London Sightseeing Tour** (☎ 020/8877–1722) offers passengers a good introduction to the city from double-decker buses. Tours run daily every 12 minutes or so, departing from Baker Street (Madame Tussaud's), Marble Arch (Speakers' Corner), Piccadilly (Haymarket), or Victoria (Victoria Street). The 21 stops include most of the major sights, such as St. Paul's and Westminster Abbey, and you may hop off to view the sights and then get back on the next bus. Tickets (£12) can be bought from the driver. **The Big Bus Company** (☎ 020/8944–7810) runs a similar operation with a Red and Blue tour. The Red is a two-hour tour with 18 stops, and the Blue, one hour with 13. Both start from Marble Arch, Speakers' Corner. These tours include stops at such places as St. Paul's Cathedral and Westminster Abbey. Prices and pickup points vary according to the sights visited, but many pickup points are at major hotels. **Evan Evans** (☎ 020/8332–2222) offers good bus tours. Another reputable agency that operates bus tours is **Frames Rickards** (☎ 020/7837–3111).

By Canal. In summer narrow boats and barges cruise London's two canals, the Grand Union and Regent's Canal; most vessels operate on the latter, which runs between Little Venice in the west (the nearest tube is Warwick Ave. on the Bakerloo Line) and Camden Lock (about 200 yards north of Camden Town tube station). **Canal Cruises** (☎ 020/7485–4433) offers three or four cruises daily from March through October on the *Jenny Wren* and all year on the cruising restaurant *My Fair Lady*. **Jason's Trip** (☎ 020/7286–3428) operates one-way and round-trip narrow-boat cruises on this route. Trips last 1½ hours. The **London Waterbus Company** (☎ 020/7482–2660) operates this route year-round with a stop at London Zoo: Trips run daily from April through October, and weekends only from November through March.

By River. All year boats cruise up and down the Thames, offering a different view of the London skyline. In summer (April–October) boats run more frequently than in winter—call to check schedules and routes. For trips from Charing Cross to Greenwich Pier, call **Catamaran Cruisers** (☎ 020/7839–3572) or **Westminster Passenger Boat Services** (☎ 020/7930–4097). **City Cruises** (☎ 020/7488–0344) go from Westminster to the Tower and the Thames Barrier, while **Thames Barrier Cruises** (☎ 020/7930–3373) also feature a special package cruise to the Millennium Dome, complete with tea and admission and with stop-offs planned at convenient points for visitors, such as Bankside and London Bridge. A **Sail and Rail** ticket combines the modern wonders of Canary Wharf and Docklands development by Docklands Light Railway with the history of the riverside by boat. Tickets are available year-round from Westminster Pier or Tower Gateway (☎ 020/7363–9700). Upstream destinations include Kew, Richmond, and Hampton Court. Most of the launches have a public-address system and provide a running commentary on passing points of interest. Depending upon the destination, river trips may last from one to four hours. For more information call **Thames Cruises** (☎ 020/7928–9009).

Excursions. LT, Evan Evans, and Frames Rickards (☞ By Bus, *above*) all offer day excursions (some combine bus and boat) to places of interest within easy reach of London, such as Windsor, Hampton Court, Oxford, Stratford-upon-Avon, and Bath. Prices vary and may include lunch and admission prices or admission only. Alternatively, make your own way, cheaply, to many of England's attractions on **Green Line Coaches** (☎ 020/8668–7261).

On Foot. One of the best ways to get to know London is on foot, and there are many guided and themed walking tours from which to choose. **The Original London Walks** (☎ 020/7624–3978) and **Citisights** (☎ 020/8806–4325) are just two of the better-known firms, but your best bet is to peruse the variety of leaflets at a London Tourist Information Centre. The duration of the walks varies (usually one–three hours), and you can generally find one to suit even the most specific of interests— Shakespeare's London, or a Beatles's Magical Mystery Tour, or, even— gasp!—a Jack the Ripper tour.

If you'd rather explore on your own, then the City of London Corporation has laid out a **Heritage Walk** that leads through Bank, Leadenhall, and Monument; follow the trail by the directional stars set into the sidewalks. A map of this walk can be found in *A Visitor's Guide to the City of London,* available from the City Information Centre across from St. Paul's Cathedral. The **Silver Jubilee Walkway** covers 16 km (10 mi) and is marked by a series of silver crowns set into the sidewalks; Parliament Square makes a good starting point. **The Thames Path** is a new National Trail, some 291 km (180 mi) from the river's source in Gloucestershire to the Thames Barrier; for information, call London Docklands Visitor Centre (☎ 020/7512–1111). Several guides offering further walks are available in bookshops. One of the latest and most fascinating is *Secret London* by Andrew Duncan (New Holland).

TRAVEL AGENCIES
American Express (⊠ 6 Haymarket, SW1, ☎ 020/7930–4411; ⊠ 89 Mount St., W1, ☎ 020/7499–4436). **Thomas Cook** (⊠ 4 Henrietta St., WC2, ☎ 020/7379–0685; ⊠ 1 Marble Arch, W1, ☎ 020/7724–9483).

VISITOR INFORMATION
London Tourist Information Centre (⊠ Victoria Station Forecourt). **British Visitor Centre** (⊠ 1 Regent St., Piccadilly Circus, SW1).

Visitorcall is the London Tourist Board's 24-hour phone service—a premium-rate (39p–49p per minute) recorded information line, with different numbers for theater, events, museums, sports, getting around, and so on. To access the list of options call 0839/123456, or see the separate categories in the telephone directory.

WINDSOR TO BATH

The Thames, England's second-longest river, winds its way toward London through an accessible and gracious stretch of countryside. An excursion west from the capital, roughly following the river toward its source in the Cotswold Hills, allows you to explore such historic townships as Windsor, where the castle is still regularly used by the royal family; Oxford, home of the nation's oldest university; and Stratford-upon-Avon, Shakespeare's birthplace. Traveling south, you come to Bath, whose 18th-century streets recall an age more elegant than our own.

Windsor

★ **Windsor Castle,** 34 km (21 mi) west of London, has been a royal citadel since the days of William the Conqueror in the 11th century.

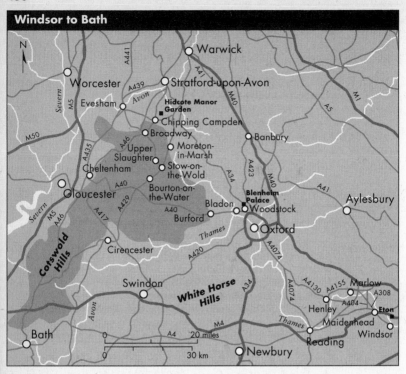

Windsor to Bath

During the 14th century Edward III revamped the old castle, building the Norman gateway, the great round tower, and new apartments. Almost every monarch since then has added new buildings or improved existing ones; over the centuries the medieval fortification has been transformed into the lavish royal palace the visitor sees today.

The devastating fire of November 1992, which started in the Queen's private chapel, totally gutted some of the State Apartments. A swift rescue response meant that, miraculously, hardly any works of art were lost. In fact some were even discovered in the restoration process, with fragments of a 17th-century mural, done for Charles II by Antonio Verrio, surfacing during the renovation on St. George's Hall. Reopened to the public in December 1997 with grand fanfare, the castle has never looked more impressive. Costing a total of £37 million, phenomenal repair work has restored the **Grand Reception Room,** the **Green and Crimson Drawing Rooms,** and the **State and Octagonal Dining Rooms** to their former, if not greater, glory. The ceiling of St. George's Hall, where the Queen gives state banquets, was completely destroyed—today, a new green oak roof, the largest hammerbeam construction roof to have been built during the 20th century, now looms magnificently over the 600-year-old hall. The private chapel of the Royal Family has also been redesigned, with a new stained-glass window commemorating the fire of 1992 and the restoration work that subsequently took place. All restored rooms, except the private chapel, are open to the public. Be aware that the State Apartments are sometimes closed when the Queen is in residence; call ahead to check.

St. George's Chapel, more than 230 ft long with two tiers of great windows and hundreds of gargoyles, buttresses, and pinnacles, is one of the noblest buildings in England. Inside, above the choir stalls, hang the banners, swords, and helmets of the Knights of the Order of the Garter, the most senior Order of Chivalry. The many monarchs buried in the chapel include Henry VIII and George VI, father of the present queen. (Note that St. George's Chapel is closed to the public on Sunday.)

The magnificent art collection at Windsor contains paintings by such masters as Rubens, Van Dyck, and Holbein; drawings by Leonardo da Vinci; and Gobelin tapestries. There are splendid views across to Windsor Great Park, the remains of a former royal hunting forest. Make time to view **Queen Mary's Dolls' House,** a charming toy country house with every detail complete, including electricity, running water, and miniature books on the library shelves. It was designed in 1921 by the architect Sir Edwin Lutyens for the present queen's grandmother.

✉ *Windsor Castle,* ☎ *01753/868286.* 🎫 *£10, £21.50 family ticket; Dolls' House £1 extra (included in family ticket), or separately (including entry to the precincts).* ☉ *Mar.–Oct., daily 10–5:30 (last admission at 4); Nov.–Feb., daily 10–4 (last entrance at 3).*

After seeing the castle stroll around the town and enjoy the shops; antiques are sold on cobbled Church Lane and Queen Charlotte Street.

A new attraction to delight children (of all ages) is a **Legoland,** set in woodland 3¼ km (2 mi) outside Windsor. Hands-on activities both indoors and out include building, driving, and boating. For more information ask at the Windsor tourist office. ✉ *B3202, Bracknell/Ascot Rd.,* ☎ *0990/040404.* 🎫 *£16.50.* ☉ *Mar.–June and Sept.–Nov., daily 10–6; July–Aug., daily 10–8.*

$$ ✕ **Ye Harte and Garter.** Right opposite Windsor Castle, in the hotel of the same name, this restaurant has a reasonably priced carvery offering a range of meats alongside the full à la carte menu. There is also a snack bar for sandwiches and light meals. ✉ *High St., Windsor,* ☎ *01753/863426. AE, DC, MC, V.*

Henley

Henley has been famous since 1839 for the rowing regatta it holds each year around the first Sunday in July. The social side of the regatta is as entertaining as the races themselves; elderly oarsmen wear brightly colored blazers and tiny caps, businessmen entertain wealthy clients, and everyone admires the ladies' fashions. The town is worth exploring for its small but good selection of specialty shops. The Red Lion Hotel near the 200-year-old bridge has been visited by kings, dukes, and writers. **St. Mary's Church** has a 16th-century "checkerboard" tower made of alternate squares of flint and stone. The **Chantry House,** built in 1420 as a school for poor boys, is an unspoiled example of the rare overhanging timber-frame design. ✉ *Hart St.,* ☎ *01491/577062.* 🎫 *Free.* ☉ *For church services or by appointment.*

Oxford

Numbers in the margin correspond to points of interest on the Oxford map.

The surest way to absorb Oxford's unique blend of history and scholarliness is to wander around the tiny alleys that link the honey-color stone buildings topped by elegant "dreaming" spires, exploring the colleges where the undergraduates live and work. Oxford University, like Cambridge University, is not a single building but a collection of 35 independent colleges; many of their magnificent chapels and dining halls are open to visitors—times and (in some cases) entry charges are displayed at the entrance lodges. Some colleges are open only in the afternoons during university semesters, when the undergraduates are in residence; access is often restricted to the chapels and dining rooms (called halls) and sometimes the libraries, too. All are closed during exams, usually from mid-April to late June, when the May Balls are held. By far the best way to gain access is to join a walking tour led by an official Blue Badge guide. These two-hour tours leave up to five times daily from the Tourist Information Centre. The main highways leading into Oxford are A4130 and A4074.

One of the most delightful walks through Oxford is along the **banks of the River Cherwell,** either through the University Parks area or through Magdalen College to Addison's Walk. Along the way you can watch the undergraduates idly punting a summer's afternoon away. Better still, rent one of these narrow flat-bottom boats yourself—but be warned: Navigating is more difficult than it looks!

❼ Ashmolean Museum. Off Broad and Magdalen streets, the Ashmolean is Britain's oldest public museum, holding noted collections of Egyptian, Greek, and Roman artifacts; Michelangelo drawings; and European silverware. ⊠ *Beaumont St.,* ☎ *01865/278000.* ▣ *Free.* ☉ *Tues. 10–5, Wed.–Sat. 10–4, Sun. 2–5.*

❹ Balliol College. The doors between the inner and outer quadrangles of Bailliol still bear the scorch marks from the flames that burned Archbishop Cranmer and Bishops Latimer and Ridley at the stake in 1555 for their Protestant beliefs. ⊠ *Broad St.* ☉ *Daily 2–5.*

❿ Bodleian Library. Begun in 1602 and one of the oldest libraries in the world, the Bodleian is housed in the spectacular Radcliffe Camera (☞ *below*) and contains an unrivaled collection of manuscripts. Limited sections of the Bodleian can be visited on a tour (☎ 01865/277188). Otherwise, the general public can only visit the Divinity School, a superbly vaulted room with changing exhibitions of manuscripts and rare books. Nearby is the **St. Aldate's Coffee House** (⊠ 94 St. Aldate's), a great place for lunch or coffee. ⊠ *Broad St.,* ☎ *01865/277165.* ☉ *Tour mid-Mar.–Oct., weekdays at 10:30, 11:30, 2, and 3; Nov.–mid-Mar., weekdays at 2 and 3; occasional Sat. morning tours.*

❸ Christ Church College. Built in 1546, Christ Church is the site of Oxford's largest quadrangle, "Tom Quad," named after the huge bell (6¼ tons) that hangs in the gate tower. Its 800-year-old chapel in one corner has been Oxford's cathedral since the time of Henry VIII. The college's medieval dining hall contains portraits of many famous alumni, including John Wesley, William Penn, and 13 of Britain's prime ministers. Lewis Carroll was a teacher of mathematics here for many years; a shop opposite the meadows in St. Aldate's was the inspiration for the shop in *Through the Looking Glass.* ⊠ *St. Aldate's.* ▣ *£3.* ☉ *Mon.–Sat. 9:30–4:30, Sun. 2–4:30.*

Christ Church Picture Gallery. In Canterbury Quadrangle, this connoisseur's delight exhibits paintings by Tintoretto, Veronese, and Van Dyck. ⊠ *Deanery Gardens,* ☎ *01865/276172.* ☉ *Mon.–Sat. 10:30–1 and 2–4:30, Sun. 2–4:30 (till 5:30 Easter–end Oct.).*

Magdalen Bridge. At the foot of this famous Oxford landmark you can rent a punt (a shallow-bottomed boat that is poled slowly up the river) for £10 an hour. You may wish, like many an Oxford student, to spend a summer afternoon punting—while dangling your champagne bottle in the water to keep it cool. ⊠ *High St.*

❶ Magdalen College. Founded in 1458, with an impressive main quadrangle and a supremely monastic air, Magdalen is one of the most impressive of Oxford's colleges; scenic highlights include the Deer Park and Addison's Walk. Graduates includes Cardinal Wolsey, Gibbon, and Oscar Wilde. ☉ *Daily 2–6.*

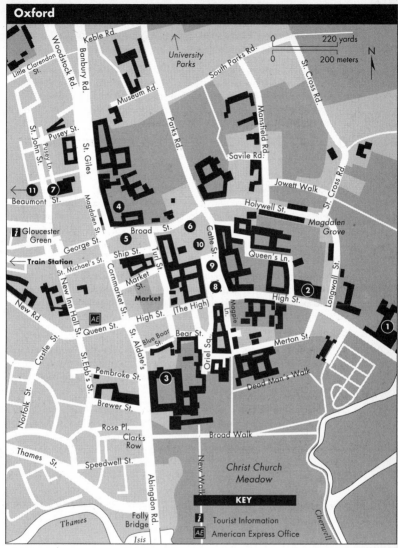

Oxford

0 ··· 220 yards
0 ··· 200 meters

N

University Parks

Keble Rd.
Woodstock Rd.
Little Clarendon St.
Banbury Rd.
Museum Rd.
St. John St.
Pusey St.
Pusey Ln.
St. Giles
Magdalen St.
Parks Rd.
South Parks Rd.
St. Cross Rd.
Savile Rd.
Mansfield Rd.
Jowett Walk
Holywell St.
Magdalen Grove
Beaumont St.
Gloucester Green
George St.
Broad St.
Catte St.
Queen's Ln.
← Train Station
Ship St.
St. Michael's St.
Cornmarket St.
Turl St.
Market St.
Market
Magpie Ln.
High St.
New Inn Hall St.
New Rd.
Castle St.
Queen St.
St. Aldate's
St. Ebb's St.
High St. (The High)
Blue Boar St.
Bear St.
Oriel Sq.
Merton St.
Dead Man's Walk
Norfolk St.
Pembroke St.
Brewer St.
Rose Pl.
Clarks Row
Broad Walk
Thames St.
Speedwell St.
Abingdon Rd.
New Walk
Christ Church Meadow
Thames
Folly Bridge
Isis
Cherwell

KEY

Tourist Information

American Express Office

Ashmolean Museum, **7**
Balliol College, **4**
Bodleian Library, **10**
Christ Church College, **3**
Magdalen College, **1**
Oxford Story, **5**

Radcliffe Camera, **9**
St. Edmund Hall, **2**
Sheldonian Theatre, **6**
University Church, **8**
Worcester College, **11**

⑤ The **Oxford Story.** This multimedia presentation explores the university's 800-year history. ⊠ *Broad St.,* ☎ *01865/790055.* ⊙ *Apr.–June and Sept.–Oct., daily 9:30–5; Jul.–Aug., daily 9:30–7; Nov.–Mar., daily 10–4.*

⑨ **Radcliffe Camera.** Located behind University Church, this striking English Baroque structure is adorned with marble urns, massive columns, and one of the largest domes in Britain. Other than for access to the world-famous Bodleian Library (☞ *above*), the structure is not open to the public.

② **St. Edmund Hall.** Adjacent to Magdalen College on High Street, St. Edmund Hall has one of the smallest and most picturesque quadrangles, with an old well in the center. ⊙ *Daily 1 PM to dusk.*

⑥ **Sheldonian Theatre.** Famous 17th-century architect Christopher Wren designed this to look like a semicircular Roman amphitheater, complete with front gate topped by gigantic busts of the ancient emperors. ⊠ *Broad St.,* ☎ *01865/277299.* ⊙ *Mon.–Sat. 10–12:30 and 2–4:30 (mid-Nov.–Feb. until 4). Closed 10 days at Christmas and Easter, also for student events.*

⑧ **University Church.** Officially known as St. Mary the Virgin, this church is near the center of Oxford, and its 14th-century tower provides a splendid panoramic view of the city's famous skyline. The interior of the church is crowded with 700 years of funeral monuments. ☎ *01865/ 243806.* ⊙ *Tower daily 9:15–7, 9:15–5 Oct.–Easter.*

⑪ **Worcester College.** Noted for its wide lawns, colorful cottage garden, and large lake, this college was built on the site of a former college, founded in 1283, and numbers Thomas De Quincey and other luminaries among its alumni. ⊠ *Worcester St.*

$$$ ✕ **Elizabeth's.** These small, elegant dining rooms in a 16th-century bishop's palace overlook Christ Church and have the best views of any restaurant in Oxford. Salmon quenelles and roast lamb are among the Spanish chef's specialties. ⊠ *82 St. Aldate's,* ☎ *01865/242230. Reservations essential. AE, DC, MC, V. Closed Mon.*

$$ ✕ **Gee's.** This brasserie in a conservatory, formerly a florist's shop, is just north of the town center. The menu offers French and English dishes, including a good fish selection, and the place is popular with both town and gown. ⊠ *61 Banbury Rd.,* ☎ *01865/553540. AE, MC, V.*

$ ✕ **Munchy Munchy.** A constantly changing menu of spicy Indonesian dishes and a good selection of fresh fruit and vegetables make this a refreshing and popular spot. The surroundings are unpretentious and the prices are reasonable. ⊠ *6 Park End St.,* ☎ *01865/245710. MC, V. Closed Sun., Mon.*

$$$$ 🏨 **Old Parsonage.** It's rare to find an attractive country house–hotel, with stone gables and mullion windows, in the middle of a city, but that is just what awaits at the Old Parsonage. It was established in 1660 and was completely restored and refurbished in 1991. Open fires, fascinating pictures, comfortable rooms, and immaculate service make this a hotel to remember. The rates are at the bottom of its price category. ⊠ *1 Banbury Rd., OX2 6NN,* ☎ *01865/310210,* 🆋 *01865/311262. 30 rooms. Restaurant. AE, DC, MC, V.*

$$$–$$$$ 🏨 **The Randolph.** Oxford's only large central hotel has undergone extensive restoration of its beautiful Victorian Gothic interior (unfortunately, this has not extended to some of the very squeaky floorboards, an annoyance at night). It's across from the Ashmolean Museum. ⊠ *Beaumont St., OX1 2LN,* ☎ *01865/247481,* 🆋 *01865/791678. 104 rooms, 4 suites. Restaurant. AE, DC, MC, V.*

$$$ ☐ **Eastgate Hotel.** This welcoming hotel has the traditional style of an inn. Flanked by ancient university buildings and colleges, it is a good place to get an insight into university life. ☒ *The High, OX1 4BE,* ☎ *01865/ 248244,* ☒ *01865/791681. 62 rooms. Restaurant. AE, DC, MC, V.*

Woodstock

★ **Blenheim Palace,** about 13 km (8 mi) north of Oxford on A44 (Woodstock Road), is the most spectacular house in England, even beating Buckingham Palace and Windsor Castle for sheer grandeur and majesty. A vast pile of towers, colonnades, and porticoes, Blenheim was built in neoclassical style during the early 18th century by the architect Sir John Vanbrugh; it stands in 2,500 acres of beautiful gardens created later in the 18th century by the English landscape gardener "Capability" Brown. Soldier and statesman John Churchill, first duke of Marlborough, built the house on land given to him by Queen Anne as a reward for his defeat of the French at the Battle of Blenheim in 1704. The house is filled with fine paintings—don't miss the grand John Singer Sargent portrait of the ninth Duke and his wife, Consuelo Vanderbilt— tapestries, and furniture. Winston Churchill, a descendant of Marlborough, was born in the palace; some of his paintings are on display, and there is an exhibition devoted to his life. A cafeteria is on the grounds, as is a famous topiary maze, butterfly house, and other amusements. ☒ *Woodstock,* ☎ *01993/811091.* ☐ *House, £8.50.* ☺ *Mid-Mar.–Oct., 10:30–4:45; grounds open year-round 9–4:45.*

Sir Winston Churchill (1874–1965) is buried in the nearby village of **Bladon.** His grave in the small tree-lined churchyard is all the more touching for its simplicity.

Just outside the back gates of Blenheim Palace is the village of **Woodstock**—extraordinarily civilized, it's filled with beautiful shops, some elegant 18th-century buildings, and historic hotels, such as The Bear (☎ 01993/811511), The Feathers (☎ 01993/812291), and the Blenheim Guest House and Tea Rooms (☎ 01993/813810), the last set just outside the imperial back gates of the palace. Stay here instead of in Oxford and take the 15-minute bus ride back and forth to the college town.

Stratford-upon-Avon

Numbers in the margin correspond to points of interest on the Stratford-upon-Avon map.

A34 runs northwest from Oxford and Blenheim across the Cotswold Hills to Stratford-upon-Avon, the hometown of William Shakespeare. Even without its most famous son, Stratford would be worth visiting. The town's timbered buildings bear witness to its prosperity during the 16th century, when it was a thriving craft and trading center. Attractive buildings from the 18th century add to the town's historic feel.

The main places of Shakespearean interest are run by the **Shakespeare Birthplace Trust** (☎ 01789/204016). They all have similar opening times, and you can get a combination ticket for them all—£11—or pay separate entry fees if you want to visit only one or two. ☺ *Shakespeare's Birthplace and Anne Hathaway's Cottage: mid-Mar.–mid-Oct., Mon.– Sat. 9–5, Sun. 9:30–5; mid-Oct.–mid-Mar., Mon.–Sat. 9:30–4, Sun. 10– 4. Nash's House, Hall's Croft, and Mary Arden's House: mid-Mar.– mid-Oct., Mon.–Sat. 9:30–5, Sun. 10–5; mid-Oct.–mid-Mar., 10–4, Sun. 10:30–4. Last entry for all sights 30 mins before closing.*

★ ❸ **Anne Hathaway's Cottage.** Set in Shottery on the edge of the town, this is the early home of the playwright's wife. With a storybook thatched roof, this house is one of the most picturesque sights in all

464

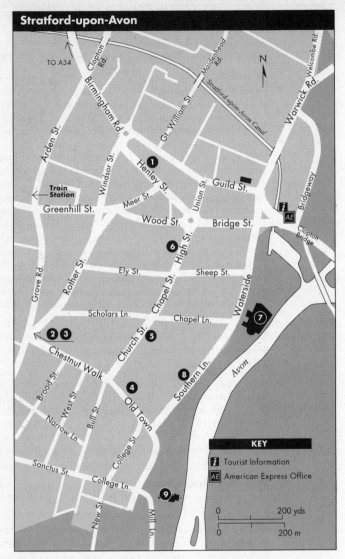

Stratford-upon-Avon

KEY

i Tourist Information

AE American Express Office

Britain. *Cottage La., Shottery,* ☎ *01789/292100. A Shakespeare Birthplace Trust property.*

⑤ **Guildhall Grammar School.** Along the main thoroughfare of Church Street are almshouses built by the Guild of the Holy Cross during the early 15th century. Farther along is the town school, which Shakespeare probably attended as a boy, and which is—four centuries later—still used to educate the youths of Stratford. ⊠ *Church St., near Chapel La.,* ☎ *01789/293351.* ☉ *Easter and summer school vacations, daily 10–6.*

④ **Hall's Croft.** A fine Tudor town house, this was the home of Shakespeare's daughter Susanna and her doctor husband; it is furnished in the decor of the day. The doctor's dispensary and consulting room can also be seen. ⊠ *Old Town. A Shakespeare Birthplace Trust property.*

⑥ **Harvard House.** Next to the Garrick Inn, Harvard House is a half-timbered 16th-century structure that was home to Catherine Rogers, mother of the John Harvard who founded Harvard University in 1636. Unfortunately, the house is virtually unfurnished. ⊠ *High St.* ⊘ *May–Sept. Contact the Shakespeare Centre for hrs.*

❾ Holy Trinity Church. Close to the Royal Shakespeare Theatre and along the banks of the Avon, this is where Shakespeare and his wife are buried. ⊠ *Trinity St.*

❷ Mary Arden's House. Originally a farmhouse, the girlhood home of Shakespeare's mother, this house is now an extensive museum of farming and country life, and it's beautifully evocative of the times in which Shakespeare lived. The black-and-white timbered house was built in the 16th century, and many of the original outbuildings are intact, together with a 600-nesting-hole dovecote. The garden is planted with trees mentioned in Shakespeare's plays. ⊠ *Wilmcote (5½ km/3½ mi northwest of Stratford, off A3400 and A46); reachable by train in a few minutes from Stratford. A Shakespeare Birthplace Trust property.*

❽ The Other Place. This new auditorium for experimental productions stands just down the street from the Royal Shakespeare Theatre. ⊠ *Waterside, Stratford-upon-Avon, Warwickshire CV37 6BB,* ☎ *01789/ 295623.*

❼ Royal Shakespeare Theatre. The most famous Shakesperian theater in the world occupies a perfect position on the banks of the Avon—try to see a performance if you can. The company (always referred to as the RSC) performs several Shakespeare plays each season, as well as scripts by a wide variety of other playwrights, between March and January. For a fascinating insight into how the theater operates, join one of the backstage tours, led twice daily (four times on Sunday). Beside the main theater is the smaller **Swan.** Modeled on an Elizabethan theater, the Swan stages productions in the round. The Swan also provides entry to the RSC Collection, comprising paintings, props, and memorabilia; visit it either on one of the backstage tours or on your own. It's best to book well in advance for RSC productions, but a very few tickets for the day of performance are always available, and it is also worth asking if there are any returns. ⊠ *The Royal Shakespeare Theatre, Stratford-upon-Avon, Warwickshire CV37 6BB,* ☎ *01789/ 295623 (programs available starting Feb.); 01789/412602 for details on backstage tours and RSC Collection.*

★ **❶ Shakespeare Birthplace and Centre.** This holy shrine for Shakespeare lovers also contains a small museum with costumes used in the BBC's versions of the plays and an exhibition of the playwright's life and work. ⊠ *Henley St. A Shakespeare Birthplace Trust property.*

$$$ ✕ Box Tree Restaurant. In the Royal Shakespeare Theatre, this elegant restaurant overlooks the river and is a favored spot for pre- and post-theater dining. Specialties include roast rack of lamb and grilled Scotch beef fillet. ⊠ *Waterside,* ☎ *01789/293226. AE, MC, V. Closed when theater is closed.*

$$ ✕ The Opposition. Located near the Royal Shakespeare Theatre, the Opposition caters to the pre- and post-theater dining crowd (as do all sensible restaurants in Stratford). It is extremely popular with the locals, so book in advance. The American and Continental dishes change each month—if you're lucky there will be Cajun chicken. ⊠ *13 Sheep St.,* ☎ *01789/269980. Reservations essential. MC, V.*

$ ✕ The Slug and Lettuce. Don't let the name put you off—this pine-paneled pub serves excellent meals. Long-standing favorites are chicken breast baked in avocado and garlic, and poached cushion of salmon. ⊠ *38 Guild St.,* ☎ *01789/299700. Reservations essential. MC, V.*

\$\$\$ 🏠 **Falcon County Hotel.** Licensed as an alehouse since 1640, it still has a friendly inn atmosphere. The heavily beamed rooms in the older part are small and quaint; those in the modern extension are in standard international style. ⊠ *Chapel St., CV37 6HA,* ☎ *01789/279953,* 𝐅𝐀𝐗 *01789/414260. 73 rooms. Restaurant. AE, DC, MC, V.*

\$\$\$ 🏠 **Shakespeare Hotel.** For a touch of typical Stratford, stay at this timbered Elizabethan town house in the heart of the town, close to the theater and to most of the attractions. It has been luxuriously modernized while still retaining its Elizabethan character. ⊠ *Chapel St., CV37 6ER,* ☎ *01789/294771,* 𝐅𝐀𝐗 *01789/415411. 63 rooms. AE, DC, MC, V.*

\$\$ 🏠 **Caterham House.** Built in 1830, this elegantly furnished building is within an easy walk of the theater. You may spot an actor or two among the guests. ⊠ *58 Rother St., CV37 6LT,* ☎ *01789/267309,* 𝐅𝐀𝐗 *01789/414836. 10 rooms with bath or shower. MC, V.*

Warwick

Warwick, some 13 km (8 mi) north of Stratford along A46, is an unusual mixture of Georgian redbrick and Elizabethan half-timber buildings, although some unattractive postwar developments have spoiled the town center. **Warwick Castle** is one of the finest medieval structures of its kind in England, towering on a precipice above the River Avon. Most of the present buildings date from the 14th century. The interior contains magnificent collections of armor, paintings, and furniture, and a waxworks display by Madame Tussaud's. Outside, peacocks strut in the 60 acres of landscaped riverside gardens. A restored Victorian boathouse has a flora-and-fauna exhibition and a nature walk. ⊠ *Castle Hill,* ☎ *01926/495421.* 🎟 *£9.25 (£9.95 July and Aug.).* ⊙ *Easter–Oct., daily 10–6; Nov.–Easter, daily 10–5 (last entry 30 mins before closing).*

The Cotswolds

Near the spires and shires of Shakespeare Country is a region that conjures up "olde Englande" at its most blissfully rural: the Cotswolds. If you've come in search of picture-postcard English countryside, with soft rolling hills and mellow stone-built villages, this is your destination. From Stratford take an easy detour via A3400 and B4632 into this region, which is marked by high, bare hills patterned by patches of ancient forest and stone walls that protect the sheep that have grazed here from the earliest times.

The gateway to the Cotswolds is **Cheltenham,** once the rival of Bath in its Georgian elegance. Although it's now marred by modern developments, there are still some fine examples of the Regency style in its graceful secluded villas, lush gardens, and leafy crescents and squares (☞ Windsor to Bath map, *above*). If you visit this historic health resort in the spring or summer—take either M4 and M5 north from Bath, or M5 south from Birmingham, turning east on A40—be sure to explore elegant Landsdowne Terrace, Pittville Spa, Sherborne Walk, and Montpellier Walk. Cheltenham may look in part like a Gilbert & Sullivan stage set but it is also home to the progressive **Cheltenham Festival of Literature,** held in October.

From Cheltenham, take B4632 to reach the Cotswolds proper. Two kilometers (1 mile) southeast of Winchcombe is **Sudeley Castle,** the home and burial place of Catherine Parr (1512–48), Henry VIII's last wife. Now restored by the Dent-Brocklehurst family, the Tudor-age mansion is surrounded by the most beautiful rose gardens in England, where Shakespeare performances are given in the summer. ⊠ *Winchcombe,* ☎ *01242/604357.* ⊙ *Castle: end Mar.–end Oct., daily 10:30–5:30; gardens, plant center, and shop: Mar.–end Oct., daily 10:30–5:30.*

Just 5 km (3 mi) northeast of Sudeley Castle is the tiny village of Stanway, landmarked by **Stanway House,** which dates from the Jacobean era and familiar to many, thanks to its starring role in many TV dramas, including *The Buccaneers.* J. M. Barrie, author of *Peter Pan,* often rented this house during summer and his thatched-roof cricket pavilion adorns the grounds. ⊠ *Stanway,* ☎ *01386/584469.* 🎫 *£3.* ⊙ *Aug.–Sept., Tues., Thurs. 2–5 (Wed. by appt. only for groups of at least 20).*

★ Two kilometers (1 mile) to the north of Stanway lies the storybook hamlet of Snowshill. Here lies the perfect Cotswold house, **Snowshill Manor,** a 17th-century house overflowing with the amazing collections of bric-a-brac formed by Charles Paget Wade. ⊠ *Snowshill,* ☎ *01386/852410.* ⊙ *Apr.–Oct., Wed.–Mon. 1–5.*

Three kilometers (2 miles) north of Snowshill lies **Broadway,** the Cotswold town to end all Cotswold towns. William Morris first discovered this village in the late 19th century and art lovers have journeyed there ever since to enjoy its many picturesque houses, tea parlors, and antiques shops. North of Broadway along the B4081 is the Cotswolds in a microcosm, the idyllic town of **Chipping Campden,** announced from afar by the soaring steeple of **St. James.** Look for the group of almshouses built in 1624 on High St. and raised above street level and for the gabled **Market Hall** built three years later by Sir Baptiste Hycks for the sale of local produce. The historic **Silk Mill** has been renovated for crafts shops.

★ Six kilometers (4 miles) outside Chipping Campden is **Hidcote Manor Garden,** a 20th-century garden created around a Cotswold manor house (not open to the public). The lovely garden—which some connoisseurs consider the finest in Britain—consists of a series of open-air rooms divided by walls and hedges, each in a different style. Nearby is the fairy-tale hamlet of Hidcote Bartrim. ⊠ *Hidcote Bartrim,* ☎ *01386/ 438333.* ⊙ *Apr.–May and Aug.–Sept., Sat.–Mon., Wed., Thurs. 11– 7; June–July, Sat.–Thurs. 11–7; Oct., Sat.–Mon., Wed., Thurs. 11–6. Last entrance 1 hr before sunset.*

South of Hidcote is **Stow-on-the-Wold,** the highest, as well as the largest, town in the Cotswolds. Built around a wide square, Stow's imposing golden stone houses have been discreetly converted into a good number of quality antiques stores. Six kilometers (4 miles) southeast of Stow is **Bourton-on-the-Water,** the most classic of the Cotswold "water" villages. The River Windrush runs through town, crossed by low stone bridges. Follow the stream and its ducks to the old mill, now home to the **Cotswold Motor Museum and Exhibition of Village Life,** to enjoy exhibits of vintage cars and recreated stores. ⊠ *The Old Mill,* ☎ *01451/821255.* ⊙ *Feb.–Nov., daily 10–6.*

$$$ 🏨 **Lygon Arms.** Mullioned windows, a gorgeous 17th-century stone
★ facade, baronial fireplaces, and rooms that once sheltered Charles I and Oliver Cromwell make this the most luxurious hotel of the Cotswolds. However, some of the modern additions are way too glitzy for this part of the country. On the main street of Broadway, the inn also has 3 acres of private gardens. ⊠ *High St., Broadway WR12 7DU,* ☎ *01386/ 852255,* ℻ *01386/858611. 65 rooms. Restaurant, indoor pool. AE, DC, MC, V.*

$$$ 🏨 **Queen's Hotel.** Overlooking Imperial Gardens from the center of Cheltenham's Promenade, this classic Regency building has welcomed visitors since 1838. Decor is very British. ⊠ *The Promenade, Cheltenham GL50 1NN,* ☎ *01242/224145,* ℻ *01242/224145. 77 rooms. Restaurant. MC, V.*

$$ 🏠 **Coombe House.** This neat guest house has comfortable bedrooms, an attractive garden, and ample parking. ⊠ *Rissington Rd., Bourton-on-the-Water GL54 2DT,* ☎ *01451/821966,* 🗚 *01451/810477. 7 rooms. AE, MC, V.*

Bath

Numbers in the margin correspond to points of interest on the Bath map.

Bath lies at the southern end of the Cotswolds (at the end of A46), some 113 km (70 mi) from Stratford. A perfect 18th-century city, perhaps the best preserved in all Britain, it is a compact place, easy to explore on foot; the museums, elegant shops, and terraces of magnificent town houses are all close to one another. Bath's golden age came about when the city became England's fashionable center for taking the waters. The architect John Wood created a harmonious vision from the mellow local stone, building beautifully executed terraces and crescents throughout the city. After promenading through the town, stop at either the Pump Room (⊠ Abbey Churchyard) for morning coffee or afternoon tea in grand surroundings (perhaps listening to the music of a string quartet), or Sally Lunn's (⊠ North Parade Passage), where the famous Sally Lunn bun is still baked.

❷ Abbey. Next to the Pump Room is the town abbey, built in the 15th century. There are superb fan-vaulted ceilings in the nave and a multimedia show about the abbey's history in the adjacent Heritage Vaults. ⊠ *Abbey Churchyard.* ⊘ *Abbey: daily 9:30–4:30; Heritage Vaults: Mon.–Sat. 10–4.*

❺ Assembly Rooms. Near the Circus, these Assembly Rooms are frequently mentioned by Jane Austen in her novels of early 19th-century life. Housed in a neoclassical mansion, the salons now house a Museum of Costume that displays dress styles from Beau Nash's day to the present. ⊠ *Bennett St.,* ☎ *01225/477785.* 🎟 *£8.70 combined ticket with Roman Baths.* ⊘ *Mon.–Sat. 10–5, Sun. 11–5.*

★ ❸ The Circus. The heart of Georgian Bath is the perfectly proportioned Circus, begun in 1754. Three perfectly proportioned Georgian terraces outline the round garden in the center; to the north of Saw Close, other Georgian cityscapes are on view at Queen Square and Gay Street.

❽ Holburne Museum and Crafts Study Centre. Housed in an elegant 18th-century building, this museum contains a superb collection of 17th- and 18th-century fine art, silverware, and decorative arts. ⊠ *Great Pulteney St.,* ☎ *01225/466669.* ⊘ *Easter–mid-Nov., Mon.–Sat. 11–5, Sun. 2:30–5:30; mid-Nov.–mid-Dec. and mid-Feb.–Easter, Tues.–Sat. 11–5, Sun. 2:30–5:30.*

★ ❹ No. 1 Royal Crescent. Bath's most fashionable address is now home to a museum that offers a delightful peek into the gracious lifestyles of the Age of Enlightenment. It is furnished as it might have been when Beau Nash, the master of ceremonies and arbiter of 18th-century Bath society, lived in the city. ☎ *01225/428126.* ⊘ *Mid-Feb.–Oct., Tues.–Sun. 10:30–5; Nov., Tues.–Sun. 10:30–4 (last admission 30 mins before closing).*

❼ Pulteney Bridge. One of the most charming and picturesque sights in Bath is this 18th-century span, whose design was based on the Ponte Vecchio of Florence. Lined with little shops, the bridge is the only work of Robert Adam in the city. At the western end is the Victoria Art Gallery.

❶ Roman Baths Museum. It was the Romans who first took the waters at Bath, building a temple in honor of their goddess Minerva and a so-

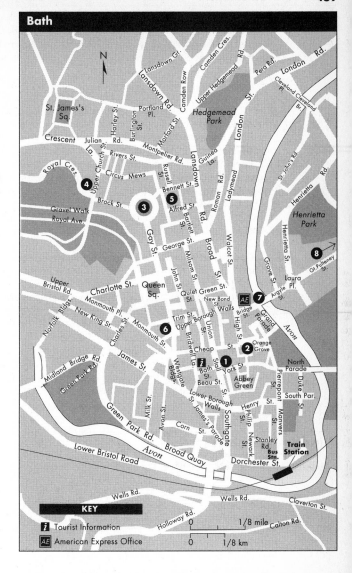

Bath

KEY

ℹ️ Tourist Information

AE American Express Office

0   1/8 mile

0   1/8 km

phisticated series of baths to make full use of the curative hot springs. To this day, these springs gush from the earth at a constant temperature of 115.7°F (46.5°C). Underneath the 18th-century Pump Room, you can see the excavated remains of almost the entire baths complex. ✉ *Abbey Churchyard,* ☎ *01225/477785.* 💷 *£6.70, £8.70 combined ticket for Roman Baths and Museum of Costume.* ☺ *Apr.–July and Sept., daily 9–6; Aug., daily 9–6 and 8 PM–10 PM; Oct.–Mar., daily 9:30–5.*

❻ **Theatre Royal.** This theater opened in 1805 and was restored in 1982. Next door the former home of Beau Nash—the dictator of fashion for mid-18th-century society in Bath—and his mistress Juliana Popjoy is now a restaurant called Popjoy's (☞ *below*).

$$ ✕ **Number Five.** This candlelit bistro off Pulteney Bridge has a relaxed ambience and offers tasty homemade soups or more elaborate dishes, such as roast quail on wild rice and char-grilled loin of lamb. ✉ *5 Argyle St.,* ☎ *01225/444499. AE, DC, MC, V. Closed Sun. No lunch Mon.*

$$ ✕ **Popjoy's Restaurant.** Beau Nash entertained the best of 18th-century society here, and Popjoy's retains its air of elegance. Diners can choose between dining on the ground floor or upstairs in a lovely Georgian drawing room. ⊠ *Sawclose*, ☎ *01225/460494. Reservations essential. AE, DC, MC, V. Closed Sun.*

$$ ✕ **Pump Room.** In addition to the famous morning coffee, lunches, and afternoon tea served here—often to music by a string trio—the adjoining Terrace Restaurant has views over Bath, and is also open for evening meals during the Bath Festival, and in August and December. Lines can be long; reservations are a must for evening. ⊠ *Abbey Churchyard*, ☎ *01225/444477. AE, MC, V. No dinner.*

$$$$ 🏨 **Royal Crescent.** The ultimate in luxury living, in a gracious, lavishly
★ converted building, the hotel stands on one of England's most famous terraces. Each bedroom has been individually designed to recapture the elegance of Bath's heyday. The hotel's formal Dower House restaurant wins consistent praise. ⊠ *16 Royal Crescent, BA1 2LS*, ☎ *01225/ 739955*, FAX *01225/339401. 25 rooms, 19 suites. Restaurant. AE, DC, MC, V.*

$$$ 🏨 **Queensberry Hotel.** In a quiet residential street near the Circus, this
★ intimate, elegant hotel is in three 1772 town houses built by the architect John Wood for the Marquis of Queensberry. Renovations have preserved the Regency touches, and below stairs, the Olive Tree restaurant serves English and Mediterranean dishes. ⊠ *Russell St., BA1 2QF*, ☎ *01225/447928*, FAX *01225/446065. 22 rooms with bath. Restaurant, bar. MC, V. Closed Dec. 24–30.*

$$ 🏨 **Paradise House.** It's a steep uphill climb from the center of Bath, but you'll be rewarded by a wonderful prospect of the city from the upper stories of this Georgian guest house. It features open fires in winter and a lush, secluded garden for the spring and summer. ⊠ *88 Holloway, BA2 4PX*, ☎ *01225/317723*, FAX *01225/482005. 8 rooms with bath or shower. AE, MC, V.*

Windsor to Bath Essentials

Getting Around

BY BUS

Regular long-distance services leave from Victoria Coach Station. **National Express** (☎ 0990/808080) has runs on the route. **Oxford Bus Company** (☎ 020/8668–7261) serves the region. The **Green Line** (☎ 020/8668-7261) bus leaves from Eccleston Bridge, behind London's Victoria train station, *not* from the Coach Station itself. Make sure you catch the fast direct service, which takes 45 minutes and runs hourly; the stopping services take up to 1¼ hours.

BY CAR

M4 and M40 are the main highways out of London serving Oxford, the Cotswolds, and Bath. Once you're clear of London, take to the country roads and explore tiny villages and the best of the English countryside.

BY TRAIN

Windsor is easy to reach by train from London, either from Waterloo direct to Windsor and Eton Riverside (50 minutes), or from Paddington to Windsor Central, changing at Reading (45 minutes); there are two trains per hour on each route. Regular fast trains run from Paddington to Oxford and Bath, and less frequent and slower services requiring at least one change, to Stratford. For information, call 0345/ 484950. An alternative route to Stratford is from London's Euston Station to Coventry, from which there are hourly bus connections on the Stratford Blue line; call 01788/535555 for details.

Guided Tours

Evan Evans (☎ 020/8332–2222) operates daily one-day tours to Oxford, Stratford, and the Cotswolds. **Frames Rickards** (☎ 020/7837–3111) runs full-day sightseeing tours to Windsor, Stratford-upon-Avon, Oxford, and Bath. **Golden Tours** (☎ 020/7233–7030) runs four-day trips to Oxford, Stratford, and the Cotswolds from London. **Guide Friday** (Windsor and Oxford, ☎ 01865/790522; Stratford, ☎ 01789/294466) offers excellent open-top bus tours of Windsor, Oxford, the Cotswolds, and Shakespeare Country.

Visitor Information

Bath (✉ The Colonnades, 11–13 Bath St., ☎ 01225/477101). **Oxford** (✉ The Old School, Gloucester Green, ☎ 01865/726871). **Stow-on-the-Wold** (✉ Hollis House, The Square, ☎ 01451/831082). **Stratford** (✉ Bridgefoot, next to Clopton Bridge, ☎ 01789/293127). **Warwick** (✉ The Court House, Jury St., ☎ 01926/492212). **Windsor** (✉ 24 High St., ☎ 01753/852010).

CAMBRIDGE

Cambridge, home of England's second-oldest university, is an ideal place to explore. There have been students here since the late 13th century, and virtually every generation after that has produced fine buildings, often by the most distinguished architects of its day. The result is a compact gallery of the best of English architecture. There is also good shopping in the city, and you can enjoy relaxing riverside walks. Cambridge is 87 km (54 mi) north of London, 66 km (41 mi) northwest of Colchester, and 102 km (63 mi) southwest of Norwich.

Exploring Cambridge

Numbers in the margin correspond to points of interest on the Cambridge map.

The university is in the very heart of Cambridge. It consists of a number of colleges, each of which is a separate institution with its own distinct character. Undergraduates join an individual college and are taught by dons, who are known as "fellows." Each college is built around a series of courts, or quadrangles; because students and fellows live in these quadrangles, access is sometimes restricted, especially during examination weeks. Visitors are not normally allowed into college buildings other than chapels, halls, and some libraries; some colleges levy an admission charge for certain buildings. Public visiting hours vary dramatically from college to college, and it's best to call ahead or to check first with the city tourist office. Some general guidelines for visiting hours, however, can be noted. Colleges close to visitors during the main exam time, late May to mid-June. Term-time (when classes are in session) means October to December, January to March, and April to June, while summer term, or vacations, run from July to September. If you have time, there's no better way to absorb Cambridge's unique atmosphere than by hiring a punt at Silver Street Bridge or at Magdalene Bridge and navigating down past St. John's or upstream to Grantchester, the pretty village made famous by the poet Rupert Brooke.

❿ Emmanuel College. Evident throughout much of Cambridge, the master hand of Christopher Wren designed the chapel and colonnade of Emmanuel College, founded in 1584. The college was an early center of Puritan learning; among the portraits of famous members of the college hanging in Emmanuel Hall is one of John Harvard, founder of Harvard University. ✉ *St. Andrew's St.,* ☎ *01223/334200.*

Cambridge

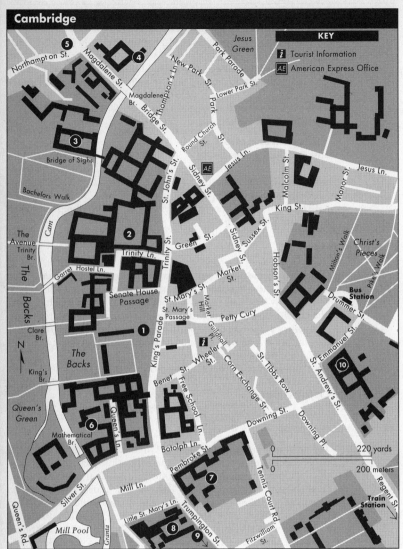

KEY

i Tourist Information

AE American Express Office

Jesus Green

Northampton St.

Magdalene St.

Magdalene Br.

Bridge St.

New Park St.

Park Parade

Jesus Green

Thompson's Ln.

Lower Park St.

Round Church St.

St. John's St.

Sidney St.

Jesus Ln.

AE

Malcolm St.

Manor St.

Jesus Ln.

Bridge of Sighs

Bachelors Walk

King St.

Christ's Pieces

The Cam

The Avenue

Trinity Br.

Trinity Ln.

Green St.

Sidney St.

Sussex St.

Hobson's St.

Milton's Walk

Pike's Walk

Bus Station

Drummer St.

The Backs

Garret Hostel Ln.

Senate House Passage

St. Mary's St.

St. Mary's Passage

Petty Cury

Market St.

Market Hill

Guildhall St.

St. Emmanuel St.

Clare Br.

King's Br.

N

The Backs

King's Parade

Wheeler St.

Benet St.

Free School Ln.

Corn Exchange St.

St. Tibbs Row

St. Andrew's St.

Queen's Green

Mathematical Br.

Queen's Ln.

Botolph Ln.

Pembroke St.

Downing St.

Downing Pl.

0   220 yards

0   200 meters

Silver St.

Mill Ln.

Little St. Mary's Ln.

Trumpington St.

Tennis Court Rd.

Regent St.

Train Station

Queen's Rd.

Mill Pool

Granta

Fitzwilliam St.

Emmanuel
College, **10**

Fitzwilliam
Museum, **9**

Kettle's Yard, **5**

King's College, **1**

Magdalene College, **4**

Pembroke College, **7**

Peterhouse
College, **8**

Queen's College, **6**

St. John's College, **3**

Trinity College, **2**

⑨ Fitzwilliam Museum. Cambridge's most renowned museum contains outstanding art collections (including paintings by Constable, Gainsborough, and the French Impressionists) and antiquities (especially from ancient Egypt). The coffee shop here is an excellent choice for a pastry or a light lunch. ⊠ *Trumpington St.,* ☎ *01223/332900.* ▣ *Free; donation requested.* ⊙ *Tues.–Sat. 10–5, Sun. 2:15–5.*

⑤ Kettle's Yard. Originally a private house owned by a former curator of London's Tate Gallery, Kettle's Yard is home to a fine permanent collection of 20th-century art, sculpture, furniture, and decorative arts. A separate gallery provides space for a regular program of exhibitions. ⊠ *Castle St.,* ☎ *01223/352124.* ▣ *Free.* ⊙ *House: Tues.–Sun. 2–4; gallery: Tues.–Sat. 12:30–5:30, Sun. 2–5:30.*

★ **① King's College.** The high point of King's—and possibly of Cambridge—is its chapel, started by Henry VI in 1446, a masterpiece of late-Gothic architecture, with a great fan-vaulted ceiling supported only by a tracery of soaring side columns. Behind the altar hangs Rubens's painting, *Adoration of the Magi.* Every Christmas Eve the college choir sings the Festival of Nine Lessons and Carols, which is broadcast all over the world. The novelist E. M. Forster, who wrote *Howards End* and *A Passage to India,* studied at King's, as did the war poet Rupert Brooke. King's runs down to the **"Backs,"** the tree-shaded grounds on the banks of the River Cam, which is the background of many of the colleges. ⊠ *King's Parade,* ☎ *01223/331447.* ⊙ *Chapel: term time, Mon. 9:30–4:30, Tues.–Fri. 9:30–3:30, Sat. 9:30–3:15, Sun. 1:15–2:15; summer, Mon.–Sat. 9:30–4:30, Sun. 1:15–2:15 and 5–5:30.*

④ Magdalene College. Across Magdalene (pronounced "maudlin") Bridge, a cast-iron 1820 structure, is Magdalene College, distinguished by pretty redbrick courts. It was a hostel for Benedictine monks for over 100 years before the college was founded in 1542. The college's **Pepys Library** contains the books and desk of the 17th-century diarist Samuel Pepys. Admission to the library is free and it's open April–September, Monday–Saturday 11:30–12:30 and 2:30–5:30; October–March, Monday–Saturday 2:30–3:30. ⊠ *Magdalene St.,* ☎ *01223/332100.*

⑦ Pembroke College. The first court of Pembroke College (1347) has some buildings dating from the 14th century. On the south side Christopher Wren's chapel—his first major commission, completed in 1665—looks like a distinctly modern intrusion. You can walk through the college, around a delightful garden, and past the fellows' bowling green. ⊠ *Trumpington St.,* ☎ *01223/338100.*

⑧ Peterhouse College. Cambridge's oldest college was founded in 1281 by the Bishop of Ely. Parts of the dining hall date from 1290; the chapel, in late Gothic style, dates from 1632. On the river side of the buildings is a large and tranquil deer park. ⊠ *Trumpington St.,* ☎ *01223/ 338200.*

⑥ Queen's College. One of the most eye-catching colleges, Queen's (1446) is named after the respective consorts of Henry VI and Edward IV. The college's Mathematical Bridge (best seen from the Silver Street road bridge) is an arched wooden structure that was originally held together by gravitational force; when it was taken apart to see how Isaac Newton did it, no one could reconstruct it without using nails. The present bridge, dating from 1902, is securely bolted. ⊠ *Queen's La.,* ☎ *01223/ 335511.* ⊙ *Daily 1:45–4:30.*

③ St. John's College. St. John's is Cambridge's second-largest college, founded in 1511 by Henry VII's mother, Lady Margaret Beaufort. The famous copy of the Bridge of Sighs in Venice is here, reaching across the Cam to the mock-Gothic New Court (1825). ✉ *St. John's St.,* ☎ *01223/338600.* ⏱ *Weekdays 10–5:30, weekends 9:30–5:30.*

② **Trinity College.** This is the largest college, with almost 700 undergraduates, established by Henry VIII in 1546. It has a handsome 17th-century Great Court, around which are sited the chapel, hall, gates, and a magnificent library by Christopher Wren—colonnaded and seemingly constructed as much of light as of stone. In the massive gatehouse is Great Tom, a large clock that strikes each hour and that figured in the race around the quadrangle at the heart of the movie *Chariots of Fire.* Prince Charles was an undergraduate here in the late 1960s. ✉ *St. John's St.,* ☎ *01223/338400.* ⏱ *College: daily 10–6; library: weekdays noon–2, Sat. in term time 10:30–12:30.*

$$–$$$ ✕ **Midsummer House.** A classy restaurant set beside the River Cam,
★ Midsummer House is lovely in summer. There's a comfortable conservatory. Set-price menus for lunch and dinner offer a selection of robust yet sophisticated European and Mediterranean dishes. Choices might include tender lamb or the best from the fish market adorned with inventively presented vegetables. ✉ *Midsummer Common,* ☎ *01223/ 369299. Reservations essential. AE, DC, MC, V. Closed Mon. No lunch Sat. No dinner Sun.*

$$ ✕ **Three Horseshoes.** This is an early 19th-century thatched cottage. The menu in the busy—sometimes crowded—pub-restaurant and conservatory sets out a tempting range of beautifully presented dishes. The emphasis is on modern British cuisine, for example, char-grilled meats or roast fish accompanied by sun-dried tomatoes, polenta, and olives. ✉ *Madingley (5 km/3 mi west of Cambridge),* ☎ *01954/210221. Reservations essential. AE, DC, MC, V. No dinner Sun.*

$–$$ ✕ **Brown's.** This huge, airy French-American–style brasserie-diner was converted from the outpatient department of the old Addenbrooke's Hospital opposite the Fitzwilliam Museum. Large fans still keep things cool in the pale yellow dining room. The wide-ranging menu runs from toasted tuna sandwiches, steak-mushroom-and-Guinness pie, hamburgers, and salads to venison or gigot of lamb; check the daily specials, too—there's usually fresh fish and pasta. ✉ *23 Trumpington St.,* ☎ *01223/461655. AE, MC, V.*

$$$$ 🏨 **Garden House Hotel.** Set among the colleges, this luxurious, mod-
★ ern hotel makes the most of its peaceful riverside location—it even rents out its own punts. Its gardens, lounge, cocktail bar, and conservatories all have river views, as do most of the smart guest rooms—if you want one, ask when you make your reservation. A leisure center incorporates an indoor swimming pool, a gym, a sauna, and a steam room. ✉ *Granta Pl., Mill La., CB2 1RT,* ☎ *01223/259988,* 🆑 *01223/ 316605. 118 rooms. Restaurant, pool. AE, DC, MC, V.*

$$$ 🏨 **Arundel House.** This hotel occupies a converted terrace of Victorian houses overlooking the river Cam and Jesus Green, while a pleasing conservatory and patio-garden out back offers a calm hideaway. The bedrooms are comfortably furnished with locally made mahogany furniture; Continental breakfast is included in the room rate, though a full breakfast is available for an extra charge. ✉ *53 Chesterton Rd., CB4 3AN,* ☎ *01223/367701,* 🆑 *01223/367721. 105 rooms with bath or shower. Restaurant. AE, DC, MC, V.*

Cambridge Essentials

Getting Around

BY BUS
There are 14 buses daily from Victoria Coach Station that take just under two hours. Call 0990/808080.

M11 is the main highway from London to Cambridge. The main car-rental companies have offices in Cambridge.

Half-hourly trains from London's Liverpool Street Station and King's Cross Station run to Cambridge. For information call 0345/484950. Average journey time varies from 50 minutes to 1½ hours, depending on the day of week or time of day.

Guided Tours

The **Cambridge Tourist Information Centre** offers two-hour guided walking tours of the city and the colleges daily; tickets (£5.75) are available up to 24 hours in advance from the city tourist information center. Various theme tours are also offered, including combined walking/punting tours and 1½-hour evening pub tours. Booking is essential—the tours are very popular. **Guide Friday** (☎ 01223/362444), in Cambridge, operates a city open-top bus tour every 15 minutes throughout the day (October–May, half-hourly); tickets (£7.50) can be bought from the driver, the office at Cambridge train station, or Cambridge Tourist Information Center. You can join the tours at the station or at any of the specially marked bus stops throughout the city.

Visitor Information

Cambridge (✉ Wheeler St., off King's Parade, ☎ 01223/322640, FAX 01223/463385).

YORK

Once England's second city in terms of population and importance, the ancient town of York has survived the ravages of time, war, and industrialization to remain one of northern Europe's few preserved walled cities. It was King George VI, father of the present queen, who remarked that the history of York is the history of England. Even in a brief visit to the city, you can see evidence of life from every era since the Romans, not only in museums but also in the very streets and houses. York—41 km (25 mi) northeast of Leeds, 133 km (82 mi) south of Newcastle—is surrounded by some of the grandest countryside England has to offer. A fertile plain dotted with ancient abbeys and grand aristocratic mansions leads westward to the hidden valleys and jagged, windswept tops of the Yorkshire Dales and northward to the brooding mass of the North York Moors. This is a land quite different from the south of England—it's friendlier, emptier, and less aggressively materialistic.

Exploring York

Numbers in the margin correspond to points of interest on the York map.

You can get a first, memorable overview of the city by taking a stroll along the **city walls.** Originally they were earth ramparts erected by York's Viking kings to repel raiders; the present stone structure dates from the 14th century. A narrow paved walk runs along the top (originally 5 km, or 3 mi, in circumference), passing over York's distinctive fortified gates or "bars" and providing delightful views across rooftops and gardens. Following an afternoon exploring the city, you can head for **Betty's,** on St. Helens Square—a York institution since 1912, it serves refreshing teas with a splendid selection of cakes.

★ ❸ **Castle Museum.** A debtor's prison during the 18th century, this museum now offers a number of detailed exhibitions and re-creations, including a cobblestone Victorian street complete with crafts shops; a

York

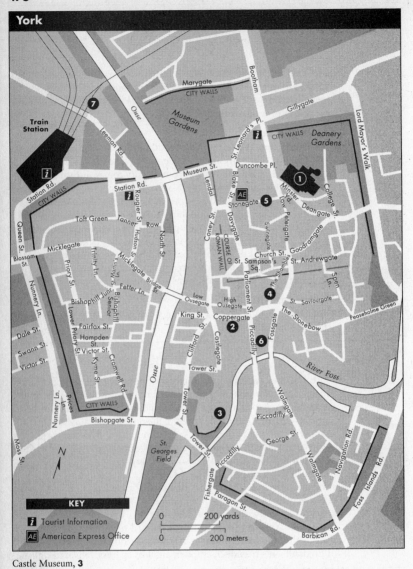

KEY

i Tourist Information

AE American Express Office

0 — 200 yards

0 — 200 meters

Castle Museum, **3**

Jorvik Viking
Centre, **2**

Merchant
Adventurers' Hall, **6**

National Railway
Museum, **7**

Shambles, **4**

Stonegate, **5**

York Minster, **1**

working water mill; and, most important, the Coppergate Helmet, a 1,200-year-old Anglo-Saxon helmet, one of only three ever found. ⊠ *Clifford St.,* ☎ *01904/653611.* ☉ *Apr.–Oct., Mon.–Sat. 9:30–5:30, Sun. 10–5:30; Nov.–Mar., Mon.–Sat. 9:30–4, Sun. 10–4.*

❷ **Jorvik Viking Centre.** On this authentic Viking site, you can take another journey into history—whisked back in little "time cars" to the sights, sounds, and even the smells of a Viking street, which archaeologists have re-created in astonishing detail. ⊠ *Coppergate,* ☎ *01904/ 653211.* ☉ *Apr.–Oct., daily 9–7; Nov.–Mar., daily 9–5:30 (last admission 2 hrs before closing).*

❻ **Merchant Adventurers' Hall.** A superb medieval building (1357–68), this hall was built and owned by one of the richest medieval guilds; it contains the largest timber-frame hall in York. ⊠ *Fossgate,* ☎ *01904/ 654818.* ☉ *Mid-Mar.–mid-Nov., daily 8:30–5; mid-Nov.–mid-Mar., Mon.–Sat. 8:30–3:30.*

❼ **National Railway Museum.** Britain's national collection of locomotives forms part of this complex, the world's largest train museum. Among the exhibits are gleaming giants of the steam era, including *Mallard,* holder of the world speed record for a steam engine (126 mph). The museum lies just outside the city walls, by the train station. ⊠ *Leeman Rd.,* ☎ *01904/621261.* ☉ *Daily 10–6.*

★ ❹ **Shambles.** Within York's city walls the narrow streets still follow the complex medieval pattern. In the heart of the city is the Shambles, a particularly well-preserved example; the half-timbered shops and houses have such large overhangs that you can practically reach from one second-floor window to another.

❺ **Stonegate.** This is a narrow pedestrian street of 18th-century (and earlier) shops and courts. Along a narrow passage off Stonegate, at 52A, you will find the remains of a 12th-century Norman stone house—one of the very few surviving in England.

★ ❶ **York Minster.** The glory of York, this is the largest Gothic church in England and one of the finest in Europe. The 14th-century nave has soaring columns and intricate tracery, the choir screen portrays whimsical images of the kings of England, and the mighty rose window— just one of 128 stained-glass windows in the Minster—commemorates the marriage of Henry VII and Elizabeth of York. Visit the exquisite 13th-century **Chapter House** and the Roman and Saxon remains in the **Undercroft Museum and Treasury.** The 275 steps of the **Central Tower** lead to an unrivaled view of the city and the countryside beyond. The **Crypt** contains some of the cathedral's oldest and most valuable treasures, among them the Romanesque 12th-century statue of a heavy-footed Virgin Mary. ⊠ *Duncombe Pl., York Minster Undercroft Museum and Treasury, Chapter House, Crypt, and Central Tower,* ☎ *01904/624426.* ⊡ *Minster free; donation appreciated.* ☉ *Minster: summer, daily 7 AM–8:30 PM; winter, daily 7–6. Undercroft, Chapter House, Crypt, and Central Tower:* ☉ *summer, Mon.–Sat. 10–5:30, Sun. 1–5:30; winter, Mon.–Sat. 10–4:30, Sun. 1–4:30.*

$$–$$$ ✕ **19 Grape Lane.** The narrow, slightly cramped restaurant is housed
★ in a typically leaning timbered York building in the heart of town. It serves modern English food from a blackboard of such specials as grilled wild boar sausages, and the substantial puddings are always a treat. ⊠ *19 Grape La.,* ☎ *01904/636366. MC, V. Closed Sun., 1 wk at Christmas, 2 wks in Feb., 2 wks in Sept.*

$–$$ ✕ **Pierre Victoire.** At lunchtime in this airy brasserie you can feast on a set three-course menu of simple French food, one of the city's best bargains. At dinner prices increase, but not outrageously so, while the dishes become more elaborate: Choose from warming seasonal soups, confit of duck, or that old brasserie standby, *moules mariniere* (mussels). ⊠ *2 Lendal,* ☎ *01904/655222. MC, V.*

$$$–$$$$ ⊞ **Dean Court.** This large Victorian house once provided accommodation for the clergy of York Minster, which looms just across the road. Refurbished to a high quality, it now has comfortably furnished rooms with plump sofas, TVs, and fine views overlooking the Minster. The restaurant serves good English cuisine, including a hearty Yorkshire breakfast. ⊠ *Duncombe Pl., YO1 2EF,* ☎ *01904/625082,* FAX *01904/ 620305. 40 rooms. Restaurant. AE, DC, MC, V.*

$$–$$$ ⊞ **Savages.** Despite its name, this small hotel on a leafy road near the town center is eminently refined, with a reputation for attentive service. Once a Victorian home, it has a stylish and comfortable interior, and there's a bar in which to relax. ⊠ *15 St. Peter's Grove, Clifton, YO3 6AQ,* ☎ *01904/610818,* FAX *01904/627729. 21 rooms with bath or shower. Restaurant. AE, DC, MC, V.*

$ ⊞ **Abbey Guest House.** This pretty, no-smoking, terraced guest house—formerly an artisan's house—is a 10-minute walk from the train station and town center. Although small, it's very clean and friendly, with a peaceful garden right on the river and ducks pottering about outside. Picnic lunches and evening meals can be arranged on request. ⊠ *14 Earlsborough Terr., Marygate, YO3 7BQ,* ☎ *01904/627782. 7 rooms, 2 with bath. AE, MC, V.*

Side Trips: Fountains Abbey and Castle Howard

★   Thirty-two kilometers (21 miles) northwest of York, along B6265, you'll find that the majestic ruins of **Fountains Abbey,** with its own high tower and soaring 13th-century arches, make a striking picture on the banks of the river Skell. Founded in 1132, the abbey still possesses many of its original buildings, and the National Trust operates highly informative free guided tours around them; tours run April–October only, usually at 1:30, 2:30, and 3:30. The extensive ruins are set beside an 18th-century water garden and deer park, **Studley Royal,** combining lakes, ponds, and even a diverted river, while waterfalls splash around classical temples, statues, and a grotto. ⊠ *Off B6265,* ☎ *01765/608888 or 01765/601005 (weekends).* ☉ *Jan.–Mar., daily 10–5 (or dusk); Apr.–Sept., daily 10–7; Oct.–Dec., daily 10–5 (or dusk). Closed Fri. Nov.–Jan.*

Newby Hall—reached along pleasant country roads 5 km (3 mi) east of Fountains Abbey—has some restored interiors by the 18th-century master architect Robert Adam and some equally celebrated gardens with a collection of rare roses. There is a handy restaurant. ⊠ *Skelton-on-Ure,* ☎ *01423/322583.* ☉ *Easter–Oct., Tues.–Sun., grounds 11–5, house noon–5.*

★   Nineteen kilometers (12 miles) southeast of Helmsley and 24 km (15 mi) northeast of York is **Castle Howard,** one of the grandest and most opulent stately homes in Britain. Its magnificent skyline is punctuated by stone chimneys and a graceful central dome. Many people know it best as Brideshead, the home of the Flyte family in Evelyn Waugh's tale of aristocratic woe, *Brideshead Revisited;* this was where much of the TV series was filmed. The audacity and confidence of the great Baroque house are startling, proclaiming the wealth and importance of the Howards and the utter self-assurance of its architect, Sir John Vanbrugh. Castle Howard took 60 years to build (1699–1759) and it was worth every year. A magnificent central hallway dwarfs all visitors, and there is no shortage of grandeur elsewhere: vast family portraits, delicate marble fireplaces, immense tapestries, and a great many marble busts. Outside, the stately theme continues in one of the most stunning neo-classical landscapes in England. ✉ *Coneysthorpe,* ☎ *01653/648333.* 🎫 *House and gardens £7.* ⊘ *House: mid-Mar.–Oct., daily 11–4:30; grounds: daily 10–5.*

York Essentials

Getting Around

BY BUS

National Express (☎ 0990/808080) buses to York leave from London's Victoria Coach Station. Average travel time is 4½ hours to York.

BY CAR

Take the A1, the historic main route from London to the north, which branches east onto the A64 near Tadcaster for the final 19 km (12 mi) to York. Alternatively, take the M1, then M18, and finally the A1. The drive from London takes a minimum of four hours.

BY TRAIN

Great North-Eastern Railways (☎ 0345/484950) serves York from London King's Cross. Journeys on the fastest trains take two hours.

Guided Tours

Guide Friday (✉ De Grey Rooms, Exhibition Sq., ☎ 01904/640896) runs frequent city tours of York that allow you to get on and off the bus as you please (£7.50, £5.50 if booked in advance). It also conducts tours of the surrounding countryside, including Fountains Abbey and Castle Howard. **Yorktour** (☎ 01904-641737) also offers tours to Castle Howard. The **York Association of Voluntary Guides** (✉ De Grey Rooms, Exhibition Sq., ☎ 01904/640780) arranges short walking tours around the city each morning at 10:15, with additional tours at 2:15 PM from April through October, and one at 7 PM from July through August.

Visitor Information

De Grey Rooms (✉ Exhibition Sq., North Yorkshire, YO1 2HB, ☎ 01904/621756). **York railway station** (☎ 01904/621756). **Adjunct office** (✉ 20 George Hudson St., ☎ 01904/554488).

THE LAKE DISTRICT

The poets Wordsworth and Coleridge can probably be held responsible for the development of the Lake District as a tourist destination. They, and other English men of letters, found it an inspiring setting for their work—and fashion, and thousands of visitors, have followed. The district, created in the 1970s as a national park from parts of the old counties of Cumberland, Westmorland, and Lancashire, combines so much that is magnificent in mountain, lake, and dales that new and entrancing vistas open out at each corner of the road. In addition to Wordsworth and Coleridge, other literary figures who made their homes in the region include De Quincey, Ruskin, Arnold, and the children's writer Beatrix Potter. Today, travelers find this region one of England's most peaceful destinations. Walking is perhaps the best way to discover the delights of this area.

The Lake District lies in the northwest of England, the entire region contained within the county of Cumbria. The major gateway from the south is Kendal; from the north, the gateway is Penrith—both are on the M6 motorway. The southern lakes and valleys contain the most popular destinations, notably the largest body of water, Windermere, as well as such quintessential Lake District towns and villages as

Kendal, Bowness, Ambleside, Grasmere, Elterwater, Coniston, and Hawkshead. Among the northern lakes, south of Keswick and Cockermouth, you have the best chance to get away from the crowds and soak up the Lake District experience.

Kendal

The ancient town of Kendal—113 km (70 mi) north of Manchester—was one of the most important textile centers in northern England before the Industrial Revolution. Away from the busy main road, you'll discover narrow, winding streets and charming courtyards, many dating from medieval times.

Take a stroll along the River Kent, where—close to the Parish Church—you can visit the 18th-century **Abbott Hall.** Here the **Museum of Lakeland Life and Industry** offers interesting exhibits on blacksmithing, wheelwrighting, farming, weaving, printing, local architecture, and regional customs. ⊠ *Kirkland,* ☎ *01539/722464.* ☉ *Apr.–Oct., daily 10:30–5; Nov.–Mar., daily 10:30–4.*

At the northern end of town the **Kendal Museum** details splendidly the flora and fauna of the Lake District. It also contains displays on Alfred Wainwright, the region's most avid chronicler of countryside matters, who died in 1991. His multivolume Lake District walking guides are famous the world over; you'll see them in every local book and gift shop. ⊠ *Station Rd.,* ☎ *01539/721374.* ☉ *Apr.–Oct., daily 10:30–5; Nov.–Mar., daily 10:30–4.*

$ ✕🏠 **The Punch Bowl Inn.** Hidden along a country road in the hamlet of Crosthwaite, 8 km (5 mi) west of Kendal, the Punch Bowl—formerly a 16th-century coaching inn—delights with its inspired Modern British food (reservations essential) and comfortable rooms. Fresh fish, local lamb, warming soups, and rich desserts all hit the spot. There are just three rooms; book well in advance. ⊠ *Crosthwaite, near Kendal (off A5074), LA8 8HR,* ☎ *015395/68237,* 🖷 *015395/68875. 3 rooms. Restaurant. MC, V.*

Windermere

★ Windermere, 16 km (10 mi) northwest of Kendal on the A591, makes a natural touring base for the southern half of the Lake District—split between the part of town around the station (known as Windermere) and the prettier lakeside area ½ km (¼ mi) away, called Bowness-on-Windermere. A minibus (every 20 minutes in summer, hourly the rest of the year), leaving from outside Windermere train station, links the two. Although Windermere's marinas and piers have some charm, you can bypass the busier stretches of shoreline by walking beyond the boat houses, from where there's a fine view across the lake. A **ferry** crosses the water at this point to reach Far Sawrey and the road to Hawkshead; the crossing takes just a few minutes. ☉ *Ferries run every 20 mins Mon.–Sat. 6:50 AM–9:50 PM, Sun. 9:10 AM–9:50 PM; Oct.–Easter until 8:50 PM.*

$$ ✕ **Porthole Eating House.** In an intimate 18th-century house in the cen-
★ ter of Bowness, the small restaurant has a largely Italian menu with homemade pasta and excellent meat and fish dishes. In winter a large open fire adds to the ambience. ⊠ *3 Ash St., Bowness-on-Windermere,* ☎ *015394/42793. AE, DC, MC, V. Closed Tues. and mid-Dec.–late Feb. No lunch Sat.*

$$$$ ✕🏠 **Miller Howe.** This small, white Edwardian country-house hotel is
★ beautifully situated, with views across Windermere to the Langdale Pikes. The bedrooms have exceptional individual style—fresh and dried flowers are everywhere. The outstanding restaurant (reservations essential; jacket and tie) is renowned for its experimental, almost theatrical take

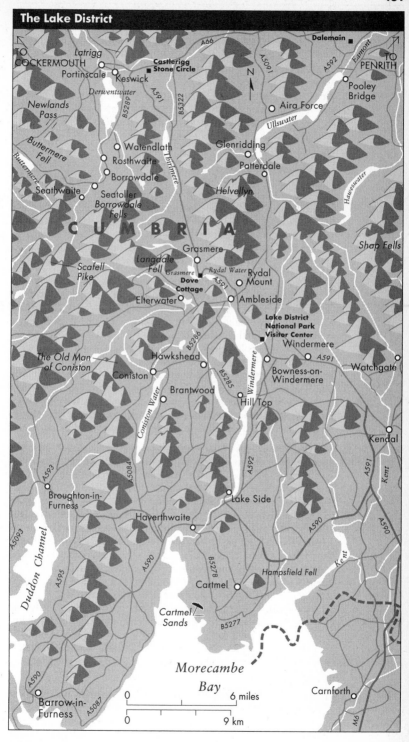

The Lake District

on British cuisine—every night is a new performance. Menus change with the season. The room rate includes breakfast and dinner. ⊠ *Rayrigg Rd., Bowness-on-Windermere LA23 1EY,* ☏ *015394/42536,* 🖷 *015394/ 45664. 13 rooms. Restaurant. AE, DC, MC, V. Closed Jan.*

$ 🏠 **Brendan Chase.** This well-maintained lodging is in the heart of Windermere's B&B-land, not far from the train station but about 2 km (1 mi) or so from the lake—though some rooms have distant water views. A full breakfast (English or vegetarian) sets you up for the day. ⊠ *1–3 College Rd., Windermere LA23 1BU,* ☏ *015394/45638. 8 rooms, 3 with bath. No credit cards.*

Brockhole

Five kilometers (3 miles) northwest of Windermere on the A591, a magnificent lakeside mansion houses the **Lake District National Park Visitor Centre,** which offers a fine range of exhibitions about the Lake District, including useful interpretative displays about the local ecology, flora, and fauna. The gardens are at their best in the spring, when floods of daffodils cover the lawns and the azaleas burst into bloom. ⊠ *Ambleside Rd.,* ☏ *015394/46601.* 🎟 *Free.* ☉ *Easter–late Oct., daily 10–5.*

Ambleside

The small town of Ambleside sits at the head of Lake Windermere—6½ km (4 mi) north of Brockhole, along the A591—making it a popular center for Lake District excursions. The town suffers terribly from tourist overcrowding in high season; Wednesday is particularly busy, when the local market takes place. However, it's easy enough to escape the crowds. Follow A593 west out of Ambleside and take the turning for the nearby village of **Elterwater,** a good stop for hikers. The B5343 continues west from here to **Langdale Fell,** where you can take one of several excellent walks: There are information boards at the various parking places and no more comforting resting place than the hiker's bar of the **Old Dungeon Ghyll Hotel** (⊠ on B5343, west of Elterwater), where the roaring fireplace rapidly dries out wet walking gear.

$$ ✕ **Glass House.** This exciting conversion of an old watermill switches from a café by day to a thoroughly modern restaurant by night—with Mediterranean flavors, panfried fish, and char-grilled meats forming the mainstay of the menu. ⊠ *Rydal Rd.,* ☏ *015394/32137. Reservations essential for dinner. MC, V.*

$$ ✕🏠 **Britannia Inn.** The Britannia is a friendly inn in the heart of splen-
★   did walking country, with quaint little rooms and hearty homemade English food served in the bar. The four guest rooms across the road in the Maple Tree Corner annex are a few pounds cheaper, but you'll have to walk over to the inn for breakfast. ⊠ *Elterwater, on B5343, 6 km/4 mi west of Ambleside, LA22 9HP,* ☏ *015394/37210,* 🖷 *015394/37311. 13 rooms, 9 with shower. Restaurant. MC, V.*

$ 🏠 **3 Cambridge Villas.** Ambleside abounds in inexpensive B&Bs, but you'd be hard pressed to find a more welcoming spot than this—a lofty Victorian house right in the center, with hosts who know a thing or two about local walks. ⊠ *Church St. LA22 9DL,* ☏ *015394/32307. 8 rooms, 4 with shower. No credit cards. Closed Dec.–Jan.*

Rydal Mount

If there's one poet associated with the Lake District, it is William Wordsworth, who made his home at Rydal Mount, 2 km (1 mi) northwest of Ambleside, from 1813 until his death 37 years later. Wordsworth and his family moved to these grand surroundings when he was nearing the height of his career, and his descendants still live here, surrounded by his furniture, portraits, and the 4½-acre garden laid out by the poet himself. ⊠ *Rydal, Ambleside,* ☏ *015394/33002.* ☉ *Mar.–Oct., daily 9:30–5; Nov.–Feb., Wed.–Mon. 10–4. Closed 3 wks in Jan.*

Grasmere

The heart of Wordsworth country, Grasmere is one of the most typical of Lake District villages, sited on a tiny, wood-fringed lake 2 km (1 mi) north of Dove Cottage, 6½ km (4 mi) northwest of Ambleside, and made up of crooked lanes lined with charming slate-built cottages. Since Wordsworth lived on the town's outskirts for almost 50 years— at Rydal Mount (☞ *above*) and Dove Cottage (☞ *below*), he, his wife Mary, his sister Dorothy, and his daughter Dora are buried in Grasmere churchyard.

★ **Dove Cottage** is the leading literary shrine of the Lake District. Located 2½ km (1½ mi) northwest of Rydal Mount, this was Wordsworth's home from 1799 until 1808, and the tiny house still contains many personal belongings. Dove Cottage is also headquarters of the Centre for British Romanticism, which documents the literary contributions made by Wordsworth and his sister Dorothy, Samuel Taylor Coleridge, Thomas De Quincey, and Robert Southey. ⊠ *The Wordsworth Trust, Dove Cottage, Grasmere LA22 9SH,* ☎ *015394/35544.* ☼ *Mid-Feb.–mid-Jan., daily 9:30–5.*

$$$ ✕⌂ **The Swan.** The handsome, flower-decked, 300-year-old Swan, a former coaching inn on the main road just outside Grasmere, keeps a fire in the lounge grate, an oak-beam restaurant ($$) serving Lake District specialties, and elegant guest rooms that combine space with fine views of the surrounding fells. ⊠ *Grasmere, on the A591, LA22 9RF,* ☎ *015394/35551,* ℻ *015394/35741. 36 rooms. Restaurant. AE, DC, MC, V.*

$ ⌂ **Banerigg House.** You don't have to spend a fortune to find appealing lakeside lodgings in Grasmere. This turn-of-the-century family house, 1½ km (¾ mi) south of the village, offers well-appointed, no-smoking rooms, most with lake views. ⊠ *Lake Rd., LA22 9PW,* ☎ *015394/35204. 7 rooms, 5 with bath. No credit cards.*

Coniston

Formerly a copper-mining village, Coniston is now a small lake resort and boating center at the foot of **The Old Man of Coniston** (2,635 ft), 13 km (8 mi) south of Grasmere. Tracks lead up from the village past an old mine to the peak, which you can reach in about two hours, though many experienced hikers include the peak in an enervating seven-hour circular walk from the village.

★ Just outside Coniston is **Brantwood,** the home of Victorian artist, critic, and social reformer John Ruskin (1819–1900). Here, in the rambling white 18th-century house, you'll find a collection of Ruskin's own paintings, drawings, and books. The extensive grounds were laid out by Ruskin himself. It's an easy drive to Brantwood from Coniston, but it's much more agreeable to travel here by ferry across the lake. Services are with either the Coniston Launch (Easter–October, hourly departures; fewer sailings in winter) or the steam yacht *Gondola* (April–October, four–five trips daily), both departing from Coniston Pier. ⊠ *Brantwood,* ☎ *015394/41396.* ☼ *Mid-Mar.–mid-Nov., daily 11–5:30; mid-Nov.–mid-Mar., Wed.–Sun. 11–4.*

Hawkshead

Just outside the attractive village of Hawkshead, **Hill Top** was the home of children's author and illustrator Beatrix Potter, most famous for her *Peter Rabbit* stories. Now run by the National Trust, the tiny house is a popular—and often crowded—spot; admission has to be strictly controlled. Try to avoid visiting on summer weekends and during school vacations. The house is 3 km (2 mi) south of Hawkshead on the B5285, though you can also approach via the car ferry from Bowness-on-Windermere. ✉ *Near Sawrey, Ambleside,* ☎ *015394/36269.* ⊗ *Apr.–Oct., Sat.–Wed. 11–5.*

Ullswater

Hemmed in by towering hills, Ullswater, 10 km (6 mi) southwest of Penrith along A592, is the region's second-largest lake, enjoying a spectacular setting. Some of the finest views are from A592 as it hugs the lake's western shore, through Glenridding and Patterdale at the southern end. Here, you're at the foot of Helvellyn (3,118 ft), which lies to the west. Arduous footpaths run from the road between Glenridding and Patterdale and pass by Red Tarn, at 2,356 ft the highest Lake District tarn.

Aira Force, 8 km (5 mi) north of Patterdale, just off the A592, is a spectacular series of waterfalls pounding through a wooded ravine to feed into Ullswater. From the parking lot (parking fee charged), it's a 20-minute walk to the falls—bring sturdy shoes in wet weather. Just above Aira Force in the woods of Gowbarrow Park, William Wordsworth and his sister Dorothy were walking on April 15, 1802. Dorothy remarked that she had never seen "daffodils so beautiful." Two years later Wordsworth was inspired by his sister's words to write one of the best-known lyric poems in English, "I Wandered Lonely as a Cloud."

Keswick

The great Lakeland mountains of Skiddaw and Blencathra brood over the gray slate houses of Keswick (pronounced "Kezzick"), 22 km (14 mi) west of Ullswater, on the scenic shores of Derwentwater. As many of the best hiking routes radiate from here, it is more of a touring base than a tourist destination. People stroll the congested, narrow streets in boots and corduroy hiking trousers, and there are plenty of mountaineering shops in addition to hotels, guest houses, pubs, and restaurants.

★ To understand why **Derwentwater** is considered one of England's finest lakes, take a short walk from the town center to the lake shore, and follow the Friar's Crag path—about 15 minutes' level walk from the center of Keswick. This pine-tree-fringed peninsula is a favorite vantage point, with its view over the lake, the surrounding ring of mountains, and many tiny wooded islands. Ahead you will see the crags that line the **Jaws of Borrowdale** and overhang a dramatic mountain ravine—the perfect setting for a Romantic painting or poem. Between late March and November, cruises set off every hour in each direction from a wooden dock at the lake shore.

$$$ ✕▦ **Keswick Country House Hotel.** Built to serve railroad travelers during the 19th century, the Keswick has all the grandeur and style of that age, although it has been modernized. The room rate includes dinner, as well as breakfast, though you can opt for a stay without dinner if you wish. ✉ *Station Rd., CA12 4NQ,* ☎ *017687/72020,* 🆉 *017687/71300. 74 rooms. Restaurant. AE, DC, MC, V.*

$–$$ ✕▦ **Highfield Hotel.** Overlooking the lawns of Hope Park, a few minutes' walk from lake or town, this family-run hotel preserves such features as its idiosyncratic turret rooms and even a former attached chapel, now used as a four-poster bedroom. Dinner serves up Lake District delights. ✉ *The Heads, CA12 5ER,* ☎ *017687/72508. 19 rooms. Restaurant. MC, V. Closed mid-Nov.–Jan.*

Cockermouth

This attractive little town, 22 km (14 mi) northwest of Seatoller, at the confluence of the Derwent and Cocker rivers, is slightly larger than Keswick and has a maze of narrow streets that's a delight to wander.

It was the birthplace of William Wordsworth and his sister Dorothy, whose childhood home, **Wordsworth House,** is a typical 18th-century north-country gentleman's home, now owned by the National Trust. ⊠ *Main St.,* ☏ *01900/824805.* ⊘ *Apr.–Oct., weekdays 11–5; July–Aug., also Sat. 11–5.*

Lake District Essentials

Getting Around

BY BOAT

Windermere Lake Cruises (☏ 015394/43360) employs its handsome fleet of modern launches and vintage cruisers—the largest ships on the lake—in regular service between Ambleside, Bowness, Brockhole, and Lakeside. A Freedom of the Lake ticket (£9.50) gives unlimited travel on any of the ferries for 24 hours.

BY BUS

National Express (☏ 0990/808080) serves the region from London's Victoria Coach Station. Average travel time to Kendal is just over 7 hours; to Windermere, 7½ hours; and to Keswick, 8¼ hours. **Stagecoach Cumberland** (☏ 01946/63222) operates year-round throughout the Lake District, with reduced service on weekends and bank holidays. A One-day Explorer Ticket (£5.50) is valid on all routes.

BY CAR

Take M1 north from London to M6, leaving at exit 36 and joining A590/A591 west (around the Kendal bypass to Windermere) or at exit 40, joining A66 directly to Keswick and the northern lakes. Travel time to Kendal is about four hours, to Keswick five–six hours. Car-rental companies are few and far between in the Lakes; rent in London or York before your trip.

Roads within the region are generally good, although many of the minor routes and mountain passes can be steep and narrow. Warning signs are normally posted if snow has made a road impassable. In July and August and during public holiday weekends, expect heavy traffic.

BY TRAIN

InterCity West Coast serves the region from London's Euston Station (☏ 0345/484950). Take an InterCity train bound for Carlisle, Edinburgh, or Glasgow, and change at Oxenholme for the branch line service to Kendal and Windermere. Average travel time to Windermere (including the change) is 4½ hours. The **Lakeside & Haverthwaite Railway Co.** (☏ 015395/31594) runs vintage steam trains in summer (and at Christmas) between Lakeside and Haverthwaite along Lake Windermere's southern tip.

ON FOOT

Every hamlet, village, and town provides scores of walking opportunities; stores throughout the region stock the right equipment, books, and maps. Always check on weather conditions before setting out, as mist or rain can roll in without warning. For short, local walks consult the tourist information centers, which can provide maps, guides, and advice. The other main source of information is the **Lake District National Park Visitor Centre** (☞ Brockhole, *above*).

Guided Tours

From Easter until October, the **National Park Authority** (☏ 015394/46601) at Brockhole, near Windermere, arranges half-day or full-day walks introducing you to the history and natural beauties of the Lake District. **Mountain Goat Holidays** (☏ 015394/45161) provides half- and full-day minibus sightseeing tours with skilled local guides.

Visitor Information

The Cumbria Tourist Board (⊠ Ashleigh, Holly Rd., Windermere, Cumbria LA23 2AQ, ☏ 015394/44444). **Ambleside** (⊠ Central Buildings, Market Cross, ☏ 015394/32582). **Grasmere** (⊠ Red Bank Rd., ☏ 015394/35245). **Kendal** (⊠ Town Hall, Highgate, ☏ 01539/725758). **Keswick** (⊠ Moot Hall, Market Sq., ☏ 017687/72645). **Windermere** (⊠ The Gateway Centre, Victoria St., ☏ 015394/46499).

EDINBURGH

Scotland and England *are* different—and let no Englishman tell you otherwise. Although the two nations have been united in a single state since 1707, Scotland retains its own marked political and social character, with, for instance, legal and educational systems quite distinct from those of England. Indeed, since July 1999 there has been once again a Scottish Parliament, which at present sits in the Assembly Hall on the Mound. In late 2001, the Parliament will move to its permanent home in a building designed by Barcelona architect Enric Miralles, on a site adjacent to the Palace of Holyroodhouse. With its castle surmounting a long-dead volcano and the survival of a large number of outstanding stone buildings carrying echoes of the nation's history, Edinburgh ranks among the world's greatest capital cities.

Exploring Edinburgh

Numbers in the margin correspond to points of interest on the Edinburgh map.

The key to understanding Edinburgh is to make the distinction between the Old and New towns. Until the 18th century the city was confined to the rocky crag on which its castle stands, straggling between the fortress at one end and the royal residence, the Palace of Holyroodhouse, at the other. In the 18th century, during a civilizing time of expansion known as the "Scottish Enlightenment," the city fathers fostered the construction of another Edinburgh, one a little to the north. In 1767 the competition to design the New Town was won by a young and unknown architect, James Craig. His plan was for a grid of three east–west streets, balanced at each end by a grand square. The plan survives today, despite all commercial pressures. Princes, George, and Queen streets are the main thoroughfares, with St. Andrew Square at one end and Charlotte Square at the other. The mostly residential New Town, with elegant squares, classical facades, wide streets, and harmonious proportions, remains largely intact and lived-in today.

⓭ **Arthur's Seat.** The open grounds of Holyrood Park enclose Arthur's Seat, Edinburgh's distinctive, originally volcanic minimountain, with steep slopes and miniature crags. ⊠ *Holyrood Park.*

★ ⓰ **Calton Hill.** Steps and a road lead up to splendid views north across the Firth (estuary) of Forth to the Lomond Hills of Fife, and south to the Pentland Hills. Among the various monuments on Calton Hill are a partial reproduction of Athens's **Parthenon**, begun in 1824 but left incomplete because the money ran out; the **Nelson Monument;** and the **Royal Observatory.** ⊠ *North side of Regent Rd.*

⓫ **Canongate Kirk.** In the graveyard of this church, built in 1688, are buried some notable Scots, including the economist Adam Smith and the poet Robert Fergusson. ⊠ *Canongate.*

⓲ **Charlotte Square.** The centerpiece of the New Town opens out at the western end of George Street. The palatial facade of the north side was designed by the great Scottish neoclassical architect, Robert Adam. The

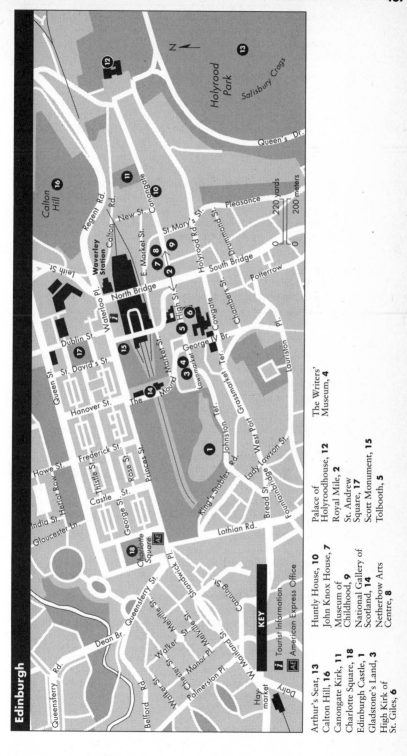

Edinburgh

Holyrood Park
Salisbury Crags
Queen's Dr.

Calton Hill
Regent Rd.
Calton Rd.
New St.
Canongate
St. Mary's St.
Waverley Station
Leith St.
E. Market St.
North Bridge
Waterloo Pl.
Dublin St.
St. David's St.
Queen St.
Hanover St.
High St.
Cowgate
George IV Br.
Lawnmarket
Market St.
The Mound
Holyrood Rd. St.
South Bridge
Pleasance
South Drummond St.
Chambers St.
Potterrow
Lauriston
Frederick St.
Howe St.
Thistle St.
Rose St.
Princes St.
Castle St.
George St.
India St.
Heriot Row
Gloucester Ln.
Hanover St.
King's Stables Rd.
Johnston Ter.
Grassmarket
Lady Lawson St.
West Port
Bread St.
Fountainbridge
Lothian Rd.
Charlotte Square
Canning St.
Shandwick Pl.
Queensferry St.
Melville St.
Stafford St.
Walker St.
Manor Pl.
Palmerston Pl.
Maitland St.
W. Maitland St.
Belford Rd.
Queensferry Rd.
Dean Br.
Hay market
Dairy
Queensferry Rd.

Laurie Ter.

0   220 yards
0   200 meters

KEY

i Tourist Information

AE American Express Office

Arthur's Seat, **13**
Calton Hill, **16**
Canongate Kirk, **11**
Charlotte Square, **18**
Edinburgh Castle, **1**
Gladstone's Land, **3**
High Kirk of
St. Giles, **6**

Huntly House, **10**
John Knox House, **7**
Museum of
Childhood, **9**
National Gallery of
Scotland, **14**
Netherbow Arts
Centre, **8**

Palace of
Holyroodhouse, **12**
Royal Mile, **2**
St. Andrew
Square, **17**
Scott Monument, **15**
Tolbooth, **5**

The Writers'
Museum, **4**

elegant **Georgian House** (National Trust for Scotland) is furnished to show the domestic arrangements of a prosperous late-18th-century Edinburgh family. ✉ *7 Charlotte Sq.,* ☎ *0131/225–2160.* ⊙ *Apr.–Oct., Mon.–Sat. 10–5, Sun. 2–5 (last admission 4:30).*

★ ❶ **Edinburgh Castle.** The brooding symbol of Scotland's capital and the nation's martial past, the castle dominates the city center. Its attractions include the city's oldest building—the 11th-century **St. Margaret's Chapel**; the **Crown Room**, where the Regalia of Scotland are displayed; **Old Parliament Hall**; and **Queen Mary's Apartments**, where Mary, Queen of Scots, gave birth to the future King James VI of Scotland (who later became James I of England). In addition military features of interest include the **Scottish National War Memorial** and the **Scottish United Services Museum**. The **Castle Esplanade**, the wide parade ground at the entrance to the castle, hosts the annual Edinburgh Military Tattoo—a grand military display staged during a citywide festival every summer (☞ The Arts, *below*). ✉ *Castlehill,* ☎ *0131/668–8800.* ✇ *£6.50.* ⊙ *Apr.–Sept., daily 9:30–5:15; Oct.–Mar., daily 9:30–4:15.*

❸ **Gladstone's Land.** This six-story property cared for by the National Trust for Scotland dates from 1620. It has an arcaded front and first-floor entrance typical of the period and is furnished in the style of a merchant's house of the time; there are magnificent painted ceilings. ✉ *377B Lawnmarket,* ☎ *0131/226–5856.* ⊙ *Easter–Oct., Mon.–Sat. 10–5, Sun. 2–5 (last entrance 4:30).*

❻ **High Kirk of St. Giles.** Often called St. Giles's Cathedral, this historic structure dates back to the 12th century; the impressive choir was built during the 15th century. ✉ *High St.,* ☎ *0131/225–4363.* ✇ *Donation suggested.* ⊙ *Mon.–Sat. 9–5 (7 in summer), Sun. 1–5 and for services.*

❿ **Huntly House.** Built in 1570, this museum presents Edinburgh history and social life. ✉ *142 Canongate,* ☎ *0131/529–4143.* ✇ *Free.* ⊙ *Mon.–Sat. 10–5, Sun. during festival 2–5.*

❼ **John Knox House.** Its traditional connections with Scotland's celebrated religious reformer are tenuous, but this 16th-century dwelling gives a flavor of life in the Old Town during Knox's time. ✉ *45 High St.,* ☎ *0131/556–2647.* ⊙ *Mon.–Sat. 10–5 (last admission 4:30).*

❾ **Museum of Childhood.** Even adults may well enjoy this celebration of toys. The museum was the first in the world to be devoted solely to the history of childhood. ✉ *42 High St.,* ☎ *0131/529–4142,* FAX *0131/558–3103.* ✇ *Free.* ⊙ *Mon.–Sat. 10–5, Sun. during festival 2–5.*

★ ⓮ **National Gallery of Scotland.** Works by the old masters and the French Impressionists and a good collection of Scottish paintings make this one of Britain's best national galleries. It is small enough to be taken in easily on one visit. There may be a charge for special exhibitions. ✉ *The Mound,* ☎ *0131/556–8921.* ✇ *Free.* ⊙ *Mon.–Sat. 10–5, Sun. 2–5. Print Room: weekdays 10–noon and 2–4, by arrangement.*

❽ **Netherbow Arts Centre.** In addition to the art gallery there are a theater and a café here. ✉ *43 High St.,* ☎ *0131/556–9579.* ⊙ *Mon.–Sat. 10–5 (last admission 4:30).*

★ ⓬ **Palace of Holyroodhouse.** Still the Royal Family's official residence in Scotland, the palace came into existence originally as a guest house for the Abbey of Holyrood, founded in 1128 by Scottish king David I. It was extensively remodeled by Charles II in 1671. The state apartments, with their collections of tapestries and paintings, can be visited. ✉ *East* *end of Canongate, ☎ 0131/556–7371; 0131/556–1096 recorded information. ⊙ Apr.–Oct., daily 9:30–5:15; Nov.–Mar., daily 9:30–3:45. Closed during royal and state visits.*

② **Royal Mile.** The backbone of the Old Town, the Royal Mile starts immediately below the Castle Esplanade (☞ **Edinburgh Castle,** *above*). It consists of a number of streets running into one another—Castlehill, Lawnmarket, High Street, and Canongate—leading downhill to the **Palace of Holyroodhouse.** The many original Old Town "closes," narrow alleyways enclosed by high tenement buildings, reward exploration with a real sense of the former life of the city. ⊠ *Between Edinburgh Castle and the Palace of Holyroodhouse.*

⑰ **St. Andrew Square.** The most notable building on this square at the eastward termination of George Street is the Georgian headquarters of the **Royal Bank of Scotland,** with a lavishly decorated central banking hall. ⊠ *St. Andrew Sq., ☎ 0131/556–8555. ⊙ Mon.–Tues., Thurs.–Fri. 9:15–4:45, Wed. 10–4:45.*

⑮ **Scott Monument.** This unmistakable 200-ft-high Gothic spire was built in the 1840s to commemorate Sir Walter Scott (1771–1832), the celebrated novelist of Scots history. Currently closed for renovation, the monument can only be viewed from outside. ⊠ *Princes St., ☎ 0131/529–4068.*

⑤ **Tolbooth.** A heart shape set in the cobbles of High Street marks the site of the 15th-century Tolbooth, the center of city life—and original inspiration for Sir Walter Scott's novel *The Heart of Midlothian*—until its demolition in 1817. ⊠ *High St.*

④ **The Writers' Museum.** Housed in Lady Stair's House, a town dwelling of 1622, this museum recalls Scotland's literary heritage with exhibits on Sir Walter Scott, Robert Louis Stevenson, and Robert Burns. ⊠ *Lady Stair's Close, Lawnmarket, ☎ 0131/529–4901. ☐ Free. ⊙ Mon.–Sat. 10–5, Sun. during festival 2–5.*

Dining and Lodging

Edinburgh's restaurants make the most of Scotland's excellent game, fish, shellfish, beef, and lamb. For details and price-category definitions, *see* Dining *in* Great Britain A to Z, *above.*

Much of Edinburgh's accommodations are very central, with New Town bed-and-breakfast establishments being especially convenient. For details and price-category definitions, *see* Lodging *in* Great Britain A to Z, *above.*

$$$$ ★ ✕ **La Pompadour.** The decor in this hotel-restaurant, with its subtle plasterwork and rich murals, is inspired by the France of Louis XV. A sophisticated French menu is accented with Scottish delicacies. ⊠ *Caledonian Hotel, Princes St., ☎ 0131/459–9988. Reservations essential. Jacket and tie. AE, DC, MC, V. No lunch weekends.*

$$$$ ✕ **Witchery by the Castle.** Jack Nicholson was the most recent star to be spotted in this spooky haunt, which comes complete with lugubrious, cavernous interior set with flickering candles, broomsticks, and cabalistic insignia. However, there's nothing spooky about the excellent Scottish-accented French food. ⊠ *352 Castlehill, Royal Mile, ☎ 0131/225–5613. Reservations essential. AE, DC, MC, V.*

$$$ ★ ✕ **Jackson's Restaurant.** Set in the historic Old Town halfway down the Royal Mile, this intimate and candlelit spot offers good Scots fare. Aberdeen Angus steaks and Border lamb are excellent; there are vegetarian and seafood specialties, too. ⊠ *2 Jackson Close, 209–213 High St., ☎ 0131/225–1793. Reservations essential. AE, MC, V.*

$$ ✕ **The Dome.** The splendid interior of this former bank—splendid is the word, thanks to the painted plasterwork and central dome—provides an elegant backdrop for relaxed dining. Or you just might opt for a drink at the central bar, a favored spot for sophisticates to wind down after work. The toasted BLT sandwiches are almost big enough for two, but if you're even more ravenous, the eclectic menu offers many other options. ⊠ *14 George St. EH2 2PF,* ☎ *0131/624–8624. AE, DC, MC, V.*

$$ ✕ **Howie's.** Howie's is a simple neighborhood bistro. The steaks are tender Aberdeen beef, the Loch Fyne herring are sweet-cured to Howie's own recipe, and the clientele is lively. ⊠ *75 St. Leonard's St.,* ☎ *0131/668–2917, MC, V, no lunch Mon.;* ⊠ *63 Dalry Rd.,* ☎ *0131/313–3334, MC, V, no lunch Mon.;* ⊠ *208 Bruntsfield Pl.,* ☎ *0131/221–1777, MC, V;* ⊠ *4/6 Glanville Pl., Stockbridge,* ☎ *0131/225–5553, MC, V.*

$–$$ ✕ **Petit Paris.** Serving classic French farmhouse cuisine, Petit Paris is rather appropriately situated in the area of the Old Town where the agricultural market was once held. Offerings on the menu might include cassoulet, Toulouse sausage, *boudin* (black pudding sausage), or quail, as well as more standard fare such as steak. ⊠ *38 Grassmarket,* ☎ *0131/226–2442, MC, V.*

$ ✕ **Beehive Inn.** One of the oldest pubs in the city, the Beehive snuggles in the Grassmarket, under the majestic shadow of the castle. The upstairs Rafters restaurant lies hidden in an attractive and spacious attic room, crammed with weird and wonderful junk. Open only for dinner, it features mostly steaks and fish: Try the charcoal-grilled Scottish salmon. ⊠ *18/20 Grassmarket,* ☎ *0131/225–7171. AE, DC, MC, V. No lunch.*

$$$$ ▥ **Caledonian Hotel.** "The Caley" echoes the days of the traditional great railway hotel, though the neighboring station has long since been demolished. The imposing Victorian decor has been lovingly preserved and embellished. There are also three excellent restaurants: ☞ **La Pompadour,** *above;* **Chisholms,** offering a less pricey Scottish menu; and **Henry J. Bean's,** a U.S.-style diner. ⊠ *Princes St., EH1 2AB,* ☎ *0131/459–9988,* ℻ *0131/225–6632. 246 rooms. 3 restaurants. AE, DC, MC, V.*

$$$$ ▥ **Channings.** Five Edwardian terraced houses have become an elegant
★   hotel in an upscale neighborhood minutes from Princes Street. Restrained colors, antiques, quiet rooms, and great views towards Fife (from the north-facing rooms) set the tone. The Brasserie offers excellent value, especially at lunchtime; try the hot-smoked salmon with coriander and saffron risotto. ⊠ *12–16 South Learmonth Gardens, EH4 1EZ,* ☎ *0131/315–2226,* ℻ *0131/332–9631. 48 rooms with bath or shower. Restaurant. AE, DC, MC, V.*

$$$ ▥ **17 Abercrombie Place.** An exceptional standard is set at this Geor-
★   gian terraced B&B in the center of the New Town. There are stunning views from the top-floor rooms. The host and the hostess both enjoy meeting guests and are very helpful and, unusually for this part of town, there is off-street car parking. ⊠ *17 Abercrombie Pl., EH3 6LB,* ☎ *0131/557–8036,* ℻ *0131/558–3453. 10 rooms with bath or shower. Dining room. MC, V.*

$$ ▥ **Stuart House.** Within 15 minutes' walk of the city center, this B&B
★   is in a Victorian terraced house with some fine plasterwork. The decor suits the structure: Bold colors, floral fabrics and generously curtained windows combine with antique and traditional-style furniture and chandeliers to create an opulent ambience. Smoking is not permitted. ⊠ *12 E. Claremont St., EH7 4JP,* ☎ *0131/557–9030,* ℻ *0131/557–0563. 7 rooms with bath or shower. AE, DC, MC, V.*

In case you want to see the world.

At American Express, we're here to make your journey a smooth one. So we have over 1,700 travel service locations in over 130 countries ready to help. What else would you expect from the world's largest travel agency?

do more **Travel**

In case you want to be welcomed there.

We're here to see that you're always welcomed at establishments everywhere. That's why millions of people carry the American Express® Card – for peace of mind, confidence, and security, around the world or just around the corner.

do more

To apply, call 1 800 THE-CARD
or visit www.americanexpress.com

In case you're running low.

We're here to help with more than 190,000 Express Cash locations around the world. In order to enroll, just call American Express at 1 800 CASH-NOW before you start your vacation.

do more AMERICAN EXPRESS

Express Cash

And in case you'd rather be safe than sorry.

We're here with American Express® Travelers Cheques. They're the safe way to carry money on your vacation, because if they're ever lost or stolen you can get a refund, practically anywhere or anytime. To find the nearest place to buy Travelers Cheques, call 1 800 495-1153. Another way we help you do more.

do more®

Travelers Cheques

The Arts

The **Edinburgh International Festival,** a celebration of music, dance, and drama staged each summer (August 13–September 2 in 2000), draws international artists of the highest caliber. The **Festival Fringe** (information: ⊠ 180 High St., ☎ 0131/226–5257; 0131/226–5259 during festival only, ℻ 0131/220–4205), the unruly child of the official festival, spills out of halls and theaters all over town, offering visitors a cornucopia of theatrical and musical events of all kinds—some so weird that they defy description. At the official festival you'll see top-flight performances by established artists, while at a Fringe event you might catch a new star, or a new art form, or a controversial new play. Advance information, programs, and ticket sales for the festival are available from the **Edinburgh International Festival Office** (⊠ Castlehill, EH1 1ND, ☎ 0131/473–2001, ℻ 0131/473–2003).

The **Edinburgh Military Tattoo** (information: Edinburgh Military Tattoo Office, ⊠ 32 Market St., EH1 1QB, ☎ 0131/225–1188, ℻ 0131/225–8627) may not be art, but it is certainly entertainment. This celebration of martial music and skills (in 2000, held August 4–26) is set on the Castle Esplanade. Dress warmly for late-evening shows. Even if it rains, the show most definitely goes on! Away from the August–September festival overkill, **Shoots and Roots** (☎ 0131/557–1050), the Edinburgh Folk Festival, takes place over Easter weekend and also the third weekend in November (in 2000: November 17–20). This is the premier festival for Scottish folk music and folk crossover with other musical genres (jazz, classical etc.).

The List, available from newsagents throughout the city, as well as *The Day by Day List* and *Events 2000,* available from the Information Centre, carry the most up-to-date details about cultural events. *The Scotsman,* an Edinburgh daily, also carries reviews in its arts pages on Monday and Wednesday, and daily during the festival.

Edinburgh Essentials

Arriving and Departing

Regular service is operated by **National Express** (☎ 0990/808080, ℻ 0141/332–8055) between Victoria Coach Station, London, and St. Andrew Square bus station, Edinburgh, twice a day. The journey takes approximately eight hours.

London and Edinburgh are 656 km (407 mi) apart; allow a comfortable nine hours for the drive. The two principal routes to the Scottish border are A1 (mostly a small but divided road) or the eight-lane M1, then M6. From there, the choice is between the four-lane highway A74, which can be unpleasantly busy, followed by A701 or A702, or the slower but much more scenic A7 through Hawick. All the main car-rental agencies have offices in Edinburgh.

British Airways (☎ 0345/222111) operates a shuttle service from London's Heathrow Airport to Edinburgh; reservations are not necessary. Flying time from London is one hour, 15 minutes. **British Midland** (☎ 0345/554554) also flies from Heathrow. **KLM UK** flies from Stansted (☎ 01279/680500) to Edinburgh (☎ 0345/666777). **EasyJet** (☎ 0990/292929) offers bargain fares from London Luton to Edinburgh. Transatlantic flights direct to Scotland use Glasgow Airport, with regular rail connections to Glasgow city center and on to Edinburgh.

Regular trains run from London's King's Cross Station (☎ 0345/
484950) to Edinburgh Waverley; the fastest journey time is just over
four hours.

Getting Around

BY BUS

Lothian Regional Transport (✉ 27 Hanover St., ☎ 0131/555–6363; ✉
Waverley Bridge, ☎ 0131/554–4494), operating dark-red-and-white
buses, is the main operator within Edinburgh. A **Day Saver Ticket**
(£2.40), allowing unlimited one-day travel on the city's buses, can be
purchased in advance.

BY CAR

Driving in Edinburgh has its quirks and pitfalls, but competent drivers should not be intimidated. Metered parking in the center city is scarce
and expensive, and the local traffic wardens are alert. Note that illegally parked cars are routinely wheel-clamped and towed away, and
getting your car back will be expensive. After 6 PM the parking situation improves considerably, and you may manage to find a space quite
near your hotel, even downtown. If you park on a yellow line or in a
resident's parking bay, be prepared to move your car by 8 AM the following morning, when the rush hour gets under way.

BY TAXI

Taxi stands can be found throughout the downtown area, most conveniently at the west end of Princes Street, South St. David Street, and
North St. Andrew Street (the latter two just off St. Andrew Sq.), Waverley Market, Waterloo Place, and Lauriston Place. You can also hail
any taxi displaying an illuminated FOR HIRE sign.

Contacts and Resources

CONSULATE

U.S. Consulate General (✉ 3 Regent Terr., ☎ 0131/556–8315).

EMERGENCIES

Police, ambulance, fire (☎ 999). **Pharmacy: Boots** (✉ 48 Shandwick
Pl., west end of Princes St., ☎ 0131/225–6757).

GUIDED TOURS

Orientation. Lothian Regional Transport (☞ Getting Around By Bus,
above) operates tours in and around the city.

Walking. The Cadies and Witchery Tours (✉ 352 Castlehill, 3rd floor,
☎ 0131/225–6745) offers a highly popular murder and mystery tour,
and historical and other special-interest tours.

VISITOR INFORMATION

Edinburgh and Scotland Information Centre (✉ 3 Princes St., ☎ 0131/
557–1700, FAX 0131/473–3881) is adjacent to Waverley Station.

Greece (Ellada)

BULGARIA

FORMER YUGOSLAV
REPUBLIC OF
MACEDONIA

ALBANIA

Stavrou
Sidirokastro
Serres
Philippi
Kilkis
Eleftheroupoli
Amfipoli
Kavala
Edessa
Gianitsa
E86
Florina
Alexandria
Thessaloniki
Kastoria
Veria
Thermi
Nea
Apollonia
Moun
Ptolemaïda
Polygyros
Vatopedio
Pennir
Monk
Kozani
Katerini
Ormylia
iirion
E75
Siatista
Gulf of
Thermaikos
Dafni
Mou
Grevena
Mount
Olympus
Gulf of Kassandra
Ath
Konitsa
Elassona
Kalithea
Delvinakio
Meteora
Paliouri
Metsovo
Kalambaka
Tirnavos
Kerkira
Ioanina
Agia
Corfu
Igoumenitsa
Trikala
Larissa
Mount
Pelion
Paramythia
Karditsa
Volos
SPORADES
E951
Arta
Stavros
Farsala
Parga
Aliki
Almiros
Skiathos
Preveza
Lamia
Skopelos
Karpenissi
Lefkas
Skyro
Vassiliki
Agrinio
Orhomenos
EVIA
Kephalonia
Ithaki
Delphi
Arahova
Kymi
Nafpaktos
Itea
Livadia
Halkida
Messolongi
E55
Galaxidi
E75
Lixouri
Sami
Patras
Gulf of Corinth
Thebes
Diakofto
Megara
Rafina
Killini
Corinth
Piraeus
Athens
Kary
Loutra
Nemea
Glyfada
Zakynthos
Amalias
Mycenae
Voula
Lavrio
Kea
Zakynthos
Pyrgos
Argos
Aegina
Poros
Sounio
Kaïafas
Olympia
Tripoli
Nauplion
Tolo
Andritsena
Ermioni
Kythnos
Kyparissia
PELOPONNESE
Spetses
Hydra
Serifos
Messini
Sparta
Leonidio
Gargaliani
Kalamata
Geraki
Pilos
Mystras
Kyparissi
Methoni
Koroni
Skala
Areopoli
Gythio
Monemvassia
Milos

Ionian Sea

Agia Pelagia
Kythira
Kythira

Mediterranean Sea

Hania

0 ———— 100 miles
0 ———— 150 km

CRETE

14 GREECE

ATHENS, THE NORTHERN PELOPONNESE, MAINLAND GREECE, CORFU, THE AEGEAN ISLANDS

It can be disorienting for a visitor conditioned by museums, textbooks, and college Greek to arrive in Athens and find the natives roaring around in sports cars and talking about the latest nouvelle restaurant. The Greeks provide the vibrant color that has long since vanished from classical monuments once saturated with pigment, blue, gold, and vermilion, under the eye-searing Aegean sun.

The land itself is a stunning presence, dotted with cypress groves, vineyards, and olive trees; carved into gentle bays or dramatic coves bordered with startling white sand; or articulated into rolling hills and rugged mountain ranges that plunge into the sea. In Greece, indeed, you cannot travel far across the land without encountering the sea, or far across the sea without encountering one of its roughly 2,000 islands. Approximately equal in size to New York State and roughly the size of England, Greece has 15,019 km (9,312 mi) of coastline, more than any other country of its size. The sea is everywhere, not on three sides only but at every turn, reaching into the shoreline like a probing hand. This natural beauty and the sharp, clear light of sun and sea, combined with plentiful archaeological treasures, make Greece one of the world's most inviting and rewarding countries to visit.

Western poetry, music, architecture, politics, medicine, law—all had their birth centuries ago in Greece. Among the mountains of mainland Greece are Mt. Olympus, whose cloud-capped peak was the fabled home of the Greek gods, and Mt. Parnassus, favorite haunt of the sun god, Apollo, and the nine Muses. Romantic and beautiful remains of the ancient past—the Acropolis and the Parthenon, the temples of Delphi, the Tombs of the Kings in Mycenae—and later Byzantine churches, Crusader castles and fortresses, and Turkish mosques dot the country.

Of the many hundreds of islands and islets scattered across the Aegean Sea, in the east, and the Ionian Sea, in the west, fewer than 250 are still inhabited. This world of the farmer, fisherman, and seafarer has largely been replaced by the world of the tourist. More than 10 mil-

Black Sea

T U R K E Y

Istanbul

Kastanies

Xanthi Komotini Didymotiho
T H R A C E EO51

Avdira
Makri Alexandroupoli

Thassos

Samothrace

Sea of
Marmara

ount Athos
nninsula-
onk's Republic
on
Mount
thos

Limnos

■ **Troy**

S

Lesvos Mytilini

Aegean Sea

Plomari

T U R K E Y

Hios Hios
Mesta
Pirgi

Izmir (Smyrna)

ystos

Andros
Andros

Samos

Samos

■ **Ephesus**

Ikaria

Tinos

Pythagorio

Ermoupoli Tinos
Syros
Mykonos

Agios
Kirykos

Delos
Patmos

Paros

Naxos

Leros

Bodrum
(Halicarnassus)

Kos

C Y C L A D E S Amorgos

Kos

Ios
Astypalea

Nissyros

Symi

Rhodes

Oia Fira
Santorini Anafi

Tilos Kameiros ■

Halki

Lindos

D O D E C A N E S E

Rhodes

Sea of Crete

Karpathos

thymnon Heraklion
Mallia
Knossos
Agios Nikolaos
Phaestos Ierapetra

Siteia

Kassos

lion vacationers visit Greece each year, almost doubling the entire native population. Once-idyllic beaches have become overcrowded and noisy, and fishing harbors have become flotilla-sailing centers. But traditional Greece survives: Pubs and bars stand next door to *ouzeri* (informal eateries that serve appetizers and ouzo), *kafeneia* (Greek coffee houses) are as popular as discos, and pizza and hamburger joints must compete with tavernas.

Although mass tourism has transformed the main centers, it is still possible to strike out and discover your own place among the smaller islands and the miles of beautiful mainland coastline. Except for an occasional scarcity of accommodations, especially in high summer, this is the ideal way to see traditional Greece. If you explore this fascinating country with open eyes, you'll enjoy it in all its forms: its slumbering cafés and buzzing tavernas; its elaborate religious rituals; its stark, bright beauty; and the generosity and curiosity of its people.

GREECE A TO Z

Customs

For details on imports and duty-free limits, *see* Customs & Duties *in* Chapter 1. You may bring in only one each of such expensive portable items as camcorders and computers. You should register these with Greek Customs upon arrival, to avoid any problems when taking them out of the country again. Foreign banknotes amounting to more than $2,500 must be declared for re-export, although there are no restrictions on traveler's checks; foreign visitors may export no more than 100,000 dr. in Greek currency.

Dining

The principal elements of Greek cuisine are fresh vegetables, such as eggplant, tomatoes, and beans, inventively combined with lots of olive oil and seasoned with lemon juice, garlic, onion, and oregano. Let your senses guide you—visit the kitchen and point to what looks appetizing; try the regional specialties and barrel wine whenever possible. Your best bet is to choose the tavernas and slightly more upscale *estiatoria* (restaurants) that are frequented by most Greeks. Both serve oven-baked dishes and stove-top stews called *magirefta,* prepared in advance and often served at room temperature. If you're in a fish taverna, ask to see the daily catch to check for freshness, choose your fish, and have it weighed before it's cooked; prices are by the kilo. Another alternative is an ouzeri or *mezedopolion,* where you order plates of appetizers, called *mezedes,* instead of an entrée. Traditional fast food in Greece consists of the gyro (slices of grilled meat with tomato and onions in pita bread), souvlakia (shish kebab), and pastries known as *pites,* filled with a variety of stuffings (spinach, cheese, or meat)—but hamburgers and pizzas are also found everywhere.

MEALTIMES

Lunch in Greek restaurants is served from 12:30 until 3. Dinner begins at about 9 and is served until 1 in Athens and until midnight outside Athens.

RATINGS

Prices are per person and include a first course, main course, dessert, VAT, and service charge. They do not include drinks or tip.

CATEGORY	ATHENS/ MAIN ISLAND TOWNS	OTHER AREAS
$$$$	over 15,000 dr.	over 14,000 dr.
$$$	10,000 dr.–15,000 dr.	9,000 dr.–14,000 dr.
$$	5,500 dr.–10,000 dr.	5,000 dr.–9,000 dr.
$	under 5,500 dr.	under 5,000 dr.

WHAT TO WEAR

Throughout the Greek islands you can dress informally for dinner, even at expensive restaurants; in Athens, jackets are appropriate at the top-price restaurants.

Language

English is widely spoken in hotels and elsewhere, especially by young people, and even in out-of-the-way places someone is always happy to lend a helping word. In this guide names are given in the Roman alphabet according to the Greek pronunciation.

Lodging

Greece offers a range of lodgings from Spartan campgrounds to family-run pensions to luxurious resorts complete with a pseudo village (bakery, church, café) on the premises. If you plan to visit during Easter week (Catholic or Orthodox) or from mid-June through August, reserve well in advance. In August on the islands, even the most basic rooms are hard to find, as that's when most Greeks take their monthlong vacation. Off-season, you usually can negotiate room rates.

CAMPING

There are numerous privately owned campgrounds, with amenities ranging from basic to elaborate (those operated by the tourist organization are cushier than most). Contact the **Greek Camping Association** (⊠ Solonos 102, 10680 Athens, ☎ FAX 01/362–1560) or the Greek National Tourist Organization (EOT; ☞ Visitor Information *in* Athens Essentials, *below*) for more information.

HOTELS

Greek hotels are classified by the government as De Luxe (L) and A–E. Within each category quality varies greatly, but prices usually don't. Still, you may come across an A-class hotel that charges less than a B-class, depending on facilities. In this guide hotels are classified according to price. All $$$$ and $$$ hotels are assumed to have air-conditioning and, unless indicated, all have private baths.

Prices quoted by hotels usually include service, local taxes, and VAT; many include breakfast. Often you can negotiate the price, sometimes by eliminating breakfast. The official price should be posted on the back of the door or inside a closet. Booking a room through a travel agency may reduce the price substantially. During high season larger resort hotels may insist that guests take half board.

RATINGS

Prices quoted are for a double room in high season, including taxes but not breakfast unless so indicated.

CATEGORY	COST
$$$$	over 55,000 dr.
$$$	33,000 dr.–55,000 dr.
$$	18,000 dr.–33,000 dr.
$	under 18,000 dr.

RENTED ROOMS AND APARTMENTS

Most areas have pensions—usually clean, bright, and recently built—and self-catering apartments. Owners wait for tourists at the harbor, and signs in English throughout villages indicate rooms available. Accommodations are harder to find in smaller resort towns during the winter and beginning of spring. You can pick up (at kiosks and foreign-language bookstores) an English-language copy of *Holiday Rentals in Greece: Rooms, Studios and Apartments* (published by Touristiki Ekdotiki), which includes photos and details on prices and facilities. Check the rooms first, for quality and location. Also, make sure you feel comfortable with the owners if they live on the premises.

TRADITIONAL SETTLEMENTS

State organized, these establishments house guests in buildings representative of the local architecture. Many settlements are described in a free brochure from EOT (☞ Visitor Information *in* Athens Essentials, *below*), as well as in the English-language *Traditional Inns in Greece: Alternative Forms of Tourism* (published by Vertical Advertising-Publishing), available in foreign-language bookstores.

YOUTH HOSTELS

Hostels operate in major tourist areas but often close from season to season, so contact the **Greek Youth Hostel Organization** (✉ Damareos 75, 11633 Athens, ☎ 01/751–9530, ℻ 01/751–0616). The **YWCA** (✉ Amerikis 11, 10672 Athens, ☎ 01/362–4291 through 01/362–4293, ℻ 01/362–2400) puts up overnight female guests.

Mail

POSTAL RATES

Airmail letters and postcards for delivery within Europe cost 170 dr. for 20 grams and 270 dr. for 50 grams; for outside Europe 200 dr. for 20 grams and 300 dr. for 50 grams. All parcels must be inspected; bring them open and with wrapping materials to the nearest post office. In Athens parcels that weigh more than 2 kilograms (4½ pounds) must be brought to Mitropoleos 60 or to the Spiromiliou arcade off Voukourestiou Street.

RECEIVING MAIL

Letters are often lost in the mail; it's best to send important items registered. Most post offices are open weekdays 8–2. In Athens the **main offices** (✉ Aiolou 100 and on ✉ Syntagma Square at Mitropoleos) stay open late (weekdays 7:30 AM–8 PM, Saturday 7:30–2, Sunday 9–2). You can have your mail addressed to "poste restante" and sent to any post office in Greece (in Athens: ✉ Aiolou 100, Athens 10200), where you can pick it up once you show your passport. Or have it mailed to American Express offices (✉ Ermou 2, Athens 10563). The service is free for holders of American Express cards or traveler's checks. Other AmEx offices are located in Thessaloniki, Patras, Corfu, Rhodes, Santorini, Mykonos, Skiathos, and Heraklion in Crete.

Money Matters

COSTS

Fluctuations in currency make it impossible to do accurate budgeting in advance; watch the exchange rates. On the whole, Greece offers good value compared with many other European countries. A modest hotel in a small town will charge only slightly lower rates than a modest hotel in Athens, with the same range of amenities. The same is true of restaurants. Car rentals are costly in Greece, but taxis, public transportation, and ferries are inexpensive even for long-distance runs.

CURRENCY

The Greek monetary unit is the drachma (dr.). Banknotes are in denominations of 100, 200, 500, 1,000, 5,000, and 10,000 dr.; coins, 5, 10, 20, 50, and 100. At press time (summer 1999), there were approximately 318 dr. to the U.S. dollar, 216 dr. to the Canadian dollar, 498 dr. to the pound sterling, 212 dr. to the Australian dollar, 168 dr. to the New Zealand dollar, and 413 to the Irish punt. Daily exchange rates are prominently displayed in banks.

At a central-city café you can expect to pay about 800 dr.–1,000 dr. for a cup of coffee (Greek coffee is always cheaper), 700 dr.–900 dr. for a bottle of beer, 500 dr. for a soft drink, and around 850 dr. for a grilled cheese sandwich. A 2-km (1-mi) taxi ride costs about 500 dr. Admission to most museums and archaeological sites is free on Sunday from November through March.

By law a service charge is figured into the price of a meal, but unless the waiter was rude or inept, it is customary to leave an additional 8%–10%. Tip porters 150 dr.–200 dr. per bag; in better hotels maids get about 200 dr. per day. For taxi drivers Greeks usually round off the fare to the nearest 100 dr. Hairdressers receive 10%. In legitimate theaters tip ushers 100 dr.; at the cinema give 100 dr. if you take a program. On cruises cabin and dining-room stewards get about 600 dr. per day; guides receive about the same.

National Holidays

January 1; January 6 (Epiphany); March 13 (Clean Monday and first day of Lent); March 25 (Independence Day); April 28 (Good Friday); April 30 (Greek Easter Sunday); May 1 (Greek Easter Monday and Labor Day); June 18 (Pentecost); August 15 (Assumption); October 28 (Ochi Day); December 25–26.

Opening and Closing Times

Office and shopping hours vary from season to season. Check with your hotel for up-to-the-minute information on opening and closing times. **Banks** are open weekdays 8–2, except Friday, when they close at 1:30; they are closed weekends and public holidays. In Athens two branches of the National Bank of Greece have extended hours: services other than foreign exchange (⊠ Aiolou 86, off Omonia Square, ☎ 01/334–1000), open weekdays 6 PM–8 PM; foreign exchange only (⊠ Karageorgi Servias 2, Syntagma, ☎ 01/334–0500), open Monday–Thursday 3:30–6:30, Friday 3–6:30, Saturday 9–3, Sunday 9–1. Even smaller towns have at least one bank with an ATM. **Museums and archaeological sites** are open daily 8–3 off-season, or winter (October–mid-April). Depending on available personnel, sites usually stay open longer mid-April–September, sometimes as late as 8 PM in July and August. Many museums are closed one day a week, usually Monday. **Shops** are usually open Monday through Saturday 9–3 (8:30–3 mid-April–September) and Tuesday, Thursday, and Friday 5 PM–8:30 (5:30–9 in summer). Supermarkets are open weekdays, with reduced hours on Saturday. In tourist areas like Athens's Plaka, souvenir shops stay open late.

Shopping

Prices in large stores are fixed. Bargaining may take place in small, owner-managed souvenir and handicrafts shops and in antiques shops. In flea markets bargaining is expected.

You are required to have an export permit (not normally given if the piece is of any value) for antiques and Byzantine icons, but replicas can be bought fairly cheaply, although even these require a certificate stating they are copies.

SALES-TAX REFUNDS

Prices quoted in shops include the value-added tax (VAT). You may get a VAT refund on products worth 40,000 dr. or more (including VAT) bought in Greece from licensed stores, which usually display the Tax-Free Shopping sticker. Ask the shop to complete a refund form called a Tax-Free check, which Greek Customs will stamp after viewing the item to make sure you are exporting it. Send the refund form back to the shop for repayment by check or credit card.

Telephoning

COUNTRY CODE

The country code for Greece is 30. When dialing Greece from outside the country, drop the first zero in the regional telephone code. Mobile phone numbers begin with 093, 0932, and 094 codes.

INTERNATIONAL CALLS

You can buy phone cards (☞ *below*) with 100 units (1,700 dr.) and 500 units (7,000 dr.) for use at card phones. You might also go to the local OTE (Hellenic Telecommunications Organization) office for convenience and privacy. There is a three-minute minimum charge for operator-assisted station-to-station calls, a four-minute minimum for person-to-person connections. For an **AT&T** long-distance operator, dial 00/800–1311; for **MCI,** 00/800–1211; for **Sprint,** 00/800–1411. For operator-assisted calls in English, dial ☎ 161 or 162.

LOCAL CALLS

Many kiosks have pay telephones for local calls only. You pay the kiosk owner 20 dr. per call after you've finished. It's easier to buy a phone card from an OTE office, kiosks, or convenience shops, and use it at card phones. For calls within Greece, the price is reduced by about 30% weekdays 3 PM–5 PM and 10 PM–8 AM, and on weekends from 3 PM Saturday to 8 AM Monday.

Transportation

In Greek addresses, the word "street" is not used; the abbreviation for the word "Platia" (square) is Pl. In city addresses, the name of the district follows the name of the street.

BY BOAT

Frequent car ferries and hydrofoils leave from Piraeus, the port of Athens, for the central and southern Aegean islands and Crete. Boats to such nearby islands as Evia, Andros, Mykonos, and Tinos also leave from Rafina, east of Athens. Ships to the Ionian islands usually sail from Patras and Igoumenitsa. Buy your tickets two or three days in advance, especially if you are traveling in summer or taking a car. Reserve your return journey or continuation soon after you arrive. Timetables change frequently, and boats may be delayed by weather conditions, so your plans should be flexible.

BY BUS

Travel with the regional KTEL bus network is inexpensive, usually comfortable, and relatively fast. Bus timetables are available from EOT offices (☞ Visitor Information, *below*). In summer and on holiday weekends, make reservations or buy tickets a few days before your planned trip. Board early, as passengers often have a loose attitude about assigned seating; if smoking bothers you, get a seat away from the driver, who is exempt from the no-smoking regulations. For bus stations, ☞ By Bus *in* Arriving and Departing *in* Athens Essentials, *below*.

BY CAR

Breakdowns. The **Automobile and Touring Club of Greece** (ELPA, ✉ Athens Tower, Messoghion 2–4, 11525 Athens, ☎ 01/748–8800, FAX

01/778–6642; emergency, ☎ 104 throughout Greece) assists tourists with breakdowns free of charge if they belong to AAA or to ELPA (29,500 dr. per year, good throughout Europe); otherwise, there is a charge. ELPA also provides tourist information (☎ 174) to drivers.

Gasoline. At press time gas cost about 200 dr. a liter. Gas pumps and service stations are everywhere, and lead-free gas is widely available. In rural areas and on the islands many stations are closed evenings.

Parking. In Greece's half-dozen large cities, downtown street parking and lots are hard to find. It's often cheaper to leave your car at the hotel and take a cab or bus. Elsewhere, parking is easy.

Road Conditions. Greece has one of the highest ratios in Europe of collisions to the number of cars on the road. The National Road can be nightmarish with its inadequate signposting, remarked lanes, and constant repair work; tolls range from 250 dr. to 900 dr., depending on the distance traveled. You also need nerves of steel to drive in the cities, but many country roads, though narrow, are free of traffic.

Rules of the Road. Non-EU citizens must have an international driver's license. Driving is on the right, and although seat belts are compulsory, don't expect this or any other driving rule to be obeyed. The speed limit is 120 kph (74 mph) on the National Road (follow the temporary speed signs where it's under repair); 90 kph (54 mph) outside built-up areas; and 50 kph (31 mph) in town.

BY MOTORCYCLE AND BICYCLE

Dune buggies, bicycles, mopeds, and motorcycles can be rented on the islands. Use extreme caution. Helmets, technically compulsory for motorcyclists, are not usually available, and injuries are common.

BY PLANE

Air Greece (⌗ Nikis 20, Syntagma, Athens, ☎ 01/325–5011) flies from Athens to Rhodes, Heraklion, and Hania in Crete, and between these destinations. **Cronus Airlines** (⌗ Othonos 10, Syntagma, Athens, ☎ 01/331–5515) flies regularly from Athens to Thessaloniki. **Olympic Airways** (⌗ Fillelinon 15, near Syntagma, Athens, ☎ 01/966–6666 for reservations) has service between Athens and most large cities and islands in Greece.

For information on arrivals and departures for Olympic Airways flights (West Terminal), call ☎ 01/936–3363 through 01/936–3366; for other carriers (East Terminal), call ☎ 01/969–4466 for departures and ☎ 01/969–4531 for arrivals. For information on flights using the New Charter Terminal (Terminal B), just before the East Terminal on the former U.S. military base, call ☎ 01/997–2686 and 01/997–2581.

BY TRAIN

The main **railway** line runs north from Athens, dividing into three lines at Thessaloniki. The main line continues to Belgrade, a second line goes east to the Turkish border and Istanbul, and a third line heads northeast to Bulgaria. The Peloponnese in the south is served by a narrow-gauge line dividing at Corinth into the Mycenae–Argos section and the Patras–Olympia–Kalamata section. Call ☎ 01/529–7777 for general information and timetables or ☎ 145 for a recorded departure timetable (in Greek) of trains within Greece; call ☎ 147 for information on trains to Europe and Russia.

Visitor Information

Tourist police, at most popular tourist sites, can answer questions in English about transportation, steer you to an open pharmacy or doctor, and locate phone numbers of hotels, rooms, and restaurants. There are **Greek National Tourist Organization (EOT)** offices throughout the country. Often more helpful are **municipal tourism offices** (☞ Visitor Information *in each* Essentials *section, below*).

Weather

May, June, September, and October are the most temperate and least-crowded months to visit Greece. The heat can be unpleasant in July and August, especially in Athens. On the islands a brisk northwesterly wind, the *meltemi,* can make life more comfortable. The winter months tend to be damp and cold virtually everywhere.

CLIMATE

The following are the average daily maximum and minimum temperatures for Athens.

Jan.	55F	13C	May	77F	25C	Sept.	84F	29C
	44	6		61	16		67	19
Feb.	57F	14C	June	86F	30C	Oct.	75F	24C
	44	6		68	20		60	16
Mar.	60F	16C	July	92F	33C	Nov.	66F	19C
	46	8		73	23		53	12
Apr.	68F	20C	Aug.	92F	33C	Dec.	58F	15C
	52	11		73	23		47	8

ATHENS

Athens is a village that outgrew itself, spreading from the original settlement at the foot of the Acropolis. In 1834, when it became the capital of modern Greece, the city had a population of fewer than 10,000. Now it houses more than a third of the entire Greek population—around 4.3 million. A modern concrete city has engulfed the old village and sprawls for 388 square km (244 square mi), covering almost all the surrounding plain from the sea to the encircling mountains. The city is has an air-pollution problem, caused mainly by traffic fumes; in an attempt to lessen the congestion, private cars are forbidden in central Athens on alternate workdays. Still, Athens's vibrancy makes it one of the most exciting cities in Europe, and the sprawling cement has failed to overwhelm the astonishing reminders of the fabled ancient metropolis.

Although Athens covers a huge area, the major landmarks of the ancient Greek, Roman, and Byzantine periods are close to the modern city center. You can stroll from the Acropolis to the other sites, taking time to browse in shops and relax in cafés and tavernas along the way. The Acropolis and Filopappou, two craggy hills sitting side by side; the ancient and Roman agoras (marketplaces); and Kerameikos, the first cemetery, form the core of ancient and Roman Athens.

Exploring Athens

Numbers in the margin correspond to points of interest on the Athens map.

The central district of modern Athens is small, stretching from the Acropolis to Mt. Lycabettus, with its small white church on top. The layout is simple: Three parallel streets—Stadiou, Panepistimiou, and Akademias—link two main squares—Syntagma and Omonia. Try to wander off this beaten tourist track: Seeing the Athenian butchers in the central market near Monastiraki sleeping on their cold marble slabs during the heat of the afternoon siesta may give you more of a feel for the city than looking at hundreds of fallen pillars. In summer closing times often depend on the site's available personnel, but throughout the year, arrive at least 45 minutes before the official closing time to ensure that you can buy a ticket. Flash photography is forbidden in museums.

❻ Agios Eleftherios (St. Eleftherios). What's fascinating about the city's former cathedral is that the walls of this 12th-century Byzantine church incorporate reliefs—fanciful figures and zodiac signs—from buildings that date back to the Classical period. The church is also known as Little Mitropolis and Panagia Gorgoepikoos (Virgin Who Answers Prayers Quickly), based on its 13th-century icon, said to perform miracles. ⊠ *Pl. Mitropolis,* ☎ *no phone.* ⌷ *Free.* ☼ *Hrs depend on services, but usually open daily 8–1.*

★ ❶ Akropolis (Acropolis). The Athenians built this complex during the 5th century BC to honor the goddess Athena, patron of the city. It is now undergoing conservation as part of an ambitious 20-year rescue plan launched with international support in 1983 by Greek architects. The first ruins you'll see are the **Propylaia,** the monumental gateway that led worshipers from the temporal world into the spiritual world of the sanctuary; now only the columns of Pentelic marble and a fragment of stone ceiling remain. Above, to the right, stands the graceful **Naos Athenas Nikis** or **Apterou Nikis** (Wingless Victory). The temple was mistakenly called the latter because common tradition often confused Athena with the winged goddess Nike. The elegant and architecturally complex **Erechtheion,** most sacred of the shrines of the Acropolis and later turned into a harem by the Turks, has emerged from repair work with dull, heavy copies of the caryatids (draped maidens) supporting the roof. The **Acropolis Museum** (☞ Museo Akropoleos, *below*) houses five of the six originals, their faces much damaged by acid rain. The sixth is in the British Museum in London.

The **Parthenonas** (Parthenon) dominates the Acropolis and indeed the Athens skyline. Designed by Ictinus, with Phidias as master sculptor, it was completed in 438 BC and is the most architecturally sophisticated temple of that period. Even with hordes of tourists wandering around the ruins, it still inspires wonder. The architectural decorations were originally painted vivid red and blue, and the roof was of marble tiles, but time and neglect have given the marble pillars their golden-white shine, and the beauty of the building is all the more stark and striking. The British Museum houses the largest remaining part of the original 532-ft frieze (the Elgin Marbles). The building has 17 fluted columns along each side and eight at the ends; these were cleverly made to lean slightly inward and to bulge, counterbalancing the natural optical distortion. The Parthenon was made into a brothel by the Romans, a church by the Christians, and a mosque by the Turks. The Turks also stored gunpowder in the Propylaia. When this was hit by a Venetian bombardment in 1687, 28 columns of the Parthenon were blown out and a fire raged for two days, leaving the temple in its present condition. ⊠ *Top of Dionyssiou Areopagitou,* ☎ *01/321–4172.* ☼ *May–Oct., weekdays 8–7, weekends 8–2:30; Nov.–Apr., daily 8–2:30.*

❹ Archaia Agora (Ancient Agora). Now a sprawling confusion of stones, slabs, and foundations, this was the civic center and focal point of community life in ancient Athens, where Socrates met with his students while merchants haggled over the price of olive oil. It is dominated by the best-preserved Doric temple in Greece, the **Hephaisteion,** built during the 5th century BC. Nearby, the Stoa Attalou (Stoa of Attalos II), reconstructed in the mid-1950s by the American School of Classical Studies in Athens, houses the **Museo tis Agoras** (Museum of Agora Excavations). The museum offers a glimpse of everyday life in ancient Athens, its objects ranging from a child's terra-cotta chamber pot to

504

the shards (*ostraka,* from which the word "ostracism" is derived) used in secret ballots to recommend banishment of Themistocles and other powerful citizens. ⊠ *Three entrances: from Monastiraki, on Adrianou; from Thission, on Apostolos Pavlou; from Acropolis, on descent along Ag. Apostoli;* ☎ *01/321–0185.* ⊙ *Tues.–Sun. 8–2:30.*

❸ Areios Pagos (Areopagus). From this rocky outcrop, ancient Athens's supreme court, you can view the Propylaia, the Agora, and the modern city. Legend claims it was here that Orestes was tried for the murder of his mother, and much later St. Paul delivered his Sermon to the Unknown God, so moving that a senator named Dionysius was converted and became the first bishop of Athens. ⊠ *Opposite Acropolis entrance.* ⊠ *Free.* ⊙ *Always open.*

★ ⓲ Ethniko Archaiologiko Museo (National Archaeological Museum). Among the collection of antiquities are the sensational archaeological finds of Heinrich Schliemann in 1874 at Mycenae; 16th-century BC frescoes from the Akrotiri ruins on Santorini; and the 6½-ft-tall bronze sculpture *Poseidon,* an original work of circa 470 BC, which was found in the sea off Cape Artemision in 1928. ⊠ *28 Oktovriou (Patission) 44, 10-min walk north of Pl. Omonia,* ☎ *01/821-7717.* ⊙ *May–Oct., Mon. 12:30–7, Tues.–Fri. 8–7, weekends 8–2:30; Nov.–Apr., Mon. 10:30–5, Tues.–Sun. 8–2:30.*

★ ⓮ Goulandri Museo Kikladikis ke Ellinikis Archaias Technis (Goulandris Museum of Cycladic and Greek Ancient Art). The collection spans 5,000 years, with nearly 100 exhibits of the Cycladic civilization (3000–2000 BC), including many of the marble figurines that so fascinated such artists as Picasso and Modigliani. ⊠ *Neofitou Douka 4 or Irodotou 1,* ☎ *01/722-8321.* ⊙ *Mon. and Wed.–Fri. 10–4, Sat. 10–3.*

❽ Irodion (Odeon of Herod Atticus). This hauntingly beautiful 2nd-century AD theater was built Greek-style into the hillside but with typical Roman archways in its three-story stage building and barrel-vaulted entrances. Now restored, it hosts Athens Festival performances (☞ The Arts, *below*). ⊠ *Dionyssiou Areopagitou across from Propylaia,* ☎ *01/323-2771.* ⊙ *Open only to audiences during performances.*

★ ⓯ Likavitos (Mt. Lycabettus). Athens's highest hill borders Kolonaki, a residential quarter worth a visit if you enjoy window-shopping and people-watching. A steep funicular climbs to the summit, crowned by whitewashed Agios Giorgios chapel. The view from the top—pollution permitting—is the finest in Athens. ⊠ *Base: 10-min walk northeast of Syntagma; funicular every 10 min from Ploutarchou 1 at Aristippou (take minibus 060 from Pl. Kolonaki and walk up stairs);* ☎ *01/722-7065.* ⊙ *Fri.–Wed. 9:30 AM–midnight (9 AM–12:30 AM in summer), Thurs. 11:15 AM–midnight (11:30 AM–12:30 AM in summer). Closed Feb.*

❺ Monastiraki. The old Turkish bazaar area takes its name from Panayia Pantanassa Church, commonly called Monastiraki (Little Monastery); it once flourished as a convent, perhaps dating from the 10th century. Near the church stands the Tzistarakis Mosque (1759), exemplifying the East-West paradox that characterizes Athens. But the district's real draw is the Sunday flea market, centered on tiny Abyssinia Square and running along Ifestou and Kynetou streets where Greeks bargain with wildly gesturing hands and dramatic facial expressions. Everything's for sale, from gramophone needles to old matchboxes, from nose rings to lacquered eggs and cool white linens. ⊠ *South of junction Ermou and Athinas Sts.*

★ ❷ Museo Akropoleos (Acropolis Museum). Tucked into one corner of the Acropolis, this institution contains superb sculptures, including the caryatids and a collection of colored *korai* (statues of women dedicated by worshipers to Athena, patron of the ancient city). ⊠ *Southeastern corner of Acropolis,* ☎ *01/323–6665.* ⊙ *Mon. 11–6:30 (11–2:30 in winter), Tues.–Sun. 8–6:30 (8–2:30 in winter).*

⑫ Panathinaiko Stadio (Panathenaic Stadium). A reconstruction of the ancient Roman stadium in Athens, this gleaming white marble structure was built for the first modern Olympic Games in 1896 and seats 80,000 spectators. ⊠ *Near junction Vas. Konstantinou and Vas. Olgas,* ☎ *no phone.* 🎟 *Free.* ⊙ *Daily 9–2.*

⑩ Pili tou Adrianou (Hadrian's Arch). Built in AD 131–32 by Emperor Hadrian to show where classical Athens ended and his new city, Hadriaopolis, began, the Roman archway with Corinthian pilasters bears an inscription on the side facing the Acropolis that reads, THIS IS ATHENS, THE ANCIENT CITY OF THESEUS. But the side facing the Temple of Olympian Zeus proclaims, THIS IS THE CITY OF HADRIAN AND NOT OF THESEUS. ⊠ *Junction Vas. Amalias and Dionyssiou Areopagitou.* 🎟 *Free.* ⊙ *Always open.*

★ **❼ Plaka.** Stretching east from the Agora, this is almost all that's left of 19th-century Athens, a lovely quarter with winding walkways, neoclassical houses, and such sights as the **Museo EllinikisLaikis Technis** (Greek Folk Art Museum; ⊠ Kidathineon 17, ☎ 01/322–9031; ⊙ Tues.–Sun. 10–2), with a collection dating from 1650, and the Roman Agora's **Aerides** (Tower of the Winds; ⊠ Pelopidas and Aiolou, ☎ 01/324–5220; ⊙ Tues.–Sun. 8–2:30), a 1st-century BC water clock. Just down the street from the Tower of the Winds in a neoclassical mansion is the delightful **Museo Ellinikon Laikon Musikon Organon** (Museum of Popular Greek Musical Instruments; ⊠ Diogenous 1–3, ☎ 01/325–0198; ⊙ Tues. and Thurs.–Sun. 10–2, Wed. 12–6), which gives a crash course in the development of Greek music, with three floors of instruments and headphones so visitors can appreciate recorded sounds made by such unusual organs as goatskin bagpipes and the Cretan lyra. Admission is free. The **Mnimeio Lysikratous** (Monument of Lysikrates; ⊠ Herefondos and Lysikratous Sts.) is one of the few surviving tripods on which stood the award given to the producer of the best play in the Dionyssia festival. Above Plaka, at the northeastern base of the Acropolis, is **Anafiotika,** the closest thing you'll find to a village in Athens. Take time to wander among its whitewashed, bougainvillea-framed houses and tiny churches.

⑪ Stiles Olymbiou Dios or Olymbion (Temple of Olympian Zeus). Begun during the 6th century BC, this temple was larger than all other temples in Greece when it was finally completed 700 years later. It was destroyed during the invasion of the Goths in the 4th century; only a few towering, sun-browned columns remain. ⊠ *Vas. Olgas 1,* ☎ *01/922–6330.* ⊙ *May–Oct., Tues.–Sun. 8:30–3; Nov.–Apr., 8–2:30.*

⑯ Syntagma (Constitution Square). At the top of the square stands the **Vouli** (Parliament), formerly the royal palace, completed in 1838 for the new monarchy. From the Parliament you can watch the changing of the Evzone honor guard at the **Mnimeio Agnostou Stratiotou** (Tomb of the Unknown Soldier), with its text from Pericles's famous funeral oration and a bas-relief of a dying soldier modeled after a sculpture on the Temple of Aphaia in Aegina. The most elaborate ceremony takes place on Sunday, when the sturdy young guards don their *foustanellas* (kilts) with 400 pleats, one for each year of the Ottoman occupation. The procession usually arrives in front of Parliament at 11:15 AM. On the square's southern side sits the lush **Ethnikos Kipos** (National Garden), its dense foliage, gazebos, and trellised walkways offering a quick escape from the center's bustle. ⊠ *Corner of Vas. Sofias and Vas. Amalias.*

❾ Theatro Dionyssou (Theater of Dionysus). In this theater dating from about 330 BC, the ancient dramas and comedies were performed in conjunction with bacchanalian feasts. The throne in the center was reserved for the priest of Dionysus: It is adorned with regal lions' paws, and the back is carved with reliefs of satyrs and griffins. ⊠ *Dionyssiou Areopagitou opposite Mitsaion,* ☎ 01/322–4625. ☉ *Daily 8:30–2:30.*

⓱ Vivliothiki, Panepistimio, Akademia (Old University complex). These three dramatic buildings belong to the University of Athens, designed by the Hansen Brothers in the period after independence and built of white Pentelic marble, with tall columns and decorative friezes. In the center is the Senate House of the university; on the right is the Academy, flanked by statues of Athena and Apollo; and on the left is the National Library. ⊠ *Panepistimiou between Ippokratous and Sina,* ☎ *Library, 01/361–4413; Panepistimio, 01/361–4301; Akademia, 01/360–0207 and 01/360–0209.* ▧ *Free.* ☉ *Library: Mon.–Thurs. 9–8, Fri.–Sat 9–2. Other buildings: weekdays 9–2. Library closed Aug.*

⓭ Vizantino Museo (Byzantine Museum). Housed in an 1848 mansion built by an eccentric French aristocrat, the museum has a unique collection of icons, re-creations of Greek churches throughout the centuries, and a very beautiful 14th-century Byzantine embroidery of the body of Christ, in gold, silver, yellow, and green. Sculptural fragments provide an excellent introduction to Byzantine architecture. ⊠ *Vas. Sofias 22,* ☎ 01/721–1027. ☉ *May–Oct., Tues.–Sun. 8:30–3; Nov.–Apr., 8–2:30.*

Dining and Lodging

Search for places with at least a half dozen tables occupied by Athenians—they're discerning customers. For details and price-category information, *see* Dining *in* Greece A to Z, *above.* It's always advisable to reserve a room. Hotels are clustered around the center of town and along the seacoast toward the airport. Modern hotels are more likely to be air-conditioned and to have double-glazed windows; the center of Athens can be so noisy that it's hard to sleep. For details and price-category definitions, *see* Lodging *in* Greece A to Z, *above.*

$$$$ ✕ **Bajazzo.** This is the only restaurant in Athens that has been accorded
★ international praise. In a neoclassical house with wooden floors and furniture, gilt-edged mirrors, fresh flowers, and pale colors set the formal tone. Chef Klaus Feuerbach creates imaginative, beautifully presented dishes. Appetizers might include seafood tart in fish velouté or crab with banana wrapped in mango slices. For delectable main courses you may choose among beef fillets in Metaxa sauce, goose with quince, almond-laced shrimp strudel, and lamb stuffed with scallops. Try the mouthwatering chocolate concoctions or the lighter pear mousse with meringue for dessert. ⊠ *Anapafseos 14, Mets,* ☎ 01/921–3013. *Reservations essential. AE, DC, MC, V. Closed Sun. No lunch.*

$$$$ ✕ **Vardis.** A meal at this French restaurant is worth the ride to the northern suburb of Kifissia. The chef is committed to the classics and to quality ingredients—he brings in sweetwater crayfish from Orhomenos and tracks down rare large shrimp from Thassos island. The clientele may be a little sedate, but the food dazzles. Especially good are the warm foie gras with dried fig puree, the superb crayfish linguine, and the tournedos Rossini served with a demi-glace enriched with foie gras. ⊠ *Diligianni 66 in Pentelikon Hotel, Kefalari, Kifissia,* ☎ 01/623–0650 *through 01/623–0656. Reservations essential. AE, DC, MC, V. Closed Sun. and Aug. No lunch.*

$$$–$$$$ ✕ **To Varoulko.** Chefs Lefteris Lazarou and Fabrizio Buliani try to outdo
★ each other nightly, with magnificent results. You can sample such ap-
petizers as sturgeon-filled phyllo triangles or carpaccio made from
petrobarbouno (a kind of rock fish). Although the restaurant is most
famous for monkfish, it offers a mind-boggling array of other seafood
dishes: swordfish with porcini mushrooms; baby squid with pesto; lob-
ster with wild rice, celery, and champagne sauce; and cabbage trans-
formed into heady dolmades filled with crayfish and leeks. ⊠ *Deligeorgi
14, Piraeus,* ☎ *01/411–2043 and 01/422–1283. Reservations essen-
tial. AE, DC, MC, V. Closed Sun. and Aug. No lunch.*

$$$ ✕ **Azul.** The space may be a bit cramped, but the food is heavenly. Start
with mushrooms stuffed with nuts and *anthotiro* cheese (soft, mild,
low-fat white cheese made from goat and sheep milk), or salmon and
trout in pastry with champagne sauce. The spaghetti à la *nona* (god-
mother) with chamomile, Gorgonzola, and bacon is an unparalleled
combination. Other memorable dishes are beef fillet with raisins and
cedar needles, and chicken prepared with lemon leaves. In summer, Azul
sets up tables outside. ⊠ *Haritos 43, Kolonaki,* ☎ *01/725–3817.
Reservations essential. AE, DC, V. Closed last 3 wks in Aug. No lunch.*

$$$ ✕ **Boschetto.** The restaurant pampers diners with its park setting, ex-
pert maître d', and creative Italian nouvelle food. The specialty here
is fresh pasta, such as airy cappellini with crab and sautéed tomatoes,
or ravioli with duck livers and truffle zabaglione. Entrées may include
sea bass grilled in a salt crust, venison with pomegranate sauce, and
beef fillet with black truffles and red wine. End your meal with the bit-
tersweet chocolate mousse followed by the finest espresso in Athens.
The tables tend to be close together; reserve near the window or in the
courtyard during the summer. ⊠ *Alsos Evangelismos, Hilton area,* ☎
*01/721–0893 and 01/722–7324. Reservations essential. AE, V. Closed
Sun. and 2 wks in Aug. No lunch weekends.*

$$$ ✕ **Spondi.** This vaulted stone-interior restaurant suggests a medieval
wine cellar, with heavy candlesticks and massive wood furniture, but
the cuisine is delightfully contemporary. Savor the foie gras terrine or
the more complex sweetbread-oyster mushroom tart. Try such entrées
as tuna grilled with mint and coriander, saltimbocca of red mullet with
wild mushroom ravioli, pappardelle and lobster in a cognac-port sauce,
or lamb with apple puree and Calvados. For dessert: white chocolate
mousse. In good weather, you can sit in the bougainvillea-draped
courtyard. ⊠ *Pirronos 5, Pangrati,* ☎ *01/756–4021 and 01/752–
0658. Reservations essential. DC, MC, V. No lunch.*

$$–$$$ ✕ **Kollias.** Friendly owner Tassos Kollias creates his own dishes, rang-
ing from the humble to the aristocratic: fried whole squid in its ink;
sea urchin salad; lobster with lemon, balsamic vinegar, and a shot of
honey. He's known for bringing in the best-quality catch, whether mullet from Messolonghi or oysters culled by Kalymnos sponge divers, and
his prices are usually 25% lower than most fish tavernas. A fitting end
to the meal: fresh *loukoumades* (sweet fritters) or *bougatsa* (custard
in phyllo). Ask for directions when you call—even locals get lost trying to find this obscure street in the working-class quarter of Piraeus.
⊠ *Stratigou Plastira 3, near jct Dramas and Kalokairinou, Tabouria,*
☎ *01/461–9150 and 01/462–9620. Reservations essential weekends.
AE, DC, MC, V. Closed Sun. and Aug. No lunch.*

$$–$$$ ✕ **Thalassinos.** In a neoclassical house, linen tablecloths, mirrors, a
wooden chest of drawers behind the bar, and frescoes on the ceiling
evoke the atmosphere of an old French restaurant. Fine, rare appetizers include salted eel from Komotini and house-made seafood *pastourmas*
(dried, cured, spicy meat or seafood), excellent with a shot of icy
tsipouro (a liqueur similar to raki). Hot entrées may be red mullet stuffed
with arugula, sorrel, and olives, and garlic shrimp baked amid layers

of potato. Desserts may include dried figs stewed in *mavrodaphni* (deep red, sweet dessert wine from the Patras region). ⊠ *Tsakalof 36A, Kolonaki*, ☎ 01/361–4695. *Reservations essential. AE, DC, V. Closed mid-June–Aug. No dinner Sun.*

$$ ✕ **Stous 7 Anemous.** The decor is a bit of postmodern pastiche, but the playful food with intense flavors is impressive here. For appetizers try the fried Dodoni feta wrapped in sesame-enhanced crust and served with marinated tomatoes and walnut sauce, or the prosciutto with sweet red peppers and *ladotiri* (Mytilini cheese) in phyllo. Main dishes include moist pork fillet with a dense coffee–black currant sauce; chicken with shrimp and pistachios doused with brandy; grilled tuna with tomato, thyme, and chamomile; and salmon, monkfish, and shrimp poached in lettuce leaves. End your meal with the almond pastry (*amigdaloto*) with tsipouro. ⊠ *Astiggos 17 (from Ermou 121), Monastiraki*, ☎ 01/324–0386. *Reservations essential. AE, DC, MC, V. Closed Aug.*

$$ ✕ **Tade Efi Anna.** Near the end of the Ermou pedestrian zone, this restaurant serves Greek regional cuisine with a modern touch. Try *Melitzanes amigdalou* (thinly sliced eggplant layered with tomatoes and cheese with a thick topping of crushed almonds). The rabbit is cooked with cinnamony plums and fresh spinach, and the chicken fillet is first wrapped around Gruyère, then baked in a crust of pistachios. ⊠ *Ermou 72, Monastiraki*, ☎ 01/321–3652. *V. Closed Mon. and Aug.*

$$ ✕ **Vlassis.** Relying on recipes from Thrace, Roumeli, Thessaly, and the
★   islands, the chefs whip up Greek home cooking in generous portions. Musts are pastitsio (made here with bits of lamb liver), *lahanodolmades* (cabbage rolls), goat with oil and oregano, and octopus *stifado* (stew), tender and sweet with lots of onions. ⊠ *Paster 8, Platia Mavili (near American embassy)*, ☎ 01/646–3060. *Reservations essential. No credit cards. Closed Aug.–mid-Sept. No dinner Sun.*

$ ✕ **Karavitis.** A neighborhood favorite, this taverna near the Olympic Stadium has warm-weather garden seating and a winter dining room decorated with huge wine casks. Classic Greek cuisine is well prepared here, including pungent *tzatziki* (yogurt-garlic dip), *bekri meze* (lamb chunks in a spicy red sauce), and *stamnaki* (beef baked in a clay pot). ⊠ *Arktinou 35 and Pausaniou 4, Pangrati*, ☎ 01/721–5155. *No credit cards. Closed around Aug. 15. No lunch.*

$ ✕ **Margaro.** Near Piraeus, next to the Naval Academy, this popular no-nonsense fish taverna serves just four items, along with excellent barrel wine: fried crayfish, fried red mullet, fried *marida* (a small white fish), and huge Greek salads. Tables on the terrace offer a view of the busy port. If it's crowded, you may be asked to go into the kitchen and prepare your own salad! Try to arrive between 6 and 8 PM, before Greeks eat dinner; reservations are not accepted. ⊠ *Hatzikyriakou 126, Piraeus*, ☎ 01/451–4226. *No credit cards. Closed Sun. and Aug.*

$ ✕ **O Platanos.** Set in a picturesque courtyard, this is one of Plaka's old-
★   est yet least touristy tavernas. The waiters are fast but far from ingratiating, and the place is packed with Greeks. Don't miss the oven-baked potatoes, roast lamb, green beans in savory olive oil, and exceptionally cheap but delicious barrel retsina. ⊠ *Diogenous 4, Plaka*, ☎ 01/322–0666. *No credit cards. Closed Sun. and 2 wks in Aug.*

$ ✕ **To Ouzadiko.** This unpretentious mezedopolion has a cozy interior (old posters, abundant wood, small marble tables), friendly service, and enticing mezedes. Depending on what the owner bought at market that morning, you may find delicious *tsigerosarmadakia* (Thessaloniki mini meat pies), the juiciest *keftedes* (meatballs), duckling with rice and chestnuts, black-eyed peas cooked with fresh greens, and juicy rooster with onions. ⊠ *Karneadou 25–29 in Lemos shopping mall atrium, Kolonaki*, ☎ 01/729–5484. *Reservations essential for dinner. DC, MC, V. Closed Sun. and last 2 wks Aug.*

$$$$ ★   🏨 **Andromeda Athens Hotel.** On a quiet street near the U.S. Embassy, this small, luxury hotel caters to business travelers, but the meticulous service and sumptuous decor of Persian carpets, Italian pastels, and designer furniture have a universal appeal. The restaurant has excellent Italian cuisine. The hotel also operates a property across the street with 12 executive suites (one- and two-room apartments), which include refrigerator, microwave, and a pay TV system. ⊠ *Timoleondos Vassou 22, Pl. Mavili, 11521,* ☎ *01/643–7302,* FAX *01/646–6361. 20 rooms, 6 suites, 4 penthouses. Restaurant. AE, DC, MC, V.*

$$$$ ★   🏨 **Athens Hilton.** A 200-year-old olive tree with a Turkish cannonball in its branches adds an earthy touch to the marble lobby. About a 20-minute walk from Syntagma, this is still one of the city's top hotels after nearly 30 years; a shuttle takes guests downtown during the day. The rooms, in muted colors, all have balconies and double-glazed windows, as well as fine views of either the Acropolis or Mt. Ymittos. The Galaxy bar has an outdoor terrace overlooking an Athens panorama. ⊠ *Vas. Sofias 46, 11528,* ☎ *01/725–0201, 800/445–8667 from U.S. and Canada,* FAX *01/725–3110. 454 rooms, 19 suites. 3 restaurants, pool. AE, DC, MC, V.*

$$$$ 🏨 **Grande Bretagne.** Built in 1842, the G. B. is an Athens landmark, and its guest list testifies to its colorful history, with such visitors as Edith Piaf, Jackie Kennedy, royalty, and rock stars. A face-lift in 1992 restored the hotel: The lobby has Oriental rugs, tapestries, and ornate chandeliers, and the coveted Syntagma rooms have large balconies and Acropolis views. There are also "Smart" rooms, with desk, printer, fax, photocopier, and a direct telephone line, and a no-smoking floor. ⊠ *Vas. Georgiou A' 1, Syntagma, 10563,* ☎ *01/333–0000, 01/331–5555 through 01/331–5559 for reservations,* FAX *01/322–8034, 01/322–2261 for reservations. 364 rooms, 23 suites. Restaurant. AE, DC, MC, V.*

$$$$ 🏨 **Holiday Inn.** The light, modern rooms, renovated in 1998, have voice mail, satellite TV, video, hair dryer, computer hookups, and express checkout. The Executive Rooms on the fifth and sixth floors have private balconies and extra amenities. The rooftop pool sits alongside a snack bar and a restaurant open summer evenings. ⊠ *Mihalakopoulou 50, Ilisia, 11528,* ☎ *01/724–8322 through 01/724–8329,* FAX *01/724–8187. 189 rooms, 3 suites. Restaurant, pool. AE, DC, MC, V.*

$$$$ 🏨 **N. J. V. Athens Plaza.** At an exclusive Syntagma Square address, the fresh, spacious rooms, in gray and burgundy, come equipped with minibar, direct-dial phones, Internet facilities, and large marble bathrooms with phone extensions. The few rooms in the back are quieter, but even those on the front are fine, due to double glazing and air-conditioning. The suites on the eighth and ninth floors have sitting areas, breathtaking Acropolis views, and interiors decked out with designer fabrics and furnishings. ⊠ *Vas. Georgiou A' and Stadiou, Pl. Syntagma, 10564,* ☎ *01/325–5301,* FAX *01/323–5856. 182 rooms, 25 suites. Restaurant. AE, DC, MC, V.*

$$$–$$$$ 🏨 **Kefalari Suites.** In a turn-of-the-century building among the neoclassical mansions and tree-lined boulevards of the suburb of Kifissia, the hotel offers imaginative suites at prices lower than those of downtown deluxe hotels. The suites include kitchenettes with utensils, refrigerators, satellite TV, minibars, and verandas or balconies; guests share the sundeck, which has a whirlpool tub. Continental deluxe breakfast (cheese and cold cuts) is included in the room rate. ⊠ *Pentelis 1 and Kolokotroni, Kefalari, Kifissia 14562,* ☎ *01/623–3333,* FAX *01/623–3330. 13 suites. AE, DC, MC, V.*

$$$ 🏨 **Electra Palace.** At the edge of Plaka, this hotel has cozy rooms in warm hues with satellite TVs, hair dryers, and balconies for comparatively low prices. Rooms from the fifth floor up are smaller but have larger balconies. The renovated roof garden has a bar, a pool and whirl-

pool tub, barbecue in summer, and stunning Acropolis views. Buffet breakfast is included in the price. ⊠ *Nikodimou 18, Plaka, 10557,* ☎ *01/324–1401 through 01/324–1410,* ℻ *01/324–1875. 101 rooms, 5 suites. Restaurant, pool. AE, DC, MC, V.*

$$ ⊞ **Acropolis View Hotel.** Major sights are just a stone's throw away
★ from this hotel tucked into in a quiet neighborhood below the Acropolis. About half of the agreeable rooms with balconies have Parthenon views. There is a roof garden, staff members in the homey lobby are efficient, and full breakfast is included in the price. ⊠ *Webster 10, Acropolis, 11742,* ☎ *01/921–7303, 01/921–7304, or 01/921–7305,* ℻ *01/923–0705. 32 rooms. Air-conditioning. AE, MC, V.*

$$ ⊞ **Astor.** The Astor is convenient, with amenities such as TV, hair dryers, and air-conditioning. The rooms were renovated in 1998; request one above the sixth floor for a memorable view of the Acropolis. You can also take in the view during the buffet breakfast (included), served on the roof garden of the restaurant. ⊠ *Karageorgi Servias 16, Syntagma, 10562,* ☎ *01/335–1000,* ℻ *01/325–5115. 131 rooms. Restaurant, air-conditioning. AE, DC, V.*

$$ ⊞ **Hotel Achilleas.** This modern, family-owned hotel is just a few minutes from Syntagma but priced at the low end of its category. It has plain but spacious, airy rooms with TV, direct-dial phones, and air-conditioning, and on the top floor, two rooms share a bath. Breakfast, included in the price, is served in an interior courtyard filled with jungly plants and marble-topped blue tables. ⊠ *Lekka 21, Syntagma, 10562,* ☎ *01/322–5826, 01/322–8531, or 01/323–3197,* ℻ *01/322–2412. 34 rooms. Air-conditioning. AE, DC, MC, V.*

$$ ⊞ **Plaka Hotel.** Close to the ancient sights and the Monastiraki Square metro, this hotel has a roof garden overlooking the Plaka district's rooftops to the Parthenon. Double-glazed windows cut down the noise; the highest floors are the quietest. All rooms, done in blue and white, have TV and are simply furnished; those in back from the fifth floor up have the best Acropolis views. ⊠ *Kapnikareas 7 and Mitropoleos, Plaka, 10556,* ☎ *01/322–2096 through 01/322–2098,* ℻ *01/322–2412. 67 rooms. Air-conditioning. AE, DC, MC, V.*

$–$$ ⊞ **Acropolis House.** Ensconced in a 19th-century Plaka residence, this pension is frequented by artists and academics, who appreciate its large rooms, original frescoes, and genteel owners. All rooms have private bathrooms, though about 10 have their bath immediately outside in the hallway. Some rooms have air-conditioning, and a full breakfast is included in the price. ⊠ *Kodrou 6–8, Plaka, 10558,* ☎ *01/322–2344 and 01/322–6241,* ℻ *01/324–4143. 20 rooms. V.*

$ ⊞ **Adams Hotel.** Favored by young people for its clean rooms and good value, this quiet hotel sits across from Ayia Aikaterini church in Plaka. Most of the rooms have balconies and many, including all on the top floor, enjoy splendid views of the Acropolis. All but nine rooms have air-conditioning; four cheaper rooms have their private bath outside the room. ⊠ *Herefondos 6 at Thalou, Plaka, 10558,* ☎ *01/322–5381 and 01/324–6582,* ℻ *01/323–8553. 14 rooms. Air-conditioning. V.*

$ ⊞ **Art Gallery Pension.** On a side street not far from the Acropolis, this friendly, handsome house has an old-fashioned look, with family paintings on the muted white walls, comfortable beds, hardwood floors, and ceiling fans. Many rooms have balconies with views of Filopappou or the Acropolis. ⊠ *Erecthiou 5, Koukaki, 11742,* ☎ *01/923–8376 and 01/923–1933,* ℻ *01/923–3025. 19 rooms, 2 suites. No credit cards. Closed Nov.–Feb.*

$ ⊞ **Attalos Hotel.** The hotel has a rooftop garden, and many rooms have fine views of the Acropolis or Lycabettus; about 12 include balconies. Try to get a room in the back, where street noise is less, though it's also reduced by double-glazed windows. ⊠ *Athinas 29, Monastiraki,*

10554, ☎ 01/321–2801 *through* 01/321–2803, ℻ 01/324–3124. *80 rooms. Air-conditioning.* V.

Nightlife and the Arts

The English-language newspapers *Athens News* and *Kathemerini,* inserted in the *International Herald Tribune,* list current performances, gallery openings, and films.

The Arts

The **Athens Festival** (box office, ✉ Arcade at Stadiou 4, ☎ 01/322–1459) runs from late June through September with concerts, opera, ballet, folk dancing, and drama. Performances are in various locations, including the theater of Herod Atticus (Irodion; ☎ 01/323–2771 box office) below the Acropolis and Mt. Lycabettus (☎ 01/722–7233 box office). Tickets range in price from 4,000 dr. to 20,000 dr. and are available a few days before the performance.

The **Krystalleia Festival** stages local and international musical and dance groups from June through July and September in the stately Plakendias mansion (✉ 16 km/10 mi northeast of Athens on Mt. Pendeli). The concurrent **Pendelis Festival** (end July and Sept.) focuses on classical music, often importing international orchestras to take advantage of the acoustics of the Megaron (☞ Concerts and Operas, *below*). For information on the festivals, contact EOT (☞ Visitor Information *in* Athens Essentials, *below*) or the Megaron (☎ 01/804–2575). Tickets run from 2,000 dr. to 4,000 dr. and are usually sold at major record stores in downtown Athens.

Though rather corny, the **sound-and-light shows** (✉ Pnyx theater box office off Dionyssiou Areopagitou opposite Acropolis ☎ 01/922–6210), held April–October nightly at 9, display the Acropolis with dramatic lighting and a brief narrated history. The box office opens 8:20 PM, admission is 1,500 dr., and performances are in English.

CONCERTS AND OPERAS

Greek and world-class international orchestras perform September through June at the **Megaron Athens Concert Hall** (✉ Vas. Sofias and Kokkali, ☎ 01/728–2333, ℻ 01/728–2300; downtown box office, ✉ Arcade at Stadiou 4). Information and tickets are available weekdays 10–4; prices range from 2,500 dr. to 20,000 dr.

DANCE

The lively **Dora Stratou Troupe** (✉ Theater, Filopappou Hill, ☎ 01/921–4650, 01/324–4395 offices, ℻ 01/324–6921) performs Greek and Cypriot folk dances in authentic costumes. Tickets cost 3,500 dr. Performances are from end of May to end of September, Tuesday–Sunday 10:15 PM and Wednesday and Sunday 8:15.

FILM

Almost all Athens cinemas now show foreign films; *The Athens News,* the *Kathemerini* insert in the *International Herald-Tribune,* and *Hellenic Times* list them in English. Tickets run about 1,800 dr.–2,000 dr.

Nightlife

Athens has an active nightlife: Most bars stay open at least until 3 AM and often central squares are crowded with revelers. Drinks are rather steep (about 1,800 dr.–2,000 dr.) but generous. Often there is a surcharge on weekends at the most popular clubs, which also have bouncers. Few clubs take credit cards for drinks. In summer many downtown dance clubs move to the seaside. Ask your hotel for recommendations and check ahead for summer closings. For a uniquely Greek evening visit a club featuring *rembetika* music, a type of blues, or the popular *bouzoukia* (clubs with live bouzouki music). In the larger venues, there is usually a per-person minimum or an overpriced, second-rate prix-fixe menu; a bottle of whiskey costs about 30,000 dr.

BARS

Balthazar (⊠ Tsoha 27, Ambelokipi, ☎ 01/644–1215 and 01/645–2278), in a neoclassical house, has a lush garden courtyard and subdued music. Fairly new but sure to endure, **Banana Moon** (⊠ Vas. Olgas 1, Zappio, ☎ 01/321–5414) offers both a lively bar with a glamorous crowd and quieter tables set among the trees of the National Gardens; in winter the bar moves to Kolonaki. Cinema stars, romancing couples, girlfriends, the local Lotto vendor—all show up at **En Delfois** (⊠ Skoufa 75 on Delfon pedestrian zone, Kolonaki, ☎ 01/360–8269) for its see-and-be-seen atmosphere in a friendly setting with good snacks, eclectic music played at conversational level, and generous drinks. **Folie** (⊠ Eslin 4, Ambelokipi, ☎ 01/646–9852) has a congenial crowd of all ages dancing to reggae, Latin, funk, and ethnic music. Of the new bars for the under-40 crowd, **Kingsize** (⊠ Amerikis 3, Syntagma, ☎ 01/323–2500 and 01/ 323–2506) is especially popular; the music is techno, progressive, and house. Gregarious **Memphis** (⊠ Ventiri 5, Ilisia, behind Hilton, ☎ 01/722–4104) is an Athens classic for rock and occasional live music. With low-key music and a romantic park setting, **Parko** (⊠ Eleftherias Park, Ilisia, ☎ 01/722–3784) is a summer favorite. **Plus Soda** (⊠ Ermou 161, Thissio, ☎ 01/345–6187) draws an under-40 crowd with techno, progressive, and house. To enjoy Greek *kefi* (high spirits), visit the always-packed **Vareladiko Klassikon** (⊠ Distomou and E. Zanni 1, Piraeus, ☎ 01/422–7500 through 01/ 422–7502), where you'll see frenzied table dancing to Greek hits.

BOUZOUKIA

Apollon Palace (⊠ Syngrou 259, Nea Smyrni, ☎ 01/942–4267 and 01/942–5780) is the most popular place with Athenians who want to hear Greece's singing stars, such as Antonis Remos and Lambis Livieratos; it's also the most expensive, with a 7,500 dr. per-person minimum. Decadence reigns at **Posidonio** (⊠ Posidonios 18, Elliniko, ☎ 01/894–1033) as diners dance the seductive *tsifteteli*.

LIVE ROCK, JAZZ, BLUES

The laid-back **Blues Hall** (⊠ Ardittou 44, Mets, ☎ 01/924–7448 and 01/921–8282) hosts small groups. Small groups also play the sophisticated **Half Note** (⊠ Trivonianou 17, Mets, ☎ 01/921–3310 and 01/ 923–2460). The lively **Hi-Hat Cafe** (⊠ Dragoumi 28 and Krousovou 1, Hilton, ☎ 01/721–8171) hosts international artists. Most big names in popular music perform at the informal **Rodon Live** (⊠ Marni 24, Platia Vathis, ☎ 01/524–7427).

REMBETIKA CLUBS

Rembetika, the blues sung by refugees from Asia Minor who came to Greece in the 1920s, still enthralls Greeks. At **Stathmos** (⊠ Mavromateon 22, Pedion Areos, ☎ 01/883–2392), the band usually starts off slowly, but by 1 AM is wailing to a packed dance floor. At **Stoa Athanaton** (⊠ Sofokleous 19, Central Market, ☎ 01/321–4362 and 01/321–0342), in a renovated warehouse, the authentic music of popular *rembetis* Bobis Goles draws audience participation.

Shopping

Antiques

Pandrossou Street in Monastiraki is especially rich in shops selling small antiques and icons. Keep in mind fakes are common and that you must have government permission to export objects from the Classic, Hellenistic, Roman, or Byzantine periods. For serious antiques collecting, head to **Martinos** (✉ Pandrossou 50, ☎ 01/321–2414). **Motakis** (✉ Pl. Abyssinia 3 in basement, ☎ 01/321–9005) sells antiques and other beautiful old objects. At **Nasiotis** (✉ Ifestou 24, ☎ 01/321–2369) you may uncover interesting finds in a basement stacked with engravings, old magazines, and books, including first editions.

Flea Markets

The **Sunday-morning flea market** (✉ Pandrossou and Ifestou Sts.) sells everything from secondhand guitars to Russian caviar. However little it costs, you should haggle. On weekdays in **Ifestou,** where coppersmiths have their shops, you can pick up copper wine jugs, candlesticks, and cookware for next to nothing.

Gift Ideas

Better tourist shops sell copies of traditional Greek jewelry; silver filigree; Skyrian pottery; onyx ashtrays and dishes; woven bags; attractive rugs, including flokatis; worry beads in amber or silver; and blue-and-white amulets to ward off the *mati* (evil eye). Reasonably priced natural sponges from Kalymnos also make good gifts. **George Goutis** (✉ Pandrossou 40, Monastiraki, ☎ 01/321–3212) has an eclectic assortment of costumes, embroidery, and old, handcrafted silver items. **Ilias Kokkonis** (✉ Stoa Arsakeiou 8, Omonia; enter from Panepistimiou or Stadiou; ☎ 01/322–1189 and 01/322–6355) stocks any flag you've hankered after—large or small, from any country. **Mati** (✉ Voukourestiou 20, Syntagma, ☎ 01/362–6238) has finely designed amulets to battle the evil eye, as well as a collection of monastery lamps and candlesticks. **Karamichos Mazaraki** (✉ Voulis 31–33, Syntagma, ☎ 01/323–9428) offers a large selection of flokatis and will ship.

Greeks spend hours heatedly playing *tavli,* or backgammon. To take home a set of your own, look for the hole-in-the-wall, no-name shop affectionately called **Baba** (✉ Ifestou 30, Monastiraki, ☎ 01/321–9994), which sells boards and pieces in all sizes and designs. For an inexpensive gift pick up some freshly ground Greek coffee at **Miseyiannis** (✉ Levendis 7, Kolonaki, ☎ 01/721–0136).

Handicrafts

The **Kentro Ellinikis Paradosis** (Center of Hellenic Tradition; ✉ Mitropoleos 59 or Pandrossou 36, Monastiraki, ☎ 01/321–3023) is an outlet for quality handicrafts. The **Organismos Ethnikos Pronoias** (National Welfare Organization; ✉ Vas. Sofias 135, Ambelokipi, ☎ 01/646–0603; ✉ Ipatias 6 and Apollonos, Plaka, ☎ 01/321–8272) displays work by Greek craftspeople—stunning handwoven carpets, flatweave kilims, hand-embroidered tablecloths, and flokatis.

At **Amorgos** (✉ Kodrou 3, Plaka, ☎ 01/324–3836) the owners make wooden furniture using motifs from regional Greek designs. They also sell needlework, hanging ceiling lamps, shadow puppets, and other decorative accessories. The Greek cooperative **EOMMEX** (✉ Mitropoleos 9, Syntagma, ☎ 01/323–0408) operates a showroom with folk and designer rugs made by more than 30 weavers around the country.

Jewelry

Prices for gold and silver are much lower in Greece than in many Western countries, and jewelry is of high quality. Many shops in Plaka carry original-design pieces available at a good price if you bargain hard enough. For more expensive items, the Voukourestiou pedestrian mall off Syntagma Square has a number of the city's leading jewelry shops: The baubles at **J. Vourakis & Fils** (✉ Voukourestiou 8, ☎ 01/323–1258) are both unique modern designs and older, collector's items. **Xanthopoulos** (✉ Voukourestiou 4, ☎ 01/322–6856) carries diamond necklaces, magnificently large gems, and the finest pearls; you can also order custom-made jewelry.

Some of the most original work in gold can be had at **Fanourakis** (⊠ Patriarchou Ioakeim 23, Kolonaki, ☎ 01/721–1762; ⊠ Evangelistrias 2, Center, ☎ 01/324–6642), where contemporary Athenian artists use gold almost like a fabric—creasing, scoring, and fluting it. **LALAoUNIS** (⊠ Panepistimiou 6, Syntagma, ☎ 01/362–4354 and 01/361–1371) showcases pieces by Ilias Lalaounis, who takes his ideas from nature, biology, and ancient Greek pieces.

The **Benaki Museum gift shop** (⊠ Koumbari 1and Vas. Sofias, Kolonaki, ☎ 01/362–7367) has finely rendered copies of classical jewelry. The **Goulandris Cycladic Museum** (⊠ Neofitou Douka 4, Kolonaki, ☎ 01/724–9706) also carries modern versions of classic jewelry designs.

Music

CDs of Greek music are much cheaper before they've been exported. One of the biggest selections, along with knowledgeable English-speaking staff, is at the **Virgin Megastore** (⊠ Stadiou 7–9, Syntagma, ☎ 01/331–4788 through 01/331–4796), where you can listen before you purchase.

Side Trips

Mikrolimano

The pretty, crescent-shape harbor of Mikrolimano is famous for its many seafood restaurants. Although it has become increasingly touristy, its delightful atmosphere remains intact, and the harbor is crowded with elegant yachts. Terraces of lovely houses are tucked up against the hillsides. Take the Metro from Monastiraki Square to the Neo Faliron train station; it's only five minutes' walk from there.

Moni Kaisarini

Outside central Athens, on the slopes of Mt. Ymittos (ancient Mt. Hymettus), stands **Moni Kaisariani** (Kaisariani Monastery), one of the city's
★ most evocative Byzantine remains. The well-restored 11th-century monastery, built on the site of a sanctuary of Aphrodite, has some beautiful frescoes dating from the 17th century. Nearby is a basilica and a picnic site with a superb panorama of the Acropolis and Piraeus. Take a taxi or Bus 224 (in front of the Byzantine museum) to the end of the line, then walk 35 minutes along the paved road that climbs Mt. Ymittos. ⊠ *Ethnikis Antistaseos,* ☎ *01/723–6619.* ☉ *Monastery: Tues.– Sun. 8–2:30; grounds: daily sunrise–sunset.*

Athens Essentials

Arriving and Departing

BY BOAT

Most ships from the Greek islands dock at Piraeus (port authority; ☎ 01/422–6000 and 01/51–1311), 10 km (6 mi) from the center. EOT (☞ Visitor Information, *below*) distributes boat schedules updated every Wednesday, as well as a booklet, *Greek Travel Routes: Domestic Sea Schedules;* you can also call a daily Greek recording (☎ 143) for departure times. From the main harbor you can take the nearby Metro right into Omonia Square. The trip takes 25 minutes and costs 120 dr. A taxi takes longer because of traffic and costs around 1,900 dr. As the driver may wait until he fills the taxi with several passengers headed in the same direction, it's faster to walk to the main street and hail a cab there. If you arrive by hydrofoil in the smaller port of Zea Marina, take Bus 905 or Trolley 20 to the Metro. At Rafina port (☎ 0294/22–300), which serves some of the closer Cyclades and Evia, taxi are hard to find.

KTEL buses (⌧ slightly uphill from port, ☎ 01/821–0872) leave every 30 minutes from 5:40 AM until 9:30 PM and cost 500 dr.

BY BUS

Greek buses serving parts of northern Greece, including Thessaloniki, and the Peloponnese (Nauplion, Epidavros, Mycenae) arrive at Terminal A (⌧ Kifissou 100, ☎ 01/512–4910). Those traveling from Evia, most of Thrace, and central Greece, including Delphi, pull in to Terminal B (⌧ Liossion 260, ☎ 01/831–7153 except weekends, when you must call each region's ticket counter for information; EOT provides a phone list; ☞ Visitor Information, *below*). From Terminal A, take Bus 051 to Omonia Square; from Terminal B, take Bus 24 downtown. To get to the stations, catch Bus 051 at Zinonos and Menandrou off Omonia Square for Terminal A and Bus 024 on Amalias Avenue in front of the National Gardens for Terminal B. International buses drop their passengers off on the street, usually in the Omonia or Syntagma Square areas or at Stathmos Peloponnisos.

BY CAR

You enter Athens by the Ethniki Odos (or National Road, as the main highways going north and south are known) and then follow signs for the center. Leaving Athens, routes to the National Road are marked with signs in English; they usually name Lamia for the north and Corinth or Patras for the southwest.

BY PLANE

Ellinikon Airport (⌧ Vas. Georgiou B' 1, ☎ 01/936–3363 for West Terminal; 01/969–4466 for East Terminal; 01/997–2686 and 01/997–2581 for the New Charter Terminal) lies about 10 km (6 mi) from the city center.

Between the Airport and Downtown. An express **bus** service connects the East and West terminals, Syntagma Square, Omonia Square, and Piraeus. Between the terminals and Athens, the express bus (No. 091) runs around the clock, about every 30 minutes. You can catch the bus on Syntagma Square between Ermou and Mitropoleos streets or off Omonia Square on Stadiou and Aiolou. From the airport terminals to Piraeus (Pl. Karaiskaki), the express bus (No. 019) leaves about every hour, day and night. The fare is 250 dr., 500 dr. after midnight until 5 AM (check with EOT, ☞ Visitor Information, *below,* for schedules). It's easier to take **taxis:** about 2,200 dr. to Piraeus; 1,200 dr. between terminals; 2,400 dr. to the center, more if there is traffic. The price goes up by about two-thirds between midnight and 5 AM.

BY TRAIN

Athens has two railway stations, side by side, not far from Omonia Square off Diliyianni street. International trains and those coming from north of Athens use **Stathmos Larissis** (☎ 01/823–7741). Take Trolley 1 from the terminal to Omonia Square. Trains from the Peloponnese use the marvelously ornate **Stathmos Peloponnisos** (☎ 01/513–1601). To Omonia and Syntagma squares take Bus 057. As the phones are almost always busy, it's easier to get departure times from the main information phone service (☞ By Train *in* Transportation *in* Greece A to Z, *above*) or buy tickets at a **railway office** downtown (⌧ Sina 6, ☎ 01/362–4402 through 01/362–4406; ⌧ Filellinon 17, ☎ 01/323–6747 and 01/323–6273; or ⌧ Karolou 1, ☎ 01/522–4302 for the Peloponnese, 01/522–2491 for northern Greece).

Getting Around

Many of the sights and most of the hotels, cafés, and restaurants are within a fairly small central area. It's easy to walk everywhere, though sidewalks are often obstructed by parked cars.

BY BUS

EOT (☞ Visitor Information, *below*) can provide bus information, as can the Organization for Public Transportation (✉ Metsovou 15, ☎ 01/883–6076), open weekdays 7:30–3, and Metsovou 185, open weekdays 7:30–3 and 7 PM–9 PM). The fare on buses and trolleys is 120 dr.; monthly passes are sold at the beginning of each month for 5,000 dr. (bus and trolley). Purchase tickets at curbside kiosks or from booths at terminals. Validate your ticket in the orange machines when you board to avoid a fine. Buses run from the center to all suburbs and nearby beaches from 5 AM until about midnight. For suburbs north of Kifissia, change at Kifissia's main square, Platia Platanou. Most buses to the east Attica coast, including those for Sounion (☎ 01/823–0179; 1,150 dr. for inland route and 1,200 dr. on coastal road), and Marathon (☎ 01/821–0872; 750 dr.), leave from the KTEL terminal (✉ Platia Aigyptiou, corner Mavromateon and Alexandras near Pedion Areos park).

BY METRO

An electric (partially underground) railway runs from Piraeus to Omonia Square and then on to Kifissia, with downtown stops at Thission, Monastiraki, Omonia, and Platia Victorias (near the National Archaeological Museum). The fare is 120 dr. for two zones, or 180 dr. for three zones. You can buy a monthly pass covering the Metro, buses, and trolleys for 8,000 dr. at the beginning of each month. Validate your ticket by stamping it in the orange machines at the entrance to the platforms, or you will be fined.

BY TAXI

Although you can find an empty taxi, it's often faster to call out your destination to one carrying passengers; if the taxi is going in that direction, the driver will pick you up. Most drivers speak basic English. The meter starts at 200 dr., and even if you join other passengers, you must add this amount to your final charge. The minimum fare is 500 dr. The basic charge is 66 dr. per km (½ mi); this increases to 130 dr. between midnight and 5 AM. There are surcharges for holidays (120 dr.), trips to and from the airport (300 dr.), and rides to, but not from, the port, train stations, and bus terminals (150 dr.). There is also a 50 dr. charge for each suitcase over 10 kilograms (22 pounds), but drivers expect 100 dr. for each bag they place in the trunk anyway. Waiting time is 2,200 dr. per hour. Make sure drivers turn on the meter and use the high tariff ("Tarifa 2") only after midnight; if you encounter trouble, threaten to go to the police. Radio taxis charge an additional 300 dr. for the pickup or 600 dr. for a later appointment. Some reliable services are Athina 1 (☎ 01/921–7942 and 01/922–5755), Ellas (☎ 01/645–7000 and 01/801–4000), Kosmos (☎ 1300), and Parthenon (☎ 01/581–4711, 01/581–1809, and 01/582–1292).

Contacts and Resources

EMBASSIES

U.S. (✉ Vasilissis Sofias 91, ☎ 01/721–2951). **Canadian** (✉ Gennadiou 4, ☎ 01/727–3400). **U.K.** (✉ Ploutarchou 1, ☎ 01/723–6211 through 01/723–6219 and 01/727–2600). **Australian** (✉ Soutsou 37, ☎ 01/645–0404. **Irish** (✉ Vas. Konstantinou 7, ☎ 01/723–2771). **Commonwealth Countries representative** (✉ Kifissias 268, ☎ 01/687–4700).

EMERGENCIES

Police: Tourist police (✉ Dimitrakopoulou 77, Koukaki, ☎ 171); for auto accidents, city police (☎ 100). **Fire** (☎ 199). **Ambulance** (☎ 166; taxi often faster). Not all hospitals are open nightly (☎ 106 for a Greek listing); ask your hotel to check for you. The *Athens News* often lists available emergency hospitals, as do most Greek newspapers. **Coast Guard** (☎ 108). **Doctor:** Most hotels will call one for you; or contact your embassy. A Greek recording (☎ 105) lists doctors available 2 PM–7 AM, Sunday, and holidays. **Dentist:** Ask your hotel or embassy. **Pharmacy:** Many pharmacies in the center have someone who speaks English. Try Mantika (⊠ Stadiou 41 between Omonia and Syntagma, ☎ 01/331–2060 and 01/331–2061) or Thomas (⊠ Papadiamantopoulou 6, near Hilton and Holiday Inn, ☎ 01/721–6101). For late-night pharmacies dial ☎ 107 (Greek) or check the *Athens News*.

ENGLISH-LANGUAGE BOOKSTORES
Booknest (⊠ Folia tou Bibliou, Panepistimiou 25–29, ☎ 01/322–9560). **Compendium** (⊠ Nikis 28, upstairs, ☎ 01/322–1248). **Eleftheroudakis** (⊠ Nikis 4, near Syntagma, ☎ 01/322–9388; ⊠ Panepistimiou 17, ☎ 01/331–4180). **Pantelides** (⊠ Amerikis 9–11, ☎ 01/362–3673).

GUIDED TOURS
Excursions. A one-day tour to Delphi costs 21,000 dr., with lunch included, 18,000 without lunch; a two-day tour to Mycenae, Nauplion, and Epidauros costs 31,500 dr., including half board in first-class hotels; and a full-day cruise from Piraeus, visiting the islands of Aegina, Poros, and Hydra, costs 19,000 dr., including buffet lunch on the ship (☞ Guided Tours *in* Mainland Greece Essentials, *below*).

Orientation. All tour operators offer a four-hour morning bus tour of Athens, including a guided tour of the Acropolis and its museum (10,000 dr.). Make reservations at your hotel or at a travel agency; many are situated around Filellinon and Nikis streets off Syntagma Square.

Personal Guides. All the major tourist agencies can provide English-speaking guides for personally organized tours, or call the **Union of Guides** (⊠ Apollonas 9A, ☎ 01/322–9705, ℻ 01/323–9200). Hire only those licensed by the EOT; a four-hour tour including the Acropolis and its museum costs about 26,000 dr.

Special-Interest. For folk dancing take a four-hour evening tour (April–October; 9,700 dr.) that begins with a sound-and-light show of the Acropolis and goes on to a performance of Greek folk dances in the open-air theater nearby. Another tour offers a dinner show at a taverna in the Plaka area for around 13,600 dr. For efficient service, go first to **CHAT Tours** (☞ Travel Agencies, *below*). For organized adventure travel, contact **Trekking Hellas** and **F-Zein** (☞ Travel Agencies, *below*).

Travel Agencies
American Express (⊠ Ermou 2, ☎ 01/324–4975, ℻ 01/322–7893). **CHAT Tours** (⊠ Stadiou 4, ☎ 01/322–2886, ℻ 01/323–5270). **Condor Travel** (⊠ Stadiou 43, ☎ 01/321–2453 and 01/321–6986, ℻ 01/321–4296). **F-Zein** (⊠ Syngrou 132, 5th floor, ☎ 01/921–6285, ℻ 01/922–9995). **Key Tours** (⊠ Kallirois 4, ☎ 01/923–3166, ℻ 01/923–2008). **Travel Plan** (⊠ Christou Lada 9, ☎ 01/323–8801 through 01/323–8804 and 01/323–0224, ℻ 01/322–2152). **Trekking Hellas** (⊠ Fillelinon 7, 3rd floor, ☎ 01/331–0323 through 01/331–0326, ℻ 01/323–4548; offices also in Thessaloniki and Kalambaka).

Visitor Information
EOT (⊠ Amerikis 2, near Syntagma, ☎ 01/331–0561 and 01/331–0562; ⊠ East Terminal—Arrivals—of Ellinikon Airport, ☎ 01/961–2722 and 01/961–4500; ⊠ Piraeus, EOT Building, 1st floor, Zea Marina, ☎ 01/452–2591).

THE NORTHERN PELOPONNESE

Suspended from the mainland of Greece like a large leaf, the ancient land of Pelops offers beautiful scenery—rocky coasts, sandy beaches, mountains—and a fascinating variety of ruins: temples, theaters, mosques, churches, palaces, and medieval castles built by crusaders. Legend and history meet a few miles south of the isthmus of Corinth, in Mycenae, where Agamemnon, Elektra, and Orestes played out their grim family tragedy. This city dominated the entire area from the 18th through the 12th centuries BC and may even have conquered Minoan Crete. After German archaeologist Heinrich Schliemann's excavations in 1874 uncovered gold-filled graves and a royal palace, Mycenae became a world-famous archaeological site.

Exploring the Northern Peloponnese

From Athens, head west across the Corinth Canal (84 km/52 mi) to ancient Corinth (detour off the National Road; otherwise you'll whiz by the Canal on the new bridge before you know it). Head south to Mycenae (4 km/2½ mi off the road at Fichtion), and then turn off at Argos via Tiryns for Nauplion (63 km/39 mi from Corinth). The ancient theater of Epidauros is another 26 km (16 mi) west. From Epidauros you can return to Athens, joining the National Road at Corinth, or backtrack to Argos, where the road continues through the rugged mountains of Arcadia to ancient Olympia (191 km/118 mi from Argos). North of Olympia (122 km/76 mi) lies Patras, from where you can return to Athens on the National Road, an exceptionally beautiful drive along the coast. If you want to go on to Delphi (☞ Mainland Greece, *below*), cross the gulf at Rion-Antirion en route.

Corinth

★ When you cross the **Gefira Isthmou** or **Isthmos** (Corinth Canal), you will have entered the Peloponnese. The ancients once winched their ships across a paved slipway nearby, then talked for centuries about carving a canal through the limestone. The modern throughway was completed in 1893; you can watch the ships go by from the narrow bridge, 60 m (197 ft) above the water.

At the site of **Archaia Korinthos** (Ancient Corinth) lie remains of the Doric **Naos Apollonos** (Temple of Apollo), built during the 6th century BC and one of the few buildings that still stood when Julius Caesar decided to restore Corinth. A **museum** contains finds from the excavations. ⊠ *9 km (6 mi) west of Corinth*, ☎ *0741/31–207 and 0741/31–480 (24 hrs).* ☉ *May–Oct., daily 8–7; Nov.–Apr., daily 8–5.*

Looming over ancient Corinth, the limestone **Acrocorinthos** (Acrocorinth) was one of the best naturally fortified citadels in Europe, where citizens retreated in times of invasions and earthquakes. Built on ancient foundations, the remains indicate the many additions made by Romans, Franks, Venetians, and Turks. Take a taxi from ancient Corinth (about 1,500 dr.) or follow the signs by car. ⊠ *Take road outside the museum in ancient Corinth 4 km/2.5 mi. up to tourist pavilion at Acrocorinth gate.* ☎ *0741/31–266 and 0741/31–443.* ☜ *Free.* ☉ *May–Oct., daily 8–7; Nov.–Apr., daily 8–5.*

★ Mycenae

Ancient Mykines (Mycenae) was the fabulous stronghold of the Achaean kings of the 13th century BC. Destroyed in 468 BC, it was forgotten until 1874 when Heinrich Schliemann, who had discovered the ruins of ancient Troy, uncovered the remains of this fortress city. Mycenae was the seat of the doomed House of Atreus—of King Agamemnon and

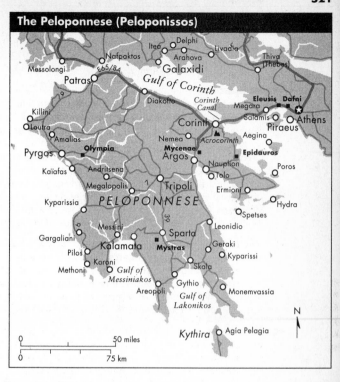

The Peloponnese (Peloponissos)

his wife, Clytemnestra (sister of Helen of Troy), and of their ill-fated children, Orestes and Elektra. When Schliemann uncovered six shaft graves (so named because the kings were buried standing up) of the royal circle, he was certain that one was the tomb of Agamemnon. The gold masks and diadems, daggers, jewelry, and other treasures found in the graves are now in the National Archaeological Museum in Athens. The new local **museum** is dedicated to archaeological studies. You'll also see the monumental **Pili ton Leonton (Lion Gate)**, dating from 1250 BC, the **castle ruins** crowning the bleak hill, and the astounding beehive tomb **Thisavros tou Atrea** (Treasury of Atreus), built into the hillside outside the massive fortification walls, all remnants of the first great civilization in continental Europe. ☎ 0751/76–585. ⊙ *May–Oct., daily 8–sundown; Nov.–Apr., daily 8–5.*

Argos

One of the oldest continuously inhabited towns in Greece and prominent during the 8th century BC, Argos has a grand central square and an **archaeological museum,** which displays Neolithic pottery, Roman objects, and finds from the Mycenaean tombs. ⊠ *Platia Argos on Vas. Olgas pedestrian zone,* ☎ *0751/68–819.* ⊙ *Tues.–Sun. 8–2:30.*

$ ✕ **I Spilia.** This countryside taverna is known for its specialty, *bogana,* baby lamb slow-cooked in a wood-burning oven that is sealed airtight with mud, giving the meat a wonderful smoky flavor. (Call ahead to make sure the chef saves you some.) He makes over 30 local specialties, including wild artichoke salad. ⊠ *Tripoleos 165, 3 km (2 mi) from Argos on old national road to Tripolis,* ☎ *0751/62–300; 0751/29–913 before 5 PM. No credit cards. No lunch Sun.*

Tiryns

Homer described Tirintha (Tiryns) as "the wall-girt city" for its ramparts, built of gigantic limestone blocks (the largest weighs 15 tons), which ancients thought could be handled only by giants. The remains, including the walls, date mostly from the 13th century BC, when Tiryns was one of the most important Mycenaean cities. ⊠ *On hill behind Tiryns jail, 4 km (2½ mi) before Nauplion,* ☎ *0752/22–657.* ⊙ *May–Oct., daily 8–7; Nov.–Apr., daily 8–5.*

★ Nauplion

A favorite weekend getaway for Athenians, Nauplion is a picturesque town on the Gulf of Argos, dominated by brooding Venetian fortifications. Modern Greece's first king lived for a year or two within the walls of the high fortress, **Palamidi,** when Nauplion was the capital of Greece. His courtiers had to climb 999 steps to reach him; you can still climb the long staircase (steps begin near the Cultural Center and the courts) or drive up to the fortress. Guards on this large site generally stop letting visitors in one hour before closing time, and they usher out all visitors 15 minutes before the gates close. ⊠ *Above town,* ☎ *0752/ 28–036.* ⊙ *May–Oct., daily 8–7; Nov.–Apr., daily 8–2:30.*

Wander for at least a few hours through the **Palia Poli** (Old Town)'s narrow streets and shady squares, lined with a mix of Venetian, Turkish, Frankish, and Byzantine buildings. The Venetian naval arsenal on the main town square houses an **archaeological museum** with Mycenaean finds, including a 7th-century BC Gorgon mask from Tiryns. ⊠ *East side of Pl. Constitution,* ☎ *0752/27–502.* ⊙ *Tues.–Sun. 8–2:30.*

$$ ✕ **Savouras.** The best-known seafood taverna in town, Savouras continues to maintain its high standards of freshness and simple but successful presentations of such specialties as grilled cod, as well as more expensive catch—red mullet, pandora, dorado. ⊠ *Bouboulinas 79,* ☎ *0752/27–704. No credit cards. Closed Mon. Nov.–Apr.*

$ ✕ **Karamanlis (O Kanaris).** A favorite with former Greek president Karamanlis, this taverna near the courthouse is crowded at lunch with civil servants who come for its tasty magirefta. The fish soup makes a good appetizer, as do the melt-in-your-mouth *gigantes yiachni* (giant beans with fresh tomato), followed by savory beef *yiouvetsi* (lamb or beef baked with orzo-shaped noodles). ⊠ *Bouboulinas 1,* ☎ *0752/27– 668. No credit cards. Closed Greek Easter.*

$ ✕ **Omorfo Tavernaki.** Snug and inviting, this mezedopolion serves up such appetizers as *tiroboukies* (cheese "bites") and croquettes made from wild greens, as well as some unusual dishes, such as Constantinople souvlaki, marinated in yogurt and garlic. ⊠ *Vas. Olgas and Kotsonopoulou 1,* ☎ *0752/25–944. Reservations essential weekends. No credit cards. No lunch.*

$$$$ ⊞ **Candia House.** This beautifully decorated hotel 17 km (10½ mi) south
★ of Nauplion on Candia Beach weds good taste with comfort. Fresh flowers, antiques, paintings by Greek artists, and handcrafted mirrors are just some of the special touches. Other facilities include a playroom with board games, a sauna, and a gym. The "bio-breakfast" included in the price offers fresh vegetable dishes, salads, and homemade bread. ⊠ *Candia-Irion, 21100,* ☎ *0752/94–060 through 0752/94–063,* FAX *0752/94–480; off-season:* ☎ *01/347–1503; 094/841–864 after 3* PM; FAX *01/347–4732. 10 suites. Restaurant, pool. AE, DC, MC, V. Closed Nov.–Mar. except Christmas wk.*

$$$ ⊞ **Amalia.** The Amalia occupies a fine neoclassical building in large gardens 3 km (2 mi) outside town, on the sea and close to the beach, on the way to ancient Tiryns. The public rooms are spacious and comfortable, and service is attentive. A buffet breakfast is included. ⊠ *National Rd. to Argos outside Nauplion, 21100,* ☎ *0752/24–401; 01/ 323–7301 reservations,* FAX *0752/24–400; 01/323–8792 reservations. 174 rooms, 1 suite. 3 restaurants, pool. AE, DC, MC, V.*

$$ ⊞ **O Nausimedon.** Just a few minutes' walk from the Old Town, this
★ lovely hotel is in a refurbished 19th-century residence. Most of its high-
ceilinged rooms have antiques accompanied by such modern ameni-
ties as air-conditioning and TV. The quiet house sits across from the
city park and is fronted by a large garden with palms. Full breakfast
with homemade sweets is included in the price. ⊠ *Sidiras Merarhias
9, 21100,* ☎ *0752/25–060,* ℻ *0752/26–913. 12 rooms, 2 studios. Air-
conditioning. V.*

$–$$ ⊞ **Byron.** This gracious hotel in the Old Town is in a rose-and-blue
18th-century house. Rooms include minibars, hair dryers, and op-
tional TV and air-conditioning (1,500 dr. and 2,000 dr. daily, respectively). The owners have added another building (yellow with green
shutters), with four rooms that have Jugendstil furniture, TV, and air-
conditioning. Guests eat breakfast on a terrace overlooking the town
and the gulf. ⊠ *Platonos 2, Platia Agios Spiridonos, 21100,* ☎ *0752/
22–351,* ☎ ℻ *0752/26–338. 18 rooms. AE, MC, V.*

Epidauros

Epidauros was the sanctuary of Asklepios, the Greek god of healing.
You can visit the foundations of the temples and ancient hospital, as
★ well as the **museum.** The site you must not miss is the ancient **open-
air theater,** which seats 14,000. In summer, during the Festival of Ancient Drama, plays are staged here (☞ Nightlife and the Arts of the
Northern Peloponnese, *below*), but it merits a visit at any time of year.
The acoustics are so good that you can sit in the top row and hear a
whisper on stage. ☎ *0753/22–009.* ☉ *Theater: May–Oct., daily 8–7;
Nov.–Apr., daily 8–5. Museum: May–Oct., Tues.–Sun. 8–7, Mon.
noon–6; Nov.–Apr., Tues.–Sun. 8–5, Mon. noon–5.*

Olympia

Just east of the modern village of Olympia, a few miles from the sea,
★ lies **Archaia Olympia** (Ancient Olympia), where the Olympic Games were
first held in 776 BC. A huge assembly hall was built here to hold the
10,000 representatives of the Arcadian League. The games continued
to be celebrated every four years until AD 393, when the Roman emperor Theodosius I, a Christian, banned these "pagan rites." Women
were excluded from watching the games under penalty of death; women's
games were held a few weeks earlier. Archaeologists still uncover statues and votive offerings among the pine trees surrounding the **stadium,**
the imposing ruins of the **Naos Dios** (Temple of Zeus), and the **Heraion**
(Temple of Hera) within the sacred precinct. The **museum,** which lies
a few hundred meters north of the sanctuary, includes pedimental sculptures from the Zeus temple and the 4th-century BC head of the Hera
cult statue and a well-preserved Hermes sculpted by Praxiteles, both from
the Heraion. *Stadium/site,* ☎ *0624/22–517; museum, 0624/22–742.* ☉
*Site: May–Oct., weekdays 8–7, weekends 8–2:30; Nov.–Apr., weekdays
8–5. Museum: May–Oct., Mon. 12:30–7, Tues.–Sun. 8–7; Nov.–Apr.,
Mon. 10:30–5, Tues.–Fri. 8–5, weekends 8–2:30.*

$$ ✕ **O Kladeos.** Named for the river it borders, this *koutouki* (a tiny eatery)
is big with locals. Sit near the fireplace in winter, in the shade of the
plane tree in summer. The food is simple but classic Greek: codfish with
garlic dip, fried squid, lamb in oil-oregano sauce, and *patsa,* a tripe
soup said to cure all ills. ⊠ *Ancient Olympia beside river,* ☎ *0624/
23–322. No credit cards. Closed Oct.–Apr. No lunch.*

$$ ✕ **Taverna Ambrosia.** Although there are no grilled meats, this taverna
★ offers excellent magirefta like *papoutsakia* (sliced eggplant topped
with minced meat), *briam* (like ratatouille), baked tomatoes and peppers stuffed with rice, and the specialty, lamb stewed in lemon sauce.

✉ *Off main road between ancient and modern Olympia near train station, Oikismou Kambo,* ☎ *0624/23–414. AE, MC, V.*

$$ ✕ **Thraka.** This family-run taverna has a large variety of home-cooked food including *lahanodolmades* (cabbage leaves stuffed with minced meat), and beef stifado made with vinegar and garlic. The two kinds of baklava are from the family's pastry shop. ✉ *Vasiliou Bakopanou and Praxitelis Kondili,* ☎ *0624/22–575, 0624/22–475 off-season. AE, MC, V. Closed Nov.–Mar. (meals by special arrangement).*

$ ✕ **Bacchus.** If you're at the ancient site and want to break for lunch, follow signs to the nearby village of Miraka, recently renamed Archaia (ancient) Pissa. You can try such hearty dishes as rooster with hand-made noodles called *hilopites* (order one day before), charcoal-broiled chicken, lamb or goat in oregano sauce, and spit-roasted meats on weekends. ✉ *Archaia Pissa, 3 km (2 mi) outside Olympia, turnoff on Tripolis Rd.,* ☎ *0624/22–498. V. No lunch Dec.–Jan.*

$$ 🏨 **Hotel Europa.** Run by the gracious Spiliopoulos family, this Best Western hilltop hotel overlooks ancient Olympia, the mountains of Arcadia, Alfios Valley, and the distant sea. Rooms have flokati rugs, marble bathrooms, hair dryers, and TVs; most face the pool. Buffet breakfast is included for all rates. ✉ *Off road to ancient Olympia, at Oikismou Drouba, 27065,* ☎ *0624/22–650, FAX 0624/23–166. 42 rooms. Restaurant, pool. AE, DC, MC, V.*

$$ 🏨 **Olympic Village.** Popular with groups, the hotel has simple rooms with views of the surrounding vineyards, all new beds, wooden furniture, and comfortable public spaces. American breakfast is included, and the restaurant serves excellent Greek food such as *arnaki fricassee* (lamb with spinach and rice). ✉ *Pyrgos-Olympia road (about 300 yards from site), 27065,* ☎ *0624/22–211, FAX 0624/22–812. 51 rooms. Restaurant, air-conditioning, pool. AE, V. Closed Nov.–Feb.*

$ 🏨 **Pelops.** The Australian owner has taken a standard '60s Greek hotel, across from the main church, and decorated each room differently, with knickknacks, chintz, and lace curtains, producing an old-fashioned feel. Rooms have orthopedic mattresses and telephones; most have balconies. The vine-shaded bar is open in summer. ✉ *Varela 2, 27065,* ☎ *0624/22–543 and 0624/22–792, FAX 0624/22–213. 25 rooms. Restaurant. MC, V. Closed Nov.–Feb.*

Patras

Patras, the third-largest city in Greece and its main western port, is the business hub of the Peloponnese. The city's prettiest features are its arcaded streets and its squares surrounded by neoclassical buildings. The Byzantine **Kastro** (fortress), built on the site of the ancient acropolis, affords a fine view along the coast. **Agiou Andrea** (Cathedral of St. Andrew; ✉ west side of harbor at end of Agiou Andreou, ☎ 061/330–644), open daily 7:30 AM–8 PM, reputedly the largest in Greece and built on the site of the crucifixion of St. Andrew, is also worth exploring. Its treasure is the saint's silver-mounted skull, returned to Patras in 1964 after 500 years in St. Peter's Cathedral, Rome.

Eight kilometers (5 miles) outside Patras is the **Achaia Clauss Winery,** founded in the mid-1800s by Baron von Klauss. You can take a tour and sample the area's mavrodafni wine, a dessert wine named for the Baron's love, who died prematurely. Take Bus 7 from the Platia Georgiou stop on Kanakari Street, get off at the Kato Filagio stop, and walk 766 yards, or take a taxi (1,000 dr.–1,300 dr.). ✉ *Achaia,* ☎ *061/325–051.* 🎟 *Free.* ☉ *May–Oct., daily 10–7; Nov.–Apr., daily 9–5.*

$$ ✕ **Ditis.** When the diver-owner closes up shop in summer to indulge
★ his love of the sea, locals mourn. The humble decor of his fish taverna belies the masterful seafood dishes he prepares: delectable *kakavia* (Greek

fish stew); crayfish with pepperoncini; and anchovies cooked with carrot, dill, and fennel. The fresh local fish includes sargus, pandora, and gildhead, depending on the season. ⊠ *Norman and Gambetta 44,* ☎ *061/432–554. No credit cards. Closed Sun. and July–Aug.*

$$ ✕ **Majestic.** Diners choose from an eclectic mix of Greek, French, and Italian dishes at this restaurant on one of Patras's main squares. Fresh seafood, such as dorado and swordfish, top the list, while other reliables include pork chops simmered in wine, rooster baked with noodles, and octopus marinated in vinaigrette. ⊠ *Agiou Nikolaou 2, Platia Trion Simmachon,* ☎ *061/222–792. AE, DC, MC, V.*

$$ ✕ **Petrino.** Wood, stone, and a live palm tree dominate this restaurant,
★ which serves creative Mediterranean cuisine. Try the lamb with green peppers; crayfish with sun-dried tomatoes; or chicken Narcissus—stuffed with shrimp, wrapped in a spinach leaf, and sprinkled with poppy seeds. ⊠ *Agiou Nikolaou 17,* ☎ *061/620–255. DC, V. Closed July–Aug.*

$ ✕ **Lavyrinthos (Taverna tou Antipa).** This classic taverna with wine barrels, old lamp fixtures, and a cozy loft serves such traditional Greek dishes as rabbit in lemon and pungent homemade potato salad. After your meal be sure to try a shot of *detoura,* a local liqueur similar to cognac and flavored with cinnamon and clove. ⊠ *Poukevil 44 near Platia Vas. Olgas,* ☎ *061/226–436. No credit cards.*

$$$ ⊞ **Astir.** This large, stylish hotel on the waterfront near the center of town has such amenities as a piano bar, a roof garden with sparkling sea views, and a sauna. A buffet breakfast is included. ⊠ *Ag. Andreou 16, 26223,* ☎ *061/277–502 and 061/276–311,* FAX *061/271–644. 120 rooms. 2 restaurants, pool. AE, DC, MC, V.*

$$$ ⊞ **Porto Rio Hotel and Casino.** Play a set of tennis or a round of beach
★ volleyball, go for an afternoon dip, then head for the casino at this 35-acre beachside hotel complex across from a small medieval fort at Rion, about 8 km (5 mi) from Patras. Most rooms have outstanding views. American breakfast is included. ⊠ *Rio-Patroon National Rd., 26500,* ☎ *061/992–212,* FAX *061/992–115. 235 rooms, 13 suites, 48 bungalows. Restaurant, 2 pools. AE, DC, MC, V.*

$$ ⊞ **Rannia.** The Rannia stands on Queen Olga Square, the loveliest plaza in Patras. It's just two blocks from the waterfront and within walking distance of the bus and train stations. The clean, quiet rooms all have balconies. ⊠ *Riga Fereou 53, Platia Vas. Olgas, 26500,* ☎ *061/220–114,* ☎ FAX *061/220–537. 30 rooms. Air-conditioning. V.*

$ ⊞ **Hotel Saint George.** The city's smallest and most recently built hotel is clean and central—just a few blocks from the bus station. Nearly all the balconied rooms overlook the harbor or Trion Simmachon square. A few rooms have air-conditioning for an extra charge (4,000 dr.–5,000 dr.). ⊠ *Agiou Andreou 73, 26221,* ☎ *061/225–092,* FAX *061/273–905. 23 rooms. No credit cards.*

Nightlife and the Arts of the Northern Peloponnese

The **Festival of Ancient Drama** in the theater at Epidauros takes place from mid-July to mid-September; the smaller Micro Theatro (Little Theater) of ancient Epidauros nearby simultaneously hosts concerts and dance performances. Tickets can be bought at both theaters before performances (☎ 0753/22–006 for box office) or in advance from the festival box office in Athens (⊠ Stadiou 4, ☎ 01/322–1459). A venue modeled on an ancient theater but with state-of-the-art lighting and sound near the Olympia sanctuary hosts the summer **Festival Olympias,** an eclectic mix of performances ranging from Paco Pena to the White Oak Dance Project. Ticket booths are located throughout the region, or call the Floca community offices (☎ 0624/22–751). Patras also stages a **summer arts festival** July through August. Check with the Patras International Festival office (⊠ Koryllon 2, Old Municipal Hospital, Old Town, ☎ 061/279–008) for details. A few weeks before Greek Orthodox Lent, Patras holds **Carnival** celebrations, including Sunday's Grand Parade, with entrants competing for the best costume. Buy tickets for Grand Parade seats at the kiosk in Vas. Georgiou Square or at the Carnival office in the Municipal Cultural Center (⊠ Koryllon 2, Old Municipal Hospital, Old Town, ☎ 061/226–063).

Northern Peloponnese Essentials

Getting Around

BY BOAT

In summer hydrofoils leave Zea Marina in Athens for Nauplion; it's a good idea to reserve a seat (☎ 01/429–0001 through 01/429–0010.)

BY BUS

The regional bus associations (KTEL) run frequent service from Athens to Nauplion (where you change for Mycenae), Epidauros, Corinth, Patras, and Olympia.

BY CAR

The roads are fairly good, and driving can be the most enjoyable (if not economical) way to see the area, once you get off the National Road.

BY TRAIN

You can take a train from Athens to Corinth, where the route splits, heading either south to Argos, Mycenae, and Nauplion, or west along the coast to Patras, and then south to Pyrgos and the branch line to Olympia. There is a substantial discount on round-trip tickets.

Guided Tours

Available tours include one-day (with lunch, 21,000 dr.; without lunch 18,000 dr.) or two-day (31,500 dr.) trips to Mycenae, Nauplion, and Epidauros; four-day trips to those sites, as well as Olympia and Delphi (99,800 dr.); and a five-day excursion to all major sites in the Peloponnese, as well as Delphi and Meteora (139,000 dr.). **CHAT Tours** (⊠ 4 Stadiou, Athens, ☎ 01/322–2886, ℻ 01/323–5270). **Key Tours** (⊠ Kallirois 4, Athens, ☎ 01/923–3166, ℻ 01/923–2008).

Visitor Information

Nauplion: tourist information (⊠ 25th Martiou across from OTE, ☎ 0752/24–444); tourist police (⊠ P. Koundourioti 14 in police station, ☎ 0752/28–131). **Olympia:** municipal tourist information office (⊠ Kondili 75, ☎ 0624/23–100); tourist police (⊠ Spiliopoulou 5, ☎ 0624/22–550 and 0624/22–100). **Patras:** EOT (⊠ Filopimenos 26, ☎ 061/620–353); tourist police (⊠ Norman and Iroon Politechniou—harbor welcome station— ☎ 061/451–833 and 061/451–893); Olympic Airlines (⊠ Aratou 17–19, Platia Vas. Olgas, ☎ 061/222–901); Automobile and Touring Club of Greece (⊠ Patroon Athinon 18, ☎ 061/425–411 and 061/426–416).

MAINLAND GREECE

The dramatic rocky heights of mainland Greece provide an appropriate setting for humanity's attempt to approach divinity. The ancient Greeks placed their gods on snowcapped Mt. Olympus and chose the precipitous slopes of Parnassus, "the navel of the universe," as the site for Delphi, their most important religious center. Many centuries later, pious Christians built a great monastery (Hosios Loukas) in a remote mountain valley. Others settled on the rocky peninsula of Athos, the Holy Mountain. Later, devout men established themselves precari-

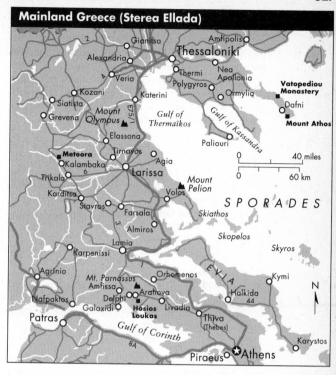

Mainland Greece (Sterea Ellada)

ously on top of strange, towerlike rocks and, to be closer to God, built such monasteries as those at Meteora, which remain among the most spectacular sights in Greece.

Exploring Mainland Greece

En route to Delphi from Athens via the National Road, take the turnoff for the ancient city of Thiva (Thebes), 90 km/56 mi northwest of Athens. After detouring to the monastery of Hosios Loukas (turn off at Distomo village, 20 km/12 mi from Livadia), continue to Delphi. The road climbs a spur of Mt. Parnassus, past Arahova, known for its lively après-ski scene and handmade rugs of brightly colored wools; it also offers a better range of dining and lodging options than Delphi, if you're staying in the area. From Arahova it's a short, spectacular drive through the Pleistos gorge to the ancient site (179 km/111 mi northwest of Athens). After Delphi the road descends in sharp bends to lackluster Lamia (another 82 km/51 mi), then heads northwest to Kalambaka and Meteora (139 km/86 mi from Lamia).

Thiva

Thiva (Thebes), of which little remains, was the birthplace of legendary Oedipus, who unwittingly fulfilled the prophecy of the Delphic Oracle by slaying his father and marrying his mother.

Hosios Loukas

★ Nestled in a serene upland valley is **Moni Osiou Louka** (Monastery of Hosios Loukas), a fine example of Byzantine architecture and decoration. Built during the 11th century to replace the earlier shrine of a local saint, it has some of the world's finest Byzantine mosaics. ☎ 0267/ 22–797. ☉ *May–mid-Sept., daily 8–2 and 4–7; mid-Sept.–mid-Nov., and Mar.–Apr., daily 8–6; mid-Nov.–Feb., daily 8–5.*

★ **Delphi**

At the edge of Delphi loom the Phaedriades, twin cliffs split by the Castalian spring. It was here that pilgrims to the Delphic Oracle came for purification. To the ancient Greeks Delphi was the center of the universe, because two eagles released by the gods at opposite ends of the earth met here. For hundreds of years the worship of Apollo and the pronouncements of the oracle made Delphi the most important religious center of ancient Greece. When first excavated in 1892, most of the ruins were found to date from the 5th through the 3rd centuries BC. As you walk up the **Iera Odos** (Sacred Way) to the **Naos Apollonos** (Temple of Apollo), the **theater,** and the **stadium,** you'll see Mt. Parnassus above; silver-green olive trees below; and, in the distance, the blue Gulf of Itea. East of the main site, about 500 ft down the road, is the area with the temple of **Athena Pronaia,** from which many of the museum's best sculptures came; the **gymnasium;** and the **Tholos,** the rotunda. If you come here in the early morning or evening, avoiding the busloads of tourists, you will feel the power and beauty of the place. ☎ 0265/82–312 and 0265/82–313. ☉ May–Oct., weekdays 7:30–8; Nov.–Apr., weekdays 8–2:30.

Don't miss the bronze charioteer (early 5th century BC) in the **Delphi Museum.** Other works of art here include a statue of Antinoüs, Emperor Hadrian's lover; fragments of a 6th-century BC silver-plated bull, the largest example of an ancient statue in precious metal, and the stone omphalos, representing the navel of the earth. ☎ 0265/82–312 and 0265/82–313. ☉ May–Oct., weekdays 7:30–8; Nov.–Apr., 8–2:30.

$ ✗ **Karaouli.** This warm, low-key taverna serves delicious regional cuisine along with barrel wine from Distomo: the lightest cabbage rolls, spicy local sausage and spit-roasted meats (kontosouvli), baked red peppers stuffed with four cheeses, roasted formaella (a local cheese), and tiganopsomo (cheese bread). For dessert: a large portion of creamy sheep yogurt topped with quince preserves. ⊠ Elef. Venizelou, Arahova, ☎ 0267/31–001. No credit cards. Closed mid-June to mid-Sept.

$ ✗ **Sunflower.** You'll find the classic Greek dishes well prepared here and reasonably priced—dolmades, tzatziki, a rich bean soup called fassolada—but the restaurant is known for its savory bourekakia, pastries stuffed with cheese and minced meat. ⊠ Vas. Pavlou and Friderikis 33, Delphi, ☎ 0265/82–442. AE, V. Closed weekdays Nov.–Feb.

$ ✗ **Taverna P. Dasargiris (Barba Yiannis).** In a town that once counted its wealth by the size of its flocks, the oldest taverna is fittingly known for its meat dishes—lamb with oregano and beef in red sauce, both served with homemade noodles. Sample the pastries filled with mountain greens; grilled beef patties stuffed with formaella, Gouda, or kefalograviera cheese; and the dark red local wine, brusco. ⊠ Arahova–Delfon 56, ☎ 0267/31–291. No credit cards. No lunch May–Oct.

$$ ✗⊞ **Hotel Anemolia Best Western.** At this homey hotel on a bluff at
★ the edge of Arahova, most of the large guest rooms have a view of the Amphissa plain from their balconies; some days you can see as far as the Peloponnese. All of the comfortable rooms have TV and some have bathtubs instead of showers; the eight newest rooms have fireplaces but no balconies. The lobby has a large fireplace and country antiques. The indoor pool is usable year-round; other facilities include a bar, sauna, hydromassage, and exercise room. Buffet breakfast is included in the price. ⊠ Arahova–Delfon, Arahova 32004, ☎ 0267/31640, FAX 0267/31–642. 63 rooms. Restaurant, pool. AE, DC, MC, V.

$$ ⊞ **Apollo.** Owned and operated by a husband-and-wife team, this hotel is lovely. The saloni (living room) here has traditional wall hangings and old prints among its carefully selected furnishings. The cheerful rooms have light-wood furniture set off by blue quilts and striped

curtains, with pretty bathroom tiles, hair dryers, TVs, and minibars. Many have wood balconies with black-iron railings, and a full breakfast is included. ⊠ *Vas. Pavlou and Friderikis 59B, Delphi 33054,* ☎ *0265/82–580 and 0265/82–244,* ℻ *0265/82–455. 21 rooms. Air-conditioning. MC, V. Closed weekdays Jan.–mid-Mar.*

$$ 🏨 **Villa Filoxenia-Apollo.** Rustic, charming, and lovingly decorated, this young hotel has such amenities as electronic keys and air-conditioning, a game area, and a lounge with fireplace. Rooms include TVs, minibars, and hair dryers; most have balconies and a view. Full breakfast is included. ⊠ *Vas. Pavlou and Friderikis 15, Delphi 33054,* ☎ *0265/ 83–114,* ℻ *0265/82–455. 14 rooms. Air-conditioning. MC, V. Closed weekdays Jan.–mid-Mar.*

$ 🏨 **Acropole.** This friendly, family-run hotel has a garden and a spectacular view—dramatic mountainside and a sea of olive groves. The rooms are furnished with carved Skyrian pieces, traditional linens, and paintings of the islands. All rooms have satellite TV, direct-dial phones, and hair dryers. ⊠ *Filellinon 13, 33054,* ☎ *0265/82–675,* ℻ *0265/ 83–171. 42 rooms. Air-conditioning. AE, DC, MC, V.*

Meteora

Kalambaka serves as the base for visits to the monasteries of Meteora, which sit atop gigantic pinnacles that tower almost 1,000 ft above the plain. Monks and supplies once reached the top on ladders or in baskets; now steps are cut into the rocks, and some of the monasteries can easily be reached by car. Of the original 24 monasteries, only six can now be visited. Appropriate dress for women requires skirts to the knee (not shorts), and men should wear long pants. The fortresslike **Varlaam** monastery (☎ 0432/22–277; closed Fri.—Thurs.–Fri. in winter), is easy to reach and has beautiful Byzantine frescoes. For an idea of what living in these monasteries was like 300 years ago, climb the steep rock steps to the **Megalo Meteoron** (☎ 0432/22–278; closed Tues.–Wed. in winter). Allow time for the trek up if it's nearing midday or evening closing time. ☉ *May–Oct., daily 9–1 and 3–6; Nov.– Apr., daily 9–1 and 3–5.*

In Kalambaka stop at the **Koimisis tis Theotokou** (Dormition of the Virgin), built during the first half of the 12th century by Emperor Manuel Comnenos, though some historians believe it was founded during the 7th century on the site of a temple of Apollo (classical drums and other fragments are incorporated into the walls). The church also has vivid 16th-century frescoes. ⊠ *North end of town; follow signs from Platia Riga Fereou,* ☎ *0432/24–962.* ☉ *May–Oct., daily 7 AM–1 PM and 3 PM–7 PM; Nov.–Apr., daily 7 AM–10 AM and 3:30–6:30 PM.*

$$ ✕ **Restaurant Meteora.** A local favorite since 1925, this family restau-
★ rant on the upper square relies on the cooking of matriarch Ketty Gertzou, who prepares such dishes as *soutzoukakia* (spicy minced meat patties), lamb fricassee, stifado, *ladera* (vegetables cooked in olive oil), and chicken or pork in wine with green peppers and garlic. ⊠ *Ekonomou 4, on Platia Dimarchiou,* ☎ *0432/22–316. No credit cards. Closed Nov.– Mar. No dinner.*

$–$$ ✕ **Ziogas.** Master-griller Grigoris chooses only the freshest local meats and barbecues them to perfection over burning wood—try the pork chops, the lamb ribs, or the succulent *kokkoretsi* (spit-roasted meat roll made of lamb entrails). ⊠ *On Patriarchou Dimitriou (road from Kalambaka to Meteora), Kastraki,* ☎ *0432/22–286. No credit cards. No lunch Mon.–Sat. No dinner Sun.*

$ ✕ **To Lakario.** At this *tsipouradiko,* mezedes are served with carafes of tsipouro, a liqueur similar to raki. The day's plates may include leek pie, charcoal-grilled potatoes, codfish with garlic dip, *pipernati* (baked eggplant, peppers, and cheese), and a seasonal local specialty, *bit-sivissia* (tasty lamb bits with oregano). ✉ *28 Oktovriou 38,* ☎ *0432/24–871. No credit cards. Closed Greek Easter Sun.*

$$$ 🏨 **Amalia.** The area's best hotel is about 4 km (2½ mi) outside Kalam-
★ baka. The low-lying complex has spacious, handsomely decorated public rooms with touches such as Byzantine-style frescoes, as well as a garden. The rooms are done in soothing colors and have large beds, art prints, and wooden balconies. Buffet breakfast is included. ✉ *Trikalon 14, 42200,* ☎ *0432/72–216 and 0432/72–217,* 🖷 *0432/72–457; reservations,* ☎ *01/323–7301,* 🖷 *01/323–8792. 169 rooms, 2 suites. Restaurant, pool. AE, DC, MC, V.*

$$ 🏨 **Hotel Antoniadi.** This reliable hotel in Kalambaka has pastel-hued rooms with carpeting, minibars, color TVs, and hair dryers. Many rooms have a view of the Meteora rocks. During the sweltering summers the hotel opens its rooftop pool. ✉ *Trikalon 148, 42200,* ☎ *0432/24–387,* 🖷 *0432/24–319 and 0432/23–419. 69 rooms. Restaurant, air-condi-tioning, pool. V.*

$ 🏨 **Kastraki.** Step out on the balcony and bid good morning to the mas-
★ sive rocks that seem to loom over this great little hotel in a village on the road from Kalambaka to Meteora. It is efficiently run by a pair of friendly and helpful brothers. ✉ *Patriarchou Dimitriou, 42200 Kas-traki,* ☎ *0432/75–336,* ☎ 🖷 *0432/75–335. 28 rooms. V.*

Mainland Greece Essentials

Getting Around
Although it's easiest to visit the region by **car,** there is very good **train** and **bus** service between the main towns, and between each town and Athens.

Guided Tours
Call travel agencies in Athens for tours of mainland Greece, such as a two-day trip to the Meteora monasteries (36,500 dr.), a three-day trip to Delphi and Meteora (76,000 dr.), and a six-day excursion to north-ern Greece including Delphi, Meteora, Thessaloniki and its outlying archaeological sites (197,500 dr.) (☞ Travel Agencies *in* Athens Es-sentials, *above*). **Trekking Hellas** (✉ Rodou 11, Kalambaka, ☎ 🖷 0432/75–214) offers numerous outdoor travel excursions, ranging from canyoning to rafting.

Visitor Information
Delphi: municipal tourist office (✉ Vas. Pavlou and Friderikis 12, ☎ 0265/82–900); tourist police (✉ Aggelos Sikelianou 3, ☎ 0265/82–222). **Meteora:** tourist information office (✉ Kondili 38; summer in-formation kiosk: Platia Dimarchiou, Kalambaka, ☎ 0432/75–306); tourist police (✉ Pindou and Ioanninon, Kalambaka, ☎ 0432/22–813).

CORFU

Temperate, multihued Corfu—of emerald mountains; turquoise wa-ters lapping rocky coves; ocher and pink buildings; shimmering silver olive leaves; scarlet roses, bougainvillea, jacaranda, and lavender wis-teria spread over cottages—could have inspired Impressionism. The is-land—which lies strategically in the northern Ionian Sea at the entrance to the Adriatic, opposite northwestern Greece and Albania—has a colorful history reflecting the commingling of Corinthians, Romans, Goths, Normans, Venetians, French, Russians, and British. Today, more than a million visitors a year—most from England and many from Europe—enjoy, and in summer, crowd its evocative capital city, iso-lated beaches, stylish restaurants, and resorts. The island combines neoclassic villas and eco-sensitive resorts, horse-drawn carriages and Jaguars—simplicity and sophistication—in an alluring mix. Its desirability, however, makes it expensive. The island of Corfu is small enough to cover completely in a few days. Roads vary from gently winding to spiraling, but they're generally well marked, and all lead to Corfu town, which recalls a stage set for a Verdi opera.

East coast mid-island, **Corfu** town occupies the central prong of a three-pronged peninsula. On the southern prong is Paleopolis (Old Town) and on the northern is the Old Fort (now the backdrop for summer sound-and-light shows), walled in the 8th century. The remains of the medieval Venetian town here are scanty. If you arrive from Igoumenitsa or Patras, on mainland Greece, your ferry will dock at the **Old Port** on the north side of town, west of the **New Fortress** (1577–78) (⊠ on promontory northwest of the old fortress and medieval town), built by the Venetians and expanded by the French and the British to protect the town from a possible Turkish invasion. You can now wander through the maze of tunnels, moats, and fortifications.

The **Esplanade** (⊠ between Old Fortress and old town), the huge open parade ground on the land side of the canal, is central to the life of the town, and one of the most beautiful *spianadas* (esplanades) in Greece. It is bordered on the west by a street lined with seven- and eight-story Venetian and English Georgian houses, and arcades, called the **Liston** (modeled, by the French under Napoléon, on the Parisian Rue de Rivoli). Cafés spill out into the passing scene, and Corfiot celebrations, games, and trysts occur in the sun and shadows.

The oldest cultural institution in modern Greece, the **Corfu Reading Society**, contains archives (dating back several centuries) of the Ionian islands. In the early 19th century, Corfu was the literary center of Greece. One of the island's loveliest buildings, it has an exterior staircase leading up to a loggia. ⊠ *Kapodistriou.* ⊙ *Daily 9–1, Thurs., Fri. 5–8 also.*

The **Garrison Church of St. George** (1830) in the Old Fortress has a Doric portico. In summer there's folk dancing, and in August sound-and-light shows relate the fortress's history. The views from here, east to the Albanian coast and west over the town, are splendid. ⊠ *In middle of Old Fortress.* ⊠ *Free.* ⊙ *8–7.*

$$$ ✕ **Aegli.** This 35-year-old restaurant on the Liston serves more than 100 different dishes, both local and international. The tables in front overlook the nonstop parade on the promenade. ⊠ *Liston,* ☎ *0661/31949. AE, DC, MC, V. Closed Dec.–Feb.*

$$$ ✕ **The Venetian Well.** On the most charming little square in the old town, built around a 17th-century well, this romantic restaurant—its staff tiptoes around lingering lovers—seems too evocative and perfect to be true. The dining rooms in the handsome Venetian building are painted the classic Greek blue. Creative entrées might include duck with kumquats or wild boar. ⊠ *Pl. Kremasti,* ☎ *0661/44761. AE, DC, MC, V.*

$ ✕ **O Yiannis.** One of the nicest in Corfu, this restaurant is unpretentious and full of locals. It's also cheap: You'll be hard-pressed to tally up 3,000 dr. on the great barrel wine and wonderful food. Check out the ancient photos of Corfu's old-timers. ⊠ *Sophia Kremona and Iassonos-Sossipatrou 30, Anemomilos,* ☎ *0661/31066. Reservations not accepted. No credit cards.*

$$$$ ▦ **Corfu Palace.** Overlooking the bay, 100 yards from the center of town, this elegant hotel is one of the most beautiful in all of Greece. *Tasteful* and *comfortable* best describe its old-world grandeur. The spacious rooms, furnished in various styles (Louis XIV and Empire), have TVs and wide balconies with splendid views. The hotel also has two

of Corfu's most luxurious restaurants. ⊠ *Democratias 2, 49100,* ☎ *0661/39485,* ℻ *0661/31749. 110 rooms. 2 restaurants, outdoor pool, indoor pool. AE, DC, MC, V.*

$$$ 🏨 **Cavalieri Hotel.** In this venerable, eight-story building on the arcade of the Liston, get a room on the fourth or fifth floor with a number ending in 2, 3, or 4 for a breathtaking view of the Old Fort. The building is swank, yet graceful and chock-full of history. Have a drink at the usually empty but delightful English-style wood-paneled bar. Best of all is the roof garden, which offers light meals and the most remarkable view in town. ⊠ *4 Kapodistriou, 49100,* ☎ *0661/39041,* ℻ *0661/ 39336. 50 rooms. Restaurant. AE, DC, MC, V.*

$ 🏨 **Hotel Konstantinoupoulis.** A hotel for more than 200 years, this can be most ambitiously called traditional. But rooms are reasonably clean and acceptable if you're on a budget. It's opposite the dock for car ferries to the islands, with a great view of the old port. ⊠ *Zavitsianou 11, Old Port, 49100,* ☎ *0661/39826. 44 rooms, shared baths. No credit cards.*

Kanoni

Outside Corfu town, at Kanoni, the site of the ancient capital, you may behold the most famous view on Corfu. A French cannon once stood in this hilly landscape, which is now built up and often noisy because of the nearby airport. From Kanoni, against the backdrop of the green slopes of Mount Ayia Deka, is the serene view of two tiny islets: One, **Moni Viahernes,** is reached by causeway. The other islet, **Pontikonisi** (Mouse Island), has a **white convent** and, beyond, tall cypresses guarding the **13th-century chapel.** You can take a little launch or pedal boat to visit it—or even swim there.

Elsewhere in the environs outside Corfu town are two fabled palaces and gardens open to visitors: **Mon Repos,** built by Robert Adam in 1831, used by English Lord High Commissioners, and birthplace of England's Prince Philip, and, in the village of Gastouri, **Achilleion,** the Greek retreat of Empress Elizabeth of Austria.

Corfu Essentials

Getting Around

BY BOAT

Passenger ships stop at Corfu twice a week, April to October. **Minoan Lines** (⊠ Akti Poseidonos 28, Piraeus, ☎ 01/411–8211 through 01/ 411–8216, ℻ 01/411–8631) runs the ship service. Ferries from Igoumenitsa on the mainland leave every hour in summer and every two hours off-season, landing in Corfu town (two hours) and in Lefkimmi, at the southern tip of Corfu (45 minutes).

BY BUS

KTEL Corfu buses (☎ 0661/39985 and 0661/37186) leave Athens (☎ 01/512–9443) three or four times a day. Bus travel on Corfu is inexpensive, and the bus network covers the island. The **Spilia** (⊠ Avramiou, ☎ 0661/30627) bus company's terminal is at the New Port. Buses also run from the **San Rocco** (⊠ Pl. San Rocco, ☎ 0661/31595) bus company's depot.

BY CAR

By car, the best route from Athens is the National Road via Corinth to the Rion/Antirion ferry, then to Igoumenitsa (472 km/274 mi), where you take the ferry to Corfu. Call the **Touring Club of Greece** (☎ 104) for information.

Guided Tours

Many agencies run half-day tours of Old Corfu town, and tour buses go daily to all the sights on the island. Tickets and information are available at travel agencies all over town.

Visitor Information

Greek National Tourist Organization (GNTO or EOT; ⊠ Kapodistriou 1, ☎ 0661/37520, 0661/37638, or 0661/37639, ℻ 0661/30298). **Tourist Police** (⊠ Kapodistriou 1, ☎ 0661/30265).

THE AEGEAN ISLANDS

The islands of the Aegean have colorful legends of their own—the Minotaur in Crete; the lost continent of Atlantis, which some believe was Santorini; and the Colossus of Rhodes, to name a few. Mykonos has windmills, dazzling whitewashed buildings, hundreds of tiny red-domed churches on golden hillsides, and small fishing harbors. Visitors to Santorini sail into a vast volcanic crater and anchor near the island's forbidding cliffs. Crete, with its jagged mountain peaks, olive orchards, and vineyards, contains the remains of the Minoan civilization. In Rhodes a bustling modern town surrounds a walled medieval city and a castle.

Mykonos

Mykonos's chief village, also called Mykonos, is the Cyclades' best preserved; it is a maze of narrow, flagstone streets lined with two-story whitewashed houses, many with flower-filled balconies, outdoor stairways, and blue or red doors and shutters. Every morning women scrub the sidewalks and streets in front of their homes, undaunted by passing donkeys. During the 1960s the bohemian jet set discovered Mykonos, and many old houses are now shops, restaurants, bars, or discos; the nightlife, both gay and straight, is notorious. The rich arrive by yacht, the middle class by plane, the backpackers and Athenians by boat. It is *the* holiday destination for the young, lively, and liberated.

If you stay more than a day, pay a quick visit to the **archaeological museum** to get a sense of the island's history; the most significant local find is a 7th-century BC *pithos* (storage jar) showing the Greeks emerging from the Trojan Horse. ⊠ *East end of port, ☎ 0289/22–325.* ☉ *Tues.–Sun. 8:30–3.*

From the museum stroll down to the esplanade, where islanders promenade in the evening, or meander through the town, whose confusing layout evolved to foil pirates. In a picturesque neighborhood called **Venetia** (Little Venice) at the southwest end of the port, a few of the old houses have been turned into stylish bars, and wooden balconies hang over the water. In the distance, lined up like toy soldiers on the high hill, are the **Mykonos windmills**; until 40 years ago, wind power was used to grind the island's grain.

Mykoniots claim that 365 churches and chapels dot their landscape, one for each day of the year. The most beautiful, **Paraportiani** (Our Lady of the Postern Gate; ⊠ Anargon), is really three churches imaginatively combined, like a confectioner's dream gone mad.

$$$ ✕ **Chez Cat'rine.** This is the Cyclades' fanciest restaurant. Inside, the islands' whitewashed walls and archways combine with a French château feeling—reflecting the cuisine. Among the well-prepared French and Greek dishes are tournedos, langoustines, and seafood soufflé. The restaurant (also spelled "Katrin") has an ace sommelier. ⊠ *Delos and Drakopoulou, ☎ 0289/22–169. Reservations essential. AE, MC, V. Closed Nov.–Apr. No lunch.*

The Aegean Islands (Ta Nissia tou Aegaiov)

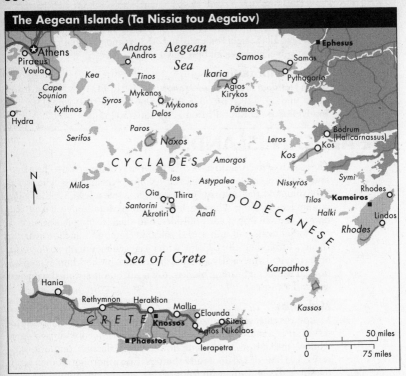

Athens
Piraeus
Voula
Cape Sounion
Kythnos
Hydra
Kea
Tinos
Syros
Serifos
Milos
Andros
Andros
Mykonos
Delos
Paros
Naxos
CYCLADES
Ios
Astypalea
Oia
Santorini
Akrotiri
Thira
Anafi
Aegean Sea
Ikaria
Agios Kirykos
Pátmos
Amorgos
Samos
Samos
Pythagorio
■ **Ephesus**
Leros
Kos
Kos
Nissyros
Tilos
Kameiros
Halki
Bodrum (Halicarnassus)
Symi
Rhodes
Rhodes
Lindos
DODECANESE
Sea of Crete
Karpathos
Kassos
Hania
Rethymnon
Heraklion
Mallia
Elounda
Sifeia
Knossos
Phaestos
CRETE
Agios Nikolaos
Ierapetra
N

0   50 miles
0   75 miles

$$ ✕ Chrisanthos. The clean lines of this sparkling white taverna with red shutters and blue chairs reflect the exquisite simplicity of its food: tomatoes stuffed with capers, risotto with cuttlefish ink, homemade french fries cooked in olive oil, and spaghetti *thanatos* made with female lobster. ⊠ *Ftelia,* ☎ *0289/71–535. V. Closed Nov.–Apr.*

$$ ✕ Spilia. Tucked into a seaside cave on a rock ledge, this family operation (dad fishes, mom cooks) lets you choose lobster and other live seafood kept in the nearby tide pool to go with appetizers like grilled octopus, crunchy cheese pies, or mussels in cream with fennel. If you're on foot and not pulling up in your yacht, follow the signs from the beach off the distant fishing hamlet of Kalafati. ⊠ *Kalafati, below Hotel Anastassia,* ☎ *0289/71–205. No credit cards. Closed Nov.– Apr.*

$$$$ ✕🏨 Kivotos ClubHotel. The hotel, a member of the Small Luxury Hotels of the World, has rooms that view the yachts on Ornos bay (about 3½ km/2 mi from Chora), its own beach, fitness center, and squash court, and even a schooner you can rent for the day. Built on several levels, the hotel has elaborate stone mosaics and much sculpture. The restaurant's dishes are artfully presented—the chicken stuffed with feta and tomato comes with a spoon each of fava, lentils, and tzatziki. ⊠ *Ornos Bay, 84600,* ☎ *0289/24–094,* FAX *0289/22–844; Athens,* ☎ *01/724–6766,* FAX *01/724–9203. 26 rooms, 4 suites. Restaurant, pool. AE, DC, MC, V. Closed mid-Oct.–Apr.*

$$$$ 🏨 Cavo Tagoo. This medley of cream-color cubical suites perched above a small beach has been much praised for its architecture. The hotel is about 10 minutes' walk from the port; all rooms have balconies or terraces with superb sea views. Its restaurant serves excellent haute Mediterranean cuisine. ⊠ *Road to Ayios Stefanos, 84600 Chora; 400 yards from town;* ☎ *0289/23–692,* FAX *0289/24–923; Athens,* ☎ *01/643–0233,* FAX *01/644–5237. 67 rooms, 5 suites. Restaurant, seawater pool. DC, MC, V. Closed Nov.–mid-Apr.*

$$ 🏨 **Kouneni Hotel.** The Kouneni is a casual, family-run hotel in the town center that's quieter than most. It is set in a cool green garden, an ideal place to linger over the full breakfast that's included in the price. Rooms are fairly large and look out on the garden. ⊠ *Tria Pigadia, 84600, opposite public school,* ☎ *0289/22–301 and 0289/23–311,* FAX *0289/26–559. 19 rooms. No credit cards.*

$ 🏨 **Philippi.** With a lovely flower garden whose scent permeates the immaculate rooms, this hotel is in the town center. With or without bath, rooms are the same price, so book early. ⊠ *Kalogera 35, 84600 Chora,* ☎ *0289/22–294,* FAX *0289/24–680. 13 rooms, 4 with bath. Air-conditioning. No credit cards. Closed Nov.–Mar.*

Delos

★ Thirty minutes by caïque from Mykonos, little dry Delos was the islands' ancient religious center, sacred to Apollo and Artemis. Its **Exedra ton Leonton** (Terrace of the Lions), a weathered row of nine Naxian marble sculptures from the 7th century BC, overlooks the dried-up sacred lake. Another highlight is a group of houses of the Hellenistic and Roman periods, with their fine floor mosaics *in situ.* Museum, theater, houses—the site is endlessly rich and needs exploring time. *Boats leave Mykonos in morning and return at 1, depending on winds.* ☎ *0289/ 22–259.* ⊙ *Tues.–Sun. 8:30–3.*

★ Santorini

The best way to approach Santorini, or Thira, is to sail into its spectacular bay, once the vast crater of the volcano, and dock beneath its black and red cliffs, which rise up to 1,000 ft above the sea. Passenger ferries dock at the grungy new port, Athinios, where visitors are met by buses, taxis, and hotel touts. The houses and churches of the main town, **Fira,** cling inside the rim in dazzling white contrast to the somber cliffs. The ride to Fira takes about a half hour, and from there you can make connections to **Oia,** the serene town at the northern tip. Though crowded in summer, tiny Oia, pictured on dozens of advertisements for Greece, is famous for its marine sunset. Be sure to try the local wines—a number of wineries offer tours and tastings (Antinopoulos is a good bet). The volcanic soil produces a unique range of flavors, from light and dry to rich and aromatic.

The island's volcano erupted violently about 1500 BC, destroying its Minoan civilization. At **Akrotiri,** on the south end of Santorini, the remains of a Minoan city buried by volcanic ash are being excavated. The site, once a prosperous town some think is the legendary Atlantis, is remarkably well preserved. Its charming frescoes are in Athens but the island wants them back. ☎ *0286/81–366.* ⊙ *Tues.–Sun. 8:30–3.*

At **Archaia Thira** (Ancient Thira), a clifftop site on the east coast of the island, a town founded before the 9th century BC has a theater, agora, houses, fortifications, and temples. Though only foundations remain, it is very romantic; you can easily imagine its famed dances performed by naked youths. ☎ *No phone.* ⊡ *Free.* ⊙ *Tues.– Sun. 8:30–3.*

$$$ ✕ **Domata.** Named for the revered Santorini tomato, this sleek restaurant has Aegean-inspired cuisine created by the same chef who spends winters at Vitrina, a noted Athens restaurant. Start with the mussels in white sauce and capers, or onions stuffed with sun-dried tomatoes, then move on to such entrées as crayfish with saffron or the heartier ribs marinated in fennel seed, ouzo, and yogurt. ⊠ *Monolithos,* ☎ *0286/ 32–069. MC, V. Closed Sept.–May.*

$$$ ✕ **Selene.** At this longtime favorite overlooking the bay, the creative cooking develops traditional Santorini fare into Mediterranean elegance. The favaballs with tomato caper sauce and *Brodedo* (fish, squid, oc-

topus, prawns, and other shellfish in a clay pot) are both based on local recipes. ⊠ *Fira,* ☎ *0286/22–249. MC, V. Closed Nov.–Mar.*

$$ ✕ **Camille Stefani.** On the seaside walkway of black Kamari beach, below
★ ancient Thira, is one of the island's best restaurants. It serves seafood and Greek and Continental cuisine. Begin with the *lahanodolmades* (stuffed cabbage), a plate of fava, and moist tomato croquettes, and continue with one of the 16 versions of beef, pork, or chicken fillet. Try a glass of the mellow Santorini Lava red wine. Locals eat here. ⊠ *Beach road, Kamari,* ☎ *0286/31–716. AE, DC, MC, V. Closed Dec.–mid-Feb.*

$ ✕ **1800.** A group of new restaurants has sprung up in rapidly devloping Oia, but this elegant old favorite, in an atmospheric captain's mansion, holds its own. Veal with tomato sauce and eggplant, zucchini pie with cheese and onions—everything is good. ⊠ *Main pedestrian lane, Oia,* ☎ *0286/71–485. AE, DC, MC, V. Closed mid-Nov.–mid-Apr.*

$ ✕ **Nikolas.** This simple, congenial taverna is one of the few places in
★ town that stays open in winter. Arrive early, as the cook runs out of food around midnight. The menu on the chalkboard offers barrel wine and a delicious choice of classic Greek dishes, including stifado, stuffed cabbage rolls, and mountain greens. ⊠ *Erithrou Stavrou, Fira,* ☎ *0286/24–550. No credit cards.*

$$$$ 🛏 **Perivolas Traditional Houses.** Built into the cliffside at the outskirts of beautiful Oia, these authentic cave houses, some of them 200 and 300 years old, have been restored and individually decorated in Cycladic style. They overlook the sea and offer comfortable accommodations complete with kitchenettes and terraces. ⊠ *84702 Oia,* ☎ *0286/71–308,* FAX *0286/71–309. 16 houses. Pool. No credit cards. Closed Nov.–Mar.*

$$$ 🛏 **Aigialos Traditional Houses.** These former cave houses have been
★ redesigned, each differently, with traditional elegance, privacy, and comfort. Balconies overlook the bay, flowers decorate the rooms, and all the amenities are discretely present. ⊠ *Follow signs from Hypapantis walkway, 84700 Fira,* ☎ *0286/25–191,* FAX *0286/22856. 16 houses. AE, MC, V. Closed Nov.–mid-Apr.*

$$$ 🛏 **Atlantis Villas.** If you don't mind stairs, descend to this beautiful hotel on Oia's cliffside, 600 ft above the sea, which offers separate apartments of varied configuration with splendid sunset sea views, comfort, quiet, and amenities. ⊠ *Down from main walkway, 84702 Oia,* ☎ *0286/71–214,* FAX *0286/71–312. 20 houses. Pool. AE, DC, MC, V. Closed mid-Oct.–mid-Apr.*

$–$$ 🛏 **Delfini II.** Near Fira's center, this hotel has rooms decorated with old handcrafted objects and ceramics. Rooms include refrigerators; apartments have kitchens and private balconies. Guests in the rooms make use of the terrace with a sea view, an umbrella pergola, and sun beds. ⊠ *Between cathedral and Ayios Minas church, 84700 Fira,* ☎ *0286/ 22–780,* FAX *0286/22–780; 0286/22–371 off-season. 4 rooms, 3 apartments. No credit cards. Closed Nov.–Mar.*

Rhodes

The large island of Rhodes, 11 km (7 mi) off the coast of Turkey, is the chief island of the Dodecanese. The northern end is one of Greece's major vacation centers. The island is large and not always beautiful, but it has fine beaches, ancient ruins, and an excellent climate. It makes a good base for visiting other islands of the Dodecanese, with their mixture of Aegean and Turkish architecture.

The town of Rhodes has an attractive harbor with fortifications; the gigantic bronze statue of the Colossus of Rhodes, incorrectly rumored to have straddled the entrance, was one of the wonders of the ancient world. The **Old Walled City** is full of crooked, cobbled streets and echoes of antiquity. It's also full of the trappings of tourism, mainly evident in pubs and bars that cater to the large European market. The Old Town was built by crusaders—the Knights of St. John—on the site of an ancient city. The knights ruled the island from 1309 until they were defeated by the Turks in 1522.

On the Street of the Knights stands the Knights' Hospital. Behind it ★ the **archaeological museum** has ancient pottery and sculpture, including two voluptuous statues of Aphrodite. ⊠ *Platia Mouseiou (Museum Square), reached by wide staircase from Hospital,* ☎ *0241/31– 048.* ⊙ *May–Oct., Tues.–Fri. 8 AM–9 PM, weekends 8:30–3; Nov.–Apr., Tues.–Fri. 8–2:40, weekends 8:30–3.*

The medieval **Palati ton Ippoton** (Palace of the Knights), destroyed in 1856 by a gunpowder explosion, was restored by the Italians as a summer retreat for Mussolini. It is now a museum. Note its splendid Hellenistic and Roman floor mosaics. ⊠ *Ippoton,* ☎ *0241/23–359.* ⊙ *May– Oct., Tues.–Fri. 8–7, weekends 8:30–3; Nov.–Apr., Tues.–Fri. 8:30–2:40, weekends 8:30–3.*

★ The **walls** of Rhodes's Old Town are among the greatest medieval monuments in the Mediterranean. For 200 years the knights strengthened them, making them up to 40 ft thick in places and curving the surfaces to deflect cannonballs. You can take a walk on about half of the 4-km (2½-mi) road along the top of the fortifications. The tour begins from the courtyard of the Palace of the Knights at the end of Ippoton Street. ⊠ *Old Town,* ☎ *0241/23–359.* ⊙ *Tours Tues. and Sat. 2:45 (arrive at least 15 mins early).*

★ The enchanting village of **Lindos** ornaments the eastern coast. You can climb the winding path and steep stairs to the ruins of the ancient acropolis, **Akropoli tis Archaias Lindou.** The sight of its beautiful colonnade— part of the sanctuary to Athena Lindaia—with the sea far below is unforgettable. Look for little St. Paul's Harbor, beneath the cliffs of the acropolis; seen from above, it appears to be a lake, as rocks obscure its entrance. ⊠ *Above town,* ☎ *0241/75–674.* ⊙ *May–Oct., Tues.– Sun. 8–6; Nov.–Apr., Tues.–Sun. 8:30–2:40.*

$$$$ ✕ **Alexis.** The owners spare no effort to present the very best seafood— ★ whether fresh lobster, mussels from nearby Simi steamed with onion, fennel, and white wine, or such specialties as sea urchin, limpets, and sea snail. ⊠ *Sokratous 18, Old Town,* ☎ *0241/29–347. Reservations essential. AE, MC, V. No lunch June–Aug.*

$$$$ ✕ **Ta Kioupia.** Antique farm implements hang on the walls at this Rhodes landmark, and tables are elegantly set with linens, fine china, and crystal. Food arrives on large platters, and for a fixed price you select what pleases your eye: carrot bread, pine-nut salad, oven-baked meatballs with leeks, *tiropites* (four-cheese pie), and rooster kebab. ⊠ *Tris, about 7 km (4¼ mi) from Rhodes town,* ☎ *0241/91–824. Reservations essential. AE, V. Closed Jan. No lunch.*

$$ ✕ **Dinoris.** In a cavernous hall built in 1530 as a stable for the knights, this establishment has long specialized in fish. For mezes try the variety platter of *psarokeftedakia* (fish balls made from a secret recipe), mussels, shrimp, and lobster. ⊠ *Platia Mouseiou 14A, Old Town,* ☎ *0241/25–824. Reservations essential Mar.– Sept. AE, MC, V.*

$$ ✕ **Palia Istoria.** Ensconced in an old house with genteel murals, this ★ mezedopolion is a visual treat. Entrées include pork tenderloin in wine, fresh salmon in champagne sauce, and shrimp ouzo with orange juice. A taxi ride here from the center costs about 700 dr. ⊠ *Mitropoleos 108 and Dendrinou, Ayios Dimitrios,* ☎ *0241/32–421. Reservations essential. MC, V. Closed Dec. 15–Jan. 15. No lunch.*

$ ✕ **Taverna Nisiros.** Once the home of an Aga, this simple taverna dishes up traditional Greek fare in the large courtyard or in the cozy interior decorated with sheep bells and kilims. Sample the strong barrel wine or a fiery souma (or raki). ⊠ *Ayiou Fanouriou 45–47, Old Town,* ☎ *0241/31–471. AE, MC, V.*

$$$$ ★ 🖬 **Grecotel Rhodos Imperial.** The buildings zigzag down the hillside like stacked red, blue, and yellow boxes. Linked by a pedestrian tunnel to the beach, the resort is just 4 km (2½ mi) from Rhodes town. Guests can play tennis, jet ski and windsurf, rent a mountain bike, or just amble along in pedal boats. The crisp, modern rooms all have balconies, about two-thirds of them with sea views (about 9,000 dr. more). ⊠ *Ialyssou Ave., Box 316, 85100 Ixia,* ☎ *0241/75–000,* FAX *0241/76–690; Athens,* ☎ *01/725–0920,* FAX *01/725–7671. 402 rooms, 42 suites. 3 restaurants, 3 pools. AE, DC, MC, V. Closed Nov.–mid-Mar.*

$$$–$$$$ 🖬 **Grand Hotel.** This resort hotel in Rhodes town offers easy access to the beach across the street and the casino next door, the Old Town (20 minutes on foot), and the New Town's vibrant nightlife. Although about three-fourths of the rooms have been renovated, the best are in the newer wings. Rooms have balconies with either a sea or a garden view, there is a tennis court and an exercise room, and the main pool is Olympic-size. ⊠ *Akti Miaouli 1, 85100 Rhodes,* ☎ *0241/26–284,* FAX *0241/35–589; Athens,* ☎ *01/2917002,* FAX *01/291–7672. 379 rooms, 18 suites. 2 restaurants, 4 pools. AE, DC, MC, V.*

$$$ 🖬 **S. Nikolis' Hotel.** This small hotel within the Old Town is away from the most crowded tourist area. The rooms, in several 14th-century buildings, are outfitted with dark, rustic furniture, TV, hair dryers, air-conditioning (except in the apartments, which have fans), and refrigerators; they look out toward the spacious courtyard or the old city walls. Depending on the suite, different "honeymoon" features include a whirlpool tub, king- or queen-size beds, bathtub, loft, and balconies. A roof terrace lets guests enjoy a view over the town with the buffet breakfast. ⊠ *Ippodamou 61, 85100 Rhodes,* ☎ *0241/34–561,* FAX *0241/32–034. 10 rooms, 8 suites, 4 apartments. Restaurant. AE, DC, MC, V.*

$$ 🖬 **Spartalis Hotel.** Convenient if you have to catch a boat from the harbor, this is in Rhodes's New Town. Many rooms in the simple but lively hotel have balconies overlooking the bay, and there is a terrace for breakfast. The rooms on the street are noisy. ⊠ *Plastira 2, 85100 Rhodes,* ☎ *0241/24–371,* FAX *0241/20–406. 79 rooms. AE, DC, MC, V. Closed Nov.–Mar.*

Crete

Greece's largest island, lying in the south Aegean, was the center of Europe's earliest civilization, the Minoan, which flourished from about 2000 BC to 1200 BC. Crete was struck a mortal blow in about 1450 BC by an unknown cataclysm, perhaps political.

★ The most important Minoan objects are in the **archaeological museum** in Heraklion, Crete's largest (and least attractive) city. The museum's treasures include the frescoes and ceramics from Knossos and Agia Triada depicting Minoan life, the snake goddesses, and the Phaestos disc, with Europe's first writing. ⊠ *Xanthoudidou 1, Platia Eleftherias,* ☎ *081/226–092.* ☉ *May–Oct., Mon. 12:30–7, Tues.–Sun. 8–7; Nov.–Apr., Mon. 12:30–5, Tues.–Sun. 8–5.*

Not far from Heraklion is the partly reconstructed, sublimely evoca-
★ tive palace of **Knossos.** From 2000 to 1400 BC it was the chief site of Europe's first civilization. Note the simple throne room, with its tiny gypsum throne, pipes for running water, and splendid decorations. Its complexity and rituals probably suggested the myth of the Minotaur: The monstrous man-bull, offspring of Queen Pasiphae and a white bull, was confined by King Minos to the labyrinth. ☎ *081/231–940.* ☉ *May–Oct., daily 8–7; Nov.–Apr., daily 8–5.*

In addition to archaeological treasures, Crete has beautiful snow-capped mountain scenery and many beach resorts along the north coast. **Mallia,** in addition to another extensive palace ruin, has good sandy beaches. Two other highly developed beach resorts, Ayios Niko-laos and the nearby Elounda, lie farther east.

Western Crete, with soaring mountains, deep gorges, and rolling olive orchards, is much less visited. The region is rich in Byzantine churches, Venetian monasteries, and interesting mountain villages. The town of ★ **Rethymnon** is dominated at its western end by the **Fortezza,** one of the largest and best-preserved Venetian castles in Greece. In the town's old section, you'll come across carved-stone Renaissance doorways belonging to vanished mansions; fountains; wooden Turkish houses; and one of the few surviving minarets in Greece. It belongs to the **Neratzes mosque,** and you can climb its 120 steps for a panoramic view. The carefully restored Venetian **loggia** is the clubhouse of the local nobility. The small Venetian **harbor,** with its 13th-century lighthouse, comes to life in summer, with restaurant tables cluttering the quayside.

★ **Hania** is one of the most attractive towns in Greece. Work your way through the covered market, then through the maze of narrow streets to the waterfront. Walk along the inner harbor, past the Venetian ar-senals and around to the old lighthouse, for a magnificent view of the town with the White Mountains looming beyond. Behind the outer har-bor, Theotokopoulou and Zambeliou streets lead you into the alleys where almost all the houses are Venetian or Turkish, and to the **ar-chaeological museum.** The finds come from all over western Crete: The painted Minoan clay coffins and elegant Late Minoan pottery indicate the region's Bronze Age wealth. ⊠ *Halidon 24,* ☎ *0821/90–334.* ☉ *May–Oct., Tues.–Sun. 8:30–7; Nov.–Apr., Tues.–Sun. 8:30–3.*

In summer boat service operates along the southwest coast, stopping at **Paleochora,** the area's main resort. **Elafonissi** islet has white-sand beaches and black rocks set in a turquoise sea (to get there you wade across a narrow channel). A good road on the west coast from Ela-fonissi north accesses beaches that are rarely crowded even in summer, ★ including **Falasarna,** near Crete's northwest tip.

$$ ✕ **Vaonakis.** The lively owner is known for his *leventia* (big-hearted ★ manliness) and his taverna's fine cooking: memorable Cretan mezedes, such as handmade dolmades with tomato and carrot; fried *galantera,* made with the intestines of milk-fed lamb; and pepper croquettes with white cheese, fried eggplants, and baby squash. Leave room for the *mizithrokaltsouna* (pastries filled with sweet local ricotta and served hot with honey). ⊠ *Pigianos Kambos, Rethymnon, near El Greco Hotel,* ☎ *0831/72–252. No credit cards. No lunch weekdays Oct.–Mar.*

$$ ✕ **Vassilis.** Watch the boats bobbing along the jetty at this congenial taverna. Don't miss the daily fish soup and such Cretan dishes as *koukouvayia* (a local roll soaked in wine, tomato, oil, and herbs). The owners also make their own rosé. ⊠ *Nearchou 10, old harbor, Rethym-non,* ☎ *0831/22–967. V.*

$–$$ ✕ **Samaria.** The taverna has a loyal clientele who yearn for Greek food the way their grandmothers used to make it: *stamnas* (meat, usually beef, oven-cooked with carrots and potatoes in individual ceramic bowls), soutzoukakia, stuffed tomatoes, and creamy pastitsio (try a quar-ter kilo), ideal with the barrel retsina. The taverna stays open until very late. ⊠ *El. Venizelou 39–40, Rethymnon,* ☎ *0831/24–681. V.*

$ ✕ **Kyriakos.** This popular taverna with pink tablecloths and green chairs offers fish and such Cretan specialties as snail stew with *pligouri* (cracked wheat), artichokes with broad beans, small eggplants with feta, and *tiropitakia* (pies with honey and creamy, mild Cretan cheese). ⊠

Dimokratias 53, Heraklion, ☎ 081/224–649. AE, DC, V. No dinner Sun. June–Sept.; no dinner Wed. Oct.–May.

$$ ✕🏨 **Doma.** This converted 19th-century mansion on the outskirts of Hania has the welcoming atmosphere of a private home: The sitting room has a fireplace and armchairs with embroidered scarlet bolsters. The dining room, where the owner serves dinner on request (lamb cooked with white wine and Cretan mountain herbs, for example), has a memorable view across the bay to the old town. Many rooms have air-conditioning; ask for one overlooking the garden to reduce street noise. ⊠ *El. Venizelou 124, 73100 Hania, ☎ 0821/51–772, ℻ 0821/41–578. 25 rooms, 3 suites. Dining room. MC, V. Closed Nov.–Mar.*

$$$$ 🏨 **Elounda Beach.** This is one of Greece's most renowned seaside re-
   ★   sorts, 9 km (7 mi) north of Ayios Nikolaos. The complex, set in beautiful grounds—the pool is cleverly landscaped among carob trees—includes a miniature Greek village, complete with kafenion and church, minigolf, two beaches, and a disco. Many of the suites—bliss!—have their own swimming pool. ⊠ *Elounda, 72053, ☎ 0841/41–412, ℻ 0841/41–373; Athens, ☎ 01/360–7120, ℻ 01/360–3392. 120 rooms, 43 bungalows, 37 suites, 27 suite-bungalows. 4 restaurants, pool. AE, DC, MC, V. Closed Nov.–Mar.*

$$–$$$ 🏨 **Mythos Suites Hotel.** A former 16th-century manor, this hotel near the cathedral has hardwood floors and beam ceilings, ceramic tiles, and remnants of the original massive stonework. The air-conditioned rooms are traditionally furnished, with brass beds in the two-floor maisonettes. All rooms, which overlook the small sunny courtyard pool, include a fully equipped kitchen. Only the maisonettes have balconies. ⊠ *Platia Karaoli-Dimitriou 12, 74100 Rethymnon, ☎ 0831/53–917, ☎ ℻ 0831/51–036. 1 apartment, 3 studios, 6 maisonettes. Pool. AE, DC, MC, V. Closed Nov.–Mar.*

$$ 🏨 **Atrion.** Nestled in a quiet street behind Heraklion's historical museum, this well-run hotel has rooms in shades of blue with heavy wood furniture and TVs. Drinks are served evenings in the tiny patio-garden. ⊠ *9 K. Paleologou, 71202 Heraklion, ☎ 081/229–225, ℻ 081/223–292. 65 rooms. Restaurant, air-conditioning. AE, DC, MC, V.*

$$ 🏨 **Casa Delfino.** This tranquil hotel in the heart of Hania's old town
   ★   was once part of a Venetian Renaissance palace; you can still see the original stonework throughout the building and the beautiful pebble mosaic in the atrium. Set around a courtyard, the rooms are decorated in cool pastel colors. Four apartments, available at a higher price, are decorated with 17th-century objects and may have such features as a private terrace, sea view, or hydromassage. ⊠ *Theofanous 9, Palea Poli, 73100 Hania, ☎ 0821/93–098, ℻ 0821/96–500. 16 rooms. Air-conditioning. AE, DC, MC, V.*

$ 🏨 **Nostos.** Dating from the 1400s, this building seems to have housed
   ★   all the peoples who passed through Hania: the renovated Venetian palazzo contains remains of an Ottoman bath and living quarters; it was also the site of the town's first Orthodox church. The roof garden is resplendent with honeysuckle, bougainvillea, and grapes. Antique kitchenware adorns the breakfast room. All rooms have balconies and fans; two have sea views. ⊠ *Zambeliou 42–46, Palio Limani, 73131 Hania, ☎ ℻ 0821/94–740. 12 studios. MC, V.*

Aegean Islands Essentials

Getting Around

`BY BOAT`

The simplest way to visit the Aegean Islands is by **cruise ship.** These usually stop at the four most popular islands—Mykonos, Rhodes, Crete, and Santorini. Car and passenger **ferries** sail to these destinations from Piraeus. Boats for Mykonos also leave from Rafina, 32 km (20 mi) north of Athens. En route from Piraeus you pass one of the great sights of Greece: the Temple of Poseidon looming on a hilltop at Cape Sounion.

BY PLANE

There is also frequent **air** service from Athens to each island, but in summer and on holidays it's vital to book well in advance.

Guided Tours

AEGEAN CRUISES

From April through October many cruises go to the islands from Piraeus. Try **Golden Sun Cruises** (✉ Akti Miaouli 71, Piraeus, ☎ 01/428–7894, ℻ 01/428–7898), or **Royal Olympic Cruises** (✉ Akti Miaouli 87, Piraeus, ☎ 01/429–0700 reservations, ℻ 01/429–0638). Most cruise agencies also have downtown Athens representatives.

Visitor Information

Crete: EOT (✉ Kriari 40, Megaron Pantheon building, Hania, ☎ 0821/92–943, ☎ ℻ 0821/92–624; ✉ Xanthoudidou 1, Heraklion, ☎ 081/244–462, 081/228–225, or 081/228–203; ✉ El. Venizelou beach road, Rethymnon, ☎ 0831/29–148); tourist police (✉ Karaiskaki 60, Hania, ☎ 0821/73–333; ✉ Dikaiosinis 10, Heraklion, ☎ 081/283–190 and 081/ 289–614; ✉ El. Venizelou beach road next to EOT, Rethymnon, ☎ 0831/28–156); ELPA (✉ G. Papandreou 46–50 and Knossos, Heraklion, ☎ 081/289–440). **Mykonos:** Hotel Reservations office (✉ Port, next to tourist police, ☎ 0289/24–540); Association of Rental Rooms and Apartments (✉ Port, next to tourist police, ☎ 0289/24–860); tourist police (✉ Port, ☎ 0289/22–482). **Rhodes:** EOT (✉ Archbishop Makarios and Papagou, Rhodes town, ☎ 0241/23–655); municipal tourism office (✉ Platia, Rimini, ☎ 0241/35–945), closed November–March; tourist police (✉ Archbishop Makarios and Papagou, entrance on Karpathou, Rhodes town, ☎ 0241/27–423). **Santorini:** tourist police (✉ next to KTEL bus station, ☎ 0286/22– 649).

15 HUNGARY

BUDAPEST, THE DANUBE BEND, LAKE BALATON

Hungary sits, proudly but precariously, at the crossroads of Central Europe, having retained its own identity despite countless invasions and foreign occupation by great powers of the East and West. Its industrious, resilient people have a history of brave but doomed uprisings: against the Turks in the 17th century, the Habsburgs in 1848, and the Soviet Union in 1956. Each upheaval has resulted in a period of readjustment, a return to politics as the art of the possible.

The '60s and '70s saw matters improve politically and materially for most Hungarians. Communist party leader János Kádár remained relatively popular at home and abroad, allowing Hungary to improve trade and relations with the West. The bubble began to burst during the 1980s, however, when the economy stagnated and inflation escalated. The peaceful transition to democracy began when young reformers in the party shunted aside the aging Mr. Kádár in 1988 and began speaking openly about multiparty democracy, a market economy, and cutting ties with Moscow. Events quickly gathered pace, and by spring 1990, as the Iron Curtain disappeared, Hungarians went to the polls in the first free elections in 40 years. A center-right government took office, sweeping away the Communists and their renamed successor party, the Socialists, who finished fourth. Ironically, four years later, in the nation's next elections, Hungarians voted out the ailing center-right party in favor of none other than the Hungarian Socialist party, which ruled in coalition with the Free Democrats until it was ousted again in the 1998 elections. Voting the center-right FIDESZ party, led by 35-year-old Viktor Orbán, into power, the nation has chosen an entirely new generation to take it into the new millennium.

In bald mathematical terms, the total area of Hungary (Magyarország) is less than that of Pennsylvania. Two rivers cross the country: The Duna (Danube) flows from the west through Budapest on its way to the southern frontier, the smaller Tisza from the northeast across the Great Plain (Nagyalföld). Western Hungary is dominated by the largest lake in Central Europe, Lake Balaton. Although overdevelopment is advancing, the northern lakeshore is still dotted with Baroque villages and old-world spas, and the surrounding hills are covered with vineyards. In eastern Hungary, the Nagyalföld is steeped in the romantic culture of the Magyars (the Hungarians' name for themselves), with its spicy food, strong wine, and proud *csikós* (horsemen).

However, it is Budapest, a city of more than 2 million people, that draws travelers from all over the world. Bisected by the Danube, the city has a split personality; villas and government buildings cluster in the hills of Buda to the west, whereas an imposing array of hotels, restaurants, and shopping areas crowd the flatlands of Pest.

Hungarians, known for their hospitality, love talking with foreigners. Hungarians of all ages share a deep love of music, and wherever you go you will hear it, whether it's opera performed at Budapest's imposing opera house or simply Gypsy violinists serenading you at dinner.

HUNGARY A TO Z

Customs

Objects for personal use may be imported freely. If you are over 16, you may also bring in 250 cigarettes or 50 cigars or 250 grams of tobacco, plus 2 liters of wine, 1 liter of spirits, 5 liters of beer, and 0.25 liters of perfume. A customs charge is made on gifts valued in Hungary at more than 27,000 Ft.

Keep receipts of any purchases from Konsumtourist, Intertourist, or Képcsarnok Vállalat. A special permit is needed for works of art, antiques, or objects of museum value. You are entitled to a VAT refund on new goods (i.e., not works of art, antiques, or objects of museum value) valued at more than 50,000 Ft.; *see* Shopping, *below*.

For further customs information, inquire at the **Hungarian Customs Office** (⊠ IX, Mester u. 7, Budapest, ☎ 1/218–0017). If you have trouble communicating, ask **Tourinform** (☎ 1/317–9800) for help.

Dining

Although prices are steadily increasing, plenty of good, affordable restaurants offer a variety of Hungarian dishes. Meats, rich sauces, and creamy desserts predominate, but you can also find salads, even out of season. Bypass the usual red-or-white question and order *Egri Bikavér*, or "bull's blood," Hungary's best-known red wine, with any meal. A regular restaurant is likely to be called either a *vendéglő* or an *étterem*. You also have the option of eating in a *büfé* (snack counter), an *eszpresszó* (café), or a *söröző* (pub). Be sure to visit a *cukrászda* (pastry shop). Keep in mind that typical Hungarian breakfasts consist of cold cuts and bread; if the start of your day requires specially prepared omelets or blueberry muffins, be sure to inquire about your hotel's breakfast offerings ahead of time.

One caveat: Many restaurants have a fine-print policy of charging for each slice of bread consumed from the bread basket. General overcharging is not unheard of, either. Authorities in Budapest, however, have been cracking down on establishments reported for overcharging. Don't order from menus without prices, and don't accept dining or drinking invitations from women hired to lure people into shady situations.

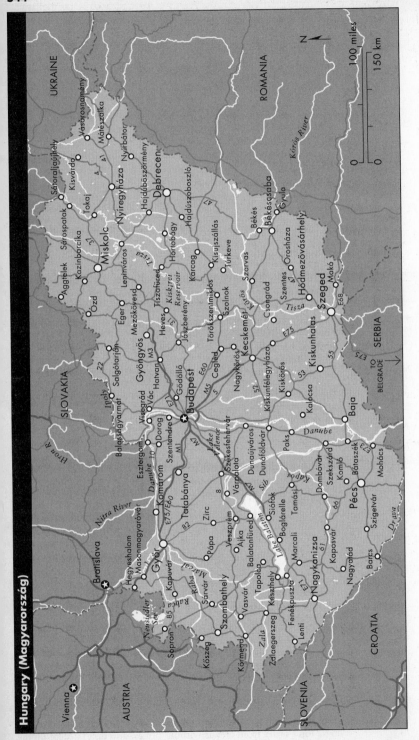

Hungary (Magyarország)

MEALTIMES

Hungarians eat dinner early—you risk offhand service and cold food after 9 PM. Lunch, the main meal for many, is served from noon to 2. Some restaurants are introducing simple breakfast menus catering to Western travelers and expats.

RATINGS

Prices are per person and include a first course, main course, and dessert, but no wine or tip. Prices in Budapest tend to be a good 30% higher than elsewhere in Hungary.

CATEGORY	COST
$$$$	over 3,500 Ft.
$$$	2,500 Ft.–3,500 Ft.
$$	1,500 Ft.–2,500 Ft.
$	under 1,500 Ft.

WHAT TO WEAR

At most moderately priced and inexpensive restaurants, casual but neat dress is acceptable. In more expensive establishments, especially in Budapest, a jacket and a tie are sometimes required.

Language

Hungarian (Magyar) tends to look and sound intimidating to English-speakers at first because it is not an Indo-European language. Generally, older people speak some German, and many younger people speak at least rudimentary English, which has become the most popular language to learn. It's a safe bet that anyone in the tourist trade will speak at least one of the two languages.

Lodging

Lodging ranges from sophisticated hotels to guest houses, private rooms, and campsites. Unless otherwise noted, rooms include bath.

CAMPING

Most of the some 300 campsites in Hungary are open from May through September. As rates are no longer regulated, prices vary. An average rate is about 800 Ft. a day per site in Budapest and the Balaton region, slightly less elsewhere, plus an accommodations fee—about 500 Ft. per person per night. Children under 14 often get a 50% reduction. Camping is forbidden except in designated areas. For information contact travel agencies or **Tourinform** (☞ Visitor Information, *below*), where you can pick up a detailed map locating campsites around the country.

GUEST HOUSES AND PRIVATE LODGINGS

Also called *panziók* (pensions), small guest houses lying just outside the heart of the city or town provide simple accommodations well suited to people on a budget. These usually include a private bathroom, and many also offer breakfast. A room for two in Budapest with breakfast and private bath will run around the equivalent of $70 per night in peak season, less at other times. Arrangements can be made through local tourist offices or travel agents abroad.

In the provinces rooms that you are offered directly are likely to be clean and in a relatively good neighborhood. Look for a placard reading either SZOBA KIADÓ or—in German—ZIMMER FREI (room for rent). The rate per night for a double room in Budapest or at Lake Balaton is $20–$30 (which usually includes the use of a bathroom but not breakfast). Reservations can also be made by any tourist office.

HOTELS

Don't expect a bargain on your hotel room in Budapest: High-season rates at established hotels rival those of most Western capitals. There are few expensive hotels outside Budapest, but the moderately priced hotels are generally comfortable and well run. Unless otherwise noted, breakfast is not included.

RATINGS

The following price categories are for a double room with bath and breakfast, VAT included, during the peak season; rates are markedly lower off-season and in the countryside, sometimes under $20 for two. For single rooms with bath, count on about 80% of the double-room rate. As most large hotels require payment in hard currency, rates are given in dollars below.

CATEGORY	BUDAPEST	BALATON AND DANUBE BEND
$$$$	over $200	over $70
$$$	$140–$200	$50–$70
$$	$80–$140	$30–$50
$	under $80	under $30

During the peak season (June through August), full board may be compulsory at some of the Lake Balaton hotels, although this is increasingly rare. During the off-season (in Budapest, September through March; at Lake Balaton and the Danube Bend, May and September), rates can be considerably lower than those given above and are frequently negotiable.

RENTALS

Apartments in Budapest and cottages at Lake Balaton, available for short- and long-term rental, can make the most economic lodging for families. Contact tourist offices in Hungary and abroad for rates and reservations. A Budapest apartment may cost anywhere from $40 to $60 a day; a luxury cottage for two on Lake Balaton costs about the same. You can make bookings in Budapest at the **Tribus Hotel Service** (⊠ V, Apáczai Csere János u. 1, ☎ 1/318–4848 or 1/318–5776, ℻ 1/317–9099), which is open 24 hours a day. Although some enterprising locals stand outside tourist offices and offer tourists their apartments for lower than official rates, it's less risky if you go the official route. Other rental agencies in Budapest are **IBUSZ's main office** (⊠ V, Ferenciek tere 10, ☎ 1/318–6866) and **Cooptourist** (⊠ I, Attila u. 107, ☎ 1/375–2846 or 1/375–2937). **Amadeus Apartments** (⊠ VIII, Üllői út 197, ☎ 30/942–2893, ℻ 1/302–8268) oversees five apartments that cost roughly $45 a night (two-night minimum), including airport transport.

YOUTH HOSTELS

Most hostels in Budapest are in university dorms and open only when school is not in session (typically July and August). Hostels have no age limits or membership requirements, and they offer a 10% discount to HI cardholders. Most have no curfews and offer 24-hour reception service. The **Hungarian Youth Hostel Federation** (⊠ VII, Almássy téri Szabadidő központ, Almássy tér 6, 4th floor, ☎ ℻ 1/352–1572, ext. 203 or 204) in Budapest publishes an informative, annual directory of hostels throughout the country and provides information. Budapest's two main hostel agencies are **Universum Ltd.** (⊠ Báthory László u. 18, H-1029 Budapest, ☎ ℻ 1/275–7046) and **Mellow Mood Kft.** (⊠ Dózsa György út 152, H-1134 Budapest, ☎ 1/340–8585 or 1/329–8644, ☎ ℻ 1/320–8425). Both companies operate year-round hostels, as well as summer-only. Be sure to book in advance in summer.

Hostels are uncommon outside Budapest, but some towns open their university dorms to travelers during July and August; inquire at the local tourist office. The atmosphere and price at these dorms is about the same as at a hostel.

Mail

Two post offices, Keleti (Eastern; ⊠ VII, Baross tér 11c) and Nyugati (Western; ⊠ VI, Teréz körút 51), are open 24 hours. Each is near one of Budapest's main train stations.

POSTAL RATES

Postage for an airmail letter to the United States costs about 130 Ft; an airmail letter to the United Kingdom and elsewhere in Western Europe costs about 120 Ft. Airmail postcards to the United States cost about 100 Ft and to the United Kingdom and elsewhere in Western Europe, about 90 Ft.

RECEIVING MAIL

General delivery service is available through any post office in Budapest, including the main downtown branch (⊠ Magyar Posta 4. sz., H-1052 Budapest, Városház utca 18); the envelope should have your name written on it, as well as "posta maradó" (poste restante) in large letters. The roman numeral prefix listed in a Budapest address refers to one of the city's 22 districts.

Money Matters

BANK MACHINES AND TRAVELER'S CHECKS

Eurocheque holders can cash personal checks in all banks and in most hotels. Many banks now also cash American Express and Visa traveler's checks. American Express has a full-service office in Budapest (⊠ V, Deák Ferenc u. 10, ☎ 1/235–4330 travel service; 1/235–4311 cardmember services; FAX 1/267–2029); a smaller branch on Castle Hill—in the Sisi Restaurant (☎ 1/224–0118), closed January–February—offers mostly only currency exchange. Hungary's first Citibank (⊠ V, Vörösmarty tér 4) offers full services to account holders, including a 24-hour ATM.

Hundreds of ATMs have appeared throughout the capital and in other major towns. Some accept Plus network bank cards and Visa credit cards, others Cirrus and MasterCard. You can withdraw forints only (automatically converted at the bank's official exchange rate) directly from your account; most levy a 1% or $3 service charge. Many cash-exchange machines, into which you feed paper currency for forints, have also sprung up.

COSTS

The forint was significantly devalued over the last few years and continues its decline, but inflation has dramatically decreased to around 10% from an annual rate of more than 25%. Although you receive more forints for your dollar, prices have risen to keep up with inflation. Nevertheless, even with inflation and the 25% value-added tax (VAT) in the service industry, enjoyable vacations with all the trimmings remain less expensive than in nearby Western European cities such as Vienna.

CREDIT CARDS

Most credit cards are accepted, but don't rely on them in smaller towns or less expensive accommodations and restaurants. The full-service American Express office (☞ Bank Machines and Traveler's Checks, *above*) in Budapest also dispenses cash to its cardholders.

CURRENCY

The unit of currency is the forint (Ft.). There are bills of 200, 500, 1,000, 2,000, 5,000, and 10,000 forints and coins of 1, 2, 5, 10, 20, 50, and 100 forints. Do not accept the now-defunct 100-Ft. bills. At press time (summer 1999) the exchange rate was approximately 243 Ft. to the U.S. dollar, 165 Ft. to the Canadian dollar, 381 Ft. to the pound sterling,

162 Ft. to the Australian dollar, and 129 Ft. to the New Zealand dollar. Note that official exchange rates are adjusted at frequent intervals.

There is still a black market in hard currency, but changing money on the street is risky and illegal, and the bank rate almost always comes close. Stick with banks and official exchange offices.

SAMPLE PRICES
Cup of coffee, 100 Ft.; bottle of beer at a bar or restaurant, 300 Ft.–400 Ft.; soft drinks, 150 Ft.; 2-km (1-mi) taxi ride, 150 Ft.; museum admission 100–300 Ft.

TIPPING
Four decades of socialism didn't alter the Hungarian habit of tipping. Hairdressers and taxi drivers expect 10% to 15% tips, while porters should get a dollar or two or a few hundred forints. Cloakroom attendants receive 100 to 200 Ft., as do gas pump attendants if they wash your windows or check your tires. Unless otherwise noted, gratuities are not automatically included in restaurant bills; when the waiter arrives with the bill, you should immediately add a 10%–15% tip to the amount and pay the waiter, as it is not customary to leave a tip on the table. If a Gypsy band plays exclusively for your table, you can leave 200 Ft. in the plate provided.

National Holidays
January 1; March 15 (Anniversary of 1848 Revolution); April 23–24 (Easter and Easter Monday); May 1 (Labor Day); June 11–12 (Pentecost); August 20 (St. Stephen's and Constitution Day); October 23 (1956 Revolution Day); December 24–26.

Opening and Closing Times
Banks are generally open weekdays 8–2 or 3, often with a one-hour lunch break around noon; most close at 1 on Friday. **Museums** are generally open daily 10–6 and are closed on Monday; many stop selling admission 30 minutes before closing. Note that some museums change their opening and closing times by an hour or so at the beginning and end of peak seasons based on visitor traffic; it's prudent to double-check hours. Many have free admission one day a week; see individual listings in tours below, but double-check, as the days tend to change. **Department stores** are open weekdays 10–5 or 6, Saturday until 1. **Grocery stores** are generally open weekdays 7–6 or 7, Saturday until 1; **"nonstops"** or *éjjeli-nappali* (24-hour convenience stores) are (theoretically) open 24 hours.

Shopping
SALES-TAX REFUNDS
You are entitled to a VAT refund on new goods (i.e., not works of art, antiques, or objects of museum value) valued at more than 50,000 Ft. (VAT inclusive). Cash refunds are given only in forints. If you made your purchases by credit card, you can file for a credit to your card or to your bank account (again in forints), but this process is slow at best. If you intend to apply for the credit, make sure you get customs to stamp the original purchase invoice before you leave the country. For more information pick up a tax refund brochure from any tourist office or hotel, or contact **Intel Trade Rt.** (⊠ Budapest I, Csalogány u. 6-10, ☎ 1/201–8120 or 1/356–9800) or **Global Refund Magyarország Rt.** (⊠ Budapest II, Bég u. 3–5, ☎ 1/212–4906).

Telephoning
COUNTRY CODE
The country code for Hungary is 36.

INTERNATIONAL CALLS

Direct calls to foreign countries can be made from Budapest and all major provincial towns by dialing 00 and waiting for the international dialing tone; on pay phones the initial charge is 60 Ft. To reach an **AT&T** long-distance operator, dial 00–800–01111; for **MCI,** dial 00–800–01411; for **Sprint,** dial 00–800–01877.

LOCAL CALLS

The cost of a three-minute local call is 20 Ft. Pay phones use 10, 20, and 50 Ft. coins. Most towns in Hungary can be dialed direct—dial 06 and wait for the buzzing tone, then dial the local number. It is unnecessary to use the city code, 1, when dialing within Budapest.

Gray, card-operated telephones are common in Budapest and the Balaton region. The cards—available at post offices, newsstands, and kiosks—come in units of 50 (800 Ft.) and 120 (1,800 Ft.) calls.

While Hungary's telephone system continues to be modernized, phone numbers are subject to change—usually without forewarning and sometimes several times. A recording in Hungarian and English may provide the new number. If you're having trouble getting through, ask your concierge to check the number.

OPERATORS

Operator-assisted international calls can be made by dialing 190; for operator-assisted calls within Hungary, dial 191. Dial 198 for directory assistance throughout the country. Operators are unlikely to speak English. A safer bet is to consult *The Phone Book,* an English-language yellow pages–style telephone directory that also has cultural and tourist information; it's free in most major hotels, at many restaurants, and at English-language bookstores.

Transportation

Roman numeral prefixes in Budapest addresses refer to one of the city's 22 districts. (Full postal addresses do not cite a Roman numeral, as the district is indicated by the zip code.) Getting around is easier if you learn a few basic terms: *utca* (abbreviated *u.*) and *út,* which mean "street" and "road," respectively; *tér* or *tere* (square); and *körút* (ring).

BY BICYCLE

A land of rolling hills and flat plains, Hungary lends itself to bicycling. For brochures and general information on bicycling conditions and suggested routes, try Tourinform (☞ Visitor Information, *below*) or contact the **Magyar Kerékpáros Túrázók Szövetsége** (Bicycle Touring Association of Hungary; ⊠ V, Bajcsy-Zsilinszky út 31, 2nd floor, apt. 3, H-1052 Budapest, ☎ 1/332–7177).

BY BOAT

Boat travel is possible in many parts of Hungary. Budapest, of course, straddles a major international waterway—the Danube. Vienna is six hours away by hydrofoil, and many Hungarian resorts are accessible by either hydrofoil or boat. For information about excursions or pleasure cruises, contact **MAHART Tours** (⊠ V, Belgrád rakpart, H-1056 Budapest, ☎ 1/318–1704 or 1/318–1586).

BY BUS

Long-distance buses link Budapest with many main cities in Eastern and Western Europe. Services to the eastern part of the country leave from Népstadion station (⊠ IX, Hungária körút 46–48, ☎ 1/252–4496). Buses to the west and south leave from the main Volán bus station (⊠ V, Erzsébet tér, ☎ 1/317–2966) in the Inner City. Buses are inexpensive and tend to be crowded, so reserve your seat.

BY CAR

To drive in Hungary, U.S. and Canadian visitors are supposed to have an International Driver's License—although their domestic licenses are usually accepted—and U.K. visitors may use their own domestic licenses.

Breakdowns. The Magyar Autó Klub (Hungarian Automobile Club; ⊠ Budapest XIV, Francia út 38/B, ☎ 1/212–2821) runs a 24-hour "Yellow Angels" breakdown service.

Gasoline. Gas stations are plentiful in and around major cities, and major chains have opened modern full-service stations on highways in the provinces. A gallon of *ólommentes benzin* (unleaded gasoline) costs about 180 Ft. per liter and is usually available at all stations, as is diesel.

Road Conditions. There are three classes of roads: highways or "motorways" (designated by the letter M and a single digit), secondary roads (designated by a two-digit number), and minor roads (designated by a three-digit number). Highways and secondary roads are generally well maintained. Minor roads vary; tractors and horse-drawn carts may slow you down in rural areas. Tolls on major highways help fund the upgrading of many of the country's motorways.

Rules of the Road. Drive on the right. Unless otherwise noted, the speed limit in developed areas is 50 kph (30 mph), on main roads 80–100 kph (50–62 mph), and on highways 120 kph (75 mph). Keep alert: Speed limit signs are scarce compared to those in the United States. Seat belts are compulsory, as is the use of headlights (except in developed areas), and drinking alcohol is prohibited—there is a zero tolerance policy, and the penalties are severe.

BY TRAIN

Travel by train from Budapest to other large cities or to Lake Balaton is cheap and efficient. Remember to take a *gyorsvonat* (express train) and not a *személyvonat* (local), which can be extremely slow. A *helyjegy* (seat reservation), which costs about 350 Ft., is advisable for all Inter-City trains, which provide rapid, express service among Hungary's major cities.

Only Hungarian citizens are entitled to student discounts; non-Hungarian senior citizens (men over 60, women over 55), however, are eligible for a 20% discount. For more information about rail travel contact the MÁV Passenger Service (⊠ Budapest VI, Andrássy út 35; ☎ 1/461–5500 international information; ☎ 1/461–5400 domestic information).

Visas

Only a valid passport is required of U.S., British, and Canadian citizens. For additional information contact the **Hungarian Embassy** in the United States (⊠ 3910 Shoemaker St. NW, Washington, DC 20008, ☎ 202/362–6730), in Canada (⊠ 299 Waverley St. Ottawa, Ontario K2P 0V9, ☎ 613/230–9614), in London (⊠ 35b Eaton Pl., London SW1X 8BY, ☎ 0171/235–5218), or in Australia (⊠ 17 Beale Crescent Deakin Act., Canberra 2600, ☎ 6126/282–3226).

Visitor Information

Tourinform (⊠ Sütő u. 2, H-1052 Budapest, ☎ 1/317–9800).

Weather

Many of Hungary's major fairs and festivals take place in the spring and fall. During July and August, Budapest can be hot and the resorts at Lake Balaton crowded, so spring (May) and the end of summer (September) are the ideal times to visit.

CLIMATE

The following are average daily maximum and minimum temperatures for Budapest.

Jan.	34F	1C	May	72F	22C	Sept.	73F	23C
	25	– 4		52	11		54	12
Feb.	39F	4C	June	79F	26C	Oct.	61F	16C
	28	– 2		59	15		45	7
Mar.	50F	10C	July	82F	28C	Nov.	46F	8C
	36	2		61	16		37	3
Apr.	63F	17C	Aug.	81F	27C	Dec.	39F	4C
	45	7		61	16		30	– 1

BUDAPEST

Exploring Budapest

Budapest, lying on both banks of the Danube, unites the hills of Buda and the wide boulevards of Pest. Though it was the site of a Roman outpost during the 1st century, the modern city was not actually created until 1873, when the towns of Óbuda, Pest, and Buda were joined. The resulting capital is the cultural, political, intellectual, and commercial heart of the nation; for the 20% of the nation's population who live here, anywhere else is just "the country."

Much of the charm of a visit to Budapest consists of unexpected glimpses into shadowy courtyards and long vistas down sunlit cobbled streets. Although some 30,000 buildings were destroyed during World War II and in 1956, the past lingers on in the often crumbling architectural details of the antique structures that remain and in the memories and lifestyles of Budapest's citizens.

The principal sights of the city fall roughly into three areas, each of which can be comfortably covered on foot. The Budapest hills are best explored using public transportation. Many street names have been changed since 1989 to purge all reminders of the Communist regime—you can sometimes still see the old name, negated with a victorious red *x*, next to the new. The 22 districts of Budapest are referred to in addresses with Roman numerals, starting with I for the Várhegy (Castle Hill) district; V, VI, and VII indicate the main downtown areas.

Várhegy
Numbers in the margin correspond to points of interest on the Budapest map.

Most of Buda's main sights are on Várhegy (Castle Hill), a long, narrow plateau laced with cobblestone streets, clustered with beautifully preserved baroque, Gothic, and Renaissance houses, and crowned by the stately Royal Palace. Painstaking reconstruction work has been in progress here since the area was nearly leveled during World War II.

⑤ Hadtörténeti Múzeum (Museum of Military History). The collection here includes uniforms and regalia, many belonging to the Hungarian generals who took part in the abortive uprising against Austrian rule in 1848. Other exhibits trace the military history of Hungary from the original Magyar conquest in the 9th century up to the middle of this century. English-language tours can be arranged in advance. ⊠ *I, Tóth Árpád sétány 40,* ☎ *1/356–9522.* ۞ *Apr.–Oct., Tues.–Sun. 10–6; Nov.–mid-Dec. and Feb.–Mar., Tues.–Sun. 10–4. Closed mid-Dec.–Jan.*

★ ③ Halászbástya (Fishermen's Bastion). This wondrous porch overlooking Pest and the Danube was built at the turn of the century as a lookout tower to protect what was once a thriving fishing settlement. Its neo-Romanesque columns and arches frame views over the city and the river. ⊠ *I, Behind Mátyás templom.* ۞ *Free in winter.*

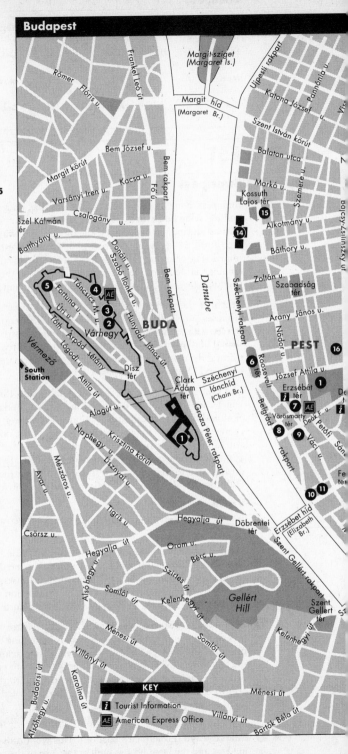

Budapest

KEY

ℹ Tourist Information

AE American Express Office

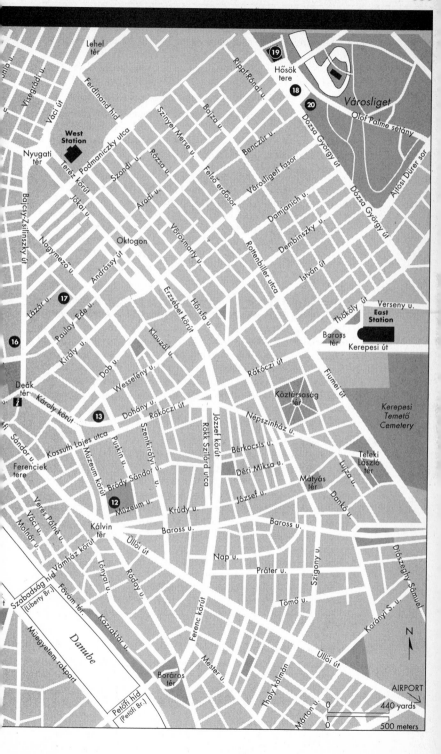

★ ❶ **Királyi Palota** (Royal Palace, also known as Buda Castle). The Nazis made their final stand here and left it a blackened wasteland. Under the rubble archaeologists discovered the medieval foundations of the palace of King Matthias Corvinus, who, during the 15th century, presided over one of the most splendid courts in Europe. The rebuilt palace is now a vast museum complex and cultural center. ⊠ *I, south of Szent György tér.*

In the castle's northern wing, the **Ludwig Múzeum** (Ludwig Museum) houses a collection of more than 200 pieces of Hungarian and contemporary world art, including works by Picasso and Lichtenstein. ⊠ *I, Buda Castle (Wing A), Dísz tér 17,* ☎ *1/375–7533.* ⊑ *Free Tues.* ☉ *Tues.–Sun. 10–6.*

The central section of the palace houses the **Magyar Nemzeti Galéria** (Hungarian National Gallery), which exhibits a wide range of Hungarian fine art. Names to look for are Munkácsy, a 19th-century Romantic painter, and Csontváry, an early Surrealist admired by Picasso. Tours for up to five people with an English-speaking guide can be booked in advance. ⊠ *I, Buda Castle (Wing C), Dísz tér 17,* ☎ *1/375–7533.* ☉ *Mid-Mar.–Oct., Tues.–Sun. 10–6; Nov.–mid-Mar., Tues.–Sun. 10–4; some special exhibits 10–6.*

The **Budapesti Történeti Múzeum** (Budapest History Museum), the southern block of the palace, displays a fascinating new permanent exhibit of the city's history from Buda's liberation from the Turks in 1686 through the 1970s. The 19th- and 20th-century photos and videos of the castle, the Chain Bridge, and other Budapest monuments here can provide a helpful orientation to the city. Down in the cellars are the original medieval vaults of the palace, a palace chapel, and more royal relics. ⊠ *I, Buda Castle (Wing E), Szt. György tér 2,* ☎ *1/375–7533.* ☉ *Mar.–mid-May, Wed.–Mon. 10–6; mid-May–mid-Sept., daily 10–6; mid-Sept.–Oct., Wed.–Mon. 10–6; Nov.–Feb., Wed.–Mon. 10–4.*

★ ❷ **Mátyás templom** (Matthias Church). This venerable church with its distinctive roof of colored, diamond-pattern tiles and skeletal Gothic spire dates from the 13th century. Built as a mosque by the Turks, it was destroyed and reconstructed during the 19th century, only to be bombed during World War II. Only the south porch survives from the original structure. The Habsburg emperors were crowned kings of Hungary here, the last of them, Charles IV, in 1916. High mass is held every Sunday at 10 AM with an orchestra and choir, and organ concerts are often held in the summer on Friday at 8 PM. Visitors are asked to remain at the back of the church during services (it's least intrusive to come after 9:30 AM weekdays and between 1 PM and 5 PM Sunday and holidays). Saturday is a popular wedding day; visitors are asked to be respectful. ⊠ *I, Szentháromság tér 2,* ☎ *1/355–5657.* ⊑ *Free, except during concerts.* ☉ *Church: Daily 7 AM–8 PM; Treasury: Daily 9:30–5:30.*

❹ **Zenetörténeti Múzeum** (Museum of Music History). The handsome, 18th-century gray-stone palace that once belonged to the noble Erdődy family hosts intimate recitals of classical music and displays rare manuscripts and antique instruments. ⊠ *I, Táncsics Mihály u. 7,* ☎ *1/214–6770.* ☉ *Mid-Mar.–mid-Dec., Tues.–Sun. 10–6.*

The Heart of the City

Pest fans out from the Belváros (Inner City), which is bounded by the Kiskörút (Little Ring Road). The Nagykörút (Grand Ring Road) describes a wider semicircle from the Margaret Bridge to the Petőfi Bridge.

⓫ Belvárosi plébánia templom (Inner-City Parish Church). The oldest church in Pest dates from the 12th century. The structure incorporates a succession of Western architectural styles as well as preserving a Muslim prayer niche from the time when the Turks ruled the country. Liszt, who lived only a few yards away, often played the organ here. ⊠ *V, Március 15 tér 2.*

★ **Korzó.** This elegant promenade runs south along the Pest side of the river, providing views of Castle Hill, the Chain Bridge, and Gellért Hill on the other side of the Danube. ⊠ *V, from Eötvös tér to Március 15 tér.*

★ **⓱ Magyar Állami Operaház** (Hungarian State Opera House). Flanked by a pair of marble sphinxes, this 19th-century neo-Renaissance treasure was the crowning achievement of architect Miklós Ybl. It has been restored to its original ornate glory—particularly inside. The best way to view the inside is to attend a ballet or opera, but there are no performances from around mid-July to late September, except for the weeklong BudaFest international opera and ballet festival in mid-August. ⊠ *VI, Andrássy út 22,* ☎ *1/331–2550; 1/332–8197 for tours. Foreign-language tours (45 min) daily, 3 PM and 4 PM, meet at the Sphinx statue in front of opera house.*

⓬ Magyar Nemzeti Múzeum (Hungarian National Museum). The stern, classical edifice was built between 1837 and 1847. On its steps, on March 15, 1848, Petőfi Sándor recited his revolutionary poem, the *"Nemzeti Dal"* ("National Song"), declaring "By the God of Magyar, / Do we swear, / Do we swear, chains no longer / Will we wear." This poem, along with the "12 Points," a formal list of political demands by young Hungarians, called upon the people to rise up against the Hapsburgs. Celebrations of the national holiday—long banned by the Communist regime—are now held here (and throughout the city) every year on March 15. The museum's most sacred treasure, the Szent Korona (Holy Crown)—the one that looks like a great golden soufflé resting on a Byzantine band of enamel, pearls, and other gems—lies with a host of other royal relics in the domed Hall of Honor. The museum's epic Hungarian history exhibition includes exhibits chronicling the end of Communism and the much-celebrated exodus of the Russian troops. ⊠ *IX, Múzeum körút 14–16,* ☎ *1/338–2122.* ☉ *Mid-Mar.–mid-Oct., Tues.–Sun. 10–6; mid-Oct.–mid-Mar., Tues.–Sun. 10–5.*

❿ Március 15 tér (March 15 Square). This square is not particularly picturesque, but it commemorates the 1848 struggle for independence from the Hapsburgs with a statue of the poet Petőfi Sándor, who died in a later uprising. On March 15, the national holiday commemorating the revolution, the square is packed with patriotic Hungarians. ⊠ *V, end of Apácai Csere János u. just north of Erzsébet Bridge.*

⓭ Nagy Zsinagóga (Great Synagogue). Europe's largest synagogue was built between 1844 and 1859 in a Byzantine-Moorish style. Desecrated by German and Hungarian Nazis, it underwent years of massive restorations, completed in fall of 1996. Liszt and Saint-Saëns are among the great musicians who have played the synagogue's grand organ. ⊠ *VII, Dohány u. 2–8,* ☎ *1/342–1335.* ☉ *Mid-Mar.–Nov., Mon.–Thurs. 10–5, Fri. 10–3, Sun. 10–1. Closed Jewish holidays.*

★ **⓯ Néprajzi Múzeum** (Museum of Ethnography). Elegant both inside and out, this museum has impressive, exhaustive exhibits—captioned in English—of folk costumes and traditions. These are the authentic pieces you can't see in tourist shops. ⊠ *V, Kossuth Lajos tér 12,* ☎ *1/332–6340.* ☉ *Mar.–Oct., Tues.–Sun. 10–6; Nov.–Feb., Tues.–Sun. 10–5.*

⑭ **Országház** (Parliament). The riverfront's most striking landmark is the imposing neo-Gothic Parliament, now minus the red star on top. Still a workplace for the nation's legislators, it is open for tours only. ⊠ *V, Kossuth Lajos tér. For tours: IBUSZ Travel,* ☎ *1/317–8343.*

❻ **Roosevelt tér** (Roosevelt Square). On this picturesque square opening onto the Danube you'll find the 19th-century neoclassical **Magyar Tudományos Akadémia** (Hungarian Academy of Sciences), and the 1907 **Gresham Palota** (Gresham Palace), a crumbling tribute to the age of Art Nouveau. ⊠ *V, at Pest end of Széchenyi lánchíd (Chain Bridge).*

★ **Széchenyi lánchíd** (Chain Bridge). The most beautiful of the Danube's eight bridges, the Széchenyi lánchíd was built twice: once in the 19th century and again after it was destroyed by the Nazis. Luckily, its classic, symmetrical design was left unchanged. ⊠ *Spanning the Danube between I, Clark Ádám tér, and V, Roosevelt tér.*

⑯ **Szent István Bazilika** (St. Stephen's Basilica). Dark and massive, the 19th-century basilica is one of the chief landmarks of Pest. It was planned early in the 19th century as a neoclassical building, but by the time it was completed more than 50 years later, it was decidedly neo-Renaissance. The mummified right hand of St. Stephen, Hungary's first king and patron saint, is preserved in the Szent Jobb chapel; the guard will illuminate it for you for a minimal charge. A climb up to the cupola (or a lift on the elevator) affords a sweeping city view. As restorations are under way, with a target completion date of 2010, some part of the structure is likely to be under scaffolding when you visit. ⊠ *V, Szt. István tér,* ☎ *1/317–2859.* ⊙ *Church: Mon.–Sat. 7–7, Sun 1–7. Szt. Jobb Chapel: Apr.–Sept., Mon.–Sat. 9–5, Sun. 1–5; Oct.–Mar., Mon.–Sat. 10–4, Sun. 1–4. Cupola: Apr. and Sept.–Oct., daily 10–4:30; May–Aug., daily 9–6.*

❾ **Váci utca** (Váci Street). Lined with expensive boutiques and dozens of souvenir shops, this pedestrian-only thoroughfare is Budapest's most upscale shopping street, and one of its most kitschy tourist areas. Váci utca's stretch south of Kossuth Lajos utca was transformed into another pedestrian-only zone in 1996, making the total length extend from Vörösmarty tér to the Szabadság Bridge. ⊠ *V, south from Vörösmarty tér.*

❽ **Vigadó tér** (Vigadó Square). This square, opening onto a grand Danube view, is named for the **Vigadó concert hall** (☞ Nightlife and the Arts, *below*). The hall was built in an eclectic mix of Byzantine, Moorish, and Romanesque styles; the façade even draws upon the ceremonial knots from the uniforms of the Hungarian hussars. Liszt, Brahms, and Bartók all performed here. Completely destroyed during World War II, it has been faithfully rebuilt. ⊠ *V, off the Korzó, between Vigadó u. and Deák Ferenc u.*

❼ **Vörösmarty tér** (Vörösmarty Square). In this handsome square in the heart of the Inner City, street musicians and sidewalk cafés combine to make one of the liveliest, albeit sometimes too touristy, atmospheres in Budapest. It's a great spot to sit and relax—but prepare to be approached by caricature artists and money changers. ⊠ *V, at northern end of Váci u.*

Hősök tere and Városliget

⑱ **Hősök tere** (Heroes' Square). Budapest's grandest boulevard of music and mansions, Andrássy út, ends appropriately at this sweeping piazza flanked by the Szépművészeti Múzeum (☞ *below*) and the Műcsarnok (☞ *below*). In the center stands the 120-ft bronze **Millenniumi Emlékmű** (Millennium Monument), begun in 1896 to commemorate the 1,000th anniversary of the Magyar Conquest and now newly shining in celebration of yet another 100 years. Statues of Árpád and six other founders of the Magyar nation occupy the base of the monument, while Hungary's greatest rulers and princes stand between the columns on either side. ⊠ *VI, Andrássy út at Dózsa György út.*

㉑ Műcsarnok (Palace of Exhibitions). This striking 1895 structure on Heroes' Square schedules exhibitions of contemporary Hungarian and international art and a rich series of films, plays, and concerts. ⊠ *XIV, Dózsa György út 37,* ☎ *1/343–7401.* ☉ *Tues.–Sun. 10–6.*

★ **㉑ Szépművészeti Múzeum** (Fine Arts Museum). An entire section of this Heroes' Square museum is devoted to Egyptian, Greek, and Roman artifacts, including many rare pieces of Greco-Roman ceramics. The institution's collection of Spanish paintings is among the best of its kind outside Spain. ⊠ *XIV, Dózsa György út 41,* ☎ *1/343–9759.* ☉ *Tues.– Sun. 10–5:30.*

★ **Városliget** (City Park). Just behind Heroes' Square, this park harbors Budapest's zoo, the state circus, an amusement park, and the outdoor swimming pool of the Széchenyi mineral baths. Inside is **Vajdahunyad Vár** (Vajdahunyad Castle), an art historian's Disneyland, created for the millennial celebration in 1896 and incorporating architectural elements typical of various periods of Hungary's history all in one complex. ⊠ *XIV, between Dózsa György út and Hungária körút, and Vágány u. and Ajtósi Dürer sor.*

Elsewhere in the City

Aquincum. The reconstructed remains of the capital of the Roman province of Pannonia, dating from the 1st century AD, lie in northern Budapest's Óbuda district. A varied selection of artifacts and mosaics has been unearthed, giving a tantalizing inkling of what life was like on the northern fringes of the Roman empire. The on-site **Aquincum Museum** displays the dig's most notable finds. ⊠ *III, Szentendrei út 139,* ☎ *1/250–1650.* ☉ *Mid-Apr.–end Apr. and Oct., Tues.–Sun. 10– 5; May–Sept., Tues.–Sun. 10–6. Grounds open at 9.*

Jánoshegy (János Hill). A *libegő* (chairlift) will take you to the summit, the highest point in Budapest, where you can climb a lookout tower for the best view of the city. ⊠ *Take Bus 158 from Moszkva tér to last stop, Zugligeti út,* ☎ *1/395–6494 or 1/376–3764.* ☉ *Mid-May–mid-Sept., daily 9–5; mid-Sept.–mid-May (depending on weather), daily 9:30– 4. Closed alternate Mon.*

Szobor Park (Statue Park). For a look at Budapest's too-recent Iron Curtain past, make the 30-minute trip out to this open-air exhibit cleverly nicknamed "Tons of Socialism." Forty-two Communist statues and memorials that once dominated the city have been exiled here since the political changes in 1989. You can wander among mammoth figures of Lenin and Marx while listening to songs from the Hungarian and Russian workers' movement blaring from loudspeakers. To get here by public transport, take the yellow Volánbus from stall 6 at Kosztolányi Dezső ter. ⊠ *XXII, Balatoni út, corner of Szabadkai út,* ☎ ⬛ *1/227– 7446.* ☉ *Mid-Mar.–Oct., daily 10–dusk; Nov.–mid-Mar., weekends 10– dusk.*

Dining and Lodging

Private restaurateurs are breathing excitement into the Budapest dining scene. You can choose from Chinese, Mexican, Italian, French, Indian, or various other cuisines—there are even vegetarian restaurants. Or you can stick to solid, traditional Hungarian fare. Be sure to check out the less expensive spots favored by locals. If you get a craving for sushi or tortellini, consult the restaurant listings in *The Budapest Sun* or *Where Budapest* magazine (☞ Visitor Information *in* Budapest Essentials, *below*). For details and price-category definitions, *see* Dining in Hungary A to Z, *above*.

Some 30 million tourists come to Hungary every year, and the boom has encouraged hotel building; yet there is sometimes a shortage of rooms, especially in summer. If you arrive in Budapest without a reservation, go to the 24-hour Tribus Hotel Service or to one of the tourist offices at any of the train stations or at the airport. For details and price-category definitions, *see* Lodging *in* Hungary A to Z, *above*.

$$$$ ✕ **Gundel.** George Lang, Hungary's best-known restaurateur, show-
★ cases his country's cuisine at this turn-of-the-century palazzo in City Park. Dark-wood paneling, rich navy-blue and pink fabrics, paintings by exemplary Hungarian artists, and tables set with Zsolnay porcelain make the oversize dining room plush and handsome. Violinist György Lakatos, of the Lakatos Gypsy musician dynasty, strolls from table to table playing folk music. Waiters in black tie serve traditional favorites such as tender beef tournedos topped with goose liver and forest mushroom sauce or excellent fish specialties. ⊠ *XIV, Állatkerti út 2,* ☎ *1/321–3550. Reservations essential. AE, DC, MC, V. Closed daily 4–6:30.*

$$$$ ✕ **Vadrózsa.** This restaurant in a romantic old villa in Buda's exclusive Rózsadomb district is elegant to the last detail—even the service is white glove—and the garden is delightful in summer. Kitchen fortes include venison and a variety of grilled fish; the house specialty, grilled goose liver, is exquisite. ⊠ *II, Pentelei Molnár u. 15,* ☎ *1/326–5817. Reservations essential. AE, DC, MC, V. Closed daily 3–7 and mid-July–end July.*

$$$–$$$$ ✕ **Kacsa.** Hungarian and international dishes with a focus on duck are done with a light touch, with quiet chamber music in the background, in this small, celebrated restaurant just a few steps from the river. Try the crisp wild duck stuffed with plums. ⊠ *II, Fő u. 75,* ☎ *1/201–9992. Reservations essential. AE, DC, MC, V. Closed daily 3–6 and weekends lunch.*

$$$–$$$$ ✕ **Múzeum.** Named for its location just steps from the National Museum, this elegant salon with mirrors, mosaics, and swift-moving waiters serves authentic Hungarian cuisine with a lighter touch. The salads are fresh, the Hungarian wines excellent, and the chef dares to be creative. ⊠ *VIII, Múzeum körút 12,* ☎ *1/267–0375. AE. Closed Sun.*

$$$ ✕ **Kisbuda Gyöngye.** This Budapest favorite, hidden away on a small street in Óbuda, is filled with mixed antique furniture, and its walls are covered with a patchwork of antique carved wooden cupboard doors. Try the fresh trout smothered in cream sauce with mushrooms and capers. ⊠ *III, Kenyeres u. 34,* ☎ *1/368–6402 or 1/368–9246. Reservations essential. AE, DC, MC, V. Closed Sun.*

$$$ ✕ **Lou Lou.** Since it opened in 1995, this convivial bistro tucked onto
★ a side street near the Danube has been the hottest restaurant in Budapest. Framed prints, low lighting, and candles conjure a tasteful, elegantly romantic atmosphere. Blending local and Continental cuisines, the menu includes excellent rack of lamb and succulent fresh salmon with lemongrass; the Dijon-spiced venison fillets with wild berry sauce are a standout. ⊠ *V, Vigyázó Ferenc u. 4,* ☎ *1/312–4505. Reservations essential. AE. Closed daily 3–7; Sat. lunch; Sun.*

$$$ ✕ **Művészinas.** Walls hung with framed vintage prints and photos, antique vitrines filled with old books, and tall slender candles on the tables create a romantic, old-world ambience in this bustling, bistrolike restaurant in the heart of Pest. Dozens of Hungarian specialties fill the long menu, from sirloin "Budapest style" (smothered in a goose liver,

mushrooms, and sweet-pepper ragout) to spinach-stuffed turkey breast in fragrant garlic sauce. Crepes with a seasonal fruit sauce are a sublime dessert. ⊠ *VI, Bajcsy-Zsilinszky út 9,* ☎ *1/268–1439. Reservations essential. AE, MC, V.*

$$–$$$ ✕ **Bagolyvár.** George Lang opened this restaurant next door to his gastronomic palace, Gundel (☞ *above*), in 1993. The immaculate dining room with soaring beamed ceilings has a familial yet professional atmosphere, and the kitchen produces first-rate daily menus of home-style Hungarian specialties. Soups, served in shiny silver tureens, are particularly good. Musicians entertain with cimbalom (gypsy dulcimer) music nightly from 7 PM. In warm weather there is outdoor dining on a roomy back patio. ⊠ *VI, Állatkerti körút 2,* ☎ *1/343–0217. AE, DC, MC, V.*

$$ ✕ **Café Kör.** Vaulted ceilings, low lighting, wood floors with Oriental-★ style rugs render a warm and classy atmosphere. Service is excellent. The kitchen has won tremendous popularity for its lighter touch on Hungarian and Continental meat dishes and ample salads. Daily specials are listed in marker on a giant pad of paper on the wall. The Kör appetizer platter, generously piled with patés, brie, vegetables, goose liver, salmon, and more, is perfect for sharing. Avoid the tables by the bathroom doors and immediately at the entrance. ⊠ *V, Sas u. 17,* ☎ *1/311–0053. Reservations essential. No credit cards. Closed Sun.*

$–$$ ✕ **Náncsi Néni.** "Aunt Nancy's" out-of-the-way restaurant is irresistibly cozy. The dining room feels like a country kitchen: Chains of paprikas and garlic dangle from the low wooden ceiling and shelves along the walls are crammed with jars of home-pickled vegetables that you can purchase to take home. On the Hungarian menu (large portions!), turkey dishes are given a creative flair, such as breast fillets stuffed with apples, peaches, mushrooms, cheese, and sour cream. Special touches include an outdoor garden in summer and free champagne for all couples in love. ⊠ *II, Ördögárok út 80,* ☎ *1/397–2742. Reservations essential in summer. AE, MC, V.*

$ ✕ **Tüköry Söröző.** At this traditional Hungarian spot, courageous carnivores can sample the beefsteak tartare, topped with a raw egg; many say it's the best in town. ⊠ *V, Hold u. 15,* ☎ *1/269–5027. No credit cards. Closed weekends.*

$$$$ ▥ **Budapest Hilton.** Built in 1977 around a 13th-century monastery ★ adjacent to the Matthias Church, this perfectly integrated architectural wonder overlooks the Danube from the best site on Castle Hill. Every ample, contemporary room has a remarkable view; all were further improved by renovations in 1999. Service is of the highest caliber. ⊠ *I, Hess András tér 1–3, H-1014,* ☎ *1/214–3000; 800/445–8667 in U.S. and Canada,* FAX *1/488–6688. 295 rooms, 27 suites. 3 restaurants, air-conditioning. AE, DC, MC, V.*

$$$$ ▥ **Danubius Hotel Gellért.** Built in 1918 in the *Jugendstil* (Art Nouveau style), this grand old lady with its double-deck rotunda sits regally at the foot of Gellért Hill. One of Hungary's most prized spa hotels, it also houses wonderfully ornate thermal baths—free to guests. Rooms range from palatial suites to awkward, tiny spaces and have either early 20th-century furnishings, including some authentic Jugendstil pieces, or newer, more basic contemporary decor. Rooms that face the building's inner core are drastically less expensive, but cramped and viewless. Now part of the Danubius hotel chain, the Gellért has begun an ambitious overhaul, adding air-conditioning and refurnishing all rooms in the mood of the original eclectic-flourished Jugendstil. Inquire about completed rooms when you reserve. Breakfast is included in the room rates. ⊠ *XI, Gellért tér 1, H-1111,* ☎ *1/385–2200,* FAX *1/366–6631. 199 rooms, 13 suites. Restaurant, 2 pools. AE, DC, MC, V.*

$$$$ ⚏ **Hotel Inter-Continental Budapest.** Formerly the Forum Hotel, this
★ boxy, modern riverside hotel consistently wins applause for its superior business facilities, friendly service, and gorgeous views across the
Danube to Castle Hill. Sixty percent of the rooms face the river (and
are slightly more expensive than those that don't). The hotel café, Bécsi
Kávéház, is locally renowned for its pastries—and the hotel's fitness
facilities are similarly excellent. ☒ *V, Apáczai Csere János u. 12–14,
Box 231, H-1368,* ☎ *1/327–6333,* ℻ *1/327–6357. 392 rooms, 16 suites.
2 restaurants, air-conditioning, pool. AE, DC, MC, V.*

$$$$ ⚏ **Kempinski Hotel Corvinus Budapest.** Afternoon chamber music sets
★ the tone at this sleek luxury hotel, a favorite of visiting VIPs. Rooms
are spacious, with elegant contemporary decor accented by geometric
blond-and-black Swedish inlaid woods. The large, sparkling bathrooms
are the best in Budapest. ☒ *V, Erzsébet tér 7–8, H-1051,* ☎ *1/429–3777;
800/426–3135 in the U.S. and Canada,* ℻ *1/429–4777. 337 rooms, 28
suites. 2 restaurants, air-conditioning, pool. AE, DC, MC, V.*

$$$ ⚏ **Budapest Marriott.** At this sophisticated yet friendly hotel near
downtown Pest, every detail sparkles, including the marble floors and
dark-wood paneling in the lobby. Stunning vistas open from every guest
room, the ballroom, and even the fitness room. Most rooms have a
balcony. Fitness facilities are outstanding. ☒ *V, Apáczai Csere János
u. 4, H-1364,* ☎ *1/266–7000; 800/831–4004 in U.S. and Canada,* ℻
*1/266–5000. 362 rooms, 20 suites. 3 restaurants, air-conditioning.
AE, DC, MC, V.*

$$$ ⚏ **Danubius Grand Hotel.** Set on a car-free island in the Danube and
connected to a bubbling thermal spa (free for guests), the Danubius
(formerly Ramada) Grand feels removed from the city but is still only
a short taxi- or bus-ride away. This venerable hotel, built in 1873, has
been completely modernized, yet retains its period look, with high ceilings and old-world furnishings. Room prices include breakfast. ☒
XIII, Margit-sziget, H-1138, ☎ *1/329–2300; 1/353–3029 for reservations,* ℻ *1/329–3923. 164 rooms, 10 suites. Restaurant, pool. AE,
DC, MC, V.*

$$–$$$ ⚏ **Astoria.** Revolutionaries and intellectuals once gathered in the mar-
ble-and-gilt Art Deco lobby here. Rooms are Empire-style and renovations have not obscured their charm. In fact, the addition of
soundproofing was essential, as the Astoria stands at a busy downtown
intersection. Breakfast is included in the room rates. ☒ *V, Kossuth Lajos
u. 19–21, H-1053,* ☎ *1/317–3411,* ℻ *1/318–6798. 25 rooms, 5 suites.
Restaurant. AE, DC, MC, V.*

$$ ⚏ **Alba Hotel.** Tucked into an alleyway at the foot of Castle Hill, this
spotless, modern hotel is a short walk via the Chain Bridge from busi-
ness and shopping districts. Rooms are snug and quiet, with white and
pale-gray contemporary decor and quintessentially Budapestian views
over rooftops and chimneys. Half of the rooms have bathtubs. A buf-
fet breakfast is included in the room price. ☒ *I, Apor Péter u. 3, H-
1011,* ☎ *1/375–9244,* ℻ *1/375–9899. 50 rooms with bath, 45 with
shower. Air-conditioning. AE, DC, MC, V.*

$$ ⚏ **Victoria.** The stately Parliament building is visible from every room
★ of this relatively young establishment right on the Danube. The absence
of conventioneers is a plus, and the location—an easy walk from Castle Hill and downtown Pest—couldn't be better. Room rates include
breakfast. ☒ *I, Bem rakpart 11, H-1011,* ☎ *1/457–8080,* ℻ *1/457–
8088. 27 rooms, 1 suite. Air-conditioning. AE, DC, MC, V.*

$ ⚏ **Kulturinnov.** One wing of a magnificent 1902 neo-Baroque castle
★ now houses basic budget accommodations. Rooms come with two or
three beds and are clean and delightfully peaceful; breakfast is included in the rates. The neighborhood—one of Budapest's most famous
squares in the luxurious castle district—is magical. ☒ *I, Szenthárom-*

ság tér 6, H-1014, ☎ *1/355–0122 or 1/375–1651,* ⅋ *1/375–1886. 16 rooms. AE, DC, MC, V.*

$ ▦ **Molnár Panzió.** Fresh air, peace, and quiet reign at this immaculate guest house high above Buda on Széchenyi Hill. Rooms in the octagonal main house are polyhedral, clean, and bright; most have distant views of Castle Hill and Gellért Hill, and some have balconies. Eight rooms added next door in 1997 are more private and have superior bathrooms. Service is both friendly and professional, and the restaurant is first rate. A Finnish sauna and garden setting add to the pension's appeal. Eight rooms have air-conditioning. ✉ *XII, Fodor u. 143, H-1124,* ☎ *1/395–1873,* ☎ ⅋ *1/395–1872. 23 rooms. Restaurant. AE, DC, MC, V.*

Nightlife and the Arts

The Arts

The English-language *The Budapest Sun* lists some of the week's entertainment and cultural events. *Where Budapest,* free in most hotels, is a richer source, but only comes out once a month. Hotels and tourist offices distribute the monthly *Programme,* which contains details of all cultural events in the city. Buy tickets at venue box offices, your hotel desk, many tourist offices, or ticket agencies, among them the **National Philharmonic Ticket Office** (✉ V, Mérleg u. 10, ☎ 1/318–0281) and the **Vigadó Ticket Office** (✉ V, Vörösmarty tér 1, ☎ 1/327–4322).

Arts festivals begin to fill the calendar in early spring. The season's first and biggest, the **Budapest Spring Festival** (early to mid-March), showcases Hungary's best opera, music, theater, fine arts, and dance, as well as visiting foreign artists. The weeklong **BudaFest** opera and ballet festival (mid-August) takes place at the Opera House. Information and tickets are available from ticket agencies (☞ *above*).

CONCERTS AND MUSICALS

Several excellent orchestras, such as the Budapest Festival Orchestra, are based in Budapest. Concerts frequently include works by Hungarian composers Bartók, Kodály, and Liszt. **Liszt Ferenc Zeneakadémia** (Franz Liszt Academy of Music; ✉ VI, Liszt Ferenc tér 8, ☎ 1/342–0179) is Budapest's premier classical concert venue; orchestra and chamber music performances take place in its splendid main hall. Classical concerts are also held at the **Pesti Vigadó** (Pest Concert Hall; ✉ V, Vigadó tér 2, ☎ 1/318–9167). The **Régi Zeneakadémia** (Old Academy of Music; ✉ VI, Vörösmarty u. 35, ☎ 1/322–9804) is a smaller venue for chamber music. The 1896 **Vígszínház** (Comedy Theater; ✉ XIII, Pannónia út 1, ☎ 1/329–2340) presents mostly musicals. Operettas and Hungarian renditions of popular Broadway musicals are staged at the **Operett Színház** (Operetta Theater; ✉ VI, Nagymező u. 19, ☎ 1/332–0535).

OPERA AND DANCE

Budapest has two opera houses, one of which is the gorgeous neo-Renaissance **Magyar Állami Operaház** (Hungarian State Opera House; ✉ VI, Andrássy út 22, ☎ 1/331–2550). There's also the plainer **Erkel Színház** (Erkel Theater; ✉ VIII, Köztársaság tér, ☎ 1/333–0540).

From May through September, displays of Hungarian folk dancing take place at the **Folklór Centrum** (Folklore Center; ✉ XI, Fehérvári út 47, ☎ 1/203–3868). The Hungarian State Folk Ensemble performs regularly at the **Budai Vigadó** (✉ I, Corvin tér 8, ☎ 1/201–5846). There are regular participatory folk-dance evenings—with instructions for beginners—at district cultural centers; consult the entertainment listings of *Where Budapest* for schedules and locations, or check with a hotel concierge.

Nightlife

Budapest is a lively city by night. Establishments stay open well past midnight and Western European–style bars and British-style pubs have sprung up all over the city. For quiet conversation, hotel bars are a good choice, but beware of the inflated prices. Expect to pay cash for your night on the town. The city also has its share of seedy go-go clubs and "cabarets," some of which have been shut down for scandalously excessively billing and physical intimidation and assault. Avoid places where women lingering nearby "invite" you in, and never order without first seeing the price.

BARS

The most popular of Budapest's Irish pubs and a favorite expat watering hole is **Becketts** (✉ V, Bajcsy-Zsilinszky út 72, ☎ 1/311–1035), where Guinness flows freely amid polished-wood and brass decor. A hip, low-key crowd mingles at the stylish **Café Incognito** (✉ VI, Liszt Ferenc tér 3, ☎ 1/351–9428), with low lighting and funky music kept at a conversation-friendly volume by savvy DJs. **Café Pierrot** (✉ I, Fortuna u. 14, ☎ 1/375–6971), an elegant café and piano bar on a small street on Castle Hill, is well suited for a secret rendezvous.

CASINOS

Most casinos are open daily from 2 PM until 4 or 5 AM and offer gambling in hard currency—usually dollars—only. The **Gresham Casino** (✉ V, Roosevelt tér 5, ☎ 1/317–2407) is in the Gresham Palace at the Pest end of the Chain Bridge. Sylvester Stallone is alleged to be an owner of the popular **Las Vegas Casino** (✉ V, Roosevelt tér 2, ☎ 1/317–6022), in the Atrium Hyatt Hotel. In an 1879 building designed by the prolific architect Miklós Ybl, who also designed the Hungarian State Opera House, the **Várkert Casino** (✉ I, Miklós Ybl tér 9, ☎ 1/202–4244) is the most attractive in the city.

JAZZ AND ROCK CLUBS

A welcoming, gay-friendly crowd flocks to late-night hot spot **Café Capella** (✉ V, Belgrád rakpart 23, ☎ 1/318–6231) for glittery drag shows (held a few nights per week) and DJ'd club music. With wrought-iron and maroon-velvet decor, the stylish but unpretentious **Fél 10 Jazz Club** (✉ VIII, Baross u. 30, ☎ 06/60–318–467) has a dance floor and two bars on three open levels. **Made Inn** (✉ VI, Andrássy út 112, ☎ 1/311–3437), open Wednesday–Saturday, in an old stone mansion near Heroes' Square, has elaborate decor, a large covered-terrace bar, and a disco dance floor packed with local and international beautiful people.

Shopping

You'll find plenty of expensive boutiques, folk art and souvenir shops, and classical record shops on or around **Váci utca,** Budapest's pedestrian-only promenade. Browsing among some of the smaller, less touristy, more typically Hungarian shops in Pest—on the **Kiskörút** (Small Ring Boulevard) and **Nagykörút** (Great Ring Boulevard)—may prove more interesting and less pricey. Artsy boutiques are springing up in the section of district V south of Ferenciek tere toward the Danube and around Kálvin tér. **Falk Miksa utca,** north of Parliament, is home to some of the city's best antiques stores. You'll also encounter Transylvanian women dressed in colorful folk costume standing on busy sidewalks selling their own handmade embroideries and ceramics at rock-bottom prices. Look for them at **Moszkva tér, Jászai Mari tér,** outside the **Kossuth tér Metro,** and around **Váci utca.**

A good place for special gifts, **Holló Műhely** (✉ V, Vitkovics Mihály u. 12, ☎ 1/317–8103) sells the work of László Holló, a master wood craftsman who has resurrected traditional motifs and styles of earlier centuries. There are lovely hope chests, chairs, jewelry boxes, candlesticks, and more, all hand carved and hand painted with cheery folk motifs—a predominance of birds and flowers in reds, blues, and greens.

Stores specializing in Hungary's excellent wines have become a trend in Budapest over the past few years. Among the best of them is the store run by the **Budapest Bortársaság** (Budapest Wine Society; ⊠ I, Batthyány u. 59, ☎ 1/212–0262). The cellar shop, at the base of Castle Hill, always has an excellent selection of Hungary's finest wines, chosen by the wine society's discerning staff, who will happily help you with your purchases. Tastings are held Saturday afteroons.

Markets

The magnificent, cavernous, three-story **Vásárcsarnok** (Central Market Hall; ⊠ IX, Vámház körút 1–3) teems with shoppers browsing among stalls packed with salamis, red paprika chains, and other enticements. Upstairs you can buy folk embroideries and souvenirs.

A good way to find bargains (and adventure) is to make an early morning trip out to **Ecseri Piac** (⊠ IX, Nagykőrösi út—take Bus 54 from Boráros tér), a vast, colorful, chaotic flea market on the outskirts of Budapest. Try to go Saturday morning when by far the most vendors are out. Foreigners are a favorite target for overcharging, so prepare to be tough when bargaining.

Budapest Essentials

Arriving and Departing

BY BUS

Most buses to Budapest from the western region of Hungary and from Vienna arrive at **Erzsébet tér station** (⊠ V, Erzsébet tér, ☎ 1/317–2966) downtown.

BY CAR

The main routes into Budapest are the M1 from Vienna (via Győr), the M5 from Kecskemét, the M3 from near Gyöngyös, and the M7 from the Balaton region.

BY PLANE

The only nonstop service between Budapest and the United States is aboard **Malév** (☎ 06/40–212–121 toll free; 1/235–3804 for tel. sales and information). Tickets for this flight can also be booked through Delta Airlines, which purchases seats on the Malév flight.

Hungary's international airport, **Ferihegy** (☎ 1/296–9696), is about 22 km (14 mi) southeast of the city. All **Malév** flights operate from Terminal 2a; other airlines use the new Terminal 2b. For same-day flight information call the airport authority (☎ 1/296–7155), where operators theoretically speak some English.

Between the Airport and Downtown. Minibuses marked LRI CENTRUM-AIRPORT-CENTRUM leave every half hour from 5:30 AM to 9:30 PM for the Erzsébet tér station (Platform 1) in downtown Budapest. The trip takes 30–40 minutes and costs around 700 Ft. The modern minivans of the reliable **LRI Airport Shuttle** (☎ 1/296–8555 or 1/296–6283) take you to any destination in Budapest, door to door, for around 1,400 Ft., even less than the least expensive taxi—and most employees speak English. At the airport buy tickets at the LRI counter in the arrivals hall near baggage claim; for your return trip call ahead for a pick-up. There are also approved **Airport Taxi** (☎ 1/282–2222) stands outside both terminals, with fixed rates based on which district you are going to. The cost to the central districts is about 3,700 Ft. Going to the airport, the cost is 1,990 Ft. from Pest, 2,490 Ft. from Buda; call one day ahead to arrange for a pick-up.

BY TRAIN

Call the MÁV Passenger Service (☞ Transportation *in* Hungary A to Z, *above*) for train information. Call one of the three main train stations in Budapest for information during off-hours (8 PM–6 AM): **Déli** (Southern; ⊠ XII, Alkotás u., ☎ 1/375–6293), **Keleti** (Eastern; ⊠ VII, Rákóczi út, ☎ 1/313–6835), and **Nyugati** (Western; ⊠ V, Nyugati tér, ☎ 1/349–0115). Trains for Vienna usually depart from Keleti station, those for Lake Balaton from Déli.

Getting Around

Budapest is best explored on foot. The maps provided by tourist offices are not very detailed, so arm yourself with one from any of the bookshops in Váci utca or from a stationery shop or newsstand.

BY BICYCLE

On Margaret Island in Budapest, **Bringóhintó** (⊠ Hajós Alfréd sétány 1, across from the Thermal Hotel, ☎ 1/329–2072) rents four-wheeled pedaled contraptions called *Bringóhintós,* as well as traditional two-wheelers; mountain bikes cost about 650 Ft. per hour, 1,200 Ft. for 24 hours. For more information about renting in Budapest, contact **Tourinform** (⊠ V, Sütő u. 2, ☎ 1/317–9800).

BY PUBLIC TRANSPORTATION

The Budapest Transportation Authority (BKV) runs the public transportation system—the Metro (subway) with three lines, buses, streetcars, and trolleybuses—and it's cheap, efficient, and simple to use. Most of it closes down around 11:30 PM, but certain trams and buses run on a limited schedule all night. A *napijegy* (day ticket) costs about 700 Ft. (three-day "tourist ticket," around 1,400 Ft.) and allows unlimited travel on all services within the city limits. Metro stations or newsstands sell single-ride tickets for about 90 Ft. You can travel on all trams, buses, and on the subway with this ticket, but you can't change lines or direction.

Bus, streetcar, and trolleybus tickets must be canceled on board—watch how other passengers do it. Metro tickets are canceled at station entrances. Plainclothes agents wearing red armbands do frequent spot checks, often targeting tourists, and you can be fined 1,200 Ft. if you don't have a canceled ticket.

BY TAXI

Taxis are plentiful and are a good value, but be careful to avoid the also plentiful rogue cabbies. The city of Budapest recently established a tariff ceiling for taxi drivers. For a hassle-free ride, avoid unmarked "freelance" taxis; stick with those affiliated with an established company. Rather than hailing a taxi in the street, your safest bet is to do what the locals do and order one by phone; a car will arrive in about five to 10 minutes. The average initial charge is 120 Ft., to which is added about 130 Ft. per km (½ mi) plus 30 Ft. per minute of waiting time. The best rates are offered by **Citytaxi** (☎ 1/211–1111) and **Fötaxi** (☎ 1/222–2222).

Contacts and Resources

EMBASSIES

U.S. (⊠ V, Szabadság tér 12, ☎ 1/267–4400). **Canadian** (⊠ Mailing address: XII, Budakeszi út 32; ⊠ Street address: XII, Zugligeti út 51–53, ☎ 1/275–1200). **U.K.** (⊠ V, Harmincad u. 6, ☎ 1/266–2888). **Australian** (⊠ XII, Királyhágó tér 8–9, ☎ 1/201–8899).

Police (☎ 107). **Ambulance** (☎ 104 or 1/311–1666; 1/200–0100 private, English-speaking). **Doctor** (☎ 1/325–9999 private, English-speaking). **24-hour pharmacies** (**Gyógyszertár,** in Pest, ☎ 1/311–4439; in Buda, ☎ 1/355–4691).

ENGLISH-LANGUAGE BOOKSTORES

Bestsellers (⊠ V, Október 6 u. 11, ☎ 1/312–1295). **Central European University Academic Bookshop** (⊠ V, Nádor u. 9, ☎ 1/327–3096).

GUIDED TOURS

Boat. From late March through October boats leave from the quay at Vigadó tér on 1½-hour cruises between the railroad bridges north and south of the Árpád and Petőfi bridges, respectively. The trip, organized by **MAHART Tours** (☎ 1/318–1704), runs only on weekends and holidays until late April, then once or twice a day, depending on the season; the trip costs around 800 Ft.

Excursions. Excursions farther afield include daylong trips to the *Puszta* (Great Plain), the Danube Bend, and Lake Balaton. **IBUSZ Travel** (☞ Visitor Information, *below*) offers trips to the Buda Hills and stays in many of Hungary's historic castles and mansions.

Orientation. Cityrama (⊠ V, Báthori u. 22, ☎ 1/302–4382) offers a three-hour city bus tour (about 5,000 Ft. per person). Year-round, **IBUSZ Travel** (☞ Visitor Information, *below*) sponsors three-hour bus tours of the city that cost about 5,000 Ft; starting from Erzsébet tér, they take in parts of both Buda and Pest.

Special-Interest. IBUSZ Travel (☞ Visitor Information, *below*), Cityrama (☞ Orientation, *above*), and Budapest Tourist (☞ Visitor Information, *below*) organize a number of unusual tours, including horseback riding, bicycling, and angling, as well as visits to the National Gallery. These tour companies will provide personal guides on request. Also check at your hotel's reception desk. **The Chosen Tours** (⊠ XII, Pagony u. 40, ☎ FAX 1/355–2202) offers an excellent three-hour combination bus and walking tour (about $17), "Budapest Through Jewish Eyes," highlighting the sights and cultural life of the city's Jewish community.

TRAVEL AGENCIES

American Express (⊠ V, Déak Ferenc u. 10, ☎ 1/235–4330). **Getz International** (⊠ V, Falk Miksa u. 5, ☎ 1/269–3728 or 1/312–0649). **Vista** (⊠ VI, Andrássy út 1, ☎ 1/269–6032 or 1/269–6033).

VISITOR INFORMATION

Tourinform (⊠ V, Sütő u. 2, ☎ 1/317–9800). **Tourism Office of Budapest** (⊠ VI, Liszt Ferenc tér 11, ☎ 1/322–4098, FAX 1/342–2541, info@budtour.hu; ⊠ VII, Király u. 93, ☎ 1/352–1433; ⊠ VI, Nyugati pályaudvar (Western Railway Station), ☎ 1/302–8580). **IBUSZ Travel** (main branch, ⊠ V, Ferenciek tere 10, ☎ 1/318–6866; 1/317–8343 or 1/317–7767 tours and programs; one central branch, ⊠ V, Vörösmarty tér 6, Budapest, ☎ 1/317–0532). **Tribus Hotel Service** (⊠ V, Apáczai Csere János u. 1, ☎ 1/318–4848 or 1/318–5776). **Budapest Tourist** (⊠ V, Roosevelt tér 5, ☎ 1/317–3555).

The English-language weekly *The Budapest Sun* covers news, business, and culture and carries tips for visitors. The monthly *Where Budapest* is another good source.

The Tourism Office of Budapest (☞ *above*) has developed the **Budapest Card,** which entitles holders to unlimited travel on public transportation; free admission to many museums and sights; and discounts on various purchases, entertainment events, tours, meals, and services from participating businesses. The cost is 2,450 Ft. for two days, 2,950 Ft. for three days; one card is valid for an adult plus a child under 14.

THE DANUBE BEND

About 40 km (25 mi) north of Budapest, the Danube abandons its eastward course and turns abruptly south toward the capital, cutting through the Börzsöny and Visegrád hills. In this area, the Danube Bend, are the Baroque town of Szentendre, the hilltop castle ruins and town of Visegrád, and the cathedral town of Esztergom.

Here, in the heartland, are traces of the country's history—the remains of the Roman empire's frontiers, the battlefields of the Middle Ages, and relics of the Hungarian Renaissance. Just 40 minutes or 21 km (13 mi) north of Budapest, Szentendre is a popular day trip. To visit the entire area, two days, with a night in Visegrád or Esztergom, would be a better way to savor its charms.

★ Szentendre

The lively, flourishing artists' colony of Szentendre was first settled by Serbs and Greeks fleeing the advancing Turks during the 14th and 17th centuries. The narrow cobbled streets are lined with cheerfully painted houses, many now containing art galleries. Unfortunately, tacky souvenir shops have appeared, and in summer, the streets swarm with tourists. Part of the town's artistic reputation can be traced to the ceramic artist Margit Kovács, whose pottery blended Hungarian folk art traditions with motifs from modern art. The **Kovács Margit Múzeum** (Margit Kovács Museum), in a small, 18th-century merchant's house, is devoted to her work. ⊠ *Vastag György u. 1*, ☎ *26/310–244*. ⊙ *Mid-Mar.–Oct., daily 10–6; Nov.–mid-Mar., Tues.–Sun. 10–4. Note: last tickets sold 30 min before closing.*

The **Szabadtéri Néprajzi Múzeum** (Open-Air Ethnography Museum) re-creates Hungarian peasant life and folk architecture of the 19th century. Crafts demonstrations are held in summer. ⊠ *Szabadság Forrás út*, ☎ *26/312–304*. ⊙ *Apr.–Oct., Tues.–Sun. 9–5.*

$$ ✕ **Rab Ráby.** This popular restaurant, decorated with wood beams and myriad eclectic antiques, is a great place for fish soup and fresh grilled trout. ⊠ *Péter Pál u. 1*, ☎ *26/310–819. Reservations essential in summer. No credit cards.*

$$ 🏠 **Bükkös Panzió.** Impeccably clean, this stylishly modernized old house is on a small canal just a few minutes' walk from the town center. The narrow staircase and small rooms give it a homey feel. Rates include breakfast. ⊠ *Bükkös part 16, H-2000*, ☎ *26/312–021*, ☎ FAX *26/310–782. 16 rooms. Restaurant. MC, V.*

Visegrád

This hilly village presided over by a mountaintop fortress was the seat of the kings of Hungary during the 14th century. The ruins of the palace of King Matthias on the main street have been excavated and reconstructed; there are jousting tournaments on the grounds of the fortress in June and a medieval festival in July. A winding road leads up to the haunting late-medieval fortress, **Fellegvár** (Citadel), from which you have a fine view of the Danube Bend. ☎ *26/398–101*. ⊙ *Mid-Mar.–Oct., daily 10–5; Nov.–mid-Mar., weekends 10–dusk, in good weather.*

$$$ 🏠 **Silvanus.** Set high up on Fekete hill, this hotel is renowned for its spectacular views and offers hiking trails through the forest. Rooms are bright and clean. A buffet breakfast is included in the rates. ⊠ *Feketehegy, H-2025*, ☎ FAX *26/398–311 or 26/398–170. 88 rooms, 5 suites. Restaurant. AE, MC, V.*

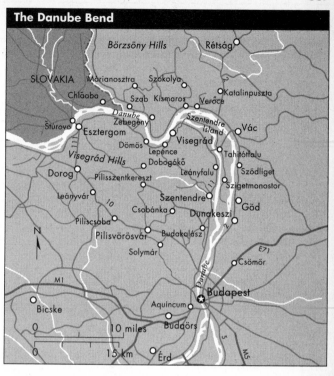

The Danube Bend

$ 🏠 **Haus Honti.** This intimate, alpine-style pension, named for its owner, József Honti, is in a quiet neighborhood close to the Danube ferry. A stream running near the house amplifies the country atmosphere. ✉ *Fő u. 66 H-2025,* ☎ FAX *26/398–120. 27 rooms. No credit cards.*

Esztergom

This primarily Baroque town stands on the site of a Roman fortress. St. Stephen, the first Christian king of Hungary, was crowned here in the year 1000. The kings are long gone, but Esztergom is still the home of the archbishop of Esztergom, the cardinal primate, head of the Catholic church in Hungary.

★ Thousands of pilgrims visit the imposing **Bazilika** (basilica), the largest in Hungary, which stands on Vár-domb (Castle Hill) overlooking the town. It was here that the anti-Communist cleric, Cardinal József Mindszenty, was finally reburied in 1991, ending an era of religious intolerance and persecution. The cathedral also houses a valuable collection of ecclesiastical art. ✉ *Szt. István tér,* ☎ *33/411–895.* 🎫 *Free.* 🕐 *Mar.–Oct., daily 9–4:30; Nov.–Dec., Tues.–Sun. 11–3:30. Closed Jan.–Feb. and Good Fri./Sat.*

The **Keresztény Múzeum** (Museum of Christian Art) is in the Primási Palota (Primate's Palace). It is one of the finest art galleries in Hungary, with a large collection of early Hungarian and Italian paintings. The Italian collection, coupled with the early Renaissance paintings from Flanders and the Lower Rhine, provides insights into the transition of European sensibilities from medieval Gothic to the humanistic Renaissance. ✉ *Mindszenty tér 2,* ☎ *33/413–880.* 🕐 *Mid-Mar.–Sept., Tues.–Sun. 10–6; Oct.–Dec., early Mar.–mid-Mar., Tues.–Sun. 10–5.*

$$ ✗ **Primáspince.** This restaurant's vaulted ceilings and exposed brick walls make a charming setting for refined Hungarian fare. Game dishes

are a specialty. ⊠ *Szt. István tér 4,* ☎ *33/313–495. AE, DC, MC, V. No dinner Jan.–Feb.*

$ ✕ **Fili Falatozó.** Be prepared for a hefty meat-and-potatoes meal. The location is on Esztergom's most pleasant old cobblestone street, just a short stroll from the Danube. ⊠ *Pázmány Péter u. 1,* ☎ *33/312–534. Reservations not accepted. No credit cards. Closed Jan.–Feb. and Mon. in Oct.–Mar.*

$$ ⛉ **Alabárdos Panzió.** Downhill from the Basilica, this cozy, remodeled house provides an excellent view of Castle Hill. Rooms (doubles and quads) are small, but less cramped than at other pensions. Breakfast is included in the rates. ⊠ *Bajcsy-Zsilinszky u. 49, H-2500,* ☎ ᴲᴬˣ *33/ 312–640. 21 rooms. No credit cards.*

$$ ⛉ **Ria Panzió.** In this small, friendly guest house near the cathedral, all rooms face a garden courtyard. Rates include breakfast. ⊠ *Batthyány u. 11–13, H-2500,* ☎ *33/313–115,* ᴲᴬˣ *33/401–429. 13 rooms. No credit cards.*

The Danube Bend Essentials

Getting Around

The best way to get around on the Danube is by boat or hydrofoil. The three main centers—Szentendre, Esztergom, and Visegrád—all have connections with one another and with Budapest. Contact MA-HART Tours (☎ 1/318–1704) for schedules. Regular bus service connects all three with one another and with Budapest. Szentendre is most easily reached by HÉV commuter rail, departing from the Batthyány tér Metro in Budapest; the trip takes about 40 minutes and costs around 250 Ft.

Guided Tours

IBUSZ Travel (☎ 1/317–8343 or 1/317–7767) organizes daylong bus trips from Budapest along the Danube stopping in Esztergom, Visegrád, and Szentendre. **Cityrama** (☎ 1/302–4382) runs full-day bus tours to Visegrád, Esztergom, and Szentendre, returning to Budapest by boat, from May through September on Saturday. Both tours include lunch and admission fees.

Visitor Information

Budapest (Tourinform, ⊠ V, Sütő u. 2, ☎ 1/317–9800). **Esztergom** (Grantours, ⊠ Széchenyi tér 25, ☎ ᴲᴬˣ 33/413–756; Komtourist, ⊠ Lőrinc u. 6, ☎ 33/312–082). **Szentendre** (Tourinform, ⊠ Dumsta J. u. 22, ☎ ᴲᴬˣ 26/317–965).

LAKE BALATON

Lake Balaton, the largest lake in Central Europe, stretches 80 km (50 mi) across western Hungary. It is within easy reach of Budapest. Sometimes known as the nation's playground, it helps to make up for Hungary's much-lamented lack of coastline. On its hilly northern shore, ideal for growing grapes, is Balatonfüred, the country's oldest spa town.

The national park on the Tihany Peninsula is just to the south, and regular boat service links Tihany and Balatonfüred with Siófok on the southern shore. This shore is flatter and more crowded with resorts, cottages, and high-rise hotels once used as Communist trade-union retreats. The south shore's waters are even shallower than those of the north: You can walk out for nearly 2 km (1 mi) before they deepen.

The region grows more crowded every year (July and August are the busiest times), but a few steps along any side road will still lead you

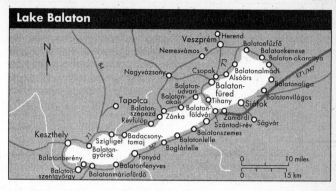

Lake Balaton

to a serene landscape of vineyards and old stone houses. A circular tour taking in Veszprém, Balatonfüred, and Tihany could be managed in a day, but two days, with a night in Tihany or Balatonfüred, would be more relaxed and allow for detours to Herend and its porcelain factory, or to the castle at Nagyvázsony.

Veszprém

★ Hilly Veszprém, though not on the lake itself, is the center of cultural life in the Balaton region. **Veszprémi Várhegy** (Castle Hill) is the most attractive part of town, north of Szabadság tér. **Hősök Kapuja** (Heroes' Gate), at the entrance to the Castle, houses a small exhibit on Hungary's history. Just past the gate and down a little alley to the left is the **Tűztorony** (Fire Tower); note that the lower level is medieval while the upper stories are Baroque. There is a good view of the town and surrounding area from the castle balcony. Tower: ⊙ *May–Oct., daily 10–6.*

Vár utca, the only street in the castle area, leads to a small square in front of the **Püspök Palota** (Bishop's Palace) and the cathedral; outdoor concerts are held here in summer. Vár utca continues past the square up to a terrace erected on the north staircase of the castle. Stand beside the modern statues of St. Stephen and his queen, Gizella, for a far-reaching view of the old quarter of town.

$ ✕ **Club Skorpio.** This city-center eatery might look like an Alpine hut, but the excellent menu offers grilled meats and specialties such as sliced duck breast in green peppercorn sauce. ⊠ *Virág Benedek út 1,* ☎ *88/420–319. No credit cards.*

$ ✕ **Diana.** Just a little southwest of the town center, it's worth the trip
★ if you want to experience the old-fashioned charm of a small provincial Hungarian restaurant. The fish and game specialties are always good. There is also a 10-room pension on the premises. ⊠ *József Attila u. 22,* ☎ *88/421–061. No credit cards.*

Herend

Herend is the home of some of Hungary's most renowned hand-painted porcelain. The Herendi Porcelángyár factory, founded in 1839, displays many rare pieces in its **museum.** The museum is closed for renovations from October 1999 until early May 2000. ⊠ *Kossuth Lajos u. 144,* ☎ *88/261–144.* ⊙ *Apr., Mon.–Sat. 8:30–4; May–Sept., daily 8:30–4; Oct.–mid-Dec. and Feb.–Mar., weekdays 10–3.*

Balatonfüred

Balatonfüred first grew famous as a spa catering to people suffering from heart disease, but thanks to its good beaches and proximity to Budapest, it's now the most popular resort on the lake. The town also lies in one of Hungary's finest wine-producing regions. In the main square, strong-smelling medicinal waters bubble up under a colonnaded pavilion. Down at the shore, the Tagore sétány (Tagore Promenade) is a wonderful place to stroll and watch the swans glide by.

$$ ✕ **Baricska Csárda.** From its perch atop a hill at the southwestern end of town, this rambling, reed-thatched inn overlooks vineyards toward the river. The hearty fare includes roasted trout and *fogas* (a freshwater fish of the Balaton region), and desserts crammed with sweet poppy-seed filling. In summer colorful Gypsy wedding shows are held nightly. ⊠ *Baricska dülő, off Rt. 71 (Széchenyi út) behind the Shell station,* ☎ *87/343–105. AE, V. Closed mid-Nov.–mid-Mar.*

$$ ✕ **Tölgyfa Csárda.** A prime hilltop location gives this tavern breathtaking views over the steeples and rooftops of Balatonfüred and the Tihany peninsula. The menu and decor are the equals of a first-class Budapest restaurant, and there's live Gypsy music in the evening. ⊠ *Meleghegy hill (at end of Csárda u.),* ☎ *87/343–036. No credit cards. Closed late Oct.–mid-Apr.*

$$$$ ▥ **Annabella.** The cool, spacious guest quarters in this Miami-style highrise are especially pleasant in summer. Overlooking the Tagore Promenade and Lake Balaton, it has access to excellent water-sports facilities. All rooms have balconies; for the best vistas, request a room on a high floor with a view of the Tihany peninsula. Room rates include breakfast. Five suites have air-conditioning. ⊠ *Deák Ferenc u. 25, H-8230,* ☎ *87/342–222,* ℻ *87/483–029. 383 rooms, 5 suites. 3 restaurants, 2 pools. AE, DC, MC, V. Closed mid-Oct.–mid-Apr.*

$$$ ▥ **Park.** Hidden on a side street in town but close to the lakeshore, this family-run spot is noticeably calmer than Füred's bustling main hotels. Rooms are large and bright, with high ceilings and tall windows. However, the decor is uninspired, Eastern Bloc style, with low, narrow beds and plain green and brown upholstery. Suites have large, breezy balconies but small bathrooms. ⊠ *Jókai u. 24, H-8230,* ☎ ℻ *87/343–203 or 87/342–005. 38 rooms, 3 suites. Restaurant. No credit cards. Closed late Oct.–late Mar.*

Tihany

★ A short trip by boat or car takes you from Balatonfüred to the **Tihanyi fél-sziget** (Tihany Peninsula), a national park rich in rare flora and fauna. As you walk from the ferry port, follow green markers to the Oroszkút (springs) or red ones to the top of Csúcs-hegy, where there is a great view of the lake.

★ The village of Tihany, with its **Bencés Apátság** (Benedictine Abbey), is on the lake's northern shore. The abbey building houses a **museum** with exhibits related to the Balaton area. Also worth a look are the pink angels floating on the ceiling of the abbey church. Organ concerts are held weekend nights in July and the first half of August. ⊠ *Első András tér 1,* ☎ *87/448–405 abbey; 87/448–650 museum.* ☉ *May–Sept., Mon.–Sat. 9–6, Sun. 11–6; Nov.–Mar., Mon.–Sat. 10–3, Sun. 11–3; Apr. and Oct., Mon.–Sat. 10–4:30, Sun. 11–4:30; open holidays year-round from 11 (after mass).*

$$ ✕ **Pál Csárda.** Two thatched cottages house this simple restaurant, where cold fruit soup and fish stew are the specialties. You can eat in the garden, which is decorated with gourds and strands of peppers. ⊠ *Visszhang u. 19,* ☎ *87/448–605. Reservations not accepted. AE, MC, V. Closed Oct.–Mar.*

$ ✕ **Halásztanya.** The location on a twisting, narrow street and evening Gypsy music contribute to the popularity of this restaurant, which specializes in fish. ⊠ *Visszhang u. 11,* ☎ *87/448–771. Reservations not accepted. AE, MC, V. Closed Nov.–Easter.*

$$$$ ⚅ **Kastély.** Lush, landscaped gardens surround this stately neo-Baroque
★ mansion on the water's edge. Inside, it's all understated elegance; rooms
have soaring ceilings and beautiful views. Next door, a newer, less attractive building houses the Kastély's sister, the Park Hotel, which has
less expensive but ugly rooms. Breakfast is included in the rates. ✉
Fürdőtelepi út 1, H-8237, ☎ *87/448–611,* FAX *87/448–409. 25 rooms,
1 suite. Restaurant. AE, DC, MC, V. Closed mid-Oct.–mid-Apr.*

$$ ⚅ **Kolostor.** Cozy, wood-paneled rooms are built into an attic above
a popular restaurant and brewery in the heart of Tihany village. Rates
include breakfast. ✉ *Kossuth u. 14, H-8237,* ☎ FAX *87/448–009. 5
rooms. Restaurant. MC, V. Closed Nov.–Mar.*

Lake Balaton Essentials

Getting Around

Trains from Budapest serve all the resorts on the northern shore; a sep-
arate line links the resorts of the southern shore. Highway 71 runs along
the northern shore; M7 covers the southern. Buses connect most re-
sorts, and regular ferries link the major ones. On summer weekends
traffic can be heavy, and driving around the lake can take quite a while;
because of the crowds, you should also book bus and train tickets in
advance. In winter, schedules are curtailed, so check ahead.

Guided Tours

IBUSZ Travel has several tours to Balaton from Budapest; inquire at
the main office in Budapest (☞ Visitor Information *in* Budapest Es-
sentials, *above*). Other tours more easily organized from hotels in the
Balaton area include boat trips to vineyards and folk music evenings.

Visitor Information

Budapest (Tourinform, ✉ V, Sütő u. 2, ☎ 1/317–9800). **Balatonfüred**
(Balatontourist, ✉ Tagore sétány 1, ☎ 87/343–471 or 87/342–822;
Tourinform, ✉ Petőfi u. 8, ☎ 87/342–237). **Tihany** (Tourinform, ✉
Kossuth u. 20, ☎ 87/448–804; Tihany Tourist, ✉ Kossuth u. 11, ☎
87/448–481). **Veszprém** (Tourinform, ✉ Óváros tér 2, ☎ 88/404–548).

Don't be fooled by its name. Iceland is anything but icy, with only about 10% of the country covered by glaciers. Considering the high latitude, summers in Iceland are relatively warm, and the winter climate is milder than New York's. Coastal farms lie in green, pastoral lowlands where cows, sheep, and horses graze alongside raging streams.

Iceland's chilly name can be blamed on Hrafna-Flóki, a 9th-century Norse settler who failed to store up enough fodder to see his livestock through their first winter. Leaving in a huff, he passed a fjord filled with pack ice and cursed the country with a name that has stuck for 1,100 years.

The second-largest island in Europe, Iceland lies in the middle of the North Atlantic, where the warm Gulf Stream from the south meets cold currents from the north, creating a choice breeding ground for fish, which provide the nation with 80% of its export revenue. Iceland itself emerged from the bed of the Atlantic Ocean as a result of volcanic activity, which is still going on. Every five years, on average, this fire beneath the earth breaks the surface in the form of an eruption, sometimes even below glaciers. The fiery forces also heat the hot springs and geysers that bubble and spout in many parts of the country. The springs, in turn, provide hot water for public swimming pools and heating for most homes and buildings, helping to keep the air smogless. Hydropower, generated by harnessing some of the country's many rivers, is another main energy source, so pollution from fossil fuels is at a minimum.

Except for fish and agricultural products, almost all consumer goods are imported, making the cost of living high. Economic stability and reforms in recent years, however, have been bringing prices down to make them competitive with the rest of Scandinavia and not so different from those of Europe in general.

The first permanent settlers came from Norway in 874, though a handful of Irish monks are thought to have arrived a century earlier. In 1262, Iceland came under foreign rule, by Norway and later Den-

Iceland (Ísland)

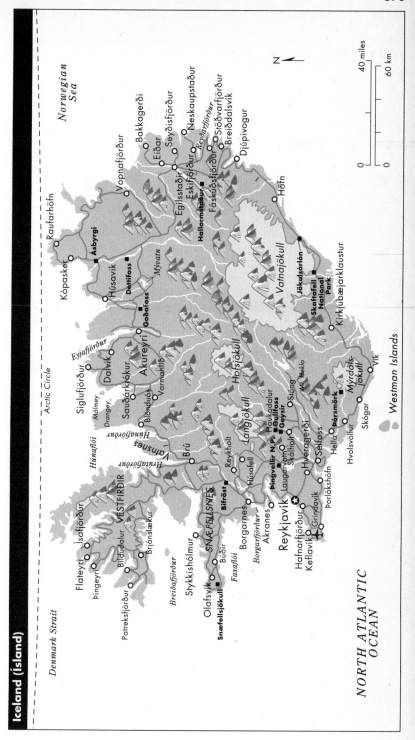

mark, and did not regain full independence until 1944. Today, almost 60% of the country's 273,000 people live in the greater Reykjavík area.

ICELAND A TO Z

Customs

Tourists can bring in 6 liters of beer or 1 liter of wine containing up to 21% alcohol, 1 liter of liquor with up to 47% alcohol, and 200 cigarettes.

Dining

Restaurants are small and diverse. You can expect superb seafood, beef, and lamb, and the fresh fish is not to be missed—surely some of the best you'll ever have. In addition to a growing array of award-winning cheeses, dairy products include the unique *skýr* (say skeer), a thick, creamy, protein-rich dairy product, which is available plain, or with various fruits. It's almost a staple, for many a busy Icelander virtually lives off skýr. Besides native cuisine, ethnic eateries range from Asian, Mexican, and Indian to French and Italian. Pizzas, hamburgers, and a tasty local version of the hot dog, with fried onions, are widely available. Most restaurants accept major credit cards.

MEALTIMES

Dinner, served between 6 and 9, is the main meal. A light lunch is usually served between noon and 2. Most restaurants are open from mid-morning until midnight.

RATINGS

The following ratings are for a three-course meal for one person. Prices include taxes and service charges but not wine or cocktails.

CATEGORY	REYKJAVÍK	OTHER AREAS
$$$	over IKr4,000	over IKr3,500
$$	IKr3,000–IKr4,000	IKr2,500–IKr3,500
$	under IKr3,000	under IKr2,500

WHAT TO WEAR

Neat, casual dress is acceptable in all but the most expensive restaurants, where jacket and tie are recommended.

Language

The official language is Icelandic, a highly inflected North Germanic tongue that is little changed from that originally spoken by the island's Norse settlers. In fact, an official committee invents new words for modern usage to keep Icelandic pure. Never fear though, English is widely understood and spoken, particularly by the younger generations.

Lodging

Hotels are clean, quiet, and friendly. Reykjavík and most villages also have guest houses and private accommodations.

If you tour Iceland on your own, get a list of hotels and guest houses in the various regions from the **Tourist Information Center** and additional lodging information from the **Iceland Tourist Bureau** (ITB; ☞ Visitor Information, *below*). Icelandair has now taken over operation of the former Edda hotels. A Sleep-As-You-Please voucher is available from **Samvinn Travel** (✉ Austurstræti 12, IS-101 Reykjavík, ☎ 569–1010 or 569–1070), entitling holders to stay at a selection of hotels and guest houses all over Iceland; it costs IKr10,000 for seven nights.

FARM HOLIDAYS

Farm holidays are an excellent way to become acquainted with Iceland: Some 120 participating farms are listed with **Icelandic Farm Hol-**

idays (✉ Hafnarstræti 1, IS-101 Reykjavík, ☎ 562–3640, FAX 562–3644).
Many offer fishing, guided tours, and horseback riding.

Information on the 30 hostels around the country can be obtained from
the **Icelandic Youth Hostel Association** (✉ Sundlaugavegur 34, IS-105
Reykjavík, ☎ 553–8110, FAX 588–9201).

HUTS
Outside Reykjavík, the **Icelandic Touring Club** (✉ Mörkin 6, IS-108 Reykjavík, ☎ 568–2533, FAX 568–2535) operates several variously spartan
huts for mountaineers and hikers in remote areas, available all year
except spring; club members get discounts and have priority.

RATINGS
Prices are for two people sharing a double room.

CATEGORY	REYKJAVÍK	OTHER AREAS
$$$	over IKr11,000	over IKr9,000
$$	IKr8,000–IKr11,000	IKr6,000–IKr9,000
$	under IKr8,000	under IKr6,000

Mail

POSTAL RATES
Airmail letters cost IKr65 to the United States and IKr45 to Europe.

RECEIVING MAIL
You can have your mail sent to the post office in any town or village
in Iceland. In Reykjavík, have mail sent to the downtown post office
(✉ R/O Pósthússtræti, IS-101 Reykjavík).

Money Matters

COSTS
As with many islands, Iceland is on the expensive side. Hotels and restaurants cost about 20% more in Reykjavík than elsewhere in the country. Ironically, though, prestige goods, such as Armani clothes, Rolex
watches, and top fashion labels in perfumes and jewelry, are often cheaper
once the value-added tax is refunded. The built-in airport departure
tax is IKr1,340.

CURRENCY
The Icelandic monetary unit is the króna (plural krónur), which is equal
to 100 aurar, and is abbreviated kr locally and IKr internationally. Coins
are the IKr1, 5, 10, 50, and 100. There are krónur bills in denominations of 500, 1,000, 2,000, and 5,000. At press time (summer
1999), the rate of exchange was IKr75 to the U.S. dollar, IKr51 to the
Canadian dollar, IKr117 to the pound sterling, IKr50 to the Australian
dollar, and IKr40 to the New Zealand dollar, but some fluctuation
occurs. No limitations apply to the import and export of currency.
Foreign currency is easily exchanged for krónur at Icelandic banks.
In fact, krónur are essentially unavailable abroad, so attempts to exchange at home are bound to be futile. Major credit cards are widely
accepted.

SAMPLE PRICES
Cup of coffee or soft drink, IKr150; bottle of beer, IKr300; sandwich
or snack, IKr300; 3-km (2-mi) taxi ride, IKr500.

TIPPING
Tipping is not customary in Iceland.

National Holidays

January 1; April 20–24 (Easter); April 20 (first day of summer—Icelanders are Europe's most optimistic nation); May 1 (Labor Day);

June 1 (Ascension); June 4 (Seamen's Day); June 11–12 (Pentecost); June 17 (National Day); August 7 (public holiday); December 24 (from noon)–26; December 31 (New Year's Eve, half-day off).

Opening and Closing Times

Banks are open weekdays 9:15–4. Some branches are also open Thursday 5–6. The **bank at Hotel Loftleiðir** (✉ Reykjavík Airport, IS-101 Reykjavík, ☎ 505–0900) is open weekends for foreign exchange only. Currency exchange is provided by **The Change Group** (✉ Bankastræti 2, Reykjavík, ☎ 552–3735), open May–September, daily 8:30–8, and October–April, 8:30–6. **Museums** are usually open 1–4:30, but some open as early as 10 and others stay open until 7. Some may be closed Monday. **Shops** are open weekdays 9–6 and Saturday 9–noon, and shopping malls Monday–Saturday 10–6. Grocery stores stay open later, including Sunday afternoon.

Shopping

SALES-TAX REFUNDS

A 24.5% *virðisaukaskattur* (value-added tax or VAT), abbreviated VSK, applies to most goods and services. It is usually included in prices; if not, that fact must be stated explicitly. Foreign visitors can claim a partial refund on the VAT, which accounts for 19.68% of the purchase price of most goods and services. Fifteen percent of the purchase price for goods is refunded, provided you buy at least IKr5,000 worth of goods at one time. Souvenir stores issue "tax-free checks" that allow foreign visitors to collect the VAT rebates; these rebates are obtained when departing, in the duty-free store at Keflavík Airport. To qualify, keep your purchases in tax-free packages (except woolens), and show them to customs officers at the departure gate along with a passport and the tax-free check.

Telephoning

Iceland's phone system is entirely digital and the country is part of the Nordic Automatic Mobile Telephone System (NTM) and the GSM global mobile phone network. Coverage for phones with NTM capability includes all but the highest remote glacial areas of Iceland, whereas the GSM system, as of press time, includes mostly the coastal populated areas around the country but is expanding incrementally. Mobile phones are ubiquitous. The ITT modem jack is fast becoming a standard connection in lieu of the Ericsson plug.

COUNTRY CODE

The country code for Iceland is 354. Iceland has only one area code, built in to the system; dial the seven-digit number immediately after the country code, without any extra numbers. All numbers outside Reykjavík begin with the number 4; numbers starting with 85 or 89 indicate mobile phones, which may have iffy reception if the location is remote.

INTERNATIONAL CALLS

For assistance with overseas calls dial 115; for direct international calls dial 00. To reach a long-distance operator in the United States from Iceland, you can use an international access code: **AT&T** (☎ 800–9001); **MCI** (☎ 999–002); or **Sprint** (☎ 800–9003).

LOCAL CALLS

Pay phones take IKr10 and IKr50 coins and are found in hotels, some shops, and post offices; bus station pay phones have become targets for vandals and may be nonfunctional. Outdoor telephone booths in towns and villages are sparse. Phone cards cost IKr500 and are sold at post offices, hotels, and some stores. For operator assistance with local calls dial 119; for information dial 118; for collect calls dial 115.

Transportation
BY BOAT

The **Herjólfur** (✉ Básaskersbryggja, IS-900 Westman Islands) ferry travels to the Westman Islands from Þorlákshöfn on the south coast. The **MS Fagranes** (☎ 456–3155) links several Western Fjord villages with Ísafjörður. The car and passenger ferry **Baldur** (at Stykkishólmur, ☎ 438–1120, FAX 438–1093; at Brjánslæk, ☎ 456–2020) links the Western Fjords with the village of Stykkishólmur on the Snæfellsnes peninsula of the west coast. The Faroese Smyril Line calls during summers at the east coast town of Seyðisfjörður, sailing from Bergen, Norway, Hanstholm, Denmark, and the Shetland Islands.

The East. In summer the North Atlantic ferry *Norröna* sails from the Faroe Islands, Denmark, and Norway to Seyðisfjörður (720 km/450 mi east of Reykjavík). For information contact **Smyril Line Passenger Department** (✉ Box 370, FR-110 Torshavn, Faroes). **Norröna ferðaskrifstofan** (✉ Laugavegur 3, IS-101 Reykjavík, ☎ 562–6362, FAX 552–9450) also provides information.

BY BUS

An extensive network of buses serves most parts of Iceland; services are intermittent in winter, and some routes are operated only in summer. Many cross-country buses have bike racks should weather or saddle leather become tiresome for bicyclists. Another option, the Air Bus Rover package, allows travelers to fly one way and return by coach. The bus network is operated from **Bifreiðastöð Íslands** (BSÍ, ✉ Vatnsmýrarvegur 10, ☎ 552–2300, FAX 552–9973); its terminal is on the northern rim of Reykjavík Airport. Guided bus tours are a good option (☞ Guided Tours *in* Reykjavík Essentials, *below*).

BY CAR

An international driver's license is required. Most of the Ring Road, which encircles the island, is two-lane asphalt. Other roads can be bumpy, often along gravel, dirt, or lava track—but the scenery is worth it. Be alert for loose livestock. Although rural service stations and garages are few and far apart, the main roads are patrolled, and fellow motorists are helpful. A four-wheel-drive vehicle is vital for remote roads such as those in the highlands, which may not be passable at all until early July. If you drive over the highlands, it is best to travel in convoy, especially when crossing unbridged rivers. For information on road conditions and the availability of gasoline off the beaten track, call **Vegagerð Ríkisins** (Public Roads Administration; ☎ 563–1500).

There are car rental agencies at Keflavík International Airport, in Reykjavík, and in many towns.

BY PLANE

Daily flights go to most of the larger towns. Although plane travel is a bit expensive, special family fares and vacation tickets are available, and stiffening competition had prices declining at press time.

Visitor Information
Tourist Information Center (✉ Bankastræti 2, IS-101 Reykjavík, ☎ 562–3045, FAX 562–3057). **Iceland Tourist Bureau** (✉ Skógarhlíð 18, IS-101 Reykjavík, ☎ 562–3300, FAX 562–5895). **Icelandic Tourist Board** (✉ Gimli, Lækjargata 3, IS-101 Reykjavík, ☎ 552–7488, FAX 562–4749; info@icetourist.is, http://www.icetourist.is).

Weather
Although it is a great year-round destination, Iceland is best for visiting from May to mid-November. From June through July, the sun barely sets. In December the sun shines for only three hours a day, but on clear,

cold evenings any time from September through March you may see the Northern Lights dancing among the stars.

Weather in Iceland is unpredictable: in June, July, and August, sunny days alternate with spells of rain showers, crisp breezes, and driving winds. Winter temperatures fluctuate wildly—it can be as high as 50°F (10°C) or as low as −14°F (−10°C).

CLIMATE

Iceland enjoys a temperate ocean climate with cool summers and relatively mild winters. The climate in the north is stable and continental, the south fickle and maritime.

Below are average daily maximum and minimum temperatures for Reykjavík.

Jan.	35F	2C	May	50F	10C	Sept.	52F	11C
	28	− 2		39	4		43	6
Feb.	37F	3C	June	54F	12C	Oct.	45F	7C
	28	− 2		34	7		38	3
Mar.	39F	4C	July	57F	14C	Nov.	39F	4C
	30	− 1		48	9		32	0
Apr.	43F	6C	Aug.	56F	14C	Dec.	36F	2C
	33	1		47	8		29	− 2

REYKJAVÍK

Reykjavík has a small, safe city center, clean air, and plenty of open spaces. Their diet of fresh local seafood from the pollution-free waters may give a clue to Icelanders' longevity and attractiveness as a people. For a city of 110,000, Reykjavík offers an astonishingly wide range of artistic events—the main cultural season is winter, but there's always plenty going on in summer as well. Reykjavík hosts a two-week arts festival in June (in even-numbered years), with a strong international flavor. Most nightlife is in or near the city center; it's liveliest on weekends, especially near the turn of the month when paychecks help fuel the festivities. If weather is good, this can make for a carnival-like atmosphere, with perhaps thousands spilling into Lækjatorg Square when pubs and restaurants begin closing at 3 AM. To limit the potential for crime in the center, video cameras have been placed at strategic intervals so police can monitor the situation.

Exploring Reykjavik

Numbers in the margin correspond to points of interest on the Reykjavík map.

Old Midtown, the capital's original core, is the city's highlight, with classic buildings, a park, museums, shops, galleries, and a plethora of cafés. Between the Second World War and the mid-'60s, a middle belt of residential neighborhoods, such as Vesturbæ, was established. Extending from the once separate community of Seltjarnarnes, well west of Old Midtown, to the salmon-populated Elliðaá River in the east, these areas have small, inviting parks. Many larger homes have established gardens with lovely flower beds and large trees, by Icelandic standards. Since the late '60s, distant suburbs, such as the intimidating Breiðholt, have sprung up as far as 8 km (5 mi) from the center of town. Recognizable by their large, modern apartment buildings, auto repair garages, office furniture stores, and the occasional small collections of convenience shops, these austere areas offer few attractions.

Old Midtown can be easily browsed on foot; if you prefer, the city's bus system is an efficient option. Sightseeing tours are also available.

⑯ Árbæjarsafn (Open-Air Folk Museum). This authentic "village" of relocated 18th- and 19th-century houses, 20 minutes southeast of downtown, is well worth the trip. ⊠ *Árbær, Bus 10 from Hlemmur bus station,* ☎ *577–1111.* ⊙ *June–Aug., Tues.–Sun. 10–6 and by appointment.*

⑫ Arnarhóll. A statue of the Viking **Ingólfur Arnarson,** Iceland's first settler in 874, dominates this hill, from which you can share his view of Reykjavík more than 1,100 years after his arrival. To the north is the ultramodern, glossy-black **Seðlabanki** (Central Bank). Behind Ingólfur is the copper-green **High Courts** building nestled beside the old **National Library** building, which dates from the beginning of the 20th century. ⊠ *Arnarhóll Hill.*

⑮ Ásmundarsafn (Ásmundur Sveinsson Sculpture Museum). Some originals by this sculptor (1896–1982), depicting ordinary working people, myths, and folktale episodes, are exhibited in the museum's gallery and studio as well as in the surrounding garden and chosen spots in Reykjavík. ⊠ *v/Sigtún, 5-min ride from Hlemmur Station on Bus 5,* ☎ *553–2155.* ⊙ *June–Sept., daily 10–4; Oct.–May, daily 1–4.*

★ ❶ Austurvöllur (East Field). This small square in Old Midtown is truly the heart of Reykjavík. The 19th-century **Alþingishús** (Parliament House), one of the oldest stone buildings in Iceland, faces the square. A heroic statue of Jón Sigurðsson (1811–79), the nationalist who led Iceland toward independence, stands in the square's center. ⊠ *Bounded by Kirkjustræti, Thorvaldsstræti, Vallarstræti, and Pósthússtræti.*

❼ Bernhöftstorfa. Picturesque, two-story, mid-19th-century wooden houses typify this small hill, which overlooks Lækjargata, the main street linking the peaceful park and Tjörnin Lake with the busy city center. ⊠ *Just east of Lækjargata and just south of Bankastræti.*

❷ Dómkirkjan (Lutheran Cathedral). This small, charming 18th-century stone church, with a treasured baptismal font carved by sculptor Bertel Thorvaldsen (1768/70?–1844), is a short block north from Tjörnin Lake. One corner of the lake is fed by warm water that does not freeze, creating an oasis for birds year-round. ⊠ *Austurvöllur,* ☎ *551–2113.* ⊙ *Mon. and Tues.–Fri. 9–5, Wed. 10–5 unless in use for services.*

⑲ Hallgrímskirkja (Hallgrím's Church). Forty years in the making, this church was finally completed in the 1980s. Its 210-ft gray concrete tower, visible from almost anywhere in the city, is open to the public, allowing a panoramic view of the city and its expansive suburbs. ⊠ *Top of Skólavörðustígur,* ☎ *551–0745.* ⊙ *May–Sept., daily 9–6; Oct.–Apr., daily 10–6.*

⑭ Höfði. Mikhail Gorbachev and Ronald Reagan met here for the Reykjavík Summit of 1986. Rumored to be haunted, the house is now city property, serving as a venue for special city business and receptions. It is decorated with some of the city's art holdings and open to the public in summer, on the first Sunday of each month. ⊠ *Near junction of Borgartún and Nótún.*

⑩ Íslenska Óperan (Icelandic Opera). Reminiscent of an old-fashioned movie house, this building was, in fact, Iceland's first cinema. The resident company performs here in winter. ⊠ *Ingólfsstræti,* ☎ *551–1475.*

⑰ Kjarvalsstaðir (Reykjavík Municipal Art Museum). This municipal art museum named for Jóhannes Kjarval (1885–1972), the nation's best-known painter, displays the artist's lava landscapes, portraits, and images of mystical beings. It also shows works by Icelandic contemporary

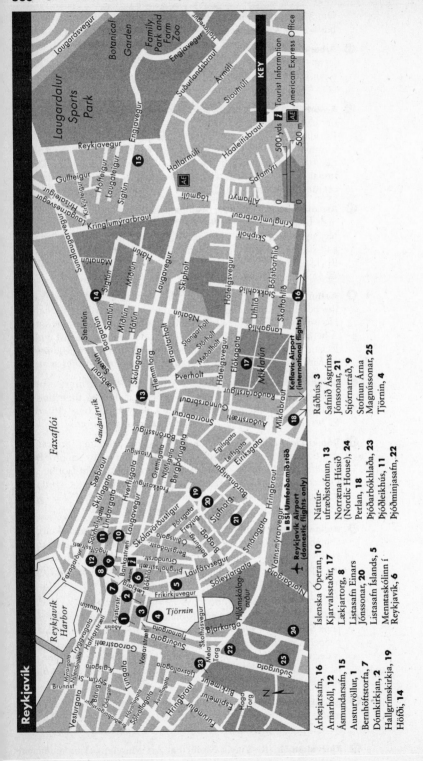

Reykjavik

580

Reykjavik Harbor

Faxaflói

Laugardalur Sports Park

Botanical Garden

Family Park and Farm Zoo

Tjörnin

→ Keflavik Airport (international flights)

→ Reykjavik Airport (domestic flights only)

■ BSI Umferðamiðstöð

Árbæjarsafn, **16**
Arnarhóll, **12**
Ásmundarsafn, **15**
Austurvöllur, **1**
Bernhöftstorfa, **7**
Dómkirkjan, **2**
Hallgrímskirkja, **19**
Höfði, **14**

Íslenska Óperan, **10**
Kjarvalsstaðir, **17**
Lækjartorg, **8**
Listasafn Einars Jónssonar, **20**
Listasafn Íslands, **5**
Menntaskólinn í Reykjavik, **6**

Náttúrufræðistofnun, **13**
Norræna Húsið (Nordic House), **24**
Perlan, **18**
Þjóðarbókhlaða, **23**
Þjóðleikhús, **11**
Þjóðminjasafn, **22**

Ráðhús, **3**
Safnið Ásgríms Jónssonar, **21**
Stjórnarráð, **9**
Stofnun Árna Magnússonar, **25**
Tjörnin, **4**

artists and great masters, as well as visiting art collections. ⊠ *Flóka-gata, Miklatún Park,* ☎ *552–6131.* ⊙ *Daily 10–6.*

⑧ Lækjartorg (Brook Square). Now a focal point in Reykjavík's other-wise rambling city center, this square opens onto **Austurstræti,** a semi-pedestrian shopping street. A brook once drained Tjörnin Lake into the sea (hence the name). ⊠ *Junction of Bankastræti and Lækjargata.*

⑳ Listasafn Einars Jónssonar (National Gallery of Einar Jónsson). Cubic and fortresslike, this building was once the home and studio of Iceland's leading early 20th-century sculptor (1874–1954). His monumental works explore profound symbolic and mystical subjects. The sculpture garden is always open. ⊠ *Njarðargata,* ☎ *551–3797.* ⊙ *June–mid-Sept., Tues.–Sun. 1:30–4; mid-Sept.–Nov. and Feb.–May, weekends 1:30–4.*

⑤ Listasafn Íslands (National Gallery). A collection of Icelandic art fills the stately white building overlooking Tjörnin Lake. ⊠ *Fríkirkjuve-gur 7,* ☎ *562–1000.* ⊙ *Tues.–Sun. noon–6.*

⑥ Menntaskólinn í Reykjavík (Reykjavík Grammar School). Many grad-uates from the country's oldest educational institution, established in 1846, have gone on to dominate political and social life in Iceland. ⊠ *Corner of Amtmannsstígur and Lækjargata.*

⑬ Náttúrufræðistofnun (Museum of Natural History). One of the last great auks is on display here, as well as several exhibits that focus on Ice-landic natural history. It is just across from the west entrance to the Hlemmtorg terminus of the city's bus system. ⊠ *Hlemmtorg, Hver-fisgata 116,* ☎ *562–9822.* ⊙ *Tues., Thurs., and weekends 1:30–4.*

㉔ Norræna Húsið (Nordic House). Designed by Finnish architect Alvar Aalto, this blue-and-white Scandinavian cultural center hosts exhibitions, lec-tures, and concerts; it has a library and a coffee shop. ⊠ *Sæmundargata,* ☎ *551–7030.* ⊙ *Coffee shop, daily 9–5; exhibitions, daily 2–7.*

⑱ Perlan. The gleaming glass dome perches like a space station high on a hill atop six huge hot-water towers that provide hot water for much of the capital area. The wooded slopes below draw walkers and run-ners. Two man-made geysers—one inside, which spouts about every five minutes, and Strókur on the south slope, which spouts, without pumps, on the same pressure and release system as in nature—com-plement the site. Also inside you'll find a balcony with splendid views, a coffee shop, an ice-cream bar, and a fine restaurant with the same name (☞ Dining and Lodging, *below*). ⊠ *Öskjuhlíð Hill,* ☎ *562–0200.* ⊙ *Daily 11:30–10.*

㉓ Þjóðarbókhlaða (National and University Library). Clad in red alu-minum, this edifice—completed in 1994—is hard to miss. It houses the substantial collection from the now-closed Landsbókasafnið (Old Na-tional Library). ⊠ *Arngrímsgata, corner of Suðurgata and Hringbraut,* ☎ *563–5600.* ⊙ *Weekdays 9–7, Sat. 10–5.*

⑪ Þjóðleikhús (National Theater). The interior of this basalt-black struc-ture reflects the natural polygonal lava columns occurring in Iceland. It is a venue for the biennial June Reykjavík Arts Festival and, from fall to spring, diverse cultural events and theatrical presentations. ⊠ *Hverfisgata 19,* ☎ *551–1200.*

㉒ Þjóðminjasafn (National Museum). On display are Viking artifacts, na-tional costumes, weavings, carvings, and silver works. It is closed for renovations until 2001. ⊠ *Suðurgata 141,* ☎ *530–2200.* ⊙ *After June 2000: Mid-May–mid-Sept., Tues.–Sun. 11–5; late Sept.–early May, Tues., Thurs., and weekends noon–5.*

❸ **Ráðhús** (Reykjavík City Hall). Inside are a tourist information desk, a large-scale relief map of Iceland, and a coffee shop. Modern architecture and nature meet here—not only at Tjörnin Lake (☞ *below*), but at the entrance from Vonarstræti; water seeping down one wall mimics nature, and moss clings to the stone structure. ⊠ *Bounded by Fríkirkjuvegur, Vonarstræti, and Tjarnargata,* ☎ *563–2000.* ☉ *Weekdays 8:20–4:15; coffee shop, weekdays 11–6, weekends noon–6.*

㉑ **Safn Ásgríms Jónssonar** (Ásgrímur Jónsson Collection). Works by this well-regarded post–Impressionist-period painter (1876–1958) are displayed in his house, left otherwise untouched since his death. ⊠ *Bergstaðastræti 74,* ☎ *551–3644.* ☉ *June–Aug., Tues.–Sun. 1:30–4; Sept.–Nov. and Feb.–May, weekends 1:30–4.*

❾ **Stjórnarráð** (Government House). Ironically once a jail, this white, 18th-century building now houses the offices of Iceland's prime minister. ⊠ *Lækjartorg, on seaward side of Bankastræti.*

㉕ **Stofnun Árna Magnússonar** (Árni Magnússon Manuscript Institute). Named for Árni Magnússon (1663–1730), who was instrumental in collecting and preserving priceless manuscripts, this facility houses what is arguably Iceland's greatest cultural treasure trove. Ancient volumes, some in calfskin or vellum and quite ornate, contain many of the sagas and much of the mythical poetry that established medieval Icelandic literature as some of the greatest in the world. ⊠ *Suðurgata, University of Iceland,* ☎ *525–4010.* ☉ *Mid-June–Sept., Mon.–Sat. 2–6 or by appointment.*

❹ **Tjörnin.** This natural, somewhat bottle-shaped shallow lake is a haven for a variety of birds, from majestic swans to elegant but tenacious Arctic terns. In colder winters, skaters venture out. At the southeast end of the lake, **Hljómskálagarður Park** is a fine spot to relax and breathe in the fresh air. ⊠ *Bounded by Tjarnargata on west, Fríkirkjuvegur/Sóleyjargata on east, and traversed at bottleneck by Skothúsvegur.*

Dining and Lodging

Most Reykjavík restaurants offer excellent seafood and lamb dishes. Winter menus often include sumptuous game, such as goose, ptarmigan, or reindeer. Lavish winter holiday buffets offer innumerable varieties of seafood, meats, and desserts. Evening reservations are necessary on weekends in the better restaurants. Some offer discount lunch specials or tourist menus. For details and price-category definitions, *see* Dining *in* Iceland A to Z, *above.*

Hotels run the gamut from elegant to simple, classic to modern. For details and price-category definitions, *see* Lodging *in* Iceland A to Z, *above.*

$$$ ✕ **Gallery at Hótel Holt.** The walls of this distinguished hotel dining room are covered with Icelandic art from the owner's private collection. You can indulge in such mouthwatering seafood as gravlax and grilled halibut, and there's a fabulous wine list to match. ⊠ *Holt Hotel, Bergstaðastræti 37,* ☎ *552–5700. AE, DC, MC, V.*

$$$ ✕ **Perlan.** In this rather formal revolving restaurant under the Perlan
★ dome, you may pay a bit more for the food—including Icelandic fish and lamb dishes—but the splendid view, especially at sunset, more than justifies the expense. ⊠ *Öskjuhlíð,* ☎ *562–0200. AE, DC, MC, V. No lunch.*

$$ ✕ **Oðinsvé.** On the ground floor of a hotel with the same name, this cozy restaurant serves Scandinavian-French–style fare, mostly seafood and lamb. ⊠ *Oðinstorg,* ☎ *552–5090. AE, DC, MC, V.*

$$ ✕ **Þrír Frakkar Hjá Úlfari.** Housed in an unassuming red building in an older part of town, this restaurant offers great beef dishes and unique seafood, including whale meat. The bright, cozy annex looks upon a tiny tree-filled park. ⊠ *Baldursgata 14,* ☎ *552–3939. DC, MC, V.*

$$ ✕ **Við Tjörnina.** The imaginative Icelandic seafood here includes marinated cod cheeks and *tindabikkja* (starry ray) with grapes, capers, and Pernod. It's on the second floor of a typical early 20th-century corrugated-iron–clad house. ⊠ *Templarasund 3,* ☎ *551–8666. AE, MC, V.*

$ ✕ **Hornið.** Pizzas and pasta are the draw, but good meat and fish dishes are also served at this cosmopolitan bistro. ⊠ *Hafnarstræti 15,* ☎ *551–3340. AE, DC, MC, V.*

$ ✕ **Potturinn og Pannan.** The service at this small restaurant on the edge of the downtown area is efficient and friendly. Lamb, fish, and American-style salads are the best bets. ⊠ *Brautarholt 22,* ☎ *551–1690. AE, MC, V.*

$$$ ▥ **Hótel Borg.** Elegant Art Deco rooms retain their original unique style but are equipped with many handy gadgets, including CD players and coffeemakers. ⊠ *Pósthússtræti 11, IS-101,* ☎ *551–1440,* 𝔽𝔸𝕏 *551–1420. 26 rooms, 4 suites. Restaurant, bar. AE, D, MC, V.*

$$$ ▥ **Hótel Esja, Icelandair Hotel.** Renovated in 1997, this hotel, with its Planet Pulse health facility, puts a strong emphasis on pampering its guests and is unique in offering a wide variety of exercise and spalike therapies, even personal trainers. Rooms in the box layer-cake building of blue panels and glass are appealingly decorated in neutral colors; those facing north have a view of the hotel's namesake mountain. ⊠ *Suðurlandsbraut 2, IS-108,* ☎ *505–0950,* 𝔽𝔸𝕏 *505–0955. 160 rooms, 12 suites. Restaurant. AE, DC, MC, V.*

$$$ ▥ **Hótel Holt.** One of Reykjavík's finest, the Holt has excellent service and an exquisite restaurant (☞ *above*). Rooms are on the small side but, like the aptly named Gallery Restaurant, they're warmed by works of leading Icelandic artists. It's in a central residential neighborhood. ⊠ *Bergstaðastræti 37, IS-101,* ☎ *552–5700,* 𝔽𝔸𝕏 *562–3025. 40 rooms, 14 suites. Restaurant. AE, DC, MC, V.*

$$$ ▥ **Hótel Reykjavík.** This hotel is convenient to the Reykjavík Municipal Art Museum. Its unimposing facade incorporates a vertical wedge of windows to channel light inward; rooms have smart Nordic-style furnishings. Under the same roof are a Korean café and a steak house—both good. ⊠ *Rauðarárstígur 39, IS-105,* ☎ *562–6250,* 𝔽𝔸𝕏 *562–6350. 53 rooms, 7 suites. 2 restaurants. AE, DC, MC, V.*

$$$ ▥ **Radisson SAS Hótel Saga.** All the rooms above the fourth floor in this business-oriented hotel have spectacular views. There is a full range of services, and the location is convenient to most museums, shops, and restaurants. ⊠ *Hagatorg, IS-107,* ☎ *552–9900,* 𝔽𝔸𝕏 *562–3980. 216 rooms. Restaurant. AE, DC, MC, V.*

$$ ▥ **FossHótel City Reykjavík.** On a quiet street, this hotel stands in a row of plain residential buildings a few minutes' walk from midtown. The rooms are modest but fully appointed and bright. The elevator is a plus. ⊠ *Ránargata 4A, IS-101,* ☎ *511–1155,* 𝔽𝔸𝕏 *552–9040. 31 rooms. Restaurant. AE, DC, MC, V. Closed winter.*

$$ ▥ **Hotel Garður.** A student residence, convenient to the National Museum, downtown, and other attractions, it is open as a hotel only in summer when students flee. The rooms are basic but modernized. ⊠ *Hringbraut, IS-107,* ☎ *551–5656. 44 rooms with shared bath and shower. AE, DC, MC, V. Closed winter. Book through Hotel Cabin,* ☎ *511–6030,* 𝔽𝔸𝕏 *511–6031.*

$$ ▥ **Hotel Leifur Eiríksson.** Opposite the entrance to the hilltop Hallgrím's Church, this utilitarian hotel is an easy walk from all the city's main attractions. ⊠ *Skólavörðustígur 45, IS-101,* ☎ *562–0800,* 𝔽𝔸𝕏 *562–0804. 29 rooms. Restaurant, bar. AE, DC, MC, V.*

$$ 🏨 **Lind.** The Lind indulges in few frills but offers plenty of clean rooms. It's near the Hlemmur bus station and is a 10-minute walk from downtown. ⊠ *Rauðarárstígur 18, IS-105,* ☎ *562–3350,* FAX *562–3351. 44 rooms. Restaurant. AE, DC, MC, V.*

$ 🏨 **Smárar Guest House.** Rooms here are simple and clean, with washbasins and access to a fully equipped kitchen. ⊠ *Snorrabraut 52, near Hlemmur bus station, IS-105,* ☎ *562–3330. 18 rooms without bath. MC, V.*

Shopping

The main shopping street starts at Lækjatorg (say, *Like*-ya-torg), heads up the hill as Bankastræti, and continues on to become Laugavegur, where Skólavörðustígur angles in, descending from the huge Hallgrímskirkja. Skólavörðustígur has been pleasantly reborn as a center for distinctive custom jewelry, Icelandic-designed fashions, arts, crafts, and leatherwork. Attractive Icelandic woolen goods and handicrafts are sold in shops on Aðalstræti, Hafnarstræti, and Vesturgata.

For bargain woolens, it might well be worth following Vesturlandsvegur about 25 minutes north from Reykjavík to the **Álafoss Verksmiðjusala** (Álafoss Factory Store; ⊠ turn right at third traffic circle in Mossfelsbær, ☎ 566–6303). At the **Handknitting Association of Iceland** (⊠ Skólavörðustígur 9, ☎ 552–1890), you can buy high-quality hand knits through a knitters' cooperative. **The Kringlan Mall** (⊠ jct Miklabraut and Kringlumýrarbraut) is an option for homesick mall rats. **Rammagerðin** (⊠ Hafnarstræti 19, ☎ 551–7910) stocks a wide range of Icelandic clothes and souvenirs. For other bargains, try the weekend **flea market** (⊠ Kolaportið, at harborside in the rear of the Customs House on Geirsgata) between 11 and 5.

Reykjavík Essentials

Arriving and Departing

BY PLANE

Flights from the United States and Europe arrive at **Keflavík Airport** (☎ 505–0500), 50 km (31 mi) south of Reykjavík. **Reykjavík Airport** (☎ 569–4100) is the central hub of domestic air travel in Iceland. For reservations and information, contact Air Iceland (☎ 570–3030) or Íslandsflug (☎ 561–6060).

Between Keflavík Airport and Downtown. Buses connect with all flights to and from Keflavík. The drive takes 45 minutes and costs IKr700. **Flybus,** from Reykjavík Excursions (☎ 562–1011), has terminals at Hótel Loftleiðir and Hótel Esja. **Taxis** are also available; they cost at least IKr4,500.

Getting Around

BY BUS

Midtown Reykjavík is served by two main bus stop zones: Lækjatorg and Hlemmur bus station. These punctuate the popular shopping street, Laugavegur, at its beginning and midpoint and are stops on routes to the suburbs and neighboring metro communities.

Buses run from 7 AM to around midnight, some slightly later on weekends. The flat fare for Reykjavík and suburbs is IKr120 for adults. Exact change is required. Strips of tickets are available from bus drivers and at bus stations. If you need to change buses (once, within a half hour), ask for a *skiptimiða* (free transfer ticket, pronounced *skiff*-tee-mee-tha).

Rates start at about IKr300; few in-town taxi rides exceed IKr700. **BSR** (☎ 561–0000 or 561–1720). **Bæjarleiðir** (☎ 553–3500). **Hreyfill** (☎ 588–5522).

Contacts and Resources

U. S. (✉ Laufásvegur 21, IS-101, ☎ 562–9100). **Canadian Consulate** (✉ Suðurlandsbraut 10, IS-101, ☎ 568–0820). **U. K.** (✉ Laufásvegur 31, IS-108, ☎ 550–5100).

Police, ambulance, and fire (☎ 112). **Doctors and dentists** (☎ 569–6600 or 552–1230). **Pharmacies** operate in shifts at night and on weekends; for information, ☎ 551–8888.

Bókabúð Steinars (✉ Bergstaðastræti 7, ☎ 551–2030). **Eymundsson-Penninn** (✉ Austurstræti 18, ☎ 511–1130 or 511–1140; ✉ Kringlan 4-6, South Mall, ☎ 533–1130). **Mál og menning** (✉ Laugavegur 18, ☎ 552–4240).

Guided tours can be an alternative to driving the rougher roads. Day excursions and longer journeys by coach and/or plane are an excellent way to relax and enjoy Iceland's spectacular scenery. Destinations include Akureyri, Mývatn, Höfn, Snæfellsnes, the Westman Islands, and the West Fjords.

Most longer tours operate between June and September and cost from IKr25,000 to IKr150,000 per person, including accommodations and three meals a day. On some tours you'll stay in hotels; on others you'll sleep in tents. Tours typically last from three to 19 days.

Tours can be booked from abroad through **Icelandair** (☎ 505–0200) or travel agencies. **Guðmundur Jónasson Travel** (✉ Borgartún 34, IS-105, ☎ 511–1515) is an experienced agency. The **Iceland Tourist Bureau** (☞ Visitor Information, *below*) is a well-established agency. For information on other tour operators, contact the **Icelandic Tourist Board** (✉ Gimli, Lækjargata 3, IS-101, ☎ 552–7488, FAX 562–4749).

Samvinn Travel (✉ Austurstræti 12, IS-101, ☎ 569–1010 or 569–1070, FAX 569–1095 or 552–7796). **Úrval–Útsýn Travel** (✉ Lágmúli 4, IS-108, ☎ 569–9300, FAX 588–0202).

The city-run **Tourist Information Center** (✉ Bankastræti 2, IS-101, ☎ 562–3045, FAX 562–3057). The private, commercial **Iceland Tourist Bureau** (✉ Skógarhlíð 18, IS-101, ☎ 562–3300, FAX 562–5895, itb@itb.is, http://www.arctic.is/itb/). The national, state-run **Icelandic Tourist Board** (✉ Gimli, Lækjargata 3, IS-101, ☎ 552–7488, FAX 562–4749, info@ icetourist.is, http://www.icetourist.is).

THE COUNTRYSIDE

Incredible natural contrasts appear throughout Iceland's beautiful countryside. Magnificent and diverse fjords impart a scenic wrinkle to all coasts excepting the south, which is marked with sprawling plains, foothills, and bizarre black sands crowned by pristine white glaciers. The interior highlands, a challenge to reach, are raw wonderlands of panoramas and solitude. You are never far from cool waterfalls, spurting hot springs, or snowcapped summits.

The amount of countryside you can cover naturally depends on time. Day trips from Reykjavík can easily be expanded to a few rewarding days in the neighboring southern or western regions. To circle the country via the Ring Road (Road 1), allow at least a week—this will give you time to explore some of the spectacular attractions along the way. There can be up to 80 km (50 mi) between towns and accommodations.

The South

You reach the rich piedmont and coastal farmlands of the south by descending the plateau east of Reykjavík along the Ring Road. Look sharp offshore toward the southeast on your way down, and you may see the Vestmannaeyjar (Westman Islands) in the distance on the horizon. This region, laced by major rivers with some of the country's best-known waterfalls, like majestic Gullfoss and wide-open Skógafoss, is charged with numerous hot springs, including Geysir, the original namesake of the spouting natural wonders.

Crowning the countryside are many noteworthy peaks. Mt. Hekla, once said to be where lost souls were banished, is alive and well—it last erupted in 1991. The volcanic network under Europe's largest glacier, Vatnajökull, is also active. Resulting meltwater from a 1996 eruption created a peculiar, though temporary, sculpture garden of ice. Still remaining are huge boulders and the vast, expanded black sands of Skeiðarásandur, which cover a sizable part of the central south coast. Skiers, snowmobilers, and ice climbers need not despair, as Vatnajökull is larger than all of mainland Europe's glaciers combined. Don't miss the unique geology and flora and fauna of Skaftafell National Park, Iceland's first, with Mt. Hvannadalshnjúkur, Iceland's highest peak, just beyond its borders.

Hveragerði

Hveragerði, about 40 km (25 mi) east of Reykjavík, has hot springs and fruit and vegetable greenhouses. An unabashed tourist stop is **Eden,** where homegrown bananas have astonished visitors for years. A newly opened art gallery, **Listaskálinn** (⊠ Austurmörk 2, ☎ 483–5071) shows local and traveling art and is a nice stop for coffee.

$$$ ☷ **Hótel Örk.** The rooms here are expensive, but meals in the ground-floor restaurant are reasonable. Three- to seven-day "spa cure" retreat packages are worthwhile. ⊠ *Breiðamörk 1, IS-810,* ☎ *483–4700,* ℻ *483–4775. 81 rooms. Restaurant, pool. AE, DC, MC, V.*

$ ☷ **Ból Youth Hostel.** Rooms in this standard youth hostel have one to five beds and kitchen facilities. There is also a guest house with doubles and a shower. ⊠ *Hveramörk 14, IS-810,* ☎ *483–4198,* ℻ *483–4088. 20 beds. MC, V. Closed mid-Sept.–mid-May.*

Selfoss

Selfoss, on the turbulent Ölfusá River, is the south's largest community. With many diverse services, it is home to the nation's largest dairy plant.

$$$ ☷ **Hótel Selfoss.** Just off the river, this hotel is a perfect base for sojourns to inland sites or to the coast. The restaurant is the town's best eatery. ⊠ *Eyravegur 2, IS-800,* ☎ *482–2500,* ℻ *482–2524. 20 rooms. Restaurant. AE, DC, MC, V.*

Skógar

Skógar, 120 km (75 mi) east of Selfoss, is a small crossroads settlement near one of the country's many spectacular waterfalls, **Skógafoss.** What you see from the roadside is actually the last in a long series of cascades and plunging rapids that reward the hiker.

$$ ▥ **Hôtel Edda Skógar.** Close to the Skógafoss waterfall, this airy summer hotel has views of the sea, mountains, and glaciers. ⊠ *Skógar, IS-861 Hvolsvöllur,* ☎ *487–8870,* ℻ *187–8870. 34 rooms without bath. Restaurant. AE, MC, V. Closed Sept.–May.*

Kirkjubæjarklaustur

Aptly named Kirkjubæjarklaustur (or church farmstead cloister) was the site of a medieval convent. When the volcano Laki erupted in 1783, it produced the greatest amount of lava from a single eruption in recorded history, its deposits greatly shaping the landscape. A tiny chapel commemorates the priest whose prayers are said to have stopped the lava before it reached habitation. Two waterfalls and an August chamber music festival are among local attractions. Visit the **Kirkjubæjarstofa** (Kirkjubæjar Center; ⊠ Klausturvegur 2, IS–880 Kirkjubæjarklaustur, ☎ 487–4645) for exhibits on regional nature and culture.

$$ ▥ **Hotel Kirkjubæjarklaustur, Icelandair Hotel.** This excellent facility is one of the few in the chain open year-round. For liquid and mealtime refreshment, head to the restaurant and bar in the newer building. ⊠ *Klausturvegur 6, IS-880,* ☎ *487–4799,* ℻ *487–4614. 73 rooms, 57 with shower. Restaurant, pool. AE, MC, V.*

Skaftafell National Park

From the foot of the Skaftafellsjökull you can pass over lowland sands into lush foothills to Svartifoss, with its polygonal lava sides, and up to hidden glacial canyons and stunning mountaintops. If you're lucky, you will glimpse Iceland's highest summit, Mt. Hvannadalshnjúkur, rising 6,950 ft just outside the park borders. About 32 km (20 mi) east of the park is the adventure world of the **Jökulsárlón**; you can tour the glacial lagoon's eerie ice floes by boat (☞ Guided Tours *in* The Countryside Essentials, *below*).

$$ ▥ **Hôtel Skaftafell.** Expanded in late 1998, this hotel has a setting near breathtaking Skaftafell National Park that is matched by few other Icelandic hotels. Rooms come in three price options: contemporarily furnished with private bath, spartan rooms without bath, and, lastly, similar rooms without bed linens for which you provide a sleeping bag. The latter two groups share bathrooms, but kitchen facilities are a plus. A travel shop, a gas station, and a campsite are also on the property. ⊠ *Skaftafell, Fagurhólsmýri, IS-785,* ☎ *478–1945,* ℻ *478–1946. 53 rooms, 43 with bath. Restaurant. MC, V.*

$ ⚠ **Skaftafell National Park Campground and Service Center.** This sprawling campground has excellent facilities. ⊠ *Skaftafell National Park, Rte 998 off Ring Road,* ☎ *478–1627. MC, V. Closed Sept.–June.*

Höfn

Höfn, the major port community of the southeast, offers a fine view of Europe's largest glacier, **Vatnajökull,** and the adjacent mountains.

$$$ ▥ **FossHótel Vatnajökull.** Though opened only in 1996, this hotel with spectacular views of the glacier already has a nationwide reputation for quality accommodations and excellent food, including fine meat and seafood. ⊠ *Lindarbakka, Hornafjörður, IS-780,* ☎ *478–2555,* ℻ *478–2444. 26 rooms. Restaurant. AE, DC, MC, V.*

$$$ ▥ **Hôtel Höfn, Icelandair Hotel.** A prominent hilltop location affords splendid views either to nearby mountains or to the sea from rooms furnished in contemporary Scandinavian decor. This clean and comfortable hotel has a restaurant with good service and tasty dishes, especially the lobster. You can order fast food at the grill. ⊠ *Hornafjörður, IS-780,* ☎ *478–1240,* ℻ *478–1996. 40 rooms, 32 with bath. Restaurant, grill. AE, DC, MC, V.*

Westman Islands

This cluster of islets off Iceland's south coast again became the focus of world attention as Keiko, the Orca whale that starred in the movie *Free Willy*, was brought to **Heimaey,** the largest of the Westman Islands. In a roomy sea-pen he has thrived from the day he arrived, chatting with dolphins, porpoises, and other small whales and re-learning how to catch his own food. Most of the 5,000 residents of the main isle of Heimaey have returned since the 1973 evacuation when the local volcano awoke rather violently after a nap of several thousand years. Heimaey has one of Iceland's best natural history museums, the **Fiska-og Náttúrugripasafn** (Fish- and Nature-Research Center); its fine research aquarium was a feature pivotal to returning the whale Keiko to the Icelandic waters from which he came in the 1970s. ⊠ *Heiðarvegi 12,* ☎ *481–1997.* ⊙ *May–Aug., daily 11–5; Sept.–Apr., weekends 3–5.*

On the first weekend of August, islanders celebrate the 1874 grant of Icelandic sovereignty with a huge festival in the town of Vestmannaeyjar, on Heimaey. The population and hundreds of visiting revellers move into a tent city in the **Herjólfsdalur** (Herjólf's Valley), a short distance west of town, for an extended weekend of bonfires, firewater, dance, and song.

The nearby isle of **Surtsey,** which erupted on the scene as a new island in 1963, is an ecological research preserve, closed to visitors.

The East

Numerous busy fishing towns and villages dot Iceland's east coast north of Höfn. As the names Stöðvarfjörður, Fáskrúðsfjörður, and Reyðarfjörður testify, each village has its own fjord. Farming thrives in the valleys, which enjoy almost Continental summers. The Ring Road ties the inland hub Egilsstaðir to the southeastern coastal villages, and secondary roads make outlying communities accessible.

Djúpivogur

Some of the oldest buildings in Djúpivogur, a fishing village since about 1600, date from the 1788–1920 Danish monopoly. Nearby, basaltic Mt. Búlandstindur, legendary as a force of mystical energy, rises to 6,130 ft.

$ ⌂ **Berunes Youth Hostel.** This small summer hostel offers lodging for 25 people in two-, three-, and four-person rooms. There are two separate cottages for five and seven people. ⊠ *Beruneshreppur, IS-765,* ☎ FAX *478–8988. 32 beds. No credit cards. Closed mid-Sept.–mid-May.*

$ ⌂ **Hótel Framtíð.** An annex and a larger dining room, all in warm, square-hewn Finnish timber, have refreshed this friendly harborside hotel. The newer rooms have a country look. ⊠ *Vogaland 4, IS-765,* ☎ *478–8887,* FAX *478–8187. 10 rooms without bath. Restaurant. AE, MC, V.*

Breiðdalsvík

Commerce in this tiny village of a few hundred souls dates from 1883. Hugging the shore on its own small inlet, the hamlet is gradually growing, thanks to its good harbor.

$$ ⌂ **Hótel Bláfell.** The small hotel has a cozy, rustic interior and an award-winning seafood restaurant. ⊠ *Sólvellir 14, IS-760,* ☎ *475–6770,* FAX *475–6668. 15 rooms, 7 with bath. Restaurant. AE, MC, V.*

Seyðisfjörður

Although it may be hard to believe now, the quaint village of Seyðisfjörður was one of Iceland's major trade ports in the 1800s, when tall sailing ships plied the crowded fjord. A number of beautiful wooden houses and buildings in Norwegian style attest to its affluent past. Nowadays, the ferry *Norröna* (☞ Transportation *in* Iceland A to Z, *above*) cruises into the harbor regularly during summer, disgorging visitors and vehicles from Europe.

$$ ⊞ **Hótel Snæfell.** In a classic Norse-style wooden house, this hotel over-looking a dramatic view of the fjord puts on a huge buffet on Wednes-days, accompanied by live music. Rooms are tidy and cozy but not lavish. ⊠ *Austurvegur 3, IS-710,* ☎ *472–1460,* FAX *472–1570. 9 rooms. Restaurant. AE, MC, V.*

Egilsstaðir

Egilsstaðir is the major commercial hub of the eastern sector, with an airport approved for international flights. The town straddles the Ring Road and lies on the eastern shore of Lake Lögurinn, the reputed home of a wormlike serpent that guards a treasure chest.

In summer at nearby **Eiðar**—just north of Egilsstaðir on the Borgarfjörður Road, a local theater and dance troupe performs weekly in an intimate, open-air setting. Performances are in Icelandic, but English summaries are available. For information contact Philip Vogler (⊠ Dalskógar 12, IS-700 Egilsstaðir, ☎ 471–1673, FAX 471–2190). The nation's largest forest, **Hallormsstaðarskógur,** is 25 km (15 mi) south of Egilsstaðir. Native birch and planted aspen, larch, and spruce have grown tall here. As with the entire region, it is ideal for hikers and horseback riders.

$$ ⊞ **FossHótel Hallormsstaður.** New in 1998, this hotel is set in one of Iceland's largest forests and is part of the year-round Foss chain. ⊠ *IS-707 Hallormsstaður,* ☎ *562–3350. 36 rooms. Restaurant. AE, MC, V.*

$$ ⊞ **Hótel Hérað, Icelandair Hotel.** Opened in 1998, this pleasant hotel in a valley has views of the nearby countryside. It's convenient to Egilsstaðir's shopping center and pool. ⊠ *IS-700 Egilsstaðir,* ☎ *471–2770,* FAX *471–2771. 36 rooms. Restaurant. AE, MC, V.*

The North

The entire length of the north coast is deeply gouged by fjords, from Vopnafjörður in the east to Hrútafjörður (Rams' Fjord) at the western end. In fact, Eyjafjörður, the country's longest, dips far inward to Akureyri, the "Capital of the North." In the region's midsection, large, well-established farms, some dating from Viking times, have thrived in the shelter of long fertile valleys, whose rivers attract salmon fishers.

Húsavík

Húsavík is a charming port on the north coast with a bustling harbor and a timber church dating from 1907. Handy to a nearby winter sports area, it is also a good base for summer hiking. Whale watchers have had amazing success (99.5%) on tours aboard restored oak boats (☞ Guided Tours *in* The Countryside Essentials, *below*). The new **Hvalamiðstöð á Húsavík** (Húsavík Whale Center) has exhibits on Iceland's past history as a whaling nation and on the natural history of these behemoths of the depths. ⊠ *Sólbrekku 21,* ☎ *464–2520.* ☉ *May and Aug., daily 9–7; June and July, daily 9* AM*–10* PM*; mid-Sept.–Apr., upon request.*

The true natural jewel of this area is **Mývatn,** a lake 54 km (33 mi) south-east of Húsavík, with its fascinating "false craters" and varied, abundant birdlife. Among the species, the harlequin duck and barrow's goldeneye are found nowhere else in Europe. Bring head nets if you visit in summer, because the lake is rightly named for midges, huge swarms of which are essential in the bird food chain and a bit of a nuisance to humans.

Not far from Mývatn, shrub lands, lava barrens, and black sands are traversed in places by rivers with impressive waterfalls. At **Goðafoss** (Waterfall of the Gods), 52 km (32 mi) southwest of Húsavík, looping north along the Tjörnes Peninsula, the last Viking follower of the pagan Norse faith tossed his icons into the waterfall when forced to accept Christianity. Thundering **Dettifoss,** on the Jökulsá (Glacier River) 97 km (60 mi) southeast of Húsavík via the Tjörnes Peninsula, is Europe's most powerful waterfall, and its canyon is a national park. Also protected is the nearby promontory **Ásbyrgi,** which, according to legend, is a giant hoofprint left by Sleipnir, the eight-legged horse of the ancient Norse god Óðinn.

$$$ 🏨 **Hótel Reynihlíð.** This popular hotel provides a helpful tourist information service and a restaurant for hungry travelers. Guests' comfort and convenience are paramount in this beautiful setting. ✉ *Mývatn, IS-660 Reykjahlíð,* ☎ *464–4170,* 🅵🅰🆇 *464–4371. 41 rooms. Restaurant. AE, DC, MC, V.*

$$ 🏨 **Hótel Húsavík.** A favorite of skiers, this sizable hotel has 10 rooms with balconies and many that have views to either the sea or the mountains. Car rental, whale-watching tours, and a host of seasonal activities can be booked from the hotel. Delicious seafood dishes are cooked up in the restaurant. ✉ *Ketilsbraut 22, IS-640,* ☎ *464–1220,* 🅵🅰🆇 *464–2161. 44 rooms. Restaurant. MC, V.*

$$ 🏨 **Hótel Reykjahlíð.** This small, peaceful hotel south of Húsavík near Mývatn has a prime lakeside location, meaning bird-watchers can spot most of the lake's main species right from their windows. All rooms are good-sized with baths and essential furnishings, but it is nature that supplies the luxury here. ✉ *Mývatn, IS-660 Reykjahlíð,* ☎ *464–4142,* 🅵🅰🆇 *464–4336. 9 rooms. Restaurant. MC, V.*

Akureyri

Akureyri's natural surroundings are unrivaled by those of any other Icelandic town. Several late-19th-century wooden houses give the city center a sense of history, as well as architectural variety. **Lystigarðurinn** (Arctic Botanic Gardens) has more than 400 species of Arctic flora native to Iceland. ✉ *Eyrarlandsvegur.* ☉ *Daily 8* AM*–11* PM.

With the northernmost 18-hole golf course in the world, Akureyri hosts the **Arctic Open Golf Tournament** each year around midsummer. For information, call the Iceland Tourist Bureau (☞ Visitor Information *in* Iceland A to Z, *above*).

$$$ 🏨 **FossHótel KEA.** This centrally located, first-class hotel has an excellent ground-level restaurant, Rósagarðarin, serving haute cuisine, plus an inexpensive cafeteria on the lower level. ✉ *Hafnarstræti 87-89, IS-602,* ☎ *460–2000,* 🅵🅰🆇 *460–2060. 95 rooms. Restaurant. AE, DC, MC, V.*

$$$ 🏨 **Hótel Norðurland.** Rooms here are pleasantly decorated with Danish furnishings. A sitting room has an impressive view. ✉ *Geislagata 7, IS-600,* ☎ *462–2600,* 🅵🅰🆇 *462–7962. 38 rooms. Restaurant. AE, DC, MC, V.*

$$ 🏨 **Hótel Edda.** This summer hotel in a school dormitory is known for its quality service. ✉ *Menntaskólinn, IS-600,* ☎ *461–1434. 79 rooms, 7 with bath. Restaurant. AE, MC, V. Closed Sept.–mid-June.*

$ 🏨 **Lónsá Farm Holidays.** This accommodation is spartan, but kitchen facilities are available. ✉ *Glæsibæjarhreppur, IS-601,* ☎ 🅵🅰🆇 *462–5037. 14 rooms without bath. MC, V.*

Sauðárkrókur

In summer, boat trips from the large coastal town of Sauðárkrókur to Drangey and the Málmey Islands offer striking views of the fjord and bird cliffs. Drangey, which requires a bit of climbing, is not for anyone leery of heights.

$$ 🏨 **FossHótel Áning.** Views from the tidy, though bare, rooms of this good-size summer hotel are of either the nearby mountains or the fjord. Hiking, golf, horseback riding, boat tours, and river rafting can be arranged from here. ✉ *Sæmundarhlíð, IS-550,* ☎ *453–6717 or 453–5940,* FAX *453–6087. 65 rooms. Restaurant. MC, V.*

Blönduós

The largest town on the west end of the north coast is nestled beneath gently rolling hills at the mouth of the glacially chalky Blanda. Though unsightly shrimp and shellfish processing plants and small industrial businesses mark the landscape here, from Blönduós it is an easy drive to neighboring picturesque valleys.

$$ 🏨 **Gistihús Sveitasetrið, Blönduós.** This small hotel, in the old center of town, is a stone's throw from the seashore. Fresh trout and salmon are specialties at the large restaurant. ✉ *Aðalgata 6, IS-540,* ☎ *452–4126,* FAX *452–4989. 18 rooms, 11 with shower. Restaurant. AE, MC, V.*

The West

The west is dramatically diverse. It encompasses the northwest dragon head—the rugged Vestfirðir (West Fjords) where, at Europe's westernmost part, seabirds vastly outnumber people. Due south is the long arm of the Snæfellsnes Peninsula, with awe-inspiring Snæfellsjökull at its tip. South of the peninsula is Borgarfjörður, where rich farmlands steeped in the history of the Viking sagas still fire visitors' imaginations.

Ísafjörður

The uncrowned capital of the West Fjords and one of the most important fishing towns in Iceland hosts a renowned Easter week ski meet. This is a convenient jumping-off point for tours to Hornstrandir, the splendidly peaceful and desolate land north of the 66th parallel inhabited by millions of seabirds.

$$$ 🏨 **Hótel Ísafjörður.** A stone's throw from the sea, this hotel is great for families. The modern structure has rooms decorated in modern Scandinavian style. The restaurant offers a wide variety of excellent seafood. ✉ *Silfurtorg 2, IS-400,* ☎ *456–4111,* FAX *456–4767. 32 rooms. Restaurant. AE, MC, V.*

Stykkishólmur

Stykkishólmur is an active port community on the peninsula's north coast, with a well-sheltered natural harbor. Classic timber houses, dating from as early as 1828, reveal its distinguished past, when many of the now-abandoned islets of Breiðafjörður were settled.

Snæfellsjökull

Literally the high point on the Snæfellsnes Peninsula is Snæfellsjökull, entry point in Jules Verne's novel *Journey to the Center of the Earth.* This beautiful glacier-covered conical summit, according to local legend, possesses mysterious energies and is home to hidden folk.

$$ 🏨 **Hótel Búðir.** The rustic hotel is under the magical Snæfellsjökull and close to a beach of black lava and golden sand. The stellar restaurant here specializes in nouveau interpretations of seafood and regional lamb—all laced with local herbs and veggies. ✉ *Staðarsveit, IS-355 Snæfellsnes,* ☎ *435–6700,* FAX *435–6701. 26 rooms, 6 with bath. Restaurant. MC, V. Closed Oct.–Apr.*

Ólafsvík

Commerce has been carried on in this small village, under the north shoulder of Snæfellsjökull, since 1687. From here you can hike to the top of the glacier or arrange snowmobile tours. Call the Tourist Information Center (☎ 436–1543).

$$ 🏨 **Höfði Guest house.** This family-style, harborside hotel has a small restaurant that serves up fresh local fare such as trout and halibut. ⊠ *Ólafsbraut 20, IS-355,* ☎ *436–1650,* ℻ *436–1651. 14 rooms without bath. Restaurant. AE, MC, V.*

Borgarnes

Borgarnes, the major town of the Borgarfjörður district, is unique in Iceland as being the only sizable coastal town that does *not* rely on fishing for its livelihood, turning instead to commerce and agriculture-related businesses.

$$$ 🏨 **Hótel Borgarnes.** Daylight through large windows fills the neutral-color interiors of the newer rooms of this hotel. A number of south-facing rooms overlook the fjord, with views of nearby mountains. It's a good bet for dependable food and service. ⊠ *Egilsgata 14–16, IS-310,* ☎ *437–1119,* ℻ *437–1443. 75 rooms. Restaurant. AE, DC, MC, V.*

The Countryside Essentials

Dining and Lodging

Because most restaurants outside Reykjavík are in hotels, there are no separate restaurant listings in the regional coverage. For details and price-category definitions, *see* Dining *and* Lodging *in* Iceland A to Z, *above.*

Guided Tours

THE SOUTH

Boat tours can be arranged on arrival at the **Jökulsárlón** glacial lagoon (call Fjölnir Torfason, ☎ 478–1065, or Skaftafell National Park, ☎ 478–1627). **Jórvik Aviation** (⊠ Box 5308, Reykjavík, ☎ 562–5101) offers spectacular sightseeing flights to Skaftafell National Park and environs. **Öræfaferðir** (⊠ 785 Fagurhólsmýri, Hofsnes-Öræfi, Fagurhólsmýri, ☎ 478–1682), a father-son outfit, puts together tours ranging from introductory ice climbing to assaults on the summit of Iceland's highest mountain to bird-watching.

Topp Ferðir (⊠ Lindarbakka, Höfn in Hornafjörður, ☎ 478–2666) has glacier jeep tours leaving from Hotel Vatnajökull. **Westman Islands Travel Service** (⊠ Herjólfsgötu 4, Westman Islands, ☎ 481–2922) offers informative, reasonably priced sightseeing trips by boat and bus in the Westman Islands.

THE NORTH

In Húsavík, **Norður Sigling—North Sailing** (⊠ Box 122, IS-640 Húsavík, ☎ 464–2350) offers whale-watching aboard three classic oak ships.

THE WEST

Eyjaferðir (⊠ Egilshús, Stykkishólmur, ☎ 438–1450) runs boat tours. Snowmobile trips to the top of Snæfellsjökull for groups can be arranged at **Snjófell** (⊠ Arnarstapi, ☎ 435–6783). **West Tours** (⊠ Box 37, Ísafjörður, ☎ 456–5111) runs hiking and mountaineering trips to the inhabitable parts of Strandasýsla.

Visitor Information

Akureyri (⊠ Hafnarstræti 82, ☎ 462–7733). **Egilsstaðir** (⊠ Egilsstaðir Campsite, ☎ 471–2320). **Höfn** (⊠ Höfn Campsite, Hafnarbraut, ☎ 478–1701). **Húsavík** (⊠ Safnarhús Húsavíkur Library/Museum, ☎ 464–1173). **Ísafjörður** (⊠ Hafnarstræti 6, ☎ 456–5121). **Kirkjubæjarklaustur** (⊠ Community Center, Klausturvegur 10, ☎ 487–4620).

Mývatn (⊠ Eldá Travel, Mývatnssveit, ☎ 464–4220); June–August contact **Reykjahlíðarskóli School** (☎ 464–4390), 9 AM–10 PM. **Ólafsvík** (☎ 436–1543). **Selfoss** Tryggvaskáli (⊠ Next to Ölfusá River bridge, ☎ 482–1704). **Seyðisfjörður** Austfar (⊠ Fjarðargata 8, ☎ 472–1111).

17 IRELAND

DUBLIN, DUBLIN TO CORK, CORK TO GALWAY, GALWAY TO DONEGAL, BELFAST

For a small island country isolated on the westernmost extreme of the continent, Ireland has nevertheless managed to strut its way around the European stage. Economically it has traditionally been a mere understudy to the great European powers (especially Great Britain); politically its influence is minimal, and yet everyone knows of the Irish, and they all cast a slightly envious eye at this mysterious island of romance.

Never more so than now. A major influx of money from the European Union over the last decade has substantially enlivened Ireland's economy, particularly in the booming capital city of Dublin. One-third of the country's very young population lives in the city, which is as much a college town as a center of government. Galleries, art-house cinemas, elegant shops, coffeehouses, and a stunning variety of restaurants are springing up on almost every street, transforming the provincial capital that once suffocated Joyce into a city every bit as cosmopolitan as the Paris to which he fled.

The pace of life outside Dublin is even more relaxed. Indeed, the farther you travel from the metropolis, the more you'll be inclined to linger. Apart from such sporting attractions as championship golf, horse racing, angling, and the native games of hurling and Gaelic football, the thing to do in Ireland is to stop, take a deep breath of some of the best air in the western world, and look around.

The lakes of Killarney—a chain of azure lakes surrounded by wild, boulder-strewn mountains—are justifiably among the country's most famous attractions. The Ring of Kerry is a gift from the gods to touring motorists, an out-and-back, daylong adventure through lush green mountain and valley, and on down to the sea. By contrast the lunar landscape of County Clare's eerie limestone desert, the Burren, must be explored on foot if you're to enjoy its rare alpine and Mediterranean flowers. Likewise, if you want to stand on the summit of the Cliffs of Moher to watch the Atlantic breakers bite into the ancient rocks 710 ft below, you'll have to get out of your car—even in the rain, and it often rains in Clare. If you love history, there are plenty of delightful castles and great stately houses peppering the banks of the old River Shannon, the spine of the nation. Throughout the country, prehistoric and early Christian ruins and remains hint at the awesome age of civilization on this ancient island. Alternatively you could just visit a bookstore and pick up anything by the great writers of Ireland; let James Joyce, William Butler Yeats, John Millington Synge, or Seamus Heaney be your travel guide, as you seek out the places made famous in their works.

IRELAND A TO Z

Addresses

We have tried to provide full addresses for hotels, restaurants, and sights, though many of Ireland's villages and towns are so tiny they barely have street names, much less house numbers. If in doubt, ask for directions.

Customs

For details on imports and duty-free limits, *see* Customs & Duties *in* Chapter 1.

Dining

Ireland is in the throes of a food revolution. Many of today's Irish chefs are young and have traveled widely and absorbed the best influences of Europe, North America, and the Pacific Rim. The result is a pan-European, postmodern cuisine that has moved beyond the age-old roast-beef-and-Yorkshire-pudding habit of the old Anglo-Irish country houses. In its place an innovative, indigenous style is emerging, marrying simple treatments of traditional courses—nettle soup, oysters, wild salmon—with more exotic dishes featuring unusual combinations of the best local, often organic, ingredients.

Despite the new sophistication, there are many examples of traditional cooking, particularly in pubs serving lunches of Irish stew, boiled bacon and cabbage, or steamed mussels. Pubs are one of the pillars of Irish society, worth visiting as much for conversation and music as for drinking. The national drink, Guinness, is a pitch-black, malted stout, one of the great beers of the world.

Hotel dining rooms vary in quality, but the best country-house hotels offer some of the finest dining in Europe, and most of these welcome guests, whether you're staying overnight or not.

MEALTIMES

Always check breakfast times in advance. It's usually 8–10, but some hotels serve from 7 to 11. Most offer a full Irish breakfast, with cereal, followed by bacon, eggs, sausage, and, sometimes, black and white pudding. Lunch, from noon to 2 (or even 3), is a leisurely affair. Some hotels serve afternoon tea and scones. Most people go out for dinner after 8; if you want to eat earlier, watch for "early bird" menus, typically served from 6:30 to 7:30.

RATINGS

Prices are per person and include an appetizer, main course, and dessert, but no wine or tip. Many restaurants also have à la carte menus allowing you to select only the main course or even two appetizers. Sales tax is included in the price. Many places add a 10%–15% service charge—if not, a 10% tip is fine.

CATEGORY	COST
$$$$	over IR£25
$$$	IR£20–IR£25
$$	IR£15–IR£20
$	under IR£15

WHAT TO WEAR

People dress up for dinner at the top restaurants, but a jacket is ordinarily sufficient. Ties are rarely essential. Nice casual wear is usually acceptable.

Language

Officially, Irish (Gaelic) is the first language of the Republic, but the everyday language of the vast majority of Irish people is English. Except for the northwest and parts of Connemara, where many signs are not translated, most signs in the country are written in Irish with an English translation underneath. There is one important exception to this rule, with which you should familiarize yourself: FIR (pronounced fear) and MNÁ (pronounced muh-*naw*) translate, respectively, into "men" and "women." The *Gaeltacht* (pronounced *gale*-tocked)—areas in which Irish *is* the everyday language of most people—comprises only 6% of the land, and all its inhabitants are, in any case, bilingual.

Lodging

Accommodations in Ireland range from deluxe castles and stately homes to thatched cottages and farmhouses to humble bed-and-breakfasts. Standards everywhere are high, and they—along with prices—continue to rise. The days of considering Ireland your basic bargain destination are long gone. Pressure on hotel space reaches a peak between June and September, but it's a good idea to make reservations in advance at any time of the year, particularly at the more expensive spots. Rooms can be reserved directly from the United States and elsewhere; ask your travel agent for details. Local tourist board offices can also make reservations, as can the Bord Fáilte's (the Irish Tourist Board, pronounced Board *Fall*-cha) **Central Credit Card Reservations Service** (⊠ Suffolk St., Dublin 2, ☎ 01/605–7777 in Ireland, 011800/668–96866 from the U.S., 𝖥𝖠𝖷 01/605–7787). Bord Fáilte has an official grading system and publishes a detailed price list of all approved accommodations, including hotels, guest houses, farmhouses, B&Bs, and hostels. No hotel may exceed this price without special authorization from Bord Fáilte; prices must also be displayed in every room. Don't hesitate to complain either to the manager or to Bord Fáilte, or both, if prices exceed this maximum.

In general, hotels charge per person. In most cases (but not all, especially in more expensive places), the price includes a full breakfast. VAT is included, but some hotels—again, usually the more expensive ones—add a 10%–15% service charge. This should be mentioned in their price list. If it's not, a tip of between 10% and 15% is customary—if you think the service is worth it. In $$ and $ hotels, be sure to specify whether you want a private bath or shower; the latter is cheaper. Off-season (October–May) prices are reduced by as much as 25%.

BED-AND-BREAKFASTS

Bed-and-breakfast means just that. The bed can vary from a four-poster in the wing of a castle to a feather bed in a whitewashed farmhouse or the spare bedroom of a modern home. Rates are generally around IR£18 per person, though these can vary significantly. Although many larger B&Bs have rooms with bath or shower, in some you'll have to use the bathroom in the hall.

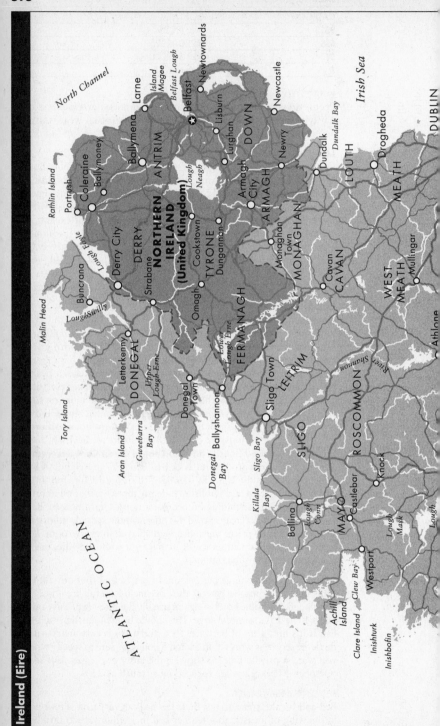

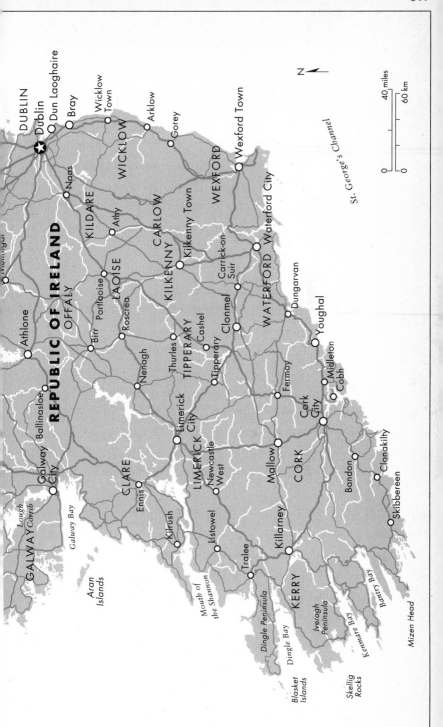

CAMPING

Ireland has a variety of beautifully sited campgrounds and trailer parks, but be prepared for wet weather! All are listed in *Caravan and Camping in Ireland,* available from Bord Fáilte (☞ Visitor Information, *below*).

GUEST HOUSES

Some smaller hotels are graded as guest houses. To qualify, they must have at least five bedrooms, but in major cities they often have many more. A few may have restaurants; those that do not will often provide evening meals by arrangement. Otherwise these rooms can be as comfortable as those of a regular hotel, and in major cities they offer very good value for the money, compared with the $ hotels.

RATINGS

Prices are for two people in a double room, based on high season (June–mid-September) rates.

CATEGORY	COST
$$$$	over IR£180
$$$	IR£140–IR£180
$$	IR£100–IR£140
$	under IR£100

Mail

POSTAL RATES

Airmail rates to the United States, Canada, and the Commonwealth are 45p for letters and postcards. Letters and postcards to Britain and continental Europe cost 32p.

RECEIVING MAIL

A general delivery service is operated free of charge from Dublin's **General Post Office** (⊠ O'Connell St., Dublin 1, ☎ 01/705–7000).

Money Matters

COSTS

Dublin is expensive—an unfortunate state of affairs that manifests itself most obviously in hotel rates and restaurant menus. You can generally keep costs lower if you visit Ireland on a package tour. Alternatively, consider staying in a guest house or one of the multitude of B&Bs; they provide an economical and atmospheric option (☞ Lodging, *above*). The rest of the country—with the exception of the better-known hotels and restaurants—is less expensive than Dublin. That the Irish themselves complain bitterly about the high cost of living is partly attributable to the rate of value-added tax (VAT)—a stinging 21% on "luxury" goods and 12½% on hotel accommodations. Some sample costs make the point. For instance, while a double room in a moderately priced Dublin hotel will cost about IR£90, with breakfast sometimes another IR£9 per person, the current rate for a country B&B is around IR£16 per person. Modest, small-town hotels generally charge around IR£25 per person.

CURRENCY

The unit of currency in Ireland is the pound, or punt (pronounced poont), written as IR£ to avoid confusion with the pound sterling. The currency is divided into the same denominations as in Britain, with IR£1 divided into 100 pence (written *p*). The North uses British currency; Irish *punts,* or pounds, are not accepted. Although the Irish pound is the only legal tender currency in the Republic, U.S. dollars and British currency are often accepted in large hotels and shops licensed as bureaux de change. Banks give the best rate of exchange. There is likely to be some variance in the rates of exchange between Ireland and the United Kingdom (which includes Northern Ireland). Change U.K. pounds at a bank when you get to Ireland (pound coins not accepted); change Irish pounds before you leave. Ireland is now a member of the European Monetary Union (EMU) and as of January 1, 1999, all prices are quoted in pounds and euros. January 2002 is to see the introduction of the euro coins and notes and the gradual withdrawal of the local currency. The rate of exchange at press time (summer 1999) was 77 pence to the U.S. dollar, 52 pence to the Canadian dollar, IR£1.21 to the British pound sterling, 51 pence to the Australian dollar, and 41 pence to the New Zealand dollar.

SAMPLE PRICES

Cup of coffee, 80p; pint of beer, IR£2.20; Coca-Cola, 95p; a sandwich, IR£1.80; 2-km (1-mi) taxi ride, IR£4.

National Holidays

January 1 (New Year's); March 17 (St. Patrick's Day); April 21 (Good Friday); April 24 (Easter Monday); May 1 (May Day); June 7 (Whit Monday); August 2 (August Holiday); October 25 (October Holiday); and December 25–26 (Christmas and St. Stephen's Day). If you're planning a visit at Easter, remember that theaters and cinemas are closed for the last three days of the preceding week.

Opening and Closing Times

Banks are open weekdays 10–4, and until 5 on Thursday. In small towns they may close for lunch from 12:30 to 1:30. **Museums** are usually open weekdays 10–5, Saturday 10–1, and Sunday 2–5. Always make a point of checking, however, as hours can change unexpectedly. **Shops** are open Monday–Saturday 9–5:30, closing earlier on Wednesday, Thursday, or Saturday, depending on the locality. Many shops, however, remain open until 9 PM on Thursday.

Shopping

SALES-TAX REFUNDS

Visitors from outside Europe can take advantage of the "cash-back" system on value-added tax (VAT) in two ways. The first is by having your invoice receipt stamped by customs on departure and mailing it back to the store for VAT refund. You must, however, verify at the time of purchase that the store operates by this system. The second and more popular option is by using one of the private cash-back companies, which charge a commission. **Europe Tax-free Shopping** offers customers their cash back at Dublin and Shannon airports when they present a Europe Tax-free Shopping voucher that has been filled out by the retailer at the point of sale. Other companies operate a cash-back system whereby you return your voucher just before you depart or when you arrive home, and you receive the VAT refund by mail, or it can be credited directly to your credit card.

Telephoning

COUNTRY CODE

The country code for the Republic of Ireland is 353 and for Northern Ireland it's 44.

INTERNATIONAL CALLS

For calls to the United States and Canada, dial 001 followed by the area code. For calls to the United Kingdom, dial 0044 followed by the number, dropping the beginning zero. For long-distance operators: **AT&T** (☎ 1–800/550–000); **MCI** (☎ 1–800/551–001); **Sprint** (☎ 1–800/552–001).

LOCAL CALLS

Pay phones can be found in all post offices and most hotels and bars, as well as in street booths. Local calls cost 20p for three minutes, calls within Ireland cost about 80p for three minutes, and calls to Britain cost about IR£2 for three minutes. Telephone cards are available at post offices and most newsagents. Prices range from IR£2 for 10 units to IR£8 for 50 units. Card booths are as common as coin booths. Rates go down by about a third after 6 PM and all day Saturday and Sunday.

Tipping

Some hotels and restaurants will add a service charge of about 12% to your bill, so tipping isn't necessary unless you've received particularly good service. But if there is no service charge, you might want to add a minimum of about 10% to the total. You don't tip in pubs, but if there is waiter service in a bar or hotel lounge, leave about 50p. Tip taxi drivers about 10% of the fare if the taxi has been using its meter. For longer journeys, where the fare is agreed in advance, a tip will not be expected unless some kind of commentary (solicited or not) has been provided. In luxury hotels porters and bellhops will expect IR£1; elsewhere, 50p is adequate. Hairdressers normally expect a tip of about IR£1.

Transportation

BY BICYCLE

Biking can be a great way to get around Ireland. For information about renting bikes, contact the Bord Fáilte (☞ Visitor Information, *below*). Rates average IR£8 per day or IR£40 per week. You must pay a IR£30 deposit. Be sure to make reservations, especially in July and August. If you rent a bike in the Republic, you may *not* take it into Northern Ireland; nor may you take a bike rented in Northern Ireland into the Republic.

BY BOAT

Exploring Ireland's lakes, rivers, and canals is a delightful, offbeat way to get to know the country. Motor cruisers can be chartered on the Shannon, the longest river in the British Isles. Bord Fáilte (☞ Visitor Information, *below*) has details of the wide choice of trips and operators available. For drifting through the historic Midlands on the Grand Canal and River Barrow, contact **Celtic Canal Cruisers** (✉ 24th Lock, Tullamore Co. Offaly, ☎ 0506/21861).

BY BUS

Bus Eireann (Irish Bus; ☎ 01/836–6111) runs bus service in the Republic. The 15-day Rambler ticket gives unlimited travel by bus in the Republic and is an excellent value at IR£98 (IR£130 for all of Ireland). It can be purchased from any city bus terminal and is valid for travel on any 15 days in a 30-day period. The provincial bus system operated by Bus Eireann is widespread—more so than the train system—although service can be infrequent in remote areas. In Northern Ireland, all buses are operated by the state-owned **Ulsterbus** (☎ 01232/333–000). *See* By Train, *below,* for details of combined train and bus discount tickets.

BY CAR

Parking. Parking in towns (especially Dublin) can be difficult. Signs with the letter P indicate parking lots, but if there's a stroke through the P, keep away or you'll collect a stiff fine, normally around IR£15. After 6 PM, restrictions are lifted. Give lot attendants about 50p when you leave.

Road Conditions. Ireland is one country in which a car is more or less essential to really get around. Despite improvements in public transportation, both the train and bus networks are limited, and many of the most intriguing regions are accessible only by car. Distances in Ireland seem short, but roads are narrow and often twisty and hilly, and side attractions are numerous, so you should aim for a daily mileage of no more than 240 km (149 mi). You'll find that driving past an ever-changing and often dramatic series of unspoiled landscapes is very much part of the fun. There's a bonus in the fact that traffic is normally light, though you can easily find yourself crawling down country lanes behind an ancient tractor or a flock of sheep. This is not a country for you if you've got a taste for life in the fast lane.

All principal roads are designated by the letter N, meaning National Primary Road. Thus, the main highway north from Dublin is N1, the main highway northwest is N2, and so on. Brand-new divided highways, or motorways—designated by blue signs and the letter M—take the place of some N roads. They are the fastest way to get from one point to another, but use caution, as they can end as abruptly as they begin. Road signs are usually in both Irish and English; in the northwest and Connemara, most are in Irish only, so make sure you have a good road map. A sensible rule to follow at unmarked intersections is: Keep going straight if there's no sign directing you to do otherwise. Distances on the green signposts are in kilometers; white signposts give distances in miles.

Rules of the Road. Driving is on the left. There is a general speed limit of 96 kph (60 mph) on most roads; in towns, the limit is 48 kph (30 mph). In some areas, the limit is 64 kph (40 mph); this is always clearly posted. At traffic circles (roundabouts), which are the main form of interchange, traffic from the right takes priority. Seat belts must be worn by the driver and front-seat passengers. Children under 12 must ride in the back. The new (and controversial) drunk-driving laws are strict, restricting the driver to less than one pint of beer.

BY PLANE
Distances are not great in Ireland, so airplanes play only a small role in internal travel. There are daily flights from Dublin to Shannon, Cork, Waterford, Kerry, Knock, and Galway; all flights take about 30 minutes. There is frequent service to the Aran Islands, off Galway Bay, from Connemara Airport, Galway. The flight takes five minutes.

BY TRAIN
The Irish Republic's train services are generally reliable, reasonably priced, and comfortable, though trains in Ireland travel more slowly than other places in Europe. **Iarnód Eireann** (Irish Rail; ☎ 01/836–6222) and Bus Eireann are independent components of the state-owned public transportation company Coras Iompair Eireann (CIE). All the principal towns are easily reached from Dublin, though services between provincial cities are roundabout. To reach Cork City from Wexford, for example, you have to go via Limerick Junction. It is often quicker, though perhaps less comfortable, to take a bus. Most mainline trains have two classes: standard and superstandard. Round-trip tickets are usually cheapest.

In Northern Ireland, train service is run by **Northern Ireland Railways** (☎ 01232/899–411), all operating out of Belfast's **Central Station** (☎ 01232/899–400). These are north to Derry, via Ballymena and Coleraine; east to Bangor along the shores of Belfast Lough; and south to Dublin and the Irish Republic.

Discount Passes. Eurailpasses are not valid in Northern Ireland. The **Irish Explorer Rail & Bus Pass**, for use on Ireland's railroads, bus system, or both, covers all the state-run and federal railways and bus lines throughout the Republic of Ireland. It does not apply to the North or to transportation within the cities. The **Emerald Isle Card** offers unlimited bus and train travel anywhere in Ireland and Northern Ireland, valid within cities as well. In Northern Ireland, **Rail Runabout** tickets entitle you to seven days' unlimited travel on scheduled rail services April–October. Even if you have a rail pass, be sure to book seats ahead of time.

Visitor Information

For information on travel in the Irish Republic, contact the **Irish Tourist Board,** known as Bord Fáilte (pronounced "Board Falcha"): **Canada** (⊠ 160 Bloor St. E, Suite 1150, Toronto, Ontario M4W 1B9, ☎ 416/929–2779, FAX 416/929–6783); **U.K.** (⊠ Ireland House, 150 New Bond St., London W1Y 0AQ, ☎ 0171/493–3201, FAX 0171/493–9065); **U.S.** (⊠ 345 Park Ave., New York, NY 10154, ☎ 212/418–0800 or 800/223–6470, FAX 212/371–9052).

Information on travel in the North is available from the **Northern Ireland Tourist Board**: **Canada** (⊠ 111 Avenue Rd., Suite 450, Toronto, Ontario M5R 3J8, ☎ 416/925–6368, FAX 416/961–2175); **U.K.** (⊠ 4–12 Lower Regent St., London BW1Y 4PQ, ☎ 0171/839–8417); **U.S.** (⊠ 551 5th Ave., Suite 701, New York, NY 10176, ☎ 212/922–0101 or 800/326–0036, FAX 212/922–0099).

Weather

June to mid-September is Ireland's high season, but the country's attractions are not as dependent on the weather as those in most other northern European countries, and the scenery is just as attractive in the off-peak times of fall and spring. Accommodations are more economical in winter, although some—particularly in the west and the northwest—are closed from October through March. In all seasons you can expect rain, although the sun is often out moments after a squall passes.

CLIMATE

Winters are mild though wet; summers can be warm and sunny, but there's always the risk of a sudden shower. No one ever went to Ireland for a suntan. The following are the average daily maximum and minimum temperatures for Dublin.

Jan.	46F	8C	May	60F	15C	Sept.	63F	17C
	34	1		43	6		48	9
Feb.	47F	8C	June	65F	18C	Oct.	57F	14C
	35	2		48	9		43	6
Mar.	51F	11C	July	67F	19C	Nov.	51F	11C
	37	3		52	11		39	4
Apr.	55F	13C	Aug.	67F	19C	Dec.	47F	8C
	39	4		51	11		37	3

DUBLIN

Today, Europe's most intimate capital has become a boomtown—the soul of the Republic of Ireland is in the throes of what may be the nation's most dramatic period of transformation since the Georgian era. Dublin is riding the back of the Celtic Tiger (as the roaring Irish economy has been nicknamed) and massive construction cranes are hovering over both shiny new hotels and old Georgian houses. Irish culture is hot: Patriot Michael Collins has become a Hollywood box-office star, Frank McCourt's *Angela's Ashes* has conquered American best-seller lists and the movie version is being filmed in Ireland, and *Riverdance* has become a worldwide old Irish mass jig. Because of these and other attractions, travelers are coming to Dublin in ever-greater numbers, so don't be surprised if you stop to consult your map in Temple Bar—the city's most happening neighborhood—and are swept away by the ceaseless flow of bustling crowds. Dublin has become a colossally entertaining, engaging city—all the more astonishing considering its gentle size. The quiet pubs and little empty backstreets might be harder to find now that Dublin has been "discovered," but a bit of effort and research can still unearth the old "Dear Dirty Dumpling," a city that Joyce was so found of.

Exploring Dublin

Numbers in the margin correspond to points of interest on the Dublin map.

Originally a Viking settlement, Dublin sits on the banks of the River Liffey, which divides the city north and south. The liveliest round-the-clock spots, including Temple Bar and Grafton Street, are on the south side, although a variety of construction projects on the north side are helping to reinvigorate these areas. The majority of the city's most notable buildings date from the 18th century—the Georgian era—and, although many of its finer Georgian buildings disappeared in the redevelopment of the '70s, enough remain, mainly south of the river, to recall the elegant Dublin of centuries past. Literary Dublin can still be recaptured by following the footsteps of Leopold Bloom's progress, as described in James Joyce's *Ulysses*. Trinity College, alma mater of Oliver Goldsmith, Jonathan Swift, and Samuel Beckett, among others, is a green, Georgian oasis, alive with students.

Trinity and St. Stephen's: The Georgian Heart of Dublin

South of the Liffey are graceful squares and fashionable terraces from Dublin's elegant heyday and, interspersed with some of the city's leading sights, this area is perfect for an introductory city tour. You might begin at O'Connell Bridge—as Dublin has no central focal point, most natives regard it as the city's Piccadilly Circus or Times Square—then head south down Westmoreland Street to Parliament House. Continue on to Trinity College—the Book of Kells, Ireland's greatest artistic treasure, is on view here; then eastward to Merrion Square and the National Gallery; south to St. Stephen's Green and Fitzwilliam Square; west to Dublin's two beautiful cathedrals—Christ Church and St. Patrick's; and end with supper in a Temple Bar restaurant overlooking the Liffey.

➋ **Bank of Ireland.** With a grand facade of marble columns, the Bank of Ireland is one of Dublin's most striking buildings. Across the street from the front entrance to Trinity College, the Georgian structure was once the home of the Irish Parliament. Built in 1729, it was bought by the Bank of Ireland in 1803. Hurricane-shape rosettes adorn the coffered ceiling in the pastel-hued, colonnaded, clerestoried main banking hall, once the Court of Requests where citizens' petitions were heard. Just down the hall is the original House of Lords, with tapestries, an oak-panel nave, and a 1,233-piece Waterford glass chandelier; ask a guard to show you in. Visitors are welcome during normal banking hours; a brief guided tour is given every Tuesday at 10:30, 11:30, and 1:45. ⊠ *2 College Green,* ☎ *01/677–6801.* ☉ *Weekdays 10–4 (Thurs. until 5).*

⓱ **Christ Church Cathedral.** Although St. Patrick's Cathedral is Dublin's grandest house of worship, Christ Church is actually the flagship of the Church of Ireland—it, not St. Patrick's, stood initially within the walls of the city. Construction was begun in 1172 by Strongbow, a Norman baron and conqueror of Dublin for the English crown, but an 1875 renovation to the exterior gave Christ Church much the look it has

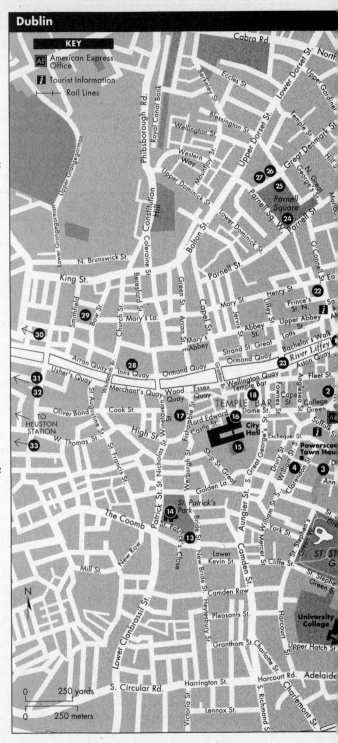

Dublin

KEY

AE American Express Office

i Tourist Information

Rail Lines

0   250 yards

0   250 meters

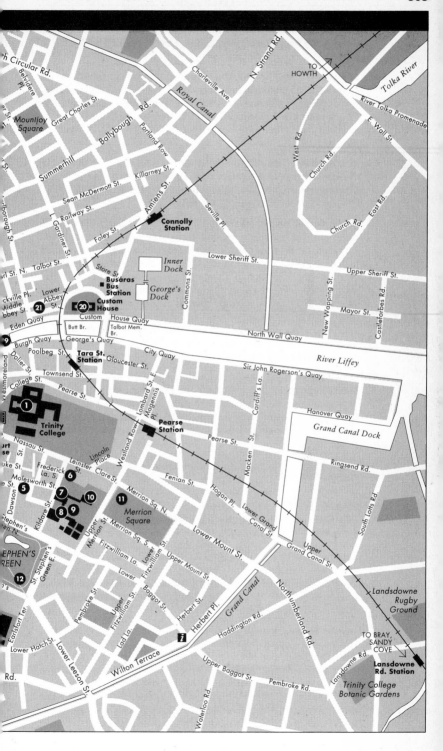

today. The vast, sturdy **crypt,** with its 12th- and 13th-century vaults, is Dublin's oldest surviving structure and the building's most notable feature. ⊠ *Christ Church Pl. and Winetavern St.,* ☎ *01/677–8099.* ☉ *Daily 10–5.*

⑯ City Hall. Facing the Liffey from the top of Parliament Street, this grand Georgian municipal building (1769–79), once the Royal Exchange, was designed by Thomas Cooley. It has a central rotunda encircled by 12 columns, a fine mosaic floor, and 12 frescoes depicting Dublin legends and ancient Irish historical scenes. ☎ *01/679–6111.* ☉ *Weekdays 9–1, and 2:15–5.*

❹ Civic Museum. Built in 1765–71 as an assembly house for the Society of Artists, the museum displays drawings, models, maps of Dublin, and other civic memorabilia. ⊠ *58 S. William St.,* ☎ *01/679–4260.* ☜ *Free.* ☉ *Tues.–Sat. 10–5:45, Sun. 11–2.*

⑮ Dublin Castle. Neil Jordan's film *Michael Collins* captures this structure's near-indomitable status in the city. Just off Dame Street behind City Hall, the grounds of the Castle encompass a number of buildings, including the **Record Tower,** a remnant of the original 13th-century Norman castle that was the seat of English power in Ireland for almost 7½ centuries, as well as various 18th- and 19th-century additions. The lavishly furnished **state apartments** are now used to entertain visiting heads of state. Guided tours run every half hour, but the rooms are closed when in official use, so call first. The **Castle Vaults** now hold an elegant little patisserie and bistro. ⊠ *Castle St.,* ☎ *01/677–7129.* ☉ *Weekdays 10–5, weekends 2–5.*

❻ Genealogical Office. The reference library here is a good place to begin ancestor tracing. It also houses the **Heraldic Museum,** where displays of flags, coins, stamps, silver, and family crests highlight the uses and development of heraldry in Ireland. ⊠ *2 Kildare St.,* ☎ *01/661–8811.* ☜ *Free.* ☉ *Office: weekdays 10–5, Sat. 10–12:30; guided tours by appointment. Museum: Mon.–Wed, 10–8:30, Thurs.–Fri. 10–4:30, Sat. 10–12:30.*

★ ❸ Grafton Street. Open only to pedestrians, brick-lined Grafton Street is one of Dublin's vital spines: the most direct route between the front door of Trinity College and Stephen's Green; the city's premier shopping street, off which radiate smaller streets housing stylish shops and pubs; and home to many of the city's street musicians and flower sellers. Browse through the Irish and international designer clothing and housewares at **Brown Thomas,** still Ireland's most elegant department store despite its recent move from its quaint old building to a newly designed store across the street. The **Powerscourt Town House** is a shopping arcade installed in the covered courtyard of one of Dublin's most famous Georgian mansions.

❾ Leinster House. When it was built in 1745 it was the largest private residence in Dublin. Today it is the seat of Dáil Eireann (pronounced dawl Erin), the Irish House of Parliament. The building has two facades: the one facing Merrion Square is designed in the style of a country house; the other, in Kildare Street, is in the style of a town house. ⊠ *Kildare St.,* ☎ *01/618–3000.* ☉ *Tours: Mon. and Fri. by prior arrangement (when Parliament is not in session). Dáil visitors' gallery: access with an introduction from a member of Parliament.*

⑬ Marsh's Library. A short walk west from Stephen's Green and accessed through a tiny but charming cottage garden lies a gem of old Dublin: the city's—and Ireland's—first public library, opened in 1701 to "All Graduates and Gentlemen." Its interior has been left practically unchanged since it was built—it still contains "cages" into which scholars who wanted to peruse rare books were locked. (The cages were to discourage students who, often impecunious, may have been tempted to make the books their own.) ✉ *St. Patrick's Close,* ☎ *01/454–3511.* ⊙ *Mon. and Wed.–Fri. 10–12:45 and 2–5, Sat. 10:30–12:45.*

★ ⑪ **Merrion Square.** Created between 1762 and 1764, this tranquil Georgian square is lined on three sides by some of Dublin's best-preserved Georgian town houses. Even when the flower gardens are not in bloom, the vibrant green grounds, dotted with sculpture and threaded with meandering paths, are worth a walk. **No. 1,** at the northwest corner, was the home of Sir William and Sperenza Wilde, Oscar's parents. ✉ *East end of Nassau St.* ⊙ *Daily sunrise–sunset.*

★ ⑩ **National Gallery of Ireland.** On the west side of Merrion Square, this 1854 building contains the country's finest collection of old masters—great treasures include Vermeer's incomparable *Woman Writing a Letter* (twice stolen from Sir Alfred Beit and now safe at last), Gainsborough's *Cottage Girl,* and Caravaggio's *The Arrest of Christ.* The gallery's restaurant is one of the city's best spots for an inexpensive, top-rate lunch. Free guided tours are available on Saturday at 3 PM and on Sunday at 2:15, 3, and 4. ✉ *Merrion Sq. W,* ☎ *01/661–5133.* ▦ *Free.* ⊙ *Mon.–Sat 10–5:30, Thurs. until 8:30, Sun. 2–5.*

⑦ **National Library.** The collections here include first editions of every major Irish writer. Temporary exhibits are held in the entrance hall, off the colonnaded rotunda. The main reading room, opened in 1890, has a dramatic dome ceiling. ✉ *Kildare St.,* ☎ *01/661–8811.* ▦ *Free.* ⊙ *Mon. 10–9, Tues.–Wed. 2–9, Thurs.–Fri. 10–5, Sat. 10–1.*

⑧ **National Museum.** On the other side of Leinster House from the National Library, the museum is most famous for its spectacular collection of Irish artifacts from 6000 BC to the present, including the Tara Brooch, the Ardagh Chalice, the Cross of Cong, and a fabled hoard of Celtic gold jewelry. It also houses an important collection of Irish decorative arts and a replica of a small Viking boat. ✉ *Kildare St.,* ☎ *01/660–1117.* ▦ *Free.* ⊙ *Tues.–Sat. 10–5, Sun. 2–5.*

⑲ **O'Connell Bridge.** Strange but true: The main bridge spanning the Liffey is wider than it is long. The north side of the bridge is dominated by an elaborate memorial to Daniel O'Connell, "The Liberator," erected as a tribute to the great 19th-century orator's achievement in securing Catholic Emancipation in 1829. Today **O'Connell Street,** one of the widest in Europe, is less a street to loiter in than to pass through on your way to elsewhere. **Henry Street,** to the left just beyond the General Post Office, is, like a downscale Grafton Street, a busy pedestrian thoroughfare where you'll find throngs of Dubliners out doing their shopping. A few steps down Henry Street off to the right is the colorful **Moore Street Market,** where street vendors recall their most famous ancestor, Molly Malone, by singing their wares—mainly flowers and fruit—in the traditional Dublin style.

⑤ **Royal Irish Academy.** The country's leading learned society houses important manuscripts in its 18th-century library. Just below the academy is the **Mansion House,** the official residence of the Lord Mayor of Dublin. Its Round Room, the site of the first assembly of Dáil Eireann in January 1919, is now used mainly for exhibitions. ✉ *19 Dawson St.,* ☎ *01/676–2570.* ▦ *Free.* ⊙ *Weekdays 9:30–5:30.*

⑭ **St. Patrick's Cathedral.** Legend has it that St. Patrick baptized many converts at a well on the site of the cathedral during the 5th century. The building dates from 1190 and is mainly early English Gothic in style.

At 305 ft, it is the longest church in the country. During the 17th century Oliver Cromwell, dour ruler of England and no friend of the Irish, had his troops stable their horses in the cathedral. It wasn't until the 19th century that restoration work to repair the damage was begun. St. Patrick's is the national cathedral of the Anglican church in Ireland and has had many illustrious deans. The most famous was Jonathan Swift, author of *Gulliver's Travels,* who held office from 1713 to 1745. Swift's tomb is in the south aisle. Memorials to many other celebrated figures from Ireland's past line the walls. ✉ *Patrick St.,* ☎ *01/475–4817.* ☉ *May and Sept.–Oct., weekdays 9–6, Sat. 9–5, Sun. 10–11 and 12:30–3; June–Aug., weekdays 9–6, Sat. 9–4, Sun. 9:30–3 and 4:15–5:15; Nov.–Apr., weekdays 9–6, Sat. 9–4, Sun. 10–11 and 12:30–3.*

⑫ St. Stephen's Green. Dubliners call it simply Stephen's Green; green it is—strikingly so, year-round (you can even spot a palm tree or two). The north side is dominated by the magnificent **Shelbourne Hotel** (☞ Lodging, *below*). A drink in one of its two bars, thronged after work, or afternoon tea in the elegant Lord Mayor's Room is the most financially painless way to soak in the old-fashioned luxury.

★ ⑱ Temple Bar. Dublin's hippest neighborhood—bordered by Dame Street to the south, the Liffey to the north, Fishamble Street to the west, and Westmoreland Street to the east—is the city's version of the Latin Quarter, the playing ground of "young Dublin." Representative of the improved fortunes of the area, with its narrow, winding pedestrian-only cobblestone streets, is the **Clarence** (✉ 6–8 Wellington Quay, ☎ 01/670–9000), a favorite old Dublin hotel now owned by Bono and the Edge of U2. The area is chock-full of small, hip stores, art galleries, and inexpensive restaurants and pubs. The **Irish Film Centre** (✉ 6 Eustace St., ☎ 01/679–5744) is emblematic of the area's vibrant mix of high and alternative culture.

★ ❶ Trinity College. Ireland's oldest and most famous college is the heart of college-town Dublin. Trinity College, Dublin (officially titled Dublin University but familiarly known as Trinity), was founded by Elizabeth I in 1592 and offered a free education to Catholics—providing they accepted the Protestant faith. As a legacy of this condition, until 1966 Catholics who wished to study at Trinity had to obtain a dispensation from their bishop or face excommunication. Today more than 70% of Trinity's students are Catholics, an indication of how far away those days seem to today's generation.

The pedimented, neoclassical Georgian facade, built between 1755 and 1759, consists of a magnificent portico with Corinthian columns. The design is repeated on the interior, so the view from outside the gates and from the quadrangle inside is the same. On the quad's lawn are statues of two of the university's illustrious alumni—statesman Edmund Burke and poet Oliver Goldsmith. Other famous students include the philosopher George Berkeley (who gave his name to the northern California city), Jonathan Swift, Thomas Moore, Oscar Wilde, John Millington Synge, Bram Stoker, Edward Carson, and Samuel Beckett. The 18th-century building on the left, just inside the entrance, is the **chapel.** There's an identical building opposite, the **Examination Hall.** The oldest buildings are the library in the far right-hand corner, completed in 1712, and a 1690 row of redbrick buildings known as the **Rubrics,** which contain student apartments.

Ireland's largest collection of books and manuscripts is housed in **Trinity College Library,** entered through the library shop. Its principal treasure is the Book of Kells, generally considered the most striking manuscript ever produced in the Anglo-Saxon world. Only a few pages from the 682-page, 9th-century gospel are displayed at a time, but an informative exhibit has reproductions of many of them. At peak hours you may have to wait in line to enter the library; it's less busy early in the day. Don't miss the grand and glorious Long Room, an impressive 213 ft long and 42 ft wide, which houses 200,000 volumes in its 21 alcoves. ☎ 01/677–2941. ⊙ Mon.–Sat. 9:30–4:45, Sun. noon–4:30.

In the Thomas Davis Theatre in the Arts Building, the **"Dublin Experience"** is an audiovisual presentation devoted to the history of the city over the last 1,000 years. ☎ 01/677–2941. ⊙ May–Oct., daily 10–5; shows every hr on the hr.

North of the Liffey

The Northside city center is a mix of densely thronged shopping streets and run-down sections of once-genteel homes, which are now being bought up and renovated. There are some classic sights in the area, including gorgeous Georgian monuments—the Custom House, the General Post Office, Parnell Square, and the Hugh Lane Gallery—and two landmarks of literary Dublin, the Dublin Writers Museum and the James Joyce Cultural Center, hub of Bloomsday celebrations. A good way to begin is by heading up O'Connell Street to Parnell Square and the heart of James Joyce Country.

㉑ **Abbey Theatre.** Ireland's national theater was founded by W. B. Yeats and Lady Gregory in 1904. The original building was destroyed in a fire in 1951; the present, rather austere theater was built in 1966. It has some noteworthy portraits and mementos in the foyer. Seats are usually available for about IR£12; all tickets are IR£8 for Monday performances. ⊠ Lower Abbey St., ☎ 01/878–7222.

㉒ **Custom House.** Extending 375 ft on the north side of the Liffey, this is the city's most spectacular Georgian building (1781–91), the work of James Gandon, an English architect. The central portico is linked by arcades to the pavilions at each end. A statue of Commerce tops the graceful copper dome; statues on the main facade are based on allegorical themes. Republicans set the building on fire in 1921, but it was completely restored; it now houses government offices and a visitor center that is open to the public. ⊠ Custom House Quay, ☎ 01/679–3377. ⊙ Weekdays 9:30–5, weekends 2–5.

★ ㉖ **Dublin Writers Museum.** Two restored 18th-century town houses on the north side of Parnell Square, an area rich in literary associations, lodge one of Dublin's finest cultural sights. Rare manuscripts, diaries, posters, letters, limited and first editions, photographs, and other mementos commemorate the lives and works of the nation's greatest writers, including Joyce, Shaw, Wilde, Yeats, and Beckett. The bookshop and café make this an ideal place to spend a rainy afternoon. ⊠ 18–19 Parnell Sq. N, ☎ 01/872–2077. ⊙ June–Aug., Mon.–Sat., 10–6, Sun. 11–5; Sept.–May, Mon.–Sat. 10–5, Sun. 11–5.

㉒ **General Post Office.** The GPO (1818), still a working post office, is one of the great civic buildings of Dublin's Georgian era, but its fame derives from the role it played during the Easter Rising. Here, on Easter Monday, 1916, the Republican forces stormed the building and issued the Proclamation of the Irish Republic. After a week of shelling, the GPO lay in ruins; 13 rebels were ultimately executed. Most of the original building was destroyed; only the facade—in which you can still see the scars of bullets on its pillars—remained. ⊠ O'Connell St., ☎ 01/872–8888. ⊙ Mon.–Sat. 8–8, Sun. 10:30–6:30.

㉓ **Ha'penny Bridge.** This heavily trafficked footbridge crosses the Liffey at a prime spot: Temple Bar is on the south side, and the bridge provides the fastest route to the thriving Mary and Henry Street shopping areas to the north. Until early in this century, a half-penny toll was charged to cross it. Yeats was one among many Dubliners who found this too high a price to pay—more a matter of principle than of finance—and so made the detour via O'Connell Bridge.

★ **㉗ Hugh Lane Municipal Gallery of Modern Art.** The imposing Palladian facade of this town house, once the home of the Earl of Charlemont, dominates the north side of Parnell Square. Sir Hugh Lane, a nephew of Lady Gregory (Yeats's patron), collected Impressionist paintings and 19th-century Irish and Anglo-Irish works. Among them are canvases by Jack Yeats (W. B.'s brother) and Paul Henry. ⊠ *Parnell Sq., ☎ 01/874–1903.* ▦ *Free.* ☉ *Tues.–Thurs. 9:30–6 (Apr.–Aug. Thurs. 9:30–8), Fri.–Sat. 9:30–5, Sun. 11–5.*

㉕ Parnell Square. This is the north side's most notable Georgian square and one of Dublin's oldest. Because fashionable hostesses liked passersby to be able to peer into the first-floor reception rooms of the elegant brick-face town houses and admire the distinguished guests, their windows are much larger than the others.

㉔ Rotunda Hospital. Founded in 1745 as the first maternity hospital in Ireland or Britain, it is now most worth a visit for its **chapel,** with elaborate plasterwork, appropriately honoring motherhood. The **Gate Theater** (☞ Nightlife and the Arts, *below*), housed in an extension, attracts large crowds to its fine repertoire of classic Irish and European drama. ⊠ *Parnell St., ☎ 01/873–0700.*

Dublin West

If you're not an enthusiastic walker, hop a bus or find a cab to take you to these sights in westernmost Dublin.

㉘ Four Courts. Today the seat of the High Court of Justice of Ireland, the Four Courts are James Gandon's second Dublin masterpiece, built between 1786 and 1802. The courts were destroyed during the "Troubles" of the '20s and restored by 1932. Its distinctive copper-covered dome atop a colonnaded rotunda makes this one of Dublin's most recognizable buildings. You are allowed to listen in on court proceedings, which can often be interesting, educational, even scandalous. ⊠ *Inns Quay, ☎ 01/872–5555.* ☉ *Daily 10:30–1 and 2:15–4.*

★ **㉝ Guinness Brewery.** Founded by Arthur Guinness in 1759, Ireland's all-dominating brewery is on a 60-acre spread west of Christ Church Cathedral; it is the most popular tourist destination in town. The brewery itself is closed to the public, but the **Hop Store,** part museum and part gift shop, puts on an 18-minute audiovisual show. After the show you get two complimentary glasses (or one pint) of the famous black stout. ⊠ *Crane St., ☎ 01/453–3645.* ☉ *Apr.–Sept., Mon.–Sat. 9:30–5, Sun. 10:30–4:30; Oct.–Mar., Mon.–Sat. 9:30–4, Sun. noon–4.*

㉜ Kilmainham Gaol. This grim, forbidding structure was where leaders of the 1916 Easter Uprising, including Pádrig Pearse and James Connolly, were held before being executed. A guided tour and a 30-minute audiovisual presentation relate a graphic account of Ireland's political history over the past 200 years from a Nationalist viewpoint. ⊠ *Inchicore Rd., ☎ 01/453–5984.* ☉ *Apr.–Sept., daily 9:30–5; Oct.–Mar., weekdays 9:30–4, Sun. 10–5.*

★ **㉚ Phoenix Park.** Europe's largest public park encompasses 1,752 acres of verdant lawns, woods, lakes, playing fields, a zoo, a flower garden, and two residences—those of the president of Ireland and the American ambassador. A 210-ft-tall obelisk, built in 1817, commemorates the Duke of Wellington's defeat of Napoléon. It is a jogger's paradise, but Sunday is the best time, when all kinds of games are likely to be in progress.

㉙ Old Jameson Distillery. The birthplace of one of Ireland's best whiskeys has been fully restored and offers a fascinating insight into the making of *uisce batha*, or "holy water," as whiskey is known in Irish. There is a 40-minute guided tour of the old distillery, a 20-minute audiovisual tour, and a complimentary tasting. ⊠ *Bow St.,* ☎ *01/807–2355.* ⊙ *Daily 9:30–5:30; tours are every ½ hr.*

★ ㉛ Royal Hospital Kilmainham. A short ride by taxi or bus from the city center, this structure is regarded as the most important 17th-century building in Ireland. Completed in 1684 as a hospice for soldiers, it survived into the 1920s as a hospital. The ceiling of the Baroque chapel is extraordinary. It now houses the **Irish Museum of Modern Art,** which displays works by such non-Irish greats as Picasso and Miró but concentrates on the work of Irish artists. ⊠ *Kilmainham La.,* ☎ *01/ 612–9900.* ⊠ *Free.* ⊙ *Exhibitions: Tues.–Sat. 10–5:30, Sun. noon–5:30; museum tours: Wed., Fri. 2:30, Sat. 11:30; historical tours: Sun. 2–4:30.*

Dining

Beyond the restaurants recommended here, the area between Grafton Street and South Great George's Street has many to offer, as does Temple Bar, just across Dame Street. You'll find a pub—if not two or three—on almost every block (☞ Nightlife and the Arts, *below,* for additional pub listings). For details and price-category definitions, *see* Dining *in* Ireland A to Z, *above.*

$$$$ ✕ Le Coq Hardi. John Howard has been running one of the best restaurants in Dublin in this Georgian house for many years. One of his signature dishes—a little old-fashioned, perhaps, but still popular—is Coq Hardi chicken, stuffed with potatoes and mushrooms, wrapped in bacon before going into the oven, and finished off with a dash of Irish whiskey. ⊠ *35 Pembroke Rd., Ballsbridge,* ☎ *01/668–9070. Reservations essential. AE, DC, MC, V. Closed Sun.*

$$$$ ✕ Patrick Guilbaud. Everything is French here, including the eponymous
★ owner, his chef, and the maître d'. Guillaume Le Brun's cooking is a fluent expression of modern French cuisine—not particularly flamboyant, but coolly professional. ⊠ *Hotel Merrion, Merrion St.,* ☎ *01/ 676–4192. AE, DC, MC, V. Closed Sun., Mon., and late Dec.–mid-Jan.*

$$$$ ✕ Peacock Alley. In the elegant Fitzwilliam Hotel on St. Stephen's Green
★ is this stylish 120-seat dining room with a white-tiled open kitchen at the rear. Chef Conrad Gallagher is a passionate cook, who builds up food on the plate and garnishes with painterly precision. His strikingly inventive dishes include deep-fried crab cakes with *katifi* (shredded phyllo pastry), and daube of pot-roasted beef. ⊠ *Fitzwilliam Hotel, 47 S. William St.,* ☎ *01/662–0760. Reservations essential. AE, DC, MC, V.*

$$$$ ✕ Thornton's. Chef-owner Kevin Thornton is as restrained and clas-
★ sical in his approach as the Peacock Alley's Conrad Gallagher is flamboyant. In a house on the north bank of the Grand Canal, the space is coolly understated; the service is French and quite formal. ⊠ *1 Portobello Rd.,* ☎ *01/454–9067. Reservations essential. AE, DC, MC, V. Closed Sun. No lunch.*

$$$ ✕ The Commons Restaurant. This restaurant is in a large, elegant room with French windows in the basement of Newman House, where James Joyce was a student at the original premises of University College Dublin. The seasonal menu encompasses a light treatment of classical themes. ⊠ *85–86 St. Stephen's Green,* ☎ *01/478–0530. AE, DC, MC, V. Closed Sun. No lunch Sat.*

$$$ ✕ **Cooke's Café.** Johnny Cooke has turned this city-center, Californian–Mediterranean-style bistro into a cool spot. It's busy and service can be slow; the outdoor seating on nice summer days is a consolation. ⊠ *14 S. William St.,* ☎ *01/679–0536. AE, DC, MC, V. No lunch.*

$$$ ✕ **L'Ecrivain.** Paintings of Beckett and other Irish writers hang on the walls
★ of chef-owner Derry Clarke's restaurant. The food is serious—disciplined and restrained, with the emphasis on fresh Irish produce. ⊠ *109a Lower Baggot St.,* ☎ *01/661–1919. AE, DC, MC, V. Closed Sun.*

$$–$$$ ✕ **Bruno's.** At this Italian-Mediterranean bistro on one of the busiest corners in Temple Bar, enjoy simple but stylish dishes ranging from starters of fresh crab claws with chilies, lemongrass, and tomato concassé, to main dishes of chargrilled chicken with raisins, dried prunes, Moroccan semolina, and walnut dressing. ⊠ *30 Essex St. E,* ☎ *01/670–6767. AE, MC, DC, V. Closed Sun.*

$$ ✕ **Chapter One.** In the vaulted, stone-walled basement of the Dublin Writers Museum, this is one of the most notable restaurants in northside Dublin. Dishes include pressed duck and black pudding terrine with a pear chutney, and grilled black sole with ravioli stuffed with salmon mousse. ⊠ *18–19 Parnell Sq.,* ☎ *01/873–2266. AE, DC, MC, V. Closed Sun. No lunch Sat., no dinner Mon.*

$$ ✕ **Eden.** At this popular brasserie-style restaurant overlooking one of Temple Bar's main squares, chef Eleanor Walsh creates such dishes as a vegetarian buckwheat pancake filled with garlic, spinach, and cheddar, and duck leg confit with lentils. ⊠ *Meeting House Sq.,* ☎ *01/670–5372. Reservations essential. AE, MC, V.*

$–$$ ✕ **The Side Door.** This stylish restaurant has oak floors, cream walls, Art Deco–style tables and chairs, and an eclectic but good menu of grilled meats and international-influenced dishes. Designer beers and a good wine list complement the food nicely. ⊠ *Shelbourne Hotel, 27 St. Stephen's Green,* ☎ *01/676–6471. AE, DC, MC, V.*

$ ✕ **Caviston's.** The Cavistons have been dispensing recipes for years from their fish counter and delicatessen in Sandycove, just south of the ferry port of Dun Laoghaire, 30 minutes by taxi or DART train south of Dublin. The fish restaurant next door is a lively and intimate spot. ⊠ *59 Glasthule Rd., Dun Laoghaire,* ☎ *01/280–9120. MC, V. Closed Sun., Mon., and late Dec.–early Jan. No dinner.*

$ ✕ **Milano.** In a well-designed dining room with lots of brio, choose from a tempting array of inventive, thin-crust pizzas. There are two locations. ⊠ *38 Dawson St.,* ☎ *01/670–7744;* ⊠ *18 Essex St. E, Temple Bar,* ☎ *01/670–3384. AE, MC, V.*

Pub Food

Most pubs serve food at lunchtime, some throughout the day. Food ranges from hearty soups and stews to chicken curries, smoked salmon salads, and sandwiches. Expect to pay IR£4–IR£5 for a main course. Many pubs do not take credit cards.

✕ **Davy Byrne's.** James Joyce immortalized Davy Byrne's in *Ulysses.* Nowadays it's more akin to a cocktail bar than a Dublin pub, but it's good for fresh and smoked salmon, salads, and a hot daily special. ⊠ *21 Duke St.,* ☎ *01/671–1298.*

✕ **John M. Keating.** For a real Irish pub lunch, this old-timer at the corner of Mary and Jervis streets can't be beat. ⊠ *14 Mary St./23 Jervis St.,* ☎ *01/873–1567.*

✕ **Kitty O'Shea's.** Kitty O'Shea's cleverly, if a little artificially, re-creates the atmosphere of old Dublin. ⊠ *23–25 Grand Canal St.,* ☎ *01/660–9965.*

✕ **Old Stand.** Conveniently close to Grafton Street, the Old Stand serves grilled food, including steaks. ⊠ *37 Exchequer St.,* ☎ *01/677–0823.*

✕ **Porterhouse.** Ireland's first brew pub has an open kitchen and a dazzling range of beers—from pale ales to dark stouts. ☒ *16–18 Parliament St.,* ☎ *01/679–8847.*

✗ **Stag's Head.** The Stag's Head is a favorite of Trinity students and businesspeople who come for one of the best pub lunches in the city. ☒ *1 Dame Ct.,* ☎ *01/679–3701.*

Cafés

Though Dublin has nowhere near as many cafés as pubs, it's easier than ever to find a good cup of coffee at most hours of the day or night.

✗ **Bewley's Coffee House.** The granddaddy of the capital's cafés, Bewley's has been supplying Dubliners with coffee and buns for more than a century. ☒ *78 Grafton St., 13 S. Great George's St., and 12 Westmoreland St.; all* ☎ *01/677–6761.*

✗ **Kaffe Moka.** One of Dublin's hottest haunts for the caffeine-addicted, this spot has three hyper-stylish floors and a central location in the heart of the city center. ☒ *39 S. William St.,* ☎ *01/679–8475.*

✗ **Thomas Read's.** By day it's a café, by night a pub. Its large windows overlooking a busy corner in Temple Bar make it a great spot for people-watching. ☒ *123 Parliament St.,* ☎ *01/677–1487.*

Lodging

On the lodging front Dublin is in the midst of a major hotel boom. For value stay in a guest house or a B&B; both tend to be in suburban areas—generally a 10-minute bus ride from the center of the city. **Bord Fáilte** (☞ Visitor Information *in* Dublin Essentials, *below*) can usually help find you a place to stay if you don't have reservations. For details and price-category definitions, *see* Lodging *in* Ireland A to Z, *above*.

$$$$ ▦ **Conrad.** A subsidiary of Hilton Hotels, the Conrad is aimed at the international business executive. The seven-story redbrick and smoked-glass building is just off Stephen's Green. The spacious rooms are done in light brown and pastel greens. Alfie Byrne's, the main bar, attempts to re-create a traditional Irish pub atmosphere. ☒ *Earlsfort Terr., Dublin 2,* ☎ *01/676–5555,* ℻ *01/676–5424. 182 rooms, 9 suites. 2 restaurants, bar, exercise room. AE, DC, MC, V.*

$$$$ ▦ **Merrion.** Four exactingly restored Georgian town houses make up
★ part of one of the capital's newest—and perhaps most luxurious—hotels. The stately rooms have been richly appointed in classic Georgian style down to the last detail. Leading Dublin restaurateur Patrick Guilbaud's (☞ Dining, *above*) eponymous restaurant is here. ☒ *Upper Merrion St., Dublin 2,* ☎ *01/603–0600,* ℻ *01/603–0700. 127 rooms, 18 suites. 2 restaurants, 2 bars. AE, DC, MC, V.*

$$$$ ▦ **Shelbourne Hotel.** Old-fashioned luxury prevails at this magnificent
★ showplace, which has presided over Stephen's Green since 1824. Each room has its own fine, carefully selected furnishings. Those in front overlook the green; rooms in back, without a view, are quieter. The restaurant, 27 The Green, is one of the most elegant rooms in Dublin; Lord Mayor's Room, off the lobby, is a perfect rendezvous spot and serves a lovely afternoon tea. ☒ *27 Stephen's Green, Dublin 2,* ☎ *01/676–6471, 800/543–4300 in U.S.,* ℻ *01/661–6006. 194 rooms, 9 suites. 2 restaurants, 2 bars. AE, DC, MC, V.*

$$$$ ▦ **Westbury.** This comfortable, modern hotel is right off the city's shopping mecca, Grafton Street. The spacious main lobby, where you can have afternoon tea, is furnished with antiques and large sofas. Rooms are rather utilitarian; the suites, which combine European decor with Japanese prints and screens, are more inviting. The flowery Russell Room serves formal lunches and dinners; the Sandbank, a seafood bar, is less enticing. ☒ *Grafton St., Dublin 2,* ☎ *01/679–1122,* ℻ *01/679–7078. 203 rooms, 8 suites. 2 restaurants, bar. AE, DC, MC, V.*

$$$ 🏨 **Hibernian.** An early 20th-century Edwardian nurses' home was converted into this hotel in 1993; the distinctive red-and-amber brick facade has been retained. Every room is a different shape, though all are done in light pastels with deep-pile carpets. Public rooms are slightly small, but are attractive in cheerful chintz and stripes. ⊠ *Eastmoreland Pl., off Upper Baggot St., Dublin 4,* ☎ *01/668–7666,* FAX *01/660–2655. 40 rooms. Restaurant, bar. AE, DC, MC, V.*

$$$ 🏨 **Jurys and The Towers.** These adjacent, seven-story hotels, a short cab ride from the center of town, are popular with businesspeople and vacationers. They both have more atmosphere than most comparable modern hotels, though the Towers has an edge over Jurys, its older (it dates from 1962), larger, less expensive companion. ⊠ *Pemroke Rd., Ballsbridge, Dublin 4,* ☎ *01/660–5000,* FAX *01/660–5540. Jurys: 300 rooms, 3 suites; the Towers: 100 rooms, 4 suites with kitchenettes. 3 restaurants, indoor/outdoor pool. AE, DC, MC, V.*

$$ 🏨 **Ariel Guest House.** Dublin's leading guest house is a block from the
★ elegant Berkeley Court, a 10-minute walk from Stephen's Green, and close to a DART stop. Rooms in the main house are lovingly filled with antiques; 13 rooms at the back of the house are more spartan; all are immaculate. Owner Michael O'Brien is an extraordinarily helpful and gracious host. ⊠ *52 Lansdowne Rd., Dublin 4,* ☎ *01/668–5512,* FAX *01/668–5845. 40 rooms. Breakfast room, wine bar. MC, V.*

$$ 🏨 **Central Hotel.** Established in 1887, this grand, old-style redbrick hotel is in the heart of the city. Rooms are small but have high ceilings and tasteful if practical furnishings. Adjacent to the hotel is Molly Malone's Tavern, a lively hotel-bar. ⊠ *1–5 Exchequer St., Dublin 2,* ☎ *01/679–7302,* FAX *01/679–7303. 67 rooms, 3 suites. Restaurant, 2 bars. AE, DC, MC, V.*

$$ 🏨 **Lansdowne.** In the leafy suburb of Ballsbridge, southeast of the city center, but within walking distance, is this small, friendly hotel. The cozy rooms are Georgian style. The basement bar is a popular hangout for local businesspeople and fans of the international rugby matches held at nearby Lansdowne Road. Parker's Restaurant specializes in steaks and seafood. ⊠ *27 Pembroke Rd., Dublin 4,* ☎ *01/668–2522,* FAX *01/668–5585. 39 rooms. Restaurant. AE, DC, MC, V.*

$ 🏨 **Dublin International Youth Hostel.** In a converted convent north of Parnell Square, near the Mater Hospital, this hostel has dormitory accommodations (up to 25 people per room) and family-size rooms for up to four people. It's a spartan, low-cost alternative to hotels. If you're not a member of the youth hostelling organization, you can stay for a small extra charge. ⊠ *61 Mountjoy St., Dublin 1,* ☎ *01/830–1766,* FAX *01/830–1600. 380 beds. Restaurant. MC, V.*

$ 🏨 **Jurys Christchurch Inn.** Expect few frills at this functional budget hotel (part of an otherwise upscale hotel chain), where there's a fixed room rate for up to three adults or two adults and two children. The biggest plus: the pleasant location, facing Christ Church Cathedral and within walking distance of most city-center attractions. Rooms are in pastel colors and have utilitarian furniture. The bar serves a pub lunch, and the restaurant, breakfast and dinner. ⊠ *Christchurch Pl., Dublin 8,* ☎ *01/454–0000,* FAX *01/454–0012. 182 rooms. Restaurant, bar. AE, DC, MC, V.*

$ 🏨 **Mount Herbert Guest House.** Close to the luxury hotels in the tree-lined inner suburb of Ballsbridge, a 10-minute DART ride from Dublin's center, the Mount Herbert is popular with budget-minded Americans. Rooms are small, but all have 10-channel TVs and hair dryers. There's no bar on the premises, but there are plenty to choose from nearby. ⊠ *7 Herbert Rd., Ballsbridge, Dublin 4,* ☎ *01/668–4321,* FAX *01/660–7077. 200 rooms. Restaurant, sauna. AE, DC, MC, V.*

$ 🏠 **Number 31.** Two Georgian mews strikingly renovated in the early
★   '60s by Ireland's leading modern architect as his own home are now
connected via a small garden to the grand town house they once served;
together they form a marvelous guest house a short walk from Stephen's
Green. New owners Deirdre and Noel Comer offer gracious hospitality and made-to-order breakfasts. ⊠ *31 Leeson Close, Dublin 2,* ☎
01/676–5011, ℻ *01/676–2929. 19 rooms. AE, MC, V.*

Nightlife and the Arts

The weekly magazines *In Dublin* and *The Big Issue* (at newsstands)
contain comprehensive details of upcoming events, including ticket availability. *The Event Guide* also lists events, and is free at many pubs and
cafés. In peak season, consult the free Bord Fáilte leaflet "Events of
the Week."

Cabarets
The following all have cabaret shows, with dancing, music, and traditional Irish song. They are open only in peak season (roughly May–
October; call to confirm). **Abbey Tavern** (⊠ Howth, Co. Dublin, ☎
01/839–0307). **Doyle Burlington Hotel** (⊠ Upper Leeson St., ☎ 01/660–
5222). **Jurys Hotel** (⊠ Pembroke Rd, Ballsbridge, ☎ 01/660–5000).

Classical Music
The **National Concert Hall** (⊠ Earlsfort Terr., ☎ 01/475–1666), just
off Stephen's Green, is home to the National Symphony Orchestra of
Ireland, and is Dublin's main theater for classical music of all kinds.
St. Stephen's Church (⊠ Merrion Sq., ☎ 01/288–0663) has a regular
program of choral and orchestral events.

Nightclubs
The Kitchen (⊠ Essex St., ☎ 01/677–6635) is part-owned by U2 and
attracts a young, vibrant clientele. **Lillie's Bordello** (⊠ Grafton St., ☎
01/679–9204) is a favorite with celebs and their admirers. **Rí Ra** (⊠
Dame Court, ☎ 01/677–4835) means "uproar" in Irish, and on most
nights the place does go a little wild; it's one of the best spots for no-
frills, fun dancing in Dublin.

Pubs
Check advertisements in evening papers for folk, ballad, Irish traditional, or jazz music performances. The pubs listed below generally have
some form of musical entertainment. For details on pubs serving food,
see Dining, *above.* The **Brazen Head** (⊠ 20 Lower Bridge St., ☎ 01/
677–9549)—Dublin's oldest pub, dating from 1688—has music every
night. President Bill Clinton dropped in at **Cassidy's** (⊠ 42 Lower Camden St., ☎ 01/475–1429) for a pint of stout during his visit to Dublin.
Doheny & Nesbitt's (⊠ 5 Lower Baggot St., ☎ 01/676–2945) is frequented by local businesspeople, politicians, and legal eagles. In the
Horseshoe Bar (⊠ Shelbourne Hotel, St. Stephen's Green, ☎ 01/676–
6471) you can eavesdrop on Dublin's social elite. **Kehoe's** (⊠ 9 S. Anne
St., ☎ 01/677–8312) is popular with students, artists, and writers. Locals and tourists bask in the theatrical atmosphere of **Neary's** (⊠ 1
Chatham St., ☎ 01/676–2807). **O'Donoghue's** (⊠ 15 Merrion Row,
☎ 01/661–4303) features some form of musical entertainment on
most nights. The **Palace Bar** (⊠ 21 Fleet St., ☎ 01/677–9290) is a journalists' haunt.

Theaters
Ireland has a rich theatrical tradition. The **Abbey Theatre** (⊠ Marl-
borough St., ☎ 01/878–7222) is the home of Ireland's national theater company, its name forever associated with J. M. Synge, W. B.
Yeats, and Sean O'Casey. The **Peacock Theatre** (☞ Abbey Theatre, *above*)

is the Abbey's more experimental small stage. The **Gaiety Theatre** (⊠ S. King St., ☎ 01/677–1717) features musical comedy, opera, drama, and revues. The **Gate Theatre** (⊠ Cavendish Row, Parnell Sq., ☎ 01/874–4045) is an intimate spot for modern drama and plays by Irish writers. The **Olympia Theatre** (⊠ Dame St., ☎ 01/677–7744) has comedy, vaudeville, and ballet performances. The **Project Arts Centre** (⊠ 39 E. Essex St., ☎ 01/679–6622) is an established fringe theater.

Shopping

The rest of the country is well supplied with crafts shops, but Dublin is the place to seek out more specialized items—antiques, traditional sportswear, haute couture, designer ceramics, books and prints, silverware and jewelry, and designer hand-knit items.

Shopping Centers and Department Stores

The shops north of the river—many of them chain stores and lackluster department stores—tend to be less expensive and less design-conscious. The one exception is the **Jervis Shopping Center** (⊠ Jervis St. at Mary St., ☎ 01/878–1323), the city's newest major shopping center. Also on the north side, **Clery's** (⊠ O'Connell St., directly opposite the GPO, ☎ 01/878–6000) was once the city's most fashionable department store and is still worth a visit, despite its rapidly aging decor. **Arnotts** (⊠ Henry St., ☎ 01/805–0400) is Dublin's largest department store and carries a good range of cut crystal. **Brown Thomas** (⊠ Grafton St., ☎ 01/605–6666) is Dublin's most elegant department store. **St. Stephen's Green Center** (⊠ St. Stephen's Green, ☎ 01/478–0888) contains 70 stores, large and small, in a vast Moorish-style glass-roof building.

Shopping Districts

Grafton Street is the most sophisticated shopping area in Dublin's city center. **Molesworth Street** and **Dawson Street** are the places to browse for antiques. **Nassau Street** and **Dawson Street** are for books; the smaller side streets are good for jewelry, art galleries, and old prints. The pedestrianized **Temple Bar** area, with its young, offbeat ambience, has a number of small art galleries, specialty shops (music and books), and inexpensive, trendy clothing shops. The area is further enlivened by buskers (street musicians) and street artists.

Bookstores

Fred Hanna's (⊠ 29 Nassau St., ☎ 01/677–1255) sells old and new books, with a good choice of books on travel and Ireland. **Hodges Figgis** (⊠ 56–58 Dawson St., ☎ 01/677–4754) is Dublin's leading independent, with a café on the first floor. **Waterstone's** (⊠ 7 Dawson St., ☎ 01/679–1415) is the Dublin branch of the renowned British chain.

Gift Items

Blarney Woollen Mills (⊠ Nassau St., ☎ 01/671–0068) has a good selection of tweed, linen, and woolen sweaters. **Dublin Woolen Mills** (⊠ Metal Bridge Corner, 41 Lower Ormond Quay, ☎ 01/677–5014), at Ha'penny Bridge, sells hand-knit and other woolen sweaters at competitive prices. **Kevin & Howlin** (⊠ Nassau St., ☎ 01/677–0257) carries tweeds for men. **Kilkenny Shop** (⊠ Nassau St., ☎ 01/677–7066) is good for contemporary Irish-made ceramics, pottery, and silver jewelry. **McDowell** (⊠ 3 Upper O'Connell St., ☎ 01/874–4961), in business for over 100 years, is a popular jewelry shop. **Tierneys** (⊠ St. Stephen's Green Centre, ☎ 01/478–2873) carries a good selection of crystal, china, claddagh rings, pendants, and brooches.

Outdoor Markets

Moore Street, behind the Ilac Center (⊠ Henry St.), a large mall, is open from Mondays to Saturdays, 9–6; stalls lining both sides of the street sell fruits and vegetables. A variety of bric-a-brac is sold at the **Liberty Market** on the north end of Meath Street, open on Fridays and Saturdays, 10–6, and Sundays, noon–5:30. The indoor **Mother Redcap's Market,** opposite Christ Church, is open Fridays, Saturdays, and Sundays, 10–5; come here for antiques and bric-a-brac.

Side Trips from Dublin

The **Hill of Tara,** 33 km (21 mi) northwest of Dublin, was the religious and cultural capital of Ireland in ancient times. Its importance waned with the arrival of Christianity during the 5th century, and today its crest is, appropriately enough, crowned with a statue of the man who brought Christianity to Ireland—St. Patrick.

It was in the 8th-century abbey in **Kells,** 64 km (40 mi) north of Dublin, that the Book of Kells was completed; a facsimile can be seen in **St. Columba's Church.** Among the remains of the abbey are a well-preserved round tower and a rare example of a stone-roof church dating from the 9th century.

Dublin Essentials

Arriving and Departing

BY BUS

The central bus station is **Busaras** (✉ Store St. near the Custom House); some buses also terminate near O'Connell Bridge. **Dublin Bus** (☎ 01/873–4222) provides city service, including transport to and from the airport. **Bus Eireann** (☎ 01/836–6111) provides express and provincial service.

BY CAR

The main access route from the north is N1; from the west, N4; from the south and southwest, N7; from the east coast, N11. All routes have clearly marked signs indicating the center of the city: AN LÁR. The M50 motorway encircles the city from Dublin Airport in the north to Tallaght in the south.

BY FERRY

Irish Ferries (✉ Merrion Row, ☎ 01/661–0511) and **Stena Sealink** (✉ Ferryport, Dun Laoghaire, ☎ 01/204–7777) have regular car and passenger service between Dublin and Wales (Holyhead). Irish Ferries sails directly into Dublin port. Stena Sealink docks in Dublin port (3½-hour service to Holyhead) and in Dun Laoghaire (High Speed Service, known as "HSS," which takes 99 minutes). Prices and departure times vary according to season, so call to confirm. In summer, reservations are strongly recommended. Dozens of taxis wait to take you into town from both ports, or you can take DART or a bus to the city center.

BY PLANE

All flights arrive at **Dublin Airport,** 10 km (6 mi) north of town.

Between the Airport and Downtown. Buses leave every 20 minutes from outside the Arrivals door for the central bus station in downtown Dublin. The ride takes about 30 minutes, depending on the traffic, and the fare is IR£2.50. A taxi ride into town will cost from IR£10 to IR£14, depending on the location of your hotel; be sure to ask in advance if the cab has no meter (☞ Getting Around by Taxi, *below*).

BY TRAIN

Irish Rail (✉ 35 Lower Abbey St., ☎ 01/836–6222 for information) provides train service throughout the country. Dublin has three main stations. **Connolly Station** (✉ at Amiens St.) is the departure point for Belfast, the east coast, and the west. **Heuston Station** (✉ at Kingsbridge) is the departure point for the south and southwest. **Pearse Station** (⊠ on Westland Row) is for Bray and connections via Dun Laoghaire to the Liverpool/Holyhead ferries.

Getting Around

Dublin is small as capital cities go—the downtown area is compact— and the best way to soak in the full flavor of the city is on foot.

BY BUS

Most city buses originate in or pass through the area of O'Connell Street and O'Connell Bridge. If the destination board indicates AN LÁR, that means that the bus is going to the city center. Timetables (IR£2.50) are available from **Dublin Bus** (⊠ 59 Upper O'Connell St., ☎ 01/873–4222); the minimum fare is 55p.

BY CAR

The number of cars in Ireland has grown exponentially in the last few years, and nowhere has their impact been felt more than in Dublin, where the city's complicated one-way streets are often congested. Avoid driving a car in the city except to get you into and out of it, and be sure to ask your hotel or guest house for clear directions when you leave.

BY TAXI

Official licensed taxis, metered and designated by roof signs, do not cruise; they can be found beside the central bus station, at train stations, at O'Connell Bridge, Stephen's Green, College Green, and near major hotels. The initial charge is IR£1.80 with an additional charge of about IR£1.60 per 2 km (1 mi) thereafter; the fare is displayed in the cab. (Make sure the meter is on.) Hackney cabs, which also operate in the city, have neither roof signs nor meters, and will sometimes respond to hotels' requests for a cab. Negotiate the fare before your journey begins.

BY TRAIN

An electric train commuter service, **DART,** serves the suburbs out to Howth, on the north side of the city, and to Bray, County Wicklow, on the south side. Fares are about the same as for buses. Street-direction signs to DART stations read STAISIUN/STATION.

Contacts and Resources

EMBASSIES

Australian (⊠ Fitzwilton House, Wilton Terr., ☎ 01/676–1517). **Canada** (⊠ 65 St. Stephen's Green, ☎ 01/478–1988). **U.K.** (⊠ 29 Merrion Rd., ☎ 01/205–3700). **U.S.** (⊠ 42 Elgin Rd., Ballsbridge, ☎ 01/668–8777).

EMERGENCIES

Police (☎ 999). **Ambulance** (☎ 999). **Dentist** (☎ 01/662–0766). **Doctor** (☎ 01/679–0700). **Pharmacy** (⊠ Hamilton Long, 5 Upper O'Connell St., ☎ 01/874–8456).

GUIDED TOURS

Excursions. Bus Eireann (☎ 01/836–6111) and **Gray Line Tours** (☎ 01/670–8822) have daylong tours into the surrounding countryside and longer tours elsewhere; the price includes accommodations, breakfast, and admission costs.

Orientation. Dublin Bus (☎ 01/873–0000) and **Gray Line Tours** (☎ 01/670–8822) organize bus tours of Dublin and its surrounding areas. From mid-April through September Dublin Bus runs a continuous guided open-top bus tour (IR£5) that allows you to hop on and off the bus as often as you wish and visit some 15 sights along its route.

Special-Interest. Elegant Ireland (☎ 01/475–1665) arranges tours for groups interested in architecture and the fine arts; these include visits with the owners of some of Ireland's stately homes and castles.

Walking Tours. The tourist office has leaflets giving information on a selection of walking tours, including "Literary Dublin," "Georgian Dublin," and "Pub Tours." **Bord Fáilte** (☞ Visitor Information, *below*) has a "Tourist Trail" walk, which takes in the main sites of central Dublin and can be completed in about three hours, and a "Rock 'n Stroll" tour, which covers the city's major pop and rock music sites.

TRAVEL AGENCIES

American Express (✉ 116 Grafton St., ☎ 01/677–2874). **Thomas Cook** (✉ 118 Grafton St., ☎ 01/677–1721).

VISITOR INFORMATION

In addition to the main office (☞ Visitor Information *in* Ireland A to Z, *above*), you can find visitor information offices in the entrance hall of the headquarters of **Bord Fáilte** (✉ Baggot St. Bridge, ☎ 1850/230–330); open weekdays 9:15–5:15. **Dublin Tourism** also has visitor information at the airport (arrivals level), open daily 8 AM–10 PM; and at the Ferryport, Dun Laoghaire; open daily 10 AM–9 PM.

DUBLIN TO CORK

One good way to see the country is to drive southwest from Dublin to Cork, the Republic's second-largest city. On the way, you'll see the lush green fields of Ireland's famous stud farms and imposing Cashel, where Ireland built its reputation as the "Land of Saints and Scholars" while most of Europe was slipping into the Dark Ages.

Naas

The road to Naas (pronounced *nace*) passes through the area known as The Pale—that part of Ireland in which English law was formally acknowledged up to Elizabethan times. The aesthetically mundane seat of County Kildare and a thriving market town in the heartland of Irish thoroughbred country, Naas is full of pubs filled with jockeys discussing the merits of their stables. Naas has its own small racecourse, but **Punchestown Racecourse** (3 km/2 mi from Naas) has a wonderful setting amid rolling plains and is famous for its steeplechases.

The Curragh

The Curragh, 8 km (5 mi) southwest of Naas, just beyond the end of the bypass M7 and bisected by the main N7 road, is the biggest area of common land in Ireland, containing about 31 square km (12 square mi) and devoted mainly to grazing. It's also Ireland's major racing center, home to the **Curragh Racecourse** (☎ 045/441–205), where the Irish Derby and other international horse races are run. In addition, the Irish army trains here, at the **Curragh Main Barracks.**

Kildare Town

The thriving economy of Kildare, 5 km (3 mi) from the Curragh on M7, is based on horse breeding. The town is also where St. Brigid founded a religious settlement in the 5th century; **St. Brigid's Cathedral** (✉ off Market Sq.) is a restoration of a 13th-century building.

If you're a longtime horse aficionado, or just curious, the **National Stud Farm,** a main center of Ireland's racing industry, is well worth a visit. Also on the grounds, the **National Stud Horse Museum** recounts the history of the horse in Ireland. ✉ *South of Kildare Town about 2½ km/1½ mi, clearly signposted to left of market square,* ☎ 045/521617. ☉ *Mid-Feb.–mid-Nov., daily 9:30–6.*

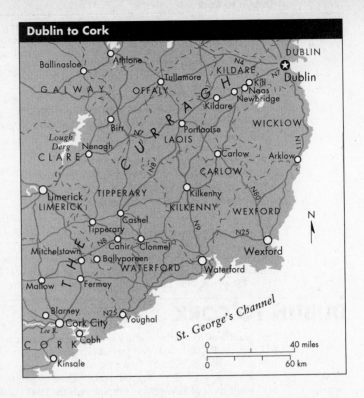

Dublin to Cork

★ The elegant **Japanese Gardens,** adjacent to the National Stud Farm, were laid out between 1906 and 1910 and are considered among the finest in Europe. ⊠ *South of Kildare Town about 2½ km/1½ mi, clearly signposted to left of market square,* ☎ *045/521617.* ☉ *Mid-Feb.– mid-Nov., daily 9:30–6.*

Cashel

Cashel is a market town on the busy Cork–Dublin road, which, in spite of the incessant heavy traffic running through it, retains some interesting Victorian shopfronts on its Main Street. The town has a lengthy history as a center of royal and religious power.

★ The awe-inspired, oft-mist-shrouded **Rock of Cashel** is one of Ireland's most visited sites. The rock itself, which is a short walk to the north of the town, rises as a giant, circular mound 200 ft above the surrounding plain; it is crowned by a tall cluster of gray monastic remains. The kings of Munster held it as their seat for about seven centuries, and it was here that St. Patrick reputedly plucked a shamrock from the ground, using it as a symbol to explain the mystery of the Trinity, giving Ireland, in the process, its universally recognized symbol. ☎ 062/61437. ☉ *Mid-Mar.–mid-June, daily 9:30–5:30; mid-June–mid-Sept., daily 9–7:30; mid-Sept.–mid-Mar., daily 9:30–4:30.*

$$$ ✕ **Chez Hans.** Fresh local produce cooked with a French accent is served in this converted chapel at the foot of the famous rock. ⊠ *Rockside,* ☎ *062/61177. MC, V. Closed Sun., Mon., first 3 wks in Jan. No lunch.*

$$$$ ✕⊞ **Cashel Palace.** Although in the town center, this magnificently restored 18th-century bishop's palace has great views of the Rock of Cashel from its back rooms. Inexpensive light meals are served all day in its bistro-style cellar restaurant. ⊠ *Main St., Cashel, Co. Tipperary,* ☎ *062/62707,* ℻ *062/61521. 13 rooms. 2 restaurants. AE, DC, MC, V.*

Cahir

Cahir (pronounced *care*) is a popular stopping place to break the Dublin–Cork journey. **Cahir Castle,** the town's main attraction, is a massive limestone structure dating from 1164 and built on rock in the middle of the river. There are regular guided tours and an audiovisual display in the lodge. ☎ 052/41011. ☉ *Apr.–June and late Sept.–mid-Oct., daily 10–6; June–mid-Sept., daily 9–7:30; late Oct.–Mar., daily 10–1 and 2–4:30.*

$ 🖭 **Kilcoran Lodge Hotel.** This handsome, sprawling, 19th-century former hunting lodge sits amid beautiful countryside 6 km (4 mi) outside Cahir on the main Cork–Dublin (N8) road. Rooms facing the front have the best views of the beautiful, heather-covered slopes; all have Victorian-style furnishings and comfortable beds. ⊠ *Cahir Co. Tipperary,* ☎ 052/41288, 🖬 052/41994. 23 *rooms. Restaurant, bar.* AE, DC, MC, V.

Cork City

The road enters Cork City along the banks of the River Lee. In the center of Cork, the Lee divides in two, giving the city a profusion of picturesque quays and bridges. The name Cork derives from the Irish *corcaigh* (pronounced *corky*), meaning a marshy place. The city received its first charter in 1185 and grew rapidly during the 17th and 18th centuries with the expansion of its butter trade. It is the major metropolis of the south and, with a population of about 175,000, the second-largest city in Ireland. The main business and shopping center of Cork lies on the island created by the two diverging channels of the Lee, and most places of interest are within walking distance of the center. **Patrick Street** is the focal point; here you'll find the city's major department stores, **Roches** and **Brown Thomas.** If you look up above the plate-glass shop facades, you'll see examples of the bowfront Georgian windows that are emblematic of old Cork.

The famous bell tower of **St. Anne's Church,** the 120-ft **Shandon Steeple,** is on a hill across the river to the north of Cork's main shopping area. Shaped like a pepper pot, it houses the bells immortalized in the song "The Bells of Shandon." You can climb the tower, and ring the bells over Cork. ⊠ *Church St.* ☉ *May–Oct., Mon.–Sat. 9:30–5; Nov.–Apr., Mon.–Sat. 10–3:30.*

The liveliest place in town to shop is the pedestrian-only **Paul Street** area, near the city center parking lot. Housed in the 1724 building that was once the city's Custom House, the **Crawford Art Gallery,** at the top of Paul Street, has an excellent collection of 18th- and 19th-century views of Cork and adventurous exhibits by modern artists. ⊠ *Emmet Pl.,* ☎ 021/427–3377. 🖾 *Free.* ☉ *Weekdays 10–5, Sat. 9–1.*

$$$ ✕ **The Ivory Tower.** Seamus O'Connell, the young chef-owner of this restaurant off Patrick Street, concocts such adventurous dishes as tagliatelle of flashed squid, and wild pheasant tamale. The bare boards and stick-back chairs are enlivened by original works of art. ⊠ *35 Princes St.,* ☎ 021/427–4665. MC, V. *Closed Sun., Mon.*

$ ✕ **Isaac's.** In an old warehouse, this popular spot has modern art on
★ the walls and Mediterranean-influenced food. Excellent local produce is used in such starters as warm potato salad with smoked bacon, and black pudding. ⊠ *48 MacCurtain St.,* ☎ 021/450–3805. MC, V.

$$$ ✕🖭 **Arbutus Lodge.** This hillside hotel—only a five-minute drive from the city center—makes you feel like you're a guest in a fancy, private home. Although at press time the Arbutus was on the market, its new owners should continue to maintain the same standards of excellence. Airy guest rooms have fine antiques and original paintings. The out-

standing restaurant serves French-Irish haute cuisine. ✉ *Middle Glanmire Rd., Montenotte,* ☎ *021/450–1237,* ℻ *021/450–2893. 16 rooms, 4 suites. Restaurant. AE, DC, MC, V. Closed 1 wk at Christmas.*

$$$$ ⊞ **Hayfield Manor.** This fine, luxury hotel is built to resemble an old country house. It's beside the university campus, five minutes' drive from the city center. ✉ *Perrott Ave., College Rd.,* ☎ *021/431–5600,* ℻ *021/431–6839. 53 rooms. Restaurant, bar. AE, DC, MC, V.*

$ ⊞ **Victoria Lodge.** Built in the early 20th century as a Capuchin monastery, this well-appointed B&B is a five-minute drive from the town center; it's also on several bus routes. Guest rooms are simple but comfortable, with views of the grounds. ✉ *Victoria Cross, Co. Cork,* ☎ *021/454–2233,* ℻ *021/454–2572. 30 rooms. AE, MC, V.*

Cobh and Fota Island

If you're American and have Irish roots, chances are your ancestors were among the thousands who sailed from the port of Cork. Cobh (pronounced *cove*), as it is known nowadays, is an attractive, hilly town, dominated by its 19th-century cathedral. From Cork, follow the signposts for Waterford on N25 along the northern banks of the River Lee. Alternatively, a suburban rail service leaves from Cork's **Kent Station** (☎ 021/506–766 for schedule) with stops in Cobh and Fota Island. In
★ the old Cobh railway station, the **Queenstown Project** re-creates the experience of the emigrants who left the town between 1750 and the mid-20th century. It also tells the stories of the great transatlantic liners, including the *Titanic,* whose last port of call was Cobh, and the *Lusitania,* which was sunk by a German submarine off this coast on May 7, 1915. ✉ ☎ *021/481–3591.* ☉ *Feb.–Nov., daily 10–6.*

Part of the **Fota Demesne,** a large estate on the Cobh side of Cork, consists of a magnificent arboretum. Also on the estate is the 238-square-km (70-acre) **Fota Wildlife Park,** an important breeding center for cheetahs and wallabies. ☎ *021/481–2678.* ☉ *Mid-Mar.–Sept., daily 10–6.*

$$$ ✕⊞ **Ballymaloe House.** One of Ireland's best known and loved coun-
★ try houses, Ballymaloe has, for 50 years, been the home of the Allen family, who welcome guests with gracious aplomb. Each guest room is an elegant variation on country-house style. Myrtle, the doyenne of Irish cooking, presides over the outstanding dining room. ✉ *Shanagarry, Midleton,* ☎ *021/465–2531,* ℻ *021/465–2021. 32 rooms. Restaurant, pool. AE, DC, MC, V. Closed Dec. 24–27.*

Blarney

Just north of Blarney is **Blarney Castle**—or what remains of it: The ruined central keep is all that's left of this mid-15th-century stronghold. The walls of the castle contain the famed **Blarney Stone,** in a wall below the castle's battlements; kissing the stone, it is said, endows you with the fabled "gift of gab." To kiss the stone, you must lie down on the battlements, and lean your head way back. Nobody knows how the tradition originated, but Elizabeth I is credited with giving the word *blarney* to the language when, commenting on the unfulfilled promises of Cormac MacCarthy, Lord Blarney of the time, she remarked, "This is all Blarney; what he says, he never means." ✉ *Blarney Castle,* ☎ *021/438–5252.* ☉ *Mon.–Sat. 9–sundown, Sun. 9–5:30.*

Dublin to Cork Essentials

Getting Around

BY BICYCLE

Bicycles can be rented from **Rothar Cycle Tours** (✉ 2 Bandon Rd., Cork City, ☎ 021/431–3133).

BY BUS

Bus Éireann (☎ 01/836–6111, 061/313333, 021/508–188, or 066/23566) operates Expressway services from Dublin to Cork City. **Cork City Main Bus Terminal** (✉ Parnell Pl., ☎ 021/450–8188).

BY CAR

From Dublin, pick up N8 in Portlaoise for Cork City (257 km/160 mi); the journey time is about 3½ hours. A car is the ideal way to explore this area. Roads are generally small, with two lanes (one in each direction). All the main car-rental firms have desks at Cork Airport. Be sure to get a map of Cork City's complicated one-way street system.

BY PLANE

Cork Airport (☎ 021/431–3131), 5 km (3 mi) south of Cork City on the Kinsale road, is used primarily for flights to and from the United Kingdom. Regular 30-minute internal flights are scheduled between Shannon and Dublin, Shannon and Cork, and Cork and Dublin.

BY TRAIN

The terminal in Cork City is **Kent Station** (☎ 021/450–6766 for information). There's direct service from Dublin and Tralee and a suburban line to Cobh.

Guided Tours

Arrangements Unlimited (✉ 1 Woolhara Park, Douglas, Cork City, Co. Cork, ☎ 021/429–3873, FAX 021/429–2488) can arrange special-interest tours of the region for small or large groups. **Bus Eireann** (☎ 021/450–6066) operates a number of city tours and regional excursions from Parnell Place in Cork City.

Visitor Information

Cahir (✉ Castle St., Co. Tipperary, ☎ 052/41453); open April–September. **Cashel** (✉ Town Hall, Co. Tipperary, ☎ 062/61333, FAX 062/61789); open April–September. **Cork City** (✉ Grand Parade, Cork City, ☎ 021/273–251, FAX 021/273–504); open year-round.

CORK TO GALWAY

The trip from Cork north to Galway is about 300 km (186 mi) and includes stops in Killarney and Limerick. The Shannon region around Limerick is littered with castles, both ruined and restored. Along the way, the Cork–Killarney road passes through the west Cork Gaeltacht—a predominantly Irish-speaking region—and begins its climb into the Derrynasaggart Mountains.

Killarney

Killarney Town itself is an undistinguished market town, well developed to handle the crowds that gather here in peak season. They come to drink in the famous scenery, located out of town toward the lakes that lie in a valley running south between the mountains. Part of Killarney's lake district is within the **Killarney National Park.** At the heart of the park is the 10,000-acre **Muckross Estate,** which is open daily, daylight hours. Cars are not allowed in the estate, so if you don't want to walk, rent a bicycle in town or take a trip in a jaunting car—a small two-wheel horse-drawn cart whose operators can be found at the gates to the estate and in Killarney. At the center of the estate is **Muckross House,** a 19th-century manor that contains the **Kerry Country Life Experience.** On the adjoining grounds is an old-world farm. ☎ 064/31440. ☉ Sept.–June, daily 9–5:30; July–Aug., daily 9–7. Closed 1 wk at Christmas.

Cork to Galway

To get an idea of the splendor of the lakes and streams—and of the massive glacial sandstone and limestone rocks and lush vegetation that characterize the Killarney district—take a daylong tour of the **Gap of Dunloe,** as well as the **Upper Lake, Long Range, Middle and Lower lakes,** and **Ross Castle.** The central section, the Gap of Dunloe, is not suitable for cars, but horses and jaunting cars are available at **Kate Kearney's Cottage,** which marks the entrance to the gap.

$$$ ✕ **The Strawberry Tree.** Imaginative, rustic-style Irish cooking is the star of this tiny, upstairs restaurant with character. Downstairs, Yer Man's Pub, a minuscule Olde Village Pub, is a good choice for lunchtime bar-food specials. ✉ *24 Plunkett St., Co. Kerry,* ☎ *064/32688. AE, DC, MC, V. Closed Dec.–Jan.*

$$ ✕ **Gaby's Seafood.** Tile floors, pine booths, and red gingham table-cloths are the hallmarks of the cheerful, informal decor. Fresh seafood simply prepared is the specialty. ✉ *17 High St.,* ☎ *064/32519. AE, DC, MC, V. Closed Mon. No lunch Sun.*

$$$$ ✕🏨 **Aghadoe Heights.** Its location on a bluff (4 km/2½ mi outside town on the Tralee side, signposted off the N22) translates into unforget-table lake views—especially from the aerie of the famous hotel restau-rant, Frederick's. The luxurious interior is a pleasant combination of the antique and the modern. Two-thirds of the bedrooms have lake views, and all are relatively large. (The hotel will be closed November '99–April 2000 for renovation.) ✉ *Aghadoe Heights, Co. Kerry,* ☎ *064/ 31766,* FAX *064/31345. 60 rooms, 3 suites. Restaurant, bar. AE, DC, MC, V.*

$$ 🏨 **Arbutus.** A good budget hotel in the town center, Arbutus has been in the same family since it was built more than 60 years ago. Ask for a room in the newer second-story section. Its quiet bar draws a local crowd. ✉ *College St., Co. Kerry,* ☎ *064/31037,* FAX *064/34033. 44 rooms. Restaurant, bar. AE, DC, MC, V.*

Ring of Kerry

Running along the perimeter of the Iveragh Peninsula, the dramatic Ring of Kerry is probably the single most popular tourist route in Ireland. Stunning mountain and coastal views are around almost every turn. The only drawback: On a sunny day, it seems like half the tourists in Ireland are there. It's a daylong drive (176 km/109 mi round-trip) from Killarney; leave by N71 (the Kenmare road).

Kenmare

Kenmare is a small, mainly 19th-century market town at the head of Kenmare Bay. Across the water, as you drive out along the Iveragh Peninsula, are views of the gray-blue mountain ranges of the Beara Peninsula.

$$$$ ✕🏨 **Park Hotel.** Spacious rooms with late-Victorian antiques and Italian-marble-tile bathrooms distinguish this fine country-house hotel. Local
★ ingredients and seafood star on the restaurant's sophisticated Irish-Continental menu (a jacket and tie are required). ✉ *Kenmare, Co. Kerry,* ☎ *064/41200,* 🖷 *064/41402. 50 rooms with bath. Restaurant, bar. AE, DC, MC, V. Closed Jan.–mid-Apr.*

Sneem

Sneem, on the estuary of the River Ardsheelaun, is one of the prettiest villages in Ireland. Look for "the pyramids" (as they are known locally), 12-ft-tall, traditional stone structures that look old but were completed in 1990 by Kerry-born artist James Scanlon.

Caherdaniel

The **Derrynane House** was once the home of the 19th-century politician and patriot Daniel O'Connell, "The Liberator." The south and east wings of the house are open to visitors and still contain much of the original furniture and other items associated with O'Connell. ☎ *066/947–5113.* ☾ *Jan.–Mar., Nov., and Dec., weekends 1–5; Apr. and Oct., Tues.–Sun. 1–5; May–Sept., Mon.–Sat. 9–6, Sun. 11–7.*

Dingle

If time and weather are on your side, turn off the main Killorglin–Tralee road and make a tour of the **Dingle Peninsula**—one of the wildest and least spoiled regions of Ireland. Take in **Connor Pass, Mount Brandon, Gallarus Oratory,** and stop in **Dunquin** to hear some of Ireland's best traditional musicians.

Dingle Town itself is a handy touring base with crafts shops, seafood restaurants, and pubs; still, its main streets—The Mall, Main and Strand streets, and The Wood—can be covered in less than an hour.
★ For an adventure off the beaten path, take a boat ride to the **Blasket Islands** and spend a few blissful hours wandering along the cliffs.

$$ ✕ **Beginish.** The food at this outstanding restaurant imaginatively in-
★ terprets French nouvelle cuisine; specialties include brill fillets on leek fondue, and fillet of lamb. ✉ *Green St.,* ☎ *066/915–1588. AE, DC, MC, V. Closed Mon. and mid-Nov.–mid-Mar.*

$$$ ✕🏨 **Dingle Skellig.** A five-minute walk from the town center, this hotel-restaurant is a showcase of Irish craft, art, and design. More than half the spacious rooms have sea views (ask for these when reserving). The Coastguard Restaurant is the town's only water's-edge eatery; seafood is the specialty. ✉ *Dingle Town, Co. Kerry,* ☎ *066/915–1144,* 🖷 *066/915–1501. 110 rooms. Restaurant, indoor pool. AE, DC, MC, V. Closed early Jan.–mid-Feb.*

$ 🏨 **Greenmount House.** This impeccably kept, modern B&B a short walk from the town center is renowned for its imaginative breakfasts. ✉ *Gortanora, Dingle Town, Co. Kerry,* ☎ *066/915–1414,* 🖷 *066/915–1974. 12 rooms. MC, V.*

Tralee

County Kerry's capital and its largest town, Tralee has neither ruins nor quaint architecture, yet it makes a go at attracting visitors without them. Tralee has long been associated with its annual festival, during which, every September, a young woman of Irish descent is chosen to be the "Rose of Tralee." The **Kerry County Museum**, Tralee's major cultural attraction, traces the history of Kerry's people from 5000 BC to the present. ⊠ *Ashe Memorial Hall, Denny St.,* ☎ *066/712–7777.* ⊙ *Mon.–Sat. 10–6 (10–8 in Aug.).*

Adare

Adare is one of Ireland's most picture-perfect towns. A bit of England in the Old Sod, it has storybook thatch-roof cottages and Tudor-style churches. Visit the **Adare Heritage Centre** for a look back at the town's picturesque history. A seasonal tourist office is open here, May through October. ⊠ *Main St.,* ☎ *061/396666.* ⊙ *May–June, Sept.–Oct., daily 9–6; July–Aug., daily 9–7.*

$$$ ▥ **Dunraven Arms.** Although Adare Manor, a Tudor-Gothic castle just across the road, is swankier, you get a warmer welcome at this old coaching inn. It's a handy first stop when arriving at Shannon Airport, about 40 km (25 mi) northwest. Guest rooms, decorated with antiques, are comfortable. ⊠ *Adare, Limerick,* ☎ *061/396633,* ℻ *061/396541. 76 rooms. Restaurant, bar, indoor pool. AE, DC, MC, V.*

Limerick City

Limerick is an industrial port and the fourth-largest city in the Republic (population 60,000). The area around the cathedral and the castle is the old part of the city, dominated by mid-18th-century buildings with fine Georgian proportions. Economic investment is helping to spiff up its former image as an unattractive city marked by high unemployment and a high crime rate. Frank McCourt's 1996 memoir *Angela's Ashes*— set in Limerick, where McCourt grew up desperately poor—has also helped to pique interest in the city.

In the Old Customs House on the banks of the Shannon in the city center, the **Hunt Museum** has the finest collection of Celtic and medieval treasures outside the National Museum in Dublin. ⊠ *Rutland St.,* ☎ *061/312833.* ⊙ *May–Sept., Mon.–Sat. 10–5, Sun. 2–5; Oct.–Apr., Tues.–Sat. 10–5, Sun. 2–5.*

First built by the Normans in the early 1200s, **King John's Castle** still bears traces on its north side of the 1691 bombardment. Climb the drum towers for a good view of the town and the Shannon. Inside, exhibitions illustrate the history of Limerick. ⊠ *Castle St.,* ☎ *061/411201.* ⊙ *Apr.–Sept., daily 9:30–5; Oct.–Mar., weekends 9:30–5.*

★ **Bunratty Castle,** 18 km (10 mi) west of Limerick City on N18, is one of four castles in the area that have nightly medieval banquets. The castle, once the stronghold of the princes of Thomond, is the most complete and—despite its ye-Olde-World banquets—authentic medieval castle in Ireland, restored in such a way as to give an idea of life during the 15th and 16th centuries. The **Folk Park** on its grounds has farm buildings and crafts shops typical of the 19th century. ☎ *061/361511.* ⊙ *Daily 9:30–dusk (last entry 1 hr before closing).*

$$$$ ▥ **Castletroy Park.** High standards of comfort are the rule at this well-
★ designed modern hotel on the outskirts of town. ⊠ *Dublin Rd.,* ☎ *061/ 335566,* ℻ *061/331117. 107 rooms. 2 restaurants, indoor pool. AE, DC, MC, V.*

$$ ▥ **Greenhills.** This suburban, modern low rise is convenient for Shannon Airport and also makes a good touring base. The friendly owner-

manager welcomes families. ✉ *Ennis Rd.,* ☎ *061/453033,* FAX *061/453307. 55 rooms. Restaurant, indoor heated pool. AE, DC, MC, V.*

★ Ennis

Ennis, 37 km (23 mi) northwest of Limerick, and the principal town of County Clare, is a pleasant if unremarkable market town that's often bustling. It has always fostered traditional music, especially fiddle playing and step dancing; at the end of May, it's the gathering place for the **Fleadh Nua** (pronounced fla-nooa), a festival of Irish music.

$$$$ ✕⌂ **Carnelly House.** This 250-year-old Queen Anne–style, redbrick house is an elegant, convenient base (it's 5 km/3 mi south of Ennis, 16 km/10 mi from Shannon Airport). The large, comfortable guest rooms have canopied or four-poster beds and bucolic views over the 100-acre estate. Dishes such as rack of lamb with garlic and rosemary, and pheasant in port figure on the menu. ✉ *Clarecastle, Co. Clare,* ☎ *065/682–8442,* FAX *065/682–9222. 5 rooms. Horseback riding, fishing. MC, V.*

Corofin

If you're searching for your Irish roots, Corofin's **Clare Heritage Center** has a genealogical service and information about doing research yourself. It also has displays on the history of the West of Ireland in the 19th century. ☎ *065/683–7955.* ☉ *Apr.–Oct., daily 10–6; Nov.–Mar. (genealogy service only) weekdays 9–5; museum by appointment.*

Lisdoonvarna

Lisdoonvarna is a small spa town with several sulfurous and iron-bearing springs with radioactive properties. Its buildings reflect a mishmash of mock-architectural styles, which, depending on your taste, is either lovably kitschy or unappealingly tacky. The town has developed something of a reputation over the years as a matchmaking center, with bachelor farmers and single women converging here each year in late September for a Bachelors' Festival.

$ ⌂ **Ballinalacken Castle.** It's not a castle, but a converted Victorian shooting lodge on 100 acres of wildflower meadows, commanding a breathtaking view of the Atlantic. Rooms are modest but full of character. ✉ *Co. Clare,* ☎ *065/707–4025,* FAX *065/707–4025. 12 rooms. Restaurant. MC, V. Closed early Oct.–Mar.*

$ ⌂ **Sheedy's Spa View.** Originally a 17th-century farmhouse, this small, friendly, family-run hotel is only a short walk from both the town center and the spa wells. Rooms are simple, spotlessly clean, and well cared for. French-Irish cuisine is served at the award-winning, moderately priced Orchid Restaurant. ✉ *Co. Clare,* ☎ *065/707–4026,* FAX *065/707–4555. 11 rooms. Restaurant, bar, tennis court. AE, DC, MC, V. Closed Oct.–Mar.*

The Burren

In the northwest corner of County Clare, the Burren (from the Irish word for "stony rock") is a strange, rocky, limestone district—and a superb nature reserve, with a profusion of wildflowers that are at their best in late May. Huge colonies of birds—puffins, kittiwakes, shags, guillemots, and razorbills—nest along its coast. The **Burren Display Center** in Kilfenora explains the extraordinary geology and wildlife of the area in a simple audiovisual display. ☎ *065/708–8030.* ☉ *Mid-Mar.–May and Sept.–Oct., daily 10–5; June–Aug., daily 10–6.*

★ The Cliffs of Moher

One of Ireland's most breathtaking natural sites, the majestic Cliffs of Moher rise vertically out of the sea in a wall that stretches over a long 8-km (5-mi) swath and as high as 710 ft. **O'Brien's Tower** is a defiant, broody sentinel built at their highest point. The **visitor center,** at the base of the cliffs, beside the parking lot, has a tearoom and is a good refuge from passing rain squalls. It's open mid-February–April, daily 10–5; May, June, and September, daily 10–6; July–August, daily 9:30–6:30. On a clear day the Aran Islands are visible from the cliffs, and in summer there are regular day trips to them from **Doolin,** a tiny village that claims three of the best pubs in Ireland for traditional music.

Ballyvaughan

A pretty waterside village with views of Galway Bay and the Aran Islands, Ballyvaughan makes a good base for exploring the Burren. At nearby **Ailwee Cave,** you can take a guided tour into the underworld of the Burren, where 3,415 ft of cave, formed millions of years ago, can be explored. ☎ 065/707–7036. ⊙ *Early Mar.–June and Sept.–early Nov., daily 10–6 (last tour 5:30); July–Aug., daily 10–7 (last tour 6:30).*

$$ ✕⊞ **Hyland's Hotel.** Travelers have been looked after for 250 years at this comfortable, family-run coaching inn. The cheerful, unpretentious restaurant specializes in local seafood and lamb. ⊠ *Co. Clare,* ☎ *065/707–7037,* FAX *065/707–7131. 31 rooms. Restaurant. AE, MC, V. Closed Jan.*

Kinvara

The picture-perfect village of Kinvara is worth a visit, thanks to its gorgeous bay-side locale, great walking and sea angling, and numerous pubs. The town is best known for its early August sailing event, **Cruinniú na mBád** (Festival of the Gathering of the Boats). On a rock north of Kinvara Bay, the 16th-century **Dunguaire Castle** stands commanding the approaches from Galway Bay. ⊠ *Co. Galway,* ☎ *091/637108.* ⊙ *May–Sept., daily 9:30–5; banquets at 5:30 and 8:30.*

Clarinbridge

Clarinbridge hosts Galway's annual **Oyster Festival,** which is held in September and features the superlative products of the village's oyster beds.

$ ✕ **Moran's of the Weir.** This waterside traditional thatched cottage is one of Ireland's simplest yet most famous seafood eateries. The specialty here is oysters, but crab, prawns, mussels, and smoked salmon are also served. ⊠ *The Weir, Kilcolgan, Co. Galway,* ☎ *091/796113. AE, MC, V.*

Cork to Galway Essentials

Getting Around

BY BUS

Bus Éireann (☎ 01/836–6111, 061/313–333, 021/508–188, or 066/23566) operates Expressway services from Dublin to Limerick City and Tralee, and from Dublin, Cork City, and Limerick City to Ennis and Galway City. Information is also available at local tourist offices.

BY CAR

Though it's possible to explore the region by local and intercity bus services, you will need plenty of time; a car makes getting around much easier. All major rental companies have facilities at Shannon Airport. **Avis** (☎ 064/36655, 091/568–886) and **Budget** (☎ 064/34341, 091/566–376) also have facilities in Killarney.

BY PLANE

The most convenient international airport is **Shannon** (☎ 061/471–444), 25 km (16 mi) east of Ennis. **Galway Airport** (☎ 091/752–874), near Galway City, is used mainly for internal flights, with steadily increasing U.K. traffic.

Trains run from Cork to Tralee, via Killarney, and from Cork to Limerick City. Trains for Galway City leave from Dublin's Heuston Station.

Guided Tours

Bus Eireann organizes day tours by bus from the Killarney and Tralee train stations; check with the tourist office or rail station for details. **Destination Killarney** (☎ 064/32638) arranges tours of Killarney and the Gap of Dunloe. **Shannon Castle Tours** (☎ 061/360–788) has "Irish Nights" in Bunratty Folk Park or takes you to a medieval banquet at Bunratty Castle. **CIE** has two full-day tours, one covering Connemara and the other the Burren. Tours run from early June to late September only. Book in advance at Galway City's **Ceannt Railway Station** (☎ 091/562–000) or the **Salthill TIO** (☎ 091/520–500).

Visitor Information

All visitor information offices are open weekdays 9–6 and Saturday 9–1: **Ennis** (⊠ Clare Rd., Co. Clare, ☎ 065/682–8366). **Killarney** (⊠ Aras Failte, Beech Rd., ☎ 064/31633, FAX 064/34506). **Limerick City** (⊠ Arthur's Quay, ☎ 061/317–522, FAX 061/317–939). **Shannon Airport** (☎ 061/471–664). **Tralee** (⊠ Ashe Memorial Hall, ☎ 066/712–1288).

GALWAY TO DONEGAL

The trip from Galway to Donegal takes you through the rugged landscape of Connemara to the fabled Yeats country in the northwest and then skirts the borders of Northern Ireland. Although it passes through some of the wildest, loneliest, and most dramatic parts of Ireland, it takes in Galway City, which today has become a hip and happening mini-Dublin.

Galway City

As almost any Galwegian will tell you, theirs is the fastest-growing city in all of Ireland. Nonetheless, its heart is a warren of compact streets. The city's medieval heritage is everywhere apparent, particularly in and around its main pedestrian-oriented street—the name of which changes from Williamsgate to William to Shop to High to Quay. For many Irish people, Galway is a favorite weekend getaway—it's in a beautiful spot, on the north shore of Galway Bay, where the River Corrib flows from Lough Corrib out into the sea. It's also a university town: University College Galway (or UCG as it's locally known) is a center for Gaelic culture. The town, too, has long attracted writers, artists, and musicians, who keep the traditional music pubs lively year-round—the de facto centers of culture.

On the west bank of the Corrib estuary, just outside of the town walls, is **Claddagh,** said to be the oldest fishing village in Ireland. **Salthill Promenade** is the place "to sit and watch the moon rise over Claddagh, and see the sun go down on Galway Bay"—in the words of the city's most famous song.

$$$ ✕ **Drimcong House.** A 300-year-old lakeside house 13 km (8 mi) from
★ Galway City is the home of one of Ireland's most highly regarded restaurants. Chef-owner Gerry Galvin fashions the finest local, organic ingredients into extraordinarily inventive dishes. ⊠ *Northwest on N59,* ☎ *091/555–115. AE, DC, MC, V. Closed Sun., Mon., and Christmas–mid-Mar. No lunch.*

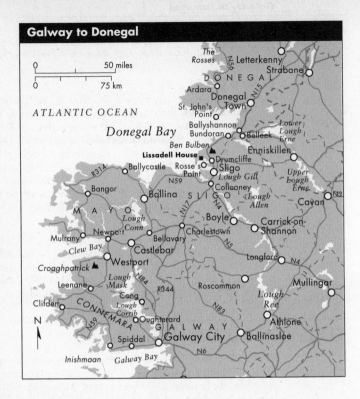

Galway to Donegal

ATLANTIC OCEAN

Donegal Bay

$$$ ✗ **Nimmo's.** Swiss chef Stephan Zeltner presides over a spacious sec-ond-floor dining room (a separately run wine bar is downstairs) in an old stone riverside building. Appropriately, fresh fish is a feature of the menu, as are hearty meat dishes and local produce. ⊠ *Spanish Arch, Galway,* ☎ *091/563–565. AE, DC, MC, V. Closed Sun. No lunch.*

$$ ✗ **Malt House.** This cheerful pub-restaurant tucked away in an alley off High Street in the center of old Galway has long been popular for good food—steaks, rack of lamb, prawns panfried in garlic butter—served in pleasantly informal surroundings. ⊠ *Olde Malte Mall, High St., Galway,* ☎ *091/567–866. AE, DC, MC, V. Closed Sun. Oct.–Apr.*

$$$ 🏨 **Ardilaun House.** This lovely, 19th-century house is at the end of a tree-lined avenue in a quiet suburb, midway between the city center and the Salthill promenade. For views of the bay, book an even-num-bered room on the top floor; other rooms, which are just as pleasant, overlook the flower garden. ⊠ *Taylor's Hill, Co. Galway,* ☎ *091/521–433,* FAX *091/521–546. 81 rooms, 7 suites. Restaurant, 2 bars, indoor pool. AE, DC, MC, V.*

$$$ 🏨 **Galway Great Southern.** Expect to rub elbows with many native Irish visiting Galway at this grand, old-fashioned hotel presiding over Eyre Square. Rooms have high ceilings and Georgian-style furniture. A pianist often graces the spacious lobby, which, like the two bars, is a popular gathering spot. ⊠ *Eyre Sq., Co. Galway,* ☎ *091/564–041,* FAX *091/566–704. 115 rooms. Restaurant, 2 bars, indoor pool. AE, DC, MC, V.*

$ 🏨 **Jurys Galway Inn.** At the foot of Galway's busy main Quay Street, this modern, four-story hotel offers good-quality budget accommodation. Each room is big enough for three adults, or two adults and two chil-dren. ⊠ *Quay St., Co. Galway,* ☎ *091/566–444,* FAX *091/568–415. 128 rooms. Restaurant, bar. AE, DC, MC, V.*

The Aran Islands

Jutting from a belligerent ocean, the Aran Islands—Inishmore, Inishmaan, and Inisheer—are remote western outposts of the ancient province of Connaught. The islands have been populated for thousands of years, and the Irish-speaking inhabitants have adhered to the traditions of their ancestors. The best time to visit the islands is May and early June while the unusual, Burren-like flora is at its best and before the bulk of the visitors arrive.

★ **Rossaveal,** a port on the coast road beyond Spiddle, is the handiest port for a trip to the Aran Islands, 48 km (30 mi) off the coast. **Inis Meáin (Inishmaan),** the middle island, is the most unspoiled of the three; it's here that the traditional Aran lifestyle is most evident. Boats depart for Inishmaan from Rossaveal and less frequently from Galway. You can also fly daily from the **Connemara Airport** (☎ 091/593–034).

Connemara

Bordered by the long expanse of Lough Corrib on the east and the deeply indented, jagged coast of the Atlantic on the west, rugged, desolate western County Galway is known as Connemara. It's an area of spectacular, almost myth-making geography—of glacial lakes; gorgeous, silent mountains; lonely roads; and hushed, uninhabited boglands. In the midst of this wilderness, you'll find few people. In the off-season, especially, you're far more likely to come across sheep than another car.

Two main routes—one inland, the other coastal—lead through Connemara. To take the inland route, leave Galway City on the well-signposted outer-ring road and follow signs for N59—Moycullen, Oughterard, and Clifden. If you choose to go the coastal route, you'll travel due west from Galway City to Rossaveal on R336 through Salthill, Barna, and Spiddle.

Clifden

The principal town of Connemara, Clifden has an almost alpine setting, nestling on the edge of the Atlantic with a spectacular mountain backdrop. A good selection of small restaurants, lively bars with music most nights in the summer, some very pleasant accommodations, and excellent walks make the town a popular base, especially in July and August. A short (2-km/1-mi) walk along the beach road through the grounds of the ruined **Clifden Castle** is the best way to explore the seashore.

Kylemore Abbey, about 15 minutes from Clifden on N59, is one of the most photographed castles in all of Ireland. The vast Gothic-Revival, turreted, gray-stone castle was built as a private home between 1861 and 1868. Today it's the home of Benedictine nuns. Three reception rooms and the main hall are open to the public, as are a crafts center and simple cafeteria. ⊠ *Kylemore,* ☎ *095/41146.* ⊙ *Crafts shop: mid-Mar.–Oct., daily 10–6; cafeteria: Easter–Nov., daily 9:30–6; grounds: daily 9–dusk, exhibition: daily 9–5:30; gardens: Easter–Nov., daily 9–5:30.*

$–$$ ✕⊞ **Erriseask House.** This rambling, modern house, on the rocky seashore of Mannin Bay, is a stylish, comfortable accommodation. Owner-chef Stefan Matz has won many awards for his fine cooking; freshly turf-smoked fillet of beef is a house specialty. ⊠ *Ballyconneely, Co. Galway,* ☎ *095/23553,* 𝕱𝕬𝕏 *095/23639. 8 rooms, 5 suites. Restaurant. AE, DC, MC, V. Closed Nov.–Mar.*

Letterfrack

The 5,000-acre **Connemara National Park** lies just southeast of the village of Letterfrack (14 km/9 mi north of Clifden on N59). The park's **visitor center** covers the area's history and ecology. You can also get details on the many excellent walks and beaches in the area. ☎ 095/41054. ☉ *Park: accessible at all times; visitor center: Apr., May, Sept., daily 10–5:30; June, daily 10–6:30; July and Aug., daily 9:30–6:30.*

$$$ ✕▥ **Renvyle House.** The extraordinary setting—a lake is at the front
★ door and the Atlantic Ocean is at the back—distinguishes this country house. The elegant rooms all have breathtaking views. The cheerful, softly lit restaurant's table d'hôte menu emphasizes fresh local fish and lamb. ⊠ *Renvyle, Co. Galway,* ☎ *095/43511,* 𝖥𝖠𝖷 *095/43515. 65 rooms. Restaurant, pool. AE, DC, MC, V. Closed Jan.–Feb.*

Westport

Westport is a quiet, mainly 18th-century town overlooking Clew Bay—a wide expanse of water studded with nearly 400 islands. The distinctive silhouette of **Croagh Patrick,** a 2,540-ft mountain, dominates the town. Today some 25,000 pilgrims climb it on the last Sunday in July in honor of St. Patrick, who is believed to have spent 40 days fasting on its summit in AD 441. Whether he did or not, the climb is an exhilarating experience and can be completed in about three hours; it should be attempted only in good weather, however.

$$ ✕ **Asgard.** On the Quay, a short distance from the town center, this pub serves award-winning food in both its downstairs bar and its more formal, upstairs restaurant. ⊠ *The Quay, Westport,* ☎ *098/25319. AE, DC, MC, V.*

$$ ▥ **Delphi Lodge.** In the heart of spectacular mountains-and-lakes scenery, this sporting lodge is heavily stocked with fishing paraphernalia. The owner, Peter Mantle, is a valuable storehouse of information and stories. Guests dine together. ⊠ *6 km (4 mi) off N59, northwest of Leenane, Co. Mayo,* ☎ *095/42211,* 𝖥𝖠𝖷 *095/42296. 12 rooms. Restaurant, bar. MC, V. Closed mid-Dec.–mid-Jan.*

$$ ▥ **Olde Railway Hotel.** This Victorian hotel on the town center's tree-lined mall offers both character and comfort. ⊠ *The Mall, Co. Mayo,* ☎ *098/25605,* 𝖥𝖠𝖷 *098/25090. 24 rooms. Restaurant. AE, DC, MC, V. Closed mid-Jan.–mid-Feb.*

Sligo

County Sligo is noted for its seaside resorts, the famous golf course at Rosses Point (just outside Sligo Town), and its links with Ireland's most famous 20th-century poet, W. B. Yeats. **Sligo Town** is the best place to begin a tour of Yeats Country. In the throes of an economic boom, Sligo retains all the charm of smaller, sleepier villages, yet by day it's as lively and crowded as Galway City. The **Niland Gallery** houses one of Ireland's largest collections of works by the poet's brother, Jack B. Yeats, as well as memorabilia of Yeats the poet. Yeats's grave is in Drumcliffe, beneath the slopes of Ben Bulben, just north of town. ⊠ *Stephen St.,* ☎ *071/42212.* ☉ *Library: Tues.–Fri. 10–5, Sat. 10–1 and 2–5; museum: June–Sept., Tues.–Sat. 10–noon and 2–4:50; Oct.–mid-Dec. and mid-Mar.–May, Tues.–Sat. 2–4:50.*

★ From Sligo, you can take a boat or drive up to **Lough Gill** and see the **Lake Isle of Innisfree** and other places immortalized in Yeats's poetry. Fourteen km (9 mi) northwest of Sligo Town is **Lissadell House,** a substantial mansion dating from 1830 that features prominently in Yeats's writings. It was the home of Constance Gore-Booth, later Countess Markeviecz, who took part in the 1916 uprising. ☎ *071/63150.* ☉ *June–mid-Sept., Mon.–Sat. 10:30–12:30 and 2–4:30.*

$ ✗ **Bistro Bianconi.** The decor is all white: blond wood and white-tile floors. But the food is a colorful array of gourmet pizzas, baked in the wood-burning oven with toppings both traditional and innovative. ✉ *44 O'Connell St., Sligo Town,* ☎ *071/41744. AE, MC, V. No lunch.*

$$$ ✗🏨 **Markree Castle.** A pastoral, 1,000-acre estate is home to this 17th-century, family-owned hotel in a castle. Public rooms share a comfortable informality; guest rooms are idiosyncratic. The kitchen offers up an excellent table d'hôte menu and on Sunday, a traditional lunch attracts a sizable, family-oriented crowd. ✉ *Off N4, south of Sligo Town,* ☎ *071/67800, 800/223–6510 in the U.S.,* 🖷 *071/67840. 30 rooms. Restaurant. AE, DC, MC, V.*

Donegal Town

Donegal is the gateway to the magnificent Northwest, with its rugged coastline and dramatic highlands. The town is centered around the triangular Diamond, where three roads converge (N56 to the west, and N15 to the south and the northeast) and the mouth of the River Eske pours gently into Donegal Bay. Near the north corner of the Diamond is **Donegal Castle,** built by clan leader Hugh O'Donnell in the 1470s. Ruins of the **Franciscan abbey,** founded in 1474 by Hugh O'Donnell, are a five-minute walk south of town at a spectacular site perched above the Eske.

$ ✗ **Blueberry Tea Room.** This pleasant restaurant and café is just across the street from Donegal Castle. ✉ *Castle St.,* ☎ *073/22933. V. Closed Sun. mid-Sept.–May.*

$$$$ ✗🏨 **St. Ernan's House.** On its own wooded tidal island in Donegal Bay,
★ five minutes south of town, St. Ernan's is one of the most spectacularly situated country houses in all of Ireland. Guest rooms are simple but elegant, with antiques and views of the bay. Dinner in the intimate dining room is prepared in Irish country-house style. ✉ *St. Ernan's Island, Co. Donegal,* ☎ *073/21065,* 🖷 *073/22098. 12 rooms. Dining room. MC, V. Closed Nov.–Easter.*

$ ✗🏨 **Castle Murray House Hotel.** The original house has been extended and modernized to take full advantage of the exceptional panoramic views of the bay and distant mountains. The restaurant is renowned for its superb French cuisine. ✉ *St. John's Point, Dunkineely, Co. Donegal (21 km/13 mi west of Donegal Town),* ☎ *073/37022,* 🖷 *073/37330. 10 rooms. Restaurant. MC, V. Closed entirely mid-Jan.–mid-Feb. and Mon.–Tues. Oct.–mid-Jan. and mid-Feb.–Easter*

Galway to Donegal Essentials

Getting Around

BY BICYCLE

Bikes can be rented from **Celtic Cycles** (✉ Victoria Pl., Galway City, ☎ 091/566–606); **Gary's Cycles** (✉ Quay St., Sligo, ☎ 071/45418); or **John Mannion** (✉ Railway View, Clifden, ☎ 095/21160).

BY BUS

Bus Eireann (☎ 01/836–6111) travels all over the region. **McGeehan Coaches** (☎ 075/46150) services County Donegal locally.

BY CAR

In Galway, cars can be rented from **Avis** (☎ 091/568–886); **Budget** (☎ 091/566–376 or 091/564–570); and **Murray's** (☎ 091/562–222). Taxis do not operate on meters; agree on the fare beforehand.

BY TRAIN

Trains to Galway, Westport, and Sligo operate from Dublin's Heuston or Connolly (Sligo) stations. There is no train service north of Sligo.

Guided Tours

CIE Tours International operates day tours of Connemara out of Galway City and bus tours into the Donegal highlands from Sligo train station; details are available from local tourist offices. **CIE/Bus Eireann** (☎ 01/830–2222) and **Gray Line** (☎ 01/661–9666) organize tours of the Boyne Valley and County Meath out of Dublin.

Visitor Information

All offices are open weekdays 9–6 and Saturday 9–1. **Galway City** (✉ off Eyre Sq., ☎ 091/563–081, 🖷 091/565–201). **Sligo Town** (✉ Temple St., ☎ 071/61201, 🖷 071/60360). **Westport** (✉ The Mall, ☎ 098/25711, 🖷 098/26709).

BELFAST

Belfast is the capital of Northern Ireland, a province under the rule of the United Kingdom. The hardheaded and industrious Scots-Presbyterians, imported to make Ulster a bulwark against Ireland's Catholicism, have had a profound and ineradicable effect on the place. The North seems to have more factories, neater-looking farms, better roads, and—in its cities—more of the two-story, redbrick houses typical of Great Britain than does the Republic.

Belfast was a great Victorian success story, an industrial boomtown whose prosperity was built on trade—especially linen and shipbuilding (the *Titanic* was built here). For the last two decades, however, news about Belfast was news about the Troubles. But the 1994 cease-fire began to change that, and on July 20, 1997, the cease-fire was officially reestablished. Like other cities in the throes of a major historical transition, it's a fascinating place to visit.

The city is fairly compact; its center is made up of roughly three contiguous areas that are easy to navigate on foot, though from the south end to the north it's about an hour's leisurely walk. At Belfast's southern end, the **Queen's University area** is easily the most appealing part of the city. This is where you'll find the university, the Botanic Gardens, fine 19th-century buildings, and many good pubs, restaurants, and B&Bs. Between University Street and Shaftesbury Square is the **Golden Mile,** with hotels, major civic and office buildings, and some restaurants, cafés, and stores. City Hall marks the northern boundary of the Golden Mile and the southern end of the (theoretically) pedestrian-only **central district,** which extends from Donegall Square north almost to St. Anne's Cathedral; this is the old heart of Belfast. Behind St. Anne's is the **Cathedral Quarter,** a maze of cobbled streets that the city plans to transform over the next few years.

$$$–$$$$ ✕ **Roscoff.** Celebrity TV chefs Paul and Jeanne Rankin run this acclaimed
★   Golden Mile spot. The long, stylish room has a modern, minimalist decor, sort of like the Rankins's cuisine. Dishes are often Asian-influenced, such as pork with ginger, and roast monkfish with grilled tomatoes and black beans. The Rankins travel frequently, and the overall standards tend to suffer in their absence. ✉ *Shaftesbury Sq. at end of Great Victoria St.,* ☎ *01232/331–532. AE, DC, MC, V. Closed Sun. No lunch Fri.*

$–$$ ✕ **The Strand.** In the University area, this dark and intimate bistro with candlelighted tables attracts students and professors with its adventurous and unusual menu. Recommended dishes include Irish lamb noisettes and baked eggplant. ✉ *12 Stranmillis Rd.,* ☎ *01232/682–266. AE, DC, MC, V.*

$$$$ ⬚ **The McCausland Hotel.** Clean, simple lines, and an aura of sump-tuous minimalism are the hallmarks of this pair of 1867 grain ware-houses that have been turned into a luxury hotel. Guest rooms are more traditional country-cottage style. ⬚ *34–38 Victoria St., Belfast, Co. Antrim BT1 3GH,* ☎ *01232/220–200,* FAX *01232/220–220. 60 rooms. AE, DC, MC, V. Closed late Dec.*

$$–$$$ ⬚ **Ash-Rowan Guest House.** This outstanding B&B in a spacious Vic-★ torian home has guest rooms in tasteful, individual style; each has a pri-vate bath and TV. ⬚ *Mrs. E. Hazlett, 12 Windsor Ave., Belfast BT9 6EE,* ☎ *01232/661–758,* FAX *01232/663–227. 5 rooms. MC, V. Closed Dec.*

$$–$$$ ⬚ **Madison's.** A few minutes' walk from the university, this hotel is done in a modish Barcelona-inspired take on Art Nouveau. Rooms, in cool yellows and rich blues, are sparely furnished but comfortable. ⬚ *59 Botanic Ave., Belfast BT7 1JL,* ☎ *01232/330–040,* FAX *01232/328–007. 35 rooms. Restaurant, bar. AE, MC, V.*

Belfast Essentials

Getting Around

BY BUS

Northern Ireland's bus company, **Ulsterbus** (☎ 01232/333–000), and the Republic's **Bus Éireann** (☎ 01/836–6111 in Dublin) both run di-rect services between Dublin and Belfast. The main bus stations in Belfast are **Europa Buscentre** (⬚ Glengall St., ☎ 01232/333–000) and **Laganside Buscentre** (⬚ Donegall Quay, ☎ 01232/320–111).

BY CAR

Many roads from the Republic into Northern Ireland were once closed for security reasons, but all are now open, leaving you with a score of legitimate crossing points to choose from. Army checkpoints at all ap-proved frontier posts are rare, and few customs formalities are observed. The fast N1/A1 road connects Belfast to Dublin (160 km/100 mi) with an average driving time of just over two hours.

BY PLANE

Belfast International Airport at Aldergove (☎ 01849/422–888) is the North's principal air arrival point, 30½ km (19 mi) from Belfast. **Belfast City Airport** (☎ 01232/457–745) is the second airport, 6½ km (4 mi) from the city; it receives flights only from the United Kingdom.

BY TRAIN

The Dublin–Belfast Express train is operated by both railways (travel time is about two hours): **Northern Ireland Railways** (☎ 01232/899–411) and **Irish Rail** (Iarnrod Éireann; ☎ 01/836–6222). Belfast's main station is the misnamed **Central Station** (⬚ E. Bridge St., ☎ 01232/899–411); a free shuttle bus service will drop you off at City Hall or Ulsterbus's city-center **Europa Buscentre** (☎ 01232/333–000). Or you can change trains for the de facto city-center **Great Victoria Street Sta-tion** (⬚ Great Victoria St., ☎ 01232/230–671).

Contacts and Resources

CAR RENTALS

All the major car-rental agencies have branches at the Belfast Interna-tional Airport; some also have branches at the Belfast City Airport. If you're planning to take a rental car across the border into the Republic, inform the company and check its insurance procedures.

EMERGENCIES

Police, fire, ambulance, and coast guard (☎ 999 toll-free in all of North-ern Ireland). **Belfast's main police station** (⬚ 6–10 N. Queen St., ☎ 01232/650–222).

GUIDED TOURS
Citybus (⊠ Milewater Rd., ☎ 01232/458–484) runs a Belfast City Tour.
Ulsterbus (⊠ Milewater Rd., ☎ 01232/333–000) operates half-day or
full-day trips (June–September) from Belfast to surrounding areas.

VISITOR INFORMATION
Northern Ireland Tourist Board Information Centre (⊠ Wellington
Pl./Queen St., ☎ 01232/246–609, FAX 01232/312–424).

18 ITALY

ROME, FLORENCE, TUSCANY, MILAN, VENICE, CAMPANIA

Where else in Europe can you find the blend of great art, delicious food and wine, and sheer verve that awaits you in Italy? This Mediterranean country has made a profound contribution to Western civilization, producing some of the world's greatest thinkers, writers, politicians, saints, and artists. Impressive traces of their lives and works can still be seen in Italy's great buildings and lovely countryside.

The whole of Italy is one vast attraction, but the triangle of its most-visited cities—Rome (Roma), Florence (Firenze), and Venice (Venezia)—represents the great variety found here. In Rome and Florence, especially, you can feel the uninterrupted flow of the ages, from the Classical era of the ancient Romans to the bustle and throb of contemporary life being lived in centuries-old settings. Venice, by contrast, seems suspended in time, the same today as it was when it held sway over the eastern Mediterranean and the East. Each of these cities reveals a different aspect of the Italian character: the Baroque exuberance of Rome, Florence's serene stylishness, and the dreamy sensuality of Venice.

Trying to soak in Italy's rich artistic heritage poses a challenge. The country's many museums and churches draw hordes of visitors, all wanting to see the same thing at the same time. From May through September, the Sistine Chapel, Michelangelo's *David*, Piazza San Marco, and other key sights are more often than not swamped by mobs of tourists. Try to see the highlights at off-peak times. If they are open during lunch, this is often a good time. Again, relax: Seeing some attractions—such as the scrubbed facades of Rome's glorious Baroque churches—entails no opening hours and no lines at all.

It's important to be attentive to matters of personal security in certain parts of the country; always be on guard against pickpockets and purse snatchers in the main tourist cities and in Naples. Especially in Rome and Florence, watch out for bands of gypsy children, expert at lifting wallets. Keep the children at a distance, and don't be shy about shouting at them to stay away. Small cities and towns are usually safe.

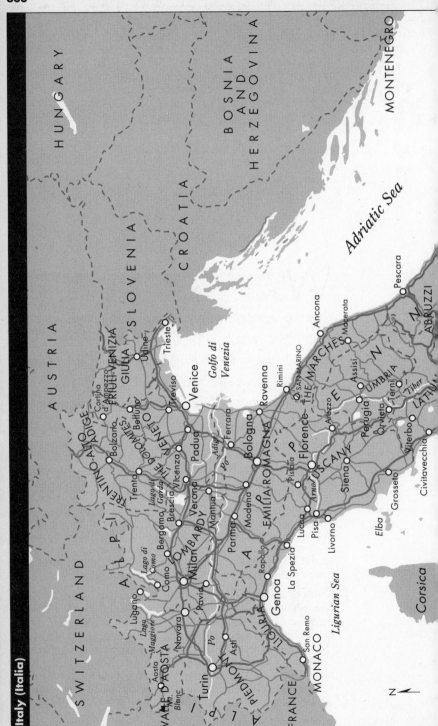

Italy (Italia)

HUNGARY

AUSTRIA

SWITZERLAND

SLOVENIA

CROATIA

BOSNIA
AND
HERZEGOVINA

MONTENEGRO

Adriatic Sea

FRIULI-VENEZIA
GIULIA

TRENTINO-ALTO ADIGE

VALLE D'AOSTA

Mont
Blanc

Aosta

A L P S

Lago
Maggiore

Lugano

Lago di
Como

Como

Bergamo

Novara

Turin

Asti

PIEDMONT

P o

FRANCE

MONACO

San Remo

LIGURIA

Genoa

Rapallo

La Spezia

Ligurian Sea

Corsica

Elba

Livorno

Pisa

Lucca

Pistoia

Arno

TUSCANY

Siena

Grosseto

Florence

EMILIA-ROMAGNA

Modena

Parma

Mantua

Po

Verona

Brescia

Lago di
Garda

Trento

Bolzano

THE DOLOMITES

Cortina
d'Ampezzo

Belluno

VENETO

Vicenza

Padua

Adige

Ferrara

Bologna

Ravenna

Rimini

SAN MARINO

THE MARCHES

Ancona

Macerata

Assisi

Perugia

UMBRIA

Arezzo

Orvieto

Terni

Tiber

Viterbo

LATIUM

Civitavecchia

Pescara

ABRUZZI

Treviso

Udine

Trieste

Venice

Golfo di
Venezia

LOMBARDY

Milan

Pavia

N

N

E

Z

Corsica

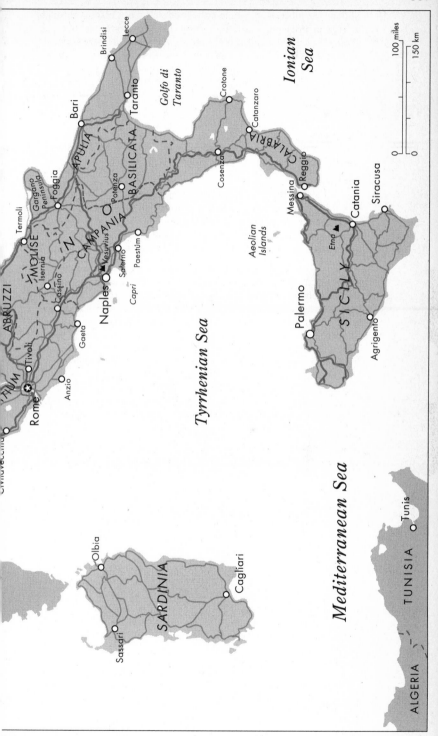

Making the most of your time in Italy doesn't mean rushing through it. To gain a rich appreciation for Italy, don't try to see everything all at once. Practice the Italian-perfected *il dolce far niente*—the sweet art of idleness—which might mean skipping a museum to sit at a table in a pretty café, enjoying the sunshine and a cappuccino. Art—and life—are to be enjoyed, and the Italians can show you how.

ITALY A TO Z

Customs

For details on imports and duty-free limits, *see* Customs & Duties *in* Chapter 1.

Dining

Generally speaking, a *ristorante* pays more attention to decor and service than does a *trattoria,* which is simpler and often family run. An *osteria* used to be a simple tavern, though now the term may be used to designate a chic and expensive eatery. A *tavola calda* offers hot dishes and snacks, with seating. A *rosticceria* offers the same to take out.

The menu is always posted in the window or just inside the door of an eating establishment. Check to see what is offered, and note whether there are charges for *coperto* (cover) and *servizio* (service), which will increase your check amount. The coperto charge has been abolished in many eating places. Many restaurants offer a *menu turistico,* usually a complete dinner, limited to a few entrées, at a reasonable price (including taxes and service, usually with beverages extra). Tap water is safe in large cities and almost everywhere else unless noted *non potabile*. Bottled mineral water is available everywhere, *gassata* (with bubbles) or *non gassata* (without bubbles). If you prefer tap water, ask for *acqua semplice*. Note that many restaurants close from Christmas through the first week in January and for a good part of August.

MEALTIMES

Lunch is served in Rome from 1 to 3, dinner from 8 to 10:30 and sometimes later. Service begins and ends a half hour earlier in Florence and Venice and later in the south. Practically all restaurants close one day a week; some close for winter or summer vacations.

RATINGS

Prices are per person and include first course, main course, dessert or fruit, and house wine, where available.

CATEGORY	ROME, MILAN*	OTHER AREAS
$$$$	over 120,000 lire	over 100,000 lire
$$$	70,000 lire–120,000 lire	60,000 lire–80,000 lire
$$	40,000 lire–70,000 lire	30,000–60,000
$	under 40,000 lire	under 30,000 lire

Note that restaurant prices in Venice can be slightly higher than those in Rome and Milan; in small cities prices are usually lower.

WHAT TO WEAR

Except for restaurants in the $$$$ and occasionally in the $$$ categories, where jacket and tie are advisable, neat, casual attire is acceptable.

Language

Italy is accustomed to English-speaking tourists, and in major cities you will find that many people speak at least a little English. In smaller hotels and restaurants and on public transportation, a basic knowledge or knowing just a few phrases of Italian comes in handy.

Lodging

Italy, especially Rome, Florence, and Venice, offers a good choice of accommodations, though rooms tend to be small. Room rates are on a par with those of most European capitals, although porters, room service, and in-house laundering are disappearing in all but the most elegant hotels. Taxes and service are included in the room rate. Although breakfast is usually quoted in the room rate, it's actually an extra charge that you can decline. The desk might not be happy about it, but make your preference clear when booking or checking in. Air-conditioning also may be an extra charge. Rooms, except where noted, have a private bath with shower. Specify if you care about having either a bathtub or shower, as not all rooms have both. In $$ and $ places showers may be the drain-in-the-floor type guaranteed to flood the bathroom. In older hotels room quality may be uneven; if you don't like the room you're given, ask for another. This applies to noise, too; some front rooms are bigger and have views but get street noise. Train stations in major cities have hotel-reservation service booths.

CAMPING

Italy has a wide selection of campgrounds, and the Italians themselves have taken to camping, which means that beach or mountain sites will be crammed in July and August. A *carnet* (permit) is required; get one from your local association before leaving home. You can buy a campsite directory such as the detailed guide published by the Touring Club Italiano (available in bookstores in Italian only) or obtain the free directory of campsites published by the Federazione Italiana del Campeggio (✉ Casella Postale 23, 50041 Calenzano, Florence, ☎ 055/882391, FAX 055/8825918) in tourist information offices or by mail from the organization.

HOTELS

Italian hotels are classified by regional tourist boards from five-star (deluxe) to one-star (modest hotels and small inns). The established price of the room appears on a rate card on the back of the door of your room or inside the closet door, though you may be able to get a lower rate by asking. Any variations above the posted rate should be cause for complaint and should be reported to the manager and the police. Sheraton, Forte, Jolly, Space, Atahotels, Best Western, Holiday Inn, and Italhotels are among the reliable chains or groups operating in Italy. Several Relais & Châteaux hotels are noted for individual atmosphere, personal service, and luxury; they are also expensive. The AGIP chain is found mostly on main highways. The Family Hotels group, composed mostly of small $$ and $ family-run hotels, offers good value, reliability, and special attention to families. Standards in one-star hotels are very uneven. At best, rooms are usually spotlessly clean but basic, with soft beds and shower and toilets down the hall.

Low-season rates do not officially apply in Rome, Florence, and Milan, but you can usually bargain for discounted rates in Rome and Milan in summer and during weekends (when business travelers are few) and in Florence in winter. Ask for *"la tariffa scontata."* You can save on hotel accommodations in Venice and in such resorts as Sorrento and Capri during their low seasons—the winter (with the exception of Christmas holidays and Carnival in Venice), early spring, and late-autumn months.

RATINGS

The following price categories are determined by the cost of two people in a double room.

CATEGORY	ROME, MILAN*	OTHER AREAS
$$$$	over 600,000 lire	over 450,000 lire
$$$	350,000 lire–600,000 lire	300,000 lire–450,000 lire
$$	250,000 lire–350,000 lire	200,000 lire–300,000 lire
$	under 250,000 lire	under 200,000 lire

As with restaurant prices, the cost of hotels in Venice may be slightly more than those shown here.

RENTALS AND AGRITOURISM

Short or long rental stays in town apartments or in rural villas or farms are a good option for families traveling with children and others who value independence and want a taste of living Italian-style. Agritourism, or staying on a working farm, usually for a week or more, is growing in popularity in rural areas throughout Italy, especially in Tuscany and Umbria. Agritourism accommodations range in style from rustic simplicity to country chic, and prices vary accordingly. Contact local APT tourist offices or the only agritourist agency that offers booking service in Italy (Agriturist, ✉ Piazza San Firenze 3, 50122 Florence, ☎ 055/287838, FAX 055/2302285). Alternatively, you can buy *Guida all'Ospitalità Rurale,* compiled by Agriturist, which includes over 1,600 farms in Italy. Although it is available in Italian only, pictures and the use of international symbols describing facilities make the guide a good tool to use. You can get the guide from major bookstores.

Mail

The Italian mail system is notoriously erratic and can be excruciatingly slow. Until a trend toward greater efficiency is confirmed, allow up to 15 days for mail to and from the United States and Canada and almost as much to and from the United Kingdom.

POSTAL RATES

Airmail letters and postcards (lightweight stationery) to the United States and Canada cost 1,300 lire for the first 20 grams, 2,700 lire for up to 40 grams, and 3,100 lire for up to 50 grams. Always stick a blue airmail tag (available at post offices) on your mail, or write "airmail" in big, clear characters to the side of the address. Postcards and letters (for the first 20 grams) to the United Kingdom, as well as to any other EU country, including Italy, cost 800 lire. In addition to post offices, you can buy stamps at tobacconists.

RECEIVING MAIL

Mail can be sent to American Express offices; service is free if you are a card member. You can send mail to Italian post offices, marked "fermo posta" and addressed to you c/o Palazzo delle Poste, with the name of the city in which you will pick it up. You must show your passport and pay a small fee.

Money Matters

COSTS

Venice, Milan, Florence, and Rome are the more expensive Italian cities to visit. Taxes are usually included in hotel bills; a cover charge may appear as a separate item in restaurant checks, as does the service charge, usually about 15%, if added. There is a 19% tax on car rentals, usually included in the rates.

CURRENCY

The unit of currency in Italy is the lira (plural, lire). There are bills of 1,000, 2,000, 5,000, 10,000, 50,000, 100,000, and 500,000 lire (impossible to change, except in banks); coins are worth 50, 100, 200, 500, and 1,000 lire. In 1999 the euro was introduced as a banking currency, but the lire is still the currency in use on a day-to-day basis. At press time (summer 1999) the exchange rate was about 1,891 lire to the U.S. dollar, 1,289 lire to the Canadian dollar, and 2,955 lire to the pound sterling.

When your purchases run into hundreds of thousands of lire, beware of being shortchanged, a dodge that is practiced at ticket windows, toll booths, and cashiers' desks, as well as in shops and even in banks. *Always count your change before you leave the counter.* Always carry some smaller-denomination bills for sundry purchases; you're less likely to be shortchanged, and you won't have to face the eye-rolling dismay of cashiers reluctant to change large-denomination bills.

Credit cards are generally accepted in shops and hotels, but may not always be welcome in restaurants, so always look for card logos displayed in windows or ask when you enter to avoid embarrassing situations. When you wish to leave a tip beyond the 15% service charge that is usually included with your bill (☞ Tipping, *below*), leave it in cash rather than adding it to the credit card slip.

SAMPLE PRICES
A cup of espresso enjoyed while standing at a bar costs from 1,000 to 1,500 lire, the same cup served at a table, triple that. A bottle of beer costs from 2,500 to 3,800 lire, a soft drink about 2,500 lire. A *tramezzino* (small sandwich) costs about 2,500 lire, a more substantial one about 3,500 to 5,000 lire. You will pay about 15,000 lire for a short taxi ride. Admission to a major museum is about 12,000 lire.

TIPPING
Tipping practices vary depending on where you are. Italians tip smaller amounts in small cities and towns, often not at all in cafés and taxis north of Rome. The following guidelines apply in major cities.

In restaurants a 15% service charge is usually added to the total; it's customary to give the waiter an additional 5% to 10%, depending on the service and on the quality of the meal. Charges for service are included in all hotel bills, but smaller tips to staff members are appreciated. In general, in a $$ hotel, chambermaids should be given about 1,000 lire per room per day, 4,000–5,000 lire per week; bellhops should get 1,000 to 2,000 lire. Tip a minimum of 1,000 lire for room service and valet service. Tip breakfast waiters 500 lire per day per table (at end of stay). These amounts should be increased by 40% in $$$ hotels, doubled in $$$$ hotels. Give the concierge about 15% of the bill for services. Tip doormen about 500 lire for calling a cab.

Taxi drivers are happy with 5%–10%, although Italians never tip them. Porters at railroad stations and airports charge a fixed rate per suitcase; tip an additional 500 lire per person, more if the porter is very helpful. Tip service-station attendants 1,000 lire if they are especially helpful. Tip guides about 2,000 lire per person for a half-day tour, more if they are very good.

National Holidays
January 1; January 6 (Epiphany); April 23 and 24 (Easter Sunday and Monday); April 25 (Liberation Day); May 1 (May Day); August 15 (Assumption, known as Ferragosto); November 1 (All Saints' Day); December 8 (Immaculate Conception); December 25–26.

The feast days of patron saints are observed locally. Many businesses and shops may be closed in Florence, Genoa, and Turin on June 24 (St. John the Baptist); in Rome on June 29 (Sts. Peter and Paul); in Palermo on July 15 (Santa Rosalia); in Naples on September 19 (San Gennaro); in Bologna on October 4 (San Petronio); in Trieste on November 3 (San Giusto); and in Milan on December 7 (St. Ambrose).

Venice's feast of St. Mark is April 25, the same as Liberation Day, and November 21 (Madonna della Salute).

Opening and Closing Times

Banks are open weekdays 8:30–1:30 and 2:45–3:45. **Churches** are usually open from early morning to noon or 12:30, when they close for about two hours or more, opening again in the afternoon until about 7 PM. **National museums** are usually open from 9 AM until 2 and are often closed on Monday, but there are many exceptions, especially at major museums. **Non-national museums** have entirely different hours, which may vary according to season. Most major archaeological sites are open every day from early morning to dusk, except some holidays. At all museums and sites, ticket offices close an hour or so before official closing time. Always check with the local tourist office for current hours and holiday closings. **Shops** are open, with individual variations, from 9 to 1 and from 3:30 or 4 to 7:30 or 8. They are open from Monday through Saturday, but close for a half day during the week; for example, in Rome most shops (except food shops, which close on Thursday afternoon, and hairdressers, which close all day Monday) are closed on Monday morning (all shops close Saturday afternoon in July and August), though a 1995 ordinance allows greater freedom. Some tourist-oriented shops and department stores—in downtown Rome, Florence, and Venice—are open all day, every day.

Shopping

SALES-TAX REFUNDS

Getting a refund of Italy's value-added tax is complicated. Foreign tourists who have spent more than 300,000 lire (before tax) in one store can take advantage of it, however. At the time of purchase, with passport or ID in hand, ask the store for an invoice describing the article or articles and the total lire amount. If your destination when you leave Italy is a non-EU country, you must have the invoice stamped at customs upon departure from Italy; if your destination is another EU country, you must obtain the customs stamp upon departure from that country. Once back home—and within 90 days of the date of purchase—you must send the stamped invoice back to the store, which should forward the IVA rebate directly to you. If the store participates in the Europe Tax-Free Shopping System (those that do display a sign to the effect), things are simpler. The invoice provided is a Tax-Free Check in the amount of the tax refund, which can be cashed at the Tax-Free Cash Refund window in the transit area of major airports and border crossings.

Telephoning

COUNTRY CODE

The country code for Italy is 39. You no longer drop the "0" in the regional code when calling Italy.

INTERNATIONAL CALLS

To place an international call, insert a phone card, dial 00, then the country code, area code, and phone number. The cheaper and easier option, however, will be to use your AT&T, MCI, or Sprint calling card. For **AT&T USADirect,** dial access number ☎ 172–1011; for **MCI Call USA,** access number ☎ 172–1022; for **Sprint Express,** access number ☎ 172–1877. You will be connected directly with an operator in the United States. You can make collect calls from any phone by dialing ☎ 172–1011, which will get you an English-speaking operator. For information and operators in Europe and the Mediterranean area, dial ☎ 15; for intercontinental service, dial ☎ 170.

LOCAL CALLS

LOCAL CALLS

For all local calls, you must dial the regional area codes, even in cities. Most local calls cost 200 lire for two minutes. Pay phones take either 100-, 200-, or 500-lire coins or *schede telefoniche* (phone cards), purchased in bars, tobacconists, post offices, and TELECOM offices in either 5,000- 10,000-, or 15,000-lire denominations. To activate cards, tear off the marked corner. For information and operators in Europe and the Mediterranean area, dial 15; for intercontinental service, dial 170.

Transportation

BY BOAT

Ferries connect the mainland with all the major islands. Car ferries operate to Sicily, Sardinia, Elba, Ponza, Capri (though taking a car here is not advised), and Ischia, among others. Lake ferries connect the towns on the shores of the Italian lakes: Como, Maggiore, Garda, and Iseo.

BY BUS

Regional bus companies provide service throughout Italy. Route information and timetables are usually available at tourist information offices and travel agencies, or at bus company ticket offices. One of the interregional companies providing long-distance service is **SITA** (⊠ Viale Cadorna 105, Florence, ☎ 055/483651).

BY CAR

The Autostrada del Sole (A1, A2, and A3) crosses the country from north to south, connecting Milan to Reggio Calabria. The A4 from west to east connects Turin to Trieste.

Breakdowns. Dial 116 for towing and repairs; breakdown service (emergency repairs and towing on an autostrada) is free for tourists with foreign license plates or with cars rented in Italy that have breakdown insurance. Dial 113 for an ambulance and highway police.

Gasoline. Gas costs the equivalent of more than $4 per U.S. gallon, or about 1,900 lire per liter. Except on the autostrade, most gas stations are closed Sunday; they also close from 12:30 PM to 3:30 PM and at 7 PM for the night. Most gas stations do not accept credit cards. Self-service pumps, which usually accept only 10,000 lire notes, can be found in most cities and towns.

Parking. Check with your hotel to determine the best place to park. Parking is greatly restricted in the center of most cities. Parking in a ZONA DISCO is for limited periods. City garages cost up to 30,000 lire per day.

Road Conditions. The extensive autostrada network (toll superhighways) connecting all major towns is complemented by equally well-maintained but toll-free *superstrade* (express highways), *strade statali* (main roads), and *strade provinciali* (secondary roads). All are clearly signposted and numbered. The ticket issued on entering an autostrada must be returned on leaving, along with the toll. On some shorter autostrade, mainly connections, the toll is payable on entering. Have small bills and change handy for tolls; shortchanging is a risk, so always count your change before leaving the toll booth. If you will be using autostrade extensively, buy a Viacard—an automatic toll card—for 50,000 or 100,000 lire at autostrada locations. Some automatic booths also take an array of credit cards.

Rules of the Road. Driving is on the right. The speed limit on an autostrada is 130 kph (81 mph). It is 110 kph (70 mph) on state and provincial roads, unless otherwise marked. Other regulations are largely as in the United States except that the police have the power to levy severe on-the-spot fines. Italians drive fast and impatiently; don't be surprised when, on a windy two-lane highway, drivers zip into the ongo-ing-traffic lane to pass you if you are going too slowly.

BY PLANE
Alitalia and some privately owned companies such as **Meridiana** and **Air One,** in addition to other European airlines, provide service through-out Italy. Most of them offer several types of discount fares; inquire at travel agencies or at Alitalia agencies in major cities.

BY TRAIN
The fastest trains on the FS (Ferrovie dello Stato), the state-owned rail-road, are the Eurostar trains, for which you pay a supplement and for which seat reservations are required in both first and second class and are included in the cost of the ticket. Also fast are Intercity (IC) and Eurocity (EC) trains, for which you pay a supplement in both classes and for which reservations may be required. Trains designated *inter-regionale* are slower, making more stops. *Regionale* trains are locals, serving a single region. Throughout Italy, call ☎ 1478/880880 toll free daily 7 AM–9 PM for train information in Italian. If you plan on a lot of train traveling, the complete FS train schedule, sold at news stalls, is a good investment.

You can buy tickets and make seat reservations at travel agencies dis-playing the FS symbol up to two months in advance, thereby avoid-ing long lines at station ticket windows. **All tickets must be date-stamped in the small yellow or red machines near the tracks before you board.** Once stamped, your ticket is valid for six hours if your destination is within 200 km (124 mi) and for 24 hours for destinations beyond that; you can get on and off at will for the duration of the ticket's validity. If you don't stamp your ticket in the machine, you must actively seek out a conductor to validate the ticket on the train, paying an extra 10,000 lire for the service. If you merely wait in your seat for him to collect your ticket, unless the train is overcrowded, you might risk a heavier fine (30,000 lire), depending on how "understanding" the controller is. You will pay a hefty surcharge if you purchase your ticket on board the train. Tickets for destinations within a 200-km (125-mi) range can be purchased at any *tabacchi* (tobacconist) inside the station. There is a refreshment service on all long-distance trains. Tap water on trains is not drinkable. Carry compact bags for easy overhead storage. Trains are very crowded at holiday times; always reserve, at all times of year.

Visitor Information
In Italy regional and local agencies, either the **Azienda di Promozione Turistica** (APT or AST) or the **Ente Provinciale per il Turismo** (EPT), as well as municipal tourist offices and others known as **Informazione e Accoglienza Turistica** (IAT) or **Pro Loco** in small towns, provide help-ful information.

Weather
The best months for good-weather sightseeing are April, May, June, September, and October, usually pleasant and not too hot. In general the northern half of the peninsula and the entire Adriatic Coast, with the exception of Apulia, are rainier than the rest of Italy. In Venice, fog and high tides are likely to be part of the landscape between November and February.

CLIMATE
The hottest months are July and August, when brief afternoon thun-derstorms are common in inland areas. Winters are relatively mild in most places on the tourist circuit, but there are always some rainy spells. The following are average daily maximum and minimum temperatures for Rome and Milan.

ROME

Jan.	52F	11C	May	74F	23C	Sept.	79F	26C
	40	5		56	13		62	17
Feb.	55F	13C	June	82F	28C	Oct.	71F	22C
	42	6		63	17		55	13
Mar.	59F	15C	July	87F	30C	Nov.	61F	16C
	45	7		67	20		49	9
Apr.	66F	19C	Aug.	86F	30C	Dec.	55F	13C
	50	10		67	20		44	6

MILAN

Jan.	40F	5C	May	74F	23C	Sept.	75F	24C
	32	0		57	14		61	16
Feb.	46F	8C	June	80F	27C	Oct.	63F	17C
	35	2		63	17		52	11
Mar.	56F	13C	July	84F	29C	Nov.	51F	10C
	43	6		67	20		43	6
Apr.	65F	18C	Aug.	82F	28C	Dec.	43F	6C
	49	9		66	16		35	2

ROME

Antiquity is taken for granted in Rome, where successive ages have piled the present on top of the past—building, layering, and overlapping their own particular segments of Rome's 2,500 years of history to form a remarkably varied urban complex. Most of the city's major sights are in the *centro storico* (historic center), which is between the long, straight Via del Corso and the Tiber River, and *Roma antica* (ancient Rome), site of the Roman Forum and Colosseum, and around which the other sections of the city grew up through the ages: medieval Rome, which covered the horn of land that pushes the Tiber toward the Vatican and extended across the river into Trastevere; and Renaissance Rome, which was erected upon medieval foundations and extended as far as the Vatican, with beautiful villas created in what were then the outskirts of the city.

Exploring Rome

Numbers in the margin correspond to points of interest on the Rome map.

The layout of the *centro storico* is highly irregular, but several landmarks serve as orientation points to identify the areas that most visitors come to see: the Colosseum, Pantheon, Piazza Navona, St. Peter's Basilica, the Spanish Steps, and the Terme di Caracalla. You'll need a good map to find your way around; newsstands offer a wide choice. Energetic sightseers will walk a lot, a much more pleasant way to see the city now that some traffic has been barred from the center of town during the day; others might choose to take taxis, buses, or the Metro. If you are in Rome during a hot spell, do as the Romans do: Start out early in the morning, have a light lunch and a long siesta during the hottest hours, then resume sightseeing in the late afternoon and end your evening with a leisurely meal outdoors, refreshed by cold Frascati wine and the *ponentino,* the cool evening breeze.

Ancient Rome

❼ Arco di Costantino (Arch of Constantine). The best preserved of Rome's triumphal arches, this 4th-century BC monument is covered with reliefs depicting Constantine's victory over Maxentius at the Milvian

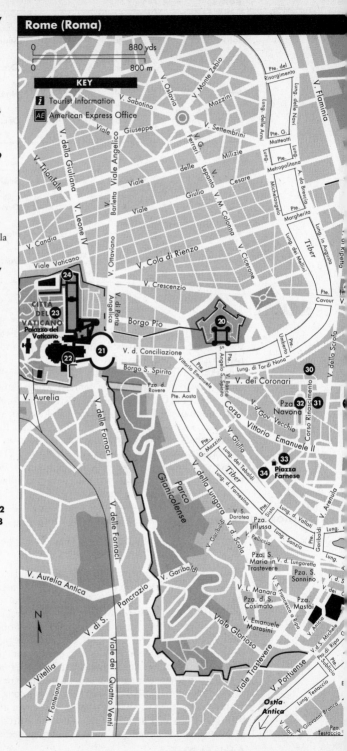

Rome (Roma)

KEY

ℹ️ Tourist Information

AE American Express Office

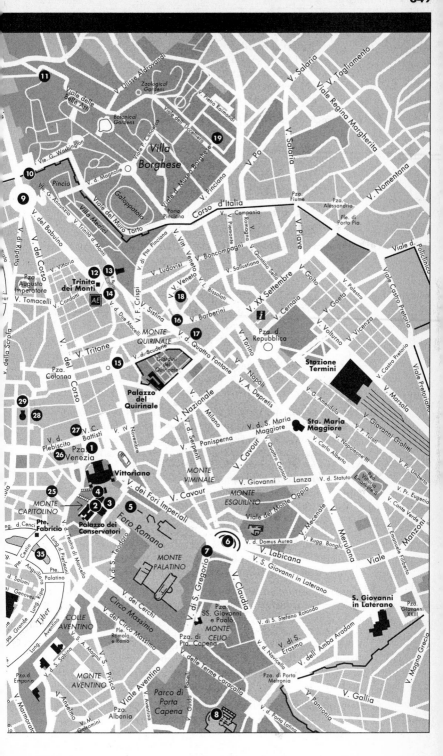

Bridge. Just before this battle in AD 312, Constantine had a vision of a cross in the heavens and heard the words: "In this sign thou shalt conquer." The victory led not only to the construction of this majestic marble arch but also to a turning point in the history of Christianity: Soon afterward a grateful Constantine decreed that it was a lawful religion and should be tolerated throughout the empire. ⊠ *Piazza del Colosseo at end of Via di San Gregorio.*

❷ Campidoglio (Capitoline Hill). In the square on the Capitoline Hill, the majestic ramp and beautifully proportioned piazza are the handiwork of Michelangelo (1475–1564), who also designed the facades of the three palaces, two of which house the Capitoline Museums. Palazzo Senatorio, at the center, is still the ceremonial seat of Rome's City Hall; it was built over the Tabularium, where ancient Rome's state archives were kept. The statue at the center of the square is a copy of an ancient Roman bronze of Marcus Aurelius (AD 120–180). ⊠ *Piazza del Campidoglio.*

★ ❻ Colosseum (Colosseo). Massive and majestic, this ruin is ancient Rome's most famous monument, inaugurated in AD 80 with a program of games and shows that lasted 100 days. Before the imperial box, gladiators would salute the emperor and cry, *"Ave, imperator, morituri te salutant"* (Hail, emperor, men soon to die salute thee); it is said that when one day they heard the emperor Claudius respond, "or maybe not," they became so offended that they called a strike. The Colosseum could hold more than 50,000 spectators; it was faced with marble, decorated with stuccos, and had an ingenious system of awnings to provide shade. It was built in just eight years. The Colosseum takes its name from a colossal, 118-ft statue of Nero that stood nearby. ⊠ *Piazza del Colosseo,* ☎ *06/7004261.* ☉ *Mon.–Sat. 9–2 hrs before sunset, Sun. 9–1.*

❸ Musei Capitolini (Capitoline Museums). The **Museo Capitolino** and **Palazzo dei Conservatori,** the palaces flanking Palazzo Senatorio on the Campidoglio (☞ above), form a single museum holding some fine classical sculptures, including the gilded bronze equestrian statue of Marcus Aurelius that once stood on the pedestal in the piazza, as well as the *Dying Gaul,* the *Capitoline Venus,* and a fascinating series of portrait busts of ancient philosophers and emperors. In the courtyard of Palazzo dei Conservatori on the right of the piazza, you can use the mammoth fragments of a colossal statue of the emperor Constantine (circa 280–336). Inside you will find splendidly frescoed salons still used for municipal ceremonies, as well as sculptures and paintings. ⊠ *Piazza del Campidoglio,* ☎ *06/67102071.* ☒ *Free last Sun. of month.* ☉ *Tues.–Sun. 9–7.*

❶ Piazza Venezia. Considered the geographical heart of the city, the square is dominated by the enormous marble monument honoring the first king of unified Italy, Vittorio Emanuele II (1820–78). It also holds the Tomb of the Unknown Soldier. The piazza takes its name from Palazzo Venezia, once Mussolini's headquarters. His most famous speeches were delivered from the balcony to the roaring crowds below. ⊠ *Square at intersection of Via del Corso, Via del Plebiscito, and Via del Fori Imperiali.*

❺ Roman Forum (Foro Romano). In the valley below the Campidoglio, what was once a marshy hollow important only as a crossroads and marketplace became the political, commercial, and social center of Rome, containing public meeting halls, shops, and temples. As Rome declined, these monuments lost their importance and were eventually destroyed by fire or the invasions of barbarians. Rubble accumulated (though much of it was carted off later by medieval home builders as construction material), and the site reverted to marshy pastureland; sporadic excavations began at the end of the 19th century. You don't really have to try to make sense of the mass of marble fragments scattered over the area of the Roman Forum. Just consider that 2,000 years ago this was the center of the Mediterranean world. Wander down the **Via Sacra** and climb the **Colle Palatino** (Palatine Hill), where the emperors had their palaces and where 16th-century cardinals strolled in elaborate Italian gardens. From the belvedere you have a good view of the **Circo Massimo** (Circus Maximus). Audio guides are available at the bookshop-ticket office at the Via dei Fori Imperiali entrance. ⊠ *Entrances at Via dei Fori Imperiali and Piazza del Colosseo,* ☎ *06/6990110.* ☞ *Forum: free.* ⊙ *Mon.–Sat. 9–2 hrs before sunset, Sun. 9–1.*

❹ **Santa Maria d'Aracoeli.** The 13th-century church on the Campidoglio can be reached by a long flight of steep stairs or, more easily, by way of the stairs on the far side of the Museo Capitolino. Stop in to see the medieval pavement, the Renaissance gilded ceiling that commemorates the victory of Lepanto, and the Pinturicchio (1454–1513) frescoes. ⊠ *Piazza Aracoeli,* ☎ *06/6798155.* ⊙ *Oct.–May, daily 7–noon and 4–6; June–Sept., daily 7–noon and 4–6:30.*

❽ **Terme di Caracalla** (Baths of Caracalla). The scale of the towering ruins of ancient Rome's most beautiful and luxurious public baths hint at their past splendor. Inaugurated by Caracalla in 217, the baths were used until the 6th century. An ancient version of a swank athletic club, the baths were open to all, though men and women used them separately; citizens could bathe, socialize, and exercise in huge pools and richly decorated halls and libraries. ⊠ *Via delle Terme di Caracalla,* ☎ *06/5758626.* ⊙ *Apr.–Sept., Tues.–Sat. 9–6, Sun.–Mon. 9–1; Oct.–Mar., Tues.–Sat. 9–3, Sun.–Mon. 9–1.*

Piazzas and Fountains

⑭ **Fondazione Keats-Shelley Memorial** (Keats and Shelley Memorial House). To the right of the Spanish Steps is the house where Keats (1795–1821) died; the building is now a museum of Keats memorabilia and it also houses a library of works by Romantic authors. ⊠ *Piazza di Spagna 26, next to the Spanish Steps,* ☎ *06/6784235.* ⊙ *June–Sept., weekdays 9–1 and 3–6; Oct.–May, weekdays 9–1 and 2:30–5:30.*

★ ⑮ **Fontana di Trevi** (Trevi Fountain). A spectacular fantasy of mythical sea creatures and cascades of splashing water, this fountain is one of Rome's Baroque greats. The fountain as you see it was completed in the mid-1700s, but there had been a drinking fountain on the site for centuries. Pope Urban VIII (1568–1644) almost sparked a revolt when he slapped a tax on wine to cover the expenses of having the fountain repaired. Legend has it that visitors must toss a coin into the fountain to ensure their return to Rome. ⊠ *Piazza di Trevi.*

⑲ **Galleria Borghese.** At the southeast corner of Villa Borghese, a park studded with pines and classical statuary, is this gallery created by Cardinal Scipione Borghese in the early 17th century as a showcase for his fabulous collection of ancient sculpture and Baroque painting. One of the noteworthy additions to the collections over the centuries, the reclining statue of Pauline Borghese by Canova (1757–1822) continues to seduce visitors. Among some extraordinary works by Bernini (1598–1680), the unforgettable *Apollo and Daphne* shows how the artist transformed marble into flesh and foliage. The picture collection is no less impressive, with works by Caravaggio (1573–1610), Raphael (1483–1520), and Titian (circa 1488–1576). You must make reservations. ⊠ *Piazza Scipione Borghese, off Via Pinciana,* ☎ *06/8548577; 06/32810 reservations.* ⊙ *Tues.–Sun. 9–7.*

⓫ Museo Etrusco di Villa Giulia (Etruscan Museum of Villa Giulia). Pope Julius III (1487–1555) built this gracious Renaissance villa as a summer retreat. It now holds a world-class museum where you can delve into the world of the Etruscans, who inhabited Italy in pre-Roman times and have left fascinating evidence of their relaxed lifestyle attuned to the pleasures of the senses. You'll observe smiles as enigmatic as that of the Mona Lisa on deities and other figures in terra-cotta, bronze, and gold. ⊠ *Piazza di Villa Giulia 9*, ☎ *06/3201951.* ⊘ *Tues.–Sat. 9–7, Sun. 9–2.*

⓱ Palazzo Barberini (Barberini Palace). Rome's most splendid 17th-century palace houses the **Galleria Nazionale di Arte Antica.** Its gems include Raphael's *La Fornarina* and many other fine paintings, some lavishly frescoed ceilings, and a charming suite of rooms decorated in 1782 on the occasion of the marriage of a Barberini heiress. ⊠ *Via Quattro Fontane 13*, ☎ *06/9538100.* ⊘ *Mid-Sept.–mid-Nov. and mid-Mar.–May, daily 9–6; June–mid-Sept., daily 9–7:30; mid-Nov.–mid-Mar., daily 9–4.*

⓰ Piazza Barberini. This busy crossroads has two fountains by Bernini: the jaunty **Fontana del Tritone** (Triton Fountain) in the middle of the square and the **Fontana delle Api** (Fountain of the Bees) at the corner of Via Veneto. Decorated with the heraldic Barberini bees, this latter shell-shape fountain bears an inscription that was immediately regarded as an unlucky omen by the superstitious Romans, for it erroneously stated that the fountain had been erected in the 22nd year of the reign of Pope Urban VIII, who commissioned it, whereas in fact the 21st anniversary of his election was still some weeks away. The wrong numeral was hurriedly erased, but to no avail: Urban died eight days before the beginning of his 22nd year as pontiff. ⊠ *Square at intersection of Via del Tritone, Via Vittorio Veneto, and Via Barberini.*

❾ Piazza del Popolo. Designed by neoclassic architect Giuseppe Valadier in the early 1800s, this square is one of the largest and airiest in Rome. The 3,000-year-old obelisk in the middle was brought to Rome from Egypt by the emperor Augustus, and it once stood in the Circus Maximus. ⊠ *Square at southern end of Via Flaminia and northern end of Via del Corso.*

⓬ Piazza di Spagna. The square is the heart of Rome's chic shopping district and a popular rendezvous spot, especially for the young people who throng the Spanish Steps on evenings and weekend afternoons. In the center of the elongated square, at the foot of the Spanish Steps, is the **Fontana della Barcaccia** (Old Boat) by Pietro Bernini (Gian Lorenzo's father). ⊠ *Southern end of Via del Babuino and northern end of Via Due Macelli.*

⓲ Santa Maria della Concezione. In the crypt under the main Capuchin church skeletons and scattered bones of some 4,000 dead Capuchin monks are arranged in odd decorative designs, a macabre practice peculiar to the Baroque age. ⊠ *Via Veneto 27*, ☎ *06/4871185.* ⊘ *Fri.–Wed. 9–12 and 3–6.*

❿ Santa Maria del Popolo. This medieval church rebuilt by Bernini in Baroque style is rich in art; the pièces de résistance: two stunning Caravaggios in the chapel to the left of the main altar. You'll find it tucked away in the corner of Piazza del Popolo next to the monumental Renaissance city gate. ⊠ *Piazza del Popolo*, ☎ *06/3610836.* ⊘ *Mon.–Sat. 7–noon and 4–7, Sun. 8–2.*

★ **⓭ Spanish Steps.** The 200-year-old staircase got its name from the nearby Spanish Embassy to the Holy See (the Vatican), though the staircase was built with French funds in 1723, as the approach to the French church of **Trinità dei Monti** at the top of the steps. The steps are banked with blooming azaleas from mid-April to mid-May. ⊠ *Piazza di Spagna and Piazza Trinità dei Monti.*

Castel Sant'Angelo and the Vatican

⑳ Castel Sant'Angelo (Sant'Angelo Castle). Transformed into a formidable fortress, this castle was originally built as the tomb of Emperor Hadrian (AD 76–138) in the 2nd century AD. In its early days it looked much like the Augusteo (Tomb of Augustus), which still stands in more or less its original form across the river. Hadrian's Tomb was incorporated into the city's walls and served as a military stronghold during the barbarian invasions. According to legend it got its present name in the 6th century, when Pope Gregory the Great, passing by in a religious procession, saw an angel with a sword appear above the ramparts to signal the end of the plague that was raging. Enlarged and fortified, the castle became a refuge for the popes, who fled to it along the Passetto, an arcaded passageway that links it with the Vatican.

Inside the castle you see ancient corridors, medieval cells, and Renaissance salons, a museum of antique weapons, courtyards piled with stone cannonballs, and terraces with great views of the city. There's a pleasant bar with outdoor tables. The highest terrace of all, under the bronze statue of the legendary angel, is the one from which Puccini's heroine Tosca threw herself to her death. **Ponte Sant'Angelo,** the ancient bridge spanning the Tiber in front of the castle, is decorated with lovely Baroque angels designed by Bernini. ⊠ *Lungotevere Castello 50,* ☎ *06/6819111.* ☉ *Tues.–Sun. 9–7; longer hrs in summer.*

㉓ Giardini Vaticani (Vatican Gardens). The attractively landscaped gardens can be seen in a two-hour tour that shows you a few historical monuments, fountains, and the lovely 16th-century house of Pius IV (1499–1565) designed by Pirro Ligorio (1500–83), as well as the Vatican's mosaic school. Vistas from within the gardens give you a different perspective of the basilica itself. You should make reservations two or three days in advance. ⊠ *Tickets: Piazza San Pietro,* ☎ *06/69884466.* ☜ *18,000 lire.* ☉ *Tours Apr.–Oct., Mon., Tues., Thurs.–Sat. at 10; Nov.–Mar., Sat. at 10, weekdays by request for groups.*

㉔ Musei Vaticani (Vatican Museums). The accumulated collections of humanity's artistic history are housed here, from the Egyptians to the present, boasting such masterpieces as Michelangelo's frescoes in the Sistine Chapel. The collections cover nearly 8 km (5 mi) of displays, so if you are visiting St. Peter's and the museums on the same day, you can save yourself the 15-minute walk between the two by taking the shuttle bus (2,000 lire) that operates during museum opening hours, except on Wednesday. The ride gives you a glimpse of the Giardini Vaticani (☞ *above*). Posters at the museum entrance plot out a choice of four color-coded itineraries; the shortest takes about 90 minutes, the longest more than four hours, depending on your rate of progress. No ★ matter which tour you take, it will include the famed **Sistine Chapel** (Cappella Sistina). In 1508 Pope Julius II (1443–1513) commissioned Michelangelo to paint the more than 10,000 square ft of the chapel's ceiling. For four years Michelangelo dedicated himself to painting in the fresco technique, over fresh plaster, and the result was a masterpiece. Cleaning has removed centuries of soot and revealed the original and surprisingly brilliant colors of the ceiling and the *Last Judgment.* You can try to avoid the tour groups by going early or late, allowing yourself enough time before the closing hour. In peak season the crowds definitely detract from your appreciation of this outstanding artistic achievement. To make sense of the figures on the ceiling, buy an illustrated guide or rent an audio guide. A pair of binoculars also helps.

Some of the highlights that might be of interest on your first tour are
the reorganized Egyptian collection and the *Laocoön*, the *Belvedere
Torso*, which inspired Michelangelo, and the *Apollo Belvedere*. The
Stanze di Raffaello (Raphael Rooms) are decorated with masterful fres-
coes, and there are more of Raphael's works in the **Pinacoteca** (Picture Gallery). At the Quattro Cancelli, near the entrance to the Picture
Gallery, a rather spartan cafeteria provides basic refreshments. ⊠ *Viale
Vaticano,* ☎ *06/69883041.* 🎫 *Free last Sun. of month.* ☉ *Easter wk
and mid-Mar.–Oct., weekdays 8:45–3:45, Sat. 8:45–12:45; Nov.–mid-
Mar. (except Easter), Mon.–Sat. 8:45–12:45; last Sun. of every month
8:45–12:45. Closed religious holidays (Jan. 1 and 6, Feb. 11, Mar. 19,
Easter Sun. and Mon., May 1, Ascension Thurs., Corpus Christi, June
29, Aug. 15 and 16, Nov. 1, Dec. 8, Dec. 25 and 26) and Sun., excepting last Sun. of month. Note: Ushers at the entrance of St. Peter's
Basilica and the Vatican Museums will not allow entry to persons
with inappropriate clothing (no bare knees or shoulders).*

㉑ **Piazza San Pietro** (St. Peter's Square). Completed in 1667, the vast, oval-
shape square in front of St. Peter's basilica opens at the western end
of Via della Conciliazione, the broad avenue created by Mussolini's
architects by razing blocks of old houses. This opened up a vista of
the basilica, giving the eye time to adjust to its mammoth dimensions,
and thereby spoiling the effect Bernini sought. He enclosed his huge
square in the embrace of mammoth quadruple colonnades. Look for
the stone disks in the pavement halfway between the fountains and the
obelisk. From these points the colonnades seem to be formed of a single row of columns all the way around. The square was designed to
accommodate crowds, and it has held up to 400,000 people at one time.
At noon on Sunday when he is in Rome, the pope appears at his third-
floor study window in the **Palazzo Vaticano,** to the right of the basilica, to bless the crowd in the square.

Since the Lateran Treaty of 1929, Vatican City has been an independent and sovereign state, which covers about 108 acres and is surrounded
by thick, high walls. Its gates are watched over by the Swiss Guards,
who still wear the colorful dress uniforms designed by Michelangelo.
Sovereign of this little state is John Paul II, 264th pope of the Roman
Catholic Church. For many visitors a **papal audience** is the highlight
of a trip to Rome. Mass audiences take place on Wednesday morning
in a modern audience hall (capacity 7,000) off the left-hand colonnade
or in St. Peter's Square. Tickets are necessary, but you can also see the
Pope when he appears at the window of the Vatican Palace to bless
the crowd in the square below at noon on Sunday. He also blesses the
public on summer Sundays when he's at the papal residence at Castel
Gandolfo. For audience tickets write or fax well in advance indicating the date you prefer, language you speak, and hotel in which you
will stay. Or, apply for tickets in person on the Monday or Tuesday
before the Wednesday audience. ⊠ *Prefettura della Casa Pontificia,
00120 Vatican City,* ☎ *06/69883017,* 📠 *06/69885863.* ☉ *Mon. and
Tues. 9–1.*

★ **㉒** **St. Peter's Basilica** (Basilica di San Pietro). In all of its staggering
grandeur and magnificence, St. Peter's Basilica is best appreciated as
the lustrous background for ecclesiastical ceremonies thronged with
the faithful. The original basilica was built during the early 4th century AD by the emperor Constantine, above an earlier shrine that supposedly marked the burial place of St. Peter. After more than a thousand
years, the old basilica was so decrepit it had to be torn down. The task
of building a new, much larger one took almost 200 years, and em-
ployed the architectural geniuses of Alberti (1404–72), Bramante

(1444–1514), Raphael, Peruzzi (1481–1536), Antonio Sangallo the Younger (1483–1546), and Michelangelo, who died before the dome he had planned could be completed. The structure was finally finished in 1626.

Among the most famous works of art is Michelangelo's *Pietà* (1498), seen in the first chapel on the right just as you enter the basilica. Michelangelo carved four statues of the Pietà; this one is the earliest and best known, two others are in Florence, and the fourth, the *Rondanini Pietà*, is in Milan. At the end of the central aisle is the bronze statue of St. Peter, its foot worn by centuries of reverent kisses. The bronze throne above the altar in the apse was created by Bernini to contain a simple wood-and-ivory chair once believed to have belonged to St. Peter. Bernini's bronze baldachin over the papal altar was made with metal stripped from the portico of the Pantheon at the order of Pope Urban VIII, one of the powerful Roman Barberini family. His practice of plundering ancient monuments for material with which to carry out his grandiose schemes inspired the famous quip, *"Quod non fecerunt barbari, fecerunt Barberini"* ("What the barbarians didn't do, the Barberini did").

As you stroll up and down the aisles and transepts, observe the fine mosaic copies of famous paintings above the altars, the monumental tombs and statues, and the fine stucco work. Stop at the **Museo Storico** (Historical Museum), which contains some priceless liturgical objects. ☉ *Apr.–Sept., daily 9–6; Oct.–Mar., daily 9–5.*

The entrance to the so-called **Grotte Vaticane** (Vatican Grottoes), crypts containing chapels and the tombs of various popes, is in one of the huge piers at the crossing. It's best to leave this visit for last, as the crypt's only exit takes you outside the church. It occupies the area of the original basilica, over the necropolis, the ancient burial ground where evidence of what may be St. Peter's burial place has been found. ☉ *Apr.–Sept., daily 7–6; Oct.–Mar., daily 7–5.*

To see the roof and dome of the basilica, take the elevator or climb the stairs in the courtyard near the exit from the Vatican Grottoes. From the roof you can climb a short interior staircase to the base of the dome for an overhead view of the basilica's interior. Then, only if you are in good shape should you attempt the very long, strenuous, and claustrophobic climb up the narrow stairs to the balcony of the lantern atop the dome, where you can look down on the Giardini Vaticani (Vatican Gardens) and out across all of Rome. ⊠ *Entrance in courtyard to the left as you leave the basilica.* ☉ *Apr.–Sept., daily 8–6; Oct.–Mar., daily 8–5.*

Free 60-minute tours of St. Peter's Basilica are offered in English daily (usually starting about 10 AM and 3 PM, and at 2:30 PM Sunday) by volunteer guides. They start at the information desk under the basilica portico. At the Ufficio Scavi you can book special tours of the necropolis. Note that entry to St. Peter's, the Musei Vaticani (Vatican Museums, ☞ *above*), and the Gardens (☞ *above*) is barred to those wearing shorts, miniskirts, sleeveless T-shirts, and otherwise revealing clothing. Women can cover bare shoulders and upper arms with scarves; men should wear full-length pants or jeans. ⊠ *Piazza San Pietro,* ☎ *06/69884466.* ☉ *Apr.–Sept., daily 7–7; Oct.–Mar., daily 7–6. Closed during ceremonies in the piazza. Necropolis (left beyond Arco delle Campane entrance to Vatican):* ☎ *06/69885318. Apply a few days in advance to Ufficio Scavi, or try in morning for the same day. Office hrs Mon.–Sat. 9–5; closed Sun.*

Old Rome

㉝ Campo dei Fiori (Field of Flowers). This square is the site of a crowded and colorful daily morning market. The hooded bronze figure brooding over the piazza is philosopher Giordano Bruno (1548–1600), who was burned at the stake here for heresy in 1600. ⊠ *Piazza Campo dei Fiori.*

㉖ Chiesa del Gesù. This huge 16th-century church is a paragon of the Baroque style and the tangible symbol of the power of the Jesuits, who were a major force in the Counter-Reformation in Europe. Its interior gleams with gold and precious marbles, and it has a fantastically painted ceiling that flows down over the pillars, merging with painted stucco figures to complete the three-dimensional illusion. ⊠ *Piazza del Gesù,* ☎ 06/697001. ⊙ *Mon.–Sat. 6–noon and 4–7, Sun. 4–5.*

㉕ Fontana delle Tartarughe (Turtles). This pretty 16th-century bronze fountain by Giacomo della Porta (circa 1537–1602)—the turtles were added probably by Bernini in 1658—is in the heart of Rome's former Jewish Ghetto, a neighborhood with medieval inscriptions and friezes on the old buildings on Via Portico d'Ottavia, and the remains of the Teatro di Marcello (Theater of Marcello), a theater built by Julius Caesar to hold 20,000 spectators. ⊠ *Piazza Mattei.*

㉗ Galleria Doria Pamphili. You can visit this rambling palazzo, still the residence of a princely family, to view the gallery housing the family's art collection and also some of the magnificently furnished private apartments. ⊠ *Piazza del Collegio Romano 2,* ☎ 06/6797323. ⊙ *Fri.–Wed. 10–5; private-apartments tours 10–noon.*

㉟ Isola Tiberina (Tiberina Island). Built in 62 BC, Rome's oldest bridge, the **Ponte Fabricio,** links the Ghetto neighborhood on the Tiber's left bank to this little island, home to the city hospital and the church of San Bartolomeo. The island has been dedicated to healing ever since a temple to Aesculapius was erected here in 291 BC. **Ponte Cestio** links the island with the Trastevere section on the right bank.

OFF THE
BEATEN PATH

Ostia Antica (Ancient Ostia) – The well-preserved Roman port city of Ostia Antica, near the sea, is a parklike archaeological site analogous to Pompeii and much easier to get to from Rome. There's a regular train service from the Ostiense Station (Piramide Metro stop). ⊠ *Via dei Romagnoli, Ostia Antica, not far from Fiumicino Airport,* ☎ 06/5651405. ⊙ *Daily 9–1 hr before sunset.*

㉚ Palazzo Altemps. A 15th-century patrician dwelling, the palace has been beautifully restored and is now a showcase for the sculpture collection of the **Museo Nazionale Romano.** Informative labels in English make it easy to appreciate such famous sculptures as the amazingly intricate carved reliefs on the *Ludovisi Sarcophagus* and the *Galata,* representing the heroic death of a barbarian warrior. ⊠ *Piazza Sant'Apollinare 46,* ☎ 06/6833759. ⊙ *Tues.–Sun. 9–7.*

㉞ Palazzo Farnese. Now the French Embassy, one of the most beautiful of Rome's many Renaissance palaces, dominates Piazza Farnese, where Egyptian marble basins from the Terme di Caracalla have been transformed into fountains. ⊠ *Piazza Farnese.*

㉙ Pantheon. Originally built in 27 BC by Augustus's general Agrippa and totally rebuilt by Hadrian in the 2nd century AD, this is one of Rome's finest, best-preserved, and perhaps least appreciated ancient monuments. You don't have to look far past the huge columns of the portico and the original bronze doors to find the reason for its astounding architectural harmony: The diameter of the soaring dome is exactly equal to the height of the walls. The hole in the ceiling is intentional: The oculus at the apex of the dome signifies the "all-seeing eye of heaven." In ancient times the entire interior was encrusted with rich decorations of gilt bronze and marble that were plundered by later emperors and popes. Note the bronze doors: They are originals. ⊠ *Piazza della Rotonda,* ☎ *06/68300230.* ☉ *Mon.–Sat. 9–6:30, Sun. 9–1.*

★ ㉜ **Piazza Navona.** This elongated 17th-century piazza traces the oval form of the underlying Circus of Diocletian. At the center Bernini's lively **Fontana dei Quattro Fiumi** (Four Rivers) is a showpiece. The four statues represent rivers in the four corners of the world: the Nile, with its face covered in allusion to its then unknown source; the Ganges; the Danube; and the River Plate, with its hand raised. And here we have to give the lie to the legend that this was Bernini's mischievous dig at Borromini's design of the facade of the church of **Sant'Agnese in Agone,** from which the statue seems to be shrinking in horror. The fountain was created in 1651; work on the church's facade began a year or two later. The piazza dozes in the morning, when little groups of pensioners sun themselves on the stone benches and children pedal tricycles around the big fountain. In the late afternoon the sidewalk cafés fill up for the aperitif hour, and in the evening, especially in good weather, the piazza comes to life with a throng of street artists, vendors, tourists, and Romans out for their evening *passeggiata* (promenade). ⊠ *North of Corso Vittorio Emanuele and west of Corso Rinascimento.*

㉛ **San Luigi dei Francesi.** The clergy of San Luigi considered Caravaggio's roistering and unruly lifestyle scandalous enough, but his realistic treatment of sacred subjects—seen in three paintings in the last chapel—was just too much for them. They rejected his first version of the altarpiece and weren't particularly happy with the other two works either. Thanks to the intercession of Caravaggio's patron, an influential cardinal, they were persuaded to keep them—a lucky thing, since they are now recognized to be among the artist's finest paintings. Have a few 500-lire coins handy for the light machine. ⊠ *Piazza San Luigi dei Francesi,* ☎ *06/688271.* ☉ *Fri.–Wed. 7:30–12:30 and 3:30–7, Thurs. 7:30–12:30.*

㉘ **Santa Maria sopra Minerva.** Rome's only major Gothic church takes its name from the temple of Minerva over which it was built. Inside are some beautiful frescoes by Filippo Lippi (1406–69); outside there is a charming elephant by Bernini with an obelisk on its back. ⊠ *Piazza della Minerva,* ☎ *06/6793926.* ☉ *Daily 7–noon and 4–7.*

Dining and Lodging

Rome has no shortage of restaurants, especially those that serve various Italian regional cuisines. The most expensive restaurants usually offer interpretations of Italian and international specialties with a flourish of linen and silver, followed up by a whopping *conto* (check). If you want typical Italian cooking and lower prices, try a more moderately priced ristorante or a trattoria, usually a smallish and unassuming, often family-run place. Although McDonald's colonized the whole country in the 1980s, Rome still offers a variety of fast-food places that serve Italian fare, called *tavola calda* or *rosticceria,* where you can get anything from a fruit salad and fresh spinach to lasagne and fish such as deep-fried cod fillets. Cheap ethnic places are proliferating, especially around the Termini area, but sadly the quality too often matches the price. On the whole, pizza to go (*al taglio*), which comes thick and with tasty toppings, or a crispy crust, Roman-style pizza from a Trastevere pizzeria are the best low-budget treats in town. During August and over Christmas many restaurants close for vacation. For details and price-category information, *see* Dining *in* Italy A to Z, *above.*

Hotels listed are within walking distance of at least some sights and handy to public transportation. Those in the $$ and $ categories do not have restaurants but serve Continental breakfast. Rooms facing the street may get traffic noise throughout the night, and few hotels in the lower price categories have double-glazed windows. Ask for a quiet room—or bring earplugs. Always make reservations, even if only a few days in advance, by phone or fax. Always inquire about special low rates. Should you find yourself in the city without reservations, however, contact **HR** (✉ Termini Station; Aeroporto Fiumicino, ☎ 06/6991000), a hotel reservation service, or **EPT** (✉ Via Parigi 5, ☎ 06/48899253, 𝖥𝖠𝖷 06/4819316; ✉ Near Piazza della Repubblica, Aeroporto Fiumicino, ☎ 06/65956074; ✉ Stazione Termini, ☎ 06/4871270). The Rome municipal tourist information booths (☞ Visitor Information *in* Rome Essentials, *below*) will also help you find a room. For details and price-category definitions, *see* Lodging *in* Italy A to Z, *above*.

$$$$ ✕ **La Pergola.** High atop Monte Mario, the Cavalieri Hilton's (☞ *below*)
★   rooftop restaurant commands sweeping views onto the city below. The warmly elegant dining room has trompe l'oeil ceilings, handsome wood paneling, and large windows. Celebrated Wunder-chef Heinz Beck is a skilled technician, and brings Rome its finest example of Mediterranean *alta cucina* (haute cuisine). ✉ *Cavalieri Hilton, Via Cadlolo 101,* ☎ *06/3509221. Reservations essential. Jacket and tie. AE, DC, MC, V. Closed Sun.–Mon. No lunch.*

$$$$ ✕ **La Rosetta.** In 1992 chef-owner Massimo Riccioli took the nets and
★   fishing gear off the classic cherry-wood walls of his parents' trattoria to create what is widely known as the place to go in Rome to eat first-rate fish. Start with *ricci di mare* (sea urchins), *vongole veraci* (sautéed clams), or a variety of delicately marinated fish; move on to perfectly grilled seafood or a poached fillet. Desserts (made in house) are worth saving room for. ✉ *Via della Rosetta 9,* ☎ *06/68308841. Dinner reservations essential. Closed Sun. and 2–3 wks in Aug. No lunch Sat. AE, DC, MC, V.*

$$$ ✕ **Checchino dal 1887.** Literally carved out of a hillside made of potsherds from Roman times, Checchino serves the most traditional Roman cuisine—carefully prepared and served without fanfare—in a clean, sober environment. The slaughterhouses of the Testaccio quarter are long gone, but you can still try the variety of meats that make up the soul of Roman cooking, including *trippa* (tripe) and *coratella* (sweetbreads). There's also plenty to choose from for those uninterested in innards. Desserts are very good. ✉ *Via di Monte Testaccio 30,* ☎ *06/5746318. AE, DC, MC, V. Closed Mon., Aug., and during Christmas. No dinner Sun.*

$$$ ✕ **Da Checco er Carettiere.** Maybe this is what all Italian restaurants once looked like: an aging doorman, garlic braids hanging from the ceiling, black-and-white photos in small frames lining the wood-paneled walls. At this third-generation, family-run Trastevere institution you'll find all the Roman standards, solidly prepared with good-quality ingredients, plus plenty of local vegetables and an unusually good selection of fish. ✉ *Via Benedetta 10,* ☎ *06/5817018. AE, DC, MC, V. Closed Mon. No dinner Sun.*

$$–$$$ ✕ **Dal Bolognese.** This classic restaurant is a trendy choice for a leisurely lunch between sightseeing and shopping. An array of contemporary paintings decorates the dining room but the real attraction is the lovely piazza—prime people-watching real estate. As the name of the restaurant promises, the cooking here adheres to the hearty tradition of Bologna, with delicious homemade *tortellini in brodo* (filled pasta in broth), fresh pastas in creamy sauces, and *bollito misto* (steam-

ing trays of boiled meats). ✉ *Piazza del Popolo 1,* ☎ *06/3611426. AE, MC, V. Closed Mon. and Aug.*

$$ ✕ **Colline Emiliane.** Behind an opaque glass facade not far from Piazza Barberini are a couple of plain dining rooms, where you are served light homemade pastas, *tortelli di zucca* (pumpkin-filled ravioli), and meats ranging from *giambonetto di vitello* (roast veal) to *cotoletta alla bolognese* (fried veal cutlet with cheese and prosciutto). Family-run, it's quiet and soothing. ✉ *Via San Nicolò da Tolentino 26,* ☎ *06/4818564. Reservations essential. AE, DC, MC, V. Closed Sun. and Aug.*

$$ ✕ **Il Cardinale.** This serene little restaurant turns out fanciful, lightened-up Roman fare, beautifully presented on king-size plates. Oil paintings and enlarged old photos of Roman landmarks are hung against golden damask wall coverings and chairs and couches are covered in a pretty floral print. The menu speaks of composed salads, vegetable soups, and such pastas as vermicelli *cacio e pepe* (thin spaghetti with pecorino cheese and black pepper) or *ravioli di borragine* (ravioli filled with borage leaves), and various vegetable *sformati* (flans). ✉ *Via delle Carceri 6,* ☎ *06/6869336. AE, DC, MC, V. Closed Sun.*

$$ ✕ **Myosotis.** Myosotis is the sequel to a successful restaurant on the ★ outskirts of town run by the Marsilis. The menu rides that delicate line between tradition and innovation, focusing more on the freshness and quality of the ingredients than on elaborate presentation. Fresh pasta gets special attention: It's rolled out by hand to order for the *stracci alla delizia di mare* (roughly cut, diamond-shape pasta with seafood). There's a wide choice of fish, meat, and seasonal veggies to choose from. ✉ *Via della Vaccarella 3/5,* ☎ *06/2053943. AE, DC, MC, V. Closed Mon. and 2 wks in Aug.*

$$ ✕ **Papà Baccus.** Italo Cipriani, owner of Rome's best Tuscan restaurant, takes his meat as seriously as any Tuscan, using real Chianina beef for the house special, *bistecca alla fiorentina* (grilled, thick bone-in steak). Cipriani brings many ingredients from his hometown in northern Tuscany. Try the sweet and delicate prosciutto from Pratomagno. The welcome here is warm, the service excellent, and the decor has the feel of an upscale trattoria. ✉ *Via Toscana 36,* ☎ *06/42742808. AE, DC, MC, V. Closed Sun., 2 wks in Aug., and during Christmas. No lunch Sat.*

$–$$ ✕ **Antico Arco.** Run by three friends with a passion for wine and fine ★ food, the Antico Arco has quickly won the hearts of Roman foodies with great invention and moderate prices. Particularly good are such starters as *sformato di finocchi in salsa d'arancia* (fennel flan with orange sauce) and such second courses as *petto d'anatra con salsa di lamponi* (duck breast with raspberry sauce). Don't miss dessert. ✉ *Piazzale Aurelio 7,* ☎ *06/5815274. AE, DC, MC, V. Closed Mon. No lunch Tues.–Sat.*

$–$$ ✕ **Dal Toscano.** The hallmarks of this great family-run Tuscan trattoria ★ near the Vatican are friendly and speedy service, an open wood-fired grill, and such classic dishes as *ribollita* (a dense bread and vegetable soup) and the prized bistecca alla fiorentina. Wash it all down with a strong Chianti. All desserts are yummy and homemade. ✉ *Via Germanico 58,* ☎ *06/39725717. DC, MC, V. Closed Mon., Aug., and 2 wks in Dec.*

$ ✕ **Dar Poeta.** Romans drive across town for great pizza from this neighborhood joint in Trastevere. Maybe it's the dough—it's made from a secret blend of flours reputed to be easier to digest than the crust of the competition. For dessert try the unusual calzone with Nutella (a gooey, delicious chocolate hazelnut spread) and ricotta. ✉ *Vicolo del Bologna 45,* ☎ *06/5880516. Reservations not accepted. AE, MC, V. Closed Mon. No lunch.*

$ ✗ **Il Simposio di Costantini.** At the classiest wine bar in town—done out in wrought-iron vines, wood paneling, and velvet—choose from about 30 wines in *degustazione* (available by the glass) or order a bottle from a list of over a thousand Italian and foreign labels sold in the shop next door. Food is appropriately fancy: marinated and smoked fish, composed salads, fine salami and cured meats (classical and wild), terrines and pâtés, and stellar cheeses. ✉ *Piazza Cavour 16, near the Vatican,* ☎ *06/3211502. AE, MC, V. Closed Sun. and Aug. No lunch Sat.*

$ ✗ **Perilli.** A bastion of authentic Roman cooking and trattoria charm since 1911 (the decor has changed very little), this is the place to go to try rigatoni *con pajata* (with veal's intestines)—if you're into that sort of thing. Otherwise the carbonara and *all'amatriciana* (spicy tomato sauce with pancetta) are classics. The house wine is a golden nectar from the Castelli Romani. ✉ *Via Marmorata 39,* ☎ *06/5742415. No credit cards. Closed Wed.*

$$$$ 🏨 **Eden.** Under the aegis of the Forte hotel group, the historic Eden, ★ a haunt of Hemingway, Ingrid Bergman, and Fellini, merits superlatives for dashing elegance and stunning vistas of Rome from the rooftop restaurant and bar (also from some of the most expensive rooms). Precious but discreet antique furnishings, sensuous Italian fabrics, fine linen sheets, and marble baths whisper understated opulence. ✉ *Via Ludovisi 49, 00187,* ☎ *06/478121,* 🅵🅰🆇 *06/4821584. 101 rooms, 11 suites. Restaurant. AE, DC, MC, V.*

$$$$ 🏨 **Hassler.** You can expect a cordial atmosphere and superb service at this hotel at the top of the Spanish Steps. The public rooms have an extravagant, somewhat dated decor, especially the clubby winter bar, garden bar, and the glass-roofed lounge, with gold marble walls and hand-painted tile floors. Elegant bedrooms are decorated in a variety of classic styles (the best feature the frescoed walls). ✉ *Piazza Trinità dei Monti 6, 00187,* ☎ *06/699340,* 🅵🅰🆇 *06/6789991. 85 rooms, 15 suites. Restaurant. AE, MC, V.*

$$$ 🏨 **Dei Borgognoni.** This quietly chic hotel near Piazza Colonna is as central as you could want, yet the winding byway stage set gives you a sense of being off the beaten track. The centuries-old building provides spacious lounges, a glassed-in garden, and rooms well arranged to create an illusion of space, though they are actually compact. The hotel has a garage (fee), a rarity in such a central location. ✉ *Via del Bufalo 126, 00187,* ☎ *06/69941505,* 🅵🅰🆇 *06/69941501. 50 rooms. AE, DC, MC, V.*

$$$ 🏨 **Farnese.** An early 20th-century-style mansion, the Farnese is in a ★ quiet but central residential district. Art Deco–style furniture is mixed with enchanting fresco decorations amidst its compact rooms, plenty of lounge space, and a roof garden. ✉ *Via Alessandro Farnese 30, 00184,* ☎ *06/3212553,* 🅵🅰🆇 *06/3215129. 21 rooms, 2 suites. AE, DC, MC, V.*

$$ 🏨 **Britannia.** A quiet locale off Via Nazionale is only one of the at- ★ tractions of this small and special hotel, where you will be coddled with luxury touches such as English-language dailies and local weather reports delivered to your room each morning. The well-furnished rooms (two with a rooftop terrace), frescoed halls, and lounge (where a rich breakfast buffet is served) attest the management really cares about superior service and value. ✉ *Via Napoli 64, 00184,* ☎ *06/4883153,* 🅵🅰🆇 *06/4882343. 33 rooms, 1 suite. AE, DC, MC, V.*

$$ 🏨 **La Residenza.** A converted town house near Via Veneto, this hotel offers good value and first-class comfort at reasonable rates. Public areas are spacious and furnished nicely and have a private-home atmosphere. Guest rooms are comfortable and have large closets and TVs. The hotel's clientele is mainly American. Rates include a generous buffet breakfast. ✉ *Via Emilia 22, 00187,* ☎ *06/4880789,* 🅵🅰🆇 *06/ 485721. 21 rooms, 7 suites. AE, MC, V.*

$$ ▦ **Scalinata di Spagna.** An old-fashioned pensione loved by genera-
tions of romantics, this tiny hotel is booked solid for months ahead.
Its location at the top of the Spanish Steps, inconspicuous little entrance,
quaint hodgepodge of old furniture, and view from the terrace where
you breakfast make it seem like your own special, exclusive inn. ✉ *Pi-
azza Trinità dei Monti 17, 00187,* ☎ *06/6793006,* ℻ *06/69940598.
16 rooms. MC, V.*

$ ▦ **Amalia.** The Consoli family—Amalia and her brothers—run this small
hotel, a former pensione, near the Vatican and the Cola di Rienzo shop-
ping district. On several floors of a 19th-century building, it has 21
restyled rooms with gleaming marble bathrooms. The Ottaviano stop
of Metro A is a block away. ✉ *Via Germanico 66, 00192,* ☎ *06/
39723356,* ℻ *06/39723365. 30 rooms, 7 without bath. AE, MC, V.*

$ ▦ **Margutta.** This small hotel near the Spanish Steps and Piazza del
★ Popolo has an unassuming lobby but bright, attractive bedrooms with
wrought-iron bedsteads and modern baths. ✉ *Via Laurina 34, 00187,*
☎ *06/3223674,* ℻ *06/3200395. 21 rooms. AE, DC, MC, V.*

$ ▦ **Romae.** Near Termini Station, this mid-size hotel has clean, spacious
rooms with light-wood furniture and small but bright bathrooms. The
congenial, helpful management offers special winter rates and welcomes
families. Low rates that include breakfast make this a good deal. ✉
Via Palestro 49, 00185, ☎ *06/4463554,* ℻ *06/4463914. 38 rooms.
AE, MC, V.*

Nightlife and the Arts

You will find information on scheduled events and shows at EPT and
municipal tourist offices or booths. The biweekly booklet "Un Ospite
a Roma," free from concierges at some hotels, is another source of in-
formation, as is "Wanted in Rome," published on Wednesday, avail-
able at newsstands. There are listings in English in the back of the weekly
"RomaC'è" booklet, with handy bus information for each listing; it
is published on Thursday and sold at newsstands. If you want to go
to the opera, the ballet, or a concert, it's best to ask your concierge to
get tickets for you. They are sold at box offices only, just a few days
before performances.

The Arts

CONCERTS

The main concert hall is the **Accademia di Santa Cecilia** (✉ Via della
Conciliazione 4, ☎ 06/68801044). There are many concerts year-
round; look for posters or for schedules in the publications mentioned
above.

FILM

The only English-language movie theater in Rome is the **Pasquino** (✉
Piazza Sant'Egidio, near Piazza Santa Maria in Trastevere, ☎ 06/
5803622). The program is listed in Rome's daily newspapers. Several
other movie theaters show films in English on certain days of the
week; the listings in "RomaC'è" are reliable.

OPERA

The opera season runs from November or December through May, and
performances are staged in the **Teatro dell'Opera** (✉ Piazza Beniamino
Gigli, ☎ 06/48160255 or 06/481601). From May through August, the
spectacular performances are held in the open air. After having been
evicted from the ancient ruins of the Terme di Caracalla, temporary
venues have been created in Villa Borghese and most recently at one
end of the Stadio Olimpico, Rome's soccer stadium.

Nightlife

Rome's "in" nightspots change like the flavor of the month, and many fade into oblivion after a brief moment of glory. The best places to find an up-to-date list are the weekly entertainment guide "Trovaroma," published each Thursday in the Italian daily *La Repubblica,* and "RomaC'è," the weekly guide sold at newsstands.

BARS

One of the grandest places for a drink in well-dressed company is **Le Bar** (⊠ Via Vittorio Emanuele Orlando 3, ☎ 06/47091) of Le Grand Hotel. **Jazz Cafè** (⊠ Via Zanardelli 12, ☎ 06/6861990), near Piazza Navona, is an upscale watering hole. **Flann O'Brien** (⊠ Via Napoli 29, ☎ 06/4880418), one of a plethora of pubs that now monopolize the bar scene in Rome, has the feel of a good Irish pub but also serves a decent cappuccino. **Trinity College** (⊠ Via del Collegio Romano 6, near Piazza Venezia, ☎ 06/6786472) has two floors of Irish pub trappings, with plenty o' gift of the gab and background music until 3 AM.

DISCOS AND NIGHTCLUBS

Testaccio's three-floor **The Saint** (⊠ Via Galvani 46, ☎ 06/5747945) has two discos designated "Paradiso" and "Inferno" (Heaven and Hell). You might spot an American celeb at **Gilda** (⊠ Via Mario de' Fiori 97, ☎ 06/6784838), with a disco, piano bar, and live music. It's closed Monday and jackets are required. Just as exclusive is **Bella Blu** (⊠ Via Luciani 21, ☎ 06/3230490), a Parioli club that caters to Rome's thirtysomething elite.

MUSIC CLUBS

For the best live music, including jazz, blues, rhythm and blues, African, and rock, go to **Big Mama** (⊠ Vicolo San Francesco a Ripa 18, ☎ 06/5812551). Live performances of jazz, soul, and funk by leading musicians draw celebrities to **Alexanderplatz** (⊠ Via Ostia 9, in the Vatican area, ☎ 06/39742171). The music starts about 10 PM, and you can have supper while you wait.

Shopping

Via Condotti, directly across from the Spanish Steps, and the streets running parallel to Via Condotti, as well as its cross streets, form the most elegant and expensive shopping area for clothes and accessories in Rome. Lower-price fashions may be found on display at shops on **Via Frattina** and **Via del Corso.** Romans in the know do much of their shopping along **Via Cola di Rienzo** and **Via Nazionale.** For prints browse among the stalls at **Piazza Fontanella Borghese** or stop in at the shops in the Pantheon area. For minor antiques **Via dei Coronari** and other streets in the Piazza Navona area are good. The most prestigious antiques dealers are situated in **Via del Babuino** and its environs. The open-air markets at **Campo de' Fiori** and in many neighborhoods throughout the city provide an eyeful of local color.

Rome Essentials

Arriving and Departing

BY PLANE

Rome's principal airport is **Aeroporto Leonardo da Vinci,** usually known as **Fiumicino** (⊠ 29 km/18 mi southeast of Rome, ☎ 06/65953640 for flight information). The smaller **Ciampino** (⊠ On the edge of Rome, ☎ 06/794941 for flight information) is used as an alternative by international and domestic lines, especially for charter flights.

Between the Airport and Downtown. To get to downtown Rome from **Fiumicino** you have a choice of two trains. Ask at the airport (at EPT or train information counters) which one takes you closest to your hotel. The nonstop Airport-Termini express takes you directly to Track 22 at Termini Station, Rome's main train terminal, well served by taxis and the hub of Metro (subway) and bus lines. The ride to Termini takes 30 minutes; departures are hourly, beginning at 7:50 AM, with the final departure at 10:05 PM. Tickets cost 13,000 lire. The other airport train (FM1) runs to Tiburtina station in Rome and beyond to Monterotondo, a suburban town to the east. The main stops in Rome are at the Trastevere, Ostiense, and Tiburtina stations. At each of these you can find taxis and bus and/or Metro connections to various parts of Rome. This train runs from 6:35 AM to 12:15 AM, with departures every 20 minutes. The ride to Tiburtina takes 40 minutes. Tickets cost 7,000 lire. For either train you buy your ticket at an automatic vending machine (you need Italian currency). There are ticket counters at some stations (Termini Track 22, Trastevere, Tiburtina). Remember to **date-stamp your ticket in one of the yellow machines near the track.**

A taxi to or from Fiumicino costs about 70,000 to 80,000 lire, including supplements. At a booth inside the terminal you can hire a four- or five-passenger car with driver for a little more. If you decide to take a taxi, use only the yellow or the newer white cabs, which must wait outside the terminal; make sure the meter is running. Gypsy cab drivers solicit your business as you come out of customs; they're not reliable, and their rates may be rip-offs. **Ciampino** is connected with the Anagnina Station of the Metro A by bus (runs every half hour). A taxi between Ciampino and downtown Rome costs about 35,000 lire.

BY TRAIN

Termini Station is Rome's main train terminal, although the Tiburtina, Ostiense, and Trastevere stations serve some long-distance trains, many commuter trains, and the FM1 line to Fiumicino Airport. For train information call ☎ 1478/88088 toll free, or try the English-speaking personnel at the information office in Termini, or at any travel agency. Tickets and seats can be reserved and purchased at travel agencies bearing the FS (Ferrovie dello Stato) emblem. Tickets can be purchased up to two months in advance. Short-distance tickets are also sold at tobacconists and ticket machines in the stations.

Getting Around

Rome's integrated Metrebus transportation system includes buses and trams (ATAC), Metro and suburban trains and buses (COTRAL), and some other suburban trains (FS) run by the state railways. A ticket valid for 75 minutes on any combination of buses and trams and one admission to the Metro costs 1,500 lire (time-stamp your ticket when boarding the first vehicle; you're supposed to stamp it again if you board another vehicle just before the ticket runs out, but few do). Tickets are sold at tobacconists, newsstands, some coffee bars, automatic ticket machines in Metro stations, some bus stops, and at ATAC and CO-TRAL ticket booths. A BIG tourist ticket, valid for one day on all public transport, costs 6,000 lire. A weekly ticket (Settimanale, also known as CIS) costs 24,000 lire and can be purchased only at ATAC and Metro booths.

BY BICYCLE

Pedaling through Villa Borghese, along the Tiber, and through city center when traffic is light is a pleasant way to see the sights, but remember: Rome is hilly. Rental concessions are at the Piazza di Spagna and Piazza del Popolo Metro stops, and at Largo San Silvestro and Largo Argentina. You will also find rentals at Viale della Pineta and Viale del Bambino on the Pincio. **Collalti** (⊠ Via del Pellegrino 82, just off Campo de' Fiori, ☎ 06/68801084) leases and repairs bikes. **St. Peter's**

Motor Rent (✉ Via di Porta Castello 43, near St. Peter's, ☎ 06/6875714) also rents bikes.

BY BUS
Orange ATAC (☎ 167/431784) city buses (and a few streetcar lines) run from about 6 AM to midnight, with night buses (indicated N) on some lines. When entering a bus, remember to board at the rear and exit at the middle. Bus lines 117 and 119, with compact electric vehicles, make a circuit of limited but scenic routes in downtown Rome. They can save you from a lot of walking, and you can get on and off as you please.

BY CAR
If you come by car, put it in a parking space (and note that parking in central Rome is generally either metered or prohibited) or a garage, and use public transportation. If you plan to drive into or out of the city, take time to study your route, especially on the GRA (Grande Raccordo Anulare, a beltway that encircles Rome and funnels traffic into the city, not always successfully). The main access routes to Rome from the north are the A1 autostrada from Florence and Milan and the Aurelia highway (SS 1) from Genoa. The principal route to or from points south, such as Naples, is the A2 autostrada.

BY METRO
The Metro is the easiest and fastest way to get around, but the network has limited stops. It opens at 5:30 AM, and the last train leaves each terminal at 11:30 PM. Metro A runs from the eastern part of the city to Termini Station and past Piazza di Spagna and Piazzale Flaminio to Ottaviano-S. Pietro, near St. Peter's and the Vatican museums. Metro B serves Termini, the Colosseum, and Tiburtina Station (where the FM1 Fiumicino Airport train stops).

BY MOPED
You can rent a moped or scooter and mandatory helmet at **Scoot-a-Long** (✉ Via Cavour 302, ☎ 06/6780206). **St. Peter Moto** (✉ Via di Porta Castello 43, ☎ 06/6875714) also rents equipment.

BY TAXI
Taxis wait at stands and, for a small extra charge, can also be called by telephone. The meter starts at 4,500 lire; there are supplements for service after 10 PM, on Sunday and holidays, and for each piece of baggage. Use the yellow or the newer white cabs only, and be very sure to check the meter. To call a cab dial ☎ 06/3570, 06/5551, 06/4994, or 06/88177.

Contacts and Resources
EMBASSIES
U.S. (✉ Via Veneto 121, ☎ 06/46741). **Canadian** (✉ Via Zara 30, ☎ 06/445981). **U.K.** (✉ Via XX Settembre 80a, ☎ 06/4825441).

EMERGENCIES
Police (☎ 113). **Ambulance** (☎ 1188 or 06/5510): Say "Pronto Soccorso" and be prepared to give your address. **Hospitals** (Salvator Mundi Hospital, ☎ 06/588961; Rome American Hospital, ☎ 06/22551). **Pharmacies** are open 8:30–1 and 4–8. Some stay open all night, and all open Sunday on a rotation system; a notice of the neighborhood pharmacies open all night is posted at each pharmacy.

ENGLISH-LANGUAGE BOOKSTORES
Economy Book and Video Center (✉ Via Torino 136, ☎ 06/4746877). **Anglo-American Bookstore** (✉ Via della Vite 102, ☎ 06/6795222). **Corner Bookstore** (✉ Via del Moro 48, Trastevere, ☎ 06/5836942).

Excursions. Most operators offer half-day excursions to Tivoli to see the Villa d'Este's fountains and gardens; **Appian Line**'s (⊠ Via Barberini 109, ☏ 06/4884151) and **CIT**'s (⊠ Piazza della Repubblica 64, ☏ 06/47941) half-day tours to Tivoli also include Hadrian's Villa and its impressive ancient ruins. Most operators have all-day excursions to Assisi, to Pompeii and/or Capri, and to Florence. For do-it-yourself excursions to Ostia Antica and other destinations, pick up information at the EPT information offices (☞ Visitor Information, *below*).

Orientation. American Express (⊠ Piazza di Spagna 38, ☏ 06/67641) **CIT** (☞ *above*). **Appian Line** (☞ *above*). **ATAC** (Information booth, Termini Station).

Walking. Secret Walks (⊠ Viale Medaglie d'Oro 127, 00136 Rome, ☏ 06/39728728) conducts small groups on theme walks led by English-speaking city experts; they can also arrange excursions. **Scala Reale** (⊠ Via Varese 52, 00185 Rome, ☏ 06/44700898) also has English-language tours. For more information contact city tourist offices.

American Express (⊠ Piazza di Spagna 38, ☏ 06/67641). **CIT** (⊠ Piazza della Repubblica 64, ☏ 06/47941). **CTS** (youth and budget travel, discount fares; ⊠ Via Genova 16, ☏ 06/46791, 06/4679271 for information).

EPT (Rome Provincial Tourist Agency, ⊠ main office: Via Parigi 5, 00185, ☏ 06/48899253; ⊠ Termini Station, ☏ 06/4871270; ⊠ Fiumicino Airport, ☏ 06/65956074). **City tourist information booths** (⊠ Largo Goldoni, corner of Via Condotti; Via del Corso in the Spanish Steps area; Via dei Fori Imperiali, opposite the entrance to the Roman Forum; Via Nazionale, at Palazzo delle Esposizioni; Piazza Cinque Lune, off the north end of Piazza Navona).

FLORENCE

One of Europe's preeminent treasures, Florence draws visitors from all over the world. Its historic center has 15th-century palazzi lining its narrow streets. The plain and sober facades often give way to delightful courtyards. With the exception of a very few buildings, the classical dignity of the High Renaissance and the exuberant invention of the Baroque are not to be found here. The typical Florentine exterior gives nothing away, as if obsessively guarding secret treasures within. The treasures, of course, are very real. And far from being a secret, they are famous the world over. The city is an artistic treasure trove of unique and incomparable proportions. A single historical fact explains the phenomenon: Florence gave birth to the Renaissance.

Exploring Florence

Numbers in the margin correspond to points of interest on the Florence map.

Founded by Julius Caesar, Florence was built in the familiar grid pattern common to all Roman colonies that makes it easy to explore. Except for the major monuments, which are appropriately imposing, the buildings are low and unpretentious and the streets are narrow. At times Florence can be a nightmare of mass tourism. Plan, if you can, to visit the city in late fall, early spring, or even in winter to avoid the crowds. For 15,000 lire you can purchase a special museum ticket valid for six months at six city museums, including the Palazzo Vecchio and the Museum of Santa Maria Novella. Inquire at any city museum.

Piazza del Duomo and Piazza della Signoria

★ ❸ **Battistero** (Baptistery). In front of the Duomo is the octagonal baptistery, one of the city's oldest (modern excavations suggest its foundations date from the 4th to 5th and the 8th to 9th centuries) and most beloved buildings, where since the 11th century Florentines have baptized their children. The interior dome mosaics are famous but cannot outshine the building's renowned gilded bronze east doors (facing the Duomo). The work of Lorenzo Ghiberti (1378–1455), dubbed the "Gates of Paradise" by Michelangelo, the doors are the most splendid of the Baptistery's three doors. A luminous copy replaces the original, removed to the Museo dell'Opera del Duomo (☞ *below*). ⊠ *Piazza del Duomo,* ☎ *055/2302885.* ۞ *Mon.–Sat. 1:30–6:30, Sun. 8:30–1:30.*

❷ **Campanile** (Bell tower). Giotto (1266–1337) designed the early 14th-century bell tower, richly decorated with colored marbles and sculpture reproductions; the originals are in the Museo dell'Opera del Duomo (☞ *below*). The 414-step climb to the top is less strenuous than that to the cupola on the Duomo (☞ *below*). ⊠ *Piazza del Duomo,* ☎ *055/2302885.* ۞ *Apr.–Oct., daily 9–6:50; Nov.–Mar., daily 9–4:20.*

★ ❶ **Duomo.** Cattedrale di Santa Maria del Fiore is dominated by a cupola representing a landmark in the history of architecture. The cathedral itself was begun by master sculptor and architect Arnolfo di Cambio in 1296, and its construction took 140 years to complete. Gothic architecture predominates; the facade was added in the 1870s but is based on Tuscan Gothic models. Inside, the church is cool and austere, a fine example of the architecture of the period. Take a good look at the frescoes of equestrian figures on the left wall; the one on the right is by Paolo Uccello (1397–1475), the one on the left by Andrea del Castagno (circa 1419–57). The dome frescoes by Vasari take second place to the dome itself, Brunelleschi's (1377–1446) greatest architectural and technical achievement. It was also the inspiration behind such later domes as the one Michelangelo designed for St. Peter's in Rome and even the Capitol in Washington. You can visit early medieval and ancient Roman remains of previous constructions excavated under the cathedral. And you can climb to the cupola gallery, 463 exhausting steps up between the two layers of the double dome for a fine view. ⊠ *Piazza del Duomo,* ☎ *055/2302885.* ۞ *Mon.–Sat. 10–5 (1st Sat. of month 10–3:30), Sun. 1–5. Cupola (entrance in left aisle of cathedral): weekdays 9:30–7 and Sat. 8:30–5 (1st Sat. of month 8:30–3:20).*

★ ❾ **Galleria degli Uffizi** (Uffizi Gallery). The Uffizi Palace was built to house the administrative offices of the Medici, onetime rulers of the city. Later their fabulous art collection was arranged in the Uffizi Gallery on the top floor, which was opened to the public in the 17th century—making this the world's first modern public gallery. It houses Italy's most important collection of paintings. The emphasis is on Italian art of the Gothic and Renaissance periods. Make sure you see the works by Giotto, and look for Botticelli's (1445–1510) *Birth of Venus* and *Primavera* in Rooms X–XIV, Michelangelo's *Holy Family* in Room XXV, and the works by Raphael next door. In addition to its art treasures, the gallery offers a magnificent close-up view of the Palazzo Vecchio tower from the little coffee bar at the end of the corridor. Notoriously long lines can be avoided by purchasing tickets in advance from Consorzio ITA. ⊠ *Loggiato Uffizi 6,* ☎ *055/23885; 055/2347941 Consorzio ITA (advance tickets).* ۞ *Nov.–Mar., Tues.–Sat. 8:30–7, Sun. 8:30–1:50; Apr.–Oct., Mon.–Sat. 8:30–10, Sun. 8:30–8.*

8 **Loggia del Mercato Nuovo** (Loggia of the New Market). Tiers of souvenirs and straw and leather goods are crammed into this historic open-air marketplace. Along with the goods, a main attraction is a copy of Pietro Tacca's bronze *Porcellino* (Little Pig) fountain, which is itself a 17th-century copy of an ancient Roman work now in the Uffizi. Touching the pig is said to bring good luck. ⊠ *Via Calimala.* ⊙ *Tues.–Sat. 8–7, Mon. 9:30–7.*

★ **4** **Museo dell'Opera del Duomo** (Cathedral Museum). The museum contains some superb sculptures by Donatello (circa 1386–1466) and Luca della Robbia (1400–82)—especially their *cantorie*, or singers' galleries—and an unfinished *Pietà* by Michelangelo that was intended for his own tomb. ⊠ *Piazza del Duomo 9,* ☎ *055/2302885.* ⊙ *Mar.–Oct., Mon.–Sat. 9–7:30; Nov.–Feb., Mon.–Sat. 9–7.*

10 **Museo di Storia della Scienza** (Museum of the History of Science). You don't have to know a lot about science to appreciate the antique scientific instruments presented here in informative, eye-catching exhibits. From astrolabes and armillary spheres to some of Galileo's own instruments, the collection is one of Florence's lesser-known treasures. ⊠ *Piazza dei Giudici 1,* ☎ *055/2398876.* ⊙ *Mon., Wed., Fri. 9:30–1 and 2–5; Tues., Thurs., Sat. 9:30–1.*

5 **Orsanmichele.** For centuries this was an odd combination of first-floor church and second-floor granary. The statues in the niches on the exterior (many of which are now copies) constitute an anthology of the work of eminent Renaissance sculptors, including Donatello, Ghiberti, and Verrocchio (1435–88). The tabernacle inside is an extraordinary piece by Andrea Orcagna (1308–68). Some of the original statues can be seen in the Museo Nazionale del Bargello (☞ *below*) and the Palazzo della Signoria (☞ *below*). ⊠ *Via Calzaiuoli,* ☎ *055/ 284944.* ⊙ *Daily 9–noon and 4–6. Closed 1st and last Mon. of month.*

7 **Palazzo Vecchio** (Old Palace). Also called Palazzo della Signoria, this massive, fortresslike city hall was begun in 1299 and was taken over, along with the rest of Florence, by the Medici family. Inside, the impressive, frescoed salons and the *studiolo* (small study) of Francesco I are the main attractions. ⊠ *Piazza della Signoria,* ☎ *055/2768465.* ◩ *Free Sun.* ⊙ *Mon.–Wed. and Fri.–Sat. 9–7, Thurs. 8–1, Sun. 8–1.*

6 **Piazza della Signoria.** This is the heart of Florence and the city's largest square. In the pavement in the center of the square a slab marks the spot where Savonarola, the reformist monk who urged the Florentines to burn their pictures, books, musical instruments, and other worldly objects, was hanged and then burned at the stake as a heretic in 1498. The square, the *Fontana di Nettuno* (Neptune) by Ammanati (1511–92), and the surrounding cafés are popular gathering places for Florentines and for tourists who come to admire the Palazzo della Signoria, the copy of Michelangelo's *David* standing in front of it, and the sculptures in the 14th-century Loggia dei Lanzi, including a copy of Cellini's famous bronze *Perseus Holding the Head of Medusa.*

San Marco, San Lorenzo, Santa Maria Novella, Santa Croce

★ **16** **Cappelle Medicee** (Medici Chapels). This extraordinary chapel, part of the San Lorenzo complex, contains the tombs of practically every member of the Medici family, and there were a lot of them, for they guided Florence's destiny from the 15th century to 1737. Cosimo I (1519–74), a Medici whose acumen made him the richest man in Europe, is buried in the crypt beneath the **Cappella dei Principi** (Chapel of the Princes), and Donatello's tomb is next to that of his patron, Cosimo Il Vecchio (1389–1464). Upstairs is a dazzling array of colored mar-

668

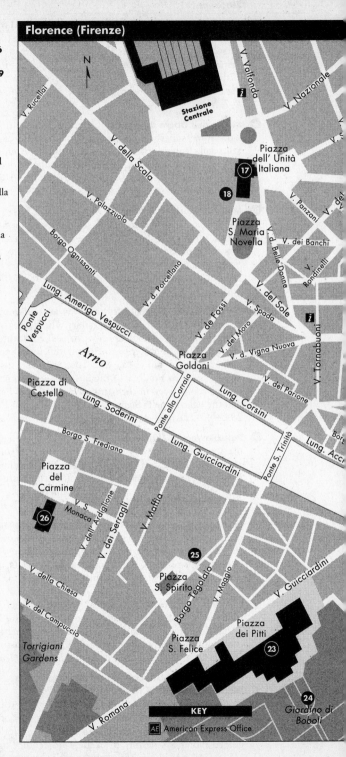

Florence (Firenze)

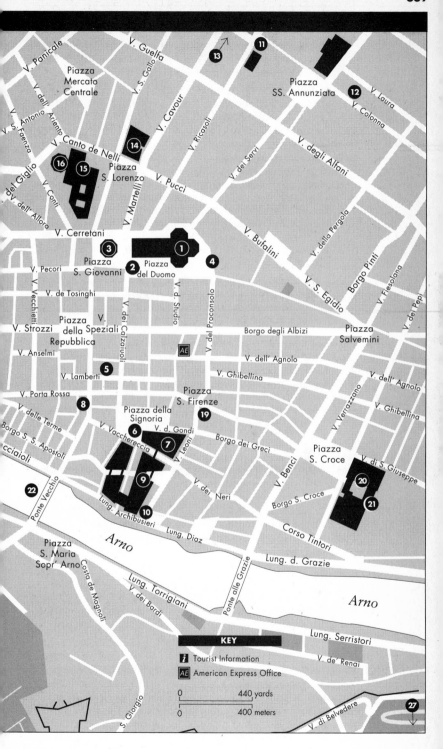

V. Panicale

V. Guelfa

Piazza Mercato Centrale

V. S. Gallo

V. dell' Ariento

V. Canto de Nelli

Canto de Nelli

V. S. Antonio

V. S. Faenza

V. del Giglio

V. Conti

V. dell' Alloro

13

11

Piazza SS. Annunziata

12 V. Laura

V. Colonna

V. Cavour

V. Ricasoli

V. dei Servi

V. degli Alfani

V. della Pergola

14

16 **15**

Piazza S. Lorenzo

V. Pucci

V. Martelli

V. Cerretani

3 **1**

Piazza S. Giovanni

2 Piazza del Duomo

4

V. Bufalini

V. S. Egidio

Borgo Pinti

V. Fiesolana

V. dei Pepi

V. Pecori

V. de Tosinghi

V. Vecchietti

Piazza della Repubblica

V. Strozzi

V. Speziali

V. Anselmi

V. dei Calzaiuoli

V. d. Studio

V. del Proconsolo

Borgo degli Albizi

Piazza Salvemini

AE

5

V. Lamberti

V. Ghibellina

V. dell' Agnolo

V. dell' Agnolo

V. Porta Rossa

8

V. delle Terme

Borgo S. S. Apostoli

-cciaioli

Piazza S. Firenze

19

Piazza della Signoria

6 V. d. Gondi

7 V. Leoni

V. Vacchereccia

Borgo dei Greci

V. Banci

V. Verrazzano

V. Ghibellina

Piazza S. Croce

V. di S. Giuseppe

9

V. dei Neri

20

22

Ponte Vecchio

10

Lung. Archibusieri

Lung. Diaz

Borgo S. Croce

21

Corso Tintori

Arno

Piazza S. Maria Sopr' Arno

Costa de Magnoli

Lung. Torrigiani

V. dei Bardi

Ponte alle Grazie

Lung. d. Grazie

Arno

Lung. Serristori

V. de' Renai

KEY

i Tourist Information

AE American Express Office

0   440 yards

0   400 meters

S. Giorgio

V. di Belvedere

27

ble panels. Michelangelo's **Sagrestia Nuova** (New Sacristy) tombs of Giuliano and Lorenzo de' Medici are adorned with the justly famed sculptures of *Dawn* and *Dusk*, *Night* and *Day*. ⊠ *Piazza Madonna degli Aldobrandini, San Lorenzo,* ☎ *055/2388602.* ☉ *Daily 8:30–1:50. Closed 1st, 3rd, and 5th Mon. and 2nd and 4th Sun. of month.*

★ ⑪ **Galleria dell'Accademia** (Accademia Gallery). Michelangelo's *David* is a tour de force of artistic conception and technical ability, for he was using a piece of stone that had already been worked on by a lesser sculptor. Take time to see the forceful *Slaves*, also by Michelangelo; their rough-hewn, unfinished surfaces contrast dramatically with the highly polished, meticulously carved *David*. Michelangelo left the *Slaves* "unfinished," it is often claimed, to accentuate the figures' struggle to escape the bondage of stone. Actually, he simply abandoned them because his patron changed his mind about the tomb monument for which they were planned. Try to be first in line at opening time or go shortly before closing time so you can get the full impact without having to fight your way through the crowds. ⊠ *Via Ricasoli 60,* ☎ *055/2388609.* ☉ *Nov.–Mar., Tues.–Sat. 8:30–7, Sun. 8:30–1:50; Apr.–Oct., Tues.– Sat. 8:30–10, Sun. 8:30–8.*

⑫ **Museo Archeologico** (Archaeological Museum). Fine Etruscan and Roman antiquities and a pretty garden are the draw here. ⊠ *Via della Colonna 36,* ☎ *055/2478641.* ☉ *Tues.–Sat. 9–2, and 1st, 3rd, and 5th Mon. and 2nd and 4th Sun. of the month 9–1.*

㉑ **Museo dell'Opera di Santa Croce e Cappella dei Pazzi** (Museum of Santa Croce and Pazzi Chapel). From the cloister of the monastery adjacent to Santa Croce you can visit the small museum and see what remains of the Giotto crucifix irreparably damaged by a flood in 1966, when water rose to 16 ft in parts of the church. The **Cappella dei Pazzi** in the cloister is an architectural gem by Brunelleschi. The interior is a lesson in spatial equilibrium and harmony. ⊠ *Piazza Santa Croce,* ☎ *055/244619.* ☉ *Thurs.–Tues. 10–12 and 3–5.*

⑬ **Museo di San Marco.** A former Dominican monastery houses this museum, which contains many stunning works by Fra Angelico (1400– 55). Within the same walls where the unfortunate Savonarola, the monastery's prior, later contemplated the sins of the Florentines, Fra Angelico went humbly about his work, decorating many of the otherwise austere cells and corridors with brilliantly colored frescoes on religious subjects. Look for his masterpiece, the *Annunciation*. Together with many of his paintings arranged on the ground floor, just off the little cloister, they form a fascinating collection. ⊠ *Piazza San Marco 1,* ☎ *055/2388608.* ☉ *Daily 8:30–1:50. Closed 1st, 3rd, and 5th Sun. and 2nd and 4th Mon. of month.*

⑱ **Museo di Santa Maria Novella.** Adjacent to the church, this museum is worth a visit for its serene atmosphere and the faded Paolo Uccello frescoes from Genesis. ⊠ *Piazza Santa Maria Novella 19,* ☎ *055/ 282187.* ☉ *Mon.–Thurs. and Sat. 9–2, Sun. 8–1.*

★ ⑲ **Museo Nazionale del Bargello.** This grim, fortresslike palace served in medieval times as a residence of Florence's chief magistrate and later as a prison. It is now a treasure trove of Italian Renaissance sculpture. In this historic setting you can see masterpieces by Donatello, Verrocchio, Michelangelo, and other major sculptors amid an eclectic array of arms and ceramics. For Renaissance enthusiasts this museum is on a par with the Uffizi. ⊠ *Via del Proconsolo 4,* ☎ *055/2388606.* ☉ *Daily 8:30–1:50, Tues. and Sat. 2–5. Closed 1st, 3rd, and 5th Sun. and 2nd and 4th Mon. of month.*

⓮ Palazzo Medici-Riccardi. Few tourists get to see Benozzo Gozzoli's (1420–97) glorious frescoes in the tiny second-floor chapel of this palace, built in 1444 for Cosimo de' Medici (Il Vecchio, 1389–1464). Glimmering with gold, they represent the journey of the Magi as a spectacular cavalcade with cameo portraits of various Medici and the artist himself. ☒ *Via Cavour 1,* ☎ *055/2760340.* ☉ *Mon.–Tues., Thurs.–Sat. 9–1 and 3–6, Sun. 9–1.*

⓯ San Lorenzo. The facade of this church was never finished, but the Brunelleschi interior is elegantly austere. Stand in the middle of the nave at the entrance, on the line that stretches to the high altar, and you'll see what Brunelleschi achieved with the grid of inlaid marble in the pavement. Every architectural element in the church is placed to create a dramatic effect of single-point perspective. The **Sagrestia Vecchia,** decorated with stuccoes by Donatello, is attributed to Brunelleschi. ☒ *Piazza San Lorenzo,* ☎ *055/216634.* ☉ *Daily 7–noon and 3:30–6:30.*

★ **⓴ Santa Croce.** The mighty church of Santa Croce was begun in 1294 and has become a kind of pantheon for Florentine greats; monumental tombs of Michelangelo, Galileo (1564–1642), Machiavelli (1469–1527), and other Renaissance luminaries line the walls. Inside are two chapels frescoed by Giotto and another painted by Taddeo Gaddi (1300–66), as well as an *Annunciation* and crucifix by Donatello. But it is the scale of this grandiose church that proclaims the power and ambition of medieval Florence. ☒ *Piazza Santa Croce,* ☎ *055/244619.* ☉ *Apr.–Sept., 8–6:45, Sun. 3–5:30.*

⓱ Santa Maria Novella. A Tuscan interpretation of the Gothic style, this handsome church should be viewed from the opposite end of Piazza Santa Maria Novella for the best view of its facade. Inside are some famous paintings, especially Masaccio's (1401–28) *Trinity,* a Giotto crucifix in the sacristy, and Ghirlandaio's frescoes in the **Capella Maggiore.** At press time, the church was closed for restoration until 2000. ☒ *Piazza Santa Maria Novella,* ☎ *055/210113.* ☉ *Mon.–Sat. 7–12 and 3–6, Sun. 3–5.*

The Oltrarno

⓴ Giardini Boboli (Boboli Gardens). The main entrance to this garden on a landscaped hillside is in the right wing of Palazzo Pitti. The garden was laid out in 1549 for Cosimo I's wife, Eleanora of Toledo, and was further developed by later Medici dukes. ☒ *Piazza dei Pitti,* ☎ *055/213440.* ☉ *Nov.–Mar., daily 9–4:30; Apr.–Oct., daily 9–5:30.*

㉓ Palazzo Pitti. This enormous palace is a 15th-century extravaganza the Medici acquired from the Pitti family shortly after the latter had gone deeply into debt to build the central portion. The Medici enlarged the building, extending its facade along the immense piazza. Solid and severe, it looks like a Roman aqueduct turned into a palace. The palace houses several museums: The **Museo degli Argenti** (Silver Museum) displays the fabulous Medici collection of objects in silver and gold; another has the collections of the **Galleria d'Arte Moderna** (Gallery of Modern Art), which was closed for restoration at press time. The most famous museum, though, is the **Galleria Palatina** (Palatine Gallery), with an extraordinary collection of paintings, many hung frame-to-frame in a clear case of artistic overkill. Some are high up in dark corners, so try to go on a bright day. ☒ *Piazza Pitti,* ☎ *055/210323. Museo degli Argenti:* ☉ *Nov.–Mar., Wed. and Fri.–Mon. 8:30–1:50, Tues. and Thurs. 8:30–5; Apr.–Oct., Wed. and Fri.–Mon. 8:30–3:30, Tues. and Thurs. 2–5. Closed 2nd and 4th Sun. and 1st, 3rd, and 5th Mon. of month. Galleria Palatina:* ☉ *Nov.–Mar., Tues.–Sat. 8:30–7, Sun. 8:30–1:50; Apr.–Oct., Tues.–Sat. 8:30–10, Sun. 8:30–8.*

★ **㉒ Ponte Vecchio** (Old Bridge). Florence's oldest bridge appears to be just another street lined with goldsmiths' shops until you get to the middle and catch a glimpse of the Arno below. Spared during World War II by the retreating Germans (who blew up every other bridge in the city), it also survived the 1966 flood. It leads into the **Oltrarno,** where the atmosphere of old-time Florence is preserved amid fascinating crafts workshops. ⊠ *East of Ponte Santa Trinita and west of Ponte alle Grazie.*

㉗ San Miniato al Monte. One of Florence's oldest churches, this charming green-and-white marble Romanesque edifice is full of artistic riches, among them the gorgeous Renaissance chapel where a Portuguese cardinal was laid to rest in 1459 under a ceiling by Luca della Robbia. ⊠ *Viale Michelangelo, or take stairs from Piazzale Michelangelo,* ☎ *055/ 2342731.* ⊙ *Daily 8–7.*

㉖ Santa Maria del Carmine. The church is of little architectural interest but of immense significance in the history of Renaissance art. It contains the celebrated frescoes painted by Masaccio in the **Cappella Brancacci.** The chapel was a classroom for such artistic giants as Botticelli, Leonardo da Vinci (1452–1519), Michelangelo, and Raphael, since they all came to study Masaccio's realistic use of light and perspective and his creation of space and depth. ⊠ *Piazza del Carmine,* ☎ *055/2382195.* ⊙ *Mon. and Wed.–Sat. 10–5, Sun. 1–5.*

㉕ Santo Spirito. Its plain, unfinished facade is less than impressive, but this church is important as one of Brunelleschi's finest architectural creations. It contains some superb paintings, including a *Madonna* by Filippo Lippi. Santo Spirito is the hub of a colorful, trendy neighborhood of artisans and intellectuals. An outdoor market enlivens the square every morning except Sunday; in the afternoon, pigeons, pet owners, and pensioners take over. ⊠ *Piazza Santo Spirito,* ☎ *055/210030.* ⊙ *Thurs.–Tues. 8:30–12 and 4–6, Wed. 8:30–12, Sun. 4–6.*

Dining and Lodging

Mealtimes in Florence are from 12:30 to 2:30 and 7:30 to 9 or later. Reservations are always advisable; to find a table at inexpensive places, get there early. For details and price-category definitions, *see* Dining *in* Italy A to Z, *above.*

With mass tourism and trade fairs, hotel rooms are at a premium in Florence for most of the year. Reserve well in advance. If you arrive without a reservation, the **Consorzio ITA** office in the train station (⊠ Stazione Centrale di Santa Maria Novella), open 8:20 AM–9 PM, can help you, but there may be a long line (take a number and wait). Now that much traffic is banned in the downtown area, many central hotel rooms are quieter. Local traffic and motorcycles can still be bothersome, however, so check the decibel level before you settle in. From November through March ask for special low winter rates. For details and price-category definitions, *see* Lodging *in* Italy A to Z, *above.*

$$$$ ✕ **Enoteca Pinchiorri.** A sumptuous Renaissance palace with high fres-
★ coed ceilings and bouquets in silver vases is the setting for this restaurant, one of the best and most expensive in Italy. It serves a Tuscan menu and a special degustation menu, plus a variety of fish, game, and meat dishes à la carte. Of the splendid combinations, a favorite is the *ignudi*—ricotta and cheese dumplings with a lobster and coxcomb fricassee. ⊠ *Via Ghibellina 87,* ☎ *055/242777. Reservations essential. AE, MC, V. Closed Sun., Aug., and 10 days during Christmas. No lunch Mon. or Wed.*

$$$ ✕ **Alle Murate.** This sophisticated restaurant features creative versions of classic Tuscan dishes. The main dining room has a rich, uncluttered look, with warm wood floors and paneling and soft lights. In a smaller adjacent room called the *vineria,* you get the same splendid service and substantially reduced prices. Be warned that there's no middle ground with the wine list—only a smattering of inexpensive offerings before it soars to exalted heights. ⊠ *Via Ghibellina 52/r,* ☎ *055/240618. AE, DC, MC, V. Closed Mon. No lunch.*

$$$ ✕ **Cibrèo.** The food at this classic Florentine trattoria is fantastic, from
★ the first bite of seamless, creamy *crostini di fegatini* (savory Tuscan chicken liver spread on grilled bread) to the last bite of one of the melt-in-your-mouth-good desserts. If you thought you'd never try tripe, let alone like it, this is the place to lay any doubts to rest: The cold tripe salad with parsley and garlic is an epiphany. ⊠ *Via dei Macci 118/r,* ☎ *055/2341100. Reservations essential. AE, DC, MC, V. Closed Sun., Mon., July 25–Sept. 5, and Dec. 31–Jan. 7.*

$$ ✕ **Cammillo.** This bustling trattoria just on the other side of the Arno has been in the capable hands of the Masiero family for three generations, and in its present venue since 1945. Their farm in the country supplies the olive oil and wines for the restaurant, which marry nicely with the wide-ranging list of Tuscan specialities on the menu. Reservations are advised. ⊠ *Borgo Sant'Jacopo 57/r,* ☎ *055/212427. AE, DC, MC, V. Closed Wed., 15 days in Aug., and 15 days Dec.–Jan.*

$$ ✕ **La Giostra.** La Giostra, which means "carousel" in Italian, is owned
★ and run by Prince Dimitri Kunz d'Asburgo Lorena. It has a clubby feel, with white walls and tablecloths and dim lighting accented with a few tiny blue lights twinkling on the ceiling. The unusually good pastas may require some explanation from Dimitri or Soldano, the prince's good-looking twin sons. In perfect English they'll describe a favorite dish, such as the *carbonara di tartufo,* decadently rich spaghetti with eggs and white truffles. Leave room for dessert: This might be the only show in town with a sublime tiramisu and a wonderfully gooey Sacher torte. ⊠ *Borgo Pinti 12/r,* ☎ *055/241341. AE, MC, V.*

$$ ✕ **Pallottino.** With its tile floor, photograph-filled walls, and wooden tables, Pallottino is the quintessential Tuscan trattoria, with such hearty, heartwarming classics as *pappa al pomodoro* (a tomato and bread soup) to *peposo alla toscana* (beef stew laced with black pepper). Their lunch special—*primo and secondo* (first and second courses)— could be, at 10,000 lire, the best bargain in town. ⊠ *Via Isola delle Stinche 1/r,* ☎ *055/289573. AE, DC, MC, V. No credit cards at lunch. Closed Mon. and Aug. 1–20.*

$$ ✕ **Toscano.** A small table attractively set in a show window identifies this restaurant near Palazzo Medici-Riccardi. Prominently displayed on a counter near the entrance are cured meats and plates glistening with vegetables. Terra-cotta tile floors and beamed ceilings further typify a Tuscan trattoria, but the pink tablecloths, arty photos, and a touch of creative cuisine take it out of the ordinary. The kitchen prides itself on top-quality meat; try *spezzatino peposo* (beef stew with black pepper and a wine sauce). ⊠ *Via Guelfa 70/r,* ☎ *055/215475. AE, DC, MC, V. Closed Tues. and Aug.*

$ ✕ **Baldovino.** This lively, brightly hued trattoria across the street from Santa Croce is the brainchild of David and Catherine Gardner, two Scottish expats. In addition to turning out fine pizzas, Baldovino offers some tasty antipasti (like their plate of smoked salmon and tuna) and *insalatone* ("big salads"), as well as various pasta dishes and grilled meats—and they do it till the wee hours. It's a good idea to reserve ahead. ⊠ *Via S. Guiseppe, 22/r,* ☎ *055/241773. AE, DC, MC, V. Closed Mon. and 2 wks in Aug.*

$ ✕ **La Maremmana.** The owners and chef here have been working together for 19 years, and it shows. The space is light and cheery—with white walls, tile floor, and pink tablecloths, giving the place a warm glow. Dead center is an impressive array of antipasti, which whet the taste buds for the glories that follow, such as spaghetti *alla vongole* (with tiny clams) and grilled meats. ⊠ *Via dei Macci 77/r,* ☎ *055/241226. MC, V. Closed Sun.*

$$$$ ⛉ **Excelsior.** The neo-Renaissance Excelsior, housed in a 13th-century convent that once was the residence of Josephine Bonaparte, has painted wooden ceilings, stained glass, and acres of Oriental carpets strewn over marble floors in the public rooms. Opulent furnishings adorn the guest rooms, some with elegant balconies overlooking the river or a Florentine panorama. ⊠ *Piazza Ognissanti 3, 50123,* ☎ *055/264201,* FAX *055/210278. 168 rooms. Restaurant. AE, DC, MC, V.*

$$$$ ⛉ **Grand.** Facing its sister hotel, the smaller Excelsior (☞ *above*),
★ across the expanse of Piazza Ognissanti, the Grand exudes old-world grace with its posh amenities. Sumptuous Renaissance style prevails, enriched with distinctive Florentine fabrics. Guest rooms are imperial or Florentine in style, many with frescoes or canopied beds. Bathrooms are swathed in marble. ⊠ *Piazza Ognissanti 1, 50123,* ☎ *055/288781,* FAX *055/217400. 107 rooms. Restaurant, bar. AE, DC, MC, V.*

$$$$ ⛉ **Hotel Lungarno.** Rooms and suites in this hotel across the Arno from the Palazzo Vecchio and the Duomo have private terraces jutting out over the river. The very chic decor approximates a breezily elegant home, with lots of crisp white fabrics trimmed in blue. Four suites in a 13th-century tower preserve exposed stone walls and old archways. More than 100 paintings and drawings—from Picassos to Cocteaus—hang in hallways, bedrooms, even bathrooms. The lobby bar has a wall of windows and a sea of white couches that make it one of the nicest places in the city to stop for a drink. ⊠ *Borgo San Jacopo 14, 50125,* ☎ *055/27261,* FAX *055/ 268437. 61 rooms, 11 suites. Restaurant, bar. AE, DC, MC, V.*

$$$$ ⛉ **Plaza Hotel Lucchesi.** Elegant without being ostentatious, this hotel
★ is right on the Arno near Santa Croce. Bedrooms are spacious and quiet (double glazing throughout), and the lounges and piano bar are a favorite rendezvous for Florentines. Front bedrooms have views of the river; rear rooms on the top floor have balconies and knockout views of Santa Croce. ⊠ *Lungarno della Zecca Vecchia 38, 50122,* ☎ *055/ 26236,* FAX *055/2480921. 97 rooms. Restaurant. AE, DC, MC, V.*

$$$ ⛉ **Brunelleschi.** This unique hotel in the heart of Florence encom-
★ passes a Byzantine tower, medieval church, and an 18th-century palazzo. Sections of ancient stone walls and brick arches set off the tasteful contemporary decor in the public rooms. Bedrooms have textured, coordinated fabrics in soft colors; the beige marble bathrooms are stately. ⊠ *Piazza Sant'Elisabetta, off Via dei Calzaiuoli, 50122,* ☎ *055/ 290311,* FAX *055/219653. 94 rooms. Restaurant. AE, DC, MC, V.*

$$$ ⛉ **Hermitage.** Comfort and charm are the attributes of this hotel occupying the top six floors of a palazzo next to the Ponte Vecchio and the Uffizi. The inviting living room overlooking the Arno, flowered roof terrace, and well-lighted bedrooms are as lovely as a well-kept Florentine villa. Double glazing and attentive maintenance sustain the relaxing ambience. ⊠ *Vicolo Marzio 1, Piazza del Pesce, Ponte Vecchio, 50122,* ☎ *055/287216,* FAX *055/212208. 28 rooms. AE, MC, V.*

$$$ ⛉ **Monna Lisa.** Staying here is like living in an aristocratic palace in
★ the heart of Florence. American visitors in particular are fond of its smallish but homey bedrooms and sumptuously comfortable sitting rooms. Ask for a room on the quiet 17th-century courtyard, especially the one with the delightful balcony. A lavish buffet breakfast is included in the price. Reserve well in advance. ⊠ *Borgo Pinti 27, 50121,* ☎ *055/2479751,* FAX *055/2479755. 30 rooms. AE, DC, MC, V.*

$$–$$$ 🏨 **Loggiato dei Serviti.** You'll find the Loggiato dei Serviti tucked under an arcade in one of the city's quietest and most attractive squares. With its vaulted ceilings and tasteful antique furnishings, this 19th-century town house hotel is a real find if you want to get the genuine Florentine feel while enjoying modern creature comforts. ⊠ *Piazza Santissima Annunziata 3, 50122,* ☎ *055/2398280,* 🅵🅰🆇 *055/289595. 29 rooms. AE, DC, MC, V.*

$$ 🏨 **Alessandra.** The location, a block from the Ponte Vecchio, and clean, ample rooms make this a good choice for basic accommodations at reasonable rates. The English-speaking staff make sure guests are happy. ⊠ *Borgo Santi Apostoli 17, 50123,* ☎ *055/283438,* 🅵🅰🆇 *055/210619. 25 rooms, 9 without bath. AE, MC, V. Closed Dec. 15–26.*

$$ 🏨 **Hotel Ritz.** Set amid a row of buildings facing the Arno, this family-managed hotel has been decorated to make you feel as if you are a guest in a pretty, 19th-century Florentine home with 20th-century amenities. Most of the rooms have lovely views of either the Arno or the domed, red-roofed "skyline" of Florence. ⊠ *Lungarno Zecca Vecchia 24, 50122,* ☎ *055/2340650,* 🅵🅰🆇 *055/240863. 30 rooms. AE, DC, MC, V.*

$$ 🏨 **Hotel Torre Guelfa.** Hidden just steps from the Ponte Vecchio, this small hotel has guest rooms in a Florentine palazzo and rooftop bar in its 13th-century tower. The owners have worked to make it feel like a private residence, complete with canopy beds in some of the guest rooms. ⊠ *Borgo S.S. Apostoli 8, 50123,* ☎ *055/2396338,* 🅵🅰🆇 *055/2398577. 12 rooms. Bar. AE, MC, V.*

$$ 🏨 **Morandi alla Crocetta.** This charming and distinguished residence ★ near Piazza Santissima Annunziata was once a monastery, and access is up a flight of stairs. It is furnished in the classic style of a gracious Florentine home, and guests feel like privileged friends of the family. Small and exceptional, it is also a good value and must be booked well in advance. ⊠ *Via Laura 50, 50121,* ☎ *055/2344747,* 🅵🅰🆇 *055/2480954. 9 rooms. AE, DC, MC, V.*

$$ 🏨 **Pendini.** The atmosphere of an old-fashioned Florentine pensione is intact here; bedrooms have floral wallpaper, pastel carpeting, and modern baths. Public rooms have a belle-epoque look, with some antiques. It's central, and off-season rates here are a real bargain. ⊠ *Via Strozzi 2, 50123,* ☎ *055/211170,* 🅵🅰🆇 *055/281807. 42 rooms. AE, DC, MC, V.*

$$ 🏨 **Porta Faenza.** A hospitable Italian-Canadian couple owns and manages this conveniently positioned hotel near the station. Spacious rooms in Florentine style and sparkling bathrooms that, though compact, have such amenities as hair dryers make this a good value. The staff is helpful and attentive to your needs. ⊠ *Via Faenza 77, 50123,* ☎ *055/284119,* 🅵🅰🆇 *055/210101. 15 rooms. AE, DC, MC, V.*

$$ 🏨 **Villa Azalee.** In a residential area about five minutes from the train station, this century-old mansion is set in a large garden. It has a private-home atmosphere and comfortable living rooms. Rooms are decorated individually and are air-conditioned. ⊠ *Viale Fratelli Rosselli 44, 50123,* ☎ *055/214242,* 🅵🅰🆇 *055/268264. 24 rooms. AE, DC, MC, V.*

$ 🏨 **Bellettini.** Very central, this small hotel occupies two floors of an ★ old but well-kept building near San Lorenzo in an area with many inexpensive eating places. Rooms are ample, with Venetian or Tuscan decor, and bathrooms are modern. The management is friendly and helpful. ⊠ *Via dei Conti 7, 50123,* ☎ *055/213561,* 🅵🅰🆇 *055/283551. 27 rooms, 4 without bath. AE, DC, MC, V.*

$ 🏨 **Nuova Italia.** Near the main train station and within walking distance of the sights, this homey hotel in a dignified palazzo is run by a genial English-speaking family. Rooms are clean and simply furnished, and they have triple-glazed windows to ensure restful nights. ⊠ *Via*

Faenza 26, 50123, ☎ *055/268430,* ᶠᴬˣ *055/210941. 20 rooms. AE, MC, V.*

Nightlife and the Arts

The Arts

FILM

You can find movie listings in *La Nazione,* the daily Florence newspaper. English-language films are shown Tuesday through Sunday evenings at the **Cinema Astro** (✉ Piazza San Simone near Santa Croce); on Monday at the **Odeon** (✉ Piazza Strozzi); and on Wednesday at the **Goldoni** (✉ Via dei Serragli).

MUSIC

Most major musical events are staged at the **Teatro Comunale** (✉ Corso Italia 16, ☎ 055/2779236). The box office (closed Sunday and Monday) is open from 9 to 1, and a half hour before performances. It's best to order your tickets by mail, however, as they're difficult to come by at the last minute. Amici della Musica (Friends of Music) puts on a series of concerts at the **Teatro della Pergola** (✉ Box office, Via della Pergola 10a/r, ☎ 055/2479652). For program information contact the **Amici della Musica** (✉ Via Sirtori 49, ☎ 055/608420) directly.

Nightlife

BARS

The bar in the lobby of the **Excelsior** (✉ Piazza Ognissanti 3, ☎ 055/264201) attracts locals as well as business travelers and tourists. **The Jazz Club** (✉ Via Nuova dei Caccini 3, ☎ 055/2479700) offers good live jazz in a surprisingly well-ventilated club near the Duomo.

NIGHTCLUBS

The River Club (✉ Lungarno Corsini 8, ☎ 055/282465), closed Sunday, has winter-garden decor and a large dance floor. **Meccanò** (✉ Cascine park, Viale degli Olmi 1, ☎ 055/331371), closed Sunday, offers a multimedia experience, with videos, art, and music in a high-tech disco with a late-night restaurant, the Pomodoro d'Acciaio. **Hurricane Roxy** (✉ Via Il Prato 58/r, ☎ 055/2103999) serves a light lunch during the day but in the evening there's a deejay, good music, and welcoming atmosphere. **Maramao** (✉ Via dei Macci 79, ☎ 055/244341) teems with young Florentines out until the wee hours. **Space Electronic** (✉ Via Palazzuolo 37, ☎ 055/2393082), closed Monday October–February, is exactly what its name implies: ultramodern and psychedelic. **Yab** (✉ Via Sassetti 5/r, ☎ 055/282018), closed Sunday and Monday, is another futuristic disco popular with the young jet set.

Shopping

Markets

The **Mercato di San Lorenzo** (✉ Piazza San Lorenzo and Via dell'Ariento) is a fine place to browse for buys in leather goods and souvenirs; it's open Tuesday–Saturday 8–7 (June–September, Sunday 8–7). Don't miss the indoor, two-story **Mercato Centrale** (✉ Piazza del Mercato Centrale), near San Lorenzo, open in the morning Monday–Saturday.

Shopping Districts

Via Tornabuoni is the high-end shopping street. **Via della Vigna Nuova** is just as fashionable. Goldsmiths and jewelry shops can be found on and around the **Ponte Vecchio** and in the **Santa Croce** area, where there is also a high concentration of leather shops and inconspicuous shops selling gold and silver jewelry at prices much lower than those of the elegant jewelers near Ponte Vecchio. The monastery of **Santa Croce** (✉ Via San Giuseppe 5/r and Piazza Santa Croce 16) houses a leather-working school and showroom. Antiques dealers can be found in and around the center, but are concentrated on **Via Maggio** in the Oltrarno area. **Borgo Ognissanti** is also home to shops selling period decorative objects.

Florence Essentials

Arriving and Departing

BY CAR

The north–south access route to Florence is the Autostrada del Sole (A1) from Milan or Rome. The Florence–Mare autostrada (A11) links Florence with the Tyrrhenian coast, Pisa, and the A12 coastal autostrada. Parking in Florence is severely restricted.

BY PLANE

The airport that handles most arrivals is **Aeroporto Galileo Galilei** (⊠ Pisa, ☎ 050/500707), more commonly known as **Aeroporto Pisa-Galilei.** Some domestic and European flights use Florence's **Aeroporto Vespucci** (⊠ Peretola, ☎ 055/373498).

Between the Airport and Downtown. Pisa-Galilei Airport is connected to Florence by train direct to the Stazione Centrale di Santa Maria Novella. Service is hourly throughout the day and takes about 60 minutes. When departing, you can buy train tickets for the airport and check in for all flights leaving from Aeroporto Pisa-Galilei at the Florence Air Terminal at Track 5 of Santa Maria Novella. Aeroporto Vespucci is connected to downtown Florence by SITA bus.

BY TRAIN

The main station is **Stazione Centrale di Santa Maria Novella** (☎ 1478/88088 toll free). Florence is on the main north–south route between Rome, Bologna, and Milan or Venice. High-speed Eurostar trains reach Rome in less than two hours and Milan in less than three.

Getting Around

BY BICYCLE

Alinari (⊠ Via Guelfa 85/r, ☎ 055/280500). **Motorent** (⊠ Via San Zanobi 9/r, ☎ 055/490113).

BY BUS

Bus maps and timetables are available for a small fee at the Azienda Transporti Autolinee Fiorentine (ATAF, ⊠ near Stazione Centrale di Santa Maria Novella; Piazza del Duomo 57/r) city bus information booths. The same maps may be free at visitor information offices. **ATAF** city buses run from about 5:15 AM to 1 AM. Buy tickets before you board the bus; they are sold at many tobacco shops and newsstands. The cost is 1,500 lire for a ticket good for one hour, 2,500 lire for two hours, and 5,800 lire for four one-hour tickets, called a *multiplo*. A 24-hour tourist ticket (*turistico*) costs 6,000 lire. For excursions outside Florence, for instance, to Siena, you take **SITA** (bus terminal, ⊠ Via Santa Caterina da Siena 17, near the Stazione Centrale di Santa Maria Novella). The **CAP** bus terminal (⊠ Via Nazionale 13) is also near the train station.

BY MOPED

Try **Alinari** or **Motorent** (☞ By Bicycle, *above*).

BY TAXI

Taxis (☎ 055/4798 or 055/4390) wait at stands and you can call them. Use only authorized cabs, which are white with a yellow stripe or rectangle on the door. The meter starts at 4,500 lire, with extra charges for nights, holidays, or radio dispatch.

It is easy to find your way around in Florence with the help of the many landmarks. Major sights can be explored on foot, as they are packed into a relatively small area. Wear comfortable shoes. The system of street addresses is unusual, with commercial addresses (those with an *r* in them, meaning *rosso,* or red) and residential addresses numbered separately (32/r might be next to or a block away from plain 32).

Contacts and Resources

CONSULATES

U.S. (⊠ Lungarno Vespucci 38, ☎ 055/2398276). **Canadian** citizens should contact their embassy in Rome (☞ Rome Essentials, *above*). **U.K.** (⊠ Lungarno Corsini 2, ☎ 055/284133).

EMERGENCIES

Police (☎ 113). **Ambulance** (☎ 118 or 055/212222). **Tourist Medical Service** (⊠ Viale Lorenzo il Magnifico, ☎ 055/475411). **Pharmacies** are open Sunday and holidays by rotation. Signs posted outside pharmacies list those open all night and on weekends. The pharmacy at Santa Maria Novella train station is always open.

ENGLISH-LANGUAGE BOOKSTORES

BM Bookshop (⊠ Borgo Ognissanti 4/r, ☎ 055/294575). **Paperback Exchange** (⊠ Via Fiesolana 31/r, ☎ 055/2478154). **Seeber** (⊠ Via Tornabuoni 70/r, ☎ 055/215697).

GUIDED TOURS

Excursions. Operators offer a half-day excursion to Pisa, usually in the afternoon, costing about 48,000 lire, and a full-day excursion to Siena and San Gimignano, costing about 68,000 lire. Pick up a timetable at ATAF information offices near the train station, at SITA (⊠ Via Santa Caterina da Siena 17, ☎ 055/214721), or at the APT tourist office (☞ Visitor Information, *below*).

Orientation. A bus consortium (through hotels and travel agents) offers tours in air-conditioned buses covering the important sights in Florence with a trip to Fiesole. The cost is about 48,000 lire for a three-hour tour, including entrance fees, and bookings can be made through travel agents.

Special-Interest. Inquire at travel agents or at **Agriturist Regionale** (⊠ Piazza San Firenze 3, ☎ 055/287838) for visits to villa gardens around Florence from April through June, or for visits to farm estates during September and October.

TRAVEL AGENCIES

American Express (⊠ Via Guicciardini 49/r, ☎ 055/288751; ⊠ Via Dante Alighieri 14/r, ☎ 055/2382876). **CIT** (⊠ Piazza Stazione 51/4, ☎ 055/284145 or 055/212606). **Micos Travel Box** (⊠ Via dell'Oriuolo 50–52/r, ☎ 055/2340228).

VISITOR INFORMATION

Azienda Promozione Turistica (APT; ⊠ Via Manzoni 16, 50121, ☎ 055/2346284).

TUSCANY

Tuscany is a blend of rugged hills, fertile valleys, and long stretches of sandy beach that curve along the west coast of central Italy and fringe the pine-forested coastal plain of the Maremma. The gentle, cypress-studded green hills may seem familiar: Leonardo and Raphael often painted them in the backgrounds of their masterpieces. Cities and towns here were the cradle of the Renaissance, which during the 15th century flourished most notably in nearby Florence. Come to Tuscany to enjoy its unchanged and gracious atmosphere of good living, and, above all, its unparalleled artistic treasures, many still in their original tiny old churches and patrician palaces.

Prato

Since the Middle Ages, Prato, 21 km (13 mi) northwest of Florence, has been Italy's major wool-producing center, and it remains one of the world's largest manufacturers of cloth. Ignore the drab industrial outskirts and devote some time to the fine old buildings in the downtown area, crammed with artwork commissioned by Prato's wealthy merchants during the Renaissance. Though in ruins, the formidable **Castello** (Castle) built for Frederick II Hohenstaufen, adjacent to Santa Maria delle Carceri, is an impressive sight, the only castle of its type to be seen outside southern Italy. ⊠ *Piazza Santa Maria delle Carceri,* ☎ *0574/38207.* ⊉ *Free.* ☉ *Mon. and Wed.–Sat. 8:30–12:30 and 3–5:30, Sun. 9–12.*

The **Duomo,** erected during the Middle Ages, was decorated with paintings and sculptures by some of the most illustrious figures of Tuscan art. Among them was Fra Filippo Lippi, who executed scenes from the life of St. Stephen on the left wall and scenes from the life of John the Baptist on the right in the **Cappella Maggiore** (Main Chapel). Bring a flashlight—there's no illumination provided. ⊠ *Piazza del Duomo,* ☎ *0574/26234.* ☉ *Daily 7:30–noon and 3:30–6:30.*

In the former bishop's palace, now the **Museo dell'Opera del Duomo** (Cathedral Museum), you can see the original reliefs by Donatello for the Pulpit of the Holy Girdle (Mary's belt, supposedly given to the apostle Thomas as evidence of her assumption into heaven; the relic is kept in a chapel of the cathedral). ⊠ *Piazza del Duomo 49,* ☎ *0574/29339.* ☉ *Mon. and Wed.–Sat. 9:30–12:30 and 3–6:30, Sun. 9:30–12:30.*

The church of **Santa Maria delle Carceri** was built by Giuliano Sangallo in the 1490s, and is a landmark of Renaissance architecture. ⊠ *Piazza Santa Maria delle Carceri, off Via Cairoli and southeast of the cathedral.*

$$–$$$ ✗ **Osvaldo Baroncelli.** Polished wooden floors, subtly striped chairs, and
★ pale sponged walls bespeak the seriousness of this restaurant, which has been in the Baroncelli family for 50 years, and in that time they've perfected their menu. You'll be tempted to eat all of the perfectly fried olives that arrive warm, but save room for what's to come. The pastas are house made—the *tortelli di branzino* (tortelli stuffed with sea bass) is wonderful. Reservations are advised. ⊠ *Via Fra Bartolomeo 13,* ☎ *0574/23810. AE, MC, V. Closed Aug. 7–21. No lunch Sat.*

Pistoia

A floricultural capital of Europe, Pistoia—about 15 km (9 mi) northwest of Prato—is surrounded by greenhouses and plant nurseries. Flowers aside, Pistoia's main sights are all in the historic center with superb examples of Romanesque architecture. The Romanesque **Duomo** is flanked by a bell tower begun in the 12th century and faces the unusual Gothic baptistery. Inside the cathedral in a side chapel dedicated to San Jacopo (St. James, the patron saint of Pistoia), there's a massive **silver altar** that alone makes the stop in Pistoia worthwhile. Nearly 200 years in the making, it's an incredible piece of workmanship, begun in 1287. ⊠ *Piazza del Duomo,* ☎ *0573/25095.* ☉ *Daily 9–noon and 4–7.*

North of the cathedral, the **Spedale del Ceppo** (Hospital of the Tree Trunk), founded in the 13th century, gets its name from the hollow trunk in which offerings were placed. On the facade is a superb frieze

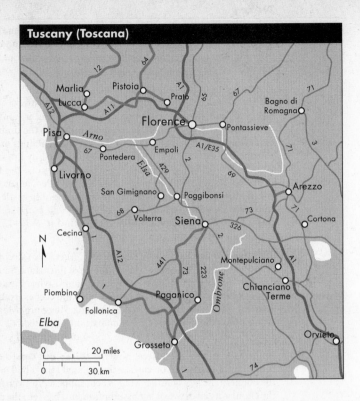

Tuscany (Toscana)

by Giovanni della Robbia (1469–1529) that was completed by the workshop of Santi and Benedetto Buglioni in 1527. ✉ *Piazza dell'Ospedale, Via delle Pappe.*

An architectural gem revealed in green-and-white marble, the medieval church of **San Giovanni Fuorcivitas** holds a *Visitation* by Luca della Robbia (1400–82), a painting attributed to Taddeo Gaddi, and a holy-water font that may have been executed by Giovanni Pisano (circa 1270–1348). ✉ *Via Cavour.*

Though it is not as grand as the silver altar in the cathedral, many consider Pistoia's greatest art treasure to be Giovanni Pisano's powerfully sculpted pulpit executed between 1298 and 1301 in the church of **Sant'Andrea.** ✉ *Via Sant'Andrea,* ☎ *0573/21912.* ⊙ *Daily 8–1 and 3–5:30.*

$$ ✕ **S. Jacopo.** This charming restaurant near the Duomo has white walls, tile floors, and a gracious host in Bruno Lottini. The food is as welcoming as he: Bread, flecked with olives, is baked on the premises and arrives hot. Regional favorites include *maccheroni S. Jacopo*, wide ribbons of house-made pasta with a duck *ragù* (sauce), and they can turn out perfectly grilled squid as well. Save room for dessert, especially the apple strudel. ✉ *Via Crispi 15,* ☎ *0573/27786. AE, DC, MC, V. Closed 15 days in Aug. No lunch Mon. and Tues.*

Lucca

Any tour of Tuscany should include Lucca, with its handful of marvelously elaborate Romanesque churches and late-19th-century and early 20th-century Liberty facades along the Fillungo, its main shopping thoroughfare. Because few cars are allowed in the historic center, the city is easy to get around in—and a pleasure. For that very reason it's an excellent alternative to, or side trip from, Pisa, just 22 km (14 mi) away.

First enjoy the views of Lucca and countryside from the parklike 16th-century ramparts. Then explore the churches that look suspiciously like oversized marble wedding cakes. A forest of columns fronts the 11th-century **Duomo**; inside is the 15th-century tomb of Ilaria del Carretto by Jacopo della Quercia (1374–1438). ⊠ *Piazza San Martino,* ☎ *0583/490530.* ⊙ *Apr.–Oct., daily 7–7; Nov.–Mar., daily 7–5.*

Piazza del Mercato preserves the oval form of the Roman amphitheater over which it was built; an outdoor market bustles here on weekdays. The church of **San Frediano** is graced with an austere facade ornamented by 13th-century mosaic decoration. Inside, check out the exquisite reliefs by Jacopo della Quercia in the last chapel on the left and the bizarre mummy of St. Zita, patron saint of domestic servants. ⊠ *Piazza San Frediano.* ⊙ *Daily 7:30–12 and 3–5, holidays 9–1 and 3–6.*

One of the most fanciful facades in central Italy can be seen on the front of the church of **San Michele in Foro,** adorned with a marriage of arches and columns crowned by a statue of St. Michael. The church is an exceptional example of the Pisan Romanesque style and the decorative flair peculiar to Lucca. ⊠ *Piazza San Michele.* ⊙ *Daily 7:30–12:30 and 3–6.*

The **Villa Reale** (Royal Villa), at Marlia, 8 km (5 mi) west of Lucca, was once the home of Napoléon's sister, and has been restored by the Counts Pecci-Blunt. It is celebrated for its spectacular gardens, originally laid out in the 16th century, and redone in the middle of the 17th century. Gardening buffs adore the legendary **Teatro di Verdura,** a theater carved out of hedges and topiaries; a music festival is usually held here during July and August. ⊠ *Via Villa Reale, Marlia,* ☎ *0583/30108.* ⊙ *Mar.–Nov., tours 10, 11, 3, 4, 5, 6; Dec.–Feb., open by previous appointment only. Closed Dec.–Feb.*

$$ ✕ **Buca di Sant'Antonio.** Buca di Sant'Antonio has been around for more ★ than two centuries, and it's easy to see why. A white-walled interior adorned with copper pots, expertly prepared food, and an able staff make dining here a real treat. The menu offers something for everyone, from simple pasta dishes to more daring dishes such as roast *capretto* (kid) with herbs. ⊠ *Via della Cervia 3,* ☎ *0583/55881. AE, DC, MC, V. Closed Mon. and last 3 wks in July. No dinner Sun.*

$$ ✕ **Il Giglio.** Just off Piazza Napoleone, this restaurant has quiet, late-19th-century charm and classic cuisine. It's a place for all seasons, with a big fireplace and an outdoor terrace in summer. Among the local specialties are *farro garfagnino* (a thick soup made with grain and beans), and *coniglio con olive* (rabbit stew with olives). ⊠ *Piazza del Giglio 3,* ☎ *0583/494058. AE, DC, MC, V. Closed Wed. and 2 wks in Feb. No dinner Tues.*

$-$$$ 🏠 **Villa La Principessa.** This pretty 19th-century country mansion, 3½ ★ km (2 mi) outside Lucca, is an exclusive hotel with a deluxe annex, Locanda L'Elisa. All rooms are individually and tastefully decorated. Antique floors, furniture, and portraits set the tone, and the restaurant is known for its fine Tuscan dishes. ⊠ *Massa Pisana, 55050,* ☎ *0583/370037,* ℻ *0583/379136. 40 rooms. Restaurant, outdoor pool. AE, DC, MC, V. Closed Nov.–Mar.*

$ 🏠 **Piccolo Hotel Puccini.** Just a few steps away from the busy square and church of San Michele, this little hotel is quiet and calm. It also offers parking (which must be reserved in advance) at a reasonable fee, which is a great advantage. ⊠ *Via di Poggio, 9, 55100,* ☎ *0583/55421,* ℻ *0583/55421. 14 rooms. AE, DC, MC, V.*

Pisa

If you cut through the kitschy atmosphere around the Leaning Tower, Pisa has much to offer. Its cathedral-baptistery-tower complex in Piazza dei Miracoli is among the most dramatic in Italy, and the Piazza dei Cavalieri is a superb example of a Renaissance piazza. Pisa's treasures are more subtle than Florence's, to which it is inevitably compared. Pisa usually emerges the loser, and it shouldn't. Though it sustained heavy damage during World War II, many of its beautiful Romanesque structures are still preserved.

The **Battistero** (Baptistery) in front of the cathedral is known mainly for its graceful form and for the pulpit carved by Giovanni Pisano's father, Nicola (1220–78). The Baptistery was begun in 1153 but not completed until 1400. Ask one of the ticket takers if he'll sing for you inside the Baptistery. The acoustics are remarkable; a tip of 5,000 lire is appropriate. ⊠ *Piazza dei Miracoli.* ☉ *Apr.–Sept., daily 8–7:40; Oct.–Mar., daily 9–4:40.*

The **Camposanto** (Cemetery) is said to be filled with earth brought back from the Holy Land by Crusaders. Important frescoes, notably the *Drunkenness of Noah* by Renaissance artist Benozzo Gozzoli and a 14th-century *Triumph of Death*, are within. ⊠ *Piazza dei Miracoli.* ☉ *Apr.–Sept., daily 8–7:40; Oct.–Mar., daily 9–5:40.*

★ Pisa's **Duomo** is elegantly simple, its facade decorated with geometric and animal shapes. The cavernous interior is supported by a series of 68 columns, while the pulpit is a prime example of Giovanni Pisano's work and one of the major monuments of the Italian Gothic style. Be sure to note the suspended lamp that hangs across from the pulpit. Known as Galileo's Lamp, it's said to have inspired his theories on pendular motion. ⊠ *Piazza del Duomo.* ☉ *Apr.–Sept., Mon.–Sat. 10–7:40, Sun. 1–5; Oct.–Mar., daily 10–12:30 and 3–5:30.*

$$$ ✕ **Al Ristoro dei Vecchi Macelli.** The 18-year-old "Inn by the Old Slaughterhouse" got its name from being down the street from an old slaughterhouse, but a calm serenity pervades. Such earthy connotations aside, the food is sophisticated and special, served in white-tablecloth surroundings. You can order a fixed-price seafood or meat menu or choose dishes à la carte. The *coniglio disossato e farcito con salsa di tartufo* (boneless rabbit stuffed with truffle sauce) is a winner. Reservations are advised. ⊠ *Via Volturno 49,* ☎ *050/20424. AE, DC, MC, V. Closed Wed. and Aug. 10–25. No lunch Sun.*

$$ ✕ **Osteria dei Cavalieri.** This charming white-walled osteria, a few steps from Piazza dei Cavalieri, is reason enough to come to Pisa. On offer are exquisitely grilled fish dishes, vegetarian dishes, and *tagliata,* thin slivers of rare beef. Finish your meal with a lemon sorbet bathed in Prosecco, and walk away feeling like you've eaten like a king at plebeian prices. ⊠ *Via San Frediano 16,* ☎ *055/580858. AE, DC, MC, V. Closed Sun. and July 25–Aug. 25. No lunch Sat.*

Siena

One of Italy's best-preserved medieval towns, Siena is rich both in works of art and in expensive antiques shops. Built on three hills, Siena is not an easy town to explore, for everything you'll want to see is either up or down a steep hill or stairway and many hotels are outside the old walls. But it is worth every ounce of effort. Siena really gives you the chance of seeing and feeling what the Middle Ages must have been like: dark fortresslike stone palaces, Gothic church portals, and narrow streets leading to airy squares. Siena was a center of learning and art during the Middle Ages, and almost all the public buildings and churches in the town have enough artistic or historical merit to be worth visiting.

You can buy a combined ticket for admission to the Biblioteca Piccolomini and Museo dell'Opera Metropolitana.

One of the finest Gothic cathedrals in Italy, Siena's **Duomo** is unique in displaying a mixture of religious and civic ornamentation on both its interior and exterior. The unique inlaid marble floors and Nicola Pisano's (circa 1220–1284) pulpit, carved about 1265, are highlights. The animated frescoes of papal history in the **Biblioteca Piccolomini** (Piccolomini Library), with an entrance off the left aisle of the cathedral, were painted by Pinturicchio. ⊠ *Piazza del Duomo,* ☎ *0577/ 283048.* ☉ *Mid-Mar.–Oct., daily 9–7:30; Nov.–mid-Mar., daily 10–1 and 2:30–5.*

The **Museo dell'Opera del Duomo** (Cathedral Museum) contains some fine works of art, notably a celebrated *Maestà* by Duccio di Buoninsegna. ⊠ *Piazza del Duomo,* ☎ *0577/283048.* ☉ *Nov.–mid-Mar., daily 9–1:30; mid-Mar.–Oct., daily 9–7:30.*

★ The 13th-century **Palazzo Pubblico** (City Hall) dominates Piazza del Campo and houses the Museo Civico (Civic Museum), where there are noteworthy frescoes. ⊠ *Piazza del Campo,* ☎ *0577/292263.* ☉ *Mar.– Apr., Mon.–Sat. 9:30–6:30; Nov.–early Jan., Mon.–Sat. 9:30–1:30.*

★ Fan-shaped, sloping **Piazza del Campo** is Siena's main center of activity, with 11 streets leading into it. Farsighted planning has preserved it as a medieval showpiece. This is the venue for the famous **Palio,** a breakneck, 90-second horse race that takes place twice each year, on July 2 and August 16. The **Torre del Mangia** (Bell Tower) of the Palazzo Pubblico (☞ *above*) offers a wonderful view (you'll have to climb 503 steps to reach it, however). ⊠ *Piazza del Campo.* ☉ *Daily 10–1 hr before sunset.*

$$$ ✕ **Antica Trattoria Botteganova.** Just outside the city walls, north toward Chianti, the Botteganova is arguably the best restaurant in Siena. The interior, with high vaulting, is relaxed yet classy, and the service is first rate. Clean flavors, balanced combinations, and inviting presentations are paramount on the menu that changes often; but some frequently appear—try the delicious, light potato gnocchi with a sweet red onion sauce. ⊠ *Strada Chiantigiana 29, 2 km (1 mi) north of Siena,* ☎ *0577/284230. AE, DC, MC, V. Closed Mon.*

$$ ✕ **Osteria Le Logge.** Just off Piazza del Campo, this is a fine choice for an informal but memorable meal. Get there early to claim a table. Among the specialties are *malfatti all'Osteria* (ricotta and spinach dumplings in cream sauce) and tagliata *alla rucola* (with arugula). ⊠ *Via del Porrione 33,* ☎ *0577/48013. AE, DC, MC, V. Closed Sun., 2 wks in June and Nov.*

$$ ✕ **Tullio Tre Cristi.** To find this historic trattoria, take Via dei Rossi from Via Banchi di Sopra. Even though it was discovered by tourists long ago, it remains true to typical Sienese cooking and atmosphere. Try spaghetti *alle briciole,* a poor-man's pasta with bread crumbs, tomato, and garlic. ⊠ *Vicolo di Provenzano 1,* ☎ *0577/280608. MC, V. Closed Tues.*

$$$$ ☶ **Certosa di Maggiano.** A 14th-century Carthusian monastery less than
★ 2 km (1 mi) southeast of Siena has been converted into a luxe oasis furnished in impeccable style. The bedrooms have every comfort, and the atmosphere is that of an aristocratic family villa. In warm weather breakfast is served on the patio next to the garden aburst with roses, peonies, and zinnias. ⊠ *Strada di Certosa 82, 53100,* ☎ *0577/288180,* FAX *0577/288189. 18 rooms. Restaurant, pool. AE, DC, MC, V.*

$$$ ☶ **Duomo.** Occupying the top floor of a 17th-century building in the
★ center of Siena, near Piazza del Campo, the hotel is quiet and is fur-

nished in a neat contemporary style, with traces of the past showing in the artfully exposed brickwork in the breakfast room. Many rooms have superb views of the city's towers and the hills beyond. ⊠ *Via Stalloreggi 38, 53100,* ☎ *0577/289088,* ☒ *0577/43043. 23 rooms. AE, DC, MC, V.*

$$$ ▦ **Park.** Just outside the walls of the old city, this is a handsome and sprawling 15th-century villa on its own well-equipped grounds, with a nine-hole golf course. The furnishings in the public areas strike an elegant balance between antique charm and patrician comfort. Comfortable guest rooms have bold, dark fabrics, mirrors, and modern appointments. ⊠ *Via di Marciano 18, 53100,* ☎ *0577/44803,* ☒ *0577/49020. 69 rooms. Restaurant, pool. AE, DC, MC, V.*

$$ ▦ **Antica Torre.** A cordial young couple runs this hotel in a restored centuries-old tower a 10-minute walk from Piazza del Campo. Rooms are smallish and are furnished sparingly but in good taste. Beam ceilings throughout and original brick vaults here and there are reminders of the tower's venerable history. ⊠ *Via Fieravecchia 7, 53100,* ☎ ☒ *0577/222255. 8 rooms. AE, MC, V.*

San Gimignano

San Gimignano-of-the-Beautiful-Towers—to use its original name—is perhaps the most delightful of the Tuscan medieval hill towns, 31 km (20 mi) northwest of Siena. There were once more than 70 tall towers here, symbols of power for the wealthy families of the Middle Ages. Fifteen still stand, giving the town its unique skyline. The main street leads directly from the city gates to Piazza della Cisterna, with a quaint wellhead, and Piazza del Duomo.

The walls of the **Collegiata** (Church), and those in the **Cappella della Santa Fina** chapel dedicated to Santa Fina, are decorated with radiant frescoes by Domenico Ghirlandaio; at press time, the frescoes were being restored. (Have plenty of 100-lire coins at hand for the light machines; to get a closer look at the chapel frescoes, buy a ticket for the Municipal Museum in Palazzo del Popolo.) From the steps of the church you can observe the town's countless crows as they circle the tall towers. In the pretty courtyard on the right as you descend the church stairs, there's a shop selling Tuscan and Deruta ceramics, which you'll also find in other shops along the Via San Giovanni. ⊠ *Piazza del Duomo,* ☎ *0577/940316.* ☉ *Daily 9:30–12:30 and 3–5:30.*

$$$ ✕ **Bel Soggiorno.** Bel Soggiorno is attached to a small hotel. It has fine views, refectory tables set with linen and candles, and leather-covered chairs. Specialties are *zuppa medioevale* (soup of mushrooms, truffle, grain, and potatoes) and *sorpresa in crosta* (spicy rabbit stew in a bread crust). ⊠ *Via San Giovanni 91,* ☎ *0577/940375. AE, DC, MC, V. Closed Mon. and Jan.–Feb.*

$$ ✕ **La Mangiatoia.** In this rustic trattoria off Via San Matteo prices are more moderate than at places with a view. The kitchen turns out simple country cooking. ⊠ *Via Mainardi 5,* ☎ *0577/941528. MC, V. Closed Tues., 3 wks in Nov., and 1 wk in Jan.*

$$ ▦ **Pescille.** This rambling stone farmhouse, about 3 km (2 mi) outside San Gimignano, with a good view of the town, has been restored as a hotel and furnished in attractive chic rustic style. ⊠ *Località Pescille, 53037,* ☎ *0577/940186,* ☒ *0577/940186. 50 rooms. Pool. AE, DC, MC, V. Closed Nov.–mid-Mar.*

Arezzo

To appreciate Arezzo you have to delve into the town's historic core, ignoring the industrialized suburbs. The city is one of Italy's three major gold jewelry production centers. In the old, upper town are an array of medieval and Renaissance buildings and a piazza that is a compendium of several eras. Tuscan art treasures abound in Arezzo, including frescoes by Piero della Francesca (1420–92), stained glass, and ancient Etruscan pottery. In the old part of Arezzo, the poet Petrarch (1304–74), the artist Vasari (1511–74), and the satirical author Pietro Aretino (1492–1556) all lived.

The fine Gothic **Duomo** is decorated with richly colored 16th-century stained-glass windows and an eye-level fresco of a tender Magdalen by Piero della Francesca next to the large marble tomb near the organ. ⊠ *Piazza del Duomo,* ☏ *0575/23991.* ⊙ *Daily 7–12:30 and 3–6:30.*

Piazza Grande is an attractive, sloping square where an extensive open-air fair of antiques and old bric-a-brac is held the first weekend of every month. The shops around the piazza also specialize in antiques, with prices lower than those you will encounter in Florence. The colonnaded apse and bell tower of the Romanesque church of **Santa Maria della Pieve** grace one end of this pleasant piazza. ⊠ *Via dei Pileati, end of Corso Italia,* ☏ *0575/377678.* ⊙ *Daily 8–1 and 3–7.*

Next to what's left of an ancient **Roman amphitheater** and near the train station is the **Museo Archeologico** (Archaeological Museum), with a rich collection of Etruscan art, artifacts, and pottery. Reproductions of the latter by contemporary Arezzo artisans are sold in local ceramic shops. ⊠ *Via Margaritone 10,* ☏ *0575/20882.* ⊙ *Mon.–Sat. 9–2, Sun. 9–1.*

★ In the church of **San Francesco** are famous frescoes by Piero della Francesca, painted between 1452 and 1466 and depicting *The Legend of the True Cross* on three walls of the choir. Though part of the frescoes may be hidden from view while restoration work takes place, it is possible to go up on the scaffolding to view at eye level part of this magnificent fresco cycle. ⊠ *Via Cavour,* ☏ *0575/20630.* ⊙ *Daily 2–7.*

$$ ✕ **Buca di San Francesco.** Travelers and passing celebrities come to this
★ rustic and historic cellar restaurant for the 13th-century cantina atmosphere, but locals love it for the food, especially ribollita and *sformato di verdure* (vegetable flan). ⊠ *Piazza San Francesco 1,* ☏ *0575/23271. AE, DC, MC, V. Closed Tues. and 2 wks in July. No dinner Mon.*

$$ ✕ **L'Agania.** The main draw to this central osteria is not its plain wood paneling and cheap furniture, but its good, inexpensive dishes such as *cinghiale* (wild boar), both as a second course and in a savory sauce with pasta. Also try the *griffi,* which is actually veal cheek in a tasty sauce with tomatoes and spices. ⊠ *Via Mazzini 10,* ☏ *0575/ 295381. AE, DC, MC, V. Closed Mon. and 2nd wk in June.*

$$ ▥ **Continental.** The circa-1950 Continental has fairly spacious rooms decorated in white and bright yellow, spic-and-span bathrooms, and the advantage of a central location within walking distance of all major sights. ⊠ *Piazza Guido Monaco 7, 52100,* ☏ *0575/20251,* FAX *0575/350485. 74 rooms. AE, DC, MC, V.*

Cortona

Cortona, about 30 km (19 mi) south of Arezzo, has a peculiarly Tuscan brand of charm. This well-preserved, unspoiled medieval hill town is known for its excellent small picture gallery and a number of fine antiques shops, as well as for its colony of foreign residents. The approach to Cortona from the east passes the Renaissance church of **Santa Maria del Calcinaio**. The heart of Cortona is formed by **Piazza della Repubblica** and the adjacent **Piazza Signorelli**.

The **Museo Diocesano** (Diocesan Museum) houses an impressive number of large and splendid paintings by native son Luca Signorelli (1445 to 1450–1523), as well as a beautiful *Annunciation* by Fra Angelico, a delightful surprise in this small, eclectic town. ⊠ *Piazza del Duomo 1,* ☎ *0575/62830.* ☉ *Nov.–Mar., Tues.–Sun. 10–1 and 3–5; Apr.–Oct., Tues.–Sun. 9:30–1 and 3:30–7.*

Picturesque **Palazzo Pretorio** (Praetorian Palace) houses a museum with a representative collection of Etruscan bronzes. Climb its centuries-old stone staircase to the **Museo dell'Accademia Etrusca** (Gallery of Etruscan Art). ⊠ *Piazza Signorelli 9,* ☎ *0575/630415.* ☉ *Apr.–Sept., Tues.–Sun. 10–1 and 4–7; Oct.–Mar., Tues.–Sun. 9–1 and 3–5.*

$$ ✕ **Tonino.** The place to eat in Cortona, it's known for its delicious an-
★ tipasto and for succulent steaks of Chianina beef. It's best on week-days, when it's quieter. Both service and food have a touch of class. The dining rooms, on two floors, have large picture windows overlooking the valley. ⊠ *Piazza Garibaldi,* ☎ *0575/630500. AE, DC, MC, V. Closed Tues.*

Tuscany Essentials

Getting Around

BY BUS

Buses are a good alternative to driving; the region is crisscrossed by bus lines, which in some cases offer more frequent local service than trains, especially from Florence to Prato, a half-hour trip, and from Florence to Siena, which can take from 1¼ (by express bus) to 2 hours.

BY CAR

The best way to see the region is by car, taking detours to hill towns and abbeys. Roads throughout Tuscany are in good condition, though often narrow. The A1 autostrada links Florence with Arezzo and Chiusi (where you turn off for Montepulciano). A toll-free superstrada links Florence with Siena. For Chianti wine country scenery, take the S222 south of Florence through the undulating hills between Strada in Chianti and Greve in Chianti.

BY TRAIN

The main train network connects Florence with Arezzo and Prato. Another main line runs to Pisa, and a secondary line goes from Prato to the coast via Lucca. Trains also connect Siena with Pisa, a two-hour ride. Call ☎ 1478/88088 toll free for train information.

Guided Tours

American Express (⊠ Via Guicciardini 49/r, ☎ 055/288751) operates one-day excursions to Siena and San Gimignano out of Florence. **CIT** (⊠ Via Cavour 54/r, ☎ 055/294306) operates regional tours, too.

Visitor Information

Arezzo (⊠ Piazza della Repubblica 28, ☎ 0575/377678). **Cortona** (⊠ Via Nazionale 72, ☎ 0575/630352). **Lucca** (⊠ Piazzale Verdi, ☎ 0583/419689). **Pisa** (⊠ Piazza del Duomo 8, ☎ 050/560464). **Pistoia** (⊠ Palazzo dei Vescovi, ☎ 0573/21622). **Prato** (⊠ Via Cairoli 48, ☎ 0574/24112). **San Gimignano** (⊠ Piazza del Duomo, ☎ 0577/940008).

MILAN

Milan, capital of all that is new in Italy, has a history spanning back at least 2,500 years. Its fortunes ever since, both as a great commercial trading center and as the object of regular conquest and occupation, are readily explained by its strategic position at the center of the Lombard Plain.

Exploring Milan

Numbers in the margin correspond to points of interest on the Milan map.

Virtually every invader in European history—Gaul, Roman, Goth, Longobard, and Frank—as well as every ruler of France, Spain, and Austria, has taken a turn at ruling the city and the region. So if you are wondering why so little seems to have survived from Milan's antiquity, the answer is simple—war. Thanks to the great family dynasties of the Visconti and the Sforza, however, there are still great Gothic and Renaissance treasures to be seen, including Leonardo's unforgettable *The Last Supper.* And thanks to new lords—Valentino and Armani among them (and alas a martyr: Versace's tragic murder has done little to stem the tide of his influence)—the city now dazzles as the design and fashion center of the world. Old and new come together at Milan's La Scala—Europe's most important opera house—where audiences continue to set sail for passion on the high C's.

❼ Basilica di Sant'Ambrogio (St. Ambrose). Noted for its medieval architecture, the church was consecrated by St. Ambrose in AD 387, and is the model for all Lombard Romanesque churches. Ancient pieces inside include a remarkable 9th-century altar in precious metals and enamels and some 5th-century mosaics. ☒ *Piazza Sant'Ambrogio,* ☎ *02/ 86450895.* ☉ *Mon.–Sat. 9:30–12 and 2:30–6:30.*

❺ Castello Sforzesco. Surrounded by a moat, this building is a somewhat sinister 19th-century reconstruction of the imposing 15th-century fortress built by the Sforzas, who succeeded the Viscontis as lords of Milan. It now houses wide-ranging collections of sculptures, antiques, and ceramics, including Michelangelo's *Rondanini Pietà,* his last work, left unfinished at his death. ☒ *Piazza Castello,* ☎ *02/76002378.* ☒ *Free.* ☉ *Tues.–Sun. 9:30–5:30.*

★ ❶ Duomo. The massive Duomo, a mountain of marble fretted with statues, spires, and flying buttresses, sits—in all its Gothic drama—in the heart of Milan. The **Madonnina,** a gleaming gilt statue on the highest spire, is a city landmark. Take the elevator or walk up 158 steps to the roof for a view of the Lombard Plain and the Alps beyond. Dating from the 4th century, the **Baptistery** ruin is beneath the piazza; enter through the Duomo. ☒ *Piazza del Duomo,* ☎ *02/86463456.* ☉ *Mar.–Oct., daily 9–5:30; Nov.–Feb., daily 9–4:30.*

★ ❷ Galleria Vittorio Emanuele. In this spectacularly extravagant late-19th-century, glass-top, barrel-vaulted tunnel, Milanese and visitors stroll, window shop, and sip pricey cappuccinos at trendy cafés. ☒ *Piazza del Duomo, beyond the northern tip of cathedral's facade.* ☉ *Daily 9:30–1 and 3:30–7.*

★ ❹ Pinacoteca di Brera (Brera Painting Gallery). One of Italy's great fine art collections includes works by Mantegna (1431–1506), Raphael, and Titian. Most are of a religious nature, confiscated during the 19th century when many religious orders were suppressed and their churches closed. ☒ *Via Brera 28,* ☎ *02/722631.* ☉ *Tues.–Sat. 9–5:30, Sun. 9–12:45.*

❽ San Lorenzo Maggiore (Older San Lorenzo). Sixteen ancient Roman columns line the front of this sanctuary; 4th-century mosaics still survive in the Chapel of St. Aquilinus. ☒ *Corso di Porta Ticinese.* ☉ *Daily 9–1 and 3–7.*

❾ San Satiro (St. Satyr). This church is another architectural gem in which Bramante's perfect command of proportion and perspective, char-

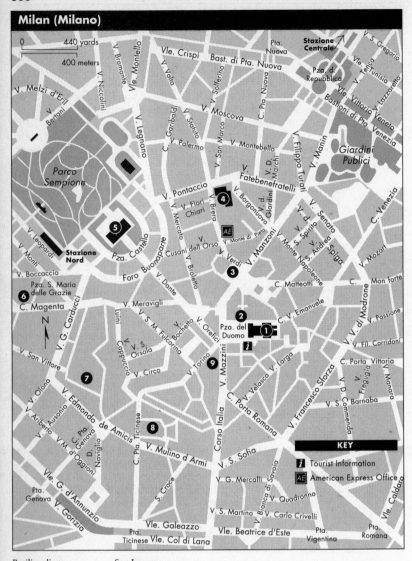

Milan (Milano)

0   440 yards
        400 meters

V. Melzi d'Eril
V. Bertoni
Parco Sempione
V. Leopardi
V. Monti
V. Boccaccio
Pza. S. Maria delle Grazie
C. Magenta
V. G. Carducci
V. San Vittore
V. Olona
V. Edmondo de Amicis
V. Ariberto
Ausonio
V. M. d'Oggioni
Pta. J. Genova
Naviglio D.
Vle. G. d'Annunzio
Pta. Genova
V. Gorizia

V. Bramante
V. Niccolini
V. Montello
V. Legnano
C. Garibaldi
V. Statuto
V. Palermo
Pza. Castello
Stazione Nord
Foro Buonaparte
V. Dante
V. Meravigli
V. S. M. Fulcorina
V. S. Orsola
V. Cappuccio
V. Circo
Luini
V. Bochetto
V. Orefici
V. Torino
C. Pta. Ticinese
V. Mulino d'Armi
S. Croce
Vle. Galeazzo
Pta. Ticinese
Vle. Col di Lana

Vle. Crispi
V. Vola
Bast. di Pta. Nuova
Pta. Nuova
V. Moscova
V. San Marco
V. Montebello
V. Pontaccio
V. Fiori Chiari
Brera
Mercato
Cusani
V. dell'Orso
V. Broletto
V. Mazzini
Pza. del Duomo
Pza. d. Repubblica
Stazione Centrale

C. Pta. Nuova
V. Solferino
V. Filippo Turati
Fatebenefratelli
V. d. Giardini
V. Borgonuovo
V. Monte di Pietà
V. Verdi
V. Manzoni
V. Monte Napoleone
C. Matteotti
C. V. Emanuele
C. P. V. Velasca
V. Larga
C. Porta Romana
Corso Italia
V. S. Sofia
V. G. Mercalli
V. S. Martino
V. Carlo Crivelli
Vle. Beatrice d'Este
Bianca di Savoia
V. S. Quadronno
Pta. Vigentina

Giardini Publici
V. S. Gregorio
V. Lecco
Tunisia
Vle. Vittorio Veneto
V. Lazzaretto
Bastioni di Pta. Venezia
C. Venezia
V. Mozart
Mon forte
C. Porta Vittoria
Manara
Freguglia
V. S. Commenda
V. D. Commenda
Pta. Romana
Vle. Caldara

V. d. Senato
V. S. Spirito
V. S. Andrea
Spiga
V. di Passione
V. Fil. Corridoni
V. Francesco Sforza

KEY

ℹ️ Tourist Information
AE American Express Office

Basilica di
Sant'Ambrogio, **7**

Castello Sforzesco, **5**

Duomo, **1**

Galleria Vittorio
Emanuele, **2**

Pinacoteca di Brera, **4**

San Lorenzo
Maggiore, **8**

San Satiro, **9**

Santa Maria delle
Grazie, **6**

Teatro alla Scala, **3**

acteristic of the Renaissance, made a small interior seem extraordinarily spacious and airy. ⊠ *Via Torino.* ☉ *9–dusk.*

★ ⑥ **Santa Maria delle Grazie** (Madonna of Grace). Although portions of this church were designed by Bramante, it plays second fiddle to the **Cenacolo Vinciano,** the former rectory next door, where, over a three-year period, Leonardo da Vinci painted his megafamous *The Last Supper.* The fresco has suffered more than its share of disasters, beginning with the experiments of the artist, who used untested pigments that soon began to deteriorate. *The Last Supper* is now a mere shadow of its former self, despite meticulous, slow restoration. Visitors are limited in time and number; lines can be long. ⊠ *Piazza Santa Maria delle Grazie 2,* ☎ *02/4987588.* ☉ *Tues.–Sun. 8–1:45.*

⑤ **Teatro alla Scala.** In this world-famous institution, Verdi established his reputation and Maria Callas sang her way into opera lore. Its rich history is displayed in the attached **Museo Teatrale alla Scala.** The theater will close for renovations in 2001, after the events to mark the centenary of Verdi's death. ⊠ *Piazza della Scala,* ☎ *02/8053418.* ☉ *Mon.–Sat. 9–noon and 2–6 (May–Oct., Sun. 9:30–noon and 2:30–5). Closed occasionally during rehearsals.*

Dining and Lodging

Lombardy is home to some of Italy's freshest waters and in the south some of the best pastureland, so you can be sure restaurants have choice selections of meats and fish. All are paired nicely with the crisp wines of the region. For details and price-category information, *see* Dining *in* Italy A to Z, *above.*

If Rome is the administrative and political capital of Italy, Milan is the bustling business heart. As such, hotels are plentiful, with efficient service and for those hotels in the $$ and up categories, excellent standards. Stay as close to the city center as possible and always book well in advance. For details and price-category information, *see* Lodging *in* Italy A to Z, *above.*

$$$$ ✕ **Savini.** Red carpets and cut-glass chandeliers characterize this typ-
★ ical old-world Milanese restaurant with dining rooms spread over three floors. There's also a "winter garden" from which patrons can people-watch Galleria shoppers. The Milanese *risotto al salto* (rice cooked as a pancake, tossed in the pan) is excellent here, as is the *cotoletta di vitello* (breaded veal cutlets). ⊠ *Galleria Vittorio Emanuele,* ☎ *02/72003433. AE, DC, MC, V. Closed Sun. and 10 days in Aug.*

$$$–$$$$ ✕ **Boeucc.** Milan's oldest restaurant is not far from La Scala and is sub-
★ tly lighted, with fluted columns, chandeliers, thick carpet, and a garden for warm-weather dining. You'll savor typical Milanese foods and such exotica as *penne al branzino e zucchine* (penne with sea bass and zucchini sauce) and *gelato di castagne con zabaglione caldo* (chestnut ice cream with hot zabaglione). ⊠ *Piazza Belgioioso 2,* ☎ *02/76020224. Reservations essential. AE. Closed Sat., Aug., and Dec. 24–Jan. 2. No lunch Sun.*

$$ ✕ **Al Cantinone.** Opera goers still go to the Cantinone bar for a drink after the final curtain, just as they did a century ago. The decor is basic, the atmosphere lively, the service fast, and the food reliable. The proprietor stocks 240 different wines. Try the *cotoletta al Cantinone* (veal cutlets with mushrooms, olives, and a cream and tomato sauce). ⊠ *Via Agnello 19,* ☎ *02/86461338. AE, MC, V. Closed Sun., Aug., and Dec. 24–Jan. 5. No lunch Sat.*

$$ ✕ **Antica Trattoria della Pesa.** The late-19th-century decor and atmosphere, dark wood paneling, and old-fashioned lamps still look much as they must have when this eatery opened 100 years ago. This is authentic Old Milan, and the menu is right in line, with risotto, minestrone, and osso buco. ⊠ *Viale Pasubio 10,* ☎ *02/6555741. AE, DC, MC, V. Closed Sun., 2 wks in Aug., and Dec. 23–Jan. 6.*

$$ ✕ **Trattoria Milanese.** Between the Duomo and the Basilica of Sant'Ambrogio, this small, popular trattoria has been run by the same family for more than 60 years. It's invariably crowded, especially at dinner, when the regulars love to linger. Food is classic regional in approach, with risotto and *cotoletta alla milanese* (veal Milanese style) good choices. ⊠ *Via Santa Marta 11,* ☎ *02/86451991. DC, MC, V. Closed Tues., Aug., and Dec. 24–Jan. 6.*

$–$$ ✕ **Bistrot di Gualtiero Marchesi/Brunch.** Atop the Rinascente department store off Piazza del Duomo, this brunch eatery, bar, and bistro is supervised by the well-known chef Gualtiero Marchese and offers a variety of menus with a full range of prices. A bonus is a great view of the Duomo's spires. ⊠ *La Rinascente, Piazza Duomo,* ☎ *02/ 877120. AE, DC, MC, V. Closed Sun. No lunch Mon.*

$ ✕ **La Bruschetta.** A winning partnership of Tuscans and Neapolitans runs this tiny, busy, and first-class pizzeria near the Duomo. It features the obligatory wood-burning oven, though there are plenty of other dishes to choose from as well—try the spaghetti *alle cozze e vongole* (with mussels and clams) or the grilled and skewered meats. ⊠ *Piazza Beccaria 12,* ☎ *02/8692494. MC, V. Closed Mon., 3 wks in Aug., and Dec. 24–Jan. 3.*

$ ✕ **La Giara.** This tavern with bare wooden tables and benches features a limited selection of southern Italian specialties, notably a varied vegetable antipasto. Meat is grilled on a range at the front of the restaurant and served with crusty bread and dense olive oil from the Puglia region. You may be asked to share a table. ⊠ *Viale Monza 10, near Piazzale Loreto,* ☎ *02/26143835. No credit cards. Closed Wed., Aug., and Dec. 23–Jan. 6. No lunch Tues.*

$$$$ 🏨 **Duomo.** Just 20 yards from the cathedral, this hotel's first- through
★ third-floor rooms all look out onto the church's Gothic gargoyles and pinnacles. The rooms are spacious and snappily furnished in contemporary style. ⊠ *Via San Raffaele 1, 20121,* ☎ *02/8833, ℻ 02/ 86462027. 153 rooms. Restaurant. AE, DC, MC, V.*

$$$$ 🏨 **Four Seasons.** The elegant restoration of a 14th-century monastery on an exclusive shopping street in the center of Milan has produced a precious gem—with the highest rates in the city. The hotel blends European class with American comfort. Individually furnished rooms have opulent marble bathrooms; most rooms face the quiet courtyard. Il Teatro serves dinner only. ⊠ *Via Gesù 8, 20121,* ☎ *02/77088, ℻ 02/ 77085000. 98 rooms. 2 restaurants. AE, DC, MC, V.*

$$$$ 🏨 **Palace.** This truly elegant hotel, part of ITT-Sheraton's Luxury Col-
★ lection, is one of the finest the city has to offer, with a personalized, attentive service to match, and elegantly outfitted and upholstered guest rooms. ⊠ *Piazza della Repubblica 20, 20124,* ☎ *02/6336, ℻ 02/654485. 216 rooms. Restaurant, bar. AE, DC, MC, V.*

$$$$ 🏨 **Pierre.** Luxury keynotes rooms individually furnished with elegant fabrics and an assortment of modern and antique furniture. Electronic gadgetry controls curtains and lights. You'll find the Pierre near the medieval Sant'Ambrogio church. ⊠ *Via De Amicis 32, 20123,* ☎ *02/ 72000581, ℻ 02/8052157. 49 rooms. Restaurant. AE, DC, MC, V.*

$$$$ 🏨 **Principe di Savoia.** The pulse of the most fashionable and glitzy hotel
★ in Milan is largely driven by the fashion and expense-account set. Dark-wood paneling and period furniture, brass lamps, and a stucco lobby are all reminiscent of early 1900s Europe. ⊠ *Piazza della Re-*

pubblica 17, 20124, ☎ 02/6230, FAX 02/6595838. 287 rooms. Restaurant. AE, DC, MC, V.

$$ 🏨 **Canada.** This friendly, small, rather nondescript hotel close to Piazza del Duomo offers standard hotel trappings at a nice price. ✉ Via Santa Sofia 16, 20122, ☎ 02/58304844, FAX 02/58300282. 35 rooms. AE, DC, MC, V.

$$ 🏨 **Casa Svizzera.** A faithful clientele considers this one of Milan's best moderately priced small hotels, so it's advisable to make early reservations. The location, adjacent to the Duomo and a few yards from the Galleria, is central and handy to Metro and bus lines. The soundproofed rooms burst forth with sunny floral prints. ✉ Via San Raffaele 3, 20121, ☎ 02/8692246, FAX 02/72004690. 45 rooms. AE, DC, MC, V. Closed Aug. and Dec. 24–Jan. 6. ·

$$ 🏨 **Gritti.** This bright, clean hotel has a cheerful feel. Rooms are adequate, with picturesque views from the upper floors over the tile roofs to the gilt Madonnina atop the Duomo, only a few hundred yards away. ✉ Piazza Santa Maria Beltrade 4 (north end of Via Torino), 20123, ☎ 02/801056, FAX 02/8901099. 48 rooms. AE, DC, MC, V.

$ 🏨 **London.** Close to the Duomo, the London has clean, good-size, simply furnished rooms and an English-speaking staff. ✉ Via Rovello 3, 20121, ☎ 02/72020166, FAX 02/8057037. 29 rooms. MC, V. Closed Aug. and Dec. 23–Jan. 3.

$ 🏨 **San Francisco.** In a residential area between the central station and the university, this medium-size pension is handy to subway and bus lines. It also has the advantages of a friendly management, rooms that are bright and clean, and a charming garden. ✉ Viale Lombardia 55, 20131, ☎ 02/2361009, FAX 02/26680377. 31 rooms. AE, DC, MC, V.

Nightlife and the Arts

The Arts

Milan's most famous spectacle, **Teatro alla Scala** (✉ Piazza della Scala, Ufficio Biglietteria, Via Filodrammatici 2, ☎ 02/72003744) presents some of the world's most impressive operatic productions. The opera season begins December 7 (St. Ambrose Day) and ends in May. The concert season runs from May to the end of June and from September through November. There is a brief ballet season in September. Programs are available at principal travel agencies and tourist information offices in Italy and abroad.

Tickets are usually hard to come by, but your hotel may be able to help obtain them. For information on schedules, ticket availability, and how to buy tickets, the **Infotel Scala Service** (✉ Teatro alla Scala, Ufficio Biglietteria, Via Filodrammatici 2, ☎ 02/72003744, FAX 02/8607787) operates (with English-speaking staff) at the ticket office, and is open daily noon–6. Telephone bookings are not accepted, but travelers from abroad can book in advance—within a short specified period before each presentation (these dates are published at the beginning of the season)—through postal bookings, for which a certain percentage of tickets are set aside, allocated on a first-come, first-served basis. Apply for a reservation by mail (☞ above) or fax with return fax number (also denoting time and date of transmission). You may also be able to book at CIT (☞ Contacts and Resources in Milan Essentials, below) or other travel agencies (no more than 10 days before performance) for a 15% advance booking charge.

Nightlife

El Brellin (✉ Vicolo Lavandai at the corner of Alzaia Naviglio Grande, ☎ 58101351) is one of many bars in the Navigli district; it's closed Sunday. Upscale, intimate nightcaps are sipped at **Momus** (✉ Via Fiori

Chiari 8, ☎ 02/8056227) in the Brera quarter; it is closed Monday. **Le Scimmie** (✉ Via Ascanio Sforza 49, ☎ 02/89402874) delivers cool jazz in a relaxed atmosphere. The pricey nightclub **Stage** (✉ Galleria Manzoni, off Via Monte Napoleone, ☎ 02/76021071) serves dinner on Tuesday in digs great for dancing; it's closed Sunday. **Rock Hollywood** (✉ Via Como 15/c, ☎ 02/6598996) is the "in" place for the fashion set.

Shopping

Milan being one of the most renowned fashion centers in the world, it comes as no surprise that the majority of shops sell clothing—designer names with designer price tags. Milan's most elegant shopping streets are **Via Monte Napoleone, Via Manzoni, Via della Spiga,** and **Via Sant'Andrea.** Head for **Corso Buenos Aires,** near the central train station, if the chic goods of other areas are a shock to your purse.

Milan Essentials

Arriving and Departing

As Lombardy's capital and the most important financial and commercial center in northern Italy, Milan is well connected with Rome and Florence by fast and frequent rail and air service. Flights in and out of Milan during winter months are often prone to delay due to heavy fog.

BY CAR

From Rome and Florence take the A1 Autostrada. From Venice take the A4. Due to bans on parking throughout Milan center, it's easier to park on the outskirts and use public transportation.

BY PLANE

Aeroporto Milano Linate (✉ 11 km/7 mi east of Milan, ☎ 02/74852200) handles mainly domestic and European flights. **Aeroporto Malpensa** (✉ 50 km/30 mi northwest of the city, ☎ 02/74852200) services intercontinental flights. For air-traffic information for both airports and information on connections with Milan, call ☎ 02/74851.

Between the Airport and Downtown. Buses connect both airports with Milan, stopping at the central station and at the Porta Garibaldi station. Fare from Linate is 5,000 lire on the special airport bus or 1,500 lire on municipal Bus 73 (to Piazza San Babila); from Malpensa, 13,000 lire. A taxi from Linate to the center of Milan costs about 30,000 lire; from Malpensa, about 130,000 lire.

BY TRAIN

The main train station is **Milano Centrale** (✉ Piazzale Duca d'Aosta, ☎ 1478/88088). Several smaller stations handle commuter trains. Rapid Intercity trains connect Rome and Milan daily, stopping in Florence and/or Bologna; a nonstop Intercity leaves Rome or Milan morning and evening, taking about four hours.

Getting Around

BY BUS AND STREETCAR

Buy tickets at newsstands, tobacco shops, and bars. The fare is 1,400 lire. One ticket is valid for 75 minutes on all surface lines and one subway trip. Daily tickets valid for 24 hours on all public transportation lines are sold at the Duomo Metro station ATM (city transport authority) information office, and at Milano Centrale Metro station. Twenty-four-hour tickets cost 5,000 lire; 48-hour tickets 9,000 lire.

BY METRO

Milan's subway network, the Metropolitana, is modern, fast, and easy to use. MM signs mark Metropolitana stations. There are, at present, three lines. The ATM has an information office (✉ Mezzanine of the

Duomo Metro station, ☎ 02/875495). Tickets are sold at newsstands at every stop, and in ticket machines *for exact change only.* The fare is 1,500 lire, and the subway runs from 6:20 AM to midnight.

BY TAXI
Use yellow cabs (☎ 02/6767, 02/8585, or 02/8388) only. They wait at stands or can be called in advance.

Contacts and Resources

CONSULATES
U.S. (⌧ Via Principe Amedeo 2, ☎ 02/290351). **Canadian** (⌧ Via Pisani 19, ☎ 02/6697451). **U.K.** (⌧ Via San Paolo 7, ☎ 02/723001).

EMERGENCIES
Police (☎ 02/113). **Ambulance** (☎ 02/7733). **Carabinieri** (military police, ☎ 02/112). **Hospital and Doctor** (☎ 02/113).

GUIDED TOURS
Excursions. April through September, **Autostradale** (⌧ Via Pompeo Marchesi 55, ☎ 02/48203177) offers an all-day tour of Lake Maggiore, including a boat trip to the Borromean Islands and lunch. The cost is about 130,000 lire. **Autostradale Viaggi** (⌧ Piazza Castello 1, ☎ 02/166845010) operates similar tours.

Orientation. Three-hour morning or afternoon sightseeing tours depart Tuesday to Sunday from Piazzetta Reale (⌧ Next to the Duomo); they cost about 50,000 lire and tickets can be purchased from APT offices (☞ *below*) or aboard the bus.

TRAVEL AGENCIES
Compagnia Italiana Turismo (CIT, ⌧ Galleria Vittorio Emanuele, ☎ 02/863701). **American Express Travel Agency** (⌧ Via Brera 3, ☎ 02/809645).

VISITOR INFORMATION
Main tourist offices (⌧ Stazione Centrale, ☎ 02/72524370). **APT Offices** (⌧ Palazzo del Turismo, Via Marconi 1, ☎ 02/72524301).

VENICE

Venice—La Serenissima, the Most Serene—is disorienting in its complexity, an extraordinary labyrinth of narrow streets and waterways, opening now and again onto an airy square or broad canal. Many of its magnificent palazzi are slowly crumbling; though this sounds like a recipe for a down-at-the-heels slum, somehow in Venice the shabby, derelict effect is magically transformed into one of supreme beauty and charm, rather than horrible urban decay. The place is romantic, especially at night when the lights from the vaporetti and the stars overhead pick out the gargoyles and arches of the centuries-old facades. For hundreds of years Venice was the unrivaled mistress of trade between Europe and the Orient, and the staunch bulwark of Christendom against the tide of Turkish expansion. Though the power and glory of its days as a wealthy city-republic are gone, the art and exotic aura remain.

Exploring Venice

Numbers in the margin correspond to points of interest on the Venice map.

To enjoy the city you will have to come to terms with the crowds of day-trippers, who take over the center around San Marco from May through September and during Carnival. Hot and sultry in summer,

Venice is much more welcoming in early spring and late fall. Romantics like it in the winter, when prices are much lower, the streets are often deserted, and the sea mists impart a haunting melancholy to the *campi* (squares) and canals. Piazza San Marco is the pulse of Venice, but after joining with the crowds to visit the Basilica di San Marco and the Doge's Palace, strike out on your own and just follow where your feet take you—you won't be disappointed.

San Marco and San Polo

★ ❸ **Basilica di San Marco** (St. Mark's Basilica). Half Christian church, half Middle Eastern mosque, this building was conceived during the 11th century to hold the relics of St. Mark the Evangelist, the city's patron saint. Its richly decorated facade is surmounted by copies of four famous gilded bronze horses (the originals are in the basilica's upstairs museum). Inside, golden mosaics cover walls and vaults, lending an extraordinarily exotic aura. Be sure to see the **Pala d'Oro,** an eye-filling 10th-century altarpiece in gold and silver studded with precious gems and enamels. From the atrium climb the steep stairway to the museum: The bronze horses alone are worth the effort. ⊠ *Piazza San Marco,* ☎ *041/5225205.* ⬚ *Free for Basilicata.* ☉ *Mon.–Sat. 9:45–4:30, Sun. 1–4:30; last entry 30 mins before closing.*

★ ❺ **Campanile di San Marco** (St. Mark's Bell Tower). This bell tower is a reconstruction of the 1,000-year-old tower that collapsed one morning in 1912, practically without warning. Fifteenth-century clerics found guilty of immoral acts were suspended in wooden cages from the tower, sometimes to live on bread and water for as long as a year, sometimes to die of starvation and exposure. Look for them in Carpaccio's paintings of the square that hang in the Accademia. You can take the elevator up to the top for a pigeon's-eye view of Venice. ⊠ *Piazza San Marco,* ☎ *041/5224064.* ☉ *June–Sept., daily 9:30–10; Oct.–May, daily 9:30–4:15; last entry 30 mins before closing. Closed 2 wks in Jan.*

❷ **Museo Correr.** Upstairs here you will find an eclectic collection of historical objects and a picture gallery of fine 13th- to 17th-century paintings. ⊠ *Piazza San Marco, Ala Napoleonica,* ☎ *041/5225625.* ☉ *Apr.– Oct., daily 9–7; Nov.–Mar., daily 9–5; last entry 1 hr before closing.*

★ ❹ **Palazzo Ducale** (Doge's Palace). During Venice's heyday, this was the epicenter of its great empire. More than just a palace, it was a combination White House, Senate, Supreme Court, torture chamber, and prison. The building's exterior is striking; the lower stories consist of two rows of fragile-seeming arches, and above rests a massive pink-and-white marble wall whose solidity is barely interrupted by its six great Gothic windows. The interior is a maze of vast halls, monumental staircases, secret corridors, and sinister prison cells. The palace is filled with frescoes, paintings, and a few examples of statuary by some of the Renaissance's greatest artists. Don't miss the famous view from the balcony, overlooking the piazza and St. Mark's Basin and the church of San Giorgio Maggiore across the lagoon. ⊠ *Piazzetta San Marco,* ☎ *041/5224951.* ☉ *Apr.–Oct., daily 9–7; Nov.–Mar., daily 9–5; last entry 1½ hrs before closing.*

★ ❶ **Piazza San Marco.** In the most famous piazza in Venice, pedestrian traffic jams clog the surrounding byways and even pigeons have to fight for space. Despite the crowds, San Marco is the logical starting place from which to explore the city. The short side of the square opposite the Basilica of San Marco is known as the **Ala Napoleonica,** a wing built by order of Napoléon to complete the much earlier palaces on either side of the square, enclosing it to form what he called "the most beautiful drawing room in all of Europe."

6 **Santa Maria Gloriosa dei Frari.** This vast, soaring Gothic brick church known simply as I Frari contains a number of the most sumptuous, important pictures in Venice. Paradoxically, as the principal church of the Franciscans it is austere in design, suitably reflecting the order's vows of poverty. Chief among the works are the magnificent Titian altarpiece, the immense *Assumption of the Virgin,* over the main altar. Titian was buried here at the ripe old age of 88, the only one of 70,000 plague victims to be given a personal church burial. ⊠ *Campo dei Frari, San Polo,* ☎ *041/5222637.* ⊘ *Mon.–Sat. 9–6, Sun. 1–6.*

7 **Scuola Grande di San Rocco** (School of St. Rocco). In the 1500s Tintoretto embellished the school with more than 50 canvases; they are an impressive sight, dark paintings aglow with figures hurtling dramatically through space amid flashes of light and color. The *Crucifixion* in the Albergo (the room just off the great hall) is held to be his masterpiece. ⊠ *Campo di San Rocco, San Polo,* ☎ *041/5234864.* ⊘ *Dec.–Feb., Mon.–Fri. 10–1, weekends 10–4; Mar. and Nov., daily 10–4; Apr.–Oct., daily 9–5:30.*

Grand Canal and Cannaregio

Set off on a boat tour along the Grand Canal, which serves as Venice's main thoroughfare. The canal winds in the shape of a backwards S for more than 3½ km (2 mi) through the heart of the city, past some 200 Gothic and Renaissance palaces. Your vaporetto tour will give you an idea of the opulent beauty of the palaces and a peek into the side streets and tiny canals where the Venetians go about their daily business.

13 **Ca' d'Oro.** The most flowery palace on the canal now houses the Galleria Franchetti. ⊠ *Galleria Franchetti, Calle della Ca' d'Oro, 3933 Cannaregio,* ☎ *041/5238790.* ⊘ *Daily 9–2.*

11 **Ca' Foscari.** This 15th-century Gothic structure was once the home of Doge Foscari, who was unwillingly deposed and died the following day. Today it's the headquarters of Venice's university. ⊠ *Fondamenta Ca' Foscari.*

★ **10** **Ca' Rezzonico.** The most spectacular palace in all of Venice was built between the mid-17th and 18th centuries and is now a museum of sumptuous 18th-century Venetian paintings and furniture. The museum will be closed for restoration through 2000. ⊠ *Fondamenta Pedrocco, 3136 Dorsoduro,* ☎ *041/2410100.* ⊘ *Sun.–Thurs. 10–7, Fri.–Sat. 10–10; last entry 30 mins before closing. Closed for restoration.*

8 **Collezione Peggy Guggenheim.** The late heiress's exceptional modern art collection—with works by Picasso, Kandinsky, Ernst, Pollock, and Motherwell—is housed in the incomplete Palazzo Venier dei Leoni. ⊠ *Calle San Cristoforo, 701 Dorsoduro,* ☎ *041/5206288.* ⊘ *Wed.–Mon. 11–6.*

★ **9** **Gallerie dell'Accademia** (Accademia Gallery). Hanging in this museum is unquestionably the most extraordinary collection of Venetian art in the world. Works range from 14th-century Gothic to the Golden Age of the 15th and 16th centuries, including oils by Giovanni Bellini (1430–1516), Giorgione (1477–1511), Titian, and Tintoretto (1518–94), and superb later works by Veronese (1528–88) and Tiepolo (1696–1770). ⊠ *Campo della Carità, Dorsoduro,* ☎ *041/5222247.* ⊘ *Tues.–Sat. 9–7, Sun. and Mon. 9–2; longer hrs June–Sept.*

15 **Palazzo Labia.** Within the walls of this sumptuous palazzo you'll find the prettiest ballroom in Venice, magnificently adorned with Giambattista Tiepolo's 18th-century frescoes of Anthony and Cleopatra. This palace, once the home of Venice's most ostentatiously rich family, is now the Venetian headquarters of RAI, Italy's National Broad-

Venice (Venezia)

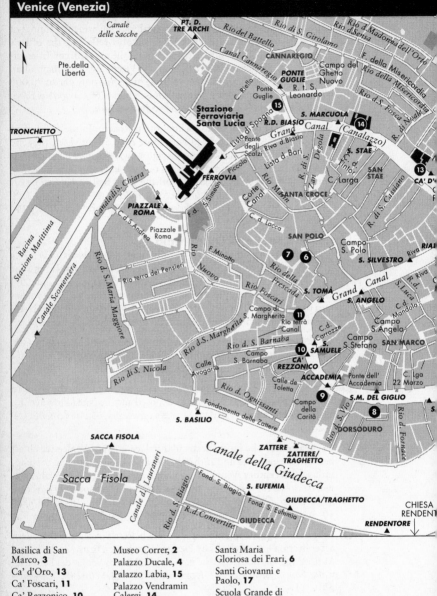

Basilica di San Marco, **3**

Ca' d'Oro, **13**

Ca' Foscari, **11**

Ca' Rezzonico, **10**

Campanile di San Marco, **5**

Collezione Peggy Guggenheim, **8**

Gallerie dell'Accademia, **9**

Museo Correr, **2**

Palazzo Ducale, **4**

Palazzo Labia, **15**

Palazzo Vendramin Calergi, **14**

Piazza San Marco, **1**

Ponte di Rialto, **12**

Santa Maria dei Miracoli, **18**

Santa Maria Formosa, **16**

Santa Maria Gloriosa dei Frari, **6**

Santi Giovanni e Paolo, **17**

Scuola Grande di San Rocco, **7**

Torcello, **19**

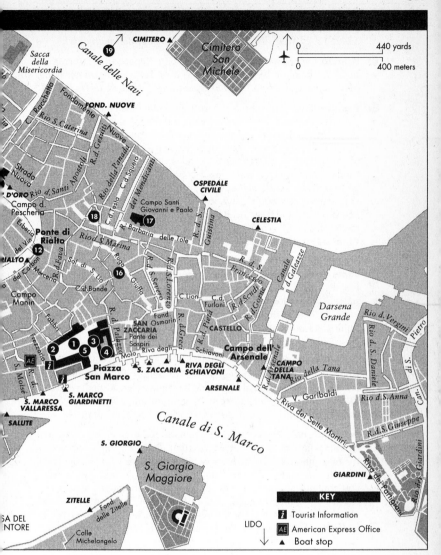

Sacca
della
Misericordia

CIMITERO ▲

Cimitero
San
Michele

Canale delle Navi

19

0 _____ 440 yards
0 _____ 400 meters

Rio S. Caterina

Racchetta

Fondamenta

FOND. NUOVE ▲

R. d. Gesuiti Nuova

C. d. Teatro

C. d. Savoro

dei Mendicanti

della Panada

Strada
Nuova

D'ORO ▲

Rio d. Santi Apostoli

Campo d.
Pescheria

Erberia

del Vin

**Ponte di
Rialto**

12

RIALTO ▲

del Carbon

Mercerie

Riod S. Marina

C. d. Bande

Ruga
Giuffa

Sal. di S. Lio

Campo
Manin

Fabbri

Frezzaria

R. d. Fava

Lista

18

17

Calle Barbaria

16

R. d. S. Severo

R. d. S. Lorenzo

Fond.
S. Osmarin

Ponte dei
Sospiri

**OSPEDALE
CIVILE** ▲

Campo Santi
Giovanni e Paolo

delle Tole

C. Lion

C. d.
Furlani

R. d. Piovan

R. d. Grea

CASTELLO

R. d. S.
Giustina

R. d. S.
Francesco

R. d. Scudi

R. d. Gorne

Canale
d. Galeazze

CELESTIA ▲

**Darsena
Grande**

Rio d. Vergini

R. d. S. Daniele

di d. S. Pietro

2

1

5

3

4

**SAN
ZACCARIA**

Riva degli

Schiavoni

Molo

Riva degli

**Piazza
San Marco**

AE

i

i

R. d. Palazzo

S. ZACCARIA

**RIVA DEGLI
SCHIAVONI**

**Campo dell'
Arsenale**

**CAMPO
DELLA
TANA**

R. d'Arsenale

Rio della Tana

V. Garibaldi

Rio d. S. Anna

R. d. S. Giuseppe

Carr.

R. d. S. Anna

R. d. S.

**S. MARCO
GIARDINETTI**

**S. MARCO
VALLARESSA**

R. d. Moise

ARSENALE

Riva dei Sette Martiri

Riva dei Part(?)giani

Rio d. Giardini

SALUTE ▲

Canale di S. Marco

S. GIORGIO ▲

GIARDINI

**S. Giorgio
Maggiore**

Ci

ZITELLE ▲

Fond.
delle Zitelle

LIDO

↓

A DEL
NTORE

Calle
Michelangelo

KEY	
i	Tourist Information
AE	American Express Office
▲	Boat stop

casting Corporation, which occasionally hosts concerts in the Tiepolo ballroom. ⊠ *Campo San Geremia, near the train station,* ☎ *041/ 5242812.* ☾ *Wed., Thurs., and Fri. 3–4 (by appointment only).*

⑭ Palazzo Vendramin Calergi. This opulent Renaissance structure is noted as the place Wagner (1813–83) died. It's also the winter home of the municipal casino. ⊠ *2040 Cannaregio, 30133,* ☎ *041/5297111.*

★ ⑫ Ponte di Rialto (Rialto Bridge). Street stalls hung with scarves and gondolier's hats signal the heart of Venice's shopping district. Cross over the bridge, and you'll find yourself on the edge of the famous market. Try to visit the Rialto market (open Tuesday–Saturday mornings; fish market closed Monday) when it's in full swing, with fruit and vegetable vendors hawking their wares in a cacophony of sights and sounds. Not far beyond is the fish market, where you'll probably find sea creatures you've never seen before (and possibly won't want to see again). Ruga San Giovanni and Ruga del Ravano, beside the market, will bring you face to face with scores of shops. Start from the Salizzada San Giovanni side of the bridge.

North of San Marco

⑱ Santa Maria dei Miracoli. Perfectly proportioned and sheathed in marble, the church embodies all the classical serenity of the early Renaissance. The interior of this late-15th-century building is decorated with marble reliefs by the church's architect, Pietro Lombardo, and his son Tullio. ⊠ *Campo dei Miracoli,* ☎ *041/5235293.* ☾ *Mon.–Sat. 10–5, Sun. 1–5.*

⑯ Santa Maria Formosa. This graceful white marble church, built by Mauro Coducci in 1492, was grafted onto 11th-century foundations. Inside is a hodgepodge of Renaissance and Baroque styles. A small vegetable market bustles in the square weekday mornings. ⊠ *Campo Santa Maria Formosa,* ☎ *041/5234645.* ☾ *Mon.–Sat. 10–5, Sun. 1–5.*

⑰ Santi Giovanni e Paolo. A massive Dominican church of Santi Giovanni e Paolo—known in the slurred Venetian dialect as San Zanipolo—is the twin (and rival) of the Franciscan Santa Maria Gloriosa dei Frari. The church is a kind of pantheon of the doges (25 are buried here), and contains a wealth of artwork. Outside in the campo stands Verrocchio's magnificent equestrian monument of **Bartolomeo Colleoni** (1400–75), who fought for the Venetian cause during the mid-1400s. ⊠ *Campo SS. Giovanni e Paolo,* ☎ *041/5237510.* 🎫 *Free.* ☾ *Mon.– Sat. 8–12:30 and 3–6, Sun. 3–6.*

Venetian Lagoon

⑲ Torcello. Discover the Venetian equivalent of World's End on this magical island in the Venetian lagoon. Settled 1,500 years ago and a thriving city during the Byzantine era, the island is now deserted, but art lovers still make pilgrimages to it because of its two great 11th-century churches. Locanda Cipriani, a restaurant favored by Hemingway and the Duke of Windsor, still lures gourmands. Katharine Hepburn and Rossano Brazzi fell in love during a picnic on Torcello in the film classic *Summertime.* Take Vaporetto 12 from Fondamente Nuove to get to the island. The cathedral of **Santa Maria Assunta** has a world-famous mosaic of the Virgin. ☎ *041/730084.* ☾ *June–Sept., daily 10:30–5:45; Oct.–May, daily 10–12:15 and 2–4:45.*

Dining and Lodging

Venetians love seafood, and it figures prominently on most restaurant menus, sometimes to the exclusion of meat dishes. Fish is generally expensive, however, and you should bear this in mind when ordering: The price given on menus for fish as a main course is often per 100 grams, not the total cost of what you are served, which could be two or three times that amount. City specialties also include *pasta e fagioli* (pasta and bean soup), risotto, and the delicious *fegato alla veneziana* (liver with onions) served with grilled polenta. For details and price-category definitions, *see* Dining *in* Italy A to Z, *above*.

Space in the time-worn, but renovated palaces-cum-hotels is at a premium in this city, and even in the best hotel rooms can be small and offer little natural light. Preservation restrictions on buildings often preclude the installation of such things as elevators and air-conditioning systems. So don't come to Venice expecting to find the standard modern hotel room. On the other hand, Venice's luxury hotels can offer rooms of fabulous opulence and elegance, and even in the more modest hotels you can find comfortable rooms of great charm and character, sometimes with stunning views. Venice attracts visitors year-round, although the winter months, with the exception of Carnival time, are generally much quieter, and most hotels offer lower rates during this period. It is always worth booking in advance, but if you haven't, AVA (Venetian Hoteliers Association) booths (☞ Contacts and Resources *in* Venice Essentials, *below*) will help you find a room after your arrival in the city. For details and price-category definitions, *see* Lodging *in* Italy A to Z, *above*.

$$$$ ✕ **Grand Canal.** The Hotel Monaco and Grand Canal's restaurant is a favorite among Venetians, who enjoy the sunny canal-side terrace, with views across the mouth of the Grand Canal to Giorgio Maggiore, and the cozy dining room in winter. Here you can taste well-prepared Venetian seafood specialties, such as *scampi alla Busera* (shrimp in cognac sauce, served with rice), and savory meats. Pasta is made fresh daily on the premises, as is the marinated smoked salmon. ⊠ *Hotel Monaco and Grand Canal, Calle Vallaresso, 1325 San Marco,* ☎ *041/5200211. Jacket required for dinner. AE, DC, MC, V.*

$$$$ ✕ **La Caravella.** La Caravella is reminiscent of an old Venetian sailing ship's dining saloon, with lots of authentic touches, and has a pretty garden courtyard used during summer. The menu is long and slightly intimidating, though the highly competent maître d' will advise you well. The *granseola* (crab) is marvelous in any of several versions. ⊠ *Calle Larga XXII Marzo, 2397 San Marco,* ☎ *041/5208901. AE, DC, MC, V.*

$$$–$$$$ ✕ **Da Arturo.** The tiny Da Arturo is a refreshing change from the numerous seafood restaurants of which Venetians are so fond. The cordial proprietor prefers, instead, to offer varied and delicious seasonal vegetable and salad dishes, or tasty, tender and generous meat courses like *braciola alla veneziana* (pork chop schnitzel with vinegar). ⊠ *Calle degli Assassini, 3656 San Marco,* ☎ *041/5286974. Reservations essential. No credit cards. Closed Sun. and 4 wks in Aug.*

$$$–$$$$ ✕ **Osteria Da Fiore.** Long a favorite with Venetians, Da Fiore has been
★ discovered by tourists, so reservations are imperative. It's known for its excellent seafood dinners, which might include such specialties as *pasticcio di pesce* (fish pie) and *seppioline* (little cuttlefish). Not easy to find, it's just off Campo San Polo. ⊠ *Calle dello Scaleter, 2202/A San Polo,* ☎ *041/721308. Reservations essential. AE, DC, MC, V. Closed Sun., Mon., Aug. 10–early Sept., and Dec. 25–Jan. 15.*

$$$ ✕ **Fiaschetteria Toscana.** Once the storehouse of a 19th-century wine merchant from Tuscany, this popular restaurant has long been a favorite of Venetians and visitors from terra firma. Courteous, cheerful waiters serve such specialties as *rombo* (turbot) with capers, an exceptionally good *pasta alla buranella* (pasta with shrimp, au gratin), and zabaglione. ⊠ *Campo San Giovanni Crisostomo, 5719 Cannare-*

gio, ☎ 041/5285281. AE, DC, MC, V. Closed Tues. and 4 wks in July and Aug.

$$–$$$ ✕ **Al Covo.** This small osteria changes its menu according to the day's
★ bounty—mostly local seafood caught just hours before. Cesare Benelli and his American wife, Diane, insist on only the freshest ingredients and claim to not use butter or animal fats. Try the *zuppa di pesce* (fish broth) followed by the fish of the day either grilled, baked, or steamed. The flexible tasting menu at lunch is a good deal. ✉ *Campiello della Pescaria, 3968 Castello,* ☎ *041/5223812. No credit cards. Closed Wed. and Thurs., 1 wk in Aug., and 1 month between Dec. and Jan.*

$$ ✕ **Locanda Montin.** Peggy Guggenheim used to wine and dine the greatest artists of the 20th century here. Since those days, Montin has become more of an institution, less a bohemian hangout. Service can be erratic, but crowds still pack the place to enjoy the rigatoni *ai quattro formaggi* (with four cheeses, mushrooms, and tomato) and antipasto Montin. ✉ *Fondamenta di Borgo, 1147 Dorsoduro,* ☎ *041/5227151. AE, DC, MC, V. Closed Jan. 7–26, Wed., and 15 days in Aug. No dinner Tues.*

$$ ✕ **Vini da Gigio.** An attractive, friendly, and family-run establishment, this trattoria is found on the quayside of a canal, just off the Strada Nuova. Customers appreciate the affable service and tasty homemade pasta, fish, and meat dishes and good draft wine. The barroom is pleasant and casual for lunch. ✉ *Fondamenta de la Chiesa, 3628A Cannaregio,* ☎ *041/5285140. AE, DC, MC, V. Closed Mon., last 2 wks in Jan.–Feb., and last 2 wks in Aug.*

$–$$ ✕ **Al Mondo Novo.** In this fish restaurant you can get *cape sante* (pilgrim scallops) and *cape longhe* (razor clams), risotto and pasta dishes, charcoal-grilled fish, and a less-expensive tourist menu. ✉ *Salizzada San Lio, 5409 Castello,* ☎ *041/5200698. AE, MC, V.*

$ ✕ **L'Incontro.** This trattoria has a faithful clientele drawn in by good food (excellent meat, but no fish) at reasonable prices. Menu choices include freshly made Sardinian pastas, juicy steaks, wild duck, boar, and (with advance notice) roast suckling pig. L'Incontro is between San Barnaba and Campo Santa Margherita. ✉ *Rio Terrá Canal, 3062A Dorsoduro,* ☎ *041/5222404. AE, DC, MC, V. Closed Mon., 2 wks in Jan., and 2 wks in Aug.*

$$$$ ▦ **Cipriani.** A sybaritic oasis of stunningly decorated rooms and suites with marble whirlpool baths, the Cipriani is located across St. Mark's Basin on the island of Giudecca, offering a panorama of romantic views of the entire lagoon. Some rooms have pretty garden patios. The subtly integrated 17th-century-style Palazzo Vendramin, an annex of seven suites and three double rooms, is open all year. ✉ *Giudecca 10, 30133,* ☎ *041/5207744,* FAX *041/5203930. 54 rooms, 50 suites. Restaurant, indoor pool. AE, DC, MC, V. Closed Dec.–Apr.*

$$$$ ▦ **Danieli.** Parts of this rather large hotel are built around a 15th-century palazzo bathed in sumptuous Venetian colors. The downside is the Danieli also has several modern annexes that some find bland and impersonal and the lower-price rooms can be exceedingly drab. Still, celebrities and English-speaking patrons crowd its sumptuous four-story-high lobby, chic salons, and dining terrace with a fantastic view of St. Mark's Basin. ✉ *Riva degli Schiavoni, 4196 Castello, 30122,* ☎ *041/ 5226480,* FAX *041/5200208. 219 rooms, 11 suites. Restaurant. AE, DC, MC, V.*

$$$$ ▦ **Gritti Palace.** This haven of pampering is like an aristocratic private
★ home, with fresh flowers, fine antiques, lavish appointments, and old-world service. The dining terrace overlooking the Grand Canal is best in the evening when boat traffic dies down. ✉ *Campo Santa Maria del Giglio, 2467 San Marco, 30124,* ☎ *041/794611,* FAX *041/5200942. 87 rooms, 6 suites. Restaurant. AE, DC, MC, V.*

$$$–$$$$ ⊞ **Metropole.** Guests can step from their water taxi or gondola into
★ the lobby of this small, very well-run hotel, rich in precious antiques,
just five minutes from Piazza San Marco. Many rooms have a view of
the lagoon, others overlook the garden at the back, and all are furnished
with style. ⊠ *Riva degli Schiavoni, 4149 Castello, 30122,* ☎ *041/
5205044,* ℻ *041/5223679. 67 rooms, 7 suites. Restaurant. AE, DC,
MC, V.*

$$$ ⊞ **Londra Palace.** You get the obligatory view of San Giorgio and St.
Mark's Basin at this distinguished hotel whose rooms are decorated
in dark paisley prints, with such sumptuous touches as canopied beds.
A neoclassical touch has been imparted into the rooms, with light pastel colors and plenty of marble. French chefs preside over Les Deux
Lions restaurant, and the piano bar is open late. ⊠ *Riva degli Schiavoni, 4171 Castello, 30122,* ☎ *041/5200533,* ℻ *041/5225032. 36
rooms, 17 suites. Restaurant. AE, DC, MC, V.*

$$ ⊞ **Accademia.** Hidden within the heart of Venice, this miniature Pal-
★ ladian villa—complete with canal-side garden—is the city's most en-
chanting hotel. There's plenty of atmosphere here, with just a touch
of romance. Many rooms overlook the gardens, where you can sit in
warm weather. ⊠ *Fondamenta Bollani, 1058 Dorsoduro, 30123,* ☎
041/5210188, ℻ *041/5239152. 27 rooms, 2 without bath. AE, DC,
MC, V.*

$$ ⊞ **Ala.** The Ala is between San Marco and Santo Stefano, a few steps
from the Santa Maria del Giglio vaporetto stop. Some rooms are large
with coffered ceilings and old-style furnishings; smaller ones have
more modern decor and orthopedic beds. Breakfast is served in a beautiful room overlooking a small canal. ⊠ *2494 San Marco, 30124,* ☎
041/5208333, ℻ *041/5206390. 85 rooms. AE, DC, MC, V.*

$$ ⊞ **Wildner.** Right between the super deluxe Danieli and Londra ho-
tels, this pleasant family-run, unpretentious pensione enjoys the same
views. Rooms are spread over four floors (no elevator), half with a view
of San Giorgio; the others (cooler and quieter in summer) look out onto
Campo San Zaccaria. ⊠ *Riva degli Schiavoni, 4161 Castello, 30122,*
☎ *041/5227463,* ℻ *041/5265615. 16 rooms. AE, DC, MC, V.*

$–$$ ⊞ **Paganelli.** The lagoon views here so impressed Henry James that
he wrote the Paganelli up in the preface to his *Portrait of a Lady.* This
charming, small hotel on the waterfront has an annex on the quiet square
of Campo San Zaccaria, and is tastefully decorated in Venetian style.
⊠ *Riva degli Schiavoni, 4687 Castello, 30122,* ☎ *041/5224324,* ℻
041/5239267. 22 rooms, 3 without bath. AE, MC, V.

$ ⊞ **Bucintoro.** Whistler once stayed here, and today the Bucintoro is still
favored by artists, drawn by the lagoon views from every room. Slightly
off the tourist track, this friendly, family-run hotel has clean and simple rooms. The price is unbeatable for such spectacular vistas. ⊠ *Riva
San Biagio, 2135 Castello, 30122,* ☎ *041/5223240,* ℻ *041/5235224.
28 rooms, 3 without bath. Restaurant. No credit cards. Closed mid-
Dec.–early Feb.*

$ ⊞ **Locanda Fiorita.** Just off Campo Santo Stefano, near the Accademia
Bridge, you'll find this welcoming hotel tucked away in a sunny little
square where breakfast is served in summer. The rooms have beamed
ceilings and are simply furnished. ⊠ *Campiello Novo o dei Morti, 3457/
A San Marco, 30124,* ☎ *041/5234754,* ℻ *041/5228043. 18 rooms,
4 without bath. AE, MC, V. Closed 2 wks in Jan.*

Nightlife and the Arts

Your hotel concierge may be able to secure you tickets (or advice on
how to get them) for some arts events going on around town.

The Arts

The **Biennale,** a cultural institution, organizes many events throughout the year, including the film festival, which begins at the end of August. The big Biennale international art exhibition, usually held from mid-June to the end of September, has been held since 1993 on odd-numbered years at the **Giardini di Castello** (Castello Gardens).

CONCERTS

Regular concerts are held at the Pietà Church, with an emphasis on Vivaldi, and at San Stae and San Barnaba. Concerts, sometimes free, are also held by visiting choirs and musicians in other churches. For information on these often impromptu events, ask at the APT office and look for posters on walls and in restaurants and shops. **Kele e Teo Agency** (✉ Ponte dei Bareteri, 4930 San Marco, ☎ 041/5208722, FAX 041/5208913) handles tickets for several musical events.

OPERA

Because of the devastating fire that destroyed **Teatro La Fenice** in January 1996, opera and concert performances were rescheduled in various venues. At press time restoration work (helped in large part by donations from opera lovers around the world) had begun, and the theater was scheduled to reopen by 2000. In the meantime, opera, symphony and ballet performances are held year-round at the **Palafenice** near the Tronchetto parking area. Call ☎ 041/5204010 for ticket information, or go to the Cassa di Risparmio bank, on Campo San Luca (☎ 041/5210161).

Nightlife

The **Martini Scala Club** (✉ Calle del Cafetier, 1077 San Marco, ☎ 041/5224121) is an elegant piano bar with a restaurant. Tunes start at 10 PM and go until the wee hours. For dancing try the **Disco Club Piccolo Mondo** (✉ 1056/A Dorsoduro, ☎ 041/5200371), near the Accademia Gallery. **Fiddler's Elbow** (✉ Strada Nuova, 3847 Cannaregio, ☎ 041/5239930) offers all the typical trappings of an Irish pub: gab, grub, and frothy Guinness.

Shopping

At **La Scialuppa** (✉ Calle delle Saoneri, 2695 San Polo) you'll find hand-carved wooden models of gondolas and their graceful oar locks known as *forcole*. **Norelene** (✉ Calle della Chiesa, 727 Dorsoduro, near the Guggenheim) has stunning hand-painted fabrics that make wonderful wall hangings or elegantly styled jackets and chic scarves. **Venetia Studium** (✉ Calle Larga XXII Marzo, 2430 San Marco) is famous for Fortuny-inspired lamps and elegant scarves.

Glass

There's a lot of cheap Venetian glass for sale; if you want something better, try **l'Isola** (✉ 2084 San Marco), where Carlo Moretti's chic, contemporary designs are on display. **Domus** (✉ Fondamenta dei Vetrai, Murano) has a good selection of glass and is on the island of Murano.

Shopping Districts

Le Mercerie, along with the Frezzeria and Calle dei Fabbri, are some of Venice's busiest streets and lead off of Piazza San Marco.

Venice Essentials

Arriving and Departing

BY CAR

If you bring a car to Venice, you will have to pay for a garage or parking space during your stay. Warning: Do not be waylaid by illegal con artists often wearing fake uniforms who may try to flag you down and offer to arrange parking and hotels. Continue on until you reach the automatic ticket machines.

Parking at **Piazzale Roma** (✉ Autorimessa Comunale, end of S11 road) costs between 15,000 and 25,000 lire. The private **Garage San Marco** (✉ Piazzale Roma, end of S11 road) costs between 34,000 and 46,000 lire per 24 hours, depending on the size of the car. To reach the privately run **Tronchetto** parking area, follow the signs to turn right before Piazzale Roma. Parking here costs 25,000 lire per 24 hours. (Do not leave valuables in the car. There is a left-luggage office, open daily 8–8, next to the Pullman Bar on the ground floor of the municipal garage at Piazzale Roma.) The AVA (☞ Visitor Information, *below*) has arranged a discount of around 5,000 lire per day for hotel guests who use the official Tronchetto parking facility. Ask for a voucher on checking into your hotel. Present the voucher at Tronchetto when you pay the parking fee. A vaporetto (No. 82) runs from Tronchetto to Piazzale Roma and Piazza San Marco (also to the Lido in summer). In thick fog or when tides are extreme, a bus runs instead to Piazzale Roma, where you can pick up a vaporetto.

BY PLANE

Aeroporto Marco Polo (✉ 10 km/6 mi northeast of Venice on the mainland, ☎ 041/2609260 flight information).

Between the Airport and Downtown. The most direct way is by the **Cooperativa San Marco** (✉ just off Piazza San Marco, ☎ 041/5222303) launch, with regular scheduled service throughout the day, until midnight; it takes about an hour to get to the landing, stopping at the Lido on the way, and the fare is 17,000 lire per person, including bags. Blue **ATVO** buses make the 25-minute trip in to Piazzale Roma, where the road to Venice terminates; the cost is 5,000 lire. From Piazzale Roma visitors will most likely have to take a vaporetto to their hotel (☞ Getting Around, *below*). **Water taxis** (slick high-power motorboats called *motoscafi*) should cost about 130,000 lire. **Land taxis** are available, running the same route as the buses; the cost is about 60,000 lire.

BY TRAIN

Make sure your train goes all the way to the **Stazione Ferroviaria Santa Lucia** (✉ Venice's northwest corner, ☎ 1478/88088 toll free). Some trains leave passengers at the **Stazione Ferroviaria Venezia-Mestre** (✉ on the mainland, ☎ 1478/880880 toll free). All trains traveling to and from Santa Lucia stop at Mestre, so to get from Mestre to Santa Lucia, or vice versa (a 10-minute trip), take the first available train, remembering there is a *supplemento* (extra charge) for traveling on Intercity, Eurocity, and Eurostar trains, and that if you board one of these trains without having paid in advance for this part of the trip, you are subject to a hefty fine. Since most tourists arrive in Venice by train, tourist services are conveniently located at Santa Lucia, including an **APT** information booth (☎ 041/5298727) and baggage depot. If you need a hotel room, the station has an **AVA** booth (☞ Visitor Information, *below*). Directly outside the train station are the main vaporetto landing stages; from here, vaporetti can transport you to your hotel's general neighborhood. Be prepared with advance directions from the hotel and a good map.

Getting Around

First-time visitors find that getting around Venice presents some unusual problems: the complexity of its layout (the city is made up of more than 100 islands, all linked by bridges); the bewildering unfamiliarity of waterborne transportation; the apparently illogical house numbering system and duplication of street names in its six districts; and the necessity of walking whether you enjoy it or not. It's essential to have a good map showing all street names and water bus routes; buy one at any newsstand.

BY GONDOLA

If you mustn't leave Venice without treating yourself to a gondola ride, take it in the quiet of the evening, when the churning traffic on the canals has died down, the palace windows are illuminated, and the only sounds are the muted splashes of the gondolier's oar. Make sure he understands that you want to see the *rii,* or smaller canals, as well as the Grand Canal. There's supposed to be a fixed minimum rate of about 120,000 lire for 50 minutes, and a nighttime supplement of 30,000. Come to terms with your gondolier *before* stepping into his boat.

BY TRAGHETTO

Few tourists know about the two-man gondolas that ferry people across the Grand Canal at various fixed points. It's the cheapest and shortest gondola ride in Venice, and it can save a lot of walking. The fare is 700 lire, which you hand to one of the gondoliers when you get on. Look for TRAGHETTO signs.

BY VAPORETTO

ACTV water buses run the length of the Grand Canal and circle the city. There are several lines, some of which connect Venice with the major and minor islands in the lagoon. The fare is 6,000 lire on all lines. A 24-hour tourist ticket costs 18,000 lire, a three-day ticket 35,000 lire, and a seven-day ticket 60,000 lire; these are especially worthwhile if you are planning to visit the islands. ACTV information is available by calling ☎ 041/5287886, daily from 7:30 AM to 8 PM. Free timetables are available at the ticket office at Piazzale Roma. Timetables are posted at every landing stage, but there is not always a ticket booth operating. After 9 PM, tickets are available on the boats, but you must immediately inform the controller that you need a ticket. For this reason it may be useful to buy a *blocchetto* (book of tickets) in advance. Landing stages are clearly marked with name and line number, but check before boarding, particularly with the 52 and 82, to make sure the boat is going in your direction.

Line 1 is the Grand Canal local, calling at every stop, and continuing via San Marco to the Lido. (The trip takes about 45 minutes from the station to San Marco.) **Line 41** and **Line 42** follow long loop routes in opposite directions: Take Line 41 from San Zaccaria to Murano, but Line 42 from Murano to San Zaccaria; Line 42 from San Zaccaria to the Redentore, but Line 41 from the Redentore back to San Zaccaria. **Line 51** runs from the railway station to San Zaccaria via Piazzale Roma and Zattere and continues to the Lido. **Line 52** goes along the same route but in the opposite direction, so from the Lido it makes stops at the Giardini, San Zaccaria, Zattere, Piazzale Roma, the train station, Fondamente Nuove (where boats leave for the islands of the northern lagoon), San Pietro, and back to the Lido. **Line 82** runs in a loop from San Zaccaria to Giudecca, Zattere, Piazzale Roma, the train station, Rialto (with fewer stops along the Grand Canal than Line 1), back to San Zaccaria, and out to the Lido.

BY WATER TAXI

Motoscafi, or taxis, are excessively expensive, and the fare system is as complex as Venice's layout. A minimum fare of about 50,000 lire gets you nowhere, and you'll pay three times as much to get from one end of the Grand Canal to the other. *Always agree on the fare before starting out.* It's probably worth considering taking a water taxi only if you are traveling in a small group. Contact the **Cooperativa San Marco** (☎ 041/5222303).

ON FOOT
This is the only way to reach many parts of Venice, so wear comfortable shoes. Invest in a good map that names all the streets, and count on getting lost more than once.

Contacts and Resources

CONSULATES
U.K. (⊠ Campo della Carità, 1051 Dorsoduro, ☎ 041/5227207). There is no U.S. or Canadian consular service in Venice. The nearest consulates are in Milan (☞ Contacts and Resources *in* Milan Essentials, *above*).

EMERGENCIES
Police (☎ 113). **Ambulance** (☎ 118). **Carabinieri** (☎ 112). **Doctor** (emergency room, Venice's hospital, ☎ 041/5230000).

Pharmacies are open weekdays 9–12:30 and 3:45–7:30 and Saturday 9–12:45; a notice telling where to get late-night and Sunday service is posted outside every pharmacy. **Farmacia Italo-Inglese** (⊠ Calle della Mandola, 3717 San Marco, ☎ 041/5224837). **Farmacia Internazionale** (⊠ Calle Larga XXII Marzo, 2067 San Marco, ☎ 041/5222311).

GUIDED TOURS
Excursions. The **Cooperativa San Marco** (⊠ Just off San Marco, ☎ 041/5222303, 041/5235775) organizes tours of the islands of Murano, Burano, and Torcello departing April–September daily at 9:30 and 2:30, October–March 1 daily departure at 2 PM, from the landing stage in front of Giardini Reali near Piazza San Marco. Tours last about 3½ hours and cost about 25,000 lire. However, tours tend to be annoyingly commercial and emphasize glass factory showrooms where you are pressured to buy, often at higher than standard prices. **American Express** (⊠ Salizzada San Moisè, 1471 San Marco, ☎ 041/5200844, FAX 041/5229937) books a day trip to Padova by boat along the Brenta River, with stops at three Palladian villas. The tours run three days a week from March to November; the cost is about 120,000 lire per person (the return, by bus, is included), and bookings need to be made the day before.

Orientation. American Express (☞ *above*) and other operators offer two-hour walking tours of the San Marco area, taking in the basilica and the Doge's Palace. The cost is about 45,000 lire, including admission. From April 25 through November 15, American Express offers an afternoon walking tour that ends with a short gondola ride (about 40,000 lire).

Personal Guides. American Express (☞ *above*) can provide guides for walking or gondola tours of Venice, or cars with driver and guide for excursions on the mainland. Pick up a list of licensed guides and their rates from the main **IAT** office (⊠ San Marco 71/F, near the Museo Correr, ☎ 041/5298740), or directly contact the **Guides' Association** (⊠ 750 San Marco, near San Zulian, ☎ 041/5209038, FAX 041/5210762).

Special-Interest. Some tour operators offer group gondola rides with a serenade. The cost is about 50,000 lire. During the summer free guided tours of the Basilica di San Marco are offered by the Procuratoria; information is available at a desk in the atrium of the church. From June through August there are several tours daily, except Sunday, and some tours are in English.

American Express (✉ Salizzada San Moisè, 1471 San Marco, ☎ 041/5200844, FAX 041/5229937). **CarlsonWagon-Lit** (✉ Piazzetta dei Leoncini, 289 San Marco, ☎ 041/5223405, FAX 041/5228508).

IAT Information booths (✉ Santa Lucia train station, ☎ 041/5298727; ✉ 71/f San Marco, near the Museo Correr, ☎ 041/5298740; Lido in summer, ✉ Gran Viale S. Maria Elisabetta 6A, ☎ 041/5265721, FAX 041/5298720).

AVA (Venetian Hoteliers Association, ☎ 041/715016) has a booth at Stazione Ferroviaria Santa Lucia; other satellite locations are at piazzale Roma and Marco Polo airport. Alternatively, you can call AVA's toll-free number, ☎ 1678/43006, daily 8 AM–9 PM.

CAMPANIA

Campania, the region comprised of Naples, the Amalfi coast, and the surrounding sun-drenched area is where most people's preconceived ideas of Italy become a reality. You'll find lots of beaches, good food that relies heavily on tomatoes and mozzarella, acres of classical ruins, and gorgeous scenery. The exuberance of the locals doesn't leave much room for efficient organization, however, and you may have to revise your concept of real time; here minutes dilate into hours at the drop of a hat.

Once a city that rivaled Paris as a brilliant and refined cultural capital, Napoli (Naples) is afflicted by acute urban decay and chronic delinquency. You need patience, stamina, and a degree of caution to visit Naples on your own, but it's worth it for those who have a sense of adventure and the capacity to discern the enormous riches the city has accumulated in its 2,000-year history.

If you want the fun without the hassle, skip Naples and head for Sorrento, Capri, and the Amalfi coast, legendary haunts of the sirens who tried to lure Odysseus off course. Sorrento is touristy but has some fine old hotels and beautiful views; it's a good base for a leisurely excursion to Pompeii. Capri is a pint-size paradise, though sometimes too crowded for comfort, and the Amalfi coast offers enchanting towns and spectacular scenery.

Naples

Founded by the Greeks, Naples became a playground of the Romans and was ruled thereafter by a succession of foreign dynasties, all of which left traces of their cultures in the city and its environs. The most splendid of these rulers were the Bourbons, who were responsible for much of what you will want to see in Naples. Among the greatest relics of Bourbon powers in Naples is the 17th-century **Palazzo Reale** (Royal Palace), still furnished in the lavish Baroque style that suited them so well. ✉ *Piazza del Plebiscito*, ☎ *081/5808111.* ☉ *Thurs.–Fri. and Mon.–Tues. 9–2, weekends 9–7.*

On the heights of the Vomero hill, the bastions of **Castel Sant'Elmo** (✉ Largo San Martino), open Tuesday through Sunday 9–2, occupy an evocative position with distant views over Naples and its bay. You can reach it by the **Montesanto funicular,** near Piazza Dante.

Also known as the Maschio Angioino, the massive stone **Castel Nuovo** was built by the city's Aragon rulers during the 13th century; inside, the city's **Museo Civico** comprises mainly local artwork from the 15th to the 19th centuries, and there are also regular exhibitions. ✉ *Castel Nuovo, Piazza Municipio*, ☎ *081/7952003.* ☉ *Mon.–Sat. 9–7, Sun. 9–1.*

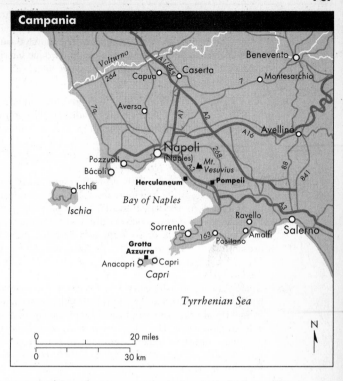

The **Certosa di San Martino,** a Carthusian monastery restored during the 17th century, contains an eclectic collection of Neapolitan landscape paintings, royal carriages, and *presepi* (Christmas crèches). Check out the view from the balcony off Room 25. The museum lies on the Vomero Hill, close by the Castel Sant'Elmo. ✉ *Certosa di San Martino,* ☎ *081/5781769.* ⏰ *Tues.–Sun. 9–2.*

★ The **Museo Archeologico Nazionale** is generally dusty and unkempt, but it holds one of the world's great collections of antiquities. Greek and Roman sculptures, vividly colored mosaics, countless objects from Pompeii and Herculaneum, and an equestrian statue of the Roman emperor Nerva are all worth seeing. ✉ *Piazza Museo,* ☎ *081/440166.* ⏰ *Aug.–Sept., Mon.–Sat. 9–10, Sun. 9–6; Oct.–July, Wed.–Mon. 9–2.*

★ The **Museo di Capodimonte** is housed in an 18th-century palace built by Bourbon king Charles III, and surrounded by a vast park that affords sweeping views of the bay. The picture gallery is devoted to work from the 13th to the 18th centuries, including many familiar works by Dutch and Spanish masters, as well as by the great Italians. Other rooms contain an extensive collection of porcelain and majolica from the various royal residences, some produced in the Bourbons' own factory right here on the grounds. ✉ *Parco di Capodimonte,* ☎ *081/ 7441307.* ⏰ *Tues.–Sun. 10–7.*

Santa Chiara, built during the early 1300s in Provençal Gothic style, is opposite Gesù Nuovo. A favorite Neapolitan song celebrates the quiet beauty of its cloister, decorated in delicate floral tiles. ✉ *Piazza Gesù Nuovo,* ☎ *081/5526209.* ⏰ *Apr.–Sept., daily 8:30–noon and 4–7; Oct.–Mar., daily 8:30–noon and 4–6.*

Via Toledo (runs north–south connecting Piazza Dante, Piazza del Gesù, and Piazza del Plebiscito), also known as Via Roma, is great for strolling and watching the antics of the Neapolitans, whose daily lives are fraught with theatrical gestures and fiery speeches. They all seem to be actors in their own human comedy. The church **Gesù Nuovo,** with oddly faceted stone facade and elaborate Baroque interior, is off Via Toledo. ⊠ *Via Benedetto Croce, Piazza Gesù Nuovo,* ☎ *081/5518613.* ⊙ *Daily 9–1 and 4–7 (Oct.–Mar. until 6).*

$$$ ✕ **La Sacrestia.** This lovely restaurant above Mergellina has a fine view from the delightful summer terrace. Traditional Neapolitan specialties of the day might be baked or steamed sea bass and linguine *in salsa di scorfano* (with scorpion-fish sauce). ⊠ *Via Orazio 116,* ☎ *081/ 7611051. AE, DC, MC, V. Closed Sun. (July–Aug.) and 2 wks in mid- Aug. No lunch Mon. No dinner Sun.*

$$ ✕ **Ciro a Santa Brigida.** This no-frills restaurant is a favorite with businesspeople, artists, and journalists. Tables are arranged on two levels, and the decor is classic trattoria. This is the place to try traditional Neapolitan *sartù di riso* (a rich rice dish with meat and peas) and *melanzane alla parmigiana* or *scaloppe alla Ciro* (eggplant or veal with prosciutto and mozzarella). There's pizza, too. ⊠ *Via Santa Brigida 71, off Via Toledo,* ☎ *081/5524072. AE, DC, MC, V. Closed Sun. and 2 wks in Aug.*

$$$$ 🏨 **Excelsior.** On the shore drive the Excelsior has splendid views of the bay from its front rooms. Spacious bedrooms are well furnished in informal floral prints or more formal Empire style; all have a comfortable, traditional air. The salons are formal, with chandeliers and wall paintings, and the excellent Casanova restaurant is elegant. ⊠ *Via Partenope 48, 80121,* ☎ *081/7640111,* 𝔽𝔸𝕏 *081/7649743. 136 rooms. Restaurant. AE, DC, MC, V.*

$$ 🏨 **Jolly Ambassador.** This hotel occupies the top 14 floors of a down-
★ town skyscraper, and its rooms and roof restaurant have wonderful views of Naples and the bay. It's furnished in the functional, modern style typical of this reliable chain, which promises comfort and efficiency in a city where these are scarce commodities. ⊠ *Via Medina 70, 80133,* ☎ *081/416000,* 𝔽𝔸𝕏 *081/5518010. 251 rooms. Restaurant. AE, DC, MC, V.*

$ 🏨 **Rex.** On the first two floors of an Art Nouveau building, the hotel, in a fairly quiet spot near the Santa Lucia waterfront, reveals a haphazard collection of 1950s modern, fake period pieces, and even some folk art. ⊠ *Via Palepoli 12, 80132,* ☎ *081/7649389,* 𝔽𝔸𝕏 *081/7649227. 38 rooms. Bar. AE, DC, MC, V.*

Herculaneum

★ Hercules is reputed to have founded Herculaneum (Ercolano), just 10 km (6 mi) southeast of Naples. The elite Roman resort was devastated by the same volcanic eruption that buried Pompeii in AD 79. Excavations have revealed that many died on the shore in an attempt to escape, as a slow-moving mud slide embalmed the entire town by covering it with a 36-ft-deep blanket of volcanic ash and ooze. Though devastating for Herculaneum's residents, it has helped to preserve the site in pristine condition for nearly two millennia. ⊠ *Corso Ercolano,* ☎ *081/7390963.* ⊙ *Daily 9–1 hr before sunset (ticket office closes 2 hrs before sunset).*

Pompeii

★ An estimated 2,000 of Pompeii's residents perished on that fateful August day. The ancient city of Pompeii was much larger than Herculaneum, and excavations have progressed to a much greater extent, though the remains are not as well preserved, due to some 18th-century scavenging for museum-quality artwork, most of which you are able to see at Naples's Museo Archeologico Nazionale (☞ *above*). This prosperous Roman city had an extensive forum, lavish baths and temples, and patrician villas richly decorated with frescoes. It's worth buying a detailed guide of the site to gain an understanding of the ruins and their importance. Be sure to see the **Villa dei Misteri** (Villa of the Mysteries), with frescoes some 1,900 years old that still retain rich detail and color depth. Have lots of small change handy to tip the guards at the more important houses so they will unlock the gates for you. ⊠ *Pompeii Scavi,* ☎ *081/8610744.* ⊘ *Daily 9–1 hr before sunset (ticket office closes 2 hrs before sunset).*

Sorrento

In the not-too-distant past, small Sorrento was a genteel resort for the fashionable elite. Now the town, 28 km (17 mi) southwest of Pompeii, has spread out along the crest of its fabled cliffs. The once-secret haunts for the few tourists who came for the magnificent coastline have been long discovered, now ravaged by package tours. But truly, nothing can dim the delights of the marvelous climate and view of the Bay of Naples. For the best views go to the **Villa Comunale,** near the old church of San Francesco (in itself worth a visit). **Museo Correale,** in an attractive 18th-century villa, retains a collection of decorative arts and paintings of the Neapolitan school. ⊠ *Via Correale.* ⊘ *Wed.–Mon. 9–2.*

\$\$ ✕ **Antica Trattoria.** Garden dining at this homey, hospitable spot is a joy in summer. Classic *pennette al profumo di bosco* (mini-penne with a creamy mushroom and ham sauce), sometimes pricey fish, and *gamberetti freschi Antica Trattoria* (shrimp in a tomato sauce) are among the house specialties. ⊠ *Via Giuliani 33,* ☎ *081/8071082. AE, DC, MC, V. Closed Mon. and 4 wks Jan.–Feb.*

\$\$ ✕ **Gigino.** Just off the central Piazza Tasso, this is one of Sorrento's best inexpensive and informal eateries. The fixed-price menu at lunch is an especially good value. ⊠ *Via degli Archi 15,* ☎ *081/8781927. MC, V. Closed Tues. and Jan.–Feb.*

\$\$ ✕ **Parrucchiano.** One of the town's best and oldest, Parrucchiano features greenhouse-type dining rooms dripping with vines and dotted with plants. Among the antipasti, try the *panzerotti* (pastry crust filled with mozzarella and tomato), and for a main course, the scaloppe *alla sorrentina,* again with mozzarella and tomato. ⊠ *Corso Italia 71,* ☎ *081/ 8781321. MC, V. Closed Wed. Nov.–Mar.*

\$\$\$–\$\$\$\$ ▥ **Excelsior Vittoria.** In the heart of Sorrento, this hotel right on the cliff has Art Nouveau furnishings, some very grand, though faded. Tenor Enrico Caruso's bedroom is preserved as a relic; guest bedrooms are spacious and elegant in a late-19th-century way. ⊠ *Piazza Tasso 34, 80067,* ☎ *081/8071044,* ☒ *081/8771206. 110 rooms. Restaurant, pool. AE, DC, MC, V.*

\$\$\$ ▥ **Bellevue Syrene.** This exclusive hotel is set in a cliff-top garden close to the center of Sorrento. It retains its solid, old-fashioned comforts and sumptuous charm, with Victorian nooks and alcoves, antique paintings, and exuberant frescoes. ⊠ *Piazza della Vittoria 5, 80067,* ☎ *081/8781024,* ☒ *081/8783963. 73 rooms. Restaurant, bar. AE, DC, MC, V.*

\$\$ ▥ **Eden.** Central but quiet within its own gardens, the Eden has recently been overhauled and its facilities improved. Guest rooms are bright and modern, among them 18 fully equipped mini-apartments. ⊠ *Via Correale 25, 80067,* ☎ *081/8781909,* ☒ *081/8072016. 63 rooms. Restaurant, pool. AE, DC, MC, V.*

\$ ▥ **City.** The central position and excellent value for money are the best reasons to stay in this modest establishment, close to the bus and train stations. Bedrooms are small and functional, but it's relaxed and the management is always ready with information and advice. ⊠ *Corso Italia 221, 80067,* ☎ ☒ *081/8772210. 13 rooms. AE, MC, V.*

Capri

No matter how many day-trippers crowd onto the island, no matter how touristy certain sections have become, Capri remains one of Italy's loveliest places. Incoming visitors disembark at Marina Grande, from where you can take some time out for an excursion to the **Grotta Azzurra** (Blue Grotto). Be warned that this must rank as one of the country's all-time great rip-offs: Motorboat, rowboat, and grotto admissions are charged separately, and if there's a line of boats waiting, you'll have little time to enjoy the grotto's marvelous colors. At Marina Grande you can also take a boat excursion around the island. A cog railway or bus service takes you up to the deliberately commercial and self-consciously picturesque **Capri Town**, where you can stroll through the **Piazzetta**, a choice place from which to watch the action, and window-shop expensive boutiques. The **Giardini di Augusto** (Gardens of Augustus; ⊠ Via Matteotti) have gorgeous views. To get away from the crowds, hike to **Villa Jovis,** one of the many villas that Roman emperor Tiberius built on the island. The walk takes about 45 minutes, with pretty views all the way and a final spectacular vista of the entire Bay of Naples and part of the Gulf of Salerno. ⊠ *Villa Jovis, Via Tiberio,* ☎ *081/8370381.* ☉ *Daily 9–1 hr before sunset.*

★

You can take the bus or a jaunty open taxi to **Anacapri** and look for the little church of **San Michele** (⊠ Off Via Orlandi), where a magnificent hand-painted majolica tile floor shows you an 18th-century vision of the Garden of Eden; it's open Easter–October, daily 9–7, November–Easter, daily 10–3. **Villa San Michele** is the charming former home of Swedish scientist-author Axel Munthe. ⊠ *Via Axel Munthe,* ☎ *081/837401.* ☉ *May–Sept., daily 9–6; Nov.–Feb., daily 10:30–3:30; Mar., daily 9:30–4:30; Apr. and Oct., daily 9:30–5.*

$$–$$$ ✕ **La Capannina.** Only a few steps away from Capri's social center, the Piazzetta, La Capannina has a delightful vine-hung courtyard for summer dining and a reputation as one of the island's best eating places. Antipasto features fried ravioli and eggplant stuffed with ricotta, and house specialties include chicken, scaloppine, and a refreshing, homemade lemon liqueur called *limoncello.* ⊠ *Via Botteghe 14,* ☎ *081/ 8370732. AE, DC, MC, V. Closed Wed. Oct.–May and mid-Jan.– mid-Mar.*

$$ ✕ **Al Grottino.** This small family-run restaurant, with a handy loca-
★ tion near the Piazzetta, displays autographed photographs of celebrity customers. House specialties are gnocchi with tomato sauce and mozzarella and linguine *ai gamberetti* (with shrimp sauce). ⊠ *Via Longano 27,* ☎ *081/8370584. AE, MC, V. Closed Tues. and Nov. 3–Mar. 20.*

$$ ✕ **Da Gemma.** One of Capri's favorite places for a homey atmosphere and a good meal, Da Gemma features *pappardelle all'aragosta* (wide pasta ribbons with lobster) and fritto misto. If you're on a budget, forgo the fish that you pay for by weight—it's always expensive. Pizza makes a great starter. ⊠ *Via Madre Serafina 6,* ☎ *081/8370461. AE, DC, MC, V. Closed Mon. Oct.–Apr. and 4 wks Jan.–Feb.*

$$$$ ▥ **Quisisana.** One of Italy's poshest hotels is right in the center of the town of Capri. The rooms are spacious, and many have arcaded balconies with views of the sea; the decor is traditional or contemporary, with some antique accents. From the small terrace at the entrance you can watch all Capri go by, but the enclosed garden and pool in the back are perfect for getting away from it all. The bar and restaurant are casual in a terribly elegant way. ⊠ *Via Camerelle 2, 80073,* ☎ *081/ 8370788,* ⅣⅩ *081/8376080. 149 rooms. Restaurant, pool. AE, DC, MC, V. Closed Nov.–mid-Mar.*

$$$–$$$$ ▥ **Villa Brunella.** The glassed-in bar of this family-run hotel is on the lane
★ leading to Punta Tragara and the Faraglioni. From that level you descend

to the restaurant, and then to the rooms and the pool on lower levels. Furnishings are tastefully casual and comfortable, the views serendipitous. ⊠ *Via Tragara 24, 87003,* ☎ *081/8370122,* ℻ *081/8370430. 20 rooms. Restaurant, pool. AE, DC, MC, V. Closed Nov.–Mar.*

$$$ 🏨 **Villa Sarah.** Just a 10-minute walk from the Piazzetta, the Sarah is a whitewashed Mediterranean villa with bright, simply furnished rooms. There's a garden and small bar, but no restaurant. ⊠ *Via Tiberio 3/A, 87003,* ☎ *081/8377817,* ℻ *081/8377215. 20 rooms. AE, DC, MC, V. Closed Nov.–Mar.*

Positano

★ Positano's jumble of pastel houses, topped by whitewashed cupolas, clings to the mountainside above the sea. The town—the prettiest along this stretch of coast—attracts a sophisticated group of visitors and summer residents who find that its relaxed and friendly atmosphere more than compensates for the sheer effort of moving about this exhaustingly vertical town, most of whose streets are stairways. This former fishing village has now opted for the more regular and lucrative rewards of tourism and commercialized fashion. Practically every other shop is a boutique displaying locally made casual wear. The beach is the town's main focal point, with a little promenade and a multitude of café-restaurants.

$$ ✕ **'O Capurale.** Among all the popular restaurants on the beach promenade, 'O Capurale (just around the corner) has the best food and lowest prices. Tables are set under vines on a breezy sidewalk in the summer, upstairs and indoors in winter. Spaghetti *con melanzane* (with eggplant) and crepes *al formaggio* (with cheese) are tasty. ⊠ *Via Regina Giovanna 12,* ☎ *089/875374. AE, DC, MC, V. Closed Nov.–mid-Feb.*

$$$$ 🏨 **Le Sirenuse.** The most fashionable hotel in Positano, in an 18th-century villa, has been in the same family for eight generations. The hotel is set into the hillside overlooking Positano's harbor. Most of the bedrooms face the sea—these are the best. Because of the hotel's location, the dining room is like a long, closed-in terrace overlooking the village of Positano. The cuisine ranges from acceptable to excellent. ⊠ *Via Cristoforo Colombo 30, 84017,* ☎ *089/875066,* ℻ *081/811798. 62 rooms. Restaurant, bar. AE, DC, MC, V.*

$$$$ 🏨 **San Pietro.** Perched on the side of a cliff, this opulent hotel is eclectic and airy, with unusual antiques and, everywhere, hanging bougainvillea. The guest rooms are tastefully appointed but the stupendous window views steal the show. Verdant with plants, the light, open dining room offers fine Italian cuisine. An elevator takes guests to the hotel's small beach area. ⊠ *Via Laurito 2, 84017,* ☎ *089/875455,* ℻ *089/811449. 60 rooms. Restaurant. AE, DC, MC, V. Closed Nov.–Mar.*

$$$ 🏨 **Palazzo Murat.** The location is perfect, in the heart of town, near the beachside promenade and set within a walled garden. The old wing is a historic palazzo, with tall windows and wrought-iron balconies; the newer wing is a whitewashed Mediterranean building with arches and terraces. You can relax in antiques-strewn lounges or on the charming vine-draped patio. ⊠ *Via dei Mulini 23, 84017,* ☎ *089/875177,* ℻ *089/811419. 32 rooms. Restaurant, bar. AE, DC, MC, V. Closed Jan.–Mar.*

$ 🏨 **La Fenice.** Paradise found. This tiny and unpretentious hotel beck-
★ ons with bougainvillea-laden vistas, castaway cottages, and a turquoise pool, all perched over a private beach. Guest rooms—accented with coved ceilings, whitewashed walls, and native folk art—are simple havens of tranquility (book the best, those closest to the sea, only if you can handle *very* steep walkways). Situated on the peaceful outskirts of town, this is happily open year-round. ⊠ *Via G. Marconi 4, 84017,* ☎ *089/875513,* ℻ *089/811309. 10 rooms. Pool. No credit cards.*

Amalfi

The coastal drive down to the resort town of Amalfi provides some of the most dramatic and beautiful scenery you'll find in all of Italy. Amalfi itself is a charming maze of covered alleys and narrow byways straggling up the steep mountainside. The **piazza** just below the cathedral forms the town's heart—a colorful assortment of pottery stalls, cafés, and postcard shops grouped around a venerable old fountain. The exterior of the **cathedral** is its most impressive feature. The **cloisters,** with whitewashed arches and palms, are worth a glance, and the small **museum** in the adjoining crypt could really inspire you to climb up all those stairs. ☎ 089/871059. ⊙ *Duomo: Apr.–Oct., daily 7:30 AM–8 PM; Nov.–Mar., daily 7:30–noon and 3–7. Cloisters and museum: Apr.–Oct., daily 9–9; Nov.–Mar., daily 10–12:30 and 2:30–5:30.*

$$ ✕ **La Caravella.** Tucked away under some arches lining the coast road, the Caravella has a nondescript entrance but a pleasant interior decorated with paintings of old Amalfi. It's small and intimate, and proprietor Franco describes the cuisine as *"sfiziosa"* (taste tempting). Specialties include linguine *alla colatura di alici* (with anchovies) based on a medieval recipe and *calamari ripieni* (stuffed squid). ⊠ *Via M. Camera 12,* ☎ *089/871029. AE, MC, V. Closed Nov. and Tues. (except Aug.).*

$$$$ ⌂ **Santa Caterina.** A large mansion perched above terraced and flow-
★ ered hillsides on the coast road just outside Amalfi proper, the Santa Caterina is one of the best hotels on the entire coast. The rooms are tastefully decorated, and most have small terraces or balconies with great views. There are lounges and terraces for relaxing, and an elevator whisks guests down to the seaside saltwater pool, bar, and swimming area. Amid lemon and orange groves are two romantic villa annexes. ⊠ *Strada Amalfitana 9, 84011,* ☎ *089/871012,* FAX *089/871351. 54 rooms. Restaurant, pool. AE, DC, MC, V.*

Ravello

★ Ravello is not actually on the coast, but on a high mountain bluff overlooking the sea 8 km (5 mi) north of Amalfi. The road up to it is a series of switchbacks, and the village itself clings precariously on the mountain spur. The village flourished during the 13th century and then fell into a tranquility that has remained unchanged for the past six centuries. The town center is Piazza del Duomo, with its **cathedral,** founded in 1087. Note the fine bronze 12th-century doors and, inside, two pulpits richly decorated with mosaics: One depicting the story of Jonah and the whale; the other, more splendid mosaic is carved with fantastic beasts and rests on a pride of lions. Composer Richard Wagner once stayed in Ravello, and today there is a Wagner festival every summer on the garden terrace of the 11th-century **Villa Rufolo.** There is a Moorish cloister with interlacing pointed arches, beautiful gardens, an 11th-century tower, and a belvedere with a fine view of the coast. ⊠ *Piazza del Duomo,* ☎ *089/857657. ⊙ Apr.–Sept., daily 9–8; Oct.–Mar., daily 9–6 or sunset.*

At the entrance to the **Villa Cimbrone** complex is a small cloister that looks medieval but was actually built in 1917, with two bas-reliefs: one representing nine Norman warriors, the other illustrating the seven deadly sins. Then, the long avenue leads through peaceful gardens scattered with grottoes, small temples, and statues to a belvedere and terrace where, on a clear day, the view stretches out over the Mediterranean Sea. ⊠ *Via Santa Chiara,* ☎ *089/857459. ⊙ Daily 8:30–1 hr before sunset.*

$$$$ ⊞ **Hotel Palumbo.** Of all the hotels on the Amalfi coast, the Hotel Palumbo is the most genteel, and one of the most costly. Occupying a 12th-century patrician palace furnished with antiques and provided with modern comforts, this hotel has an elegant, warm atmosphere. You won't quickly forget the lovely garden terraces, breathtaking views, and sumptuous upstairs dining room. Some of the bedrooms are small, but they are full of character. The rooms facing the sea are the choice ones— and the more expensive (those in the modern annex are considerably cheaper). Note that you are required to take half- or full-board lodging at all times. ⊠ *Via Toro 28, 84010,* ☎ *089/857244,* FAX *089/ 858133. 8 rooms. Restaurant. AE, DC, MC, V.*

Campania Essentials

Getting Around

BY BOAT
Most boats and hydrofoils for the islands and the Sorrento peninsula leave from the Molo Beverello Pier (⊠ near Naples's Piazza Municipio); there's also a hydrofoil station at Mergellina Pier.

Hydrofoils. Caremar (☎ 081/5513882). **Linee Marittime Veloci** (LMV, ☎ 081/5527209). **SNAV** (☎ 081/7612348).

Passenger and Car Ferries. Service is frequent. **Caremar** (☞ *above*). **Linee Marittime Veloci** (☞ *above*).

BY BUS
SITA (☎ 081/5522176 for information).

BY CAR
The Naples–Pompeii–Salerno toll road has exits at Herculaneum and Pompeii and connects with the tortuous coastal road to Sorrento and the Amalfi coast at the Castellammare exit. Parking within Naples is not recommended: Window smashing and robbery are not uncommon.

BY HELICOPTER
From May through September there's direct helicopter service (☎ 081/5841481 for information) between Capodichino and Capri or Ischia.

BY PLANE
There are several daily flights between Rome and Naples's **Aeroporto Capodichino** (⊠ 8 km/5 mi north of downtown Naples, ☎ 081/ 7896259).

BY TRAIN
Stazione Centrale (⊠ Piazza Garibaldi, ☎ 1478/88088 for toll-free information). A great number of trains run between Rome and Naples every day; Intercity trains make the journey in less than two hours. There are several stations in Naples, and a network of suburban trains connects the city with diverse points of interest in Campania, most usefully the **Circumvesuviana line** (☎ 081/7722444), which runs to Herculaneum (Ercolano), Pompeii, and Sorrento. Naples has a **Metropolitana** (subway); though it's old and trains are infrequent, it beats the traffic. The fare is 1,500 lire.

Guided Tours
One-, two-, or three-day guided tours of the area depart from Rome. **American Express** (☎ 06/67641). **Carrani** (☎ 06/4880510 and 06/ 4742501). **Appian Line** (☎ 06/4884151). From Naples you can choose from a wide range of half-day and all-day tours on the mainland and to the islands. **Tourcar** (⊠ Piazza Matteotti 1, ☎ 081/5520429). **STS** (⊠ Piazza Medaglie d'Oro 41, ☎ 081/5789292).

Visitor Information

Capri (✉ Marina Grande pier, ☎ 081/8370634; ✉ Piazza Umberto I, Capri Town, ☎ 081/8370686). **Naples** (EPT, ✉ Piazza dei Martiri 58, ☎ 081/405311; ✉ Stazione Centrale, ☎ 081/268779; ✉ Stazione Mergellina, ☎ 081/7612102; ✉ Aeroporto Capodichino, ☎ 081/7805761; Azienda Autonoma di Soggiorno, Cura e Turismo, AASCT, ✉ Piazza del Gesù, ☎ 081/5523328). **Sorrento** (✉ Via De Maio 35, ☎ 081/8074033).

19 LUXEMBOURG

When you try to locate Luxembourg on a map, look for "Lux." at the heart of Western Europe. Even abbreviated, the name runs over—west into Belgium, east into Germany, south into France—as the country's influence has done for centuries. The Grand Duchy of Luxembourg is a thriving, Rhode Island–size land that contains variety and contrasts out of all proportion to its size.

It has a wild and beautiful highland country studded with castles, rich in history. It has legendary vineyards producing great wines and a lovely farmland called Le Bon Pays. And, of course, it has its capital, with an ancient fortress towering above the south central plain. Seen through early morning mists, Luxembourg City revives the magic of Camelot. Yet it is actually the nerve center of a thousand-year-old seat of government, a bustling and important element of the European Union (EU), a spot where the past still speaks, the present interprets, and the future listens.

One of the smallest countries in the United Nations, Luxembourg comprises only 2,587 square km (999 square mi). It is dwarfed by its neighbors, yet from its history of invasion, occupation, and siege, you might think the land covered solid gold. Starting in AD 963, when Charlemagne's descendant Sigefroid started to build his castle atop the promontory of the Bock, the duchy encased itself in layer upon layer of fortifications until by the mid-19th century its very impregnability was considered a threat. The Castle of Luxembourg was ultimately dismantled in the name of peace, its neutrality "guaranteed" by the 1867 Treaty of London. But the Grand Duchy was to be invaded twice again, in 1914 and 1940. Its experiences during World War II convinced Luxembourg of the necessity to cooperate with all its neighbors to avoid conflicts. The entire country now flaunts new wealth, new political muscle, and the highest per capita income in Europe. Luxembourg bristles with international banks—enough to rival Switzerland—and just outside the Old City, a new colony has been populated by *fonctionnaires* of the EU, the successor of the Common Market.

There is an old saying that describes the life of the Luxembourgers—
or *Luxembourgeois,* if you prefer the more elegant French appellation:
"One Luxembourger, a rose garden; two Luxembourgers, a kaf-
feeklatsch; three Luxembourgers, a band." This is a country of parades
and processions, good cheer, and a hearty capacity for beer and Moselle
wine. In its traditions, values, and politics, Luxembourg remains more
conservative than its neighbors. This may occasionally seem stifling to
the younger generation of Luxembourgeois, but to the majority of their
elders these attitudes express the age-old national motto, *Mir wëlle bleiwe
wat mir sin* ("We want to remain what we are").

LUXEMBOURG A TO Z

Customs
For information on customs regulations, *see* Customs & Duties *in* Chapter 1.

Dining
Restaurants in Luxembourg combine Gallic quality with Teutonic
quantity. The best deals are at lunch, when you can find a plat du jour
or *menu* (two or three courses included in the price) at bargain rates.
Pizzerias, found everywhere, offer an inexpensive alternative.

MEALTIMES
Most hotels serve breakfast until 10. Luxembourgers shut down their
computers at noon to rush home for a two-hour lunch. Dinner is eaten
a bit earlier than in neighboring countries, generally between 7 and 10.

RATINGS
Prices quoted are per person and include a first course, main course,
and dessert, but not wine. Service (10%) and sales tax (3%) are included in quoted prices.

CATEGORY	COST
$$$$	over Flux 3,000
$$$	Flux 1,500–Flux 3,000
$$	Flux 750–Flux 1,500
$	under Flux 750

WHAT TO WEAR
Stylish, casual dress is expected in most restaurants; when in doubt,
err on the side of formality. In expensive French restaurants, formal
dress (jacket and tie) is taken for granted.

Language
Native Luxembourgers speak three languages fluently: Luxembourgish
(a Germanic language salted with French), German, and French. Many
also speak English.

Lodging
CAMPING
The Grand Duchy is probably the best-organized country in Europe
when it comes to camping. It offers some 120 sites, all with full amenities. Listings are published annually by the National Tourist Office (☞
Visitor Information, *below*).

HOTELS
Most hotels in Luxembourg City are relatively modern and range from
the international style to smaller, family-run establishments. Weekdays,
Luxembourg City hotels are often full of business travelers, who depart on Friday; many hotels offer reduced rates on weekends.

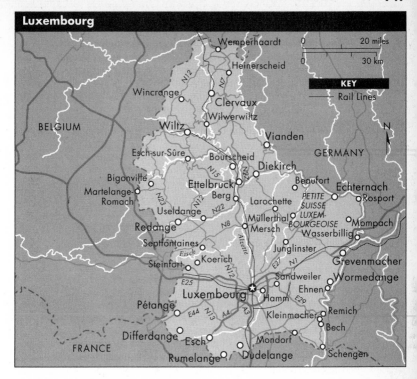

Luxembourg

RATINGS

Price categories are for a double room. Service (10%) and sales tax (3%) are included in posted rates. Check for special rates when making reservations.

CATEGORY	COST
$$$$	over Flux 8,000
$$$	Flux 5,000–Flux 8,000
$$	Flux 2,500–Flux 5,000
$	under Flux 2,500

YOUTH HOSTELS

Inexpensive youth hostels are plentiful; many are housed in historic buildings. For information contact **Centrale des Auberges Luxembourgeoises** (✉ Rue du Fort Olisy 2, L-2261 Luxembourg City, ☎ 225588).

Mail

POSTAL RATES

Airmail postcards and letters to North America weighing less than 20 grams cost Flux 25. Letters and postcards to the United Kingdom cost Flux 16.

RECEIVING MAIL

Mail can be sent in care of BBL Travel American Express (✉ 3 rue Jean Piret, L-2350 Luxembourg City). This service is free for holders of American Express credit cards or traveler's checks.

Money Matters

COSTS

Luxembourg is a highly developed and sophisticated country with a high standard and cost of living. Prices in the countryside are slightly lower than in Luxembourg City.

CURRENCY
In Luxembourg, as in Belgium, the unit of currency is the franc (abbreviated *Flux*). Luxembourg issues its own currency in bills of 100, 1,000, and 5,000 francs and coins of 1, 5, 20, and 50 francs. Belgian currency can be used freely in Luxembourg, and the two currencies have the same value. At press time (summer 1999), the exchange rate was Flux 40.3399 to the euro, Flux 39 to the U.S. dollar, Flux 30 to the Canadian dollar, Flux 62 to the pound sterling, Flux 26 to the Australian dollar, and Flux 21 to the New Zealand dollar.

SAMPLE PRICES
Cup of coffee, Flux 55–Flux 80; glass of beer, Flux 55–Flux 70; movie admission, Flux 250–Flux 300; 5-km (3-mi) taxi ride, Flux 800.

TIPPING
In hotels and restaurants, taxes and service charges are included in the bill. If you wish to tip further, round off the total to the nearest Flux 100. Bellhops and doormen appreciate a tip of Flux 50 to Flux 100. Porters at the railway station (whose services can be reserved on ☎ 4990–5574) charge Flux 50 per bag, max charge Flux 150. Taxi drivers expect a tip; add about 15% to the amount on the meter.

National Holidays
January 1; March 7 (Carnival); April 24 (Easter Monday); May 1 (May Day); June 1 (Ascension); June 12 (Pentecost Monday); June 23 (National Day); August 15 (Assumption); November 1 (All Saints' Day); November 2 (All Souls' Day); December 25–26 (Christmas). Note: When a holiday falls on a Sunday, the following Monday is automatically a national holiday.

Opening and Closing Times
Banks are generally open weekdays 8:30–4, though some close for lunch (noon–2). In Luxembourg City, an automatic exchange machine located in the Rue de la Reine accepts banknotes of most foreign currencies. **Museums'** opening hours vary, so check individual listings. Most are closed Monday, and in the countryside some also close for lunch (noon–2). **Shops** and department stores are generally open Monday 2–6 and Tuesday–Saturday 9–6. Some close for lunch (noon–2). A few small family businesses are open Sunday 8–noon.

Shopping
SALES-TAX REFUNDS
Purchases of goods for export may qualify for a Value Added Tax refund of 15%. For more information, *see* Money *in* Chapter 1.

Telephoning
COUNTRY CODE
The country code for Luxembourg is 352. Note that there are no area codes within the Grand Duchy.

INTERNATIONAL CALLS
The cheapest way to make an international call is to dial direct from a public phone. To reach an **AT&T** long-distance operator, dial 0800–0111; for **MCI**, dial 0800–0112; for **Sprint**, dial 0800–0115.

LOCAL CALLS
You can find public phones on the street and in city post offices. A local call costs a minimum of Flux 5 from a public phone (slightly more from restaurants and gas stations). Post offices sell Telekaart, in denominations from Flux 250 to Flux 750, which can be used in nearly half the country's phone booths. To place operator-assisted calls, dial 0010.

Visitor Information

Office Nationale du Tourisme (National Tourist Office; main branch, ✉ Gare Centrale, ☎ 481199; head office, ✉ B.P. 1001, L-1010 Luxembourg City, ☎ 428282–1, FAX 4282–8238; airport branch, ☎ 4282–8221).

Weather

The main tourist season in Luxembourg is from early May through October, with spring and fall the most rewarding seasons. In the hilly north there is frequently snow in winter.

CLIMATE

In general, temperatures in Luxembourg are moderate. Be sure to pack rain gear. The following are the average daily maximum and minimum temperatures for Luxembourg.

Jan.	37F	3C	May	65F	18C	Sept.	66F	19C
	29	– 1		46	8		50	10
Feb.	40F	4C	June	70F	21C	Oct.	56F	13C
	31	– 1		52	11		43	6
Mar.	49F	10C	July	73F	23C	Nov.	44F	7C
	35	1		55	13		37	3
Apr.	57F	14C	Aug.	71F	22C	Dec.	39F	4C
	40	4		54	12		32	0

LUXEMBOURG CITY

As you arrive in the capital of Luxembourg from the airport and cross the vast span of the Grande Duchesse Charlotte Bridge, you're greeted by an awe-inspiring panorama of medieval stonework fortifications fronted by massive gates. Then, after a left turn that swings you into the Boulevard Royal, you're back in the 20th century of BMW and Mercedes cars and glittering glass-and-concrete office buildings. A block away, in the Old City, the sedate pace of a provincial picture-book town delightfully returns.

Exploring Luxembourg City

Numbers in the margin correspond to points of interest on the Luxembourg City map.

The military fortifications and the Old Town, with its cobbled streets and inviting public squares, make for terrific exploring. In 1994 the United Nations Educational, Scientific, and Cultural Organization (UNESCO) declared these areas part of the world's cultural heritage.

★ ⓭ **Bock.** This stony promontory is Luxembourg's raison d'être. Jutting up dramatically above the valley, the Bock once supported the castle built by the first Duke of Luxembourg in AD 963. Taking in vertiginous views of the valley, you'll see the **Plateau du Rham** across the way, on the right, and before it, the massive towers of Duke Wenceslas's fortifications, which were built in 1390. The blocklike *casernes* (barracks) were added during the 17th century by the French. From the Bock you can gain access to fascinating 18th-century military tunnels. At the entrance, the **Crypte Archéologique du Bock** (Archaeological Crypt) offers an audiovisual presentation providing a brief history of Luxembourg from the 10th to the 15th centuries. ✉ *Montée de Clausen*, ☎ *226753.* ☉ *Mar.–Oct., daily 10–5.*

❽ **Boulevard Royal.** Luxembourg's mini–Wall Street, once the site of the fortress's main moat, curves around the west and north sides of the

Luxembourg City (Luxembourg Ville)

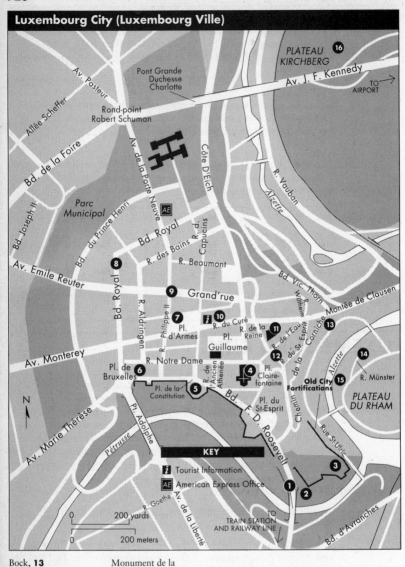

KEY

- 🛈 Tourist Information
- AE American Express Office

0 — 200 yards

0 — 200 meters

TO TRAIN STATION AND RAILWAY LINE

TO AIRPORT

PLATEAU KIRCHBERG

PLATEAU DU RHAM

Old City Fortifications

Av. Pasteur
Allée Scheffer
Bd. de la Foire
Bd. Joseph II
Pont Grande Duchesse Charlotte
Rond-point Robert Schuman
Parc Municipal
Av. de la Porte Neuve
Côte D'Eich
Av. J. F. Kennedy
R. Vauban
Alzette
Bd. du Prince Henri
Bd. Royal
R. des Bains
R. d. Capucins
R. Beaumont
Av. Emile Reuter
Bd. Royal
R. Aldringen
R. Philippe II
Grand'rue
R. du Curé
R. de la Reine
R. de l'Eau
R. du St-Esprit
Bd. Vic. Thorn
R. Wiltheim
Corniche Montée de Clausen
Pl. d'Armes
Pl. Guillaume
Av. Monterey
R. Notre Dame
Pl. de Bruxelles
R. de l'Ancien Athénée
Pl. Claire-fontaine
Pl. de la Constitution
Chemin de la Corniche
Bd. F. D. Roosevelt
Pl. du St-Esprit
Alzette
R. Münster
Av. Marie Thérèse
Pétrusse
Bd. Adolphe
R. Goethe
Av. de la Liberté
Rue St-Ulric
Bd. d'Avranches

N

Old City. It is lined with as many of the duchy's 225 financial institutions as could be crowded into five blocks.

⑤ Casemates de la Pétrusse (Pétrusse casemates). During the many phases of the fortress-city's construction, the rock itself was hollowed out to form a honeycomb of underground passages. Those facing the Pétrusse Valley go back to the Spanish occupation during the 17th century. ⊠ *Pl. de la Constitution,* ☎ *222809.* ⊙ *Mar.–Oct., daily 10–5.*

⑥ Casino Luxembourg. Far from being a gaming establishment, this gracious hall, where Liszt played his last public concert, is now a gallery where contemporary art exhibitions are mounted. ⊠ *Rue Notre-Dame 41,* ☎ *225045.* ⊙ *Wed.–Mon. 11–6 (Thurs. until 8).*

④ Cathédrale Notre-Dame. Luxembourg's 17th-century cathedral is still the scene of national pilgrimage during the two weeks beginning on the third Sunday after Easter. It has an extravagantly carved portal and a fine Baroque organ gallery, both the work of Daniel Muller. In the crypt are the tombs of members of the present ruling dynasty as well as that of John the Blind (1296–1346), the gallant count of Luxembourg and king of Bohemia who fell at the Battle of Crécy in France during the Hundred Years' War. ⊠ *Rue Notre-Dame (Crypt entrance Bd. F. D. Roosevelt).* ☜ *Free.* ⊙ *Crypt: Easter–Oct., weekdays 10–5, Sat. 8–6, Sun. 10–6; Nov.–Easter, weekdays 10–11:30 and 2–5, Sat. 8–11:30 and 2–5, Sun. 10–5.*

③ Citadelle du St-Esprit (Citadel of the Holy Spirit). This 17th-century citadel was built during a French occupation by Maréchal Vauban (1633–1707), Louis XIV's chief military engineer, in the typical style of thrusting wedges. From the "prow" you have a panoramic view of the three spires of the cathedral, the Alzette River, and the white tower of the European Parliament secretariat. ⊠ *Plateau du St-Esprit.*

⑭ Église de St-Jean Baptiste (Church of St. John the Baptist). This Baroque church on the shore of the Alzette River was formerly part of a Benedictine abbey. Among its treasures are a cycle of the Stations of the Cross made of Limoges enamel and a Black Madonna once thought to provide protection against the plague. The riverside passageway outside the church has an awe-inspiring view of the cliffs. ⊠ *Rue Münster.*

⑨ Grand' Rue. The city's main upscale shopping street runs west to east from Boulevard Royal to Rue du Fossé. The pedestrian mall is lined with luxury boutiques and tempting patisseries, adding to the Luxembourg bourgeois touch.

⑩ Maquette de la Forteresse (Scale Model of the Fortress). This model is a copy of one (now in Paris) made of the fortress-city for Napoléon in 1804, when the fortified complex was at the peak of its glory. ⊠ *Rathskeller, Rue du Curé,* ☎ *222809.* ⊙ *School holidays (Easter wks, Whitsun wk, mid-July–mid-Sept.), daily 10–5.*

② Monument de la Solidarité Nationale (Monument to National Unity). Luxembourg was the only occupied country during World War II to stage a general strike against its occupiers. Hitler annexed the Grand Duchy and drafted its young men into the German army. This moving memorial honors Luxembourg's World War II casualties. Within the stark walls is a small, stained-glass chapel housing a symbolic tombstone. ⊠ *Kanounenhiwel, Plateau du St-Esprit.*

★ **⑫ Musée d'Histoire de la Ville de Luxembourg** (Luxembourg City Historical Museum). Oft postponed, this exciting, interactive museum opened in 1996 to rave reviews. It explores the wealth of the city's history over 1,000 years, and visitors are provided with electronic cards to use the many touch-sensitive screens in their language of choice. A marriage of ancient buildings and contemporary technology, the museum invites visitors to descend in time and space in a panoramic elevator the size of an exhibition hall. ⊠ *Rue du St-Esprit 14,* ☎ *229050–1 (direct information line).* ⊙ *Tues.–Sun. 10–6 (Thurs. 10–8).*

★ ⑮ **Le Natur Musée au Grund** (Museum of Natural History). Opened in 1996, the museum was formerly a women's prison. The building, dating from 1308, now houses collections and displays that explain the environment, past and present. The museum stands on the bank of the Alzette River in the heart of the **Grund**; to get here in comfort, take the elevator from the Plateau du St-Esprit. ⊠ *Rue Münster 23,* ☎ *462233–1 (direct information line).* ⊙ *Mid-Sept.–May, Tues.–Fri. 2–6, Sat. 10–6; June.–mid-Sept., Tues.–Sun. 10–6.*

⑪ **Palais Grand-Ducal** (Palace of the Grand Dukes). This restored palace is the city residence of the grand ducal family. Parts date from the 16th century, notably the section that once served as the town hall; a distinct Spanish-Moorish influence is obvious in the elaborate facade. Tickets for guided tours (often sold out) are available only at the City Tourist Office (☞ Visitor Information *in* Contacts and Resources, *below*). ⊠ *Rue du Marché-aux-Herbes.* ⊙ *Guided tours only; mid-July–mid-Aug., in English, Mon.–Fri. 1–4, Sat. 10.*

❼ **Place d'Armes.** Lined with symmetrical plane trees and strung with colored lights, this is the city's liveliest and most welcoming square. A bandstand (concerts are often held here on summer evenings), sidewalk cafés, fast-food joints, and a twice-monthly flea market constantly lure natives and tourists alike. From its southeast corner, a passage leads to the more dignified **Place Guillaume**, with the Hôtel de Ville (Town Hall); there's a farmers' market Wednesday and Saturday mornings. Next, continuing southeasterly, comes the elegant, sloping **Place Clairefontaine**, adorned with a graceful statue of the much-loved Grande Duchesse Charlotte, who ruled from 1919 to 1964.

⑯ **Plateau Kirchberg.** Several European Union institutions, some major banks, the country's new Auchan shopping center, and the 10-screen Utopolis cinema complex lie in this district. ⊠ *Across Grande Duchesse Charlotte Bridge. Bus 18 (direction Domaine du Kiem) from Bd. Royal loops around area.*

❶ **Viaduc.** The 19th-century bridge is also known as the *Passerelle* (footbridge), although it carries vehicular traffic from the railway station. A good starting point for exploring Luxembourg City, it spans the valley of the Pétrusse (now more a brook than a river), which has become a beautiful park. ⊠ *From Av. de la Gare to Plateau du St-Esprit.*

Dining and Lodging

Today, leading chefs are taking traditional Luxembourg specialties— *jambon d'Ardennes* (pearly pink raw-smoked ham served cold with pickled onions), *treipen* (blood pudding), and *écrevisses* (crayfish)—and giving them all a newer-than-now nouvelle spin. In the process, Luxembourg City is becoming a true capital *gastronomique*. Keep in mind that many upscale places offer a reasonably priced menu at lunch. For more details and price-category definitions, *see* Dining *in* Luxembourg A to Z, *above.*

Hotels in the city center are more convenient to exploring than those clustered around the train station. There are also large, modern hotels near the airport and on the Plateau Kirchberg. For details and price-category definitions, *see* Lodging *in* Luxembourg A to Z, *above.*

$$$$ ✕ **Clairefontaine.** The tastefully discreet luxury of this dining spot on
★ the city's most attractive square draws government ministers, visiting
dignitaries, and well-heeled gourmands. Chef-owner Tony Tintinger's
inspirations include foie gras specialties, innovative fish dishes (soufflé of langoustines perfumed with anise), and such game offerings as
tournedos of doe with wild mushrooms. ⊠ *Pl. de Clairefontaine 9,* ☎
*462211. Reservations essential. Jacket and tie. AE, DC, MC, V. Closed
Sun.–Mon., 3 wks in Aug., 1st wk in Nov. No lunch Sat.*

$$$ ✕ **Jan Schneidewind.** The chef-owner of this bandbox bistro serves ex-
★ cellent stuffed North Sea crab, panfried garlic-scented monkfish, and
other seafood specialties. In August, this is virtually the only top-rank
restaurant in town that stays open. ⊠ *Rue du Curé 20,* ☎ *222618.
AE, DC, MC, V. Closed Mon., Feb. No lunch weekends.*

$$$ ✕ **La Lorraine.** Outstanding seafood is the specialty of this restaurant
strategically situated on the Place d'Armes. A retail shop around the
corner shows off the freshness of its wares. Baked skate (in hazelnut
butter with capers) and puff pastry with sole and morels are good bets.
⊠ *Pl. d'Armes 7,* ☎ *474620. AE, DC, MC, V. Closed Sun., mid-Aug.–
Sept. 5.*

$$ ✕ **Club 5.** With a branch in the heart of the old town and another at
the Utopolis cinema complex on the Kirchberg, this is a popular restau-
rant with locals and visitors. In a relaxed French bistro setting the wait-
ers serve tasty dishes such as carpaccio. The tablecloths are brown paper
and come complete with crayons for diners to draw with. ⊠ *Rue du
Fossé 23,* ☎ *472973. MC, V. Closed Sun.*

$$ ✕ **Lëtzebuerger Kaschthaus.** One of the country's great chefs, Lea
★ Linster, owns this farmhouse-restaurant, which celebrates local culi-
nary traditions: green-bean soup, sweetbreads vol-au-vent, sausage
with savory lentils. Print linens, stenciled wallpaper, and ceramic flooring add up to a comfortable, retro setting. Its authenticity makes the
special trip 10 km (6 mi) south of the city worthwhile. ⊠ *Rte. de Bet-
tembourg 4, Hellange,* ☎ *516573. Reservations essential. AE, DC, MC,
V. Closed Tues., 3 wks in Aug./Sept. No lunch Mon.–Wed.*

$$ ✕ **Mousel's Cantine.** Right next to the great Mousel brewery, this
fresh, comfortable café serves up heaping platters of local specialties—
braised and grilled ham, sausage, broad beans, and fried potatoes—
accompanied by crockery steins of creamy *Gezwickelte Béier* (unfiltered
beer). ⊠ *Montée de Clausen 46,* ☎ *470198. MC, V. Closed Sun.*

$$ ✕ **Times.** On a pedestrian street of art galleries and boutiques you'll
also find excellent-value food. The narrow dining room lined with glass
and Canadian cherry wood is often crowded with artists and journalists. The cuisine tends toward ambitious creations that change daily,
such as fillet of suckling pig flavored with tea. ⊠ *Rue Louvigny 8,* ☎
222722. AE, V. Closed Sun.

$ ✕ **Ems.** Everybody in Luxembourg vies for one of the vinyl booths in
★ this unpretentious but lively establishment. Its vast portions of mussels in a rich wine-and-garlic broth are best accompanied by french fries
and a bottle of sharp, cold, and inexpensive Auxerrois or Rivaner. Ems
is open until 1 AM. Reservations are essential on weekends. ⊠ *Pl. de
la Gare 30,* ☎ *487799. AE, DC, MC, V. No lunch Sat.*

$ ✕ **Oberweis.** Luxembourg's most famous patisserie also serves light
lunches. You select your meal at the counter (quiche lorraine, spinach
pie, and the like), and it is served at your table. ⊠ *Grand'Rue 19–20,*
☎ *470703. Reservations not accepted. AE, DC, MC, V. Closed Sun.*

$$$$ 🏨 **Le Royal.** In the city center, on Luxembourg's Wall Street and within
★ steps of parks, shopping, and the Old Town, Le Royal is the best
choice for luxury. It's solid, modern, and sleek, with pleasant lobbies
on each floor. A wing added in 1997 has an exotic winter garden and
a deluxe restaurant, La Pomme Cannelle. ⊠ *Bd. Royal 12, L-2449,*

☎ 2416161, ℻ 225948. *190 rooms, 20 suites. 2 restaurants, bar, indoor pool, beauty salon, health club. AE, DC, MC, V.*

$$$ 🏨 **Cravat.** This charming Luxembourg relic straddles the valley and the Old Town in the best location in the city. Though corridors have a dated air, guest rooms are fresh and welcoming in a variety of tastefully retro styles. The Art Deco coffee shop has been freshened up but still draws fur-hatted ladies to tea. The prime minister and his cabinet may turn up in the hotel tavern on Friday afternoons. Buffet breakfast is included in the rate. ⊠ *Bd. F. D. Roosevelt 29, L-2450,* ☎ *221975,* ℻ *226711. 60 rooms. 2 restaurants. AE, DC, MC, V.*

$$$ 🏨 **Parc Belair.** This privately owned, family-run hotel a few blocks from the city center stands on the edge of the Parc de Merl. Rooms are a warm beige; those on the park are the quietest. The complex includes a separate restaurant with an outdoor café. A substantial buffet breakfast is included. The restaurant serves dinner only. ⊠ *Av. du X Septembre 109, L-2551,* ☎ *442323,* ℻ *444484. 52 rooms, 19 suites. Restaurant. AE, DC, MC, V.*

$$ 🏨 **Hotel le Châtelet.** At the edge of a quiet residential area, this pleasant hotel has stone and terra-cotta floors, double windows, Oriental rugs, and tropical plants. Rooms are furnished in knotty pine and have new tile baths. The three rooms in the adjoining annex cost slightly less. Breakfast is included. ⊠ *Bd. de la Pétrusse 2, L-2320,* ☎ *402101,* ℻ *403666. 40 rooms. Restaurant. AE, DC, MC, V.*

$$ 🏨 **Ibis.** The Luxembourg franchise of this French hotel chain is across the street from the airport, with direct access to the motorway. You can walk from the airport or call the hotel to send its free shuttle. Not strong on personality, it does provide honest value for the money. Family rooms sleeping up to four are available. The forest begins just behind the hotel. ⊠ *Rte. de Trèves, L-2632 Findel,* ☎ *438801,* ℻ *438802. 120 rooms. Restaurant. AE, DC, MC, V.*

$$ 🏨 **Italia.** This is a find: a former private apartment house converted into hotel rooms, some with plaster detailing and vintage cabinetry. Rooms are solid and freshly furnished, all with tile bathrooms. The restaurant downstairs is one of the city's better Italian eateries. ⊠ *Rue d'Anvers 15–17, L-1130,* ☎ *486626,* ℻ *480807. 20 rooms. Restaurant. AE, DC, MC, V.*

$$ 🏨 **La Cascade.** A turn-of-the-century villa has been converted into a
★ hotel of considerable charm and elegance. There's a good French restaurant and a lovely terrace overlooking the Alzette River. A bus stops outside to take you to the city center, just over 2 km (1 mi) away. ⊠ *Rue de Pulvermuhl 2, L-2356,* ☎ *428736,* ℻ *424788. 9 rooms. Restaurant. AE, DC, MC, V.*

$$ 🏨 **Sieweburen.** At the northwestern end of the city is this attractively rustic hotel, opened in 1991; the clean, large rooms have natural-wood beds and armoires. There's a playground in front and woods in the back. The brasserie-style tavern, older than the rest of the property, is hugely popular, especially when its terrace is open. ⊠ *Rue des Septfontaines 36, L-2534,* ☎ *442356,* ℻ *442353. 14 rooms. Restaurant. MC, V. Closed 3 wks late Dec.–early Jan.*

$ 🏨 **Carlton.** In this vast 1918 hotel near the train station, you'll find roomy, quiet quarters. The beveled glass and the oak parquet and terrazzo floors are original—but so are the toilets, all down the hall. Each room has antique beds, floral-print comforters, and a sink; wooden floors, despite creaks, are white-glove clean. ⊠ *Rue de Strasbourg 9, L-2561,* ☎ *299660,* ℻ *299664. 50 rooms without toilet, 8 with shower. No credit cards.*

Shopping

Luxembourg City's principal shopping areas comprise the **Grand'Rue** and its side streets, the recently revamped **Gare** area, and the **Auchan** shopping center on Kirchberg. Jewelry and designer fashions are particularly well represented. Luxembourg chocolates, called *knippercher,* are popular purchases at the best pastry shops. Luxembourg's most famous product is porcelain from **Villeroy & Boch** (⊠ Rue du Fossé 2, ☏ 463343). Feast your eyes on their tableware, crystal, and cutlery at the glitzy main store, then buy—at a 20% discount—at the excellent second-quality factory outlet to the northwest of the city center (⊠ Rue Rollingergrund 330, ☏ 468211).

Side Trips

The northern highlands that comprise the celebrated Ardennes plateau were the hunting ground of emperors and dukes and have been fought over from time immemorial to World War II. Castles punctuate its hills and dominate the valleys; rocky rivers and streams pour off its slopes. In contrast, the Petite Suisse, to the northeast of the capital, presents a more smiling face. It's a hilly area of leafy woods, rushing brooks, and old farms, ideal for rustic picnics and great hiking. An easy hour's drive from Luxembourg City will take you to any of the towns except Clervaux, which is a bit farther.

Diekirch

In the Ardennes, Diekirch has a lovely little Romanesque church, **Eglise St-Laurent** (St. Lawrence's), with Merovingian tombs, and (south of town) the **Devil's Altar,** a Celtic dolmen. The **Musée National d'Histoire Militaire** (National Military History Museum) mainly commemorates the Battle of the Bulge, the last German counteroffensive, which began just before Christmas, 1944. ⊠ *Bamertal 10,* ☏ *808908.* ⏲ *Apr.– Oct., daily 10–6; Nov.–Mar., daily 2–6.*

Vianden

★ The medieval **Château de Vianden** is the most romantic sight in the Grand Duchy. Rearing up on a hill above the tiny village, and replete with conical spires and massive bulwarks, it vividly recalls Luxembourg's feudal past. This was the last bit of Luxembourg soil to be liberated by U.S. troops toward the end of World War II. ⊠ *Grand'Rue,* ☏ *849291.* ⏲ *Apr.–Sept., daily 10–6; Mar. and Oct., daily 10–5; Nov.– Feb., daily 10–4.*

Clervaux

Surrounded by deep-cleft hills, the town is noted for the 12th-century **Château de Clervaux,** which has become the permanent home for Luxembourg-born Edward Steichen's "Family of Man," arguably the greatest photographic exhibit ever assembled. Franklin Delano Roosevelt's ancestor, Philip de Lannoi, set forth from this castle in 1621 to seek his fortune in America. ⊠ *Grand'Rue,* ☏ *522–4241.* ⏲ *Mar.– Dec., Tues.–Sun. 10–6.*

Bourscheid

★ The romantic ruins of the **Château de Bourscheid** loom 500 ft above the River Sûre, commanding three valleys. Restorations have made the rambling towers and walls more accessible. ⊠ *Bourscheid Moulin-Plage,* ☏ *990570.* ⏲ *Apr., daily 11–5; May–June and Sept., daily 10–6; July– Aug., daily 10–7; Oct., daily 11–4; Nov.–Mar., weekends 11–4.*

Echternach

Echternach's cobbled market square is a mix of Gothic arcades and medieval town houses. The River Sûre here forms the border with Germany, and large numbers of tourists cross over on weekends. Some 15,000 pilgrims participate every year in a dancing procession on the Tuesday after Pentecost, ending at the **Basilique St-Willibrord,** whose crypt, open daily 9:30–6:30, contains the tomb of the great English missionary St. Willibrord (658–739). Painstakingly detailed reproductions of the illuminated manuscripts of the Echternach School are displayed in the **Musée de l'Abbaye** (Abbey Museum). ⊠ *Parvis de la Basilique 11,* ☎ *727472.* ⊙ *Apr.–Oct., daily 10–noon and 2–6; Nov.–Mar., weekends 2–5.*

Moselle

On the eastern border with Germany, this wide river turns into Luxembourg's seaside come the summer months with promenading and jet skiing. The banks of the river are covered with vineyards where the Luxembourg Moselle wine and sparkling wine (crement) are grown. Famous for sparkling wines, the **Bernard Massard** cellars are open for tours and tastings. ⊠ *8, rue Pont, Grevenmacher,* ☎ *7505451.* ⊙ *Daily 9:30–6.*

The valley can be best appreciated from aboard the **MS *Princess Marie-Astrid,*** which cruises along the Moselle. ⊠ *Rte. du Vin 10, Grevenmacher,* ☎ *758275.*

Luxembourg City Essentials

Arriving and Departing

BY PLANE

All international flights arrive at Luxembourg's **Findel Airport,** 6 km (4 mi) northeast of the city.

Between the Airport and Downtown. Bus 9 links the airport, the city center, and the main bus depot, next to the train station. Tickets cost Flux 40. A taxi costs Flux 700–Flux 800. If you are driving, follow the signs for the CENTRE VILLE (city center).

BY TRAIN

Luxembourg is served by frequent direct trains from Paris (four hours) and Brussels (three hours). From Amsterdam (six hours), the journey is via Brussels. There are connections from most German cities via Koblenz. Outside Luxembourg City, three major train routes extend to the north, south, and east. All services are from the **Gare Centrale** (☎ 4990–4990).

Getting Around

BY BICYCLE

Bicycling is an excellent way to see the city and outlying areas. Bikes can be rented in Luxembourg City at **Velo en Ville** (⊠ Bisserwee 8, ☎ 4796–2383) from April through October.

BY BUS

Luxembourg City has highly efficient bus service (for information: Aldringen Center, underground station off Boulevard Royal; 10-ride ticket, Flux 320).

BY CAR

On-street parking in Luxembourg City is difficult. If you're in Luxembourg for a day, use one of the underground parking lots or park at the Parking Glacis next to the Municipal Theater, five minutes' walk from the city center. If you arrive from the west, use the free Parking Stade (opposite the Stadium) on Route d'Arlon and take the shuttle bus (Flux 40) to town. If you arrive from France, look for the park-and-ride facility Sud; from Germany, look for Kirchberg-FIL. You need local currency for the bus ride.

Taxi (☎ 480058 or 482233) stands are near the Gare Centrale and the main post office; it is almost impossible to hail one in the street.

Contacts and Resources

EMBASSIES

U.S. (✉ Bd. Emmanuel Servais 22, ☎ 460123). **Canadian:** In Belgium (✉ Av. de Tervuren 2, 1040 Brussels, ☎ 00322/741–0611). **Irish** (✉ 28 Rte. D' Arlon, ☎ 450610). **U.K.** (✉ Bd. F. D. Roosevelt 14, ☎ 229864).

EMERGENCIES

Police (☎ 113). **Ambulance, Doctor, Dentist** (☎ 112). **Pharmacies** in Luxembourg stay open nights on a rotation system; see signs listing late-night facilities outside each pharmacy.

ENGLISH-LANGUAGE BOOKS

For books and magazines in English, try **Magasin Anglais** (✉ Allée Scheffer 13, ☎ 224925). The English-language paper, *Luxembourg News,* published on Thursdays, is available from newsagents in the city.

GUIDED TOURS

Orientation. Sales-Lentz (☎ 461818–1) runs 2¼-hour city bus tours, April–mid-November, from the war memorial on Place de la Constitution and from the bus station, as well as a 4¾-hour tour to Château de Vianden on weekends May–September. A guided walking tour called "City Promenade" (☎ 222809), held November–Easter, Monday, Wednesday, Saturday, and Sunday at 2, leaves from Place d'Armes. **Pétrusse Express** (☎ 461617) guided mini-train tours of the Old Town and the Pétrusse Valley operate from the Place de la Constitution April–October.

★ **Special Interest.** The **Wenzel Walk** allows visitors to experience 1,000 years of history in 100 minutes. The walk starts at the Bock promontory and leads over medieval bridges and past ancient ruins. The City Tourist Office (☞ Visitor Information, *below*) can provide a guide.

Self-Guided Tours. The **Luxembourg Card** provides admission to 31 major attractions in the capital and countryside and use of public transport throughout the Grand Duchy. For one person it costs Flux 350 for one day, 600 for two days, and 850 for three days; family cards are twice the price. Cards can be bought in hotels and tourist offices.

TRAVEL AGENCIES

BBL Travel American Express (✉ 3 rue Jean Piret, ☎ 4924041). **Carlson/Wagonlit** (✉ Grand'Rue 105, ☎ 460315). **Connections** (including youth travel; ✉ Grand'Rue 70, ☎ 229933).

VISITOR INFORMATION

Luxembourg City Tourist Office (✉ Pl. d'Armes, ☎ 222809). **Beaufort** (✉ Rue de l'Eglise 9, ☎ 836081). **Bourscheid** (✉ Château, ☎ 990564). **Clervaux** (✉ Château, ☎ 920072). **Diekirch** (✉ Esplanade 1, ☎ 803023). **Echternach** (✉ Porte St-Willibrord, Basilique, ☎ 720230). **Vianden** (✉ Maison Victor Hugo, Rue de la Gare 37, ☎ 834257).

20 MALTA

VALLETTA, AROUND THE ISLANDS

Hulking megalithic temples, ornate Baroque churches, narrow old-world streets, and hilltop citadels are Malta's human legacy. Dizzying limestone cliffs, sparkling Mediterranean seas, and charming rural landscapes make up its natural beauty. Its three main islands—Malta, Gozo, and Comino—offer history, swimming, spectacular coastal views, and culinary delights.

In its 7,000 years of human habitation, Malta has been overrun by every major Mediterranean power: Phoenicians, Carthaginians, Romans, Byzantines, and Arabs; French, Germans, Aragonians, and the Knights of the Order of St. John of Jerusalem; Napoleon, the British, and now European tourists. The Germans and Italians tried to take it in World War II—their air raids were devastating—but could not.

The islands' history with the Knights of the Order of St. John has given them their lasting character. Charles V of Spain, 410 years before the Axis powers' assault, granted Malta to the Knights after the Ottoman Turks chased the military order of hospitalers out of Rhodes. In 1565, when the forces of Suleyman the Magnificent laid siege to the islands, it was the Knights' turn, with the faithful backing of the Maltese, to send the Turks packing.

The handsome limestone buildings and fortifications that the wealthy Knights left behind are all around the islands. Malta has plenty of modern development, too—all the more reason to stick to the historic sights on Malta and head to quieter Gozo to relax and to enjoy the sea. You'll need at least four days to see Malta and Gozo; allow two or more for taking in Malta's splendid past, then make your way to Gozo for a few days of the good life.

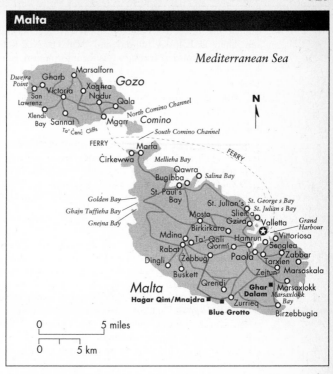

MALTA A TO Z

Customs

You may bring into Malta, duty-free, 200 cigarettes, one bottle of liquor, one bottle of wine, and one bottle of perfume. Up to Lm 50 in currency may be brought in.

Dining

Traditional Maltese cuisine is Sicilian and Moorish in origin, but Italian food is on most restaurant menus as well. Locally caught fish is a specialty. The national dish is *fenek* (rabbit); *braġjoli* (beef olives) and *lampuki* (fish) pie are runners-up. Pastry coats fish, vegetables, cheese, and pasta dishes. Soups, *minestra* (minestrone) and *aljotta* (fish soup) especially, are common, delicious with daily baked crusty Maltese bread. Capers, the buds of the *caperis specicum* shrub that is native to the islands, are widely used. Native wine is abundant and inexpensive; look for medium-dry whites. Cisk lager is a local favorite, and try Hop Leaf pale ale for something with a bit more bite.

RATINGS

Prices are per person for a three-course meal, not including wine and tip.

CATEGORY	COST
$$$$	over Lm 10
$$$	Lm 7–Lm 10
$$	Lm 4–Lm 7
$	under Lm 4

WHAT TO WEAR

A jacket and tie are appropriate in higher-priced restaurants. Otherwise, casual dress is acceptable. Skirts covering the knees or pants and covered shoulders are appropriate attire for churches.

Guided Tours

Sightseeing tours are arranged by local travel agents and the large hotels. There are half-day, full-day, and "Malta by Night" bus tours; rates vary. Contact tourist offices (☞ Visitor Information, *below,* and in Valletta *and* Gozo and Comino Essentials, *below*) for details. **Malta Air Charter** (☎ 557905 or 662211) runs helicopter tours of the islands. Beware of cheap tours: Officially licensed guides should wear an identification tag.

Language

English and Malti, a Semitic language with Roman script, are the official languages. Malti pronunciations are as follows: *ċ* = ch (as in Ċirkewwa), *ġ* = j (Ħaġar), *ħ* = a barely perceptible h (Hal Saflieni), *j* = y (Dwejra), *M*=im (Mdina), *x*=sh (Marsaxlokk), *ż* = ts (Żebbuġ), and the plain *g* and *q* are silent, as in Għarb ("arb") and Ħaġar Qim ("*ha*jar eem").

Lodging

Aside from the larger resort hotels in Buġibba and Sliema, quality accommodations in Malta can be difficult to find. Often, the inexpensive lodgings are run down, the mid-priced scarce, and the high-end inconsistent and short on service. Malta's tourist office (☞ Visitor Information, *below*) has a brochure listing all hotels and apartment hotels on the islands. On Gozo the best bet is to rent a farmhouse or villa where you can fix your own meals. The limestone houses can be anywhere from 300 years to one month old; newer ones tend to be on the edges of towns. Insist on clear photographs and details in writing before sending a deposit.

RATINGS

Prices are for two people sharing a double room.

CATEGORY	COST
$$$$	over Lm 50
$$$	Lm 25–Lm 50
$$	Lm 12–Lm 25
$	under Lm 12

Mail

Airmail letters to the United States and Canada cost 22¢; postcards cost 22¢. Airmail letters and postcards to the United Kingdom cost 16¢.

Money Matters

COSTS

Malta is among the least expensive holiday destinations in Europe, though with the rapid development of tourism, prices are inevitably rising. Prices in Sliema and in Valletta, the capital, are slightly higher than those elsewhere in the islands.

CURRENCY

The unit of currency is the Maltese lira (Lm), also sometimes referred to as the pound; it's divided into 100 cents. There are Lm 2, 5, 10, and 20 bills. The 1¢ coin is bronze, and other coins—2¢, 5¢, 10¢, 25¢, 50¢, and Lm 1—are silver. At press time (summer 1999) the exchange rate was Lm 0.41 to the U.S. dollar, Lm 0.28 to the Canadian dollar, Lm 0.64 to the pound sterling, Lm 0.27 to the Australian dollar, Lm 0.22 to the New Zealand dollar, and 0.53 to the Irish punt.

SAMPLE PRICES

In Maltese currency: a cup of coffee, 35¢; a bottle of beer, 35¢; a soft drink, 30¢; a sandwich, 90¢; an individual pizza, Lm 1.70.

A tip of 10% is expected when a service charge is not included.

National Holidays

January 1; February 10 (St. Paul's Shipwreck); March 19 (St. Joseph's Day); March 31 (Freedom Day); April 21 (Good Friday); May 1 (Worker's Day); June 7 (Commemoration of First Maltese Nationalist Protest); June 29 (Sts. Peter and Paul); August 15 (Assumption, or Santa Marija); September 8 (Our Lady of Victories); September 21 (Independence Day); December 8 (Immaculate Conception); December 13 (Republic Day); December 25.

Opening and Closing Times

Banks are generally open Monday–Saturday 8–2; from June through August they're open Friday until 4. Banks in tourist areas also stay open weekdays until 4 from June through August. The currency-exchange booth at the airport is open 24 hours, and there are ATMs in tourist areas. **Museums** run by Malta's Museums Department (☎ 233821) are open as follows: October–mid-June, Monday–Saturday 8–5; Sunday 8–4:15; mid-June–September, daily 7:45–2. Gozo museums: October–March, Monday–Saturday 8:30–4:30, Sunday 8:30–3; April–mid-June and mid–end September, Monday–Saturday 8:30–6:30, Sunday 8:30–3; mid-June–mid-September, Monday–Saturday 8:30–7, Sunday 8:30–3. All museums are closed on public holidays. Other museums' hours may vary slightly, so check locally. **Shops** are open Monday–Saturday 9–1 and 4–7.

Telephoning

COUNTRY CODE
The country code for Malta is 356.

INTERNATIONAL CALLS
Overseas operator, 194. **International dialing access code,** 00. For an **AT&T** long-distance operator, dial 0800–890110.

LOCAL CALLS
Operator, 190. Public phones are mostly operated by phone cards, which may be purchased at many shops for Lm 2 and Lm 3.

Transportation

BY BOAT
Daily car and passenger **ferries** (☎ 243964 in Malta, ☎ 556114 or ☎ 556743 in Gozo) run year-round from Ċirkewwa (northwest Malta) to Mġarr Harbor on Gozo. One service leaves weekdays from Pietà (near Valletta) for Gozo. Commuter ferry service links Sliema to Valletta. An express **hydrofoil** service operates from Pietà.

BY BUS
Most routes across the island start at Valletta (Terminal: ✉ Triton Fountain Sq., just outside main City Gate, ☎ 225916). Local fares on Malta's colorful fleet of new and retro buses are remarkably cheap: 11¢ for most trips, 13¢ for longer rides. With the help of the tourism bureau's map of the islands, on which bus routes are marked, and the Public Transportation Association's (☎ 250007/8) schedule listing the stops for each bus number (plus a little bit of luck) you can get almost anywhere on the island.

BY CAR
Driving is on the left, and in spite of the well-signposted routes, challenging. Speed limits are 40 kph (25 mph) in towns, 65 kph (40 mph) elsewhere. British driver's licenses are acceptable; Americans must have international licenses.

Malta Air Charter (☎ 557905 or 662211) makes the 10-minute flight
to and from Gozo several times daily.

Visitor Information

National Tourism Organization–Malta (⊠ 280 Republic St., Valletta CMR
02, ☎ 224444/5).

Weather

Late April into June and late September through October have pleasantly warm weather, and the sea is delightful. Mid-June to early September can be too hot for comfort; November through March tends to be
cool and occasionally rainy.

CLIMATE
The following are the average daily maximum and minimum temperatures for Valletta.

Jan.	58F	14C	**May**	71F	22C	**Sept.**	81F	27C
	50	10		61	16		7	22
Feb.	59F	15C	**June**	79F	26C	**Oct.**	75F	24C
	51	11		67	19		66	19
Mar.	61F	16C	**July**	84F	29C	**Nov.**	67F	20C
	52	11		72	22		60	16
Apr.	65F	18C	**Aug.**	85F	29C	**Dec.**	61F	16C
	56	13		73	23		54	12

VALLETTA

Malta's capital, the minicity of Valletta, has ornate palaces and museums protected by massive fortifications of honey-color stone. Houses
along the narrow streets have overhanging wooden balconies for people-watching from indoors. Generations ago they gave housebound
women a window on the world of the street.

Exploring Valletta

The main entrance to town is through the City Gate (where all bus routes
end), which leads onto Triq Repubblika (Republic Street), the spine of
the grid-pattern city and the main shopping street. Triq Sala Mercante
(Merchant Street) parallels Repubblika to the east and is also good for
strolling. From these two streets, cross streets descend toward the
water; some are stepped. Valletta's compactness makes it ideal to explore on foot. Before setting out along Republic Street, stop at the tourist
information office (just inside the city gate) for maps, brochures, and
a copy of *What's On.*

Barrakka ta' Fuq (Upper Barrakka Gardens). Where Knights once
honed their fencing skills under a covered loggia (now open to the sky),
a troupe of cats and some greenery occupy this lofty lookout over the
Grand Harbor and the Three Cities across the water. ⊠ *Southeastern
heights of city off Castile Sq.* ☉ *Dawn to dusk.*

★ **Casa Rocca Piccola.** The exquisitely cultured current owners, Nicolas
and Frances De Piro d'Amico Inguanez, host tours of the last of the
patrician houses still nobly occupied. The treasures inside chart the history of the house, from a portable Baroque chapel for baptisms to a
painting of "Miss Electricity," commissioned to mark the local contribution of an ambitious ancestor. ⊠ *74 Triq Repubblika,* ☎ *231796.*
☉ *Guided tours Mon.–Sat. 10, 11, noon, 1.*

Forti Sant'Iermu (Fort St. Elmo). Built in 1552 by the knights to defend the harbor, it was completely destroyed during the siege of 1565 and rebuilt by succeeding military leaders. Today part of the fort houses the **War Museum** (☏ 222430), with its collection of military objects related to World War II, including an Italian E-Boat and one of the three Gloster Gladiator biplanes that defended the island. ⊠ *St. Elmo Pl., Valletta. Fort:* ☏ *226400.* ▱ *Free.* ☉ *Fort: Mid-June–Sept., daily 7:45–2; Oct.–mid-June, Mon.–Sat. 8:15–5, Sun. 8:15–4:15. Museum:* ☞ *Opening and Closing Times in Malta A to Z, above.*

★ **Konkatidral ta' San Gwann** (St. John's co-Cathedral). Functional in design but lavishly decorated, the Order of St. John's own church (1578) is Malta's most important treasure. The Knights' colored-marble tombstones on the floor are gorgeous. Each of the side chapels was decorated by a national hostel of the Knights. Many of the paintings and the decoration scheme are by the island's beloved 17th-century painter Mattia Preti (b. 1613). The cathedral **museum** has illuminated manuscripts and a rich collection of Flemish tapestries. ⊠ *Pjazza San Gwann.* ☉ *Weekdays 9:30–4:30, weekends 9:30–1.*

Manoel Theater. If you are here in opera season, don't miss a show at the third-oldest theater in Europe, which had its opening night on January 9, 1732. Intimate and splendidly decorated, it was designed after Palermo's theater at the time. ⊠ *Old Theater St. at Old Bakery St.,* ☏ *246389.* ☉ *Guided tours weekdays 10:45 and 11:30, Sat. 11:30.*

★ **Muzew Arkejologiku** (National Museum of Archaeology). Housed in the Auberge de Provence (the hostel of the knights from Provence), the museum has an excellent collection of finds from Malta's many prehistoric sites—Tarxien, Haġar Qim, and the Hypogeum at Paola. ⊠ *Triq Repubblika,* ☏ *233821.* ☉ ☞ *Opening and Closing Times in Malta A to Z, above.*

★ **Palazz tal-Gran Mastri** (Grand Masters' Palace). Malta's parliament meets here, and Malta's president sometimes uses one of the palace rooms. Completed in 1574, the palace has a unique collection of Gobelin tapestries; the main hall is decorated with frescoes depicting the history of the knights and the Great Siege. On view are works by Ribera, Van Loo, and Batoni. At the back of the building is the **Armoury of the Knights,** with exhibits of arms and armor down through the ages. ⊠ *Palace Sq., Triq Repubblika,* ☏ *221221.* ☉ ☞ *Opening and Closing Times in Malta A to Z, above.*

Sacra Infermeria (Hospital of the Knights). This gracious building near the seawall has been converted into the Mediterranean Conference Center. For an introduction to the island, see the "Malta Experience," a multimedia presentation on the history of Malta that is given here daily on the hour. ⊠ *Mediterranean St.,* ☏ *243776.* ☉ *Weekdays 9–4.*

★ **San Pawl Nawfragu** (St. Paul's Shipwreck Church). The importance of the Apostle Paul to the Maltese explains the work lavished on this Baroque marvel—its raised central vault, oval dome, and marble columns. The *os brachii* (arm bone) relic of San Pawl is in a chapel on the right, a splendid gated chapel is on the left, and a baptismal font stands by the door. ⊠ *Triq San Pawl just north of Triq Santa Lucija.* ☉ ☞ *Opening and Closing Times in Malta A to Z, above.*

Dining and Lodging

$$$$ ✕ **The Carriage.** It feels like a prohibition-era secret when you ride the private elevator to the top floor, where you seem to be joining a stylish international party. Window tables have splendid views. Warm service

brings you ambitious fare that sometimes disappoints. ✉ *22/5 Valletta Buildings, South St.,* ☎ *247828. Reservations essential. Jacket and tie. AE, DC, MC, V. Closed Sun., Mon. No dinner Tues., Wed. No lunch Sat.*

$$$ ✗ **Giannini.** Atop the quiet west end of Valletta's mighty bastions, this is among the city's most reserved and elegant restaurants. Leading politicians and the fashionable set dine here on haute Maltese-Italian cuisine. There is a lounge downstairs; the restaurant is on the fifth floor. ✉ *23 Windmill St.,* ☎ *237121. Reservations essential. AE, DC, MC, V. No dinner Sun.–Thurs., no lunch weekends.*

$$ ✗ **Caffe Cordina.** On the ground floor of the original treasury of the
★ Knights is Malta's finest café. Since 1837, this ornate, vaulted confectionery has produced hot, savory breakfast pastries, *Gaquata-ghasel* (honey rings), and dozens of other mouthwatering treats—as well as the best espresso and cappuccino on the island. ✉ *244/45 Triq Republika,* ☎ *234385. AE, DC, MC, V.*

$$ ✗ **Trattoria Palazz.** In a golden limestone cellar beneath the city's public library, which the Knights of Malta built over 270 years ago, this tiny, romantic hideaway cooks up tasty Maltese/Italian dishes. Specials and recommendations are your best bet here. ✉ *43 Old Theater St.,* ☎ *226611. Reservations essential. AE, DC, MC, V. Closed Sun.*

$ ✗ **Lantern.** Two brothers run this friendly spot. The interior of the 18th-century town house on Valletta's western heights is spare but chummy, and the traditional Maltese food is flavorful. ✉ *20 Sappers St.,* ☎ *237521. V. Closed Sun.*

$ ✗ **Pizzeria Bologna.** This very casual spot serves delicious pizza and at lunch creative sandwiches on local *ftjra* ("ftee-ra," a wide sandwich roll)—with what the owner calls the "freshest and finest quality food possible." ✉ *60 Triq Repubblika,* ☎ *238014. No credit cards. Closed Sun.*

$$$$ 🏨 **Hotel Phoenicia.** The grande dame of Malta is just outside Valletta's City Gate and across from the busy bus terminus. Nonetheless, you can enjoy attractive lounges, a stunning dining room, and very well-appointed guest rooms (standard rooms can be small). Service is inconsistent—from professional to haughty and surly. ✉ *The Mall, Floriana VLT 16,* ☎ *225241,* 🖷 *235254. 136 rooms. 2 restaurants, 2 bars, pool, shops. AE, DC, MC, V.*

$$ 🏨 **Castille.** In a 16th-century former palazzo, this slightly worn—sagging mattresses and not-so-nice bathrooms—hotel is by far the best bet for inexpensive accommodations in Valletta. Rooms are spacious, with good windows, and the staff is friendly. Book at least three months ahead. ✉ *Castille Sq., VLT 07,* ☎ *243677 or 243678,* 🖷 *243679. 38 rooms. Rooftop restaurant, café. AE, DC, MC, V.*

$$ 🏨 **Osborne.** In budget-hotel-starved Valletta, the Osborne provides a foothold within the city walls. The spacious lounge downstairs and the rooftop sundeck are filled with adventuresome European travelers, but the rooms are smoked-in, dark, and worn. ✉ *50 South St., VLT 11,* ☎ *243656,* 🖷 *232120. 60 rooms. Restaurant. AE, DC, V.*

Shopping

Valletta's main shopping street, **Triq Repubblika,** is lined with touristy shops—pick up postcards and film here, then venture onto side streets for a look at everyday Maltese wares. The **Government Craft Center** (✉ Pjazza San Gwann) has traditional handmade goods. At the **open-air market** (Triq Sala Mercate), with some haggling you may snap up a good bargain.

Valletta Essentials

Arriving and Departing

BY BOAT

Virtú (☎ 318854, FAX 345221) runs express passenger ferries (Lm 21–Lm 36) most days of the week between Malta and Catania, Syracusa, and Pozzallo (separately) on Sicily. Summer and winter schedules vary.

BY PLANE

Air Malta runs a weekly direct flight from New York in conjunction with **Balkan Airlines** and, along with several other airlines, regular flights from London, Paris, Frankfurt, Athens, and Rome to Luqa Airport (☎ 249600), 6 km (4 mi) south of Valletta.

Between the Airport and Downtown. Local Bus 8 (11¢) passes through Luqa on its way to Valletta, with a stop at the airport every 10 or 15 minutes. Taxis (Lm 8–Lm 10) are also available.

Getting Around

BY BUS

Bus 98 (11¢) circles the perimeter of the city every hour from the terminus by the City Gate. Buses do not run on streets within the city.

BY TAXI

Metered taxis are plentiful. Be sure the meter is switched on when your trip starts, or bargain first. Tip the driver 10%.

Contacts and Resources

CONSULATES AND HIGH COMMISSIONS

U.S. Embassy (✉ 2nd floor, Development House, St. Anne St., Floriana, ☎ 235960).

BRITISH HIGH COMMISSION

(✉ 7 St. Anne St., Floriana, ☎ 233134).

EMERGENCIES

Police (☎ 191). **Ambulance** (☎ 196). **Fire Brigade** (☎ 199). **Hospital: St. Luke's** (✉ Gwardamangia, ☎ 241251).

GUIDED TOURS

Orientation. One-hour boat tours of Valletta's Grand Harbour leave regularly from Sliema jetty. Buy tickets at most travel agencies or on the boat.

Personal Guides. Licensed guides can be hired through local travel agencies.

TRAVEL AGENCIES

American Express (representative; ✉ Brockdorff, 14 Zachary St., Valletta, ☎ 232141). **Thomas Cook** (✉ Il-Pjazzetta, Tower Rd., Sliema, ☎ 344225). Local agencies have desks at most hotels.

VISITOR INFORMATION

Valletta (✉ 1 City Gate Arcade, ☎ 237747; ✉ Luqa Airport, ☎ 249600; or ✉ 280 Republic St., ☎ 224444 or 228282). **St. Julian's** (✉ Ballutta Bay, ☎ 342671 or 342672).

AROUND MALTA

The conurbation around Valletta varies in character. The Three Cities area has its old-world charms, while the semi-urban sprawl of Sliema and St. Julian's is becoming increasingly commercialized with new hotels and expanding shopping areas. Southern and eastern Malta has prehistoric sites, as well as the stunning cliffs and waters around the Blue Grotto. The ancient and silent walled city of Mdina rises out of the center of the island. On the way to the ferry on the northwest end, parallel rift valleys alternate fertile terrain with barren, exposed hills, and sandy or rocky coastline. Alas, the cities in this direction, such as Buġibba, Qawra, and Mellieha, have largely been done in by interchangeable international resorts with no real Maltese character.

The Three Cities

East across the Grand Harbor from Valletta, the three cities of **Vittoriosa, Senglea,** and **Conspicua** are where the Knights of the Order of St. John first settled—and where crucial fighting took place in the Great Siege of the Turks in 1565. Vittoriosa, also called Birgu, is named for the victory over the Turkish navy. The 5 km (3 mi) of great walls around the cities are the Cotonera Lines, built in the 1670s.

In **Vittoriosa/Birgu** in early October, hundreds of actors stage a Grand Master's crossing of the harbor and monastery doors on Triq San Lawrenz open to the public for the **Birgu Festa.** On the narrow streets north of the main square you can loop from the Triq La Vallette to the Triq Majjistral on the right. Triq It-Tramuntana takes you past Baroque doorways, the Knights' Auberge d'Angleterre (Inn of England), and a Saracen-style house that is thought to be from the 1200s.

Below Birgu's main square, **Knisja ta' San Lawrenz** is the city's finest church, with the 17th-century painter Mattia Preti's *Martyrdom of San Lawrenz.* ⊠ *Triq San Lawrenz.*

The displays in Birgu's **Il-Palazz Ta l-Inkwizitur** (Inquisitor's Palace) reveal less-discussed aspects of less-tolerant times in Malta. ⊠ *Triq San Lawrenz.*

At the tip of **Senglea, Gardjola Garden,** once a high fort, has great views and a turret carved with a vigilant eye and ear.

Sliema and St. Julian's

Sliema's shoreline is an almost-flashy commercial strip, and is Malta's best spot for designer clothes shopping. St. Julian's Bay has a number of excellent Italian restaurants and waterfront cafés. Heavily trafficked Paceville, just beyond St. Julian's, is where Malta's club-goers party at night. The town of Ta' Xbiex is equipped for yachts.

$$$$ ✕ **Barracuda.** Perched precariously on columns and commanding a superb view of St. Julian's Bay, this old house holds one of Malta's most delightful and efficiently run restaurants. Seafood is the drawing card here—choose from a variety caught the same day served with such sauces as cucumber and mint or tomatoes, black olives, and capers. ⊠ *194/ 5 Main St., St. Julian's,* ☎ FAX *331817. AE, DC, MC, V.*

$$$$ ✕ **San Giuliano.** The large, second-story dining room overlooking Spinola Bay in St. Julian's permits some of the swankiest dining in Malta. The Italian chef prepares a delicious array of antipasti and knows that truly fresh fish caught the same day needs little fussing. ⊠ *Spinola Bay, St. Julian's,* ☎ *332000. Reservations essential. AE, DC, MC, V. No lunch Mon.*

$$ ✕ **Ta' Kolina.** The only point of culinary interest on Sliema's waterfront, this untrendy spot serves traditional Maltese dishes—such as *timpana* (baked pasta covered with pastry), fresh cheese salad, braġjoli, and octopus. ⊠ *151 Tower Rd., Sliema,* ☎ *335106. AE, DC, MC, V. No lunch.*

Paola and Tarxien

★ Here the **Hal Saflieni Hypogeum,** a massive labyrinth of underground chambers, was used for burials more than 4,000 years ago. Many of the chambers are decorated with red ocher or fine carvings. ⊠ *On road to Santa Licija,* ☎ *233821.* ☉ *By appointment.*

The three interconnecting **Tarxien Temples** have curious carvings, oracular chambers, and altars, all dating from about 2800 BC. Nearby are remains of an earlier temple from about 4000 BC. ✉ *Behind Paola's Church of Christ the King.* ✆ ☞ *Opening and Closing Times* in *Malta A to Z, above.*

Marsaxlokk

At the fishing and resort town Marsaxlokk on the southeast coast you can see the *luz zu,* Malta's multicolored, traditional fishing boat. Its vertical prow has Phoenician ancestry.

$$ ✕ **Ix-Xlukkajr.** Seafood is the draw at the seemingly unpronounceable, harborside "Ish-Shlu-Kayre." Octopus marinated in garlic sauce is a wonderful cold starter. Try the whole-fish specials and for dessert, homemade prickly pear and kiwi ice creams. ✉ *Village Sq.,* ☎ *612109. MC, V. Closed Wed.*

Għar Dalam

The semifossilized remains of long-extinct species of dwarf elephants and hippopotamuses that roamed the island some 125,000 years ago were found in a **cave** here. The fossils are now on display in the small **museum** (☞ Opening and Closing Times *in* Malta A to Z, *above*).

Għajn Tuffieħa Bay

This secluded sandy beach on the northwestern side of Malta is wonderful for a calm afternoon by the sea. The sometimes bumpy bus (routes 47 and 52) ride takes you through the rolling countryside, which is patchworked with ancient stone walls and occasional fields of root crops.

Zurrieq

On the way to Zurrieq from Valletta you will pass limestone quarries, where fruit tree orchards are planted, protected from the wind, after the limestone is exhausted. On the far side of town, **Wied-iz-Zurrieq** (Zurrieq valley) runs along the road to a lookout over the towering walls of the Blue Grotto's bay. Across the water, tiny **Filfla,** flat-topped from British Air Force target practice, is the smallest of the Maltese islands.

★ The turnoff for the **Blue Grotto** is 1 km (½ mi) beyond the lookout. A steep road takes you to the rocky inlet where noisy boats (Lm 2.50) leave for the grottoes (there are many) and the stained-glass-blue waters that splash their walls. Bring a bathing suit in case the water is calm enough for swimming. ✉ *Coast Rd.*

★ The 4,800-year-old **Haġar Qim** ("ha-jar eem") gives a clear picture of the massive scale of Malta's ancient sandstone temples. The altars are well preserved, but the decoration (some of which is a reproduction)
★ is pitted. From the temple of **Mnajdra** ("mna-ee-dra"), on the edge of a hill by the sea, views are superb. The temple is encircled by hard coralline limestone walls and has the typical, cloverlike trefoil plan. ✉ *Coast Rd.* ✆ ☞ *Opening and Closing Times* in *Malta A to Z, above.*

Dingli

With a car, you can drive south from Mdina to Dingli for a tour of the countryside, a look at the cliffs, and a tree fix at **Buskett Gardens.** Buskett Gardens surround **Verdala Castle,** which the Knights built as a hunting lodge during the 16th century. Now the President of Malta uses it to host distinguished visitors. It is not open to the public. ✉ *Buskett Rd.* ✆ *Gardens, daily 9–6.*

Mdina

★ In Malta's ancient, walled capital—the longtime stronghold of Malta's nobility—traffic is limited to residents' cars, and the noise of the world outside doesn't penetrate the thick, golden walls. The quiet streets are lined with sometimes block-long, still-occupied noble palaces.

At the café **Fontanella** (⊠ 1 Bastion St., ☎ 454264) you can have huge slices of delicious cake and an open view of the surrounding towns.

★ The serene, Baroque **Il-Katidral Ta' l-Imdina** (Cathedral of St. Peter and St. Paul) contains Mattia Preti's 17th-century painting, *The Shipwreck of St. Paul.* In the **Cathedral Museum** are Dürer woodcuts and illuminated manuscripts. ⊠ *Archbishop Sq.,* ☎ 454679. ☉ *Mon.–Sat. 9–1 and 1:30–4.*

Rabat

The town's name means suburb—of Mdina, in this case. The beautiful **Knysja San Pawl** (St. Paul's Church; ⊠ Parish Sq.) stands above a grotto where St. Paul reputedly took refuge after his shipwreck on Malta.

Catacombs run under much of Rabat. Up Triq Santa Agatha from Parish Square, the **Catacombs of St. Paul** are clean of bones but full of carved-out burial troughs. Don't forget the way out when you set off to explore. **St. Agatha's Crypt and Catacombs,** farther up the street, were beautifully frescoed between 1200 and 1480, then defaced (literally) by Turks in 1551. ⊠ *St. Agatha St.* ☉ ☞ *Opening and Closing Times* in *Malta A to Z, above.*

Mosta

The **Rotunda** (Church of St. Mary) has one of the largest unsupported domes in Europe, after St. Peter's in Rome and Hagia Sophia in Istanbul. A German bomb fell through the roof during World War II—without detonating. ⊠ *Rotunda Sq. (Buses 53 and 57).* ☉ *Daily 9–12 and 3–6.*

GOZO AND COMINO

Gozo is a place to relax. Spend a morning in the walled, hilltop Cittadella, stroll around Victoria's narrow limestone-walled streets, look inside splendid local churches, then head down for a swim at Ramla Bay or a boat ride from the Inland Sea at Dwejra ("dway-ra"). You can take great walks along the cliffs of Ta' Ćenċ ("ta chench") and San Lawrenz/Dwejra or hike past the centuries-old salt pans west of Marsalforn at Qbajjar.

Gozo has some superb restaurants, and local bakeries turn out tasty, crusty round loaves. The island's traditional craft is lace making, practiced by a diminishing number of older women who still make time for the intricacy of this labor of love. Gozitan men love to hunt, and native and migratory birds are either caged or shot. Most of the waist-high stone structures that dot Gozo's fields are blinds, and on autumn hunting season mornings you'll hear the sporadic pop of rifles. The island has become increasingly popular for diving, especially at Xlendi Bay (☞ *below*). The ferry docks at Mġarr Harbour, but this part of Gozo is unrepresentative. Go elsewhere.

Xagħra

The parish **Church of Our Lady of Victories** has two clock towers. One clock has the correct time, the other is deliberately wrong to fool the devil. In the cliffs to the west is reputedly **Calypso's Cave,** of Homer's *Odyssey* fame, viewable only from a platform a good distance away.

★ Imagine domes rising from the heavy stone walls of eastern Xagħra's 5,800-year-old **Ggantija Temples,** and you will get a sense of their original power. Each bears the classic five-apse plan that is the signature of Maltese megalithic temples. ⊠ *Xagħra plateau.* ☉ ☞ *Opening and Closing Times* in *Malta A to Z, above.*

$$ ✕ **Oleander.** Mario Attard prepares sophisticated, authentic local food
★ at this village square restaurant. The fresh tomato soup and pasta with anchovies, tomatoes, and black olives are spectacular. ⊠ *10 Victory Sq.,* ☎ *557230. AE, MC, V. Closed Mon.*

$ ✕ **Gester Restaurant.** This old-time luncheonette is run by sisters
★ Gemma and Ester, who serve delicious, homey Gozitan food. Try peppered local sheep's milk cheese, rabbit in rich tomato sauce, lasagna, and the meadlike local "wine." For dessert have Mr. Rapa's ice cream, from down the street; it's the best in Malta. ⊠ *8th September Ave.,* ☎ *556621. No credit cards. Closed Sun. No dinner.*

$$$ ⊞ **Cornucopia.** This sprawling complex of hotel rooms, bungalows, and farmhouses lies on the western flank of town. Valley view rooms (24 and 47 are the best), bungalows, and farmhouses are spacious and pleasant. Avoid all others. ⊠ *10 Gnien Imrik St., Xagħra XRA 102,* ☎ *556486 or 553866,* ᴵᴬˣ *552910. 45 rooms, 2 suites, 11 bungalows, 2 farmhouses, 2 apts. Restaurant, 3 pools. AE, DC, MC, V.*

Nadur

Gozo's second-largest town has a substantial parish church with a colored Italian marble interior and French stained-glass windows.

★ Baker Joe at **Mekren's Bakery** (⊠ Triq Tal-Hanaq, 50 yards down the road to Ramla after first intersection in Nadur) makes some of Gozo's best bread—for 11¢ a loaf—and occasionally whips up sweet pastry or pizza.

Outside Nadur are two small beaches that were once considered secret. Anything but that now, tiny **San Blas Bay** to the north is accessed by a *very* steep descent on foot past citrus groves. **Hondoq Bay,** to the east through the town of Qala, faces Comino. The beach isn't gorgeous, but the swims to rocky inlets are delightful.

Ramla Bay

The ocher-color sands at Ramla Bay cover Gozo's largest and most popular beach, which is ideal for swimming.

$ ✕ **Il-Werqa.** When the sunshine and the sea are no longer enough at this popular beach, take a few steps over to the fish shack with the cactus sign for its "special fish dinner," in which only today's catch is served. ⊠ *Ramla Bay Beach,* ☎ *559723. No credit cards. Closed mid-Nov.– Easter.*

Victoria

Gozo's capital is a charming old city with warrens of narrow streets, a hilltop Cittadella, and two main squares—Pjazza Independenza beneath the Cittadella and Pjazza San Franġisk. The splendid Baroque **Bażilika San Ġorġ** (St. George's Basilica; ⊠ down Triq San Ġiżepp from Pjazza Indepenża) has the most beautiful interior on Gozo. The original city here is the walled, hilltop **Cittadella.** It has steep, winding streets and great views from its ramparts. The **katidral**'s dome fell in a 1693 earthquake; it is now simulated by a trompe l'oeil painting. A museum displays the cathedral's ceremonial silver. The intriguing **Muzew Tal-Folklor** (Folklore Museum; ⊠ Triq Milite Bernardo) occupies three medieval houses. The **Muzew Tal-Arkeologija** (Archaeological Museum; ⊠ Triq il-Katidral) exhibits objects from various ancient periods (☞ Opening and Closing Times *in* Malta A to Z, *above*).

The street to the left of the katidral (☞ *above*) leads to the **Cittadella Boutique** (⊠ 4 Fosse St., ☎ 555953), closed Sunday, a one-stop shop for high-quality local lacework and nicely packaged food items. It also serves light lunches of tomatoes, cheese, bread, and wine.

$$$ ✕ **Brookie's.** In a stone farmhouse under the western walls of the Cittadella, Brookie's prepares some of the island's priciest and richest fare (cream is a favorite ingredient). A popular bar is on site, as well as a terrace and patio for drinks. Service can be erratic. ⊠ ½ *Triq Wied Sara,* ☎ *559524. AE, DC, MC, V. Closed Mon.*

$$–$$$ 🏨 **Paradise Travel and Property Services, Ltd.** This realtor has stun-
★ ning farmhouses to rent. Be specific with your request: number of guests, old or new farmhouse, necessity of pool (usually unheated), telephone service, size of town, and so on. Linen and weekly maid service is provided. Paradise can also arrange car rentals. ⊠ *38 St. Sabina Sq., VCT 102,* ☎ *562025,* 🖷 *562026. 15 self-catering farmhouses. AE, MC, V.*

Sannat

Sannat is a quiet town due south of Victoria where lace makers work along the streets and the church is Baroque. Beyond town, park your car along the dirt road and continue north and west for the spectacular Ta' Ċenċ cliffs and wildflowers in the fields around them.

Palazzo Palina (☎ 556474), to the right of the Hotel Ta' Ċenċ (☞ *below*) entrance, an early 18th-century manor house built in the time of Grand Master Ramon Perellos Y Rocaful, contains some of its original furnishings. Tours can be arranged for hotel guests, or stop by in the morning to see if a caretaker is in.

$$$$ 🏨 **Hotel Ta' Ċenċ.** Near the windy southern cliffs of Gozo, the under-stated hotel has an exclusivity unique for Malta. In spite of poorly lit rooms, not enough staff, and the unkempt peripheries of the property, the hotel is a quiet, memorable place to relax for a few days. There is private swimming at a rocky inlet a 10-minute drive away. ⊠ *Ta' Ċenċ, near Sannat, VCT 112,* ☎ *556819 or 556830,* 🖷 *558199. 59 rooms, 21 suites, 4 apts. Restaurant, 2 pools. AE, DC, MC, V.*

Xlendi Bay

The miniature, fjordlike Xlendi Bay (that's "shlendi") is home to fishermen and an abundance of holiday flats that have come close to spoiling this splendid place. The promenade along the water is lined with cafés, and on Sunday families traditionally parade here in their finest.

Ghajn il-Kbira (The Great Fountain; ⊠ Fontana, between Victoria and Xlendi Bay) was built during the 15th century to provide fresh spring water and laundry facilities for nearby Gozitans. Today, though it is still used for its original intent, you're just as likely to see a car being washed.

Malta's history, geography, and clear blue sea provide excellent opportunities for underwater exploration. Contact **St. Andrew's Divers' Cove Ltd.** (⊠ St. Simon St., Xlendi Bay, and Shore St., Mġarr Harbour, ☎ 551301, 🖷 561548).

$$$ 🏨 **St. Patrick's Hotel.** This well-maintained midsize hotel stands steps
★ away from the bay. It is architecturally consistent with its surroundings in town, even to the balconied facade. Harbor view rooms are the best; avoid claustrophobic courtyard rooms. ⊠ *Xlendi Bay, VCT 115,* ☎ *562951 or 562952,* 🖷 *556598. 40 rooms, 4 penthouse rooms. Restaurant. AE, MC, V.*

Marsalforn and Qbajjar

On a bay north of Victoria, this former fishing village is a tourist factory out of character with the rest of the island. On the coast west of Marsalforn, past Qbajjar ("by-*jar*"), is a stretch of salt pans dating from the time of the Knights. June through September, troughs cut into the limestone flats are filled with seawater, left to evaporate, then scraped for the salt left behind. The coarse crystals are excellent for cooking. In season you can buy salt along the road here from the gatherers.

$$$$ ✕ **Auberge Ta' Frenċ.** In an atmospheric limestone farmhouse, this French-inspired restaurant has Gozo's most refined service and classic cuisine. Seafood dishes are best here. ⊠ *Marsalforn Rd.,* ☎ *553888. Reservations essential. AE, DC, MC, V. Closed Tues. and weekdays Jan.–Feb.*

Għarb

This far-west island village is one of the prettiest on Gozo. Its central square has a particularly handsome church. If the privately owned, 28-room **Għarb Folklore Museum** (⊠ 99 Pjazza il-Knisja, ☎ 561929) isn't busy, chances are you'll see the quirky owner on the street flagging down cars.

$$–$$$ ✕ **Jeffrey's.** Chef/owner Jeffrey's interpretations of Gozitan classics in
★ this romantic find are superb: a delicate brine-free fish soup, succulent braciola, and rabbit in a white wine and garlic sauce. Jeffrey harvests produce from his own farm and herbs from outside the kitchen. ⊠ *10 Triq L-Għarb,* ☎ *561006. Reservations essential. AE, MC, V. Closed Sun. and Nov.–Easter. No lunch.*

San Lawrenz and Dwejra

The **cliffs of San Lawrenz and Dwejra** ("dway-ra") are spectacular—especially at sunset. From Għarb, follow signs for the hamlet of San Lawrenz. Park where the road turns to dirt at the town's end and follow the road for a km (½ mi) or so.

★ A must on Gozo is a ride (Lm 5 per boat) from the tiny **Inland Sea** through a natural tunnel under the cliffs out to the sea. Have the boatman loop around Dwejra Point to see the **Azure Window and Fungus Rock,** a huge limestone arch with unique rock formations extending from the cliffs. You can also walk to the window and the rock.

Comino

The 1-sq-mi island is populated by a handful of people year-round. Day trippers walk the dirt paths and swim in the beautiful but overcrowded **Blue Lagoon,** whose underwater grottoes scuba divers love to explore.

$$$$ ☷ **Comino Hotel.** Functionally modern, the Comino is the only hotel on the island. In spite of its private beach, abundant water sports, and a spirited new manager, the hotel needs to update rooms, public spaces, and furnishings. Day use of facilities is also available. ⊠ *Gozo Channel, SPB 10,* ☎ *529821,* FAX *529826. 95 rooms, 45 bungalows. Restaurant, 2 pools. AE, DC, MC, V. Closed mid-Nov.–end Mar.*

Gozo and Comino Essentials

Getting Around

BY BOAT

Hourly ferries leave from Ġrkewwa on Malta for Mġarr Harbour on Gozo. Passenger fares are Lm 1.75; car fares are Lm 5.75. Less frequent ferries go to Comino from Ġrkewwa and from Mġarr Harbor for Lm 2.

BY BUS

A rather unreliable bus service (☎ 562040) connects Victoria with the major towns in Gozo. A bus from the harbor to Victoria runs according to the ferry schedule.

BY TAXI OR RENTAL CAR

Mario's Taxi and Rent a Car (✉ Victoria, ☎ 557242, FAX 551827). **Mgàrr Rent a Car** (✉ Mgàrr Harbour, ☎ 556081 or 556098). Ask about jeeps if you want to venture to Gozo's more remote sites—some of the island's roads are extremely bumpy and rutted.

Contacts and Resources

EMERGENCIES

Police (☎ 191). **Ambulance** (☎ 196). **Fire Brigade** (☎ 199). **Hospital: Craig Hospital** (☎ 561600).

GUIDED TOURS

Xlendi Pleasure Cruises' (✉ Xlendi Bay, ☎ 559967, FAX 555667) 40-ft *Gozo Princess* circles Gozo and Comino, stopping at scenic spots. The Lm 10.50 fare includes buffet meals, and you can swim from the boat.

VISITOR INFORMATION

Mgàrr Harbour (✉ Mgàrr Harbor, ☎ 553343). **Victoria** (✉ Palm St., ☎ 561419).

21 THE NETHERLANDS

AMSTERDAM; HISTORIC HOLLAND; THE HAGUE, DELFT, AND ROTTERDAM

The bucolic images of windmills and wooden shoes that brought tourism here in the decades after World War II have little to do with the Netherlands of the '90s. Sure, tulips grow in abundance in the bulb district of Noord- and Zuid-Holland provinces, but today's Netherlands is no backwater operation: This tiny nation has an economic strength and cultural wealth that far surpass its size and population.

Sophisticated, modern Netherlands has more art treasures per square kilometer than just about any other country on earth, as well as a large number of ingenious, energetic citizens with a remarkable commitment to quality, style, and innovation. The 41,526 square km (15,972 square mi) of the Netherlands are just about half the area of the state of Maine or half the area of Scotland, and its population of 15 million is slightly less than that of the state of Texas or half the population of London. Formerly home to the most successful seafaring merchants, the country is still one of the world's most important distribution and transport hubs, and the banks have invested this wealth around the world. The country encourages internal accomplishments as well, particularly of a cultural nature. In the country, within a 120-km (75-mi) radius, are 10 major art museums and several smaller ones that together contain the world's richest and most comprehensive collection of Western art masterpieces from the 15th to the 20th centuries. In the same small area are a half dozen performance halls offering music, dance, and internationally known performing arts festivals.

The marriage of economic power and cultural wealth is nothing new to the Dutch; during the 17th century, for example, money raised through their colonial outposts overseas was used to buy or commission portraits and paintings by young artists such as Rembrandt, Hals, Vermeer, and Van Ruysdael. But it was not only the arts that were encouraged: The Netherlands was home to the philosophers Descartes, Spinoza, and Comenius; the jurist Grotius; the naturalist Van Leeuwenhoek, inventor of the microscope; and others like them who flourished in the country's enlightened tolerance. The Netherlands continues to subsidize its artists and performers, supporting an educational system in which creativity in every field is respected and nourished.

The Netherlands is the delta of Europe, located where the great Rhine and Maas rivers and their tributaries empty into the North Sea. Near the coast, it is a land of flat fields and interconnecting canals; in the center it is surprisingly wooded, and in the far south are rolling hills. About half of the Netherlands is below sea level.

Amsterdam is the focal point of the country's culture, as well as of a 60-km (37½-mi) circle of cities, known as the Randstad (agglomeration of cities), that includes The Hague (the Dutch seat of government and the world center of international justice), Rotterdam (the industrial center of the Netherlands and the world's largest port), and the historic cites of Haarlem, Leiden, Delft, and Utrecht.

The northern and eastern provinces are rural and quiet; the southern provinces that hug the Belgian border are lightly industrialized and sophisticated. The great rivers that cut through the heart of the country provide both geographical and sociological borders. The area "above the great rivers," as the Dutch phrase it, is peopled by tough-minded and practical Calvinists; to the south are more ebullient Catholics. A tradition of tolerance pervades this densely populated land; aware that they cannot survive alone, the Dutch are bound by common traits of ingenuity, personal honesty, and a bold sense of humor.

THE NETHERLANDS A TO Z

Customs
For imports and duty-free limits, *see* Customs & Duties *in* Chapter 1.

Dining
The Dutch enjoy a wide variety of cuisines from traditional Dutch to Indonesian—the influence of the former Dutch colony. Breakfast includes several varieties of bread, butter, jam, ham, cheese, chocolate, boiled eggs, juice, and steaming coffee or tea. Lunch tends to be a *broodje* (sandwich) from the great selection of delicatessens. Dutch specialties for meals later in the day include *erwtensoep* (rich, thick pea soup with pieces of tangy sausage or pigs' knuckles) and *stamppot* (mashed potatoes and greens with *worst* [sausage]); both are usually served only in winter. *Haring* (herring) is particularly popular, especially the "new herring" caught between May and September and served raw, with a garnish of onions and pickles. At Indonesian restaurants, the chief item is *rijsttafel* (rice table), a meal made up of rice and 20 or more small meat, seafood, or vegetable dishes, many of which are hot and spicy. Eating places range from snack bars, fast-food outlets, and modest local cafés to haute cuisine restaurants of international repute. Of special note are the *bruin cafés* (brown cafés), characterful, traditional pubs that normally serve snack-type meals. The indigenous Dutch liquor is potent and warming *jenever* (gin), both "old" (matured) and "young."

MEALTIMES
Lunchtime in this grab-a-broodje culture is between 12:30 and 1. The Dutch eat dinner at around 6 or 7 PM, especially in the country and smaller cities, so many restaurants close at about 10 PM and accept final orders at 9. In larger cities dining hours vary, and some restaurants stay open until midnight.

RATINGS
Prices are per person including three courses (appetizer, main course, and dessert), service, and sales tax but not drinks. For budget travel-

The Netherlands (Nederland)

North Sea

Wadden Islands

Schiermonnikoog

Ameland

Terschelling

Dokkum

Groningen

Delfzijl

Winschoten

Vlieland

Leeuwarden

Drachten

Assen

Harlingen

Bolsward

Emmen

Texel

Sneek

Waddenzee

Den Helder

IJsselmeer

Hoogeveen

Enkhuizen

Meppel

Zwolle

Almelo

Alkmaar

Hoorn

Lelystad

Hengelo

Zaanstad

Purmerend

Deventer

Enschede

Haarlem

Amsterdam

Bussum

Apeldoorn

Winterswijk

Hilversum

Amersfoort

Arnhem

Doetinchem

Leiden

Utrecht

Oude Rijn

Rijn

Tiel

Nijmegen

Rhine

GERMANY

Den Haag
(The Hague)

Delft

Lek

Oss

Rotterdam

Waal

's Hertogenbosch

Veghel

Dordrecht

Maas

Haringvliet

Overflakkee

Grevelingen

Breda

Tilburg

Eindhoven

Schouwen/
Duiveland

Steenbergen

Weert

Roermond

Oosterschelde

Bergen op Zoom

Tholen

Walcheren

Goes

Beveland

Middelburg

Westerscheld

Breskens

Terneuzen

Antwerp

Sittard

Aachen

Maastricht

Vaals

BELGIUM

Liège

KEY

Ferry

0   40 miles

0   60 km

Brussels

ers, many restaurants offer a tourist menu at an officially controlled price, currently Fl. 25.

CATEGORY	AMSTERDAM/ MAIN CITIES	OTHER AREAS
$$$$	over Fl. 100	over Fl. 85
$$$	Fl. 70–Fl. 100	Fl. 55–Fl. 85
$$	Fl. 40–Fl. 70	Fl. 35–Fl. 55
$	under Fl. 40	under Fl. 35

WHAT TO WEAR

Jacket and tie are advised for restaurants in the $$$$ and $$$ categories. The tolerant Dutch accept casual outfits in most eateries.

Language

Dutch is a difficult language for foreigners, but the Dutch are fine linguists, so almost everyone speaks at least some English, especially in larger cities and tourist centers.

Lodging

The Netherlands has a wide range of accommodations, from the luxurious Dutch-owned international Golden Tulip hotel chain to traditional, small-town hotels and family-run guest houses. For young or adventurous travelers, the provinces abound with modest hostels, campgrounds, and rural bungalows. Bed-and-breakfast establishments are in short supply and must be booked well ahead at local tourist offices.

B&B RESERVATION AGENCIES

VVV (☞ Visitor Information, *below*) provides lists of B&B and "pension" accommodations, which can work out to be much cheaper than hotel accommodations, while introducing you to Dutch domestic life in the flesh. **Bed & Breakfast Holland** (✉ Theophile de Bockstraat 3, 1058 TV, Amsterdam, ☎ 020/6157527, ℻ 020/6691573) also provides B&B addresses in cities and rural areas around the country.

HOTELS

Dutch hotels are generally clean, if not spotless, no matter how modest their facilities, and service is normally courteous and efficient. There are many moderate and inexpensive hotels, most of which are relatively small. In the provinces, the range of accommodations is more limited, but there are friendly, inexpensive family-run hotels that are usually centrally located. Some have good—if modest—dining facilities. Hotels generally quote room prices for double occupancy, and rates often include breakfast, service charges, and VAT.

To book hotels in advance, you can use the free **Netherlands Reservation Center** (✉ Box 404, 2260 AK Leidschendam, ☎ 070/4195544, ℻ 070/4195519), open weekdays 8–8, Saturday 8–2. For a small fee, tourist offices can usually make reservations at short notice. Bookings must be made in person, however.

RATINGS

Prices are for two persons sharing a double room.

CATEGORY	AMSTERDAM/ MAIN CITIES	OTHER AREAS
$$$$	over Fl. 500	over Fl. 350
$$$	Fl. 300–Fl. 500	Fl. 200–Fl. 350
$$	Fl. 200–Fl. 300	Fl. 150–Fl. 200
$	under Fl. 200	under Fl. 150

Mail
POSTAL RATES
The Dutch postal system is as efficient as the telephone network. Air-mail letters to the United States cost Fl. 1.60 for the first 20 grams; postcards cost Fl. 1.60; aerograms cost Fl. 1.30. Airmail letters to the United Kingdom cost Fl. 1 for the first 20 grams; postcards cost Fl. 1; aerograms cost Fl. 1.30.

RECEIVING MAIL
If you're uncertain where you'll be staying, have mail sent to "poste restante, Hoofd Postkantoor" in major cities along your route (making sure that your name and initials are clear and correctly spelled), or to American Express offices, where a small fee is charged on collection to non–American Express customers.

Money Matters
COST
The Netherlands is prosperous, with a high standard of living, so overall costs are similar to those in other northern European countries. Prices for hotels and services in major cities are 10% to 20% higher than those in rural areas. Amsterdam and The Hague are the most expensive. Hotel and restaurant service charges and the 6% value-added tax (VAT) are usually included in the prices quoted.

The cost of eating varies widely, from a snack in a bar or a modest restaurant offering a *dagschotel* (day special) or "tourist menu" at around Fl. 25 to the considerable expense of gourmet cuisine. A traditional Dutch breakfast is often included in the overnight hotel price.

CURRENCY
The unit of currency in the Netherlands is the guilder, written as NLG (for Netherlands guilder), Fl., or simply F. (from the centuries-old term for the coinage, florin). Each guilder is divided into 100 cents. Bills are in denominations of 10, 25, 50, 100, 250, and 1,000 guilders. Denominations over Fl. 100 are rarely seen, and many shops refuse to change them. Coins are 1, 2.5, and 5 guilders and 5, 10, and 25 cents. Don't confuse the 1- and 2.5-guilder coins and the 5-guilder and 5-cent coins. Bills have a code of raised dots that can be identified by touch.

At press time (summer 1999), the exchange rate for the guilder was Fl. 2.15 to the U.S. dollar, Fl. 1.46 to the Canadian dollar, Fl. 3.36 to the pound sterling, Fl. 1.43 to the Australian dollar, and Fl. 1.14 to the New Zealand dollar.

MUSEUM ADMISSIONS
The **Museumjaarkaart,** which can be purchased from most museums and all VVV tourist offices, provides a year's free or discounted admission to about 450 museums. It costs Fl. 55, Fl. 45 if you're over 55, and Fl. 25 if you're under 18. A photo and passport are required for purchase. Nearly all museums participate.

SAMPLE PRICES
Half bottle of wine, Fl. 25; glass of beer, Fl. 3.50; cup of coffee, Fl. 3; ham and cheese sandwich, Fl. 5; 2-km (1-mi) taxi ride, Fl. 12.

TIPPING
Hotels and restaurants almost always include 10%–15% service and 6% VAT in their charges. Give a doorman Fl. 3 for calling a cab. Bellhops in first-class hotels should be tipped Fl. 2 for each bag they carry. Hat-check attendants expect at least Fl. 1, and washroom attendants get 50¢. Taxis in almost every town have a tip included in the meter charge, but you round the fare to the next guilder nevertheless.

National Holidays

January 1; April 23–24 (Easter); April 30 (Queen's Day); May 5 (Liberation); June 1 (Ascension); June 11–12 (Pentecost/Whitsunday and Monday); December 25–26.

Opening and Closing Times

Banks are open weekdays 9–4. GWK Border Exchange Offices at major railway stations and Schiphol Airport are open Monday–Saturday 8–8 and Sunday 10–4. GWK offices in major cities or at border checkpoints are open 24 hours. **Museums** in Amsterdam are open all week. Elsewhere they close on Monday, but there are exceptions, so check with local tourist offices. In rural areas, some museums close or operate shorter hours in winter. Usual hours are 10–5. **Shops** are open weekdays and Saturday 8:30 or 9–5:30 or 6, but outside the cities some close for lunch. Department stores and most shops do not open on Monday until 1 PM. Late-night shopping usually can be done until 9 PM on Thursday or Friday. Sunday opening, from noon to 5, varies from city to city.

Shopping

SALES-TAX REFUNDS

Purchases of goods in one store on one day amounting to Fl. 300 or more qualify for a value-added tax, called BTW (VAT), refund of 17.5%, which can be claimed at the airport or main border crossing when you leave the Netherlands, or by mail. This arrangement is only valid if you export the goods within 30 days. Ask the salesperson for a VAT refund form when you buy anything that may qualify.

Telephoning

COUNTRY CODE

The country code for the Netherlands is 31. When dialing a number in the Netherlands from outside the country, drop the initial 0 from the local area code.

INTERNATIONAL CALLS

Direct-dial international calls can be made from any phone booth. To reach an **AT&T** long-distance operator, dial 0800/022–9111; for **MCI**, dial 0800/022–9122; for **Sprint,** dial 0800/022–9119.

LOCAL CALLS

All towns and cities have area codes that are used only when you are calling from outside the area. All public phone booths require phone cards. Phone cards may be purchased from post offices, railway stations, and newsagents for Fl. 10 or Fl. 25. Pay phones in bars and restaurants take 25¢ or Fl. 1 coins, but rates are often hiked. Dial 0800/0410 for an English-speaking operator.

Transportation

BY BICYCLE

The Netherlands is a cyclist-friendly country with specially designated cycle paths, signs, and picnic areas. Bikes can be rented at train stations in most cities and towns, and Dutch trains are cycle-friendly, too, with extra-spacious entryways designed to accommodate bicycles. You will need an extra ticket for the bike, however. There are some restrictions on carrying bicycles on trains, so check first. Advice on rentals and routes is available from offices of the Netherlands Board of Tourism in North America or in the Netherlands (☞ Visitor Information, *below*), or from local tourist offices.

BY BUS

The Netherlands has an excellent bus network between and within towns. Bus excursions can be booked on the spot and at local tourist offices.

In major cities, the best buy is a *strippenkaart* ticket (Fl. 11.50), which can be used for all bus, tram, and metro services. Each card has 15 strips, which are canceled either by the driver as you enter the bus or by the stamping machine at each door of the tram. More than one person can travel on a strippenkaart—it just gets used up more quickly. You can buy it at train stations, post offices, some tourist offices, in Amsterdam at the public transport (GVB) ticket office in the plaza in front of the central railway station, and at many newsagents. A *dagkaart,* a travel-anywhere ticket (Fl. 12, one day; Fl. 16, two days; Fl. 19.75, three days), covers all urban bus/streetcar routes. National public transport information is available from ☎ 0900/9292, at a cost of 75¢ per minute.

BY CAR

Breakdowns. Experienced, uniformed mechanics of the **Wegenwacht** patrol the highways in yellow cars 24 hours a day. Operated by the Royal Dutch Touring Club (ANWB), they will help if you have car trouble. On major roads, ANWB also maintains phone boxes from which you can call for assistance. Otherwise call 0800/0888. To use these services, you may be asked to take temporary membership in ANWB.

Gasoline. Gas, *benzine* in Dutch, costs around Fl. 2.12 per liter for regular, Fl. 2.08 for super unleaded, and Fl. 1.45 for diesel.

Parking. Parking in the larger towns is difficult and expensive, with illegally parked cars quickly towed away or subject to a wheel clamp. Fines for recovery can top Fl. 300. Consider parking on the outskirts and using the efficient public transportation. Watch for blue P&R (Park and Ride) signs on ring roads and approach roads to major towns.

Road Conditions. The Netherlands has one of the best road systems in Europe. Multilane expressways (toll-free) link major cities, but the smaller roads and country lanes provide more picturesque routes. In towns, many of the streets are narrow, and you'll have to contend with complex one-way systems and cycle lanes. Be particularly vigilant for cyclists; they're ubiquitous, and they assume you'll give them the right of way. Information about weather and road conditions—in Dutch— can be obtained by calling 0900/9622 (75¢ per minute).

Rules of the Road. The speed limit on expressways is 120 kph (75 mph); on city streets and in residential areas it is 50 kph (30 mph) or less, according to the signs. Driving is on the right.

BY PLANE

KLM Royal Dutch Airlines, under the banner of CityHopper, operates several domestic services connecting major cities. In this small country, however, you'd probably travel just as fast by car or train.

BY TRAIN

Fast, frequent, comfortable trains operate throughout the country. All trains have first- and second-class cars, and many intercity trains have buffet or dining-car services. Sometimes one train contains two separate sections that divide during the trip, so be sure you are in the correct car for your destination.

At railway stations, look for blue columns marked REISWIJZER ("Route Finder"). For Fl. 1.25, paid with a telephone card, you can get a printout in English with door-to-door travel information that includes stops and connections on trains, buses, and trams.

Fares. To get the best value out of rail travel, purchase a pass. The Benelux Tourrail can be bought abroad, but the other passes are available only in the Netherlands. A Holland Rail Pass (known in the Netherlands as a Euro Domino Holland) ticket allows unlimited travel throughout the Netherlands for 3, 5, or 10 days within any 30-day period. A Transport Link ticket, which offers free travel on buses and trams as well, may be bought in conjunction with the Holland Rail Pass. Your rail pass is also valid on Interliner, a fast bus network that operates 16 intercity lines. Other options are a Dagkaart (one-day, travel-anywhere ticket) and, from June through August, a Zomertoer (summer tour) ticket for 3 days' travel in a 10-day period offers excellent value. Netherlands Board of Tourism (NBT) and Netherlands Railways (NS) offices abroad have information on train services. Your passport may be needed when you purchase these tickets. Rail Idee tickets include entry to tourist attractions with train, boat, and bus transportation, usually with a reduction of 20%. Ask about these fares at railway information bureaus or local tourist offices.

Visitor Information

Netherlands Board of Tourism (⊠ Box 404, 2260 AK Leidschendam, Holland, ☎ 070/419–5544, ℻ 070/3202611). **VVV** (acronym for national tourist offices; telephone inquiries, ☎ 0900/4004040, Fl. 1 per minute) has branches even in smaller towns.

Weather

The prime tourist season in the Netherlands runs from April through October and peaks during school vacation periods (Easter, July, and August), when hotels may impose a 20% surcharge. Dutch bulb fields bloom from late March to the end of May; hotels tend to fill up then, too. June is the ideal time to catch the warm weather and miss the crowds, but every region of the Netherlands has its season. Delft is luminous after a winter storm, and fall in the Utrecht countryside can be as dramatic as it is in New England.

CLIMATE

Summers are generally warm, but beware of sudden showers and blustery coastal winds. Winters are chilly and wet but are not without clear days. If the canals freeze over, then they immediately fill with keen skaters, the learners pushing along chairs. After a cloudburst, notice the watery quality of light that inspired Vermeer and other great Dutch painters. The following are the average daily maximum and minimum temperatures for Amsterdam.

Jan.	40F	4C	May	61F	16C	Sept.	65F	18C
	34	1		50	10		56	13
Feb.	41F	5C	June	65F	18C	Oct.	56	13C
	34	1		56	13		49	9
Mar.	47F	8C	July	70F	21C	Nov.	47F	8C
	38	3		59	15		41	5
Apr.	52F	11C	Aug.	68F	20C	Dec.	41F	5C
	43	6		59	15		36	2

AMSTERDAM

Amsterdam is a gem of a city for the visitor. Small and densely packed with fine buildings, many dating from the 17th century or earlier, it is easily explored on foot or by bike.

Exploring Amsterdam

The old heart of the city consists of canals, with narrow streets radiating out like the spokes of a wheel. The hub of this wheel and the most convenient point to begin sightseeing is Centraal Station. Across the street, in the same building as the Old Dutch Coffee House, is a tourist information office. The Rokin, once an open canal, is the main route from Centraal Station via the Dam to the Muntplein. Amsterdam's key points of interest can be covered within two or three days, including visits to one or two of the important museums and galleries. The city center is broken up into districts that are easily covered on foot.

Around the Dam

Numbers in the margin correspond to points of interest on the Amsterdam map.

★ ⑭ **Anne Frankhuis** (Anne Frank House). Immortalized by the poignant diary kept by the young Jewish girl from 1942 to 1944, when she and her family hid here from the German occupying forces, this canal-side house also has an educational exhibition and documents about the Holocaust and civil liberty. ✉ *Prinsengracht 263,* ☎ *020/5567100.* ☉ *June–Aug., Mon.–Sat. 9–7, Sun. 10–7; Sept.–May, Mon.–Sat. 9–5, Sun. 10–5.*

⑩ **Beurs van Berlage** (Berlage's Stock Exchange). This impressive building, completed in 1903, was designed by Hendrik Petrus Berlage (1856–1934), whose principles were to guide modernism; the building's function was fundamental to the design. The sculpture and rich decoration of the plain brick interior are among modernism's embryonic masterpieces. It now houses two concert halls, a large exhibition space, and its own museum, which also offers the chance to climb the 39-m- (138-ft-) high tower for its superb views. ✉ *Damrak 277,* ☎ *020/6265257.* ☉ *Museum: Tues.–Sun. 10–4.*

❶ **Centraal Station** (Central Station). The flamboyant redbrick and stone portal was designed by P. J. H. Cuijpers (1827–1921) and built in 1884–89. It provides an excellent viewpoint for both the Beurs van Berlage and the Scheepvaarthuis, two of the city's best examples of early 20th-century architecture. Compare it with Cuijpers's other significant contribution to Amsterdam's architectural heritage—the Rijksmuseum. ✉ *Stationsplein.*

⑪ **Dam** (Dam Square). This is the broadest square in the old section of the town. Fishermen used to come here to sell their catch. Today it is a busy crossroads, circled with shops and bisected by traffic; it is also a popular spot for outdoor performers. At one side of the square stands a simple monument to Dutch victims of World War II. Eleven urns contain soil from the 11 provinces of the Netherlands, while a 12th contains soil from the former Dutch East Indies, now Indonesia. ✉ *Jct. Rokin, Damrak, Moses en Aaronstraat, and Paleisstraat.*

❻ **De Waag** (The Weighhouse). Dating from 1488, this turreted, redbrick monument dominates the Nieuwmarkt (New Market) in the oldest part of Amsterdam. Once the headquarters for ancient professional guilds, the building now is home to the Society for Old and New Media, which hosts occasional exhibitions in the magnificently restored **Theatrum Anatomicum**, up the winding stairs. ✉ *Nieuwmarkt,* ☎ *020/5579844.*

⑬ **Het Koninklijk Paleis te Amsterdam** (Royal Palace in Amsterdam). The vast, well-proportioned classical structure dominating the Dam was completed in 1655. It is built on 13,659 pilings sunk into the marshy soil. The great pediment sculptures are an allegorical representation of Amsterdam surrounded by Neptune and mythological sea creatures. Filled with opulent 18th- and early 19th-century furnishings, it is the official royal residence but is used only on high state occasions. ✉ *Dam,* ☎ *020/6248698.* ☉ *Tues.–Thurs. 1–4; daily 12:30–5 in summer. Occasionally closed for state events.*

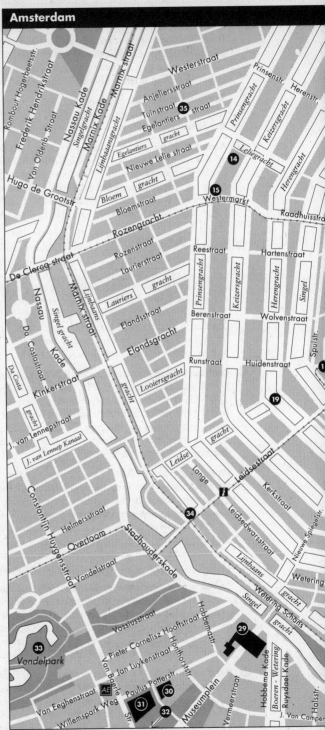
Amsterdam

Het IJ

CENTRAAL STATION
Front

de Ruyterkade

Oosterdokskade

Oosterdok

Open Haven

Prins Hendrikskade

Nieuwendijk

Singel

Spuistr.

Damrak

Oudebrugsteeg

Beursstraat

Warmoesstraat

Nieuwendijk

Zeedijk

Oudezijds Kolk

Geldersekade

Prins Hendrikskade

Binnen kant

eilandsgracht

Oude waal

Recht Boomssloot

Koningstr.

St. Antoniesbreestr.

Oude

Schans

Oosterdokskade

Rapenburg

Nieuwe Uilenburgerstraat

Uilenburgergracht

Valkenburgerstraat

Rapenburgergracht

Anne

rankstr.

Wertheim Park

Plantage parklaan

Plantage Middenlaan

NIEUW-MARKT

Nieuwezijdsvoorburgwal

Dam

Rokin

Damstraat

Zijds Voorburgwal

Achter burgwal

Oude Hoogstr.

Zijds

Oude

Kloveniersburgwal

Raamgr.

nenburgwal

Jodenbreestraat

Mr. Visser-plein

Muiderstraat

gracht

Kalverstraat

Nes

Nieuwe Doelenstr.

burgwal

Groen

Staalstraat

Zwa

Amstel

Amstel

Nieuwe Amstel

Heren

WATERLOOPLEIN

Spui

Rokin

Singel

Reguliersdwarsstraat

Rembrandt plein

Amstelstr.

Blauwbrug

Nieuwe

Nieuwe

Nieuwe

Nieuwe

Keizersgracht

Kerkstraat

Prinsengracht

Nieuwe Achter

Valckenierstraat

Weesperstraat

Vijzelstraat

Heren

gracht

Keizersgracht

Prinsengracht

Reguliers

gracht

Utrechtsestraat

Kerkstraat Magere Brug

Amstel

Utrechtse dwarsstraat

Amstel

WEESPERPLEIN

Sarphatistraat

Vijzelgracht

Noorderstr.

Nieuwe Looiersstr.

dwarstr.

Frederiks plein

Sarphatistraat

Mauritskade

Wetering Pl.

Weteringschans

Nicolaas Witsen Kade

Stadhouderskade

str.

F. Bol Straat

KEY

American Express Office

Tourist Information

Metro Stops

Metro Lines

Tram Lines

Railroad

0   220 yards

0   200 meters

N

⑨ Museum Amstelkring. The facade carries the inscription *"Ons Lieve Heer Op Solder"* ("Our Lord in the Attic"). In 1578 Amsterdam embraced Protestantism and outlawed the church of Rome. The municipal authorities were so tolerant that secret Catholic chapels were allowed to exist; at one time there were 62 in Amsterdam alone. One such chapel was established in the attics of these three neighboring canal-side houses, built around 1661. The lower floors were used as ordinary dwellings, while services were held in the attics regularly until 1888, the year the St. Nicolaaskerk was consecrated for Catholic worship. Of interest are the Baroque altar with its revolving tabernacle, the swinging pulpit that can be stowed out of sight, and the upstairs gallery with its displays of religious artifacts. ⊠ *Oudezijds Voorburgwal 40,* ☏ *020/ 6246604.* ⊘ *Mon.–Sat. 10–5, Sun. 1–5.*

⑤ Nederlands Scheepvaartmuseum (Netherlands Maritime Museum). This former naval warehouse maintains a collection of restored vessels, including a replica of a three-masted VOC (Verenigde Oostindische Compagnie—Dutch East India Company) trading ship from 1749. The museum explains the whole history of Dutch shipping, from dugout canoes right through to modern container ships, with maps, paintings, and models. ⊠ *Kattenburgerplein 1,* ☏ *020/5232222.* ⊘ *Mon.–Sat. 10–5, Sun. and holidays 12–5.*

☝ ③ newMetropolis Science & Technology Center. This stunning, modern, interactive museum was designed by Renzo Piano, architect of the Pompidou Center in Paris. The building's colossal, copper-clad volume rises from the harbor waters like the hull of a ship. Hands-on exhibits for young and old range from elementary physics to the latest technological gadgets. The rooftop terrace offers a superb panoramic view across the city. ⊠ *Oosterdok 2, Prins Hendrikkade,* ☏ *020/5313233.* ⊡ *Fl. 23.50.* ⊘ *Daily 10–6.*

⑫ Nieuwe Kerk (New Church). This huge Gothic structure was gradually expanded until 1540, when it reached its present size. Gutted by fire in 1645, it was reconstructed in an imposing Renaissance style, as interpreted by strict Calvinists. The superb oak pulpit, the 14th-century nave, the stained-glass windows, and the great organ (1645) are all shown to great effect on national holidays, when the church is bedecked with flowers. As befits the Netherlands' national church, the Nieuwe Kerk is the site of all coronations, most recently that of Queen Beatrix in 1980. In democratic Dutch spirit, the church is also used as a meeting place, has a lively café, and hosts temporary exhibitions and concerts. ⊠ *Dam,* ☏ *020/6268168.* ⊡ *Free, except for special exhibitions.* ⊘ *Daily 11–5; exhibitions daily 10–6.*

⑧ Oude Kerk (Old Church). The city's oldest house of worship dates from the early 14th century, but it was badly damaged by iconoclasts after the Reformation. The church still retains its original bell tower and a few remarkable stained-glass windows. The tower overlooks a typical view of Old Amsterdam. Rembrandt's wife, Saskia, is buried here. ⊠ *Oudekerksplein 23,* ☏ *020/6258284.* ⊘ *Apr.–Oct., Mon.–Sat. 11–5, Sun. 1–5; Nov.–Mar., Sun.–Fri. 1–5, Sat. 11–5.*

⑦ Rosse Buurt (red-light district). This area is defined by two of the city's oldest canals. In the windows at canal level, women in sheer lingerie slouch, stare, or do their nails. The area can be shocking, with its sex shops and porn shows, but is generally safe, although midnight walks down dark side streets are not advised. If you do explore the area, watch for purse snatchers and pickpockets. ⊠ *Bordered by Oudezijds Voorburgwal and Oudezijds Achterburgwal.*

❹ Scheepvaartshuis (Shipping Offices). Designed (1911–16) by J. M. der Mey and the Van Gendt brothers, this office building is the earliest example of the Amsterdam School's unique building style. The fantastic facade is richly decorated in brick and stone, with lead and zinc roofing pouring from on high. ✉ *Prins Hendrikkade 108–119.*

❷ Schreierstoren (Weepers' Tower). Facing the harbor stands a lookout tower, erected in 1480, for women whose men were out at sea. A tablet marks the point from which Henrik (a.k.a. Henry) Hudson set sail on the *Half Moon* on April 4, 1609, on a voyage that eventually took him to what is now New York and the river that bears his name. A recently opened café allows you to appreciate some of the historic, wood-beamed interior. ✉ *Prins Hendrikkade 94–95.*

⓯ Westerkerk (West Church). The church's 279-ft tower is the city's highest; it also has an outstanding carillon. Rembrandt (1606–69) and his son Titus are buried in the church, which was completed as early as 1631. In summer you can climb to the top of the tower for a fine view over the city. ✉ *Prinsengracht (corner of Westermarkt),* ☎ *020/ 6247766.* ⏰ *Tower: June–Sept., Tues.–Wed. and Fri.–Sat. 2–5.*

South of the Dam

⓰ Amsterdam Historisch Museum (Amsterdam Historical Museum). The museum traces the city's history from its origins as a fishing village through the 17th-century Golden Age of material and artistic wealth to the decline of the trading empire during the 18th century. A display of old maps, documents, and paintings, often aided by a commentary in English, tells the story. In the courtyard off Kalverstraat a striking Renaissance gate (1581) guards a series of tranquil inner courtyards. In medieval times, this area was an island devoted to piety. Today the bordering canals are filled in. ✉ *Kalverstraat 92,* ☎ *020/5231822.* ⏰ *Weekdays 10–5, weekends 11–5.*

★ ⓱ Begijnhof (Beguine Court). This is an enchanting, enclosed square of almshouses founded in 1346 that is a surprising oasis of peace just a stone's throw from the city's hectic center. The Beguines were women who chose to lead a form of convent life, often taking the vow of chastity. The last Beguine died in 1974 and her house, Number 26, has been preserved as she left it. Number 34, dating from the 15th century, is the oldest house, and the only one to retain its wooden Gothic facade. A small passageway and courtyard link the Begijnhof to the Amsterdam Historisch Museum (☞ *above*). ✉ *Begijnhof 29,* ☎ *020/6233565.* ✍ *Free.* ⏰ *Daily 9–dusk.*

㉑ Bloemenmarkt (Flower Market). Here, floating stalls carry a bright array of freshly cut flowers and foliage, as well as an enviable variety of bulbs and plants. ✉ *Along Singel Canal, from Muntplein to Koningsplein.* ⏰ *Mon.–Sat. (occasionally Sun.) 9:30–5.*

⓱ Engelse Kerk (English Church). This church was given to Amsterdam's English and Scottish Presbyterians early in the 17th century. On the church wall and in the chancel are tributes to the Pilgrim Fathers who sailed from Delftshaven (present-day Delfshaven, in Rotterdam) to the New World in 1620. Opposite the church is another of the city's secret Catholic chapels, whose exterior looks as though it were two adjoining houses, built in 1671. ✉ *Begijnhof* (☞ *above*).

★ ⓳ Gouden Bocht (Golden Bend). The Herengracht (Gentlemen's Canal) is the city's most prestigious canal. The stretch of the canal from Leidsestraat to Huidenstraat is named for the sumptuous patrician houses with double staircases and grand entrances that line it. Seventeenth-century merchants moved here from the Amstel River to escape the byproducts of their wealth: noisy warehouses, unpleasant brewery smells, and the risk of fire in the sugar refineries. The Herengracht houses display the full range of Amsterdam architectural detailing, from gables in a variety of shapes to elaborate Louis XIV–style cornices and frescoed ceilings. They are best seen from the east side of the canal. ⊠ *Herengracht—Leidsestraat to Huidenstraat.*

20 **Munttoren** (Mint Tower). Built in 1620 at this busy crossroads, the graceful tower that was later added to this former royal mint has a clock and bells that still seem to mirror the Golden Age. There are frequent carillon recitals. ⊠ *Muntplein.*

22 **Museum Willet-Holthuysen.** Built in 1690, the elegant residence was bequeathed to the city of Amsterdam on condition that it be retained as a museum. It provides a peek into the lives of the city's well-heeled merchants. The rooms are elegantly furnished in an opulent Louis XVI style. ⊠ *Herengracht 605,* ☎ *020/5231870.* ☉ *Weekdays 10–5, weekends 11–5.*

18 **Spui** (sluice). In the heart of the university area, the lively square was a center for revolutionary student rallies in 1968. Now you'll find bookstores and bars, including cozy brown cafés. ⊠ *Jct. Nieuwezijds Voorburgwal, Spuistraat, and Singel Canal.*

Jewish Amsterdam

The original settlers in the Jodenbuurt (old Jewish Amsterdam) were wealthy Sephardic Jews from Spain and Portugal, later followed by poorer Ashkenazic refugees from Germany and Poland. At the beginning of the 20th century this was a thriving community of Jewish diamond polishers, dyers, and merchants.

23 **Jodenbreestraat.** During World War II this street marked the southwestern border of the *Joodse wijk* (Jewish neighborhood), by then an imposed ghetto. The character of the area was largely destroyed by highway construction in 1965 and more recently by construction of both the Metro and the Muziektheater/Stadhuis complex (☞ *below*).

27 **Joods Historisch Museum** (Jewish Historical Museum). A complex of three ancient synagogues, places of worship that once served a community of 100,000 Jews, shrunk to fewer than 10,000 after 1945, is now a museum. Founded by American and Dutch Jews, it displays religious treasures in a clear cultural and historical context. As the synagogues lost most of their treasures in the war, their architecture and history are more compelling than the exhibits. ⊠ *Jonas Daniël Meijerplein 2–4,* ☎ *020/6269945.* ☉ *Daily 11–5.*

25 **Muiderstraat.** This pedestrian area east of Waterlooplein retains much of the neighborhood's historic atmosphere. Notice the gateways decorated with pelicans, symbolizing great love; according to legend, the pelican will feed her starving young with her own blood. ⊠ *Muiderstraat/Waterlooplein.*

★ **24** **Museum het Rembrandthuis** (Rembrandt's House). From 1639 to 1658, Rembrandt lived at Jodenbreestraat 4. For more than 20 years the ground floor was used by the artist as living quarters; the sunny upper floor was his studio. It contains a superb collection of his etchings as well as work by his contemporaries. The modern new wing next door houses a multimedia auditorium, two new exhibition spaces, and a shop. From St. Antonies Sluis bridge, just by the house, there is a canal view that has barely changed since Rembrandt's time. ⊠ *Jodenbreestraat 4–6,* ☎ *020/6249486.* ☉ *Mon.–Sat. 10–5, Sun. 1–5.*

28 **Muziektheater/Stadhuis** (Music Theater/Town Hall complex). Amsterdammers come to the town hall section of the building by day to obtain driver's licenses, pick up welfare payments, and get married. They return by night to the rounded, marble-clad facade overlooking the Amstel river to see opera and ballet performed by the Netherlands' finest companies. You can wander into the town hall for a look at some interesting sculptures and other displays. A guided tour of the Muziektheater takes you around the dressing rooms, dance studios, backstage, and even to the wig department. ⊠ *Amstel 3,* ☎ *020/5518054.* ☉ *Guided tours Wed. and Sat. at 3.*

★ **26** **Portugese Israelitische Synagoge** (Portuguese Israelite Synagogue). As one of Amsterdam's four neighboring synagogues, this was part of the largest Jewish religious complex in Europe. The beautiful, austere interior of the 17th-century building is still intact, even if the building itself is marooned on a traffic island. ⊠ *Mr. Visserplein 3,* ☎ *020/ 6245351.* ☉ *Apr.–Oct., Sun.–Fri. 10–12:30 and 1–4; Nov.–Mar., Mon.–Thurs. 10–12:30 and 1–4, Fri. 10–12:30 and 1–3, Sun. 10–noon.*

The Museum Quarter

32 **Concertgebouw** (Concert Hall). The sounds of the country's foremost orchestra, the world-famous Concertgebouworkest, resonate in this imposing, classical building. The smaller of the two auditoriums is used for chamber music and solo recitals. The main hall hosts world-class concerts. ⊠ *Concertgebouwplein 2–6,* ☎ *020/6718345.*

34 **Leidseplein.** This square is the pulsing heart of the city's nightlife. In summer you can enjoy the entertainment of street performers on the many café terraces. ⊠ *Jct. Leidsestraat, Marnixstraat, and Weteringschans.*

★ **29** **Rijksmuseum** (State Museum). Allow at least an hour or two to explore the main collection of Dutch paintings at the most important of Dutch museums, and a whole morning or afternoon if you want to visit other sections. The museum was founded in 1808, but the current, rather lavish building dates from 1885, designed by the architect of Centraal Station, P. J. H. Cuijpers. As well as Italian, Flemish, and Spanish paintings, there are also vast collections of furniture, textiles, ceramics, sculpture, and prints. The museum's fame, however, rests on its unrivaled collection of Dutch 16th- and 17th-century masters. Of Rembrandt's masterpieces, *The Nightwatch,* concealed during World War II in caves in Maastricht, was misnamed because of its dull layers of varnish; in reality it depicts the Civil Guard in daylight. Also worth searching out are Frans Hals's family portraits, Jan Steen's drunken scenes, Van Ruysdael's romantic but menacing landscapes, and Vermeer's glimpses of everyday life bathed in his limpid light. The Zuid Vleugel (South Wing) houses a freshly displayed treasure trove of Eastern art. ⊠ *Stadhouderskade 42,* ☎ *020/6732121.* ☉ *Daily 10–5.*

31 **Stedelijk Museum** (Museum of Modern Art). The museum has a stimulating collection of modern art and ever-changing displays of the works of contemporary artists. Before viewing the paintings of Cézanne, Chagall, Kandinsky, and Mondriaan, check the list of temporary exhibitions in Room 1. ⊠ *Paulus Potterstraat 13,* ☎ *020/5732911.* ☉ *Apr.–Sept., daily 10–5; Oct.–Mar., daily 11–5.*

★ **30** **Van Gogh Museum.** This museum contains the world's largest collection of the artist's works—200 paintings and nearly 500 drawings—as well as works by some 50 of his contemporaries. There are usually very well presented temporary exhibitions. The modern, airy building was designed by Gerrit Rietvelt (1888–1964) and completed in 1972. The low entrance foyer opens into a high, skylit exhibition space. The new wing is a spaceship-like stone and titanium oval structure designed by the Japanese architect Kisho Kurokawa. The renovated main building and the newly built wing were to reopen in mid-1999. Connected to the main building by an underground walkway, the wing provides space to exhibit Van Gogh's prints and accommodate temporary exhibitions. ⊠ *Paulus Potterstraat 7,* ☎ *020/5705200.* ☉ *Daily 10–5.*

🖑 ㉝ **Vondelpark.** Amsterdam's central park is an elongated rectangle of paths, lakes, and pleasant, shady greenery. A monument honors the 17th-century epic poet Joost van den Vondel, after whom the park is named. There are special children's areas with paddling pools and sandboxes. From June through August, the park hosts free outdoor concerts and plays Wednesday through Sunday. ⊠ *Stadhouderskade.*

The Jordaan

㉟ **Jordaan.** In this old part of Amsterdam the canals and side streets are named for trees, flowers, and plants. When it was the French quarter of the city, the area was known as *le jardin* (the garden), a name that over the years has become Jordaan. The best time to explore the district is on a Sunday morning or in the evening. The Jordaan has attracted many artists and is something of a bohemian quarter, where run-down buildings are being converted into restaurants, antiques shops, boutiques, and galleries. ⊠ *Bordered by Prinsengracht, Lijnbaansgracht, Brouwersgracht, and Raadhuisstraat.*

Dining and Lodging

Health-conscious Amsterdammers prefer set menus and early dinners. The blue-and-white TOURIST MENU sign in a restaurant guarantees an economical (Fl. 25) yet imaginative set menu created by the head chef. For traditionalists the NEDERLANDS DIS soup tureen sign is a promise of regional recipes and seasonal ingredients. "You can eat in any language" is the city's proud boast, so when Dutch restaurants are closed, Indonesian, Chinese, and Turkish restaurants are often open. For details and price-category definitions, *see* Dining *in* The Netherlands A to Z, *above.*

Accommodations are tight from Easter to summer, so early booking is advised. For details and price-category definitions, *see* Lodging *in* The Netherlands A to Z, *above.*

$$$$ ✕ **La Rive.** This world-class restaurant is fit for royalty. The French
★   cuisine, with an awe-inspiring "truffle menu" of dishes prepared with exotic (and expensive) ingredients, can be tailored to meet your every whim. Epicureans should inquire about the "chef's table": With a group of six you can sit at a table alongside the open kitchen and watch chefs prepare and describe each of your courses. ⊠ *Amstel Inter-Continental Hotel* (☞ *below*), *Professor Tulpplein 1,* ☎ *020/6226060. Jacket and tie. AE, DC, MC, V.*

$$$$ ✕ **'t Swarte Schaep.** The Black Sheep is named after a proverbial
★   17th-century sheep that roamed the area. With its creaking boards and array of copper pots, the interior is reminiscent of a ship's cabin. The Dutch chef uses seasonal ingredients to create classic dishes with regional flourishes. Choices include scallops wrapped in bacon for starters and fillet of beef with hazelnuts as a filling main course. ⊠ *Korte Leidsedwarsstraat 24,* ☎ *020/6223021. Reservations essential. Jacket and tie. AE, DC, MC, V.*

$$$–$$$$ ✕ **Excelsior.** The restaurant at the Hôtel de l'Europe (☞ *below*) offers
★   a varied menu of French cuisine based on local ingredients prepared by chef Jean Jacques Menanteau. There are no fewer than 15 splendid set menus. Service is discreet and impeccable, and the view over

the Amstel River, to the Muntplein on one side and the Muziektheater on the other, is the best in Amsterdam. ⊠ *Hôtel de l'Europe, Nieuwe Doelenstraat 2–4,* ☎ *020/6234836. Reservations essential. Jacket and tie. AE, DC, MC, V. No lunch Sat.*

$$$ ✕ **De Silveren Spiegel.** In an alarmingly crooked 17th-century house, ★ you can have an outstanding meal while you enjoy the personal attention of the owner at one of just a small cluster of tables. Local ingredients such as Texel lamb and wild rabbit are cooked with subtlety and flair. ⊠ *Kattengat 4–6,* ☎ *020/6246589. Jacket and tie. AE, MC, V.*

$$$ ✕ **Le Tout Court.** This small, meticulously appointed restaurant serves seasonal specialties (spring lamb, summer fruits, game in autumn and winter) personally prepared by owner-chef John Fagel, who mixes generous Dutch helpings with rich sauces. Lighter main courses include poached turbot. The restaurant draws Amsterdam's media set. ⊠ *Runstraat 13,* ☎ *020/6258637. AE, DC, MC, V. Closed Sun.–Mon.*

$$–$$$ ✕ **Dynasty.** Surrounded by luxurious oriental furniture and murals, you can savor subtly spiced Pan-Asian dishes from Thailand, Malaysia, and China. Main-course delicacies include mixed seafood in banana leaves and succulent duck and lobster on a bed of watercress. In one of the city's most active nightlife areas, it can get very busy, but service is always impeccable. ⊠ *Reguliersdwarsstraat 30,* ☎ *020/6268400. Jacket required. AE, DC, MC, V. Closed Tues. No lunch.*

$$–$$$ ✕ **Eerste Klas.** Amsterdam's best-kept secret is in the most obvious of places: the former first-class waiting lounge of the central train station. Classic dark-wood paneling and soft interior lighting create the perfect hideaway from the city's hustle and bustle. A continental brasserie-like menu includes tasty salads, steaks, and fish dishes. ⊠ *Stationsplein 15, Spoor 2b,* ☎ *020/6250131. Jacket and tie. AE, DC, MC, V.*

$$–$$$ ✕ **Lonny's.** Lonny Gerungan's family have been cooks on Bali for gen-★ erations—even preparing banquets for visiting Dutch royals. His plush restaurant in Amsterdam, draped in silky fabrics, serves the finest authentic Indonesian cuisine. Staff are dressed in exuberant traditional Balinese costumes. Even the simplest rijsttafel is a feast of more than 15 delicately spiced dishes. ⊠ *Rozengracht 46–48,* ☎ *020/6238950. Reservations essential. AE, DC, MC, V.*

$$–$$$ ✕ **Lucius.** Outstanding fish and seafood are simply served in an informal brasserie setting. Choices range from grilled lobster to more adventurous creations such as sea bass with buckwheat noodles and mushrooms. As you tuck into your fish, its live cousins eye you from a tank along the wall. ⊠ *Spuistraat 247,* ☎ *020/6241831. AE, DC, MC, V. Closed Sun. No lunch.*

$$–$$$ ✕ **Oesterbar.** The Oyster Bar specializes in seafood, grilled, baked, or fried. The upstairs dining room is more formal than the downstairs bistro, but prices don't vary. The sole is prepared in four different ways, or you can try the local specialties such as halibut and eel; oysters are a stimulating, if pricey, appetizer. ⊠ *Leidseplein 10,* ☎ *020/6232988. AE, DC, MC, V.*

$$–$$$ ✕ **Pier 10.** Perched on the end of a pier behind Centraal Station, this ★ intimate restaurant was built in the '30s as a shipping office. Water laps gently just beneath the windows as the harbor lights twinkle in the distance. The chef's special salads are lavish affairs, and the vegetable side orders are carefully steamed to perfection. Other culinary adventures might include a handsome platter of dove, duck, and partridge with cranberry sauce. ⊠ *De Ruyterkade Steiger 10,* ☎ *020/ 6248276. Reservations essential. AE, MC, V. No lunch.*

$$ ✕ **De Knijp.** Traditional Dutch food is served here in a traditional Dutch environment. The mezzanine level is especially cozy. Alongside tamer dishes, there are seasonal game specialties including wild boar ham with red cabbage and fillet of hare. After-midnight dinner draws

concertgoers from the neighboring Concertgebouw. ⊠ *Van Baerlestraat 134,* ☎ *020/6720077. AE, DC, MC, V.*

$$ ✕ **In de Waag.** The lofty, beamed interior below the Theatrum Anatomicum (☞ De Waag *in* Exploring Amsterdam, *above*) has been converted into a grand café and restaurant. The reading table harbors computer terminals for Internet enthusiasts. Dinnertime brings a seasonal selection of French-influenced continental cuisine to be savored by candlelight. ⊠ *Nieuwmarkt 4,* ☎ *020/5579844. AE, MC, V.*

$$ ✕ **Kantjil en de Tijger.** This lively Indonesian restaurant is a favorite with the locals and close to the bars on the Spui. The menu is based on three different rijsttafel, with a profusion of meat and vegetable dishes varying in flavor from coconut-milk sweetness to peppery hot. ⊠ *Spuistraat 291/293,* ☎ *020/6200994. AE, DC, MC, V. No lunch.*

$$ ✕ **Rose's Cantina.** A perennial favorite of the sparkling set, it offers spicy Tex-Mex food, lethal cocktails, and a high noise level. Pop in for a full meal or a late afternoon drink, and in fine summer weather call ahead to book a table on the terrace overlooking the elegant gardens of Herengracht's mansions. ⊠ *Reguliersdwarsstraat 38,* ☎ *020/6259797. Weekend reservations essential. AE, DC, MC, V.*

$$ ✕ **Toscanini.** This cavernous, noisy Italian restaurant has superb cui-
★ sine and an enthusiastic regular clientele. Try a selection of antipasti appetizers followed by fresh pasta or the simple fish and meat dishes, all expertly prepared with the day's best fresh produce. ⊠ *Lindengracht 75,* ☎ *020/6232813. Reservations essential. No credit cards. No lunch.*

$ ✕ **Het Gasthuys.** In this bustling restaurant you'll be served handsome portions of traditional Dutch home cooking—choice cuts of meat with excellent fries and piles of mixed salad. Sit at the bar or take a table high up in the rafters at the back. In summer the enchanting terrace on the canal side opens. ⊠ *Grimburgwal 7,* ☎ *020/6248230. No credit cards.*

$ ✕ **Pancake Bakery.** Here's a chance to try a traditionally Dutch way of keeping eating costs down. The name of the game is pancakes—laden with savory cheese and bacon or fruit and liqueur. ⊠ *Prinsengracht 191,* ☎ *020/6251333. Reservations not accepted. AE, MC, DC, V.*

$$$$ ▦ **Amstel Inter-Continental.** Amsterdam's grande dame opened in 1867
★ and was spectacularly renovated in late 1992. The interior creates a Dutch atmosphere with a European touch. The spacious rooms have Oriental rugs, brocade upholstery, Delft lamps, and a color scheme inspired by the warm, earthy tones of Makkum pottery. The Amstel is frequented by many of the nation's top businesspeople and sometimes hosts members of the royal family. ⊠ *Professor Tulpplein 1, 1018 GX,* ☎ *020/6226060,* ℻ *020/6225808. 58 rooms, 21 suites. 2 bars, 2 restaurants. AE, DC, MC, V.*

$$$$ ▦ **Golden Tulip Barbizon Palace.** The newest Golden Tulip hotel in Amsterdam combines past and present with fantasy and flair. The modern entrance blends in with the 17 neighboring monumental houses that the hotel occupies; inside, a towering atrium stretches across the length of the hotel. The Restaurant Vermeer serves haute cuisine. ⊠ *Prins Hendrikkade 59–72, 1012 AD,* ☎ *020/5564564,* ℻ *020/6243353. 256 rooms, 7 suites, 11 apartments. 2 restaurants, bar, café. AE, DC, MC, V.*

$$$$ ▦ **Grand Hotel Krasnapolsky.** The fine old-world hotel is enhanced by the Winter Garden restaurant ($$), which dates from 1818. In 1995 the hotel expanded into the building next door, increasing its size by half and replacing the bland decor with stylish period furnishings. The cosmopolitan atmosphere carries through all the rooms, with decor ranging from Victorian to Art Deco. ⊠ *Dam 9, 1012 JS,* ☎ *020/5548080,* ℻ *020/6261570. 429 rooms, 36 apartments. 4 restaurants, bar. AE, DC, MC, V.*

$$$$ 🏨 **Grand Westin Demeure Amsterdam.** In 1991 Amsterdam's former city hall was converted into a luxury hotel. Parts of this elegant building date from the 16th century, but most of it belongs to the early 20th, when the country's best artists and architects were commissioned to create a building the city could be proud of. Features include a mural by Karel Appel, Jugendstil stained-glass windows, and Gobelin tapestries. The palatially luxurious reception areas and rooms have hosted Michael Jackson as well as visiting presidents. The kitchen of the brasserie-style restaurant, Café Roux, is supervised by the incomparable Albert Roux. ⊠ *Oudezijds Voorburgwal 197, 1001 EX,* ☎ *020/5553111,* 𝔽𝔸𝕏 *020/5553222. 138 rooms, 29 suites, 11 apartments. Restaurant, bar, indoor pool. AE, DC, MC, V.*

$$$$ 🏨 **Hôtel de l'Europe.** Behind the stately facade of this building dating
★ from the end of the 19th century is a full complement of modern facilities, as befits a hotel often ranked among the world's best. The rooms are larger than usual for Amsterdam, and each is decorated according to its shape and location. Bright rooms overlooking the Amstel are done in pastel colors; others have warm, rich colors and antiques. Apart from its world-renowned Excelsior restaurant (☞ *above*), the hotel houses a sophisticated leisure complex. ⊠ *Nieuwe Doelenstraat 2–8, 1021 CP,* ☎ *020/6234836,* 𝔽𝔸𝕏 *020/6242962. 80 rooms, 20 suites. Restaurant, indoor pool. AE, DC, MC, V.*

$$$$ 🏨 **Pulitzer.** The Pulitzer is one of Europe's most ambitious hotel
★ restorations, using the shells of a block of 24 17th- and 18th-century merchants' houses. Inside, the refined atmosphere is sustained by the modern art gallery and the lovingly restored brickwork, oak beams, and split-level rooms: No two are alike, and many rooms have antique furnishings to match the period architectural features. ⊠ *Prinsengracht 315–331, 1016 GZ,* ☎ *020/5235235,* 𝔽𝔸𝕏 *020/6276753. 218 rooms, 7 suites, 5 apartments. Restaurant, indoor pool. AE, DC, MC, V.*

$$$ 🏨 **Ambassade.** With its beautiful canal-side location, its Louis XV–
★ style decoration, and its Oriental rugs, the Ambassade seems more like a stately home than a hotel. Service is attentive and room prices include breakfast in an elegant room overlooking the canal. For other meals, the neighborhood has a good choice of restaurants. ⊠ *Herengracht 341, 1016 AZ,* ☎ *020/6262333,* 𝔽𝔸𝕏 *020/6245321. 46 rooms, 5 suites, 1 apartment. Bar. AE, DC, MC, V.*

$$ 🏨 **Atlas Hotel.** Known for its friendly atmosphere, this small hotel is in Amsterdam's most prestigious neighborhood, just a block from the Vondelpark (☞ Exploring Amsterdam, *above*). The moderate-size rooms are decorated in a comfortable, modern style. The main museums are within easy walking distance. ⊠ *Van Eeghenstraat 64, 1071 GK,* ☎ *020/6766336,* 𝔽𝔸𝕏 *020/6717633. 23 rooms. Restaurant, bar. AE, DC, MC, V.*

$$ 🏨 **Canal House Hotel.** The American owners opt for antiques rather than televisions as furnishings in this canal-side hotel to create a real sense of sleeping in the 17th century. Spacious rooms overlook the canal or the illuminated garden. A hearty Dutch breakfast served in the breakfast room is included in the price. Children under age 14 are not permitted. ⊠ *Keizersgracht 148, 1015 CX,* ☎ *020/6225182,* 𝔽𝔸𝕏 *020/6241317. 26 rooms. AE, DC, MC, V.*

$–$$ 🏨 **Agora.** The cheerful bustle of the nearby Singel flower market is re-
★ flected in this small hotel in an 18th-century house. Rooms are light and spacious, some decorated with vintage furniture; the best overlook the canal or the university. The Agora has a considerate staff, and the neighborhood is relaxed. Book well in advance. ⊠ *Singel 462, 1017 AW,* ☎ *020/6272200,* 𝔽𝔸𝕏 *020/6272202. 15 rooms, 13 with bath or shower. AE, DC, MC, V.*

$–$$ ☷ **Hotel Seven Bridges.** Named for the view from its front steps, this small canal-house hotel has rooms decorated with individual flair. Oriental rugs warm wooden floors, and there are comfy antique armchairs and marble washstands. The Rembrandtsplein is nearby. For a stunning view, request a canal-side room. One of the pleasures here is breakfast in bed. There are four attic rooms full of character that have shared bath facilities. ⊠ *Reguliersgracht 31, 1017 RK,* ☎ *020/6231329. 10 rooms, 6 with shower or bath. AE, MC, V.*

$ ☷ **Amstel Botel.** The floating hotel moored near Centraal Station is an appropriate place to stay in watery Amsterdam. The rooms are small and basic, but the large windows offer fine views across the water to the city. Make sure you don't get a room on the land side of the vessel, or you'll end up staring at a postal sorting office. ⊠ *Oosterdokskade 2, 1011 AE,* ☎ *020/6264247,* FAX *020/6391952. 176 rooms with shower. AE, DC, MC, V.*

$ ☷ **Hotel de Filosoof.** On a quiet street near Vondelpark, the hotel attracts artists, thinkers, and people looking for something a little unusual. Each room is decorated in a different philosophical or cultural motif—such as an Aristotle room and a Goethe room adorned with texts from *Faust.* ⊠ *Anna van den Vondelstraat 6, 1054 GZ,* ☎ *020/ 6833013,* FAX *020/6853750. 29 rooms, 24 with bath. AE, MC, V.*

$ ☷ **Hotel Washington.** On a peaceful street, the hotel is just a few blocks from the museum quarter. Many of the world's top musicians find it the ideal place to reside when in Amsterdam. Period furniture and attentive service lend this small establishment a homey feel. All except the cheaper upper-floor rooms have bath or shower and toilet. ⊠ *Frans van Mierisstraat 10, 1071 RS,* ☎ *020/6796754,* FAX *020/ 6734435. 24 rooms, 19 with bath or shower. AE, DC, MC, V.*

Nightlife and the Arts

The Arts

The arts flourish in cosmopolitan Amsterdam. The best sources of information about performances are the *Time Out Amsterdam* listings on the Internet (http://www.timeout.nl). *De Uit Krant* is available in Dutch and covers practically every event. The monthly, English-language *What's On in Amsterdam* is published by the VVV tourist office, where you can also secure tickets for the more popular events. Tickets must be booked in person from Monday through Saturday, 10–4. You can also find the latest information and make personal or phone bookings for a small charge at the **Amsterdam Uitburo** (⊠ Stadsschouwburg, Leidseplein 26, ☎ 0900/0191, 75¢ per minute, 9–9 daily).

CLASSICAL MUSIC

The **Concertgebouw** (⊠ Concertgebouwplein 2–6, ☎ 020/6718345) is the home of one of Europe's finest orchestras. A smaller hall in the same building hosts chamber music, recitals, and even jam sessions. While ticket prices for international orchestras are high, most concerts are good value, and Wednesday midday concerts are free.

FILM

The greatest concentration of movie theaters is around Leidseplein and near Muntplein. Most foreign films are subtitled rather than dubbed. The largest theater (seven screens) in the city is the **City 1–7** (⊠ Kleine Gartmanplantsoen 13–25, ☎ 020/6234579). The Art Deco–era **Tuschinski** (⊠ Reguliersbreestraat 26, ☎ 020/6262633) is the most beautiful.

OPERA AND BALLET

The Dutch national ballet and opera companies perform in the **Muziektheater** (⊠ Waterlooplein, ☎ 020/6255455). Guest companies from other countries perform here during the three-week Holland Festival in June. The country's smaller regional dance and opera companies usually include performances at the **Stadsschouwburg** (Municipal Theater; ⊠ Leidseplein 26, ☎ 020/6242311) in their schedules.

THEATER

Young American comedians living in Amsterdam have created **Boom Chicago** (⊠ Leidsepleintheater, Leidseplein 12, ☎ 020/5307300), improvised comedy with a local touch. For experimental theater, dance, and colorful cabaret in Dutch, catch the shows at **Felix Meritis House** (⊠ Keizersgracht 324, ☎ 020/6231311). Along the **Nes** you'll find eight different performance spaces for theater and dance. The main theater ticket booking office is at the **De Brakke Grond** (⊠ Nes 45, ☎ 020/6229014), which is also the Flemish Cultural Center.

Nightlife

Amsterdam has a wide variety of dance clubs, bars, and exotic shows. The more respectable—and expensive—after-dark activities are in and around Leidseplein and Rembrandtsplein; fleshier productions are on Oudezijds Achterburgwal and Thorbeckeplein. Most bars and clubs are open every night from 5 PM to 2 AM or 5 AM. On weeknights very few clubs charge admission, though the livelier ones sometimes ask for a "club membership" fee of Fl. 20 or more.

CAFÉS AND BARS

Amsterdam, and particularly the Jordaan (☞ Exploring Amsterdam, *above*), is renowned for its brown cafés, so named because of the rich wooden furnishings and—some say—the centuries-old pipe-tobacco stains on the ceilings. There are also grand cafés, with spacious interiors, snappy table service, and well-stocked reading tables. Two other variants of Amsterdam's buzzing bar are the *proeflokalen* (tasting houses) and *brouwerijen* (breweries). The Dutch have a relaxed tolerance of the dreaded weed, to be encountered in "coffee shops" with the green leaves of the marijuana plant showing in the window.

Among more fashionable cafés is **Caffe Esprit** (⊠ Spui 10, ☎ 020/6221967), serving delicious burgers and fine lunches; it is often used as a venue for radio and television interviews. The beamed interior of **De Admiraal Proeflokaal en Spijhuis** (⊠ Herengracht 319, ☎ 020/6254334) is an intimate setting to enjoy the head-warming selection of award-winning *genevers* (gins). **De Gijs** (⊠ Lindegracht 249, ☎ 020/6380740) is an atmospheric example of the brown café. **De Jaren** (⊠ Nieuwe Doelenstraat 20, ☎ 020/6255771), a spacious grand café with a canal-side terrace, attracts smart young businesspeople, arts and media workers, and trendy types. If Continental lagers no longer tickle your fancy, then the home-brewed selection of beers at **Maximiliaan Amsterdams Brouwhuis** (⊠ Kloveniersburgwal 6, ☎ 020/6266280) are well worth sampling. At the **Rooie Nelis** (⊠ Laurierstraat 101, ☎ 020/6244167), you can spend a rainy afternoon chatting with friendly strangers over homemade meatballs and a beer or apple tart and coffee. **Tweede Kamer** (⊠ Heisteeg 6, just off the Spui, ☎ no phone), named for parliament's lower house, offers chess and backgammon in a convivial, civilized atmosphere permeated with the smoke of hemp.

CASINO

Holland Casino (⊠ Max Euweplein 62, ☎ 020/6201006), just off Leidseplein, has blackjack, roulette, and slot machines in elegant, canal-side surrounds. You'll need your passport to get in, and although you don't have to wear a tie, sneakers will not get you past the door; the minimum age is 18.

DANCE CLUBS

Dance clubs tend to fill up after midnight. The cavernous **Escape** (⊠ Rembrandtsplein 11–15, ☏ 020/6221111) has taken on a much hipper mantle. The **iT** (⊠ Amstelstraat 24, ☏ 020/6250111) is gay on Saturday. It's primarily straight on Thursday, Friday, and Sunday—but could never be accused of being straitlaced. **RoXY** (⊠ Singel 465, ☏ 020/6200354) is the current hot spot, though you need to be a member or impressively dressed to get in. **Seymour Likely Too** (⊠ Nieuwezijds Voorburgwal 161, ☏ 020/4205663), opened by a group of artists, is guaranteed to have a lively, trendy crowd hopping to the latest music.

GAY AND LESBIAN BARS

Amsterdam has a vibrant gay and lesbian community, concentrated on Warmoesstraat, Reguliersdwarsstraat, Amstelstraat, and Kerkstraat near Leidseplein. The **Gay & Lesbian Switchboard** (☏ 020/6236565) has friendly operators who provide information on the city's nightlife and other advice for gay or lesbian visitors. The **COC** (⊠ Rozenstraat 14, ☏ 020/6263087), the Dutch lesbian and gay political organization, operates a coffee shop and weekend discos.

JAZZ CLUBS

The **Bimhuis** (⊠ Oude Schans 73–77, ☏ 020/6233373) has long offered the best jazz and improvised music in town. The adjoining BIM café has a magical view across the Oude Schans canal.

Café Meander (⊠ Voetboogsteeg 5, ☏ 020/6258430) caters to a younger crowd with traditional jazz to the latest in hip-hop and experimental crossover streams.

ROCK CLUBS

Melkweg (⊠ Lijnbaansgracht 234, ☏ 020/6248492), a big draw in the flower-power era, has made a successful comeback as a major rock and pop venue with its large, new auditorium; it also has a gallery, theater, cinema, and café. The **Paradiso** (⊠ Weteringschans 6–8, ☏ 020/6264521), converted from a church, is a vibrant venue for rock, New Age, and even contemporary classical music.

Shopping

Amsterdam is a cornucopia of interesting markets, quirky specialty shops, antiques, art, and diamonds.

Department Stores

De Bijenkorf (⊠ Dam 1), the city's number-one department store, is excellent for contemporary fashions and furnishings. **Maison de Bonneterie en Pander** (⊠ Rokin 140–142; ⊠ Beethovenstraat 32) is the Queen Mother of department stores—gracious, genteel, and understated. The well-stocked departments of **Vroom & Dreesmann** (⊠ Kalverstraat 201) carry all manner of goods.

Gift Ideas

DIAMONDS

Since the 17th century, "Amsterdam cut" has been synonymous with perfection in the quality of diamonds. At the diamond-cutting houses, the craftsmen explain how the diamond's value depends on the four cs—carat, cut, clarity, and color—before encouraging you to buy. There is a cluster of diamond houses on the Rokin.

PORCELAIN

The Dutch have been producing Delft, Makkum, and other fine porcelain for centuries. **Focke & Meltzer** (⊠ P. C. Hooftstraat 65–67, ☏ 020/6642311) stores have been selling it since 1823. Pieces range from affordable, newly painted tiles to expensive Delft blue-and-white pitchers.

Markets

Antiekmarkt De Looier (✉ Elandsgracht 109) is a bustling, warrenlike market, with little stalls selling everything from expensive antiques and art to kitschy bricabrac; it's open Sunday–Wednesday 11–5, Thursday 11–9. In summer, you'll find etchings, drawings, and watercolors at the Sunday **art markets** on Thorbeckeplein and the Spui. The **Bloemenmarkt** (flower market) on the Singel has bulbs and cut flowers. On Saturday the Noordermarkt and Nieuwmarkt host an **organic farmers' market,** with essential oils and other New Age fare alongside oats, pulses, and vegetables. A small but choice **stamp market,** open Wednesday and Saturday 1–4, is held on the Nieuwezijds Voorburgwal. Amsterdam's lively **Waterlooplein flea market,** open Monday–Saturday 9:30–4, next to the Muziektheater is the ideal spot to rummage for secondhand clothes, inexpensive antiques, and other curiosities.

Shopping Districts

The Jordaan and the quaint streets crisscrossing the main ring of old canals are a treasure trove of trendy small boutiques and unusual crafts shops. Leidsestraat, Kalverstraat, Utrechtsestraat, and Nieuwendijk, Amsterdam's chief shopping districts, have largely been turned into **pedestrian-only areas.** The imposing new **Kalvertoren** shopping mall (✉ Kalverstraat, near Munt) has a rooftop restaurant with magnificent views of the city. **Magna Plaza** shopping center (✉ Nieuwezijds Voorburgwal 182), built inside the glorious old post office behind the Royal Palace at the Dam, is *the* place for A-to-Z shopping in a huge variety of stores. The **Spiegelkwartier** (✉ Nieuwe Spiegelstraat and Spiegelgracht), just a stone's throw from the Rijksmuseum, is Amsterdam's antiques center, with galleries for wealthy collectors as well as old curiosity shops. **P. C. Hooftstraat,** and also Van Baerlestraat and Beethovenstraat, are the homes of haute couture and other fine goods. **Rokin** is hectic with traffic and houses a cluster of boutiques and renowned antiques shops selling 18th- and 19th-century furniture, antique jewelry, Art Deco lamps, and statuettes. **Schiphol Airport** tax-free shopping center is often lauded as the world's best.

Amsterdam Essentials

Arriving and Departing

BY PLANE

Most international flights arrive at Amsterdam's Schiphol Airport. Immigration and customs formalities on arrival are relaxed, with no forms to be completed.

Between the Airport and Downtown. The best link is the direct rail line to the central train station, where you can get a taxi or tram to your hotel. The train runs every 10 to 15 minutes throughout the day and takes about a half hour. Make sure you buy a ticket before boarding: Ruthless conductors will happily impose a fine. Second-class single fare is Fl. 6.25. Taxis from the airport to central hotels cost about Fl. 60.

BY TRAIN

The city has excellent rail connections with the rest of Europe, including the high-speed **Thalys** service to Brussels and Paris (☎ 0900/9296, 50¢ per minute) with a journey time of just over four hours. It is now possible to travel by train to London, by either the Eurostar channel tunnel link or the High Speed Sea service, in less than seven hours. Centraal Station (✉ Stationsplein; international service information, ☎ 0900/9296, 50¢ per minute, long wait) is in the center of town.

Getting Around

BY BICYCLE

Rental bikes are widely available for around Fl. 12.50 per day with a Fl. 50–Fl. 200 deposit and proof of identity. Several rental companies are close to the central train station; ask at tourist offices for details. Lock your bike whenever you park it, preferably to something immovable. Also, check with the rental company to see what your liability is under their insurance terms.

BY BOAT

The **Canalbus** (Fl. 19.50 for a hop-on, hop-off day card) travels between the central train station and the Rijksmuseum. The **Museum Boat** (Fl. 22; ☞ Guided Tours, *below*) stops near major museums.

BY CAR

The city's concentric ring of canals, one-way systems, hordes of cyclists, and lack of parking facilities make driving here unappealing. It's best to put your car in one of the parking lots on the edge of the old center and abandon it for the rest of your stay.

BY METRO, TRAM, AND BUS

A zonal fare system is used. Tickets (starting at Fl. 3) are available from automatic dispensers on the Metro or from the drivers on trams and buses; or buy a money-saving strippenkaart (☞ Transportation, By Bus, *in* The Netherlands A to Z, *above*). Even simpler is the dagkaart, which covers all city routes for Fl. 12. These discount tickets can be obtained from the main GVB ticket office, open weekdays 7–7 and weekends 8–7, in front of Centraal Station and from many newsstands, along with route maps of the public transportation system. The Circle Tram 20 goes both ways around a loop that passes close to most of the main sights and offers a hop-on, hop-off ticket for one to three days.

BY TAXI

Taxis are expensive: A 5-km (3-mi) ride costs around Fl. 15. Taxis are not usually hailed on the street but are picked up at stands near stations and other key points. Alternatively, you can dial 020/6777777. Water taxis (☎ 020/6222181) are more expensive: Standard-size water taxis—for up to eight people—cost Fl. 90 for a half hour, including pick-up charge, and Fl. 30 per 15 minutes thereafter.

ON FOOT

Amsterdam is a compact city of narrow streets and canals, ideal for exploring on foot. The tourist office issues seven excellent guides in English that detail walking tours around the center.

Contacts and Resources

CONSULATES

U.S. (⊠ Museumplein 19, ☎ 020/6645661). **Canadian** (⊠ 7 Sophialaan, The Hague, ☎ 070/3614111). **U.K.** (⊠ Koningslaan 44, ☎ 020/6764343). **Australia** (⊠ Carnegielaan 12, The Hague, ☎ 070/310–8200). **Ireland** (⊠ Dr. Kuyperstraat 9, The Hague, ☎ 070/363–0993). **New Zealand** (⊠ Carnegielaan 10, The Hague, ☎ 070/346–9324).

EMERGENCIES

Police (☎ 112). **Ambulance** (☎ 112). **Central Medical Service** (☎ 020/5923434) will give you names and opening hours of duty pharmacists and dentists as well as doctors outside normal surgery hours.

ENGLISH-LANGUAGE BOOKSTORES

American Book Center (⊠ Kalverstraat 185, ☎ 020/6255537). **Athenaeum Boekhandel** (⊠ Spui 14, ☎ 020/6233933). **English Bookshop** (⊠ Lauriergracht 71, ☎ 020/6264230). **Waterstone's** (⊠ Kalverstraat 152, ☎ 020/6383821).

Bike. From April through October, guided bike tours are an excellent way to discover Amsterdam. There are also supervised tours to the idyllic countryside and quaint villages just north of the city. The three-hour city tour costs Fl. 30, and the 6½-hour countryside tour costs Fl. 42.50, arranged by **Yellow Bike Guided Tours** (⊠ Nieuwezijds Kolk 29, ☎ 020/6206940).

Boat. The most enjoyable way to get to know Amsterdam is on a boat trip along the canals. Departures are frequent from points opposite Centraal Station, along the Damrak, and along the Rokin and Stadhouderskade (near the Rijksmuseum). For a tour lasting about an hour, the cost is around Fl. 12.50, but the student guides expect a small tip for their multilingual commentary. A candlelight dinner cruise costs upward of Fl. 39.50. Trips can be booked through the tourist office.

At **Canal-Bike** (⊠ Corner Leidsestraat and Keizersgracht, Leidsekade, Stadhouderskade opposite Rijksmuseum, Prinsengracht opposite Westerkerk; ☎ 020/6239886), a pedal boat for four costs Fl. 20.50 per hour.

The **Museum Boat** (⊠ Stationsplein 8, ☎ 020/6222181) combines a scenic view of the city with seven stops near 20 museums. Tickets, good for the day and including discounted entry to museums, are Fl. 25.

Bus. Guided bus tours also provide an excellent introduction to Amsterdam. A bus-and-boat tour includes the inevitable trip to a diamond factory. Costing Fl. 25–Fl. 35, the comprehensive 3½-hour tour can be booked through **Key Tours** (⊠ Dam 19, ☎ 020/6235051) or **Lindbergh** (⊠ Damrak 26–27, ☎ 020/6222766).

Travel Agencies
American Express (⊠ Damrak 66, ☎ 020/5207777; ⊠ Van Baerlestraat 39, ☎ 020/6738550). **Holland International** (⊠ Leidseplein 23, ☎ 020/6262660). **Key Tours** (⊠ Dam 19, ☎ 020/6235051). **Reisburo Arke** (⊠ Damrak 90, ☎ 020/5550888). **Thomas Cook** (Bureau de Change, ⊠ Leidseplein 31a, ☎ 020/6267000; ⊠ Dam 23–25, ☎ 020/6250922; ⊠ Damrak 1, ☎ 020/6203236).

Visitor Information
VVV Amsterdam Tourist Office (⊠ Stationsplein 10, in front of Centraal Station in Old Dutch Coffee House, and on Spoor 2 [Platform 2] inside the station itself; ☎ 0900/4004040, Fl. 1 per minute, electronic queue—long wait).

HISTORIC HOLLAND

Between the historic towns, you'll see some of the Netherlands' windmill-dotted landscape and pass through centers of tulip-growing and cheese production. Apeldoorn is 90 km (56 mi) east of Amsterdam along highway A1, where the national park and royal palace are day trips in themselves. Amersfoort is an optional stop-off on the way. Arnhem is 15 km (9 mi) south of Apeldoorn on the A90, for trips to the open-air museum with children during summer months. The historically important centers of Utrecht, Gouda, and Leiden form an arc from the Groene Hart (Green Heart) of Holland toward the coast. Utrecht is 40 km (25 mi) southeast of Amsterdam on the A2. West of Utrecht, 36 km (22 mi) along the A12, you'll come to Gouda. Heading north on N11, you'll come to the ancient city of Leiden. The bulb fields of Lisse are halfway between Haarlem and Leiden, taking the N208 or the H206 coastal route. Haarlem, with its major museums, is 20 km (12 mi) directly west of Amsterdam on the A5.

Amersfoort

Although Amersfoort, east of Amsterdam on the way to Apeldoorn, is now a major industrial town, it has managed to retain much of its medieval character and charm. It is also the birthplace of the modern painter Piet Mondriaan (1872–1944). A double ring of canals surrounds the town's old center. The **Hovik** canal was once the harbor and loading quay. The **Koppelport** (⊠ Kleine Spui), an imposing water gate across the Eem, dates from 1400. The turreted **Kamperbinnenpoort** (⊠ Langstraat) is a land gate surviving from the 15th century. The graceful 335-ft-high **Onze Lieve Vrouwetoren** (Tower of Our Lady; ⊠ Breestraat) on a Gothic church has musical chimes that ring every Friday between 10 and 11 AM.

Museum Flehite, with its unusual medieval collections, gives a fascinating insight into the history of the town, augmented by a large model of the Old Town. In the associated **St. Pieters-en-Bloklands Gasthuis,** a hospice founded in 1390, are a chapel and a medieval room. ⊠ *Westsingel 50,* ☎ *033/4619987.* ۞ *Tues.–Fri. 10–5, weekends 2–5.*

The **Culinair Museum Mariënhof** (Culinary Museum) traces the history of eating and drinking, from prehistoric hunters and early agriculture, via the Roman period, through to the present day. The Mariënhof was a convent during the 16th century. ⊠ *Kleine Haag 2,* ☎ *033/4631025.* ۞ *Tues.–Fri. 10–5, weekends 2–5.*

Apeldoorn

★ The main attraction at Apeldoorn is the **Rijksmuseum Paleis Het Loo** (Het Loo Palace National Museum). Built during the late 17th century for William III, this former royal palace was the summer residence for the House of Orange from 1684 to 1972. It has been beautifully restored to illustrate the domestic surroundings enjoyed by the House of Orange for more than three centuries. The museum, housed in the stables, has a fascinating collection of royal memorabilia, including cars and carriages, furniture and photographs, and silver and ceramics. The formal gardens and the surrounding parkland have attractive walks. ⊠ *Amersfoortseweg 1,* ☎ *055/5772400.* ۞ *Tues.–Sun. 10–5.*

★ The **Nationale Park De Hoge Veluwe** (Hoge Veluwe National Park) is an area of moorlands, dense woods, and open meadows lying in the triangle formed by Arnhem, Apeldoorn, and Ede. At the entrance to the park are free white bikes for everybody's use or touring cars costing Fl. 25. ⊠ *5 km (3 mi) south of Apeldoorn on N304.* ۞ *Oct.–Mar., daily 9–6; Apr.–May, daily 8–8; June–Sept., daily 8 AM–10 PM.*

★ The **Kröller-Müller Museum** lies in the woods in the middle of the Hoge Veluwe park. The museum displays one of the finest collections of modern art in the world. It possesses 278 works by Vincent van Gogh, as well as paintings, drawings, and sculptures by such masters as Seurat, Redon, Braque, Picasso, and Mondriaan. The building, too, is part of the experience; it seems to bring the museum's wooded setting right into the galleries with you. ⊠ *National Park De Hoge Veluwe, 5 km (3 mi) from Apeldoorn on N304,* ☎ *0318/591241.* ۞ *Tues.–Sun. 10–5; sculpture garden, Apr.–Oct., Tues.–Sun. 10–4:30.*

$$$$ ✕ **De Echoput.** Near Rijksmuseum Paleis Het Loo (☞ *above*), this delightful restaurant is a member of the Alliance Gastronomique Néerlandaise, a guarantee of an excellent, classic French meal. Game from the surrounding forest is a specialty. An attractive terrace overlooks fountains and greenery for summer dining. ⊠ *Amersfoortseweg 86,* ☎ *055/5191248. Reservations essential. Jacket and tie. AE, DC, MC, V. Closed Mon. No lunch Sat.*

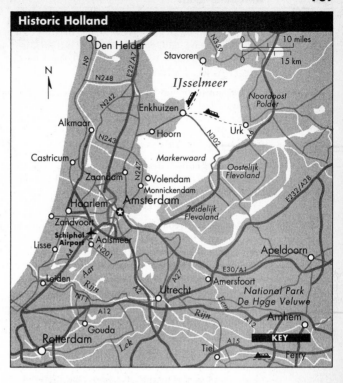

Historic Holland

Den Helder
Stavoren
N9
E22/A7
N248
N242
IJsselmeer
N
Enkhuizen
Alkmaar
N243
Hoorn
Urk
N302
A6
Castricum
Markerwaard
Noordoost Polder
Zaandam
N247
Volendam
Oostelijk Flevoland
Monnickendam
E232/A28
Haarlem
Amsterdam
Zuidelijk Flevoland
Zandvoort
Schiphol Airport
Aalsmeer
Apeldoorn
Lisse
A4
N201
Leiden
Aar
Rijn
A27
E30/A1
Amersfoort
National Park De Hoge Veluwe
N11
A2
Utrecht
Eem
A12
Arnhem
A12
Gouda
Rijn
Lek
Rotterdam
A15
KEY
Tiel
Ferry

0   10 miles
0   15 km
N50

$$$ 🏨 **Bilderberg Hotel de Keizerskroon.** In style and amenities it is a business hotel; in comfort and cordiality, a traveler's hotel; and in setting—at the edge of the town on a quiet street leading toward the woods—a weekend getaway. Three suites have an open hearth and a Jacuzzi. ⊠ *Koningstraat 7, 7315 HR,* ☎ *055/5217744,* 🗏 *055/5214737. 91 rooms, 6 suites. Restaurant, indoor pool. AE, DC, MC, V.*

Arnhem

☾ If you have children in tow, consider a visit to the **Nederlands Openlucht Museum** (Open-Air Museum) in Arnhem. In a 44-acre park, the curators have brought together original buildings and furnishings from all over the Netherlands to establish a comprehensive display of Dutch rural architectural styles and to depict traditional ways of living. There are farmhouses and barns, workshops, and windmills—animals, too. ⊠ *Schelmseweg 89,* ☎ *026/3576111.* ⊙ *Apr.–Oct., daily 10–5.*

Utrecht

The city of Utrecht was formerly the academic and religious center of the Netherlands. The gabled houses of Nieuwegracht, the canals with their sluice gates, the 13th-century wharves and storage cellars of Oudegracht, and an abundance of Gothic churches are just some of the city's key attractions. Utrecht hosts a number of internationally respected festivals, especially the annual Holland Festival of Early Music in the last week of August. If you arrive by rail, you pass through the enormous and ugly Vredenburg shopping center on the way to the beautiful, tree-lined old town.

The main cathedral square is a good point for orientation. The **Domkerk** is a late-Gothic cathedral with a series of fine stained-glass windows. The **Domtoren** (cathedral tower) opposite was connected to the cathedral until a hurricane hit in 1674. It's open April–October, weekdays 10–5, weekends noon–5; November–March, weekends noon–5.

The bell tower is the country's tallest, and its 465 steep steps lead to a magnificent view. A guide is essential in the tower's labyrinth of steps and passageways. ⊠ *Domplein*, ☎ *030/2310403.* ☉ *Tours on the hr: May–Sept., weekdays 10–5, Sat. 10–3:30, Sun. 2–4; Oct.–Apr., weekdays 11–4, Sat. 11–3:30, Sun. 2–4.*

★ ☾ The **Rijksmuseum van Speelklok tot Pierement** (National Museum of Mechanical Musical Instruments) is devoted to music machines—from music boxes to street organs and even musical chairs. During the tour music students play some of the instruments. ⊠ *Buurkerkhof 10*, ☎ *030/2312789.* ☉ *Tues.–Sat. 10–5, Sun. 1–5.*

The **Museum Catharijneconvent** (Catherine's Convent Museum) contains the country's largest display of medieval art in addition to its collection of holy relics and vestments. ⊠ *Nieuwegracht 63*, ☎ *030/ 2313835.* ☉ *Tues.–Fri. 10–5, weekends 11–5.*

The **Centraal Museum** houses a rich collection of contemporary art, especially applied arts, and exhibits about the city. Amid the clutter is a Viking ship (discovered in 1930) and a 17th-century dollhouse with period furniture, porcelain, and miniature old master paintings. ⊠ *Agnietenstraat 1*, ☎ *030/2362362.* ☉ *Tues.–Sat. 10–5, Sun. noon–5.*

An important part of the museum's collection is a 15-minute walk away in Utrecht's eastern suburbs, the **Rietveld-Schröderhuis** (Rietveld-Schröder House). In 1924 architect Gerrit Rietveld (1888–1964), working with Truus Schröeder, designed what is considered to be the architectural pinnacle of de Stijl (The Style). The use of primary colors (red, yellow, blue) and black and white, as well as the definition of interior space, is unique and innovative even today. ⊠ *Prins Hendriklaan 50a*, ☎ *030/2362310.* ☉ *Wed.–Sat. 11–4:30, Sun. 1:30–4:30; by appointment only.*

$$–$$$ ✕ **Polman's Huis.** A comfortable classic café welcomes you to this restaurant; beyond, the spacious dining room has an incredibly high, cherub-decked ceiling. Attentive service accompanies well-prepared international cuisine, influenced by Asian as well as European palates. Vegetables are either steamed to perfection or given an exotic twist. ⊠ *Keistraat 2*, ☎ *030/2313368. Reservations essential. AE, DC, MC, V.*

$ ✕ **De Soepterrine.** This snug restaurant offers 10 varieties of steaming homemade soups, including Dutch specialties such as thick *erwtensoep* (green pea soup). Each bowl comes with crusty bread and herb butter. Quiches and generous salads fill up extra corners. ⊠ *Zakkendragerssteeg 40*, ☎ *030/2317005. Reservations not accepted. AE, MC, DC, V.*

$$ ▥ **Malie Hotel.** The Malie is in a 19th-century row house on a quiet, leafy street a 15-minute walk from the old center. Rooms are vividly decorated though simply furnished. The breakfast room overlooks a garden and terrace. ⊠ *Maliestraat 2–4, 3581 SL*, ☎ *030/2316424*, ⅏ *030/2340661. 29 rooms with bath or shower. AE, DC, MC, V.*

Gouda

Gouda is famous for its cheese. Brightly colored farm wagons arrive loaded with cheeses for the morning *Kaasmarkt* (Cheese Market; open July–August, Thursday 10–noon). In the ornate, Baroque **Waag** (weigh house) overlooking the marketplace, the **Kaasexposeum** (cheese exhibition) explains the history of cheese and dairy products. ⊠ *Markt 35–36*, ☎ *0182/529996.* ☉ *Apr.–Oct., Mon.–Sat. 10–5, Sun. noon–5.*

Sint Janskerk (Church of St. John) on the market square holds carillon concerts in summer; it's open July–August, daily, 12:30. The structure you see today was built during the 16th century. It has the longest nave in the country and 64 glorious stained-glass windows, the oldest of which is from 1555. ⊠ *Achter de Kerk 16,* ☎ *0182/512684.* ☾ *Mar.– Oct., Mon.–Sat. 9–5; Nov.–Feb., Mon.–Sat. 10–4.*

The **Stedelijk Museum Het Catharina Gasthuis** (Catharina Hospice Municipal Museum) is a former hospital. In it are many unusual exhibits, including a fearsome medieval torture chamber and an equally horrific operating room. ⊠ *Oosthaven 10/ Achter de Kerk 14,* ☎ *0182/ 588440.* ☾ *Mon.–Sat. 10–5, Sun. noon–5.*

\$\$ ✗ **Goudsche Salon.** Wooden floors and a big table of newspapers and magazines contribute to the friendly atmosphere here. A good-value, seasonally changing set menu may include such delights as peppery rabbit stew. ⊠ *Wijdstraat 13,* ☎ *0182/512330. MC, V. Closed Tues.*

Leiden

Leiden is renowned for its spirit of religious and intellectual tolerance and for its university and royal connections. The university was founded by William the Silent as a reward to Leiden for its victory over the Spanish in the 1573–74 siege. During the war the dikes were opened and the countryside flooded so that the rescuing navy could sail right up to the city walls. The unusual **De Burcht** (The Keep; ⊠ Burgsteeg 14), a man-made mound that formed part of the city's early fortifications, affords a spectacular view of the city.

The Pilgrim Fathers stayed in Leiden before they set out for Delftshaven on the first stage of their arduous voyage to the New World. Documents relating to their stay are now kept in the vaults of the **Stedelijk Museum De Lakenhal** (☞ *below*). The Public Reading Room of the **Stadsarchief** (City Record Office), however, has facsimiles of documents and other material of historical interest. ⊠ *Dolhuissteeg 7,* ☎ *071/ 5120191 or 071/5165355.* ☾ *Weekdays 9:30–5, Sat. 9–12:15.*

The **Leiden American Pilgrim Museum,** opened in 1997, displays a historic furniture collection in a 16th-century house, along with copies of documents relating to the Pilgrim Fathers. ⊠ *Beschuitsteeg 9,* ☎ *071/5122413.* ☾ *Wed.–Sat. 1–5.*

Founded in 1590, the **Hortus Botanicus** (botanical gardens) are among the oldest in the world. The highlights are ancient trees, a faithful reconstruction of a 16th-century garden, an herb garden, a Japanese garden, and an orangery. ⊠ *Rapenburg 73,* ☎ *071/5120748.* ☾ *Mon.– Sat. 9–5, Sun. and holidays 10–5.*

Stedelijk Museum De Lakenhal (Cloth Hall Municipal Museum), a textile and antiques museum and art gallery, occupies a classical building constructed in 1639 for cloth merchants. Pride of place in the collection goes to the Dutch 16th- and 17th-century paintings, with works by Steen, Dou, Rembrandt, and, above all, Lucas van Leyden's *Last Judgment* (1526)—the first great Renaissance painting executed in what is now the Netherlands. Other rooms are devoted to furniture and to the history of Leiden's medieval guilds: the drapers, tailors, and brewers. ⊠ *Oude Singel 28–32,* ☎ *071/5165360.* ☾ *Tues.–Fri. 10–5, weekends and holidays noon–5.*

★ ♻ **Molenmuseum de Valk** (Windmill Museum) is housed in a windmill built in 1747, which was worked by 10 generations of millers until 1964. The seven floors contain the original machinery, an old forge, and living quarters. ⊠ *2e Binnenvestgracht 1,* ☎ *071/5165353.* ☾ *Tues.–Sat. 10–5, Sun. 1–5.*

St. Pieterskerk (St. Peter's Church) is associated closely with the Pilgrim Fathers, who worshiped here, and with their spiritual leader,

John Robinson, who is buried here. An imposing structure, inside and out, it is surrounded by quaint, cobbled streets. ⊠ *Pieterskerkhof 1a,* ☏ *071/5124319.* ⊘ *Daily 1:30–6.*

A narrow street by the **Persijnhofje** alms house (⊠ Kloksteeg 21), dating from 1683, leads to the tree-lined **Rapenburg** canal, crossed by triple-arch bridges and bordered by stately 18th-century houses.

The **Rijksmuseum van Oudheden** (National Museum of Antiquities) is the country's leading archaeological museum. The prize exhibit is the entire 1st-century Temple of Taffeh, donated by the Egyptian government. There is also a floor devoted to finds in the Netherlands. ⊠ *Rapenburg 28,* ☏ *071/5163163.* ⊘ *Tues.–Fri. 10–5, weekends and holidays noon–5.*

$$ ✗ **Stadscafé Restaurant van der Werff.** From the Art Nouveau interior you can see the De Valk windmill framed across the water. The restaurant serves café fare throughout the day but in the evening offers an appetizing and adventurous dinner menu based on traditional Dutch cuisine. ⊠ *Steenstraat 2,* ☏ *071/5130335. AE, DC, MC, V.*

$–$$ ✗ **Annie's Verjaardag.** A vaulted cellar full of students and a canalside terrace make Annie's attractive in all weather. The selection of salads and baguettes is usually accompanied by a daily special, such as mussels or jugged hare. ⊠ *Oude Rijn 1a,* ☏ *071/5125737. Reservations not accepted. MC, V.*

$–$$ ✗🏨 **Nieuw Minerva.** This family-run hotel is a conversion of eight 15th-century buildings. The original part of the hotel is decorated in Old Dutch style; the newer part is better equipped but has slightly less character. Many rooms overlook a quiet tributary of the Rhine. The restaurant caters to most tastes and pockets; the excellent three-course tourist menu has vegetarian as well as meat and fish selections. ⊠ *Boommarkt 23, 2311 EA,* ☏ *071/5126358,* 🖷 *071/5142674. 38 rooms, 30 with bath or shower. Restaurant. AE, DC, MC, V.*

$$ 🏨 **Hotel De Doelen.** The spartan decor of this small hotel is in keeping with its origins as a 17th-century patrician's house, but the rooms are comfortable and modern, some still furnished in period style. ⊠ *Rapenburg 2, 2311 EV,* ☏ *071/5120527,* 🖷 *071/5128453. 16 rooms with bath or shower. AE, DC, MC, V.*

Lisse

The **Keukenhof,** a 70-acre park and greenhouse complex, is planted each year to create a special exhibition of flowering bulbs (in spring only) between Leiden and Haarlem. The world's largest flower show draws huge spring crowds to its regimental lines of tulips, hyacinths, and daffodils. (A lazier way to see the flowers is from the windows of the Leiden–Haarlem train.) ⊠ *N208, Lisse,* ☏ *0252/465555.* ⊘ *Late Mar.–late May, daily 8–7:30.*

Aalsmeer

Flowers are big business to the Dutch, and the Netherlands has the world's largest complex of flower auction houses. The biggest of these facilities (it also is the single largest in the world) is the **Bloemenveiling** (flower auction) in Aalsmeer, close to Schiphol International Airport and Amsterdam. In a building the size of three football fields, three auction rooms function simultaneously. Get there early; it's all over by 10 AM. ⊠ *Legmeerdijk 313,* ☏ *0297/334567.* ⊘ *Weekdays 7:30 AM–11:30 AM. Closed weekends and holidays.*

Haarlem

With buildings notable for their secret inner courtyards and pointed gables, Haarlem can resemble a 17th-century canvas, even one by Frans Hals, the city's greatest painter. The area around the **Grote Markt** (market square) provides an architectural stroll through the 17th and 18th centuries. Some of the facades are adorned with such homilies as, "The body's sickness is a cure for the soul."

The **Vleeshal** (meat market), close to the Stadhuis (town hall), has an especially fine gabled front. The building dates from the early 1600s and is now used as the **Archeologisch Museum Haarlem** (Haarlem Archaeological Museum), with local history and computer simulations of finds. ⊠ *Grote Markt 16.* ▣ *Free.* ☉ *Wed.–Sun. 1–5.*

The **Grote Kerk** (cathedral) is also known as the St. Bavo, to whom it is dedicated. Built between 1400 and 1550, it houses one of the world's finest organs, which has 5,000 pipes and was played by both Mozart and Handel. An annual organ festival is held here in July. ⊠ *Grote Markt,* ☎ *023/5330877.* ☉ *Apr.–Aug., Mon.–Sat. 10–4; Sept.–Mar., Mon.–Sat. 10–3:30.*

The **Teylers Museum** claims to be the oldest museum in the country. It was founded by a wealthy merchant in 1778 as a museum of science and the arts; it now houses a fine collection of the Hague school of painting as well as drawings and sketches by Michelangelo, Raphael, and other non-Dutch masters. As the canvases in this building are shown in natural light, try to visit on a sunny day. ⊠ *Spaarne 16,* ☎ *023/ 5319010.* ☉ *Tues.–Sat. 10–5, Sun. 1–5.*

The **Frans Hals Museum,** in what was a 17th-century hospice, contains a marvelous collection of works by Hals (1585–1666); his paintings of the guilds of Haarlem are particularly noteworthy. The museum also has works of the artist's 17th-century contemporaries. ⊠ *Groot Heiligland 62,* ☎ *023/5164200.* ☉ *Mon.–Sat. 11–5, Sun. 1–5.*

$$ ✕ **Café Restaurant Brinkman.** This elegant, classic grand café overlooks the magnificent Grote Kerk. You can while away the afternoon over a single coffee or choose from a wide menu of casseroles and grills with salad. ⊠ *Grote Markt 9–13,* ☎ *023/5323111. AE, DC, MC, V.*

$$$ ▢ **Golden Tulip Lion d'Or.** Just five minutes from the old city center and conveniently near the railway station, this comfortable but unprepossessing hotel offers a full range of luxuries. Special weekend deals include reduced room rates, gourmet evening meals, and free cocktails. ⊠ *Kruisweg 34–36, 2011 LC,* ☎ *023/5321750,* ☏ *023/5329543. 32 rooms, 2 suites. Restaurant. AE, DC, MC, V.*

Historic Holland Essentials

Getting Around
The most convenient way to explore the countryside is by rented car from Amsterdam. All the towns listed above can also be reached by bus or train. Check with the tourist office in Amsterdam for help in planning your trip, or inquire at Centraal Station.

Guided Tours
The towns of Historic Holland are covered, in various combinations, by organized bus tours out of Amsterdam. Brochures for tour operators are available from the **VVV Amsterdam Tourist Offices** (☞ Visitor Information *in* Amsterdam Essentials, *above*).

The VVV office in Utrecht (☞ *below*) organizes several excursions, including a boat trip along the canals and a sightseeing flight over the city. There are also day trips to country estates, castles, and gardens.

Visitor Information
In towns such as Apeldoorn and Gouda, which have few good hotels, B&B accommodations can be booked through the VVV.

Amersfoort (VVV, ✉ Stationsplein 9–11, ☎ 0900/1122364, Fl. 1 per minute). **Apeldoorn** (VVV, ✉ Stationstraat 72, ☎ 0900/1681636, 80¢ per minute). **Gouda** (VVV, ✉ Markt 27, ☎ 0182/513666). **Haarlem** (VVV, ✉ Stationsplein 1, ☎ 0900/6161600, Fl. 1 per minute). **Leiden** (VVV, ✉ Stationsplein 210, ☎ 0900/2222333, Fl. 1 per minute). **Lisse** (VVV, ✉ Grachtweg 53a, ☎ 0252/414262). **Utrecht** (VVV, ✉ Vredenburg 90, ☎ 0900/4141414, 50¢ per minute).

THE HAGUE, DELFT, AND ROTTERDAM

The royal, diplomatic, and governmental seat of Den Haag or 's-Gravenhage (The Hague) is the Netherlands' most dignified and spacious city. Its close neighbor is the leading North Sea beach resort of Scheveningen. Also nearby are Delft, a historic city with many canals and ancient buildings, and the energetic and thoroughly modern international port city of Rotterdam.

These cities are all linked by excellent train service. The Hague and Delft, only 14 km (9 mi) from each other, are both about 60 km (37 mi) southwest of Amsterdam and can be reached within an hour by fast, frequent trains. Rotterdam is a quarter of an hour farther.

By road The Hague is 50 km (31 mi) southwest of Amsterdam using the A4, then the A44. Delft is 60 km (37 mi) southwest of Amsterdam on the A4, then the A13, via The Hague. The A13 is also the trunk road to Rotterdam, 13 km (8 mi) farther south. Rotterdam is just 73 km (45 mi) south of Amsterdam.

The Hague

During the 17th century, when Dutch maritime power was at its zenith, The Hague was known as "the Whispering Gallery of Europe" because it was thought to be the secret manipulator of European politics. The Hague remains a powerful world diplomatic and juridical capital, as well as the seat of government for the Netherlands.

The city's heart is the **Hofvijver** (court pond), a still, reflecting pond filled with water lilies. It was originally a moat to protect the gracious

★ **Binnenhof** (Inner Court or Parliament Buildings) complex. The Hague was established in 1250, when William II built a castle on this site. At the center is the late-13th-century **Ridderzaal** (Knights' Hall). Inside are vast beams spanning a width of 59 ft, flags, and stained-glass windows. The two government chambers sit in separate buildings on either side of the Ridderzaal; when Parliament is not in session they can be visited by guided tour. Tours in English are conducted by **Stichting Bezoekerscentrum Binnenhof** (Binnenhof Visitors Center), just to the right of the Ridderzaal. ✉ *Binnenhof 8a*, ☎ *070/3646144 for tour reservations.* 🎫 *Parliament exhibition free.* ☉ *Mon.–Sat. 10–4.*

★ The **Mauritshuis** (Maurits House), a small, well-proportioned palace on the far side of the Binnenhof, dates from 1644. This former royal residence is one of the finest small art museums in the world. It contains a feast of art from the 17th century, including six works by Rembrandt van Rijn (1606–1669); of these the most powerful is *The Anatomy Lesson of Dr. Tulp,* a theatrical work depicting a dissection of the lower arm. Also here are the celebrated *Girl Wearing a Turban* and the glistening *View of Delft* by Jan Vermeer (1632–75), famous for his brilliant ability to capture the fall of light. ✉ *Korte Vijverberg 8*, ☎ *070/3023456.* ☉ *Tues.–Sat. 10–5, Sun. 11–5.*

Lange Voorhout is a large L-shape boulevard close to the Mauritshuis and Parliament buildings. During the 19th century, horse-drawn trams clattered along its cobbles and deposited dignitaries outside the vari-

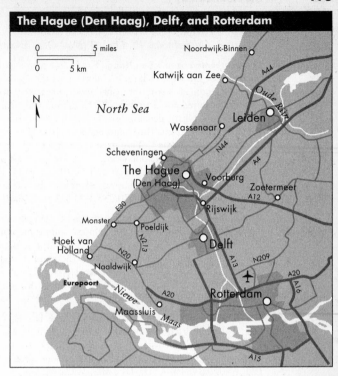

The Hague (Den Haag), Delft, and Rotterdam

ous palaces, which are now inhabited by embassies. The **Hoge Raad** (Supreme Court; ✉ Lange Voorhout 34) once belonged to William I, the first king of the Netherlands. With its clumsy skewed redbrick gable, the **Rode Kruis** (Dutch Red Cross) headquarters at No. 6 seems out of place on this stately avenue.

The **Kloosterkerk** (cloister church; ✉ Lange Voorhout 4, corner Parkstraat), built in 1400, is The Hague's oldest church. In spring the adjoining square is covered with yellow and purple crocuses; on Thursday in summer it is the setting for a colorful antiques market.

Panorama Mesdag is a 400-ft painting-in-the-round that shows the nearby seaside town of Scheveningen as it looked in 1880. Hendrik Mesdag (1831–1915), a late-19th-century marine painter, used the muted colors of the Hague school in his calming seascape, as well as special perspective techniques. ✉ *Zeestraat 65,* ☎ *070/3106665.* ☼ *Mon.–Sat. 10–5, Sun. noon–5.*

Museum Mesdag (Mesdag Museum), the painter's former home, contains works by H. W. Mesdag and members of The Hague school interspersed with those of Corot, Courbet, and Rousseau. These delicate landscapes represent one of the finest collections of Barbizon School painting outside France. ✉ *Laan van Meerdervoort 7f,* ☎ *070/5705200.* ☼ *Tues.–Sun. noon–5.*

The **Vredespaleis** (Peace Palace) is a monument to world peace through negotiation. Following the first peace conference at The Hague in 1899, the Scottish-American millionaire Andrew Carnegie donated $1.5 million for the construction of a building to house an international court. The interior and furniture display an eclectic mix of works donated by participating nations from around the world. Today the **International Court of Justice,** currently in session for the trial of war criminals from former Yugoslavia, has its headquarters here. ⊠ *Carnegieplein 2,* ☎ *070/3469680.* ⊙ *May–Oct., weekdays 10–4; Nov.–Apr., weekdays 10–3. Guided tours 10, 11, 2, 3 (May–Oct., also at 4).*

The **Gemeentemuseum Den Haag** (The Hague Municipal Museum) is the home of the world's largest collection of the work of Piet Mondriaan, including his last, unfinished work, *Broadway BoogieWoogie,* recently acquired for a massive $20 million. The exhibition traces Mondriaan's stylistic development from figurative painting to refined, minimalist abstraction. The Hague School of painters is also amply represented, as well as the CoBrA artist Karel Appel. In addition to magnificent arts-and-crafts collections, there are two vast collections of musical instruments—European and non-European. H. P. Berlage's 1935 building itself is a fascinating example of the International Style. ⊠ *Stadhouderslaan 41,* ☎ *070/3381111.* ⊙ *Tues.–Sun. 11–5.*

⊙ **Madurodam,** between The Hague and Scheveningen (☞ *below*), is a miniature Netherlands where the country's important buildings are duplicated at a scale of 1:25. No detail has been forgotten, from the lighthouse and 4½-km (3-mi) train track to the hand-carved furniture in the gabled houses. ⊠ *George Maduroplein 1, The Hague,* ☎ *070/ 3553900.* ⊠ *Fl. 19.50.* ⊙ *Sept.–Mar., daily 9–5; Apr.–June 9–8; July–Aug., daily 9 AM–10 PM.*

$$$ ✕ **Da Roberto.** Popular with politicians and The Hague's business elite, Roberto's is a quiet and comfortable restaurant where all the adventure goes into the cuisine. Italian standards and some ambitious variations are treated to elegant nouvelle cuisine presentation. ⊠ *Noordeinde 196,* ☎ *070/3464977. AE, DC, MC, V. Closed Sun.*

$$–$$$ ✕ **Bistromer.** A notch above most other seafood restaurants in The
★ Hague, Bistromer has a menu that ranges from the North Sea to the Mediterranean. Portions are generous, and the food is cooked to perfection. There's a wood-paneled dining room for snug winter meals and an attractive glassed-in terrace for the summer. ⊠ *Javastraat 9,* ☎ *070/3607389. AE, DC, MC, V. Closed lunch weekends.*

$$–$$$ ✕ **Djawa.** Whether or not it is a result of the city's diplomatic heritage is unknown, but The Hague is said to have the Netherlands' highest concentration of Indonesian restaurants. Among them is this cozy, family-run neighborhood place not far from the center. ⊠ *Mallemolen 12a,* ☎ *070/3635763. AE, DC, MC, V. No lunch.*

$$–$$$ ✕ **Le Haricot Vert.** What was built in 1638 as a staff house for the nearby palace is nowadays an intimate, candlelit restaurant in the city center. Succulent meats swimming in sauce appear on large white plates with a colorful tangle of vegetables. Owner Herman van Overdam chats at diners' tables or flits back into the kitchen to create one of his sinfully laden dessert platters. ⊠ *Molenstraat 9a–11,* ☎ *070/3652278. AE, DC, MC, V. No lunch Sun.–Mon.*

$$$$ ✕🏨 **Hotel Des Indes.** At the end of one of The Hague's most prestigious squares, the Des Indes is grace and gentility supreme. The once-private mansion was built for grand balls and entertainments; the rooms are arranged around the glamorous, marble-walled foyer. For more than 100 years it has hosted ambassadors and kings, dancers and spies. Rooms are spacious and classically styled; one suite offers a spectacular view across the city toward the coast. The historic restaurant ($$$), frequented by diplomats, serves French-style haute cuisine amid the glitter of crystal and silver. ⊠ *Lange Voorhout 54–56, 2514 EG,* ☎ *070/3632932,* 𝖥𝖠𝖷 *070/3451721. 70 rooms, 6 suites. Restaurant, bar. AE, DC, MC, V.*

$$$ ✕🏨 **Corona.** Overlooking a charming square in the center of the city, this hotel has rooms decorated in a restful scheme of white, cream, and

dove gray. Mouthwatering dishes from the restaurant's excellent French kitchen include lamb with forest mushrooms and wild duck with sage and thyme. The brasserie serves sandwiches and light meals. ⊠ *Buitenhof 39–42, 2513 AH,* ☎ *070/3637930,* FAX *070/3615785. 26 rooms. Restaurant, bar. AE, DC, MC, V.*

$$ ⊞ **Hotel Sebel.** In a largely residential district between the city center and the Peace Palace, Hotel Sebel provides a convenient stopover for businesspeople and for visitors on vacation. The rooms are invitingly spacious and light, and have marble bathrooms. ⊠ *Zoutmanstraat 38, 2518 GR,* ☎ *070/3608010,* FAX *070/3455855. 27 rooms. Bar, breakfast room. AE, DC, MC, V.*

Scheveningen

Scheveningen is adjacent to The Hague on the North Sea coast, with the **Scheveningse Bosjes** (Scheveningen Woods) separating it from the capital. A fishing village since the 14th century, Scheveningen became a popular beach resort during the 19th century. The beach itself, protected from tidal erosion by stone jetties, slopes gently into the sea in front of a high promenade that protects the boulevard and everything behind it from winter storms. The surface of the beach is fine sand, and you can bicycle or walk for kilometers to the north.

The **Pier,** completed in 1962, stretches 1,220 ft into the sea. The four circular buildings at its end contain a sun terrace and restaurant, an observation tower, an amusement center with a children's play area, and an underwater panorama. ⊠ *Northern end of Boulevard.*

☾ **Sea Life Scheveningen** on the beachfront is an ingeniously designed aquarium complex with a transparent underwater tunnel. You walk through it as if you were on the sea floor, with sharks, rays, eels, and octopuses swimming inches above your head. ⊠ *Strandweg 13,* ☎ *070/3542100.* ☉ *Sept.–June, daily 10–6; July–Aug., daily 10–8.*

$$$$ ⊞ **Kurhaus Hotel.** At the turn of the century this imposing spa hotel stood alone at the center of the beach as a fashionable resort. Now it is modern and bustling, with a casino among its new attractions. There is a fancifully painted ceiling over the large central court and a buffet restaurant. Rooms have tasteful neoclassical furnishings. ⊠ *Gevers Deynootplein 30, 2586 CK,* ☎ *070/4162636,* FAX *070/4162646. 231 rooms, 10 suites. 2 restaurants. AE, DC, MC, V.*

Delft

Probably no town in the Netherlands is more intimate, more attractive, or more traditional than this mini-metropolis, whose famous blue-and-white earthenware is popular throughout the world. Compact and easy to explore despite its web of canals, Delft is best discovered on foot—although canal-boat excursions are available April through October, and horse-drawn trams leave from the marketplace. Every street is lined with attractive Gothic and Renaissance houses.

In the marketplace, the only lively spot in this tranquil town, stands the **Nieuwe Kerk** (New Church), built during the 14th century, with its tall Gothic spire and a 48-bell carillon. The crypt contains the remains of all members of the royal family since King William I ascended the throne in the mid-16th century. ⊠ *Markt,* ☎ *015/2123025.* ☉ *Tower: Mar.–Oct., Mon.–Sat. 9–6; Nov.–Feb., Mon.–Sat. 11–4.*

The **Stedelijk Museum Het Prinsenhof** (Prinsenhof Municipal Museum) was formerly the Convent of St. Agatha, founded in 1400; it was here that William of Orange was murdered in 1584. The chapel dates from 1471; its interior is remarkable for the wooden statues under the vaulting ribs. Today the Prinsenhof's collection includes 16th- and 17th-century paintings by Delft masters, local silverware, and Delft ceramics. The **Volkenkundig Museum Nusantara** (Nusantara Ethnographic Museum), part of the same complex, has a collection of objects from the former Netherlands colonies in Indonesia. ⊠ *St. Agathaplein 1,* ☎ *015/ 2602358.* ⏰ *Tues.–Sat. 10–5, Sun. 1–5.*

The **Oude Kerk** (Old Church), a vast Gothic monument from the 13th century, overlooks the Oude Delft canal, the city's oldest waterway. The beautiful tower, surmounted by a brick spire, lists somewhat alarmingly. ⊠ *Heilige Geest Kerkhof,* ☎ *015/2123015.* ⏰ *Apr.–Nov., Mon.–Sat. 10–5.*

The timbered rooms of the **Lambert van Meerten Museum** have been filled with an extensive collection of old Dutch and foreign tiles and Delft pottery since the museum was founded in the home of this successful 19th-century industrialist in 1908. ⊠ *Oude Delft 199,* ☎ *015/ 2602358.* ⏰ *Tues.–Sat. 10–5, Sun. 1–5.*

When decorated porcelain brought to the Netherlands from China on East India Company ships during the 17th century became so popular that Dutch potters felt their livelihood threatened, they set about creating pottery to rival the Chinese product. This resulted in Delftware. Only two manufacturers still make hand-painted Delftware: **De Delftse Pauw** (⊠ Delftweg 133, ☎ 015/2124920), open April–mid-October, daily 9–4:30 and mid-October–March, weekdays 9–4:30, weekends 11–1, and **De Porceleyne Fles** (⊠ Rotterdamsweg 196, ☎ 015/2560234), open April–October, Monday–Saturday 9–5, Sunday 9:30–5 and November–March, Monday–Saturday 9–5.

$$$ ✕ **L'Orage.** This canal-side restaurant serves up delicious fish steeped in tantalizing sauces. Chef/owner Jannie Munk is French influenced but bases many of her dishes on recipes from her native Denmark. Main courses might include grilled bass served on a bed of risotto and sundried tomatoes. ⊠ *Oude Delft 111b,* ☎ *015/2123629. Reservations essential. Jacket and tie. AE, DC, MC, V. Closed Mon.*

$–$$ ✕ **Spijshuis De Dis.** Seafood is a house specialty at this favorite neighborhood spot, where a friendly staff serves typically Dutch cuisine. The mussels with garlic sauce are delicious, and you can try such delicacies as roast quail. ⊠ *Beestenmarkt 36,* ☎ *015/2131782. Reservations essential for lunch. AE, MC, V. Closed Wed.*

$ ✕▥ **Hotel de Plataan.** Converted in 1994 from a rather grand old post
★ office building, the hotel was decorated by a local artist in 1950s-style cream and green. Most rooms have a kitchen nook. You can also have meals in Het Establissement, an excellent restaurant that serves meaty casseroles as well as imaginative vegetarian dishes. ⊠ *Doelenplein 9– 10, 2611 BP,* ☎ *015/2126046,* ⅎ𝕏 *015/2157327. 23 rooms, 2 suites. Restaurant. AE, DC, MC, V.*

$$–$$$ ▥ **Hotel De Ark.** This bright, airy hotel in the center of old Delft comprises three canal houses joined so that nearly every room has a view of either the canal or the large garden in back. Rooms are clean and modern. ⊠ *Koornmarkt 59–65, 2611 EC,* ☎ *015/2157999,* ⅎ𝕏 *015/ 2144997. 16 rooms, 9 apartments. AE, DC, MC, V.*

$$ ▥ **Hotel Leeuwenbrug.** On one of the prettiest canals in Delft, this traditional Dutch family-style hotel is in a former patrician mansion and an annex. The mansion is simpler, with smaller rooms; the annex is more contemporary and businesslike. You can breakfast overlooking the canal; rooms on the top floor of the annex overlook the city. ⊠ *Koornmarkt 16, 2611 EE,* ☎ *015/2147741,* ⅎ𝕏 *015/2159759. 37 rooms with bath or shower. Bar. AE, MC, V.*

Rotterdam

Rotterdam is one of the few thoroughly modern cities in the Netherlands and the site of the world's largest and busiest port. Art lovers know the city for its extensive and outstanding collection of art; philosophers recall it as the city of Erasmus. Representative of the city's adventuresome modern architecture is the **Erasmusbrug** (Erasmus Bridge), an extraordinary, single-span pylon bridge over the Maas river, nicknamed "the swan." This forms the main link with the **Kop van Zuid,** Rotterdam's phenomenal ongoing development project in former docklands on the south bank.

In the city center a most intriguing series of cube-shape apartments balance on a tall stem. One of these precarious-looking houses, the **Kijk-Kubus** (literally, viewing cube), just east of the center, is open to the public. ✉ *Overblaak 70,* ☎ *010/4142285.* ⊙ *Mar.–Nov., Mon.–Fri 10–5, weekends 11–5; Dec.–Feb., Fri.–Sun. 11–5.*

The biggest surprise in Rotterdam is the remarkable 48-km- (30-mi-) long **Europoort** (Europort; ✉ Willemsplein), which handles more than 300 million tons of cargo every year and more ships than any other port in the world. It is the delta for three of Europe's most important rivers (the Rhine, the Waal, and the Maas). You can get to the piers by tram or Metro (blue line to the Leuvehaven station) from the train station. The 1¼-hour harbor tour (☞ Guided Tours, *below*) illuminates Rotterdam's vital role in world trade.

You can also survey the harbor from the vantage point of the **Euromast** observation tower. Get there via the RET Metro red line to Dijkszicht. ✉ *Parkhaven 20,* ☎ *010/4364811.* ⊙ *Mar.–June and Sept., daily 10–7; July and Aug., Sun. and Mon. 10–7, Tues.–Sat. 10 AM–10:30 PM; Oct.–Feb., daily 10–5.*

The inner harbor's hodgepodge of cranes, barges, steamships, and old shipbuilding machinery looking like a maritime junkyard is a work in progress: Volunteers are restoring the vessels and machinery. The open-air museum of shipbuilding, shipping, and communications is part of the **Maritiem Museum Prins Hendrik** (Prince Henry Maritime Museum), housed in a large gray building at the head of the quay. Moored in the inner harbor adjacent to the museum is the historic 19th-century Royal Dutch Navy warship, *De Buffel.* Within the museum are exhibits devoted to the history and activity of the great port outside. ✉ *Leuvehaven 1,* ☎ *010/4132680.* ⊙ *Sept.–June, Tues.–Sat. 10–5, Sun. 11–5; July–Aug., Mon.–Sat. 10–5, Sun. 11–5.*

The **Museumpark,** an easy stroll along the canal from Eendrachtsplein Metro station, is a welcome contrast to the industrial might of the Europoort and the Netherlands' maritime history. Three of Rotterdam's ★ art institutions are sited around these landscaped gardens. The **Boymans Van Beuningen Museum** has an Old Arts section that includes the work of Bruegel, Bosch, and Rembrandt, as well as a renowned print gallery with works by artists such as Dürer and Cézanne. Dali and Magritte mix with the Impressionists in the Modern Arts collection. ✉ *Museumpark 18–20,* ☎ *010/4419400.* ⊙ *Tues.–Sat. 10–5, Sun. and holidays 11–5.*

The **Nederlands Architectuurinstituut** (Netherlands Institute of Architecture), designed by Jo Coenen, hosts innovative exhibitions and lectures in the field of architecture, town and country planning, and interior design from the 1800s to the present. ✉ *Museumpark 25,* ☎ *010/4401200.* ⊙ *Tues.–Sat. 10–5, Sun. and holidays 11–5.*

The **Kunsthal** (Art Hall) in Museumpark mounts all manner of major temporary exhibitions —from prehistoric bones to Picasso retrospectives to avant-garde rows of compact cars. ⊠ *Kunsthal: Westzeedijk341,* ☎ *010/4400300.* ⊘ *Tues.–Sat. 10–5, Sun. and holidays 11–5.*

Delfshaven—spelled Delftshaven when the Pilgrims set sail from here— is the last remaining nook of old Rotterdam. Rows of gabled buildings and a windmill line the waterfront. Today Delfshaven is an up-and-coming area of trendy galleries, cafés, and restaurants. ⊠ *From Delfshaven Metro station, double back along Schiedamseweg, then turn right down Aelbrechtskolk.*

$$-$$$ × **Heerenhuis De Heuvel.** Resplendent beside a lake in the city's Maas Park, this airy 19th-century building has the sunniest terrace in town. In one wing is a restaurant serving such tantalizing dishes as cod with sesame seeds or lamb with anchovy butter. In the café on the other side of the building, the same kitchen serves inexpensive, lighter meals. ⊠ *Baden-Powelllaan 12,* ☎ *010/4364249. AE, DC, MC, V.*

$$-$$$ × **Loos.** The stylish brasserie is in one of the city's few remaining old neighborhoods. The fare is adventurous French-influenced Dutch, with such dishes as braised calf's tail with truffle sauces. ⊠ *Westplein 1,* ☎ *010/4117723. AE, MC, V. No lunch weekends.*

$$ × **Inn the Picture.** This trendy café offers a wide selection of typical Dutch fare. The salads are especially inviting. In summer tables afford a view of passing crowds in the shopping district. ⊠ *Karel Doormanstraat 294,* ☎ *010/4117723. AE, DC, MC, V.*

$$-$$$ × **Hotel New York.** The twin towers of the Hotel New York have been a feature of Rotterdam's skyline for almost a century. In the days of transatlantic liners it was the head office of the Holland-America Line. Some rooms retain the original walnut paneling and restored Art Nouveau carpets, while others are modern in design. Downstairs, the huge café-restaurant serves everything from English afternoon tea to a choice of five different types of oysters. ⊠ *Koninginnenhoofd 1, 3072 AD,* ☎ *010/4390500,* FAX *010/4842701. 72 rooms with shower or bath, 1 apartment. Restaurant. AE, DC, MC, V.*

$ **Hotel Van Walsum.** This pleasant, family-run hotel is just around the corner from Rotterdam's main museums. The small restaurant overflows into the garden in good weather. ⊠ *Mathenesserlaan 199–201, 3014 HC,* ☎ *010/4363275,* FAX *010/4364410. 18 rooms, 1 apartment. Restaurant. AE, DC, MC, V.*

The Hague, Delft, and Rotterdam Essentials

Getting Around

The heart of The Hague and Delft are compact enough to be explored on foot. Scheveningen is reached from The Hague's center by bus or tram; public transportation is more convenient than driving because of severe parking problems at the resort. The RET Metro is an easy-to-use option for getting around Rotterdam; the two main branches (north–south and east–west) cross in the heart of the business district.

Guided Tours

ORIENTATION

Sightseeing tours of **The Hague** can be arranged by or through the main VVV tourist office next to the train station (☞ Visitor Information, *below*). The 2½- to 3-hour "Royal Bus Tour" from outside the office at 1 PM every day from April through September takes passengers past Queen Beatrix's residences. **Scheveningen** is for walkers. The Scheveningen VVV office (☞ Visitor Information, *below*) has information about coastal strolls. **Delft** is best seen on foot. The VVV Delft Tourist Office (☞ Visitor Information, *below*) organizes tours. From April through September daily two-hour bus tours of **Rotterdam** are conducted by the VVV Rotterdam Tourist Office (☞ Visitor Information, *below*) from the office at 1:30 PM.

BOAT

From **The Hague,** various boat companies run short day trips and longer candlelight dinner cruises. These can be booked at The Hague tourist office (☞ Visitor Information, *below*) or through **De Haagse Rederij** (✉ Spui 256, ☎ 070/3462473). In **Scheveningen** there are fishing-boat tours around the Dutch coast; contact **Sportsviscentrum Trip 30** (☎ 070/3541122). In **Delft,** the tourist office (☞ Visitor Information, *below*) organizes boat tours along the unspoiled canal system. You can cruise the port of **Rotterdam** on a basic tour of 1¼ hours (year-round) or choose one that lasts as long as nine hours (midsummer only), with **Spido Rondvaarten** (✉ Willemsplein, ☎ 010/4135400), the main boat company. They also operate 2½-hour summer evening music-and-dinner cruises of the inner harbor. The pier can be reached by taking the RET Metro blue line toward Spijkenisse to the Leuvehaven station and walking to the end of the boulevard.

Visitor Information

Delft (✉ Markt 83–85, ☎ 015/2126100). **The Hague** (✉ Babylon Center, Koningin Julianaplein 30, next to the train station, ☎ 0900/3403505, 75¢ per minute). **Rotterdam** (✉ Coolsingel 67, ☎ 0900/4034065, 50¢ per minute). **Scheveningen** (✉ Gevers Deynootweg 1134, ☎ 0900/3403505, 75¢ per minute).

NORWAY

OSLO; THE COAST ROAD TO STAVANGER; THROUGH TELEMARK TO BERGEN; ABOVE BERGEN: THE FAR NORTH

O n Norway's dramatic west coast, deep fjords knife into steep mountain ranges. Inland, cross-country ski trails follow frozen trout streams, and downhill trails slice through forests that are carpeted with wildflowers and berries in summer. In older villages, wooden houses spill down toward docks where Viking ships were once moored. Small fishing boats, pleasure craft, and large industrial oil tankers dot the maritime horizon.

Inhabited since 1700 BC, Norway is today a peaceful nation, but from the 8th to the 10th century AD, the Vikings marauded as far afield as Seville and the Isle of Man and engaged in vicious infighting at home. This fierce spirit remained alive, despite Norway's subsequent centuries of subjugation by the Danes and Swedes. Independence came early in the 20th century but was tested during World War II, when the Germans occupied the country. Norwegian Resistance fighters rose to the challenge, eventually sabotaging Nazi efforts to develop atomic weapons.

The foundations for modern Norwegian culture were laid in the 19th century, during the period of union with Sweden, which lasted until 1905. Oslo blossomed at this time, and Norway produced its three greatest men of arts and letters: composer Edvard Grieg (1843–1907), playwright Henrik Ibsen (1828–1906), and painter Edvard Munch (1863–1944). Other notable Norwegians of this period were the polar explorers Roald Amundsen and Fridtjof Nansen.

The fjords, however, are Norway's true claim to fame. They were formed during an ice age a million years ago, when the ice cap created enormous pressure by burrowing deep into existing mountain-bound riverbeds. There was less pressure along the coast, so the entrances to most fjords are shallow, about 500 ft, while inland depths reach as much as 4,000 ft. Although Norway's entire coastline is notched with fjords, the most breathtaking sights are on the west coast between Stavanger and Trondheim, and the northern Helgeland coastline to the Lofoten Islands. From

North Cape

Vardø

Vadsø

Hammerfest

Kirkenes

ATLANTIC
OCEAN

Alta

Masi

Tromsø

Kantokeino

FINLAND

Harstad

Bardu

Norwegian
Sea

Narvik

Svolvoer

Lofoten

Vestfjorden

Bodø

Fauske

Saltdal

Arctic   Circle

Mo i Rana

Umbukta

Sandnessjøen

Mosjøen

Brønnøysund

E6

SWEDEN

Gulf of Bothnia

Vikna

Namsos

Steinkjer

Trondheim

Meråker

Støren

Kristiansund N.

70 Oppdal

Molde

Røros

Ålesund

E6o

Tynset

Dombås

Otta

Nordfjord

Koppang

Florø

Jostedalsbreen

Rena

Lillehammer

Sognefjorden

Laka
Mjøsa

Hamar

Voss

E68

Eidsvoll

Bergen

Hønefoss

Hardangerfjorden

40

Oslo

Baltic Sea

Kongsberg

Sarpsborg

Haugesund

Drammen

Larvik

Fredrikstad

Skien

Oslofjorden

Stavanger

Sandefjord

Egersund

Evje

Arendal

Grimstad

Skagerrak

Kattegat

Mandal

Kristiansand S.

0   200 miles
0   300 km

the sheltered villages deep in fjord country to the wildest windswept plateaus in Finnmark, Norway's natural beauty captivates both visitors and residents, transforming many into serious outdoor enthusiasts.

NORWAY A TO Z

Customs

Residents of non-European countries who are over 18 may import duty-free into Norway 400 cigarettes or 500 grams of other tobacco products. Residents of European countries who are over 18 may import 200 cigarettes or 250 grams of other tobacco goods. Anyone can bring in souvenirs, gifts, perfume, and eau de cologne to a value of NKr 5,000 after being out of the country for more than 24 hours. Within 24 hours, you may bring in goods duty free valued up to NKr 2,000. Anyone over 20 may bring in 1 liter of liquor, 1 liter of wine, and 2 liters of beer or 2 liters of wine and 2 liters of beer. Travelers who are at least 18 years old may bring in 2 liters of wine and 2 liters of beer.

Dining

The Norwegian diet emphasizes protein and carbohydrates. Breakfast is usually a large buffet of smoked fish, cheeses, sausage, cold meats, and whole-grain breads accompanied by tea, coffee, or milk. Lunch is simple, usually *smørbrød* (open-face sandwiches). Restaurant and hotel dinners are usually three-course meals, often starting with soup and ending with fresh fruit and berries. Meals are generally expensive, so take hotel breakfast when it's offered. Spirits are not served on Sunday, although beer and wine are available in most establishments. Alcohol is very expensive and, except in restaurants, is sold only during strictly regulated hours at state-owned *vinmonopol* stores. When dining out, take note that laws relating to drinking and driving are very strict; you should never drink without having a designated driver.

MEALTIMES

Lunch is from noon to 3 at restaurants featuring a *koldtbord*—a Scandinavian buffet, primarily for special occasions and visitors. Dinner has traditionally been early, but in hotels and major restaurants it is now more often from 6 to 11.

RATINGS

Prices are per person and include a first course, main course, and dessert, without wine or tip (☞ Tipping *in* Money Matters, *below*).

CATEGORY	COST
$$$$	over NKr 450
$$$	NKr 300–Nkr 450
$$	NKr 150–Nkr 300
$	under NKr 150

WHAT TO WEAR

Unless otherwise indicated, jacket and tie or high-fashion casual wear are recommended for restaurants in the $$$$ and $$$ price categories; during the summer, neat casual dress is acceptable in most places.

Language

There are two official forms of the Norwegian language—*bokmål* and *nynorsk*—along with many dialects. As is typical of Scandinavian languages, Norwegian's additional vowels—æ, ø, and å—come at the end of the alphabet in the phone book.

English is the main foreign language taught in schools, and movies, music, and TV reinforce its popularity. It is widely spoken by people in larger cities and most commercial establishments.

Lodging

CAMPING

There are 1,160 registered campsites in the country, many in spectacular surroundings. Prices vary according to the facilities provided: A family with a car and tent can expect to pay about NKr 80–NKr 150 per night. Some campsites have log cabins available from between NKr 20 and NKr 600 per night. *Camping Norway* is available from tourist offices and the **Norges Automobil Forbund** (NAF; ⊠ Storgt. 2, 0155 Oslo, ☎ 22341400).

HOTELS

Accommodations in Norway are usually spotless, and smaller establishments are often family-run. Service is attentive and considerate, right down to blackout curtains to block out the midnight sun. The **Fjord Pass** (⊠ Fjord Tours, Box 1752, 5024 Bergen, ☎ 55326550), which costs about NKr 75 (around $10), is valid for discounts at 250 establishments. Hotels in larger towns have special summer rates from late June to early August, and some chains have their own discount offers— see Norway's annual accommodation guide at tourist offices. Discounts in smaller hotels are offered to guests staying several days; meals are then included in the rate.

RATINGS

Prices are summer rates for two people in a double room with bath, and include breakfast, service, and taxes.

CATEGORY	MAJOR CITIES	OTHER AREAS
$$$$	over NKr 1,300	over NKr 1,000
$$$	NKr 1,000–NKr 1,300	NKr 850–NKr 1,000
$$	NKr 800–NKr 1,000	NKr 650–NKr 850
$	under NKr 800	under NKr 650

RENTALS

Norwegians escape to *hytter* (mountain cabins) whenever they have the chance. Stay in one for a week or two and you'll see why—magnificent scenery, pure air, edible wild berries, and a chance to hike, fish, or cross-country ski. For information on renting cabins, farms, or private homes, write to **Den Norske Hytteformidling A.S.** (⊠ Box 3404, Bjølsen, 0406 Oslo, ☎ 22356710), or get the brochure "Norsk Hytteferie" from tourist offices. An unusual alternative is to rent a *rorbu* (fisherman's dwelling) in the northerly Lofoten Islands. Contact **Destination Lofoten** (⊠ Box 210, 8301 Svolvær, ☎ 76073000).

YOUTH HOSTELS

Norway has about 100 youth hostels; some are schools or farms in winter. Members of the Youth Hostel Association (YHA) get a discount. Contact **Norske Vandrerhjem** (NoVa; ⊠ Dronningensgt. 26, 0154 Oslo, ☎ 23139300). International YHA guides are available to members in the United Kingdom and North America (☞ Student Travel *in* Chapter 1). There are no age restrictions for membership.

Mail

Opening times for post offices can vary throughout the country, but in general they are open weekdays 9–5 and Saturday 10–2. They cash traveler's checks, exchange foreign currency, and provide postal services.

POSTAL RATES

Letters and postcards to the United States cost NKr 6 for the first 20 grams. The rate within Europe is NKr 5.50 for the first 20 grams.

RECEIVING MAIL

If you're uncertain about where you'll be staying, have your mail marked "poste restante" and sent to the town where you plan to pick

it up. Your last name should be underlined. The service is free; letters
are directed to the nearest main post office, where you'll need your passport to pick up your mail. American Express offices will also hold mail
(nonmembers pay a small fee on collection).

Money Matters

COSTS

Norway has a high standard—and cost—of living, but there are ways
to save money by taking advantage of special offers for accommodations and travel during the tourist season and on weekends.

CURRENCY

The unit of currency in Norway is the krone, written as Kr. on price
tags but officially NOK (bank designation), NKr, or kr. The krone is
divided into 100 øre. Bills of NKr 50, 100, 200, 500, and 1,000 are in
general use. Coins are in denominations of 50 øre and 1, 5, 10, and 20
kroner. Credit cards are accepted in most hotels, stores, restaurants, and
many gas stations and garages, but generally not in smaller shops and
inns in rural areas. The exchange rate at press time (summer 1999) was
NKr 7.88 to the U.S. dollar, NKr 5.36 to the Canadian dollar, NKr 12.31
to the pound sterling, NKr 5.22 to the Australian dollar, and NKr 4.15
to the New Zealand dollar.

SAMPLE PRICES

Cup of coffee, NKr 12–NKr 25; ½ liter of beer, NKr 35–NKr 50; soft
drink, NKr 15–NKr 25; ham sandwich, NKr 30–NKr 50; taxi base rates
in Oslo: Nkr 35–Nkr 55, depending on time of day and whether you
phone for or hail the cab.

TIPPING

A 10%–12% service charge is added to most bills at hotels and restaurants. If you have had exceptional service, then give an additional 5%–
10% tip. Round off a taxi fare to the next higher unit, or a little more
if the driver has been particularly helpful with luggage. If the porter
helps with your luggage, give Nkr 15–NKr 20. Tip with kroner only.

National Holidays

January 1; April 16 (Palm Sunday); April 20–21, 23–24 (Easter); May
1 (Labor Day); May 17 (Constitution Day); June 1 (Ascension); June
11–12 (Pentecost); December 25–26.

Opening and Closing Times

Banks are open weekdays 8–3:30, in summer 8:15–3. **Museums** are usually open Tuesday–Sunday 10–3 or 4. **Shops** are usually open weekdays 9 or 10–5 (Thursday until 7 or 8) and Saturday 9–3 or 4, though
times vary. Shopping malls are often open until 8 on weeknights.

Shopping

GIFT IDEAS

Prices of handmade articles are government controlled, and selection
is widest in Oslo, so that's the best place to do your shopping: Pewter,
silver, glass, sheepskin, leather, painted wood decorations, kitchenware,
knitwear, and wall hangings all make special souvenirs.

SALES-TAX REFUNDS

Much of the 23% Norwegian value-added tax (VAT) will be refunded
to visitors who spend more than NKr 308 in any single store. Ask for
a special tax-free check and show your passport to confirm that you
are not a resident. All purchases must be sealed and presented together
with the tax-free check at the tax-free counter at foreign ferry ports
and at airports and border posts. The VAT will be refunded, minus a
service charge. You can get general information about the tax-free system by calling ☎ 67149901.

Telephoning

Domestic rates are reduced 5 PM–8 AM weekdays and all day on weekends. Cheap rates for international calls apply only after 10 PM. Avoid using room phones in hotels. In the public booths you can find card phones or coin phones. Be sure to read the instructions; some phones require the coins to be deposited before dialing, some after. You can buy telephone cards at Narvesen kiosks or at the post office. The largest coins generally accepted are NKr 10, although some new phones take NKr 20 coins. Most older phones take only NKr 1 or NKr 5 coins. The minimum deposit is NKr 2 or NKr 3, depending on the phone.

COUNTRY CODE

The international country code for Norway is 47.

INTERNATIONAL CALLS

These can be made from any pay phone. For calls to North America, dial 00–1, then the area code and number. When dialing the United Kingdom, omit the initial zero of the area code (for Central London you would dial 00 followed by 44, then 171 and the local number). To reach an **AT&T** long-distance operator, dial 80019011.

LOCAL CALLS

Area codes are not used in Norway. The cost of calls within the country varies according to distance: In Oslo, the cost goes up according to the amount of time used after the three-minute flat fee. The Oslo phone book has dialing information in English.

OPERATORS AND INFORMATION

For local information, dial 180. For international information, dial 181. For international collect calls, dial 115.

Transportation

The Norwegian words for street (gate or gata), road (veien), avenue (aveny), and square (plass) are abbreviated gt., vn., av., and pl.

BY BUS

The Norwegian bus network makes up for some limitations of the country's train system, and several routes are particularly scenic. For example, the **Nord-Norge Buss Service** (North Norway bus service; ✉ 8400 Sortland, ☎ 76111111) goes from Fauske (on the train line to Bodø) to Sortland; from Sortland the **Tromsø–innland rutebil** (Tromsø-inland coach; ☎ 77852100) goes right up to Kirkenes on the Russian-Norwegian border. Buses leave the Oslo area from **Bussterminalen** (Bus Terminal; ✉ Galleri Oslo, Schweigaardsgt. 10, ☎ 23002400), close to Oslo's Sentralstasjonen (Oslo S or Central Station).

BY CAR

Breakdowns. Norges Automobil Forbund (NAF) patrols main roads and has emergency telephones on mountain roads. For NAF 24-hour service, dial 80032900, 80033880 or 22341600.

Gasoline. Gas costs 8 NKr –9 NKr per liter and diesel costs 7NKr –8 NKr per liter. Gas stations are not hard to find in remote areas.

Parking. Street parking in cities and towns is clearly marked. There are also municipal parking lots. You cannot park on main roads or on bends. Check the leaflet *Parking in Oslo,* available free from the tourist office, at toll stations, and at the City Hall; or ask at your hotel.

Road Conditions. Away from the major routes, roads are narrow and winding, so don't expect to average more than 50–70 kph (30–40 mph), especially in fjord country. Even the best roads suffer from frost, and mountain passes may be closed in winter. Snow tires (preferably studded) are advised in winter in most areas; if you're renting a car, choose a smaller model with front-wheel drive.

Rules of the Road. Driving is on the right. The speed limit is 90 kph (55 mph) on highways, 80 kph (50 mph) on main roads, 50 kph (30 mph) in towns, and 30–40 kph (18–25 mph) in residential areas. The use of headlights at all times is mandatory. For assistance contact **Norges Automobil Forbund** (NAF—the Norwegian Automobile Association, ✉ Storgt. 2, 0155 Oslo, ☎ 22341400). It is important to remember to yield to the vehicle approaching from the right. Passing areas on narrow roads are marked with a white *M* (for *møteplass*) on a blue background.

BY FERRY

Norway's long, fjord-indented coastline is served by an intricate and essential network of ferries and passenger ships. A wide choice of services is available, from simple hops across fjords (saving many kilometers of traveling) and excursions among the thousands of islands to luxury cruises and long journeys up the coast. Most ferries carry cars. Reservations are required on journeys of more than one day but are not needed for simple fjord crossings. Fares and exact departure times depend on the season and the availability of ships. Contact **Nortra** (Norwegian Travel Association) or the **Norway Information Centre** for details (☞ Visitor Information, *below*.)

One of the world's great sea voyages is aboard one of the mail-and-passenger Hurtigruta ships that run up the Norwegian coast from Bergen to Kirkenes, well above the Arctic Circle. Contact the **Bergen Line** (✉ 405 Park Ave., New York, NY 10022, ☎ 800/323–7436; Tromsø Main Office, ☎ 77648200 or 76967600).

BY PLANE

Fares are high, so be sure to ask about the special rates available year-round within Norway. For longer distances, flying can be cheaper than driving a rented car, given the cost of gas and incidentals. Inquire about "Visit Norway" and "Visit Scandinavia" passes, which provide relatively cheap domestic-flight coupons. Contact the following Norwegian airlines for more information: **SAS** (✉ Oslo S or Central Station; beginning of Karl Johans Gt., ☎ 81003300); **Braathens SAFE AS** (Oslo S or Central Station, ☎ 81001200); **Norsk Air** (✉ Torp Airport, Sandefjord, ☎ 33482600); **Widerøe** (✉ Volls vei 6, Box 131, 1324 Lysaker, ☎ 67596600).

BY TRAIN

Trains are punctual and comfortable, and most routes are scenic. Lines fan out from Oslo and leave the coastline (except in the south) to buses and ferries. Reservations are required on all *ekspresstog* (express trains) and night trains. The Oslo–Bergen route is especially beautiful, and the Oslo–Trondheim–Bodø route takes you within the Arctic Circle. Do not miss the side trips from Myrdal to Flåm from the Oslo–Bergen line, and Dombås to Åndalsnes from the Oslo–Trondheim line. **NSB** (Norwegian rail system; ☎ 81500888) trains leave Oslo from Sentralstasjonen (Oslo S or Central Station; ✉ Jernbanetorget, beginning of Karl Johans Gt.).

Fares. In addition to the Europe-wide passes (Eurail and Inter-Rail), **ScanRail passes,** good in Norway, Sweden, Denmark, and Finland, are also available. ScanRail passes offer unlimited travel in a set number of travel days within a specified period. They are available in the United States through Rail Europe (☎ 914/682–2999) and DER Travel Service (☎ 310/479–4411). A **Norway Rail Pass** is available with a choice of one or two weeks' unlimited rail travel or three travel days within a month within Norway. In the United States the ticket is available through DER Travel Service, Rail Europe, and ScanAm (☎ 201/835–7070 or 800/545–2204), and in London through NSB Travel. **Reduced fares** during off-peak times ("green" routes) are also available if booked in advance. These can be purchased in Norway only.

Visitor Information

Nortra (Norwegian Travel Association; ✉ Drammensvn. 40, Postboks 2893, Solli, 0230 Oslo, ☎ 22925200). **Norway Information Centre** (✉ Vestbanepl. 1, 0250 Oslo, ☎ 22830050; 82060100 within Norway; ✉ Oslo Sentralstasjonen/Central Station, East of Strandgt.). **Trafikanten** (✉ Oslo Sentralstasjonen/Central Station, East of Strandgt., ☎ 22177030, or 177 for Oslo public transportation).

Weather

Norway is an important winter sports center. January, February, and early March are good skiing months, and hotel rooms are plentiful then. Avoid late April, when sleet, rain, and repeated thaws and refreezings may ruin the good skiing snow and leave roads—and spirits—in bad shape. The country virtually closes down for the five-day Easter holiday, when Norwegians make their annual migration to the mountains. If you plan to visit at this time, reserve well in advance. May is one of the best times to visit—the days are long and sunny, cultural life is still going strong, and *Syttende mai* (Constitution Day, May 17), with all its festivities, is worth a trip in itself. Norwegians tend to take their vacations in July and the first part of August. Summers are generally mild. With the midnight sun, even in the "southern" city of Oslo, night seems more like twilight around midnight, and dawn comes by 2 AM. The weather can be fickle, and rain gear and sturdy waterproof shoes are recommended even in summer.

CLIMATE

The following are the average daily maximum and minimum temperatures for Oslo.

Jan.	28F	– 2C	May	61F	16C	Sept.	60F	16C
	19	– 7		43	6		46	8
Feb.	30F	– 1C	June	68F	20C	Oct.	48F	9C
	19	– 7		50	10		38	3
Mar.	39F	4C	July	72F	22C	Nov.	38F	3C
	25	– 4		55	13		31	– 1
Apr.	50F	10C	Aug.	70F	21C	Dec.	32F	0C
	34	1		54	12		25	– 4

OSLO

Although it is one of the world's largest capital cities in area, Oslo has only about 500,000 inhabitants. In recent years the city has become more lively: Shops are open later, and plentiful pubs, cafés, and restaurants are crowded at all hours, especially later in the week.

Exploring Oslo

Numbers in the margin correspond to points of interest on the Oslo map.

The downtown area is compact, but the city limits include forests, fjords, and mountains, giving Oslo a pristine airiness that complements its urban dignity. Explore downtown on foot, then venture beyond via bus, streetcar, or train.

★ ❿ **Aker Brygge** (Aker Wharf). The quayside shopping and cultural center, with a theater, cinemas (including an IMAX film theater), and galleries among the stores, restaurants, and cafés, is a great place to linger late into summer nights. It's in the central harbor—the heart of Oslo and head of the fjord. ✉ *Off Dokkvn.*

❾ **Akershus Slott** (Akershus Castle). This fortified harbor-front castle was built in 1299 and restored in 1527 by Christian IV of Denmark (Denmark then ruled Norway) after it was damaged by fire. Christian laid out the present city of Oslo (naming it Christiania, after himself) around his new residence; Oslo's street plan still follows his design. Some rooms are open for guided tours, and the grounds form a park. Also on the grounds are the **Forsvarsmuséet** (Defense Museum; ☎ 23093582) and **Hjemmefrontmuseum** (Resistance Museum; ☎ 23093138). Both give you a feel for the Norwegian fighting spirit throughout history and especially during the German occupation, when the Nazis set up headquarters on this site and had a number of patriots executed here. ✉ *Festningspl.; castle,* ☎ *22412521; Forsvarsmuséet,* ☎ *29093582; Hjemmefrontmuséet,* ☎ *23093138.* ◷ *Castle: May–mid-Sept., Mon.–Sat. 10–4, Sun. 12:30–4; Sept. and Apr., Sun. 12:30–4; guided tours May–Sept., Mon.–Sat. 11, 1, and 3, Sun. 1 and 3. Forsvarsmuséet: June–Aug., weekdays 10–6, weekends 11–4; Sept.–May, weekdays 10–3, weekends 11–4. Hjemmefrontmuseum: mid-Apr.–mid-June, Mon.–Sat. 10–4, Sun. 11–4; mid-June–Aug., daily 11–5; Sept., Mon.–Sat. 10–4, Sun. 11–4; Oct.–mid-Apr., daily 11–4.*

❼ **Astrup Fearnley Muséet.** This private museum collection was founded by a leading Oslo shipping family and has an impressive permanent display of post-war and contemporary works of art and sculptures by Norwegian and international artists, including pieces by the celebrated British artist Damien Hirst. Special exhibitions and guided tours are held regularly throughout the year. ✉ *Grev Wedels Pl. 9,* ☎ *22936060 or 22936015.* ◷ *Tues.–Sun. 12–4.*

Bygdøy. In summer, ferries make the seven-minute run from Rådhusbryggen (City Hall Wharf) across the fjord to the Bygdøy peninsula, where there are several museums (☞ *Fram*-Muséet, *Kon-Tiki* Muséet, Norsk Folkemuseum, Vikingskiphuset, *below*) and some popular beaches. You can also take Bus 30 (from the National Theater or the Central Station). ◷ *Ferries run May–Sept., daily every ½ hr 8:15–5:45.*

❶❾ **Ekebergsletta Parken.** The oldest traces of human habitation in Oslo are the 5,000-year-old carvings on **runic stones** across the road from this park; they are marked by a sign reading FORTIDSMINNE. ✉ *Karlsborgvn.; take Trikk (tram) 18 or 19 east from National Theater or Central Station to Sjømannsskolen stop.*

❶❻ **Fram-Muséet** (*Fram* Museum). Housed in a triangular building, the museum is devoted to the polar ship *Fram*, the wooden vessel that belonged to explorer Fridtjof Nansen. In 1893 Nansen led an expedition that reached latitude 86°14′N, farther north than any European had been at that time. Active in Russian famine-relief work, Nansen received a Nobel Peace Prize in 1922. You can board the ship and imagine yourself in one of the tiny berths with a force-9 gale blowing outside and the temperature dozens of degrees below freezing. ✉ *Bygdøynes,* ☎ *22438370.* ◷ *Mar.–Apr., daily 11–3:45; May and Sept., daily 10–4:45; June–Aug., daily 9–5:45; Oct., daily 10–3:45; Nov., weekends 11–2:45; Dec.–Feb., weekends 11–3:45.*

❷ **Historisk Museum** (Historical Museum). In addition to displays of daily life and art from the Viking period, the museum has an ethnographic section with a collection related to the great polar explorer Roald

Amundsen, the first man to reach the South Pole. ⊠ *Frederiksgt. 2,* ☎ *22859964.* ⊙ *Mid-May–mid-Sept., Tues.–Sun. 11–3; mid-Sept.–mid-May, Tues.–Sun. 12–3.*

Karl Johans Gate (Karl Johan's Street). Oslo's main street runs right through the center of town, from the Oslo S Station uphill to the Royal Palace. Half its length is closed to automobiles but it still bustles with many of the city's shops and outdoor cafés.

★ ⑮ ***Kon-Tiki Muséet*** (*Kon-Tiki* Museum). Take the ferry from Rådhusbryggen (City Hall Wharf) to the museum where Thor Heyerdahl's *Kon-Tiki* raft and his reed boat *RA II* are on view. He crossed the Pacific on the former and the Atlantic on the latter. ⊠ *Bygdøynesvn. 36,* ☎ *22438050.* ⊙ *Oct.–Mar., daily 10:30–4; Apr.–May and Sept., daily 10:30–5; June–Aug., daily 9:30–5:45.*

★ ⑰ **Munch-Muséet** (Munch Museum). In 1940, four years before his death, Edvard Munch bequeathed much of his work to the city; the museum opened in 1963, the centennial of his birth. Although only a fraction of its 22,000 items—books, paintings, drawings, prints, sculptures, and letters—are on display, you can still get a sense of the tortured Expressionism that was to have such an effect on European painting. ⊠ *Tøyengt. 53; Bus 29 from Rådhuset or T-bane from Nationaltheatret to Tøyen in northeast Oslo,* ☎ *22673774.* ⊙ *June–mid-Sept., daily 10–6; late Sept.–May, Tues., Wed., Fri., Sat. 10–4, Thurs., Sun. 10–6.*

🖐 ⑧ **Muséet for Samtidskunst** (Museum of Contemporary Art). Housed in the Norwegian Art Nouveau former Bank of Norway building, the museum displays Norwegian and international contemporary art. You will also find a library, a cafeteria, and a book shop. ⊠ *Bankpl. 4,* ☎ *22335820.* ⊙ *Tues., Wed., Fri. 10–5, Thurs. 10–8, Sat. 11–4, Sun. 11–5. Guided tours weekends at 2. Special children's tours first Sun. in month at 1. Group tours and theme tours can be arranged.*

❸ **Nasjonalgalleriet** (National Gallery). Norway's largest public gallery has a small but high-quality selection of paintings by European artists, and there's an impressive collection of works by Scandinavian Impressionists. Here you can see Edvard Munch's most famous painting, *The Scream.* ⊠ *Universitetsgt. 13,* ☎ *22200404.* ⊙ *Mon., Wed., Fri. 10–6, Thurs. 10–8, Sat. 10–4, Sun. 11–4.*

❹ **Nationaltheatret** (National Theater). Statues of Bjørnstjerne Bjørnson, the nationalist poet who wrote Norway's anthem, and Henrik Ibsen, who wrote the plays *Peer Gynt, A Doll's House, Hedda Gabler,* and other classics, watch over Nationaltheatret. Ibsen worried that his works, packed with allegory, myth, and sociological and emotional angst, might not have appeal outside Norway. As it happened, they changed the face of modern theater around the world. ⊠ *Stortingsgt. 15,* ☎ *22412710.*

★ 🖐 ⑬ **Norsk Folkemuseum** (Norwegian Folk Museum). Take the ferry from Rådhusbryggen (City Hall Wharf) and walk up a well-marked road to see centuries-old historic farmhouses that have been collected from all over the country and reassembled in this large park. A whole section of 19th-century Oslo was moved here, as was a 12th-century wooden stave church. ⊠ *Museumsvn. 10,* ☎ *22123700.* ⊙ *Jan.–mid-May, Mon.–Sat. 11–3, Sun. 11–4; mid-May–mid-June, daily 10–5; mid-June–Aug., daily 10–6; early Sept., daily 10–5; mid-Sept.–Dec., Mon.–Sat. 11–3, Sun. 11–4.*

❻ **Oslo Domkirke** (Oslo Cathedral). Consecrated in 1697 and subsequently much renovated, this rather austere cathedral is modest compared to those of other European capitals, but the interior is rich with

792

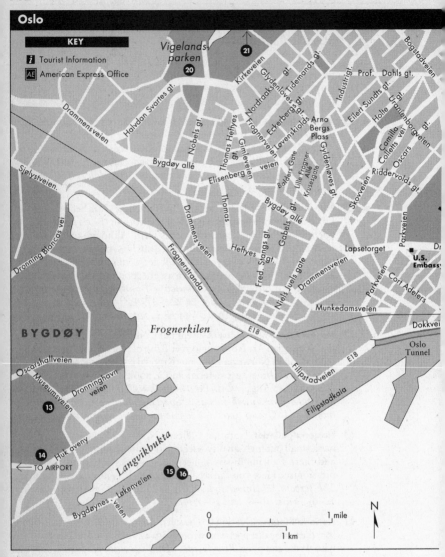

Aker Brygge, **10**

Akershus Slott, **9**

Astrup Fearnley
Muséet, **7**

Ekebergsletta
Parken, **19**

Fram-Muséet, **16**

Historisk Museum, **2**

Holmen-
kollbakken, **21**

Kon-Tiki
Muséet, **15**

Munch-Muséet, **17**

Muséet for
Samtidskunst, **8**

Nasjonalgalleriet, **3**

Nationaltheatret, **4**

Norsk
Folkemuseum, **13**

Oslo Domkirke, **6**

Oslo Ladegård, **18**

Oslo Rådhus, **12**

Slottet, **1**

Stenersenmuséet, **11**

Stortinget, **5**

Vigelandsparken, **20**

Vikingskiphuset, **14**

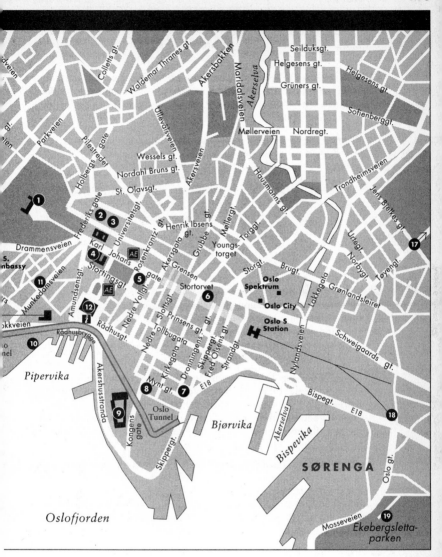

treasures, such as the Baroque carved wooden altarpiece and pulpit. The ceiling frescoes by Hugo Lous Mohr were done after World War II. Look for arcades, small restaurants, and street musicians behind the cathedral. ⊠ *Stortorvet 1.* ⊙ *Weekdays 10–4.*

⑱ Oslo Ladegård (The Manor). Now owned by the city council, this museum has scale models of old Oslo on the site of the 13th-century Bispegård (Bishop's Palace). ⊠ *St. Hallvards Plass, Oslgt. 13,* ☎ *22194468.* ⊙ *May–Sept., guided tours Wed. at 6 and Sun. at 1, and on request; book in advance.*

⑫ Oslo Rådhus (City Hall). Designed by architects Arnstein Arneberg and Magnus Poulsson, the impressive redbrick city hall opened officially on May 15, 1950. The courtyard friezes portraying scenes from Norwegian folklore literally pale in comparison to the marble-floored inside halls, where murals and frescoes bursting with color depict daily life, historical events, and Resistance activities in Norway. The elegant main hall has been the venue for the Nobel Peace Prize Ceremony since 1991. ⊠ *Rådhuspl.,* ☎ *22861600.* ⊡ *Free.* ⊙ *May–Aug., Mon.–Sat. 9–5, Sun. noon–5; Sept.–Apr., Mon.–Sat. 9–4, Sun. 12–4. Tours weekdays 10, noon, and 2.*

★ **① Slottet** (Royal Palace). This neoclassical structure, completed in 1848, is as sober, sturdy, and unpretentious as the Norwegian character. The surrounding park is open to the public, though the palace is not. The changing of the guard takes place daily at 1:30. When the king is in residence—signaled by a red flag—the Royal Guard strikes up the band. ⊠ *Drammensvn. 1,* ☎ *22048700.*

⑪ Stenersenmuséet (The Stenersen Museum). The museum shows a representative collection of Norwegian art from 1850 to 1970, featuring works by Amaldus Nielsen, Ludvig O. Ravensberg, and Rolf E. Stenersen. In addition the museum hosts special exhibitions, generally in photography and Nordic modern art. ⊠ *Munkedamsv. 15,* ☎ *22839560.* ⊙ *Tues., Thurs. 11–7; Wed., Fri., Sun. 11–5.*

⑤ Stortinget (Parliament). Built in 1866 by Swedish architect Emil Langelot, this bow-front, yellow-brick building is open to visitors by request when Parliament is not in session. A guide will take you around the frescoed interior and into the debating chamber. ⊠ *Karl Johans Gt. 22,* ☎ *22313050.* ⊡ *Free.* ⊙ *Guided tours July–Aug.; public gallery, weekdays when parliament is in session.*

★ **⑳ Vigelandsparken** (Frogner Park/Vigeland's Park). Don't leave Olso before pondering Gustav Vigeland's sculptures—192 of them, with a total of 650 figures—in this park in northwest Oslo. Two works in particular continue to spark metaphysical ruminations: *Wheel of Life,* a circle in stone depicting the stages of human life, and *The Monolith,* nearly 50 ft high and covered with more than 100 linked human forms. The nearby Vigeland Museum, open-air restaurants, tennis courts, and swimming pools provide additional diversions. ⊠ *Kirkevn. and Middelthunsgt.; Trikk 12 or 15 or T-bane trains 1, 2, 3, 4, 5, or 8 to Majorstuen.*

★ **⑭ Vikingskiphuset** (Viking Ship Museum). Three remarkably intact 9th-century ships last used by Vikings on the shores of the Oslofjord as royal burial chambers are the treasures of this cathedral-like museum. Also on display are riches that accompanied the royal bodies on their last voyage. The ornate craftsmanship evident in the ships and jewelry dispels any notion that the Vikings were skilled only in looting and pillaging. ⊠ *Huk Av. 35,* ☎ *22438379.* ⊙ *Nov.–Mar., daily 11–3; Apr. and Oct., daily 11–4; May–Aug., daily 9–6; Sept., daily 11–5.*

Elsewhere in Oslo

㉑ **Holmenkollbakken** (Holmenkollen Ski Museum and Ski Jump). At 203 ft above ground level, Holmenkollen's ski jump is among the world's highest and the site of an international contest each March. Carved into the rock at the base is the Ski Museum. The scenic ½-hour train ride from downtown Oslo to the jump sweeps up from underground to 1,322 ft above sea level. ⊠ *Kongevn. 5, Holmenkollen; Frogner-seter/Holmenkollen T-bane train from Nationaltheatret, to Holmenkollen; walk uphill to the jump;* ☎ *22923200.* ⊙ *Oct.–Apr., daily 10–4; May and Sept., daily 10–5; June–Aug., daily 9–8.*

Dining and Lodging

Oslo's chefs are gaining recognition worldwide. Norwegian cuisine, based on products from the country's waters and farmland, is now firmly ingrained in the culinary melting pot. Menus change daily, weekly, or according to the season in many Oslo restaurants. For details and price-category information *see* Dining *in* Norway A to Z, *above.*

Lodging in the capital is expensive. Prices for downtown accommodations are high, even for B&Bs, although just about all hotels have weekend, holiday, and summer rates (25%–50% reductions). Taxes and service charges, unless otherwise noted, are included. Breakfast is usually included also, but be sure to ask before booking your room. If you arrive and need a hotel the same day, ask about last-minute prices, which are generally discounted. The helpful accommodations bureau of the **Norway Information Centre** (☞ Visitor Information *in* Oslo Essentials, *below*) in Oslo's Sentralstasjonen (Oslo S or Central Station) can help you find a room; apply in person and pay a fee of NKr 20. If you are planning your trip from home, call **ScanAm** (in the U.S., ☎ 973/835–7070 or 800/545–2204) and ask about the Oslo Package, which combines an Oslo Card (☞ Getting Around *in* Oslo Essentials, *below*) with discounted room rates for almost all of Oslo's better hotels. For details and price-category information, *see* Lodging *in* Norway A to Z, *above.*

$$$$ ✕ **Bagatelle.** Bagatelle was the first restaurant with a Norwegian chef
★ serving Norwegian food to receive international recognition. Choose the seven-course menu for the full range of chef Hellstrøm's talents. The chairs are comfortable, service is impeccable, and Norwegian contemporary art adorns the walls. The fish soup is a highlight. ⊠ *Bygdøy allé 3,* ☎ *22446397. AE, DC, MC, V. Closed Sun. No lunch.*

$$$$ ✕ **D'Artagnan.** Stellar French-inspired food and excellent service make
★ this a place to remember. Try chef Freddie Nielsen's copious Grand Menu if you're famished. Otherwise, try the beef; you can literally cut it with a fork. **A Touch of France** (☎ 22425697, $$), downstairs from D'Artagnan, is a French-style brasserie run by the same chef. The bouillabaisse is outstanding. ⊠ *Øvre Slottsgt. 16,* ☎ *23100160. Reservations essential. AE, DC, MC, V.*

$$$$ ✕ **De Fem Stuer.** Chef Frank Halvorsen prepares food that is even bet-
★ ter than the view from this restaurant near the Holmenkollen ski jump. Modern versions of Norwegian classics focus on fish and game. ⊠ *Holmenkollen Park Hotel, Kongevn. 26,* ☎ *22922734. AE, DC, MC, V.*

$$$$ ✕ **Feinschmecker.** In the fashionable Frogner area, only minutes from the center of town, this restaurant specializes in modern Scandinavian cuisine. ⊠ *Balchensgt. 5,* ☎ *22441777. Reservations essential. AE, DC, MC, V. Closed Sun.*

$$$ ✕ **Babette's Gjestehus.** This intimate restaurant has an international menu with a French accent. ⊠ *Rådhuspassasjen,* ☎ *22416464. Reservations essential. AE, DC, MC, V. Closed Sun. No lunch.*

$$$ ✕ **Theatercafeen.** One of the last Viennese-style cafés in northern Eu-
★ rope, this is a favorite with the literary and entertainment crowd. The
pastry chef here also makes desserts for Norway's royal family. ⊠ *Hotel
Continental, Stortingsgt. 24/26,* ☎ *22824050. AE, DC, MC, V.*

$$ ✕ **Det Gamle Raadhus.** The "old city hall," Oslo's oldest restaurant,
is in a building that dates from 1641. Specialties include seafood casse-
role. ⊠ *Nedre Slottsgt. 1,* ☎ *22420107. AE, DC, MC, V. Closed Sun.*

$$ ✕ **Dinner.** Though its name does not identify the restaurant as specializing
★ in Szechuan-style cuisine, this is the best place for Chinese food, both
hot and not so pungent. The mango pudding dessert is wonderful. ⊠
Stortingsgt. 22, ☎ *22426890. AE, DC, MC, V. No lunch.*

$$ ✕ **Frognerseteren.** This restaurant specializing in fish and reindeer
looks down on the city from just above the Holmenkollen ski jump.
The upstairs room has the same view as the more expensive panorama
veranda, and there is outdoor seating. ⊠ *Holmenkollenvn. 200,* ☎
22140550. DC, MC, V.

$$ ✕ **Kastanjen.** The short menu at this stylish neighborhood bistro
changes often and offers all seasonal ingredients. The three-course
prix-fixe dinner is an excellent value. ⊠ *Bygdøy allé 18,* ☎ *22434467.
AE, DC, MC, V. Closed Sun. and 2 wks in July.*

$ ✕ **Lofotstua.** This rustic fish restaurant has a cozy atmosphere and good
food. Typical specialties include fresh cod and seafood from the Lo-
foten Islands in northern Norway. ⊠ *Kirkevn. 40,* ☎ *22469396. AE,
DC, MC, V. Closed weekends, July, Easter, and Christmas.*

$ ✕ **Vegeta.** Take advantage of the all-you-can-eat specials at this veg-
etarian spot. The restaurant is next to the Nationaltheatret bus and
trikk station. ⊠ *Munkedamsvn. 3B,* ☎ *22834020. Reservations not
accepted. AE, DC, V.*

$$$$ ▥ **Grand Hotel.** It's hard to beat the Grand's site on Oslo's main
★ street, opposite Parliament. The hotel has comforts and history to
match its name. Palmen, just off the lobby, is where Oslo matrons sip
afternoon tea. ⊠ *Karl Johans Gt. 31, 0159,* ☎ *22429390,* FAX *22421225.
287 rooms, 50 suites. 3 restaurants, indoor pool. AE, DC, MC, V.*

$$$$ ▥ **Holmenkollen Park Rica.** The imposing building in the old roman-
★ tic folkloric style stands near the ski jump in Holmenkollen. The rooms
are bright, and most have balconies with excellent views of the city and
the fjord. ⊠ *Kongevn. 26, 0390,* ☎ *22922000,* FAX *22146192. 221
rooms. 2 restaurants, indoor pool. AE, DC, MC, V.*

$$$$ ▥ **Hotel Continental.** The Brockmann family, owners of the hotel since
★ 1900, have succeeded in combining the rich elegance of the turn of the
century with modern, comfortable living. Antique furniture and shiny
white porcelain fixtures add a distinctive touch to the impeccably dec-
orated rooms. The property stands in the heart of Oslo, between the Royal
Palace and the City Hall. ⊠ *Stortingsgt. 24–26, 0161,* ☎ *22824000,* FAX
22429689. 140 rooms, 19 suites. 3 restaurants. AE, DC, MC, V.

$$$$ ▥ **Radisson SAS Scandinavia Hotel.** The SAS, across from the Royal
Palace, is a comfortable business hotel with impeccable service, including
an airport bus that stops right outside. ⊠ *Holbergs Gt. 30, 0166,* ☎
22113000, FAX *22113017. 488 rooms, 3 suites. 2 restaurants, indoor
pool. AE, DC, MC, V.*

$$$ ▥ **Bondeheimen.** Established to provide "down-home" accommoda-
tions for farmers on business in the big city, this may be Oslo's most
Norwegian hotel. The rooms are simple and comfortable. ⊠
Rosenkrantz' Gt. 8, 0159, ☎ *22429530,* FAX *22419437. 81 rooms.
Restaurant. AE, DC, MC, V.*

$$$ ▥ **Radisson SAS Park Royal Hotel.** This clean, efficient hotel sits in
Fornebu park by the shores of the Oslo fjord, 15 minutes from Oslo's
center. ⊠ *Fornebuparken, Box 1324, 1324 Lysaker,* ☎ *67120220,* FAX
67120011. 254 rooms, 14 suites. Restaurant. AE, DC, MC, V.

$$ 🏨 **Ambassadeur.** On a quaint residential street, this hotel has individually
★ designed rooms and personalized service. ⊠ *Camilla Colletts vei 15,
0266,* ☎ *22441835,* FAX *22444791. 33 rooms, 8 suites. Indoor pool.
AE, DC, MC, V.*

$$ 🏨 **Rainbow Cecil Tulip Hotel.** Known for its copious breakfast table,
this hotel is right in the heart of town near the Parliament building.
⊠ *Stortingsgt. 8, 0130,* ☎ *22427000,* FAX *22422670. 112 rooms. AE,
DC, MC, V.*

$$ 🏨 **Stefan.** The service is cheerful and accommodating in this hotel in
the center of town. Be sure to sample traditional Norwegian dishes at
Oslo's best buffet lunch, served in the restaurant on the top floor. ⊠
Rosenkrantz' Gt. 1, 0159, ☎ *22429250,* FAX *22337022. 138 rooms.
Restaurant. AE, DC, MC, V.*

$ 🏨 **Gabelshus Hotel.** Only five minutes from the center of town on an
attractive side street in Frogner, Gabelshus has the feel of a large coun-
try house. The rooms are spacious and airy. ⊠ *Gabels Gt. 16, 0272,*
☎ *22552260,* FAX *22442730. 43 rooms. Restaurant. AE, DC, MC, V.*

$ 🏨 **Munch.** This B&B near the National Gallery has large, spartan
rooms. ⊠ *Munchsgt. 5, 0165,* ☎ *22424275,* FAX *22206469. 180 rooms.
AE, DC, MC, V.*

$ 🏨 **Oslo Vandrerhjem Haraldsheim.** Oslo's youth hostel is one of Eu-
rope's largest. Most rooms have four beds; those in the new wing all
have showers. Breakfast is included. ⊠ *Haraldsheimvn. 4, 0409; Trikk
10 or 11 to Sinsen;* ☎ *22222965,* FAX *22221025. 270 beds. V.*

$ 🏨 **Rainbow Gyldenløve.** Freshly decorated rooms are offered here at
a reasonable price. Just outside are many shops and cafés. ⊠ *Bogstadvn.
20, 0355,* ☎ *22601090,* FAX *22603390. 168 rooms. AE, DC, MC, V.*

Nightlife and the Arts

The Arts

Considering the city's small population, Oslo has a surprisingly rich
arts scene. Check the monthly "What's On in Oslo," available at the
Norway Information Centre (☞ Visitor Information *in* Oslo Essentials,
below).

FILM

All films are screened in the original language with Norwegian subti-
tles. Oslo has one of Europe's best cinema collections, with 30 screens.
Call ☎ 82030000 for schedules for: **Coloseum** (⊠ Fr. Nansensv. 6, Ma-
jorstua); **Eldorado** (⊠ Torggt. 9); **Felix** (⊠ Bryggetorget, Akerbrygge);
Klingenberg (⊠ Olav V'sgt. 4); and **Saga** (⊠ Stortingsgt. 28). For al-
ternative and classic films, try **Cinemateket** (⊠ Dronningensgt. 16, ☎
22474505), the city's only independent cinema.

MUSIC

Oslo's modern **Konserthuset** (⊠ Munkedamsvn. 14, ☎ 23113100) is
the home of the Oslo Philharmonic. A smaller hall in the same build-
ing has folk dancing, held Monday and Thursday at 9 in July and Au-
gust. At **Den Norske Opera** (The Norwegian Opera House; ⊠ Storgt.
23, ☎ 22429475), performances usually start at 7:30; it's closed in
July and August. **Cosmopolite Club** (⊠ Industrigaten 36, ☎ 22690198)
has international acts regularly, ranging from folk to jazz. **Oslo Spek-
trum** (⊠ Sonja Henies plass 2, ☎ 22052900) is a large indoor show
and concert venue. **Rockefeller/John Dee** (⊠ Torggt. 16, ☎ 22203232)
has concerts featuring well-known pop and rock acts.

THEATER

Winter is *the* cultural season, when the **Nationaltheatret** (National The-
ater; ☞ Exploring Oslo, *above*) presents modern plays (all in Norwe-
gian), classics, and a good sampling of Ibsen. **Det Norske Teatret** (The

Norwegian Theater; ⊠ Kristian IV's Gt. 8, ☎ 22424344), one of Europe's most modern theater complexes, has musicals and plays (all in Norwegian).

Nightlife

NIGHTCLUBS AND BARS

Barock-Restauranthuset (⊠ Universitetsgt. 26, ☎ 22424420), complete with elegant chandeliers and blaring techno pop, is where Oslo's young and beautiful people choose to dance. **Baronen og Baronessen** (⊠ Stortingsgt. 10, ☎ 22420470), a combination discotheque, piano bar, and restaurant, is one of the few places serving food until 4 AM. Students frequent the informal and intimate **Ett Glass** (⊠ Karl Johansgt. 23, ☎ 22334079) café. Media people and students hang out at **Galleriet** (⊠ Kristian IV's Gt. 12, ☎ 22422936), a three-story disco with live music sessions on the third floor. **Karl Johans Gate** is a lively and drunken place into the wee hours, with loads of music cafés and clubs, as well as more conventional nightspots. Dress codes apply at **Lipp** (⊠ Olav V's Gt. 2, ☎ 22824060), a popular upscale predinner drinks bar (for people over 24); Lipp's restaurant serves international cuisine. **Smuget** (⊠ Rosenkrantz' Gt. 22, ☎ 22425262) is a combination discotheque and bar with live rock and blues bands most nights of the week.

Outdoor Activities and Sports

The forests within Oslo's vast city limits include 11 sports chalets geared toward exercise and the outdoors. You'll find outstanding walking and skiing trails around **Skullerudstua** and **Skistua.** Small passenger ferries run between Vippetangen and the islands that dot Oslo fjord, including **Hovedøya,** which has the ruins of a medieval monastery and swimming possibilities. On Bygdøy you will find **Huk,** the area's most popular beach. Contact **Oslo Kommune** (⊠ Forestry Services, Skogvesenet, ☎ 22082200) for more information. For winter or summer "safaris" through the forest by Land Rover, contact the **Norway Information Centre** (☞ Visitor Information *in* Oslo Essentials, *below*).

Shopping

Many of the larger stores are in the pedestrian-only areas between Stortinget and the cathedral. Shops stay open until 5 or 6 on weekdays, 7 or 8 on Thursdays, and 2 or 3 on Saturdays. Stores hold extended hours the first Saturday of the month, known as "Super Saturday." One of Oslo's newest shopping areas, **Aker Brygge** (⊠ waterfront), a complex of booths, offices, and sidewalk cafés, is especially lively in summer and spring. The **Basarhallene** (⊠ at back of the cathedral) is an art and handicrafts boutique center just around the corner from the many outdoor vendors and shops that line the pedestrian part of Karl Johans Gate. Check out the many shops and galleries on **Bogstadveien/Hegdehaugsveien** (⊠ runs from Majorstua to Parkvn.).

Department Stores and Malls

Glasmagasinet (⊠ Stortorvet 9, ☎ 22908900), open weekdays 10–7 and Saturday 10–6, has a large assortment of wares in 50 different stores, including souvenirs, glassware, and silver and pewter jewelry. **Gunerius** (⊠ Storgt. 32, ☎ 22170571), open weekdays 9–7 and Saturday 9–6, has a restaurant and 21 shops, including a big low-price grocery store in the cellar. Oslo's largest shopping mall, **Oslo City** (⊠ opposite Sentralstasjonen/Central Station, ☎ 22938050), open weekdays 9–9 and Saturday 9–7, has more than 100 stores and businesses including a bank, a travel agency, and a grocery store on the lower level. **Paléet** (⊠ Karl Johans Gt., ☎ 22417086), open weekdays 10–8 and Saturday 10–5, is an elegant indoor shopping center with 45 shops and 12 restaurants. **Steen & Strøm** (⊠ Kongengsgt. 23, ☎ 22100250), open weekdays 10–7 and Saturday 10–6, is an exclusive department store with six floors and 58 different shops plus a cafeteria.

Flea Markets

Every Saturday during spring, summer, and fall, there is a flea market at **Vestkanttorget** (⊠ 2 blocks east of Frogner Park, junction of Professor Dahls Gt. and Eckerbergs Gt.). Check the papers for local *loppemarkeder* (flea markets) in schools and outdoor squares around town.

Side Trips

Høvikodden

Just outside Oslo is the **Henie-Onstad Kunstsenter** (Henie-Onstad Art Center), which displays an impressive collection of important works by Léger, Munch, Picasso, Bonnard, and Matisse. The center was a gift from the Norwegian Olympic skater Sonja Henie and her husband, shipowner Niels Onstad. ⊠ *About 12 km (7 mi) southwest of Oslo on E18,* ☎ *67543050.* ⊙ *Tues.–Thurs. 9–9, Fri.–Mon. 11–6.*

Vinterbro

☺ **Tusenfryd** is Norway's largest amusement park, with more than 50 attractions, including carousels, a roller coaster, games, an outdoor stage, shops, and restaurants. Don't miss **Vikingelandet** (Viking Land), which re-creates life during the time of the Vikings, with trading centers, boat building, a blacksmith, jewelry making, and farm animals. One of the "Vikings" will also help you try your talent as an archer, or you can join "Leif Eriksson" on an expedition in the depths of a mountain cave. ⊠ *1433 Vinterbro, about 20 km (12 mi) southeast of Oslo on E18,* ☎ *64946363.* ⊙ *Tusenfryd: May–early June and mid-Aug.–mid-Sept., weekends 10:30–7; June 6–mid-Aug., daily 10:30–7. Vikingelandet: 2 wks in mid-June, weekdays 10:30–3, weekends 1–7; last wk in June–mid-Aug., daily 1–7.*

Lillehammer

At the top of the long finger of Lake Mjøsa, Lillehammer is reached by train from the Sentralstasjonen (Central Station) in about two hours. A paddle steamer, *D/S Skibladner,* travels the length of the lake (six hours each way) in summer, making several stops. At the site of the 1994 Winter Olympics, Lillehammer's Olympic bobsled track, **Hunderfossen** (⊠ about 5 km/3 mi north of town), is open for runs; you can book at the **Lillehammer Tourist Office** (⊠ Lilletorget, ☎ 61259299). Lillehammer is also home of **Maihaugen** (⊠ Maihaugvn. 1, ☎ 61288900), one of the largest open-air museums in northern Europe. More than 100 old buildings have been relocated here, along with workshop interiors, antique tools, and the like.

Oslo Essentials

Arriving and Departing

BY PLANE
Gardermoen Airport (⊠ 37 km/23 mi north of Oslo) is Oslo's main airport.

Between the Airport and Downtown. Taxis between downtown and Gardermoen cost between Nkr 700 and Nkr 800. **Flybussen** (airport bus; ☎ 67596220) takes about 40 minutes from Galleri Oslo shopping center, stopping at Jernbanetorget (Central Station—Oslo S); the fare is Nkr 55. The high-speed **Airport Train** carries passengers from Central Station to Gardermoen in 30 minutes; fares run about Nkr 70.

Trains on international or domestic long-distance and express routes arrive at Oslo's **Sentralstasjon** (Oslo S or Central Station; ⊠ east of Strandgt.). Suburban trains depart from the Sentralstasjon, Stortinget, and the Nationaltheatret stations.

Getting Around

Oslo Kortet (the Oslo Card)—valid for one, two, or three days—entitles you to free entrance to museums, public swimming pools, and the racetrack; unlimited travel on the Oslo transport system and Norwegian Railways commuter trains within the city limits; free parking on municipal streets and in some lots; and discounts at various stores, cinemas, and sports centers. You can get the card at Oslo's tourist information offices and hotels (☞ Visitor Information, *below*). A one-day card costs Nkr 150; two-day, Nkr 220; three-day, Nkr 250. A one-day family card costs Nkr 350.

If you're using public transportation only occasionally, you can get tickets (Nkr 18) at bus and subway (T-bane) stops. For Nkr 40, the **Dags Kort** (One-day Card) gives 24 hours' unlimited travel on all public transportation, including the summer ferries to Bygdøy, Hovedøya, Langøya, and Gressholmen. The **Flexikort** gives you eight rides on the subway, bus, or trikk (the name given to Oslo's extensive tram network) for Nkr 110, including transfers.

Taxis can be hailed on the street when the roof light is on, found at taxi stands, or ordered by phone (☎ 22388090), though during peak hours you may have to wait.

Contacts and Resources

U.S. (⊠ Drammensvn. 18, ☎ 22448550). **Canadian** (⊠ Oscarsgt. 20, ☎ 22995300). **U.K.** (⊠ Thos. Heftyesgt. 8, ☎ 23132700). **Australian Consulate** (⊠ Jernbanetorget 2, 0106 Oslo, ☎ 22414433).

Police (☎ 112 or 22669050). **Ambulance** (☎ 113 or 94208000). **Emergency Clinic: Oslo Legevakt** (☎ 22118080). **Dentist** (☎ 22176566). **Pharmacy: Jernbanetorgets Apotek** (☎ 22412482), open 24 hours.

Erik Qvist (⊠ Drammensvn. 16, ☎ 22542600, near U.S. Embassy). **Tanum Libris** (⊠ Karl Johans Gt. 37–41, ☎ 22411100).

Forest. The Norway Information Centre (☎ 22830050; ☞ Visitor Information, *below*) can arrange four- to eight-hour motor safaris through the forests surrounding Oslo.

Orientation. Båtservice Sightseeing (⊠ Rådhusbryggen 3, ☎ 22200715) has a bus tour, five cruises, and one combination tour. **HMK Sightseeing** (⊠ Hegdehaugsvn. 4, ☎ 22208206) offers several bus tours in and around Oslo.

Personal Guides. The Norway Information Centre can provide an authorized city guide for your own private tour. **OsloTaxi** (⊠ Trondheimsvn. 100, ☎ 22388070) also gives private tours.

Sleigh Rides. In winter you can ride an old-fashioned sleigh or a horse through Hallingdal, northwest of the Oslo, with **Vangen Skistue** (⊠ Laila and Jon Hamre, Fjell, 1404 Siggerud, ☎ 64865481).

Street Train. Starting at noon and continuing at 45-minute intervals until 10 PM, the **Oslo Train,** which looks like a chain of dune buggies, leaves Aker Brygge for a 30-minute ride around the town center. Ask at the Norway Information Centre (☞ Visitor Information, *below*).

POST OFFICE

The **Oslo Hoved Post Kontor** (Oslo Main Post Office; ✉ Dronningensgt. 15) is open weekdays 8–6, Saturday 10–3.

TRAVEL AGENCIES

Bennett (✉ Linstowsgt. 6, ☎ 22597800). **NSB Reisebyr AS** (✉ Storgt. 10 b, ☎ 23151550). **Winge** (American Express, ✉ Karl Johans Gt. 33/ 35, ☎ 22004500).

VISITOR INFORMATION

Nortra (Norwegian Travel Association; ✉ Drammensvn. 40, Postboks 2893, Sentrum, 0230 Oslo, ☎ 22925200). **Norway Information Centre** (✉ Vestbanepl. 1; Sentralstasjon/Central Station, east of Strandgt., ☎ 22830050). For information on public transportation call **Trafikanten** (✉ Oslo Sentralstasjonen/Central Station, east of Strandgt., ☎ 22177030 or 177).

THE COAST ROAD TO STAVANGER

Route E18 parallels the coast of Sørlandet, or Southern Norway, south of Oslo toward the busy port of Kristiansand. Beyond the city, the coast curves west and north to Stavanger. After Flekkefjord, follow the coast road (Route 44) past the fishing port of Egersund to Ogna, and then on to Stavanger. Sørlandet's whaling business has given way to canneries, lumber, paper production, and petrochemicals. Yet the beauty of this 608-km (380-mi) route remains, and you'll find seaside towns, rocky headlands, and stretches of forest (fjord country does not begin until north of Stavanger). Travel between towns takes less than an hour in most cases. South of Stavanger is flat and stony Jæren, the largest expanse of level terrain in this mountainous country. The mild climate and the absence of good harbors caused the people here to turn to agriculture, and the kilometers of stone walls are a testament to their labor. It is also possible to reach Stavanger on an inland route through Telemark.

Drammen

Drammen lies on the shore of the wide Drammen River, 45 km (28 mi) long and popular for its salmon and trout fishing. The river was the city's main street during the centuries when the production of wood products (paper and cellulose) were the chief industries in Drammen. From May 10 through August you can join a five-hour guided tour aboard the 114-year-old sailing ship *Christiane* (☎ 95887560 for tours), which sails south from Drammen to the attractive little village of Holmsbu. Holmsbu has a restaurant overlooking the small harbor and a number of attractive arts and crafts shops.

The center of Drammen has a great variety of shops and restaurants. **Bragernes Torg** is home to a sizable farmer's market. This large square is lined by several buildings dating from just after 1866, when a huge fire devastated the entire district. **Drammens Teatret,** also built after the great fire, has an impressive collection of ceiling paintings and crystal chandeliers. Designed by Emil Langlet, it was completed in 1870.

$$ ✕ **Spiraltoppen Café.** You'll find excellent views and food here atop Bragernes Hill. ✉ *Bragernesåsen,* ☎ *32837815. Reservations not accepted. AE, DC, MC, V.*

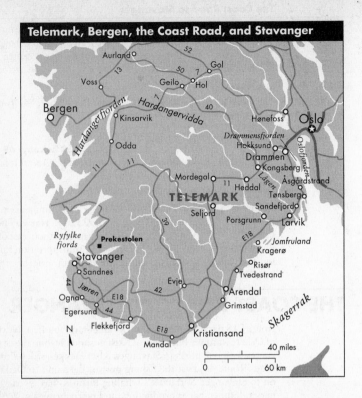

Telemark, Bergen, the Coast Road, and Stavanger

\$\$ 🏨 **Rica Park Hotel.** This comfortable and central hotel has traditional Norwegian decor. ⊠ *Gamle Kirkepl. 3, 3019,* ☎ *32838280,* FAX *32893207. 96 rooms, 2 suites. 2 restaurants. AE, DC, MC, V.*

Åsgårdstrand

Edvard Munch painted many of his best works in Åsgårdstrand, where he spent seven summers in a small yellow frame house. **Munchs lille hus** is open to visitors during the summer. ⊠ *Munchsgt.,* ☎ *33031708.*

Tønsberg

Tønsberg was founded in 871, during the Viking Age, or possibly earlier; it is the site of the Oseberg Viking ship, discovered in 1903. Shipping, commerce, and culture prospered in Tønsberg from the Viking Age until the rise of Oslo as Norway's capital during the 14th century. Later, Tønsberg had a resurgence as a thriving whaling port during the 1700s. Today, on steep **Slottsfjellet** (Castle Hill; ⊠ next to Tønsberg train station), the ruins of **Tønsberghus,** an extensive fortress and abbey, evoke the Middle Ages, when Tønsberg was the administrative center for the Norwegian kings. A model of Tønsberghus stands in the lookout tower, finished in time to commemorate the town's millennium. The tower also affords a panoramic view of Oslo fjord and the surrounding mountains.

Sandefjord

Attractive Sandefjord is a port that served as the base for the Norwegian whaling fleet until after World War II, when large-scale competition from the Soviet Union and Japan made the operation uneconomical. The port remains a busy depot for timber shipping.

\$\$–\$\$\$ ✕ **Ludl's Gourmet Odd Ivar Solberg.** Chef Solberg has taken over chef
★ Ludl's duties preparing fish specialties in one of the best restaurants outside Oslo. The eight- and five-course menus are excellent choices. ⊠ *Rådhusgt. 7,* ☎ *33462741. AE, DC, MC, V. Closed Sun.*

\$\$\$ **▣ Rica Park Hotel.** The imposing Rica Park, one of the best hotels in
★ Norway, overlooks Sandefjord's harbor. The rooms are large and comfortable, and the service is flawless. ⊠ *Strandpromenaden 9, 3200,* ☎
33465550, ℻ *33447500. 179 rooms. Restaurant. AE, DC, MC, V.*

Larvik

Larvik is the terminus for ferries to Frederikshavn, Denmark. It once
looked to whaling for its livelihood but now concentrates on lumber
and ferrying.

The **Larvik Sjøfarts Museum** (Maritime Museum), in the former customs house, chronicles Larvik's seafaring history. ⊠ *Kirkestredet 5,*
☎ *33130404.* ⊙ *Check with tourist office (☞ Visitor Information* in
The Coast Road to Stavanger Essentials, below).

\$\$ **▣ Quality Grand Hotel Farris.** Spotless rooms and attentive service are
what you'll find at this large hotel overlooking the fjord. Sample the
local fish soup and smoked meat platters in the hotel's restaurant. ⊠
Storgt. 38–40, 3256, ☎ *33187800,* ℻ *33187045. 88 rooms. Restaurant. AE, DC, MC, V.*

Risør

The coastal village of Risør is a sailing center; its picturesque harbor
is lined with with white-painted 19th-century patrician houses. If
you're here in August, don't miss the town's wooden sailboat festival.

Arendal

Between 1850 and 1886, Arendal was one of the most important seafaring towns in Scandinavia. You can still discern a bit of that era in
the tidy cottages and grandiose captains' houses within shouting distance of the docks. Explore Arendal's **Tyholmen quarter,** the oldest part
of the town, for a glimpse into this 19th-century world.

Arendals Rådhus (Arendal's City Hall) was created by the Danish architect Peder Krog Bonsach Jessen and constructed between 1812 and
1815. Originally built as a private home for one of Arendal's wealthy
ship owners, it was converted to City Hall in 1844. Arendal hosts a
popular speedboat race every summer.

\$\$ **✕ Madam Reiersen.** Good, traditional Norwegian food is served at this
informal waterfront restaurant. ⊠ *Nedre Tyholmsvn. 3,* ☎ *37021900.*
Reservations essential on weekends. AE, DC, MC, V.

\$\$\$\$ **▣ Clarion Tyholmen Hotel.** This maritime hotel is in the heart of the
old town, which is filled with well-preserved, brightly painted houses.
The views of the fjord are splendid. ⊠ *Teaterpl. 2, 4801,* ☎ *37026800,*
℻ *37026801. 60 rooms. 2 restaurants. AE, DC, MC, V.*

Kristiansand

The largest town in Sørlandet, Kristiansand has important air, sea, road,
and rail links. It was laid out during the 17th century in a grid pattern, with the imposing **Christiansholm Festning** (fort) guarding the eastern harbor approach.

☾ The open-air **Vest-Agder Fylkesmuseum** (County Museum) has 30 old
buildings and farms rebuilt in the local style of the 18th and 19th centuries. ⊠ *Kongsgård; Rte. E18, east of Kristiansand;* ☎ *38090228.* ⊙
Sept.–mid-June, Sun. noon–5 or by appointment.

Kristiansand Cannon Museum has the last remaining 38-cm caliber cannon in the world. The huge cannon installations were built by the Germans during World War II. ⊠ *South of town, off E39,* ☎ *38085090.*
⊙ *May–Oct., Thurs.–Sun. 11–6; mid-June–Aug., daily 11–6.*

Ⓒ Children love the **Kristiansand Dyrepark** (Kristiansand Zoo), with five
separate parks, including a water park, a forested park, an entertainment park, and a zoo. There's also **Kardemomme By** (Cardamom
Town), a replicated storybook village. ⊠ *4609 Kardemomme By,* ☎
38049700. ☒ *NKr 185.* ⊘ *Jan.–mid-June and mid-Aug.–Dec., daily
10–3; mid-June–mid-Aug., daily 9–6.*

$$ ✕ **Sjøhuset.** Seafood and fish are the best bets in this rustic waterfront
restaurant. ⊠ *Østre Strandgt. 12a,* ☎ *38026260. Reservations not ac-
cepted. AE, DC, MC, V.*

$$$ ▥ **Rica Travel Hotel.** Only a stone's throw from the town hall and cathe-
dral, this hotel is also close to the harbor beach. Breakfast and evening
buffet are included Monday through Thursday. ⊠ *Dronningens Gt.
66, 4602,* ☎ *38021500,* ℻ *38020119. 47 rooms. Restaurant. AE, DC,
MC, V.*

Mandal

Norway's most southerly town is famous for its beach, salmon, and
18th- and 19th-century houses. Seafood lovers flock here for the shellfish festival held on the second weekend in August.

Flekkefjord

The road climbs and weaves its way through steep, wooded hills before descending to the fishing port of Flekkefjord, with its charming
Hollenderbyen, or Dutch Quarter.

Ogna

Ogna is known for the stretch of beautiful and unspoiled sandy beach
that has inspired so many Norwegian artists, among them Kitty Kjel-
land.

★ Stavanger

Stavanger is a former trading town that became a focus (some envi-
ronmentalists say victim) of the oil boom. It is now the fourth-largest
city in Norway. Drilling platforms and oil tankers take the place of fishing boats in the harbor. In sharp contrast to the new high-rise complexes,
there is an old quarter with narrow, cobbled lanes and clapboard houses
at odd angles. The town is believed to date from the 8th century.

Stavanger's Anglo-Norman **Domkirke** (cathedral), next to the central
market, was established in 1125 by the English bishop of Winchester.
Norway and England had strong trading and ecclesiastical links throughout the Middle Ages. ⊠ *City center, next to pond, Breiavatnet.*

Ledaal is a fine patrician mansion where the royal family resides when
visiting Stavanger. ⊠ *Eiganesvn. 45,* ☎ *51520618.* ⊘ *Mid-June–mid-
Aug., daily 11–4; mid-Aug.–mid-June, Sun. 11–4.*

Breidablikk manor house (designed by the architect Henrik Nissen) was
built by a Norwegian shipping magnate between 1881 and 1882. An
outstanding example of Norwegian "Swiss style" architecture, it has
been perfectly preserved. ⊠ *Eiganesvn. 40A,* ☎ *51523115.* ⊘ *Mid-
June–mid-Aug., daily 11–4; mid-Aug.–mid-June, Sun. 11–4.*

Ⓒ **Ullandhaug** is a reconstructed Iron Age farm. ⊠ *Grannesvn., Ullandhaug,* ☎ *51846061.* ⊘ *Mid-June–Aug., daily 11–4; early May–mid-
June and Sept., Sun. noon–4.*

The **Norsk Hermetikkmuseum** (Canning Museum) in the heart of Old
Stavanger is a reconstructed sardine factory that was in use between
1890 and 1920. ⊠ *Øvre Strandgt. 88A,* ☎ *51534989.* ⊘ *Sun. 11–4.*

The **Utvanndrings Sentre** (Norwegian Emigration Center) specializes
in genealogy and family research, helping to bridge the gap between

Norway and the families of emigrants. ⊠ *Nedre Strandgt. 31,* ☎ *51538860,* ⅏ *51538863.* ⊙ *Weekdays 9–3.*

The **Ryfylke fjords** north and east of Stavanger form the southern end of the fjord country. The city is a good base for exploring this region, with the "white fleet" of low-slung sea buses making daily excursions into even the most distant fjords of Ryfylke. Great for a heart-stopping view is **Prekestolen** (Pulpit Rock), a huge cube of rock with a vertical drop of 2,000 ft. You can join a tour to get here or you can do it on your own from mid-June to late August by taking the ferry from Fiskepiren across Hildefjorden to Tau, riding a bus to the Pulpit Rock Lodge, and walking 1½ to two hours to the rock.

$$$ 🏨 **Comfort Hotel Grand.** On the edge of the town center, this hotel doesn't aim to be fancy: Rooms are comfortable and bright, done in white and pastels. In summer the rates drop significantly. ⊠ *Klubbgt. 3, 4012,* ☎ *51895800,* ⅏ *51895710. 90 rooms. AE, DC, MC, V.*

$$–$$$ 🏨 **Skagen Brygge.** In three rehabilitated old sea houses, almost all rooms are different, from modern to old-fashioned maritime with exposed beams and brick-and-wood walls. The hotel can make reservations for you at any of 14 restaurants in the area and put the tab on your bill. ⊠ *Skagenkaien 30, 4006,* ☎ *51894100,* ⅏ *51850001. 106 rooms. Turkish bath. AE, DC, MC, V.*

The Coast Road to Stavanger Essentials

Getting Around

BY BUS
Local buses cover the entire route, but they take much longer than the train. For details on fares and schedules, check with the tourist offices listed below or the Norway Information Centre in Oslo (☞ Visitor Information *in* Oslo Essentials, *above*).

BY CAR
Driving gives you the chance to stop at coastal villages that are either not served by trains or have only sporadic service. The route is simple: E18 as far as Flekkefjord, then Route 44 to Stavanger.

BY TRAIN
The Sørland line leaves from Oslo Central Station and goes all the way to Stavanger via Kristiansand. It has five departures daily to Kristiansand; three continue to Stavanger. The Oslo–Drammen stretch is an engineering feat that includes Norway's longest tunnel, an 11-km (7-mi) bore through sheer rock.

Guided Tours
In summer a daily boat excursion sets out from Oslo southwest to the coastal resorts of Kragerø, the long, thin island of Jomfruland, and Risør. You return the same day, and refreshments are served on board. Contact the Norway Information Centre (☞ Visitor Information *in* Oslo Essentials, *above*).

Visitor Information
Arendal (⊠ Friholmsgt. 1, ☎ 37005544). **Drammen** (⊠ Rådhuset, ☎ 32806210). **Flekkefjord** (⊠ Main St., ☎ 38322131). **Kristiansand** (⊠ Dronningensgt. 2, ☎ 38121314). **Larvik** (⊠ Storgt. 48, ☎ 33139100). **Mandal** (⊠ Bryggetgt., ☎ 38260820). **Risør** (⊠ Strandgaten, ☎ 37152270). **Stavanger** (⊠ Rosenkildehuset, Rosenkildetorget 1, ☎ 51859200). **Tønsberg** (⊠ Nedre Langgt. 36B, ☎ 33310220).

THROUGH TELEMARK TO BERGEN

Bergen is Norway's second-largest city. To get here from Oslo, drive west through Telemark, a region marked by steep valleys, pine forests, lakes, and fast-flowing rivers full of trout. Morgedal, the cradle of skiing, is here. At the Haukeligrend crossroads, Route 11 really begins to climb, and you'll see why the Norwegians are so proud of keeping this route open all year. Hardangervidda, a wild mountain area and national park, was the stronghold of Norway's Resistance fighters during World War II. Farther west is the beautiful Hardangerfjord. Few places on earth match western Norway—the fabled land of the fjords—for spectacular scenic beauty.

Fjord transportation is good, as crossing fjords is a necessary as well as scenic way to travel in Norway. Hardangerfjorden, Sognefjord, and Nordfjord are three of the deepest and most popular.

Kongsberg

Kongsberg, founded in 1624 next to the fast-flowing Lågen River as a silver-mining town, is one of the gateways to Telemark. Forests give way to rocky peaks and desolate spaces farther into the plateau. Although there is no more mining, the old mines at Saggrenda are open for guided tours; contact the tourist office (☞ Visitor Information *in* Through Telemark to Bergen Essentials, *below*). In the town center is an 18th-century rococo church, which reflects the town's former source of wealth—silver. The **Norsk Bergverksmuseum** (Norwegian Mining Museum) includes the **Sølvverkets Samlinger** (Silver Mines Collection), the **Kongsberg Skimuseum** (Ski Museum), and **Den Kongelige Mynts Museum** (Royal Mint Museum). ✉ *Hyttegt. 3,* ☎ *32723200.* ☉ *Mid-May–mid-Aug., weekdays 10–6, weekends 10–4; mid–late Aug., daily 10–4; Sept., daily noon–4; Oct.–mid-May, Sun. noon–4. Otherwise by appointment.*

$$ ✗ **Gamle Kongsberg Kro.** Hearty Norwegian dishes are served at this café near Nybrofossen (the Nybro waterfall). ✉ *Thornesvn. 4,* ☎ *32731633. DC, MC, V.*

★ Heddal

Heddal is the first stop in Telemark. Here you'll find the **Heddal Kirke** (Heddal Church), Norway's largest stave church, built in 1147. Stave churches are built with wooden planks staked vertically into the ground or base and usually have some carved ornamentation on the doors and around the aisle. These churches date from the medieval period and are found almost exclusively in southern Norway. ☎ *35020400.*

Seljord

The attractive village of Seljord, on a lake of the same name, has ornamented wooden houses and a medieval church. The countryside by the lake is richer than that on the Telemark plateau; meadows and pastureland run down to the lakefront. Before you descend toward Seljord, you'll see the Lifjell area's highest peak, **Røydalsnuten** (4,235 ft), on the left.

Morgedal

It was here in the 19th century that Sondre Nordheim developed the Telemark method of skiing. You can get the full story of that development at **Olav Bjåland Museum** (✉ opposite Morgedal Turisthotell, ☎ 35054250), named for the South Polar explorer and ski hero. The museum is open daily May–mid-June, 11–4, mid-June–mid-August, 9–7, and 11–4 during the last two weeks of August.

Kinsarvik

The attractive village of Kinsarvik is on the Sørfjord. For the best view of the junction of the Sørfjord and the mighty Hardangerfjord, take the ferry to Utne. On the dramatic 30-minute ferry crossing, you will come to understand why this area was such a rich source of inspiration for Romantic composer Edvard Grieg.

$$$$ ⊞ **Utne Hotel.** The white frame house dates from 1722, making this
★ hotel one of the oldest in Norway. The wood-paneled, hand-painted dining room is decorated with copper pans, old china, and paintings. ⊠ *5797 Utne,* ☎ *53666983,* FAX *53666950. 22 rooms with bath or shower. Restaurant. AE, DC, MC, V.*

$$$ ⊞ **Best Western Kinsarvik Fjord Hotel.** This handsome hotel near the busy ferry port offers good views of Hardangerfjord and the glacier. The rooms are bright and spacious. ⊠ *5780 Kinsarvik,* ☎ *53663100,* FAX *53663374. 70 rooms. Restaurant. AE, DC, MC, V.*

★ Bergen

The road descends tortuously into Bergen, the capital of the fjords and Norway's second-largest city (pop. 219,000). As one of the nine European Cities of Culture for the year 2000, Bergen is presenting three season-based programs of art and folk festivals (ask for details at the tourist office). The town was founded in 1070, and before oil brought an influx of foreigners to Stavanger, Bergen was the most international Norwegian city, having been an important trading and military center when Oslo was still an obscure village. A member of the medieval Hanseatic League, it offered an ice-free harbor and convenient trading location on the west coast. Natives of Bergen still think of Oslo as a dour provincial town.

Despite numerous fires in its past, much of medieval Bergen has survived. Seven surrounding mountains set off the weathered wooden houses, cobbled streets, and Hanseatic-era warehouses of **Bryggen** (the harbor area).

The best way to get a feel for Bergen's medieval trading heyday is to visit the **Hanseatisk Museum.** One of the oldest and best-preserved of Bergen's wooden buildings, it is furnished in 16th-century style. ⊠ *Bryggen,* ☎ *55316710.* ⊙ *May–Aug., daily 10–5; Sept.–Apr., weekdays 11–3, Sat. noon–3, Sun. noon–4.*

Rosenkrantztårnet (the Rosenkrantz tower) is part of the **Bergenhus Festning** (Bergenhus Fortress), the 13th-century fortress guarding the harbor entrance. The tower and fortress were destroyed during World War II but were meticulously restored during the 1960s and are now rich with furnishings and household items from the 16th century. ⊠ *Bergenhus,* ☎ *55314380.* ⊙ *Mid-May–mid-Sept., daily 10–4; mid-Sept.–mid-May, Sun. noon–3, or upon request.*

From behind Bryggen you can walk through the meandering back streets to the popular **Fløybanen** (Fløyen Funicular), which climbs a steep 1,070 ft to the top of Fløyen, one of the seven mountains guarding the city. ⊠ *Øvregt.* ⊙ *May–Sept., weekdays every ½ hr 7:30 AM–11 PM, Sat. 8 AM–midnight, Sun. 9 AM–midnight.*

★ **Troldhaugen** (Troll Hill) manor on Nordås Lake, once home to Edvard Grieg, is now a museum that incorporates a new chamber-music hall. Recitals are held from late June to mid-August (Wed. and Sun. 7:30 PM, Sat. 2). ⊠ *Troldhaugsvn., Hop,* ☎ *55910710.* ⊙ *Jan.–Mar., weekdays 10–2; early Apr. and Oct.–Nov., weekdays 10–2, Sat. noon–4, Sun. 10–4; mid-Apr.–Sept., daily 9–6. Closed Dec.*

$$$$ ✕ **Lucullus.** This French-inspired seafood restaurant is, appropriately enough, in the Hotel Neptun. It has an excellent wine cellar, with special emphasis on white wines to go with the fish. ☒ *Walckendorffsgt. 8,* ☎ *55901000,* ⛶ *55233202. AE, DC, MC, V. Closed Sun. and in the winter.*

$$$ ✕ **Finnegaardstue.** This classic Norwegian restaurant near Bryggen has
★ four snug, intimate rooms. Some of the timber interior dates from the 18th century. The emphasis here is on seafood, but the venison and reindeer are outstanding. Traditional Norwegian desserts, such as cloudberries and cream, are irresistible. ☒ *Rosenkrantz' Gt. 6,* ☎ *55550300,* ⛶ *55315811. AE, DC, MC, V. Closed Sun.*

$$–$$$ ✕ **Munkestuen Café.** This tiny mom-and-pop place is a hometown leg-
★ end. Try the monkfish with hollandaise sauce or the fillet of roe deer with morels. Reserve a table early; they can be booked up to four weeks in advance. ☒ *Klostergt. 12,* ☎ *55902149. Reservations essential. AE, DC, MC, V. Closed weekends and 3 wks in July. No lunch.*

$$$$ 🏨 **Augustin.** This small but excellent hotel in the center of town has been restored to its original late–Art Nouveau character, complete with period furniture in the lobby. ☒ *C. Sundtsgt. 22–24, 5004,* ☎ *55304000,* ⛶ *55304010. 82 rooms. Restaurant. AE, DC, MC, V.*

$$–$$$$ 🏨 **Radisson SAS Hotel.** This hotel on the harbor is near a section of old, well-preserved warehouses and buildings. Ravaged by nine fires since 1170, the warehouses have been rebuilt each time in the same style, which SAS has incorporated into its design. ☒ *Bryggen, 5003,* ☎ *55573000,* ⛶ *55324808. 273 rooms. 2 restaurants. AE, DC, MC, V.*

$–$$ 🏨 **Rainbow Hotel Bryggen Orion.** Facing the harbor in the center of town, the hotel is surrounded by Bergen's most famous sights. The rooms are decorated in warm, sunny colors. ☒ *Bradbenken 3, 5003,* ☎ *55318080,* ⛶ *55329414. 229 rooms. Restaurant. AE, DC, MC, V.*

Through Telemark to Bergen Essentials

Getting Around

BY BUS
Buses in the region rarely run more than twice a day; schedules are available at tourist offices or **Nor-Way Bussekspress** (☒ Bussterminalen, Galleri Oslo, ☎ 22330190). All buses serving the Bergen region depart from Bergen's **central bus station** (☒ Strømgaten 8, ☎ 177).

BY CAR
E18 goes from Oslo to Drammen and Route 11 from Drammen to Haukeli. From Haukeli to Kinsarvik you take Route 13. After the ferry crossing, Kinsarvik–Utne–Kvandal, you follow Route 7 to Bergen.

BY PLANE
Flesland Airport is 20 km (12 mi) south of Bergen.

BY TRAIN
For Bergen, the **Bergensbanen** has five departures daily, plus an additional one on Sunday, in both directions on the Oslo–Bergen route. The only train service in the southern part of Telemark is the Oslo–Stavanger line (via Kristiansand).

Guided Tours

Bergen is the gateway to the fjords, and excursions cover most towns in the western part of the region as well as the fjords farther north. Contact the tourist information offices (☞ *below*) for details of these constantly changing tours.

Visitor Information
Bergen (✉ Bryggen 7, ☎ 55321480). **Kinsarvik** (✉ Public Library bldg./mid-June–mid-Aug., ☎ 53663112). **Kongsberg** (✉ Storgt. 35, ☎ 32735000).

ABOVE BERGEN: THE FAR NORTH

The fjords continue northward from Bergen all the way to Kirkenes, on Norway's border with the Republic of Russia. In the north you can hike, climb, fish, bird-watch (seabirds), see Samiland—the land of the Sami ("Lapps")—or experience the unending days of the midnight sun in June and July. The Lofoten Islands present the grand face of the "Lofoten Wall"—a rocky massif surrounded by the sea and broken into six pieces. Svolvær, the most populated island, has a thriving summer artists' colony. It's also known for Lofotfisket, a winter cod-fishing event.

The major towns north of Bergen are Ålesund, Kristiansund, Molde, and Trondheim. In Northern Norway the major towns are Bodø, Narvik, Harstad, Tromsø, Hammerfest, and Kirkenes. Cheaper accommodations are the rule in the north, whether you stay in hotels, cabins, campsites, guest houses, or *rorbuer*—fishermen's huts next to the sea with modern facilities.

★ Ålesund

Ålesund's pride is its unique, internationally recognized collection of Art Nouveau buildings constructed between 1904 and 1907 after the Great Fire. Romantic and colorful, these buildings line the narrow streets of the old town. Also attractive is **Brosundet** (the old harbor). This area on the west coast of Norway was one of the first places exposed after the Ice Age. Excavations in the Skjonghelleren cave on the nearby island of Valderøy have given evidence of stone-age settlements that lived off plentiful fishing. Even today, much of the town's income derives from the fishing industry. *Klipfisk* (split, dried cod), which is exported worldwide, is the main ingredient for *bacalao*, a popular local dish whose name derives from the Portuguese for salted cod, and whose preparation was learned from Portuguese fishermen. **Atlantic Sea Park** (☎ 70128200), 3 km (2 mi) west of Ålesund, has the largest aquarium in Scandinavia and is open all year.

$$ ✗ **Fjellstua.** This mountaintop restaurant has tremendous views over the surrounding peaks, islands, and fjords. The main dining room serves the widest variety of dishes and homemade desserts. ✉ *Fjellstua*, ☎ 70126582. AE, DC, MC, V. Closed Dec.–early Feb.

$$ ✗ **Sjøbua.** On an old wharf at Brunholmen, Sjøbua offers an excellent seafood selection. You can even pick your own dinner from a saltwater aquarium. ✉ *Brunholmgt. 1,* ☎ 70127100. AE, DC, MC, V.

$$$ ▥ **Comfort Home Hotel Bryggen.** This dockside warehouse converted into a hotel has splendid views over the water. ✉ *Apotekergt. 1–3, 6004,* ☎ 70126400, FAX 70121180. 85 rooms. AE, DC, MC, V.

$$ ▥ **Quality Scandinavie Hotel.** The impressive building dates from 1905. The rooms are decorated in blue, peach, and green, with reproduction Biedermeier furniture. ✉ *Løvenvoldgt. 8, 6002,* ☎ 70123131, FAX 70132370. 65 rooms. 2 restaurants. AE, DC, MC, V.

Trondheim

Trondheim sits at the southern end of Norway's widest fjord, Trondheimsfjord. This water-bound city, the third largest in the country, is where Norwegian rulers are traditionally crowned. It has a historic fish market worth seeing, as well as Scandinavia's two largest wooden buildings. One is a student dormitory and the other is the rococo **Stiftsgården,** built between 1774 and 1778, which became a royal palace in 1906. It is one of the highlights of Norwegian architecture, but the architect is unknown. Construction of Scandinavia's largest medieval building, **Nidaros Domkirke** (Nidaros Cathedral), first started in 1070, but it suffered numerous burnings-down and was not finally completed until 1969. The cathedral has attracted pilgrims for centuries. ✉ *Kongsgårdsgt. 2,* ☎ *73538480.* ☉ *May–late June, 9–3; late June–late Aug., 9–6; late Aug.–late Sept., 9–3; late Sept.–Apr., 12–2:30.*

$$$ ✕ **Bryggen.** A feast of Norwegian specialties is served at this popular
★ restaurant near the Gamle Bybro (Old Town Bridge). There's also a cheaper brasserie, a lively pub, and a private dining room. ✉ *Øvre Bakklandet 66,* ☎ *73874242. AE, DC, MC, V.*

$$$ ✕ **Dickens.** In a 17th-century building in the Bryggen section of town, this charming restaurant is decorated in traditional Norwegian style. The menu includes national dishes as well as a variety of international specialties. ✉ *Kjøpmannsgt. 63,* ☎ *73515750. AE, DC, MC, V.*

$$ ✕ **Tavern på Sverresborg.** Outside the city, at the open-air Folk Mu-
★ seum, this restaurant serves Norwegian specialties. ✉ *Sverresborg,* ☎ *73520932. AE, DC, MC, V.*

$$ 🏨 **Comfort Home Hotel Bakeriet.** The hotel is housed in a building that
★ opened as a bakery in 1897. Few rooms look alike, but all are large and stylish in their simplicity, with natural wood furniture and beige-and-red textiles. A light evening meal is included in the room rate. ✉ *Brattørgt. 2, 7010,* ☎ *73525200,* 🆁🆇 *73502330. 109 rooms. AE, DC, MC, V.*

$$ 🏨 **Radisson SAS Royal Garden Hotel.** Trondheim's finest hotel has good facilities for sports and fitness, as well as features useful to guests with disabilities. Enjoy music in the hotel's jazz club. ✉ *Kjøpmannsgt. 73, 7001,* ☎ *73803000,* 🆁🆇 *73803250. 297 rooms. Restaurant, indoor pool. AE, DC, MC, V.*

$–$$ 🏨 **Hotel Ambassadeur.** Take in the dramatic view of fjord and coastline from the roof terrace of this hotel, about 300 ft from the market square. Breakfast and a light evening meal (weekdays only) are included. ✉ *Elvegt. 18, 7013,* ☎ *73527050,* 🆁🆇 *73527052. 34 rooms. AE, DC, MC, V.*

Bodø

The last stop on the European rail system, Bodø is the first major town above the Polar Circle and, with its 40,000 inhabitants, the second-largest city in Northern Norway. Bodø's modern airport has frequent flights daily serving most of the country. *Hurtigruten* (the Coastal Express ship) calls in twice a day, and a ferry will take you from Bodø straight to the Lofoten islands. For boat excursions to coastal bird colonies on **Værøya,** Bodø is also the best base. While the city was bombed by the Germans in 1940, postwar reconstruction gave rise to the bustling modern city center, replete with lively shopping streets, a marina, and good restaurants and accommodations. A war memorial stands outside the stunning, contemporary **Bodø Domkirke** (Bodø Cathedral), its spire separated from the main building; inside are rich modern tapestries. **Norsk Luftfarts Museum** (the Norwegian Aviation Museum) is divided into military and civilian sections. Among the attractions are an American U-2 spy plane, a Junkers JU 52, a Catalina anti-submarine aircraft, and the Mosquito Bomber. Try the flight simulator. ✉ *Olav V's Gt.* ☉ *Mid-June–mid-Aug., weekdays and Sun. 10–8, Sat. 10–5; mid-Aug.–mid-June, Tues., Wed., Fri. 10–4, Thurs. 10–7, Sat. 10–5, Sun. 11–6.*

Saltstraumen, the world's strongest tidal current, has inspired tales of ships' being sucked down in its maelstrom (whirlpool). It is one of nature's wonders as well as a paradise for anglers. A new visitor's center opened here in 1996. ✉ *33 km (20 mi) south of Bodø,* ☎ *75560655.*

WITHOUT KODAK MAX
photos taken on 100 speed film

TAKE PICTURES. FURTHER.™

© Eastman Kodak Company, 1999. Kodak, Max and Take Pictures. Further. are trademarks.

Ever see someone

waiting for the sun to come out

while trying to photograph

a charging rhino?

WITH KODAK MAX
photos taken on Kodak Max 400 film

New!
Kodak Max film:

Now with better color, Kodak's maximum versatility film gives you great pictures in sunlight, low light, action or still.

It's all you need
to know about film.

www.kodak.com

Kjærringøy Gamle Handelssted (Kjærringøy Old Trading Post) is 40 km (25 mi) north of Bodø. It has one of Norway's most important collections of buildings preserved from the 19th century, capturing part of the history of north Norwegian coastal life and culture. The Norwegian author Knut Hamsun developed a special relationship to Kjerringøy, which became the setting for some of his best literary descriptions. For more information contact **Destination Bodø AS** (⊠ Box 514, Sjøgt. 21, 8001 Bodø, ☏ 75526000).

$$$ ⊞ **Radisson SAS Hotel.** This grand hotel pulses with life and has enough amenities—like bowling and live music—to keep you solidly entertained. The rooms are well supplied and the service is impeccable. ⊠ *Storgt. 2, 8006,* ☏ *75524100,* FAX *75527493. 190 rooms. 2 restaurants, bar. AE, DC, MC, V.*

$$ ⊞ **Quality Hotel Diplomat** Located centrally near the harbor, this comfortable hotel has a sauna, a solarium, and a gymnasium. ⊠ *Sjøgt. 23A, 8006,* ☏ *75527000,* FAX *75547089. 113 rooms. 2 restaurants, bar. AE, DC, MC, V.*

$ ⊞ **Norrøna Hotell.** This bed-and-breakfast is comfortable, with a good view of the sea. ⊠ *Storgt. 4B, 8006,* ☏ *75525550,* FAX *75523388. 99 rooms. Restaurant. AE, DC, MC, V.*

★ Lofoten Islands

The Lofoten Islands archipelago is a 190-km (118-mi) chain of mountaintops rising from the bottom of the sea north of Bodø. In summer the local farms, fjords, and fishing villages become a major tourist magnet. Between January and March, thousands of fishermen from all over the country head for Lofoten to the annual Lofoten Fishery, the world's largest annual cod-fishing event. **Svolvær,** the main town and administrative center for the villages on Lofoten Islands, is connected with the other islands by express boat and ferry, and by coastal steamer and air to Bodø. It has a thriving summer art colony. **Lofotr** (Viking Museum of Borg; ⊠ 8360 Bøstad, ☏ 76084900), 67 km (42 mi) south of Svolvær on Route E10, has a reconstruction of a Viking chieftain's homestead. The year 900 is re-created inside, with a flickering fireplace and cod liver oil lamps. You may also bump into the chieftain himself; he tells many stories of raids and expeditions. The **midnight sun** is visible in Lofoten from May 27 to July 17. The best places to view it are Unstad and Eggum on **Vestvågøy** and Gimsøy and Laukvik on **Vågan.** It is also worth taking a fishing boat trip to see the impressive **Refsvikhula Cave.**

Narvik

Narvik is a rebuilt city, an ice-free seaport, and a major iron ore shipping center. An excellent railway connects it to the mines across the Swedish border. **Krigsminnemuséet** (the War Memorial Museum) has gripping displays on wartime intrigue and suffering. ⊠ *Kongensgt., near the main square,* ☏ *76944426.* ☉ *Mar.–mid-June and mid-Aug.–Sept., daily 11–2; mid-June–mid-Aug., daily 10–10. Closed Oct.–Feb., except for tours arranged by special appointment.*

$$$ ⊞ **Grand Royal Hotel.** An eager-to-please staff serves you at this handsome hotel near the train station. There are many possibilities for skiing and fishing nearby. ⊠ *Kongensgt. 64, 8500,* ☏ *76941500,* FAX *76945531. 107 rooms. 2 restaurants. AE, DC, MC, V.*

Harstad

Northeast of Lofoten on Hinnøya, Norway's largest island, is Harstad, where the population of 23,000 swells to 42,000 during the annual June cultural festival and the July deep-sea fishing festival.

Tromsø

Farther north on the mainland is Tromsø, self-dubbed "the Paris of the North" for its nightlife inspired by the midnight sun. Looming over the remote arctic university town are 6,100-ft peaks with permanent snowcaps. Tromsø trails off into the islands: Half the 50,000 inhabitants of the town live offshore. Be sure to see the spectacular **Ishavskatedral** (Arctic Cathedral), with its eastern wall made entirely of stained glass. Coated in aluminum, the **Tromsø bridge** has triangular peaks that make a bizarre mirror for the midnight sun.

Part of Tromsø University, **Tromsø Museum** concentrates on science, the Sami, and northern church art. ⊠ *Lars Thøringsvei 10, Folkeparken; take Bus 28;* ☎ *77645000.* ☉ *June–Aug., daily 9–9; Sept.–May, weekdays 8:30–3:30, Sat. noon–3, Sun. 11–4.*

$$$$ 🏨 **Radisson SAS Hotel Tromsø.** Rooms in this central hotel have great views over the shoreline. ⊠ *Sjøgt. 7, 9001,* ☎ *77600000,* 𝔽𝔸𝕏 *77685474. 195 rooms. 3 restaurants. AE, DC, MC, V.*

$$ 🏨 **Comfort Saga Hotel.** On a pretty town square, this hotel has quiet and comfortable, if basic, rooms. Its restaurant serves affordable, hearty meals. ⊠ *Richard Withs Pl. 2, 9008,* ☎ *77681180,* 𝔽𝔸𝕏 *77682380. 66 rooms, 3 suites. Restaurant. AE, DC, MC, V.*

Hammerfest

With 10,000 inhabitants, Hammerfest is the world's northernmost town. Founded in 1789, it is an elegant, festive-looking port. In the late 19th century fire razed it to the ground, and years later, defeated German troops destroyed the town as they retreated. Modern Hammerfest is the natural starting point for exploring Finnmark.

Discover **Sami culture** and try traditional Sami food while sitting on reindeer skins on a trip to a *mikkelgammen* (Sami turf hut) just outside town through Hammerfest Turist AS (☎ 78412185). The city is also home to **Isbjørn Klubben** (the Royal and Ancient Polar Bear Society), which has taxidermic displays of polar bears and other Arctic animals. ⊠ *Town Hall ground floor,* ☎ *78413100.* 🎟 *Free.* ☉ *June–Aug., weekdays 7–7, weekends 10–5, Sept.–May, daily 11:30–1:30.*

The Far North Essentials

Getting Around

BY CAR
E6 and its feeder roads are the only routes available north of Trondheim, where the country narrows dramatically.

BY SHIP
One of the best ways to travel in northern Norway is aboard a **Hurtigruta** (two coastal steamer companies in Tromsø: ☎ 77648200 or 76967600), which starts out in Bergen and turns around 2,000 nautical km (1,250 mi) farther north at Kirkenes. Many steamers run this route, so you can stay in port for any length of time and pick up the next one coming through. Major tourist offices have schedules, and reservations are essential as far as a year in advance (☞ Visitor Information, *below*).

BY TRAIN
A major train route runs from Oslo to Trondheim, then to Bodø (Norland Line). From Bodø tours go to the Lofoten by ferry. To reach the Nordkapp (North Cape), the northernmost mainland point in Norway and Europe, you must continue your trip by bus from Fauske. With a Scanrailpass you get 50% discount on the buses. From Narvik a train

to Sweden departs twice a day. In summer a special day trip through wild and beautiful scenery takes you to the Swedish border.

Visitor Information

Ålesund (✉ Rådhuset, ☏ 70121202). **Bodø** (✉ Sjøgt. 21, ☏ 75526000). **Hammerfest** (✉ 9600, ☏ 78412185). **Harstad** (✉ Torvet 8, ☏ 77018989). **Lofoten** (✉ 8300 Svolvær, ☏ 76073000). **Narvik** (✉ Kongensgt. 66, ☏ 76943309). **Tromsø** (✉ Storgt. 61, ☏ 77610000). **Trondheim** (✉ Munkegt. 19, ☏ 73929400).

23 POLAND

WARSAW, KRAKÓW AND ENVIRONS, GDAŃSK AND THE NORTH

Poles are fond of quoting, with a wry grimace, the old Chinese curse, "May you live in interesting times." The times were certainly interesting in 1990s Poland, the home of the Solidarity political/labor/social movement that sent shock waves through the Soviet Bloc in 1980, and the first Eastern European state to shake off Communist rule. But as the grimace implies, being on the firing line of history—something that the Poles are well used to—can be uncomfortable.

You will be constantly reminded that the return to free-market capitalism after more than 45 years of state socialism is an experiment on an unprecedented scale that has brought hardships for millions but also benefits for a growing percentage of the population. With 39 million inhabitants living in a territory of 318,400 sq km (121,000 sq mi), Poland in the 1990s was suspended between the Old World and the New, and the images can be confusing. Bright, new, privately owned shops with smiling assistants carry on business in shabby buildings that have not been renovated for decades. Billboards advertise goods that most Poles cannot afford. Many key public services have deteriorated as local authorities make valiant attempts to satisfy an increasingly demanding electorate with woefully insufficient funds. In 1998, however, the government approved sweeping reform programs in the fields of education, health care, and social security.

The official trappings of the Communist state were quickly dismantled after the Solidarity victory in the 1989 elections. But Communism never sat easily with the Poles. It represented yet another stage in their age-old struggle to retain their identity in the face of pressure from large and powerful neighbors to the west and east. Since its foundation as a unified state on the great north European plain during the 10th century, Poland has lain at the heart of Europe, precisely at the halfway point on a line drawn from the Atlantic coast of Spain to the Ural Mountains. This has never been an enviable position. During the Middle Ages Poland fought against German advance; in the Golden Age of Polish history during the 16th and 17th centuries—of which you will be reminded by splendid Renaissance buildings in many parts of the country—Poland pushed eastward against her Slavic neighbors, taking Kiev and dreaming of a kingdom that stretched from the Baltic to the Black Sea. By the end of the 18th century Poland's territories were divided among the Austrian, Prussian, and Russian empires.

During the 20th century Poland fell victim to peculiarly vicious forms of dictatorship—from both the right and the left: the brutal Nazi occupation, and imposition of Soviet rule. Poland's ancient cities—Kraków, Warsaw, Gdańsk—tell much of the tale of European history and culture. Its countryside offers unrivaled opportunities to escape from the present. Paradoxically, Communism—which after 1956 dropped attempts to collectivize agriculture and left the Polish farmer on his small, uneconomical plot—has left rural Poland in something of a time warp. Despite pollution, cornflowers still bloom, storks perch atop untidy nests by cottage chimneys, and horsepower still frequently comes in the four-legged variety. While the Poles have a certain wary reserve, they will win you over with their strong individualism—expressed through their well-developed sense of humor and their capacity for conviviality.

It's likely to take several generations before the physical and psychological traces of 45 years of Soviet rule fade and at least 20 years until Poland "catches up" with the poorest EU member in terms of standard of living. Nevertheless, Poland became a NATO member in 1999. Parliamentary elections in fall 1997 returned a center-right coalition with deep roots in the Solidarity movement to power, where it "cohabits" with a post-Communist President.

POLAND A TO Z

Customs
Persons over 18 may bring in duty-free: personal belongings, including musical instruments, one computer, one radio, one camera with 24 rolls of film; up to 250 cigarettes, 50 cigars, 1 liter of spirits, 2 liters of wine, and 5 liters of beer. Goods with a value of 70 euros may be brought into the country. The foreign currency limit is now 5,000 euros, but it must be declared on arrival. Further customs information can be obtained in Warsaw by calling ☎ 022/650–28–73.

Dining
Polish food and drink are basically Slavic with Baltic overtones. The emphasis is on soups and meat (especially pork), as well as freshwater fish. Cream is a staple, and pastries are rich and often delectable. The most popular soup is *barszcz* (known to many Americans as borscht), a clear beet soup often served with such Polish favorites as sausage, cabbage, potatoes, sour cream, coarse rye bread, and beer. Other typical dishes are *pierogi,* which may be stuffed with savory or sweet fillings; *gołąbki* (cabbage leaves stuffed with minced meat); *bigos* (sauerkraut with meat and mushrooms); and *flaki* (a tripe soup). Polish beer is excellent; vodka is a specialty and is often downed before, during, and after meals.

Zajazdy (roadside inns) and *bar mleczny* (milk bars), which are often less expensive than regular restaurants, serve more traditional food. As elsewhere in Central Europe, cafés are a way of life in Poland and often serve delicious homemade pastries and ice cream.

Poland (Polska)

MEALTIMES

Poles eat their main meal at around 2 PM with a light supper at about 8 PM. Restaurants—especially in major cities—open around noon for lunch and serve dinner between 7 PM and 10 PM. Although many restaurants in the provinces close around 10 PM, more cosmopolitan establishments stay open until 11 PM or later. Most hotel restaurants serve the evening meal until 10:30.

RATINGS

Prices are per person and include three courses and service but not drinks.

CATEGORY	WARSAW/KRAKÓW	OTHER AREAS
$$$$	zł 100–200	over zł 60
$$$	zł 50–zł 100	zł 40–zł 60
$$	zł 25–zł 50	zł 20–zł 40
$	under zł 25	under zł 20

In Warsaw and Kraków formal dress is customary at $$$ and $$$$ restaurants. Casual dress is appropriate elsewhere.

Language
Polish is a Slavic language that uses the Roman alphabet but has several additional characters and diacritical marks. Because it has a high incidence of consonant clusters, most English speakers find it a difficult language to decipher, much less pronounce. Many older Poles speak German; the younger generation usually knows some English. In larger cities English is increasingly common, especially in hotels, but you may have difficulty in the countryside.

Lodging
Acceptable lodging can be found even in remote corners of the country. For luxurious, world-class accommodations you'll have to wait several more years before being satisfied with offerings outside Warsaw.

HOTELS
The government rates hotel accommodations with from one to five stars. A tourism law that took effect in July 1998 sets standards for each rating where none previously existed. Note that even the best hotels in Poland do not boast five stars—usually because they don't want to pay the 22% value-added tax that accompanies the honor.

Orbis hotels, owned by the state tourist office and currently undergoing privatization, have almost all been accorded three or four stars and guarantee a reasonable standard of cleanliness and service (although they tend to lack character). Most of them range in price from $$ to $$$$; the chain includes a number of foreign-built luxury hotels. In recent years Orbis hotels have faced competition from a growing number of privately owned lodgings, often part of international chains and mostly in the top price range.

Municipal hotels and Dom Turysty hotels are run by local authorities or the Polish Tourist Association. They are often rather old and can have limited bath and shower facilities. Standards are improving as many undergo renovations; prices are in the $$ category.

PRIVATE ACCOMMODATIONS
Rooms can be arranged either in advance through a travel agent or on the spot at the local tourist information office. Villas, lodges, rooms, or houses are available. Daily rates vary from about $8 for a room to more than $150 for a villa.

RATINGS
The following chart is based on a rate for two people in a double room with bath or shower and breakfast. These prices are in U.S. dollars; many hotels in Poland quote prices in American dollars or German marks because of the fluctuations in Polish currency.

CATEGORY	COST
$$$$	over $200
$$$	$100–$200
$$	$50–$100
$	under $50

ROADSIDE INNS
Many roadside inns are quite attractive, offering inexpensive food and guest rooms at moderate rates.

Mail

POSTAL RATES

Airmail letters abroad cost about zł 1.60 (depending on weight); post-cards, zł 1.10. Post offices are open weekdays 8–8. At least one post office is open 24 hours in every major city. In Warsaw the 24-hour post office is at ✉ ul. Świętokrzyska 31.

Money Matters

COSTS

Inflation in Poland is high by Western standards, although the rate has fallen to about 10% annually. Prices are highest in the big cities, especially Warsaw.

CREDIT CARDS

Major credit cards are accepted in all major hotels, in the better restaurants and nightclubs, and for other tourist services. In small cafés and shops, especially in the provinces, credit cards are not accepted.

CURRENCY

The monetary unit in Poland is the złoty (zł), which is divided into 100 groszy (gr). Since the currency reform of 1994, there are notes of 10, 20, 50, 100, and 200 złotys, and coins in values of 1, 2, and 5 złotys and 1, 2, 5, 10, and 50 groszys. At press time (summer 1999), the exchange rate was zł 3.90 to the U.S. dollar, zł 2.66 to the Canadian dollar, zł 6.10 to the pound sterling, zł 2.58 to the Australian dollar, and zł 2.06 to the New Zealand dollar.

The złoty is exchangeable at a free-market rate in banks and at *kantory* (private exchange bureaus), which sometimes offer slightly better rates than do banks and are usually open until 8 PM. There are also cash machines throughout the country that accept most major credit cards as long as you have a PIN number. (Bankomat currently has more than 500 machines in Poland.)

SAMPLE PRICES

A cup of coffee, zł 3–zł 7; a bottle of beer, zł 4–zł 8; a soft drink, zł 2–zł 5; a ham sandwich, zł 4–zł 6; a 2-km (1-mi) taxi ride, zł 5.20.

TIPPING

At restaurants, if service is not included, waiters get a standard 10% of the bill. On smaller bills, round upward to the nearest zł or two. Hotel porters and doormen get about zł 2 per bag.

National Holidays

January 1; April 23–24 (Easter); May 1 (Labor Day); May 3 (Constitution Day); June 22 (Corpus Christi); August 15 (Assumption); November 1 (All Saints' Day); November 11 (Independence Day; rebirth of the Polish state in 1918); December 25, 26 (Christmas).

Opening and Closing Times

Banks are open weekdays 8 or 9–3 or 6. **Museum** hours vary greatly but are generally Tuesday–Sunday 10–5. Among **shops,** food shops are open weekdays 7–7, Saturday 7–1 or 2; many are now open on Sunday, and there are a few all-night stores in most central shopping districts. Other stores are open weekdays 11–7 and Saturday 9–1 or 2.

Precautions

Tap water in major cities is unsafe to drink, so ask for bottled mineral water. Beware of meat dishes served in cheap snack bars.

Telephoning

COUNTRY CODE

The international country code for Poland is 48. When dialing a number in Poland from outside the country, drop the initial 0 from the local area code.

INFORMATION

For local directory information, dial 913; for Poland-wide directory information and dialing codes, dial 912; for international information and codes, dial 908.

INTERNATIONAL CALLS

Post offices and first-class hotels have booths at which you can use your calling card or pay after completing your call. To place a call via **AT&T** USA Direct, dial 0–0800–111–1111. For **MCI,** dial 0–0800–111–2122. For **Sprint Global One,** dial 0–0800–111–3115.

LOCAL CALLS

Most public phones in Poland now take phone cards, which can be used for either local or long-distance calls. The cards, which cost zł 5.80, zł 11.59, or zł 23.18, are sold at kiosks and post offices. When making a long-distance call, first dial 0, wait for the dial tone, then dial the rest of the number. To place a domestic long-distance call to a number without a direct-dial facility, dial 900.

Transportation

BY BUS

PKS (☎ 9433) is the national bus company. **Polski Express** (☎ 022/620–03–30) is private and much nicer. Both offer long-distance service to most cities. Express buses, on which you can reserve seats, are somewhat more expensive than trains but often—except in the case of a few major intercity routes—get to their destinations more quickly. For really out-of-the-way destinations, the bus is often the only means of transportation. Bus stations are usually quite near railway stations. Tickets and information are best obtained from any travel agency, hotel, or the bus station itself.

BY CAR

Breakdowns. Poland's **Motoring Association** (PZMot) offers breakdown, repair, and towing services to members of various international insurance organizations; check with Orbis (☞ Travel Agencies *in* Warsaw Essentials, *below*) before you leave home. Carry a spare-parts kit. For emergency road help call 981.

Car Rentals. You can rent cars at international airports or through most travel agents. Rates tend to be high but vary according to season, car model, and mileage. Fly-drive vacations are also available.

Gasoline. The price of gas is about zł 22 for 10 liters of high octane. Filling stations are located every 30 km (19 mi) or so and are usually open 6 AM–10 PM. More and more bright, clean, full-service 24-hour stations are opening each year, and they're often accompanied by fast-food restaurants or grocery stores.

Road Conditions. Despite the extensive road network, a major increase in traffic in the 1990s and the lack of divided highways have made driving in Poland extremely dangerous. Minor roads tend to be narrow and encumbered with horse-drawn carts, bicycles, and pedestrians. If you're in a hurry, stick to roads marked E (express roads that in theory lead to a border of Poland) or A (domestic express roads).

Rules of the Road. Driving is on the right. The speed limit on highways is 110 kph (68 mph) and on roads in built-up areas, 60 kph (37 mph).

A built-up area is marked by a white rectangular sign with the name of the town on it.

BY PLANE

LOT, Poland's national airline, operates daily flights linking eight main cities: Warsaw, Kraków, Gdańsk, Wrocław, Szczecin, Poznań, Katowice, and Rzeszów. Fares begin at about $80 round-trip from Warsaw. Tickets and information are available from LOT or any travel agent. Be sure to book well in advance, especially for the summer season.

BY TRAIN

Poland's **PKP** railway network is extensive and relatively inexpensive. Most trains have first- and second-class accommodations, but Western visitors usually prefer to travel first-class. You should arrive at the station well before departure time. The fastest trains are intercity and express trains, which require reservations. Orbis and other travel agents furnish information, reservations, and tickets. If you're traveling on overnight trains, reserve a berth in a first-class sleeping car or second-class couchette. Long-distance trains carry buffets.

Fares. Polish trains run at three speeds—*ekspresowy* (express), *pośpieszny* (fast), and *osobowy* (slow)—and fares vary accordingly. You pay more for intercity and express, and round-trip tickets are priced at precisely double the one-way fare.

Visas

Citizens of the United States and the United Kingdom do not need visas for entry to Poland; Canadian citizens and citizens of other countries that have not yet abolished visas for Poles must apply to the Polish Consulate General in any country. (At present, Canadians must pay the equivalent of 89 Canadian dollars, and more for multiple-entry visas.) Visitors from Canada and other countries who are required to have visas must complete one application form and provide two photographs; allow one to two weeks for processing. Such visas for Canadians are now issued for 180 days but can be extended in Poland through the local province police headquarters.

Visitor Information

There is no national tourist office in Poland. State-run tourist offices are listed in individual cities' Essentials sections (☞ *below*).

Weather

The main tourist season runs from May through September. The best times for sightseeing are late spring and early fall. Major cultural events usually take place in the cities during the fall. The early spring is often wet and windy.

CLIMATE

Below are the average daily maximum and minimum temperatures for Warsaw.

Jan.	32F	0C	May	67F	20C	Sept.	66F	19C
	22	− 6		48	9		49	10
Feb.	32F	0C	June	73F	23C	Oct.	55F	13C
	21	− 6		54	12		41	5
Mar.	42F	6C	July	75F	24C	Nov.	42F	6C
	28	− 2		58	16		33	1
Apr.	53F	12C	Aug.	73F	23C	Dec.	35F	2C
	37	3		56	14		28	− 3

WARSAW

At the end of World War II Warsaw lay in ruins, a victim of systematic Nazi destruction. Only one-third of its prewar population survived the German occupation. The experience is visible everywhere in the memorial plaques describing mass executions of civilians and in the bullet holes still on the facades of some buildings. However, Varsovians painstakingly rebuilt their beloved Old Town, reconstructing it from old prints and paintings. The result, an area whose buildings are painted in warm pastel colors, is remarkable. Surrounding the old districts, however, is the modern Warsaw, built since the war in utilitarian Socialist and later styles, giving it a certain "Soviet" feel.

Exploring Warsaw

Numbers in the margin correspond to points of interest on the Warsaw map.

The sights of Warsaw are all relatively close to one another, making most attractions accessible on foot. A walking tour of the old historic district takes about two hours. A walk along the former Royal Route—the Trakt Królewski—which stretches south from Castle Square down Krakowskie Przedmieście, through Nowy Świat and on along Aleje Ujazdowskie, which is considered by many locals to be Warsaw's finest street, is also worthwhile. Lined with magnificent buildings and embassies, it has something of a French flavor. The Muranów district is the site of Jewish Warsaw.

Stare Miasto (Old Town) and Nowego Miasto (New Town)

❼ Barbakan (Barbican). This pinnacled redbrick gate is a fine example of a 16th-century defensive fortification. From here you can see the partially restored wall that was built to enclose the Old Town and enjoy a splendid view of the Vistula River, with the district of Praga on its east bank. ⊠ *Ul. Freta.*

❸ Bazylika Świętego Jana (Cathedral of St. John). The oldest church in Warsaw, it dates from the 14th century. Several Polish kings were crowned here. ⊠ *Ul. Świętojańska 8.*

❿ Kościół Najświętszej Marii Panny (St. Mary's Church). This is the oldest church in the New Town, built as a parish church for the district by the princes of Mazovia in the early 15th century. St. Mary's has been destroyed and rebuilt many times throughout its history. The Gothic bell tower dates from the early 16th century. ⊠ *Ul. Przyrynek 2.*

❻ Muzeum Historyczne Warszawy (Historical Museum of Warsaw). This excellent museum detailing the history of the city has a 20-minute movie, *Warsaw Remembers,* describing the history of Warsaw, mostly made up of old footage. It is shown in English on Tuesdays at noon. ⊠ *Rynek Starego Miasta 28,* ☎ *022/635–16–25.* ⊙ *Tues., Thurs. 11–5; Wed., Fri. 10–3:30; weekends 10:30–4:30.*

❺ Muzeum Literatury Adama Mickiewicza (Adam Mickiewicz Museum of Literature). This museum contains manuscripts, mementoes, and portraits of Polish writers. ⊠ *Rynek Starego Miasta 20,* ☎ *022/831–40–61.* ⊙ *Mon., Tues., Fri. 10–3; Wed., Thurs., Sat. 11–6; Sun. 11–5. Closed 1st Sun. of month.*

❽ Muzeum Marii Skłodowskiej-Curie (Marie Curie Museum). In this beige-and-rose-color stone house the Nobel prize winner for physics (1903)—for the discovery of radium and polonium (named after

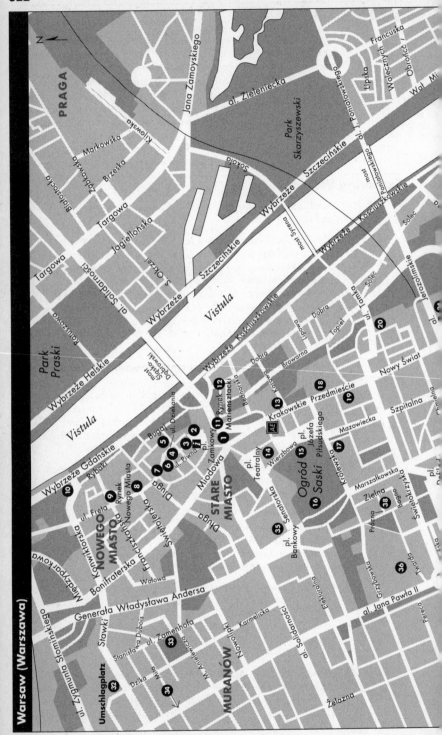

823

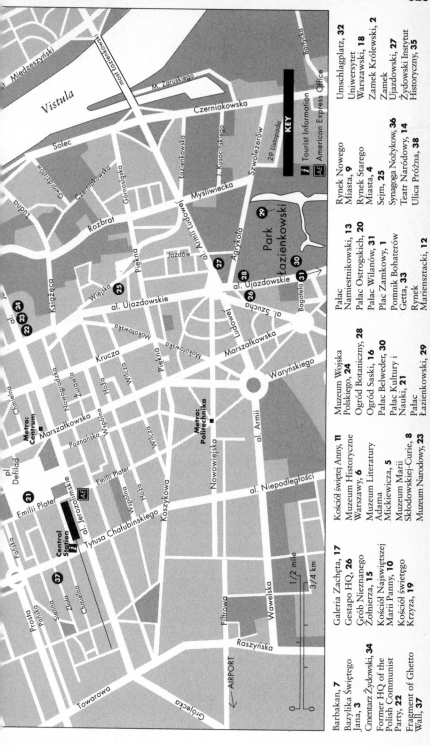

KEY

i Tourist Information

AE American Express Office

Barbakan, **7**
Bazylika Świętego Jana, **3**
Cmentarz Żydowski, **34**
Former HQ of the Polish Communist Party, **22**
Fragment of Ghetto Wall, **37**

Galeria Zachęta, **17**
Gestapo HQ, **26**
Grób Nieznanego Żołnierza, **15**
Kościół Najświętszej Marii Panny, **10**
Kościół świętego Krzyża, **19**

Kościół świętej Anny, **11**
Muzeum Historyczne Warszawy, **6**
Muzeum Literatury Adama Mickiewicza, **5**
Muzeum Marii Skłodowskiej-Curie, **8**
Muzeum Narodowy, **23**

Muzeum Wojska Polskiego, **24**
Ogród Botaniczny, **28**
Ogród Saski, **16**
Pałac Belweder, **30**
Pałac Kultury i Nauki, **21**
Pałac Łazienkowski, **29**

Pałac Namiestnikowski, **13**
Pałac Ostrogskich, **20**
Pałac Wilanów, **31**
Plac Zamkowy, **1**
Pomnik Bohaterów Getta, **33**
Rynek Mariensztacki, **12**

Rynek Nowego Miasta, **9**
Rynek Starego Miasta, **4**
Sejm, **25**
Synagoga Nożyków, **36**
Teatr Narodowy, **14**
Ulica Próżna, **38**

Umschlagplatz, **32**
Uniwersytet Warszawski, **18**
Zamek Królewski, **2**
Zamek Ujazdowski, **27**
Żydowski Instytut Historyczny, **35**

Poland)—and chemistry (1911) was born. ✉ *Ul. Freta 16,* ☎ *022/831–80–92.* ☉ *Tues.–Sat. 10–4, Sun. 10–2.*

❶ Plac Zamkowy (Castle Square). Here a slender column supports the statue of Zygmunt (Sigismund) **III Wasa,** king of Poland and Sweden, who moved the country's capital from Kraków to Warsaw in the early 17th century. The city's oldest monument, it was the first to be rebuilt after World War II. ✉ *Junction ul. Miodowa and Krakowskie Przedmieście.*

❾ Rynek Nowego Miasta (New Town Square). The center of the New Town is slightly more irregular and relaxed than its Old Town counterpart (☞ *below*). The town was founded at the turn of the 15th century. Rebuilt after World War II in 18th-century style, the **Nowe Miasto** district has a more spacious feeling to it. ✉ *Off ul. Freta.*

★ ❹ Rynek Starego Miasta (Old Town Market Square). In summer the square is full of open-air cafés and tubs of flowering plants; the inevitable artists display their talents for tourists year-round. At night the brightly lighted Rynek is the place to go for good food and atmosphere. The streets of the **Stare Miasto** have colorful medieval houses, cobblestone alleys, uneven roofs, and wrought-iron grillwork. ✉ *Junction ul. Piedarska and ul. Świętojańska.*

★ ❷ Zamek Królewski (Royal Castle). The princes of Mazovia first built a residence here during the 14th century; its present Renaissance form dates from the reign of King Sigismund III, who needed a magnificent palace for his new capital. Reconstructed later than the Old Town, in the 1970s, the castle now gleams as it did in its earliest years, with gilt, marble, and wall paintings; it houses impressive art collections—including views of Warsaw by Canaletto's nephew Bernardo Bellotto (known in Poland as "Canaletto"), which were used to help rebuild the city after the war. ✉ *Pl. Zamkowy 4,* ☎ *022/657–21–70.* ☉ *Tues.–Sat. 10–4, Sun. 11–4; tours available in English.*

Trakt Królewski (The Royal Route)

All towns with kings had their Royal Routes; the one in Warsaw stretched south from Castle Square down Krakowskie Przedmieście, through Nowy Świat and on along Aleje Ujazdowskie to Łazienki Park. Some of Warsaw's finest churches and palaces are along this route.

㉒ Former headquarters of the Polish Communist Party. This large, solid, gray building, erected in the Socialist-Realist architectural style, now, ironically, houses banks and the Warsaw Stock Exchange. ✉ *Corner Al. Jerozolimskie and Nowy Świat.*

⑰ Galeria Zachęta (Zachęta Gallery). Built during the last years of the 19th century by the Society for the Encouragement of the Fine Arts, the gallery was the site of the assassination of the first president of the post–World War I Polish Republic, Gabriel Narutowicz, by a right-wing fanatic in 1922. It has no permanent collection but organizes thought-provoking special exhibitions—primarily modern art and photography—in high, well-lit halls. It also has an excellent bookshop. ✉ *Pl. Małachowskiego 3,* ☎ *022/827–69–09.* ☉ *Tues.–Sun. 10–6.*

㉖ Gestapo Headquarters. Now the Ministry of National Education, the building also houses a small museum that recalls the horrors that took place behind its peaceful facade. ✉ *Al. Szucha 25,* ☎ *022/629–49–19.* ☉ *Wed. 9–5; Thurs., Sat., 9–4; Fri. 10–5; Sun. 10–4.*

⑮ Grób Nieznanego Żołnierza (Tomb of the Unknown Soldier). The only surviving fragment of an early 18th-century Saxon palace, which was blown up by the Nazis in 1944, now honors Poland's war dead.

Ceremonial changes of the guard take place here at noon on Sunday; the Polish Army still uses the goose step. ⊠ *Pl. Piłsudskiego.*

⑲ Kościoł świętego Krzya (Holy Cross Church). Inside is a pillar in which the heart of the great Polish composer Frédéric Chopin is entombed. The golden altar contrasts with the entirely white interior. Opposite the church is a statue of the astronomer Nicolaus Copernicus, who was born in Poland. ⊠ *Ul. Krakowskie Przedmieście 3.*

⑪ Kościół świętej Anny (St. Anne's Church). Originally built in 1454, it was rebuilt in high Baroque style during the 17th century. A plaque on the wall outside marks the spot where Pope John Paul II celebrated mass in 1980, during his first visit to Poland after his election to the papacy. ⊠ *Ul. Krakowskie Przedmieście 68.*

★ **㉓ Muzeum Narodowe** (National Museum of Warsaw). The spacious, sky-lighted museum has an impressive collection of Polish and European paintings, Gothic icons, and works from antiquity. ⊠ *Al. Jerozolimskie 3,* ☎ *022/629–30–93.* ☉ *Tues., Wed., Fri. 10–4; Thurs. noon–5; weekends 10–5.*

㉔ Muzeum Wojska Polskiego (Polish Army Museum). With exhibits of weaponry, armor, and uniforms tracing Polish military history across the past 10 centuries, it captures the romance of the subject. Even if the museum is closed, stroll past the gates to see the military helicopters, airplanes, and tanks parked outside. ⊠ *Al. Jerozolimskie 3,* ☎ *022/629–52–71.* ☉ *Wed.–Sun. 10–4.*

㉘ Ogród Botaniczny (Botanical Gardens). These beautiful plantings belonging to the University were laid out in 1818. Note the neoclassical Observatory. ⊠ *Al. Ujazdowskie 4.*

⑯ Ogród Saski (Saxon Gardens). The palace park was designed by French and Saxon landscape gardeners; the gardens still contain 18th-century sculptures, a man-made pond, and a sundial. ⊠ *Corner ul. Marszałkowska and ul. Królewska.*

㉚ Pałac Belweder (Belvedere Palace). This 18th-century former residence and office of the President was vacated in 1995 by former president Lech Wałesa, who declared Pałac Namiestnikowski (☞ *below*) the new official presidential residence. The building could become a museum in the next few years. ⊠ *Ul. Belwederska 2.*

㉑ Pałac Kultury i Nauki (Palace of Culture and Science). With ironic humor, locals tell you that the best vantage point from which to admire their city is atop the 37-story Palace of Culture and Science. Why? Because it is the only point from which you can't see the Palace of Culture and Science. This wedding-cake-style skyscraper was a personal gift from Stalin. It is Warsaw's best example of early 1950s "Socialist Gothic" architecture. ⊠ *Pl. Defilad 1,* ☎ *022/656–60–20.* ☉ *Mon–Sat. 9–4, Sun. 10–4.*

★ **㉙ Pałac Łazienkowski** (Łazienki Palace). Set inside the wonderfully landscaped French-style **Park Łazienkowski**, the palace, a gem of the Polish neoclassical style, was the private residence of Stanisław August Poniatowski, the last king of Poland. It overlooks a lake stocked with huge carp. To many Varsovians, this park provides the ideal respite from their concrete housing blocks. At the impressionistic Chopin monument nearby, wonderful open-air concerts take place on summer Sundays. ⊠ *Ul. Agrykola 1,* ☎ *022/621–62–41.* ☉ *Tues.–Sun. 9:30–3.*

⑬ Pałac Namiestnikowski (Namiestnikowski Palace). Built during the 17th century by the Radziwiłł family (into which Jacqueline Kennedy's sister, Lee, later married), this palace at one time functioned as the administrative office of the tsarist occupiers. In 1955 the Warsaw Pact was signed here, and now the palace serves as the official residence of Poland's president. In the forecourt is an equestrian statue of Prince Józef Poniatowski, a nephew of the last king of Poland, and one of Napoléon's marshals. ⊠ *Krakowskie Przedmieście 46–48.*

㉒ Pałac Ostrogskich (Ostrogski Palace). Headquarters of the Chopin Society, the 17th-century mansion towers impressively above the street. The best approach is along the steps from ulica Tamka. During the 19th century the Warsaw Conservatory was housed here (Paderewski was one of its students); now used for Chopin concerts, it has a small museum with mementoes of the composer. ⊠ *Ul. Okólnik 1,* ☎ *022/827–54–71.* ☉ *Mon.–Sat. 10–2, Thurs. 12–6.*

★ **㉛ Pałac Wilanów** (Wilanow Palace). Built by King Jan Sobieski, who in 1683 stopped the Ottoman advance on Europe at the Battle of Vienna, the palace later passed into the hands of Stanisław Kostka Potocki. Potocki amassed a major art collection and was responsible for the layout of the palace gardens. He opened Poland's first public museum here in 1805. The palace still holds much of the original furniture; there's also a striking display of 16th- to 18th-century Polish portraits on the first floor. Outside, to the left of the main entrance, is a romantic park with pagodas, summerhouses, and bridges overlooking a lake. There's also a **gallery** of contemporary Polish art on the grounds, and the stables to the right of the entrance house a **poster museum.** ⊠ *Ul. Wiertnicza 1, 10 km (6 mi) from town center,* ☎ *022/42–07–95.* ☉ *Museum: Wed.–Mon. 9:30–2:30; park: Wed.–Mon. until dusk.*

㉑ Rynek Mariensztacki (Mariensztat Square). At the bottom, and to the left of, a steeply sloping, cobbled street lies a quiet, leafy 18th-century square that is worth a detour. ⊠ *Ul. Bednarska.*

㉕ Sejm. The Polish Houses of Parliament, with their round, white debating chamber, were built during the 1920s, after the rebirth of an independent Polish state. ⊠ *Ul. Wiejska 4–6.*

⑭ Teatr Narodowy (Opera House and National Theater). This columned theater was built in the 1820s and reconstructed after World War II. It has a grand dome that is adorned inside with abstract constellation art. ⊠ *Pl. Piłsudskiego,* ☎ *022/826–32–88.*

⑱ Uniwersytet Warszawski (University of Warsaw). Established in 1816, the university has been a center for independent political thinking; most student protests have started here. Near the university, in the small garden opposite ulica Bednarska, stands a monument to the great Polish poet Adam Mickiewicz. It was here that Warsaw University students gathered in March 1968, after a performance of Mickiewicz's until-then banned play, *Forefathers' Eve,* and set in motion the events that led to the toppling of Poland's longtime Communist leader Władysław Gomułka. ⊠ *Krakowskie Przedmieście 26–28,* ☎ *022/620–03–81.*

㉗ Zamek Ujazdowski (Ujazdów Castle). Reconstructed in the 1980s, it is now the home of the **Centrum Sztuki Współczesnej** (Center for Contemporary Art), which hosts a variety of exhibitions by Polish, European, and North American artists. At the back, a terrace looks over formal gardens laid out down to the Vistula. ⊠ *Al. Ujazdowskie 6,* ☎ *022/628–12–71.* ☉ *Tues.–Thurs. and weekends 11–5, Fri. 11–9.*

The Muranów District

The Muranów district is the historic heart of the old prewar Warsaw Jewish district and ghetto under the Nazi regime. In April 1943 the Jewish resistance began the Warsaw Ghetto uprising, which was put down by the Nazis with unbelievable ferocity; the Muranów district was flattened. Today there are only bleak gray apartment blocks here.

㉞ **Cmentarz Żydowski** (Jewish Cemetery). This active cemetery is an island of continuity amid destruction. It survived the war, and although badly neglected during the postwar period, is gradually being restored. Fine 19th-century headstones testify to the Jewish community's important role in Polish history and culture. ✉ *Ul. Okopowa 49–51.*

㊲ **Fragment of Ghetto Wall.** In the courtyard of this building, through the archway on the right, stands a 9½-ft-tall fragment of the ghetto wall that existed for one year from November 1940. ✉ *Ul. Złota 60.*

㉝ **Pomnik Bohaterów Getta** (Heroes of the Warsaw Ghetto). The simple monument to the heroes of the Warsaw Ghetto is a slab of dark granite with a bronze bas-relief. A monument—inscribed in Hebrew and Polish—also marks the site of the house at ulica Miła 18 in which the command bunker of the uprising was concealed. ✉ *Ul. Zamenhofa, between ul. Anielewicza and ul. Lewartowskiego.*

㊱ **Synagoga Nożykow** (Nozyk Synagogue). Founded in 1900 by Zelman and Ryfka Nożyk, the synagogue survived the war and is now the only active synagogue in Warsaw. ✉ *Ul. Twarda 6.*

㊳ **Ulica Próżna** (Próżna Street). This is the only thoroughfare in Jewish Warsaw where tenement buildings have been preserved on both sides of the street. The Lauder foundation plans to restore the street to its original state. No. 9 belonged to Zelman Nożyk.

㉜ **Umschlagplatz.** From this rail terminus, hundreds of thousands of the ghetto's inhabitants were shipped in cattle cars to the extermination camp of Treblinka, about 100 km (60 mi) northeast of Warsaw. The school building to the right of the square was used to detain those who had to wait overnight for transport, and the beginning of the rail tracks survives on the right. At the entrance to the square is a **symbolic gateway**, erected in 1988 as a memorial on the 45th anniversary of the uprising. The first names of deportees are inscribed on the walls. ✉ *Corner ul. Stawki and ul. Dzika.*

㉟ **Żydowski Instytut Historyczny** (Jewish Historical Institute). Some 3 million Polish Jews were put to death by the Nazis during World War II, ending the enormous Jewish contribution to Polish culture, tradition, and achievement. The Institute houses a genealogy project that acts as a clearinghouse of information on archival sources and on the history of towns and villages in which Polish Jews lived. The Institute also houses a **museum** with photographs and displays of artifacts recalling a lost world. The nearby Sony building stands on the site of Warsaw's largest synagogue, which was blown up by the Nazis in May of 1943 as a triumphal finale to the liquidation of the Jewish ghetto. ✉ *Ul. Tłomackie 3/5,* ☎ *022/827–92–21.* ⏲ *Institute, weekdays 9–3.*

Dining and Lodging

More and more interesting restaurants have opened up throughout the city, but some of the most atmospheric dining rooms are still to be found on and around the Rynek Starego Miasta (Old Town Square) in the Old Town. Reservations for dinner can be made by telephone (by your hotel receptionist if you don't speak Polish); in the case of expensive and fashionable restaurants, this is essential. For details and price-category definitions, *see* Dining *in* Poland A to Z, *above.*

Orbis hotels are reliable, offering standardized, functional rooms. Most show signs of wear, but bathrooms have often been renovated to Western European standards. Private accommodations are cheap and hospitable. Information and reservations are available through the Center for Tourist Information (☞ Visitor Information *in* Warsaw Essentials, *below*), or through Syrena (✉ ul. Krucza 17, ☎ 022/628–75–40, which arranges for rooms in private homes). Some hotels have lower prices during the winter months. For details and price-category definitions, *see* Lodging *in* Poland A to Z, *above*.

$$$$ ✕ **Belvedere.** Housed in the elegant, romantic, 19th-century orangery in Łazienki Park, the restaurant has tables set among palms and waterfalls. The overpriced menu offers such traditional dishes as sliced breast of duck with a fruit sauce or, for a French touch, veal medallions in French pastry. ✉ *Łazienki Królewskie, entrance from ul. Parkowa*, ☎ *022/41–48–06. Reservations essential. AE, DC, MC, V.*

$$$ ✕ **Bazyliszek.** Dimly lighted, the Bazyliszek excels in boar, venison, and duck. At the same address are the restaurant's seafood venture, Fisherman (☎ 022/831–38–50), and a café and snack bar downstairs. ✉ *Rynek Starego Miasta 3/9*, ☎ *022/831–18–41. AE, DC, MC, V.*

$$$ ✕ **Café Ejlat.** This Warsaw institution reopened in 1998 after renovations and real-estate complications. Owned by the Polish-Israeli Friendship Society, the café has a menu rich in Jewish specialties, including a halvah dessert, and contemporary Polish dishes. ✉ *Al. Ujazdowskie 47*, ☎ *022/628–54–72. AE, DC, MC, V.*

$$$ ✕ **Karczma Gessler.** Bathed in candlelight, this restaurant occupies a
★   splendid brick cellar with vaulted ceilings. Delicious soups and meat offerings are prepared according to rural Polish recipes. Music students often entertain with old Polish tunes. The bakery upstairs has a wide array of pastries plus coffee. ✉ *Rynek Starego Miasta 21*, ☎ *022/831–16–61. Reservations essential. AE, DC, MC, V.*

$$$ ✕ **Restauracja Polska.** Decorated with antiques, floral prints, and
★   fruits, the restaurant is a treat for the senses. The specialty here is nouvelle Polish cuisine, and the service is excellent. The royal carp with sour cream sauce is an update of the country's classic Christmas dish. ✉ *Ul. Nowy Świat 21*, ☎ *022/828–38–77. AE, DC, MC, V.*

$$ ✕ **Menora.** Poland's only kosher restaurant stands on the dilapidated Plac Grzybowski, opposite the Jewish Theater and synagogue. Among the traditional dishes are *kreplach* (crepes with meat filling) and apple cake. ✉ *Pl. Grzybowski 2*, ☎ *022/620–37–54. AE, DC, MC, V.*

$$ ✕ **Pod Samsonem.** This simple, pre-war Jewish-style (nonkosher) restaurant serves terrific traditional Polish food, but don't expect service with a smile. Order the borscht with dumplings. ✉ *Ul. Freta 3/5*, ☎ *022/831–17–88. AE, DC, MC, V.*

$$ ✕ **Qchnia Artystyczna.** This artsy place at the back of the Ujazdowski Castle is not for the stodgy. The service is terrible, but the mainly vegetarian menu is creative and filling. Sample the *naleśniki* (crepes stuffed with sweet cheese or fruit). In summer, outdoor tables overlook a magnificent view of the park. ✉ *Ujazdowski Castle, Al. Ujazdowskie 6*, ☎ *022/625–76–27. AE, DC, MC, V.*

$ ✕ **Czytelnik.** Intellectuals and politicians from the Parliament next door hang out at this cafeteria-style restaurant/café with homemade, upscale milk bar cuisine: classic Polish soups, such as tomato and mushroom, and cutlets of various meats, from veal to pork to chicken. ✉ *Ul. Wiejska 12a*, ☎ *022/628–14–41. No credit cards. No dinner.*

$$$$ 🏠 **Bristol.** Since reopening in 1992 after a decade of renovation, Warsaw's most famous hotel has reclaimed its tradition of luxury and elegance. Built in 1901 and once partially owned by Ignacy Paderewski, the pianist who was Poland's prime minister in 1919–20, the Bristol is again the posh place to stay in the capital. The decidedly Polish Sunday brunch includes a caviar bar. ✉ *Krakowskie Przedmieście 42–44*,

00–325, ☎ *022/625–25–25,* FAX *022/625–25–77. 163 rooms, 43 suites. 2 restaurants, pool. AE, DC, MC, V.*

$$$$ ☷ **Marriott.** This Marriott was completed in 1989, and at 40 stories (20 make up the hotel; the rest are set aside for office and retail shopping space), the building is among the tallest in Warsaw. Its Italian resturant, Parmizzano's, is among the best of its kind in the city. Cafe Vienna, on the mezzanine level, is a popular meeting place. ✉ *Al. Jerozolimskie 65–79, 00–697,* ☎ *022/630–63–06,* FAX *022/630–52–39. 487 rooms, 34 suites. 3 restaurants, pool. AE, DC, MC, V.*

$$$$ ☷ **Sheraton.** Finished in 1996, this hotel stands near the Parliament
★ and Embassy Row. The tastefully decorated rooms overlook a beautiful square. Hotel service is impeccable, and there are small but excellent exercise facilities in the basement. ✉ *Ul. Prusa 2, 00–493,* ☎ *022/657–61–00,* FAX *022/657–62–00. 331 rooms, 21 suites. 2 restaurants. AE, DC, MC, V.*

$$$$ ☷ **Victoria Inter-Continental.** The main advantage of this large 1970s hotel is its location near the Old Town. It has the full range of Inter-Continental facilities. Ask for a room facing Victory Square. ✉ *Ul. Królewska 1, 00–065,* ☎ *022/657–80–11,* FAX *022/657–80–57. 347 rooms, 13 suites. 3 restaurants, pool. AE, DC, MC, V.*

$$$ ☷ **Hotel Europejski.** This late-19th-century hotel has views overlooking the Royal Route. Rooms are spacious, and the location is so good that you may not mind the slightly shabby furnishings. ✉ *Krakowskie Przedmieście 13, 00–065,* ☎ *022/826–50–51,* FAX *022/826–11–11. 224 rooms, 13 suites. Restaurant. AE, DC, MC, V.*

$$ ☷ **Dom Chłopa.** This renovated 1950s hotel has bright, pine-furnished rooms with gleaming bathrooms. It is a five-minute walk from the primary shopping streets and the National Philharmonic. If you don't mind the noisy clientele of the nightclub on the ground floor, it's good value. ✉ *Pl. Powstańców Warszawy 2, 00–030,* ☎ *022/625–15–45,* FAX *022/ 625–21–40. 282 rooms. Restaurant. AE, DC, MC, V.*

$$ ☷ **MDM.** The rooms are slightly dreary, with brown bedspreads, but the place is clean and the bathrooms are up to Western standards. For a downtown hotel, you can't beat the price. The central location can be noisy, so request a room on one of the higher floors. ✉ *Pl. Konstytucji 1, 00–647,* ☎ *022/621–62–11,* FAX *022/621–41–73. 105 rooms, 5 suites. Restaurant. AE, DC, MC, V.*

Nightlife and the Arts

The Arts

The monthly *Warsaw Insider,* available at most major hotels, is the best English-language source. If you read Polish, *Gazeta Wyborcza* and the monthly *IKS (Informator Kulturalny Stolicy)* have extensive listings. Cultural information is available by phone (☎ 022/629–84–89). Tickets can be ordered at your hotel, at the theater, or through the ticket office **Zasp** (✉ Al. Jerozolimskie 25, ☎ 022/621–93–83).

CONCERTS

The **National Philharmonic** (✉ Ul. Sienkiewicza 10, ☎ 022/826–72–81) is Poland's best concert hall. The **Royal Castle** (✉ Pl. Zamkowy 4, ☎ 022/657–21–70) has regular concerts in its stunning Great Assembly Hall. In summer free Chopin concerts are held at the Chopin monument in **Łazienki Park** on Sunday. Summer Chopin concerts also take place at **Żelazowa Wola** (☎ 046/863–33–00), the composer's birthplace, 58 km (36 mi) west of Warsaw.

OPERA

Teatr Wielki (✉ Pl. Teatralny 1, ☎ 022/826–32–88) hosts the Grand Theater of Opera and Ballet. Its stage is one of Europe's largest. The beautiful, intimate **Opera Kameralna** (⊠ Al. Solidarności 76b, ☎ 022/831–22–40) theater is not to be missed.

There are still 17 major theaters in Warsaw, despite large cuts in state funding, attesting to Poles' love of this art form. The **Globe Theatre Group** (☎ 022/620–44–29) has a varied contemporary English-language repertory. **Teatr Narodowy** (⊠ Pl. Teatralny 1, ☎ 022/826–32–88) is the oldest in Poland (it opened in 1765). **Żydowski Theater** (⊠ Pl. Grzybowski 12/16, ☎ 022/620–70–25), Warsaw's Jewish Theater, stages performances in Yiddish.

Nightlife

BARS

Harenda (⊠ Krakowskie Przedmieście 4/6, ☎ 022/826–29–00), with an outdoor terrace in summer, is open until 3 AM; jazz is played almost every night in the cellar bar. The **John Bull Pub** (⊠ Ul. Jezuicka 4, ☎ 022/831–37–62) is a comfortable Old Town pub that serves English draft beers. The Irish-owned **Morgan's** (⊠ Ul. Okólnik 1, ☎ 022/826–81–38), below the Pałac Ostrogskich, stays open until the wee hours.

CABARET

Variétes (⊠ Ul. Królewska 1, ☎ 022/657–84–84), at the Victoria Inter-Continental Hotel, includes a dinner and floor show. Other major hotels have nightclubs that present jazz and/or striptease. Check listings.

CAFÉS

Warsaw's *kawiarnia* (cafés), which move outdoors in summer, are busy meeting places, serving coffee and pastries in Central European style. **Café Blikle** (⊠ Nowy Świat 35, ☎ 022/826–66–19) is a traditional, fashionable hangout on Warsaw's main shopping street; try the *pączki* (Polish doughnuts). **E. Wedel** (⊠ Ul. Szpitalna 8, ☎ no phone), a venerable Warsaw institution, is best known for its thick, incredibly rich hot chocolate. **Nowe Miasto** (⊠ Nowego Miasta 13/15, ☎ 022/831–43–79), a vegetarian café-cum-restaurant, is on the restored, quiet New Town Square. The large, bustling **Nowy Świat** (⊠ Nowy Świat 63, ☎ 022/826–58–03) is good for people-watching and has a selection of foreign-language newspapers. The tiny, four-table **Pożegnanie z Afrika** (Out of Africa; ⊠ Ul. Freta 4/6, ☎ no phone) café has aromatic coffees from all over the world, but a limited selection of pastries. **Słodkie Fukier** (⊠ Ul. Mokotowska 45, ☎ 022/622–49–34) serves delicious pastries and good coffee. The menu at **Time Café** (⊠ Al. Jana Pawła 36, ☎ 022/604–817–244) offers full breakfasts, as well as panini sandwiches and salads.

DANCE CLUBS

Barbados (⊠ Ul. Wierzbowa 9, ☎ 022/827–71–61) draws corporate types to its small dance floor. The cavernous **Ground Zero** (⊠ Ul. Wspólna 62, ☎ 022/625–43–80), a former bomb shelter, caters to crowds of varying ages; it has its own eatery, the Warsaw Tortilla Factory. The elegant **Panorama Club** (⊠ Al. Jerozolimskie 65/79, ☎ 022/630–74–35), on the top floor of the Marriott, is very expensive. **Riviera Remont** (⊠ Ul. Waryńskiego 12, ☎ 022/825–74–97) showcases live music acts, ranging from blues to rock. **Scena** (⊠ Ul. Armii Ludowej 3/5, ☎ 022/625–35–10) attracts aspiring Polish actors and models. **Tango** (⊠ Ul. Smolna 15, ☎ 022/622–19–19) is an upmarket disco and cabaret.

JAZZ CLUBS

Akwarium (⊠ Ul. Emilii Plater 49, ☎ 022/620–50–72), a popular jazz club, may be in a new location in 2000. The cozy **Kawiarnia Literacka**

(⊠ Krakowskie Przedmieście 87/89, ☏ 022/828–89–95), overlooking Castle Square, has classic jazz on Sunday evenings.

Shopping

Nowy Świat, Krakowskie Przedmieście, and ulica Chmielna are lined with boutiques selling good-quality leather goods, silver and amber jewelry, clothing, and trinkets. For the best selection of Polish wood carvings, including animals and nativity scenes, go to **Arex** (⊠ Ul. Chopina 5B, ☏ 022/629–66–24). Try the **Cepelia** stores (⊠ Pl. Konstytucji 5, ☏ 022/621–26–18; ⊠ Rynek Starego Miasta 10, ☏ 022/831–18–05) for handicrafts such as glass, enamelware, amber, and hand-woven wool rugs. **Desa** (⊠ Ul. Marszałkowska 34, ☏ 022/621–66–15) specializes in antiques (objects from before 1945 cannot be legally exported). **Galeria Plakatu** (⊠ Rynek Starego Miasta 23, ☏ 022/831–93–06) has an excellent selection of Polish posters, many of which celebrate National Theater performances.

Warsaw Essentials

Arriving and Departing
BY BUS

Warsaw's central **bus terminal** is at ⊠ Aleje Jerozolimskie 144.

BY CAR

Seven main access routes lead to the center of Warsaw. Highways E30 and E77 are the main arteries from the West.

BY PLANE

International flights arrive at Warsaw's **Okęcie Airport** (⊠ Port Lotniczy, ☏ 022/650–42–20) just southwest of the city. Terminal 1 serves international flights; Terminal 2, next door, serves domestic flights.

Between the Airport and Downtown. The airport–city bus (about every 20 minutes from Platform 4; costs zł 5.60) and public Bus 175 (every 15 minutes; costs zł 1.40) run past almost all major downtown hotels. The trip takes about 25 minutes.

Avoid at all costs taxi drivers who approach you inside and those parked outside the arrivals hall. Your best bet is to go upstairs to the departure drop-off and flag down a taxi (if the driver cannot take you, ask him to call one) or call ☏ 919 for a radio taxi (fare about zł 35). Some of the hotels will also pick you up (fare about zł 45).

BY TRAIN

Trains to and from Western Europe arrive at **Dworzec Centralny** (Central Station; ⊠ Al. Jerozolimskie 54, ☏ 022/620–03–61 local train information; 022/620–45–12 international train information) in the center of town. For tickets contact a travel agent or your hotel or go to the train station.

Getting Around
BY BUGGY

Horse-drawn carriages can be rented at a negotiated price at the Old Town Market Square or Castle Square. Prices vary, but the average rate is zł.60 for a ride around the entire Old Town area.

BY SUBWAY

Warsaw's subway opened in spring 1995. The single line runs 17½ km (11 mi) from the southern suburbs to the city center (Natolin to the Palace of Culture and Science), with an extension to ulica Świętokrzyska that opened in mid-1999. It is clean and fast, costs the same as the tram and bus, and uses the same tickets, which you cancel at the entrance to the station. Trains run every five minutes during rush hours, every 15 minutes during off-peak hours.

BY TAXI

Taxis are still relatively cheap—about zł 3.60 for the first km (½ mi) and zł 1.60 for each additional km (½ mi)—and are readily available at taxi stands. Most major hotels have their own monogrammed fleets, but expect to pay more than you would for the efficient radio taxi service (☎ 919, English spoken), which is also considerably cheaper than taxis at stands.

BY TRAM AND BUS

Though often crowded, trams and buses are the cheapest way of getting around. They (including express buses) cost zł 1.40. Night buses run between 11:15 PM and 4:45 AM and require three tickets. Tickets must be bought in advance from **Ruch** newsstands. You must cancel your own ticket in a machine on the tram or bus when you get on; watch how others do it. Beware of very professional pickpockets.

Contacts and Resources

EMBASSIES AND CONSULATES

U.S. (⊠ Al. Ujazdowskie 29–31, ☎ 022/628–30–41). **Canadian** (⊠ Ul. Matejki 1/5, ☎ 022/629–80–51). **U.K.** (⊠ Al. Róż 1, ☎ 022/628–10–01). **U.K. Consulate** (⊠ Ul. Emilii Plater 28, ☎ 022/625–30–99). **Australian** (⊠ Ul. Estońska 3/5, ☎ 022/617–6081/5).

EMERGENCIES

Police (☎ 997). **Ambulance** (☎ 999). **Doctor** (☎ 999, or call your embassy or the **American Medical Center** (AMC; ☎ 0602/243–024 [24 hours]). **Pharmacies** in Warsaw stay open late on a rotational system. Signs listing the nearest open facility are posted outside every pharmacy. There is also a **24-hour pharmacy** upstairs in the Central Train Station (⊠ Al. Jerozolimskie 54, ☎ 022/825–69–84).

ENGLISH-LANGUAGE BOOKSTORES

American Bookstore (⊠ Ul. Koszykowa 55, ☎ 022/660–56–37). **Bookland** (⊠ Al. Jerozolimskie 61, ☎ 022/646–57–27). **Empik** (⊠ Ul. Nowy Swiat 15/17, ☎ 022/627–06–50).

GUIDED TOURS

Bus tours of the city depart in the morning and afternoon from major hotels. **Mazurkas Travel** (⊠ Ul. Długa 8/14, ☎ 022/635–66–33) offers an excellent selection of tours around the city. **Orbis** (☞ Travel Agencies, *below*) also has half-day excursions into the surrounding countryside. **Our Roots** (☞ Travel Agencies, *below*) offers four-hour tours of Jewish Warsaw.

TRAVEL AGENCIES

American Express (⊠ Krakowskie Przedmieście 11, ☎ 022/635–20–02; Marriott Hotel, ⊠ Al. Jerozolimskie 65/79, ☎ 022/630–69–52; for lost or stolen cards, call ☎ 022/625–40–30 from 6 AM to 2 AM). **Carlson Wagonlit Travel** (⊠ Ul. Nowy Świat 64, ☎ 022/826–04–31). **Orbis** (⊠ Ul. Bracka 16, ☎ 022/826–02–71; ⊠ Ul. Marszałkowska 142, ☎ 022/827–80–31). **Our Roots–Jewish Information and Tourist Bureau** (⊠ Ul. Twarda 6, ☎ 022/620–05–56).

VISITOR INFORMATION

Center for Tourist Information (⊠ Pl. Zamkowy 1, ☎ 022/635–18–81). **Warsaw Tourist and Cultural Information** (⊠ Central Train Station, Al. Jerozolimskie 54, ☎ 022/524–51–84). **Warsaw Tourist Information Center** (☎ 9431).

KRAKÓW

Kraków, once the capital of Poland (before losing the honor to Warsaw in 1611), and seat of the country's oldest university, is one of the few Polish cities that escaped devastation during World War II. Today Kraków's fine ramparts, towers, facades, and churches, illustrating seven centuries of Polish architecture, have earned its Old Town a listing by UNESCO as one of the 12 great historic cities of the world.

The city's location—about 270 km (167 mi) south of Warsaw—makes it a good base for hiking and skiing trips in the mountains of southern Poland. Within exploring range from Kraków are, in addition, the Polish shrine to the Virgin Mary at Częstochowa, and a grim reminder of man's capacity for inhumanity at Auschwitz (Oświęcim).

Exploring Kraków

Numbers in the margin correspond to points of interest on the Kraków map.

It seems a miracle that the marvelous old city of Kraków escaped World War II virtually undamaged. The city has three basic districts for touring: the Old Town, the Jewish quarter, and the Wawel. Each area can be seen in a half day or so, but more time can easily be spent.

❶ Barbakan (The Barbican). This imposing, round, redbrick 15th-century fortress was part of the old city defense system. It stands in Planty Park, which, circling the Old Town, replaces the old walls, which were torn down in the mid-19th century. ⊠ *Ul. Basztowa.*

❷ Brama Floriańska (St. Florian's Gate). The surviving fragment of the city wall opposite the Barbakan, where students and amateur artists like to hang their paintings for sale in the summer, contains the renaissance Municipal Arsenal. ⊠ *Ul. Pijarska.*

❾ Collegium Maius (Greater College). The pride of the oldest building of the world-renowned **Jagiellonian University**, founded in 1364, is the Italian-style arcaded courtyard. A **museum** here contains the Copernicus globe, the first on which the American continents were shown, as well as astronomy instruments from the time of Kraków's most famous graduate. ⊠ *Ul. Jagiellońska 15,* ☎ *012/422–05–49 (museum).* ☉ *Courtyard: Mon.–Sat. 8–6; museum: Mon–Fri. 11–2:30, Sat. 11–1:30 (call ahead for tours in English).*

❺ Kościół Mariacki (Church of the Virgin Mary). Every hour, four short bugle calls drift down from the spire of this church. The notes are a centuries-old tradition that honors a trumpeter whose throat was pierced by an enemy arrow as he was warning his fellow citizens of an impending Tartar attack. Inside the church is a 15th-century wooden altarpiece—the world's largest—carved by Veit Stoss. The saints' faces are reputedly those of local burghers. ⊠ *Rynek Główny.*

⓫ Kościół na Skałce (Church on the Rock). This Pauline Church is the center of the cult of St. Stanisław, an 11th-century bishop and martyr. Starting in the 19th century, it became the last resting place for well-known Polish writers and artists; among those buried here are the composer Karol Szymanowski (1882–1937) and the poet and painter Stanisław Wyspiański (1869–1907). ⊠ *Ul. Skałeczna and ul. Paulińska.*

❼ Muzeum Narodowy (National Museum). The highlights of this museum are Polish Art Nouveau and 20th-century painting, as well as historic arms and uniforms. ⊠ *Al. 3 Maja 1,* ☎ *012/634–33–77.* ☉ *Tues.–Sun. 10–3:30, Wed. 10–6.*

834

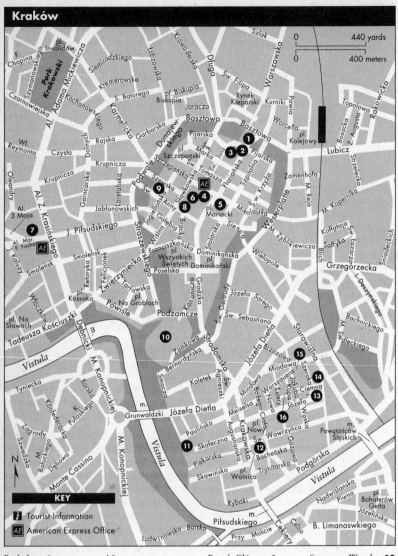

Barbakan, **1**

Brama Floriańska, **2**

Collegium Maius, **9**

Kościół Mariacki, **5**

Kościół na Skałce, **11**

Muzeum
Narodowy, **7**

Pałac
Czartoryskich, **3**

Ratusz, **12**

Rynek Główny, **4**

Stara Synagoga, **14**

Sukiennice, **6**

Synagoga Izaaka, **16**

Synagoga Remuh, **15**

Synagoga Wyoska, **13**

Wawel, **10**

Wieża Ratuszowa, **8**

★ **❸ Pałac Czartoryskich** (Czartoryski Palace). This branch of the National Museum, partially housed in the **Municipal Arsenal,** is one of the best art collections in Poland. Among its treasures is Leonardo da Vinci's *Lady with an Ermine.* ⊠ *Ul. Św. Jana 19,* ☏ *012/422–55–66.* ☉ *Tues.–Sun. 10–3:30, Fri. 10–6.*

⓬ Ratusz (City Hall of Kazimierz). The building is in the Kazimierz district of Kraków, which was once a town in its own right, chartered in 1335 and named for its founder, Kazimierz the Great. After 1495, when they were expelled from Kraków by King John Albert, this was the home of Kraków's Jews. The 15th-century town hall on the town square, now the **Muzeum Etnograficzne** (Ethnographic Museum), displays a well-mounted collection of regional folk art. ⊠ *Pl. Wolnica,* ☏ *012/656–28–63.* ☉ *Mon. 10–6; Wed., Thurs., and Fri. 10–3; weekends 10–2.*

❹ Rynek Główny (Main Market Square). This is one of the largest and finest Renaissance squares in Europe. ⊠ *Center of Old Town at ul. Floriańska and Św. Anny.*

⓮ Stara Synagoga (Old Synagogue). This synagogue was built during the 15th century and reconstructed in Renaissance style following a fire in 1557. Here, in 1794, Tadeusz Kościuszko successfully appealed to the Jewish community to join in the national insurrection. The synagogue now houses the **Museum of the History and Culture of Kraków Jews.** ⊠ *Ul. Szeroka 24,* ☏ *012/422–09–62.* ☉ *Sat.–Thurs. 9–3, Fri. 11–6. Closed 1st weekend of mo.*

❻ Sukiennice (Cloth Hall). In the center of the main square stands a covered market hall built during the 14th century but remodeled during the Renaissance. The ground floor, open Monday–Saturday 10–6, Sunday 10–5, is still in business, selling trinkets and folk-art souvenirs. On the second floor, in a branch of the **National Museum,** you can view a collection of 19th-century Polish painting. ⊠ *Rynek Główny,* ☏ *012/422–11–66.* ☉ *Tues.–Sun. 10–3:30, Thurs. 10–6.*

⓰ Synagoga Izaaka (Isaac Synagogue). Reopened in 1997 after three years of renovation, this Renaissance-era synagogue has Roman columns separating the women's gallery from the main room. Two short films, *The Jewish District of Kraków* (1936) and *Removal to the Kraków Ghetto* (1941), are continuously shown at the site. ⊠ *Ul. Kupa 18,* ☏ *012/ 602–300–277.* ☉ *Sun.–Fri. 9–7, except Jewish holidays.*

⓯ Synagoga Remuh (Remuh Synagogue). This tiny 16th-century synagogue is still used for worship. The cemetery, used by the Jewish community from 1533 to 1799, is the only well-preserved Renaissance Jewish burial ground in Europe. The so-called New Cemetery (⊠ Ul. Miodowa), which contains many old headstones, was established in the 19th century. ⊠ *Ul. Szeroka 40.* ☉ *Sun.–Fri. 9–4, except Jewish holidays.*

⓭ Synagoga Wysoka (High Synagogue). This late-16th-century synagogue has a prayer room on the second floor. ⊠ *Ul. Józefa 38.*

★ **❿ Wawel.** Unveiled in 1998 after extensive restoration work, this impressive castle complex of Gothic and Renaissance buildings stands on fortifications dating from the 8th century. Inside the castle is a **museum** with an exotic collection of Oriental tents captured from the Turks at the Battle of Vienna in 1683 as well as rare 16th-century Flemish tapestries. **Katedra Wawelska** (Wawel Cathedral) is where, until the 18th century, Polish kings were crowned and buried. Until 1978 the cathedral was the principal church of Archbishop Karol Wojtyła, now Pope John Paul II. ⊠ *Ul. Grodzka,* ☏ *012/422–51–55.* ☉ *Tues.–Sun. 10–3.*

⑧ **Wieża Ratuszowa** (Town Hall Tower). Across from the Cloth Hall is all that remains of the 16th-century town hall. Art exhibitions are held here in summer. ⊠ *Rynek Główny.*

Dining and Lodging

For details and price-category definitions, *see* Dining and Lodging *in* Poland A to Z, *above.*

Hotel rooms are in short supply in Kraków, especially during the busy summer season, when it is absolutely essential to book well in advance. Rooms facing the street in the Old Town are often noisy at night.

$$$$ ✕ **Hawelka.** Established in 1876 as a breakfast house by the merchant Antoni Hawelka, this Kraków institution specializes in Polish cuisine. The restaurant on the ground floor is casual and cheaper than the one upstairs, officially called Tetmajerowska. ⊠ *Rynek Główny 34,* ☎ *012/ 422–47–53. AE, DC, MC, V.*

$$$$ ✕ **Wierzynek.** It was in a restaurant on this site, after a historic meeting in 1364, that the king of Poland wined and dined the Holy Roman Emperor Charles IV, five kings, and a score of princes. The current establishment serves traditional Polish specialties and excels in soups and game. ⊠ *Rynek Główny 15,* ☎ *012/422–10–35. AE, DC, MC, V.*

$$$ ✕ **Chimera.** The vaulted ceilings and simple furnishings here are in sharp contrast to the creative cuisine, which adds a continental flair to Polish game dishes. Try the roast venison in juniper sauce or the goose á la Dijon. The bar in the cellar hosts blues and folk music. ⊠ *Ul. Świętej Anny 3,* ☎ *012/423–21–78. AE, DC, MC, V.*

$$$ ✕ **Pod Aniołami.** In summer the restaurant is in a courtyard; in win-
★ ter it moves into a cozy cellar. The country-style kitchen turns out home-made bread and hearty entrées. The chef will roast an entire pig for a group. ⊠ *Ul. Grodzka 35,* ☎ *012/421–39–99. No credit cards.*

$$ ✕ **Kabaret Loch Camelot.** This little café is on a small street right off the main square. If you can get a table and a waiter's attention, it's a good place to get a glass of wine and soak up the lively atmosphere. It's also open in the morning for coffee. ⊠ *Ul. Tomasza 17,* ☎ *022/ 421–01–23. No credit cards.*

$ ✕ **Jama Michalikowa.** Kraków's most famous café serves good coffee and excellent, homemade ice cream. The decor pays homage to the site's cabaret days. ⊠ *Ul. Floriańska 45,* ☎ *012/422–15–61. No credit cards.*

$$$ ▦ **Continental.** The first Holiday Inn in Eastern Europe, this high-rise hotel is bland but comfortable. Its location, on the far side of Kraków Common, is a short taxi ride from the Old Town. Athletic facilities, such as horseback riding stables, are nearby. ⊠ *Ul. Armii Krajowej 11, 30–150,* ☎ *012/637–50–44,* 𝔽𝔸𝕏 *012/637–59–38. 305 rooms. Restaurant, pool. AE, DC, MC, V.*

$$$ ▦ **Cracovia.** Large and Orbis-run, this five-story 1960s hotel is one of the few likely to have space during the busy summer months. The rooms are small and standardized but comfortable. Unfortunately, the hotel overlooks a traffic-laden square, but it also faces the National Museum. ⊠ *Al. Marszałka F. Focha 1, 30–111,* ☎ *012/422–86–66,* 𝔽𝔸𝕏 *012/421– 95–86. 427 rooms. Restaurant. AE, DC, MC, V.*

$$$ ▦ **Forum.** Opened in 1988, this charmless Orbis hotel stands on the south bank of the Vistula, commanding a fine view of Wawel Castle. It's a bit far from the Old Town but has good exercise facilities and a large selection of shops. There's also underground parking and a car wash. ⊠ *Ul. Marii Konopnickiej 28, 30–302,* ☎ *012/261–92–12,* 𝔽𝔸𝕏 *012/269–00–80. 277 rooms. Restaurant, pool. AE, DC, MC, V.*

$$$ ☷ **Francuski.** Just inside the Old Town's ramparts, this small, turn-of-the-century hotel stands on a quiet street. The atmosphere is intimate and the service friendly. The rooms are small but elegant in a homey, Eastern European way. The restaurant is tranquil and plush. ✉ *Ul. Pijarska 13, 31–015,* ☎ *012/422–51–22,* FAX *012/422–52–70. 42 rooms. Restaurant. AE, DC, MC, V.*

$$$ ☷ **Grand.** An air of Regency elegance predominates at this late-19th-
★ century hotel in the Old Town, although some Art Nouveau stained-glass windows have been preserved on the first floor. Rooms have reproduction period furniture and modern bathrooms and facilities. ✉ *Ul. Sławkowska 5–7, 31–014,* ☎ *012/421–72–55,* FAX *012/421–83–60. 56 rooms. Restaurant. AE, DC, MC, V.*

$$ ☷ **Pollera.** This 150-year-old hotel is a bit on the shabby side but is a good value because of its location. The bathrooms were modernized in 1998, and the bedrooms received a facelift in 1999. ✉ *Ul. Szpitalna 30, 31–024,* ☎ *012/422–10–44,* FAX *012/422–13–89. 42 rooms. Restaurant. AE, DC, MC, V.*

$$ ☷ **Saski.** Quaint and unpretentious, the Saski seems less hotel than it does early 1900s residence, although a stupendous pre-war elevator takes you to your room. Some of the spacious rooms were redecorated in 1997 and 1998. The small, dark restaurant is mainly frequented for breakfast. ✉ *Ul. Sławkowska 3, 31–014,* ☎ *012/421–42–22,* FAX *012/ 421–48–30. 63 rooms. Restaurant. AE, DC, MC, V.*

Side Trips

Oświęcim (Auschwitz)

About 50 km (30 mi) west of Kraków is Oświęcim, better known by its German name, Auschwitz. Here 4 million victims, mostly Jews, were executed by the Nazis in the Auschwitz and Birkenau concentration camps. **Auschwitz** is now a museum, with restored crematoria and barracks housing dramatic displays of Nazi atrocities. The buildings at **Birkenau,** a 15-minute walk away, have been left just as they were found in 1945 by the Soviet Army. Oświęcim itself is an industrial town with good connections from Kraków; buses and trains leave Kraków periodically, and signs in Oświęcim direct visitors to the former camp. ✉ *Ul. Więźniów Oświęcimia 20,* ☎ *033/843–21–33.* ◔ *Auschwitz: Nov.–Mar., daily 8–3; Apr. and Oct., daily 8–5; May and Sept., daily 8–6; June–Aug., daily 8–7. Birkenau: daily, sunrise–sunset.*

Wieliczka

About 8 km (5 mi) southeast of Kraków is the oldest salt mine in Europe, in operation since the 13th century. The mine is on the Unesco World Cultural Heritage list and is famous for its magnificent underground chapel hewn from crystal rock, the **Chapel of the Blessed Kinga** (Queen Kinga was a 14th-century Polish queen, later beatified). ✉ *Ul. Daniłowicza 10,* ☎ *012/278–73–34.* ◔ *Daily 8–4.*

Częstochowa

About 120 km (70 mi) from Kraków and reachable by regular trains and buses, Częstochowa is the home of the holiest shrine in a country that is some 95% Catholic. Inside the 14th-century **Pauline Monastery** on Jasna Góra (Light Hill) is the *Black Madonna,* a painting of Our Lady of Częstochowa attributed by legend to St. Luke. Here an invading Swedish army met heroic resistance from the Poles in 1655.

$ ☷ **Polonia.** The humble but charming Polonia makes a good base for exploring the Monastery, and as most of the guests are pilgrims, the atmosphere is a mixture of piety and good fun. ✉ *Ul. Piłsudskiego 9, 42–200,* ☎ *034/324–23–88,* FAX *034/365–11–05. 62 rooms. Restaurant. AE, DC, MC, V.*

Wadowice

About 40 km (25 mi) southwest of Kraków is the little town of Wad-owice, birthplace of Pope John Paul II. You can visit the **Muzeum Wadowice** (Wadowice Museum), dedicated to his life, in the house where he grew up. ⊠ *Ul. Kościelna 7,* ☎ *033/823–26–62.* ☉ *Tues.–Sun. 9–noon and 2–5.*

Kraków Essentials

Consulate

U.S. (⊠ Ul. Stolarska 9, ☎ 022/429–66–55, FAX 022/421–82–92).

Getting Around

The **bus** station is across the street from the train station (☞ *below*). By **car** Kraków can be reached on major highways—E7 direct from Warsaw and E40 from Częstochowa. The city can be reached by **plane** with direct flights from many major European cities and most Polish cities (airport information, ☎ 012/411–67–00). **Trains** link Kraków with most major destinations in Poland; the station, Kraków Główny (⊠ Pl. Kolejowy 1, ☎ 012/422–22–48, international information), is in the city center near the Old Town.

Guided Tours

Bus or walking tours of Kraków and its environs are provided by Orbis and other travel agencies (☞ *below*). Jardan Tours (☞ *below*) specializes in "Schindler's List" tours. Horse-drawn carriages can be rented at the main market square for a negotiated price.

Travel Agencies

Jardan Tours (⊠ Ul. Szeroka 2, ☎ 012/421–71–66). **Orbis** (⊠ Rynek Główny 41, ☎ 012/422–40–35; ⊠ Al. Marszałka F. Focha 1, ☎ 012/421–98–80).

Visitor Information

Częstochowa: Częstochowa Informacja Turystyczna (⊠ Al. Najświętszej Marii Panny 64, ☎ 034/324–13–60). **Kraków:** Jewish Cultural Center (⊠ Ul. Rabina Mieselsa 17, ☎ 012/423–55–95). Kraków 2000 Cultural Information Center (⊠ Ul. Świętej Jana 2, ☎ 012/421–77–87). Waweltur (⊠ Ul. Pawia 8, ☎ 012/422–19–21).

GDAŃSK AND THE NORTH

In contrast to Kraków and the south, Poland north of Warsaw is a land of castles, dense forests and lakes, and fishing villages and beaches. If you don't have a car, consider going straight to Gdańsk and making excursions from there.

Exploring Gdańsk and the North

By car from Warsaw, follow routes E77 and E62 through Płock. Con-tinue through Włocławek to Toruń, where you can stay overnight. The route leading north from Toruń to Gdańsk passes through some of the oldest towns in Poland. Along the way are many medieval castles, manor houses, and churches that testify to the wealth and strategic importance of the area. Two short detours are a must: One is to Kwidzyń, to see the original 14th-century castle and cathedral complex, which is open to the public. The other is to Malbork (☞ *below*).

For a different route back to Warsaw, follow highway E77 southeast along the edge of Poland's scenic lake district. The area is rich in nat-ural and historic attractions. A side trip 42 km (26 mi) east of Ostróda

Gdańsk and the North

takes you to the medieval town of Olsztyn. Another diversion, 17 km (10½ mi) west of Olsztynek, is the site of the Battle of Grunwald.

Gdańsk

Gdańsk, once the Free City of Danzig, contains another of Poland's beautifully restored old towns, displaying a rich heritage of Gothic, Renaissance, and Mannerist architecture. In 1997 Gdańsk celebrated its 1,000th anniversary. This is where the first shots of World War II were fired and where the first free trade union in the Soviet bloc, Solidarity, was born after strikes in August 1980. The city's Old Town has a wonderful collection of historic town houses and narrow streets. Splendid **ulica Długa** (best for shopping) and Długi Targ are great starting points for walks into other districts. The evocative **Pomnik Solidarnosci** (Solidarity Monument)—erected in honor of workers killed by the regime during strikes in 1970—stands outside the former Lenin shipyards. The nearby town of **Sopot** is Poland's most charming pre-war seaside resort.

$$$ ✕ **Euro.** Paisley prints and dark wood give this restaurant a tasteful look, matched by its classic menu. The pork chop stuffed with plums is a regional dish. ⊠ *Ul. Długa 79/80,* ☎ *058/305–23–83. AE, DC, MC, V.*

$$$ ✕ **Major.** Superbly located on Gdańsk's main pedestrian shopping street, this restaurant specializes in seafood but also serves excellent meat dishes, such as filet mignon in a wood mushroom sauce. Heavily draped in green curtains, the restaurant is reminiscent of many formal Polish eateries, but the atmosphere is lively. ⊠ *Ul. Długa 18,* ☎ *058/301–10–69. AE, DC, MC, V.*

$$$ ✕ **Pod Łososiem.** The name of this restaurant refers to salmon, which, if available on the day you visit, is highly recommended. Other fish and wild fowl such as duck and pheasant are good choices, too. The

decor is overdone, but the service is pleasant. The famous Gdańsk liqueur "Goldwasser" used to be made in the basement. ⊠ *Ul. Szeroka 54,* ☎ *058/301–76–52. AE, DC, MC, V.*

$$ ✕ **Tawerna.** For traditional Polish and Germanic dishes such as pork
★ cutlets and seafood, try this well-established restaurant overlooking the river. Yes, it's touristy, but the food is delicious. ⊠ *Ul. Powroźnicza 19–20, off Długi Targ,* ☎ *058/301–92–48. AE, DC, MC, V.*

$$$$ ✕▥ **Villa Hestia.** Built in 1894, the Sopot villa that houses this elegant
★ restaurant is an architectural and artistic treasure. Still, the atmosphere is comfortable and the service is superb. The French-accented menu, based on Polish specialties, changes with every season. The villa is also a guest house for a very luxurious night's sleep. ⊠ *Ul. Władysława IV 3/5, 81–703 Sopot,* ☎ *058/551–21–00,* ℻ *058/551–02–55. 2 rooms, 3 suites. Restaurant. AE, DC, MC, V.*

$$$ ▥ **Hanza.** Opened in 1998, this luxury hotel overlooks the picturesque harbor in Gdańsk. Its ultramodern decor is softened by the use of warm colors and recessed lighting. The increasingly popular restaurant specializes in continental cuisine. ⊠ *Ul. Tokarska 6, 80–888,* ☎ *058/305–34–27,* ℻ *058/305–33–86. 60 rooms. Restaurant. AE, DC, MC, V.*

$$$ ▥ **Hewelius.** This 18-story hotel is within walking distance of the Old Town and is also close to the train and bus stations. The spacious, blandly furnished rooms have most modern conveniences. ⊠ *Ul. Heweliusza 22, 80–861,* ☎ *058/301–56–31,* ℻ *058/301–19–22. 281 rooms. Restaurant. AE, DC, MC, V.*

$$ ▥ **Grand.** With its magnificent location on the Bay of Gdańsk in the charming German-era seaside resort of Sopot, this pre-war hotel is well worth the short commute. The rooms could have been restored more authentically, but the view from the restaurant is great. ⊠ *Ul. Powstańców Warszawy 12/14, 81–718 Sopot,* ☎ *058/551–00–41,* ℻ *058/551–61–24. 112 rooms. Restaurant. AE, DC, MC, V.*

$$ ▥ **Marina.** Built in 1982, this modern high-rise hotel is a short taxi ride from the center of Sopot. Upper floors have splendid ocean views, as the hotel is right on the beach. ⊠ *Ul. Jelitkowska 20, 80–342,* ☎ *058/553–20–79,* ℻ *058/553–04–60. 193 rooms. Restaurant, pool. AE, DC, MC, V.*

Site of the Battle of Grunwald

In 1410, in what was possibly the greatest battle of the Middle Ages, Władysław Jagiełło and his Polish-Lithuanian army annihilated the Grand Master of the Teutonic Order, Ulrich von Jungingen, and thousands of his knights. A small museum on the site explains the course of the battle. ⊠ *17 km (11 mi) west of Olsztynek off Rte. 537.* ☉ *May–Sept., daily 10–6.*

Olsztyn

Olsztyn, which was badly damaged during World War II, is more of a jumping-off point for the Mazurian Lakes region than a place of interest in its own right. The **Rynek** (market place) in the Old Town is worth a short stroll. The town's 14th-century **castle** contains a museum, open Tuesday–Sunday 10–4, dedicated to local culture, and **Copernicus's quarters** on the first floor, where he lived for three years.

$$ ▥ **Orbis Novotel.** This standard 1970s hotel is typical of the kind found in Poland. It is the most comfortable lodging in the area, set in beautiful surroundings on the shores of Lake Ukiel. Water sports and horseback riding facilities are nearby. ⊠ *Ul. Sielska 4A, 10–802,* ☎ *089/527–40–81,* ℻ *089/527–54–03. 97 rooms. Restaurant. AE, DC, MC, V.*

Olsztynek

This otherwise drab town contains the **Muzeum Budownictwa Ludowego** (Museum of Folk Buildings, or Skansen), a collection of historic timber buildings, including a thatched-roof church. The region's Lithuanian influence is evident, particularly in the museum's colorful mill. ⊠ *Ul. Sportowa 21,* ☎ *089/519–21–64.* ☉ *Mid-Apr.–Aug., daily 9–3; Sept., Tues.–Sun. 9–3.*

★ **Malbork**

This huge, redbrick, turreted castle was one of the most powerful strongholds in medieval Europe. From 1308 to 1457 it was the residence of the Grand Masters of the Teutonic Order. The Teutonic Knights were a thorn in Poland's side until their defeat at the Battle of Grunwald (☞ *above*) in 1410. Inside Malbork Castle is a museum with beautiful examples of amber—including lumps as large as melons and pieces containing perfect specimens of prehistoric insects. ⊠ *Rte. 50, 58 km (36 mi) southeast of Gdańsk,* ☎ *055/272–33–64.* ☉ *Museum: Oct.–Apr., Tues.–Sun. 9–3; May–Sept., Tues.–Sun. 9–5; grounds: Oct.–Apr., daily 9–3; May–Sept., daily 9–6.*

Płock

Once you get through Płock's industrial area, you will find a lovely medieval city that was, for a short time, the capital of Poland. The 12th-century **Katedra** (cathedral), where two Polish kings are buried, has a **Muzeum Diecezjalne** (Diocesan Museum) that displays a collection of religious art as well as local folk pieces. In the remains of the dramatic 14th-century **Teutonic castle** is the **Muzeum Mazowieckie** (Mazovian Museum), with one of the best Art Nouveau collections in Poland.

Toruń

Toruń, birthplace of Nicolaus Copernicus, is a medieval city that grew wealthy due to its location on the north–south trading route along the Vistula. In 1998 Torun was placed on the Unesco World Cultural Heritage List. Its **Old Town** district is a remarkably successful blend of Gothic buildings—churches, the town hall, and burghers' residences—and Renaissance and Baroque patrician houses. The town hall tower (1274) is the oldest in Poland. Don't leave without trying some of Toruń's gingerbread and honey cakes.

$$ ✕ **Petite Fleur.** In a cozy, redbrick cellar, this restaurant serves Polish and French specialties with care. The six-room guest house upstairs opened in summer 1998. ⊠ *Ul. Piekary 25,* ☎ *056/663–54–54. No credit cards.*

$$ ✕ **Zajazd Staropolski.** Excellent meat dishes and soups are served in a restored 17th-century interior. The restaurant, which is part of a small hotel, is only one block from Toruń's Old Town Square. ⊠ *Ul. Żeglarska 10/14,* ☎ *056/622–60–60. AE, DC, MC, V.*

$$$ 🏨 **Helios.** This friendly, medium-size Orbis hotel in the city center is walking distance from the Old Town. Request a room with a renovated bathroom—it's worth the higher rate. ⊠ *Ul. Kraszewskiego 1, 87–100,* ☎ *056/655–54–16,* 📠 *056/655–54–29. 108 rooms. Restaurant. AE, DC, MC, V.*

$$ 🏨 **Kosmos.** A functional 1960s hotel, Kosmos had a face-lift in 1998. It is near the Vistula river, in the city center. ⊠ *Ul. Popiełuszko 2, 87–100,* ☎ *056/622–89–00,* 📠 *056/622–13–41. 58 rooms. Restaurant. AE, DC, MC, V.*

Gdańsk and the North Essentials

Getting Around

Gdańsk is a major transportation hub, with an international airport just outside town (and good bus connections to downtown) and major road and rail connections with the rest of the country.

Guided Tours

Orbis and other travel agencies (☞ Travel Agencies *in* Warsaw Essentials, *above*) arrange group and individual package tours of Warsaw, Toruń, Gdańsk, Poznań, and the surrounding areas.

Visitor Information

Gdańsk (Orbis, ✉ Ul. Heweliusza 22, ☎ 058/301–21–32). **Olsztyn** (Orbis, ✉ Ul. Dąbrowszczaków 1, ☎ 089/527–46–74). **Płock** (✉ Hotel Tetropol, Al. Jachowicza 49, ☎ 024/262–94–97). **Toruń** (✉ Ul. Piekary 37/39, ☎ 056/622–37–46; Orbis, ✉ Ul. Mostowa 7, ☎ 056/655–48–63).

24 PORTUGAL

LISBON; THE ESTORIL COAST, SINTRA, AND QUELUZ; THE ALGARVE

Clinging to the western cusp of the continent, insulated from Spain's arid plains and burning sun, Portugal is one of Europe's great surprises. It is a land of fine food and wine, spectacularly sited castles, medieval hilltop villages, and excellent beaches, but Portugal is also a land of myriad and delightful distinctions.

The landscape unfolds in astonishing variety from a mountainous, green interior to a sweeping coastline—and Celtic and Moorish influences are evident in the land, its people, and their tongue. Given its long Atlantic coastline, it isn't surprising that Portugal has been a maritime nation for most of its tumultuous history. From the charting of the Azores archipelago in 1427 to the discovery of Japan in 1542, Portuguese explorers unlocked the major sea routes to southern Africa, India, eastern Asia, and the Americas. This great era of exploration, known as the *descobrimentos*, reached its height during the 15th century under the influence of Prince Henry the Navigator. The glories of the Portuguese empire were relatively short lived, however, and the next several centuries saw dynastic instability, extravagant spending by feckless monarchs, natural disasters, and foreign invasion. The 20th century brought little change, and not until a bloodless coup in 1974 deposed the ruling right-wing dictatorship was democracy established and the process of modernization begun.

Today Portugal is a stable country, its people keen to share in the prosperity offered by developments within the European Union (EU). Given the relatively short time since the revolution, this stability demonstrates the inherent strengths of the Portuguese psyche. Political confidence couldn't have been maintained without improvements in the economy, and there have been great strides forward since 1974—the highway system, in particular, has been completely overhauled as money from Brussels has been used to modernize the country's infrastructure. One effect of this regeneration is that Portugal has become more expensive over the last few years.

Following its 1994 stint as European City of Culture, Portugal's capital city—Lisbon—moved firmly into the international limelight during 1998 when it hosted the World Exposition (Expo '98), the last great world expo of the 20th century. A startling regeneration program has improved the city center, its transportation, and public buildings. Meanwhile, over at the former Expo site—reclaimed dockland a little northeast of the city's center—the attractions in the renamed Parque das Nações (Park of the Nations) include riverside restaurants, exhibitions, concerts, a cable car ride, and the stupendous Lisbon Oceanarium, the expo's erstwhile centerpiece. Portugal's centuries-old capital is an engaging mixture of modernity and mellow age, where graceful old buildings hold their own with modern high-rise development. The city's coastal and wooded environs give it an added dimension.

In the country's south, the sun-swept beaches of the Algarve are one of Europe's most popular vacation areas. Off the beaten track, you'll be rewarded with glimpses of a traditional life and culture shaped by memories of empire and tempered by the experience of revolution.

PORTUGAL A TO Z

Customs
See Customs & Duties *in* Chapter 1.

Dining
Seafood is a staple; *sardinhas assadas* (fresh-grilled sardines) are a local favorite. *Bacalhau* (dried salt cod) appears on all menus in a number of mouthwatering guises. Freshly caught lobster, crab, shrimp, tuna, sole, and squid are widely available. *Caldeirada* is a piquant seafood stew; in an *arroz de marisco,* seafood stew is mixed with rice. In the Algarve *cataplana* is a must—a delectable mixture of clams, ham, tomatoes, onions, garlic, and herbs, named for the covered copper pan in which it's cooked. Meat lovers wax rhapsodic over char-grilled *frango* (chicken)—usually served with very hot *piri-piri* (chili) sauce—northern-style *leitão da bairrada* (roast suckling pig); *coelho á caçadora* (rabbit with potatoes, onions, garlic, and a splash of wine); and the tasty *linguiça* (spiced sausages) and *presunto* (cured) ham. *Porco alentejana* (pork with clams) is a tasty southern specialty that's found all over the country; *cozido á Portuguesa* (Portuguese stew—a boiled selection of meat, offal, and root vegetables) is similarly ubiquitous, though more of an acquired taste. Desserts include *doces de ovos* (egg-and-sugar confections), *pudim flan* (egg custard), egg and almond tarts, and fruit. Water is safe, but you may prefer bottled water—*sem gas* for still, *com gas* for fizzy.

Unless noted, reservations are not necessary. Less expensive meals in Portugal are served in a *churrascaria* (grill house), a *tasca* (tavern), or a *cervejaria* (beer hall–restaurant). A seafood specialist is a *marisqueira.* In *adegas típicas* (wine cellars), you dine on Portuguese specialties, drink wine, and listen to traditional *fado* music. At all restaurants be wary of eating anything brought as an appetizer that you didn't order. You'll be charged extra, even if you eat just one olive.

MEALTIMES
Most hotels serve breakfast until 10. Lunch usually begins around 1 PM; dinner is served at about 8 PM.

RATINGS
Prices are per person, without alcohol. Taxes and service are usually included, but a tip of 5%–10% is always appreciated.

Portugal

0 — 50 miles
0 — 50 km

ATLANTIC OCEAN

Valença
Viana do Castelo
Minho
Lima
Barcelos
Póvoa de Varzim
Vila do Conde
Oporto
Espinho
Serra do Gerês N103
Braga
Guimarães
Amarante
Penafiel
A3/IP1
Douro
Tâmega
Chaves
Bragança
Mirandela
Vila Real
A4/IP4
Douro
N102/IP2
Sabor
Mogadouro
Duoro
Lamego
Moimenta da Beira
Oliveira dos Azeméis
S. Pedro do Sul
Vouga
Albergaria-a-Velha
Aveiro
Viseu
IP5
Pinhel
Mealhada
Mira
Cantanhede
Figueira da Foz
Sta. Comba Dão
Coimbra
Arganil
Mondego
Serra da Estrela
Guarda
Covilhã
Fundão
Penamacor
Zêzere
A1/IP1/E1
N109
N10
Pombal
Serra da Gardunha
N233
Leiria
Nazaré
Batalha
Ourém
Tomar
Fátima
IP6
Proença-a-Nova
IP2
Castelo Branco
Alcobaça
Caldas da Rainha
Óbidos
Sra. do Aire
Abrantes
Tagus N118
Nisa
Aveiras de Cima
Torres Vedras
Mafra
Torres Novas
Santarém
Tejo
Ponte de Sor
Portalegre
Sintra
N8
Vila Franca de Xira
Sorraia
Avis
Lisbon
N10
Cascais
Estoril
Montemor-o-Novo
Arraiolos
A6/IP1
Estremoz
Elvas
Sra. de Ossa
Vila Viçosa
Guadiana
SPAIN
Seixal
Setúbal
A2/E1
Sado
A2
Alcácer do Sal
Évora
Reguengos
IP2
Cabo Espichel
← TO THE AZORES
N2
IP1/E1
Ferreira do Alentejo
Moura
Sines
Cabo de Sines
Santiago do Cacem
Beja
Serpa
Vilaverde de Ficalho
← TO MADEIRA ISLAND
Odemira
Ourique
N122
Castro Verde
Chança
Mira
Mértola
Almodôvar
Guadiana
N120
Monchique
ALGARVE
Portimão
EN125
IP1
S. Brás de Alportel
Vila do Bispo
Cabo de S. Vicente
Sagres
Lagos
Albufeira
Tavira
Vila Real de S. António
Faro
Olhão

CATEGORY	COST
$$$$	over 6,000$00
$$$	4,500$00–6,000$00
$$	3,000$00–4,500$00
$	under 3,000$00

WHAT TO WEAR

Neatness will suffice for all but the most formal occasions; jacket and tie are advised for city restaurants in the $$$$ category; otherwise, casual dress is acceptable.

Language

For English-speakers, Portuguese is difficult to pronounce and understand (most people speak quickly and elliptically); if, however, you have a fair knowledge of a Latin language, you may be able to read a little Portuguese. Just be aware that, with some cognates, appearances can be deceptive—it's best to double-check terms in a pocket Portuguese-English dictionary. In large cities and major resorts many people speak English and, occasionally, French or Spanish.

Lodging

Portugal has many lodging options and some of the lowest rates in Europe. The government grades hotels with one to five stars; there are also small, family-owned, city-center *pensões* (pensions); rooms in country manor houses; villas, holiday apartments, and campsites; and luxury *pousadas* (tourist hotels) in historic buildings. Rates depend on location and time of year. In the Algarve in winter, particularly January–March, room prices drop by as much as 40%. In high season (summer, Easter, and Christmas) you'll need to book ahead.

Tourist offices can help with reservations and will provide lists of the local hostelries without charge. In Lisbon there are hotel reservations desks at the airport and at the downtown tourist information center. If you arrive at a resort in summer without a reservation, you may be offered an inexpensive *quarto* (room) at a rail or bus station; always see the room before agreeing to take it.

CAMPING

There are more than 150 campsites throughout the country, with a large concentration in the Algarve. Most are owned and run by local municipal governments. The main private operating chain is **Orbitur** (⊠ Rua Diogo do Couto 1–8, 1100 Lisbon, ☎ 01/815–4871); most local tourist offices can direct you to specific sites. For additional information contact **Federação Portuguesa do Campismo** (⊠ Av. Cel. Ed. Galhardo 24, 1170 Lisbon, ☎ 01/812–6900).

COUNTRY AND MANOR HOUSES

Many splendid country homes, manor houses, and historic buildings are accessible through a variety of programs in which private homeowners offer you a room, breakfast, and sometimes dinner (on request). Properties are inspected and approved by the government and then advertised by a variety of private agencies. The Portuguese National Tourist Office in your home country (☞ Visitor Information *in* Chapter 1) can provide more information in advance of your trip; in Portugal tourist offices can advise about the most attractive local possibilities.

HOTELS AND POUSADAS

As well as regular hotels, many towns also have smaller inns called *estalagems* or *albergarias,* which usually provide breakfast only.

The 44 state-subsidized pousadas, in castles or old monasteries or in newer buildings on sites that have a particularly fine view, are luxury properties—though rates in low season can make them a remarkably good value. Contact **Enatur Pousadas de Portugal** (✉ Av. Santa Joana Princesa 10, 1700 Lisbon, ☎ 01/844–2001, FAX 01/844–2085), or the national tourist organization in your home country.

PENSIONS

The mainstay of budget accommodation in Portugal is the *pensão,* or pension, rated up to four stars and sometimes including meals in the price; depending on the rating, size, and location, pensão rooms come with or without private baths or showers; air-conditioning is standard only in the higher-category accommodations. A *residencial* (between a pensão and a hotel) has similar facilities and, again, is found in most towns and larger villages; breakfast is usually included.

RATINGS

Prices quoted are for two people in a double room based on high-season rates, including tax and service.

CATEGORY	COST
$$$$	over 35,000$00
$$$	25,000$00–35,000$00
$$	15,000$00–25,000$00
$	under 15,000$00

Mail

In Lisbon the post office in the Praça dos Restauradores is open daily 8 AM–10 PM, and there's a 24-hour post office at the airport. Main post offices in towns are open weekdays 8:30–6; offices in rural areas close for lunch and at 6 PM on weekdays and aren't open on weekends.

You can have mail sent care of American Express (✉ Top Tours, Av. Duque de Loulé 108, 1000 Lisbon, ☎ 01/315–5885, FAX 01/315–5873). Elsewhere in the country, post offices in major towns offer "held mail" services (you simply have letters sent to you labeled "poste restante" at a particular post office address).

Money Matters

COSTS

The most expensive areas are Lisbon, the Algarve, and the tourist resorts along the Tagus estuary; the least expensive are country towns. A sales, or value-added, tax (called IVA) of either 5% (for basic foodstuffs, medicines, and accommodation), 12% (restaurant bills), or 17% (other goods and services, including car rentals) is included in the price of most items.

CURRENCY

The unit of currency in Portugal is the escudo, which is divided into 100 centavos. Escudos come in bills of 500$00, 1,000$00, 2,000$00, 5,000$00, and 10,000$00. (In Portugal the dollar sign stands between the escudo and the centavo.) Owing to the complications of dealing with millions of escudos, 1,000$00 is always called a *conto,* so 10,000$00 is referred to as 10 contos. Coins come in denominations of 1$00, 2$50, 5$00, 10$00, 20$00, 50$00, 100$00, and 200$00.

At press time (summer 1999), the exchange rate was about 195$97 to the U.S. dollar, 133$25 to the Canadian dollar, and 306$14 to the pound sterling. You can change money in hotels and in larger shops and restaurants, but banks and *cambios* (exchange offices) usually give better rates.

SAMPLE PRICES

Cup of coffee, 100$00–200$00; bottle of beer, 150$00; soft drink, 125$00–175$00; bottle of house wine, 600$00–800$00; 2-km (1-mi) taxi ride, 450$00; city bus ride, 150$00; museum entrance, 250$00–500$00.

Service is included in bills at hotels and most restaurants. In hotels give the porter who carries your luggage 200$00 and leave the maid who cleans your room 200$00 a day. If you dine regularly in the hotel, give your waiter between 500$00 and 1,000$00 at the end of your stay; give the wine waiter somewhat less if you order wine with every meal. Otherwise tip 5%–10% on restaurant bills, except at inexpensive establishments, where you may just leave any coins given in change. Taxi drivers get 10%; cinema and theater ushers who seat you, 50$00; train and airport porters, 100$00 per bag; hairdressers, around 10%.

National Holidays

January 1; April 21 (Good Friday); April 25 (Anniversary of the Revolution); May 1 (Labor Day); June 22 (Corpus Christi); June 10 (National Day); August 15 (Assumption); October 5 (Day of the Republic); November 1 (All Saints' Day); December 1 (Independence Day); December 8 (Immaculate Conception); December 25.

Opening and Closing Times

Banks are open weekdays 8:30–3. There are automatic currency-exchange machines in Lisbon (around the Praçado Comércio and Praça dos Restauradores) and in other cities. **Museums** are usually open 10–12:30 and 2–5. Most close on Sunday afternoon, and all close Monday. Most **palaces** close on Tuesday. **Shops** are open weekdays 9–1 and 3–7, Saturday 9–1. Shopping malls in Lisbon and other cities remain open until 10 PM or midnight and are often open on Sunday.

Shopping

Bargaining is not the practice in city stores or shops, though it is sometimes possible in flea markets and antiques shops. The **Centro de Turismo Artesanato** (⊠ Rua Castilho 61, 1200 Lisbon, ☎ 01/386–0879) will ship goods abroad. By air to the United States, parcels take about three weeks; by sea, two months.

For non-EU residents, the IVA tax paid on individual items that cost more than 11,700$00 can be reclaimed if you buy them in a tax-free associated shop. Ask for a special *Tax-Free Shopping Cheque* at the shop and get it stamped by airport customs, and the money will be refunded at the tax-free desk at Lisbon airport.

Telephoning

Portugal has been updating its phone system since 1987, causing phone numbers to change throughout the country. The changes made up to press time (spring 1999) have been incorporated in this chapter, but a small percentage of the country's phone numbers are still slated to change. If you dial an old number, in most cases you will reach a recording stating the new number; however, unless you're dialing a large tourism-oriented establishment or major international corporation, the message will be given only in Portuguese.

The country code for Portugal is 351. When dialing a number in Portugal from outside the country, drop the initial 0 in the regional code.

You can make international and collect calls from most public phones as well as from main post offices, which almost always have a supply of phone cabins (you're assigned a booth, and you pay at the end of the call). In larger towns you may be able to charge calls that cost more than 500$00 to your MasterCard or Visa. Some phone booths accept international calls. For the operator, dial 099 (Europe, Algeria, Morocco, and Tunisia) or 098 (rest of the world). Access numbers to reach American long-distance operators are: for **AT&T,** 050–171288; for **MCI,** 050–171234; for **Sprint,** 050–171877.

LOCAL CALLS

Older-style pay phones take 10$00, 20$00, and 50$00 coins; the newer models (with instructions in English) take 100$00 and 200$00 coins as well; 10$00 is the minimum payment for short local calls. POR-TUGAL TELECOM card phones will accept plastic phone cards of 50 or 120 units; you can buy these cards at post and phone offices and most tobacconists and newsagents.

Transportation

BY BUS

Several private operators provide regular service from Lisbon's main **bus terminal** (⊠ Av. Casal Ribeiro 18, ☎ 01/354–5439) to destinations throughout Portugal. One major company, **Renex** (⊠ Rua dos Arameiros 15, ☎ 01/888–2829), operates from a different address and offers services to northern towns and the Algarve. At either terminal it's wise to buy tickets a day in advance. It's three hours to Oporto and five hours to the Algarve. For information on particular routes, contact the main tourist office in Lisbon; for tickets visit the terminals themselves or any travel agency (☞ Lisbon Essentials, *below*).

BY CAR

Breakdowns. All large garages in and around towns have breakdown services, and you'll see orange emergency (SOS) phones along turnpikes and highways. The national automobile organization, **Automóvel Clube de Portugal** (⊠ Rua Rosa Araújo 24/26, 1200 Lisbon, ☎ 01/318–0100) provides reciprocal membership with AAA and other European automobile associations.

Gasoline. Gas prices are among the highest in Europe: around 168$00 per liter for regular, 162$00 for unleaded 95 octane, and 169$00 for unleaded 98 octane. Many gas stations are self-service, and credit cards are widely accepted.

Parking. Parking lots and underground garages abound in major cities, but those in Lisbon and Oporto are no longer cheap. It's often difficult to find a parking space near city-center hotels, though increasingly common parking meters are improving the situation.

Road Conditions. The turnpikes and main highways that link Lisbon with Cascais, the Algarve, Oporto, and other main cities are in good shape. Minor roads are often poor and winding with unpredictable surfaces. The local driving may be faster and less forgiving than you're used to, and other visitors in rental cars on unfamiliar Algarve roads can cause problems: Drive carefully.

EN 125, the principal east–west Algarve highway, has been widened and resurfaced, and construction of the new IP1 Algarve highway—named the Via Infante D. Henrique, after Prince Henry the Navigator—from the Spanish border to Albufeira, has eliminated many of the formerly horrendous bottlenecks. In the north the IP5 shortens the drive from Aveiro to the border with Spain, near Guarda, but should be driven on with great care. A major revamp is scheduled to eliminate dangerous hills and curves. IP4 connects Oporto through Vila Real to once-remote Bragança.

The A2–A6 turnpike system south from Lisbon currently reaches Estremoz on its way to the Spanish frontier at Badajoz and Alcacer do

Sal en route to the Algarve. There's good, fast access to Setúbal and to Évora and other Alentejo towns, though rush hour traffic on the 25 de Abril bridge across the Tagus can be frustrating. An alternative is to take the 17-km- (11-mi-) long Vasco da Gama bridge (opened 1998) across the Tagus estuary to Montijo and then link up with south-bound and eastbound roads.

Rules of the Road. Driving is on the right. At the junction of two roads of equal size, traffic coming from the right has priority. Vehicles already in a traffic circle have priority over those entering it from any point. The use of seat belts is obligatory. Horns should not be used in built-up areas, and a reflective red warning triangle sign, for use in a break-down, must be carried. The speed limit on turnpikes is 120 kph (74 mph); on other roads it is 90 kph (56 mph), and in built-up areas, 50 kph–60 kph (30 mph–36 mph).

BY PLANE

The internal air services of **TAP Air Portugal** (✉ Praça Marquês de Pom-bal 3, 1200 Lisbon, ☎ 01/386–4080) are good. Other internal services are provided by **Portugália** (☎ 01/843–7000) and **SATA-Air Açores** (☎ 096/22311)—which flies to the Azores—both of whose schedules change according to season.

BY TRAIN

For such a small country Portugal has a very extensive rail system. Trains are clean and leave on time, but there are few express runs except the one between Lisbon and Oporto, which takes just over three hours for the 338-km (210-mi) journey, and the one between Lisbon and the Al-garve (four hours to Faro, five hours to Lagos). You should buy tick-ets and reserve seats (at stations or through travel agents) two or three days in advance. Advance reservations are essential on Lisbon–Oporto express trains; on the Algarve rail line you can simply buy tickets on the day of travel.

International Services. Trains to Madrid, Paris, and other parts of Eu-rope depart from the Santa Apolonia Station in Lisbon, Campanhã in Oporto, and Coimbra (Paris only).

Train Passes. Special **tourist passes** are available through travel agents or at main train stations, valid for periods of 7, 14, or 21 days for first- and second-class travel on any domestic train service; mileage is un-limited. At press time (spring 1999), the cost was 18,000$00 for 7 days, 30,000$00 for 14 days, and 42,000$00 for 21 days.

Visitor Information
Green Line (tourist help line, within Portugal, ☎ 800/296–296).

Weather
The tourist season runs from spring through autumn, but some parts of the country—especially the Algarve, which has 3,000 hours of sun-shine annually—are balmy even in winter. Hotel prices are greatly re-duced between November and February, except in Lisbon, where business visitors keep rates uniformly high throughout the year.

CLIMATE

Portugal's climate is temperate year-round. Even in August, the hottest month, the Algarve and the Alentejo are the only regions where the midday heat may be uncomfortable, but in these regions you can go to the beaches to swim and soak up the sun. What rain there is falls from November through June; December and January can be chilly at times, even on the Algarve, and very wet to the north, but there's no snow except in the mountains of the Serra da Estrela in the northeast.

The almond blossoms and vivid wildflowers that cover the countryside start to bloom early in February.

The following are the average daily maximum and minimum temperatures for Lisbon.

LISBON

Jan.	57F	14C	May	71F	21C	Sept.	79F	26C
	46	8		55	13		62	17
Feb.	59F	15C	June	77F	25C	Oct.	72F	22C
	47	8		60	15		58	14
Mar.	63F	17C	July	81F	27C	Nov.	63F	17C
	50	10		63	17		52	11
Apr.	67F	20C	Aug.	82F	28C	Dec.	58F	15C
	53	12		63	17		47	9

LISBON

Spread out over a string of hills to the north of the Tagus River estuary, Portugal's capital presents unending treats for the eye. Its wide boulevards are bordered by black-and-white mosaic sidewalks made of tiny cobblestones called *calçada*. Modern, pastel-color apartment blocks vie for attention with Art Nouveau structures covered with decorative tiles. Winding, hilly streets provide scores of *miradouros,* vantage points that offer spectacular views of the river and the city.

With a population of around a million, Lisbon is a small capital by European standards. Its center stretches north from the spacious Praça do Comércio, one of the largest riverside squares in Europe, to the Rossío, a smaller square lined with shops and sidewalk cafés. This district, known as the Baixa (Lower Town), is one of the earliest examples of town planning on a large scale. The grid of parallel streets between the two squares was built after an earthquake and tidal wave destroyed much of the city in 1755. The Alfama, the old Moorish quarter that survived the earthquake, lies just east of the Baixa, and the Bairro Alto—an 18th-century quarter of restaurants, bars, and clubs—just to the west; Belém, a district containing many royal palaces and museums, lies another 5 km (3 mi) to the west. A similar distance northeast of the center, the riverside Expo site has the Lisbon Oceanarium—Europe's largest aquarium—as its major attraction.

Lisbon is not easy to explore on foot. The steep inclines of many streets present a tough challenge to the casual visitor, and places that appear to be close to one another on a map are sometimes on different levels. Yet the effort is worthwhile—judicious use of trams, the funicular railway, and the majestic city-center *elevador* (vertical lift) make walking tours enjoyable even on the hottest summer day.

Castelo de São Jorge and the Alfama

Numbers in the margin correspond to points of interest on the Lisbon map.

The Moors, who imposed their rule on most of the southern Iberian Peninsula during the 8th century, left their mark on Lisbon. Their most visible traces are the imposing castle, set on one of the city's highest hills, and the Alfama, a district of narrow streets that wind up toward it. This jumble of steep, stepped alleys and whitewashed houses with flower-laden balconies and red-tile roofs is notoriously easy to get lost in, though it's relatively compact. Its down-to-earth charm is most apparent in June, during the festivals of the *Santos Populares* (Popular

Saints), when the entire quarter turns out to eat, drink, and be merry. The best way to tour the area is to take Tram 28, Bus 37, or a taxi up to the castle and then walk down.

★ ❶ **Castelo de São Jorge** (St. George's Castle). Although the castle is Moorish in construction, it stands on the site of a fort used by the Visigoths as early as the 5th century. The main walls enclose the ruins of a Muslim palace that served as the residence of Portuguese kings until the 16th century; the outer walls encompass the (restored) medieval church of Santa Cruz, a few simple houses, and souvenir shops. Inside the main gate are well-tended grounds and terraces with panoramic city views. There are entrances to the castle from Largo do Chão da Feira or Largo do Menino de Deus. ⊠ *Rua da Costa do Castelo,* ☎ *no phone.* ⊡ *Free.* ⊙ *Apr.–Sept., daily 9–9; Oct.–Mar., daily 9–7.*

❷ **Miradouro de Santa Luzia.** Hop off Tram 28 at the miradouro for one of the most sweeping views of the Alfama and the Tagus River. The little terrace garden by the Santa Luzia Church catches the sun all day. ⊠ *Largo da Santa Luzia.*

❸ **Museu da Marioneta** (Puppet Museum). The intricate workmanship that went into the creation of the puppets on display here is remarkable. ⊠ *Largo Rodrigues de Freitas 19,* ☎ *01/886–5794.* ⊙ *Tues.–Sun. 10–12:30 and 2–6.*

❹ **Museu de Artes Decorativas** (Museum of Decorative Arts). Housed in a splendid 18th-century mansion with period furnishings, the museum puts on temporary exhibitions of its art and furniture. It also conducts workshops that teach threatened handicrafts—bookbinding, carving, and cabinetmaking. ⊠ *Largo das Portas do Sol 2,* ☎ *01/886–2183.* ⊙ *Tues.–Sun. 10–5.*

❺ **Museu Nacional do Azulejo** (National Tile Museum). This museum, installed in the cloisters of the 16th-century Madre de Deus convent complex, holds a major and extremely lovely collection of 15th- to 20th-century tiles. They trace the development of the art in Portugal from its introduction into Iberia by the Moors. The convent church has a sumptuously decorated 18th-century interior with a splendid rococo altarpiece. ⊠ *Rua da Madre de Deus 4,* ☎ *01/814–7747.* ⊙ *Tues., Thurs.–Sun. 10–6; Wed. 2–6.*

★ ❻ **Sé** (Cathedral). Founded in 1150 to commemorate the defeat of the Moors three years earlier, the Sé has an austere Romanesque interior and a beautiful 13th-century cloister. The treasure-filled sacristy contains the relics of the martyr St. Vincent. ⊠ *Largo da Sé,* ☎ *01/886–6752.* ⊡ *Free.* ⊙ *Cathedral: daily 9–noon and 2–6. Sacristy: daily 10–1 and 2–6.*

The Baixa and the Modern City

The Baixa, Lisbon's main shopping and banking district, opens on its northwestern end into the Praça dos Restauradores, the beginning of modern Lisbon, with Avenida da Liberdade running northwest to the green expanses of the Parque Eduardo VII.

❾ **Avenida da Liberdade.** A stroll along the city's main avenue, from the Praça dos Restauradores to the Parque Eduardo VII, takes about 30 minutes, though you may want to stop at an open-air café in the esplanade that runs down the center of the tree-lined avenue. ⊠ *Between Praça dos Restauradores and Parque Eduardo VII.*

❼ **Baixa** (Lower Town). The Baixa's various streets once housed trades and crafts now reflected in the street names: Rua dos Sapateiros (Cob-

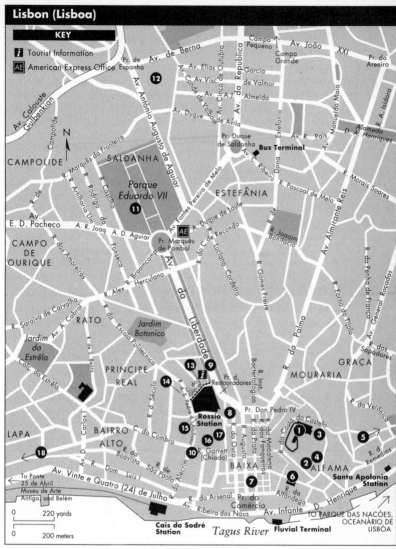

Lisbon (Lisboa)

KEY

i Tourist Information
AE American Express Office

Avenida da
Liberdade, **9**

Baixa, **7**

Castelo de São
Jorge, **1**

Chiado, **10**

Elevador da
Glória, **13**

Elevador de Santa
Justa, **17**

Fundação Calouste
Gulbenkian, **12**

Igreja de São
Roque, **15**

Igreja do Carmo, **16**

Instituto do Vinho do
Porto, **14**

Miradouro de Santa
Luzia, **2**

Museu da
Marioneta, **3**

Museu de Artes
Decorativas, **4**

Museu Nacional de
Arte Antiga, **18**

Museu Nacional do
Azulejo, **5**

Parque
Eduardo VII, **11**

Rossío, **8**

Sé, **6**

blers' Street), Rua da Prata (Silversmiths' Street), and Rua do Ouro (Gold-smiths' Street). Scattered throughout are shoe shops, glittering jewelry stores, and a host of cafés and delicatessens that sell wines, cheeses, and pastries. ⊠ *Between the river and Rossío.*

⑩ Chiado. This chic district is home to some of the city's most fashion-able shops. Rua Garrett, in particular, the Chiado's principal street, is lined with old department stores and a series of comfortable, turn-of-the-century, wood-paneled coffee shops. Most famous is the **Brasileira** (⊠ Rua Garrett 120, ☎ 01/346–9541), closed Sunday, which has a life-size statue of Fernando Pessoa, Portugal's national poet, seated at one of the sidewalk tables. ⊠ *Western side of Baixa.*

★ **⑫ Fundação Calouste Gulbenkian** (Calouste Gulbenkian Foundation). This cultural trust houses a museum of art and artifacts collected by Armenian oil magnate Calouste Gulbenkian (1869–1955). It displays superb Greek and Roman coins, Persian carpets, Chinese porcelain, and paint-ings by such old masters as Rembrandt and Rubens, as well as im-pressionist and pre-Raphaelite works. The complex also includes a good modern art museum and two concert halls that host music and ballet festivals in winter and spring. ⊠ *Av. de Berna 45 (Metro: Palhavã),* ☎ 01/795–0236. ⚑ *Free Sun.* ⊙ *June–Sept., Tues., Thurs., Fri., and Sun. 10–5; Wed. and Sat. 2–7:30; Oct.–May, Tues.–Sun. 10–5.*

⑪ Parque Eduardo VII (Edward VII Park). The city's main park was named in honor of King Edward VII of England, who visited Lisbon in 1903. Rare flowers, trees, and shrubs thrive in both the *estufa fria* (cold greenhouse) and the *estufa quente* (hot greenhouse). ⊠ *Parque Eduardo VII (Metro: Rotunda),* ☎ 01/388–2278. ⊙ *Apr.–Sept., daily 9–6; Oct.–Mar., daily 9–5.*

⑧ Rossio. Lisbon's main square since the Middle Ages is officially known as Praça Dom Pedro IV (whom the central statue commemorates). Renowned sidewalk cafés line the east and west sides of the square. ⊠ *Praça Dom Pedro IV.*

Bairro Alto and Lapa

Lisbon's Bairro Alto (Upper Town) is largely made up of 18th- and 19th-century buildings that house a mixture of restaurants, theaters, nightclubs, churches, bars, and antiques shops. You can approach and leave the district by funicular railway and by street elevator.

⑬ Elevador da Glória. One of the finest approaches to the Bairro Alto is via the funicular railway on the western side of Avenida da Liberdade, by Praça dos Restauradores. The ascent takes about a minute; you are let out at the São Pedro de Alcântara miradouro, facing the castle and the Alfama. ⊠ *Calçada da Glória,* ☎ 01/363–2044. ⊙ *Daily 7 AM–midnight.*

⑰ Elevador de Santa Justa. The elevator—enclosed in a Gothic-style tower created by Raul Mesnier, a Portuguese protégé of Gustave Eif-fel—connects the Bairro Alto with Rua da Santa Justa in the Baixa. ⊠ *Largo do Carmo,* ☎ 01/363–2044. ⊙ *Daily 7 AM–midnight.*

⑭ Igreja de São Roque. The the plain exterior of the Church of St. Roque belies its rich interior. Its flamboyant 18th-century **Capela de São João Baptista** (Chapel of St. John the Baptist) is adorned with rare stones and mosaics that resemble oil paintings. The **Museu de Arte Sacra** (Mu-seum of Sacred Art) next door displays 16th- to 18th-century paintings. ⊠ *Largo Trinidade Coelho,* ☎ 01/346–0361. ⚑ *Church and museum free.* ⊙ *Church: daily 8:30–5; museum: Tues.–Sun. 10–1 and 2–5.*

⑯ Igreja do Carmo (Carmelite Church). The sacristy and nave of this church, the only sections to survive the 1755 earthquake, house the quirky **Museu Arqueológico** (Archaeological Museum), filled with everything from Roman coins to medieval sarcophagi. ⊠ *Largo do Carmo,* ☎ *01/346–0473.* ☉ *Apr.–Sept., daily 10–6; Oct.–Mar., daily 10–1 and 2–5.*

⑮ Instituto do Vinho do Porto (Port Wine Institute). Inside the cozy, club-like lounge you can sample the different types and vintages of Portugal's most famous beverage from the Institute's formidably well-stocked cellars. The five main types are white (an extra-dry aperitif, not for purists), tawny, ruby, late-bottled vintage, and vintage. ⊠ *Rua S. Pedro de Alcântara 45,* ☎ *01/347–5707.* ☉ *Mon.–Sat. 10–10.*

⑱ Museu Nacional de Arte Antiga (National Museum of Art). In a 17th-century palace in the wealthy district of Lapa, midway between the Baixa and Belém, this museum was founded in 1884 and fully restored in 1994. It has a beautifully displayed collection of Portuguese art, mainly 15th–19th centuries, whose highlight is the St. Vincent Altarpiece (1467–70) by Nuno Gonçalves. Foreign masterpieces include Dürer's St. Jerome, and the fascinating Japanese lacquered "namban" screens depicting the arrival of the Portuguese in Japan in the 16th century. ⊠ *Rua das Janelas Verdes (Bus 27 and Bus 49),* ☎ *01/396–4151.* ☉ *Tues. 2–6, Wed.–Sun. 10–6.*

Belém

Numbers in the margin correspond to points of interest on the Belém map.

To see the best examples of that uniquely Portuguese, late-Gothic architecture known as Manueline, head for Belém, at the southwestern edge of Lisbon. If you're traveling in a group of three or four, taxis are the cheapest way to get here; otherwise take Tram 15 from the Praça do Comércio for a more scenic, if bumpier, journey.

㉑ Monumento dos Descobrimentos (Monument to the Discoveries). Erected in 1960, the tall, white, angular slab at the water's edge—a modern tribute to the seafaring explorers—stands at what was the departure point for many a voyage. Take the elevator to the top for river views. ⊠ *Av. de Brasília,* ☎ *no phone.* ☉ *Tues.–Sun. 9:30–7.*

★ **⑲ Mosteiro dos Jerónimos** (Jerónimos Monastery). This structure was conceived and planned by King Manuel I at the beginning of the 16th century to commemorate the discoveries of Vasco da Gama. Construction, begun in 1502, was financed by treasures brought back from the Portuguese "discoveries" in Africa, Asia, and South America. ⊠ *Praça do Império,* ☎ *01/362–0034.* ☒ *Church free; cloister free Sun.* ☉ *June–Sept., Tues.–Sun. 10–6:30; Oct.–May, Tues.–Sun. 10–1 and 2:30–5.*

⑳ Museu de Marinha (Maritime Museum). The huge collection here reflects Portugal's long seafaring tradition. The exhibits range from early maps, model ships, and navigational instruments to fishing boats and royal barges. ⊠ *Praça do Império (west end Jerónimos Monastery),* ☎ *01/362–0010.* ☒ *Free Sun. 10–1.* ☉ *Tues.–Sun. 10–6.*

㉓ Museu Nacional dos Coches (National Coach Museum). One of the largest collections of coaches in the world is housed in a former riding school. The oldest conveyance on display was made for Philip II of Spain in the late 16th century, but the most stunning exhibits are three golden Baroque coaches made in Rome for King John V in 1716. ⊠ *Praça Afonso de Albuquerque,* ☎ *01/361–0850.* ☒ *Free Sun. 10–1.* ☉ *June–Sept., Tues.–Sun. 10–1 and 2:30–6:30; Oct.–May, Tues.–Sun. 10–1 and 2:30–5:30.*

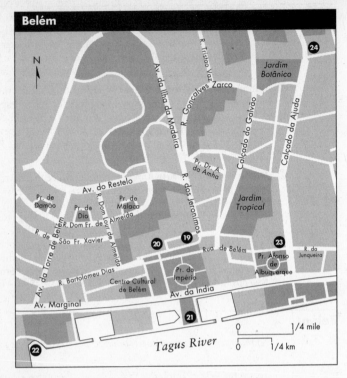

Belém

---

24 Palácio da Ajuda (Ajuda Palace). Once a royal residence, this building now contains a collection of 18th- and 19th-century paintings, furniture, and tapestries. ⊠ *Calçada da Ajuda,* ☎ *01/363–7095.* ☜ *Free Sun. 10–2. Guided tours arranged on request.* ☉ *Thurs.–Tues. 10–5.*

★ **22 Torre de Belém** (Belém Tower). The balconies and domed turrets of the fanciful Torre de Belém make this perhaps the purest Manueline structure in the country. Although it was built during the early 16th century on an island in the middle of the Tagus River, the tower now stands near its north bank—the river has changed course over the centuries. ⊠ *Av. da India,* ☎ *01/301–6892.* ☉ *June–Sept., Tues.–Sun. 10–6:30; Oct.–May, Tues.–Sun. 10–1 and 2:30–5.*

Parque das Nacões

An ambitious urban-renewal project 5 km (3 mi) northeast of the city center is revitalizing a 5-km- (3-mi-) long stretch of riverfront by building on the infrastructures left in place after Expo '98. The leisure-oriented part of the development is called Parque das Nacões, and its attractions include Europe's biggest oceanarium (☞ *below*), restaurants, acres of landscaped parkland, a theater, a 10,000-seat indoor stadium, exhibition halls, a marina, and a scenic cable-car ride. The area is easy to reach on the subway to Oriente, or, if you're driving up from the south or east, on the 16-km (9-mi) Ponte Vasco da Gama (Vasco da Gama Bridge) that now spans the Tagus.

Oceanário de Lisboa. (Lisbon Oceanarium). This stunning glass-and-stone structure, rising from the river and reached by footbridge, is the largest aquarium in Europe. It contains 25,000 fish, seabirds, and mammals and is the first aquarium to incorporate selected world ocean habitats (North Atlantic, Pacific, Antarctic, and Indian Ocean) within one complex. ⊠

Doca dos Olivais, Esplanada Dom Carlos I, ☎ *01/891–7002, 01/891–7006, 01/891–7007, or 01/891–7008.* ⊙ *Daily 10–6.*

Dining and Lodging

Most of Lisbon's restaurants offer an *ementa turistica* (tourist menu), usually at lunchtime. Meals vary in quality but generally include three courses, a drink, and coffee, all for about 3,000$00. Accommodations range from some of the major international chain hotels to charming little family-run establishments. For peak season reserve well in advance. For details and price-category definitions, *see* Dining *and* Lodging *in* Portugal A to Z, *above.*

$$$–$$$$ ✕ **O Terraço.** The quality of the dishes that come off the restaurant's grill matches the quality of the view over the city from the top floor of the Tivoli Lisboa hotel. Choices include huge shrimp with spicy oil, prime rib, lamb cutlets, or the freshest of fish. ✉ *Av. da Liberdade 185,* ☎ *01/319–8900. Reservations essential. AE, DC, MC, V.*

$$$–$$$$ ✕ **Sua Excêlencia.** There's no written menu in this cozy Lapa district
★ restaurant. The English-speaking owner talks you through the outstanding Portuguese dishes available. ✉ *Rua do Conde 34,* ☎ *01/390–3614. MC, V. Closed Wed. and Sept. No lunch weekends.*

$$$–$$$$ ✕ **Tagide.** Delicious Portuguese food and wine are served in this fine old tiled house that looks out over the Baixa and the river. Try to secure a window table. ✉ *Largo Academia das Belas Artes 18–20, at bottom of Rua Ivens,* ☎ *01/342–0720. Reservations essential. AE, DC, MC, V. Closed weekends.*

$$$–$$$$ ✕ **Tavares Rico.** A seasonal, French-inspired menu, an excellent wine
★ list, and handsome Edwardian furnishings have made this dining room (established as a café in the 18th century) one of Lisbon's most famous restaurants. ✉ *Rua Misericórdia 37,* ☎ *01/342–1112. Reservations essential. AE, DC, MC, V. Closed Sat. No lunch Sun.*

$$–$$$$ ✕ **Gambrinus.** Noted for its fish and shellfish, it is among Lisbon's older restaurants. To enter, you pass through an inconspicuous door off a busy street and into one of its small, wood-paneled dining rooms. ✉ *Rua das Portas de S. Antão 23–25,* ☎ *01/346–8974 or 01/342–1466. AE, DC, MC, V.*

$$–$$$$ ✕ **Pap' Açorda.** Art and media types scramble for the closely packed
★ tables in this former bakery at the heart of the Bairro Alto. It serves cutting-edge versions of Portuguese classics—grilled sea bass, breaded veal cutlets, and *açorda,* a bread-based seafood dish. ✉ *Rua da Atalaia 57,* ☎ *10/346–4811. Reservations essential. AE, DC, MC, V.*

$$–$$$$ ✕ **Solmar.** This large restaurant near Restauradores is best known for its seafood, but try the wild boar or venison in season. ✉ *Rua das Portas de S. Antão 108,* ☎ *01/342–3371. AE, DC, MC, V.*

$–$$$ ✕ **Bota Alta.** This tiny, wood-paneled tavern is one of the Bairro Alto's
★ oldest eating places; lines form outside the door by 8 PM. The menu is strong on traditional Portuguese dishes—bacalhau cooked in cream, homemade sausages, steaks in wine sauce, or grilled fish. ✉ *Travessa da Queimada 37,* ☎ *01/342–7959. MC, V. Closed Sun. No lunch Sat.*

$–$$$ ✕ **O Madeirense.** In a rustic-style room, the traditional Madeiran *espedata* (skewer of fillet steak) is hung from a stand above the table so that you can serve yourself. ✉ *Loja 3027, Amoreiras Shopping Center, Av. Eng. Duarte Pacheco,* ☎ *01/381–3147. AE, DC, MC, V.*

$$ ✕ **Comida de Santo.** Lively Brazilian music and excellent Brazilian food served in an attractive, brightly painted dining room ensure a steady repeat clientele. ✉ *Calçada Eng. Miguel Pais 39,* ☎ *01/396–3339. Reservations essential. AE, DC, MC, V.*

$–$$ ✕ **Bonjardim.** Known as "Rei dos Frangos" (King of Chickens), it specializes in the spit-roasted variety. Just off the Restauradores, it's very crowded at peak hours. ⊠ *Travessa S. Antão 11,* ☎ *01/342–4389. AE, DC, MC, V.*

$–$$ ✕ **Cantinho da Paz.** This joyful mom-and-pop establishment on the edge of the Bairro Alto specializes in the cuisine of Goa. The shrimp curry is rich in coconut and cream; the *balichão* shrimp is tangier and hotter. ⊠ *Rua da Paz 4, off Rua dos Poiais de São Bento,* ☎ *01/396–9698. Reservations essential Sun. V. Closed Mon.*

$–$$ ✕ **Cervejaria Trindade.** Expect hearty Portuguese cuisine served in a
★ 19th-century Lisbon beer hall adorned with colorful tiles. It special-izes in seafood and has a garden for summer dining. ⊠ *Rua Nova da Trindade 20,* ☎ *01/342–3506. AE, DC, MC, V.*

$–$$ ✕ **Sinal Vermelho.** This Bairro Alto restaurant updates the traditional Lisbon adega. Start with a plate of clams drenched in oil and garlic and follow with the fresh fish, which is rarely disappointing. ⊠ *Rua das Gáveas 89,* ☎ *01/346–1252. Weekend reservations essential. AE, MC, V. Closed Sun.*

$–$$ ✕ **Vá e Volta.** This is a splendid place for one-plate Bairro Alto fare—fried or grilled meat or fish dishes served with gusto and good humor. ⊠ *Rua do Diario de Notícias 100,* ☎ *01/342–7888. AE, MC, V. Closed Mon.*

$ ✕ **As Barrigas.** Here the house specialty is a rich *arroz de polvo* (rice with octopus). There are also steaks, fish of the day, and other Bairro Alto tavern standards. And the name? It means "the stomachs," which you'll appreciate once you've feasted on the large portions. ⊠ *Travessa da Queimada 31,* ☎ *01/347–1220. V.*

$$$$ ⊞ **Lisboa Sheraton and Towers.** A typical Sheraton hotel, it has a huge reception area and medium-size rooms. The deluxe units in the Tow-ers section, which has a separate reception desk and a private lounge, are about the same size but are more luxuriously appointed and have better views. ⊠ *Rua Latino Coelho 1, 1000,* ☎ *01/357–5757,* FAX *01/354–7164. 381 rooms. 2 restaurants, pool. AE, DC, MC, V.*

$$$$ ⊞ **Ritz Four Seasons.** One of the finest hotels in Europe, the Ritz is
★ renowned for its excellent service. The large, handsomely decorated guest rooms all have terraces, and the public rooms are elegantly ap-pointed with tapestries, antique reproductions, and fine paintings. ⊠ *Rua Rodrigo da Fonseca 88, 1070,* ☎ *01/383–2020,* FAX *01/383–1783. 304 rooms. Restaurant. AE, DC, MC, V.*

$$$–$$$$ ⊞ **Park Atlantic.** The rooms in this distinctive luxury hotel are on the small side, but they're soundproof and attractively decorated; those on the front overlook the Parque Eduardo VII. ⊠ *Rua Castilho 149, 1070,* ☎ *01/383–0400,* FAX *01/383–3231. 330 rooms. Restaurant. AE, DC, MC, V.*

$$$–$$$$ ⊞ **Tivoli Lisboa.** Facing Lisbon's main avenue, this comfortable, well-
★ run establishment has a large public area furnished with inviting arm-chairs and sofas. The guest rooms are all pleasant, but those in the rear are quieter. ⊠ *Av. da Liberdade 185, 1250,* ☎ *01/319–8900,* FAX *01/319–8950. 327 rooms. Restaurant, pool. AE, DC, MC, V.*

$$$ ⊞ **As Janelas Verdes.** This late-18th-century mansion has marvelously
★ restored, individually furnished rooms. You can eat breakfast in an ivy-covered patio garden. Reservations are vital at this hotel; it's as pop-ular as it is small. ⊠ *Rua das Janelas Verdes 47, 1200,* ☎ *01/396–8143,* FAX *01/396–8144. 17 rooms. Dining room. AE, DC, MC, V.*

$$$ ⊞ **Fenix.** At the top of Avenida da Liberdade, this elegant hotel has large guest rooms—many with fine views over the restored square in front—and a pleasant basement Spanish restaurant. ⊠ *Praça Marquês de Pombal 8, 1250,* ☎ *01/386–2121,* FAX *01/386–0131. 119 rooms. Restaurant. AE, DC, MC, V.*

$$$ ⊞ **Lisboa Plaza.** At this comfortable family-owned hotel behind Avenida da Liberdade, the staff is friendly and helpful. Pastel colors, prints on the walls, dried flower arrangements, and smart, well-stocked bathrooms all add to the charm. The room rate covers an excellent buffet breakfast. ☒ *Travessa do Salitre 7, 1250,* ☎ *01/346–3922,* FAX *01/347– 1630. 106 rooms. Restaurant. AE, DC, MC, V.*

$$$ ☷ **York House.** This atmospheric residential hotel, built as a convent
★ in the 17th century, is in a shady garden at the top of a long flight of steps. It has a good restaurant, and full or half board is available. Book well in advance: The place is small and has a loyal following. ☒ *Rua das Janelas Verdes 32, 1200,* ☎ *01/396–2435,* FAX *01/397–2793. 34 rooms. Restaurant. AE, DC, MC, V.*

$$ ☷ **Albergaria Senhora do Monte.** Four of the rooms in this unpreten-
★ tious little hotel in the oldest part of town have terraces that offer some of the loveliest views of Lisbon—though these rooms fall into a higher price category. Other rooms are less exalted, but the top-floor grill has a wide window. ☒ *Calçada do Monte 39, 1100,* ☎ *01/886–6002,* FAX *01/887–7783. 28 rooms. Restaurant. AE, DC, MC, V.*

$$ ☷ **Flamingo.** A good-value choice near the top of the Avenida da Liberdade, this hotel has simply furnished, slightly old-fashioned rooms; those in the front are noisy. ☒ *Rua Castilho 41, 1250,* ☎ *01/ 386–2191,* FAX *01/386–1216. 39 rooms. Restaurant. AE, DC, MC, V.*

$$ ☷ **Principe Real.** There's a real old-fashioned warmth and charm—from the rattling elevator to the lovely antique furniture in the rooms—at this small hotel close to the botanical gardens. And each day starts with the glorious views accompanying the complimentary buffet breakfast in the top-floor restaurant. ☒ *Rua da Alegria 53, 1250,* ☎ *01/346– 0116,* FAX *01/342–2104. 23 rooms. Restaurant. AE, DC, MC, V.*

$ ☷ **Aljubarrota.** An effusive welcome awaits you in this fourth-floor pensão (no elevator) in the Baixa. The small rooms have linoleum floors, but they're carefully maintained, and antique tiles on the walls and old bedsteads add character. Tiny little balconies in some offer neck-craning views over the rooftops to the castle. ☒ *Rua da Assunção 53, 1100,* ☎ *01/346–0112. 15 rooms. No credit cards.*

$ ☷ **Casa de São Mamede.** One of the first private houses to be built in Lisbon after the 18th-century earthquake, São Mamede has been handsomely restored and transformed into a relaxed guest house. Only breakfast is served, but you're just a 10-minute walk from the Bairro Alto. ☒ *Rua da Escola Politécnica 159, 1250,* ☎ *01/396–3166,* FAX *01/ 395–1896. 28 rooms. MC, V.*

$ ☷ **Hotel Borges.** This dependable, old-fashioned Chiado district hotel has good service, a breakfast room, and a charm that transcends its limited facilities. ☒ *Rua Garrett 108–110, 1200,* ☎ *01/346–1951,* FAX *01/342–6617. 99 rooms. Breakfast room. MC, V.*

$ ⛺ **Lisboa Camping.** In the pine woods of a park on the western outskirts of the city, this large campground reopened in 1998 after a thorough face-lift. Amenities include two tennis courts, a children's play park, minigolf, a roller skating rink, a recreation room with TV, and a supermarket. ☒ *Parque Florestal de Monsanto, 1500,* ☎ *01/760– 2061. 171 serviced trailer sites, 400 tent sites, 70 serviced cabins. Restaurant, pool. AE, MC, V.*

Nightlife and the Arts

Lisbon has an extensive arts-and-nightlife scene. You'll find listings of music, theater, film, and other entertainment in the monthly *Agenda Cultural* booklet, available from the tourist office. The Friday editions of the *Diario de Notícias* and *O Independente* newspapers also contain listings magazines.

The Arts

Classical music, opera, and ballet are presented in the beautiful **Teatro Nacional de Opera de São Carlos** (⊠ Rua Serpa Pinto 9, ☎ 01/346–5914). Classical music and ballet are also staged from autumn through summer by the **Fundação Calouste Gulbenkian** (⊠ Av. Berna 45, ☎ 01/793–5131). Of particular interest is the annual Early Music and Baroque Festival presented in churches and museums around Lisbon every spring. The **Centro Cultural de Belém** (⊠ Praça do Império, ☎ 01/361–2400) hosts a full range of concerts and exhibitions. Free recitals take place regularly at the Igreja do Carmo and Igreja de São Roque in the Bairro Alto, and at the Sé. Plays are performed in Portuguese at the **Teatro Nacional de D. Maria II** (⊠ Praça Dom Pedro IV, ☎ 01/347–2246) from August through June.

All films shown in Lisbon appear in their original language with Portuguese subtitles. There are movie houses on Avenida da Liberdade, as well as at the **Amoreiras shopping center** (⊠ Av. Eng. Duarte Pacheco, ☎ 01/383–1275) and at the **Colombo shopping center** (⊠ Av. Col. Militar, Benfica, ☎ 01/711–3200).

Nightlife

DANCE CLUBS AND BARS

The main districts for bars and discos are the Bairro Alto, the Avenida 24 de Julho, running west from Cais do Sodré Station, and the waterfront between the same station and the Ponte 25 de Abril, where converted warehouses and other former dock facilities in the Alcântara, Santo Amaro, and Rocha Conde de Obidos docks have become fashionable late-opening bars and discos. In the Bairro Alto, the best place to start a night out is the refined **Instituto do Vinho do Porto** (⊠ Rua de São Pedro de Alcântara 45, ☎ 01/347–5707), where you choose from a menu of port wines. **Pavilhão Chines** (⊠ Rua Dom Pedro V 89, ☎ 01/342–4729) is decorated with bric-a-brac from around the world. Typical of the more youthful Bairro Alto joints is the boisterous **Três Pastorinhos** (⊠ Rua da Barroca 111–113, ☎ 01/341–4301). In the dockside development near Cais do Sodré, restaurant-bars like **Rock City** (⊠ Rua Cintura do Porto de Lisboa, Armazém 225, ☎ 01/342–8636) are the rage; this one has a garden and is open until 4 AM for steaks, drinks, and live music. The **Kapital** (⊠ Av. 24 de Julho 68, ☎ 01/395–5963) attracts trendy Lisboetas. **Memorial** (⊠ Rua Gustavo Sequeira 42, ☎ 01/396–8891) is popular with gay and lesbian visitors. **Trumps** (⊠ Rua Imprensa Nacional 104b, ☎ 01/397–1059) is the city's biggest gay dance club.

MUSIC CLUBS

Most of the adegas típicas or wine cellars, where you can not only drink wine but also dine on Portuguese specialties and listen to haunting fado melodies, are scattered throughout the Alfama and Bairro Alto districts. The singing starts at 10 PM, and reservations are advised. The **Adega do Machado** (⊠ Rua do Norte 91, ☎ 01/342–8713) is a reliable fado spot in the Bairro Alto. For reasonable food, as well as entertaining singing by a number of people, including one of the cooks, visit the **Adega do Ribatejo** (⊠ Rua Diário de Notícias 23, Bairro Alto, ☎ 01/346–8343). In the Alfama **Parreirinha d'Alfama** (⊠ Beco do Espírito Santo 1, ☎ 01/886–8209) is considered one of the best fado clubs. Lisbon's top spot for live jazz is **The Hot Clube** (⊠ Praça da Alegria 39, ☎ 01/346–7369), closed Sunday–Wednesday, where sessions don't usually begin until 11 PM.

Shopping

Flea Markets

A **Feira da Ladra** (flea market) takes place on Tuesday morning and all day Saturday in the Largo de Santa Clara behind the Church of São Vicente, near the Alfama district.

Gift Ideas

HANDICRAFTS

For embroidered goods and baskets from the Azores, try **Casa Regional da Ilha Verde** (⊠ Rua Paiva de Andrade 4, Chiado). **Casa Ribeiro da Silva** (⊠ Travessa Fiéis de Deus 69, Bairro Alto) is the place to go for handcrafted pottery. **Fábrica Sant'Ana** (⊠ Rua do Alecrim 95, Bairro Alto) sells wonderful hand-painted ceramics and tiles. For fine porcelain visit **Vista Alegre** (⊠ Largo do Chiado 18 and Rua Ivens 52, Bairro Alto). **Viúva Lamego** (⊠ Largo do Intendente and Calçada do Sacramento 29) has the largest selection of tiles and pottery.

JEWELRY AND ANTIQUES

Most of the antiques shops are along the Rua Escola Politénica, Rua Dom Pedro IV, Rua da Misericórdia, and Rua do Alecrim. **Antonio da Silva** (⊠ Praça Luis de Camões 40), at the top of the Chiado, specializes in antique silver and jewelry. Look for Portuguese gold and silver filigree work at **Sarmento** (⊠ Rua Aurea 251), in the Baixa.

LEATHER GOODS

Shoe stores abound in Lisbon, and some of the better shops can make shoes to order. You can buy leather gloves at a variety of specialty shops on Rua do Carmo and Rua Aurea. Fine leather handbags and luggage are sold at **Casa da Siberia** (⊠ Rua Augusta 254, Baixa). Visit **Ulisses** (⊠ Rua do Carmo 87, Chiado) for a fine selection of gloves.

Shopping Districts

Since the fire that destroyed much of the **Chiado** in 1988, reconstruction has progressed. The beautifully renovated **Eden** building (⊠ Av. da Liberdade) is an Art Deco triumph containing a Virgin Megastore, an aparthotel, and a small shopping center. Another important shopping area is in the **Baixa** quarter (between the Rossío and the River Tagus). On Avenida Engenheiro Duarte Pacheco, west of Parque Eduardo VII, the blue-and-pink towers of the **Amoreiras,** a huge shopping center, dominate the Lisbon skyline. **Colombo,** in the suburb of Benfica and reached directly by metro (Col. Militar–Luz), is the largest shopping mall on the Iberian peninsula.

Lisbon Essentials

Arriving and Departing

BY BUS

International buses, and most from the north or the Algarve, arrive at the city's **main bus terminal** (⊠ Av. Casal Ribeiro 18, ☎ 01/354–5439), a few minutes' walk from Saldanha metro station; taxis line up outside the terminal. You may also arrive at the **Renex bus terminal** (⊠ Campo Cebolas, ☎ 01/887–4871) near the cathedral. From it you can walk down to the main Avenida Infante d'Henrique and catch Bus 9, 39, 46, or 90 to the central Praça dos Restauradores.

BY PLANE

Lisbon's **Portela Airport** (☎ 01/841–3700 or 01/840–2262) is on the northern edge of the city, about a 20-minute drive from the center.

Between the Airport and Downtown. The **Aerobus** runs every 20 minutes, 7 AM–9 PM, from outside the airport into the city center; tickets available from the driver, cost 430$00 or 1,000$00 and provide one and three days' travel, respectively, on all of Lisbon's buses and trams. **Taxis** are cheap: the fare into Lisbon is about 1,500$00–2,000$00, and to Estoril or Sintra, 6,000$00. For luggage in the trunk, add another 300$00. No trains or subways link the airport and the city, but there are car-rental desks at the airport.

BY TRAIN

International trains from Paris and Madrid arrive at the spectacular **Oriente Station,** built in 1998 with excellent bus, subway, and taxi connections to all parts of the city. They continue on to the older **Santa Apolonia** terminal (☎ 01/888–4025), just east of the city center. To get from Santa Apolonia to the central Praça dos Restauradores by public transport, take Bus 9, 39, 46, or 90.

Getting Around

Lisbon is a hilly city, and the sidewalks are paved with cobblestones, so walking can be tiring, even when you're wearing comfortable shoes. However, buses, trams, and the metro (subway) system connect all parts of the city. A pass for unlimited rides on buses or trams costs 430$00 for one day's travel (*bilhete um dia*), 1,000$00 for three days (*bilhete tres dias*); the four-day (1,640$00) or seven-day (2,320$00) **Passe Turistico** (Tourist Pass) is also valid on the metro and the Santa Justa elevator and Gloria and Bica funiculars. You can buy Tourist Passes at the Cais do Sodré Station train station, Restauradores metro station, and other terminals. Otherwise, you pay a flat fee of 160$00 to the driver every time you ride a bus, tram, the Santa Justa elevator, or the funiculars; it's better to buy your ticket in advance from a kiosk, in which case the 160$00 ticket is valid for two separate journeys.

The **Lisboa Card** costs 1,700$00 (24 hrs), 2,800$00 (48 hrs), or 3,600$00 (72 hrs) and gives unlimited travel on the city's public transportation system, as well as entrance to the city's museums. Buy it from the **Municipal Council Tourist Office** (✉ Rua Jardim do Regedor 51, ☎ 01/343–3672) or at the **Jerónimos Monastery** in Belém (☞ Exploring Belém, *above*).

BY BUS AND TRAM

Buses and trams operate 6:30 AM–midnight. Try Tram 28 for an inexpensive tour of the city; buses to Costa da Caparica and Setúbal cross the Tagus bridge. In summer old-fashioned trams run on tours through the city (2,800$00 per person), departing from Praçca do Comércio; call the public transportation company, **Carris** (☎ 01/361–3053).

BY FERRY

Ferries cross the Tagus River from the Fluvial Terminal, adjacent to Praça do Comércio, to the suburb of Cacilhas, known for its fish restaurants, and to the towns of Seixal, Montijo, and Barreiros. The six-minute crossing (daily 7 AM–9:30 PM) to Cacilhas costs 100$00 one way. Car-carrying ferries also run to Cacilhas from the quay at Cais do Sodré (10 minutes, 100$00 person, 250$00 car) and from Belém to Porto Brandão, another fish restaurant mecca (15 minutes, 110$00). Even if gastronomy is not your main concern, these river trips are worth it for the fine views they afford of the city. For details about two-hour cruises on the Tagus River, contact **Transtejo** (☎ 01/887–5058). Services operate from April through October.

BY SUBWAY

The subway, called the **Metropolitano** (☎ 01/355–8457), operates 6:30 AM–1 AM. It has recently been extended to connect the Cais do Sodré train station with the rest of the network, and now it also runs out to the Oriente station at the former Expo site. Individual tickets cost 100$00; a 10-ticket strip, a *caderneta*, is 800$00. Unlimited use daily tickets cost 250$00. Watch out for pickpockets during rush hour.

BY TAXI

Taxis have a lighted sign on their green roofs. Stands are in the main squares, or you can flag one cruising by (difficult late at night). Taxis are metered and take up to four passengers at no extra charge. Rates start at 300$00, with an extra charge for luggage.

Contacts and Resources

EMBASSIES

U.S. (✉ Av. Forças Armadas, ☎ 01/727–3300). **Canadian** (✉ Av. da Liberdade 144-3, ☎ 01/347–4892). **U.K.** (✉ Rua São Bernado 33, ☎ 01/392–4000).

EMERGENCIES

SOS Emergencies (☎ 112). **Police** (☎ 01/346–6141). **Ambulance** (☎ 01/301–7777 or 01/942–1111). **Doctor:** British Hospital (✉ Rua Saraiva de Carvalho 49, ☎ 01/395–5067). **Pharmacies** are open weekdays 9–1 and 3–7, and Saturday 9–1. A notice on the door indicates the nearest one open on weekends or after hours; a similar list appears in Lisbon's daily newspapers.

GUIDED TOURS

Orientation and Excursions. A half-day tour of Lisbon costs about 6,000$00; a full-day trip north to Obidos, Nazaré, and Fatima runs about 15,000$00 (including lunch), as does a full day east along the "Roman Route" to Évora and Monsaraz. As the tours are so similar, several companies have joined together in one organization: **Citirama** (✉ Av. Praia da Vitória 12-b, ☎ 01/355–8569 or 01/355–8564) has details about all the possible excursions. You can reserve through Citirama or any travel agent or hotel.

Personal Guides. Contact the main **Lisbon Tourist Office** (☞ Visitor Information, *below*) or the **Syndicate of Guide Interpreters** (✉ Rua do Telhal 4, ☎ 01/346–7170). The front desk at your hotel may also have a list of bilingual guides. Beware of unauthorized guides who try to "guide" you to a particular shop or restaurant.

TRAVEL AGENCIES

Abreu (✉ Av. da Liberdade 158–160, ☎ 01/347–6441). **Marcus & Harting** (✉ Rossío 45–50, ☎ 01/346–9271). **Top Tours** (✉ Av. Duque de Loulé 108, ☎ 01/315–5877).

VISITOR INFORMATION

Lisbon Tourist Office: main (Palácio Foz, Praça dos Restauradores, at Baixa/Lower Town end of Avenida da Liberdade, ☎ 01/346–3643); airport (☎ 01/849–3689).

THE ESTORIL COAST, SINTRA, AND QUELUZ

Extending 32 km (20 mi) west of Lisbon is a stretch known as the Estoril Coast. Over the years the Casino at Estoril and the beaches, both there and in Cascais, have served as playgrounds for the wealthy. To the north of Cascais and Estoril lie the lush mountains of Sintra and, to the northeast, the historic town of Queluz, dominated by its 18th-century rococo palace and formal gardens. The villas, châteaus, and luxury *quintas* (country properties) of Sintra contrast notably with Cascais and Estoril, where life revolves around the sea.

The Estoril Coast, Sintra, and Queluz

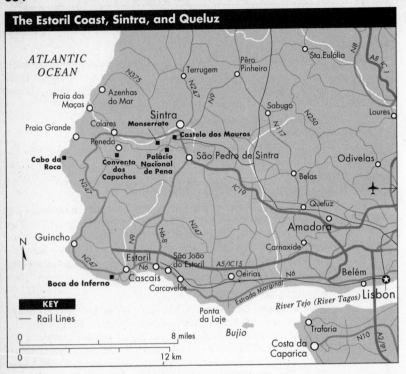

Sporting possibilities abound: golf courses, horseback riding, fishing, tennis, squash, swimming, Grand Prix racing, mountain climbing, and country walks. Beaches vary in both quality and cleanliness, though more and more display the blue Council of Europe flag, which signals a high standard of unpolluted water and sands. The waters off Cascais and Estoril are calm. To the north, around Guincho's rocky promontory and along the Praia de Maças coast, the Atlantic is often windswept and rough but provides good surfing and windsurfing.

Estoril

Estoril, 26 km (16 mi) west of Lisbon, is filled with grand homes and gardens. Many of its large mansions date from the 19th century, when the town was a favorite with the European aristocracy. People-watching is the favored pastime, and one of the best places for it is on the seafront Tamariz esplanade. The best and longest local beach is at adjacent Monte Estoril, which adjoins Estoril's beach.

The town's **casino**, with its gaming rooms, restaurants, cinema, floor show, and bars, is not just the glittering hub of Estoril's nightlife; it also houses one of Portugal's major art galleries and hosts, sponsors, and co-sponsors cultural events ranging from handicraft shows to ballet and concerts. Admission to the casino complex is free, though it costs 500$00 to enter the gaming rooms; taking in dinner and a floor show can cost up to 9,000$00. ⊠ *Parque do Estoril,* ☎ *01/468–4521.* ⊙ *Casino and restaurant 3 PM–3 AM; floor show nightly, 11.*

$$$–$$$$ ✕ **Estoril Mandarim.** Part of the Casino Estoril complex, this luxury Chinese restaurant aimed from the start to position itself among Europe's finest, with top Canton chef U Peng Kuan to oversee its elaborate menu of 119 items. It is also one of the few Chinese restaurants in Europe to offer a top-quality Chinese wine list. The food is Can-

tonese, with outstanding seafood, poultry, beef, and vegetarian specialities. ⊠ *Casino Estoril, Parque do Estoril,* ☎ *01/468–4521. AE, DC, MC, V. Closed Tues.*

$$–$$$$ ✕ **A Choupana.** Just outside town toward Lisbon, this restaurant overlooks the beach, putting its picture windows to good use with views of Cascais Bay. You can sample high-quality fresh seafood and other local dishes such as the cataplana of chicken and clams. ⊠ *Estrada Marginal, São João de Estoril,* ☎ *01/468–3099. AE, DC, MC, V. Closed Mon.*

$$–$$$$ ✕ **The English Bar.** This mock-Tudor establishment serves good Portuguese and French-influenced cuisine in friendly, comfortable surroundings. There are beautiful views over the beach to Cascais and an excellent wine list. ⊠ *Av. Saboia, off Av. Marginal, Monte Estoril,* ☎ *01/468–0413. AE, DC, MC, V. Closed Sun.*

$–$$$ ✕ **Restaurante Frolic.** The friendly restaurant-bar has a covered, outdoor terrace. Try the delectable cakes, or stop longer for a Portuguese meal or a pizza. ⊠ *Av. Clotilde,* ☎ *01/468–1219. AE, DC, MC, V.*

$$$$ ✕⊡ **Hotel Palácio.** During World War II, exiled European aristocrats
★ came here to wait out the war in grand style. Rooms are splendidly appointed, and those on the first, third, and fifth floors have balconies; public areas are decorated with monumental columns, tiled floors, and chandeliers. The elegant Four Seasons restaurant ($$–$$$$) serves buffets around the garden pool in summer and seeks perfection with the freshest of foods—the menu changes with the season. ⊠ *Parque do Estoril, 2765,* ☎ *01/468–0400,* ℻ *01/468–4867. 162 rooms. Restaurant, pool. AE, DC, MC, V.*

★ Cascais

Once a mere fishing village, Cascais (3¼ km/2 mi west of Estoril)—with three small, sandy bays—is now a heavily developed resort. Even so, it has retained some of its small-town character, seen at its best around the harbor and in the streets and squares off Largo 5 Outubro, where you'll find lace shops, cafés, and restaurants galore.

The most visited local attraction is the forbiddingly named **Boca do Inferno** (Mouth of Hell), just 2 km (1¼ mi) west of Cascais, where the sea pounds into an impressive natural grotto. ⊠ *Estrada da Boca do Inferno.* ▣ *Free.*

The **Igreja de Nossa Senhora da Assunção** (Church of Our Lady of the Assumption) has paintings by the Portuguese 17th-century artist Josefa de Óbidos. ⊠ *Largo da Assunção,* ☎ *no phone.* ▣ *Free.* ☉ *Daily 9–1 and 5–8.*

One of Cascais's elegant 19th-century town houses now serves as the charming **Museu Conde de Castro Guimarães** (Museum of the Counts of Guimarães), which displays 18th- and 19th-century paintings, ceramics, furniture, and archaeological artifacts that were excavated nearby. The gem of the collection is an illumination from a 16th-century manuscript with a rare, contemporary view of Lisbon. The museum is set in the attractive grounds of the **Parque do Marechal Carmona** (Marechal Carmona Park), open daily 9–6, in which you'll find a shallow lake, a café, and a small zoo. ⊠ *Estrada da Boca do Inferno,* ☎ *01/482–5407.* ▣ *Free Sun.* ☉ *Tues.–Sun. 11–12:30 and 2–5.*

$–$$$$ ✕ **Beira Mar.** Tucked behind the fish market, the Beira Mar serves a wide variety of fish and meat dishes—be careful when choosing shellfish as it's sold by weight and can be very pricey. The atmosphere is comfortable and unpretentious. ⊠ *Rua das Flores 6,* ☎ *01/483–0152. AE, DC, MC, V. Closed Tues.*

$–$$$ ✕ **João Padeiro.** This town-center restaurant serves the best sole in the region—and other seafood as well—in cheerful surroundings. ⊠ *Rua Visconde da Luz 12,* ☎ *01/483–0232. AE, DC, MC, V. Closed Sun.*

$$$$ ✕⌂ **Hotel Albatroz.** On a rocky outcrop, this attractive old house, con-
★ verted from an aristocrat's summer residence, is the most luxurious of Cascais's hotels. Though enlarged and modernized, it has retained its character, with charming bedrooms and a pleasant terrace bar. The restaurant ($$–$$$$) offers superior sea views; it specializes in fish dishes, such as local grilled sole or baked cod stuffed with ham. ⊠ *Rua Frederico Arouca 100, 2750,* ☎ *01/483–2821,* ⒡⒜⒳ *01/484–4827. 40 rooms. Restaurant, pool. AE, DC, MC, V.*

$ ⌂ **Solar Dom Carlos.** This delightful inn tucked into a quiet back street is the most appealing budget bet in town. Dating from the 16th century, it was formerly a nobleman's mansion and any lingering mustiness is the smell of history, not neglect—the traditionally tiled floors and walls positively gleam. ⊠ *Rua Latina Coelho 8, 2750,* ☎ *01/482–8115,* ⒡⒜⒳ *01/486–5115. 18 rooms. MC, V.*

Guincho

There's a superb, wide beach (overlooked by several seafood restaurants) at Guincho (11 km/7 mi northwest of Cascais), where rollers from the Atlantic pound onto the sand even on the calmest of days, providing perfect conditions for windsurfing. But beware: The undertow at Guincho beach is notoriously dangerous, and even the best swimmers should take heed.

$$$–$$$$ ✕⌂ **Hotel do Guincho.** This small, luxurious hotel built in an old fort overlooks one of the most beautiful stretches of Portugal's Atlantic coast. The rooms are small but luxuriously equipped in a mixture of period styles; the views they afford of the rocky shoreline are spectacular. The spacious, elegantly furnished restaurant ($$$–$$$$) is clearly the hub of the establishment. The cooking is nouveau-ish French, coordinated by Strasbourg chef and restaurateur Antoine Westermann and prepared by another Alsatian specialist, resident chef Marc Ouedec. Among the best on the extensive menu: *carrè de veau, ratatouille et pomme de terre au thym* (roast veal, ratatouille, and thyme-flavored potato cakes) and *marmite de poissons et gambas* (fish soup). ⊠ *Estrada do Guincho, 2750 Cascais,* ☎ *01/487–0491,* ⒡⒜⒳ *01/487–0431. 29 rooms. Restaurant, bar. AE, DC, MC, V.*

Cabo da Roca

The windswept Cabo da Roca (20 km/12 mi northwest of Cascais; 15 km/9 mi west of Sintra) and its lighthouse mark continental Europe's westernmost point. As with many similar places, tourist stalls take advantage of its popularity and offer shell souvenirs and other gimmicks, while an information desk and gift shop sells a certificate that verifies your visit.

★ Convento dos Capuchos

In 1560 Franciscan monks built the Convento dos Capuchos (Capuchin Convent) deep in the hills of the Serra de Sintra (Sintra Mountains) 6 km (4 mi) northeast of Cabo da Roca, 9 km (5½ mi) southwest of Sintra. The tiny friary, no longer inhabited, whose 12 diminutive cells are hacked out of solid rock, is lined with cork for warmth and insulation. ⊠ *Signposted off Rte. N247,* ☎ *01/923–0137.* ☉ *June–Sept., daily 10–6; Oct.–May, daily 10–5.*

Monserrate

This botanical wonderland 5 km (3 mi) northeast of Convento dos Capuchos and 4 km (2½ mi) west of Sintra was laid out by Scottish gardeners in the mid-1800s. It surrounds an exotic and architecturally extravagant domed Moorish-style palace (closed to visitors). In addition to a dazzling array of other plant species, the gardens have one of the largest collections of fern varieties in the world. ⊠ *Estrada da Monserrate,* ☎ *01/923–1201.* ۞ *June–Sept., daily 9–7; Oct.–May, daily 10–5.*

★ Sintra

One of Portugal's oldest towns, beautiful Sintra (30 km/19 mi northwest of Lisbon, 13 km/8 mi north of Estoril) was the summer residence of early Portuguese kings and aristocrats. By the 18th and 19th centuries its charms became widely known as English travelers, poets, and writers—including an enthusiastic Lord Byron—were drawn by the region's beauty. If you're in the area on the second or fourth Sunday of the month, visit the **Feira de Sintra** (Sintra Fair) in the nearby village of São Pedro de Sintra, 2 km (1¼ mi) to the southeast.

The 8th-century **Castelo dos Mouros** (Moors' Castle) defied hundreds of invaders until it was conquered by Dom Afonso Henriques in 1147. Follow the steep, partially cobbled road up to the ruins or rent a horse-drawn carriage in Sintra. From the castle's serrated walls, you can see why its Moorish architects chose the site. The views falling away on all sides are breathtaking. ⊠ *Estrada da Pena.* ☜ *Free.* ۞ *June–Sept., daily 10–7; Oct.–May, daily 10–5.*

★ At the center of the Old Town stands the 14th-century **Palácio Nacional de Sintra** (Sintra Palace). This twin-chimney building, a combination of Moorish and Gothic architectural styles, was once the summer residence of the House of Avis, Portugal's royal line. Today it's a museum (guided tours only) exhibiting some fine examples of Moorish-Arabic *azulejos* (tiles). ⊠ *Largo Rainha D. Amelia,* ☎ *01/923–0085.* ☜ *Free Sun.* AM. ۞ *Thurs.–Tues. 10–1 and 2–5.*

★ The **Palácio Nacional de Pena** (Pena Palace), an extravaganza built by the king consort Ferdinand of Saxe-Coburg in 1840, is a cauldron of clashing styles, from Arabian to Victorian, and was home to the last kings of Portugal. It's surrounded by a park filled with trees and flowers brought from every corner of the Portuguese empire by Dom Fernando, consort to Dona Maria II, in the 1840s. It's a long but pleasant walk to the palace from Sintra (about 1½ hours); there's also hourly bus service from Sintra train station and town center. ⊠ *Estrada da Pena,* ☎ *01/923–0227.* ☜ *Free Sun. 10–2.* ۞ *June–Sept., Tues.–Sun. 10–6:30; Oct.–May, Tues.–Sun. 10–1 and 2–5.*

$$–$$$$ ✗ **Solar de São Pedro.** Highly recommended by its habitués, this restaurant specializes in Portuguese and French country cooking. Its English-speaking host adds to the warm, friendly atmosphere. ⊠ *Largo da Feira 12, São Pedro de Sintra,* ☎ *01/923–1860. AE, DC, MC, V. Closed Wed.*

$–$$ ✗ **Alcobaça.** Classic Portuguese cooking is offered at this central, very reasonably priced restaurant. Try the grilled chicken or the arroz de marisco. ⊠ *Rua das Padarias 7–11,* ☎ *01/923–1651. MC, V. No credit cards.*

$$$$
★ 🏠 **Palácio de Seteais.** This luxurious former palace set on its own grounds 1 km (½ mi) from Sintra was built by the Dutch consul in Portugal during the 18th century. Its stately rooms are decorated with delicate wall and ceiling frescoes, and it houses a splendid restaurant. ⊠ *Rua Barbosa do Bocage 8, 2710,* ☎ *01/923–3200,* ℻ *01/923–4277. 30 rooms. Restaurant, pool. AE, DC, MC, V.*

$$
★ 🏠 **Quinta das Sequóias.** Reservations are essential at this lovely antiques-filled manor house set on gardens down a side road. It's just over 1 km (½ mi) from Sintra and makes an excellent touring base; time in

the whirlpool tub or the sauna here is a wonderful way to unwind from a day of sightseeing. Dinner is served if ordered in advance. ⊠ *Apartado 4, 2710,* ☎ 🅵🅰🆇 *01/923–0342. 6 rooms. Pool. AE, DC, MC, V.*

$$ 🔳 **Tivoli Sintra.** From its perch in the center of Sintra, the Tivoli has views over the nearby valleys. The smart rooms provide space and comfort in equal measure. ⊠ *Praça da República, 2710,* ☎ *01/923–3505,* 🅵🅰🆇 *01/923–1572. 75 rooms. Restaurant. AE, DC, MC, V.*

Queluz

The town of Queluz, 15 km (9 mi) east of Sintra and 15 km (9 mi) northwest of Lisbon, is accessible by train directly from Lisbon or by way of the IC19/N249 road, which runs between Lisbon and Sintra.

★ Once you turn off the main road, it's hard to miss the magnificent **Palácio Nacional de Queluz** (Queluz Palace). Inspired in part by Versailles, this salmon-pink rococo palace was begun by Dom Pedro III in 1747 and took 40 years to complete. The formal landscaping and waterways surrounding it are the work of the French designer Jean-Baptiste Robillon. Restored after a fire in 1934, the palace is now used for formal banquets and music festivals and as housing for visiting heads of state. You can walk through its more elegant rooms, among them the Music Salon, the Hall of the Ambassadors, and the mirrored Throne Room with its crystal chandeliers and gilt trim. ⊠ *Rte. IC19,* ☎ *01/435–0039.* ☉ *Wed.–Mon. 10–1 and 2–5.*

$$$ ✕🔳 **Pousada de Dona Maria I.** The old servants' quarters, beneath the
★ clock tower opposite the Queluz palace, have undergone a stunning refurbishment: Marble hallways lined with prints of old Portugal give way to high-ceiling rooms whose reproduction furniture carefully follows 18th-century fashion. Across the road in the old palace kitchens, the Restaurante de Cozinha Velha ($$–$$$$, reservations essential) takes full advantage of its heritage. The cooking hits the mark; a spicy cataplana of salmon, monkfish, clams, and shrimp is just one superb main course. ⊠ *Rte. IC19, 2745,* ☎ *01/435–6158,* 🅵🅰🆇 *01/435–6189. 24 rooms. Restaurant. AE, DC, MC, V.*

The Estoril Coast, Sintra, and Queluz Essentials

Getting Around

Although the best way to reach Cascais, Estoril, and Sintra is by train from Lisbon, there are some useful bus connections between towns. The area is served by three main roads: the often congested four-lane coastal highway (the N6 Avenida Marginal), the IC19/N249 to Sintra, and the A5 expressway, which links Lisbon with Cascais.

At Cascais the **bus** terminal (☎ 01/483–6357) outside the train station operates regular summer services to Guincho (journey time 15 minutes) and Sintra (40 minutes). From the bus terminal outside the Sintra train station, there's regular year-round service to Cascais and Estoril (1 hour), as well as to the Moorish Castle and Pena Palace.

A commuter **train** leaves every 15 to 30 minutes (5:30 AM–2:30 AM) from Cais do Sodré Station in Lisbon for the trip to Estoril and on to Cascais, four stops farther. A one-way ticket costs 185$00. Trains from Lisbon's Rossío station run every 15 minutes to Queluz (155$00), taking 20 minutes, and on to Sintra (185$00), which takes 40 minutes. For current information about train services, call ☎ 01/888–4025.

Guided Tours

Most travel agents and guided-tour operators (☞ Lisbon Essentials, *above*) can reserve you a place on a guided tour, or you can contact the reception desk of your hotel. Half-day trips to Queluz, Sintra, or

Estoril, or a tour of the area's royal palaces, cost around 8,000$00; nine-hour tours of Mafra, Sintra, and Cascais cost 13,000$00, including lunch.

Visitor Information
Cascais (⊠ Rua Visconde da Luz 14, ☎ 01/486–8204). **Estoril** (⊠ Arcadas do Parque, ☎ 01/466–3813). **Sintra** (⊠ Praça da República 3, ☎ 01/923–1157 or 01/924–1700; 01/924–1623 train station).

THE ALGARVE

The Algarve, Portugal's southernmost region, encompasses some 240 sun-drenched km (150 mi) of coastline, making it a top destination for foreign visitors. Since the 1960s it has been heavily developed and in certain areas, apartment complexes, hotels, and restaurants sprout from every bay and cliff top. There are, however, still fishing villages and secluded beaches that remain untouched, while the attractions in even the most developed resorts are well known—clean, sandy beaches; excellent sports facilities; championship golf courses; and plenty of color in the local markets, cafés, and restaurants. The drive to Albufeira from Lisbon takes about four hours; allow another hour to reach either Faro or Lagos. (Note that regional authorities are currently working to improve the clarity and quality of directional signs along roads—welcome news for visitors to the Algarve— but signposting remains inadequate.)

Monte Gordo
Pine woods and orchards break up the flat landscape around Monte Gordo, a town of brightly colored houses with extensive tourist facilities 4 km (2½ mi) west of Vila Real de Santo António, a town—laid out in an 18th-century grid pattern similar to that of the Baixa district in Lisbon—near the Spanish border. There's a long stretch of beach here. Other local beaches to the west, such as Praia Verde and Manta Rota, are equally attractive—you should have little trouble finding a spot on the sand, perhaps having a lunch of grilled sardines at one of the numerous beach bar-restaurants.

$ ✕ **Mota.** The Mota is a lively, unpretentious seafood restaurant with a covered terrace right on the ocean. ⊠ *On beach at Monte Gordo,* ☎ *081/512340. AE, DC, MC, V.*

$$ ▦ **Alcazar.** This attractive hotel has unusual architecture and interior design—the sinuous arches and low molded ceilings suggest the inside of a cave or an Arab tent. ⊠ *Rua de Ceuta 9, 8900,* ☎ *081/512184,* FAX *081/512242. 95 rooms. Restaurant, pool. AE, DC, MC, V.*

Tavira
A tuna-fishing port at the mouth of the River Gilão 20 km (12 mi) west of Monte Gordo, Tavira has numerous attractions: cobbled old town streets, a seven-arch Roman bridge, old Moorish defense walls crowning the central hill, and a series of interesting churches—not least, **Santa Maria do Castelo** (St. Mary of the Castle), built on the site of a former mosque. There are good sand beaches on nearby **Ilha da Tavira** (Tavira Island), which you can reach by ferry from the jetty at Quatro Águas (⊠ 2 km/1¼ mi east of town center)—it runs May–mid-October, every 30–60 minutes and charges 200$00 round-trip—and from a quay in the center of town (⊠ between Roman bridge and market); it runs May–mid-October, every 15 minutes and charges 150$00 round-trip.

Olhão
Founded during the 18th century, the fishing port and market town of Olhão, 22 km (14 mi) west of Tavira, is notable for its North African-

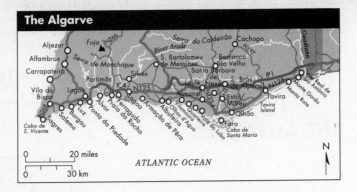

The Algarve

style architecture (cube-shape whitewashed buildings) and some of the best food markets in the Algarve (next to the harbor). There are also ferries (✉ jetty east of town gardens) from Olhão to the nearby sandy islands of **Armona** and **Culatra,** both of which have excellent beaches. Schedules are available at the tourist office (☞ Visitor Information *in* Algarve Essentials, *below*).

Faro

Founded by the Moors, Faro—provincial capital of the Algarve—was taken by Afonso III in 1249, ending the Arab domination of Portugal. It's a modern center 9 km (6 mi) west of Olhão, full of restaurants that offer international cuisines. There's also a smart marina.

★ The best of the sights is surely the **Capela dos Ossos** (Chapel of the Bones) in the **Igreja do Carmo** (Carmelite Church), decorated with human bones taken from the monks' cemetery. ✉ *Largo do Carmo,* ☎ *no phone.* ☾ *Weekdays 10–1 and 2:30–5, Sat. 10–1.*

★ In the older district, the **Cidade Velha,** you can see remnants of medieval walls and gates. One of the old gates, the **Arco da Vila,** with a white marble statue of St. Thomas Aquinas in a niche at the top, leads to the grand Largo da Sé (Cathedral Square). Surrounded by orange trees in the square, you'll find the restored Gothic Sé (Cathedral), whose stunning interior is decorated with 17th-century tiles. ✉ *Largo da Sé,* ☎ *089/806632.* ☾ *Mon.–Fri. 10–5, Sat. 10–5 if no weddings.*

Perhaps the most fascinating museum in town is the **Museu Etnológico** (Ethnological Museum), which displays an ethnographical collection showing just how much the Algarve has changed since the 1960s. There are displays relating to lace making, embroidery, and fishing, plus the restored interior of an old-time general store. ✉ *Rua do Pé da Cruz,* ☎ *no phone.* ☾ *Weekdays 10–6.*

The old town's **Museu Municipal** (Municipal Museum), housed in a former convent, has a section devoted to the Roman remains found at nearby Milreu (☞ *Estói, below*). ✉ *Largo D. Afonso III,* ☎ *089/822042.* ☾ *Weekdays 9:30–12:30, 2–5.*

There's a large sand beach on Faro Island, the **Praia de Faro,** which is connected by road (Bus 16 from the harbor gardens). Or you can take the ferry from the jetty below the old town to the beach at Farol on Culatra Island (☞ *Olhão, above*).

$$$ ✕ **Cidade Velha.** Occupying an 18th-century house inside the old town walls, this intimate restaurant serves excellent international cuisine. ✉ *Rua Domingos Guieiro 19,* ☎ *089/827145. AE, MC, V. Closed Sun. No lunch June–Sept.*

$$ ✕ **Dois Irmãos.** A friendly staff in this central, cheery setting serves up an array of cataplana dishes. Save room for the homemade *pudim caseiro* (crème caramel). ⊠ *Largo do Terreiro do Bispo 13,* ☎ *089/803912. AE, DC, MC, V.*

$$$$ ✕☷ **Hotel La Reserve.** This intimate luxury hotel in Santa Barbara, in
★ the hills, 10 km (6 mi) inland from Faro and set in a 6-acre park, offers high-class apartment accommodations, including small duplexes with verandas and sea views. Don't pass up the restaurant (reservations essential; closed Tuesday; no lunch), which serves elegant cuisine with a French accent; local game is a specialty, and the wine list is very good. ⊠ *Santa Barbara de Nexe, 8000,* ☎ *089/999494,* 𝔽𝔸𝕏 *089/ 999402. 12 studios, 8 duplexes. Restaurant, pool. AE, DC, MC, V.*

$$ ☷ **Hotel Eva.** This well-appointed, modern hotel overlooks the yacht basin. The best rooms, with spacious balconies, face the sea; there's a shuttle to the beach. ⊠ *Av. da República 1, 8000,* ☎ *089/803354,* 𝔽𝔸𝕏 *089/802304. 150 rooms. Restaurant, pool. AE, DC, MC, V.*

Estói

The charming small village of Estói, 9 km (5½ mi) north of Faro, on a signposted branch road off the N2, is the setting for the 18th-century **Palácio do Visconde de Estói** (Palace of the Counts of Estói). The palace itself is closed to the public, but you can stroll around its gardens. ⊠ *Rua da Barroca,* ☎ *089/97282.* ☷ *Free.* ☉ *Tues.–Sat. 9–12:30 and 2–5:30.*

A 10-minute walk down the main road from town lie extensive 1st-century **Roman ruins** at **Milreu.** ⊠ *Estói,* ☎ *089/997823.* ☉ *Tues.– Sun. 9:30–12:30 and 2–5.*

Loulé

This little market town in the hills 17 km (10 mi) northwest of Faro, along the N125–4, was once a Moorish stronghold and is now best known for its crafts and the decorative white chimneys of its houses. In its narrow streets you can usually see coppersmiths and leather workers toiling in their workshops. You can also visit the partially restored ruins of a medieval Saracen **castle,** inside which is the town's **museum.** ⊠ *Rua D. Paio Peres Correia.* ☷ *Free.* ☉ *Weekdays 9–5:30, Sat. 10–5:30.*

The 13th-century **parish church,** decorated with handsome tiles and wood carvings, contains an unusual wrought-iron pulpit. ⊠ *Largo da Matriz.* ☷ *Free.* ☉ *At discretion of priest.*

Almansil/Vale do Lobo/Quinta do Lago

East of the nondescript town of Almansil, 13 km (8 mi) west of Faro, the 18th-century Baroque chapel of **São Lourenço** (St. Lawrence) is filled with blue-and-white tile panels and intricate gilt work. The cottages beside it have been transformed into a lovely art gallery. ⊠ *N125,* ☎ *089/395475.* ☉ *Mon.–Sat. 10–1 and 2–5.*

The nearest beach is about 6 km (4 mi) southwest of the São Lourenço chapel, where the upscale resort of **Vale do Lobo** sits in exclusive isolation. To the southeast of the chapel is the equally grand **Quinta do Lago** resort, known for its golf, leisure activities, and hotel.

$$$$ ☷ **Le Meridien Dona Filipa.** The Dona Filipa has a lavish interior, pleasant rooms, and first-rate service. Set on extensive, beautifully landscaped grounds near the beach, the hotel houses a chic restaurant that offers an excellent international menu. There are tennis courts on the premises, and discount fees for nearby golf courses are available. ⊠ *Vale do Lobo, 8235 Almansil,* ☎ *089/394141,* 𝔽𝔸𝕏 *089/394288. 147 rooms. Restaurant, pool. AE, DC, MC, V.*

Vilamoura

Vilamoura, 10 km (6¼ mi) west of Almansil, is a highly developed resort. In addition to modern luxury hotels and a casino, it has a large yacht marina, several golf courses, a major tennis center, one of Europe's largest shooting centers, and other sports facilities. The beach is a splendid stretch, and there's more good sand just 4 km (2½ mi) to the east at the neighboring market town of Quarteira, once a quiet fishing village but now a bustling high-rise resort.

$$$$ 🏨 **Hotel Vilamoura Marinotel.** Built around 1970 and one of the flagships of the Algarve's fleet of luxury hotels, the Marinotel was completely refurbished and modernized in 1997. The rooms are spacious and handsomely furnished. The hotel overlooks the Vilamoura marina and has gardens leading down to the beach. If you don't feel up to the short stroll, there are pools to tempt you on the way. ⊠ *Vilamoura, 8125 Quarteira,* ☎ *089/389988,* FAX *089/389869. 193 rooms, 16 suites. 3 restaurants, bar, 2 pools. AE, DC, MC, V.*

$$$ 🏨 **Hotel Dom Pedro Golf.** In the heart of this successful vacation complex, the Dom Pedro is close to the casino and not far from the beach. Each room is attractively furnished and has its own balcony, and you can take advantage of golf privileges, tennis courts, and the hotel's own health club. ⊠ *Vilamoura, 8125 Quarteira,* ☎ *089/300700,* FAX *089/ 300701. 263 rooms. Restaurant, pool. AE, DC, MC, V.*

Albufeira

Once an attractive fishing village, Albufeira, 10 km (6¼ mi) west of Vilamoura, has mushroomed into a large, brash resort. But with its steep, narrow streets and hundreds of whitewashed houses clutching the slopes, Albufeira retains a distinctly Moorish flavor. Among its attractions are a lively fish market (held daily), stunning caves and grottoes along the local coast, and plenty of nightlife.

$$$ ✕ **Cabaz da Praia.** This long-established restaurant has a spectacular view of the main beach from its cliff-side terrace. There's fine French-Portuguese cooking here—fish soup, imaginatively served fish plates, and chicken with seafood. ⊠ *Praça Miguel Bombarda 7,* ☎ *089/ 512137. AE, MC, V. Closed Dec. No lunch Sat.*

$$$ ✕ **La Cigale.** Nine kilometers (5½ miles) east of Albufeira, overlooking its own little beach, this restaurant—one of the best—offers both French and Portuguese cuisine. ⊠ *Olhos d'Agua,* ☎ *089/501637. AE, DC, MC, V. Closed Dec.–Feb.*

$$–$$$ ✕ **A Ruína.** A rustic restaurant on the beach, built on several levels, this is the place for good views and charcoal-grilled seafood. ⊠ *Cais Herculano, Praia dos Pescadores,* ☎ *089/512094. AE, DC, MC V.*

$$$$ 🏨 **Sheraton Algarve.** This luxury hotel occupies a spectacular cliff-top ★ site 8 km (5 mi) east of town. It overlooks the sea and has direct access to a very fine beach on an exterior elevator. The architecture and decor blend traditional Moorish-style courtyards, fountains, and terraces with fine Portuguese tiles and furnishings. Up-to-the-minute facilities include a sauna, a nine-hole golf course, tennis courts, and an exercise room. An excellent buffet breakfast is included in the room rate. ⊠ *Praia da Falésia, 8200 Albufeira,* ☎ *089/500100,* FAX *089/ 501950. 215 rooms. Restaurant, 3 pools. AE, DC, MC, V.*

$$$ 🏨 **Hotel Cerro Alagoa.** The smartly decorated guest rooms here have private balconies; be sure to request a sea view. It's a 10-minute walk to the town center, but there's courtesy bus service to both Albufeira and the local beaches. ⊠ *Via Rápida, 8200,* ☎ *089/5802100,* FAX *089/ 580–2199. 310 rooms. Restaurant, pool. AE, DC, MC, V.*

Armação de Pêra

The straggling resort of Armação de Pêra, 14 km (8 mi) west of Albufeira, has one of the longest beaches in the Algarve, a wide sandy strand with a pretty promenade. Local boats take sightseers on cruises to the caves and grottoes along the shore.

$$ ✕ **A Santola.** This well-established restaurant overlooking the beach is the best in town. Try the excellent cataplana. ⊠ *Largo da Fortaleza,* ☎ *082/312332. MC, V. Closed Sun.*

$$$–$$$$ ⊞ **Vila Vita Parc.** The pampering begins as soon as you pass through the wrought-iron gates. Gentle colors, fireplaces, dark woods, and the feel of an exclusive oasis run throughout this superb cliff-top resort. There's golf and tennis, while landscaped gardens wind down to two sequestered beaches. ⊠ *Alporchinhos (Box 196), 8365,* ☎ *082/315310,* FAX *082/315333. 172 rooms, 10 suites, 5 villas. 6 restaurants, 3 pools. AE, DC, MC, V.*

$–$$$ ⊞ **Hotel Garbe.** The bar, lounge, and restaurant—all with terraces that provide views of the sea—take full advantage of the superb location of this squat, white, central hotel. Rooms are modern and smartly furnished, and steps lead from the hotel down to the beach. ⊠ *Av. Marginal, 8365,* ☎ *082/315187,* FAX *082/315087. 152 rooms. Restaurant, pool. AE, DC, MC, V.*

Portimão

Portimão, 15 km (9 mi) west of Armação de Pêra, is the most important fishing port in the Algarve; it's cheerful and busy with shops and open-air cafés. There was a settlement here at the mouth of the River Arade even before the Romans arrived. Restaurants along the quay are pleasant spots to sample the local specialty: charcoal-grilled sardines with chewy fresh bread and red wine.

$$ ✕ **A Lanterna.** This well-run restaurant is just over the bridge at Parchal, on the Ferragudo side of town. Its specialty is duck, but you might also try the exceptional fish soup or smoked fish. ⊠ *Largo 1Ž Dezembro,* ☎ *082/423948. AE, MC, DC, V. Closed Sun. No lunch.*

$$$$ ⊞ **Le Meridien Penina.** This impressive golf hotel, on 360 well-main-
★ tained, secluded acres off the main road between Portimão and Lagos, has spacious, elegant public rooms, pleasant guest rooms (many with balconies), and attentive service. Rooms in the back of the hotel face the Serra de Monchique and have the best views. The excellent golf courses were designed by Henry Cotton, and greens fees are waived for hotel guests, who also have full access to an impressive range of activities and facilities. ⊠ *Montes de Alvor, 8500,* ☎ *082/415415,* FAX *082/415000. 192 rooms. Restaurant, pool. AE, DC, MC, V.*

Praia da Rocha

Now dominated by high-rise apartments and hotels, this was the first spot in the Algarve (3 km/2 mi south of Portimão) to be developed as a resort. It has an excellent beach, made more interesting by its wall of huge, colored rocks worn into odd shapes by sea and wind.

$$ ✕ **Safari.** This lively Portuguese seafront restaurant behind the cathedral has a distinctly African flavor. Seafood and delicious Angolan recipes are specialties. ⊠ *Rua António Feu,* ☎ *082/423540. AE, DC, MC, V.*

$$–$$$$ ⊞ **Hotel Algarve-Casino.** A modern hotel, the Algarve-Casino is perched atop a cliff. Decorated in Moorish style, it has good-size rooms and an attentive staff. Leisure facilities are particularly comprehensive here, and there's easy access to the fine beach below. The on-site casino has international shows and gaming rooms. ⊠ *Av. Tomás Cabreira, 8500,* ☎ *082/415001,* FAX *082/415999. 209 rooms. Restaurant, 2 pools. AE, DC, MC, V.*

$-$$ ⌶ **Hotel Bela Vista.** Tasteful decor and such magnificent appointments as traditional tiles and stained-glass panels help to make this small beach-front hotel the delight that it is. Relax on the terrace that overlooks the beach; in summer the hotel has live music performances. ⌂ *Av. Tomás Cabreira, 8500,* ☎ *082/424055,* FAX *082/415369. 14 rooms. AE, DC, MC, V.*

Silves

Once the Moorish capital of the Algarve, Silves, 18 km (11 mi) north-east of Portimão, along the N124-1, ceased to be important after it was almost completely destroyed by the 1755 earthquake. The 12th-cen-
★ tury sandstone **castelo** (castle), with its impressive parapets, was re-stored in 1835 and still dominates the town. ⌂ *Castelo do Silves,* ☎ *082/445624.* 🎫 *Free.* 🕑 *Daily 9–7.*

Below the fortress stands the 12th- to 13th-century **Santa Maria da Sé** (Cathedral of St. Mary), which was built on the site of a Moorish mosque. ⌂ *Rua da Sé.* 🎫 *Free.* 🕑 *Mon.–Sat. 8:30–6, Sun. 8:30–1.*

The excellent **Museu Arqueológico** (Archaeological Museum), below the cathedral, displays artifacts from prehistoric times through the 17th century. ⌂ *Rua das Portas de Loulé 14,* ☎ *082/442020.* 🕑 *Mon.–Sat. 10–12:30 and 2–6.*

Lagos

Lagos—western terminus of the coastal railway that runs from Vila Real de Santo António—is a bustling holiday resort whose main pedes-trian streets are lined with shops, restaurants, and bars. It's still an im-portant fishing port, too, with an attractive harbor and a modern marina, though it's the amazing nearby cove beaches that attract the holiday crowds. The prettiest, the Praia de Doña Ana, is just a 30-minute walk away, along the cliff top. Lagos has a venerable history (Henry the Navigator maintained a base here), most evident in its imposing **city walls**, which still survive, and its 17th-century harborside **fort** at **Ponta da Bandeira.** ⌂ *Av. dos Descobrimentos.* 🕑 *Tues.–Sat. 10–1 and 2–6, Sun. 10–1.*

The 18th-century Baroque **Igreja de Santo António** (Church of St. An-thony) is renowned for its exuberant carved and gilt wood decoration. The **Museu Regional** (Regional Museum) at the church houses an ex-traordinary jumble of exhibits, including mosaics and archaeological and ethnographical items. ⌂ *Rua General Alberto Silveira,* ☎ *082/ 762301.* 🕑 *Tues–Sun. 9:30–12:30 and 2–5.*

$$$ ✕ **Dom Sebastião.** Portuguese cooking and charcoal-grilled specials are
★ the main attractions at this cheerful restaurant. It has a wide range of aged Portuguese wines. ⌂ *Rua 25 de Abril 20,* ☎ *082/762795. AE, DC, MC, V. Closed Oct. 1999–Apr. 2000.*

$$$ ✕ **No Patio.** You'll find some fine food, indeed, at this cheerful restau-rant with an attractive patio. It's run by a Danish couple, Bjarne and Gitte, and the fare is international with a Scandinavian accent. Spe-cialties include tenderloin of pork with a Madeira and mushroom sauce. ⌂ *Rua Lançarote de Freitas 46,* ☎ *082/763777. AE, MC, V.*

$$$ ⌶ **Hotel de Lagos.** This modern hotel stands out at the eastern edge
★ of the Old Town, within easy walking distance of all the sights and restaurants. From its terraced rooms you look down at the pool or across the river to the coast. Traditional tiles are effectively used throughout, even on lamps and tabletops. A shuttle bus runs to the beach, where the hotel has outstanding club facilities. ⌂ *Rua Nova da Aldeia, 8600 Lagos,* ☎ *082/769967,* FAX *082/769920. 317 rooms. 2 restaurants, 2 pools. AE, DC, MC, V.*

Sagres

On the windy headland at Sagres, 30 km (19 mi) west of Lagos (take the N268 south from the N125 at Vila do Bispo), some contend that Prince Henry established his famous school of navigation—the first of its kind—in the 15th century. A small road leads across a promontory hundreds of feet above the sea, through the tunnel-like entrance to the

★ **Fortaleza de Sagres.** Here you can experience the crashing of waves, the howl of the wind, and centuries of nautical history at the site where Henry the Navigator's memory is preserved. Recent renovations transformed the on-site youth hostels into an exhibition center and cafeteria, restored the 16th-century church, and created parking areas outside the fort. Fishermen still come here to tempt fate and cast their long lines from the surrounding cliffs. ☎ *082/620140.* ☼ *May–Sept., daily 10–8:30; Oct.–Apr., daily 10–6:30.*

$–$$ ✕🏠 **Pousada do Infante.** Housed in a sprawling structure with a red-
★ tile roof, this pousada affords spectacular views of the sea and craggy rock cliffs. The moderate-size rooms are well appointed and have small balconies. The restaurant offers excellent fresh fish, good desserts, and more marvelous sea views. ⊠ *8650 Sagres,* ☎ *082/624222,* 🗚 *082/624225. 39 rooms. Restaurant, pool. AE, DC, MC, V.*

★ Cabo de São Vicente

There are spectacular views from Cabo de São Vicente (Cape St. Vincent), 6 km (4 mi) west of Sagres. This point, the most southwesterly tip of Europe, is sometimes called *o fim do mundo* (the end of the world). The lighthouse at Cabo de São Vicente is said to have the strongest reflectors in Europe, casting a beam some 96 km (60 mi) out to sea; it's open to the public.

Algarve Essentials

Getting Around

The main east–west highway in the Algarve is the two-lane N125, which extends from Vila Real de Santo António, on the Spanish border, to Sagres. This road doesn't run right along the coast, but turnoffs to beachside destinations are posted along the route. A four-lane motorway, the IP1/E1, several miles inland, runs parallel to the coast from the suspension bridge at the Spanish border west to Albufeira, where it joins the main road to Lisbon. Daily bus and rail service connects Lisbon with the major towns in the Algarve; trips take four to six hours.

TAP Air Portugal and Portugalia have daily flights to Faro, the capital of the Algarve, from Lisbon (a 45-minute trip; ☞ *also* Transportation *in* Portugal A to Z, *above*), and there are frequent flights to Faro from most European capitals.

Guided Tours

Organized guided bus tours of some of the more noteworthy villages and towns depart from Faro, Vilamoura, Albufeira, Portimão, and Lagos.

Visitor Information

Albufeira (⊠ Rua 5 de Outubro, ☎ 089/585279), **Armação de Pêrá** (⊠ Av. Marginal, ☎ 082/312145), **Faro** (⊠ Rua da Misericórdia 8/12, ☎ 089/803604; ⊠ airport, ☎ 089/818582), **Lagos** (⊠ Largo Marquês de Pombal, ☎ 082/763031), **Loulé** (⊠ Edifico do Castelo, ☎ 089463900), **Monte Gordo** (⊠ Av. Marginal, ☎ 081/544495), **Olhão** (⊠ Largo da Lagoa, ☎ 089/713936), **Portimão** (⊠ Largo 1 de Dezembro, ☎ 082/419131), **Praia da Rocha** (⊠ Av. Tomás Cabreira, ☎ 082/419132), **Silves** (⊠ Rua 25 de Abril, ☎ 082/442255), and **Tavira** (⊠ Rua da Galeria 9, ☎ 081/322511).

25 ROMANIA

BUCHAREST, THE BLACK SEA COAST AND DANUBE DELTA, TRANSYLVANIA

Though Romania can be a challenging destination, it is among the most beautiful countries in Eastern Europe. Its attractions are varied, from summer play on the Black Sea coast to winter skiing in the rugged Carpathian Mountains. The medieval towns and rural villages of Romania are among the least spoiled in Europe.

Romania, made up of the provinces of Walachia, Moldavia, and Transylvania, borders Ukraine, Moldova, Bulgaria, Serbia, and Hungary. With a population of 23 million, Romania is a Latin island in a sea of Slavs and Magyars—its people are the descendants of the Dacian tribe and of the Roman soldiers who garrisoned this province of the Roman Empire. Barbarian invasions, struggles against the Turks, the Austro-Hungarian domination of Transylvania, and a strong French cultural influence have all shaped Romanian culture. Famous natives of what is now Romania include Androcles (famed for his care of a lion), Romanian-born French playwright Eugène Ionesco, writer and Nobel Peace Prize winner Elie Wiesel, the modern sculptor Constantin Brancuşi, and the prominent 20th-century composer George Enescu.

Romania's largest metropolis, Bucharest, may appear unwelcoming, but its wide, tree-lined avenues and hidden charm can outweigh the effects of rows of drab buildings and depressing neighborhoods. The Romanian Riviera on the Black Sea enjoys unfailing popularity, as do the spectacular wildlife sanctuaries of the nearby Danube Delta. Transylvania is famous for the Dracula legend and its related sights, but the region is also home to Hungarian and German populations with distinctive folk traditions.

The overthrow of the Ceauşescu regime in December 1989 ushered in the country's shift toward Western-style democracy and a market economy. Such adversities as bread lines, food shortages, and empty store shelves have been replaced with rapidly rising prices, which trouble many Romanians and frustrate the current government.

Romania (România)

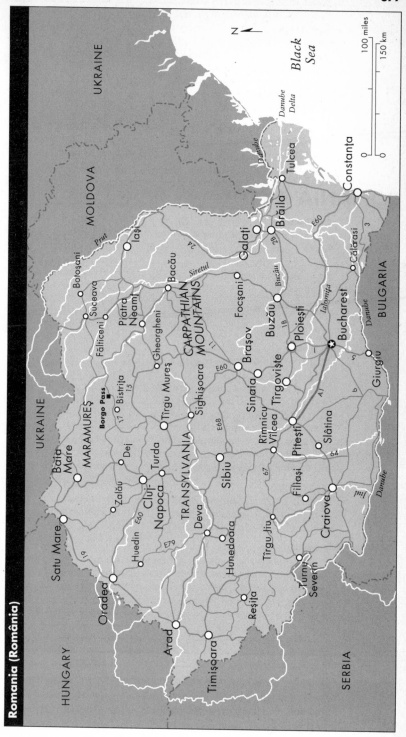

UKRAINE

HUNGARY

UKRAINE

MOLDOVA

Black
Sea

Danube
Delta

Tulcea

Constanța

Brăila

Galați

Danube

Satu Mare

Baia
Mare

MARAMUREȘ

Borgo Pass

Botoșani

Suceava

Fălticeni

Iași

Piatra
Neamț

Gheorgheni

Bacău

CARPATHIAN
MOUNTAINS

Focșani

Buzău

Ploiești

Bucharest

BULGARIA

Zalău

Dej

Bistrița

Tîrgu Mureș

Sighișoara

Brașov

Sinaia

Tîrgoviște

Giurgiu

Oradea

Huedin

Cluj-
Napoca

Turda

TRANSYLVANIA

Sibiu

Rîmnicu
Vîlcea

Pitești

Slatina

Călărași

Arad

Deva

Hunedoara

Tîrgu Jiu

Filiași

Craiova

Danube

Timișoara

Reșița

Turnu
Severin

SERBIA

Prut

Siretul

Buzău

Ialomița

Danube

Danube

Jiu

Black Sea

100 miles

150 km

As Romania is among the poorest countries in Europe, petty theft remains a widespread problem; try to conceal jewelry and valuables as best you can. Be sure to drink bottled water or mineral water *(apa minerala),* which is readily available. You should bring an emergency supply of toilet paper, a full first-aid kit, a flashlight for poorly lighted streets and corridors, and, in summer, insect repellent. While many pharmacies carry an assortment of Western medications and vitamins, most medical facilities do not meet Western standards.

Romania is likely to remain underexplored until the serious problems caused by the former Ceauşescu regime are resolved. In the meantime, you will experience a part of Europe that has largely eschewed the technological advances and social reforms of the late 20th century.

ROMANIA A TO Z

Customs

You may bring in a personal computer and printer, 2 cameras, 10 rolls of film, 1 small camcorder/video camera and VCR, 10 rolls of video film, a typewriter, binoculars, a radio/tape recorder, a small television set, a bicycle, a stroller, 200 cigarettes, 2 liters of liquor, and 4 liters of wine or beer. Gifts are permitted, though you may be charged duty on some electronic goods. Souvenirs and gifts may be taken out of Romania, provided their value not exceed 50% of the currency you have changed legally—so keep all receipts.

Dining

Bucharest is in the throes of a restaurant renaissance. French, German, Italian, Mexican, Middle Eastern, and Asian restaurants are thriving. Traditional Romanian foods are *mamaliga* (corn porridge often smothered with sour cream and cheese), *sarmale* (cabbage rolls filled with meat and rice), *ciorbă* (a slightly spicy and sour soup stock), and sheep-milk cheeses. Favored meats are usually pork or beef. Outside the capital, options are limited and some restaurants may not even have printed menus. In order to avoid being overcharged, ask for prices before you eat. Street vendors sell fragrant offerings like *covrigi* (giant pretzels) and roasted chestnuts.

MEALTIMES

Outside Bucharest and the Black Sea and Carpathian resorts, many restaurants will have stopped serving by 9 PM, although an increasing number have begun staying open until 11 PM or later.

RATINGS

Prices are per person and include first course, main course, and dessert. Because high inflation means local prices frequently change, ratings are given in U.S. dollars, which remain constant. Your bill will be in lei.

CATEGORY	COST
$$$$	over $30
$$$	$20–$30
$$	$10–$20
$	under $10

WHAT TO WEAR

Jacket and tie are advised for the best restaurants and business lunches and dinners. Casual dress is appropriate at other times.

Guided Tours

Guided tours run the gamut from chauffeured sight-seeing drives in Bucharest to more ambitious expeditions to the Danube Delta. A major travel agency and tour operator is **Oficiul National de Turism— ONT** (⊠ B-dul Gen. Magheru 7, Bucharest, ☎ 01/313–0474, 🖷 01/

312–2594; ⊠ Otopeni Airport; ⊠ Gara de Nord); office signs in most Romanian towns read AGENŢIA DE TURISM).

Language

If you speak a Romance language, Romanian is likely to sound pleasantly familiar. French is widely spoken and understood in Romanian cities, German and Russian less so. Romanians involved with the tourist industry usually speak English.

Lodging

The Romanian Tourism License and Control Department oversees hotel ranking and licensing, rating hotels with from one to five stars. Though accommodations have undergone major improvements, lodging is not Romania's forte. Prices are highly variable depending on booking arrangements. Prepaid arrangements through travel agencies abroad often entitle you to discounted prices. Some packages, such as fly-drive holidays, come with bed-and-breakfast accommodation vouchers. Most state-run facilities accept vouchers; in deluxe hotels you pay a little extra. You can also book accommodations directly with hotels (which may require reservations by fax) or through travel agencies. Avoid the cheap and often cheerless hotels used by many Romanians; you may encounter perilous conditions. Rooms in private homes, which can be booked through some private agencies, are a good alternative to hotels. Private citizens come to railway stations and offer spare rooms in their homes; use discretion and be prepared to bargain.

HOTELS

Standards of facilities, including plumbing and hot water, improve rapidly through the categories but may not be ideal even in expensive lodgings. Ask at the front desk when hot water will be available. Whatever class of property you choose, do not leave valuables in your room and, on departure, check your bill for unnecessary charges.

RATINGS

The following hotel price categories are for two people in a double room. Rates usually include breakfast. Because of inflation, ratings are given according to hard-currency equivalents. There is a dual price system in which foreigners are charged a much higher rate than Romanians; the higher price may not be displayed. Though the government has discouraged this practice, many hotels and museums continue to charge foreigners higher rates in order to survive. Room rates in Bucharest are much higher than those in the rest of the country.

CATEGORY	BUCHAREST	OUTSIDE BUCHAREST
$$$$	over $200	over $120
$$$	$125–$200	$80–$120
$$	$70–$125	$50–$80
$	under $70	under $50

RENTALS

Rustic cottages may be rented at such ski resorts as Sinaia and Poina Braşov. Details are available from Romanian tourist offices abroad or local offices in Bucharest (☞ Contacts and Resources *in* Bucharest Essentials, *below*).

Mail

Postal codes exist but are not used in Romania. Rates increase regularly, so check before you post.

Money Matters

COSTS

Prices in Western-style establishments can be as high as those in Western Europe, though typical Romanian restaurants and hotels offer reasonable costs. Prices of basic items are often as high as those in the West.

CREDIT CARDS
Though major credit cards are now relatively commonplace in large hotels, restaurants, and shops, they are not accepted in most independent establishments or in the countryside, nor are traveler's checks.

CURRENCY
The unit of currency is the leu (plural lei). There are coins of 20, 50, and 100 lei. Banknotes come in denominations of 200, 500, 1,000, 5,000, 10,000, 50,000, and 100,000 lei (introduced in 1998). Do not expect to be given change of less than 100 lei. Inflation and frequent price increases are expected to continue; costs are therefore best calculated in convertible hard currencies such as U.S. dollars, German marks, or Swiss francs. As the U.S. dollar is the most readily negotiated currency, it is a good idea always to keep some with you, especially in smaller denominations. At press time (summer 1999), the official exchange rate was approximately 15,503 lei to the U.S. dollar, 10,541 lei to the Canadian dollar, and 24,215 lei to the pound sterling.

An increasing number of licensed *casă de schimb* (exchange offices) compete to offer rates far better than the official rate available at banks, the airport, the train station, or in hotels. Do not deal with the dangerous black market. Retain all exchange receipts, as you may need to prove your money was changed legally, and you must produce these receipts to exchange lei back into hard currency upon departure from Romania. By law, foreigners must pay for everything except air tickets in lei, though hard currency is widely accepted in most hotels and in some restaurants. You may not import or export lei.

SAMPLE PRICES
Museum admission usually costs between 10,000 and 50,000 lei; a bottle of imported beer in a restaurant, around 30,000 lei; a 2-km (1-mi) taxi ride, about 25,000 lei.

TIPPING
Most Romanians do not tip, but it is generally expected of foreigners. A 10% tip is welcomed and appreciated (especially by taxi drivers).

National Holidays
January 1–2 (New Year's); May 1 (Orthodox Easter Monday and Labor Day); December 1 (National Day); December 25–26 (Christmas); December 31 (New Year's Eve).

Opening and Closing Times
Banks are open weekdays 9–12:30. Exchange office hours vary, but most are open weekdays 9–7 and Saturday 9–1; some are open until 7 on Saturday and 1 on Sunday. **Museums** are usually open 10–6, closed on Monday (and sometimes Tuesday). **Shops** are generally open weekdays 10–6. Most state-owned shops close at 2 on Saturday, though private shops stay open until 5 on Saturday and 2 on Sunday.

Shopping
An influx of private shops has introduced additional style and choice to Romania. Bargains can be found on Oriental-style and flat-weave rugs, wool sweaters, crystal, porcelain, and glassware. Traditional folk crafts—painted eggs, handmade lace, and embroidered items—are sold in *Artizanat* stores, in shopping areas and museums. Keep receipts of all purchases, regardless of their legal export status.

Telephoning

COUNTRY CODE

The country code for Romania is 40. When dialing Romania from outside the country, drop the initial 0 from the regional code.

INTERNATIONAL CALLS

Direct-dial international calls can be made from hotels, the train station, the phone company building on Bucharest's Calea Victoriei, and local post offices (☞ Local Calls, *below*). To place long-distance calls out of Romania, dial 00, then the country code and number. To place a call from Romania via an **AT&T** USADirect international operator, dial 01–800–4288; for **MCI**, dial 01–800–1800; for **Sprint**, dial 01–800–0877. For international information, dial 971.

LOCAL CALLS

While the Romanian telephone system is old and overextended, it has become much easier to use in the past few years. Most public telephones are orange and require a phone card, which can be purchased at the post office. Older, coin-operated telephones at roadsides, airports, and train stations usually work only for local calls; these phones use the obscure 20-lei coins, although some require 50- or 100-lei coins. You can also make local or long-distance calls at the post office. In larger towns, private business offices offer phone, fax, and telex services.

The area code for Bucharest is 1, and telephone numbers in the city have 2, 3, 4, 6, or 7 as a prefix, followed by a six-digit number. Long-distance calls within Romania should be prefixed with a 0 followed by the area code for the county or region. For information in Romania, your hotel's front desk or phone book is often your best bet. In Bucharest, dial 9; for internal long distance, dial 991; for local information, dial 951 (the operators sometimes speak English).

Transportation

BY BOAT

Regular passenger services operate on various sections of the Danube; tickets are available at the ports (e.g., Giurgiu, Turnu Severin).

BY BUS

Bus stations, or *autogara,* are usually near train stations. Buses are generally crowded and far from luxurious. Tickets go on sale at stations up to two hours before departure.

BY CAR

An International Driver's Permit is required for all drivers from outside the country for stays of more than 30 days.

Car Rentals. Avis has offices at Bucharest's Otopeni Airport (☎ 01/230–0054) and in various hotels. **Budget** is in the Hotel Dorobanţi (✉ Calea Dorobantilor 1–7, Bucharest, ☎ 01/210–2867) and at Otopeni Airport. **Hertz** (✉ Regina Maria 1, ☎ 01/337–3932) is also at the airport and in the Hotel Dorobanţi (☞ *above*).

Gasoline. State gas stations, usually at the edge of towns on main roads, remain scarce. The many new private gas stations charge a bit more than the state stations. Most gas stations sell regular (90-octane), premium (98-octane), *motorina* (diesel), and *fară plumb* (unleaded). Prices remain low compared to those of Western Europe.

Road Conditions. A network of main roads covers the country, though the majority only allow for a single lane in each direction. Potholes are common, and a few roads are not paved at all. Farm machinery, slow-moving trucks, horses and carts, and herds of animals often block roads. At night cars without headlights often drive along poorly lit or unlit roads, an enduring legacy of the Ceauşescu regime.

Rules of the Road. Drive on the right and observe the speed limits: 40 kph (37 mph) in built-up areas and 80 kph–90 kph (50 mph–55 mph) on all other roads. Traffic signs are the same as those used in most of Western Europe. Driving after drinking any alcohol is prohibited. Seat belts are obligatory in the front seat of vehicles, with the exception of taxis. Spot checks are frequent; police can levy on-the-spot fines. Most fines are minimal, but the seat belt fine is approximately $50.

BY PLANE

Tarom operates daily flights to major Romanian cities from Bucharest's Baneasa Airport. In summer additional flights link Constanţa with major cities, including Cluj and Iaşi. Be prepared for delays and cancellations. For domestic flights, go to Piaţa Victoriei 1, Bucharest (☎ 01/659–4125). International flights can be booked at the central reservations office (✉ Str. Brezoianu 10, Bucharest, ☎ 01/615–0499 or 01/613–4295, FAX 01/613–0363) and at some major hotels.

BY TRAIN

Romanian Railways (CFR) operates an extensive network of trains. *Rapid* and *accelerat* trains are the fastest, with limited stops; *personal* trains are slow and have many stops. *Expres* designates special international express trains, such as the Dacia Expres to Vienna. First class is worth the extra cost. A *vagon de dormit* (sleeper) or cheap *cuşeta*, with bunk beds, is available on longer journeys. It is always advisable to reserve a seat, but you cannot buy the ticket itself at a train station more than one hour before departure. If your reserved seat is already occupied, it may have been sold twice. To buy a ticket ahead of time in Bucharest, contact either a travel agency or the CFR Advance Booking Office (✉ Str. Brezoianu 10, ☎ 01/614–5528). You will be charged a small commission, but the process is less time-consuming than buying your ticket at the station.

Visas

U.S. citizens need only a valid passport to enter Romania for up to 30 days, but border guards may try to extort money from you anyway; be firm. If you're traveling on a British, Australian, or New Zealand passport, you must pay $31 for a 30-day tourist card when you cross the border. Canadians must pay $33. There is no application, you don't need any photos—just hand the border guard your money. They prefer U.S. dollars but will accept British pounds or German marks.

Visitor Information

Oficiul de Promovare a Turismului—OPT (Romanian Tourism Promotion Office; ✉ Str. Apolodor 17, 5th floor, Bucharest, ☎ 094/655011).

Weather

Bucharest is at its best during the spring and fall. The Black Sea resorts open in mid- to late May and close at the end of September. Developed ski resorts in the Carpathians, such as Poiana Braşov and Sinaia, are increasingly popular in winter months.

CLIMATE

The Romanian climate is temperate and generally free of extremes, but snow as late as April is not unknown, and the lowlands can be very hot in midsummer. The following are the average daily maximum and minimum temperatures for Bucharest.

Jan.	34F	1C	May	74F	23C	Sept.	78F	25C
	19	– 7		51	10		52	11
Feb.	38F	4C	June	81F	27C	Oct.	65F	18C
	23	– 5		57	14		43	6
Mar.	50F	10C	July	86F	30C	Nov.	49F	10C
	30	– 1		60	16		35	2
Apr.	64F	18C	Aug.	85F	30C	Dec.	39F	4C
	41	5		59	15		26	– 3

BUCHAREST

According to legend the capital's name comes from one of the first inhabitants of the area, a shepherd named Bucur. The name Bucureşti was first used officially in 1459 by Vlad Ţepeş, the real-life Count Dracula. Two centuries later, this citadel on the Dîmboviţa River became the capital of Walachia, and after another 200 years, it was named the capital of Romania. Bucureşti gradually developed into a center of trade and gracious living, with ornate and varied architecture, landscaped parks, busy, winding streets, and wide boulevards. The city was known before World War II as the Paris of the Balkans, but much of its glory now lies buried under decades of neglect and political turmoil.

Nicolae Ceauşescu's megalomaniacal drive to redevelop the capital involved the forced displacement of thousands of people and the demolition of many priceless early houses, churches, synagogues, and other irreplaceable buildings. Piaţa Unirii (Unirii Plaza) was the hub of his enormously expensive and impractical vision. Lined with ornate, gilded fountains, the lengthy Bulevardul Unirii leads west from the plaza to the enormous, unfinished Palace of Parliament, still flanked by construction cranes. The massive diversion of resources weakened the city's infrastructure, but now efforts are underway to remedy the situation. Bucharest nevertheless contains a good selection of places of historical interest, cafés, cinemas, and performance halls.

Exploring Bucharest

The high-rise Hotel Inter-Continental dominates the main intersection at Piaţa Universităţii; northward, up the main shopping streets Bulevardul Nicolae Bălcescu and Bulevardul General Magheru, only the occasional older building survives. Along Calea Victoriei, however, you can savor Bucharest's grander past, especially at the former royal palace opposite the Romanian Senate (formerly Communist Party headquarters) in Piaţa Revoluţiei and near the beautifully restored domed National Library. South of Bulevardul Regina Elisabeta along Calea Victoriei is the busy Lipscani trading district, a remnant of the Old City.

Historic Bucharest

Numbers in the margin correspond to points of interest on the Bucharest map.

❹ Biserica din Curtea Veche (Church of the Princely Court). The oldest church in Bucharest is ocher with cross-hatched onion domes. This important center of worship was founded in the 16th century beside the Princely Court. ⊠ *Str. Selari.*

❺ Curtea Veche (Princely Court). The Princely Court now houses **Muzeul Curtea Veche–Palatul Voievodal**, a museum exhibiting the recently renovated remains of the palace built by Vlad Ţepeş during the 15th century. Tours of the court provide insight into the legend of Dracula. ⊠ *Str. Iuliu Maniu 31.*

Bucharest (București)

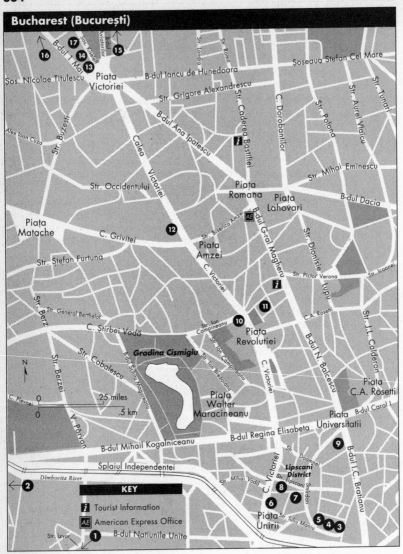

Arcul de Triumf, **16**

Ateneul Român, **11**

Biserica din Curtea Veche, **4**

Biserica Stavropoleos, **7**

Curtea Veche, **5**

Hanul lui Manuc, **3**

Lipscani, **8**

Muzeul Colecțiilor de Artă, **12**

Muzeul de Artă al României, **10**

Muzeul de Istorie al orasului Bucurestului, **9**

Muzeul de Știinţe Naturale Grigore Antipa, **13**

Muzeul National de Istorie, **6**

Muzeul Satului Romanesc, **17**

Muzeul Ţăranului Român, **14**

Muzeul Zambaccian, **15**

Palatul Cotroceni, **2**

Palatul Parlamentului, **1**

❸ **Hanul lui Manuc** (Manuc's Inn). A small hotel and tolerable restaurant operate out of this renovated inn, built in 1808 by a wealthy Armenian merchant named Manuc around a courtyard in traditional Romanian fashion. The 1812 Russian-Turkish Peace Treaty was signed here. ⊠ *Str. Iuliu Maniu 62–64,* ☎ *01/613–1415.*

★ ❷ **Palatul Cotroceni** (Cotroceni Palace). On the Dîmbovița River corniche near the Botanical Gardens, this grand building was once the royal residence. Reservations are required for visits. The **Cotroceni National Museum** is in the lower level; ask what's on display here. ⊠ *B-dul Gen. 1,* ☎ *01/221–1200.*

★ ❶ **Palatul Parlamentului** (Parliament Palace). This mammoth structure is among the largest buildings in the world; it is as deep as it is high. Originally meant to house Ceaușescu and his government offices, the unfinished structure is currently the home of the Romanian parliament. The building is closed to visitors during government functions. ⊠ *South entrance, Calea 13 Septembrie.* ☉ *Daily 10–4.*

Lipscani District

❼ **Biserica Stavropoleos** (Stavropoleos Church). This small, exquisite church combines late-Renaissance and Byzantine styles with elements of Romanian folk art. Inside are superb wood and stone carvings and an ornate iconostasis (the painted screen that partitions off the choir). The inside walls of the church, covered with beautiful frescoes that had turned black from age and pollution, are currently undergoing extensive restoration. ⊠ *Str. Stavropoleos.*

❽ **Lipscani.** This district is home to a bustling bazaar of narrow streets, open stalls, and small artisans' shops. In Hanul cu Tei, off Strada Lipscani, you'll find many galleries and shops dealing in traditional crafts and gifts. ⊠ *Str. Lipscani.*

❾ **Muzeul de Istorie al orasului Bucurestului** (Bucharest History Museum). The artifacts, costumes, and pictures in this modern museum capture the rich history of Romania's capital from ancient times to World War I. ⊠ *B-dul I. C. Brătianu,* ☎ *01/315–6858.* ☉ *Tues.–Sun. 10–5.*

❻ **Muzeul Național de Istorie** (National History Museum). This vast, somewhat dreary museum contains an enormous collection dating from the Neolithic period to the 1920s. The Treasury has a stunning trove of gold objects and precious stones—royal crowns, weapons, plates, and jewelry—dating from the 4th millennium BC through the 20th century. ⊠ *Calea Victoriei 12,* ☎ *01/315–7056.* ☉ *Treasury, Tues.–Sun. 10–5, last ticket 4 PM; museum, Wed.–Sun. 10–4.*

Around Bucharest

⑯ **Arcul de Triumf.** The Arcul de Triumf was built in 1922 to commemorate the Allied victory in World War I. Originally constructed of wood and stucco, it was rebuilt during the 1930s and carved by some of Romania's most talented sculptors. ⊠ *Head of Șos. Kiseleff.*

⑪ **Ateneul Român** (Romanian Athenaeum). The restored Ateneul concert hall, with its Baroque dome and Greek columns, has survived much upheaval since 1888; it is still home to the George Enescu Philharmonic Orchestra. ⊠ *Str. Franklin 1,* ☎ *01/315–6875.*

⑫ **Muzeul Colecțiilor de Artă** (Museum of Art Collections). This institution, an affiliate of the National Art Museum, houses an impressive collection of Romanian Art from the 19th and 20th centuries as well as carpets, furniture, and icons painted on glass. ⊠ *Calea Victoriei 111,* ☎ *01/650–6132.* 🎫 *Free Wed.* ☉ *Wed.–Sun. 10–6; last admission at 5.*

🔟 **Muzeul de Artă al României** (National Art Museum). Sculptures by Brancuşi and paintings from the Brueghel school are among the works here. During ongoing restoration, only small exhibits are on display; the major part of the original collection can be viewed at the Muzeul Colecţiilor de Artă (☞ *above*). ☒ *Calea Victoriei 49,* ☎ *01/315–5193.* 🎟 *Free Wed.* ☺ *Wed.–Sun. 10–6; last admission at 5.*

⓭ **Muzeul de Ştiinţe Naturale Grigore Antipa** (Natural History Museum). Natural wildlife exhibits from around Romania and the rest of the world are on display in realistic settings. ☒ *Şos. Kiseleff 1,* ☎ *01/312–8863.* ☺ *Tues.–Sun. 10–5.*

★ ☙ ⓱ **Muzeul Satului Romanesc** (Romanian Village Museum). This fabulous open-air museum near Herăstrău Lake is home to more than 300 representations of folk style and architecture taken from peasant villages of different regions and periods. ☒ *Şos. Kiseleff 28,* ☎ *01/222–9110.* ☺ *Oct.–mid-May, daily 8–4; mid-May–Sept., daily 9–7.*

★ ⓮ **Muzeul Ţăranului Român** (Museum of the Romanian Peasant). Peasant costumes, icons, carpets, and other artifacts from rural life are vividly displayed, along with interiors from two 19th-century wooden churches. ☒ *Şos. Kiseleff 3,* ☎ *01/650–5360.* ☺ *Tues.–Sun. 10–6.*

⓯ **Muzeul Zambaccian** (Zambaccian Museum). This unassuming, though lovely, Romanian home contains an astounding collection of art: Works by Romanian artists hang alongside paintings by Cézanne, Matisse, Pissarro, and Renoir—all gathered by Armenian-Romanian businessman K. H. Zambaccian. ☒ *Str. Muzeul Zambaccian 21,* ☎ *01/212–1919.* 🎟 *Free Wed.* ☺ *Wed.–Sun. 10–6.*

Dining and Lodging

Bucharest's restaurant boom has given rise to a host of delightfully decorated establishments that offer enjoyable, inexpensive fare. You'll find food kiosks, cafés, grills, fast-food chains, and restaurants sprinkled throughout the city. Be sure to check your bill, as it is not uncommon for restaurants to try to overcharge foreigners. Some places will serve wine and water only by the bottle and not by the glass. Romanian coffee is served with grounds; instant coffee is called *ness*.

More private hotels are appearing throughout Bucharest. Competition has prompted a boost in service and an improvement in amenities. Hotels fill up quickly during the tourist season and expositions; book early if you can. For details and price-category definitions, *see* Dining *and* Lodging *in* Romania A to Z, *above.*

$$$$ ✕ **Korea House.** You can sample authentic spicy food in this highly regarded Asian restaurant. The fish and seafood are particular favorites; try the squid in a piquant brown sauce. ☒ *Str. Cimpina 53,* ☎ *01/666–5283. No credit cards.*

$$$$ ✕ **Velvet.** Delicately prepared lobster, pheasant, duck, and lamb await you at Velvet, one of the first restaurants in Bucharest to offer haute cuisine in a formal setting. ☒ *Ştirbei Vodă 2–4,* ☎ *01/311–1736. Reservations essential. AE, DC, MC, V.*

$$$ ✕ **La Premiera.** Just behind the National Theater, this restaurant of-
★   fers a superb mix of international cuisine. The walls are decorated with scenes of Bucharest during the 1920s and '30s. ☒ *Str. Tudor Arghezi 16,* ☎ *01/312–4397. Reservations essential. AE, MC, DC, V.*

$$–$$$ ✕ **Café de la Joie.** This café hidden in the basement of a small apart-
★   ment building on a tiny street behind the Bucharest History Museum is perhaps the most congenial restaurant in Bucharest. The menu changes daily, offering freshly prepared delicacies like fondue and

shrimp quiche. ⊠ *Str. Biblotecci 4,* ☎ *01/315–0937. Reservations essential. No credit cards.*

$$ ✕ **Bistro Atheneu.** A favorite among both Romanians and expatriates,
★   this Paris-style bistro prepares traditional Romanian dishes such as liver in mushroom sauce, steak, and grilled chicken. If the bistro is full, walk around the corner to its sister restaurant, Taifas (⊠ Str. G. Clemenceau 6, ☎ 01/311–3204). ⊠ *Str. Episcopiei 3,* ☎ *01/313–4900. Reservations essential. No credit cards.*

$$ ✕ **Piccolo Mondo.** This haven of Lebanese cuisine serves kebabs, hum-
★   mus, tabouleh, *fettouche* (a flavorful Middle Eastern salad), spicy chicken, and a variety of other Middle Eastern dishes. A few Italian and Romanian items are also available. ⊠ *Str. Clucerului,* ☎ *01/223–2225. MC, V.*

$$ ✕ **Sydney.** This bar and restaurant offers grilled meats, a salad bar, generous Mexican dishes, and the best cheesecake in Bucharest. There is a wide choice of drinks, including many exotic cocktails and imported beers. ⊠ *Calea Victoriei 222,* ☎ *01/312–9670. AE, V.*

$–$$ ✕ **Casa Veche.** In warm weather, this restaurant's convivial patio is the perfect spot for enjoying wood-oven pizza topped with spinach and ricotta or *quattro formaggi* (Brie, mozzarella, Camembert, and goat cheese). ⊠ *Str. Georges Enescu 15–17,* ☎ *01/312–5816. Reservations essential. AE, MC, V.*

$$$$ 🏨 **Athenée Palace Hilton.** The spacious rooms at this historic hotel are fresh and immaculate; the service is first-rate. ⊠ *Str. Episcopiei 1–3,* ☎ *01/315–1212,* ℻ *01/315–2121. 257 rooms, 15 suites. 3 restaurants. AE, DC, MC, V.*

$$$$ 🏨 **Hotel Sofitel.** On the edge of the city en route to the airport, the
★   Sofitel is a Western oasis in Bucharest. ⊠ *B-dul Expoziţiei 2,* ☎ *01/223–4000,* ℻ *01/222–4650. 91 rooms, 12 suites. 2 restaurants. AE, DC, MC, V.*

$$$ 🏨 **Lido.** In the center of the city, this prewar hotel has been privatized and renovated to offer comfortable rooms and good facilities. ⊠ *B-dul Gen. Magheru 5,* ☎ *01/614–4930,* ℻ *01/312–6544. 107 rooms, 12 suites. Restaurant, pool. AE, DC, MC, V.*

$$ 🏨 **Casa Victor.** Unlike some drab, state-run establishments, this sim-
★   ple hotel near the Arcul de Triumf offers room rates that include cable television, a refrigerator, and a generous breakfast. ⊠ *Str. Emanoil Porumbaru 44,* ☎ *01/222–91830,* ℻ *01/222–5723. 12 rooms, 8 suites. Restaurant. No credit cards.*

$$ 🏨 **Hotel Bulevard.** Across the street from the impressive Military Cir-
★   cle building, this welcoming hotel has graciously decorated rooms that flaunt French Louis XIV furniture and dark red curtains. ⊠ *B-dul Regina Elisabeta 21,* ☎ *01/615–3300,* ℻ *01/312–3923. 82 rooms, 7 suites. Restaurant, bar. No credit cards.*

$ 🏨 **Triumf.** On a small park near the Arcul de Triumf, this economical, comfortable hotel once served the Communist elite. The more expensive rooms are mini-apartments. ⊠ *Şos. Kiseleff 12,* ☎ *01/222–3172,* ℻ *01/223–2411. 97 rooms, 3 suites. Restaurant. MC, V.*

Nightlife and the Arts

The Arts

The **Romanian Athenaeum** (⊠ Str. Franklin 1, ☎ 01/315–6875) is Bucharest's concert hall, where the George Enescu Philharmonic Orchestra performs regularly. Inside the **Teatrul Naţional** (National Theater; ⊠ Piaţa Universitatii, ☎ 01/614–1717), you can see performances by the Ion Dacian Operetta. The **Opera Română** (⊠ B-dul Mihail Kogălniceanu 70, ☎ 01/314–6980) stages good operas. At the **Radio**

Hall (✉ Str. Gen. Berthelot 62–64, ☎ 01/222–4714) you can hear classical music performed by local and visiting musicians.

Nightlife

As Romania's nightlife continues to blossom, new bars and clubs are opening throughout the capital. For a Romanian feel, head to the Lipscani district and the subterranean **Club A** (✉ Str. Blanari 14, ☎ 01/315–6853), where university students crowd the dance floor and enjoy inexpensive beer. **The Harp** (✉ Str. Bibescu Vodă 1, ☎ 01/222–9473) Irish pub, a favorite of the Bucharest expatriate community, serves a variety of imported beers. For a lively Romanian bar with good music, try the **Laptaria Enache** (Milk Bar; ✉ Teatrul Național, ☎ 01/315–8508) after 11 PM. If dancing is part of your weekend plan, head to the **Salsa You and Me** (✉ Str. 11 Iunie 51, ☎ 01/335–5640), where an international crowd moves to a lively Latin beat. The new hot spot, **Terminus** (✉ Str. George Enescu 54A, ☎ 01/659–7606), attracts an animated group of foreigners and Romanians.

One of the older and better known of Bucharest's 16 casinos is the **Casino Victoria** (✉ Calea Victoriei 174, ☎ 01/659–4913), which also offers a dinner show. Gambling is available in both dollars and lei; admission and drinks are free.

All foreign films in Bucharest are shown in their original language with Romanian subtitles. One good theater is **Cinema Patria** (✉ B-dul Gen. Magheru 12–14, ☎ 01/211–8625). Just down the street is the clean **Cinema Scala** (✉ B-dul Gen. Magheru 2–3, ☎ 01/211–0372).

If you cannot survive in Romania without e-mail, head to the internet center in the **Institut Français** (French Institute; ✉ B-dul Dacia 77, ☎ 01/210–0224), which also houses a charming restaurant, a French film theater, and a space for art exhibits.

Shopping

You may legally export art bought at the **Apollo** gallery, in the National Theater building (☞ The Arts *in* Nightlife and the Arts, *above*) or in the galleries of the fascinating **Hanul cu Tei** (✉ off Str. Lipscani).

For local folk arts and crafts, look for *Artizanat* stores, which specialize in embroidered decorations, dolls, masks, and other crafts made by Romanian peasants. Be sure to consider the carpets, ceramics, and figurines in the **Magazin Amintiri** (✉ Str. Gabroveni 20) in the Lipscani district. Try the Artizanat store in the **Muzeul Satului Romanesc** (Romanian Village Museum; ✉ Şos. Kiseleff 28, ☎ 01/222–9110) or in the **Muzeul Țăranului Român** (Museum of the Romanian Peasant; ✉ Şos. Kiseleff 3, ☎ 01/650–5360).

Romania is well known for its handwoven carpets. For export they must be purchased from an authorized retailer such as **Covoare** (✉ B-dul Unirii 13, ☎ 01/336–2174).

Crystal, porcelain, and china can be great values in Romania. **Sticerom S.A.** (✉ Str. Selari 9–11, ☎ 01/315–7504, and Str. Soarelui 3–5, ☎ 01/314–4066) specializes in magnificent items at unbelievably low prices.

For a truly unique shopping experience, explore the department store **Magizinul Unirea** (✉ B-dul Unirii), a Communist-era labyrinth of counters and racks selling everything from CDs to carpets. In contrast, the **World Trade Center** (✉ B-dul Expoziției 2) is a small version of a Western shopping mall.

The main food market is **Piaţa Amzei,** which offers a variety of cheeses, fruits, and flowers and provides a glimpse of animated Romanians bargaining for food.

Bucharest Essentials

Arriving and Departing

BY CAR

Three main routes lead into the city—E70 from the Hungarian border to the west, E60 via Braşov from the north, and E70/E85 from Bulgaria and the south. Streets have few signs and many are one-way.

BY PLANE

All international flights to Romania land at Bucharest's **Otopeni Airport** (☎ 01/230–0042), 16 km (9 mi) north of the city.

Between the Airport and Downtown. Express **Bus** 783 leaves the airport every 30 minutes between 7 AM and 10 PM, stopping in the main squares before terminating in Piaţa Unirii. The journey takes an hour and costs 6,000 lei round-trip. A shuttle service connects the airport to the center of Bucharest: For $10 a person, **Sky Services** (☎ 01/232–9691) takes passengers to Bucharest's main hotels and the train station. Your hotel can arrange transport by **car** from the airport. **Taxi** drivers at the airport seek business aggressively and usually demand payment in dollars; the cost is about $20–$30 with tip.

BY TRAIN

There are five main stations in Bucharest; international lines operate from **Gara de Nord** (✉ B-dul Gara de Nord, ☎ 01/952). For tickets and information, go to the **CFR Advance Booking Office** (✉ Str. Brezoianu 10, ☎ 01/614–5528).

Getting Around

Bucharest is spacious and sprawling. Though the old heart of the city and the two main arteries running the length of it are best explored on foot, long, wide avenues and vast squares make some form of transportation necessary. It is generally safe on the streets at night, but watch out for potholes and vehicles without headlights.

BY BUS, TRAM, AND TROLLEY BUS

Surface transit may sometimes be uncomfortable and crowded, but service is extensive. A one-way ticket can be purchased for 1,400 lei from kiosks near bus stops or from tobacconists; validate your ticket when you board. There are also *abonaments* (day and week passes). You can pay your fare on board the more expensive **maxi taxis** (minibuses that stop on request) and **express buses.** The system shuts down at midnight, though buses become scarce around 11 PM.

BY SUBWAY

Three subway lines serve the city. Change is available from kiosks inside stations. The present price is 3,300 lei for one round-trip ticket. The system closes at 11 PM.

BY TAXI

While you can hail a taxi in the street, you'll get better taxi rates if you call a dispatcher at ☎ 01/941, 945, 953, or 985. Some operators may speak English, but it might be easier to ask the staff at your hotel or a restaurant to call for you. A taxi ride is relatively inexpensive; nevertheless, you should negotiate a price before getting in or ask the driver to turn on the meter.

Contacts and Resources

U.S. (✉ Tudor Arghezi, ☎ 01/210–4042). **U.K.** (✉ Str. J. Michelet 24, ☎ 01/312–0303). **Canadian** (✉ Str. N. Iorga 36, ☎ 01/222–9845). **Australian** (Honorary Consular Section, ✉ 124A Str. Mihai Eminescu, 3rd floor, Apt. 8, Bucharest, ☎ 041/210–6027).

Police (☎ 955). **Ambulance** (☎ 961). **Fire** (☎ 981). Each sector of Bucharest has a 24-hour pharmacy; ask at your hotel or call ☎ 961.

Carpatours (✉ Ion Mihalache 16, ☎ 01/311–0509). **National Tourism Office—ONT** (✉ B-dul Gen. Magheru 7, Bucharest, ☎ 01/313–0474, FAX 01/312–2594).

Bucharest Central Post Office (✉ Matei Millo 10, ☎ 01/614–4054).

Magellan Tourism (✉ B-dul Gen. Magheru 12–14, ☎ 01/211–9650, FAX 01/210–4903). **Medair Travel and Tourism** (✉ Str. N. Bălcescu 16, ☎ 01/312–0699, FAX 01/312–7033). **National Tourism Office—ONT** (☞ Guided Tours, *above*.) **Romantic Travel** (✉ Str. Mamulari 4, ☎ 01/310–0401, ☎ FAX 01/312–3056).

Oficiul de Promovare a Turismului—OPT (Romanian Tourist Promotion Office; ✉ Str. Apolodor 17, 5th Floor, Bucharest, ☎ 094/655–011). Front desks in main hotels also dispense brochures and information.

THE BLACK SEA COAST AND DANUBE DELTA

The southeastern Dobrogea region, only 45 minutes by air from Bucharest (210 km/130 mi by road), has been important throughout Romania's long history. Within a clearly defined area are the historic port of Constanţa; the Romanian Riviera; the Murfatlar vineyards; Roman, Greek, and earlier ruins; and the Danube Delta, which has become one of Europe's leading wildlife sanctuaries. The rapid development of the resorts and increasing interest in the delta region have led to improvement of tourist facilities and transport.

Constanţa

Romania's second-largest city has the busy, polyglot flavor characteristic of so many seaports. The poet Ovid was exiled here from Rome in AD 8; a statue of him presides over one of the city's squares.

Famous for its large mosaic floor, the **Edificiu Roman cu Mozaic** (✉ Piaţa Ovidiu 1) is a Roman complex of warehouses and shops from the 4th century. The **Parcul Arheologic** (Archaeology Park; ✉ B-dul Republicii) contains artifacts from the 3rd and 4th centuries, including the remains of Roman baths. Modern attractions in Constanţa include the **Acvariul** (Aquarium; ✉ Str. Februarie 16) and the **Delfinariul** (Dolphinarium; ✉ B-dul Mamaia 265).

The **Muzeul Naţional de Istorie şi Arheologie** (National History and Archaeological Museum) displays statues from the Neolithic Hamangian culture (4000–3000 BC) as well as Greek and Roman artifacts. ✉ Piaţa Ovidiu 12, ☎ 041/618763. ☉ Tues.–Sun. 10–6.

$$$ ✕ **Cazinou.** The turn-of-the-century former casino near the aquarium is ornately decorated. You'll find an adjoining bar by the sea; seafood

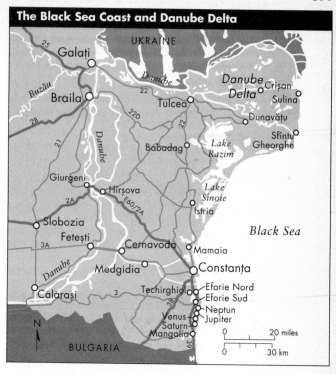

The Black Sea Coast and Danube Delta

dishes are the house specialties. ✉ *Str. Februarie 16,* ☎ *041/617416. No credit cards.*

$$ ✕ **Veneţia.** A variety of pasta dishes emerges from the kitchen of this
★ friendly Italian restaurant right off Piaţa Ovidiu. ✉ *Str. Mircea cel Bu-trin 5,* ☎ *041/617390. No credit cards.*

$$$ ⊞ **Palace.** Near the city's historic center, this gracious renovated hotel
has a good restaurant. A terrace overlooks the sea and the tourist port
of Tomis. ✉ *Str. Remus Opreanu 5–7,* ☎ *041/614696,* FAX *041/617532. 102 rooms, 9 suites. Restaurant. No credit cards.*

Eforie Nord, Neptun, Jupiter, Venus, Saturn, and Mangalia

A string of seaside resorts lies just south of Constanţa. Eforie Nord is
an up-to-date thermal treatment center; named to evoke the coast's Greco-
Roman past, Neptun, Jupiter, Venus, and Saturn were built during the
1960s. The old port of Mangalia is the southernmost resort.

You can take excursions from the seaside resorts to the **Podgorile Mur-fatlar** (Murfatlar Vineyards) for wine tasting. Visits to the ruins of the
Roman town at **Trophaeum Trajani** (Trajan's Trophy) can also be arranged.

$$$ ✕⊞ **Panoramic.** Seaside rooms in this beachfront hotel have magnif-
★ icent views. The restaurant offers good Romanian cuisine. ✉ *Olimp–Neptun,* ☎ *041/731356. 418 rooms. Restaurant, pool. AE, MC, V.*

$ ⊞ **Moldova.** One of many inexpensive hotels near the beach, Moldova
has somewhat run-down rooms, but they are clean and the staff is
friendly. ✉ *Olimp–Neptun,* ☎ *041/731916. 466 rooms. Restaurant. No credit cards.*

Mamaia

The largest of the Black Sea resort areas, Mamaia is on a strip of land
bordered on one side by fine Black Sea beaches and on the other by

the fresh waters of Mamaia Lake. All the resorts along this stretch of the coast have high-rise modern apartments, villas, restaurants, nightclubs, and discos. There are early morning sea-fishing expeditions as well as cruises down the coast to Mangalia and along the new channel that links the Danube with the Black Sea near Constanţa.

Just 60 km (37 mi) north of Mamaia is **Istria,** which was founded in 600 BC by Greek merchants from Miletus. There are traces of early Christian churches, baths, and even entire neighborhoods here.

Between Mamaia and the Danube Delta town of Tulcea lies **Babadag.** According to local legend, Jason and the Argonauts cast anchor here during their search for the mythical Golden Fleece.

$$$ ☒ **Rex.** A former residence of King Carol, this is the largest and grand-
★   est of all the hotels in Mamaia. The rooms are spacious and clean, and the staff is very attentive. ⊠ *Mamaia,* ☎ *041/831595,* ☒ *041/831690. 90 rooms. Restaurant, pool. AE, DC, MC, V.*

$ ☒ **Lido.** This hotel stands next to an outdoor pool near the beach at the north end of Mamaia's resort district. ⊠ *Mamaia,* ☎ *041/831555. 129 rooms. Restaurant, pool. No credit cards.*

Tulcea

Tulcea is the main town of the Danube Delta and the gateway to the region. Built on seven hills and influenced by Turkish architectural styles, this former market town is now an important sea and river port. It is the center of the Romanian fish industry, famous for processing caviar-bearing sturgeon.

The **Muzeul Deltei Dunării** (Danube Delta Museum) provides a good introduction to the flora, fauna, and way of life of the communities in the region. ⊠ *Str. Grigore Antipa 2,* ☎ *040/515866.* ◷ *Tues.–Sun. 11–4.*

$$ ☒ **Delta.** On the bank of the Danube, this spacious, modern hotel has good facilities. ⊠ *Str. Isaacei 2,* ☎ *040/514720,* ☒ *040/516260. 117 rooms. Restaurant. V.*

The Danube Delta

The **Delta Dunării** (Danube Delta) is Europe's largest wetlands reserve, covering 4,357 square km (1,676 sq mi), with a sprawling, watery wilderness that stretches from the Ukrainian border to a series of lakes north of the Black Sea resorts. Romanians have committed themselves to the restoration and preservation of this treasure. While it is home to birds such as the pelican, the Danube Delta is also a refuge for hundreds of species of migratory birds, some from as far away as China and India.

As the Danube approaches the Delta Dunării, it divides into three branches. The northernmost branch forms the border with Ukraine, the middle arm leads to the busy port of Sulina, and the southernmost arm meanders gently toward the little port of Sfintu Gheorghe, a simple holiday spot. From these channels, countless canals widen into tree-fringed lakes and water-lily pools; sand dunes and lush forests are among the region's natural treasures.

$$ ☒ **Lebăda.** This not-very-comfortable hotel is the only one convenient for fishing trips into the more remote parts of the delta. ⊠ *Sulina Canal, mi 14.5, Crişan,* ☎ *040/543778. 74 rooms. Restaurant. No credit cards.*

Black Sea Coast and Danube Delta Essentials

Getting Around

Travel in this area involves several hours on the road; allow more than one day for a substantive trip.

Guided Tours

Most hotels in the Black Sea region arrange guided tours throughout the area. Individual and group tours can also be prearranged through travel agencies in Bucharest.

Visitor Information

Constanța (OPT, ⊠ Str. Traian 36, bl. C1, apt. 31, ☎ 094/655–004; Danubius, ⊠ B-dul Ferdinand 22/36, ☎ 041/615836). **Mamaia** (ATI— Carpați, ⊠ B-dul Tomis 46, ☎ 041/614861, FAX 041/611429). **Tulcea** (OPT, ⊠ Str. Pacii 20, ☎ 094/655–010; Europolis, ⊠ Str. Pacii 20, ☎ 040/512443).

TRANSYLVANIA

Transylvania, Romania's western province, contains some of Europe's most beautiful and unspoiled villages and rural landscapes. The Carpathian Mountains, which separate Transylvania from Walachia and Moldavia, shielded the province from the Turks and Mongols during the Middle Ages. Germans and Hungarians settled here during this period, building spectacular castles, towns, and churches. Since the 1980s many ethnic Germans have emigrated, but Transylvania, which was ruled by Hungary until 1920, is still home to a large Hungarian minority and to many of Romania's 2 million ethnic Gypsies. You can best explore the countryside by taking day trips from a major town such as Sibiu, Sinaia, or Brașov.

Sinaia

Prior to World War II and the abdication of Romania's royal family, Sinaia was a summer retreat for the aristocracy. On the mountainside stand many grand summer homes from this period, as well as the **Sinaia Minastire,** which has operated as a monastery since 1695.

Just up the hill from the monastery is **Castelul Peleș** (Peleş Palace), a 19th-century Bavarian-style palace that served as the summer residence of Romania's first Hohenzollern king, Carol I; inside hang many originals by Gustav Klimt. Tours are available in English. ⊠ *Str. Peleşului 2; take Str. Manastirii uphill and follow signs to castle;* ☎ *044/310918.* ♡ *Wed.–Sun. 9–3.*

Castelul Pelisor (Pelisor Palace), the summer home of the second Hohenzollern king, Ferdinand, lies just above Peleş Palace. Tours in English are available. ⊠ *Str. Peleşului,* ☎ *044/310918.* ♡ *Wed.–Sun. 9–3.*

$$$$ 🏨 **Holiday Inn Resort Sinaia.** One of the grandest provincial hotels in
★ Romania, this resort has a pool and spa, as well as an elegant restaurant serving Romanian fare. ⊠ *Str. Toporasilor 1A,* ☎ *044/310440,* FAX *044/310551. 142 rooms, 6 suites. Restaurant. AE, MC, V.*

$ 🏨 **Economat.** Built in the same Bavarian style as the nearby Peleş Palace, this simple, comfortable hotel is surrounded by mountains. The restaurant serves Romanian and French specialties. ⊠ *Str. Peleşului 2,* ☎ *044/311151,* FAX *044/311150. 40 rooms. Restaurant. MC, V.*

Bran

Some locals claim that Vlad Țepeş once lived in the beautifully preserved **Castelul Bran** (Castle Bran), built in 1377; Vlad's castle actually lies in ruins farther west in Transylvania. Bran was a trading post during the Middle Ages; nowadays the town's parking lot hosts a lively market. ⊠ *Str. Principală (Rte. DN 73),* ☎ *068/236538.* ♡ *Tues.–Sun. 8–4:30.*

Brașov and Poiana Brașov

To enjoy Brașov, stroll through **Piața Sfatului,** the bustling cobblestone square at the heart of the old Germanic city, formerly an important medieval trade center. **Casa Sfatului** (⊠ Piaţa Sfatului; ☉ Tues.–Sun. 8–4) was once the town hall of old Braşov. Built in 1420, it now houses a historical museum. Just off Piaţa Sfatului is the spiraling tower of the Gothic **Biserica Neagră** (Black Church). The 15th-century masterwork acquired its name after a fire in 1689 left it black and charred. Currently it is undergoing massive renovation. Opposite the Black Church is **Strada Republicii,** a pedestrian street that provides shopping opportunities.

For a breathtaking view of Braşov, ride the **Telecabina Timpa** (⊠ Str. Romer), a cable car that runs to the top of Mount Timpa, open Tuesday–Sunday 10–6. To find the cable car, leave Piaţa Sfatului on Strada Apollonia Hirscher; take a left on to Strada Castelului; the next right is Strada Romer, which leads to the cable car. Just below the entrance to Telecabina Timpa are some of the remains of the old Braşov city wall. A stroll along the wall will take you to the **Bastionul Ţesătorilor** (Weaver's Bastion), which now holds a museum that is occasionally open to the public.

A 10-minute drive, or bus ride (No. 2), from Braşov on St. Stejărişului brings you to **Poiana Braşov,** a mountaintop ski resort that embraces several good restaurants and hotels. In winter Poiana Braşov offers some of the best skiing in Romania, though trails are not groomed and ski lifts are limited. In summer you can follow well-marked hiking trails along the spectacular mountainsides. From the top of the mountain, you'll have a stunning view of the Transylvania Plains. Local peasants sell handmade wool sweaters in the central parking lot. ⊠ *Agenţa Poiana Braşov,* ☎ *068/262389.*

$$ ✕ **Coliba Haiducilor.** In this classic Romanian lodge, whose walls are
★   decorated with hunting trophies, traditional song and dance transport you to an earlier era. Waiters dressed in peasant costume serve boar, bear, venison, and chicken. ⊠ *Poiana Braşov,* ☎ *068/262137. Reservations essential. No credit cards.*

$$ ✕ **Sura Dacilor.** Built to look like a traditional Romanian hunting
★   lodge, this restaurant offers garlic chicken, grilled meats, salad, and ciorbă. ⊠ *Poiana Braşov,* ☎ *068/262327. No credit cards.*

$$$$ 🏨 **Alpin.** Comfort, cleanliness, and service define this hotel at the zenith of Piana Braşov; most rooms have breathtaking views. ⊠ *Poina Braşov,* ☎ *068/262343,* FAX *068/150427. 130 rooms. Restaurant, pool. AE, MC, V.*

$$ 🏨 **Casa Viorel.** Every room in this irreproachable hotel is immaculate,
★   with a balcony and view of the mountains; the service is superb. During ski season, the hotel requires minimum stays of one week. ⊠ *Poiana Braşov,* ☎ *068/262024,* FAX *068/262148. 10 rooms, 2 suites. No credit cards.*

$$ 🏨 **Centrul De Echitatie** (Equitation Center). Head for this resort's stable if you'd like to explore the mountainous countryside on horseback or take a sleigh ride. You can rent a clean villa and enjoy barbecues in the woods. The center is on the bus line to Braşov and within walking distance of all facilities in Poiana Braşov. ⊠ *Poiana Braşov,* ☎ *068/ 262161. 10 1- and 2-bedroom villas. No credit cards.*

Sighişoara

Sighişoara's enchanting stone towers and spires can be seen from a great distance. Above the modern town is an exceptionally well-preserved medieval **citadel.** Walking up from the city center, you enter the citadel through the 14th-century **Bastionul de Ceas** (clock tower), which is 60 m (195 ft) tall. The clock still works, complete with rotating painted wooden figures, one for each day of the week. The tower houses the town's **Muzeul de Istorie** (History Museum), which includes some moving photographs of the 1989 revolution that led to the execution of Nicolae and Elena Ceauşescu. From the wooden gallery at the top of the tower, you can appreciate a vista of terra-cotta roofs and painted houses. ⊠ *Pta. Muzeului.* ◷ *Tues.–Sun. 9–3:30.*

Along narrow, cobbled streets lined with faded pink, green, and ocher houses, you'll come to a covered staircase that leads to the 14th-century **Berglorcje** (Gothic Church) and the **Cimitir de Germania** (German Cemetery), a testament to the town's settlers that extends over the hilltop beyond the city walls. ⊠ *Str. Sçolii, Str. Tamplarilor.*

$–$$ ✕ **Restaurentul Cetaţe (Casa Vlad Dracul).** Occupying a house where the father of Vlad Ţepeş (Count Dracula) once lived, this two-story bar and restaurant is the best place in town for a traditional Romanian meal. ⊠ *Str. Cositorarilor 5,* ☎ *065/771596. No credit cards.*

$ 🏨 **Rex.** This clean, modern hotel is the most appealing establishment in town, a few minutes' walk from the center. ⊠ *Str. Dumbravei 18,* ☎ 𝖥𝖠𝖷 *065/166615. 24 rooms. Restaurant. No credit cards.*

Sibiu
Known as Hermannstadt to the Germans, who founded the city in 1143, Sibiu was the Saxon hub in Transylvania. Even though few ethnic Germans remain, the city's atmosphere is still distinctly German or Central European. The old part of the town centers around the magnificent **Piaţa Mare** (Great Square) with its painted 17th-century town houses. The **Biserica Romano Catolică** (Roman Catholic Church) on the square is a splendid high-Baroque building. Also on the square is the **Brukenthal Museum,** in the palace of its founder, Samuel Brukenthal, Habsburg governor from 1777 to 1787; one of the most extensive collections of silver, paintings, and furniture in Romania is on display.

The second center of the old town is **Piaţa Mica** (Small Square), next to which stands the **Biserica Luthero,** a massive 14th- to 15th-century edifice with a simple, stark interior.

$$ 🏨 **Împăratul Romanilor.** In the heart of town, the century-old Romanilor is among Romania'a best provincial hotels. Rooms are at-
★ tractively decorated with paintings and locally made furniture. The restaurant has a lively floor show and discotheque on weekends. ⊠ *Calea Dumbravii 2–4,* ☎ *069/218100,* 𝖥𝖠𝖷 *069/210125. 182 rooms. Restaurant. MC, V.*

Transylvania Essentials
Getting Around
Transylvania's rich rural life is best explored by car. Regular rail travel is available to most Transylvanian towns (☞ Transportation *in* Romania A to Z, *above*).

Guided Tours
Many travel agencies in Bucharest, and those in many hotels throughout Transylvania, offer guided tours of the region. The **Transylvanian Society of Dracula** (⊠ Str. George Călinescu 20, Apt. 28, Bucharest, ☎ 𝖥𝖠𝖷 01/231–4022) arranges unique "Dracula" tours.

Visitor Information
Braşov (OPT, ⊠ Str. Harmanulul 50, apt. 11, ☎ 094/655007; ⊠ Aro-Palace, B-dul Eroilor 9, ☎ 068/142840, 𝖥𝖠𝖷 068/150427). **Sibiu** (OPT, ☎ 094/655008; ⊠ Str. Cetăţii 1, ☎ 069/211788, 𝖥𝖠𝖷 069/217933).

SLOVAKIA

BRATISLAVA, THE HIGH TATRAS
AND EASTERN SLOVAKIA

Despite more than 70 years of common statehood with the Czech Republic, not to mention centuries spent under Hungarian and Habsburg rule, Slovakia has shaped a distinct cultural profile. The country's farmlands stretch to an important mountain range. Its culture, steeped in folk tradition, is particularly rich.

Although they speak a language closely related to Czech, the Slovaks have a strong sense of national identity. United with the Czechs during the 9th century as part of the Great Moravian Empire, the Slovaks were conquered a century later by the Magyars and remained under Hungarian domination until 1918. The Hungarians were not alone in infiltrating the country; after the Tatar invasions of the 13th century, many Saxons were invited to resettle the land and develop the economy. During the 15th and 16th centuries, Romanian shepherds migrated from Walachia into Slovakia. The merging of these varied groups with the resident Slavs further enriched the native folk culture.

Bratislava, the capital of Hungary for nearly 250 years until 1784, and now the capital of the new Slovak republic, was once a city filled with picturesque streets and Gothic churches. Forty years of Communist rule hid its ancient beauty behind hulking, and now dilapidated, futuristic structures. The streets of the Old Town, however, have undergone rapid revitalization.

The peaks of the High Tatras are a major draw. The smallest Alpine range in the world, the Tatras rise magnificently from the foothills of northern Slovakia. Hikers and skiers are the chief visitors here. The area's subtler attractions—the exquisite medieval towns of the Spiš region below the Tatras and the beautiful 18th-century wood churches farther east—are definitely worth the trip.

SLOVAKIA A TO Z

Customs
Enter valuable items such as jewelry or laptops on arrival on your customs declaration, so that you encounter no problems with customs of-

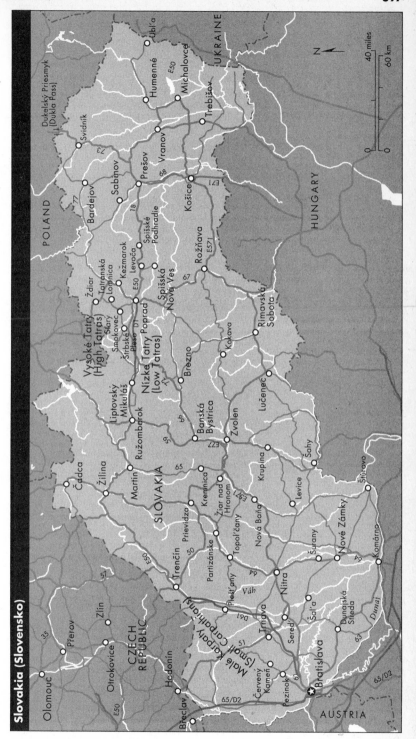

Slovakia (Slovensko)

ficials on departure. U.S. or EU citizens over 18 years old can bring in 250 cigarettes (or their equivalent in tobacco), 2 liters of wine, 1 liter of spirits, and ½ liter of eau de cologne.

There is no limit on the amount of goods purchased for noncommercial use, but to be on the safe side, keep all receipts. You can export antiques (i.e., items more than 50 years old) with a special opinion from a commission at the National Relic and Landscape Center (Bratislava, ☎ 07/54774444). Commission opinion is based on a court-expert opinion submitted by you; for a list of court experts, call the department of experts and interpreters at the Regional Court in Bratislava (✉ Krajský Súd, Záhradnícka 10, 81366, ☎ 07/55424060, 07/55574176, or 07/55423954, ext. 210).

Dining
In Slovakia you can choose from a variety of ambiences—restaurants, *vináreň* (wine cellars), beer taverns, cafeterias, and a growing number of coffee shops and snack bars. Most restaurants are remarkably inexpensive, but the free market is pushing up prices.

Typical main dishes are roast pork, duck, or goose, served with sauerkraut and some type of dumpling or potatoes, generally with a rich gravy. Peppers frequently spice up bland entrées. Look for *bryndzové halušky*, a tasty Slovak noodle dish with sheep cheese. Green vegetables and salads come pickled. Be sure to try *palacinky*, a delicious treat of crepes stuffed with fruit and cream or jam.

MEALTIMES
Lunch is usually from 11:30 to 2 or 3; dinner from 6 to 9:30 or 10. Some places are open all day, and in Bratislava it may be easier to find a table during off-hours.

RATINGS
Prices are reasonable by American standards, even in the more expensive restaurants. The following prices are for meals made up of a first course, main course, and dessert (excluding wine and tip).

CATEGORY	COST
$$$$	over 600 Sk
$$$	400 Sk–600 Sk
$$	200 Sk–400 Sk
$	under 200 Sk

WHAT TO WEAR
A jacket is suggested for higher-priced restaurants. Otherwise, casual dress is acceptable.

Language
Slovak, a western-Slavic tongue related to both Czech and Polish, is the official language of Slovakia. English is popular among young people, but German is still the most useful language for visitors.

Lodging
Slovakia has a few new hotels, and many of the older hotels have been privatized by local entrepreneurs as recently as 1997 and 1998. Bratislava and the High Tatras have the highest hotel rates in Slovakia—but prices drop dramatically in the rest of the country. Shortages of hotel rooms are common during the peak season, so make reservations well in advance. Many private room agencies are in operation, and as long as you arrive in a city before 9 PM, you should be able to get a room. Brace yourself for inconveniences from faulty plumbing to indifferent reception clerks. Unless otherwise noted, rooms include bath.

CAMPING

In summer signs that announce *Autokemping* (campsites) crop up along major highways like mushrooms after rain. Campsites open year-round are extremely scarce. Plumbing is often primitive, and hot water is a blessing, not a given. The main Satur Tours and Travel office in Bratislava (☞ Visitor Information, *below*) has a rudimentary country-wide directory.

HOTELS

Satur Tours and Travel (☞ Visitor Information, *below*) officially grades hotels from one to four stars in accordance with norms that are not identical with international standards.

PRIVATE ACCOMMODATIONS

Satur (☞ Visitor Information, *below*) can help you find a private room in Bratislava and other large cities. These accommodations are invariably cheaper (around $20) and often more comfortable than hotels, though you may have to sacrifice some privacy. You can also wander the main roads looking for signs reading ROOM FREE, or more frequently, in German, ZIMMER FREI or PRIVATZIMMER.

RATINGS

Prices are for double rooms, generally not including breakfast. Prices at the lower end of the scale apply off-season. At certain periods, such as Easter or during festivals, rates may increase by 15%–25%.

CATEGORY	COST
$$$$	over 3,200 Sk
$$$	1,600 Sk–3,200 Sk
$$	480 Sk–1,600 Sk
$	under 480 Sk

Mail

POSTAL RATES

First-class (airmail) letters to the United States and Canada cost 16 Sk up to 20 grams, postcards 10 Sk. Airmail (first-class) letters to the United Kingdom cost 12 Sk up to 20 grams, postcards 7 Sk.

RECEIVING MAIL

Mail can be marked "poste restante" and sent to the main post office in Bratislava (✉ Hlavná pošta, Nám. SNP 35, ☎ 07/59393111 or 07/54434055); there's no charge.

Money Matters

COSTS

Costs are highest in Bratislava and only slightly lower in the High Tatra resorts and main spas. The least expensive areas are central and eastern Slovakia.

CURRENCY

The unit of currency in Slovakia is the crown, or koruna, written as Sk, and divided into 100 halierov. There are bills of 20, 50, 100, 200, 500, 1,000, and 5,000 Sk, and coins of 10, 20, and 50 halierov and 1, 2, 5, and 10 Sk.

At press time (summer 1999), the rate of exchange was 44 Sk to the U.S. dollar, 30 Sk to the Canadian dollar, 69 Sk to the pound sterling, 29 Sk to the Australian dollar, and 23 Sk to the New Zealand dollar.

SAMPLE PRICES

Cup of coffee, 10 Sk–20 Sk; beer (½ liter), 20 Sk; Coca-Cola, 15 Sk–20 Sk; ham sandwich, 30 Sk; 2-km (1-mi) taxi ride, 150 Sk. Admission to museums and castles ranges from 10 Sk to 50 Sk.

TIPPING

Although many Slovaks still tip in restaurants by rounding up the bill to the nearest multiple of 10, higher tipping is beginning to catch on. For good service, 10% is considered an appropriate gratuity on very large tabs. Tip porters and room service 20 Sk. In taxis round up the bill to the nearest multiple of 10. Give tour guides and helpful concierges between 20 Sk and 30 Sk for services rendered.

National Holidays

January 1 (day of founding of the Slovak Republic); January 6 (12th Night); April 21 and 24 (Good Friday and Easter Monday); May 1 (Labor Day); May 8 (Liberation of the Republic); July 5 (Sts. Cyril and Methodius); August 29 (anniversary of the Slovak National Uprising); September 1 (Constitution Day); September 15 (Our Lady of Sorrows); November 1 (All Saints' Day); December 24–26.

Opening and Closing Times

Banks are open weekdays 8–4; they remain open through the general lunch hour. **Museums** are usually open Tuesday–Sunday 10–5. **Shops** are generally open weekdays 9–6 and stay open slightly later on Thursday; some close between noon and 2. Many are also open Saturday 9–noon (department stores, 9–4) and, in big cities, on Sunday.

Passport and Visa information

Entry without a visa is permitted for citizens of the United States (up to 30 days), United Kingdom (6 months), and Canada (90 days). Citizens of Australia and New Zealand need a visa for any visits.

Telephoning

If you plan to make several calls, buy a phone card. You can buy one at most newsstands or at any post office for 100 and 150 Sk; the cards can be used for both local and out-of-town calls.

COUNTRY CODE

The country code for Slovakia is 421. When dialing a number from outside the country, drop the initial zero from the regional code.

INTERNATIONAL CALLS

You can automatically dial many countries, including North America and the United Kingdom, from public pay phones. You can also call from Telefón/Telegraf (✉ Kolárska 12, Bratislava, ☎ 07/363400), a public communications office with phone booths inside and out. It's open weekdays 7 AM–9 PM and weekends 8 AM–8 PM. For international inquiries dial 0139 or 0149 for the United States, Canada, or the United Kingdom. To place a call via an **AT&T** USA Direct international operator, dial 00–421–00101; for **MCI,** dial 001–881–422–0042; for **Sprint,** dial 001–881–824–9242.

LOCAL CALLS

These cost 2 Sk from a pay phone. Public phones on street corners are often out of order. Try a hotel. For information call 120 or 121.

Transportation

The most common words you'll find on street signs are *ulica* (street, abbreviated *ul.*) and *námestie* (square, abbreviated *nám.*).

BY BUS

Bus and tram service in Bratislava is very cheap and reasonably frequent, and you can use it to reach any of the places in the tours below. The timetables can be confusing, so be sure to confirm your itinerary. The bus network in the rest of Slovakia is dense, but service to the smaller towns can be infrequent.

Breakdowns. In Bratislava or elsewhere contact the 24-hour repair service (☎ 154). The *Auto Atlas SR* (available at bookstores) has a list of emergency road-repair numbers in various towns. If you have an accident and need an ambulance, call the emergency number: ☎ 155.

Gasoline. Gasoline is expensive. Service stations are usually along main roads on the outskirts of towns and cities. Finding a station in Bratislava can be difficult, so fill up on the freeway as you approach the city. Lead-free gasoline, known as "natural," is still available only at select stations.

Road Conditions. Main roads are often narrow but adequate. Traffic is light, especially away from main centers. Outside Bratislava, a car is especially useful in central and eastern Slovakia, where many of the sights are difficult to reach by public transportation.

Rules of the Road. Drive on the right. Speed limits are 60 kph (37 mph) in built-up areas, 90 kph (55 mph) on open roads, 110 kph (68 mph) on expressways, and 130 kph (80 mph) on highways. Seat belts are compulsory; drinking and driving is strictly prohibited.

Tatra Air (☎ 07/43292306) has flights from Bratislava to Košice three times daily on weekdays and once on Saturday and Sunday. **TLS Air** (☞ Guided Tours *in* The High Tatras and Eastern Slovakia Essentials, *below*) provides charter flights from Poprad to any airport within Slovakia.

Train service is erratic to all but the largest cities—Bratislava, Poprad, Prešov, Košice, and Banská Bystrica. Make sure to take the express trains marked R or the fast Intercity trains. Reliable, if slow, electric rail service connects Poprad with the resorts of the High Tatras. If you're going just to the Tatras, an electric train will get you there.

Visitor Information
Satur Tours and Travel (main office, ✉ Jesenského 5, Bratislava, ☎ 07/54410133 or 07/54410129, FAX 07/54410136).

Weather
Organized sightseeing tours generally run from April or May through October. Some monuments, especially castles, either close entirely or have shorter hours in winter. Hotel rates drop off-season except during festivals. In winter (December–February), skiers from all over Eastern Europe crowd the slopes and resorts of the High Tatra mountains. Visit the mountains in late spring (May or June) or fall and you'll have the hotels and restaurants pretty much to yourself.

The following are the average daily maximum and minimum temperatures for Bratislava.

Jan.	36F	2C	May	70F	21C	Sept.	72F	22C
	27	− 3		52	11		54	12
Feb.	39F	4C	June	75F	24C	Oct.	59F	15C
	28	− 2		57	14		45	7
Mar.	48F	9C	July	79F	26C	Nov.	46F	8C
	34	1		61	16		37	3
Apr.	61F	16C	Aug.	79F	26C	Dec.	39F	4C
	43	6		61	16		32	0

BRATISLAVA

In Bratislava you'll find high-rise housing projects, faded supermodern structures, and less-than-inspiring monuments. But everywhere you look new shops are opening and older buildings are under renovation—as if the capital's residents are trying to forget as quickly as possible the past 40 years of playing second fiddle to Prague.

Exploring Bratislava

Numbers in the margin correspond to points of interest on the Bratislava map.

Despite its charms, there's no denying that Bratislava is intensely industrial. Avoid the newer, and shabbier, parts of the city and head toward the Danube River to discover the peace and beauty of the Staré Mesto (Old Town) and its Gothic and Renaissance architectural treasures. Walking between the major sites will take just an hour or two.

⑩ Dóm svätého Martina (St. Martin's Cathedral). Construction of this massive Gothic church, with its 280-ft gold-trimmed steeple, began during the 14th century. Between the 16th and 19th centuries, 17 Hungarian monarchs were crowned here. ⊠ *Rudnayovo nám.,* ☎ *07/ 54431359.* ☉ *Weekdays 10–11:30 and 2–6, Sat. 10–noon, Sun. 2–4:30.*

❼ Hlavné námestie (Main Square). This enchanting square in Old Town is lined with old houses and palaces that represent architectural styles from Gothic (No. 2), through Baroque (No. 4) and Rococo (No. 7), to a wonderfully decorative example of Art Nouveau (No. 10). ⊠ *Bordered by Radničná ul. and Rybárska brána.*

❾ Hrad (Castle). Bratislava's castle has been continually rebuilt since its original fortifications were laid in the 9th century. The Hungarian kings expanded the castle into a royal residence, and the Habsburgs turned it into a very successful defense against the Turks. Its current design, square with four corner towers, stems from the 17th century, although the existing castle had to be completely rebuilt after a disastrous fire in 1811. In the castle you'll find the **Slovenské národné múzeum** (Slovak National Museum). The exhibits cover crafts, historic furniture and clocks, and silver treasure. ⊠ *Zámocká ul.,* ☎ *07/54411444.* ☉ *Castle and museum: Tues.–Sun. 9–5.*

❷ Hurbanovo námestie (Hurban Square). This busy square hides the entrance to the Old Town. A small bridge, decorated with statues of St. John Nepomuk and St. Michael, takes you over the old moat, now blossoming with trees and fountains, into the intricate barbican and past Michalská brána (Michael's Gate; ☞ *below).* ⊠ *Jct. Obchodná, Suché mýto, Michalská, and Námestie SNP.*

❹ Jezuitský kostol (Jesuit Church). Wild with Baroque detailing on the inside, this church was originally built by Protestants who, in 1636, received an imperial concession for a place of worship on the condition that it have no tower. ⊠ *Hlavné nám,* ☎ *no phone.* ☉ *Mass: weekdays 6:30, 3:15, 4, and 6; Sun. and holidays at 7, 9, 11, 5, and 6.*

❽ Kostol Klarisiek (Church and Monastery of the Poor Clares). Go through the arched passageway at the back of the Baroque **Palác Uhorskej kráľovskej komory** (Hungarian Royal Chamber) on Michalská ulica and you'll come to this church and convent on a tiny square. The one-nave, Gothic church is small but still imposing, due to its richly decorated spire. ⊠ *Farská ul.,* ☎ *no phone.*

Dóm svätého
Martina, **10**

Hlavné
námestie, **7**

Hrad, **9**

Hurbanovo
námestie, **2**

Jezuitský
kostol, **4**

Kostol
Klarisiek, **8**

Michalská
brána, **3**

Námestie
SNP, **1**

Nový Most, **11**

Primaciálny
palác, **5**

Stará
radnica, **6**

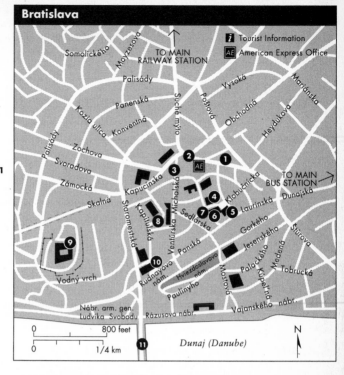

❸ **Michalská brána** (Michael's Gate). Topped with a copper onion dome and a statue of St. Michael, this 500-year-old gate at one entrance to Old Town is the only remainder of Bratislava's three original city gates. ✉ *Hurbanovo nám.*

❶ **Námestie SNP** (SNP Square). An abbreviation for *Slovenské Národné Povstanie* (Slovak National Uprising), "SNP" appears on streets, squares, bridges, and posters throughout Slovakia. The anti-Nazi resistance movement involved partisan fighting in Slovakia's mountainous areas during the final years of World War II. On the monument that commemorates it in this square, you can often see the Slovak flag (red, blue, and white with a double cross) flying from a partisan's gun. In 1992 the square was the center for demonstrations in support of Slovak independence. ✉ *Bordered by Obchodná ul. and Poštová ul.*

⏲ ⓫ **Nový Most** (New Bridge). This futuristic bridge, opened in 1972, was formerly known as Most SNP. The steps under the passageway and up the other side lead in the direction of the historic castle. ✉ *Between Staromestská ul. and Panónska cesta.*

❺ **Primaciálny palác** (Primates' Palace). Go through the back entrance of the Old Town Hall (☞ *below*) to find the **Primaciálne námestie** (Primates' Square), which is dominated by the glorious pale pink, classical elegance of the Palace. In the dazzling Hall of Mirrors Napoléon and Habsburg Emperor Francis I signed the Peace of Bratislava of 1805, following Napoléon's victory at the Battle of Austerlitz. ✉ *Primaciálne nám. 1,* ☎ *07/54435151 or 07/59356166.* ⊙ *Tues.–Sun. 10–5.*

❻ **Stará radnica** (Old Town Hall). A colorful jumble of Gothic and Renaissance arcades, archways, and audience halls makes up the Old Town Hall. Walk through the vaulted passageway with early Gothic ribbing into a cheerful Renaissance courtyard. (The hall's interior is not open to the public.) Toward the back of the courtyard, you'll find the entrance to the **Mestské múzeum** (City Museum), which documents Bratislava's rocky past. ⊠ *Primaciálne nám. Museum:* ☎ *07/54435800.* ☉ *Tues.–Sun. 10–5; wine-growing, pharmacy, and art crafts exhibitions, Mon., Wed.–Sun. 10–5.*

Dining and Lodging

When it's time to eat, you can be happy that you're in Bratislava. The long-shared history with Hungary gives Slovak cuisine an extra fire. Bratislava's proximity to Vienna, moreover, has lent a bit of grace and charm to the city's eateries. You'll find a variety of meat dishes, all spiced to enliven the palate and served (if you're lucky) with the special noodles Slovaks call *halušky*. Keep in mind that the city's many street stands offer a price-conscious alternative to restaurant dining. Try some *langoš*—flat, deep-fried, and delicious pieces of dough, which can be seasoned with garlic and other toppings. For details and price-category definitions, *see* Dining *in* Slovakia A to Z, *above*.

On the whole, Bratislava's hotels are no bargain, and new properties are few and far between. If you're on a budget, investigate the accommodation services at the Bratislava Tourist Information branch in the main train station (⊠ Hlavná stanica, Predstaničné nám., ☎ 07/395904)—but stay near the city center, as the fringe areas are a vast sea of block housing. For details and price-category definitions, *see* Lodging *in* Slovakia A to Z, *above*.

$$$$ ✕ **Arkadia.** Arkadia's several dining rooms range from intimate to boisterous and are decorated with period 19th-century furnishings. Come here by taxi and after fortifying yourself with steak or shish kebab, enjoy the 15-minute and mostly downhill walk back into town. ⊠ *Zámocké schody,* ☎ *07/54435650. AE, DC, MC, V.*

$$$ ✕ **Kláštorná Vináreň.** This Old Town monastery offers subterranean
★ meals in its vaulted cellars. When ordering *čikós tokáň* (a potent mixture of pork, onions, and peppers), keep a glass of mellow red wine and a fire hose on hand. *Bravčové ražniči* (a tender pork shish kebab with fried potatoes) is milder. It is the only downtown place with live violin, accordion, and bass folk music at night. ⊠ *Františkánska ul. 2,* ☎ *07/54430430. AE, MC, V. Closed Sun.*

$$$ ✕ **Slovenská Reštaurácia.** Here you'll find the widest choice of genuine Slovak meals in Bratislava. The traditional decor evokes Slovak folk art, unlike the live piano music in the evening. ⊠ *Hviezdoslavovo nám. 20,* ☎ *07/54434883. DC, MC, V.*

$$ ✕ **Chez David.** The draw here is kosher food downtown in calm surroundings. Try a delicious duck in *sholet* (thick bean sauce made of milk, flour, and whole beans) with Austrian wine. David has a great kitchen and a knowledgeable staff. ⊠ *Zámocká 13,* ☎ *07/54413824. AE, DC, MC, V. Closed Sat. No dinner Fri.*

$$ ✕ **Modrá Gula.** At the top of the Slovenská sporiteľňa bank headquarters building, the rounded restaurant, furnished with metal and blue glass, has a fresh, clean feel. The windows and in summer the terrace afford a good view of downtown. Try a garlic soup served in a bosniak bread. ⊠ *Suché mýto 6,* ☎ *07/58504007. AE, DC, MC, V.*

$$ ✕ **Modrá Hviezda.** A small wine cellar, the "Blue Star" concentrates on regional fare. Try the *Bryndzový posúch* (baked sheep-cheese pie) and *Mamičkina špecialita* ("Mother's favorite dish"; stewed beef with sour-cream sauce, potato-dough fritters, and cranberries). ⊠ *Beblavého 14,* ☎ *54432747. No credit cards.*

$ ✕ **Café Meyer.** Opened in 1997 at the same location downtown as its namesake after more more than a century, this café has brought back with it the Austrian flavor of Pressburg (as Bratislava was known to the Austrians). The great variety of delicious cakes filled with cream and fruit is a reminder of the former owner Julius Meyer, a candy supplier to the emperor's court. Its late hours make it an ideal place for a post-theater dinner of such dishes as Wiener schnitzel or hot strudels filled with vegetables, cabbage, spinach, or meat and covered with a vegetable sauce. In July and August, you can sit outside under umbrellas. ⊠ *Hlavné nám. 4,* ☎ *07/54411741. No credit cards.*

$ ✕ **Prešporská kúria.** The large restaurant, dining hall, and snack bar is housed in three wooden buildings. The cuisine is rich Central European: meats served with potatoes, rice, or dumplings plus vegetable salads. The wooden tables and chairs are simplified Slovak folk art. In summer you can sit outdoors, where wine and beer are served in plastic cups. ⊠ *Dunajská 21–23,* ☎ *07/367981. AE, DC, MC, V.*

$ ✕ **Stará Sladovňa.** This beer hall is known lovingly, and fittingly, as "Mamut" (the word for Mammoth, a huge and ungainly beast) to Bratislavans. Locals come here for the Bohemian beer on tap and for inexpensive, filling meals. The place, which has billiards and slot machines on two floors, seats almost 1,000, so don't worry about reservations. ⊠ *Cintorínska ul. 32,* ☎ *07/321151. No credit cards.*

$$$$ 🏨 **Danube.** Opened in 1992, this French-run hotel on the bank of the
★ Danube has superior facilities and service. The modern rooms are done in tasteful pastels; the public areas gleam. ⊠ *Rybné nám. 1, 81338,* ☎ *07/59340000,* FAX *07/54414311. 264 rooms, 16 suites. 2 restaurants, pool. AE, DC, MC, V.*

$$$$ 🏨 **Hotel Forum Bratislava.** The Forum, opened in 1989 in downtown Bratislava, houses three restaurants—French, Slovak, and Hungarian— and several cafés and bars. Rooms are bright and, thanks to twice-daily maid service, very clean. Request a room with a view of the castle or Old Town. ⊠ *Hodžovo nám. 2, 81625,* ☎ *59348111,* FAX *54414645. 179 rooms, 14 suites. 3 restaurants, pool. AE, DC, MC, V.*

$$ 🏨 **Grémium.** This small, bright, affordable pension is in the center of
★ Bratislava's Old Town. The friendly staff serves a terminally arty clientele. A Continental breakfast is included in the room rate. Rooms have showers, not tubs. ⊠ *Gorkého ul. 11, 81103,* ☎ *07/54131026,* FAX *07/54430653. 5 rooms, 1 suite. Restaurant. AE, MC, V.*

$$ 🏨 **Hotel Turist.** Modern, no-frills, and pleasant, this hotel is a short hop from the city center. A winter stadium and a swimming pool (open in summer) are nearby. Rooms have showers, not tubs. ⊠ *Ondavská ul. 5, 82505,* ☎ *07/55572789,* FAX *07/50238263. 95 rooms. No credit cards.*

$ 🏨 **Penzión SlovAir.** In this apartment building only 1 km (½ mi) from Bratislava airport, the three-room apartments all have kitchens. The clean units have simply upholstered wooden furniture. ⊠ *Ivánska cesta 81, 82312,* ☎ *07/43422123,* FAX *07/43423032. 10 apartments. No credit cards.*

Nightlife and the Arts

For listings of events look in Bratislava's English-language newspaper, *The Slovak Spectator,* or ask at **Bratislava Tourist Information** (BIS; ☞ Visitor Information *in* Bratislava Essentials, *below*).

The Arts

The **Slovak Philharmonic Orchestra** puts on excellent concerts at the Reduta (⊠ Medená 3, ☎ 07/54433351 or 07/54433352). **Slovenské Národné Divadlo** (Slovak National Theater; ⊠ Hviezdoslavo nám. 1, ☎ 07/54430069 or 07/54430402) offers high-quality opera and ballet performances at bargain prices.

Nightlife

Bratislava hosts an annual jazz festival in the fall, but the city lacks a
good venue for regular jazz gigs. The **Aligátor** (✉ Laurinská 7, ☎ 07/
54418611), downtown, plays rock on Tuesday and blues on Thursday. The **Čierny Havran Club** (Black Raven, ✉ Biela ul. 6, ☎ 07/
54430717) occasionally has local jazz acts. Good Guinness beer is served
at the Irish pub **Dubliner** (✉ Sedlárska ul. 6, ☎ 07/54410706), which
has a nonsmoking corner. For American-style hard rock try the **Harley-
Davidson Club** (✉ Rebarborova ul. 1, ☎ 07/43191095); take Trolleybus
220 from behind the Tesco department store and get off at Ružinovský
cintorín (Ružinov Cemetery). **Hysteria Pub** (✉ Odbojárov 9, ☎ 07/
44454495) plays rock and dance music.

Shopping

You will find folk art and souvenir shops along **Obchodná ulica** (Shopping Street) as well as on Námestie SNP (☞ Exploring Bratislava, *above*).
Stores tend to come and go in this fast-changing city.

There are several **Dielo** (✉ Obchodná 27, Obchodná 33, Nám. SNP
12) stores that sell works by Slovak artists and craftspeople at reasonable
prices. **Folk, Folk** (✉ Rybárska Brána 2) deals in Slovak folk art, including crystal, pottery, handwoven tablecloths, wooden articles, and
dolls in folk costumes. **ÚLUV** (✉ Nám. SNP 12) has hand-painted
table pottery and vases, wooden figures, and folk costumes.

Bratislava Essentials

Arriving and Departing

BY BUS

Buses run frequently between Prague and Bratislava; the trip costs around
300 Sk and takes about five hours. From Vienna there are four buses
a day from Autobusbahnhof Wien-Mitte; the trip takes between 1½
and 2 hours. The **Autobusová Stanica** (Bus Station; ✉ Mlynské nivy
ul., ☎ 0984/222222) in Bratislava is outside the city center; take Trolleybus 217 to Hodžovo námestie in the direction of the Hrad (Castle).

BY CAR

Good highways link Prague and Bratislava via Brno (D1 and D2); the
315-km (195-mi) journey takes about 3½ hours. From Vienna (A4 and
then Rte 8) the 60-km (37-mi) trip takes 1½ hours.

BY PLANE

The most convenient international airport for Slovakia is Vienna's
Schwechat Airport, approximately 60 km (37 mi) from Bratislava. Nine
buses a day run from Schwechat to Bratislava, or you can even take a
taxi; the journey takes just over an hour, depending on the border crossing. From Prague's Ruzyně Airport you can take a Tatra Air, or ČSA
flight to Bratislava; the flight takes about an hour. A Tatra Air flight
from Zürich to Bratislava takes about two hours.

BY TRAIN

Bratislava's train station is **Hlavná stanica** (✉ Predstaničné nám., ☎
07/50584488, 50584484, or 398651). The tourist information office
(☎ 07/395904) here provides traveling tips and helps find accommodation in the city. Reasonably efficient train service connects Prague
and Bratislava (five–six hours). Unless you crave adventure, take the
Intercity trains for their speed and safety. There are several trains a day
to and from Vienna (just over an hour) and Budapest (three hours),
and one train from Krakow to Bratislava (5½ hours).

Getting Around

BY BUS

Bus, trolleybus, and tram service in Bratislava is cheap, fairly frequent, and convenient for getting to the main sights. Buy tickets ahead of time at any newsstand or at automatic ticket dispensers for 7 Sk each and stamp them when you enter the bus, trolleybus, or tram.

BY CAR

Driving can be difficult in Bratislava and parking spaces are at a premium in the city center; foot power is the best way to get around. You can rent a car either at Satur (☞ Visitor Information, *below*) or at the Forum Bratislava and Danube hotels (☞ Dining and Lodging, *above*). Watch out for no-parking zones or you get the boot and have to pay a hefty fine to have it removed.

Contacts and Resources

EMBASSIES

U.S. (✉ Hviezdoslavovo nám. 4, ☎ 07/54430861, ℻ 07/54418861). **Canadian** (✉ Mišíkova 28/d, ☎ 07/352175 or 07/352177, ℻ 07/399995). **U.K.** (✉ Panská 16, ☎ 07/54417688 or 07/54419633, ℻ 07/54410002).

EMERGENCIES

Police (☎ 158). **Ambulance** (☎ 155). **Pharmacies:** *Lekárne* (pharmacies) take turns staying open late or on Sunday; a list is posted at each pharmacy. For after-hours service, ring the bell; you will be served through a little hatch door. **Lekáreň pod Manderlom** (✉ Nám. SNP 20, ☎ 07/54432952); **Lekáreň** (✉ Palackého 10, ☎ 07/54419665).

ENGLISH-LANGUAGE BOOKSTORE

Big Ben (✉ Michalská 1, ☎ 07/54433632).

GUIDED TOURS

The best tours of Bratislava are offered by Bratislava Tourist Information (BIS; ☞ Visitor Information, *below*), which can arrange a tour in a vintage coach or with an individual guide for a very reasonable price. Both BIS and Satur (☞ Visitor Information, *below*) offer one-day tours of castles and the Small Carpathian mountains close to Bratislava.

VISITOR INFORMATION

Bratislava Tourist Information (BIS, ✉ Klobučnícka 2, ☎ 07/54434370). **Satur Tours and Travel** (main office, ✉ Jesenského 5, ☎ 07/367645).

THE HIGH TATRAS AND EASTERN SLOVAKIA

In the High Tatras region are some of the best hotels in the country (often with saunas to pamper tired skiers), good orientation tours, and stunning mountain scenery laced with well-marked walking trails. Finding a satisfying meal in the Tatras can be difficult, especially in late fall, when some restaurants close. One bright spot is shish kebab made on a *koliba* (open-faced grill). Both an electric train network and a winding highway (Route 537) link the industrial center of Poprad with the resorts on the lower slopes of the High Tatras.

In the brooding towns of the Spiš region just south and east of the High Tatras (on a map look for the prefix "Spišský" preceding a town name), isolation and economic stagnation have preserved a striking mix of Gothic and Renaissance architecture—Gothic churches with Renaissance bell towers attached are typical of the area. These towns do tend to be short on creature comforts.

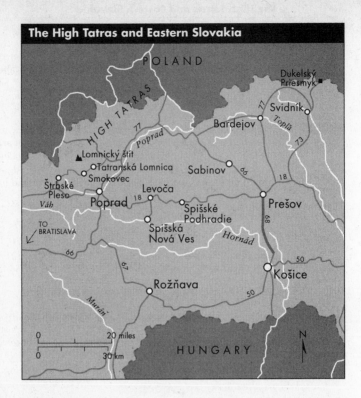

The High Tatras and Eastern Slovakia

East of Spiš, the Šariš region is permeated with a unique legacy of 17th- and 18th-century Orthodox and Greek Catholic (Uniate) wooden churches. The splendid walled town of Bardejov makes the best center from which to explore. In contrast, Nazi and Soviet tanks, trenches, and planes, kept as a reminder of the fighting that took place here in 1944, are concentrated near the Slovakia–Poland border at the Dukelský Priesmyk (Dukla Pass).

Spišská Sobota

The beautiful medieval suburb of Spišská Sobota seems light-years away from the Communist apartment blocks of its industrial neighbor Poprad. Once a hub of the historic Spiš empire, the village is rife with steep shingled roofs, high timber-framed gables, and arched brick doorways. The lovely old square—a nearly perfect ensemble of Renaissance houses—has a Romanesque church, **Kostol svätého Juraja** (St. George's Church; ⊠ Sobotské nám., ☎ no phone), rebuilt during the early 16th century. The church's ornate altar is the work of Pavol of Levoča, one of the great wood-carvers of the 16th century. The neighboring **Múzeum** (museum; ⊠ Sobotské nám. 33, ☎ no phone) collection focuses on local history, including the career of Pavol of Levoča. At press time the museum was closed for reconstruction.

Levoča

★ One of the most famous Spiš towns is Levoča, whose layers of Renaissance-on-Gothic architecture are undergoing restoration. The row of facades in Námestie Majstra Pavla, the main square, is particularly striking, especially those of Nos. 43, 45, 47, and 49. **Kostol svätého Jakuba** (St. Jacob's Church) on the main square has an astounding concentration of Gothic religious art, including work by Spiš artist Pavol of Levoča. His carved-wood high altar is monumental in size and exquisite in detail. ⊠ *Nám. Majstra Pavla*, ☎ *no phone.*

Just 16 km (10 mi) east from Levoča along Route 18 is one of the largest castles in Europe: **Spišský hrad** (Spiš Castle). The beautiful views relieve the grim atmosphere of the museum's display of torture devices. ⊠ *On hill above town of Spišské Podhradie,* ☎ *0966/512786.* ⊙ *June–Aug., daily 9–6; May, Sept., and Oct., Tues.–Sun. 9–5.*

$$$ ⊡ **Hotel Satel.** Inside an 18th-century mansion, the Satel centers around a picturesque courtyard that conjures up all the charm of fairy-tale Levoča. The guest rooms are bright and modern. ⊠ *Nám. Majstra Pavla 55, 05401,* ☎ *0966/4512943,* 𝔽𝔸𝕏 *0966/4514486. 21 rooms, 2 suites. Restaurant. AE, DC, MC, V.*

$$ ⊡ **Hadušovský Penzión.** Close to the Spiš Castle and 12 km (8 mi) from the ski resort of Plejsy near Krompachy, this pension in a two-story family house offers cozy rooms, horseback riding, and horse-drawn cross-country skiing. ⊠ *Hodkovce 14, Spišské Vlachy, 05361,* ☎ *0965/495129,* 𝔽𝔸𝕏 *0965/495546. 2 suites. No credit cards.*

Smokovec

Smokovec is really three resorts in one: Starý (Old), Nový (New), and Horný (Upper). Starý Smokovec is an excellent place to start exploring the Tatras' hiking trails. Some of the more traveled paths lead to waterfalls, a turn-of-the-century chalet, and alpine lakes. A funicular at Hrebienok can take you back to Starý Smokovec. As soon as there's sufficient snow on the ground, the resort is crammed with skiers (equipment can be rented at Tatrasport Adam & Andreas: ⊠ Pekná Vyhliadka, Horný Smokovec, ☎ 0969/422110).

$$ ✕ **Restaurant Koliba.** This restaurant's koliba turns out excellent beef, venison steak with cranberry sauce and red wine, and *kapustová polievka* (sauerkraut soup with mushrooms and sausage). A local Gypsy band plays here every night. ⊠ *Downhill from train station,* ☎ *0969/422204. No credit cards. Closed Sun., Apr.–Dec.*

$$$ ⊡ **Grand Hotel.** The town's oldest hotel has an air of faded fin de siè-
★ cle elegance. Large rooms have high ceilings, and some have their own balcony. A filling buffet breakfast is included in the rate. ⊠ *Starý Smokovec, 06201,* ☎ *0969/422154,* 𝔽𝔸𝕏 *0969/422157. 78 rooms, some with bath; 5 suites. Restaurant, pool. AE, DC, MC, V.*

Tatranská Lomnica

Tiny out-of-the-way Tatranská Lomnica is a peaceful, but still convenient, spot for hiking and skiing. The **Magistrale** trail (24 km/15 mi) begins behind the Grandhotel Praha (☞ *below*). Skirting the tree line, you'll see dwarf pines and spectacular views—with relatively little exertion. At the **Múzeum Tatranského Národného Parku** (Museum of the Tatra National Park), startlingly realistic mounted animals dominate the first floor, while exhibits on local peasant life wait upstairs. ☎ *0969/ 467951.* ⊙ *Weekdays 8–noon and 1–4:30, weekends 8–noon.*

$$ ✕ **Zbojnícka Koliba.** This tavern offers a small range of Slovak specialties prepared over an open fire amid rustic decor and accompanied by Gypsy music. ⊠ *Near Grandhotel Praha, Tatranská Lomnica,* ☎ *0969/467630. No credit cards. No lunch.*

$$$ ⊡ **Grandhotel Praha.** The multiturreted, turn-of-the-century hotel has
★ spacious, traditionally decorated guest rooms. The restaurant has an unusual air of elegance. ⊠ *Tatranská Lomnica, 05960,* ☎ *0969/ 467941,* 𝔽𝔸𝕏 *0969/467891. 83 rooms, 7 suites. Restaurant. AE, DC, MC, V.*

Bardejov

Once astride the trade routes between Poland and Russia, Bardejov revolves around its beautiful main square. On the south side of the square is the **Šarišské múzeum** (Šariš Museum), filled with 16th- to

19th-century religious art from local Russian Orthodox churches. ⊠ *Radničné nám. 13,* ☎ *0935/4746038.* ☉ *Daily (except Mon.) 8–noon, 12:30–4.*

Kostol svätého Egídia (St. Egidium Church), on the main square, is an almost purely Gothic building inside and out. Nearly a dozen perfectly preserved Gothic side altars line the nave. ⊠ *Radničné nám. 3,* ☎ *0935/722595.* ☉ *Tues.–Sun., summer 9–5:30, winter 10–4.*

$ ⌹ **Roland.** This pension is right at the main square, on the second floor of a brick municipal building. It is nevertheless quiet at night. ⊠ *Radničné nám. 25, 08501 Bardejov,* ☎ *0935/4748538. 3 suites. Restaurant. No credit cards.*

$ ⌹ **Športhotel.** The rectangular building with a gray facade built in 1989 sits on the Topla River bank, among tennis and volleyball playgrounds, just seven minutes from Bardejov's beautiful main square. ⊠ *Kutuzovova 34, 08501 Bardejov,* ☎ *0935/724949,* FAX *0935/728208. 20 rooms, only showers, no tubs. Restaurant. No credit cards.*

The High Tatras and Eastern Slovakia Essentials

Getting Around
Many of the towns in this region have no formal street names; instead, they usually have signs pointing to hotels, restaurants, and museums.

BY CAR
Driving is the quickest and most convenient way to see eastern Slovakia—sometimes it's the only way to reach small villages. Route 537 is the main road between Poprad and the High Tatras resort towns.

BY PLANE
Tatra Air has flights from the capital to Košice (☞ Transportation *in* Slovakia A to Z, *above*).

BY TRAIN OR BUS
Trains and buses run frequently except weekends. The electric trains that run between Poprad and the resort towns in the High Tatras leave from the upper platforms of Poprad's main train station, Železničná stanica Poprad-Tatry (⊠ Wolkerova 496, ☎ 092/62509).

Guided Tours
Satur's (Headquarters, ⊠ Miletičova 1, Bratislava 82472, ☎ 07/55422828) seven-day Grand Tour of Slovakia, which leaves from Bratislava every other Saturday from June through September, stops in the High Tatras and a few other towns in eastern Slovakia. The Satur office in Starý Smokovec (☎ 0969/422710 or 0969/422497) is also helpful in arranging tours of the Tatras and the surrounding area. **TLS Air** (Poprad airport, ☎ 092/61626, 0905/342425, or 092/63875) offers a biplane flight over the Tatras from Poprad airport.

Visitor Information
Bardejov (⊠ Radničné nám. 21, ☎ 0935/186). **Smokovec** (⊠ Starý Smokovec, ☎ 0969/186). **Štrbské Pleso** (⊠ Štrbské Pleso, ☎ 0969/492391). **Tatranská Lomnica** (☎ 0969/467951).

27 SLOVENIA

Surging peaks, mysterious caves, and a coast dotted with well-preserved Venetian cities of old are the attractions of Slovenia. The combination of alpine, plain, and coastal geography allows both morning skiing high in the Julian Alps and views of sunset on the Adriatic on the same day. Slovenes' love of their natural surroundings is reflected in the motto they use for their country (fully half of which is covered by forests): A Green Piece of Europe.

Slovenia's northern border is lined with the jagged peaks of the Karavanke Mountains. The Julian Alps, capped by majestic Mt. Triglav (Three Heads), which rises to 9,393 ft, dominate the northwest. Eastward, the mountains gradually descend to the great Hungarian plain. Lovely lakes nestle in thickly wooded mountain valleys, and vineyards cover low-lying hills farther east.

Slovenia has from earliest times been a frontier region. The Romans came from the coast and marched north; Germanic tribes propelled themselves south. Later Slovenia became a province of Charlemagne's empire; next it served as the Hapsburg empire's bulwark against the Turks. The years during World War II, when Slovenia was annexed by Hitler and Mussolini, were filled with both heroic and unspeakable acts. After World War II, as part of Yugoslavia, Slovenia was at the vanguard of the movement toward democracy and self-determination following Tito's death.

The 2 million Slovenes held a national referendum on December 23, 1990, voting for independence and sovereignty from Yugoslavia, and proclaimed their independence on June 26, 1991. Slovenia gained recognition from other nations and soon set about becoming an active member of the family of European states. Following 500 years as part the Austro-Hungarian Empire, Slovenes have perfectly combined Austrian efficiency and organization with a genuine and captivating Slavic friendliness. Slovenia's small size (about half the area of Switzer-

Slovenia (Slovenija)

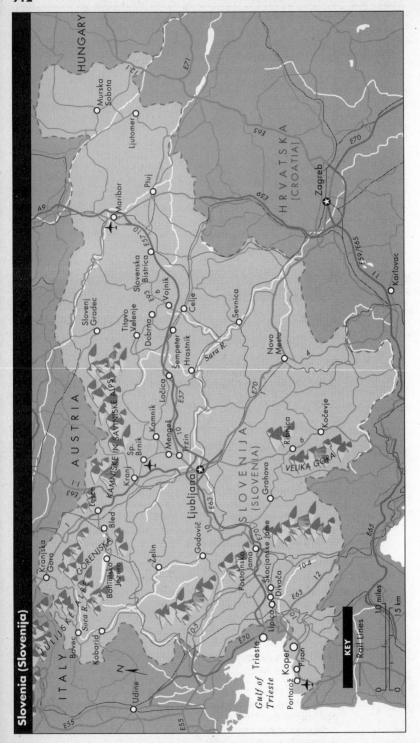

KEY
Rail Lines

land) can be an advantage: From the centrally located capital, Ljubljana, everything in the country is no more than a three-hour drive.

SLOVENIA A TO Z

Customs

Duty-free allowances are: 1 carton of cigarettes, 1 liter of spirits, 2 liters of wine. The export of historical artifacts is strictly forbidden.

Dining

When you look at a menu remember two key words: regional and seasonal. This is the best way to eat in Slovenia. There are no pretensions at the table and full respect is paid to traditional peasant dishes. To really get down to basics, eat in a country *gostilna* (inn). Typical dishes are *krvavice* (black pudding) served with *žganci* (polenta), or sausages served with sauerkraut. Another favorite is *bograč*, a peppery stew similar to Hungarian goulash, made from either horse meat or beef. Coffee shops serve the delicious calorie-laden *prekmurska gibanica*, a layered cake combining curd cheese, walnuts, and poppy seeds. Another national favorite is *potica*, a rolled cake filled with either walnuts, chocolate, poppy seeds, or raisins. Slovenes enjoy drinking and produce some excellent wines, notably the red *Teran*, and the white *Laški Rizling*.

RATINGS

Prices are for a three-course meal for one person, not including drinks or tip.

Category	Cost
$$$	over SIT4,000
$$	SIT2,500–SIT4,000
$	under SIT2,500

WHAT TO WEAR

Casual dress is acceptable in many restaurants in Slovenia, but Slovenes do tend to dress more formally when going out for the evening.

Language

Slovene is the chief language. In the eastern part of the country signs are posted in Slovene and Hungarian; on the Adriatic coast both Slovene and Italian are officially used. English, German, and Italian are spoken in many places.

Lodging

Don't expect Slovenia to be a cheap option: Prices are comparable to those in western Europe. During the high season (June–September), many hotels, particularly on the coast, become fully booked.

HOTELS

Many hotels have been upgraded: They are clean, smartly furnished, and well run. Establishments built under socialism are highly equipped with extras such as saunas and sports facilities but tend to be gargantuan structures lacking in soul. Older hotels dating back to the turn of the century are more romantic. Most establishments add a 30% surcharge for stays of fewer than three days.

PRIVATE LODGINGS

This is the cheapest option. Prices vary depending on region and season. Contact local Tourist Information Centers for details.

RATINGS

CATEGORY	COST
$$$$	over SIT25,000
$$$	SIT18,000–SIT25,000
$$	SIT10,000–SIT18,000
$	under SIT10,000

TOURIST FARMS

Staying on a working farm offers the chance to experience rural life first hand. "Agritourism" is growing in popularity, especially in the Gorenjska region. This is an ideal solution for families with children. Contact the Association of Tourist Farms of Slovenia (⌑ Trnoveljska 1, 3000 Celje, ☎ 063/345–21, ℻ 063/344–04).

YOUTH HOSTELS

During the summer break, university dorms in Ljubljana and Maribor are open to visitors. There are also a number of youth hostels, generally in country areas, that cater to hikers. For information contact Hosteling International Slovenia (YHA; ⌑ Kocenova 2, 3000 Celje, ☎ 063/ 484–111, ℻ 063/442–870).

Mail

Airmail postage to the United States is SIT99 for a letter, SIT89 for a postcard. Airmail postage in Europe is SIT80 for a letter, SIT70 for a postcard. Post offices are open weekdays 8–6 and Saturday 8–noon. Stamps are also sold at hotels, newsstands, and kiosks.

Money Matters

COSTS

Costs in general are comparable to those in western Europe. Notable exceptions are public transport, alcohol, and cigarettes, all of which are cheaper here. Typical prices are: cup of coffee, SIT150; glass of beer (draught), SIT200; slice of cake, SIT200; bottle of wine (house wine), SIT1500; sandwich, SIT350; admission to museums, SIT300.

CURRENCY

The monetary unit in Slovenia is the Slovenian tolar (SIT). One Slovenian tolar is divided into 100 stotin. There are notes of SIT10,000, SIT5,000, SIT1,000, SIT500, SIT200, SIT100, SIT50, SIT20, and SIT10 and coins of 5, 2 and 1 Slovenian tolar and 50 stotin. Exchange rates at press time (summer 1999) were SIT188 to the U.S.$, SIT294 to the £ sterling, SIT128 to the C$, SIT125 to the A$, and SIT99 to the NZ$.

TIPPING

Tax is already included in listed prices. As tips are not included in bills, a 10% tip is customary; if service is especially good, tip 15%.

National Holidays

January 1–2; February 8 (Prešeren Day, Slovene cultural day); April 23 and 24 (Easter Sunday and Monday); April 27 (National Resistance Day); May 1 and 2 (Labor Day); June 25 (Slovenia National Day); August 15 (Assumption); October 31 (Reformation Day); November 1 (All Saints' Day); December 25; December 26 (Independence Day).

Opening and Closing Times

Most **banks** should be open weekdays 9–12 and 2–4:30, Saturday 9–11. You can also change money at exchange desks in hotels, gas stations, tourist agencies, supermarkets, and small exchange offices. The main **museums** are open Tuesday–Sunday 10–6. Larger **shops** are open Monday–Saturday 10–6, smaller ones may open mornings only 10–2. Most are closed Sunday.

Telephoning

COUNTRY CODE

The country code for Slovenia is 386.

INTERNATIONAL CALLS

To make international calls, dial 00 and then the appropriate country code. International calls can be made from local telephones or at the post office. To call collect dial 901. For international directory inquiries dial 989.

LOCAL CALLS

Pay phones take telephone cards. These can be purchased at post offices and kiosks. Lower rates apply from 10 PM to 7 AM and all day Sunday. For local directory inquiries dial 988.

Transportation

In Slovenian the words for street (*ulica*) and drive (*cesta*) are abbreviated *ul.* and *c. Nabrežje* (abreviated *nab.*) means embankment. The word for square is *trg.*

BY BOAT

Between Easter and the last week of October the **Prince of Venice** (Kompas Turizem; ✉ Obala 41, 6320 Portorož, ☎ 066/747–032) hydrofoil makes regularly scheduled trips between Venice and Portorož.

From late May to late September, the Italian firm **Adriatica** (Maona; ✉ Cankarievo nab. 7, 6330 Piran, ☎ 066/746–228) runs a round-trip service from Trieste, calling at Piran and stopping at several towns on the Croatian Adriatic coast.

BY BUS

Intercity bus service is regular, cheap, and efficient, reaching even the most outlying mountain villages. For information contact **Ljubljana bus station** (✉ Trg OF 5, ☎ 061/133–6136).

BY CAR

An international driver's license is required in Slovenia. Main roads between large towns are comparable to those in western Europe. Highways charge a toll depending on route and distance traveled. The main highways between Ljubljana and the Austrian and Italian borders have recently been widened. A tunnel speeds traffic through the Karavanke Alps between Slovenia and Austria. From Vienna the passage is by way of Maribor to Ljubljana, with a highway from Graz to Celje. Slovenia's roads also connect with Italy's autostrada. Road conditions are good. Gasoline costs SIT80 per liter. Rental for a mid-size car costs US$112 (SIT18,500) for 24 hours, with unlimited mileage and leaving a credit card as deposit.

BY PLANE

There are no direct flights between Slovenia and the United States. **Adria Airways** (✉ Gosposvetska 6, 1000 Ljubljana, ☎ 061/313–312), the Slovene national airline, offers regular flights to most major European cities. Austrian Airlines has daily flights from Vienna; Aeroflot and Swissair also have good connections.

BY TRAIN

The internal rail network is limited, but trains are cheap and efficient. Daily trains link Slovenia with Austria, Italy, Hungary, and Croatia. Many are overnight trains with sleeping compartments. For information contact **Ljubljana Train Station** (✉ Trg OF 6, ☎ 061/131–5167).

Visas

No visas are necessary for holders of valid passports from the United States, Canada, the United Kingdom, mainland European countries,

Australia, New Zealand, or the Republic of Ireland. South African nationals, however, must have a 3-month tourist visa.

Visitor Information

Slovenian Tourist Board (✉ Dunajska 156, Ljubljana, ☎ 061/1891–840, 🖷 061/1891–841). Each region has its own Tourist Information Center (TIC).

Weather

The tourist season runs throughout the year, though prices tend to be lower from November through March. Late spring and fall are best, usually warm enough for swimming but not uncomfortably hot.

CLIMATE

Weather in Slovenia can vary greatly depending upon what part of the country you are in. Temperatures are colder and precipitation tends to be higher in the alpine regions, while the summers on the coast can be quite hot. Ljubljana and the Pannonian plain have less extreme variations in weather. The following are the average temperatures for Ljubljana.

Jan.	32F	0C	May	59F	14.5C	Sept.	59F	15C
Feb.	37F	2.5C	June	65F	18C	Oct.	49F	9C
Mar.	43F	6C	July	70F	20C	Nov.	40F	4C
Apr.	49F	9C	Aug.	68F	19C	Dec.	32F	0C

LJUBLJANA

The capital of the republic of Slovenia is on occasion referred to as "Ljubljana the beloved," a play on words: *Ljubljena* means "beloved"; change one letter, and you have the name Ljubljana.

In 34 BC, the Romans founded Emona on this site. Traces of the Roman occupation have been preserved in sections of walls and a complex of foundations complete with mosaics. Slovenes settled here in the 7th century. Later, under the German name Laibach, this became the capital of the Duchy of Carniola, which in 1335 passed into the hands of the House of Habsburg. From then until the end of World War I Ljubljana remained part of the Habsburg monarchy. In 1849 the railway linking Vienna and Trieste reached Ljubljana, establishing it as a major center of commerce, industry, and culture.

Influences from the past are apparent in the Ljubljana of today, although you will have to pass through concentric circles like the growth rings of a tree in order to reach the romantic heart of the original old town. Vast industrial complexes and high-rise apartments form the outermost ring. "Downtown," composed mainly of modern office buildings, is also spread out.

To reach the old, romantic Ljubljana, follow one of the city's main commercial streets, Miklošičeva Cesta, south from the railway station, eventually passing a series of palatial three- and four-story structures in florid Art Nouveau style (Jugendstil), topped by cupolas, spires, and ornate statuary, facades adorned with extravagant arches, balustrades, and curlicue details. Miklošičeva reaches the River Ljubljanica at Prešernov Trg, the square named for Slovenia's greatest poet, France Prešeren (1800–49), whose bronze statue stands here. This expansive, traffic-free square, the banks of the river, and old Ljubljana are the places where this lively city is at its most animated. The narrow cobblestone passageways through the medieval quarter and its 19th-century adjuncts evoke a calmer, quieter time. Here students pedal bicycles to and from

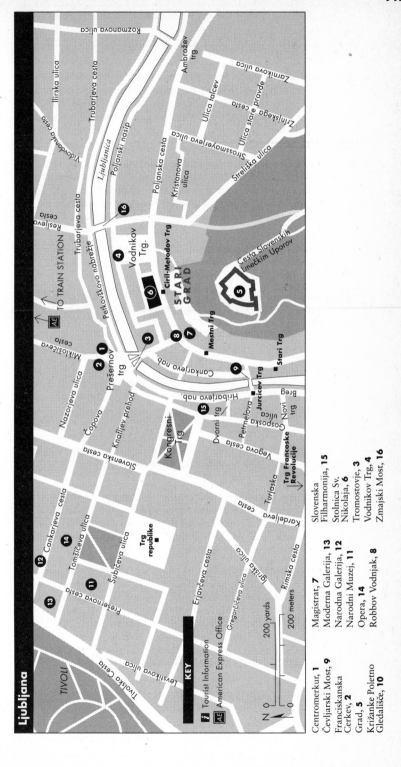

Ljubljana

KEY

ℹ️ Tourist Information

AE American Express Office

0 — 200 yards
0 — 200 meters

N

Centromerkur, **1**
Čevljarski Most, **9**
Franciskanska
Cerkev, **2**
Grad, **5**
Križanke Poletno
Gledališče, **10**

Magistrat, **7**
Moderna Galerija, **13**
Narodna Galerija, **12**
Narodni Muzej, **11**
Opera, **14**
Robbov Vodnjak, **8**

Slovenska
Filharmonija, **15**
Stolnica Sv.
Nikolaja, **6**
Tromostovje, **3**
Vodnikov Trg, **4**
Zmajski Most, **16**

classes. Along Mestni and Stari Trg green hills rise straight up behind
the curve of steeply pitched tile roofs.

Exploring Ljubljana

① Centromerkur. This magnificent Vienna Secessionist–style building,
dating from 1903, is the oldest department store in town. The entrance,
off Prešernov trg, bears a flaring iron butterfly-wing portal and is
topped by a statue of Mercury. Inside, extraordinarily graceful curved
wrought-iron stairways lead to upper floors. ⊠ *Trubarjeva 1,* ☎ *061/
126–3170.*

⑨ Čevljarski Most (Shoemaker's Bridge). Taking its name from the cob-
blers who once plied their trade here, this was formerly a wooden structure lined with craftsmen's huts. The present ferroconcrete bridge,
with more than a dozen Corinthian columns topped by stone spheres,
was built in 1931 to plans by the architect Jože Plečnik (1872–1957).
⊠ *Pod Tranco.*

Ciril-Metodov Trg (Cyril Methodius Square). This thoroughfare, lined
with fine old palaces, leads from the cathedral to the heart of old Ljubljana. ⊠ *Jct. Mestni trg, Vodnikov trg, and Sritarjeva ul.*

② Franciskanska Cerkev (Franciscan Church). This massive, pink, high-
Baroque church was built between 1646 and 1660. The main altar is
by Francesco Robba (1698–1757), dating from 1736. The three sets
of stairs in front serve as a popular meeting place for students. ⊠
Prešernov trg 4. ☉ *Daily 8–6.*

⑤ Grad (Castle). Although Ljubljana Castle dates from the early 16th century, the tower was added in the mid-19th century, and a park on the
castle hill was landscaped in the 1930s by Plečnik. The magnificent setting affords splendid views down across the old town, with its red roofs,
spires, and green cupolas, and the river, with its bridges—all silhouet-
ted against the backdrop of the Julian Alps. The castle courtyard is used
for occasional concerts, and the ramparts shelter a restaurant and a
café. ⊠ *Up hill from Vodnikov trg via Studentovska ul.,* ☎ *061/1327–
216.* ☉ *Mon.–Fri, and Sun 11–6.*

Jurcicev Trg. In late afternoon and early evening, as the globular lights
of Čevljarski Most (☞ *above*) come on and are reflected in the water,
this small square rimmed with boutiques and several cafés is Ljubljana
at its brightest and most appealing. ⊠ *West end of Čevljarski Most at
jct. of Petrnelova and Breg Hribarjevo nab.*

⑩ Križanke Poletno Gledališče. (Monastery of the Holy Cross Summer
Theater). While the former Teutonic Knights' monastery in whose
courtyard it stands dates from the 18th century, the Summer Theater
itself was completed in 1976, to plans drawn up by the architect Jose
Plec(h)nik between 1950 and 1956. This open-air space, which provides seating for 1,400, has a movable roof to ensure that performances can continue if it rains. The annual International Summer
Festival and the Jazz Festival are both held here. ⊠ *Trg Francoske Revolucije.*

⑦ Magistrat (Town Hall). Behind the building's heavy facade a passageway leads to an internal courtyard where a statue of Hercules keeps company with a fountain bearing a Narcissus figure. On the walls of the
courtyard, murals depict historic battles for the town. ⊠ *Mestni trg 1.*

Mestni Trg (Town Square). This cobbled, traffic-free square extends into
the oldest part of the city, past onetime town houses and patrician palaces
now divided into functional apartments but still presenting marvelously

ornate facades; carved oak doors with great brass handles are framed within columns, and second and third floors are decorated with balustrades, statuary, and intricate ironwork. Narrow passageways connect with inner courtyards in one direction and run to the riverfront in the other. Street-level floors contain boutiques, antiques shops, or art galleries. ✉ *Jct. Ciril-Metodov trg, Stritarjeva ul., and Stari trg.*

⑬ Moderna Galerija (Modern Gallery). The strikingly modern one-story structure contains a selection of paintings, sculpture, and prints by Slovenian 20th-century artists. In odd-numbered years it also hosts the International Biennale of Graphics. ✉ *Cankarjeva 15,* ☎ *061/214–106.* ⊘ *Tues.–Sat. 10–6, Sun. 10–1.*

⑫ Narodna Galerija (National Gallery). The imposing turn-of-the-century building houses a survey of Slovene art from the 13th through the early 20th century. ✉ *Cankarjeva 20,* ☎ *061/1263–109.* ⊘ *Tues.–Sat. 10–6, Sun. 10–1.*

⑪ Narodni Muzej (National Museum). Of the archaeological finds in the collection here, the greatest treasure is the Vace Situle, a bronze urn discovered in Vace in Slovenia. Dating from the 5th century BC, it is a striking example of Illyrian workmanship. ✉ *Muzejski 1,* ☎ *061/ 1264–098.* ⊘ *Tues.–Sat. 10–6, Sun. 10–1.*

⑭ Opera. This neo-Renaissance palace with an ornate facade topped by an allegorical sculpture group was erected in 1892. The Opera, home to the Slovene National Opera and Ballet Theater, was originally built for the Theater of the County of Carniola during the time when, as part of the Austro-Hungarian Empire under the Habsburgs, Ljubljana was the county's administrative center. ✉ *Župančičeva 1,* ☎ *061/ 1254–840.* ⊘ *Weekdays 11–1, and 1 hr before performances.*

⑧ Robbov Vodnjak (Robba's Fountain). When the Slovenian Baroque sculptor Francesco Robba saw Bernini's "Fountain of the Four Rivers" on Piazza Navona during a visit to Rome, he was inspired to create this allegorical representation of the three main Kranjska rivers—the Sava, the Krka, and the Ljubljanica—that flow through Slovenia. ✉ *Mestni trg.*

⑮ Slovenska Filharmonija (Slovenian Philharmonic Hall). The hall was built in 1891 for one of the oldest music societies in the world, established in 1701. Associates of the orchestra have included Hadyn, Brahms, Beethoven, Mahler, and Paganini. ✉ *Kongresni trg 10,* ☎ *061/ 311–892.*

Stari Trg (Old Square). More a narrow street than a square, Stari Trg is lined with cafés and small restaurants; in good weather tables are set out on the cobblestones. ✉ *Mestni trg and Cankarjevo nab.*

⑥ Stolnica Sv. Nikolaja (Cathedral of St. Nicholas). Overlooking Vodnikov trg, the Baroque church was built between 1701 and 1708. The cupola was added in 1836. In 1996 in honor of the Pope's visit, new bronze doors were added: The main door tells the story of Christianity in Slovenia, while the side door portrays the history of the Ljubljana Diocese. ✉ *Dolničarjeva 1,* ☎ *061/310–684.* ⊘ *Daily 7–noon and 3–7.*

Trg Francoske Revolucije (French Revolution Square). This square is dominated by Plečnik's **Ilirski Steber** (Illyrian Column), erected in 1929 to commemorate the brief tenure of Napoléon's Illyrian Provinces regime in Slovenia. ✉ *Jct. Rimska c. and Vegova c.*

Trg Republike (Republic Square). The heart of Ljubljana's cultural life, this square is where old and new parts of the city merge in an unlikely mix of glass-and-steel skyscrapers and the city's chief cultural institutions (museums, concert halls, small theaters) on the north side and the preserved remains of the ancient Roman city of **Emona** (between Erjavčeva Cesta and Gregorčičeva ul.) on the south. ⊠ *Jct. Šubičeva ul. and Valvazorjeva ul.*

❸ Tromostovje (Triple Bridge). Passing over the River Ljubljanica from Prešernov trg to the old town, this splendid structure takes the fortress on 1,233-ft-high Grajski Hrib (Castle Hill) as its backdrop. The three bridges started as a single span, but in 1931 the two graceful outer arched bridges, designed by Plečnik, were added. ⊠ *Pres(h)ernov trg at north end; Stritarjeva ul. at Cankarjevo nab. at south end.*

❹ Vodnikov Trg (Vodnik Square). The big and bustling flower, fruit, and vegetable market is held here six days a week. An elegant riverside colonnade designed by Plečnik runs the length of the market, and a bronze statue of the Slovene poet Valentin Vodnik, after whom the square is named, overlooks the scene. ⊠ *Resleva c. and Poljanska c.* ☉ *Market, Mon.–Sat., 7–6.*

⓰ Zmajski Most (Dragon's Bridge). Four fire-breathing winged dragons crown the corners of this spectacular concrete and iron structure. ⊠ *Resljeva ul.*

Dining and Lodging

You can eat well in Ljubljana, but it won't be cheap. The restaurants listed here serve traditional Slovenian dishes. Meanwhile, foreign restaurants are on the rise: Italian, Chinese, and Mexican predominate. For a lunchtime snack visit the Vodnikov market. Choose from tasty fried squid and whitebait in the riverside arcade by the fish section, or freshly baked pies and cakes at the bakeries on the square.

The hotels listed here are clustered conveniently around Miklošičeva cesta, the main axis running from the train station down to the Triple Bridge. Ljubljana is expensive, but standards are high. In summer you can opt for private accommodation or university dorms for better deals. Ask at the TIC kiosk in the train station.

$$$ ✕ **Rotovz.** In the old quarter, this restaurant has tables beneath umbrellas on the cobblestones in summer and serves meals in the dark wood interior in colder weather. Order *pastrmka* (trout) with parsley potatoes or a frog-leg specialty, along with crisp salad and a bottle of first-rate Slovenian wine. ⊠ *Mestni trg 2,* ☎ *061/212–839. AE, DC, MC, V. Closed Sun.*

$$$ ✕ **Spajza.** Tucked into a rose-tone building in the old district, this restaurant has the best decor in the city in a winding series of rooms full of color and knickknacks. Excellent food selections may include venison in cognac sauce with fresh asparagus or pasta with mushrooms and zucchini. ⊠ *Gornji trg 28,* ☎ *061/125–3094. AE, DC, MC, V. Closed Sun.*

$$$ ✕ **Vinoteka.** This fine restaurant in the Ljubljana trade fair complex offers the best national dishes, such as grilled seafood with lemon, as well as vegetarian food. It also serves a great selection of Slovenian wines. ⊠ *Dunajska 18,* ☎ *061/131–5015. AE, DC, MC, V. Closed Sun.*

$$ ✕ **AS.** Opened in 1998, this restaurant just off Prešernov trg has become an instant success. Serving seafood specialties in old-fashioned style, AS attracts a young and lively crowd. ⊠ *Knafljev prehod,* ☎ *061/ 125–8822. AE, DC, MC, V.*

$$ ✕ **Figovec.** Renowned for horse meat, this restaurant also serves roasts such as suckling pig, duck, and goose. The wood-paneled interior creates a dark but intimate atmosphere. There's live music on Friday. ✉ *Gosposvetska 1,* ☏ *061/126–5000. AE, DC, MC, V. Closed Sun. evening.*

$ ✕ **Pivnica Kratchowill.** This microbrewery is a designer bar and restaurant: terra-cotta floor, ocher walls, blue details, and discreet lighting. Besides the classic beer sausage and sauerkraut, the menu offers game dishes, tasty pastas, and a salad bar. The beer, brewed on the premises, is excellent. It's a real find in such proximity to the train station. ✉ *Kolodvorska 14,* ☏ *061/133–3114. AE, DC, MC, V.*

$ ✕ **Zlata Ribica.** Ideal for the Sunday flea market, this popular bar and bistro is frequented by boisterous stall holders and antiques buffs. The sound menu includes black pudding, squid, and mushroom omelet. Check out the mulled wine drink list at the bar in winter. ✉ *Cankarjevo nab. 5,* ☏ *061/221–367. AE, DC, MC, V. Closed Sat. and Sun. after 3.*

$$$ 🏨 **Best Western Slon Hotel.** Close to the river, this older hotel was completely renovated in 1996. It is on the site of a famous mid-16th-century inn and maintains an atmosphere of traditional hospitality. The breakfast here is among the finest in the city. The rooms are comfortable but not special. ✉ *Slovenska 34, 1000,* ☏ *061/170–1100,* FAX *061/ 217–164. 185 rooms. 2 restaurants. AE, DC, MC, V.*

$$$ 🏨 **Grand Hotel Union.** This turn-of-the-century hotel occupies a magnificent Jugendstil structure. The lobby and the main-floor café have been tastefully renovated, as have the rooms. ✉ *Miklošičeva 1, 1000,* ☏ *061/125–4133,* FAX *061/217–910. 233 rooms, 6 suites. 2 restaurants. AE, DC, MC, V.*

$$ 🏨 **Hotel Turist.** The rooms are basic, but this hotel is conveniently in the city center. Service is satisfactory at best. ✉ *Dalmatinova 15, 1000,* ☏ *061/132–2343,* FAX *061/319–291. 190 rooms. 2 restaurants. AE, DC, MC, V.*

$ 🏨 **Hotel Bellevue.** In Tivoli Park, this former villa has an air of bygone luxury fallen into decadence. The high-ceiling rooms and dining terrace give the place grandeur, while the lumpy mattresses and peeling paintwork keep the prices low. ✉ *Pod gozdom 2, 1000,* ☏ *061/133– 4049,* FAX *061/133–4057. 19 rooms. Restaurant. AE, DC, MC, V.*

Nightlife and the Arts

The Arts

Ljubljana's **International Summer Festival** (✉ Trg Francoske Revolucije 1–2, ☏ 061/126–4340), running through July and August, is held in Plečnik's open-air Križanke Theater. Musical, theatrical, and dance performances attract acclaimed artists from all over the world.

Nightlife

In recent years Ljubljana has become more international and more commercial. Nightclubs, bars, and restaurants open and close, changing hands from one month to the next. The best long-standing nightclub in town is **Eldorado** (✉ Nazorjeva 4, ☏ 061/126–2126). **K4** (✉ Kersnikova 4, ☏ 061/131–7010), a student-run nightclub attached to the university, is something of an institution, attracting a young and lively crowd. **Jazz Club Gojo** (✉ Beethovnova 8, ☏ 061/125–3206) boasts a framed letter from U.S. President Clinton accepting, "subject to his schedule," an open invitation to play the sax here.

Shopping

The Sunday morning flea market is held on Cankarjevo nabrežje, near the Triple Bridge.

Ljubljana Essentials

Arriving and Departing

BY CAR

See Transportation *in* Slovenia A to Z, *above.*

BY PLANE

Ljubljana's airport is at **Brnik** (☎ 064/222–700), 22 km (14 mi) north of the city. A shuttle bus runs between the airport and Ljubljana and other nearby destinations.

BY TRAIN

The **train station** (⊠ Trg OF 6, ☎ 061/131–5167), close to the city center, has a tourist information office to help travelers find accommodations in hotels, pensions, and apartments.

Getting Around

BY BUS

Tokens are sold at kiosks and post offices. As you board the bus, drop the token into the box by the driver. The cost is a little higher if you pay in change. During the day buses operate every half hour and cover an extensive network; at night they are less frequent.

BY TAXI

Private taxis operate 24 hours a day. Telephone (☎ 061/9700, 061/9701, to 061/9709 inclusive) from your hotel or hail one in the street. Drivers are bound by law to display and run a meter.

Contacts and Resources

EMBASSIES AND CONSULATES

U.S. (⊠ Pražakova 4, ☎ 061/301–427, FAX 061/301–401). **Canadian** (⊠ Miklošičeva 19, ☎ 061/130–3570, FAX 061/130–3575). **U.K.** (⊠ Trg republike 3/IV, ☎ 061/125–7191, FAX 061/125–0174). **Australian Consulate** (Trg Republike 3/XII, ☎ 061/125–4252, FAX 061/126–4721).

EMERGENCIES

Police (☎ 113). **Ambulance, fire brigade** (☎ 112). **Doctor: Ljubljana Emergency Medical Services** (☎ 061/323–060). **Pharmacies:** 24-hour pharmacy, **Lekarna Miklošič** (⊠ Miklošičeva 24, ☎ 061/314–558).

ENGLISH-LANGUAGE BOOKSTORES

Cankarjeva založba/Oxford Center (⊠ Kopitarjeva 2, ☎ 061/324–568). **MK Knjigarna Konzorcij** (⊠ Slovenska 29, ☎ 061/125–0196).

GUIDED TOURS

Informative and amusing sightseeing walks, organized by Ljubljana Promotion Center, depart from the Magistrat (Town Hall; ⊠ Mestni trg 1), June–September, daily at 5; October–May, Sunday at 11.

VISITOR INFORMATION

Turistično Informacijski Center (Tourist Information Center, TIC; ⊠ Mačkova 1, ☎ 061/133–0111).

MOUNTAINS AND LAKES

Northwest of Ljubljana lies a region of mountain and lakeside resorts, complete with thermal springs, ski trails, and historic religious shrines. The Julian Alps, lying at the junction of the borders of Italy, Austria, and Slovenia, are contained within Triglav National Park. The resort centers of Bled and Bohinj lie beside the lakes of Bled and Bohinj respectively, while Krajnska Gora is an alpine resort.

Bled

Bled, 50 km (31 mi) northwest of Ljubljana, is among the most magnificently situated mountain resorts in Europe. The healing powers of its thermal springs were known during the 17th century; in the early 19th century the aristocracy arrived to bask in Bled's tranquil Alpine setting. Since the mid-1970s a spate of new hotels and a wide range of recreational facilities have sprung up in Bled, including an 18-hole golf course. Rowing, hiking, swimming, boating, biking, tennis, and horseback riding are important here. In winter there's skiing and ice-skating at the nearby high-altitude resort of Zatrnik.

Blejsko Jezero (Lake Bled), surrounded by forests, is nestled within a rim of mountains, with a castle on one side and a promenade beneath stately chestnut trees on the other. Horse-drawn carriages clip-clop along the promenade while swans glide on the water. On a minuscule island in the lake the lovely **Cerkov Svetega Martina** (St. Martin's pilgrimage church) rises from within a circle of red roofs and trees. Graceful, old-fashioned canopied wooden boats called *pletna,* propelled by oarsmen standing aft, carry passengers to the island.

☾ The stately 16th-century **Grad** (Castle) perches above the lake at the summit of a steep cliff, against the backdrop of the Julian Alps and Mt. Triglav. You can climb up to the castle for fine views of the lake, the resort, and the surrounding countryside. ☏ *064/741–230.* ☾ *Mar.–Oct., daily 8–7; Nov.–Feb., daily 9–4.*

☾ The **Vintgar Gorge** was cut between precipitous cliffs by the clear river Radovna, which flows down numerous waterfalls and through pools and rapids. The trip in the gorge leads over bridges and along wooden walkways and galleries. ✉ *5 km (3 mi) northeast of Bled on road to Pokljuka/Zg. Gorje.*

\$\$\$ ✕ **Gostilna Lectar.** At this restaurant with a cozy country-inn atmosphere, you can choose from an impressive array of Slovenian national dishes and wines. Try the pumpkin soup, the "peasant's plate" (buckwheat dumplings, mixed smoked meats, potatoes, and fresh steamed vegetables), and the apple strudel, for a cross section of local cuisine. ✉ *Linhartov trg 2, Radovljica, 9 km/5½ mi south of Bled on Rte. E61,* ☏ *064/715–642. AE, DC, MC, V.*

\$\$ ✕ **Ribic.** At this small restaurant the fish selection is excellent and very fresh. The pink tablecloths and polished silver cutlery create an unnecessarily staid atmosphere, but the view of the lake makes up for it. ✉ *C. Svobode 27,* ☏ *064/778–66. AE, DC, MC, V.*

\$ ✕ **Gostilna pri Planincu.** This friendly joint keeps busy year-round. Locals meet here for morning coffee or a bargain set-menu lunch, or just to drink the cheapest beer in town. While rowdy farmers occupy the front bar, lovers share a candlelit supper in the dining room. Portions are "for people who work all day": roast chicken and chips, steak and mushrooms, black pudding and turnip. Walnut *štrukle* (dumplings) are served with cream. ✉ *Grajska 8,* ☏ *064/741–613. AE, DC, MC, V.*

\$ ✕ **Mlino.** Follow the lakeside footpath 20 minutes from the center of Bled to reach this informal family restaurant. Try the Mlino Plate: A mixed platter of barbecued meats served with *djevec* (rice cooked with vegetables). There is a special menu for children, and boats are for hire on the lake. ✉ *C. Svobode 45,* ☏ *064/741–404,* ☒ *064/741–506. AE, DC, MC, V.*

\$\$\$\$ ▨ **Vila Bled.** Yugoslavia's late president Tito used this former royal residence on the lake as a hunting lodge. It was converted into a luxurious small-scale hotel in 1984 and became part of the Relais et Chateaux association in 1987. Among the elegant touches are hand-embroidered linen sheets, Art Deco furnishings, antique rugs, Oriental vases, and original art. ⊠ *C. Svobode 26, 4260, ☎ 064/7915, ﬀ 064/741–320. 10 rooms, 20 suites. Restaurant. AE, DC, MC, V.*

$$$ 🏨 **Grand Hotel Toplice.** This elegant, old-fashioned, ivy-covered resort hotel has been favored by British visitors since the 1920s. Directly on the lake, the main building has balconies and big windows that offer dramatic views of the castle and the Julian Alps. The rooms, the lounges, and the bar are all furnished with antiques and heirloom rugs. ⊠ *C. Svobode 20, 4260, ☎ 061/7910, ﬀ 061/741–841. 206 rooms. Restaurant, indoor pool. AE, DC, MC, V.*

$ 🏨 **Bledec Youth Hostel.** Just five minutes from the lake and 10 minutes from the castle, Bledec is one of the cleanest and most comfortable youth hostels in Europe. ⊠ *Grajska cesta 17, 4260, ☎ 064/745–250. 13 rooms. Restaurant, bar. MC. Closed Nov.*

Bohinjsko Jezero

A 26-km (16-mi) drive west from Bled will take you to Bohinjsko Jezero (Lake Bohinj) in **Triglavski Narodni Park** (Triglav National Park). In a valley surrounded by the steep walls of the Julian Alps, at an altitude of 1,715 ft, this deep-blue, 4½-km- (3-mi-) long lake is even more dramatically situated than Bled (☞ *above*) and not nearly as developed.

At the lakeside, the small, exquisite 15th-century Gothic church of **Sveti Janez** (St. John), with a fine bell tower, contains a number of notable 15th- and 16th-century frescoes.

At the west end of the lake a cable car leads up **Mt. Vogel** to a height of 5,035 ft. Here you have spectacular views of the Julian Alps massif and the Bohinj valley and lake. From the cable-car base the road continues 5 km (3 mi) beyond the lake to the point where the waters of the Savica make a tremendous leap over a 195-ft waterfall.

$$ 🏨 **Hotel Bellevue.** As the name suggests, Bellevue affords wonderful views down over the lake. Agatha Christie fell in love with this old-fashioned hotel and stayed one month here while working on *Murder on the Orient Express*. ⊠ *Ribčev Laz 65, 4265, ☎ 064/723–331, ﬀ 064/723–684. 76 rooms. AE, DC, MC, V.*

Kranjska Gora

Kranjska Gora, 39 km (24 mi) northwest of Bled, is one of the largest winter tourist centers in Slovenia, in the dramatic setting of some of the country's highest peaks. In summer the resort caters mainly to hiking and mountaineering enthusiasts.

A spectacular side trip from Kranjska Gora is the drive over the **Vršič Pass,** at 5,252 ft, and the descent into the beautiful Soca Valley, winding through the foothills to the west of Mt. Triglav, occasionally plunging through tunnels along the way. You reach the rustic mountain resort of **Bovec** after 44 km (27 mi). From here the road follows the magnificent turquoise-color Soča River (Isonzo, in Italian) running parallel to the border. Farther along the road is **Kobarid** (Caporetto in Italian), where the **Kobarid Museum** recalls the World War I struggles that took place here.

Gorenjska Essentials

Arriving and Departing

BY BUS

Hourly buses link Ljubljana to Bled, Bohinj, and Kranjska Gora.

BY CAR

From Ljubljana a toll road (E63) runs 42 km (26 mi) northwest past Kranj; from there a recently reconditioned road (E651) leads to the resorts of Bled and Kranjska Gora.

Getting Around

BY BICYCLE

You can rent mountain bikes at Bohinjsko Jezero through **Alpinum** (⌧ Ribčev Laz 50, ☎ 064/723–441).

ON FOOT

Gorenjska offers unspoiled countryside and magnificent mountain walks. Trails are well marked. Local Tourist Information Centers can supply maps and further details.

Guided Tours

Alpinum (☎ 064/723–441) organizes guided mountain-hiking and climbing tours as well as rafting trips. **Slovenijaturist** (☎ 061/314–284) arranges a trip on a steam locomotive, following the Bohinj line, which runs through the Soca valley, operating mid-June to mid-September every Thursday.

Visitor Information

In the Bohinj area many families let out rooms to visitors. The prettiest villages are Stara Fužina and Srednja Vas. Contact the Bohinj Tourist Information Center for details.

Bled (⌧ C. Svobode 15, 4260 Bled, ☎ 064/741–122). **Bohinj** (⌧ Ribčev Laz 48, 4265 Bohinjsko Jezero, ☎ 064/723–370). **Kranjska Gora** (⌧ Ticarjeva 2, 4280 Kranjska Gora, ☎ 064/881–768).

KARST AND COAST

Karst

The name of this limestone plateau between Ljubljana and the coast is the source of the word karst, which describes a geological phenomenon whose typical features include sinkholes, underground caves, and streams.

Postojnska Jama

The Postojnska Jama (Postojna Caves) are among the largest and most extraordinary caves in the world, with 23 km (14 mi) of labyrinthine underground passageways and chambers on two levels, of which the first 7 km (4½ mi) are easily accessible and illuminated by electric light. The passage by train and on foot takes you through a succession of extraordinary rock formations of rare beauty and color. In keeping with the strangeness of this underground world are the snakelike creatures, the size of a pencil, called Proteus Anguineus, on view in a floodlit aquarium in the Great Hall. Eyeless and colorless because of countless millennia of life in total darkness, the proteus is both fish and mammal, a biological conundrum that can live up to 60 years. The cave temperature averages 8°C (46°F) year-round; in summer it can seem chilly. You can rent woolen cloaks at the entrance. One-and-a-half-hour tours leave every half hour in summer, hourly the rest of the year. ⌧ *Jamska c. 30, Postojna,* ☎ *067/25–041.* ▨ *SIT1,900.* ۞ *May–Sept., daily 8:30–6; Apr. and Oct., daily 8:30–5; Nov.–Mar., weekdays 9:30–1:30, weekends 9:30–3.*

Škocjanske Jame

The Škocjanske Jame (Škocjan Caves) at Divača are included on UNESCO's list of World Natural and Cultural Heritage sites. These caves require walking, but the beauty of the caverns makes the effort worthwhile. One-hour tours leave hourly. ⌧ *Matavun 12, 6215 Divača,* ☎ *067/601–22.* ▨ *SIT1,700.* ۞ *June–Sept., daily 10–6; Apr., May, Oct., tours daily 10, 1, and 5; Nov.–Mar., tours weekdays 10, weekends 10 and 3.*

Lipica

The **Kobilarna Lipica** (Lipica Stud Farm) in Sežana is the birthplace of the Lipizzaner white horses. Founded in 1580 by the Austrian Archduke Karl II, the farm still supplies Lipizzaners to the Spanish Riding School in Vienna. Lipica has developed into a modern sports complex, with two hotels, an indoor riding arena, a swimming pool, and a golf course. The stables are open to the public, and riding classes are available at all levels. ⊠ *Lipica 5, 6210 Sežana,* ☎ *067/315–80.* ☉ *Stables, July–Aug., daily 9–6; Apr.–June and Sept.–Oct., daily 10–5; Nov.–Mar., daily 11–3. Dressage performances, Apr.–Oct., Fri. and Sun. 3.*

Coast

Backed by a hilly hinterland planted with olive groves and vineyards, this strip of coast southwest of Ljubljana was once under the control of the Republic of Venice. Rich merchants built their villas here; the indelible mark of Venetian architecture has remained. The four towns of Koper, Izola, Piran, and Potorož dominate the 42 km (26 mi) of coastline. Koper is Slovenia's largest port for seagoing vessels and cargo ships. Potorož and the smaller medieval city of Piran are the resort centers.

Portorož

Known for its thermal spas, Portorož has a pleasant Mediterranean climate. Its situation on a south-facing slope keeps the city warm and blocks cold northern air even in winter. In summer vacationers fill the town in pursuit of the pleasures of the sea and the healing spas.

$$$ 🏨 **Hotel Palace.** At this modern hotel resort complex the elegant thermal spa recreation center offers massages and medical treatments. Rooms are comfortable and service professional. ⊠ *Obala 45, 6320,* ☎ *066/747–380,* 🖷 *066/747–002. 150 rooms. Restaurant, 1 outdoor and 1 indoor pool. AE, DC, MC, V.*

Piran

The medieval walled Venetian town of Piran is the jewel of the Slovenian coast, perched on a small, triangular peninsula pointing into the Adriatic Sea. Its narrow, winding, covered walkways are hardly wider than the span of outstretched arms. The main square, Piazza Tartini, opens out onto a charming harbor and is presided over by a hilltop Romanesque church.

Karst and Coast Essentials

Arriving and Departing

BY BOAT
See Transportation *in* Slovenia A to Z, *above.* There are four marinas (Izola, Koper, Piran, and Potorož) to choose from if you arrive on a private or rented yacht.

BY BUS
Buses connect the region to Ljubljana and to Trieste in Italy.

BY CAR
A drive of 52 km (32 mi) west from Ljubljana on the toll road (marked A-10) will bring you to the Karst region; 125 km (78 mi) southwest of Ljubljana (via the A-10) lies the Adriatic Coast.

BY PLANE
The region is served by **Portorož Airport** (☎ 066/790–01).

All trains from Ljubljana to Venice pass through the Karst region, stopping at Postojna and Divača. A train from Ljubljana to Koper serves the coast.

Visitor Information

Along the coast private lodgings offer a cheap alternative to hotels. Owners usually live on the ground floor and let rooms or apartments upstairs. Contact local Tourist Information Centers for details. **Lipica** (⊠ Lipica 5, ☎ 067/315–80). **Portorož** (⊠ Obala 16, ☎ 066/747–015). **Postojna** (⊠ Jamska c. 30, ☎ 067/250–41).

MARIBOR

Eastern Slovenia's chief city is next to the Austrian border, 128 km (79 mi) from Ljubljana. Straddling the Drava River, Maribor was founded during the 11th century under the name Marburg an der Drau (Marburg on the Drava). For centuries it served as a bastion against the repeated tides of Turkish conquest that swept into Central Europe. The old town north of the Drava has retained its pre-20th-century look, with ornate 18th- and 19th-century town houses and patrician palaces typical of Imperial Austria. Traffic-free narrow streets lead down to the riverside, where a number of fine old buildings have been restored and much of the waterfront along the former defensive walls outfitted with bars, terrace cafés, restaurants, and boutiques. The countryside south of the city is a land of vineyards and apple orchards.

Along the left bank of the river stands a restored ancient tower, **Sodni Stolp** (Tower of Justice). Near the tower, the facade of the **Stara Trta** (Vojasniska Ulica 8) inn is covered with grapevines said to be the oldest continuously producing vines in Europe, from which a small quantity of wine has been made annually for more than 400 years. Their yearly production is measured at no more than 45–50 kg (100–110 lb) of grapes, bottled as Somotska Crnina. A second historic tower, **Vodni Stolp** (Water Tower), now houses the **Vinoteka Slovenskih** (⊠ Usnjarska 10, ☎ 062/277–43), the wine shop of the regional wine-producing cooperative, where you can sample and purchase the best of local wines.

One street back from the waterfront, the **Kuzno Znamenje** (Plague Memorial) stands before the 16th-century **Razstavni** (Town Hall; ⊠ Glavni trg), which has an unusual Renaissance balcony. A passage through the Town Hall courtyard leads to the **Stolnica** (cathedral) in a small park next to the pedestrian precinct.

The **Grad** (castle) has Renaissance and Baroque elements grafted onto its original Gothic core, built in 1478. The castle houses the **Pokrajinski Muzej** (Regional Museum), with archaeological and ethnographic exhibits, collections of regional costumes and uniforms, Roman relics, an art gallery, and a collection of arms and armor. The main salon, where Franz Liszt gave recitals, is decorated with frescoes and ceiling paintings. ⊠ Grajska ul. 2, ☎ 062/218–51. ☉ Mid-Apr.–Nov., Tues.–Sat. 9–5, Sun. 10–2.

$$$ 🏨 **Best Western Slavija.** This modern white high-rise hotel qualifies as the best by far in Maribor, with a spacious lobby and comfortably decorated rooms. ⊠ Vita Kraigherja 3, 2000, ☎ 062/213–661, FAX 062/222–857. 120 rooms. Restaurant. AE, DC, MC, V.

$$ 🏨 **Hotel Orel.** The four-story prewar building on the main square has a pleasant restaurant at street level. The rooms are acceptable and the service is friendly. ⊠ Grajski trg 3a, 2000, ☎ 062/261–71, FAX 062/284–97. 146 rooms, 7 suites. Restaurant. AE, DC, MC, V.

Maribor Essentials

Arriving and Departing

BY CAR

To reach Maribor from Ljubljana take the E57.

BY PLANE

Maribor Airport (☎ 062/691–541).

BY TRAIN

Regular service links Ljubljana and Maribor; several international trains continue to Graz and Vienna.

Visitor Information

In summer, university dorms are open to visitors, offering a cheap alternative to hotels. Ask at the Tourist Information Center for details. **Maribor** (✉ Glavni trg 15, ☎ 062/211–262).

28 SPAIN

Spain is much more than flamenco, bullfights, and white hillside villages—it is soaring cathedrals, narrow lanes twisting through medieval towns, delicious food, spirited nightlife, and great art. Spain's master artists range from El Greco, Velázquez, and Goya to Picasso, Miró, and Dalí.

As any Spaniard is quick to point out, Spain is really several countries in one, each with its own proud character, its own distinctive cuisine, and sometimes even its own language. Andalusia, in the south, comes closest to postcard images of Spain: rolling hills dotted with whitewashed villages and olive trees. Andalusia's capital, Seville, is known for flamenco music and dance; for the girls dressed in ruffled polka-dot dresses at its April Fair; and for the solemn processions of penitents during Semana Santa (Holy Week). The region is also marked by its Moorish heritage, and remnants of its Islamic past abound, from the red-and-white striped arches of Córdoba's mosque to Spain's most important monument, Granada's Alhambra Palace. Andalusia is known more for tapas than for gourmet cuisine; provincial specialties include mounds of fried fish and shellfish called *frituras,* olives, cured ham, and the sherries of Jerez. On the Andalusian coast, the famed Costa del Sol, you can join the jet set at Marbella or, if you're feeling adventurous, cross the Strait of Gibraltar to explore northern Morocco.

Spain's vast center is still shaped by its role as a battlefield for centuries of contests between Moorish and Christian armies. Turreted castles look out over the bleak plains of Castile–La Mancha, the land of Don Quixote, and Castile–León, once known as Old Castile. Castile is home to Toledo, where Jews, Moors, and Christians lived and worked together before the Christian Reconquest of the 15th century; and medieval jewels like Segovia, the university city of Salamanca, and the fortress town of Ávila. The people of Castile are as simple, warm, and hearty as their cuisine—huge portions of roast lamb or suckling pig washed down with red wine from the Valdepeñas or Ribera del Duero regions.

At the hub of it all is Madrid, one of the liveliest capitals in Europe. Madrid is the seat of the Spanish government, a center for the national

Spain (España)

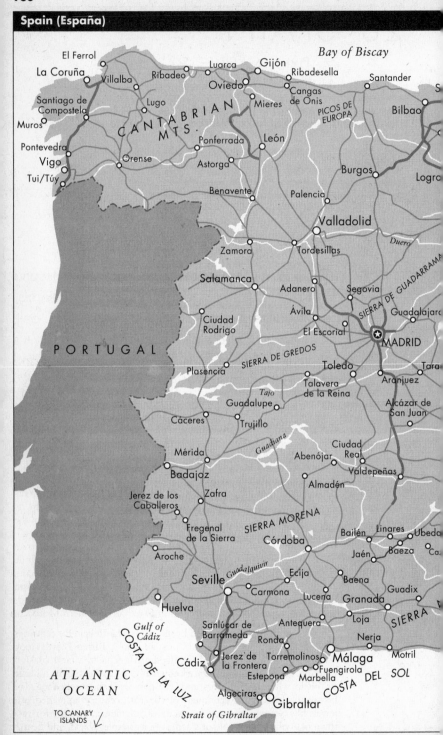

Bay of Biscay

El Ferrol
La Coruña
Villalba
Ribadeo
Luarca
Gijón
Ribadesella
Santander
Santiago de
Compostela
Lugo
Oviedo
Mieres
Cangas
de Onis
PICOS DE
EUROPA
Bilbao
Muros
CANTABRIAN
MTS.
León
Pontevedra
Orense
Ponferrada
Logro
Vigo
Astorga
Burgos
Tui/Túy
Benavente
Palencia
Valladolid
Zamora
Tordesillas
Duero
Salamanca
Adanero
Segovia
SIERRA DE GUADARRAMA
Ciudad
Rodrigo
Ávila
Guadalajara
El Escorial
MADRID
PORTUGAL
Plasencia
SIERRA DE GREDOS
Toledo
Tara
Talavera
de la Reina
Aranjuez
Tajo
Guadalupe
Alcázar de
San Juan
Cáceres
Trujillo
Mérida
Guadiana
Ciudad
Real
Badajoz
Abenójar
Zafra
Almadén
Valdepeñas
Jerez de los
Caballeros
SIERRA MORENA
Fregenal
de la Sierra
Córdoba
Bailén
Linares
Ubeda
Aroche
Jaén
Baeza
Ca
Seville
Guadalquivir
Ecija
Baena
Guadix
Huelva
Lucena
Granada
Carmona
Gulf of
Cádiz
Sanlúcar de
Barrameda
Antequera
Loja
SIERRA
COSTA DE LA LUZ
Ronda
Nerja
Jerez de
la Frontera
Torremolinos
Málaga
Motril
ATLANTIC
OCEAN
Cádiz
Fuengirola
Estepona
Marbella
COSTA DEL SOL
Algeciras
Gibraltar
TO CANARY
ISLANDS
Strait of Gibraltar

FRANCE

San
Sebastián ○Fuenterrabia

○Roncesvalles

ANDORRA

Vitoria ○Pamplona

P Y R E N E E S

○Jaca

ogroño ○Seu d'Urgell Figueres/
Figueras

○Huesca ○Girona/Gerona

○Tudela ○Barbastro Vich/Vic

Soria Ebro Manresa COSTA
BRAVA

Zaragoza Montserrat ▲

○Calatayud ○Lérida Barcelona

RRAMA ○Daroca ○Alcañiz Tarragona

○Medinaceli Caminreal COSTA DORADA

Tajo ○Tortosa

lajara ○Monreal
del Campo Balearic
Sea

○Teruel La Jana ○Vinaròs TO
MENORCA →

Tarancón ○Cuenca COSTA DEL AZAHAR ○Castellón
de la Plana Palma

de Sagunto Golfo de
Valencia Majorca

○Requena Valencia Ibiza

Jucar BALEARIC
ISLANDS

○Albacete ○Eivissa
Formentera

Alcaraz ○Hellín Alicante Menorca

Segura Elche COSTA BLANCA Ciutadella Mahón

beda Orihuela

○Cazorla Murcia

Lorca Manga del
Mar Menor

Cartagena COSTA
CALIDA Mediterranean
Sea

A NEVADA COSTA DE ALMERIA

○Almería

ALGERIA

N

0   100 miles
0   150 km

media, and the home of dozens of embassies, but its sophistication is largely a veneer. Scratch the surface, and beyond Madrid's designer boutiques and chic restaurants you'll find a simple Castilian town. Life here is lived in cafés and rustic taverns; all it takes to become a local is to duck inside.

Madrid is also a magnet for art lovers, with three world-class museums—the Prado, the Reina Sofía, and the Thyssen-Bornemisza—all along a 1-km (½-mi) stretch of leafy promenade. The city's restaurants serve good food from all of Spain's regions, but are probably best known for their seafood, which arrives daily from the coasts and has earned landlocked Madrid an affectionate reputation as Spain's biggest port.

Catalonia—with a population of 6 million Catalan speakers—is Spain's richest and most industrial region. Its capital, Barcelona, rivals Madrid for power and is generally regarded as the winner in culture and chic. Barcelona's tree-lined streets, Art Nouveau architecture, and renovated waterfront still gleam from the scouring they received for the 1992 Summer Olympics—an event that not only focused the world's attention on this Mediterranean port, but also provided the city with new museums, sports facilities, and restaurants. The spirit of turn-of-the-century modernist architect Antoni Gaudí lives on both in his Sagrada Familia church, which is still unfinished, and in the Catalans' general passion for stylish design.

Since Franco died in 1975, and since the country joined the European Union in 1986, Spain has been forced to modernize. The most obvious improvements for the traveler are the fast new nationwide network of superhighways and the high-speed AVE train linking Seville and Córdoba to Madrid. Happily, though, Spain's uniqueness has not been tossed aside in the rush toward the 21st century. Fewer Spaniards take a siesta these days, but shops still close at midday, and three-hour lunches are commonplace. Young adults still live with their parents until marriage. Bullfight fans are not giving in to animal-rights activists. And flamenco is making a comeback with young rock-and-rollers.

Most exciting for anyone vacationing in Spain is the Spaniards' insistence on enjoying life. This may mean strolling in the park with the family on a Sunday afternoon, lingering over a weekday lunch, or socializing with friends until dawn. A zest for living life to its fullest is Spain's greatest contribution to Europe.

SPAIN A TO Z

Customs
For details on imports and duty-free limits, *see* Customs & Duties *in* Chapter 1.

Dining
Spain offers a choice of restaurants, tapas bars, and cafés. Restaurants are strictly for lunch and dinner; they do not serve breakfast. Tapas bars are ideal for a glass of wine or beer accompanied by an array of appetizers. Cafés, called *cafeterías,* are basically coffee shops that serve snacks, light meals, tapas, and pastries along with coffee, tea, and alcoholic drinks. They also serve breakfast and are perfect for afternoon tea or a cup of thick, creamy hot chocolate.

MEALTIMES
Mealtimes in Spain are much later than in any other European country. Lunch begins between 1 and 2:30, usually around 2, and around 3 on Sunday. Dinner is usually available from 8:30 on, but it's more often taken at 10, especially in larger cities and resorts. Lunch is the

main meal. Tapas bars are busiest between noon and 2 and from 8 PM on. Cafés are usually open from around 8 AM to midnight.

Tap water is safe to drink in all but the remotest villages. In Madrid tap water is excellent; in Barcelona it's safe and getting tastier. However, most Spaniards drink bottled mineral water; ask for either *agua sin gas* (without bubbles) or *agua con gas* (with bubbles). A good paella should be served only at lunchtime and should be prepared to order (usually 30 minutes); beware paella dinners (tourist traps) or prices that look too good to be true.

Spanish restaurants are officially classified from five forks down to one fork, with most places earning two or three forks. In our rating system, prices are per person and include a first course, main course, and dessert, but not wine or tip. Sales tax (IVA) is usually included in the menu price; check the menu for *IVA incluído* or *IVA no incluído*. When it's not included, an additional 7% will be added to your bill. Most restaurants offer a prix-fixe menu called a *menú del día*; however, this is often offered only at lunch, and at dinner tends to be a reheated version of the same. *Menús* are usually the cheapest way to eat; à la carte dining is more expensive. Service charges are never added to your bill; leave around 10%, less in $ restaurants and bars.

CATEGORY	COST
$$$$	over 9,000 ptas.
$$$	6,000 ptas.–9,000 ptas.
$$	3,000 ptas.–6,000 ptas.
$	under 3,000 ptas.

Paella—a mixture of saffron-flavored rice with seafood, chicken, sausage, and vegetables—is Spain's national dish. Gazpacho, a cold soup usually made of crushed garlic, tomatoes, and olive oil and garnished with diced vegetables, is a traditional Andalusian dish, served mainly in summer. Galicia and the Basque country are the country's gourmet centers, and both serve outstanding fish and seafood; if you can spend time in these northern provinces, indulge in a *fuente de marisco* (mixed shellfish/seafood platter). Asturias is famous for its *fabadas* (bean stews), cider, and dairy products; Extremadura for its hams and sausages; and Castile for its roasts, especially *cochinillo* (suckling pig), *cordero* (lamb), and *perdiz* (partridge). The best wines are those from the Rioja and Penedés regions. Valdepeñas is a pleasant table wine, and most restaurants serve a perfectly acceptable house wine; ask for *vino de la casa* (say *tinto* for red and *blanco* for white). *Un café solo* is a small, black espresso coffee, and the tasty *café con leche* is coffee with cream, somewhat like *café au lait*. Weaker, black, American-style coffee is hard but not impossible to come by; essentially watered-down espresso, it's known as *café americano*.

In $$$$ and $$$ restaurants, jacket and tie are appropriate but by no means the norm. Elsewhere, casual dress is fine.

Language

Spanish (called Castellano, or Castilian) is not the principal language throughout Spain. The Basques speak Euskera; in Catalonia, you'll hear Catalan; and in Galicia, Gallego. However, almost everyone in these regions also speaks and understands Spanish. If your Spanish breaks down, you should have no trouble finding people who speak English in major cities and coastal resorts, but you won't necessarily be able to count on the bus driver or the passerby on the street. Fortunately, Spanish is fairly easy to pick up, and your efforts to speak the local tongue are bound to be graciously received.

Lodging

Spain has a wide range of accommodations, including luxury palaces, medieval monasteries, converted 19th-century houses, modern hotels, coastal high-rises, and inexpensive hostels in family homes. Rates are always quoted per room, not per person. Single occupancy of a double room costs 80% of the usual price. Breakfast is rarely included in the quoted room rate. The quality of rooms, particularly in older properties, can be uneven; always ask to see your room *before* you sign the acceptance slip. If you want a private bathroom in a less expensive hotel, state your preference for shower or bathtub; the latter usually costs more, though many hotels have both. All hotels and hostels are listed with their rates in the annual *Guía de Hoteles,* available from bookstores and kiosks or for perusal in local tourist offices.

CAMPING

There are about 540 campgrounds in Spain, with the highest concentration along the Mediterranean coast. The season runs from April through October, though some places are open year-round. In summer, especially in August, the best campsites fill with Spanish families who move in with what seems like their entire household. Campgrounds are listed in the annual publication *Guía de Campings,* available from bookstores or tourist offices, and the Tourist Office of Spain has additional information. Reserve the most popular seaside sites with the campground itself or through **Federación Española de Campings** (✉ Príncipe de Vergara 85, 2°-dcha, Madrid 28006, ☎ 91/562–9994).

HOTELS AND HOSTELS

Hotels are officially classified from five stars (the highest) to one star. Although quality is a factor, the ratings mainly indicate how many facilities the hotel offers. *Hostales* are rated from three stars to one star; these are not the youth hostels associated with the word in most countries, but are usually family homes converted to provide accommodations in one part of the building. A hotel with an *R* on its blue plaque is classified as a *residencia,* and may offer breakfast and cafeteria facilities. A three-star hostel is usually comparable to a two-star hotel; two- and one-star hostels offer basic accommodations.

The main hotel chains are Barceló, Husa, Iberotel, Meliá Sol, Tryp, and the state-run *paradores* (paradors; state-run hotels). Holiday Inn, InterContinental, and Forte also own some of the best hotels in Madrid, Barcelona, and Seville; only these, the paradors, and the recently organized Estancias de España, a group of lodgings in historic buildings, have any special character. The others mostly provide clean, comfortable accommodation in the two- to four-star range.

At many hotels, rates can vary dramatically according to the time of year. The hotel year is divided into *temporada alta, media,* and *baja* (high, mid-, and low season); high season usually covers summer, Easter, and Christmas plus the major fiestas. IVA is rarely included in the quoted room rates, so expect an additional 7% to be added to your bill. Service charges are not included.

PARADORS

Spain has about 100 state-owned and -run paradors, many of which are in magnificent medieval castles or convents. Most of these are relatively luxurious and are priced accordingly. All have restaurants that serve some regional specialties, and you can stop in for a meal or a drink without spending the night. Breakfast, however, is an expensive buffet, and you'll do better to go down the street for a cup of coffee and a roll. Paradors are often booked far in advance; for more information or to make reservations, contact **Paradores** (✉ Requena 3, Madrid 28013, ☎ 91/516–6666, ⅏ 91/516–6657, www.parador.es), **Marketing Ahead Inc.** (✉ 433 5th Ave., New York, NY 10016, ☎ 212/686–9213 or 800/223–1356, ⅏ 212/686–0271), or **Keytel International** (✉ 402 Edgware Rd., London W2 1ED, ☎ 0171/402–8182, ⅏ 0171/724–9503). These firms also have extensive information on—and can reserve—other fine lodgings.

RATINGS

Prices are for two people in a double room, not including breakfast.

CATEGORY	MAJOR CITY	OTHER AREAS*
$$$$	over 20,000 ptas.	over 18,000 ptas.
$$$	14,000 ptas.–20,000 ptas.	12,000 ptas.–18,000 ptas.
$$	9,000 ptas.–14,000 ptas.	7,000 ptas.–12,000 ptas.
$	under 9,000 ptas.	under 7,000 ptas.

In Gibraltar, $$$: £65–£75 ($104–$120); $$: £40–£46 ($64–$74); not including tax.

VILLAS

Villas are plentiful all along the Mediterranean coast. A few agencies rent cottages in Cantabria and Asturias, on the north coast; check with the Tourist Office of Spain.

Mail

POSTAL RATES

At press time the following rates were in effect: To the United States, airmail letters up to 20 grams and postcards each cost 115 ptas. To the United Kingdom and other European countries (both EU and non-EU), letters up to 20 grams and postcards each cost 70 ptas. Within Spain, letters and postcards each cost 35 ptas. Mailboxes are yellow with red stripes; use the slot marked EXTRANJERO for mail going abroad. Buy your *sellos* (stamps) at a *correos* (post office) or in an *estanco* (tobacco shop).

RECEIVING MAIL

Because mail delivery in Spain can be slow and unreliable, it's best to have your mail sent to American Express. An alternative is to have mail held at a Spanish post office; have it addressed to *lista de correos* (poste restante) in a town you'll be visiting. The address should include the name of the province in parentheses—e.g., Marbella (Málaga). You'll need to show your passport to claim your mail. American Express charges $2 per letter for noncardholders.

Money Matters

CHANGING MONEY

The word to look for is CAMBIO (exchange). Most Spanish banks take a 1½% commission, though some less scrupulous places charge more; always check, as rates can vary widely. To change money in a bank, you need your passport and plenty of patience, because filling out the forms takes time. Hotels offer rates lower than banks, but they rarely charge a commission, so you may well break even. Restaurants and stores, with the exception of those catering to the tour-bus trade, generally do not accept payment in dollars or traveler's checks. If you have a credit card with a Personal Identification Number (PIN), you'll most likely be able to get cash advances at cash machines.

COSTS

The days when Spain was Europe's bargain basement are truly over; the cost of living here is now on a par with that of most European nations. In recent years, however, currency fluctuations have increased the buying power of those visiting from North America and the United Kingdom.

Most hotels, restaurants, and stores accept payment by credit card. Visa is the most widely accepted card, followed by MasterCard (called EuroCard in Spain). More-expensive establishments may also take American Express and Diners Club.

Spain's unit of currency is the peseta (pta.). Bills are worth 10,000, 5,000, 2,000, and 1,000 ptas.; coins are worth 500, 200, 100, 50, 25, 10, 5, and 1 pta. At press time (summer 1999) the exchange rate was about 163 ptas. to the U.S. dollar, 111 ptas. to the Canadian dollar, and 254 ptas. to the pound sterling.

Visitors may take any amount of foreign currency in bills or traveler's checks into Spain, as well as any amount of pesetas. When leaving Spain you may take out only 100,000 ptas. per person in Spanish banknotes and foreign currency up to the equivalent of 500,000 ptas., unless you can prove you declared the excess at customs on entering the country.

A cup of coffee costs between 125 ptas. (if you're standing) and 150 ptas. (if you're seated); a Coke, 150 ptas.; a small draft beer, 125 ptas.; a glass of wine in a bar, 100 ptas.; a sandwich 300–450 ptas.; a local bus or subway ride 125–200 ptas.; a 2-km (1-mi) taxi ride, about 400 ptas.

Spaniards appreciate being tipped, but they don't expect American rates. By law, restaurants and hotels are not allowed to add a service charge to your bill, but, confusingly, your bills for both will probably say *servicios e impuestos incluídos* (service and tax included). In restaurants, ignore this unhelpful snippet and leave 10% if you've had a full meal. In humbler eateries, bars, and cafés, leave 5%–10% or round the bill up to the nearest 100 ptas. Tip taxi drivers about 5%–10% when they use the meter, otherwise nothing—they'll have seen to it themselves. Train and airport porters usually operate on a fixed rate of 60 ptas.–100 ptas. a bag. Hotel porters get 100 ptas.–150 ptas. for carrying bags, and waiters get the same for room service. If you stay in a hotel more than two nights, it's customary to tip the maid 100 ptas. per night.

National Holidays

In 2000, major holidays are January 1; January 6 (Epiphany); April 21 (Good Friday); April 23 (Easter); May 1 (May Day); July 25 (St. James's Day); August 15 (Assumption); October 12 (National Day); November 1 (All Saints' Day); December 6 (Constitution); December 8 (Immaculate Conception); December 25.

Opening and Closing Times

Banks are open Monday–Saturday 9–2 from October through June; in summer they are closed on Saturday. Hours for **museums and churches** vary; most are open in the morning, but most museums close one day a week, often Monday. **Stores** are open weekdays from 9 or 10 until 1:30 or 2, then in the afternoon from around 5 to 8. In some cities, especially in summer, stores close on Saturday afternoon.

Shopping

Value-added tax, called IVA, is levied on most goods and services. It's 7% at hotels and restaurants (except on the Canary Islands, where it's

4%) and 16% on car rentals. A number of shops, particularly large stores and boutiques, offer a 16% IVA refund on purchases of over 15,000 ptas.—you show your passport, fill out a form, and the store mails the refund to your home. You can also present your original receipt in the IVA office in the airport; customs signs the original and gives it back to you to mail to the vendor or, for a credit-card refund, to the national IVA office.

Telephoning

COUNTRY CODE
The country code for Spain is 34.

INTERNATIONAL CALLS
You can call abroad from any pay phone marked TELÉFONO INTERNACIONAL. Use 50-pta. (or 100-pta., if the phone takes them) coins initially, then coins of any denomination to prolong your call. Dial 07, wait for the tone to change, then dial 1 for the United States, 0101 for Canada, or 44 for the United Kingdom, followed by the area code and number. For lengthy calls, go to the *telefónica,* a phone office found in all sizable towns: Here an operator assigns you a private booth and collects payment at the end of the call. This is the cheapest and by far the easiest way to call overseas, and you can charge calls costing more than 500 ptas. to Visa or MasterCard.

LOCAL CALLS
There are three types of pay phones in Spain, all of them bright green or dull blue. The most common kind has a digital readout, so you can see your money ticking away. You need at least 25 ptas. for a local call, 75 ptas. to call another province. Insert coins and wait for a dial tone. (At older models you line coins up in a groove on top of the dial, and they drop down as needed.)

Newer pay phones take only phone cards, which can be purchased at any tobacco shop in denominations of 1,000 or 2,000 ptas.

Note that to call anywhere within Spain—even locally—you need to dial the area code first. All provincial codes begin with a 9.

OPERATORS AND INFORMATION
For the operator and directory information for any part of Spain, dial 1003. The international information and assistance operator is at 025 (some operators speak English). If you're in Madrid, dial 008 to make collect calls to countries in Europe; 005 for the rest of the world. Private long-distance companies have special access numbers: **AT&T** (☏ 900/990011), **MCI** (☏ 900/990014), and **Sprint** (☏ 900/990013).

Transportation
In addresses, the word *Calle* (Street) is abbreviated *C.*

BY BUS
Spain has an excellent bus network, but there is no national or nationwide bus company; there are simply numerous *empresas* (private regional bus companies). Buses tend to be more frequent than trains, are sometimes cheaper, and often allow you to see more of the countryside. Some of those on major routes are now quite luxurious; but although they designate no-smoking seats, it's hard to cordon smoke in a bus, so you may be in for a smokier ride than you're used to. On major routes and at holiday times, buy your ticket a day or two in advance. Some cities have central bus stations, but in many of these, including Madrid and Barcelona, buses leave from various boarding points; always check with the local tourist office. Unlike train stations, bus stations usually have facilities for luggage storage.

BY CAR

Gasoline. Gas costs about 120 ptas. per liter for super (octane) and 115 ptas. per liter for regular. *Sin plomo* (unleaded) gas is now available at a steadily increasing number of pumps. Most pumps have attendant service, but there's no need to tip for a simple fill-up. Most gas stations accept credit cards.

Parking. Parking restrictions should be checked locally. In many cities a blue line on the street indicates parking for residents only; other cars are towed promptly. Thefts are common, so it's safer to leave your car in one of the many staffed parking lots; charges are reasonable.

Road Conditions. Roads marked *A* (*autopista*) are toll roads. *N* stands for national or main roads, and *C* for country roads. Spain's huge road-improvement scheme has been largely completed, but many N roads are still single-lane, and the going can be slow. Tolls vary but are high; for example: Bilbao–Zaragoza 3,010 ptas., Salou–Valencia 2,150 ptas., Seville–Jerez 610 ptas., and Santiago–La Coruña 510 ptas.

Rules of the Road. Spaniards drive on the right. The use of horns and high-beam headlights is forbidden in cities. Front seat belts are compulsory. Children under age 10 may not ride in front seats. At traffic circles, cars already in the circle have right of way. Your home driver's license is essential and must be carried with you at all times, along with your car insurance and vehicle registration. If you are bringing your own car into Spain, you will also need an International Driving License and a proof-of-insurance Green Card. Speed limits are 120 kph (74 mph) on *autopistas,* 100 kph (62 mph) on N roads, 90 kph (56 mph) on C roads, and 60 kph (37 mph) in cities unless otherwise signposted.

BY PLANE

Iberia and its subsidiary **Aviaco** operate a wide network of domestic flights, linking all of Spain's major cities and the Balearic Islands. Domestic airfares are high by U.S. standards, although deregulation is pushing prices lower. A frequent shuttle service connects Madrid and Barcelona. Iberia has its own offices in most major Spanish cities and acts as agent for Aviaco. In Madrid, Iberia headquarters are at Velázquez 130 (☎ 91/411–1011 for domestic reservations, ☎ 91/329–4353 for international, or call Info-Iberia for flight information, ☎ 91/329–5767). You can also book flights at most travel agencies. **Air Europa** (☎ 91/305–8159 and 91/559–1500) and **Spanair** (☎ 91/393–6735) offer slightly cheaper service between Madrid and Barcelona as well as flights to the Canary Islands. For information on other airlines' flights to and within Spain, call the airline itself, or call the Madrid airport (☎ 91/305–8343, -44, -45, or -46) and ask for your airline.

BY TRAIN

The Spanish railroad system—usually known by its initials, RENFE—operates several different types of trains: Talgo (ultramodern), electric unit expresses (ELT), diesel rail cars (TER), and ordinary *expresos* and *rápidos*. Fares are determined by the kind of train as well as the distance traveled. Of the long-distance trains, Talgos are by far the quickest, most comfortable, and most expensive of the lot; *expresos* and *rápidos* are the slowest and cheapest. The high-speed Alto Velocidad Español (AVE) runs between Madrid and Seville in just 2½ hours, with a stop in Córdoba; fares vary, but the AVE can cost almost as much as flying. A few lines, such as the narrow-gauge FEVE routes along the north coast and the Costa Blanca, do not belong to the RENFE network and do not accept international rail passes.

The **RENFE Tourist Card,** on sale to anyone who lives outside Spain, buys you unlimited distance over 3, 5, or 10 days' travel. Contact the Span-

Finally, a travel companion that doesn't snore on the plane or eat all your peanuts.

When traveling, your MCI WorldCom Card is the best way to keep in touch. Our operators speak your language, so they'll be able to connect you back home—no matter where your travels take you. Plus, your MCI WorldCom Card is easy to use, and even earns you frequent flyer miles every time you use it. When you add in our great rates, you get something even more valuable: peace-of-mind. So go ahead. Travel the world. MCI WorldCom just brought it a whole lot closer.

You can even sign up today at www.mci.com/worldphone or ask your operator to make a collect call to 1-410-314-2938.

EASY TO CALL WORLDWIDE

1. Just dial the WorldPhone access number of the country you're calling from.
2. Dial or give the operator your MCI WorldCom Card number.
3. Dial or give the number you're calling.

France ◆	0-800-99-0019
Germany	0800-888-8000
Ireland	1-800-55-1001
Italy ◆	172-1022
Spain	900-99-0014
Sweden ◆	020-795-922
Switzerland ◆	0800-89-0222
United Kingdom To call using BT	0800-89-0222
To call using CWC	0500-89-0222

For your complete WorldPhone calling guide, dial the WorldPhone access number for the country you're in and ask the operator for Customer Service. In the U.S. call 1-800-431-5402.

◆ Public phones may require deposit of coin or phone card for dial tone.

EARN FREQUENT FLYER MILES

AmericanAirlines
AAdvantage

Continental Airlines
OnePass

▲ Delta Air Lines
SkyMiles

✈ MILEAGE PLUS.
United Airlines

U·S AIRWAYS
DIVIDEND MILES

MCI WorldCom, its logo and the names of the products referred to herein are proprietary marks of MCI WorldCom, Inc. All airline names and logos are proprietary marks of the respective airlines. All airline program rules and conditions apply.

The first thing you need overseas is the one thing you forget to pack.

FOREIGN CURRENCY DELIVERED OVERNIGHT

Chase Currency To Go® delivers foreign currency to your home by the next business day*

It's easy—before you travel, call 1-888-CHASE84 for delivery of any of 75 currencies

Delivery is free with orders of $500 or more

Competitive rates— without exchange fees

You don't have to be a Chase customer—you can pay by Visa® or MasterCard®

 CHASE

THE RIGHT RELATIONSHIP IS EVERYTHING.®

1•888•CHASE84
www.chase.com

ish National Tourist Office for a list of agencies or call RENFE in Madrid at ☎ 011–34/1–563–0202.

Visitor Information

For the Tourist Office of Spain in your home country, *see* Visitor Information *in* Chapter 1. For general information on travel within Spain, call Turespaña's information line (☎ 901/300600). For regional and city tourist offices, *see* Visitor Information *in* the Essentials section for the relevant geographic region, *below*.

Weather

The tourist season runs from Easter to mid-October. The best months for sightseeing are May, June, September, and early October, when the weather is usually pleasant and sunny without being unbearably hot. In July and August, try to avoid Madrid and the inland cities of Andalusia, where the heat can be stifling and many places close down at 1 PM. Air-conditioning is not widely used. The one exception to Spain's high summer temperatures is the north coast, where the climate is similar to that of northern Europe.

Seasonal events can clog parts of the country, and major fiestas, such as Pamplona's running of the bulls (July 6–15), cause prices to soar. In 2000 Semana Santa (Holy Week) is the third week of April; this is the time to catch some of Spain's most spectacular fiestas.

CLIMATE

The following are average daily maximum and minimum temperatures for Madrid.

Jan.	47F	9C	May	70F	21C	Sept.	77F	25C
	35	2		50	10		57	14
Feb.	52F	11C	June	80F	27C	Oct.	65F	18C
	36	2		58	15		49	10
Mar.	59F	15C	July	87F	31C	Nov.	55F	13C
	41	5		63	17		42	5
Apr.	65F	18C	Aug.	85F	30C	Dec.	48F	9C
	45	7		63	17		36	2

MADRID

Smack in the heart of Spain at 2,120 ft above sea level, Madrid is the highest capital in Europe, and fittingly one of the continent's most vibrant cities. Madrileños are vigorous, joyful people, famous for their ability to defy the need for sleep; they embrace their city's cultural offerings and make enthusiastic use of its cafés and bars. If you can match this energy, you'll take in Madrid's museum mile, with more masterpieces per foot than anywhere else in the world; regal Madrid, with its sumptuous palaces and posh boutiques; medieval Madrid, with its dark, narrow lanes; *and* Madrid after midnight, where today's action is.

Exploring Madrid

Numbers in the margin correspond to points of interest on the Madrid map.

You can see important parts of the city in one day if you stop only to visit the Prado and Royal Palace. Two days should give you time for browsing. You can begin in the Plaza Atocha (Glorieta del Emperador Carlos V), at the bottom of the Paseo del Prado.

★ ❶ **Centro de Arte Reina Sofía** (Queen Sofía Arts Center). Spain's Queen Sofía opened this center in 1986, and it quickly became one of Europe's most dynamic venues—a Spanish rival to Paris's Pompidou Center. A converted hospital, the center houses painting and sculpture, including works by Joan Miró and Salvador Dalí as well as Picasso's *Guernica,* the painting depicting the horrific April 1937 carpet bombing of the Basque country's traditional capital by Nazi warplanes aiding Franco in the Spanish Civil War. ⊠ *Main entrance, C. de Santa Isabel 52,* ☎ *91/467–5062.* ⌑ *Free Sat. after 2:30 and all day Sun.* ☉ *Mon., Wed.–Sat. 10–9; Sun. 10–2:30.*

❿ **Convento de las Descalzas Reales** (Convent of the Royal Barefoot Nuns). Founded by Juana de Austria, daughter of Charles V, this convent is still in use. Over the centuries, the nuns—daughters of royalty and nobility—have endowed it with an enormous wealth of jewels, religious ornaments, superb Flemish tapestries, and the works of such master painters as Titian and Rubens. A bit off the main track, it's one of Madrid's better-kept secrets. Your ticket includes admission to the nearby, but less interesting, **Convento de la Encarnación.** ⊠ *Plaza de las Descalzas 3,* ☎ *91/542–0059.* ☉ *Tues.–Thurs. and Sat. 10:30–12:30 and 4–5:30, Fri. 10:30–12:30, Sun. 11–1:30.*

❼ **Fuente de la Cibeles** (Cybele's Fountain). Cybele, the Greek goddess of fertility and unofficial emblem of Madrid, languidly rides her lion-drawn chariot here, watched over by the mighty Palacio de Comunicaciónes, a splendidly pompous, cathedral-like post office. Fans of the home football team, Real Madrid, used to celebrate major victories by splashing in the fountain, but police now blockade it during big games. The fountain stands in the center of **Plaza de la Cibeles,** one of Madrid's great landmarks, at the intersection of the city's two main arteries. ⊠ *Meeting of Castellana and C. de Alcalá.*

★ ❷ **Museo del Prado** (Prado Museum). On the old cobblestone section of the Paseo del Prado you'll find Madrid's number-one cultural site, one of the world's most important art museums. Plan to spend at least a day here; it takes at least two days to view the museum's treasures properly. Brace yourself for crowds. The greatest treasures—the Velázquez, Murillo, Zurbarán, El Greco, and Goya galleries—are all on the upper floor. Two of the best works are Velázquez's *Surrender of Breda* and his most famous work, *Las Meninas,* awarded a room of its own. The Goya galleries contain the artist's none-too-flattering royal portraits, his exquisitely beautiful *Marquesa de Santa Cruz,* and his famous *Naked Maja* and *Clothed Maja,* for which the 13th duchess of Alba was said to have posed. Goya's most moving works, the *Second of May* and the *Fusillade of Moncloa* or *Third of May,* vividly depict the sufferings of Madrid patriots at the hands of Napoléon's invading troops in 1808. Before you leave, feast your eyes on Hieronymus Bosch's flights of fancy, *Garden of Earthly Delights* and the triptych *The Hay Wagon,* both on the ground floor. The museum was scheduled to unveil an extra 20,000 square ft of exhibition space in summer 1999, much of which will be occupied by long-forgotten masterpieces by Zurbarán and Pereda. ⊠ *Paseo del Prado s/n,* ☎ *91/420–3768.* ⌑ *Free Sat. after 2:30 and all day Sun.* ☉ *Tues.–Sat. 9–7, Sun. 9–2.*

❹ **Museo Thyssen-Bornemisza.** Opened in 1992 in the elegant Villahermosa Palace, this museum has plenty of airy spaces and natural light. The ambitious collection—800 paintings—attempts to trace the history of Western art through examples from each important movement, beginning with 13th-century Italy. Among the museum's gems are the *Portrait of Henry VIII,* by Hans Holbein (purchased from the late Princess Diana's grandfather, who used the money to buy a new

Bugatti sports car). Two halls are devoted to the Impressionists and post-Impressionists, with works by Pissarro as well as Renoir, Monet, Degas, Van Gogh, and Cézanne. The more recent paintings include some terror-filled examples of German expressionism, but these are complemented by some soothing Georgia O'Keeffes and Andrew Wyeths. ⊠ *Paseo del Prado 8,* ☎ *91/369–0151.* ☉ *Tues.–Sun. 10–7.*

★ ⑬ **Palacio Real** (Royal Palace). This magnificent granite-and-limestone pile was begun by Philip V, the first Bourbon king of Spain, who was always homesick for his beloved Versailles and did his best to re-create its opulence and splendor. To judge by the palace's 2,800 rooms, with their lavish rococo decorations, precious carpets, porcelain, timepieces, mirrors, and chandeliers, his efforts were successful. From 1764, when Charles III first moved in, until the coming of the Second Republic and the abdication of Alfonso XIII in 1931, the Royal Palace proved a very stylish abode for Spanish monarchs; today, King Juan Carlos, who lives in the far less ostentatious Zarzuela Palace outside Madrid, uses it only for official state functions. Allow 1½–2 hours for a visit that includes the Royal Pharmacy and other outbuildings. The **Royal Carriage Museum,** which belongs to the palace, has a separate entrance on Paseo Virgen del Puerto. One of its highlights is the wedding carriage of Alfonso XIII and his English bride, Victoria Eugenia (granddaughter of Queen Victoria), which was damaged by a bomb tossed in the Calle Mayor during the couple's wedding procession in 1906. Another is the chair that carried the gout-stricken Emperor Charles V to his retirement at the remote monastery of Yuste. The museum has been closed for several years for restoration; inquire at the Royal Palace about its reopening. ⊠ *Bailén s/n,* ☎ *91/542–0059.* ☉ *Mon.–Sat. 9–6, Sun. 9–3. Closed during official receptions.*

★ ☾ ❺ **Parque del Retiro** (Retiro Park). Once a royal retreat, Retiro is Madrid's prettiest park. Visit the beautiful rose garden, **La Rosaleda;** enjoy street musicians and magicians; row a boat around El Estanque; and wander past the park's many statues and fountains. Look particularly at the monumental **statue of Alfonso XII,** one of Spain's least notable kings (though you wouldn't think so from the statue's size), or wonder at the **Monument to the Fallen Angel**—Madrid claims the dubious honor of being the only capital to have a statue dedicated to the Devil. The **Palacio de Velázquez** and the beautiful, glass-and-steel **Palacio de Cristal,** built as a tropical plant house during the 19th century, now host occasional art exhibits. ⊠ *Between C. Alfonso XII and Avda. de Menéndez Pelayo below C. de Alcalá.* ☉ *Daylight hrs.*

⑫ **Plaza de la Villa** (City Square). This plaza's notable cluster of buildings includes some of the oldest houses in Madrid. The **Casa de la Villa,** Madrid's city hall, was built in 1644 and has also served as the city prison and the mayor's home. Its sumptuous salons are occasionally open to the public; ask about guided tours, which are sometimes given in English. An archway joins the Casa de la Villa to the **Casa Cisneros,** a palace built in 1537 for the nephew of Cardinal Cisneros, primate of Spain and infamous inquisitor general. Across the square is the **Torre de Lujanes,** one of the oldest buildings in Madrid; it once imprisoned Francis I of France, archenemy of the Emperor Charles V. ⊠ *C. Mayor between C. Santiago and C. San Nicholas.*

★ ⑪ **Plaza Mayor** (Great Square). Without a doubt the capital's architectural showpiece, the Plaza Mayor was built in 1617–19 for Philip III—the figure astride the horse in the middle. The plaza has witnessed the canonization of saints, the burning of heretics, fireworks, and bullfights, and is still one of Madrid's great gathering places. ⊠ *South of C. Mayor, west of Cava San Miguel.*

Centro de Arte
Reina Sofía, **1**

Convento de las
Descalzas Reales, **10**

Fuente de la Cibeles, **7**

Museo del Prado, **2**

Museo Thyssen-
Bornemisza, **4**

Palacio Real, **13**

Parque del Retiro, **5**

Plaza de la Villa, **12**

Plaza Mayor, **11**

Puerta de Alcalá, **6**

Puerta del Sol, **9**

Real Academia de
Bellas Artes de San
Fernando (RA de BA
de SF), **8**

Ritz, **3**

Teatro Real, **14**

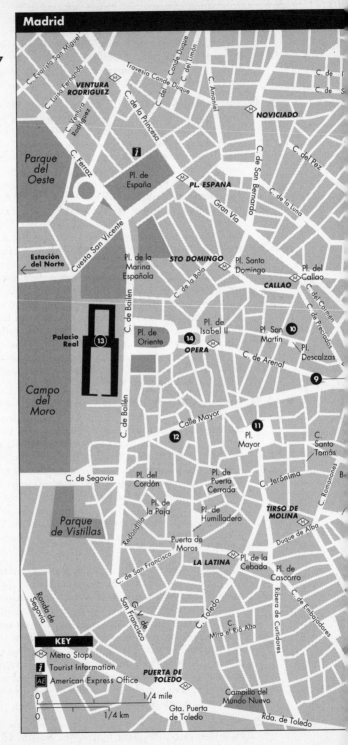

Madrid

C. Evaristo San Miguel
C. Luisa Fernanda
C. de Ventura Rodríguez
VENTURA RODRIGUEZ
Travesía Conde Duque
Conde Duque
C. del Limón
C. Amaniel
C. de la Princesa
C. de S
C. de
NOVICIADO
C. del Pez
C. Ferraz

Parque del Oeste

i

Pl. de España
PL. ESPAÑA
Gran Vía
C. de San Bernardo
C. de la Luna

← **Estación del Norte**

Cuesta San Vicente

Pl. de la Marina Española
STO DOMINGO
Pl. Santo Domingo
Pl. del Callao
CALLAO
C. de la Bola
C. del Carmen
C. de Preciados

C. de Bailén
Pl. de Oriente
14
OPERA
Pl. de Isabel II
Pl. San Martín **10**
Pl. Descalzas
C. de Arenal
9

Palacio Real 13

Campo del Moro

C. de Bailén
Calle Mayor
Pl. Mayor **11**
C. Santo Tomás

12

C. de Segovia
Pl. del Cordón
Pl. de Puerta Cerrada
C. Jerónima
C. de Romanones
B

Parque de Vistillas
Redondilla
Pl. de la Paja
Pl. de Humilladero
TIRSO DE MOLINA
Duque de Alba

Puerta de Moros
C. de San Francisco
LA LATINA
Pl. de la Cebada
Pl. de Cascorro
Ribera de Curtidores
C. de Embajadores

Ronda de Segovia
G. V. de San Francisco
C. de Toledo
C. Mira el Río Alto

KEY
Ⓜ Metro Stops
i Tourist Information
AE American Express Office

0 _____ 1/4 mile
0 _____ 1/4 km

PUERTA DE TOLEDO
Campillo del Mundo Nuevo
Gta. Puerta de Toledo
Rda. de Toledo

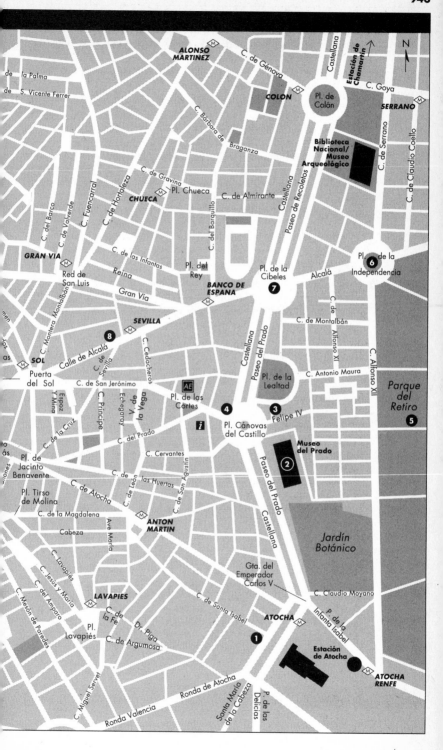

N

Estación de Chamartín

ALONSO MARTINEZ

C. de Génova

C. Goya

COLON

Pl. de Colón

SERRANO

de la Palma

de S. Vicente Ferrer

C. de Serrano

C. Bárbara de Braganza

Biblioteca Nacional/ Museo Arqueológico

C. de Gravina

CHUECA

Pl. Chueca

C. de Almirante

C. de Claudio Coello

C. del Barco

C. de Valverde

C. de Hortaleza

C. del Barquillo

Castellana

Paseo de Recoletos

C. Fuencarral

GRAN VIA

C. de las Infantas

Pl. del Rey

Pl. de la Cibeles

Red de San Luis

Reina

BANCO DE ESPAÑA

Alcalá

Pl. de la Independencia

6

Gran Vía

7

C. de Montalbán

C. Mantera Montalbán

SEVILLA

8

C. Cedacheros

C. de Sevilla

Castellana

Paseo del Prado

C. de

Alfonso XI

C. Antonio Maura

Parque del Retiro

SOL

Calle de Alcalá

Puerta del Sol

C. de San Jerónimo

Pl. de las Cortes

AE

Pl. de la Lealtad

C. de Alfonso XII

Espoz Y Mina

C. Príncipe

Echegaray

C. V. de la Vega

4

Felipe IV

3

Pl. Cánovas del Castillo

5

C. de la Cruz

C. del Prado

i

C. Cervantes

Museo del Prado

Pl. de Jacinto Benavente

C. de León

las Huertas

2

C. de San Agustín

Pl. Tirso de Molina

C. de Atocha

ANTON MARTIN

Jardín Botánico

C. de la Magdalena

Cabeza

Ave María

C. Lavapiés

C. Jesús y María

C. del Amparo

LAVAPIES

C. de la fe

Dr. Piga

Gta. del Emperador Carlos V

C. Claudio Moyano

C. Mesón de Paredes

Pl. Lavapiés

C. de Argumosa

C. de Santa Isabel

ATOCHA

1

P. de la Infanta Isabel

Estación de Atocha

ATOCHA RENFE

C. Miguel Servet

Ronda de Atocha

Santa María de la Cabeza

P. de las Delicias

Ronda Valencia

⑥ Puerta de Alcalá (Alcalá Gate). Built in 1779 for Charles III, the grandiose gateway dominates the Plaza de la Independencia. A customs post once stood beside the gate, as did the old bullring until it was moved to its present site, Las Ventas, in the 1920s. At the turn of the century, the Puerta de Alcalá more or less marked the eastern edge of Madrid. ⊠ *Plaza de la Independencia.*

⑨ Puerta del Sol (Gate of the Sun). The old gate disappeared long ago, but you're still at the very heart of Madrid here, and indeed the very heart of Spain: kilometer distances for the whole nation are measured from the zero marker in front of the police headquarters. The square was expertly revamped in 1986 and now accommodates both a copy of **La Mariblanca** (a statue that adorned a fountain here 250 years ago) and, at the bottom of Calle Carmen, the much-loved statue of the **bear and strawberry tree**. The Puerta del Sol is inextricably linked with the history of Madrid and of Spain; a half century ago, a generation of literati gathered in Sol's long-gone cafés to thrash out the burning issues of the day. Nearly 200 years ago, the square witnessed the patriots' uprising immortalized by Goya in his painting *The Second of May.* ⊠ *Meeting of C. Mayor and C. Alcalá.*

⑧ Real Academia de Bellas Artes de San Fernando (St. Fernando Royal Academy of Fine Arts). Second only to the Prado in the Madrid art stakes, this fine-arts gallery focuses on the masters: Velázquez, El Greco, Murillo, Zurbarán, Ribera, and Goya. ⊠ *Alcalá 13,* ☎ *91/522–0046.* 🎫 *Free weekends.* ⊙ *Tues.–Fri. 9:30–4:30, Sat.–Mon. 9:30–2.*

③ Ritz. Alfonso II built Madrid's grande dame in 1910, when he realized that his capital had no hotels elegant enough to accommodate his wedding guests. The garden is a wonderfully aristocratic place to lunch in summer. ☞ Dining and Lodging, *below.* ⊠ *Plaza de Lealtad 5.*

⑭ Teatro Real (Royal Theater). This neoclassical theater was built in 1850 and was long a cultural center for *Madrileño* society. Plagued by disasters more recently, including fires, a bombing, and profound structural problems, the house went dark in 1988. Closed for almost a decade for restoration, it reopened to worldwide fanfare in October 1997. Now replete with golden balconies, plush seats, and state-of-the-art stage equipment for operas and ballets, the theater is a modern showpiece with its vintage appeal intact. ⊠ *Plaza de Isabel II,* ☎ *91/516–0600 or 91/516–0660.*

Bullfighting

Madrid's bullfighting season runs from March through October. Fights are held on Sunday and sometimes also on Thursday; starting times vary between 4:30 and 7 PM. The height of taurine spectacle comes with the San Isidro festivals, in May, which usher in three weeks of daily bullfights. The bullring is at **Las Ventas,** formally known as the Plaza de Toros Monumental (⊠ Alcalá 237, ☎ 91/356–2200, metro: Ventas). You can buy your ticket here shortly before the fight or, for a 20% surcharge, at the agencies that line Calle Victoria, just off Carrera San Jerónimo and Puerta del Sol.

Dining and Lodging

For details and price-category definitions, *see* Dining *and* Lodging *in* Spain A to Z, *above.* Note that some restaurants close for Holy Week.

$$$$ ✕ **Horcher.** In a luxurious mansion at the edge of Retiro Park, this clas-
★ sic restaurant is renowned for its hearty but elegant fare, served with impeccable style in an intimate dining room. Specialties include wild

boar, venison, and roast wild duck with almond croquettes. The star appetizer is lobster salad with truffles. Other dishes, such as stroganoff with mustard, pork chops with sauerkraut, and a chocolate-covered fruit-and-cake dessert called *baumkuchen,* reflect the restaurant's German roots. A wide selection of French and German wines rounds out the menu. ☒ *Alfonso XII 6,* ☎ *91/522–0731. Reservations essential. AE, DC, MC, V. Closed Sun. No lunch Sat.*

$$$$ ✕ **Viridiana.** The trendiest of Madrid's haute cuisine restaurants, Viridiana is decorated in black and white and has the relaxed atmosphere of a bistro. Iconoclast chef Abraham García creates a new menu every two weeks, dreaming up such varied fare as red onions stuffed with *morcilla* (black pudding); soft flour tortillas wrapped around marinated fresh tuna; and filet mignon in white-truffle sauce. The tangy grapefruit sherbet for dessert is a marvel. ☒ *Juan de Mena 14,* ☎ *91/531–5222. Reservations essential. AE, MC, V. Closed Sun. and Aug.*

$$$$ ✕ **Zalacaín.** A deep-apricot color scheme, set off by dark wood and gleaming silver, makes this restaurant look like an exclusive villa. Zalacaín introduced nouvelle cuisine to Spain and continues to set the pace after 20 years at the top—splurge on such dishes as prawn salad in avocado vinaigrette, scallops and leeks in Albariño wine, and roast pheasant with truffles. A prix-fixe tasting menu allows you to sample the restaurant's best for about 6,500 ptas. Service is somewhat stuffy, and jackets are required. ☒ *Alvarez de Baena 4,* ☎ *91/561–5935. Reservations essential. AE, DC, V. Closed Sun. and Aug. No lunch Sat.*

$$$ ✕ **El Cenador del Prado.** The Cenador's innovative menu has French and
★ Asian touches, as well as exotic Spanish dishes that rarely appear in restaurants. The house specialty is *patatas a la importancia* (sliced potatoes fried in a sauce of garlic, parsley, and clams); other possibilities are shellfish consommé with ginger ravioli, veal and eggplant in béchamel, or wild boar with prunes. For dessert try the *cañas fritas,* a cream-filled pastry once served only at Spanish weddings. Settings are a Baroque salon and a plant-filled conservatory. ☒ *C. del Prado 4,* ☎ *91/429–1561. AE, DC, MC, V. Closed Sun. and Aug. 1–15. No lunch Sat.*

$$$ ✕ **Gure-Etxea.** In the heart of Old Madrid, on the Plaza de la Paja, this is one of the capital's most authentic Basque restaurants. The ground-floor dining room is airy, high-ceilinged, and elegant; brick walls line the lower level, giving it a rustic, farmhouse feel. As in the Basque country, you are waited on only by women. Classic dishes include *bacalao al pil-pil* (spicy cod fried in garlic and oil—making the "pil-pil" sound), *rape en salsa verde* (monkfish in garlic-and-parsley sauce), and for dessert *leche frita* (fried custard). On weekdays the lunch menu includes a hearty and inexpensive daily special. ☒ *Plaza de la Paja 12,* ☎ *91/365–6149. AE, DC, V. Closed Sun. and Aug. No lunch Mon.*

$$$ ✕ **La Trainera.** La Trainera is all about fresh seafood. With nautical decor and a maze of little dining rooms, this informal restaurant has reigned as the queen of Madrid's fish houses for decades. Crab, lobster, shrimp, mussels, and a dozen other types of shellfish are served by weight in *raciónes,* and while Spaniards often share several plates of these delicacies as their entire meal, the grilled hake, sole, or turbot makes an unbeatable second course. Skip the house wine and go for a bottle of Albariño from the cellar. ☒ *Lagasca 60,* ☎ *91/576–8035. AE, MC, V. Closed Sun. and Aug.*

$$$ ✕ **Paradís.** One of the most talked-about restaurants of the moment, Paradís serves avant-garde Catalan cuisine in a stylish, sophisticated setting. Chef Francisco Patón changes his menu daily, with an emphasis on freshness rather than spices or sauces. Carpaccio with almonds, an assortment of sautéed mushrooms, and *bacalao de Girona* (cod in the traditional style of this Catalan town) are a few examples of his simple yet brilliant work. Night owls can bask in the luxury of a gourmet midnight meal: Dinner is served until 2 AM on weekends. ⊠ *Marqués de Cuba 14,* ☎ *91/429–7303. Reservations essential. AE, DC, V. Closed Mon. No lunch Sun.*

$$ ✕ **Casa Botín.** Just off the Plaza Mayor, Madrid's oldest and most fa-
★ mous restaurant has been catering to diners since 1725. Its decor and food are traditionally Castilian, as are the wood-fire ovens used for cooking. *Cochinillo asado* (roast suckling pig) and *cordero asado* (roast lamb) are the specialties. The restaurant was a favorite of Hemingway's and is somewhat touristy, but it's still fun. Try to get a table in the basement or the upstairs dining room. ⊠ *Cuchilleros 17,* ☎ *91/ 366–4217. Reservations essential. AE, DC, MC, V.*

$$ ✕ **La Gamella.** American-born chef Dick Stephens has created a new
★ reasonably priced menu at this hugely popular spot. The sophisticated rust-red dining room, batik tablecloths, oversize plates, and attentive service remain the same, but much of the nouvelle cuisine has been replaced by more traditional fare, such as chicken in garlic, beef bourguignon, or steak tartare à la Jack Daniels. A few signature dishes—such as sausage-and-red-pepper quiche and, for dessert, bittersweet chocolate pâté—remain, and the lunchtime menú del día is a great value at 1,700 ptas. ⊠ *Alfonso XII 4,* ☎ *91/532–4509. AE, DC, MC, V. Closed Sun., Mon., and Aug. 15–31. No lunch Sat.*

$$ ✕ **Nabucco.** Had enough Spanish food for the moment? With pastel-washed walls and subtle lighting from gigantic, wrought-iron candelabras, this pizzeria and trattoria is a trendy but elegant haven in gritty Chueca. Fresh bread sticks and garlic olive oil show up within minutes of your arrival. The spinach, ricotta, and walnut ravioli is heavenly, and this may be the only Italian restaurant in Madrid where you can order (California-style?) barbecued-chicken pizza. Considering the ambience and quality, the bill is a pleasant surprise. ⊠ *Hortaleza 108,* ☎ *91/310–0611. AE, MC, V.*

$ ✕ **Casa Mingo.** Resembling an Asturian cider tavern, the bustling Casa
★ Mingo is built into a stone wall beneath the Norte train station. The only dishes offered are succulent roast chicken, sausages, and salad, all washed down with *sidra* (hard cider). Normally, you'll share long plank tables with other diners; in summer, tables appear on the sidewalk. ⊠ *Paseo de la Florida 2,* ☎ *91/547–7918. No credit cards.*

$ ✕ **Gula Gula.** Artsy students and local yuppies fill up this small, brightly painted, chic eatery nightly, so come early or make a reservation. Just opened in 1998 between the lively Plaza Santa Ana and the Paseo del Prado, Gula Gula draws its trendy crowd with sponge-painted walls, funky candles, and eclectic wall hangings. The imaginative pan-European cuisine includes innovative twists on Spanish specialties, like a spinach tortilla with a hint of nutmeg, or garlic shrimp (normally a tapa) with angel-hair pasta. ⊠ *Infante 5,* ☎ *91/ 420–2919. AE, DC, MC, V.*

$ ✕ **La Biotika.** A vegetarian's dream, this small, cozy restaurant in the heart of the bar district (just east of Plaza Santa Ana) serves macrobiotic vegetarian cuisine every day of the week. Enormous salads, hearty soups, fresh bread, and creative tofu dishes make dining here a flavorful experience. A small market at the entrance sells macrobiotic groceries. ⊠ *Amor de Dios 3,* ☎ *91/429–0780. No credit cards.*

$$$$ 🏨 **Palace.** Built in 1912, Madrid's most famous grand hotel is a Belle Epoque creation of Alfonso XIII and has hosted the likes of Marlon Brando, Rita Hayworth, and Salvador Dalí. In 1995 the hotel was aquired by the Sheraton, and by 1998 it had completed its first restoration in 85 years. The guest rooms now meet today's highest standards; banquet halls and lobbies have been lovingly beautified; and the facade has been finely restored. The Palace is more charming and stylish than ever—and while the glass dome over the lounge remains exquisitely

original, the windows in the guest rooms are now exquisitely double-glazed. ✉ *Plaza de las Cortes 7, 28014,* ☎ *91/429–7551,* FAX *91/429–8266. 436 rooms, 45 suites. Restaurant. AE, DC, MC, V.*

$$$$
★ ⚑ **Ritz.** Spain's most exclusive hotel is elegant and aristocratic, with beautiful rooms, spacious suites, and sumptuous public salons furnished with antiques and handwoven carpets. The restaurant is justly famous, and the garden terrace is the perfect setting for summer dining. Weekend brunch is accompanied by harp music, and weekend tea or supper by chamber music from February through May. Near the Parque del Retiro and overlooking the Prado, the Ritz offers unadulterated luxury. ✉ *Plaza Lealtad 5, 28014,* ☎ *91/521–2857,* FAX *91/532–8776. 158 rooms. Restaurant. AE, DC, MC, V.*

$$$$ ⚑ **Santo Mauro.** Once the Canadian embassy, this turn-of-the-20th-century neoclassical mansion is now an intimate luxury hotel. The architecture is accented by contemporary furniture (such as suede armchairs) in such hues as mustard, teal, and eggplant. Twelve guest rooms are in the main building, which also has a popular gourmet restaurant; the others are in a new annex and are split-level, with stereos and VCRs. Request a room with a summer terrace overlooking the gardens. ✉ *Zurbano 36, 28010,* ☎ *91/319–6900,* FAX *91/308–5477. 37 rooms. Restaurant. AE, DC, MC, V.*

$$$$ ⚑ **Villa Magna.** Renowned in the early '90s as the favorite of visiting financiers and reclusive rock stars, the Villa Magna has been humbled by competition, and its reputation for ultraexclusivity has faded with the decor of its green-and-white lobby. Still, it's one of Madrid's top luxury hotels, its modern facade belying an exquisite interior furnished with 18th-century antiques. Set in a delightful garden, it offers all the amenities you'd expect from an internationally known hotel. ✉ *Paseo de la Castellana 22, 28046,* ☎ *91/576–7500,* FAX *91/575–3158. 164 rooms, 18 suites. Restaurant. AE, DC, MC, V.*

$$$$ ⚑ **Villa Real.** English antiques and 19th-century Aubusson tapestries set the tone in the lobby of this very personal hotel. The emphasis is on service and luxurious details, such as three telephones in every room and teletext service on TV. Decor in the rooms is somewhat clubby, with leather sofas and dark-red floral fabrics. The hotel looks over the Plaza de las Cortes and is convenient to almost everything. ✉ *Plaza de las Cortes 10, 28014,* ☎ *91/420–3767,* FAX *91/420–2547. 94 rooms, 20 suites. Restaurant. AE, DC, MC, V.*

$$$ ⚑ **El Prado.** Wedged in among the classic buildings of Old Madrid, this slim hotel is within stumbling distance of Madrid's best bars and nightclubs. Rooms are soundproofed with double-pane glass and are surprisingly spacious. Appointments include pastel floral prints and gleaming marble baths. ✉ *Prado 11, 28014,* ☎ *91/429–0234,* FAX *91/429–2829. 47 rooms. AE, DC, MC, V.*

$$$ ⚑ **Reina Victoria.** One of Madrid's most historic and best-loved ho-
★ tels, the Reina Victoria faces two of the city's liveliest squares. Once a haven for bullfighters, it now attracts a more upscale clientele. Rooms are large and comfortable and have magnificent views, especially those overlooking the Plaza Santa Ana. ✉ *Plaza del Ángel 7, 28014,* ☎ *91/531–4500,* FAX *91/522–0307. 200 rooms. Restaurant. AE, DC, MC, V.*

$$ ⚑ **Carlos V.** If you like to be right in the center of things, hang your hat at this classic hotel on a pedestrian street: It's just a few steps away from the Puerta del Sol, Plaza Mayor, and Descalzas Reales convent. A suit of armor guards the tiny lobby, while crystal chandeliers add elegance to the second-floor lounge. All rooms are bright and carpeted, and the price is right. ✉ *Maestro Victoria 5, 28013,* ☎ *91/531–4100,* FAX *91/531–3761. 67 rooms. AE, DC, MC, V.*

$$ ⊡ **Inglés.** This budget favorite once drew such writers and artists as Virginia Woolf. Though dreary, the rooms are comfortable enough, and the location is key: a short walk from the Puerta del Sol in one direction, the Prado in the other. Inexpensive restaurants and distinctive bars are close at hand. ⊠ *Echegaray 8, 28014,* ☎ *91/429–6551,* FAX *91/420–2423. 58 rooms. AE, DC, MC, V.*

$$
★ ⊡ **Paris.** You can't get more central than this: For a remarkably fair price, the Paris offers delightful old-world charm right at the corner of the busy Puerta del Sol and Calle de Alcalá. The odd-shape rooms are clean, spacious, and decked out in orange bedspreads and curtains. The lobby is dark, woody, and somehow redolent of times long past. There's no bar, but three meals are served in the bright, second-floor restaurant. All in all, it's an unusual deal. ⊠ *Alcalá 2, 28014,* ☎ *91/ 521–6496,* FAX *91/531–0188. 114 rooms. Restaurant. MC, V.*

$ ⊡ **Mora.** Right across the Paseo del Prado from the Botanical Garden, the Mora rewards your journey with a sparkling, faux-marble lobby and bright, carpeted hallways. Rooms are simple but large and comfortable. Those on the street have great views of the garden and Prado through soundproof, double-pane windows. For breakfast and lunch, the attached café is excellent, affordable, and popular with locals. ⊠ *Paseo del Prado 32, 28014,* ☎ *91/420–1569,* FAX *91/420–0564. 61 rooms. AE, DC, MC, V.*

$ ⊡ **Villar.** All of these rooms are pleasant, clean, and tastefully furnished, with antique beds and armoires, but the eight rooms with balconies are the best: Laden with flowers, the balconies overlook lively Calle Príncipe and have corner views of the Plaza Santa Ana, including the well-heeled crowds arriving at the Teatro Español. The area's best bargain, Villar is on the second floor of a beautiful old building with a marble foyer and winding staircase. ⊠ *C. Príncipe 18, 28014,* ☎ *91/ 531–6600,* FAX *91/521-5073. 34 rooms, 18 with bath. AE, DC, MC, V.*

Nightlife and the Arts

The Arts

Details of all cultural events are listed in the daily newspaper *El País* or in the weekly *Guía del Ocio*.

CONCERTS AND OPERA

Madrid's main concert hall is the **Auditorio Nacional de Madrid** (⊠ Príncipe de Vergara 146, ☎ 91/337–0100, metro: Cruz del Rayo). Beneath the Plaza de Colón, the underground **Centro Cultural de la Villa** (⊠ Plaza de Colon s/n, ☎ 91/575–6080 for tickets, 91/553–2526 for info) hosts an eclectic variety of performances, from gospel, spiritual, and blues festivals to Celtic dance. For ballet or opera, catch a performance at the legendary **Teatro Real** (⊠ Plaza de Isabel II, ☎ 91/516–0606), whose splendid facade dominates the Plaza de Oriente.

FILM

Foreign films are mostly dubbed into Spanish, but movies in English are listed in *El País* or *Guía del Ocio* under "VO" (*versión original*). A dozen or so theaters now show films in English. Leading VO theaters include **Alphaville** (⊠ Martín de los Heroes 14, off Plaza España, ☎ 91/559–3836) and **Cines Renoir** (⊠ Martín de los Heroes 12, off Plaza España, ☎ 91/559–5760). The **Filmoteca Cine Doré** (⊠ Santa Isabel 3, ☎ 91/369–1125) is a city-run institution showing different classic VO films every day. Your best bet for first-run films in the original is the **Multicines Ideal** (⊠ Doctor Cortezo 6, ☎ 91/369–2518).

THEATER

If language is no problem, check out the fringe theaters in Lavapiés and the Centro Cultural de la Villa (☎ 91/575–6080), beneath the Plaza

Colón, and the open-air events in Retiro Park. The **Círculo de Bellas Artes** (⊠ Marqués de Casa Riera 2, off Alcalá 42, ☎ 91/360–5400) is a leading theater. The **Teatro Español** (⊠ Príncipe 25 on Plaza Santa Ana, ☎ 91/429–6297) stages Spanish classics. The **Teatro María Guerrero** (⊠ Tamayo y Baus 4, ☎ 91/319–4769), the home of the Centro Dramático Nacional, stages plays by García Lorca. Most theaters have two curtains, at 7 PM and 10:30 PM, and close on Monday. Tickets are inexpensive and often easy to come by on the night of the performance.

ZARZUELA

Zarzuela, a combination of light opera and dance that's ideal for non–Spanish speakers, is performed at the **Teatro Nacional Lírico de la Zarzuela** (⊠ Jovellanos 4, ☎ 91/524–5400). The season runs from October through July.

Nightlife
BARS AND CAFÉS

Mesónes. The most traditional and colorful taverns are on Cuchilleros and Cava San Miguel, just west of Plaza Mayor, where you'll find a whole array of *mesónes* with such names as Tortilla, Champiñón, and Boqueron. These are the places to start your evening out in Madrid; many serve tapas and raciónes and close around midnight, when crowds move on to bars and nightclubs.

Old Madrid. Wander the narrow streets between Puerta del Sol and Plaza Santa Ana—most are packed with traditional tapas bars. The **Cervecería Alemana** (⊠ Plaza Santa Ana 6, ☎ 91/429–7033) is a beer hall founded over 100 years ago by Germans and patronized, inevitably, by Ernest Hemingway. **El Abuelo** (⊠ Victoria 6, ☎ no phone), or "Grandpa," serves only two tapas, but does them better than anyone else: grilled shrimp and shrimp sautéed in garlic. **La Trucha** (⊠ Manuel Fernández y González 3, ☎ 91/532–0890) is a small, cheery, traditional bar packed with locals. For a more tranquil atmosphere try the lovely, old, tiled bar **Viva Madrid** (⊠ Fernández y González 7, ☎ 91/429–3640) early in the evening.

Calle Huertas. Once lined with turn-of-the-20th-century bars playing guitar or chamber music, Calle Huertas now has more nightclubs than any other street in Madrid. **Casa Alberto** (⊠ C. Huertas 18), a quiet restaurant-tavern with brick walls, has a good selection of draft beers, and tapas. **La Fídula** (⊠ C. Huertas 57, ☎ 91/429–2947) maintains a traditional feel. For zest, try the discobar **La Fontanería** (⊠ Huertas 38, ☎ 91/369–4904), where the action lasts until 4 AM.

Plaza Santa Bárbara. Just off Alonso Martínez, this area is packed with fashionable bars and beer halls. Stroll along Santa Teresa, Orellana, Campoamor, or Fernando VI and take your pick. The **Cervecería Santa Bárbara** (☎ 91/319–0449), in the plaza itself, is one of the most colorful, a popular beer hall with a good range of tapas.

Cafés. Madrid has no lack of old-fashioned cafés, with dark-wood counters, brass pumps, marble-top tables, and plenty of atmosphere. **Café Comercial** (⊠ Glorieta de Bilbao 7, ☎ 91/521–5655) is a typical spot in the classic style. **Café Gijón** (⊠ Paseo de Recoletos 21, ☎ 91/521–5425) is a former literary hangout and the most famous of the old cafés; it's now just one of many terrace cafés that line the Castellana. **Café León** (⊠ Alcalá 57) is just up from Cibeles. **El Espejo** (⊠ Paseo de Recoletos 31, ☎ 91/308–2347) has Art Nouveau decor and an outdoor terrace in summer. For a late-night coffee, or something stronger, stop into the Baroque **Palacio de Gaviria** (⊠ Arenal 9, ☎ 91/526–8089), a restored 19th-century palace that often has live jazz. "International" parties are held every Thursday night.

Berlin (⊠ Costanilla de San Pedro 11, ☎ 91/366–2034) opens at 9:30 for a dinner that's tasty by most cabaret standards, followed by rib-ald comedy, chorus girls, and dancing until 4 AM. **Florida Park** (⊠ Avda. Menéndez Pelayo, at C. Ibiza, ☎ 91/573–7805), in the Parque del Retiro, offers dinner and a show with ballet, flamenco, or Spanish dance.

Nightlife—or *la marcha,* as the Spanish fondly call it—reaches legendary heights in Spain's capital. Smart, trendy dance clubs filled with well-heeled Madrileños are everywhere. For adventure, try the scruffy bar district in Malasaña, around the Plaza Dos de Mayo, where smoky hangouts line Calle San Vicente Ferrer. The often seedy haunts of Chueca are notorious for thrill-seekers (watch your purse), but classy cafés and trendy live music venues occasionally break up the alleys of tattoo parlors, boutiques, techno discos, and after-hours clubs.

Amadis (⊠ Covarrubias 42, under Luchana Cinema, ☎ 91/446–0036) has concerts, dancing, and telephones on every table, encouraging people to call each other with invitations to dance. You must be over 25 to enter. The well-heeled crowd likes **Archy's** (⊠ Marqués de Riscal 11, ☎ 91/310–5008). Salsa has become a fixture in Madrid; check out the most spectacular moves at **Azucar** (Sugar; ⊠ Paseo Reina Cristina 7, ☎ 91/501–6107). **El Clandestino** (⊠ Barquillo 34, ☎ 91/521–5563) is low-key: Choose from mellow jazz or house and ambient music. Madrid's hippest new club for wild, all-night dancing to an international music mix is **El Sol** (⊠ C. Jardines 3, ☎ 91/532–6490). **Fortuny** (⊠ Fortuny 34, ☎ 91/319–0588) attracts a celebrity crowd, especially in summer, when the lush outdoor patio is open. The door is ultraselective. **Joy Eslava** (⊠ Arenal 11, ☎ 91/366–3733), a downtown disco in a converted theater, is an old standby. **Pacha** (⊠ Barceló 11, ☎ 91/466–0137), one of Spain's infamous chain discos, is always energetic. **Torero** (⊠ Cruz 26, ☎ 91/523–1129) is for the beautiful people—quite literally: A bouncer allows only those judged *gente guapa* (beautiful people) to enter.

Madrid has an array of flamenco shows. Some are good, but many are aimed at the tourist trade. Dinner tends to be mediocre and over-priced, though it ensures the best seats; otherwise, opt for the show and a *consumición* (drink) only, usually starting around 11 PM and costing 3,000 ptas.–3,500 ptas. **Arco de Cuchilleros** (⊠ Cuchilleros 7, ☎ 91/364–0263) is one of the better and cheaper venues. **Café de Chini-tas** (⊠ Torija 7, ☎ 91/559–5135) is reasonably authentic. **Casa Patas** (⊠ Cañizares 10, ☎ 91/369–0496) is a major showplace; it offers good, if somewhat touristy, flamenco and tapas all at reasonable prices. **Corral de la Morería** (⊠ Morería 17, ☎ 91/365–8446) invites well-known stars to perform with the resident group.

The city's best-known jazz venue is **Café Central** (⊠ Plaza de Angel 10, ☎ 91/369–4143). **Café del Foro** (⊠ San Andrés 38, ☎ 91/445–3752) is a friendly club with live music nightly. Another well-known spot is **Clamores** (⊠ Albuquerque 14, ☎ 91/445–7938). **Populart** (⊠ Huertas 22, ☎ 91/429–8407) features blues, Brazilian music, and salsa. Seasonal citywide festivals also present excellent artists; check the local press for listings and venues.

Shopping

The main shopping area in central Madrid surrounds the pedestrian streets **Preciados** and **Montera,** off the Gran Vía between Puerta del

Sol and Plaza Callao. The **Salamanca** district, just off the Plaza de Colón, bordered roughly by Serrano, Goya, and Conde de Peñalver, is more elegant and expensive; just west of Salamanca, the shops on and around Calle Argensola, just south of Calle Génova, are on their way upmarket. **Calle Mayor** and the streets to the east of **Plaza Mayor** are lined with fascinating old-fashioned stores straight out of the 19th century.

Antiques

The main areas for antiques are the Plaza de las Cortes, the Carrera San Jerónimo, and the Rastro flea market, along the Ribera de Curtidores and the courtyards just off it.

Boutiques

Calle Serrano has the widest selection of smart boutiques and designer fashions—think Prada, Armani, and Donna Karan New York, as well as renowned Spanish designers such as Josep Font-Luz Diaz. Worth special trips are several posh boutiques. **Adolfo Dóminguez** (⊠ Serrano 96, ☎ 91/576–7053; ⊠ C. Orense, ☎ 91/576–0084), one of Spain's top designers, has several boutiques in Madrid. **Jesús del Pozo** (⊠ Almirante 9, ☎ 91/531-3646) is one of Spain's premier young fashion designers, a scion of Spanish style for both men and women. **Loewe** (⊠ Serrano 26, ☎ 91/577–6056; ⊠ Gran Vía 8, ☎ 91/522–6815) is Spain's most prestigious leather store. **Seseña** (⊠ De la Cruz 23, ☎ 91/531–6840) has outfitted Hollywood stars (and, on occasion, Hillary Rodham Clinton) since the turn of the 20th century. **Sybilla** (⊠ Jorge Juan 12, ☎ 91/578–1322) is the studio of Spain's best-known woman designer, whose fluid dresses and hand-knit sweaters in natural colors and fabrics have made her a favorite with model Helena Christensen.

Several upscale shopping centers group a variety of exclusive shops stocked with unusual clothes and gifts: **Centro Comercial ABC** (⊠ Paseo de la Castellana 34); **Galerías del Prado** (⊠ Plaza de las Cortes 7, on the lower level of the Palace Hotel); and **Los Jardines de Serrano** (⊠ corner of C. Goya and Claudio Coello). South of the city center an old factory building has been transformed into the ultraslick, government-subsidized **Mercado Puerta de Toledo** (⊠ Ronda de Toledo 1). For street-chic fashion closer to medieval Madrid, check out the window displays at the **Madrid Fusion Centro de Moda** (⊠ Plaza Tirso de Molina, 15, ☎ 91/369–0018), where up-and-coming Spanish labels like Instinto, Kika, and Extart fill five floors with faux furs, funky jewelry, and the city's most eccentric selection of shoes.

Department Stores

El Corte Inglés (⊠ Preciados 3, ☎ 91/532–8100; ⊠ Goya 76, ☎ 91/577–7171; ⊠ Goya 87, ☎ 91/432–9300; ⊠ Princesa 42, ☎ 91/542–4800; ⊠ Serrano 47, ☎ 91/432–5490; ⊠ La Vaguada Mall, ☎ 91/387–4000; ⊠ Parquesur Mall, ☎ 91/558–4400; ⊠ Raimundo Fernández Villaverde 79, ☎ 91/556–2300) is Spain's biggest, brightest, and most successful chain store. **Marks & Spencer** (⊠ C. Serrano 52, ☎ 91/431–6760), a British department store, specializes in woolens, underwear, and gourmet foods.

Food and Flea Markets

The **Rastro,** Madrid's most famous flea market, operates on Sunday from 9 to 2 around the Plaza del Cascorro and the Ribera de Curtidores. A **stamp and coin market** is held on Sunday morning in the Plaza Mayor. Mornings, take a look at the colorful food stalls inside the 19th-century glass-and-steel **San Miguel** market, also near the Plaza Mayor. There's a **secondhand-book market** most days on the Cuesta Claudio Moyano, near Atocha Station.

Gift Ideas

No special crafts are associated with Madrid itself, but traditional Spanish goods are sold in many stores. El Corte Inglés (☞ *above*) stocks a good selection of Lladró **porcelain,** as do several specialty shops on the Gran Vía and the Plaza de España, behind the Plaza Hotel. Department stores stock good displays of **fans,** but for superb examples, try the long-established Casa Diego, in Puerta del Sol. Two stores opposite the Prado on Plaza Cánovas del Castillo, Artesanía Toledana and El Escudo de Toledo, have a wide selection of **souvenirs,** especially Toledo swords, marquetry ware, and pottery. Carefully selected **handicrafts** from all over Spain—ceramics, furniture, glassware, rugs, embroidery, and more—are sold at **Artespaña** (✉ Hermosilla 14, ☎ 91/435–0221). **Casa Julia** (✉ Almirante 1, ☎ 91/522–0270, FAX 91/521–3137) is an artistic showcase, with two floors of tasteful antiques, paintings by up-and-coming artists, and furniture in experimental designs.

Madrid Essentials

Arriving and Departing

BY BUS

Madrid has no central bus station. Check with the tourist office for departure points for your destination. The **Estación del Sur** (✉ Méndez Álvaro s/n, ☎ 91/468–4200, metro: Palos de la Frontera) serves Toledo, La Mancha, Alicante, and Andalucía. **Auto-Rés** (✉ Plaza Conde de Casal 6, ☎ 91/551–7200, metro: Conde de Casal) serves Extremadura, Cuenca, Salamanca, Valladolid, Valencia, and Zamora. Auto-Rés has a central ticket and information office at Salud 19 (☎ 91/551–7200), just off Gran Vía, near the Hotel Arosa. The Basque country and most of north-central Spain are served by **Auto Continental** (✉ Avda. de America 34, ☎ 91/356–2307, metro: Ríos Rosas). For Àvila, Segovia, and La Granja, use **Empresa La Sepulvedana** (✉ Paseo de la Florida 11, ☎ 91/530–4800, metro: Norte). **Empresa Herranz** (✉ C. Reina Victoria 3, ☎ 91/890–4100, metro: Moncloa) serves El Escorial and the Valley of the Fallen. **La Veloz** (✉ Avda. Mediterraneo 49, ☎ 91/409–7602, metro: Conde de Casal) serves Chinchón.

BY CAR

The main roads are: north–south, the Paseo de la Castellana and Paseo del Prado; east–west, Calle de Alcalá, Gran Vía, and Calle de la Princesa. The M30 circles Madrid, and the M40 is an outer ring road about 12 km (7 mi) farther out. For Burgos and France, drive north up the Castellana and follow the signs for the NI. For Barcelona, head up the Castellana to Plaza Dr. Marañón, then right onto María de Molina and the NII; for Andalusia and Toledo, head south down Paseo del Prado, then follow the signs to the NIV and N401, respectively. For Segovia, Ávila, and El Escorial, head west along Princesa to Avenida Puerta de Hierro and onto the NVI–La Coruña.

BY PLANE

All international and domestic flights arrive at Madrid's Barajas Airport (☎ 91/305–8343), 16 km (10 mi) northeast of town just off the NII Barcelona highway. For information on arrivals and departures, call the airport at ☎ 91/305–8343, or call **Info-Iberia** (☎ 91/329–5767) or the airline concerned (☞ Air Travel *in* Chapter 1).

Between the Airport and Downtown. Buses leave the national and international terminals every 15 minutes from 5:40 AM to 2 AM for the downtown bus terminal at Plaza de Colón, just off the Paseo de la Castellana. The ride takes about 20 minutes, and the fare at press time was 450 ptas. Most city hotels are then only a short taxi or metro ride away. The fastest and most expensive route into town is by taxi (usually about

1,500 ptas., but up to 2,000 ptas. plus tip in traffic). Pay the metered amount plus the 350-pta. surcharge and 150 ptas. for each suitcase. By car take the NII (which becomes Avenida de América) into town, then head straight into Calle María de Molina and left on either Calle Serrano or the Castellana.

BY TRAIN

Madrid has three railroad stations. **Chamartín** (⊠ Avda. Pío XII, ☎ 91/315–9976), in the northern suburbs beyond the Plaza de Castilla, is the main station, with trains to France and the north (including Barcelona, Ávila, Salamanca, Santiago, and La Coruña). Most trains to Valencia, Alicante, and Andalusia leave from Chamartín but stop at Atocha station as well. **Atocha** (⊠ Glorieta del Emperador Carlos V, southern end of Paseo del Prado, ☎ 91/328–9020) sends trains to Segovia, Toledo, Granada, Extremadura, and Lisbon. A convenient metro stop (Atocha RENFE) connects the Atocha rail station to the city subway system. The old Atocha station, designed by Eiffel, is Madrid's terminal for high-speed AVE service to Córdoba and Seville. **Norte** (or Príncipe Pío; ⊠ Paseo de la Florida, above Campo del Moro) serves the residential suburbs.

For all train information call or visit the **RENFE offices** (⊠ Alcalá 44, ☎ 91/563–0202 Spanish; 91/328–9020 English, if speaker is available); open weekdays 9:30–8. There's another RENFE office in the International Arrivals Hall at Barajas Airport, or you can purchase tickets at any of the three main stations or from travel agents displaying the blue and yellow RENFE sign.

Getting Around

Madrid is a fairly compact city, and most of the main sights can be visited on foot. If you're staying in one of the modern hotels in northern Madrid, however, off the Castellana, you may need to use the bus or subway. Some rough guidelines: The walk from the Prado to the Royal Palace at a comfortable sightseeing pace, but without stopping, takes around 30 minutes; from Plaza del Callao on Gran Vía to the Plaza Mayor, about 15 minutes.

BY BUS

City buses are red and generally run from 6 AM to midnight (some stop earlier). The flat fare is 130 ptas. Route plans are displayed at *paradas* (bus stops), and a map of the entire system is available from Empresa Municipal de Transportes (EMT) booths on Plaza de la Cibeles, Callao, or Puerta del Sol. You can save money by buying a **Bonobus** (670 ptas.), good for 10 rides, from EMT booths or any tobacco shop.

BY METRO

The metro offers the simplest and quickest means of transport and operates from 6 AM to 1:30 AM. Metro maps are available from ticket offices, hotels, and tourist offices. The flat fare at press time was 130 ptas. a ride; a 10-ride ticket, 670 ptas. Carry some change (5, 25, 50, and 100 ptas.) for the ticket machines, especially after 10 PM; the machines make change and allow you to skip long ticket lines.

BY TAXI

Madrid has more than 18,000 taxicabs, and fares are low by New York or London standards. The meter starts at 175 ptas.; each additional km (½ mi) costs 70 ptas. The average city ride costs about 500 ptas., and there is a surcharge of 150 ptas. between 11 PM and 6 AM and on holidays. A supplemental fare of 150 ptas. applies to trips to the bullring or football matches, and there is an additional charge of 150 ptas. per suitcase. The airport surcharge is 400 ptas. Cabs available for hire display a LIBRE sign during the day and a green light at night. They hold four passengers. Make sure the driver turns the meter on when you start your ride; tip 5%–10% of the fare. To radio a cab call **Tele-Taxi** (☎ 91/445–9008 or 91/448–4259).

Contacts and Resources

EMBASSIES

U.S. (✉ Serrano 75, ☎ 91/577–4000). **Australia** (✉ Paseo de la Castellana 143, ☎ 91/579–0428). **Canada** (✉ Núñez de Balboa 35, ☎ 91/431–4300). **New Zealand** (✉ Plaza de La Lealtad 2, ☎ 91/523–0226). **U.K.** (✉ Fernando el Santo 16, ☎ 91/319–0200).

EMERGENCIES

112 is the **general emergency number** in all EU nations (akin to 911 in the U.S.). **Police** (emergencies, ☎ 091; Municipal Police, ☎ 092 for towed cars or traffic accidents). **Ambulance** (☎ 061, 91/522–2222, or 91/588–4400). **Emergency clinics:** Hospital 12 de Octubre (☎ 91/390–8000), La Paz Ciudad Sanitaria (☎ 91/358–2600). **English-speaking doctors: British-American Medical Unit** (☎ 91/435–1823). **Pharmacies:** List of pharmacies open 24 hours (*farmacias de guardia*) published daily in El País.

ENGLISH-LANGUAGE BOOKS

Booksellers (✉ José Abascal 48, ☎ 91/442–8104). **Casa del Libro** (✉ Maestro Victoria 3, ☎ 91/521–4898). **The International Bookshop** (✉ Campomanes 13, ☎ 91/541–7291). **Turner's English Bookshop** (✉ Génova 3, ☎ 91/319–0926).

GUIDED TOURS

Orientation. Julià Tours (✉ Gran Vía 68, ☎ 91/559–9605). **Pullmantur** (✉ Plaza de Oriente 8, ☎ 91/541–1807). **Trapsatur** (✉ San Bernardo 23, ☎ 91/302–6039). All three run the same tours, conducted in Spanish and English. Reserve directly with the offices above, through any travel agent, or through your hotel. Departure points are the addresses above, though you can often arrange to be picked up at your hotel. Tours leave in morning, afternoon, and evening and cover various selections of sites and activities. Trapsatur also runs the Madridvision bus, which makes a one-hour tour of the city with recorded commentary in English. No reservation is necessary; catch the bus in front of the Prado every 1½ hours beginning at 10 AM, from Tuesday through Sunday. There are no buses on Sunday afternoon. A round-trip ticket costs 1,500 ptas., and a two-day pass, 2,200 ptas. If you want a personal tour with a local guide, contact the **Asociación Profesional de Informadores** (✉ Ferraz 82, ☎ 91/542–1214 or 91/541–1221).

Walking and Special-Interest. The Municipal Tourist Office (✉ Plaza Mayor 3) leads English-language tours of Madrid's old quarter every Saturday morning at 10. The **ayuntamiento** (city hall) has a popular selection of Spanish bus and walking tours under the name "Discubre Madrid." Walking tours depart most mornings and visit many hidden corners as well as major sights; options include "Madrid's Railroads," "Medicine in Madrid," "Goya's Madrid," and "Commerce and Finance in Madrid." Schedules are listed in the "Discubre Madrid" leaflet available from the municipal tourist office. Tickets can be purchased at the Patronato de Turismo (✉ C. Mayor 69, ☎ 91/588–2906).

Excursions. Julià Tours, Pullmantur, and **Trapsatur** (☞ *above*) run full- or half-day trips to El Escorial, Ávila, Segovia, Toledo, and Aranjuez, and in summer to Cuenca and Salamanca. Summer weekends, the popular *Tren de la Fresa* (Strawberry Train) takes passengers from the old Delicias Station to Aranjuez (known for its production of strawberries) on a 19th-century train. Tickets can be obtained from RENFE offices (☞ Arriving and Departing by Train, *above*), travel agents, and the Delicias Station (⊠ Paseo de las Delicias 61). Other one- or two-day excursions by train are available on summer weekends. Contact RENFE for details.

TRAVEL AGENCIES

American Express (⊠ Plaza de las Cortes 2, ☎ 91/322–5445). **Carlson Wagons-Lits** (⊠ Paseo de la Castellana 96, ☎ 91/563–1202). **Pullmantur** (⊠ Plaza de Oriente 8, ☎ 91/541–1807).

VISITOR INFORMATION

Madrid tourist office (⊠ Torre de Madrid, Plaza de España, C. de la Princesa 1, ☎ 91/541–2325) is the best place for comprehensive information. The **Madrid Provincial Tourist Office** (⊠ Duque de Medinacelli 2, ☎ 91/429–4951) is also helpful. The **municipal tourist office** (⊠ Plaza Mayor 3, ☎ 91/366–5477) is centrally located, but hordes of tourists tend to deplete its stock of brochures. The **airport tourist office** (⊠ International Arrivals Hall, Barajas Airport, ☎ 91/305–8656) has a convenient visitors' center.

CASTILE

The beauty and romantic histories of the towns around Madrid rank them among Spain's greatest sights. Ancient Toledo, Spain's former capital; the great palace-monastery of El Escorial; Segovia's Roman aqueduct and fairy-tale Alcázar; the imposing medieval walls of Ávila; and the magnificent Plaza Mayor of the old university town of Salamanca all lie within an hour or two of the capital.

All of these towns, with the possible exception of Salamanca, are easy day trips from Madrid. But if you've had your fill of Spain's booming capital, you'll find it far more rewarding to leave Madrid altogether and tour from one town to another, spending a night or two in classically Spanish Castile (Castilla). After the day-trippers have gone home, you can enjoy the real charm of these provincial communities and wander at leisure through their medieval streets.

Toledo

If you're driving, head south from Madrid on the N401. About 20 minutes from the capital, look left for a prominent rounded hill topped by a statue of Christ. This is **El Cerro de los Angéles** (Hill of the Angels), the geographical center of the Iberian Peninsula. After 90 minutes of drab, industrial scenery, the unforgettable silhouette of Toledo suddenly rises before you, with the imposing bulk of the Alcázar and the slender spire of the cathedral dominating the skyline. This former capital, where Moors, Jews, and Christians once lived in harmony, is now a living national monument, holding all the elements of Spanish civilization in hand-carved, sun-mellowed stone. For a stunning view, and to capture the beauty of Toledo as El Greco knew it, begin with a panoramic drive around the Carretera de Circunvalación, crossing over the Alcántara bridge and returning by way of the bridge of San Martín. As you gaze at the city rising like an island in its own bend of the Tagus, you may notice how little its skyline has changed in the four centuries since El Greco painted *Storm over Toledo*.

Toledo is a small city steeped in history and full of magnificent buildings. It was the capital of Spain under both Moors and Christians until Philip II moved the capital to Madrid in 1561. Begin your visit with a drink in one of the many terrace cafés on the central **Plaza Zocódover**; study a map and try to get your bearings, for a veritable labyrinth confronts you as you try to find your way to Toledo's great treasures. While

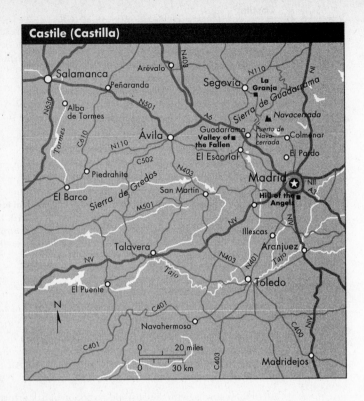

Castile (Castilla)

here search the square's pastry shops for Toledo's typical *mazapanes* (marzipan candies).

Toledo's 13th-century **cathedral** is one of the greatest in Spain, and the seat of the Cardinal Primate. Somber but elaborate, it blazes with jeweled chalices, gorgeous ecclesiastical vestments, historic tapestries, some 750 stained-glass windows, and paintings by Tintoretto, Titian, Murillo, El Greco, Velázquez, and Goya. The cathedral has two surprises: a **Mozarabic chapel,** where mass is still celebrated on Sunday according to an ancient Mozarabic rite from the days of the Visigoths (AD 419–711); and its unique **Transparente,** an ornate Baroque roof that gives a theatrical glimpse of heaven as the sunlight pours down through a hole to a mass of figures and clouds. ⊠ *Arco de Palacio 2,* ☎ *925/222241.* ☉ *Mon.–Sat. 10:30–1 and 3:30–6 (3:30–7 in summer), Sun. 10:30–1:30 and 4–6 (4–7 in summer).*

The tiny chapel of **Santo Tomé,** which houses El Greco's (1541–1614) masterpiece, *The Burial of the Count of Orgaz,* captures some of the incredible spirit of the Greek painter who adopted Spain, and Toledo in particular, as his home. Do you recognize the sixth man from the left in the painting's earthly contingent? Or the young boy in the left-hand corner? The first is El Greco himself, the second his son Jorge Manuel—embroidered on the boy's handkerchief you'll see *1578,* the year of his birth. ⊠ *Plaza del Conde 1,* ☎ *925/256098.* ☉ *Daily 10–6:45.*

Casa de El Greco (El Greco's House) has copies of the artist's works. The museum next door contains some originals, including a panorama of Toledo with the Hospital of Tavera in the foreground. ⊠ *Samuel Levi s/n,* ☎ *925/224006.* ☉ *Tues.–Sat. 10–2 and 4–6, Sun. 10–2.*

The splendid **Sinagoga del Tránsito** (Tránsito Synagogue) was commissioned in 1366 by Samuel Levi, chancellor to Peter the Cruel. The synagogue bears Christian and Moorish as well as Jewish influences in its architecture and decoration; notice the stars of David interspersed with the arms of Castile and León. The small **Museo Sefardí** (Sephardic Museum) chronicles Toledo's former Jewish community. ⊠ *C. Samuel Levi s/n, corner of Reyes Católicos,* ☎ *925/223665.* ☉ *Tues.– Sat. 10–2 and 4–6, Sun. 10–2.*

Santa María la Blanca (St. Mary the White) was originally a synagogue, founded in 1203. Stormed in the early 15th century by a Christian mob led by St. Vincent Ferrer, it was then consecrated as a church. Except for the 16th-century altarpiece, however, the architecture is neither Jewish nor Christian but Moorish; the interior has five naves, horseshoe arches, and capitals decorated with texts from the Koran. ⊠ *Reyes Católicos 4,* ☎ *925/227257.* ☉ *Daily 10–2 and 3:30–6 (4–7 in summer).*

Ferdinand and Isabella began **San Juan de los Reyes,** a beautiful Gothic church with fine cloisters, in 1476. The iron manacles on the outer walls were placed there for posterity by Christians freed by the Moors. The Catholic Monarchs originally intended to be buried here, but their great triumph at Granada in 1492 changed their plans. ⊠ *Reyes Católicos,* ☎ *925/223802.* ☉ *Daily 10–1:45 and 3:30–5:45 (6:45 in summer).*

The **Museo de la Santa Cruz** (Museum of the Holy Cross) has some splendid El Grecos. ⊠ *Cervantes 3, off Plaza de Zocódover,* ☎ *925/ 221036.* ☉ *Mon. 10–2 and 4–6:30, Tues.–Sat. 10–6:30, Sun. 10–2.*

The **Hospital de Tavera** (Tavera Hospital), outside the city walls, houses the **Duque de Lema** museum in its southern wing. The most important works in this miscellaneous collection are El Greco's *Baptism of Christ* and Alonso de Berruguete's exquisitely carved tomb of Cardinal Tavera. ⊠ *Cardenal Tavera 2,* ☎ *925/220451.* ☉ *Daily 10–1:30 and 3:30–6.*

$$$$ ✗ **Cason López.** No other restaurant in town offers such a combination of ambience and cuisine. A vaulted foyer leads to an enclosed patio with marble statues, twittering caged birds, a fountain, and abstract religious paintings. The market-based menu features the finest Castilian and Continental cuisine. Starters like garlic-ravioli soup are followed by hearty second courses, like braised rabbit with mustard sauce and mashed potatoes. Plum-and-cheese mousse with ice cream is one way to round out this superb meal. The lunchtime *menu del día* is 3,800 ptas. ⊠ *Sillería 3,* ☎ *925/254774. AE, DC, MC, V.*

$$$ ✗ **Asador Adolfo.** Toledo's most famous restaurant, near the cathe-
★ dral, is known for its gratifying combination of good food, service, and old-world charm. Parts of the building date from the 14th century; the dining room retains its original wood-beam ceiling and traces of original murals. Try the superb roast meat and the *tempura de flor de calabacín* (zucchini-flower tempura). ⊠ *C. de la Granada 6 and Hombre de Palo 7,* ☎ *925/227321. AE, DC, MC, V. No dinner Sun.*

$$ ✗ **La Abadía.** Perfect for a light lunch, a sandwich, or a round of tapas, this stylish bar-restaurant has vaulted stone ceilings and a huge, old wooden door. The dining room downstairs specializes in shish kebabs, grilled meats, and salads. ⊠ *Plaza San Nicolás, Núñez de Arce 3,* ☎ *925/251140. MC, V. No dinner.*

$$ ✗ **Venta de Aires.** This century-old inn on the edge of town, not far from the Tajo River, is where Toledanos go to eat partridge. Steaks and lamb are also expertly prepared. ⊠ *Circo Romano 35,* ☎ *925/220545. AE, DC, MC, V.*

$$$ ▤ **Parador Nacional de Toledo.** The best and most expensive hotel in
★ Toledo, the Conde de Orgaz is one of Spain's most highly respected paradors. It's a modern structure built in the traditional Toledan style; perched on a hill across the river (a 15-minute drive from the city cen-

ter), it commands magnificent views of the city. Book well in advance. ✉ *Cerro del Emperador s/n, 45001,* ☎ *925/221850,* 🖷 *925/225166. 77 rooms. Pool. AE, DC, MC, V.*

$$ 🏨 **Hostal del Cardenal.** Built during the 18th century as a summer palace for a cardinal, this quiet and beautiful hotel has some rooms that overlook a wooded garden. It's hard to believe that the highway is so close by. ✉ *Paseo de Recaredo 24, 45004,* ☎ *925/224900,* 🖷 *925/222991. 27 rooms. Restaurant. AE, DC, MC, V.*

$$ 🏨 **Pintor El Greco.** Next door to the famous painter's house/museum, this friendly hotel fills a building that was once a 17th-century bakery. The interior is warm and modern, with some antique touches such as exposed brick vaulting and terra-cotta tile floors. ✉ *Alamillos del Tránsito 13, 45002,* ☎ *925/214250,* 🖷 *925/215819. 33 rooms. AE, DC, MC, V.*

El Escorial

In the foothills of the Guadarrama Mountains, 50 km (31 mi) northwest of Madrid, and 120 km (74 mi) from Toledo, stands the Monastery of San Lorenzo del Escorial, the burial place of Spanish kings and queens. Built by the religious fanatic Philip II as a memorial to his father, Charles V, El Escorial is a vast, rectangular structure, conceived and executed with a monotonous magnificence worthy of the Spanish royal necropolis: It was designed by Juan de Herrera, Spain's greatest Renaissance architect. The **Panteón Real** (Royal Pantheon) contains the tombs of all the monarchs since Carlos I save three. Only those queens who bore sons who were later crowned lie in the same crypt; the others, along with royal sons and daughters who never ruled, lie in the nearby **Panteón de los Infantes** (Princes' Pantheon). The monastery's other highlights are Philip II's magnificent **library**, with 40,000 rare volumes and 2,700 illuminated manuscripts, including the diary of St. Teresa, and the **royal apartments.** Compare the spartan private apartment of Philip II, including the simple bedroom in which he died in 1598, with the beautiful carpets, porcelain, and tapestries with which his less austere successors embellished the rest of his somber commission. ✉ *Junction Rtes. C600 and M505, NW of Madrid,* ☎ *91/890–5905.* ☉ *Tues.– Sun. 10–6 (7 in summer), last entry 45 mins before closing.*

$$$$ ✕ **Charolés.** This elegant restaurant has a terrace above the street for
★ summer dining. Its meat dishes are famous throughout the region; try the *charolés a la pimienta* (peppered steak). Fresh fish is brought in daily from Spain's north coast. ✉ *Floridablanca 24,* ☎ *91/890–5975. Reservations essential. AE, DC, MC, V.*

$$$ ✕ **Parrilla Príncipe.** The scents of roast kid, lamb, chicken, and pork sausage draw crowds with big appetites to this specialist in succulent barbecue. Airier and more modern that most local taverns, the restaurant adds vegetarian paella and pasta to its meat menu. ✉ *Floridablanca 6,* ☎ *91/890–1611. AE, DC, MC, V. Closed Tues.*

$$ ✕ **Mesón de la Cueva.** Founded in 1768, this atmospheric *mesón* has several small, rustic dining rooms. It's a must for ambience—and the food is tasty, too. ✉ *San Antón 4,* ☎ *91/890–1516. No credit cards. Closed Mon.*

$$$ 🏨 **Victoria Palace.** The rooms at the back of this grand old hotel near the monastery have balconies and a splendid view toward Madrid. There's also a garden. ✉ *Juan de Toledo 4, 28200,* ☎ *91/890–1511,* 🖷 *91/890–1248. 89 rooms. Pool. AE, DC, MC, V.*

$$ 🏨 **Miranda Suizo.** With its dark-wood fittings, marble café tables, and main-street location, this charming hotel is straight out of the 19th century. The guest rooms are comfortable. ✉ *Floridablanca 20, 28200,* ☎ *91/890–4711,* 🖷 *91/890–4358. 52 rooms. AE, DC, MC, V.*

★ **Segovia**

The golden-stone market town of Segovia has outstanding medieval and Roman monuments, embroideries, and textiles, and excellent cuisine. Note that until 2001, however, you will have to view many of Segovia's monuments from a distance. The city's historic sights are undergoing a massive restoration project, which has several areas roped off or surrounded by scaffold and cranes.

The majestic **Roman aqueduct,** its huge granite blocks held together without mortar, greets you at the entrance to Segovia. At its foot is a small bronze statue of Romulus and the wolf, presented by Rome in 1974 to commemorate the 2,000-year history of Spain's greatest surviving Roman monument.

The **Ronda de Santa Lucía** leads to the most romantic view of the Alcázar, perched high on its rock like the prow of a mighty ship. Return via the Carretera de los Hoyos for yet another magical view, this time of the venerable cathedral rising from the ramparts.

Calle Real, the main shopping street, passes the Romanesque church of **San Martín,** with a porticoed outer gallery.

Plaza Mayor, with colorful ceramic shops (good bargains) and pleasant cafés, is set against a backdrop of ancient arcaded houses and one of the loveliest Gothic cathedrals in Spain.

Segovia's **cathedral** was the last Gothic cathedral to be built in Spain (the first was in nearby Ávila). Begun in 1525 by order of Charles V, it has a golden and harmonious interior, illuminated by 16th-century Flemish windows. Its museum, off the cloister, has the first book printed in Spain (1472) and a 17th-century ceiling paneled in white and gold, a splendid example of Mudéjar *artesonado* work. ⊠ *Marqués del Arco 1, Plaza Mayor,* ☎ *921/435325.* ☉ *June–Sept., daily 9–7; Oct.–May, daily 9:30–6.*

The turreted **Alcázar** is largely a fanciful re-creation from the 1880s; the original 13th-century castle was destroyed by fire in 1862. However, the view from its ramparts—and, even better, from its tower if you can manage the 156 steps—is breathtaking. The Alcázar served as a major residence of the Catholic Monarchs; here Isabella met Ferdinand, and from here she set out to the Plaza Mayor to be crowned Queen of Castile. The interior successfully illustrates the dawn of Spain's Golden Age. ⊠ *Plaza de la Reina Victoria Eugenia s/n,* ☎ *921/ 460759.* ☉ *May–Sept., daily 10–7; Oct.–Apr., daily 10–6.*

$$–$$$ ✕ **Casa Duque.** At the end of Segovia's main shopping street, this restaurant has several floors of beautifully decorated traditional dining rooms. It is the main rival to the famous Mesón de Cándido (☞ *below*). There's plenty of local atmosphere, and the food is pure Castilian—roasts are the house specialty. ⊠ *Cervantes 12,* ☎ *921/462487. AE, DC, MC, V.*

$$–$$$ ✕ **Mesón de Cándido.** Normally tucked cozily under the aqueduct,
★ Segovia's most prestigious restaurant looks less inviting while the Plaza de Azoguejo is torn up by bulldozers, but the dining rooms are still full of medieval atmosphere and Castilian memorabilia. Specialties are *cochinillo asado* (roast suckling pig) and *cordero asado* (roast lamb), both succulent. ⊠ *Plaza Azoguejo 5,* ☎ *921/425911. Reservations essential. AE, DC, MC, V.*

$$ ☷ **Infanta Isabel.** Right on a corner of the Plaza Mayor, this small, central hotel has a Victorian feel and great views of the cathedral. Guest rooms are feminine and light, with painted white furnishings. ⊠ *Is-*

abel la Católica, 40001, ☎ *921/461300,* FAX *921/462217. 29 rooms. AE, DC, MC, V.*

$$ ✕ **La Oficina.** Just off the Plaza Mayor, traditional Castilian dishes are served in two delightful dining rooms that date back to 1893. ✉ *Cronista Lecea 10,* ☎ *921/460286. AE, DC, MC, V.*

$$ ✕⊞ **Las Sirenas.** A few steps from the Plaza Mayor, this elegant hotel has one of Segovia's best locations. The furnishings are slightly faded, but old-fashioned charm and splendid views of the church of San Martín make it a hard-to-beat value. ✉ *Juan Bravo 30, 40001,* ☎ *921/ 462663,* FAX *921/462657. 36 rooms. Restaurant. AE, DC, MC, V.*

$$ ⊞ **Parador Nacional de Segovia.** To the north of town, this modern
★ parador offers comfortable, spacious rooms and pools. The views of the city are magnificent, especially at night. The restaurant serves excellent Castilian food. ✉ *Carretera de Valladolid s/n (off the N601 toward Valladolid), 40003,* ☎ *921/443737,* FAX *921/437362. 113 rooms. Restaurant, indoor and outdoor pools. AE, DC, MC, V.*

Ávila

At nearly 4,100 ft above sea level, Ávila is the highest provincial capital in Spain. Alfonso VI and his son-in-law, Count Raimundo de Borgoña, rebuilt the town and walls in 1090, bringing it permanently under Christian control. It is these walls, the best-preserved military installations of their kind in Spain, that give Ávila its special medieval quality. Thick and solid, with 88 towers tufted with untidy storks' nests, they stretch for 2½ km (1½ mi) around the entire city and make an ideal focus for the start of your visit. For a superb overall view, drive out to the **Cuatro Postes** (Four Posts), ¾ km (½ mi) out on the road to Salamanca. Ávila's other claim to fame is St. Teresa the Mystic, who lived much of her life here in the 16th century.

The **Basílica de San Vicente,** just outside the walls, is one of Ávila's finest Romanesque churches, erected on the spot where St. Vincent and his sisters Sabina and Cristeta were martyred in AD 306. Here, too, St. Teresa is said to have experienced the vision that told her to reform the Carmelite order. ✉ *Plaza de San Vicente,* ☎ *920/255230.* ☉ *Tues.–Sun. 10–2 and 4–8.*

Ávila's oldest and most rewarding ecclesiastical monuments predate St. Teresa. The impregnable hulk of the **cathedral** resembles a fortress as much as a house of God. Though of Romanesque origin—the Romanesque sections are recognizable by their red-and-white stonework—it is usually cited as Spain's first Gothic cathedral. Inside is the ornate alabaster tomb of Cardinal Alonso de Madrigal, a 15th-century bishop whose swarthy complexion earned him the nickname of "El Tostado" (the toasted one). ✉ *Plaza de la Catedral,* ☎ *920/211641.* ☉ *Daily 10–1:30 and 3:30–6:30.*

The **Convento de Santa Teresa** stands on the site of the saint's birthplace, with an ornate Baroque chapel and a museum with some of Teresa's relics: her rosary, books, walking stick, sandal sole, and preserved ring finger, wearing her wedding ring. ✉ *Plaza de la Santa, inside the southern gate,* ☎ *920/211030.* ☉ *Daily 9:30–1:30 and 3:30–7:30.*

The **Monasterio de Santo Tomás** was built between 1482 and 1493 by Ferdinand and Isabella, who used it as a summer palace. It houses the tomb of their only son, Prince Juan, who died at the age of 19 while a student at Salamanca; and the tomb of the notorious Inquisitor General Tomás de Torquemada. ✉ *Plaza Granada 1,* ☎ *920/220400.* ☉ *Cloister daily 10–1 and 4–7; museum daily 11–1 and 4–6.*

You can relax in the pleasant **Plaza de Santa Teresa,** with outdoor cafés and a statue of the saint erected for Pope John Paul's visit in 1982.

$$ ✕ **El Molino de la Losa.** On a quiet spit of land in the Adaja River, this
★ restaurant occupies a restored 15th-century mill and has splendid
views of Ávila's walls. In summer you can have a drink and enjoy some
tapas outside by the duck pond. Specialties include lamb roasted in a
medieval-style wood oven and fresh river trout. ⊠ *Bajada de la Losa
12,* ☎ *920/211101. AE, MC, V. Closed Mon. in winter.*

$$ ✕ **Las Canselas.** Push your way past the bar to the dining room, where
tables are heaped with combo platters of roast chicken, french fries,
and sunny-side-up eggs. Don't be daunted by the no-nonsense servers
or the volume of the Spanish being shouted around; do as the locals
do and relax with a *caña* (small shot of beer). ⊠ *Cruz Viejo 6,* ☎ *920/
220068. AE, V. Closed Mon. No dinner Sun.*

$$ ✕ **Mesón del Rastro.** This ancient inn tucked into the city walls is Ávila's
★ most atmospheric place to dine. Local specialties include *ternera* (veal)
and *yemas de Santa Teresa,* a dessert made from candied egg yolks. ⊠
Plaza del Rastro 4, ☎ *920/211218. AE, DC, MC, V.*

$$$ ▦ **Meliá Palacio de los Velada.** A beautifully restored 16th-century palace
★ houses Ávila's top hotel, ideally located in the heart of the city, beside
the cathedral. You can relax between sightseeing excursions in the lovely
palace courtyard. The attractive rooms are modern and comfortable,
and have all the amenities. ⊠ *Plaza de la Catedral 10, 05001,* ☎ *920/
255100,* FAX *920/254900. 85 rooms. Restaurant. AE, DC, MC, V.*

$$$ ▦ **Parador Nacional de Ávila.** Superbly set in a 15th-century palace
just inside the city's northern walls, this parador has rooms decorated
in traditional Castilian style and spacious, modern bathrooms. Some
rooms also have four-poster beds and views of the city walls. The at-
tractive dining room serves local dishes, and the garden sometimes per-
mits access to the walls. ⊠ *Marqués Canales de Chozas 2, 05001,* ☎
920/211340, FAX *920/226166. 62 rooms. Restaurant. AE, DC, MC, V.*

★ Salamanca

Salamanca is an ancient and gorgeous city, and even your first glimpse
of it is bound to be unforgettable. In the foreground as you approach
is the sturdy 15-arch Roman bridge, and above this—dominating the
view—soar the city's old houses and the golden walls, turrets, and domes
of its plateresque cathedrals. The word *plateresque* comes from *plata*
(silver), implying that the stone is chiseled and engraved as intricately
as that delicate metal. Today, as centuries ago, the University of Sala-
manca is the dominant influence here, creating an intellectual atmo-
sphere and a stimulating arts scene.

The west facade of the Dominican **Monasterio de San Esteban**
(Monastery of St. Stephen) is superbly plateresque. ⊠ *Plaza Concilio
de Trento s/n,* ☎ *923/215000.* ☉ *Daily 9–1 and 4–7.*

Salamanca has two distinct, adjoining **cathedrals,** the **Catedral Vieja**
(Old Cathedral) and the grandly carved **Catedral Nueva** (New Cathe-
dral). Inside the sturdy Romanesque walls of the old cathedral is a stun-
ning altarpiece with 53 painted panels. Within the splendid **cloister** are
a worthy collection of religious art and the **Capilla de Santa Bárbara**
(Chapel of St. Barbara, or Degree Chapel) where anxious students sought
help the night before their final exams. ⊠ *Plá y Deniel s/n,* ☎ *923/
217476.* 🎟 *New Cathedral free.* ☉ *New Cathedral daily 10–1 and 4–
6; Old Cathedral daily 10–12:30 and 4–5:30.*

Founded by Alfonso IX in 1218, the **universidad** (university) of Sala-
manca is to Spain what Oxford is to England. On the famous facade
of the **Escuelas Mayores,** a profusion of plateresque carving surrounds
the medallions of Ferdinand and Isabella. See if you can find the fa-
mous frog and skull, said to bring good luck to students taking exams.
Inside, the **Sala de Fray Luis de León** (Friar Luis's lecture room) has

been untouched since the days of that great scholar, and the prestigious **library** holds some 50,000 parchment and leather-bound volumes. ✉ *Patio de Las Escuelas,* ☎ *923/294400, ext. 1150.* ☉ *Weekdays 9:30– 1:30 and 4–7:30, Sat. 9:30–1:30 and 4–7, Sun. 10–1.*

The elegant, 18th-century **Plaza Mayor** is Salamanca's crowning glory. Built by Alberto and Nicolás Churriguera, it is widely thought the most beautiful Plaza Mayor in Spain. Here you can browse in stores offering typical *charro* jewelry (silver and black flower heads), head down the adjoining streets in search of colorful tapas bars, or just relax and watch the world go by at an outdoor café.

$$$ ✕ **Chez Victor.** If you're tired of Castilian cuisine, try this chic place, where chef-owner Victoriano Salvador adapts French food to Spanish tastes. Sample the *patatas rellenas de bacalao* (potatoes stuffed with salt cod) and outstanding desserts, especially the rasberry-walnut *tarta de chocolate* with fresh whipped cream. ✉ *Espoz y Mina 26,* ☎ *923/ 213123. AE, DC, MC, V. Closed Sun. July and Aug.*

$$ ✕ **Chapeau.** This chic spot offers both meat and fish carefully roasted
★ in its wood-fire ovens. Try the *pimientos relleños* (stuffed peppers) and, for dessert, the orange mousse. ✉ *Gran Vía 20,* ☎ *923/271833. AE, DC, MC, V. No dinner Sun.*

$$ ✕ **Río de la Plata.** This tiny, long-standing basement restaurant just off Calle de San Pablo retains a warm, old-fashioned character with a fireplace and a local crowd. The food—good-quality fish and meat— is simple but carefully prepared. ✉ *Plaza del Peso 1,* ☎ *923/219005. AE, MC, V. Closed Mon. and July.*

$$$–$$$$ 🏨 **Gran Hotel.** The grande dame of Salamanca's hotels offers stylishly Baroque lounges and refurbished, yet old-fashioned, oversize rooms just steps from the Plaza Mayor. ✉ *Poeta Iglesias 5, 37001,* ☎ *923/ 213500,* 🖷 *923/213501. 140 rooms. Restaurant. AE, DC, MC, V.*

$$$ 🏨 **Palacio de Castellanos.** Housed in an immaculately restored 15th-century palace, this hotel has an exquisite interior patio and an equally beautiful restaurant. ✉ *San Pablo 58, 37001,* ☎ *923/261818,* 🖷 *923/ 261819. 63 rooms. Restaurant. AE, DC, MC, V.*

$$ 🏨 **Hostal Plaza Mayor.** Steps from the Plaza Mayor, this agreeable hostelry has small but modern rooms. The potential drawback is noise on Friday and Saturday nights, when student *tunas* (strolling musicians) sing guitar ballads at nearby cafés until the wee hours. Reserve ahead. ✉ *Plaza del Corrillo 20, 37008,* ☎ *923/262020,* 🖷 *923/217548. 19 rooms. Restaurant. MC, V.*

Castile Essentials

Arriving and Departing
Trains to Toledo leave from Madrid's Atocha Station; to Salamanca from Chamartín Station; and to Ávila, Segovia, and El Escorial from both stations, although sometimes more frequently from Chamartín. For schedules and reservations call RENFE (☎ 91/328–9020).

Getting Around
BY BUS

All towns are linked by buses; local tourist offices can advise on schedules. Each town has a central bus station. **Ávila** (✉ Avda. de Madrid, ☎ 920/220154). **Salamanca** (✉ Filiberto Villalobos 71, ☎ 923/236717). **Segovia** (✉ Paseo Ezequiel González, ☎ 921/427725). **Toledo** (✉ Ronda de Castilla la Mancha, off the road from Madrid, ☎ 925/223641).

BY CAR

The N403 from Toledo to Ávila passes through spectacular scenery in the Sierra de Gredos, as does the C505 from Ávila to El Escorial. From

El Escorial to Segovia, both the Puerto de León and Puerto de Navac-
errada mountain passes offer magnificent views. The N501 from Ávila
to Salamanca takes you across the tawny plain of Castile.

BY TRAIN
There's a direct train line between El Escorial, Ávila, and Salamanca;
otherwise, train connections are poor, and you'll do better by bus.

Visitor Information

Ávila (⊠ Plaza de la Catedral 4, ☎ 920/211387). **El Escorial** (⊠ Florid-
ablanca 10, ☎ 91/890–1554). **Salamanca** (⊠ Casa de las Conchas,
Rúa Mayor s/n, ☎ 923/268571; information booth, ⊠ Plaza Mayor).
Segovia (⊠ Plaza Mayor 10, ☎ 921/460334). **Toledo** (⊠ Puerta de
Bisagra, ☎ 925/220843).

BARCELONA

Barcelona, capital of Catalunya (Catalonia), thrives on its business acumen and industrial muscle. The hardworking citizens of this thriving
metropolis are proud to have and use their own language—street
names, museum exhibits, newspapers, radio programs, and movies are
all in Catalan. An important milestone here was the city's long-awaited
opportunity to host the Olympic Games, in summer 1992; the Olympics
were of singular importance in Barcelona's modernization. Their legacy
includes a vastly improved ring road and several other highways; four
new beaches; and an entire new neighborhood in what used to be the
run-down industrial district of Poble Nou. In addition, the promontory of Montjuïc has a new sports stadium, several swimming pools,
and an adjoining marina. Few cities can rival the medieval atmosphere
of the Gothic Quarter's narrow alleys, the elegance and distinction of
the Moderniste (Art Nouveau) Eixample, or the many fruits of Gaudí's
whimsical imagination. Extraordinarily endowed with 2,000 years of
art and architecture, Barcelona remains a world center for design.

Exploring Barcelona

*Numbers in the margin correspond to points of interest on the Barcelona
map.*

It should take you two full days of sightseeing to complete the following
tour. The first part covers the Gothic Quarter, the Picasso Museum,
and the Rambla. The second part takes you to Passeig de Gràcia and
the church of the Sagrada Família; and the third, to Montjuïc.

The Barri Gòtic (Gothic Quarter) and La Rambla

★ **❶** **Catedral de la Seu** (Cathedral). Citizens of Barcelona gather on Sunday morning to dance the *sardana*, a symbol of Catalan identity, on
Plaça de la Seu, in front of the cathedral. The elaborate Gothic structure was built between 1298 and 1450, though the spire and Gothic
facade were not added until 1892. Inside, highlights are the beautifully
carved **choir stalls;** Santa Eulàlia's tomb in the crypt; the battle-scarred
crucifix from Don Juan's galley in the naval battle of Lepanto, in the
Capella de Lepanto (Lepanto Chapel); and the cloisters. ⊠ *Plaça de
la Seu,* ☎ *93/315–1554.* 🎫 *Free.* ☉ *Daily 7:45–1:30 and 4–7:45.*

⓬ **Gran Teatre del Liceu.** Barcelona's famous opera house was tragically gutted by fire in 1994 but has finally reopened, a modern replica of its original self. Built between 1845 and 1847, the old Liceu was one of the world's
most beautiful opera houses, with ornamental gilt and plush red-velvet
fittings. Anna Pavlova danced here in 1930, and Maria Callas sang here
in 1959. ⊠ *Rambla de los Capuchinos 63,* ☎ *93/318–9122.*

❾ Monument a Colom (Columbus Monument). You can ride an elevator to the top for a commanding view of the city and port. Columbus faces out to sea, pointing, ironically, east toward Naples. Nearby you can board the cable car to cross the harbor to Barceloneta or catch it in the other direction up Montjuïc. ⊠ *Bottom of the Rambla.* ☉ *Tues.–Sat. 10–2 and 3:30–6:30, Sun. 10–7.*

⓯ Museu d'Art Contemporani (MACBA; Museum of Contemporary Art). Designed by American Richard Meier, the new contemporary-art museum is an important addition to Barcelona's treasury of art and architecture. Located in the once rough-and-tumble Raval district, it and the neighboring **Centre de Cultura Contemporània** (CCCB; Center for Contemporary Culture) have reclaimed important buildings and spaces as part of the city's renewal of its historic quarters and traditional neighborhoods. ⊠ *Plaça dels Àngels 1,* ☎ *93/412–0810.* ☉ *Tues.–Fri. noon–8, weekends 10–3.*

❷ Museu Frederic Marès. Here you can browse for hours among the miscellany assembled by sculptor/collector Frederic Marès, including everything from polychrome crucifixes to hat pins, pipes, and walking sticks. ⊠ *Plaça Sant Iu 5,* ☎ *93/310–5800.* ▥ *Free 1st Sun. of month.* ☉ *Tues.–Sat. 10–5, Sun. 10–2.*

❿ Museu Marítim (Maritime Museum). Housed in the 13th-century Drassanes Reiales (Royal Shipyards), this museum is packed with ships, figureheads, and nautical paraphernalia. You can pore over early navigation charts, including a map by Amerigo Vespucci and the 1439 chart of Gabriel de Valseca, the oldest chart in Europe. ⊠ *Plaça Portal de la Pau 1,* ☎ *93/318–3245.* ▥ *Free 1st Sun. of month.* ☉ *Tues.–Sat. 10–2 and 4–7, Sun. 10–2.*

★ ❺ Museu Picasso. Two 15th-century palaces provide a striking setting for these collections of Picasso's early art, donated in 1963 and 1970 by Picasso's secretary and then by the artist himself. The works range from childhood sketches to exhibition posters done in Paris shortly before the artist's death. In rare abundance are the Rose Period and Blue Period paintings and the variations on Velázquez's *Las Meninas.* ⊠ *Carrer Montcada 1519,* ☎ *93/319–6310.* ▥ *Free 1st Sun. of month.* ☉ *Tues.–Sat. 10–8, Sun. 10–3.*

★ ❹ Palau de la Música (Music Palace). Attend a performance at Domènechi Montaner's fantastic Moderniste concert house. ⊠ *Sant Francesc de Paula 2, off Via Laietana,* ☎ *93/268–1000.*

⓮ Palau de la Virreina. Built by a one-time Spanish viceroy to Peru in 1778, this building is now a major exhibition center. Check to see what's showing while you're in town. ⊠ *Rambla de les Flors 99,* ☎ *93/301–7775.* ☉ *Tues.–Sat. 10–2 and 4:30–9, Sun. 10–2, Mon. 4:30–9. Last entrance 30 mins before closing.*

★ ⓫ Palau Güell. Gaudí built this mansion between 1886 and 1890 for his patron, Count Eusebi de Güell. It's the only Gaudí house open to the public and one of the highlights on the Ruta Modernista. ⊠ *Nou de la Rambla 3,* ☎ *93/317–3974.* ☉ *Weekdays 10–1:30 and 4–6:30.*

⓰ Plaça de Catalunya. This intersection is the business center and transport hub of the modern city. ⊠ *Top of the Rambla.*

❸ Plaça del Rei. Several historic buildings surround what is widely considered the most beautiful square in the Gothic Quarter. Following Columbus's first voyage to America, the Catholic Kings received him in the **Saló de Tinell,** a magnificent banquet hall built in 1362. Other ancient buildings around the square are the **Palau del Lloctinent** (Lieutenant's Palace); the 14th-century **Capella de Santa Àata** (Chapel of St. Agatha), built right into the Roman city wall; and the **Palau Padellàs** (Padellàs Palace), which houses the **Museu d'Història de la Ciutat** (City History Museum). ⊠ *Plaça del Rei,* ☎ *93/315–1111.* ☉ *Tues.– Sat. 10–2 and 4–8, Sun. 10–2:30.*

❽ Plaça Reial. In this neoclassical 19th-century square, arcaded houses overlook the wrought-iron **Font de les Tres Gràcies** (Fountain of the Three Graces) and lampposts designed by a young Gaudí in 1879. Despite its spotty population, the plaza retains a certain elegance. The most colorful time to come is Sunday morning, when crowds gather at the stamp and coin market. ⊠ *C. Colom, off Rambla.*

❼ Plaça Sant Jaume. This impressive square in the heart of the Gothic Quarter was built in the 1840s, but the two imposing buildings facing each other across it are much older. The 15th-century **ajuntament** (city hall) has an impressive black and gold mural (1928) by Josep María Sert (who also painted the murals in New York's Waldorf-Astoria) and the famous **Saló de Cent,** the first European parliament, from which the Council of One Hundred ruled the city from 1372 to 1714. To visit the interior, you'll need to arrange permission in the protocol office. The **Palau de la Generalitat,** seat of the Autonomous Catalonian Government, is a 15th-century palace open to the public on special days or by arrangement. ⊠ *Junction of C. de Ferràn and C. Jaume I.*

⓭ Rambla St. Josep. This stretch of the boulevard is one of the most fascinating. The colorful paving stones on the Plaça de la Boquería were designed by Joan Miró. Glance up at the swirling Moderniste dragon and the Art Nouveau street lamps; then take a look inside the bustling **Boquería Market** and the **Antiga Casa Figueras,** a vintage pastry shop on the corner of Petxina, with a splendid mosaic facade. ⊠ *Between Plaça de la Boquería and Rambla de les Flors.*

★ ❻ Santa Maria del Mar (St. Mary of the Sea). Simply the best example of Mediterranean Gothic architecture, this church is widely considered Barcelona's loveliest. It was built between 1329 and 1383 in fulfillment of a vow made a century earlier by James I to build a church for the Virgin of the Sailors. The structure's simple beauty is enhanced by a colorful rose window and slender soaring columns. ⊠ *Plaça Santa Maria.* ☉ *Weekdays 9–12:30 and 5–8.*

Eixample

Above the Plaça de Catalunya you enter modern Barcelona and an elegant area known as the Eixample, built in the late 19th century as part of the city's expansion scheme. Much of the building here was done at the height of the Moderniste movement, a Spanish and mainly Catalan version of Art Nouveau, whose leading exponents were the architects Luís Domènech i Montaner, Josep Puig i Cadafalch, and Antoni Gaudí. The main thoroughfares are the Rambla de Catalunya and the Passeig de Gràcia, both lined with some of the city's most elegant shops and cafés. Moderniste houses are among Barcelona's drawing cards. For the Ruta Modernista tour of the city's main Art Nouveau sights, stop at the Casa Lleó Morera (⊠ Passeig de Gràcia 35, 3rd floor).

★ ⓲ Casa Milà. This Gaudí house is known as **La Pedrera** (stone quarry). Its remarkable curving stone facade, with ornamental balconies, ripples its way around the corner of the block. In the attic of La Pedrera is the superb **Espai Gaudí,** Barcelona's only museum dedicated exclusively to the architect's work. ⊠ *Passeig de Gràcia 92,* ☎ *93/484–5995.* ☉ *Tues.–Sun. 10–8; guided tours Tues.–Fri. 6 PM.*

966

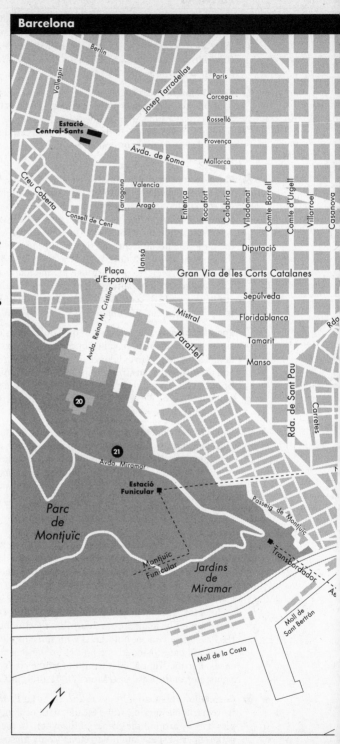

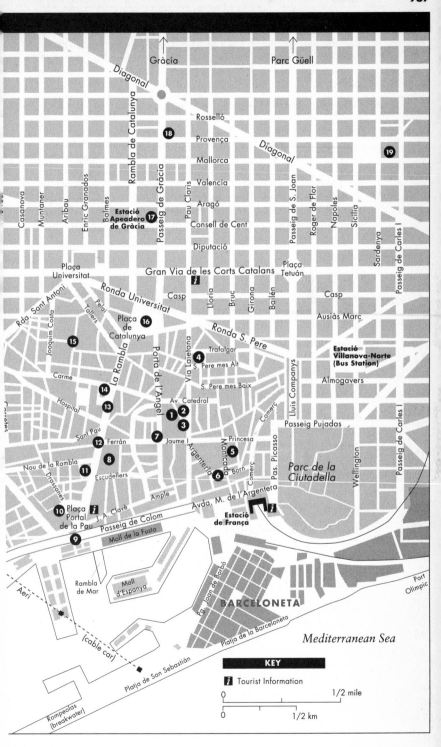

Gràcia

Parc Güell

Diagonal

Rosselló

Provença

Mallorca

Valencia

Aragó

Consell de Cent

Diputació

Diagonal

Rambla de Catalunya

Passeig de Gràcia

Pau Claris

Passeig de S. Joan

Roger de Flor

Napoles

Sicília

Sardenya

Passeig de Carles I

18

19

Casanova

Muntaner

Aribau

Enric Grandos

Balmes

**Estació
Apeadero
de Gràcia**

17

Plaça
Universitat

Gran Via de les Corts Catalans

Plaça
Tetuán

i

Ronda Universitat

Casp

Lloria

Bruc

Girona

Bailén

Casp

Ausiàs Marc

Rda. Sant Antoni

Joaquim Costa

Tallers

Pelai

Plaça
de
Catalunya

16

Porta de l'Angel

Via Laietana

Ronda S. Pere

**Estació
Villanova-Norte
(Bus Station)**

Almogavers

15

La Rambla

Carme

Trafalgar

S. Pere mes Alt

S. Pere mes Baix

4

Lluís Companys

Hospital

14

13

Av. Catedral

1 2

3

Comerç

Passeig Pujadas

Sant Pau

Carrelat

12

Ferràn

8

7

Jaume I

Argentería

Princesa

Montcada

5

Born

Comerç

Wellington

Passeig de Carles I

Nou de la Rambla

Drassanes

11

Escudellers

6

*Parc de la
Ciutadella*

10

Plaça
Portal
de la Pau

A. Clavé

i

Ample

Passeig de Colom

Avda. M. de l'Argentera

Comerç

Pas. Picasso

**Estació
de França**

i

9

Moll de la Fusta

Aeri

Rambla
de Mar

Moll
d'Espanya

Pg. Joan de Borbó

Port
Olímpic

BARCELONETA

Platja de la Barceloneta

Mediterranean Sea

(cable car)

Platja de San Sebastián

Rompeolas
(breakwater)

⑰ **Mançana de la Discòrdia** (Block of Discord). The name is a pun on the word *mançana,* which means both "block" and "apple." The houses here are quite fantastic: The floral **Casa Lleó Morera** (No. 35) is by Domènech i Montaner, the pseudo-Gothic **Casa Amatller** (No. 41) is by Puig i Cadafalch, and No. 43 is Gaudí's **Casa Batlló.** ✉ *Passeig de Gràcia, between Consell de Cent and Aragó.*

★ ⑲ **Temple Expiatori de la Sagrada Família** (Expiatory Church of the Holy Family). Barcelona's most eccentric landmark was designed by Gaudí but remained far from finished upon his death in 1926, when he was run over by a tram and died unrecognized in a pauper's hospital. This striking creation causes consternation, wonder, shrieks of protest, and cries of rapture, and the angular figures on the western facade (by sculptor Joseph Maria Subirach) do nothing to quell the controversy. An elevator can take you to the top of one of the towers for a magnificent view of the city. Gaudí is buried in the crypt. ✉ *C. de Sardenya between C. de Mallorca and C. de Provença,* ☎ *93/455–0247.* ☯ *Sept.– May, daily 9–7; June–Aug., daily 9–9.*

Montjuïc

The hill of Montjuïc is thought to have been named for the Jewish cemetery once located here. Montjuïc has a fortress, delightful gardens, a model Spanish village, an illuminated fountain, the Mies van der Rohe Pavilion, and a cluster of museums—all of which could keep you busy for several days. The 1992 Olympics were held here.

★ ㉑ **Fundació Miró** (Miró Foundation). A gift from the artist Joan Miró to his native city, this is one of Barcelona's most exciting galleries, with many of its exhibition spaces devoted to Miró's droll, colorful works. ✉ *Av. de Miramar,* ☎ *93/329–1908.* ☯ *Tues., Wed, Fri., Sat. 11–7, Thurs. 9:30–7, Sun. 10:30–2:30.*

★ ⑳ **Museu Nacional d'Art de Catalunya** (National Museum of Catalan Art). In the **Palau Nacional** atop a long flight of steps up from the Plaça Espanya, the collection of Romanesque and Gothic art treasures, medieval frescoes, and altarpieces—most from small churches and chapels in the Pyrenees—is simply staggering. The museum's last renovation was directed by architect Gae Aulenti, who also remodeled the Musée d'Orsay, in Paris. ✉ *Montjuïc,* ☎ *93/423–7199.* ☯ *Tues.–Sat. 10–7, Thurs. 10–9, Sun. 10–2:30.*

Elsewhere in Barcelona

Barceloneta. Take a stroll around what was once the fishermen's quarter, built in 1755. There are no-frills fish restaurants on the Passeig Joan de Borbó. Hike out to the end of the *rompeolas* (breakwater), extending 4 km (2½ mi) southeast into the Mediterranean, for a panoramic view of the city and a few breaths of fresh air. The modernized port is home to the Aquarium, one of Europe's best; the Maregmagnum shopping center; the IMAX wide-format cinema; the newly opened World Trade Center; and numerous bars and restaurants. The 1992 Olympic Village, now a hot tapas and nightlife spot, is up the beach to the north and is easily identifiable by the enormous, gold, Frank Gehry–designed fish sculpture next to the Hotel Arts. ✉ *Below Estació de França and Ciutadella Park.*

Gràcia. This small, once-independent village within the city is a warren of narrow streets whose names change at every corner. Here you'll find tiny shops that sell everything from old-fashioned tin lanterns to feather dusters. ✉ *Around C. Gran de Gràcia above Diagonal.*

★ **Parc Güell.** This park in the upper part of town is Gaudí's magical attempt at creating a garden city. ⊠ *C. D'Olot s/n*, ☉ *May–Aug., daily 10–9; Sept.–Apr., daily 10–7.*

Bullfighting

Bullfights are held on Sunday between March and October at the **Monumental** (⊠ Gran Via and Carles I); check the newspaper for details. To avoid paying a markup, go to the official ticket office (⊠ Muntaner 24, near Gran Via, ☎ 93/453–3821). The **Bullfighting Museum** at the ring is open March–October, daily 10–1 and 5:30–7.

Dining and Lodging

For details and price-category definitions, *see* Dining *in* Spain A to Z, *above.*

Hotels around the Rambla and in the Gothic Quarter have generous helpings of old-world charm but are weaker on creature comforts; those in the Eixample are mostly '50s or '60s buildings, often more recently renovated; and the newest hotels are out along the Diagonal or beyond, with the exception of the Hotel Arts, in the Olympic Port. The Airport and Sants Station have hotel-reservation desks. For details and price-category definitions, *see* Lodging *in* Spain A to Z, *above.*

$$$$ ✕ **Botafumeiro.** Barcelona's most exciting seafood restaurant, this
★ Galician spot never fails. Open continuously from 1 PM to 1 AM, Botafumeiro is always filled with ecstatic people in mid-feeding frenzy. It's expensive, but without question a great value. ⊠ *Gran de Gràcia 81,* ☎ *93/218–4230. AE, DC, MC, V. Closed Aug. 5–25.*

$$$$ ✕ **Jean Luc Figueras.** Every restaurant that Jean Luc Figueras has touched has shot straight to the top of the charts. This one, installed in an elegant Gràcia town house that was once couturier Cristóbal Balenciaga's studio, may be the best of all. For an extra $20 or so, the taster's menu is the best choice. ⊠ *C. Santa Teresa 10,* ☎ *93/415–2877. Reservations essential. AE, DC, MC, V. Closed Sun. No lunch Sat.*

$$$ ✕ **Can Gaig.** This traditional Barcelona restaurant is well known to Catalonian gastronomes. The market-fresh ingredients combine seafood with upland products in innovative ways. Try the roast partridge with bacon from free-range Iberian pork. ⊠ *Passeig Maragall 402,* ☎ *93/429–1017. AE, DC, MC, V. Closed Mon. and Aug. No dinner holidays.*

$$$ ✕ **El Racó de Can Freixa.** This is one of Barcelona's hottest new places, with young chef Ramón Freixa taking his father José María's work in new directions. The cuisine is innovative and yet traditionally Catalan; try one of the game specialties in season. ⊠ *Sant Elíes 22,* ☎ *93/ 209–7559. Reservations essential. AE, DC, MC, V.*

$$$ ✕ **El Tragaluz.** This is an excellent choice if you've been prowling the Eixample and find yourself in the grip of a design rush. The roof opens up to the stars in summer, and everything from chairs to utensils has been cleverly invented by some playful designer. There's even good food—modern and light, but hearty. ⊠ *Passatge de la Concepció 5,* ☎ *93/ 487–0196. AE, DC, MC, V. Closed Jan. 5. No lunch Mon.*

$$$ ✕ **Tram-Tram.** With chef Isidro Soler at the helm in the kitchen and
★ Reyes Lizán as hostess and pastry chef, Tram-Tram is one of Barcelona's culinary highlights. The excursion northwest to the villagelike suburb of Sarrià is a delight. Order the taster's menu and let Isidro take care of you—you won't regret it. ⊠ *Major de Sarrià 121,* ☎ *93/204–8518. AE, MC, V. Closed Sun. and Dec. 24–Jan. 6.*

$$ ✕ **Los Caracoles.** Just below the Plaça Reial is Barcelona's best-known tourist haunt, crawling with Americans having a terrific time. Its walls are hung thick with photos of bullfighters and visiting celebrities; its

specialties are mussels, paella, and of course, *caracoles* (snails). ⊠ *Escudellers 14,* ☎ *93/309–3185. AE, DC, MC, V.*

$$ ✕ **Set Portes.** With plenty of old-world charm, this delightful restau-
★ rant near the waterfront has been going strong since 1836. The cook-
ing is Catalan, the portions enormous, and specialties are paella *de
pescado* (with seafood) and *zarzuela Set Portes* (a mixed grill of
seafood). The restaurant serves nonstop from 1 PM to 1 AM. ⊠ *Passeig Isabel II 14,* ☎ *93/319–3033. AE, DC, MC, V.*

$ ✕ **Agut.** Simple, hearty Catalan fare awaits you in this unpretentious
restaurant in the lower reaches of the Gothic Quarter. Founded in 1924,
Agut has kept its popularity. There's plenty of wine to go with the tra-
ditional home cooking, along with a family warmth that always makes
the place exciting. ⊠ *Gignàs 16,* ☎ *93/315–1709. AE, MC, V. Closed
Mon. and July. No dinner Sun.*

$ ✕ **El Convent.** This small, friendly restaurant hidden behind the Bo-
★ quería Market is a real find, known better to locals than to visitors.
Its traditional Catalan home cooking, huge desserts, and swift, personable
service all make it a good value. ⊠ *Jerusalem 12,* ☎ *93/301–6208.
Reservations not accepted. AE, DC, MC, V. Closed Sun.*

$ ✕ **La Fonda.** This is one of the Camós family's three budget restau-
rants. The other two are in neighboring Plaça Reial: Les Quinze Nits
(⊠ Plaça Reial 6) and Hostal de Rita (⊠ Carrer Arago 279, near the
corner of Arago and Pau Claris). Be early (1 for lunch, 8 for dinner),
as long lines tend to form. ⊠ *Escudellers 10,* ☎ *93/301–7515. Reser-
vations not accepted. AE, DC, MC, V.*

$$$$ ▦ **Condes de Barcelona.** The Condes is one of Barcelona's most pop-
★ ular hotels, so rooms must be booked well in advance. The decor is
stunning, with marble floors and columns, an impressive staircase, and
an outstanding bar area. Guest rooms are on the small side. ⊠ *Passeig de Gràcia 75, 08008,* ☎ *93/484–8600,* ℻ *93/488–0614. 183 rooms.
Restaurant. AE, DC, MC, V.*

$$$$ ▦ **Hotel Arts.** This luxurious skyscraper, a Ritz-Carlton property, over-
looks Barcelona from the Olympic Port, providing unique views of the
Mediterranean, the city, and the mountains behind. A short taxi ride
from the city center, it's virtually a world of its own. Rooms are ul-
tramodern, with pale wood, Bang & Olufsen CD players, and Frette
linens. Three restaurants serve Mediterranean cuisine, Californian
cooking, and tapas, like *gambas al ajillo* (baby shrimp fried in garlic).
At press time, rumors had a grand casino opening beneath the hotel.
⊠ *C. de la Marina 19–21, 08005,* ☎ *93/221–1000,* ℻ *93/221–1070.
399 rooms, 56 suites. 3 restaurants, pool. AE, DC, MC, V.*

$$$$ ▦ **Hotel Claris.** Widely considered Barcelona's best hotel, the Claris is
a fascinating mélange of design and tradition. The rooms come in 60
different layouts, all decorated in a classical, 18th-century English
style. Wood and marble furnishings and decorative details are every-
where, and you can dip into a Japanese water garden, a first-rate
restaurant, and a rooftop pool—all near the center of Barcelona. ⊠
Carrer Pau Claris 150, 08009, ☎ *93/487–6262,* ℻ *93/215–7970. 106
rooms, 18 suites. Restaurant, pool. AE, DC, MC, V.*

$$$$ ▦ **Majestic.** Right in the thick of the Eixample shopping district, sur-
rounded by high-style boutiques and within sight of two Gaudí cre-
ations, the newly refitted Majestic is a good choice. The rooms are lovely,
painted in soothing pastels and decorated very tastefully. ⊠ *Passeig
de Gráia 70, 08008,* ☎ *93/488–1717,* ℻ *93/488–1880. 335 rooms.
Restaurant, pool. AE, DC, MC, V.*

$$$$ ▦ **Princesa Sofía.** The most convenient hotel to the airport, the Sofía
is removed from the hue and cry of downtown. For business and con-
venience, it's one of the city's best options. ⊠ *Plaça Pius XII 4, 08028,*

☎ 93/330–7111, FAX 93/411–2106. *505 rooms. 3 restaurants, 2 pools. AE, DC, MC, V.*

$$$$ ⌂ **Rey Juan Carlos I–Conrad International.** Towering over the western
★ end of Avinguda Diagonal, this skyscraper is as much a commercial complex as a luxury hotel: art, jewelry, furs, caviar, flowers, fashions, and even limousines are for sale or hire on site. The lush garden, including a swan-dappled pond, has an Olympic-size pool, and Barcelona's finest in-town country club, El Polo, spreads luxuriantly out beyond. There are two restaurants: Chez Vous, with French cuisine, and Café Polo, with a sumptuous buffet and an American bar. ⊠ *Av. Diagonal 661671, 08028,* ☎ 93/448–0808, FAX 93/448–0607. *375 rooms, 40 suites. 2 restaurants, pool. AE, DC, MC, V.*

$$$$ ⌂ **Ritz.** This classic hotel has new management and has maintained or
★ even heightened its splendor. The entrance lobby is awe inspiring; the rooms spacious, and furnished with Regency furniture; and the service excellent. ⊠ *Gran Via 668, 08010,* ☎ 93/318–5200, FAX 93/318–0148. *158 rooms. Restaurant. AE, DC, MC, V.*

$$$ ⌂ **Colón.** This cozy, older hotel has a unique charm and intimacy rem-
★ iniscent of an English country hotel. Rooms are comfortable and taste-ful. The location, right in the heart of the Gothic Quarter, is ideal, and front rooms overlook the cathedral and square. ⊠ *Avda. Catedral 7, 08002,* ☎ 93/301–1404, FAX 93/317–2915. *147 rooms. Restaurant. AE, DC, MC, V.*

$$ ⌂ **Gran Vía.** Architectural features are the charm of this 19th-century mansion. The original chapel has been preserved, and you can break-fast in a hall of mirrors, climb a Moderniste staircase, and make calls from elaborate Belle Epoque phone booths. ⊠ *Gran Vía 642, 08007,* ☎ 93/318–1900, FAX 93/318–9997. *53 rooms. AE, DC, MC, V.*

$$ ⌂ **San Agustín.** Just off the Rambla in the leafy square of the same name,
★ this inn has long been a favorite for musicians performing at the nearby Liceu opera house. Rooms are modest in size but charmingly decorated. The staff is helpful and polite. ⊠ *Plaça de Sant Agustí 3, 08001,* ☎ 93/318–1708, FAX 93/317–2928. *77 rooms. AE, DC, MC, V.*

$ ⌂ **Continental.** Something of a legend among cost-conscious travelers, this comfortable hostel with canopied balconies stands at the top of the Rambla, just below Plaça Catalunya. The rooms are homey and comfortable, the staff is friendly, and the location is ideal. Buffet break-fasts are a plus. ⊠ *Rambla 138, 08002,* ☎ 93/301–2508, FAX 93/302–7360. *35 rooms. AE, DC, MC, V.*

$ ⌂ **Jardí.** The rooms at this budget hotel are small but have new bath-rooms, powerful showers, and, in most cases, views over the charm-ing, traffic-free Plaça del Pi and Plaça Sant Josep Oriol. Noise can be a problem. The quietest rooms are the highest, but you have to walk up to them; there's no elevator. ⊠ *Plaça Sant Josep Oriol 1, 08002,* ☎ 93/301–5900, FAX 93/318–3664. *40 rooms. AE, DC, MC, V.*

Nightlife and the Arts

The Arts

To find out what's on, look in the daily papers or the weekly *Guía del Ocio. Actes a la Ciutat* is a weekly list of cultural events published by City Hall and available from its information office on Plaça Sant Jaume, or at the Palau de la Virreina (☞ Exploring Barcelona, *above*). *El País* lists all events of interest on its *agenda* page.

CONCERTS

Catalans are great music lovers. Their main concert hall is the **Palau de la Música** (☞ Exploring Barcelona, *above*), whose ticket office is open weekdays 11–1 and 5–8 and Saturday 5–8. You can usually buy tickets just before the concert. Sunday-morning concerts (11 AM) are a local tradition. Musical events are also held (free) in City Hall's **Saló de Cent** every other Thursday at 8, as well as in some of Barcelona's best architectural venues, such as the church of Santa Maria del Mar and others. The city's opera house, the newly rebuilt **Liceu,** is thriving.

DANCE

L'Espai de Dansa i Mùsica de la Generalitat de Catalunya (⊠ Travessera de Gràcia 63, ☎ 93/414–3133), usually listed simply as "L'Espai" (The Space), is now Barcelona's prime venue for ballet and contemporary dance. **El Mercat de les Flors** (⊠ Lleida 59, ☎ 93/426–1875), not far from Plaça d'Espanya, always has a rich program of modern dance and theater.

FILM

Several theaters show foreign movies in their original languages—indicated by "VO," or *versión original.* A few of the best are the Olympic Port's 15-screen **Icaria Yelmo** (⊠ Salvador Espriu 61, ☎ 93/221–7585), **Capsa** (⊠ Pau Claris 134, ☎ 93/215–7393), and the Gràcia neighborhood's **Verdi** (⊠ Verdi 32, Gràcia, ☎ 93/237–0516).

THEATER

Most plays are in Catalan, but Barcelona is also known for its experimental theater and its mime troupes. The best-known modern theaters are the **Teatre Lliure** (⊠ Montseny 47, Gràcia, ☎ 93/218–9251), **El Mercat de les Flors** (☞ Dance, *above*), **Teatre Romea** (⊠ Hospital 51, ☎ 93/317–7189), **Teatre Tívoli** (⊠ Casp 10, ☎ 93/412–2063), **Teatre Poliorama** (⊠ Rambla Estudios 115, ☎ 93/317–7599), and **Teatre Nacional de Catalunya** (⊠ Plaça de les Arts 1, ☎ 93/900–121133).

Nightlife

BARS

Champagne Bars. *Xampanyerías,* serving sparkling Catalan *cava,* are a Barcelona specialty. **El Xampanyet** (⊠ Montcada 22, ☎ 93/319–7003), near the Picasso Museum, serves cava, cider, and tapas in a lively setting. **La Cava del Palau** (⊠ Verdaguer i Callis 10, ☎ 93/310–0938), near the Palau de la Música, has a wide selection of cavas, wines, and cocktails.

Cocktail Bars. The **Passeig del Born,** near the Picasso Museum, is lined with bars. **Dry Martini** (⊠ Aribau 162, ☎ 93/217–5072) has more than 80 different gins. **El Copetín** (⊠ Passeig del Born 19, ☎ 93/317–7585) has exciting decor and good cocktails. **Miramelindo** (⊠ Passeig del Born 15, ☎ 93/319–5376) offers a large selection and often jazz. **El Paraigua** (⊠ Plaça Sant Miquel, behind City Hall, ☎ 93/217–3028) serves cocktails in a stylish setting with classical music.

Tapas Bars. Cal Pep (⊠ 8 Plaça de les Olles, ☎ 93/319–6183), near Santa Maria del Mar, is a popular spot, with the best and freshest selection of tapas. **Carrer de la Mercé** is all tapas bars, across from the Moll de la Fusta, from Correos (the post office) down to the Iglesia de la Mercé. **Casa Tejada** (⊠ Tenor Viñas, near Plaça Francesc Macià, ☎ 93/200–7341) has some of the finest nibbles in town. **Sagardi** (⊠ Argenteria 62, ☎ 93/319–9993), near Santa Maria del Mar, and **El Irati** (⊠ Cardenal Casañas 17, ☎ 93/302–3084), just off Plaça del Pi, are two excellent new Basque bars. The bars on the east side of Passeig de Gràcia are not the city's best, as they generally microwave pre-prepared food; **La Tramoia,** at Rambla de Catalunya and Gran Via (☎ 93/412–3634), is a happy exception.

CABARET

Barcelona City Hall (⊠ Rambla de Catalunya 2–4, access through New Canadian Store, ☎ 93/317–2177) offers sophisticated cabaret in a beautiful music hall.

CAFÉS

Carrer Petritxol (from Portaferrissa to Plaça del Pi) is famous for its *chocolaterías* (serving hot chocolate, tea, coffee, and pastries) and tearooms. The **Café de l'Opera** (⊠ Rambla 74, ☎ 93/317–7585), across from the Liceu opera house, is a perennial hangout, open daily until 2 AM. **Café Zurich** (⊠ Plaça de Catalunya 1, ☎ 93/302–4140), at the head of the Rambla, is Barcelona's number-one rendezvous spot. Picasso hung out at **Els Quatre Gats** (⊠ Montsió 3, ☎ 93/302–4140).

DISCOS AND NIGHTCLUBS

El Otro (⊠ Valencia 166, ☎ 93/323–6759) draws both young and not-so-young. **La Tierra** (⊠ Aribau 230, ☎ 93/200–7346) welcomes all ages, even those over 35. At **Luz de Gas** (⊠ Muntaner 246, ☎ 93/209–7711), guitar and soul are followed by wild abandon. **Oliver y Hardy** (⊠ Diagonal 593, next to Barcelona Hilton, ☎ 93/419–3181) is popular with over-35s. **Otto Zutz** (⊠ Lincoln 15, just below Via Augusta, ☎ 93/238–0722) is a top spot. **Up and Down** (⊠ Numancia 179, ☎ 93/280–2922), pronounced "pendow," is a lively classic.

FLAMENCO

El Patio Andaluz (⊠ Aribau 242, ☎ 93/209–3378) is a solid option but rather expensive. **Los Tarantos** (⊠ Plaça Reial 17, ☎ 93/318–3067) was the most happening flamenco spot at press time. **Tablao del Carmen** (⊠ Arcs 9, Poble Espanyol, ☎ 93/325–6895) is a solid runner-up.

JAZZ CLUBS

The **Barcelona Pipa Club** (⊠ Plaça Reial 3, ☎ 93/302–4732) hosts visiting artists. The Gothic Quarter's **Harlem Jazz Club** (⊠ Comtessa Sobradiel 8, ☎ 93/310–0755) is small but sizzling. **Jamboree** (⊠ Plaça Reial 17, ☎ 93/301–7564), downstairs from Los Tarantos (☞ Flamenco, *above*), has regular jazz performances.

Ports and Beaches

Barcelona's waterfront was overhauled in the 1990s. The **Port Vell** (Old Port) now includes an extension of the Rambla, the **Rambla de Mar,** which crosses the inner harbor from just below the Columbus Monument. This boardwalk connects the Rambla with the **Moll d'Espanya,** which in turn comprises a shopping mall, restaurants, an aquarium, a cinema, and two yacht clubs. A walk around Port Vell leads past the marina to Passeig Joan de Borbó, both lined with restaurants and their outdoor tables. From here you can go south out to sea along the *rompeolas,* a 3-km (2-mi) excursion, or north (left) down the San Sebastián beach to the Passeig Marítim, which leads to the **Port Olímpic.** Except for the colorful inner streets of Barceloneta, the traditional fisherman's quarter, this new construction is largely devoid of character. Take the Golondrinas boat (☞ Getting Around by Boat, *below*) to the end of the breakwater and walk into Barceloneta for some paella.

Beaches

Starting at the southern end of the city is the **Platja (Beach) de Sant Sebastià,** a nudist enclave, followed by **La Barceloneta, Passeig Marítim, Port Olímpic, Nova Icaria,** and **Bogatell.** Topless bathing is the rule. Water quality is officially tested and rated as acceptable, but you should still have a careful look before you dive; some days are better than others.

Shopping

Elegant shopping districts are the Passeig de Gràcia, Rambla de Catalunya, and the Diagonal. For more affordable, old-fashioned, and typically Spanish-style shops, explore the area between the Rambla and Via Laietana, especially around Carrer de Ferràn. The area around Plaça del Pi from Boquería to Portaferrisa and Canuda is well stocked with youthful fashion stores and imaginative gift shops.

Barcelona has several shopping plazas: **Les Glories** (⊠ Avda. Diagonal 208, Plaça de les Glories, ☎ 93/486–0639), **L'Illa** (⊠ Diagonal 545, between Numancia and Entenza, ☎ 93/444–0000), and **Maremagnum** (⊠ Moll d'Espanya s/n, Port Vell, ☎ 93/225–8100). Try **Carrer Tuset,** north of Diagonal between Aribau and Balmes, for small boutiques.

Antiques

Carrer de la Palla and Banys Nous, in the Gothic Quarter, are lined with antiques shops where you'll find old maps, books, paintings, and furniture. An **antiques market** is held every Thursday in front of the Cathedral. The **Centre d'Antiquaris** (⊠ Passeig de Gràcia 57, ☎ 93/215–4499) has some 75 antiques stores. **Gothsland** (⊠ Consell de Cent 331, ☎ 93/488–1922) specializes in Moderniste designs.

Boutiques

Fashionable boutiques line Passeig de Gràcia and Rambla de Catalunya. Others are on Gran Via between Balmes and Pau Claris, and on the Diagonal between Ganduxer and Passeig de Gràcia. **Adolfo Domínguez** (⊠ Passeig de Gràcia 89, Valencia 245, ☎ 93/487–3687) is one of Spain's top clothing designers. **Loewe** (⊠ Passeig de Gràcia 35, Diagonal 570, ☎ 93/216–0400) is Spain's top leather store. **Joaquín Berao** (⊠ Rosselló 277, ☎ 93/218–6187) is a top jewelry designer. **Zapata** (⊠ Buenos Aires 64, at Diagonal, ☎ 93/430–4785) is a major jewelry dealer.

Department Stores

With four locations in Barcelona alone, **El Corte Inglés** (⊠ Plaça de Catalunya 14, ☎ 93/302–1212; ⊠ Porta de l'Angel 19–21, ☎ 93/306–3800; ⊠ Av. Francesc Macià 58, ☎ 93/419–2020; ⊠ Diagonal 617, near María Cristina metro stop, ☎ 93/419–2828) is Spain's great consumer emporium. Both Plaça Catalunya's Mançana de Oro and L'Illa (☞ *above*) include **Marks & Spencer** and **FNAC** stores.

Food and Flea Markets

The **Boquería Market** (⊠ on Rambla between Carme and Hospital) is an exuberant cornucopia, a colorful display of both food and humanity; it's open every day except Sunday. **Els Encants** (⊠ end of Dos de Maig, on the Plaça Glòries Catalanes), Barcelona's wild-and-woolly flea market, is held every Monday, Wednesday, Friday, and Saturday, 8–7. **Sant Antoni Market** (⊠ end of Ronda Sant Antoni) is an old-fashioned food and clothes market, best on Sunday when there's a secondhand **book market** with old postcards, press cuttings, lithographs, and prints. There's a **stamp and coin market** (⊠ Plaça Reial) on Sunday morning. An **artists' market** (⊠ Placeta del Pi, just off Rambla and Boquería) sets up on Saturday morning.

Gift Ideas

No special handicrafts are associated with Barcelona, but you'll have no trouble finding typical Spanish goods anywhere in town. **Xavier Roca i Coll** (⊠ Sant Pere mes Baix 24, off Via Laietana, ☎ 93/215–1052) specializes in silver models of Barcelona's buildings.

If your friends back home like fashion and jewelry, you're in the right city—Barcelona makes all the headlines on Spain's booming fashion front. Barcelona and Catalonia passed along a playful sense of design even before Antoni Gaudí began creating shock waves over a century ago. A number of stores and boutiques specialize in design items (jewelry, furnishings, knickknacks). **Bd** (Barcelona Design; ⊠ Mallorca

291293, ☎ 93/458–6909) offers reproduction furniture from many designers. **Dos i Una** (✉ Rosselló 275, ☎ 93/217–7032) is a good source of clever gifts. **Vinçon** (✉ Passeig de Gràcia 96, ☎ 93/215–6050) has a huge selection of stylish housewares.

Barcelona Essentials

Arriving and Departing

BY BUS

Barcelona has no central bus station, but all buses operate either from the old Estació Vilanova, generally known as **Estació del Norte** (✉ end of Av. Vilanova, ☎ 93/893–5312), or from the **Estació Autobuses de Sants** (✉ C. Viriato, next to Sants Central train terminal, ☎ 93/490–0202). **Julià** (✉ Ronda Universitat 5, ☎ 93/317–6454) runs buses to Zaragoza and Montserrat. **Alsina Graëlls** (✉ Ronda Universitat 4, ☎ 93/265–6866) runs to Lérida and Andorra.

BY PLANE

All international and domestic flights arrive at **El Prat de Llobregat** airport (☎ 93/478–5000 or 93/478–5032), 14 km (8½ mi) south of Barcelona just off the main highway to Castelldefels and Sitges. For information on arrival and departure times, call the airport or Info-Iberia (☎ 93/412–5667).

Between the Airport and Downtown. The airport-to-city **train** leaves every 30 minutes between 6:30 AM and 11 PM, costs about 350 ptas., and reaches the Barcelona Central (Sants) Station in 15 minutes and Plaça de Catalunya, in the heart of the old city (at the head of La Rambla), in 20–25 minutes. From there a short taxi hop of 350 ptas.–500 ptas. will take you from Plaça Catalunya to most of central Barcelona's hotels. The **Aerobus** service connects the airport with Plaça Catalunya every 15 minutes between 6:25 AM and 11 PM; the fare of 475 ptas. can be paid with all international credit cards. RENFE also provides a bus service to the Central Station during the night hours. A **taxi** from the airport to your hotel, including airport and luggage surcharges, will cost about 3,000 ptas.

BY TRAIN

The **Sants Central Station** (✉ Plaça Països Catalans, ☎ 93/490–0202, 24-hr RENFE information line) is Barcelona's main train station, serving international and national destinations as well as suburban areas. The old and elegant **Estació de França** (✉ Av. Marquès de l'Argentera, ☎ 93/490–0202, 24-hr RENFE information) now serves as the main terminal for certain trains to France and some express trains to points in Spain. Inquire at the tourist office (☞ Visitor Information *in* Contacts and Resources, *below*) for current travel information and to find out which station you need. Many trains also stop at the **Passeig de Gràcia underground station** (✉ Passeig de Gràcia and C. Aragó, ☎ 93/488–0236); this station is closer to the Plaça de Catalunya and Rambla area than Sants. Tickets and information are available here, but luggage carts are not.

Getting Around

Modern Barcelona, the Eixample—above the Plaça de Catalunya—is built on a grid system; the Gothic Quarter, from the Plaça de Catalunya to the port, is a warren of narrow streets. You'll need a good map to get around. Almost all sightseeing can be done on foot, but you may need to use taxis, the metro, or buses to link certain areas, depending on how much time you have. From mid-May to mid-October look for **Bus Turistic 100** for low-cost transport between the sights.

El Consorci Turisme de Barcelona (Barcelona Tourism Consortium; ⊠ Plaça de Catalunya 17, lower level, ☎ 906/301282) sells 24-, 48-, and 72-hour versions of the very worthwhile **Barcelona Card.** For 2,500, 3,000, or 3,500 ptas., travelers get unlimited travel on all public transport as well as discounts at 27 museums, 10 restaurants, 14 leisure spots, 20 stores, and various other services including walking tours, the airport shuttle, the bus to Tibidabo, and the Tombbus between Barcelona's key shopping areas.

BY BOAT

Golondrinas boats operate short harbor trips from the Portal de la Pau near the Columbus Monument daily 10–8 in summer, 10 AM–1:30 PM, weekends only, in winter. A one-way ticket lets you off at the end of the breakwater for a 4-km (2½-mi) stroll, surrounded by the Mediterranean, back into Barceloneta.

BY BUS

City buses run from about 5:30 or 6 AM to 10:30 PM, though some stop earlier. There are also night buses to certain destinations. The flat fare is 155 ptas. Route plans are displayed at bus stops. You can purchase a **tarjeta multiviatge,** good for 10 rides, at the transport kiosk on Plaça de Catalunya (750 ptas.).

BY CABLE CAR AND FUNICULAR

Montjuïc Funicular is a cog railroad that runs from the junction of Avenida Parallel and Nou de la Rambla to the Miramar Amusement Park on Montjuïc; it's open 10:45 AM–8 PM, except in summer (late June to mid-Sept.), when it runs 11 AM–10 PM. A **teleferico** (cable car) runs from the amusement park up to Montjuïc Castle; it runs Oct.–June 21, weekends 11–2:45 and 4–7:30; June 22–Sept., daily 11:30–9.

The **Transbordador Aeri Harbor Cable Car** runs from Miramar on Montjuïc to the Torre de Jaume I across the harbor on Barcelona *moll* (quay), and on to the Torre de Sant Sebastià at the end of Passeig Joan de Borbó in Barceloneta. You can board at either stage. ⚏ *1,500 ptas.* ☺ *Oct.–June, weekdays noon–5:45, weekends noon–6:15; June–Oct., daily 11–9.*

To reach Tibidabo summit, take either Bus 58 or the Ferrocarrils de la Generalitat train from Plaça de Catalunya to Avenida Tibidabo, then the *tramvía blau* (blue tram) to Peu del Funicular, and the **Tibidabo Funicular** from there to the Tibidabo Fairground. The funicular runs every half hour from 7:15 AM to 9:45 PM.

BY METRO

The subway is the fastest and easiest way to get around. You can pay a flat fare of 150 ptas. or buy a **tarjeta multiviatge,** good for 10 rides (780 ptas.). Maps of the system are available at main metro stations and branches of the Caixa savings bank.

BY TAXI

Taxis are black and yellow. When available for hire, they show a LIBRE sign in the daytime and a green light at night. The meter starts at 315 ptas., and there are supplements for luggage (100 ptas. per case), and for rides from the airport, a station, or the port (varies according to zone). There are cab stands all over town; cabs may also be flagged down on the street. Taxi drivers in Barcelona are nearly always pleasant, helpful, and fair, and don't care much about tips one way or the other.

Contacts and Resources

CONSULATES

U.S. (⊠ Passeig Reina Elisenda 23, ☎ 93/280–2227). **Australia** (⊠ Gran Viá Carles III 98, ☎ 93/330–9496). **Canada** (⊠ Via Augusta 125, ☎

93/209–0634). **New Zealand** (⊠ Travessera de Gràcia 64, ☎ 93/209–0399). **U.K.** (⊠ Diagonal 477, ☎ 93/419–9044).

112 is the **general emergency number** in all EU nations (akin to 911 in the U.S.). **Police** (National Police, ☎ 091; Municipal Police, ☎ 092). **Medical emergencies** (☎ 061). **Pharmacies** (☎ 010). **Tourist Attention** (⊠ La Rambla 43, ☎ 93/317–7016, 24-hr assistance for crime victims).

ENGLISH-LANGUAGE BOOKSTORES

BCN Books (⊠ Aragó 277, ☎ 93/487–3123) is one of Barcelona's top spots for books in English. **Come In** (⊠ Provença 203, ☎ 93/253–1204) is another good option for English books. **El Corte Inglés** (☞ Department Stores *in* Shopping, *above*) sells English guidebooks and novels, but the selection is limited. For variety, try **The English Bookshop** (⊠ Entençan 63, ☎ 93/425–4466). The bookstore at the **Palau de la Virreina** (☞ Exploring Barcelona, *above*) has good books on art, design, and Barcelona.

GUIDED TOURS

El Consorci Turisme de Barcelona (Barcelona Tourism Cortium; ⊠ Plaça de Catalunya 17, lower level, ☎ 906/301282) leads walking tours of the Gothic Quarter in English at 10 AM on Saturday. The tour costs 1,000 ptas. and includes a visit to the Town Hall.

Orientation. City sightseeing tours are run by **Julià Tours** (⊠ Ronda Universitat 5, ☎ 93/317–6454). **Pullmantur** (⊠ Gran Viá de les Corts Catalanes 635, ☎ 93/318–5195) also has city sightseeing. Tours leave from the above terminals, though you may be able to arrange a pickup at your hotel. Both agencies offer the same tours at the same prices. A morning sightseeing tour visits the Gothic Quarter and Montjuïc; an afternoon tour concentrates on Gaudí and the Picasso Museum. You can visit Barcelona's Olympic sites from May through October.

Excursions. Trips out of town are run by **Julià Tours** and **Pullmantur** (☞ *above*). The principal attractions are a half-day tour to Montserrat to visit the monastery and shrine of the famous Black Virgin; a full-day trip to the Costa Brava resorts, including a boat cruise to the Medes Isles; and, from June through September, a full-day trip to Andorra for tax-free shopping.

SPECIAL-INTEREST AND WALKING TOURS

La Ruta del Modernismo (the Route of Modernism), created by Barcelona's *ayuntamiento,* connects some 50 key sites in the city's rich trove of Art Nouveau architecture. Everything from Gaudí's first lamppost to the colossal Sagrada Família to the odd Moderniste pharmacy or bakery is included, along with guided visits of key sites not open to the general public. The Palau Güell (⊠ Carrer Nou de Rambla 3–5, ☎ 93/317–3974) is "kilometer zero" for the tour; you can also buy the multiple ticket at the Casa Lleó Morera (⊠ Passeig de Gràcia 35, 3rd floor, ☎ 93/488–0139). Tickets are 1,500 ptas. Both offices are open Monday–Saturday 10–7.

TRAVEL AGENCIES

American Express (⊠ Roselló 257, corner of Passeig de Gràcia, ☎ 93/217–0070). **Bestours** (⊠ Diputación 241, ☎ 93/487–8580). **Viajes Iberia** (⊠ Rambla 130, ☎ 93/317–9320). **Wagons-Lits Cook** (⊠ Passeig de Gràcia 8, ☎ 93/317–5500).

VISITOR INFORMATION

Information on Barcelona: Centre d'Informació Turistic de Barcelona (⊠ Plaça de Catalunya 17, lower level; ☎ 906/301282 within Spain;

☎ 93/304–3421 from overseas, ℻ 93/304–3155). **Sants** train station (☎ 93/491–4431). **França** train station (☎ 93/319–5758). **El Prat Airport** (☎ 93/478–4704). **Ajuntament** (✉ Plaça Sant Jaume, ☎ 93/402–7000, ext. 433). **Palau de la Virreina** (cultural information; ✉ Rambla 99, ☎ 93/301–7775). **Palau de Congressos** (during special events and conferences; ✉ Avda. María Cristina, ☎ 93/423–3101, ext. 8356). **Information on Catalonia and Spain: El Prat Airport** (☎ 93/478–4704). **Centre d'Informació Turística** (✉ Palau Robert, Passeig de Gràcia 107, at Diagonal, ☎ 93/238–4000). **General information:** dial 010.

ANDALUSIA

Stretching from the dark mountains of the Sierra Morena in the north, west to the plains of the Guadalquivir valley, and south to the mighty, snowcapped Sierra Nevada, Andalusia (Andalucía) rings with echoes of the Moors. Creating a kingdom they called Al-Andalus, these North African Muslims ruled southern Spain for almost 800 years, from their conquest of Gibraltar in 711 to their expulsion from Granada in 1492. To this day the cities and landscapes of Andalusia are rich in their legacy: Córdoba's breathtaking mosque, Granada's magical Alhambra Palace, and Seville's landmark Giralda tower were the inspired creations of Moorish architects and craftsmen working for Al-Andalus's Arab emirs. Outside the cities, brilliant white villages—with narrow streets, heavily grilled windows, and whitewashed facades, all clustered around cool private patios—and the wailing songs of flamenco, vaguely reminiscent of the muezzin's call to prayer, all stem from centuries of Moorish occupation.

The downside to a visit here, especially to Seville, is that petty crime is not uncommon, and thieves often prey on tourists. Purse-snatching and thefts from cars, even when drivers are in them, are depressingly familiar. *Always* keep your car doors *and* trunk locked. *Never* leave valuables in your car. Leave your passport, traveler's checks, and credit cards in your hotel's safe, *never* in your room. Don't carry expensive cameras or wear jewelry. Take only the minimum amount of cash with you.

Seville

Numbers in the margin correspond to points of interest on the Seville map.

Lying on the banks of the Guadalquivir River, 538 km (334 mi) southwest of Madrid, Seville (Sevilla)—Spain's fourth-largest city and the capital of Andalusia—is one of the most alluring cities in Europe. Famous in the arts as the home of the sensuous Carmen and the amorous Don Juan—and celebrated in real life for its spectacular Semana Santa (Holy Week) processions and April Fair—Seville is the urban embodiment of Moorish Andalusia.

★ ❸ **Alcázar.** The high, fortified walls of this Moorish palace belie the exquisite delicacy of its interior. It was built by Peter the Cruel—so known because he murdered his stepmother and four of his half brothers—who lived here with his mistress, María de Padilla, from 1350 to 1369. Don't mistake this for a genuine Moorish palace, as it was built more than 100 years after the reconquest of Seville; rather, its style is Mudéjar—built by Moorish craftsmen working under orders of a Christian king. The Catholic Kings (Ferdinand and Isabella)—whose only son, Prince Juan, was born in the Alcázar in 1478—added a wing to serve as the administrative center for their New World empire, and Charles V enlarged it further for his marriage celebrations in 1526. Pedro's Mudéjar palace centers around the beautiful **Patio de las Doncellas** (Court

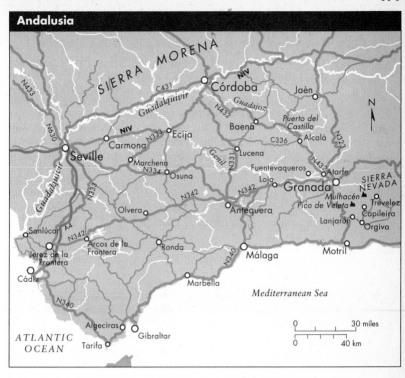

of the Damsels), whose name pays tribute to the annual gift of 100 virgins to the Moorish sultans whose palace once stood here. Resplendent with lacelike stucco and gleaming *azulejo* (tile) decorations, the patio is immediately reminiscent of Granada's Alhambra and is in fact the work of Granada artisans. Opening off this patio are the **Salón de Embajadores,** where Charles V married Isabel of Portugal, and the apartments of María de Padilla.

The fragrant **Alcázar Gardens** are planted with jasmine and myrtle; there's also an orange tree said to have been planted by Peter the Cruel, and a lily pond well stocked with fat, contented goldfish. The end of your visit brings you to the **Patio de las Banderas** for an unrivaled view of the Giralda. ⊠ *Plaza del Triunfo,* ☎ 95/450–2324. ☉ *Tues.–Sat. 9:30–5, Sun. 9:30–1:30.*

★ ❹ **Barrio de Santa Cruz.** With its twisting alleyways, cobbled squares, and whitewashed houses, this intriguing neighborhood is the perfect setting for an operetta. Once the home of Seville's Jewish population, it was much favored by 17th-century nobles and today boasts some of the most expensive properties in Seville. Romantic images of Spain come to life here: Every house gleams white or deep ocher, wrought-iron grilles adorn the windows, and balconies and patios are bedecked with geraniums and petunias. Ancient bars nestle side-by-side with antiques shops. Don't miss the bar **Casa Román,** in Plaza de los Venerables, its ceilings hung thick with some of the best hams in Seville; or the **Hostería del Laurel,** next door, where in summer you can dine in one of the loveliest squares in the city. Souvenir shops and excellent ceramics shops surround the **Plaza Doña Elvira,** where young Sevillanos gather to play guitars around the fountain and *azulejo* benches. In the **Plaza Alianza,** with its well-stocked antiques shops, a simple crucifix hangs on a wall, framed in a profusion of bougainvillea. ⊠ *North of Alcázar Gardens.*

6 **Calle Betis.** An early evening stroll along this street on the far side of the Guadalquivir is a delight. The vista of sparkling water and palm-lined banks is stunning. ⊠ *Between San Telmo and Isabel II bridges.*

★ **1** **Cathedral.** Seville's massive cathedral was begun in 1402, a century and a half after Ferdinand III seized Seville from the Moors, and took more than a century to build. It's the largest and highest cathedral in Spain, the largest Gothic building in the world, and the world's third-largest church after St. Peter's in Rome and St. Paul's in London. As if that weren't enough, it has the world's largest carved wooden altarpiece. Despite all this, the inside can be dark and gloomy, with too many overly ornate Baroque trappings. Seek out the beautiful Virgins by Murillo and Zurbarán. In a silver urn before the high altar rest the precious relics of Seville's reconquerer, Ferdinand III. The mortal vestiges of Christopher Columbus are said to be enshrined in the flamboyant mausoleum in the south aisle. Borne aloft by statues representing the four medieval kingdoms of Spain, perhaps the great voyager has found peace at last, after the transatlantic quarrels that carried his body from Valladolid to Santo Domingo and from Havana to Seville. ⊠ *Plaza Virgen de los Reyes,* ☎ *95/456–3321.* ◷ *Mon.–Sat. 10:30–5, Sun. 2–6, and mass.*

★ **2** **Giralda.** A splendid example of Moorish art, the tower, adjacent to the cathedral, is now the symbol of Seville. Originally the minaret of Seville's great mosque, the Giralda was incorporated by the Christians into their new cathedral after the Reconquest and later topped by a bell tower and weather vane. In place of steps, 35 sloping ramps climb the 230 ft to the viewing platform; St. Ferdinand is said to have ridden his horse to the top to admire the view of the city he had just conquered. Seven centuries later, your view of the Golden Tower and shimmering Guadalquivir is just as beautiful. Try to see the Giralda at night, too, when floodlights cast a different magic on this Islamic gem. ⊠ *Plaza Virgen de los Reyes,* ☎ *95/456–3321.* ◷ *Mon.–Sat. 10:30–5, Sun. 2–6.*

9 **Museo de Bellas Artes** (Museum of Fine Art). *Sevillanos* claim that their museum is second only to Madrid's Prado in Spanish art. Opened in 1841, it occupies the former convent of La Merced Calzada. The excellent collection, presented in chronological order on two floors, includes works by Murillo, Zurbarán, Velázquez, Valdés Leal, and El Greco. ⊠ *Plaza del Museo,* ☎ *95/422–0790.* ◷ *Tues. 3–8, Wed.–Sat. 9–8, Sun. 9–3.*

5 **Parque de María Luisa** (María Luisa Park). The gardens here are a wonderful blend of formal design with wild vegetation, shady walkways, and sequestered nooks. In the 1920s the park was redesigned to house the 1929 Hispanic-American exhibition; the villas you see here today are the fair's remaining pavilions. The centerpiece of the exhibition was the grandiose pavilion of Spain at the monumental **Plaza de España.** At the opposite end of the park you can feed the hundreds of white doves that gather around the fountains of the lovely **Plaza de América.** Two of the pavilions here now house the **Museo Arqueológico** (Archaeological Museum; ☎ 95/423–2401), open Tuesday 3–8, Wednesday–Saturday 9–8, Sunday 9–2:30; and the **Museo de Artes y Costumbres Populares** (Museum of Folklore; ☎ 95/423–2576), open Wednesday–Saturday 9–8, Sunday 9–2:30. ⊠ *Park entrance, Glorieta San Diego.*

8 **Plaza de Toros Real Maestranza** (Maestranza Bullring). Sevillanos have spent many a thrilling Sunday afternoon in this bullring, built between 1760 and 1763. *Corridas* (bullfights) are held from Easter through October; the best are during the April Fair. Buy tickets in ad-

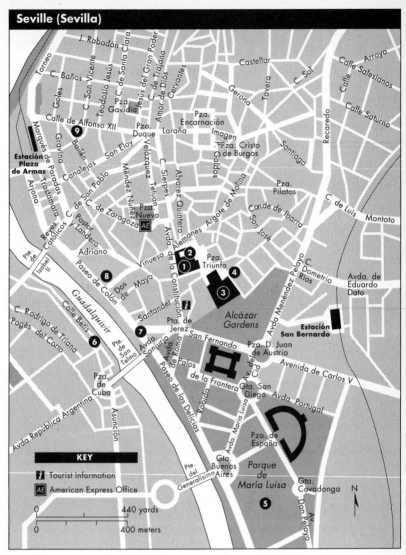

Seville (Sevilla)

vance at the ring or from the kiosks on Calle Sierpes (these charge a commission). You can visit the ring and the small **museum** year-round. ✉ *Paseo de Colón 12,* ☎ *95/422–4577.* ⊙ *Daily 9:30–2 and 3–6 (mornings only on bullfight days).*

❼ Torre de Oro (Tower of Gold). Built by the Moors in 1220, this 12-sided structure is visible from both sides of the river. During the day you can enjoy a nice view from the tower, which also houses a small naval museum. ✉ *Paseo de Colón, between C. Santander and C. Almirante Lobo,* ☎ *95/422–2419.* ⊙ *Tues.–Fri. 10–2, weekends 11–2.*

Seville's regular flamenco clubs cater largely to tourists and cost a little over 3,000 ptas. per person, but their shows are colorful and serve as a good introduction for the uninitiated. **El Arenal** (✉ Rodo 7, ☎ 95/421–6492) is a flamenco club in the back of the picturesque Mesón Dos de Mayo. You can catch flamenco and other regional dances nightly at **El Patio Sevillano** (✉ Paseo de Colón 11, ☎ 95/421–4120), which mainly serves tour groups. **Los Gallos** (✉ Plaza Santa Cruz 11, ☎ 95/421–6981), an intimate club in the heart of the Barrio Santa Cruz, offers fairly pure flamenco.

$$$ ✕ **Egaña-Oriza.** Egaña-Oriza is one of Seville's most fashionable and ★ acclaimed restaurants. The menu changes with the seasons, but might include *lomos de lubina con salsa de erizos de mar* (sea bass with sea-urchin sauce) or *solomillo con foie natural y salsa de ciruelas* (fillet steak with foie gras and plum sauce). ✉ *San Fernando 41,* ☎ *95/422–7211. AE, DC, MC, V. Closed Sun. and Aug. No lunch Sat.*

$$$ ✕ **La Albahaca.** Set in an attractive old house in the heart of the Barrio Santa Cruz, the Albahaca offers plenty of style and atmosphere and original, imaginative cuisine. Specialties are *lubina al horno con sofrito de ciruelas y almendras* (baked sea bass with plum and almond sauce) and *filetitos de ciervo con salsa de hongos* (venison medallions with wild mushroom sauce). ✉ *Plaza Santa Cruz 12,* ☎ *95/422–0714. AE, DC, MC, V. Closed Sun.*

$$$ ✕ **La Isla.** In the center of town between the cathedral and the Convent of La Caridad, La Isla has long been famous for its superb seafood and paella. ✉ *Arfe 25,* ☎ *95/421–5376. AE, DC, MC, V.*

$$$ ✕ **San Marco.** The brothers Ramacciotti serve Italian-influenced cuisine in an 18th-century mansion with a classic Andalusian patio—a wonderful spot for a summer meal. Try the *raviolis rellenos de gambas y pesto* (ravioli stuffed with shrimp and pesto), *cordero relleno de espinacas y setas* (lamb with spinach and forest mushrooms), or any of a delectable array of desserts. ✉ *Cuna 6,* ☎ *95/421–2440. AE, DC, MC, V.*

$$ ✕ **Enrique Becerra.** This small, cozy restaurant is a short walk from ★ the cathedral. Its lively, crowded bar decorated with Sevillian ceramic tiles is a meeting place for locals, who enjoy its excellent selection of tapas. The menu concentrates on traditional Andalusian home-cooked dishes. ✉ *Gamazo 2,* ☎ *95/421–3049. AE, DC, MC, V. Closed Sun.*

$$ ✕ **La Judería.** This bright, modern restaurant on a side street off Avenida Menendez Pelayo has gained recognition for the quality of its Spanish and international cuisine and reasonable prices. Fish dishes from the north of Spain and meat from Ávila are specialties. Try *cordero lechal asado* (roast baby lamb) or *urta a la Roteña* (a bream dish from Rota, on the Costa de la Luz—cooked with brandy, peppers, onions, and tomatoes). ✉ *Cano y Cueto 13,* ☎ *95/441–2052. Reservations essential. AE, DC, MC, V. Closed Mon. and Aug.*

$$ ✕ **Mesón Don Raimundo.** In an old convent close to the cathedral, the ★ Mesón has deliberately Sevillian atmosphere and decor. Its bar is the perfect place to sample some splendid tapas, and the restaurant, when not catering to tour groups, is one of Seville's most delightful. ⊠ *Argote de Molina 26,* ☏ *95/422–3355. AE, DC, MC, V.*

$–$$ ✕ **El Bacalao.** This popular fish restaurant, opposite the church of Santa Catalina, is in an Andalusian house decorated with ceramic tiles. As the name suggests, the house specialty is *bacalao* (salt cod); try it *con arroz* (with rice) or al pil-pil. ⊠ *Plaza Ponce de León 15,* ☏ *95/421–6670. AE, DC, MC, V. Closed Mon., late July, and early Aug.*

$$$$ 🏨 **Alfonso XIII.** This ornate Mudéjar-style palace was built for King
★ Alfonso XIII's visit to the 1929 exhibition. It's worth a visit just for its splendid Moorish decor, including beautiful stained glass and the colorful ceramic tiles typical of Seville. ⊠ *San Fernando 2, 41004,* ☏ *95/422–2850,* 𝔽𝔸𝕏 *95/421–6033. 127 rooms, 19 suites. Restaurant, pool. AE, DC, MC, V.*

$$$$ 🏨 **Tryp Colón.** The rooms and suites have been very comfortably mod-
★ ernized while retaining much of their old-fashioned style. You're right in the heart of town, near the main shopping area; and on the premises you can dine in the elegant El Burladero restaurant or the more casual La Tasca. ⊠ *Canalejas 1, 41001,* ☏ *95/422–2900,* 𝔽𝔸𝕏 *95/422–0938. 204 rooms, 14 suites. 2 restaurants. AE, DC, MC, V.*

$$$ 🏨 **Doña María.** Near the cathedral, the Doña María is one of Seville's most charming hotels. Some rooms are small and plain; others are tastefully furnished with antiques. Room 310 has a four-poster double bed, 305 has two single four-posters, and both have spacious bathrooms. There's no restaurant, but a breakfast buffet is served. The rooftop pool has a good view of the Giralda, just a stone's throw away. ⊠ *Don Remondo 19, 41004,* ☏ *95/422–4990,* 𝔽𝔸𝕏 *95/421–9546. 69 rooms. Pool. AE, DC, MC, V.*

$$$ 🏨 **Las Casas de la Judería.** In the heart of the Barrio de Santa Cruz, this labyrinthine hotel occupies three of the quarter's old palaces, each arranged around inner courtyards. The spacious guest rooms are dressed in tasteful pastels and decorated with prints of Seville. ⊠ *Callejón de Dos Hermanas, 41004,* ☏ *95/441–5150,* 𝔽𝔸𝕏 *95/442–2170. 41 rooms, 16 suites. AE, DC, MC, V.*

$$ 🏨 **Bécquer.** Conveniently near the main shopping areas, this relatively modern hotel prides itself on attentive service. It's one of the best mid-range options, with comfortable rooms decorated in traditional Spanish style. There's also a parking garage. ⊠ *Reyes Católicos 4, 41001,* ☏ *95/422–8900,* 𝔽𝔸𝕏 *95/421–4400. 116 rooms, 2 suites. AE, DC, MC, V.*

$$ 🏨 **Giralda.** The Giralda is comfortable and functional, with spacious, light rooms. It lies on the edge of the old city, in a cul-de-sac off Avenida Recaredo, and caters largely to tour groups. Rooms on the fifth floor are best. ⊠ *Sierra Nevada 3, 41003,* ☏ *95/441–6661,* 𝔽𝔸𝕏 *95/441–9352. 101 rooms, 5 suites. Restaurant. AE, DC, MC, V.*

$ 🏨 **Internacional.** If you want an inexpensive alternative, head for this old-world, family-run hotel in the narrow streets of the old town, near the Casa de Pilatos. The rooms are very plain, but the service is friendly. ⊠ *Aguilas 17, 41003,* ☏ 𝔽𝔸𝕏 *95/421–3207. 24 rooms. DC, MC, V.*

Carmona

Thirty kilometers (19 miles) east of Seville, the NIV brings you to Carmona. This unspoiled Andalusian town of Roman and Moorish origin has a wealth of Mudéjar and Renaissance churches and its streets of whitewashed houses. At the entrance to the town stands the church of **San Pedro,** begun in 1466, whose extraordinary interior is an unbroken mass of sculptures and gilded surfaces, and whose tower, erected in 1704, is an unabashed imitation of Seville's Giralda. Opposite this is the **Alcázar de Abajo** (Lower Fortress), a Moorish fortification built on Roman foundations. In the tower beside the gate is the tourist office. Carmona's most affecting monument is its splendid

Roman necropolis, where in huge underground chambers some 900 family tombs, dating between the 2nd and 4th centuries AD, were chiseled out of the rock. ⊠ *C. Enmedio,* ☎ *95/414–0811.* ☉ *Mid-June–mid-Sept., Tues.–Sat. 9–2, Sun. 10–2; mid-Sept.–mid-June, Tues.–Fri. 10–2 and 4–6, weekends 10–2.*

$$$$ 🏨 **Casa de Carmona.** If you want to relax like royalty, do it at one of
★ the most stunning hotels in all of Spain. The 16th-century palace of Lasso de la Vega was renovated in the late 1980s, and today you'll find beautifully furnished rooms decorated with fine art, rich fabrics, and antiques. ⊠ *Plaza de Lasso 1, 41410,* ☎ *95/414–3300,* FAX *95/419–0189. 30 rooms, 3 suites. Restaurant, pool. AE, DC, MC, V.*

$$$ 🏨 **Parador Alcázar del Rey Don Pedro.** The beauty of this modern
★ parador, completely renovated in 1998, is its splendid, peaceful setting, in the ruins of the old Moorish Alcázar on top of the hill above Carmona. The views across the vast fertile plain below are magnificent. ⊠ *Alcázar, 41410,* ☎ *95/414–1010,* FAX *95/414–1712. 63 rooms. Restaurant, pool. AE, DC, MC, V.*

Jerez de la Frontera

One hundred kilometers (60 miles) south of Seville, Jerez is world headquarters for **sherry.** The word *sherry,* first heard in Great Britain in 1608, is in fact an English corruption of this town's old Moorish name, Xeres; today, names such as González Byass and Domecq are just as inextricably linked with Jerez. The town's wine-making tradition dates from Roman times and continued under the Moors despite the Koran's condemnation of alcohol.

At any given time more than half a million barrels of sherry are maturing in Jerez's vast, aboveground wine cellars. Most ***bodegas*** (wineries) welcome visitors, but it's wise to phone ahead for an appointment. If you take a tour, a guide will explain the *solera* method of blending old wine with new, and the importance of the *flor* (a sort of yeast that forms on the surface of the wine as it ages) in determining the kind of sherry. You can finish by sampling generous amounts of pale, dry fino, nutty amontillado, or rich, deep oloroso, and of course you'll be welcome to purchase a few bottles at interesting prices in the shop.

Founded in 1730, **Domecq** (☎ 956/151000) is Jerez's oldest bodega and makes the world's best-selling brandy, Fundador, as well as sherry. Other wineries worth visiting are **Sandeman** (☎ 956/301100), **Harveys** (☎ 956/151000), and **Wisdom and Warter** (☎ 956/184306). If you only have time for one, tour the prestigious **González Byass,** home of Tío Pepe (☎ 956/357000).

The **Real Escuela Andaluza del Arte Ecuestre** (Royal Andalusian School of Equestrian Art) stands on the grounds of the Recreo de las Cadenas, a splendid 19th-century palace. Every Thursday (Tuesday and Thursday in summer) the Cartujana horses—a cross between the native Andalusian workhorse and the Arabian—and skilled riders in 18th-century riding costume demonstrate intricate dressage techniques and jumping in the spectacular show "Como Bailan los Caballos Andaluces." ⊠ *Avda. Duque de Abrantes,* ☎ *956/307798.* ☉ *Nov.–Feb., Thurs. 12; Mar–Oct., Tues. and Thurs. 12 (reservations essential).*

$$$ ✕ **Gaitán.** Within walking distance of the riding school, Gaitán's white walls and brick arches are adorned with colorful ceramic plates and photos of famous diners. The menu is Andalusian, with a few Basque dishes. In season, *setas* (wild mushrooms) make a delicious starter. ⊠ *Gaitán 3,* ☎ *956/345859. AE, DC, MC, V. No dinner Sun.*

$$$ ✕ **La Mesa Redonda.** Just off Avenida Alvaro Domecq, this small, friendly restaurant serves classic Jerez dishes in what feels like a fam-

ily dining room. There are only eight tables; the round one at the end of the room gives the restaurant its name. The menu changes constantly; your best bet is to take the advice of the chef's wife, Margarita—who also has an encyclopedic knowledge of Spanish wines. ⊠ *Manuel de la Quintana 3,* ☎ *956/340069. AE, DC, MC, V. Closed Sun.*

$$$ ✕⊡ **Jerez.** This luxury hotel is a low, white building in the residential neighborhood north of town. The bar and elegant restaurant overlook the terrace, pool, and big, leafy garden, and all public rooms are light and airy. The best bedrooms overlook the pool and garden. ⊠ *Avda. Alvaro Domecq 35, 11405,* ☎ *956/300600,* FAX *956/305001. 116 rooms, 4 suites. Restaurant, pool. AE, DC, MC, V.*

$ ⊡ **Ávila.** Centrally located but tucked away on a side street, this friendly hotel is a good value. Guest rooms have basic furnishings and tile floors, with beds on the small side. The lobby is joined by a TV lounge and bar, providing a convenient break spot. ⊠ *Ávila 3, 11401,* ☎ *956/334808,* FAX *956/336807. 32 rooms. Bar, breakfast room. AE, DC, MC, V.*

Córdoba

Numbers in the margin correspond to points of interest on the Córdoba map.

Ancient Córdoba (138 km [86 mi] northwest of Seville), city of the caliphs and one of Spain's oldest cities, is the greatest urban embodiment of Andalusia's Moorish heritage. Moorish emirs and caliphs held court here from the 8th to the 11th centuries, and the city became one of the Western world's greatest centers of art, culture, and learning. Moors, Christians, and Jews lived together in peace here.

② **Judería.** The medieval Jewish quarter is packed with houses, museums, and monuments that best typify Córdoba's storied past. The municipal tourist office is on the **Plaza Judá Leví.** ⊠ *Around C. Judíos.*

④ **Maimónides.** A statue of the great Jewish philosopher stands in Plaza Tiberiades.

★ **①** **Mezquita** (Mosque). Founded by Abd ar-Rahman I (756–788), Córdoba's justly famous mosque was completed by Al Mansur (976–1002) around 987. As you step inside you'll face a forest of gleaming pillars of precious marble, jasper, and onyx, rising to the red-and-white horseshoe arches characteristic of Moorish architecture. Not even the heavy Baroque cathedral that Charles V built in its midst—and later regretted—can detract from the extraordinary art of the Moorish craftsmen. The mosque once housed the original copy of the Koran and a bone from the arm of the prophet Mohammad, relics that drew thousands of pilgrims before St. Ferdinand reconquered Córdoba for the Christians in 1236. The building opens onto the **Patio de los Naranjos** (Orange Tree Courtyard) and the bell tower, which was the mosque's minaret. ⊠ *Torrijos and Cardinal Herrero,* ☎ *957/470512.* ☉ *Mon.–Sat. 10–7; Sun. for morning mass and 3:30–5:30 (3:30–7 in summer).*

Near the mosque, the streets of Torrijos, Cardenal Herrero, and Deanes are lined with tempting souvenir shops specializing in local handicrafts, especially the filigree silver and embossed leather for which Córdoba is known.

③ **Museo Taurino** (Museum of Bullfighting). Two delightful old mansions house this well-presented collection of memorabilia, paintings, and posters by early 20th-century Córdoban artists. Some rooms are dedicated to great Córdoban *toreros*—one holds the hide of the bull that killed the legendary Manolete in 1947. ⊠ *Plaza Maimónides,* ☎ *957/*

Córdoba

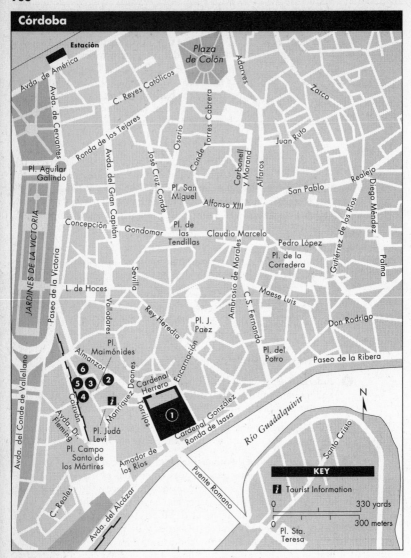

Juderîa, **2**

Maimónides, **4**

Mezquita, **1**

Museo Taurino, **3**

Synagogue, **5**

Zoco, **6**

201056. ⊘ *May–Sept., Tues.–Sat. 9:30–1:30 and 5–8, Sun. 9:30–3; Oct.–Apr., Tues.–Sat. 10–1:30 and 5–7, Sun. 10–3.*

⑤ Synagogue. Córdoba's was the only synagogue in Andalusia to survive the expulsion of the Jews in 1492. One of only three remaining ancient synagogues in Spain—the other two are in Toledo—it has some fine Hebrew and Mudéjar stucco tracery and a women's gallery. ⊠ *C. Judíos,* ☎ *957/202928.* ⊘ *Tues.–Sat. 10–2 and 3:30–5:30, Sun. 10–1:30.*

⑥ Zoco. Formerly the Arab souk, this courtyard has pleasant shops and stalls, and a bar that opens in summer. ⊠ *Near synagogue.*

$$$ ✕ **El Caballo Rojo.** The Red Horse, near the mosque, is Córdoba's
★ longest-established restaurant. The decor resembles a cool Andalusian patio, and the menu features such traditional specialties as *rabo de toro* (bull's tail), *salmorejo* (a thick local version of gazpacho, with chunks of ham and egg), and other exotic creations inspired by Córdoba's Moorish heritage. ⊠ *Cardenal Herrero 28,* ☎ *957/478001. AE, DC, MC, V.*

$$ ✕ **El Blasón.** This charming restaurant has earned its reputation for fine food and unbeatable ambience. Tucked into an old inn with a pleasant tapas patio and a whole array of restaurants upstairs, it serves specialties like *salmón con naranjas* (salmon in oranges) and *musclo de oca al vino afrutado* (leg of goose in fruited wine). ⊠ *José Zorrilla 11,* ☎ *957/480625. AE, DC, MC, V.*

$$ ✕ **El Churrasco.** In the heart of the Judería, this atmospheric restaurant
★ has a patio and a colorful tapas bar. The steak is the best in town, and the grilled fish is super-fresh. Specialties are *churrasco* (a pork dish in pepper sauce) and an excellent *salmorejo.* In a separate house, two doors down the street, is the restaurant's formidable wine cellar, which is also a small museum. Ask your waiter to take you there before or after your meal. ⊠ *Romero 16,* ☎ *957/290819. AE, DC, MC, V. Closed Aug.*

$$ ✕ **La Almudaina.** This attractive restaurant is in a 15th-century house and former school that overlooks the Alcázar at the entrance to the Judería. It has an Andalusian patio, and the decor and cooking are both typical of Córdoba. ⊠ *Campo Santo de los Mártires 1,* ☎ *957/474342. AE, DC, MC, V. Closed Aug. No dinner Sun.*

$$$–$$$$ ⊞ **Conquistador.** This delightful contemporary hotel on the east side
★ of the mosque is built in Andalusian Moorish style, with a charming patio and ceramic decor. Rooms at the front have small balconies overlooking the walls of the mosque, which are floodlit at night. ⊠ *Magistral González Francés 15, 14003,* ☎ *957/481102,* ℻ *957/ 474677. 99 rooms, 3 suites. AE, DC, MC, V.*

$$ ⊞ **Marisa.** This hotel fills a charming, old Andalusian house whose location—in the heart of the old town, overlooking the mosque's Patio de los Naranjos—is its prime virtue. The decor is quaint and charming, and the rates reasonable. ⊠ *Cardenal Herrero 6, 14003,* ☎ *957/ 473142,* ℻ *957/474144. 28 rooms. AE, DC, MC, V.*

OFF THE BEATEN PATH | If you're traveling between Córdoba and Granada, you might want to stop for a drink and wander the narrow streets and squares of **Baena,** a picturesque Andalusian town of white houses clustered on a hillside.

Granada

Numbers in the margin correspond to points of interest on the Granada map.

The graceful city of Granada, 166 km (103 mi) southeast of Córdoba, rises onto three hills dwarfed by the mighty snowcapped peaks of the Sierra Nevada, on which lie the highest roads in Europe. Atop one of these hills, the pink-gold Alhambra Palace, at once terribly imposing yet infinitely delicate, gazes out across the rooftops and gypsy caves of the Sacromonte to the fertile plain, rich in orchards, tobacco fields, and poplar groves. Granada was the Moors' last stronghold, their most cherished city; it fell finally to the Catholic Kings in January 1492.

4 **Albaicín.** Narrow streets wind up steep slopes in the old Moorish quarter, a fascinating mixture of dilapidated white houses and beautiful *cármenes*, luxurious villas with fragrant gardens. Make your way up to the small plaza in front of **San Nicolás** church for an unforgettable view of the Alhambra—particularly at night, when the palace is floodlit.

3 **Alcaicería.** The narrow streets of the old Arab silk exchange now draw souvenir hunters.

★ **5** **Alhambra.** From the Plaza Nueva the Cuesta de Gomérez climbs steeply toward the grandest and most stunning Moorish monument in all of Andalusia. If you're in the mood for a long walk, follow the promenade where the Duke of Wellington planted shady elms and Washington Irving tarried among the gypsies, from whom he learned the Moorish legends so evocatively recounted in his *Tales of the Alhambra*. Otherwise, take the minibus from the Plaza Nueva, or drive to the main ticket office. The number of visitors at any one time is restricted, and your ticket will show your alloted entry time (if you have a long wait, first visit the **Alcazaba** next to the main palace, and the Generalife gardens, below). You can also reserve tickets in advance by phone (below). Once you are inside the Alhambra, the legends of the Patio of the Lions, the Hall of the Two Sisters, and the murder of the Abencerrajes spring to life amid a profusion of lacy walls, frothy stucco, gleaming tiles, and ornate domed ceilings. In this realm of myrtles and fountains, festooned arches, and careful inscriptions, every corner holds its secret. Here the emirs installed their harems, awarded their favorites the most lavish of courts, and bathed in marble baths. In the midst of so much delicacy, the Baroque palace of Charles V would seem an intrusion—heavy and incongruous—were it not for its splendid acoustics, which make it the perfect setting for Granada's summer music festival. Wisteria, jasmine, and roses line your route from the Alhambra to the **Generalife**, the caliphs' summer retreat, where crystal drops shower from slender fountains against a background of stately cypresses. The sweeping view includes the clustered white houses of the Albaicín; the Sacromonte, riddled with gypsy caves; and the bulk of the Alhambra towering above the city. ⊠ *Enter on Cuesta de Gomérez,* ☎ *958/221503 and 958/220912; for advance reservations, 902/224460.* ☉ *Mar.–Oct., Mon.–Sat. 9–8, Sun. 9–7; floodlit visits Tues., Thurs., and Sat. 10 PM–midnight. Nov.–Feb., daily 9–6; floodlit visits Sat. 8 PM–10 PM. Ticket office opens 30 mins before opening time and closes 1 hr before closing.*

★ **1** **Capilla Real** (Royal Chapel). This ornate Gothic masterpiece is the burial shrine of Ferdinand and Isabella, who have lain here since 1521, later joined by their daughter Juana la Loca, mother of Holy Roman Emperor Charles V. ⊠ *C. Oficios,* ☎ *958/229239.* ☉ *Mar.–Sept., Mon.–Sat. 10:30–1 and 4–7; Oct.–Feb., Mon.–Sat. 10:30–1 and 3:30–6:30.*

2 **Cathedral.** Commissioned in 1521 by Charles V, Granada's cathedral is a grandiose and gloomy monument, not completed until 1714 but still surpassed in beauty and historic value by the neighboring Royal Chapel—which, despite the emperor's plans, still houses the tombs of his illustrious grandparents. ⊠ *Gran Vía de Colón 5,* ☎ *958/222959.* ☉ *Mar.–Sept., Mon.–Sat. 10:30–1 and 4–7, Sun. 4–7; Oct.–Feb., Mon.–Sat. 10:30–1:30 and 3:30–6:30, Sun. 3:30–6.*

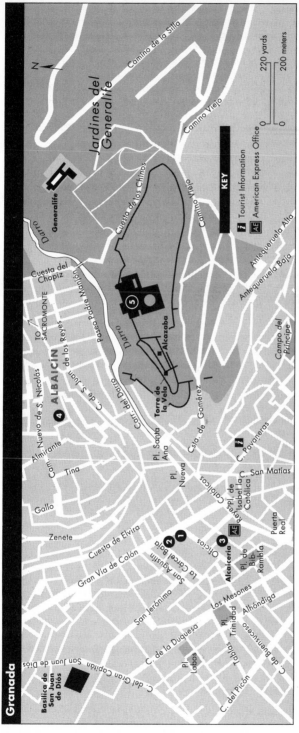

Granada

Basílica de San Juan de Diós

Jardines del Generalife

Generalife

Camino de la Silla

Camino Viejo

Camino Viejo

Cuesta de los Chinos

KEY

ⓘ Tourist Information

AE American Express Office

Antequeruela Alta

Antequeruela Baja

Campo del Príncipe

220 yards

200 meters

Cuesta del Chapiz

Paseo Padre Manjón

TO SACROMONTE

ALBAICÍN

C. Nuevo de S. Nicolás

Darro

Alcazaba

Torre de la Vela

Carr. del Darro

C. de S. Juan de los Reyes

Almirante

Cam.

Tina

Gallo

Zenete

Pl. Santa Ana

Pl. Nueva

Csta. de Gomérez

C. Pavaneras

San Matías

Pl. Isabel la Católica

Reyes Católicos

Oficios

Cuesta de Elvira

Gran Vía de Colón

San Agustín

La Cárcel Baja

Alcaicería

Pl. de Bib-Rambla

Puerta Real

San Jerónimo

Los Mesones

Pl. Trinidad

Alhóndiga

C. del Gran Capitán   San Juan de Diós

C. de la Duquesa

Pl. Lobos

Tablas

C. del Picón

C. de Bensucese

Albaicín, **4**

Alcaicería, **3**

Alhambra, **5**

Capilla Real, **1**

Cathedral, **2**

The province of Granada was also the home of the poet Federico García Lorca. García Lorca was born on June 5, 1898, in the village of **Fuentevaqueros,** 10 km (6 mi) west of Granada; his childhood home is now a **museum** (⊠ Poeta García Lorca 4, ☎ 958/516453). On the outskirts of Granada is the Lorca family's summer residence, **Huerta del San Vicente,** now also a museum and a cultural center with exhibits on Lorca and his time (⊠ C. de la Virgen Blanca, ☎ 958/258466). Just outside this village, 9 km (5½ mi) northeast of Granada, is **Víznar,** where the poet was executed at the outbreak of the Spanish Civil War in 1936. He is probably buried here, in a common grave; a memorial park commemorates him.

There are several "impromptu" flamenco shows in the caves of the Sacromonte, but these can be little more than tourist traps. Go only if you're accompanied by a Spanish friend who knows his or her way around or with a tour organized by a local agency. **Jardines Neptuno** (⊠ C. Arabial, ☎ 958/522533) is a colorful flamenco club catering mainly to tourists. **Reina Mora** (⊠ Mirador de San Cristóbal, ☎ 958/276690), though somewhat smaller than Jardines Neptuno, offers regular flamenco shows known as *tablaos.*

$$$ ✕ **Carmen de San Miguel.** The crux of this restaurant is its superb setting, perched on the Alhambra hill (beside the Hotel Alhambra Palace) in a villa with an outdoor terrace and magnificent views over Granada. The food is average continental cuisine. ⊠ *Paseo Torres Bermejas 3,* ☎ *958/226723. AE, DC, MC, V. Closed Sun.*

$$$ ✕ **Cunini.** Right in the center of town, near the cathedral, this restaurant has long been valued for the quality of its seafood. Try one of the mixed-fish platters, either fried (*fritura mixta*) or grilled (*parrillada*). The long tapas bar up front is popular with locals, the dining room in back small and cozy. ⊠ *Pescadería 9,* ☎ *958/250777. AE, DC, MC, V. Closed Mon.*

$$ ✕ **Los Manueles.** This old inn is one of Granada's long-standing traditions. The walls have ceramic tiles, and the ceiling is hung with hams. There's lots of atmosphere, good old-fashioned service, and plenty of traditional Granadan cooking. ⊠ *Zaragoza 2,* ☎ *958/223413. AE, DC, MC, V.*

$$ ✕ **Sevilla.** A colorful restaurant in the Alcaicería, beside the cathedral, it has a superb tapas bar at the entrance. The dining room is picturesque, if rather small and crowded. The menu can be somewhat tourist-oriented, but the *sopa sevillana* (fish soup) is excellent. ⊠ *Oficios 12,* ☎ *958/221223. AE, DC, MC, V. Closed Mon. No dinner Sun.*

$$$$ 🏨 **Parador de San Francisco.** Magnificently set in an old convent within the Alhambra precincts, San Francisco is the most popular parador in Spain. Queen Isabella was entombed here before the completion of the Royal Chapel. The rooms in the old section are the most elaborate; all need to be reserved four–six months in advance. ⊠ *Alhambra, 18008,* ☎ *958/221440,* 🖷 *958/222264. 36 rooms. Restaurant. AE, DC, MC, V.*

$$$–$$$$ 🏨 **Alhambra Palace.** This flamboyant, ocher-red, Moorish-style palace
★ was built around 1910 and sits halfway up the hill to the Alhambra. The mood is busier than at the more isolated parador, but the decor offers rich carpets, tapestries, and Moorish tiles. The best rooms overlook the town. The terrace is the perfect place for an early evening drink as the sun sets over the Sierra Nevada. ⊠ *Peña Partida 2, 18009,* ☎ *958/221468,* 🖷 *958/226404. 122 rooms, 13 suites. Restaurant. AE, DC, MC, V.*

$$ 🏨 **América.** Here's a simple but charming hotel within the Alhambra precincts: The location is magnificent, and you can linger over breakfast on a delightful patio. It's popular, so reserve months in advance.

⊠ *Real de la Alhambra 53, 18009,* ☎ *958/227471,* ℻ *958/227470. 14 rooms. Restaurant. No credit cards. Closed Nov.–Feb.*

$$ 🏠 **Inglaterra.** At this period house just above Gran Vía de Colón, old-world charm is combined with modern comforts. ⊠ *Cetti Meriem 4, 18010,* ☎ *958/221558,* ℻ *958/227100. 36 rooms. AE, DC, MC, V.*

$$ 🏠 **Reina Cristina.** This hotel occupies an old house near the lively and central Plaza de la Trinidad. A marble stairway leads to the rooms, which are simply but cheerfully furnished with red curtains and red-and-white-checked bedspreads. ⊠ *Tablas 4, 18002,* ☎ *958/253211,* ℻ *958/ 255728. 43 rooms. Restaurant, bar, cafeteria. AE, DC, MC, V.*

Andalusia Essentials

Arriving and Departing

Seville, Córdoba, and Granada all lie on direct train routes from Madrid. Service is frequent from both Chamartín and Atocha stations in Madrid, and includes overnight trains (to Seville and Granada), slower day trains, and express Talgos. In addition the high-speed AVE train connects Seville, Córdoba, and Atocha station on entirely new track; it's more expensive than any other train, but it's a pleasant whiz of a ride and cuts the inter-province travel time down to 2½ hours. Most bus service from Madrid to Andalusia operates out of the Estación del Sur (☞ Arriving and Departing *in* Madrid, *above*). If you have a car, follow the NIV, which takes you through the scorched orange plains of La Mancha to Córdoba, then along the Guadalquivir River to Seville. The N323 road, which splits from the NIV at Bailén, takes you past lovely olive groves and rolling hills to Granada.

Getting Around

BY BUS

Seville has two bus stations, **Estación del Prado de San Sebastián** (⊠ C. Manuel Vázquez Sagastizábal s/n, ☎ 95/441–7111) and **Estación Plaza de Armas** (⊠ Cristo de la Expiración, by Cachorro Bridge, ☎ 95/490–8040), closer to downtown. Ask the tourist office which one serves your destination. In Granada, the main bus station is on ⊠ Carretera de Jaén, ☎ 958/185011. Córdoba has no central bus depot, so ask the tourist office for the appropriate company and location.

BY CAR

Driving in Andalusia is all about winding roads and rolling olive groves. Consider renting a car.

BY TRAIN

Seville and Córdoba are linked by direct train service. Buses are a better choice between either of them and Granada, as trains are relatively slow and infrequent and often involve a time-consuming change. Seville's main train station is **Santa Justa** (⊠ Avda. Kansas City, ☎ 95/ 454–0202; RENFE office: ⊠ Zaragoza 29, ☎ 95/422–2693). Granada's train station is at the end of Avenida Andaluces (RENFE office: ⊠ Reyes Católicos 63, ☎ 958/271272). Córdoba's train station is on the Glorieta Conde de Guadalorce (RENFE office: ⊠ Ronda de los Tejares 10, ☎ 957/475884).

Guided Tours

Guided tours of Seville, Córdoba, and Granada are run by **Julià Tours** (☎ 91/571–8696), **Pullmantur** (☎ 91/541–1807), and **Trapsatur** (☎ 91/542–6666), departing from either Madrid or from Costa del Sol resorts; check with travel agents. In Seville you may find group excursions to the sherry *bodegas* and equestrian museum in Jerez.

Visitor Information

Córdoba (⊠ Plaza de Judá Leví, ☎ 957/200522). **Granada** (⊠ Plaza Mariana Pineda 10, ☎ 958/223528; ⊠ Corral del Carbón, C. Mariana Pineda, ☎ 958/225990). **Jerez** (⊠ Larga 35, ☎ 956/331150). **Seville** (⊠ Avda. Constitución 21, ☎ 95/422–1404; Costurero de la Reina: ⊠ Paseo de las Delícias 9, ☎ 95/423–4465).

COSTA DEL SOL

Ah, the Costa del Sol, where impoverished fishing villages of the 1950s are now retirement colonies and package-tour havens for northern Europeans and Americans. Fear not; behind the concrete monsters are old cottages, villas, and gardens resplendent with jasmine and bougainvillea. The sun still sets over miles of beaches, and the lights of small fishing craft still twinkle in the distance. The primary diversion here is indolence—swimming and sunning—but when you need something to do, you can head inland to historic Ronda and the white villages of Andalusia or take a day trip to Gibraltar or Tangier.

Exploring the Costa del Sol

Nerja

Nerja is a small but expanding resort town that so far has escaped the worst excesses of development. Its growth has been largely confined to village-style complexes outside town, such as El Capistrano. There's
★ pleasant bathing here, though the sand is gray and gritty. The **Balcón**
★ **de Europa** is a fantastic lookout, high above the sea. The **Cuevas de Nerja** (a series of stalactite caves) lie off the road to Almuñecar and Almería; a kind of vast underground cathedral, they contain the world's largest known stalactite (203 ft long). ☎ 95/252–9520. ⊘ Sept.–June, daily 10–2 and 4–6:30; July–Aug., daily 10:30–2 and 4–8.

$$ ✕ **Casa Luque.** One of the most authentically Spanish of Nerja's restaurants occupies a charming old Andalucían house behind the church of Balcón de Europa. Meat and game are featured, but good fresh fish is also served. ⊠ Plaza Cavana 2, ☎ 95/252–1004. AE, DC, MC, V.

$$ ✕ **Udo Heimer.** A genial German is your host at this Art Deco villa; his menu is a combination of traditional German dishes and local produce. Try pumpkin stuffed with ham or prawns wrapped in bacon and served in a curried banana sauce. ⊠ Pueblo Andaluz 27, ☎ 95/252–0032. AE, DC, MC, V. No lunch in summer.

$$$ ⌂ **Parador de Nerja.** A modern structure surrounded by a leafy gar-
★ den on the cliff's edge, this parador offers rooms with balconies overlooking the garden and, obliquely, the sea; those in the newer, single-story wing open onto their own patios. An elevator takes you down to the beach. ⊠ Almuñecar, 8, Nerja 29780, ☎ 95/252–0050, FAX 95/252–1997. 73 rooms. Restaurant, pool. AE, DC, MC, V.

$$$ ⌂ **Paraiso del Mar.** An erstwhile private villa was expanded to accommodate this 12-room hotel perched on the edge of a cliff overlooking the sea east of the Balcón de Europa. Some rooms have terraces, four have hot tubs, and most have sea views; prices vary accordingly. ⊠ Prolongación del Carabeo 22, 29780, ☎ 95/2521621, FAX 95/252–2309. 11 rooms, 1 suite. Pool. AE, DC, MC, V. Closed mid-Nov–mid-Dec.

Málaga

Málaga (544 km [337 mi] south of Madrid) is a busy port city with ancient streets and lovely villas surrounded by exotic foliage. The central Plaza de la Marina, overlooking the port, is a pleasant place for a drink. The main shops are along the Calle Marqués de Larios.

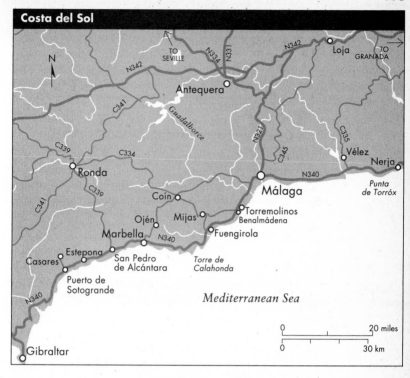

Costa del Sol

Málaga's **cathedral,** built between 1528 and 1782 on the site of the former mosque, is unfinished, its construction funds having mysteriously dried up. (One story has it that the money was donated instead to the American Revolution.) Because it's missing one of its twin towers, the cathedral is known as *La Manquita* (the one-armed lady). The lovely, enclosed choir, which somehow survived the burnings of the civil war, is the work of the great 17th-century artist Pedro de Mena. The adjoining **museum** has art and religious artifacts. ⊠ *C. de Molina Larios,* ☎ *95/221–5917.* ☉ *Mon.–Sat. 9–6:45.*

The **Alcazaba** (fortress) was begun in the 8th century, when Málaga was the most important port in the Moorish kingdom. Both the fortress and the ruins of the Roman amphitheater at its entrance were undergoing restoration in 1999; ask which parts are open to the public. The inner palace dates from the 11th century, when the Moorish emirs camped out here for a time after the breakup of the caliphate in Córdoba. ⊠ *Entrance on Alcazabilla.* ☉ *Wed.–Mon. 9:30–7.*

It takes some energy to climb from the Alcazaba to the summit of **Gibralfaro.** (You can also drive, by way of Calle Victoria, or take the parador minibus that leaves roughly every 1½ hours from near the cathedral on Molina Lario.) Gibralfaro's fortifications were built for Yusuf I in the 14th century—the Moors called it Jebelfaro, which means "rock of the lighthouse," after the beacon that stood here to guide ships into the harbor and warn of invasions by pirates. The beacon is gone, but the parador makes a delightful place for a drink or a meal and has some stunning views.

$$$ ✕ **Café de Paris.** The owner of this stylish restaurant in the Paseo Marítimo area was once a chef at Maxim's. The *menú de degustación* (tasting menu) lets you try a little of everything. Specialties include *rodaballo*

con espinacas (turbot and spinach). ✉ *Vélez Málaga 8,* ☎ *95/222–5043. Reservations essential. AE, DC, MC, V. Closed Sun.*

$$ ✕ **Casa Pedro.** Casa Pedro can get crowded; Malgueños have been flocking to this no-frills fish restaurant for more than 50 years. In the seaside suburb of El Palo, the restaurant has a huge, bare dining room that overlooks the ocean. Try joining the local families who come for lunch on Sunday. ✉ *Quitapenas 121, El Palo beach,* ☎ *95/229–0013. AE, DC, MC, V. No dinner Mon.*

$$ ✕ **Rincón de Mata.** This is one of the best of many restaurants in the pedestrian shopping streets between Calle Larios and Calle Nueva. The menu is more original than most, with house specialties such as *tunedor* (calf in sauce). In summer tables appear on the sidewalk. ✉ *Esparteros 8,* ☎ *95/221–3135. AE, DC, MC V.*

$ ✕ **La Cancela.** At this colorful restaurant in the center of town, just off Calle Granada, you can dine indoors or alfresco. The Spanish menu includes *riñones al jerez* (kidneys sauteed with sherry) and *cerdo al vino de Málaga* (pork with Málaga wine sauce). ✉ *Denís Belgrano 5,* ☎ *95/222–3125. AE, DC, MC, V.*

$$$ ▦ **Larios.** Málaga's newest hotel opened in 1994, in an elegant, restored building on the central Plaza de la Constitución. Rooms have light wood, cream-color fabrics, and black-and-white photographs. ✉ *Marqués de Larios 2, 29005,* ☎ *95/222–2200,* ℻ *95/222–2407. 34 rooms, 6 suites. Restaurant, meeting room. AE, DC, MC, V.*

$$$ ▦ **Parador de Málaga-Gibralfaro.** In a small wood on top of Gibral-
★ faro—3½ km (2 mi) above the city—this cozy parador offers spectacular views over the city and bay. Guest rooms have a pleasant mixture of modern comforts and Spanish charm. ✉ *Monte de Gibralfaro, 29016,* ☎ *95/222–1902,* ℻ *95/222–1904. 38 rooms. Restaurant, pool. AE, DC, MC, V.*

$$ ▦ **Las Vegas.** In a pleasant, if somewhat tumultuous, part of town just east of the center, this convenient hotel has a dining room overlooking the Paseo Marítimo, a large leafy garden, and a pool. Rooms at the back enjoy ocean views. ✉ *Paseo de Sancha 22, 29016,* ☎ *95/221–7712,* ℻ *95/222–4889. 107 rooms. Restaurant, pool. AE, DC, MC, V.*

$ ▦ **Venecia.** This four-story hotel has a central location on the Alameda Principal, next to the Plaza de la Marina. The rooms are simply furnished but spacious. ✉ *Alameda Principal 9, 29001,* ☎ *95/221–3636.* ℻ *95/221–3637. 40 rooms. AE, DC, MC, V.*

Torremolinos and Benalmádena

As you approach Torremolinos through an ocean of concrete blocks, it's hard to grasp that it was once an inconsequential fishing village. Today this grossly overdeveloped resort is a prime aesthetic example of 20th-century tourism run amok (despite a helpful cleanup in 1996). The town center, with its brash Nogalera Plaza, is full of overpriced bars and restaurants. Far more attractive is the district of La Carihuela, farther west, below the Avenida Carlota Alexandra—here you'll find some old fishermen's cottages, excellent seafood restaurants, and a traffic-free esplanade for an enjoyable stroll on a summer evening. La Carihuela merges with the coastal resort of Benalmádena-Costa, which has a lively yacht harbor and marina; at the western end of the resort is the Torrequebrada casino and golf course, while inland is the surprisingly unspoiled village of Benalmádena itself.

$$$ ✕ **Ventorillo de la Perra.** This old inn (built in 1785) is 3 km (2 mi) from the center of Torremolinos, on the road inland to Arroyo de la Miel. A cozy, rustic atmosphere prevails in both the dining room and the bar; the ceiling in the latter is hung with hams. The menu mixes Malagueño specialties and general Spanish fare with international favorites. ⊠ *Avda. Constitución, Arroyo de la Miel*, ☎ *95/244–1966. AE, DC, MC, V. Closed Mon.*

$$ ✕ **Casa Guaquin.** Casa Guaquin is widely known as the best seafood restaurant in the area. Changing daily catches and stalwarts like *coquinas al ajillo* (wedge-shell clams in garlic sauce) are served on a seaside patio. ⊠ *Paseo Marítimo 63*, ☎ *95/238–4530. AE, MC, V. Closed Thurs. and mid-Dec.–mid-Jan.*

$$ ✕ **Europa.** A short walk from the Carihuela, this villa has pleasant international dining in leafy surroundings—it's in the middle of a large garden. On Sunday local families flock here for a leisurely lunch. ⊠ *Via Imperial 32*, ☎ *95/238–8022. AE, DC, MC, V.*

$$ ✕ **Juan.** Juan is a great place to dine in summer, with a sunny outdoor patio facing the sea. Specialties include the great Costa del Sol standbys: *sopa de mariscos* (shellfish soup), *dorada al horno* (oven-roasted giltheads), and *fritura malagueña* (Málaga's fried fish). ⊠ *Paseo Marítimo 29, La Carihuela*, ☎ *95/238–5656. AE, DC, MC, V.*

$$$ ▦ **Cervantes.** This busy, cosmopolitan hotel in the heart of town has comfortable rooms, good service, and an excellent restaurant on the top floor. ⊠ *Las Mercedes s/n, 29620*, ☎ *95/238–4033*, 𝐅𝐀𝐗 *95/238–4857. 397 rooms. Restaurant, 2 pools. AE, DC, MC, V.*

$$ ▦ **Tropicana.** On the beach at the far end of the Carihuela is this comfortable, relaxing resort hotel with several good restaurants nearby. ⊠ *Trópico 6, 29620*, ☎ *95/238–6600*, 𝐅𝐀𝐗 *95/238–0568. 84 rooms. Pool. AE, DC, MC, V.*

$ ▦ **Miami.** Set in an old Andalusian villa in a shady garden west of the
★ Carihuela, Miami is an oasis in the desert of concrete. ⊠ *Aladino 14, 29620*, ☎ *95/238–5255. 26 rooms. Pool. No credit cards.*

Fuengirola and Mijas

Head west from Torremolinos for the similar but more staid resort of Fuengirola, a retirement haven for Britons and Americans. A short drive from Fuengirola up into the mountains takes you to the picturesque
★ and oft-photographed village of **Mijas.** Though the vast and touristy main square may seem like an extension of the Costa's tawdry bazaar, Mijas does have hillside streets of whitewashed houses whose authentic village atmosphere survived the tourist boom of the '60s largely unscathed. You can visit the bullring, the nearby church, and the chapel of Mijas's patroness, the Virgen de la Peña (to the side of the main square), and shop for quality gifts and souvenirs.

$$ ✕ **Mirlo Blanco.** Here, in a large Andalusian townhouse overlooking the square, you can sample Basque dishes, such as *txangurro* (crab) and *merluza a la vasca* (hake with asparagus, eggs, and clam sauce). The decor and ambience are both pleasantly busy, and in warm weather, you can dine on the terrace overlooking the square. ⊠ *Plaza Constitución 13*, ☎ *95/248–5700. AE, DC, MC, V.*

$$ ✕ **Portofino.** This lively restaurant, one of Fuengirola's best, is camouflaged among the brash souvenir shops and fast-food joints on the seafront promenade, just east of the port. The menu is international. ⊠ *Paseo Marítimo 29*, ☎ *95/247–0643. AE, DC, MC, V. Closed Mon. No lunch July–mid-Sept.*

$$$$ ▦ **Byblos Andaluz.** You won't miss any comforts in this luxury spa
★ hotel, set in a huge garden of palms, cypresses, and fountains. The restaurant, Le Nailhac, is known for its French cuisine and can also provide special, low-calorie meals. ⊠ *Mijas-Golf, Fuengirola, 29640*, ☎ *95/247–3050*, 𝐅𝐀𝐗 *95/247–6783. 109 rooms, 35 suites. 2 restaurants, indoor and outdoor pools. AE, DC, MC, V.*

$$$ ▦ **Mijas.** This beautifully situated hotel at the entrance to Mijas has views of the hillsides stretching down to Fuengirola and the Mediter-

ranean. ⊠ *Urb. Tamisa, 29650,* ☎ *95/248–5800,* FAX *95/248–5825. 99 rooms, 4 suites. Restaurant, 2 pools. AE, DC, MC, V.*

Marbella and Estepona

Marbella is the most fashionable resort area on the Costa del Sol. It smacks a bit of the Florida land boom, and the town's otherwise charming ancient Moorish quarter is crowded with both upmarket boutiques and T-shirt-and-fudge shops; but when people speak of Marbella, they refer both to the town and to the resorts, some more exclusive than others. These stretch some 8 km (5 mi) east of town, between the highway and the beach, and west to San Pedro de Alcántara and Estepona. If you're vacationing in southern Spain, this is the place to stay: In one place you've got championship golf courses and tennis courts, yacht harbors, waterfront cafés, and shopping arcades.

Marbella's Golden Mile (which is, in fact, 5 km/3 mi), with its mosque, Arab banks, and residence of Saudi Arabia's King Fahd, illustrates the ever-growing influence of wealthy Arabs in this playground of the rich. In the plush marina, **Puerto Banús,** flashy yachts, fashionable people, and expensive restaurants form a glittering parade that outshines even St. Tropez.

Estepona is set back from the main highway and lacks the hideous highrises of Torremolinos and Fuengirola. It's not hard to see the original outlines of this old fishing village. Wander the streets of the Moorish village, around the central food market and the church of **San Francisco,** and you'll find a pleasant contrast to the excesses up the coast.

$$$$ ✕ **El Portalón.** Opposite the Marbella Club hotel, this attractive restaurant, with a light, glassed-in dining room, combines two extremes of the culinary spectrum: hearty Castilian roasts and innovative *cocina de mercado,* based on whatever ingredients are freshest at the market. ⊠ *Carretera de Cádiz, Km 178,* ☎ *95/282–7880. AE, DC, MC, V.*

$$$$ ✕ **La Meridiana.** A favorite with the local jet set, La Meridiana is just west of town and is famous for its original Bauhaus architecture and the superb quality and freshness of its ingredients. ⊠ *Camino de la Cruz,* ☎ *95/277–6190. Reservations essential. AE, DC, MC, V. Closed Jan. No lunch June–Aug., or Mon.–Tues. Sept.–May.*

$$$ ✕ **Santiago.** This busy place is known as the best fish restaurant in Marbella, but you can pursue excellent meat dishes as well. ⊠ *Paseo Marítimo 5,* ☎ *95/277–0078. AE, DC, MC, V. Closed Nov.*

$$$$ ✕🏨 **Las Dunas.** This spectacular hotel, opened in 1997, rises like a multicolor apparition next to the beach midway between Estepona and Marbella. The setting is palatial, with trickling fountains and generous use of exotic plants. ⊠ *La Boladilla Baja, Ctra de Cádiz Km 163, 29689,* ☎ *95/279–4345,* FAX *95/279–4825. 34 rooms, 39 suites, 33 apartments. 2 restaurants, pool, exercise room. AE, DC, MC, V.*

$$$$ 🏨 **Los Monteros.** On the road to Málaga, 2½ km (1¼ mi) east of Mar-
★ bella, this deluxe hotel offers top-notch facilities, including golf, tennis, pools, horseback riding, and gourmet dining in the famous El Corzo Grill. ⊠ *Urb. Los Monteros, Carretera N340, Km 187, 29600,* ☎ *95/ 277–1700,* FAX *95/282–5846. 159 rooms, 10 suites. 3 restaurants, 1 indoor and 2 outdoor pools. AE, DC, MC, V.*

$$$$ 🏨 **Marbella Club.** The grande dame of Marbella tends to attract an older clientele. The bungalow-style rooms run from small to spacious, and the decor varies considerably, so specify the type you prefer. The grounds are exquisite. Breakfast is served on a patio where songbirds flit through the vegetation. ⊠ *Carretera de Cádiz, Km 178, 29600,* ☎ *95/282–2211,* FAX *95/282–9884. 90 rooms, 36 suites, 10 bungalows. Restaurant, 2 pools. AE, DC, MC, V.*

$$$$ ⊞ **Puente Romano.** A spectacular, modern hotel and apartment com-
★   plex of low, white stucco buildings 3¼ km (2 mi) west of Marbella (on
the road to Puerto Banús), this "village" has a Roman bridge in its beautifully landscaped grounds as well as two pools, a tennis club, squash
courts, and a nightclub. ⊠ *Carretera de Cádiz, Km 177, 29600,* ☎
95/282–0900, ℻ *95/277–5766. 149 rooms, 77 suites. 2 restaurants,
2 pools. AE, DC, V.*

$$–$$$ ⊞ **El Fuerte.** The best of the few hotels in the center of Marbella, this
one has comfortable rooms with sea views. The 1950s-style building
sits in a large garden with an outdoor pool. ⊠ *Avda. El Fuerte s/n,
29600,* ☎ *95/286–1500,* ℻ *95/282–4411. 261 rooms, 2 suites. Restaurant, indoor and outdoor pools. AE, DC, MC, V.*

Ronda

You arrive in Ronda (61 km [38 mi] northwest of Marbella) via a spectacular mountain road from San Pedro de Alcántara, between Marbella and Estepona. Ronda is one of the oldest towns in Spain and the
last stronghold of the storied Andalusian bandits. The town's most dra-
★   matic feature is its ravine, known as **El Tajo,** which is 915 ft across and
divides the old Moorish town from the "new town" of El Mercadillo.
Spanning the gorge is the amazing **Puente Nuevo,** built between 1755
and 1793, whose parapet offers dizzying views of the River Guadalevin,
far below. Ronda's breathtaking setting and ancient houses are its
chief attractions. Stroll the old streets of **La Ciudad**; drop in at the historic **Reina Victoria** hotel, built by the English from Gibraltar as a fashionable resting place on their Algeciras-Bobadilla railroad line. Visit
the **bullring,** one of the oldest and most beautiful in Spain; Ronda's
most famous native son, Pedro Romero (1754–1839), father of modern bullfighting, is said to have killed 5,600 bulls here during his 30-
year career. The **museum** inside has posters dating back to the very first
fights held in this ring in May 1785. The ring is privately owned now,
but three or four fights are still held in the summer; tickets are exceedingly
difficult to come by (☎ 95/287–4132); it's open daily 10–6:30 (10–8
in summer). Above all, don't miss the cliff-top walk and the gardens
of the **Alameda del Tajo** (Tajo Park), where you can feast on one of
the most dramatic views in all of Andalusia.

$$$ ✕ **Tragabuches.** Opened in 1998, this stylish restaurant around the cor-
ner from Ronda's parador and the tourist office features interesting
decor which, like the food, combines traditional and modern ingredi-
ents. Try the *menú de degustación,* a taster's menu of five courses plus
two desserts. ⊠ *José Aparicio 1,* ☎ *95/219–0291. AE, DC, MC, V.
Closed Mon. No dinner Sun.*

$$ ✕ **Pedro Romero.** Located opposite the bullring, this restaurant is, not
surprisingly, packed with colorful taurine decor. The restaurant serves
traditional regional recipes; the *tocinillo del cielo al coco* (sweet caramel
custard flavored with coconut) is a treat. ⊠ *Virgen de la Paz 18,* ☎
95/287–1110. AE, DC, MC, V.

$$$ ✕⊞ **Parador de Ronda.** One of Spain's newest paradors stands at the
very edge of the Tajo gorge, with a modern interior concealed within
the shell of the old town hall. The rooms are spacious and comfort-
able, and the restaurant is justifiably famous. ⊠ *Plaza de España, 29400,*
☎ *95/287–7500,* ℻ *95/287–8188. 62 rooms, 8 suites. Restaurant, pool,
meeting room. AE, DC, MC, V.*

$$ ⊞ **Polo.** A cozy, old-fashioned hotel in the center of town, Polo has a
reasonably priced restaurant. The staff is friendly, and the rooms are
simple but comfortable. ⊠ *Mariano Souvirón 8, 29400,* ☎ *95/287–
2447,* ℻ *95/287–2449. 33 rooms. Restaurant. AE, DC, MC, V.*

Casares

Nineteen kilometers (11¾ miles) northwest of Estepona, the mountain village of Casares lies high in the Sierra Bermeja. Streets lined with ancient white houses perch on the slopes beneath a ruined Moorish castle. Stop for a breather, admire the view of the Mediterranean, and check out the village's thriving ceramics industry.

Between Estepona and Gibraltar the highway is flanked by new and prosperous vacation developments known as *urbanizaciones*. The architecture here is much more in keeping with traditional Andalusian style than the earlier, concrete stuff. Near Gibraltar, Sotogrande—a millionaires' paradise—is the home of the Puerto de Sotogrande Marina and the Valderrama golf course, which hosted the 1997 Ryder Cup.

Gibraltar

Numbers in the margin correspond to points of interest on the Gibraltar map.

To enter Gibraltar simply walk or drive across the border at **La Línea** and show your passport. There may be border delays for cars, and traffic in Gibraltar is congested, so unless you have a good reason for driving it is best to leave your car in a guarded car park in La Línea, walk across the border and take a taxi or bus from there. In theory, drivers need an International Driver's License, insurance certificate, and registration book; play it safe and bring these documents with you to avoid a possible hefty fine. In practice, these requirements are usually waived. Flights leave London for Gibraltar daily; as yet there are no flights from Spanish airports, but there are plenty of bus tours from Spanish cities. Julià Tours, Pullmantur, and many smaller agencies run daily tours to Gibraltar (except Sunday) from most Costa del Sol resorts. Portillo runs an inexpensive daily tour to Gibraltar from the Torremolinos bus station, and you can always take the regular Portillo bus to La Línea and walk across the border. Once you reach Gibraltar the official language is English, and the currency is the British pound, but Spanish and pesetas are also widely accepted.

The Rock of Gibraltar acquired its name in AD 711, when it was captured by the Moorish chieftain Tarik at the beginning of the Arab invasion of Spain. It became known as Jebel Tariq (Rock of Tariq), later corrupted to Gibraltar. After successive periods of Moorish and Spanish domination, Gibraltar was captured by an Anglo-Dutch fleet in 1704 and ceded to the British by the Treaty of Utrecht in 1713. This tiny British colony, whose impressive silhouette dominates the strait between Spain and Morocco, is a rock just 5⅓ km (3⅗ mi) long, ¾ km (½ mi) wide, and 1,394 ft high.

Upon entering Gibraltar, you have to cross the airport runway on the narrow strip of land that links the Rock with La Línea, in Spain. A good way to see all the sights is the **Official Rock Tour,** available by minibus or taxi.

❾ Apes' Den, near the Wall of Charles V, can be reached by car or cable car. The famous Barbary apes are a breed of cinnamon-color, tailless monkeys, natives of the Atlas Mountains in Morocco. Legend holds that as long as the apes remain, the British will continue to hold the Rock. Winston Churchill himself ordered the maintenance of the ape colony when its numbers began to dwindle during World War II.

❶ Catalan Bay. If you turn left (east) at Devil's Tower Road just after you enter Gibraltar, you'll reach a small fishing village founded by Genoese settlers during the 18th century and now one of the Rock's most picturesque resorts.

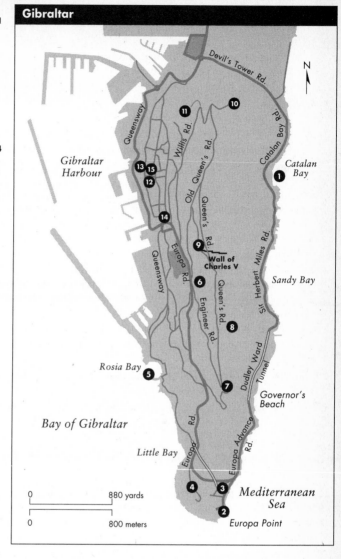

Gibraltar

🔟 **Gibraltar Museum.** Exhibits recall the history of the Rock throughout the ages. ✉ *Bomb House La.,* ☎ *9567/74289.* ⏰ *Weekdays 10–6, Sat. 10–2.*

🔟 **Great Siege Tunnel.** These huge galleries at the northern end of the Rock were carved out during the Great Siege of 1779–83, when the French and Spanish attacked. In 1878 the Governor, Lord Napier of Magdala, entertained ex-President Ulysses S. Grant here at a banquet in St. George's Hall. From here the Holyland Tunnel leads out to the east side of the Rock, above Catalan Bay.

❼ Jews' Gate. Drive down Engineer Road for an unbeatable lookout point over the docks and Bay of Gibraltar to Algeciras. Here you can access the **Upper Nature Preserve,** which includes St. Michael's Cave, the Apes' Den, the Great Siege Tunnel, and the Moorish Castle (☞ *below*). The preserve is open daily 10–sunset.

⑮ Koehler Gun. Standing in Casemates Square, this is an impressive example of the type of gun developed during the Great Siege. ⊠ *Northern end of Main St.*

⑪ Moorish Castle. This refuge was built by chieftain Tarik's successors. The present **Tower of Homage** was rebuilt by the Moors in 1333. Admiral Rooke hoisted the British flag from its top when he captured the Rock in 1704, and it has flown here ever since. ⊠ *Willis Rd.*

⑭ Nefusot Yehudada Synagogue. The synagogue is worth a look for its inspired design. ⊠ *Line Wall Rd.*

❸ Nun's Well. The Nun's Well is an ancient Moorish cistern. ⊠ *Europa Flats.*

❷ Punta Grande de Europa (Europa Point). Stop here at the Rock's southernmost tip to admire the view across the strait to the coast of Morocco, 22½ km (14 mi) away. You are standing on what in ancient times was called one of the two Pillars of Hercules. (The second pillar was just across the water, in Morocco—a mountain between the cities of Ceuta and Tangier.) Plaques explain the history of the gun installations here.

❺ Rosia Bay. This is where Admiral Nelson's flagship, HMS *Victory,* was towed after the Battle of Trafalgar, in 1805. Aboard were the battle's casualties, now buried in **Trafalgar Cemetery** (⊠ southern edge of town), and the body of Nelson himself, preserved in a barrel of rum. Nelson was taken to London for burial.

❽ St. Michael's Cave. A series of underground chambers adorned with stalactites and stalagmites, the cave makes a wonderful setting for concerts, ballet, and drama. ⊠ *Off Queen's Rd.*

❹ Shrine of Our Lady of Europe. The shrine has been venerated by sailors since 1462. ⊠ *Europa Flats.*

❻ Stakis International Casino. Perched above the Alameda Gardens, the casino is open for gaming daily until 4 AM. Dress is "smart casual." ⊠ *Europa Rd.,* ☎ *9567/76666.*

⑫ Town of Gibraltar. Britain's dignified Regency architecture blends with the shutters, balconies, and patios of southern Spain in this colorful, congested confluence. Apart from the attraction of shops, restaurants, and pubs on Main Street, you can visit some of the following: the **Governor's Residence**; the **Law Courts**, where the famous case of the *Mary Celeste* sailing ship was heard in 1872; the Anglican **Cathedral of the Holy Trinity**; and the Catholic **Cathedral of St. Mary the Crowned.**

$$$ ✕ **La Bayuca.** One of the Rock's best-established restaurants, La Bayuca is renowned for its onion soup and Mediterranean dishes. Prince Charles and Prince Andrew have dined here while on naval service. ⊠ *21 Turnbull's La.,* ☎ *9567/75119. AE, DC, MC, V. Closed Tues. No lunch Sun.*

$–$$ ✕ **Strings.** This popular bistro serves an English-style menu, with daily specials chalked up on a blackboard. ⊠ *44 Cornwall's La.,* ☎ *9567/78800. AE, MC, V. Closed Sun.*

$$$$ 🏨 **The Eliott.** The Rock's most modern hotel, the Eliott is right in the center of the town in what used to be the Gibraltar Holiday Inn. The rooms are functional and comfortable. ⊠ *2 Governor's Parade,* ☎ *9567/70500,* FAX *9567/70243. 114 rooms, 2 suites. Pool, sauna. AE, DC, MC, V.*

$$$ 🏨 **The Rock.** Overlooking the town and harbor, the refurbished Rock
★ is spiffy enough to qualify as a truly international hotel while preserving something of its colonial English background. Pink, peach, and beach predominate in the rooms and restaurant, accessorized by ceiling fans. ⊠ *3 Europa Rd.,* ☎ *9567/73000,* FAX *9567/73513. 112 rooms, 8 suites. Restaurant, pool. AE, DC, MC, V.*

$$ ☒ **Bristol.** This colonial-style hotel is in the heart of town, just off Gibraltar's main street. Rooms are large and comfortable, and the tropical garden is a real haven if you're craving some peaceful isolation. ☒ *10 Cathedral Sq.,* ☎ *9567/76800,* FAX *9567/77613. 60 rooms. Pool. AE, DC, MC, V.*

Costa del Sol Essentials

Arriving and Departing

BY PLANE

Daily flights on Iberia and Aviaco connect Málaga with Madrid and Barcelona. Air Europa and Spanair also schedule wallet-friendly flights. Iberia (☎ 95/213–6166), British Airways, and numerous charter airlines offer frequent service from London; most other major European cities also have direct air links. You'll have to connect in Madrid if you're flying from the United States. **Málaga Airport** (☎ 95/224–8804) is 12 km (7 mi) west of the city; city buses run from the airport to the city every 30 minutes, 6:30 AM–midnight, and cost 150 ptas. The Portillo bus company (☎ 95/236–0191) has frequent service from the airport to Torremolinos. A suburban train serving Málaga, Torremolinos, and Fuengirola also stops at the airport every half hour, though the station is a long walk from the terminal.

BY TRAIN

From Madrid, Málaga is served by half a dozen rapid trains daily.

Getting Around

BY BUS

Buses are the best means of transportation along the Costa del Sol (as well as from Seville or Granada). Málaga's long-distance station is on the Paseo de los Tilos (☎ 95/235–0061); nearby, on Muelle de Heredía, a smaller station serves suburban destinations. The main bus company serving the Costa del Sol is **Portillo** (offices at the bus station, ☎ 95/236–0191). **Alsina-Gräells** (at the station, ☎ 95/231–8295) goes to Granada, Córdoba, Seville, and Nerja.

BY TRAIN

The train station in Málaga (☒ Explanada de la Estación, ☎ 95/236–0202) is a 15-minute walk from the city center, across the river. The **RENFE** office (☒ Strachan 2, ☎ 95/221–4127) is more convenient for tickets and information.

Guided Tours

Numerous companies, including **Julià Tours** and **Pullmantur,** lead one- and two-day excursions from all Costa del Sol resorts to such places as Seville, Granada, Córdoba, Ronda, Gibraltar, and Tangier. Your hotel desk or any travel agent can arrange a reservation.

Visitor Information

The most helpful tourist offices (by far) are in Málaga and Marbella. The Málaga office covers the entire province.

Estepona (☒ Paseo Marítimo Pedro Manrique, ☎ 95/280–0913). **Fuengirola** (☒ Avda. Jesús Santos Rein 6, ☎ 95/246–7457). **Gibraltar** (☒ Cathedral Sq., ☎ 9567/74950). **Málaga** (☒ Pasaje de Chinitas 4, ☎ 95/221–3445, and at the airport in both national and international terminals). **Marbella** (☒ Glorieta de la Fontanilla, ☎ 95/282–2818). **Nerja** (☒ Puerta del Mar 2, ☎ 95/252–1531). **Ronda** (☒ Plaza de España 1, ☎ 95/287–1272). **Torremolinos** (☒ Ayuntamiento, C. Rafael Quintana, ☎ 95/237–9511).

EXCURSION TO MOROCCO

The crossing to Morocco, just 14 km (9 mi) across the Strait of Gibraltar, may be the longest short trip on the globe: A 90-minute boat ride from Algeciras to Tangier replaces postmodern Europe with seemingly timeless North Africa.

Islam is the state religion here, and Arabic is the official language, but you'll also hear French, Berber, Spanish, and English. Berbers, Romans, Vandals, and Arabs inhabited Morocco in the country's early history, but incessant conflict between Arabs and Berbers left Morocco ripe for invasion. After expelling the Moors from the Iberian Peninsula, Spain and Portugal attacked the Moroccan coast. Other European countries, including Germany and France, fought for control of Morocco until 1956, when all foreign rights were relinquished except for those to the Western Sahara, which is still disputed territory.

Tangier

Be prepared for Tangier: It's bedlam. The hustlers seem to be able to smell new arrivals. Do not take a volunteer guide; act as if you know exactly where you're going. As you emerge from the port, walk to the right up the Rue Portugal and duck into the beautiful **American Legation Museum.** Continue up the hill through a small gate in the medina wall to the **Fondouk Market,** where you will be surrounded by the color and vitality—men and women with bright *djellabas* (full-length robes with pointed hoods)—that inspired Delacroix, Regnault, Fortuny, and so many others to make Morocco a leitmotif. A left on Rue de la Liberté leads up to Place de France and the sumptuous **French consulate.** Another left on Boulevard Pasteur takes you down past a belvedere to the **tourist office.**

Walk down the **Grand Socco** (large market) through the pointed archway to the **Petit Socco** (small market) into the heart of Tangier's old city and artisan district. Uphill to the left is the **Place de la Kasbah,** where a belvedere has views over the port across to Tarifa.

$$$$ ✕⌂ **El Minzah Hotel.** Ask any native where the best place in town is—for either dining *or* lodging—and the immediate answer will be the El Minzah. Lovely studded wooden doors, hotel staff in Ottoman costumes, and fine views over the Mediterranean to the Iberian Peninsula prove them right. ⊠ *85 Rue de la Liberté,* ☎ *09/935885,* ℻ *09/934546. 100 rooms. Restaurant, pool. AE, DC, MC, V.*

$$ ⌂ **Hotel Continental.** Overlooking the port from the edge of the medina, this wonderful palace, built in 1888, is the best buy in Tangier for aesthetes and dreamers—and really, who else goes to Morocco? Bertolucci stayed in Room 108 while shooting *The Sheltering Sky.* Monsieur Abdessalam is a gracious host. ⊠ *36 Rue Dar el Baroud,* ☎ *09/931024,* ℻ *09/931143. 15 rooms with bath, 30 rooms share 10 baths. AE, DC, MC, V.*

$ ⌂ **Hotel Muniria.** William Burroughs wrote *Naked Lunch* in Room 9, now the home of Madame Rabia, the lovely owner. Room 8 overlooks the Bay of Tangier. Rue Magellan can be tricky to find. ⊠ *2 Rue Magellan,* ☎ *09/935337. 6 rooms with bath, 2 rooms share a bath. No credit cards.*

Casablanca

Casablanca, a booming metropolis of 3.5 million, is bound to disappoint cineasts and romantics hoping to bump into Bergman and Bogart. The closest they'll get: At the counterfeit Rick's Bar, in the Hyatt Regency, waiters take orders in trench coats and fedoras. The **Grande Mosquée Hassan II,** however, will not disappoint. Opened in 1994, it's

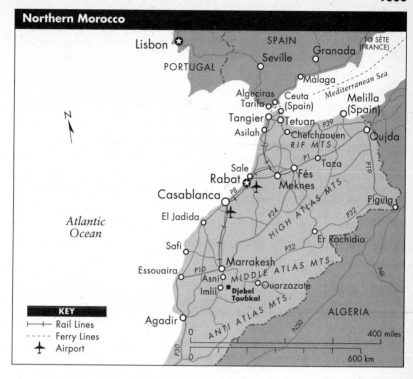

Northern Morocco

the world's third-largest mosque (after those in Mecca and Medina), with room for 25,000 worshipers inside—where the glass floor reveals the ocean below—and 80,000 in the courtyard. The 650-ft minaret is Morocco's tallest structure. Casablanca's **Corniche** is a pleasant promenade; the **spice market** in the medina is another attraction.

$$ ✕ **Al Mounia.** The best spot in Casablanca for authenticity and value, Al Mounia serves the classic Moroccan specialties: *pastilla* (pigeon pie), *harira* (lentil, chickpea, and meat soup), *tajines* (meat or fish stewed in almonds, plums, and/or vegetables), *mechoui* (roast lamb), and couscous. ⊠ *95 Rue du Prince Moulay Abdallah,* ☎ *02/222669. AE, DC, MC, V. Closed Sun.*

$$$$ ✕🏨 **Royal Mansour.** One of Morocco's top hotels, the Royal Mansour is a treat: Fabulous food is served in a lush garden courtyard to live Cole Porter tunes, and a rooftop *hammam* (Turkish bath). ⊠ *27 Av. des F.A.R.,* ☎ *02/313011,* 𝐅𝐀𝐗 *02/312583. 159 rooms, 23 suites. 3 restaurants. AE, DC, MC, V.*

$$ 🏨 **Hotel Moussafir.** New, impeccably clean, and well situated near the Casa-Voyageurs train station, the Moussafir is about one-tenth as expensive as the Royal Mansour and not nearly as far removed in quality. ⊠ *Bd. Bahmir,* ☎ *02/401984,* 𝐅𝐀𝐗 *02/400799. 99 rooms. Restaurant. AE, DC, MC, V.*

Marrakesh

The tumultuous and panoramic **Djemâa el Fna** (Assembly of the Dead) square, the highlight of a visit to Marrakesh, is a sensorial feast. Great clouds of aromatic smoke from the outdoor kitchens in the center of the square combine with the sounds of Berber musicians and storytellers, the muezzin's eerie call to prayer, snake charmers' flutes, and water vendors' bells. Scribes and clients confer intimately in the shade of umbrellas, tooth pullers are surrounded by even rows of molars, the snowcapped Atlas peaks rise behind the 800-year-old Kotoubia minaret, and the warmth of the fires meets the cool evening breeze from the mountains (Marrakesh is equidistant from the Atlantic and the Sahara).

$$$$ ✕ **Dar Marjana.** You'll feel like you've walked into a Delacroix paint-
★   ing. Excellent cuisine, beautiful surroundings, Nubian waiters uniformed in rich greens, belly dancing, and folk music combine for a true tour de force. ✉ *15 Derb Sidi Ali Tair, Bab Doukkala,* ☎ *04/445773. MC, V. Closed Tues. No lunch.*

$$$$ ✕⌂ **La Mamounia.** Everyone from Winston Churchill to Bryan Ferry has loved this unique oasis within an oasis. One of the most famous hotels in the world, La Mamounia is worth every one of the many nickels it costs. The grounds, facilities, service, and taste are sensational, and you're walking distance from Djemâa el Fna square. ✉ *Av. Bab Jdid,* ☎ *04/448981,* 𝔽𝔸𝕏 *04/444940. 171 rooms, 57 suites, 3 villas. 5 restaurants, pool. AE, DC, MC, V.*

Fez

Traditionally considered Morocco's intellectual and spiritual capital, Fez can at first seem almost too quiet after tumultuous Marrakesh. Whereas the latter is a crossroads between the Berber Sahara and black Africa from one direction and Islam and the Orient from the other, Fez is more refined, Islamic, Mediterranean, even Andalusian. The 9th-century medina, **Fez el Bali** (Old Fez), is a labyrinth of mosques (360 of them), *medersas* (medieval residential colleges), shops, and artisans. Nowhere in Morocco is a good guide more indispensable.

Fez's architectural treasures are many: carving and tilework, the **water clock,** the **Kairaouine Mosque,** and **Kairaouine University,** which, founded during the 9th century, predates Bologna's university by 200 years and Oxford's by 300. The souks and *fondouks* are all hauntingly ancient and aesthetically perfect.

$$ ✕ **Al Andalus.** On the airport road in the modern part of town, this excellent spot is a local secret. Owner Hilali Fouad's collection of curios and antiques is as enticing as the food. ✉ *34 Rte. d'Immouzzer,* ☎ *05/603162,* 𝔽𝔸𝕏 *05/600548. AE, DC, MC, V.*

$$$$ ✕⌂ **Hotel Merinides.** This spectacular hotel is usually booked well in advance. The views over Fez el Bali from the pool, nicely raised above the fray, are unique. ✉ *Borj Nord,* ☎ *05/646040,* 𝔽𝔸𝕏 *05/645225. 79 rooms, 11 suites. 2 restaurants, pool. AE, DC, MC, V.*

$$–$$$$ ⌂ **Palais Jamai.** This elegant 120-year-old palace at the edge of Fez el Bali was once the residence of the Vizir Jamai. For a combination of comfort and medina atmosphere, it's the best place to stay in Fez. ✉ *Bab Guissa,* ☎ *05/634331,* 𝔽𝔸𝕏 *05/635096. 123 rooms, 14 suites. 2 restaurants, pool. AE, DC, MC, V.*

Morocco Essentials

You will not need a visa, you *can* drink the water, and the time is usually one hour behind Spain. Women traveling alone or without men will have difficulty and should hire an official guide from the tourist office, wear conservative clothing, and be on guard at all times. The country code for Morocco is 212; drop the zero in the area code when calling from outside the country.

Getting Around

BY BOAT

From Algeciras to Tangier, **Transmediterranea** (in Algeciras, ✉ Recinto del Puerto s/n, ☎ 95/666–3850; in Madrid, ✉ C. Pedro Muñoz Seca 2, ☎ 91/431–0700; in Tangier, ✉ 31 Av. de la Résistance, ☎ 09/941101) has a 90-minute hydrofoil and a two-hour car ferry. The slow boat is

bigger, more stable, and offers better views than the somewhat claustrophobic hydrofoil. Having your passport stamped and getting your
yellow exit card before you leave the boat can save you an hour or more.

BY BUS

Bus stations: **Casablanca** (✉ 23 Rue Leon l'Africain, ☎ 02/268061).
Fez (✉ Av. Mohammed V, ☎ 05/622041). **Marrakesh** (✉ Bab Doukkala,
☎ 04/433993). **Tangier** (✉ Av. des F.A.R., ☎ 09/932415).

BY CAR

Only by car can you fully appreciate Morocco's panoramas, but Moroccan roads are challenging. In addition to poor surfaces, there is
bumper-car confusion. Some roads in the south seem to be designed
for only one-and-a-half cars; one or both approaching vehicles need
to give way. Spare parts are hard to come by, so rent from a reputable
international agency. **Casablanca: Budget** (✉ Torres de los Habous,
Av. des F.A.R., ☎ 02/313945). **Hertz** (✉ 25 Rue Foucault, ☎ 02/
484710). **Fez: Avis** (✉ 50 Bd. Chefchaouen, ☎ 05/626746). **Budget**
(✉ Bureau Grand Hotel, Av. Chefchaouen, ☎ 05/620919). **Hertz** (✉
Hotel de Fez, Av. des F.A.R., ☎ 05/622812). **Marrakesh: Budget** (✉
213 Av. Mohammed V, ☎ 04/434604). **Hertz** (✉ 157 Av. Mohammed
V, ☎ 04/434680). **Tangier: Budget** (✉ 79 Av. du Prince, Moulay Ab-
dallah, ☎ 09/937994). **Hertz** (✉ 36 Av. Mohammed V, ☎ 09/933322).

BY PLANE

Royal Air Maroc (☎ 800/344–6726 in the U.S., ☎ 91/547–7905 in
Madrid) and **Iberia** (☎ 800/772–4642 in the U.S.; 902/400500 in
Spain) fly to Casablanca from Madrid in 90 minutes. The former has
comprehensive domestic service.

BY TRAIN

Trains from Tangier to Casablanca leave at 4 PM and arrive six hours
later. There are two stations in **Casablanca,** the Gare du Port (also called
Casa–Port, ☎ 02/223011) and the Gare des Voyageurs (also called Casa–
Voyageurs, ☎ 02/243818). The latter serves Marrakesh and the south.
Fez (☎ 05/625001), **Marrakesh** (☎ 04/447768), and **Tangier** (☎ 09/
931201) have their own stations as well.

Guided Tours

Most Moroccan cities have a swarm of very insistent, unofficial
"guides." The best way to get rid of these volunteers, who may falsely
assure you that all hotels are full and take you to shops where they get
commissions on purchases, is to ignore them and pretend you know
exactly where you're going. If you do want a guide, hire a cheaper and
better one at the local tourist office.

Visitor Information

U.S. (✉ 20 E. 46th St., Suite 1201, New York, NY 10017, ☎ 212/
557–2520). **U.K.** (✉ 205 Regent St., W1R 7DE, London, ☎ 0171/437–
0073). **Madrid** (✉ C. Ventura Rodríguez, 28008, ☎ 91/542–7431).
Casablanca (✉ 55 Rue Omar Slaoui, ☎ 02/271177). **Fez** (Place de la
Résistance, ☎ 05/623460). **Marrakesh** (✉ 176 Bd. Mohammed V, ☎
04/432097; ✉ Place Abdel–Moumen Ben Ali, ☎ 04/431088). **Tangier** (✉ 29 Bd. Pasteur, ☎ 09/938239).

CANARY ISLANDS

Closer to North Africa than to mainland Spain, the ruggedly exotic
Canary Islands are becoming a year-round destination for sunseekers
and nature lovers alike. The Canaries lie 112 km (70 mi) off the coast
of southern Morocco and enjoy mild, sunny weather throughout the
year, except for the north coast of Tenerife. Each of the seven volcanic

islands in this archipelago is distinct: Some have lush tropical vegetation, poinsettias as tall as trees, and banana plantations, while others are so arid as to resemble an exotic moonscape of lava rock and sand dunes. Between them the islands are home to six national parks and dozens of other protected ecological zones; Tenerife has Spain's highest peak, Mt. Teide (12,198 ft), capped with snow for much of the year. Depending on the island, you can explore caves once inhabited by ancient tribal dwellers called the Guanches, hike through mist-shrouded forests of virgin laurel trees, eat meats grilled over the heat of a volcanic crater, or scuba dive off long stretches of unspoiled coastline.

Tenerife

Of all the Canary Islands, Tenerife is the most popular and has the greatest variety of scenery. Its beaches are small, though, with volcanic black sand or sand imported from the Sahara Desert.

Most tourists stay in the south coast's **Playa de las Américas,** in the island's most arid and barren zone. Chock-a-block with hotels, it's popular with young couples and singles, and offers little apart from sprawling hotel pools and sizzling nightlife.

An hour northeast by superhighway is Tenerife's capital, **Santa Cruz.** No whitewashed villas or sleepy streets here; instead, imagine all the traffic, action, and crowds of an important shipping port. Santa Cruz throws one of Spain's wildest pre-Lenten Carnival fiestas.

The **Museo de la Naturaleza y el Hombre** (Museum of Nature and Man) contains ceramics and mummies from the Stone Age Guanches. ⊠ *Fuentes Morales s/n,* ☎ *922/209320.* ۞ *Tues.–Sun. 10–8.*

The best sight in Santa Cruz is the colorful weekday-morning market, **Mercado de Nuestra Señora de Africa,** where you can buy everything from tropical fruits and flowers to canaries and parrots. ⊠ *Avda. de San Sebastín.* ۞ *Mon.–Sat. 5 AM–noon.*

Santa Cruz's beach, **Las Teresitas,** is about 7 km (4½ mi) northeast of the city, near the town of San Andrés, and is popular with local families. It was created with imported white sand from the Sahara.

Also north of Santa Cruz are the university town of La Laguna and the island's first resort village, **Puerto de la Cruz.** High-rise hotels and hawkers of plastic bananas are encroaching on the village's atmosphere, but it still has a tropical, flower-filled central square.

★ Inland, the road from Orotava rises through banana plantations, almond groves, and pine forests to the entrance to **Mt. Teide National Park.** The visitors' center, open daily 9–2, offers trail maps, guided hikes, educational videos, and bus tours. Before arriving at the foot of the mountain, you pass through a stark landscape called Las Cañadas del Teide, a violent jumble of rocks and minerals created by millions of years of volcanic activity. For 2,000 ptas. a cable car will take you within 534 ft of the top of Mt. Teide, where you'll have good views of the southern part of the island and neighboring Gran Canaria. The cable car operates daily 9–5; the last trip leaves at 4.

The north-coast town of **Icod de los Vinos** boasts a 3,000-year-old, 57-ft-tall dragon tree once worshiped by the ancient Guanches, and a plaza surrounded by typical Canarian houses with wooden balconies.

Farther west, **Garachico** is the most peaceful and best preserved village on this touristy isle.

$$$$ ✕ **El Coto de Antonio.** One of the finest restaurants in the Canaries, El
★   Coto de Antonio puts a gourmet spin on local dishes. In a setting as

cozy as a tavern, you can relax over an earthenware pot of succulent seafood stew enhanced with potatoes, yams, blanched *gofio* (a traditional corn-and-barley pudding), and cheese; or the house specialty: *pejines* (similar to sardines) dried in the sun, soaked in liquor, and served flambé at your table. ⊠ *General Goded 13,* ☎ *922/272105. AE, DC, MC, V. Closed Sun.*

$$ ✕ **La Masia del Mar.** There's no menu here; you simply point and choose from a vast array of fresh fish and shellfish in a refrigerated case. Add a salad and a bottle of white wine to the order, then find a seat on the wide terrace overlooking Las Caletas cove (about 5 km/3 mi west of Playa de las Americas) and enjoy a simple feast. ⊠ *Caleta de Adeje,* ☎ *922/710895. AE, DC, MC, V.*

$$$$ ⌂ **Hotel Gran Melia Bahía del Duque.** This sprawling hotel is a jumble of pastel houses and palaces, with Renaissance windows, loggias, and quiet courtyards. Rooms have oversize beds, summery wicker and pine furnishings, and rich architectural details such as scalloped plasterwork and hand-painted ceramics. ⊠ *Carretera Bajada la Caleta, Km 2, Costa Adeje 38670,* ☎ *922/713000,* ℻ *922/712369. 362 rooms. 5 restaurants, 4 pools. AE, DC, MC, V.*

$$ ⌂ **Hotel Monopol.** One of Puerto de la Cruz's first inns, this hotel has welcomed guests for over a century. Before that it was a private home (built in 1742) in the Canarian patio style. Tropical plants fill the center courtyard. Rooms are simple but have good views of the sea or the main plaza. ⊠ *Quintana 15, Puerto de la Cruz, 38400,* ☎ *922/384611,* ℻ *922/370310. 110 rooms. Restaurant, pool. AE, DC, MC, V.*

Gran Canaria

The place to be in the '60s and '70s, Gran Canaria has better beaches than Tenerife. Most visitors base themselves in the south-coast resorts **Playa del Inglés** and **Maspalomas,** where the white-sand beach extends for 4 km (2½ mi).

Gran Canaria's central highlands provide a glimpse of rural island life: The road passes through numerous villages, and it's common to see farmers walking along the road laden with burlap sacks of potatoes. The highest point on the island, **Mirador Los Pechos,** has magnificent vistas.

Gran Canaria's capital, **Las Palmas,** the largest city in the Canaries, is a multicultural whirlwind, overrun with sailors, tourists, traffic, and shoppers. Despite the somewhat seedy center, Las Palmas does have an interesting and beautiful old quarter, La Vegueta. Here you can wander cobblestone streets and visit the **Casa Museo Colón** (Columbus House and Museum), where the explorer is said to have stayed when he stopped to repair the mast on the *Pinta.* ⊠ *C. Colón 1,* ☎ *928/311255.* ▭ *Free.* ☺ *Weekdays 9–6, Sat. 9–3 (Sat. 9–2 in Aug.).*

It's quite a walk to the other end of town and the beach, so you may want to jump on one of the many canary-yellow buses, named *guaguas* (pronounced "wawas") in honor of the ancestral Guanches. Take the guagua to **Parque Santa Catalina;** lines 2, 3, and 30 link the old town and the port. The real jewel of the capital is **Las Canteras beach,** a sparkling-clean strand of white sand perfect for swimming or strolling.

$$ ✕ **Tenderete II.** Local cuisine is cherished at this unassuming little restaurant in a shopping center, one of the few in the Canaries to serve *gofio,* a traditional corn-and-barley pudding. Typical Canarian soups and stews are always available for the first course; the main course is always fish, grilled or baked in rock salt. ⊠ *Avda. de Tirajana, Edificio Aloe, Maspalomas,* ☎ *928/761460. AE, DC, MC, V.*

$$$ ⌂ **Hotel Palm Beach.** One of the islands' most sophisticated hotels, the Palm Beach rests in the middle of a 1,000-year-old palm oasis at the edge of Maspalomas Beach. The spacious rooms have bamboo furniture, marble baths, and terraces overlooking the sea or the pool. ⊠ *Avda. del Oasis s/n, Maspalomas, 35106,* ☎ *928/140806,* FAX *928/ 141808. 358 rooms. Restaurant, pool. AE, DC, MC, V.*

Lanzarote

Stark and dry, with landscapes of volcanic rock, Lanzarote enjoys good beaches and tasteful architecture—low-rise, with a green-and-white color scheme—the latter due to the efforts of the late artist César Manrique, a Lanzarote native revered for single-handedly saving the island from mass development.

★ ✕ In Costa Teguise the **Jameos del Agua** (water cavern) is a natural wonder created when molten lava streamed through an underground tunnel and hissed into the sea. The site features an auditorium with fantastic acoustics, and a restaurant and bar. ⊠ *Rte. GC710, 21 km (13 mi) north of Arrecife,* ☎ *928/835010.* ☉ *Daily 9:30–6:45; Tues., Fri., and Sat. also 7 PM–3 AM.*

★ The **Parque National Timanfaya,** popularly known as the "fire mountains," takes up much of the southern part of the island. Here you can have a camel ride, take a guided coach tour of the volcanic zone, and eat lunch at one of the world's most unusual restaurants, El Diablo (☎ 928/840057), where meat is cooked over the crater of a volcano using the earth's natural heat.

$–$$ ✕ **La Era.** One of only three buildings to survive the eruption of the volcano that wiped out the town of Yaiza in 1730, this farmhouse restaurant offers country-style tabletops arranged around a center patio. It's a great place to try regional dishes such as goat stew, or Canarian cheeses. ⊠ *Barranco 3, behind the city hall (Ayuntamiento), Yaiza,* ☎ *928/ 830016. AE, DC, MC, V.*

$$$$ ✕🏨 **Meliá Salinas.** Built around an interior tropical garden, the Meliá Salinas offers a chance to rub elbows with vacationing business and political leaders from all over Europe. Rooms have a tropical feel, and all have large, flower-filled terraces that face the sea. The hotel's restaurant, **La Graciosa**—the poshest on Lanzarote—overlooks the garden. A German chef prepares international dishes from fresh island ingredients: think giant prawns, duck breast in plum sauce, and halibut wrapped in chard. ⊠ *Costa Teguise, 35509,* ☎ *928/590040,* FAX *928/ 590390. 310 rooms. 3 restaurants, pool. AE, DC, MC, V.*

Fuerteventura

The island of Fuerteventura was only recently discovered by tourists—mostly Germans—who now come to windsurf, and to enjoy the dunes of **Corralejo** and the endless white-sand beaches of the **Sotovento** coast. Diving is good along the lengthy and lonely **Jandía Peninsula,** while the arid interior is largely the domain of goatherds.

La Palma

Known as the garden isle, La Palma has luxuriant foliage, tropical storms, rainbows, and black crescents of beach, the most popular of which is

★ **Los Cancajos.** The capital, **Santa Cruz de la Palma,** was burned to the ground by pirates in 1533; it was rebuilt with royal assistance, and today remains one of the most beautiful and harmonious examples of Spanish colonial architecture.

Canary Islands Essentials

Arriving and Departing

BY BOAT

Transmediterranea (☎ 91/423–8832 in Madrid) operates a slow, comfortable ferry between Cádiz and the Canary Islands.

BY PLANE

Iberia and its sister carrier **Aviaco** have several direct flights daily to Tenerife, Gran Canaria, and Lanzarote from most cities in mainland Spain. The other islands can be reached by connecting flights or hydrofoil. **Air Europa** and **Spanair** serve the Canaries from Madrid and Barcelona at slightly lower prices.

From the United States, **Air Europa** (☎ 212/888–7010 in New York) flies directly to Tenerife once a week.

Getting Around

BY BOAT

Transmediterranea operates interisland car ferries. Trips often take all night; ferries have sleeping cabins. The company also runs a passenger-only hydrofoil service three times a day between Las Palmas and Tenerife. One hydrofoil a day links southern Fuerteventura with Las Palmas and Tenerife.

BY BUS

In Tenerife buses meet all arriving Iberia flights at Reina Sofía airport and transfer passengers to the bus terminal in the outskirts of Santa Cruz de Tenerife.

BY CAR

Most people rent a car or Jeep for at least part of their stay, as driving is by far the best way to explore the countryside. Reservations are necessary only during the Christmas and Easter holidays. **Hertz** and **Avis** have representatives on every island, though you'll get better rates from the Spanish company **Cicar** (☎ 928/802790), with offices at all the airports.

BY PLANE

All the Canary Islands except La Gomera are served by air. Tenerife has two airports: Reina Sofía, in the south, and Los Rodeos, in the north. As a general rule long-distance flights arrive at the southern terminal and interisland flights use the northern one. Driving time from one airport to the other is 1½ hours.

Airport information: **Tenerife** (✉ Reina Sofía, ☎ 922/759200; ✉ Los Rodeos, ☎ 922/234346). **Gran Canaria** (☎ 928/579000). **Lanzarote** (☎ 928/811450). **Fuerteventura** (☎ 928/860600). **La Palma** (☎ 922/411540).

Guided Tours

One-day tours of Tenerife and excursions to other islands can be arranged through **Viajes Insular** (☎ 922/380262 in Puerto de la Cruz), which has branches on all islands except La Gomera and El Hierro.

Visitor Information

Each of the Canary Islands has its own tourist office. **Tenerife** (✉ Plaza de España 1, Santa Cruz, ☎ 922/239811). **Gran Canaria** (✉ Parque Santa Catalina, Las Palmas, ☎ 928/264623). **Lanzarote** (✉ Parque Municipal, Arrecife, ☎ 928/80157). **La Palma** (✉ Palacio Salazar, C. Real s/n, Santa Cruz de la Palma, ☎ 922/412106).

SWEDEN

STOCKHOLM, UPPSALA AND THE FOLKLORE DISTRICT, THE WEST COAST, AND THE GLASS COUNTRY

The natural beauty of Sweden, with its glaciered mountains, vast forest tracts, thousands of lakes and rivers, and unspoiled archipelagoes, stands in stark contrast to the cosmopolitan lifestyle of Swedish towns and cities.

Sweden is Europe's fourth-largest coutry, encompassing an area of 457,013 square km (173,665 square mi). Watch its environment change dramatically as you travel from the barren Arctic north to the fertile plains of the south, a distance measuring nearly 1,600 km (1,000 mi). Still, Sweden is home to only 8.9 million people. The main centers of population lie south of the province of Dalarna, less than halfway up the country. The railway line that runs 2,128 km (1,322 mi) from Trelleborg, in the far south, to Riksgränsen, in the north, is the world's longest stretch of continuously electrified track. Traveling it takes more than 35 hours.

Sweden is a land of contrasts. It has short, warm summers and long, dark, cold winters. Ancient Viking rune stones and 19th-century landmarks coexist with modern skyscrapers. Socialism exists side by side with staunch royalism. Shop windows, full of the latest in consumer goods, attract shoppers who are as at home in the city as they are in the countryside. Swedes seem to like this diversity, big-city living contrasting with the silence of the countryside. Sweden is also a clean country; it is possible to fish for salmon, trout, and the odd sturgeon right in the center of Stockholm, just a stone's throw away from the Royal Palace. In Göteborg's busy harbor, you can watch fish jump out of the water—fish that are also sold at the local market. In downtown Malmö, startlingly large hares hop around in the parks.

Once the dominant power of the Nordic region, Sweden has always been politically independent. During the cold war, it was largely successful in retaining its position as a neutral trading partner of both superpowers. The economic recession of the late 1980s forced Sweden to rethink its comprehensive welfare system, making changes down to its very foundations. When the country developed one of Europe's largest budget deficits, the fragile conservative coalition that had defeated the long-incumbent Social Democrats in 1991 attempted further cutbacks.

Sweden (Sverige)

The Social Democrats' power was restored in 1994, but cutbacks have continued at an ever-increasing pace. Sweden joined the European Union (EU) in January 1995, following a closely won referendum preceded by a heated debate. While the domestic benefits of membership have been slow in showing themselves, Sweden has quickly become an influential and respected member of this often divided organization.

SWEDEN A TO Z

Customs
For details on imports and duty-free limits, *see* Customs & Duties *in* Chapter 1.

Dining
Traditional Swedish restaurants are giving way to myriad international culinary influences. Fast-food outlets abound, but an impressive range of eateries—from top-class establishments to less expensive places for lunch or a snack—can suit even the most fickle palates and every budget.

Restaurants all over the country specialize in *husmanskost* (home cooking), based on traditional Swedish recipes. Sweden is world famous for its *smörgåsbord,* a word now internationally used as a synonym for diversity. This tempting buffet of hot and cold dishes, usually with a strong emphasis on seafood, notably herring, has something to tickle all taste buds. You can usually find an authentic smörgåsbord, and eat as much as you wish, for SKr 200–SKr 300. Hotels sometimes serve a smörgåsbord-style breakfast, often included in the room price.

MEALTIMES
Swedes eat early. Lunch is served from 11 AM, and outside the main cities restaurants often close at 9 PM or don't even open for dinner. In the large cities there are plenty of places to eat, although it is advisable to make reservations at the more popular establishments, especially on weekends.

RATINGS
Prices are per person and include a first course and main course, but no drinks. Service charges and *moms* (value-added tax) are included in the check, but it is common to tip 5%–10%.

CATEGORY	COST
$$$$	over SKr 500
$$$	SKr 250–SKr 500
$$	SKr 120–SKr 250
$	under SKr 120

WHAT TO WEAR
Except for the most formal restaurants, where a jacket and a tie are preferable, casual—or casual chic—attire is perfectly acceptable.

Language
Swedish is closely related to Danish and Norwegian. After "z," the Swedish alphabet has three extra letters, "å," "ä," and "ö." Note that the letter *w*, which only appears in names, is pronounced like a *v*. Most Swedes speak English.

Lodging
Sweden offers a variety of accommodations from simple bed-and-breakfasts, campsites, and hostels to hotels of the highest international standard. Major hotels in larger cities cater mainly to business clientele and can be expensive; weekend rates are more reasonable. Prices

are usually on a per-room basis and include all taxes, service charges, and breakfast. Apart from the more modest inns and the cheapest budget establishments, private baths and showers are standard. Whatever their size, Swedish hotels provide scrupulously clean accommodation and courteous service. Sweden virtually shuts down during the entire month of July, so make your hotel reservations in advance, especially if you're staying outside the city areas during July and early August.

CAMPING

Camping is popular in Sweden. About 750 officially approved sites dot the country, most next to the sea or a lake and offering such activities as windsurfing, horseback riding, and tennis. They are generally open between June 1 and September 1, although some stay open year-round. A free, abbreviated list of sites is published in English by the **Sveriges Campingvårdernas Riksförbund** (Swedish Campsite Owners' Association, ⊠ Box 255, 451 17 Uddevalla, ☏ 0522/642440, FAX 0522/642430).

CHALET RENTAL

At 250 chalet villages with high standards, accommodations can often be arranged on the spot at tourist offices. **Scandinavian Seaways** (☏ 031/650600) in Göteborg arranges package deals that combine a ferry trip from Britain across the North Sea and a stay in a chalet village.

HOTELS

You can contact major hotel groups through their central reservations services: **Best Western** (☏ 08/330600 or 020/792752), **Radisson SAS** (☏ 020/797592), **Scandic** (☏ 08/6105050), and **Sweden Hotels** (☏ 08/7898900).

You'll find comprehensive information about hotel facilities and prices in the official annual guide *Hotels in Sweden*, published by and available free from the Swedish Travel and Tourism Council (☞ Visitor Information, *below*). The **Sweden Hotels** group has about 100 independently owned hotels and its own classification scheme—*A, B,* or *C*—based on facilities. **Countryside Hotels** (⊠ Box 69, 830 13 Åre, ☏ 0647/51860, FAX 0647/51920), 35 select resort hotels, may be restored manor houses or centuries-old inns. **Hotellcentralen** (⊠ Central Station, 111 20, ☏ 08/7892456, FAX 08/7918666) is an independent agency that makes advance telephone reservations for hotels in Stockholm.

RATINGS

Prices are for two people in a double room, based on standard rates; tax and breakfast are included.

CATEGORY	COST
$$$$	over SKr 1,400
$$$	SKr 1,100–SKr 1,400
$$	SKr 850–SKr 1100
$	under SKr 850

Mail

POSTAL RATES

Airmail letters and postcards to the United States and Canada weighing less than 20 grams cost SKr 8. Postcards and letters within Europe cost SKr 5.

RECEIVING MAIL

If you're uncertain where you will be staying, have your mail addressed to "poste restante" and sent to S-101 10 Stockholm. Collection is at Post Office Stockholm 1 (⊠ Drottningg. 53, ☏ 08/7814682). American Express (☞ Travel Agency *in* Stockholm Essentials, *below*) offers a poste-restante service free to cardholders and for a small fee to others.

Money Matters

COSTS

Sweden is looked upon as an expensive country, although prices are generally in line with the European average. Restaurant prices can be high, but bargains exist: In cities look for the lunch *dagens rätt* (dish of the day), about SKr 60–SKr 70. Also, check for a recommended two- or three-course menu. Hotels are at their priciest fall through spring; many have special low summer and weekend winter rates. Heavy taxes and excise duties make liquor prices among the highest in Europe.

CURRENCY

The unit of currency in Sweden is the krona (plural kronor), which is divided into 100 öre and is written as SKr, SEK, or kr. Coins come in values of 50 öre and 1, 5, or 10 kronor; bills come in denominations of 20, 100, 500, and 1,000 kronor. Traveler's checks and foreign currency can be exchanged at banks all over Sweden and at post offices displaying the NB EXCHANGE sign. At press time (summer 1999), the exchange rate was SKr 8.50 to the U.S. dollar, SKr 5.78 to the Canadian dollar, SKr 13.27 to the pound sterling, SKr 5.62 to the Australian dollar, and SKr 4.48 to the New Zealand dollar.

SAMPLE PRICES

Cup of coffee, SKr 15–SKr 25; beer, SKr 30–SKr 49; soda, SKr 15–SKr 25; ham sandwich, SKr 25–SKr 50; individual pizza, SKr 45–SKr 55; 2-km (1-mi) taxi ride, SKr 40–SKr 70 (depending on the taxi company, day, and time).

TIPPING

Tipping in Sweden has become more common in recent years. At hotels it is customary to tip the porter about SKr 5 per item. For taxi rides, SKr 5 to SKr 10 is usual. A potentially unpleasant feature of the Swedish restaurant scene is that you must often check your coat or sports jacket, regardless of whether you wish to do so; the tip (or cost) for this is usually SKr 10.

National Holidays

January 1; January 6 (Epiphany); April 21 (Good Friday); April 24 (Easter Monday); May 1 (Labor Day); May 13 (Ascension); June 23 (Midsummer Evening); June 24 (Midsummer Day); November 4 (All Saints' Day); December 24–26. Hotels and restaurants may close for some of these holidays and for the week between Christmas and New Year's.

Opening and Closing Times

Banks are open weekdays 9:30–3; some stay open until 5 in larger cities. Banks at Stockholm's Arlanda Airport and Göteborg's Landvetter Airport are open every day, with extended hours. Forex and Valuta Specialisten **currency-exchange offices** operate in downtown Stockholm, Göteborg, and Malmö, also with extended hours. **Museum** hours vary widely, but most are open weekdays 10–4 or 10–5, weekends 11–4; they may close on Monday. **Shops** are generally open weekdays 9 or 9:30–6 and Saturday 9–1 or 9–4. Some department stores remain open until 8 or 9 on certain evenings, and some are also open Sunday noon–4 in major cities. Many supermarkets open on Sunday. Sweden's **Systembolaget,** the state-run liquor store and only place to buy wine, hard alcohol, or class III beer, is open weekdays 9–6. Expect a long line on Friday evenings.

Shopping

Swedish goods are internationally renowned for their style and quality. Best buys are glassware, jewelry, stainless steel, pottery and ceramics, leather goods, and textiles. You will find a wide selection of top-quality goods, including Swedish-designed clothing, at such major stores as NK, PUB, and Åhléns, which have branches all over the country.

For glassware at bargain prices, head for the Glass Country (☞ The West Coast and the Glass Country, *below*). The major glassworks have large factory outlets where you can pick up seconds at prices well below normal retail. For clothing, the best centers are Borås and Ullered, not far from Göteborg, where you can find bargains from the leading mail-order and discount companies. In rural areas, head to the local Hemslöjd craft centers for high-quality clothing, woodwork, and needlework.

SALES-TAX REFUNDS

Many Swedish shops participate in the tax-free shopping program, enabling visitors to claim a refund of most of the *moms* (value-added tax) paid, a rate of about 25%. Participating shops display a distinctive black, blue, and yellow sticker in the window. (Some stores offer the service only on purchases amounting to more than SKr 200.) The cashier will wrap and seal your purchase and give you a "Tax-Free Shopping Check" equivalent to the tax paid minus a handling charge. This check can be cashed when you leave Sweden and show your unopened packages, either at the airport or aboard ferries. If you're packing your purchases in a suitcase, you can show them at the "Tax-Free" counter at Arlanda airport's check-in lobby and get your refund before you check your luggage. You need your passport when making your purchase and claiming your refund.

Telephoning

COUNTRY CODE

The country code for Sweden is 46. When dialing Sweden from outside the country, drop the first zero in the regional telephone code.

INTERNATIONAL CALLS

These can be made from any pay phone. For calls to the United States and Canada, dial 00, then 1 (the country code), then wait for a second dial tone before dialing the area code and number. When dialing the United Kingdom, omit the initial zero on area codes (for Central London you would dial 009 followed by 44, wait for the second tone, then dial 207 and the local number). You can make international calls from **Telebutik** offices. To reach an **AT&T** long-distance operator, dial 020/795611; for **MCI,** 020/795922; and for **Sprint,** 020/799011.

LOCAL CALLS

Sweden has plenty of pay phones; to use them you'll need SKr 1, 5, or 10 coins, as a local call costs SKr 2. You can also purchase a *telefonkort* (telephone card) from a Telebutik, hospital, or *Pressbyrån* store for SKr 35, SKr 60, or SKr 100. The card can provide a savings if you make numerous domestic calls and is indispensable when you're faced with one of the many public phones that accept only cards. Telephone numbers beginning with 020 are toll-free within Sweden.

OPERATORS AND INFORMATION

For international calls, the operator assistance number is 0018; directory assistance, which costs SKr 15 per minute, is 07977. Within Sweden, dial 90130 for operator assistance and 07975 for directory assistance (this service is free from public phones).

Transportation

The basic street sign terms you'll come across are *gatan* (street, abbreviated to *g.*), *vägen* (road, abbreviated to *v.*) and *gränd* (lane, shortened to *gr.*).

BY BICYCLE

Cycling is popular in Sweden, and the country's uncongested roads and many cycle paths make it ideal for extended bike tours. Bicycles can be rented throughout the country; inquire at tourist information offices. Rental costs average around SKr 80 per day or SKr 400 per week. The **Swedish Touring Club** (STF) in Stockholm (✉ Kungsg. 2, Box 25, 101 20, ☏ 08/4632200 or 020/292929, ℻ 08/6781958) can give you information about cycling packages that include bike rental, overnight accommodation, and meals. **Cykelfrämjandet** (National Cycle Association; ✉ Torsg. 31, Box 6027, 102 31 Stockholm, ☏ 08/321680, ℻ 08/310503) has information in English and German about cycling trips around Sweden.

BY BOAT

A classic Swedish boat trip is the four-day journey along the Göta Canal between Göteborg and Stockholm, operated by **Göta Canal Steamship Company** (✉ Box 272, 401 24 Göteborg, ☏ 031/806315, ℻ 031/158311). Children must be at least eight years old to ride aboard the steamship.

BY BUS

Sweden has excellent express bus service that provides inexpensive and relatively speedy transportation around the country. An information and booking office is at the front of Stockholm's station, **Cityterminalen** (✉ Klarabergsviadukten 72, bookings, ☏ 020/640640, *wait on the line for English service*). **Swebus** and **Wasatrafik** run daily; other private companies operate weekends only. In the far north, postal buses delivering mail to remote areas also carry passengers, providing an offbeat, inexpensive journey.

BY CAR

Breakdowns. The **Larmtjänst** organization (✉ Stockholm headquarters, ☏ 08/7837000), run by a confederation of Swedish insurance companies, provides 24-hour breakdown service.

Gasoline. Sweden has some of the highest gasoline prices in Europe, about SKr 8 per liter, depending on the grade. Gas stations are self-service: Pumps marked SEDEL are automatic and accept SKr 20 and SKr 100 bills; pumps marked KASSA are paid for at the cash desk; the KONTO pumps are for customers with Swedish gas credit cards.

Parking. Park on the right-hand side of the road, but if you want to park overnight, particularly in suburban areas, be sure not to do so the night the street is being cleaned; circular signs with a red border indicate when this occurs. Timed ticket machines and, sometimes, meters operate in larger towns, usually between 8 AM and 6 PM. The fee varies from about SKr 5 to SKr 30 per hour; parking is free on weekends. Parking garages in urban areas are mostly automated, often with machines that accept credit cards; LEDIGT on a garage sign means space is available. On the street, a circular sign with a red border and a red diagonal on a blue background means parking is prohibited; a yellow rectangle with a red border means restricted parking. Beware: Fines for parking violations are very high in Sweden. City "Trafikkarta" maps, available at many gas stations, include English explanations of parking signs and systems.

Road Conditions. Sweden has an excellent network of more than 80,000 km (50,000 mi) of highways. The fastest routes are those with numbers prefixed with an *E* (for "European"). Road E4, for instance, covers the entire distance from Helsingborg, in the south, to Stockholm, and on to Sundsvall and Umeå, in the north, finishing at Haparanda, on the Finnish border. All main and secondary roads are well surfaced, but some minor roads, particularly in the north, are gravel.

Rules of the Road. Drive on the right and, no matter where you sit in a car, you must wear a seat belt. You must also have at least low-beam headlights on at all times. Signs indicate five basic speed limits, ranging from 30 kph (19 mph) in school or playground areas to 110 kph (68 mph) on long stretches of *E* roads.

BY PLANE

Most major cities are served by **SAS** (☎ 020/727000) and smaller, independent airlines. From Stockholm, there are flights to more than 30 points around the country. SAS offers cut-rate round-trip fares every day on selected flights.

BY TRAIN

Frequent trains link Stockholm with Göteborg and Malmö. First- and second-class cars are provided on all main routes, and sleeping cars are available in both classes on overnight trains. Most long-distance trains have a buffet car and a playground car for kids. Seat reservations are advisable, and on some trains—indicated with *R, IN,* or *IC* on the timetable—mandatory. Reservations (☎ 020/757575 Swedish recorded message, wait to be served by operator) can be made right up to departure. Couchette reservations on the regular train cost SKr 95 and beds from SKr 180. The Swedish rail network also operates high-speed **X2000** trains from Stockholm to Göteborg, Falun, Malmö, Jönköping and Sundsvall, and from Göteborg to Malmö.

For SKr 150 you can buy a **Reslustkort** (wanderlust card), which gets you 50% reductions on *röda platser* ("Red," or off-peak, seats). Red seats have to be booked at least seven days in advance. **ScanRail** passes allow unlimited train travel throughout Sweden, as well as Denmark, Finland, and Norway. Limited ferry passage in and beyond Scandinavia is also included. The pass is available for 21 days or five days of travel within 15 days. In the United States, call RailEurope (☎ 800/438–7245) or DER (☎ 800/782–2424).

Visitor Information
Swedish Travel and Tourism Council (✉ Kungsg. 36, Box 3030, 103 61 Stockholm, ☎ 08/7255500, ℻ 08/7255531).

Weather
The tourist season runs from mid-May through mid-September; many attractions, however, close in late August, when the schools reopen at the end of the Swedish vacation season. The weather can be glorious in the spring and fall, when fewer visitors are around.

CLIMATE

Sweden has typically unpredictable north European summer weather, but, as a general rule, it is likely to be warm but not hot from May until September. In Stockholm, the weeks just before and after midsummer offer almost 24-hour light, while in the far north, above the Arctic Circle, the sun doesn't set between the end of May and the middle of July.

The following are the average daily maximum and minimum temperatures for Stockholm.

Jan.	30F	– 1C	**May**	58F	14C	**Sept.**	60F	15C
	23	– 5		43	6		49	9
Feb.	30F	– 1C	**June**	67F	19C	**Oct.**	49F	9C
	22	– 5		51	11		41	5
Mar.	37F	3C	**July**	71F	22C	**Nov.**	40F	5C
	26	– 4		57	14		34	1
Apr.	47F	8C	**Aug.**	68F	20C	**Dec.**	35F	3C
	34	1		55	13		28	– 2

STOCKHOLM

Stockholm stands on 14 islands surrounded by water so clean that you can fish and swim in the heart of the city. This cultivated, civilized city has many parks, squares, and wide streets, providing welcome calm in what has become a bustling metropolis. Modern glass and steel buildings abound in the city center, but you are seldom more than a five-minute walk from twisting, medieval streets and water views.

The first written mention of Stockholm dates from 1252, when a powerful regent named Birger Jarl built a fortified castle here. This strategic position, where the fresh waters of Lake Mälaren meet the brackish Baltic Sea, prompted King Gustav Vasa to take over the city in 1523, and King Gustavus Adolphus to make it the heart of an empire a century later.

During the Thirty Years' War (1618–48), Sweden became an important Baltic trading state, and the city gained a reputation as a commercial center. By the beginning of the 18th century, however, Swedish influence had begun to wane, and Stockholm's development slowed. It did not pick up again until the Industrial Revolution, when the hub of the city moved north from the Gamla Stan (Old Town) area.

Exploring Stockholm

Numbers in the margin correspond to points of interest on the Stockholm map.

Stockholm's main attractions are concentrated in a relatively small area, and the city itself can be explored in just a few days. If you have only limited time in Stockholm, give priority to a tour of Stockholm's Gamla Stan (Old Town), a labyrinth of narrow medieval streets, alleyways, and quiet squares on the island just south of the city center. Be sure to visit the large island of Djurgården. Although it's only a short walk from the city center, the most pleasant way to approach it is by ferry from Skeppsbron, in Gamla Stan.

🖐 ⑬ **Gröna Lund Tivoli.** Stockholm's only amusement park is a family favorite, with traditional rides and new attractions on the waterfront each season. ⊠ *Djurgårdsv.*, ☎ *08/6707600.* ⊙ *Late Apr.–early Sept. Prices and hrs subject to change; call ahead.*

⑨ **Historiska Museet** (Historical Museum). The museum houses some remarkable gold and silver treasures dating from the Swedish Viking era. ⊠ *Narvav. 13–17*, ☎ *08/7839400.* ⊙ *Tues.–Sun. 11–5, Thurs. 11–8. Closed Mon.*

★ 🖐 ⑩ **Junibacken.** This fairy-tale house lets you travel in small carriages through the world of children's book writer Astrid Lindgren, creator of the irrepressible character Pippi Longstocking. ⊠ *Galärvarsv.*, ☎ *08/6600600.* ⊙ *June–Aug., Mon.–Sat. 9–6, Sun. 10–6; Sept.–May, Wed.–Sun. 10–5.*

★ ③ **Kungliga Slottet** (Royal Palace). Visit at noon and watch the time-honored, yet now superfluous changing of the smartly dressed guards. You can wander at will into the palace courtyard and the building itself. The **Livrustkammaren** (Royal Armory) has an outstanding collection of weaponry and royal regalia. The **Skattkammaren** (Treasury) houses the Swedish crown jewels, including the regalia used for the coronation of King Erik XIV in 1561. You can also visit the **Representationsvåningen** (State Apartments), where the king swears in each successive government. ⊠ *Gamla Stan*, ☎ *08/6664466.* ⊙ *Late Apr.–early Sept. Prices and hrs subject to change; call ahead.*

❻ Kungsträdgården (King's Garden). Originally built as a royal kitchen garden, Kungsträdgården was turned into a public park in 1562. In summer you can watch people playing open-air chess with giant chess pieces. In winter the park has a skating rink. ⊠ *Between Hamng. and the Royal Opera in the city center.*

❽ Moderna Museet (Museum of Modern Art). In a 1998 building designed by Rafael Moneo, the museum displays works by Picasso, Kandinsky, Dali, Brancuşi, and other international artists. You can also view paintings and sculptures created by prominent Swedish artists. ⊠ *Skeppsholmen,* ☎ *08/6664250.* ☉ *Tues.–Thurs. 11–10, Fri.–Sun. 11–6.*

❼ National Museet (National Museum). The works of important old masters, including Rembrandt, and those of many Swedish artists line the walls here. ⊠ *Södra Blasieholmshamnen,* ☎ *08/6664250.* ☉ *Wed., Fri.–Sun. 11–5; Tues., Thurs. 11–8.*

ⓒ **⓫ Nordiska Museet** (Nordic Museum). The museum shows how Swedes have lived during the past 500 years. On permanent display are peasant costumes, folk art, and items from the Sami (Lapp) culture. On the ground floor, there's a delightful "village life" play area. ⊠ *Djurgårdsv. 6–16,* ☎ *08/6664600.* ☉ *Tues.–Sun. 11–5; July, daily 10–5.*

❷ Riddarholms kyrkan (Riddarholm Church). A legion of Swedish kings is buried in this magnificent sanctuary, a Greyfriars monastery dating from 1270. ⊠ *Riddarholmen, Gamla Stan,* ☎ *08/4026000.* ☉ *June–Aug., Mon.–Sat. 11–4, Sun. noon–4; May and Sept., Wed. and weekends noon–3.*

★ ⓒ **⓮ Skansen.** More than 150 reconstructed traditional buildings from all over Sweden and a variety of handicraft displays and demonstrations form this large, open-air folk museum. There is a zoo, with native Scandinavian lynxes, wolves, and elks, as well as an aquarium and an old-style *tivoli* (amusement park). Snack kiosks and a pleasant restaurant make it easy to spend a whole day. ⊠ *Djurgårdsslätten 49–51,* ☎ *08/ 4428000.* ☉ *Sept.–Apr., daily 9–5; May–Aug., daily 9 AM–10 PM. Prices and hrs subject to change; call ahead.*

★ **❶ Stadshuset** (City Hall). Architect Ragnar Östberg's ornate 1923 facade is a Stockholm landmark. Lavish mosaics adorn the walls of the **Gyllene Salen** (Golden Hall), and the **Prinsens Galleri** (Prince's Gallery) holds a collection of large murals by Prince Eugen, brother of King Gustav V. Take the elevator halfway up, then climb the rest of the way to the top of the 348-ft tower for a magnificent view of the city. ⊠ *Hantverkarg. 1,* ☎ *08/50829000.* ☉ *Tours: daily at 10 and noon; also at 11 and 2 in summer. Tower: May–Sept., daily 10–4:30.*

❹ Storkyrkan (Cathedral). In this 15th-century Gothic cathedral in central Gamla Stan, you will find the *Parhelion*, a painting of Stockholm dating from 1520, the oldest in existence. ⊠ *Trångsund 1,* ☎ *08/ 7233000.*

❺ Stortorget. Danish King Christian II ordered a massacre in this square in 1520 that triggered a revolt and the founding of the sovereign state of Sweden. ⊠ *Gamla Stan, just southwest of Kungliga Slottet.*

★ **⓬ Vasamuseet.** The 17th-century warship *Vasa* sank ignominiously in Stockholm Harbor on its maiden voyage in 1628 because it was not carrying sufficient ballast. Forgotten for centuries, the largely intact vessel was recovered from the sea in 1961 and now stands sentinel over the harbor in this striking museum; film presentations and exhibits are also on site. ⊠ *Galärvarvet,* ☎ *08/6664800.* ☉ *Daily 10–5, Wed. 10–8.*

Stockholm

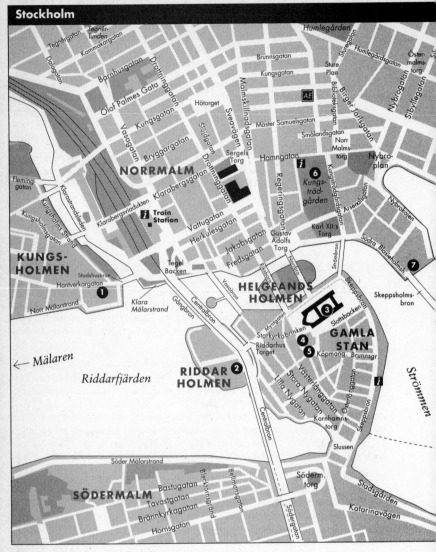

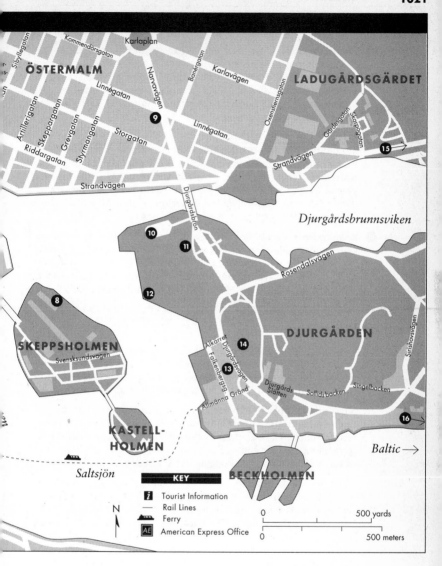

ÖSTERMALM

Kommendörsgatan

Karlaplan

LADUGÅRDSGÄRDET

Sibyllegatan

Linnégatan

Narvavägen

Banérgatan

Karlavägen

Karlavägen

Oxenstiernsgatan

Gärdesgatan

Storgatan

9

Artillerigatan

Skeppargatan

Grevgatan

Styrmangatan

Storgatan

Linnégatan

Strandvägen

15

Riddargatan

Strandvägen

Djurgårdsbron

Djurgårdsbrunnsviken

10

11

Rosendalsvägen

12

8

DJURGÅRDEN

Sirishovsvägen

SKEPPSHOLMEN

Svensksundsvägen

Alkärret

Djurgårdsvägen

14

Falkenbergsg

13

Djurgårds Slätten

Soffiasbacken

Singelbacken

Allmänna Gränd

KASTELL-
HOLMEN

16

Baltic →

Saltsjön

KEY

BECKHOLMEN

N

i Tourist Information

— Rail Lines

Ferry

AE American Express Office

0   500 yards

0   500 meters

Västerlånggatan. The main street of Gamla Stan brims with boutiques and antiques shops.

🔟 **Waldemarsudde.** Once the summer residence of Prince Eugen (1865–1947), this museum offers a significant collection of Nordic paintings dating from 1880 to 1940, as well as the prince's own works. ⊠ *Prins Eugens väg 6,* ☎ *08/6622800.* ☼ *June–Aug., Wed. and Fri.–Sun. 11–5, Tues. and Thurs. 11–8; Sept.–May, Tues.–Sun. 11–4. Prices and hrs subject to change; call ahead.*

Elsewhere in Stockholm

Bergianska Botaniska Trädgården (Bergianska Botanical Garden). North of the city center, the garden has the world's largest display of water lilies. There are plants from all over the world at the **Victoria House.** ⊠ *Frescati,* ☎ *08/162853.* 🎫 *Free to park.* ☼ *Greenhouse, daily 11–5; herbal garden, daily 8–5; Victoria House, May–Sept., daily 11–5; park always open.*

🔟 **Kaknästornet** (the Kaknäs TV Tower). Just shy of 508 ft, the tower on Gärdet is the tallest structure in Scandinavia. From its top you have a magnificent view of the city and the surrounding archipelago. Facilities include a cafeteria, restaurant, and gift shop. ⊠ *Ladugårdsgärdet, Bus 69 from Sergels Torg,* ☎ *08/7892435.* ☼ *May–Aug., daily 9 AM–10 PM; Sept.–Apr., daily 10–9.*

Dining and Lodging

Stockholm has one of the highest densities of restaurants per capita in Europe. Lunch is generally served between 11 and 2; if you're looking for value dining, make lunch your big meal. For details and price-category information, *see* Dining *in* Sweden A to Z, *above.*

Stockholm has plenty of hotels in higher price brackets, but summer rates—some as much as 50% off—can make even very expensive hotels affordable. The major chains also offer bargain plans on weekends throughout the year and weekdays in summer. For details and price-category information, *see* Lodging *in* Sweden A to Z, *above.*

More than 50 hotels offer the "Stockholm Package," providing one night's lodging at between SKr 398 and SKr 890 per person and including breakfast and a Stockholmskortet (☞ Getting Around *in* Stockholm Essentials, *below*). The package is available June through mid-August, at Christmas and Easter, and Friday through Monday year-round; get details from Hotellcentralen (☞ Lodging *in* Sweden A to Z, *above*) and American Express travel agency (☞ Contacts and Resources *in* Stockholm Essentials, *below*). If you arrive in Stockholm without a hotel reservation, Hotellcentralen can arrange accommodation for you.

$$$$ ✕ **Operakällaren.** One of Stockholm's best-known traditional restaurants is found in the elegant Opera House. With both Scandinavian and Continental cuisine on its menu, it is famed for its smörgåsbord, available from June 1st, with seasonal variations, through Christmas. In summertime you can dine on the veranda. ⊠ *Operahuset, Jakobs Torg 2,* ☎ *08/6765800. AE, DC, MC, V. Main dining room closed July.*

$$$$ ✕ **Ulriksdals Wärdshus.** Top-notch service, a beautiful location—in a castle park on the outskirts of town—and a noteworthy Swedish and international menu highlighting a lunchtime smörgåsbord all make this worth a splurge. Built in 1868, the restaurant was once a country inn, and it hasn't lost a bit of its country hospitality. ⊠ *Ulriksdals Slottspark, Solna,* ☎ *08/850815. AE, DC, MC, V. No dinner Sun.*

$$$ ✕ **Clas på Hörnet.** Just outside the city center, this small, intimate es-
★ tablishment occupies the ground floor of a restored 200-year-old
town house, now a hotel (☞ *below*). It serves international and
Swedish cuisine. ✉ *Surbrunnsg. 20,* ☎ *08/165136. AE, DC, MC, V.
Closed July.*

$$$ ✕ **Den Gyldene Freden.** Once a favorite haunt of Stockholm's artists
★ and composers, this restaurant, dating from 1722, has an Old Town
ambience. Every Thursday, the Swedish Academy meets for lunch on
the second floor. The menu offers a tasteful combination of French and
Swedish cuisines. ✉ *Österlångg. 51,* ☎ *08/249760. AE, DC, MC, V.
Closed Sun. and July. No lunch except Sat.*

$$$ ✕ **Il Conte.** A warm, Italian-style restaurant close to Stockholm's most
elegant avenue, Strandvägen, Il Conte has delicious Italian dishes and
wines served by an attentive staff. The restaurant is tastefully decorated
to create an alluring, refined atmosphere. ✉ *Grevg. 9,* ☎ *08/6612628.
Reservations essential. AE, DC, MC, V. Call for closing dates.*

$$$ ✕ **Nils Emil.** Frequented by members of the Swedish royal family,
this elegant but unpretentious restaurant is noted for its delicious
Swedish cuisine and generous helpings. Paintings of the Stockholm
archipelago decorate the walls. ✉ *Folkungag. 122, Södermalm,* ☎
*08/6407209. Reservations essential. AE, DC, MC, V. Closed July.
No lunch Sat.*

$$$ ✕ **Stallmästaregården.** This historic inn with an attractive courtyard
★ and garden sits in Haga Park, just north of Norrtull, about 15 min-
utes by car or slightly longer by bus from the city center. In summer
fine French and Swedish cuisine is served in the courtyard overlook-
ing Brunnsviken lake. ✉ *Norrtull, near Haga, Bus 52 to Stallmästaregår-
den,* ☎ *08/6101300. AE, DC, MC, V. Closed Sun.*

$$$ ✕ **Wedholms Fisk.** You can only get fresh fish and shellfish at this open,
high-ceiling restaurant near Berzelli Park, across from the Royal Dra-
matic Theater. The tartare of salmon and the grilled sole are noteworthy,
and portions are generous. The Scandinavian artwork on display is part
of the owner's personal collection. ✉ *Nybrokajen 17,* ☎ *08/6117874.
AE, DC, MC, V. Closed Sun. and July.*

$$ ✕ **Eriks Bakficka.** A favorite among locals, Eriks is a block from ele-
gant Strandvägen and a few steps down from street level. The restau-
rant serves a wide variety of Swedish dishes; the pub section has a
lower-priced menu. The same owner operates Eriks in Gamla Stan, one
of Stockholm's most exclusive restaurants. ✉ *Fredrikshovsg. 4,* ☎ *08/
6601599. AE, DC, MC, V. Closed July.*

$$ ✕ **Gondolen.** Suspended under the gangway of the Katarina elevator
at Slussen square, Gondolen has a magnificent view over the harbor,
Mälaren, and the Baltic. The cuisine is international with a range of
prix-fixe menus available. ✉ *Stadsgården 6,* ☎ *08/6417090. AE, DC,
MC, V. Closed Sun.*

$$ ✕ **Koh Phangan.** Creative food is served until midnight at this lively
Thai restaurant, where you'll be seated in individual "huts," each with
a special name and style. Sign up for a table on the chalkboard next
to the bar when you arrive. While you can expect a wait on weekends,
the food and atmosphere are well worth a visit. ✉ *Skånag. 57,* ☎ *08/
6426865,* 𝖥𝖠𝖷 *08/6426568. AE, DC, MC, V.*

$$ ✕ **Martini.** This Italian restaurant is a great place to eat; patrons line
up for a seat in summer, when the terrace is open. The main restau-
rant is below street level, but light colors and a bustling atmosphere
make it cheerful. ✉ *Norrmalmst. 4,* ☎ *08/6798220. AE, DC, MC, V.*

$$ ✕ **Sturehof.** Opened before the turn of the century, Sturehof is one of
Sweden's oldest fish restaurants. It has a refurbished (1996) bistro/pub,

but the nautically inspired ambience of the main restaurant has been preserved. ⊠ *Stureplan 2*, ☎ *08/6798750. AE, DC, MC, V.*

$ ✕ **Örtagården.** One floor up from Östermalms Saluhall market is this attractive, vegetarian buffet of soups, salads, hot dishes, and homemade bread plus a 5-SKr bottomless cup of coffee—in a turn-of-the-century atmosphere. ⊠ *Nybrog. 31,* ☎ *08/6621728. AE, MC, V.*

$$$$ ▥ **Amaranten.** Not far from the central train station, Amaranten is a large, modern hotel. Rooms with air-conditioning and sound-proofing are available at a higher rate. ⊠ *Kungsholmsg. 31, 104 20,* ☎ *08/6541060,* FAX *08/6526248. 410 rooms. Restaurant, pool. AE, DC, MC, V.*

$$$$ ▥ **Berns Hotell.** This cozy, yet subtly ultramodern hotel occupies a mid-19th-century building that was turned into a hotel in 1989. Its Art Deco, Italian-inspired design means no carpets, just exquisite wooden floors. ⊠ *Näckströmsg. 8, 111 47,* ☎ *08/56632200,* FAX *08/56632201. 65 rooms. Restaurant. AE, DC, MC, V.*

$$$$ ▥ **Continental.** In the city center across from the train station, the Continental is a reliable hotel that's especially popular with Americans. ⊠ *Klara Vattugränd 4, 101 22,* ☎ *08/244020,* FAX *08/4113695. 268 rooms. Restaurant. AE, DC, MC, V.*

$$$$ ▥ **Diplomat.** This elegant hotel near the city center, Djurgården, and
★ the open-air museum Skansen offers magnificent views over central Stockholm. The turn-of-the-century town house was used by embassies in the 1930s; in 1966 it was converted into a hotel. Try the Teahouse Restaurant and the upstairs bar. ⊠ *Strandv. 7C, 104 40,* ☎ *08/6635800,* FAX *08/7836634. 133 rooms. Restaurant. AE, DC, MC, V.*

$$$$ ▥ **Grand.** Each year the large, old world–style Grand accommodates the current Nobel Prize winners. The waterfront hotel dates from 1874 and stands opposite the Royal Palace in the center of town; request a room with a view of the water. The two restaurants—French and Swedish—offer harbor views, and the bar serves light snacks. ⊠ *Blasieholmshamnen 8, 103 27,* ☎ *08/6793500,* FAX *08/6118686. 319 rooms. 2 restaurants. AE, DC, MC, V.*

$$$$ ▥ **Lady Hamilton.** As charming, desirable, and airily elegant as its name-
★ sake, the Lady Hamilton opened in 1980 as a modern hotel inside a 15th-century building. Swedish antiques accent the light, natural-tone decor in all the guest rooms and common areas. The subterranean sauna rooms provide a chance to take a dip in the building's original, medieval well. ⊠ *Storkyrkobrinken 5, 111 28,* ☎ *08/234680,* FAX *08/ 4111148. 34 rooms. AE, DC, MC, V.*

$$$$ ▥ **Radisson SAS Strand.** This gracious, old-world hotel was built in 1912 and modernized in 1983. No two rooms are alike; all are furnished with antiques. The hotel's Italian restaurant has a superb wine list. ⊠ *Nybrokajen 9, 103 27,* ☎ *08/6787800,* FAX *08/6112436. 148 rooms. Restaurant. AE, DC, MC, V.*

$$$$ ▥ **Reisen.** This 17th-century building, on the waterfront in Gamla Stan, has been a hotel since 1819; it has a fine restaurant, a grill, tea and coffee service in the library, and a good piano bar. The swimming pool was installed beneath surviving medieval arches in the structure's foundations. ⊠ *Skeppsbron 12–14, 111 30,* ☎ *08/223260,* FAX *08/201559. 114 rooms. 3 restaurants, pool. AE, DC, MC, V.*

$$$$ ▥ **Scandic Hotel Slussen.** A modern hotel with a panoramic view of Gamla Stan and City Hall, the Scandic is on Stockholm's trendy south side. Two big attractions are the Couronne d'Or French eatery and a cellar with wines for tasting, some dating from 1650. ⊠ *Guldgr. 8, 104 65,* ☎ *08/51735300,* FAX *08/6428358. 264 rooms. 2 restaurants, pool. AE, DC, MC, V.*

$$$ ▥ **Birger Jarl.** Just outside the city center, this contemporary, conservative, thickly carpeted refuge is for business travelers, conferences, and tourists requiring unfussy comforts. Breakfast is an extensive buffet just off the lobby, but room service is also available. Rooms are not large, but they are well furnished; four family-style rooms have extra floor space and sofa beds. ⊠ *Tuleg. 8, 104 32, Bus 46 to Stureplan,* ☎ *08/6741000,* ℻ *08/6737366. 225 rooms. AE, DC, MC, V.*

$$$ 🖪 **Clas på Hörnet.** An 18th-century inn converted into a small hotel
★ in 1982, Clas på Hörnet is not far from the city center. Its rooms, furnished with period antiques, go quickly. If you can't reserve a night's lodging, at least have a meal in the excellent restaurant (☞ *above*). ⊠ *Surbrunnsg. 20, 113 48,* ☎ *08/165130,* ℻ *08/6125315. 10 rooms. Restaurant. AE, DC, MC, V.*

$$$ 🖪 **Gamla Stan.** This quiet, cozy hotel is in one of Gamla Stan's 17th-century houses. Each room is uniquely decorated. ⊠ *Lilla Nyg. 25, 111 28,* ☎ *08/7237250,* ℻ *08/7237259. 51 rooms. AE, DC, MC, V.*

$$$ 🖪 **Lydmar Hotel.** Just opposite Humlegården in the center of Stockholm lies this modern hotel, a 10-minute walk from the downtown hub of Sergels Torg. The lobby lounge is alive on weekends with the latest jazz sounds. ⊠ *Stureg. 10, 114 36,* ☎ *08/56611300,* ℻ *08/56611301. 56 rooms, 5 junior suites. AE, DC, MC, V.*

$$$ 🖪 **Prize.** This sleek hotel has ultramodern rooms as compactly efficient as overnight train compartments. Some have no windows but are fitted with backlit shoji screens to simulate daylight. The hotel occupies part of the World Trade Centre, above one end of the Central Train Station, but a shock-absorbent base eliminates noise and vibrations from the trains below. ⊠ *Kungsbron 1, 111 22,* ☎ *08/56622200,* ℻ *08/56622444. 158 rooms. AE, DC, MC, V.*

$$$ 🖪 **Sergel Plaza.** This basic, modern downtown hotel has a relaxing atmosphere, a piano bar just behind the light, spacious lobby, and an executive floor, a casino, and a body care center. The restaurant offers international haute cuisine. ⊠ *Brunkebergstorg 9, 103 27,* ☎ *08/226600,* ℻ *08/215070. 406 rooms, 11 suites. Restaurant. AE, DC, MC, V.*

$$$ 🖪 **Stockholm Plaza Hotel.** On one of Stockholm's foremost streets for shopping and entertainment, this turn-of-the-century building is furnished in an old-style, elegant manner and has reasonable-size rooms. ⊠ *Birger Jarlsg. 29, 103 95,* ☎ *08/56622000,* ℻ *08/56622020. 151 rooms. Restaurant, bar, sauna. AE, DC, MC, V.*

$$ 🖪 **Alexandra.** Serving a business clientele in the Södermalm district, this small hotel is only five minutes by subway from the city center. The rooms are light and airy. ⊠ *Magnus Ladulåsg. 42, 118 27,* ☎ *08/840320,* ℻ *08/7205353. 74 rooms. AE, DC, MC, V.*

$$ 🖪 **Arcadia.** On a hilltop near a large waterfront nature preserve, this converted dormitory is still within 15 minutes of downtown by bus or subway, or 30 minutes on foot along pleasant shopping streets. Rooms are furnished in a spare, neutral style, with plenty of natural light. ⊠ *Körsbärsv. 1, 114 89, Bus 43 to Körsbärsvägen,* ☎ *08/160195,* ℻ *08/166224. 82 rooms. Restaurant. AE, DC, MC, V.*

$$ 🖪 **August Strindberg.** A narrow, frescoed corridor leads from the street to the flagstone courtyard, into which the hotel's restaurant expands in summer. New parquet flooring and high ceilings distinguish the rooms, which are otherwise plainly furnished. Kitchenettes are available; some rooms can be combined into family apartments. The four floors have no elevator. ⊠ *Tegnérg. 38, 113 59,* ☎ *08/325006,* ℻ *08/209085. 19 rooms. Restaurant. AE, DC, MC, V.*

$$ 🖪 **Långholmen.** This former prison (built in 1724) was converted into a combined hotel and hostel in 1989. The island on which it sits has popular beaches and a prison museum. ⊠ *Långholmen, Box 9116, 102 72,* ☎ *08/6680500,* ℻ *08/7208575. 101 rooms. 3 restaurants. AE, DC, MC, V.*

$$ \boxed{\text{T}} \text{ **Örnsköld.** Just behind the Royal Dramatic Theater in the heart of}$$
★ the city, this gem has the atmosphere of an old private club, with a brass-and-leather lobby and Victorian-style furniture in the moderately spacious, high-ceiling rooms. Rooms over the courtyard are quieter, but those facing the street are sunnier. ⊠ *Nybrog. 6, 114 34,* ☎ *08/ 6670285,* FAX *08/6676991. 30 rooms. AE, MC, V.*

$ ◲ ***Gustav af Klint.*** A "hotel ship" moored at Stadsgården quay, near Slussen subway station, the *Gustav af Klint* is divided into a hotel and a hostel. The rooms are small but clean, with bunk-style beds in both the hotel and hostel rooms; the shared bathrooms are spotless and accessible. You can dine on deck in summer. ⊠ *Stadsgårdskajen 153, 116 45,* ☎ *08/6404077,* FAX *08/6406416. 8 hotel cabins, 120 hostel beds. Restaurant. AE, MC, V.*

Nightlife and the Arts

The Arts

Stockholm's theater and concert season runs from September through May, so you won't find many big-name artists in summer except during the Stockholm Water Festival in August. For a list of events, pick up the free booklet *Stockholm This Week,* available from hotels and tourist information offices. For tickets to theaters and shows try **Biljettdirekt** at Sweden House (☞ Stockholm Tourist Centre *in* Visitor Information *in* Stockholm Essentials, *below*) or any **post office.**

CONCERTS

The city's main concert hall is **Konserthuset** (⊠ Hötorget 8, ☎ 08/ 102110), home of the Stockholm Philharmonic Orchestra. Also look in the local press for events at **Berwaldhallen** (⊠ Strandv. 69, ☎ 08/ 7845000). In summer many city parks have free concerts; listings appear in the "Events" section of *Stockholm This Week.*

FILM

English and American films predominate, screened with the original soundtrack and Swedish subtitles. Programs are listed in the local evening newspapers, although movie titles are usually given in Swedish. **Filmstaden Sergel** (⊠ Hötorget, ☎ 08/56260000) has 18 cinemas under one roof. Most cinemas take reservations over the phone, and the latest releases may well be sold out. The city's annual **Stockholms Filmfestival** is held in early November, screening new and classic films from all over the world.

OPERA

Operan (the Royal Opera House; ⊠ Jakobs Torg 2, ☎ 08/248240) lies just across the water from the Royal Palace. The season runs from mid-August to early June and offers world-class performances. The exquisite **Drottningholms Slottsteater** (Drottningholm Court Theater; ⊠ Drottningholm, ☎ 08/6608225) presents opera, ballet, and orchestral music from May to early September; the original 18th-century stage machinery is still used in these productions. Drottningholm, the royal residence, is reached by subway and bus or by special theater-bus (which leaves from the Grand Hotel or opposite the Central Train Station). Boat tours run here in summer (☞ Contacts and Resources *in* Stockholm Essentials, *below*).

THEATER

Stockholm has some 20 theaters. **Kungliga Dramatiska Teatern** (Dramaten: the Royal Dramatic Theater, ⊠ Nybroplan, ☎ 08/6670680), with great gilded statues at Nybroplan, stages international productions in Swedish. **Vasa Teatern** (⊠ Vasag. 19–21, ☎ 08/248240) offers whimsical Swedish comedies. Musicals are presented regularly at several city theaters. Productions by the **English Theatre Company** are occasionally staged at various venues in Stockholm; check the local press for details.

Nightlife

BARS AND NIGHTCLUBS

The Red Room, on the second floor of the renovated restaurant/bar **Berns' Salonger** (⊠ Berzelli Park 9, ☎ 08/6140550), is where playwright August Strindberg once held court. **Café Opera** (⊠ Operahuset, Gustav Adolfs Torg, ☎ 08/6765807) is a favorite meeting place of the suit-and-tie set; at the waterfront end of Kungsträgården, it has the longest bar in town, plus dining, roulette, and dancing after midnight. **Mosebacke Etablissement** (⊠ Mosebacke Torg 3, ☎ 08/6419020) is a combined indoor theater and outdoor café with a spectacular view of the city. Royalty and other dignitaries mingle at **Riche** (⊠ Birger Jarlsg. 4, ☎ 08/6117022); the grand bar's pedigree stretches back to 1893. **Snaps Bar and Bistro** (⊠ Götg. 48, ☎ 08/6402868) is a bar, restaurant, and nightclub with two floors for dancing. **Sture Compagniet** (⊠ Stureg. 4, ☎ 08/6117800) is good for drinking and dancing. **Tiger** (⊠ Kungsg. 18 12–14, ☎ 08/244700) is a multilevel club and restaurant—with a Latin touch.

Pubs now abound in Stockholm. Watch for happy hour, when drinks are cheap. Irish beer enthusiasts rally at **Dubliner** (⊠ Smålandsg. 8, ☎ 08/6797707). **Limerick** (⊠ Tegnérg. 10, ☎ 08/6734398) is a favorite Hibernian spot. The **Tudor Arms** (⊠ Grevg. 31, ☎ 08/6602712) is just as popular as when it opened in the '70s.

CABARET

Stockholm's biggest nightclub, **Börsen** (⊠ Jakobsg. 6, ☎ 08/7878500), has high-quality Swedish and international cabaret. **Wallmans Salonger** (⊠ Teaterg. 3, ☎ 08/6116622) offers an unforgettable cabaret experience; reservations are essential.

DANCING

Bäckahästen (⊠ Kungsg. 56, ☎ 08/4115180) is lively on weekends. **Karlson & Co** (⊠ Kungsg. 56, ☎ 08/54512140) is a pub, restaurant, and nightclub. **Penny Lane** (⊠ Birger Jarlsg. 29, ☎ 08/201411) pulls in all ages with music from the '70s.

JAZZ CLUBS

Fasching (⊠ Kungsg. 63, ☎ 08/216267) is Stockholm's largest jazz club, offering both jazz and soul. **Nalens** (⊠ Stora Nyg. 5, ☎ 08/4533400) is a jazz and dance club with performances and dancing four or five nights a week. Tickets for concerts are available through BiljettDirekt (☎ 077/1707070); most shows cost SKr 100 or less.

Shopping

Department Stores

NK (⊠ Hamng. 18–20, ☎ 08/7628000) is a high-class galleria. **PUB** (⊠ Hötorget, ☎ 08/239915) has 42 boutiques. **Åhléns City** (⊠ Klarabergsg. 50, ☎ 08/6766000) is a traditional department store.

Food and Flea Markets

One of the largest flea markets in northern Europe, the **Loppmarknaden,** is held in the parking garage of the Skärholmen shopping center, a 20-minute subway ride from downtown (SKr 10 on weekends; weekdays 11–6, Sat. 9–3, and Sun. 10–3). Beware of pickpockets. For a real Swedish food market with such specialties as marinated salmon and reindeer try **Östermalms Saluhall** (⊠ at Hötorget), open Monday 10–6, Tuesday 9–6, and Saturday 9–3; from late June through August, the Saturday market is open 9–2. Another good bet is **Hötorgshallen** (⊠ at Hötorget), open August–April, Monday–Thursday 10–6, Friday 10–6:30, Saturday 10–4; May–July, weekdays 10–6, Saturday 10–1; it's under Filmstaden Sergel (☞ Film *in* Nightlife and the Arts, *above*).

Gift Ideas

Stockholm shops have the best in Swedish design and elegance. The choice and price of Swedish and international brand name items, particularly glass, porcelain, furs, jewelry, and leather goods, make a day's shopping a must (☞ Shopping *in* Sweden A to Z, *above*).

Glassware

Duka (⊠ Sveav. 24/26, ☎ 08/104530) specializes in crystal as well as porcelain. **Gustavsbergs Fabriksbod** (⊠ Odelbergs Väg 13, Gustavsberg, ☎ 08/57035655) just outside the city is a factory shop of quality. For the best buys try **Nordiska Kristall** (⊠ Kungsg. 9, ☎ 08/104372).

Handicrafts

A good center for all kinds of Swedish wood and metal handicrafts is **Svensk Hemslöjd** (⊠ Sveav. 44, ☎ 08/232115). **Svenskt Hantwerk** (⊠ Kungsg. 55, ☎ 08/214726) has Swedish folk costumes and handicraft souvenirs from different parts of Sweden. For elegant home furnishings and timeless fabrics, try **Svenskt Tenn** (⊠ Strandv. 5A, ☎ 08/6701600), best known for its selection of designer Josef Franck's furniture and fabrics.

Shopping Districts

Shop till you drop means hitting the stores along **Hamngatan** with a vengeance. The **Gamla Stan** area is best for antiques shops, bookshops, and art galleries. **Sturegallerian** (⊠ Stureg.) is an elegant covered shopping gallery on the site of the former public baths at Stureplan.

Side Trips

★ Skärgården

You could sail forever among the 24,000 islands of Stockholm's Skärgården (archipelago). But if you don't have a boat, then purchase the Båtluffarkortet (Inter-Skerries Card, ⊜ SKr 250) from early June to mid-August, which gives you 16 days' unlimited travel on Waxholmsbolaget (Waxholm Steamship Company) boats. Get the card at Excursion Shop at Sweden House or at the Waxholm Steamship Company terminal (☞ Getting Around by Boat *in* Stockholm Essentials, *below*).

Fjäderholmarna

☺ The group of four islands known as Fjäderholmarna (the Feather Islets) lies only 20 minutes by boat from the city center. They were formerly a restricted military zone but are now a haven of restaurants, cafés, a museum depicting life in the archipelago, an aquarium with many species of Baltic marine life, handicraft studios, shops, and a pirate-ship playground. Boats leave from Slussen, Strömkajen, and Nybroplan (April 29–September 17); contact the **Strömma Kanalbolaget** (Strömma Canal Company; ☞ Getting Around by Boat *in* Stockholm Essentials, *below*) or Fjäderholmarna information (☎ 08/7180100).

Mariefred

In Mariefred, on the southern side of Lake Mälaren about 64 km (40
★ mi) from Stockholm, **Gripsholm Slott** (Gripsholm Castle), with its drawbridge and four massive round towers, is one of Sweden's most romantic castles. Following the destruction of a castle from the 1380s, King Gustav Vasa built the present structure in 1577. It now houses the state portrait collection, some 3,400 paintings. ☎ *0159/10194.* ☉ *May–Aug., daily 10–4; Sept., Tues.–Sun. 10–4; Oct.–Apr., weekends noon–3.*

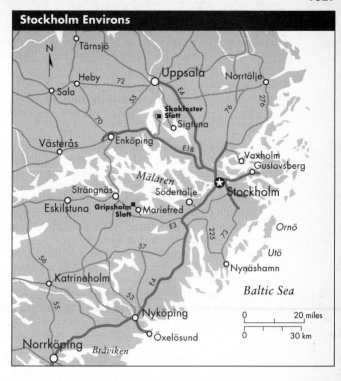

Stockholm Environs

An unforgettable boat journey on the recently restored vintage steamer **Mariefred,** the last coal-fired ship on Lake Mälaren, is the best way to get to Gripsholm, but you can also take the train. ✉ *Boat departs quay next to City Hall,* ☎ *08/6698850.* 🎫 *SKr 170 round-trip.* ☉ *Mid-May– late Aug., Tues.–Sun. 10 AM (returns 4:30).*

Skokloster

Built by the Swedish field marshal Carl Gustav Wrangel, **Skokloster Slott** (Skokloster Castle) contains many of his trophies from the Thirty Years' War. The palace, about 70 km (44 mi) from Stockholm in Skokloster, also displays one of the largest private collections of arms in the world, as well as some magnificent Gobelin tapestries. Next door to the palace is a **motor museum** housing Sweden's largest collection of vintage cars and motorcycles. ☎ *018/386077.* ☉ *May–Aug., daily 11– 4; Sept. and Oct., weekdays 1–2, Sat. and Sun. 1–4.*

Skokloster is easily reached by boat. The route follows the narrow inlets of Lake Mälaren along the "Royal Waterway." It stops at **Sigtuna,** an ancient trading center. You can get off the boat here to visit the town, which has medieval ruins and an 18th-century town hall. For boat information contact the **Strömma Kanalbolaget.** ✉ *Boats depart from Stadshusbron (City Hall Bridge,* ☎ *08/58714000).* 🎫 *SKr 165 round-trip.* ☉ *Early June–mid.-Aug., Tues.–Thurs. and weekends.*

Stockholm Essentials

Arriving and Departing

BY BUS

All major bus lines arrive at the **Cityterminalen** (✉ next to the train station). Bus tickets are also sold at the railroad reservations office.

BY CAR

One of the two main access routes from the west and south is the **E20** main highway from Göteborg. The other is the **E4** from Helsingborg, continuing as the main route to Sundsvall, the far north, and Finland. All routes to the CENTRUM (city center) are well marked.

BY PLANE

International flights arrive at **Arlanda Airport** (✉ 40 km/25 mi north of city). For information on arrival and departure times, call the individual airlines.

Between the Airport and Downtown. The airport is linked to Stockholm by a major highway. Buses depart for **Cityterminalen** from the international and domestic terminals every 10–15 minutes between 6:30 AM and 11 PM. The ride costs SKr 60 per person. A bus-taxi package is available from the bus driver at prices ranging from SKr 150 per person to SKr 220; additional passengers in a group pay only the bus portion of the fare. Ask the bus driver for details. For bus information call the SL, the **Stockholm Transit Authority** (☎ 08/6001000). A **taxi** directly from the airport will cost around SKr 435 (be sure to ask the driver if he offers a "fixed-price" airport-to-city rate before you get into the taxi). Look for Taxi Stockholm and Taxi Kurir cabs and ask the cab line attendant for help. Illegal taxis abound. The **SAS limousine service** operates a shared taxi service at SKr 263 per person to any point in greater Stockholm. Limousine rental is SKr 616. The *moms* (VAT; ☞ Shopping *in* Sweden A to Z, *above*) will be deducted if the limousine is booked ahead of time through a travel agent in connection with an international arrival.

BY TRAIN

Both long-distance and commuter trains arrive at Stockholm Central Station on Vasagatan, a main boulevard in the heart of the city. For train information and ticket reservations 6 AM–11 PM, call 020/757575 (recorded message, wait for assistance). There is a ticket and information office at the station where you can make reservations. Automatic ticket-vending machines are also available.

Getting Around

Maps and timetables for all city transportation networks are available from the **Stockholm Transit Authority** (SL) information desks (✉ Sergels Torg; Stockholm Central Station; Slussen in Gamla Stan; information ☎ 08/6001000).

Stockholmskortet (the Stockholm card) grants unlimited transportation on city subway, bus, and rail services, and free admission to 70 museums and several sightseeing trips. The card costs SKr 199 for 24 hours, SKr 398 for two days, and SKr 498 for three days. It is available at the tourist information centers at Sweden House, Kaknästornet (TV tower; ☞ Visitor Information, *below*), and at Hotellcentralen at the central train station (☞ Lodging *in* Sweden A to Z, *above*).

BY BOAT

Waxholmsbolaget (Waxholm Steamship Company) terminal (✉ Strömkajen, in front of Grand Hotel, ☎ 08/6795830). **Strömma Kanalbolaget** (Strömma Canal Company; ✉ boats depart from Stadshusbron/City Hall Bridge, ☎ 08/58714000).

BY BUS AND SUBWAY

The SL operates both the bus and subway systems. Tickets for the two networks are interchangeable. The subway system, known as T-banan (*T* stands for tunnel), is the easiest and fastest way to get around. Station entrances are marked with a blue T on a white background. Trains run frequently between 5 AM and 2 AM. The comprehensive bus network serves out-of-town points of interest, such as Waxholm, with its historic fortress, and Gustavsberg, with its porcelain factory. In greater Stockholm there are a number of night-bus services.

Bus and subway fares are based on zones, starting at SKr 14, good for travel within one zone, such as downtown, for one hour. You pay more if you travel in more than one zone. Single tickets are available at station ticket counters, but it is cheaper to buy the **SL Tourist Card,** which is valid on buses and the subway and also gives free admission to a number of sights and museums (though not as many as the Stockholmskortet). It can be purchased at Pressbyrån newsstands and SL information desks and costs SKr 60 for 24 hours or SKr 120 for 72 hours. Also available from the Pressbyrån newsstands are SKr 95 coupons, good for at least 10 bus or subway rides in the central zone.

BY TAXI
Typically, a trip of 10 km (6 mi) will cost SKr 97 between 9 AM and 4 PM on weekdays, SKr 107 on weekday nights, and SKr 114 on weekends. It can be difficult to hail a taxi on the street, so call ahead if possible. Call **Taxi Stockholm** (☏ 08/150000), **Taxikurir** (☏ 08/300000), or **Taxi 020** (☏ 020/939393).

BY TRAIN
SL runs commuter trains from Stockholm Central Station to a number of nearby locales, including Nynäshamn, a departure point for ferries to the island of Gotland. Trains also run from the Slussen station to the fashionable seaside resort of Saltsjöbaden.

Contacts and Resources
EMBASSIES
U.S. (✉ Strandv. 101, ☏ 08/7835300). **Canadian** (✉ Tegelbacken 4, ☏ 08/4533000). **U.K.** (✉ Skarpög. 6–8, ☏ 08/6719000). **Australian** (✉ Sergelstorg 12, ☏ 08/6132900).

EMERGENCIES
Police (☏ 08/4010000; 112, emergencies only). **Ambulance** (☏ 112). **Doctor** (Medical Care Information, ☏ 08/6541117). **Private clinic** (✉ City Akuten, ☏ 08/4122960). **Dentist** (☏ 08/6541117, 8 AM–9 PM; 08/6449200, 9 PM–8 AM). **24-hour Pharmacy** (C. W. Scheele, ☏ 08/4548130).

ENGLISH-LANGUAGE BOOKSTORES
Akademibokhandeln (✉ Mäster Samuelsg. 32, ☏ 08/6136100).

GUIDED TOURS
Boat. Take a boat trip through the **archipelago** with the Strömma Kanalbolaget (Strömma Canal Company) or the Waxholm Steamship Company (☞ Getting Around, *above*). Trips range from one to three hours each way. One-day excursions include Waxholm, Utö, Sandhamn, and Möja. Conventional sightseeing tours include a one-hour **city tour** run by Strömma Kanalbolaget and leaving from the Nybroplan quay every hour on the half hour between 10:30 and 5:30 in summer. Don't miss the boat trip to the 17th-century palace of **Drottningholm.** Trips depart every hour on the hour from 10 to 4 and at 6 PM during the summer from City Hall Bridge (Stadshusbron). Other trips go from Stadshusbron to the ancient towns of **Sigtuna and Vaxholm.** By changing boats you can continue to Uppsala to catch the train back to Stockholm. Information is available from the Strömma Kanalbolaget (☞ Getting Around, *above*) or the Stockholm Tourist Centre at Sweden House (☞ Visitor Information, *below*).

Orientation. More than 35 different tours—by foot, boat, bus, or a combination of these—are available throughout the summer. Some take only 30 minutes, others an entire day. A 90-minute coach tour, costing SKr 120, runs daily. Tickets are available from the Excursion Shop at Stockholm Tourist Centre (☞ Visitor Information, *below*).

Personal Guides. Guide Centralen (✉ Sweden House, Hamng. 27, Box 7542, 103 93, ☎ 08/7892496) at the Stockholm Information Service offers individual guides and group bookings.

Special Interest. Special-interest tours in the Stockholm area include spending a weekend at a cabin in the archipelago, renting a small fishing or sailing boat, visiting the Gustavsberg porcelain factory, and more. Call the Tourist Centre at Sweden House (☞ Visitor Information, *below*) for details.

TRAVEL AGENCY
American Express (✉ Birger Jarlsg. 1, ☎ 08/6797880, FAX 08/7969533).

VISITOR INFORMATION
Stockholm Tourist Centre (✉ Sweden House, Kungsträdgården, Hamng. 27, ☎ 08/7892490). **Stockholm Information Service** (✉ Sweden House, Excursion Shop, Box 7542, 103 93, ☎ 08/7892415). **Stockholm Central Station** (✉ Vasag., ☎ 020757575). **City Hall** (summer only; ✉ Hantverkarg. 1, ☎ 08/50829000). **Kaknästornet** (TV Tower; ✉ Ladugårdsgärdet, ☎ 08/7892435). **Fjäderholmarna** (☎ 08/7180100).

UPPSALA AND THE FOLKLORE DISTRICT

The "Folklore District" is essentially the provinces of Dalarna and Värmland. With its rural ambience, it's the best place to discover some of the country's most interesting traditions. Dalarna, which has its own special style of handicrafts, can be reached via the ancient city of Uppsala. Return to Stockholm through the Bergslagen region, the heart of the centuries-old Swedish iron industry.

★ **Uppsala**

Uppsala is well worth exploring. **Gamla Uppsala** (Old Uppsala) is dominated by three huge burial mounds dating from the 5th century. The first Swedish kings, Aun, Egil, and Adils, were all buried here. The church next to the burial mounds was the seat of Sweden's first archbishop, built on the site of a former pagan temple. At the adjacent Odinsborg restaurant you can sample local mead brewed from a 14th-century recipe. Check all prices and times listed below with the local tourist office, as they are subject to change.

The impressive **Domkyrka** (cathedral), with its twin towers that dominate the skyline, has been the seat of the archbishop of the Swedish church for 700 years. Its present appearance owes much to major restoration work completed during the late 19th century. At the **Cathedral Museum** in the north tower, you can see one of Europe's finest collections of ecclesiastical textiles. ✉ *Domkyrkoplan,* ☎ *018/187166.* ☉ *Cathedral: daily 8–6; museum: May–Aug., daily 9–4:30; Sept.–Apr., Sun. 12:30–3.*

Strategically positioned atop a hill, the august **Uppsala Slott** (Uppsala Castle) was built during the 1540s by King Gustav Vasa. Having broken his ties with the Vatican, the king was eager to show who was actually running the country; he even arranged to have the cannons aimed directly at the archbishop's palace. ✉ *Borggården,* ☎ *018/544810.* ☉ *Mid-Apr.–mid-June, daily 11–3; mid-June–mid-Aug., daily 10–5.*

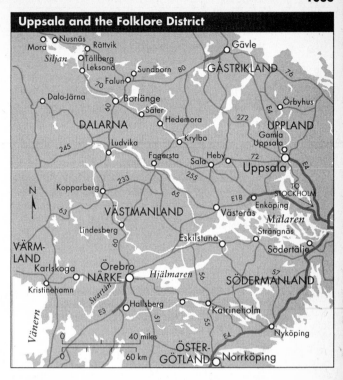

Uppsala and the Folklore District

Uppsala Universitetet (Uppsala University) is Scandinavia's oldest, founded in 1477. Beneath the cupola of the university's venerable **Gustavianum**, near the cathedral, is the anatomical theater, where public dissections of executed convicts were a popular 17th-century tourist attraction. ⊠ *Akademig. 3,* ☎ *018/4710000.* ☉ *Mid-May–mid-Sept., daily 11–4.*

One of the most famous people to emerge from Uppsala was Carl von Linné, known as Linnaeus. A professor of botany during the 1740s, he developed the system of plant and animal classification still used today. Visit the **gardens** he designed, as well as his former residence, **Linni Trädgården,** now a museum. ⊠ *Svartbäcksg. 27,* ☎ *018/109490 garden; 018/136540 museum.* ☉ *Garden: May–Aug., daily 9–9; Sept., daily 9–7; museum: June–Aug., Tues.–Sun. noon–4; May and Sept., weekends noon–4.*

$$$ ✕ **Domtrappkällaren.** One of the city's most popular restaurants,
★ Domtrappkällaren is in a 14th-century cellar near the cathedral. The menu includes both French and Swedish fare. ⊠ *St. Eriksgr. 15,* ☎ *018/ 130955,* 𝙵𝙰𝚇 *018/101740. Reservations essential. AE, DC, MC, V. Closed Sun.*

$$$$ ⊡ **Gillet.** Operated by the Sweden Hotels group, Uppsala's largest hotel was opened in 1971 and renovated most recently in 1996. Its lobby is decorated with marble. ⊠ *Dragarbrunnsg. 23, 751 42,* ☎ *018/155360,* 𝙵𝙰𝚇 *018/153380. 160 rooms. 2 restaurants, pool. AE, DC, MC, V.*

$$ ⊡ **Grand Hotel Hörnan.** An old-world hotel opened in 1906, the Grand Hotel Hörnan is in the city center near the train station, with a view of the castle and the cathedral. ⊠ *Bangårdsg. 1, 753 20,* ☎ *018/ 139380,* 𝙵𝙰𝚇 *018/120311. 37 rooms. AE, DC, MC, V. Closed July.*

Säter

Säter, one of the best-preserved wooden villages in Sweden, sits north-west of Uppsala on the way to Dalarna in farming country.

Falun

Probably the best place to stay in Dalarna is Falun, the province's cap-ital. Here you can visit the **Falu Koppargruva** (Great Pit), a hole cre-ated in 1687 when an abandoned copper mine collapsed. There are actually still working mines in the area and guided tours (requiring good shoes) into some of the old shafts. ⊠ *Ask at tourist board on Stora Torget (main square) for directions.* ⊙ *May–Aug., daily 10–4:30; Sept.–mid-Nov. and Mar.–Apr., weekends 12:30–4:30.*

The **Storamuseum** tells the story of the local mining industry. ☎ *023/ 15825 or 023/711475.* ⊙ *May–Aug., daily 10–4:30; Sept.–Apr., daily 12:30–4:30.*

$$$ 🏨 **Hotel Win.** In the town center, this cozy hotel built in traditional Dalarna style is filled with antique furnishings. ⊠ *Bergskolegr. 7, 791 26,* ☎ *023/63600,* FAX *023/22524. 88 rooms. Restaurant. AE, DC, MC, V.*

$$ 🏨 **Hotel Falun.** This cozy hotel built in the 1950s is in the center of town. The front desk closes at 9 PM. ⊠ *Centrumhuset, Trotzg. 16, 791 71,* ☎ *023/29180,* FAX *023/13006. 25 rooms, 16 with shower. AE, DC, MC, V.*

★ Sundborn

Just outside Falun, at Sundborn, is the former home of Swedish artist Carl Larsson, **Carl Larsson Gården.** Here, in an idyllic lakeside setting, you can see a selection of his paintings, which owe much to local folk-art traditions. His great-grandchildren still use the house on occasion. ⊠ *Carl Larssonsv. 12,* ☎ *023/60053 in summer, 023/60069 in win-ter.* ⊙ *May–Sept., daily 10–5; Oct.–Apr., Tues. at 11; tours only, in groups of 15 every 10 mins (may be a wait in summer).*

Tällberg

The real center of Dalarna folklore is the area around Lake Siljan, by far the largest of the 6,000 lakes in the province. The attractive lake-side village of Tällberg is a good starting point for a tour.

$$ 🏨 **Åkerblads.** Near the shores of Lake Siljan, the hotel offers a gen-★ uine experience of rural Sweden. In a typical Dalarna farmstead, parts of which date from the 16th century, it is run by the 19th generation of the Åkerblad family and has been a hotel since 1910. ⊠ *Sjögatu, 793 70,* ☎ *0247/50800,* FAX *0247/50652. 58 rooms with bath, 6 rooms with shared WC/shower. Restaurant. AE, DC, MC, V.*

Mora

Mora is the home of the artist Anders Zorn (1860–1920), famous for his distinctive and tasteful paintings of robust, naked women in rural surroundings. His house and **Zorn Museet** (the Zorn Museum), exhibiting his paintings, are open to the public. ⊠ *Vasag. 36,* ☎ *0250/16560.* ⊙ *House: guided tours only, call for information and times; museum: May 15–Sept. 15, Mon.–Sat. 9–5, Sun. 11–5; Sept. 16–May 14, Mon.–Sat. noon–5, Sun. 1–5.*

$$ 🏨 **Siljan.** Named for the nearby lake, the Siljan is a small but up-to-★ date hotel. ⊠ *Morag. 6, 792 01,* ☎ *0250/13000,* FAX *0250/13098. 43 rooms with shower, 2 with WC only. Restaurant. AE, DC, MC, V.*

Rättvik

At midsummer in Rättvik, hundreds of people wearing traditional costumes arrive in longboats to attend midsummer church services—a time-honored tradition. Twelve-man longboat races are held in summer. The *Gustav Vasa* vintage steamboat has trips with nightly dancing and prawn dinners.

Nusnäs

Nusnäs is the home of the brightly colored Dalarna handmade wooden horses, known as *Dalahästar*. Red or blue and painted with traditional floral patterns, the only real Dala horses are made here. One of the biggest workshops is Nils Olsson (⊠ Edåkersv. 17, ☎ 0250/37200).

Ludvika

This town is an important center of the old Bergslagen mining region, which stretches from the forests of Värmland in the west to the coastal gorges in the east. Ludvika has a notable open-air mining museum, the **Gammelgården**. ⊠ *Nilsnilsg. 7,* ☎ *0240/10019.* ⊙ *June 1–Sept. 3, daily 11–6.*

The **Lokmuseet** (Railway Engine Museum) showcases three steam turbine–driven engines once used to pull trains filled with iron ore, the only ones of their kind in the world. ⊠ *Signposted,* ☎ *0240/20493.* ⊙ *June 1–Sept. 3, daily 10–6.*

The poet Dan Andersson lived in **Luosastugan** (Luosa Cottage) in the early part of the century. Music and poetry festivals are held in Andersson's memory in nearby towns. ⊠ *Signposted,* ☎ *0240/86050 (tourist office).* ⊙ *Mid-May–Aug., daily 11–5.*

$$$ 🏨 **Grand.** A modern-style hotel, the Grand enjoys a central location. ⊠ *Eriksg. 6, 771 31,* ☎ *0240/18220,* 📠 *0240/611018. 102 rooms. Restaurant. AE, DC, MC, V.*

$ 🏨 **Rex.** Built in 1960, the Rex is a basic modern hotel near the city center. ⊠ *Engelbrektsg. 9, 771 30,* ☎ *0240/13690. 28 rooms, 15 with shower. AE, DC, MC, V. Closed 1 wk in July.*

Örebro

Örebro nestles on the western edge of Lake Hjälmaren. It received its charter during the 13th century, becoming an important trading center for the farmers and miners of the Bergslagen region. Rising from a small island in the Svartån (Black River), right in the center of town, is the imposing **Örebro slott** (Örebro castle), parts of which date from the 13th century. The castle is now the residence of the regional governor and has an excellent restaurant, Slottskrogen. ⊠ *Kanslig.,* ☎ *019/ 212121 (Örebro Tourist Information).* ⊙ *Call ahead for hrs.*

In the **Wadköping** district, just east of the castle, a number of old houses and crafts workshops have been painstakingly preserved. At the north end of town is **Svampen** (the Mushroom), a 193-ft-tall water tower. From the top (reached by elevator), you can enjoy a magnificent view of the surrounding countryside. ⊙ *Apr. 30–Sept. 4, daily 10–8.*

$$ ✕ **Cajsa Warg.** This excellent restaurant is named after the Swedish woman who reportedly wrote one of the earliest Swedish cookbooks about 250 years ago. Some of her recipes can be sampled here. ⊠ *Kanslig.,* ☎ *019/168020. AE, DC, MC, V.*

$$$ 🏨 **Scandic Grand.** In the heart of town, the Grand is Örebro's largest hotel. Built in 1985, it offers all the modern comforts. ⊠ *Fabriksg. 23, 70008,* ☎ *019/150200,* 📠 *019/185814. 219 rooms. 2 restaurants. AE, DC, MC, V.*

$$$ 🏨 **Stora Hotellet.** Across the street from the castle on the Svartån, this Best Western hotel is one of the oldest in Sweden, dating from 1858. It has a cozy 13th-century cellar restaurant, the Slottskällaren, and an English pub, the Bishop's Arms. ⊠ *Drottningg. 1, 701 45,* ☎ *019/ 124360,* 📠 *019/6117890. 103 rooms. Restaurant. AE, DC, MC, V.*

Uppsala and the Folklore District Essentials

Getting Around

The train from Stockholm to Uppsala takes only 50 minutes, and service is fairly frequent. For information about bus travel, call Dalatrafik (☎ 020/232425). A car will give you the flexibility to explore some of the attractions not so easily accessible by public transportation; the drive to Uppsala, via the E4, is about 71 km (44 mi).

Guided Tours

Uppsala is compact enough to explore on foot, and guided sightseeing tours are available; call the Guide Service (Uppsala Tourist Information office, ☎ 018/274800). For guided tours of the district, contact the Falun tourist office (☞ *below*), which has both package tours and personalized services.

Visitor Information

Falun (✉ Stora Torget, ☎ 023/83637). **Ludvika** (✉ Fredsg. 10, ☎ 0240/86050). **Mora** (✉ Ångbåtskajen, ☎ 0250/26550). **Örebro** (✉ Slottet, ☎ 019/212121). **Rättvik** (✉ Torget, ☎ 0248/70200). **Uppsala** (✉ Fyris Torg 8, ☎ 018/274800).

THE WEST COAST AND THE GLASS COUNTRY

Göteborg (Gothenburg) is an important Swedish port on the North Sea. North and south of the city lie scenic stretches of the country's western coast. Inland are the lakes and forests of the Glass Country, and beyond stands the medieval fortress town of Kalmar, on the east coast.

Göteborg

This attractive harbor city is Sweden's second largest, well worth a stop. A quayside jungle of cranes and warehouses attests to the city's industrial life, yet within a 10-minute walk of the waterfront is an elegant modern city of broad avenues, green parks, and gardens. As in Stockholm, the major attractions are gathered in an accessible central area. There is an excellent streetcar network and, in summer, sightseeing tours on a vintage open-air streetcar.

Once known as "Little London" because British merchants invested heavily in developing Göteborg during the 19th century, it could have more accurately been called "Little Amsterdam," for the city was in fact laid out during the 17th century by Dutch architects, who gave it its extensive network of straight streets divided by canals. Only one major canal survives; you can explore it by sightseeing boat. Gothenburgians fondly refer to these short and squat (so that they can pass under the city's 20 low bridges) boats as *paddan* (toads). Passengers embark for the one-hour boat tour at the **Paddan terminal.** ✉ *Kungsportsplatsen.* ⊙ *Departures: late Apr.–late June and mid-Aug.–early Sept., daily 10–5; late June–mid-Aug., daily 10–9; early Sept.–Oct. 1, daily noon–3. Closed Oct.–late Apr.*

★ Running through the heart of Göteborg is **Kungsportsavenyn,** commonly called Avenyn (the Avenue). This broad, tree-lined boulevard is lined with many brand-name stores, boutiques, and eateries, making for a very Continental atmosphere, especially in summer. Avenyn ends at **Götaplatsen,** where there is a **grand theater,** a **concert hall,** an **art museum,** and a **library** that has a wide selection of English-language newspapers.

☾ Just a stone's throw away from Götaplatsen is the **Liseberg amusement park** (✉ Öregrytev. 5).

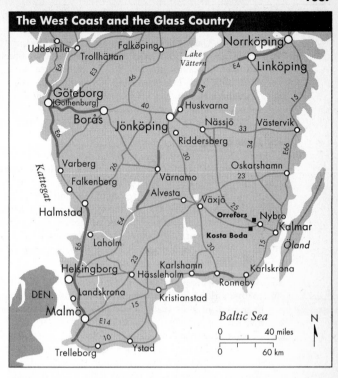

The West Coast and the Glass Country

Trädgårdsföreningen (The Garden Association) maintains an attractive park with a magnificent Palm House, built in 1878 and recently restored, and a butterfly house containing 40 different species. ⊠ *Just off Kungsportsavenyn,* ☎ *031/611911 Butterfly House.* ☉ *Park: daily 7–8; Palm House: daily 10–4; Butterfly House: Oct.–Mar., Tues.–Sun. 10–3; Apr., Tues.–Sun. 10–4; May and Sept., daily 10–4; June–Aug., daily 10–5.*

For shopping, try **Nordstan** (⊠ entrances on Köpmansg., Nils Ericsonsg., Kanaltorgsg., and Östra Hamng.), a covered complex of shops near the train station.

The **Maritima Centrum** (Maritime Center), at the harbor near the Nordstan shopping complex, provides a chance to explore a number of historic vessels, among them a destroyer, a lightship, a trawler, and several tugboats. ⊠ *Packhuskajen 8,* ☎ *031/105950.* ☉ *Mar.–Apr. and Sept.–Nov., daily 10–4; May–June, daily 10–6; July, daily 10–9; Aug., daily 10–6.*

$$$$ ✕ **Sjömagasinet.** In a renovated 200-year-old shipping warehouse,
★ this waterfront restaurant has a view of the harbor and the suspension bridge; in summer an outdoor terrace provides even better views. The regular menu features seafood. ⊠ *Klippanskulturreservat,* ☎ *031/ 246510,* FAX *031/245539. Reservations essential. AE, DC, MC, V.*

$$$ ✕ **Räkan.** The informal Räkan makes the most of an unusual gimmick.
★ The tables are arranged around a long tank, and if you order shrimp, the house specialty, they arrive at your table in radio-controlled boats you navigate yourself. ⊠ *Lorensbergsg. 16,* ☎ *031/169839,* FAX *031/ 186418. Reservations essential. AE, DC, MC, V. No lunch weekends.*

$$$$ 🏨 **Sheraton Hotel and Towers.** Opened in 1986, this is Göteborg's most
★ modern and spectacular international-style hotel. It has an atrium lobby with a central fountain. The international-style restaurant changes its menu from French to Asian to Italian, for example, each month. ⊠

Södra Hamng. 59–65, 401 24, ☎ *031/806000,* FAX *031/159888. 344 rooms. Restaurant. AE, DC, MC, V.*

$$$ ⊞ **Eggers.** Dating from 1859 (renovated in 1997), the Best Western
★ Eggers has more old-world character than other hotels in the city. Most rooms are furnished with antiques. ⊠ *Drottningtorget, 401 25,* ☎ *031/806070,* FAX *031/154243. 67 rooms. AE, DC, MC, V.*

$$$ ⊞ **Liseberg Heden.** Not far from the Liseberg amusement park, this is a modern family hotel. ⊠ *Sten Stureg., 411 38,* ☎ *031/7506900,* FAX *031/7506930. 159 rooms. Restaurant. AE, DC, MC, V.*

Jönköping

Jönköping is an attractive town on the southern shore of Lake Vättern, Sweden's second-largest lake. The town is distinguished not only by its age—it celebrated the 700th anniversary of its founding in 1984—but also as the birthplace of the match-manufacturing industry, established here during the 19th century. **Tändsticksmuseet** (the Match Museum), built on the site of the first factory, has exhibits on the development and manufacture of matches. ⊠ *Tändsticksgr. 7,* ☎ *036/105543.* ☉ *June–Aug., weekdays 10–5, weekends 10–3; Sept.–May, Tues.–Thurs. noon–4, weekends 11–3.*

$$ ✕ **Mäster Gudmunds Källare.** This particularly inviting restaurant is
★ cozily nestled beneath the vaults of a 16th-century-style cellar and is only two minutes from the train station. The cuisine is typically Swedish. ⊠ *Kapellg. 2,* ☎ *036/100640. AE, DC, MC, V.*

$$$ ⊞ **John Bauer Hotel.** This modern Best Western, named for a local artist famous for his fairy-tale depictions of trolls and mystical landscapes, lies close to the center of town and overlooks Munksjön lake. ⊠ *Södra Strandg. 15, 550 02,* ☎ *036/349000,* FAX *036/349050. 100 rooms. Restaurant. AE, DC, MC, V.*

Växjö

The nub of Sweden's Glass Country is Växjö, the main town in Kronoberg County. On the second Sunday in August, Växjö celebrates "Minnesota Day." Swedes and Swedish-Americans come together to commemorate their common heritage with American-style square dancing and other festivities. Some 10,000 Americans visit Växjö each year, drawn here by a desire to see where their ancestors emigrated from during the 19th century. The **Utvandrareshus** (Emigrants' House, ⊠ Vilhelm Mosbergsg. 4, ☎ 0470/20120), in the town center, tells the story of the migration period, when close to a million Swedes—a fourth of the entire population—set sail for the promised land across the sea. The museum has exhibits about the rigors of their journey, and people of Swedish descent can trace their ancestry in an archive and research center.

★ Manufacture of Swedish **glass** dates back to the middle of the 16th century, when Venetian glassblowers were first invited to the Swedish court. About 200 years passed before glassmaking became a major Swedish industry. Because the dense forests between Växjö and Kalmar offered an unlimited supply of wood for firing furnaces, the glass industry was centered here. All the major Swedish glass companies, including **Orrefors** (⊠ follow signposts, ☎ 0481/34195 or 0481/34000 for tours), which celebrated its 100th anniversary in 1998, and **Kosta Boda** (⊠ follow signposts, ☎ 0481/24030 or 0481/34500 for tours), still operate in this area, and their plants are open to the public; their factory shops sometimes give huge discounts. As there is no regular local bus service, you'll need a car to get around.

$$$ ⊞ **Statt.** A conveniently located traditional hotel, this Best Western attracts tour groups. The building dates from 1853; the rooms themselves are modern but classic and were completely renovated in 1996. The hotel

has a cozy Irish pub and two restaurants. ⊠ *Kungsg. 6, 352 33,* ☎ *0470/ 13400,* 𝔽𝔸𝕏 *0470/44837. 124 rooms. 2 restaurants. AE, DC, MC, V.*

$ 🏨 **Esplanad.** This small family hotel in the center of town offers the basic amenities. ⊠ *Norra Esplanaden 21A, 352 31,* ☎ *0470/22580,* 𝔽𝔸𝕏 *0470/26226. 27 rooms, most with shower. MC, V.*

Kalmar

★ In this bustling coastal town the imposing 12th-century **Kalmar Slott** (Kalmar Castle) stands as a reminder of the time when Kalmar was the "lock and key" of Sweden. Situated on the eastern coast, it was often attacked by Baltic raiders. Most of the present-day castle stems from the days of King Gustav Vasa, who rebuilt the fortress during the 16th century. ⊠ *Slottsv.,* ☎ *0480/56450.* ☉ *mid-June–mid-Aug., Mon.–Sat. 10–6, Sun. 12–6; Apr.–mid-June and mid-Aug.–Oct., weekdays 10–4, weekends 12–4; Nov.–Mar., Sun. 1–3.*

$$$$ 🏨 **Slottshotellet.** Occupying a gracious old house on a quiet street, Slottshotellet faces a waterfront park and is a few minutes' walk from both the train station and Kalmar Castle. Inside, modern facilities are wrapped in a 19th-century atmosphere. Restaurant service is offered on the terrace in summer. ⊠ *Slottsv. 7, 392 33,* ☎ *0480/88260,* 𝔽𝔸𝕏 *0480/88266. 36 rooms. Restaurant. AE, DC, MC, V.*

$$$ 🏨 **Stadshotellet.** This Best Western in the town center is a large hotel done in traditional English style with smartly decorated rooms. The main building dates from 1907. ⊠ *Stortorget 14, 392 32,* ☎ *0480/ 15180,* 𝔽𝔸𝕏 *0480/15847. 139 rooms. Restaurant. AE, DC, MC, V.*

The West Coast and the Glass Country Essentials

Getting Around

The best and cheapest way to get around Göteborg is with the **Göteborg Card.** It provides free travel on all public transportation, free parking, and free admission to the Liseberg amusement park and all city museums. The card costs SKr 75 for 24 hours.

BY CAR

By car, Göteborg is 478 km (297 mi) west of Stockholm along the E20.

BY PLANE

SAS operates hourly flights to Göteborg from Stockholm's Arlanda Airport between 7 AM and 10 PM on weekdays, less frequently on weekends. The flight takes 55 minutes.

BY TRAIN

Regular train services depart from Stockholm's Central Station for Göteborg every hour. Normal travel time is about 4½ hours. Daily high-speed **X2000** trains also operate between the two cities. These shave a bit more than an hour off the normal journey time, but cost more. Seat reservations are compulsory on all trains to Göteborg.

Guided Tours

Summer sightseeing tours around Göteborg usually begin at the city tourist office on Kungsportsplatsen 2 (reserve tickets at the office in advance). Tour boats run frequently in summer; a central reservations service (☎ 031/609660) will book you with either Paddans Sightseeing or Börjessons Sightseeing.

Visitor Information

Göteborg (⊠ Kungsportsplatsen 2, ☎ 031/612500). **Kalmar** (⊠ Larmg. 6, ☎ 0480/15350). **Växjö** (⊠ Kungsg. 11, ☎ 0470/41410).

30 SWITZERLAND

ZÜRICH, GENEVA, LUZERN, LUGANO, BERN, ZERMATT

The Swiss keep coziness under strict control: An electric eye beams open a sliding glass door into a room of carved wood, copper, and old-fashioned rafters. That is the paradox of the Swiss, whose primary impulses pitch high-tech urban efficiency against rustic Alpine comfort.

Alcohol here is measured with scientific precision into glasses marked for 1 or 2 centiliters (⅓ or ⅔ ounces), and the local wines come in graduated carafes reminiscent of laboratory beakers. And as for passion—well, the "double" beds have separate mattresses and sheets tucked firmly down the middle. Politically isolated, culturally self-contained, Switzerland remains economically aloof . . . even Europhobic. As their neighbors pull their wagons in a circle, sweeping away borders to present a unified front to the world, the Swiss continue to choose their apples from bins marked *Inland* (domestic), leaving the *Ausland,* or imported, varieties to humbly rot. Yet Switzerland is many different countries. Not far from the hum of commerce in the streets of Zürich you can listen to the tinkle of cowbells on the slopes of the Klewenalp. While fur-wrapped and bejeweled socialites shop in Geneva, the women of Appenzell, across the country, stand beside their husbands on the Landsgemeinde-Platz, raising their hands to vote—a right they won only in 1990.

Switzerland combines most of the attractions of its larger European neighbors—Alpine grandeur, urban sophistication, ancient villages, exhilarating ski slopes, and all-around artistic excellence. It's the heartland of the Reformation, the homeland of William Tell; its cities are full of historic landmarks, its countryside strewn with castles. The varied cuisine reflects French, Italian, and German influences.

All these assets have made Switzerland a major tourist destination, and the Swiss are delighted to pave the way. A welcoming if reserved people, many of them are well versed in English. Their hotels and inns are famous for cleanliness and efficiency, and the notoriously high prices do mirror the quality you'll receive in return.

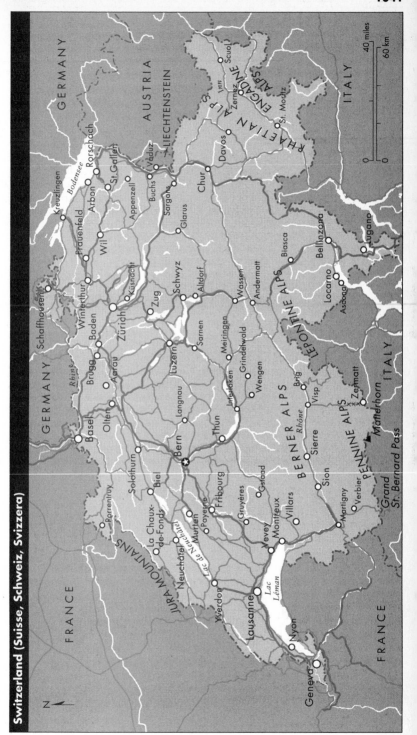

Switzerland (Suisse, Schweiz, Svizzera)

SWITZERLAND A TO Z

Customs
For details on imports and duty-free limits, *see* Customs & Duties *in* Chapter 1.

Dining
Because the Swiss are so good at preparing everyone else's dishes, it is sometimes said that they have none of their own, but there definitely is a distinct and characteristic Swiss cuisine. Switzerland produces great cheeses—Gruyère, Emmentaler, Appenzeller, and Vacherin—that form the basis of many dishes. Raclette is cheese melted over a fire and served with potatoes and pickles. Fondue is either a bubbling pot of melted cheeses flavored with garlic and kirsch, into which you dip chunks of bread, or a pot of boiling broth into which you dip various meats. *Rösti* is shredded potato sauteed until golden brown. Other Swiss specialties are *geschnetzeltes Kalbfleisch* (veal bits in cream sauce with mushrooms), Italian-style polenta in the Ticino, and fine game in autumn. A wide variety of Swiss sausages makes for filling, inexpensive meals, and in every region the breads are varied and superb.

Dining options range from luxury establishments to modest cafés, *stübli* (tavern-cafés), and restaurants specializing in local cuisine. In resorts especially, most restaurants are associated with hotels, and the half-pension plan includes a simple, hot meal in the room rate.

MEALTIMES
At home, the main Swiss meal of the day is lunch, followed by a light snack in the evening. Restaurants are open at midday and at night; often limited menus are offered all day. Watch for *Tagesteller* or *plats du jour* (prix-fixe lunch platters or menus), enabling you to a taste of the best restaurants without paying high à la carte rates.

RATINGS
Prices are per person, including tip and taxes, but not wine and coffee.

CATEGORY	ZÜRICH/GENEVA	OTHER AREAS
$$$$	over 90 SF	over 70 SF
$$$	50 SF–90 SF	40 SF–70 SF
$$	30 SF–50 SF	20 SF–40 SF
$	under 30 SF	under 20 SF

WHAT TO WEAR
Jacket and tie are suggested for restaurants in the $$$$ and $$$ categories (except in more relaxed ski resorts); casual dress is acceptable elsewhere.

Language
French is spoken in the southwest, around Lake Geneva, and in the cantons of Fribourg, Neuchâtel, Jura, Vaud, and the western portion of Valais; Italian is spoken in the Ticino; and German is spoken everywhere else—in more than 70% of the country, in fact. (Keep in mind that the Swiss versions of these languages can sound very different from those spoken in France, Italy, and Germany.) The Romance language called Romansh has regained a firm foothold throughout the Upper and Lower Engadine regions of the canton Graubünden, where it takes the form of five different dialects. English, however, is spoken widely. Many signs are in English as well as in the regional language, and all hotels, restaurants, tourist offices, train stations, banks, and shops have at least a few English-speaking employees.

Lodging

Switzerland's accommodations range from the most luxurious hotels to more practical rooms in private homes. Pick up the free "Schweizer Hotelführer" (Swiss Hotel Guide) from Switzerland Tourism (☞ Visitor Information *in* Chapter 1). The guide lists all members of the Swiss Hotel Association (SHA).

Most hotel rooms have private bath and shower; those that don't, noted below, are usually considerably cheaper. Remember that the no-nonsense Swiss sleep in separate beds or, at best, a double with separate bedding. For a standard double bed, request a "French bed" or a *lit matrimoniale*. Service charges and taxes are included in the price quoted. Breakfast is usually included. In resorts especially, half pension (choice of a noon or evening meal) may be included in the room price. If you choose to eat à la carte or elsewhere, the management, if notified in advance, will usually reduce your price.

CHALETS

Off-season, per-day prices for a furnished chalet for four are around 50 SF per person; in peak season, prices double. You may save money if you write directly to the village or resort you wish to rent in. Pick up an illustrated brochure from the **Touring Club Swiss** (⊠ Ch. de Blandonnet 4, C.P. 820, CH-1214 Vernier, ☎ 022/4172727, FAX 022/4172020). You can also get a brochure offering apartment rentals with hotel services at **Utoring AG** (⊠ Buckhauserstr. 26, CH-8048 Zürich, ☎ 01/4972763, FAX 01/4972721). In the United States write to **Interhome** (⊠ 36 Carlos Dr., Fairfield, NJ 07006). In Britain, contact **Interhome** (⊠ 383 Richmond Rd., Twickenham, Middlesex TW1 2EF).

HOTELS

The Swiss Hotel Association grades from one to five stars. Always confirm the price before you register, and check the posted price in your room. Often, rates will be quoted on a per-person basis; single rooms are about two-thirds the price of doubles, but this can vary considerably. Romantik Hotels and Restaurants and Relais & Châteaux have premises in either historic houses or houses with some special character. First-class Relais du Silence hotels are usually isolated in a peaceful setting. The Check-In E and G (*einfach und gemütlich*, or "Simple and Cozy") Hotels are dependable small hotels, boardinghouses, and mountain lodges.

RATINGS

Prices are for two people in a double room with bath or shower, including taxes, service charges, and breakfast.

CATEGORY	ZÜRICH/GENEVA	OTHER AREAS
$$$$	over 450 SF	over 300 SF
$$$	250 SF–450 SF	200 SF–300 SF
$$	120 SF–250 SF	120 SF–200 SF
$	under 120 SF	under 120 SF

Mail

POSTAL RATES

Mail rates are divided into first class "A" (air mail) and second class "B" (surface). Letters and postcards to the United States up to 20 grams cost 1.80 SF first class, 0.90 SF second class; to the United Kingdom, 1 SF first class, 0.80 SF second class.

RECEIVING MAIL

If you're uncertain where you'll be staying, you can have your mail, marked "poste restante" or "postlagernd," sent to any post office in Switzerland. The sender's name and address must be on the back, and you'll need identification to collect it. You can also have your mail sent to American Express. This service is free to those holding American Express cards or traveler's checks; others are charged a small fee.

Money Matters

Most major credit cards are generally, though not universally, accepted at hotels, restaurants, and shops. Traveler's checks are almost never accepted outside banks.

COSTS

Switzerland's high standard of living is reflected in its prices. You'll pay more for luxury here than in almost any other European country. Though annual inflation has been less than 2% for years, and the dollar has regained its strength against the SF, Switzerland's exorbitant cost of living makes travel noticeably expensive. You'll find plenty of reasonably priced digs and eats, however, if you look for them.

Zürich and Geneva are Switzerland's priciest cities, followed by Basel, Bern, and Lugano. Price tags at resorts—especially the better-known Alpine ski centers—rival those in the cities. Off the beaten track and in the northeast prices drop considerably.

CURRENCY

The unit of currency is the Swiss franc (SF), divided into 100 centimes (in Suisse Romande) or rappen (in German Switzerland). There are coins of 5, 10, 20, and 50 rappen/centimes and of 1, 2, and 5 francs. Bills come in denominations of 10, 20, 50, 100, 200, and 1,000 francs. At press time (summer 1999), the Swiss franc stood at 1.57 SF to the U.S. dollar, 1.06 SF to the Canadian dollar, 1.03 SF to the Australian dollar, 0.82 SF to the New Zealand dollar, and 2.44 SF to the pound sterling.

SAMPLE PRICES

Cup of coffee, 3 SF; bottle of beer, 3.50 SF; soft drink, 3.50 SF; sausage and Rösti, 16 SF; 1⅓-km (1-mi) taxi ride, 12 SF (more in Geneva, Lugano, or Zürich).

TIPPING

Although restaurants include service charges of 15% along with the taxes in bills, a small tip is still expected: 1 SF or 2 SF per person for a modest meal, 5 SF for a first-class meal, and 10 SF at an exclusive gastronomic mecca in the $$$$ range. When possible, tip in cash. Elsewhere, give bathroom attendants 1 SF and hotel maids 2 SF. Theater and opera-house ushers get 2 SF. Hotel porters and doormen should get about 2 SF per bag in an upscale hotel; 1 SF elsewhere. Airport porters receive 5 SF per bag.

National Holidays

January 1–2; April 21 (Good Friday); April 23–24 (Easter Sunday and Monday); June 2 (Ascension); June 11–12 (Whitsunday/Pentecost); August 1 (National Day); December 25–26. May 1 (Labor Day) is celebrated in French-speaking areas.

Opening and Closing Times

Banks are open weekdays 8:30–4:30 or 5 but are often closed at lunch. **Museum** times vary considerably, though many close on Monday. Check locally. **Shops** are generally open 8–noon and 1:30–6:30. Some close Monday morning and at 5 on Saturday. In cities, many large stores do not close for lunch. There is a trend toward late shop hours, usually on Thursday or Friday evening.

Shopping

SALES-TAX REFUNDS

A 7.5% value-added tax (VAT) is included in the price of all goods. Nonresidents spending at least 550 SF at one time at a particular store may get a VAT refund. To obtain a refund, pay by credit card; at the time of purchase, the store clerk should fill out and give you a red form and keep a record of your credit card number. When leaving Switzerland, you must hand deliver the red form to a customs officer—at the customs office at the airport, or, if leaving by car or train, at the border. Customs will process the form and return it to the store, which will refund the tax by crediting your card.

Telephoning

COUNTRY CODE

The country code for Switzerland and Liechtenstein is 41. When dialing Switzerland from outside the country, drop the initial zero from the area code.

INTERNATIONAL CALLS

To dial international numbers directly from Switzerland, dial 00 before the country's code. If a number cannot be reached directly, dial ☎ 1141 for a connection. Dial ☎ 1159 for international numbers and information. Calls from booths in train stations and post offices are far cheaper than those made from hotels. A phone card, available in 5 SF, 10 SF, and 20 SF units at the post office or train station, allows you to call from any adapted public phone. Note that fewer and fewer public phones accept coins. International access codes for the major telephone companies will put you directly in touch with an operator who will place your call: for **AT&T,** dial ☎ 155/0011; for **MCI,** dial ☎ 155/0222; for **Sprint,** dial ☎ 155/9777. International telephone rates are generally lower between 3 PM and 7 PM, 8 AM and 10 AM, on weekends, and on holidays. Calls to the United States and the United Kingdom cost 0.75 SF per minute.

LOCAL CALLS

There is direct dialing to every location in Switzerland. For local codes, consult the pink pages of the telephone book; for international country and city codes, consult the phone book's green pages.

Transportation

BY BICYCLE

Bikes can be rented at all train stations and returned to any station (though there's a service charge of 6 SF per bike for returning the bike to a different station). Rates for standard bikes are 20 SF per half day, 26 SF per day, and 100 SF per week. Mountain bikes are 25 SF per half day, 32 SF per day, or 128 SF per week. Groups get reductions according to the number of bikes. Individuals must make a reservation by 6 PM the day before they plan to use the bike, groups a week in advance. There is a daily charge of 15 SF to transport a bicycle on a train.

BY BOAT

Drifting across a Swiss lake and stopping off here and there at picturesque villages makes for a relaxing day trip, especially if you are lucky enough to catch one of the elegant old paddle steamers (although there is a supplemental charge). Trips are scheduled on most of the lakes, with increased service in summer. Unlimited travel is free to holders of the Swiss Pass (☞ By Train, *below*). For those not traveling by train, there is also a **Swiss Boat Pass** (35 SF), which allows half-fare travel on all lake steamers for the entire calendar year.

BY BUS

Switzerland's famous yellow postal buses link main cities with villages off the beaten track. Both postal and city buses follow posted schedules to the minute. Free timetables can be picked up at any post office.

The Swiss Pass (☞ By Train, *below*) allows you unlimited travel on postal buses, which venture well beyond the rail routes. "The Best River and Lakeside Walks," a free booklet available from Switzerland Tourism (☞ Visitor Information, *below,* and *in* Chapter 1), describes 28 walks you can enjoy by hopping on and off postal buses. Most walks take about three hours.

Breakdowns. Assistance is available by telephone: Dial ☎ 140 and ask for *Strassenhilfe/Secours routier.*

Gasoline. *Sans plomb* or *bleifrei* (lead-free) gasoline costs 1.11 SF per liter; super costs 1.21 per liter. Leaded regular is no longer available.

Parking. Areas are clearly marked. Note that when parking in a blue or red zone, a "disque" (provided in rental cars or available from banks or police stations) must be placed clearly in the front window noting the time of arrival; this will automatically tell you how long you may use the space. Parking in public lots normally costs about 2 SF per hour.

Road Conditions. Conditions are usually excellent due to well-surfaced roads. Note that roads—especially in the mountains—wind about considerably. Don't plan to achieve high average speeds. When estimating likely travel times, look carefully at the map: There may be only 32 km (20 mi) between one point and another, but there could also be a mountain pass along the way. There is a well-developed highway network, though some notable gaps still exist in the south along an east–west line, roughly between Lugano and Sion. Under some mountain passes, there are tunnels through which cars are transported by train while passengers remain inside—an experience not unlike riding through the world's longest car wash. A combination of steep or winding routes and hazardous weather conditions may close some roads during the winter, especially over mountain passes. Dial ☎ 163 for bulletins and advance information on road conditions.

Rules of the Road. Drive on the right. In built-up areas, the speed limit is 50 kph (30 mph), and on main highways, it's 120 kph (75 mph). On other roads outside built-up areas, the limit is 80 kph (50 mph). Fines for speeding are exorbitant and foreigners are required to pay on the spot—in cash. Children under 12 are not permitted to sit in the front seat. The use of seat belts in both the front and rear seats is mandatory. Driving with parking lights is prohibited, and the use of headlights is mandatory during heavy rain and in road tunnels. To use the main highways, you must display a sticker or *vignette,* which you can buy for 40 SF from Switzerland Tourism (☞ Visitor Information, *below,* and *in* Chapter 1) before you leave home, at the border stations when you enter the country, or at post offices and most gas stations. Cars rented in Switzerland already have these stickers. Traffic going up a mountain has priority, except when postal buses are coming down (signs showing a yellow post horn against a blue background indicate that postal buses have right-of-way). During the winter, snow chains are advisable—sometimes mandatory. They can be rented in all areas, and snow-chain service stations have signs reading SERVICE DE CHAÎNES À NEIGE or SCHNEEKETTENDIENST.

Swissair (☎ 800/221–4750 in the U.S.; 020/7434–7300 in the U.K.) connects airports in Zürich, Basel, and Geneva. The airline's in-house tour operator, **Swisspack,** arranges flexible packages (✉ 106 Calvert St., Harrison, NY 10528, ☎ 800/688–7947) for the independent traveler who flies at least one way between North America and Europe on Swissair. **Crossair** (☎ 020/7439–4144 in the U.K., ☎ 084/8852000 toll free within Switzerland) is Switzerland's domestic airline, servicing local airports and various Continental cities as well, including Rome, Barcelona, Berlin, Amsterdam, and London.

Swiss trains are swift (except through the mountains), immaculate, and punctual. Don't linger between international connections: Swiss Federal Railways (CFF/SBB) runs a tight ship. If you plan to use the trains extensively, get a comprehensive timetable (*Offizieles Kursbuch* or *Horaire*), which costs 16 SF, or a portable, pocket version called the *Reka* for 12 SF. A useful booklet, "Switzerland by Rail," available from Switzerland Tourism (☞ Visitor Information, *below,* and *in* Chapter 1), describes passes, itineraries, and discounts available to rail travelers. Apply for tickets through your travel agent or **Rail Europe** (☎ 800/438–7245).

Inter-City or **Express** trains are the fastest, stopping only at principal towns. A *Regionalzug/Train Régional* is a local train, often affording the most spectacular views. Meals, snacks, and drinks are provided on most main services. Seat reservations are useful during rush hours and high season, especially on international trains and in second class.

Fares offer many extras for visitors. The **Swiss Pass** is the best value, offering unlimited travel on Swiss Federal Railways, postal buses, lake steamers, and the local bus and tram services of 30 cities. It also gives reductions on many privately owned railways, cable cars, and funiculars. Available from Switzerland Tourism (☞ Visitor Information, *below,* and *in* Chapter 1) and from travel agents outside Switzerland, the card is valid for 4 days (216 SF second class, 324 SF first class), 8 days (270 SF second class, 388 SF first class), 15 days (314 SF second class, 454 SF first class), or one month (430 SF second class, 626 SF first class). There is also a three-day **Flexi Pass** (216 SF second class, 324 SF first class), which offers the same unlimited travel options as a regular Swiss Pass for any three days within a 15-day period. In some popular tourist areas, **Regional Holiday Season Tickets,** issued for 15 days, give five days of free travel by train, postal buses, steamers, and mountain railways, with half fare for the rest of the validity of the card. Central Switzerland offers a similar pass for seven days, with two days of free travel. Prices vary widely, depending upon the region and period of validity. Travelers holding tickets or passes on Swiss Federal Railways can forward their luggage to their final destination.

The **Swiss Half-Fare Travel Card** allows half-fare travel for 30 days (90 SF) or one year (150 SF). The **Swiss Card,** which can be purchased in the United States through Rail Europe (✉ 226–230 Westchester Ave., White Plains, NY 10604, ☎ 800/438–7245) and at train stations at the Zürich and Geneva airports and in Basel, is valid for 30 days and grants full round-trip travel from your arrival point to any destination in the country, plus a half-price reduction on any further excursions during your stay (144 SF second class, 175 SF first class). For more information, get the free "Swiss Travel System" or "Discover Switzerland" brochures from Switzerland Tourism (☞ Visitor Information, *below,* and *in* Chapter 1). You can get information from **Swiss Federal Railways** by phone (☎ 1572222; 1.19 SF/min).

Visitor Information
Switzerland Tourism (✉ Tödistr. 7, Postfach, CH-8027 Zürich, ☎ 01/2881111, FAX 01/2881205).

Weather
Switzerland attracts visitors year-round. Winter sports begin around Christmas and usually last until mid-April, depending on snow conditions. The countryside is a delight in spring, when wildflowers are

in bloom, and foliage colors (and clear skies) in fall rival those in New England. In the Ticino, or the Italian-speaking region, and around Lake Geneva (Lac Léman), summer lingers late: There is often sparkling weather in September and October.

CLIMATE

Summer is generally warm and sunny, though the higher you go, the cooler it gets, especially at night. Winter is cold everywhere: In low-lying areas it is frequently damp and overcast; in the Alps, days are brilliantly clear but cold and snowy—especially above 4,600 ft.

Summer and winter, some areas of Switzerland are subject to an Alpine wind that blows from the south and is known as the *Föhn*. It brings clear but somewhat oppressive weather, which the Swiss claim causes headaches. The only exception to these more general weather patterns is the Ticino; protected by the Alps, it has a positively Mediterranean climate—even in winter.

The following are the average daily maximum and minimum temperatures for Zürich.

Jan.	36F	2C	May	67F	19C	Sept.	69F	20C
	26	– 3		47	8		51	11
Feb.	41F	5C	June	73F	23C	Oct.	57F	14C
	28	– 2		53	12		43	6
Mar.	51F	11C	July	76F	25C	Nov.	45F	7C
	34	1		56	14		35	2
Apr.	59F	15C	Aug.	75F	24C	Dec.	37F	3C
	40	– 4		56	14		29	– 2

ZÜRICH

Zürich is not what you'd expect. Stroll around on a fine spring day and you'll ask yourself if this can really be one of the great business centers of the world: the glistening lake, swans on the river, sidewalk cafés, hushed old squares of medieval guild houses. There's not a gnome—a mocking nickname for a Swiss banker—in sight. For all its economic importance, this is a place where people enjoy life.

Zürich started in 15 BC as a Roman customs post on the Lindenhof overlooking the River Limmat, but its growth really began around the 10th century AD. It became a free imperial city in 1336, a center of the Reformation in 1519, and gradually assumed commercial importance during the 1800s. Today the Zürich stock exchange is fourth in the world, and the city's extraordinary museums and galleries and luxurious shops along the Bahnhofstrasse, Zürich's 5th Avenue, attest to its position as Switzerland's cultural—if not political—capital.

Exploring Zürich

Numbers in the margin correspond to points of interest on the Zürich map.

Although Zürich is Switzerland's largest city, it has a population of only 360,000 and is small by European standards. That's one of its nicest features: It's small enough to be explored comfortably on foot. The Limmat river, crisscrossed with lovely low bridges, bisects the city. On the left bank are the Hauptbahnhof, the main train station, and the Bahnhofplatz, a major urban crossroads and the source of the world-famous luxury shopping street, Bahnhofstrasse. The right bank constitutes the younger, livelier section of the Old Town, also known as Niederdorf.

⑨ Altstadt. Zürich's Old Town is a maze of well-preserved medieval streets. Along Rindermarkt, Napfplatz, and Kirchgasse you'll find charming old houses. ⊠ *Near Rathaus.*

❷ Bahnhofstrasse. Zürich's principal boulevard offers concentrated luxury shopping, while much shifting and hoarding of the world's wealth takes place discreetly behind the upstairs windows of the banking institutions. Below the Bahnhofstrasse, vaults that once stored great piles of gold and silver now stand empty—the long-standing story of a subterranean treasure trove was quashed by a local journalist allowed access to the vaults in mid-1998. (The precious metals were moved several years ago.) ⊠ *Runs north–south, west of Limmat.*

★ **❺ Fraumünster.** Of the church spires that are Zürich's signature, the Fraumünster's is the most delicate, a graceful sweep to a narrow spire. The Romanesque, or pre-Gothic, choir has stained-glass windows by Chagall. ⊠ *Stadthausquai.* ⊙ *May–Sept., Mon.–Sat. 9–6; Oct., Mon.– Sat. 10–5; Nov.–Feb., Mon.–Sat. 10–4; Mar.–Apr., Mon.–Sat. 10–5.*

⑫ Graphische Sammlung (Graphic Collection). This impressive collection of the Federal Institute of Technology displays portions of its vast holdings of woodcuts, etchings, and engravings by European masters such as Dürer, Rembrandt, Goya, and Picasso. ⊠ *Rämistr. 101,* ☎ *01/ 6324046.* ◪ *Free.* ⊙ *Weekdays 10–5, Wed. until 8.*

★ **⑩ Grossmünster** (Large Church). During the 3rd century AD, St. Felix and his sister Regula were martyred nearby by the Romans. Legend maintains that having been beheaded, they then walked up the hill carrying their heads and collapsed on the spot where the Grossmünster now stands. On the south tower of this 11th-century structure you can see a statue of Charlemagne (768–814), who is said to have founded the church when his horse stumbled on the same site. In the 16th century, the Zürich reformer Huldrych Zwingli preached sermons here that were so threatening in their promise of fire and brimstone that Martin Luther himself was frightened. ⊠ *Zwinglipl.,* ☎ *01/2526144.* ⊙ *Late Mar.–Oct., daily 9–6; Nov.–Mar., daily 10–5.*

★ **⑪ Kunsthaus.** With a varied, high-quality permanent collection of paintings—medieval, Dutch and Italian Baroque, and Impressionist, the Kunsthaus is Zürich's best art museum. There's a rich collection of works by Swiss artists, though some could be an acquired taste. Besides those of Ferdinand Hodler (1853–1918), there are darkly ethereal paintings by Johann Heinrich Füssli and a terrifying *Walpurgisnacht* by Albert Welti. Other European artists, including Picasso, Klee, Degas, Matisse, Kandinsky, Chagall, and Munch, are all satisfyingly represented. ⊠ *Heimpl. 1,* ☎ *01/2516765.* ⊙ *Tues.–Thurs. 10–9, Fri.–Sun. 10–5.*

🖰 **❸ Lindenhof.** On this quiet square are the remains of the original Roman customs house and fortress, and the imperial medieval residence. A fountain commemorates the day in 1292 when Zürich's women saved the city from the Hapsburgs. As the story goes, the town was on the brink of defeat when its women donned armor and marched to the Lindenhof. On seeing them, the enemy thought they were faced with another army and promptly beat a strategic retreat. ⊠ *Bordered by Fortunag. to west and intersected by Lindenhofstr.*

❽ Rathaus (Town Hall). Zürich's 17th-century town hall is strikingly Baroque, with its interior as well preserved as its facade. There's a richly decorated stucco ceiling in the Banquet Hall and a fine ceramic stove in the government council room. ⊠ *Limmatquai 55.* ⊙ *Tues., Thurs., and Fri., 10–11:30.*

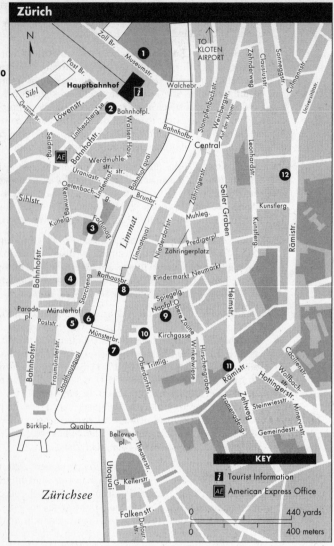

Zürich

④ St. Peters Kirche (St. Peter's Church). Zürich's oldest parish church, with a 13th-century tower, has the largest clock face in Europe. ⊠ *St. Peterhofstatt.* ⊙ *Weekdays 8–6, Sat. 8–4.*

★ ☺ ① Schweizerisches Landesmuseum (Swiss National Museum). In a gargantuan neo-Gothic building, this museum possesses an enormous collection of objects dating from the Stone Age to modern times, including costumes, furniture, early watches, and a great deal of military history, including thousands of toy soldiers reenacting battles. ⊠ *Museumstr. 2,* ☎ *01/2186511.* ☞ *Free.* ⊙ *Tues.–Sun. 10:30–5.*

⑦ Wasserkirche (Water Church). This is one of Switzerland's most delicate late-Gothic structures; its stained glass is by Giacometti. Next door is the **Helmhaus,** an exhibit space for up-and-coming Zürich artists. ⊠ *Limmatquai 31.* ⊙ *Wed. 9–11 and 2–5.*

⑥ Zunfthaus zur Meisen. Erected for the city's wine merchants during the 18th century, this Baroque guildhall today houses the Landesmuseum's

exquisite ceramics collection. ⊠ *Münsterhof 20,* ☎ *01/2212807.* 🖼
Free. ☉ *Tues.–Sun. 10:30–5.*

Elsewhere in Zürich

Museum Rietberg. A wonderful representation of art from India, China, Africa, Japan, and Southeast Asia is displayed in the neoclassic Villa Wesendonck, where Richard Wagner once lived (as in *Wesendonck Songs*). ⊠ *Gablerstr. 15; take Tram 7 from city center;* ☎ *01/2024528.* ☉ *Tues.–Sun. 10–5.*

Dining and Lodging

You're likely to be served seconds in Zürich's generous restaurants, where the rest of your Rösti and geschnetzeltes Kalbfleisch simmer in copper pans by your table while you relish the hefty first portion. This is a Germanic city, but its status as a minor world capital means international cuisines can be sampled. However, the cash register rings portentously when the waiter places your order. For savings, watch for posted *Tagesteller* (daily, prix-fixe special) lunches. For details and price-category definitions *see* Dining *in* Switzerland A to Z, *above.*

Zürich has an enormous range of hotels, from chic and prestigious to modest. Prices tend to be high, but you will get what you pay for: Quality and good service are guaranteed. Deluxe hotels—the five-star landmarks—average between 450 SF and 600 SF per night for a double, and you'll be lucky to get a shower and toilet in your room for less than 140 SF. For details and price-category definitions, *see* Lodging *in* Switzerland A to Z, *above.*

$$$$ ✕ **La Rotonde.** Even when it's not illuminated by candlelight, the Dolder Grand Hotel's (☞ *below*) haute-cuisine restaurant is one of the city's most grandiose spots. Housed in a great arc of a room, La Rotonde provides sweeping lake views. The atmosphere is formal, the staff attentive to a fault, the culinary style traditional French with a fashionably light touch—sweetbreads on a bed of gnocchi with asparagus and truffles, for instance. ⊠ *Kurhausstr. 65,* ☎ *01/2516231. Reservations essential. Jacket and tie. AE, DC, MC, V.*

$$$$ ✕ **Petermann's Kunststuben.** This is one of Switzerland's gastronomic
★ meccas, and although it's south of the city center—in Küssnacht on the lake's eastern shore—it's more than worth the 8-km (5-mi) pilgrimage. The ever-evolving menu may include lobster with artichoke and almond oil, or Tuscan dove with pine nuts and herbs. Come here for serious, world-class food—and prices to match. ⊠ *Seestr. 160, Küssnacht,* ☎ *01/9100715. Reservations essential. AE, DC, MC, V. Closed Sun. and Mon., 2 wks in Feb., and 3 wks in late summer.*

$$$–$$$$ ✕ **Kronenhalle.** From Stravinsky, Brecht, and Joyce to Nureyev,
★ Deneuve, and Saint-Laurent, this beloved landmark has always drawn a stellar crowd for its genial, formal but relaxed atmosphere, hearty cooking, and astonishing collection of 20th-century art. Try the herring in double cream, tournedos with truffle sauce, or duck *à l'orange* with red cabbage and *Spätzli* (tiny dumplings). Be sure to have a cocktail in the adjoining bar: *Le tout* Zürich drinks here. ⊠ *Rämistr. 4,* ☎ *01/2516669. Reservations essential. AE, DC, MC, V.*

$$$ ✕ **Blaue Ente.** Part of a shopping gallery in a converted mill south of
★ the city center, this modern, upscale restaurant and bar draw well-dressed crowds. In a setting of whitewashed brick and glass, with jazz filtering through from the adjoining bar, guests sample a pot-au-feu of clams, prawns, and saffron, or lamb with potato pancakes and eggplant. Take Tram 2 toward Wildbachstrasse. ⊠ *Seefeldstr. 223,* ☎ *01/ 4227706. Reservations essential. AE, DC, MC, V.*

$$$ ✕ **Veltliner Keller.** Though its rich, carved-wood decor borrows from Graubündner Alpine culture, this ancient dining spot is no tourist-trap transplant: The house, built in 1325, has functioned as a restaurant since 1551. There is a definite emphasis on the heavy and the meaty, but the kitchen is flexible and reasonably deft with more modern favorites as well: grilled salmon, veal steak with Gorgonzola, and dessert mousses. ⊠ *Schlüsselg. 8,* ☎ *01/2254040. AE, DC, MC, V.*

$$ ✕ **Oepfelchammer.** This was once the haunt of Zürich's beloved writer
★   Gottfried Keller, and it still draws unpretentious literati. The bar is dark and riddled with graffiti, with sagging timbers and slanting floors; the welcoming little dining rooms have carved oak paneling, coffered ceilings, and damask linens. The traditional meats—calf's liver, veal, tripe in white wine sauce—come in generous portions; salads are fresh and seasonal. It's always packed and service can be slow. ⊠ *Rindermarkt 12,* ☎ *01/2512336. MC, V. Closed Sun., Mon.*

$$ ✕ **Opus.** Bathed in this restaurant's bookish hum, you can enjoy a chic supper of Italian-inspired specialties: olive risotto with shrimp, duck breast with orange and balsamic vinegar sauce. A three-course lunch menu is good value, especially the vegetarian version. On some winter weekends, there's a hip salon/cabaret show between courses. ⊠ *Pfalzg. 1,* ☎ *01/2115917. AE, DC, MC, V.*

$$ ✕ **Zunfthaus zur Zimmerleuten/Käferstube.** While the pricier Zunfthaus
★   upstairs is often overwhelmed with conference crowds, at substreet level a cozy, candlelit haven dubbed "coopers' pub" serves intimate, atmospheric meals in a dark-beamed, old-Zurich setting. Standard dishes have enough novelty to stand apart: wild boar steak with red bilberry sauce, roast pork with smoked bacon, and homemade cinnamon ice cream with wine-poached pear. ⊠ *Limmatquai 40,* ☎ *01/2520834. AE, DC, MC, V.*

$–$$ ✕ **Adler's Swiss Chuchi.** A bit of a shock in a black-leather-and-nose-ring neighborhood, this squeaky-clean, Swiss-kitsch restaurant features an airy, modern decor, with carved fir, Alpine-rustic chairs, Big Boy–style plastic menus, and good home-cooked national specialties. Excellent lunch menus are rock-bottom cheap and served double-quick; nights are reserved for fondue. ⊠ *Roseng. 10,* ☎ *01/2669696. AE, DC, MC, V.*

$–$$ ✕ **Bierhalle Kropf.** Under the mounted boar's head and restored cen-
★ ☻   tury-old murals, businesspeople, workers, and shoppers share crowded tables to feast on generous hot dishes and a great selection of sausages. The *Leberknödli* (liver dumplings) are tasty, *Apfelköchli* (fried apple slices) tender and sweet, and the service as wisecracking-cranky as in a New York deli. ⊠ *In Gassen 16,* ☎ *01/2211805. AE, DC, MC, V. Closed Sun.*

$–$$ ✕ **Zeughauskeller.** Built as an arsenal in 1487, this enormous stone
★   and beam hall offers hearty meat platters and a variety of beers and wines amid comfortable, friendly chaos. The waitstaff is harried and brisk, especially at lunchtime, when crowds are thick with locals—don't worry, just roll up your sleeves and dig in. ⊠ *Bahnhofstr. 28, at Paradepl.,* ☎ *01/2112690. AE, DC, MC, V.*

$ ✕ **Reithalle.** In a downtown theater complex behind the Bahnhofstrasse, this old military horse barn now serves as a noisy and popular restaurant, with candles perched on the mangers and beams and heat ducts exposed. Young locals share long tables arranged mess-hall style to sample French and Italian specialties, many vegetarian, and an excellent, international blackboard list of wines. ⊠ *Gessnerallee 8,* ☎ *01/ 2120766. AE, MC, V.*

$$$$ ▥ **Baur au Lac.** This is the highbrow patrician of Swiss hotels, with
★   luxurious but low-key facilities—like the Rolls-Royce limousine service. Its broad back is turned to the commercial center, while its front rooms overlook the lake, canal, and manicured lawns of the hotel's

private park. The decor is posh, discreet, and firmly fixed in the Age of Reason. ⊠ *Talstr. 1, CH-8022,* ☎ *01/2205020,* ℻ *01/2205044. 108 rooms, 17 suites. 2 restaurants. AE, DC, MC, V.*

$$$$ 🏠 **Dolder Grand.** A cross between Camp David and Maria Theresa's
★ summer palace, this sprawling Victorian fantasy-palace sits high on a wooded hill over Zürich, quickly reached from Römerhof by funicular railway (free for guests). It's a picturesque hodgepodge of turrets, cupolas, half-timbering, and mansards; the uncompromisingly modern wing was added in 1964, but from inside the connection is seamless. Its restaurant La Rotonde excels in traditional French cuisine (☞ *above*). ⊠ *Kurhausstr. 65, CH-8032,* ☎ *01/2693000,* ℻ *01/2693001. 149 rooms, 34 suites. Restaurant, pool. AE, DC, MC, V.*

$$$$ 🏠 **Widder.** One of the city's most captivating hotels, the Widder rev-
★ els in the present while preserving the past. Ten adjacent medieval houses were gutted and combined to create it. Behind every door is a fascinating mix of old and new—a guest room could pair restored 17th-century frescoes with a leather bedspread, halogen bell jars, and a private fax. ⊠ *Rennweg. 7, CH-8001,* ☎ *01/2242526,* ℻ *01/2242424. 42 rooms, 7 suites. 2 restaurants. AE, DC, MC, V.*

$$$ 🏠 **Florhof.** This is an anti-urban hotel, a gentle antidote to the bustle
★ of downtown commerce. In a quiet residential area by the Kunstmuseum, this Romantik property pampers guests with its polished wood, blue-willow fabrics, and wisteria-sheltered garden. ⊠ *Florhofsg. 4, CH-8001,* ☎ *01/2614470,* ℻ *01/2614611. 33 rooms, 2 suites. Restaurant. AE, DC, MC, V.*

$$$ 🏠 **Neues Schloss.** Now managed by the Arabella-Sheraton chain, this small, intimate hotel in the business district, southeast of Paradeplatz, offers a warm welcome and dark, classic decor, the result of a complete refurbishment in early 1999. ⊠ *Stockerstr. 17, CH-8022,* ☎ *01/2869400,* ℻ *01/2869445. 58 rooms. Restaurant. AE, DC, MC, V.*

$$$ 🏠 **Splügenschloss.** Befitting its age, this Relais & Châteaux property maintains its ornate, antiques-filled decor. One room is completely paneled in Alpine-style pine; others are decorated in fussy florals. Its location southeast of the Neues Schloss may be a little out of the way for tourists, but atmosphere buffs will find it worth the effort. ⊠ *Splügenstr. 2, CH-8002,* ☎ *01/2899999,* ℻ *01/2899998. 50 rooms, 2 suites. Restaurant. AE, DC, MC, V.*

$$$ 🏠 **Zum Storchen.** In a stunning central location, tucked between
★ Fraumünster and St. Peters Kirche, this 600-year-old structure has become an impeccable modern hotel. It has warmly appointed rooms, some with French windows opening over the Limmat, and a lovely restaurant with riverfront terrace seating. ⊠ *Weinpl. 2, CH-8001,* ☎ *01/2272727,* ℻ *01/2272700. 73 rooms. Restaurant. AE, DC, MC, V.*

$$ 🏠 **Haus zum Kindli.** This charming little bijou hotel could pass for a 3-D Laura Ashley catalog, with every cushion and bibelot as artfully styled as a magazine ad. The result is welcoming, intimate, and a sight less contrived than most cookie-cutter hotel decors. At the Opus restaurant downstairs, guests earn 10% off menu prices, though you may have to vie with crowds of locals for a table (☞ *above*). ⊠ *Pfalzg. 1, CH-8001,* ☎ *01/2115917,* ℻ *01/2116528. 21 rooms. Restaurant. AE, DC, MC, V.*

$$ 🏠 **Rössli.** This ultrasmall but friendly hotel is set in the heart of Oberdorf. The chic white-on-white decor mixes stone and wood textures with bold textiles and mosaic bathrooms. Extras include safes and bathrobes—unusual in this price range. Some singles are tiny, but all have double beds. ⊠ *Rösslig. 7, CH-8001,* ☎ *01/2522121,* ℻ *01/2522131. 16 rooms, 1 suite. AE, DC, MC, V.*

$ 🏠 **Leoneck.** From the cowhide-covered front desk to the edelweiss-print curtains, this budget hotel wallows in its Swiss roots, but balances this with no-nonsense conveniences: new tile baths (with cow-print shower curtains), murals, and built-in pine furniture. It's one stop from the Central tram stop, two from the Bahnhof. ⊠ *Leonhardst. 1, CH-8001,* ☎ *01/2542222,* ℻ *01/2542200. 65 rooms. AE, DC, MC, V.*

$ 🏨 **Limmathof.** This spare but welcoming city hotel inhabits a handsome historic shell and is ideally placed on the Limmatquai, minutes from the Hauptbahnhof. Rooms have tile bathrooms and plump down quilts. There's an old-fashioned Weinstube (pub) as well as a new vegetarian restaurant that doubles as the breakfast room. ⊠ *Limmatquai 142, CH-8023,* ☎ *01/2614220,* ℻ *01/2620217. 62 rooms. Restaurant. AE, DC, MC, V.*

$ 🏨 **St. Georges.** This simple former pension has a bright lobby and breakfast space; rooms are milky white-on-white. A few now offer full bathrooms, but the majority, under 100 SF, have shower and toilet down the hall. ⊠ *Weberstr. 11, CH-8004,* ☎ *01/2411144,* ℻ *01/2411142. 40 rooms, 11 with bath. AE, MC, V.*

Nightlife and the Arts

Zürich has a lively nightlife scene, largely centered in the Niederdorf area on the right bank of the Limmat. And despite its small population, Zürich is a big city when it comes to the arts; it supports a top-ranked orchestra, an opera company, and a theater. For information on goings-on, check *Zürich News,* published weekly in English and German. Also check "Züri-tipp," a German-language supplement to the Friday edition of the daily newspaper *Tages Anzeiger.* Tickets to opera, concert, and theater events can also be bought from the tourist office, while tickets for almost any event can be purchased in advance by telephone from **Fastbox** (☎ 0848/800800) or **Ticketline** (☎ 01/2256060). Depending on the event, **Musik Hug** (⊠ Limmatquai 28–30, ☎ 01/2694100) makes reservations. Also try **Jecklin** (⊠ Rämistr. 30, ☎ 01/2537676).

The Arts

During July or August, the **Theaterspektakel** takes place, with circus tents housing avant-garde theater and experimental performances on the lawns by the lake at Mythenquai. The Zürich Tonhalle Orchestra, named for its concert hall **Tonhalle** (⊠ Claridenstr. 7, ☎ 01/2063434), was inaugurated by Brahms in 1895 and enjoys international acclaim. Tickets sell out quickly, so book directly through the Tonhalle. The music event of the year is the **Züricher Festspiele** (Zürich International Festival), when, from late June to mid-July, orchestras and soloists from all over the world perform, and plays and exhibitions are staged. Book well ahead. Details are available from Info- und Ticketoffice (⊠ Postfach 6036, CH-8023, ☎ 01/2154030).

Nightlife

BARS AND LOUNGES

Champagnertreff in the Hotel Central (⊠ Central 1, ☎ 01/2515555) is a popular neo–Art Deco piano bar with several champagnes available by the glass. The **Jules Verne Panorama Bar** (⊠ Uraniastr. 9, ☎ 01/2111155) shakes up cocktails with a wraparound downtown view. The narrow bar at the **Kronenhalle** (⊠ Rämistr. 4, ☎ 01/2516669) draws mobs of well-heeled locals and internationals. Serving a young, arty set until 4 AM, **Odéon** (⊠ Am Bellevue, ☎ 01/2511650) is a cultural and historic landmark (Mata Hari danced here).

DANCING

The medieval-theme **Adagio** (⊠ Gotthardstr. 5, ☎ 01/2063666) offers classic rock, jazz, and tango to well-dressed thirtysomethings. **Kaufleuten** (⊠ Pelikanstr. 18, ☎ 01/2211505) is a landmark dance club that draws a well-dressed, upwardly mobile crowd. **Mascotte** (✉ The-aterstr. 10, ☎ 01/2524481) draws all ages on weeknights, a young crowd on weekends, for funk and soul.

JAZZ CLUBS

Casa Bar (✉ Münsterg. 30, ☎ 01/2612002) is, arguably, Zürich's most famous jazz club. The **Widder Bar** (✉ Widderg. 6, ☎ 01/2242411), in the Hotel Widder (☞ Dining and Lodging, *above*), attracts local celebrities with its 800-count "library of spirits" and international jazz groups.

Shopping

One of the broadest assortments of watches in all price ranges is avail-able at **Bucherer** (✉ Bahnhofstr. 50, ☎ 01/2112635). **Heimatwerk** (✉ Rennweg 14 and Bahnhofstr. 2, ☎ 01/2115780) specializes in Swiss handicrafts, all of excellent quality. **Jelmoli** (✉ Seideng. 1, ☎ 01/2204411), Switzerland's largest department store, carries a wide range of tasteful Swiss goods. You can snag some of last season's fashions at deep discounts at **Lagerverkauf** (✉ Weinpl. 10, ☎ 01/2128318), which jumbles chichi brands on thrift-shop style racks. If you have a sweet tooth, stock up on truffles at **Sprüngli** (✉ Paradepl., ☎ 01/2244646). The renowned chocolatier **Teuscher** (✉ Storcheng. 9, ☎ 01/2115153) concocts a killer champagne truffle. For the latest couture, go to one of a dozen **Trois Pommes** (✉ Storcheng. 6/7, ☎ 01/2110239) boutiques featuring top-name designers such as Versace or Armani.

Side Trip from Zürich: Liechtenstein

For an international day trip out of Zürich, dip a toe into tiny Liecht-enstein: There isn't room for much more. Just 80 km (50 mi) south-east on the Austrian border, this miniature principality covers a scant 158 square km (61 square mi). An independent nation since 1719, Liecht-enstein has a customs union with Switzerland, which means they share trains, currency, and diplomats—but not stamps, which is why collectors prize the local releases. It's easiest to get there by car, since Swiss trains pass through without stopping. If you're using a train pass, ride to Sar-gans or Buchs. From there, local postal buses deliver mail and passengers across the border to Liechtenstein's capital, Vaduz.

Exploring Liechtenstein

Green and mountainous, with vineyards climbing its slopes, greater Liechtenstein is best seen by car; however, the postal buses are prompt and their routes are extensive.

VADUZ

In fairy-tale Vaduz, Prince Johannes Adam Pius still lives in the Cas-tle, a massive 16th-century fortress perched high on the cliff above the city. Only honored guests of the prince tour the interior, but its exte-rior and the views from the grounds are worth the climb. In the mod-ern town center, head for the tourist information office to have your passport stamped with the Liechtenstein crown. Upstairs, the **Liecht-ensteinische Staatliche Kunstsammlung** (Liechtenstein State Museum of Art) showcases various segments of the vast collection. ✉ *Städtle 37, ☎ 075/2322341. ⊙ Apr.–Oct., daily 10–noon and 1:30–5:30; Nov.–Mar., daily 10–noon and 1:30–5.*

On the same floor, the **Briefmarkenmuseum** (Stamp Museum) attracts philatelists from all over the world to see the 300 frames of beautifully designed and relatively rare stamps. ✉ *Städtle 37, ☎ 075/2366105. ▨ Free. ⊙ Apr.–Oct., daily 10–noon and 1:30–5:30; Nov.–Mar., daily 10–noon and 1:30–5.*

The **Liechtensteinisches Landesmuseum** (National Museum) will be closed for structural repair until 2001. Its collection includes church carvings, ancient coins, and arms. ✉ *Städtle 43,* ☎ *075/22310.*

BEYOND VADUZ

In **Schaan,** just north of Vaduz, visit the Roman excavations and the parish church built on the foundations of a Roman fort. Or drive southeast of the capital to the chalets of picturesque **Triesenberg** for spectacular views of the Rhine Valley. **Malbun** is a sun-drenched ski bowl with comfortable slopes and a low-key ambience.

$ ✕ **Wirthschaft zum Löwen.** It may be tiny, but Liechtenstein has a cui-
★ sine of its own, and this is the place to try it. In a farmhouse on the Austrian border, the friendly Biedermann family serves pungent *Sauerkäse* (sour cheese) and *Käseknöpfli* (cheese dumplings), plus lovely meats and the local crusty, chewy bread. ✉ *Schellenberg,* ☎ *075/3731162. No credit cards.*

$$$$ ✕🍽 **Real.** Surrounded by slick modern decor, you'll find rich, old-style
★ Austrian-French cuisine in all its buttery glory. It's prepared these days by Martin Real, son of the unpretentious former chef, Felix Real—who, in his retirement, presides over the 20,000-bottle wine cellar. The menu offers game, seafood, soufflés, and an extraordinary wine list. Downstairs is a more casual stübli for those who don't feel like get-ting dressed up. Upstairs is a baker's dozen of small, airily decorated rooms. ✉ *Städtle 21, Vaduz FL-9490,* ☎ *075/2322222,* 🆔 *075/2320891. 11 rooms, 2 suites. Restaurant. AE, DC, MC, V.*

$$$$ 🍽 **Park-Hotel Sonnenhof.** A garden oasis commanding a superb view of the valley and mountains beyond, this hillside retreat in a residen-tial district offers discreet luxury minutes from downtown Vaduz. Some rooms open directly onto the lawns; others have balconies. The excellent restaurant is open only to guests. ✉ *Mareestr. 29, Vaduz FL-9490,* ☎ *075/2321192,* 🆔 *075/2320053. 17 rooms, 12 suites. Restau-rant, indoor pool. AE, DC, MC, V.*

$$ 🍽 **Engel.** On the main tourist street, its café bulging with bus-tour crowds, this simple hotel manages to maintain a local, comfortable am-bience. ✉ *Städtle 13, Vaduz FL-9490,* ☎ *075/2361717,* 🆔 *075/2331159. 20 rooms. 2 restaurants. AE, DC, MC, V.*

Liechtenstein Essentials

VISITOR INFORMATION

Tourist Office (✉ Städtle 37, Box 139, Vaduz FL-9490, ☎ 075/2321443).

Zürich Essentials

Arriving and Departing

BY BUS

All bus services to Zürich will drop you at the **Hauptbahnhof** (✉ City center). There are also hotel bus services that charge 22 SF per person.

BY CAR

Highways link Zürich to France, Germany, and Italy. The quickest ap-proach is from Germany; the **A5** autobahn reaches from Germany to Basel, and the **A2** expressway leads from Basel to Zürich. The **A3** ex-pressway feeds into the city from the southeast.

BY PLANE

Zürich-Kloten (☎ 1571060) is Switzerland's most important airport. Several airlines fly directly to Zürich from major cities in the United States, Canada, and the United Kingdom. Swissair flies nonstop from major international cities. "Fly–Rail Baggage" allows Swissair passengers departing Switzerland to check their bags at any of 120 rail or postal bus stations throughout the country; luggage is automatically transferred to the airplane. At many Swiss railway stations, passengers may complete all check-in procedures for Swissair flights, including picking up their boarding pass and checking their bags.

BY TRAIN

Zürich is the northern crossroads of Switzerland, with swift and punctual trains arriving from Basel, Geneva, Bern, and Lugano. All routes lead to the **Hauptbahnhof** (✉ Between Museumstr. and Bahnhofpl., ☎ 01/1572222).

Getting Around

The city's transportation network is excellent.

BY BUS AND TRAM

VBZ Züri-Linie (Zürich Public Transport) buses and trams run from 5:30 AM to midnight, every six minutes on all routes at peak hours, and about every 12 minutes at other times. Before you board the bus, you must buy your ticket from one of the automatic vending machines found at every stop. An all-day pass is a good buy at 7.20 SF. Free route plans are available from VBZ offices and larger kiosks.

BY TAXI

Taxis are very expensive, with an 8 SF minimum.

Contacts and Resources

CONSULATES

Contact the **U.S.** embassy in Bern (✉ Jubiläumsstr. 93, ☎ 031/3577011). Contact the **Canadian** embassy in Bern (✉ Kirchenfeldstr. 88, ☎ 031/3573200). There is a **British** consulate in Zürich (✉ Minervastr. 117, ☎ 01/3833560).

EMERGENCIES

Police (☎ 117). **Ambulance** (☎ 144). **Doctor/Dentist Referral** (☎ 01/2616100). **Pharmacy: Bellevue** (✉ Theaterstr. 14, ☎ 01/2525600) offers an all-night service.

ENGLISH-LANGUAGE BOOKS

English-language magazines are available at most large kiosks, especially in the Hauptbahnhof. **Payot** (✉ Bahnhofstr. 9, ☎ 01/2115452). **Orell Füssli** (✉ Füsslistr. 4, ☎ 01/2211060).

GUIDED TOURS

Orientation. Three bus tours are available. The daily "Sights of Zürich" tour (32 SF) gives a good general idea of the city in two hours. "In and Around Zürich" covers more ground and includes an aerial cableway trip to Felsenegg; it takes 2½ hours and costs 39 SF for adults. The daily "Cityrama" tour hits the main sights, then visits Rapperswil, a nearby lakeside town; it costs 35 SF. All tours start from the Hauptbahnhof. Contact the tourist office (☞ Visitor Information, *below*) for reservations.

Walking. Daily from May to October, two-hour conducted walking tours (18 SF) start at the train station. You can join a group with English-language commentary, but the times vary, so call ahead. This tourist office service (☞ Visitor Information, *below*) also offers day trips by coach to Luzern, up the Rigi, Titlis, or Pilatus mountains, and the Jungfrau.

TRAVEL AGENCIES

American Express (✉ Uraniastr. 14, ☎ 01/2287777). **Kuoni Travel** (✉ Bahnhofpl. 7, ☎ 01/2243333).

VISITOR INFORMATION

Tourist office (✉ Bahnhof, ☎ 01/2154000). **Hotel reservations** (☎ 01/2154040, FAX 01/2154044).

GENEVA

Nestled between the Jura and the Alps at the southwestern tip of Lake Geneva (Lac Léman), Geneva is the most cosmopolitan and graceful of Swiss cities. Just a stone's throw from the French border, this French-speaking city is tied to the water: Mansarded mansions stand guard beside the River Rhône, yachts bob, gulls dive, and Rolls-Royces purr beside manicured lakeside promenades. The combination of Swiss efficiency and French savoir faire gives the city a chic polish, and the infusion of international blood from the United Nations adds a heterogeneity that is rare in cities with a population of only 180,000.

Headquarters of the World Health Organization and the International Red Cross, Geneva has long been known for enlightened tolerance. It gave refuge to writers Voltaire, Hugo, and Stendhal, as well as to religious reformers Calvin and Knox. Rousseau was born here; Byron, Shelley, Wagner, and Liszt all fled to Geneva from scandal elsewhere.

A Roman seat for 500 years (from 120 BC), then home to early Burgundians, and ruled by bishop-princes into the 16th century, Geneva fended off the greedy dukes of Savoy until 1603. Under the guiding fervor of Calvin in the 16th century, Geneva rejected Catholicism and became a stronghold of Protestant reform. In 1798 the city fell to the French, then made overtures to the Swiss Confederation as Napoléon's star waned. Geneva finally joined the Confederation as a canton in 1815.

Exploring Geneva

Numbers in the margin correspond to points of interest on the Geneva map.

Geneva follows the tapering shores of Lake Geneva as it narrows back into the Rhône river between the pont du Mont-Blanc and the pont de la Coulouvrenière. Thus Geneva is both a river town and a lake town; its Rive Droite (Right Bank, on the north side) and Rive Gauche (Left Bank, on the south side) have distinct identities. Most of the central city's best is concentrated on the Rive Gauche, but the Rive Droite encompasses the International Area and many handsome hotels. Most of the main neighborhoods, including the Old Town, are easily toured on foot. To visit the International Area, a modern section north of the pont du Mont-Blanc, you'll need to take a bus or a cab.

⑫ Auditoire de Calvin (Protestant Lecture Hall). In this Gothic, former Catholic chapel, Jean Calvin taught missionaries his doctrines of puritanical reform and founded what became Geneva's university. From 1556 to 1559 the Scots reformer John Knox also preached here. Today English, Dutch, and Italian services are held Sunday. ⊠ *Pl. de la Taconnerie,* ☎ *022/3118533.* ☉ *Weekdays 2–5.*

⑩ Cathédrale St-Pierre (St. Peter's Cathedral). Begun in 1160, this Gothic cathedral's aesthetic balance was tipped when a sternly beautiful but incongruous neoclassic facade was added in the 18th century. The austerity of the nave reflects the change of role from a Catholic cathedral to a Protestant church, stripped of its icons by followers of Calvin. You can climb the north tower for a panoramic city view; underneath the cathedral are archaeological excavations (☞ site archéologique, *below*). ⊠ *Cour Saint-Pierre,* ☎ *022/3117575.* ☉ *Oct.–May, Mon.–Sat.10–noon and 2–5, Sun. 11–12:30 and 1:30–5; June–Sept., Mon.–Sat. 9–7, Sun. 11–7.*

★ ⑭ Collections Baur. This graceful mansion exhibits businessman Alfred Baur's Asian object collection of rose and celadon porcelains from China, medieval Japanese stoneware, Samurai swords, and much more. ✉ *8 rue Munier-Romilly,* ☎ *022/3461729.* ⏲ *Tues.–Sun. 2–6.*

7 **Hôtel de Ville** (Town Hall). The political seat since 1455, this still-active Town Hall shelters the Alabama Hall, where, on August 22, 1864, 16 countries signed the Geneva Convention, laying the foundation of the International Red Cross. The tourist office (☞ Geneva Essentials, *below*) leads tours on weekdays from June to October and Saturday year-round. ✉ *2 rue de l'Hôtel-de-Ville,* ☎ *022/9097000.*

★ 8 **Maison Tavel** (Tavel House). Geneva's oldest house traces the development of urban life in the city from the 14th to the 19th centuries. Several rooms have period furnishings; others display artifacts ranging from medieval grafitti to a garishly painted miter, worn by convicted pimps in Calvin's day. ✉ *6 rue du Puits-St-Pierre,* ☎ *022/3102900.* *Free.* ⏲ *Tues.–Sat. noon–5, Sun. 10–5.*

★ 4 **Monument de la Réformation** (Monument of the Reformation). Conceived on a grand scale and erected between 1909 and 1917, this group of larger-than-life granite statues pays homage to such Protestant pioneers as Bèze, Calvin, Farel, and Knox. It's flanked by memorials to kingpins Ulrich Zwingli and Martin Luther. ✉ *Parc des Bastions.*

★ 13 **Musée d'Art et d'Histoire** (Museum of Art and History). This mother lode of world culture, built in 1910, presents its enormous archaeological, applied arts, and Beaux Arts collections as a walk through time. Among its holdings are the largest collection of Egyptian art in Switzerland, 17th-century weapons, and a full room of Alpine landscapes by Swiss painter Ferdinand Hodler. ✉ *2 rue Charles-Galland,* ☎ *022/4182600.* *Free.* ⏲ *Tues.–Sun. 10–5.*

★ 5 **Musée d'Art Moderne et Contemporain** (Museum of Modern and Contemporary Art). The concrete floors and fluorescent lighting from this former factory frame this gritty collection of stark, mind-stretching, post-1965 art. The building's spare, bleak lines highlight works by Gordon Matta-Clark, Jenny Holzer, Sol Le Witt, and Jean-Michel Basquiat. To get here from the train station, take Bus 1 (direction Rive) to the École de Médécine. Walk back one block and turn left down rue des Vieux-Grenadiers. The entrance is the last doorway on the right. ✉ *10 rue des Vieux-Grenadiers,* ☎ *022/3206122.* ⏲ *Wed.–Sun. noon–6, Tues. noon–9.*

★ 9 **Musée Barbier-Mueller** (Barbier-Mueller Museum). Since 1907 Josef Mueller and his family have acquired a staggering number of fine "primitive" pieces from Africa, Oceania, Southeast Asia, and the Americas. A small but dynamic selection is on view at any given time; labels in English guide visitors from ivory fly-whisk handles from Zaire to massive carved masks from New Ireland. ✉ *10 rue Calvin,* ☎ *022/3120270.* ⏲ *Daily 11–5.*

★ 15 **Musée International de la Croix-Rouge** (International Red Cross Museum). State-of-the-art media technology illuminates human kindness in the face of disasters both natural and man-made. The sometimes grim displays include a reconstruction of a 9- by 6½-ft concrete prison cell that once held 17 political prisoners. The masterpiece of the exhibition is the astonishing Mur du Temps (Wall of Time), a simple time line that traces, year by year, wars and natural disasters that have killed over 100,000 people. Commentary is available in English. ✉ *17 av. de la Paix,* ☎ *022/7489511.* ⏲ *Wed.–Mon. 10–5.*

2 **Musée Rath** (Rath Museum). Switzerland's first fine-art museum, built in 1826, hosts three major temporary exhibitions of archaeology and

1060

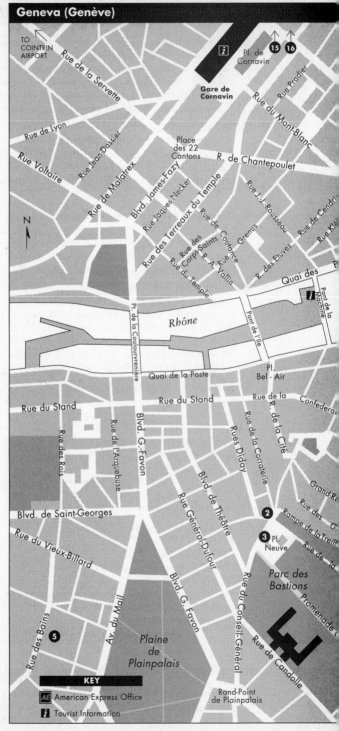

Geneva (Genève)

TO
COINTRIN
AIRPORT

Rue de la Servette

Rue de Lyon

Rue Voltaire

Rue Jean-Dassier

Rue de Malatrex

Pl. de
Cornavin

15 16

Gare de
Cornavin

Rue Pradier

Rue du Mont-Blanc

Place
des 22
Cantons

R. de Chantepoulet

Blvd. James-Fazy

Rue Jaques-Necker

Rue des Terreaux du Temple

Rue de Coutance

Rue J.-J.-Rousseau

Rue de Cendri

Rue Kle

Grenus

Rue des
Corps-Saints

R. A. Vallin

Rue du Temple

R. des Étuves

Quai des

Pont de la
Machine

Pt. de la Coulouvrenière

Rhône

Pont de l'Ile

Quai de la Poste

Pl.
Bel - Air

Rue du Stand

Rue du Stand

Rue de la

R. de la Cité

Confédera

Rue du Stand

Rue des Rois

Rue de l'Arquebuse

Blvd. G.-Favon

Rues Diday

Rue de la Corraterie

Grand-R

Rue des G

Rampe de la Treitt

Rue de la

2

3 Pl.
Neuve

Blvd. de Saint-Georges

Rue du Vieux-Billard

Rue Général-Dufour

Blvd. de Théâtre

Blvd. G. Favon

Rue du Conseil-Général

Parc des
Bastions

Promenade

Rue des Bains

Av. du Mail

5

Plaine
de
Plainpalais

Rue de Candolle

Rond-Point
de Plainpalais

KEY

AE American Express Office

i Tourist Information

contemporary art each year. ⊠ *Pl. Neuve,* ☎ *022/4183340.* ⊙ *Tues. and Thurs.–Sun. 10–5, Wed. noon–9.*

★ **⑯ Palais des Nations** (Palace of Nations). The period detail alone—bronze torchères, allegorical murals—merit a visit to the European headquarters of the United Nations. The Assembly Hall has hosted scores of world leaders; the Council on Disarmament meets in the Council Chamber. ⊠ *Palais des Nations, 14 av. de la Paix,* ☎ *022/9074896.* ⊙ *Apr.–June and Sept.–Oct., daily 10–noon and 2–4; July–Aug., daily 9–6; Nov.–Mar., weekdays 10–noon and 2–4.*

★ **❻ Place du Bourg-de-Four.** Once a Roman cattle market, later flooded by Protestant refugees, this Genevois crossroads is now a charming mix of scruffy bohemia, genteel tradition, and slick gentrification. ⊠ *Intersection of rue Verdaine, rue des Chaudronniers, rue Etienne-Dumont, and rue de l'Hôtel-de-Ville.*

★ **❸ Place Neuve.** On this lyrical square stands a marvelous opera house, the **Grand Théâtre,** flanked by the Musée Rath (*above*) and the Conservatoire de Musique. ⊠ *Intersection of bd. du Théâtre, rue de la Corraterie, rue de la Croix-Rouge, and rue Bartholoni.*

❶ Pont du Mont-Blanc (Mont-Blanc Bridge). From the middle of this bridge—the spectacular focal point of traffic—you can see the snowy peak of Mont Blanc. Between March and October you'll have a fine view of the **Jet d'Eau,** Europe's tallest fountain, gushing 475 ft up. ⊠ *Joins rue du Mont-Blanc with quai Général-Guisan.*

☁ **⑪ Site archéologique** (archaeological site). Archaeologists found layer upon layer of history when they tunneled under the Cathédrale St-Pierre (☞ *above*) in 1976; excavations continue to this day. You can peer at remnants of a 4th-century Christian sanctuary, an 11th-century crypt, and striking 5th-century mosaic floors. ⊠ *6 cour St-Pierre, under Cathédrale St-Pierre,* ☎ *022/3117575.* ⊙ *June–Sept., Tues.–Sun. 11–5:30; Oct.–May, Tues.–Sat. 2–5, Sun. 10–noon and 2–5.*

Dining and Lodging

Geneva is a true gastronomic crossroads. Its restaurants excel in everything from *haute gastronomie* to fusion experiments. The city's traditional cuisine is earthy and rich, with seasonal dishes such as *cardon* (cardoon, a locally grown, artichokelike vegetable) baked in a gratin with cream and Gruyère, and lake fish such as *omble* (char). *Longeole* (unsmoked pork sausage with cabbage and fennel), *pieds de cochon* (pigs' feet), and *fricassée de porc* (pork simmered in wine) are other favorites. Many restaurants close on weekends, particularly on Sunday night. For details and price-category definitions, *see* Dining *in* Switzerland A to Z, *above.*

Hotel prices in Geneva are on a par with those in most European capitals, but many luxury hotels offer lower weekend prices or group rates. Since it's a popular convention center, you'll need to book well in advance; blocks of rooms can be snatched up quickly. For details and price-category definitions, *see* Lodging *in* Switzerland A to Z, *above.*

$$$$ ✕ **Les Continents.** Chef Patrick Domon apprenticed with Fredy Girardet
★ and earned his wings in London, Hong Kong, and Singapore; the expert touch and Asian influences come through in ever-changing dishes such as chilled breast of pigeon in lemon, filet mignon with truffles and candied onions, and pineapple soufflé with rum and tropical fruit. The interior is most dignified: Victorian wood panels, creamy linen, and chandeliers. ⊠ *Hotel Inter-Continental, 7–9 chemin du Petit-Sacon-*

nex, ☎ *022/9193350. Reservations essential. AE, DC, MC, V. Closed weekends.*

$$$$ ✕ **Le Lion d'Or.** Cologny is Geneva's Beverly Hills with a view, and this
★ culinary landmark takes full advantage of its real estate—its summer
terrace overlooks the city. While the decor models Louis XV, local
celebrity chefs Gilles Dupont and Tommy Birne give their seasonal menus
a modern edge. Duck wings with foie gras and fricassee of lobster with
lemon and endive are highlights, as are warm soufflés from the dessert
cart. The bistro next door shares the restaurant's kitchen, not its
prices—grab a cab and come for lunch. ⊠ *5 pl. Pierre-Gautier, Cologny,*
☎ *022/7364432. AE, DC, MC, V. Closed weekends.*

$$$ ✕ **L'Ange du Dix Vins/Le Dix Vins.** Chef Réné Fracheboud's innova-
tive kitchen serves two crowds, one in the main restaurant, the other
in the cozy, antiques-cluttered bistro next door. Novel specialties are
vividly flavored with curry oil, cocoa, and even coffee. Prices are com-
parable between the two restaurants. ⊠ *31/29 rue Jacques Dalphin,*
Carouge, ☎ *022/3420318. AE, MC, V. Closed Sun., weekends Jan.–*
Aug. No lunch Sat. Sept.–Dec.

$$$ ✕ **Boeuf Rouge.** In a kitschy, fin-de-siècle setting, this popular spot de-
★ livers the real thing: rich, unadulterated Lyonnaise cuisine. Try the hand-
stuffed pistachio sausage; *boudin noir* (blood sausage) with apples; or
tender *quenelles de brochet* (pike). There's an unusual selection of chestnut and citrus mousses for dessert. ⊠ *17 rue Alfred-Vincent,* ☎ *022/*
7327537. AE, DC MC, V. Closed weekends.

$$$ ✕ **La Favola.** Run by a young Ticinese chef from Locarno, this quirky
★ little restaurant may be the most picturesque in town. The tiny dining
room, at the top of a vertiginous spiral staircase, strikes a delicate bal-
ance between rustic and fussy. The food aptly mixes country simple
and city chic: Homemade pastas melt on the tongue, the carpaccio is
paper thin, and the tiramisu is divine. ⊠ *15 rue Calvin,* ☎ *022/*
3117437. No credit cards. Closed Sun. No lunch Sat.

$$ ✕ **Le Lyrique.** In this relaxed café-brasserie, portraits of Beethoven, Verdi,
★ Strauss, and Liszt watch over pre-theater diners as they choose between
homemade pasta with scampi, summer gazpacho, or a nuanced steak
tartare. Though it's normally closed on weekends, an exception is
made for performance dates at the Grand Théâtre, which is just across
the square. ⊠ *12 bd. du Théâtre,* ☎ *022/3280095. AE, DC, MC, V.*

$$ ✕ **L'Opera Bouffe.** This extremely popular spot offers excellent bistro
★ dishes, many with an exotic twist courtesy of the Syrian chef. The set-
ting is chic and postmodern, with wine stacked floor to ceiling and opera
trilling in the background. ⊠ *5 av. de Frontenex,* ☎ *022/7366300. AE,*
DC, MC, V. Closed Sun., Mon. No lunch Sat.

$$ ✕ **Le Pied-de-Cochon.** Crowded, noisy, smoky, and packed shoulder-
to-shoulder, this lively bistro is anchored by its ancient beams and worn
zinc bar. Among the simple, regional dishes are *longeole, boudin noir,*
and *pieds de cochon* (pigs' feet)—grilled, poached, or boned. ⊠ *4 pl.*
du Bourg-de-Four, ☎ *022/3104797. AE, DC, MC, V.* .

$ ✕ **L'Echalotte.** Polished wood banquettes, good food, and low prices
★ draw local artists and journalists to this comfortable spot. The menu
stretches from vegetarian options to *abats* (organ meats); such dishes
as buttery *crème de courge* (pumpkin soup), grilled shrimp with fresh
thyme, and a rich chocolate terrine are served with casual flair. ⊠ *17*
rue des Rois, ☎ *022/3205999. MC, V. Closed weekends.*

$ ✕ **Taverne de la Madeleine.** Tucked behind l'Église de la Madeleine,
this local, friendly, alcohol-free café claims to be the oldest eatery in
Geneva. Relax over homemade choucroute, generous summer salads,
or fresh-baked fruit tarts in the charming Victorian dining room upstairs. Hot food is served until 9 PM in summer, only until 4 PM on Sat-

urday and in winter. ✉ *20 rue Toutes-âmes,* ☎ *022/3106070. MC, V. Closed Sun.*

$$$$ 🏨 **Beau-Rivage.** Hushed and genteel, this grand old Victorian palace maintains much of its original 1865 splendor: Rooms have period furniture, dramatic swagged fabrics, and enormous baths. Suites and front doubles overlook Mont-Blanc. In 1898, Empress Elizabeth of Austria died here after being stabbed only 300 ft away. ✉ *13 quai du Mont-Blanc, CH-1201,* ☎ *022/7166666,* 🖷 *022/7166060. 91 rooms, 6 suites. Restaurant. AE, DC, MC, V.*

$$$$ 🏨 **Des Bergues.** Creamy fabrics, graceful statues, and unpretentious, ★ friendly service give the oldest of Geneva's grand hotels an inner glow. The 19th-century architectural details and Louis-Philippe elegance mesh seamlessly with modern conveniences like private fax machines and Internet connections. The air is thick with discretion; registering guests are seated in the low-key marble lobby as if they were shopping for jewels. The sunny Le Pavillon serves an extraordinary afternoon tea. ✉ *33 quai des Bergues, CH-1201,* ☎ *022/7315050,* 🖷 *022/ 7321989. 104 rooms, 14 suites. 2 restaurants. AE, DC, MC, V.*

$$$$ 🏨 **Les Armures.** This 17th-century architectural treasure reveals charming original stonework, frescoes, and stenciled beams while still providing impeccable modern comforts. Intimate rooms are embellished with slick marble baths. Its casual restaurant is an Old Town must. Two very quiet rooms give onto a tiny inner courtyard; those overlooking rue du Perron have picturesque cobblestone views. ✉ *1 rue du Puits-St-Pierre, CH-1204,* ☎ *022/3109172,* 🖷 *022/3109846. 24 rooms, 4 suites. Restaurant. AE, DC, MC, V.*

$$$ 🏨 **Ambassador.** Don't let the airport-lounge lobby fool you—each room ★ in this central Right Bank hotel is fresh and colorful. Many of the huge doubles would be called suites elsewhere, and bathrooms gleam with white tile. You'll pay more for a room with a view, but it's worth it to see the sun rise over the Old Town across the river. ✉ *21 quai des Bergues, CH-1211,* ☎ *022/7317200,* 🖷 *022/7389080. 83 rooms. Restaurant. AE, DC, MC, V.*

$$–$$$ 🏨 **Le Montbrillant.** Nineteenth-century stone walls and beams accent the clean lines and crisp, blue-gray trim of this family-run hotel near the train station. If you plan to stay a few days, request one of the spacious fifth-floor studios—these have kitchenettes, dormer windows, and cathedral ceilings. The third floor is off limits to smokers. ✉ *2 rue de Montbrillant, CH-1201,* ☎ *022/7337784,* 🖷 *022/7332511. 58 rooms, 24 studios. 2 restaurants. AE, DC, MC, V.*

$$ 🏨 **Montana.** The warm welcome from the multilingual staff sets this spot heads above its neighbors. Two rooms still have two-way shoe-shine doors from 1957—but the property is up-to-date with in-room cable TV and Internet connections. Windows on all but the top floor are soundproof. The hotel is just a block from the train station. ✉ *23 rue des Alpes, CH-1201,* ☎ *022/7320840,* 🖷 *022/7382511. 40 rooms. AE, DC, MC, V.*

$$ 🏨 **Suisse.** This corner hotel across from the train station makes the ★ most of itself. The narrow lobby is brightly sponge-painted; colorful trompe l'oeil scenes decorate the elevator doors; a model tall ship or clipper greets you on the landing of each floor. The sunny, spacious rooms are soundproof, with generously sized bathrooms. ✉ *10 pl. de Cornavin, CH-1201,* ☎ *022/7326630,* 🖷 *022/7326239. 57 rooms. Restaurant. AE, DC, MC, V.*

$ 🏨 **Bel'Espérance.** The Salvation Army owns this former *foyer pour dames* ★ (ladies' boardinghouse) tucked away near place du Bourg-de-Four. Its conference facilities, bright yellow and blue rooms, tiled baths, and graceful Louis Philippe–style breakfast salon put it in the league of much pricier hotels. Monthly rates, nonsmoking rooms, and communal kitchen space are available. There's a no-alcohol policy. ⊠ *1 rue de la Vallée, CH-1204,* ☎ *022/8183737,* FAX *022/8183773. 38 rooms, 2 studios. AE, DC, MC, V.*

$ ☎ **De la Cloche.** Think of yourself as a privileged boarder in this once-
★ luxurious first-floor apartment. It's been carved into eight bedrooms that share toilets down the hall. The homey decor (flocked wallpaper, crowded bookcases, creaky parquet floors) matches the spirit. ⊠ *6 rue de la Cloche, CH-1201,* ☎ *022/7329481,* FAX *022/7381612. 8 rooms, 4 with bath. AE, DC, MC, V.*

Nightlife and the Arts

Geneva Agenda, which has weekly listings of concerts, exhibitions, and performances, is available free in tourist information booths and most hotels. It's bilingual (English/French).

The Arts

The **Grand Théâtre** (⊠ pl. Neuve, ☎ 022/4183000) stages a full-scale production roughly every six weeks between September and June. The luscious red velvet and cutting-edge technical facilities date from a 1998 restoration. The list of artists who have performed with **L'Orchestre de la Suisse Romande** in the gilt-and-velvet **Victoria Hall** (⊠ 14 rue Général-Dufour, ☎ 022/8070017) since 1918 reads like a who's who of classical music.

Nightlife

Le Baroque (⊠ 12 pl. de la Fusterie, ☎ 022/3110515) draws chic young bankers with its opulent decor. For a quiet drink, the piano bars of luxury hotels like the Beau-Rivage (☞ Dining and Lodging, *above*) are hard to beat. For dancing, **Arthur's** (⊠ 20 rte. de Pré-Bois, ☎ 022/7917700) spins house music and packs some 1,500 people into its multilevel dance areas. **La Clémence** (⊠ 20 pl. du Bourg-de-Four, ☎ 022/3122498) fills with university students and explodes into the street. You'll find live rhythm and blues during the week (and a black tie crowd) at **Griffin's** (⊠ 36 bd. Helvétique, ☎ 022/7351218). Try **L'Interdit** (⊠ 18 quai du Seujet, ☎ 022/7389091) for Versace-esque style and classic disco.

Geneva Essentials

Arriving and Departing

BY BUS

Long-distance buses generally use the **Gare Routière de Genève** (bus station, ⊠ pl. Dorcière, ☎ 022/7320230).

BY CAR

Since Geneva sits on the border of the French Alps, entry from the French autoroutes is very convenient; the French **A40** links Geneva to Chamonix and the French Alps as well as Annecy, Lyon, and Grenoble. From within Switzerland, enter from the north via the **A1** expressway from Lausanne.

BY PLANE

Cointrin (⊠ 5 km/3 mi northwest of city center, ☎ 022/7177111), Geneva's airport, is served by several airlines with direct flights from New York and London. Swissair also operates hourly connector flights to its hub in Zürich. Crossair, Switzerland's domestic airline, connects Geneva with Basel, Zürich, Lugano, and most major European cities.

Between the Airport and Downtown. Cointrin has a direct rail link with the **Gare Cornavin** (☎ 022/1572222), the city's main train station. Trains run about every 15 minutes from 5:45 AM to midnight. The trip takes about six minutes; the fare is 5 SF. There is also regular city **bus**

service between the airport and downtown. The bus takes about 20 minutes, and the fare is 2.20 SF. Some hotels provide their own shuttle service. **Taxis** are plentiful but expensive; you'll pay at least 25 SF to reach the city center, plus a 1 SF charge for each piece of luggage.

BY TRAIN

All services—domestic and international—use the **Gare Cornavin** (⊠ pl. Cornavin, ☎ 022/1572222). Direct express trains arrive from most Swiss cities every hour and the French TGV provides a fast link to Paris.

Getting Around

BY BUS AND TRAM

There are scheduled services by local buses and trams every few minutes on all routes. Before you board, you must buy your ticket from one of the vending machines at the stop (they have English instructions). For 2.20 SF you can use the system for one hour, changing as often as you like between buses, trams, or the Mouettes Genevoises (☞ Guided Tours, *below*). To save money and time, buy a **carte journalière**, a ticket for all-day unlimited city-center travel for 5 SF; these are available at most newsstands and the *transports publics genevois* booths at the train station and the Cours de Rive. Travel with a Swiss Pass is free (☞ Transportation by Train *in* Switzerland A to Z, *above*).

BY TAXI

Taxis are expensive. There is a 6.30 SF minimum charge per passenger just to get into the cab, plus a 2.70 SF-per-km (½ mi) charge, which climbs to 3.30 SF in the evening and on Sunday.

Contacts and Resources

CONSULATES

U.S. (⊠ 29 rte. de Pré-Bois, ☎ 022/7981615). **Canada** (⊠ 1 rue du Pré de la Bichette, ☎ 022/9199200). **U.K.** (⊠ 37–39 rue de Vermont, ☎ 022/9182400). **Australia** (⊠ 2 chemin des Fins, ☎ 022/7999100). **New Zealand** (⊠ 28A chemin du Petit-Saconnex, ☎ 022/7349530).

EMERGENCIES

Police (☎ 117). **Ambulance** (☎ 144). **Hospital** (⊠ Hôpital Cantonal, 24 rue Micheli-du-Crest, ☎ 022/3723311). **Doctor referral** (☎ 022/3202511). **Pharmacies** (☎ 111).

GUIDED TOURS

Boat. In good weather take one of the many boat tours around the lake, from a quick half-hour trip to a daylong cruise to Montreux and back: **Mouettes Genevoises** (☎ 022/7322944); **Swissboat** (☎ 022/7324747); or **Compagnie Générale de Navigation** (☎ 022/3125223).

Orientation. Two-hour bus-and-minitrain tours of Geneva, operated by **Key Tours** (☎ 022/7314140), leave from the bus station in place Dorcière daily at 2 PM and also at 10 AM May–October. You may opt to catch the minitrain (independent of the bus tour) at place Neuve for a trip around the Old Town.

Walking. The Tourist Office (☞ *below*) offers a series of daily two-hour group walks following itineraries that range from "Historic Edifices" to "International Geneva." Fees start at 35 SF per person; there's a minimum of two people. The Tourist Office also provides audio tours (in English) of the Old Town that cover 26 points of interest; they include a map, cassette, and player. Rental is 10 SF, plus a refundable deposit of 50 SF.

VISITOR INFORMATION

Office du Tourisme de Genève (Tourist Office; ⊠ 18 rue du Mont-Blanc, ☎ 022/9097000; ⊠ Cointrin arrivals terminal, ☎ 022/9097045;

✉ Gare Cornavin, ☎ 022/9097050; ✉ Pont de la Machine, ☎ 022/3119827). **Information by mail** (✉ 10 rte. de l'Aéroport, Case Postale 596, CH-1215, Genève 15, ☎ 022/9297000, FAX 022/9297011).

LUZERN

As you cruise down the leisurely sprawl of the Vierwaldstättersee, mist rising off the gray waves, mountains—great loaflike masses of forest and stone—looming above the clouds, it's easy to understand how Wagner could have composed his *Siegfried Idyll* in his mansion beside this lake. This is inspiring terrain, romantic and evocative. When the waters roil up you can hear the whistling chromatics and cymbal clashes of Gioacchino Rossini's thunderstorm from his 1829 opera, *Guillaume Tell*. It was on this lake, after all, that William Tell—the beloved, if legendary, Swiss national hero—supposedly leapt from the tyrant Gessler's boat to freedom. And it was in a meadow nearby that three furtive rebels and their cohorts swore an oath by firelight and planted the seed of the Swiss Confederation.

Exploring Luzern

Numbers in the margin correspond to points of interest on the Luzern map.

Luzern's Old Town straddles the waters of the River Reuss where it flows out of the Vierwaldstättersee, its more concentrated section occupying the river's right bank. There are a couple of passes available for discounts for museums and sights in the city. One is a museum pass that costs 25 SF and grants free entry to all museums for one month. If you are staying in a hotel, you may also want to pick up a special visitor's card; once stamped by the hotel, it entitles you to discounts at most museums and other tourist-oriented businesses as well. You can get both passes at the tourist office (☞ Luzern Essentials, *below*).

Altes Rathaus (Old Town Hall). This relic facing the end of a modern bridge, the Rathaus-Steg, was built between 1599 and 1606 in the late-Renaissance style. ✉ *Rathausquai, facing end of bridge, Rathaus-Steg.*

❶ Am Rhyn-Haus (Am Rhyn House). Also known as the Picasso Museum, the compact Renaissance-style building has an impressive collection of late paintings by Picasso. ✉ *Furreng. 21,* ☎ *041/4101773.* ۞ *Apr.–Oct., daily 10–6; Nov.–Mar., daily 11–1 and 2–4.*

❾ Bourbaki-Panorama. An enormous conical wooden structure was created in 1876–78 as a genuine, step-right-up tourist attraction. Its conical roof covers a sweeping, wraparound epic painting of the French Army of the East retreating into Switzerland at Verrières—a famous episode in the Franco-Prussian War. ✉ *Löwenpl.,* ☎ *041/4109942.* ۞ *May–Sept., daily 9–6; Mar., Apr., and Oct., daily 9–5.*

❺ Franziskanerkirche (Franciscan Church). More than 700 years old, this church retains its 17th-century choir stalls and carved wooden pulpit despite persistent modernization. ✉ *Franziskanerpl., just off Münzg.*

⓫ Gletschergarten (Glacier Garden). The bedrock of this 19th-century tourist attraction was excavated between 1872 and 1875 and has been dramatically pocked and polished by Ice Age glaciers. A private museum on the site displays impressive relief maps of Switzerland. ✉ *Denkmalstr. 4,* ☎ *041/4104340.* ۞ *May–mid-Oct., daily 8–6; Mar., Apr., and mid-Oct.–mid-Nov., daily 9–5; mid-Nov.–Feb., Tues.–Sat. 10:30–4:30, Sun. 10–5.*

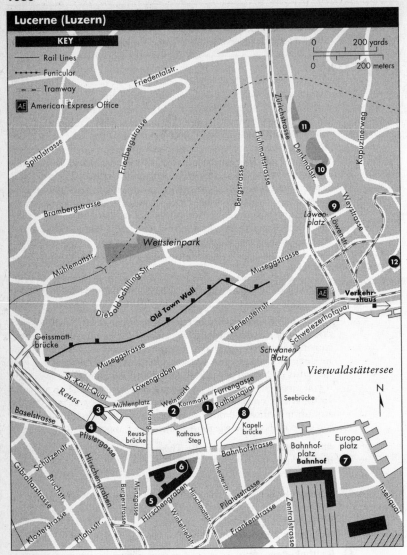

Lucerne (Luzern)

KEY

— Rail Lines
••••• Funicular
⊷⊷ Tramway
AE American Express Office

Friedentalstr.

Spitalstrasse

Brambergstrasse

Friedbergstrasse

Mühlemattstr.

Wettsteinpark

Diebold Schilling-Str.

Old Town Wall

Museggstrasse

Geissmatt-brücke

St.-Karli-Quai

Reuss

Löwengraben

Mühlenplatz

Baselstrasse

Schützenstr.

Gibraltarstrasse

Klosterstrasse

Pilatusstr.

Bruchstr.

Hirschengraben

Pfistergasse

Reuss-brücke

Krang

Rathaus-Steg

Münzgasse

Hirschengraben

Burgerstrasse

Winkelriedstr.

Hirschmattstr.

Theaterstr.

Weinmarkt

Kornmarkt

Furrengasse

Rathausquai

Kapell-brücke

Bahnhofstrasse

Pilatusstrasse

Frankenstrasse

Bergstrasse

Fluhmattstrasse

Museggstrasse

Hertensteinstr.

Zürichstrasse

Denkmalstr.

Löwen-platz

Weystrasse

Löwenstr.

Kapuzinerweg

Schwanen-Platz

Schweizerhofquai

AE **Verkehr-shaus**

Seebrücke

Vierwaldstättersee

Bahnhof-platz
Bahnhof

Europa-platz

Zentralstrasse

Inseliquai

N

0 — 200 yards
0 — 200 meters

4 **Historisches Museum** (Historical Museum). Dating from 1567, this building was an armory and today exhibits city sculptures, Swiss arms, and flags; reconstructed rooms depict rural and urban life. ⊠ *Pfisterg. 24,* ☎ *041/2285424.* ⊙ *Tues.–Fri. 10–noon and 2–5, weekends 10–5.*

12 **Hofkirche** (Collegiate Church). Founded in 750 as a monastery, this Gothic structure was destroyed by fire in 1633 and rebuilt in late-Renaissance style. The 80-rank organ (1650) is one of Switzerland's finest. ⊠ *St. Leodegarstr. 13.*

★ **6** **Jesuitenkirche** (Jesuit Church). Constructed in 1667–78, this Baroque edifice reveals a symmetrical entrance flanked by two onion-dome towers, added in 1893. The vast interior, restored to mint condition, is a rococo explosion of gilt, marble, and epic frescoes. ⊠ *Banhofstr., just west of Rathaus-Steg.*

★ **8** **Kapellbrücke** (Chapel Bridge). It snakes diagonally across the water and, when first built during the early 14th century, served as the dividing line between the lake and the river. Its shingled roof and grand stone water tower (now housing a souvenir stand) are to Luzern what the Matterhorn is to Zermatt—but considerably more vulnerable, as was proved by a fire in 1993. Almost 80% of this fragile monument was destroyed, including many of the 17th-century paintings inside; the original 111 gable panels painted by Heinrich Wägmann during the 17th century have been replaced with polychrome copies. The paintings depict scenes from the history of Luzern and Switzerland, legendary exploits of the city's patron saints—St. Leodegar and St. Mauritius, and coats of arms of local patrician families. ⊠ *Between Seebrücke and Rathaus-Steg bridges, connecting Rathausquai and Bahnhofstr.*

★ **7** **Kultur- und Kongresszentrum** (Culture and Conference Center). Architect Jean Nouvel's masterful design fits this glass and steel building smoothly into its ancient milieu; immense sheets of glass mirror the picture-postcard surroundings. Its concert hall has acoutics so perfect you can hear the proverbial pin drop. The annual, high-profile International Music Festival is held here. ⊠ *Europapl.,* ☎ *041/2201717.*

★ **10** **Löwendenkmal** (Lion Monument). The evocative monument commemorates the 760 Swiss guards and their officers who died defending Louis XVI of France at the Tuileries in Paris in 1792. Carved out of a sheer sandstone face by Lucas Ahorn of Konstanz, this 19th-century wonder is a simple image of a dying lion, his chin sagging on his shield, a broken stump of spear in his side. The Latin inscription translates: "To the bravery and fidelity of the Swiss." ⊠ *Denkmalstr.*

3 **Spreuerbrücke.** This narrow, weathered, all-wood covered bridge dates from 1408. In its center is a lovely 16th-century chapel looking back on the Old Town. Its interior gables hold a series of eerie, well-preserved paintings by Kaspar Meglinger of the *Dance of Death*; they date from the 17th century, though their style and inspiration—tracing to the plague that devastated Luzern and all of Europe during the 14th century—are medieval. ⊠ *Between Geissmattbrücke and Reussbrücke bridges, connecting Zeughaus Reuss-Steg and Mühlenpl.*

2 **Weinmarkt** (Wine Market). One of the loveliest of Luzern's several fountain squares, this former site of the wine market drew visitors from across Europe from the 15th to the 17th centuries to witness its passion plays. Its Gothic central fountain depicts St. Mauritius, patron saint of warriors, and its surrounding buildings are flamboyantly frescoed in 16th-century style. ⊠ *Sq. just west of Kornmarkt, north of Metzgerrainle.*

Elsewhere in Luzern

★ **Verkehrshaus.** The Swiss Transport Museum is one of Luzern's (if not Switzerland's) greater attractions. Easily reached by steamer, car, or Bus 2, it's almost a world's fair in itself, with a complex of buildings and exhibitions both indoors and out, including dioramas, live demonstrations, an IMAX theater, and a "Swissorama" (360° screen) film about Switzerland. Every mode of transit is discussed, from stagecoaches and bicycles to jumbo jets and space capsules. If you're driving, turn east at the waterfront and follow the signs. ⊠ *Lidostr. 5,* ☎ *041/3704444.* 🔄 *16 SF.* ☉ *Mar.–Oct., daily 9–6; Nov.–Feb., daily 10–5.*

Dining and Lodging

Rooted in the German region of Switzerland and surrounded by farmland, central Switzerland has a native cuisine that's best described as down-home and hearty. Luzern takes pride in its *Kügelipaschtetli,* puff pastry nests filled with tiny veal meatballs, mushrooms, cream sauce, occasionally raisins, and bits of chicken, pork, or sweetbreads. Watch for lake fish such as *Egli* (perch), *Hecht* (pike), *Forelle* (trout), and *Felchen* (whitefish). A Luzern tradition offers them sautéed and sauced with tomatoes, mushrooms, and capers. For details and price-category definitions *see* Dining *in* Switzerland A to Z, *above.*

Unlike most Swiss cities, Luzern has its high and low seasons, and lodgings drop prices considerably in winter. For details and price-category definitions *see* Lodging *in* Switzerland A to Z, *above.*

$$$$ ★ ✕ **Wilden Mann.** Both dining rooms here—one formal, the other cozily old-fashioned—are excellent, combining old-style local cooking with French cuisine. The Bürgerstube is all dark beams and family crests, while the Liedertafel dining room has soft candlelight and a vaulted ceiling. In both spots the menus and prices are the same; try the smoked salmon tartare wrapped in Rösti with dill sauce or the duck breast with dandelion honey and balsamic vinegar. ⊠ *Bahnhofstr. 30,* ☎ *041/2101666. AE, DC, MC, V.*

$$$ ★ ✕ **Rotes Gatter.** This chic restaurant in the Des Balances hotel (☞ *below*) has a combination as desirable as it is rare: soigné decor, shimmering river views, and a sophisticated menu with fish dishes such as curry cream scallops, or the house specialty, meat and fish fondue. There's a more casual, less-expensive bistro area as well. ⊠ *Weinmarkt,* ☎ *041/4103010. AE, DC, MC, V.*

$$ ★ ✕ **Galliker.** Step past the ancient facade into an all-wood room roaring with local action. Brisk, motherly waitresses serve the dishes Mutti used to make: Fresh *Kutteln* (tripe) in rich white wine sauce with cumin seeds; real *Kalbskopf* (chopped fresh veal head) served with heaps of green onions and warm vinaigrette; and their famous simmered-beef pot-au-feu. ⊠ *Schützenstr. 1,* ☎ *041/2401002. AE, DC, MC, V. Closed Sun., Mon., and 3 wks in Aug.*

$$ ✕ **Rebstock/Hofstube.** Across from the Hofkirche, this kitchen offers modern, international fare, including rabbit, lamb, and organic vegetarian specialties. The lively bentwood brasserie hums with locals lunching by the bar, while the more formal, old-style restaurant glows with wood and brass under a low-beamed herringbone-patterned ceiling. ⊠ *St. Leodegarpl. 3,* ☎ *041/4103581. AE, DC, MC, V.*

$ ✕ **Pfistern.** One of the architectural focal points of the Old Town waterfront, this floridly decorated former guildhall offers a good selection of moderately priced meals in addition to higher-priced standards. Lake fish and *pastetli* (meat pies made with puff pastry) are good local options. ⊠ *Kornmarkt 4,* ☎ *041/4103650. AE, DC, MC, V.*

$$$$ ✕▯▯ **Palace Hotel.** This waterfront hotel drinks in the broadest possible lake views. Built in 1906, it has been brilliantly refurbished so that its classical look has a touch of postmodernism. Rooms are large enough for a game of badminton and picture windows afford sweeping views of Lake Luzern and Mt. Pilatus. The hotel's elegance infuses its excellent restaurant, Mignon, as well. (Reservations are essential.) ✉ *Haldenstr. 10, CH-6002,* ☎ *041/4100404,* ▯▯ *041/4101504. 178 rooms, 45 suites. Restaurant. AE, DC, MC, V.*

$$$$ ▯▯ **Château Gütsch.** Any antiquity in this "castle" (built as a hotel in 1888) is strictly contrived, but honeymooners, groups, and determined romantics in search of a storybook Europe enjoy the Disneyland-like experience. The turrets and towers are worthy of mad Ludwig of Bavaria; a hodgepodge of relics lines the cellars, crypts, and corridors; and beyond the magnificent hilltop site is a private forest. ✉ *Kanonenstr., CH-6002,* ☎ *041/2494100,* ▯▯ *041/2494191. 28 rooms, 3 suites. 2 restaurants, pool. AE, DC, MC, V.*

$$$ ▯▯ **Des Balances.** This 19th-century riverfront property gleams with
★ style. State-of-the-art tile baths, up-to-date pastel decor, and one of the best sites in Luzern (in the heart of the Old Town) make this the slickest in its price class. The restaurant, Rotes Gatter, is so good, you may want to eat every meal in the hotel. ✉ *Weinmarkt, CH-6000,* ☎ *041/4103010,* ▯▯ *041/4106451. 50 rooms, 7 suites. Restaurant. AE, DC, MC, V.*

$$$ ▯▯ **Wilden Mann.** The city's best-known hotel offers its guests a gra-
★ cious and authentic experience of Old Luzern, with stone, beams, brass, and burnished wood everywhere. Standard rooms have a prim 19th-century look. The hotel's reputation is matched by its restaurants (☞ *above*). ✉ *Bahnhofstr. 30, CH-6003,* ☎ *041/2101666,* ▯▯ *041/ 2101629. 35 rooms, 8 suites. 2 restaurants. AE, DC, MC, V.*

$$ ▯▯ **Des Alpes.** This historic hotel, with a terrific riverfront location in the bustling heart of the Old Town, has an interior resembling a laminate-and-vinyl chain motel. Rooms are generously proportioned, tidy, and sleek; front doubles, several with balconies, overlook the water and the promenade. ✉ *Rathausquai 5, CH-6003,* ☎ *041/4105825,* ▯▯ *041/4107451. 45 rooms. 2 restaurants. AE, DC, MC, V.*

$$ ▯▯ **Krone.** Spotless and modern, this hotel softens its edges with pastel linens and walls; along the interior walls you may find a stone prayer shrine retained from the original structure. The rooms facing the Weinmarkt have high ceilings and tall windows that let in floods of sunshine. Rooms to the back are less bright but a little larger. The restaurant has a no-alcohol policy. ✉ *Weinmarkt 12, CH-6004,* ☎ *041/4194400,* ▯▯ *041/4194490. 25 rooms. Restaurant. AE, DC, MC, V.*

$ ▯▯ **Schlüssel.** This spare, no-nonsense little lodging on the Franziskanerplatz attracts young bargain hunters. It's a pleasant combination of tidy new touches (quarry tile, white paint) and antiquity: You can have dinner in a low, cross-vaulted "crypt" and admire the fine old lobby beams. ✉ *Franziskanerpl. 12, CH-6003,* ☎ *041/2101061,* ▯▯ *041/ 2101021. 11 rooms. Restaurant. AE, DC, MC, V.*

$ ▯▯ **Tourist.** Despite its friendly, collegiate atmosphere, this cheery
★ dormlike spot is anything but a backpackers' flophouse. It has a terrific setting around the corner from the Old Town. The coed four-bed, shared-bath dorms (sex-segregated in high season) draw sociable travelers with their rock-bottom prices; there are also seven private-bath doubles. ✉ *St. Karli Quai 12, CH-6003,* ☎ *041/4102474,* ▯▯ *041/4108414. 35 dormitory rooms, 7 doubles with bath. AE, DC, MC, V.*

Nightlife and the Arts

For information on its concerts and other performances throughout the year, consult the German/English *Luzern City Guide* published by the city seasonally; it's available at the tourist office (☞ Luzern Essentials, *below*).

The Arts

The Allgemeine Musikgesellschaft Luzern (AML), the local orchestra in residence, offers a season of concerts from October through June. These are held in the **Kunsthaus** (⊠ Moosstr. 15, ☎ 041/2105050). Luzern hosts the **International Music Festival** for three weeks in August every year. Performances take place at the Kultur- und Kongresszentrum (☞ Exploring Luzern, *above*). For more information, contact Internationale Musikfestwochen (⊠ Hirschmanttstr. 13, CH-6002 Luzern, ☎ 041/2264400).

Nightlife

BARS AND LOUNGES

Château Gütsch (⊠ Kanonenstr., ☎ 041/2494141) draws a sedate dinner-and-dancing crowd. The **National Hotel** (⊠ Haldenstr. 4, ☎ 041/4190909) serves drinks in both its glossy American-style bar and its imposing lobby lounge. The **Palace Hotel** (⊠ Haldenstr. 10, ☎ 041/4100404) has two American-style bars.

CASINO

The most sophisticated nightlife in Luzern is found in the **Casino** (⊠ Haldenstr. 6, ☎ 041/4185656), a turn-of-the-century building on the northern shore by the grand hotels. You can visit the Gambling Room (5 SF limit, federally imposed), dance in the **Vegas** club, or have a Swiss meal in **Le Chalet** while watching a folklore display.

FOLKLORE

Nightboat (⊠ Landungsbrücke 6, ☎ 041/3194978) sails nightly May through September at 8:45, offering drinks, meals, and a folklore show. The **Stadtkeller** (⊠ Sternenpl. 3, ☎ 041/4104733) transports you to the Valais Alps for cheese, yodeling, and dirndled dancers.

Shopping

Luzern no longer produces embroidery or lace, but you can find Swiss crafts of the highest quality, and watches in all price categories. **Bucherer** (⊠ Schwanenpl., ☎ 041/3697700) represents Piaget and Rolex. **Gübelin** (⊠ Schweizerhofquai 1, ☎ 041/4105142) is the exclusive source for Audemars Piguet, Patek Philippe, and its own house brand. **Ordning & Reda** (⊠ Hertensteinstr. 3, ☎ 041/4109506) is a Swedish stationer whose store is filled with brightly colored, handmade, recycled paper products. At **Sturzenegger** (⊠ Schwanenpl. 7, ☎ 041/4101958), you'll find St.-Gallen-made linens and embroidered niceties.

Luzern Essentials

Arriving and Departing

BY CAR

It's easy to reach Luzern from Zürich by road, approaching from the national expressway **A3** south, connecting to the **A4** via the secondary E41, in the direction of Zug, and continuing on A4 to the city (roads are well marked). Approaching from the southern St. Gotthard Pass route, or after cutting through the Furka Pass by rail ferry, you'll descend below Andermatt to Altdorf, where a view-stifling tunnel sweeps you through to the shores of the lake and on to the city. Arriving from Basel in the northwest, it's a clean sweep on the **A2** into Luzern.

BY PLANE

The nearest international airport is **Kloten** in Zürich (✉ 54 km/33 mi northeast of Luzern, ☎ 1571060). Swissair flies in most often from the United States and the United Kingdom. Easy rail connections, departing hourly, whisk you on to Luzern within 50 minutes.

BY TRAIN

Luzern functions as a rail crossroads, with express trains connecting hourly from Zürich and every two hours from Geneva, the latter with a change at Bern. For rail information, call the **Swiss Federal Railways** (☎ 1572222).

Getting Around

Luzern's modest scale allows you to explore most of the city easily on foot, but you will want to resort to mass transit to visit such noncentral attractions as the Verkehrshaus (Swiss Transport Museum).

BY BOAT

It's a crime to see this city and the surrounding mountainous region only from the shore; some of its most impressive landscapes can be seen from the deck of one of the cruise ships that ply the Vierwaldstättersee (Lake Lucerne). The boats of the Schiffahrtsgesellschaft des Vierwaldstättersees (☎ 041/3676767) operate on a standardized, mass-transit-style schedule, crisscrossing the lake and stopping at scenic resorts and historic sites. The Swiss Pass entitles you to free rides; the Swiss Boat Pass (☞ Transportation by Boat *in* Switzerland A to Z, *above*) gives you a discount.

BY BUS

The city bus system offers easy access to sights throughout the urban area. If you're staying in a Luzern hotel, you will be eligible for a special **Guest-Ticket,** offering unlimited rides for two days for a minimal fee of 8 SF.

BY TAXI

Given the small scale of the Old Town and the narrowness of most of its streets, taxis can prove a pricey encumbrance.

Contacts and Resources

EMERGENCIES

Police (☎ 117). **Medical, dental, and pharmacy referral** (☎ 111). **Auto breakdown: Tourist Club of Switzerland** (☎ 140); **Swiss Automobile Club** (☎ 041/2100155).

GUIDED TOURS

Orientation. The City Tourist Office (☞ *below*) offers a two-hour guided walking tour of Luzern with English commentary.

VISITOR INFORMATION

City Tourist Office (✉ Frankenstr. 1, near the Bahnhof, ☎ 041/4107171). **Tourist information center** (with accommodation service; ✉ Schweizerhofquai 2). **Central Switzerland Tourism Association** (✉ Verkehrsverband Zentralschweiz, ✉ Alpenstr. 1, Luzern, ☎ 041/4184080).

LUGANO

Because of the beautiful, sparkling bay of the Lago di Lugano and dark, conical mountains rising up on either side, Lugano is often referred to as "the Rio of the Old World." The largest city in the Ticino—Switzerland's Italian-speaking region—Lugano has not escaped some of the overdevelopment inevitable in a successful resort town. There's bumper-to-bumper traffic, right up to the waterfront, much of it manic Italian–style; and concrete high-rise hotels crowd the waterfront, with balconies skewed to a view no matter what the aesthetic cost.

Even so, the view from the waterfront is unforgettable, the boulevards are fashionable, and the Old Quarter is still reminiscent of sleepy old towns in Italy. And the sacred *passeggiata*—the early evening stroll to see and be seen—asserts the city's true personality as a graceful, sophisticated old-world resort—not Swiss, not Italian . . . just Lugano.

Exploring Lugano

Numbers in the margin correspond to points of interest on the Lugano map.

❽ Castagnola Parks. The **Parco degli Ulivi** (Olive Park) spreads over the lower slopes of Monte Brè and offers a romantic landscape of silvery olive trees mixed with cypress, laurel, and wild rosemary; you enter it from the Gandria footpath (Sentiero di Gandria). **Parco San Michele** (St. Michael Park), also on Monte Brè, has a public chapel and a broad terrace that overlooks the city; the lake; and, beyond, the Alps. From Cassarate, walk up the steps by the lower terminus of the Monte Brè funicular. ▱ *Free.*

❺ Cattedrale di San Lorenzo (Cathedral of St. Lawrence). With its graceful Renaissance facade, this cathedral contains noteworthy frescoes inside and a lovely view outside. ⊠ *Via Cattedrale.* ▱ *Free.*

★ ❻ Chiesa di Santa Maria degli Angioli (Church of St. Mary of the Angels). Dating from 1455, this church has frescoes of the *Passion* and *Crucifixion* by Bernardino Luini (1475–1532). ⊠ *Piazza Luini.* ▱ *Free.*

❼ Giardino Belvedere (Belvedere Gardens). Here you'll see 12 modern sculptures with palms, camellias, oleanders, and magnolias. At the far west end there's public bathing on the Riva Caccia. ⊠ *Quai Riva Antonio Caccia.* ☉ *Daily.*

❸ Lido. Along the lake the municipal stretch of sandy beach includes several swimming pools (heated in spring and autumn), and a restaurant. ⊠ *Entrance on right off Viale Castagnola,* ☎ *091/9714041.* ▱ *7 SF.* ☉ *May and Sept., daily 9:30–6; July and Aug. daily 9–7.*

❷ Museo Cantonale di Storia Naturale (Cantonal Museum of Natural History). This museum in the Parco Civico (☞ *below*) has exhibits on the region's fossils, plants, and mushrooms. ⊠ *Viale Cattaneo 4 (on the grounds of the Parco Civico),* ☎ *091/9115380.* ▱ *Free.* ☉ *Tues.–Sat. 9–noon and 2–5.*

🐾 ❶ Parco Civico (Town Park). With its cacti, exotic shrubs, and more than 1,000 varieties of roses, this first-rate park also holds fountains, statues, an aviary, a tiny "deer zoo," and a fine view of the bay from its peninsula. Music and events take place here during fair-weather months. **Villa Ciani** has paintings and sculptures from Tintoretto to Giacometti. ⊠ *Area south of Viale Carlo Cattaneo, east of Piazza Castello.*

★ ❹ Piazza della Riforma. Stronghold of Lugano's Italian culture, here you'll encounter modish locals socializing in outdoor cafés. From the piazza one can enter the **Old Town** and follow the steep, narrow streets lined with chic Italian clothing shops and small markets offering pungent local cheeses and porcini mushrooms. Many festivals and concerts take place here. ⊠ *Town center.*

★ ❾ Villa Favorita. This splendid 16th-century mansion in Castagnola houses a portion of the extraordinary private art collection of the Baron von Thyssen-Bornemisza. Among the artists represented are Lucien Freud, Edward Hopper, Franz Marc, Jackson Pollock, and Andrew Wyeth. The villa gardens are lush with native and exotic flora. Call ahead; opening hours and entrance fees can change during spe-

Lugano

Lago di Lugano

KEY

ℹ️ Tourist Information

0	440 yards
0	400 meters

cial exhibitions. ⊠ *Strada Castagnola, Via Rivera 14,* ☎ *091/9721741.* ▨ *12 SF; 5 SF for park only.* ⊙ *Easter–Oct., Fri.–Sun. 10–6.*

Dining and Lodging

The Ticinese were once poor mountain people, so their cuisine shares the earthy delights of the Piemontese: polenta, gnocchi, game, and mushrooms. But as in all prosperous resorts, the mink-and-Vuarnets set draws the best in upscale international cooking. Prix-fixe lunches are almost always cheaper, so dine as the Luganese do—before your siesta. That way you can sleep off the fruity local merlot wine before the requisite *passeggiata* through the piazza. For details and price-category definitions, *see* Dining *in* Switzerland A to Z, *above*.

There are few inexpensive hotels in downtown Lugano, but a brief drive into the surrounding countryside increases your options. Since this is a summer resort, many hotels close for the winter, so call ahead. For details and price-category definitions, *see* Lodging *in* Switzerland A to Z, *above*.

$$$$ ✕ **Al Portone.** Silver and lace dress up the stucco and stone, but the
★ ambience here is strictly easy. Chef Roberto Galizzi creates *nuova cucina* (nouvelle cuisine, Italian-style) with ambition and flair, putting local spins on classics such as roast veal kidneys with balsamic vinegar, pasta with white beans and lobster, and seafood carpaccio. ⊠ *Viale Cassarate 3, Lugano/Cassarate,* ☎ *091/9235511. Reservations essential. AE, DC, MC, V. Closed Sun. and Mon.*

$$$$ ✕ **Santabbondio.** Ancient stone and terra-cotta blend with pristine pas-
★ tels in this upgraded grotto, where superb and imaginative new Franco-Italian dishes are served in intimate, formal little dining rooms and on a flower-filled terrace. Watch for lobster risotto, eggplant ravioli, or scallops in orange-basil sauce. It's a cab ride from town, toward the airport, but worth the trip. ⊠ *Via Fomelino 10, Lugano/Sorengo,* ☎ *091/9932388. AE, DC, MC, V. Closed Mon., 1st wk in Jan. and last wk in Feb. No lunch Sat., no dinner Sun.*

$$$ ✕ **Galleria.** Though the setting aspires to formal hauteur, with contemporary appointments, modern art, and jacket-clad guests, family warmth and vigor peek through the veneer, and in the end this is a comfortable place for good, middle-class Italian cooking. ⊠ *Via Cantonale, Lugano/Manno,* ☎ *091/6108761. AE, DC, MC, V. Closed Sun. and the 2nd and 3rd wks of Aug.*

$$$ ✕ **Locanda del Boschetto.** The grill is the first thing you see in this no-
★ nonsense restaurant specializing in simple but sensational seafood *alla griglia* (grilled). Crisp linens contrast with rustic wood touches, and the low-key service is helpful and down-to-earth. ⊠ *Via Boschetto 8,* ☎ *091/9942493. AE, DC, MC, V. Closed Mon. and first ½ Nov.*

$–$$ ✕ **Da Raffaelle.** Having a meal in this family-run Italian restaurant feels like being let in on a neighborhood secret. Start with a pasta, then try something from the grill, like *gamberoni all griglia* (grilled shrimp). The restaurant is just outside the city in a residential neighborhood, but easily reached by car or by bus 8 or 9 from the train station to the Viganello stop. ⊠ *Contrada dei Patrizi 8/via Pazzalino, Viganello,* ☎ *091/9716614. AE, MC, V. Closed Sun., last wk. of July and 1st two wks. of Aug. No lunch Sat.*

$ ✕ **Grotto Figini.** This is the real thing. In a short stretch of woods on a hill in Gentilino, above Lugano-Paradiso, locals gather here for a *boccalino* of good merlot and a satisfying, rib-sticking meal of polenta and grilled meats. Don't expect English or other tourists. ⊠ *Via ai Grotti,* ☎ *091/9946497. V. Closed Mon., mid-Dec.–Feb.*

$ ✕ **La Tinera.** This tiny tavern crowds loyal locals, tourists, and fami-
★ lies onto wooden benches for authentic regional specialties, hearty meats,
and pastas. It's tucked down an alley off Via Pessina in the Old Town.
Regional wine is served in traditional ceramic bowls. ⊠ *Via dei Gorini
2,* ☎ *091/9235219. AE, DC, MC, V. Closed Sun. and Aug.*

$$$$ ▥ **Ticino.** This warmly appointed, 500-year-old palazzo, protected as
★ a historical monument, is in the heart of the Old Town, just steps away
from the funicular to the station. Shuttered windows look out from
every room onto a glassed-in garden and courtyard, and vaulted halls
are lined with art and antiques. There are nonsmoking rooms available, and there's a two-night minumum stay. ⊠ *Piazza Cioccaro 1, CH-
6901,* ☎ *091/9227772,* FAX *091/9236278. 18 rooms, 2 suites. Restaurant.
AE, DC, MC, V. Closed Jan.*

$$$$ ▥ **Villa Principe Leopoldo/Hotel Montalbano.** This sumptuously ap-
★ pointed Relais & Châteaux garden mansion sits on the "Collina d'Oro"
(Golden Hill), offering guests magnificent lake, garden, or pool views.
There are scads of facilities, including a fitness room, sauna, and tennis. ⊠ *Via Montalbano 5, CH-6900,* ☎ *091/9858855,* FAX *091/9858825.
70 rooms, 4 suites. 3 restaurants, pool. AE, DC, MC, V.*

$$$–$$$$ ▥ **Du Lac.** This discreet, simple hotel offers you true lakefront luxury
for your money. All rooms face the lake, but the sixth floor is the qui-
etest. The hotel has a private swimming area on the lake, plus a num-
ber of such pampering facilities as a sauna and massage. ⊠ *Riva
Paradiso 3, CH-6902 Lugano/Paradiso,* ☎ *091/9941921,* FAX *091/
9941122. 52 rooms, 1 suite. Restaurant, pool. AE, DC, MC, V. Closed
Jan.–mid-Mar.*

$$$ ▥ **Alba.** This solid little hotel, surrounded by landscaped grounds, is
★ ideal for lovers with a sense of camp or honeymooners looking for pri-
vacy. It's lavish in the extreme—mirrors, gilt, plush, and crystal fill the
public areas, and the beds are all ruffles and swags. ⊠ *Via delle Scuole
11, CH-6902 Lugano-Paradiso,* ☎ *091/9943731,* FAX *091/9944523.
25 rooms, 1 suite. Restaurant, outdoor pool. AE, DC, MC, V.*

$$$ ▥ **International au Lac.** This is a big, old-fashioned, friendly city hotel,
half a block from the lake, with many lake-view rooms. It's next to
Santa Maria degli Angioli, on the edge of the Old Town. ⊠ *Via Nassa
68, CH-6901,* ☎ *091/9227541,* FAX *091/9227544. 80 rooms. Restau-
rant, pool. AE, DC, MC, V. Closed Nov.–Easter.*

$$$ ▥ **Park-Hotel Nizza.** This former villa affords panoramic views from
★ its perch on the lower slopes of San Salvatore; it's an uphill hike from
town. The mostly small rooms are decorated in styles ranging from repro-
antique to modern; there is no extra charge for lake views. A cozy bar
overlooks the lake, and a good restaurant serves vegetables from its
own garden and even wine from its own vineyards—alfresco, when
weather permits. There are some nonsmoking rooms, and one of the
restaurants is nonsmoking as well. A shuttle provides service to the nearby
town Paradiso. ⊠ *Via Guidino 14, CH-6902,* ☎ *091/9941771,* FAX *091/
9941773. 29 rooms. 2 restaurants, outdoor pool, indoor pool. AE, MC,
V. Closed mid-Dec.–mid-Mar.*

$$ ▥ **San Carlo.** The San Carlo offers one of the better deals in this high-
priced town: It's small, clean, quiet, and newly renovated. The loca-
tion's great too—right on the main pedestrian shopping street, a block
from the waterfront, and just 150 yards from the funicular that takes
you to the railway station. ⊠ *Via Nassa 28, CH-6901,* ☎ *091/9227107,*
FAX *091/9228022. 22 rooms. AE, DC, MC, V.*

$ ▥ **Dishma.** The welcoming owners of this hotel make it a bargain worth
seeking out. The rooms are clean and bright, with flowers on the bal-
conies; public rooms are a riot of colors, souvenirs, and knick-knacks.
The restaurant is nonsmoking (rare in these parts). ⊠ *Vicolo Geretta*

6, CH-6902 Lugano-Paradiso, ☎ *091/9942131,* 🖷 *091/9941503. 35 rooms. Restaurant. AE, MC, V. Closed Dec.–Feb.*

$ 🏨 **Zurigo.** Handy to parks and shopping, this spartan hotel near the Palais Congrès offers quiet comfort at rock-bottom rates, even in high season. ✉ *Corso Pestalozzi 13, CH-6900,* ☎ *091/9234343,* 🖷 *091/9239268. 28 rooms. AE, DC, MC, V. Closed Nov.–mid-Mar.*

Lugano Essentials

Arriving and Departing

BY CAR

There are fast, direct highways from both Milan and Zürich. If you are planning to drive from Geneva, check weather conditions with the automobile associations beforehand.

BY PLANE

There are short connecting flights by **Crossair**—the Swiss domestic network—to Aeroporto Lugano-Agno (☎ 091/6101212) from Zürich, Geneva, Basel, and Bern, as well as from Paris, Nice, Rome, Florence, and Venice. The nearest intercontinental airport is **Malpensa**, about 50 km (31 mi) northwest of Milan, Italy.

Between the Airport and Downtown. There is no regular bus service between the local airport and central Lugano, 7 km (4 mi) away, but there is a shuttle bus which operates on request (☎ 079/2214243). A taxi ride costs about 30 SF to the center.

BY TRAIN

There's a train from Zürich every hour; the trip takes about three hours. If you're coming from Geneva, you can catch the Milan express at various times, changing at Domodossola and Bellinzona. During the day, there's a train every hour from Milan's Stazione Centrale; the trip takes about 1½ hours. Always keep passports handy and confirm times with the **Swiss Federal Railways** (☎ 1572222).

Getting Around

BY BOAT

The **Navigation Company of Lake Lugano** (☎ 091/9715223) offers cruise-boat excursions around the bay to the romantic fishing village of Gandria and to the Villa Favorita. You may use these like public transit, following a schedule and paying according to distance, or look into special tickets: Seven consecutive days' unlimited travel costs 58 SF, three days' within a week costs 51 SF; an all-day pass costs 32 SF.

BY BUS

Well-integrated services run regularly on all local routes. Buy your ticket from the machine at the stop before you board.

BY TAXI

Though less expensive than in Zürich or Geneva, taxis are still not cheap, with a 10 SF minimum. To order a cab, call 091/9712121 or 091/9719191.

BY TRAIN

The **Regional Holiday Season Ticket** gives unlimited free travel for seven consecutive days on most rail and steamer routes and a 50% or 25% discount on longer trips in Lugano. Available at the Tourist Office, they cost 92 SF (82 SF for Swiss Pass holders). They can be used with or without a Swiss Pass (☞ Transportation *in* Switzerland A to Z, *above*). The newest version offers any three out of seven days free on most routes, with 50% or 25% reductions on the remaining four days. It costs 70 SF (62 SF for Swiss Pass holders).

Contacts and Resources

Police (☎ 117). **Ambulance** (☎ 144). **Civic hospital** (☎ 091/8056111). **Dental clinic** (☎ 091/9350180).

The Tourist Office has information about hiking tours into the mountains surrounding Lugano; it offers a wonderful packet of topographical maps and itineraries. Cycling maps are also available. There are bus trips to Locarno, Ascona, Lake Como, Lake Maggiore, Milan, Venice, St. Moritz, Florence, the Alpine passes, and the Italian market in Como.

Lugano Tourism (Tourist Office; ✉ Palazzo Civico, CH-6901, ☎ 091/9133232, ℻ 091/9227653).

BERN

No cosmopolitan nonsense here: Local specialties are fatback and sauerkraut, the annual fair celebrates the humble onion, and the president takes the tram to work. Walking down medieval streets past squares teeming with farmers' markets and cafés full of shirtsleeved politicos, you might forget the city of Bern is the federal capital—indeed, the geographic and political hub—of a sophisticated nation.

Bern earned its pivotal position with a combination of muscle and influence dating from the 12th century, when the Holy Roman Emperor Berchtold V established a fortress on this gooseneck in the River Aare. By the 15th century the Bernese had overcome the Burgundians to expand their territories west to Geneva. Napoléon suppressed them briefly—from 1798 until his defeat in 1815—but by 1848 Bern was back in charge as the capital of the Swiss Confederation. Yet today it's not the massive Bundeshaus (Houses of Parliament) that dominates the city but instead its perfectly preserved arcades and fountains—all remnants of its heyday as a medieval power. They're the reason UNESCO granted Bern World Cultural Heritage status, along with the Egyptian pyramids, Rome, Florence, and the Taj Mahal.

Exploring Bern

Numbers in the margin correspond to points of interest on the Bern map.

Bern's easily walkable streets seem to follow the river's flow, running in long parallels east to the Old Town. The Old Town was founded on the farthest tip and grew westward; its towers mark those stages of growth like rings on a tree. The city is crisscrossed by *Lauben* (arcades) that shelter stores of every kind and quality.

★ **❽ Bärengraben** (Bear Pits). According to legend, Berchtold V named Bern after the first animal he killed while hunting. It was a bear; in those days the woods were full of them. Live mascots have been on display here since the late 1400s. Pampered and well-fed on carrots, they caper and roll for tourists year-round. ✉ *South side of Nydeggbrücke.*

★ **❸ Bundeshaus** (Capitol). This hulking, domed building is the beating heart of the Swiss Confederation and meeting place for the Swiss National Council. Free guided tours include entry to the parliamentary chambers. ✉ *Bundespl.,* ☎ *031/3228522.* ☉ *Free tours daily at 9, 10, 11, 2, 3, and 4 (Sun. until 3). Can vary according to Parliament sessions.*

❶ Heiliggeistkirche (Church of the Holy Ghost). This broad Baroque edifice, finished in 1729, stands at odds with both the modern and the medieval in Bern. ⊠ *Spitalg. 44, across from Hauptbahnhof.*

★ **⓬ Historisches Museum** (Historical Museum). This daunting Victorian sprawl houses a prehistoric collection, 15th-century Flemish tapestries, and Bernese sculptures as well as 15th- and 16th-century stained-glass windows. Don't miss the novel three-way portrait of Calvin, Zwingli, and Luther. ⊠ *Helvetiapl. 5,* ☎ *031/3507711.* ⊘ *Tues.–Sun. 10–5.*

❺ Kornhaus (Granary). Its magnificent vaulted cellar, now a popular restaurant (☞ Kornhauskeller *in* Dining and Lodging, *below*), once held the city government's wine stores. Extensive renovations took place throughout 1998; it now houses the Forum for Media and Design, which hosts exhibitions on architecture, photography, contemporary media, and applied arts. ⊠ *Kornhauspl. 18,* ☎ *031/3129110.* ⊘ *Tues.–Fri. 10–7, weekends 10–5.*

⓫ Kunsthalle (Art Gallery). This groundbreaking contemporary art venue displays the works of living artists, usually before you've heard of them. Built in 1918 in heroic classical style to boost local artists—Kirchner, Klee, Hodler—it grew to attract the young Kandinsky, Mirò, Cy Twombly—and a parade of newcomers of strong potential. ⊠ *Helvetiapl. 1,* ☎ *031/3510031.* ⊘ *Tues. 10–9, Wed.–Sun. 10–5.*

★ **❷ Kunstmuseum** (Art Museum). Established for the promotion of Swiss artists, this landmark art museum houses an exceptional group of works by Ferdinand Hodler, including some enormous allegories. Fans of Paul Klee have hit the jackpot: the world's largest collection of his work, with more than 2,000 pieces. There is also an impressive collection of old masters and Impressionists, and a constant turnover of temporary exhibitions. ⊠ *Hodlerstr. 8–12,* ☎ *031/3110944.* ⊘ *Tues. 10–9, Wed.–Sun. 10–5.*

★ **❾ Münster** (Cathedral). Begun in 1421, Bern's famous cathedral was planned on lines so spacious that half the population could worship in it at one time; its construction went on for centuries. It has an outstanding, brightly painted portal (1490) depicting the Last Judgment, and there are stunning stained-glass windows, both originals and period reproductions. The steeple, added in 1893, is the tallest in Switzerland. ⊠ *Münsterpl. 1,* ☎ *031/3110572.* ⊘ *Easter Sun.–Oct. 31, Tues.–Sat. 10–5, Sun. 11:30–5; Nov.–Easter Sun., Tues.–Fri. 10–noon and 2–4, Sat. 10–noon and 2–5, Sun. 11:30–2.*

⓯ Museum für Kommunikation (Museum of Communication). This high-concept museum (formerly the Schweizerisches PTT Museum) has detailed documents, art, and artifacts relating to the history of the mails in Switzerland. There's a magnificent stamp and postmark collection. ⊠ *Helvetiastr. 16,* ☎ *031/3575555.* ⊘ *Tues.–Sun. 10–5.*

★ **⓮ Naturhistorisches Museum** (Museum of Natural History). Considered one of Europe's finest museums of natural history, this institution has a huge display area with a slick, skylit wing. It features enormous wildlife dioramas and a splendid collection of Alpine minerals. ⊠ *Bernastr. 15,* ☎ *031/3507111.* ⊘ *Mon. 2–5, Tues. and Thurs.–Fri. 9–5, Wed. 9–8, weekends 10–5.*

❼ Nydeggkirche (Nydegg Church). Built between 1341 and 1571 on the foundations of Berchtold V's ruined fortress, this ancient church marks the founding place of Bern. ⊠ *Nydegg.,* ☎ *031/3116102.* ⊘ *Daily 10–noon and 2–5:30. Closed Sun. afternoon.*

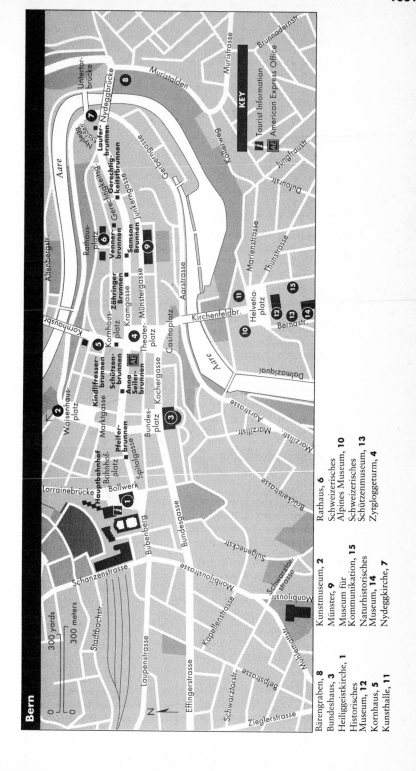

Bern

300 yards
300 meters

Lorrainebrücke
Aare
Untertor-
brücke
Muristalden
Brunnadernstr.
Murisfrasse
Nydeggbrücke
Nydeggkirche
Läufer-
brunnen
Gerechtig-
keitsbrunnen
Gerechtigkeitsg.
Gerbergasse
Junkerngasse
Altenbergstr.
Rathaus-
platz
Venner- Gerechtig-
brunnen keitsbrunnen
Samson
Brunnen
Aarstrasse
Kollerweg
Jungfraustr.
Dufourstr.
Marienstrasse
Thunstrasse
KEY
i Tourist Information
AE American Express Office
Kornhausbr.
Zähringer
Brunnen
Kornhaus Kramgasse
platz
Münstergasse
Münster-
platz
Casinoplatz
Theater-
platz
Aarstrasse
Kirchenfeldbr.
Helvetia-
platz
Bernastr.
Aare
Dalmaziquai
Marzilistr.
Marzilistr.
Aarstrasse
Waisenhaus-
platz
Kindlifresser- brunnen
Marktgasse
Schützen-
brunnen
AE
Anna
Seiler-
brunnen
Kochergasse
Bundes-
platz
Brückenstrasse
Pfeifer-
brunnen
Spitalgasse
Bubenberg
Hauptbahnhof
Bahnhof
platz
Bollwerk
i
Bundesgasse
Schanzenstrasse
Stadtbachstr.
Laupenstrasse
Effingerstrasse
Schwarztorstr.
Kapellenstrasse
Belpstrasse
Zieglerstrasse
Monbijoustrasse
Sulgeneckstr.
Schwarztor-
strasse
Monbijou-
str.
Mühlemattstr.
N

⑥ Rathaus (City Hall). Seat of both the city and cantonal governments, this stately Gothic edifice was built after the great fire of 1405. ✉ *Rathauspl. 2.*

⑩ Schweizerisches Alpines Museum (Swiss Alpine Museum). This arcane but eye-opening museum has old photos, topographical maps, and reliefs illustrating the history of mountain climbing. There's an enormous model of the Berner Oberland under a magnificent Hodler mural of the tragic conquest of the Matterhorn. ✉ *Helvetiapl. 4,* ☎ *031/3510434.* ☉ *Late Feb.–mid-Oct., Mon. 2–5, Tues.–Sun. 10–5; mid-Oct.–late Feb., Mon. 2–5, Tues.–Sun. 10–noon and 2–5.*

⑬ Schweizerisches Schützenmuseum (Swiss Rifle Museum). This unusual (but very Swiss) cultural center traces the development of firearms since 1817 and celebrates Swiss marksmanship beyond the apple-splitting accuracy of William Tell. ✉ *Bernastr. 5,* ☎ *031/3510127.* 🎫 *Free.* ☉ *Tues.–Sat. 2–4, Sun. 10–noon and 2–4.*

★ ④ Zytgloggeturm (Clock Tower). This mighty landmark, Bern's oldest building, was built as a city gate in 1191 but transformed by the addition of an astronomical clock in 1530. At four minutes to the hour every hour, a delightful group of mechanical figures parades out of the clock; a knight above the circling figures hammers out the hour, and Father Time, on a throne in the middle, beats time with a scepter in one hand and an hourglass in the other. ✉ *Kramg., between Theaterpl. and Kornhauspl.*

Dining and Lodging

Although Bern teeters between two cultures politically, Teutonic conquers Gallic when it comes to cuisine. Dining here is usually a down-to-earth affair, with Italian home cooking a popular alternative to meat and potatoes. Specialties include the famous *Bernerplatte* (sauerkraut with boiled beef, fatty pork, sausages, ham, and tongue), normally served in heaping portions, and the Berner version of *Ratsherrtopf*, traditionally enjoyed by the town councilors: veal shank cooked in white wine, butter, and sage. For details and price-category definitions, *see* Dining *in* Switzerland A to Z, *above.*

There's no shortage of comfortable, central hotels in Bern; most are concentrated in the Old Town and make pedestrian tourism a breeze. Rooms are hard to find when Parliament is in session. For details and price-category definitions, *see* Lodging *in* Switzerland A to Z, *above.*

$$$$ ✕ Bellevue-Grill. When Parliament is in session, this haute-cuisine
★ landmark turns into a political clubhouse. The menu leans to luxury; unusual dishes might include beef fillet with truffle pasta or roast breast of duck with a hint of coffee in the sauce. ✉ *Kocherg. 3–5,* ☎ *031/3204545. Reservations essential. AE, DC, MC, V.*

$$$$ ✕ Schultheissenstube. The intimate, rustic dining room of the Schweiz-
★ erhof hotel (☞ *below*) looks less like a gastronomic haven than a country pub. Yet the cooking is sophisticated, international, and imaginative, such as lightly smoked lamb with saffron lentils. ✉ *Bahnhofpl. 11,* ☎ *031/3268080. Reservations essential. Jacket and tie in dining room. AE, DC, MC, V. Closed Sun. and July.*

$$$ ✕ Jack's Brasserie. Locally known as the Stadt Restaurant, this bustling brasserie in the Schweizerhof hotel (☞ *below*) has high ceilings, wainscoting, and roomy banquettes. You can settle in for a smartly served repertoire of French classics with a light touch or an impressive Sunday brunch. ✉ *Bahnhofpl. 11,* ☎ *031/3268080. AE, DC, MC, V.*

$$$ ✕ Zimmermania. This deceptively simple bistro has been in business
★ for over 150 years and is a local favorite for authentic French bour-

geois cooking. Try their cheese soufflé or veal kidneys in mustard sauce, and be sure to ask for the separate, special French wine list. ⊠ *Brunng. 19,* ☎ *031/3111542. AE, MC, V. Closed Sun.–Mon.*

$$–$$$ ✕ **Kornhauskeller.** The spectacular vaulted ceilings and magnificent fres-
★ coes of this old city wine cellar would be reason enough to visit—but after an extensive revamp in late 1998, the fare has been brought up to par as well. The menu goes all over the map, from local fare to French, Italian, even Asian cuisine; there's also a whiskey lounge and humidor. ⊠ *Kornhauspl. 18,* ☎ *031/3277272. AE, DC, MC, V.*

$$ ✕ **Della Casa.** Affectionately nicknamed "Delli," this unadorned fa-
★ vorite has been serving locals for over a century in its rowdy, yellowed stübli and wood-paneled upstairs rooms. It's an unofficial Parliament headquarters, with generous local and Italian specialties—a good place to try the Bernerplatte. ⊠ *Schauplatzg. 16,* ☎ *031/3112142. AE, DC, MC, V. Closed Sun. No dinner Sat.*

$$ ✕ **Harmonie.** Run by the same family since 1900, this leaded-glass and old-wood café-restaurant serves inexpensive basics alongside pricier heavy-meat dinners: sausage-and-Rösti, *Käseschnitte* (cheese toast), *Bauernomelette* (farm-style omelet with bacon, potatoes, onions, and herbs), and fondue. It's lively, a little dingy, and foreigner-friendly. ⊠ *Hotelg. 3,* ☎ *031/3113840. MC, V. Closed Sun. No dinner Sat., no lunch Mon.*

$$ ✕ **Lorenzini.** In a town where the cozy or stuffy holds sway, this hip,
★ bright spot stands apart. Changing menus represent the specialties of different Italian regions; the homemade pastas are delicious. The clientele is a mix of voguish yuppies; the café-bar downstairs draws the young and even more seriously chic. ⊠ *Theaterpl. 5,* ☎ *031/3117850. AE, DC, MC, V. Closed Sun.*

$$ ✕ **Menuetto.** A reaction against meaty Bern cuisine, this refreshing vegetarian oasis represents the city's (also very Germanic) Green side, serving sophisticated, imaginative cooking—*Rouladen* (roulades) of spinach and feta with tamari-sweetened beer sauce. ⊠ *Münsterg. 47 and Herreng. 22 (2 entrances),* ☎ *031/3111448. AE, DC, MC, V. Closed Sun.*

$–$$ ✕ **Klötzlikeller.** This cozy wine cellar dates from 1635 and is the oldest in Bern. Since 1885 only unmarried women have been permitted to own and run the place—a tradition begun by the daughters of Mr. Klötzli himself. A changing menu of regional dishes and wines make this restaurant unique. ⊠ *Gerechtigkeitsg. 62,* ☎ *031/3117456. AE, MC, V. Closed Sun.–Mon.*

$$$$ ⊞ **Schweizerhof.** More intimate than the Bellevue-Grill (☞ *above*), this
★ landmark offers quarters that are roomy and luxuriously appointed (most double rooms are the size of junior suites and, starting at 350 SF, represent a great value). You might be assigned to one of four ultramodern rooms; or you might find a Sheraton chair keeping company with a pair of giant porcelain Dalmatians. ⊠ *Bahnhofpl. 11, CH-3001,* ☎ *031/3268080,* 𝖥𝖠𝖷 *031/3268090. 70 rooms, 15 suites. 2 restaurants. AE, DC, MC, V.*

$$$ ⊞ **Belle Epoque.** This novel hotel is more suggestive of fin de siècle Paris
★ than you might expect in Germanic Bern: Every inch of the arcaded row house is filled with authentic Art Nouveau and Jugendstil antiques. Despite the historic look, amenities, including white-tile baths and electric blinds, are state-of-the-art. ⊠ *Gerechtigkeitsg. 18, CH-3011,* ☎ *031/3114336,* 𝖥𝖠𝖷 *031/3113936. 14 rooms, 2 suites. AE, DC, MC, V.*

$$$ ⊞ **Bern.** Behind a severe and imposing neoclassical facade, this onetime theater and formerly modest hotel is now a sleek, modern business-class lodging, with air-shaft gardens supplying light to the inner rooms. ⊠ *Zeughausg. 9, CH-3011,* ☎ *031/3292222,* 𝖥𝖠𝖷 *031/3292299. 98 rooms, 1 suite. 2 restaurants. AE, DC, MC, V.*

$$$ 📷 **Innere Enge.** The building's 18th-century origins and Jugendstil updates are discreetly discernible in this quiet spot just outside the city center. Guest rooms are spacious, light, and airy thanks to generous windows that face the Bernese Alps. Marian's Jazzroom, in the Louis Armstrong Bar, features top jazz acts. Take Bus 21 ("Bremgarten") from the train station. ✉ *Engestr. 54, CH-3012,* ☎ *031/3096111,* FAX *031/ 3096112. 13 rooms, 15 suites. 2 restaurants. AE, DC, MC, V.*

$$ 📷 **Krebs.** A tidy, small Swiss hotel being steadily upgraded, the Krebs
★ is solid and impeccable, thanks to the ownership's eye for detail. The older rooms are spare but pristine; the newer, no-smoking rooms are freshly done with pastels and polished granite. ✉ *Genferg. 8, CH-3001,* ☎ *031/3114942,* FAX *031/3111035. 46 rooms. AE, DC, MC, V.*

$$ 📷 **Zum Goldener Adler.** From the outside, this 1764 building looks like
★ a patrician town house, but its interior is modern and modest, with linoleum baths and severe Formica furniture. The ambience is comfortable and familial nonetheless; it's been in the same family for 100 years. ✉ *Gerechtigkeitsg. 7, CH-3011,* ☎ *031/3111725,* FAX *031/ 3113761. 16 rooms. Restaurant. AE, DC, MC, V.*

$ 📷 **Goldener Schlüssel.** This is a bright, tidy spot with wood, crisp linens, and tile baths. It's in the heart of the Old Town, so the rooms are quieter in the back. The inexpensive restaurant serves home-cooked meat-and-Rösti favorites. The rooms without bath are a bargain. ✉ *Rathausg. 72, CH-3011,* ☎ *031/3110216,* FAX *031/3115688. 29 rooms, 22 with bath. Restaurant. AE, MC, V.*

$ 📷 **Landhaus.** This 90-year old apartment building in the Old Town
★ has been freshly renovated into a simple, clean, and bright hotel/hostel with natural-wood floors and soothing pastel walls. Pick from a dorm-style cubicle to a double room with shower; value-for-money wise, there isn't a better bargain in town. Cook for yourself in the community kitchen, or dine at the hotel's trendy (and popular) restaurant. ✉ *Altenbergst. 46, CH-3013,* ☎ *031/3314166,* FAX *031/3326904. 4 rooms, 3 4- and 6-bed dormitories. Restaurant. AE, DC, MC, V.*

Nightlife and the Arts

This Week in Bern, edited every week by the tourist office, carries listings on concerts, museums, and nightlife; it's available at the tourist office (☞ Visitor Information *in* Bern Essentials, *below*) and hotels.

The Arts

The **Bern Symphony Orchestra** (☎ 031/3114242 for tickets) is the city's most notable musical institution. Concerts take place at the **Casino** (✉ Casinopl.) and the **Stadttheater** (✉ Kornhauspl. 20). There also is a five-day **International Jazz Festival** every April or May, with tickets available at Ticket Corner, located at the Schweizerischer Bankverein (Swiss Bank Corporation; ✉ Bärenpl., ☎ 031/3362539).

Bern's resident opera company is famous for its adventurous production standards. Performances are at the **Stadttheater** (✉ Kornhauspl. 20, ☎ 031/3110777); tickets are sold next door (✉ Kornhauspl. 18) weekdays 10–6:30, Saturday 10–4, and Sunday 10–12:30.

Nightlife

BARS AND LOUNGES

On the ground floor of the little hotel **Belle Epoque** (✉ Gerechtigkeitsg. 18, ☎ 031/3114336), there's a lovely small bar where you can drink while surrounded by Art Nouveau treasures. The chic bar **CoCo** (✉ Genferg. 10, ☎ 031/3111551) has faux-Gauguin murals on the walls and a classy decor. For history, head for **Klötzlikeller** (✉ Gerechtigkeitsg. 62), said to be the oldest wine bar in Bern (☞ Dining and Lodging, *above*).

DANCING

Babalu (⊠ Gurteng. 3, ☎ 031/3110808) draws crowds for dancing with live music. With a revolving stage and multiple bars, the popular **Mocambo** (⊠ Aarbergerg. 61, ☎ 031/3115041) keeps going until at least 3 AM. Places for dancing often also have a separate "cabaret," but it's not exactly for Liza Minnelli; it's normally a strip joint.

Bern Essentials

Arriving and Departing

BY CAR

Bern is connected conveniently by expressway to Basel via **A1**, to the Berner Oberland via **A6**, and to Lac Léman and thus Lausanne, Geneva, and the Valais via **A12**.

BY PLANE

Belp (☎ 031/9602111) is a small airport, 9 km (5½ mi) south of the city, with flights to and from most European capitals. A bus from the airport to the train station costs 14 SF, a taxi about 35 SF.

BY TRAIN

Bern is a major link between Geneva, Zürich, and Basel, with fast connections running usually every hour from the enormous central station, **Hauptbahnhof** (⊠ Bahnhofpl.). Bern is the only European capital to have three high-speed trains: the **ICE**, the **TGV**, and the **Pendolino**. The ICE from Berlin takes 9 hours; the TGV from Paris takes 4½ hours; the Pendolino from Milan takes 3–4 hours.

Getting Around

BY BUS AND TRAM

The bus and tram service in Bern is excellent; fares range from 1.50 SF to 2.40 SF. Buy individual tickets from the dispenser at the tram or bus stop. Visitor cards for unlimited rides are available for 6 SF a day at the tourist office in the Hauptbahnhof (☞ Visitor Information, *below*) or at the public-transportation ticket office in the passageway leading down to the Hauptbahnhof (take the escalator in front of Loeb's department store and turn right through the Christoffel Tower). A Swiss Pass (☞ Transportation *in* Switzerland A to Z, *above*) allows you to travel free.

BY TAXI

This extravagant alternative to walking costs between 12 SF and 15 SF across town.

Contacts and Resources

EMBASSIES

U.S. (⊠ Jubiläumsstr. 93, ☎ 031/3577011). **Canadian** (⊠ Kirchenfeldstr. 88, ☎ 031/3573200). **U.K.** (⊠ Thunstr. 50, ☎ 031/3597700).

EMERGENCIES

Police (☎ 117). **Ambulance** (☎ 144). **Doctor/Dentist** (☎ 031/3119211). **All-night pharmacy** (☎ 031/3112211).

GUIDED TOURS

Walking. A tour around the Old Town, covering all the principal sights, is offered for 12 SF by the tourist office (☞ Visitor Information, *below*); it lasts almost two hours, generally starting at 2 PM daily, but frequency varies according to season and demand.

Bus tour. A two-hour, English-commentary bus tour around the Old Town, covering all the principal sights, is offered by the tourist office for 22 SF.

VISITOR INFORMATION

Berne Tourismus (⊠ Hauptbahnhof, Bahnhofpl., ☎ 031/3281212).

ZERMATT

Reaching an altitude of 5,300 ft, Zermatt offers the ultimate Swiss-Alpine experience: spectacular mountains, a roaring stream, state-of-the-art transport network, and a broad range of high-quality accommodations—some of them rich in rusticity—plus 230 km (143 mi) of downhill runs and 7 km (4 mi) of cross-country trails. But its
★ greatest claim to fame remains the **Matterhorn** (14,690 ft), which attracts swarms of package-tour sightseers pushing shoulder to shoulder to get yet another shot of this genuine wonder of the Western world.

Exploring Zermatt

Zermatt lies in a hollow of meadows and trees ringed by mountains—among them the broad **Monte Rosa** (14,940 ft) with its tallest peak, the **Dufourspitze** (at 15,200 ft, the highest point in Switzerland), of which visitors hear relatively little, so all consuming is the cult of the Matterhorn. Walking down the main street, Bahnhofstrasse, you'll be deluged by Matterhorn images: on postcards, on beer steins, on candy wrappers. But the Matterhorn deserves idolatry: Though it has become an almost self-parodying icon, like the Eiffel Tower or the Statue of Liberty, this distinctive, snaggletoothed pyramid thrusting upward in solitary splendor is even more impressive than the photographs suggest.

Despite its celebrity mountain, Zermatt remains a resort with its feet on the ground. It is as protective of its regional quirks as it is of its wildlife and its tumbledown *mazots* (grain-storage sheds raised on stone bases to keep the mice away), which hunker between the glass-and-concrete chalets like old tenements trapped between skyscrapers. Streets twist past weathered wood walls and flower boxes until they break into open country that inevitably slopes uphill.

The cog railway between Visp and Zermatt began disgorging summer tourists in 1891, but it was not until 1927 that it also plowed through in wintertime. What had drawn the first tourists and made Zermatt a household word was Edward Whymper's spectacular—and catastrophic—conquest of the Matterhorn in 1865. Whymper and his band of six managed to reach the summit, but then tragedy struck. On the treacherous descent, four of the men lost their footing and snapped their safety rope, pulling each other 4,000 ft to their death. One of the bodies was never recovered, but the others remain in the grim little cemetery behind the church in the village center.

To experience the exhilaration of standing on top of the world without risking life or limb, you can take the trip up the **Gornergrat** on the *Gornergratbahn,* which does double duty as ski transport and a sightseeing excursion. Completed in 1898 and the highest exposed rail system in Europe, it connects out of the main Zermatt station and climbs slowly up the valley to the **Riffelberg,** which at 8,471 ft offers wide-open views of the Matterhorn. From **Rotenboden,** at 9,248 ft, a short downhill walk leads to the **Riffelsee,** with its pristine reflections of the famous peak. At the end of the 9-km (5½-mi) line, passengers pour onto the observation terraces of the Gornergrat (10,269 ft), to take in majestic views of Gorner glacier, the Matterhorn, Monte Rosa, and scores of other peaks. Be sure to bring warm clothes, sunglasses, and sturdy shoes. ⊠ *Leaves from Zermatt Station.* 🚠 *63 SF round-trip; 37 SF one-way up and ski or hike down.* ☉ *Departures every 24 mins* 7 AM–7 PM.

Skiing

Zermatt's skiable terrain lives up to its reputation: It is said to guarantee skiers 7,216 ft of vertical drop no matter what the snowfall—

an impressive claim. This royal plateau has several less-than-perfect features, however, not least of which is the separation of the skiable territory into three sectors. **Sunegga-Blauherd-Rothorn** culminates at an elevation of 10,170 ft. **Gornergrat-Stockhorn** (11,155 ft) is the second. The third is the region dominated by the **Klein Matterhorn;** to go from this sector to the others you must return to the bottom of the valley and lose considerable time crossing town to reach the lifts to the other elevations. The solution is to ski for a whole day in the same area, especially during high season (mid-December to the end of February, or even until Easter if the snow cover is good). A ski school (Skischulbüro; ☎ 027/9662466) runs during the high season. A one-day lift ticket costs 60 SF; a six-day pass costs 296 SF.

Dining and Lodging

Perched at the German end of the mostly French canton of Valais, Zermatt offers a variety of French and German cooking, from veal and Rösti to raclette and fondue. Specialties often feature pungent mountain cheese: *Käseschnitte,* for instance, are substantial little casseroles of bread, cheese, and often ham, baked until the whey saturates the crusty bread and the cheese browns to gold. Air-dried beef is another Valais treat; it's served in thin, translucent slices, with gherkins and crisp pickled onions. Alas, McDonald's has infiltrated this once-isolated retreat, and you now have to climb or ski to find memorable, cut-above dining outside the hotels—which do offer considerable variety. For details and price-category definitions, *see* Dining *in* Switzerland A to Z, *above.*

At high season—Christmas and New Year's, Carnaval to Easter, and late summer—Zermatt's high hotel prices rival those of Zürich and Geneva. But read the fine print carefully when you plan your visit: Most hotels include half pension in their price, offering breakfast and your choice of a noon or evening meal. Hotels that call themselves "garni" do not offer pension dining plans. For details and price-category definitions, *see* Lodging *in* Switzerland A to Z, *above.* Since Zermatt is for the most part a one-street town, street addresses are rarely used. However, hotels are signposted throughout the town.

$$-$$$ ✕ **Grill-Room Stockhorn.** The tantalizing aromas of pungent cheese and roasting meat on the open grill should sharpen your hunger the moment you step inside this low-slung restaurant. This is a great place to fortify yourself with regional dishes; the service and the clientele are equally lively. ☎ 027/9671747. *AE, MC, V. Closed May and Oct.*

$$ ✕ **Findlerhof.** This mountain restaurant in tiny Findeln is perched high
★ between the Sunnegga and Blauherd ski areas. The Matterhorn views from the wraparound dining porch are astonishing, and the food surprisingly fresh and creative. Franz and Heidi Schwery tend their own Alpine garden to provide spinach for the bacon-crisped salad, and rhubarb and berries for their hot desserts. It's about 30 minutes' walk down from the Sunnegga Express stop, and another 30 minutes back down to Zermatt. ⊠ *Findeln,* ☎ 027/9672588. *No credit cards. Closed May–mid-June, mid-Oct.–Nov.*

$$ ✕ **Zum See.** Beyond Findeln, in a tiny village by the same name, Zum
★ See has become something of an institution, serving light meals of a quality and level of inventiveness that would merit acclaim even if the restaurant weren't in the middle of nowhere at 5,794 ft. Regional specialties include wild mushrooms in pastry shells to rabbit, Rösti, and *foie de veau* (calves' liver). ⊠ *Zum See,* ☎ 027/9672045. *No credit cards. Closed May–June and Oct.–mid-Nov.*

$$$$ ✕🏠 **Monte Rosa.** This was the first inn in Zermatt, and the home base
★ of Edward Whymper when he conquered the Matterhorn in 1865. Be-

hind its graceful shuttered facade you will find flagstone floors, brass, stained and beveled glass, honey-gold pine, fireplaces, and an elaborate Victorian dining hall, fully restored. Dinner is a five-course candlelight affair that could have been styled for a Merchant Ivory film. The bar is an après-ski must. Guests have access to the sports facilities at Mont Cervin (☞ *below*), and all Seiler restaurants on the members' "Dine-Around" plan. ✉ *CH-3920*, ☎ *027/9663333*, ℻ *027/ 9671160. 44 rooms, 5 suites. Restaurant. AE, DC, MC, V.*

$$$–$$$$ ✕🏨 **Julen.** For this hotel's radical 1998 room renovation, it shunned
★ the usual regional kitsch in favor of a century-old spruce wood decor coupled with primary-color carpets and silk curtains. A three-floor sports center includes an elaborate Roman bath room. Besides a restaurant serving international cuisine, there's a welcoming stübli with unusual lamb dishes (such as lamb's tongue in capers) made from local family-owned flocks. ✉ *CH-3920*, ☎ *027/9667000*, ℻ *027/9667676. 27 rooms, 5 suites. 2 restaurants, indoor pool. AE, DC, MC, V.*

$$$$ 🏨 **Mont Cervin.** One of the flagships of the Seiler dynasty, this is a sleek,
★ luxurious, and urbane mountain hotel. Built in 1852, it's unusually low slung for a grand hotel, with dark beams and classic decor; a few rooms are full of rustic stucco and carved blond wood. A fire in 1998 destroyed the old restaurant; the new one is lighter in decor and tone—now a jacket and tie are required only for the Friday gala buffet. The "Residence," across the street through a handy tunnel, offers chic, luxurious apartments. ✉ *CH-3920*, ☎ *027/9668888*, ℻ *027/9672878. 101 rooms, 40 suites. 2 restaurants, indoor pool. AE, DC, MC, V. Closed May–mid-June and mid-Oct.–Nov.*

$$$$ 🏨 **Zermatterhof.** If you can afford no-limits luxury then this faultless
★ hotel has a lot to offer. Rooms in multifarious shades and styles of wood have either granite or marble bathrooms where you can lie back and enjoy the ultimate in alpine decadence—nibbling a Matterhorn-shape chocolate while soaking in a whirlpool bath. There are plenty of facilities, including an indoor pool, health club, and sauna. The formal restaurant, for guests only, has superb French- and Italian-influenced cuisine. ✉ *CH-3920*, ☎ *027/9666600*, ℻ *027/9666699. 60 rooms, 26 suites. 2 restaurants. AE, DC, MC, V.*

$–$$$ 🏨 **Romantica.** Among the scores of anonymously modern hotels cloned all over the Zermatt plain, this modest structure—unremarkable at first glance—offers an exceptional location directly above the town center. Its tidy, bright gardens and flower boxes, its game trophies, and its old-style granite stove give it personality, and the plain rooms benefit from big windows and balconies. You can also stay in one of the two *Walliserstudel*, 200-year-old, tiny (but charming) huts in the hotel's garden. Views take in the mountains, though not the Matterhorn, over a graceful clutter of stone roofs. ✉ *CH-3920*, ☎ *027/9662650*, ℻ *027/ 9662655. 13 rooms. AE, DC, MC, V.*

$–$$$ 🏨 **Touring.** Its reassuringly traditional architecture and snug, sunny rooms full of pine, combined with an elevated position apart from town and excellent Matterhorn views, make this an appealing choice. A sunny enclosed playground has lounge chairs for parents. ✉ *CH-3920*, ☎ *027/9671177*, ℻ *027/9674601. 21 rooms. 2 restaurants. MC, V.*

$$ 🏨 **Alphubel.** Although it's surrounded by other hotels and just steps from the main street, this modest, comfortable pension feels off the beaten track, offering large sunny balconies in its south-side rooms. The interior—a little institutional—lets you know that the place was built in 1954, but there's a sauna in the basement available to guests for a slight surcharge. ✉ *CH-3920*, ☎ *027/9673003*, ℻ *027/9676684. 31 rooms. Restaurant. AE, MC, V.*

$–$$ 🏨 **Mischabel.** One of the least, if not *the* least, expensive hotels in this pricey resort town, the Mischabel provides comfort, atmosphere, and a central situation few places can match at twice the price: Southern balconies frame a perfect Matterhorn view—the higher the better. Creaky, homey, and covered with *Arvenholz* (Alpen pine) aged to the color of toffee, its rooms have sinks only and share the linoleum-lined showers on every floor. A generous daily menu, for guests only, caters to families and young skiers on the cheap. ⊠ *CH-3920,* ☎ *027/ 9671131,* 𝔽𝔸𝕏 *027/9676507. 28 rooms. Restaurant. MC, V.*

Nightlife

GramPi's Bar (☎ 027/9677788), on the main drag, is a lively, young bar where you can get into the mood for dancing downstairs with a Lady Matterhorn cocktail. **T-Bar** (☎ 027/9674000), below the Pollux hotel, plays more varied music than the generic disco-pap of most ski resort nightspots, and its walls and ceilings are interestingly hung with antique skiing equipment.

Zermatt Essentials

Arriving and Departing

Zermatt is a car-free resort isolated at the end of the Mattertal, a rugged valley at the eastern end of the Alpine canton of Valais.

BY CAR

A good mountain highway cuts south through the Mattertal valley from Visp, the crossroads of the main Valais east–west routes. You can drive up the valley as far as Täsch, but there you must abandon your car in a large parking lot and catch the train for the cogwheel climb into Zermatt.

BY PLANE

The airports of Zürich and Geneva are roughly equidistant from Brig, but by approaching from Geneva you can avoid crossing mountain passes.

BY TRAIN

The **Brig-Visp-Zermatt Railway,** a private narrow-gauge system, runs from Brig to Visp, connecting on to Zermatt. All major rail routes connect through Brig, whether you approach from Geneva or Lausanne in the west, from the Lötschberg line that tunnels through from Kandersteg and the Bernese Oberland, or from the connecting Simplon Pass from Italy.

Getting Around

Because Zermatt permits no private cars, electric taxi shuttles operated by hotels are the only means of transportation. The village is relatively small and easily covered on foot.

BY CABLE CAR AND MOUNTAIN RAIL

Hiking and skiing are Zermatt's raisons d'être, but you can get a head start into the heights by riding part of the sophisticated network of cable cars, lifts, cog railways, and even an underground metro that carry you above the village center into the wilderness. Excursions to the Klein Matterhorn and Gornergrat are particularly spectacular.

Contacts and Resources

EMERGENCIES

Police (☎ 027/9666920). **Ambulance** (☎ 027/9672000).

VISITOR INFORMATION

Verkehrsbüro Zermatt (⊠ Bahnhofpl., CH-3920, ☎ 027/9670181).

31 TURKEY

ISTANBUL, THE AEGEAN COAST, THE MEDITERRANEAN COAST, CENTRAL ANATOLIA AND CAPPADOCIA

Turkey is one place to which the phrase "East meets West" really applies. It is in Turkey's largest city, Istanbul, that the continents of Europe and Asia come together, separated only by the Bosporus, which flows 29 km (18 mi) from the Black Sea to the Sea of Marmara. On the vibrant streets of this city of 12 million people, miniskirts and trendy boots mingle with head scarves and prayer beads.

Although 97% of Turkey's landmass is in Asia, Turkey began facing West politically in 1923, when Mustapha Kemal, better known as Atatürk, founded the modern republic. He transformed the remnants of the shattered Ottoman Empire into a secular state with a Western outlook. So thorough was this changeover—culturally, politically, and economically—that in 1987, 49 years after Atatürk's death, Turkey applied to the European Union (EU) for full membership. Currently, though, the country is experiencing an identity crisis that could lead to social and political upheavals, particularly over the role of Islam in public life and the recognition of minority rights.

For 16 centuries Istanbul, originally known as Byzantium, played a major part in world politics: first as the capital of the Eastern Roman Empire, when it was known as Constantinople, then as capital of the Ottoman Empire, the most powerful Islamic empire in the world, when it was renamed Istanbul. Atatürk moved the capital to Ankara at the inception of the Turkish Republic.

The legacies of the Greeks, Romans, Ottomans, and numerous other civilizations have made the country a vast outdoor museum. The most spectacular of the reconstructed classical sites are along the western Aegean coast and the southwest Mediterranean coast, which are lined with magnificent sandy beaches and sleepy little fishing villages, as well as busy resorts with sophisticated facilities for travelers.

If you have time—an extra five to seven days—an excursion inland to central Anatolia and the eroded lunar valleys of the Cappadocia area

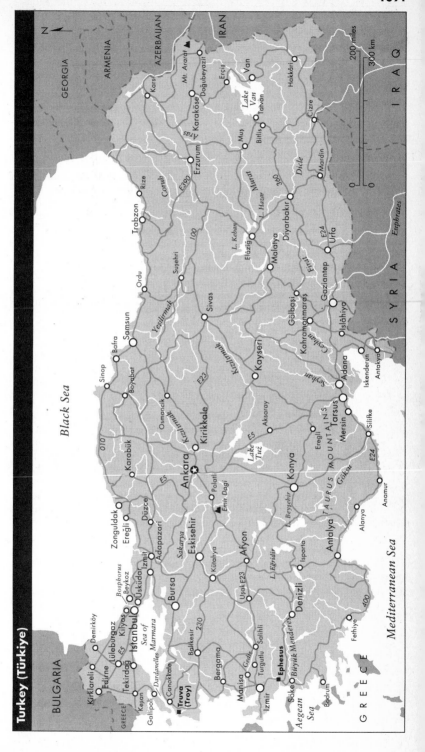

Turkey (Türkiye)

will give you a glimpse at some of the enormous diversity of the landscapes and people of Turkey.

TURKEY A TO Z

Customs

Turkish customs officials rarely look through tourists' luggage on arrival. You are allowed to bring in 400 cigarettes, 50 cigars, 200 grams of tobacco, 1.5 kilograms of instant coffee, 500 grams of tea, and 2.5 liters of alcohol. An additional 600 cigarettes, 100 cigars, or 500 grams of tobacco may be imported if purchased at the Turkish duty-free shops on arrival. Register all valuable personal items in your passport on entry. Items at duty-free shops in airports are usually less expensive here than in duty-free shops in other European airports or in-flight offerings. Turkey is extremely tough on anyone attempting to export antiques without authorization or on anyone caught with illegal drugs, regardless of the amount.

Dining

The Turkish people are justly proud of their cuisine. In addition to the blends of spices used, the food is also extremely healthy, full of fresh vegetables, yogurt, legumes, and grains, not to mention fresh seafood, roast lamb, and kebabs made of lamb, beef, or chicken. Because Turkey is predominantly Muslim, pork is not readily available. But there's plenty of alcohol, including local beer and wine, which are excellent and inexpensive. Particularly good wines are Villa Doluca and Kavaklidere, available in *beyaz* (white) and *kırmızı* (red). The most popular local beer is Efes Pilsen. The national alcoholic drink, *rakı*, is made from grapes and aniseed. Turks mix it with water or ice and sip it throughout their meal or serve it as an aperitif.

Many hotel restaurants have English-language menus and usually serve a bland version of Continental cuisine. Far more adventurous and tasty are meals in *restorans* and in *lokantas* (Turkish restaurants). Most lokantas do not have menus because they serve only what's fresh and in season, which varies daily. At lokantas you simply sit back and let the waiter bring food to your table, beginning with a tray of mezes (appetizers). You point to the dishes that look inviting and take as many as you want. Then you select your main course from fresh meat or fish—displayed in glass-covered refrigerated units—which is then cooked to order, or from a steam table laden with casseroles and stews. For lighter meals there are *kebabcıs*, tiny restaurants specializing in kebabs served with salad and yogurt, and *pidecis*, selling *pides,* a pizzalike snack of flat bread topped with butter, cheese, egg, or ground lamb and baked in a wood-burning oven.

MEALTIMES

Lunch is generally served from noon to 3 and dinner from 7 to 10. In cities you can find restaurants or cafés open almost any time of day or night, but in villages, finding a restaurant open at odd hours can be a problem. In more conservative areas restaurants often close during daylight hours in the Islamic holy month of Ramadan (varies from year to year; Nov. 30–Dec. 31, 2000), when many Muslims fast.

PRECAUTIONS

Although tap water is heavily chlorinated, it is often not safe to drink in cities and resorts. It's best to play it safe and drink *maden suyu* (bottled mineral water) or regular *şişe suyu* (bottled water), which is better tasting and inexpensive.

Prices are per person and include an appetizer, main course, and dessert. Wine and gratuities are not included.

CATEGORY	MAJOR CITIES	OTHER AREAS
$$$$	over $40	over $30
$$$	$25–$40	$20–$30
$$	$12–$25	$10–$20
$	under $12	under $10

WHAT TO WEAR

Except for the pricier restaurants, where jacket and tie are appropriate, informal dress is acceptable at restaurants in all price categories.

Language

Atatürk launched language reforms that replaced Arabic script with the Latin-based alphabet. English and German are widely spoken in cities and resorts. In villages and remote areas you'll have a hard time finding anyone who speaks anything but Turkish. Try learning a few basic Turkish words; it will be appreciated.

Lodging

Accommodations range from international luxury chains in Istanbul, Ankara, and İzmir to comfortable, family-run *pansiyons* (guest houses). Plan ahead for the peak summer season, when resort hotels are often booked solid by tour companies. Turkey does not have central hotel reservations offices.

Hotels are officially classified in Turkey as HL (luxury), H1 to H5 (first- to fifth-class); motels, M1 to M2 (first- to second-class); and P, pansiyons. The classification is misleading because the lack of a restaurant or a lounge automatically relegates the establishment to the bottom of the ratings. A lower-grade hotel may actually be far more charming and comfortable than one with a higher rating. There are also many local establishments that are licensed but not included in the official ratings list. You can obtain their names from local tourist offices.

Rates vary from $10 to more than $200 a night for a double room. In less expensive hotels the plumbing and furnishings will probably leave much to be desired. You can find very acceptable, clean double rooms with bath for between $30 and $70, with breakfast included. Room rates are displayed in the reception area. It is accepted practice in Turkey to ask to see the room in advance.

RATINGS

Prices are for two people in a double room, including 20% VAT and a 10%–15% service charge.

CATEGORY	MAJOR CITIES	OTHER AREAS
$$$$	over $200	over $150
$$$	$100–$200	$100–$150
$$	$60–$100	$50–$100
$	under $60	under $50

Mail

Post offices are painted bright yellow and have PTT (Post, Telegraph, and Telephone) signs on the front. The major ones are open Monday–Saturday from 8 AM to 9 PM, Sunday from 9 to 7. Smaller branches are open Monday–Saturday 8–4:30.

If you're uncertain where you'll be staying, have mail addressed to "post restante" and sent to Merkez Postanesi (central post office) in the town of your choice.

Money Matters

COSTS

Turkey is among the least expensive of the Mediterranean countries. Inflation has hovered between 60% and 100% for more than a decade, but frequent devaluations of the lira keep prices fairly stable when measured against foreign currencies. Prices in this chapter are quoted in U.S. dollars, which indicate the real cost to the visitor more accurately than do the constantly increasing lira prices.

CURRENCY

The monetary unit is the Turkish lira (TL), which comes in bank notes of 50,000, 100,000, 250,000, 500,000, 1,000,000 and 5,000,000. Coins come in denominations of 5,000, 10,000, 25,000, 50,000, and 100,000. At press time (summer 1999), the exchange rate was 425,850 TL to the U.S. dollar, 289,540 TL to the Canadian dollar, and 664,974 TL to the pound sterling. These rates are subject to continual fluctuation, so check close to the time of your departure. Major credit cards and traveler's checks are widely accepted in hotels, shops, and expensive restaurants in cities and resorts, but rarely in villages and small shops and restaurants.

There are no problems changing money back from Turkish lira to other currencies. But because the value of Turkish currency can sometimes fall significantly over a very short period, it is advisable to change enough money for only a few days at a time.

Foreign exchange bureaus are now widespread in Turkey's major cities and resorts (they usually have a sign saying DÖVIZ, Turkish for "Foreign Exchange"). Exchange rates can usually be seen on an electronic display just inside the door. Rates may vary slightly between exchange bureaus but are always better than bank rates and considerably more attractive than rates offered in hotels.

SAMPLE PRICES

Coffee can range from about 30¢ to $2.50 a cup, depending on whether it's the less expensive Turkish coffee or American-style coffee and whether it's served in a luxury hotel or a café; tea, 20¢ to $2.50 a glass; local beer, $1–$5; soft drinks, $1–$4; lamb shish kebab, $1.50–$7; taxi, approximately $1 for 2 km (1 mi) (prices are 50% higher between midnight and 6 AM).

TIPPING

Except at the cheapest restaurants, a 10%–15% charge is added to the bill. As the money does not necessarily find its way to the waiter, leave an additional 10% on the table or hand it to the waiter. In top restaurants waiters expect tips of between 10% and 15%. Hotel porters expect between $1 and $4 and the chambermaid about $2. Taxi drivers don't expect tips, although they are becoming accustomed to foreigners' giving them something. Round off the fare to the nearest 50,000 TL. At Turkish baths the staff that attends you expects to share a tip of 30%–35% of the bill. Don't worry about missing them—they'll be lined up expectantly on your departure.

National Holidays

January 1; January 9–11 (Şeker Bayramı, "sugar feast," a three-day celebration marking the end of Ramadan); March 18–21(Kurban

Bayramı, an important sacrificial feast celebrating Abraham's willingness to sacrifice his son to God); April 23 (National Sovereignty and Children's Day); May 19 (National Youth and Sports Day); August 30 (Victory Day); October 29 (Republic Day).

Note: The Islamic religious holidays of Şeker Bayramı and Kurban Bayramı follow the lunar calendar and move forward by approximately 10 days each year. The dates given above are for 2000. Many shops and companies close at midday on the day before the official beginning of Şeker Bayramı and Kurban Bayramı.

Opening and Closing Times

Banks are generally open weekdays, 8:30 or 9–noon and 1:30–5, although increasingly banks are remaining open at lunchtime. Foreign exchange bureaus normally remain open from 9:30 or 10 AM to 6 PM. **Mosques** are usually open to the public, except during *namaz* (prayer hours), which are observed five times a day. These times are based on the position of the sun, so they vary throughout the seasons between the following hours: sunrise (5–7), lunchtime (noon–1), afternoon (3–4), sunset (5–7), bedtime (9–10). Prayers last 30–40 minutes. **Museums** are generally open Tuesday–Sunday, 9:30–4:30, and closed Monday. **Palaces** are open Friday–Wednesday, 9:30–4:30, and closed Thursday. Most **shops** are open Monday–Saturday, 9:30–1 and 2–7. There are some exceptions in the major shopping areas in large cities and resort areas, where shops stay open until 9 PM. Most are closed Sunday, although small grocery stores and a few other stores in the main shopping areas remain open seven days a week.

Shopping

BARGAINING

The best part of shopping in Turkey is visiting the *bedestans* (bazaars), all brimming with copper and brass items, hand-painted ceramics, alabaster and onyx goods, fabrics, richly colored carpets, and relics and icons trickling in from the former Soviet Union. The key word for shopping in the bazaars is "bargain." You must be willing to bargain, and bargain hard. It's great fun once you get the hang of it. As a rule of thumb offer 50% less after you're given the initial price and be prepared to go up by about 25% to 30% of the first asking price. It is often advisable to get up to leave, as the best price is invariably the one called as you disappear around the corner. You can always think about it for two minutes and, if you are happy about it, return and accept. It's both bad manners and bad business to underbid grossly or to start bargaining if you're not serious about buying. Outside the bazaars prices are usually fixed, although in resort areas some shopkeepers may be willing to bargain if you ask for a "better price." Part of the fun of roaming through the bazaars is having a free glass of *çay* (tea), which vendors will offer you whether you're a serious shopper or just browsing. Beware of antiques: Chances are you will end up with an expensive fake, but even if you do find the genuine article, it's illegal to export antiques of any type.

SALES-TAX REFUNDS

Value-added tax (VAT) is nearly always included in the price. You can claim back the VAT if you buy articles from authorized shops. The net total value of articles subject to VAT on your invoice must be more than a specified amount, depending on the nature of the goods, and these articles must be exported within three months of purchase. The invoice must be stamped by customs. Otherwise, mail the stamped invoice back to the dealer within one month of departure and the dealer should send back a check.

Telephoning

Note: All telephone numbers in Turkey have seven local digits plus three-digit city codes. Intercity calls are preceded by 0. One of Istanbul's area codes is 212; be sure to dial the country code first if you are calling from outside Turkey—otherwise you may reach New York City!

Pay phones are blue, push-button models. Many take *jetons* (tokens) although increasingly, particularly in large cities, they are being replaced with phones that take phone cards or, to a lesser extent, credit cards. Multilingual directions are posted in phone booths.

Turkey's two GSM mobile telephone service providers have reciprocal agreements with most of their European counterparts, enabling subscribers to use the Turkish GSM network during their stay in the country. But most subscribers to U.S. and Canadian cellular telephone service providers are currently unable to log on to the Turkish network.

COUNTRY CODE

The country code for Turkey is 90. When dialing a number in Turkey from outside the country, drop the initial 0 from the local area code.

INTERNATIONAL CALLS

For all international calls dial 00, then dial the country code, area or city code, and the number. You can use the higher-price cards for this, or reach an international operator by dialing 132. To reach an **AT&T** long-distance operator, dial 00800–12277, for **MCI**, dial 00800–11177, and for **Sprint**, 00800–14477.

LOCAL CALLS

Tokens can be purchased for 7¢ at post offices and, for a couple of cents more, at street booths. If you need operator assistance for long-distance calls within Turkey, dial 131. For intercity automatic calls, dial 0, then dial the city code and the number. Tokens are available for 25¢ and 80¢ for long-distance calls. Far more practical than the tokens are telephone cards, available at post offices for $2 for 30 units, $3.50 for 60 units, and $5 for 100 units.

Telephone numbers in European and Asian Istanbul have different codes: The code for European Istanbul (for numbers beginning with 2, 5, or 6) is 0/212; for Asian Istanbul (for numbers that start with 3 or 4), dial 0/216.

Transportation

BY BOAT

A car ferry and cruise service is operated out of Istanbul by **Turkish Maritime Lines.** Cruises are in great demand, so make your reservations well in advance, either through the main office (✉ Rıhtım Cad. 1, Karaköy, ☎ 212/249–9222 or 212/293–7454) in Istanbul or through Sunquest Holidays Ltd. (✉ Aldine House, Aldine St., London W12 8AW, ☎ 0181/800–5455) in London. The Black Sea Ferry sails from May through September from Istanbul to Samsun and Trabzon and back, from Karaköy Dock in Istanbul. One-way fares to Trabzon are about $30 for a reclining seat, $40–$95 for cabins, and $50 for cars. The Istanbul-to-İzmir car ferry departs three days a week. The price of a one-way ticket with no meals included varies between $40 and $125, plus $40 for a car.

BY BUS

Buses, which are run by private companies, are much faster than trains and provide excellent, inexpensive service. Buses are available, almost around the clock, between all cities and towns. They are fairly comfortable and many are air-conditioned. Companies have their own fixed fares for different routes. Istanbul to Ankara, for instance, varies from $8 to $13; Istanbul to İzmir varies from $11 to $16. *Şişe suyu* (bottled water) is included in the fare. You can purchase tickets at stands in a town's *otogar* (central bus terminal) or at branch offices in city centers. All seats are reserved. There are small variations in fares among the different companies, but it is usually worth paying the 3%–5% extra for companies such as Varan, Ulusoy, and Kamil Koç. Many buses between major cities are double-deckers and all of those operated by the larger companies have toilets. Companies such as Varan, Ulusoy, and Kamil Koç offer no-smoking seating. For very short trips or getting around within a city, take minibuses or a *dolmuş* (shared taxi). Both are inexpensive and comfortable.

BY CAR

Breakdowns. Before you start out, check with your hotel or a tourist information office about how, in case of an emergency, to contact one of the road rescue services available on some highways. Turkish mechanics in the villages will usually manage to get you going again, at least until you reach a city for full repairs. In the cities, entire streets are given over to car-repair shops. Prices are not high, but it's good to give a small tip to the person who does the actual repair work. If you're not in the shop during the repairs, take all car documents with you. The **Touring and Automobile Club** (TTÖK, ☎ 212/282–8140) gives information about driving in Turkey and has a repair service.

Gasoline. Throughout the country Shell, Total, Elf, and British Petroleum, as well as two Turkish oil companies, have gas stations that are open 24 hours on the main highways. Others are open from 6 AM to 10 PM.

Road Conditions. Turkey has very good main roads—37,500 km (25,000 mi) of well-maintained, paved highways—but signposts are few, lighting is scarce, and city traffic is chaotic. City streets and highways are jammed with vehicles operated by high-speed drivers who constantly blast their horns. In Istanbul it's safer and faster to drive on the modern highways. Avoid the many small one-way streets; you never know when someone is going to barrel down one of them in the wrong direction. Better yet, use public transportation or take taxis. Parking is a big problem in the cities and larger towns.

Rules of the Road. The best way to see Turkey is by car, but be warned that it has one of the highest accident rates in Europe. In general, Turkish driving conforms to Mediterranean customs, with driving on the right and passing on the left. But watch out for drivers passing on a curve or on the top of a hill. Other hazards are peasant carts and motorcycles weaving in and out of traffic. Archaeological and historical sites are indicated by yellow signposts.

BY PLANE

Turkish Airlines (THY; ✉ Taksim Sq., Istanbul, ☎ 212/252–1106; 212/663–6363, reservations by phone) operates an extensive domestic network. There are at least 14 flights daily on weekdays between Istanbul and Ankara, as well as less-frequent flights to other major cities. In summer additional flights between the cities and coastal resorts are added. Try to arrive at the airport at least 45 minutes before your flight because security checks, which are rigidly enforced, can be time-consuming. Checked luggage is placed on trolleys on the tarmac and must be identified by boarding passengers before it is put on the plane. Unidentified luggage is left behind and checked for bombs or firearms.

Istanbul Airlines (✉ Cumhuriyet Cad. 289, Harbiye, 80230, Istanbul, ☎ 212/231–7526), Turkey's largest privately owned carrier, has also started domestic flights between major cities. Prices are 10%–15% lower than THY's, but flights are less frequent.

BY TRAIN

Although there are trains labeled express, the term is usually a misnomer. These trains have several long-distance routes, but they tend to be slow. The best daily trains between Istanbul and Ankara are the Başkent Expres and the Faith Expres. The overnight Yataklı Ankara Expres has luxurious sleeper cars; the Anadolu Expres has cheaper, less comfortable berths. There are overnight trains to Pamukkale as well as daily trains to Edirne from Sirkeci station in Istanbul. Dining cars on some trains have waiter service and serve surprisingly good and inexpensive food.

Fares. Train fares tend to be lower than bus fares. Seats on the best trains, as well as those with sleeping berths, should be reserved in advance. In railroad stations, buy tickets at windows marked ANAHAT GISELERI. Travel agencies carrying the TCDD (State Railways) sign and some post offices sell train tickets, too.

Visas

U.S. citizens not arriving on a cruise line need visas. These are most easily obtained at the port of entry—just be sure to have cash (U.S. $20). Canadian tourists do not need visas. Visas are required for visitors from the U.K.—obtain them at the port of entry for £10 or from any Turkish consulate (the rate will be somewhat higher).

Weather

The height of the tourist season runs from April through October. July and August are the busiest and warmest months. April through June and September and October are the best months to visit archaeological sites or Istanbul and the Marmara area because the days are cooler and the crowds are smaller.

CLIMATE

The Mediterranean and Aegean coasts have mild winters and hot summers. You can swim in the sea from late April through October. The Black Sea coast is mild and damp, with a rainfall of 90 inches a year.

The following are the average daily maximum and minimum temperatures for Istanbul.

Jan.	46F	8C	May	69F	21C	Sept.	76F	24C
	37	3		53	12		61	16
Feb.	47F	9C	June	77F	25C	Oct.	68F	20C
	36	2		60	16		55	13
Mar.	51F	11C	July	82F	28C	Nov.	59F	15C
	38	3		65	18		48	9
Apr.	60F	16C	Aug.	82F	28C	Dec.	51F	11C
	45	7		66	19		41	

ISTANBUL

Istanbul is noisy, chaotic, and exciting. Spires and domes of mosques and medieval palaces dominate the skyline. At dawn, when the muezzin's call to prayer rebounds from ancient minarets, many people are heading home from the nightclubs and bars, while others are kneeling on their prayer rugs, facing Mecca.

Day and night, Istanbul has a schizophrenic air. Women in jeans, business suits, or elegant designer outfits pass women wearing the long skirts and head coverings that villagers have worn for generations. Donkey-drawn carts vie with old Chevrolets and Pontiacs or shiny Toyotas and BMWs for dominance of the loud, narrow streets. The world's most fascinating Asian bazaar competes with Western boutiques for your time and attention.

Exploring Istanbul

Ironically, Istanbul's Asian side is filled with Western-style sprawling suburbs, while its European side contains Old Istanbul—an Oriental wonderland of mosques, opulent palaces, and crowded bazaars. The Golden Horn, an inlet 6½ km (4 mi) long, flows off the Bosporus on the European side, separating Old Istanbul from New Town. The center of New Town is Beyoğlu, a district filled with a combination of modern and turn-of-the-century hotels, banks, and shops grouped around Taksim Square. There are three bridges spanning the Golden Horn: the Atatürk, the Galata, and the Haliç.

The historic Galata Bridge (the original structure has been replaced by a modern drawbridge) is a central landmark and a good place to get your bearings. From here, you can see the city's layout and its seven hills. The bridge will also give you a taste of Istanbul's frenetic street life. It's filled with peddlers selling everything from pistachio nuts and spices to curly-toed slippers fancy enough for a sultan; fishermen grill their catch on coal braziers and sell them to passersby. None of this sits well with motorists, who blast their horns constantly, usually to no avail. If you want to orient yourself in a quieter way, take a boat trip from the docks on the Eminönü side of the Galata Bridge up the Bosporus.

Old Istanbul (Sultanahmet)

Numbers in the margin correspond to points of interest on the Istanbul map.

★ ❷ **Arkeoloji Müzesi** (Archaeological Museum). This museum houses a fine collection of Greek and Roman antiquities, including finds from Ephesus and Troy. Admission to the Archaeological Museum is also good for entrance to the **Eski Şark Eserleri Müzesi** (Museum of the Ancient Orient), with Sumerian, Babylonian, and Hittite treasures; and the **Çinili Köşkü** (Tiled Pavilion), which houses ceramics from the early Seljuk and Osmanli empires. ⊠ *Gülhane Park,* ☎ *212/520–7740.* ☉ *Tues.– Sun. 9:30–4:30; ticket office 9:30–4.*

★ ❸ **Aya Sofya** (Hagia Sophia, Church of the Divine Wisdom). One of the world's greatest examples of Byzantine architecture, it was built in AD 532 under the supervision of Emperor Justinian. The third church on the site, it took 10,000 men five years to complete it. The first was built in 360; both it and its successor were destroyed by fire. The dome of the current church was the world's largest until the dome at St. Peter's Basilica was built in Rome 1,000 years later. Aya Sofya was the cathedral of Constantinople for nearly 1,000 years, surviving earthquakes and looting Crusaders until 1453, when it was converted into a mosque by Mehmet the Conqueror. Minarets were added by succeeding sultans. Aya Sofya originally had many mosaics depicting Christian scenes, which were plastered over by Süleyman I, who felt they were inappropriate for a mosque. In 1935 Atatürk converted Aya Sofya into a museum. Shortly after that American archaeologists discovered the mosaics, which were restored and are now on display. According to legend, the Sacred Column in the north aisle "weeps water" that can work miracles. It's so popular that over the centuries believers have worn a hole through the marble and brass column. You can stick your finger in it and make a wish. ⊠ *Aya Sofya Meyd.,* ☎ *212/522–1750.* ☉ *Tues.– Sun. 9:30–4:30.*

Arkeoloji Müzesi, **2**
Aya Sofya, **3**
Çiçek Pasajı, **14**
Dolmabahçe Cami, **15**
Dolmabahçe Sarayı, **16**
Galata Kulesi, **12**
Hippodrome, **5**
İstanbul Üniversitesi, **9**
İstiklâl Caddesi, **13**
Kapalı Aya Sota, **8**
Mısır Çarşısı, **11**
Süleymaniye Cami, **10**
Sultan Ahmet Cami, **4**
Topkapı Saray, **1**
Türk Ve Islâm Eserleri Müzesi, **6**
Yerebatan Sarnıcı, **7**

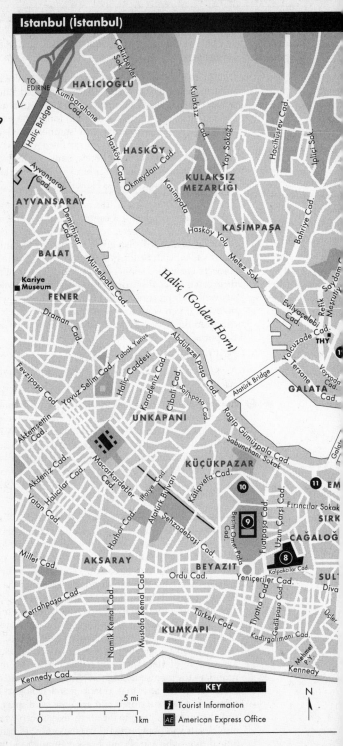

Istanbul (İstanbul)

⑤ Hippodrome. Once a Byzantine stadium with 100,000 seats, it was the focal point for city life, including chariot races, circuses, and public executions. Disputes between rival groups of supporters of chariot teams often degenerated into violence. In AD 531, 30,000 people died in the Hippodrome in what came to be known as the Nike riots. The original shape of the Hippodrome is still clearly visible. The monuments that can be seen today—the **Dikilitaş** (Egyptian Obelisk), the **Örme Sütun** (Column of Constantinos), and the **Yılanlı Sütun** (Serpentine Column) taken from the Temple of Apollo at Delphi in Greece—formed part of the central barrier around which the chariots raced. ⊠ *Sultanahmet Meyd.* 🎟 *Free.* ☉ *24 hrs.*

⑨ İstanbul Üniversitesi (Istanbul University). The main campus of one of Istanbul's leading universities is worth visiting for its magnificent Ottoman gateway and quiet walkways. ⊠ *Fuat Paşa Cad., Beyazit.* 🎟 *Free.* ☉ *Open dawn–dusk.*

★ **⑧ Kapalı Çarşısı** (Grand Bazaar, also known as the Covered Bazaar). This maze of 65 winding, covered streets hides 4,000 shops, tiny cafés, and restaurants, believed to be the largest number under one roof anywhere in the world. Originally built by Mehmet the Conqueror in the 1450s, it was ravaged by two modern-day fires, one in 1954 that nearly destroyed it, and a smaller one in 1974. In both cases the bazaar was quickly rebuilt. It's filled with thousands of curios, including carpets, fabrics, clothing, brass ware, furniture, icons, and gold jewelry. ⊠ *Yeniçeriler Cad. and Fuatpaşa Cad.* 🎟 *Free.* ☉ *Apr.–Oct., Mon.–Sat. 8:30–7; Nov.–Mar., Mon.–Sat. 8:30–6:30.*

★ **⑪ Mısır Çarşısı** (Egyptian Bazaar). Built during the 17th century to provide rental income for the upkeep of the Yeni Mosque, the Egyptian Bazaar was once a vast pharmacy, filled with burlap bags overflowing with herbs and spices for folk remedies. Today, you're more likely to see bags full of fruit, nuts, royal jelly from the beehives of the Aegean coast, and white sacks spilling over with culinary spices. Some shopkeepers will offer you tastes of energizing pastes, such as *macun,* as well as dried fruits or other Turkish delights. Nearby are equally colorful fruit and fish markets. ⊠ *Sabunchanı Sok., Eminönü.* ☉ *Mon.–Sat. 8–7.*

★ **⑩ Süleymaniye Cami** (Mosque of Süleyman). Sinan, the 16th-century architectural genius who masterminded more than 350 buildings and monuments under the direction of Süleyman the Magnificent, designed this mosque. It is his grandest and most famous monument. The mosque serves as the burial site of both Sinan and his patron, Süleyman. ⊠ *Süleymaniye Cad., near Istanbul University's north gate.* 🎟 *Free.* ☉ *Daily except prayer hrs.*

④ Sultan Ahmet Cami (Blue Mosque). With its shimmering blue tiles, 260 stained-glass windows, and six minarets, Sultan Ahmet is as grand and beautiful a monument to Islam as Aya Sofya was to Christianity. Mehmet Ağa, also known as Sedefkar (Worker of Mother of Pearl), built the mosque during the reign of Sultan Ahmet I in eight years, beginning in 1609, nearly 1,100 years after the completion of Aya Sofya. His goal was to surpass Justinian's masterpiece, and some believe he succeeded. Press through the throngs and enter the mosque at the side entrance that faces Aya Sofya. Remove your shoes and leave them at the entrance. Immodest clothing is not allowed, but an attendant will lend you a robe if he feels you are not dressed appropriately. **Hünkar Kasrı** (the Carpet and Kilim Museum; ☎ 212/518–1330) is in the mosque's stone-vaulted cellars and upstairs at the end of a stone ramp, where the sultans rested before and after their prayers; call for hours. ⊠ *Sultanahmet Meyd.* 🎟 *Free.* ☉ *Daily 9–5.*

★ ❶ **Topkapı Saray** (Topkapı Palace). The number-one attraction in Istanbul stands on Seraglio Point in Old Istanbul, known as Sultanahmet. The palace, which dates from the 15th century, was the residence of a number of sultans and their harems until the mid-19th century. To avoid the crowds try to get here by 9:30 AM, when the gates open. If you're arriving by taxi, tell the driver you want the *Topkapı Saray* in Sultanahmet, or you could end up at the remains of the former Topkapı bus terminal on the outskirts of town.

Sultan Mehmet II built the first palace during the 1450s, shortly after the Ottoman conquest of Constantinople. Over the centuries, sultan after sultan added ever more elaborate architectural fantasies, until the palace eventually ended up with more than four courtyards and some 5,000 residents, many of them concubines and eunuchs. Topkapı was the residence and center of bloodshed and drama for the Ottoman rulers until the 1850s, when Sultan Abdül Mecit moved with his harem to the European-style Dolmabahçe Palace farther up the Bosporus coast.

In Topkapı's outer courtyard are the **Aya İrini** (Church of St. Irene), open only during festival days for concerts, and the **Merasim Avlusu** (Court of the Janissaries), originally for members of the sultan's elite guard.

Adjacent to the ticket office is the **Bab-i-Selam** (Gate of Salutation), built in 1524 by Süleyman the Magnificent, who was the only person allowed to pass through it. In the towers on either side, prisoners were kept until they were executed beside the fountain outside the gate in the first courtyard. In the second courtyard, amid the rose gardens, is the **Divan-i-Humayun,** the assembly room of the council of state, once presided over by the *grand vizier* (prime minister). The sultan would sit behind a latticed window, hidden by a curtain so no one would know when he was listening, although occasionally he would pull the curtain aside to comment.

One of the most popular sections of Topkapı is the **Harem,** a maze of nearly 400 halls, terraces, rooms, wings, and apartments grouped around the sultan's private quarters on the west side of the second courtyard. Forty rooms are restored and open to the public. Next to the entrance are the quarters of the eunuchs and about 200 of the lesser concubines, who were lodged in tiny cubicles, as cramped and uncomfortable as the main rooms of the Harem are large and opulent. Tours begin every half hour. Only a limited number are taken on each tour. During the height of the tourist season it is advisable to try to buy a ticket for the harem tour soon after you enter the palace.

In the third courtyard is the **Hazine Dairesi** (Treasury), four rooms filled with jewels, including two uncut emeralds, each weighing 3½ kilograms (7.7 pounds), that once hung from the ceiling. Here, too, is the dazzling emerald dagger used in the movie *Topkapı* and the 84-carat "Spoonmaker" diamond that, according to legend, was found by a pauper and traded for three wooden spoons.

In the fourth and last courtyard of the Topkapı Palace are small, elegant summer houses, mosques, fountains, and reflecting pools scattered amid the gardens on different levels. Here you will find the **Rivan Köşk,** built by Murat IV in 1636 to commemorate the successful Rivan campaign. In another kiosk in the gardens, called the **İftariye** (Golden Cage), the closest relatives of the reigning sultan lived in strict confinement under what amounted to house arrest. The custom began during the 1800s after the old custom of murdering all possible rivals to the throne had been abandoned. The confinement of the heirs apparently helped keep the peace, but it deprived them of any chance to prepare themselves for the formidable task of ruling a great empire. ⊠ *Top-kapı Palace,* ☎ *212/512–0480.* ⊙ *Wed.–Mon. 9:30–4:30.*

❻ Türk Ve İslâm Eserleri Müzesi (Museum of Turkish and Islamic Arts). The museum is housed in Ibrahim Paşa Palace, once the grandiose residence of the son-in-law and grand vizier of Süleyman the Magnificent, Ibrahim Paşa, who was executed when he became too powerful for Süleyman's liking. The collection gives a superb insight into the lifestyles of Turks of every level of society, from the 8th century to the present. ⊠ *Atmeydanı 46, Sultanahmet,* ☎ *212/518–1385 or 212/518–1805.* ⊙ *Tues.–Sun. 9–4.*

★ ❼ Yerebatan Sarnıcı (the Sunken Palace, also known as the Basilica Cistern). This underground cistern was probably first excavated by Emperor Constantine in the 4th century and then enlarged by Emperor Justinian in the 6th century. It has 336 marble columns rising 26 ft to support Byzantine arches and domes. The cistern was always kept full as a precaution against long sieges. Its echoing vastness and the reflections of the columns in the dark water give it a haunting, cathedral-like beauty, and it is a welcome relief from the heat and noise above ground. ⊠ *Yerebatan Cad.,* ☎ *212/522–1259.* ⊙ *Daily 9–4:30.*

New Town

New Town is the area on the northern shore of the Golden Horn, the waterway that cuts through Istanbul on the European side of the Bosporus.

⓮ Çiçek Pasajı (Flower Arcade). Here you'll find a lively blend of tiny restaurants, bars, and street musicians. ⊠ *Çiçek Pasajı, off İstiklâl Cad., Galatasaray.*

★ ⓯ Dolmabahçe Cami (Dolmabahçe Mosque). Founded by Valide Sultan Bezmialem, mother of Abdül Mecit I, it was completed in 1853; the 88-ft-tall clock tower was built a year later. ⊠ *Dolmabahçe Cad.* ☎ *Free.* ⊙ *Daily except prayer hrs.*

⓰ Dolmabahçe Sarayi (Dolmabahçe Palace). Built in 1853, it was, until the declaration of the modern republic in 1923, the residence of the last sultans of the Ottoman Empire. It was also the residence of Atatürk, who died here in 1938. The palace, floodlit at night, is an extraordinary mixture of Hindu, Turkish, and European styles of architecture and interior design. Queen Victoria's contribution to the lavishness was a chandelier weighing 4½ tons. Guided tours of the palace take about 80 minutes. ⊠ *Dolmabahçe Cad.,* ☎ *212/258–5544.* ⊙ *Apr.–Oct. 9–4; Nov.–Mar. 9–3. Closed Mon. and Thurs.*

⓬ Galata Kulesi (Galata Tower). It was built by the Genoese in 1349 as part of the fortifications for their quarter of the Byzantine city. In this century it served as a fire lookout until 1960. Today it houses a restaurant and nightclub (☞ *Nightlife and the Arts, below*), and a viewing tower. ⊠ *Büyük Hendek Cad., Galata,* ☎ *212/245–1160.* ⊙ *Daily 9–8.*

⓭ İstiklâl Caddesi. Formerly known as La Grande Rue de Pera, İstiklâl Caddesi was the most fashionable street in the city during the 19th and early 20th centuries. Pedestrianized and lined with shops, restaurants, banks, and cafés in turn-of-the-century buildings, the street teems with every human element in Turkey's cultural melting pot, dodging the restored 19th-century tram that runs from Tünel to Taksim Square. In the side streets you'll find Greek and Armenian churches, bars, and other establishments; in the narrow, poorer residential alleys, you'll see children playing and laundry hanging between the old buildings. ⊠ *İstiklâl Cad., Beyoğlu.*

Dining and Lodging

Most major hotels have dining rooms serving bland international cuisine. It's far more rewarding to eat in Turkish restaurants. For details and price-category definitions, *see* Dining *in* Turkey A to Z, *above.*

The top hotels are mainly around Taksim Square in New Town. Hotels generally include the 15% VAT and a service charge of 10% to 15% in the rate. In Old Istanbul, the Aksaray, Laleli, Sultanahmet, and Beyazit areas have many conveniently located, inexpensive small hotels and family-run pansiyons. For details and price-category definitions, *see* Lodging *in* Turkey A to Z, *above.* **Note: telephone numbers below are in Istanbul; if you're calling from outside Turkey dial the country code first!**

$$$$ ✕ **Körfez.** The specialty here is seafood dishes such as bass baked in salt. The garden setting on the waterfront is very romantic. The restaurant has a boat that ferries you across the Bosporus from Rumeli Hisarı. ⊠ *Körfez Cad. 78, Kanlıca,* ☎ *216/413–4314. Reservations essential. AE, DC, MC, V. Closed Mon.*

$$$$ ✕ **Le Select.** Located in an elegant villa in the upmarket Levent neighborhood, Le Select lives up to its name by offering a sumptious selection of Turkish, French and Russian cuisine. House specialties include marinated salmon, sea bass with thyme, and steak in wine sauce. ⊠ *Manolya Sokak 21, Levent,* ☎ *212/268–2120. Reservations essential. AE, MC, V.*

$$$$ ✕ **Tuğra.** This spacious and luxurious restaurant in the historic Çirağan Palace serves the most delectable of long-savored Ottoman recipes, including slices of tender beef cooked in paper, air-dried beef cooked in vine leaves, and desserts such as quince tart in cinnamon syrup. The Bosporus view is framed by the palace's marble columns; the high ceilings support dazzlingly crafted glass chandeliers. ⊠ *Çirağan Cad. 84, Beşiktaş,* ☎ *212/258–3377. Reservations essential. Jacket required. AE, DC, MC, V. No lunch.*

$$$ ✕ **Beyti.** Over 50 years old, this classy, sprawling eatery is famous for inventing the *beyti kebabı* (spicy, skewered meatballs wrapped in pita) but also offers a range of other tasty meat dishes and salads to a clientele ranging from Turkish celebrities and business leaders to middle-class families. ⊠ *Orman Caddesi 8, Florya,* ☎ *212/663–2990. AE, MC, V.*

$$$ ✕ **Develi Restaurant.** Established in 1912, the Develi specializes in dishes from southeast Anatolia, which are traditionally more spicy than those from the west of the country. Try the *patlıcan kebap* (kebab with eggplants) or the *fıstıklı kebap* (kebab with pistachios). ⊠ *Balıkpazarı, Gümüşyüzük Sok. 7, Samatya,* ☎ *212/529–0833. AE, MC, V.*

$$$ ✕ **Divan.** Enjoy Turkish and international haute cuisine, elegant surroundings, and excellent service at this restaurant in the Divan hotel. Specialties include *islim kebap* (lamb covered with eggplant and served with Turkish rice). ⊠ *Cumhuriyet Cad. 2, Elmadağ,* ☎ *212/231–4100. AE, DC, MC. Closed Sun.*

$$ ✕ **Çatı.** On the seventh floor of a building in a Beyoğlu side street, this place serves a range of excellent hot and cold Turkish cuisine and a good open buffet. Its lofty location provides a rare opportunity to appreciate the architectural splendors of İstiklâl Caddesi. ⊠ *Orhan Apaydın Sok. 20/7, İstiklâl Cad., Beyoğlu,* ☎ *212/251–0000. MC, V. Closed Sun.*

$$ ✕ **Dört Mevsim** (Four Seasons). The restaurant, in a large Victorian building, is noted for its blend of Turkish and French cuisine and for its owners, Gay and Musa, an Anglo-Turkish couple who opened it in 1965. On any given day you'll find them in the kitchen overseeing such delights as shrimp in cognac sauce and baked marinated lamb. ⊠ *İstiklâl Cad. 509, Beyoğlu,* ☎ *212/293–3941. AE, DC, MC, V. Closed Sun.*

\$\$ ✕ **Dünya.** The busy traffic of the adjacent Ortaköy Square and waiters balancing appetizer trays is countered by the picturesque Bosporus
view, which on summer nights includes many passing pleasure boats.
The grilled *cupra* (bream) is a must, and the mezes are always fresh
and delicious. ✉ *Salhane Sok. 10, Ortaköy,* ☎ *212/258–6385. V.*

\$\$ ✕ **İmroz.** Tucked away in a side street of similar restaurants behind the
★ *Balık Pazarı* (Fish Market) in Beyoğlu, this is one of last Greek tavernas
in Istanbul. The menu offers high-quality fish and meat dishes. Wooden
tables and faded photographs contribute to the cozy, relaxed atmosphere. ✉ *Nevizade Sokak 24, Beyoğlu,* ☎ *212/249–9073. MC, V.*

\$\$ ✕ **Rejans.** Founded by two Russians and a Crimean fleeing the Bol-
shevik revolution, and now run by their widows, this restaurant has
excellent Russian food and lemon vodka, as well as Turkish dishes. The
decor has remained basically unchanged since the 1930s. ✉ *Emir
Nevrut Sok. 17, İstiklâl Cad., Beyoğlu,* ☎ *212/244–1610 or 212/
243–3882. Reservations essential Fri. and Sat. V. Closed Sun.*

\$ ✕ **Hacıbaba.** This large, cheerful-looking place has a summer terrace
★ overlooking an old Greek church. Fish, meat, and a wide variety of
vegetable dishes are on display for your selection. Before you choose
your main course, you'll be offered a tray of mezes that can be a meal
in themselves. ✉ *İstiklâl Cad. 49, Taksim,* ☎ *212/244–1886 or 212/
245–4377. AE, MC, V.*

\$ ✕ **Hacı Salih.** This tiny, family-run restaurant has only 10 tables, so
★ you may have to line up and wait—but it's worth it. Traditional Turkish food is the fare, with special emphasis on vegetable dishes and lamb.
Alcohol is not served. ✉ *Anadolu Pasajı 201, off İstiklâl Cad., Beyoğlu,* ☎ *212/243–4528. No credit cards. Closed Sun. No dinner.*

\$ ✕ **Yakup 2.** This cheerful hole-in-the-wall is smoky and filled with lo-
cals rather than tourists. It can get loud, especially if there is a soccer
game on TV. From the stuffed peppers to the *tereyağlı börek* (buttered
pastries) and octopus salad, the mezes are above average. ✉ *Asmalı
Mescit Sok. 35–37, Beyoğlu,* ☎ *212/249–2925. AE, V.*

\$\$\$\$ 🛏 **Çırağan Palace.** The 19th-century Ottoman palace is the city's most
★ luxurious hotel. The setting is exceptional, right on the Bosporus; the
outdoor pool is on the water's edge. Most rooms are in the new wing
(ask for a renovated one), though there are 12 suites in the palace. ✉
Çırağan Cad. 84, Beşiktaş, 80700, ☎ *212/258–3377,* 🖷 *212/259–6686.
287 rooms, 28 suites. 4 restaurants, pool. AE, DC, MC, V.*

\$\$\$\$ 🛏 **Hyatt Regency.** This massive but tasteful pink building, reminiscent
of Ottoman splendor, houses one of the city's newer upscale hotels.
Many rooms have views of the Bosporus. The interior has plush carpeting and the decor is a combination of earth tones in many textures.
The restaurants serve a range of Asian, Turkish, and Italian foods. ✉
Taşkışla Cad., Taksim, 80090, ☎ *212/225–7000,* 🖷 *212/225–7007.
360 rooms. 3 restaurants, pool. AE, DC, MC, V.*

\$\$\$\$ 🛏 **Istanbul Hilton.** One of the best hotels in the chain, it is decorated
with Turkish rugs and large brass urns. Ask for a room overlooking
the Bosporus. ✉ *Cumhuriyet Cad., Harbiye, 80200,* ☎ *212/231–
4650,* 🖷 *212/240–4165. 501 rooms. 4 restaurants, 2 pools. AE, DC,
MC, V.*

\$\$\$\$ 🛏 **Pera Palace.** A grand hotel with a genuinely Turkish feel, the Pera
★ Palace was built in 1892 to accommodate guests arriving on the *Orient Express.* The likes of Atatürk, Agatha Christie, Mata Hari, and even
Greta Garbo have slept here. Although it has been modernized for comfort, the hotel has retained its original Victorian elegance. Many old
features, such as a magnificent antique elevator, are still in working
order. ✉ *Meşrutiyet Cad. 98, Tepebaşı, 80050,* ☎ *212/251–4560,* 🖷
212/251–4089. 145 rooms. Restaurant. AE, DC, MC, V.

$$$$ ⊞ **Swissôtel.** Near the city center in a hilltop wood, this hotel has views
★ across the Bosporus and beyond to the Sea of Marmara. It also has
lavish amenities, including excellent sports facilities and a range of French,
Turkish, Japanese, Chinese, and Swiss cuisine at its many restaurants.
⊠ *Bayıldim Cad. 2, Maçka, 80680,* ☎ *212/259–0101,* ℻ *212/259–*
0105. 500 rooms, 17 suites, 50 executive rooms. 10 restaurants, 2 pools.
AE, DC, MC, V.

$$$ ⊞ **Ayasofia Pansiyons.** These guest houses are part of a project under-
taken by the Touring and Automobile Club to restore a little street of
historic wooden houses along the outer wall of Topkapı Palace. One of
the houses has been converted into a library and the rest into pansiyons,
furnished in late Ottoman style. In summer tea and refreshments are served
in the gardens. ⊠ *Soğukçeşme Sok., Sultanahmet, 34400,* ☎ *212/513–*
3660, ℻ *212/513–3669. 64 rooms. 2 restaurants. AE, MC, V.*

$$$ ⊞ **Divan Hotel.** Quiet, but close enough to Taksim Square, this reno-
vated old hotel has some rooms with private terraces overlooking the
Bosporus. All are clean and functionally furnished. The restaurant is
renowned for impeccably prepared Turkish and international dishes.
⊠ *Cumhuriyet Cad. 2, Elmadağ, 80200,* ☎ *212/231–4100,* ℻ *212/*
248–8527. 180 rooms, 8 suites. 2 restaurants. AE, DC, MC.

$$$ ⊞ **Yeşil Ev** (Green House). Practically next door to the Blue Mosque,
★ this 19th-century building is decorated in old-fashioned Ottoman style
with lace curtains and latticed shutters. Its high-walled garden restau-
rant is a verdant and peaceful oasis in the midst of frenetic Istanbul.
⊠ *Kabasakal Cad. 5, Sultanahmet, 34400,* ☎ *212/517–6785,* ℻ *212/*
517–6780. 20 rooms with shower. 2 restaurants. AE, MC, V.

$$ ⊞ **Büyük Londra.** This Victorian hotel has grown old gracefully. Furnishings are heavy and traditional. ⊠ *Meşrutiyet Cad. 117, Tepebaşi,*
80050, ☎ *212/293–1619,* ℻ *212/245–0671. 54 rooms. Restaurant.*
AE, MC, V.

$$ ⊞ **Hotel Barin.** Modern, clean, and comfortable, with good, friendly
service, the Barin caters to business travelers as well as tourists. ⊠ *Fevziye*
Cad. 7, Şehzadebaşı, 34470, ☎ *212/513–9100,* ℻ *212/526–4440. 65*
rooms. AE, MC, V.

$$ ⊞ **Richmond.** A turn-of-the-century building on İstiklâl Caddesi was
renovated to create this comfortable hotel. Downstairs is the Lebon
patisserie, a remake of the 19th-century pastry shop that once operated here and an excellent place to watch the world pass by. ⊠ *İstik-*
lâl Cad. 445, Tepebaşi, 80070, ☎ *212/252–5460,* ℻ *212/252–9707.*
109 rooms. 2 restaurants. AE, V.

$ ⊞ **Berk Guest House.** An English-speaking woman, Yeşim Evrensel,
runs this tidy little inn with adequate if unexceptional rooms. Three
have balconies overlooking a garden. ⊠ *Kutlugün Sok. 27, Sultanah-*
met, 34400, ☎ *212/516–9671,* ℻ *212/517–7715. 9 rooms with*
shower. No credit cards.

$ ⊞ **Hotel Empress Zoe.** Named for an empress who ruled Byzantium
★ during the 11th century, this unusual property is decorated with murals and paintings in that era's style. Rooms, of varying configurations,
are brightened with colorful embroidered textiles—some have views.
The American owner, Ann Nevans, can help out with personalized
itineraries of the nearby Sultanahmet sights and beyond. ⊠ *Akbıyık*
Cad., Adliye Sok. 10, Sultanahmet, 34400, ☎ *212/518–2504,* ℻ *212/*
518–5699. 19 rooms. MC, V.

Nightlife and the Arts

The Arts

Entertainment in Istanbul ranges from the Istanbul International Festival—held late June through mid-July and attracting internationally

renowned artists and performers—to local folklore and theatrical groups, some amateur, some professional. Because there is no central ticket agency, ask your hotel for help getting tickets. You can also get them at the box office or through a local tourist office. For tickets to the **Istanbul International Festival,** contact the Istanbul Foundation for Culture and Arts (✉ Kültür ve Sanat Vakfı, İstiklâl Cad., Luvr Apt. 146, Beyoğlu, 80070, ☎ 212/293–3133). Tickets can also be purchased at ticket booths outside some of the venues. Performances, which include modern and classical music, ballet, opera, and theater, are given throughout the city in historic buildings, such as the Church of St. Irene and Rumeli Castle. The season at the city of Istanbul's **Cemal Resit Rey Concert Hall** (☎ 212/231–5498) runs from September through May and includes classical, jazz, and rock music, as well as ballet performed by visiting and local groups.

CONCERTS

From October through May, the Istanbul State Symphony gives performances at the main concert hall, **Atatürk Kültür Merkezi** (✉ box office, Taksim Sq., ☎ 212/251–5600); tickets are also available here for concerts at Cemal Resit Rey Concert Hall. Ballet and dance companies perform at this hall, too.

Nightlife

BARS

Bebek Bar (✉ Bebek Ambassadeurs Hotel, Cevdet Paşa Cad. 113, Bebek, ☎ 212/263–3000) has views over the Bosporus and draws locals from the neighborhood and nearby Bosporus University. Sophisticated **Beyoğlu Pub** (✉ İstiklâl Cad. 140/7, Beyoğlu, ☎ 212/252–3842), behind an arcade off İstiklâl Caddesi, has a pleasant first-story garden and a discreet indoor bar. **Hayal Kahvesi** (✉ Büyük Parmakkapı Sok. 19, Beyoğlu, ☎ 212/244–2558) is a bohemian side-street bar with wooden furniture, lace curtains, and live music. The fin-de-siècle decor of the **Orient Express Bar** (✉ Pera Palace Hotel, Meşrutiyet Cad. 98, Tepebaşı, ☎ 212/251–4560) distills the atmosphere of old Istanbul with the lingering presence of the rich, powerful, and famous who once played here. With its British pub atmosphere and range of imported beers and malt whiskies the **Sherlock Holmes** (✉ Çalıkuşu Sokak 5, ☎ 212/281–6372) has become a popular haunt for local yuppies and expatriates alike. **Tribunal** (✉ İstiklâl Cad. Muammer Karaca Cikmazi 3, ☎ 212/249–7179) once served as a French court and retains the original inlaid brick ceiling.

DANCE CLUBS

Çubuklu 29 (✉ Paşabahçe Yolu, Çubuklu, ☎ 216/322–2829), by the Bosporus on the Asian side, is open mid-June through September. **Deep** (✉ Nispetiye Caddesi 32, Etiler, ☎ 212/287–5785) is a lively late-night disco-bar attracting an affluent, dance-crazy clientele of all ages. **Hayal Kahvesi** (✉ Burunbahçe, Çubuklu, ☎ 216/413–6880), a huge, restaurant/bar/disco complex on the Asian shore of the Bosporus, has dancing to live jazz or rock on Friday or Saturday (summer only). The loud and lively three-story **Kemancı Rock-Bar** (✉ Taksim Sitesi, Sıraselviler 69, Taksim, ☎ 212/245–3048 or 212/251–3015) is a favorite with students, who dance to live rock and blues bands. **Şaziye** (✉ Abdi İpekçi Cad. 24–26, Maçka, ☎ 212/232–4155 or 212/231–1401) turns into a disco with Turkish pop music or live Turkish pop stars after 11:30 PM.

JAZZ CLUBS

Q Jazz Bar (✉ Çırağan Cad. 84, Beşiktaş, ☎ 212/236–2489 or 212/236–2131), the Çırağan Hotel's luxurious jazz bar, has some of the classiest music in town—at equally classy prices. **Tepe Bar Lounge** (✉ Marmara Hotel, Taksim Sq., ☎ 212/251–4696), on the top floor of the

Marmara Hotel, has a 360-degree view of Istanbul, as well as local and visiting musicians.

NIGHTCLUBS

Galata Tower (✉ Kuledibi, ☎ 212/245–1160) serves dinner followed by a Turkish show and dancing. **Kervansaray** (✉ Cumhuriyet Cad. 30, Elmadağ, ☎ 212/247–1630) has dining, dancing, and belly-dancing shows. The revue at **Regine's** (✉ Cumhuriyet Cad. 16, Elmadağ, ☎ 212/247–1630) is the spot for some of Istanbul's best-known belly dancers and big dance production numbers.

Shopping

Districts and Malls

In New Town, stores and boutiques line İstiklâl Caddesi, which runs off Taksim Square, and Rumeli, Halaskargazi, and Valikonağı Caddeleri, north of the Istanbul Hilton. Two streets in the Kadiköy area with good shops are Bağdat and Bahariye Caddeleri. **Akmerkez,** the newest of the malls in Etiler, has luxury and designer wear. **Ataköy Shopping and Tourism Center** is a large mall near the airport. In Altunizade on the Asian side, the slick **Capitol** mall has movies and entertainment, too.

Gift Ideas

The **Grand Bazaar** (☞ Exploring Istanbul, *above*) is what it sounds like: a smattering of all things Turkish—carpets, brass, copper, jewelry, textiles, and leather goods. **Tünel Square,** a quick Metro ride up from Karaköy, is a quaint group of stores with old prints, books, and artifacts. **Çukurcuma,** in the back streets of Beyoğlu, contains several shops specializing in maps and odds and ends from the late 19th and early 20th centuries.

Markets

Balıkpazarı (fish market) is in Beyoğlu Caddesi, off İstiklâl Caddesi. A bustling clutter of narrow covered streets, **Balıkpazarı** contains stalls and tiny stores, selling everything from spices, vegetables, and fruit to fish, cooked meats, and even pork. Turkish traders are joined by new arrivals from the former Soviet Union at a flea market held in **Beyazit Square,** near the Grand Bazaar, every Sunday starting at about 10 AM; here you can find everything from cheap electronic goods to Soviet army boots and hats. A crafts market, with street entertainment, is open on Sunday along the Bosporus at **Ortaköy.** A weekend crafts market takes place on **Bekar Sokak,** off İstiklâl Caddesi.

Istanbul Essentials

Arriving and Departing

BY BUS

Esenler terminal, northwest of the city center, is the destination for buses arriving in Istanbul. From the terminal, the major bus companies offer free minibus service to centers such as Sultanahmet, Taksim, and Aksaray. The Hızlı Tren (rapid train) also connects the terminal to Aksaray, though it is often very crowded and can be extremely hot in summer. A few buses from Anatolia arrive at **Harem terminal,** on the eastern shore of the Bosporus. If you arrive with baggage, it is much easier to take a taxi, which will cost about $8 to Taksim from the Esenler terminal and about $5 to Old Istanbul.

BY CAR

If you drive in from the west, take the busy E5 highway, also called Londra Asfaltı, which leads from Edirne to Atatürk Airport and on through the city walls at Cannon Gate (Topkapı). E5 heading out of Istanbul leads into central Anatolia and on to Iran and Syria. You can also take one of the numerous car ferries that ply the Sea of Marmara and the Dardanelles from Kabataş Dock, or try the overnight ferry to İzmir, which leaves from Sarayburnu.

BY PLANE

All international and domestic flights arrive at Istanbul's **Atatürk Airport.** For arrival and departure information call the individual airline or the airport's information desk (☎ 212/663–6400).

Between the Airport and Downtown. Shuttle buses run from the airport's international and domestic terminals to the Turkish Airlines (THY) terminal in downtown Istanbul, at Cumhuriyet Caddesi, near the THY Taksim office. Buses depart for the airport at the same address on the hour every hour from 7 AM to 11 PM. After that, departure time depends on demand. Allow at least 45 minutes for the bus ride. Plan to be at the airport two hours before your international flight because of the lengthy security and check-in procedures. The ride from the airport into town takes from 30 to 40 minutes, depending on traffic. Taxis charge about $15 to Taksim Square and $11 to Sultanahmet.

BY TRAIN

Trains from the west arrive at **Sirkeci Station** (☎ 212/527–0050 or 212/527–0051) in Old Istanbul. Eastbound trains to Anatolia depart from **Haydarpasa station** (☎ 216/336–0475) on the Asian side.

Getting Around

The best way to get to the various magnificent monuments in Sultanahmet in Old Istanbul is to walk; they're all within easy distance of one another. Dolmuş vehicles and taxis are plentiful, inexpensive, and more comfortable than city buses. A tram system runs from Topkapı, via Sultanahmet, to Sirkeci. The Tünel, a tiny underground train, is handy for getting up the steep hill from Karaköy to the bottom of İstiklâl Caddesi. It runs every 10 minutes and costs about 25¢. Trams run the length of İstiklâl Caddesi from Taksim to Tünel and cost about 25¢.

BY BOAT

Many ferries run between the Asian and European continents. *Deniz otobüsü* (sea buses; ☎ 216/362–0444) run between the continents, as well as to destinations such as the Princes' Islands; they are fast and efficient. For an inexpensive ride take the boat in the direction of *Anadolu Kavağı,* along the Bosporus to its mouth at the Black Sea. The boat leaves year-round from the Eminönü Docks, next to the Galata Bridge on the Old Istanbul side, at 10:30 AM and 1:30 PM, with two extra trips on weekdays and four extra trips on Sunday from April through September. The fare is $6 (round-trip). The trip takes 1¾ hours one way. You can disembark at any of the stops and return by land if you wish. Regular ferries depart from Kabataş Dock, near Dolmabahçe Palace on the European side, to Üsküdar on the Asian side; and also from Eminönü Docks 1 and 2, near Sirkeci station (☎ 212/244–4233).

BY BUS

You need to buy a ticket before boarding a bus. Individual tickets or books of 10 can be purchased at ticket stands around the city. Shoeshine boys or men on the street will also sell them to you for a few cents more. Fares are about 25¢ per ride. On the city's orange privatized buses (Halk Otobüsü), you pay for tickets on the bus. The London-style double-deckers operate along a scenic route between Sultanahmet and Emigran on the Bosporus and between Europe and Asia and cost about $1 one way.

BY DOLMUŞ

These are shared taxis operating between set destinations throughout the city. Dolmuş stops are indicated by a blue-and-white sign with a large D. The destination is shown on either a roof sign or a card in the front window. Until the mid-1990s all the dolmuş were classic American cars from the 1950s, but they have now been nearly all been replaced by modern yellow minibuses.

BY TAXI

Taxis are inexpensive and metered. As most drivers do not speak English and may not know the street names, write down the street you want, the nearby main streets, and the name of the area. Although tipping is not expected, you should round off the fare to the nearest 50,000 TL.

Contacts and Resources

Note: all telephone numbers below are in Istanbul and must be preceded by the country code if you are dialing from outside Turkey!

CONSULATES

U.S. (⊠ Meşrutiyet Cad. 104–108, Tepebaşi 80050, Beyoğlu, ☎ 212/251–3602). **U.K.** (⊠ Meşrutiyet Cad. 34, Tepebaşı 80050, Beyoğlu, ☎ 212/293–7540). **Canadian** (⊠ Büyükdere Cad. 107/3, Bengün Han, 80300, Gayrettepe, ☎ 212/272–5174). **Australia** (⊠ Tepecik Yokuşu 58, Etiler, 80630, ☎ 212/257–7050). **Ireland** (Honorary; ⊠ Cumhuriyet Cad. 26, Harbiye, 80200, ☎ 212/246–6025).

EMERGENCIES

Tourism Police (☎ 212/527–4503). **Ambulance** (☎ 112). **Doctors: American Hospital** (⊠ Güzelbahçe Sok. 20, Nişantaşı, 80200, ☎ 212/231–4050 through 231–4069); **International Hospital** (Yesilyurt, ☎ 212/663–3000). **Pharmacies** (☎ 118, for 24-hour pharmacy in each neighborhood; notice in window of every pharmacy lists name and address of nearest all-night shop); in center, **Taksim** (⊠ İstiklâl Cad. 17, Taksim, 80060, ☎ 212/2244–3195).

ENGLISH-LANGUAGE BOOKSTORES

ABC Bookshop (⊠ İstiklâl Cad. 461, Tünel, ☎ 212/249–2414). **D & R** (⊠ Nispetiye Cad., Etiler, ☎ 212/263–2914). **Homer** (⊠ Yeni Çarşı Cad. 28A, Galatasaray, ☎ 212/249–5902). **Robinson Crusoe** (⊠ İstiklâl Cad. 389, Tünel, ☎ 212/293–6968 or 212/293–6977).

GUIDED TOURS

Tours can be arranged through travel agencies (☞ Travel Agencies, *below*). Most companies have a half- or full-day "Classical Tour." The half-day tour includes Aya Sofya, the Museum of Turkish and Islamic Arts, the Hippodrome, Yerebatan Saray, and the Blue Mosque; the full-day tour, in addition to the above sights, includes Topkapı Palace, the Süleymaniye Mosque, the Covered or Egyptian Bazaar, and lunch.

TRAVEL AGENCIES

Fest (⊠ Barbaros Bulvarı 85, A Daire 13, Beşiktaş, ☎ 212/258–2589 or 212/258–2573). **Intra** (⊠ Halaskargazi Cad. 111/2, Harbiye, ☎ 212/247–8174 or 212/240–3891). **Plan Tours** (⊠ Cumhuriyet Cad. 131/1, Elmadağ, ☎ 212/230–2272 or 212/230–8118). **Setur** (⊠ Cumhuriyet Cad. 107, Harbiye, ☎ 212/230–0336). **Türk Express** (American Express Travel Service representative; ⊠ Istanbul Hilton, Cumhuriyet Cad., Harbiye, ☎ 212/241–0248 or 212/241–0249). **Vip Tourism** (⊠ Cumhuriyet Cad. 269/2, Harbiye, ☎ 212/241–6514).

VISITOR INFORMATION

Official tourist offices in Istanbul: **Atatürk Airport** (☎ 212/663–6400); the **Istanbul Hilton** (☎ 212/233–0592); **Karaköy Yolcu Salonu,** International Maritime Passenger Terminal (☎ 212/249–5776); **pavilion** (✉ Divan Yolu Cad. 3, Sultanahmet, ☎ 212/518–1802 or 212/518–8754).

THE AEGEAN COAST

Some of the finest ancient Greek and Roman cities, including the fabled Pergamum, Ephesus, Aphrodisias, and Troy, are found in this region of Turkey. Watch for the ubiquitous bright yellow road signs pointing to historic sites or to those currently undergoing excavation. There are so many Greek and Roman ruins, in fact, that some haven't yet been excavated and others are going to seed. Grand or small, all the sites are steeped in atmosphere and are best visited early in the morning or late in the afternoon, when crowds are smaller. Escape the heat of the day on one of the sandy beaches along the coast.

It makes sense to begin your exploration of the Aegean Coast in the north at inland Bursa, moving west to Gallipoli and Canakkale at the Dardanelles. Farther south, past Troy, is the city of Izmir. Follow the southern coast down to Bodrum, with a detour inland to the ruins at Aphrodisias and the natural hot springs of Pamukkale. You'll need 8–10 days to cover the region thoroughly.

Bursa

The first capital of the Ottoman Empire, Bursa is known as Yeşil (Green) Bursa. The name derives from its many trees and parks and from its **Yeşil Cami** (Green Mosque) and **Yeşil Türbe** (Green Mausoleum). ★ Both mosque and mausoleum derive their names from the green tiles that line their interiors. ✉ *Yeşil Cad. (Green Ave.).* ⌨ *Free.* ☉ *Daily except prayer hrs.*

The town square, called Heykel, which means "statue," is named for its statue of Atatürk. Off Heykel is the **Ulu Cami** (Great Mosque) with its distinctive silhouette of 20 domes. ✉ *Atatürk Cad.* ⌨ *Free.* ☉ *Daily except prayer hrs.*

Bursa is also the site of **Uludağ** (Great Mountain), Turkey's most popular ski resort. To fully appreciate why the town is called Green Bursa, take a ride on the *teleferik* (cable car; ✉ Namazgah Cad.) up the mountain for a panoramic view.

$$ ✕ **Cumurcul.** In a converted old house, this restaurant is a local favorite. Grilled meats and fish are attentively prepared. ✉ *Çekirge Cad.,* ☎ *224/235–3707 or 224/235–3373. V.*

$ ✕ **Kebabcı İskender.** Bursa is famous for the dish served here, *İskender kebab* (Alexander's kebab—slivers of skewer-grilled meat served with tomato sauce and yogurt). ✉ *Ünlü Cad. 7, Heykel,* ☎ *224/221–4615. No credit cards.*

$$$$ ▥ **Çelik Palace.** After you've indulged at this posh hotel's restaurant, ★ casino, and clubs, enjoy the crowning luxury: a dip in the domed, Roman-style thermal pool. The place has a lively 1930s design scheme, and some rooms have balconies. ✉ *Çekirge Meyd. 79, 16000,* ☎ *224/233–3800,* ꜰꜱ *224/236–1910. 173 rooms. Restaurant. AE, DC, MC, V.*

$$ ▥ **Ada Palas.** There are thermal baths on every floor of this Çekirge hotel, and the price tag is lower than that at the nearby Çelik. Rooms are unexceptional but in good condition. ✉ *Murat Cad. 21, Çekirge 16000,* ☎ *224/233–3990,* ꜰꜱ *224/236–4656. 36 rooms. Restaurant. V.*

Çanakkale and Gallipoli

Çanakkale is the guardian of the Dardanelles, the narrow straits that separate Europe from Asia and connect the Aegean Sea with the Sea of Marmara. This strategic point has been fought over since the days of the Trojan War. During World War I Britain and France tried to breach

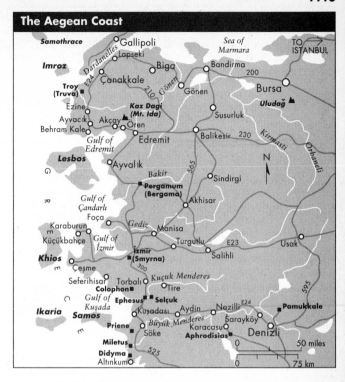

The Aegean Coast

Samothrace · Gallipoli
Dardanelles · Lapseki
Sea of Marmara
TO ISTANBUL
Imroz · Biga · Bandirma
Çanakkale · Göner · Gönen · 200 · Bursa
Troy (Truva) · Kaz Daği (Mt. Ida) · Uludağ
Ezine · Akçay · Ören · Susurluk · Kirmasti
Ayvacık · Edremit · Balikesir · 230 · Orhaneli
Behram Kale · Gulf of Edremit
Lesbos · Ayvalık · Bakir · Sindirgi
Pergamum (Bergama) · Akhisar
Gulf of Çandarlı · Foça
Karaburun · Gediz · Manisa
Küçükbahçe · Gulf of İzmir · Turgutlu · E23 · Salihli · Usak
Khios · Çeşme · İzmir (Smyrna)
Seferihisar · Torbalı · Küçük Menderes
Colophon · Tire
Gulf of Kuşada · Ephesus · Selçuk
Ikaria · Samos · Kuşadası · Aydın · Nazilli · E24 · Pamukkale
Priene · Büyük Menderes · Sarayköy
Miletus · Söke · Karacasu · Denizli
Didyma · Aphrodisias
Altınkum · 525
0 · 50 miles
0 · 75 km

Çanakkale's defenses in the unsuccessful Gallipoli campaign. They were defeated by the strategy of Mustafa Kemal—the man who would later be called Atatürk. Thirty-one beautifully tended **military cemeteries** of the Allied dead from World War I line the battlefields.

Nowadays Çanakkale is a drab agricultural center and garrison town, but it serves as the gateway to historic Gallipoli, on the north side of the Dardanelles. At Cape Helles there is a massive, four-pillared memorial to Turkey's war dead. Half-day excursions to Gallipoli are organized by **Troy-Anzac Tours** (⊠ İskele Meyd., south side near clock tower, Çanakkale, ☎ 286/217–5849).

$$ ▦ **Akol.** This modern hotel is perched on the waterfront in Çanakkale; ask for a room with a terrace overlooking the Dardanelles. ⊠ *Kordonboyu, Çanakkale, 17100,* ☎ *286/217–9456,* FAX *286/217–2897. 135 rooms, 2 suites. Restaurant, pool. AE, MC, V.*

$$ ▦ **Büyük Truva.** Near the center of Çanakkale, the Truva is an excellent base for sightseeing. Rooms are clean and functional and have large windows. ⊠ *Cevatpaşa Mah. Mehmet Akif Ersoy Cad. 2 Kordonboyu, Çanakkale, 17000,* ☎ *286/217–1024,* FAX *286/217–0903. 66 rooms. Restaurant. V.*

Troy

Long thought to be simply an imaginary city from Homer's *Iliad*, **Troy** (Truva in Turkish, Ilion in Greek) was excavated in the 1870s by Heinrich Schliemann, a German amateur archaeologist. He also found the remains of nine successive civilizations, one on top of the other, dating back 5,000 years. Considering Troy's fame, the site is surprisingly small. It's best to take a guided tour to appreciate fully the significance of this discovery and the unwavering passion of the man who proved that Troy was not just another ancient myth. ⊠ *Follow signs from Rte. E87, 32 km (20 mi) south of Çanakkale.* ⊙ *Daily 8–7.*

$ ⊞ **Tusan.** Along the beachfront north of Troy at Güzelyalı, and framed by a pine forest, this is one of the most attractive hotels in the area. Be certain to reserve well in advance. ⌧ *Güzelyalı, 17001,* ☎ *286/232–8210 or 286/232–8746/47,* ℻ *286/232–8226. 64 rooms. Restaurant. MC, V. Closed Nov.–Feb.*

Ayvalık

The charming, sleepy coastal resort just south of the Gulf of Edremit has some of the best examples of 19th-century Greek domestic architecture found anywhere in the Aegean. From Ayvalık you can take boats to **Ali Bey Adası,** a tiny island with pleasant waterfront restaurants, and to the Greek island of Lesbos.

$$ ⊞ **Büyük Berk.** Part of a larger complex, this modern hotel sits on Ayvalık's best beach, about 3¼ km (2 mi) from the center of town. ⌧ *Sarımsaklı Plaj, 10425,* ☎ *266/324–1045,* ℻ *266/324–1194. 180 rooms. Restaurant, pool. No credit cards. Closed Oct.–Mar.*

$ ⊞ **Ankara Oteli.** On Sarımsaklı beach, just a few feet from the surf, the Ankara Oteli is the cheapest option. Although rooms are nondescript, they do have balconies; book ahead to get one facing the beach. ⌧ *Sarımsaklı Plaj, 10425,* ☎ *266/324–1195 or 266/324–1048,* ℻ *266/324–0022. 108 rooms. Restaurant. No credit cards. Closed Nov.–Mar.*

Pergamum

The windswept ruins of Pergamum (Bergama in Turkish) are among the most spectacular in Turkey. Pergamum's glory peaked during the Greek Attalid dynasty (241 BC–133 BC), when it was one of the world's most magnificent architectural and artistic centers—especially under the rule of Eumenes II, who lavished his great wealth on the city. When the mad Attalus III died, he bequeathed the entire kingdom to Rome.

Because the attractions are spread out over several kilometers, it's best to take a taxi from one site to the next. The most noteworthy places are the **Asklepieion,** the **Ethnological Museum,** the **Red Hall,** and the **Acropolis.** The most famous building at the **Acropolis** is the **library,** which once contained a collection of 200,000 books, all on papyrus. The library's collection was second only to the one in Alexandria, Egypt. ☉ *Apr.–Oct., daily 8:30–6:30; Nov.–Mar., daily 8:30–5:30.*

$$ ⊞ **Hotel İskender.** Although it's plain and modern, this place is right in the center of town and has air-conditioning. The outdoor restaurant serves tasty fresh mezes and grilled foods. ⌧ *İzmir Cad. Ilica Önü Mev., Bergama 35700,* ☎ *232/633–2123 or 232/632–9711,* ℻ *232/632–9710. 60 rooms. 2 restaurants, air-conditioning. MC, V.*

$$ ⊞ **Tusan Bergama Moteli.** Just off the main road to Bergama, this hotel has simple but clean rooms. Its location isn't that convenient if you don't have a car. The real draw, though, is a pool fed by hot springs. ⌧ *İzmir Yolu, Çatı Mev., Bergama 35700,* ☎ *232/667–2236,* ℻ *232/633–1938. 44 rooms. Restaurant, pool. No credit cards. Closed Nov.–Apr.*

İzmir

Turkey's third-largest city is also its most Mediterranean in feel. Called Smyrna by the Greeks, it was a vital trading port that was often ravaged by wars and earthquakes. The city was almost completely destroyed by a fire in 1922 during the final stages of Turkey's War of Independence against Greece. It was quickly rebuilt and became known by its Turkish name, İzmir. Today it's a lively, modern city filled with wide boulevards, apartment houses, and office buildings. At the center of the city is **Kültürpark,** a large green park that is the site of İzmir's industrial fair from late August to late September (a time when most hotels are full).

Atop İzmir's highest hill is the **Kadifekale** (Velvet Fortress), built in the 3rd century BC by Lysimachos. It is easily reached by dolmuş and is one of the few ancient ruins that was not destroyed in the fire. At the foot of the hill is the restored **Agora,** the market of ancient Smyrna. The modern-day marketplace is in **Konak Square,** a maze of tiny streets filled with shops and covered stalls. ⊙ *Mon.–Sat. 8–8.*

$$$$ 🏨 **İzmir Hilton.** At 34 stories, the Hilton is one of the Aegean coast's tallest buildings. Striking and modern, the structure looms over the city center. From the 10-story atrium to the rooftop restaurant, the public spaces are suitably grand. Guest rooms are plush and have thick floral comforters and matching drapes. ⊠ *Gazi Osman Paşa Bul. 7, 35210,* ☎ *232/441–6060,* FAX *232/441–2277. 381 rooms. 4 restaurants, pool. AE, DC, MC, V.*

$$$ 🏨 **Mercure Konak Hotel.** This hotel right on the water has lots of cool marble and greenery. Guest rooms have full-size beds, plush carpeting, and big windows with views. The city's museums are within easy walking distance. ⊠ *Mithatpasa Cad. 128,, 35210,* ☎ *232/489–1500,* FAX *232/489–1709. 80 rooms. Restaurant. AE, MC, V.*

$–$$ 🏨 **Kismet.** Tastefully decorated, the Kismet is a quiet, comfortable hotel with friendly service. ⊠ *1377 Sok. 9, Alsancak 35210,* ☎ *232/463–3850,* FAX *232/421–4856. 62 rooms. Restaurant. AE, MC, V.*

Kuşadası

One of the most popular tourist resorts in the Mediterranean, Kuşadası has grown in less than 30 years from a fishing village into a sprawling town. Although geared to serving thousands of tourists who visit the nearby ruins and beaches, the busy town maintains an easy pace.

$$ ✕ **Ali Baba Restaurant.** The focus is on fish at this simply styled (starched white tablecloths, wooden chairs) waterfront spot with a peaceful view of the bay. Try the marinated octopus salad or the fried calamari, followed by a grilled version of whatever has just been caught. ⊠ *Belediye Turistik Çarşısı 5,* ☎ *256/614–1551. Reservations essential. MC, V.*

$$ ✕ **Alize.** A five-minute walk from the waterfront, this excellent bistro
★ more than makes up for its lack of a sea view with a superb range of meat, fish, and pasta dishes and live acoustic music in the evenings. It's a favorite hangout for locals, particularly the young trendy set, for whom it doubles as a café and a bar. ⊠ *Karagöz Sok. 67, Sağlık Cad.,* ☎ *256/612–0360. MC, V.*

$$$ 🏨 **Club Kervansaray.** In a refurbished 300-year-old caravansary, this hotel in the center of town is Ottoman in style and loaded with charm and atmosphere. Its restaurant has a floor show and there's dancing after dinner in the courtyard, where the camels were once kept. ⊠ *Atatürk Bul. 2, 09400,* ☎ *256/614–4115,* FAX *256/614–2423. 26 rooms. Restaurant. AE, DC, MC, V.*

$$$ 🏨 **Kismet.** Although it's small, this hotel is run on a grand scale. It's
★ surrounded by beautifully maintained gardens on a promontory overlooking the marina on one side and the Aegean on the other. Ask for rooms in the garden annex. Reservations are a must. ⊠ *Akyar Mev., Türkmen Mahallesi, 09400,* ☎ *256/614–2005,* FAX *256/614–4914. 96 rooms. Restaurant. MC, V. Closed Jan.–Mar.*

$$ 🏨 **Efe Otel.** Located on the waterfront a little beyond the path to Pigeon Island, the Efe is clean and comfortable. Ask for a room with a balcony and a view over Pigeon Island. ⊠ *Guvercin Ada Cad. 37, 09400,* ☎ *256/614–3661,* FAX *256/614–3662. 44 rooms. MC, V.*

Ephesus and Selçuk

Ephesus is the showpiece of Aegean archaeology and one of the grandest reconstructed ancient sites anywhere in the world. Created by the Ionians in the 11th century BC, Ephesus became a powerful trading port and the sacred center for the cult of Artemis, Greek goddess of chastity, the moon, and hunting. The Ionians built a temple in her honor, one of the Seven Wonders of the Ancient World. Later the city received a visit from St. Paul, who spent two years preaching here and established one of the first Christian communities on the Aegean coast. Over the centuries, heavy silting of the old port finally led to the city's being abandoned; the ancient site now lies 3 km (2 mi) inland. Allow yourself one full day for Ephesus. The city is especially appealing out of season, when it can seem like a ghost town with its shimmering, long, white marble road grooved by chariot wheels. Some of the splendors here include the two-story **Library of Celsus**; houses of nobles, with their terraces and courtyards; a 25,000-seat **amphitheater,** still used today during the Selçuk Ephesus Festival of Culture and Art; remains of the municipal baths; and a brothel. ✉ *4 km (2½ mi) west of Selçuk on Selçuk–Ephesus rd.,* ☎ *232/892–6402.* ☉ *Apr.–Sept., daily 8:30–6; Oct.–Mar., daily 8:30–5.*

In Selçuk, east of Ephesus, on Ayasoluk Hill, stands the restored **Basilica of St. John** (St. Jean Anıtı), containing the tomb of the apostle. Near the entrance to the basilica is the **Ephesus Museum,** with two statues of Artemis. The museum also has marvelous frescoes and mosaics among its treasures. ☉ *Basilica and museum, Tues.–Sun. 8:30–6.*

St. Paul and St. John preached in both Ephesus and Selçuk and changed the cult of Artemis into the cult of the Virgin Mary. **Meryemana,** 5 km (3 mi) from Ephesus, has the **House of Mary,** thought by some to have been the place where St. John took the mother of Jesus after the crucifixion and from which some believe she ascended to heaven. ☉ *Daily 7:30–sunset.*

$$ ⚑ **Kale Han.** In a refurbished stone building, this is one of the nicest hotels in town, managed by a very welcoming family. Rooms are simple, with bare, whitewashed walls and dark timber beams. The restaurant serves salads and grilled meats such as kebabs, meatballs, shish, mixed grill and chicken around the clock. ✉ *Atatürk Cad. 49, Selçuk 35920,* ☎ *232/892–6154,* ℻ *232/892–2169. 50 rooms with shower, 4 with bath. Restaurant, pool. MC, V.*

$ ⚑ **Victoria Hotel.** A tidy, cheerful hostelry in the center of town, it's named for the four years that the owners spent in England. Rooms have whitewashed walls and honey trim. In summer most have delightful views of storks nesting on a nearby aqueduct. ✉ *Cengiz Topel Cad. 4, Selçuk 35920,* ☎ *232/892–3203,* ℻ *232/892–3204. 24 rooms. Restaurant. No credit cards.*

Priene

Priene, which sits atop a steep hill, was an artistic and cultural center during the Hellenistic period. Its main attraction is the **Temple of Athena,** a spectacular sight, with its five fluted columns and its backdrop of mountains and the fertile plains of the Meander River. The city also has a small amphitheater, gymnasium, council chambers, marketplace, and stadium. ☉ *Daily 8:30–6.*

Miletus

A thriving port made Miletus one of the greatest commercial centers of the ancient Greek world. It was the first Greek city to use coins for money. It also became an Ionian intellectual center and home to such philosophers as Thales, Anaximander, and Anaximenes, all of whom made contributions to mathematics and the natural sciences. The city's most magnificent building is the **Great Theater,** a remarkably intact amphitheater first built by the Ionians and enlarged by the Romans to seat

25,000. Climb to the highest seats in the amphitheater for a view across the city to the bay. ☉ *Tues.–Sun. 8:30–6.*

Didyma

Once home to one of the most famous oracles in the ancient world, Didyma was a holy sanctuary dedicated to Apollo. It's still possible to follow the 32 km (20 mi) path of what was known as the Sacred Way, leading from the coast at Miletus to the site of the oracle at Didyma's **Temple of Apollo.** Under the temple courtyard is a network of corridors whose walls would throw the oracle's voice into deep and ghostly echoes. The messages would then be interpreted by the priests. Fragments of bas-relief include a gigantic head of Medusa and a small statue of Poseidon and his wife, Amphitrite. ☉ *Daily 8:30–6.*

Pamukkale

The place first appears as an enormous chalky white cliff rising some 330 ft from the plains. Mineral-rich volcanic spring water cascades over basins and natural terraces, crystallizing into white stalactites—curtains of solidified water seemingly suspended in air. The hot springs in the area were popular with the ancient Romans, who believed them to have curative powers. Many of Pamukkale's small hotels surround the hot springs. People still believe that the waters cure a variety of ailments, including rheumatism. Farther down in the village are inexpensive pansiyons, some also with hot springs. You can see the remains of Roman baths among the ruins of nearby **Hierapolis.**

★ It's best to stay in Pamukkale overnight before heading on to the ruins of **Aphrodisias,** a city of 60,000 dedicated to Aphrodite, the Greek goddess of love and fertility. It thrived from 100 BC to AD 500. Aphrodisias is reached via Karacasu, a good place to stop for lunch; fresh trout is the local specialty. Aphrodisias is filled with marble baths, temples, and theaters, all overrun with wild blackberries and pomegranates. Across a field sprinkled with poppies and sunflowers is a well-preserved **stadium,** which was built for 30,000 spectators.

$$–$$$ 🏨 **Tusan.** The best feature of this hotel is its pool, one of the most inviting in the area. The one-story building is at the top of a steep hill. Rooms are basic and comfortable. ⊠ *Pamukkale, Denizli 20280,* ☎ *258/272–2010,* ℻ *258/272–2059. 47 rooms. Restaurant, pool. MC, V.*

Aegean Coast Essentials

Getting Around

The E24 from Çanakkale follows the coast until it turns inland at Kuşadası to meet the Mediterranean again at Antalya. All the towns on the itinerary are served by direct bus routes, and there are connecting services to the ancient sites.

Guided Tours

Travel agencies in all the major towns organize tours of the historic sites. Travel agencies along Teyyare Caddesi in Kuşadasi arrange escorted tours to Ephesus; Priene, Miletus, and Didyma; and Aphrodisias and Pamukkale.

Visitor Information

Ayvalık (⊠ Yat Limanı Karşisi, 10400, ☎ 266/312–2122). **Bergama** (⊠ Hükümet Binasıı, Zemin Kat, B Blok, 35700, ☎ 232/633–1862). **Bursa** (⊠ Ulu Cami Parkı, Atatürk Cad. 1, 16020, ☎ 224/221–2359). **Çanakkale** (⊠ İskele Meyd. 67, 17000, ☎ 286/217–1187). **Çeşme** (⊠ İskele Meyd. 8, 35948, ☎ 232/712–6653). **İzmir** (⊠ Gaziosmanpaşa Bul. 1/1DC, 35340, ☎ 232/489–9278 or 232/445–7390). **Kuşadası** (⊠ İskele Meyd., 09400, ☎ 256/614–1103).

THE MEDITERRANEAN COAST

Until the mid-1970s, Turkey's southwest coast was inaccessible to all but the most determined travelers—those intrepid souls in four-wheel-drive vehicles or on the backs of donkeys. Today well-maintained highways wind through the area and jets full of tourists arrive at the Dalaman Airport.

Thanks to strict developmental control, the area has maintained its Turkish flavor, with low, whitewashed buildings and tile roofs. The beaches are clean, and you can swim and snorkel in turquoise waters so clear that it is possible to see fish 20 ft below. There are excellent outdoor cafés and seafood restaurants, and no shortage of bars, discos, or nightclubs. But the region isn't just about untainted beaches and charming fishing villages. It also contains ancient cities of Greek, Roman, Arab, Seljuk, Armenian, crusader, and Byzantine vintage.

Seven full days should give you enough time to travel the 560-km (350-mi) route from Bursa to Antalya, stopping at the highlights in between.

Bodrum

Sitting between two crescent-shape bays, Bodrum, known as Halicarnassos in antiquity, was one of the first Greek colonies in Asia, founded around 1000 BC. In modern times it has long been the favorite haunt of the Turkish upper classes. Today the elite are joined by thousands of foreign visitors, and the area is rapidly filling with hotels and guest houses, cafés, restaurants, and discos. Many compare it to St. Tropez on the French Riviera. Fortunately, it is still beautiful and unspoiled, with gleaming, whitewashed buildings covered with bougainvillea and magnificent unobstructed vistas of the bays. People flock to Bodrum not for its beach, which is a disappointment, but for its fine dining and nightlife. Beautiful **beaches** can be found in the outlying villages on the peninsula—Torba, Türkbükü, Yalıkavak, Turgutreis, Akyarlar, Ortakent, Bitez, and Gümbet. Easy to reach by minibus or dolmuş, these villages are about an hour's drive away and have clean hotels and plenty of outdoor restaurants.

One of the outstanding sights in Bodrum is **Bodrum Kalesi** (Bodrum Castle), known as the Castle of St. Peter. Standing between the two bays, the castle was built by crusaders during the 15th century. It has beautiful gardens and a **Museum of Underwater Archaeology.** ⊠ *Kale Cad.,* ☏ *252/316–2516.* ☉ *Tues.–Sun. 8:30–noon and 1–5.*

$$$ ✕ **Club Pirinç.** This restaurant serves Turkish-French cuisine and has a pleasant bar, as well as nine guest rooms and a swimming pool. ⊠ *Yeni Çarşi 8, Akçabuk Mev., Kumbahçe,* ☏ *252/316–2902. No credit cards.*

$$ ✕ **Kortan.** This seaside fish restaurant with white tablecloths and candles overlooks the bay. Try the calamari and octopus salad. ⊠ *Cumhuriyet Cad. 32,* ☏ *252/316–1241. Reservations essential in summer. AE, MC, V.*

$$$ 🏨 **Manastır Hotel Bodrum.** The bar in this comfortable whitewashed-stucco Mediterranean-style hotel was once the site of a monastery. Front rooms have balconies and look out on the Petronion; all are cool and spacious, with whitewashed walls and tasteful, modern furnishings. ⊠ *Barış Sitesi Mev., Kumbahçe 48400,* ☏ *252/316–2854,* 𝔽𝔸𝕏 *252/316–2772. 59 rooms. 2 restaurants, pool. AE, DC, V.*

$ 🏨 **Hotel Anka.** This hilltop hotel, just 2 km (1 mi) from the city center, has commanding views of the Bodrum bay. Rooms, in whitewashed bungalows, are simple and clean and have balconies. The staff is warm. ⊠ *Eskiçeşme Mah. Asarlik Mev., Gümbet 48400,* ☏ *252/316–8217,* 𝔽𝔸𝕏 *252/316–6194. 85 rooms. Restaurant, pool. AE, D, MC, V.*

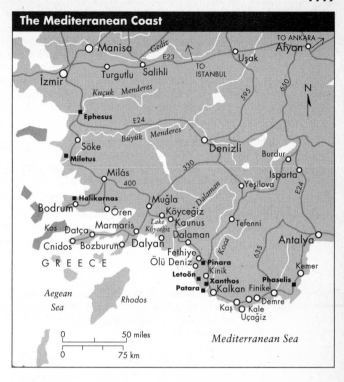

The Mediterranean Coast

Marmaris

Built on the site of the ancient Greek city of Phryscus, Marmaris has developed into a sophisticated resort with boutiques, elegant restaurants, plenty of nightlife, and some of the best sailing in the Mediterranean. Nearby are quiet villages that are easy to reach by boat or taxi. The remains of Phryscus can be see on **Asar Tepe,** a hill 1½ km (1 mi) north of the modern town.

★ At **Knidos,** on the end of the peninsula, you can see the ruins of Aphrodite's circular temple and an ancient theater. By road Knidos is a very rough 108 km (67 mi) from Marmaris; it's easier and quicker to take a boat. **Turunç,** 16 km (10 mi) from Marmaris, is also worth a day trip, especially for its beaches.

Dalyan

Tombs from the Carian civilization of the first millennium BC are carved into the cliff that rises behind the Dalyan River in the fishing town of Dalyan, 20 minutes' drive from the airport in Dalaman. The town makes a good base for exploring the 4th-century BC city of **Kaunos,** 10 km (6 mi) to the west. It costs about $20 to rent a boat with a boatman to sail from Dalyan to the ruins and unspoiled **İstuzu beach.** You can also reach freshwater **Lake Köyceğiz** by boat through the reed beds of the Dalyan delta. This entire area is a wildlife preserve, filled with such birds as kingfishers, kestrels, egrets, and cranes.

$$$ ⛫ **Hotel Özay.** This quiet, modern, efficiently run lakeside hotel is surrounded by lush greenery and palm trees. Daily boat tours of the lake are available, and Turkish belly-dancing shows take place at night. ⊠ *Kordon Boyu 11, Köyceğiz 48800,* ☎ *252/262–4300,* ℻ *252/262–2000. 34 rooms. Restaurant, pool. MC, V.*

$$ ⛫ **Dalyan Hotel.** Comfortable and clean, with views across Lake Köyceğiz to the tombs, the Dalyan is surrounded by trees on the shore

of the lake. It has an excellent restaurant and a friendly, attentive staff. ⊠ *Yalı Sok., Maras Mahalli, Dalyan 48840,* ☎ *252/284–2239,* FAX *252/ 284–2240. 20 rooms with shower. 2 restaurants, pool. AE, MC, V.*

$$ ⊞ **Hotel Assyrian.** Beautifully situated at the edge of town with views across the delta, the Assyrian consists of whitewashed single-story units with wooden trims in the style of the local architecture and offers free boat rides to the turtle beaches and medicinal mud baths. ⊠ *Maraş Mahallesi, Dalyan 48800,* ☎ *252/284–3232,* FAX *252/284– 3244. 34 rooms. Restaurant, pool. MC, V.*

Ölü Deniz

One of Turkey's greatest natural wonders is Ölü Deniz, an azure lagoon flanked by long, white beaches. There are a few wooden chalets in campgrounds and one beachfront hotel. Opposite the beach are small restaurants with rooftop bars, many with live music all night long.

$$$$ ✕ **Beyaz Yunus.** Wicker chairs and wooden floors fill this domed
★ restaurant, whose name means "white dolphin." The most elegant restaurant in the area, it commands a promontory overlooking the sea. Continental and Turkish cuisines are imaginatively prepared and presented. ⊠ *On bay of Belcekiz, near Padirali,* ☎ *252/617–0068. No credit cards. Closed Nov.–Mar.*

$ ✕ **Asmali Restaurant.** On the road to the Meri Oteli (☞ *below*), this family-run restaurant serves homemade dishes, which vary from day to day, and cold mezes, grilled meats, and fish. It has a beautiful garden terrace with overhanging vines. ⊠ *On road to Meri Oteli,* ☎ *no phone. No credit cards.*

$$–$$$ ⊞ **Meri Oteli.** On a steep incline above the lagoon, this hotel is made up of a series of bungalows with rooms that are a bit down-at-the-heel though clean. But it's the only place to stay at the lagoon. ⊠ *Olüdeniz, Fethiye 48300,* ☎ *252/617–0001,* FAX *252/617–0010. 84 rooms. Restaurant. MC, V.*

Pinara

In ancient times Pinara was one of the most important cities of the former Roman province of Lycia. Near the **ruins** of the ancient city, up a steep and strenuous dirt road, are nearly 200 Roman tombs cut honeycomb-fashion into the face of the cliffs. ⊠ *Southeast of Fethiye, near Rte. 400.* ☺ *Daily 8:30–sunset.*

Xanthos

Xanthos was one of the most important cities in the Roman province of Lycia. Its inhabitants developed a fearsome reputation for bravery, twice burning down their own city rather than surrender. The **ruins** of the city lie down a rough road, but it's still well worth the bumpy ride to see the acropolis, the Tomb of Harpies, some plaster-cast reliefs, and ruins of some Byzantine buildings. ⊠ *Off Rte. 400 from Kinik.* ☺ *Daily 8:30–sunset.*

Patara

Two thousand years ago, Patara, port city of Xanthos, was among the busiest ports in the region. Hannibal and St. Paul both visited, and St. Nicholas, the future Santa Claus, was born here. Today you will find **ruins** scattered around the marshes and sand dunes. The area's long, wide **beaches** remain unspoiled despite the fact that they attract hundreds of Turkish families and tourists.

Kalkan

With its red-tile roofs and waterfront restaurants, Kalkan is the picture of a perfect Mediterranean fishing village. Nearby **beaches** have made it a popular base for exploring the region.

$$ ☶ **Hotel Pirat.** On the waterfront, this large, modern hotel consists of a cluster of three-story buildings. Each room has its own private terrace. ⊠ *Kalkan Marina, 07960,* ☎ *242/844–3178,* ℻ *242/844–3183. 136 rooms. 2 restaurants, 3 pools. AE, MC, V.*

$–$$ ☶ **Kalkan Han.** A rambling old house in the back part of the village, the Kalkan Han has a special treat: a roof terrace with sweeping views of the bay, a perfect place to enjoy breakfast. ⊠ *Köyiçi Mev., 07960,* ☎ *242/844–3151,* ℻ *242/844–2059. 12 rooms, 2 suites. Restaurant, pool. No credit cards. Closed Nov.–Apr.*

Kaş

Kaş is rapidly developing from a sleepy resort into a major yachting center. Luxury hotels have replaced many of the tiny houses on the hills, though there are still plenty of old-fashioned, budget-priced pansiyons. One of the attractions here is a day trip by boat to the underwater city of **Kekova,** where you can look overboard and see ancient Roman and Greek columns that were once part of a thriving city before the area was flooded. Kekova is especially popular with scuba divers and snorkelers, but to scuba dive or fish in this area, a permit must be obtained from the directorate of the harbor and from the directorate of the ministry of tourism. Boats leave daily at 9:30 and cost about $15.

$$ ✕ **Mercan.** On the eastern side of the harbor, this place serves good, basic Turkish food in an open-air setting. The menu includes whole lamb on a spit, fish, and lobster, as well as vegetarian choices. ⊠ *Hükümet Cad., Cumhuriyet Meyd.,* ☎ *242/836–1209. MC, V.*

$$ ☶ **Anı Motel.** From both the rooms and the terrace bar of this hotel in a restored old building you get beautiful views of the sea and the town of Kaş. Traditional furnishings enliven the clean, whitewashed walls. ⊠ *Recep Bilgin Cad. 12/B, 07580,* ☎ *242/836–1791,* ℻ *242/836–1791. 10 rooms. AE, MC, V.*

$ ☶ **Medusa Hotel.** On a cliff overlooking the sea, this picturesque hotel is also a diving school. Front rooms have expansive ocean views, and back rooms face the mountains. ⊠ *Küçükçakil 61, 07580,* ☎ *242/836–1440,* ℻ *242/836–1441. 40 rooms. 2 restaurants, pool. No credit cards.*

Phaselis

Phaselis is the site of some of the most romantic ruins in Turkey. The Roman agora, theater, aqueduct, and a necropolis with fine sarcophagi are scattered throughout the pine woods that surround the **Temple of Athena.** Overgrown streets descend to the sparkling waters of the Mediterranean, which are ideal for swimming.

Kemer

This town is a center of intensive tourist development, with hotels and restaurants, a well-equipped marina, and club-style holiday villages that may make you forget you're in Turkey.

Antalya

The resort of Antalya is a good base for several worthwhile excursions to major **archaeological sites** at Perge, Aspendos, Side, and Termessos. The city, built around a restored harbor, is filled with narrow streets lined with small houses, restaurants, and pansiyons. On the hilltop are tea gardens where you can enjoy tea made in an old-fashioned samovar and look across the bay to the Taurus Mountains. To the right of the port is the 13th-century **Yivli Minare** (Fluted Minaret). The first-rate **Antalya Müzesi** (Antalya Museum) displays Turkish crafts, costumes, and artifacts from the classical Greek and Roman eras. ⊠ *Konyaaltı Cad., west of town,* ☎ *242/241–4528.* ☉ *Tues–Sun. 9–6.*

$–$$ ✕ **Sini.** This beautiful, wood-decorated restaurant integrates Turkish *sulu yemekleri* (literally, dishes with water)—a style of home cooking

in which meats and vegetables are simmered slowly in various sauces—
into fine dining. Just point to what you want. Note that no alcohol is
served and that although it is supposed to be open 24 hours, it isn't.
✉ *Hükümet Cad. 34,* ☎ *242/241–1912 or 242/241–1163. MC, V.*

$$$$ 🏨 **Talya.** At this luxurious resort you reach the private beach by tak-
★ ing an elevator down the side of the cliff. Every angle gives a view of
the sea. The hotel is usually full in high season, so plan ahead. ✉ *Fevzi
Çakmak Cad. 30, 07100,* ☎ *242/248–6800,* ℻ *242/241–5400. 204
rooms. 3 restaurants, pool. AE, DC, MC, V.*

$$ 🏨 **Tütav Türk Evleri** Part of the old Kaleiçi district, this hotel consists
of a row of restored Turkish houses joined together. Well-tended gar-
dens surround the inn and its popular restaurant, which is known for
delectable fish stew. ✉ *Mermerli Sok. 2, 07100,* ☎ *242/248–6478,* ℻
242/241–9419. 20 rooms. Restaurant, pool. AE, MC, V.

$ 🏨 **Ottoman House Pansiyon.** This pansiyon in the old town is trimmed
in honey-color wood with Turkish tiles everywhere. Ask for a room
overlooking the garden. ✉ *Mermerli Banyo Sokak 8, 07100,* ☎ *242/
242–6630.* ℻ *242/247–6258. 14 rooms with shower. Restaurant,
pool. MC, V.*

Termessos
Writers in antiquity referred to Termessos as the "Eagle's Nest." It's
not hard to see why. The only access is a stiff but rewarding climb up
a steep, rocky path. Perched on the top of the mountain, the ruins offer
views that are among the most dramatic in Turkey. Difficulty of ac-
cess means that much of the site is romantically overgrown, while large
areas, including virtually the entire Roman city, have never been ex-
cavated. You can see an amphitheater built on the mountainside. Or-
ganized tours to Termessos leave from Antalya. ✉ *Korkuteli, Rte. 350
off Rte. E87, northwest of Antalya.* 🎫 *Free.* 🕐 *Daily 9–5:30.*

Perge
The ruins of the ancient city of Perge, northeast of Antalya, include a
superb amphitheater, well-preserved thermal baths, a restored colonnaded
street, and a Roman basilica, where St. Paul preached his first sermon
in AD 45. ✉ *North off Rte. 400 at Aksu turnoff.* 🕐 *Daily 9–5:30.*

★ Aspendos
This site contains Turkey's best-preserved Roman amphitheater. The
acoustics are so fine that modern-day performers don't need micro-
phones or amplifiers. ✉ *North off Rte. 400 at turnoff past Belkis.* 🕐
Daily 9–5:30.

Mediterranean Coast Essentials

Getting Around
BY BOAT
There are many coves and picnic areas along the coast, accessible only
by boat. For a small fee local fishermen will take you to and from the
coves; you can also take one of the many water taxis. Or charter a
small yacht, with or without skipper, at the marinas in Bodrum and
Marmaris. One of the most enjoyable ways to see the coast is to take
a one- or two-week **Blue Voyage** cruise on a *gulet*, a wooden craft with
a full crew. For information contact the following Blue Voyage agen-
cies: in the United States, Club Voyages (✉ 43 Hooper Ave., Atlantic
Highlands, N.J. 07716, ☎ 732/291–8228); in the United Kingdom,
Explore (✉ 1 Frederick St., Aldershot, Hants GU11 1LQ, ☎ 012/5231–
9448), Simply Turkey (✉ 8 Chiswick Terr., Acton La., London W4,
☎ 0181/747–1011), and Falcon Sailing (✉ 13 Hillgate St., London
W8, ☎ 0171/727–0232).

BY CAR

Although the highways between towns are well maintained, the smaller roads are usually unpaved and very rough.

Visitor Information

Local tourist offices list all the guided tours for the area and will also arrange for local guides. **Antalya** (⊠ Cumhuriyet Cad., Özel İdare Altı 2, 07040, ☎ 242/241–1747). **Bodrum** (⊠ Barış Meyd. 12, 48400, ☎ 252/316–1091). **Dalaman** (⊠ Dalaman Airport, 48770, ☎ 252/692–5291). **Datça** (⊠ İskele Mah. Hükümet Binası, 48900, ☎ 252/712–3163 or 252/712–3546). **Kaş** (⊠ Cumhuriyet Meyd. 5, 07580, ☎ 242/836–1238). **Marmaris** (⊠ İskele Meyd. 2, 48700, ☎ 252/412–1035).

CENTRAL ANATOLIA AND CAPPADOCIA

The archaeological sites of Central Anatolia abound with well-preserved Roman architecture. Cappadocia, an area in the eastern part of Anatolia filled with ruins of ancient civilizations, has changed little over the centuries. People still travel between their farms and villages in horse-drawn carts, women drape their houses with strings of apricots and peppers for drying in the sun, and nomads pitch their black tents beside sunflower fields and cook on tiny fires that send smoke billowing through the tops of the tents.

Ankara

From the time it was founded in about 1200 BC through its gradual decline under the Ottomans, Ankara, now Turkey's capital, had an illustrious, yet strife-filled existence. By the early 20th century it was little more than a dusty provincial town, the perfect site for Atatürk to build his new capital and establish the new Turkish Republic. It was at the **Cumhuriyet Müzesi** (Republic Museum; ⊠ Cumhuriyet Bul. off Ulus Meyd., ☎ 312/310–5361) in 1920 that Atatürk was elected chairman of the Grand National Assembly, which would organize the new nation. Housed in a restored 15th-century *bedestan* (covered bazaar and inn) is the superb **Ankara Anadolu Medeniyetleri Müzesi** (Museum of Anatolian Civilizations; ⊠ Gözcü Sok., ☎ 312/324–3160).

$$$$ 🏨 **Ankara Hilton SA.** The luxurious 16-story Hilton in a quiet, hilly
★ neighborhood on Embassy Row provides many amenities and a view to boot. ⊠ *Tahran Cad. 12, Kavaklıdere, 06700,* ☎ *312/468–2888,* FAX *312/468–0909. 324 rooms. 2 restaurants. AE, DC, MC, V.*

$$ 🏨 **King Hotel.** The central location, the helpful staff, the above-aver-
★ age restaurant, and the clean rooms with typical hotel decor (a plus in Turkey) all make this hotel a great deal. ⊠ *Güvenlik Cad. 13, Aşağıayrancı, 06540,* ☎ *312/418–9099,* FAX *312/417–0382. 36 rooms, 3 suites. Restaurant. AE, DC, MC, V.*

Konya

Konya has always been the religious capital of Turkey. During the Ottoman Empire it was the center of the Islamic mystical order known to the West as the Whirling Dervishes. The order was founded in the 13th century by Celaleddin Rumi, or Mevlâna, a Muslim mystic, who said, "There are many ways of knowing God. I choose the dance and music." The **Mevlâna Müzesi** (Mevlâna Museum; Mevlâna Meyd., ☎ 332/331–1215) contains the **Mevlâna Türbesi** (Tomb of Mevlâna Celaleddin), as well as displays that illustrate the dervishes' way of life. You can still see the dervishes whirl to the sounds of a flute at the annual commemorative rites held in Konya in early December. Tickets

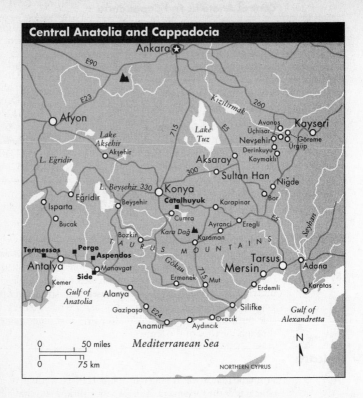

Central Anatolia and Cappadocia

are available from travel agencies or from the Konya tourist information office (☞ Visitor Information, *below*).

$ ✕ **Hanedan.** Kebabs are the order of the day at Hanedan. Highly recommended are the *tandır* (baked lamb) and the *inegöl köfte* (grilled meatballs). ⊠ *Mevlâna Cad.,* ☎ *332/351–4546. No credit cards.*

Cappadocia

Over the centuries the softness of the volcanic rock in the Cappadocia region has been ideal for hollowing out cave dwellings and forming defenses from invading armies. They were begun as early as the 5th century BC. From the 7th through the 10th centuries AD, inhabitants of the Christian kingdom of Cappadocia took refuge from Arab raiders in about 40 underground cities, with some structures as deep as 20 stories underground. The largest of these cities housed 20,000 people. Each had dormitories, dining halls, sewage disposal systems, ventilation chimneys, a cemetery, and a prison. Large millstones sealed off the entrances from enemies.

The magical landscape of Cappadocia consists roughly of the triangular area between **Kayseri** in the west, **Nevşehir** in the center, and **Niğde** in the south. Within that triangle **Ürgüp** is the center from which to explore the villages on your own or arrange tours; it is the best place to shop. Because the Cappadocia area is so vast, you'll need at least two days to see the main sights.

In the ruins of the underground city of **Derinkuyu** (⊠ Rte. 765, 30 km/19 mi south of Nevşehir, ☎ 384/381–3194) is an unusual Greek church that is underground and carved out of rock. Equipped with a flashlight, explore the stairways and corridors of the underground city of

★ **Kaymaklı** (⊠ Rte. 765, 21 km/13 mi south of Nevşehir, ☎ 384/218–2500). ☉ *Daily 8–5 for both cities.*

Some of the earliest relics of Christianity can be found in the **Göreme Valley,** a few kilometers east of Nevşehir. There are dozens of old churches and monasteries covered with frescoes. For a history of the area, visit the **Göreme Açık Hava Müzesi** (Göreme Open-Air Museum). ✉ *1 km (½ mi) outside Göreme village on Ürgüp Rd.* ➧ *Free.* ☉ *Daily 8:30–5:30.*

★

$$$$ ⌂ **Ataman.** Run by tourist guide Abbas and his wife, Şermin, this hotel is built into the face of a rock. Rooms have kilims and handicrafts. Room rates include breakfast and dinner. ✉ *Göreme 50180,* ☎ *384/271–2310,* FAX *384/271–2313. 38 rooms. Restaurant. MC, V.*

$$ ⌂ **Alfina.** For the ultimate Cappadocia experience try this hotel, where the rooms are carved out of volcanic rock. Even with a small window in every room it still feels as if you are sleeping in a cave, albeit a fully equipped one. ✉ *İstiklal Cad., Ürgüp Girişi 27, Ürgüp 50400,* ☎ *384/ 341–4822,* FAX *384/341–2424. 26 rooms. MC, V. Closed Nov.–Mar.*

Central Anatolia and Cappadocia Essentials

Getting Around

BY BUS

A good bus network links most towns and cities; fares are reasonable.

BY CAR

There are good roads between Istanbul and the main cities of Anatolia—Ankara, Konya, and Kayseri. The highways are generally well maintained and lead to all the major sites. Minor roads are full of potholes and are very rough. On narrow winding roads, look out for oncoming trucks.

BY TAXI

Drivers are usually willing to take you to historical sites out of town for reasonable fares.

BY TRAIN

Although there is frequent train service between the main cities, it is almost nonexistent between small towns. It's much quicker to take a bus.

Guided Tours

If you are driving, consider hiring a guide for about $15 to $30 a day. Local tourist offices (☞ *below*) and hotels can recommend guides and excursions.

Visitor Information

Aksaray (✉ Ankara Cad. Dinçer Apt. 2/2, 68000, ☎ 382/212–5651). **Ankara** (✉ Gazi Mustafa Kemal Bul. 121, Tandoğan, 06050, ☎ 312/ 229–2631). **Kayseri** (✉ Kağnı Pazari 61, 38000, ☎ 352/222–3903). **Konya** (✉ Mevlâna Cad. 65, Karatay, 42030, ☎ 332/351–1074). **Nevşehir** (✉ Atatürk Bul., 50130, ☎ 384/213–3659). **Ürgüp** (✉ Kayseri Cad. 37, 50200, ☎ 384/341–4059).

WORDS AND PHRASES

CZECH

English	Czech	Pronunciation
Basics		
Yes/No	Ano/ne	**ah**-no/neh
Please	Prosím	**pro**-seem
Thank you	Děkuji	**dyek**-oo-yee
You're welcome (it's nothing)	Není zač	**neh**-nee **zahtch**
Pardon me	Pardon	**par**-don
Hello/Good morning	Dobry den	**dob**-ree den
Good evening	Dobry večer	**dob**-ree **ve**-chair
Goodbye	Na shledanou	Na **sled**-ah-noh
Numbers		
0	Nula	**noo**-la
1	Jeden, jedna, jedno	ye-**den, yed**-nah, **yed**-no
2	Dva, dvě	dvah, dvyeh
3	Tři	tshree
4	Čtyři	ch'**ti**-zhee
5	Pět	pyet
6	Šest	shest
7	Sedm	**sed**-oom
8	Osm	**oh**-soom
9	Devět	**deh**-vyet
10	Deset	**deh**-set
20	Dvacet	**dvaht**-set
50	Padesát	**pah**-deh-**saht**
100	Sto	sto
1,000	Tisíc	**tee**-seets
Days of the Week		
Sunday	neděle	**neh**-dyeh-leh
Monday	pondělí	**pon**-dye-lee
Tuesday	útery	**oo**-teh-ree
Wednesday	středa	**stshreh**-da
Thursday	čtvrtek	ch't'v'**r**-tek
Friday	pátek	**pah**-tek
Saturday	sobota	**so**-boh-ta

Useful Phrases

Do you speak English?	Mluvíte anglicky?	**mloo**-vit-eh ahng-**glit**-ski
I don't understand.	Nerozumím.	**neh**-rohz-oom-eem
I don't know.	Nevím.	**neh**-veem
Excuse me. Where is the . . .	Promiňte, prosím. Kde je . . .	**pro**-meen-teh **pro**-seem g'deh yeh
bus stop?	autobusová zastávka?	**ow**-to-boos-oh-vah zah-**stahv**-kah
bank?	banka?	**bahn**-ka
subway station?	stanice metra?	**stah**-nit-seh **meh**-trah
Where is the rest room?	Kde jsou toalety, prosím?	g'deh so twa-**leh**-tee **pro**-seem
On the right	Napravo	**na**-pra-vo
On the left	Nalevo	**na**-leh-vo
I would like this.	Chtěl bych tohle.	kh'**tyel** bikh **toh**-hleh
How much?	Kolik?	**ko**-lik
I would like a room.	Chtěl (Chtěla) bych pokoj.	kh'**tyel** (kh'**tyel**-ah) bikh **poh**-koy

Dining Out

Waiter, the menu, please.	Pane vrchní! Jídelní lístek, prosím.	**pah**-neh **verkh**-nee **yee**-dell-nee **lis**-tek **pro**-seem
The wine list, please.	Líst vin, prosím. (or, vinny listek).	leest vin **pro**-seem **vin**-nee **lis**-tek
What's the specialty of the day?	Jaká je dnešní specialitá?	**ya**-ka yeh **dnesh**-nee spet-sya-lih-**tah**
The check, please.	Účet, prosím.	**oo**-chet **pro**-seem
Is the tip included?	Je záhrnuto zpropítně?	yeh **za**-her-noo-toh **zpro**-peet-nyeh
Napkin	Ubrousek	**oo**-bro-sek

DANISH

English	Danish	Pronunciation

Basics

Yes/no	Ja/nej	yah/nie
Thank you	Tak	tak
You're welcome	Selv tak	**sell** tak
Excuse me (to apologize)	Undskyld	**unsk**-ul
Hello	Hej	hi
Goodbye	Farvel	fa-**vel**
Today	I dag	ee **day**
Tomorrow	I morgen	ee **morn**
Yesterday	I går	ee **gore**

Vocabulary

Numbers

1	Een/eet	een/eet
2	To	toe
3	Tre	tre
4	Fire	fear
5	Fem	fem
6	Seks	sex
7	Syv	syoo
8	Otte	**oh**-te
9	Ni	nee
10	Ti	tee

Days of the Week

Sunday	søndag	**soo**(n)-day
Monday	mandag	**man**-day
Tuesday	tirsdag	**tears**-day
Wednesday	onsdag	**ons**-day
Thursday	torsdag	**trs**-day
Friday	fredag	**free**-day
Saturday	lørdag	**lore**-day

Useful Phrases

Do you speak English?	Taler du engelsk?	**te**-ler doo **in**-galsk
I don't understand.	Jeg forstår ikke.	yi fahr-store **ick**
I don't know.	Det ved jeg ikke.	deh **ved** yi ick
I am American/British.	Jeg er amerikansk/britisk.	yi ehr a-mehr-i-**kansk**/bri-**tisk**
Please call a doctor.	Kan du ringe til en læge.	can **doo** rin-geh til en lay-eh
Do you have a vacant room?	Har du et værelse?	har **doo** eet va(l)r-sa
How much does it cost?	Hvad koster det?	va cos-ta **deh**
It's too expensive.	Det er for dyrt.	deh ehr **fohr** dyrt
Beautiful	Smukt	smukt
Help!	Hjælp!	yelp
Stop!	Stop!	stop
How do I get to . . .	Hvordan kommer jeg til . . .	vore-**dan** kom-mer yi til
the train station?	banegarden?	**ban** eh-gore-en
the post office?	postkontoret?	**post**-kon-toh-raht
the tourist office?	turistkonoret?	too-**reest**-kon-tor-et
the hospital?	hospitalet?	hos-peet-**tal**-et
Does this bus go to . . . ?	Går denne bus til . . .	**goh** den-na boos til
Where is the W.C.?	Hvor er toilettet?	vòr **ehr** toi-le(tt)-et

| On the left | Til venstre | til **ven**-strah |
| On the right | Till højre | til **hoy**-ah |

Dining Out

Please bring me . . .	Må jeg få . . .	mo yi foh
Menu	Menu	me-**nu**
Napkin	Serviet	serv-**eet**
Bread	Brød	brood
Water/bottled water	Vand	van
The check, please.	Må jeg bede om regningen.	mo yi bi(d) om **ri**-ning

DUTCH

English	Dutch	Pronunciation

Basics

Yes/no	Ja, nee	yah, nay
Please	Alstublieft	**ahls**-too-bleeft
Thank you	Dank u	**dahnk** oo
Excuse me, sorry	Pardon	pahr-**don**
Good morning	Goede morgen	**hoh**-deh **mor**-ghen
Goodbye	Dag	dah

Numbers

1	Een	ehn
2	Twee	tveh
3	Drie	dree
4	Vier	veer
5	Vijf	vehf
6	Zes	zehss
7	Zeven	**zeh**-vehn
8	Acht	ahkht
9	Negen	**neh**-ghen
10	Tien	teen

Days of the Week

Sunday	zondag	**zohn**-dagh
Monday	maandag	**mahn**-dagh
Tuesday	dinsdag	**dinns**-dagh
Wednesday	woensdag	**voons**-dagh
Thursday	donderdag	**don**-der-dagh
Friday	vrijdag	**vreh**-dagh
Saturday	zaterdag	**zah**-ter-dagh

Useful Phrases

| Do you speak English? | Spreekt U Engels? | sprehkt oo **ehn**-gls |

I don't understand.	Ik begrijp het niet.	ihk be-**ghrehp** het neet
I don't know.	Ik weet niet.	ihk **veht** ut neet
I'm American/English.	Ik ben Amerikaans/Engels.	ihk ben am-er-ee-**kahns/ehn**-gls
Where is . . .	Waar is . . .	vahr iss
the train station?	het station?	heht stah-**syohn**
the post office?	het postkantoor?	het **pohst**-kahn-tohr
the hospital?	het ziekenhuis?	het **zeek**-uhn-haus
Where are the restrooms?	Waar is de WC?	**vahr** iss de **veh**-seh
Left/right	Links/rechts	leenks/rehts
How much is this?	Hoeveel kost dit?	hoo-**vehl** kohst deet
It's expensive/cheap	Het is te duur/goedkoop	het ees teh **dour/hood**-kohp
I am ill/sick.	Ik ben ziek.	ihk behn zeek
Help!	Help!	help
Stop!	Stoppen!	**stop**-pen

Dining Out

Bill/check	De rekening	de **rehk**-en-eeng
Bread	Brood	brohd
I'd like to order	Ik wil graag bestellen	ihk veel khrah behs-**tell**-en
Menu	Menu/kaart	men-**oo**/kahrt
Napkin	En servet	ehn ser-**veht**
Please give me . . .	Mag ik [een] . . .	mahkh ihk [ehn]

FINNISH

English	Finnish	Pronunciation

Basics

Yes/no	Kyllä/Ei	**kue**-la/ee
Please	Olkaa hyvä	**ol**-kah **hue**-va
Thank you very much.	Kiitoksia paljon	**kee**-tohk-syah **pahl**-yon
You're welcome.	Olkaa hyvä	**ol**-kah **hue**-va
Excuse me. (to get by someone)	Anteeksi Suokaa	**ahn**-teek-see **soo**-oh-kah
(to apologize)	anteeksi	**ahn**-teek-see
Hello	Hyvää päivää terve	**hue**-va **paee**-va **tehr**-veh
Goodbye	Näkemiin	**na**-keh-meen
Today	Tänään	**ta**-naan
Tomorrow	Huomenna	**hoo**-oh-men-nah
Yesterday	Eilen	**ee**-len

Numbers

1	Yksi	**uek**-see
2	Kaksi	**kahk**-see
3	Kolme	**kohl**-meh
4	Neljä	**nel**-ya
5	Viisi	**vee**-see
6	Kuusi	**koo**-see
7	Seitsemän	**sate**-seh-man
8	Kahdeksan	**kah**-dek-sahn
9	Yhdeksän	**uef**-dek-san
10	Kymmenen	**kue**-meh-nen

Days of the Week

Sunday	sunnuntai	**soon**-noon-tie
Monday	maanantai	**mah**-nahn-tie
Tuesday	tiistai	**tees**-tie
Wednesday	keskiviikko	**kes**-kee-veek-koh
Thursday	torstai	**tohrs**-tie
Friday	perjantai	**pehr**-yahn-tie
Saturday	lauantai	**loo**-ahn-tie

Useful Phrases

Do you speak English?	Puhutteko englantia?	**poo**-hoot-teh-koh **ehng**-lahn-tee-ah
I don't speak . . .	En puhu suomea . . .	ehn **poo**-hoo **soo**-oh-mee-ah
I don't know.	En tiedä.	ehn **tee**-eh-da
I am American/ British.	Minä olen amerikkalainen/ englantilainen.	**mee**-na **oh**-len **ah**-mehr-ee-kah-lie-nehn/**ehn**-glahn-tee-lie-nehn
Please call a doctor.	Haluan kutsua lääkärin.	**hah**-loo-ahn **koot**-soo-ah **lay**-ka-reen
Do you have a vacant room?	Onko teillä vapaata huonetta?	**ohn**-koh **teel**-la **vah**-pah-tah **hoo**-oh-neht-tah?
How much does it cost?	Paljonko tämä maksaa?	**pahl**-yohn-koh **ta**-ma **mahk**-sah
It's too expensive.	Se on liian kallis.	**say** ohn **lee**-ahn **kah**-lees
Beautiful	Kaunis	**kow**-nees
Help!	Auttakaa!	**ow**-tah-kah
Stop!	Seis!/ Pysähtykää!	say(s) **peu**-sa-teu-kay
How do I get to . . .	Voitteko sanoa miten pääsen . . .	**voy**-tay-koh **sah**-noh-ah **mee**-ten **pay**-sen
the train station?	asema (pääsen asemalle)?	**ah**-say-mah (**pay**-sen **ah**-say-mah-lay)

the post office?	posti (paasen postiin)?	**pohs**-tee (**pay**-sen **pohs**-teen)
the hospital?	sairaala (pääsen sairaalaan)?	**sigh**-rah-lah (**pay**-sen **sigh**-rah-lahn)
Does this bus go to . . . ?	Kulkeeko tämä bussi-n . . . ?	**kool**-kay-koh **ta**-ma **boo**-see-n
Where is the W.C.?	Missä on W.C.?	**mee**-sa ohn **ves**-sah
On the left	Vasemmalle	**vah**-say-mahl-lay
On the right	Oikealle	**ohy**-kay-ah-lay

Dining Out

Please bring me . . .	Tuokaa minulle . . .	**too**-oh-kah **mee**-new
Menu	Ruokalista	**roo**-oh-kah-lees-tah
Napkin	Lautasliina	**low**-tahs-lee-nah
Bread	Leipä	**lay**-pa
Butter	Voi	**voh**(ee)
Water/bottled water	Vesi/ kivennäisvesi	**veh**-see/**kee**-ven-eyes-veh-see
The check, please.	Lasku, olkaa hyvä/Saanko maksaa.	**lahs**-kew, **ohl**-kah **heu**-va/**sahn**-koh **mahk**-sah

FRENCH

English	**French**	**Pronunciation**
Basics		
Yes/no	Oui/non	wee/nohn
Please	S'il vous plaît	seel voo **play**
Thank you	Merci	mair-**see**
Excuse me, sorry	Pardon	pahr-**dohn**
Good morning/ afternoon	Bonjour	bohn-**zhoor**
Goodbye	Au revoir	o ruh-**vwahr**
Mr. (Sir)	Monsieur	muh-**syuh**
Mrs. (Ma'am)	Madame	ma-**dam**
Miss	Mademoiselle	mad-mwa-**zel**
Numbers		
1	Un	uhn
2	Deux	deuh
3	Trois	twah
4	Quatre	**kaht**-ruh
5	Cinq	sank
6	Six	seess
7	Sept	set
8	Huit	wheat
9	Neuf	nuf
10	Dix	deess

20	Vingt	vehn
21	Vingt-et-un	vehnt-ay-**uhn**
50	Cinquante	sang-**kahnt**
100	Cent	sahn
1,000	Mille	meel

Days of the Week

Sunday	dimanche	dee-**mahnsh**
Monday	lundi	luhn-**dee**
Tuesday	mardi	mahr-**dee**
Wednesday	mercredi	mair-kruh-**dee**
Thursday	jeudi	zhuh-**dee**
Friday	vendredi	vawn-druh-**dee**
Saturday	samedi	sahm-**dee**

Useful Phrases

Do you speak English?	Parlez-vous anglais?	par-lay **voo** ahn-**glay**
I don't understand.	Je ne comprends pas.	zhuh nuh kohm-**prahn** pah
I don't know.	Je ne sais pas.	zhuh nuh say **pah**
I'm American/British.	Je suis américain/anglais.	zhuh sweez a-may-ree-**kehn**/ahn-**glay**
Yesterday	Hier	yair
Today	Aujourd'hui	o-zhoor-**dwee**
Tomorrow	Demain	duh-**mehn**
What is it?	Qu'est-ce que c'est?	kess-kuh-**say**
Where is . . .	Où est . . .	oo ay
the train station?	la gare?	la gar
the subway station?	la station de métro?	la sta-**syon** duh may-**tro**
the post office?	la poste?	la post
the bank?	la banque?	la bahnk
the hospital?	l'hôpital?	lo-pee-**tahl**
Where are the rest rooms?	Où sont les toilettes?	oo sohn lay twah-**let**
Left/right	A gauche/à droite	a goash/a drwaht
I'd like . . .	Je voudrais . . .	zhuh voo-**dray**
a room	une chambre	ewn **shahm**-bruh
I'd like to buy . . .	Je voudrais acheter . . .	zhuh voo-**dray** ahsh-**tay**
How much is it?	C'est combien?	say comb-bee-**ehn**
A little/a lot	Un peu/beaucoup	uhn peuh/bo-**koo**
More/less	Plus/moins	plu/mwehn
I am ill/sick.	Je suis malade.	zhuh swee ma-**lahd**
Help!	Au secours!	o suh-**koor**
Stop!	Arrêtez!	a-reh-**tay**

Dining Out

A bottle of . . .	Une bouteille de . . .	ewn boo-**tay** duh
Bill/check	L'addition	la-dee-see-**ohn**
Bread	Du pain	dew pan
Dish of the day	Le plat du jour	luh plah dew **zhoor**
Fixed-price menu	Le menu	luh muh-**new**
I'd like to order.	Je voudrais commander.	zhuh voo-**dray** ko-mahn-**day**
Is service/the tip included?	Est-ce que le service est compris?	ess kuh luh sair-**veess** eh comb-**pree**
Menu	La carte	la cart
Napkin	Une serviette	ewn sair-vee-**et**
Please give me . . .	Donnez-moi . . .	doe-nay-**mwah**
Waiter!/Waitress!	Monsieur!/ Mademoiselle!	muh-**syuh**/ mad-mwa-**zel**
Wine list	La carte des vins	la cart day **van**

GERMAN

English	German	Pronunciation
Basics		
Yes/no	Ja/nein	yah/nine
Please	Bitte	**bit**-uh
Thank you (very much)	Danke (vielen Dank)	**dahn**-kuh (**fee**-lun dahnk)
Excuse me	Entschuldigen Sie	ent-**shool**-de-gen zee
Good day	Guten Tag	**goo**-ten tahk
Good bye	Auf Wiedersehen	auf **vee**-der-zane
Mr./Mrs.	Herr/Frau	hair/frau
Miss	Fräulein	**froy**-line
Numbers		
1	Ein(s)	eint(s)
2	Zwei	tsvai
3	Drei	dry
4	Vier	fear
5	Fünf	fumph
6	Sechs	zex
7	Sieben	**zee**-ben
8	Acht	ahkt
9	Neun	noyn
10	Zehn	tsane
Days of the Week		
Sunday	Sonntag	**zone**-tahk
Monday	Montag	**moan**-tahk
Tuesday	Dienstag	**deens**-tahk

Wednesday	Mittwoch	**mit**-vokh
Thursday	Donnerstag	**doe**-ners-tahk
Friday	Freitag	**fry**-tahk
Saturday	Samstag/ Sonnabend	**zahm**-stakh/ **zonn**-a-bent

Useful Phrases

Do you speak English?	Sprechen Sie Englisch?	**shprek**-un zee **eng**-glish?
I am American/ British.	Ich bin Amerikaner(in)/ Engländer(in).	ich bin a-mer-i- **kahn**-er(in)/**eng**- glan-der(in)
Where are the rest rooms?	Wo ist die Toilette?	vo ist dee twah-**let**-uh
Left/right	links/rechts	links/rechts
Where is . . .	Wo ist . . .	**vo** ist
the train station?	der Bahnhof?	dare **bahn**-hof
the subway station?	die U-Bahn- Station?	dee oo-bahn-**staht**- sion
the post office?	die Post?	dee **post**
the bank?	die Bank?	dee **banhk**
the hospital?	das Krankenhaus?	dahs **krahnk**-en- house
I'd like to have . . .	Ich hätte gerne . . .	ich **het**-uh **gairn**-uh . . .
a room	ein Zimmer	ine **tsim**-er
a ticket	eine Karte	I-nuh **cart**-uh
How much is it?	Wieviel kostet das?	**vee**-feel **cost**-et dahs?
I am ill/sick.	Ich bin krank.	ich bin krahnk
Help!	Hilfe!	**hilf**-uh
Stop!	Halt!	hahlt

Dining Out

A bottle of . . .	Eine Flasche . . .	I-nuh **flash**-uh
Bill/check	Die Rechnung	dee **rekh**-nung
Do you have . . . ?	Haben Sie . . . ?	**hah**-ben zee
I'd like to order . . .	Ich möchte bestellen . . .	ich **mush**-tuh buh-shtel-en . . .
Menu	Die Speisekarte	dee **shpei**-zeh-car-tuh
Napkin	Die Serviette	dee zair-vee-**eh**-tuh

GREEK

The phonetic spelling used in English differs somewhat from the internationalized form of Greek place names. There are no long and short vowels in Greek; the pronunciation never changes. Note, also, that the accent is a stress mark, showing where the stress is placed in pronunciation.

Basics

Yes, no	Málista or Né, óchi
Good morning, Good day	Kaliméra

Good evening, Good night	Kalispéra, Kaliníchta
Goodbye	Yá sas
Mister, Madam, Miss	Kírie, kiría, despiní
Please	Parakaló
Excuse me	Me sinchórite or signómi
Thank you	Efcharistó

Numbers

1	Éna
2	Dío
3	Tría
4	Téssera
5	Pénde
6	Éxi
7	Eptá
8	Októ
9	Enéa
10	Déka
50	Penínda
100	Ekató
200	Diakóssia
1,000	Hília
2,000	Dió hiliádes

Days of the Week

Sunday	Kyriakí
Monday	Deftéra
Tuesday	Tríti
Wednesday	Tetárti
Thursday	Pémpti
Friday	Paraskeví
Saturday	Sávato

Useful Phrases

Do you speak English?	Miláte angliká?
I don't understand.	Dén katalavéno.
Which is the road to . . . ?	Piós íne o drómos giá . . . ?
Where is the toilet?	Póu íne í toaléta?
Ladies, men	Ginekón, andrón
How much?	Pósso?
To the right, to the left	Dexiá, aristerá
Where is . . .	Pou íne . . .
the bank?	i trápeza?
the post office?	to tachidromío?
How much is it?	Pósso káni? (or kostízi)

Dining Out

Waiter	Garsón
The menu, please.	To katálogo, parakaló.
Fixed-price menu	Menú
Red wine, white wine	Kokivó krasí, áspro krasí
Unresinated wine	Krasí aretsínato
Greek (formerly Turkish) coffee	Ellenikó kafé

HUNGARIAN

English	Hungarian	Pronunciation
Basics		
Yes/No	Igen/Nem	**ee**-gen/nem
Hello (good day)	Jó napot/Jó napot kivánok	**yoh** nuh-poht/**yoh** nuh-poht **kee**-vah-nohk
Good-bye	Viszontlátásra	**vee**-sohnt-lah-tahsh-ruh
Ma'am	Asszonyom	**uhs**-sohn-yohm
Miss	Kisasszony	**keesh**-uhs-sohny
Mr./Sir	Uram	**oor**-uhm

To address someone as Mrs., add the suffix "né" to the last name. Mrs. Kovács is then "Kovácsné." To address someone as Mr., use the word "úr" after the last name. Mr. Kovács is then "Kovács úr."

Please	Kérem szépen	**kay**-rem **say**-pen
Thank you	Köszönöm	**ku(r)**-su(r)-nu(r)m
You're welcome	Kérem szépen	**kay**-rem **say**-pen
Pardon me	Bocsánat	**boh**-chah-nuht

Numbers

0	Nulla	**nool**-luh
1	Egy	edge
2	Kettő	**ket**-tu(r)
3	Három	**hah**-rohm
4	Négy	naydge
5	Öt	u(r)t
6	Hat	huht
7	Hét	hayt
8	Nyolc	nyohlts
9	Kilenc	**kee**-lents
10	Tíz	teez
20	Húsz	hooss
50	Ötven	**u(r)t**-ven
100	Száz	sahz
1,000	Ezer	**e**-zer

Days of the Week

Sunday	Vasárnap	**vuh**-shahr-nuhp
Monday	Hétfő	**hayt**-fu(r)
Tuesday	Kedd	ked
Wednesday	Szerda	**ser**-duh
Thursday	Csütörtök	**chew**-tur-tu(r)k
Friday	Péntek	**payn**-tek
Saturday	Szombat	**sohm**-buht

Useful Phrases

Do you speak English?	Beszél angolul?	**be**-sayl **uhn**-gohl-ool
I don't understand.	Nem értem.	nem **ayr**-tem
I don't know.	Nem tudom.	**nem** too-dohm
Excuse me, where is the . . .	Bocsánat, hol van a . . .	**boh**-chah-nuht **hohl** vuhn uh
bus stop?	buszmegallo?	**booss**-meg-ahl-loh
subway station?	metro?	**met**-roh
bank?	bank?	**buhnk**
post office?	pósta?	**pohsh**-tuh
Where is the toilet?	Hol van a toálet (WC)?	**hohl** vuhn uh **toh**-ah-let (**vay**-tsay)
To the right	Jobbra	**yohb**-bruh
To the left	Balra	**buhl**-ruh
How much?	Mennyi?	**men**-nyee
I would like a room.	Kérek egy szobát.	**kay**-rek edge **soh**-baht

Dining Out

| Waiter | Pincér | **peen**-sayr |
| Waitress | Pincérnő | **peen**-sayr-nu(r) |

(Waiters and waitresses are more likely to respond to the request "Kérem" [**kay**-rem], which means "please.")

I would like the menu, please.	Kérem az étlapot.	**kay**-rem uhz **ayt**-luhp-oht
The wine list, please.	Kérem a borlapot.	**kay**-rem uh **bohr**-luhp oht
The specialty of the day	A mai ajánlat	uh **muh**-ee **uhy**-ahn-luht
The check, please.	Kérem szépen a számlát.	**kay**-rem **say**-pen uh **sahm**-laht
Is the tip included?	Benne van a borravallo?	**ben**-ne vuhn uh **bohr**-ruh-vuhl-loh
Napkin	Szalvéta	**suhl**-vay-tuh
Mineral water	Ásványvíz	**ahsh**-vahn'y-veez

ICELANDIC

English	Icelandic	Pronunciation

Basics

Yes/no	Já/nei	yow/nay
Thank you very much	Kærar þakkir takk	**kie**-rahr **thah**-kihr **ta**hkk
You're welcome	Ekkert að-þakka	**ehk**-kehrt ath **thah**-ka
Excuse me (to get by someone)	Afsakið	**ahf**-sah-kith(e)
(to apologize)	Fyrirgefið	**feer**-ee-geh-vith(e)
Hello	Góðan dag	goh-than **dahgh**
Goodbye	Bless	bless
Today	Í dag	**ee dahgh**
Tomorrow	Á morgun	ow **mohr**-gun
Yesterday	Í gær	ee **gah-eer**

Numbers

1	Einn	ehnn
2	Tveir	**tveh**-eer
3	Þrír	threer
4	Fjórir	**fyohr**-eer
5	Fimm	fehm
6	Sex	sex
7	Sjö	sy-uh
8	Átta	**owt**-tah
9	Níu	**nee**-uh
10	Tíu	**tee**-uh

Days of the Week

Sunday	sunnudagur	**soon**-noo-dah-gur
Monday	mánudagur	**mown**-ah-dah-gur
Tuesday	þriðjudagur	**thrithe**-yoo-dah-gur
Wednesday	miðvikudagur	**meethe**-veek-uh dah-gur
Thursday	fimmtudagur	**feem**-too-dah-gur
Friday	föstudagur	**fuhs**-too-dah-gur
Saturday	laugardagur	**loy**-gahr-dah-gur

Useful Phrases

Do you speak English?	Talar þú ensku?	**tah**-lahr thoo **ehn**-skoo
I don't understand.	Ég skil ekki.	yeh **skeel ehk**-keh
I don't know.	Ég veit ekki.	yeh **vayt ehk**-keh
I am American/ British.	Ég er ameriskur/ breskur.	yeh ehr **ah**-mehr eeskur/**brehs**-koor
Please call a doctor.	Viltu hringja í lækni, takk.	veel-too **hreeng**-yah ee **lahk**-nee **tah**-kk

Do you have a vacant room?	Átt pú laust herbergi?	owt thoo laysht **hehr**-behr-ghee
How much does it cost?	Hvað kostar Það?	kvathe kohs-tahr thathe
It's too expensive.	Það er of dýt.	thathe ehr ohf deert
Beautiful	Fallegur/t	**fahl**-lehg-oor
Help!	Hjálp!	hyalp
Stop!	Stopp!	stohp
How do I get to . . .	Hvernig kemst ég . . .	**kvehr**-neeg kehmst **yehg**
the post office?	á pósthúsið	ow pohst-hoos-ihthe
the hospital?	á spitalan	ow **spee**-tah-lahn
Does this bus go to . . . ?	Fer Þessi vagn . . . ?	fehr **thehs**-see **vakn**
Where is the W.C.?	Hvar er salerni?	kvahr ehr sahl-ehr-nihthe
On the left	til vinstri	teel **veen**-stree
On the right	til hægri	teel **hie**-ree

Dining Out

Please bring me . . .	Get ég fengið . . .	geht yehg fehn-gihthe
Menu	Matseðil	**maht**-seh-theel
Napkin	Servetta	sehr-**veht**-tah
Bread	Brauð	braythe
Water/bottled water	Vatn	vahtn
The check, please.	Reikninginn.	takk **rehk**-nihn-ghihn

ITALIAN

English	Italian	Pronunciation
Basics		
Yes/no	Sí/No	see/no
Please	Per favore	pear fa-**vo**-ray
Thank you	Grazie	**grah**-tsee-ay
You're welcome	Prego	**pray**-go
Excuse me, sorry	Scusi	**skoo**-zee
Good morning/ afternoon	Buon giorno	bwohn **jor**-no
Good evening	Buona sera	**bwoh**-na **say**-ra
Good bye	Arrivederci	a-ree-vah-**dare**-chee
Mr. (Sir)	Signore	see-**nyo**-ray
Mrs. (Ma'am)	Signora	see-**nyo**-ra
Miss	Signorina	see-nyo-**ree**-na
Hello (over the phone)?	Pronto?	**proan**-to

Numbers

1	Uno	**oo**-no
2	Due	**doo**-ay
3	Tre	tray
4	Quattro	**kwah**-tro
5	Cinque	**cheen**-kway
6	Sei	say
7	Sette	**set**-ay
8	Otto	**oh**-to
9	Nove	**no**-vay
10	Dieci	dee-**eh**-chee
20	Venti	**vain**-tee
50	Cinquanta	cheen-**kwahn**-ta
100	Cento	**chen**-to
10,000	Diecimila	dee-eh-chee-**mee**-la
100,000	Centomila	chen-to-**mee**-la

Days of the Week

Sunday	domenica	doe-**men**-ee-ca
Monday	lunedì	loo-neh-**dee**
Tuesday	martedì	mahr-teh-**dee**
Wednesday	mercoledì	mare-co-leh-**dee**
Thursday	giovedì	jo-veh-**dee**
Friday	venerdì	ven-air-**dee**
Saturday	sabato	**sah**-ba-toe

Useful Phrases

Do you speak English?	Parla inglese?	**par**-la een-**glay**-zay
I don't understand.	Non capisco.	non ka-**peess**-ko
I don't know.	Non lo so.	noan lo **so**
I'm American/British.	Sono americano/a Sono inglese.	**so**-no a-may-ree-**kah**-no/a **so**-no een-**glay**-zay
What is it?	Che cos'è?	kay ko-**zay**
Where is . . .	Dov'è . . .	doe-**veh**
the train station?	la stazione?	la sta-tsee-**oh**-nay
the subway station?	la metropolitana?	la may-tro-po-lee-**tah**-na
the post office?	l'ufficio postale?	loo-**fee**-cho po-**stah**-lay
the bank?	la banca?	la **bahn**-ka
the hospital?	l'ospedale?	lo-spay-**dah**-lay
Where are the rest rooms?	Dov'è il bagno?	doe-**vay** eel **bahn**-yo
Left/right	A sinistra/a destra	a see-**neess**-tra/ a **des**-tra

I'd like . . .	Vorrei . . .	vo-**ray**
a room	una camera	**oo**-na **kah**-may-ra
How much is it?	Quanto costa?	**kwahn**-toe **coast**-a
A little/a lot	Poco/tanto	**po**-ko/**tahn**-to
More/less	Più/meno	pee-**oo**/**may**-no
I am sick.	Sto male.	sto **mah**-lay
Help!	Aiuto!	a-**yoo**-toe
Stop!	Alt!	ahlt

Dining Out

A bottle of . . .	Una bottiglia di . . .	**oo**-na bo-**tee**-lee-ah dee
Bill/check	Il conto	eel **cone**-toe
Fixed-price menu	Menù a prezzo fisso	may-**noo** a **pret**-so **fee**-so
I'd like . . .	Vorrei . . .	vo-**ray**
Is service included?	Il servizio è incluso?	eel ser-**vee**-tzee-o ay een-**kloo**-zo
Menu	Il menù	eel may-**noo**
Napkin	Il tovagliolo	eel toe-va-lee-**oh**-lo
Waiter/Waitress	Cameriere/ cameriera	ka-mare-**yer**-av/ ka-mare-**yer**-a
Wine list	La lista dei vini	la **lee**-sta **day**-ee **vee**-nee

NORWEGIAN

English	Norwegian	Pronunciation
Basics		
Yes/no	Ja/nei	yah/nay
Please	Vær så snill	**vehr** soh snihl
Thank you very much	Tusen takk	**tews**-sehn tahk
You're welcome	Vær så god	**vehr** soh goo
Excuse me	Unnskyld	**ewn**-shewl
Hello	God dag	goo **dahg**
Goodbye	Adjø	ah-**dyur**
Today	I dag	ee **dahg**
Tomorrow	I morgen	ee **moh**-ern
Yesterday	I går	ee **gohr**

Numbers		
1	En	ehn
2	To	too
3	Tre	treh
4	Fire	**feer**-eh
5	Fem	fehm
6	Seks	sehks

7	Syv, sju	shew
8	Åtte	**oh**-teh
9	Ni	nee
10	Ti	tee

Days of the Week

Sunday	sondag	**suhn**-dahg
Monday	mandag	**mahn**-dahg
Tuesday	tirsdag	**teesh**-dahg
Wednesday	onsdag	**oonss**-dahg
Thursday	torsdag	**tohsh**-dahg
Friday	fredag	**fray**-dahg
Saturday	lørdag	**loor**-dahg

Useful Phrases

Do you speak English?	Snakker De engelsk?	snahk-kerr dee **ehng**-ehlsk
I don't understand.	Jeg forstår ikke.	yay fosh-**tawr** **ik**-keh
I don't know.	Jeg vet ikke.	yay veht **ik**-keh
I am American/ British.	Jeg er amerikansk/ engelsk.	yay ehr ah-mehr-ee-**kahnsk**/**ehng**-ehlsk
Please call a doctor.	Vær så snill og ring etter en lege.	vehr soh snihl oh ring **eht**-ehr ehn **lay**-geh
Do you have vacant room?	Har du et rom som er ledig?	yay vil **yehr**-neh hah eht room
How much does it cost?	Hva koster det?	vah **koss**-terr deh
It's too expensive.	Det er for dyrt.	deh ehr for **deert**
Beautiful	Vakker	**vah**-kehr
Help!	Hjelp!	yehlp
Stop!	Stopp!	stop
How do I get to . . .	Hvor er . . .	voor ehr
the train station?	jernbanestasjonen?	yehrn-bahn-eh sta-**shoon**-ern
the post office?	posthuset?	**pohsst**-hewss
the hospital?	sykehuset?	**see**-keh-hoo-seh
Does this bus go to . . . ?	Går denne bussen til . . . ?	gohr **den**-nah boos teel
Where is the W.C.?	Hvor er toalettene?	voor ehr too-ah-**leht**-te-ne
On the left	Til venstre	teel **vehn**-streh
On the right	Til høyre	teel **hooy**-reh

Dining Out

Menu	Meny	meh-**new**
Napkin	Serviett	ssehr-**vyeht**
Bread	Brød	brur

Water/bottled water	Vann	vahn
The check, please.	Jeg vil gjerne betale.	yay vil **yehr**-neh beh-**tah**-leh

POLISH

English	Polish	Pronunciation
Basics		
Yes/no	Tak/nie	tahk/nye
Please (or "You're welcome")	Proszę	**pro**-sheh
Thank you	Dziękuję	dzhen-**koo**-yeh
Excuse me	Przepraszam	psheh-**prah**-shahm
Hello/Good morning	Dzień dobry	**dzhehn dohb**-ree
Goodbye	Do widzenia	doh vee-**dzehn**-yah
To a woman; Ms.	Pani	**pahn**-ee
To a man; Mr.	Panu	**pahn**-oo
Good evening	Dobry wieczór	**dohb**-ree **vyeh**-choor
Numbers		
0	Zero	**zeh**-roh
1	Jeden	**yeh**-den
2	Dwa	**dvah**
3	Trzy	**tchee**
4	Cztery	**chteh**-ree
5	Pięć	**pyehnch**
6	Sześć	**shayshch**
7	Siedem	**shyeh**-dem
8	Osiem	**oh**-shyem
9	Dziewięć	**dzhyeh**-vyehnch
10	Dziesięć	**dzhyeh**-shehnch
20	Dwadzieścia	dvah-**dzheh**-shchah
50	Pięćdziesiąt	pyehnch-**dzheh**-shont
100	Sto	stoh
1,000	Tysiąc	**tee**-shonch
100,000	Sto Tysiąc	stoh **tee**-shonch
Days of the Week		
Sunday	niedziela	nyeh-**dzhy'e**-la
Monday	poniedziałek	poh-nyeh-**dzhya**-wek
Tuesday	wtorek	**ftohr**-ek
Wednesday	środa	**shroh**-da
Thursday	czwartek	**chvahr**-tek
Friday	piątek	**pyohn**-tek
Saturday	sobota	soh-**boh**-ta

Useful Phrases

Do you speak English?	Czy pan (pani) mówi po angielsku?	**chee** pahn (**pahn**-ee) **moo**-vee po-ahn-**gyel**-skuu
I don't understand.	Nie rozumiem.	**nyeh** rohz-**oo**-myehm
I don't know.	Nie wiem.	**nye**-vyehm
Where is . . .	Gdzie jest . . .	**gdzhyeh** yest
the bus stop?	przystanek autobusowy?	pshee-**stahn**-ehk a'oo-toh-boo-**soh**-vee
the train station?	dworzec kolejowy?	**dvoh**-zhets koh-lay-**oh**-vee
the bank?	bank?	bahnk
Where is the toilet?	Gdzie jest toaleta?	**gdzhyeh** yest toh-ah-**lyet**-ah
To the right/left	Na prawo/lewo	nah **prah**-voh/ **lyeh**-voh
I (m/f) would like this.	Chciałbym (Chciałabym) to.	**kh'chow**-beem (kh'chow-**ah**-beem) toh
I (m/f) would like to reserve a room.	Chciałbym (Chciałabym) zamówić pokój.	**kh'chow**-bim (kh'chow-**ah**-bim) zah-**moo**-veech **poh**-kooy
How much is it?	Ile to kosztuje?	**ee**-leh to kosh-**too**-yeh

Dining Out

The menu, please.	Proszę menu.	**proh**-sheh **men**-yoo
The wine list, please.	Proszę kartę win.	**proh**-sheh **kahr**-teh **veen**
The specialty of the day	Danie gotowe	**dahn**-yeh goh-**toh**-veh
The check, please.	Proszę rachunek.	**proh**-sheh rah-**kh'oon**-ehk
Is the tip included?	Czy napiwek jest wliczony?	**chee** nah-**pee**-vehk yest vlee-**chohn**-ee
Napkin	Serwetka	ser-**vyet**-kah
Black coffee	Czarną kawę	**chahrn**-ohn **kah**-veh
Mineral water	Wodę mineralną	**voh**-deh mee-nehr-**ahl**-nohn
How much?	Ile?	**ee**-leh

PORTUGUESE

English	Portuguese	Pronunciation
Basics		
Yes/no	Sim/Não	**see**ing/**nown**
Please	Por favor	pohr fah-**vohr**
Thank you (very much)	(Muito) obrigado	(**moo**yn-too) o-bree **gah**-doh
You're welcome	De nada	day **nah**-dah

Excuse me	Com licença	con lee-**ssehn**-ssah
Good morning!	Bom dia!	bohn **dee**-ah
Good afternoon!	Boa tarde!	**boh**-ah **tahr**-dee
Good evening!	Boa noite!	**boh**-ah **noh**ee-tee
Goodbye!	Adeus!/Até logo!	ah-**deh**oos/ah-**teh loh**-go
Mr./Mrs.	Senhor/Senhora	sen-**yor**/sen-**yohr**-ah
Miss	Senhorita	sen-yo-**ri**-tah
Hello (on the telephone)	Alô	ah-**low**

Numbers

1	Um/uma	oom/**oom**-ah
2	Dois	**doh**ees
3	Três	**treh**ys
4	Quatro	**kwa**-troh
5	Cinco	**seen**-koh
6	Seis	**seh**ys
7	Sete	**seh**-tee
8	Oito	**oh**ee-too
9	Nove	**noh**-vee
10	Dez	**deh**-ees
20	Vinte	**veen**-tee
50	Cinquenta	seen-**kwehn**-tah
100	Cem	**seh**-ing
1,000	Mil	meel
1,000,000	Um milhão	oom mee-lee-**ahon**

Days of the Week

Sunday	Domingo	doh-**meehn**-goh
Monday	Segunda-feira	seh-**goon**-dah **fey**-rah
Tuesday	Terça-feira	**tehr**-sah **fey**-rah
Wednesday	Quarta-feira	**kwahr**-tah **fey**-rah
Thursday	Quinta-feira	**keen**-tah **fey**-rah
Friday	Sexta-feira	**sehss**-tah **fey**-rah
Saturday	Sábado	**sah**-bah-doh

Useful Phrases

Do you speak English?	Fala inglês?	**fah**-lah een-**glehs**?
I don't understand (you).	Não lhe entendo.	nown ly**eh** ehn-**tehn**-doh
I don't know.	Não sei.	nown say
I am American/British.	Sou americano/inglês.	sow a-meh-ree-**cah**-noh/een-**glehs**
What is it?	O que é isso?	oh **keh** eh **ee**-soh
Where is . . .	Onde é . . .	**ohn**-deh eh

the train station?	a estação de trem?	ah es-tah-**sah**-on deh train
the subway station?	a estação de metrô?	ah es-tah-**sah**-on deh meh-**tro**
the post office?	o correio?	oh coh-**hay**-yoh
the bank?	o banco?	oh **bahn**-koh
the hospital?	o hospital?	oh ohss-pee-**tal**
the bathroom?	o banheiro?	oh bahn-**yey**-roh
Left/right	Esquerda/ direita	ehs-**kehr**-dah/ dee-**ray**-tah
I'd like to buy . . .	Gostaria de comprar . . .	gohs-tah-**ree**-ah deh cohm-**prahr** . . .
How much is it?	Quanto custa?	**kwahn**-too **koos**-tah
A little/a lot	Um pouco/muito	oom **pohw**-koh/ **mooyn**-too
Please call a doctor.	Por favor chame um médico.	pohr fah-**vohr shah**-meh oom **meh**-dee-koh
Help!	Socorro!	soh-**koh**-ho

Dining Out

A bottle of . . .	Uma garrafa de . . .	**oo**mah gah-**hah**-fah deh
Bill/check	A conta	ah **kohn**-tah
Is the tip included?	A gorjeta esta incluída?	ah gohr-**jyeh**-tah ehss-**tah** een-clue-**ee**-dah
Menu	Menu/ cardápio	me-**noo**/ kahr-**dah**-peeoh
Mineral water	Água mineral	**ah**-gooah mee-neh-**rahl**
Napkin	Guardanapo	gooahr-dah-**nah**-poh
Please give me . . .	Por favor me dê . . .	pohr fah-**vohr** mee **deh**
Waiter!	Garçon!	gahr-**sohn**
Wine	Vinho	**vee**-nyoh

SPANISH

English	Spanish	Pronunciation
Basics		
Yes/no	Sí/no	see/no
Please	Por favor	pohr fah-**vohr**
Thank you (very much)	(Muchas) gracias	(**moo**-chas) **grah**-see-as
You're welcome	De nada	deh **nah**-dah
Excuse me	Con permiso	con pehr-**mee**-so
Good morning!	¡Buenos días!	**bway**-nohs **dee**-ahs
Goodbye!	¡Adiós!/ ¡Hasta luego!	ah-dee-**ohss**/ **ah**-stah-**lwe**-go

Mr./Mrs.	Señor/Señora	sen-**yor**/sen-**yohr**-ah
Miss	Señorita	sen-yo-**ree**-tah
Hello (on the telephone)	Diga	**dee**-gah

Numbers

1	Un, uno	oon, **oo**-no
2	Dos	dohs
3	Tres	tress
4	Cuatro	**kwah**-tro
5	Cinco	**sink**-oh
6	Seis	saice
7	Siete	see-**et**-eh
8	Ocho	**o**-cho
9	Nueve	new-**eh**-veh
10	Diez	dee-**es**
20	Veinte	**vain**-teh
50	Cincuenta	seen-**kwen**-tah
100	Cien	see-**en**
500	Quinientos	keen-**yen**-tohss
1,000	Mil	meel

Days of the Week

Sunday	Domingo	doh-**meen**-goh
Monday	Lunes	**loo**-ness
Tuesday	Martes	**mahr**-tess
Wednesday	Miércoles	me-**air**-koh-less
Thursday	Jueves	hoo-**ev**-ess
Friday	Viernes	vee-**air**-ness
Saturday	Sábado	**sah**-bah-doh

Useful Phrases

Do you speak English?	¿Habla usted inglés?	**ah**-blah oos-**ted** in-**glehs**
I don't understand (you).	No entiendo.	no en-tee-**en**-doh
I don't know.	No sé.	no seh
I am American/British.	Soy americano (americana)/inglés(a).	soy ah-meh-ree-**kah**-no (ah-meh-ree-**kah**-nah)/in-**glehs**(ah)
Yes, please/No, thank you	Sí, por favor/No, gracias	**see** pohr fah-**vor**/no **grah**-see-ahs
Yesterday/today/tomorrow	Ayer/hoy/mañana	ah-**yehr**/oy/mahn-**yah**-nah
What is it?	¿Qué es esto?	keh es **es**-toh
Where is . . .	¿Dónde está . . .	**dohn**-deh es-**tah**
the train station?	la estación del tren?	la es-tah-see-**on** del **train**
the subway	la estación del	la es-ta-see-**on** del

station?	metro?	**meh**-tro
the post office?	la oficina de correos?	la oh-fee-**see**-nah deh-koh-**reh**-os
the bank?	el banco?	el **bahn**-koh
the hospital?	el hospital?	el ohss-pee-**tal**
the bathroom?	el baño?	el **bahn**-yoh
Left/right	Izquierda/derecha	iss-key-**er**-dah/ dare-**eh**-chah
I'd like . . .	Quisiera . . .	kee-see-**ehr**-ah
a room.	un cuarto/una habitación.	oon **kwahr**-toh/ **oo**-nah ah-bee-tah-see-**on**
I'd like to buy . . .	Quisiera comprar . . .	kee-see-**ehr**-ah kohm-**prahr**
How much is it?	¿Cuánto cuesta?	**kwahn**-toh **kwes**-tah
A little/a lot	Un poquito/ mucho	oon poh-**kee**-toh/ **moo**-choh
More/less	Más/menos	mahss/**men**-ohss
Please call a doctor.	Por favor llame un medico.	pohr fah-**vor** ya-meh oon **med**-ee-koh
Help!	¡Ayuda!	ah-**yoo**-dah

Dining Out

A bottle of . . .	Una bottella de . . .	**oo**-nah bo-**teh**-yah deh
A glass of . . .	Un vaso de . . .	oon **vah**-so deh
Bill/check	La cuenta	lah **kwen**-tah
Bread	El pan	el pahn
Menu of the day	Menú del día	meh-**noo** del **dee**-ah
Fixed-price menu	Menú fijo o turistico	meh-**noo fee**-hoh oh too-**ree**-stee-coh
Is the tip included?	¿Está incluida la propina?	es-**tah** in-cloo-**ee**-dah lah pro-**pee**-nah
Menu	La carta, el menú	lah **cart**-ah, el meh-**noo**
Napkin	La servilleta	lah sehr-vee-**yet**-ah
Please give me	Por favor déme	pohr fah-**vor deh**-meh
Waiter!/Waitress!	¡Por favor Señor/Señorita!	pohr fah-**vor** sen-**yor**/ sen-yor-**ee**-tah

SWEDISH

English	Swedish	Pronunciation
Basics		
Yes/no	Ja/nej	yah/nay
Please	Var snäll; Var vänlig	vahr snehll vahr vehn-leeg
Thank you very much	Tack så mycket	tahk soh **mee**-keh
You're welcome	Var så god	vahr shoh **goo**

Excuse me (to get by someone)	Ursäkta	oor-**shehk**-tah
(to apologize)	Förlåt	fur-**loht**
Hello	God dag	goo **dahg**
Goodbye	Adjö	ah-**yoo**
Today	I dag	ee **dahg**
Tomorrow	I morgon	ee **mor**-ron
Yesterday	I går	ee **gohr**

Numbers

1	Ett	eht
2	Två	tvoh
3	Tre	tree
4	Fyra	fee-rah
5	Fem	fem
6	Sex	sex
7	Sju	shoo
8	Åtta	oht-tah
9	Nio	nee
10	Tio	tee

Days of the Week

Sunday	söndag	**sohn**-dahg
Monday	måndag	**mohn**-dahg
Tuesday	tisdag	**tees**-dahg
Wednesday	onsdag	**ohns**-dahg
Thursday	torsdag	**tohrs**-dahg
Friday	fredag	**freh**-dahg
Saturday	lördag	**luhr**-dahg

Useful Phrases

Do you speak English?	Talar ni engelska?	tah-lahr nee **ehng**-ehl-skah
I don't understand.	Jag förstår inte.	yah fuhr-**stohr** **een**-teh
I don't know.	Jag vet inte.	yah **veht een**-teh
I am American/ British.	Jag är amerikan/ engelsman.	yah ay ah-mehr-ee-**kahn/ehng**-ehls-mahn
Please call a doctor.	Jag vill skicka efter en läkare.	yah veel **shee**-kah **ehf**-tehr ehn **lay**-kah-reh
Do you have a vacant room?	Har Ni något rum ledigt?	hahr nee noh-goht **room leh**-deekt
How much does it cost?	Vad kostar det?/ Hur mycket kostar det?	vah **kohs**-tahr deh/hor **mee**-keh **kohs**-tahr deh
It's too expensive.	Den är för dyr.	dehn ay foor **deer**
Beautiful	Vacker	**vah**-kehr
Help!	Hjälp!	yehlp

Stop!	Stopp, stanna!	stop, **stahn**-nah
How do I get to . . .	Kan Ni visa mig vägen till . . .	kahn nee **vee**-sah may **vay**-gehn teel
the train station?	stationen?	stah-**shoh**-nehn
the post office?	posten?	**pohs**-tehn
the hospital?	sjukhuset?	**shyook**-hoo-seht
Does this bus go to . . . ?	Går den här bussen till . . . ?	gohr dehn hehr **boo**-sehn teel
Where is the W.C.?	Var är toalett/ toaletten	vahr ay twah-**leht**
On the left	Till vänster	teel **vehn**-stur
On the right	Till höger	teel **huh**-gur

Dining Out

Please bring me . . .	Var snäll och hämta åt mig . . .	vahr snehl oh **hehm**-tah oht may
Menu	Matsedeln	maht-seh-dehln
Napkin	En servett	ehn sehr-**veht**
Bread	Bröd	bruh(d)
Water	Vatten	vaht-n
The check, please.	Får jag be om notan.	fohr yah beh ohm **noh**-tahn

TURKISH

English	Turkish	Pronunciation
Basics		
Yes/no	Evet/hayir	**eh**-vet/**haw**-yer
Please	Lütfen	**lewt**-fen
Thank you	Tesekkür ederim	tay-shake-**cure** eh-day-**reem**
Sorry	Pardon	**pahr**-doan
Good morning	Günaydin	goo-eye-**den**
Good day	Iyi günler	ee-yee gewn-**lair**
Goodbye	Allahaismarladik	**allah**-aw-ees-mar- law-deck
	Güle güle	**gew**-leh- **gew**-leh

Numbers

1	Bir	beer
2	Iki	ee-**kee**
3	Üc	ooch
4	Dört	doort
5	Beş	besh
6	Alti	awl-tuh
7	Yedi	yed-dy
8	Sekiz	sek-**kez**
9	Dokuz	doh-**kooz**

10	On	own
20	Yirmi	yeer-mee
50	Elli	el-leeh
100	Yüz	yewz
1,000	Biņ	bin

Days of the Week

Sunday	Pazar	Poz-**ahr**
Monday	Pazartesi	Poz-**ahr**-tes-sy
Tuesday	Sali	Saul-luh
Wednesday	Çarşamba	Char-shom-**bah**
Thursday	Perşembe	Pair-shem-**beh**
Friday	Cuma	**Joom**-ah
Saturday	Cumartesi	Joom-**ahr**-tes-sy

Useful Phrases

Do you speak English?	Ingilizce biliyormusunuz?	in-**gee-leez**-jay bee-lee-**your**-moo-soo-noose
I don't understand.	Anlamiyorum.	On-**lah**-muh-your-oom
I don't know.	Bilmiyorum.	**beel**-meeh-your-oom
I'm American/British.	Amerikahyim Ingilizim.	ahm-ay-**ree**-kah-lew-yum **een**-gee-leez-um
What is it?	Nedir?	**neh**-deer
Where is . . .	Nerede . . .	**nay**-ray-deh
the train station?	tren istasyonu?	tee-**rehn** ees-**taws**-yone-oo
the subway station?	metro duraği?	metro doo-**raw**-ugh
the post office?	postane?	post-**ahn**-eh
the bank?	banka?	**bahn**-kah
the hospital?	hastane?	hoss-**taw**-neh
Where are the rest rooms?	Tuvalet nerede?	too-vah-**let** nay-ray-deh
Left/right	Sağ/sol	Saw/soul
I'd like . . .	Istiyorum . . .	**ess**-tee-your-room
a room.	bir oda.	beer oh-**dah**
I'd like to buy . . .	Almak istiyorum . . .	ahl-**mock** ees-tee-your-room
How much is it?	Fiyati ne kadar?	fee-yacht-eh **neh** kah-dar
It's expensive/cheap.	Pahaih/ucuz.	pah-hah-**luh**/oo-**jooz**
More/less	Daha çok/daha az	da-ha choke/da-ha oz
I am ill/sick.	Hastayim.	**hahs**-tah-yum
Help!	Imdat!	eem-**dot**
Stop!	Durun!	Doo-**roon**

Dining Out

A bottle of . . .	Bir şişe . . .	**beer** she-shay
A glass of . . .	Bir bardak . . .	beer **bar**-dock
Bill/check	Hesap	heh-**sop**
Bread	Ekmek	**ek**-mek
Fixed-price menu	Fiks menü	fix meh-**new**
I'd like to order . . .	Ismarlamak isterim . . .	us-mahr-lah-**muck** ee-stair-em
I'd like . . .	Isterim . . .	ee-stair-**em**
Is service/the tip included?	Servis fiyata dahil mi?	service **fee**-yah-tah dah-hee-**mee**
It's good/bad	Güzel/güzel değil	gew-**zell**/gew-**zell day**-eel
Menu	Menü	meh-**new**
Napkin	Peçete	**peh**-che-teh
Please give me . . .	Lutfen bana verirmisiniz . . .	**loot**-fen bah-nah vair-**eer**-mee-see-niz

Vocabulary

INDEX

DATE DUE

This item is Due on
or before Date shown.